The Broadview Anthology of

RESTORATION & EARLY
EIGHTEENTH-CENTURY DRAMA

"THE DUKE'S THEATRE IN DORSET GARDENS"

(reproduced by permission of the Folger Shakespeare Library)

The Broadview Anthology of

RESTORATION & EARLY EIGHTEENTH-CENTURY DRAMA

J. DOUGLAS CANFIELD

GENERAL EDITOR

MAJA-LISA VON SNEIDERN, ASSISTANT EDITOR

BROADVIEW ANTHOLOGIES OF ENGLISH LITERATURE

broadview press

National Library of Canada Cataloguing in Publication

Main entry under title:

The Broadview anthology of Restoration and early eighteenth-century English drama

(Broadview anthologies of English literature)
Includes index.

ISBN 1-55111-270-1

1. English drama – Restoration, 1660-1700.   2. English drama – 18th century.   3. English drama (Comedy).
I. Canfield, J. Douglas (John Douglas), 1941-   .   II. von Sneidern, Maja-Lisa.   III. Series.

PR1265.B76 2001   822'.408   C2001-930330-0

Broadview Press Ltd. is an independent, international publishing house, incorporated in 1985. Broadview believes in shared ownership, both with its employees and with the general public; since the year 2000 Broadview shares have traded publicly on the Toronto Venture Exchange under the symbol BDP.

We welcome comments and suggestions regarding any aspect of our publications–please feel free to contact us at the addresses below or at broadview@broadviewpress.com.

North America
PO Box 1243, Peterborough, Ontario, Canada K9J 7H5
3576 California Road, Orchard Park, NY, USA 14127
Tel: (705) 743-8990; Fax: (705) 743-8353
email: customerservice@broadviewpress.com

UK, Ireland, and continental Europe
NBN Plymbridge
Estover Road, Plymouth PL6 7PY
Tel: + 44 (0) 1752 202301; Fax: + 44 (0) 1752 202331
Fax Order Line: + 44 (0) 1752 202333
Customer Service: cservs@nbnplymbridge.com
Orders: orders@nbnplymbridge.com

Australia and New Zealand
UNIREPS, University of New South Wales
Sydney, NSW, 2052
Tel: 61 2 9664 0999; Fax: 61 2 9664 5420
email: info.press@unsw.edu.au

www.broadviewpress.com

Broadview Press Ltd. gratefully acknowledges the financial support of the Government of Canada through the Book Publishing Industry Development Program for our publishing activities.

Cover design by George Kirkpatrick

PRINTED IN CANADA

For
Paul
Hunter

The editors gratefully acknowledge the conscientious work of our contributing editors—and that of Broadview Press in general and Eileen Eckert and Dawn Huck in particular. Thanks also to Danika Brown and Elise Marubbio for research assistance. Special thanks to Derek Hughes.

Contents

Plays by genre and subperiod

Introduction

This anthology of English drama covers the years 1660 to 1737, with a glance at the resurrection of its kind of comedy toward the end of the eighteenth century. The years 1660 and 1737 mark major political events that affected the theater in England: the restoration of the monarchy in 1660 after the commonwealth of the mid-seventeenth century (an event that also restored public theaters to London) and the Licensing Act of 1737 (an event that marked the stifling of creativity through government censorship). Just as the closing of the public theaters in 1642 was a political act (the emerging powers buttressed their right to rule with a claim of moral superiority above the Court and its decadent entertainments), so their restoration was a political act: the triumphant Court gave patents to political supporters to run two theaters, aptly named the King's and the Duke's for the restored King Charles II and his brother, James, the duke of York. Thus the theaters were reopened rather explicitly as ideological state apparatuses, for the plays, subject to state censorship through the offices of Master of the Revels and the Lord Chamberlain (though exercised rather mildly except in times of political crisis), were expected to inculcate into their audiences the ideology that attempted to naturalize the right of the monarchists to rule.

Thanks to the "Puritans," who had torn most of them down, the new companies had no adequate theaters and had to make shift with tennis courts. They also had no new plays to hand and so had to make shift with the repertory of plays from before the Civil Wars. It is no accident that this repertory was dominated by the Elizabethan/Jacobean playwrights, William Shakespeare and John Fletcher, both of whose plays generally affirmed aristocratic, monarchist ideology. The new plays of the 1660s were often adaptations of earlier Cavalier drama, particularly its tragicomic romances about lost, dispossessed heirs to thrones and estates. One of the more original genres, the rhymed heroic play, with roots in Cavalier drama and in French drama witnessed by the Court in exile, was also, in the main, a form of romance with political ramifications. Both heroic and tragicomic romance usually restored the dispossessed to positions of power they merited by birth. Comedies too were political, uniting aristocratic couples whose inborn wit and energy entitle them to inherit and make new heirs for the estates that were the backbone of the political economy of the English aristocracy. The comedies also regularly disciplined Puritans and Cits, opponents of the Court who, because of religious or economic ties to new sources of power especially in the City of London, had demanded participation in their own government but were now caricatured as vain, hypocritical, vulgar, and eminently unworthy to rule. Paradoxically, these 1660s comedies were leavened by a folk energy that disrupted the very status hierarchy being reaffirmed, as enterprising soldiers and commoners and thieves and whores often stole the show and sometimes even estates themselves. And occasional tragedies allowed villains with enormous energy to get away with murder and to indict the ruling aristocracy with ideological hypocrisy.

The Restoration political compromise between the competing oligarchies of the civil war period began to unravel almost as soon as it was made. Just as Charles I had courted alliance with Catholic France and tried to run the country without Parliament, so did Charles II, especially in the infamous secret Treaty of Dover (1670), which in return for financial aid from Louis XIV promised to return England to the Catholic fold. James was already a Catholic, and Charles promised to declare his own conversion when it would not be too politically disruptive. Parliament was prorogued during the second half of the '70s, and Charles ran the country with subsidies from France. The country became suspicious, and the time was ripe for the Popish Plot of 1678.

After Henry VIII broke England away from the Roman Catholic Church in the middle of the sixteenth century, the Pope had, in effect, declared war: England was to be returned to the fold no matter how. Hence "Bloody" Mary I and her purges of Protestants; hence the attempted invasion of England by Mary's husband, King Philip II of Spain, which ended with the defeat of the Spanish Armada in 1588; hence Guy Fawkes and the Jesuit Gunpowder Plot to blow up Parliament in 1605; hence the Vatican's offer to finance a Catholic invasion of England to keep Charles I on the throne during the Civil Wars. Paranoid Protestants blamed Catholics for the Great Fire of London in 1666. So the rumor in 1678 of a Catholic plot to assassinate the king, murder Protestants, and invade England through Ireland was not so far-fetched. Titus Oates, who claimed to be a doctor of divinity, was the star witness, denouncing putative conspirators right and left. Indeed, several English Catholics were executed. The scare led powerful groups to agitate for the exclusion of the Catholic James from succession to the throne, to which he was heir-presumptive because Charles had no legitimate children, though he had several bastards. Hence the Exclusion Crisis of 1679-81, when opponents of the Court attempted not only to exclude James but have one of Charles's bastards, James Scott, duke of Monmouth, declared heir-apparent. Charles had repeatedly to prorogue or dissolve Parliament. By the dismissal of his last Parliament at Oxford in 1681, Charles won a Pyrrhic victory. He had to rely increasingly on France until his death in 1685, when James himself won a Pyrrhic victory over Monmouth, who was defeated and executed. The days of the monarchists were numbered. Immediately after the birth of a son to James II and his second (Catholic) wife, Maria of Modena, he was forced to abandon the throne to his Protestant daughter Mary and her Protestant Dutch husband, William of Orange. They became the co-sovereigns William III and Mary II in what their winning side dubbed the Glorious Revolution of 1688.

These major political events of course affected the drama. Already in the early 1670s comedies began to portray anti-bourgeois sentiments more aggressively. Puritan and Cit wives and daughters were seduced by Cavaliers whose *droit du seigneur* bestowed upon their actions not just impunity but the patina of a kind of benevolence: they were not only giving the women what they wanted but they were ennobling their backward City breed. Cit-cuckolding plays increased as the '70s careened on through the Popish Plot to the Exclusion Crisis. Heroic romances and tragedies portrayed political crises of succession, especially in adaptations of Shakespeare's history plays. As in Shakespeare's Roman tragedies (several of which were also adapted at this time), some Restoration neoclassical tragedies portrayed societies in crisis precisely because they did not have clear traditions to resolve the problem of succession; others presented protagonists great but flawed and unable to bequeath to their states political stability; still others (a rare few) portrayed a republican alternative to monarchism. A few comedies and dramatic satires enacted intra-class strife and exposed the fissures beneath the ostensibly smooth surface of the old ideology.

The Act of Settlement of the Revolution, with its accompanying Bill of Rights, did not mark a middle-class revolution, as was formerly assumed by historians. There was no Reign of Terror; the aristocracy persisted; land remained the symbol of wealth and power. Wealth of estates increased through enclosing lands and putting them into production and through improving yield. Much of this growth depended on infusions of money from trade, and power itself shifted from one oligarchy to another more responsive to the increasing wealth of the rising merchant class. Government monopolies were broken, resulting in virtual free trade. A national bank and the National Debt were instituted (1694), providing low-interest loans and venture capital for both government and industry. Paper money and checks increased the fluidity of the economic system. Wars were fought on the Continent that had serious ramifications for colonial trade. Victories under John Churchill, later duke of Marlborough, in the War of the Spanish Succession brought England much of New France and the *asiento*, the right to the exclusive slave trade with Spanish America. By the end of the Revolution period (1714), the wealth was increasingly invested in stocks and the moneyed interest came to dominate the landed interest. England, united formally with Scotland in 1707, was on the verge of becoming the empire of Great Britain.

The new ruling oligarchy required an ideology that embodied a new ethos (character) and ethics (morality). Revolution drama helped constitute it. Worth was increasingly portrayed as based no longer on birth but on merit. Heroic romances and political tragedies generally replace passionate, self-indulgent protagonists with stoic, self-controlled protagonists. Protagonists of personal tragedies are more often the victims of economic circumstance. And comic protagonists are not rewarded for their wit and sexual energy but for their good nature and generosity, a term that shifts from referring to nobility to referring to moral action: benevolence. A theory that maintains the essential goodness of human nature, benevolence emerged from the writings of the Latitudinarian divines (who would emphasize the broad latitudes of Christianity) and was codified by the third earl of Shaftesbury in the early eighteenth century. It formed the basis of this new comedy, a comedy based on an ethic of sentiment, of feelings. In such comedy, the Restoration comic libertine is bifurcated into an effete beau, who is easily defeated, and a downright villain, who is—not so easily—defeated, who stands for the rapacity of Lockean unlimited acquisition. From between these two husks emerges a good husband who is also a good husbandman—of his estate for the good of the new Nation. Comedy also becomes less about the socializing of the centrifugal sexual energy of the male rake than the socializing of the centrifugal sexual energy of the female coquette.

This movement in comedy was part of a general reform movement, summoned forth by the new King William himself: "We most earnestly Desire, and shall Endeavour a General Reformation of the Lives and Manners of all Our Subjects, as being that which must Establish Our Throne, and Secure to Our People their Religion, Happiness and Peace, all which seem to be in great Danger at this time, by reason of that overflowing of Vice, which is too Notorious in this as well as other Neighbouring Nations." The king's call was met by the establishment of societies for the reformation of manners. As today, such societies focused not on real corruption but on surface and style: in the drama, on satiric portrayals of the ruling establishment and its supporting clerics and on sexual "immorality." One of the most notorious attacks was the Reverend Jeremy Collier's *Short View of the Immorality, and Profaneness of the English Stage* (1698), the importance of which was less causal than symptomatic.

Dramatic theory accompanied this shift from aristocratic to bourgeois ethos. Following the Aristotelian tradition that had come to them from Italian and French "neoclassicism," Restoration dramatic theory legitimated a tragedy that portrayed "great people," because they were the only people whose fall might concern the audience, and that instilled in the audience not only Aristotle's pity and fear but also admiration for the great heroics as well as great passions of such protagonists. Restoration comedy was theorized in the manner of Molière: *corriger les hommes en les divertissant*. But the entertaining correction of vices and folly seems a theory more honored in the breach than in the observance and more designed to placate Puritan hostility than to accurately legitimate the practice of Restoration comedy. Theorists like Dryden actually spent more time celebrating Restoration drama in relation to previous English and current French practice. Its superiority was said to reside in its wit and elegant dialogue and its eschewing of vulgarities. At the same time, the theorists celebrated the "mixed way" of the English: their blurring of generic boundaries in the very popular mode of tragicomedy. Farce they explained as a sop to unsophisticated audience taste.

There lurks in this aristocratic theory an acceptance of a surplus exuberance that allows explicitly for genre—and implicitly for class—mixing: tragicomedies and comedies are invaded by successful, applauded disrupters from below. In a sense, it is bourgeois theory that demands purity, as if the taste Dryden pointed to is the cultural status symbol par excellence for the nouveaux riches. Thus neoclassical theory, as it develops toward the end of the Restoration and is adapted from a new wave of French theory, demands a purer adherence to Aristotle in terms of the dramatic unities of time, place, and action, for instance, and in terms of decorum of character and genre. That decorum will cleanse the stage of improprieties and vulgarities. Just as Joseph Addison and Richard Steele would attempt to mold the taste of the new ruling class through a series of essays in their periodicals, *The Tatler* and *The Spectator*, so dramatic theorists would attempt to justify a drama that invokes not so much admiration for heroic action and passion nor contempt for vice and folly but sympathy for models of exemplary behavior under stress, the register of which would gradually open to include merchants and even apprentices and servants.

This new decorum blurred generic distinctions between tragedy and comedy. And with regard to tragedy, Revolution theory introduced a strict interpretation of an old doctrine: poetical justice. Aristotle himself had argued that the fall of a totally good man would scandalize us because it could challenge the justice of the gods. The tragic protagonist, therefore, must not be perfect; his fall must be justified by at least a *hamartia*, an error in judgment. English Renaissance and Restoration dramatic practice portrayed a version of retributive justice: the evil are punished or disciplined (either onstage or in prophecy); the good may suffer in this life, but be rewarded

in the next. The Revolution theorists insisted that such justice must be distributive: the evil must be punished and the good rewarded onstage. Again, a rule more honored in the breach, but as early as 1680 the ending of *King Lear* was altered so that Lear lives and Cordelia is happily married to Edgar—all so as not to violate our sense of decorum, here the decorum of God's justice.

Revolution comedies occasionally subvert the new order. Comic protagonists sometimes succeed because they parasitically feed off the new political economy, whose meritocratic rhetoric occludes those left out, who must resort to crime and trickery. Sometimes they make a mockery of bourgeois systems of order, from residual status hierarchy, to gender distinctions that deny equality and agency, to the military, with its impressment of a displaced surplus labor pool. Especially interesting are comedies and satires (both comical and tragical) that attack the institution of marriage, retained in the bourgeois ideology because power and property are still, in the main (despite the ideology of meritocracy and egalitarianism) transmitted through patrilineal genealogy. Women remain the sacred transmitters and must therefore be chaste—and monogamous. Some comedies indulge the fantasy of no-fault divorce. Some satires close with women standing alone in bas relief, their marital problems unresolved and unresolvable. Tragical satires attack the republican system as no more efficacious than the monarchal. One menippean, absurdist satire portrays usurpers as not accountable in a world where God himself is sheer Will-to-Power.

These trends continue after 1714-15, when occurred these three crucial events: the death of Mary II's younger sister, Anne, the last of the Stuart monarchs; the succession of the Hanoverian dynasty, distantly related to the Stuarts through marriage; and the failure of The Fifteen, a revolution that attempted, once again with Catholic backing, to restore James II's son, now called James III by his supporters, termed

Jacobites. Both this failure and this successful succession mark the full triumph of the Revolutionary Settlement; Parliament, backed by the army, clearly had the power to make or break a king. And they mark the dawn of the era of the strong chief minister, as this office took shape under the hands of Sir Robert Walpole, who consolidated the new constitutional monarchy at home and the new empire abroad. The new wealth called for new laws protecting property. Named for blackfaced Robin Hoods in the countryside, the infamous Black Act was passed in 1724, making most crimes against property, even the pettiest, capital, and giving rise to England's "Hanging Judge" and "Albion's Fatal Tree"—the gallows. The new oligarchy cut the slack built into the previous system for the poor and let it out to themselves. Although the act was repealed a short time later, it and other oppressive acts by the Walpole government, including the most successful intelligence agency until the twentieth century, gave rise to an opposition press and opposition literature, championed by the Scriblerists (named for their fictional blockhead creation, Martinus Scriblerus), who included Jonathan Swift, Alexander Pope, and John Gay.

Early Georgian drama (named after the Georges of the House of Hanover, who became England's monarchs for the rest of the eighteenth century) solidified bourgeois ideology, by extending tragedy and tragicomic romance, for example, to include as spokesmen for the new ethos (and for its discrimination from the aristocratic ethos) positive merchant characters with such telling names as Mr. Sealand and Mr. Thorowgood. Industry and prudence become key words. Wealth from the colonies (first the Indies, later India itself) is laundered, as it were, by crossing the seas to the metropolis. The appropriation of resources from them is justified in the name of superior culture, civilization, not to mention technology. Effete beaux of the decadent aristocracy continue to be defeated, while good husbands, in both senses of the word, continue to win wives, sometimes by bold strokes.

Even the Georgian heroic romance *Lucius*, however, continues to reveal the ineluctable Oedipal crisis of the patrilineal monarchy to which England stubbornly clings: the only way to the throne is over the dead body of the father. This repressed truth lurks at the heart of English heroic romance and tragedy. It surfaces with a vengeance around the time of the Exclusion Crisis. And it rears its beheaded ghost again around the time of The Fifteen.

One of the great delights of early Georgian theater is the invention of the ballad opera, precursor to the modern musical. In the hands of its greatest practitioners, John Gay and Henry Fielding, it strips bare the hypocrisy of the new bourgeois ethos, embodied in Walpole and his agents and placemen, revealing the inherent rapacity of capitalism (as well as its frightful instability, as witnessed in the stock-market crash of 1720 known as the "South Sea Bubble") and escaping into the fantasies of art. Gay's *Polly*, unstaged but immensely popular in print, like Thomas Southerne's *Oroonoko* before it, reveals the ugly truth behind bourgeois cultural imperialism: that its ideology is bankrupt and untrue. The only nobles on the planet may well be the supposed savages, and they are headed toward the hinterlands to escape civilization.

Walpole could not stand such severe criticism, so at the very moment of his own demise (he lost power steadily after the death of his chief supporter at Court, George II's Queen Caroline, in 1737) he engineered the passage of the Licensing Act, which enforced zero tolerance for criticism of the ministry and effectively disciplined playwrights into conformity. In the atmosphere of crisis brought on by the American Revolution and the Gordon (anti-Catholic) Riots in the late 1770s and early 1780s, a few playwrights tried to resuscitate the theater by departing from sentimental comedy and returning to the greatest contribution of Restoration and Revolution drama, what Oliver Goldsmith called "laughing"—that is, satirical—comedy (though neither the departure nor the return was radical).

* * *

The Restoration theater itself, as it moved from the tennis courts to new buildings, implemented new designs and innovations. The typical theater comprised stage and backstage, pit, boxes, and galleries. Backstage contained the tiring rooms where actors and actresses dressed and made up, and they were the site of visitations by VIPs. This interaction between company and members of the audience continued on the stage itself, where some of the bolder young aristocrats might actually bring benches and sit and where the long apron allowed an immediacy and intimacy between actor and audience. Proscenium arches came to frame the action. Extending out from the arch into the architecture of the boxes were structures containing doors and balconies with windows. Moveable scenery became possible by sliding multiple pairs of screens or flats, representing different scenes, along grooves in the stage floor. These flats could be opened or "drawn" to reveal another scene upstage up to a final set scene, with cutouts to imply three-dimensional depth. As the theaters became more elaborate, they were capable of raising and lowering all kinds of "machines" with various "engines" operating on a pulley system. Such by the early 1670s were the Duke's Company's new theater in Dorset Garden and the King's Company's new Theater Royal in Drury Lane, designed by the great architect, Christopher Wren. These two theaters were the model for the theaters of the eighteenth century. Indeed, Drury Lane remained active as the most famous of London theaters. In the early eighteenth century another great architect, John Vanbrugh, designed the elegant Haymarket theater, which proved to be too grand for drama and housed mainly operas, which were becoming the new fad. Dorset Garden, in the meantime, fell into desuetude. When Betterton and Barry led their rebellion against the patent theaters, they were forced to return to—and renovate—the old Lincoln's Inn Fields tennis court.

The majority of the audience of Restoration drama sat either in the pit immediately in front of the stage or in galleries that tiered up and back. In the pit and middle gallery vendors, including prostitutes, plied their wares. In the upper gallery servants could sit at reduced prices. The boxes along the sides and across the back of the pit under the galleries were reserved for the upper crust, including members of the royal family, who often attended—and whose patronage was both indispensable and conveniently protective from residual antitheatrical prejudice. This Restoration audience was not limited to Court and the fashionable Town (and their servants), however: it contained increasing numbers of the middling sort, from wealthy merchants down to apprentices. During the eighteenth century, the royal family was less in evidence, the middling sorts more.

One of the more interesting aspects of theater history of the period is the gradual resistance to control, culminating in the repression of the Licensing Act of 1737. After finances and politics conspired to collapse the two patent companies into the United Company in 1682, the management of that company eventually devolved into the hands of Christopher Rich, a professional manager with no experience in the theater. When leading actors Thomas Betterton and Elizabeth Barry and their followers broke away in 1695, they established a tradition of actor managers. Rich was ousted as manager of Drury Lane in 1707 and replaced by another group of actor managers. Meanwhile, smaller non-patent theaters began to proliferate, the most interesting being the Little Haymarket, where Henry Fielding staged plays attacking the Walpole administration. By 1737 Walpole had had enough; the Licensing Act restricted London theater once again to two patented houses (Drury Lane, run by Colley Cibber and his fellow actors, and the new Covent Garden Theater, run by Rich's son John), though entrepreneurs like Samuel Foote developed elaborate ways to get around the laws in lesser venues around town. Out of such venues came the most successful actor-manager of the mid-eighteenth century, David Garrick. But the enforcer of the theatrical ideological state apparatus became virtually directly the far more powerful Lord Chamberlain, who eventually quashed the upstarts.

It is essential to remember that the London stage was a profit-seeking enterprise, financed by wealthy investors, who were the major shareholders. Some of the leading actors and even playwrights held shares as well, but the majority of the workers in the theater were hirelings. In general during the period 1660–1737, theater was a profitable enterprise for the shareholders. Ticket prices early were four shillings for the boxes, two for the pit, one and a half for the middle gallery, and one for the upper. As audiences began demanding and theaters providing more elaborate productions, including operas and even entre acte and afterpiece pantomimes and entertainments, prices began to rise (though interesting subversions persisted, like not having to pay for attending only one act or getting a partial refund by leaving before the afterpiece). Playwrights were not usually shareholders or on salary, and they made a mere pittance from book sales, so their major income came from either wealthy patrons—a capricious lot—or benefit performances: if a play succeeded well enough to be extended to a third night, the profit went to the playwright. If he or she was really lucky, the play might extend to a sixth or a ninth night. Gay's *Beggar's Opera* had such a spectacular run that it is said to have made Gay rich and Rich gay.

* * *

One of the most important innovations of the Restoration stage was the presence of actresses. Previously in public theater in England the roles of women were played by boys. Like today's film stars, beautiful actresses were a great attraction. With their low-cut dresses they could show off their bosoms, and when they played "breeches" roles, they could show off their legs. They were not just objectified by the gaze of the audience, however; in their reciting of prologues and epilogues, in their asides, and merely in their making eye contact with the audience, they conveyed their personalities and enacted their own gaze of agency. And they enacted roles of significant agency, from queens to more private women of powerful passion and intelligence.

Great actresses earned important places in the repertory companies: the Marshall sisters, Rebecca and Anne, who dominated heroic roles in the early decades; Nell Gwynn, Charles II's mistress, who immortalized the witty heroine of the gay, lively couple that became a staple of comedy; Katherine Corey, the premier comedienne; Elizabeth Barry, the prima donna in the best sense, who became a manager of the breakaway company after the Revolution; her stage antagonist Anne Bracegirdle and her stage descendent Anne Oldfield; Letitia Fenton, who made a career acting Gay's Polly Peachum; the irrepressible Charlotte Charke, whose outrageous energy could not be contained within legitimate theater. The leading ladies were paired with brilliant leading men (and were sometimes married to them, as in the case of Susanna and William Mountfort): Charles Hart, the other half of the early gay couple; Thomas Betterton, the Olivier of his time; wild Jack Verbruggen and handsome Robert Wilks, who played the dashing young men of Revolution comedy and tragedy; Barton Booth, whose specialty was Shakespeare. Not to be left unmentioned are the great comic actors John Lacy, Edward Angel, Thomas Jevon, Cave Underhill, Jo Haines, and especially, James Nokes and Anthony Leigh. These comedians energized the ubiquitous farce of this comedy in ways we can now only imagine by analogy with W. C. Fields, Laurel and Hardy, Abbott and Costello, Guinness and Sellers, Belushi and Aykroyd and Murray, Chapman and Gilliam and Cleese and Idle.

Procedures

This anthology attempts to provide as many plays as feasible, especially from the aesthetically richest genres (comedy and satire) and subperiods (Restoration and Revolution) with a modicum of apparatus (general introduction, genre headnotes, individual play headnotes, explanatory and textual notes). Accordingly, we have included as many different authors as feasible, doubling (or in the case of Dryden, tripling) up only when a playwright excelled in more than one genre (Behn, Otway, Lee, Southerne, Rowe, Gay). We might have included more Dryden, who excelled in virtually every genre (*The Conquest of Granada*, for example, among heroic romances), but that would probably have cost us any Orrery; other playwrights who excelled in more than one genre might have been doubled up (Crowne, Trotter, and Howard, respectively, in political and personal tragedy and corrective satire, for example). And of course the great comic playwrights Etherege, Wycherley, Shadwell, Southerne, Vanbrugh, Congreve, Farquhar, Fielding, and Sheridan (and of course Behn) wrote more than one comic or satiric masterpiece. But we couldn't include everything, and we are grateful to Broadview Press that we have been allowed to include so much.

So that students might study chronological development within genres, we have organized the plays by genre and by subperiod within each genre. The subperiods represent times of relative political coherence: Restoration, 1660–1688; Revolution, 1689–1714; Early Georgian, 1715–1737; Later Georgian. We have fudged in a couple of instances: Lee's *Lucius Junius Brutus* and Shadwell's *A True Widow*, though produced during the Restoration, are proto-Whig and therefore belong in the Revolution group; Addison's *Cato* is on the cusp of the Hanoverian succession, providing a republican ideology that helped effect it in the face of Jacobite resistance. For the convenience of teachers and students, we have also provided a chronological table of contents.

Keeping in mind the primary audience for this text, students, we have tried to provide competently edited texts, modernized for their convenience. We have generally employed first editions, unless another edition demanded precedence, checking them against other early editions that might be presumed to have authority and against modern editions (whose scholarship has been enormously beneficial). We have kept textual annotation to a minimum, noting only substantive variants adopted or substantive variants of interest in other editions unadopted. We have simplified and often silently corrected and repositioned stage directions, though we have set major additions in brackets. We have also so marked additions to dramatis personae, to act and scene divisions, and to settings.

In order to maximize space for plays, we have omitted dedications and prefaces, referring to salient features occasionally in our headnotes. We have also eschewed the reproduction of the lists of all actors and actresses, mentioning only noteworthy names in headnotes. Those who wish to know more may consult such standard references as *The London Stage* and *A Biographical Dictionary of Actors, Actresses, Musicians, Dancers, Managers & etc.* More reluctantly, we have, in the main, omitted prologues and epilogues, since, witty and entertaining as they are, they rarely contribute to the thematics of the plays to which they are attached but rather most often carry on a banter with the audience over the state of the theater, the plight of actors, and so forth. Occasionally we have printed some on the grounds that they importantly relate to the thematics of the plays, to important political contexts, or to significant aesthetic developments. And we have retained (and translated) epigraphs.

We have omitted theoretical and practical texts about the theater; instead we refer students to the Garland series, *The English Stage: Attack and Defense, 1577–1730*. And we have eschewed a bibliography, although we have already mentioned here some of the standard reference works. Criticism is always both ephemeral and incremental; thus, bibliographies are always outdated—and hence increasingly misleading—during the life of an anthology. Students should have recourse to the various bibliographies on the drama and the dramatists—some reference books themselves, others carried in journals, from general bibliographies, like the *MLA International Bibliography*, to specialized, like *The Scriblerian* and *Restoration: Studies in English Literary Culture, 1660–1700*.

We have not glossed words that are in *Webster's Tenth Collegiate Dictionary*, readily available online. We have glossed words and facts not readily available to students, and we have provided a glossary of words not in the dictionary that appear in more than one play, and words that, although in the dictionary, have secondary meanings not readily apparent to students, and we have marked them in the text with asterisks; for example, *want** as *lack*, *parts** as *talents*, *glass** as *mirror*. We have not so marked repeated instances of such words when they follow hard upon one we have just marked. When Town and City refer to Westminster and London, we have capitalized them (and have also glossed their first use in each play) because they are specific, proper names for important geographical locations in these plays. Other important locations are also in our glossary: for example, the New Exchange, the Tower, St. James's Park.

We have modernized and regularized spelling and punctuation, although occasionally an old spelling will be retained for its dialectal flavor or its sound (especially in verse). We have retained dashes mostly to indicate pregnant pauses or (when preceded by another mark of punctuation) to indicate a change of subject or object of address. We have generally not emended grammar, but we have corrected foreign words and phrases, unless the mistakes are thematic, characteristic. We have occasionally emended a line for metrics' sake (preferably with warrant), but never by introducing elisions not in the original: students of foreign as well as English poetry quickly learn to perform such elisions themselves if only *sotto voce*.

We have regularized certain distinctions: for example, "Hah" is an exclamation, "ha" part of a laugh; "aye" is an affirmation, "ay" a sigh. Others we have collapsed as trivial: for example, we have changed all instances of "O" to "Oh." We have retained (or sometimes introduced) capitals in personifications: for example, "Heaven," "Love," "Fortune," "Nature," "Death" (but when the devil is part of a cliché, we have left him lower case).

Our principle throughout these procedures has been readability. We are not insensitive to original aspects of texts that might have facilitated performance, for example, punctuation that might have indicated phrasing. But we also know that published texts are not based, in the main, upon prompters' copies: those heavily marked with pointings and marginal stage directions—and excisions—all perhaps extraneous to the original script. Printed texts bear no absolute connection to plays as they were performed, any more than film scripts do today. Plays are always collaborative enterprises, refined through production, even from one night to another. If these texts are readable and therefore intelligible, they can provide the basis for performances in which the director—or the student—will decide how the lines should be read, how the play should be blocked and staged, how the sets would look, if only in his or her head.

One last word of justification for our enterprise here: We have tried, as have the best of our predecessors, to provide soundly edited and annotated texts. Others have provided texts, sometimes with a claim to inclusivity, with not so careful attention to the copytext chosen or to subsequent substantive emendations. For example, one series's reprint of *The Way of the World* is based upon a pirated Dublin edition. We do not claim that our texts are definitive. Students should have recourse to such editions, if they exist. But we do claim that ours are solid and, in some instances, are the only modern scholarly editions.

In short, we hope we have been of service to teachers, to students, to lovers (amateurs) of English drama.

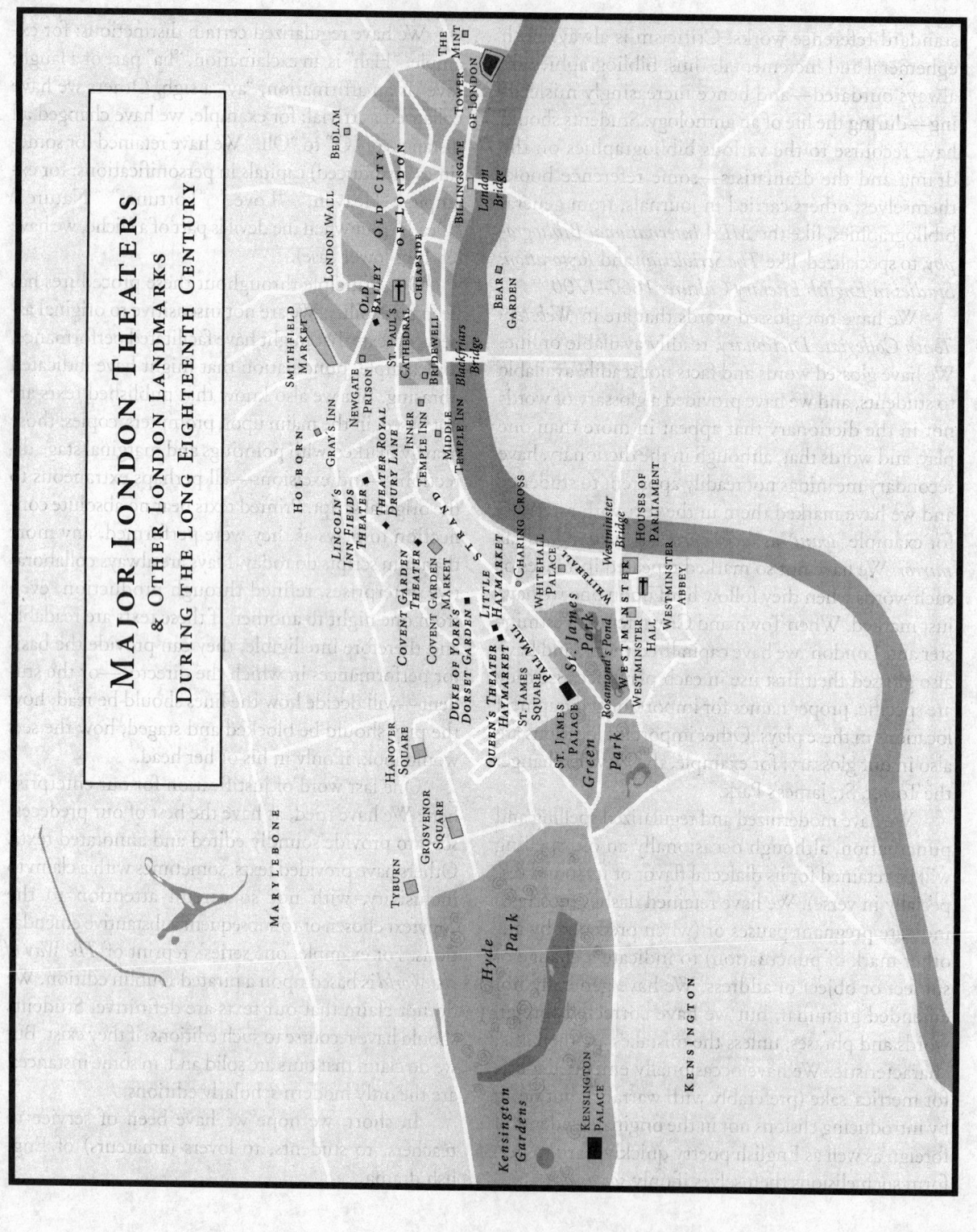

MAJOR LONDON THEATERS
& OTHER LONDON LANDMARKS
DURING THE LONG EIGHTEENTH CENTURY

Heroic Romance

Heroic romance pits heroes, representing hegemonic cultural values, against forces portrayed by that culture as threatening. Often those forces are figured as monstrous, foreign, other, but they are what Freud called *unheimlich*: seemingly strange but really at home in us. English baroque drama (late 16th to early 18th century) specialized in the character type of the Machiavel, the unscrupulous statesman or even prince (modeled after Florentine philosopher Niccolò Machiavelli's infamous treatise of that name, which preached that the end justifies the means). Juxtaposed to such unscrupulousness is the heroic code of virtue, honor, loyalty—supposedly underwritten by God. In the Restoration and early eighteenth century, a crucial issue in such plays, as one would expect given the political background, is who has the right to rule and why. Post-Revolution heroic romance begins to give us rulers who rule by merit and not by birth, who may even be outsiders. But the spectre of parricide remains, for the way to the throne lies over the dead body of the king, and playwrights still had to negotiate the Oedipal crisis.

The History of Henry the Fifth[a]

by Roger Boyle, First Earl of Orrery (1621–1679)

edited by Stephan P. Flores

With the première of *Henry the Fifth* in early August 1664 at the Duke's theater in Lincoln's Inn Fields, Roger Boyle, first earl of Orrery, publicly inaugurated the influential mode of rhymed heroic romance. Orrery had already written a rhymed play at the request of Charles II: *The Generall*—a heroic drama in rhymed iambic-pentameter couplets—was produced by the King's Company, opening in September 1664 at the Bridges Street playhouse. Samuel Pepys described the more popular *Henry the Fifth* as "the most full of heighth and raptures of wit and sense, that ever I heard" (13 August 1664). Following a highly successful first run, the play was revived several times in the 1660s, including a performance at court.

Orrery's play is not an adaptation of Shakespeare's historical drama. The play's dramatic action and dialogue often represent both Henry's desire to restore England's sovereignty over France and the heroic worth and legitimacy of such desire. King Henry asserts the Plantagenets' hereditary rights to three French provinces, and by extension, to the French crown. Such claims are expressed, ensured, and perhaps enforced through a series of obligations and conquests that produce military and romantic success. Orrery depicts Henry winning and wooing France and his subjects, particulary through the king's courtship of Princess Katherine, through his friendship with Owen Tudor—who is also his romantic rival for Katherine—and through declamations, debates, and political intrigues that ultimately culminate in providing for Henry's eventual accession to the French throne.

The cultural significance of these relations of love, honor, and friendship may thus be considered in the context of the play's—and the genre's—preoccupation with questions of royal prerogatives and succession, with concerns over reciprocal obligations and trust, and with how such dynastic settlements engage in the politics of sexual difference and exchange under Stuart patriarchalism. Playgoers surely were impressed as well by seeing lead actors Betterton, Harris, and Smith in the royal coronation robes, a sign of Charles II's friendly patronage, especially of the soldier, statesman, and playwright, Orrery himself.

During the Interregnum, the Irish born Roger Boyle, baron of Broghill, avoided going to prison for supporting the exiled Charles II, served in turn on Cromwell's cabinet council and in Parliament, advised Cromwell to accept the crown, suggested that Cromwell marry his daughter Frances to Charles II, and later worked with others to help restore Charles and the monarchy. Following his restoration, Charles II appointed Boyle Lord Justice in Ireland and Governor of Limerick, as well as Lord President of Munster; he created him earl of Orrery; and in due course he made him a member of the King's Privy Council. Orrery's heroic romance demonstrates the legacies of the English civil wars, the promise of the restored monarchy, and the pursuit of political settlements and stability that persists into the Exclusion Crisis of the early 1680s.

DRAMATIS PERSONAE

[MEN]

King Henry the Fifth.
Duke of Bedford, his brother.
Duke of Exeter, his uncle.
Earl of Warwick.
Archbishop[b] of Canterbury.
Owen Tudor, the King's favorite.
The Dauphin.[1]
Duke of Burgundy.
Earl of Chareloys, his son.
Constable of France.
De Chastel, the Dauphin's creature.[2]
Bishop of Arras.
Count of Blamount.
Monsieur Colemore.
Heralds.
Guards.

[WOMEN]

Queen of France.
Princess Katherine, her daughter.
Princess Anne of Burgundy.
The Countess of La Marr.
French Ladies.

[THE SCENE: FRANCE.]

The History of Henry the Fifth.

Act I, [scene i. The royal pavilion in the
English camp at Agincourt.]

*Enter King Henry the Fifth, the Duke of Exeter, the Duke
of Bedford, and Owen Tudor, with their attendants.*

KING.

This is the day in which our valor must
Prove to the French, our claim to France is just;
Since 'twill no other way be understood,

It must be writ in characters of blood.
By injuries they us to battle call;   5
Denying us our part, they forfeit all.
'Tis fit in number they should us exceed,
That odds the French against the English need;
That odds which both obliges them and me,
Brings them to fight, and us to victory.   10

EXETER.

Heav'n left us purposely but few for fight
To show the world, by your success, your right.

BEDFORD.

They seem t'acknowledge Heav'n is not their friend,
Since on their boasted numbers they depend,
Which when their cause is reckoned, we should   15
  prize,
As Heav'n accounts them, for a sacrifice.

Enter Earl of Warwick.

EXETER.

The Earl of Warwick in his looks does bring
Some news of high importance to the King.

WARWICK.

Arm! Arm! Great sir, the foe is in our view
And has a herald sent to challenge you.   20

KING.

Tell him, I in this field possess all France,
From which I'll ne'er retire, but may advance.
In vain they threaten war or promise peace,
They boast their numbers, which we wish not less;
They are enow both to destroy and save,   25
But were they more, they here might find a grave.
Take care the herald so rewarded be
That he may know his message pleases me.
Under their standards, as I ordered you,
Are all my troops fixed in the form I drew?   30

WARWICK.

They are, and like one face, all looks agree,
Resolving and foretelling victory.

KING.

Whoe'er a room to other thoughts affords
Injures our quarrel* and mistakes our swords.

WARWICK.

How short a time and narrow space of ground   35
Is't 'twixt your conquest and your being crowned?

KING.

To make both shorter, I will straight advance

---

1 Dauphin] Charles, third son of Charles VI ("the Mad"),
   heir apparent and future Charles VII (1422-1461)

2 De Chastel … creature] Tannegui du Châtel, an adherent of the Constable of France and the Armagnac party
   who saved the Dauphin's life and became his chief ad-
   viser (Clark)

And by two titles[3] wear the crown of France.
—Uncle, to your command with speed repair.
—The right wing, brother, does expect your care.　40
Both to the field of battle lead the way,
Whilst but a moment I with Tudor stay.

Exeunt Exeter, Bedford, and Warwick.

Oh my best friend! Thy sadness I must blame:
Canst thou now think on anything but fame?

TUDOR.

When I reflect how many dangers still　45
You must attempt, how many more you will—

KING.

Reflect on dangers which must glory win.

TUDOR.

Excuse me, if my duty makes me sin:
Since I no other way can grateful prove,
I'll rather show my fear, than hide my love.　50

KING.

That I to thee may proofs of mine dispense,
I now stay here, though glory calls me hence:
When fame, when life, and empire are at stake,
All thoughts of those for thee I can forsake.
Banish thy grief by thinking on that praise　55
Which shall thy name so high in battle raise
That all my future favors men may say
Are not what I bestow but what I pay.

TUDOR.

What you have said and done brings me relief;
This day I will deserve your love or grief.　60

KING.

Speak not of grief, but think on that applause
Which Heav'n does still* allow the juster cause.

TUDOR. [*Aside.*]

Why should he be by too much courage lost
Of whom alone this world has cause to boast?

Exeunt.

[SCENE ii. The Dauphin's residence
in a provincial town.]

Enter Dauphin and De Chastel.

DAUPHIN.

Let me despise what I can ne'er obtain:
I'll live retired since I'm denied to reign.

My mother, having got the regency,[4]
Does either hate or is afraid of me,
But I perceive by my retirement here,　5
I shun her malice and suppress her fear.
I shall (if I to Paris now return)
Her hatred feel, or which is worse, her scorn.

DE CHASTEL.

But shall our Dauphin, the undoubted heir,
Sit idly peaceful in an active war　10
And let his enemy the throne ascend?

DAUPHIN.

He who my wrongs revenges is my friend.
De Chastel, you have often heard me plead
That in this war I might the army lead;
On me so high a trust she'll not bestow,　15
And any other trust I think too low:
A prince whose soul as well as birth is great,
If he in glory cannot shine, should set.
From courts I am condemned to villages,
From noble toils of war t'ignoble ease,　20
Where undisturbed I'll for her hatred grieve,
And honor makes me rather choose to live
Equal with men not worth the governing
Than be at court and there not be a king.

DE CHASTEL.

Though I confess her usage, sir, has been　25
Such as not fits a mother or a queen,
Yet sir, consider, whilst from her you fly,
You more exalt the Duke of Burgundy.

DAUPHIN.

That fatal name my fury does advance:
'Twas he who murthered royal Orléans,[5]　30

---

3 two titles] both by right (see headnote) and by conquest

4 reign ... regency] Beginning in 1392 Charles "the Mad" suffered from recurring bouts of insanity, and during much of his reign (1380-1422) the houses of Burgundy and Orléans contended for power and influence. The Dauphin antagonized his mother, who eventually lent her support to John "the Fearless," duke of Burgundy (cousin to Charles VI). In 1417, Charles VI's consort and queen, Isabella of Bavaria, declared herself regent in opposition to the leader of the Orléanists, Bernard VII, count of Armagnac. Imprisoned by Count Bernard and the Dauphin, Isabella (also known as Isabel) was rescued by the duke of Burgundy. These events, including the Dauphin's own assumption of the title of regent, occurred two years after the battle of Agincourt.

And though the Queen recover my esteem,
No palace can have space for me and him.
DE CHASTEL.
Return the sooner to revenge that blood.
No man has well his int'rest understood
Who to enjoy it scrupled at the way: 35
He who builds high must low foundations lay.
I by the Queen for your return am sent;
Her harsh behavior she does now repent.
By kind submissions you may rule her heart,
And what's denied by kindness, gain by art;   40
With small compliance you'll suppress her hate,
When Nature's judge and Duty advocate.
Your absence, sir, has cast your party down:
Few follow those on whom the Prince does frown.
DAUPHIN.
Thou in all storms hast been my constant friend;   45
I'll on thy wisdom and thy care depend.
'Tis just I should to thy advice submit,
For he who makes my fate should govern it.
DE CHASTEL.
With this glad news I will outride the post,
And ere you come to court I'll clear the coast.   50

Exeunt.

[SCENE iii. Audience chamber in the
royal palace at Paris.]

*Enter the Queen of France, Princess Katherine, Princess
Anne of Burgundy,6 Duke of Burgundy, and their train.*

QUEEN.
This is the day Alanson7 sent us word
He would our fate determine by the sword,
Which he has hastened, hearing by his spies
The plague had so impaired our enemies
That more delay would make our princes dream   5
They should not come to kill but bury them

And France would be obliged for her defense,
Not to their swords, but to that pestilence.
BURGUNDY.
Since from th'Eternal Pow'r that rod is sent,
Why from his hand take we the punishment?   10
And this insulting, madam, makes me fear
Our ruin rather than our triumph near:
Those English swords on which he sets no price
Lately cut down our *Flower de Luces* twice,8
And to King Edward's piety9 we owe   15
The miracle that now again they grow.
QUEEN.
France justly might the English valor dread
Were it again by that great Monarch led;
We fear him less who now that crown does wear,
His wildness, not his courage, brings him here.   20
BURGUNDY.
Whilst his prodigious father10 was alive,
Some youthful signs of wildness he did give,
But when he early on his throne was placed,
A kingly soul his royal title graced,
And then whatever misbecoming thing   25
Lived in the prince, was buried in the king.
Nought should in us low thoughts of him persuade
Who does himself subdue and France invade.

Enter a French lady.

LADY.
The Count of Blamount from the camp with news
Does wait without and for admittance sues.   30
QUEEN.
Blamount so soon returned? Let him appear.

Enter Blamount.

Ill news is swifter than the wings of fear.
His looks to me a sad account have given.
Where is Alanson?

---

5 he who … Orléans] In 1407, Burgundy arranged for the
   assassination of his cousin Louis, duc d' Orléans, who
   was also the frequent companion and reputed lover of
   Queen Isabella.
6 Anne of Burgundy] Burgundy's daughter was Catherine.
   To avoid confusion, Orrery calls her "Anne" to distinguish her from the French princess of the same name.
7 Alanson] John, duke of Alençon, French general at
   Agincourt slain by Henry V in personal combat after he
   had split the king's helmet by a blow of his sword.

8 Flower de Luces twice] Fleurs-de-lis, the heraldic device
   of the royal family of France. The French suffered two
   previous famous defeats by the English under Edward III
   and his son the Black Prince in the battles of Crécy
   (1346) and Poitiers (1356).
9 Edward's piety] By signing the treaty of Brétigni (8 May
   1360), Edward III renounced his claims to the crown of
   France (his mother Isabella was the daughter of Philip
   IV the Fair).
10 prodigious father] Henry Bolingbroke became Henry IV
    (1399-1413) after deposing Richard II.

BLAMOUNT.

    Madam, he's in Heav'n: 35
    That glory cannot be to him denied
    Who for his country lived and for it died.

QUEEN.

    The brave Alanson dead! By what mischance?

BLAMOUNT.

    By the most signal that e'er fell on France.

QUEEN.

    Without disguise the naked truth declare, 40
    Before my grief be turned into despair.

BLAMOUNT.

    Last night both camps so near each other lay,
    As we not more for triumph longed than day;
    The mighty Martel lead not braver men,
    When he at Tours subdued the Saracen 45
    And with their blood washed France,[11] than did
      resort
    To the unhappy fields of Agincourt,
    Where many then with joyful shouts did greet
    The rising Sun who ne'er should see him set.
    A while both armies on each other gazed, 50
    Both at th'intended slaughter seemed amazed.

QUEEN.

    Could those who oft have bloody battles won
    Stand long amazed at ills which must be done?

BLAMOUNT.

    War's cheerful music now fills every ear,
    Whilst death more gaudy did than life appear. 55
    For various ensigns did unfold such pride
    That all seemed bridegrooms there, and Death
      the bride.
    The noble order in each squadron seen,
    The many warriors of a haughty mien,
    The prouder horses chafing to be rid, 60
    Who breathed the combat as their riders did,
    Made all confess that war gave death a grace
    And has its charms as well as beauty has.
    After a little pause they both advance,
    One to preserve, th'other to conquer France: 65
    Those who did proudly think the foe would yield
    Saw him draw up with order in the field

[11] Martel … France] Charles Martel achieved a lasting vic-
    tory over a large force of Saracens near Tours in 732 and
    thus stopped the advance of Islam into western Europe.

    And by a King advanced whose hand and head
    All the defects supplied of those he led.

QUEEN.

    How! Did young Henry dare to meet you then? 70
    We heard diseases had consumed his men.

BLAMOUNT.

    The courages of all the English dead
    Were to those few then living newly fled:
    So thin, so harrassed all his squadrons were
    As we did pity them we used to fear, 75
    For it is equally as strange to say
    That they durst fight as that they won the day.
    But Fame can want* no theme when she does sing
    Of English swords led by an English king,
    Nor was he only in the battle known 80
    By his bright armor, which like lightning shone,
    But did with nobler marks his valor grace,
    Still* being seen where foremost danger was.
    Alanson, who observed this wondrous king
    Courage to his and fear to ours did bring, 85
    Made fighting single with him his high aim
    And in a battle to a duel came.

QUEEN.

    By an attempt so noble and sublime
    He showed as much as I believed of him.

BLAMOUNT.

    Both nations at a sight so great and rare 90
    Their bloody swords suspended in the air
    And by a general silence made it known
    They in their leaders' fate would see their own.
    But though Alanson did stupendous things,
    A subject's sword could not resist a king's: 95
    Angels are guardians of that sacred name.

BURGUNDY.

    Yet by his death he got a deathless fame.

BLAMOUNT.

    That loss invaded all to that degree
    As we more fought for death than victory,
    For many worthies waited on his fall: 100
    The Constable of France, the Admiral,
    The Duke of Brabant, and the Duke of Bar.
    Promiscuous killing now disgraced the war:
    So glutted was the thirsty victor's sword
    As now the spacious world cannot afford, 105
    After so many heroes drowned in gore,
    Unless of English, one brave worthy more.

QUEEN.
　That nation still too highly you esteem.
BURGUNDY.
　Ourselves we best excuse in praising them.
BLAMOUNT.
　Now only horror, death, confusion reigns　　110
　And covers Agincourt's unhappy plains;
　Here corpses lie, where squadrons lately stood;
　Standards and ensigns there lie rolled in blood;
　Here woods of lances o'er the fields are spread,
　And dying men lie groaning o'er the dead.　　115
QUEEN.
　If truth consents to what you now relate,
　From this black day France may her ruin date.
BLAMOUNT.
　This is not all the destiny of France:
　The Dukes of Bourbon and of Orléans,
　The Lords of Domcourt, Humiere, Harcourt, Salt-　　120
　Roy, Fauconbridge, Noel, and Beausiquault,
　And many more of signal worth and race*
　The conqueror's triumphal chariot grace.
　But Bondile, who this day first turned his back,
　In hopes to wash away a stain so black　　125
　Assaulted with a loud and furious cry
　The unguarded baggage of the enemy.
　The King supposed new troops had took the field
　And ordered straight all pris'ners to be killed:
　What Bondile thus at first and last did do　　130
　Made Henry happy and yet cruel too,
　But 'twas a cruelty ourselves did cause
　And which his judgment took from safety's laws.
　For shameful was our fate, the pris'ners there
　Surpassed in number those who victors were.12　　135
QUEEN.
　Could nothing less than this Heav'n's wrath abate?
　It made us agents to our own dire fate.
BURGUNDY.
　The Destinies were never so severe:
　The fault, as well as loss, they make us bear,

---

12 the King … victors were] On October 25, 1415, when
　Henry feared an imminent attack from French troops who
　were plundering their tents, he ordered French prisoners
　to be killed. While the 6000 English troops were greatly
　outnumbered by the 20,000 French, contemporary esti-
　mates of the total of French prisoners make them 1500.

And by so strange a ruin make us know　　140
This empire to one field her fall may owe.
Were those renowned commanders now alive,
They might the fortune of lost France revive
And by their swords restore her dying fame.
BLAMOUNT.
　All those are living which I last did name:　　145
　The King did rather hazard a gained field
　Than suffer chiefs so noble to be killed
　And but with half his army did advance,
　Twice in one day, to act the fate of France,
　Leaving the rest to guard them where they stood.　　150
BURGUNDY.
　His valor sheds, his mercy spares our blood.
BLAMOUNT.
　Young Tudor, madam, much renowned you know,
　To whom all France her gratitude does owe,
　For he, when all did danger's face decline,
　Met it to serve the Princess Katherine.　　155
　He 'gainst my will this hated life did save,
　And when he heard those orders Henry gave,
　Fearing their rigor might extend to me,
　Above my hope or wish did set me free;
　He told me as we parted that he knew　　160
　I had the honor to belong to you. (Bowing to
　　Princess Katherine.)
QUEEN.
　'Tis Heav'n has strucken us, and when we know
　That hand, who dares want* patience for the blow?
　My lord, 'tis needful I resolve with speed
　Who shall the fatal Constable succeed.　　165
BURGUNDY.
　And counsel needful is how far 'tis fit
　After defeat to struggle or submit.
QUEEN.
　Assemble straight. Heav'n does occasion give
　Of mourning yet allows no time to grieve.
Exeunt Queen, Burgundy, Blamount, and lady.
PRINCESS ANNE.
　Madam, methought when Tudor's name you heard,　　170
　A new vermilion in your face appeared;
　That word did raise a trouble there as great
　As you discovered* hearing our defeat.
　Though these are signs that Love does for him sue,
　Yet to our friendship there is so much due　　175
　That from my height of faith I'll not descend;

I'll rather blame my eyes than doubt* my friend
And think I saw not that which I did see
Rather than fear you hide yourself from me.
PRINCESS KATHERINE.
　Ah, how this soft concernment shows you just!　　　180
　For what can be too precious for your trust?
　I must confess I blushed when he was named,
　But it was scorn, not love, my face inflamed,
　That any but a king, and crowned with bays,
　Presumed so high as me his thoughts to raise.　　　185
　That secret now shall be to you revealed
　Which only through your absence was concealed:
　With so much grief I did your absence mourn,
　When to your father's court you did return,
　That the same day I to St. Germain went　　　190
　To give in that retreat my sorrows vent.
　A storm o'ertook us as we thither passed;
　Rain made the rising flood to swell so fast
　That of the bridge it did the mast'ry get;
　An arch was borne away, and we with it.　　　195
PRINCESS ANNE.
　Madam, I heard that ev'n that sad mischance
　Did frighten you less than it frighted France.
PRINCESS KATHERINE.
　Tudor, whom Fortune led that way, descried
　What many more with vain compassion spied;
　They at the horror of my danger wept,　　　200
　He from the bridge into the river leapt
　And stemmed the raging current, till he bore
　My breathless body to the neighboring shore.
　Him to the court this timely service brought,
　In whom so many charms concurring wrought　　　205
　As I can scarce without some blushes own
　That I did grieve he sat not on a throne.
　For to a princess, who like me would do,
　He who a throne does want,* wants all things too.
PRINCESS ANNE.
　Ah Madam! Love, if it be strong and true,　　　210
　Levels the pow'rful down to those that sue,
　And when by inclination we are steered,
　Only what that does speak is fully heard.
PRINCESS KATHERINE.
　Tudor soon changed his cheerful brow at court;
　To unfrequented groves he did resort;　　　215
　Whilst others did rejoice, he sighing mourned
　And all his freedom into bondage turned.

This new distemper to a habit grew;
His mirth was ever feigned, his sorrows true.
The cause of this when I desired to know,　　　220
He made no answer but did sigh and bow;
By no reply he would his silence break.
PRINCESS ANNE.
　In such a silence he did more than speak.
PRINCESS KATHERINE.
　Ah! So he did, but yet I must confess
　I knew not Love could speak yet hold its peace.　　　225
　I urged to be informed; he sighed and then
　Looked often on me and looked down again,
　Then said, "You force me, madam, to a strait:
　To disobey you or deserve your hate;
　One of these evils does engage me now;　　　230
　Silence the first, speaking the last will do,
　But I implore you will not think it fit
　To force me unto speech then punish it."
PRINCESS ANNE.
　Against your justice, madam, 'twas a crime
　To punish what you did constrain from him.　　　235
PRINCESS KATHERINE.
　Then he his passion for me did declare
　With words and gestures, which so mournful were,
　As straight I did by my experience prove,
　That pity was no way to bring in love.
　A hundred things he said, but I was so　　　240
　Offended with myself and with him too:
　First, that his words I had constrained from him;
　Then that he could be guilty of that crime,
　As I forgot ev'n all he did relate
　But these few words, which I shall ne'er forget:　　　245
　"Love, of a wondrous birth, cannot expire,
　Which strangely in the water first took fire."
PRINCESS ANNE.
　None, madam, but a lover will believe
　That flames in water can their birth receive.
PRINCESS KATHERINE.
　'Tis true, but those bold words which then he spoke　250
　Did soon my indignation so provoke
　That never any crime can raise it higher.
　I bid him instantly from court retire.
　'Twould grieve your patience if I should declare
　All that he said his trespass to repair;　　　255
　Let it suffice that after that black night
　I never did admit him to my sight,

Nor will I tell you how he sought relief
And vainly since hath almost died with grief.
PRINCESS ANNE.
  Did you not give him then some sighs by stealth   260
  And wish his sickly mind a little health?
PRINCESS KATHERINE.
  All that 't had been injustice to deny.
PRINCESS ANNE.
  Sure that was love?
PRINCESS KATHERINE.
                    Oh no! 'Twas charity.
  Love is a flame which nothing can control;   265
  As souls to bodies are, love's to the soul:
  A pow'r which does all other powers o'erturn
  And cannot be concealed when it does burn.
  Had that been love, which is mistook by you,
  Tudor had seen and I had felt it too.   270
  But term it what you please, it cannot be,
  Whilst I have pow'r to rule it, love in me.
PRINCESS ANNE.
  Love to his height oft by degrees does rise;
  Sometimes it storms a bosom by surprise.
  Love moves not ever in one constant road;   275
  Oft, like a child, he acts, then like a god.
  And by your easy ruling him, you may
  Mistake his power for what is but his play.
PRINCESS KATHERINE.
  I doubt* you'd have me think I am in love.
PRINCESS ANNE.
  I rather would my fear of it remove.   280
PRINCESS KATHERINE.
  No, though I were, so much I owe my fame
  That to my birth I would resign my flame.
PRINCESS ANNE.
  May I, with safety, build on what you say?
PRINCESS KATHERINE.
  If my own heart deceive me not, you may.
PRINCESS ANNE.
  Then I will tell you something which, perhaps,   285
  If you are cured, will hinder your relapse.
  When dreadful Henry to this war was bent,
  The royal Bedford to my father sent[13]

13 Bedford ... sent] Before invading France, Henry V sent
  the duke of Bedford to parley with the duke of Burgundy,
  who also tried to arrange a marriage between his daughter and Henry. Orrery invents the romance between Bedford and Anne.

  Offers of power and treasure, with design
  To make him in this last invasion join.   290
  My father to his Burgundy retired,
  Having rejected what the duke desired,
  But said, since here unjustly we retain
  Anjou, rich Normandy, and Aquitaine,
  He would, if rend'ring these might peace advance,   295
  Persuade in England, and prevail in France.
PRINCESS KATHERINE.
  We then have done th'injurious Henry wrong:
  Do all these provinces to him belong?
PRINCESS ANNE.
  France can no other title there pretend
  But what, force having got, arms must defend.   300
PRINCESS KATHERINE.
  My grief for our defeat shall then grow less;
  Since we want* justice, we should want* success.
PRINCESS ANNE.
  But since to me your secrets you declare,
  'Tis equal you in mine should have a share.
  Ah Madam! Do not wonder if my heart,   305
  Which was entirely yours when we did part,
  Is from that high and blest condition flown:
  I, blushing, say, 'tis now no more my own.
  The Duke of Bedford, by the noblest force
  That e'er subdued a heart into remorse,   310
  Did with such joint success act his design,
  That I took his and then resigned him mine.
PRINCESS KATHERINE.
  Dear Princess, I shall now admire no more
  What you have mentioned of Love's art and power,
  Nor that so high in that discourse you went,   315
  Since you but spoke your own experiment.
PRINCESS ANNE.
  If madam, you had present been to see
  The softness of those charms which conquered me,
  You'd wonder more that long I held the field
  Than that at last I willingly did yield.   320
PRINCESS KATHERINE.
  The English archers may victorious grow
  Where Love begins the conquest with his bow.
PRINCESS ANNE.
  After we had this sacred friendship made,
  He told me, though his brother would invade
  This kingdom to regain what was his due,[14]   325

14 his due] Henry laid claim to Normandy, Touraine, and

Yet the chief conquest he designed was you;
He told me too, though England still affords
Beauties resistless as the English swords,
Yet none of them prevailed, though ne'er so bright,
Like your victorious picture at first sight.   330
Then he implored that, when to you I came,
I would prepare you to receive his flame:
A flame which all things else must needs outdo,
Since by him cherished and inspired by you.
This, madam, was the cause why I have pressed   335
To find if e'er your heart were prepossessed.
Let France, by you, be freed from her distress:
This happy union will procure her peace.

PRINCESS KATHERINE.

If me he loved, her blood he then would spare;
Love's gentle voice is never heard in war.   340

PRINCESS ANNE.

Yet like a king to you he does pretend:
Glory he makes his way and Love his end.

PRINCESS KATHERINE.

Where blood does cry, can I a lover hear?

PRINCESS ANNE.

When glory pleads, what then can stop your ear?

Enter a lady.

LADY.

Madam, the council is assembled now,   345
And ere it sits, the Queen would speak with you.

PRINCESS KATHERINE.

I come: too long by Love we have been stayed;
I will consider all that you have said.

PRINCESS ANNE.

Madam, be pleased to think upon it so
That France to you may her redemption owe.   350

Exeunt.

Act II, [scene i. The royal pavilion
in the English camp at Agincourt.]

*Enter the King, Duke of Exeter, Duke of Bedford, Earl
of Warwick, and Tudor.*

Maine (former Angevin holdings), to new territories, and
to the French crown itself, citing a right of inheritance
from his great grandfather, Edward III. In January, 1415,
Henry again pressed these claims, and in exchange, also
offered marriage to Princess Catherine. Charles VI refused these demands.

KING.

My lord of Warwick, you may give to all
The French of note the rites of funeral;
It is a debt which to the dead we pay,
Rewarding courage ev'n in those we slay.

WARWICK.

It shall be done.   5

KING.

              Brother, it will be fit
The pris'ners you to stronger guards commit;
They shall a court within our army see
And in it nothing want* but liberty.

BEDFORD.

They shall be safe yet have some freedom too.   10

KING.

Uncle, the great request I make to you
Is to preserve our wounded men with care;
'Tis by their courage we victorious are.

EXETER.

They shall be served with all they can desire;
We must that valor serve which you admire.   15

Exeunt Exeter, Bedford, and Warwick.

TUDOR.

Though this great day th'expecting world may see
Your title both to France and victory,
And though no conqueror alive or dead
With nobler wreaths did ever crown his head,
Yet pardon me if I presume to say   20
I see a sadness misbecomes this day.
This day, in which your friends and foes confess
Nothing can make you greater, nothing less:
So fixed are Fortune's wheels they cannot turn.
Then sir, permit only the French to mourn;   25
The loss of York and Suffolk, though too great,
Should not outweigh your enemies' defeat.
If, sir, your wars cost not some lives like these,
You would not conquests make but miracles.
Who in his prince's service finds a grave   30
Rather our envy than our grief should have,
And fighting in your sight, who for you dies^c
Is blest enough without such obsequies:
If to their death such envied grief you give,
You'll make us then repent that we do live.   35
Sir, for the living's sake your grief decline
And let your looks clear as your glories shine.

KING.

    So great a loss as is above relief
    Even on this day might justify my grief.
    He who of friendship knows the sacred ties   40
    Will value more his friends than victories,
    But that just sorrow, which thou wouldst remove,
    Is not a tribute paid to death but love;
    If fame or power only in me did sway,
    I could not have been seen in clouds today;   45
    'Tis love's fierce fire which does my heart devour,
    Less to be quenched than heats of fame or power.

TUDOR.

    She must do more than woman e'er could do,
    Resisting such a king and conqueror too;
    You, though her eyes should brightest beams emit,   50
    May safe in shades under your laurels sit.

KING.

    My laurels might a safe refreshment prove
    To any other heat but that of love;
    Their sacred force 'gainst thunder only lies,
    Not against lightning shot from conqu'ring eyes,   55
    Whose pow'r, like that of lightning, I have felt:
    My breast they wound not, yet my heart they melt.

TUDOR.

    May I not know who does my King subdue?

KING.

    Saying I love, I need not tell thee who:
    Who of the planets speaks of brightest beams   60
    Need not say after, 'tis the sun he means.

TUDOR.

    The sun by all is mentioned at one rate,
    But fancy alters beauty's estimate;
    Were it not fancy which that value gave,
    All lovers then would but one mistress have.   65

KING.

    Such adoration fancy cannot raise
    As to this beauty sight and reason pays,
    For he whose heart love can to ashes turn
    Must feel her eyes alone have right to burn.
    But that this ignorance thou may'st decline,   70
    Know I adore the Princess Katherine.
    Love's rebels by her eyes are kept in awe;
    She reigns in France spite of the Salic Law.[15]

---

15 Salic Law] medieval French law denying inheritance to
   women

TUDOR.

    Will not love's heat make glory's flame expire?

KING.

    No Tudor, it will rather raise it higher,   75
    For none should aim at this exalted state
    Who makes not glory first his advocate.
    This was the cause when Charles, her father, sent
    Ambassadors my conquest to prevent
    And this bright beauty offered for my bride,   80
    But with her, as her dowry, France denied.
    I shunned the match, knowing her beauties were
    No price for peace but the reward of war.
    My vows and passion she might justly scorn
    Did I not crown her queen where she was born   85
    And raise her boundless beauties to supply
    What a rude law does to her sex deny.

TUDOR.

    Perhaps your flame had with more luster shone
    Had you for it declined the Gallic throne:
    For love of her to quit in France your right   90
    Is more than 'tis to conquer it in fight,
    Nor can you hope her passion's flame to raise
    When with her country's blood you stain your bays.

KING.

    Dear Tudor, I perceive, because thou art
    A subject, thou mistak'st a monarch's heart.   95
    Those who from royal veins derive their blood
    Find only in a throne what's great and good;
    Sure nature in her would much rather see
    Her son than brother rule this monarchy.

TUDOR.

    A love like this was never known before: 100
    The father you'll depose, the child adore.
    Your love will be in proofs of hatred shown;
    You on her country's ruins build her throne.
    This strange design, sir, does my wonder raise.

KING.

    A love like mine moves not in common ways: 105
    Such unexampled things I'll strive to do
    That, when I reach to what I now pursue,
    When men name one who loved to a degree
    Ne'er known before, they'll say he loved like me.
    Prepare thyself to go within an hour   110
    To the French court as my ambassador
    And let them know if they resign up France
    (Mine both by conquest and inheritance),

They shun such force as cannot be withstood,
They show their justice, and they spare their blood. 115
Success now asks but what I asked before.

TUDOR.

He that at first asked all can ask no more.
Much is not in the proffer I shall make.

KING.

Yes, it is much to ask what I can take
And to accept from them that crown which I 120
Have giv'n me from the hand of Victory.
Tudor, in this they cannot but confess
I make my mercy hinder my success.

TUDOR.

It might be then convenient that I tried
T'obtain with France the Princess for your bride: 125
Since you as well for her as France contend,
Without her you'll not reach your noblest end.

KING.

She justly, Tudor, might my passion hate
If love's high int'rest I should mix with state.
If I this great concern by treaty move, 130
'Twill be below her beauty and my love.
That blessing must in nobler ways be sought;
Though Heav'n may be bestowed, 'tis never bought.
But that which chiefly makes me send thee now
Is that my friend should let my princess know 135
My flames are such as martyred saints sustain:
The glory of them takes away the pain. (*Exit.*)

TUDOR.

Was ever such a curse imposed by Fate?
His favor wounds much deeper than his hate.
I must unworthy or else wretched prove, 140
Be false to honor or else false to love.
To which of both shall I precedence give?
I'm killed by this, by that unfit to live.
But stay! Why should not I, even I alone,
Raise love and honor to a height unknown? 145
If, for his sake, my passion I forego,
In that great act I pay him all I owe:
Who for his king against his love does act
Pays debts much greater than he can contract.
Nor are these all th'advantages will flow 150
From that great action I intend to do.
If I her right above my love prefer,
In that, by losing, I shall merit her.
And to obtain, not merit her, will prove

Less than to lose her and deserve her love. 155
'Tis worthy of my flame, and of her eyes,
To make love be to love a sacrifice.

Exit.

[Scene ii. Audience chamber
in the royal palace at Paris.]

*Enter Queen, Duke of Burgundy, the Constable, Earl
of Chareloys, and the Count de Chastel.*

QUEEN.

The fatal cause why we assemble now
We by the worst of sad experience know.
Heav'n does at once on this our empire shower
All the fierce marks of anger and of power.
The King, my lord, whose head and heart and hand 5
Should be employed our ruin to withstand,
Under his old disease still worser grows,
Yields to his pain as France does to his foes.
Yet is he not unhappy in that state
Which makes him not to feel the wounds of Fate. 10
The Dauphin, whose green years make him unfit
In such a storm at empire's helm to sit,
Yet for that great and dang'rous place does press
And, missing it, forsakes us in distress.
As these two miseries assault us here, 15
So th'English late success fills all with fear.
Yet France, surviving such destructive blows,
Ev'n in her ruin still her greatness shows.
By your wise help she hopes yet to be freed,
And on your breasts she leans her weary head. 20
Shall we again by battle try our fate?
Or with the English king capitulate?

CONSTABLE.

Our shoulders but attend for heavier weight,
If in the field we shun to try our fate.
For doubtless, madam, he less virtue shows 25
Who yields to than who falls by Fortune's blows.
Rome, though she lost four fields to Hannibal,
Her valor raised ev'n in her fortune's fall.
Her steady virtue did all storms suppress
And made her Empress of the universe. 30
I would not doubt but we at length should find
A Roman fate, had we a Roman mind.

DE CHASTEL.

Those who too hastily with victors treat
Make them too proud who were before too great.

Such condescension would to fear dispose   35
Your subjects' hearts and elevate your foes'.
Let not posterity have cause to say
That you lost France—and lost her in one day.
CONSTABLE.
The chance of arms are still* alternative:
Fortune one day does take, next day does give,   40
And all the English fame will be o'erthrown
If we of twenty fields can win but one.
All thoughts of treaties, madam, then despise,
Which but excuses fear whilst we seem wise.
BURGUNDY.
Madam, what the great Constable does say   45
Becomes that place you raised him to this day:
He, who the head of all your armies is,
Safe counsels should obey but not advise.
If to my judgment you will please to trust,
Choose not what great appears but what is just.   50
Madam, it is alone by arms you reign
O'er Anjou, Normandy, and Aquitaine;
Those three, the noblest provinces of France,
Are th'English king's confessed inheritance.
Whatever of prescription gown-men16 write,   55
Yet length of time changes not wrong to right.
Why should you not, ere things are desp'rate grown,
By giving what is his, preserve your own?
Keeping those countries will at last be found
A gangrene: the corrupt will eat the sound.   60
CHARELOYS.
Justice is more than but an empty word;
Therefore, whilst that assists the English sword,
Success will always to their side resort,
And every field will be an Agincourt.
BURGUNDY.
Can councils prosp'rous be or armies strong,   65
Both aiming to perpetuate a wrong?
If after this fair offer he pursue
The war, our swords will act what his does now.
If he accepts it (as no doubt he must),
You will be safe as soon as you are just.   70
Pursue the acts of justice; those alone
Have pow'r to save and to exalt a throne.

Enter Blamount.

---

16 gown-men] university educated legal and historical scholars

BLAMOUNT.
Young Tudor is arrived and craves to be
With speed admitted to your Majesty.
By those few words which have between us passed   75
I find his message does require some haste.
QUEEN.
Know you what 'tis which does him hither bring?
BLAMOUNT.
Some overtures of peace from th'English king.
    (*Whispers in the Queen's ear.*)
QUEEN.
Yes, I consent, and give her notice I
Expect she should receive him civilly.   80

Exit Blamount.

My lords, I find your judgments various are:
Two are for treaty, th'other two for war.
Such reasons you for both opinions give
That I, with reason, either may receive.
But Tudor being come does surely bring   85
Something important from the English king.
'Tis fit our resolutions we defer
Till I his bus'ness in his message hear.

Exeunt.

[Scene iii. Princess Katherine's chamber
in the royal palace.]

Enter Princess Katherine and Blamount.

BLAMOUNT.
Madam, what I have said the Queen will own.
PRINCESS KATHERINE.
What? That with Tudor I should speak alone?
BLAMOUNT.
He for that honor, madam, now does stay.
PRINCESS KATHERINE.
Since by the Queen commanded, I obey.

Exit Blamount. Enter Tudor.

TUDOR.
Though, madam, this high honor does excel   5
What deeds can merit or what words can tell,
It shall no cause of new presumption be;
I'll not repeat what you condemned in me.
I then presumed to tell you of a fire
Your eyes did in a subject's heart inspire,   10

But madam, now th'assurance which I bring
Is that your beauties have subdued a king:
A King renowned by all the voice of fame;
The least he has of monarch is the name.
He only love and glory does pursue,   15
Which makes him conquer France and yield to you.
And by th'unhappi'st of his subjects says,
He at your feet his heart and laurel lays.
Judge what his virtues are, and what my fate,
Which makes his rival turn his advocate.   20

PRINCESS KATHERINE.
Tudor, what first you spoke made me not fear
That rival was a word I e'er should hear.
For you in that repeat the past offence,
Which made me lately banish you from hence.
If, by his worth, your king claims my esteem,   25
Why grieve you that you plead to gain it him?

TUDOR.
Ah madam, may I not your pardon crave
For grieving when I part from all I have?
A father when he sees his only son
Condemned to death for what he could not shun   30
(Though to the right of justice he submit)
May well be pardoned if he mourns for it.
By double dictates, madam, I am led:
My loss makes me lament, my justice plead.
But all my sorrows soon will lose their name   35
If you raise him for whom I ruined am:
A prince who only does, as his just due,
Deserve to love you and be loved by you.

PRINCESS KATHERINE.
Has yet the Queen aught of this business known?

TUDOR.
I had but leave to wait on you alone.   40
Those common paths of kings mine will not tread,
To see by picture and by proxy wed.
He'll make his court at an unusual rate;
His is a love of liking, not of state.
He^d says, he does not for a mistress sue   45
To France but humbly begs yourself of you.

PRINCESS KATHERINE.
I but by picture did to him appear.

TUDOR.
Yes, he has seen you in my character.*
'Tis far above the labored art of man
To draw a mistress as a lover can.   50
Your picture took his sight, but you will find

My words alone did captivate his mind.
Though you may think the pencil's pow'r is great,
It aims to paint a fire but not a heat,
Much less a heat which does from love arise   55
And which is kindled by his mistress's eyes.
The pencil to my words resigned the place;
Those drew your soul, that painted but your face.
Madam, 'twas I who told him how your mind
With greater luster than your beauty shined;   60
That from the charms of your discourse and shape
Men could no more than from your eyes escape.
And I may justly, madam, be afraid
He saw, in me, you acted all I said,
And to revenge that which you called a crime,   65
I on this embassy am sent by him.

PRINCESS KATHERINE.
Tudor, into a new relapse you fall.
You seemed to mourn at your love's funeral,
And I on that assurance pardoned you.

TUDOR.
I told you what was then, not what is now.   70
If other words have wandered in my talk,
The ghost then of my murdered love did walk,
And like a ghost to none it shall appear
But before you, who are the murtherer.

PRINCESS KATHERINE.
If you'll to my esteem yourself restore,   75
Let me by it be visited no more.

TUDOR.
Madam, I'll strive t'obey you from this hour.
But since the dead have o'er their ghosts no power,
If mine again the trespass should commit,
My last request is that you'll pardon it   80
And to so sad a love some sorrow give,
Which troubles you when dead as when alive.
But for my king I must my suit renew
And beg to know what I must say from you.
If to accept his passion you incline,   85
You'll make his happiness your own and mine.
Since you deny what for myself I move,
Let me, against myself, successful prove.

PRINCESS KATHERINE.
You may acquaint the King all you have said
Have in my thoughts a fit impression made;   90
That I (as all who have but heard his name)
Believe his merit has acquired his fame,
Though I with passion wish that he had chose

To raise his glory on remoter foes.
I never more can his address receive   95
Till from the Queen he has procured me leave.

TUDOR.
Why do you, madam, words so cruel speak?
Make him not for you to another seek,
Since in that way should he successful prove,
'Twill rather show you can obey than love.   100
Only to you let him his blessings own.

PRINCESS KATHERINE.
I have declared my resolution.

TUDOR.
To what then must the wretched Tudor trust?

PRINCESS KATHERINE.
To find his cure in what he grants is just.

TUDOR.
How can that heal him which does make his wound?   105
Yet to obey you, madam, he is bound.
But if hereafter you should chance to hear
Some dying sighs which may offend your ear,
Forced from him by the fiercest grief's assault,
Be pleased to pity not condemn the fault. (*Exit.*)   110

PRINCESS KATHERINE.
Oh! Why is love called Nature's highest law,
When title, man's invention, does it awe?
But 'tis the strength which reason does impart
That makes my blood give rules thus to my heart.
If Nature reason on us did bestow,   115
Love, Nature's dictate, 'twould not overthrow.
But reason is a bright resistless fire
Which Heav'n, not Nature, does in us inspire.
It is not Nature's child, but Nature's king
And o'er love's heights does us to glory bring.   120
As bodies are below and souls above,
So much should reason be preferred to love.
Since glory is the soul's most proper sphere,
It does but wander when it moves not there.
This makes that king, who courts me, France subdue   125
And makes me fly what else I would pursue.

[*Exit.*]

Act III, [scene i. The royal pavilion
in the English camp at Agincourt.]

Enter King Henry and Tudor.

TUDOR.
What I have said shows all that I have done;

The daughter by the mother must be won.
Those, sir, who, serving Heav'n, to Heav'n pretend,
By others' mediation reach that end.
She makes the Queen bestow her for your wife   5
That you may owe the Queen more than your life.ᵉ

KING.
That obligation, Tudor, I'll decline.
She shall be all her own that must be mine.
'Tis for her glory she herself should give
The greatest gift that I can e'er receive.   10
If from her will I differ, can she hate
My being for her int'rest obstinate?

Tudor offers to speak.
Go! What I told thee, Tudor, must be done:
He ne'er meets honor who does danger shun.

TUDOR.
A subject must not with his king contend.   15

KING.
My subject? Thou art more: thou art my friend!
Make haste! For I will only stay behind
Till I have orders for the treaty signed.

Exeunt several ways.

[Scene ii. A lobby in the royal palace at Paris.]

Enter Duke of Burgundy and Chareloys.

BURGUNDY.
No son, the treaty must not so proceed,
Lest of my help the Queen should have no need:
That envied pow'r which makes me useful here
Is the effect not of her love but fear;
Whilst things continue in their present state,   5
I can dispose of France and England's fate.
The greatest skill that I would wish from Heav'n
Is in a war to keep the scale so even
As neither party ever may prevail
But by his help whose hand does hold the scale.   10
Whilst these two mighty kingdoms disagree,
I keep in safety my own Burgundy.

CHARELOYS.
Have you forgot that vow, sir, which you made
To the English king when France he did invade?
That vow is to your honor still a debt.   15

BURGUNDY.
A statesman all but int'rest may forget
And only ought in his own strength to trust:

'Tis not a statesman virtue to be just.

CHARELOYS.
    Those words which lately you in council said
    Have on my breast a deep impression made.   20
    You urged that acts of justice are alone
    What can preserve or must exalt a throne.
    Is your own counsel by yourself despised?

BURGUNDY.
    I then for others, not myself, advised.
    Reason should still* appoint us what to do.   25

CHARELOYS.
    You'll find that reason has religion too,
    Which is by interchange of justice shown,
    Doing to all what to yourself is done.

BURGUNDY.
    You measure reason with a crooked line.

CHARELOYS.
    High reason to religion does incline.   30

BURGUNDY.
    Aye son, reason of cloisters, not of state:
    Pow'r seldom is religious to that height.
    Religion, too, not reason is but faith.

CHARELOYS.
    I fear, sir, if such dang'rous ways you choose,
    Instead of ruling both, you both will lose.   35

BURGUNDY.
    A harder game than this I twice have played,
    And though by Fortune I was still* betrayed,
    Yet still to greater pow'r I reached at length:
    Antaeus-like,[17] by falling, I got strength.
    Besides, De Chastel, by much art and pain,   40
    Has brought the Dauphin back to court again,
    Who offers, if I'll urge the Queen for war,
    We equally betwixt us two shall share
    All armies and all governments in France,
    And he'll forget the death of Orléans.   45

CHARELOYS.
    Oh sir, from such an offered friendship fly;
    What only int'rest ties it will untie.
    And I presume, though you restored him France,
    He'll ne'er forget the death of Orléans.
    I wish Heav'n sooner may forgive it you.   50

_____

17 Antaeus] A giant son of Earth, whose strength was re-
    newed so long as he touched the ground; Heracles held
    Antaeus aloft and strangled him.

BURGUNDY.
    Alas young man, if you but truly knew
    What pow'rful charms on sweet revenge do wait,
    You would have acted what you think you hate.

CHARELOYS.
    Beware, sir, I beseech you then in time,
    Lest his revenge may seem as sweet to him.   55

BURGUNDY.
    These tender thoughts are graceful in a son!
    I have our[f] interest, you your duty shown.
    I'll hear their offers, though I them refuse;
    When all is offered, I the best will choose.

Exeunt.

        [Scene iii. The Dauphin's chamber
            in the royal palace.]

Enter the Dauphin and De Chastel.

DE CHASTEL.
    Sir, I believe you now no longer fear
    That on vain hopes I begged your presence here.
    The Queen, while you retired, had by her arts
    So robbed you of your future subjects' hearts
    That 'twas your presence only could restore   5
    Them to that duty which they owe to power.
    Sir, Fortune too begins to pay her debts,
    For the Burgundian with your servant treats,
    And such an ear to my discourse he lent
    As makes me more than hope a good event.   10
    And, as a proof he liked what I did speak,
    He vowed he would the English treaty break.
    Nor is this all: the Countess of La Marr
    (To whom your sister grows particular)
    I have entirely wrought to favor you: 15
    She told me, and th'intelligence is new,
    That Blamount from the Queen has gained free leave
    Your sister shall a single audience give
    To one whom Henry sent with privacy.

DAUPHIN.
    His love for her will fatal be to me,   20
    Unless th'effects of it I soon prevent.

DE CHASTEL.
    I therefore have obtained La Marr's consent
    That you, concealed, shall in that room remain
    Where she this messenger will entertain.
    By that concealment you may clearly know   25

The roots of their designs and how they grow.

DAUPHIN.

Heav'n for my mother's faults makes me amends
In sending me a friend who gets me friends.
I feared my sister's pride, my mother's hate,
The English king's great love, and greater fate,   30
Helped by the subtle head of Burgundy,
Might by a fatal marriage ruin me.
But this permission thou for me hast got
May teach me both to know and break the plot.
When does this love-ambassador appear?   35

DE CHASTEL.

They every moment, sir, expect him here.

DAUPHIN.

Then it is fit I instantly repair
To that concealment promised by La Marr.

Exeunt.

[Scene iv. The Queen's chamber in the royal palace.]

Enter the Queen and the Great Constable.

QUEEN.

Yes, I have seen the Dauphin, but methought,
Though he has humbler gestures with him brought,
Shaping his looks to what he gently said,
Yet old resentments clearly he betrayed.
But yet, perhaps, those charms which courts attend   5
May to some mildness his fierce nature bend.
I will apply all that is taught by art
Or wiser nature to reclaim his heart.
'Tis fit you know, ere you begin to treat,
The King of England's passion is so great   10
For my unmarried daughter that I hear
He'll quit all he does claim to marry her.
That this is true the duke does undertake,
And you great use may of that passion make.

CONSTABLE.

Madam! 'Tis strange, for she was then as fair   15
When offered to him to prevent a war.

QUEEN.

He that by rules can judge a lover's heart
Has brought into the world an unknown art.
But having heard me, you must now be gone.
Should the duke know we two had been alone   20
(You having both ta'en solemn leave of me),
It might in him create a jealousy.

Exeunt.

[Scene v. Princess Katherine's chamber
in the royal palace.]

Enter Princess Katherine and King Henry incognito.

KING.

Madam, when first my king from Tudor heard
That you your person to the Queen referred,
He sent me hither humbly to desire
You'd to your eyes be just and to his fire
And would believe this right to both is due,   5
That he his fate should only learn from you.
He'll but from you receive his destiny,
Whether you'll make him live or have him die.

PRINCESS KATHERINE.

That answer, which by Tudor you have known,
Is, sir, my final resolution.   10
Nothing can e'er persuade me to forsake
Results which duty and my reason make.

KING.

Let him not be a double sacrifice:
You killed him with your words and with your eyes.
Heav'n meant that beauty, Nature's greatest force,   15
Having exceeding pow'r, should have remorse.
Valor, and it, the world should so enjoy,
As both might overcome but not destroy.

PRINCESS KATHERINE.

He who in fight has all the French o'er-thrown
Cannot be killed by words spoke but by one.   20

KING.

Yet he who has in France a conqu'ring pow'r
With joy does own you as his conqueror.
And, that you may not doubt that this is true,
He is in person come to tell it you! (*Takes off his
disguise.*)
I was Love's heretic till you I saw   25
In that which Tudor said and art did draw;
Now like an heretic I treated am
By Love, who has condemned me to the flame.
Your picture to resist I wanted* skill;
T'oppose th'original I want* the will.   30
Believe what of myself is told by me.

PRINCESS KATHERINE.

The King of England! Sure it cannot be!

KING.

Madam! By doubting add not to his pain;
You cannot but know him in whom you reign.

PRINCESS KATHERINE.
  Since he 'twixt France and all her safety stands,   35
  How dares he trust his person in her hands?
KING.
  He who adores you and dares tell you so,
  What is there after which he dare not do?
PRINCESS KATHERINE.
  To what a strait, sir, have you brought me to:
  I must be false to France or false to you.   40

The Dauphin discovers* himself.

DAUPHIN.
  I will enlarge you though you wicked grow
  In calling that a strait which was not so:
  For she who doubts if evil she should act,
  Does, in that very doubt, a guilt contract.
  No wonder now that France is fall'n so low,   45
  The daughter of it treating thus our foe.
PRINCESS KATHERINE.
  Brother! I nothing of his coming knew;
  His being here surprised me more than you.
DAUPHIN.
  Sister, when he revealed himself, your eyes
  Showed greater signs of liking than surprise,   50
  And, to convince me clearly of your crime,
  You doubted if you should discover* him.
KING. [*Aside.*]
  I shall want* patience to attend this storm!
PRINCESS KATHERINE.
  The only fault you should in me reform
  Is that I doubted whether I should do   55
  As it became the sister, sir, of you.
  But to the King Heav'n will this truth aver,
  I ne'er would have revealed his being here.
  My father's virtue to the world is known,
  Who to my falsehood would not owe his throne.   60
  If acts of treachery he does not hate,
  What he now suffers he deserves from Fate.
  Since, by fair war, France now assaulted is,
  Let her sink lower or by virtue rise.
  To abject deeds I'll never condescend   65
  Nor make the means unworthy of the end.
KING. [*Aside.*]
  Virtue a higher pitch did never rise;
  It has a luster which outshines her eyes.
  —Madam, in saying what you pleased to say,

  You broke that silence my respects did pay.   70
  —And now, sir, something I shall let you see
  To make you grant you injured her and me.
DAUPHIN.
  Have you a passport then for coming here?
KING. (*Pointing to his sword.*)
  This is my passport to go everywhere!
  Whoe'er a passport such as this can show   75
  Will find all places safe or make 'em so.
  And sir, it is by this that you must swear
  Not to reveal what you discovered here:
  This must be sworn, and sworn without a pause.
DAUPHIN.
  You should subdue me ere you give me laws.   80
  Yet, I will swear, but 'tis that to this chance
  I owe the pow'r to pay my debts to France.
  Debts, which so weighty were as I did bow
  More under them than France does under you;
  Those debts which by a cruel mother's sway   85
  Till now I to my birth could never pay.
  Fortune! And sister! Here I pardon you,
  For all you did and all that you would do!
  Since through her blindness and your treachery,
  Myself I single in condition see   90
  To make our France such a revenge receive
  As all her swords in battle could not give.
  I only grieve one false to France and me
  Should of that justice th'only witness be,
  But yet that cause of grief should disappear,   95
  Since seeing of your death will punish her.
KING.
  Oh could I justly think myself so blest
  That what relates to me could touch her breast,
  Though I should perish in this present strife,
  My death would be more happy than my life.   100
  But since no service I have paid her yet
  Can make me hope a happiness so great,
  I'll strive to merit that which you but fear
  By now revenging what you said to her!
  But yet, we should not fight, she being by.   105
DAUPHIN.
  That is the reason why you here must die. (*Draws his sword.*)
KING.
  Then, madam, you'll forgive me, if I now (*Draws.*)
  Defend that life which does belong to you.

PRINCESS KATHERINE. [*Aside.*]
　Oh heavens! Whom shall I call? Perhaps I may,
　Saving my brother's life, the King betray. (*Exit,*　110
　　and enters again with La Marr.)
　You broke your trust. Think on the King's high
　　worth.
LA MARR.
　Blamount's without and stays to lead him forth!
The King closes with the Dauphin.
PRINCESS KATHERINE.
　Go open straight the garden gallery,
　Keep for the King's escape that passage free.
　First for my brother in the lobby stay.　115
LA MARR.
　When he is gone I'll shut it with this key. (*Exit.*)
The King disarms him.
PRINCESS KATHERINE.
　My brother is disarmed! What shall I do?
KING.
　Your life, young Prince, is at my mercy now.
PRINCESS KATHERINE.
　Sir, for my brother's life let me implore;
　Nature speaks now as honor did before!　120
KING.
　I to your pleasure ever will submit.
　—'Tis to your blood you owe my sparing it.
　Your life I give you at the Princess' word,
　And for her sake, I here restore your sword.
　But sir, remember y'are obliged by me　125
　No more t'invade your sister's privacy
　Nor practice to obstruct that passion's way
　Which is a debt so due as I must pay.
　These not observing, my revenge shall prove
　As strong to you as she shall find my love.　130
　But if in both your courtesy be shown,
　What here has passed shall vanish as unknown.
DAUPHIN.
　Your fortune, sir, is great o'er France and me;
　Great is your promise too of secrecy.
　But if I can myself with silence please,　135
　You may thank that and not your menaces. (*Exit.*)
PRINCESS KATHERINE.
　I'll follow him t'observe which way he takes,
　Whilst for the King she the other passage makes.
　—Sir, you should stay awhile; I'll straight return!
　　(*Exit.*)

KING.
　Oh heavens! Why have I given her cause to mourn?　140
　Blamount, whose conduct did me hither bring,
　Will surely with a friend, and with a king,
　His promise keep, which was to see me out.
　I cannot his unblemished honor doubt.
　But I will stay to speak with her though all　145
　The world were to be buried in my fall.

Enter Princess Katherine.

　Madam, can you the cause in me forgive
　Which gave you terrors here and made you grieve?
　When you he injures not, much more than me,
　Your presence will his sanctuary be.　150
PRINCESS KATHERINE.
　I will forgive you, sir, all terrors here,
　If by your quick return you'll end my fear.
　To all your longer stay alarms will give;
　My brother's nature is vindicative:
　I fear from his revenge all that is ill,　155
　Here, where he wants* no pow'r to act his will.
KING.
　A greater ruin, madam, I foresee
　Than he, though in this place, can cast on me,
　If I from hence should to my camp remove
　Before I know how you receive my love.　160
PRINCESS KATHERINE.
　The first day, sir, you'll think it were unfit
　I should do more than only know of it.
　Nor have you any reason to despair,
　When for your safety I express my care.
KING.
　Virtue may make you be my safety's friend,　165
　But to what's dearer to me I pretend.*
　My safety lies not in my going hence
　But in that blessing you may here dispense.
　I would not safety without that enjoy,
　And with it, naught my safety can destroy.　170
PRINCESS KATHERINE.
　I will say anything you'll have me say
　Rather than keep you here in ruin's way.
　But yet, that what I speak may not appear
　To be the dictates only of my fear,
　If you were gone, I'd̥ to myself confess　175
　Such virtue and respect you did express,
　That what I thought an age had not the power

To act in me you acted in one hour.
Now sir, you should retire and give a maid
The ease to blush alone for what she said.   180
KING.
Madam, I go, but go so charmed from hence,
Both by your eyes and virtue's influence,
That 'tis impossible for me to know
To which I most of adoration owe.
But if the humblest duty, highest fire,   185
Which man e'er showed or love did e'er inspire,
Can be oblations fitting to be paid,
You'll ne'er need blush for what you now have said.

Enter La Marr.

LA MARR.
Sir, Blamount stays for you. This is your way!
PRINCESS KATHERINE.
She is your guide, take heed, sir, of delay!   190
Exeunt La Marr and the King.
Who can or love or reason's pow'r express?
One oft does more than th'other, often less.
Reason makes me a subject's passion fly;
Love o'er a King gains such a victory
As makes him venture life, and, what is far   195
More great, his growing glories of the war,
That he his passion only might relate
And from my lips might hear his doubtful fate.
Sure to return some love for love so great
Is not to give a gift but pay a debt.   200

Exit.

[Scene vi. The Dauphin's chamber
in the royal palace.]

Enter Dauphin and De Chastel.

DAUPHIN.
Oh friend, if I had killed him in that fight,
My glory I had raised to such a height
That, maugre all my mother's arts and hate,
I had restored and I had ruled the state.
All their successes had with him been dead,   5
For he's his army's soul as well as head.
Why did my stars so fair a hope afford
(Leaving, oh France, thy fortune to my sword!)
Yet not to kill or perish by my foe,
But both my life and sword I to him owe?   10

DE CHASTEL.
Your mind, sir, is too great to feel despair
For one ill chance in duel or in war.
DAUPHIN.
To be o'ercome would be the greatest curse,
If to outlive that fate were not a worse.
The first, perhaps, was Fortune's fault alone,   15
But friend, the last too clearly is my own.
DE CHASTEL.
If of that stain your heart has such a sense,
Let's wash it off in's blood ere he go hence.
DAUPHIN.
Should the first act of life which he did give
Meanly the giver of his life deprive?   20
Because blind Fortune guilty is to me,
Shall I, to my own self, more guilty be?
No, my De Chastel, though he be my foe,
Yet he hath still* most gen'rously been so,
And by no acts of mine he ne'er shall die,   25
Unless by such as raised him up so high.
DE CHASTEL.
Let me then, single, your revenge pursue.
DAUPHIN.
Who to a crime consents does act it too.
If it were fit, the act itself I'd do,
And what's unfit shall not be done by you.   30
DE CHASTEL.
I hope, sir, then the treaty I begun
Will put you in so high a posture soon
That the disgrace, which but a few now sees,
Shall in the eyes of crowds of witnesses
Be so washed off as shall your sorrow cure.   35
DAUPHIN.
Thy hope's uncertain, my disgrace is sure.
But what of good is meant for me by Fate
Thou ought'st to hasten, or 'twill come too late.

Exeunt.

[Scene vii. A lobby in the royal palace.]

Enter Warwick, and Tudor disguised.

WARWICK.
Blamount desired us to expect him here.
TUDOR.
The King did never show us how to fear,
Else we should tremble now at Blamount's stay.

WARWICK.
　Would love had led the King a safer way.
　Kings, in whose chances nations fall or rise,　　5
　Hazard too much in private gallantries;
　The odds against them checks their luck and skill.
TUDOR.
　'Tis true, but love's great gamesters reckon still*
　(Whilst boldly they the stake that's fairest choose)
　What they may win and not what they may lose.　10

Enter Blamount.

BLAMOUNT.
　The King hath sent for you. I'll bring you straight
　Where he is safe out of the reach of Fate.
　You must to horse. I'll tell you what has passed.
TUDOR.
　You free us from a pain too great to last.

Exeunt.

[Scene viii. Princess Katherine's chamber
in the royal palace.]

Enter Princess Katherine and Princess Anne.

PRINCESS KATHERINE.
　My fear did then my reason overthrow;
　I could scarce think, much less know what to do.
PRINCESS ANNE.
　Why did you not by positive commands
　Restrain at least the King of England's hands?
PRINCESS KATHERINE.
　Should I so much my brother's safety prize　　5
　As to procure it by mean remedies?
　Ah! Since 'twas only love brought Henry here,
　Should I have made love his murderer?
　The Dauphin to the King injurious was:
　Heaven would not let those wrongs unpunished pass.　10
PRINCESS ANNE.
　His wrongs more than your own your anger move.
PRINCESS KATHERINE.
　That's what I owe my virtue, not his love.
PRINCESS ANNE.
　I doubt* the Dauphin some rash thing will do.
PRINCESS KATHERINE.
　La Marr was to attend our interview,
　Who did, corrupted by De Chastel, bring　　15
　The Dauphin to observe me with the King.
　I from the terror of their fight did fly
　And met her, who to salve her treachery
　(Having a full command of all the keys),

Disposed their passage forth by sev'ral ways.　　20
　Blamount with all the friends that he could get,
　I have engaged to second his retreat.
　I hope my care in that will happy prove.
PRINCESS ANNE.
　Where there is so much care there is some love.
PRINCESS KATHERINE.
　I know not whether it be love or no,　　25
　But such great things he did both say and do
　That I, dear friend, insensibly am led
　To think that may be true which now you said.
　Who can, when such a victor will advance,
　Resist that virtue which does conquer France?　　30
PRINCESS ANNE.
　The proof he lately gave you of his flame,
　Madam, is such as is above a name.
　All trodden ways in love he does despise
　As things below his passion and your eyes.
PRINCESS KATHERINE.
　Condemn not then my being in some pain　　35
　Till I assurance of his safety gain,
　Which blessing that I may the sooner know,
　This proof of friendship mine does beg of you,
　That we dividedly ourselves concern
　Which of us first the welcome news shall learn.　　40
PRINCESS ANNE.
　I'll still* obey whatever you command,
　And what I hear you straight shall understand.
PRINCESS KATHERINE.
　May Heaven so guide the King that I may hear
　He is beyond the prospect of my fear!

Exeunt.

Act IV, [scene i.[18] A council pavilion.]

18 Act IV, scene i] Orrery combines several historic episodes
　in this scene. The speeches of Canterbury, Exeter, and
　Bedford are based upon the Archbishop of Canterbury's
　address to Parliament at London in 1414, in which Hen-
　ry's claims to the French crown and territories were set
　forth. In 1419, the Earl of Warwick and English ambas-
　sadors met a similar delegation led by the duke of Bur-
　gundy at Provins to arrange a meeting between Henry V
　and Charles VI to discuss terms for peace. On May 31,
　1419, Henry V met with Queen Isabel, Catherine, and
　Burgundy, but they did not reach an agreement.

The curtain being drawn up, the Duke of Burgundy,
the Constable, Earl of Chareloys, and the Bishop of
Arras are seen sitting at one side of a table, attended by
the French officers of state; on the other side are seated
the Duke of Exeter, Duke of Bedford, the Archbishop of
Canterbury, and the Earl of Warwick, attended by the
English officers of state.[h]

BURGUNDY.
Since all, my lords, is done by us and you
Which is, as previous to a treaty, due,
Delays in the affair should be abhorred;
Those impious are when peace may be restored.
Therefore, my lords, 'twere fit you would express   5
On what conditions you will grant a peace.
EXETER.
Those who our right and strength well understand
Need not be told that we all France demand.
CONSTABLE.
You would by mere demand a conquest make;
No treaty gives all that success can take.   10
This high resolve does more become the field:
'Tis nobler all to lose than all to yield.
BEDFORD.
And you'll confess it is more nobly done
By arms than treaty to regain a throne,
But yet my brother thought a treaty good,   15
That his French subjects might preserve their blood.
ARCHBISHOP.
That king proves well the justice of his claim
Who for his subjects' sakes is deaf to fame.
CHARELOYS.
Had we no plea but what prescription gives,
That were enough whilst any Frenchman lives.   20
WARWICK.
In pleading so, my lord, yourselves you wrong;
That can no title be but to the strong.
For what can a protective aid afford
Against the clearest right and sharpest sword?
ARRAS.
From what pretence soe'er a claim you draw,   25
France knows no right above her Salic Law:
A law which is both rational and old;
It never was by time or force controlled.
EXETER.
You but imperfectly your story know,

Or speaking thus, you hope that we do so.   30
That law (if made) was passed on Sala's banks
And was not made for France but for the Franks,
A German people who in camps were bred
And therefore still* renounced a female head.
BEDFORD.
A law which only from armed tumults rose   35
And which Heaven's law and Nature's does oppose.
My lord of Canterbury 'tis in you
To speak how France we challenge as our due.
ARCHBISHOP.
Philip the Fourth, as your own stories tell,
Had Louis, Philip, Charles, and Isabel;   40
Edward the Second did his daughter wed;
His sons did all to the French crown succeed.
Who, no sons leaving, Philip, the uncle's son,[19]
Did from the father's daughter take the crown
And kept it during injured Edward's life,   45
To whom 'twas due, in justice, by his wife.
That Edward dead, Edward the Third, his son,
Did in his mother's right demand this crown.
Crécy and Poitiers to the world declare
How Heav'n esteemed his sword in that just war.   50
Death, Nature's conqueror, did him subdue
And his great son, the greater of the two.
Soon after, civil wars[20] our isle destroyed:
Our swords against ourselves were long employed.
Whilst sick with civil war, pride's worst disease,   55
We bled in France and lost three provinces.
But now when those intestine wars are done,
We come here to receive or take our own.
BEDFORD.
You boast your Salic Law so just and old
That it by time or force was ne'er controlled.   60
But tell, I pray, what part of it decreed

---

[19] the uncle's son] Philip Valois, nephew to Philip IV, upon
Charles IV's death in 1328 became king Philip VI by lat-
eral succession. Edward III initially accepted Philip VI as
king, but revived his own claim to the French throne on
October 7, 1337, asserting that the Salic Law excluded
females but not their male descendants.

[20] civil wars] early War of the Roses (White=York,
red=Lancaster), from Henry V's father's (a Lancastrian)
seizing the throne from Richard II (a Yorkist) in 1399 to
recent rebellions against him, after which Henry V
consolidated power upon Henry IV's death in 1413.

That Martel should King Childerick succeed?
Or how it could, if not by wrested shift,
Make Capet successor to Lewis the Fifth,
When Charles of Lorraine should have filled the   65
    place,
The first heir-male left of your royal race?*[21]

EXETER.

'Tis true, the States[22] of France by their decree
Did call King Capet to the monarchy.
Who wisely then did royal int'rest save,
Making them think that what they paid, they gave,   70
For so to his just right he joined their power,
By which he vanquished his competitor.
Thus when by arms the Salic Law was tried,
Heaven judged the title to the female side,
For the chief right which Capet had to plead   75
Was that he did King Lewis's sister wed.

ARCHBISHOP.

From this great Capet, who that law repealed,
All your succeeding kings their crown have held.
By which, my lords, we think we clearly show,
If then his claim was good, ours now is so.   80

WARWICK.

Or if you grant the States by their decree
Can give to whom they will this monarchy,
If you their pow'r so highly will advance,
We need but conquer to have right to France.

BURGUNDY.

Since you, my lords, so pry into our right,   85

How comes your red-rose now to rule your white?
Blame not what France to that Duke Charles has
    done
When a Lancastrian head does wear your crown.
What by both sides may equally be said
That neither, as his proper right, can plead.   90
But if your roses Heav'n should e'er unite,
Then you may challenge France with better right.
None of the present line we will admit;
The house of York can only plead for it.

EXETER.

All of that house allow my nephew's right,   95
And under him they for this empire fight.
If Fate should them to England's throne advance,
They shall possess, with it, the throne of France:
By them as subjects he is served and feared.

BURGUNDY.

When they are kings again they shall be heard.   100
My lords, that all this vain discourse may cease,
What say you if, t'induce you to a peace,
We give your king the Princess Katherine
And with her such vast treasure we assign
As may forever all your title buy   105
To Anjou, Aquitaine, and Normandy?

BEDFORD.

How came such abject offers in your thought?
One ought not to be sold, nor th'other bought.

BURGUNDY.

Then know, my lords, the war you must pursue;
The sword must end what treaty could not do.   110

He rises and the rest after him.

EXETER.

'Tis to the sword we must have our recourse!
Where right's denied, 'tis justice to use force.

BEDFORD.

Pepin and Capet such sharp swords did draw,
As twice repealed this pagan Salic Law.
My brother then may charge it as your crime   115
If he presume to do it the third time.
His sword you'll quickly feel as sharp as theirs,
Since force must plead the right of female heirs.
My lords, farewell! We cannot here agree!

Salutes the English lords.

But they'll begin th'ensuing war at sea.   120

---

21 royal race] Pepin the Short, son of Charles Martel, the
    first Carolingian ruler to assume the title of king (751-
    768), usurped the throne from the Merovingian
    Childeric III, supposedly claiming blood descent from
    Blithild, daughter of the Merovingian king, Clothaire I
    (558-561). When Louis V died without direct heirs, the
    nobles and church officials passed over Louis's uncle,
    Charles, duke of Lorraine, to elect Hugh Capet (987-
    996), a descendant through his mother of Otto II, son
    of Robert the Strong, duke of the Franks, thus found-
    ing the Capetian dynasty. Hugh Capet also claimed de-
    scent from the Carolingian line through Lingard,
    daughter of Carloman (882-84), grandson of Charle-
    magne.
22 States] First formally convened by Philip IV in 1302, the
    Estates General represented the three estates or classes of
    the clergy, the nobility, and commons.

Their fleet's prepared and, by this morning post,
Our navy too does call me to the coast.

Exeunt.

[Scene ii. Audience chamber
in the royal palace at Paris.]

Enter the Queen and Countess of La Marr.

LA MARR.

So far this treaty has already gone
That the Burgundian did assure your son
The English treaty never should succeed,
Which with the Dauphin's passion so agreed
As he has offered him to share all France   5
And to forget the death of Orléans.
This, madam, but too clearly lets you see
They mean to force you from the Regency,
Which the false duke soon after will enjoy:
First he'll divide and then your house destroy.   10

QUEEN.

This service, my La Marr, is far above
All presents I can make you but my love.
I thought De Chastel had so fierce a mind
As he to love could never have inclined,
But in that thought I find I injure you: 15
This conquest only to your eyes is due.

LA MARR.

Madam, 'twas only love which could have pressed
This fatal secret from De Chastel's breast.
Nor would I e'er to him have faithless been
But to save France and to preserve my queen.   20

QUEEN.

Thy queen, half lost, thy friendship does restore,
And yet thy friendship must oblige her more.

*Enter Burgundy and Constable. The Queen casts her
eyes on Burgundy.*

That haughty Burgundy shall shortly mourn.
—Kind cousin! You have made a quick return.

BURGUNDY.

The dukes of Bedford and of Exeter,   25
Joined with their talking bishop, did appear
So much averse to all that we could speak
As we in duty did the treaty break:
Duty to you. We offered all you sent,
But only France can give their pride content.   30

QUEEN.

Since these bold foes take pleasure to make war
(Proud that they dare do worse than others dare,
And prouder with success), let us provide
T'advance our merit and debase their pride.

BURGUNDY.

Madam, in this just cause I shall afford   35
Th'assistance of my counsel and my sword.

QUEEN.

It is on those my chief dependence lies,
For you, my lord, both pow'rful are and wise.
Prepare for action and let treaties cease:
The wise may lose by war, fools lose by peace.   40

BURGUNDY.

The better to obey what you desire,
Excuse me, madam, if I now retire. (*Exit.*)

QUEEN.

He being gone, my lord, I'll let you know
What France and I do to this lady owe:
The duke has broke the English treaty now   45
That to the Dauphin he may keep his vow,
And false De Chastel made 'em both agree
Out of my hands to force the regency.
And then between themselves they are to share
The high employments both of peace and war.   50

CONSTABLE.

This duke does all my faculties amaze:
Yet still* he loved to walk in crooked ways.

QUEEN.

They all shall sink and their own ruin find
Within that depth which they for me designed.
My secretary Perrot understands   55
The art of counterfeiting seals and hands:
I'll make him straight write to the English King,
As from the duke, proposing everything
Which false De Chastel offered from my son.
Yet when all promised by the King is done,   60
Though less than what my son did e'er propose,
Him he'll forsake and with the English close.
La Marr shall entertain De Chastel so
As of the duke he may suspicious grow.

LA MARR.

Some doubts which seem perplexed I will unfold;   65
I'll say, he with the King does treaty hold.

QUEEN.

Which can no other way be brought to light

But by those letters ta'en which he may write:
These letters shall, though forged, authentic seem
And must be intercepted too by him.   70

LA MARR.
This will between them raise a jealousy.

CONSTABLE.
And when that seed is sown, 'twill never die.
The Dauphin's soul I never understood
If he revenge not this affront with blood.

QUEEN.
My lord, withdraw, and write with instant care   75
The letter for Du Perrot.

Exit Constable.
You, La Marr,
Shall soothe De Chastel with your former art
And subtly play yourself in all your part.

Exit La Marr.
Great troubles to a throne the way prepare,
And greater troubles must preserve us there.   80
Yet the ambitious envy those who reign:
They know the pomp of crowns, but not the pain.

Exit.

[Scene iii. Princess Katherine's
chamber in the royal palace.]

Princess Katherine meeting Princess Anne.

PRINCESS KATHERINE.
Madam, what news?

PRINCESS ANNE.
                    The worst that I could bring:
They have dissolved the treaty with the King.
Peace is quite fled, which did before but hide
Her cheerful face. The sword must all decide.   5
Thou forward hope, War's voice has called thee back!

PRINCESS KATHERINE.
I ne'er could think suspense was such a rack.

PRINCESS ANNE.
Suspense, in any thing, a pain does prove,
But turns a torment when 'tis mixed with love.

Enter La Marr in haste.

LA MARR.
Madam, I doubt* the Queen and duke have heard   10
Of that disguise in which the King appeared.
The busy whisp'rers run from place to place,
And fear, or news, is seen in every face.

Small parties meet, then to a throng they grow,
As clouds unite before a storm does blow.   15

Enter Blamount.

BLAMOUNT.
Madam, I left the Dauphin with the Queen;
They have this morning in a tempest been.
Their meeting was both violent and short:
Your brother instantly will leave the court.
He said he would no longer vainly strive,   20
But boldly take what some deny to give.
Safely the duke th'event of this attends,
And his apartment fills with guards and friends.

Enter Earl of Chareloys.

CHARELOYS.
Madam, just now I from the Dauphin came:
His friends are kindled with his anger's flame.   25
He is to sudden execution bent
To deeds so swift as he'll too late repent.
He puts on wings for what he will pursue
And says my father does usurp his due.
And fierce De Chastel too (which all admire)   30
Against his nature strives to quench this fire.

Enter French lady.

LADY.
Madam, you are expected by the Queen.

PRINCESS KATHERINE.
This storm will fall as soon as it is seen.
My lord, I'll strive to make the Queen apply
To this distemper a quick remedy.   35

CHARELOYS.
I'll still near my suspicious father stay:
Too much suspicion does itself betray.

PRINCESS ANNE.
Brother, I'll follow! Madam, we in vain
In storms of love of other storms complain.
Love's Queen did rise from the tempestuous sea,   40
Which shows that love in storms must ever be.

Exeunt.

[Scene iv. Tudor's pavilion in the English camp.]

Enter Tudor.

TUDOR.
By what the King related I may see
The Princess is forever lost to me.
'Tis evident she has her love resigned

To his great title and his greater mind.
Why should I thus what she has done deplore?   5
She did but that which I had done before.
But Fate, thou art unjust in making me
To quit the love yet keep the jealousy,
Which is of love's fair tree the foulest fruit:
A branch whose nourishment offends the root.   10
Shall jealousy a pow'r o'er judgment gain,
Though it does only in the fancy reign?
With knowledge thou art inconsistent still:*
The mind's foul monster whom fair truth does kill.
Thy tyranny subverts even Nature's laws,   15
For oft thou hast effects without a cause.
And, which thy strength or weakness does detect,
Thou often hast a cause without effect.
In all thou dost, thou ever dost amiss,
Seest what is not or seest not that which is.   20
Whilst thou dost live, sickness does thee pursue,
And he who cures thee needs must kill thee too.

Enter King.

KING.
    Tudor! You must not think my friendship rude
    Though it pursue you to your solitude.
    Some fatal sorrow has your heart oppressed;   25
    Divide it and send half into my breast.
TUDOR.
    What is it can invade me in excess
    But joy whilst I your favor, sir, possess?
KING.
    If my warm favor has your blessing made,
    Why leave you then that sun to seek this shade?   30
TUDOR.
    Sir, from your bounties I retire to show
    I would prevent th'increase of what I owe.
    I study here to pay my former score,
    And I avoid your making of it more.
KING.
    Tudor, I no such answer will admit;   35
    I must be paid with truth and not with wit.
    The truth of friendship has forsook the earth:
    Thou dost dissemble thy accustomed mirth.
    A sudden sigh does thy feigned smiles detect:
    Nature betrays more art than I suspect.   40
TUDOR.
    Let me not, sir, be for that shape despised
    In which I am, ev'n to myself, disguised.

KING.
    Friendship above all ties does bind the heart,
    And faith in friendship is the noblest part.
    'Tis ill, unasked, not to have told your pain   45
    But worse, when asked, if you excuses feign.
    Farewell, frail man, our friendship here must end.
    You wrong your honor when you wrong a friend.
        (*King offers* to go out.)
TUDOR.
    Stay sir, and to your virtue I'll unfold
    The saddest story that was ever told.   50
KING.
    Why with thy king should there such trifling be,
    With friendship too, which sacred is as he?
TUDOR.
    My grief is yet close pris'ner in my breast;
    Whilst there confined, 'twill only me molest
    But may disquiet you when got from home.   55
    Complaints, when past relief, grow troublesome.
KING.
    That grief does far all other griefs transcend
    Which greater grows when trusted to a friend.
    Friendship in noble hearts would never reign
    If friendship's duty should be friendship's pain. 60
    For ease of sorrow friends from Heaven were sent.
    Tudor, dispatch, and try th'experiment.
TUDOR.
    Why should you press me, sir? It will not out.
KING.
    Those fear their cure who their physicians doubt.
TUDOR.
    Force me not, sir, to tell you what can be   65
    No ease to you and yet a rack to me.
KING.
    Tell it I say!
TUDOR.
                I'll tell it though I die—
    I am in love.
KING.
                In love? And so am I.   70
    Is this the strangest story e'er was known?
TUDOR.
    Pray Heav'n you think not so ere it be done.
KING.
    Proceed.

TUDOR.

         She, sir, who does my heart subdue
Is by my friend adored with passion too,   75
And which is worse, his passion he did tell
To me ere mine I durst to him reveal.
And worser yet, that friend does me employ
T'assist his love whilst I my own destroy.
I lose my mistress if I condescend   80
To this; not doing it, I lose my friend.
But which is worst of all, I'll not deny
He does deserve her so much more than I
That should she, for my sake, make him despair,
She must be more unjust than she is fair,   85
And whilst she does admit of my address,
The wrong I do destroys my happiness.

KING.

'Tis difficult. What hast thou fixed upon?

TUDOR.

What I thought just I have already done.

KING.

Why then is so much time in sorrow spent?   90
For what is justly done canst thou repent?

TUDOR.

In what I did such justice I have shown
That I would do't again, were it undone.
But sir, I cannot yet that grief remove
Which springs from friendship that contests with love,   95
As after storms the sea does troubled show,
Though the fierce winds, which moved it, cease to
     blow.

KING.

No wonder grief's wild sea so high is wrought
Since in your breast friendship and love have fought.
But tell me now thy friend's and mistress' name   100
For whom yourself you nobly overcame.
He who you think deserves much more than you
I must conclude deserves my friendship too.

TUDOR.

Oh sir! In that your pardon I implore:
Too much is said; force me to say no more.   105

KING.

Tudor, that man must high in merit be
For whom you'll do more than you'll trust with me.

TUDOR. (*Kneels.*)

Forgive me, sir, if more I dare not say:
Let me in silence mourn my life away.

KING.

Rise, but no more I thee my friend will call,   110
For he's no friend, if not a friend in all.
In part thou show'st me what I whole would see:
A half friend's worse than a whole enemy.
Thy silence by a stricter way I'll break.
By thy allegiance I command thee speak!   115

TUDOR.

Oh do not think my soul is sunk so low
That aught can act what friendship could not do.

KING.

Thy want* of it, this passion from me draws:
Excuse th'effects of which thou art the cause.
No longer, Tudor, at this rate contend   120
With him who is thy King, and more, thy friend.
    (*Embraces him.*)

TUDOR.

The charming name of friend will make me speak
When, even my King, could not my silence break.
You are that friend whose name I would conceal;
Who is the mistress then I need not tell.   125
She too did this revealment, sir, constrain:
What but my pain could have disclosed my pain?

KING.

Oh why so late dost thou this truth avow?

TUDOR.

I fear too early I have told it now.

KING.

Thus to have used thy friendship breeds a pain   130
Which nothing can transcend but her disdain.

TUDOR.

But had I told it sooner, sir, to you,
Could you have then done more than you can now,
Since all I ask, for what you make me say,
Is but your pardon that I durst obey?   135

KING.

My ignorance alone has made me do
What love itself could not have forced me to.

TUDOR.

Though, sir, the charms of lovers' hopes are sweet,
Yet mine I freely prostrate at your feet.

KING.

My rival thus in love thou shun'st to be,   140
Yet thus in honor dost out-rival me.
I to no monarch e'er that glory gave,
Much less my subject shall that glory have.

If, Tudor, you would now suppress your flame
To show your friendship or exalt your fame,   145
That act on neither score I will allow,
For I'm in both as much concerned as you.
So greatly, Tudor, thou hast done for me
As naught can pay it but the same for thee.

TUDOR.

I cannot, sir, imagine your design.   150

KING.

To be your advocate as you were mine
And give you leave your passion to pursue,
And which is more, I do command you, too.

TUDOR.

Forgive me if this offer I refuse.

KING.

Resolve to take it or thy King to lose.   155

TUDOR.

Then I'll embrace it and dispute no more.
And give me leave a pardon to implore
From all the better world who lovers are,
From all who shall be so, and all that were,
That I against them did so guilty prove   160
As to consider aught in love, but love.

KING.

Tudor, this gallantry obliges more
Than all thy pleading for me did before.
But if I ever can attend again
That sov'reign beauty which does o'er us reign,   165
I'll give her then such characters* of thee
As shall outspeak what thou hast said of me.
We then will be each other's advocate
And from her sentence each receive his fate.

TUDOR.

Though this is more than I could hope, yet still   170
That which revives my hopes, my hopes does kill.
For when describing me, you please to add
All that you think is likely to persuade.
Even that a surer way will rather prove
To show your virtue than advance my love.   175

KING.

Fear not, you may succeed: though drawing you,
I shall but copy what for me you drew.

TUDOR.

Yet those will find, who justly balance things,
I only subjects taught, but you teach kings!

Exeunt.

Act V, [scene i. The royal pavilion in the English camp.]

Enter the King, the Duke of Exeter, the Duke of Bedford, and Tudor.

KING.

Our good successes come together still,
And as the good concur, so do the ill.
I have observed it, uncle, have not you?

EXETER.

'Tis, sir, as worthy notice as 'tis true.

KING.

This seems, methinks, t'accuse their ignorance   5
Who attribute our great events to chance.
For though it may, when slowly one event
Follows another, look like accident,
Yet when together many swiftly join,
It shows a power which rules us by design.   10
Whilst we succeed at land, to Heav'n we owe
The triumph of a naval overthrow.23
Brother, your tongue may claim the right alone
To tell what Heav'n by your brave hand has done.

BEDFORD.

But little fame, where many conqu'rors were,   15
Could justly fall to any single share.
When we had sailed your fleet in sight of France,
From the Seine's mouth the French did straight
    advance:
Their number pleased us whom it meant to fright;
We joyed at anything that made them fight.   20
But whilst to gain the wind both navies plied,
Both to the southward a third fleet descried,
Whose course, by bearing, to our fleet was bent:
We thought to them, they feared to us, 'twas sent.
When drawing near us, 'twas perceived by all   25
Their flags displayed the arms of Portugal.

---

23 naval overthrow] Bedford's victory over the French navy
at the mouth of the Seine in spring 1416 was in relief of
the besieged Harfleur. The Count of Narbon commanded the French navy. In 1418 a Portuguese fleet
aided the English siege of Rouen by preventing French
vessels from entering the Seine. As Clark notes, Orrery
transfers Portugal's actions to the previous battle while
placing this victory near the later date.

That prosp'rous king, your kinsman[24] and your
  friend,
His royal navy to your aid did send,
Hearing the French had rigged a numerous fleet.
KING.
This shows his friendship, like his virtue, great.   30
I am obliged, and more I could not be
Than by a debt great as your victory.
BEDFORD.
The valiant Bourbon, Admiral of France,
Shrunk not at this but swiftlier did advance.
That shout with which we did their navy greet,   35
Th'affrighted shore did echo to their fleet.
At the first shock, some ships we sunk and burned;
Our order soon was to a chaos turned.
The Portugals still like the English fought,
Envying our valor or else by it taught.   40
A thousand deeds were worthy in that fight,
Though not, sir, of your hands yet of your sight.
But what the French performed, worthy your praise,
Served but the more your glory, sir, to raise.
For your resistless genius* there did reign   45
And made us gather laurels on the main:
As prosp'rous stars, though absent to the sense,
Bless those they shine for by their influence.
Five hundred ships were sunk or taken there,
Whose flags seem wreaths for you, the conqueror.   50
KING.
This high success at sea, which Heav'n has sent,
Has made me master of that element.
When monarchs have at land a battle lost,
It may, to raise new troops, some treasure cost.
But to repair lost fleets is not so cheap;   55
Woods are a crop which men but once can reap.
That prince whose flags are bowed to on the seas
Of all kings' shores keeps in his hand the keys:
No king can him, he may all kings invade,
And on his will depends their peace and trade.
Trade, which does kings' and subjects' wealth   60
  increase;

---

24 kinsman] Behind the action of Orrery's play runs a contemporary political analogy that surfaces here: Charles
II's brother, James, duke of York, was Admiral of the
Fleet; Charles had just married Catherine of Braganza,
a Portuguese princess.

Trade, which more necessary is than peace.
EXETER.
If the world's trade may to our hand be brought,
Though purchased by a war, 'tis cheaply bought.
TUDOR.
He who an island rules and not the sea
Is not a king and may a pris'ner be.   65
BEDFORD.
In this victorious fleet your parliament
Have such supplies of men and treasure sent
That France will now in humble posture seek
The treaty which her former pride did break.
KING.
Those loyal limbs[i] will not their head forsake;   70
My glory they their own kind int'rest make.
Their love does with their duty nobly strive,
And giving thus, unasked, they doubly give.
—Oh Tudor! Though my sword at land and sea
Does conquer others, Love does conquer me.   75
Whilst under his resistless pow'r I groan,
Fate cannot make me joyful with a crown.
TUDOR.
May still* the greatness of your fame increase,
And for your quiet, may your love grow less.

Enter Warwick.

WARWICK.
From the French court Count Blamount, sir, is sent   80
And newly is alighted at your tent.
KING.
Admit him, but he soon may hasten home
If from the false Burgundian he is come:

Exit Warwick.

A prince worthy of nothing but of hate,
Early in promise, in performance late;   85
He cheaply rates my honor with his own
And meanly thinks that I would sell a crown.
In wronging his high birth he injures me
And gives my sword a right to Burgundy.

Enter Warwick, Blamount, Chareloys disguised.

BLAMOUNT.
If a surprising wonder may be news,   90
Such as does joy and horror too infuse,
I bring it, sir, for he whose head and sword

Made war and peace the creatures of his word,
The great Burgundian, who in France did reign,
Is by appointment of the Dauphin slain.[25]   95

KING.

Heaven's hand is sure, though it the stroke defer.

BLAMOUNT.

The face of France does full of change appear.

KING.

This murder sudden was. But what late crime
Could urge the Dauphin thus to murder him?

BLAMOUNT.

The duke (who said, treaties would ne'er advance   100
That peace with you which was desired by France)
Did therefore for the Dauphin's friendship sue.
Iyon appointed was for interview,
To which the duke did instantly repair,
There to resolve how to contrive the war.   105
The Dauphin met at the appointed time,
But whilst the duke humbly saluted* him,
De Chastel, unprovoked by deed or word,
In the duke's heart did sheath his guilty sword.
And then the Dauphin publicly did own   110
That this strange act by his command was done
And said it was a justice due to France
Because the duke had murdered Orléans.

KING.

Through what false optics do men's passions look?
In this wild justice he out-sinned the duke.   115

BLAMOUNT.

De Chastel talked (though few did credit it)
Of letters taken which the duke had writ
And, the express confessed,ʲ to you were meant,
In which he offered (if you would consent
To what he there, sir, did propose to you)   120
He would unthrone the King and Dauphin too.

KING.

I by the duke have been so coarsely used

That what he had proposed I had refused.
Will not the son revenge the father's fall?

Chareloys pulls off his diguise.

CHARELOYS.

Yes sir, and does for your assistance call.   125
The blood of sov'reign princes basely spilt
Calls loud to monarchs to revenge the guilt.
My reason, not my passion, makes me fly
From a false friend to a brave enemy.
If you'll revenge high blood, ignobly shed,   130
The crown of France I'll settle on your head.
And when you wed the Princess Katherine,
The States shall then entail it on your line.
Of those most are my friends and my allies,
And they are all so noble and so wise   135
That with one voice they will aloud disdain
The proud injustice of a murd'rer's reign.

KING.

Your father's faults I'll cast into his grave
And will revenge that blood I could not save.
And since you are so generous* and just   140
That without treaty you my honor trust,
You shall, sir, on a king's unblemished word
Enjoy my friendship and engage my sword.

CHARELOYS.

Where faith is wanting* this would satisfy,
On which, as on truth's pillars, I rely.   145

KING.

Th'example of your worth will make a friend.
But what, sir, does the Dauphin now intend?

CHARELOYS.

This fatal murder, sir, he did design
Just when the Queen, the Princess Katherine,
My sister Anne, and I (t'avoid the heat   150
And noise of Paris) did to Meaux retreat.
Some troops to seize on us he thither sent.
One of their leaders (as to Meaux they went,
Being my private friend) did by a post
Tell me, unless we fled, we all were lost   155
And that we should not then t'wards Paris fly,
For on that road some other troops did lie
To intercept us if we thither fled.

KING.

This root of mischief soon will shoot and spread.

---

25 slain] Burgundy, who had allied with the queen to regain
Paris from the Armagnacs in 1418, met the Dauphin on
10 September 1419 at the bridge of Montereau, where
the river Yonne falls into the Seine. Du Châtel struck
Burgundy with a battle-axe, thereby avenging his former
master, Louis of Orléans; the Dauphin's followers also ran
the duke through with their swords. In consequence, the
new duke of Burgundy, Philip the Good, aligned his
party with the English.

CHARELOYS.

    At this I found the Queen's amazement great,   160

    For being now cut off from her retreat,

    Her wisdom could not teach her what to do.

    I then proposed we all should fly to you

    As the securest way to 'scape his rage

    And so your virtue by our trust engage: 165

    Virtue so known as would her fears control.

KING.

    Trust is the strongest bond upon the soul:

    That sacred tie has virtue oft begot;

    It binds where 'tis and makes it where 'twas not.

CHARELOYS.

    I said she might, to break her son's design,   170

    Give you for bride the Princess Katherine

    And urge th'Estates t'entail the crown on you:

    This to your right, that to your love, is due.

    This done, what could resist your arms and mine?

    As she considered how she should incline,   175

    Clermount came in, disguised, in whose known

      care

    Her wealth and jewels lay, who did declare

    Her treasure was surprised by some who said

    That they the Dauphin in that act obeyed,[26]

    Who would employ that wealth, vilely procured,   180

    So as that France should have her peace assured.

KING.

    The Dauphin, in his rage or want, has done

    What was below him as a prince or son.

CHARELOYS.

    Though she this wrong and loss did calmly bear,

    Yet the high dictates of revenge and fear   185

    Made her resolve immediately to do

    What I with reason first advised her to.

    And now at Troyes the Queen and Princess are,

    To which the Dauphin will transport the war.

    A garrison of mine secures that town,   190

    And since 'tis mine you know it is your own.

KING.

    'Tis chiefly to your favor I must owe

    My being blest in love and conquest too.

CHARELOYS.

    'Twere fit, sir, that you sent some troops of horse

    The garrison of Troyes to reinforce.   195

KING.

    I'll lead them, sir, myself. All that are mine

    In France are but the guards of Katherine.

    My duty else she might in question bring.

CHARELOYS.

    'Tis spoken like a lover and a king.

    Blamount I'll send before that she may know   200

    What honor to her you intend to do.

Exit Blamount.

    When you to Troyes are come, it shall appear

    I will perform more than I promised here.

KING.

    You may augment my debt as you think fit,

    But nothing can increase my sense of it,   205

    Unless your favor, sir, I could incline

    To make my brother's joys keep time with mine:

    His love to Princess Anne wants* your consent.

CHARELOYS.

    She made me in their loves her confidant,

    And in your brother I shall think her blest.[27]   210

KING.

    This, sir, unites our bloods and interest.

BEDFORD.

    This grant (great Prince) my happiness secures.

KING.

    It makes my happiness as much as yours.

    —Now, Tudor, if our prosp'rous stars design

    That we shall both see beauteous Katherine,   215

    I will perform all that I promised thee,

    And when thy story she has heard from me

    (In which by all her truth I'll do thee right),

    We then our supplications will unite

    That she (our judge) will only him prefer   220

    Whom she believes is least unworthy her,

    Without regarding in the cause we bring

    That thou my subject art or I thy king.

TUDOR.

    In virtue, sir, so much you me outshine

    That you all other motives may decline.   225

---

26 obeyed] As Clark notes, the Dauphin seized the queen's treasures in 1417, acting on information supplied by the Count of Armagnac.

27 blest] John of Lancaster, duke of Bedford married a sister of Philip of Burgundy.

KING.

Brother, 'tis fit the duke, with you and I,
Should on the Princess wait immediately.
Tudor's brigade the Princess' guard shall be,
And with the army you must follow me.

Exeunt.

[Scene ii. Audience chamber
in the royal palace at Troyes.]

Enter Queen, Princess Katherine, Princess Anne,
Countess La Marr.

QUEEN.

Our sins make us defenseless, and we fly
For our protection to our enemy.
Thy laws, oh Heav'n, have I offended so
That thou hast made my son my greatest foe?
Into the world I have the monster brought,   5
And now no suff'rings can transcend that fault.

PRINCESS KATHERINE.

Madam, you make, whilst thus you bear his crime,
Our grief more just for you than yours for him.

LA MARR.

If he should hear you grieve in this excess,
The triumph of his malice would increase.   10

PRINCESS ANNE.

My duty has th'assault of grief withstood,
For since his fury shed my father's blood,
That wasted time which you employ to grieve
I to designed revenge more justly give.
Let all your sorrow in such thoughts expire.   15

QUEEN.

Grief is the fuel and revenge the fire.

PRINCESS ANNE.

Think then on all the crimes which he has done
And let those thoughts cancel the name of son.

QUEEN.

Since fall'n so low from what is great or good,
I hate his crimes more than I love his blood.   20

Enter Blamount.

BLAMOUNT.

Madam, my duty has provoked my speed.
The King and duke most strictly are agreed,
And both this night will wait upon you here.

QUEEN.

This happy news suppresses all my fear

And makes me hope, assisted by their fate,   25
That I shall live to punish what I hate.

BLAMOUNT.

Those troops, now on their march, he does design
As guards t'attend the Princess Katherine
And therefore would not send but leads them here,
That his respect and love may both appear.   30

QUEEN.

We were, when to this monarch we did trust,
Kind to ourselves and to his virtue just.
—Blamount, for his reception straight prepare
All that can joy and our respect declare.
—Daughter, you must a while retire with me;   35
I have some words which need your privacy.

Exeunt.

[Scene iii. A lobby in the palace
of the Estates General at Paris.]

Enter Constable and Bishop of Arras.

ARRAS.

Our Ecclesiastic States are all agreed:
This day the Dauphin for his bloody deed
Will summoned be to answer what was done.[28]

CONSTABLE.

I have the Peers to that conclusion won,
And those who represent the Commons too   5
Will now not slowly yield to what we do.
I'll lose my judgment if he dares appear.

ARRAS.

He loses his, and life, in coming here;
This murder has incensed them to the height.

CONSTABLE.

All hate a prince who violates his faith.   10
The people's temper does occasion give
T'obey those orders we did now receive.
I find already that the most incline
The King should marry Princess Katherine
And on their issue would the crown entail.   15

---

28 what was done] Clark notes that on 22 September 1419
the three estates met in Paris and swore "to prosecute the
cause of vengeance and reparation against those guilty of
the death and homicide of the late duke of Burgundy."
Henry's succession to the crown of France, however, was
not determined at this assembly.

ARRAS.

    The Dauphin's crime will make that King prevail.

CONSTABLE.

    Rather than bow beneath a murd'rer's pow'r

    Let's to the throne advance our conqueror:

    The Queen and duke expect it at your hands.

ARRAS.

    I never durst obey unjust commands.   20

CONSTABLE.

    Do you then think that those commands are such?

ARRAS.

    If you think so, my lord, you wrong me much.

    My judgment by a better guide was led

    When I your annals and records had read:

    For then I doubted* that since Charles the Fair[29]   25

    Our kings insensibly usurpers were.

    The crown (if truth did dictate what I read)

    Belonged to the victorious Edward's head,

    Which no prescription from his line should take.

    I'll therefore to this change no scruple make.   30

    But if the Dauphin were the rightful heir,

    You might of my obedience then despair,

    For reason's maxim I must ever own:

    No king can make a forfeit of his crown.

    Much less can I admit the States' decree   35

    Has power to give away this monarchy.

CONSTABLE.

    My justice shall, now I am taught by you,

    Perform what I resolved revenge should do.

    My lord, let's go where all our friends are met,

    And jointly pay to Heav'n this double debt.   40

Exeunt.

[Scene iv. Audience chamber
in the royal palace at Troyes.]

Enter King, Princess Katherine, Tudor.

KING.

    Madam, I have injurious been to him

    As far as ignorance could make a crime:

    I did employ him in my suit to you

    But knew not then that he adored you too.

    But I declare (which some amends may be)   5

---

29 Since Charles the Fair] since Charles was succeeded in
    1328 by Philip of Valois instead of by the son of Isabella's
    husband, Edward III of England.

    That he, at least, in all things equals me

    Unless in title, but 'tis greater far

    A crown to merit than a crown to wear.

    Can title in that balance e'er prevail

    Where love is merit and you hold the scale?   10

    I waive whatever may your favor move

    Except the title of the highest love.

    —Speak for thyself if I have lessened thee.

TUDOR.

    Only my silence, sir, should plead for me.

KING.

    Thy love, when I employed thee, was unknown: 15

    I minded no man's sorrows but mine own

    Nor, where so many shafts were shot in me,

    Could think any before had wounded thee.

TUDOR.

    All, sir, that in my cause is said by you

    At once is for me and against me too.   20

    Howe'er, I'll rather speak than quite despair,

    Since she is just and you my rival are,

    Yet sir, this diff'rence to my case is due,

    You speak for me, but I resign for you.

PRINCESS KATHERINE.

    He who resigns his love, though for his king,   25

    Does, as he is a lover, a low thing

    But, as a subject, a high crime does do,

    Being at once subject and rebel too,

    For whilst to regal pow'r he does submit,

    He casts off love, a greater pow'r than it.   30

TUDOR.

    I fear you now are glad of a pretence

    To punish what you cannot recompense.

    Else would you think love's pow'r I do not know

    Because my love all others does outgo?

    If I by that seem guilty in your eye,   35

    Oh happy guilt which raises love so high!

    For I but show in what I now have done

    That I your int'rest prize above my own.

PRINCESS KATHERINE.

    But justly I admire how you can prove

    So true to friendship and so false to love;   40

    Since in effect they both are but the same,

    Only the sex gives them a diff'rent name.

TUDOR.

    You friendship tax for being too sublime

    And make its duty ev'n to love a crime.

PRINCESS KATHERINE.

    Your king does give you a brave* rival's leave,   45
    But you seem loth that license to receive.
    Of these, which for my wonder is more fit:
    The leave he gave or your not using it?

TUDOR.

    The giver may such gifts as these esteem:
    I can, but by refusing, merit them,   50
    And madam, since 'tis evident that you
    Can never pay what to us both is due,
    Why will you call that act in me a crime
    By which we both may justice do to him?
    Nor blame me that my friendship's debt I paid   55
    By thus resigning what I never had.
    Let me my death without reproaches crave.

PRINCESS KATHERINE.

    At once you my disdain and pardon have.

TUDOR.

    But why should you disdain that which to you
    Obedience shows, to him my duty too?   60

PRINCESS KATHERINE.

    It is a duty he will not receive.

TUDOR.

    But you, to love you, have denied me leave.

PRINCESS KATHERINE.

    He who makes love* at a true lover's height
    Does ne'er ask leave but takes it as his right.

TUDOR.

    Have you designed in what you'd have me do   65
    To make me lose my king and mistress too?
    In losing of the last I'm so accursed
    As you'll in pity let me keep the first.

PRINCESS KATHERINE.

    I'd have you, sir, in that which I intend
    Express that you did merit such a friend.   70
    I would have had you too, to let him see
    That you were not unworthy to love me.
    But making such an ill retreat, you seem
    No more to merit bravely me or him.
    What greater thing or meaner* could you do   75
    Than dare at once to love and quit me too?
    I would have had you like yourself appear
    And not with friendship's name disguise your fear
    Nor tell him he to your respect does owe
    That which alone my justice does bestow.   80
    I would have had you nobly fall by it

    And not thus meanly, uncompelled, submit.

TUDOR.

    Madam, with you no longer I'll contend,
    Since in the way we differ, not the end.
    —Sir, though she thinks my condemnation fit,   85
    Yet without sighs I to her doom submit,
    For one joy's loss another joy secures:
    What loses me her favor merits yours.

KING.

    Whilst, Tudor, you for me your claim deny,
    I gain the field and you the victory: 90
    Yours is the nobler, mine the happier share,
    I'm the obliged, but you th'obliger are.

PRINCESS KATHERINE.

    In leaving me, as worthy of your friend,
    You to the utmost rate my worth commend.
    Whilst with that value I to him am brought,   95
    You show a friendship worthy to be sought.
    Be but my friend, as you to him have been,
    Letting out love to keep your friendship in,
    And make forsaken love contented seem;
    Then I'll your friendship, sir, like love esteem.[30]   100

Enter Queen, Chareloys, Duke of Bedford, and Princess Anne.

QUEEN.

    I'm come to tell you, sir, that we have signed
    All that can France to your protection bind.
    The States have judged to banishment my son
    And, as we promised, have entailed the crown.

CHARELOYS.

    And sir, in all their names, one from each State,   105
    Attending both your thrones, shall supplicate
    That they in public their decree may give,
    Which only from their justice you receive.

QUEEN.

    That public form, sir, may a little wait
    Till we your^k nuptial rites shall celebrate;   110
    My thoughts are fully to my daughter known.

KING.

    But from herself would I might know her own.

PRINCESS KATHERINE.

    I of your love shall too unworthy be
    When I deny that it has conquered me.

---

[30] love esteem] Queen Dowager after Henry V's death,
Catherine of Valois married Owen Tudor secretly in the
early 1430s.

KING.

  He who the glory has to conquer you   115
  Does, without war, more than the world subdue.

BEDFORD.

  Heav'n meant not you alone should happy be.
  Behold, sir, what it has reserved for me,
  Confirmed by her and by her brother too.

CHARELOYS.

  The gift is perfect when allowed by you.   120

KING.

  I can but add the ceremonial part;
  You had the substance when you had the heart.

PRINCESS ANNE.

  I cannot add to what I gave before
  Unless in saying I could give no more.

QUEEN.

  Crowds of impatient subjects wait within   125
  To see the nuptials of their king and queen:
  The sacred prelate in the temple stays
  And longs to mingle myrtle with your bays.
  It were offensive to admit delay.
  —She, sir, will follow when I lead the way.   130

Exeunt.

  [Scene v. The Dauphin's pavilion in his camp.]

Enter the Dauphin.

DAUPHIN.

  Revenge and pride my reason have betrayed,
  And both have ruled what both should have
      obeyed.
  This duke did with his life his sins resign,
  Which in his blood are written down for mine.
  Revenge! Of all thy charms, oh let me find   5
  But one t'appease the tempest of my mind.
  Let none to the success of mischief trust;
  I'll rather be unhappy than unjust.

Enter De Chastel hastily.

DE CHASTEL.

  You cannot your new levies now employ   10
  To storm or to besiege the Queen in Troyes.
  Sir, to prevent* our courage and her fear,
  The King of England is in person there.
  The bride's prepared, the King and duke agreed;
  The trembling States have treach'rously decreed   15

  During your father's life the King shall be
  Admitted to a boundless regency.
  And after his decease their law declares
  The crown shall fall to Henry and his heirs.
  The Queen (to whom they vast revenues give)   20
  Will, quitting pow'r, rich and obscurely live.

DAUPHIN.

  Can her revenge alone incline her to
  What right and nature could not make her do?

DE CHASTEL.

  Spend not that time in blaming what she does,
  Which Fortune for a fair retreat allows.   25
  The Duke of Exeter with all his horse
  Directly to your camp now bends his course.
  Th'alarm of such a growing force so near
  Gave your new troops a good excuse for fear.
  O'ertake your time before it runs too far.   30
  Sir, 'tis a granted principle in war
  That chiefs not strong enough t'engage in fight
  Should still* retire before the foe's in sight.
  Of all war's tasks the hardest is retreat,
  Where fear does our worst foe, disorder, meet.   35
  Retire, sir, lest men say we proudly stayed
  Too long for those of whom we were afraid.

DAUPHIN.

  Must the first act which I designed to do
  Be foiled and ere it is attempted too?

DE CHASTEL.

  Let not one look of Fortune cast you down: 40
  She were not Fortune if she still* did frown.
  Such as do braveliest bear her scorns a while
  Are those on whom, at last, she most will smile.

DAUPHIN.

  Raise then the camp! Fortune, that leads the way
  Of time's whole progress, can give us a day.   45

Exeunt.
The curtain falls.

  [Scene vi. The gates of the royal palace at Troyes.]

Two heralds appear opposite to each other in the
balconies near the stage.

FIRST HERALD.

  Herald! What summons have you to proclaim?
  Whom would you summon now, and in whose
      name?

SECOND HERALD.

    All that are English, all that are French, appear!

FIRST HERALD.

    I am to summon those great nations here.

SECOND HERALD.

    And I must summon them to come before

    Henry the Fifth, both king and conqueror.   5

    All that are English, all that are French, appear!

FIRST HERALD.

    Behold your king and queen! behold! and hear!

    You prelates of the church are summoned all

    And every member ecclesiastical.   10

SECOND HERALD.

    And every noble too and commoner!

FIRST HERALD.

    He that is French or English and not here

    In person or in public deputy

    Shall, though alive, in law not living be.

SECOND HERALD.

    Henry the Fifth is now to take the crown   15

    Of France, not as if giv'n him, but his own.

FIRST HERALD.

    That crown shall still* descend to all his line

    As heirs or not as heirs of Katherine.

SECOND HERALD.

    He that is French or English now attend!

FIRST HERALD.

    Or else he is no liegeman nor no friend.   20

        [Scene vii. The Hall of State
        in the royal palace at Troyes.]

*The curtain is drawn up. The curtain being lifted up,
there appear the King, Princess Katherine, Queen
Mother, Princess Anne, Chareloys, and all the English
and the French Nobility and officers of state and others
according to their places.*

CHARLELOYS.

    The deputies, sent by the Three Estates,

    Wait for admittance at your palace gates.

KING.

    My lord, with all the public forms of care

    Let all my officers their way prepare.

*All the officers designed for that purpose, then orderly
go out.*

    If aught this day my blessings could abate,   5

    'Tis that they are ill husbanded by Fate.

    For madam, I am now too happy grown

    By gaining in one day you and a throne.

    The first felicity I found so vast

    As takes away my relish of the last.   10

*Enter the distinct trains of the deputies from the Three
Estates, the King's officers, and last of all, the three
deputies, the Bishop of Arras for the ecclesiastics, the
Constable for the peers, and Monsieur Colemore for the
people.*

ARRAS.

    Great King, th'Estates of France have sent us three

    To pay their duties in this just decree:[31]

    Fixing the crown on you and on that line

    Which Heav'n in favor shall to both design.

    Who knows what wonders such a line may do   15

    As is from beauties drawn and conqu'rors too,

    In which Heav'n all those princes will unite

    Who to this empire have or claim a right?

    We by the Dauphin's bloody deed did see

    That he but falsely claimed what he would be.   25

    For we admired* one born to fill this throne

    Could act his crime and then that crime could own.

    But searching our records, we found at last

    That a long error as a truth has passed:

    For he who flies now justice does advance   30

    Is Charles of Valois, not the son of France.

    From those records the learned clearly tell

    Your ancient title by Queen Isabel,

    By whom you to this crown are lawful heir:

    New rights we grant not but the old declare.   35

    This just decree, in which they pay that debt,

    We humbly prostrate at your royal feet.

    I from the clergy come, to whom is given

    The lasting pow'r of legates sent from Heav'n:

    Their pray'rs will make you conquer when you fight,   40

    And in their voice Heav'n does allow you right.

CONSTABLE.

    I from the nobles come, who still* are born

---

31 just decree] The Treaty of Troyes, signed in the cathedral
    of Troyes on 21 May 1420, disinherited the Dauphin and
    declared Henry V of England regent and heir to the
    French throne.

To save their monarchs and their courts adorn,
And still* are certain of th'incessant care
Of palaces and dangers of the war.   45
They in their sphere should still* continue bright
Since they from kings derive their borrowed light.

COLEMORE.

I from the people come, who always are
The hands as nobles are the heads of war.
And when the glorious toils of war shall cease,   50
Their hands are no less useful, sir, in peace.

ARRAS.

And all the three do with one voice confess
They in their duty find their happiness.

They give the parchment.

KING.

Th'Estates I hope, my lords, shall ne'er repent
What I receive and they have freely sent.   55
English and French now but one people are,
And both shall have my equal love and care.
But Charles of Valois we shall soon destroy,
And by his ruin France shall peace enjoy.[32]
Since now 'gainst so much guilt we are to fight,   60
We may depend on conquest as our right.
Our swords should only miracles produce
Now we have joined the Cross and Fleur de Luce.
'Twere sin the help of Fortune to implore
To crown that head your hands have crowned before.   65

Exeunt omnes.

FINIS.

---

32 peace enjoy] When Henry V and Charles VI died in
1422, Henry's infant son Henry VI became heir to both
realms. Charles VII governed southern France as the
Dauphin, and his reign continued the Valois monarchy
(1422-1461); he was not formally crowned until 1429.

Textual Notes

a Copytext is the first edition, a 1668 folio (F1), corrected
according to its errata sheet. Also consulted, the second
edition, a 1668 folio (F2), and a modern edition of 1937
(Clark), which examines subsequent folio editions of
1669 (F3), 1672 (F4), 1677 (F5), and 1690 (F6); a 1739
collected edition (C); and five manuscripts (mss). For the
exact location of the mss readings, consult Clark. Inter-
polations of act and scene divisions and settings follow
Clark.

b Archbishop] F6, C, Clark; Bishop F1-5

c And … who for you dies] F2-6, C, Clark; Who … does
for you die F1; F1 errata changes "Who" to "And" but
does not emend the rest of the line.

d He] Clark (from mss); And F1-6, C

e She makes … your life.] Clark (from mss); *om.* F1-6, C

f our] F1; your F2-6, C, Clark

g I'd] Clark (mss); I'll F1-6, C

h officers of state] Clark (mss); *om.* F1-6, C

i loyal limbs] C, Clark (mss); Royal Limbs F1-6

j And, the express confessed] Clark (mss); Th'express
confest that they to you F1-6, C

k your] Clark (mss); our F1-6, C

Tamerlane[a]

by Nicholas Rowe (1674-1718)

edited by J. Douglas Canfield

Nicholas Rowe's *Tamerlane*, first performed in late 1701, was the second most popular tragedy (or serious play), outside of Shakespeare, on the eighteenth-century English stage. Its popularity is due in no small measure to its obvious political allegory, wherein Tamerlane is a thinly veiled, idealized portrait of William III and Bajazet a thinly veiled, demonized portrait of Louis XIV. It was played nearly every year for the next seventy-five on the anniversaries of William's birth (November 4) and his landing in England to accept the throne (November 5), which also happened to be, appropriately for a nation trying desperately to avoid a Catholic succession, Guy Fawkes Day, that is, the day Fawkes in a Jesuit plot was to blow up Parliament in 1605.

Rowe in his dedication to the Whiggish marquis of Hartington (later duke of Devonshire) lifts the veil of his allegory:

> Some people (who do me a very great honor in it) have fancied that in the person of Tamerlane I have alluded to the greatest character of the present age. … There are many features, 'tis true, in that great man's life not unlike His Majesty: his courage, his piety, his moderation, his justice, and his fatherly love of his people, but above all, his hate of tyranny and oppression and his zealous care for the common good of mankind carry a large resemblance of him. Several incidents are alike in their stories, and there wants* nothing to His Majesty but such a deciding victory as that by which Tamerlane gave peace to the world. That is yet to come. But I hope we may reasonably expect it from the unanimity of the present Parliament and so formidable a force as that unanimity will give life and vigor to.

For his purpose of idealization, Rowe distorts history: neither Tamerlane nor William was such a saint. Indeed, the real Tamerlane, or Timur Lenk (Timur the Lame), was a late fourteenth-century neo-Mongol (though actually Turkic by birth, hence called the Tartar) who savagely reestablished Mongol hegemony from India to Asia Minor, building towers out of the decapitated heads of his victims. In a single, decisive campaign in 1402 he defeated Bajazet, or Bayezid I, who had just led the Ottoman Turks to consolidate Anatolia behind Timur's back, so to speak. Rowe calls for such a decisive victory by William over Louis in the War of the Spanish Succession.

Lest we wonder how Rowe could so have distorted history and so have departed from the portrayal of Tamburlaine by Christopher Marlowe in his Elizabethan play of that title, it is important to note that Rowe's Tamerlane was filtered through the idealizing lenses of Richard Knolles's *General Historie of the Turkes* (1603) and Samuel Clarke's *Life of Tamerlane the Great* (1653). Probably for his own anti-Turkish purpose (the Turks were knocking down the walls of cities in central Europe during the seventeenth century), Knolles fashioned Tamerlane as a "Scourge of God" against a demonic Bajazet and even a benevolent monarch with sympathy to Christianity. Following hints in both Knolles and Clarke, Rowe further distinguishes Tamerlane from the fiercer, Turkic Tartars by making his origins Parthian, hence Persian, Indo-European, less Other.

Rowe combines contemporary anti-French sentiment with continuing anti-Turkish sentiment, for his Prince Axalla is modeled on Prince Eugene of Savoy, who, before he joined William in his wars against the French, had been fighting with the Holy Roman Emperor against the Turks in Austria and Hungary and the Balkans. But Rowe's purpose is not merely war-inspired propaganda. It is to fashion an ideal, constitutional, bourgeois monarch, who works hand-in-glove with his "senate" or parliament, and an ethos where worth is based not so much on birth as on merit.

Rowe's play succeeded not just because of its politics or ideology but also because of brilliant acting by Betterton in the role of Tamerlane, Verbruggen in the role of Bajazet, Barry in the role of Arpasia, Powell in the role of Moneses, Bracegirdle in the role of Selima, and Booth in the role of Axalla. The play was produced by Betterton and Barry's company at their breakaway theater in Lincolns Inn Fields. They inaugurated the greatest heroic romance of the century.

Prologue[1]

Of all the Muses' various labors, none
Have lasted longer or have higher flown
Than those that tell the fame by ancient heroes won.
With pleasure Rome and great Augustus heard
Arms and the man sung by the Mantuan bard;[2]   5
In spite of time, the sacred story lives,
And Caesar and his Empire still survives.
Like him (though much unequal to his flame)
Our author makes a pious prince[3] his theme.
High with the foremost names in arms he stood,   10
Had fought[4] and suffered for his country's good,
Yet sought not fame but peace in fields of blood.
Safe under him his happy people sate
And grieved at distance for their neighbors' fate.
Whilst with success a Turkish monarch[5] crowned,   15
Like spreading flame, deformed the nations round;
With sword and fire he forced his impious way
To lawless pow'r and universal sway.
Some abject states for fear the tyrant join;
Others for gold their liberties resign,   20
And venal princes sold their right divine,

Till Heaven, the growing evil to redress,
Sent Tamerlane to give the world a peace.
The hero, roused, asserts the glorious cause
And to the field the cheerful soldier draws.   25
Around in crowds his valiant leaders wait,
Anxious for glory and secure of Fate,
Well pleased once more to venture on his side
And prove that faith again, which had so oft been tried.
The peaceful fathers who in senates[6] meet   30
Approve an enterprise so just, so great,
While with their prince's arms their voice thus joined
Gains half the praise of having saved mankind.
Ev'n in a circle where, like this, the fair
Were met, the bright assembly did declare   35
Their house with one consent were for the war.
Each urged her lover to unsheath his sword
And never spare a man who broke his word.
Thus fired, the brave on to the danger press;
Their Arms were crowned abroad with just success   40
And blest at home with beauty and with peace.

DRAMATIS PERSONAE

[MEN]

Tamerlane.
Bajazet, Emperor of the Turks.
Axalla, an Italian prince, general and favorite of
    Tamerlane.
Moneses, a Grecian prince and a Christian.
Stratocles, his friend.
Prince of Tanais,[7] kinsman and general to
    Tamerlane.

---

1 Prologue] spoken by Betterton
2 Rome ... bard] Virgil, born in Mantua, wrote the *Aeneid*, whose famous opening phrase is *arma virumque* (arms and the man), to celebrate the incipient Roman Empire under Octavius, known as Caesar Augustus.
3 prince] William III
4 fought] Tamerlane fought in Asia Minor; his allegorical counterpart here, William III, fought in the War of the League of Augsburg in the 1690s and now in the War of the Spanish Succession at the turn of the century, both attempts by William and his allies to contain French expansionism.
5 Turkish monarch] Bajazet, or Bayezid I (1389-1403)

6 senates] allegorically, parliaments
7 Tanais] ancient Greek colony on the Don River in southwestern Russia, having become by Tamerlane's time the Genoese colony of Tana

Omar, a Tartar general.
Mirvan,
Zama, Parthian generals to Tamerlane.
Haly, favorite eunuch to Bajazet.
A Turkish dervish.
Parthian and Tartar soldiers.
Mutes belonging to Bajazet.
Other Attendants.

WOMEN

Arpasia, a Grecian princess.
Selima, daughter of Bajazet.

SCENE: TAMERLANE'S CAMP,
NEAR ANGORIA IN GALATIA.[8]

Tamerlane.

… *Magnus ad altum*
Fulminat Euphraten bello, Victorque volentes
Per Populos dat jura, viamq; affectat Olympo.
Virg. Georg. 4[9]

Act I. Before Tamerlane's tent.

Enter the Prince of Tanais, Zama, and Mirvan.

PRINCE OF TANAIS.
Hail to the sun! from whose returning light
The cheerful soldiers' arms new luster take
To deck the pomp of battle. Oh, my friends!
Was ever such a glorious face of war?
See from this height how all Galatia's plains   5
With nations numberless are covered o'er,
Who, like a deluge, hide the face of earth
And leave no object in the vast horizon
But glitt'ring arms and skies.
ZAMA.
⠀⠀⠀⠀⠀⠀⠀⠀⠀Our Asian world   10
From this important day expects a lord;
This day they hope an end of all their woes,

---

8 Angoria in Galatia] or Angora, modern Ankara, capital
⠀⠀of Turkey, in the northwest region once known as
⠀⠀Galatia
9 *Magnus … Georg. 4*] Virgil, *Georgics* 4.560-62: The
⠀⠀Great One from on high lights up the Euphrates Valley
⠀⠀with war; the Victor gives laws to a willing people and
⠀⠀seeks the path to Olympus.

Of tyranny, of bondage, and oppression
From our victorious emp'ror, Tamerlane.
MIRVAN.
Well has our holy Alha marked him out   15
The scourge of lawless pride and dire ambition,
The great avenger of the groaning world.
Well has he worn the sacred cause of justice
Upon his prosp'rous sword. Approving Heav'n
Still* crowned the righteous warrior with success,   20
As if it[b] said, "Go forth, and be my champion,
Thou most like me of all my works below."
PRINCE OF TANAIS.
No lust of rule (the common vice of kings),
No furious zeal inspired by hot-brained priests,
Ill hid beneath religion's specious name,   25
E'er drew his temperate courage to the field.
But to redress an injured people's wrongs,
To save the weak one from the strong oppressor,
Is all his end of war, and when he draws
The sword to punish, like relenting Heav'n,   30
He seems unwilling to deface his kind.
MIRVAN.
So rich his soul in every virtuous grace
That, had not Nature made him great by birth,
Yet all the brave* had sought him for their friend.
The Christian prince Axalla, nicely* bred   35
In polished arts of European courts,
For him forsakes his native Italy
And lives a happy exile in his service.
PRINCE OF TANAIS.
Pleased with the gentle* manners of that prince,
Our mighty lord is lavish to his friendship,   40
Though Omar and the Tartar lords repine
And loudly tax their monarch as too partial.
ZAMA.
Ere the mid hour of night, from tent to tent,
Unwearied, through the num'rous host he passed,
Viewing with careful eyes each several quarter,   45
Whilst from his looks, as from divinity,
The soldiers[c] took presage and cried, "Lead on,
Great Alha, and our Emperor, lead on
To victory and everlasting fame."
MIRVAN.
Hear you of Bajazet?   50
PRINCE OF TANAIS.
⠀⠀⠀⠀⠀⠀⠀⠀⠀Late in the evening

A slave of near attendance on his person
'Scaped to our camp: from him we learned the
  tyrant,
With rage redoubled, for the fight prepares;
Some accidental passion fires his breast   55
(Love, as 'tis thought, for a fair Grecian captive)
And adds new horror to his native fury.
For five returning suns, scarce was he seen
By any the most favored of his court,
But in lascivious ease amongst his women
Lived from the war retired or else, alone   60
In sullen mood, sate meditating plagues
And ruin to the world, till yester morn,
Like fire that lab'ring upwards rends the earth,
He burst with fury from his tent, commanding
All should be ready for the fight this day.   65

ZAMA.

I know his temper well, since in his court,
Companion of the brave Axalla's embassy,
I oft observed him: proud; impatient
Of aught superior, ev'n of Heav'n, that made him;
Fond of false glory, of the savage pow'r   70
Of ruling without reason, of confounding
Just and unjust by an unbounded will;
By whom religion, honor, all the bands
That ought to hold the jarring world in peace
Were held the tricks of state, snares of wise princes 75
To draw their easy neighbors to destruction.

MIRVAN.

Thrice by our law and Prophet has he sworn,
By the world's Lord and Maker, lasting peace[10]
With our great master and his royal friend,
The Grecian Emperor;[11] as oft, regardless   80
Of plighted faith, with most unkingly baseness
He's ta'en the advantage of their absent arms,
Without a war proclaimed or cause pretended,

To waste with sword and fire their fruitful fields:
Like some accursèd fiend who, 'scaped from hell,   85
Poisons the balmy air through which he flies,
He blasts the bearded corn* and loaded branches,
The lab'ring hind's best hopes, and marks his way
  with ruin.

PRINCE OF TANAIS.

But see! his fate, the mighty Tamerlane,
Comes like the proxy of inquiring Heav'n   90
To judge and to redress.

*Flourish of trumpets. Enter Tamerlane, guards, and
other attendants.*

TAMERLANE.

Yet, yet a little, and destructive slaughter
Shall rage around and mar this beauteous prospect;
Pass but an hour, which stands betwixt the lives
Of thousands and eternity. What change   95
Shall hasty Death make in yon glitt'ring plain?
Oh thou fell monster War! that in a moment
Lay'st waste the noblest part of the creation,
The boast and masterpiece of the great Maker,
That wears in vain th'impression of his image,   100
Unpriviledged from thee.

(*To the Prince, Zama, and Mirvan.*)

Health to my[d] friends, and to our arms, success,
Such as the cause for which we fight deserves.

PRINCE OF TANAIS.

Nor can we ask beyond what Heav'n bestows,
Preventing* still* our wishes. See, great sir!   105
The universal joy your soldiers wear,[e]
Omen of prosp'rous battle.
Impatient of the tedious night, in arms
Watchful they stood, expecting opening day,
And now are hardly by their leaders held   110
From darting on the foe, like a hot courser
That, bounding, paws the mold'ring soil, disdaining
The rein that checks him, eager for the race.

TAMERLANE.

Yes, Prince, I mean to give a loose to War:
This morn, Axalla, with my Parthian horse,   115
Arrives to join me: he who, like a storm,
Swept with his flying squadrons all the plain[12]

---

10 Thrice ... peace] In his political allegory "Rowe is prob-
    ably thinking of the Treaty of Aix-la-Chapelle (1688),
    the Treaty of Nimegwen (1678) and the Partition Trea-
    ties (1698 and 1700)" (Sutherland).
11 Grecian Emperor] probably alluding to the Holy Ro-
    man Emperor, Leopold I, who in the late seventeenth
    century (along with Prince Eugene) fought against the
    Turks in central Europe; no Byzantine emperor fought
    on the side of Timur.

---

12 Swept ... plain] "Rowe may here intend a reference to
    the battle of Chiari, when Eugene routed the French

Between Angoria's walls and yon tall mountains
That seem to reach the clouds. And now he comes,
Loaden with spoils and conquest, to my aid.   120

Flourish of trumpets.

ZAMA.

These trumpets speak his presence—

*Enter Axalla with soldiers. Moneses, Stratocles, and
Selima, prisoners. Axalla kneels to Tamerlane.*

TAMERLANE.

Welcome! thou worthy partner of my laurels,
Thou brother of my choice, a band more sacred
Than nature's brittle tie. By holy friendship!
Glory and fame stood still for thy arrival;   125
My soul seemed wanting* in its better half
And languished for thy absence, like a prophet
That waits the inspiration of his god.

AXALLA.

My emperor! my ever royal master!
To whom my secret soul more lowly bends   130
Than forms of outward worship can express.
How poorly does your soldier pay this goodness,
Who wears his every hour of life out for you?
Yet 'tis his all, and what he has he offers.
Nor now disdain t'accept the gift he brings,   135
This earnest of your fortune. See, my lord,
The noblest prize that ever graced my arms.
—Approach, my fair.

TAMERLANE.

                        This is indeed to conquer,
And well to be rewarded for thy conquest: 140
The bloom of opening flow'rs, unsullied beauty,
Softness, and sweetest innocence she wears
And looks like Nature in the world's first spring.
But say, Axalla—

SELIMA. (*Kneeling to Tamerlane.*)

                        Most renowned in war,   145
Look with compassion on a captive maid,
Though born of hostile blood, nor let my birth,
Derived from Bajazet, prevent that mercy
Which every subject of your fortune finds.
War is the province of ambitious man,   150

Who tears the miserable world for empire,
Whilst our weak sex, incapable of wrong,
On either side claims privilege of safety.

TAMERLANE. (*Raising her.*)

Rise, royal maid, the pride of haughty power
Pays homage, not receives it from the fair.   155
Thy angry father fiercely calls me forth
And urges me unwillingly to arm.
Yet, though our frowning battles menace death
And mortal conflict, think not that we hold
Thy innocence and virtue as our foe.   160
Here, till the fate of Asia is decided,
In safety stay. Tomorrow is your own.
Nor grieve for who may conquer or who lose:
Fortune on either side shall wait thy wishes.

SELIMA.

Where shall my wonder and my praise begin!   165
From the successful labors of thy arms?
Or from a theme more soft and full of peace,
Thy mercy and thy gentleness? Oh, Tamerlane!
What can I pay thee for this noble usage
But grateful praise? So Heav'n itself is paid.   170
—Give peace, ye Pow'rs above, peace to mankind,
Nor let my father wage unequal war
Against the force of such united virtues.

TAMERLANE.

Heaven hear thy pious wish!—But since our prospect
Looks darkly on futurity till Fate   175
Determine for us, let thy beauty's safety
Be my Axalla's care, in whose glad eyes
I read what joy the pleasing service gives him.

(*To Axalla.*)

Is there amongst thy other pris'ners aught
Worthy our knowledge?   180

AXALLA. (*Pointing to Moneses.*)

                        This brave man, my lord,
With long resistance held the combat doubtful.
His party, pressed with numbers, soon grew faint
And would have left their charge an easy prey,
Whilst he alone, undaunted at the odds   185
Though hopeless to escape, fought well and firmly
Nor yielded till, o'ermatched by many hands,
He seemed to shame our conquest whilst he
    owned it.

TAMERLANE.

Thou speak'st him as a soldier should a soldier,

---

under Villeroy (Sept. 1, 1701). The event was still recent, and in everyone's mind" (Sutherland).

Just to the worth he finds. (*To Moneses.*) I would   190
    not war
With aught that wears thy virtuous stamp of
    greatness.
Thy habit speaks thee Christian—nay, yet more,
My soul seems pleased to take acquaintance with
    thee,
As if allied to thine: perhaps 'tis sympathy
Of honest minds, like strings wound up in music,   195
Where by one touch both utter the same harmony.
Why art thou then a friend to Bajazet?
And why my enemy?

MONESES.
               If human wisdom
Could point out every action of our lives   200
And say, "Let it be thus, in spite of Fate
Or partial Fortune," then I had not been
The wretch I am.

TAMERLANE.
The brave meet every accident
With equal minds. Think nobler of thy foes   205
Than to account thy chance in war an evil.

MONESES.
Far, far from that: I rather hold it grievous
That I was forced ev'n but to seem your enemy.
Nor think the baseness of a vanquished slave
Moves me to flatter for precarious life   210
Or ill-bought freedom when I swear, by Heav'n,
Were I to choose from all mankind a master,
It should be Tamerlane.

TAMERLANE.
               A noble freedom
Dwells with the brave, unknown to fawning   215
    sycophants,
And claims a privilege of being believed.
I take thy praise as earnest of thy friendship.

MONESES.
Still you prevent* the homage I should offer,
Oh royal sir! let my misfortunes plead
And wipe away the hostile mark I wore: 220
I was, when not long since my fortune hailed me
Blessed to my wish, I was the Prince Moneses,
Born and bred up to greatness. Witness: the blood
Which through successive heroes' veins allied
To our Greek emperors rolled down to me,   225
Feeds the bright flame of glory in my heart.

TAMERLANE.
Ev'n that, that princely tie should bind thee to me,
If virtue were not more than all alliance.

MONESES.
I have a sister (Oh severe remembrance!),
Our noble house's, nay, her sex's pride.   230
Nor think my tongue too lavish if I speak her
Fair as the fame of virtue and yet chaste
As its cold precepts, wise beyond her sex
And blooming youth, soft as forgiving mercy,
Yet greatly brave and jealous for her honor.   235
Such as she was, to say I barely loved her
Is poor to my soul's meaning. From our infancy
There grew a mutual tenderness between us
Till, not long since, her vows were kindly plighted
To a young lord, the equal of her birth.   240
The happy day was fixed and now approaching,
When faithless Bajazet (upon whose honor,
In solemn treaty giv'n, the Greeks depended)
With sudden war broke in upon the country,
Secure of peace and for defence unready.   245

TAMERLANE.
Let majesty no more be held divine,
Since kings, who are called gods, profane themselves.

MONESES.
Among the wretches whom that deluge swept
Away to slavery, myself and sister,
Then passing near the frontiers to the court   250
(Which waited for her nuptials) were surprized
And made the captives of the tyrant's power.
Soon as we reached his court, we found our usage
Beyond what we expected, fair, and noble.
'Twas then the storm of your victorious arms   255
Looked black and seemed to threaten, when he
    pressed me
(By oft repeated instances) to draw
My sword for him. But when he found my soul
Disdained his purpose, he more fiercely told me
That my Arpasia, my loved sister's fate   260
Depended on my courage shown for him.
I had long learnt to hold myself at nothing,
But for her sake, to ward the blow from her,
I bound my service to the man I hated.
Six days are passed since by the Sultan's order   265
I left the pledge of my return behind
And went to guard this princess to his camp.

The rest the brave Axalla's fortune tells you.
TAMERLANE.
Wisely the tyrant strove to prop his cause
By leaguing with thy virtue, but just Heav'n   270
Has torn thee from his side and left him naked
To the avenging bolt that drives upon him.
Forget the name of captive. And I wish
I could as well restore that fair one's freedom,
Whose loss hangs heavy on thee. Yet ere night   275
Perhaps we may deserve thy friendship nobler;
Th'approaching storm may cast thy shipwrecked
   wealth
Back to thy arms. Till that be past, since war
(Though in the justest cause) is ever doubtful,
I will not ask thy sword to aid my victory,   280
Lest it should hurt that hostage of thy valor
Our common foe detains.
MONESES.
                    Let Bajazet
Bend to his yoke repining slaves by force,
You, sir, have found a nobler way to empire,   285
Lord of the willing world.
TAMERLANE.
                    Oh, my Axalla!
Thou hast a tender soul, apt for compassion,
And art thyself a lover and a friend:
Does not this prince's fortune move thy temper?   290
AXALLA.
Yes, sir, I mourn the brave Moneses' fate;
The merit of his virtue hardly matched
With disadvent'rous[13] chance. Yet, Prince, allow me,
Allow me from the experience of a lover
To say, one person whom your story mentioned   295
(If he survive) is far beyond you wretched:
You named the bridegroom of your beauteous
   sister.
MONESES.
I did. Oh, most accurst!
AXALLA.
                    Think what he feels,
Dashed in the fierceness of his expectation   300
Then, when the approaching minute of possession
Had wound imagination to the heighth—
Think if he lives—

---

[13] disadvent'rous] unfortunate, disastrous (*OED*)

MONESES.
                    He lives, he does; 'tis true,
He lives. But how? To be a dog, and dead,   305
Were paradise to such a state as his:
He holds down life as children do a potion,
With strong reluctance and convulsive strugglings,
Whilst his misfortunes press him to disgorge it.
TAMERLANE.
Spare the remembrance. 'Tis a useless grief   310
And adds to the misfortune by repeating it.
The revolution of a day may bring
Such turns as Heav'n itself could scarce have
   promised,
Far, far beyond thy wish. Let that hope cheer thee.
—Haste, my Axalla, to dispose with safety   315
Thy beauteous charge and on the foe revenge
The pain which absence gives. Thy other care,
Honor and arms, now summon thy attendance.
—Now do thy office well, my soul, remember
Thy cause, the cause of Heaven and injured earth.   320
Oh thou Supreme! if thy great spirit warms
My glowing breast and fires my soul to arms,
Grant that my sword, assisted by thy pow'r,
This day may peace and happiness restore,
That war and lawless rage may vex thy world no more.   325

Exeunt Tamerlane, Moneses, Stratocles, Prince of
Tanais, Zama, Mirvan, and attendants. Manent
Axalla and Selima, with soldiers.

AXALLA.
The battle calls and bids me haste to leave thee.
Oh! Selima— But let destruction wait.
Are there not hours enough for blood and slaughter?
This moment shall be Love's, and I will waste it
In soft complainings for thy sighs and coldness,   330
For thy forgetful coldness. Even at Birza,
When in thy father's court my eyes first owned thee
Fairer than light, the joy of their beholding,
Ev'n then thou wert not thus.
SELIMA.
                    Art not thou changed,   335
Christian Axalla, art thou still the same?
Those were the gentle hours of peace and thou
The world's good angel that didst kindly join
Its mighty masters in harmonious friendship.
But since those joys that once were ours are lost,   340

Forbear to mention 'em, and talk of war,
Talk of thy conquest, and my chains, Axalla.
AXALLA.
    Yet I will listen, fair unkind upbraider,
Yet I will listen to thy charming accents,
Although they make me curse my fame and fortune,   345
My laurel wreaths and all the glorious trophies
For which the valiant bleed. Oh! thou unjust one,
Dost thou then envy me this small return
My niggard fate has made for all the mournings,
For all the pains, for all the sleepless nights   350
That cruel absence brings?
SELIMA.
                  Away, deceiver,
I will not hear thy soothing. Is it thus
That Christian lovers prove the faith they swear?
Are war and slavery the soft endearments   355
With which they court the beauties they admire?
'Twas well my heart was cautious of believing
Thy vows and thy protesting. Know, my conqueror,
Thy sword has vanquished but the half of Selima;
Her soul disdains thy victory.   360
AXALLA.
                Hear, sweet Heav'n,
Hear the fair tyrant, how she wrests Love's laws,
As she had vowed my ruin! What is conquest?
What joy have I from that but to behold thee,
To kneel before thee, and with lifted eyes   365
To view thee as devotion does a saint,
With awful,* trembling pleasure, then to swear
Thou art the queen and mistress of my soul.
Has not ev'n Tamerlane (whose word, next Heav'n's,
Makes Fate at second hand) bid thee disclaim   370
Thy fears? And dost thou call thyself a slave
Only to try how far the sad impression
Can sink into Axalla?
SELIMA.
          Oh, Axalla!
Ought I to hear you?   375
AXALLA.
           Come back, ye hours,
And tell my Selima what she has done.
Bring back the time when to her father's court
I came ambassador of peace from Tamerlane;
When, hid by conscious darkness and disguise,   380
I passed the dangers of the watchful guards,

Bold as the youth who nightly swam the
    Hellespont.[14]
Then, then she was not sworn the foe of love
When, as my soul confessed its flame and sued
In moving sounds for pity, she frowned rarely   385
But, blushing, heard me tell the gentle tale,
Nay, ev'n confessed and told me softly, sighing,
She thought there was no guilt in love like mine.
SELIMA.
Young and unskilful in the world's false arts,
I suffered Love to steal upon my softness   390
And warm me with a lambent, guiltless flame.
Yes, I have heard thee swear a thousand times
And call the conscious Pow'rs of heav'n to witness
The tend'rest, truest, everlasting passion.
But oh! 'tis past, and I will charge remembrance   395
To banish the fond* image from my soul.
Since thou art sworn the foe of royal Bajazet,
I have resolved to hate thee.
AXALLA.
              Is it possible!
Hate is not in thy nature; thy whole frame   400
Is harmony without one jarring atom.
Why dost thou force thy eyes to wear this coldness?
It damps the springs of life. Oh! bid me die,
Much rather bid me die, if it be true
That thou hast sworn to hate me.   405
SELIMA.
            Let life and death
Wait the decision of the bloody field,
Nor can thy fate (my conqueror) depend
Upon a woman's hate. Yet since you urge
A power which once perhaps I had, there is   410
But one request that I can make with honor.
AXALLA.
Oh, name it! say—
SELIMA.
           Forego your right of war,
And render me this instant to my father.
AXALLA.
Impossible! The tumult of the battle   415
That hastes to join cuts off all means of commerce
Betwixt the armies.

---

14 youth ... Hellespont] Leander, Greek youth in love with
    the priestess Hero, who performed this feat guided by
    the light from her tower

SELIMA.

              Swear then to perform it,
Which way soe'er the chance of war determines,
On my first instance.   420

AXALLA.

               By the sacred majesty
Of Heav'n to whom we kneel, I will obey thee.
Yes, I will give thee this severest proof
Of my soul's vowed devotion: I will part with thee
(Thou cruel, to command it!) I will part with thee, 425
As wretches that are doubtful of hereafter
Part with their lives—unwilling, loth and fearful,
And trembling at futurity. But is there nothing,
No small return that honor can afford
For all this waste of love?   430

SELIMA.

                  The gifts of captives
Wear somewhat of constraint, and generous* minds
Disdain to give where freedom of the choice
Does but seem wanting.*

AXALLA.

                 What! not one kind look? 435
Then thou art changed indeed.

Trumpets.

Hark! I am summoned,
And thou wilt send me forth like one unblessed,
Whom Fortune has forsaken and ill* Fate
Marked for destruction. Thy surprising coldness 440
Hangs on my soul and weighs my courage down,
And the first feeble blow I meet shall raze me
From all remembrance. Nor is life or fame
Worthy my care, since I am lost to thee. (*Going.*)

SELIMA.

Hah! Goest thou to the fight?   445

AXALLA.

                I do. Farewel!

SELIMA.

What! and no more? A sigh heaves in my breast
And stops the struggling accents on my tongue,
Else, sure, I should have added something more
And made our parting softer.   450

AXALLA.

                   Give it way.
The niggard honor, that affords not love,
Forbids not pity—

SELIMA.

               Fate perhaps has set
This day the period of thy life and conquests, 455
And I shall see thee borne at evening back
A breathless corse—oh! Can I think on that
And hide my sorrows? No, they will have way,
And all the vital air that life draws in
Is rendered back in sighs.   460

AXALLA.

The murmuring gale revives the drooping flame
That at thy coldness languished in my breast.
So breathe the gentle zephyrs on the spring
And waken every plant and od'rous flower,
Which winter frosts had blasted, to new life. 465

SELIMA.

To see thee for this moment, and no more—
Oh! help me to resolve against this tenderness
That charms my fierce resentments and presents
    thee
Not as thou art, mine and my father's foe,
But as thou wert when first thy moving accents 470
Won me to hear; when, as I list'ned to thee,
The happy hours passed by us unperceived,
So was my soul fixed to the soft enchantment.

AXALLA.

Let me be still the same, I am, I must be.
If it were possible my heart could stray, 475
One look from thee would call it back again
And fix the wanderer forever thine.

SELIMA.

Where is my boasted resolution now? (*Sinking
   into his arms.*)
Oh! Yes! Thou art the same; my heart joins with thee
And to betray me will believe thee still.* 480
It dances to the sounds that moved it first
And owns at once the weakness of my soul:
So when some skilful artist strikes the strings,
The magic numbers[15] rouse our sleeping passions
And force us to confess our grief and pleasure. 485
Alas! Axalla, say, dost thou not pity
My artless innocence and easy fondness?
Oh! turn thee from me, or I die with blushing.

AXALLA.

No, let me rather gaze, forever gaze,

---

15 numbers] musical notes

And bless the newborn glories that adorn thee;　490
From every blush that kindles in thy cheeks
Ten thousand little loves and graces spring
To revel in the roses.

Trumpets.

　　　　　　　　　　'Twonnot be,
This envious trumpet calls and tears me from thee—　495
SELIMA.
　My fears increase and doubly press me now.
　I charge thee, if thy sword comes cross my father,
　Stop for a moment, and remember me.
AXALLA.
　Oh! doubt not but his life shall be my care,
　Even dearer than my own—　500
SELIMA.
　　　　　　　　　　Guard that (for me) too.
AXALLA.
　Oh, Selima! thou hast restored my quiet.
　The noble ardor of the war, with love
　Returning brightly, burns within my breast
　And bids me be secure of all hereafter.　505
　So cheers some pious saint a dying sinner
　(Who trembled at the thought of pains to come)
　With Heav'n's forgiveness and the hopes of mercy:
　At length the tumult of his soul appeased
　And every doubt and anxious scruple eased,　510
　Boldly he proves the dark, uncertain road;
　The peace his holy comforter bestowed
　Guides and protects him, like a guardian god. (*Exit.*)
SELIMA.
　In vain all arts a lovesick virgin tries,
　Affects to frown and seem severely wise,　515
　In hopes to cheat the wary lover's eyes.
　If the dear youth her pity strives to move
　And pleads, with tenderness, the cause of love,
　Nature asserts her empire in her heart
　And kindly[16] takes the faithful lover's part.　520
　By Love herself and Nature thus betrayed,

16　kindly] may still retain its older senses: (1) in accordance with nature; naturally; by natural disposition; characteristically; (2) in the way suitable or appropriate to the nature of the thing; properly, fittingly; in later use, esp. said of processes which successfully follow their natural course (*OED*)

No more she trusts in Pride's fantastic aid
But bids her eyes confess the yielding maid.

Exit Selima, guards following.

　　　Act II, scene i. Tamerlane's Camp.

Enter Moneses.

MONESES.
　The dreadful business of the war is over,
　And Slaughter, that from yester morn till even
　With giant steps passed striding o'er the field
　Besmeared and horrid with the blood of nations,
　Now weary sits among the mangled heaps　5
　And slumbers o'er her prey, while from this camp
　The cheerful sounds of "Victory and Tamerlane"
　Beat the high arch of heav'n. Deciding Fate,
　That crowns him with the spoils of such a day,
　Has given it as an earnest of the world,　10
　That shortly shall be his.

Enter Stratocles.

　　　　　　　　　　My Stratocles!
　Most happily returned. Might I believe
　Thou bring'st me any joy?
STRATOCLES.
　　　　　　　　　　With my best diligence
　This night I have enquired of what concerns you.　15
　Scarce was the sun, who shone upon the horror
　Of the past day, sunk to the western ocean,
　When, by permission from the Prince Axalla,
　I mixed among the tumult of the warriors
　Returning from the battle: here a troop　20
　Of hardy Parthians, red with honest wounds,
　Confessed the conquest they had well deserved;
　There a dejected crew of wretched captives,
　Sore with unprofitable hurts and groaning
　Under new bondage, followed sadly after　25
　The haughty victor's heels. But that which fully
　Crowned the success of Tamerlane was Bajazet,
　Fall'n, like the proud archangel[17] from the heighth
　Where once (even next to Majesty Divine)
　Enthroned he sat, down to the vile descent　30
　And lowness of a slave. But oh! to speak
　The rage, the fierceness, and the indignation—
　It bars all words and cuts description short.

17　proud archangel] Satan

MONESES.
    Then he is fall'n! that comet which on high
    Portended ruin; he has spent his blaze   35
    And shall distract the world with fears no more.
    Sure it must bode me well, for oft my soul
    Has started into tumult at his name,
    As if my guardian angel took th'alarm
    At the approach of somewhat mortal to me.   40
    But say, my friend, what hear'st thou of Arpasia?
    For there my thoughts, my every care is centered.
STRATOCLES.
    Though on that purpose still* I bent my search,
    Yet nothing certain could I gain but this,
    That in the pillage of the Sultan's tent   45
    Some women were made pris'ners, who this morning
    Were to be offered to the Emperor's view;
    Their names and qualities,[18] though oft enquiring,
    I could not learn.
MONESES.
                    Then must my soul still labor   50
    Beneath uncertainty and anxious doubt,
    The mind's worst state. The tyrant's ruin gives me
    But a half-ease.
STRATOCLES.
                    'Twas said, not far from hence
    The captives were to wait the Emperor's passage. 55
MONESES.
    Haste me to find the place.——Oh! my Arpasia!
    Shall we not meet? Why hangs my heart thus heavy
    Like death within my bosom? Oh! 'tis well
    The joy of meeting pays the pangs of absence,
    Else who could bear it?   60
    When thy loved sight shall bless my eyes again,
    Then I will own I ought not to complain,
    Since that sweet hour is worth whole years of pain.

Exeunt.

Scene ii. The inside of a magnificent tent.

*Symphony of warlike music. Enter Tamerlane, Axalla,
Prince of Tanais, Zama, Mirvan, soldiers, and other
attendants.*

AXALLA.
    From this auspicious day the Parthian name

_____

18 qualities] social ranks

    Shall date its birth of empire and extend,
    Even from the dawning east to utmost Thule,
    The limits of its sway.
PRINCE OF TANAIS.
                            Nations unknown,   5
    Where yet the Roman eagles never flew,
    Shall pay their homage to victorious Tamerlane,
    Bend to his valor and superior virtue,
    And own that conquest is not giv'n by Chance
    But (bound by fatal and resistless merit)   10
    Waits on his arms.
TAMERLANE.
                        It is too much, you dress me
    Like an usurper in the borrowed attributes
    Of injured Heav'n: Can we call conquest ours?
    Shall man, this pigmy with a giant's pride,   15
    Vaunt of himself and say, "Thus have I done this"?
    Oh! vain pretence to greatness! Like the moon,
    We borrow all the brightness which we boast,
    Dark in ourselves and useless. If that Hand
    That rules the fate of battles strike for us,   20
    Crown us with fame, and gild our clay with honor,
    'Twere most ungrateful to disown the benefit
    And arrogate a praise which is not ours.
AXALLA.
    With such unshaken temper of the soul
    To bear the swelling tide of prosp'rous fortune 25
    Is to deserve that fortune. In adversity
    The mind grows tough by buffeting the tempest,
    Which, in success dissolving, sinks to ease
    And loses all her firmness.
TAMERLANE.
                            Oh, Axalla!   30
    Could I forget I am a man, as thou art,
    Would not the winter's cold or summer's heat,
    Sickness or thirst and hunger, all the train
    Of nature's clamorous appetites (asserting
    An equal right in kings and common men)   35
    Reprove me daily? No, if I boast of aught,
    Be it to have been Heaven's happy instrument,
    The means of good to all my fellow creatures:
    This is a king's best praise.

Enter Omar.

OMAR. (*Bowing to Tamerlane.*)
                            Honor and Fame   40

Forever wait the Emperor; may our Prophet
Give him ten thousand thousand days of life
And every day like this. The captive Sultan,
Fierce in his bonds and at his fate repining,
Attends your sacred will.   45

TAMERLANE.

                         Let him approach.

Enter Bajazet and other Turkish prisoners in chains,
with a guard of soldiers.

When I survey the ruins of this field,
The wild destruction which thy fierce ambition
Has dealt among mankind (so many widows
And helpless orphans has thy battle made   50
That half our eastern world this day are mourners),
Well may I in behalf of heav'n and earth
Demand from thee atonement for this wrong.

BAJAZET.

Make thy demand to those that own thy power.
Know, I am still beyond it, and though Fortune   55
(Curse on that changeling deity of fools!)
Has stripped me of the train and pomp of greatness,
That outside of a king, yet still my soul,
Fixed high and of itself alone dependent,
Is ever free and royal and ev'n now,   60
As at the head of battle, does defy thee.
I know what pow'r the chance of war has giv'n
And dare thee to the use on't. This vile speeching,
This after-game[19] of words is what most irks me;
Spare that, and for the rest, 'tis equall all—   65
Be it as it may.

TAMERLANE.

                    Well was it for the world
When on their borders neighboring princes met
Frequent in friendly parle, by cool debates
Preventing wasteful war; such should our meeting   70
Have been, hadst thou but held in just regard
The sanctity of leagues so often sworn to.
Canst thou believe thy Prophet (or what's more,
That Pow'r Supreme which made thee and thy
     Prophet)
Will, with impunity, let pass that breach   75
Of sacred faith given to the royal Greek?

BAJAZET.

Thou pedant talker! Hah! art thou a king,
Possessed of sacred power, Heav'n's darling attribute,
And dost thou prate of leagues and oaths and
     prophets?
I hate the Greek (perdition on his name!),   80
As I do thee, and would have met you both
(As Death does human nature) for destruction.

TAMERLANE.

Causeless to hate is not of human kind;[20]
The savage brute, that haunts in woods remote
And desert wilds, tears not the fearful traveler   85
If hunger or some injury provoke not.

BAJAZET.

Can a king want* a cause when empire bids
Go on? what is he born for but ambition?
It is his hunger, 'tis his call of nature,
The noble appetite which will be satisfied   90
And, like the food of gods, makes him immortal.

TAMERLANE.

Henceforth I will not wonder we were foes,
Since souls that differ so by nature hate,
And strong antipathy forbids their union.

BAJAZET.

The noble fire that warms me does indeed   95
Transcend thy coldness. I am pleased we differ
Nor think alike.

TAMERLANE.

                    No—for I think like man,
Thou like a monster, from whose baleful presence
Nature starts back, and though she fixed her stamp 100
On thy rough mass and marked thee for a man,
Now conscious of her error, she disclaims thee
As formed for her destruction.
'Tis true, I am a king, as thou hast been:
Honor and glory, too, have been my aim.   105
But though I dare face death and all the dangers
Which furious War wears in its bloody front,
Yet would I choose to fix my fame by peace,
By justice, and by mercy and to raise
My trophies on the blessings of mankind,   110
Nor would I buy the empire of the world
With ruin of the people whom I sway
Or forfeit of my honor.

---

19 after-game] a second game played in order to reverse or
improve the issues of the first (*OED*)

20 kind] nature, essence

BAJAZET.

                              Prophet, I thank thee.
Damnation! Couldst thou rob me of my glory   115
To dress up this tame king, this preaching dervish?
—Unfit for war, thou shouldst have lived secure
In lazy peace and with debating senates
Shared a precarious scepter, sate tamely still,
And let bold factions canton[21] out thy power   120
And wrangle for the spoils they robbed thee of,
Whilst I (curse on the power that stops my ardor!)
Would, like a tempest, rush amidst the nations,
Be greatly terrible, and deal, like Alha,
My angry thunder on the frighted world.   125

TAMERLANE.

The world! 'twould be too little for thy pride:
Thou wouldst scale heav'n.

BAJAZET.

                              I would. Away: my soul
Disdains thy conference.

TAMERLANE.

                              Thou vain, rash thing,   130
That with gigantic insolence hast dared
To lift thy wretched self above the stars
And mate with pow'r almighty: thou art fallen!

BAJAZET.

'Tis false! I am not fall'n from aught I have been;
At least my soul resolves to keep her state   135
And scorns to take acquaintance with ill* fortune.

TAMERLANE.

Almost beneath my pity art thou fallen,
Since, while th'avenging Hand of Heav'n is on thee
And presses to the dust thy swelling soul,
Foolhardy, with the stronger thou contendest.   140
To what vast heights had thy tumultuous temper
Been hurried if success had crowned thy wishes?
Say, what had I to expect if thou hadst conquered?

BAJAZET.

Oh, glorious thought! By Heav'n! I will enjoy it,
Though but in fancy; imagination shall   145
Make room to entertain the vast idea.
Oh! had I been the master but of yesterday,
The world, the world had felt me. And for thee,
I had used thee as thou art to me—a dog,
The object of my scorn and mortal hatred: 150

---

21 canton] to quarter, divide, usually with *out* (*OED*)

I would have taught thy neck to know my weight
And mounted from that footstool to my saddle;
Then, when thy daily servile task was done,
I would have caged thee for the scorn of slaves
Till thou hadst begged to die, and ev'n that mercy   155
I had denied thee. Now thou know'st my mind,
And question me no farther.

TAMERLANE.

                              Well dost thou teach me
What justice should exact from thee. Mankind
With one consent cry out for vengeance on thee;   160
Loudly they call to cut off this league-breaker,
This wild destroyer, from the face of earth.

BAJAZET.

Do it, and rid thy shaking soul at once
Of its worst fear.

TAMERLANE.

                              Why slept the thunder   165
That should have armed thy idol deity
And given thee power, ere yester sun was set,
To shake the soul of Tamerlane? Hadst thou an arm
To make thee feared, thou shouldst have proved it
     on me
Amidst the sweat and blood of yonder field   170
When through the tumult of the war I sought thee,
Fenced in with nations.

BAJAZET.

                              Curse upon the stars
That fated us to different scenes of slaughter!
Oh! could my sword have met thee—   175

TAMERLANE.

                              Thou hadst then,
As now, been in my power and held thy life
Dependent on my gift.—Yes Bajazet,
I bid thee, live: so much my soul disdains
That thou shouldst think I can fear aught but Heav'n.   180
Nay more: Couldst thou forget thy brutal fierceness
And form thyself to manhood, I would bid thee
Live and be still a king, that thou mayst learn
What man should be to man, in war rememb'ring
The common tie and brotherhood of kind.   185
—This royal tent, with such of thy domestics
As can be found, shall wait upon thy service,
Nor will I use my fortune to demand
Hard terms of peace, but such as thou mayst offer
With honor, I with honor may receive.   190

Tamerlane signs to an officer, who unbinds Bajazet.

BAJAZET.

Hah! say'st thou!—no!—our Prophet's vengeance
  blast me
If thou shalt buy my friendship with thy empire.
Damnation on thee! thou smooth, fawning talker!
Give me again my chains, that I may curse thee
And gratify my rage. Or, if thou wilt,   195
Be a vain fool and play with thy perdition:
Remember, I'm thy foe and hate thee deadly.
Thy folly on thy head!

TAMERLANE.

                        Be still my foe.
Great minds (like Heav'n) are pleased in doing good,   200
Though the ungrateful subjects of their favors
Are barren in return. Thy stubborn pride,
That spurns the gentle office of humanity,
Shall in my honor own and thy despite
I have done as I ought. Virtue still* does   205
With scorn the mercenary world regard,
Where abject souls do good and hope reward;
Above the worthless trophies men can raise
She seeks not honors, wealth, nor airy praise,
But with herself, herself the goddess pays.   210

*Exeunt Tamerlane, Axalla, Prince of Tanais, Mirvan,
Zama, and attendants. Manent Bajazet, Omar, guards.*

BAJAZET.

Come, lead me to my dungeon, plunge me down
Deep from the hated sight of man and day,
Where (under covert of the friendly darkness)
My soul may brood at leisure o'er its anguish.

OMAR.

Our royal master would with noble usage   215
Make your misfortunes light; he bids you hope—

BAJAZET.

I tell thee, slave, I have shook hands with hope,
And all my thoughts are rage, despair, and horror.

Enter Haly, Arpasia, and women attendants.

Hah! wherefore am I thus? Perdition seize me,
But my cold blood runs shiv'ring to my heart   220
As at some phantom, that in dead of night
With dreadful action stalks around our beds.
The rage and fiercer passions of my breast
Are lost in new confusion.—Arpasia!—Haly!

HALY.

Oh, Emperor! for whose hard fate our Prophet   225
And all the heroes of thy sacred race*
Are sad in paradise, thy faithful Haly
(The slave of all thy pleasures) in this ruin,
This universal shipwreck of thy fortunes,
Has gathered up this treasure for thy arms.   230
Nor ev'n the victor, haughty Tamerlane
(By whose command, once more, thy slave
  beholds thee),
Denies this blessing to thee but with honor
Renders thee back thy queen, thy beauteous bride.

BAJAZET.

Oh! had her eyes with pity seen my sorrows,   235
Had she the softness of a tender bride,
Heav'n could not have bestowed a greater blessing,
And love had made amends for loss of empire.
But see what fury dwells upon her charms!
What lightning flashes from her angry eyes!   240
With a malignant joy she views my ruin.
Ev'n beauteous in her hatred, still she charms me
And awes my fierce, tumultuous soul to love.

ARPASIA.

And dar'st thou hope, thou tyrant! ravisher!
That Heav'n has any joy in store for thee?   245
Look back upon the sum of thy past life,
Where tyranny, oppression and injustice,
Perjury, murders swell the black account,
Where lost Arpasia's wrongs stand bleeding fresh,
Thy last recorded crime. But Heav'n has found thee;   250
At length the tardy vengeance has o'erta'en thee.
My weary soul shall bear a little longer
The pain of life to call for justice on thee,
That once complete, sink to the peaceful grave
And lose the memory of my wrongs and thee.   255

BAJAZET.

Thou rail'st! I thank thee for it. Be perverse,
And muster all the woman in thy soul,
Goad me with curses, be a very* wife,
That I may fling off this tame love and hate thee.

Enter Moneses. Bajazet starting.

Hah! Keep thy temper, heart, nor take alarm   260
At a slave's presence.

MONESES.

It is Arpasia! Leave me, thou cold fear.

Sweet as the rosy morn she breaks upon me,
And sorrow, like the night's unwholesome shade,
Gives way before the golden dawn she brings.   265
BAJAZET. (*Advancing towards him.*)
    Hah, Christian! Is it well that we meet thus?
    Is this thy faith?
MONESES.
                    Why does thy frowning brow
    Put on this form of fury? Is it strange
    We should meet here, companions in misfortune,   270
    The captives of one common chance of war?
    Nor shouldst thou wonder that my sword has failed
    Before the fortune of victorious Tamerlane,
    When thou with nations like the sanded shore,
    With half the warring world upon thy side   275
    Couldst not stand up against his dreadful battle,
    That crushed thee with its shock. Thy men can
        witness,
    Those cowards that forsook me in the combat,
    My sword was not unactive.
BAJAZET.
                        No, 'tis false.   280
    Where is my daughter, thou vile Greek? Thou hast
    Betrayed her to the Tartar, or even worse,
    Pale with thy fears, didst lose her like a coward
    And, like a coward now, wouldst cast the blame
    On Fortune and ill* stars.   285
MONESES.
    Hah! said'st thou like a coward?
    What sanctity, what majesty divine
    Hast thou put on to guard thee from my rage,
    That thus thou dar'st to wrong me?
BAJAZET.
                            Out, thou slave,   290
    And know me for thy lord—
MONESES.
                        I tell thee, tyrant,
    When in the pride of pow'r thou sat'st on high,
    When like an idol thou wert vainly worshipped
    By prostrate wretches, born with slavish souls,   295
    Ev'n when thou wert a king, thou wert not more
    Nor greater than Moneses, born of a race*
    Royal and great as thine: What art thou now, then?
    The fate of war has set thee with the lowest,
    And captives (like the subjects of the grave),   300
    Losing distinction, serve one common lord.

BAJAZET.
    Braved by this dog! now give a loose to rage
    And curse thyself, curse thy false, cheating Prophet.
    Hah! Yet there's some revenge.— Hear me, thou
        Christian:
    Thou left'st that sister with me— Thou impostor!   305
    Thou boaster of thy honesty! thou liar!
    But take her to thee back.
    —Now to explore my prison. If it holds
    Another plague like this, the restless damned
    (If muftis[22] lie not) wander thus in hell: 310
    From scorching flames to chilling frosts they run,
    Then from their frosts to fires return again,
    And only prove variety of pain.
Exeunt Bajazet and Haly.
ARPASIA.
    Stay, Bajazet, I charge thee by my wrongs!
    Stay, and unfold a tale of so much horror   315
    As only fits thy telling.—Oh, Moneses!
MONESES.
    Why dost thou weep? why this tempestuous passion
    That stops thy falt'ring tongue short on my name?
    Oh, speak! unveil this mystery of sorrow
    And draw the dismal scene at once to sight.   320
ARPASIA.
    Thou art undone, lost, ruined, and undone.
MONESES.
    I will not think 'tis so while I have thee,
    While thus 'tis giv'n to fold thee in my arms,
    For while I sigh upon thy panting bosom,
    The sad remembrance of past woes is lost.   325
ARPASIA.
    Forbear to sooth thy soul with flatt'ring thoughts
    Of evils overpassed and joys to come:
    Our woes are like the genuine shade beneath,
    Where Fate cuts off the very hopes of day
    And everlasting night and horror reign.   330
MONESES.
    By all the tenderness and chaste endearments
    Of our past love, I charge thee, my Arpasia,
    To ease my soul of doubts. Give me to know
    At once the utmost malice of my fate.
ARPASIA.
    Take then thy wretched share in all I suffer,   335

---

22 muftis] Muslim priests or expounders of the law (*OED*)

Still partner of my heart. Scarce hadst thou left
The Sultan's camp when the imperious tyrant,
Soft'ning the pride and fierceness of his temper,
With gentle speech made offer of his love.
Amazed, as at the shock of sudden death,   340
I started into tears and often urged
(Though still* in vain) the difference of our faiths.
At last, as flying to the utmost refuge,
With lifted hands and streaming eyes, I owned
The fraud which, when we first were made his   345
   pris'ners,
Conscious of my unhappy form and fearing
For thy dear life, I forced thee to put on:
Thy borrowed name of brother, mine of sister,
Hiding beneath that veil the nearer tie
Our mutual vows had made before the priest.   350
Kindling to rage at hearing of my story,
"Then be it so," he cried. "Think'st thou thy vows
Giv'n to a slave shall bar me from thy beauties?"
Then bade the priest pronounce the marriage rites,
Which he performed whilst, shrieking with despair,   355
I called in vain the Pow'rs of heav'n to aid me.

MONESES.
Villain! Imperial villain! Oh—the coward!
Awed by his guilt, though backed by force and power,
He durst not to my face avow his purpose,
But in my absence, like a lurking thief,   360
Stole on my treasure and at once undid me.

ARPASIA.
Had they not kept me from the means of death
(Forgetting all the rules of Christian suffering),
I had done a desperate murder on my soul
Ere the rude slaves that waited on his will   365
Had forced me to his—

MONESES.
                Stop thee there, Arpasia,
And bar my fancy from the guilty scene.
Let not thought enter, lest the busy mind
Should muster such a train of monstrous images   370
As would distract me. Oh! I cannot bear it.
Thou lovely hoard of sweets, where all my joys
Were treasured up, to have thee rifled thus!
Thus torn untasted from my eager wishes!
But I will have thee from him. Tamerlane   375
(The sovereign judge of equity on earth)
Shall do me justice on this mighty robber
And render back thy beauties to Moneses.

ARPASIA.
And who shall render back my peace, my honor,
The spotless whiteness of my virgin soul?   380
Ah! no, Moneses—think not I will ever
Bring a polluted love to thy chaste arms.
I am the tyrant's wife (Oh, fatal title!)
And, in the sight of all the saints, have sworn,
By honor, womanhood, and blushing shame,   385
To know no second bride-bed but my grave.

MONESES.
I swear, it must not be, since still my eye
Finds thee as heavenly white, as angel pure,
As in the earliest hours of life thou wert,
Nor art thou his but mine: thy first vow's mine,   390
Thy soul is mine—

ARPASIA.
                Oh! think not that the power
Of most persuasive eloquence can make me
Forget I have been another's, been his wife.
Now by my blushes, by the strong confusion   395
And anguish of my heart, spare me, Moneses,
Nor urge my trembling virtue to the precipice.
Shortly (oh! very shortly) if my sorrows
Divine aright and Heav'n be gracious to me,
Death shall dissolve the fatal obligation   400
And give me up to peace, to that blest place
Where the good rest from care and anxious life.

MONESES.
Oh! teach me, thou fair saint, like thee to suffer;
Teach me with hardy piety to combat
The present ills; instruct my eyes to pass   405
The narrow bounds of life, this land of sorrow,
And with bold hopes to view the realms beyond,
Those distant beauties of the future state.
Tell me, Arpasia, say what joys are those
That wait to crown the wretch who suffers here.   410
Oh! tell me, and sustain my failing faith.

ARPASIA.
Imagine somewhat exquisitely fine,
Which fancy cannot paint, which the pleased mind
Can barely know, unable to describe it;
Imagine, 'tis a tract of endless joys   415
Without satiety or interruption;
Imagine, 'tis to meet, and part no more.

MONESES.
Grant, gentle Heaven, that such may be our lot!

Let us be be blest together.—Oh, my soul!
Build on that hope, and let it arm thy courage   420
To struggle with the storm that parts us now.

ARPASIA.

Yes! my Moneses, now the surges rise,
The swelling sea breaks in between our barks
And drives us to our fate on different rocks.
Farewell—my soul lives with thee—   425

MONESES.

                                        Death is parting,
'Tis the last sad adieu 'twixt soul and body,
But this is somewhat worse— My joy, my comfort,
All that was left in life fleets after thee.
My aching sight hangs on thy parting beauties,   430
Thy lovely eyes all drowned in floods of sorrow!
So sinks the setting sun beneath the waves
And leaves the traveler in pathless woods,
Benighted and forlorn. Thus with sad eyes
Westward he turns to mark the light's decay   435
Till, having lost the last, faint glimpse of day,
Cheerless, in darkness, he pursues his way.

Exeunt Moneses and Arpasia severally.

Act III, scene i. The inside of the royal tent.

Enter Axalla, Selima, and women attendants.

AXALLA.

Can there be aught in love beyond this proof,
This wondrous proof I give thee of my faith:
To tear thee from my bleeding bosom thus,
To rend the strings of life to set thee free
And yield thee to a cruel father's power,   5
Foe to my hopes? What canst thou pay me back,
What but thyself (thou angel) for this fondness?

SELIMA.

Thou dost upbraid me, beggar as I am,
And urge me with my poverty of love.
Perhaps thou think'st 'tis nothing for a maid   10
To struggle through the niceness* of her sex,
The blushes and the fears, and own she loves.
Thou think'st 'tis nothing for my artless heart
To own my weakness and confess thy triumph.

AXALLA.

Oh! yes, I own it, my charmed ears ne'er knew   15
A sound of so much rapture, so much joy.
Not voices, instruments, not warbling birds,

Not winds, not murmuring waters joined in consort,
Not tuneful nature, not th'according spheres[23]
Utter such harmony as when my Selima   20
With downcast looks and blushes said, "I love."

SELIMA.

And yet thou say'st I am a niggard to thee.
I swear, the balance shall be held between us
And Love be judge if after all the tenderness,
Tears, and confusion of my virgin soul   25
Thou shouldst complain of aught, unjust Axalla!

AXALLA.

Why was I ever blest? Why is remembrance
Rich with a thousand pleasing images
Of past enjoyments, since 'tis but to plague me?
When thou art mine no more, what will it ease me   30
To think of all the golden minutes past,
To think that thou wert kind and I was happy,
But, like an angel fall'n from bliss, to curse
My present state and mourn the heav'n I've lost.

SELIMA.

Hope better for us both, nor let thy fears,   35
Like an unlucky omen, cross my way.
My father, rough and stormy in his nature,
To me was always gentle and, with fondness
Paternal, ever met me with a blessing.
Oft when offence had stirred him to such fury   40
That not grave counselors for wisdom famed
Nor hardy captains that had fought his battles
Presumed to speak but, struck with awful* dread,
Were hushed as death, yet has he smiled on me,
Kissed me, and bade me utter all my purpose,   45
Till with my idle prattle I had soothed him
And won him from his anger.

AXALLA.

                                        Oh! I know
Thou hast a tongue to charm the wildest tempers:
Herds would forget to graze and savage beasts   50
Stand still and lose their fierceness but to hear thee,
As if they had reflection and by reason
Forsook a less enjoyment for a greater.
But oh! when I revolve each circumstance,

---

23 according spheres] The planets themselves were said to
orbit embedded in spheres that together (along with the
sphere of the fixed stars) made heavenly music, which
only the purest of mortals could hear.

My Christian faith, my service closely bound 55
To Tamerlane, my master and my friend—
Tell me (my charmer) if my fears are vain.
Think what remains for me if the fierce Sultan
Should doom thy beauties to another's bed.

SELIMA.

'Tis a sad thought, but to appease thy doubts, 60
Here, in the awful* sight of Heav'n, I vow,
No pow'r shall e'er divide me from thy love,
Ev'n duty shall not force me to be false.
My cruel stars may tear thee from my arms
But never from my heart. And when the maids 65
Shall yearly come with garlands of fresh flow'rs
To mourn with pious office o'er my grave,
They shall sit sadly down and weeping tell
How well I loved, how much I suffered for thee
And, while they grieve my fate, shall praise my 70
    constancy.

AXALLA.

But see, the Sultan comes! My beating heart
Bounds with exulting motion; hope and fear
Fight with alternate conquest in my breast.
Oh! Can I give her from me? yield her up?
Now mourn, thou God of Love, since Honor 75
    triumphs
And crowns his cruel altars with thy spoils.

Enter Bajazet.

BAJAZET.

To have a nauseous courtesy forced on me,
Spite of my will, by an insulting foe—
Hah! they would break the fierceness of my temper
And make me supple for their slavish purpose. 80
Curse on their fawning arts. From Heav'n itself
I would not on such terms receive a benefit
But spurn it back upon the giver's hand.

SELIMA. (*Comes forward and kneels to Bajazet.*)

My lord, my royal father.

BAJAZET.

                          Hah! what art thou? 85
What heavenly innocence? that in a form
So known, so loved, hast left thy paradise
For joyless prison, for this place of woe?
Art thou my Selima?

SELIMA.

                     Have you forgot me? 90

Alas! my piety is then in vain.
Your Selima, your daughter whom you loved,
The fondling once of her dear father's arms,
Is come to claim her share in his misfortunes,
To wait and tend him with obsequious duty, 95
To sit and weep for every care he feels,
To help to wear the tedious minutes out,
To soften bondage and the loss of empire.

BAJAZET.

Now by our Prophet! If my wounded mind
Could know a thought of peace, it would be now. 100
Ev'n from thy prating infancy thou wert
My joy, my little angel; smiling comfort
Came with thee still* to glad me. Now I'm cursed
Ev'n in thee too. Reproach and infamy
Attend the Christian dog to whom thou wert trusted 105
To see thee here—'twere better see thee dead.

AXALLA.

Thus Tamerlane to royal Bajazet
With kingly greeting sends: "Since with the brave
(The bloody bus'ness of the fight once ended)
Stern hate and opposition ought to cease, 110
Thy queen already to thy arms restored,
Receive this second gift, thy beateous daughter,
And if there be aught farther in thy wish,
Demand with honor and obtain it freely."

BAJAZET.

Bear back thy fulsome greeting to thy master; 115
Tell him I'll none on't. Had he been a god,
All his omnipotence could not restore
My fame diminished, loss of sacred honor,
The radiancy of majesty eclipsed.
For aught besides, it is not worth my care. 120
Thy giver and his gifts are both beneath me.

AXALLA.

Enough of war the wounded earth has known;
Weary at length and wasted with destruction,
Sadly she rears her ruined head to show
Her cities humbled and her countries spoiled 125
And to her mighty masters sues for peace.
Oh, Sultan! by the Power Divine I swear!
With joy I would resign the savage trophies
In blood and battle gained, could I atone
The fatal breach 'twixt thee' and Tamerlane, 130
And think a soldier's glory well bestowed
To buy mankind a peace.

BAJAZET.

                  And what art thou,
That dost presume to mediate 'twixt the rage
Of angry kings?   135

AXALLA.

                    A prince, born of the noblest
And of a soul that answers to that birth,
That dares not but do well. Thou dost put on
A forced forgetfulness thus not to know me,
A guest so lately to thy court, then meeting   140
On gentler terms—

SELIMA.

                       Could aught efface the merit
Of brave Axalla's name? Yet when your daughter
Shall tell how well, how nobly she was used,
How light this gallant prince made all her bondage, 145
Most sure the royal Bajazet will own
That honor stands indebted to such goodness,
Nor can a monarch's friendship more than pay it.

BAJAZET.

Hah! Know'st thou that, fond* girl? Go—'tis not
    well—
And when thou couldst descend to take a benefit 150
From a vile Christian and thy father's foe,
Thou didst an act dishonest to thy race.*
Henceforth, unless thou mean'st to cancel all
My share in thee and write thyself a bastard,
Die, starve, know any evil, any pain,   155
Rather than taste a mercy from these dogs.

SELIMA. (*Weeping.*)

Alas! Axalla!

AXALLA.

                  Weep not, lovely maid.
I swear, one pearly drop from those fair eyes
Would overpay the service of my life;   160
One sigh from thee has made a large amends
For all thy angry father's frowns and fierceness.

BAJAZET.

Oh my curst fortune! Am I fall'n thus low?
Dishonored to my face? Thou earthborn thing,
Thou clod! how hast thou dared to lift thy eyes 165
Up to the sacred race* of mighty Ottoman,
Whom kings, whom ev'n our Prophet's holy
    offspring
At distance have beheld? and what art thou?
What glorious titles blazon out thy birth,
Thou vile obscurity, hah? Say, thou base one. 170

AXALLA.

Thus challenged virtue, modest as she is,
Stands up to do herself a common justice,
To answer and assert that inborn merit,
That worth, which conscious to herself she feels.
Were honor to be scanned by long descent   175
From ancestors illustrious, I could vaunt
A lineage of the greatest and recount
Among my fathers names of ancient story,
Heroes and godlike patriots,* who subdued
The world by arms and virtue and, being Romans, 180
Scorned to be kings. But that be their own praise.
Nor will I borrow merit from the dead,
Myself an undeserver. I could prove
My friendship such as thou might'st deign t'accept
With honor when it comes with friendly office 185
To render back thy crown and former greatness.
And yet ev'n this, ev'n all is poor, when Selima
With matchless worth weighs down the adverse scale.

BAJAZET.

To give me back what yesterday took from me
Would be to give like Heaven when, having finished 190
This world (the goodly work of his creation),
He bid his favorite, man, be lord of all.
But this—

AXALLA.

             Nor is this gift beyond my power:
Oft has the mighty master of my arms   195
Urged me with large ambition to demand
Crowns and dominions from his bounteous pow'r.
'Tis true, I waived the proffer and have held it
The worthier choice to wait upon his virtues,
To be the friend and partner of his wars,   200
Than to be Asia's lord. Nor wonder then
If in the confidence of such a friendship,
I promise boldly for the royal giver
Thy crown and empire.

BAJAZET.

                    For our daughter thus 205
Mean'st thou to barter? hah! I tell thee, Christian,
There is but one, one dowry thou canst give,
And I can ask, worthy my daughter's love.

AXALLA.

Oh! name the mighty ransom, task my power,
Let there be danger, difficulty, death   210
T'enhance the price.

BAJAZET.

            I take thee at thy word:
Bring me the Tartar's head.

AXALLA.

                  Hah!

BAJAZET.

                       Tamerlane's,   215
That death, that deadly poison, to my glory.

AXALLA.

    Prodigious! Horrid!

SELIMA.

              Lost! forever lost!

BAJAZET.

    And couldst thou hope to bribe me with aught else?
With a vile peace patched up on slavish terms?   220
With tributary kingship? No—to merit
A recompense from me, sate my revenge.
The Tartar is my bane, I cannot bear him.
One heav'n and earth can never hold us both;
Still shall we hate and with defiance deadly   225
Keep rage alive till one be lost forever:
As if two suns should meet in the meridian
And strive in fiery combat for the passage.
—Weep'st thou, fond* girl? Now as thy king and father
I charge thee, drive this slave from thy remembrance.   230
Hate shall be pious in thee. (*Laying hold on her hand.*) Come and join
To curse thy father's foes.

SELIMA.

              Undone forever!
Now tyrant duty, art thou yet obeyed?
There is no more to give thee.—Oh, Axalla.   235

Bajazet leads out Selima, she looking back on Axalla.

AXALLA.

    'Tis what I feared. Fool that I was t'obey!
The coward Love, that could not bear her frown,
Has wrought his own undoing. Perhaps ev'n now
The tyrant's rage prevails upon her fears:
Fiercely he storms; she weeps and sighs and trembles   240
But swears at length to think on me no more.
He bade me take her. But oh, gracious honor!
Upon what terms? My soul yet shudders at it
And stands but half recovered of her fright.
The head of Tamerlane! monstrous impiety!   245

Bleed, bleed to death, my heart, be virtue's martyr.
Oh Emperor, I own I ought to give thee
Some nobler mark, than dying, of my faith.
Then let the pains I feel my friendship prove:
'Tis easier far to die than cease to love.   250

Exit.

Scene ii. Tamerlane's camp.

Enter severally Moneses and Prince of Tanais.

MONESES.

    If I not press untimely on his leisure,
You would much bind a stranger to your service
To give me means of audience from the Emperor.

PRINCE OF TANAIS.

    Most willingly, though for the present moment
We must entreat your stay: he holds him private.   5

MONESES.

    His council, I presume—

PRINCE OF TANAIS.

                 No, the affair
Is not of earth but heav'n: a holy man
(One whom our Prophet's law calls such), a dervish,
Keeps him in conference.   10

MONESES.

               Hours of religion,
Especially of princes, claim a reverence
Nor will be interrupted.

PRINCE OF TANAIS.

              What his business
Imports we know not, but with earnest suit   15
This morn he begged admittance. Our great master
(Than whom none bows more lowly to high heaven)
In reverend regard holds all that bear
Relation to religion and, on notice
Of his request, received him on the instant.   20

MONESES.

    We will attend his pleasure.

Exeunt. Enter Tamerlane and a dervish.

TAMERLANE.

    Thou bring'st me thy credentials from the highest,
From Alha and our Prophet: speak thy message.
It must import the best and noblest ends.

DERVISH.

    Thus speaks our holy Mahomet, who has giv'n thee   25

To reign and conquer: Ill dost thou repay
The bounties of his hand; unmindful of
The fountain whence thy streams of greatness flow,
Thou hast forgot high Heav'n, hast beaten down
And trampled on religion's sanctity.   30
TAMERLANE.
Now as I am a soldier and a king
(The greatest names of honor), do but make
Thy imputation out, and Tamerlane
Shall do thee ample justice on himself,
So much the sacred name of Heav'n awes me.   35
Could I suspect my soul of harboring aught
To its dishonor, I would search it strictly
And drive th'offending thought with fury forth.
DERVISH.
Yes, thou hast hurt our holy Prophet's honor
By fost'ring the pernicious Christian sect: 40
Those whom his sword pursued with fell destruction
Thou tak'st into thy bosom to thy councils;
They are thy only friends. The true believers
Mourn to behold thee favor this Axalla.
TAMERLANE.
I fear me thou outgo'st the Prophet's order   45
And bring'st his venerable name to shelter
A rudeness ill becoming thee to use
Or me to suffer. When thou nam'st my friend,
Thou nam'st a man beyond a monk's discerning,
Virtuous and great, a warrior and a prince.   50
DERVISH.
He is a Christian: there our law condemns him,
Although he were ev'n all thou speak'st and more.
TAMERLANE.
'Tis false: no law divine condemns the virtuous
For differing from the rules your schools devise.
Look round, how Providence bestows alike   55
Sunshine and rain, to bless the fruitful year,
On different nations, all of different faiths.
And (though by several names and titles worshipped)
Heav'n takes the various tribute of their praise,
Since all agree to own, at least to mean,   60
One best, one greatest, only Lord of all.
Thus when he viewed the many forms of nature,
He found that all was good and blessed the fair
    variety.
DERVISH.
Most impious and profane! Nay, frown not, Prince.

Full of the Prophet, I despise the danger   65
Thy angry power may threaten. I command thee
To hear and to obey, since thus says Mahomet:
Why have I made thee dreadful to the nations?
Why have I giv'n thee conquest? but to spread
My sacred law ev'n to the utmost earth   70
And make my holy Mecca the world's worship?
Go on, and wheresoe'er thy arms shall prosper,
Plant there the Prophet's name; with sword and fire
Drive out all other faiths, and let the world
Confess him only.   75
TAMERLANE.
                        Had he but commanded
My sword to conquer all, to make the world
Know but one Lord, the task were not so hard;
'Twere but to do what has been done already,
And Philip's son[24] and Caesar did as much.   80
But to subdue th'unconquerable mind;
To make one reason have the same effect
Upon all apprehensions; to force this
Or this man just to think as thou and I do—
Impossible! Unless souls were alike   85
In all, which differ now like human faces.
DERVISH.
Well might the Holy Cause be carried on,
If Mussulmen did not make war on Mussulmen.
Why hold'st thou captive a believing monarch?
Now, as thou hop'st to 'scape the Prophet's curse,   90
Release the royal Bajazet and join
With force united to destroy the Christians.
TAMERLANE.
'Tis well: I have found the cause that moved thy
    zeal.
What shallow politician set thee on
In hopes to fright me this way to compliance?   95
DERVISH.
Our Prophet only—
TAMERLANE.
                        No—thou dost belie him,
Thou maker of new faiths! that dar'st to build
Thy fond* inventions on religion's name.
Religion's luster is by native innocence   100
Divinely pure and simple from all arts.

---

24 Philip's son] Alexander the Great, son of Philip of
Macedon

You daub and dress her like a common mistress,
The harlot of your fancies, and by adding
False beauties, which she wants* not, make the world
Suspect her angel's face is foul beneath   105
And wonnot bear all lights. Hence! I have found
      thee.

DERVISH. (*Aside.*)
I have but one resort. Now aid me, Prophet.
—Yet have I somewhat further to unfold:
Our Prophet speaks to thee in thunder—thus—
      (*Draws a concealed dagger and offers* to stab
      Tamerlane.*[25]*)

TAMERLANE. (*Wresting the dagger from him.*)
No, villain, Heav'n is watchful o'er its worshippers   110
And blasts the murderer's purpose. Think thou,
      wretch,
Think on the pains that wait thy crime, and tremble
When I shall doom thee—

DERVISH.
                              'Tis but death at last,
And I will suffer greatly for the cause   115
That urged me first to the bold deed.

TAMERLANE.
                              Oh, impious!
Enthusiasm* thus makes villains martyrs.
(*Pausing.*)
It shall be so.—To die! 'twere a reward.
Now learn the difference 'twixt thy faith and mine: 120
Thine bids thee lift thy dagger to my throat;
Mine can forgive the wrong and bid thee live.
Keep thy own wicked secret and be safe.
If thou continu'st still to be the same,
'Tis punishment enough to be a villain;   125
If thou repent'st, I have gained one to virtue
And am, in that, rewarded for my mercy.
Hence! from my sight!

Exit dervish.
It shocks my soul to think
That there is such a monster in my kind.   130
Whither will man's impiety extend?
Oh gracious Heav'n! dost thou withhold thy thunder
When bold assassins take thy name upon 'em
And swear they are the champions of thy cause?

---

25 *Draws … Tamerlane*] Sutherland notes that several attempts were made on William III's life.

Enter Moneses.

MONESES. (*Kneeling.*)
Oh, Emperor! before whose awful* throne   135
Th'afflicted never kneel in vain for justice,
Undone and ruined, blasted in my hopes,
Here let me fall before your sacred feet
And groan out my misfortunes, till your pity
(The last support and refuge that is left me)   140
Shall raise me from the ground and bid me live.

TAMERLANE.
Rise, Prince, nor let me reckon up thy worth
And tell how boldly that might bid thee ask,
Lest I should make a merit of my justice,
The common debt I owe to thee, to all,   145
Ev'n to the meanest* of mankind, the charter
By which I claim my crown and Heav'n's protection.
Speak then as to a king, the sacred name
Where pow'r is lodged for righteous ends alone.

MONESES.
One only joy, one blessing, my fond heart   150
Had fixed its wishes on, and that is lost:
That sister, for whose safety my sad soul
Endured a thousand fears—

TAMERLANE.
                              I well remember,
When, ere the battles joined, I saw thee first: 155
With grief uncommon to a brother's love
Thou told'st a moving tale of her misfortunes
Such as bespoke my pity. Is there aught
Thou canst demand from friendship? ask, and
      have it.

MONESES.
First, oh let me entreat your royal goodness,   160
Forgive the folly of a lover's caution
That forged a tale of falsehood to deceive you.
Said I she was my sister? Oh! 'tis false.
She holds a dearer interest in my soul
Such as the closest ties of blood ne'er knew: 165
An int'rest such as pow'r, wealth, and honor
Can't buy, but love, love only can bestow.
She was the mistress of my vows, my bride,
By contract mine, and long ere this the priest
Had tied the knot forever, had not Bajazet—   170

TAMERLANE.
Hah! Bajazet! If yet his pow'r withholds
The cause of all thy sorrows, all thy fears,

Ev'n gratitude for once shall gain upon him,
Spite of his savage temper, to restore her.
This morn a soldier brought a captive beauty,   175
Sad though she seemed, yet of a form most rare,
By much the noblest spoil of all the field.
Ev'n Scipio[26] or a victor yet more cold
Might have forgot his virtue at her sight.
Struck with a pleasing wonder, I beheld her,   180
Till by a slave that waited near her person
I learned she was the captive Sultan's wife;
Strait[27] I forbid my eyes the dangerous joy
Of gazing long and sent her to her lord.

MONESES.
There was Moneses lost. Too sure my heart   185
(From the first mention of her wondrous charms)
Presaged it could be only my Arpasia.

TAMERLANE.
Arpasia! didst thou say?

MONESES.
                                             Yes, my Arpasia.

TAMERLANE.
Sure I mistake, or fain I would mistake thee.   190
I named the queen of Bajazet, his wife.

MONESES.
His queen! His wife! he brings that holy title
To varnish o'er the monstrous wrongs he has done me.

TAMERLANE.
Alas! I fear me, Prince, thy griefs are just;
Thou art indeed unhappy.   195

MONESES.
                                             Can you pity me
And not redress? (Kneeling.) Oh, royal Tamerlane!
Thou succor of the wretched, reach thy mercy
To save me from the grave and from oblivion.
Be gracious to the hopes that wait my youth.   200
Oh! let not sorrow blast me, lest I wither
And fall in vile dishonor. Let thy justice
Restore me my Arpasia. Give her back,
Back to my wishes, to my transports give her,

To my fond, restless, bleeding, dying bosom.   205
Oh! give her to me yet while I have life
To bless thee for the bounty. Oh, Arpasia!

TAMERLANE.
Unhappy royal youth, why dost thou ask
What honor must deny? Hah! Is she not
His wife, whom he has wedded, whom enjoyed?   210
And wouldst thou have my partial friendship break
That holy knot which, tied once, all mankind
Agree to hold sacred and undissolvable?
The brutal violence would stain my justice
And brand me with a tyrant's hated name   215
To late posterity.

MONESES.
                                             Are then the vows,
The holy vows we registered in heav'n,
But common air?

TAMERLANE.
                                             Could thy fond love forget   220
The violation of a first enjoyment?
—But sorrow has disturbed and hurt thy mind.

MONESES.
Perhaps it has, and like an idle madman
That wanders with a train of hooting boys,
I do a thousand things to shame my reason.   225
Then let me fly and bear my follies with me
Far, far from the world's sight. Honor and fame,
Arms and the glorious war shall be forgotten;
No noble sound of greatness or ambition
Shall wake my drowsy soul from her dead sleep   230
Till the last trump do summon.[28]

TAMERLANE.
                                             Let thy virtue
Stand up and answer to these warring passions
That vex thy manly temper. From the moment
When first I saw thee, something wondrous noble   235
Shone through thy form and won my friendship
   for thee
Without the tedious form of long acquaintance.
Nor will I lose thee poorly for a woman.
Come, droop no more, thou shalt with me pursue
True greatness till we rise to immortality.   240
Thou shalt forget these lesser cares, Moneses,
Thou shalt, and help me to reform the world.

---

26 Scipio] Scipio Africanus the Elder, Roman hero of the
   Second Punic War because he defeated the great
   Carthaginian general, Hannibal; noted for his stoicism
   (as recently portrayed by Nathaniel Lee in *Sophonisba*)

27 Strait] *straight*: Immediately, without delay; also *strait* as
   an adverb: with rigorous exactness; with strict correctness (*OED*)

28 last trump do summon] the trumpet that will summon
   from the grave all souls on Doomsday

MONESES.

So the good genius* warns his mortal charge
To fly the evil fate that still pursues him
Till it have wrought his ruin. Sacred Tamerlane,   245
Thy words are as the breath of angels to me.
But oh! too deep the wounding grief is fixed
For any hand to heal.

TAMERLANE.

                              This dull despair
Is the soul's laziness. Rouse to the combat,   250
And thou art sure to conquer. War shall restore thee;
The sound of arms shall wake thy martial ardor
And cure this amorous sickness of thy soul,
Begun by sloth and nursed by too much ease.
The idle God of Love supinely dreams   255
Amidst inglorious shades and purling streams;
In rosy fetters and fantastick chains
He binds deluded maids and simple swains
With soft enjoyments, woos 'em to forget
The hardy toils and labors of the great.   260
But if the warlike trumpet's loud alarms
To virtuous acts excite and manly arms,
The coward boy avows his abject fear;
On silken wings sublime he cuts the air,
Scared at the noble noise and thunder of the war.   265

Exeunt.

Act IV, scene i. Bajazet's tent.

Enter Haly and the dervish.

HALY.

To 'scape with life from an attempt like this
Demands my wonder justly.

DERVISH.

                              True, it may;
But 'tis a principle of his new faith;
'Tis what his Christian favorites have inspired,   5
Who fondly make a merit of forgiveness
And give their foes a second opportunity
If the first blow should miss.—Failing to serve
The Sultan to my wish and ev'n despairing
Of further means t'effect his liberty,   10
A lucky accident retrieved my hopes.

HALY.

The Prophet and our master will reward
Thy zeal in their behalf. But speak thy purpose.

DERVISH.

Just ent'ring here I met the Tartar general,   15
Fierce Omar.

HALY.

                    He commands (if I mistake not)
This quarter of the army and our guards.

DERVISH.

The same. By his stern aspect and the fires
That kindled in his eyes I guessed the tumult   20
Some wrong had raised in his tempestuous soul.
A friendship of old date had giv'n me privilege
To ask of his concerns. In short, I learned
That, burning for the Sultan's beauteous daughter,
He had begged her as a captive of the war   25
From Tamerlane, but meeting with denial
Of what he thought his services might claim,
Loudly he storms and curses the Italian
As cause of this affront. I joined his rage
And added to his injuries the wrongs   30
Our Prophet daily meets from this Axalla.
—But see, he comes. Improve what I shall tell,
And all we wish is ours.

They seem to talk together aside. Enter Omar.

OMAR.

                    No—if I forgive it,
Dishonor blast my name. Was it for this   35
That I directed his first steps to greatness,
Taught him to climb, and made him what he is,
When our great Khan[29] first bent his eyes
    towards him
(Then petty Prince of Parthia) and, by me
Persuaded, raised him to his daughter's bed,   40
Called him his son and successor of empire?
Was it for this, that like a rock I stood
And stemmed the torrent of our Tartar lords,
Who scorned his upstart sway? When Calibes[30]
In bold rebellion drew ev'n half the provinces   45
To own his cause, I, like his better angel,
Stood by his shaking throne and fixed it fast.
And am I now so lost to his remembrance

29 Khan] Rowe writes as if there were still one great Khan
    ("Can" in the original), like Kublai a century previous.
    But the subsequent details (being raised to Khan's
    daughter's bed and a rebellion that involved "half the
    provinces") fit better with Rowe's historical allegory.

30 Calibes] one of Tamerlane's generals; advised him on
    how to overcome the Great Wall of China; nothing in
    either Knolles or Clarke indicates a feud between them.

That, when I ask a captive, he shall tell me
She is Axalla's right, his Christian minion? 50

DERVISH.

Allow me, valiant Omar, to demand,
Since injured thus, why right you not yourself?
The prize you ask is in your power.

OMAR.

                       It is,
And I will seize it in despite of Tamerlane 55
And that Italian dog.

HALY.

                    What need of force
When everything concurs to meet your wishes?
Our mighty master would not wish a son
Nobler than Omar. From a father's hand 60
Receive that daughter which ungrateful Tamerlane
Has to your worth denied.

OMAR.

                  Now by my arms,
It will be great revenge. What will your Sultan
Give to the man that shall restore his liberty, 65
His crown and give him pow'r to wreck his hatred
Upon his greatest foe?

HALY.

                All he can ask
And far beyond his wish.

Trumpets.

OMAR.

                  These trumpets speak 70
The Emperor's approach; he comes once more
To offer terms of peace. Retire—within
I will know farther—he grows deadly to me,
And curse me, Prophet, if I not repay
His hate with retribution full as mortal. 71

Exeunt.

        Scene ii. Scene draws,
    discovers* Arpasia lying on a couch.

A song[31] to Sleep.

To Thee, oh! gentle Sleep, alone
    Is owing all our peace;
By thee our joys are heightened shown;
    By thee our sorrows cease.

The nymph whose hand by fraud or force 5
    Some tyrant has possessed,
By thee obtaining a divorce,
    In her own choice is blest.

Oh! stay, Arpasia bids thee stay,
    The sadly weeping fair 10
Conjures thee not to lose in day
    The object of her care,

To grasp whose pleasing form she sought:
    That motion chased her sleep.
Thus by ourselves are oft'nest wrought 15
    The griefs for which we weep.

ARPASIA.

Oh Death! thou gentle end of human sorrows,
Still must my weary eyelids vainly wake
In tedious expectation of thy peace?
Why stand thy thousand thousand doors still* open 20
To take the wretched in, if stern religion
Guards every passage and forbids my entrance?
Lucrece* could bleed, and Portia swallow fire,[32]
When urged with griefs beyond a mortal sufferance,
But here it must not be. Think then, Arpasia, 25
Think on the sacred dictates of thy faith,
And let that arm thy virtue to perform
What Cato's daughter durst not: live, Arpasia,
And dare to be unhappy.

Enter Tamerlane and attendants.

TAMERLANE.

When Fortune smiles upon the soldier's arms 30
And adds ev'n beauty to adorn his conquest,
Yet she ordains the fair should know no fears,
No sorrows to pollute their lovely eyes
But should be used ev'n nobly, as herself,
The queen and goddess of the warrior's vows. 35
Such welcome as a camp can give, fair Sultaness,

---

had already addressed his *Epistle to* Flavia (A *New Mis-cellany* …, 1701), is perhaps the authoress; but the song is not included in her collected verses." It is still not included.

32 Portia … fire] Thus the wife of Brutus (and Cato's daughter) committed suicide in the aftermath of the assassination of Caesar.

---

31 song] identified in the text as " By a Lady." Sutherland opines: "Anne, Countess of Winchelsea, to whom Rowe

We hope you have received. It shall be larger
And better, as it may.
ARPASIA.
                              Since I have borne
That miserable mark of fatal greatness,   40
I have forgot all difference of conditions;
Scepters and fetters are grown equal to me,
And the best change my fate can bring is death.
TAMERLANE.
When sorrow dwells in such an angel form,
Well may we guess that those above are mourners.   45
Virtue is wronged, and bleeding innocence
Suffers some wondrous violation here
To make the saints look sad. Oh! teach my power
To cure those ills, which you unjustly suffer,
Lest Heav'n should wrest it from my idle hand   50
If I look on and see you weep in vain.
ARPASIA.
Not that my soul disdains the generous aid
Thy royal goodness proffers, but oh! Emperor,
It is not now in my fate to be made happy,
Nor will I listen to the coz'ner Hope   55
But stand resolved to bear the beating storm
That roars around me, safe in this alone,
That I am not immortal.—Though 'tis hard,
'Tis wondrous hard, when I remember thee
(Dear native Greece) and you, ye weeping maids,   60
That were companions of my virgin youth.
My noble parents! oh! the grief of heart,
The pangs that, for unhappy me, bring down
Their reverend ages to the grave with sorrow.
And yet, there is a woe surpassing all.   65
Ye saints and angels, give me of your constancy
If you expect I shall endure it long.
TAMERLANE.
Why is my pity all that I can give
To tears like yours? And yet I fear 'tis all,
Nor dare I ask what mighty loss you mourn,   70
Lest honor should forbid to give it back.
ARPASIA.
No, Tamerlane, nor did I mean thou shouldst.
But know (though to the weakness of my sex
I yield these tears) my soul is more than man.
Think I am born a Greek, nor doubt my virtue: 75
A Greek! from whose famed ancestors of old
Rome drew the patterns of her boasted heroes.

They must be mighty evils that can vanquish
A Spartan courage and a Christian faith.

Enter Bajazet.

BAJAZET.
To know no thought of rest! to have the mind   80
Still minist'ring fresh plagues! as in a circle
Where one dishonor treads upon another.
What know the fiends beyond it? (*Seeing Arpasia
    and Tamerlane.*) Hah! by hell!
There wanted* only this to make me mad.
Comes he to triumph here? to rob my love?   85
And violate the last retreat of happiness?
TAMERLANE.
But that I read upon thy frowning brow
That war yet lives and rages in thy breast,
Once more (in pity to the suff'ring world)
I meant to offer peace—   90
BAJAZET.
                              And mean'st thou too
To treat it with our Empress? And to barter
The spoils which Fortune gave thee for her favors?*
ARPASIA. (*Aside.*)
What would the tyrant?
BAJAZET.
                              Seek'st thou thus our friendship?   95
Is this the royal usage thou didst boast?
TAMERLANE.
The boiling passion that disturbs thy soul
Spreads clouds around and makes thy purpose dark.
Unriddle what thy mystic fury aims at.
BAJAZET.
Is it a riddle? Read it there explained,   100
There in my shame.—Now judge me thou, Oh
    Prophet
And equal Heav'n, if this demand not rage!
The peasant hind, begot and born to slavery,
Yet dares assert a husband's sacred right
And guard his homely couch from violation.   105
And shall a monarch tamely bear the wrong
Without complaining?
TAMERLANE.
                              If I could have wronged thee,
If conscious virtue and all-judging Heaven
Stood not between to bar ungoverned appetite,   110
What hindered but in spite of thee, my captive,

I might have used a victor's boundless power
And sated every wish my soul could form?
But to secure thy fears, know, Bajazet,
This is among the things I dare not do.   115
BAJAZET.
By hell, 'tis false! Else wherefore art thou present?
What cam'st thou for, but to undo my honor?
I found thee holding amorous parley with her,
Gazing and gloating[33] on her wanton eyes
And bargaining for pleasures yet to come.   120
My life, I know, is the devoted[34] price,
But take it, I am weary of the pain.
TAMERLANE.
Yet ere thou rashly urge my rage too far,
I warn thee to take heed: I am a man
And have the frailties common to man's nature;   125
The fiery seeds of wrath are in my temper
And may be blown up to so fierce a blaze
As wisdom cannot rule. Know, thou hast touched me
Ev'n in the nicest,* tenderest part, my honor.
My honor! which, like pow'r, disdains being   130
  questioned.
Thy breath has blasted my fair virtue's fame
And marked me for a villain and a tyrant.
ARPASIA.
And stand I here an idle looker on
To see my innocence murdered and mangled
By barbarous hands nor can revenge the wrong?   135

(*To Bajazet.*)

Art thou a man, and dar'st thou use me thus?
Hast thou not torn me from my native country?
From the dear arms of my lamenting friends?
From my soul's peace, and from my injured love?
Hast thou not ruined, blotted me forever,   140
And driv'n me to the brink of black despair?
And is it in thy malice yet to add
A wound more deep, to sully my white name,
My virtue?
BAJAZET.
                Yes, thou hast thy sex's virtues: 145

Their affectation, pride, ill nature, noise,
Proneness to change ev'n from the joy that
  pleased 'em.
So gracious is your idol, dear variety,
That for another love you would forego
An angel's form to mingle with a devil's.   150
Through every state and rank of men you wander,
Till ev'n your large experience takes in all
The different nations of the peopled earth.
ARPASIA.
Why sought'st thou not from thy own impious tribe
A wife, like one of these, for such thy race   155
(If human nature brings forth such) affords.
Greece, for chaste virgins famed and pious matrons,
Teems not with monsters like your Turkish wives,
Whom guardian eunuchs, haggard and deformed,
Whom walls and bars make honest* by constraint.   160
Know, I detest, like hell, the crime thou mention'st.
Not that I fear or reverence thee, thou tyrant,
But that my soul, conscious of whence it sprung,
Sits unpolluted in its sacred temple
And scorns to mingle with a thought so mean.*   165
TAMERLANE.
Oh pity! that a greatness so divine
Should meet a fate so wretched, so unequal.
(*To Bajazet.*)
Thou blind and wilful to the good that courts thee.
With openhanded bounty Heaven pursues thee
And bids thee (undeserving as thou art   170
And monstrous in thy crimes) be happy yet,
Whilst thou in fury dost avert the blessings
And art an evil genius* to thyself.
BAJAZET.
No—Thou! thou art my greatest curse on earth,
Thou, who hast robbed me of my crown and glory   175
And now pursu'st me to the verge of life
To spoil me of my honor. Thou! thou hypocrite!
That wear'st a pageant outside show of virtue
To cover the hot thoughts that glow within,
Thou rank adulterer!   180
TAMERLANE.
                      Oh! That thou wert
The lord of all those thousands that lie breathless
On yonder field of blood, that I again
Might hunt thee in the face of death and danger
Through the tumultuous battle and there force thee, 185

---

33 gloating] casting amorous or admiring glances, with *on*
   or *upon* (*OED*)
34 devoted] formally or surely consigned to evil or destruction; doomed (*OED*)

Vanquished and sinking underneath my arm,
To own thou hast traduced me like a villain.

BAJAZET.

Hah! does it gall thee, Tartar? By revenge,
It joys me much to find thou feel'st my fury!
Yes! I will echo to thee, thou adulterer!   190
Thou dost profane the name of king and soldier
And like a ruffian-bravo cam'st with force
To violate the holy marriage bed.

TAMERLANE.

Wert thou not sheltered by thy abject state,
The captive of my sword, by my just anger!   195
My breath, like thunder, should confound thy pride
And doom thee dead this instant with a word.

BAJAZET.

'Tis false! my fate's above thee, and thou dar'st not.

TAMERLANE.

Hah! dare not? Thou hast raised my pond'rous rage,
And now it falls to crush thee at a blow.   200
—A guard there.

Enter a guard; they seize Bajazet.

Seize and drag him to his fate.
Tyrant, I'll do a double justice on thee,
At once revenge myself and all mankind.

BAJAZET.

Well dost thou, ere thy violence and lust   205
Invade my bed, thus to begin with murder:
Drown all thy fears in blood and sin securely.

TAMERLANE.

Away!

ARPASIA. (*Kneeling.*)
                    Oh stay! I charge thee by renown,
By that bright glory thy great soul pursues,
Call back the doom of death!   210

TAMERLANE.

                              Fair injured excellence,
Why dost thou kneel and waste such precious
    pray'rs
(As might ev'n bribe the saints to partial justice)
For one to goodness lost, who first undid thee,   215
Who still pursues and aggravates the wrong.

BAJAZET.

By Alha, no! I will not wear a life
Bought with such vile dishonor. Death shall free me
At once from infamy and thee, thou traytress!

ARPASIA.

No matter, though the whistling winds grow loud   220
And the rude tempest roars, 'tis idle rage.
Oh! mark it not, but let thy steady virtue
Be constant to its temper: save his life,
And save Arpasia from the sport of talkers.
Think how the busy, meddling world shall toss   225
Thy mighty name about in scurril mirth,
Shall brand thy vengeance as a foul design,
And make such monstrous legends of our lives
As late posterity shall blush in reading.

TAMERLANE.

Oh matchless virtue! Yes I will obey,   230
Though laggard in the race, admiring* yet,
I will pursue the shining path thou tread'st.
—Sultan, be safe. Reason resumes her empire,

The guards release Bajazet.

And I am cool again. Here break we off,
Lest further speech should minister new rage.   235
Wisely from dangerous passions I retreat
To keep a conquest which was hard to get.
And oh! 'tis time I should for flight prepare:
A war more fatal seems to threaten there,
And all my rebel blood assists the fair.   240
One moment more, and I too late shall find
That love's the strongest pow'r that lords it o'er
    the mind.

Exit Tamerlane followed by the guards.

BAJAZET.

To what new shame, what plague am I reserved?
Why did my stars refuse me to die warm,
While yet my regal state stood unimpeached   245
Nor knew the curse of having one above me?
Then too (although by force I grasped the joy)
My love was safe nor felt the rack of doubt.
Why hast thou forced this nauseous life upon me?
Is it to triumph over me? But I will,   250
I will be free, I will forget thee all:
The bitter and the sweet, the joy and pain
Death shall expunge at once and ease my soul.
—Prophet, take notice, I disclaim thy paradise,
Thy fragrant bow'rs and everlasting shades: 255
Thou hast placed woman there, and all thy joys
    are tainted. (*Exit.*)

ARPASIA.

A little longer yet, be strong, my heart,
A little longer let the busy spirits
Keep on their cheerful round— It wonnot be:
Love, sorrow, and the sting of vile reproach, 260
Succeeding one another in their course,
Like drops of eating water on the marble,
At length have worn my boasted courage down.
I will indulge the woman in my soul
And give a loose to tears and to impatience. 265
Death is at last my due, and I will have it.
—And see, the poor Moneses comes to take
One sad adieu, and then we part forever.

Enter Moneses.

MONESES.

Already am I onward of my way.
Thy tuneful voice comes like a hollow sound 270
At distance to my ears. My eyes grow heavy,
And all the glorious lights of heav'n look dim;
'Tis the last office they shall ever do me,
To view thee once, and then to close and die.

ARPASIA.

Alas! how happy have we been, Moneses? 275
Ye gentle days, that once were ours, what joys
Did every cheerful morning bring along?
No fears, no jealousies, no angry parents,
That for unequal births or fortunes frowned,
But love, that kindly joined our hearts to bless us, 280
Made us a blessing too to all besides.

MONESES.

Oh! Cast not thy remembrance back, Arpasia,
'Tis grief unutterable, 'tis distraction!
But let this last of hours be peaceful sorrow;
Here let me kneel and pay my latest vows: 285
Be witness, all ye saints, thou Heav'n and Nature,
Be witness of my truth, for you have known it;
Be witness that I never knew a pleasure
In all the world could offer like Arpasia;
Be witness that I lived but in Arpasia; 290
And oh! be witness that her loss has killed me.

ARPASIA.

While thou art speaking, life begins to fail,
And every tender accent chills like death.
Oh! let me haste then yet, ere day declines
And the long night prevail, once more to tell thee 295

What and how dear Moneses has been to me.
What has he not been? All the names of love—
Brothers or fathers, husbands—all are poor:
Moneses is my self; in my fond heart,
Ev'n in my vital blood he lives and reigns. 300
The last dear object of my parting soul
Will be Moneses; the last breath that lingers
Within my panting breast shall sigh Moneses.

MONESES.

It is enough! Now to thy rest, my soul,
The world and thou have made an end at once. 305

ARPASIA.

Fain would I still detain thee, hold thee still,
Nor Honor can forbid that we together
Should share the poor few minutes that remain.
I swear, methinks this sad society
Has somewhat pleasing in it. Death's dark shades[35] 310
Seem as we journey on to lose their horror:
At near approach the monsters formed by fear
Are vanished all and leave the prospect clear;
Amidst the gloomy vale a pleasing scene
With flow'rs adorned and never-fading green 315
Inviting stands to take the wretched in.
No wars, no wrongs, no tyrants, no despair
Disturb the quiet of a place so fair,
But injured lovers find Elysium there.

Exeunt. Enter Bajazet, Omar, Haly, and the dervish.

BAJAZET.

Now by the glorious tomb that shrines our Prophet, 320
By Mecca's sacred temple, here I swear!
Our daughter is thy bride, and to that gift
Such wealth, such pow'r, such honors will I add
That monarchs shall with envy view thy state
And own, thou art a demigod to them. 325
Thou hast given me what I wished, power of revenge,
And when a king rewards, 'tis ample retribution.

OMAR.

Twelve Tartar lords, each potent in his tribe,
Have sworn to own my cause and draw their
        thousands
Tomorrow from th'ungrateful Parthian's side. 330

---

35 shades] both Hades and Sheol, Greek and Hebrew lands
of the dead, carry the connotation of the land of shades,
where the word means both shadows and ghosts.

The day declining seems to yield to night
Ere little more than half her course be ended:
In an auspicious hour prepare for flight;
The leaders of the troops through which we pass,
Raised by my pow'r, devoted to my service,
Shall make our passage secret and secure.   335
DERVISH.
Already, mighty Sultan, art thou safe,
Since by yon passing torch's light I guess
To his pavilion Tamerlane retires,
Attended by a train of waiting courtiers.
All who remain within these tents are thine   340
And hail thee as their lord.
  —Hah, th'Italian prince
With sad Moneses are not yet gone forth.
BAJAZET.
Hah! With our queen and daughter?
OMAR.
                                    They are ours: 345
I marked the slaves who waited on Axalla;
They, when the Emperor passed out, pressed on
And mingled with the crowd nor missed their lord.
He is your pris'ner, sir. I go this moment
To seize and bring him to receive his doom. (*Exit.*)   350
BAJAZET.
Haste, Haly, follow, and secure the Greek.
Him too I wish to keep within my power.

Exit Haly.

DERVISH.
If my dread lord permit his slave to speak,
I would advise to spare Axalla's life
Till we are safe beyond the Parthian's power: 355
Him as our pledge of safety may we hold,
And could you gain him to assist your flight,
It might import you much.
BAJAZET.
                          Thou counsel'st well,
And though I hate him, for he is a Christian   360
And to my mortal enemy devoted,
Yet to secure my liberty and vengeance
I wish he now were ours.
DERVISH.
                        And see, they come!
Fortune repents, again she courts your side,   365
And, with this first fair offering of success,

She woos you to forget her crime of yesterday.

*Enter Omar with Axalla prisoner, Selima following
weeping.*

AXALLA.
I wonnot call thee villain, 'tis a name
Too holy for thy crime: to break thy faith
And turn a rebel to so good a master   370
Is an ingratitude unmatched on earth.
The first revolting angel's pride could only
Do more than thou hast done. Thou copy'st well
And keep'st the black original in view.
OMAR.
Do, rage, and vainly call upon thy master   375
To save his minion. My revenge has caught thee,
And I will make thee curse that fond* presumption
That set thee on to rival me in aught.
BAJAZET.
Christian, I hold thy fate at my disposal.
One only way remains to mercy open: 380
Be partner of my flight and my revenge,
And thou art safe. Thy other choice is death.
OMAR.
What means the Sultan?
DERVISH. (*Aside to Omar.*)
                        I conjure you, hold—
Your rival is devoted to destruction,   385
Nor would the Sultan now defer his fate
But for our common safety. Listen further. (*Whispers.*)
AXALLA.
Then briefly thus: death is the choice I make,
Since, next to Heav'n, my master and my friend
Has interest in my life and still* shall claim it.   390
BAJAZET.
Then take thy wish.—Call in our mutes.
SELIMA.
                                      My father,
If yet you have not sworn to cast me off
And turn me out to wander in misfortune;
If yet my voice be gracious in your ears;   395
If yet my duty and my love offend not,
Oh, call your sentence back and save Axalla.
BAJAZET.
Rise, Selima, the slave deserves to die
Who durst with sullen pride refuse my mercy.
Yet for thy sake, once more I offer life.   400

SELIMA.

Some angel whisper to my anxious soul
What I shall do to save him.—Oh, Axalla!
Is it so easy to thee to forsake me?
Canst thou resolve with all this cold indifference
Never to see me more? To leave me here   405
The miserable mourner of thy fate,
Condemned to waste my widowed virgin youth,
My tedious days and nights in lonely weeping
And never know the voice of comfort more?

AXALLA.

Search not too deep the sorrows of my breast.   410
Thou say'st I am indifferent and cold.
Oh, is it possible my eyes should tell
So little of the fighting storm within?
Oh, turn thee from me, save me from thy beauties,
Falsehood and ruin all look lovely there.   415
Oh, let my lab'ring soul yet struggle through—
I will—I would resolve to die and leave thee.

BAJAZET.

Then let him die. He trifles with my favor.
I have too long attended his resolves.

SELIMA. (To Bajazet.)

Oh! stay a minute, yet a minute longer;   420
A minute is a little space in life.
There is a kind consenting in his eyes,
And I shall win him to your royal will.

(To Axalla aside.)

Oh! my Axalla, seem but to consent—
Unkind and cruel, will you then do nothing?   425
I find I am not worth thy least of cares.

AXALLA.

Oh! labor not to hang dishonor on me.
I could bear sickness, pain, and poverty,
Those mortal evils worse than death, for thee.
But this: it has the force of fate against us   430
And cannot be.

SELIMA. (To Bajazet.)

　　　　　See, see, sir, he relents;
Already he inclines to own your cause.
A little longer, and he is all yours.

BAJAZET.

Then mark how far a father's fondness yields: 435
Till midnight I defer the death he merits
And give him up till then to thy persuasion.

If by that time he meets my will, he lives;
If not, thyself shalt own he dies with justice.

AXALLA.

'Tis but to lengthen life upon the rack.   440
I am resolved already.

SELIMA.

　　　　　　　　Oh! be still,
Nor rashly urge a ruin on us both.
'Tis but a moment more I have to save thee.
—Be kind, auspicious Alha, to my pray'r.   445
More for my love than for myself I fear.
Neglect mankind awhile, and make him all thy care.

Exeunt Axalla and Selima.

BAJAZET.

Moneses! Is that dog secured?

OMAR.

　　　　　　　　　　He is.

BAJAZET.

'Tis well.—My soul perceives returning greatness,   450
As Nature feels the spring. Lightly she bounds
And shakes dishonor, like a burden, from her:
Once more imperial, awful,* and herself.
So when of old Jove from the Titans fled,
Ammon's[36] rude front his radiant face belied,   455
And all the majesty of heaven lay hid.
At length by Fate to pow'r divine restored,
His thunder taught the world to know its lord.
The god grew terrible again and was again adored.

Exeunt.

Act V. Bajazet's tent.

Enter Arpasia.

ARPASIA.

Sure 'tis a horror more than darkness brings
That sits upon the night. Fate is abroad.
Some ruling fiend hangs in the dusky air
And scatters ruin, death, and wild distraction
O'er all the wretched race of man below.   5
Not long ago a troop of ghastly slaves
Rushed in and forced Moneses from my sight.
Death hung so heavy on his drooping spirits

---

36 Ammon] Jupiter was sometimes associated with the
Egyptian king of the gods, Ammon or Amon.

That scarcely could he say, "Farewell—forever."
And yet, methinks, some gentle spirit whispers, 10
"Thy peace draws near, Arpasia, sigh no more."
—And see the king of terrors is at hand:
His minister appears.

Enter Bajazet, and Haly.

BAJAZET. (*Aside to Haly.*)
                              The rest I leave
To thy dispatch. For oh, my faithful Haly, 15
Another care has taken up thy master:
Spite of the high-wrought tempest in my soul,
Spite of the pangs which jealousy has cost me,
This haughty woman reigns within my breast.
In vain I strive to put her from my thoughts, 20
To drive her out with empire and revenge.
Still she comes back like a retiring tide
That ebbs awhile but straight returns again
And swells above the beach.

HALY.
                              Why wears my lord 25
An anxious thought for what his pow'r commands?
When in an happy hour you shall ere long
Have borne the Empress from amidst your foes,
She must be yours, be only and all yours.

BAJAZET.
On that depends my fear. Yes! I must have her. 30
I own I will not, cannot go without her.
But such is the condition of our flight
That, should she not consent, 'twould hazard all
To bear her hence by force. Thus I resolve, then,
By threats and pray'rs, by every way to move her. 35
If all prevail not, force is left at last,
And I will set life, empire on the venture
To keep her mine.—Be near, to wait my will.

Exit Haly.

When last we parted, 'twas on angry terms.
Let the remembrance die, or kindly think 40
That jealous rage is but a hasty flame
That blazes out when love too fiercely burns.

ARPASIA.
For thee to wrong me and for me to suffer
Is the hard lesson that my soul has learnt,
And now I stand prepared for all to come. 45
Nor is it worth my leisure to distinguish

If love or jealousy commit the violence;
Each have alike been fatal to my peace,
Confirming me a wretch and thee a tyrant.

BAJAZET.
Still to deform thy gentle brow with frowns! 50
And still to be perverse! It is a manner
Abhorrent from the softness of thy sex:
Women, like summer storms, awhile are cloudy,
Burst out in thunder and impetuous show'rs,
But straight the sun of beauty dawns abroad, 55
And all the fair horizon is serene.

ARPASIA.
Then to retrieve the honor of my sex
Here I disclaim that changing and inconstancy.
To thee I will be ever as I am.

BAJAZET.
Thou say'st I am a tyrant. Think so still, 60
And let it warn[h] thy prudence to lay hold
On the good hour of peace that courts thee now.
Souls formed like mine brook being scorned but ill.
Be well advised, and profit by my patience.
It is a short-lived virtue. 65

ARPASIA.
                              Turn thy eyes
Back on the story of my woes, barbarian.
Thou that hast violated all respects
Due to my sex and honor of my birth,
Thou brutal ravisher! that hast undone me, 70
Ruined my love! can I have peace with thee?
Impossible! first heav'n and hell shall join:
They only differ more.

BAJAZET.
                              I see 'tis vain
To court thy stubborn temper with endearments. 75
Resolve this moment to return my love
And be the willing partner of my flight,
Or by the Prophet's holy law! thou die'st.

ARPASIA.
And dost thou hope to fright me with that phantom?
Death! 'Tis the greatest mercy thou canst give. 80
So frequent are the murders of thy reign,
One day scarce passing by unmarked with blood,
That children, by long use, have learned to scorn it.
Know, I disdain to aid thy treacherous purpose,
And shouldst thou dare to force me, with my cries 85
I will call heaven and earth to my assistance.

BAJAZET.

Confusion! dost thou brave me? But my wrath
Shall find a passage to thy swelling heart
And rack thee worse than all the pains of death.
That Grecian dog, the minion of thy wishes,   90
Shall be dragged forth and butchered in thy sight.
Thou shalt behold him, when his pangs are
    terrible,
Then when he stares and gasps and struggles
    strongly,
Ev'n in the bitterest agony of dying,
Till thou shalt rend thy hair, tear out thy eyes,   95
And curse thy pride, while I applaud my vengeance.

ARPASIA.

Oh, fatal image! All my powers give way,
And resolution sickens at the thought;
A flood of passion rises in my breast
And labors fiercely upward to my eyes.   100
—Come, all ye great examples of my sex—
Chaste virgins, tender wives, and pious matrons—
Ye holy martyrs, who with wondrous faith
And constancy unshaken have sustained
The rage of cruel men and fiery persecution,   105
Come to my aid, and teach me to defy
The malice of this fiend. I feel, I feel
Your sacred spirit arm me to resistance.
—Yes, tyrant, I will stand this shock of Fate,
Will live to triumph over thee for a moment,   110
Then die well pleased and follow my Moneses.

BAJAZET.

Thou talk'st it well. But talking is thy privilege;
'Tis all the boasted courage of thy sex,
Though, for thy soul, thou dar'st not meet the
    danger.

ARPASIA.

By all my hopes of happiness, I dare!   115
My soul is come within her ken of heaven.
Charmed with the joys and beauties of that place,
Her thoughts and all her cares she fixes there,
And 'tis in vain for thee to rage below.
Thus stars shine bright and keep their place above, 120
Though ruffing[37] winds deform this lower world.

BAJAZET.

This moment is the trial.

---

37 ruffing] blustering (OED)

ARPASIA.

                            Let it come.
This moment, then, shall show I am a Greek
And speak my country's courage in my suffering.   125

BAJAZET.

Here, mercy, I disclaim thee.—Mark me, traitress!
My love prepares a victim to thy pride,
And when it greets thee next, 'twill be in blood.
    (Exit.)

ARPASIA.

My heart beats higher, and my nimble spirits
Ride swiftly through their purple channels round.   130
'Tis the last blaze of life: nature revives
Like a dim, winking lamp that flashes brightly
With parting light and straight is dark forever.
And see! my last of sorrows is at hand:
Death and Moneses come together to me,   135
As if my stars, that had so long been cruel,
Grew kind at last and gave me all I wish.

*Enter Moneses, guarded by some mutes, others
attending with a cup of poison and a bowstring.*

MONESES.

I charge ye, oh ye ministers of Fate,
Be swift to execute your master's will.
Bear me to my Arpasia, let me tell her   140
The tyrant is grown kind: he bids me go
And die beneath her feet. A joy shoots through
My drooping breast, as often, when the trumpet
Has called my youthful ardor forth to battle,
High in my hopes and ravished with the sound,   145
I have rushed eager on amidst the foremost
To purchase victory or glorious death.

ARPASIA.

If it be happiness, alas, to die,
To lie forgotten in the silent grave,
To love and glory lost and from among   150
The great Creator's works expunged and blotted,
Then very shortly shall we both be happy.

MONESES.

There is no room for doubt, 'tis certain bliss.
The tyrant's cruel violence, thy loss
Already seem more light, nor has my soul   155
One unrepented guilt upon remembrance
To make me dread the justice of hereafter,
But standing now on the last verge of life,

Boldly I view the vast abyss, eternity,
Eager to plunge and leave my woes behind me.   160
ARPASIA.
By all the truth of our past lives I vow,
To die appears a very nothing to me!
But oh! Moneses, should I not allow
Somewhat to love and to my sex's tenderness?
This very now I could put off my being   165
Without a groan. But to behold thee die—
Nature shrinks in me at the dreadful thought,
Nor can my constancy sustain this blow.
MONESES.
Since thou art armed for all things after death,
Why should the pomp and preparation of it   170
Be frightful to thy eyes? There's not a pain
Which age or sickness brings, the least disorder
That vexes any part of this fine frame
Is full as grievous. All that the mind feels
Is much, much more. And see, I go to prove it.   175

*Enter a mute; he signs to the rest, who proffer[38] the
bowstring to Moneses.*

ARPASIA.
Think ere we part!
MONESES.
                                Of what?
ARPASIA.
                                        Of something soft,
Tender and kind, of something wondrous sad.
Oh! my full soul!   180
MONESES.
                    My tongue is at a loss;
Thoughts crowd so fast, thy name is all I've left,
My kindest! truest! dearest! best Arpasia!

The mutes struggle with him.

ARPASIA.
I have a thousand, thousand things to utter,
A thousand more to hear yet.—Barbarous villains!   185
Give me a minute.—Speak to me, Moneses.
MONESES.
Speak to thee? 'Tis the business of my life,
'Tis all the use I have for vital air.

---

38 *proffer*] To offer (battle, injury, etc.); to attempt to in-
    flict: offer*

Stand off, ye slaves! To tell thee that my heart
Is full of thee, that ev'n at this dread moment   190
My fond eyes gaze with joy and rapture on thee.
Angels and light itself are not so fair—

Enter Bajazet, Haly, and attendants.

BAJAZET.
Hah! wherefore lives this dog? Be quick, ye slaves,
And rid me of the pain.
MONESES.
                                For only death,   195
And the last night can shut out my Arpasia.

The mutes strangle Moneses.

ARPASIA.
Oh, dismal! 'tis not to be borne. Ye moralists,
Ye talkers, what are all your precepts now?
Patience? Distraction! Blast the tyrant, blast him,
Avenging lightnings, snatch him hence, ye fiends! 200
Love! Death! Moneses! Nature can no more:
Ruin is on her, and she sinks at once. (*Sinks down.*)
BAJAZET.
Help, Haly, raise her up, and bear her out.
HALY.
Alas! she faints.
ARPASIA.
                        No, tyrant, 'tis in vain.   205
Oh! I am now beyond thy cruel power:
The peaceful slumber of the grave is on me.
Ev'n all the tedious day of life I've wandered,
Bewildered with misfortunes—
At length 'tis night, and I have reached my home. 210
Forgetting all the toils and troubles past,
Weary I'll lay me down and sleep till—oh! (*Dies.*)
BAJAZET.
Fly, ye slaves,
And fetch me cordials.—No, she shall not die.
Spite of her sullen pride, I'll hold in life   215
And force her to be blest against her will.
HALY.
Already 'tis beyond the power of art,
For see, a deadly cold has froze the blood;
The pliant limbs grow stiff and lose their use;
And all the animating fire is quenched.   220
Even beauty too is dead; an ashy pale
Grows o'er the roses; the red lips have lost

Their flagrant hew for want of that sweet breath
That blest 'em with its odors as it passed.

BAJAZET.

Can it be possible? Can rage and grief, 225
Can love and indignation be so fierce,
So mortal in a woman's heart? Confusion!
Is she escaped, then? What is royalty,
If those that are my slaves and should live for me
Can die and bid defiance to my power? 230

Enter the dervish.

DERVISH.

The valiant Omar sends to tell thy Greatness
The hour of flight is come and urges haste,
Since he descries near Tamerlane's pavilion
Bright troops of crowding torches, who from thence
On either hand stretch far into the night 235
And seem to form a shining front of battle.

(*Looking out.*)

Behold, ev'n from this place, thou mayst discern 'em.

BAJAZET.

By Alha! yes! they cast a day around 'em,
And the plain seems thick set with stars as heav'n.
Hah! or my eyes are false, they move this way. 240
'Tis certain so.—Fly, Haly, to our daughter.

Exit Haly.

Let some secure the Christian prince, Axalla.
We will be gone this minute.

Enter Omar.

OMAR.

                    Lost! Undone!

BAJAZET.

What mean'st thou? 245

OMAR.

            All our hopes of flight are lost:
Mirvan and Zama with the Parthian horse
Enclose us round; they hold us in a toil.

BAJAZET.

Hah! whence this unexpected curse of Chance?

OMAR.

Too late I learnt that early in the night 250
A slave was suffered by the Princess' order
To pass the guard; I clove the villain down
Who yielded to his flight, but that's poor vengeance.

That fugitive has raised the camp upon us
And, unperceived by favor of the night, 255
In silence they have marched to intercept us.

BAJAZET.

My daughter! oh, the traitress!

DERVISH.

                    Yet we have
Axalla in our power, and angry Tamerlane
Will buy his favorite's life on any terms. 260

OMAR.

With these few friends I have, I for a while
Can face their force. If they refuse us peace,
Revenge shall sweeten ruin, and 'twill joy me
To drag my foe down with me in my fall. (*Exit.*)

Enter Haly, with Selima weeping.

BAJAZET.

See where she comes! with well-dissembled 265
    innocence,
With truth and faith so lovely in her face,
As if she durst ev'n disavow the falsehood.
—Hop'st thou to make amends with trifling tears
For my lost crown and disappointed vengeance?
Ungrateful Selima! thy father's curse! 270
Bring forth the minion of her foolish heart;
He dies this moment.

HALY.

                    Would I could not speak
The crime of fatal love: the slave who fled,
By whom we are undone—was that Axalla. 275

BAJAZET.

Hah! say'st thou?

HALY.

                Hid beneath that vile appearance,
The Princess found a means for his escape.

SELIMA.

I am undone! ev'n nature has disclaimed me:
My father, have I lost you all? My father! 280

BAJAZET.

Talk'st thou of nature? who hast broke her bands!
Thou art my bane, thou witch! thou infant parricide!
But I will study to be strangely cruel;
I will forget the folly of my fondness,
Drive all the father from my breast, now snatch 285
    thee,
Tear thee to pieces, drink thy treacherous blood,

And make thee answer all my great revenge.
Now, now, thou traitress! (*Offers* to kill her.*)
SELIMA. (*Embraces him.*)
                  Plunge the poniard deep!
The life my father gave shall hear his summons   290
And issue at the wound. Start not, to feel
My heart's warm blood gush out upon your hands,
Since from your spring I drew the purple stream,
And I must pay it back if you demand it.
BAJAZET.
Hence! from my thoughts! thou soft, relenting   295
    weakness.
Hast thou not given me up a prey? betrayed me?
SELIMA.
Oh! not for worlds, not ev'n for all the joys
Love or the Prophet's paradise can give.
Amidst the fears and sorrows of my soul,
Amidst the thousand pains of anxious tenderness,   300
I made the gentle, kind Axalla swear
Your life, your crown, and honor should be safe.
BAJAZET.
Away! my soul disdains the vile dependence.
No, let me rather die, die like a king.
Shall I fall down at the proud Tartar's foot   305
And say, have mercy on me?
    Shout.
                  Hark, they come.
Disgrace will overtake my ling'ring hand.
Die then. Thy father's shame, and thine, die with
    thee. (*Offers* to kill her.*)
SELIMA.
For Heaven, for pity's sake!   310
BAJAZET.
                  No more, thou trifler!
She catches hold of his arm.
    Hah! dar'st thou bar my will?—Tear off her hold.
SELIMA.
What, not for life? should I not plead for life,
When Nature teaches ev'n the brute creation
To hold fast that, her best, her noblest gift?   315
Look on my eyes, whom you so oft have kissed
And swore they were your best loved queen's, my
    mother's.
Behold 'em now streaming for mercy, mercy!
Look on me, and deny me if you can;
'Tis but for life I beg. Is that a boon   320

So hard for me t'obtain? or you to grant?
Oh! spare me! spare your Selima, my father.
BAJAZET.
A lazy sloth hangs on my resolution.
It is my Selima! Hah! What, my child?
And can I murder her? Dreadful imagination!   325

Shout.

Again they come. I leave her to my foes!
—And shall they triumph o'er the race* of Bajazet?
Die, Selima!—Is that a father's voice?
Rouse, rouse my fury! yes, she dies, the victim
To my lost hopes. Out! out! thou foolish nature!   330
Justly she shares the ruin she has made.
(*To the mutes.*) Seize her, ye slaves, and strangle
    her this moment.
SELIMA.
Oh! let me die by you! behold my breast!
I wonnot shrink. Oh! save me but from these.

The mutes seize her.

BAJAZET.
Dispatch.   335
SELIMA.
                But for a moment, while I pray
That Heaven may guard my royal father.
BAJAZET.
                      Dogs!
SELIMA.
That you may only bless me ere I die.

Shout.

BAJAZET.
Ye tedious villains!* then the work is mine.   340

*As Bajazet runs at Selima with his sword, enter
Tamerlane, Axalla, etc. Axalla gets between Bajazet
and Selima, whilst Tamerlane and the rest drive
Bajazet and the mutes off the stage.*

AXALLA.
And I am come to save thee. Oh! my joy!
Be this the whitest hour of all my life.
This one success is more than all my wars,
The noblest, dearest glory of my sword.
SELIMA.
Alas, Axalla, death has been around me;   345

My coward soul still trembles at the fright
And seems but half secure ev'n in thy arms.

AXALLA.

Retire, my fair, and let me guard thee forth.
Blood and tumultuous slaughter are about us,
And danger in her ugliest forms is here,   350
Nor will the pleasure of my heart be full
Till all my fears are ended in thy safety.

*Exeunt Axalla and Selima. Enter Tamerlane, the
Prince of Tanais, Zama, Mirvan, and soldiers, with
Bajazet, Omar, and the dervish, prisoners.*

TAMERLANE.

Mercy at length gives up her peaceful scepter,
And Justice sternly takes her turn to govern.
'Tis a rank world and asks her keenest sword   355
To cut up villainy of monstrous growth.
—Zama, take care, that with the earliest dawn,
    (*Pointing to Omar and the dervish.*)
Those traitors meet the fate their treason merits.

(*To Bajazet.*)

For thee, thou tyrant, whose oppressive violence
Has ruined those thou shouldst protect at home,   360
Whose wars, whose slaughters, whose assassinations
(That basest thirst of blood, that sin of cowards),
Whose faith so often given, and always violated,
Have been th'offense of heav'n and plague of earth.
What punishment is equal to thy crimes?   365
The doom thy rage designed for me be thine:
Closed in a cage like some destructive beast,[39]
I'll have thee borne about in public view
A great example of that righteous vengeance
That waits on cruelty and pride like thine.   370

BAJAZET.

It is beneath me to decline my fate.

I stand prepared to meet thy utmost hate.
Yet think not I will long thy triumph see:
None want* the means when the soul dares be free.
I'll curse thee with my last, my parting breath   375
And keep the courage of my life in death,
Then boldly venture on that world unknown.
It cannot use me worse than this has done. (*Exit
    guarded.*)

TAMERLANE.

Behold the vain effects of earthborn pride
That scorned Heav'n's laws and all its pow'r defied, 380
That could the Hand which formed it first forget
And fondly say I made myself be great.
But justly those above assert their sway
And teach ev'n kings what homage they should pay,
Who then rule best when mindful to obey.   385

Exeunt omnes.

FINIS.

Textual Notes

a Copytext is the first edition, a 1702 quarto (Q1). Also
consulted: the second edition, a 1703 quarto (Q2); the
third edition, a 1714 dudecimo (D1); the fourth edition, a 1717 duodecimo (D2); and modern editions of
1929 (Sutherland) and 1966 (Burns).

b it] Q1, Sutherland; he Q2, D1, D2, Burns

c soldiers] Q2, D1, D2, Burns; soldier Q1, Sutherland

d my] Q1, Sutherland; our Q2, D1, D2, Burns

e soldiers wear] Q2, D1, D2, Sutherland, Burns; soldier
wears Q1

f thee] Q2, D1, D2, Sutherland, Burns; thy self Q1

g scanned] Q2, D1, D2, Sutherland, Burns; scar'd Q1

h warn] Q2, D1, D2, Sutherland, Burns; warm Q1

---

39 cage ... beast] Sutherland suggests this caging of Bajazet
like a beast is Rowe's one borrowing from Marlowe.

Lucius, The First Christian King of Britain[a]

by Delarivier Manley (ca. 1670-1724)

edited by Melinda A. Rabb

Delarivier Manley began to write for the theater in 1695. She had put aside girlhood prospects of conventional respectability, either as a maid of honor to Queen Mary of Modena or as an officer's wife, after becoming entangled in a bigamous marriage and serving some years as companion to a former mistress of King Charles II. Her first tragedy, *The Royal Mischief*, won her enough fame (or notoriety) to make her the model for the main character in a satire on women playwrights, *The Female Wits* (ca. 1696). Undaunted by public criticism, she continued to write a total of six plays, four of them produced, of which *Lucius* is the last. It was first performed on May 11, 1717, at the Royal Theater at Drury Lane with a cast of fine actors including Barton Booth as Lucius; Anne Oldfield as Rosalinda, John Mills as Arminius. Its performance marked the end of a long feud with her former friend Sir Richard Steele. After many years of wrangling over personal grievances and political antagonisms, the two writers reconciled. Manley dedicated the play to him, and Steele, the manager of the Drury Lane theater, saw to it that the ever-impecunious Manley enjoyed the rewards of a third night.

In *Lucius*, Manley adapts heroic tragedy in order to invent a unique explanation for the introduction of Christianity into England. Her drama draws very loosely on prior "histories" of the legendary monarch's religious enlightenment, according to which Lucius wrote of his interest in Christian miracles to Pope Eleutharius, who sent two priests from Rome to instruct and convert the king and his people. None of the chronicles mention a queen; rather, Lucius ends his ascetic life alone and without an heir (ca. 154).

All of Manley's possible sources include another important segment of early British history which, although it completely defies chronology when incorporated with the story of Lucius, has relevance for her reimagining of the past. Fifth-century King Vortigern, according to the chronicles, usurped the throne, abandoned Christianity, and, because of his lust for the Saxon princess Rowenne, calamitously invited the Saxons into Britain. Vortigern's good son, Vortimer, chased out the Saxons for a time, but was killed in battle. Typically, the story of evil Vortigern ends with the prophesies of Merlin, foretelling the eventual relief of national misery by Uther Pendragon and Arthur.

In Lucius' and Vortigern/Vortimer's stories, Manley found political parallels to contemporary England that were safely remote and relatively obscure. After a career of intense public controversy, including imprisonment for seditious libel, she chose a seemingly irreproachable plot, the advent of Christian faith, in which she freely conflates, inverts, and fictionalizes history, offering a final Tory fantasy about the virtues of the true royal bloodline and the dangers of foreign rule and religious dissension.

Her most striking alteration is to trace the origins of Christian Britain to a woman. Without Rosalinda, it seems, Lucius would have remained a pagan; he adores his fair queen before he adores God. Queen Rosalinda is in part a nostalgic gesture toward good and pious queen Anne, now dead along with Tory hopes of governing. But Rosalinda also represents a continuation of Manley's constant theme in all of her writing: the inseparability of sex and politics in the human struggle for power and love. The secret motives of war and of religion, the play insists, may be reduced to the contending desires of men and women. Love, in all its permutations from lust to spiritual ardor, feminizes Manley's re-creation of a national past.

DRAMATIS PERSONAE

[MEN]

    Honorius,[1] King of Gallia.

    Vortimer,[2] usurper of Britain.

    Lucius,[3] Prince of Britain.

    Arminius, Prince of Albany.[4]

    Prince of Cambria.

    Sylvius,[5] page to the Queen.

    An Alban lord.

    Flamens, guards, soldiers.

[WOMEN]

    Rosalinda, Queen of Albany and Aquitaine.[6]

    Emmelin, Princess of Gallia.

    Irene, lady to the Queen.

---

1 Honorius] The name may have been inspired by Manley's recollection of the Roman emperor in the West, Honorius (393–423).

2 Vortimer] Manley has in mind King Vortigern, although she confuses his name with his son's, Vortimer. According to early accounts of British history by chroniclers, Vortigern's reign (ca. 425) epitomized tyranny and political betrayal. After usurping the British throne, he allowed the Saxon invaders Hengest and Horsa into Britain to help him fight the Scots and Picts, and gave them grants of land. The Saxons proved themselves far more dangerous than the enemies they were supposed to suppress. In most accounts, Vortigern's love for Hengest's daughter Rowenn created an alliance which ultimately made Britain vulnerable to devastating invasion and destruction.

3 Lucius] Legendary King of Britain during the second century, Lucius became known as "Lever Maur," "the great light," because, after being converted to Christianity, he made it the national religion. Lucius died without an heir. The representation of Lucius as younger than (and possibly the son of) Vortimer/Vortigern is entirely fanciful.

4 Albany] the ancient name for modern Scotland; some early histories of Britain trace the country's founding to Brute, great-grandson of Aeneas who, after the Trojan War, fled to the islands north of Gaul. Brute had three sons, Camber, Locrine, and Albanact, among whom he divided his kingdom into Cambria or Wales, Loegria or England, and Albany.

5 Sylvius] Although listed among the men, the character of Sylvius is a woman, Alenia, princess of Albany, who has assumed male dress in order to be near Lucius.

6 Rosalinda … Aquitaine] The character of Rosalinda has no historical precedent. She is depicted as daughter to

Lucius, The First Christian King of Britain.

Act I. The palace garden.

Enter Lucius and Arminius.

ARMINIUS.

    Why does the conqu'ring Lucius[7] now despond?

    Why does my Lord with secret sorrow mourn?

    Why thus averse to every sound of joy

    When Fortune crowns you with her choicest favors,

    Makes you the soldiers' pride, and wish of beauty? 5

    The coldest maid that ever graced a court,

    At your approach, drops all her haughty airs,

    New rolls her eyes, new coins her face[8] in smiles,

    And her long-practiced scorn is then no more.

LUCIUS.

    Oh, Albany! I cannot bear thy search. 10

ARMINIUS.

    I must proceed and name the beauteous queen.

LUCIUS.

    Hah! say'st thou? What of her, Arminius?

ARMINIUS.

    The mourning Rosalind in sorrow dressed

    Can charm beyond the gaudy smiles of others.

LUCIUS.

    I view indeed the captive queen[9] with pity. 15

ARMINIUS.

    My friend, does she not rule thy soul?

LUCIUS.

    She does! She does! My charming queen reigns here,

    Triumphant in her native throne, my heart.

    Diffusive is her sway. War yields to love,

---

    the King of Albany (Scotland) and widow of Otharius, the King of Aquitaine (in southwestern France).

7 Lucius] Manley credits Lucius with playing a decisive role in driving the Romans out of Britain and in a territorial war between two brothers, Honorius of Gaul and Otharius of Aquitaine.

8 new coins her face] a metaphor derived from the practice of minting new coins with the face of the currently reigning monarch.

9 captive Queen] Rosalind is taken prisoner after the defeat of Aquitaine by the joint forces of Gaul, Albany, Cambria, and Britain.

Nor know I any wish, but for her beauty.   20

ARMINIUS. (*Aside.*)

Oh sure despair as certain death for me!

LUCIUS.

Why sighs my friend? Is she not heav'nly fair?

ARMINIUS.

Oh, guardian Powers of Britain, save him now!

Oh, save the lovely youth from pleasing ruin!

—Hast thou forgot? Alas, the Queen's a Christian,   25

Apostate to our altars and our worship.[10]

LUCIUS.

In her alone all my devotion centers.

My heart (when I such wondrous charms survey)

In her adores the All-creating Power.

Nor can perfections, great as hers, mislead.   30

She cannot be mistaken, cannot err,

Or if she could, with Rosalind to err

Were better than believing with another!

ARMINIUS.

Beware the mischiefs which attend her love.

Thy father, styled the cruel king of Britain,   35

Is to the Christian sect a most invet'rate foe.

LUCIUS.

Love were not love could it admit of fear.

ARMINIUS.

Think how, when lord of Verulam, he slew

The good, the rightful majesty of Britain,

Slew, at a peaceful banquet, that brave monarch.[11]   40

The Queen (scarce up from childbed of a son,

Who soon expired) he forced to his loathed bed,

In hopes the prince of Cambria, her brother,

Would prove a friend to his bold usurpation.[12]

And yet Heav'n smiled upon the horrid nuptials   45

And blest the tyrant with the god-like Lucius.

LUCIUS.

Though sprung from one, I have no tyrant's soul.

Am I to blame? Could I direct my birth?

Could I concur to be? Was the choice mine?

My mother early paid the debt of nature: 50

Of me she died. May that atone the crime

Of wedding with her husband's murderer.

ARMINIUS.

Still, there's a secret will thy hopes destroy:

Thy father does himself the Queen adore.

His love began soon after thou wert sent   55

To aid the Gallic King against his brother.[13]

LUCIUS.

Oh fatal war! Would I had never seen it.

ARMINIUS.

Thy father, at a royal interview,

Received a dart from Rosalinda's eyes,

The beauteous heiress of my uncle's crown,   60

Then to the King of Aquitaine betrothed.

He strove in vain to cross the promised nuptials,

For his own bed courting the destined bride.

Long enmity between the Picts and Britons,

Their native hate, and contract with Otharius,   65

Caused the refusal of your father's suit.

LUCIUS.

The fame of this affront reached us abroad.

ARMINIUS.

Love was the secret motive of the war.

Hence he invaded Albany with fury,

And with my uncle's death the slight revenged.   70

How has he galled the Picts with heavy yokes!

How every day oppressed our conquered people!

How in these foreign wars and distant climes

Forced us for him to carry hated arms!

Eager to prosecute his furious love,   75

He crossed the seas to make the Queen a widow.

Too well his chance in war succeeded here;

Otharius, he was slain, and we the victors.

---

10 Christian … worship] The non-Christian characters in the play refer either to Roman gods, such as Jove, or northern gods, such the Merlin-like wizard from Norway, Almerin; both systems of belief predate Christianity and its eventual dissemination throughout the Roman Empire. Periodic persecution of Christians in Britain is well-documented, and the play's allusions to events of both the second and the fifth centuries conflate two periods especially hostile to Christianity.

11 Verulam … monarch] the Roman district Verulamium, corresponding to modern St. Albans, northwest of London; King Alban was a Christian martyr, killed during the reign of Diocletian.

12 Queen … usurpation] The chroniclers of early British history recount numerous stories that might provide precedent for the political rape of Lucius' mother.

13 Gallic king … brother] Honorius against his brother Otharius, King of Aquitaine and Rosalinda's husband

LUCIUS.
    This morning with the Gallic king he comes,
    Triumphant o'er the fate of Aquitaine.   80
ARMINIUS.
    Soon as your conqu'ring arms had forced this city,
    With orders I was sent to plead his love.
    But she, with indignation, has refused him.
    I dread to say how ill I have succeeded.
    His tyrant temper will not yield to reason,   85
    Nor can the name of son abate his rage.
    Cure or conceal your love, or you are lost.
LUCIUS.
    Conceal my love? Conceal a raging fire,
    Conceal the blaze when it invades the sky;
    As well unbounded storms may be concealed.   90
ARMINIUS.
    Sure this ethereal fire was struck by Jove.
    Oh no, the God of Love has greater force!
    He animates you thus, thus moves your frame
    And brings inimitable graces with him.
    Feels not the Queen the force of all those charms? 95
    A dawn of joy breaks from her gath'ring smiles
    With all the softness which foreruns her sex's
        yielding.
LUCIUS.
    Ten months I've offered ineffectual vows,
    Ten months pursued the Fair with ardent love.
    No more—the Princess Emmelin appears.   100
    I'll go this very hour and urge my fate.
    Ere my stern father comes, I must be blest,
    Be ever blest, or else be ever wretched.
    —Haste all ye loves and graces to my aid.
    Dwell on my voice and languish in my eyes.   105
    Bright Cytherea, from thy heav'n look down.
    Grant, Venus, grant that I her heart may move.
    For me, thy slave, make her thy votary.
    Propitious now, thou shalt my goddess be,
    And I'll devote my happy hours to thee. (*Exit*.) 110

Enter the Princess Emmelin.

EMMELIN.
    I met the Prince—how has thy search succeeded?
ARMINIUS.
    Alas, too well!
EMMELIN.
    And grows the hero Lucius sick for love,

That stubborn heart in camps and slaughter bred,
    Unused to beauty and its soft delights?   115
    Oh sympathy of sex! Oh force of nature!
    What haughty victor stops not at thy call?
    What courage melts not at the sight of beauty?
    Oh Rosalind, how glorious are thy chains!
    How much superior to the crowns of others!   120
ARMINIUS.
    As next of kindred to the Alban throne,
    Whilst none but elder rivals had declared,
    I had some distant hopes of being heard.
EMMELIN.
    If I have credit with the King, you shall.
    We are my brother's captives, not the Britons'. 125
    But oh, what hope hast thou to gain her heart?
    Where is the hero that dares rival Lucius?
    At the young warrior's sight, each virgin breast
    Throbs with an ecstasy unutterable.
    Scarce Venus feels more transport in her grove   130
    When kindling wishes hurry on to love.
ARMINIUS.
    I own the danger of superior charms.
    I own his power and valor, youth and form
    Are rivals to my boldest hopes.
    And yet, in counsel with my kinder stars,   135
    Cunning and conduct may outwit the hero
    And aid my feeble hand to reach his heart.
EMMELIN.
    Thou strik'st not there, Arminius. I oppose
    And, like his better genius,* guard the warrior.
    Know, I have seen him with indulgent eyes.   140
    As thou for Rosalind, I sigh for him.
ARMINIUS.
    Be he immortal then, as are your charms,
    Within that beauteous empire ever safe.
EMMELIN.
    Thou hast resolved his fate, I read thy soul.
    This ten long months I've studied thy dark breast 145
    And know the want* of virtue in thy frame,
    Which must subject thee to the mind that knows
        thee.
    Wherefore I left my modesty awhile,
    Revealed my virgin love to guard its object.
    Honorius comes, with him the British King.   150
    Protect my Lucius from his father's rage,
    Or by our nation's gods, thy queen shall know

'Twas your ill-fated arm which slew Otharius.

ARMINIUS.

    Why with reproaches does your Highness load me
    For what to you alone I have disclosed? 155
    Is this the end of all your promised favor,
    That promised favor which upheld my hopes?
    Yet wherefore should I shrink at your reproach?
    In battle, bravely did I take his life,
    That bar to Rosalinda's throne and bed. 160

EMMELIN.

    Spare but young Lucius, and your secret's safe,
    Nay, all that I can do to gain the Queen.

ARMINIUS.

    Well does the King your brother love his sister.
    Honorius rules the fate of Rosalinda.
    Direct her to my arms, and Vortimer 165
    (Whose ear I've gained by flatt'ring of his love)
    Shall give the Prince to yours.

EMMELIN.

    Oh Albany, that soars above my hopes!
    My haughty soul would not reveal its weakness,
    Yet something must be done. I'll think again. 170
    —But thou, my careful genius,* guard me well,
    And thou, my modesty, be faithful to me.
    Heave not, my bosom, when the invader's nigh.
    Throb not, fond heart, to beat to him thy secret.
    My eyes, take heed how ye my pain express, 175
    Strike not one spark that may the flame confess.
    He can't despise, who does not know our store;
    'Tis proffered love makes all our beauties poor.
    (*Exit.*)

ARMINIUS.

    Hah, is it so? Princess, I was to blame
    To think a woman's friendship void of int'rest. 180
    Th'advances which she made are now explained.
    She watched Prince Lucius with a jealous eye
    And taught ev'n me first to suspect his passion.
    Be cautious of thy fate! I fear her cunning.
    Guard thee, my heart, be wary of her search, 185
    Else shalt thou never steer amidst these dangers.

Enter Sylvius.

    Oh, Sister, I have news! The Prince of Britain
    Adores the widowed Queen of Aquitaine.
    Did thy soft sex and royal blood descend
    To wear the humble habit of a page 190

To watch each lucky minute of the fates
And let another blast thy brother's hopes?

SYLVIUS.

    I love my brother with a sister's love,
    As much as e'er a sister loved a brother.
    But when compared to what I feel for Lucius, 195
    How weak, how lambent is the kindred flame!
    Then not for thee but him I left my sex,
    Left the gay pleasures of the British court,
    Thus in a servile garb to follow Lucius,
    To hear his voice and view his lovely person, 200
    For with the dawn I took his beauties in.
    The vital air, the sighs which first I breathed
    Were all informed, were all inspired by Lucius.

ARMINIUS.

    Shall Rosalinda then possess thy lover?

SYLVIUS.

    Not till Alenia dies. 205

ARMINIUS.

    Earth, Hell, and all aërial Demons join,
    Join they with us to blast his hated passion.
    Born on the wings o'th'wind, the wizard Alm'rin,[14]
    Mighty in spells, in charms and magic lore,
    From Norway came to aid our hapless loves. 210
    Ten sleepless nights in magic rites have passed,
    And thus, this morn, he has our doom pronounced:
    "Divide the Queen and Lucius, ye are blest,
    And in his arms Alenia's grief shall rest.
    For Rosalinda thou shalt sigh no more, 215
    If thou with her canst touch thy native shore.
    But oh, be swift! Their stronger stars may join.
    Employ force, fraud. This day and night are thine."

SYLVIUS.

    The Fates are kind. Their oracle is good.

ARMINIUS.

    If scruples weak and vain sway not thy mind, 220
    Alenia, we may yet be blest. Oh say,
    Wilt thou unerring with thy brother join
    In mutual aid to gain our mutual loves?

SYLVIUS.

    Implicitly I will.

---

14 the wizard Alm'rin] possibly an anagram of Merlin, the
    wizard of Arthurian legend who first appears in chroni-
    cles of early British history as part of the story of King
    Vortigern

ARMINIUS.

              Give me thy vow.   225

SYLVIUS.

  I swear to act in concert with my brother.

ARMINIUS.

  Hold'st thou thy favor with the Queen?

SYLVIUS.

                       I do.

She calls me faithful boy, the only one

Of all her vast retinue she can trust.   230

Emboldened by this grace, I told the Queen

There was a Prince who always mourned her fate

In words so tender, with a voice so sweet,

I loved yet grieved to hear the moving story.

She asked me, all transported, "Is it Lucius?" 235

I sighed and paused, not daring then to name you.

ARMINIUS.

  Back, dearest maid, and watch their every glance.

Bring me, if possible, their very thoughts,

That all transparent I may view their souls.

Exit Sylvius.

Her heart for Lucius touched! The idol bleeds, 240

Though 'tis not fit this girl should know my purpose.

Arise, Invention, aid my lab'ring soul.

Fair are all ways which carry to the goal.

So, fired by Venus' son,[15] the thund'rer Jove,

Of right regardless, rushes on his love.   245

By fraud or force he gains the beauteous prize,

Tasting, in various forms, as various joys.[16]

Now, as Alcmene's lord, their bed he stains.

Then Spartan Leda, like a swan, he gains.

Europa by a lovely bull's betrayed,   250

And in a golden show'r th'imprisoned maid.[17]

---

15 Venus' son] Eros or Cupid

16 Jove . . . tasting in various forms as various joys] According to Greek and Roman mythology, Zeus or Jove had many love affairs with goddesses and mortals, often accomplishing his seduction or rape by altering his appearance.

17 th'imprisoned maid] Danae, imprisoned by her father Acrisius because a prophesy foretold his eventual death at the hands of his daughter's son; Jove entered her prison in the form of a golden shower and fathered Perseus, slayer of Medusa and Acrisius.

A dragon curls in bright Olympia's arms,[18]

Nor can chaste vows protect Callisto's charms.[19]

Hence men, by fraud and artifice succeed,

And Jove's example justifies the deed.   255

Exit.

Act II. [The palace.]

The Queen and Irene.

IRENE.

  Why does my charming mistress thus devote

Her beauty's bloom to sorrow, sighs, and tears?

QUEEN.

  My husband slain, my country made a prey,

My guards my jailers, ev'ry room a prison,

No faithful servant left but thee and Sylvius: 5

The rest are spies devoted to the victors.

IRENE.

  And yet those victors come to break your chains.

QUEEN.

  Alas! They come indeed but 'tis in triumph.

Honorius, called the Good, has well revenged

Th'unjust attempt which King Otharius made 10

T'enlarge his empire at his brother's cost.

Compelled to wed that most ambitious Prince,

I never knew one peaceful hour in marriage.

Honorius, by his death, the Romans vanquished,

Becomes the first sole monarch of the Gauls. 15

A widow I, without a dow'r or name,

No more the Queen of Albany or Aquitaine.

Enter Sylvius.

SYLVIUS.

  The Prince of Britain, to attend your Majesty.

QUEEN.

  Against myself my rebel passions arm.

They bound within my breast to meet this victor. 20

Were not my mind enslaved, were that but free,

---

18 a dragon curls in bright Olympia's arms] possibly Demeter, whom Jove loved in the form of a spotted snake

19 Callisto] nymph who had made a vow of chastity to Artemis; Jove assumed the appearance of Artemis in order to deceive Callisto into friendly intimacy before he raped her.

How could I brave my chains, how calm look down
On those lost glories which adorn a crown.

Enter Lucius. He kneels.

Why does the conqu'ring Prince of Britain kneel
To me, no more a queen, a wretched captive?   25
What would my lord, for I am all confusion?
LUCIUS.
I beg a parting audience, and alone.
QUEEN.
You, Sylvius and Irene, both withdraw.
SYLVIUS. (*Aside.*)
I'll bring the Prince of Albany to part ye. (*Exit
with Irene.*)
QUEEN.
Oh, my heart!—Sure, sir, I heard you not aright.   30
Where next does the victorious Lucius shine,
And which the kingdom marked for desolation?
LUCIUS.
I would, but oh, it dies upon my tongue!
To my loved queen, I would discourse of parting.
I would discourse of night and horrid gloom,   35
Of dismal groans and the deep vault of death.
And when the bitter cup of woe is full,
I'll sum it all in one, and call it parting.
QUEEN.
Beat gently, heart.—Who sends you hence, my lord?
LUCIUS.
That awful* virtue which destroys my hopes,   40
That chilling coldness which repels my flame.
Henceforth the joys of life shall charm no more;
No more the dusty field shall give delight,
Triumphant laurels, or the praise of beauty.
These robes I'll change to some poor hermit's weed,   45
And herbs and roots shall be my only food,
My daily thirst quenched from some common
stream,
No beam of light to cheer my dismal cell,
But all be dark and joyless as my fortune.
QUEEN.
Why choose you these extremes, my lord?   50
LUCIUS.
A convert to that Being which you worship
And which I with my pious queen adore,
I am a^b Christian, follower of your virtue.
At your command, I've heard these holy men,

By that good prelate Eleutherius sent,[20]   55
I've heard their potent and celestial reasons.
Enlightened from above, my glowing breast
Bids me undaunted own the sacred faith
Which, when professed, I'll take my leave forever
Of the too cruel Alban queen, forever!   60
QUEEN.
What, part, my lord, when this exalted change
(For which I bow to the informing Pow'rs)
Calls you, the first of Christian kings, to shine
O'er all the western world, like a bright star,[21]
To bless your people with eternal knowledge?   65
LUCIUS.
For you, I quit the hope of making converts,
For you, resign the foremost rank in fame,
For you, I leave the glories of a crown.
I can no more support this wretched being,
To see such charms shine forth, but not on me.   70
Oh, think how absolute my rival is!
Can I from a stern father's force preserve you,
Unless you will descend to fix my claim
And let me call you mine ere he arrive?
QUEEN. (*Aside.*)
How shall I teach my tongue against my heart?   75
LUCIUS.
Am I not worth a word, the least regard?
How many anxious days and sleepless nights
Have I devoted to afflicted beauty?
But she regardless pities not my pain,
Or she ungrateful triumphs in my ruin,   80
Though I, for her, first felt the sting of passion,
First felt the force of charms, what strong desires
And eager longings are inspired by beauty.
QUEEN.
My suff'ring heart, by sorrow quite possessed,
Can make no room for any other thought.   85
LUCIUS.
Oh, blest Otharius, happier in thy death,
More happy than the living, hated Lucius!
Therefore my heart, be this thy last effort.

---

20 holy men … sent] Pope Eleutherius, according to the
chronicles, sent two priests to instruct Lucius in Christianity.
21 like a bright star] an allusion to Lucius' epithet, Lever
Maur

Part, part, and die! From those dear eyes remove
This wretched object of despairing love.   90
QUEEN.
We cannot, must not part. Ye mighty Pow'rs,
Tear not this only good from my poor heart.
Take all besides, leave me but him alone,
And I no more will think of crowns and empires.
LUCIUS.
Oh full reward of all my former pain!   95
Oppressed, I faint beneath this flush of joy.
Oh Love, receive the honor—thou hast blest me!
Alas my queen! she sinks—she faints—she dies!
My Rosalind, my soul! return, return.
Come back, my love. Again, she breathes—she lives!   100
The roses gather to her cheeks and lips!
The kindling fire is glimm'ring in her eyes!
New warmth, new life reanimates the fair,
And with her living beauties I am blest.
QUEEN.
Oh force of modesty! Oh force of love!   105
'Tis fought, and thou hast gained the victory.
The struggle's past. Though vanquished, yet
    grown bold,
I must—I do declare—I cannot speak it.
Leave me to blush alone for this confession.
LUCIUS.
Not till the holy priest has joined our hands,   110
Oh my fair queen! This night must see me blest.
QUEEN.
Tomorrow, gentle* Lucius!
LUCIUS.
Let those who set no value on the present
With easy idleness expect tomorrow.
Suppose the King, grown furious to possess,   115
Should force you to his bed, should force his joys,
As once he did my royal suff'ring mother.
A captive you, oh how may you resist?
Think but of Lucius then and his despair.
Oh think, my queen, what I would then exchange   120
For but a moment of that precious time
You will not now employ!
The conqu'ring monarchs come, I hear their trumpets.
Oh sound, sound on! It is for Lucius' triumph.
Yield, yield, my fair, and all my fears remove.   125
Quick to thy inmost chamber, fly, my love,
Where binding vows my lasting truth shall prove.

QUEEN.
But if the cruel king command my death?
Swear, Lucius, at the peril of thy life,
To guard Rosalinda's.   130
LUCIUS.
I swear, my queen, by glory and by love,
I will protect thee, though against my father.
But now, my fair, my circling blood rebounds.
My lab'ring heart, as in the pangs of death,
Beats an alarm, and all the passions answer: 135
I can no more. Impatient of delay,
The God of Love himself prepares the way.
He brings us joys which never shall decay,
Joys which the truly constant only know,
Our All of bliss worth living for below.   140

Going, they are met by Emmelin and Arminius.

ARMINIUS. (*Aside.*)
They love! They love! I read it in their eyes.
Softness in hers and transport shine in his.
—Madam, the Princess Emmelin is come,
Moved by your sorrows to entreat her brother
(Whose captives the rough chance of war has   145
    made ye)
That Vortimer may not dispose your fate.
Should the stern Briton get you in his pow'r,
Our hopes of freeing Albany were lost.

Enter Sylvius.

SYLVIUS.
Oh, that unhappy Sylvius to his queen
Should be the speaker of Honorius's triumph!   150
The gaudy chariots have discharged their load,
And now the palace-hall receives the monarchs.
I've seen the prosp'rous laugh, the wretched mourn.
These gracing their proud victors gilded wheels
Are sent, for change of woe, to groan in dungeons.   155
How many Alban, Gaul, and Roman chiefs,
The relics of Otharius' royal power,
Shall never, never see the light again.
These tears be witness how I grieve their fate.
Pardon this tenderness—The kings have sent   160
To tell your Majesty, they wait for audience.
QUEEN.
Cousin of Albany, I pray attend them.
—Fate, thou art busy now for Rosalinda.

I've but one dear concern, one wish in life,
One secret pain, or one important joy: 165
To make the royal Lucius ever mine!
Or else, ye Pow'rs, contract my narrow span;
From your eternal loom tear short my thread:
I cannot taste of happiness without him.

Introduced by Albany and train, enter in triumph
Honorius (King of Gallia), Vortimer (King of Britain),
Prince of Cambria, attendants and guards.

HONORIUS.
Here let our triumphs end. You, beauteous queen, 170
Enough have mourned a royal husband dead.
My brother, to increase the blest is gone.
Death has atoned his breach of royal faith,
And time consents to mitigate your sorrows.
Let your sad heart, at length, give way to joy.

QUEEN.
I've all the joy that my sad state can give, 175
Since I was doomed to chains, that you're the
victor. *Honorius and Emmelin embrace.*

VORTIMER.
When you appear, who can be called victorious?
The sun, that with diffusive beams shines o'er
The rolling globe, to every age a wonder, 180
Reigns not more absolute than do your eyes.
Like him, you rule with universal sway.
Like him, you conquer all.—Rise, warlike Lucius.
We did expect an earlier meeting from thee.

LUCIUS.
Great sir, it was my post to guard the Queen. 185

PRINCE OF CAMBRIA.
My nephew, dearer than my life!

LUCIUS.
My honored uncle!

VORTIMER.
Oh Albany, thou partner of my heart,
The charmer shines on us with stronger glory,
As she'd been gathering a fresh stock of brightness. 190
How has our suit succeeded?

Vortimer talks apart to Arminius, Honorius with
Emmelin, whilst Lucius speaks aside to the Queen.

LUCIUS.
After the audience, where shall I be blest?

QUEEN.
I am going to the cell of Fabianus,
But trust not our important fate to any.

VORTIMER.
What! Lucius love the Queen? Beloved of her? 195
My lord of Albany, you have our thanks.
—We have to offer thee, King Honorius,
That which may make our league inviolable.

HONORIUS.
To which, great prince, we gladly shall accord.

VORTIMER.
When we had scarcely tasted royal pow'r, 200
The sweets of empire, or our consort's charms,
We left our crown and queen to aid this state.
Six years were wasted in the Gallic War
Without revisiting our native coast.
By us and our brave troops, thy father vanquished 205
And drove the Roman tyranny away:
The Romans, who had since great Caesar's conquest
Left ye but titular Kings and Gaul a province.

HONORIUS.
I have heard the obligation.

VORTIMER.
After his death, the warlike prince, your brother, 210
Deemed Aquitaine too small a share of empire.
With hostile arms he entered your dominions
And took you unprepared. The field he won,
Subdued your strongest cities in your sight,
Till braving foaming seas and winter storms, 215
In spite of winds or adverse deities,
Lucius transported to your shore our aid.

HONORIUS.
All this I thankfully remember.

VORTIMER.
Without a rival now you fill the throne,
Nay more, have joined your brother's crown to yours. 220
If this to our victorious arms be due,
Say, happy monarch, what may he expect
By whom you wear these benefits?

HONORIUS.
Speak, King of Britain, what is't thou wouldst ask?

VORTIMER.
For all our toils in war, our soldiers' loss, 225
Our friendly lavish waste of blood and treasure,
We ask the captive queen, that she, this night,
Set forward where our royal navy rides,

So to be wafted o'er to Britain's shore
With honor.   230
QUEEN.
Oh brother, let me lowly thus entreat,
That I may answer this tyrannic king!
With his great merit, how are you upbraided?
He has recited all his warlike deeds
To make impression on your grateful heart,   235
But sir, consider! I'm a queen was doubly crowned:
By birth and marriage, I am twice a sovereign.
Think whose I was—oh pity kindred grief
And royal woes! Mine's not a vulgar fate
To be weighed out by ev'ry common hand   240
Or at a moment's call to be determined.
VORTIMER.
What phantoms, what illusions, beauteous Queen
(By melancholy vapors fed), affright you?
Were Caesar yours and all that vast dominion
Of which he once could call himself the lord,   245
Less sure, less absolute would be your sway
Than now in Britain.
QUEEN.
In death I may possess an ample power.
'Tis there that I must follow when thou lead'st.
I had a father till thy cruel thirst   250
Of blood and empire left him but a name.
I had a husband, too, of kingly sway.
Now made an helpless orphan and a widow,
My country seized, my noble friends enslaved,
Groaning in dungeons, courting death in vain,   255
The next is mine, my fate may be the last.
In me thy tyranny will be accomplished.
VORTIMER.
In you the war, in you what's dreadful ends.
The prison doors fly open as you pass,
And the despairing captive drops his chain.   260
No more your Albans shall be counted foes
But with our Britons equally esteemed.[22]
EMMELIN.
Let me entreat, great sir, you'd not insist
So soon upon the mourning queen's departure.

---

[22] thy Albans . . . with our Britons] possibly an allusion
to the Union between England and Scotland in 1707
that combined their governments into Great Britain

VORTIMER.
Long since our adoration has been fixed   265
On an inexorable haughty fair,
Which has deferred the homage due to you.
But Lucius shall atone.—Our son, draw near.
EMMELIN.
What means the King?—Oh, my disordered
   heart!
LUCIUS.
What would my royal father?   270
VORTIMER.
Of what I wish, great sir, be this the cement,
And this between us be our pledge of peace.
Lucius, my son, the hopes and heir of Britain,
I give to the fair Princess Emmelin
To be her happy lord.   275
HONORIUS.
With the same view, I give the royal bride.
Tomorrow see their happiness complete.
Next, let us seek to soothe this lovely mourner,
Nor shouldst thou, King of Britain, bar our justice.
The Queen was not a warrior like her lord   280
Nor partner of his arms or his injustice;
Wherefore, we have resolved she shall be free.
—Madam, this moment gives you liberty,
And as our brother's royal dowager,
You've leave to sojourn in our court at pleasure.   285
EMMELIN.
For this, the mighty gods reward the King.
ARMINIUS.
And may he meet no hour of new distress.
QUEEN.
May Fortune here fix her inconstant wheel
And never know a change to your dishonor.
VORTIMER.
That she is free is what my soul designed.   290
But oh, I wished it not another's gift!
Ungrateful King, when thy last stake was set,
And Fortune threw the die of war against thee,
Did we not send thee Lucius at thy call?
Lucius, who made the haughty Roman tremble, 295
And chased him from the liquid fence of Britain.
We followed to retrieve thy lost affairs
When pale Despair filled thy distracted court,
And the bright goddess Victory
Sought to espouse thy brother.   300

HONORIUS.

Why dost thou stain the service with reproaches?
What thou hast done was like a monarch done,
As we had done for thee if thou hadst needed.

VORTIMER.

Madam, I take my leave. False King, beware.
Revenge but nods till it can safely rouse,   305
And then, unthankful monarch, thou shalt find
An injured Briton's rage.—Attend us, Albany.

Exeunt Vortimer and Arminius.

HONORIUS.

Lead to the temple, there to thank the gods
For peace, the sweet reward of victory.
He who is truly called his country's lord,   310
The end obtained, with joy returns the sword.
Superior to the glories of the field,
He makes the hero to the patriot* yield,
Forms on his people's good the king's renown,
And quits the laurel for the olive crown.23   315

Exeunt all but Lucius.

LUCIUS.

Whilst after all these storms I seek for rest
In the safe harbor of my charmer's breast,
Though foamy billows threaten from afar
And gath'ring clouds proclaim the wat'ry war,
Though waves around me dash and tempests roar,   320
I'll perish in the deep or gain the wished-for
    shore. *Exit.*

Act III. [The Palace.]

Enter Vortimer and Arminius.

VORTIMER.

What pow'r to awe the mind have women's charms,
Make the bold fearful and the coward brave!
Unequal to the fawning task, our age
Begins too late to learn the trade of courtship,
Too late to study flattery and praise,   5
Or how, with snares and art, to catch the sex.

ARMINIUS.

Deal we like statesmen for a while in cunning.
Your end but gained, no matter what the means.
If once the Queen be parted from the Prince,
The luster of a crown will soon efface   10
Th'impression made upon a woman's heart.

VORTIMER.

Instruct us how, since the ingrateful Gaul,
In spite of our desert, has dared to free her.

ARMINIUS.

Lend me your guards and straight prepare a ship
Well-manned and fitted to the nearest port.   15
I'll tell the Queen of dangers imminent,
Of plots and treason in the court against her,
Nay more, that Albany is up in arms
And ready to receive her as their queen.
Your faithful creature, when she's once embarked,   20
Dares answer with his head to land her safe
(Swift as the winds and waters will permit)
On Britain's shore.

VORTIMER.

                    How shall I praise thy care?
Who serves my heart does more than serve my   25
    crown,
A nearer, dearer interest by far.

ARMINIUS.

Give then immediate orders for our flight,
Lest Lucius, young and lucky, should prevail,
And Rosalind be made the Prince's bride.

VORTIMER.

Perish the thought. Lucius, no more my son,   30
For him I have decreed another nuptial.
He cannot, shall not dare to rival me.
Nature would plead in vain against my rage.
Within this breast, a power superior sways,
And Nature's self the laws of Love obeys.   35
Nor floods nor flames can stop his headlong course;
E'en tyrants yield to more tyrannic force. (*Exit.*)

ARMINIUS.

Our warlike Picts in arms will aid our claim
And, with unbounded joy, receive their queen.
Oh Almerin, thus far success attends us.   40
Tyrant, 'tis just I should thy hopes elude.
Whilst thou shalt vainly look for us in Britain,
With thy own sails we gain our native coast.
But how shall this proud dame be wrought to fly?

---

23 the laurel for the olive crown] Laurel was used to crown
the victor in competition; the olive branch signifies
peace.

She'll not with ease consent to part from Lucius.   45

Enter Silvius.

SYLVIUS.
  My lord, the Queen's returned and the Prince
    with her.
ARMINIUS.
  When did he meet her, Sylvius?
SYLVIUS.
  I do not know, my lord.
  She always goes in private to the cell,
  Whilst I, although her fav'rite, am excluded there.   50
ARMINIUS.
  Oh Jealousy! thou torment of the mind,
  How, in a moment, art thou entered here?
  My breast, my inward soul, is glowing hot.
  It burns, it rages with devouring fires.
SYLVIUS.
  My lord, what means this most unwonted rage?   55
ARMINIUS.
  Alas! Dost not thou see the Queen is wedded?
  This last sad hour has ruined us forever.
  Lucius was wanting* at the temple rites.
  Oh Fate! Where could he be but with the Queen?
  And she was praying with her trusty priest.   60
  But if, indeed, thou'rt wedded to my love,
  Rival, thou bed'st her not whilst I am living!
SYLVIUS.
  Sleep yet our rage and hear what I have done.
  Irene says the Queen preserves the sword
  Found in Otharius' body when he fell.   65
ARMINIUS.
  In this distracted state of our affairs
  'Tis all that Heav'n could grant.
  Wedded! Married!
  Oh who can know the double heart of woman?
  If e'er the sex be true,   70
  'Tis in an early bloom, before the mind
  Perceives the warmth of love, the taint of wishes.
  Then they'll at will ensnare, betray, destroy!
  What motley changes do their faces wear!
  How far from sight lie their deceitful souls!   75
SYLVIUS.
  You're blind with rage. I pray behold this letter.
  'Tis most exactly like the Queen's own writing,
  Scarce to be known by him who taught us both.

ARMINIUS.
  'Tis very like.
  The Queen herself can scarce this hand disown.   80
  On the success of this, this and the sword,
  Thine and thy brother's fortune hangs.
SYLVIUS.
  But if the Prince should kill me?
ARMINIUS.
  Fear not, I'll guard thy life with mine.
SYLVIUS.
  Or the Queen find the cheat?   85
ARMINIUS.
                              Suppose she should?
  She knows thee only as her page, as Sylvius,
  Not for Alenia, whom she thinks in Britain.
  Remember Almerin!
  Canst thou fear aught but losing of thy lover?   90
  She comes! My rival, too! Oh hated name!
  I rally my disordered, scattered thoughts
  And then return with arms for his destruction.

Exeunt. Lucius enters, leading the Queen.

LUCIUS.
  Sure, my fair Queen, when hearts like mine have
    touched
  The summit of their hopes, the height of bliss   95
  Collected all within, they find the joy
  Too big to be expressed but thus to speak [*Kissing
    her*],
  But thus to tell thee of thy husband's transport!
QUEEN.
  Oh that these raptures could forever last!
  Oh changing deity! Oh fickle love!   100
  Why are thy joys not permanent, as great?
LUCIUS.
  In thee forever blooming, ever young,
  Thou great renewer of the spring of love,
  Thou everlasting charmer, in thy arms,
  Though ages hence, those distant happy hours   105
  Will seem but as the first transporting moment.
QUEEN.
  Great Love, how arbitrary is thy sway!
  How dost thou give such harmony to words!
  My coldness all dissolves upon the sound.
  With conscious rising warmth my bosom glows   110
  To meet thy voice, thy breath, thy melting touches!

LUCIUS.

What hinders me to bear my yielding fair,
This blissful moment, to the royal bed?
There where the sun in all his gaudy round
Shall not behold a man so blest as Lucius.   115

QUEEN.

Loose me, my lord, or we are all undone:
Our secret told, and both the kings informed.
At the first fall of night Irene shall admit thee
Without the knowledge of another creature.

LUCIUS.

Meantime, my Queen, I'll wander in the grove   120
And count the minutes of expecting love.
On fragrant banks I'll lay me wishing down
And rave on joys which thou anon shalt crown.
For oh, 'tis pain to see and own such charms
And be delayed the blessing of thy arms,   125
To pause on beauty when desires are high
And only gaze when we should all enjoy.

Lucius leads the Queen to the scene[24]; returning, is met by Arminius.

ARMINIUS.

'Tis you, my dearest lord, I have been seeking.
I come to rail against the faithless sex.
I would inveigh against inconstant charms,   130
Against the flatt'ring gales and changing winds,
Against the April-season of the year,
Against false hopes, false vows, and falser beauty.

LUCIUS.

Arminius thus concerned, thus strangely moved,
Tears in his eyes, distraction in his looks!   135
What mean'st thou, Albany? Straight let me know.
Depend upon thy friend, upon his love.
Thou'rt next of kindred to our charming Queen
And hast a double title to our service.

ARMINIUS.

Behold, my lord, and view me as a lover,   140
As one who long has worn the victor's chain,
As one who once did think himself beloved.
But oh, no sooner did temptation come,
But the fair false one broke her promised faith

And publicly exchanged me for another.   145

LUCIUS.

The common frailty of the sex.

ARMINIUS.

To pity me, oh, make the case your own.
Give me some time for tears. Suppose your hopes
By mutual love, by mutual transports fired!
Just in the wished-for moment of possession,   150
When ev'ry eager pulse beat high with joy,
And her dear heart ready to join in rapture,
Then, then to find a rival youth preferred,
Wouldst thou not groan? Wouldst thou not weep
    like me?

LUCIUS.

Why dost thou pause?   155

ARMINIUS.

The Queen! Alas!

LUCIUS.

                    Immortal Powers! What Queen?

ARMINIUS.

The faithless Queen of Albany.

LUCIUS.

'Tis impossible! Dost thou adore her?

ARMINIUS.

Too fatally I did.   160

LUCIUS.

'Twas wronging me, when I had owned my flame.

ARMINIUS.

Long, long before she left the Alban court,
The virgin charmer's vows were mixed with mine.
False from her youth, she broke her early faith.
Soon as her father had his choice declared,   165
With easy resignation she became
The royal bride of Aquitaine.

LUCIUS.

Go on, I'll hear thee out with patience.

ARMINIUS.

What wretch like me, so doting or despairing?
I fought in war as one who longed to die.   170
Yourself can witness how I valued danger.
Otharius slain, and free to choose again,
What said she not for her late breach of faith?
How did she swear she ne'er had ceased to love,
That I was dearer to her than the light!   175
But in the tend'rest moment of her vows,
The wand'rer strayed again, and I was lost.

24 *scene*] perhaps to an upstage set, probably marked off
    with curtains or a door , perhaps merely to one of the
    side stage doors

LUCIUS.

Oh heaven and earth, sure I can bear no more!

ARMINIUS.

Of your great merit jealous, I prevailed
And from yourself drew the abhorred confession.   180
I warned you of the danger, but in vain.
I durst no more, as tender of her fame,
As willing yet to doubt of my misfortune.
For when I but reproached the wav'ring fair,
She used such various soothings to my mind,   185
Such vows that Lucius ne'er had spoke of love,
That scarce was it a merit to believe her.
Thus was my easy faith abused.

LUCIUS.

What proof hast thou of this?

ARMINIUS.

Oh I had ev'ry proof: her virgin heart,   190
Her speaking eyes, her lips, her charming tongue.
And the pale Queen of Night (on flow'ry banks,
Whilst we invoked her beams) beheld our loves;
Each happy moment witnessed to our joys:
True emblems of the sex and her frail vows,   195
For as the moon, so waned her fickle passion,
The fleeting moments bore her truth away,
And only I am left to speak her falsehood,
An hated evidence* of broken faith.
And yet some proof remains. (*Pulls a bracelet from*   200
his arm.)
This bracelet's of her hair, wove with her hand
Which, to the present, gave a double value.
View well the clasp, see her fair self enshrined,
The altar where my constant vows I paid.
These were the gifts she gave me with her heart.   205
Why do I still such worthless toys retain
When the chief jewel is recalled?
Why yet (as sacred relics of our love)
Worship the shrine of an apostate fair? (*Stamps
upon the bracelet and picture.*)
Hence, vain remembrancers of past delight,   210
I'll tread you into dust. Live, live no more!
Her faithless charms shall be revered no more!

LUCIUS.

Why dost thou tell and show these things to me?

ARMINIUS.

That you may lead me through the wand'ring maze,
That you may give me present death or ease.   215

By those true tears that truest lovers shed,
By all the sweets of Rosalinda's arms,
Have pity on my royal birth and suff'rings.
Confess what I, alas, too much suspect.
Confess you do succeed me in her favor,   220
That I may wander to the utmost verge,
That ceasing to esteem, I may despise
And ne'er regret nor see the bliss I lost.

LUCIUS.

But that thy breath has tainted her clear fame,
I should with pride allow myself the man   225
On whom the beauteous Rosalind has smiled.

ARMINIUS.

Then all is over. I've no more to manage.
Take, take that letter which has racked my soul.
It could be only writ by her to Lucius,
And yet (prepost'rous weakness of the mind)   230
So much, so blindly 'twas I loved the Queen,
That though I saw the false one's name and hand,
My doubting soul would scarce my eyes believe.
In triumph bear it to her and reproach
For me the heart of faithless Rosalinda.   235
She ne'er shall see the lost Arminius more.

LUCIUS.

Yet stay, and tell me where thou hadst this letter.

ARMINIUS.

I found it in the lodgings.
Though not inscribed to you, I thought it yours
Because writ by the Queen.   240

LUCIUS.

And yet, as sure as 'tis her character,
'Twas not addressed to me. (*Reads the letter.*)
"I will retire this evening into the grove. Do
you, my love, attend me there and destroy this
note at the command of ROSALINDA."   245

Sylvius enters and kneels.

SYLVIUS.

Most mighty lords, I beg you on my knees,
If tears, youth, innocence can move your pity,
Restore that sacred letter you were reading.
From me, heedless, it dropped. Wild with the loss,
Around the court I've wept and sought in vain   250
With utmost care and diligence to find it.
Should the Queen know it, I were lost forever.

LUCIUS.
  To whom is it addressed?
SYLVIUS.
  My lord!
LUCIUS.
  To whom wert thou to carry it?   255
SYLVIUS.
  Alas, I understand you not, my lord!
LUCIUS.
  Young traitor, speak or die.
SYLVIUS.
  Oh heav'ns! What shall I say? It is my own,
  A favor of the Queen's bestowed on me.
ARMINIUS.
  Is this the ground of her excess of grace,   260
  This the true motive of her wondrous kindness,
  The faithful Sylvius proved a minion?
LUCIUS.
  Now, where are those delights my passion formed,
  Those scenes of bliss which beauty set before me,
  So hard to gain and yet so quickly lost?   265
  Oh, that bright mind (for so it seemed to me)
  Where purity and all the virtues dwelt
  As at their native home, how tarnished, now
  Despoiled of luster, hateful to the sight!
  Farewell, enchanting sex, false are your joys.   270
  Delusion all, no happiness is in you.
  Not one was ever true, since she could fall.
  Ne'er shall my peace of mind return to bless me.
  My royal father's favor I have lost:
  Renowned, till now, for piety and duty,   275
  I broke those filial bars for faithless love;
  I've changed a parent's blessing into curses.
  My fame has taken wing and flies before me.
  My glory's blasted, all my laurels wither,
  And nothing now remains for me but vengeance   280
  On her—on him—on them—on all who
    wronged me.
  —Die, slave, and boast it in another world.
  —Arminius, why do you oppose me?
ARMINIUS.
  Were such a wretch an object fit for rage,
  Myself, as most abused, would end him.   285
LUCIUS.
  He shall not 'scape with life.

Enter the Queen.

QUEEN.
  Sure, 'tis the Prince of Britain's voice.
  Alas, against my faithful boy his sword!
  Is this well done, my lord?
  Or know ye not that he is mine?   290
LUCIUS.
  Too well, too well I know thy shame and mine.
ARMINIUS.
  (*Aside.*) Now Fortune work. It must be all confusion.
LUCIUS.
  Unworthy of my truth or tenderness,
  Think not of Lucius more, nor I of Rosalind!
  Mountains fall down; yawn wide, thou earth,   295
    between us.
  With molten waves roll up ye sulph'rous lakes.
  Divide us, earth and seas.
  Let all antipathies be reconciled,
  But ne'er the Queen of Albany to Lucius! (*Exit.*)
QUEEN.
  Oh heav'ns and earth! What can he mean, ye Pow'rs,   300
  Or said he not that we must meet no more?
ARMINIUS.
  Now, who shall dare to tell the Queen?
QUEEN.
  Alas, whence can proceed this sudden change?
  My lord of Albany, you are our kinsman,
  And Sylvius, thou art of our household sworn.   305
  By that allegiance that is due to us,
  We charge ye speak or see our face no more.
SYLVIUS.
  Perish the tongue that gives my mistress pain.
QUEEN.
  Speak, wretch, or by the Power that governs all,
  Thou'rt from our royal presence banished ever.   310
ARMINIUS.
  When I by cruel Vortimer was sent,
  First sent to court you to his curst embrace,
  What said you not against the tyrant's love,
  Which I but urged to prove your strength of mind?
  For know, young Queen, your father's ghost   315
    would rise,
  Leaving immortal peace and the blest shades
  With horrid screams to fright your impious bed,
  If e'er his murderer should clasp you there.
QUEEN.
  Shield me, ye Pow'rs, from Vortimer's curst love.

ARMINIUS.

But not his son's? Confession most abhorred!   320
The Queen with guilt turns pale. Oh, beauteous
    frailty!
How hard it is to find perfection.
Antipathy to all the hated race*
Should work your blood in agonies against 'em.

QUEEN.

You are too bold, uncalled, thus to advise.   325
Lucius, most free from his bad father's crimes,
Should not in justice suffer for another.

ARMINIUS.

With my dear uncle's death I do not charge him.
On Vortimer the weighty vengeance fall!
Lucius has guilt of an inherent dye,   330
Crimes all his own which Nature most abhors,
Such as must bar him from your arms forever.

QUEEN. (*Aside.*)

Now all that's blest forbid it!

ARMINIUS.

Madam, draw near. With steadfast eyes behold
The handle of this sword. Survey it well.   335
The high enamel where the curious workman
Has cast in miniature your father's form
Which, with the jewels that enrich the gift,
He gave me on that memorable day
When I attended you to Aquitaine.   340

QUEEN.

I well remember it. Most precious relic,
The representative of my dear father,
Alas, alas, how ye recall my woes,
How ye awake that killing pain, that grief
Which time, in part, had hushed.   345

ARMINIUS.

If for my uncle thus, what for Otharius,
By whom you were so ardently beloved?
But now prepare your courage for the shock:
Prince Lucius begged this fatal sword of me.
What can a vanquished man refuse the victor?   350
Though high as life I prized the dear remains,
Yet I was forced to give it on that morn
When last our army fought with your Otharius.

QUEEN.

Hah! Whither is he going?

ARMINIUS.

I, through the bloody field with this brave youth,   355

Moved, fighting by the warlike Lucius' side.
But his immortal deeds can scarce be told.
Let it suffice, he met the fated King,
The royal majesty of Aquitaine.
Some moments Fortune held an equal scale,   360
Which soon inclined to the young Briton's side.
Through the King's heart he thrust this Alban
    sword.
Sylvius and I the dreadful deed beheld.
The sword was broke in two; this piece with him,
The other in the wound remained.   365

QUEEN.

Oh, heav'nly Powers!

ARMINIUS.

The victor charged us to conceal the fact
Lest Vortimer (grown jealous of his glory)
Should think he had performed too well.

QUEEN.

Alas, no more! I am a wretch, Arminius.   370
Why told'st thou not thy hapless queen before?
Where was thy duty, thy allegiance then?
Thou shouldst have shown my husband's murd'rer,
That I, with detestation, might have shunned him.
Fatal neglect! Oh knowledge found too late!   375
Unhappy ignorance! Accursèd bride,
Never till now undone.

ARMINIUS.

Beholding you, Prince Lucius grew inflamed,
Which, of the secret, made him doubly careful.
Long, with painful silence, I obliged him,   380
Long labored 'twixt my friendship and my duty.
At last, grown big with our approaching hopes
(The Picts being up in arms and wanting* aid),
Duty prevailed, for I was bound to speak.
Your page attended with the sword, the Prince   385
(Coming from you) perceived it in his hand,
And conscious where it was designed, drew his
(With many foul reproaches) on the boy.
I interposed. Your majesty appeared
When Lucius, filled with jealous rage, departed.   390

QUEEN.

The world's united woes are in this breast,
And yet perhaps Arminius is mistaken.
Nay, King Otharius, too, fought in disguise.
Six were alike him armed; 'twas one of them.
I have a proof.—Irene, bring the sword   395

Found in the murdered body of my lord.
If they should join, Lucius and I must part.

ARMINIUS. (*Aside.*)

    Dear prosp'rous mischief, lag not now behind,
    And then, oh Almerin, the race is mine.

QUEEN.

    And yet it cannot be, my search rest here.   400
    Impossible! Fate cannot be so angry.
    I will not put it to the dreadful test.

The sword is brought and joined.

    Arminius does. Oh Heav'n, I can no more.
    Perish all demonstration! Unkind
    And cruel Prince, oh why dost thou destroy me   405
    And arm Otharius to my Lucius' ruin?
    My living husband's vanished by the dead.
    My lord, my Lucius, see thy wretched bride,
    The most forlorn, disconsolate of women.
    I am his wife, Arminius.   410

ARMINIUS.

    Forbid it, Hecate with all her train.
    Incessant Furies yell around such nuptials.
    Catch his deceitful soul, ye bluest plagues.
    Snatch him by piecemeals, ye avenging fiends.
    Treason and death! Oh impious parricide!   415
    What, wed Otharius' murderer,
    Possessed by one steeped in your husband's blood?

QUEEN.

    I sink—the most unhappy of my race.*
    Come near, my Sylvius, I would rest upon thee.
    Nay, Albany, thou art too good.   420
    Wilt thou weep, too?

ARMINIUS.

    These bitter tears, by strength of anguish wrung,
    Prove how Arminius loves his hapless queen.
    'Tis I must guard you from impending ruin.
    Lucius has charms to sway the strongest mind.   425
    Fly the seducer and assert your glory.
    Take scorpions to your bed but take not Lucius.
    Lucius! Triumphant in his sin, all gay in blood,
    Dreadfully gay with your dear husband's blood,
    Unprecedented horror! Fly to death   430
    But mingle not with him who slew your lord.
    Light up your torch at any other love.
    None are debarred your arms but that curst race*
    Who murdered poor Otharius and your father.

QUEEN.

    Thus greatly wretched, what can save thy queen?   435

ARMINIUS.

    Your Albans are already up in arms.
    Seize on this moment and be yet a queen,
    A virtuous, innocent, though wretched queen.
    A guard and ship stand ready for your flight
    Whilst on this royal hand once more I swear   440
    Only to live, only to die for you.
    (*Kneels, kissing her hand.*)

Enter Lucius behind.

LUCIUS.

    How wildly are we hurried by our passions!
    I was to blame not to explain my wrongs
    And tell the false one all her perjuries,
    Confront her with her minion and the letter,   445
    Till she confess our parting is but just.
    —Hah, what do I see, the faithless Rosalind
    On one reclined, the other at her feet?
    What, have they bargained to divide her favors?

QUEEN.

    Yes, I will go, lest Fate should join with Love,   450
    Lest I should wound Otharius o'er again,
    Lest I should view his murd'rer with indulgence.
    Lead, lead, Arminius,
    I'll follow thee, surrounded with misfortunes.
    —Hah! Lucius here, that bloody conqu'ror Lucius.   455
    Save me, Arminius, take me from his sight.
    My eyes, my soul is fastened! Tear me hence.
    Bear thy lost queen where tempests loudest roar
    And never let me see the cruel Lucius more.

Exeunt all but Lucius.

LUCIUS.

    Curst weakness of the mind which brought me   460
      back!
    Hence tender thoughts, hence all remains of love,
    Hence jealousy, thou certain proof of passion.
    Of hope and tenderness henceforth disarmed,
    My breast shall pant no more for faithless beauty.
    No more for perjured woman let us mourn.   465
    To war, to glory, now my heart return!
    So great Ulysses, soothed by Circe's charms,
    Sighed on her breast and melted in her arms.
    What wondrous transports did her eyes inspire?

Soft was her voice, and raging was his fire. 470
But when he found her false and cruel soul,
And in a form so fair, a mind so foul,
With glory and disdain the hero burned,
Broke her enchantments and the sex he scorned.

Exit.

Act IV. A forest.

Enter Lucius alone.

LUCIUS.

Hail to the savage horrors of this forest!
Receive into thy hospitable arms
The wretched and forsaken Lucius,
Driv'n from the commerce of all humankind
And never to return. 5
Oh impious woman, on thy nuptial day,
E'en on that day in which thy faith was plighted,
To fly and leave me in the last despair.
All joys farewell. The blossom of my youth,
Blighted by an unkindly, cruel frost, 10
Shall never spring again.
Pressed by this weight of woe, I bend to earth
From thence to rise no more,
In wilds and deserts waste my future hours,
Falling, inglorious, by a woman's falsehood. 15
Farewell, my people, whom I wished to bless
With all those virtues that best kings possess.
My fame, my passion, and my hopes resigned,
With that exalted ardor of the mind
Which swelled my soul and made it greatly dare 20
And, dauntless, bore me through the fiercest war,
In their cold bed unanimated lie
And like extinguished fires in darkness die. (*Walks
    down the scene and exits.*)

Enter at another door, Arminius and Sylvius.

ARMINIUS.

Sylvius, thus far our fortune has been fair,
But I grow jealous of a counter-turn: 25
Methinks the captain who commands the guard
Has much of Vortimer, the cunning Briton;
I more than fear it is the King himself—
The care he takes to shun my speech and eyes.
I'm caught in the same net I cast for others. 30

Enter an Alban lord.

ALBAN LORD.

My lord, 'tis certainly the King of Britain:
He bears the royal signet on his finger.
The Queen and you and we are now his captives.

ARMINIUS.

Shall Rosalinda know this fatal turn?
It will too much her tender heart affright. 35
My resolution must be very sudden.
The Gallic King hunts near; I'll hasten thither.
His guards are thrice more numerous than ours.
Sylvius, meantime, do thou the Queen amuse.
Till I return, my lord, oppose their flight. 40
She is our sovereign, thou art born her subject.
All's now at stake; kill him or fall thyself.

Exeunt omnes. Enter Vortimer.

VORTIMER.

What does Arminius mean by halting here?
With eyes that darted strong, he viewed me o'er
As he would look me through. 45
If thou hast found and yet avoid'st me, Prince,
'Tis proof thy soul had formed an enterprise
To what thou didst pretend most opposite.
I durst not yield a foe so large a trust.
'Twere weak indeed to put it in his pow'r 50
The Queen to bear away with our own ships,
To raise a war in Albany against us.
Therefore, like Jove, disguised to gain our love,
We veil our majesty and drop our thunder.
The Queen appears! That glorious prize is mine. 55

Enter the Queen.

Madam, forgive this seeming bold intrusion.
Till once embarked, your majesty's not safe.
Why do you squander time irrevocable?

QUEEN.

Arminius would awhile take shelter here.

VORTIMER.

The ports will instantly be stopped; 60
By noon your flight must be the public theme.
Yet a few hours, and you've the waves in view.

QUEEN.

Go find Arminius, tell to him thy reasons
And we will instantly depart.

Exit Vortimer.

Depart for what? or where? My torment's fixed. 65
No change of scene can vary my misfortunes.

The Princess now may gain the vows of Lucius,
That solemn faith he plighted first to me.
Their hands may join, and she have all his transports:
That height of wish, that ecstasy of soul,   70
When his bright eyes spoke better than his tongue,
Darting delight, for love was all their language!
Ah wretched Rosalinda, whither now?
Think on Otharius, there thou'rt lost indeed.
Thy lord was slain by him whom thou hast wedded.   75
Blot out with your till now unerring hand,
Blot out, ye Pow'rs, that single murd'ring thought.
Tear from the destined book25 that cursèd deed.
All other woes forever stand recorded.

Re-enter Vortimer.

VORTIMER.
Madam, the Prince is nowhere to be found.   80
We must proceed without him, or you're lost.
QUEEN.
And what art thou (unused to such a presence)
That, with rude sounds, presum'st t'affront our ears?
VORTIMER.
Come willingly, for fear you should be forced.
QUEEN.
Who waits? My guards! Arminius, help!   85
VORTIMER.
Thou call'st in vain, a greater force is here.
It is the King of Britain who conducts thee.
QUEEN.
Hah! My haughty foe, the cruel Vortimer!
VORTIMER.
You're now within my pow'r and can't escape.
QUEEN.
No! I will never stir, I'll grow to earth.   90
Heav'n, let me change my being with the brutes,26
Nay, welcome death, rather than go with thee!
VORTIMER.
Take heed how you provoke a king like me.

---

25 destined book] book in which destiny or fate is recorded
   or (pre)ordained
26 grow … brutes] Rosalinda, although a Christian, alludes
   to the fates of nymphs and mortals who were sexually
   assaulted by gods and were transformed into trees
   (Daphne) or animals (Callisto, Io—though both after
   being raped).

Mine is a surly, uninvited Cupid.
No willing harbor finds he in my breast.   95
On war, on empire, all my thoughts were fixed
Till thy malignant form intruded here.
Give me myself! I ask but to forget thee.
QUEEN.
A never-failing cure for love is absence.
VORTIMER.
Oh, 'tis a tedious one and racks the mind,   100
Nor has it wrought the wished-for cure on me!
Thou'st been my curst tormentor since the time
I first beheld thee with my foe, thy father.
Now I'll revenge me on that tyrant beauty.
QUEEN.
Oh hear me, King! I am already married.   105
VORTIMER.
Then Furies seize thy husband! What's to be done?
Yield thou to be divorced and reign our queen.
QUEEN.
Thy queen! Not to command the universe,
And yet I wish that I had never wedded.
VORTIMER.
Born of an hated race* and lost to me,   110
May I not ravish her I could not win?
May I not seize what would not be bestowed?
I dream of blest enchantment in her arms.
I restless burn and rave on furious joy.
And nothing but possession can assuage   115
The lovesick, raging fever of my soul.
QUEEN.
Ruffian, forbear! Whence comes this profanation?
VORTIMER.
Revenge and love are both in arms within.
Thy eyes and scorn burn me with different fires.
Urged on to war and eager for the conquest,   120
I cannot part inglorious from the field.

Struggles with her. She falls at his feet.

QUEEN.
Oh woe for me!
Thus far I'm vanquished and thus low subdued.
I clasp thy knees, I grasp thy feet with horror.
Do not assault the honor of thy daughter: 125
I am the wife of Lucius.
VORTIMER.
Of Lucius! Of that rebel!

Supplanted by my son! When wert thou wedded?

QUEEN.

Not one kind hour has our sad Hymen known.
Nay, scarce the moment smiled that joined our hands.   130
Successive woes have parted us already.

VORTIMER.

Thou goest with us, to see the Prince no more.
A banished traitor shall he always live.
The hour he lands in Britain, he shall die.

QUEEN.

What, your victorious, loyal, godlike son?   135

VORTIMER.

Unhappy Queen, thy praises wing his fate.
Curst as I am, thus burning for thy charms,
My vital blood, drunk up by thirsty love,
Seizes the cordial beauty to revive me.
Lucius has wedded thee but not enjoyed.   140
Possession is a better claim than his.
Then instant let me make the prize secure.
What follows, we at leisure may debate.
The present moment takes up all our thoughts.
This struggle past, we are ourself again,   145
And our heart free from an ungrateful passion.

QUEEN.

Give me my death. Be there a conqueror.
Arminius, Albany, help! Oh help!

VORTIMER.

Thou rav'st, thou call'st in vain. He hears thee not.
Rich Love, repay me now the peace I lost.   150

QUEEN.

Whom shall I next invoke, ye mighty Pow'rs?
Lucius! Where art thou now in my distress?
My lord! My Lucius! Where art thou, my Lucius?
He comes! My husband comes to save my honor.

Lucius appears at the lower end of the scene.

LUCIUS.

Through the wide echoing forests, who resounds   155
The name of Lucius? The Queen of Albany,
And in a ruffian's hand! Die, ravisher!

QUEEN.

Oh hold! Oh horror, Lucius! 'Tis against thy father.

The Queen interposes, and Lucius falls at Vortimer's feet.

LUCIUS.

What, was I armed against my royal father,

Against that precious source of my own life?   160
My heart bleeds inward at the racking thought.
If this be fear, I never feared till now.

VORTIMER.

Retire and leave us with the Queen.

LUCIUS.

Sir.

VORTIMER.

Traitor, be gone, thou hast no business here.   165

QUEEN.

Oh do not, Lucius, as you once loved virtue,
As you once loved your poor unhappy bride
Ere adverse Fate could teach thy heart to change.

VORTIMER.

Some other method must be found to part you.
        (*Exit.*)

QUEEN.

Above, to those bright mansions of the blest,   170
The grateful Rosalind her thanks returns. (*Kneels.*)
This day, in each revolving year, be praised.
Let it be marked the happy and the fair,
And may I cease to live when I profane it.

LUCIUS.

Can falsehood seem so graceful?   175

QUEEN.

To thee, my husband, next, with like regard
(The instrument of my deliverance)
I cannot say enough, my heart is thine.

LUCIUS.

Oh 'tis a very false one!

QUEEN.

Who's false, my lord?   180

LUCIUS.

The perjured Queen.

QUEEN.

Turn not on me the errors of our fate.
Joy at thy sight and for my late escape
Caused me some moments to forget my griefs,
But they return full-blown with sharp reproach.   185
Yes, Lucius, we must part. Fly hence forever.
I too must go and make my widowed bed
Where winds and seas, eternally at war,
Have left no landing-place for murderers.

LUCIUS.

The like forgetfulness has seized on me.   190
Almighty beauty quite becalms my rage.

In looking on thee, I forget thy crimes,
Forget thou gav'st my honor to the winds,
Stuck foul discredit on my spotless name,
Left me to drink the bitter dregs of wrath,   195
Of burning jealousy and cold despair,
Regardless of the right that I claimed in thee.

QUEEN.

Since I am false, have I not need to fly?
Bad woman as I am, I own my crime.
But oh, for whom is it that I am guilty?   200
In thee 'tis most inhuman to reproach me.
Thou mad'st me criminal and yet upbraid'st me.
False to Otharius, murd'ress as I am,
Ev'n now I kill him o'er again, ev'n now,
Whilst thy too gracious form is dear to sight,   205
Whilst all of thee is precious to my heart,
And love o'erwhelms resentment in my soul.

LUCIUS.

Oh well-dissembled falsehood.

QUEEN.

Fly thou, lest we should never part,
Though all regards, divine and human, plead,   210
Though blood cries out aloud, "Be gone, revenge,"
Though men and angels have decreed against thee,
Though shame, remorse, and vengeance call me
     hence,
Strong as thou art in charms, how can I go?

LUCIUS.

Yes, thou wouldst go   215
Around the world to bear my infamy,
The odious load which thou hast heaped on me,
On me, and on thyself.
Oh what art thou become? How art thou called?
The wife of Lucius, a known prostitute,   220
She who fled from him on his marriage day.
Arise, revenge! Arise and force out love.
Come indignation, honor, glory, come.
Strengthen my arm and show me how to punish.

QUEEN.

Ah Heav'ns! My lord, you will not kill your wife.   225

LUCIUS.

Is there another way to clear my honor?

QUEEN.

What have I done, or why am I suspected?

LUCIUS.

Arminius has thy virgin shame disclosed

And of thy early hours the secret practice.
With the same rage as once he loved, he hates.   230
Behold this letter—fair perdition.
A boy! A poor domestic slave! Low sin!
Vile woman! Vicious sex!
Why was I chosen, I, for this dishonor?

QUEEN.

Has trait'rous Albany traduced my virtue?   235

LUCIUS.

Thyself, against thyself. See here, these lines,
My shame and thine! This wicked scroll is thine.

QUEEN.

By heav'n and earth, it is not! I am wronged.
Hear me, my lord. Alas, where are your eyes?
What means that arm uplifted to my death?   240
Why do you stare as you were turned to stone?

LUCIUS.

An unseen Power disarms me.
I idly gaze, am lost but cannot strike.
Away, away, lest I should love to madness,
Lest I should take perdition to my bed,   245
The blot of glory, stained with abject joys.

QUEEN.

I ne'er writ this, never loved Albany,
Ne'er heard or thought I was beloved by him!
Oh torment of the mind, to be suspected,
I, who love honor, innocence, and truth   250
Next Heav'n and thee, that I should be suspected.

LUCIUS.

Is it not plain? See there thy hand, false woman.
In spite of charms, I shall relapse to rage,
In spite of love, destroy thee—let me go.
A miracle can only clear thy fame   255
And heal my wounded heart.

*As Lucius is breaking from the Queen, Sylvius enters,
his breast open, torn and bloody. He falls at the Queen's
feet. Lucius supports him.*

SYLVIUS.

Fly, madam, I am wounded unto death.
The King of Britain's sword has pierced my heart.
He's fighting with our party and must conquer.
My gracious Queen, I beg you would forgive me.   260
—Lucius, the letter thou hast seen, I wrote.
Thou wert thyself the cause—I loved thee, Lucius,
Loved thee in Britain, followed thee to Aquitaine.

Now in thy arms, unpitied, dies Alenia.
—Oh Almerin, are thus thy words explained?   265
(*Dies.*)

QUEEN.
Thy death's a miracle to clear my fame.
My jealous lord required a miracle.
It is Alenia, false Arminius' sister.
Base man! How deeply were thy treasons laid?

LUCIUS.
With conscious guilt for being so misled,   270
With conscious shame for having thus offended,
With all the penitence of men convinced
When they, like me, are tortured by remorse,
I prostrate fall to hear your equal doom.
Pronounce a sentence heavy as my crime.   275
Oh banish me from life, but not from love.
Send me to die, but not to live from you.

QUEEN.
Could Fate as easily be reconciled,
Then might we meet in joy. But oh! The Fates,
The Fates are angry with us, Lucius,   280
With thee, for murdering the brave Otharius,
With me, for wedding with his murderer!

LUCIUS.
I kill the King!
Who dares accuse the innocent?

QUEEN.
Albany does.
Arminius and Alenia saw thee kill him.   285
The sword found broken in Otharius' body
Was giv'n thee by Arminius.

LUCIUS.
Oh well-invented malice!
'Tis false, 'tis false. So may the traitor die,
Or Lucius perish.   290

QUEEN.
Didst thou not beg of him my father's sword?

LUCIUS.
Never! That villain has traduced us both.

QUEEN.
Oh I believe thee, Lucius! But the world!
Clear there thy fame, and I am still thy bride.

Enter Irene hastily.

IRENE.
Madam, the King has slain the Alban lord   295

Left by the Prince to guard your Majesty.
He has fought a bloody battle with our party,
But cruel Vortimer at length has conquered.

QUEEN.
Alas, then I am once again his captive!
Remember, Lucius, that which thou hast sworn.   300
Protect me from his love, or thou are perjured.

*Vortimer enters with soldiers. They go to seize the
Queen. Lucius draws and defends her.*

VORTIMER.
What, arm against thy king! against thy father!
Wilt thou? dar'st thou? Then kill the horrid villain
That I may curse I ever had a son.

LUCIUS.
Your life, great sir, to me be always sacred.   305
I but defend the honor of my wife.

VORTIMER.
Then soldiers, strike, strike through the traitor's
heart.

*They are going to kill the Prince. The Queen comes
from behind and interposes.*

QUEEN.
Through me you strike. I guard my husband's life.

VORTIMER.
Thee I can't hurt. My eyes disarm my hand.
—Slaves, tear him thence, but do not touch the   310
Queen,
Your lives shall answer it. But kill the rebel.

QUEEN.
Kill your son! Oh impious, curst command!
—Soldiers, stand off, or else you pass through me.

VORTIMER.
Slaves, villains, cowards, are you hers or mine?

QUEEN.
I cannot long defend him, he must fall.   315
Yield, Lucius, I release thee from thy vow.
—Oh save his life, and I'll consent to go!
Spare but thy son, I am thy willing captive.

LUCIUS.
What, hast thou giv'n thy honor for my life?
A vast exchange, and better I had died.   320

QUEEN.
My honor, no! That is the care of Heav'n.
My life I'd always give for thine.

LUCIUS.

Oh, sacred sir!

By all those ties that keep bad men from crimes,

From acting what their wicked hearts conceive, 325

I charge you not to think of violation.

I am your son. She is my wedded wife.

More were superfluous.

VORTIMER.

Away. Now for the sea.

QUEEN.

And may it with unbounded rage receive us. 330

Blow, winds, exert on us your utmost force,

All nature else be free. Plunge us beneath,

Dash us on rocks: ye cannot be too cruel.

Yet spare my husband amidst all your storms.

But for this impious king and me, 335

War, fire, fury, blood, and devastation

Pursue us, as ye did my wretched father.

O'ertake us, as ye have the slain Otharius,

And when ye come, I shall account it gain

That the curst Briton suffers in my pain. 340

Exeunt.

Act V. scene i. The outer-part of the Temple of Jupiter.
Emmelin and Arminius meeting, she with a dagger.

EMMELIN.

Unfaithful Albany, is this the trust,

Are these the promises thou mad'st to me?

I feel the strength of nations in this arm,

And thou shalt taste my dagger.

ARMINIUS.

A hand so fair should never menace danger, 5

And peace and joy should be the gifts of beauty.

Were I not yet of use to Emmelin,

I'd not oppose but meet the destined blow. (*Wrests
it from her.*)

EMMELIN.

Say, fawning traitor, hast thou not undone me?

ARMINIUS.

Why are you against your slave enraged? 10

How can your creature merit death from you?

EMMELIN.

Accomplished villain! Plead'st thou ignorance,

And Lucius (whom my soul is fond of) sentenced?

By thy curst accusation he's condemned.

Thou told'st the kings and priests he was a Christian. 15

For that he dies, nor can my brother save him.

ARMINIUS.

Oh, hear me! I have served you to the utmost.

No other way could gain him a reprieve

From Vortimer, his jealous father.

EMMELIN.

Speak on— 20

ARMINIUS.

When first the King, your brother, and myself

(With all his guards and train of noble huntsmen)

O'ertook the flying tyrant with the captives,

He halted to consider of their death.

EMMELIN.

New horror! Murder his only son! 25

ARMINIUS.

I thought what, by his loss, your heart would suffer,

And therefore sent for audience from the tyrant,

In which I soon his confidence regained.

For whilst the action passed, I boldly swore

Within the shady forest I was sleeping 30

Till wakened by Honorius' numerous train;

I was by them constrained to join his party.

EMMELIN.

Did he credit this?

ARMINIUS.

He seemed to do it, yet was all confusion,

Nay, vowed he would himself the captives slay 35

Rather than from his power they should be wrested.

EMMELIN.

Cruel tyrant! Most unnatural father!

ARMINIUS.

To gain a pause of time, some hours to serve you,

'Twas my advice that he should yield them up,

As Christian converts, to the flamens' hands; 40

From whence, he afterwards might save the Queen,

Should he design to let his rival perish.

EMMELIN.

Our laws are such, if Christians are convicted,

They must abjure or die!

The Queen by all our people is beloved, 45

For though they long have guessed she was a convert,

Till now, alas, she never was accused.

Thy breath has killed her. Thou hast slain thy Queen.

The gods will hunt thee round the world for this,

Rebel and traitor as thou art. 50

ARMINIUS.

    To you I am no traitor.

EMMELIN.

    How didst thou know that Lucius was a Christian?

ARMINIUS.

    I thought the Queen might have converted him,

    And he with pride, upon the first demand,

    Above his father's hopes, acknowledged it.   55

EMMELIN.

    This, then, is the result. But if he die

    (Mark me, my cunning lord of Albany,

    For by Diana's chastity I swear),

    I will have vengeance for the Prince's death.

ARMINIUS.

    They have refused the Druids' offered mercy.   60

    The jealous Briton urges for a sentence.

    His guards have got possession of this temple,

    Nor dares the King, for fear of popular rage,

    Wrest Christian convicts from the flamens' hands.

    What can we then project to save the Prince?   65

EMMELIN.

    The Prince of Cambria and the King my brother,

    With pressing yet unprosperous tears and prayers,

    Have sought the tyrant to release the captives,

    But by the superstitious people joined,

    He lords it here as if he were in Britain.   70

    In this extremity some hopes remain

    That we may yet surprise the British guard

    Which, if by thee and by the Prince performed,

    May from the public hate preserve my brother.

    A chosen party of the Gallic troops   75

    Have orders to obey you.

    Haste then, with these, and save the royal pris'ners.

    Relieve my love, though he be ne'er for me.

    Fly—tear him from his rival—set him free,

    Or my revenge shall center all on thee.   80

[Exeunt.]

      [Scene ii.] The curtain drawn up

        discovers* an altar to Jupiter.

Flamens attending; Lucius and the Queen under the British guard.

LUCIUS.

    Yet ere my father shall pronounce our doom,

    Let me this once enfold thee in my arms,

    Take from my wife this first and last embrace.

    Oh sweet to sense—oh yet untasted beauty!

    To die is nothing—but resigning thee,   5

    I merit more than ever man could merit.

QUEEN.

    So fast these troubled wat'ry bubbles rise,

    I cannot see thee through 'em. Oh, farewell!

LUCIUS.

    Farewell, my Queen. May the sharp pangs of death

    Fall gently on thee, as when children slumber.   10

QUEEN.

    May angels bear thee on their golden wings

    Without the intermediate pains between.

LUCIUS.

    My father comes, and now we part forever.

Enter Vortimer, priests, and train.

VORTIMER.

    Christians! Once more, do ye abjure or die?

LUCIUS.

    Die.   15

QUEEN.

    Both die.

LUCIUS. (*Kneels.*)

    But first, great sir, I beg in death forgiveness

    In what (as erring man) I have offended,

    Though never willingly did I displease

    My awful* King and father.   20

    As to my love, it was involuntary.

    Hearts do not give themselves. For that I die.

QUEEN. (*Kneels.*)

    As of my dearest lord you are the parent,

    Pardon those words I may in rage have spoke,

    But sure the provocation was extreme.   25

    I do forgive and would be so forgiven.

LUCIUS.

    I wish you length of days and to forget me.

    Forget you e'er had an unhappy son,

    But may you still,* with never-ending grief,

    Remember Rosalinda.   30

QUEEN.

    Long may you live, repenting Lucius' death.

    To you I recommend my helpless people:

    If e'er their Queen you loved (as much you

      flattered),

    Govern with clemency.

VORTIMER.

                        They shake my heart.   35
  Yet ne'er from love could pity gain the ground.
(*Aside to Lucius.*)
    Yield up thy bride to us, and thou shalt live.
    Thy cursèd marriage may be disannulled,
    And thou proclaimed our kingdom's heir.

LUCIUS.

  Forsake my wife! It is not in my pow'r.   40
  Mercy is cruelty when so disguised.

VORTIMER.

  Then thou shalt die, rebellious, hardened boy.
(*Aside to the Queen.*)
    You know your charms, exert 'em now, be mine,
    And Lucius, my curst rival, too shall live.

QUEEN.

  To save the Prince's life, I would do all   45
  But break the sacred vow I plighted to him.

VORTIMER.

  Since thus I'm braved by their fantastic passion,
  Their death shall be an instant cure for mine.
  —Take hence, to diff'rent prisons, both these
    Christians.
  The woman straight shall die by fire. But first,   50
  The common deathman riots in her charms,
  Whilst Lucius on a lofty scaffold bleeds.
  Their sentence is irrevocable.

LUCIUS.

  A queen condemned to suffer as a slave,
  Oh awful* judge! I cannot call you father.   55
  Let savage beasts hunt down my wearied life,
  Tear off my flesh, or bury me alive.
  Rack only me, and I will bless the King,
  But save, unhurt, the honor of my wife.

QUEEN.

  Sacred to virtue and immortal glory,   60
  Sacred to chaste and holy purity,
  Who is it dares to sentence our high honor?
  Our spotless fame aspires to reach the skies.
  Our life we willingly resign; there glut your rage.

VORTIMER.

  Hence. Bear 'em to their prisons.   65

QUEEN.

  Oh Lucius, Lucius, they would drag me from thee!

LUCIUS.

  Slaves, ravishers, forbear to touch my wife.

QUEEN.

  He is my lord. We cannot part and live.

LUCIUS.

  Oh Father, monarch, royal Vortimer,
  By my dear mother's honor, save the Queen's!   70

VORTIMER.

  Down, down with him to the Temple dungeon.

The stage opens, and Lucius is carried down by the priests and soldiers.

QUEEN.

  Upwards to heav'n where he shall rise a saint.
  Oh mighty Pow'rs! My breast (by you inspired)
  Foretells some miracle vouchsafed to me
  Shall guard my chastity from brutal rage.   75
  All wordly pomp I willingly forego,
  My husband, too, the dearest gift of life.
  Through fire I'll gladly pass, my faith to prove,
  If fire can save me from an impious love. (*Exit guarded.*)

VORTIMER.

  Now laugh, proud Queen, and scorn our   80
    proffered throne.

Enter Arminius.

  Lord Albany, what you advised is done.

ARMINIUS.

  It is revenge befitting a great soul.
  Oh 'twill be great, be ecstasy indeed,
  If you can personate the happy slave
  Sentenced to ravish this nice piece of beauty,   85
  And like brave Tarquin, clasp your far-famed
    Lucrece.*

VORTIMER.

  Revenge and love shall be together sated:
  Under the vile appearance of that wretch
  We will possess the fair, yet shroud our glory.

ARMINIUS.

  How bears Honorius such a foul decree?   90

VORTIMER.

  The coward Gaul durst not release the Christians,
  Durst not command, ev'n in his capital,
  Lest his good people should, forsooth, grow angry.
  We laughed to see the royal dastard's fears,
  Whilst, by our seeming zeal and gold well-placed,   95
  We gained a sentence hateful to their King.

Were she not fair, what were her gods to me?
Let nations wonder at the horrid deed.
Let all the monarchs of the world unite
To pour down vengeance on our guilty head,   100
We'll meet the torrent when we've quenched our
   flame.
Yes, Rosalind! Thy beauties are devoted:
Through laws we wade to reach thy cruel arms,
Through thy own blood to taste thy boasted charms.
If Love alone can wisest counsels blast,   105
Unpeople kingdoms, and lay nations waste,
With indignation when the god is fired,
At once by fury and revenge inspired,
Like lightning from the hand of Jove he flies;
All danger and all rule his rage defies;   110
Nor dreads the threatened vengeance of the skies.
   (*Exit.*)

ARMINIUS.
Fortune, once more, let me invoke thy aid.
Oh thou great goddess, be propitious now
And stand reversed forever!

Exit.

[Scene iii.] The dungeon.

Lucius discovered, * *Arminius enters to him.*

ARMINIUS.
Long live the Prince of Britain.
LUCIUS.
Who's there?
ARMINIUS.
A friend to Lucius.
LUCIUS.
Thou guilty, treacherous lord of Albany!
Canst thou, who wronged the Queen and   5
   wronged our fame,
Presume to be a friend? Oh for a sword!
ARMINIUS.
There, have your wish. But turn it not on me
Till Fate has leisure for so vile a life.
LUCIUS.
Speak on. What was thy errand hither?
ARMINIUS.
Hope to preserve the Queen from violation.   10
Measure my zeal by her distress. Alas,
Both are too great for words.

LUCIUS.
Albany's zeal! An ignominious traitor
Who has traduced us both, stained the Queen's glory,
And fixed on me the murder of Otharius.   15
ARMINIUS.
Wild to possess what most my soul adored,
What would not a poor, lost, despairing lover?
But oh, no more she lives for you nor me!
No more her honor lives without our succor.
By an unheard of, monstrous, vile decree,   20
A sordid slave possesses all her charms,
Unless, this instant, we the wretch can slay.
I'll lead you where you may the deed perform.
Time calls on me to head Honorius' troops,
Disposed by him and Emmelin to aid you.   25
Perhaps some lucky moment may look forth
To save her sacred life, as well as honor.
What vengeance then a noble foe can ask,
All the revenge that arm can take, be thine.
LUCIUS.
Hope once again rekindles in my soul.   30
This deed performed and the bright Queen
   preserved,
I claim the justice of thy sword. Till when,
In the ensuing tumult, spare my father.

Exeunt.

[Scene iv.] The scene shifts.

[Lucius and Arminius] re-enter.

ARMINIUS.
That door conducts you to the Queen.
The British guards are drawn around the temple.
The priests themselves, as loath to hear her shrieks,
Retire to corners to bewail th'event.
There's the way. Be sure you kill the ravisher.   5
LUCIUS.
Farewell. Inevitable death pursues him. (*Goes in.*)
ARMINIUS.
This is, indeed, a masterpiece of cunning;
This is a most accomplished strain of thought:
The father kill the son, the son the father.
Either fall, or both, but one must perish.   10
I head the Gauls and murder the survivor,
And then the crown and Queen may yet be mine.

Exit.

[Scene v.] The scene changes [to the Queen's cell].

Enter Vortimer disguised in a sordid habit. As he is going out at the opposite door, Lucius pursues him, pulls him back, and stabs him.

LUCIUS.
Stay, ruffian, take thy death from Lucius' hand.
Where is my Rosalinda? Where's my love?

The Queen enters.

My dearest Queen? The ravisher's no more.
The sordid, ignominious slave is dead.
VORTIMER.
Yet but a moment's space and I am gone.   5
The gods have proved themselves, and I am slain.
LUCIUS.
That voice has something sacred in the sound.
VORTIMER.
It is thy father. Thou hast slain me, Lucius,
Killed him who gave thee life. Curse on the deed.
    (*Dies.*)
LUCIUS.
Oh 'tis he, 'tis he, the royal Vortimer!   10
Ev'n now, his angry soul has forced its passage.
Swiftly his breath fleets upwards from my sight.
Now he arraigns me at the bar of justice.
Now he accuses his ill-fated son.
Now he pulls down the righteous vengeance on   15
    me,
Invokes the thunder and all-piercing lightning.
How full it glares on my defective sight.
O'erwhelmed by dreadful bolts, the wrath of
    Heav'n,
Down, down I sink to meet the fate of parricides.
Avenge my father's blood, despair and death.   20
A king's, a parent's blood! Despair and die! (*Falls
    in a trance.*)
QUEEN.
Oh great unhappy hero, born for woe!
Oh fatal moment that inclined thy heart
To think the wretched Rosalinda fair.
Dear, lovely eyes, admit no more of day.   25
Eternal be this lethargy of grief.
Do not return to conscious, racking thought.
He comes again to miseries untold,
To life, to sense, to reason, to distraction!

LUCIUS.
Say, thou bright fair one, who first taught me truth, 30
May not this hand avenge a parent's blood?
QUEEN.
The gates of mercy are forever shut
Against self-murderers.[27]
LUCIUS.
What, cut a father's thread
And calmly wait the breaking of my own?   35
Not years of strictest penitence can atone,
Can expiate for shedding sacred blood.
Oh King! Thy usurpation and bad deeds,
The murder of thy prince, are here revenged.
Forever scarlet, those deep-tinctured crimes   40
(By an irrevocable, righteous doom)
Have made thy son thy executioner.
On me thy sins descend. For thee I am curst.

An alarm and fighting within.

QUEEN.
Arise, my lord, new mischiefs are at hand.

Arminius enters at the head of a party.

LUCIUS.
'Tis false Arminius fighting with the guards.   45
Arminius says I slew the great Otharius.
Arminius stained the honor of the Queen.
Arminius urged me on to kill my father.
Arminius comes for payment of his crimes.
Traitor, have at thy heart!   50

Arminius goes to kill Lucius, is killed by him.

ARMINIUS.
                              Oh I am slain!
I've justly met my death from Lucius' hand.
QUEEN.
Yet, as thou hop'st for pardon of thy crimes,
If thou hast breath, tell me who killed Otharius?
ARMINIUS.
I slew your lord and fixed it upon Lucius.   55
Wild love and false ambition were my guides.
The gods forgive us all. (*Dies.*)

---

27 self-murderers] Suicide, although an honorable form of
    death according to Roman belief, is forbidden by Chris-
    tianity.

Enter the Prince of Cambria, leading Emmelin, Irene etc.

PRINCE OF CAMBRIA.
>   Dear noble youth,
> The Pow'rs have brought us to preserve thy life
> From the hard sentence of a cruel father.   60

LUCIUS.
> Oh Uncle, shroud me from an impious deed!
> Oh hide me in your bosom from the light!
> Behold that sacred body! There's my father:
> Behold in Lucius, the curst parricide.

PRINCE OF CAMBRIA.
> Vortimer slain and by my nephew's hand!   65
> Thou great, illustrious, happy, happy youth,
> The Fates have now been busy for thy glory.
> Hear all and tremble at this righteous justice:
> Thou hast slain thy father's murderer, Lucius,
> Avenged his death and punished the usurper.   70

LUCIUS.
> Oh uncle! Was not Vortimer my father?

PRINCE OF CAMBRIA.
> This monster could not have a son like Lucius.
> Thou ow'st thy birth to the late royal King,
> Whom this vile traitor at a banquet slew.
> The Queen was then in child-bed, you her offspring.   75
> To save you from a cruel tyrant's sword,
> We spread the rumor of your sudden death,
> And with feigned tears wept o'er an empty tomb.
> The war in Gallia drew him from the throne,
> In foreign fields to bury loyal chiefs   80
> Who ill could bear the murder of their king.

LUCIUS.
> But how, great sir, was I supposed his son?

PRINCE OF CAMBRIA.
> He forced a marriage with the Queen my sister.
> By my advice, you seemed to spring from thence.
> The Queen's retiredness barred intruding eyes,   85
> Till broke with sorrow, shortly she expired.
> Six years the tyrant passed in foreign war.
> At his return, I gave you to his arms,
> Who, as a forward miracle, received you.
> Thus the just Powers have led you by the hand   90
> To punish, in curst Vortimer, the man
> Who caused the death of both your royal parents.

LUCIUS.
> Oh holy angels, tune it in your choir.
> Echo it, heav'n, through all yon azure sky.
> The happy Lucius has not slain his father.   95
> To you, bright, beauteous Princess, I sue.
> To you, my noble uncle, and our friends,
> Kneel all and kiss the dust in adoration.
> Kneel all and praise the Eternal Pow'r with me.
> The happy Lucius has revenged his father.   100

QUEEN.
> My life, my honor, and my people rescued
> Could only be the work of Heav'n and Lucius.

LUCIUS.
> Once more thou art my wife.

QUEEN.
> Once more and ever be my love.

EMMELIN. (*Aside.*)
> Here, Emmelin, thy hopes of Lucius die.   105
> Be then no more misled by fatal love,
> But to Diana's train devote thyself forever.

LUCIUS. (*To Emmelin.*)
> What thanks, bright Princess, shall I pay to you
> And your great brother, who has helped to save me?
> —That I have passed the threatened storms of Fate,   110
> Avenged my parents, and preserved my wife
> Are blessings first derived to me from beauty.
> Benighted, grov'ling on my Mother Earth,
> Till beauty called, I unenlightened lay.
> By beauty led, I sought eternal day.   115
> I view those shining realms of light above
> And gain immortal happiness by love.

Exeunt omnes.

FINIS.

Textual Notes

a   The copytext is the first edition, the 1717 quarto (Q1).
    Also consulted: the 1720 quarto (Q2) and the modern
    facsimile, #253–254 in the 1989 Augustan Reprint So-
    ciety Series (Armistead and Davis).

b   a] *om.* Q1, Q2

Political Tragedy

Political tragedy focuses on conflicts that involve political systems. English baroque drama portrays monarchy and its discontents, which in Shakespeare's time are primarily dynastic, but as the period wears on, those discontents become revolutionary, threatening monarchism with republicanism. The figure of the grand, passionate aristocratic leader yields to that of the neostoic *primus inter pares* (first among equals), even as England moves to a constitutional, parliamentary monarchy. But peeping from behind the arras is the *iron law of oligarchy*, that despite protodemocratic rhetoric, power remains in the hands of the wealthy few and is put to the service of military, economic, and cultural imperialism, from Ireland to the Indies.

The Unhappy Favorite; or, The Earl of Essex[a]

by John Banks (ca. 1652-53—1706)

edited by J. Douglas Canfield

John Banks's fame in theater history rests on his contribution to the development of what Nicholas Rowe would come to call *she-tragedies*, plays which showcase beleaguered women protagonists. *The Unhappy Favorite*, produced around May of 1681, features a Queen Elizabeth torn between private passion and public responsibility. The play was performed in Drury Lane by an aging King's Company, and the role of Queen Elizabeth was played by the *grande dame* of the company, Anne Marshall Quin, one of the first English actresses on the stage, where she made her debut shortly after the Restoration and where she made her reputation primarily in heroic roles (though she played comic roles of note in her later years—like those of Angellica Bianca in Behn's *The Rover* and Lady Squeamish in Otway's *Friendship in Fashion*). After the two dramatic companies were united a year later, Elizabeth Barry took over the role and made it a favorite, especially with the Duchess of York, later James II's queen, who loaned Barry her coronation robes to play Elizabeth.

The play is about a real historical situation, though Banks grossly exaggerates his hero's actual exploits. In the late sixteenth century Robert Devereaux, the earl of Essex, indeed a favorite of Queen Elizabeth, was sent to quell an Irish rebellion led by Hugh O'Neill, earl of Tyrone. Instead of destroying him, Essex met Tyrone alone on horseback in a river bed in northern Ireland and negotiated a truce. Aware that the queen would be furious, Essex raced back to England to anticipate his detractors and explain his actions to her, brashly entering her private rooms. The queen was forced by policy to distance herself from Essex, and he finally led an ill-conceived rebellion against her. Essex capitulated, was tried and was executed as a traitor. Banks's source was not so much history, however, recorded by the great English historian Camden, as it was a highly fictionalized, romantic narrative, *The Secret History of the Most Renown'd Q. Elizabeth and E. of Essex* (pt. 1, 1650; pt. 2, 1680).

Because of its theme of rebellion, *The Unhappy Favorite* was a daring play, for in the spring of 1681 England was just emerging from the Exclusion Crisis—and political opponents of the king awaited execution for treason. Curiously, although Essex's rebellion was against a queen, his soliloquies are full of imagery suggesting rebellion against a father-figure. In a sense, then, the play features the return of the repressed: the Oedipal parricide that lurks at the heart of monarchy and that was indelibly etched in the national memory as the image of the beheaded Charles I.

The Unhappy Favorite became a favorite of theater-goers. It was one of the dozen most popular tragedies, outside of Shakespeare's, over the next one hundred years. Two of the prologues written for it, one by Dryden and one by Banks himself, seem worth including for their contextualizing aspects: Dryden's view of the play in relation to the Exclusion Crisis, and Banks's view of the play in relation to the legend of Queen Elizabeth, the Popish Plot, and to the emergence of she-tragedies and their appeal especially to women.

*Prologue, spoken to the King and Queen
at their coming to the House,
and written on purpose by Mr. Dryden.*

When first the Ark[1] was landed on the shore
And Heaven had vowed to curse the ground no
   more,
When tops of hills the longing patriarch[2] saw,
And the new scene of earth began to draw,[3]
The dove was sent to view the waves' decrease   5
And first brought back to man the pledge of
   peace:[4]
'Tis needless to apply when those appear
Who bring the olive and who plant it here.[5]
We have before our eyes the Royal Dove,
Still* Innocence is harbinger to Love.   10
The Ark is opened to dismiss the train
And people with a better race* the plain.
Tell me, you Powers, why should vain man pursue,
With endless toil, each object that is new,
And for the seeming substance leave the true—   15
Why should he quit for hopes his certain good
And loathe the manna of his daily food?
Must England still* the scene of changes be,
Tossed and tempestuous like our ambient sea?
Must still* our weather and our wills agree?   20
Without our blood our liberties we have:
Who that is free would fight to be a slave?
Or what can wars to aftertimes assure
Of which our present age is not secure?
All that our Monarch would for us ordain   25
Is but t'enjoy the blessings of his reign.

Our land's an Eden, and the main's our fence,
While we preserve our state of innocence;
That lost, then beasts their brutal force employ
And first their Lord, and then themselves destroy: 30
What civil broils have cost we know[b] too well;
Oh, let it be enough that once we fell,[6]
And every heart conspire with every tongue
Still* to have such a King, and this King long.

*Prologue, Intended to be Spoken,
Written by the Author*

'Tis said, when the renowned Augustus reigned,
That all the world in peace and wealth remained,
And though the school of action, war, was o'er,
Arms, arts, and letters then increased the more.
All these sprung from our Royal Virgin's bays   5
And flourished better than in Caesar's days,
And only in her time at once was seen
So brave a soldier, statesman,[7] and a queen.
Her reign may be compared to that above,
As the best poet,[8] Caesar's did to Jove: 10
For as great Julius built the mightiest throne
And left Rome's first large empire to his son,[9]
Under whose weight, till her, we all did groan,
So her great father was the first that struck
Rome's triple crown, but she threw off the yoke: 15
Straight at her birth new light the heav'ns adorned,
Which more than fifteen hundred years had
   mourned.[10]

---

1 Ark] Noah's Ark, landing after the Flood in Genesis
2 Patriarch] Noah/Charles
3 to draw] as in curtains (or sliding flats) drawing
4 dove … pledge of peace] Noah sent out birds to discover dry land; the dove returned with an olive branch, sign that not only was the flood over but the angry god, who destroyed his creation in disgust with their sinfulness, was appeased (Gen 8:7-11).
5 'Tis needless … here] It is unnecessary to strain to apply the lesson of the biblical parallel, since those to whom it applies, the dove who fetches the olive branch (Catherine) and the patriarch who plants it in the renewed earth (Charles), are present in the theater.

---

6 civil broils … fell] English Civil Wars of the 1640s
7 soldier, statesman] A marginal note identifies these as "Essex and Burleigh": strange praise from Banks for the statesman whom, however great in history, he portrays in his play as a villain. The marginalium may have no authority, and it may be that all three of these terms refer to Queen Elizabeth.
8 best poet] Virgil
9 son] Julius Caesar adopted Octavian, later Caesar Augustus.
10 Rome's … mourned] Banks shifts his attention to the empire of the Roman Church, symbolized in the tiara or triple crown worn by the pope, against whom rebelled, in England, Henry VIII, whose rebellion was solidified in the Elizabethan era, which ostensibly marked the end of the Dark Ages of Catholicism. Through its

[Prologue]

But hold, I'm bid to let you understand
That, when our poet took this work in hand,
He trembled straight like prophets in a dream: 20
Her awful* genius* stood and threatened him;
Her modest beauties only he has shown
And has her character* so nicely* drawn
That, if her self in purest robes of light
Should come from heav'n and bless us with her sight, 25
She would not blush to hear what he has writ.
Therefore—
To all the shining sex this play's addressed,
But more the Court, the planets of the rest:
You who on earth are man's best, softest fate, 30
So that, when Heav'n with some rough peace has
    met,
It sends him you to mold and new create.
Strange ways to virtue some may think to prove,
But yet the best and surest path is love:
Love, like the ermine,[11] is so nice a guest 35
It never enters in a vicious breast—
If you are pleased, we will be bold to say,
This modest poem is the ladies' play.

DRAMATIS PERSONAE

[MEN]

The Earl of Essex.
Earl of Southampton.[12]
Burleigh.[13]
Sir Walter Raleigh.
Lieutenant of the Tower.*
Gentlemen, guards, and attendants.

[WOMEN]

Queen Elizabeth.
Countess of Rutland, secretly married to the
    earl of Essex.[14]
Countess of Nottingham.[15]
Women.

THE SCENE: WHITEHALL* AND THE TOWER.*

The Unhappy Favorite; or, The Earl of Essex.

————qui nimios optabat Honores,
Et nimias poscebat Opes, numerosa parabat
Excelsae turris tabulata, unde altior esset
Casus & impulsae praeceps immane Ruin[a]e.
                                    Juven. *Sat.* 10.[16]

Act I. [A room in Whitehall.]

Enter Countess of Nottingham, Burleigh at several
doors, the countess reading a letter.

NOTTINGHAM.

Help me to rail, prodigious-minded Burleigh,
Prince of bold English Councils, teach me how
This hateful breast of mine may dart forth words
Keen as thy wit, malicious as thy person;
Then I'll caress thee, stroke thee into shape. 5
This rocky, dismal form of thine that holds
The most seraphic mind that ever was

---

aggressive policies of reconquest, however, Rome still threatened England in Banks's day; hence the credibility of the Popish Plot.

[11] ermine] emblem of purity (*OED*)

[12] Southampton] Henry Wriothesley, profligate courtier and the patron of William Shakespeare

[13] Burleigh] Not the more famous advisor to Queen Elizabeth, Lord Burghley, but his son, Sir Robert Cecil, earl of Salisbury, a hunchback reminiscent of Richard III. At this time Cecil was Principle Secretary to the Queen.

[14] Countess of Rutland … Essex] Essex was indeed married

secretly to Frances Walsingham Sidney, widow of Sir Philip—not the Frances Sidney who was their daughter and married to the earl of Rutland. By making Essex's wife the Countess of Rutland, Banks follows the *Secret History* in providing his hero with a much younger wife, ostensibly the widow of Rutland and not of Sidney. By the time of the action of the play, Essex's marriage was historically no longer secret, the real Countess of Essex had had her fifth child to the earl, and Rutland was alive and well enough to be a major contributor to Essex's rebellion.

[15] Countess of Nottingham] historically the wife of Charles Howard, earl of Nottingham and the Lord Admiral to whom Essex surrendered the night of his rebellion; her entanglement with both Essex and Burleigh is unhistorical, drawn from the *Secret History*.

[16] *qui nimios … 10*] Juvenal, *Satire X* 104-7: "[I]n coveting excessive honors, and seeking excessive wealth, he [Sejanus] was but building up the many stories of a lofty tower whence the fall would be the greater, and the crash of headlong ruin more terrific" (Loeb).

I'll heal and mold thee with a soft embrace;
Thy mountain back shall yield beneath these arms,
And thy pale, withered cheeks that never glow   10
Shall then be decked with roses of my own.
Invent some new, strange curse that's far above
Weak woman's rage to blast the man I love.

BURLEIGH.
What means the fairest of the Court? Say what
More cruel darts are forming in those eyes   15
To make adoring Cecil more unhappy.
If such a wretched and declared hard fate
Attends the man you love, what then, bright star,
Has your malignant beauty yet in store
For him that is the object of your scorn?[17]   20
Tell me that most unhappy, happy man,
Declare who is this most ungrateful lover.
And to obey my lovely Nottingham
I will prefer this dear cabal and her
To all the other councils in the world;   25
Nay, though the Queen and her two nations[18] called
And sinking England stood this hour in need
For this supporting head, they all should sue
Or perish all for one kind look from you.

NOTTINGHAM.
There spoke the genius* and the breath of England,   30
Thou Esculapius[19] of the Christian world!
Methinks the Queen, in all her majesty,
Hemmed with a pomp of rusty swords and duller
          brains,
When thou art absent, is a naked monarch
And fills an idle throne till Cecil comes   35
To head her councils and inspire her generals.
Thy uncouth self, that seems a scourge to Nature
For so maliciously deforming thee,
Is by the heavenly Powers stamped with a soul
That like the sun breaks through dark mists,   40
          when none
Beholds the cloud but wonders at the light.

---

17 bright star … scorn] by analogy to planets, which were
     thought sometimes to exert evil or malignant influence
     on people
18 two nations] Elizabeth was supposedly Queen of both
     England and Ireland.
19 Esculapius] or Aesculapius, mythical Greek healer, fa-
     ther of medicine

BURLEIGH.
Oh spare that angel's voice till the last day;[20]
Such heavenly praise is lost on such a subject.

NOTTINGHAM.
Let none presume to say while Burleigh lives
A woman wears the crown; Fourth Richard rather,   45
Heir to the Third in magnanimity,
In person, courage, wit, and bravery all,
But to his vices none, nor to his end,
I hope.

BURLEIGH.
          You torture me with this excess.   50
Were but my flesh cast in a purer mold,
Then you might see me blush, but my hot blood,
Burnt with continual thought, does inward glow;
Thought like the sun still* goes its daily round
And scorches, as in India, to the root.   55
—But to the wretched cause of your disturbance:
Say, shall I guess? Is Essex not the man?

NOTTINGHAM.
Oh! Name not Essex, hell and tortures rather:
Poisons and vultures to the breast of man
Are not so cruel as the name of Essex.   60
Speak, good my lord; nay, never speak nor think
Again, unless you can assuage this worse
Than Fury in my breast.

BURLEIGH.
          Tell me the cause;
Then cease your rage and study to revenge.   65

NOTTINGHAM.
My rage! It is the wing by which I'll fly
To be revenged. I'll ne'er be patient more.
Lift me, my rage, nay, mount me to the stars,
Where I may hunt this peacock though he lies
Close in the lap of Juno-Elizabeth,[21]   70
Though the Queen circles him with charms of pow'r
And hides her minion like another Circe.

BURLEIGH.
Still* well-instructed rage, but pray, disclose
The reason of the earl's misfortune.

---

20 last day] Doomsday, the Day of Judgment
21 peacock … Juno-Elizabeth] The peacock was the bird
     emblematically associated with Juno, symbolic of her
     pride.

NOTTINGHAM.

                              You are,   75

My friend, the cabinet of all my frailties;

From you, as from just Heaven, I hope for

    absolution;

Yet pray, though anger makes me red when I

Discourse the reason of my rage, be kind

And say it is my sex's modesty.   80

Know then,[22]

This base, imperious man I loved, loved so,

Till, lingering with the pain of fierce desire

And shame that strove to torture me alike,

At last I passed the limits of our sex   85

And (oh, kind Cecil, pity and forgive me)

Sent this opprobrious man my mind a slave:

In a kind* letter broke the silence of

My love, which rather should have broke my heart.

BURLEIGH.

But pray, what answer did you get from him?   90

NOTTINGHAM.

Such as has made an earthquake in my soul,

Shook every vital in these tender limbs,

And raised me to the storm you found me in.

At first he charmed me with a thousand hopes,

Else 'twas my love thought all his actions so.   95

Just now from Ireland I received this letter,

Which take and read—but now I think, you shall

    not—

I'll tear it in a thousand pieces first,

Tear it, as I would Essex with my will,

To bits, to morsels hack the mangled slave,   100

Till every atom of his cursèd body (*Tears the letter*

    in a rage.)

Severed and flew like dust before the wind.

Now do I bless the chance all else may blame

Me for: revealing of my foolish passion.

Did I e'er think these celebrated charms,   105

Which I so often have been blest and praised for,

Should once be destined to so mean a price

As a refusal! Are there friends above

That protect innocence and injured love?

Hear me and curse me straight with wrinkled age,   110

With leprosy, derision, all your plagues

On earth and hell hereafter, if I'm not revenged.

BURLEIGH. (*Aside.*)

Else say she is no woman, or no widow.[23]

—The sacred guardians of your slighted beauties

Have had more pity on their lovely charge   115

Than to behold you swallowed in his ruin.

The best and worst that Fortune could propose

To you in Essex' love was to have brought

A helpless, short-lived traitor to your arms.

NOTTINGHAM.

Hah! Traitor, say you! Speak that word again—   120

Yet do not; 'tis enough if Burleigh says it:

His wit has power to damn the man that thinks it

And t'extract treason from infected thought.

The Nation's safety like a ship he steers

When tempests blow, raised by designs of false   125

And ignorant statesmen; by his wit alone

They're all dispersed, and by his breath she sails,

His prosperous councils all her gentle gales.

Enter a gentleman.

GENTLEMAN.

My lord, the Queen expects you straight.

BURLEIGH.

                               Madam,   130

Be pleased to attend her Majesty i'th'Presence,

Where you shall hear such misdemeanors offered,

Such articles against the Earl of Essex,

As will both glad the Nation and yourself.

GENTLEMAN.

My lord, I see the haughty Earl of Southampton   135

Coming this way.

BURLEIGH.

                  Madam, retire.

NOTTINGHAM.

                        I go

With greater expectation of delight

Than a young bridegroom on his marriage night.   140

    (*Exit.*)

BURLEIGH.

Southampton! he's the chief of Essex' faction,

His friend and sworn brother, and I fear

---

22 Know then,] Like Dryden and others, Banks often uses
    truncated lines to indicate an overflow of emotion.

23 Widow] The lusty passion of widows was proverbial.

Too much a friend and partner of his revels
To be a stranger to the other's guilt.
'Tis not yet time to lop this haughty bough,   145
Till I have shaken first the tree that bears it.

Enter Southampton.

SOUTHAMPTON.
My lord, I hear unwelcome news: 'tis said
Some factious members of the House,[24] headed
By you, have voted an address for leave
T'impeach the Earl of Essex of strange articles   150
Of treason.

BURLEIGH.
　　　　　　Treason, 'tis most true, is laid
To Essex' charge, but that I am the cause
They do me wrong; th'occasion is too public:
For those dread storms in Ireland raised by him[25]
Have blown so rudely on our English coasts   155
That they have shipwrecked quite the Nation's peace
And waked its very statues to abhorring.

SOUTHAMPTON.
Mere argument, your nice* and fine distinctions
To make a good man vicious or a bad
Man virtuous, ev'n as please the sophisters.[26]   160
My lord, you are engendering snakes within you;
I fear you have a subtle, stinging heart,
And give me leave to tell you that this treason,
If any, has been hatched in Burleigh's school.
I see ambition in the fair pretence,   165
Burleigh in all its cunning, dark disguises,
And envious Cecil everywhere.

BURLEIGH.
My lord, my lord, your zeal to this bad earl
Makes you offend the Queen and all good men.
Believe it, sir, his crimes have been so noted,   170
So plain, and open to the State and her

That he can now no more deceive the eyes
Of a most gracious mistress or her Council,
Nor can she any longer, if she would,
In pity of his other parts* let Justice wink,   175
But rouse herself from cheated, slumbering Mercy
And start at his most foul ingratitude.
Nor does it well become the brave* Southampton
To plead in his behalf, for fear it pulls
Upon himself suspicion of his crimes.   180

SOUTHAMPTON. [*Aside.*]
Hold in, my fire, and scorch not through my ribs,
Quench, if thou canst, the burning, furious pain—
I cannot if I would, but must unload
Some of the torture.—Now by my wronged self
And Essex' much more wronged, I swear 'tis false,   185
False as the rules by which vile statesmen govern,
False as their arts by which the traitors rise
By cheating nations and destroying kings
And false imposing on the common crew.
Essex! By all the hopes of my immortal soul,   190
There's not one drop of blood of that brave man
But holds more honor, truth, and loyalty
Than thy whole mass besides and all thy brains
Stuffed with cabals and projects* for the Nation,
Than thou that seem'st a good St. Christopher   195
Carrying thy country's genius* on thy back,[27]
But art indeed a devil[28] and tak'st more hire
Than half the kingdom's wealth can satisfy.
I say again that thou and all thy race*
With Essex' base accusers every one   200
Put in a scale together weigh not half
The merit that's in one poor hair of his.

BURLEIGH.
Thank you, my lord. See, I can bear the scandal
And cannot choose but smile to see you rage.

SOUTHAMPTON.   205
It is because thy guilty soul's a coward
And has not spirit enough to feign a passion.

BURLEIGH.
It is the token of my innocence.

---

24 House] of Commons, which Cecil indeed manipulated
　　during the 1597 Parliament, but which had nothing to
　　do with the chastisement of Essex after his Irish fiasco
　　nor with his trial for treason. Banks is exploiting royal-
　　ist sentiment after the narrow defeat of another parlia-
　　mentary insurrection.
25 dread storms ... him] Essex's negotiation with rather
　　than defeat of the Tyrone
26 sophisters] practicers of sophistry (q.v.)

27 St. Christopher ... back] according to the legend, St.
　　Christopher carried the Christ-child across a river on his
　　shoulders.
28 devil] pronounced as a monosyllable (as in *Deel*) if nec-
　　essary, as in this instance, for the meter

But let Southampton have a special care
To keep his close designs from Cecil's way,   210
Lest he disturb the genius of the Nation
As you were pleased to call me, and beware
The fate of Essex. (*Exit.*)
SOUTHAMPTON.

                  Hah! The fate of Essex!
Thou liest, proud statesman, 'tis above thy reach,   215
As high above thy malice as is heaven
Beyond a Cecil's hopes.—Despair not, Essex,
Nor his brave friends, since a just queen's his judge:
She that saw once such wonders in thy person,
A scarce-fledged youth, as loading thee with honors,   220
At once made thee Earl Marshal, Knight o'th'Garter,
Chief Councilor, and Admiral at Sea[29]—
She comes, she comes, bright goddess of the day,
And Essex'[c] foes she drives like mists away.

*Enter the Queen, Burleigh, Lord Chancellor, Countess
of Nottingham, Countess of Essex,[d] lords and
attendants, Queen on a Chair of State, guards.*

QUEEN.
My lords, we hear not anything confirms   225
The new designs were dreaded of the Spaniards;
Our letters lately from our agent there
Say nothing of such fears, nor do I think
They dare.
BURLEIGH.

           To dare, most high, illustrious Princess,   230
Is such a virtue Spaniard never knew;
His courage is as cold as he is hot
And faith is as adulterate as his blood.
What truth can we expect from such a race
Of mongrels: Jews, Mohammadans, Goths, Moors,   235
And Indians with a few of old Castilians,
Shuffled in Nature's mold together?
That Spain may truly now be called the place
Where Babel first was built. These men
With all false tenets chopped and mashed together,   240
Sucked from the scum of every base religion,
Which they have since transformed to Romish mass,
Are now become the miter's darling sons,

And Spain is called the Pope's most Catholic King.[30]
QUEEN.
Spoke like true Cecil still, old Protestant.   245
But oh! It joys me with the dear remembrance
Of this romantic huge invasion.
From the Pope's closet,* where 'twas first begot,
Bulls, absolutions, pardons, frightful banns
Flew o'er the Continent and narrow seas   250
Some to reward and others to torment;[31]
Nay, worse, the Inquisition was let loose
To teach the very* atheists purgatory.[32]
Then were a thousand holy hands employed
As cardinals, bishops, abbots, monks, and Jesuits: 255
Not a poor mendicant or begging friar
But thought he should be damned to leave the work.
SOUTHAMPTON.
Whole shoals of benedictions were dispersed;
Nay, the good Pope himself so wearied was
With giving blessings to these holy warriors   260
That flew to him from ev'ry part as thick
As hornets to their nest, it gave his arms
The gout.
BURLEIGH.

         Oh faithless, uncourageous hands!
They should have both been burnt for heretics.   265
QUEEN.
But when this huge and mighty fleet was ready,
Altars were stripped of shining ornaments:
Their images, their pictures, palls, and hangings,
By nuns and Persians wrought,
All went to help their great Armada forth;   270
Relics of all degrees of saints

---

29 Earl-Marshall … Admiral at Sea] offices bestowed on Essex by Elizabeth: the first was honorific; the second an
order of merit; the third and fourth are self-explanatory.

30 miter's … Catholic King] a miter is a cone-shaped hat
worn by popes and bishops; "Spain" here stands for the
Spanish king, Philip II, royal consort to Elizabeth's sister, "Bloody" Mary, during her reign of Catholic terror,
and instigator of the invasion of the Armada in order
to reconquer England for the Pope. To Banks's time,
Spain remained one of England's chief rivals in the colo-
nization of and trade with the New World.

31 Bulls … torment] communications and orders and in-
dulgences from the pope, all concerning the reconver-
sion of England, up to the time of the Popish Plot

32 Inquisition … Purgatory] The Inquisition was Catholicism's repressive agent of counter reformation; purgatory
was a contested doctrine, denied by Protestants.

Were there distributed, and not a ship
Was blest without one; every sail amongst 'em
Boasted to carry, as a certain pledge
Of victory, some of the real Cross.[33]   275

SOUTHAMPTON.
Long live that day, and never be forgotten
The gallant hour when, to th'immortal fame
Of England and the more immortal Drake,[34]
That proud Armada was destroyed. Yet was
The fight not half so dreadful as th'event[35]   280
Was pleasant. When the first broadsides were given,
A tall, brave* ship, the tallest of the rest,
That seemed the pride of all their big half-moon,[36]
Whether by chance or by a lucky shot
From us, I know not, but she was blown up,   285
Bursting like thunder and almost as high,
And then did shiver in a thousand pieces,
Whilst from her belly crowds of living creatures
Broke like untimely births and filled the sky:
There might be seen a Spaniard catch his fellow   290
And, wrestling in the air, fall down together;
A priest for safety riding on a cross,
Another that had none, crossing himself;
Friars with long, big sleeves like magpies' wings
That bore them up came gently sailing down: 295
One with a Don that held him by the arms
And cried, "Confess me straight!" but as he just
Had spoke the words, they tumbled down together.

BURLEIGH.
Just Heav'n, that never ceased to have a care
Of your most gracious Majesty and kingdoms,   300
By valiant soldiers and by faithful leaders
Confounded in one day the vast designs
Of Italy and Spain against our liberties;
So may Tyrone and Irish rebels fall,
And so may all your captains henceforth prove   305

---

33 Relics … Cross] alleged remnants of saints and of holy
    accoutrements or objects, like the "true" or "real" Cross
    upon which Christ was crucified; Protestants considered
    such relics idolatrous.
34 Drake] Sir Francis Drake, hero of the battle of the Ar-
    mada—and of raids against Spanish shipping in the
    Caribbean and Spanish coastal ports
35 event] outcome
36 half-moon] Spanish galleons in a half-moon formation
    (*OED*)

To be as loyal and as stout commanders.

QUEEN.
Is there no fresher news from Ireland yet?

BURLEIGH.
None better than the last, that seems too ill
To be repeated in your gracious hearing.

QUEEN.
Why, what was that?   310

SOUTHAMPTON. (*Aside.*)
                    Now, now the subtle fiend
Begins to conjure up a storm.

BURLEIGH.
How soon your gracious Majesty forgets
Crimes done by any of your subjects.

QUEEN.
                              What?   315
That Essex did defer his journey to
The north and therefore lost the season[37] quite:
Was not that all?

BURLEIGH.
                    And that he met Tyrone
At his request and treated with him private.   320
A ford dividing them, they both rode in,
Wading their horses knee deep on each side,
But that the distance from each other was
So great, and they were forced to parley loud,
Orders were given to keep the soldiers off;   325
Nay, not an officer in all the army
But was denied to hear what passed between them.
What followed then the parley was the truce
So shameful (if I may be so bold to call
It so) both to your majesty and England.   330

QUEEN.
Enough, enough, good Cecil, you begin
To be inveterate. 'Twas his first fault,
And though that crimes done to the Nation's hurt
Admit of no excuse or mitigation
From th'author's many virtues or misfortunes,   335
Yet you must all confess that he is brave,
Valiant as any, and has done as much
For you as e'er Alcides[38] did for Greece.
Yet I'll not hide his faults, but blame him too,
And therefore I have sent him chiding letters,   340

---

37 season] for waging war, during the warmer months
38 Alcides] Hercules

Forbidding him to leave the kingdom till
He has dispatched the war and killed Tyrone.

*Enter Sir Walter Raleigh, attended by some other
members of the House [of Commons].*

BURLEIGH.
Most royal madam, here's the gallant Raleigh,
With others in commission from the House,
Who 'ttend your Majesty with some few bills   345
And humblest of addresses, that you would
Be pleased to pass 'em for the Nation's safety.
QUEEN.
Welcome, my people, welcome to your queen,
Who wishes still* no longer to be so
Than she can govern well and serve you all.   350
Welcome again, dear people, for I'm proud
To call you so, and let it not be boasting
In me to say, I love you with a greater love
Than ever kings before showered down on subjects
And that I think ne'er did a people more   355
Deserve than you. Be quick
And tell me your demands; I long to hear:
For know, I count your wants are all my own.
RALEIGH.
Long live the bright imperial Majesty
Of England, Virgin Star of Christendom,   360
Blessing and guide of all your subjects' lives,
Who wish the sun may sooner be extinguished
From the bright orb he rules in than their queen
Should e'er descend the throne she now makes
    happy.
Your Parliament, most blest of sovereigns,   365
Calling to mind the Providence of Heaven
In guarding still* your people under you
And sparing your most precious life,
Do humbly offer to your royal pleasure
Three bills to be made living acts hereafter,   370
All for the safety of your crown and life,
More precious than ten thousand of your slaves.
QUEEN.
Let Cecil take and read what they contain.
BURLEIGH. (*Takes the papers and reads the contents.*)
"An Act for settling and establishing
A strong militia out of ev'ry county,   375
And likewise for levying a new army
Consisting of six thousand foot, at least,

And horse three thousand, quickly to be ready
As a strong guard for the Queen's sacred person,
And to prevent what clandestine designs   380
The Spaniards or the Scots may have."[39]
QUEEN.
                              Thanks to
My dear and loving people: I will pass it.
BURLEIGH.
This second act is for the speedy raising
Two hundred thousand pounds to pay the army,   385
And to be ordered as the Queen shall please;
This to be gathered by a benevolence
And subsidy[40] in six months' time from hence.
QUEEN.
What mean my giving subjects! It shall pass.
BURLEIGH.
The third has several articles at large,   390
With an address[41] subscribed, most humbly offered
For the impeaching Robert, Earl of Essex,
Of several misdemeanors[42] of high treason.
QUEEN. (*Aside.*)
Hah!
This unthought blast has shocked me like an ague;   395
It has alarumed every sense and spoiled me
Of all the awful* courage of a queen,
But I'll recover.—Say, my Nottingham
And Rutland, did you ever hear the like!
But are you well assured I am awake?   400
Bless me, and say it is a horrid vision,
That I am not upon the throne.
Hah! is't not so?—Yes, traitors, I'll obey you:
    (*She rises in a rage.*)
Here, sit you in my place; take Burleigh's staff,
The Chancellor's seal, and Essex, valiant head,   405
And leave me none but such as are yourselves,
Knaves for my counsel, fools for magistrates,
And cowards for commanders—oh my heart!

---

39 Spaniards … Scots] The Spaniards still had the pope's
   injunction to reconquer England; the Scots were smarting from the execution of Elizabeth's cousin, Mary,
   Queen of Scots.
40 benevolence and subsidy] in reality, forced loans or contributions levied by the Crown on subjects (*OED*)
41 address] a formal request of the sovereign (*OED*)
42 misdemeanors] considered high, not low crimes

SOUTHAMPTON.

Oh horrid imposition on a throne!
Essex, that has so bravely served the Nation! 410
That I may boldly say, Drake did not more,
That has so often beat its foes on land,
Stood like a promontory in its defense,
And sailed with dragon's wings to guard the seas;
Essex! That took as many towns in Spain 415
As all this island holds, beggared their fleet
That came with loads of half their mines in India,[43]
And took a mighty carrack of such value
That held more gold in its prodigious deck
Than served the Nation's riot in a year. 420

QUEEN.

Ingrateful people! Take away my life;
'Tis that you'd have, for I have reigned too long.
You too well know that I'm a woman, else
You durst not use me thus. Had you but feared
Your queen as you did once my royal father, 425
Or had I but the spirit of that monarch,
With one short syllable I should have rammed
Your impudent petitions down your throats
And made four hundred of your factious crew
Tremble and grovel on the earth for fear. 430

Petitioners kneel.

RALEIGH.

Thus prostrate at your feet we beg for pardon
And humbly crave your Majesty's forgiveness.

QUEEN.

No more. Attend me in the House tomorrow.

BURLEIGH.

Most mighty Queen! Blest and adored by all,
Torment not so your royal breast with passion: 435
Not all of us, our lives, estates, and country
Are worth the least disturbance of your mind.

QUEEN.

Are you become a pleader for such traitors!
Hah! I suspect that Cecil too is envious
And Essex is too great for thee to grow: 440
A shrub that never shall be looked upon
Whilst Essex, that's a cedar, stands so nigh.
Tell me, why was not I acquainted with
This close design? For I am sure thou know'st it.

BURLEIGH.

Madam— 445

QUEEN.

Be dumb: I will hear no excuses.
—I could turn cynic and outrage the wind,
Fly from all courts, from business, and mankind,
Leave all like chaos in confusion hurled,
For 'tis not reason now that rules the world: 450
There's an order in all states but man below,
And all things else do to superiors bow;
Trees, plants, and fruits rejoice beneath the sun;
Rivers and seas are guided by the moon;
The lion rules through shades and ev'ry green, 455
And fishes own the dolphin for their queen.
But man, the verier* monster, worships still*
No god but lust, no monarch but his will.

Exeunt omnes.

Act II. [The same.]

Countess of Essex.

COUNTESS OF ESSEX.

Is this the joy of a new married life?
This all the taste of pleasures that are feigned
To flow from sweet and everlasting springs?
By what false optics do we view those sights
And by our ravenous wishes seem to draw 5
Delights so far beyond a mortal's reach
And bring 'em home to our deluded breasts?
'Tis not yet long since that blest day was past,
A day I wished that should forever last;
The night once gone, I did the morning chide, 10
Whose beams betrayed me by my Essex' side,
And whilst my blushes and my eyes he blest,
I strove to hide 'em in his panting breast,
And my hot cheeks close to his bosom laid,
Listening to what the guest within it said, 15
Where fire to fire the noble heart did burn
Close like a phoenix in her spicy urn:
I sighed and wept for joy a shower of tears
And felt a thousand sweet and pleasant fears,
Too rare for sense, too exquisite to say: 20
Pain we can count, but pleasure steals away.
But business now and envious glory's charms
Have snatched him from these ever-faithful arms:
Ambition, that's the highest way to woe,
Cruel ambition, love's eternal foe. 25

---

43 India] the Indies, especially in the New World

Enter Southampton.

SOUTHAMPTON.

  Thou dearest partner of my dearest friend,
  The brightest planet of thy shining sex,
  Forgive me for the unwelcome news I bring:
  Essex is come, the most deplored of men!

COUNTESS OF ESSEX.

  Now by the sacred joy that fills my heart,   30
  What fatal meaning can there be in that?
  Is my lord come? Say, speak.

SOUTHAMPTON.

                   Too sure he's come.
  But oh, that seas as wide as waters flow
  Or burning lakes as broad and deep as hell   35
  Had rather parted you forever,
  So Essex had been safe on th'other side.

COUNTESS OF ESSEX.

  My lord, you much amaze me.
  Pray, what of ill has happened since this morning
  That the Queen guarded him with so much mercy 40
  And then refused to hear his false impeachers?

SOUTHAMPTON.

  Too soon, alas, he's forfeited his honors,
  Places, and wealth, but more his precious life,
  Condemned by the too cruel Nation's laws
  For leaving his commission and returning,   45
  When the Queen's absolute commands forbid him.

COUNTESS OF ESSEX.

  Fond* hopes! must then our meeting prove so fatal!

SOUTHAMPTON.

  Say madam, now what help will you propose?
  Can the Queen's pity any more protect him?
  Never, it is no longer in her power.   50
  She must, though 'gainst her will, deliver him
  A sacrifice to all his greedy foes.

COUNTESS OF ESSEX.

  Where is my lord?

SOUTHAMPTON.

                 Blunt left him on the way
  And came disguised in haste to give me notice.   55

COUNTESS OF ESSEX.

  Let him go back and give my Essex warning,
  Conjuring him from us to stir no further
  But straight return to Ireland ere 'tis known
  He left the place.

SOUTHAMPTON.

              Alas, it is no secret;   60
  Besides, he left the Town* almost as soon
  As Blunt and is expected every moment.

COUNTESS OF ESSEX.

  How could it be revealed so suddenly?

SOUTHAMPTON.

  I know not that, unless from hell it came,
  Where Cecil too is privy councilor   65
  And knows as much as any devil there.
  I met the cunning fiend and Raleigh whispering,
  And the fair, treacherous Nottingham
  I saw bedecked with an ill-natured smile
  That showed malicious beauty to the height.   70

COUNTESS OF ESSEX.

  Hold, hold, my lord, my fears begin to wrack me
  And danger now in all its horrid shapes
  Stalks in my way and makes my blood run cold
  Worse than a thousand glaring spirits could do.
  Assist me straight, thou Damon to my Essex,   75
  Help me, thou more than friend in misery.
  I'll to the Queen and straight declare our marriage;
  She will have mercy on my helpless state,
  Pity these tears and all my humble postures,
  If not for me nor for my Essex' sake,   80
  Yet for the illustrious offspring that I bear.
  I'll go, I'll run, I'll hazard all this moment.
    (*Offers to be gone.*)

SOUTHAMPTON.

  Led by vain hopes, you fly to your destruction:
  There wants* but that dread secret to be known
  To tumble you forever to despair   85
  And leave you both condemned without the hopes
  Of the Queen's pity or remorse hereafter.

COUNTESS OF ESSEX.

  Cursed be the stars that flattered at our births,
  That shone so bright with such unusual luster
  As cheated the whole world into belief   90
  Our lives alone were all their chiefest care.

SOUTHAMPTON.

  Be comforted, rely on Essex' fate
  And the Queen's mercy—
  Behold she comes, our good or evil fate
  In discontented characters wrote on   95
  Her brow.

Enter the Queen, Burleigh, Countess of Nottingham, Raleigh, attendant guards.

QUEEN.
                    Is Essex then arrived?
BURLEIGH.
                                        He is.
QUEEN. (*Aside.*)
    Then he has lost me all the flattering hopes
    I ever had to save him.—Come, say you: 100
    Who else came with him?
BURLEIGH.
                            Some few attendants.
QUEEN.
    Durst the most vile of traitors serve me thus!
    Double my strength about me, draw out men,
    And set a guard before the palace gates   105
    And bid my valiant friends the citizens
    Be ready straight—I shall be murdered else.
    And, faithful Cecil, if thou lovest thy queen,
    See all this done. For how can I be safe
    If Essex that I favored seeks my life?   110
BURLEIGH.
    Will't please your Majesty to see the earl?
QUEEN.
    No.
BURLEIGH.
        Shall I publish straight your royal order
    That may forbid his coming to the Court
    Until your Majesty command him?   115
QUEEN.
                                Neither.
    How durst you seem t'interpret what's my pleasure!
    No, I will see him if 'a* comes, and then
    Leave me to act without your saucy aid,
    If I have any royal power.   120

[Exit Burleigh.]

COUNTESS OF ESSEX. (*Aside.*)
    Blest be the Queen, blest be the pitying God
    That has inspired her.
SOUTHAMPTON.
                        Most admired of queens,
    Thus low unto the ground I bend my body
    And wish I could sink lower through the earth   125
    To suit a posture to my humble heart.

I tremble to excuse my gallant friend
In contradiction to your heavenly will,
Who like a god knows all, and 'tis enough
You think him innocent, and he is so.   130
But yet your Majesty's most royal soul,
That soars so high above the humble malice
Of base and sordid wretches under you,
Perhaps is ignorant the valiant earl
Has foes, foes that are only so because   135
Your Majesty has crowned him with your favors
And lifted him so far above their sights
That 'tis a pain to all their envious eyes
To look so high above him; and of these
Some grow too near your royal person,   140
As the ill angels did at first in heaven,
And daily seek to hurt this brave man's virtue.
QUEEN.
    Help me, thou infinite Ruler of all things,
    That sees at once far as the sun displays
    And searches every soul of human kind   145
    Quick and unfelt, as light infuses beams,
    Unites and makes all contradictions center,
    And to the sense of man, which is more strange,
    Governs innumerable distant parts
    By one, entire, same Providence at once.   150
    Teach me so far thy holy art of rule,
    As in a mortal reason may distinguish
    Betwixt bold subjects and a monarch's right.

[Enter Burleigh.]

BURLEIGH.
    May't please your Majesty, the earl is come
    And waits your pleasure.   155
QUEEN.
                        Let him be admitted.
    —Now, now support thy royalty
    And hold thy greatness firm. But oh, how heavy
    A load is state where the free mind's disturbed!
    How happy a maid is she that always lives   160
    Far from high honor in a low content,
    Where neither hills nor dreadful mountains grow,
    But in a vale where springs and pleasures flow;
    Where sheep lie round, instead of subjects' throngs,
    The trees for music, birds instead of songs,   165
    Instead of Essex, one poor faithful hind,
    He as a servant, she a mistress kind,*

Who with garlands for her coming crowns her door
And all with rushes strews her little floor;
Where at their mean repast no fears attend 170
Of a false enemy or falser friend,
No care of scepters nor ambitious frights
Disturb the quiet of their sleep at nights.
—He comes, this proud invader of my rest,
'A* comes, but I intend so to receive him. 175

Enter the Earl of Essex with attendants. Essex kneels.
The Queen turns to the Countess of Nottingham.

ESSEX.
　Long live the mightiest, most adored of queens,
　The brightest power on earth that Heav'n e'er
　　formed.
　Awed and amazed the trembling Essex kneels,
　Essex, that stood the dreadful voice of cannons
　Hid in a darker field of smoke and fire 180
　Than that where Cyclops blow the forge and sweat
　Beneath the mighty hill,[44] whilst bullets round me
　Flew like the bolts of heav'n when shot with thunder
　And lost their fury on my shield and corslet,
　And stood these dangers unconcerned and dauntless. 185
　But you, the most majestic, brightest form
　That ever ruled on earth, have caught my soul,
　Surprised its virtues all with dread and wonder;
　My humble eyes durst scarcely look up to you,
　Your dazzling mien and sight so fill the place, 190
　And every part celestial rays adorn.
QUEEN. (*Aside.*)
　Hah!
ESSEX.
　'Tis said I have been guilty:
　I dare not rise, but crawl thus on the earth
　Till I have leave to kiss your sacred robe 195
　And clear before the justest, best of queens
　My wronged and wounded innocence.
QUEEN. (*Aside.*)
　What said'st thou, Nottingham? what said the earl?
ESSEX.
　What, not a word! a look! not one blest look!
　Turn, turn your cruel brow and kill me with 200
　A frown; it is a quick and surer way

To rid you of your Essex
Than banishment, than fetters, swords, or axes—
What, not that neither! Then I plainly see
My fate, the malice of enemies 205
Triumphant in their joyful faces: Burleigh
With a glad coward's smile that knows he's got
Advantage o'er his valiant foe, and Raleigh's proud
To see his dreaded Essex kneel so long,
Essex, that stood in his great mistress' favor 210
Like a huge oak, the loftiest of the wood,
Whilst they no higher could attain to be
Than humble succors[45] nourished by my root
And like the ivy twined their flatt'ring arms
About my waist and lived but by my smiles— 215
QUEEN. (*Aside.*)
　I must be gone, for if I stay, I shall
　Here wrack my conduct and my fame forever.
　Thus the charmed pilot listening to the sirens
　Lets his rich vessel split upon a rock
　And loses both his life and wealth together. 220
ESSEX.
　Still am I shunned as if I wore destruction. (*Rises.*)
　Here, here my faithful and my valiant friends,
　Dearest companions of the fate of Essex,
　Behold this bosom studdied[46] o'er with scars,
　This marble breast, that has so often held, 225
　Like a fierce battlement, against the foes
　Of England's Queen that made a hundred breaches.
　Here, pierce it straight and through this wild of
　　wounds
　Be sure to reach my heart, this loyal heart,
　That sits consulting 'midst a thousand spirits 230
　All at command, all faithful to my queen.
QUEEN. (*Aside.*)
　If I had ever courage, haughtiness,
　Or spirit, help me but now, and I am happy!
　He melts; it flows and drowns my heart with pity;
　If I stay longer, I shall tell him so. 235
　—What, is this traitor in my sight!

---

[44] Cyclops … hill] Titans Zeus allowed to stay on earth
　and forge his thunderbolts in an underground smithy

[45] succors] perhaps suckers, rootlets nourished by a main
　root

[46] studdied] may be just a misspelling or misprint for
　"studded," but it could also invite a punning reading of
　"studied": as if both contemplating and the object of
　contemplation.

All that have loyalty and love their queen,
Forsake this horrid wretch and follow me.

Exeunt Queen and her attendants; manet Essex solus.

ESSEX.
  She's gone, and darted fury as she went.
  Cruelest of queens!   240
  Not heard! Not hear your soldier speak one word!
  Essex, that once was all day listened to;
  Essex, that like a cherub held thy throne,
  Whilst thou didst dress me with thy wealthy favors,
  Cheered me with smiles, and decked me round   245
    with glories;
  Nor was thy crown scarce worshipped on thy head
  Without me by thy side, but now art deaf
  As adders,[47] winds, or the remorseless seas,
  Deaf as thy cunning sex's ears to those
  That make unwelcome love.   250
Enter Southampton.
  —What news, my friend?
SOUTHAMPTON.
  Such as I dare not tell: but pardon me,
  As an ill* bird that perches on the side
  Of some tall ship foretells a storm at hand,
  I come to give you warning of the danger.   255
  —See Cecil with a message from the Queen.
ESSEX.
  Then does my wrack come rolling on apace;
  That foul leviathan ne'er yet appeared
  Without a horrid tempest from his nostrils.

Enter to them Burleigh and Raleigh.

BURLEIGH.
  Hear, Robert, Earl of Essex,   260
  Hear what the Queen, my lord, by us pronounces:
  She now divests you of your offices,
  Your dignities of Governor of Ireland,
  Earl Marshal, Master of her Horse,[48] General
  Of all her forces both by land and sea,   265
  And Lord Lieutenant of the several counties
  Of Essex, Hereford, and Westmorland.

---

47 adders] common European vipers, proverbially associ-
    ated with deafness
48 Master of her Horse] another high military office from
    feudal days, now largely honorific

ESSEX.
  A vast and goodly sum all at one cast
  By an unlucky hand thrown quite away.
BURLEIGH.
  Also her pleasure is that in obedience   270
  To her commands you send your staff by us
  Then leave the Court and stir no farther than
  Your house till order from the Queen and Council.
ESSEX.
  Thanks, my misfortunes, for you fall with weight
  Upon me, and Fate shoots her arrows thick: 275
  'Tis hard if they not find one mortal place
  About me—
BURLEIGH.
  My lord, what shall we tell her Majesty?
  What is your answer, for the Queen expects us?
ESSEX.
  Wilt thou then promise to be just and tell her?   280
  Give her a caution of her worst of foes,
  Thy greedy self, the land's infesting giant,
  Exacting heads from her best subjects daily,
  Worse than the Phrygian Monster: he was more
  Cheaply compounded with and but devoured   285
  Seven virgins in a week and spared the rest.[49]
SOUTHAMPTON.
  Hold, my brave friend, waste not the noble breath
  Of Essex on so base and mean a subject.
[*To Raleigh.*]
  Thou traitor to thy sovereign and her kingdoms,
  More full of guilt than e'er thou didst devise   290
  To lay on Essex, whom thou fear'st and hatest.
[*To Burleigh.*]
  And thou, because thy sordid soul and person
  Ne'er fitted thee
  For gallant actions, thinkest the world so too,
  For he that looks through a foul glass that's stained 295
  Sees all things stained like the foul perspective* he
    uses:

---

49 Phrygian ... rest] Phrygian monsters are associated with
    a Mother Goddess—by extension, the Medusa; the
    Minotaur, fed seven virgins (along with seven youths)
    for appeasement, could perhaps be associated with
    Phrygia through his mother Pasiphae, daughter of
    Helios, but this is more probably a seventeenth-century
    confusion.

'Tis crime enough in any to be valiant,
To win a battle or be fortunate,
Whilst thou standst by the Queen to intercept
Or else determine favors from her hands;   300
'Tis not who is to blame or who deserves,
Nor whom the Queen would look on with a grace,
But whom proud Cecil pleases to reward
Or punish, and the valiant never 'scape thee.
Cursed be the brave that fall into such hands,   305
For cowards still are cruel and malicious.
BURLEIGH.
This I dare tell, and that Southampton said it.
SOUTHAMPTON.
And put her too in mind of thy vainglories,
Such impudence and ostentation in thee
And so much horrid pride and costliness   310
As would undo a monarch to supply.
ESSEX.
So thrives the lazy gown and such as sleep
On woolsacks and on seats of injured justice
Or learn to prate at council tables, but
How miserable is Fortune to the valiant!⁵⁰   315
Were but commanders half so well rewarded
For all their winters' camps and summers' fights,
Then they might eat, and the poor soldiers' widows
And children too might all be kept from starving.
RALEIGH.
My lord, in speaking thus you tax the Queen   320
Of weakness and injustice both and that
She favors none but worthless persons.
BURLEIGH.
Must we return this stubborn answer to her?
You'll not obey her Majesty, nor here
Resign your staff of offices to us?   325
ESSEX.
Tell her whate'er thy malice can invent,
Yet if thou say'st I'll not obey the Queen,
I tell thee, lord,
'Tis false, false as thy most inveterate soul
That looks through the foul prison of thy body   330
And curses all she sees at liberty.
I tell thee, creeping thing, the Queen's too good,

More merciful than to condemn a slave,
Much less her Essex without hearing him.
I will appeal to her.   335
BURLEIGH.
                              You'll not believe us,
Nor that it was by her command we came.
ESSEX.
I do not.
BURLEIGH.
                Fare you well, my lords.
Exeunt Burleigh and Raleigh.
ESSEX.
                                        Go thou,   340
My brave Southampton, follow to the Queen
And quickly ere my cruel foes are heard
Tell her that thus her faithful Essex says:
This star⁵¹ she decked me with and all these
    honors else,
In one blest hour when scarce my tender years   345
Had reached the age of man, she heaped upon me
As if the sun that sows the seeds of gems
And golden mines⁵² had showered upon my head
And dressed me like the bridegroom of her favor.
This thou beheldst, and nations wondered at.   350
The world had not a favorite so great,
So loved as I.
SOUTHAMPTON.
                    And I am witness too
How many gracious smiles she blest 'em with
And parted with a look with every favor   355
Was doubly worth the gift, whilst the whole Court
Was so well pleased and showed their wondrous joy
In shouting louder than the Roman bands
When Julius and Augustus were made consuls.
ESSEX.
Thou canst remember too, for all she said was signal, 360
That, at the happy time she did invest
Her Essex with this robe of shining glories,
She bade me prize 'em as I would my life,
Defend 'em as I would her crown and person.
Then a rich sword she put into my hand   365
And wished me Caesar's fortune, so she graced me.

---

50 So thrives … valiant] Essex distinguishes between *knights
of the robe* or "gown," functionaries of state and law, and
knights of the sword, the warrior class.

51 star] sign of the Order of the Garter
52 sun … mines] It was a Classical trope that the sun en-
gendered in the earth minerals and precious stones.

SOUTHAMPTON.
　　So young Alcides, when he first wore arms,
　　Did fly to kill the Erymanthean boar,[53]
　　And so Achilles, first by Thetis made
　　Immortal, hasted to the siege of Troy.[54]　　370
ESSEX.
　　Go thou, Southampton, for thou art my friend,
　　And such a friend's an angel in distress—
　　Now the false globe that flattered me is gone,
　　Thou art to me more wealth, more recompense
　　Than all the world was then—entreat the Queen　　375
　　To bless me with a moment's sight,
　　And I will lay her relics humbly down,
　　As traveling pilgrims do before the shrines
　　Of saints they went a thousand leagues to visit,
　　And her bright virgin honors all untainted:　　380
　　Her sword not spoiled with rust but wet with blood,
　　All nations' blood that disobeyed my queen;
　　This staff that disciplined her kingdoms once
　　And triumphed o'er an hundred victories;
　　And if she will be pleased to take it, say　　385
　　My life, the life of once her darling Essex.
SOUTHAMPTON.
　　I fly, my lord, and let your hopes repose
　　On the kind zeal Southampton has to serve you.
　　　　(*Exit.*)
ESSEX.
　　Where art thou, Essex! where are now thy glories!
　　Thy summers' garlands and thy winters' laurels,　　390
　　The early songs that ev'ry morning waked thee;
　　Thy halls and chambers thronged with multitudes
　　More than the temples of the Persian god
　　To worship thy uprising. And when I appeared,
　　The blushing Empress of the East, Aurora,　　395
　　Gladded the world not half so much as I.
　　Yesterday's sun saw his great rival thus,
　　The spiteful planet saw me thus adored,

And as[e] some tall-built pyramid, whose height
And golden top confronts him in his sky,　　400
He tumbles down with lightning in his rage,
So on a sudden has he snatched my garlands,
And with a cloud impaled my gaudy head,
Struck me with thunder, dashed me from the
　　heav'ns,
And oh! 'tis Doomsday now and darkness all with　　405
　　me.
Here I'll lie down—Earth will receive her son.
Take pattern all by me, you that hunt glory,
You that do climb the rounds of high ambition,
Yet when you've reached and mounted to the top,
Here you must come by just degrees at last,　　410
If not fall headlong down at once like me.
Here I'll abide close to my loving center,
For here I'm sure that I can fall no further.

Enter Countess of Essex.[f]

—Hah! what makes thou here? Tell me, fairest
　　creature,
Why art thou so in love with misery　　415
To come to be infected with my woe
And disobey the angry queen for me?
COUNTESS OF ESSEX.
　　Bless me, my angel, guard me from such sounds:
　　Is this the language of a welcome husband!
　　Are these fit words for Essex' bride to hear!　　420
　　Bride I may truly call myself, for love
　　Had scarce bestowed the blessing of one night
　　But snatched thee from these arms.
ESSEX.
　　　　　　　　　　My soul, my love!
　　Come to my breast, thou purest excellence,　　425
　　And throw thy lovely arms about my neck,
　　More soft, more sweet, more loving than the vine.[55]

They embrace.

　　Oh, I'm o'ercome with joy and sink beneath
　　Thy breast.
COUNTESS OF ESSEX.
　　　　　　　　Take me along with thee, my dear,　　430
　　My Essex, wake, my love, I say:

53　Alcides … boar] One of Hercules's (Alcides) twelve
　　labors was to capture a great boar on Mount
　　Erymanthus.
54　Achilles … Troy] Thetis, goddess of the sea, dipped her
　　heroic son into magical waters that made him invulner-
　　able (not immortal)—except for the spot where she held
　　him by his heel, where Paris mortally wounded him at
　　Troy.

55　vine] Classically, the vine's entwining itself about the
　　trunk of the elm is an emblem of marital fidelity.

I am grown jealous of each bliss without thee;
There's not a dream, an ecstasy or joy,
But I will double in thy ravished senses.
Come, let's prepare and mingle souls together;   435
Thou shalt lose nothing but a gainer be:
Mine is as full of love as thine can be.
ESSEX.
Where have I been! But yet I have thee still.
Come sit thee down upon this humble floor;
It was the first kind throne that love e'er had.   440
Thus like the first, bright couple let's embrace
And fancy all around is Paradise.
It must be so, for all is Paradise
Where thou remain'st, thou lovelier far than Eve.
COUNTESS OF ESSEX.
And thou more brave* and nobler person far   445
Than the first man, whom Heav'n's peculiar care
Made for a pattern for ingenious[56] nature,
Which ne'er till thee excelled th'original.
ESSEX.
Thus when th'Almighty formed the lovely maid
And sent her to the bower where Adam lay,   450
The first of men awaked and, starting from
His mossy, flow'ry bed whereon he slept,
Lifted his eyes and saw the virgin coming,
Saw the bright maid that glittered like a star:
Stars he had seen, but ne'er saw one so fair.   455
Thus they did meet, and thus they did embrace:
Thus in the infancy of pure desire,
Ere lust, displeasures, jealousies, and fears
Debauched the world and plagued the breast of man;
Thus in the dawn of golden time, when Love   460
And only Love taught lovers what to do.
COUNTESS OF ESSEX.
Oh thou most dear, most prized of all mankind,
I burn, I faint, I'm ravished with thy love:
The fever is too hot,
It scorches, flames like pure, ethereal fire,   465
And 'tis not flesh and blood but spirits can bear it,
And those the brightest of angelic forms.
ESSEX.
That is thyself, thy only self, thou fairest.
There's not in heav'n so bright a cherubim,
No angel there but for thy love would die;   470

The thrones[57] are all less happy there than I.
COUNTESS OF ESSEX.
Oh my best lord! the Queen, the Queen, my love!
Ah, what have we committed to undo us?
The Pow'rs are angry and have sent the Queen,
The jealous Queen of all our innocent joys,   475
To drive us from our Paradise of love,
And oh, my lord! she will not ere't be long
Allow us this poor plot, this ground to mourn on.
ESSEX.
Weep not, my soul, my love, my infinite all.
Ah, what could I express if there were words   480
To tell how much, how tenderly my thoughts
Adore thee. Ah, these tears are drops of blood,
Thy Essex' blood, my world, my heav'n, my bride.
Aye, there's the start of all my joys beside,
Blest that I am that I can call thee wife,   485
That loves so well and is so well beloved.
COUNTESS OF ESSEX.
Ah, hold, my lord, what shall I say of you,
That best deserves a love so well you speak of.
ESSEX.
Again thou weep'st. By Heav'n, there's not a tear
But weighs more than the wealth of England's crown.   490
Oh, thou bright storer of all virtues, were there
But so much goodness in thy sex besides,
It were enough to save all womankind
And keep 'em from damnation. Still thou weep'st.
Come, let me kiss thy eyes and catch those pearls.   495
Hold thy cheeks close to mine that none may fall
And spare me some of these celestial drops.
Thus as two turtles* driven by a storm,
Dropping and weary, sheltered on a bough,
Begin to join their melancholy voices,   500
Then thus they bill and thus renew their joys,
With quivering wings and cooing notes repeat
Their loves, and thus like us bemoan each other.

Enter a lady.

LADY.
Madam, the Queen expects you instantly.
COUNTESS OF ESSEX.
Ah, what would wish to be of humankind!   505
Man in his life scarce finds a moment's bliss

---

56 ingenious] creative

57 thrones] high order of angels

But counts a thousand pains for one short pleasure,
And when that comes, 'tis snatched away like ours.
ESSEX.
Go, my best hopes, obey the cruel Queen.
I had forgot. Thy love, thy beauties charmed me,   510
Dearer than Albion to the sailor's sight
Whom many years barred from his native country.
Looking on thee, I gazed my soul away
And quite forgot the dangerous wrecks below.
Farewell—nay then, thou'lt soften me to fondness—   515
The Queen may change, and we may meet again.
COUNTESS OF ESSEX.
Farewell.
ESSEX.
So have I seen a tall, rich ship of India
Of mighty bulk teeming with golden ore,
With prosperous gales come sailing nigh the shore,   520
Her train of pendants born up by the wind;
The gladsome seas, proud of the lovely weight,
Now lift her up above the sky in height,
And then as soon th'officious waves divide,
Hug the gay thing, and clasp her like a bride,   525
Whilst fishes play and dolphins gather round
And tritons with their coral trumpets sound,
Till on a hidden rock at last she's borne,
Swift as our fate, and thus in pieces torn.

Exeunt severally.

Act III, scene i. [The Queen's apartments.]

Countess of Nottingham, Burleigh.

NOTTINGHAM.
Now, famous Cecil, England owes to thee
More than Rome's state did once to Cicero pay,
That crushed the vast designs of Catiline.[58]
But what did he? Quelled but a petty consul
And saved a commonwealth,[59] but thou'st done   5
    more,
Pulled down a haughtier far than Catiline,
The Nation's sole dictator for twelve years,
And saved a queen and kingdoms by thy wisdom.
BURLEIGH.
But what the Roman Senate then allowed,
Nay and proud Cicero himself, to Fulvia,   10
Fulvia the lovely saver of her country,[60]
Must all and more be ascribed to you,
To the sole wit of beauteous Nottingham.
But I will cease and let the Nation praise thee
And fix thy statue high, as was Minerva's,   15
The great Palladium that protected Ilium.
I came t'attend the Queen, where is she gone?
NOTTINGHAM.
She went to her closet,* where she's now alone.
As she passed by, I saw her lovely eyes
Clouded in sorrow, and before she spied me,   20
Sad murmurs echoed from her troubled breast,
And straight some tears followed the mournful
    sound,
Which when she did perceive me, she'd have hid,
And with a piteous sigh she strove to wipe
The drops away, but with her haste she left   25
Some sad remains upon her dewy cheeks.
BURLEIGH.
What should the reason be!
NOTTINGHAM.
                                At Essex' answer,
What said she then?
BURLEIGH.
                            No doubt th'affront had stung her,   30
But kind Southampton, faithful to his friend
In all things, came and with a cunning tale,
Which she too willingly inclined to hear,
Turned her to mildness, and at his request
Promised to see the earl and hear him speak   35
To vindicate his crimes, which bold Southampton
Declared to be his enemies' aspersions.
And now is Essex sent for to the Court.
NOTTINGHAM.
Then I am lost, and my designs unraveled.
If once she sees him, all's undone again—   40

---

58 Cicero … Catiline] Catiline's attempt to become dictator in first-century BCE Rome was exposed by Cicero's
   famous orations to the Senate.

59 commonwealth] Rome was a republic; the word *commonwealth* invokes memories of the English Civil War.

---

60 Fulvia … country] Wife to Marc Antony, Fulvia aided
   Rome in defeating Catiline (but was not an unqualified
   hero, for she herself a decade later joined a rebellion by
   one of Pompey's sons, during which she died before
   Antony could return from Cleopatra to control his wife).

BURLEIGH.

Behold the closet opens, see, the Queen—
'Tis dangerous to interrupt her, let's retire.

NOTTINGHAM.

Be you not seen; I'll wait within her call.

Enter the Queen alone as from her closet, exit Burleigh.

QUEEN.

Where am I now? Why wander I alone?
What drags my body forth without a mind,   45
In all things like a statue, but in motion?
There's something I would say, but know not what,
Nor yet to whom. Oh wretched state of princes!
That never can enjoy, nor wish to have
What is but meanly in itself a crime,   50
But 'tis a plague and reigns through all the world.
Faults done by us are like licentious laws,
Adored by all the rabble, and are easier
And sooner far obeyed than what are honest,
And comets far less dreadful[61] than our failings. 55
—Where hast thou been?
I thought, dear Nottingham, I'd been alone.

NOTTINGHAM.

Pardon this bold intrusion, but my duty
Urges me farther. On my knees I first
Beg pardon that I am so bold to ask it,   60
Then, that you would disclose what 'tis afflicts you.
Something hangs heavy on your royal mind,
Or else I fear you are not well.

QUEEN.

                              Rise, prithee.
I am in health and thank thee for thy love,   65
Only a little troubled at my people.
I have reigned long, and they're grown weary of me.
New crowns are like new garlands, fresh, and lovely.
My royal sun declines towards its west;
They're hot and tired beneath its autumn beams.   70
Tell me, what says the world of Essex' coming?

NOTTINGHAM.

Much they do blame him for't but think him brave.

QUEEN.

What, when the traitor served me thus!

NOTTINGHAM.

                              Indeed,
It was not well.   75

QUEEN.

                    Not well? and was that all?

NOTTINGHAM.

It was a very bold and heinous fault.

QUEEN.

Aye, was it not? and such a base contempt
As he deserves to die for. Less than that
Has cost a hundred nearer favorites' heads   80
Since the first Saxon king that reigned in England,
And lately in my royal father's time,
Was not brave Buckingham for less condemned,
And lost not Wolsey all his church revenues,
Nay, and his life too, but that he was a coward   85
And durst not live to feel the stroke of justice?[62]
Thou know'st it too, and this most vile of men,
That brave Northumberland and Westmorland
For lesser crimes than his were both beheaded.[63]

NOTTINGHAM.

Most true. Can Essex then be thought so guilty   90
And not deserve to die?

QUEEN.

                    To die! to wrack,
And as his treasons are the worst of all men's,
So I will have him plagued above the rest,
His limbs cut off and placed to th'highest view,   95
Not on low bridges, gates, and walls of towns,
But on vast pinnacles that touch the sky,
Where all that pass may in derision say,
Lo there is Essex, proud, ingrateful Essex,
Essex that braved the justice of his queen.   100
Is not that well? Why dost not speak
And help thy queen to rail against this man?

---

61 comets … dreadful] Comets were thought to have dire influence on earthly events.

62 Buckingham … justice] Henry VIII had the duke of Buckingham and Cardinal Wolsey, his Chancellor of the Exchequer, cashiered for relatively minor offenses; the former was executed, the latter died before he could be.

63 Northumberland … beheaded] the earls of Northumberland and Westmorland, ironically, were executed for high treason against the Crown—the former for attempting to interfere with the succession of Mary Tudor, the latter for attempting to abet a Spanish invasion to return England to Catholicism.

NOTTINGHAM.
  Since you will give me leave, I will be plain
  And tell your Majesty what all the world
  Says of that proud, ingrateful man.   105
QUEEN.
  Do so. Prithee, what says the world of him and me?
NOTTINGHAM.
  Of you they speak no worse than of dead saints
  And worship you no less than as their god,
  Than peace, than wealth, or their eternal hopes.
  Yet do they often wish with kindest tears,   110
  Sprung from the purest love, that you'd be pleased
  To heal their grievances on Essex charged
  And not protect the traitor by your power,
  But give him up to justice and to shame
  For a revenge of all your wrongs and theirs.   115
QUEEN.
  What, would they then prescribe me rules to govern!
NOTTINGHAM.
  No more but with submission as to Heav'n.
  But upon Essex they unload reproaches
  And give him this bad character:*
  They say he is a person (bating his treasons)   120
  That in his noblest, best array of parts,*
  He scarcely has enough to make him pass
  For a brave* man, nor yet a hypocrite,
  And that he wears his greatness and his honors
  Foolish and proud as lackeys wear gay liveries.   125
  Valiant they will admit he is, but then
  Like beasts precipitately rash and brutish,
  Which is no more commendable in him
  Than in a bear, a leopard, or a wolf.
  He never yet had courage over Fortune,   130
  And which too shows his natural pride the more,
  He roars and staggers under small affronts
  And can no more endure the pain than hell.
  Then he's as covetous and more ambitious
  Than that first fiend that sowed the vice in heav'n   135
  And therefore was dethroned and tumbled thence.
  And so they wish that Essex too may fall.
QUEEN.
  Enough, th'ast railed thyself quite out of breath;
  I'll hear no more. (Aside.) Blisters upon her tongue.
  —'Tis baseness, though, in thee but to repeat   140
  What the rude world maliciously has said,
  Nor dare the vilest of the rabble think,

Much less profanely speak such horrid treasons.
  Yet 'tis not what they say, but what you'd have 'em.
NOTTINGHAM.
  Did not your Majesty command me speak?   145
QUEEN.
  I did, but then I saw thee on a sudden
  Settle thy senses all in eager postures:
  Thy lips, thy speech and hands were all prepared;
  A joyful red painted thy envious cheeks;
  Malicious flames flashed in a moment from   150
  Thy eyes like lightning from thy o'ercharged soul
  And fired thy breast, which like a hard-rammed
      piece,
  Discharged unmannerly upon my face.
NOTTINGHAM.
  Pardon, bright Queen, most royal and beloved,
  The manner of expressing of my duty,   155
  But you yourself began and taught me first.
QUEEN.
  I am his queen and therefore may have leave.
  May not myself have privilege to mold
  The thing I made and use it as I please?
  Besides, he has committed monstrous crimes   160
  Against my person and has urged me far
  Beyond the power of mortal suffering.
  Me he has wronged, but thee he never wronged.
  What has poor Essex done to thee? Thou hast
  No crown that he could hope to gain,   165
  No laws to break, no subjects to molest,
  Nor throne that he could be ambitious of.
  What pleasure couldst thou take to see
  A drowning man knocked on the head and yet
  Not wish to save the miserable wretch!   170
NOTTINGHAM.
  I was to blame.
QUEEN.
                  No more.
  Thou see'st thy queen, the world, and destiny
  Itself against this one bad man, and him
  Thou canst not pity nor excuse.   175
NOTTINGHAM.
                              Madam—
QUEEN.
  Be gone, I do forgive thee, and bid Rutland
  Come to me straight.

Exit Nottingham.

Hah! what have I disclosed?
Why have I chid my woman* for a fault   180
Which I wrung from her and committed first?
Why stands my jealous and tormented soul
A spy to listen and divulge the treasons
Spoke against Essex?—Oh, you mighty Powers!
Protectors of the fame of England's queen,   185
Let me not know it for a thousand worlds,
'Tis dangerous—but yet it will discover,*
And I feel something whispering to my reason
That says it is. Oh blotted be the name
Forever from my thoughts. If it be so,   190
And I am stung with thy almighty dart,
I'll die, but I will tear thee from my heart,
Shake off this hideous vapor from my soul,
This haughty earl, the prince of my control,
Banish this traitor to his queen's repose   195
And blast him with the malice of his foes.
Were there no other way his guilt to prove,
'Tis treason to infect the throne with love.

Enter Countess of Essex.

How now, my Rutland? I did send for you.
I have observed you have been sad of late.   200
Why wearest thou black so long? and why that cloud,
That mourning cloud about thy lovely eyes?
Come, I will find a noble husband for thee.
COUNTESS OF ESSEX.
Ah mighty princess, most adored of queens!
Your royal goodness ought to blush when it   205
Descends to care for such a wretch as I am.
QUEEN.
Why say'st thou so? I love thee well, indeed
I do, and thou shalt find by this 'tis truth.
Injurious Nottingham and I had some
Dispute, and 'twas about my lord of Essex—   210
COUNTESS OF ESSEX. (*Aside.*)
Hah!
QUEEN.
So much that she displeased me strangely,
And I did send her from my sight in anger.
COUNTESS OF ESSEX. (*Aside.*)
Oh that dear name o'th'sudden how it starts me!
Makes ev'ry vein within me leave its channel   215
To run and to protect my feeble heart,
And now my blood as soon retreats again

To crowd with blushes full my guilty cheeks.
Alas, I fear.
QUEEN.
Thou blushest at my story!   220
COUNTESS OF ESSEX.
Not I, my gracious mistress, but my eyes
And cheeks, fired and amazed with joy, turned red
At such a grace that you were pleased to show me.
QUEEN.
I'll tell thee, then, and ask thee thy advice.
There is no doubt, dear Rutland, but thou hear'st   225
The daily clamors that my people vent
Against the most unhappy Earl of Essex,
The treasons that they would impeach him of,
And which is worse, this day he is arrived
Against my strict commands and left affairs   230
In Ireland desp'rate, headless, and undone.
COUNTESS OF ESSEX.
Might I presume to tell my humble mind,
Such clamors very often are designed
More by the people's hate than any crimes
In those they would accuse.   235
QUEEN.
Thou speak'st my sense,
But oh, dear Rutland, he has been to blame.
Lend me thy breast to lean upon. Oh, 'tis
A heavy yoke they would impose on me
Their queen, and I am weary of the load   240
And want* a friend like thee to lull my sorrows.
COUNTESS OF ESSEX.
Behold these tears sprung from fierce pain and joy
To see your wondrous grief, your wondrous pity.
Oh that kind Heav'n would but instruct my
    thoughts
And teach my tongue such soft'ning, healing words   245
That it might charm your soul and cure your breast
Forever.
QUEEN.
Thou art my better angel, then,
And sent to give me everlasting quiet.
Say, is't not pity that so brave* a man   250
And one that once was reckoned as a god,
That he should be the author of such treasons!
That he, that was like Caesar and so great,
Has had the power to make and unmake kings,
Should stoop to gain a petty throne from me.   255

COUNTESS OF ESSEX.
I can't believe 'tis in his soul to think,
Much less to act a treason against you,
Your Majesty, whom I have heard him so
Commend that angels' words did never flow
With so much eloquence, so rare, so sweet,   260
That nothing but the subject could deserve.

QUEEN.
Hast thou then heard him talk of me?

COUNTESS OF ESSEX.
                                        I have,
And as of so much excellence as if
He meant to make a rare encomium on   265
The world, the stars, or what is brighter, heaven.
"She is," said he, "the goddess of her sex,
So far beyond all womankind beside,
That what in them is most adored and loved—
Their beauties, parts,* and other ornaments—   270
Are but in her the foils to greater luster,
And all perfections else, how rare soever,
Are in her person but as lesser gleams
And infinite beams that usher still the sun,
But scarce are visible amidst her other brightness.   275
And then she is so good it might be said
That, whilst she lives, a goddess reigns in England:
For all her laws are registered in heaven
And copied thence by her." But then he cried,
With a deep sigh fetched from his loyal heart,   280
"Well may the world bewail that time at last
When so much goodness shall on earth be mortal,
And wretched England break its stubborn heart."

QUEEN.
Did he say all this?

COUNTESS OF ESSEX.
                        All this! nay more,   285
A thousand times as much. I never saw him
But his discourse was still* in praise of you;
Nothing but raptures fell from Essex' tongue:
And all was still* the same, and all was you.

QUEEN.
Such words spoke loyalty enough.   290

COUNTESS OF ESSEX.
                                Then does
Your Majesty believe that he can be
A traitor?

QUEEN.
            No, yet he has broke the laws,
And I for shame no longer can protect him,   295
Nay, durst not see him!

COUNTESS OF ESSEX.
                        What, not see him, say you?
By that bright star of mercy in your soul
And listening through your eyes, let me entreat:
'Tis good, 'tis godlike and like England's queen,   300
Like only her to pity the distressed:
Will you not grant that he shall see you once?

QUEEN.
What, he
That did defy my absolute commands
And brings himself audaciously before me?   305

COUNTESS OF ESSEX.
Impute it not to that, but to his danger
That, hearing what proceedings here had passed
Against his credit and his life, he comes
Loyal, though unadvised, to clear himself.

QUEEN.
Well, I will see him then and see him straight.   310
Indeed, my Rutland, I would fain believe
That he is honest still, as he is brave.

COUNTESS OF ESSEX.
Oh nourish that most kind belief, 'tis sprung
From justice in your royal soul. Honest!
By your bright Majesty, he's faithful still;   315
The pure and virgin light is less untainted.
The glorious body of the sun breeds gnats
And insects that molest its curious beams;
The moon has spots upon her crystal face,
But in his soul are none. And for his valor,   320
The Christian world records its wondrous story;
Baseness can never mingle with such courage.
Remember what a scourge he was to rebels
And made your Majesty adored in Spain
More than their king, that bribed you with his Indies,   325
And made himself so dreadful to their fears
His very name put armies to the rout.
It was enough to say here's Essex come,
And nurses stilled their children with the fright.

QUEEN. [Aside.]
Hah! she's concerned, transported!   330
I'll try her further.—Then he has a person!*

COUNTESS OF ESSEX.

Aye, in his person, there you sum up all.
Ah, loveliest Queen, did you ere see the like?
The limbs of Mars and awful* front of Jove,
With such a harmony of parts* as put   335
To blush the beauties of his daughter Venus:
A pattern for the gods to make a perfect man by
And Michelangelo to frame a statue
To be adored through all the wond'ring world.

QUEEN. [Aside.]

I can endure no more.—Hold, Rutland,   340
Thy eyes are moist, thy senses in a hurry,
Thy words come crowding one upon another.
Is it a real passion or extorted?
Is it for Essex' sake or for thy queen's
That makes this furious transport in thy mind?   345
[Aside.] She loves him. Ah, 'tis so. What have I done?
Conjured another storm to rack my rest?
Thus is my mind with quiet never blest,
But like a loaded bark finds no repose,
When 'tis becalmed, nor when the weather blows.   350

*Enter Burleigh, Countess of Nottingham, Raleigh,
lords, attendants and guards.*

BURLEIGH.

May't please your Majesty, the Earl of Essex,
Returned by your command, entreats to kneel
Before you.

QUEEN. (Aside.)

Now hold out, my treacherous heart,
Guard well the breach that this proud man has made.   355
—Rutland, we must defer this subject till
Some other time.—Come hither, Nottingham.

Enter the earls of Essex and Southampton attended.

ESSEX.

Behold, your Essex kneels to clear himself
Before his queen and now receive his doom.

QUEEN. [Aside.]

I must divert my fears. I see he takes the way   360
To bend the sturdy temper of my heart.
—Well my lord, I see you can
Withstand my anger, as you lately boasted
You did your enemies. Were they such foes
As bravely did resist, or else the same   365
You parleyed with? It was a mighty courage.

ESSEX.

Well, well, you cruel Fates! well have you found
The way to shock the basis of a temper
That all your malice else could ne'er invent
And you, my Queen, to break your soldier's heart.   370
Thunder and earthquakes, prodigies on land
I've borne, devouring tempests on the seas,
And all the horrid strokes beside
That Nature e'er invented, yet to me
Your scorn is more. Here, take this traitor,   375
Since you will have me so, throw me to dungeons,
Lash me with iron rods fast bound in chains,
And like a fiend in darkness let me roar:
It is the nobler justice of the two.

QUEEN.

I see you want* no cunning skill to talk   380
And daub with words a guilt you would evade.
But yet, my lord, if you would have us think
Your virtues wronged, wash off the stain you carry
And clear yourself of parleying with the rebels.
(Aside.) Grant, Heav'n, he does but that, and I am   385
happy.

ESSEX.

My parleying with the enemy?

QUEEN.

Yes, your secret treating with Tyrone I mean,
And making articles with England's rebels.

ESSEX.

Is that alleged against me for a fault,
Put in your royal breast by some that are   390
My false accusers for a crime? Just Heaven!
How easy 'tis to make a great man fall:
'Tis wise, 'tis Turkish policy in courts.
For treating!
Am I not your general, and was   395
I not there by virtue of this staff?
I thought your Majesty had giv'n me power
And my commission had been absolute
To treat, to fight, give pardons, or disband:
So much and vast was my authority   400
That you were pleased to say as mirth to others,
I was the first of English kings that reigned
In Ireland.

QUEEN. (Aside.)

Oh how soon would I believe,
How willingly approve of such excuses,   405

His answers which to all the crowd are weak.
—That large commission had in it no power
That gave you leave to treat with rebels,
Such as Tyrone, and wanted* not authority
To fight 'em on the least advantage.   410

ESSEX.
                            The reason why
I led not forth the army to the north
And fought not with Tyrone was that my men
Were half consumed with fluxes and diseases
And those that lived, so weakened and unfit   415
That they could scarce defend them from the
    vultures
That took 'em for the carrion of an army.

QUEEN. (*Aside.*)
Oh, I can hold no longer: he'll not hide his guilt.
I fear he will undo himself and me.
—Name that no more, for shame of thee, the cause, 420
Nor hide thy guilt by broaching of a worse:
Fain I would tell, but whisper it in thy ear
That none besides may hear, nay not myself,
How vicious thou hast been. Say, was not Essex
The plague that first infected my poor soldiers   425
And killed 'em with diseases? Was't not he
That loitered all the year without one action,
Whilst all the rebels in the north grew bold
And rallied daily, to thy queen's dishonor?
Meanwhile, thou stood'st and saw thy army rot   430
In fenny and unwholesome camps. Thou hast,
No doubt, a just excuse for coming too,
In spite of all the letters that I sent
With my commands to hinder thee—be silent!
If thou makest more such impudent excuses,   435
Thou'lt raise an anger will be fatal to thee.

ESSEX.
Not speak! Must I be tortured on the rack
And not be suffered to discharge a groan!
Speak! Yes, I will, were there a thousand deaths
Stood ready to devour me. 'Tis too plain   440
My life's conspired, my glories all betrayed:
That vulture Cecil there with hungry nostrils
Waits for my blood, and Raleigh for my charge,
Like birds of prey that seek out fighting fields
And know when battle's near, nay, and my Queen   445
Has passed her vote, I fear, to my destruction.

QUEEN. (*Aside.*)
Oh I'm undone! How he destroys my pity!
Could I bear this from any other man?
He pulls and tears the fury from my heart
With greater grief and pain than a forked arrow   450
Is drawn from forth the bosom where 'twas lodged.
Mild words are all in vain and lost upon him.
—Proud and ingrateful wretch, how durst thou
    say it!
Know, monster, that thou hast no friend but me,
And I have no pretense for it but one,   455
And that's in contradiction to the world
That curses and abhors thee for thy crimes.
Stir me no more with anger, for thy life.
Take heed how thou dost shake my wrongs too much,
Lest they fall thick and heavy on thy head.   460
Yet thou shalt see what a rash fool thou art:
Know then that I forgive thee from this moment
All that is past and this unequaled boldness,
Give thee that life thou said'st I did conspire against.
But for your offices—   465

ESSEX. (*Lays his general's staff down.*)
I throw 'em at your feet.
Now banish him that planted strength about you,
Covered this island with my spreading laurels,
Whilst your safe subjects slept beneath their shade.
Give 'em to courtiers, sycophants and cowards   470
That sell the land for peace, and children's portions,
Whilst I retreat to Afric in some desert,
Sleep in a den and herd with valiant brutes
And serve the king of beasts. There's more reward,
More justice there than in all Christian courts: 475
The lion spared the man that freed him from
The toil,[64] but England's queen abhors her Essex.

SOUTHAMPTON.
My lord—

COUNTESS OF ESSEX. (*Aside.*)
           Ah, what will be th'event of this!

QUEEN.
Audacious traitor.   480

ESSEX.
Hah!

SOUTHAMPTON.
        My lord, my lord, recall your temper.

---

64 lion ... toil] a version of the more famous fable of the
    slave who removes the thorn from the lion's paw

ESSEX.

> You said that I was bold, but now who blames
> My rage? Had I been rough as storms and tempests,
> Rash as Cethegus, mad as Ajax was,[65]   485
> Yet this has rammed more powder in my breast
> And blown a magazine of fury up—
> A traitor! Yes, for serving you so well,
> For making England like the Roman Empire
> In great Augustus's time, renowned in peace   490
> At home and war abroad, enriching you
> With spoils both of the wealthy sea and land
> More than your Thames does bring you in an age
> And setting up your fame to such a height
> That it appears the column of the world;   495
> For tumbling down the proud rebellious earls,
> Northumberland and Westmorland, which caused
> The cutting both their heads off with an axe
> That saved the crown on yours. This Essex did,
> And I'll remove the traitor from your sight.   500
>   (*Offers to go.*)

QUEEN.

> Stay, sir, take your reward along with you—

The Queen comes up to him and gives him a box on the ear.[66]

ESSEX.

> Hah! Furies, Death, and Hell! a blow!
> Has Essex had a blow! (*Lays hand on his sword.*)
>   Hold, stop my arm
> Some god. Who is't has giv'n it me? The Queen!

SOUTHAMPTON.

> What do you mean, my lord!   505

QUEEN.

>   Unhand the villain.*
> Durst the vile slave attempt to murder me!

---

65 Rash ... Ajax] Cethegus, member of an important patrician family and descendent of a famous warrior and orator of the same name, rashly joined Catiline's conspiracy and set out to assassinate Cicero but was caught and executed. Ajax, furious that Achilles' armor was awarded to Odysseus, planned vengeance but went mad in the attempt, slaughtering sheep instead; realizing in a moment of lucidity his disgrace, he killed himself.

66 box on the ear] Queen Elizabeth actually administered this famous cuff or slap a year earlier during a quarrel with Essex over who should lead the army in Ireland.

ESSEX.

> No, y'are my queen, that charms me, but by all
> The subtlety and woman in your sex
> I swear, that had you been a man you durst not,   510
> Nay, your bold father Harry durst not this
> Have done. Why say I him? not all the Harrys[67]
> Nor Alexander's self,[68] were he alive,
> Should boast of such a deed on Essex done
> Without revenge.   515

QUEEN.

> Rail on, despair, and curse thy foolish breath.
> I'll leave thee like thy hopes at th'hour of death,
> Like the first slayer wandering with a mark,[69]
> Shunning the light and wishing for the dark
> In torments worse than hell, when thou shalt see   520
> Thou hast by this cursed chance lost Heav'n and me.

Exeunt Queen, etc. Manent Essex and Southampton.

SOUTHAMPTON.

> What have you done, my lord! Your haughty carriage
> Has ruined both yourself and all your friends.
> Follow the Queen and humbly on your knees
> Implore her mercy and confess your fault.   525

ESSEX.

> Hah! And tell her that I'll take a blow!
> Thou wouldst not wish thy friend were such a slave.
> By Heav'n, my cheek has set on fire my soul,
> And the disgrace sticks closer to my heart
> Than did the son of old Antipater's,   530
> Which cost the life of his proud master.[70] Stand off,
> Beware you lay not hands upon my ruin:
> I have a load would sink a legion that
> Should offer but to save me.

SOUTHAMPTON.

>   My lord, let us retire   535
> And shun this barbarous place.

---

67 Harrys] This would, of course, include Henry V, perhaps England's most heroic martial king.

68 Alexander's self] Alexander the Great

69 first slayer ... mark] Cain, whom God stamped with a mark to distinguish this first murderer.

70 Antipater's ... master] In Banks's *The Rival Kings*, Cassander, son of Antipater, is outraged by Alexander the Great's treatment of his own generals, including him; thus, he heads the conspiracy to poison Alexander.

ESSEX.

                    Aye, there thou say'st it—
Abhor all courts if thou art brave and wise,
For then thou never shalt be sure to rise;
Think not by doing well a fame to get,   540
But be a villain, and thou shalt be great.
Here virtue stands by'tself or not at all;
Fools have foundations, only brave* men fall.
But if ill fate and thy own merits bring
Thee once to be a favorite to a king,   545
It is a curse that follows loyalty:
Cursed in thy merits, more in thy degree,
In all the sport of Chance its chiefest aim,
Mankind's the hunt, a favorite is the game.

Exeunt.

Act IV. [A room in Whitehall.]

Countess of Nottingham, Raleigh.

NOTTINGHAM.

Sir, did you ever see so strange a scene
As Essex' boldness? Nay, and which is more
To be admired, the Queen's prodigious patience!

RALEIGH.

So strange that naught but such a miracle
Had saved him from death upon the place.   5

NOTTINGHAM.

She's of a nature wondrous in her sex,
Not hasty to admire the beauties, wisdom,
Valor, and parts* in others though extreme,
Because there's so much excellence in herself,
And thinks that all mankind should be so too.   10
But once entertained, none cherishes,
Exalts, or favors virtue more than she,
Slow to be moved, and in her rage discreet.
But then the earl's like an ungoverned steed
That yet has all the shapes and other beauties   15
That are commendable or sought in one.
His soul with sullen beams shines in itself,
More jealous of men's eyes than is the sun
That will not suffer to be looked into.
And there's a mine of sulfur in his breast,   20
Which when 'tis touched or heated, straight takes fire
And tears and blows up all his virtues with it.

RALEIGH.

Ambitious minds feed daily upon passion
And ne'er can be at rest within themselves
Because they never meet with slaves enough   25
To tread upon, mechanics to adore 'em,
And lords and statesmen to have cringes from,
Like some of those strange seas that I've been on
Whose tides are always violent and rough
Where winds are seldom blowing to molest 'em.   30
She'd done a nobler justice if instead of
That schoolboy's punishment, a blow,
She'd snatched a halberd from her nearest guard
And thrust it to his heart: For less than that
Did the bold Macedonian monarch kill   35
Clytus, his friend and braver soldier far.[71]

NOTTINGHAM.

But worse had been th'event of such a deed,
For if th'afflicted king was hardly brought
From Clytus' body, she'd have died o'er his.
But how proceed the bold rebellious lords   40
In Essex' house?

RALEIGH.

                  Still they increase in number.
The Queen has sent four of her chiefest lords,
And since, I hear, the guards are gone. 'Tis said
For his excuse that Blunt, that fiend of hell   45
And brand of all his master's wicked councils,
Has spread abroad this most abhorred of lies,
That I and the Lord Grey should join to murder
him.[72]

NOTTINGHAM.

Already then he's hunted to the toil,
Where let him roar and lash himself with fury,   50
But never, never shall get out with struggling.
Oh, it o'erjoyed th'affront within my soul
To see the man by all the world adored,

---

71 Macedonian … far] Alexander the Great, in a fit of rage,
killed his old friend, counselor, warrior, Clytus, for criti-
cizing him—as had recently been portrayed on the English stage most memorably by Nathaniel Lee in his *Rival
Queens.*

72 Blunt … him] It was Lord Grey's attack on Southampton that led to Essex's excuse of self-defense; Sir
Christopher Blunt, co-conspirator, was Essex's stepfather; Essex also implicated in the rebellion Charles
Blunt, Lord Mountjoy, erstwhile friend who had replaced him in command of the army in Ireland.

That like a comet shined above and ruled below,
To see him on a sudden from our eyes   55
Drop like a star and vanish in the ground,
To see him how he bit the cursèd torture
That durst no further venture than his lips
When he passed by the guards to hear no noise:
No "room for mighty Essex" was proclaimed;   60
No caps, no knees, nor welcomes to salute* him;
Then how he chafed and started like a deer
With the fierce dart fast sticking in his side
And finds his speedy death where'er he runs!

RALEIGH.
Behold the Queen and the whole Court appear.   65

Enter the Queen, Burleigh, lords, attendants and guards.

QUEEN.
Are the rebellious earls then apprehended?

BURLEIGH.
They are, thanks to the almighty Powers
And the eternal fortune of your Majesty.

QUEEN.
And how did you proceed with my commands?
And how did the rebels act?   70

BURLEIGH.
              Most audaciously:
The four lords, chiefest of your Private Council,
Sent thither by your Majesty's commission,
Came to the rebel's house,[73] but found the gates
Guarded and shut against them, yet at last,   75
Telling they brought a message from the Queen,
They were admitted, all besides but him
That bore the Seal before the Chancellor
Denied. Entering they saw the outward court
Filled with a number of promiscuous persons,   80
The chief of which bold traitors in the midst
Stood the two earls, of Essex and Southampton,
Of whom your faithful messengers with loud
And loyal voices did demand the cause
Of their unjust assembly, telling them   85
All real grievances should be redressed.
But straight their words were choked by louder cries,
And by the earls' command with insolence

The people drove 'em to a strong apartment
Belonging to the house, setting a guard   90
Of muskets at the door and threat'ning them
That they should there be kept close prisoners
Till the next morning that the earl returned
From visiting his friends, the Citizens.[74]

QUEEN.
Oh horrid insolence! Attempt my Council!   95
My nearest friends! (*Aside.*) Well, Essex, well,
I thank thee for the cure of my disease;
Thou goest the readiest way to give me ease.
—The City, say'st! What did he in the City?

BURLEIGH.
There, as I learned from many that confessed,   100
He was informed the Citizens would rise,
Which to promote, he went disguised like one
Whom evil Fortune had bereaved of sense
And almost seemed as pitiful a wretch
As Harpagus, that fled all o'er dismembered   105
To fond* Astyages to gain the trust
Of all his Median army to betray it.[75]
His head was bare, the heat and dust had made
His manly face compassionate to behold, which he
So well did use, that sometimes with a voice   110
That ushered tears both from himself and them
And sometimes with a popular rage he ran
With fury through the streets. To those that stood
Far off he bended and made taking signs,
To those about him raised his voice aloud   115
And humbly did beseech 'em for a guard,
Told 'em he was attempted to be murdered
By some the chief of th'Court, then counted all
   his wounds,
Unstripped his vest and showed his naked scars,
Telling them what great wonders he had done   120
And would do more to serve 'em and their children,

---

73 rebel's house] the great Essex House, a former bishop's palace, fronting on the Strand* and backing onto the Thames

74 Four lords … Citizens] Banks follows Camden's history closely: four lords of the Privy Council, led by the Lord Keeper of the Seal of England, were indeed sent to Essex House and were kept hostage while Essex sought promised support in the City.

75 Harpagus … it] Median general who in the sixth century BCE betrayed the last Median king, Astyages's army to the Achaemenid king, Cyrus II, perhaps because Astyages had murdered Harpagus's son

Begging still louder to the stinking rabble
And sweated too so many eager drops, as if
He had been pleading for Rome's consulship.
QUEEN.
   How came he taken? 125
BURLEIGH.
               After he had used
Such subtle means to gain your subjects' hearts
(Your Citizens that ever were most faithful
And too well grounded in their loyalties
To be seduced from such a queen), and finding 130
That none began to arm in his behalf,
Fear and confusion of his horrid guilt
Possessed him, and despairing of success
Attempted straight to walk through Ludgate home,
But being resisted by some companies 135
Of the trained bands that stood there in defense,
He soon retreated to the nearest stairs*
And so came back by water at the time
When your most valiant soldiers with their leader
Entered his house and took Southampton and the 140
   rest.
Th'affrighted earl, defenseless both in mind
And body, without the power to help himself,
And being full of horror in his thoughts,
Was forced to run for shelter in the room
Of a small summer house upon the Thames, 145
Which when the soldiers came to search and
   found him,
Who then had eyes and did not melt for pity!
To see the high, the gallant Essex there
Trembling and panting like the frighted quarry
Whom the fierce hawk had in his eager eye.[76] 150
QUEEN.
Hah! By my stars I think the mournful tale
Has almost made thee weep. Can Essex' miseries
Then force compassion from thy flinty breast!
'A* weeps, the crocodile weeps o'er his prey!
How wretched and how low then art thou fall'n, 155

---

[76] despairing of success ... eye] Essex abandoned his hopes
in the City but was indeed stopped at its western gate
(Ludgate); he was arrested by Nottingham, Lord Admiral, at Essex House, taken down the Thames, and temporarily lodged in (did not escape to) Lambeth House
before being imprisoned in the Tower.*

That ev'n thy barbarous hunters can neglect
Their rage and turn their cruel sport to pity!
What then must be my lot? how many sighs,
How many griefs, repentances and horrors
Must I eternally endure for this!— 160
Where is the earl?
BURLEIGH.
            Under sufficient guard
In order to his sending to the Tower.*
QUEEN.
Hah, in the Tower! How durst they send him there
Without my order? 165
BURLEIGH.
            Th'earls are yet without
In the lieutenant's custody, who waits
But to receive your Majesty's command
To carry 'em thither.
QUEEN. (Aside.)
                What shall I do now? 170
Wake me, thou watchful genius* of thy queen,
Rouse me and arm me[h] now against my foe:
Pity's my enemy and love's my foe,
And both have equally conspired with Essex.
Hah! Shall I then refuse to punish him, 175
Condemn the slave that disobeyed my orders,
That braved me to my face and did attempt
To murder me, then went about to gain
My subjects' hearts and seize my crown?
Now by my thousand wrongs 'a* dies, dies quickly, 180
And I could stab this heart, if I but thought
The traitor in it to corrupt it.—Away
And send him to the Tower with speed—yet hold.
NOTTINGHAM. (Aside.)
The Queen's distracted how to save the earl.
Her study puts my hatred on the rack. 185
QUEEN. (Aside.)
Who is it thou wouldst kill with so much haste?
Is it not Essex? Him thou didst create
And crowned his morning with full rays of honors?
Whilst he returned 'em with whole springs of laurels,
Fought for thy fame a hundred times in blood 190
And ventured twice as many lives for thee.
And shall I then for one rash act of his,
Of which I was the cruel cause, condemn him?
NOTTINGHAM. (Aside.)
Her rage ebbs out, and pity flows apace.

QUEEN. (*Aside.*)

Do what you will, my stars, do as you please,   195
Just Heav'n, and censure England's queen for it,
Yet Essex I must see, and then whoe're thou art
That when I'm dead shall call this tender fault,
This only action of my life in question,
Thou canst at worst but say that it was love,   200
Love that does never cease to be obeyed,
Love that has all my power and strength betrayed,
Love that sways wholly like the cause of things.
Kings may rule subjects, but love reigns o'er kings,
Sets bounds to Heav'n's high wrath when 'tis severe,   205
And is the greatest bliss and virtue there.
—Carry Southampton to the Tower straight,
But Essex I will see before he goes.
—Now help me, art,* check ev'ry pulse within me,
And let me feign a courage though I've none.   210

Enter Essex with guards.

Behold 'a* comes with such a pomp of misery!
Greatness in all he shows, and nothing makes
Him less, but turns to be majestic in him.
—All that are present for a while withdraw
And leave the prisoner here with me unguarded.   215

Exeunt. Manent Queen and Essex.

ESSEX. (*Kneels.*)

Thus, though I am condemned and hated by you,
A traitor by your royal will proclaimed,
Thus do I bless my queen and all those Powers
That have inspired her with such tender mercy
As once to hear her dying Essex speak   220
And now receive his sentence from your lips,
Which, let it be my life or death, they're both
Alike to me from you, my royal mistress.
And thus I will receive my doom and wish
My knees might ever till my dying minute   225
Cleave to the earth, as now they do in token of
The choicest, humblest begging of thy blessing.

QUEEN.

Pray rise, my lord. You see that I dare venture
To leave myself without a guard between us.

ESSEX.

Fairest that e'er was England's queen, you need not.   230
The time has been that Essex has been thought
A guard and, being near you, has been more

Than crowds of mercenary slaves.
And is he not so now? Oh think me rather,
Think me a traitor, if I can be so   235
Without a thought against your precious life,
But wrong me not with that: For by yourself,
By your bright self that rules o'er all my wishes,
I swear I would not touch that life to be
As great as you, the greatest prince on earth;   240
Lightning should blast me first
E'er I would touch the person of my queen
Less gentle than the breeze.

QUEEN.

Oh, y'are become a wondrous penitent,
My lord; the time has been you were not so: 245
Then you were haughty, and because you urged me,
Urged me beyond the suffering of a saint
To strike you, which[77] a king would have obeyed,
Then straight your malice led you to the City,
Tempting my loyal subjects to rebel,   250
Laying a plot how to surprise the Court,
Then seize my person with my chiefest Council
To murder them, and I to beg your mercy.
This, this the wondrous faithful Essex did,
Thou whom I raised from the vile dust of man   255
And placed thee as a jewel in my crown
And bought thee dearly for my favor, at the rate
Of all my people's grievances and curses,
Yet thou didst this, ingrateful monster, this
And all, for which as surely thou shalt die,   260
Die like the foulest and the worst ingrate.
But fetters now have humbled you, I see.

ESSEX.

Oh hear me speak, most injured Majesty,
Brightest of queens, goddess of mercy too,
Oh think not that the fear of death or prisons   265
Can e'er disturb a heart like mine or make it
More guilty or more sensible of guilt.
All that y'are pleased to say, I now confess,
Confess my misery, my crime, my shame,
Yet neither death nor hell should make me own it,   270
But true remorse and duty to yourself
And love. I dare stand candidate with Heav'n
Who loves you most and purest.

---

77 which] read *who* (Elizabeth means Essex would have
obeyed a male monarch).

QUEEN. (*Aside.*)
                  Now he awakes me,
And all my faculties begin to listen,   275
Steal to my eyes and tread soft paces to
My ears as loath to be discovered, yet
As loath to lose the Syrens' charming song.
Help me a little now, my cautious angel.
—I must confess I formerly believed so,   280
And I acknowledged it by my rewards.

ESSEX.
You have, but oh, what has my rashness done!
And what has not my guilt condemned me to!
Seated I was in heav'n, where once that angel,
That haughty spirit reigned that tempted me,   285
But now thrown down, like him, to worse than hell.

QUEEN.
Aye, think on that, and like that fiend roar still*
In torments, when thou mayst have been most
    happy.
(*Aside.*) There I outdid my strength and feel my rage
Recoil upon me, like a foolish child   290
Who, firing of a gun as much as he can lift,
Is blasted with the fury of the blow.

ESSEX.
Most blest of queens! her doom, her very anger's
    kind,
And I will suffer it as willingly
As your loud wrongs instruct you to inflict.   295
I know my death is nigh, my enemies
Stand like a guard of furies ready by you
To intercept each sigh, kind wish, or pity
Ere it can reach to heav'n in my defense
And dash it with a cloud of accusations.   300

QUEEN. (*Aside.*)
Hah! I begin to dread the danger nigh:
Like an unskillful swimmer that has waded
Beyond his depth, I'm caught and almost drowned
In pity. What! and no one near to help me!

ESSEX.
My father once too truly skilled in fate   305
In my first blooming age to rip'ning glory
Bid me beware my six and thirtieth year:
"That year," said he, "will fatal to thee prove;
Something like death or worse than death will
    seize thee."
Too well I find that cruel time's at hand,   310

For what can e'er more fatal to me prove
Than my lost fame and losing of my queen?

QUEEN. (*Aside.*)
'Tis so, 'tis true, nor is it in my power
To help him. Hah! Why is it not? What hinders?
Who dares or thinks to contradict my will?   315
Is it my subjects or my virtue stays me?
No, virtue's patient and abhors revenge,
Nay, sometimes weeps at justice. 'Tis not love—
Ah, call it anything but that: 'tis mercy,
Mercy that pities foes when in distress;   320
Mercy the heav'ns delights.
—My lord, I fear your hotspur[78] violence
Has brought you to the very brink of fate,
And 'tis not in my power, if I'd the will,
To save you from the sentence of the law.   325
The lords that are to be your equal judges
The House[79] has chose already, and tomorrow
So soon your trial is to be. The people
Cry loud for justice; therefore, I'll no more
Repeat my wrongs, but think you are the man   330
That once was loyal.

ESSEX.
Once!

QUEEN.
Hold! For that reason I will not upbraid you;
To triumph o'er a miserable man
Is base in any, in a queen far worse.   335
Speak now, my lord, and think what's in my power
That may not wrong your queen, and I will grant
    you.
(*Aside.*) So—I am sure in this I have not erred.

ESSEX.
Blest be my queen in mercy rich as Heav'n.
Now, now my chains are light. Come, welcome   340
    Death.
Come, all you spirits of immortality
And waft my soul unto his bright abode

---

78 hotspur] wild and unruly; also an allusion to the fiery
    rebel against Henry IV, Hotspur. Essex's supporters and
    enemies alike made ominous comparisons between the
    contemporary situation and that portrayed in Shake-
    speare's contemporary play about Bolingbroke's rebel-
    lion, *Richard II.*
79 House] here, the House of Lords, Essex's peers

That gives my queen this goodness.—Let me then
Most humbly and devoutly ask two things:
The first is, if I am condemned,   345
That execution may be done within
The Tower* walls, and so I may not suffer
Upon a public scaffold to the world.
QUEEN.
    I grant it. (*Aside.*) Oh, and wish I could do more.
ESSEX.
    Eternal blessings crown your royal head!   350
The next, the extremest bliss my soul can covet
And carry with it to the other world
As a firm passport to the Powers incensed:
Say you have pardoned me and have forgot
The rage, the guilt, and folly of your Essex.   355
QUEEN. (*Aside.*)
    Hah! What shall I do now!
Look to thyself and guard thy character.
    —Go, cure your fame and make yourself but
        what I wish you,
Then you shall find that I am still your queen.
But that you may not see I'm covetous   360
Of my forgiveness, take it from my heart:
I freely pardon now whate'er y'ave done
Amiss to me and hope you will be quitted;
Nay, I not only hope it, but shall pray for it.
My prayers to Heav'n shall be that you may clear   365
Yourself.
ESSEX.
                    Oh most renowned and godlike mercy!
Oh, let me go, your goodness is too bright
For sinful eyes like mine, or like the fiend
Of hell, when dashed from the ethereal light,   370
I shall shoot downwards with my weight of curses,
Cleave and be chained forever to the center.
QUEEN. (*Aside.*)
    He is going, ay, but whither? To his trial,
To be condemned, perhaps, and then to die.
If so, what mercy hast thou showed in that?   375
Pity and pardon! poor amends for life!
If those be well, a crocodile is blameless
That weeps for pity yet devours his prey.
And dare I not do more for Essex, I
That am a woman, and in womankind,   380
Pity's their nature? Therefore I'm resolved,
It shall be in's own power to save his life.

If I shall sin in this, witness just Heav'n,
'Tis mercy like yourselves that draws me to't,
And you'll forgive me, though the world may not.   385
—My lord, perhaps we ne'er may meet again,
And you in person may not have the power
T'implore what I too freely grant you; therefore,
That you may see you have not barely forced
An empty pity from me, here's a pledge: 390
(*Gives him a ring.*) I give it from my finger with
        this promise,
That whensoever you return this ring,
To grant in lieu of it whate'er you ask.
ESSEX. (*Receives it on his knees.*)
    Thus I receive it with far greater joy
Than the poor remnant of mankind that saw   395
The rainbow token in the heav'ns, when straight
The floods abated and the hills appeared,
And a new smiling world the waves brought forth.[80]
QUEEN.
    No more, be gone, fly with thy safety hence,
Lest horrid, dread repentance seize my soul   400
And I recall this strange misdeed.

Enter the rest with the guards.

                                            —Here take
Your prisoner, there he is, to be condemned
Or quitted by the law. Away with him.

Exeunt guards with the earl.

    Now, Nottingham, thy queen is now at rest,   405
And Essex' fate is now my least of troubles.

*Enter Countess of Essex running and weeping, then
kneels before the Queen and holds her by her robe.*

COUNTESS OF ESSEX.
    Where is my queen? Where is my royal mistress?
I throw myself for mercy here.
QUEEN.
                                            What mean'st thou!
COUNTESS OF ESSEX.
    Here I will kneel, here with my humble body   410

---

80 poor … forth] The "poor remnant" is Noah's party; the
rainbow is the sign of God's promise that He will never
destroy the world again by flood, even as its waters withdraw and reveal dry land (Gen 8:13-9:17).

Fast rooted to the earth as I'm to sorrow,
No moisture but my tears to nourish me,
Nor air but sighs, till I shall grow at last
Like a poor shriveled trunk blasted with age
And grief and never think to rise again   415
Till I've obtained the mercy I implore.

QUEEN.
Thou dost amaze me.

COUNTESS OF ESSEX.
Here let me grow the abject'st thing on earth,
A despised plant beneath the mighty cedar.
Yet if you will not pity me, I swear   420
These arms shall never cease, but grasping still
Your royal robe, shall hold you thus forever.

QUEEN.
Prithee, be quick and tell me what thou'dst have.

COUNTESS OF ESSEX.
I dare not, yet I must—my silence will
Be death, my punishment can be no more.   425
Prepare to hear, but learn to pity first,
For 'tis a story that will start your patience.
Oh, save the Earl of Essex, save his life,
My lord, whom you've condemned to prisons
     straight,
And save my life, who am no longer Rutland,   430
But Essex' faithful wife. He is my husband.

QUEEN.
Thy husband!

COUNTESS OF ESSEX.
                    Yes, too true it is, I fear,
By th'awful* darting fury in your eyes,
The threat'ning prologue of our utter ruins.   435
Married we were in secret ere my lord
Was sent by you t'his fatal government[81]
In Ireland.

QUEEN.
               Then thou art wedded to thy grave!
Dost think by this, in multiplying treasons[82]   440
And boldly braving me with them before

---

81 government] Essex was Lord Lieutenant of Ireland, that
    is, military governor.
82 treasons] A peer's marrying without his monarch's per-
    mission was a serious offense, for monarchs—Queen
    Elizabeth, especially—manipulated marriages among the
    nobility for political gain.

My face, to save thy wicked husband's life?
(*Aside.*) What will my restless fate do with me now!
—Why dost thou hold me so? Take off thy hands.

COUNTESS OF ESSEX.
Alas, I ask not mine: if that will please you,   445
I'll glut you with my torments, act whate'er
Your fury can invent. But 'tis for him,
My lord, my love, the soul of my desires.
My love's not like the common rate of women's';
It is a phoenix, there's not one such more: 450
How gladly would I burn like that rare bird,
So that the ashes of my heart could purchase
Poor Essex' life and favor of my princess.

QUEEN. (*Aside.*)
Would I were loose 'mong wilds or anywhere,
In any hell but this. Why say I hell?   455
Can there be melting lead or sulfur yet
To add more pain to what my breast endures!
—Why dost thou hang on me and tempt me still?

COUNTESS OF ESSEX.
Oh throw me not away. Would you but please
To feel my throbbing breast, you might perceive   460
At ev'ry name and very thought of Essex
How my blood starts and pulses beat for fear
And shake and tear my body like an earthquake.
And ah, which cannot choose but stir your heart
The more to pity me, th'unhappy, frighted infant,   465
The tender offspring of our guilty joys,
Pleads for its father in the very womb,
As now its wretched mother does.

QUEEN.
                              Quickly
Unloose her hands and take her from my sight.   470

COUNTESS OF ESSEX.
Oh, you will not—you'll hear me first and grant me,
Grant me poor Essex, life. Shall Essex live?
Say but you'll pardon him before I go—

QUEEN.
Help me. Will no one ease me of this burden?

The women take off her hold.

COUNTESS OF ESSEX.
Oh, I'm too weak for these inhuman creatures: 475
My strength's decayed, my joints and fingers numbed
And can no longer hold, but fall I must.
Thus like a miserable wretch that thinks

He's 'scaped from drowning, holding on a rock,
With fear and pain and his own weight oppressed   480
And dashed by ev'ry wave that shrinks his hold,

(She falls down with faintness.)

At length lets go and drops into the sea
And cries for help, but all in vain like me.
QUEEN.
  Be gone, and be delivered of thy shame:
  Let the vile insect live and grow to be   485
  A monster baser, hotter, worser far
  Than the ingrateful parents that begot it.
COUNTESS OF ESSEX.
  Ah cruel, most remorseless princess, hold:
  What has it done to draw such curses from you?
QUEEN.
  Go, let her be close prisoner in her chamber.   490
COUNTESS OF ESSEX.
  Since I must go and from my Essex part,
  Despair and Death at once come, seize my heart;
  Shut me from light, from day, ne'er to be seen
  By humankind, nor my more cruel queen.
  Yet bless her, Heav'n, and hear my loyal prayer: 495
  May you ne'er love like me nor ne'er despair,
  Ne'er see the man at his departing breath
  Whom you so love and fain would save from death,
  Lest Heav'n be deaf as you are to my cry
  And you run mad and be as cursed as I. (*Exit,*   500
    carried away by women.)
QUEEN. [*Aside.*]
  She's gone, but at her parting shot a truth
  Into my breast has pierced my soul.
  Why was I queen? And why was I not Rutland?
  Then had my princess, as myself did now,
  Giv'n Essex such a ring, and the reward   505
  Had then been mine as now the torment is.
  Oh, wretched state of monarchs! theirs is still*
  The business of the world and all the pains,
  Whilst happy subjects sleep beneath their gains.
  The meanest hind rules in his humble house,   510
  And nothing but the day sees what he does,
  But princes, like the Queen of Night so high
  Their spots are seen by ev'ry vulgar eye,
  And as the sun, the planets' glorious king,
  Gives life and growth to ev'ry mortal thing   515
  And by his motion all the world is blest,

Whilst he himself can never be at rest,
So if there are such blessings in a throne,
Kings rain 'em down, while they themselves have
  none.

Exeunt omnes.

Act V. [The Tower.*]

*Sir Walter Raleigh with the Queen's Guards, the
Lieutenant of the Tower.*

RALEIGH.
  Mr. Lieutenant, here expires my charge:
  I received orders from her Majesty
  And the Lord Steward[83] to return the prisoners
  Safe in your custody, and with you I leave 'em,
  With a charge to have 'em in a readiness,   5
  For execution will be very speedy.
LIEUTENANT.
  I shall, sir.

Enter the Countess of Nottingham.

RALEIGH.
              Hah! the Lady Nottingham!
  What makes her here?
NOTTINGHAM.
                      Where is my lord of Essex?   10
  I am commanded straight to speak with him
  And bring a message from her Majesty.
RALEIGH.
  Madam, what news can this strange visit bring?[i]
  How fares the Queen? Are her resolves yet steadfast?
NOTTINGHAM.
  No, when she heard that Essex was condemned,   15
  She started and looked pale, then blushing red,
  And said that execution should be straight,
  Then stopped and said she'd hear first from the earl.
  So she retired and passed an hour in thought,
  None daring t'interrupt her till in haste   20
  She sent for me, commanding me to go
  And tell my lord from her, she could resist
  No longer her subjects' loud demands for justice
  And therefore wished, if he had any reasons
  That were of weight to stay his execution,   25

---

83 Lord Steward] high officer of state, who in early times
   exercised important judicial functions

That he would send 'em straight by me, then blushed
Again and sighed and pressed my hand
And prayed me to be secret and deliver
What Essex should return in answer to her.

RALEIGH.
  I know not what she means, but doubt* th'event;   30
  You can tell best the cause of her disturbance.
  I will to Burleigh, and then both of us
  Will make attempts to recollect the Queen.

Exit Raleigh and guards.

NOTTINGHAM.
  Pray, bring me to my lord.
LIEUTENANT.
  Madam, I will acquaint him that y'are here.   35
    (*Exit.*)
NOTTINGHAM.
  Now dragons' blood distill through all my veins,
  And gall instead of milk swell up my breasts,
  That nothing of the woman may appear,
  But horrid cruelty and fierce revenge—

Enter Essex.

  He comes with such a gallantry and port,   40
  As if his miseries were harbingers
  And death the state to set his person* out.
  Wrongs less than mine, though in a tiger's breast,
  Might now be reconciled to such an object,
  But slighted love my sex can ne'er forget.   45
ESSEX.
  Madam, this is a miracle of favor,
  A double goodness in my royal mistress,
  T'employ the fair, the injured Nottingham,
  And 'tis no less in you to condescend
  To see a wretch like me that has deserved   50
  No favor at your hands.
NOTTINGHAM.
                     No more, my lord. The Queen,
  The gracious Queen, commends her pity to you,
  Pity by me that owe a great deal more,
  You know, and wish that I were once your queen   55
  To give you what my heart has had so long in store.
ESSEX.
  Then has my death more charms than life can
    promise,
  Since my queen pities me and you forgive me.

NOTTINGHAM.
  Hold, good my lord, that is not all: she sends
  To know if you can anything propose   60
  To mitigate your doom and stay your death,
  Which else can be no longer than this day;
  Next, if y'are satisfied with ev'ry passage
  In your late trial, if 'twere fair and legal,
  And if y'ave those exceptions that are real,   65
  She'll answer them.
ESSEX.
                 Still is my death more welcome,
  And life would be a burden to my soul,
  Since I can ne'er requite such royal goodness.
  Tell her, then, fair and charitable messenger,   70
  That Essex does acknowledge every crime,
  His guilt unworthy of such wondrous mercy,
  Thanks her bright justice and the lords his judges,
  For all was gracious and divine like her,
  And I have now no injustice to accuse,   75
  Nor enemy to blame that was the cause,
  Nor innocence to save me but the Queen.
NOTTINGHAM. (*Aside.*)
  Hah, is this true? How he undoes my hopes!
  —And is that all? Have you not one request
  To ask, that you can think the Queen will grant you?   80
ESSEX.
  I have, and humbly 'tis that she would please
  To spare my life; not that I fear to die,
  But in submission to her heav'nly justice.
  I own my life a forfeit to her power
  And therefore ought to beg it of her mercy.   85
NOTTINGHAM. (*Aside.*)
  If this be real, my revenge is lost.
  —Is there naught else that you rely upon,
  Only submitting to the Queen's mere mercy
  And barely asking her so great a grace?
  Have you no other hopes?   90
ESSEX.
                     Some hopes I have.
NOTTINGHAM.
  What are they, pray my lord? Declare 'em boldly,
  For to that only purpose I am sent.
ESSEX.
  Then I am happy, happiest of mankind,
  Blest in the rarest mercy of my queen   95
  And such a friend as you, blest in you both.

The ecstasy will let me hold no longer—
Behold this ring, the passport of my life.
At last y'ave pulled the secret from my heart:
This precious token,   100
Amidst my former triumphs in her favor
She took from off her finger and bestowed
On me, mark, with the promise of a queen,
Of her bright self less failing than an oracle,
That in what exigence or state soe'er   105
My life was in, that time when I gave back
Or should return this ring again to her,
She'd then deny me nothing I could ask.

NOTTINGHAM.
Oh, give it me, my lord, and quickly let
Me bear it to the Queen and ask your life.   110

ESSEX.
Hold, generous madam, I received it on
My knees, and on my knees I will restore it.
(*Kneels and gives Nottingham the ring.*)
Here take it, but consider what you take:
'Tis the life, blood, and very soul of Essex.   115
I've heard that by a skillful artist's hand
The bowels of a wretch were taken out
And yet he lived: you are that gallant artist;
Oh, touch it as you would the seals of life
And give it to my royal mistress' hand,   120
As you would pour my blood back in its empty
    channels
That gape and thirst like fishes on the ooze
When streams run dry and their own element
Forsakes 'em. If this should in the least miscarry,
My life's the purchase that the Queen will have for't.   125

NOTTINGHAM.
Doubt* you my care, my lord? I hope you do not.

ESSEX.
I will no more suspect my fate, nor you:
Such beauty and such merits must prevail.

Enter a gentleman.

GENTLEMAN.
Th'Earl of Southampton, having leave,
Desires to speak with you, my lord.   130

NOTTINGHAM.
                                        Repose
Your mind and take no thought but to be happy;
I'll send you tidings of a lasting life.

ESSEX.
A longer and much happier life attend
Both my good queen and you. (*Exit [with   135
    gentleman].*)

NOTTINGHAM.
                                Farewell, my lord—
Yes, a much longer life than thine, I hope,
And if thou chance to dream of such strange things,
Let it be there where lying poets feign
Elysium is, where myrtles lovely spread,   140
Trees of delicious fruit invite the taste,
And sweet Arabian plants delight the smell;
Where pleasant gardens dressed with curious care
By lovers' ghosts shall recreate thy fancy,
And there perhaps thou soon shalt meet again   145
With amorous Rutland, for she cannot choose
But be romantic now and follow thee.

Enter a gentlewoman.

WOMAN.
Madam, the Queen.

NOTTINGHAM.
Hah! that's unlucky. She come to the Tower!
Yet 'tis no matter: see him I am sure   150
She will not or at worst will be persuaded.

Enter the Queen.

QUEEN.
How now, dear Nottingham, hast seen the earl?
I left Whitehall because I could not rest
For crowds that holloed for their executions
And others that petitioned for the traitors.   155
Quick, tell me, hast thou done as I commanded?

NOTTINGHAM.
Yes madam, I have seen and spoke with him.

QUEEN.
And what has he said to thee for himself?

NOTTINGHAM.
At my first converse with him I did find him
Not totally despairing nor complaining,   160
But yet a haughty melancholy
Appeared in all his looks that showed him rather
Like one that had more care
Of future life than this.84

---

84 melancholy … this] Essex's religious melancholy,

QUEEN.

                           Well, but what said he,   165
When thou awaked'st him with the hopes of pity?

NOTTINGHAM.

  To my first question put by your command,
Which was to know if he were satisfied
In the proceedings of his lawful trial,
He answered with a careless tone and gesture   170
That it was true and he must needs confess
His trial looked most fair to all the world,
But yet he too well knew
The law that made his actions treason
Consulted but with foes and circumstances   175
And never took from Heav'n or Essex' thoughts
A precedent or cause that might condemn him,
For if they had the least been read in either,
They would have quickly found his innocence.

QUEEN.

  Hah!   180

NOTTINGHAM.

  That was but the prologue; mark what follows.

QUEEN.

  What, durst he be so bold to brand my justice!

NOTTINGHAM.

  I prayed that he would urge that sense no more,
But since he was condemned and stood in need
Of mercy, to implore it of your Majesty   185
And beg his life, which you would not deny,
For to that end I said that you were pleased
To send me to him, and then told him all,
Nay more than you commanded me to say.

QUEEN.

  What said he then? That altered him, I hope.   190

NOTTINGHAM.

  No, not at all, but as I've seen a lion
That has been played withal with gentle strokes
Has at the last been jested into madness,
So on a sudden started into passion
The furious earl: his eyes grew fiery red,   195
His words precipitate, and speech disordered.
"Let the Queen have my blood," said he, "'tis that

---

especially during his confinement at York House after
his original censure by the Star Chamber of the Privy
Council for his desertion of his post in Ireland, was extreme.

She longs for; pour it to my foes to drink,
As hunters, when the quarry is run down,
Throw to the hounds his entrails for reward.   200
I have enough to spare, but by the heavens
I swear, were all my veins like rivers full,
And if my body held a sea of blood,
I'd lose it all to the last innocent drop
Before I'd like a villain* beg my life."   205

QUEEN.

  Hold, Nottingham, and say th'art not in earnest.
Can this be true, so impudent a traitor!

NOTTINGHAM.

  That's but the gloss, the color of his treason,
But after, he did paint himself to th'life:
"Would the Queen," said he, "have me own a treason,   210
Impose upon myself a crime the law
Has found me guilty of by her command?
And so, by asking of my forfeit life,
Clear and proclaim her justice to the world
And stain myself forever? No, I'll die first."   215

QUEEN.

  Enough, I'll hear no more. You wrong him: 'tis
Impossible he should be such a devil!

NOTTINGHAM.

  Madam, I've done.

QUEEN.

                     I prithee pardon me.
But could he say all this!   220

NOTTINGHAM.

                    He did, and more,
But 'tis no matter, 'twill not be believed
If I should tell the half of what he uttered,
How insolent and how profane he used you.

QUEEN.

  You need not. I had rather   225
Believe it all than put you to the trouble
To tell it o'er again and me to hear it.
(*Aside.*) Then I am lost, betrayed by this false man:
My courage, power, my pity—all betrayed,
And like that giant, patriarch of the Jews,   230
Bereft at once both of his sight and strength
By treacherous foes, I wander in the dark,
By Essex weakened and by Essex blinded.
But then, as he prayed that his strength might grow
At once to be revenged on them and die,   235
So grant me Heav'n but so much resolution

To grope my way where I may lay but hold
On whatsoe'er this huge Colossus stands:
I'll pull the scaffold down, though o'er my head,[85]
And lose my life to be revenged on his.   240
—Well Nottingham, I have but one word more:
Talked not this wicked creature of no reason,
No obligation that I had to save
His life?

NOTTINGHAM.
           No, but far worse than I have told you.   245

QUEEN.
Sure thou art most unhappy in ill news!
No promise, nor no token did he speak of?

NOTTINGHAM.
Not the least word, and if there are such things,
I do suppose he keeps 'em to himself
For reasons that I know not.   250

QUEEN.
           'Tis most false:
He needs must tell thee all, and thou betray'st him.

NOTTINGHAM.
Your Majesty does me wrong—

QUEEN.
                Hear me,
Or I can hold no longer: say, sent he   255
No ring, no token, nor no message by thee?

NOTTINGHAM.
Not any, on the forfeit of my life.

QUEEN.
Thou liest. Can earth produce so vile a creature!
Hence from my sight and see my face no more—
Yet tarry, Nottingham, come back again.   260
(*Aside.*) This may be true, and I am still the wretch
To blame and to be pitied.—Prithee pardon me,
Forget my rage, thy queen is sorry for't.

NOTTINGHAM.
I would your Majesty instead of me
Had sent a person that you could confide in,   265
Or else that you would see the earl yourself.

QUEEN.
Prithee no more. Go to him!
No, but I'll send a message for his head.
His head's the token that my wrongs require
And his base blood the stream to quench my fury.   270
Prithee invent, for thou art wondrous witty
At such inventions, teach my feeble malice
How to torment him with a thousand deaths
Or what is worse than death. Speak, my Medea,
And thou wilt then oblige thy queen forever.   275

NOTTINGHAM.
First sign an order for his execution.

QUEEN.
Say it is done, but how to torture him!

NOTTINGHAM.
Then as the lords are carrying to the block,
Condoling both their sad misfortunes,
Which to departing souls is some delight,   280
Order a pardon for Southampton's life.
It will be worse than hell to Essex' soul,
Where 'tis a-going, to see his friend snatched from
    him,
And make him curse his so much pride and folly
That lost his own life in exchange for his.   285

QUEEN.
That was well thought on!

NOTTINGHAM.
             This is but the least.
The next will be a fatal stroke, a blow indeed,
A thousand heads to lose is not so dreadful:
Let Rutland see him at the very moment   290
Of her expiring husband; she will hang
Worse than his guilt upon him, lure his mind,
And pull it back to earth again, double
All the fierce pangs of thought and death upon him,
And make his loaded spirits sink to hell.   295

QUEEN.
Oh th'art the Machiavile[86] of all thy sex,
Thou bravest,* most heroic for invention!
Come, let's dispatch.

Enter Burleigh, Raleigh, lords, attendants, and guards.

---

85 giant … head] Samson, betrayed by his Philistine wife,
Delilah, and her allies, took God's revenge on the
Philistines by toppling their temple to Dagon on their
heads—as well as his (Judges 13-16); the story had re-
cently been magnificently retold in Milton's *Samson
Agonistes* (1671).

86 Machiavile] Machiavel (or Machiavelle), character type
of unscrupulous villain on Renaissance and Restoration
stages, named after Niccolò Machiavelli (q.v); Banks's
spelling seems worth preserving for its suggestiveness.

—My lords, see execution done on Essex,
But for Southampton, I will pardon him: 300
His crimes he may repent of; they were not
So great, but done in friendship to the other.
Act my commands with speed, [*Aside.*] that both
   of us
May straight be out of torment.—My Lord Burleigh
And you, Sir Walter Raleigh, see't performed. 305
I'll not return till you have brought the news.

Exeunt Queen and Nottingham.

RALEIGH.
   I would she were a hundred leagues from hence,
   Well, and the crown upon her head. I fear
   She'll not continue in this mind a moment.
BURLEIGH.
   Then't shall be done this moment.—Who attends? 310
   Bid the lieutenant have his prisoners ready.

Exit officer.

   Now we may hope to see fair days again
   In England, when this hov'ring cloud is vanished,
   Which hung so long betwixt our royal sun
   And us, but soon will visit us with smiles 315
   And raise her drooping subjects' hearts.

Enter the two earls, the lieutenant, and guards.

                                        —My lord,
   We bring an order for your execution
   And hope you are prepared, for you must die
   This very hour. 320
SOUTHAMPTON.
       Indeed, the time is sudden!
ESSEX.
   Is death th'event of all my flattered hopes!
   False sex, and queen, more perjured than them all!
   But die I will without the least complaint:
   My soul shall vanish silent as the dew 325
   Attracted by the sun from verdant fields
   And leaves of weeping flowers.—Come my dear
      friend,
   Partner in fate, give me thy body in
   These faithful arms, and oh! now let me tell thee
   And you, my lords, and Heav'n's my witness too, 330
   I have no weight, no heaviness on my soul,
   But that I've lost my dearest friend his life.

SOUTHAMPTON.
   And I protest by the same Powers divine
   And to the world, 'tis all my happiness,
   The greatest bliss my mind yet e'er enjoyed, 335
   Since we must die, my lord, to die together.
BURLEIGH.
   The Queen, my Lord Southampton, has been
      pleased
   To grant particular mercy to your person
   And has by us sent you a reprieve from death,
   With pardon of your treasons, and commands 340
   You to depart immediately from hence.[87]
SOUTHAMPTON.
   Oh my unguarded soul! Sure never was
   A man with mercy wounded so before.
ESSEX.
   Then I am loose to steer my wand'ring voyage,
   Like a glad vessel that has long been crossed 345
   And bound by adverse winds at last gets liberty
   And joyfully makes all the sail she can
   To reach its wished-for port.—Angels protect
   The Queen; for her my chiefest prayers shall be,
   That as in time sh'as spared my noble friend 350
   And owns his crimes worth mercy, may she ne'er
   Think so of me too late when I am dead.
   —Again Southampton, let me hold thee fast,
   For 'tis my last embrace.
SOUTHAMPTON.
   Oh be less kind, my friend, or move less pity, 355
   Or I shall sink beneath the weight of sadness.
   Witness the joy I have in life to part
   With you; witness these woman's throbs and tears:
   I weep that I am doomed to live without you
   And should have smiled to share the death of Essex. 360
ESSEX.
   Oh spare this tenderness for one that needs it,
   For her that I'll commit to all that I
   Can claim of my Southampton—oh, my wife!
   Methinks that very name should stop thy pity
   And make thee covetous of all as lost 365
   That is not meant to her. Be a kind friend
   To her as we have been to one another.

---

87 Lord Southampton … hence] Southampton was in fact
   reprieved, survived as a prisoner in the Tower until released by James I, of whom he became a favorite.

Name not the dying Essex to the Queen
Lest it should cost a tear, nor ne'er offend her.
SOUTHAMPTON.

  Oh stay, my lord, let me have one word more,   370
  One last farewell, before the greedy axe
  Shall part my friend, my only friend, from me
  And Essex from himself. I know not what
  Are called the pangs of death, but sure I am
  I feel an agony that's worse than death—   375
  Farewell.
ESSEX.

          Why that's well said. Farewell to thee.
  Then let us part, just like two travelers
  Take distant paths, only this difference is,
  Thine is the longest, mine the shortest way.   380
  Now let me go. If there's a throne in heaven
  For the most brave* of men and best of friends,
  I will bespeak it for Southampton.
SOUTHAMPTON.

  And I, while I have life, will hoard thy memory;
  When I am dead, we then shall meet again.   385
ESSEX.

  Till then farewell.
SOUTHAMPTON.

  Till then farewell.
ESSEX.

  Now on, my lords, and execute your office.
Exit Southampton. Enter Countess of Essex and women.
  My wife! Nay then, my stars will ne'er have done.
  Malicious planets, reign, I'll bear it all   390
  To your last drop of venom on my head.
  —Why, cruel, lovely creature, does thou come
  To add to sorrow, if't be possible,
  A figure more lamenting? Why this kindness,
  This killing kindness now at such a time   395
  To add more woes to thine and my misfortunes?
COUNTESS OF ESSEX.

  The Queen, my lord, has been so merciful,
  Or cruel, name it as you please, to let
  Me see my Essex ere he dies.
ESSEX.

          Has she?   400
  Then let's improve this very little time
  Our niggard fate allows us, for we're owing
  To this short space all the dear love we had
  In store for many happy promised years.

COUNTESS OF ESSEX.

  What hinders then but that we should be happy: 405
  Whilst others live long years and sip and taste
  Like niggards of their loves, we'll take whole drafts.
ESSEX.

  Then let's embrace in ecstasies and joys,
  Drink all our honey up in one short moment
  That should have served us for our winter store,   410
  Be lavish and profuse like wanton heirs
  That waste their whole estates at once,
  For the kind Queen takes care and has ordained
  That we shall never live to want.[88]
BURLEIGH.

          My lord,   415
  Prepare, the very utmost time's at hand,
  And we must straight perform the Queen's
    command
  In leading you to justice.
COUNTESS OF ESSEX.

  Hold, good Lucifer,
  Be kind a little and defer damnation.   420
  Thou canst not think how I will worship thee:
  No Indian shall adore thee as I will;
  Thou shalt have martyrs and whole hecatombs
  Of slaughtered innocents to suck their blood,
  Widow's estates and orphans without number,   425
  Manors and parks more than thy lust requires,
  Till thou shalt die and leave a king's estate
  Behind thee.
ESSEX.

          Prithee spare thy precious heart,
  That fluttering so with passion in thy breast   430
  Has almost bruised its tenderness to death.
COUNTESS OF ESSEX.

  Why ask I him and think of pity there!
  From him on whom kind Heav'n has set a mark,
  A heap of rubbish at the door to show
  No cleanly virtue can inhabit there—   435
  Malicious toad, and which is worse, foul Cecil,
  I tell thee Essex soon shall reign in heav'n,
  While thou shalt grovel in the den of hell,

---

88 wanton heirs … want] Ironically, a major reason for
the desperation of the historical Essex was that, out of
favor with the Court, he was on the brink of financial
disaster.

Roar like the damned, and tremble to behold him.
Go, share dominions with the powers of hell, 440
For Lucifer himself will ne'er dispute
Thy great desert in wickedness above him,
Nor who's the uglier fiend, thyself or he.

RALEIGH.
My lord, you think not of the Queen's commands,
And can you stand thus unconcerned and hear 445
Yourself so much abused?

BURLEIGH.
              Be patient, Raleigh,
The pain is all her own and hurts not Cecil.
She will be weary sooner than myself—
Poor innocent and most unhappy lady, 450
I pity her.

COUNTESS OF ESSEX.
        Why, dost thou pity me!
Nay then, I'm fall'n into a low estate
Indeed. If Hell compassionates my miseries,
They must be greater than the damned endure. 455
I prithee pardon me.—Ah my loved lord,
My heart begins to break. Let me go with thee
And see the fatal blow given to my Essex.
That will be sure to rid me soon of torments,
And 'twill be kindness in thee—do, my lord, 460
Then we shall both be quit of pain together.

ESSEX.
Ah why was I condemned to this? What man
But Essex ever felt a weight like this!

COUNTESS OF ESSEX.
Oh, we must never part. Support my head,
My sinking head, and lay it to the pulse, 465
The throbbing pulse that beats about thy heart,
'Tis music to my senses. Oh my love!
I have no tears left in me that should ease
A wretch that longs for pity; I am past
All pity, and my poor tormented heart 470
And spirits within are quite consumed, and tears,
Which is the balm, the scorpions' blood that cures
The biting pain of sorrow, quite have left me,
And I am now a wretched, hopeless creature,
Full of substantial misery without 475
One drop of remedy.

ESSEX.
           Th'art pale, thy breath
Grows chill and like the morning air on roses

Leaves a cold dew upon thy redder lips.
—She strives and holds me like a drowning wretch. 480
Oh now my lords, if pity ever blest you,
If you were never nursed by tigers, help me.
Now, now, you cruel heav'ns, I plainly see:
'Tis not your swords, your axes, nor diseases
Which make the death of man so feared and painful, 485
But 'tis such horrid accidents as these.
She opens her eyes, which with a waning look,
Like sickly stars, give a faint glimmering light.

COUNTESS OF ESSEX.
Where is my love?
Oh think not to get loose, for I'm resolved 490
To stick more close to thee than life, and when
That's going, mine shall run the race with thine,
And both together reach the happy goal.

ESSEX.
Now I am shocked: torn up and rooted all
That's human in me.—What, you merciless 495
  Heavens,
What is't that makes poor man—distracted, mad,
Profane—to curse the day, himself, the Heavens
That made him, but less miseries than mine?
Why, why, you Powers, do you exact from man
More than your world and all that live beside! 500
The sea is never calm when tempests blow;
Tall woods and cedars murmur at the wind;
And when your horrid earthquakes cleave the ground,
The center groans and Nature takes its part,
As if they did design to break your laws 505
And shake your fetters off; nay your own heavens,
When thunders roar, rebel, the sun engages,
And all the warring elements resist;
Heav'n, seas, and land are suffered to contend,
But man alone is cursed if he complain. 510
—Farewell my everlasting love, 'tis vain,
'Tis all in vain against resistless Fate
That pulls me from thee. (*Gives her a letter.*)
Here, give this paper to the Queen, which when
She reads, perhaps she will be kind to thee. 515

COUNTESS OF ESSEX.
Wilt thou not let me go?
I am prepared to see the deadly stroke,
And at that time the fatal axe falls on thee
It will be sure to cut the twisted cord
Of both our lives asunder. 520

ESSEX.

                We must part.
Thou miracle of love and virtues all,
Farewell, and may thy Essex' sad misfortunes
Be doubled all in blessings on thy soul.
Still, still thou grasps me like th'fangs of death—   525
Hah! now she faints, and like a wretch
Striving to climb a steep and slippery beach
With many hard attempts gets up and still
Slides down again, so she lets go at last
Her eager hold and sinks beneath her weight.   530
—Support her all—

BURLEIGH.

                My lord, she will recover.
Pray, leave her with her women* and make use
Of this so kind an opportunity
To part with her.   535

ESSEX.

           Cruel, hard-hearted Burleigh!
Most barbarous Cecil.

BURLEIGH.

              See, my lord,
She soon will come t'herself, and you must leave her.
—Haste, away.   540

LIEUTENANT.

Make way there.

ESSEX.

Look to her, faithful servants. While she lives,
She'll be a tender mistress to you all.
—Come, push me off then: Since I must swim o'er,
Why do I stand thus shivering on the shore?   545
'Tis but a breath, and I no more shall think,
Mix with the sun or into atoms shrink.
—Lift up thy eyes no more in search of mine
Till I am dead, then glad the world with thine.
This kiss (Oh that it would forever last!)   550
Gives me of immortality a taste—
Farewell:
May all that's past, when thou recover'st, seem
Like a glad waking from a fearful dream.

Exeunt Essex to execution, Burleigh, Raleigh, Lieutenant
and guards. Manent Countess of Essex with women.

WOMAN.

See, she revives.   555

COUNTESS OF ESSEX.

           Where is my Essex, where?

WOMAN.

Alas I fear by this time he's no more.

COUNTESS OF ESSEX.

Why did you wake me then from such bright
   objects?
I saw my Essex mount with angel wings
(Whilst I rode on the beauteous cherubim)   560
And took me on 'em, bore me o'er the world
Through everlasting skies, eternal light.

WOMAN.

Be comforted.

COUNTESS OF ESSEX.

           Sure we're the only pair
Can boast of such a pomp of misery,   565
And none was e'er substantially so cursed
Since the first couple that knew sorrow first.
Yet they were happy and for Paradise
Found a new world unskilled, unfraught with vice,
No tyrant to molest 'em nor no sword.   570
All that had life obedience did afford;
No pride but labor there and healthful pains,
Nor thief to rob them of their honest gains:
Ambition, now the plague of ev'ry thought,
Then was not known or else was unbegot.   575

Enter the Queen, Countess of Nottingham, lords and
attendants.

QUEEN.

Behold where the poor Rutland lies, almost
As dead and low as Essex in his grave
Can be, and I want* but a very little
To be more miserable than 'em both.
—Rise, rise unfortunate and mournful Rutland.   580
I know not what to call thee now, but wish
I could not call thee by the name of Essex.
Rise and behold thy Queen, I say,
That bends to take thee in her arms.

COUNTESS OF ESSEX.

Oh never think to charm me with such sounds,   585
Such hopes that are too distant from my soul,
For 'tis but preaching Heav'n to one that's damned.
Oh take your pity back, most cruel Queen,
Give it to those that want it for a cure;
My griefs are mortal; remedies are vain   590
And thrown away on such a wretch as I.
Here is a paper from my lord to you:
It was his last request that you would read it.

QUEEN.
Give't me. [*Aside.*] But how much more welcome had
The ring been in its stead. (*Reads to herself.*)   595
NOTTINGHAM. (*Aside.*)
                              Hah! I'm betrayed.
QUEEN.
Haste, see if execution yet be done.
If not, prevent it. Fly with angels' wings.
Officer goes out.
—Oh thou far worse than serpent! worse than
  woman!
—Ah Rutland, here's the cruel cause of both our   600
  woes.
Mark this, and help to curse her for thy husband:
(*Reads.*)
  "Madam, I receive my death with the
  willingness and submission of a subject, and as
  it is the will of Heaven and of your Majesty,
  with this request: that you would be pleased to   605
  bestow that royal pity on my poor wife which is
  denied to me, and my last, flying breath shall
  bless you. I have but one thing to repent of
  since my sentence, which is that I sent the ring
  by Nottingham, fearing it should once put my   610
  queen in mind of her broken vow. Essex."
Repentance, horrors, plagues, and deadly poisons
Worse than a thousand deaths torment thy soul.
NOTTINGHAM.
Madam—
QUEEN.
Condemn me first to hear the groans of ghosts,   615
The croaks of ravens, and the damned in torments,
Just Heaven, 'tis music to what thou canst utter.
Be gone. Fly to that utmost verge of earth
Where the globe's bounded with eternity,
And never more be seen of humankind,   620
Cursed with long life and with a fear to die,
With thy guilt ever in thy memory,
And Essex' ghost be still* before thy eye.
NOTTINGHAM.
I do confess—
QUEEN.
Quick, bear her from my sight. Her words are   625
  blasting;
Her eyes are basilisks; infection reigns
Where'er she breaths. Go, shut her in a cave
Or chain her to some rock whole worlds from hence,

The distance is too near. There let her live
Howling to th'seas to rid her of her pain,   630
For she and I must never meet again.
Away with her.
NOTTINGHAM.
I go, but have this comfort in my doom:
I leave you with greater plagues at home. (*Exit.*)

Enter Burleigh and Raleigh.

BURLEIGH.
Madam, your orders came too late—   635
The earl was dead.
QUEEN.
          Then I wish thou wert dead that say'st it.
But I'll be just and curse none but myself.
What said he when he came so soon to die?
BURLEIGH.
Indeed his end, made so by woeful casualties,[89]   640
Was very sad and full of pity.
But at the block, all hero he appeared
Or else, to give him a more Christian title,
A martyr armed with resolution,
Said little, but did bless your Majesty   645
And died full of forgiveness to the world,
As was, no doubt, his soul that soon expired.
QUEEN.
Come, thou choice relic of lamented Essex,
Call me no more by th'name of Queen but friend.
When thy dear husband's death revenged shall be,   650
Pity my fate, but lay no guilt on me,
Since 'tis th'Almighty's pleasure, though severe,
To punish thus his faithful regents here,
To lay on kings his hardest task of rule,
And yet has given 'em but a human soul.   655
The subtle paths of traitors' hearts to view
Reason's too dark, a hundred eyes too few,
Yet when by subjects we have been betrayed,
The blame is ours, their crimes on us are laid,
And that which makes a monarch's happiness   660
Is not in reigning well, but with success.

Exeunt omnes.

                    FINIS.

---

89 casualties] accidents, mischances: Banks probably alludes
  to the fact that it took three chops with the axe to sever
  Essex's head.

Textual Notes

a Copytext is the first edition, a 1682 quarto (Q1). Also consulted were the second edition in 1685 (Q2), the third edition in 1693 (Q3), the fourth edition in 1699 (Q4), and the seventh edition in 1712 (Q7). The only modern edition is a 1939 facsimile of Q1 (Blair).

b know] Q3, Q4; knew Q1, Q2, Q7

c Essex'] Q3; Essex's Q1, Q2, Q4, Q7

d Essex] Rutland Q1-4, Q7, as she is listed in the dramatis personae, but since Banks designates her Countess of Essex whenever she speaks—and since she is clandestinely married to Essex—we have thus regularized her name throughout.

e as] *om.* Q1-4, Q7 but demanded by both the metrics and the simile

f Countess of Essex] Earl of Rutland Q1-3; Rutland Q4, Q7; Blair emends to Countess of Rutland in a footnote.

g Indeed … well] Q1-4, Q7 print as one line, but the metrics dictate a break.

h arm me] Arme Q1; Arm Q2-4, Q7

i Madam, what news … bring?] Q2-3; Madam, / What news … bring? Q1, Q4, Q7

j awaked'st] Q4, Q7; awakest Q1-3

Lucius Junius Brutus, Father of His Country[a]

by Nathaniel Lee (ca. 1645/52-1692)

edited by Richard E. Brown

Nathaniel Lee's *Brutus*, widely regarded as one of the three leading tragedies of the Restoration, is also a great might-have-been of theatrical history. Though it was received with applause, the play was banned after six performances by the government censor—presumably because of its allusions to the Popish Plot, the Exclusion Crisis, and the tide of Whig dominance that occurred in late 1680—and was never revived. A modern controversy has arisen as to exactly how a politically sensitive London audience would have interpreted the character of Brutus, whose depiction may be seen as alluding either to Charles II or Oliver Cromwell, or to both. In this respect the play perhaps reflects an ambiguity of classical history with which Lee was familiar. The Roman writer Livy praises the legendary Brutus's execution of his rebellious sons as patriotic and exemplary, while Plutarch and Dionysius of Halicarnassus, both Greeks, describe the ancient founder of the Roman republic as inhumanly stern and his virtue difficult to appreciate.

Lee's Brutus gains further complexity from his role as a blocking figure in the melancholy romantic plot involving Titus and Teraminta and from his conduct in the wrenching interviews that prepare his son Titus to accept the death sentence. To the two strands of blank-verse political tragedy and domestic pathos Lee adds a third in the boisterous street scenes depicting the demogogue Vinditius (a satire of Titus Oates) and the Roman mob. Vinditius was played by the noted comedian James Nokes, a fact that suggests humor may have been sought in staging some of the play's spectacles, even including the parodic Mass in Act IV that features human torture and the drinking of blood.

In his day "mad Nat. Lee" was famous for the exclamatory, ungrammatical propulsion of his long speeches. This thrilling quality is sometimes evident in the oratory of *Brutus*, though in his dedication of the play to a noble patron Lee advertises his struggle to achieve a tone of stately magnificence suitable for the depiction of Roman history:

> There are some subjects that require but half the strength of a great poet, but when Greece or old Rome come in play, the nature, wit, and vigor of foremost Shakespeare, the judgment and force of Jonson with all his borrowed mastery from the ancients, will scarce suffice for so terrible a grapple. The poet must elevate his fancy with the mightiest imagination; he must run back so many hundred years, take a just prospect of the spirit of those times without the least thought of ours, for if his eye should swerve so low, his muse will grow giddy with the vastness of the distance, fall at once, and forever lose the majesty of the first design. . . . In such a writing there must be greatness of thought without bombast; remoteness without monstrousness; virtue armed with severity, not in iron bodies; solid wit without modern affectation; smoothness without gloss, speaking out without cracking the voice or straining the lungs.

Thomas Betterton, the Duke's Company's leading male actor, presumably brought to the role of Brutus his usual dignified restraint, through which he was said to be capable of expressing extraordinary emotional power. The young Elizabeth Barry's portrayal of Teraminta was surely one of the stepping stones to her success less than two years later as Belvidera in Otway's *Venice Preserved*, the crowning achievement in the female pathetic line.

DRAMATIS PERSONAE

[MEN]

Lucius Junius Brutus.
Titus.
Tiberius.
Collatinus.
Valerius.
Horatius.
Aquilius.
Vitellius.
Junius.
Fecilian priests
Vinditius.
Fabritius.
Citizens, etc.
[Mutius.]
[Herminius.]
[Lartius.]
[Flaminius.]
[Lucretius.]
[Trebonius.]
[Servilius.]
[Minutius.]
[Pomponius.]

[WOMEN]

Sempronia.
Lucrece.
Teraminta.
[Aquilia.]
[Vitellia.]

SCENE: ROME.

Lucius Junius Brutus, Father of His Country.

... *caeloque invectus aperto*
Flectit equos curruque volans dat lora secunda.
Virg. lib. 4.[1]

---

[1] *caeloque ... 4.*] Virgil, *Aeneid* I.155-156: "Soon as the Sire, looking forth upon the waters and driving under a clear sky, guides his steeds and, flying onwards, gives rein to his willing car" (Loeb). The Sire is Neptune, god of the sea, who calms a storm after Aeneas's ship is nearly wrecked during his escape from the Fall of Troy.

Act I.

Enter Titus, Teraminta.

TITUS.

Oh Teraminta, why this face of tears?
Since first I saw thee till this happy day,
Thus hast thou passed thy melancholy hours,
Ev'n in the court retired, stretched on a bed
In some dark room with all the curtains drawn,   5
Or in some garden o'er a flow'ry bank
Melting thy sorrows in the murmuring stream,
Or in some pathless wilderness a-musing,
Plucking the mossy bark of some old tree,
Or poring like a sibyl on the leaves.   10
What, now the priest should join us! Oh the gods!
What can you proffer me in vast exchange
For this ensuing night? Not all the days
Of crowning kings, of conquering generals,
Not all the expectation of hereafter,   15
With what bright Fame can give in th'other world
Should purchase thee this night one minute from me.

TERAMINTA.

Oh Titus! If since first I saw the light,
Since I began to think on my misfortunes
And take a prospect of my certain woes,   20
If my sad soul has entertained a hope
Of pleasure here or harbored any joy
But what the presence of my Titus gave me,
Add, add, you cruel gods, to what I bear
And break my heart before him.   25

TITUS.

Break first th'eternal Chain,[2] for when thou'rt gone
The world to me is chaos. Yes, Teraminta,
So close the everlasting Sisters[3] wove us,
Whene'er we part, the strings of both must crack.
Once more I do entreat thee, give the grave   30
Thy sadness. Let me press thee in my arms,
My fairest bride, my only lightness here,
Tune of my heart and charmer of my eyes,
Nay, thou shalt learn the ecstasy from me;
I'll make thee smile with my extravagant passion,   35
Drive thy pale fears away, and ere the morn

---

[2] th'eternal Chain] the Great Chain of Being, a concept of universal order popular in the Seventeenth Century
[3] Sisters] the three Fates that weave human lives

I swear, Oh Teraminta, oh my love,
Cold as thou art, I'll warm thee into blushes.
TERAMINTA.
Oh Titus! May I, ought I to believe you?
Remember, sir, I am the blood of Tarquin,⁴   40
The basest too.
TITUS.
                                    Thou art the blood of Heav'n,
The kindest influence of the teeming stars,
No seed of Tarquin. No, 'tis forged t'abuse thee.
A god thy father was, a goddess was his wife;   45
The wood nymphs found thee on a bed of roses,
Lapped in the sweets and beauties of the spring;
Diana fostered thee with nectar dews;
Thus tender, blooming, chaste, she gave thee me
To build a temple sacred to her name,   50
Which I will do and wed thee there again.
TERAMINTA.
Swear then, my Titus, swear you'll ne'er upbraid me,
Swear that your love shall last like mine forever;
No turn of state or empire, no misfortune,
Shall e'er estrange you from me. Swear, I say,   55
That, if you should prove false, I may at least
Have something still to answer to my fate;⁵
Swear, swear, my lord, that you will never hate me,
But to your death still cherish in your bosom
The poor, the fond, the wretched Teraminta.   60
TITUS.
Till death! Nay, after death if possible.
Dissolve me still* with questions of this nature,
While I return my answer all in oaths.
More than thou canst demand I swear to do.
This night, this night shall tell thee how I love thee.   65
When words are at a loss, and the mute soul
Pours out herself in sighs and gasping joys,
Life grasps the pangs of bliss and murmuring
    pleasures.
Thou shalt confess all language then is vile
And yet believe me most without my vowing.   70

Enter Brutus⁶ with a flamen.

But see, my father with a flamen here!
The court comes on; let's slip the busy crowd
And steal into the eternal knot of love.

Exeunt.

BRUTUS.
Did Sextus, say'st thou, lie at Collatia,⁷
At Collatine's house last night?   75
FLAMEN.
                                    My lord, he did,
Where he, with Collatine and many others,
Had been some nights before.
BRUTUS.
                                    Hah! If before,
Why did he come again?   80
FLAMEN.
                                    Because, as rumor spreads,
He fell most passionately in love with her.
BRUTUS.
What then?
FLAMEN.
                                    Why, is't not strange?
BRUTUS.
                                    Is she not handsome?   85
FLAMEN.
Oh, very handsome.
BRUTUS.
                                    Then 'tis not strange at all.
What, for a king's son to love another man's wife!
Why, sir, I've known the King has done the same.
Faith, I myself, who am not used to caper,   90
Have sometimes had th'unlawful itch upon me.
Nay prithee, priest, come thou and help the
    number.⁸
Hah! My old boy, the company is not scandalous;
Let's go to hell together. Confess the truth,
Didst thou ne'er steal from the gods an hour or so   95
To mumble a new prayer—
With a young fleshy whore in a bawdy corner? Hah!
FLAMEN.
My lord, your servant. [*Aside.*] Is this the fool? the
    madman?

---

4 Tarquin] the dynasty ruling Rome, associated with despotic reign
5 answer to my fate] I.e., I'll justify myself by saying I naturally believed you because you swore to be faithful.
6 *Brutus*] Latin nickname: half-wit, dullard
7 Collatia] town near Rome, home of Collatinus and his wife, Lucrece
8 help the number] add to the number

Let him be what he will, he spoke the truth.
If other fools be thus, they're dangerous fellows. 100
   (*Exit.*)

BRUTUS.
Occasion seems in view; something there is
In Tarquin's last abode at Collatine's.
Late entertained, and early gone this morning?
The matron ruffled, wet, and dropping tears,
As if she had lost her wealth in some black storm! 105
As in the body, on some great surprise,
The heart still calls from the discolored face,
From every part the life and spirits down,
So Lucrece comes to Rome and summons all her
   blood.
Lucrece is fair, but chaste as the fanned snow 110
Twice bolted o'er by the bleak northern blasts;
So lies this starry cold and frozen beauty,
Still watched and guarded by her waking virtue,
A pattern, though I fear inimitable,
For all succeeding wives. Oh Brutus! Brutus! 115
When will the tedious gods permit thy soul
To walk abroad in her own majesty
And throw this visor of thy madness from thee?
Oh, what but infinite spirit, propped by Fate
For empire's weight to turn on, could endure 120
As thou hast done the labors of an age,
All follies, scoffs, reproaches, pities, scorns,
Indignities almost to blows sustained
For twenty pressing years, and by a Roman?
To act deformity in thousand shapes 125
To please the greater monster of the two,[9]
That cries, "Bring forth the beast and let him
   tumble."
With all variety of aping madness
To bray and bear more than the ass's burden;
Sometimes to hoot and scream like midnight owls, 130
Then screw my limbs like a distorted satyr,
The world's grimace, th'eternal laughingstock
Of town and court, the block, the jest of Rome;
Yet all the while not to my dearest friend,
To my own children, nor my bosom wife 135
Disclose the weighty secret of my soul.

---

[9] a Roman? … the greater monster of the two] probably
   one of King Tarquin's sons, with whom the historical
   LJB was said to have been brought up as a playmate

Oh Rome, oh Mother, be thou th'impartial judge
If this be virtue, which yet wants* a name,
Which never any age could parallel,
And worthy of the foremost of thy sons. 140

Enter Horatius, Mutius.

MUTIUS.
Horatius, heard'st thou where Sextus was last night?
HORATIUS.
Yes, at Collatia. 'Tis the buzz of Rome.
'Tis more than guessed that there has been foul play,
Else why should Lucrece come in this sad manner
To old Lucretius' house and summon thither 145
Her father, husband, each distinct relation?

Enter Fabritius with courtiers.

MUTIUS.
Scatter it through the city, raise the people,
And find Valerius out. Away, Horatius.

[Mutius and Horatius] exeunt severally.

FABRITIUS.
Prithee, let's talk no more on't. Look, here's Lord
Brutus. Come, come, we'll divert ourselves. For 'tis 150
but just that we who sit at the helm should now and
then unruffle our state affairs with the impertinence
of a fool.——Prithee, Brutus, what's a clock?[10]
BRUTUS.
Clotho, Lachesis, Atropos;[11] the Fates are three.
Let them but strike, and I'll lead you a dance, my 155
masters.
FABRITIUS.
But hark you, Brutus, dost thou hear the news of
Lucrece?
BRUTUS.
Yes, yes, and I heard of the wager that was laid
among you, among you whoring lords at the siege 160
of Ardea[12]——hah, boy!——about your handsome
wives.

---

[10] what's a clock?] what's going on?

[11] Clotho, Lachesis, Atropos] names of the Fates: Clotho
   spins the thread, Lachesis allots it, Atropos (the inflexible) cuts it.

[12] Ardea] town in nearby Latium, conquered by Rome in
   442 BCE

FABRITIUS.

Well, and how, and how?

BRUTUS.

How you bounced from the board, took horse, and
rode like madmen to find the gentle* Lucrece at 165
Collatia. But how found her? Why, working with
her maids at midnight. Was not this monstrous
and quite out of the fashion? Fine stuff indeed for
a lady of honor, when her husband was out of the
way, to sit weaving and pinking and pricking of 170
arras?[13] Now by this light, my lord, your wife
made better use of her pincushion.

FABRITIUS.

My wife, my lord? By Mars, my wife!

BRUTUS.

Why, should she not, when all the royal nurses do
the same? What, what, my lord, did you not find 175
'em at it when you came from Collatia to Rome?
Lartius, your wife? and yours, Flaminius, with
Tullia's boys[14] turning the crystals up,[15] dashing the
windows, and the fates defying? Now by the gods, I
think 'twas civil in you, discreetly done, sirs, not to 180
interrupt 'em. But for your wife, Fabritius, I'll be
sworn for her, she would not keep 'em company.

FABRITIUS.

No, marry,* would she not; she hates debauches.
How have I heard her rail at Terentia and tell her next
her heart upon the qualms[16] that drinking wine so 185
late and tippling spirits would be the death of her.

BRUTUS.

Hark you, gentlemen, if you would but be secret
now, I could unfold such a business—my life on't,
a very plot upon the court.

FABRITIUS.

Out with it. We swear secrecy. 190

BRUTUS.

Why thus then. Tomorrow Tullia goes to the camp,
and I, being master of the household, have
command to sweep the court of all its furniture
and send it packing to the wars: pandars,
sycophants, upstart rogues; fine knaves and surly 195

---

13 pricking of arras] sewing designs on tapestry
14 Tullia's boys] Tullia, King Tarquin's wife, bore three sons.
15 turning the crystals up] overturning wine glasses
16 upon the qualms] in a fit of illness or nausea

rascals; flatterers; easy, supple, cringing, passing,
smiling villains—all, all to the wars.

FABRITIUS.

By Mars, I do not like this plot.

BRUTUS.

Why, is it not a plot? A plot upon yourselves, your
persons, families, and your relations; even to your 200
wives, mothers, sisters, all your kindred. For whores
too are included, setters[17] too, and whore-procurers;
bag and baggage—all, all to the wars. All hence, all
rubbish, lumber out, and not a bawd be left behind
to put you in hope of hatching whores hereafter. 205

FABRITIUS.

Hark, Lartius, he'll run from fooling to direct
madness and beat our brains out. The devil take
the hindmost.—Your servant, sweet Brutus, noble,
honorable Brutus.

[Fabritius and courtiers] exeunt. Enter Titus.

TITUS.

'Tis done, 'tis done, auspicious Heav'n has joined 210
us,
And I this night shall hold her in my arms.
—Oh sir!

BRUTUS.

Oh sir! That exclamation was too high.
Such raptures ill become the troubled times;
No more of 'em. And by the way, my Titus, 215
Renounce your Teraminta.

TITUS.

Hah, my lord!

BRUTUS.

How now, my boy?

TITUS.

Your counsel comes too late, sir.

BRUTUS.

Your reply, sir, 220
Comes too ill-mannered, pert and saucy, sir.

TITUS.

Sir, I am married.

BRUTUS.

What, without my knowledge?

TITUS.

My lord, I ask your pardon; but that Hymen—

---

17 setters] type of street con artists

BRUTUS.

Thou lie'st. That honorable god would scorn it. 225
Some bawdy flamen shuffled you together;
Priapus locked you, while the bacchanals
Sang your detested epithalamium.
Which of thy blood were the cursed witnesses?
Who would be there at such polluted rites 230
But goats, baboons, some chatt'ring old silenus,
Or satyrs grinning at your slimy joys?

TITUS.

Oh all the gods! My lord, your son is married
To Tarquin's—

BRUTUS.

    Bastard. 235

TITUS.

     No, his daughter.

BRUTUS.

      No matter.
To any of his blood, if it be his,
There is such natural contagion in it,
Such a congenial devil in his spirit, 240
Name, lineage, stock, that but to own a part
Of his relation is to profess thyself
Sworn slave of Hell and bondman to the Furies.
Thou art not married.

TITUS.

    Oh, is this possible? 245
This change that I behold? No part of him
The same; nor eyes, nor mien, nor voice, nor gesture!

BRUTUS.

Oh, that the gods would give my arm the vigor
To shake this soft, effeminate, lazy soul
Forth from thy bosom. No, degenerate boy, 250
Brutus is not the same: the gods have waked him
From dead stupidity* to be a sourge,
A living torment to thy disobedience.
Look on my face, view my eyes flame, and tell me
If aught thou see'st but glory and revenge, 255
A bloodshot anger, and a burst of fury,
When I but think of Tarquin.—Damn the monster.
Fetch him, you judges of th'eternal deep,
Arraign him, chain him, plunge him in double fires.
—If after this thou see'st a tenderness, 260
A woman's tear come o'er my resolution,
Think, Titus, think, my son, 'tis nature's fault,
Not Roman Brutus, but a father now.

TITUS.

Oh, let me fall low as the earth permits me
And thank the gods for this most happy change, 265
That you are now, although to my confusion,
That awful,* godlike, and commanding Brutus
Which I so oft have wished you, which sometimes
I thought imperfectly you were, or might be,
When I have taken unawares your soul 270
At a broad glance and forced her to retire.
Ah, my dear lord, you need not add new threats,
New marks of anger to complete my ruin;
Your Titus has enough to break his heart
When he remembers that you durst not trust him. 275
Yes, yes, my lord, I have a thousand frailties;
The mold you cast me in, the breath, the blood,
And spirit which you gave me are unlike
The godlike author. Yet you gave 'em, sir,
And sure, if you had pleased to honor me, 280
T'immortalize my name to after ages
By'imparting your high cares, I should have found
At least so much hereditary virtue
As not to have divulged them.

BRUTUS.

     Rise, my son, 285
Be satisfied thou art the first that know'st me.
A thousand accidents and fated causes
Rush against every bulwark I can raise
And half unhinge my soul. For now's the time
To shake the building of the Tyrant down. 290
As from Night's womb the glorious Day breaks forth
And seems to kindle from the setting stars,
So from the blackness of young Tarquin's crime
And furnace of his lust the virtuous soul
Of Junius Brutus catches bright occasion. 295
I see the pillars of his kingdom totter.
The rape of Lucrece is the midnight lantern
That lights my genius* down to the foundation.
Leave me to work, my Titus—oh my son—
For from this spark a lightning shall arise 300
That must ere night purge all the Roman air,
And then the thunder of his ruin follows.
No more, but haste thee to Lucretius.
I hear the multitude and must among them.
Away, my son. 305

TITUS.

    Bound and obedient ever. (*Exit.*)

Enter Vinditius with plebeians.

FIRST CITIZEN.

Jupiter defend us! I think the firmament is all
alight on fire.b Now neighbor, as you were saying,
as to the cause of lightning and thunder, and for
the nature of prodigies.   310

VINDITIUS.

What! A tailor, and talk of lightning and thunder?
Why, thou walking shred, thou moving bottom,
thou upright needle, thou shaving-edging skirt,
thou flip-flap of a man, thou vaulting flea, thou
nit, thou nothing, dost thou talk of prodigies when   315
I am by? *O tempora, O mores!*18 But neighbors, as
I was saying, what think you of Valerius?

ALL.

Valerius, Valerius!

VINDITIUS.

I know you are piping hot for sedition; you all gape
for rebellion. But what's the near?19 For look you,   320
sirs, we the people in the body politic are but the
guts of government; therefore, we may rumble and
grumble and croak our hearts out, if we have never
a head. Why, how shall we be nourished? Therefore
I say, let us get us a head, a head, my masters.   325

BRUTUS.

Protect me, Jove, and guard me from the phantom!
Can this so horrid apparition be,
Or is it but the making of my fancy?

VINDITIUS.

Hah, Brutus! What, where is this apparition?

FIRST CITIZEN.

This is the tribune of the Celeres,20   330
A notable headpiece, and the King's jester.

BRUTUS.

By Jove, a prodigy!

VINDITIUS.

Nay, like enough: the gods are very angry.
I know they are, they told me so themselves,
For look you, neighbors, I for my own part   335

---

18 *O tempora! O mores!*] proverbial Latin phrase expressing
disapproval: "O what times! O what customs!" From
Cicero's denunciation of Cataline's conspiracy.

19 the near] nearer to one's end or purpose (*OED*)

20 tribune of the Celeres] leader of the king's bodyguard
(an ironic position, in LJB's case)

Have seen today fourscore and nineteen prodigies
and a half.

BRUTUS.

But this is a whole one. Oh, most horrible!
Look, Vinditius, yonder, o'er that part
O'the Capitol, just, just there, man, yonder, look.

VINDITIUS.

Hah, my lord!   340

BRUTUS.

I always took thee for a quick-sighted fellow.
What, art thou blind? Why yonder, all o'fire,
It vomits lightning; 'tis a monstrous dragon.

VINDITIUS.

Oh, I see it. Oh Jupiter and Juno! By the gods I see it. 345
Oh neighbors, look, look, look on his filthy nostrils!
'T has eyes like flaming saucers and a belly
Like a burning caldron, with such a swinging tail!
And oh, a thing, a thing that's all o'fire!

BRUTUS.

Hah! Now it fronts us with a head that's marked   350
With Tarquin's name. And see, 'tis thunderstruck!
Look yonder how it whizzes through the air!
The gods have struck it down; 'tis gone, 'tis
vanquished.
Oh neighbors, what, what should this portent mean?

VINDITIUS.

Mean! Why, it's plain; did we not see the mark   355
Upon the beast? Tarquin's the dragon, neighbors,
Tarquin's the dragon, and the gods shall swinge him.

ALL.

A dragon! A Tarquin!

FIRST CITIZEN.

                        For my part, I saw nothing.

VINDITIUS.

How, rogue? Why, this is prodigy on prodigy!   360
Down with him, knock him down. What, not see
the dragon?

FIRST CITIZEN.

Mercy, I did, I did, a huge monstrous dragon.

BRUTUS.

So—not a word of this, my masters, not for your
lives.
Meet me anon at the Forum;21 but not a word.

---

21 Forum] open-air marketplace and social center of ancient Rome

Vinditius, tell 'em the tribune of the Celeres   365
Intends this night to give them an oration.

Exeunt Vinditius and rabble. Enter Lucrece, Valerius,
Lucretius, Mutius, Herminius, Horatius, Titus,
Tiberius, Collatinus.

BRUTUS.

Hah! In the open air? So near, you gods?
So ripe your judgments? Nay, then let 'em break
And burst the hearts of those that have deserved
   them.

LUCRECE.

Oh Collatine! Art thou come?   370
Alas, my husband! Oh my love! My lord!

COLLATINUS.

Oh Lucrece! See, I have obeyed thy summons;
I have thee in my arms. But speak, my fair,
Say, is all well?

LUCRECE.

            Away, and do not touch me.   375
Stand near, but touch me not.—My father too!
Lucretius, art thou here?

LUCRETIUS.

                Thou see'st I am.
Haste, and relate thy lamentable story.

LUCRECE.

If there be gods, oh, will they not revenge me?   380
Draw near, my lord, for sure you have a share
In these strange woes. Ah, sir, what have you done?
Why did you bring that monster of mankind
The other night to curse Collatia's walls?
Why did you blast me with that horrid visage   385
And blot my honor with the blood of Tarquin?

COLLATINUS.

Oh all the gods!

LUCRECE.

          Alas, they are far off,
Or sure they would have helped the wretched
   Lucrece.
Hear then, and tell it to the wond'ring world.   390
Last night the lustful, bloody Sextus came
Late and benighted to Collatia,
Intending, as he said, for Rome next morning,
But in the dead of night, just when soft sleep
Had sealed my eyes and quite becalmed my soul,   395
Methought a horrid voice thus thundered in my ear,

"Lucrece, thou'rt mine, arise and meet my arms."
When straight I waked and found young Tarquin
   by me,
His robe unbuttoned, red and sparkling eyes,
The flushing blood that mounted in his face,   400
The trembling eagerness that quite devoured him,
With only one grim slave that held a taper
At that dead stillness of the murd'ring night
Sufficiently declared his horrid purpose.

COLLATINUS.

Oh Lucrece, oh!   405

LUCRECE.

How is it possible to speak the passion,
The fright, the throes, and labor of my soul?
Ah, Collatine! Half dead I turned away
To hide my shame, my anger, and my blushes,
While he at first with a dissembled mildness   410
Attempted on my honor—
But hastily repulsed and with disdain,
He drew his sword, and locking his left hand
Fast in my hair, he held it to my breast,
Protesting by the gods, the fiends, and furies,   415
If I refused him he would give me death
And swear he found me with that swarthy slave,
Whom he would leave there murdered by my side.

BRUTUS.

Villain! Damned villain!

LUCRECE.

Ah Collatine! Oh Father! Junius Brutus!   420
All that are kin to this dishonored blood,
How will you view me now? Ah, how forgive me?
Yet think not, Collatine, with my last tears,
With these last sighs, these dying groans, I beg you,
I do conjure my love, my lord, my husband,   425
Oh think me not consenting once in thought,
Though he in act possessed his furious pleasure.
For, oh, the name, the name of an adultress—
But here I faint. Oh help me.
Imagine me, my lord, but what I was,   430
And what I shortly shall be, cold and dead.

COLLATINUS.

Oh you avenging gods! Lucrece, my love,
I swear I do not think thy soul consenting,
And therefore I forgive thee.

LUCRECE.

              Ah, my lord!   435

Were I to live, how should I answer this?
All that I ask you now is to revenge me.
Revenge me, Father, Husband, oh revenge me;
Revenge me, Brutus; you his sons, revenge me;
Herminius, Mutius, thou Horatius too,   440
And thou Valerius; all, revenge me, all—
Revenge the honor of the ravished Lucrece.

ALL.

We will revenge thee.

LUCRECE.

I thank you all, I thank you, noble Romans.
And that my life, though well I know you wish it,   445
May not hereafter ever give example
To any that, like me, shall be dishonored,
To live beneath so loathed an infamy,
Thus I forever lose it, thus set free
My soul, my life, and honor all together.   450

Stabs herself.^c

Revenge me, oh revenge, revenge, revenge. (*Dies.*)

LUCRETIUS.

Struck to the heart, already motionless.

COLLATINUS.

Oh give me way t'embalm her with my tears,
For who has that propriety of sorrow,
Who dares to claim an equal share with me?   455

BRUTUS.

That, sir, dare I, and every Roman here.
What now? At your laments, your puling sighs
And woman's drops? Shall these quit scores²² for
    blood,
For chastity, for Rome, and violated honor?
Now by the gods, my soul disdains your tears.   460
There's not a common harlot in the shambles²³
But for a drachma shall outweep you all.
Advance the body nearer. See, my lords,
Behold, you dazzled Romans, from the wound
Of this dead beauty thus I draw the dagger,   465
All stained and reeking with her sacred blood.
Thus to my lips I put the hallowed blade,
To yours, Lucretius, Collatinus yours,
To yours, Herminius, Mutius, and Horatius,
And yours, Valerius. Kiss the poniard round.   470

---

22 quit scores] make full payment
23 shambles] brothel

Now join your hands with mine and swear, swear all,
By this chaste blood, chaste ere the royal villain
Mixed his foul spirits with the spotless mass,
Swear and let all the gods be witnesses,
That you with me will drive proud Tarquin out,   475
His wife, th'imperial fury, and her sons,
With all the race;* drive 'em with sword and fire
To the world's limits, profligate accursed.
Swear from this time never to suffer them
Nor any other king to reign in Rome.   480

ALL.

We swear.

BRUTUS.

Well have you sworn, and oh, methinks I see
The hovering spirit of the ravished matron
Look down. She bows her airy head to bless you
And crown th'auspicious sacrament with smiles.   485
Thus with her body high exposed to view,
March to the Forum with this pomp of death.
Oh Lucrece! Oh!
When to the clouds thy pile of fame is raised,
While Rome is free thy memory shall be praised.   490
Senate and people, wives and virgins all
Shall once a year before thy statue fall;
Cursing the Tarquins, they thy fate shall mourn
But, when the thoughts of Liberty return,
Shall bless the happy hour when thou wert born.   495

Exeunt.

Act II. The Forum.

Tiberius, Fabritius, Lartius, Flaminius.

TIBERIUS.

Fabritius, Lartius, and Flaminius,
As you are Romans and obliged by Tarquin,
I dare confide in you. I say again,
Though I could not refuse the oath he gave us,
I disapprove my father's undertaking.   5
I'm loyal to the last and so will stand.
I am in haste and must to Tullia.

FABRITIUS.

Leave me, my lord, to deal with the multitude.

TIBERIUS.

Remember this in short: A king is one
To whom you may complain when you are wronged; 10
The throne lies open in your way for justice;

You may be angry, and may be forgiven.
There's room for favor and for benefit
Where friends and enemies may come together,
Have present hearing, present composition   15
Without recourse to the litigious laws—
Laws that are cruel, deaf, inexorable,
That cast the vile and noble all together,
Where, if you should exceed the bounds of order,
There is no pardon. Oh, 'tis dangerous   20
To have all actions judged by rigorous Law.
What, to depend on innocence alone,
Among so many accidents and errors
That wait on human life? Consider it:
Stand fast, be loyal. I must to the Queen. (*Exit.*)   25

FABRITIUS.

A pretty speech, by Mercury! Look you, Lartius,
when the words lie like a low wrestler, round, close
and short, squat, pat and pithy.

LARTIUS.

But what should we do here, Fabritius? The
multitude will tear us in pieces.   30

FABRITIUS.

'Tis true, Lartius, the multitude is a mad thing, a
strange blunder-headed monster, and very unruly.
But eloquence is such a thing, a fine, moving,
florid, pathetical speech! But see, the Hydra comes.
Let me alone. Fear not, I say, fear not.   35

Enter Vinditius with plebeians.

VINDITIUS.

Come, neighbors, rank yourselves, plant your-selves,
set yourselves in order. The gods are very angry, I'll
say that for 'em—pough, pough, I begin to sweat
already—and they'll find us work enough today, I'll
tell you that. And to say truth, I never liked Tarquin,   40
before I saw the mark in his forehead.[24] For look
you, sirs, I am a true Commonwealth's man and do
not naturally love kings, though they be good. For
why should any one man have more power than the
people? Is he bigger or wiser than the people? Has he   45
more guts or more brains than the people? What can
he do for the people that the people can't do for
themselves? Can he make corn grow in a famine?

Can he give us rain in drought? Or make our pots
boil, though the Devil piss in the fire?   50

FIRST CITIZEN.

For my part, I hate all courtiers, and I think I have
reason for't.

VINDITIUS.

Thou reason! Well, tailor, and what's thy reason?

FIRST CITIZEN.

Why sir, there was a crew of 'em t'other night got
drunk, broke my windows, and handled my wife.   55

VINDITIUS.

How, neighbors? Nay, now the fellow has reason,
look you. His wife handled! Why, this is a matter
of moment.

FIRST CITIZEN.

Nay, I know there were some of the princes, for I
heard Sextus his* name.   60

VINDITIUS.

Aye, aye, the King's sons, my life for't, some of the
King's sons. Well, these roaring lords never do any
good among us citizens: they are ever breaking the
peace, running in our debts,[25] and swingeing our
wives.   65

FABRITIUS.

How long at length, thou many-headed monster,
You bulls and bears, you roaring beasts and
     bandogs,[26]
Porters and cobblers, tinkers, tailors, all
You rascally sons of whores in a civil government,
How long, I say, dare you abuse our patience?   70
Does not the thought of rods and axes[27] fright you?
Does not our presence—hah, these eyes, these
     faces—
Strike you with trembling? Hah!

VINDITIUS.

Why, what have we here? A very spitfire, the crack-
fart of the court. Hold, let me see him nearer. Yes,   75
neighbors, this is one of 'em, one of your roaring
squires that poke us in the night, beat the watch,
and deflower our wives. I know him, neighbors,
for all his bouncing and his swearing. This is a
court pimp, a bawd, one of Tarquin's bawds.   80

---

24 mark in his forehead] the mark of a nefarious villain divinely inscribed in the forehead, as with the mark of Cain

25 running in our debts] running up debts (i.e., in taverns,
   shops, etc., which we commoners own)
26 bandogs] fierce dogs that must be tied up
27 rods and axes] Latin *fasces* (q.v.)

FABRITIUS.

Peace, thou obstreperous rascal, I am a man of honor. One of the Equestrian Order,[28] my name Fabritius.

VINDITIUS.

Fabritius! Your servant, Fabritius.—Down with him. Neighbors, an upstart rogue. This is he that was the Queen's coachman and drove the chariot over her father's body.[29] Down with him, down with 'em all—bawds, pimps, pandars.

FABRITIUS.

Oh mercy, mercy, mercy!

VINDITIUS.

Hold, neighbors, hold. As we are great, let us be just. You, sirrah, you of the Equestrian Order, knight? Now, by Jove, he has the look of a pimp; I find we can't save him. Rise, Sir Knight, and tell me before the majesty of the people, what have you to say, that you should not have your neck broke down the Tarpeian Rock,[30] your body burnt, and your ashes thrown in the Tiber?

FABRITIUS.

Oh! Oh! Oh!

VINDITIUS.

A courtier! A sheep biter.[31] Leave off your blubbering and confess.

FABRITIUS.

Oh! I will confess, I will confess.

VINDITIUS.

Answer me then: Was not you once the Queen's coachman?

FABRITIUS.

I was, I was.

VINDITIUS.

Did you not drive her chariot over the body of her father, the dead King Tullius?

FABRITIUS.

I did, I did, though it went against my conscience.

VINDITIUS.

So much the worse. Have you not since abused the good people by seducing the citizens' wives to court for the King's sons? Have you not by your bawd's tricks been the occasion of their making assault on the bodies of many a virtuous disposed gentlewoman?

FABRITIUS.

I have, I have.

VINDITIUS.

Have you not wickedly held the door while the daughters of the wise citizens have had their vessels broken up?

FABRITIUS.

Oh, I confess, many a time and often.

VINDITIUS.

For all which services to your princes, and so highly deserving of the Commonwealth, you have received the honor of knighthood?

FABRITIUS.

Mercy, mercy. I confess it all.

VINDITIUS.

Hitherto I have helped you to spell. Now pray put together for yourself and confess the whole matter in three words.

FABRITIUS.

I was at first the son of a carman,[32] came to the honor of being Tullia's coachman, have been a pimp, and remain a knight at the mercy of the people.

VINDITIUS.

Well, I am moved, my bowels[33] are stirred. Take 'em away and let 'em only be hanged. Away with 'em, away with 'em.

FABRITIUS.

Oh mercy! Help, help.

VINDITIUS.

Hang 'em, rogues, pimps; hang 'em, I say. Why look you, neighbors, this is Law, Right, and Justice. This is the people's law, and I think that's better than the arbitrary power of kings. Why, here was trial, condemnation, and execution without more ado.

---

28 Equestrian Order] the upper class

29 chariot over her father's body] Tullia, daughter of the previous king, Tullius, convinced her husband Tarquin to kill him and seize power. As the Roman historian Livy tells it, she deliberately drove over the corpse on her way to the Senate.

30 Tarpeian Rock] cliff of the Capitoline Hill from which criminals were thrown to their deaths

31 sheep biter] either a shifty, sneaking, or thievish fellow or one who runs after mutton, i.e., women (OED)

32 carman] see chair*

33 bowels] tender affections (pun intended)

[Exeunt Fabritius, Lartius, Flaminius under guard.]

—Hark, hark. What have we here? Look, look, the
tribune of the Celeres! Bring forth the pulpit, the
pulpit.   140

Trumpets sound a dead march. Enter Brutus, Valerius,
Herminius, Mutius, Horatius, Lucretius, Collatinus,
Tiberius, Titus with the body of Lucrece.

VALERIUS.

I charge you, fathers, nobles, Romans, friends,
Magistrates, all you people, hear Valerius.
This day, oh Romans, is a day of wonders;
The villainies of Tarquin are complete.
To lay whose vices open to your view,   145
To give you reasons for his banishment
With the expulsion of his wicked race,*
The gods have chosen Lucius Junius Brutus—
The stupid, senseless, and illiterate Brutus—
Their orator in this prodigious cause.   150
Let him ascend and silence be proclaimed.

VINDITIUS.

A Brutus, a Brutus, a Brutus! Silence there.
Silence, I say, silence on pain of death.

BRUTUS.

Patricians, people, friends, and Romans all,
Had not th'inspiring gods by wonder brought me   155
From clouded sense to this full day of reason,
Whence with a prophet's prospect I behold
The state of Rome and danger of the world,
Yet in a cause like this, methinks, the weak,
Enervate, stupid* Brutus might suffice.   160
Oh the eternal gods! Bring but the statues
Of Romulus and Numa,34 plant 'em here
On either hand of this cold Roman wife
Only to stand and point that public wound.
Oh Romans, oh, what use would be of tongues!   165
What orator need speak while they were by?
Would not the majesty of those dumb forms
Inspire your souls and arm you for the cause?
Would you not curse the author of the murder
And drive him from the earth with sword and fire?   170
But where, methinks I hear the people shout,

I hear the cry of Rome, where is the monster?
Bring Tarquin forth, bring the destroyer out,
By whose cursed offspring, lustful bloody Sextus,
This perfect mold of Roman chastity,   175
This star of spotless and immortal Fame,
This pattern for all wives, the Roman Lucrece
Was foully brought to a disastrous end.

VINDITIUS.

Oh neighbors, oh! I buried seven wives without
crying. Nay, I never wept before in all my life.   180

BRUTUS.

Oh the immortal gods, and thou great Stayer35
Of falling Rome, if to his own relations
(For Collatinus is a Tarquin too),
If wrongs so great to them, to his own blood,
What then to us, the nobles and the commons?   185
Not to remember you of his past crimes:
The black ambition of his furious queen,
Who drove her chariot through the Cyprian street36
On such a damned design as might have turned
The steeds of Day37 and shocked the starting gods,   190
Blest as they are, with an uneasy moment.
Add yet to this, oh! add the horrid slaughter
Of all the princes of the Roman Senate,38
Invading fundamental Right and Justice,
Breaking the ancient customs, statutes, laws   195
With positive power and arbitrary lust.
And those affairs which were before dispatched
In public by the fathers, now are forced
To his own palace, there to be determined
As he and his portentous council please.   200
But then for you.

VINDITIUS.

                              Aye, for the people, come,
And then, my myrmidons,39 to pot with him.

---

34 Romulus and Numa] legendary first and second kings
of Rome

35 great Stayer] Jupiter, the chief Roman god

36 Cyprian street] either a street named for Cyprus or a
street of prostitutes

37 turned the steeds of Day] caused the unstoppable horses
of the sun god's chariot to turn aside

38 princes of the Roman Senate] When Tarquin seized
power, he had many senators and their relatives killed,
including LJB's father and elder brother.

39 myrmidons] originally the faithful soldiers who accompanied Achilles to the Trojan War (here used comically)

BRUTUS.

 I say, if thus the nobles have been wronged,
 What tongue can speak the grievance of the people? 205

VINDITIUS.

 Alas, poor people!

BRUTUS.

 You that were once a freeborn people, famed
 In his forefathers' days for wars abroad,
 The conquerors of the world—oh Rome! oh
  Glory!—
 What are you now? What has the Tyrant made of 210
  you?
 The slaves, the beasts, the asses of the earth,
 The soldiers of the gods, mechanic laborers,
 Drawers of water, taskers, timber-fellers,
 Yoked you like bulls, his very jades for luggage,
 Drove you with scourges down to dig in quarries, 215
 To cleanse his sinks, the scavengers o'th'court,
 While his lewd sons, though not on work so hard,
 Employed your daughters and your wives at home.

VINDITIUS.

 Yes, marry* did they.

BRUTUS.

 Oh all the gods! What are you Romans? Hah! 220
 If this be true, why have you been so backward?
 Oh sluggish souls! Oh fall of former glory!
 That would not rouse unless a woman waked you!
 Behold, she comes and calls you to revenge her;
 Her spirit hovers in the air and cries, 225
 "To arms, to arms, drive, drive the Tarquins out."
 Behold this dagger taken from her wound.
 She bids you fix this trophy on your standard,
 This poniard which she stabbed into her heart,
 And bear her body in your battle's front. 230
 Or will you stay till Tarquin does return,
 To see your wives and children dragged about,
 Your houses burnt, the temples all profaned,
 The city filled with rapes, adulteries,
 The Tiber choked with bodies, all the shores 235
 And neighb'ring rocks besmeared with Roman
  blood?

VINDITIUS.

 Away, away. Let's burn his palace first.

BRUTUS.

 Hold, hold, my friends. As I have been th'inspirer
 Of this most just revenge, so I entreat you,

Oh worthy Romans, take me with you still. 240
Drive Tullia out, and all of Tarquin's race;*
Expel 'em without damage to their persons,
Though not without reproach. Vinditius, you
I trust in this. So prosper us the gods,
Prosper our cause, prosper the Commonwealth, 245
Guard and defend the liberty of Rome.

VINDITIUS.

 Liberty, liberty, liberty.

ALL.

 Liberty, etc.

Exeunt [Vinditius and plebeians].

VALERIUS.

 Oh Brutus, as a god we all survey thee.
 Let then the gratitude we should express 250
 Be lost in admiration. Well we know
 Virtue like thine—so fierce, so like the gods',
 That more than thou present'st we could not bear—
 Looks with disdain on ceremonious honors;
 Therefore, accept in short the thanks of Rome. 255
 First with our bodies thus we worship thee,
 Thou guardian genius* of the Commonwealth,
 Thou father and redeemer of thy country;
 Next we as friends with equal arms embrace thee,
 That Brutus may remember, though his virtue 260
 Soar to the gods, he is a Roman still.

BRUTUS.

 And when I am not so or once in thought
 Conspire the bondage of my countrymen,
 Strike me, you gods, tear me, oh Romans, piecemeal,
 And let your Brutus be more loathed than Tarquin. 265
 But now to those affairs that want* a view:
 Imagine then the fame of what is done
 Has reached to Ardea, whence the trembling King,
 By guilt and nature quick and apprehensive,
 With a bent brow comes post for his revenge 270
 To make examples of the mutineers.
 Let him come on.—Lucretius, to your care
 The charge and custody of Rome is given,
 While we, with all the force that can be raised,
 Waving^d the Tarquins on the common road, 275
 Resolve to join the army at the camp.
 What thinks Valerius of the consequence?

VALERIUS.

 As of a lucky hit. There is a number

Of malcontents that wish for such a time.
I think that only speed is necessary   280
To crown the whole event.
BRUTUS.
                              Go then yourself
With these assistants and make instant head
Well as you can—numbers will not be wanting*—
To Mars his* field. I have but some few orders   285
To leave with Titus that must be dispersed,
And Brutus shall attend you.
VALERIUS.
                              The gods direct you.

*Exeunt [Valerius, Herminius, Mutius, Horatius,
Lucretius, Collatinus, Tiberius] with the body of
Lucrece. Manent Brutus, Titus.*

BRUTUS.
    Titus, my son?
TITUS.
                        My ever honored lord.   290
BRUTUS.
    I think, my Titus,
Nay, by the gods, I dare protest it to thee,
I love thee more than any of my children.
TITUS.
    How, sir, oh how, my lord, have I deserved it?
BRUTUS.
    Therefore I love thee more because, my son,   295
Thou hast deserved it, for to speak sincerely,
There's such a sweetness still in all thy manners,
An air so open, and a brow so clear,
A temper so removed from villainy,
With such a manly plainness in thy dealing,   300
That not to love thee, oh my son, my Titus,
Were to be envious of so great a virtue.
TITUS.
    Oh all the gods, where will this kindness end?
Why do you thus, oh my too gracious lord,
Dissolve at once the being that you gave me,   305
Unless you mean to screw me to performance
Beyond the reach of man?
Ah why, my lord, do you oblige me more
Than my humanity can e'er return?
BRUTUS.
    Yes, Titus, thou conceiv'st thy father right.   310
I find our genii* know each other well,

And minds, my son, of our uncommon make,
When once the mark's in view, never shoot wide,
But in a line come level to the white
And hit the very heart of our design.   315
Then to the shocking purpose. Once again
I say, I swear, I love thee, oh my son.
I like thy frame; the fingers of the gods
I see have left their mastery upon thee:
They have been tapering up thy Roman form,   320
And the majestic prints at large appear.
Yet something they have left for me to finish,
Which thus I press thee to, thus in my arms
I fashion thee, I mold thee to my heart.
What? Dost thou kneel? Nay, stand up now a   325
    Roman,
Shake from thy lids that dew that hangs upon 'em,
And answer to th'austerity of my virtue.
TITUS.
    If I must die, you gods, I am prepared.
Let then my fate suffice, but do not rack me
With something more.   330
BRUTUS.
                    Titus, as I remember,
You told me you were married.
TITUS.
                              My lord, I did.
BRUTUS.
    To Teraminta, Tarquin's natural* daughter.
TITUS.
    Most true, my lord, to that poor virtuous maid,   335
Your Titus, sir, your most unhappy son,
Is joined forever.
BRUTUS.
                    No, Titus, not forever.
Not but I know the virgin beautiful,
For I did oft converse her when I seemed   340
Not to converse at all. Yet more, my son,
I think her chastely good, most sweetly framed,
Without the smallest tincture of her father.
Yet, Titus—Hah! What, man? What, all in tears?
Art thou so soft that only saying "yet"   345
Has dashed thee thus? Nay, then I'll plunge thee
    down,
Down to the bottom of this foolish stream
Whose brink thus makes thee tremble. No, my son,
If thou art mine, thou art not Teraminta's,

Or if thou art, I swear thou must not be, 350
Thou shalt not be hereafter.
TITUS.
      Oh the gods!
Forgive me, Blood and Duty, all respects
Due to a father's name. Not Teraminta's!
BRUTUS.
No, by the gods I swear, not Teraminta's! 355
No, Titus, by th'eternal Fates that hang,
I hope, auspicious o'er the head of Rome,
I'll grapple with thee on this spot of earth
About this theme till one of us fall dead.
I'll struggle with thee for this point of honor 360
And tug with Teraminta for thy heart
As I have done for Rome. Yes, ere we part,
Fixed as you are by wedlock joined and fast,
I'll set you far asunder. Nay, on this,
This spotted blade bathed in the blood of Lucrece 365
I'll make thee swear on this thy wedding night
Thou wilt not touch thy wife.
TITUS.
     Conscience, heart, and bowels,
Am I a man? Have I my flesh about me?
BRUTUS.
I know thou hast too much of flesh about thee. 370
'Tis that, my son, that and thy blood I fear
More than thy spirit, which is truly Roman.
But let the heated channels of thy veins
Boil o'er, I still am obstinate in this:
Thou shalt renounce thy father or thy love. 375
Either resolve to part with Teraminta,
To send her forth with Tullia to her father,
Or shake hands with me, part, and be accursed,
Make me believe thy mother played me false
And in my absence stamped thee with a Tarquin. 380
TITUS.
Hold, sir, I do conjure you by the gods,
Wrong not my mother, though you doom me dead.
Curse me not till you hear what I resolve;
Give me a little time to rouse my spirits,
To muster all the tyrant-man about me, 385
All that is fierce, austere, and greatly cruel
To Titus and his Teraminta's ruin.
BRUTUS.
Remember me. Look on thy father's suff'rings,
What he has borne for twenty rolling years;

If thou hast nature, worth, or honor in thee, 390
The contemplation of my cruel labors
Will stir thee up to this new act of glory.
Thou want'st* the image of thy father's wrongs;
Oh take it then, reflected with the warmth
Of all the tenderness that I can give thee. 395
Perhaps it stood in a wrong light before;
I'll try all ways to place it to advantage.
Learn by my rigorous Roman resolution
To stiffen thy unharassed infant virtue.
I do allow thee fond,* young, soft, and gentle, 400
Trained by the charms of one that is most lovely,
Yet, Titus, this must all be lost when Honor,
When Rome, the world, and the gods come to
 claim us.
Think then thou hear'st 'em cry, "Obey thy father.
If thou art false or perjured, there he stands 405
Accountable to us. But swear t'obey,
Implicitly believe him, that, if aught
Be sworn amiss, thou mayst have naught to answer."
TITUS.
What is it, sir, that you would have me swear,
That I may 'scape your curse and gain your blessing? 410
BRUTUS.
That thou this night will part with Teraminta.
For once again I swear, if here she stays,
What for the hatred of the multitude
And my resolves to drive out Tarquin's race,
Her person is not safe. 415
TITUS.
     Here, take me, sir,
Take me before I cool. I swear this night
That I will part with, oh! my Teraminta.
BRUTUS.
Swear too, and by the soul of ravished Lucrece,
Though on thy bridal night, thou wilt not touch her. 420
TITUS.
I swear, ev'n by the soul of her you named,
The ravished Lucrece, oh th'immortal gods!
I will not touch her.
BRUTUS.
     So—I trust thy virtue.
And by the gods I thank thee for the conquest. 425
Once more with all the blessings I can give thee,
I take thee to my arms. Thus on my breast,
The hard and rugged pillow of thy honor,

I wean thee from thy love. Farewell—be fast
To what thou'st sworn, and I am thine forever. (*Exit.*) 430
TITUS.
  To what thou'st sworn! Oh heaven and earth,
    what's that?
  What have I sworn? to part with Teraminta?
  To part with something dearer to my heart
  Than my life's drops? What, not this night enjoy her?
  Renounce my vows, the rights, the dues of marriage, 435
  Which now I gave her, and the priest was witness,
  Blessed with a flood that streamed from both our eyes
  And sealed with sighs and smiles and deathless kisses?
  Yet after this to swear thou wilt not touch her!
  Oh all the gods, I did forswear myself 440
  In swearing that, and will forswear again.
  Not touch her! Oh thou perjured braggart, where,
  Where are thy vaunts, thy protestations now?

Enter Teraminta.

  She comes to strike thy staggering duty down.
  'Tis fall'n, 'tis gone.—Oh Teraminta, come, 445
  Come to my arms, thou only joy of Titus.
  —Hush to my cares.—Thou mass of hoarded
    sweets,
  Selected hour of all life's happy moments,
  What shall I say to thee?
TERAMINTA.
              Say anything, 450
  For while you speak, methinks a sudden calm,
  In spite of all the horror that surrounds me,
  Falls upon every frighted faculty
  And puts my soul in tune. Oh Titus, oh!
  Methinks my spirit shivers in her house, 455
  Shrugging as if she longed to be at rest;
  With this foresight, to die thus in your arms
  Were to prevent a world of following ills.
TITUS.
  What ills, my love? What power has Fortune now
  But we can brave? 'Tis true, my Teraminta, 460
  The body of the world is out of frame,
  The vast distorted limbs are on the rack,
  And all the cable sinews stretched to bursting;
  The blood ferments, and the majestic spirit,
  Like Hercules in the envenomed shirt,[40] 465

Lies in a fever on the horrid pile.
  My father, like an Aesculapius[41]
  Sent by the gods, comes boldly to the cure—
  But how, my love? by violent remedies—
  And says that Rome, ere yet she can be well, 470
  Must purge and cast, purge all th'infected humors*
  Through the whole mass and vastly, vastly bleed.
TERAMINTA.
  Ah, Titus! I myself but now beheld
  Th'expulsion of the Queen, driv'n from her palace
  By the enraged and madding multitude, 475
  And hardly 'scaped myself to find you here.
TITUS.
  Why yet, my Teraminta, we may smile.
  Come then to bed, ere yet the night descends
  With her black wings to brood o'er all the world.
  Why, what care we? Let us enjoy those pleasures 480
  The gods have giv'n; locked in each other's arms
  We'll lie forever thus and laugh at Fate.
TERAMINTA.
  No, no, my lord. There's more than you have named;
  There's something at your heart that I must find.
  I claim it with the privilege of a wife. 485
  Keep close your joys, but for your griefs, my Titus,
  I must not, will not lose my share in them.
  Ah, the good gods, what is it stirs you thus?
  Speak, speak, my lord, or Teraminta dies.
  Oh heav'ns, he weeps! Nay, then upon my knees 490
  I thus conjure you, speak or give me death.
TITUS.
  Rise, Teraminta. Oh, if I should speak
  What I have rashly sworn against my love,
  I fear that I should give thee death indeed.
TERAMINTA.
  Against your love! No, that's impossible; 495
  I know your godlike truth. Nay, should you swear,
  Swear to me now that you forswore your love,
  I would not credit it. No, no, my lord,
  I see, I know, I read it in your eyes,
  You love the wretched Teraminta still. 500
  The very manner of your hiding it,
  The tears you shed, your backwardness to speak

---

40 envenomed shirt] Hercules' wife gave him a poisoned

shirt which clung to his body so painfully that he had
himself burned on a funeral pyre ("pile") to escape.

41 Aesculapius] god of healing

What you affirm you swore against your love
Tell me, my lord, you love me more than ever.
TITUS.
By all the gods, I do. Oh Teraminta,   505
My heart's discerner, whither wilt thou drive me?
I'll tell thee then. My father wrought me up,
I know not how, to swear I know not what,
That I would send thee hence with Tullia,
Swear not to touch thee, though my wife. Yet oh!   510
Hadst thou been by thyself and but beheld him,
Thou wouldst have thought, such was his majesty
That the gods lightened from his awful* eyes
And thundered from his tongue.
TERAMINTA.
                                        No more, my lord.   515
I do conjure you by all those Powers
Which we invoked together at the altar,
And beg you by the love I know you bear me,
To let this passion trouble you no farther.
No, my dear lord, my honored godlike husband,   520
I am your wife, and one that seeks your honor.
By Heaven, I would have sworn you thus myself.
What, on the shock of empire, on the turn
Of state and universal change of things,
To lie at home and languish for a woman!   525
No, Titus, he that makes himself thus vile,
Let him not dare pretend to aught that's princely,
But be, as all the warlike world shall judge him,
The droll of th'people and the scorn of kings.

Enter Horatius.

HORATIUS.
My lord, your father gives you thus in charge: 530
Remember what you swore. The guard is ready,
And I am ordered to conduct your bride,
While you attend your father.
TITUS.
                                        Oh Teraminta!
Then we must part.   535
TERAMINTA.
                                We must, we must, my lord.
Therefore be swift and snatch yourself away,
Or I shall die with ling'ring.
TITUS.
                                Oh, a kiss,
Balmy as cordials that recover souls,   540

Chaste as maids' sighs, and keen as longing mothers.
Preserve thyself; look well to that, my love.
Think on our covenant. When either dies,
The other is no more.
TERAMINTA.
                                I do remember,   545
But have no language left.
TITUS.
                                Yet we shall meet,
In spite of sighs we shall, at least in heaven.
Oh Teraminta, once more to my heart,
Once to my lips, and ever to my soul.   550
Thus the soft mother, though her babe is dead,
Will have the darling on her bosom laid,
Will talk and rave and with the nurses strive,
And fond it⁴² still as if it were alive,
Knows it must go, yet struggles with the crowd,   555
And shrieks to see 'em wrap it in the shroud.

Act III, scene i.

Collatinus, Tiberius, Vitellius, Aquilius.

COLLATINUS.
Th'expulsion of the Tarquins now must stand.
Their camp to be surprised while Tarquin here
Was scolded from our walls! I blush to think
That such a master in the art of war
Should so forget himself.   5
VITELLIUS.
                                Triumphant Brutus,
Like Jove when followed by a train of gods
To mingle with the Fates and doom the world,
Ascends the brazen steps o'th'Capitol
With all the humming Senate at his heels—   10
Ev'n in that Capitol which the King built
With the expense of all the royal treasure—
Ingrateful Brutus there in pomp appears
And sits the purple judge of Tarquin's downfall.
AQUILIUS.
But why, my lord, why are not you there too?   15
Were you not chosen consul by whole Rome?
Why are you not saluted too like him?
Where are your lictors? Where your rods and axes?
Or are you but the ape, the mimic god

---

⁴² fond it] dote on it

Of this new thunderer who appropriates   20
Those bolts of power which ought to be divided?
TIBERIUS.
Now by the gods, I hate his upstart pride,
His rebel thoughts of the imperial race,*
His abject soul that stoops to court the vulgar,
His scorn of princes, and his lust to th'people.   25
Oh Collatine, have you not eyes to find him?
Why are you raised, but to set off his honors—
A taper by the sun, whose sickly beams
Are swallowed in the blaze of his full glory?
He, like a meteor, wades th'abyss of light,   30
While your faint luster adds but to the beard[43]
That awes the world. When late through Rome
    he passed,
Fixed on his courser, marked you how he bowed
On this, on that side to the gazing heads
That paved the streets and all embossed the windows,   35
That gaped with eagerness to speak, but could not,
So fast their spirits flowed to admiration,
And that to joy, which thus at last broke forth:
"Brutus, God Brutus, Father of thy country!
Hail genius,* hail! Deliverer of lost Rome!   40
Shield of the Commonwealth, and sword of Justice!
Hail, scourge of tyrants, lash for lawless kings!
All hail," they cried, while the long peal of praises,
Tormented with a thousand echoing cries,
Ran like the volley of the gods along.   45
COLLATINUS.
No more on't, I grow sick with the remembrance.
TIBERIUS.
But when you followed, how did their bellying bodies
That ventured from the casements more than half
To look at Brutus, nay, that stuck like snails
Upon the walls and from the houses' tops   50
Hung down like clust'ring bees upon each other;
How did they all draw back at sight of you
To laze and loll and yawn, and rest from rapture!
Are you a man? Have you the blood of kings
And suffer this?   55
COLLATINUS.
Hah! Is he not his father?
TIBERIUS.
                    I grant he is.

Consider this and rouse yourself at home.
Commend my fire and rail at your own slackness.
Yet more: remember but your last disgrace,   60
When you proposed, with reverence to the gods,
A King of Sacrifices[44] should be chosen,
And from the consuls. Did he not oppose you,
Fearing, as well he might, your sure election,
Saying it smelt too much of royalty,   65
And that it might rub up the memory
Of those that loved the Tyrant? Nay, yet more,
That if the people chose you for the place,
The name of king would light upon a Tarquin,
Of one that's doubly royal, being descended   70
From two great princes[45] that were kings of Rome?
COLLATINUS.
But after all this, whither wouldst thou drive?
TIBERIUS.
I would to justice, for the restoration
Of our most lawful prince. Yes, Collatine,
I look upon my father as a traitor.   75
I find that neither you nor brave Aquilius
Nor young Vitellius dare confide in me.
But that you may, and firmly, to the hazard
Of all the world holds precious, once again
I say, I look on Brutus as a traitor,   80
No more my father, by th'immortal gods.
And to redeem the time, to fix the King
On his imperial throne, some means proposed
That savor of a governed policy,
Where there is strength and life to hope a fortune,   85
Not to throw all upon one desperate chance,
I'll on as far as he that laughs at dying.
COLLATINUS.
Come to my arms, oh thou so truly brave,
Thou mayst redeem the errors of thy race!*
Aquilius and Vitellius, oh embrace him   90
And ask his pardon, that so long we feared
To trust so rich a virtue. But behold,

Enter Brutus and Valerius.

---

44 King of Sacrifices] After Tarquin was deposed, this of-
     ficer (*rex sacrificulus*) was appointed to perform certain
     religious rites that had been the king's responsibility.

45 two great princes] apparently the two Tarquin kings,
     Lucius Tarquinius Priscus and his son or grandson,
     Lucius Tarquinius Superbus, the current tyrant

---

43 beard] the tail of the meteor; also a symbol of mascu-
     line power

Brutus appears. Young man, be satisfied,
I sound thy politic father to the bottom:
Plotting the assumption of Valerius,   95
He means to cast me from the consulship;
But now I heard how he cajoled the people
With his known industry and my remissness,
That still in all our votes, proscriptions, edicts
Against the King, he found I acted faintly,   100
Still closing every sentence, "He's a Tarquin."
BRUTUS.
No, my Valerius, till thou art my mate,
Joint master in this great authority,
However calm the face of things appear,
Rome is not safe. By the majestic gods   105
I swear, while Collatine sits at the helm,
A universal wrack is to be feared.
I have intelligence of his transactions.
He mingles with the young hot blood of Rome,
Gnaws himself inward, grudges my applause,   110
Promotes cabals with highest quality,*
Such headlong youth as, spurning laws and manners,
Shared in the late debaucheries of Sextus
And therefore wish the Tyrant here again.
As the inverted seasons shock wise men   115
And the most fixed philosophy must start
At sultry winters and at frosty summers,
So at this most unnatural stillness here,
This more than midnight silence through all Rome,
This deadness of discourse and dreadful calm   120
Upon so great a change, I more admire
Than if a hundred politic heads were met
And nodded mutiny to one another,
More fear than if a thousand lying libels
Were spread abroad, nay, dropped among the Senate.   125
VALERIUS.
I have myself employed a busy slave,
His name Vinditius, given him wealth and freedom
To watch the motions of Vitellius
And those of the Aquilian family.[46]
Vitellius has already entertained* him,   130
And something thence important may be gathered,
For these of all the youth of quality*
Are most inclined to Tarquin and his race*
By blood and humor.*

BRUTUS.
                              Oh Valerius!   135
That boy, observ'st thou? Oh I fear, my friend,
He is a weed, but rooted in my heart
And grafted to my stock. If he prove rank,
By Mars, no more but thus, away with him.
I'll tear him from me, though the blood should follow.   140
—Tiberius.
TIBERIUS.
My lord?
BRUTUS.
Sirrah, no more of that Vitellius;
I warned you too of young Aquilius.
Are my words wind, that thus you let 'em pass?   145
Hast thou forgot thy father?
TIBERIUS.
                              No, my lord.
BRUTUS.
Thou lie'st. But though thou 'scape a father's rod,
The consul's axe may reach thee: think on that.
I know thy vanity and blind ambition;   150
Thou dost associate with my enemies.
When I refused the consul Collatine
To be the King of Sacrifices, straight
As if thou hadst been sworn his bosom fool,
He named thee for the office. And since that,   155
Since I refused thy madness that preferment
Because I would have none of Brutus' blood
Pretend to be a king, thou hang'st thy head,
Contriv'st to give thy father new displeasure,
As if imperial toil were not enough   160
To break my heart without thy disobedience.
But by the majesty of Rome I swear,
If after double warning thou despise me,
By all the gods, I'll cast thee from my blood,
Doom thee to forks[47] and whips as a barbarian,   165
And leave thee to the lashes of the lictor.
—Tarquinius Collatinus, you are summoned
To meet the Senate on the instant time.
COLLATINUS.
Lead on. My duty is to follow Brutus.

Exeunt Brutus, Valerius, [Collatinus].

---

46 Aquilian family] a prominent Roman family that entered
   the conspiracy to return Tarquin to power

47 forks] forked stake used as a whipping post (*OED*)

TIBERIUS.

Now by those gods with which he menaced me, 170
I here put off all nature. Since he turns me
Thus desperate to the world, I do renounce him,
And when we meet again he is my foe.
All blood, all reverence, fondness be forgot.
Like a grown savage on the common wild 175
That runs at all and cares not who begot him,
I'll meet my lion sire and roar defiance,
As if he ne'er had nursed me in his den.

Enter Vinditius with the people and two Fecialian
priests[48] *crowned with laurel, two spears in their*
hands, one bloody and half burnt.

VINDITIUS.

Make way there, hey, news from the Tyrant. Here
come envoys, heralds, ambassadors—whether in 180
the gods' name or in the devils' I know not, but
here they come, your Fecialian priests. Well, good
people, I like not these priests. Why, what the devil
have they to do with state affairs? What side soever
they are for, they'll have heaven for their part, I'll 185
warrant you. They'll lug the gods in whether they
will or no.

FIRST PRIEST.

Hear, Jupiter, and thou, oh Juno, hear;
Hear, oh Quirinus;[49] hear us all you gods
Celestial, terrestrial, and infernal. 190

SECOND PRIEST.

Be thou, oh Rome, our judge. Hear, all you people.

VINDITIUS.

Fine canting rogues! I told you how they'd be
hooking the gods in at first dash. Why, the gods
are their tools and tackle; they work with heaven
and hell; and let me tell you, as things go, your 195
priests have a hopeful trade on't.

FIRST PRIEST.

I come ambassador to thee, oh Rome,
Sacred and just, the legate of the King.

SECOND PRIEST.

If we demand or purpose to require
A stone from Rome that's contrary to Justice, 200
May we be ever banished from our country
And never hope to taste this vital air.

TIBERIUS.

Vinditius, lead the multitude away.
Aquilius, with Vitellius and myself,
Will straight conduct 'em to the Capitol. 205

VINDITIUS.

I go, my lord, but have a care of 'em. Sly rogues I
warrant 'em. Mark that first priest: Do you see
how he leers? A lying elder, the true cast of a holy
juggler. Come, my masters, I would think well of
a priest, but that he has a commission to dissemble, 210
a patent hypocrite that takes pay to forge, lies by
law, and lives by the sins of the people.

Exit with people.

AQUILIUS.

My life upon't, you may speak out, and freely;
Tiberius is the heart of our design.

FIRST PRIEST.

The gods be praised. Thus then: the King commends 215
Your generous resolves, longs to be with you
And those you have engaged, divides his heart
Amongst you, which more clearly will be seen
When you have read these packets. As we go,
I'll spread the bosom of the King before you. 220

Exeunt.

Scene ii. The Senate.

BRUTUS.

Patricians, that long stood and 'scaped the Tyrant,
The venerable molds of your forefathers,
That represent the wisdom of the dead;
And you the conscript[50] chosen for the people,
Engines* of power, severest counselors, 5
Courts that examine treasons to the head,
All hail. The consul begs th'auspicious gods
And binds Quirinus by his tutelar vow
That plenty, peace, and lasting liberty

---

48 Fecialian priests] These priests performed rites celebrating the declaration of war and the making of peace (so
their laurel crowns and half-burnt spear); but Lee adds
other details to their portrayal based on English super-
stitions about Roman Catholics of his own time.

49 Quirinus] the early Roman King Romulus, now deified

50 Conscript] group of senators newly chosen to replace
those killed when Tarquin took power

May be your portion and the lot of Rome. 10
Laws, rules, and bounds prescribed for raging kings,
Like banks and bulwarks for the mother seas,
Though 'tis impossible they should prevent
A thousand daily wracks and nightly ruins,
Yet help to break those rolling inundations 15
Which else would overflow and drown the world.
Tarquin, to feed whose fathomless ambition
And ocean luxury the noblest veins
Of all true Romans were like rivers emptied,
Is cut from Rome, and now he flows full on. 20
Yet Fathers, ought we much to fear his ebb
And strictly watch the dams that we have raised.
Why should I go about?[51] The Roman people
All, with one voice, accuse my fellow consul.

COLLATINUS.

The people may; I hope the nobles will not. 25
The people! Brutus does indulge the people.

BRUTUS.

Consul, in what is right I will indulge 'em.
And much I think 'tis better so to do
Than see 'em run in tumults through the streets,
Forming cabals, plotting against the Senate, 30
Shutting their shops and flying from the town,
As if the gods had sent the plague among 'em.
I know too well, you and your royal tribe
Scorn the good people, scorn the late election,
Because we chose these fathers for the people 35
To fill the place of those whom Tarquin murdered.
And though you laugh at this——you and your train,
The irreligious, harebrained youth of Rome,
The ignorant, the slothful, and the base—
Yet wise men know, 'tis very rarely seen 40
That a free people should desire the hurt
Of common liberty. No, Collatine,
For those desires arise from their oppression
Or from suspicion they are falling to it.
But put the case that those their fears were false, 45
Ways may be found to rectify their errors.
For grant the people ignorant of themselves,
Yet they are capable of being told
And will conceive a truth from worthy men.
From you they will not, nor from your adherents, 50
Rome's infamous and execrable youth,

Foes to religion and the Commonwealth,
To virtue, learning, and all sober arts
That bring renown and profit to mankind,
Such as had rather bleed beneath a tyrant, 55
To become dreadful[52] to the populace,
To spread their lusts and dissoluteness round,
Though at the daily hazard of their lives,
Than live at peace in a free government
Where every man is master of his own, 60
Sole lord at home, and monarch of his house,
Where rancor and ambition are extinguished,
Where universal peace extends her wings
As if the Golden Age returned, where all
The people do agree and live secure, 65
The nobles and the princes loved and reverenced,
The world in triumph, and the gods adored.

COLLATINUS.

The consul, Conscript Fathers, says the people,
For divers reasons, grudge the dignity
Which I possessed by general approbation. 70
I hear their murmurs and would know of Brutus
What they would have me do, what's their desire.

BRUTUS.

Take hence the royal name, resign thy office,
Go as a friend and of thy own accord,
Lest thou be forced to what may seem thy will. 75
The city renders thee what is thy own
With vast increase, so thou resolve to go,
For till the name, the race,* and family
Of Tarquin be removed, Rome is not free.

COLLATINUS.

Brutus, I yield my office to Valerius, 80
Hoping, when Rome has tried my faith by exile,
She will recall me. So the gods preserve you.
(*Exit.*)

BRUTUS.

Welcome, Publicola,[53] true son of Rome.
On such a pilot in the roughest storm
She may securely sleep and rest her cares. 85

Enter Tiberius, Aquilius, Vitellius, and the priests.

---

51 go about] speak indirectly or unclearly

52 To become dreadful] so long as they are allowed to become dreadful

53 Publicola] nickname given to Valerius denoting his popularity and public service

FIRST PRIEST.

Hear, Jupiter, Quirinus, all you gods,
Thou Father, judge commissioned for the message,
Pater Patratus[54] for the embassy
And sacred oaths which I must swear for truth:
Dost thou commission me to seal the peace,   90
If peace they choose, or hurl this bloody spear
Half burnt in fire, if they enforce a war?

SECOND PRIEST.

Speak to the Senate and the Alban people[55]
The words of Tarquin: this is your commission.

FIRST PRIEST.

The King, to show he has more moderation   95
Than those that drove him from his lawful empire,
Demands but restitution of his own,
His royal household stuff, imperial treasure,
His gold, his jewels, and his proper state
To be transported where he now resides.   100
I swear that this is all the King requires:
Behold his signet set upon the wax;
'Tis sealed and written in these sacred tables.
To this I swear, and as my oath is just,
Sincere, and punctual, without all deceit,   105
May Jupiter and all the gods reward me.
But if I act or otherwise imagine,
Think, or design than what I here have sworn,
All you the Alban people being safe,
Safe in your country, temples, sepulchers,   110
Safe in your laws and proper household gods—
Let me alone be struck, fall, perish, die,
As now this stone falls from my hand to earth.

BRUTUS.

The things you ask, being very controversial,
Require some time. Should we deny the Tyrant   115
What was his own, 'twould seem a strange injustice,
Though he had never reigned in Rome, yet Fathers,
If we consent to yield to his demand,
We give him then full power to make a war.
'Tis known to you, the Fecialian priests,   120
No act of Senate after sunset stands.
Therefore your offers being of great moment,

We shall defer your bus'ness till the morn,
With whose first dawn we summon all the fathers
To give th'affair dispatch. So Jove protect,   125
Guard, and defend the Commonwealth of Rome.

Exeunt [Brutus and Senators]. Manent Tiberius,
Aquilius, Vitellius, and the priests.

TIBERIUS.

Now to the garden, where I'll bring my brother.
Fear not, my lord, we have the means to work him.
It cannot fail.

FIRST PRIEST.

     And you, Vitellius, haste   130
With good Aquilius, spread the news through Rome
To all of royal spirit, most to those
Young noblemen that used to range with Sextus!
Persuade a restitution of the King,
Give 'em the hint to let him in by night,   135
And join their forces with th'imperial troops,
For 'tis a shove, a push of Fate, must bear it.[56]
For you, the hearts and souls of enterprise,
I need not urge a reason after this.
What good can come of such a government   140
Where though two consuls—wise and able persons
As are throughout the world—sit at the helm,
A very trifle cannot be resolved,
A trick, a start, a shadow of a business
That would receive dispatch in half a minute   145
Were the authority but rightly placed
In Rome's most lawful King? But now no more.
The Fecialian Garden[57] is the place
Where more of our sworn function will be ready
To help the royal plot. Disperse and prosper.   150

Scene iii. The Fecialian Garden.

Titus solus.

TITUS.

She's gone, and I shall never see her more:
Gone to the camp, to the harsh trade of war,

---

54 *Pater Patratus*] Latin: Father of Fathers (addressed to the chief priest)

55 Alban people] the Romans (from Alba Longa, early joined to Rome)

56 a push of Fate, must bear it] Fate must be nudged in order for them to carry the day

57 Fecialian Garden] presumably the enclosure on the Capitoline Hill where the priests gathered sacred herbs (Loftis)

Driven from thy bed, just warm within thy breast,
Torn from her harbor by thy father's hand,
Perhaps to starve upon the barren plain—   5
Thy virgin wife, the very blush of maids,
The softest bosom sweet, and not enjoyed.
Oh the immortal gods! And as she went,
Howe'er she seemed to bear our parting well,
Methought she mixed her melting with disdain,   10
A cast of anger through her shining tears,
So to abuse her hopes and blast her wishes
By making her my bride, but not a woman!

*Enter Tiberius, Aquilius, Vitellius, and priests with
Teraminta.*

TIBERIUS.
See where he stands, drowned in his melancholy.
FIRST PRIEST.
Madam, you know the pleasure of the Queen,   15
And what the royal Tullia did command
I've sword to execute.
TERAMINTA.
                        I am instructed.
Since then my life's at stake, you need not doubt
But I will act with all the force I can.   20
Let me entreat you leave me here alone
Some minutes, and I'll call you to the conquest.

Exeunt Tiberius, Aquilius, Vitellius, priests.

TITUS.
Choose then the gloomiest place through all the
    grove,
Throw thy abandoned body on the ground,
With thy bare breast lie wedded to the dew;   25
Then, as thou drink'st the tears that trickle from thee,
So stretched, resolve to lie till death shall seize thee,
Thy sorrowful head hung o'er some tumbling stream
To rock thy griefs with melancholy sounds,
With broken murmurs and redoubled groans   30
To help the gurgling of the waters' fall.
TERAMINTA. (*Aside.*)
Oh Titus, oh, what scene of death is this!
TITUS.
Or if thy passion will not be kept in,
As in that glass* of nature thou shalt view
Thy swollen, drowned eyes with the inverted banks, 35
The tops of willows and their blossoms turned,

With all the under sky ten fathom down,
Wish that the shadow of the swimming globe
Were so indeed, that thou might'st leap at fate
And hurl thy fortune headlong at the stars.   40
Nay, do not bear it, turn thy wat'ry face
To yond misguided orb and ask the gods
For what bold sin they doom the wretched Titus
To such a loss as that of Teraminta?
Oh Teraminta! I will groan thy name   45
Till the tired Echo faint with repetition,
Till all the breathless grove and quiet myrtles
Shake with my sighs, as if a tempest bowed 'em.
Nothing but Teraminta. Oh Teraminta!
TERAMINTA.
Nothing but Titus, Titus and Teraminta!   50
Thus let me rob the fountains and the groves,
Thus gird me to thee with the fastest knot
Of arms and spirits that would clasp thee through.
Cold as thou art and wet with night's fall'n dews,
Yet dearer so, thus richly dressed with sorrows,   55
Than if the gods had hung thee round with kingdoms.
Oh Titus, oh!
TITUS.
              I find thee, Teraminta,
Waked from a fearful dream, and hold thee fast.
'Tis real, and I give thee back thy joys,   60
Thy boundless love with pleasures running o'er.
Nay, as thou art, thus with thy trappings, come,
Leap to my heart and ride upon the pants,
Triumphing thus, and now defy our stars.
But oh, why do we lose this precious moment!   65
The bliss may yet be barred if we delay,
As 'twas before. Come to thy husband's bed.
I will not think this true till there I hold thee,
Locked in my arms. Leave this contagious air;
There will be time for talk how thou cam'st hither 70
When we have been beforehand with the gods.
Till then—
TERAMINTA.
            Oh Titus, you must hear me first.
I bring a message from the furious Queen.
I promised, nay, she swore me not to touch you   75
Till I had charmed you to the part of Tarquin.
TITUS.
Hah, Teraminta! Not to touch thy husband
Unless he prove a villain?

TERAMINTA.

            Titus, no.
I'm sworn to tell you that you are a traitor   80
If you refuse to fight the royal cause.

TITUS.

Hold, Teraminta.

TERAMINTA.

            No, my lord, 'tis plain,
And I am sworn to lay my reasons home.
Rouse then, awake, recall your sleeping virtue, 85
Side with the King and arm against your father,
Take part with those that loyally have sworn
To let him in by night. Vitellius,
Aquilius, and your brother wait without;
Therefore, I charge you haste, subscribe your 90
    name [*Gives message.*]
And send your vowed obedience to the King.
'Tis Teraminta that entreats you thus,
Charms, and conjures you. Tell the royal heralds
You'll head their enterprise. And then, my lord,
My love, my noble husband, I'll obey you   95
And follow to your bed.

TITUS.

            Never, I swear.
Oh Teraminta, thou hast broke my heart.
By all the gods, from thee this was too much.
Farewell, and take this [*Returns the message.*] with 100
    thee. For thy sake
I will not fight against the King, nor for him.
I'll fly my father, brother, friends forever,
Forsake the haunts of men, converse no more
With aught that's human, dwell with endless
    darkness.
For, since the sight of thee is now unwelcome, 105
What has the world besides that I can bear?

TERAMINTA.

Come back, my lord. By those immortal Pow'rs
You now invoked, I'll fix you in this virtue.
Your Teraminta did but try how strong
Your honor stood and, now she finds it lasting, 110
Will die to root you in this solid glory.
Yes, Titus, though the Queen has sworn to end me,
Though both the Fecialians have commission
To stab me in your presence, if not wrought
To serve the King, yet by the gods I charge you 115
Keep to the point your constancy has gained.

Tarquin, although my father, is a tyrant,
A bloody, black usurper; so I beg you
Ev'n in my death to view him.

TITUS.

              Oh you gods!   120

TERAMINTA.

Yet guilty as he is, if you behold him
Hereafter with his wounds upon the earth,
Titus, for my sake, for poor Teraminta,
Who rather died than you should lose your honor,
Do not you strike him, do not dip your sword 125
In Tarquin's blood, because he was my father.

TITUS.

No, Teraminta, no. By all the gods,
I will defend him, ev'n against my father.
See, see, my love, behold the flight I take.
What all the charms of thy expected bed   130
Could not once move my soul to think of acting,
Thy tears and menaced death, by which thou striv'st
To fix me to the principles of glory,
Have wrought me off.—Yes, yes, you cruel gods,
Let the eternal bolts that bind this frame   135
Start from their order. Since you push me thus
Ev'n to the margin of this wide despair,
Behold I plunge at once in this dishonor,
Where there is neither shore nor hope of haven,
No floating mark through all the dismal vast. 140
'Tis rockless too, no cliff to clamber up
To gaze about and pause upon the ruin.

TERAMINTA.

Is then your purposed honor come to this?
What now, my lord?

TITUS.

           Thy death, thy death, my love: 145
I'll think on that and laugh at all the gods.
Glory, blood, nature, ties of reverence,
The dues of birth, respect of parents, all,
All are as this, the air I drive before me.
—What ho! Vitellius and Aquilius, come,   150
And you the Fecialian heralds, haste,
I'm ready for the leap, I'll take it with you
Though deep as to the fiends.

TERAMINTA.

           Thus hear me, Titus.

TITUS.

Off from my knees, away.   155

What on this theme, thy death? Nay, stabbed
  before me!

Enter priests with Tiberius, Aquilius, Vitellius.

Speak not, I will not know thee on this subject,
But push thee from my heart with all persuasions
That now are lost upon me.—Oh Tiberius,
Aquilius, and Vitellius, welcome, welcome.   160
I'll join you in the conjuration, come.
I am as free as he that dares be foremost.
TERAMINTA.
  My lord, my husband.
TITUS.
              Take this woman from me.
Nay, look you, sirs, I am not yet so gone,   165
So headlong neither in this damned design,
To quench this horrid thirst with Brutus' blood.
No, by th'eternal gods, I bar you that:
My father shall not bleed.
TIBERIUS.
              You could not think   170
Your brother sure so monstrous in his kind,[58]
As not to make our father's life his care.
TITUS.
Thus then, my lords, I list myself among you,
And with my style[59] in short subscribe myself
The servant to the King. My words are these: 175
"Titus to the King,
Sir, you need only know my brother's mind
To judge of me, who am resolved to serve you."
FIRST PRIEST.
'Tis full enough.
TITUS.
              Then leave me to the hire   180
Of this hard labor, to the dear bought prize
Whose life I purchased with my loss of honor.

Exeunt Tiberius, Aquilius, Vitellius, and priests.

—Come to my breasts, thou tempest-beaten flower,
Brimful of rain, and stick upon my heart.
O short-lived rose! Yet I some hours will wear thee.   185
Yes, by the gods, I'll smell thee till I languish,

---

58 so monstrous in his kind] in his species; of such a monstrous nature
59 style] stylus, writing implement

Rifle thy sweets, and run thee o'er and o'er,
Fall like the night upon thy folding beauties,
And clasp thee dead. Then like the morning sun
With a new heat kiss thee to life again   190
And make the pleasure equal to the pain.

Act IV.

Tiberius, Vitellius.

TIBERIUS.
  Hark, are we not pursued?
VITELLIUS.
              No, 'tis the tread
Of our own friends that follow in the dark.
TIBERIUS.
  What's now the time?
VITELLIUS.
              Just dead of night,   5
And 'tis the blackest that e'er masked a murder.
TIBERIUS.
It likes me better, for I love the scowl,
The grimmest lour of Fate on such a deed.
I would have all the charnel houses yawn,
The dusty urns and monumental bones   10
Removed, to make our massacre a tomb.
Hark! Who was that that holloed fire?
VITELLIUS.
              A slave
That snores i'th'hall; he bellows in his sleep
And cries, "The Capitol's o'fire."   15
TIBERIUS.
              I would it were,
And Tarquin at the gates. 'Twould be a blaze,
A beacon fit to light a king of blood
That vows at once the slaughter of the world.
Down with their temples, set 'em on a flame!   20
What should they do with houses for the gods,
Fat fools, the lazy magistrates of Rome,
Wise citizens, the politic heads o'th'people,
That preach rebellion to the multitude?
Why, let 'em off and roll into their graves.   25

*[Enter Aquilius, Trebonius, Servilius, Minutius,
Pomponius severally, some leading prisoners for sacrifice.]*

I long to be at work.—See, good Aquilius,
Trebonius too, Servilius and Minutius,

Pomponius, hail. Nay, now you may unmask,
Browbeat the Fates and say they are your slaves.
AQUILIUS.
    What are those bodies for? 30
TIBERIUS.

A sacrifice.

These were two very busy Commonwealth's men
That, ere the King was banished by the Senate,
First set the plot on foot in public meetings,
That would be holding forth 'twas possible 35
That kings themselves might err and were but men,
The people were not beasts for sacrifice;
Then jogged his brother, this crammed statesman
    here,
The bolder rogue, whom ev'n with open mouth
I heard once belch sedition from a stall. 40
Go, bear him to the priests; he is a victim
That comes as wished for them, the cooks of Heav'n,
And they will carve this brawn of fat rebellion
As if he were a dish the gods might feed on.

[Exeunt some with prisoners.]

VINDITIUS. (*From a window.*)
    Oh the gods! Oh the gods! What will they do with 45
    him? Oh these priests, rogues, cutthroats! A dish
    for the gods, but the Devil's cooks to dress him.
TIBERIUS.
    Thus then. The Fecialians have set down
A platform copied from the King's design.
The Pandane or the Romulide, the Roman, 50
Carmental, and Janiculan Ports of Rome,
The Circ, the Capitol, and Sublician Bridge[60]
Must all be seized by us that are within.
'Twill not be hard in the surprise of night
By us, the consuls' children and their nephews, 55
To kill the drowsy guards and keep the holds,

At least so long till Tarquin force his entrance
With all the royalists that come to join us.
Therefore, to make his broader squadrons' way,
Tarquinian is designed to be the entry 60
Of his most pompous and resolved revenge.
AQUILIUS.
    The first decreed in this great execution
Is here set down your father and Valerius.
TIBERIUS.
    That's as the King shall please, but for Valerius,
I'll take myself the honor of his head 65
And wear it on my spear. The Senate all
Without exception shall be sacrificed
And those that are the mutinous heads o'th'people
Whom I have marked to be the soldiers' spoil,
For plunder must be given, and who so fit 70
As those notorious limbs, your Commonwealth's
    men?
Their daughters to be ravished, and their sons
Quartered like brutes upon the common shambles.[61]
VITELLIUS.
    Now for the letters, which the Fecialians
Require us all to sign and send to Tarquin, 75
Who will not else be apt to trust his heralds
Without credentials under every hand,
The business being indeed of vast import
On which the hazard of his life and empire,
As well as all our fortunes, does depend. 80
TIBERIUS.
    It were a break to the whole enterprise
To make a scruple in our great affair.
I will sign first, and for my brother Titus,
Whom his new wife detains, I have his hand
And seal to show, as fast and firm as any. 85
VINDITIUS.
    Oh villainy! Villainy! What would they do with me
    if they should catch me peeping? Knock out my
    brains at least; another dish for the priests, who
    would make fine sauce of 'em for the haunch of a
    fat citizen! 90
TIBERIUS.
    All hands have here subscribed, and that your hearts
Prove resolute to what your hands have giv'n,

---

60 Pandane … Sublician Bridge] After naming various gates
    (ports) of Rome, Tiberius names other prominent sites
    in Rome: The Circ is the Circus Maximus, a famous
    Roman race course; the Sublician Bridge was the only
    bridge over the Tiber River until the second century
    BCE. The Tarquinian (below) is another city gate.
    Stroup and Cooke point out that the places named here
    are all found in Madeleine de Scudéry's popular seven-
    teenth-century novel *Clélie*, from which Lee derived his
    love plot and an interpretation of the historical action.

61 shambles] here, a place of mass slaughter, originally a
    meat market or a slaughterhouse

Behold the messengers of Heav'n to bind you,
Charms of religion, sacred conjurations,
With sounds of execration, words of horror,   95
Not to disclose or make least signs or show
Of what you have both heard and seen and sworn,
But bear yourselves as if it ne'er had been.
Swear by the gods celestial and infernal,
By Pluto, Mother Earth, and by the Furies,   100
Not to reveal, though racks were set before you,
A syllable of what is past and done.
—Hark, how the offered brutes begin to roar!
Oh that the hearts of all the traitor Senate
And heads of that foul hydra multitude   105
Were frying with their fat upon this pile,
That we might make an off'ring worth an empire
And sacrifice rebellion to the King.

*The scene draws, showing the sacrifice: one burning
and another crucified, the priests coming forward with
goblets in their hands filled with human blood.*

FIRST PRIEST.
    Kneel, all you heroes of this black design,
    Each take his goblet filled with blood and wine.   110
    Swear by the Thunderer, swear by Jove,
    Swear by the hundred gods above;
    Swear by Dis, by Proserpine,
    Swear by the Berecynthian queen.[62]
SECOND PRIEST.
    To keep it close till Tarquin comes   115
    With trumpets' sound and beat of drums;
    But then to thunder forth the deed,
    That Rome may blush and traitors bleed.
    Swear all.
ALL.
                We swear.   120
FIRST PRIEST.
                        Now drink the blood
    To make the conjuration good.
TIBERIUS.
    Methinks I feel the slave's exalted blood
    Warm at my heart. Oh that it were the spirits
    Of Rome's best life, drawn from her grizzled fathers!   125
    That were a draught indeed to quench ambition,
    And give new fierceness to the King's revenge.

VINDITIUS.
    Oh the gods! What, burn a man alive! Oh
cannibals, hell-hounds! Eat one man and drink
another! Well, I'll to Valerius; Brutus will not   130
believe me, because his sons and nephews are in
the business. What, drink a man's blood! Roast
him and eat him alive! A whole man roasted!
Would not an ox serve the turn? Priests to do this!
Oh you immortal gods! For my part, if this be your   135
worship, I renounce you. No, if a man can't go to
heaven unless your priests eat him and drink him
and roast him alive, I'll be for the broad way,[63] and
the Devil shall have me at a venture. (*Exit.*)

Enter Titus.

TITUS.
    What ho, Tiberius! Give me back my hand.   140
    What have you done? Horrors and midnight
        murders!
    The gods, the gods awake you to repentance,
    As they have me. Wouldst thou believe me, brother?
    Since I delivered thee that fatal scroll,
    That writing to the King, my heart rebelled   145
    Against itself; my thoughts were up in arms
    All in a roar, like seamen in a storm;
    My reason and my faculties were wracked,
    The mast, the rudder, and the tackling gone,
    My body, like the hull of some lost vessel,   150
    Beaten and tumbled with my rolling fears.
    Therefore I charge thee, give me back my writing.
TIBERIUS.
    What means my brother?
TITUS.
                        Oh Tiberius, oh!
    Dark as it seems, I tell thee that the gods   155
    Look through a day of lightning on our city.
    The heav'n's on fire, and from the flaming vault
    Portentous blood pours like a torrent down.
    There are a hundred gods in Rome tonight,
    And every larger spirit is abroad,   160

62 Berecynthian queen] Cybele, an Earth Mother goddess

63 priests eat ... the broad way] allusion to the Catholic
"sacrifice of the mass" (with its concomitant doctrine of
transubstantiation) and to Matthew 7:13: "Enter by the
narrow gate; for wide is the gate and broad is the way
that leads to destruction."

Monuments emptied, every urn is shaken
To fright the state and put the world in arms.
Just now I saw three Romans stand amazed
Before a flaming sword, then dropped down dead,
Myself untouched, while through the blazing air   165
A fleeting head, like a full riding moon,
Glanced by and cried, "Titus, I am Egeria.
Repent, repent, or certain death attends thee.
Treason and tyranny shall not prevail;
Kingdom shall be no more: Egeria says it.   170
And that vast turn imperial Fate designed
I saw, oh Titus, on th'eternal loom:
'Tis ripe, 'tis perfect, and is doomed to stand."

FIRST PRIEST.
Fumes, fumes—the phantoms of an ill digestion.
The gods are as good quiet gods as may be,   175
They're fast asleep and mean not to disturb us,
Unless your frenzy wake 'em.

TITUS.
                    Peace, fury, peace.
May the gods doom me to the pains of hell
If I enjoyed the beauties that I saved.   180
The horror of my treason shocked my joys,
Enervated my purpose, while I lay
Colder than marble by her virgin side,
As if I had drunk the blood of elephants,[64]
Drowsy mandragora, or the juice of hemlock.   185

FIRST PRIEST.
I like him not; I think we had best dispatch him.

TITUS.
Nothing but images of horror round me—
Rome all in blood, the ravished vestals raving,
The sacred fire put out, robbed mothers' shrieks,
Deaf'ning the gods with clamors for their babes   190
That sprawled aloft upon the soldiers' spears;
The beard of age plucked off by barbarous hands,
While from his piteous wounds and horrid gashes
The laboring life flowed faster than the blood.

*Enter Valerius, Vinditius with guards, who seize all but
the priests, who slip away. Vinditius follows them.*

VALERIUS.
Horror upon me! What will this night bring forth?   195

---

[64] blood of elephants] a drink that supposedly causes impotence (Stroup and Cooke)

Yes, you immortal gods, strike, strike the consul,
Since these are here. The crime will look less horrid
In me than in his sons. Titus, Tiberius!
Oh from this time let me be blind and dumb.
—But haste there, Mutius, fly, call hither Brutus,   200
Bid him forever leave the down of rest
And sleep no more. If Rome were all on fire,
And Tarquin in the streets bestriding slaughter,
He would less wonder than at Titus here.

TITUS.
Stop there, oh stop that messenger of fate.   205
Here bind, Valerius, bind this villain's hands,
Tear off my robes, put me upon the forks,
And lash me like a slave till I shall howl
My soul away, or hang me on a cross,
Rack me a year within some horrid dungeon,   210
So deep, so near the hells that I must suffer,
That I may groan my torments to the damned.
I do submit this traitor, this cursed villain,
To all the stings of most ingenious horror,
So thou dispatch me ere my father comes.   215
But hark! I hear the tread of fatal Brutus!
By all the gods and by the lowest Furies,
I cannot bear his face. Away with me,
Or like a whirlwind I will tear my way
I care not whither.   220

Exit with Tiberius.

VALERIUS.
                Take 'em hence together.

Enter Vinditius with the priests.

VINDITIUS.
Here, here, my lord, I have unkenneled two.
Those there are rascals made of flesh and blood,
Those are but men, but these are the gods' rogues.

VALERIUS.
Go, good Vinditius, haste and stop the people,   225
Get 'em together to the Capitol,
Where all the Senate with the consuls early
Will see strict justice done upon the traitors.
For thee, the Senate shall decree rewards
Great as thy service.   230

VINDITIUS.
I humbly thank your lordship. [*Aside.*] Why, what,
they'll make me a senator at least, and then a

consul. Oh th'immortal gods!—My lord, I go.—
To have the rods and axes carried before me and a
long purple gown trailing behind my honorable   235
heels. Well, I am made forever! (*Exit.*)

Enter Brutus attended.

BRUTUS.
Oh my Valerius, are these horrors true?
Hast thou, oh gods, this night emboweled me,
Ransacked thy Brutus' veins, thy fellow consul,
And found two villains lurking in my blood?   240
VALERIUS.
The blackest treason that e'er darkness brooded.
And who to hatch these horrors for the world,
Who to seduce the noble youth of Rome,
To draw 'em to so damned a conjuration,
To bind 'em too by new invented oaths,   245
Religious forms, and devilish sacrifices,
A sacrament of blood, for which Rome suffered
In two the worthiest of her martyred sons—
Who to do this but messengers from heav'n?
These holy men that swore so solemnly   250
Before the Senate, called the gods to curse 'em
If they intended aught against the state
Or harbored treason more than what they uttered?
BRUTUS.
Now all the fiends and furies thank 'em for it.
—You sons of murder that get drunk with blood,   255
Then stab at princes, poison commonwealths,
Destroy whole hecatombs of innocent souls,
Pile 'em like bulls and sheep upon your altars,
As you would smoke the gods from out their
   dwelling;
You shame of earth and scandal of the heav'ns,   260
You deeper fiends than any of the Furies,
That scorn to whisper envy, hate, sedition,
But with a blast of privilege proclaim it—
Priests that are instruments designed to damn us,
Fit speaking trumpets for the mouth of hell.   265
Hence with 'em, guards; secure 'em in the prison
Of Ancus Martius.[65] Read the packets o'er;
I'll bear it as I'm able, read 'em out.
VALERIUS.
"The sum of the conspiracy, to the King:

---

[65] Ancus Martius] an early Roman king

It shall begin with both the consuls' deaths   270
And then the Senate; every man must bleed
But those that have engaged to serve the King.
Be ready therefore, Sir, to send your troops
By twelve tomorrow night and come yourself
In person, if you'll reascend the throne.   275
All that have sworn to serve your Majesty
Subscribe themselves by name your faithful subjects:
Tiberius, Aquilius, Vetellius,
Trebonius, Servilius, Minutius,
Pomponius, and your Fecialian priests."   280
BRUTUS.
Hah! My Valerius, is not Titus there?
VALERIUS.
He's here, my lord, a paper by itself.
"Titus to the King:
Sir, you need only know my brother's mind
To judge of me, who am resolved to serve you."   285
What do you think, my lord?
BRUTUS.
                          Think, my Valerius?
By my heart, I know not.
I'm at a loss of thought and must acknowledge
The councils of the gods are fathomless.   290
Nay, 'tis the hardest task perhaps of life
To be assured of what is vice or virtue;
Whether when we raise up temples to the gods
We do not then blaspheme 'em. Oh behold me,
Behold the game that laughing Fortune plays—   295
Fate, or the will of Heav'n, call't what you please—
That mars the best designs that Prudence lays,
That brings events about perhaps to mock
At human reach and sport with expectation.
Consider this and wonder not at Brutus   300
If his philosophy seems at a stand,
If thou behold'st him shed unmanly tears
To see his blood, his children, his own bowels
Conspire the death of him that gave 'em being.
VALERIUS.
What heart but yours could bear it without breaking? 305
BRUTUS.
No, my Valerius, I were a beast indeed
Not to be moved with such prodigious suffering.
Yet after all I justify the gods
And will conclude there's reason supernatural
That guides us through the world with vast   310
   discretion,

Although we have not souls to comprehend it,
Which makes by wondrous methods the same causes
Produce effects though of a different nature.
Since then, for man's instruction and the glory
Of the immortal gods, it is decreed   315
There must be patterns drawn of fiercest virtue,
Brutus submits to the eternal doom.

VALERIUS.
May I believe there can be such perfection,
Such a resolve in man?

BRUTUS.
                  First, as I am their father,   320
I pardon both of 'em this black design,
But as I am Rome's consul, I abhor 'em
And cast 'em from my soul with detestation.
The nearer to my blood, the deeper grained
The color of their fault, and they shall bleed.   325
Yes, my Valerius, both my sons shall die.

Enter Teraminta.

Nay, I will stand unboweled by the altar,
See something dearer to me than my entrails
Displayed before the gods and Roman people—
The sacrifice of Justice and Revenge.   330

TERAMINTA.
What sacrifice, what victims, sir, are these
Which you intend? Oh you eternal Powers,
How shall I vent my sorrows! Oh my lord,
Yet ere you seal the death you have designed,
The death of all that's lovely in the world,   335
Hear what the witness of his soul can say,
The only evidence* that can or dare
Appear for your unhappy guiltless son.
The gods command you, Virtue, Truth, and Justice,
Which you with so much rigor have adored,   340
Beg you would hear the wretched Teraminta.

BRUTUS.
Cease thy laments. Though of the blood of Tarquin,
Yet more, the wife of my forgotten son,
Thou shalt be heard.

TERAMINTA.
                 Have you forgot him then?   345
Have you forgot yourself? The image of you,
The very picture of your excellence,
The portraiture of all your manly virtues,
Your visage stamped upon him—just those eyes,

The moving greatness of 'em, all the mercy,   350
The shedding goodness, not so quite severe,
Yet still most like—and can you then forget him?

BRUTUS.
Will you proceed?

TERAMINTA.
                  My lord, I will. Know then,
After your son, your son that loves you more   355
Than I love him, after our common Titus—
The wealth o'th'world unless you rob 'em of it—
Had long endured th'assaults of the rebellious,
And still kept fixed to what you had enjoined him;
I, as Fate ordered it, was sent from Tullia   360
With my death menaced, ev'n before his eyes,
Doomed to be stabbed before him by the priests
Unless he yielded not t'oppose the King.
Consider, sir, oh make it your own case:
Just wedded, just on the expected joys,   365
Warm for my bed and rushing to my arms,
So loving too, alas, as we did love—
Granted in haste, in heat, in flame of passion
He knew not what himself and so subscribed.
But now, sir, now, my lord, behold a wonder,   370
Behold a miracle to move your soul!
Though in my arms, just in the grasps of pleasure,
His noble heart struck with the thoughts of Brutus,
Of what he promised you, till then forgot,
Leaped in his breast and dashed him from   375
    enjoyment.
He shrieked, "Y'immortal gods, what have I done!
No, Teraminta, let us rather perish,
Divide forever with whole seas betwixt us,
Rather than sin against so good a father."
Though he before had barred your life and fortune,   380
Yet would not trust the traitors with the safety
Of him he called the image of the gods.

VALERIUS.
Oh saint-like virtue of a Roman wife!
Oh eloquence divine! Now all the arts
Of women's tongues, the rhetoric of the gods   385
Inspire thy soft and tender soul to move him.

TERAMINTA.
On this he roused, swore by the powers divine
He would fetch back the paper that he gave
Or leave his life amongst 'em, kept his word
And came to challenge it, but oh, too late.   390

For in the midst of all his piety,
His strong persuasions to a swift repentance,
His vows to lay their horrid treasons open,
His execration of the barbarous priests,
How he abhorred that bloody sacrament   395
As much as you and cursed the conjuration—
Vinditius came that had before alarmed
The wise Valerius, who with all the guards
Found Titus here, believed him like the rest,
And seized him too, as guilty of the treason.   400
VALERIUS.
But by the gods, my soul does now acquit him.
Blest be thy tongue, blest the auspicious gods
That sent thee, oh true pattern of perfection,
To plead his bleeding cause. There needs no more,
I see his father's moved. Behold a joy,   405
A wat'ry comfort rising in his eyes,
That says, "'Tis more than half a heav'n to hear thee."
BRUTUS.
Haste, oh Valerius, haste and send for Titus.

[Exit Valerius.]

TERAMINTA.
For Titus! Oh, that is a word too distant.
Say, for your son, for your beloved son,   410
The darling of the world, the joy of heav'n,
The hope of earth, your eyes not dearer to you,
Your soul's best wish, and comfort of your age.

Enter Titus with Valerius.

TITUS.
Ah, sir! Oh whither shall I run to hide me?
Where shall I lower fall? How shall I lie   415
More groveling in your view and howl for mercy?
Yet 'tis some comfort to my wild despair,
Some joy in death that I may kiss your feet
And swear upon 'em by these streaming tears,
Black as I am with all my guilt upon me,   420
I never harbored aught against your person.
Ev'n in the height of my full-fraught distraction,
Your life, my lord, was sacred, ever dear
And ever precious to unhappy Titus.
BRUTUS.
Rise, Titus. Rise, my son.   425
TITUS.
                         Alas, I dare not;
I have not strength to see the majesty

Which I have braved. If thus far I aspire,
If on your knees I hang and vent my groans,
It is too much, too much for thousand lives.   430
BRUTUS.
I pity thee, my son, and I forgive thee.
And that thou mayst believe my mercy true,
I take thee in my arms.
TITUS.
                         Oh all the gods!
BRUTUS.
Now rise, I charge thee on my blessing, rise.   435
TERAMINTA.
Ah! See sir, see, against his will, behold
He does obey, though he would choose to kneel
An age before you. See how he stands and trembles!
Now by my hopes of mercy, he's so lost,
His heart's so full, brimful of tenderness,   440
The sense of what you've done has struck him
        speechless,
Nor can he thank you now but with his tears.
BRUTUS.
My dear Valerius, let me now entreat thee
Withdraw awhile with gentle Teraminta
And leave us to ourselves.   445
TERAMINTA.
                         Ah sir, I fear you now,
Nor can I leave you with the humble Titus
Unless you promise me you will not chide
Nor fall again to anger. Do not, sir,
Do not upbraid his soft and melting temper   450
With what is past. Behold he sighs again!
Now by the gods that hitherto have blest us,
My heart forebodes a storm, I know not why.
But say, my lord, give me your god-like word
You'll not be cruel, and I'll not trust my heart,   455
Howe'er it leaps and fills me with new horror.
BRUTUS.
I promise thee.
TERAMINTA.
                         Why, then I thank you, sir,
Ev'n from my soul I thank you for this goodness.
The great, good, gracious gods reward and bless you.   460
Ah Titus, ah my soul's eternal treasure,
I fear I leave thee with a hard usurer,
But I perforce must trust thee. Oh farewell.

Exit with Valerius.

BRUTUS.

Well Titus, speak: How is it with thee now?
I would attend awhile this mighty motion,   465
Wait till the tempest were quite o'erblown,
That I might take thee in the calm of nature
With all thy gentler virtues brooding on thee,
So hushed a stillness, as if all the gods
Looked down and listened to what we were saying.   470
Speak then and tell me, oh my best beloved,
My son, my Titus, is all well again?

TITUS.

So well that saying how must make it nothing,
So well that I could wish to die this moment,
For so my heart with pow'rful throbs persuades me.   475
That were indeed to make you reparation,
That were, my lord, to thank you home, to die,
And that for Titus too would be most happy.

BRUTUS.

How's that, my son? Would death for thee be happy?

TITUS.

Most certain, sir. For in my grave I 'scape   480
All those affronts which I in life must look for,
All those reproaches which the eyes and fingers
And tongues of Rome will daily cast upon me,
From whom, to a soul so sensible as mine,
Each single scorn would be far worse than dying.   485
Besides, I 'scape the stings of my own conscience,
Which will forever rack me with remembrance,
Haunt me by day and torture me by night,
Casting my blotted honor in the way
Where'er my melancholy thoughts shall guide me.   490

BRUTUS.

But is not death a very dreadful thing?

TITUS.

Not to a mind resolved. No, sir, to me
It seems as natural as to be born.
Groans and convulsions and discolored faces,
Friends weeping round us, blacks, and obsequies   495
Make it a dreadful thing: the pomp of death
Is far more terrible than death itself.
Yes, sir, I call the Powers of heav'n to witness,
Titus dares die, if so you have decreed;
Nay, he shall die with joy to honor Brutus,   500
To make your justice famous through the world
And fix the liberty of Rome forever.
Not but I must confess my weakness too,

Yet it is great thus to resolve against it,
To have the frailty of a mortal man,   505
But the security of th'immortal gods.

BRUTUS.

Oh Titus, oh thou absolute young man!
Thou flatt'ring mirror of thy father's image,
Where I behold myself at such advantage!
Thou perfect glory of the Junian[66] race!*   510
Let me endear thee once more to my bosom,
Groan an eternal farewell to thy soul,
Instead of tears weep blood, if possible,
Blood, the heart blood of Brutus, on his child.
For thou must die, my Titus, die, my son: 515
I swear the gods have doomed thee to the grave.
The violated genius* of thy country
Rears his sad head and passes sentence on thee.
This morning sun that lights my sorrows on
To the tribunal of this horrid vengeance   520
Shall never see thee more.

TITUS.

               Alas, my lord!
Why are you moved thus? Why am I worth your
    sorrow?
Why should the godlike Brutus shake to doom me?
Why all these trappings for a traitor's hearse?   525
The gods will have it so.

BRUTUS.

               They will, my Titus.
Nor heav'n nor earth can have it otherwise.
Nay, Titus, mark: the deeper that I search,
My harassed soul returns the more confirmed.   530
Methinks I see the very hand of Jove
Moving the dreadful wheels of this affair
That whirl thee like a machine to thy fate.
It seems as if the gods had preordained it
To fix the reeling spirits of the people   535
And settle the loose liberty of Rome.
'Tis fixed. Oh therefore let not Fancy fond[67] thee:
So fixed thy death, that 'tis not in the power
Of gods or men to save thee from the axe.

TITUS.

The axe! Oh Heav'n! Then must I fall so basely?   540
What, shall I perish by the common hangman?

---

66 Junian] belonging to Junius (the family name)
67 fond] make a fool of (*OED*)

BRUTUS.

If thou deny me this, thou givest me nothing.
Yes Titus, since the gods have so decreed
That I must lose thee, I will take th'advantage
Of thy important fate, cement Rome's flaws,   545
And heal her wounded freedom with thy blood.
I will ascend myself the sad tribunal
And sit upon my sons—on thee, my Titus—
Behold thee suffer all the shame of death,
The lictor's lashes, bleed before the^e people,   550
Then, with thy hopes and all thy youth upon thee,
See thy head taken by the common axe
Without a groan, without one pitying tear,
If that the gods can hold me to my purpose
To make my justice quite transcend example.   555

TITUS.

Scourged like a bondman! Hah! A beaten slave!
But I deserve it all. Yet here I fail.
The image of this suff'ring quite unmans me,
Nor can I longer stop the gushing tears.
Oh sir! Oh Brutus! Must I call you Father,   560
Yet have no token of your tenderness,
No sign of mercy? What, not bate[68] me that!
Can you resolve—oh all th'extremity
Of cruel rigor!—to behold me too?
To sit unmoved and see me whipped to death?   565
Where are your bowels now? Is this a father?
Ah sir, why should you make my heart suspect
That all your late compassion was dissembled?
How can I think that you did ever love me?

BRUTUS.

Think that I love thee by my present passion,   570
By these unmanly tears, these earthquakes here,
These sighs that twitch the very strings of life.
Think that no other cause on earth could move me
To tremble thus, to sob or shed a tear,
Nor shake my solid virtue from her point   575
But Titus' death. Oh do not call it shameful,
That thus shall fix the glory of the world.
I own thy suff'rings ought t'unman me thus,
To make me throw my body on the ground,
To bellow like a beast, to gnaw the earth,   580
To tear my hair, to curse the cruel Fates
That force a father thus to drag his bowels.

---

68 bate] concede, spare

TITUS.

Oh rise, thou violated majesty,
Rise from the earth, or I shall beg those Fates
Which you would curse to bolt me to the center.   585
I now submit to all your threatened vengeance.
—Come forth, you executioners of Justice,
Nay, all you lictors, slaves, and common hangmen,
Come, strip me bare, unrobe me in his sight,
And lash me till I bleed, whip me like furies,   590
And when you've scourged me till I foam and fall,
For want of spirits groveling in the dust,
Then take my head and give it his revenge.
By all the gods, I greedily resign it.

BRUTUS.

No more, farewell, eternally farewell.   595
If there be gods, they will reserve a room,
A throne for thee in heav'n. One last embrace.
What is it makes thy eyes thus swim again?

TITUS.

I had forgot: be good to Teraminta
When I am ashes.   600

BRUTUS.

               Leave her to my care.
See her thou must not, for thou canst not bear it.
Oh for one more, this pull, this tug of heartstrings.
Farewell forever.

TITUS.

               Oh Brutus! Oh my father!   605

BRUTUS.

Canst thou not say farewell?

TITUS.

               Farewell forever.

BRUTUS.

Forever then. But oh, my tears run o'er.
Groans choke my words, and I can speak no more.

Exeunt.

Act V, scene i.

Valerius, Horatius, Herminius, Mutius.

HERMINIUS.

His sons condemned?

VALERIUS.

               Doomed to the rods and axes.

HORATIUS.

What, both of 'em?

VALERIUS.

      Both, sir, both, both his sons.

HORATIUS.

 What, Titus too?   5

VALERIUS.

      Yes sir, his darling Titus.

 Nay, though he knows him innocent as I am,

 'Tis all one, sir, his sentence stands like Fate.

HORATIUS.

 Yet I'll entreat him.

MUTIUS.

     So will I.   10

HERMINIUS.

     And I.

VALERIUS.

 Entreat him! Yes, you may, my lords, and move him

 As I have done. Why, he's no more a man;

 He is not cast in the same common mold,

 His spirit moves not with our springs and wards.[69] 15

 He looks and talks as if that Jove had sent him

 To be the judge of all the under world;

 Tells me this palace of the universe,

 With that vast moat, the ocean, running round us,

 Th'eternal stars so fiercely rolling o'er us, 20

 With all that circulation of heav'n's orbs,

 Were so established from before all ages

 To be the dowry of majestic Rome;

 Then looks as if he had a patent for it

 To take account of all this great expense 25

 And see the layings out of the round world.

HERMINIUS.

 What shall be done then? For it grieves my soul

 To think of Titus' loss.

VALERIUS.

       There is no help,

 But thus to shake your head and cross your arms 30

 And wonder what the gods and he intend.

HERMINIUS.

 There's scarce one man of this conspiracy

 But is some way related, if not nearly,

 To Junius Brutus. Some of the Aquilians

 Are nephews to him, and Vitellius' sister, 35

 The grave Sempronia, is the consul's wife.

---

69 springs and wards] parts of a mechanism. A ward is a
  notch in a key or a ridge in a metal lock that permits
  only correspondingly notched keys to enter.

VALERIUS.

 Therefore I have engaged that groaning matron

 To plead the cause of her unhappy sons.

Enter Titus with lictors.

 But see, oh gods, behold the gallant Titus,

 The mirror of all sons, the white of Virtue, 40

 Filled up with blots and writ all o'er with blood,

 Bowing with shame his body to the ground,

 Whipped out of breath by these inhuman slaves!

 Oh Titus! Is this possible? This shame?

TITUS.

 Oh my Valerius, call it not my shame; 45

 By all the gods, it is to Titus' honor.

 My constant suff'rings are my only glory.

 What have I left besides? But ask, Valerius,

 Ask these good men that have performed their duty,

 If all the while they whipped me like a slave, 50

 If when the blood from every part ran down,

 I gave one groan or shed a woman's tear.

 I think, I swear I think, oh my Valerius,

 That I have borne it well and like a Roman.

 But oh, far better shall I bear my death, 55

 Which, as it brings less pain, has less dishonor.

Enter Teraminta wounded.

TERAMINTA.

 Where is he? Where, where is this godlike son

 Of an inhuman, barbarous, bloody father?

 Oh bear me to him.

TITUS.

      Hah! My Teraminta! 60

 Is't possible? The very top of beauty,

 This perfect face drawn by the gods at council,

 Which they were long a-making, as they had reason,

 For they shall never hit the like again,

 Defiled and mangled thus! What barbarous wretch 65

 Has thus blasphemed this bright original?

TERAMINTA.

 For me it matters not, nor my abuses,

 But oh, for thee, why have they used thee thus?

 Whipped, Titus, whipped! And could the gods

  look on?

 The glory of the world thus basely used? 70

 Lashed, whipped, and beaten by these upright dogs,

 Whose souls, with all the virtue of the Senate,

Will be but foils to any fault of thine,
Who hast a beauty ev'n in thy offending.
And did thy father doom thee thus? Oh Titus, 75
Forgive thy dying part if she believes
A wretch so barbarous never could produce thee.
Some god, some god, my Titus, watched his absence,
Slipped to thy mother's bed, and gave thee to the
   world.

TITUS.

Oh this last wound, this stab to all my courage! 80
Hadst thou been well, I could have borne more
   lashes.
And is it thus my father does protect thee?

TERAMINTA.

Ah Titus! What, thy murd'rer my protector!
No, let me fall again among the people,
Let me be hooted like a common strumpet, 85
Tossed as I was and dragged about the streets,
The bastard of a Tarquin, foiled in dirt,
The cry of all those bloodhounds that did hunt me
Thus to the goal of death, this happy end
Of all my miseries, here to pant my last, 90
To wash thy gashes with my farewell tears,
To murmur, sob, and lean my aching head
Upon thy breast, thus like a cradle babe
To suck thy wounds and bubble out my soul.

Enter Sempronia, Aquilia, Vitellia, mourners, etc.

SEMPRONIA.

Come, ladies, haste, and let us to the Senate. 95
If the gods give us leave, we'll be today
Part of the council.—Oh my son, my Titus!
See here the bloody justice of a father,
See how the vengeance rains from his own bowels!
Is he not mad?—If he refuse to hear us, 100
We'll bind his hands as one bereft of reason.
Haste then.—Oh Titus, I would stay to moan thee,
But that I fear his orders are gone out
For something worse, for death to take the heads
Of all the kindred of these wretched women. 105

TERAMINTA.

Come then. I think I have some spirits left
To join thee, oh most pious, best of mothers,
To melt this rocky heart. Give me your hand:
Thus let us march before this wretched host
And offer to that god of blood our vows. 110

If there be aught that's human left about him,
Perhaps my wounds and horrible abuses,
Helped with the tears and groans of this sad troop,
May batter down the best of his resolves.

TITUS.

Hark, Teraminta. 115

TERAMINTA.

                No, my lord, away.

Exeunt [women].

TITUS.

Oh my Valerius! Was there ever day
Through all the legends of recorded time
So sad as this? But see, my father comes!

Enter Brutus, Tiberius, lictors.

Tiberius too has undergone the lash. 120
Give him the patience, gods, of martyred Titus,
And he will bless those hands that have chastised
   him.

TIBERIUS.

Enjoy the bloody conquest of thy pride,
Thou more tyrannical than any Tarquin,
Thou fiercer sire of these unhappy sons 125
Than impious Saturn or the gorged Thyestes.[70]
This cormorant sees and owns us for his children,
Yet preys upon his entrails, tears his bowels
With thirst of blood and hunger fetched from hell,
Which famished Tantalus would start to think on. 130
But end, barbarian, end the horrid vengeance
Which thou so impiously hast begun,
Perfect thy justice, as thou, tyrant, call'st it,
Sit like a fury on thy black tribunal,
Grasp with thy monstrous hands these gory heads, 135
And let thy flatt'ring orators adore thee
For triumphs which shall make thee smile at horror.

BRUTUS.

Lead to the Senate.

TIBERIUS.

                Go then to the Senate,
There make thy boast how thou hast doomed thy 140
   children

---

[70] Saturn … Thyestes] The god Saturn deliberately devoured all but one of his children (Jove escaped); the
   mortal Thyestes unknowingly ate a son or sons in a stew.

To forks and whips, for which the gods reward thee.
Away. My spirit scorns more conference with thee.
The axe will be as laughter, but the whips
That drew these stains, for this I beg the gods
With my last breath, for every drop that falls   145
From these vile wounds, to thunder curses on
    thee. (*Exit.*)
BRUTUS.
Valerius, haste, the Senate does attend us. (*Exit.*)
TITUS.
Valerius, ere you go, let me conjure thee
By all the earth holds great or honorable,
As thou art truly Roman, stamped a man,   150
Grant to thy dying Titus one request.
VALERIUS.
I'll grant thee anything, but do not talk
Of dying yet, for much I dare confide[71]
In that sad company that's gone before.
I know they'll move him to preserve his Titus,   155
For though you marked him not, as hence he parted
I could perceive with joy a silent shower
Run down his silver beard. Therefore have hope.
TITUS.
Hope, say'st thou! Oh the gods! What hope of life?
To live, to live! And after this dishonor!   160
No, my Valerius, do not make me rave,
But if thou hast a soul that's sensible,
Let me conjure thee, when we reach the Senate,
To thrust me through the heart.
VALERIUS.
                                     Not for the world.   165
TITUS.
Do't, or I swear thou hast no friendship for me.
First, thou wilt save me from the hated axe,
The hangman's hand, for by the gods I tell thee,
Thou mayst as well stop the eternal sun
And drive him back, as turn my father's purpose.   170
Next, and what most my soul entreats thee for,
I shall perhaps in death procure his pity,
For to die thus beneath his killing frown
Is damning me before my execution.
VALERIUS.
'Tis granted. By the gods, I swear to end thee,   175
For when I weigh with my more serious thought
Thy father's conduct in this dreadful justice,
I find it is impossible to save thee.
Come then, I'll lead thee, oh thou glorious victim,

Thus to the altar of untimely death,   180
Thus in thy trim, with all thy bloom of youth,
These virtues on thee whose eternal spring
Shall blossom on thy monumental marble
With never fading glory.
TITUS.
                               Let me clasp thee,   185
Boil out my thanks thus with my farewell spirits.
And now away, the taper's almost out,
Never, Valerius, to be kindled more!
Or if it be my friend, it shall continue,
Burn through all winds against the puff of Fortune,   190
To dazzle still and shine like the fixed stars
With beams of glory that shall last forever.

Exeunt.

Scene ii. The Senate.

*[Brutus, Horatius, members of their party, captive
conspirators, senators.]*

BRUTUS.
Health to the Senate! To the Fathers hail!
Jupiter, Horscius and Diespiter,
Hospital and Feretrian, Jove the Stayer,[72]
With all the hundred gods and goddesses,
Guard and defend the liberty of Rome.   5
It has been found a famous truth in story
Left by the ancient sages to their sons,
That on the change of empires or of kingdoms
Some sudden execution, fierce and great,
Such as may draw the world to admiration,*   10
Is necessary to be put in act
Against the enemies of the present state.
Had Hector, when the Greeks and Trojans met
Upon the truce and mingled with each other,
Brought to the banquet of those demigods   15
The fatal head of that illustrious whore,[73]

---

71 confide] trust or have faith (*OED*)

72 Horscius … Jove the Stayer] names and titles applied
   to Jupiter (Loftis)

73 Hector … whore] Homer's *Iliad* does not describe a
   truce during which the Greeks and Trojans mingle and
   banquet together, though there are a couple of truces.
   In Lee's passage the demigods are the ancient heroes on
   both sides; Hector is the Trojans' greatest warrior; the
   whore is Helen of Troy.

Troy might have stood till now, but that was
   wanting,*
Jove having from eternity set down
Rome to be head of all the under world.[74]
Raised with this thought and big with prophecy   20
Of what vast good may grow by such examples,
Brutus stands forth to do a dreadful justice.
I come, oh Conscript Fathers, to a deed
Wholly portentous, new, and wonderful,
Such as, perhaps, has never yet been found   25
In all memorials of former ages,
Nor ever will again. My sons are traitors,
Their tongues and hands are witnesses confessed;
Therefore, I have already passed their sentence
And wait with you to see their execution.   30

HORATIUS.
Consul, the Senate does not ask their deaths.
They are content with what's already done,
And all entreat you to remit the axe.

BRUTUS.
I thank you, Fathers, but refuse the offer.
By the assaulted majesty of Rome,   35
I swear there is no way to quit the grace,[75]
To right the Commonwealth, and thank the gods
But by the sacrificing of my bowels.
Take then, you sad revengers of the public,
These traitors hence, strike off their heads, and then   40
My sons'. No more: their doom is passed. Away.
Thus shall we stop the mouth of loud sedition,
Thus show the difference betwixt the sway
Of partial tyrants and of a freeborn people,
Where no man shall offend because he's great,   45
Where none need doubt his wife's or daughter's
   honor,
Where all enjoy their own without suspicion,
Where there's no innovation of religion,
No change of laws, nor breach of privilege,
No desperate factions gaping for rebellion,   50
No hopes of pardon for assassinates,
No rash advancements of the base or stranger
For luxury, for wit, or glorious vice,

But on the contrary a balanced trade,
Patriots* encouraged, manufactors cherished,   55
Vagabonds, walkers, drones, and swarming braves,[76]
The froth of states, scummed from the
   Commonwealth,
Idleness banished, all excess repressed,
And riots checked by sumptuary laws.
Oh Conscript Fathers, 'tis on these foundations   60
That Rome shall build her empire to the stars,
Send her commanders with her armies forth
To tame the world, and give the nations law,
Consuls, proconsuls, who to the Capitol
Shall ride upon the necks of conquered kings,   65
And when they die, mount from the gorgeous pile
In flames of spice and mingle with the gods.

HORATIUS.
Excellent Brutus! All the Senate thanks thee
And says that thou thyself art half a god.

*Enter Sempronia, Teraminta with the rest of the
mourners; Titus, Valerius, Junius.*

SEMPRONIA.
Gone, gone to death! Already sentenced! Doomed!   70
To lose the light of this dear world forever!
What, my Tiberius too? Ah, barbarous! Brutus!
Send, haste, revoke the order of their fate,
By all the pledges of our marriage bed,
If thou, inhuman judge, hast left me one   75
To put thee yet in mind thou art a father.
—Speak to him, oh you mothers of sad Rome,
Sisters and daughters, ere the execution
Of all your blood; haste, haste, and run about him,
Groan, sob, howl out the terrors of your souls,   80
Nay, fly upon him like robbed savages,
And tear him for your young.

BRUTUS.
               Away, and leave me.

SEMPRONIA.
Or if you think it better for your purpose,
Because he has the power of life and death,   85
Entreat him thus: throw all your heartless breasts
Low at his feet and like a god adore him;
Nay, make a rampier[77] round him with your bodies

---

74 Troy … under world] Lee assumes his audience's familiarity with the *Aeneid*: Troy had to fall so that Aeneas
   could escape and found Rome.
75 quit the grace] pay the debt (Loftis)

76 walkers, drones, … braves] vagrants, parasites, bullies
77 rampier] rampart

And block him up. I see he would be going,
Yet that's a sign that our complaints have moved him.   90
Continued falls of ever-streaming tears,
Such, and so many, and the chastest too
Of all the pious matrons throughout Rome,
Perhaps may melt this adamantine temper.
Not yet! Nay, hang your bodies then upon him,   95
Some on his arms and some upon his knees,
And lay this innocent about his neck,
This little smiling image of his father.
See how he bends and stretches to his bosom!
Oh all you pitying Pow'rs, the darling weeps;   100
His pretty eyes ruddy and wet with tears,
Like two burst cherries rolling in a storm,
Plead for our griefs more than a thousand tongues.

JUNIUS.
Yes, yes, my father will be good to us
And spare my brothers, oh, I know he will.   105
Why, do you think he ever was in earnest?
What, to cut off their heads? I warrant you
He will not; no, he only meant to fright 'em,
As he will me when I have done a fault.
Why Mother, he has whipped 'em for't already,   110
And do you think he has the heart to kill 'em?
No, no, he would not cut their little fingers
For all the world, or if he should, I'm sure
The gods would pay him for't.

BRUTUS.
                              What ho! Without there!   115
Slaves, villains, hah! Are not my orders heard?

HORATIUS.
Oh Brutus, see, they are too well performed![78]
See here the bodies of the Roman youth
All headless by your doom, and there Tiberius.

TERAMINTA.
See, sir, behold, is not this horrid slaughter,   120
This cutting off one limb from your own body,
Is't not enough? Oh, will it not suffice
To stop the mouth of the most bloody law?
Oh, it were highest sin to make a doubt[79]
To ask you now to save the innocent Titus;   125

---

[78] performed!] A stage direction is missing. Either the
screens draw to reveal an execution tableau, or else the
victims are brought on from the wings and displayed.

[79] to make a doubt] to hesitate

The common wish and general petition
Of all the Roman Senate, matrons, wives,
Widows, and babes—nay, ev'n the madding people
Cry out at last that treason is revenged
And ask no more. Oh therefore spare him, sir.   130

BRUTUS.
I must not hear you. Hark, Valerius.

TERAMINTA.
By all these wounds upon my virgin breast,
Which I have suffered by your cruelty,
Although you promised Titus to defend me.

SEMPRONIA.
Yet hold thy bloody hand, tyrannic Brutus,   135
And I'll forgive thee for that headless horror.
Grant me my Titus, oh in death I ask thee.
Thou hast already broke Sempronia's heart,
Yet I will pardon that, so Titus live.
Ah, cruel judge! Thou pitiless avenger!   140
What art thou whisp'ring? Speak the horror out,
For in thy glaring eyes I read a murder.

BRUTUS.
I charge thee by thy oath, Valerius,
As thou art here deputed by the gods
And not a subject for a woman's folly,   145
Take him away and drag him to the axe.

VALERIUS.
It shall be thus then—not the hangman's hand.

Runs him through. The women shriek.

TITUS.
Oh bravely struck! Thou hast hit me to the earth
So nobly that I shall rebound to heav'n,
Where I will thank thee for this gallant wound.   150

Sempronia swoons.

BRUTUS.
Take hence this woman, haste, and bear her home.
—Why, my Valerius, didst thou rob my justice?

TITUS.
I wrought him to it, sir, that thus in death
I might have leave to pay my last obedience
And beg your blessing for the other world.   155

TERAMINTA.
Oh do not take it, Titus. Whate'er comes
From such a monstrous nature must be blasting.
—Ah, thou inhuman tyrant! But, alas,

I loiter here when Titus stays for me.
—Look here, my love; thou shalt not be before   160
  me. (*Stabs herself.*)
Thus to thy arms then. Oh make haste, my Titus,
I'm got already in the grove of Death;
The heav'n is all benighted, not one star
To light us through the dark and pathless maze.
I've lost thy spirit; oh, I grope about   165
But cannot find thee. Now I sink in shadows.
    (*Dies.*)

TITUS.
I come, thou matchless virtue. Oh my heart!
Farewell, my love; we'll meet in heav'n again.
—My lord, I hope your justice is atoned;
I hope the glorious liberty of Rome,   170
Thus watered by the blood of both your sons,
Will get imperial growth and flourish long.

BRUTUS.
Thou hast so nobly borne thyself in dying
That not to bless thee were to curse myself;
Therefore, I give thee thus my last embrace,   175
Print this last kiss upon thy trembling lips,
And ere thou goest, I beg thee to report me
To the great shades of Romulus and Numa,
Just with that majesty and rugged virtue
Which they inspired and which the world has seen.   180
So, for I see thou'rt gone, farewell forever.
Eternal Jove, the king of gods and men,
Reward and crown thee in the other world.

TITUS.
What happiness has life to equal this?
By all the gods, I would not live again,   185
For what can Jove or all the gods give more,
To fall thus crowned with Virtue's fullest charms
And die thus blest in such a father's arms? (*Dies.*)

VALERIUS.
He's gone, the gallant spirit's fled forever.
—How fares this noble vessel that is robbed   190
Of all its wealth, spoiled of its topmast glory,
And now lies floating in this world of ruin?

BRUTUS.
Peace, Consul, peace, let us not soil the pomp
Of this majestic fate with woman's brawls.
Kneel, Fathers, friends, kneel, all you Roman people,   195
Hushed as dead calms, while I conceive a prayer
That shall be worthy Rome and worthy Jove.

VALERIUS.
Inspire him, gods, and thou, oh Rome, attend.

BRUTUS.
Let heav'n and earth forever keep their bound,
The stars unshaken go their constant round;   200
In harmless labor be our steel employed,
And endless peace through all the world enjoyed;
Let every bark the waves in safety plough,
No angry tempest curl the ocean's brow;
No darted flames from heav'n make mortals fear,   205
Nor thunder fright the weeping passenger;
Let not poor swains for storms at harvest mourn,
But smile to see their hoards of bladed corn;
No dreadful comets threaten from the skies,
No venom fall, nor pois'nous vapors rise.   210
Thou, Jove, who dost the fates of empires doom,
Guard and defend the liberty of Rome.

[Exeunt.]

FINIS.

Textual Notes

a Copytext is the first quarto in 1681 (Q1). Subsequent early editions all derive from Q1: a second quarto in 1708 (Q2) and three collected works, 1713 (C1), 1722 (C2), and 1734 (C3). Also consulted were two modern editions in 1954-55 (Stroup and Cooke) and in 1967 (Loftis).

b all alight on fire] all on a light fire, all editions

c *Stabs herself.*] Stroup and Cooke, Loftis; *om.* Q1

d Waving] Q1-2; Waiting C1-3, Stroup and Cooke, Loftis. "Waving" seems more likely in the sense of to make motions (with the uplifted hands or with something held in the hands) by way of signal (OED). That is, Brutus will wave off the Tarquins in a threatening manner as he passes them on the road. In the first speech of Act III (below) Collatinus refers to Tarquin as having been "scolded from our walls"—confirming the manner in which Brutus passed Tarquin as he left the city. "Waiting" for the Tarquins might suggest that Brutus intends a direct confrontation, but the conclusion to the present sentence—and the subsequent action of the play—do not indicate such a plan.

e the] C2, C3, Stroup and Cooke; *om.* Q1, Q2, C1, Loftis

Cato[a]

by Joseph Addison (1672-1719)
edited by Laura J. Rosenthal

Joseph Addison's *Cato*, based on Cato the Younger's famous suicide in resistance to capture by Caesar at Utica (in North Africa) during the Roman Republic's Civil War, became one of the most popular tragedies of the eighteenth century. Many prominent critics lavished praise upon it for its uplifting ideals; others, however, attacked it as lacking plausibility, failing to follow the rules for "correct" tragedy, and creating a figure of dubious admirability for its hero. Surely some of the play's early popularity must be attributed to the way it dovetailed with current political concerns, for both Whigs and Tories claimed it as the expression of their deepest beliefs. Specifically, the Whigs read Cato as the duke of Marlborough and the play as an argument for Britain's continued participation in the War of Spanish Succession against the threat of an aligned French and Spanish Empire through a Bourbon succession to the throne of Spain. The Tories, on the other hand, were able to read Caesar as Marlborough, advancing British imperial interests at the expense of virtue. Yet Addison did not necessarily write this play originally to comment on the controversy over continued participation in the War of Spanish Succession, for he had drafted it much earlier—a fact that did not prevent him from taking great care that his play would not offend either party and from reaping the rewards of his political acumen. *Cato*'s contemplation of the problem of liberty resonated in the American colonies as well as in Great Britain: Nathan Hale paraphrased from *Cato* when he regretted having but one life to give to his country, and George Washington had *Cato* performed at Valley Forge.

Modern critics have tended to recognize *Cato*'s importance as primarily a dramatization of party politics; aesthetically, however, *Cato* has been treated as a museum piece at best—as an interesting expression of the early eighteenth century's emulation of Roman stoicism in a play whose formality, stiffness, and apparent severe moral point offer primarily historical interest. Yet these modern views underestimate *Cato* in two significant ways. First, *Cato*'s intersection with eighteenth-century politics exceeds the specific case of Marlborough and even the conflict between Whigs and Tories, for *Cato* also explores the relationship between empire and colony. While Cato himself adheres firmly—even stubbornly—to a set of values he identifies as Roman, his young friend and ally, the African prince Juba, experiences the complexity of attachment to more than one culture. As in Thomas Southerne's (also very popular) dramatic adaptation of Aphra Behn's *Oroonoko*, the love plot brings together an African and a European. But while the romance in *Oroonoko* ends tragically, in *Cato*, despite some expressions of blatant ethnocentrism, these lovers provide a ray of hope and a possibility of reconciliation that Cato himself cannot achieve.

Second, to read this play as the simple advocacy of Roman stoicism (as the following selection from Pope's prologue invites) misses its complexity. Like all great tragedies, *Cato* has at its center a character who falls short of, rather than achieves, perfection. Cato's son Marcus certainly represents the dangers of an excess of passion; Addison, however, does not entirely condemn feelings in this play. If Marcus represents one extreme, then perhaps Cato represents the other.

Prologue by [Alexander] Pope

To wake the soul by tender strokes of art,
To raise the genius and to mend the heart,
To make mankind in conscious virtue bold,
Live o'er each scene and be what they behold:
For this the Tragic Muse first trod the stage,   5
Commanding tears to stream through every age;
Tyrants no more their savage nature kept,
And foes to virtue wondered how they wept.
Our author shuns by vulgar springs to move
The hero's glory or the virgin's love;   10
In pitying love, we but our weakness show,
And wild ambition well deserves its woe.
Here tears shall flow from a more gen'rous* cause,
Such tears as patriots* shed for dying laws.
He bids your breasts with ancient ardor rise,   15
And calls forth Roman drops from British eyes.
Virtue confessed in human shape he draws,
What Plato thought, and godlike Cato was:
No common object to your sight displays,
But what with pleasure Heav'n itself surveys;   20
A brave man struggling in the storms of Fate,
And greatly falling with a falling state!
While Cato gives his little senate laws,
What bosom beats not in his country's cause?
Who sees him act, but envies ev'ry deed?   25
Who hears him groan, and does not wish to bleed?
Ev'n when proud Caesar, 'midst triumphal cars,
The spoils of nations, and the pomp of wars,
Ignobly vain and impotently great,
Showed Rome her Cato's figure drawn in state,   30
As her dead father's rev'rend image passed,
The pomp was darkened and the day o'ercast,
The triumph ceased—tears gushed from ev'ry eye,
The world's great victor passed unheeded by;
Her last good man dejected Rome adored,   35
And honored Caesar's less than Cato's sword.

DRAMATIS PERSONAE

MEN
    Cato.[1]

Lucius, a senator.
Sempronius, a senator.
Juba,[2] Prince of Numidia
Syphax,[3] general of the Numidians
Portius and Marcus, sons of Cato.
Decius, ambassador from Caesar.
Mutineers, guards, etc.

WOMEN
    Marcia, daughter to Cato.
    Lucia, daughter to Lucius.

Scene: Utica.

Cato.

Ecce Spectaculum dignum, ad quod respiciat, intentus operis suo, Deus! Ecce par Deo dignum, vir fortis cum mala fortuna compositus […]! Non video, inquam, quid habeat in terris Jupiter pulchrius, si convertere animum velit, quam ut spectet Catonem, jam partibus non semel fractis, nihilominus inter ruinas publicas erectum. Sen. *de Divin. Prov.*[4]

---

1 Cato] M. Porcius Cato Uticensis (95-46 BCE), Cato the Younger, as opposed to his great-grandfather, Cato the Elder or the Censor. Cato was known for his strict stoicism.

2 Juba] Juba II, the king of Mauritania. Juba's father, Juba I, died in the war against Caesar, although—unlike in the play—not until after Cato's death. The historical Juba II was only a child at this time and was compelled to grace Caesar's triumph. Restored to Numidia by Octavian, he eventually became known as an excellent ruler and a man of extraordinary learning.

3 Syphax] a Numidian prince who lived about 150 years before the play's action and became famous for his military achievements

4 *Ecce … Prov.*] Seneca, *De providentia*: "But lo! here is a spectacle worthy of the regard of God as he contemplates his works; lo! here a contest worthy of God,—a brave man matched against ill-fortune, and doubly so if his also was the challenge. I do not know, I say, what nobler sight the Lord of Heaven could find on earth, should he wish to turn his attention there, than the spectacle of Cato, after his cause had already been shattered more than once, nevertheless standing erect amid the ruins of the commonwealth" (Loeb). Note that Addison has interpolated "divina" to modify Seneca's "providentia."

Act I. A large hall in the Governor's Palace.

Portius, Marcus.

PORTIUS.
  The dawn is overcast, the morning low'rs
  And heavily in clouds brings on the day,
  The great, th'important day, big with the fate
  Of Cato and of Rome.—Our father's death
  Would fill up all the guilt of civil war   5
  And close the scene of blood. Already Caesar
  Has ravaged more than half the globe and sees
  Mankind grown thin by his destructive sword.
  Should he go further, numbers would be wanting*
  To form new battles and support his crimes.   10
  Ye gods, what havoc does ambition make
  Among your works!
MARCUS.
                  Thy steady temper, Portius,
  Can look on guilt, rebellion, fraud, and Caesar
  In the calm lights of mild philosophy;   15
  I'm tortured, ev'n to madness, when I think
  On the proud victor: ev'ry time he's named,
  Pharsalia[5] rises to my view—I see
  Th'insulting tyrant prancing o'er the field
  Strowed with Rome's citizens and drenched in   20
    slaughter,
  His horse's hoofs wet with patrician blood.
  Oh Portius, is there not some chosen curse,
  Some hidden thunder in the stores of heav'n,
  Red with uncommon wrath, to blast the man
  Who owes his greatness to his country's ruin?   25
PORTIUS.
  Believe me, Marcus, 'tis an impious greatness
  And mixed with too much horror to be envied.
  How does the luster of our father's actions,
  Through the dark cloud of ills that cover him,
  Break out and burn with more triumphant   30
    brightness!
  His suff'rings shine and spread a glory round him;
  Greatly unfortunate, he fights the cause
  Of honor, virtue, liberty, and Rome.
  His sword ne'er fell but on the guilty head;
  Oppression, tyranny, and pow'r usurped   35

---

[5] Pharsalia] the city in Thessaly where Caesar defeated
  Pompey in 48 BCE

  Draw all the vengeance of his arm upon 'em.
MARCUS.
  Who knows not this? But what can Cato do
  Against a world, a base, degenerate world
  That courts the yoke and bows the neck to Caesar?
  Pent up in Utica, he vainly forms   40
  A poor epitome of Roman greatness
  And, covered with Numidian guards, directs
  A feeble army and an empty senate,
  Remnants of mighty battles fought in vain.
  By heav'ns, such virtues joined with such success   45
  Distract my very soul: our father's fortune
  Would almost tempt us to renounce his precepts.
PORTIUS.
  Remember what our father oft has told us:
  The ways of Heav'n are dark and intricate,
  Puzzled in mazes and perplexed with errors;   50
  Our understanding traces them in vain,
  Lost and bewildered in the fruitless search,
  Nor sees with how much art the windings run
  Nor where the regular confusion ends.
MARCUS.
  These are suggestions of a mind at ease.   55
  Oh Portius! Didst thou taste but half the griefs
  That wring my soul, thou couldst not talk thus
    calmly.[b]
  Passion unpitied and successless love
  Plant daggers in my heart and aggravate
  My other griefs. Were but my Lucia kind!   60
PORTIUS. (*Aside.*)
  Thou seest not that thy brother is thy rival,
  But I must hide it, for I know thy temper.
  —Now Marcus, now thy virtue's on the proof:
  Put forth thy utmost strength, work ev'ry nerve,
  And call up all thy father in thy soul;   65
  To quell the tyrant love and guard thy heart
  On this weak side, where most our nature fails,
  Would be a conquest worthy Cato's son.
MARCUS.
  Portius, the counsel which I cannot take,
  Instead of healing, but upbraids my weakness.   70
  Bid me for honor plunge into a war
  Of thickest foes and rush on certain death.
  Then shalt thou see that Marcus is not slow
  To follow glory and confess his father.
  Love is not to be reasoned down or lost   75

In high ambition and a thirst of greatness;
'Tis second life, it grows into the soul,
Warms ev'ry vein, and beats in ev'ry pulse:
I feel it here. My resolution melts—

PORTIUS.

Behold young Juba, the Numidian prince!   80
With how much care he forms himself to glory
And breaks the fierceness of his native temper
To copy out our father's bright example.
He loves our sister Marcia, greatly loves her,
His eyes, his looks, his actions all betray it.   85
But still the smothered fondness burns within him.
When most it swells and labors for a vent,
Then^c sense of honor and desire of fame
Drive the big passion back into his heart.
What! Shall an African, shall Juba's heir   90
Reproach great Cato's son and show the world
A virtue wanting* in a Roman soul?

MARCUS.

Portius, no more! Your words leave stings behind
    'em.
Whene'er did Juba or did Portius show
A virtue that has cast me at a distance   95
And thrown me out in the pursuits of honor?

PORTIUS.

Marcus, I know thy generous temper well;
Fling but th'appearance of dishonor on it,
It straight takes fire and mounts into a blaze.

MARCUS.

A brother's suff'rings claim a brother's pity.   100

PORTIUS.

Heav'n knows I pity thee: behold my eyes
Ev'n whilst I speak—Do they not swim in tears?
Were but my heart as naked to thy view,
Marcus would see it bleed in his behalf.

MARCUS.

Why then dost treat me with rebukes instead   105
Of kind, condoling cares and friendly sorrow?

PORTIUS.

Oh Marcus! Did I know the way to ease
Thy troubled heart and mitigate thy pains,
Marcus, believe me, I could die to do it.

MARCUS.

Thou best of brothers and thou best of friends!   110
Pardon a weak, distempered soul, that swells
With sudden gusts and sinks as soon in calms,

The sport of passions.—But Sempronius comes:
He must not find this softness hanging on me.
    (Exit.)

Enter Sempronius.

SEMPRONIUS. [Aside.]

Conspiracies no sooner should be formed   115
Than executed. What means Portius here?
I like not that cold youth. I must dissemble
And speak a language foreign to my heart.
—Good-morrow, Portius! Let us once embrace,
Once more embrace whilst yet we both are free.   120
Tomorrow should we thus express our friendship,
Each might receive a slave into his arms;
This sun, perhaps, this morning sun's the last
That e'er shall rise on Roman liberty.

PORTIUS.

My father has this morning called together   125
To this poor hall his little Roman senate
(The leavings of Pharsalia) to consult
If yet he can oppose the mighty torrent
That bears down Rome, and all her gods, before it,
Or must at length give up the world to Caesar.   130

SEMPRONIUS.

Not all the pomp and majesty of Rome
Can raise her senate more than Cato's presence.
His virtues render our assembly awful:*
They strike with something like religious fear
And make ev'n Caesar tremble at the head   135
Of armies flushed with conquest. Oh my Portius,
Could I but call that wondrous man my father!
Would but thy sister Marcia be propitious
To thy friend's vows, I might be blessed indeed!

PORTIUS.

Alas Sempronius, wouldst thou talk of love   140
To Marcia whilst her father's life's in danger?
Thou might'st as well court the pale trembling vestal
When she beholds the holy flame expiring.

SEMPRONIUS.

The more I see the wonders of thy race,*
The more I'm charmed. Thou must take heed, my   145
    Portius!
The world has all its eyes on Cato's son.
Thy father's merit sets thee up to view
And shows thee in the fairest point of light
To make thy virtues or thy faults conspicuous.

PORTIUS.

Well dost thou seem to check my ling'ring here 150
On this important hour—I'll straight away,
And while the fathers of the senate meet
In close debate to weigh th'events of war,
I'll animate the soldiers' drooping courage,
With love of freedom and contempt of life. 155
I'll thunder in their ears their country's cause
And try to rouse up all that's Roman in 'em.
'Tis not in mortals to command success,
But we'll do more, Sempronius: we'll deserve it.
(*Exit.*)

SEMPRONIUS.

Curse on the stripling! How he apes his sire! 160
Ambitiously sententious!—But I wonder
Old Syphax comes not; his Numidian genius
Is well disposed to mischief, were he prompt
And eager on it, but he must be spurred
And ev'ry moment quickened to the course. 165
Cato has used me ill: he has refused
His daughter Marcia to my ardent vows.
Besides, his baffled arms and ruined cause
Are bars to my ambition. Caesar's favor,
That show'rs down greatness on his friends, will
  raise me 170
To Rome's first honors. If I give up Cato,
I claim in my reward his captive daughter.
—But Syphax comes!

Enter Syphax.

SYPHAX.

                    Sempronius, all is ready:
I've sounded my Numidians, man by man, 175
And find 'em ripe for a revolt. They all
Complain aloud of Cato's discipline
And wait but the command to change their master.

SEMPRONIUS.

Believe me, Syphax, there's no time to waste:
Even whilst we speak, our conqueror comes on 180
And gathers ground upon us ev'ry moment.
Alas! Thou know'st not Caesar's active soul,
With what a dreadful course he rushes on
From war to war. In vain has nature formed
Mountains and oceans to oppose his passage; 185
He bounds o'er all, victorious in his march.
The Alps and Pyreneans sink before him;
Through winds and waves and storms he works
  his way,

Impatient for the battle. One day more
Will set the victor thund'ring at our gates. 190
But tell me, hast thou yet drawn o'er young Juba?
That still would recommend thee more to Caesar
And challenge better terms.

SYPHAX.

                    Alas, he's lost,
He's lost, Sempronius: all his thoughts are full 195
Of Cato's virtues. But I'll try once more
(For ev'ry instant I expect him here)
If yet I can subdue those stubborn principles
Of faith, of honor, and I know not what,
That have corrupted his Numidian temper 200
And struck th'infection into all his soul.

SEMPRONIUS.

Be sure to press upon him ev'ry motive.
Juba's surrender, since his father's death,
Would give up Africk into Caesar's hands
And make him lord of half the burning zone.[6] 205

SYPHAX.

But is it true, Sempronius, that your senate
Is called together? Gods! Thou must be cautious!
Cato has piercing eyes and will discern
Our frauds, unless they're covered thick with art.

SEMPRONIUS.

Let me alone, good Syphax: I'll conceal 210
My thoughts in passion ('tis the surest way);
I'll bellow out for Rome and for my country
And mouth at Caesar till I shake the senate.
Your* cold hypocrisy's a stale device,
A worn-out trick. Wouldst thou be thought in earnest? 215
Clothe thy feigned zeal in rage, in fire, in fury!

SYPHAX.

In troth, thou'rt able to instruct gray hairs
And teach the wily African deceit!

SEMPRONIUS.

Once more, be sure to try thy skill on Juba.
Meanwhile, I'll hasten to my Roman soldiers, 220
Inflame the mutiny, and underhand
Blow up their discontents till they break out,
Unlooked for, and discharge themselves on Cato.
Remember, Syphax, we must work in haste.
Oh, think what anxious moments pass between 225
The birth of plots and their last fatal periods.

---

6 half the burning zone] northern equatorial zone of Africa; that is, from the Mediterranean across the Sahara

Oh! 'Tis a dreadful interval of time,
Filled up with horror all and big with death!
Destruction hangs on ev'ry word we speak,
On ev'ry thought, till the concluding stroke   230
Determines all and closes our design. (*Exit.*)

SYPHAX.
  I'll try if yet I can reduce to reason
  This headstrong youth and make him spurn at Cato.
  The time is short, Caesar comes rushing on us—
  But hold! Young Juba sees me and approaches.   235

Enter Juba.

JUBA.
  Syphax, I joy to meet thee thus alone.
  I have observed of late thy looks are fall'n,
  O'ercast with gloomy cares and discontent.
  Then tell me, Syphax, I conjure thee, tell me,
  What are the thoughts that knit thy brow in frowns   240
  And turn thine eye thus coldly on thy prince?

SYPHAX.
  'Tis not my talent to conceal my thoughts
  Nor carry smiles and sunshine in my face
  When discontent sits heavy at my heart.
  I have not yet so much the Roman in me.   245

JUBA.
  Why dost thou cast out such ungen'rous terms
  Against the lords and sov'reigns of the world?
  Dost thou not see mankind fall down before 'em
  And own the force of their superior virtue?
  Is there a nation in the wilds of Africk   250
  Amidst our barren rocks and burning sands
  That does not tremble at the Roman name?

SYPHAX.
  Gods! Where's the worth that sets this people up
  Above your own Numidia's tawny sons!
  Do they with tougher sinews bend the bow?   255
  Or flies the javelin swifter to its mark
  Launched from the vigor of a Roman arm?
  Who like our active African instructs
  The fiery steed and trains him to his hand?
  Or guides in troops th' embattled elephant   260
  Loaden with war? These, these are arts, my Prince,
  In which your Zama does not stoop to Rome.[7]

---

7 Zama] Zama Regia, Juba I's capital city, northwest of
  Carthage—which *had* stooped to Rome when Scipio
  defeated Hannibal there

JUBA.
  These all are virtues of a meaner rank,
  Perfections that are placed in bones and nerves.
  A Roman soul is bent on higher views: 265
  To civilize the rude, unpolished world
  And lay it under the restraint of laws;
  To make man mild and sociable to man;
  To cultivate the wild, licentious savage
  With wisdom, discipline, and lib'ral arts,   270
  Th'embellishments of life. Virtues like these
  Make human nature shine, reform the soul,
  And break our fierce barbarians into men.

SYPHAX.
  Patience, kind heav'ns! Excuse an old man's warmth.
  What are these wondrous civilizing arts,   275
  This Roman polish, and this smooth behavior,
  That render man thus tractable and tame?
  Are they not only to disguise our passions,
  To set our looks at variance with our thoughts,
  To check the starts and sallies of the soul,   280
  And break off all its commerce with the tongue;
  In short, to change us into other creatures
  Than what our nature and the gods designed us?

JUBA.
  To strike thee dumb, turn up thy eyes to Cato!
  There mayst thou see to what a godlike height   285
  The Roman virtues lift up mortal man.
  While good and just and anxious for his friends,
  He's still severely bent against himself:
  Renouncing sleep and rest and food and ease,
  He strives with thirst and hunger, toil and heat,   290
  And when his fortune sets before him all
  The pomps and pleasures that his soul can wish,
  His rigid virtue will accept of none.

SYPHAX.
  Believe me, Prince, there's not an African
  That traverses our vast Numidian deserts   295
  In quest of prey and lives upon his bow
  But better practices these boasted virtues.
  Coarse are his meals, the fortune of the chase;
  Amidst the running stream he slakes his thirst,
  Toils all the day, and at th'approach of night   300
  On the first friendly bank he throws him down
  Or rests his head upon a rock till morn,
  Then rises fresh, pursues his wonted game,
  And if the following day he chance to find

A new repast or an untasted spring,   305
Blesses his stars and thinks it luxury.
JUBA.
  Thy prejudices, Syphax, won't discern
  What virtues grow from ignorance and choice
  Nor how the hero differs from the brute.
  But grant that others could with equal glory   310
  Look down on pleasures and the baits of sense;
  Where shall we find the man that bears affliction,
  Great and majestic in his griefs, like Cato?
  Heav'ns, with what strength, what steadiness of mind
  He triumphs in the midst of all his sufferings!   315
  How does he rise against a load of woes
  And thank the gods that throw the weight upon him!
SYPHAX.
  'Tis pride, rank pride, and haughtiness of soul:
  I think the Romans call it stoicism.
  Had not your royal father thought so highly   320
  Of Roman virtue and of Cato's cause,
  He had not fall'n by a slave's hand inglorious,
  Nor would his slaughtered army now have lain
  On Africk's sands, disfigured with their wounds,
  To gorge the wolves and vultures of Numidia.   325
JUBA.
  Why dost thou call my sorrows up afresh?
  My father's name brings tears into my eyes.
SYPHAX.
  Oh, that you'd profit by your father's ills!
JUBA.
  What wouldst thou have me do?
SYPHAX.
                            Abandon Cato.   330
JUBA.
  Syphax, I should be more than twice an orphan
  By such a loss.
SYPHAX.
                  Aye, there's the tie that binds you!
  You long to call him father. Marcia's charms
  Work in your heart unseen and plead for Cato.   335
  No wonder you are deaf to all I say.
JUBA.
  Syphax, your zeal becomes importunate;
  I've hitherto permitted it to rave
  And talk at large, but learn to keep it in,
  Lest it should take more freedom than I'll give it. 340
SYPHAX.
  Sir, your great father never used me thus.

Alas! He's dead! But can you e'er forget
The tender sorrows and the pangs of nature,
The fond embraces and repeated blessings,
Which you drew from him in your last farewell?   345
Still must I cherish the dear, sad remembrance
At once to torture and to please my soul.
The good old king, at parting, wrung my hand
(His eyes brimful of tears), then sighing cried,
"Prithee, be careful of my son!"—his grief   350
Swelled up so high, he could not utter more.
JUBA.
  Alas, thy story melts away my soul.
  That best of fathers! How shall I discharge
  The gratitude and duty which I owe him!
SYPHAX.
  By laying up his counsels in your heart.   355
JUBA.
  His counsels bade me yield to thy directions.
  Then Syphax, chide me in severest terms,
  Vent all thy passion, and I'll stand its shock,
  Calm and unruffled as a summer sea
  When not a breath of wind flies o'er its surface.   360
SYPHAX.
  Alas my Prince, I'd guide you to your safety.
JUBA.
  I do believe thou wouldst. But tell me, how?
SYPHAX.
  Fly from the fate that follows Caesar's foes.
JUBA.
  My father scorned to do't.
SYPHAX.
                            And therefore died.   365
JUBA.
  Better to die ten thousand thousand deaths
  Than wound my honor.
SYPHAX.
                        Rather say, your love.
JUBA.
  Syphax, I've promised to preserve my temper.
  Why wilt thou urge me to confess a flame   370
  I long have stifled and would fain conceal?
SYPHAX.
  Believe me Prince, 'tis^d hard to conquer love,
  But^e easy to divert and break its force:
  Absence might cure it, or a second mistress
  Light up another flame and put out this.   375

The glowing dames of Zama's royal court
Have faces flushed with more exalted charms.
The sun, that rolls his chariot o'er their heads,
Works up more fire and color in their cheeks:
Were you with these, my Prince, you'd soon forget   380
The pale, unripened beauties of the North.

JUBA.
'Tis not a set of features or complexion,
The tincture of a skin, that I admire.
Beauty soon grows familiar to the lover,
Fades in his eye, and palls upon the sense.   385
The virtuous Marcia tow'rs above her sex:
True, she is fair (Oh, how divinely fair!),
But still the lovely maid improves her charms
With inward greatness, unaffected wisdom,
And sanctity of manners. Cato's soul   390
Shines out in everything she acts or speaks,
While winning mildness and attractive smiles
Dwell in her looks and with becoming grace
Soften the rigor of her father's virtues.

SYPHAX.
How does your tongue grow wanton in her praise!   395
But on my knees I beg you would consider—

Enter Marcia and Lucia.

JUBA.
Hah! Syphax, is't not she? She moves this way
And with her Lucia, Lucius's fair daughter.
My heart beats thick—I prithee, Syphax, leave me.

SYPHAX. [*Aside.*]
Ten thousand curses fasten on them both!   400
Now will this woman with a single glance
Undo what I've been lab'ring all this while. (*Exit.*)

JUBA.
Hail, charming maid, how does thy beauty
    smooth
The face of war and make ev'n horror smile!
At sight of thee my heart shakes off its sorrows;   405
I feel a dawn of joy break in upon me
And for a while forget th'approach of Caesar.

MARCIA.
I should be grieved, young Prince, to think my
    presence
Unbent your thoughts and slackened them to arms,
While, warm with slaughter, our victorious foe   410
Threatens aloud and calls you to the field.

JUBA.
Oh Marcia, let me hope thy kind concerns
And gentle wishes follow me to battle!
The thought will give new vigor to my arm,
Add strength and weight to my descending sword,   415
And drive it in a tempest on the foe.

MARCIA.
My prayers and wishes always shall attend
The friends of Rome, the glorious cause of virtue,
And men approved of by the gods and Cato.

JUBA.
That Juba may deserve thy pious cares,   420
I'll gaze forever on thy godlike father,
Transplanting one by one into my life
His bright perfections till I shine like him.

MARCIA.
My father never, at a time like this,
Would lay out his great soul in words and waste   425
Such precious moments.

JUBA.
                        Thy reproofs are just,
Thou virtuous maid. I'll hasten to my troops
And fire their languid souls with Cato's virtue.
If e'er I lead them to the field, when all   430
The war shall stand ranged in its just array
And dreadful pomp, then will I think on thee!
Oh lovely maid, then will I think on thee!
And, in the shock of charging hosts, remember
What glorious deeds should grace the man who   435
    hopes
For Marcia's love. (*Exit.*)

LUCIA.
                    Marcia, you're too severe:
How could you chide the young good-natured Prince
And drive him from you with so stern an air,
A prince that loves and dotes on you to death?   440

MARCIA.
'Tis therefore, Lucia, that I chide him from me.
His air, his voice, his looks, and honest soul
Speak all so movingly in his behalf.
I dare not trust myself to hear him talk.

LUCIA.
Why will you fight against so sweet a passion   445
And steel your heart to such a world of charms?

MARCIA.
How, Lucia, wouldst thou have me sink away

In pleasing dreams and lose myself in love,
When ev'ry moment Cato's life's at stake?
Caesar comes armed with terror and revenge 450
And aims his thunder at my father's head.
Should not the sad occasion swallow up
My other cares and draw them all into it?
LUCIA.
Why have not I this constancy of mind,
Who have so many griefs to try its force? 455
Sure, nature formed me of her softest mold,
Enfeebled all my soul with tender passions,
And sunk me ev'n below my own weak sex:
Pity and love, by turns, oppress my heart.
MARCIA.
Lucia, disburthen all thy cares on me 460
And let me share thy most retired distress:
Tell me who raises up this conflict in thee?
LUCIA.
I need not blush to name them, when I tell thee
They're Marcia's brothers and the sons of Cato.
MARCIA.
They both behold thee with their sister's eyes 465
And often have revealed their passion to me.
But tell me, whose address thou favor'st most?
I long to know, and yet I dread to hear it.
LUCIA.
Which is it Marcia wishes for?
MARCIA.
                              For neither— 470
And yet for both. The youths have equal share
In Marcia's wishes and divide their sister.
But tell me, which of them is Lucia's choice?
LUCIA.
Marcia, they both are high in my esteem,
But in my love—Why wilt thou make me name him? 475
Thou know'st it is a blind and foolish passion,
Pleased and disgusted with it knows not what.
MARCIA.
Oh Lucia, I'm perplexed. Oh, tell me which
I must hereafter call my happy brother.
LUCIA.
Suppose 'twere Portius, could you blame my choice? 480
Oh Portius, thou hast stol'n away my soul!
With what a graceful tenderness he loves
And breathes the softest, the sincerest vows!
Complacency and truth and manly sweetness

Dwell ever on his tongue and smooth his thoughts. 485
Marcus is over-warm: his fond complaints
Have so much earnestness and passion in them,
I hear him with a secret kind of dread[f]
And tremble at his vehemence of temper.
MARCIA.
Alas, poor youth! How canst thou throw him 490
    from thee?
Lucia, thou know'st not half the love he bears thee;
Whene'er he speaks of thee, his heart's in flames.
He sends out all his soul in ev'ry word
And thinks and talks and looks like one transported.
Unhappy youth! How will thy coldness raise 495
Tempests and storms in his afflicted bosom!
I dread the consequence.
LUCIA.
                              You seem to plead
Against your brother Portius.
MARCIA.
                              Heaven forbid! 500
Had Portius been the unsuccessful lover,
The same compassion would have fall'n on him.
LUCIA.
Was ever virgin love distressed like mine!
Portius himself oft falls in tears before me,
As if he mourned his rival's ill success, 505
Then bids me hide the motions of my heart
Nor show which way it turns. So much he fears
The sad effects that it would have on Marcus.
MARCIA.
He knows too well how easily he's fired
And would not plunge his brother in despair 510
But waits for happier times and kinder moments.
LUCIA.
Alas, too late I find myself involved
In endless griefs and labyrinths of woe,
Born to afflict my Marcia's family
And sow dissension in the hearts of brothers. 515
Tormenting thought! It cuts into my soul.
MARCIA.
Let us not, Lucia, aggravate our sorrows,
But to the gods permit th'event of things.
Our lives, discolored with our present woes,
May still grow bright and smile with happier hours. 520
So the pure limpid stream, when foul with stains
Of rushing torrents and descending rains,

Works itself clear and, as it runs, refines,
Till by degrees, the floating mirror shines,
Reflects each flow'r that on the border grows, 525
And a new heav'n in its fair bosom shows.

Exeunt.

Act II. The Senate.[8]

[Sempronius, Lucius, and senators.]

SEMPRONIUS.
Rome still survives in this assembled senate!
Let us remember we are Cato's friends
And act like men who claim that glorious title.
LUCIUS.
Cato will soon be here and open to us
Th'occasion of our meeting. Hark! he comes! 5

A sound of trumpets.

May all the guardian gods of Rome direct him!

Enter Cato.

CATO.
Fathers, we once again are met in council.
Caesar's approach has summoned us together,
And Rome attends her fate from our resolves:
How shall we treat this bold, aspiring man? 10
Success still follows him and backs his crimes:
Pharsalia gave him Rome; Egypt has since
Received his yoke, and the whole Nile is Caesar's.
Why should I mention Juba's overthrow
And Scipio's[9] death? Numidia's burning sands 15
Still smoke with blood. 'Tis time we should decree
What course to take. Our foe advances on us
And envies us ev'n Libya's sultry deserts.
Fathers, pronounce your thoughts: Are they still fixed
To hold it out and fight it to the last? 20
Or are your hearts subdued at length and wrought
By time and ill success to a submission?
Sempronius, speak.
SEMPRONIUS.
                    My voice is still for war.
Gods, can a Roman senate long debate 25

8 Senate] The sense is a Republican Roman Senate in exile.
9 Scipio] Metellus Scipio, who aligned himself with Juba
   I, was defeated by Caesar in Africa.

Which of the two to choose, slav'ry or death!
No, let us rise at once, gird on our swords,
And, at the head of our remaining troops,
Attack the foe, break through the thick array
Of his thronged legions, and charge home upon him. 30
Perhaps some arm, more lucky than the rest,
May reach his heart and free the world from
    bondage.
Rise, fathers, rise. 'Tis Rome demands your help.
Rise, and revenge her slaughtered citizens,
Or share their fate: the corps[10] of half her senate 35
Manure the fields of Thessaly, while we
Sit here, delib'rating in cold debates
If we should sacrifice our lives to honor
Or wear them out in servitude and chains.
Rouse up, for shame! Our brothers of Pharsalia 40
Point at their wounds and cry aloud, "To battle!"
Great Pompey's shade complains that we are slow,
And Scipio's ghost walks unrevenged amongst us.
CATO.
Let not a torrent of impetuous zeal
Transport thee thus beyond the bounds of reason: 45
True fortitude is seen in great exploits
That justice warrants and that wisdom guides;
All else is tow'ring frenzy and distraction.
Are not the lives of those who draw the sword
In Rome's defense entrusted to our care? 50
Should we thus lead them to a field of slaughter?
Might not th'impartial world with reason say
We lavished at our deaths the blood of thousands
To grace our fall and make our ruin glorious?
Lucius, we next would know what's your opinion. 55
LUCIUS.
My thoughts, I must confess, are turned on peace.
Already have our quarrels* filled the world
With widows and with orphans: Scythia mourns
Our guilty wars, and earth's remotest regions
Lie half unpeopled by the feuds of Rome. 60
'Tis time to sheathe the sword and spare mankind.
It is not Caesar but the gods, my fathers,
The gods declare against us and repel
Our vain attempts. To urge the foe to battle
(Prompted by blind revenge and wild despair) 65
Were to refuse th'awards of Providence

10 corps] bodies, corpses

And not to rest in Heav'n's determination.
Already have we shown our love to Rome;
Now let us show submission to the gods.
We took up arms not to revenge ourselves   70
But free the commonwealth; when this end fails,
Arms have no further use: our country's cause,
That drew our swords, now wrests 'em from our
    hands
And bids us not delight in Roman blood
Unprofitably shed. What men could do   75
Is done already: heav'n and earth will witness,
If Rome must fall, that we are innocent.

SEMPRONIUS. (*Aside to Cato.*)

This smooth discourse and mild behavior oft
Conceal a traitor—something whispers me
All is not right—Cato, beware of Lucius.   80

CATO.

Let us appear nor rash nor diffident:
Immod'rate valor swells into a fault,
And fear, admitted into public councils,
Betrays like treason. Let us shun 'em both.
Fathers, I cannot see that our affairs   85
Are grown thus desp'rate. We have bulwarks
    round us;
Within our walls are troops inured to toil
In Africk's heats and seasoned to the sun;
Numidia's spacious kingdom lies behind us,
Ready to rise at its young prince's call.   90
While there is hope, do not distrust the gods,
But wait at least till Caesar's near approach
Force us to yield. 'Twill never be too late
To sue for chains and own a conqueror.
Why should Rome fall a moment ere her time?   95
No, let us draw her term of freedom out
In its full length and spin it to the last:
So shall we gain still one day's liberty,
And let me perish, but in Cato's judgment,
A day, an hour, of virtuous liberty   100
Is worth a whole eternity in bondage.

Enter Marcus.

MARCUS.

Fathers, this moment, as I watched the gates,
Lodged on my post, a herald is arrived
From Caesar's camp, and with him comes old
    Decius,

The Roman knight;[11] he carries in his looks   105
Impatience and demands to speak with Cato.

CATO.

By your permission, fathers, bid him enter.

Exit Marcus.

Decius was once my friend, but other prospects
Have loosed those ties and bound him fast to Caesar.
His message may determine our resolves.   110

Enter Decius.

DECIUS.

Caesar sends health to Cato.

CATO.

              Could he send it
To Cato's slaughtered friends, it would be welcome.
Are not your orders to address the Senate?

DECIUS.

My business is with Cato: Caesar sees   115
The straits to which you're driven and, as he knows
Cato's high worth, is anxious for his life.

CATO.

My life is grafted on the fate of Rome:
Would he save Cato? Bid him spare his country.
Tell your dictator[12] this, and tell him Cato   120
Disdains a life which he has pow'r to offer.

DECIUS.

Rome and her senators submit to Caesar;
Her gen'rals and her consuls are no more,
Who checked his conquests and denied his triumphs.
Why will not Cato be this Caesar's friend?   125

CATO.

Those very reasons thou hast urged forbid it.

DECIUS.

Cato, I've orders to expostulate
And reason with you, as from friend to friend:
Think on the storm that gathers o'er your head
And threatens ev'ry hour to burst upon it;   130
Still may you stand high in your country's honors:
Do but comply and make your peace with Caesar.
Rome will rejoice and cast its eyes on Cato,

---

11 knight] member of the equestrian class
12 dictator] a formal office in the Roman constitution, which Caesar held subsequently (46-44 BCE); Addison avails himself of the more modern sense: Caesar was indeed on his way to becoming a dictator in both senses.

As on the second of mankind.

CATO.

        No more! 135

I must not think of life on such conditions.

DECIUS.

Caesar is well acquainted with your virtues
And therefore sets this value on your life:
Let him but know the price of Cato's friendship
And name your terms. 140

CATO.

       Bid him disband his legions,
Restore the commonwealth to liberty,
Submit his actions to the public censure,
And stand the judgment of a Roman senate.
Bid him do this, and Cato is his friend. 145

DECIUS.

Cato, the world talks loudly of your wisdom—

CATO.

Nay more, though Cato's voice was ne'er employed
To clear the guilty and to varnish crimes,
Myself will mount the rostrum in his favor
And strive to gain his pardon from the people. 150

DECIUS.

A style like this becomes a conqueror.

CATO.

Decius, a style like this becomes a Roman.

DECIUS.

What is a Roman, that is Caesar's foe?

CATO.

Greater than Caesar, he's a friend to virtue.

DECIUS.

Consider, Cato, you're in Utica 155
And at the head of your own little senate;
You don't now thunder in the Capitol
With all the mouths of Rome to second you.

CATO.

Let him consider that who drives us hither:
'Tis Caesar's sword has made Rome's senate little 160
And thinned its ranks. Alas, thy dazzled eye
Beholds this man in a false glaring light,
Which conquest and success have thrown upon him;
Didst thou but view him right, thou'dst see him black
With murder, treason, sacrilege, and crimes 165
That strike my soul with horror but to name 'em.
I know thou look'st on me as on a wretch
Beset with ills and covered with misfortunes,

But by the gods I swear, millions of worlds
Should never buy me to be like that Caesar. 170

DECIUS.

Does Cato send this answer back to Caesar
For all his gen'rous cares and proffered friendship?

CATO.

His cares for me are insolent and vain.
Presumptuous man! The gods take care of Cato.
Would Caesar show the greatness of his soul, 175
Bid him employ his care for these my friends
And make good use of his ill-gotten pow'r
By shelt'ring men much better than himself.

DECIUS.

Your high unconquered heart makes you forget
That you're a man. You rush on your destruction. 180
But I have done. When I relate hereafter
The tale of this unhappy embassy,
All Rome will be in tears. (*Exit.*)

SEMPRONIUS.

       Cato, we thank thee.
The mighty genius of immortal Rome 185
Speaks in thy voice, thy soul breathes liberty.
Caesar will shrink to hear the words thou utter'st
And shudder in the midst of all his conquests.

LUCIUS.

The Senate owns its gratitude to Cato,
Who with so great a soul consults its safety 190
And guards our lives, while he neglects his own.

SEMPRONIUS.

Sempronius gives no thanks on this account.
Lucius seems fond of life. But what is life?
'Tis not to stalk about and draw fresh air
From time to time or gaze upon the sun; 195
'Tis to be free. When liberty is gone,
Life grows insipid and has lost its relish.
Oh, could my dying hand but lodge a sword
In Caesar's bosom and revenge my country,
By heav'ns, I could enjoy the pangs of death 200
And smile in agony.

LUCIUS.

       Others perhaps
May serve their country with as warm a zeal,
Though 'tis not kindled into so much rage.

SEMPRONIUS.

This sober conduct is a mighty virtue 205
In lukewarm patriots.*

CATO.

　　　　　　Come! No more, Sempronius,
All here are friends to Rome and to each other.
Let us not weaken still the weaker side
By our divisions.　　　　　　　　　　　　210
SEMPRONIUS.

　　　　　　Cato, my resentments
Are sacrificed to Rome—I stand reproved.
CATO.

Fathers, 'tis time you come to a resolve.
LUCIUS.

Cato, we all go into your opinion.
Caesar's behavior has convinced the Senate　　215
We ought to hold it out till terms arrive.
SEMPRONIUS.

We ought to hold it out till death. But Cato,
My private voice is drowned amid the Senate's.
CATO.

Then let us rise, my friends, and strive to fill
This little interval, this pause of life　　　　220
(While yet our liberty and fates are doubtful)
With resolution, friendship, Roman brav'ry,
And all the virtues we can crowd into it,
That Heav'n may say, it ought to be prolonged.
Fathers, farewell—the young Numidian prince　　225
Comes forward and expects to know our counsels.

Exeunt Senators. Enter Juba.

CATO.

Juba, the Roman Senate has resolved,
Till time give better prospects, still to keep
The sword unsheathed and turn its edge on Caesar.
JUBA.

The resolution fits a Roman senate.　　　　230
But Cato, lend me for a while thy patience
And condescend to hear a young man speak.
My father, when some days before his death
He ordered me to march for Utica
(Alas! I thought not then his death so near!),　　235
Wept o'er me, pressed me in his agèd arms,
And, as his griefs gave way, "My son," said he,
"Whatever fortune shall befall thy father,
Be Cato's friend; he'll train thee up to great
And virtuous deeds. Do but observe him well,　　240
Thou'lt shun misfortunes, or thou'lt learn to bear
　　'em."

CATO.

Juba, thy father was a worthy prince
And merited, alas, a better fate,
But Heav'n thought otherwise.
JUBA.

　　　　　　　　My father's fate,　　245
In spite of all the fortitude that shines
Before my face in Cato's great example,
Subdues my soul and fills my eyes with tears.
CATO.

It is an honest sorrow and becomes thee.
JUBA.

My father drew respect from foreign climes:　　250
The kings of Africk sought him for their friend;
Kings far remote that rule, as fame reports,
Behind the hidden sources of the Nile
In distant worlds on t'other side the sun—
Oft have their black ambassadors appeared,　　255
Loaden with gifts, and filled the courts of Zama.
CATO.

I am no stranger to thy father's greatness.
JUBA.

I would not boast the greatness of my father
But point out new alliances to Cato.
Had we not better leave this Utica　　　　260
To arm Numidia in our cause and court
Th'assistance of my father's pow'rful friends?
Did they know Cato, our remotest kings
Would pour embattled multitudes about him;
Their swarthy hosts would darken all our plains,　　265
Doubling the native horror of the war,
And making death more grim.
CATO.

　　　　　　　　And canst thou think
Cato will fly before the sword of Caesar?
Reduced, like Hannibal, to seek relief　　　270
From court to court and wander up and down,
A vagabond in Africk!
JUBA.

　　　　　　Cato, perhaps
I'm too officious, but my forward cares
Would fain preserve a life of so much value.　　275
My heart is wounded when I see such virtue
Afflicted by the weight of such misfortunes.
CATO.

Thy nobleness of soul obliges me.

But know, young Prince, that valor soars above
What the world calls misfortune and affliction. 280
These are not ills; else would they never fall
On Heav'n's first favorites and the best of men.
The gods, in bounty, work up storms about us
That give mankind occasion to exert
Their hidden strength and throw out into practice 285
Virtues that shun the day and lie concealed
In the smooth seasons and the calms of life.

JUBA.
I'm charmed whene'er thou talk'st! I pant for virtue!
And all my soul endeavors at perfection.

CATO.
Dost thou love watchings, abstinence, and toil, 290
Laborious virtues all? Learn them from Cato;
Success and fortune must thou learn from Caesar.

JUBA.
The best good fortune that can fall on Juba,
The whole success at which my heart aspires,
Depends on Cato. 295

CATO.
            What does Juba say?
Thy words confound me.

JUBA.
                I would fain retract them.
Give 'em me back again. They aimed at nothing.

CATO.
Tell me thy wish, young Prince; make not my ear 300
A stranger to thy thoughts.

JUBA.
                Oh! they're extravagant;
Still let me hide them.

CATO.
                What can Juba ask
That Cato will refuse! 305

JUBA.
                I fear to name it.
Marcia—inherits all her father's virtues.

CATO.
What wouldst thou say?

JUBA.
Cato, thou hast a daughter.

CATO.
Adieu, young Prince; I would not hear a word 310
Should lessen thee in my esteem. Remember
The hand of Fate is over us and Heav'n

Exacts severity from all our thoughts:
It is not now a time to talk of aught
But chains or conquest, liberty or death. (*Exit.*) 315

Enter Syphax.

SYPHAX.
How's this, my Prince! What, covered with
    confusion?
You look as if yon stern philosopher
Had just now chid you.

JUBA.
                Syphax, I'm undone!

SYPHAX.
I know it well. 320

JUBA.
            Cato thinks meanly of me.

SYPHAX.
And so will all mankind.

JUBA.
                I've opened to him
The weakness of my soul, my love for Marcia.

SYPHAX.
Cato's a proper person to entrust 325
A love-tale with.

JUBA.
                Oh! I could pierce my heart,
My foolish heart! Was ever wretch like Juba?

SYPHAX.
Alas my Prince, how are you changed of late!
I've known young Juba rise before the sun 330
To beat the thicket where the tiger slept
Or seek the lion in his dreadful haunts:
How did the color mount into your cheeks
When first you roused him to the chase! I've seen you
Ev'n in the Libyan dog-days hunt him down, 335
Then charge him close, provoke him to the rage
Of fangs and claws and, stooping from your horse,
Rivet the panting savage to the ground.

JUBA.
Prithee, no more!

SYPHAX.
                How would the old king smile 340
To see you weigh the paws, when tipped with gold,
And throw the shaggy spoils about your shoulders!

JUBA.
Syphax, this old man's talk (though honey flowed

In ev'ry word) would now lose all its sweetness.
Cato's displeased and Marcia lost forever! 345
SYPHAX.
Young Prince, I yet could give you good advice.
Marcia might still be yours.
JUBA.
                              What say'st thou, Syphax?
By heav'ns, thou turn'st me all into attention.
SYPHAX.
Marcia might still be yours. 350
JUBA.
                              As how, dear Syphax?
SYPHAX.
Juba commands Numidia's hardy troops,
Mounted on steeds unused to the restraint
Of curbs or bits and fleeter than the winds:
Give but the word, we'll snatch this damsel up 355
And bear her off.
JUBA.
                              Can such dishonest thoughts
Rise up in man! Wouldst thou seduce my youth
To do an act that would destroy my honor?
SYPHAX.
Gods! I could tear my beard to hear you talk! 360
Honor's a fine imaginary notion
That draws in raw and inexperienced men
To real mischiefs, while they hunt a shadow.
JUBA.
Wouldst thou degrade thy prince into a ruffian?
SYPHAX.
The boasted ancestors of these great men, 365
Whose virtues you admire, were all such ruffians.
This dread of nations, this almighty Rome,
That comprehends in her wide empire's bounds
All under heav'n, was founded on a rape.
Your Scipios, Caesars, Pompeys, and your Catos 370
(These gods on earth) are all the spurious brood
Of violated maids, of ravished Sabines.[13]
JUBA.
Syphax, I fear that hoary head of thine

Abounds too much in our Numidian wiles.
SYPHAX.
Indeed my Prince, you want* to know the world; 375
You have not read mankind; your youth admires
The throes and swellings of a Roman soul,
Cato's bold flights, th'extravagance of virtue.
JUBA.
If knowledge of the world makes man perfidious,
May Juba ever live in ignorance! 380
SYPHAX.
Go, go, you're young.
JUBA.
                              Gods, must I tamely bear
This arrogance unanswered! Thou'rt a traitor,
A false old traitor.
SYPHAX. (*Aside.*)
                              I have gone too far. 385
JUBA.
Cato shall know the baseness of thy soul.
SYPHAX (*Aside.*)
I must appease this storm or perish in it.
—Young Prince, behold these locks that are
    grown white
Beneath a helmet in your father's battles.
JUBA.
Those locks shall ne'er protect thy insolence. 390
SYPHAX.
Must one rash word, th'infirmity of age,
Throw down the merit of my better years?
This the reward of a whole life of service!
(*Aside.*) Curse on the boy! How steadily he hears me!
JUBA.
Is it because the throne of my forefathers 395
Still stands unfilled and that Numidia's crown
Hangs doubtful yet, whose head it shall enclose,
Thou thus presumest to treat thy Prince with scorn?
SYPHAX.
Why will you rive my heart with such expressions?
Does not old Syphax follow you to war? 400
What are his aims? Why does he load with darts
His trembling hand and crush beneath a casque
His wrinkled brows? What is it be aspires to?
Is it not this: to shed the slow remains,
His last poor ebb of blood, in your defense? 405
JUBA.
Syphax, no more! I would not hear you talk.

---

13 ravished Sabines] According to legend, Romulus, the
   founder of Rome, invited the neighboring Sabines to a
   feast, at which the Roman men captured, raped, and
   eventually married the Sabine women to increase their
   own population.

SYPHAX.

Not hear me talk! What, when my faith to Juba,
My royal master's son, is called in question?
My Prince may strike me dead, and I'll be dumb,
But whilst I live, I must not hold my tongue   410
And languish out old age in his displeasure.

JUBA.

Thou know'st the way too well into my heart;
I do believe thee loyal to thy prince.

SYPHAX.

What greater instance can I give? I've offered
To do an action which my soul abhors   415
And gain you whom you love at any price.

JUBA.

Was this thy motive? I have been too hasty.

SYPHAX.

And 'tis for this my Prince has called me traitor.

JUBA.

Sure thou mistakest; I did not call thee so.

SYPHAX.

You did indeed, my Prince, you called me traitor;   420
Nay further, threatened you'd complain to Cato.
Of what, my Prince, would you complain to Cato?
That Syphax loves you and would sacrifice
His life, nay more, his honor in your service.

JUBA.

Syphax, I know thou lov'st me, but indeed   425
Thy zeal for Juba carried thee too far.
Honor's a sacred tie, the law of kings,
The noble mind's distinguishing perfection,
That aids and strengthens virtue where it meets her
And imitates her actions where she is not: 430
It ought not to be sported with.

SYPHAX.

                              By heav'ns,
I'm ravished when you talk thus, though you
    chide me.
Alas! I've hitherto been used to think
A blind, officious zeal to serve my king   435
The ruling principle that ought to burn
And quench all others in a subject's heart.
Happy the people who preserve their honor
By the same duties that oblige their prince!

JUBA.

Syphax, thou now begin'st to speak thyself.   440
Numidia's grown a scorn among the nations

For breach of public vows. Our Punic faith
Is infamous and branded to a proverb.
Syphax, we'll join our cares, to purge away
Our country's crimes and clear her reputation.   445

SYPHAX.

Believe me, Prince, you make old Syphax weep
To hear you talk—but 'tis with tears of joy.
If e'er your father's crown adorn your brows,
Numidia will be blessed by Cato's lectures.

JUBA.

Syphax, thy hand! We'll mutually forget   450
The warmth of youth and frowardness of age:
Thy Prince esteems thy worth and loves thy person.
If e'er the scepter comes into my hand,
Syphax shall stand the second in my kingdom.

SYPHAX.

Why will you overwhelm my age with kindness?   455
My joy grows burdensome; I shan't support it.

JUBA.

Syphax, farewell. I'll hence and try to find
Some blest occasion that may set me right
In Cato's thoughts. I'd rather have that man
Approve my deeds, than worlds for my admirers.   460
    (Exit.)

SYPHAX.

Young men soon give and soon forget affronts;
Old age is slow in both—"A false old traitor!"
Those words, rash boy, may chance to cost thee dear.
My heart had still some foolish fondness for thee,
But hence! 'Tis gone. I give it to the winds—   465
Caesar, I'm wholly thine—

Enter Sempronius.

                              All hail, Sempronius!
Well, Cato's senate is resolved to wait
The fury of a siege before it yields.

SEMPRONIUS.

Syphax, we both were on the verge of fate: 470
Lucius declared for peace, and terms were offered
To Cato by a messenger from Caesar.
Should they submit, ere our designs are ripe,
We both must perish in the common wreck,
Lost in a gen'ral, undistinguished ruin.   475

SYPHAX.

But how stands Cato?

SEMPRONIUS.

                      Thou hast seen Mount Atlas:

While storms and tempests thunder on its brows
And oceans break their billows at its feet,
It stands unmoved and glories in its height.   480
Such is that haughty man; his towering soul,
'Midst all the shocks and injuries of Fortune,
Rises superior and looks down on Caesar.

SYPHAX.
But what's this messenger?

SEMPRONIUS.
               I've practiced with him   485
And found a means to let the victor know
That Syphax and Sempronius are his friends.
But let me now examine in my turn:
Is Juba fixed?

SYPHAX.
           Yes—but it is to Cato.   490
I've tried the force of ev'ry reason on him,
Soothed and caressed, been angry, soothed again,
Laid safety, life, and int'rest in his sight,
But all are vain; he scorns them all for Cato.

SEMPRONIUS.
Come, 'tis no matter, we shall do without him.   495
He'll make a pretty figure in a triumph
And serve to trip before the victor's chariot.
Syphax, I now may hope thou hast forsook
Thy Juba's cause and wishest Marcia mine.

SYPHAX.
May she be thine as fast as thou wouldst have her!   500

SEMPRONIUS.
Syphax, I love that woman; though I curse
Her and myself, yet spite of me I love her.

SYPHAX.
Make Cato sure and give up Utica,
Caesar will ne'er refuse thee such a trifle.
But are thy troops prepared for a revolt?   505
Does the sedition catch from man to man
And run among their ranks?

SEMPRONIUS.
              All, all is ready.
The factious leaders are our friends, that spread
Murmurs and discontents among the soldiers.   510
They count their toilsome marches, long fatigues,
Unusual fastings, and will bear no more
This medley of philosophy and war.
Within an hour they'll storm the senate-house.

SYPHAX.
Meanwhile I'll draw up my Numidian troops   515

Within the square to exercise their arms
And, as I see occasion, favor thee.
I laugh to think how your unshaken Cato
Will look aghast, while unforeseen destruction
Pours in upon him thus from every side.   520
So, where our wide Numidian wastes extend,
Sudden, th'impetuous hurricanes descend,
Wheel through the air, in circling eddies play,
Tear up the sands, and sweep whole plains away.
The helpless traveler, with wild surprise,   525
Sees the dry desert all around him rise,
And smothered in the dusty whirlwind dies.

Exeunt.

Act III, scene i.
[A room in the Governor's Palace.]

Marcus and Portius.

MARCUS.
Thanks to my stars, I have not ranged about
The wilds of life ere I could find a friend;
Nature first pointed out my Portius to me
And early taught me, by her secret force,
To love thy person ere I knew thy merit,   5
Till what was instinct grew up into friendship.

PORTIUS.
Marcus, the friendships of the world are oft
Confed'racies in vice or leagues of pleasure;
Ours has severest virtue for its basis,
And such a friendship ends not but with life.   10

MARCUS.
Portius, thou know'st my soul in all its weakness;
Then prithee spare me on its tender side,
Indulge me but in love, my other passions
Shall rise and fall by virtue's nicest* rules.

PORTIUS.
When love's well-timed, 'tis not a fault to love.   15
The strong, the brave, the virtuous, and the wise
Sink in the soft captivity together.
I would not urge thee to dismiss thy passion
(I know 'twere vain) but to suppress its force,
Till better times may make it look more graceful.   20

MARCUS.
Alas! Thou talk'st like one who never felt
Th'impatient throbs and longings of a soul
That pants and reaches after distant good.

A lover does not live by vulgar time.
Believe me, Portius, in my Lucia's absence   25
Life hangs upon me and becomes a burden,
And yet when I behold the charming maid,
I'm ten times more undone, while hope and fear
And grief and rage and love rise up at once
And with variety of pain distract me.   30

PORTIUS.
What can thy Portius do to give thee help?

MARCUS.
Portius, thou oft enjoy'st the fair one's presence:
Then undertake my cause and plead it to her
With all the strength and heats of eloquence
Fraternal love and friendship can inspire.   35
Tell her thy brother languishes to death
And fades away and withers in his bloom;
That he forgets his sleep and loathes his food;
That youth and health and war are joyless to him.
Describe his anxious days and restless nights   40
And all the torments that thou seest me suffer.

PORTIUS.
Marcus, I beg thee give me not an office
That suits with me so ill. Thou know'st my temper.

MARCUS.
Wilt thou behold me sinking in my woes?
And wilt thou not reach out a friendly arm   45
To raise me from amidst this plunge of sorrows?

PORTIUS.
Marcus, thou canst not ask what I'd refuse.
But here, believe me, I've a thousand reasons—

MARCUS.
I know thou'lt say my passion's out of season,
That Cato's great example and misfortunes   50
Should both conspire to drive it from my thoughts.
But what's all this to one who loves like me!
Oh Portius, Portius, from my soul I wish
Thou didst but know thyself what 'tis to love!
Then wouldst thou pity and assist thy brother.   55

PORTIUS. (Aside.)
What should I do! If I disclose my passion,
Our friendship's at an end; if I conceal it,
The world will call me false to a friend and brother.

MARCUS.
But see where Lucia, at her wonted hour,
Amid the cool of yon high marble arch,   60
Enjoys the noon-day breeze! Observe her, Portius!

That face, that shape, those eyes, that heav'n of
beauty!
Observe her well, and blame me if thou canst.

PORTIUS.
She sees us and advances—

MARCUS.
                              I'll withdraw   65
And leave you for a while. Remember, Portius,
Thy brother's life depends upon thy tongue. (Exit.)

Enter Lucia.

LUCIA.
Did not I see your brother Marcus here?
Why did he fly the place and shun my presence?

PORTIUS.
Oh Lucia, language is too faint to show   70
His rage of love; it preys upon his life:
He pines, he sickens, he despairs, he dies.
His passions and his virtues lie confused
And mixed together in so wild a tumult
That the whole man is quite disfigured in him.   75
Heav'ns! Would one think 'twere possible for love
To make such ravage in a noble soul!
Oh Lucia, I'm distressed! My heart bleeds for him.
Ev'n now, while thus I stand blest in thy presence,
A secret damp of grief comes o'er my thoughts,   80
And I'm unhappy, though thou smilest upon me.

LUCIA.
How wilt thou guard thy honor in the shock
Of love and friendship! Think betimes, my Portius,
Think how the nuptial tie that might ensure
Our mutual bliss would raise to such a height   85
Thy brother's griefs as might perhaps destroy him.

PORTIUS.
Alas, poor youth! What dost thou think, my Lucia?
His gen'rous, open, undesigning heart
Has begged his rival to solicit for him.
Then do not strike him dead with a denial,   90
But hold him up in life and cheer his soul
With the faint glimm'ring of a doubtful hope.
Perhaps, when we have passed these gloomy hours
And weathered out the storm that beats upon us—

LUCIA.
No, Portius, no! I see thy sister's tears,   95
Thy father's anguish, and thy brother's death
In the pursuit of our ill-fated loves.

And Portius, here I swear, to Heav'n I swear,
To Heav'n and all the Pow'rs that judge mankind,
Never to mix my plighted hands with thine   100
While such a cloud of mischiefs hangs about us,
But to forget our loves and drive thee out
From all my thoughts as far—as I am able.

PORTIUS.

What hast thou said! I'm thunderstruck!—Recall
Those hasty words, or I am lost forever.   105

LUCIA.

Has not the vow already passed my lips?
The gods have heard it, and 'tis sealed in Heav'n.
May all the vengeance that was ever poured
On perjured heads o'erwhelm me if I break it!

PORTIUS. (*After a pause.*)

Fixed in astonishment, I gaze upon thee,   110
Like one just blasted by a stroke from Heav'n,
Who pants for breath and stiffens, yet alive,
In dreadful looks: a monument of wrath!

LUCIA.

At length I've acted my severest part;
I feel the woman breaking in upon me   115
And melt about my heart! My tears will flow.
But oh, I'll think no more! The hand of Fate
Has torn thee from me, and I must forget thee.

PORTIUS.

Hard-hearted, cruel maid!

LUCIA.

                              Oh, stop those sounds,   120
Those killing sounds! Why dost thou frown upon
    me?
My blood runs cold, my heart forgets to heave,
And life itself goes out at thy displeasure.
The gods forbid us to indulge our loves,
But oh! I cannot bear thy hate and live!   125

PORTIUS.

Talk not of love, thou never knew'st its force.
I've been deluded, led into a dream
Of fancied bliss. Oh Lucia, cruel maid!
Thy dreadful vow, loaden with death, still sounds
In my stunned ears. What shall I say or do?   130
Quick, let us part! Perdition's in thy presence,
And horror dwells about thee!—Hah, she faints!
Wretch that I am! What has my rashness done!
Lucia, thou injured innocence! Thou best
And loveli'st of thy sex! Awake, my Lucia,   135

Or Portius rushes on his sword to join thee.
—Her imprecations reach not to the tomb;
They shut not out society in death.—
But, hah, she moves! Life wanders up and down
Through all her face and lights up ev'ry charm.   140

LUCIA.

Oh Portius, was this well? to frown on her
That lives upon thy smiles, to call in doubt
The faith of one expiring at thy feet,
That loves thee more than ever woman loved!
—What do I say? My half-recovered sense   145
Forgets the vow in which my soul is bound.
Destruction stands betwixt us! We must part.

PORTIUS.

Name not the word, my frighted thoughts run back
And startle into madness at the sound.

LUCIA.

What wouldst thou have me do? Consider well   150
The train of ills our love would draw behind it.
Think, Portius, think thou seest thy dying brother
Stabbed at his heart and all besmeared with blood,
Storming at Heav'n and thee! Thy awful* sire
Sternly demands the cause, th'accursèd cause   155
That robs him of his son! Poor Marcia trembles,
Then tears her hair, and frantic in her griefs
Calls out on Lucia! What could Lucia answer?
Or how stand up in such a scene of sorrow!

PORTIUS.

To my confusion and eternal grief   160
I must approve the sentence that destroys me.
The mist that hung about my mind clears up,
And now, athwart the terrors that thy vow
Has planted round thee, thou appear'st more fair,
More amiable and risest in thy charms.   165
Loveli'st of women! Heav'n is in thy soul,
Beauty and virtue shine for ever round thee,
Bright'ning each other! Thou art all divine.

LUCIA.

Portius, no more! Thy words shoot through my
    heart,
Melt my resolves, and turn me all to love.   170
Why are those tears of fondness in thy eyes?
Why heaves thy heart? Why swells thy soul with
    sorrow?
It softens me too much——Farewell, my Portius,
Farewell, though death is in the word, forever!

PORTIUS.

    Stay Lucia, stay! What dost thou say? Forever!   175

LUCIA.

    Have I not sworn? If, Portius, thy success
    Must throw thy brother on his fate, farewell.
    Oh, how shall I repeat the word! Forever!

PORTIUS.

    Thus o'er the dying lamp th'unsteady flame
    Hangs quiv'ring on a point, leaps off by fits,   180
    And falls again, as loath to quit its hold.
    —Thou must not go, my soul still hovers o'er thee
    And can't get loose.

LUCIA.

               If the firm Portius shake
    To hear of parting, think what Lucia suffers!   185

PORTIUS.

    'Tis true; unruffled and serene I've met
    The common accidents of life, but here
    Such an unlooked-for storm of ills falls on me,
    It beats down all my strength. I cannot bear it.
    We must not part.   190

LUCIA.

             What dost thou say? Not part?
    Hast thou forgot the vow that I have made?
    Are there not heav'ns and gods and thunder o'er us!
    —But see, thy brother Marcus bends this way!
    I sicken at the sight. Once more, farewell,   195
    Farewell, and know thou wrong'st me, if thou think'st
    Ever was love, or ever grief, like mine. (*Exit.*)

Enter Marcus.

MARCUS.

    Portius, what hopes? How stands she? Am I doomed
    To life or death?

PORTIUS.

             What wouldst thou have me say?   200

MARCUS.

    What means this pensive posture? Thou appear'st
    Like one amazed and terrified.

PORTIUS.

                I've reason.

MARCUS.

    Thy downcast looks and thy disordered thoughts
    Tell me my fate. I ask not the success   205
    My cause has found.

PORTIUS.

             I'm grieved I undertook it.

MARCUS.

    What! Does the barb'rous maid insult my heart,
    My aching heart! and triumph in my pains?
    That I could cast her from my thoughts forever!   210

PORTIUS.

    Away! You're too suspicious in your griefs.
    Lucia, though sworn never to think of love,
    Compassionates your pains and pities you.

MARCUS.

    Compassionates my pains and pities me!
    What is compassion when 'tis void of love!   215
    Fool that I was to choose so cold a friend
    To urge my cause! Compassionates my pains!
    Prithee what art, what rhet'ric didst thou use
    To gain this mighty boon? She pities me!
    To one that asks the warm returns of love,   220
    Compassion's cruelty, 'tis scorn, 'tis death—

PORTIUS.

    Marcus, no more! Have I deserved this treatment?

MARCUS.

    What have I said! Oh Portius, oh forgive me!
    A soul exasp'rated in ills falls out
    With ev'rything: its friend, its self—but hah!   225
    What means that shout, big with the sounds of
        war?
    What new alarm?

PORTIUS.

             A second, louder yet,
    Swells in the winds and comes more full upon us.

MARCUS.

    Oh, for some glorious cause to fall in battle!   230
    Lucia, thou hast undone me! Thy disdain
    Has broke my heart: 'tis death must give me ease.

PORTIUS.

    Quick, let us hence. Who knows if Cato's life
    Stand sure? Oh Marcus, I am warmed; my heart
    Leaps at the trumpet's voice and burns for glory.   235

Exeunt.

        Scene ii. [Another room in the palace.]

Enter Sempronius with the leaders of the mutiny.

SEMPRONIUS.

    At length the winds are raised, the storm blows high.
    Be it your care, my friends, to keep it up
    In its full fury and direct it right,

Till it has spent itself on Cato's head.
Meanwhile I'll herd among his friends and seem   5
One of the number that, whate'er arrive,
My friends and fellow soldiers may be safe. (*Exit.*)
FIRST LEADER.
　We all are safe: Sempronius is our friend;
　Sempronius is as brave a man as Cato.
　But hark! He enters. Bear up boldly to him;   10
　Be sure you beat him down and bind him fast.
　This day will end our toils and give us rest;
　Fear nothing, for Sempronius is our friend.

Enter Cato, Sempronius, Lucius, Portius, and Marcus.

CATO.
　Where are these bold, intrepid sons of war,
　That greatly turn their backs upon the foe   15
　And to their general send a brave defiance?
SEMPRONIUS. (*Aside.*)
　Curse on their dastard souls, they stand astonished!
CATO.
　Perfidious men! And will you thus dishonor
　Your past exploits and sully all your wars?
　Do you confess 'twas not a zeal for Rome,   20
　Nor love of liberty, nor thirst of honor,
　Drew you thus far, but hopes to share the spoil
　Of conquered towns and plundered provinces?
　Fired with such motives, you do well to join
　With Cato's foes and follow Caesar's banners.   25
　Why did I 'scape the envenomed aspic's rage
　And all the fiery monsters of the desert
　To see this day? Why could not Cato fall
　Without your guilt? Behold, ungrateful men,
　Behold my bosom naked to your swords   30
　And let the man that's injured strike the blow.
　Which of you all suspects that he is wronged
　Or thinks he suffers greater ills than Cato?
　Am I distinguished from you but by toils,
　Superior toils, and heavier weight of cares!   35
　Painful preeminence!
SEMPRONIUS. (*Aside.*)
　By heav'ns, they droop!
　Confusion to the villains! All is lost.
CATO.
　Have you forgotten Libya's burning waste,
　Its barren rocks, parched earth, and hills of sand,   40
　Its tainted air, and all its broods of poison?

Who was the first to explore th'untrodden path
When life was hazarded in ev'ry step?
Or fainting in the long, laborious march,
When on the banks of an unlooked-for stream   45
You sunk the river with repeated draughts,
Who was the last in all your host that thirsted?
SEMPRONIUS.
　If some penurious source by chance appeared,
　Scanty of waters, when you scooped it dry
　And offered the full helmet up to Cato,   50
　Did he not dash th'untasted moisture from him?
　Did he not lead you through the midday sun
　And clouds of dust? Did not his temples glow
　In the same sultry winds and scorching heats?
CATO.
　Hence, worthless men! Hence! and complain to   55
　　Caesar
　You could not undergo the toils of war
　Nor bear the hardships that your leader bore.
LUCIUS.
　See, Cato, see th'unhappy men! They weep!
　Fear and remorse and sorrow for their crime
　Appear in ev'ry look and plead for mercy.   60
CATO.
　Learn to be honest men, give up your leaders,
　And pardon shall descend on all the rest.
SEMPRONIUS.
　Cato, commit these wretches to my care.
　First, let 'em each be broken on the rack,
　Then, with what life remains, impaled and left   65
　To writhe at leisure round the bloody stake.
　There let 'em hang and taint the southern wind.
　The partners of their crime will learn obedience,
　When they look up and see their fellow-traitors
　Stuck on a fork and blackening in the sun.   70
LUCIUS.
　Sempronius, why, why wilt thou urge the fate
　Of wretched men?
SEMPRONIUS.
　　　　　　　How! Wouldst thou clear rebellion?
　Lucius (good man) pities the poor offenders
　That would imbrue their hands in Cato's blood.   75
CATO.
　Forbear, Sempronius! See they suffer death,
　But in their deaths remember they are men.
　Strain not the laws to make their tortures grievous.

Lucius, the base, degenerate age requires
Severity and justice in its rigor: 80
This awes an impious, bold, offending world,
Commands obedience, and gives force to laws.
When by just vengeance guilty mortals perish,
The gods behold their punishment with pleasure
And lay th'uplifted thunderbolt aside.   85

SEMPRONIUS.
Cato, I execute thy will with pleasure.

CATO.
Meanwhile, we'll sacrifice to liberty.
Remember, oh my friends, the laws, the rights,
The gen'rous plan of power delivered down
From age to age by your renowned forefathers   90
(So dearly bought, the price of so much blood).
Oh, let it never perish in your hands,
But piously transmit it to your children.
Do thou, great Liberty, inspire our souls
And make our lives in thy possession happy   95
Or our deaths glorious in thy just defense.

*Exeunt Cato, et [al. except] Sempronius and the leaders
of the mutiny.*

FIRST LEADER.
Sempronius, you have acted like yourself;
One would have thought you had been half in
  earnest.

SEMPRONIUS.
Villain, stand off! base, grov'ling, worthless wretches,
Mongrels in faction, poor faint-hearted traitors!   100

SECOND LEADER.
Nay, now you carry it too far, Sempronius.
Throw off the mask, there are none here but friends.

SEMPRONIUS.
Know, villains, when such paltry slaves presume
To mix in treason, if the plot succeeds,
They're thrown neglected by, but if it fails,   105
They're sure to die like dogs as you shall do.

Enter guards.
Here, take these factious monsters, drag 'em forth
To sudden death.

FIRST LEADER.
                    Nay, since it comes to this—

SEMPRONIUS.
Dispatch 'em quick, but first pluck out their tongues, 110
Lest with their dying breath they sow sedition.

Exeunt guards with the leaders. Enter Syphax.

SYPHAX.
Our first design, my friend, has proved abortive.
Still there remains an after-game to play:
My troops are mounted; their Numidian steeds
Snuff up the wind and long to scour the desert.   115
Let but Sempronius head us in our flight,
We'll force the gate where Marcus keeps his
  guard
And hew down all that would oppose our passage.
A day will bring us into Caesar's camp.

SEMPRONIUS.
Confusion! I have failed of half my purpose.   120
Marcia, the charming Marcia's left behind!

SYPHAX.
How? Will Sempronius turn a woman's slave?

SEMPRONIUS.
Think not thy friend can ever feel the soft
Unmanly warmth and tenderness of love.
Syphax, I long to clasp that haughty maid   125
And bend her stubborn virtue to my passion.
When I have gone thus far, I'd cast her off.

SYPHAX.
Well said! That's spoken like thyself, Sempronius.
What hinders then, but that thou find her out
And hurry her away by manly force?   130

SEMPRONIUS.
But how to gain admission? For access
Is given to none but Juba and her brothers.

SYPHAX.
Thou shalt have Juba's dress and Juba's guards.
The doors will open when Numidia's prince
Seems to appear before the slaves that watch   135
  them.

SEMPRONIUS.
Heav'ns, what a thought is there! Marcia's my
  own!
How will my bosom swell with anxious joy
When I behold her struggling in my arms
With glowing beauty and disordered charms,
While fear and anger with alternate grace   140
Pant in her breast and vary in her face!
So Pluto, seized of Proserpine, conveyed
To hell's tremendous gloom th'affrighted maid,
There grimly smiled, pleased with the beauteous
  prize,

Nor envied Jove his sunshine and his skies.   145

Exeunt.

Act IV, scene i. [Another room.]

Lucia and Marcia.

LUCIA.
  Now tell me, Marcia, tell me from thy soul
  If thou believ'st it possible for woman
  To suffer greater ills than Lucia suffers?
MARIA.
  Oh Lucia, Lucia, might my big-swoll'n heart
  Vent all its griefs and give a loose to sorrow,   5
  Marcia could answer thee in sighs, keep pace
  With all thy woes, and count out tear for tear.
LUCIA.
  I know thou'rt doomed alike to be beloved
  By Juba and thy father's friend, Sempronius,
  But which of these has pow'r to charm like Portius?   10
MARCIA.
  Still must I beg thee not to name Sempronius?
  Lucia, I like not that loud, boisterous man.
  Juba to all the brav'ry of a hero
  Adds softest love and more than female sweetness;
  Juba might make the proudest of our sex,   15
  Any of womankind but Marcia, happy.
LUCIA.
  And why not Marcia? Come, you strive in vain
  To hide your thoughts from one who knows too well
  The inward glowings of a heart in love.
MARCIA.
  While Cato lives, his daughter has no right   20
  To love or hate, but as his choice directs.
LUCIA.
  But should this father give you to Sempronius?
MARCIA.
  I dare not think he will, but if he should—
  Why wilt thou add to all the griefs I suffer
  Imaginary ills and fancied tortures?   25
  I hear the sound of feet! They march this way!
  Let us retire and try if we can drown
  Each softer thought in sense of present danger.
  When love once pleads admission to our hearts
  (In spite of all the virtue we can boast),   30
  The woman that deliberates is lost.

Exeunt.

Scene ii. [Continues.]

Enter Sempronius, dressed like Juba, with Numidian guards.

SEMPRONIUS.
  The deer is lodged. I've tracked her to her covert.
  Be sure you mind the word and, when I give it,
  Rush in at once and seize upon your prey.
  Let not her cries or tears have force to move you.
  —How will the young Numidian rave to see   5
  His mistress lost? If aught could glad my soul
  Beyond th'enjoyment of so bright a prize,
  'Twould be to torture that young gay barbarian.
  —But hark, what noise! Death to my hopes! 'Tis he,
  'Tis Juba's self! There is but one way left—   10
  He must be murdered and a passage cut
  Through those his guards—Hah! Dastards, do
    you tremble!
  Or act like men or by yon azure heav'n—

Enter Juba.

JUBA.
  What do I see? Who's this that dare usurp
  The guards and habits of Numidia's prince?   15
SEMPRONIUS.
  One that was born to scourge thy arrogance,
  Presumptuous youth!
JUBA.
                        What can this mean?
    Sempronius!
SEMPRONIUS.
  My sword shall answer thee. Have at thy heart.   20
JUBA.
  Nay then, beware thy own, proud, barb'rous man!

[They fight.] Sempronius falls. His guards surrender.

SEMPRONIUS.
  Curse on my stars! Am I then doomed to fall
  By a boy's hand, disfigured in a vile
  Numidian dress, and for a worthless woman?
  Gods, I'm distracted! This my close of life!   25
  Oh, for a peal of thunder that would make
  Earth, sea, and air and heav'n and Cato tremble!
    (*Dies.*)
JUBA.
  With what a spring his furious soul broke loose
  And left the limbs still quiv'ring on the ground!

Hence let us carry off those slaves to Cato 30
That we may there at length unravel all
This dark design, this mystery of fate.

Ex[eunt] Juba, with prisoners. [Manet corpus delicti.]
Enter Lucia and Marcia.

LUCIA.
Sure 'twas the clash of swords. My troubled heart
Is so cast down and sunk amidst its sorrows,
It throbs with fear and aches at every sound. 35
Oh Marcia, should thy brothers for my sake—
I die away with horror at the thought.
MARCIA.
See, Lucia, see! Here's blood! Here's blood and murder!
Hah, a Numidian! Heav'ns preserve the Prince!
The face lies muffled up within the garment. 40
But hah! Death to my sight, a diadem
And purple robes! Oh gods! 'Tis he, 'tis he!
Juba, the loveliest youth that ever warmed
A virgin's heart, Juba lies dead before us!
LUCIA.
Now, Marcia, now call up to thy assistance 45
Thy wonted strength and constancy of mind;
Thou canst not put it to a greater trial.
MARCIA.
Lucia, look there and wonder at my patience.
Have I not cause to rave and beat my breast,
To rend my heart with grief and run distracted! 50
LUCIA.
What can I think or say to give thee comfort?
MARCIA.
Talk not of comfort, 'tis for lighter ills.
Behold a sight that strikes all comfort dead.

Enter Juba, listening.

I will indulge my sorrows and give way
To all the pangs and fury of despair: 55
That man, that best of men, deserved it from me.
JUBA. [*Aside.*]
What do I hear! And was the false Sempronius
That best of men? Oh, had I fall'n like him
And could have thus been mourned, I had been
    happy!
LUCIA.
Here will I stand, companion in thy woes, 60
And help thee with my tears; when I behold

A loss like thine, I half forget my own.
MARCIA.
'Tis not in fate to ease my tortured breast.
This empty world, to me a joyless desert,
Has nothing left to make poor Marcia happy. 65
JUBA. [*Aside.*]
I'm on the rack! Was he so near her heart?
MARCIA.
Oh, he was all made up of love and charms,
Whatever maid could wish or man admire:
Delight of ev'ry eye! When he appeared,
A secret pleasure gladdened all that saw him, 70
But when he talked, the proudest Roman blushed
To hear his virtues, and old age grew wise.
JUBA. [*Aside.*]
I shall run mad—
MARCIA.
                    Oh Juba! Juba! Juba!
JUBA. [*Aside.*]
What means that voice? Did she not call on Juba? 75
MARCIA.
Why do I think on what he was! He's dead!
He's dead and never knew how much I loved him.
Lucia, who knows but his poor bleeding heart,
Amidst its agonies, remembered Marcia,
And the last words he uttered called me cruel! 80
Alas, he knew not, hapless youth, he knew not
Marcia's whole soul was full of love and Juba!
JUBA. [*Aside.*]
Where am I? Do I live! Or am indeed
What Marcia thinks! All is Elysium round me!
MARCIA.
Ye dear remains of the most loved of men! 85
Nor modesty nor virtue here forbid
A last embrace, while thus—
JUBA.
                              See, Marcia, see,
The happy Juba lives! He lives to catch
That dear embrace and to return it too 90
With mutual warmth and eagerness of love.
MARCIA.
With pleasure and amaze I stand transported!
Sure 'tis a dream! Dead and alive at once?
If thou art Juba, who lies there?
JUBA.
                                    A wretch, 95

Disguised like Juba, on a cursed design.
The tale is long, nor have I heard it out;
Thy father knows it all. I could not bear
To leave thee in the neighborhood of death,
But flew in all the haste of love to find thee.   100
I found thee weeping and confess this once
Am rapt with joy to see my Marcia's tears.

MARCIA.

I've been surprised in an unguarded hour,
But must not now go back. The love that lay
Half smothered in my breast has broke through all   105
Its weak restraints and burns in its full luster.
I cannot, if I would, conceal it from thee.

JUBA.

I'm lost in ecstasy! And dost thou love,
Thou charming maid?

MARCIA.

                    And dost thou live to ask it?   110

JUBA.

This, this is life indeed! Life worth preserving,
Such life as Juba never felt till now!

MARCIA.

Believe me, Prince, before I thought thee dead,
I did not know myself how much I loved thee.

JUBA.

Oh fortunate mistake!   115

MARCIA.

                    Oh happy Marcia!

JUBA.

My joy! My best beloved! My only wish!
How shall I speak the transport of my soul!

MARCIA.

Lucia, thy arm! Oh, let me rest upon it!—
The vital blood, that had forsook my heart,   120
Returns again in such tumultuous tides,
It quite o'ercomes me. Lead to my apartment.
Oh Prince! I blush to think what I have said,
But Fate has wrested the confession from me.
Go on and prosper in the paths of honor.   125
Thy virtue will excuse my passion for thee
And make the gods propitious to our love.

Exeunt Marcia and Lucia.

JUBA.

I am so blessed, I fear 'tis all a dream.
Fortune, thou now hast made amends for all

Thy past unkindness. I absolve my stars.   130
What though Numidia add her conquered towns
And provinces to swell the victor's triumph!
Juba will never at his fate repine;
Let Caesar have the world, if Marcia's mine.
    (*Exit.*)

Scene iii. [Continues.]

A march at a distance. Enter Cato and Lucius.

LUCIUS.

I stand astonished! What, the bold Sempronius!
That still broke foremost through the crowd of
    patriots,*
As with a hurricane of zeal transported,
And virtuous ev'n to madness—

CATO.

                    Trust me, Lucius,   5
Our civil discords have produced such crimes,
Such monstrous crimes, I am surprised at nothing.
—Oh Lucius, I am sick of this bad world!
The daylight and the sun grow painful to me.

Enter Portius.

But see where Portius comes! What means this haste? 10
Why are thy looks thus changed?

PORTIUS.

                    My heart is grieved.
I bring such news as will afflict my father.

CATO.

Has Caesar shed more Roman blood?

PORTIUS.

                    Not so.   15
The traitor Syphax, as within the square
He exercised his troops, the signal giv'n,
Flew off at once with his Numidian horse
To the south gate, where Marcus holds the watch.
I saw and called to stop him, but in vain;   20
He tossed his arm aloft and proudly told me
He would not stay and perish like Sempronius.

CATO.

Perfidious men! But haste, my son, and see
Thy brother Marcus acts a Roman's part.

Exit Portius.

—Lucius, the torrent bears too hard upon me.   25

Justice gives way to force; the conquered world
Is Caesar's: Cato has no business in it.
LUCIUS.
While pride, oppression, and injustice reign,
The world will still demand her Cato's presence.
In pity to mankind, submit to Caesar,   30
And reconcile thy mighty soul to life.
CATO.
Would Lucius have me live to swell the number
Of Caesar's slaves or by a base submission
Give up the cause of Rome and own a tyrant?
LUCIUS.
The victor never will impose on Cato   35
Ungen'rous terms. His enemies confess
The virtues of humanity are Caesar's.
CATO.
Curse on his virtues! They've undone his country.
Such popular humanity is treason.—
But see young Juba! The good youth appears   40
Full of the guilt of his perfidious subjects.
LUCIUS.
Alas, poor Prince! His fate deserves compassion.

Enter Juba.

JUBA.
I blush and am confounded to appear
Before thy presence, Cato.
CATO.
                          What's thy crime?   45
JUBA.
I'm a Numidian.
CATO.
                 And a brave one too.
Thou hast a Roman soul.
JUBA.
                       Hast thou not heard
Of my false countrymen?   50
CATO.
                       Alas young Prince,
Falsehood and fraud shoot up in every soil,
The product of all climes—Rome has its Caesars.
JUBA.
'Tis gen'rous thus to comfort the distressed.
CATO.
'Tis just to give applause where 'tis deserved: 55
Thy virtue, Prince, has stood the test of Fortune

Like purest gold, that, tortured in the furnace,
Comes out more bright and brings forth all its
    weight.
JUBA.
What shall I answer thee? My ravished heart
O'erflows with secret joy: I'd rather gain   60
Thy praise, oh Cato, than Numidia's empire.

Enter Portius hastily.

PORTIUS.
Misfortune on misfortune! Grief on grief!
My brother Marcus—
CATO.
                   Hah! What has he done?
Has he forsook his post? Has he giv'n way?   65
Did he look tamely on and let 'em pass?
PORTIUS.
Scarce had I left my father, but I met him
Borne on the shields of his surviving soldiers,
Breathless and pale and covered o'er with wounds.
Long, at the head of his few faithful friends,   70
He stood the shock of a whole host of foes.
Till, obstinately brave and bent on death,
Oppressed with multitudes, he greatly fell.
CATO.
I'm satisfied.
PORTIUS.
              Nor did he fall before   75
His sword had pierced through the false heart of
    Syphax.
Yonder he lies. I saw the hoary traitor
Grin in the pangs of death and bite the ground.
CATO.
Thanks to the gods! My boy has done his duty.
—Portius, when I am dead, be sure thou place   80
His urn near mine.
PORTIUS.
                  Long may they keep asunder!
LUCIUS.
Oh Cato, arm thy soul with all its patience.
See where the corpse of thy dead son approaches!
The citizens and senators, alarmed,   85
Have gathered round it and attend it weeping.
CATO. (*Meeting the corpse.*)
Welcome, my son! Here lay him down, my friends,
Full in my sight, that I may view at leisure

The bloody corse and count those glorious wounds.
How beautiful is death when earned by virtue! 90
Who would not be that youth? What pity is it
That we can die but once to serve our country!
Why sits this sadness on your brows, my friends?
I should have blushed if Cato's house had stood
Secure and flourished in a civil war. 95
—Portius, behold thy brother and remember:
Thy life is not thy own when Rome demands it.

JUBA. (*Aside.*)

Was ever man like this!

CATO.

                   Alas my friends!
Why mourn you thus? Let not a private loss 100
Afflict your hearts. 'Tis Rome requires our tears.
The mistress of the world, the seat of empire,
The nurse of heroes, the delight of gods,
That humbled the proud tyrants of the earth
And set the nations free, Rome is no more. 105
Oh Liberty! Oh Virtue! Oh my country!

JUBA. (*Aside.*)

Behold that upright man! Rome fills his eyes
With tears, that flowed not o'er his own dead son.

CATO.

Whate'er the Roman virtue has subdued,
The sun's whole course, the day and year, are Caesar's. 110
For him the self-devoted Decii died,
The Fabii fell, and the great Scipios[14] conquered;
Ev'n Pompey fought for Caesar. Oh my friends!
How is the toil of Fate, the work of ages,
The Roman empire fall'n! Oh cursed ambition! 115
Fall'n into Caesar's hands! Our great forefathers
Had left him nought to conquer but his country.

JUBA.

While Cato lives, Caesar will blush to see
Mankind enslaved, and be ashamed of empire.

CATO.

Caesar ashamed! Has not he seen Pharsalia? 120

LUCIUS.

Cato, 'tis time thou save thyself and us.

CATO.

Lose not a thought on me. I'm out of danger.

Heav'n will not leave me in the victor's hand.
Caesar shall never say, "I've conquered Cato."
But oh, my friends, your safety fills my heart 125
With anxious thoughts. A thousand secret terrors
Rise in my soul: how shall I save my friends!
'Tis now, oh Caesar, I begin to fear thee.

LUCIUS.

Caesar has mercy, if we ask it of him.

CATO.

Then ask it, I conjure you! Let him know 130
Whate'er was done against him, Cato did it.
Add, if you please, that I request it of him,
That I myself with tears request it of him,
The virtue of my friends may pass unpunished.
—Juba, my heart is troubled for thy sake. 135
Should I advise thee to regain Numidia
Or seek the conqueror?

JUBA.

                 If I forsake thee
Whilst I have life, may Heav'n abandon Juba!

CATO.

Thy virtues, Prince, if I foresee aright, 140
Will one day make thee great; at Rome, hereafter
'Twill be no crime to have been Cato's friend.
—Portius, draw near! My son, thou oft hast seen
Thy sire engaged in a corrupted state,
Wrestling with vice and faction. Now thou seest me 145
Spent, overpow'red, despairing of success.
Let me advise thee to retreat betimes
To thy paternal seat, the Sabine field,
Where the great Censor[15] toiled with his own hands
And all our frugal ancestors were blessed 150
In humble virtues and a rural life.
There live retired, pray for the peace of Rome.
Content thyself to be obscurely good.
When vice prevails and impious men bear sway,
The post of honor is a private station. 155

PORTIUS.

I hope my father does not recommend
A life to Portius that he scorns himself.

CATO.

Farewell, my friends! If there be any of you
That dares not trust the victor's clemency,
Know there are ships prepared by my command 160

---

14 Decii … Scipios] famous families whose members distinguished themselves defending Rome or conquering in her name

---

15 Censor] Cato's great grandfather, Cato the Elder

(Their sails already op'ning to the winds)
That shall convey you to the wished-for port.
Is there aught else, my friends, I can do for you?
The conqueror draws near. Once more farewell!
If e'er we meet hereafter, we shall meet 165
In happier climes and on a safer shore,
Where Caesar never shall approach us more.

(Pointing to the body of his dead son.)

There the brave youth, with love of virtue fired,
Who greatly in his country's cause expired,
Shall know he conquered. The firm patriot* there 170
(Who made the welfare of mankind his care),
Though still by faction, vice, and Fortune crossed,
Shall find the gen'rous labor was not lost.

Exeunt.

Act V, scene i. [A room in the palace.]

*Cato solus, sitting in a thoughtful posture: in his hand
Plato's book on the immortality of the soul.[16] A drawn
sword on the table by him.*

CATO.
It must be so—Plato, thou reason'st well!
Else whence this pleasing hope, this fond desire,
This longing after immortality?
Or whence this secret dread and inward horror,
Of falling into nought? Why shrinks the soul 5
Back on herself and startles at destruction?
'Tis the divinity that stirs within us,
'Tis Heav'n itself, that points out an hereafter
And intimates eternity to man.
Eternity! Thou pleasing, dreadful thought! 10
Through what variety of untried being,
Through what new scenes and changes must we pass!
The wide, th'unbounded prospect lies before me,
But shadows, clouds, and darkness rest upon it.
Here will I hold. If there's a Pow'r above us 15
(And that there is all Nature cries aloud
Through all her works), he must delight in virtue,
And that which he delights in must be happy.
But when or where!—This world was made for
    Caesar.
I'm weary of conjectures—this must end 'em. 20

_____
16 *Plato's ... soul*] *The Phaedo*

(Laying his hand on his sword.)

Thus am I doubly armed: my death and life,
My bane and antidote, are both before me;
This in a moment brings me to an end,
But this informs me I shall never die.
The soul, secured in her existence, smiles 25
At the drawn dagger and defies its point.
The stars shall fade away, the sun himself
Grow dim with age, and nature sink in years,
But thou shalt flourish in immortal youth,
Unhurt amidst the wars of elements, 30
The wrecks of matter, and the crush of worlds.
What means this heaviness that hangs upon me,
This lethargy that creeps through all my senses?
Nature, oppressed and harassed out with care,
Sinks down to rest. This once I'll favor her, 35
That my awakened soul may take her flight,
Renewed in all her strength and fresh with life,
An off'ring fit for Heav'n. Let guilt or fear
Disturb man's rest: Cato knows neither of 'em,
Indiff'rent in his choice to sleep or die. 40

Enter Portius.

But, hah! How's this, my son? Why this intrusion?
Were not my orders that I would be private?
Why am I disobeyed?
PORTIUS.
                        Alas, my father!
What means this sword, this instrument of death? 45
Let me convey it hence!
CATO.
                        Rash youth, forbear!
PORTIUS.
Oh, let the prayers, th'entreaties of your friends,
Their tears, their common danger, wrest it from you.
CATO.
Wouldst thou betray me? Wouldst thou give me up 50
A slave, a captive, into Caesar's hands?
Retire, and learn obedience to a father,
Or know, young man—
PORTIUS.
                        Look not thus sternly on me;
You know I'd rather die than disobey you. 55
CATO.
'Tis well! Again I'm master of myself.

Now, Caesar, let thy troops beset our gates
And bar each avenue, thy gathering fleets
O'erspread the sea and stop up ev'ry port;
Cato shall open to himself a passage   60
And mock thy hopes—h

PORTIUS.

            Oh sir! Forgive your son,
Whose grief hangs heavy on him! Oh my father!
How am I sure it is not the last time
I e'er shall call you so? Be not displeased,   65
Oh, be not angry with me whilst I weep
And, in the anguish of my heart, beseech you
To quit the dreadful purpose of your soul.

CATO.

Thou hast been ever good and dutiful. (*Embracing
him.*)
Weep not, my son. All will be well again.   70
The righteous gods, whom I have sought to please,
Will succor Cato and preserve his children.

PORTIUS.

Your words give comfort to my drooping heart.

CATO.

Portius, thou mayst rely upon my conduct.
Thy father will not act what misbecomes him.   75
But go, my son, and see if aught be wanting
Among thy father's friends; see them embarked;
And tell me if the winds and seas befriend them.
My soul is quite weighed down with care and asks
The soft refreshment of a moment's sleep. (*Exit.*)   80

PORTIUS.

My thoughts are more at ease, my heart revives.

Enter Marcia.

Oh Marcia, oh my sister, still there's hope!
Our father will not cast away a life
So needful to us all and to his country.
He is retired to rest and seems to cherish   85
Thoughts full of peace. He has dispatched me hence
With orders that bespeak a mind composed
And studious for the safety of his friends.
Marcia, take care that none disturb his slumbers.
    (*Exit.*)

MARCIA.

Oh ye immortal Powers that guard the good,i   90
Watch round his couch and soften his repose,
Banish his sorrows, and becalm his soul

With easy dreams; remember all his virtues!
And show mankind that goodness is your care.

Enter Lucia.

LUCIA.

Where is your father, Marcia? Where is Cato?   95

MARCIA.

Lucia, speak low, he is retired to rest.
Lucia, I feel a gently dawning hope
Rise in my soul. We shall be happy still.

LUCIA.

Alas, I tremble when I think on Cato,
In every view, in every thought I tremble!   100
Cato is stern and awful* as a god;
He knows not how to wink at human frailty
Or pardon weakness that he never felt.

MARCIA.

Though stern and awful to the foes of Rome,
He is all goodness, Lucia, always mild,   105
Compassionate, and gentle to his friends.
Filled with domestic tenderness, the best,
The kindest father! I have ever found him
Easy and good and bounteous to my wishes.

LUCIA.

'Tis his consent alone can make us blessed.   110
Marcia, we both are equally involved
In the same intricate, perplexed distress.
The cruel hand of Fate that has destroyed
Thy brother Marcus, whom we both lament—

MARCIA.

And ever shall lament, unhappy youth!   115

LUCIA.

Has set my soul at large, and now I stand
Loose of my vow. But who knows Cato's thoughts?
Who knows how yet he may dispose of Portius
Or how he has determined of thyself?

MARCIA.

Let him but live! Commit the rest to Heav'n.   120

Enter Lucius.

LUCIUS.

Sweet are the slumbers of the virtuous man!
Oh Marcia, I have seen thy godlike father:
Some Pow'r invisible supports his soul
And bears it up in all its wonted greatness.
A kind, refreshing sleep is fall'n upon him.   125

I saw him stretched at ease, his fancy lost
In pleasing dreams. As I drew near his couch,
He smiled and cried, "Caesar, thou canst not hurt
    me."

MARCIA.
His mind still labors with some dreadful thought.

LUCIUS.
Lucia, why all this grief, these floods of sorrow?   130
Dry up thy tears, my child, we all are safe
While Cato lives—his presence will protect us.

Enter Juba.

JUBA.
Lucius, the horsemen are returned from viewing
The number, strength, and posture of our foes,
Who now encamp within a short hour's march.   135
On the high point of yon bright western tower
We ken them from afar; the setting sun
Plays on their shining arms and burnished helmets
And covers all the field with gleams of fire.

LUCIUS.
Marcia, 'tis time we should awake thy father.   140
Caesar is still disposed to give us terms
And waits at distance till he hears from Cato.

Enter Portius.

Portius, thy looks speak somewhat of importance,
What tidings dost thou bring? Methinks I see
Unusual gladness sparkling in thy eyes.   145

PORTIUS.
As I was hasting to the port, where now
My father's friends, impatient for a passage,
Accuse the ling'ring winds, a sail arrived
From Pompey's son, who through the realms of
    Spain
Calls out for vengeance on his father's death   150
And rouses the whole nation up to arms.
Were Cato at their head, once more might Rome
Assert her rights and claim her liberty.
But hark! what means that groan! Oh, give me way,
And let me fly into my father's presence. (*Exit.*)   155

LUCIUS.
Cato, amidst his slumbers, thinks on Rome
And in the wild disorder of his soul
Mourns o'er his country. Hah! a second groan!—
Heav'n guard us all—

MARCIA.
                    Alas! 'Tis not the voice   160
Of one who sleeps! 'Tis agonizing pain,
'Tis death is in that sound—

Re-enter Portius.

PORTIUS.
                    Oh sight of woe!
Oh Marcia, what we feared is come to pass!
Cato is fall'n upon his sword—   165

LUCIUS.
                    Oh Portius,
Hide all the horrors of thy mournful tale
And let us guess the rest.

PORTIUS.
                    I've raised him up
And placed him in his chair, where, pale and faint,   170
He gasps for breath and, as his life flows from him,
Demands to see his friends. His weeping servants,
Obsequious to his orders, bear him hither.

(*The back scene opens and discovers* Cato.*)

MARCIA.
Oh Heav'n, assist me in this dreadful hour
To pay the last sad duties to my father.   175

JUBA.
These are thy triumphs, thy exploits, oh Caesar!

LUCIUS.
Now is Rome fall'n indeed!

(*Cato brought forward in his chair.*)   180

CATO.
                    Here set me down—
Portius, come near me—are my friends embarked?
Can anything be thought of for their service?   185
Whilst I yet live, let me not live in vain.
—Oh Lucius, art thou here?—Thou art too good!—
Let this our friendship live between our children;
Make Portius happy in thy daughter Lucia.
Alas, poor man, he weeps!—Marcia, my daughter—   190
—Oh, bend me forward!—Juba loves thee, Marcia.
A senator of Rome, while Rome survived,
Would not have matched his daughter with a king,
But Caesar's arms have thrown down all distinction:
Whoe'er is brave and virtuous is a Roman.—   195
—I'm sick to death—Oh, when shall I get loose

From this vain world, th'abode of guilt and sorrow!
—And yet methinks a beam of light breaks in
On my departing soul. Alas, I fear
I've been too hasty. Oh ye Pow'rs that search   200
The heart of man and weigh his inmost thoughts,
If I have done amiss, impute it not!—
The best may err, but you are good, and—oh!
    (*Dies.*)
LUCIUS.
There fled the greatest soul that ever warmed   205
A Roman breast. Oh Cato! Oh my friend!
Thy will shall be religiously observed.
But let us bear this awful* corpse to Caesar
And lay it in his sight, that it may stand
A fence betwixt us and the victor's wrath.   210
Cato, though dead, shall still protect his friends.
From hence, let fierce contending nations know
What dire effects from civil discord flow.
'Tis this that shakes our country with alarms
And gives up Rome a prey to Roman arms,   215
Produces fraud and cruelty and strife
And robs the guilty world of Cato's life.

Exeunt omnes.

FINIS.

Textual Notes

[a] Copytext is the first edition, a 1713 quarto (Q1). Also consulted were the third, fourth, and sixth quartos (Q3, Q4, Q6) and the eighth edition, a second duodecimo (D2), all published in 1713; and the modern edition by Nettleton and Case in 1939, revised by Stone in 1969, which checked all relevant editions (NCS).

[b] calmly] Q1, NCS; coldly Q3-6, D7-8

[c] Then] Q1, NCS; the Q3-6, D7-8

[d] 'tis] Qq, NCS; tho' D7-8

[e] But] Qq, NCS; 'Tis D7-8

[f] dread] Qq, NCS; horror D7-8

[g] his] Qq, NCS; your D7-8

[h] PORTIUS … hopes—] Q3 *et seq.*; *om.* Q1, Q2, and some copies of Q3

[i] good] Q1, Q2, NCS; just Q3-6, D7-8

Personal Tragedy

Personal tragedy focuses on conflicts within individuals that have consequences for those around them. Classical, Aristotelean tragedy portrays aristocratic heroes flawed at least by errors of judgment. To paraphrase *King Lear*, when they run downhill, they drag the world along. Restoration neoclassical personal tragedy retains such protagonists, whose warring passions destroy them, leaving their states unstable. But as the revolutionary period develops, protagonists become more domestic, more bourgeois; their motivation more banal, less Herculean; and the consequences of their mistakes less cosmic, less communal. What is lost shifts from the world to a happy marriage, a career, peace of mind.

All for Love; or, The World Well Lost[a]

by John Dryden (1631-1700)

edited by Tanya Caldwell

Dryden once claimed that he "never writ anything for myself but *Anthony and Cleopatra*." Whatever the sentiments of the poet laureate during the two years over which he supposedly composed the play, *All for Love* was a dramatic and a literary success from its appearance in 1677. The second of three Shakespeare adaptations that Dryden wrote (though he also looked to historical accounts and other English dramatizations of the lives and loves of Antony and Cleopatra), *All for Love* appealed to Restoration and eighteenth-century audiences in a number of ways. First, the so-called neoclassical neatness of the play went down much better than the perceived messiness of Shakespeare's *Antony and Cleopatra*, with its many scenes, widely scattered geographical locations, and ten-year time span. While Dryden's 1668 *Essay of Dramatick Poesy* had defended English drama against charges that it did not adhere to the classical unities, *All for Love* observes unity of time, place, and action—"more exactly," Dryden admits in the preface, "than, perhaps, the English theater requires." All the same, he insists in the title page and preface that the play imitates the "style" of the "divine Shakespeare," which in order best to do he has abandoned the rhyming couplets to which his audiences had become accustomed. Dryden expresses his nervousness over this switch in a prologue. Also a sign of the times in which the play was written are the themes of love vs. honor and public duty vs. private passion. The play was first performed during great political unrest and opposition to Charles II's government, and critics noticed the parallel between Antony and Charles as rulers with foreign mistresses that threatened their political stability.

The play's staging contributed to its great success right to the end of the eighteenth century (it kept *Antony and Cleopatra* from the stage and was performed 123 times between 1700 and 1800). The King's Company production of the play, which debuted on February 12, 1677, put the popular and charismatic Charles Hart and Elizabeth Boutell in the lead roles. The cat-fight between Cleopatra and Octavia must have especially delighted audiences since the aging Katherine Corey, known for her shrewish roles, played against the young, attractive Boutell. (In his preface Dryden in fact regrets bringing Octavia on stage, for this "must lessen the favor of the audience" to the love of Antony and Cleopatra.) In the eighteenth century such powerful acting teams as Barton Booth and Anne Oldfield, Spranger Barry and Peg Wolfington took over the lead roles.

DRAMATIS PERSONAE

[MEN]

Marc Antony.
Ventidius, his general.
Dollabella, his friend.
Alexas, the Queen's eunuch.
Serapion, priest of Isis.
Another priest.
Servants to Antony.

[WOMEN]

Cleopatra, Queen of Egypt.
Octavia, Antony's wife.
Charmion, Iras, Cleopatra's maids.
Antony's two little daughters.

Scene: Alexandria.

All for Love; or, The World Well Lost.

Facile est [enim] verbum aliquod ardens (ut ita dicam) notare: idque restinctis [iam] animorum incendiis irridere. Cicero[1]

Act I. Scene: the Temple of Isis.

Enter Serapion, Myris, priests of Isis.

SERAPION.

Portents and prodigies are grown so frequent
That they have lost their name. Our fruitful Nile
Flowed ere the wonted season with a torrent
So unexpected and so wondrous fierce
That the wild deluge overtook the haste   5
Ev'n of the hinds that watched it: men and beasts
Were borne above the tops of trees that grew
On th'utmost margin of the watermark.
Then with so swift an ebb the flood drove backward,
It slipped from underneath the scaly herd: 10
Here monstrous phocae[2] panted on the shore;
Forsaken dolphins there, with their broad tails,
Lay lashing the departing waves; hard by 'em,

Sea-horses[3] flound'ring in the slimy mud
Tossed up their heads and dashed the ooze about 'em.   15

Enter Alexas behind them.

MYRIS.

Avert these omens, Heav'n.

SERAPION.

Last night, between the hours of twelve and one,
In a lone isle o'th' temple while I walked,
A whirlwind rose, that with a violent blast
Shook all the dome. The doors around me clapped;   20
The iron wicket, that defends the vault
Where the long race* of Ptolemies is laid,
Burst open, and disclosed the mighty dead.
From out each monument, in order placed,
An armed ghost start[4] up; the boy-king[5] last   25
Reared his inglorious head. A peal of groans
Then followed, and a lamentable voice
Cried, "Egypt is no more." My blood ran back,
My shaking knees against each other knocked;
On the cold pavement down I fell entranced   30
And so unfinished left the horrid scene.

ALEXAS. (*Showing himself.*)

And dreamed you this? or did invent the story
To frighten our Egyptian boys withal
And train 'em up betimes in fear of priesthood?

SERAPION.

My lord, I saw you not,   35
Nor meant my words should reach your ears, but what
I uttered was most true.

ALEXAS.

A foolish dream,
Bred from the fumes of indigested feasts[6]
And holy luxury.   40

SERAPION.

I know my duty:
This goes no farther.

---

1 *Facile … Cicero*] Cicero, *Orator* viii, 27: "It is easy, indeed, to criticize some flaming word, if I may use this
expression, and to laugh at it when the passion of the
moment has cooled" (Loeb).

2 phocae] seals

3 sea-horses] hippopotami

4 start] started (an obsolete past tense form)

5 boy-king] Ptolemy XIV, last of the kings of Egypt and
Cleopatra's half-brother, whom, according to common
practice, she married when he was just eleven years old.
He died in 44 BCE, probably poisoned or done away
with by Cleopatra.

6 indigested feasts] a common explanation for bad dreams

ALEXAS.
                    'Tis not fit it should.

Nor would the times now bear it, were it true.   45
All southern, from yon hills, the Roman camp
Hangs o'er us black and threat'ning, like a storm
Just breaking on our heads.
SERAPION.
Our faint Egyptians pray for Antony,
But in their servile hearts they own Octavius.[7]   50
MYRIS.
Why then does Antony dream out his hours
And tempts not Fortune for a noble day
Which might redeem what Actium[8] lost?
ALEXAS.
He thinks 'tis past recovery.
SERAPION.
                    Yet the foe   55
Seems not to press the siege.
ALEXAS.
                  Oh, there's the wonder.
Maecenas and Agrippa,[9] who can most[10]
With Caesar, are his foes. His wife Octavia,[11]
Driv'n from his house, solicits her revenge,   60
And Dollabella, who was once his friend,
Upon some private grudge now seeks his ruin:
Yet still war seems on either side to sleep.
SERAPION.
'Tis strange that Antony, for some days past,

---

7 Octavius] Also referred to throughout the play as "Caesar," Octavius Caesar was the nephew and adopted son of Julius Caesar. At the time of the events described in the play he was one of the three rulers of Rome, or triumvirs, along with Antony and Lepidus. When Octavius became sole ruler on Antony's death, he changed his name to Augustus.

8 Actium] the famous naval battle of Actium, in which Octavius defeated Antony, took place in 31 BCE, the year before the events portrayed in this play

9 Maecenas and Agrippa] Gaius Maecenas (70-8 BCE) was Octavius' friend, political advisor, and later propaganda agent; Marcus Agrippa, famed for his military genius, commanded Octavius' troops at Actium.

10 can most] can do most

11 Octavia] Antony married Octavius' sister after the death of his wife, Fulvia, in order to strengthen his political standing in the triumvirate.

Has not beheld the face of Cleopatra,   65
But here in Isis' temple lives retired
And makes his heart a prey to black despair.
ALEXAS.
'Tis true, and we much fear he hopes by absence
To cure his mind of love.
SERAPION.
                  If he be vanquished   70
Or make his peace, Egypt is doomed to be
A Roman province, and our plenteous harvests
Must then redeem the scarceness of their soil.
While Antony stood firm, our Alexandria
Rivaled proud Rome (Dominion's other seat),   75
And Fortune, striding like a vast Colossus,[12]
Could fix an equal foot of empire here.
ALEXAS.
Had I my wish, these tyrants of all Nature
Who lord it o'er mankind, should perish, perish
Each by the other's sword, but since our will   80
Is lamely followed by our pow'r, we must
Depend on one, with him to rise or fall.
SERAPION.
How stands the queen affected?
ALEXAS.
                  Oh, she dotes,
She dotes, Serapion, on this vanquished man   85
And winds herself about his mighty ruins,
Whom would she yet forsake, yet yield him up,
This hunted prey, to his pursuer's hands,
She might preserve us all, but 'tis in vain—
This changes my designs, this blasts my counsels   90
And makes me use all means to keep him here,
Whom I could wish divided from her arms
Far as the earth's deep center. Well, you know
The state of things; no more of your ill omens
And black prognostics; labor to confirm   95
The people's hearts.

Enter Ventidius, talking aside with a gentleman of Antony's.

SERAPION.
                These Romans will o'erhear us.
But who's that stranger? By his warlike port,

---

12 like a vast Colossus] The Colossus of Rhodes, a giant statue of Apollo, straddled the entrance to the harbor.

His fierce demeanor, and erected look,
He's of no vulgar* note.   100
ALEXAS.
                    Oh 'tis Ventidius,[13]
Our emp'ror's great lieutenant in the East,
Who first showed Rome that Parthia[14] could be
   conquered.
When Antony returned from Syria last,
He left this man to guard the Roman frontiers.   105
SERAPION.
You seem to know him well.
ALEXAS.
Too well. I saw him in Cilicia[15] first,
When Cleopatra there met Antony:
A mortal foe he was to us, and Egypt.
But, let me witness to the worth I hate,   110
A braver Roman never drew a sword.
Firm to his prince, but as a friend, not slave.
He ne'er was of his pleasures, but presides
O'er all his cooler hours and morning counsels;
In short, the plainness, fierceness, rugged virtue   115
Of an old true-stamped Roman lives in him.
His coming bodes I know not what of ill
To our affairs. Withdraw, to mark him better,
And I'll acquaint you why I sought you here
And what's our present work.   120

*They withdraw to a corner of the stage, and Ventidius
with the other comes forward to the front.*

VENTIDIUS.
Not see him, say you?
I say I must, and will.

_____

13 Ventidius] The historical Publius Ventidius, a talented
   general, in fact died in 38 BCE–before the events of this
   play.
14 Parthia] a country in ancient Asia, south-east of the Cas-
   pian sea; Ventidius conquered the Parthians in 39 and
   38 BCE.
15 Cilicia] southeastern section of what is now Turkey; after the Battle at Philippi, Antony summoned Cleopatra
   hither to account for her actions during the civil war
   precipitated by Julius Caesar's assassination. This was not
   their first meeting, for Cleopatra had been Caesar's mistress in Rome; below, Antony and Cleopatra remember
   an earlier meeting yet.

GENTLEMAN.
                    He has commanded,
On pain of death, none should approach his
   presence.
VENTIDIUS.
I bring him news will raise his drooping spirits,   125
Give him new life.
GENTLEMAN.
                    He sees not Cleopatra.
VENTIDIUS.
Would he had never seen her.
GENTLEMAN.
He eats not, drinks not, sleeps not, has no use
Of anything but thought, or if he talks,   130
'Tis to himself, and then 'tis perfect raving.
Then he defies the world and bids it pass;
Sometimes he gnaws his lip and curses loud
The boy Octavius;[16] then he draws his mouth
Into a scornful smile and cries, "Take all,   135
The world's not worth my care."
VENTIDIUS.
                    Just, just his nature.
Virtue's his path, but sometimes 'tis too narrow
For his vast soul, and then he starts out wide
And bounds into a vice that bears him far   140
From his first course and plunges him in ills.
But, when his danger makes him find his fault,
Quick to observe and full of sharp remorse,
He censures eagerly his own misdeeds,
Judging himself with malice to himself   145
And not forgiving what as man he did
Because his other parts are more than man.
He must not thus be lost.

Alexas and the priests come forward.

ALEXAS.
You have your full instructions, now advance;
Proclaim your orders loudly.   150
SERAPION.
Romans, Egyptians, hear the Queen's command.
Thus Cleopatra bids, "Let labor cease.
To pomp and triumphs give this happy day
That gave the world a lord: 'tis Antony's."

_____

16 boy Octavius] Antony was twenty years older than the
   thirty-three year old Octavius.

Live, Antony, and Cleopatra live.   155
Be this the general voice sent up to Heav'n,
And every public place repeat this echo.
VENTIDIUS. (*Aside.*)
   Fine pageantry!
SERAPION.
               Set out before your doors
The images of all your sleeping fathers[17]   160
With laurels crowned; with laurels wreathe your
   posts
And strow with flow'rs the pavement; let the priests
Do present sacrifice; pour out the wine,
And call the gods to join with you in gladness.
VENTIDIUS.
   Curse on the tongue that bids this general joy.   165
Can they be friends of Antony who revel
When Antony's in danger? Hide, for shame,
You Romans, your great grandsires' images,
For fear their souls should animate their marbles
To blush at their degenerate progeny.   170
ALEXAS.
   A love which knows no bounds to Antony
Would mark the day with honors, when all Heaven
Labored for him, when each propitious star
Stood wakeful in his orb to watch that hour
And shed his better influence.* Her own birthday   175
Our Queen neglected, like a vulgar fate
That passed obscurely by.
VENTIDIUS.
               Would it had slept
Divided far from his, till some remote
And future age had called it out to ruin   180
Some other prince, not him.
ALEXAS.
            Your Emperor,
Though grown unkind, would be more gentle than
T'upbraid my Queen for loving him too well.
VENTIDIUS.
   Does the mute sacrifice upbraid the priest?   185
He knows him not his executioner.
Oh, she has decked his ruin with her love,
Led him in golden bands to gaudy slaughter,

---

17 images of all your sleeping fathers] the *imagines* or masks
   of distinguished ancestors, which were kept in noble
   Roman families

And made perdition pleasing: She has left him
The blank of what he was.   190
I tell thee, eunuch, she has quite unmanned him:
Can any Roman see and know him now,
Thus altered from the lord of half mankind,
Unbent, unsinewed, made a woman's toy,
Shrunk from the vast extent of all his honors,   195
And cramped within a corner of the world?
Oh Antony!
Thou bravest soldier, and thou best of friends!
Bounteous as Nature; next to Nature's God!
Couldst thou but make new worlds, so wouldst   200
   thou give 'em,
As bounty were thy being. Rough in battle
As the first Romans when they went to war,
Yet, after victory, more pitiful
Than all their praying virgins left at home!
ALEXAS.
   Would you could add to those more shining virtues   205
His truth to her who loves him.
VENTIDIUS.
                   Would I could not.
But wherefore waste I precious hours with thee?
Thou art her darling mischief, her chief engine,*
Antony's other fate. Go, tell thy queen   210
Ventidius is arrived to end her charms.
Let your Egyptian timbrels play alone,
Nor mix effeminate sounds with Roman trumpets.
You dare not fight for Antony; go pray,
And keep your coward's holy day in temples.   215

*Exeunt Alexas and Serapion. Enter second gentleman[b]
of Antony.*

SECOND GENTLEMAN.
   The Emperor approaches and commands,
On pain of death, that none presume to stay.
FIRST GENTLEMAN.
   I dare not disobey him. (*Going out with the other.*)
VENTIDIUS.
               Well, I dare.
But I'll observe him first unseen and find   220
Which way his humor drives: the rest I'll venture.
   (*Withdraws.*)

*Enter Antony walking with a disturbed motion before
he speaks.*

ANTONY.
> They tell me 'tis my birthday, and I'll keep it
> With double pomp of sadness.
> 'Tis what the day deserves, which gave me breath.
> Why was I raised the meteor of the world,   225
> Hung in the skies, and blazing as I traveled,
> Till all my fires were spent, and then cast downward
> To be trod out by Caesar?

VENTIDIUS. (*Aside.*)
>   On my soul,
> 'Tis mournful, wondrous mournful!   230

ANTONY.
>   Count thy gains.
> Now, Antony, wouldst thou be born for this?
> Glutton of Fortune, thy devouring youth
> Has starved thy wanting age.

VENTIDIUS. (*Aside.*)
>   How sorrow shakes him!   235
> So, now the tempest tears him up by th'roots
> And on the ground extends the noble ruin.

ANTONY. (*Having thrown himself down.*)
> Lie there, thou shadow of an emperor;
> The place thou pressest on thy mother earth
> Is all thy empire now. Now it contains thee;   240
> Some few days hence, and then 'twill be too large,
> When thou'rt contracted in thy narrow urn,
> Shrunk to a few cold ashes. Then Octavia
> (For Cleopatra will not live to see it),
> Octavia then will have thee all her own   245
> And bear thee in her widowed hand to Caesar;
> Caesar will weep, the crocodile will weep,
> To see his rival of the universe
> Lie still and peaceful there. I'll think no more on't.
> Give me some music; look that it be sad.   250
> I'll soothe my melancholy till I swell
> And burst myself with sighing–

Soft music.
> 'Tis somewhat to my humor. Stay, I fancy
> I'm now turned wild, a commoner of Nature;
> Of all forsaken, and forsaking all,   255
> Live in a shady forest's sylvan scene,
> Stretched at my length beneath some blasted oak.
> I lean my head upon the mossy bark,
> And look just of a piece, as I grew from it:
> My uncombed locks, matted like mistletoe,   260
> Hang o'er my hoary face; a murm'ring brook
> Runs at my foot.

VENTIDIUS.
>   Methinks I fancy
> Myself there too.

ANTONY.
>   The herd come jumping by me   265
> And, fearless, quench their thirst while I look on
> And take me for their fellow-citizen.
> More of this image, more; it lulls my thoughts.

Soft music again.

VENTIDIUS.
> I must disturb him; I can hold no longer. (*Stands
> before him.*)

ANTONY. (*Starting up.*)
> Art thou Ventidius?   270

VENTIDIUS.
>   Are you Antony?
> I'm liker what I was, than you to him
> I left you last.

ANTONY.
>   I'm angry.

VENTIDIUS.
>   So am I.   275

ANTONY.
> I would be private: leave me.

VENTIDIUS.
>   Sir, I love you,
> And therefore will not leave you.

ANTONY.
>   Will not leave me?
> Where have you learnt that answer? Who am I?   280

VENTIDIUS.
> My Emperor; the man I love next heaven:
> If I said more, I think 'twere scarce a sin;
> Y'are all that's good, and god-like.[c]

ANTONY.
>   All that's wretched.
> You will not leave me then?   285

VENTIDIUS.
>   'Twas too presuming
> To say I would not, but I dare not leave you,
> And 'tis unkind in you to chide me hence
> So soon, when I so far have come to see you.

ANTONY.
> Now thou hast seen me, art thou satisfied?   290
> For, if a friend, thou hast beheld enough;
> And, if a foe, too much.

VENTIDIUS. (*Weeping.*)
  Look, Emperor, this is no common dew.
  I have not wept this forty year, but now
  My mother comes afresh into my eyes;   295
  I cannot help her softness.
ANTONY.
  By Heav'n, he weeps, poor good old man, he weeps!
  The big round drops course one another down
  The furrows of his cheeks. Stop 'em, Ventidius,
  Or I shall blush to death: they set my shame,   300
  That caused 'em, full before me.
VENTIDIUS.
                              I'll do my best.
ANTONY.
  Sure there's contagion in the tears of friends:
  See, I have caught it too. Believe me, 'tis not
  For my own griefs, but thine—Nay, father.   305
VENTIDIUS.
                                    Emperor.
ANTONY.
  Emperor? Why, that's the style of victory.[18]
  The conqu'ring soldier, red with unfelt wounds,
  Salutes his general so, but never more
  Shall that sound reach my ears.   310
VENTIDIUS.
                            I warrant you.
ANTONY.
  Actium, Actium! Oh—
VENTIDIUS.
                        It sits too near you.
ANTONY.
  Here, here it lies, a lump of lead by day,
  And in my short, distracted nightly slumbers,   315
  The hag that rides my dreams—[19]
VENTIDIUS.
  Out with it; give it vent.
ANTONY.
                        Urge not my shame.
  I lost a battle.

VENTIDIUS.
            So has Julius[20] done.   320
ANTONY.
  Thou favor'st me and speak'st not half thou think'st,
  For Julius fought it out and lost it fairly,
  But Antony—
VENTIDIUS.
                  Nay, stop not.
ANTONY.
                        Antony—   325
  (Well, thou wilt have it) like a coward, fled,
  Fled while his soldiers fought; fled first, Ventidius.
  Thou long'st to curse me, and I give thee leave.
  I know thou cam'st prepared to rail.
VENTIDIUS.
                                I did.   330
ANTONY.
  I'll help thee—I have been a man, Ventidius—
VENTIDIUS.
  Yes, and a brave one, but—
ANTONY.
                        I know thy meaning.
  But I have lost my reason, have disgraced
  The name of soldier with inglorious ease.   335
  In the full vintage of my flowing honors,
  Sat still, and saw it pressed by other hands.
  Fortune came smiling to my youth, and wooed it,
  And purple greatness[21] met my ripened years.
  When first I came to empire, I was borne   340
  On tides of people, crowding to my triumphs,[22]
  The wish of nations, and the willing world
  Received me as its pledge of future peace.
  I was so great, so happy, so beloved,
  Fate could not ruin me, till I took pains   345
  And worked against my Fortune, chid her from me,
  And turned her loose; yet still she came again.
  My careless days and my luxurious nights
  At length have wearied her, and now she's gone,
  Gone, gone, divorced forever. Help me, soldier,   350

---

18 Emperor … victory.] Antony has in mind the Roman
    word *imperator*, which was bestowed upon a Roman
    general after an important victory.

19 hag that rides my dreams] the evil spirit that, it was be-
    lieved, haunts dreams, as if riding the body of the
    dreamer: hence, nightmare

20 Julius] Julius Caesar

21 purple greatness] The purple cloak or toga was worn
    only by those of the highest ranks in Roman society.

22 triumphs] A victorious Roman general was permitted a
    "triumph" or procession of his army and prisoners
    through Rome.

To curse this madman, this industrious fool,
Who labored to be wretched: prithee, curse me.
VENTIDIUS.
No.
ANTONY.
          Why?
VENTIDIUS.
                    You are too sensible already   355
Of what y'have done, too conscious of your failings,
And like a scorpion, whipped by others first
To fury, sting yourself in mad revenge.
I would bring balm and pour it in your wounds,
Cure your distempered mind, and heal your fortunes.   360
ANTONY.
I know thou wouldst.
VENTIDIUS.
                    I will.
ANTONY.
                              Ha, ha, ha, ha.
VENTIDIUS.
You laugh.
ANTONY.
          I do, to see officious love   365
Give cordials to the dead.
VENTIDIUS.
                    You would be lost then?
ANTONY.
I am.
VENTIDIUS.
          I say, you are not. Try your fortune.
ANTONY.
I have, to th'utmost. Dost thou think me desperate   370
Without just cause? No, when I found all lost
Beyond repair, I hid me from the world
And learnt to scorn it here, which now I do
So heartily, I think it is not worth
The cost of keeping.   375
VENTIDIUS.
                    Caesar thinks not so:
He'll thank you for the gift he could not take.
You would be killed like Tully,[23] would you? Do,
Hold out your throat to Caesar and die tamely.

ANTONY.
No, I can kill myself, and so resolve.   380
VENTIDIUS.
I can die with you, too, when time shall serve,
But Fortune calls upon us now to live,
To fight, to conquer.
ANTONY.
                    Sure thou dream'st, Ventidius.
VENTIDIUS.
No, 'tis you dream; you sleep away your hours   385
In desperate sloth, miscalled philosophy.
Up, up, for honor's sake; twelve legions wait you
And long to call you chief. By painful journeys
I led 'em, patient both of heat and hunger,
Down from the Parthian marches[24] to the Nile.   390
'Twill do you good to see their sunburnt faces,
Their scarred cheeks, and chapped hands; there's
          virtue in 'em.
They'll sell those mangled limbs at dearer rates
Than yon trim bands[25] can buy.
ANTONY.
                    Where left you them?   395
VENTIDIUS.
I said in Lower Syria.[26]
ANTONY.
                    Bring 'em hither;
There may be life in these.
VENTIDIUS.
                    They will not come.
ANTONY.
Why didst thou mock my hopes with promised   400
          aids
To double my despair? They're mutinous.
VENTIDIUS.
Most firm and loyal.
ANTONY.
                    Yet they will not march
To succor me. Oh trifler!
VENTIDIUS.
                    They petition   405
You would make haste to head 'em.

_____

23 Tully] Marcus Tullius Cicero, Antony's long-time enemy,
    was captured and killed by Antony's soldiers in Caieta
    in 43 BCE.

24 marches] borders
25 yon trim bands] Octavius' troops
26 Lower Syria] During Antony's time both Phoenicia and
    Judea were included in Syria.

ANTONY.
                                    I'm besieged.
VENTIDIUS.
   There's but one way shut up: How came I hither?
ANTONY.
   I will not stir.
VENTIDIUS.
                        They would perhaps desire   410
   A better reason.
ANTONY.
            I have never used[27]
   My soldiers to demand a reason of
   My actions. Why did they refuse to march?
VENTIDIUS.
   They said they would not fight for Cleopatra.   415
ANTONY.
   What was't they said?
VENTIDIUS.
   They said they would not fight for Cleopatra.
   Why should they fight indeed, to make her conquer
   And make you more a slave? to gain you kingdoms,
   Which, for a kiss at your next midnight feast,   420
   You'll sell to her? Then she new-names her jewels
   And calls this diamond such or such a tax;
   Each pendant in her ear shall be a province.
ANTONY.
   Ventidius, I allow your tongue free license
   On all my other faults, but on your life,   425
   No word of Cleopatra: She deserves
   More worlds than I can lose.
VENTIDIUS.
                              Behold, you Pow'rs,
   To whom you have intrusted humankind;
   See Europe, Afric, Asia put in balance   430
   And all weighed down by one light, worthless
      woman!
   I think the gods are Antonys, and give,
   Like prodigals, this nether world away
   To none but wasteful hands.
ANTONY.
                        You grow presumptuous.   435
VENTIDIUS.
   I take the privilege of plain love to speak.

ANTONY.
   Plain love! Plain arrogance, plain insolence:
   Thy men are cowards; thou an envious traitor,
   Who, under seeming honesty, hast vented
   The burden of thy rank, o'erflowing gall.   440
   Oh that thou wert my equal, great in arms
   As the first Caesar was, that I might kill thee
   Without a stain to honor!
VENTIDIUS.
                        You may kill me.
   You have done more already: called me traitor.   445
ANTONY.
   Art thou not one?
VENTIDIUS.
                    For showing you yourself,
   Which none else durst have done? But had I been
   That name, which I disdain to speak again,
   I needed not have sought your abject fortunes,   450
   Come to partake your fate, to die with you.
   What hindered me t'have led my conqu'ring
      eagles[28]
   To fill Octavius' bands? I could have been
   A traitor then, a glorious, happy traitor,
   And not have been so called.   455
ANTONY.
                        Forgive me, soldier:
   I've been too passionate.
VENTIDIUS.
                    You thought me false;
   Thought my old age betrayed you. Kill me, sir;
   Pray, kill me. Yet you need not; your unkindness   460
   Has left your sword no work.
ANTONY.
                        I did not think so;
   I said it in my rage: prithee forgive me.
   Why didst thou tempt my anger by discovery
   Of what I would not hear?   465
VENTIDIUS.
                        No prince but you
   Could merit that sincerity I used,
   Nor durst another man have ventured it,
   But you, ere love misled your wand'ring eyes,
   Were sure the chief and best of human race,   470

Framed in the very pride and boast of Nature,
So perfect, that the gods who formed you wondered
At their own skill, and cried, "A lucky hit
Has mended our design." Their envy hindered,   475
Else you had been immortal and a pattern,
When Heav'n would work for ostentation sake,
To copy out again.
ANTONY.
                But Cleopatra—
Go on, for I can bear it now.
VENTIDIUS.
                     No more.   480
ANTONY.
  Thou dar'st not trust my passion, but thou mayst:
Thou only lov'st; the rest have flattered me.
VENTIDIUS.
  Heav'n's blessing on your heart for that kind word.
May I believe you love me? Speak again.
ANTONY.
  Indeed I do. Speak this, and this, and this.   485
    (*Hugging him.*)
Thy praises were unjust, but I'll deserve 'em,
And yet mend all. Do with me what thou wilt;
Lead me to victory. Thou know'st the way.
VENTIDIUS.
  And, will you leave this—
ANTONY.
                Prithee do not curse her,   490
And I will leave her; though Heav'n knows, I love
Beyond life, conquest, empire, all but honor.
But I will leave her.
VENTIDIUS.
           That's my royal master.
And, shall we fight?   495
ANTONY.
            I warrant thee, old soldier,
Thou shalt behold me once again in iron
And at the head of our old troops that beat
The Parthians cry aloud, "Come, follow me."
VENTIDIUS.
  Oh now I hear my Emp'ror! In that word   500
Octavius fell. Gods, let me see that day
And, if I have ten years behind, take all;
I'll thank you for th'exchange.
ANTONY.
                 Oh Cleopatra!

VENTIDIUS.
  Again?   505
ANTONY.
         I've done: in that last sigh, she went.
Caesar shall know what 'tis to force a lover
From all he holds most dear.
VENTIDIUS.
              Methinks you breathe
Another soul: your looks are more divine;   510
You speak a hero, and you move a god.
ANTONY.
  Oh, thou hast fired me; my soul's up in arms
And mans each part about me. Once again,
That noble eagerness of fight has seized me:
That eagerness with which I darted upward   515
To Cassius' camp.[29] In vain the steepy hill
Opposed my way; in vain a war of spears
Sung round my head and planted all my shield.
I won the trenches while my foremost men
Lagged on the plain below.   520
VENTIDIUS.
             Ye gods, ye gods,
For such another hour!
ANTONY.
              Come on, my soldier!
Our hearts and arms are still the same: I long
Once more to meet our foes, that thou and I,   525
Like Time and Death, marching before our troops,
May taste fate[30] to 'em; mow 'em out a passage
And, ent'ring where the foremost squadrons yield,
Begin the noble harvest of the field.

Exeunt.   530

Act II.

Cleopatra, Iras, and Alexas.

CLEOPATRA.
  What shall I do, or whither shall I turn?
Ventidius has o'ercome, and he will go.
ALEXAS.
  He goes to fight for you.

---

29 Cassius' camp] Antony and Octavius defeated Cassius
    and Brutus at Philippi in 42 BCE.
30 taste fate] as an official taster would test food and drink
    for a monarch

CLEOPATRA.

Then he would see me ere he went to fight.
Flatter me not: if once he goes, he's lost,
And all my hopes destroyed.

ALEXAS.

Does this weak passion

Become a mighty queen?

CLEOPATRA.

I am no queen.

Is this to be a queen, to be besieged
By yon insulting Roman, and to wait
Each hour the victor's chain? These ills are small,
For Antony is lost, and I can mourn
For nothing else but him. Now come, Octavius,
I have no more to lose; prepare thy bands;
I'm fit to be a captive: Antony
Has taught my mind the fortune of a slave.

IRAS.

Call reason to assist you.

CLEOPATRA.

I have none,

And none would have: my love's a noble madness,
Which shows the cause deserved it. Moderate sorrow
Fits vulgar love, and for a vulgar man,
But I have loved with such transcendent passion,
I soared, at first, quite out of reason's view,
And now am lost above it. No, I'm proud
'Tis thus. Would Antony could see me now.
Think you he would not sigh? Though he must
   leave me,
Sure he would sigh, for he is noble-natured
And bears a tender heart: I know him well.
Ah, no, I know him not; I knew him once,
But now 'tis past.

IRAS.

Let it be past with you:

Forget him, madam.

CLEOPATRA.

Never, never, Iras.

He once was mine; and once, though now 'tis gone,
Leaves a faint image of possession still.

ALEXAS.

Think him unconstant, cruel, and ungrateful.

CLEOPATRA.

I cannot. If I could, those thoughts were vain;
Faithless, ungrateful, cruel though he be,
I still must love him.

Enter Charmion.

Now, what news, my Charmion?
Will he be kind? and will he not forsake me?
Am I to live, or die? Nay, do I live?
Or am I dead? for, when he gave his answer,
Fate took the word, and then I lived or died.

CHARMION.

I found him, madam—

CLEOPATRA.

A long speech preparing?

If thou bring'st comfort, haste, and give it me,
For never was more need.

IRAS.

I know he loves you.

CLEOPATRA.

Had he been kind, her eyes had told me so
Before her tongue could speak it. Now she studies
To soften what he said, but give me death
Just as he sent it, Charmion, undisguised
And in the words he spoke.

CHARMION.

I found him then

Incompassed round, I think, with iron statues,
So mute, so motionless his soldiers stood
While awfully he cast his eyes about,
And ev'ry leader's hopes or fears surveyed:
Methought he looked resolved, and yet not pleased.
When he beheld me struggling in the crowd,
He blushed, and bade make way.

ALEXAS.

There's comfort yet.

CHARMION.

Ventidius fixed his eyes upon my passage,
Severely, as he meant to frown me back,
And sullenly gave place. I told my message,
Just as you gave it, broken and disordered;
I numbered in it all your sighs and tears,
And while I moved your pitiful request
That you but only begged a last farewell,
He fetched an inward groan and, ev'ry time
I named you, sighed as if his heart were breaking,
But shunned my eyes, and guiltily looked down.
He seemed not now that awful[31] Antony

_____

31 awful] awe-inspiring

Who shook an armed assembly with his nod,
But making show as he would rub his eyes,
Disguised and blotted out a falling tear.
CLEOPATRA.
Did he then weep? and was I worth a tear?
If what thou hast to say be not as pleasing,   80
Tell me no more, but let me die contented.
CHARMION.
He bid me say, he knew himself so well,
He could deny you nothing if he saw you,
And therefore—
CLEOPATRA.
          Thou wouldst say, he would not see me?   85
CHARMION.
And therefore begged you not to use a power
Which he could ill resist, yet he should ever
Respect you as he ought.
CLEOPATRA.
          Is that a word
For Antony to use to Cleopatra?   90
Oh that faint word, "respect"! How I disdain it!
Disdain myself, for loving after it!
He should have kept that word for cold Octavia.
Respect is for a wife: Am I that thing,
That dull, insipid lump, without desires,   95
And without pow'r to give 'em?
ALEXAS.
          You misjudge;
You see through love, and that deludes your sight,
As what is straight seems crooked through the water.
But I, who bear my reason undisturbed,   100
Can see this Antony, this dreaded man,
A fearful slave, who fain would run away,
And shuns his master's eyes: if you pursue him,
My life on't, he still drags a chain along
That needs must clog his flight.   105
CLEOPATRA.
          Could I believe thee!
ALEXAS.
By ev'ry circumstance I know he loves.
True, he's hard pressed by int'rest and by honor;
Yet he but doubts and parleys and casts out
Many a long look for succor.   110
CLEOPATRA.
          He sends word
He fears to see my face.

ALEXAS.
          And would you more?
He shows his weakness who declines the combat,
And you must urge your fortune. Could he speak   115
More plainly? To my ears the message sounds,
"Come to my rescue, Cleopatra, come;
Come, free me from Ventidius, from my tyrant;
See me, and give me a pretense to leave him."
I hear his trumpets. This way he must pass.   120
Please you, retire a while; I'll work him first,
That he may bend more easy.
CLEOPATRA.
          You shall rule me,
But all, I fear, in vain.

Exit with Charmion and Iras.

ALEXAS.
          I fear so too,   125
Though I concealed my thoughts to make her bold.
But 'tis our utmost means, and Fate befriend it!
(*Withdraws.*)

*Enter lictors with fasces, one bearing the eagle; then
enter Antony with Ventidius, followed by other
commanders.*

ANTONY.
Octavius is the minion of blind Chance,
But holds from Virtue nothing.
VENTIDIUS.
          Has he courage?   130
ANTONY.
But just enough to season him from coward.
Oh, 'tis the coldest youth upon a charge,
The most deliberate fighter! If he ventures
(As in Illyria once they say he did
To storm a town) 'tis when he cannot choose,   135
When all the world have fixed their eyes upon him,
And then he lives on that for seven years after,
But at a close revenge he never fails.
VENTIDIUS.
I heard you challenged him.
ANTONY.
          I did, Ventidius.   140
What think'st thou was his answer? 'Twas so tame—
He said he had more ways than one to die,
I had not.

VENTIDIUS.
> Poor!

ANTONY.
> He has more ways than one,   145
> But he would choose 'em all before that one.

VENTIDIUS.
> He first would choose an ague or a fever.

ANTONY.
> No, it must be an ague, not a fever;
> He has not warmth enough to die by that.

VENTIDIUS.
> Or old age and a bed.   150

ANTONY.
> Aye, there's his choice.
> He would live, like a lamp, to the last wink,
> And crawl upon the utmost verge of life.
> Oh Hercules! Why should a man like this,
> Who dares not trust his fate for one great action,   155
> Be all the care of Heav'n? Why should he lord it
> O'er fourscore thousand men, of whom each one
> Is braver than himself?

VENTIDIUS.
> You conquered for him:
> Philippi[32] knows it; there you shared with him   160
> That empire, which your sword made all your own.

ANTONY.
> Fool that I was, upon my eagle's wings
> I bore this wren till I was tired with soaring,[33]
> And now he mounts above me.
> Good heav'ns, is this, is this the man who braves me?   165
> Who bids my age make way, drives me before him
> To the world's ridge, and sweeps me off like rubbish?

VENTIDIUS.
> Sir, we lose time; the troops are mounted all.

ANTONY.
> Then give the word to march:
> I long to leave this prison of a town,   170
> To join thy legions, and in open field,
> Once more to show my face. Lead, my deliverer.

---

32 Philippi] the battle of Philippi 42 BCE in which
Antony's troops saved Octavius' troops from being overrun by Brutus

33 upon my eagle's wings ... soaring] Aesop's fable of the
wren who was carried on the back of an eagle and then
flew higher than the eagle

Enter Alexas.

ALEXAS.
> Great Emperor,
> In mighty arms renowned above mankind,
> But, in soft pity to th'oppressed, a god,
> This message sends the mournful Cleopatra   175
> To her departing lord.

VENTIDIUS.
> Smooth sycophant!

ALEXAS.
> A thousand wishes and ten thousand prayers,
> Millions of blessings wait you to the wars;
> Millions of sighs and tears she sends you too,   180
> And would have sent
> As many dear embraces to your arms,
> As many parting kisses to your lips,
> But those, she fears, have wearied you already.

VENTIDIUS. (*Aside.*)
> False crocodile!   185

ALEXAS.
> And yet she begs not now you would not leave her;
> That were a wish too mighty for her hopes,
> Too presuming
> For her low fortune and your ebbing love;[d]
> That were a wish for her more prosp'rous days,   190
> Her blooming beauty, and your growing kindness.

ANTONY. (*Aside.*)
> Well, I must man it out. What would the Queen?

ALEXAS.
> First, to these noble warriors, who attend
> Your daring courage in the chase of fame
> (Too daring and too dang'rous for her quiet)   195
> She humbly recommends all she holds dear,
> All her own cares and fears, the care of you.

VENTIDIUS.
> Yes, witness Actium.

ANTONY.
> Let him speak, Ventidius.

ALEXAS.
> You, when his matchless valor bears him forward,   200
> With ardor too heroic, on his foes,
> Fall down, as she would do, before his feet;
> Lie in his way and stop the paths of death.
> Tell him, this god is not invulnerable,
> That absent Cleopatra bleeds in him,   205
> And, that you may remember her petition,
> She begs you wear these trifles as a pawn,

Which, at your wished return, she will redeem
  (*Gives jewels to the commanders.*)
With all the wealth of Egypt:
This to the great Ventidius she presents,   210
Whom she can never count her enemy,
Because he loves her lord.
VENTIDIUS.
                  Tell her I'll none on't.
I'm not ashamed of honest poverty:
Not all the diamonds of the East can bribe   215
Ventidius from his faith. I hope to see
These, and the rest of all her sparkling store,
Where they shall more deservingly be placed.
ANTONY.
And who must wear 'em then?
VENTIDIUS.
                The wronged Octavia.   220
ANTONY.
You might have spared that word.
VENTIDIUS.
               And he that bribe.
ANTONY.
But have I no remembrance?
ALEXAS.
                Yes, a dear one:
Your slave, the Queen—   225
ANTONY.
       My mistress.
ALEXAS.
            Then your mistress;
Your mistress would, she says, have sent her soul,
But that you had long since; she humbly begs
This ruby bracelet, set with bleeding hearts,   230
(The emblems of her own) may bind your arm.
    (*Presenting a bracelet.*)
VENTIDIUS.
Now, my best lord, in honor's name I ask you,
For manhood's sake, and for her own dear safety,
Touch not these poisoned gifts,
Infected by the sender; touch 'em not.   235
Myriads of bluest plagues lie underneath 'em,
And more than aconite has dipped the silk.[34]

---

34 aconite … silk.] Aconite was supposedly the fastest act-
    ing poison; Ventidius perhaps alludes here to the death
    of Hercules, who was poisoned when he put on the
    bloody shirt of the centaur Nessus given him by
    Deianira who hoped to gain his love.

ANTONY.
Nay, now you grow too cynical, Ventidius.
A lady's favors may be worn with honor.
What, to refuse her bracelet! On my soul,   240
When I lie pensive in my tent alone,
'Twill pass the wakeful hours of winter nights
To tell these pretty beads upon my arm,
To count for every one a soft embrace,
A melting kiss at such and such a time,   245
And now and then the fury of her love.
When—And what harm's in this?
ALEXAS.
              None, none, my lord,
But what's to her, that now 'tis past forever.
ANTONY. (*Going to tie it.*)
We soldiers are so awkward—help me tie it.   250
ALEXAS.
In faith, my lord, we courtiers too are awkward
In these affairs. So are all men indeed;
Ev'n I, who am not one. But shall I speak?
ANTONY.
Yes, freely.
ALEXAS.
          Then, my lord, fair hands alone   255
Are fit to tie it; she who sent it can.
VENTIDIUS.
Hell, Death! this eunuch pander ruins you.
You will not see her?

Alexas whispers an attendant, who goes out.

ANTONY.
           But to take my leave.
VENTIDIUS.
Then I have washed an Ethiop.[35] Y'are undone;   260
Y'are in the toils; y'are taken; y'are destroyed:
Her eyes do Caesar's work.
ANTONY.
          You fear too soon.
I'm constant to myself: I know my strength,
And yet she shall not think me barbarous neither,   265
Born in the depths of Afric. I'm a Roman,
Bred to the rules of soft humanity.
A guest, and kindly used, should bid farewell.

---

35 washed an Ethiop] proverbial for a futile task

VENTIDIUS.
    You do not know
    How weak you are to her, how much an infant;   270
    You are not proof against a smile or glance;
    A sigh will quite disarm you.
ANTONY.
                        See, she comes!
    Now you shall find your error. Gods, I thank you:
    I formed the danger greater than it was,   275
    And now 'tis near, 'tis lessened.
VENTIDIUS.
                        Mark the end yet.
Enter Cleopatra, Charmion, and Iras.
ANTONY.
    Well, madam, we are met.
CLEOPATRA.
                        Is this a meeting?
    Then we must part?   280
ANTONY.
            We must.
CLEOPATRA.
                        Who says we must?
ANTONY.
    Our own hard fates.
CLEOPATRA.
                    We make those fates ourselves.
ANTONY.
    Yes, we have made 'em; we have loved each other   285
    Into our mutual ruin.
CLEOPATRA.
    The gods have seen my joys with envious eyes;
    I have no friends in heav'n, and all the world
    (As 'twere the bus'ness of mankind to part us)
    Is armed against my love: ev'n you yourself   290
    Join with the rest; you, you are armed against me.
ANTONY.
    I will be justified in all I do
    To late posterity, and therefore hear me.
    If I mix a lie
    With any truth, reproach me freely with it;   295
    Else favor me with silence.
CLEOPATRA.
                        You command me,
    And I am dumb.
VENTIDIUS.
    I like this well: he shows authority.

ANTONY.
    That I derive my ruin   300
    From you alone—
CLEOPATRA.
                    Oh heav'ns! I ruin you!
ANTONY.
    You promised me your silence, and you break it
    Ere I have scarce begun.
CLEOPATRA.
                        Well, I obey you.   305
ANTONY.
    When I beheld you first, it was in Egypt,
    Ere Caesar saw your eyes. You gave me love
    And were too young to know it; that I settled
    Your father in his throne was for your sake.[36]
    I left th'acknowledgment for time to ripen.   310
    Caesar stepped in, and with greedy hand
    Plucked the green fruit, ere the first blush of red,
    Yet cleaving to the bough. He was my lord
    And was, beside, too great for me to rival,
    But I deserved you first, though he enjoyed you.   315
    When, after, I beheld you in Cilicia
    An enemy to Rome, I pardoned you.
CLEOPATRA.
    I cleared myself—
ANTONY.
                    Again you break your promise.
    I loved you still and took your weak excuses,   320
    Took you into my bosom, stained by Caesar,
    And not half mine: I went to Egypt with you
    And hid me from the bus'ness of the world,
    Shut out enquiring nations from my sight,
    To give whole years to you.   325
VENTIDIUS. (*Aside.*)
    Yes, to your shame be't spoken.
ANTONY.
                        How I loved,
    Witness ye days and nights and all your hours
    That danced away with down upon your feet,
    As all your bus'ness were to count my passion.   330
    One day passed by and nothing saw but love;

---

36 When … your sake.] Antony arrived in Egypt in 55
    BCE as part of a Roman army imported to restore Cleo-
    patra's father to his throne (Cleopatra was only fourteen);
    Caesar first arrived in Alexandria in 48 BCE.

Another came, and still 'twas only love.
The suns were wearied out with looking on,
And I untired with loving.
I saw you ev'ry day, and all the day,   335
And ev'ry day was still but as the first,
So eager was I still to see you more.
VENTIDIUS.
'Tis all too true.
ANTONY.
                    Fulvia, my wife,[37] grew jealous,
As she indeed had reason, raised a war   340
In Italy to call me back.
VENTIDIUS.
                    But yet
You went not.
ANTONY.
              While within your arms I lay,
The world fell mold'ring from my hands each hour   345
And left me scarce a grasp (I thank your love for't.)
VENTIDIUS.
Well pushed: that last was home.
CLEOPATRA.
                              Yet may I speak?
ANTONY.
If I have urged a falsehood, yes; else, not.
Your silence says I have not. Fulvia died   350
(Pardon, you gods, with my unkindness died).
To set the world at peace I took Octavia,
This Caesar's sister; in her pride of youth
And flow'r of beauty did I wed that lady,
Whom blushing I must praise, because I left her.   355
You called; my love obeyed the fatal summons;
This raised the Roman arms; the cause was yours.
I would have fought by land, where I was stronger;
You hindered it, yet when I fought at sea,
Forsook me fighting, and (Oh stain to honor!   360
Oh lasting shame!) I knew not that I fled,
But fled to follow you.
VENTIDIUS.
What haste she made to hoist her purple sails!
And, to appear magnificent in flight,
Drew half our strength away.   365
ANTONY.
                    All this you caused,

---

37 Fulvia] Antony married Fulvia in 46 BCE; she died in
    40 BCE.

And would you multiply more ruins on me?
This honest man, my best, my only friend,
Has gathered up the shipwrack of my fortunes;
Twelve legions I have left, my last recruits,   370
And you have watched the news and bring your eyes
To seize them too. If you have aught to answer,
Now speak, you have free leave.
ALEXAS. (*Aside.*)
                              She stands confounded:
Despair is in her eyes.   375
VENTIDIUS.
Now lay a sigh i'th'way to stop his passage:
Prepare a tear and bid it for his legions;
'Tis like they shall be sold.
CLEOPATRA.
How shall I plead my cause when you, my judge,
Already have condemned me? Shall I bring   380
The love you bore me for my advocate?
That now is turned against me, that destroys me,
For, love once past is, at the best, forgotten,
But oft'ner sours to hate: 'twill please my lord
To ruin me, and therefore I'll be guilty.   385
But could I once have thought it would have
    pleased you,
That you would pry with narrow searching eyes
Into my faults, severe to my destruction,
And watching all advantages with care
That serve to make me wretched? Speak, my lord,   390
For I end here. Though I deserve this usage,
Was it like you to give it?
ANTONY.
                         Oh you wrong me
To think I sought this parting, or desired
To accuse you more than what will clear myself   395
And justify this breach.
CLEOPATRA.
                       Thus low I thank you,
And since my innocence will not offend,
I shall not blush to own it.
VENTIDIUS.
                           After this,   400
I think she'll blush at nothing.
CLEOPATRA.
                              You seem grieved
(And therein you are kind) that Caesar first
Enjoyed my love, though you deserved it better.

I grieve for that, my lord, much more than you, 405
For had I first been yours, it would have saved
My second choice: I never had been his,
And ne'er had been but yours. But Caesar first,
You say, possessed my love. Not so, my lord:
He first possessed my person, you my love; 410
Caesar loved me, but I loved Antony.
If I endured him after, 'twas because
I judged it due to the first name of men,
And half constrained, I gave, as to a tyrant,
What he would take by force. 415

VENTIDIUS.

                  Oh siren! siren!
Yet grant that all the love she boasts were true,
Has she not ruined you? I still urge that,
The fatal consequence.

CLEOPATRA.

                The consequence indeed, 420
For I dare challenge him, my greatest foe,
To say it was designed: 'tis true I loved you
And kept you far from an uneasy wife
(Such Fulvia was).
Yes, but he'll say you left Octavia for me— 425
And can you blame me to receive that love
Which quitted such desert for worthless me?
How often have I wished some other Caesar,
Great as the first, and as the second young,
Would court my love, to be refused for you! 430

VENTIDIUS.

Words, words; but Actium, sir, remember Actium.

CLEOPATRA.

Ev'n there I dare his malice. True, I counseled
To fight at sea, but I betrayed you not.
I fled, but not to the enemy. 'Twas fear.
Would I had been a man, not to have feared, 435
For none would then have envied me your
    friendship,
Who envy me your love.

ANTONY.

               We're both unhappy:
If nothing else, yet our ill fortune parts us.
Speak: Would you have me perish by my stay? 440

CLEOPATRA.

If as a friend you ask my judgment, go;
If as a lover, stay. If you must perish—
'Tis a hard word–but stay.

VENTIDIUS.

See now th'effects of her so boasted love!
She strives to drag you down to ruin with her, 445
But could she 'scape without you, oh how soon
Would she let go her hold and haste to shore
And never look behind!

CLEOPATRA.

             Then judge my love by this.
  (*Giving Antony a writing.*)
Could I have borne 450
A life or death, a happiness or woe
From yours divided, this had giv'n me means.

ANTONY.

By Hercules, the writing of Octavius!
I know it well; 'tis that proscribing hand,[38]
Young as it was, that led the way to mine 455
And left me but the second place in murder.—
See, see, Ventidius! here he offers Egypt,
And joins all Syria to it as a present,
So, in requital, she forsake my fortunes
And join her arms with his. 460

CLEOPATRA.

             And yet you leave me!
You leave me, Antony, and yet I love you.
Indeed I do. I have refused a kingdom;
That's a trifle:
For I could part with life, with anything 465
But only you. Oh, let me die but with you!
Is that a hard request?

ANTONY.

             Next living with you,
'Tis all that Heav'n can give.

ALEXAS. (*Aside.*)

             He melts; we conquer. 470

CLEOPATRA.

No; you shall go. Your int'rest calls you hence.
Yes; your dear int'rest pulls too strong for these
Weak arms to hold you here.– (*Takes his hand.*)
Go, leave me, soldier
(For you're no more a lover), leave me dying: 475
Push me all pale and panting from your bosom,
And when your march begins, let one run after,

---

38 proscribing hand] After the assassination of Julius Caesar, Octavius and Antony drew up proscription lists of
enemies who should die.

Breathless almost for joy, and cry, "She's dead."
The soldiers shout; you then perhaps may sigh
And muster all your Roman gravity.   480
Ventidius chides, and straight your brow clears up,
As I had never been.
ANTONY.
Gods, 'tis too much; too much for man to bear!
CLEOPATRA.
What is't for me, then,
A weak, forsaken woman? and a lover?   485
Here let me breathe my last. Envy me not
This minute in your arms: I'll die apace,
As fast as e'er I can, and end your trouble.
ANTONY.
Die! Rather let me perish: loosened Nature
Leap from its hinges. Sink the props of heav'n,   490
And fall the skies to crush the nether world.
My eyes, my soul, my all!– (Embraces her.)
VENTIDIUS.
                                And what's this toy
In balance with your fortune, honor, fame?
ANTONY.
What is't, Ventidius? It outweighs 'em all;   495
Why, we have more than conquered Caesar now:
My queen's not only innocent, but loves me.
This, this is she who drags me down to ruin!
"But could she 'scape without me, with what haste
Would she let slip her hold, and make to shore,   500
And never look behind!"
Down on thy knees, blasphemer as thou art,
And ask forgiveness of wronged innocence.
VENTIDIUS.
I'll rather die than take it. Will you go?
ANTONY.
Go! Whither? Go from all that's excellent!   505
Faith, honor, virtue, all good things forbid
That I should go from her who sets my love
Above the price of kingdoms. Give, you gods,
Give to your boy, your Caesar,
This rattle of a globe to play withal,   510
This gewgaw world, and put him cheaply off;
I'll not be pleased with less than Cleopatra.
CLEOPATRA.
She's wholly yours. My heart's so full of joy
That I shall do some wild extravagance
Of love in public, and the foolish world,   515
Which knows not tenderness, will think me mad.

VENTIDIUS.
Oh women! Women! Women! All the gods
Have not such pow'r of doing good to man
As you of doing harm. (Exit.)
ANTONY.
                            Our men are armed.   520
Unbar the gate that looks to Caesar's camp.
I would revenge the treachery he meant me,
And long security makes conquest easy.
I'm eager to return before I go,
For all the pleasures I have known beat thick   525
On my remembrance: how I long for night!
That both the sweets of mutual love may try
And once triumph o'er Caesar ere[e] we die. (Exeunt.)

Act III.

At one door enter Cleopatra, Charmion, Iras, and Alexas, a train of Egyptians; at the other, Antony and Romans. The entrance on both sides is prepared by music, the trumpets first sounding on Antony's part, then answered by timbrels etc. on Cleopatra's. Charmion and Iras hold a laurel wreath betwixt them. A dance of Egyptians. After the ceremony, Cleopatra crowns Antony.

ANTONY.
I thought how those white arms would fold me in
And strain me close and melt me into love;
So pleased with that sweet image, I sprung forwards
And added all my strength to every blow.
CLEOPATRA.
Come to me, come my soldier, to my arms.   5
You've been too long away from my embraces,
But when I have you fast, and all my own,
With broken murmurs and with amorous sighs,
I'll say you were unkind and punish you
And mark you red with many an eager kiss.   10
ANTONY.
My brighter Venus!
CLEOPATRA.
                    Oh my greater Mars!
ANTONY.
Thou join'st us well, my love!
Suppose me come from the Phlegraean plains,[39]

---

39 Phlegraean plains] where Hercules helped the gods defeat the giants in battle and bury them beneath the earth

Where gasping giants lay, cleft by my sword,　15
And mountain tops pared off each other blow
To bury those I slew. Receive me, goddess:
Let Caesar spread his subtle nets, like Vulcan;[40]
In thy embraces I would be beheld
By heav'n and earth at once,　20
And make their envy what they meant their sport.
Let those who took us blush; I would love on
With awful state, regardless of their frowns,
As their superior god.
There's no satiety of love in thee:　25
Enjoyed, thou still art new; perpetual spring
Is in thy arms; the ripened fruit but falls,
And blossoms rise to fill its empty place,
And I grow rich by giving.

Enter Ventidius and stands apart.

ALEXAS.
Oh, now the danger's past, your general comes.　30
He joins not in your joys, nor minds your triumphs,
But, with contracted brows, looks frowning on,
As envying your success.
ANTONY.
Now, on my soul, he loves me, truly loves me.
He never flattered me in any vice,　35
But awes me with his virtue: ev'n this minute,
Methinks he has a right of chiding me.
Lead to the temple: I'll avoid his presence;
It checks too strong upon me.

*Exeunt the rest. As Antony is going, Ventidius pulls him
by the robe.*

VENTIDIUS.
Emperor.　40
ANTONY. (*Looking back.*)
'Tis the old argument; I prithee spare me.
VENTIDIUS.
But this one hearing, emperor.
ANTONY.
　　　　　　　　　　　Let go
My robe, or by my father Hercules—

---

40 like Vulcan] When Vulcan discovered that his wife Ve-
　nus was committing adultery with Mars, he ensnared
　them in bed in a fine, unbreakable net, inviting the other
　gods to come laugh at them.

VENTIDIUS.
By Hercules his father, that's yet greater,　45
I bring you somewhat you would wish to know.
ANTONY.
Thou see'st we are observed; attend me here,
And I'll return. (*Exit.*)
VENTIDIUS.
I'm waning in his favor, yet I love him;
I love this man, who runs to meet his ruin,　50
And sure the gods, like me, are fond of him:
His virtues lie so mingled with his crimes,
As would confound their choice to punish one
And not reward the other.

Enter Antony.

ANTONY.
　　　　　　　　　　　We can conquer,　55
You see, without your aid.
We have dislodged their troops;
They look on us at distance, and, like curs
'Scaped from the lion's paws, they bay far off
And lick their wounds and faintly threaten war.　60
Five thousand Romans with their faces upward
Lie breathless on the plain.
VENTIDIUS.
　　　　　　　　　　　'Tis well: and he
Who lost 'em could have spared ten thousand more.
Yet if, by this advantage, you could gain　65
An easier peace, while Caesar doubts the chance
Of arms!—
ANTONY.
　　　　　　　Oh think not on't, Ventidius.
The boy pursues my ruin, he'll no peace:
His malice is considerate in advantage.　70
Oh, he's the coolest murderer, so staunch,
He kills and keeps his temper.
VENTIDIUS.
　　　　　　　　　　　Have you no friend
In all his army who has pow'r to move him?
Maecenas or Agrippa might do much.　75
ANTONY.
They're both too deep in Caesar's interests.
We'll work it out by dint of sword, or perish.
VENTIDIUS.
Fain I would find some other.
ANTONY.
　　　　　　　　　　　Thank thy love.

Some four or five such victories as this   80
Will save thy farther pains.
VENTIDIUS.
Expect no more; Caesar is on his guard.
I know, sir, you have conquered against odds,
But still you draw supplies from one poor town,
And of Egyptians; he has all the world,   85
And at his back nations come pouring in
To fill the gaps you make. Pray think again.
ANTONY.
Why dost thou drive me from myself, to search
For foreign aids? to hunt my memory
And range all o'er a waste and barren place   90
To find a friend? The wretched have no friends.—
Yet I had one, the bravest youth of Rome,
Whom Caesar loves beyond the love of women;
He could resolve his mind as fire does wax,
From that hard, rugged image melt him down   95
And mold him in what softer form he pleased.
VENTIDIUS.
Him would I see, that man of all the world:
Just such a one we want.*
ANTONY.
                                        He loved me too:
I was his soul; he lived not but in me.
We were so closed within each other's breasts,   100
The rivets were not found that joined us first.
That does not reach us yet: we were so mixed,
As meeting streams, both to ourselves were lost;
We were one mass; we could not give or take   105
But from the same, for he was I, I he.
VENTIDIUS. (Aside.)
He moves as I would wish him.
ANTONY.
                                        After this,
I need not tell his name: 'twas Dollabella.
VENTIDIUS.
He's now in Caesar's camp.   110
ANTONY.
                                        No matter where,
Since he's no longer mine. He took unkindly
That I forbade him Cleopatra's sight
Because I feared he loved her. He confessed
He had a warmth which, for my sake, he stifled;   115
For 'twere impossible that two, so one,
Should not have loved the same. When he departed,

He took no leave, and that confirmed my thoughts.
VENTIDIUS.
It argues that he loved you more than her,
Else he had stayed. But he perceived you jealous   120
And would not grieve his friend; I know he loves you.
ANTONY.
I should have seen him, then, ere now.
VENTIDIUS.
                                                        Perhaps
He has thus long been lab'ring for your peace.
ANTONY.
Would he were here.   125
VENTIDIUS.
                                Would you believe he loved you?
I read your answer in your eyes: you would.
Not to conceal it longer, he has sent
A messenger from Caesar's camp with letters.
ANTONY.
Let him appear.   130
VENTIDIUS.
                        I'll bring him instantly.
Exit Ventidius and re-enters immediately with Dollabella.
ANTONY.
'Tis he himself, himself, by holy friendship! (Runs
    to embrace him.)
Art thou returned at last, my better half?
Come, give me all myself. Let me not live,f
If the bridegroom, longing for his night,   135
Was ever half so fond.
DOLLABELLA.
I must be silent, for my soul is busy
About a nobler work: she's new come home,
Like a long-absent man, and wanders o'er
Each room, a stranger to her own, to look   140
If all be safe.
ANTONY.
                        Thou hast what's left of me;
For I am now so sunk from what I was,
Thou find'st me at my lowest watermark.
The rivers that ran in and raised my fortunes   145
Are all dried up or take another course:
What I have left is from my native spring;
I've still a heart that swells in scorn of Fate
And lifts me to my banks.
DOLLABELLA.
Still you are lord of all the world to me.   150

ANTONY.

> Why, then I yet am so; for thou art all.
> If I had any joy when thou wert absent,
> I grudged it to myself; methought I robbed
> Thee of thy part. But oh my Dollabella!
> Thou hast beheld me other than I am.   155
> Hast thou not seen my morning chambers filled
> With sceptered slaves who waited to salute* me?
> With eastern monarchs, who forgot the sun
> To worship my uprising? Menial kings
> Ran coursing up and down my palace-yard,   160
> Stood silent in my presence, watched my eyes,
> And, at my least command, all started out
> Like racers to the goal.

DOLLABELLA.

>   Slaves to your fortune.

ANTONY.

> Fortune is Caesar's now, and what am I?   165

VENTIDIUS.

> What you have made yourself; I will not flatter.

ANTONY.

> Is this friendly done?

DOLLABELLA.

> Yes, when his end is so, I must join with him;
> Indeed I must, and yet you must not chide:
> Why am I else your friend?   170

ANTONY.

>   Take heed, young man,
> How thou upbraid'st my love: the Queen has eyes,
> And thou too hast a soul. Canst thou remember
> When, swelled with hatred, thou beheld'st her first,
> As accessary to thy brother's death?   175

DOLLABELLA.

> Spare my remembrance; 'twas a guilty day,
> And still the blush hangs here.

ANTONY.

>   To clear herself
> For sending him no aid, she came from Egypt.
> Her galley down the silver Cydnos[41] rowed,   180
> The tackling silk, the streamers waved with gold;
> The gentle winds were lodged in purple sails.
> Her nymphs, like Nereids,[42] round her couch
>   were placed,

---

41 Cydnos] The river Cydnus flowed through Tarsus in
   Cilicia.
42 Nereids] the 50 sea nymphs who were the daughters of
   the sea god Nereus in Greek mythology

> Where she, another sea-born Venus, lay.

DOLLABELLA.

> No more; I would not hear it.   185

ANTONY.

>   Oh, you must!
> She lay, and leant her cheek upon her hand
> And cast a look so languishingly sweet
> As if, secure of all beholders' hearts,
> Neglecting she could take 'em. Boys, like cupids,   190
> Stood fanning, with their painted wings, the winds
> That played about her face, but if she smiled,
> A darting glory seemed to blaze abroad,
> That men's desiring eyes were never wearied,
> But hung upon the object. To soft flutes   195
> The silver oars kept time, and while they played,
> The hearing gave new pleasure to the sight,
> And both to thought: 'twas heav'n, or somewhat
>   more,
> For she so charmed all hearts, that gazing crowds
> Stood panting on the shore and wanted* breath   200
> To give their welcome voice.
> Then, Dollabella, where was then thy soul?
> Was not thy fury quite disarmed with wonder?
> Didst thou not shrink behind me from those eyes
> And whisper in my ear, "Oh tell her not   205
> That I accused her of my brother's death"?

DOLLABELLA.

> And should my weakness be a plea for yours?
> Mine was an age when love might be excused,
> When kindly warmth and when my springing youth
> Made it a debt to Nature. Yours—   210

VENTIDIUS.

>   Speak boldly.
> Yours, he would say, in your declining age,
> When no more heat was left but what you forced,
> When all the sap was needful for the trunk,
> When it went down, then you constrained the course   215
> And robbed from Nature to supply desire;
> In you (I would not use so harsh a word)
> But 'tis plain dotage.

ANTONY.

>   Hah!

DOLLABELLA.

>   'Twas urged too home.   220
> But yet the loss was private that I made;
> 'Twas but myself I lost. I lost no legions;

I had no world to lose, no people's love.

ANTONY.

This from a friend?

DOLLABELLA.

               Yes, Antony, a true one;   225

A friend so tender that each word I speak

Stabs my own heart before it reach your ear.

Oh, judge me not less kind because I chide.

To Caesar I excuse you.

ANTONY.

             Oh ye gods!   230

Have I then lived to be excused to Caesar?

DOLLABELLA.

As to your equal.

ANTONY.

        Well, he's but my equal;

While I wear this, he never shall be more.

DOLLABELLA.

I bring conditions from him.   235

ANTONY.

            Are they noble?

Methinks thou shouldst not bring 'em else. Yet he

Is full of deep dissembling, knows no honor

Divided from his int'rest. Fate mistook him,

For Nature meant him for an usurer;   240

He's fit indeed to buy, not conquer, kingdoms.

VENTIDIUS.

Then, granting this,

What pow'r was theirs who wrought so hard a temper

To honorable terms!

ANTONY.

It was my Dollabella, or some god.   245

DOLLABELLA.

Nor I, nor yet Maecenas nor Agrippa:

They were your enemies, and I a friend

Too weak alone. Yet 'twas a Roman's deed.

ANTONY.

'Twas like a Roman done. Show me that man

Who has preserved my life, my love, my honor;   250

Let me but see his face.

VENTIDIUS.

         That task is mine,

And, Heav'n, thou know'st how pleasing. (*Exit.*)

DOLLABELLA.

            You'll remember

To whom you stand obliged?   255

ANTONY.

              When I forget it,

Be thou unkind, and that's my greatest curse.

My queen shall thank him too.

DOLLABELLA.

          I fear she will not.

ANTONY.

But she shall do't—the Queen, my Dollabella!   260

Hast thou not still some grudgings of thy fever?

DOLLABELLA.

I would not see her lost.

ANTONY.

         When I forsake her,

Leave me, my better stars, for she has truth

Beyond her beauty. Caesar tempted her,   265

At no less price than kingdoms, to betray me,

But she resisted all, and yet thou chid'st me

For loving her too well. Could I do so?

DOLLABELLA.

Yes, there's my reason.

Re-enter Ventidius with Octavia, leading Antony's two little daughters.

ANTONY. (*Starting back.*)

           Where?—Octavia there!   270

VENTIDIUS.

What, is she poison to you? a disease?

Look on her, view her well, and those she brings:

Are they all strangers to your eyes? has Nature

No secret call, no whisper they are yours?

DOLLABELLA.

For shame, my lord, if not for love, receive 'em   275

With kinder eyes. If you confess a man,

Meet 'em, embrace 'em, bid 'em welcome to you.

Your arms should open, ev'n without your knowledge,

To clasp 'em in; your feet should turn to wings

To bear you to 'em and your eyes dart out   280

And aim a kiss ere you could reach the lips.

ANTONY.

I stood amazed to think how they came hither.

VENTIDIUS.

I sent for 'em; I brought 'em in, unknown

To Cleopatra's guards.

DOLLABELLA.

         Yet are you cold?   285

OCTAVIA.

 Thus long I have attended for my welcome,
 Which, as a stranger, sure I might expect.
 Who am I?

ANTONY.

     Caesar's sister.

OCTAVIA.

       That's unkind!   290
 Had I been nothing more than Caesar's sister,
 Know, I had still remained in Caesar's camp,
 But your Octavia, your much injured wife,
 Though banished from your bed, driv'n from
  your house,
 In spite of Caesar's sister, still is yours.   295
 'Tis true, I have a heart disdains your coldness
 And prompts me not to seek what you should offer,
 But a wife's virtue still surmounts that pride:
 I come to claim you as my own, to show
 My duty first, to ask, nay beg, your kindness.   300
 Your hand, my lord: 'tis mine, and I will have it.
 (*Taking his hand.*)

VENTIDIUS.

 Do, take it; thou deserv'st it.

DOLLABELLA.

     On my soul,
 And so she does: she's neither too submissive,   305
 Nor yet too haughty, but so just a mean
 Shows, as it ought, a wife and Roman too.

ANTONY.

 I fear, Octavia, you have begged my life.

OCTAVIA.

 Begged it, my lord?

ANTONY.

    Yes, begged it, my ambassadress;   310
 Poorly and basely begged it of your brother.

OCTAVIA.

 Poorly and basely I could never beg;
 Nor could my brother grant.

ANTONY.

 Shall I, who to my kneeling slave could say,
 "Rise up, and be a king," shall I fall down   315
 And cry, "Forgive me, Caesar"? Shall I set
 A man, my equal, in the place of Jove,
 As he could give me being? No; that word
 "Forgive" would choke me up
 And die upon my tongue.   320

DOLLABELLA.

     You shall not need it.

ANTONY.

 I will not need it. Come, you've all betrayed me
 (My friend too!) to receive some vile conditions.
 My wife has bought me with her prayers and tears,
 And now I must become her branded slave.   325
 In every peevish mood she will upbraid
 The life she gave: if I but look awry,
 She cries, "I'll tell my brother."

OCTAVIA.

     My hard fortune
 Subjects me still to your unkind mistakes.   330
 But the conditions I have brought are such
 You need not blush to take: I love your honor
 Because 'tis mine; it never shall be said
 Octavia's husband was her brother's slave.
 Sir, you are free—free ev'n from her you loathe,   335
 For though my brother bargains for your love,
 Makes me the price and cement of your peace,
 I have a soul like yours: I cannot take
 Your love as alms, nor beg what I deserve.
 I'll tell my brother we are reconciled;   340
 He shall draw back his troops, and you shall march
 To rule the East: I may be dropped at Athens—
 No matter where, I never will complain,
 But only keep the barren name of wife
 And rid you of the trouble.   345

VENTIDIUS.

 Was ever such a strife of sullen honor!
 Both scorn to be obliged.

DOLLABELLA.

 Oh, she has touched him in the tender'st part;
 See how he reddens with despite and shame
 To be outdone in generosity!   350

VENTIDIUS.

 See how he winks! how he dries up a tear
 That fain would fall!

ANTONY.

 Octavia, I have heard you and must praise
 The greatness of your soul,
 But cannot yield to what you have proposed,   355
 For I can ne'er be conquered but by love,
 And you do all for duty. You would free me
 And would be dropped at Athens: Was't not so?

OCTAVIA.

 It was, my lord.

ANTONY.

              Then I must be obliged   360
To one who loves me not, who, to herself,
May call me thankless and ungrateful man.
I'll not endure it, no.

VENTIDIUS.

                  I'm glad it pinches there.

OCTAVIA.

    Would you triumph o'er poor Octavia's virtue?   365
That pride was all I had to bear me up,
That you might think you owed me for your life
And owed it to my duty, not my love.
I have been injured, and my haughty soul
Could brook but ill the man who slights my bed.   370

ANTONY.

    Therefore you love me not.

OCTAVIA.

                   Therefore, my lord,
I should not love you.

ANTONY.

               Therefore you would leave me?

OCTAVIA.

    And therefore I should leave you–if I could.   375

DOLLABELLA.

    Her soul's too great, after such injuries,
To say she loves, and yet she lets you see it.
Her modesty and silence plead her cause.

ANTONY.

    Oh, Dollabella, which way shall I turn?
I find a secret yielding in my soul,   380
But Cleopatra, who would die with me,
Must she be left? Pity pleads for Octavia,
But does it not plead more for Cleopatra?

VENTIDIUS.

    Justice and pity both plead for Octavia,
For Cleopatra, neither.   385
One would be ruined with you, but she first
Had ruined you; the other you have ruined,
And yet she would preserve you.
In everything their merits are unequal.

ANTONY.

    Oh, my distracted soul!   390

OCTAVIA.

               Sweet Heav'n compose it!
Come, come, my lord, if I can pardon you,
Methinks you should accept it. Look on these:

Are they not yours? or stand they thus neglected
As they are mine? Go to him, children, go;   395
Kneel to him, take him by the hand, speak to him,
For you may speak, and he may own you, too,
Without a blush, and so he cannot all
His children.[43] Go, I say, and pull him to me,
And pull him to yourselves from that bad woman.   400
You, Agrippina, hang upon his arms,
And you, Antonia, clasp about his waist.
If he will shake you off, if he will dash you
Against the pavement, you must bear it, children,
For you are mine, and I was born to suffer.   405

Here the children go to him, etc.

VENTIDIUS.

    Was ever sight so moving! Emperor!

DOLLABELLA.

    Friend!

OCTAVIA.

          Husband!

BOTH CHILDREN.

             Father!

ANTONY.

             I am vanquished: take me,   410
Octavia; take me, children; share me all.
    (*Embracing them.*)
I've been a thriftless debtor to your loves
And run out much, in riot, from your stock,
But all shall be amended.

OCTAVIA.

                Oh blest hour!   415

DOLLABELLA.

    Oh happy change!

VENTIDIUS.

             My joy stops at my tongue,
But it has found two channels here for one
And bubbles out above.

ANTONY. (*To Octavia.*)

    This is thy triumph; lead me where thou wilt,   420
Ev'n to thy brother's camp.

OCTAVIA.

               All there are yours.

Enter Alexas hastily.

---

43 he cannot … children.] Antony had three children with
    Cleopatra.

ALEXAS.

The Queen, my mistress, sir, and yours—

ANTONY.

'Tis past.g

—Octavia, you shall stay this night; tomorrow   425
Caesar and we are one.

Exit leading Octavia; Dollabella and the children follow.

VENTIDIUS.

There's news for you; run my officious eunuch,h
Be sure to be the first; haste forward;
Haste, my dear eunuch, haste! (*Exit.*)

ALEXAS.

This downright fighting fool, this thick-skulled hero,   430
This blunt, unthinking instrument of death,
With plain dull virtue has outgone my wit.
Pleasure forsook my earliest infancy;
The luxury of others robbed my cradle
And ravished thence the promise of a man: 435
Cast out from Nature, disinherited
Of what her meanest children claim by kind,
Yet greatness kept me from contempt. That's gone.
Had Cleopatra followed my advice,
Then he had been betrayed who now forsakes.   440
She dies for love, but she has known its joys.
Gods, is this just that I, who know no joys,
Must die because she loves?

Enter Cleopatra, Charmion, Iras, train.

Oh, madam, I have seen what blasts my eyes!
Octavia's here!   445

CLEOPATRA.

Peace with that raven's note.
I know it, too, and now am in
The pangs of death.

ALEXAS.

You are no more a queen;
Egypt is lost.   450

CLEOPATRA.

What tell'st thou me of Egypt?
My life, my soul is lost! Octavia has him!
Oh fatal name to Cleopatra's love!
My kisses, my embraces now are hers,
While I– But thou hast seen my rival: speak,   455
Does she deserve this blessing? Is she fair,
Bright as a goddess? and is all perfection
Confined to her? It is. Poor I was made

Of that coarse matter which, when she was finished,
The gods threw by for rubbish.   460

ALEXAS.

She's indeed a very miracle.

CLEOPATRA.

Death to my hopes, a miracle!

ALEXAS. (*Bowing.*)

A miracle—
I mean, of goodness; for in beauty, madam,
You make all wonders cease.   465

CLEOPATRA.

I was too rash.
Take this in part of recompense. But, oh, (*Giving
a ring.*)
I fear thou flatter'st me.

CHARMION.

She comes! she's here!

IRAS.

Fly, madam, Caesar's sister!   470

CLEOPATRA.

Were she the sister of the thund'rer Jove[44]
And bore her brother's lightning in her eyes,
Thus would I face my rival.

*Meets Octavia with Ventidius. Octavia bears up to her.
Their trains come up on either side.*

OCTAVIA.

I need not ask if you are Cleopatra:
Your haughty carriage—   475

CLEOPATRA.

Shows I am a queen.
Nor need I ask who you are.

OCTAVIA.

A Roman:
A name that makes, and can unmake, a queen.

CLEOPATRA.

Your lord, the man who serves me, is a Roman.   480

OCTAVIA.

He was a Roman, till he lost that name
To be a slave in Egypt, but I come
To free him thence.

CLEOPATRA.

Peace, peace, my lover's Juno.

44 sister of … Jove] Juno, Jove's wife and sister, frequently
punished her husband's lovers.

When he grew weary of that household clog,* 485
He chose my easier bonds.

OCTAVIA.
                              I wonder not
Your bonds are easy. You have long been practised
In that lascivious art: he's not the first
For whom you spread your snares. Let Caesar 490
    witness.

CLEOPATRA.
I loved not Caesar; 'twas but gratitude
I paid his love: the worst your malice can
Is but to say the greatest of mankind
Has been my slave. The next, but far above him
In my esteem, is he whom law calls yours, 495
But whom his love made mine.

OCTAVIA. (*Coming up close to her.*)
                              I would view nearer
That face which has so long usurped my right
To find th'inevitable charms that catch
Mankind so sure, that ruined my dear lord. 500

CLEOPATRA.
Oh, you do well to search, for had you known
But half these charms, you had not lost his heart.

OCTAVIA.
Far be their knowledge from a Roman lady,
Far from a modest wife. Shame of our sex,
Dost thou not blush to own those black 505
    endearments[45]
That make sin pleasing?

CLEOPATRA.
                  You may blush, who want* 'em.
If bounteous Nature, if indulgent Heav'n
Have giv'n me charms to please the bravest man,
Should I not thank 'em? Should I be ashamed 510
And not be proud? I am, that he has loved me,
And when I love not him, Heav'n change this face
For one like that.

OCTAVIA.
                  Thou lov'st him not so well.

CLEOPATRA.
I love him better and deserve him more. 515

OCTAVIA.
You do not–cannot: you have been his ruin.
Who made him cheap at Rome, but Cleopatra?

Who made him scorned abroad, but Cleopatra?
At Actium, who betrayed him? Cleopatra.
Who made his children orphans? and poor me 520
A wretched widow? Only Cleopatra.

CLEOPATRA.
Yet she who loves him best is Cleopatra.
If you have suffered, I have suffered more.
You bear the specious title of a wife
To gild your cause and draw the pitying world 525
To favor it; the world contemns poor me,
For I have lost my honor, lost my fame,
And stained the glory of my royal house,
And all to bear the branded name of mistress.
There wants but life, and that too I would lose 530
For him I love.

OCTAVIA.
                  Be't so, then; take thy wish.
(*Exit with her train.*)

CLEOPATRA.
And 'tis my wish,
Now he is lost for whom alone I lived.
My sight grows dim, and every object dances 535
And swims before me in the maze of death.
My spirits, while they were opposed, kept up;
They could not sink beneath a rival's scorn.
But now she's gone, they faint.

ALEXAS.
                  Mine have had leisure 540
To recollect their strength and furnish counsel
To ruin her who else must ruin you.

CLEOPATRA.
Vain promiser!
Lead me, my Charmion; nay, your hand too, Iras:
My grief has weight enough to sink you both. 545
Conduct me to some solitary chamber
And draw the curtains round;
Then leave me to myself, to take alone
My fill of grief.
There I till death will his unkindness weep, 550
As harmless infants moan themselves asleep.

Act IV.

Antony, Dollabella.

DOLLABELLA.
Why would you shift it from yourself on me?
Can you not tell her you must part?

---

45 charms ... black endearments] Cleopatra was thought
   to have authored a treatise on cosmetics.

ANTONY.

                        I cannot.
I could pull out an eye and bid it go,
And t'other should not weep. Oh, Dollabella,
How many deaths are in this word "Depart"!   5
I dare not trust my tongue to tell her so:
One look of hers would thaw me into tears,
And I should melt till I were lost again.

DOLLABELLA.

Then let Ventidius;   10
He's rough by nature.

ANTONY.

                 Oh, he'll speak too harshly;
He'll kill her with the news. Thou, only thou.

DOLLABELLA.

Nature has cast me in so soft a mold
That but to hear a story feigned for pleasure   15
Of some sad lover's death moistens my eyes,
And robs me of my manhood.–I should speak
So faintly, with such fear to grieve her heart,
She'd not believe it earnest.

ANTONY.

                  Therefore, therefore   20
Thou only, thou art fit. Think thyself me,
And when thou speak'st (but let it first be long),
Take off the edge from every sharper sound
And let our parting be as gently made
As other loves begin. Wilt thou do this?   25

DOLLABELLA.

What you have said so sinks into my soul
That if I must speak, I shall speak just so.

ANTONY.

I leave you then to your sad task. Farewell.
I sent her word to meet you.
    (*Goes to the door and comes back.*)
                  I forgot;   30
Let her be told I'll make her peace with mine.
Her crown and dignity shall be preserved,
If I have pow'r with Caesar. –Oh, be sure
To think on that.

DOLLABELLA.

               Fear not, I will remember.   35

Antony goes again to the door and comes back.

ANTONY.

And tell her, too, how much I was constrained;

I did not this but with extremest force.
Desire her not to hate my memory,
For I still cherish hers. –Insist on that.

DOLLABELLA.

Trust me, I'll not forget it.   40

ANTONY.

                 Then that's all.
    (*Goes out and returns again.*)
Wilt thou forgive my fondness this once more?
Tell her, though we shall never meet again,
If I should hear she took another love,
The news would break my heart. –Now I must go,   45
For every time I have returned, I feel
My soul more tender, and my next command
Would be to bid her stay, and ruin both. (*Exit.*)

DOLLABELLA.

Men are but children of a larger growth;
Our appetites as apt to change as theirs   50
And full as craving, too, and full as vain.
And yet the soul, shut up in her dark room,
Viewing so clear abroad, at home sees nothing,
But like a mole in earth, busy and blind,
Works all her folly up and casts it outward   55
To the world's open view. Thus I discovered
And blamed the love of ruined Antony,
Yet wish that I were he, to be so ruined.

Enter Ventidius above.

VENTIDIUS.

Alone? and talking to himself? concerned too?
Perhaps my guess is right; he loved her once   60
And may pursue it still.

DOLLABELLA.

              Oh friendship! friendship!
Ill canst thou answer this; and reason, worse.
Unfaithful in th'attempt; hopeless to win;
And, if I win, undone: mere* madness all.   65
And yet th'occasion's fair. What injury
To him, to wear the robe which he throws by?

VENTIDIUS.

None, none at all. This happens as I wish,
To ruin her yet more with Antony.

*Enter Cleopatra, talking with Alexas, Charmion; Iras
on the other side.*

DOLLABELLA.

She comes! What charms have sorrow on that face!   70

Sorrow seems pleased to dwell with so much
   sweetness,
Yet, now and then, a melancholy smile
Breaks loose, like lightning in a winter's night,
And shows a moment's day.

VENTIDIUS.
If she should love him too! Her eunuch there!   75
That porc'pisce bodes ill weather.[46] Draw, draw
   nearer,
Sweet devil, that I may hear.

Dollabella goes over to Charmion and Iras; seems to
talk with them.

ALEXAS.
                        Believe me; try
To make him jealous. Jealousy is like
A polished glass held to the lips when life's in doubt: 80
If there be breath, 'twill catch the damp and show it.

CLEOPATRA.
I grant you, jealousy's a proof of love,
But 'tis a weak and unavailing med'cine;
It puts out the disease and makes it show,
But has no pow'r to cure.   85

ALEXAS.
'Tis your last remedy, and strongest too.
And then this Dollabella: Who so fit
To practice on? He's handsome, valiant, young,
And looks as he were laid for Nature's bait
To catch weak women's eyes.   90
He stands already more than half suspected
Of loving you. The least kind word or glance
You give this youth will kindle him with love;
Then, like a burning vessel set adrift,
You'll send him down amain before the wind   95
To fire the heart of jealous Antony.

CLEOPATRA.
Can I do this? Ah, no; my love's so true
That I can neither hide it where it is,
Nor show it where it is not. Nature meant me
A wife, a silly, harmless, household dove,   100
Fond without art and kind* without deceit,
But Fortune, that has made a mistress of me,

Has thrust me out into the wide world, unfurnished
Of falsehood to be happy.

ALEXAS.
                    Force yourself.   105
Th'event will be, your lover will return
Doubly desirous to possess the good
Which once he feared to lose.

CLEOPATRA.
                 I must attempt it,
But oh, with what regret!   110

Exit Alexas. She comes up to Dollabella.

VENTIDIUS.
So, now the scene draws near; they're in my reach.

CLEOPATRA. (*To Dollabella.*)   115
Discoursing with my women! Might not I
Share in your entertainment?

CHARMION.
                You have been
The subject of it, madam.

CLEOPATRA.
                How! and how?   120

IRAS.
Such praises of your beauty!

CLEOPATRA.
                Mere poetry.
Your Roman wits, your Gallus and Tibullus,
Have taught you this from Cytheris and Delia.[47]

DOLLABELLA.
Those Roman wits have never been in Egypt;   125
Cytheris and Delia else had been unsung.
I who have seen–had I been a poet—
Should choose a nobler name.

CLEOPATRA.
              You flatter me.
But 'tis your nation's vice: all of your country   130
Are flatt'rers and all false. Your friend's like you.
I'm sure he sent you not to speak these words.

DOLLABELLA.
No, madam, yet he sent me—

CLEOPATRA.
             Well, he sent you—

---

46 porc'pisce bodes ill weather.] The porpoise (literally,
  pigfish) was thought to be a harbinger of storms.

47 Gallus … Delia.] Gaius Cornelius Gallus (c. 69-26
  BCE) and Albius Tibullus (48?-19 BCE) were love po-
  ets who wrote for and about their faithless mistresses
  Cytheris and Delia respectively.

DOLLABELLA.
Of a less pleasing errand. 135

CLEOPATRA.
How less pleasing?
Less to yourself, or me?

DOLLABELLA.
Madam, to both,
For you must mourn, and I must grieve to cause it.

CLEOPATRA.
You, Charmion, and your fellow, stand at a distance. 140
(*Aside.*) Hold up, my spirits.–Well, now your
mournful matter,
For I'm prepared, perhaps can guess it too.

DOLLABELLA.
I wish you would, for 'tis a thankless office
To tell ill news, and I, of all your sex
Most fear displeasing you. 145

CLEOPATRA.
Of all your sex,
I soonest could forgive you, if you should.

VENTIDIUS.
Most delicate advances! Woman! Woman!
Dear, damned, inconstant sex!

CLEOPATRA.
In the first place, 150
I am to be forsaken. Is't not so?

DOLLABELLA.
I wish I could not answer to that question.

CLEOPATRA.
Then pass it o'er because it troubles you:
I should have been more grieved another time.
Next, I'm to lose my kingdom. –Farewell, Egypt. 155
Yet, is there any more?

DOLLABELLA.
Madam, I fear
Your too deep sense of grief has turned your reason.

CLEOPATRA.
No, no, I'm not run mad; I can bear fortune,
And love may be expelled by other love, 160
As poisons are by poisons.

DOLLABELLA.
You o'erjoy me, madam,
To find your griefs so moderately borne.
You've heard the worst; all are not false like him.

CLEOPATRA.
No: Heav'n forbid they should. 165

DOLLABELLA.
Some men are constant.

CLEOPATRA.
And constancy deserves reward, that's certain.

DOLLABELLA.
Deserves it not, but gives it leave to hope.

VENTIDIUS.
I'll swear thou hast my leave. I have enough.
But how to manage this! Well, I'll consider. (*Exit.*) 170

DOLLABELLA.
I came prepared
To tell you heavy news: news which, I thought,
Would fright the blood from your pale cheeks to hear.
But you have met it with a cheerfulness
That makes my task more easy, and my tongue, 175
Which on another's message was employed,
Would gladly speak its own.

CLEOPATRA.
Hold, Dollabella.
First tell me, were you chosen by my lord,
Or sought you this employment? 180

DOLLABELLA.
He picked me out, and as his bosom friend,
He charged me with his words.

CLEOPATRA.
The message then
I know was tender, and each accent smooth,
To mollify that rugged word, "Depart." 185

DOLLABELLA.
Oh, you mistake: he chose the harshest words;
With fiery eyes and with contracted brows,
He coined his face in the severest stamp,
And fury shook his fabric like an earthquake.
He heaved for vent and burst like bellowing Etna 190
In sounds scarce human, "Hence, away forever.
Let her be gone, the blot of my renown
And bane of all my hopes.

*All the time of this speech, Cleopatra seems more and
more concerned till she sinks quite down.*
Let her be driv'n as far as men can think
From man's commerce. She'll poison to the center." 195

CLEOPATRA.
Oh, I can bear no more!

DOLLABELLA.
Help, help. Oh wretch! Oh cursèd, cursèd wretch!
What have I done?

CHARMION.
                    Help, chafe her temples, Iras.
IRAS.
    Bend, bend her forward quickly.   200
CHARMION.
                              Heav'n be praised;
    She comes again.
CLEOPATRA.
                    Oh, let him not approach me.
    Why have you brought me back to this loathed
        being,
    Th'abode of falsehood, violated vows,
    And injured love? For pity, let me go,   205
    For if there be a place of long repose,
    I'm sure I want it. My disdainful lord
    Can never break that quiet, nor awake
    The sleeping soul with hollowing in my tomb
    Such words as fright her hence. Unkind, unkind!   210
DOLLABELLA. (Kneeling.)
    Believe me, 'tis against myself I speak;
    That sure deserves belief. I injured him:
    My friend ne'er spoke those words. Oh, had you seen
    How often he came back and every time
    With something more obliging and more kind   215
    To add to what he said. What dear farewells!
    How almost vanquished by his love he parted
    And leaned to what unwillingly he left.
    I, traitor as I was, for love of you
    (But what can you not do, who made me false!)   220
    I forged that lie, for whose forgiveness kneels
    This self-accused, self-punished criminal.
CLEOPATRA.
    With how much ease believe we what we wish!
    Rise, Dollabella; if you have been guilty,
    I have contributed, and too much love   225
    Has made me guilty too.
    Th'advance of kindness which I made was feigned
    To call back fleeting love by jealousy,
    But 'twould not last. Oh, rather let me lose
    Than so ignobly trifle with his heart.   230
DOLLABELLA.
    I find your breast fenced round from human reach,
    Transparent as a rock of solid crystal,
    Seen through, but never pierced. My friend, my
        friend!
    What endless treasure hast thou thrown away

And scattered, like an infant, in the ocean,   235
    Vain sums of wealth which none can gather thence!
CLEOPATRA.
    Could you not beg
    An hour's admittance to his private ear?
    Like one who wanders through long barren wilds
    And yet foreknows no hospitable inn   240
    Is near to succor hunger,
    Eats his fill, before his painful march:
    So would I feed a while my famished eyes
    Before we part, for I have far to go,
    If death be far, and never must return.   245

Ventidius with Octavia behind.

VENTIDIUS.
    From hence you may discover—

[Dollabella] takes [Cleopatra's] hand.

                              Oh, sweet, sweet!
    Would you indeed? the pretty hand in earnest?
DOLLABELLA.
    I will, for this reward. Draw it not back,
    'Tis all I e'er will beg.   250
VENTIDIUS.
    They turn upon us.
OCTAVIA.
                    What quick eyes has guilt!
VENTIDIUS.
    Seem not to have observed 'em and go on.

They enter.

DOLLABELLA.
    Saw you the Emperor, Ventidius?
VENTIDIUS.
                              No.   255
    I sought him, but I heard that he was private,
    None with him but Hipparchus, his freedman.
DOLLABELLA.
    Know you his bus'ness?
VENTIDIUS.
                    Giving him instructions
    And letters to his brother Caesar.   260
DOLLABELLA.
                    Well,
    He must be found.

Exeunt Dollabella and Cleopatra.

OCTAVIA.

  Most glorious impudence!

VENTIDIUS.

                  She looked, methought,

As she would say, "Take your old man, Octavia;   265

Thank you, I'm better here." Well, but what use[i]

Make we of this discovery?

OCTAVIA.

                     Let it die.

VENTIDIUS.

  I pity Dollabella, but she's dangerous:

Her eyes have pow'r beyond Thessalian charms[48]   270

To draw the moon from heav'n; for eloquence,

The sea-green sirens taught her voice their flatt'ry,

And while she speaks, night steals upon the day,

Unmarked of those that hear. Then she's so charming

Age buds at sight of her and swells to youth.   275

The holy priests gaze on her when she smiles,

And with heaved hands, forgetting gravity,

They bless her wanton eyes. Even I, who hate her,

With a malignant joy behold such beauty

And, while I curse, desire it. Antony   280

Must needs have some remains of passion still,

Which may ferment into a worse relapse

If now not fully cured. I know, this minute,

With Caesar he's endeavoring her peace.

OCTAVIA.

  You have prevailed. (*Walks off.*) But for a farther   285

    purpose

I'll prove how he will relish this discovery.

What, make a strumpet's peace! It swells my heart;

It must not, shannot be.

VENTIDIUS.

                His guards appear.

Let me begin, and you shall second me.   290

Enter Antony.

ANTONY.

  Octavia, I was looking for you, my love.

What, are your letters ready? I have giv'n

My last instructions.

OCTAVIA.

             Mine, my lord, are written.

---

[48] Thessalian charms] In the Ancient world, Thessaly was
famous for as a center of witchcraft and sorcery.

ANTONY.

  Ventidius! (*Drawing him aside.*)   295

VENTIDIUS.

           My lord?

ANTONY.

           A word in private.

When saw you Dollabella?

VENTIDIUS.

             Now, my lord,

He parted hence, and Cleopatra with him.   300

ANTONY.

  Speak softly. 'Twas by my command he went,

To bear my last farewell.

VENTIDIUS. (*Aloud.*)

          It looked indeed

Like your farewell.

ANTONY.

  More softly. –My farewell?   305

What secret meaning have you in those words

Of "my farewell"? He did it by my order.

VENTIDIUS. (*Aloud.*)

  Then he obeyed your order. I suppose

You bid him do it with all gentleness,

All kindness, and all–love.   310

ANTONY.

  How she mourned, the poor forsaken creature![j]

VENTIDIUS.

  She took it as she ought; she bore your parting

As she did Caesar's, as she would another's

Were a new love to come.

ANTONY. (*Aloud.*)

          Thou dost belie her,   315

Most basely and maliciously belie her.

VENTIDIUS.

  I thought not to displease you; I have done.

OCTAVIA. (*Coming up.*)

  You seem disturbed, my lord.

ANTONY.

          A very trifle.

Retire, my love.

VENTIDIUS.

         It was indeed a trifle.   320

He sent—

ANTONY. (*Angrily.*)

         No more. Look how thou disobey'st me;

Thy life shall answer it.

OCTAVIA.

                    Then 'tis no trifle.

VENTIDIUS. (*To Octavia.*)

  'Tis less, a very nothing: you too saw it, 325
  As well as I, and therefore 'tis no secret.

ANTONY.

  She saw it!

VENTIDIUS.

              Yes. She saw young Dollabella—

ANTONY.

  Young Dollabella!

VENTIDIUS.

                Young, I think him young, 330
  And handsome too, and so do others think him.
  But what of that? He went by your command,
  Indeed 'tis probable, with some kind message,
  For she received it graciously. She smiled,
  And then he grew familiar with her hand, 335
  Squeezed it, and worried it with ravenous kisses.
  She blushed, and sighed, and smiled, and blushed
    again.
  At last she took occasion to talk softly,
  And brought her cheek up close and leaned on his;
  At which, he whispered kisses back on hers, 340
  And then she cried aloud that constancy
  Should be rewarded.

OCTAVIA.

             This I saw and heard.

ANTONY.

  What woman was it, whom you heard and saw
  So playful with my friend! Not Cleopatra?^k 345

VENTIDIUS.

  Ev'n she, my lord!

ANTONY.

           My Cleopatra?

VENTIDIUS.

  Your Cleopatra;
  Dollabella's Cleopatra;
  Every man's Cleopatra. 350

ANTONY.

          Thou lie'st.

VENTIDIUS.

  I do not lie, my lord.
  Is this so strange? Should mistresses be left
  And not provide against a time of change?
  You know she's not much used to lonely nights. 355

ANTONY.

  I'll think no more on't.
  I know 'tis false and see the plot betwixt you.
  You needed not have gone this way, Octavia.
  What harms it you that Cleopatra's just?
  She's mine no more. I see, and I forgive;
  Urge it no farther, love. 360

OCTAVIA.

             Are you concerned
  That she's found false?

ANTONY.

            I should be, were it so,
  For though 'tis past, I would not that the world
  Should tax my former choice, that I loved one 365
  Of so light note. But I forgive you both.

VENTIDIUS.

  What has my age deserved, that you should think
  I would abuse your ears with perjury?
  If Heav'n be true, she's false.

ANTONY.

           Though heav'n and earth 370
  Should witness it, I'll not believe her tainted.

VENTIDIUS.

  I'll bring you, then, a witness
  From hell to prove her so. (*Seeing Alexas just
  entering and starting back.*)
           Nay, go not back;
  For stay you must, and shall. 375

ALEXAS.

           What means my lord?

VENTIDIUS.

  To make you do what you most hate: speak truth.
  You are of Cleopatra's private counsel,
  Of her bed-counsel, her lascivious hours;
  Are conscious of each nightly change she makes, 380
  And watch her, as Chaldeans do the moon;[49]
  Can tell what signs she passes through, what day.

ALEXAS.

  My noble lord!

VENTIDIUS.

          My most illustrious pander,
  No fine set speech, no cadence, no turned periods, 385

---

49 as Chaldeans do the moon] Astrology was central to the
  worship of the Chaldeans, whose beliefs spread through
  Persia and Arabia.

But a plain homespun truth is what I ask.
I did, myself, o'erhear your queen make love
To Dollabella. Speak, for I will know,
By your confession, what more passed betwixt 'em:
How near the bus'ness draws to your employment,   390
And when the happy hour.

ANTONY.
Speak truth, Alexas. Whether it offend
Or please Ventidius, care not; justify
Thy injured queen from malice; dare his worst.

OCTAVIA. (*Aside.*)
See how he gives him courage! how he fears   395
To find her false! and shuts his eyes to truth,
Willing to be misled!

ALEXAS.
As far as love may plead for woman's frailty,
Urged by desert and greatness of the lover;
So far (divine Octavia!) may my queen   400
Stand ev'n excused to you for loving him
Who is your lord; so far, from brave Ventidius,
May her past actions hope a fair report.

ANTONY.
'Tis well and truly spoken. Mark, Ventidius.

ALEXAS.
To you, most noble Emperor, her strong passion   405
Stands not excused, but wholly justified.
Her beauty's charms alone, without her crown,
From Ind and Meroe[50] drew the distant vows
Of sighing kings, and at her feet were laid
The scepters of the earth, exposed on heaps,   410
To choose where she would reign.
She thought a Roman only could deserve her,
And, of all Romans, only Antony;
And, to be less than wife to you, disdained
Their lawful passion.   415

ANTONY.
                    'Tis but truth.

ALEXAS.
And yet, though love and your umatched desert
Have drawn her from the due regard of honor,
At last, Heav'n opened her unwilling eyes
To see the wrongs she offered fair Octavia,   420
Whose bed she lawlessly usurped.
The sad effects of this improsperous war

---

50 Ind and Meroe] India and an island in the Nile in Ethiopia

Confirmed those pious thoughts.

VENTIDIUS. (*Aside.*)
                    Oh, wheel you there?
Observe him now; the man begins to mend   425
And talk substantial reason. Fear not, eunuch;
The Emperor has giv'n thee leave to speak.

ALEXAS.
Else I had never dared t'offend his ears
With what the last necessity has urged
On my forsaken mistress. Yet I must not   430
Presume to say her heart is wholly altered.

ANTONY.
No, dare not for thy life, I charge thee dare not
Pronounce that fatal word!

OCTAVIA. (*Aside.*)
Must I bear this? Good Heav'n, afford me patience.

VENTIDIUS.
On, sweet eunuch; my dear half-man, proceed.   435

ALEXAS.
Yet Dollabella
Has loved her long. He, next my godlike lord,
Deserves her best, and should she meet his passion,
Rejected, as she is, by him she loved—

ANTONY.
Hence, from my sight, for I can bear no more.   440
Let Furies drag thee quick to hell; let all
The longer damned have rest; each torturing hand
Do thou employ, till Cleopatra comes,
Then join thou too and help to torture her.

Exit Alexas, thrust out by Antony.

OCTAVIA.
'Tis not well;   445
Indeed, my lord, 'tis much unkind to me
To show this passion, this extreme concernment
For an abandoned, faithless prostitute.

ANTONY.
Octavia, leave me. I am much disordered.
Leave me, I say.   450

OCTAVIA.
                    My lord?

ANTONY.
                    I bid you leave me.

VENTIDIUS.
Obey him, madam: best withdraw a while
And see how this will work.

OCTAVIA.

    Wherein have I offended you, my lord, 455
    That I am bid to leave you? Am I false
    Or infamous? Am I a Cleopatra?
    Were I she,
    Base as she is, you would not bid me leave you,
    But hang upon my neck, take slight excuses, 460
    And fawn upon my falsehood.

ANTONY.

                  'Tis too much,
    Too much, Octavia; I am pressed with sorrows
    Too heavy to be borne, and you add more.
    I would retire and recollect what's left 465
    Of man within to aid me.

OCTAVIA.

                You would mourn
    In private for your love, who has betrayed you.
    You did but half return to me: your kindness
    Lingered behind with her. I hear, my lord, 470
    You make conditions for her,
    And would include her treaty. Wondrous proofs
    Of love to me!

ANTONY.

            Are you my friend, Ventidius?
    Or are you turned a Dollabella, too, 475
    And let this Fury loose?

VENTIDIUS.

             Oh, be advised,
    Sweet madam, and retire.

OCTAVIA.

    Yes, I will go, but never to return.
    You shall no more be haunted with this Fury.
    My lord, my lord, love will not always last 480
    When urged with long unkindness and disdain.
    Take her again whom you prefer to me:
    She stays but to be called. Poor cozened man!
    Let a feigned parting give her back your heart, 485
    Which a feigned love first got. For injured me,
    Though my just sense of wrongs forbid my stay,
    My duty shall be yours.
    To the dear pledges of our former love
    My tenderness and care shall be transferred, 490
    And they shall cheer, by turns, my widowed nights.
    So, take my last farewell, for I despair
    To have you whole, and scorn to take you half.
        (Exit.)

VENTIDIUS.

    I combat Heav'n, which blasts my best designs:
    My last attempt must be to win her back, 495
    But oh, I fear, in vain. (Exit.)

ANTONY.

    Why was I framed with this plain honest heart,
    Which knows not to disguise its griefs and weakness,
    But bears its workings outward to the world?
    I should have kept the mighty anguish in 500
    And forced a smile at Cleopatra's falsehood:
    Octavia had believed it and had stayed.
    But I am made a shallow-forded stream,
    Seen to the bottom, all my clearness scorned,
    And all my faults exposed!—See where he comes 505

Enter Dollabella.

    Who has profaned the sacred name of friend
    And worn it into vileness!
    With how secure a brow and specious form 510
    He gilds the secret villain! Sure that face
    Was meant for honesty, but Heav'n mismatched it
    And furnished treason out with Nature's pomp
    To make its work more easy.

DOLLABELLA.

                Oh my friend! 515

ANTONY.

    Well, Dollabella, you performed my message?

DOLLABELLA.

    I did, unwillingly.

ANTONY.

             Unwillingly?
    Was it so hard for you to bear our parting?
    You should have wished it. 520

DOLLABELLA.

             Why?

ANTONY.

                Because you love me.
    And she received my message with as true,
    With as unfeigned a sorrow as you brought it?

DOLLABELLA.

    She loves you, ev'n to madness. 525

ANTONY.

               Oh, I know it.
    You, Dollabella, do not better know
    How much she loves me. And should I
    Forsake this beauty, this all-perfect creature? 530

DOLLABELLA.

  I could not, were she mine.

ANTONY.

                      And yet you first

Persuaded me: How come you altered since?

DOLLABELLA.

  I said at first I was not fit to go;

  I could not hear her sighs and see her tears,   535

  But pity must prevail. And so perhaps

  It may again for you, for I have promised

  That she should take her last farewell: and see,

  She comes to claim my word.

Enter Cleopatra.

ANTONY.

                 False Dollabella!   540

DOLLABELLA.

  What's false, my lord?

ANTONY.

               Why, Dollabella's false,

  And Cleopatra's false; both false and faithless.

  Draw near, you well-joined wickedness, you serpents

  Whom I have, in my kindly bosom, warmed   545

  Till I am stung to death.

DOLLABELLA.

            My lord, have I

  Deserved to be thus used?

CLEOPATRA.

              Can Heav'n prepare

  A newer torment? Can it find a curse   550

  Beyond our separation?

ANTONY.

             Yes, if Fate

  Be just, much greater: Heav'n should be ingenious

  In punishing such crimes. The rolling stone

  And gnawing vulture were slight pains, invented   555

  When Jove was young,[51] and no examples known

  Of mighty ills, but you have ripened sin

  To such a monstrous growth, 'twill pose[52] the gods

  To find an equal torture. Two, two such—

---

51 The rolling stone ... young] Sisyphus' punishment in
    the underworld was forever to roll a stone up a hill only
    to have it roll down again; the giant Tityus was bound
    to a rock where two vultures gnawed at his liver.

52 pose] pose a challenge to

Oh, there's no farther name! two such—to me,   560

To me, who locked my soul within your breasts,

Had no desires, no joys, no life, but you.

When half the globe was mine, I gave it you

In dowry with my heart; I had no use,

No fruit of all, but you; a friend and mistress   565

Was what the world could give. Oh Cleopatra!

Oh Dollabella! how could you betray

This tender heart, which with an infant fondness

Lay lulled betwixt your bosoms and there slept

Secure of[53] injured faith?   570

DOLLABELLA.

              If she has wronged you,

Heav'n, Hell, and you revenge it.

ANTONY.

               If she wronged me!

Thou wouldst evade thy part of guilt. But swear

Thou lov'st not her.   575

DOLLABELLA.

           Not so as I love you.

ANTONY.

  Not so! Swear, swear, I say, thou dost not love her.

DOLLABELLA.

  No more than friendship will allow.

ANTONY.

                 No more?

Friendship allows thee nothing: thou art perjured—   580

And yet thou didst not swear thou lov'dst her not,

But not so much, no more. Oh trifling hypocrite,

Who dar'st not own to her thou dost not love,

Nor own to me thou dost! Ventidius heard it;

Octavia saw it.   585

CLEOPATRA.

         They are enemies.

ANTONY.

  Alexas is not so. He, he confessed it;

  He who, next Hell, best knew it, he avowed it.

  (*To Dollabella.*) Why do I seek a proof beyond

    yourself?

  You, whom I sent to bear my last farewell,   590

  Returned to plead her stay.

DOLLABELLA.

              What shall I answer?

  If to have loved be guilt, then I have sinned,

---

53 Secure of] safe from

But if to have repented of that love
Can wash away my crime, I have repented. 595
Yet, if I have offended past forgiveness,
Let not her suffer: she is innocent.

CLEOPATRA.
Ah, what will not a woman do who loves!
What means will she refuse to keep that heart
Where all her joys are placed! 'Twas I encouraged, 600
'Twas I blew up the fire that scorched his soul
To make you jealous and by that regain you.
But all in vain: I could not counterfeit;
In spite of all the dams, my love broke o'er
And drowned my heart again. Fate took th'occasion, 5
And thus one minute's feigning has destroyed
My whole life's truth.

ANTONY.
                         Thin cobweb arts of falsehood,
Seen and broke through at first.

DOLLABELLA.
                         Forgive your mistress. 10

CLEOPATRA.
Forgive your friend.

ANTONY.
                         You have convinced yourselves;
You plead each other's cause. What witness have you
That you but meant to raise my jealousy?

CLEOPATRA.
Ourselves, and Heav'n. 15

ANTONY.
Guilt witnesses for guilt. Hence, love and friendship.
You have no longer place in human breasts;
These two have driv'n you out. Avoid my sight.
I would not kill the man whom I have loved
And cannot hurt the woman, but avoid me. 20
I do not know how long I can be tame,
For if I stay one minute more to think
How I am wronged, my justice and revenge
Will cry so loud within me that my pity
Will not be heard for either. 25

DOLLABELLA.
                         Heav'n has but
Our sorrow for our sins and then delights
To pardon erring man. Sweet mercy seems
Its darling attribute, which limits justice,
As if there were degrees in infinite 30
And infinite would rather want perfection

Than punish to extent.

ANTONY.
                         I can forgive
A foe, but not a mistress and a friend:
Treason is there in its most horrid shape 35
Where trust is greatest and the soul resigned
Is stabbed by its own guards. I'll hear no more;
Hence from my sight forever.

CLEOPATRA.
                         How? Forever!
I cannot go one moment from your sight, 40
And must I go forever?
My joys, my only joys, are centered here:
What place have I to go to? my own kingdom?
That I have lost for you. Or to the Romans?
They hate me for your sake. Or must I wander 45
The wide world o'er, a helpless, banished woman,
Banished for love of you, banished from you.
Aye, there's the banishment! Oh, hear me, hear me
With strictest justice, for I beg no favor,
And if I have offended you, then kill me, 50
But do not banish me.

ANTONY.
                         I must not hear you.
I have a fool within me takes your part,
But honor stops my ears.

CLEOPATRA.
                         For pity hear me! 55
Would you cast off a slave who followed you,
Who crouched beneath your spurn?—He has no pity!
See if he gives one tear to my departure,
One look, one kind farewell. Oh iron heart!
Let all the gods look down and judge betwixt us 60
If he did ever love!

ANTONY.
                         No more: Alexas!

DOLLABELLA.
A perjured villain!

ANTONY. (To Cleopatra.)
                         Your Alexas, yours.

CLEOPATRA.
Oh, 'twas his plot, his ruinous design, 65
T'engage you in my love by jealousy.
Hear him; confront him with me; let him speak.

ANTONY.
I have, I have.

CLEOPATRA.
                    And if he clear me not—
ANTONY.
    Your creature! one who hangs upon your smiles!   70
    Watches your eye to say or to unsay
    Whate'er you please! I am not to be moved.
CLEOPATRA.
    Then must we part? Farewell, my cruel lord,
    Th'appearance is against me and I go,
    Unjustified, forever from your sight.   75
    How I have loved, you know; how yet I love,
    My only comfort is, I know myself.
    I love you more, ev'n now you are unkind,
    Than when you loved me most; so well, so truly,
    I'll never strive against it, but die pleased   80
    To think you once were mine.
ANTONY. [*Aside.*]
    Good Heav'n, they weep at parting.
    Must I weep too? That calls 'em innocent.
    I must not weep, and yet I must, to think
    That I must not forgive.—   85
    Live, but live wretched; 'tis but just you should,
    Who made me so. Live from each other's sight.
    Let me not hear you meet: set all the earth
    And all the seas betwixt your sundered loves;
    View nothing common but the sun and skies.   90
    Now, all take several ways,
    And each your own sad fate with mine deplore:
    That you were false, and I could trust no more.

Exeunt severally.

                    Act V.

Cleopatra, Charmion, Iras.

CHARMION.
    Be juster, Heav'n: such virtue punished thus
    Will make us think that Chance rules all above
    And shuffles, with a random hand, the lots
    Which man is forced to draw.
CLEOPATRA.
    I could tear out these eyes, that gained his heart   5
    And had not pow'r to keep it. Oh the curse
    Of doting on, ev'n when I find it dotage!
    Bear witness, gods, you heard him bid me go,
    You, whom he mocked with imprecating vows
    Of promised faith.—I'll die. I will not bear it.   10

(*She pulls out her dagger, and they hold her.*) You
    may hold me—
    But I can keep my breath; I can die inward
    And choke this love.

Enter Alexas.

IRAS.
                    Help, oh Alexas, help!
    The Queen grows desperate; her soul struggles in her   15
    With all the agonies of love and rage
    And strives to force its passage.
CLEOPATRA.
                    Let me go.
    Art thou there, traitor! —Oh,
    Oh, for a little breath, to vent my rage!   20
    Give, give me way, and let me loose upon him.
ALEXAS.
    Yes, I deserve it, for my ill-timed truth.
    Was it for me to prop
    The ruins of a falling majesty?
    To place myself beneath the mighty flaw,   25
    Thus to be crushed and pounded into atoms
    By its o'erwhelming weight? 'Tis too presuming
    For subjects to preserve that willful pow'r
    Which courts its own destruction.
CLEOPATRA.
                    I would reason   30
    More calmly with you. Did not you o'errule
    And force my plain, direct, and open love
    Into these crooked paths of jealousy?
    Now, what's th'event? Octavia is removed,
    But Cleopatra's banished. Thou, thou villain,   35
    Hast pushed my boat to open sea, to prove,
    At my sad cost, if thou canst steer it back.
    It cannot be; I'm lost too far; I'm ruined.
    Hence, thou imposter, traitor, monster, devil—
    I can no more: thou and my griefs have sunk   40
    Me down so low that I want voice to curse thee.
ALEXAS.
    Suppose some shipwrecked seaman near the shore,
    Dropping and faint with climbing up the cliff:
    If, from above, some charitable hand
    Pull him to safety, hazarding himself   45
    To draw the other's weight, would he look back
    And curse him for his pains? The case is yours:
    But one step more and you have gained the height.

CLEOPATRA.

Sunk, never more to rise.

ALEXAS.

Octavia's gone, and Dollabella banished.   50
Believe me, madam, Antony is yours.
His heart was never lost, but started off
To jealousy, love's last retreat and covert,
Where it lies hid in shades, watchful in silence,
And list'ning for the sound that calls it back.   55
Some other, any man ('tis so advanced),
May perfect this unfinished work, which I
(Unhappy only to myself) have left
So easy to his hand.

CLEOPATRA.

                         Look well thou do't; else—   60

ALEXAS.

Else what your silence threatens.–Antony
Is mounted up the Pharos,[54] from whose turret
He stands surveying our Egyptian galleys
Engaged with Caesar's fleet: now death or conquest.
If the first happen, Fate acquits my promise;   65
If we o'ercome, the conqueror is yours.

A distant shout within.

CHARMION.

Have comfort, madam: Did you mark that shout?

Second shout nearer.

IRAS.

Hark! they redouble it.

ALEXAS.

                         'Tis from the port.
The loudness shows it near: good news, kind   70
    heavens!

CLEOPATRA.

Osiris make it so!

Enter Serapion.

SERAPION.

                    Where, where's the Queen?

ALEXAS.

How frightfully the holy coward stares!
As if not yet recovered of th'assault,
When all his gods, and what's more dear to him,   75
His offerings, were at stake.

_____

54 Pharos] the lighthouse at Alexandria

SERAPION.

                         Oh horror, horror!
Egypt has been; our latest hour is come;
The queen of nations from her ancient seat
Is sunk forever in the dark abyss;   80
Time has unrolled her glories to the last
And now closed up the volume.

CLEOPATRA.

                         Be more plain:
Say whence thou cam'st (though Fate is in thy face,
Which from thy haggard eyes looks wildly out   85
And threatens ere thou speak'st).

SERAPION.

                         I came from Pharos,
From viewing (spare me and imagine it)
Our land's last hope, your navy—

CLEOPATRA.

                         Vanquished?   90

SERAPION.

                         No.
They fought not.

CLEOPATRA.

                         Then they fled?

SERAPION.

                         Nor that. I saw,
With Antony, your well-appointed fleet   95
Row out, and thrice he waved his hand on high,
And thrice with cheerful cries they shouted back.
'Twas then false Fortune, like a fawning strumpet
About to leave the bankrupt prodigal,
With a dissembled smile would kiss at parting   100
And flatter to the last. The well-timed oars
Now dipped from every bank, now smoothly run
To meet the foe. And soon indeed they met,
But not as foes. In few, we saw their caps
On either side thrown up; th'Egyptian galleys   105
(Received like friends) passed through and fell
    behind
The Roman rear, and now they all come forward
And ride within the port.

CLEOPATRA.

                         Enough, Serapion:
I've heard my doom. This needed not, you gods.   110
When I lost Antony, your work was done;
'Tis but superfluous malice. Where's my lord?
How bears he this last blow?

SERAPION.

His fury cannot be expressed by words.
Thrice he attempted headlong to have fall'n   115
Full on his foes and aimed at Caesar's galley;
Withheld, he raves on you, cries he's betrayed.
Should he now find you—

ALEXAS.

                    Shun him; seek your safety
Till you can clear your innocence.   120

CLEOPATRA.

                          I'll stay.

ALEXAS.

You must not. Haste you to your monument,
While I make speed to Caesar.

CLEOPATRA.

                      Caesar! No,
I have no business with him.   125

ALEXAS.

                    I can work him
To spare your life and let this madman perish.

CLEOPATRA.

Base, fawning wretch! wouldst thou betray him too?
Hence from my sight. I will not hear a traitor;
'Twas thy design brought all this ruin on us.   130
Serapion, thou art honest. Counsel me,
But haste, each moment's precious.

SERAPION.

Retire; you must not yet see Antony.
He who began this mischief,
'Tis just he tempt the danger; let him clear you,   135
And since he offered you his servile tongue
To gain a poor precarious life from Caesar,
Let him expose the fawning eloquence
And speak to Antony.

ALEXAS.

                    Oh heavens! I dare not;   140
I meet my certain death.

CLEOPATRA.

                    Slave, thou deserv'st it.
Not that I fear my lord will I avoid him.
I know him noble: when he banished me
And thought me false, he scorned to take my life.   145
But I'll be justified, and then die with him.

ALEXAS.

Oh pity me and let me follow you.

CLEOPATRA.

To death, if thou stir hence. Speak, if thou canst,
Now for thy life, which basely thou wouldst save,
While mine I prize at this. Come, good Serapion.   150

Exeunt Cleopatra, Serapion, Charmion, Iras.

ALEXAS.

Oh that I less could fear to lose this being,
Which, like a snowball in my coward hand,
The more 'tis grasped, the faster melts away.
Poor reason! what a wretched aid art thou!
For still, in spite of thee,   155
These two long lovers, soul and body, dread
Their final separation. Let me think:
What can I say to save myself from death
No matter what becomes of Cleopatra?

ANTONY. (*Within.*)

Which way? where?   160

VENTIDIUS. (*Within.*)

                    This leads to th'monument.

ALEXAS.

Ah me! I hear him, yet I'm unprepared.
My gift of lying's gone,
And this court-devil, which I so oft have raised,
Forsakes me at my need. I dare not stay,   165
Yet cannot far go hence. (*Exit.*)

Enter Antony and Ventidius.

ANTONY.

Oh happy Caesar! Thou hast men to lead:
Think not 'tis thou hast conquered Antony,
But Rome has conquered Egypt. I'm betrayed.

VENTIDIUS.

Curse on this treach'rous train!   170
Their soil and heav'n infect 'em all with baseness,
And their young souls come tainted to the world
With the first breath they draw.

ANTONY.

Th'original villain sure no god created;
He was a bastard of the sun by Nile,   175
Aped into man, with all his mother's mud
Crusted about his soul.[55]

---

55 He was a bastard ... soul.] The muddy banks of the Nile
   were frequently thought a place where creatures were
   generated from the earth.

VENTIDIUS.
                The nation is
One universal traitor, and their queen
The very spirit and extract of 'em all.   180
ANTONY.
  Is there yet left
A possibility of aid from valor?
Is there one god unsworn to my destruction?
The least unmortgaged hope? for if there be,
Methinks I cannot fall beneath the fate   185
Of such a boy as Caesar.
The world's one half is yet in Antony,
And from each limb of it that's hewed away
The soul comes back to me.[56]
VENTIDIUS.
                There yet remain   190
Three legions in the town; the last assault
Lopped off the rest. If death be your design,
As I must wish it now, these are sufficient
To make a heap about us of dead foes,
An honest pile for burial.   195
ANTONY.
             They're enough.
We'll not divide our stars, but side by side
Fight emulous, and with malicious eyes
Survey each other's acts; so every death
Thou givest, I'll take on me as a just debt,   200
And pay thee in a soul.
VENTIDIUS.
Now you shall see I love you. Not a word
Of chiding more. By my few hours of life,
I am so pleased with this brave Roman fate
That I would not be Caesar to outlive you.   205
When we put off this flesh and mount together,
I shall be shown to all th'ethereal crowd:
"Lo, this is he who died with Antony."
ANTONY.
Who knows but we may pierce through all their
    troops
And reach my veterans yet? 'Tis worth the tempting   210
T'o'erleap this gulf of fate

---

56 The world's … me]The metaphor depends on the traditional theory of the soul's inhabiting every part of the
body, but in case of non-mortal amputations, retreating to the remainder.

And leave our wond'ring destinies behind.

Enter Alexas trembling.

VENTIDIUS.
  See, see that villain:
See Cleopatra stamped upon that face,
With all her cunning, all her arts of falsehood!   215
How she looks out through those dissembling eyes!
How he has set his count'nance for deceit
And promises a lie before he speaks!
Let me dispatch him first. (*Drawing.*)
ALEXAS.
             Oh spare me, spare me.   220
ANTONY.
  Hold, he's not worth your killing. On thy life
(Which thou mayst keep because I scorn to take it),
No syllable to justify thy Queen;
Save thy base tongue its office.
ALEXAS.
               Sir, she's gone   225
Where she shall never be molested more
By love, or you.
ANTONY.
          Fled to Dollabella!
Die, traitor; I revoke my promise; die. (*Going to
kill him.*)
ALEXAS.
  Oh hold! she is not fled.   230
ANTONY.
               She is; my eyes
Are open to her falsehood. My whole life
Has been a golden dream of love and friendship.
But now I wake, I'm like a merchant roused
From soft repose to see his vessel sinking   235
And all his wealth cast o'er. Ingrateful woman!
Who followed me but as the swallow summer,
Hatching her young ones in my kindly beams,
Singing her flatt'ries to my morning wake,
But now my winter comes, she spreads her wings   240
And seeks the spring of Caesar.
ALEXAS.
             Think not so:
Her fortunes have, in all things, mixed with yours.
Had she betrayed her naval force to Rome,
How easily might she have gone to Caesar,   245
Secure by such a bribe!

VENTIDIUS.

She sent it first,
To be more welcome after.

ANTONY.

'Tis too plain;
Else she would have appeared to clear herself.   250

ALEXAS.

Too fatally she has: she could not bear
To be accused by you, but shut herself
Within her monument, looked down and sighed,
While from her unchanged face the silent tears
Dropped, as they had not leave, but stole their   255
    parting.
Some undistinguished words she inly murmured;
At last she raised her eyes, and with such looks
As dying Lucrece* cast—57

ANTONY.

My heart forebodes—

VENTIDIUS.

All for the best; go on.   260

ALEXAS.

She snatched her poniard,
And, ere we could prevent the fatal blow,
Plunged it within her breast, then turned to me:
"Go, bear my lord," said she, "my last farewell,
And ask him if he yet suspect my faith."   265
More she was saying, but death rushed betwixt.
She half pronounced your name with her last breath
And buried half within her.

VENTIDIUS.

Heav'n be praised!

ANTONY.

Then art thou innocent, my poor dear love,   270
And art thou dead?
Oh those two words! their sound should be
    divided:
Hadst thou been false, and died; or hadst thou
    lived,
And hadst been true— But innocence and death!
This shows not well above. Then what am I,   275
The murderer of this truth, this innocence!
Thoughts cannot form themselves in words so horrid
As can express my guilt!

---

57 As dying Lucrece] Lucrece stabbed herself after she had
    been raped.

VENTIDIUS.

Is't come to this? The gods have been too gracious,
And thus you thank 'em for't?   280

ANTONY. (*To Alexas.*)

Why stay'st thou here?
Is it for thee to spy upon my soul
And see its inward mourning? Get thee hence;
Thou art not worthy to behold what now
Becomes a Roman emperor to perform.   285

ALEXAS. (*Aside.*)

He loves her still:
His grief betrays it. Good! The joy to find
She's yet alive completes the reconcilement.
I've saved myself and her. But, oh! the Romans!
Fate comes too fast upon my wit,   290
Hunts me too hard, and meets me at each
    double.58 (*Exit.*)

VENTIDIUS.

Would she had died a little sooner, though,
Before Octavia went; you might have treated.
Now 'twill look tame and would not be received.
Come, rouse yourself, and let's die warm together.   295

ANTONY.

I will not fight: there's no more work for war.
The bus'ness of my angry hours is done.

VENTIDIUS.

Caesar is at your gates.

ANTONY.

Why, let him enter;
He's welcome now.   300

VENTIDIUS.

What lethargy has crept into your soul?

ANTONY.

'Tis but a scorn of life and just desire
To free myself from bondage.

VENTIDIUS.

Do it bravely.

ANTONY.

I will, but not by fighting. Oh Ventidius!   305
What should I fight for now? My queen is dead.
I was but great for her; my pow'r, my empire
Were but my merchandise to buy her love,
And conquered kings, my factors. Now she's dead,
Let Caesar take the world—   310

---

58 double] doubling back (like a hunted animal)

An empty circle since the jewel's gone
Which made it worth my strife; my being's nauseous,
For all the bribes of life are gone away.
VENTIDIUS.
Would you be taken?
ANTONY.
                  Yes, I would be taken,   315
But as a Roman ought, dead, my Ventidius,
For I'll convey my soul from Caesar's reach
And lay down life myself. 'Tis time the world
Should have a lord and know whom to obey.
We two have kept its homage in suspense   320
And bent the globe, on whose each side we trod,
Till it was dinted inwards. Let him walk
Alone upon't; I'm weary of my part.
My torch is out, and the world stands before me
Like a black desert at th'approach of night.   325
I'll lay me down and stray no farther on.
VENTIDIUS.
I could be grieved,
But that I'll not outlive you: choose your death,
For I have seen him in such various shapes,
I care not which I take. I'm only troubled,   330
The life I bear is worn to such a rag,
'Tis scarce worth giving. I could wish, indeed,
We threw it from us with better grace;
That, like two lions taken in the toils,
We might at least thrust out our paws and wound   335
The hunters that inclose us.
ANTONY.
                  I have thought on't.
Ventidius, you must live.
VENTIDIUS.
                I must not, sir.
ANTONY.
Wilt thou not live to speak some good of me?   340
To stand by my fair fame and guard th'approaches
From the ill tongues of men?
VENTIDIUS.
                Who shall guard mine,
For living after you?
ANTONY.
              Say, I command it.   345
VENTIDIUS.
If we die well, our deaths will speak themselves
And need no living witness.

ANTONY.
                Thou hast loved me,
And fain I would reward thee. I must die:
Kill me, and take the merit of my death   350
To make thee friends with Caesar.
VENTIDIUS.
                Thank your kindness.
You said I loved you, and in recompense
You bid me turn a traitor. Did I think
You would have used me thus? that I should die   355
With a hard thought of you?
ANTONY.
                Forgive me, Roman.
Since I have heard of Cleopatra's death,
My reason bears no rule upon my tongue
But lets my thoughts break all at random out.   360
I've thought better; do not deny me twice.
VENTIDIUS.
By Heav'n, I will not.
Let it not be t'outlive you.
ANTONY.
              Kill me first,
And then die thou, for 'tis but just you serve   365
Thy friend before thyself.
VENTIDIUS.
              Give me your hand.
We soon shall meet again. Now farewell,
   Emperor. (*Embrace.*)
Methinks that word's too cold to be my last:
Since death sweeps all distinctions, farewell,   370
   friend.
That's all.—
I will not make a bus'ness of a trifle,
And yet I cannot look on you and kill you;
Pray turn your face.
ANTONY.
              I do. Strike home, be sure.   375
VENTIDIUS.
Home, as my sword will reach. (*Kills himself.*)
ANTONY.
                Oh, thou mistak'st.
That wound was none of thine; give it me back:
Thou robb'st me of my death.
VENTIDIUS.
              I do, indeed.   380
But think, 'tis the first time I e'er deceived you,

If that may plead my pardon. And you, gods,
Forgive me if you will, for I die perjured
Rather than kill my friend. (*Dies.*)

ANTONY.

Farewell. Ever my leader, ev'n in death!   385
My queen and thou have got the start of me,
And I'm the lag of honor.–Gone so soon?
Is death no more? He used him carelessly,
With a familiar kindness; ere he knocked,
Ran to the door and took him in his arms,   390
As who should say, "Y'are welcome at all hours,
A friend need give no warning." Books had
  spoiled him,
For all the learned are cowards by profession.
'Tis not worth
My farther thought, for death, for aught I know,   395
Is but to think no more. Here's to be satisfied.
    (*Falls on his sword.*)
I've missed my heart. Oh unperforming hand!
Thou never couldst have erred in a worse time.
My fortune jades me to the last, and death,
Like a great man, takes state, and makes me wait   400
For my admittance– (*Trampling within.*)
                    Some, perhaps, from Caesar.
If he should find me living, and suspect
That I played booty with my life! I'll mend
My work ere they can reach me. (*Rises upon his*   405
  knees.)

Enter Cleopatra, Charmion, Iras.

CLEOPATRA.

Where is my lord? where is he?

CHARMION.

                    There he lies,
And dead Ventidius by him.

CLEOPATRA.

My fears were prophets; I am come too late.
Oh that accursed Alexas! (*Runs to [Antony].*)   410

ANTONY.

                    Art thou living?
Or am I dead before I knew, and thou
The first kind ghost that meets me?

CLEOPATRA.

                    Help me seat him.
Send quickly, send for help.   415

They place him in a chair.

ANTONY.

                    I am answered.
We live both. Sit thee down, my Cleopatra;
I'll make the most I can of life, to stay
A moment more with thee.

CLEOPATRA.

                    How is it with you?   420

ANTONY.

'Tis as with a man
Removing in a hurry, all packed up
But one dear jewel that his haste forgot,
And he, for that, returns upon the spur:
So I come back for thee.   425

CLEOPATRA.

Too long, you heav'ns, you have been cruel to me;
Now show your mended faith, and give me back
His fleeting life.

ANTONY.

                    It will not be, my love.
I keep my soul by force.   430
Say but thou art not false.

CLEOPATRA.

                    'Tis now too late
To say I'm true: I'll prove it, and die with you.
Unknown to me, Alexas feigned my death,
Which when I knew, I hastened to prevent   435
This fatal consequence. My fleet betrayed
Both you and me.

ANTONY.

                    And Dollabella—

CLEOPATRA.

                    Scarce
Esteemed before he loved, but hated now.[m]   440

ANTONY.

Enough: my life's not long enough for more.
Thou say'st thou wilt come after: I believe thee,
For I can now believe whate'er thou say'st,
That we may part more kindly.

CLEOPATRA.

                    I will come.   445
Doubt not, my life, I'll come, and quickly too:
Caesar shall triumph o'er no part of thee.

ANTONY.

But grieve not, while thou stay'st
My last disastrous times:
Think we have had a clear and glorious day,   450

And Heav'n did kindly to delay the storm
Just till our close of ev'ning. Ten years' love,
And not a moment lost, but all improved
To th'utmost joys: What ages have we lived?
And now to die each other's, and so dying, 455
While hand in hand we walk in groves below,
Whole troops of lovers' ghosts shall flock about us,
And all the train be ours.

CLEOPATRA.
Your words are like the notes of dying swans,
Too sweet to last. Were there so many hours 460
For your unkindness, and not one for love?

ANTONY.
No, not a minute. –This one kiss–more worth
Than all I leave to Caesar. (*Dies.*)

CLEOPATRA.
Oh, tell me so again
And take ten thousand kisses for that word. 465
My lord, my lord. Speak, if you yet have being.
Sigh to me, if you cannot speak, or cast
One look. Do anything that shows you live.

IRAS.
He's gone too far to hear you,
And this you see, a lump of senseless clay, 470
The leavings of a soul.

CHARMION.
Remember, madam,
He charged you not to grieve.

CLEOPATRA.
And I'll obey him.
I have not loved a Roman not to know 475
What should become his wife; his wife, my
  Charmion,
For 'tis to that high title I aspire,
And now I'll not die less. Let dull Octavia
Survive, to mourn him dead; my nobler fate
Shall knit our spousals with a tie too strong 480
For Roman laws to break.

IRAS.
Will you then die?

CLEOPATRA.
Why shouldst thou make that question?

IRAS.
Caesar is merciful.

CLEOPATRA.
Let him be so 485

To those that want his mercy; my poor lord
Made no such cov'nant with him to spare me
When he was dead. Yield me to Caesar's pride?
What! to be led in triumph through all the streets,
A spectacle to base plebeian eyes, 490
While some dejected friend of Antony's,
Close in a corner, shakes his head and mutters
A secret curse on her who ruined him?
I'll none of that.

CHARMION.
Whatever you resolve, 495
I'll follow ev'n to death.

IRAS.
I only feared
For you, but more should fear to live without you.

CLEOPATRA.
Why, now 'tis as it should be. Quick, my friends,
Dispatch; ere this, the town's in Caesar's hands. 500
My lord looks down concerned and fears my stay,
Lest I should be surprised;
Keep him not waiting for his love too long.
You, Charmion, bring my crown and richest jewels,
With 'em, the wreath of victory I made 505
(Vain augury!) for him who now lies dead.
You, Iras, bring the cure of all our ills.

IRAS.
The aspics, madam?

CLEOPATRA.
Must I bid you twice?

Exeunt Charmion and Iras.
'Tis sweet to die when they would force life on me, 510
To rush into the dark abode of Death,
And seize him first. If he be like my love,
He is not frightful, sure.
We're now alone, in secrecy and silence,
And is not this like lovers? I may kiss 515
These pale, cold lips; Octavia does not see me,
And, oh! 'tis better far to have him thus
Than see him in her arms.–Oh welcome, welcome.

Enter Charmion and Iras.

CHARMION.
What must be done?

CLEOPATRA.
Short ceremony, friends, 520
But yet it must be decent. First, this laurel

Shall crown my hero's head: he fell not basely,
Nor left his shield behind him. Only thou
Couldst triumph o'er thyself, and thou alone
Wert worthy so to triumph.   525

CHARMION.

                          To what end
These ensigns of your pomp and royalty?

CLEOPATRA.

Dull that thou art! Why, 'tis to meet my love
As when I saw him first on Cydnos' bank,
All sparkling like a goddess. So adorned,   530
I'll find him once again; my second spousals
Shall match my first in glory. Haste, haste, both,
And dress the bride of Antony.

CHARMION.

                                    'Tis done.

CLEOPATRA.

Now seat me by my lord. I claim this place,   535
For I must conquer Caesar too, like him,
And win my share o'th'world. Hail, you dear relics
Of my immortal love!
Oh, let no impious hand remove you hence,
But rest forever here. Let Egypt give   540
His death that peace, which it denied his life.
Reach me the casket.

IRAS.

Underneath the fruit the aspic lies.

CLEOPATRA. (Putting aside the leaves.)

Welcome, thou kind deceiver!
Thou best of thieves, who, with an easy key,   545
Dost open life, and unperceived by us,
Ev'n steal us from ourselves, discharging so
Death's dreadful office better than himself,
Touching our limbs so gently into slumber
That Death stands by, deceived by his own image,   550
And thinks himself but sleep.

SERAPION. (Within.)

                          The Queen, where is she?
The town is yielded, Caesar's at the gates.

CLEOPATRA.

He comes too late t'invade the rights of death.
Haste, bare my arm, and rouse the serpent's fury.   555
        (Holds out her arm and draws it back.)
Coward flesh—
Wouldst thou conspire with Caesar to betray me,
As thou wert none of mine? I'll force thee to't

And not be sent by him,
But bring, myself, my soul to Antony. (Turns aside   560
        and then shows her arm bloody.)
Take hence; the work is done.

SERAPION. (Within.)

                          Break ope the door,
And guard the traitor well.

CHARMION.

                          The next is ours.

IRAS.

Now, Charmion, to be worthy   565
Of our great queen and mistress.

They apply the aspics.

CLEOPATRA.

Already, Death, I feel thee in my veins.
I go with such a will to find my lord
That we shall quickly meet.
A heavy numbness creeps through every limb,   570
And now 'tis at my head; my eyelids fall,
And my dear love is vanished in a mist.
Where shall I find him, where? Oh turn me to him,
And lay me on his breast.—Caesar, thy worst.
Now part us, if thou canst. (Dies.)   575

Iras sinks down at her feet and dies; Charmion stands
behind her chair as dressing her head. Enter Serapion,
two priests, Alexas bound, Egyptians.

TWO PRIESTS.

Behold, Serapion, what havoc death has made!

SERAPION.

'Twas what I feared. Charmion, is this well done?[n]

CHARMION.

Yes, 'tis well done, and like a queen, the last
Of her great race.* I follow her. (Sinks down; dies.)

ALEXAS.

                                    'Tis true,   580
She has done well: much better thus to die
Than live to make a holy-day in Rome.

SERAPION.

See, see how the lovers sit in state together,
As they were giving laws to half mankind.
Th'impression of a smile left in her face   585
Shows she died pleased with him for whom she lived
And went to charm him in another world.
Caesar's just ent'ring; grief has now no leisure.

Secure that villain, as our pledge of safety
To grace th'imperial triumph. Sleep, blest pair,   590
Secure from human chance, long ages out,
While all the storms of Fate fly o'er your tomb,
And fame to late posterity shall tell,
No lovers lived so great, or died so well.

[Exeunt.]

Finis.

Textual Notes

a The copytext is the 1678 first quarto (Q1). Also consulted were the 1692 quarto (Q2), the 1696 third quarto (Q3), the 1717 collected works (W1), the 1717 collected works (W2), and the 1984 California Edition (CE).

b *Enter second gentleman*] CE; Re-enter the Gentleman Q1, Q2; Gentlemen Q3, W1, W2
c god-like] W2, CE; good-like Q1, Q2, Q3, W1
d Too presuming … love] CE; *run-on in all early editions*
e ere] Q2, Q3, W1, W2, CE; *om.* Q1
f Come … live] CE; *all early editions separate into two lines.*
g 'Tis past] CE; *all early editions print as part of following line.*
h my … eunuch] CE; *all early editions print as a separate line.*
i Well … use] CE; *all early editions print as a separate line.*
j the … creature] CE; *all early editions print as a separate line.*
k Not Cleopatra] CE; *all early editions print as a separate line.*
l have] W2, CE; *om.* Q1, Q2, Q3, W1
m Scarce … now] CE; *all early editions print as one line.*
n Charmion … done] CE; *all early editions print as a separate line.*

The Fair Penitent[a]

by Nicholas Rowe (1674-1718)

edited by Jean I. Marsden

The Fair Penitent is the third of Nicholas Rowe's trag-edies and the first of the acclaimed "she-tragedies" on which his reputation as a dramatist rests. The play was first performed at Lincoln's Inn Fields in March of 1703, and, despite a disappointing premiere, soon became one of the most enduringly popular plays of the century. The title role was played by (and created for) Elizabeth Barry, the greatest tragic actress of her generation.

In The Fair Penitent, Rowe combines harmoni-ous blank verse with innovations in the subject mat-ter of serious drama. He rejects the emphasis on the affairs of kings and princes common to most earlier tragedies, and focuses instead on the lives of charac-ters with whom his audience could more readily iden-tify. As he famously states in his prologue, his tragedy presents "a melancholy tale of private woes" where viewers could "meet with sorrows like [their] own." Rowe does not break radically with tradition; his char-acters are well-to-do upper class citizens, but the fo-cus of the tragedy remains within the domestic rather than the political sphere. Rowe's interest in private rather than public woes and the concerns of family rather than empire foreshadows the development later in the eighteenth century of domestic tragedies such as George Lillo's The London Merchant.

Although Rowe was not the first playwright to write she-tragedy (see also Banks, The Unhappy Favorite), he became the most famed practitioner of the genre and the playwright whose name became al-most synonymous with the term (he even coined the phrase). Popular in the 1680s and 1690s, she-tragedies emphasize the suffering of a sympathetic fe-male figure, often a woman who, like Rowe's heroine

Calista, has committed a sexual sin. In The Fair Peni-tent, Rowe reinvigorates a form which by the early eighteenth century had become hackneyed and for-mulaic, using as his source an older tragedy, Philip Massinger's The Fatal Dowry (ca. 1630). In contrast to Massinger's play in which the female figure is dis-tinctly unsympathetic and appears infrequently, Rowe makes Calista the play's central focus. The lack of pathos displayed by the title character distin-guishes Rowe's play from many contemporary she-tragedies. Seduced and abandoned by the man she loves and forced into a marriage with another, she re-pents of her sin but nonetheless rebels against her fate. In fact, Calista's strong will and refusal to in-dulge in self-incrimination angered some contempo-rary playgoers, and Rowe's enemies complained that he made a "whore" his heroine. In particular they claimed that the play's title was misleading as Calista never, to their minds, truly repented. One such critic was Samuel Johnson, who, although he praised The Fair Penitent as "one of the most pleasing tragedies on the stage," nonetheless objected that Calista felt "pain from detection rather than from guilt, and ex-presses more shame than sorrow, and more rage than shame" (Lives of the Poets).

Despite such complaints, The Fair Penitent was exceeded in popularity only by the tragedies of Shakespeare and a handful of tragedies by Otway, Southerne, and Rowe himself. Calista became a stock role for all great actresses of the eighteenth century. The play also introduced the figure of Lothario, a character so vivid that his name has survived into modern usage as synonymous with the charming se-ducer.

PROLOGUE

Long has the fate of kings and empires been
The common bus'ness of the tragic scene,
As if misfortune made the throne her seat,
And none could be unhappy but the great.
Dearly, 'tis true, each buys the crown he wears,   5
And many are the mighty monarch's cares:
By foreign foes and home-bred factions pressed,
Few are the joys he knows, and short his hours of
 rest.
Stories like these with wonder we may hear,
But far remote, and in a higher sphere: 10
We ne'er can pity what we ne'er can share.
Like distant battles of the Pole and Swede,[1]
Which frugal citizens o'er coffee read,
Careless for who shall fail or who succeed.
Therefore an humbler theme our author chose,   15
A melancholy tale of private woes:
No princes here lost royalty bemoan,
But you shall meet with sorrows like your own;
Here see imperious Love his vassals treat
As hardly as Ambition does the great;   20
See how succeeding passions rage by turns,
How fierce the youth with joy and rapture burns,
And how to death, for beauty lost, he mourns.
Let no nice* taste the poet's art arraign,
If some frail vicious characters he feign: 25
Who writes should still let Nature be his care,
Mix shades with lights, and not paint all things fair,
But show you men and women as they are.
With deference to the fair he bade me say,
Few to perfection ever found the way;   30
Many in many parts are known t'excel,
But 'twere too hard for one to act all well.
Whom justly life should through each scene
 commend,
The maid, the wife, the mistress, and the friend:
This age, 'tis true, has one great instance seen,   35
And Heav'n in justice made that one a queen.[2]

---

1. Pole and Swede] In 1702-3, Charles XII of Sweden conducted a military campaign in Poland, deposing one
 Polish king and installing another.
2. queen] Queen Anne (1701-14)

DRAMATIS PERSONAE

MEN
 Sciolto, a nobleman of Genoa, father to Calista.
 Altamont, a young lord, in love with Calista
  and designed her husband by Sciolto.
 Horatio, his friend.
 Lothario, a young lord, enemy to Altamont.
 Rossano, his friend.
 Servants to Sciolto.
WOMEN
 Calista, daughter to Sciolto.
 Lavinia, sister to Altamont and wife to Horatio.
 Lucilla, confidant to Calista.

SCENE: SCIOLTO'S PALACE AND GARDEN, WITH
SOME PART OF THE STREET NEAR IT, IN GENOA.

The Fair Penitent.

Quin morere, ut merita es, ferroque averte dolorem.
Virg. *Aen.* Lib. 4.[3]

Act I, scene i. A garden belonging to Sciolto's palace.

Enter Altamont and Horatio.

ALTAMONT.
 Let this auspicious day be ever sacred,
 No mourning, no misfortunes happen on it;
 Let it be marked for triumphs and rejoicings;
 Let happy lovers ever make it holy,
 Choose it to bless their hopes and crown their wishes,   5
 This happy day that gives me my Calista.
HORATIO.
 Yes, Altamont, today thy better stars
 Are joined to shed their kindest influence on thee:
 Sciolto's noble hand, that raised thee first,
 Half dead and drooping o'er thy father's grave,   10
 Completes its bounty and restores thy name
 To that high rank and luster which it boasted
 Before ungrateful Genoa had forgot
 The merit of thy godlike father's arms;

---

3. *Quin ...* 4] Virgil, *Aeneid* IV.547: "Rather with steel
 thy guilty breast invade, / And take the fortune thou thyself hast made" (Dryden IV.789-90). Dido contemplates
 leaving Carthage with Aeneas or committing suicide.

Before that country, which he long had served 15
In watchful councils and in winter camps,
Had cast off his white age to want and wretchedness
And made their court to faction by his ruin.

ALTAMONT.

Oh great Sciolto! oh my more than father!
Let me not live, but at thy very name 20
My eager heart springs up and leaps with joy.
When I forget the vast, vast debt I owe thee—
Forget! (but 'tis impossible)—then let me
Forget the use and privilege of reason,
Be driven from the commerce of mankind 25
To wander in the desert among brutes,
To bear the various fury of the seasons,
The night's unwholesome dew and noonday's heat,
To be the scorn of earth and curse of Heav'n.

HORATIO.

So open, so unbounded was his goodness, 30
It reached ev'n me because I was thy friend.
When that great man I loved, thy noble father,
Bequeathed thy gentle sister to my arms,
His last dear pledge and legacy of friendship,
That happy tie made me Sciolto's son. 35
He called us his, and with a parent's fondness
Indulged us in his wealth, blest us with plenty,
Healed all our cares, and sweetened love itself.

ALTAMONT.

By Heav'n, he found my fortunes so abandoned
That nothing but a miracle could raise 'em: 40
My father's bounty and the state's ingratitude
Had stripped him bare, nor left him ev'n a grave;
Undone myself and sinking with his ruin,
I had no wealth to bring, nothing to succor him
But fruitless tears. 45

HORATIO.

                    Yet what thou couldst thou didst
And didst it like a son: when his hard creditors,
Urged and assisted by Lothario's father
(Foe to thy house and rival of their greatness),
By sentence of the cruel law forbid 50
His venerable corpse to rest in earth,
Thou gav'st thyself a ransom for his bones,
With piety uncommon didst give up
Thy hopeful youth to slaves who ne'er knew mercy,
Sour, unrelenting, money-loving villains, 55
Who laugh at human nature and forgiveness

And are, like fiends, the factors for destruction.
Heav'n, who beheld the pious act, approved it
And bade Sciolto's bounty be its proxy
To bless thy filial virtue with abundance. 60

ALTAMONT.

But see he comes, the author of my happiness,
The man who saved my life from deadly sorrow,
Who bids my days be blest with peace and plenty
And satisfies my soul with love and beauty.

Enter Sciolto, he runs to Altamont and embraces him.

SCIOLTO.

Joy to thee, Altamont! Joy to myself! 65
Joy to this happy morn that makes thee mine,
That kindly grants what Nature had denied me
And makes me father of a son like thee.

ALTAMONT.

My Father! oh, let me unlade my breast,
Pour out the fullness of my soul before you, 70
Show ev'ry tender, ev'ry grateful thought
This wondrous goodness stirs. But 'tis impossible,
And utterance all is vile,* since I can only
Swear you reign here, but never tell how much.

SCIOLTO.

It is enough, I know thee: thou art honest; 75
Goodness innate and worth hereditary
Are in thy mind; thy noble father's virtues
Spring freshly forth and blossom in thy youth.

ALTAMONT.

Thus Heav'n from nothing raised his fair creation
And then with wondrous joy beheld its beauty, 80
Well pleased to see the excellence he gave.

SCIOLTO.

Oh noble youth! I swear since first I knew thee,
Ev'n from that day of sorrows when I saw thee
Adorned and lovely in thy filial tears,
The mourner and redeemer of thy father, 85
I set thee down and sealed thee for my own:
Thou art my son, ev'n near me as Calista.
—Horatio and Lavinia too are mine. (*Embraces
   Horatio.*)
All are my children and shall share my heart.
But wherefore waste we thus this happy day? 90
The laughing minutes summon thee to joy
And with new pleasures court thee as they pass;
Thy waiting bride ev'n chides thee for delaying,

And swears thou com'st not with a bridegroom's
    haste.
ALTAMONT.
  Oh! could I hope there was one thought of Altamont, 95
  One kind remembrance in Calista's breast,
  The winds with all their wings would be too slow
  To bear me to her feet. For oh! my father,
  Amidst this stream of joy that bears me on,
  Blest as I am and honored in your friendship, 100
  There is one pain that hangs upon my heart.
SCIOLTO.
  What means my son?
ALTAMONT.
               When, at your intercession,
  Last night Calista yielded to my happiness,
  Just ere we parted, as I sealed my vows 105
  With rapture on her lips, I found her cold
  As a dead lover's statue on his tomb;
  A rising storm of passion shook her breast,
  Her eyes a piteous show'r of tears let fall,
  And then she sighed as if her heart were breaking. 110
  With all the tend'rest eloquence of love
  I begged to be a sharer in her grief,
  But she, with looks averse and eyes that froze me,
  Sadly replied, her sorrows were her own
  Nor in a father's pow'r to dispose of. 115
SCIOLTO.
  Away! It is the cozenage of their sex,
  One of the common arts they practice on us,
  To sigh and weep then when their hearts beat high
  With expectation of the coming joy.
  Thou hast in camps and fighting fields been bred, 120
  Unknowing in the subtleties of women:
  The virgin bride, who swoons with deadly fear
  To see the end of all her wishes near,
  When, blushing from the light and public eyes,
  To the kind covert of the night she flies, 125
  With equal fires to meet the bridegroom moves,
  Melts in his arms, and with a loose[4] she loves.

Exeunt.

      [Scene ii. The same.]

Enter Lothario and Rossano.

LOTHARIO.
  The father and the husband!
ROSSANO.
               Let them pass,
  They saw us not.
LOTHARIO.
             I care not if they did,
  Ere long I mean to meet 'em face to face 5
  And gall 'em with my triumph o'er Calista.
ROSSANO.
  You loved her once.
LOTHARIO.
            I liked her, would have married her,
  But that it pleased her father to refuse me,
  To make this honorable fool her husband. 10
  For which, if I forget him, may the shame
  I mean to brand his name with stick on mine.
ROSSANO.
  She, gentle soul, was kinder than her father.
LOTHARIO.
  She was, and oft in private gave me hearing,
  Till by long list'ning to the soothing tale 15
  At length her easy heart was wholly mine.
ROSSANO.
  I have heard you oft describe her haughty, insolent,
  And fierce with high disdain; it moves my wonder
  That virtue thus defended should be yielded
  A prey to loose desires. 20
LOTHARIO.
               Hear then, I'll tell thee.
  Once in a lone and secret hour of night,
  When ev'ry eye was closed and the pale moon
  And stars alone shone conscious of the theft,
  Hot with the Tuscan grape[5] and high in blood, 25
  Haply I stole unheeded to her chamber.
ROSSANO.
  That minute sure was lucky.
LOTHARIO.
             Oh 'twas great.
  I found the fond,* believing, lovesick maid,
  Loose, unattired, warm, tender, full of wishes; 30
  Fierceness and pride, the guardians of her honor,
  Were charmed to rest, and love alone was waking.
  Within her rising bosom all was calm

---

4 with a loose] with abandon, without restraint

5 Tuscan grape] wine from Tuscany in central Italy

As peaceful seas that know no storms and only
Are gently lifted up and down by tides.   35
I snatched the glorious, golden opportunity
And with prevailing, youthful ardor pressed her,
Till with short sighs and murmuring reluctance
The yielding fair one gave me perfect happiness.
Ev'n all the livelong night we passed in bliss,   40
In ecstasies too fierce to last forever.
At length the morn and cold indifference came;
When fully sated with the luscious banquet,
I hastily took leave and left the nymph
To think on what was past and sigh alone.   45

ROSSANO.
You saw her soon again.

LOTHARIO.
                          Too soon I saw her,
For oh! that meeting was not like the former:
I found my heart no more beat high with transport,
No more I sighed and languished for enjoyment,   50
'Twas past, and reason took her turn to reign,
While ev'ry weakness fell before her throne.

ROSSANO.
What of the lady?

LOTHARIO.
                  With uneasy fondness
She hung upon me, wept and sighed and swore   55
She was undone, talked of a priest and marriage,
Of flying with me from her father's pow'r,
Called ev'ry saint and blessèd angel down
To witness for her that she was my wife.
I started at that name.   60

ROSSANO.
                        What answer made you?

LOTHARIO.
None, but pretending sudden pain and illness
Escaped the persecution; two nights since,
By message urged and frequent importunity,
Again I saw her. Straight with tears and sighs,   65
With swelling breasts, with swooning, with
   distraction,
With all the subtleties and pow'rful arts
Of wilful woman lab'ring for her purpose,
Again she told the same dull, nauseous tale.
Unmoved, I begged her spare th'ungrateful subject   70
Since I resolved, that love and peace of mind
Might flourish long inviolate betwixt us,

Never to load it with the marriage chain;
That I would still retain her in my heart
My ever gentle mistress and my friend.   75
But for those other names of wife and husband,
They only meant ill-nature, cares, and quarrels.

ROSSANO.
How bore she this reply?

LOTHARIO.
                          Ev'n as the earth
When (winds pent up, or eating fires beneath   80
Shaking the mass) she labors with destruction.
At first her rage was dumb and wanted* words,
But when the storm found way, 'twas wild and loud.
Mad as the priestess of the Delphic god,[6]
Enthusiastic* passion swelled her breast,   85
Enlarged her voice, and ruffled all her form;
Proud, and disdainful of the love I proffered,
She called me "Villain! Monster! Base! Betrayer!"[b]
At last, in very bitterness of soul,
With deadly imprecations on herself,   90
She vowed severely ne'er to see me more,
Then bid me fly that minute. I obeyed
And, bowing, left her to grow cool at leisure.

ROSSANO.
She has relented since, else why this message
To meet the keeper of her secrets here   95
This morning?

LOTHARIO.
               See the person whom you named.
Enter Lucilla.
Well, my ambassadress, what must we treat of?
Come you to menace war and proud defiance,
Or does the peaceful olive grace your message?   100
Is your fair mistress calmer? does she soften?
And must we love again? Perhaps she means
To treat in juncture with her new ally
And make her husband party to th'agreement.

LUCILLA.
Is this well done, my lord? Have you put off   105
All sense of human nature? Keep a little,
A little pity to distinguish manhood,
Lest other men, though cruel, should disclaim you
And judge you to be numbered with the brutes.

---

6 priestess … god] The priestess of Apollo's temple at Del-
phi often spoke incoherently or in riddles.

LOTHARIO.
   I see thou'st learnt to rail.   110
LUCILLA.
                      I've learnt to weep:
   That lesson my sad mistress often gives me;
   By day she seeks some melancholy shade
   To hide her sorrows from the prying world;
   At night she watches all the long, long hours   115
   And listens to the winds and beating rain
   With sighs as loud and tears that fall as fast.
   Then ever and anon she wrings her hands
   And cries, "False! false Lothario!"
LOTHARIO.
                      Oh, no more!   120
   I swear thou'lt spoil thy pretty face with crying,
   And thou hast beauty that may make thy fortune:
   Some keeping* cardinal shall dote upon thee
   And barter his church treasure for thy freshness.
LUCILLA.
   What! shall I sell my innocence and youth,   125
   For wealth or titles, to perfidious man!
   To man! who makes his mirth of our undoing!
   The base, professed betrayer of our sex.
   Let me grow old in all misfortunes else,
   Rather than know the sorrows of Calista.   130
LOTHARIO.
   Does she send thee to chide in her behalf?
   I swear thou dost it with so good a grace
   That I could almost love thee for thy frowning.
LUCILLA.
   Read there, my lord, there, in her own sad lines,
     (*Giving a letter.*)
   Which best can tell the story of her woes,   135
   That grief of heart which your unkindness gives her.
LOTHARIO. (*Reads.*)
   "Your cruelty—obedience to my father—give my
   hand to Altamont."
   (*Aside.*) By Heav'n! 'tis well, such ever be the gifts
   With which I greet the man whom my soul hates.   140
   But to go on!
   "—Wish—heart—honor—too faithless—weak-
   ness—tomorrow—last trouble—lost Calista."
   Women, I see, can change as well as men:
   She writes me here, forsaken as I am,   145
   That I should bind my brows with mournful
      willow,*

For she has given her hand to Altamont.
   Yet tell the fair inconstant—
LUCILLA.
                     How, my lord?
LOTHARIO.
   Nay, no more angry words. Say to Calista,   150
   The humblest of her slaves shall wait her pleasure,
   If she can leave her happy husband's arms
   To think upon so lost a thing as I am.
LUCILLA.
   Alas! for pity, come with gentler looks,
   Wound not her heart with this unmanly triumph   155
   And, though you love her not, yet swear you do.
   So shall dissembling once be virtuous in you.
LOTHARIO.
   Hah! who comes here?
LUCILLA.
                 The bridegroom's friend, Horatio.
   He must not see us here. Tomorrow early   160
   Be at the garden gate.
LOTHARIO.
                   Bear to my love
   My kindest thoughts and swear I will not fail her.

Lothario, putting up the letter hastily, drops it as he goes out.

Exeunt Lothario and Rossano one way, Lucilla another.

[Scene iii. Continues.]

Enter Horatio.

HORATIO.
   Sure 'tis the very error of my eyes:
   Waking I dream, or I beheld Lothario;
   He seemed conferring with Calista's woman;*
   At my approach they started and retired.
   What business could he have here, and with her?   5
   I know he bears the noble Altamont
   Professed and deadly hate—What paper's this?
   (*Taking up the letter.*)
   Hah! To Lothario! 'Sdeath!* Calista's name!
    (*Opening it.*)
   Confusion and misfortune! (*Reads.*)
   "Your cruelty has at length determined me, and   10
   I have resolved this morning to yield a perfect
   obedience to my father and to give my hand to

Altamont, in spite of my weakness for the false
Lothario. I could almost wish I had that heart—
and that honor to bestow with it—which you   15
have robbed me of."
  Damnation! to the rest—   (*Reads again.*)
"But oh! I fear could I retrieve 'em, I should again
be undone by the too faithless, yet too lovely
Lothario. This is the last weakness of my pen,   20
and tomorrow shall be the last in which I will
indulge my eyes. Lucilla shall conduct you if you
are kind enough to let me see you; it shall be the
last trouble you shall meet with from,
    The Lost Calista."   25
The lost indeed! for thou art gone as far
As there can be perdition, fire, and sulfur:
Hell is the sole avenger of such crimes.
Oh that the ruin were but all thy own!
Thou wilt ev'n make thy father curse his age;   30
At sight of this black scroll the gentle Altamont
(For oh! I know his heart is set upon thee)
Shall droop and hang his discontented head,
Like merit scorned by insolent authority,
And never grace the public with his virtues.—   35
Perhaps ev'n now he gazes fondly on her
And, thinking soul and body both alike,
Blesses the perfect workmanship of Heav'n,
Then sighing to his ev'ry care, speaks peace
And bids his heart be satisfied with happiness.   40
Oh wretched husband! while she hangs about thee
With idle blandishments and plays the fond one,
Ev'n then her hot imagination wanders,
Contriving riot and loose scapes[7] of love,
And, while she clasps thee close, makes thee a   45
  monster.[8]
What if I give this paper to her father?
It follows that his justice dooms her dead
And breaks his heart with sorrow: hard return
For all the good his hand has heaped on us.
Hold, let me take a moment's thought.   50

Enter Lavinia.

LAVINIA.
                     My lord!
Trust me, it joys my heart that I have found you.

---

7 scapes] scenes
8 monster] man with horns, cuckold

Enquiring wherefore you had left the company
Before my brother's nuptial rites were ended,
They told me you had felt some sudden illness.   55
Where are you sick? Is it your head? your heart?
Tell me, my love, and ease my anxious thoughts,
That I may take you gently in my arms,
Sooth you to rest, and soften all your pains.
HORATIO.
It were unjust, no, let me spare my friend,   60
Lock up the fatal secret in my breast,
Nor tell him that which will undo his quiet.
LAVINIA.
What means my lord?
HORATIO.
           Hah! saidst thou my Lavinia?
LAVINIA.
Alas! you know not what you make me suffer.   65
Why are you pale? Why did you start and tremble?
Whence is that sigh? And wherefore are your eyes
Severely raised to Heav'n? The sick man thus,
Acknowledging the summons of his fate,
Lifts up his feeble hands and eyes for mercy   70
And with confusion thinks upon his audit.
HORATIO.
Oh no! thou hast mistook my sickness quite,
These pangs are of the soul. Would I had met
Sharpest convulsions, spotted pestilences,
Or any other deadly foe to life,   75
Rather than heave beneath this load of thought.
LAVINIA.
Alas, what is it? Wherefore turn you from me?
Why did you falsely call me your Lavinia
And swear I was Horatio's better half,
Since now you mourn unkindly by yourself   80
And rob me of my partnership of sadness?
Witness you holy Pow'rs, who know my truth,
There cannot be a chance in life so miserable,
Nothing so very hard but I could bear it
Much rather than my love should treat me coldly   85
And use me like a stranger to his heart.
HORATIO.
Seek not to know what I would hide from all,
But most from thee. I never knew a pleasure,
Aught that was joyful, fortunate, or good,
But straight I ran to bless thee with the tidings   90
And laid up all my happiness with thee.
But wherefore, wherefore should I give thee pain?

Then spare me, I conjure thee, ask no further,
Allow my melancholy thoughts this privilege
And let 'em brood in secret o'er their sorrows.   95
LAVINIA.
  It is enough, chide not, and all is well.
  Forgive me if I saw you sad, Horatio,
  And asked to weep out part of your misfortunes;
  I wonnot press to know what you forbid me.
  Yet, my loved lord, yet you must grant me this: 100
  Forget your cares for this one happy day;
  Devote this day to mirth and to your Altamont;
  For his dear sake let peace be in your looks.
  Ev'n now the jocund bridegroom wants* your wishes;
  He thinks the priest has but half blest his marriage   105
  Till his friend hails him with the sound of joy.
HORATIO.
  Oh never! never! never! Thou art innocent:
  Simplicity from ill, pure native truth,
  And candor of the mind adorn thee ever.
  But there are such, such false ones in the world,   110
  'Twould fill thy gentle soul with wild amazement
  To hear their story told.
LAVINIA.
                          False ones, my lord?
HORATIO.
  Fatally fair they are, and in their smiles
  The graces, little loves, and young desires inhabit,   115
  But all that gaze upon 'em are undone,
  For they are false, luxurious in their appetites,
  And all the heav'n they hope for is variety:
  One lover to another still* succeeds,
  Another, and another after that,   120
  And the last fool is welcome as the former
  Till, having loved his hour out, he gives place
  And mingles with the herd that went before him.
LAVINIA.
  Can there be such? and have they peace of mind?
  Have they in all the series of their changing   125
  One happy hour? If women are such things,
  How was I formed so different from my sex?
  My little heart is satisfied with you:
  You take up all her room, as in a cottage
  Which harbors some benighted princely stranger,   130
  Where the good man, proud of his hospitality,
  Yields all his homely dwelling to his guest
  And hardly keeps a corner for himself.

HORATIO.
  Oh were they all like thee, men would adore 'em,
  And all the bus'ness of their lives be loving;   135
  The nuptial band should be the pledge of peace,
  And all domestic cares and quarrels cease;
  The world should learn to love by virtuous rules,
  And marriage be no more the jest of fools.

Exeunt.

             Act II, scene i. A hall.

Enter Calista and Lucilla.

CALISTA.
  Be dumb forever, silent as the grave,
  Nor let thy fond, officious love disturb
  My solemn sadness with the sound of joy.
  If thou wilt soothe me, tell some dismal tale
  Of pining discontent and black despair.   5
  For oh! I've gone around through all my thoughts,
  But all are indignation, love, or shame,
  And my dear peace of mind is lost forever.
LUCILLA.
  Why do you follow still that wand'ring fire
  That has misled your weary steps and leaves you   10
  Benighted in a wilderness of woe?
  That false Lothario! Turn from the deceiver,
  Turn and behold where gentle Altamont,
  Kind as the softest virgin of our sex
  And faithful as the simple village swain   15
  That never knew the courtly vice of changing
  Sighs at your feet and woos you to be happy.
CALISTA.
  Away, I think not of him. My sad soul
  Has formed a dismal melancholy scene,
  Such a retreat as I would wish to find: 20
  An unfrequented vale, o'ergrown with trees
  Mossy and old within whose lonesome shade
  Ravens and birds ill-omened only dwell;
  No sound to break the silence, but a brook
  That bubbling winds among the weeds; no mark   25
  Of any human shape that had been there,
  Unless a skeleton of some poor wretch
  Who had long since, like me, by love undone,
  Sought that sad place out to despair and die in.
LUCILLA.
  Alas for pity!   30

CALISTA.

There I fain would hide me
From the base world, from malice, and from shame,
For 'tis the solemn counsel of my soul
Never to live with public loss of honor:
'Tis fixed to die, rather than bear the insolence   35
Of each affected she that tells my story
And blesses her good stars that she is virtuous.
To be a tale for fools! Scorned by the women
And pitied by the men! oh insupportable!

LUCILLA.

Can you perceive the manifest destruction,   40
The gaping gulf that opens just before you,
And yet rush on, though conscious of the danger?
Oh hear me, hear your ever faithful creature:
By all the good I wish, by all the ill
My trembling heart forebodes, let me entreat you   45
Never to see this faithless man again.
Let me forbid his coming.

CALISTA.

On thy life
I charge thee, no! My genius* drives me on.
I must, I will behold him once again.   50
Perhaps it is the crisis of my fate,
And this one interview shall end my cares.
My lab'ring heart, that swells with indignation,
Heaves to discharge the burden; that once done,
The busy thing shall rest within its cell   55
And never beat again.

LUCILLA.

Trust not to that:
Rage is the shortest passion of our souls;
Like narrow brooks that rise with sudden show'rs,
It swells in haste and falls again as soon;   60
Still* as it ebbs, the softer thoughts flow in,
And the deceiver Love supplies its place.

CALISTA.

I have been wronged enough to arm my temper
Against the smooth delusion. But alas!
(Chide not my weakness, gentle maid, but pity me)   65
A woman's softness hangs about me still.
Then let me blush and tell thee all my folly.
I swear I could not see the dear betrayer
Kneel at my feet and sigh to be forgiven,
But my relenting heart would pardon all   70
And quite forget 'twas he that had undone me.

LUCILLA.

Ye sacred Powers, whose gracious providence
Is watchful for our good, guard me from men,
From their deceitful tongues, their vows and flatteries;
Still* let me pass neglected by their eyes,   75
Let my bloom wither and my form decay,
That none may think it worth his while to ruin me,
And fatal love may never be my bane.

CALISTA.

Hah, Altamont! Calista now be wary
And guard thy soul's accesses with dissembling,   80
Nor let this hostile husband's eyes explore
The warring passions and tumultuous thoughts
That rage within thee and deform thy reason.

Enter Altamont.

ALTAMONT.

Be gone, my cares, I give you to the winds,
Far to be borne, far from the happy Altamont,   85
For from this sacred era of my love
A better order of succeeding days
Come smiling forward, white[9] and lucky all.
Calista is the mistress of the year:
She crowns the seasons with auspicious beauty   90
And bids ev'n all my hours be good and joyful.

CALISTA. [*Aside.*]

If I was ever mistress of such happiness,
Oh! wherefore did I play th'unthrifty fool
And, wasting all on others, leave myself
Without one thought of joy to give me comfort?   95

ALTAMONT.

Oh mighty love! Shall that fair face profane
This thy great festival with frowns and sadness!
I swear it shannot be, for I will woo thee
With sighs so moving, with so warm a transport,
That thou shalt catch the gentle flame from me   100
And kindle into joy.

CALISTA.

I tell thee, Altamont,
Such hearts as ours were never paired above:
Ill-suited to each other; joined, not matched.
Some sullen influence,* a foe to both,   105
Has wrought this fatal marriage to undo us.
Mark but the frame and temper of our minds,

_____

9 white] fortunate, happy

How very much we differ. Ev'n this day,
That fills thee with such ecstasy and transport,
To me brings nothing that should make me bless it   110
Or think it better than the day before
Or any other in the course of time
That dully took its turn and was forgotten.

ALTAMONT.

If to behold thee as my pledge of happiness,
To know none fair, none excellent beside thee;   115
If still* to love thee with unwearied constancy
Through ev'ry season, ev'ry change of life,
Through wrinkled age, through sickness and
    misfortune,
Be worth the least return of grateful love,
Oh then let my Calista bless this day,   120
And set it down for happy.

CALISTA.

                            'Tis the day
In which my father gave my hand to Altamont;
As such I will remember it forever.

Enter Sciolto, Horatio, and Lavinia.

SCIOLTO.

Let mirth go on, let pleasure know no pause,   125
But fill up ev'ry minute of this day.
'Tis yours, my children, sacred to your loves.
The glorious sun himself for you looks gay;
He shines for Altamont and for Calista.
Let there be music, let the master touch   130
The sprightly string and softly-breathing flute
Till harmony rouse ev'ry gentle passion,
Teach the cold maid to lose her fears in love
And the fierce youth to languish at her feet.
Begin, ev'n age itself is cheered with music,   135
It wakes a glad remembrance of our youth,
Calls back past joys, and warms us into transport.

Here an entertainment of music and dancing.

Song.[10]

I

Ah stay! ah turn! ah whither would you fly,
    Too charming, too relentless maid?
I follow not to conquer but to die,   140
    You of the fearful are afraid.

_____
10 Song] written by William Congreve

II
In vain I call, for she like fleeting air,
    When pressed by some tempestuous wind,
Flies swifter from the voice of my despair
    Nor casts one pitying look behind.   145

SCIOLTO.

Take care my gates be open, bid all welcome;
All who rejoice with me today are friends.
Let each indulge his genius, each be glad,
Jocund and free, and swell the feast with mirth.
The sprightly bowl shall cheerfully go round,   150
None shall be grave, nor too severely wise;
Losses and disappointments, cares and poverty,
The rich man's insolence and great man's scorn,
In wine shall be forgotten all. Tomorrow
Will be too soon to think and to be wretched.   155
Oh! grant, ye Powers, that I may see these happy,
    (*Pointing to Altamont and Calista.*)
Completely blest, and I have life enough
And leave the rest indifferently to Fate.

Exeunt. Manet Horatio.

HORATIO.

What if, while all are here intent on revelling,
I privately went forth and sought Lothario?   160
This letter may be forged: perhaps the wantonness
Of his vain youth, to stain a lady's fame;
Perhaps his malice, to disturb my friend.
Oh no! my heart forebodes it must be true.
Methought ev'n now I marked the starts of guilt   165
That shook her soul, though damned dissimulation
Screened her dark thoughts and set to public view
A specious face of innocence and beauty.
Oh false appearance! What is all our sovereignty,
Our boasted pow'r? When they oppose their arts,   170
Still* they prevail, and we are found their fools.
With such smooth looks and many a gentle word
The first fair she[11] beguiled her easy lord;
Too blind with love and beauty to beware,
He fell unthinking in the fatal snare   175
Nor could believe that such a heav'nly face
Had bargained with the Devil, to damn her
    wretched race.

Exit.

_____
11 she] Eve

Scene ii. The street near Sciolto's palace.

Enter Lothario and Rossano.

LOTHARIO.

To tell thee then the purport of my thoughts:
The loss of this fond* paper would not give me
A moment of disquiet, were it not
My instrument of vengeance on this Altamont;
Therefore, I mean to wait some opportunity   5
Of speaking with the maid we saw this morning.

ROSSANO.

I wish you, sir, to think upon the danger
Of being seen: today their friends are round 'em,
And any eye that lights by chance on you
Shall put your life and safety to the hazard.   10

They confer aside. Enter Horatio.

HORATIO.

Still I must doubt* some mystery of mischief,
Some artifice beneath: Lothario's father,
I knew him well, he was sagacious, cunning,
Fluent in words, and bold in peaceful councils,
But of a cold, unactive hand in war,   15
Yet with these coward's virtues he undid
My unsuspecting, valiant, honest friend.
This son, if fame mistakes not, is more hot,
More open, and unartful. (*Seeing him.*) Hah! he's
  here!

LOTHARIO.

Damnation! He again! This second time   20
Today he has crossed me like my evil genius.*

HORATIO.

I sought you, sir.

LOTHARIO.

                'Tis well then I am found.

HORATIO.

'Tis well you are: The man who wrongs my friend
To the earth's utmost verge I would pursue;   25
No place, though e'er so holy, should protect him;
No shape that artful fear e'er formed should hide
  him,
Till he fair answer made and did me justice.

LOTHARIO.

Hah! dost thou know me? that I am Lothario?
As great a name as this proud city boasts of.   30
Who is this mighty man, then, this Horatio,

That I should basely hide me from his anger,
Lest he should chide me for his friend's displeasure?

HORATIO.

The brave, 'tis true, do never shun the light;
Just are their thoughts, and open are their tempers; 35
Freely without disguise they love and hate;
Still* are they found in the fair face of day,
And Heav'n and men are judges of their actions.

LOTHARIO.

Such let 'em be of mine: there's not a purpose
Which my soul ever framed or my hand acted   40
But I could well have bid the world look on
And what I once durst do have dared to justify.

HORATIO.

Where was this open boldness, this free spirit,
When but this very morning I surprised thee
In base, dishonest privacy, consulting   45
And bribing a poor mercenary wretch
To sell her lady's secrets, stain her honor,
And with a forged contrivance blast her virtue?
At sight of me thou fled'st!

LOTHARIO.

                Hah! Fled from thee?   50

HORATIO.

Thou fled'st, and guilt was on thee like a thief,
A pilferer descried in some dark corner
Who there had lodged with mischievous intent
To rob and ravage at the hour of rest
And do a midnight murder on the sleepers.   55

LOTHARIO.

Slave! Villain!*— (*Offers* to draw, Rossano holds him.)

ROSSANO.

                Hold, my lord! think where you are,
Think how unsafe and hurtful to your honor
It were to urge a quarrel* in this place
And shock the peaceful city with a broil.   60

LOTHARIO.

Then since thou dost provoke my vengeance, know
I would not for this city's wealth, for all
Which the sea wafts to our Ligurian shore,
But that the joys I reaped with that fond wanton,
The wife of Altamont, should be as public   65
As is the noonday sun, air, earth, or water
Or any common benefit of nature.
Think'st thou I meant the shame should be
  concealed?

Oh no! by Hell and Vengeance, all I wanted*
Was some fit messenger to bear the news   70
To the dull, doting husband. Now I have found him,
And thou art he.
HORATIO.
                 I hold thee base enough
To break through law and spurn at sacred order
And do a brutal injury like this,   75
Yet mark me well, young lord, I think Calista
Too nice,* too noble, and too great of soul
To be the prey of such a thing as thou art.
'Twas base and poor, unworthy of a man,
To forge a scroll so villainous and loose   80
And mark it with a noble lady's name.
These are the mean, dishonest arts of cowards,
Strangers to manhood and to glorious dangers,
Who, bred at home in idleness and riot,
Ransack for mistresses th'unwholesome stews   85
And never know the worth of virtuous love.
LOTHARIO.
Think'st thou I forged the letter? Think so still,*
Till the broad shame comes staring in thy face
And boys shall hoot the cuckold as he passes.
HORATIO.
Away, no woman could descend so low: 90
A skipping, dancing, worthless tribe you are,
Fit only for yourselves. You herd together,
And when the circling glass warms your vain hearts,
You talk of beauties that you never saw
And fancy raptures that you never knew.   95
Legends of saints, who never yet had being,
Or being, ne'er were saints,12 are not so false
As the fond tales which you recount of love.
LOTHARIO.
But that I do not hold it worth my leisure,
I could produce such damning proof—   100
HORATIO.
                      'Tis false!
You blast the fair with lies because they scorn you,
Hate you like age, like ugliness and impotence.
Rather than make you blest they would die virgins

And stop the propagation of mankind.   105
LOTHARIO.
It is the curse of fools to be secure,
And that be thine and Altamont's. Dream on,
Nor think upon my vengeance till thou feel'st it.
HORATIO.
Hold sir, another word, and then farewell:
Though I think greatly of Calista's virtue   110
And hold it far beyond thy pow'r to hurt,
Yet as she shares the honor of my Altamont,
That treasure of a soldier, bought with blood
And kept at life's expense, I must not have
(Mark me, young sir) her very name profaned.   115
Learn to restrain the license of your speech;
'Tis held you are too lavish. When you are met
Among your set of fools, talk of your dress,
Of dice, of whores, of horses, and yourselves:
'Tis safer and becomes your understandings.   120
LOTHARIO.
What if we pass beyond this solemn order
And, in defiance of the stern Horatio,
Indulge our gayer thoughts, let laughter loose,
And use his sacred friendship for our mirth?
HORATIO.
'Tis well! Sir, you are pleasant—   125
LOTHARIO.
                      By the joys
Which yet my soul has uncontrolled pursued,
I would not turn aside from my least pleasure,
Though all thy force were armed to bar my way,
But like the birds, great Nature's happy   130
   commoners13
That haunt in woods, in meads, and flow'ry gardens,
Rifle the sweets and taste the choicest fruits
Yet scorn to ask the lordly owner's leave.
HORATIO.
What liberty has vain presumptuous youth,
That thou shouldst dare provoke me unchastised?   135
But henceforth, boy, I warn thee shun my walks.
If in the bounds of yon forbidden place
Again thou'rt found, expect a punishment
Such as great souls, impatient of an injury,
Exact from those who wrong 'em much, ev'n death   140

---

12 Legends … ne'er were saints] A veiled attack on Catholicism: radical European Protestants during the Reformation called the existence of saints into question, seeing
   them as another example of Catholic "idolotry."

---

13 commoners] those who have community rights such as
   the right to use common land

Or something worse: an injured husband's vengeance
Shall print a thousand wounds, tear thy fine form,
And scatter thee to all the winds of heav'n.

LOTHARIO.

Is then my way in Genoa prescribed
By a dependant on the wretched Altamont,   145
A talking sir that brawls for him in taverns
And vouches for his valor's reputation—

HORATIO.

Away, thy speech is fouler than thy manners.

LOTHARIO.

Or if there be a name more vile, his parasite,
A beggar's parasite?   150

HORATIO.

                        Now learn humanity,
    (*Offers* to strike him, Rossano interposes.)
Since brutes and boys are only taught with blows.

LOTHARIO.

Damnation!

They draw.

ROSSANO.

                    Hold, this goes no further here—
Horatio—'tis too much—already, see,   155
The crowd are gath'ring to us.

LOTHARIO.

                            Oh Rossano!
Or give me way, or thou'rt no more my friend.

ROSSANO.

Sciolto's servants too have ta'en th'alarm:[c]
You'll be oppressed by numbers. Be advised,   160
Or I must force you hence. Take't on my word,
You shall have justice done you on Horatio.
Put up, my lord.

LOTHARIO.

                This wonnot brook delay:
West of the town a mile, among the rocks,   165
Two hours ere noon tomorrow I expect thee,
Thy single hand to mine.

HORATIO.

                        I'll meet thee there.

LOTHARIO.

Tomorrow, oh my better stars! tomorrow,
Exert your influence, shine strongly for me.   170
'Tis not a common conquest I would gain,
Since love, as well as arms, must grace my triumph.

Exeunt Lothario and Rossano.

HORATIO.

Two hours ere noon tomorrow! hah! ere that
He sees Calista! oh unthinking fool—
What if I urged her with the crime and danger?   175
If any spark from Heav'n remain unquenched
Within her breast, my breath perhaps may wake it.
Could I but prosper there, I would not doubt
My combat with that loud vainglorious boaster.
Were you, ye fair, but cautious whom ye trust,   180
Did you but think how seldom fools are just,
So many of your sex would not in vain
Of broken vows and faithless men complain.
Of all the various wretches love has made,
How few have been by men of sense betrayed!   185
Convinced by reason, they your pow'r confess,
Pleased to be happy, as you're pleased to bless,
And conscious of your worth, can never love you less.

Exit.

Act III, scene i. An apartment in Sciolto's palace.

Enter Sciolto and Calista.

SCIOLTO.

Now by my life, my honor, 'tis too much.
Have I not marked thee wayward as thou art,
Perverse, and sullen all this day of joy?
When ev'ry heart was cheered and mirth went round,
Sorrow, displeasure, and repining anguish   5
Sate on thy brow like some malignant planet,
Foe to the harvest and the healthy year,
Who scowls adverse and low'rs upon the world,
When all the other stars, with gentle aspect,
Propitious shine and meaning good to man.   10

CALISTA.

Is then the task of duty half performed?
Has not your daughter giv'n herself to Altamont,
Yielded the native freedom of her will
To an imperious husband's lordly rule,
To gratify a father's stern command?   15

SCIOLTO.

Dost thou complain?

CALISTA.

                    For pity do not frown then,
If in despite of all my vowed obedience,

A sigh breaks out or a tear falls by chance.
For oh! that sorrow which has drawn your anger 20
Is the sad native of Calista's breast
And, once possessed, will never quit its dwelling
Till life, the prop of^d all, shall leave the building
To tumble down and molder into ruin.

SCIOLTO.
Now by the sacred dust of that dear saint 25
That was thy mother, by her wondrous goodness,
Her soft, her tender, most complying sweetness,
I swear some sullen thought that shuns the light
Lurks underneath that sadness in thy visage.
But mark me well, though by yon heaven I love thee 30
As much, I think, as a fond parent can,
Yet shouldst thou (which the Pow'rs above forbid)
E'er stain the honor of thy name with infamy,
I cast thee off as one whose impious hands
Had rent asunder nature's nearest ties, 35
Which once divided never join again.
Today I have made a noble youth thy husband.
Consider well his worth, reward his love,
Be willing to be happy and thou art so. (*Exit.*)

CALISTA.
How hard is the condition of our sex! 40
Through ev'ry state of life the slaves of man.
In all the dear delightful days of youth
A rigid father dictates to our wills
And deals out pleasure with a scanty hand.
To his, the tyrant husband's reign succeeds: 45
Proud with opinion of superior reason,
He holds domestic bus'ness and devotion
All we are capable to know, and shuts us,
Like cloistered idiots, from the world's acquaintance
And all the joys of freedom. Wherefore are we 50
Born with high souls but to assert ourselves,
Shake off this vile obedience they exact,
And claim an equal empire o'er the world?

Enter Horatio.

HORATIO.
She's here! yet oh! my tongue is at a loss.
Teach me, some Pow'r, that happy art of speech 55
To dress my purpose up in gracious words
Such as may softly steal upon her soul
And never waken the tempestuous passions.
By Heaven she weeps!—Forgive me, fair Calista,

If I presume on privilege of friendship 60
To join my grief to yours and mourn the evils
That hurt your peace and quench those eyes in tears.

CALISTA.
To steal unlooked for on my private sorrow
Speaks not the man of honor nor the friend
But rather means the spy. 65

HORATIO.
                                    Unkindly said!
For oh! as sure as you accuse me falsely,
I come to prove myself Calista's friend.

CALISTA.
You are my husband's friend, the friend of Altamont.

HORATIO.
Are you not one? Are you not joined by Heav'n, 70
Each interwoven with the other's fate?
Are you not mixed like streams of meeting rivers,
Whose blended waters are no more distinguished
But roll into the sea one common flood?
Then, who can give his friendship but to one? 75
Who can be Altamont's, and not Calista's?

CALISTA.
Force, and the wills of our imperious rulers,
May bind two bodies in one wretched chain,
But minds will still look back to their own choice.
So the poor captive in a foreign realm 80
Stands on the shore and sends his wishes back
To the dear native land from whence he came.

HORATIO.
When souls that should agree to will the same,
To have one common object for their wishes,
Look different ways, regardless of each other, 85
Think what a train of wretchedness ensues:
Love shall be banished from the genial¹⁴ bed,
The nights shall all be lonely and unquiet,
And ev'ry day shall be a day of cares.

CALISTA.
Then all the boasted office of thy friendship 90
Was but to tell Calista what a wretch she is.
Alas! what needed that?

HORATIO.
                              Oh! rather say,
I came to tell her how she might be happy,
To soothe the secret anguish of her soul, 95

---

¹⁴ genial] of or relating to marriage and generation

To comfort that fair mourner, that forlorn one,
And teach her steps to know the paths of peace.
CALISTA.
Say thou to whom this paradise is known,
Where lies the blissful region? Mark my way to it,
For oh! 'tis sure I long to be at rest.   100
HORATIO.
Then—to be good is to be happy. Angels
Are happier than mankind, because they are better.
Guilt is the source of sorrow: 'tis the fiend,
The avenging fiend, that follows us behind
With whips and stings. The blest know none of this   105
But rest in everlasting peace of mind
And find the height of all their heav'n is goodness.
CALISTA.
And what bold parasite's officious tongue
Shall dare to tax Calista's name with guilt?
HORATIO.
None should. But 'tis a busy, talking world,   110
That with licentious breath blows, like the wind,
As freely on the palace as the cottage.
CALISTA.
What mystic riddle lurks beneath thy words
Which thou wouldst seem unwilling to express,
As if it meant dishonor to my virtue?   115
Away with this ambiguous, shuffling phrase
And let thy oracle be understood.
HORATIO.
Lothario!
CALISTA.
                Hah! what wouldst thou mean by him?
HORATIO.
Lothario and Calista—thus they join   120
Two names which Heav'n decreed should never
    meet.
Hence have the talkers of this populous city
A shameful tale to tell for public sport
Of an unhappy beauty, a false fair one,
Who plighted to a noble youth her faith,   125
When she had giv'n her honor to a wretch.
CALISTA.
Death! and confusion! Have I lived to this?
Thus to be treated with unmanly insolence!
To be the sport of a loose ruffian's tongue!
Thus to be used! thus! like the vilest creature   130
That ever was a slave to vice and infamy.

HORATIO.
By honor and fair truth, you wrong me much,
For on my soul nothing but strong necessity
Could urge my tongue to this ungrateful office.
I came with strong reluctance, as if death   135
Had stood across my way, to save your honor,
Yours and Sciolto's, yours and Altamont's,
Like one who ventures through a burning pile[15]
To save his tender wife, with all her brood
Of little fondlings, from the dreadful ruin.   140
CALISTA.
Is this! Is this the famous friend of Altamont,
For noble worth and deeds of arms renowned?
Is this! this tale-bearing, officious fellow,
That watches for intelligence from eyes,
This wretched Argus of a jealous husband,   145
That fills his easy ears with monstrous tales
And makes him toss and rave and wreak at length
Bloody revenge on his defenseless wife,
Who guiltless dies because her fool ran mad?
HORATIO.
Alas! this rage is vain, for if your fame   150
Or peace be worth your care, you must be calm
And listen to the means are left to save 'em.
'Tis now the lucky minute of your fate:
By me your^e genius* speaks, by me it warns you
Never to see that curst Lothario more—   155
Unless you mean to be despised, be shunned
By all your virtuous maids and noble matrons,
Unless you have devoted this rare beauty
To infamy, diseases, prostitution—
CALISTA.
Dishonor blast thee, base, unmannered slave!   160
That dar'st forget my birth and sacred sex
And shock me with that rude unhallowed sound.
HORATIO.
Here kneel, and in the awful* face of Heav'n
Breathe out a solemn vow never to see
Nor think, if possible, on him that ruined thee,   165
Or by my Altamont's dear life I swear,
This paper—nay you must not fly (*Holding
    her.*)—this paper,
This guilty paper shall divulge your shame.

_____

15 pile] a large building or group of buildings

CALISTA.

What mean'st thou by that paper? What contrivance
Hast thou been forging to deceive my father,   170
To turn his heart against his wretched daughter,
That Altamont and thou may share his wealth?
A wrong like this will make me ev'n forget
The weakness of my sex.—Oh for a sword,
To urge my vengeance on the villain's^f hand   175
That forged the scroll.

HORATIO.

                Behold, can this be forged?
See where Calista's name—
    (Showing the letter near.)

CALISTA.

                To atoms thus, (Tearing it.)
Thus let me tear the vile, detested falsehood,   180
The wicked, lying evidence of shame.

HORATIO.

Confusion!

CALISTA.

               Henceforth, thou officious fool,
Meddle no more nor dare ev'n on thy life
To breathe an accent that may touch my virtue: 185
I am myself the guardian of my honor
And wonnot bear so insolent a monitor.

Enter Altamont.

ALTAMONT.

Where is my life, my love, my charming bride,
Joy of my heart, and pleasure of my eyes,
The wish, the care, and bus'ness of my youth?   190
Oh! let me find her, snatch her to my breast,
And tell her she delays my bliss too long,
Till my soft soul ev'n sickens with desire.
Disordered! and in tears! Horatio too!
My friend is in amaze! What can it mean?   195
Tell me, Calista, who has done thee wrong,
That my swift sword may find out the offender
And do thee ample justice.

CALISTA.

                Turn to him!

ALTAMONT.

Horatio!   200

CALISTA.

          To that insolent.

ALTAMONT.

                My friend!
Could he do this? He, who was half myself!
One faith has ever bound us, and one reason
Guided our wills. Have I have not found him just,   205
Honest as truth itself? And could he break
The sanctity of friendship? Could he wound
The heart of Altamont in his Calista?

CALISTA.

I thought what justice I should find from thee!
Go fawn upon him, listen to his tale,   210
Applaud his malice, that would blast my fame
And treat me like a common prostitute.
Thou art perhaps confederate in his mischief
And wilt believe the legend, if he tells it.

ALTAMONT.

Oh impious! What presumptuous wretch shall dare   215
To offer* at an injury like that?
Priesthood, nor age, nor cowardice itself
Shall save him from the fury of my vengeance.

CALISTA.

The man who dared to do it was Horatio!
Thy darling friend! 'Twas Altamont's Horatio!   220
But mark me well: while thy divided heart
Dotes on a villain that has wronged me thus,
No force shall drag me to thy hated bed,
Nor can my cruel father's pow'r do more
Than shut me in a cloister. There, well pleased,   225
Religious hardships will I learn to bear:
To fast and freeze at midnight hours of pray'r,
Nor think it hard, within a lonely cell,
With melancholy, speechless saints to dwell,
But bless the day I to that refuge ran,   230
Free from the marriage chain—and from that
    tyrant, man. (Exit.)

ALTAMONT.

She's gone, and as she went, ten thousand fires
Shot from her angry eyes, as if she meant
Too well to keep the cruel vow she made.
Now as thou art a man, Horatio, tell me,   235
What means this wild confusion in thy looks,
As if thou wert at variance with thyself,
Madness and reason combating within thee,
And thou wert doubtful which should get the better?

HORATIO.

I would be dumb forever, but thy fate   240

Has otherwise decreed it: thou hast seen
That idol of thy soul, that fair Calista;
Thou hast beheld her tears.

ALTAMONT.

                    I have seen her weep;
I have seen that lovely one, that dear Calista,   245
Complaining in the bitterness of sorrow
That thou! my friend! Horatio! thou hadst
      wronged her.

HORATIO.

That I have wronged her! Had her eyes been fed
From that rich stream which warms her heart and   250
      numbered
For ev'ry falling tear a drop of blood,
It had not been too much, for she has ruined thee,
Ev'n thee, my Altamont! She has undone thee.

ALTAMONT.

Dost thou join ruin with Calista's name?
What is so fair, so exquisitely good?   255
Is she not more than painting can express
Or youthful poets' fancy when they love?
Does she not come, like wisdom or good fortune,
Replete with blessings, giving wealth and honor?
The dowry which she brings is peace and pleasure,   260
And everlasting joys are in her arms.

HORATIO.

It had been better thou hadst lived a beggar
And fed on scraps at great men's surly doors
Than to have matched with one so false, so fatal—

ALTAMONT.

It is too much for friendship to allow thee.   265
Because I tamely bore the wrong thou didst her,
Thou dost avow the barb'rous, brutal part
And urge the injury ev'n to my face.

HORATIO.

I see she has got possession of thy heart.
She has charmed thee, like a Siren, to her bed   270
With looks of love and with enchanting sounds.
Too late the rocks and quicksands will appear:
When thou art wrecked upon the faithless shore,
Then vainly wish thou hadst not left thy friend
To follow her delusion.   275

ALTAMONT.

                    If thy friendship
Do churlishly deny my love a room,
It is not worth my keeping: I disclaim it.

HORATIO.

Canst thou so soon forget what I've been to thee?
I shared the task of nature with thy father   280
And formed with care thy unexperienced youth
To virtue and to arms.
Thy noble father, oh thou light young man!
Would he have used me thus? One fortune fed us,
For his was ever mine, mine his, and both   285
Together flourished and together fell.
He called me friend, like thee. Would he have left me
Thus? for a woman? nay, a vile one too?

ALTAMONT.

Thou canst not, dar'st not mean it. Speak again,
Say, who is vile? but dare not name Calista.   290

HORATIO.

I had not spoke at first, unless compelled
And forced to clear myself, but since thus urged,
I must avow I do not know a viler.

ALTAMONT.

Thou wert my father's friend, he loved thee well;
A kind of venerable mark of him   295
Hangs round thee and protects thee from my
      vengeance:
I cannot, dare not lift my sword against thee,
But henceforth never let me see thee more.
      (*Going out.*)

HORATIO.

I love thee still, ungrateful as thou art,
And must, and will preserve thee from dishonor,   300
Ev'n in despite of thee. (*Holds him.*)

ALTAMONT.

                    Let go my arm.

HORATIO.

If honor be thy care, if thou wouldst live
Without the name of credulous, wittol husband,
Avoid thy bride, shun her detested bed: 305
The joys it yields are dashed with poison—

ALTAMONT.

                              Off!
To urge me but a minute more is fatal.

HORATIO.

She is polluted! stained!

ALTAMONT.

                    Madness and raving!   310
But hence!

HORATIO.

            Dishonored by the man you hate—

ALTAMONT.

    I prithee loose me yet, for thy own sake,

    If life be worth the keeping—

HORATIO.

                    By Lothario.   315

ALTAMONT.

    Perdition take thee, villain,* for the falsehood.

    (*Strikes him.*)

    Now nothing but thy life can make atonement.

HORATIO.

    A blow! Thou hast used meᵷ well— (*Draws.*)

ALTAMONT.

                 This to thy heart—

HORATIO.

    Yet hold!—By Heav'n, his father's in his face.   320

    Spite of my wrongs my heart runs o'er with

        tenderness,

    And I could rather die myself than hurt him.

ALTAMONT.

    Defend thyself, for by my much wronged love,

    I swear the poor evasion shall not save thee.

HORATIO.

    Yet hold! thou know'st I dare—think how we've   325

        lived—

They fight; Altamont presses on Horatio, who retires.

    Nay! then 'tis brutal* violence! And thus,

    Thus Nature bids me guard the life she gave.

They fight. Lavinia enters and runs between their swords.

LAVINIA.

    My brother! My Horatio! is it possible?

    Oh! turn your cruel swords upon Lavinia.

    If you must quench your impious rage in blood,   330

    Behold, my heart shall give you all her store

    To save those dearer streams that flow from yours.

ALTAMONT.

    'Tis well thou hast found a safeguard; none but this,

    No pow'r on earth could save thee from my fury.

LAVINIA.

    Oh fatal, deadly sound!   335

HORATIO.

               Safety from thee!

    Away, vain boy! Hast thou forgot the reverence

    Due to my arm, thy first, thy great example,

Which pointed out thy way to noble daring

And showed thee what it was to be a man?   340

LAVINIA.

    What busy, meddling fiend, what foe to goodness,

    Could kindle such a discord? Oh! lay by

    Those most ungentle looks and angry weapons,

    Unless you mean my griefs and killing fears

    Should stretch me out at your relentless feet   345

    A wretched corse, the victim of your fury.

HORATIO.

    Ask'st thou what made us foes? 'Twas base

        ingratitude,

    'Twas such a sin to friendship as Heaven's mercy,

    That strives with man's untoward, monstrous

        wickedness,

    Unwearied with forgiving, scarce could pardon.   350

    He, who was all to me—child! brother! friend!—

    With barb'rous, bloody malice sought my life.

ALTAMONT.

    Thou art my sister, and I would not make thee

    The lonely mourner of a widowed bed;

    Therefore, thy husband's life is safe, but warn him   355

    No more to know this hospitable roof:

    He has but ill repaid Sciolto's bounty.

    We must not meet, 'tis dangerous—farewell.

He is going; Lavinia holds him.

LAVINIA.

    Stay Altamont, my brother stay, if ever

    Nature, or what is nearer much than nature,   360

    The kind consent of our agreeing minds,

    Have made us dear to one another, stay,

    And speak one gentle word to your Horatio.

    Behold, his anger melts, he longs to love you,

    To call you friend, then press you hard with all   365

    The tender, speechless joy of reconcilement.

ALTAMONT.

    It cannot, shannot be! You must not hold me.

LAVINIA.

    Look kindly then!

ALTAMONT.

             Each minute that I stay

    Is a new injury to fair Calista.—   370

    From thy false friendship to her arms I'll fly.

    There, if in any pause of love I rest,

    Breathless with bliss, upon her panting breast,

In broken, melting accents I will swear
Henceforth to trust my heart with none but her,   375
Then own the joys which on her charms attend
Have more than paid me for my faithless friend.
   (*Breaks from Lavinia and exits.*)

HORATIO.

Oh raise thee, my Lavinia, from the earth.
It is too much, this tide of flowing grief,
This wondrous waste of tears, too much to give   380
To an ungrateful friend and cruel brother.

LAVINIA.

Is there not cause for weeping? Oh Horatio!
A brother and a husband were my treasure:
'Twas all the little wealth that poor Lavinia
Saved from the shipwreck of her father's fortunes.   385
One half is lost already; if thou leav'st me,
If thou shouldst prove unkind to me, as Altamont,
Whom shall I find to pity my distress,
To have compassion on a helpless wanderer
And give her where to lay her wretched head?   390

HORATIO.

Why dost thou wound me with thy soft
   complainings?
Though Altamont be false and use me hardly,
Yet think not I impute his crimes to thee.
Talk not of being forsaken, for I'll keep thee
Next to my heart, my certain pledge of happiness.   395
Heav'n formed thee gentle, fair, and full of goodness
And made thee all my portion here on earth;
It gave thee to me as a large amends
For fortune, friends, and all the world beside.

LAVINIA.

Then you will love me still,* cherish me ever,   400
And hide me from misfortune in your bosom?
Here end my cares, nor will I lose one thought
How we shall live or purchase food and raiment.
The holy Pow'r, who clothes the senseless earth
With woods, with fruits, with flow'rs and verdant   405
   grass,
Whose bounteous hand feeds the whole brute
   creation,
Knows all our wants and has enough to give us.

HORATIO.

From Genoa, from falsehood and inconstancy,
To some more honest distant clime we'll go,
Nor will I be beholding to my country   410
For ought but thee, the partner of my flight.

LAVINIA.

Yes, I will follow thee, forsake for thee
My country, brother, friends, ev'n all I have;
Though mine's a little all, yet were it more,
And better far, it should be left for thee,   415
And all that I would keep should be Horatio.
So when the merchant sees his vessel lost,
Though richly freighted from a foreign coast,
Gladly for life the treasure he would give
And only wishes to escape, and live.   420
Gold and his gains no more employ his mind
But, driving o'er the billows with the wind,
Cleaves to one faithful plank, and leaves the rest
   behind.

Exeunt.

      Act IV, scene i. A garden.

Enter Altamont.

ALTAMONT.

With what unequal tempers are we formed!
One day the soul, supine with ease and fullness,
Revels secure and fondly* tells herself
The hour of evil can return no more;
The next, the spirits, palled and sick of riot,   5
Turn all to discord, and we hate our beings,
Curse the past joy, and think it folly all
And bitterness and anguish. Oh! last night!
What has ungrateful beauty paid me back
For all that mass of friendship which I squandered?   10
Coldness, aversion, tears, and sullen sorrow
Dashed all my bliss and damped my bridal bed.
Soon as the morning dawned, she vanished from me,
Relentless to the gentle call of love.
I have lost a friend, and I have gained—a wife!   15
Turn not to thought, my brain, but let me find
Some unfrequented shade; there lay me down
And let forgetful dullness steal upon me
To soften and assuage this pain of thinking.
   (*Exit.*)

Enter Lothario and Calista.

LOTHARIO.

Weep not, my fair, but let the God of Love   20
Laugh in thy eyes and revel in thy heart,
Kindle again his torch and hold it high

To light us to new joys, nor let a thought
Of discord or disquiet past molest thee,
But to a long oblivion give thy cares 25
And let us melt the present hour in bliss.

CALISTA.
Seek not to soothe me with thy false endearments,
To charm me with thy softness, 'tis in vain:
Thou canst no more betray, nor I be ruined.
The hours of folly and of fond* delight 30
Are wasted all and fled; those that remain
Are doomed to weeping, anguish, and repentance.
I come to charge thee with a long account
Of all the sorrows I have known already
And all I have to come: thou hast undone me. 35

LOTHARIO.
Unjust Calista! Dost thou call it ruin
To love as we have done: to melt, to languish,
To wish for somewhat exquisitely happy,
And then be blest ev'n to that wish's height?
To die with joy, and straight to live again, 40
Speechless to gaze, and with tumultuous transport—

CALISTA.
Oh! let me hear no more, I cannot bear it:
'Tis deadly to remembrance. Let that night,
That guilty night, be blotted from the year;
Let not the voice of mirth or music know it; 45
Let it be dark and desolate, no stars
To glitter o'er it; let it wish for light
Yet want* it still* and vainly wait the dawn,
For 'twas the night that gave me up to shame,
To sorrow, to perfidious, false Lothario. 50

LOTHARIO.
Hear this, ye Pow'rs, mark how the fair deceiver
Sadly complains of violated truth.
She calls me false, ev'n she, the faithless she,
Whom day and night, whom heav'n and earth
    have heard
Sighing to vow and tenderly protest 55
Ten thousand times she would be only mine.
And yet, behold, she has giv'n herself away,
Fled from my arms, and wedded to another,
Ev'n to the man whom most I hate on earth.

CALISTA.
Art thou so base to upbraid me with a crime 60
Which nothing but thy cruelty could cause?
If indignation, raging in my soul,

For thy unmanly insolence and scorn
Urged me to do a deed of desperation
And wound myself to be revenged on thee, 65
Think whom I should devote to death and hell,
Whom curse as my undoer but Lothario.
Hadst thou been just, not all Sciolto's pow'r,
Not all the vows and pray'rs of sighing Altamont,
Could have prevailed or won me to forsake thee. 70

LOTHARIO.
How have I failed in justice or in love?
Burns not my flame as brightly as at first?
Ev'n now my heart beats high, I languish for thee,
My transports are as fierce, as strong my wishes,
As if thou hadst never blest me with thy beauty. 75

CALISTA.
How didst thou dare to think that I would live
A slave to base desires and brutal* pleasures,
To be a wretched wanton for thy leisure
To toy and waste an hour of idle time with?
My soul disdains thee for so mean a thought. 80

LOTHARIO.
The driving storm of passion will have way,
And I must yield before it. Wert thou calm,
Love, the poor criminal whom thou hast doomed,
Has yet a thousand tender things to plead
To charm thy rage and mitigate his fate. 85

Enter behind them Altamont.

ALTAMONT.
I have lost my peace.—Hah! do I live and wake!

CALISTA.
Hadst thou been true, how happy had I been?
Nor Altamont but thou hadst been my lord.
But wherefore named I happiness with thee?
It is for thee, for thee, that I am curst; 90
For thee, my secret soul each hour arraigns me,
Calls me to answer for my virtue stained,
My honor lost to thee; for thee, it haunts me,
With stern Sciolto vowing vengeance on me,
With Altamont complaining for his wrongs— 95

ALTAMONT.
Behold him here— (*Coming forward.*)

CALISTA. (*Starting.*)
Ah!—

ALTAMONT.
    The wretch whom thou hast made!

Curses and sorrows hast thou heaped upon him,
And vengeance is the only good is left. (*Drawing.*) 100
LOTHARIO.
 Thou hast ta'en me somewhat unawares, 'tis true,
 But love and war take turns like day and night,
 And little preparation serves my turn,
 Equal to both and armed for either field.
 We've long been foes, this moment ends our quarrel.* 105
 Earth, Heav'n, and fair Calista judge the combat.
CALISTA.
 Distraction! Fury! Sorrow! Shame! and Death!
ALTAMONT.
 Thou hast talked too much, thy breath is poison
  to me:
 It taints the ambient air. This for my father,
 This for Sciolto, and this last for Altamont. 110

*They fight; Lothario is wounded once or twice and
then falls.*

LOTHARIO.
 Oh Altamont! thy genius* is the stronger,
 Thou hast prevailed! My fierce, ambitious soul
 Declining droops, and all her fires grow pale,
 Yet let not this advantage swell thy pride:
 I conquered in my turn, in love I triumphed. 115
 Those joys are lodged beyond the reach of fate;
 That sweet revenge comes smiling to my thoughts,
 Adorns my fall, and cheers my heart in dying. (*Dies.*)
CALISTA.
 And what remains for me? Beset with shame,
 Encompassed round with wretchedness, there is 120
 But this one way to break the toil and 'scape.

She catches up Lothario's sword and offers to kill
herself; Altamont runs to her and wrests it from her.*

ALTAMONT.
 What means thy frantic rage?
CALISTA.
                    Off! let me go.
ALTAMONT.
 Oh! thou hast more than murdered me, yet still,
 Still art thou here! and my soul starts with horror 125
 At thought of any danger that may reach thee.
CALISTA.
 Think'st thou I mean to live? to be forgiven?
 Oh! thou hast known but little of Calista.

If thou hadst never heard my shame, if only
The midnight moon and silent stars had seen it, 130
I would not bear to be reproached by them,
But dig down deep to find a grave beneath
And hide me from their beams.
SCIOLTO. (*Within.*)
                    What ho! my son!
ALTAMONT.
 It is Sciolto calls.—Come near and find me, 135
 The wretched'st thing of all my kind on earth.
CALISTA.
 Is it the voice of thunder or my father?
 Madness! Confusion! let the storm come on,
 Let the tumultuous roar drive all upon me.
 Dash my devoted bark, ye surges, break it; 140
 'Tis for my ruin that the tempest rises.
 When I am lost, sunk to the bottom low,
 Peace shall return and all be calm again.

Enter Sciolto.

SCIOLTO.
 Ev'n now Rossano leaped the garden walls—
 Hah! Death has been among you—oh my fears! 145
 Last night thou hadst a diff'rence with thy friend;
 The cause thou gav'st me for it was a damned one.
 Didst thou not wrong the man who told thee truth?
 Answer me quick—
ALTAMONT.
                    Oh! press me not to speak, 150
 Ev'n now my heart is breaking, and the mention
 Will lay me dead before you. See that body
 And guess my shame! my ruin! oh Calista!
SCIOLTO.
 It is enough! but I am slow to execute,
 And justice lingers in my lazy hand. 155
 Thus let me wipe dishonor from my name
 And cut thee from the earth, thou stain to
  goodness—

Offers to kill Calista, Altamont holds him.*

ALTAMONT.
 Stay thee, Sciolto, thou rash father, stay,
 Or turn the point on me and through my breast 160
 Cut out the bloody passage to Calista.
 So shall my love be perfect while for her
 I die, for whom alone I wished to live.

CALISTA.

No, Altamont! my heart, that scorned thy love,
Shall never be indebted to thy pity. 165
Thus torn, defaced, and wretched as I seem,
Still I have something of Sciolto's virtue.
Yes! yes my father, I applaud thy justice.
Strike home, and I will bless thee for the blow.
Be merciful and free me from my pain. 170
'Tis sharp, 'tis terrible, and I could curse
The cheerful day, men, earth, and heav'n and thee,
Ev'n thee, thou venerable, good old man,
For being author of a wretch like me.

ALTAMONT.

Listen not to the wildness of her raving, 175
Remember nature! Should thy daughter's murder
Defile that hand—so just, so great in arms—
Her blood would rest upon thee to posterity,
Pollute thy name, and sully all thy wars.

CALISTA.

Have I not wronged his gentle[16] nature much? 180
And yet behold him pleading for my life.
Lost as thou art to virtue, oh Calista!
I think thou canst not bear to be outdone.
Then haste to die, and be obliged no more.

SCIOLTO.

Thy pious care has giv'n me time to think 185
And saved me from a crime. Then rest my sword:
To honor have I kept thee ever sacred,
Nor will I stain thee with a rash revenge.
But mark me well, I will have justice done.
Hope not to bear away thy crimes unpunished. 190
I will see justice executed on thee,
Ev'n to a Roman strictness. And thou, Nature,
Or whatsoe'er thou art that plead'st within me,
Be still, thy tender strugglings are in vain.

CALISTA.

Then am I doomed to live and bear your triumph? 195
To groan beneath your scorn and fierce upbraidings,
Daily to be reproached, and have my misery
At morn, at noon and night told over to me,
Lest my remembrance might grow pitiful
And grant a moment's interval of peace: 200

---

16 gentle] the adjective contains both the older sense of
descended from a noble family and the new bourgeois
sense of *tender, non-aggressive*

Is this, is this the mercy of a father?
I only beg to die, and he denies me.

SCIOLTO.

Hence from my sight, thy father cannot bear thee.
Fly with thy infamy to some dark cell,
Where on the confines of eternal night 205
Mourning, misfortune, cares, and anguish dwell;
Where ugly shame hides her opprobrious head,
And death and hell detested rule maintain,
There howl out the remainder of thy life
And wish thy name may be no more remembered. 210

CALISTA.

Yes, I will fly to some such dismal place
And be more curst than you can wish I were.
This fatal form that drew on my undoing
Fasting and tears and hardship shall destroy,
Nor light, nor food, nor comfort will I know, 215
Nor aught that may continue hated life.
Then when you see me meager, wan, and changed,
Stretched at my length and dying in my cave
On that cold earth I mean shall be my grave,
Perhaps you may relent and sighing say, 220
At length her tears have washed her stains away,
At length 'tis time her punishment should cease:
Die, thou poor suff'ring wretch, and be at peace.
(*Exit.*)

SCIOLTO.

Who of my servants wait there?

Enter two or three servants.

On your lives 225
Take care my doors be guarded well, that none
Pass out or enter but by my appointment.

Exeunt servants.

ALTAMONT.

There is a fatal fury in your visage;
It blazes fierce and menaces destruction.
My father, I am sick of many sorrows, 230
Ev'n now my easy heart is breaking with 'em,
Yet above all, one fear distracts me most:
I tremble at the vengeance which you meditate
On the poor, faithless, lovely, dear Calista.

SCIOLTO.

Hast thou not read what brave Virginius did? 235
With his own hand he slew his only daughter

To save her from the fierce Decemvir's lust.[17]
He slew her yet unspotted to prevent
The shame which she might know. Then what
    should I do?
But thou hast tied my hand—I wonnot kill her.   240
Yet by the ruin she has brought upon us,
The common infamy that brands us both,
She shannot 'scape.

ALTAMONT.
              You mean that she shall die then?

SCIOLTO.
Ask me not what, nor how I have resolved,   245
For all within is anarchy and uproar.
Oh Altamont! what a vast scheme of joy
Has this one day destroyed! Well did I hope
This daughter would have blest my latter days,
That I should live to see you the world's wonder,   250
So happy, great, and good, that none were like you.
While I, from busy life and care set free,
Had spent the ev'ning of my age at home
Among a little prattling race* of yours:
There, like an old man, talked awhile and then   255
Lain down and slept in peace. Instead of this,
Sorrow and shame must bring me to my grave.
Oh damn her! damn her!

Enter a Servant.

SERVANT.
              Arm yourself, my lord.
Rossano, who but now escaped the garden,   260
Has gathered in the street a band of rioters
Who threaten you and all your friends with ruin,
Unless Lothario be returned in safety.

SCIOLTO.
By Heav'n, their fury rises to my wish,
Nor shall misfortune know my house alone,   265
But thou, Lothario, and thy race,* shall pay me
For all the sorrows which my age is curst with.
I think my name as great, my friends as potent,
As any in the state; all shall be summoned.
I know that all will join their hands to ours   270

---

17 Virginius … lust] Virginius stabbed his daughter Vir-
    ginia rather than allow Appius to rape her. Appius was
    one of the Decemvirs, ten men acting as the ruling au-
    thority in Rome, c. 450 BCE.

And vindicate thy vengeance. Raise the body
And bear it in; his friends shall buy him dearly:
I will have blood for ransom. When our force
Is full and armed, we shall expect thy sword
To join with us and sacrifice to justice. (*Exit.*)   275

*The body of Lothario is carried off by servants. Manet
Altamont.*

ALTAMONT.
There is a stupid* weight upon my senses,
A dismal sullen stillness that succeeds
The storm of rage and grief like silent death
After the tumult and the noise of life.
Would it were death, as sure 'tis wondrous like it,   280
For I am sick of living, my soul's palled,
She kindles not with anger or revenge.
Love was th'informing, active fire within;
Now that is quenched, the mass forgets to move
And longs to mingle with its kindred earth.   285

*A tumultuous noise, with clashing of swords, as at a
little distance. Enter Lavinia with two servants, their
swords drawn.*

LAVINIA.
Fly, swiftly fly to my Horatio's aid,
Nor lose your vain, officious cares on me.
Bring me my lord, my husband, to my arms:
He is Lavinia's life. Bring him me safe,
And I shall be at ease, be well and happy.   290

Exeunt servants.

ALTAMONT.
Art thou Lavinia? Oh! what barb'rous hand
Could wrong thy poor, defenseless innocence
And leave such marks of more than savage fury?

LAVINIA.
My brother! Oh, my heart is full of fears,
Perhaps ev'n now my dear Horatio bleeds.   295
Not far from hence, as passing to the port,
By a mad multitude we were surrounded,
Who ran upon us with uplifted swords
And cried aloud for vengeance and Lothario.
My lord with ready boldness stood the shock   300
To shelter me from danger, but in vain,
Had not a party from Sciolto's palace
Rushed out and snatched me from amidst the fray.

ALTAMONT.

    What of my friend?

LAVINIA. (*Looking out.*)

                        Hah! by my joys 'tis he,   305

He lives, he comes to bless me, he is safe!

*Enter Horatio with two or three servants, their swords
drawn.*

SERVANT.

    'Twere at the utmost hazard of your life

To venture forth again till we are stronger;

Their number trebles ours.

HORATIO.

                    No matter, let it.   310

Death is not half so shocking as that traitor.

My honest soul is mad with indignation

To think her plainness could be so abused

As to mistake that wretch and call him friend.

I cannot bear the sight.   315

ALTAMONT.

                 Open, thou earth,

Gape wide and take me down to thy dark bosom,

To hide me from Horatio.

HORATIO.

               Oh Lavinia,

Believe not but I joy to see thee safe.   320

Would our ill fortune had not drove us hither.

I could ev'n wish we rather had been wrecked

On any other shore than saved on this.

LAVINIA.

    Oh let us bless the mercy that preserved us,

That gracious Pow'r that saved us for each other,   325

And to adorn the sacrifice of praise

Offer forgiveness too. Be thou like Heav'n

And put away th'offences of thy friend

Far, far from thy remembrance.

ALTAMONT.

               I have marked him   330

To see if one forgiving glance stole hither,

If any spark of friendship were alive,

That would by sympathy at meeting glow

And strive to kindle up the flame anew.

'Tis lost, 'tis gone, his soul is quite estranged   335

And knows me for its counterpart no more.

HORATIO. [*To Lavinia.*]

    Thou know'st thy rule, thy empire in Horatio,

Nor canst thou ask in vain, command in vain,

Where nature, reason, nay where love is judge.

But when you urge my temper to comply   340

With what it most abhors, I cannot do it.

LAVINIA.

    Where didst thou get this sullen, gloomy hate?

It was not in thy nature to be thus.

Come, put it off and let thy heart be cheerful,

Be gay again, and know the joys of friendship,   345

The trust, security, and mutual tenderness,

The double joys, where each is glad for both:

Friendship, the wealth, the last retreat and strength

Secure against ill fortune and the world.

HORATIO.

    I am not apt to take a light offence   350

But patient of the failings of my friends

And willing to forgive. But when an injury

Stabs to the heart and rouses my resentment

(Perhaps it is the fault of my rude nature),

I own I cannot easily forget[h] it.   355

ALTAMONT.

    Thou hast forgot me.

HORATIO.

               No.

ALTAMONT.

                  Why are thy eyes

Impatient of me then, scornful, and fierce?

HORATIO.

    Because they speak the meaning of my heart,   360

Because they are honest and disdain a villain.*

ALTAMONT.

    I have wronged thee much, Horatio.

HORATIO.

                  True, thou hast.

When I forget it, may I be a wretch,

Vile as thyself, a false perfidious fellow,   365

An infamous, believing, British husband.[18]

ALTAMONT.

    I've wronged thee much, and Heav'n has well
        avenged it.

I have not, since we parted, been at peace

Or known one joy sincere. Our broken friendship

---

18 British husband] overly fond or lenient; British women
    were believed to have more liberties than women in
    other European countries such as Italy

Pursued me to the last retreat of love,   370
Stood glaring like a ghost, and made me cold with
   horror.
Misfortunes on misfortunes press upon me,
Swell o'er my head, like waves, and dash me down.
Sorrow, remorse, and shame have torn my soul;
They hang like winter on my youthful hopes   375
And blast the spring and promise of my year.

LAVINIA.
So flow'rs are gathered to adorn a grave,
To lose their freshness amongst bones and rottenness
And have their odors stifled in the dust.
Canst thou hear this, thou cruel, hard Horatio?   380
Canst thou behold thy Altamont undone?
That gentle, that dear youth! canst thou behold him,
His poor heart broken, death in his pale visage,
And groaning out his woes, yet stand unmoved?

HORATIO.
The brave and wise I pity in misfortune,   385
But when ingratitude and folly suffers,
'Tis weakness to be touched.

ALTAMONT.
                 I wonnot ask thee
To pity or forgive me, but confess
This scorn, this insolence of hate is just;   390
'Tis constancy of mind and manly in thee.
But oh! had I been wronged by thee, Horatio,
There is a yielding softness in my heart
Could ne'er have stood it out, but I had ran,
With streaming eyes and open arms, upon thee,   395
And pressed thee close, close!

HORATIO.
                 I must hear no more,
The weakness is contagious, I shall catch it,
And be a tame, fond* wretch.

LAVINIA.
                 Where wouldst thou go?   400
Wouldst thou part thus? You shannot, 'tis impossible,
For I will bar thy passage, kneeling thus.
Perhaps thy cruel hand may spurn me off,
But I will throw my body in thy way,
And thou shalt trample o'er my faithful bosom,   405
Tread on me, wound me, kill me ere thou pass.

ALTAMONT.
Urge not in vain thy pious suit, Lavinia,
I have enough to rid me of my pain.

Calista, thou hadst reached my heart before;
To make all sure, my friend repeats the blow.   410
But in the grave our cares shall be forgotten,
There love and friendship cease. (*Falls.*)

Lavinia runs to him and endeavors to raise him.

LAVINIA.
                 Speak to me, Altamont.
He faints! he dies!—Now turn and see thy triumph.
—My brother! But our cares shall end together;   415
Here will I lay me down by thy dear side,
Bemoan thy too hard fate, then share it with thee
And never see my cruel lord again.

Horatio runs to Altamont and raises him in his arms.

HORATIO.
It is too much to bear! Look up, my Altamont!
My stubborn, unrelenting heart has killed him.   420
Look up and bless me, tell me that thou liv'st.
Oh! I have urged thy gentleness too far.

Altamont revives.

Do thou and my Lavinia both forgive me;
A flood of tenderness comes o'er my soul.
I cannot speak—I love! forgive! and pity thee.   425

ALTAMONT.
I thought that nothing could have stayed my soul,
That long ere this her flight had reached the stars,
But thy known voice has lured her back again.
Methinks I fain would set all right with thee,
Make up this most unlucky breach, and then,   430
With thine and Heav'n's forgiveness on my soul,
Shrink to my grave and be at ease forever.

HORATIO.
By Heav'n my heart bleeds for thee. Ev'n this
   moment
I feel thy pangs of disappointed love.
Is it not pity that this youth should fail,   435
That all this wondrous goodness should be lost,
And the world never know it? oh my Altamont!
Give me thy sorrows, let me bear 'em for thee
And shelter thee from ruin.

LAVINIA.
                 Oh my brother!   440
Think not but we will share in all thy woes,
We'll sit all day and tell sad tales of love,

And when we light upon some faithless woman,
Some beauty, like Calista, false and fair,
We'll fix our grief and our complaining there;   445
We'll curse the nymph that drew the ruin on
And mourn the youth that was like thee undone.

Exeunt.

    Act V, scene i. *A room hung with black:*
      on one side, Lothario's body on a bier;
        on the other, a table with a skull and
          other bones, a book, and a lamp on it.

Calista is discovered on a couch in black, her hair
hanging loose and disordered. After music and a song,
she rises and comes forward.*

           Song.
            I
Hear, you midnight phantoms, hear:
You, who pale and wan appear
And fill the wretch, who wakes, with fear;
You, who wander, scream, and groan
Round the mansions once your own;   5
You, whom still your crimes upbraid;
You, who rest not with the dead;
From the coverts where you stray,
Where you lurk and shun the day,
From the charnel and the tomb,   10
Hither haste ye, hither come.
           II
Chide Calista for delay;
Tell her, 'tis for her you stay;
Bid her die, and come away.
See the sexton with his spade,   15
See the grave already made.
Listen, fair one, to thy knell:
This music is thy passing bell.

CALISTA.
  'Tis well! these solemn sounds, this pomp of horror,
Are fit to feed the frenzy in my soul.   20
Here's room for meditation, ev'n to madness,
Till the mind burst with thinking. This dull flame
Sleeps in the socket. Sure the book was left
To tell me something—for instruction then—
He teaches holy sorrow and contrition   25
And penitence—Is it become an art then?

A trick that lazy, dull, luxurious gownsmen
Can teach us to do over? I'll no more on't!
  (*Throwing away the book.*)
I have more real anguish in my heart
Than all their pedant discipline e'er knew.   30
What charnel has been rifled for these bones?
Fie! this is pageantry—they look uncouthly,
But what of that, if he or she that owned 'em,
Safe from disquiet, sit and smile to see
The farce their miserable relics play?   35
But here's a sight is terrible indeed:
Is this that haughty, gallant, gay Lothario,
That dear perfidious—Ah!—how pale he looks!
How grim with clotted blood, and those dead eyes!
Ascend ye ghosts, fantastic forms of night,   40
In all your diff'rent, dreadful shapes ascend
And match the present horror if you can.

Enter Sciolto.

SCIOLTO.
This dead of night, this silent hour of darkness,
Nature for rest ordained and soft repose,
And yet distraction and tumultuous jars   45
Keep all our frighted citizens awake.
The Senate, weak, divided, and irresolute,
Want* pow'r to succor the afflicted state;
Vainly in words and long debates they're wise,
While the fierce factions scorn their peaceful orders   50
And drown the voice of law in noise and anarchy.
Amidst the general wreck, see where she stands,
  (*Pointing to Calista.*)
Like Helen in the night when Troy was sacked,
Spectatress of the mischief which she made.[19]
CALISTA.
It is Sciolto! be thyself, my soul,   55
Be strong to bear his fatal indignation,
That he may see thou art not lost so far
But somewhat still of his great spirit lives
In the forlorn Calista.
SCIOLTO.
          Thou wert once   60
My daughter.

---

19 Helen ... made] See Virgil, *Aeneid* II.567-574, for the
famous description of Helen of Troy on the night Troy
was sacked.

CALISTA.

          Happy were it I had died
And never lost that name.
SCIOLTO.

               That's something yet.
Thou wert the very darling of my age: 65
I thought the day too short to gaze upon thee,
That all the blessings I could gather for thee,
By cares on earth and by my pray'rs to Heav'n,
Were little for my fondness to bestow.
Why didst thou turn to folly, then, and curse me? 70
CALISTA.
Because my soul was rudely drawn from yours,
A poor imperfect copy of my father,
Where goodness and the strength of manly virtue
Was thinly planted, and the idle void
Filled up with light belief and easy fondness.   75
It was because I loved, and was a woman.
SCIOLTO.
Hadst thou been honest,* thou hadst been a
   cherubim,
But of that joy, as of a gem long lost,
Beyond redemption gone, think we no more.
Hast thou e'er dared to meditate on death?   80
CALISTA.
I have, as on the end of shame and sorrow.
SCIOLTO.
Hah! answer me! say, hast thou coolly thought?
'Tis not the Stoic's lessons got by rote,
The pomp of words, and pedant dissertations
That can sustain thee in that hour of terror: 85
Books have taught cowards to talk nobly of it,
But when the trial comes, they start and stand aghast.
Hast thou considered what may happen after it?
How thy account may stand, and what to answer?
CALISTA.
I have turned my eyes inward upon myself,   90
Where foul offence and shame have laid all waste;
Therefore, my soul abhors the wretched dwelling
And longs to find some better place of rest.
SCIOLTO.
'Tis justly thought and worthy of that spirit
That dwelt in ancient Latian[20] breasts when Rome 95

Was mistress of the world. I would go on
And tell thee all my purpose, but it sticks
Here at my heart and cannot find a way.
CALISTA.
Then spare the telling, if it be a pain,
And write the meaning with your poniard here.   100
SCIOLTO.
Oh! truly guessed—seest thou this trembling
   hand—(*Holding up a dagger.*)
Thrice justice urged—and thrice the slack'ning
   sinews
Forgot their office and confessed the father.
At length the stubborn virtue has prevailed:
It must, it must be so—Oh! take it then, (*Giving* 105
   the dagger.)
And know the rest untaught.
CALISTA.

               I understand you:
It is but thus, and both are satisfied.

She offers to kill herself, Sciolto catches hold of her arm.

SCIOLTO.
A moment, give me yet a moment's space.
The stern, the rigid judge has been obeyed;   110
Now nature and the father claim their turns.
I have held the balance with an iron hand
And put off ev'ry tender, human thought
To doom my child to death. But spare my eyes
The most unnatural sight, lest their strings crack 115
And my old brain split and grow mad with horror.
CALISTA.
Hah! Is it possible? And is there yet
Some little, dear remain of love and tenderness
For poor, undone Calista in your heart?
SCIOLTO.
Oh! when I think what pleasure I took in thee, 120
What joys thou gav'st me in thy prattling infancy,
Thy sprightly wit and early blooming beauty,
How I have stood and fed my eyes upon thee,
Then lifted up my hands and, wond'ring, blest thee.
By my strong grief, my heart ev'n melts within me; 125
I could curse Nature and that tyrant, Honor,
For making me thy father and thy judge.
Thou art my daughter still.
CALISTA.

               For that kind word,

Thus let me fall, thus humbly to the earth, 130
Weep on your feet and bless you for this goodness.
Oh! 'tis too much for this offending wretch,
This parricide, that murders with her crimes,
Shortens her father's age and cuts him off
Ere little more than half his years be numbered. 135

SCIOLTO.

Would it were otherwise! but thou must die.

CALISTA.

That I must die! it is my only comfort:
Death is the privilege of human nature,
And life without it were not worth our taking;
Thither the poor, the pris'ner, and the mourner 140
Fly for relief and lay their burdens down.
Come then, and take me now to thy cold arms,
Thou meager shade; here let me breathe my last,
Charmed with my father's pity and forgiveness
More than if angels tuned their golden viols 145
And sung a requiem to my parting soul.

SCIOLTO.

I am summoned hence, ere this my friends expect me.
There is I know not what of sad presage
That tells me I shall never see thee more;
If it be so, this is our last farewell 150
And these the parting pangs which nature feels
When anguish rends the heartstrings—Oh! my
    daughter. (*Exit.*)

CALISTA.

Now think thou, curst Calista, now behold
The desolation, horror, blood, and ruin
Thy crimes and fatal folly spread around, 155
That loudly cry for vengeance on thy head.
Yet Heav'n, who knows our weak, imperfect
    natures—
How blind with passions and how prone to evil—
Makes not too strict enquiry for offences
But is atoned by penitence and pray'r. 160
Cheap recompense! here 'twould not be received:
Nothing but blood can make the expiation
And cleanse the soul from inbred, deep pollution.
And see, another injured wretch is come
To call for justice from my tardy hand. 165

Enter Altamont.

ALTAMONT.

Hail to you horrors! hail thou house of death!

And thou the lovely mistress of these shades,
Whose beauty gilds the more than midnight darkness
And makes it grateful as the dawn of day.
Oh! take me in a fellow-mourner with thee; 170
I'll number groan for groan, and tear for tear,
And when the fountain[i] of thy eyes are dry,
Mine shall supply the stream and weep for both.

CALISTA.

I know thee well, thou art the injured Altamont,
Thou com'st to urge me with the wrongs I 175
    ha'done thee.
But know I stand upon the brink of life
And in a moment mean to set me free
From shame and thy upbraiding.

ALTAMONT.

                            Falsely, falsely
Dost thou accuse me. When did I complain 180
Or murmur at my fate? For thee I have
Forgot the temper of Italian husbands,[21]
And fondness has prevailed upon revenge.
I bore my load of infamy with patience,
As holy men do punishments from Heav'n, 185
Nor thought it hard, because it came from thee.
Oh! then forbid me not to mourn thy loss,
To wish some better fate had ruled our loves,
And that Calista had been mine, and true.

CALISTA.

Oh! Altamont, 'tis hard for souls like mine, 190
Haughty and fierce, to yield they have done amiss.
But oh! behold my proud, disdainful heart
Bends to thy gentler virtue. Yes, I own,
Such is thy truth, thy tenderness and love,
Such are the graces that adorn thy youth, 195
That were I not abandoned to destruction,
With thee I might have lived for ages blest
And died in peace within thy faithful arms.

ALTAMONT.

Then happiness is still within our reach.
Here let remembrance lose our past misfortunes, 200
Tear all records that hold the fatal story;
Here let our joys begin, from hence go on
In long successive order.

---

21 temper of Italian husbands] who were proverbially hot-
   blooded and passionately jealous to the point of violence

CALISTA.

What! in death?

ALTAMONT.

Then art thou fixed to die? But be it so,   205
We'll go together; my advent'rous love
Shall follow thee to those uncertain beings:
Whether our lifeless shades are doomed to wander
In gloomy groves with discontented ghosts
Or whether through the upper air we fleet   210
And tread the fields of light, still* I'll pursue thee
Till Fate ordains that we shall part no more.

CALISTA.

Oh no! Heav'n has some better lot in store
To crown thee with: live, and be happy long;
Live for some maid that shall deserve thy goodness,   215
Some kind, unpracticed heart, that never yet
Has listened to the false ones of thy sex,
Nor known the arts of ours. She shall reward thee,
Meet thee with virtues equal to thy own,
Charm thee with sweetness, beauty, and with truth,   220
Be blest in thee alone, and thou in her.

Enter Horatio.

HORATIO.

Now mourn indeed, ye miserable pair,
For now the measure of your woes is full.

ALTAMONT.

What dost thou mean, Horatio?

HORATIO.

Oh! 'tis dreadful: 225
The great, the good Sciolto dies this moment.

CALISTA.

My father!

ALTAMONT.

That's a deadly stroke indeed.

HORATIO.

Not long ago he privately went forth,
Attended but by few, and those unbidden.   230
I heard which way he took and straight pursued him,
But found him compassed by Lothario's faction,
Almost alone, amidst a crowd of foes.
Too late we brought him aid and drove them back;
Ere that his frantic valor had provoked   235
The death he seemed to wish for from their swords.

CALISTA.

And dost thou bear me yet, thou patient earth?

Dost thou not labor with my murd'rous weight?
And you, ye glitt'ring, heav'nly host of stars,
Hide your fair heads in clouds, or I shall blast you,   240
For I am all contagion, death, and ruin,
And Nature sickens at me. Rest, thou world,
This parricide shall be thy plague no more:
Thus, thus I set thee free. (*Stabs herself.*)

HORATIO.

Oh! fatal rashness.   245

ALTAMONT.

Thou dost instruct me well: to lengthen life
Is but to trifle now.

Altamont offers to kill himself; Horatio prevents him
and wrests his sword from him.*

HORATIO.

Hah! what means
The frantic Altamont? Some foe to man
Has breathed on ev'ry breast contagious fury   250
And epidemic madness.

Enter Sciolto, pale and bloody, supported by servants.

CALISTA.

Oh my heart!
Well mayst thou fail, for see the spring that fed
Thy vital stream is wasted and runs low.
My father! will you now at last forgive me,   255
If after all my crimes and all your suff'rings,
I call you once again by that dear name?
Will you forget my shame and those wide wounds,
Lift up your hand and bless me ere I go
Down to my dark abode?   260

SCIOLTO.

Alas! my daughter?
Thou hast rashly ventured in a stormy sea,
Where life, fame, virtue, all were wrecked and lost.
But sure thou hast born thy part in all the anguish
And smarted with the pain. Then rest in peace,   265
Let silence and oblivion hide thy name
And save thee from the malice of posterity,
And mayst thou find with Heav'n the same
forgiveness
As with thy father here. Die, and be happy.

CALISTA.

Celestial sounds! Peace dawns upon my soul,   270
And ev'ry pain grows less.—Oh! gentle Altamont,

Think not too hardly of me when I'm gone,
But pity me. Had I but early known
Thy wondrous worth, thou excellent young man,
We had been happier both. Now 'tis too late,　　275
And yet my eyes take pleasure to behold thee:
Thou art their last dear object.—Mercy, Heav'n!
　　(*Dies.*)

ALTAMONT.

Cold! dead and cold! and yet thou art not changed,
But lovely still! Hadst thou a thousand faults,
What heart so hard, what virtue so severe,　　280
But at that beauty must of force relented,
Melted to pity, love, and to forgiveness?

SCIOLTO.

Oh! turn thee from the fatal object. Altamont,
Come near, and let me bless thee e'er I die.
To thee, and brave* Horatio, I bequeath　　285
My fortunes. Lay me by thy noble father
And love my memory as thou hast done his,
For thou hast been my son.—Oh! gracious Heav'n!
Thou that hast endless blessings still* in store
For virtue and for filial piety,　　290
Let grief, disgrace, and want be far away,
But multiply thy mercies on his head;
Let honor, greatness, goodness still* be with him
And peace in all his ways— (*Dies.*)

ALTAMONT.

　　　　　　　　　Take, take it all,　　295
To thee, Horatio, I resign the gift,
While I pursue my father and my love
And find my only portion in the grave.

HORATIO.

The storm of grief bears hard upon his youth
And bends him like a drooping flower to earth.　　300
Raise him and bear him in.

Altamont is carried off.

By such examples are we taught to prove
The sorrows that attend unlawful love:
Death or some worse misfortunes soon divide
The injured bridegroom from his guilty bride.　　305
If you would have the nuptial union last,
Let virtue be the bond that ties it fast.

Exeunt omnes.

FINIS.

Textual Notes

a Copytext is the first edition in 1703 (Q). Also consulted: the second edition in 1714 (D1), the third edition in 1718 (D2), the fourth edition in 1730 (D3), the first collected edition in 1747 (W), and modern editions in 1929 (Sutherland), in 1931 (Macmillan and Jones) and 1969 (Goldstein).

b Base! Betrayer!] Q, Dd, Sutherland; base betrayer! W, Macmillan and Jones, Goldstein.

c th'alarm] Dd, W; the alarm Q, Sutherland, Macmillan and Jones, Goldstein.

d of] Dd, W, Sutherland, Macmillan and Jones, Goldstein; *om.* Q

e your] Dd, W, Sutherland, Macmillan and Jones, Goldstein; our Q.

f villain's] Dd, W; villainous Q, Sutherland, Macmillan and Jones, Goldstein

g me] D2, D3, W, Sutherland; *om.* Q, D1, Macmillan and Jones, Goldstein

h forget] Q, D1, Sutherland, Macmillan and Jones, Goldstein; forgive D2, D3, W.

i fountain] Q1, Dd, Macmillan and Jones; fountains W, Sutherland, Goldstein

The London Merchant; or, The History of George Barnwell[a]

by George Lillo (1691-1739)
edited by Lincoln Faller

First performed at Drury Lane Theatre in June 1731, *The London Merchant* was the work of a relative unknown, in fact a jeweller by trade; it became an immediate and somewhat surprising success. Those who came to the playhouse to scoff and sneer at what they expected to be a low and vulgar entertainment, according to the oft-told story, found themselves moved instead to admiring tears. Queen Caroline requested a copy of the play within days of its premiere, and within months a "command" performance would be staged for her and George II. The play would eventually become one of the most frequently performed tragedies of the eighteenth century.

For all that, readers have had some notable difficulty appreciating it over the last two hundred years. The play's strenuous, sententious speechifying in praise of merchants and the art of merchandise, the lurid melodrama of Barnwell's seduction, of his murder of his uncle, of Millwood's apprehension—which at times can verge dangerously on farce—as well as the thinness and stiffness of its characters except Millwood and perhaps Lucy, have made it all too easy a target. Audiences in its own day were better able to value its excitements. Though somewhat of an anomaly in eighteenth-century theater, there being nothing quite like it before or after, the play does combine elements from the pathetic tradition of Otway, Southerne, and Rowe—all of whom were highly valued for their capacity to raise intense sympathy for their tragic characters—with certain qualities of heroic drama. As in tragedies of the latter kind, Barnwell faces a conflict between love and honor. In his capacity to suffer and fall, in the pain his friends feel as a result, and in their abilities, each of them, to bear up under the pressures entailed, Barnwell and his friends can seem for all their middle-class status just as important and heroic as the great.

Bourgeois is beautiful, the play seems to say. Indeed it announces a new era, characterized by a new political economy based on exchange rather than conquest, to be distinguished on a global level from the rapacious imperialism of the Spanish and, on a personal and domestic level, from Millwood's exploitation of the hapless Barnwell. Where mutuality and shared respect characterize Thorowgood's relations with both his family and the world, Barnwell and Millwood are linked only by his lust for her and her lust for money as well as revenge for the exploitation she herself has suffered. Barnwell might have married the boss's daughter, but his tragedy is that he gives up Thorowgood's world for the chaos and death of Millwood's.

Though redolent with Old Testament allusions and echoes of Shakespeare's great tragedies, *The London Merchant* offers a far more optimistic vision of human suffering and evil. Terrible as it is, Barnwell's fate opens heaven's door to him. Even Millwood might find a place there, for all her hopeless, hapless, dying agonies. People in the play are good, if given the chance, and do evil without quite wanting to or because they're overwhelmed by circumstance. However oddly conjoined to the heroicization of business and businessmen, such ideas can of course seem quite contemporary to us as heirs of progressive, bourgeois morality.

From the dedication to Sir John Eyles, Baronet,
Member of Parliament for and
Alderman of the City of London, and
Sub-Governor of the South Sea Company:

If tragic poetry be, as Mr. Dryden has somewhere said,[1] the most excellent and most useful kind of writing, the more extensively useful the moral of any tragedy is the more excellent that piece must be of its kind. 5

I hope I shall not be thought to insinuate that this ... is such; that depends on its fitness to answer the end of tragedy, the exciting of the passions in order to the correcting such of them as are criminal either in their nature or through their excess. ... 10

What I would infer is this, I think, evident truth: that tragedy is so far from losing its dignity by being accommodated to the circumstances of the generality of mankind that it is more truly august in proportion to the extent of its influence 15 and the numbers that are properly affected by it. As it is more truly great to be the instrument of good to many who stand in need of our assistance than to a very small part of that number.

If princes, etc., were alone liable to misfortunes 20 arising from vice or weakness in themselves or others, there would be good reason for confining the characters in tragedy to those of superior rank; but, since the contrary is evident, nothing can be more reasonable to proportion the remedy to the 25 disease.

... I have attempted, indeed, to enlarge the province of the graver kind of poetry and should be glad to see it carried on by some abler hand. Plays founded on moral tales in private life may 30 be of admirable use by carrying conviction to the mind with such irresistible force as to engage all the faculties and powers of the soul in the cause of virtue, by stifling vice in its first principles. They who imagine this to be too much to be attributed 35 to tragedy must be strangers to the energy of that noble species of poetry.

PROLOGUE

The tragic muse, sublime, delights to show
Princes distressed and scenes of royal woe,
In awful* pomp, majestic, to relate
The fall of nations or some hero's fate
That sceptered chiefs may by example know 5
The strange vicissitude of things below,
What dangers on security attend,
How pride and cruelty in ruin end,
Hence Providence supreme to know, and own
Humanity adds glory to a throne. 10
        In every former age and foreign tongue,
With native grandeur thus the goddess sung.
Upon our stage indeed, with wished success,
You've sometimes seen her in a humbler dress,
Great only in distress. When she complains 15
In Southerne's, Rowe's, or Otway's moving strains,
The brilliant drops that fall from each bright eye
The absent pomp with brighter gems supply.
Forgive us then, if we attempt to show
In artless strains a tale of private woe. 20
A London prentice ruined is our theme,
Drawn from the famed old song that bears his name.[2]
We hope your taste is not so high to scorn
A moral tale esteemed ere you were born,
Which for a century of rolling years 25
Has filled a thousand thousand eyes with tears.
If thoughtless youth to warn, and shame the age
From vice destructive well becomes the stage,
If this example innocence insure,
Prevent our guilt, or by reflection cure, 30
If Millwood's dreadful crimes and sad despair
Commend the virtue of the good and fair,
Though art be wanting* and our numbers fail,
Indulge th'attempt in justice to the tale.

---

[1] somewhere said] The reference, McBurney suggests, is to Dryden's quoting Aristotle to the effect that "the most perfect work of poetry is tragedy" in his *Discourse Concerning the Original and Progress of Satire* (1693); Steffenson suggests a generalized reference to claims made in Dryden's *An Essay of Dramatic Poesy* (1668).

[2] old song ... name] The inspiration if not exactly the source for Lillo's play is the popular "Ballad of George Barnwell," for which see McBurney, Appendix C.

DRAMATIS PERSONAE

MEN

> Thorowgood.
> Barnwell, uncle to George.
> George Barnwell.
> Trueman.
> Blunt.
> Officers with their attendants, keeper, and
> footmen.

WOMEN

> Maria.
> Millwood.
> Lucy.

SCENE: LONDON AND AN ADJACENT VILLAGE.

The London Merchant;
or, The History of George Barnwell.

> Learn to be wise from others' harm
> And you shall do full well.[3]

Act I, scene i. A room in Thorowgood's house.

Enter Thorowgood and Trueman.

TRUEMAN.

Sir, the packet from Genoa is arrived. (*Gives letters.*)

THOROWGOOD.

Heaven be praised, the storm that threatened our
royal mistress, pure religion, liberty and laws is for
a time diverted. The haughty and revengeful
Spaniard, disappointed of the loan on which he   5
depended from Genoa, must now attend the slow
return of wealth from his new world to supply his
empty coffers ere he can execute his purposed
invasion of our happy island,[4] by which means
time is gained to make such preparations on our   10
part as may, Heaven concurring, prevent his malice
or turn the meditated mischief on himself.

---

3 Learn … well] final lines of "Old Ballad of *The Lady's*
Fall," as Lillo names it in the text, though in a version,
according to Steffenson, somewhat at variance from
other printed versions.

4 storm … island] the attempted invasion by the Spanish
Armada in 1588, which was partly defeated by a storm

TRUEMAN.

He must be insensible indeed who is not affected
when the safety of his country is concerned. Sir,
may I know by what means? If I am too bold—   15

THOROWGOOD.

Your curiosity is laudable, and I gratify it with the
greater pleasure because from thence you may learn
how honest merchants, as such, may sometimes
contribute to the safety of their country as they do
at all times to its happiness; that if hereafter you   20
should be tempted to any action that has the
appearance of vice or meanness in it, upon
reflecting on the dignity of our profession, you
may with honest scorn reject whatever is unworthy
of it.   25

TRUEMAN.

Should Barnwell or I, who have the benefit of your
example, by our ill conduct bring any imputation
on that honorable name, we must be left without
excuse.

THOROWGOOD.

You compliment, young man.   30

Trueman bows respectfully.

Nay, I'm not offended. As the name of merchant
never degrades the gentleman, so by no means does
it exclude him. Only take heed not to purchase the
character of complaisant at the expense of your
sincerity. But to answer your question: the bank   35
of Genoa had agreed, at excessive interest and on
good security, to advance the King of Spain a sum
of money sufficient to equip his vast Armado. Of
which our peerless Elizabeth—more than in name
the mother of her people—being well informed,   40
sent Walsingham,[5] her wise and faithful secretary,
to consult the merchants of this loyal City,* who
all agreed to direct their several agents to influence,
if possible, the Genoese to break their contract
with the Spanish court. 'Tis done. The state and   45
bank of Genoa, having maturely weighed and
rightly judged of their true interest, prefer the
friendship of the merchants of London to that of

---

5 Walsingham] Sir Francis Walsingham (1530-1590) was
Secretary of State to Elizabeth I. There is no historical
evidence to support Thorowgood's story.

a monarch who proudly styles himself King of both Indies.

TRUEMAN.

Happy success of prudent councils! What an expense of blood and treasure is here saved! Excellent queen! Oh how unlike those princes who make the danger of foreign enemies a pretence to oppress their subjects by taxes great and grievous to be borne. 55

THOROWGOOD.

Not so our gracious queen, whose richest exchequer is her people's love, as their happiness is her greatest glory.

TRUEMAN.

On these terms to defend us is to make our protection a benefit worthy her who confers it and 60 well worth our acceptance.—Sir, have you any commands for me at this time?

THOROWGOOD.

Only look carefully over the files to see whether there are any tradesmen's bills unpaid. If there are, send and discharge 'em. We must not let artificers 65 lose their time, so useful to the public and their families, in unnecessary attendance.

Exit Trueman. Enter Maria.

THOROWGOOD.

Well, Maria, have you given orders for the entertainment? I would have it in some measure worthy the guests. Let there be plenty and of the 70 best, that the courtiers may[b] at least commend our hospitality.

MARIA.

Sir, I have endeavored not to wrong your well known generosity by an ill-timed parsimony.

THOROWGOOD.

Nay, 'twas a needless caution. I have no cause to 75 doubt your prudence.

MARIA.

Sir, I find myself unfit for conversation.* I should but increase the number of the company without adding to their satisfaction.

THOROWGOOD.

Nay my child, this melancholy must not be 80 indulged.

MARIA.

Company will but increase it. I wish you would

dispense with[6] my absence; solitude best suits my present temper.

THOROWGOOD.

You are not insensible that it is chiefly on your 85 account these noble lords do me the honor so frequently to grace my board. Should you be absent, the disappointment may make them repent their condescension and think their labor lost.

MARIA.

He that shall think his time or honor lost in 90 visiting you can set no real value on your daughter's company, whose only merit is that she is yours. The man of quality* who chooses to converse with a gentleman and merchant of your worth and character may confer honor by so doing, but he 95 loses none.

THOROWGOOD.

Come, come, Maria, I need not tell you that a young gentleman may prefer your conversation* to mine, yet intend me no disrespect at all. For though he may lose no honor in my company, 'tis very natural 100 for him to expect more pleasure in yours. I remember the time when the company of the greatest and wisest man in the kingdom would have been insipid and tiresome to me if it had deprived me of an opportunity of enjoying your mother's. 105

MARIA.

Yours no doubt was as agreeable to her, for generous minds know no pleasure in society but where 'tis mutual.

THOROWGOOD.

Thou knowest I have no heir, no child but thee; the fruits of many years' successful industry must 110 all be thine. Now it would give me pleasure great as my love to see on whom you would bestow it. I am daily solicited by men of the greatest rank and merit for leave to address you, but I have hitherto declined it in hopes that by observation I 115 should learn which way your inclination tends. For as I know love to be essential to happiness in the marriage state, I had rather my approbation should confirm your choice than direct it.

MARIA.

What can I say? How shall I answer as I ought this 120

---

6 dispense with] excuse

tenderness so uncommon even in the best of parents? But you are without example. Yet had you been less indulgent, I had been most wretched. That I look on the crowd of courtiers that visit here with equal esteem but equal indifference you have observed, and I must needs confess. Yet had you asserted your authority and insisted on a parent's right to be obeyed, I had submitted and to my duty sacrificed my peace. 125

THOROWGOOD.

From your perfect obedience in every other instance I feared as much and therefore would leave you without a bias in an affair wherein your happiness is so immediately concerned. 130

MARIA.

Whether from a want* of that just ambition that would become your daughter or from some other cause, I know not, but I find high birth and titles don't recommend the man who owns them to my affections. 135

THOROWGOOD.

I would not that they should, unless his merit recommends him more. A noble birth and fortune, though they make not a bad man good, yet they are a real advantage to a worthy one and place his virtues in the fairest light. 140

MARIA.

I cannot answer for my inclinations, but they shall ever be submitted to your wisdom and authority, and as you will not compel me to marry where I cannot love, love shall never make me act contrary to my duty. Sir, have I your permission to retire? 145

THOROWGOOD.

I'll see you to your chamber.

Exeunt.

Scene ii. A room in Millwood's house.

Millwood at her toilet, Lucy waiting.*

MILLWOOD.

How do I look today, Lucy?

LUCY.

Oh, killingly, madam! A little more red, and you'll be irresistible! But why this more than ordinary care of your dress and complexion? What new conquest are you aiming at? 5

MILLWOOD.

A conquest would be new indeed!

LUCY.

Not to you, who make 'em every day. But to me, well! 'Tis what I'm never to expect, unfortunate as I am. But your wit and beauty—

MILLWOOD.

First made me a wretch and still continue me so. Men, however generous or sincere to one another, are all selfish hypocrites in their affairs with us. We are no otherwise esteemed or regarded by them but as we contribute to their satisfaction. 10

LUCY.

You are certainly, madam, on the wrong side in this argument. Is not the expense all theirs? And I am sure it is our own fault if we haven't our share of the pleasure. 15

MILLWOOD.

We are but slaves to men.

LUCY.

Nay, 'tis they that are slaves most certainly, for we lay them under contribution. 20

MILLWOOD.

Slaves have no property, no, not even in themselves. All is the victor's.

LUCY.

You are strangely arbitrary in your principles, madam. 25

MILLWOOD.

I would have my conquests complete, like those of the Spaniards in the New World, who first plundered the natives of all the wealth they had and then condemned the wretches to the mines for life to work for more. 30

LUCY.

Well, I shall never approve of your scheme of government. I should think it much more politic, as well as just, to find my subjects an easier employment.

MILLWOOD.

It's a general maxim among the knowing part of mankind that a woman without virtue, like a man without honor or honesty, is capable of any action though never so vile. And yet what pains will they not take, what arts not use, to seduce us from our innocence and make us contemptible and wicked, 35 40 even in their own opinions? Then is it not just the villains to their cost should find us so? But guilt makes them suspicious and keeps them on their guard; therefore, we can take advantage only of the young and innocent part of the sex, who, having 45 never injured women, apprehend no injury from them.

LUCY.

Aye, they must be young indeed.

MILLWOOD.

Such a one, I think, I have found. As I've passed through the City,* I have often observed him 50 receiving and paying considerable sums of money; from thence I conclude he is employed in affairs of consequence.

LUCY.

Is he handsome?

MILLWOOD.

Aye, aye, the stripling is well made and has a good 55 face.

LUCY.

About—

MILLWOOD.

Eighteen—

LUCY.

Innocent, handsome, and about eighteen. You'll be vastly happy. Why, if you manage well, you may 60 keep him to yourself these two or three years.

MILLWOOD.

If I manage well, I shall have done with him much sooner. Having long had a design on him and meeting him yesterday, I made a full stop and, gazing wishfully on his face, asked him his name. 65 He blushed and, bowing very low, answered, "George Barnwell." I begged his pardon for the freedom I had taken and told him that he was the person I had long wished to see and to whom I had an affair of importance to communicate at a 70 proper time and place. He named a tavern; I talked of honor and reputation, and invited him to my house. He swallowed the bait, promised to come, and this is the time I expect him.

Knocking at the door.

Somebody knocks, d'ye hear? I am at home to 75 nobody today but him.

Exit Lucy.

MILLWOOD.

Less affairs must give way to those of more consequence, and I am strangely mistaken if this does not prove of great importance to me and him too, before I have done with him. Now, after what 80 manner shall I receive him? Let me consider. What manner of person am I to receive? He is young, innocent, and bashful; therefore, I must take care not to put him out of countenance[c] at first. But then, if I have any skill in physiognomy, he is amorous and, 85 with a little assistance, will soon get the better of his modesty. I'll e'en trust to Nature, who does wonders in these matters. If to seem what one is not in order to be the better liked for what one really is, if to speak one thing and mean the direct contrary be art in a 90 woman, I know nothing of Nature.

Enter Barnwell bowing very low. Lucy at a distance.

MILLWOOD.

Sir! The surprise and joy!

BARNWELL.

Madam.

MILLWOOD.

This is such a favor— (*Advancing.*)

BARNWELL.

Pardon me, madam— 95

MILLWOOD.

So unhoped for— (*Still advances.*)

Barnwell salutes her, and retires in confusion.*

MILLWOOD.

To see you here. Excuse the confusion.

BARNWELL.

I fear I am too bold.

MILLWOOD.

Alas, sir! I may justly apprehend you think me so. Please, sir, to sit. I am as much at a loss how to 100 receive this honor as I ought, as I am surprised at your goodness in conferring it.

BARNWELL.

I thought you had expected me. I promised to come.

MILLWOOD.

That is the more surprising. Few men are such 105 religious observers of their word.

BARNWELL.

All who are honest are.

MILLWOOD.

To one another. But we simple women are seldom thought of consequence enough to gain a place in your remembrance. (*Laying her hand on his, as if by accident.*) 110

BARNWELL. (*Aside.*)

Her disorder is so great, she don't perceive she has laid her hand on mine. Heaven! How she trembles! What can this mean!

MILLWOOD.

The interest I have in all that relates to you—the reason of which you shall know hereafter—excites 115 my curiosity. And were I sure you would pardon my presumption, I should desire to know your real sentiments on a very particular subject.

BARNWELL.

Madam, you may command my poor thoughts on any subject. I have none that I would conceal. 120

MILLWOOD.

You'll think me bold.

BARNWELL.

No, indeed.

MILLWOOD.

What then are your thoughts of love?

BARNWELL.

If you mean the love of women, I have not thought of it at all. My youth and circumstances make such 125 thoughts improper in me yet. But if you mean the general love we owe to mankind, I think no one has more of it in his temper than myself. I don't know that person in the world whose happiness I don't wish and wouldn't promote, were it in my 130 power. In an especial manner I love my uncle, and my master, but above all my friend.

MILLWOOD.

You have a friend then, whom you love?

BARNWELL.

As he does me, sincerely.

MILLWOOD.

He is no doubt often blessed with your company 135 and conversation.

BARNWELL.

We live in one house and both serve the same worthy merchant.

MILLWOOD.

Happy, happy youth! Whoe'er thou art, I envy thee, and so must all who see and know this youth. 140 What have I lost by being formed a woman! I hate my sex, my self. Had I been a man, I might, perhaps, have been as happy in your friendship as he who now enjoys it. But as it is, oh!

BARNWELL. (*Aside.*)

I never observed women before, or this is sure the 145 most beautiful of her sex.—You seem disordered, madam! May I know the cause?

MILLWOOD.

Do not ask me, I can never speak it, whatever is the cause. I wish for things impossible: I would be a servant bound to the same master, to live in one 150 house with you.

BARNWELL. (*Aside.*)

How strange and yet how kind her words and actions are! And the effect they have on me is strange. I feel desires I never knew before. I must be gone, while I have power to go.—Madam, I 155 humbly take my leave.

MILLWOOD.

You will not, sure, leave me so soon!

BARNWELL.

Indeed I must.

MILLWOOD.

You cannot be so cruel! I have prepared a poor supper, at which I promised myself your company. 160

BARNWELL.

I am sorry I must refuse the honor you designed me. But my duty to my master calls me hence. I never yet neglected his service. He is so gentle and so good a master that should I wrong him, though he might forgive me, I never should forgive myself. 165

MILLWOOD.

Am I refused, by the first man, the second favor I ever stooped to ask? Go then, thou proud, hard-hearted youth. But know, you are the only man that could be found who would let me sue twice for greater favors. 170

BARNWELL.

What shall I do! How shall I go or stay!

MILLWOOD.

Yet do not, do not leave me. I with my sex's pride would meet your scorn. But when I look upon you,

when I behold those eyes, oh! spare my tongue and let
my blushes—this flood of tears to that will force their 175
way—declare what woman's modesty should hide.

BARNWELL. [*Aside*.]

Oh heavens! She loves me, worthless as I am. Her
looks, her words, her flowing tears confess it. And
can I leave her then? Oh, never, never.—Madam,
dry up your tears. You shall command me always. 180
I will stay here forever, if you'd have me.

LUCY. (*Aside*.)

So! She has wheedled him out of his virtue of
obedience already and will strip him of all the rest,
one after another, till she has left him as few as her
ladyship or myself. 185

MILLWOOD.

Now you are kind, indeed. But I mean not to detain
you always. I would have you shake off all slavish
obedience to your master, but you may serve him still.

LUCY. (*Aside*.)

Serve him still! Aye, or he'll have no opportunity
of fingering his cash, and then he'll not serve your 190
end, I'll be sworn.

Enter Blunt.

BLUNT.

Madam, supper's on the table.

MILLWOOD.

Come sir, you'll excuse all defects. My thoughts
were too much employed on my guest to observe
the entertainment. 195

Exeunt Barnwell and Millwood.

BLUNT.

What, is all this preparation, this elegant supper,
variety of wines and music, for the entertainment
of that young fellow!

LUCY.

So it seems.

BLUNT.

What, is our mistress turned fool at last! She's in 200
love with him, I suppose.

LUCY.

I suppose not. But she designs to make him in love
with her if she can.

BLUNT.

What will she get by that? He seems underage and
can't be supposed to have much money. 205

LUCY.

But his master has, and that's the same thing, as
she'll manage it.

BLUNT.

I don't like this fooling with a handsome young
fellow. While she's endeavoring to ensnare him, she
may be caught herself. 210

LUCY.

Nay, were she like me that would certainly be the
consequence. For I confess, there is something in
youth and innocence that moves me mightily.

BLUNT.

Yes, so does the smoothness and plumpness of a
partridge move a mighty desire in the hawk to be 215
the destruction of it.

LUCY.

Why, birds are their prey as men are ours; though,
as you observed, we are sometimes caught
ourselves. But that, I dare say, will never be the case
with our mistress. 220

BLUNT.

I wish it may prove so, for you know we all depend
upon her. Should she trifle away her time with a
young fellow that there's nothing to be got by, we
must all starve.

LUCY.

There's no danger of that, for I am sure she has 225
no view in this affair but interest.

BLUNT.

Well, and what hopes are there of success in that?

LUCY.

The most promising that can be. 'Tis true, the
youth has his scruples, but she'll soon teach him
to answer them, by stifling his conscience. Oh, the 230
lad is in a hopeful way, depend upon't.

Exeunt.

Scene draws and discovers Barnwell and Millwood at
supper. An entertainment of music and singing, after
which they come forward.*

BARNWELL.

What can I answer! All that I know is that you are
fair and I am miserable.

MILLWOOD.

We are both so, and yet the fault is in ourselves.

BARNWELL.

To ease our present anguish by plunging into guilt 235
is to buy a moment's pleasure with an age of pain.

MILLWOOD.

I should have thought the joys of love as lasting
as they are great. If ours prove otherwise, 'tis your
inconstancy must make them so.

BARNWELL.

The law of Heaven will not be reversed, and that   240
requires us to govern our passions.

MILLWOOD.

To give us sense of beauty and desires and yet
forbid us to taste and be happy is cruelty to nature.
Have we passions only to torment us!

BARNWELL.

To hear you talk, though in the cause of vice, to   245
gaze upon your beauty, press your hand, and see
your snow-white bosom heave and fall enflames
my wishes. My pulse beats high, my senses all are
in a hurry, and I am on the rack of wild desire.
Yet for a moment's guilty pleasure shall I lose my   250
innocence, my peace of mind, and hopes of solid
happiness?

MILLWOOD.

Chimeras all,
          Come on with me and prove,
No joy's like womankind, no heaven like love.   255

BARNWELL.

I would not, yet must on.
Reluctant thus, the merchant quits his ease
And trusts to rocks and sands and stormy seas,
In hopes some unknown golden coast to find,
Commits himself, though doubtful, to the wind,   260
Longs much for joys to come, yet mourns those
   left behind.

Exeunt.

Act II, scene i. A room in Thorowgood's house.

Enter Barnwell.

BARNWELL.

How strange are all things round me? Like some
thief who treads forbidden ground and fain would
lurk unseen, fearful I enter each apartment of this
well-known house. To guilty love, as if that were too
little, already have I added breach of trust. A thief!   5
Can I know myself that wretched thing and look my
honest friend and injured master in the face?
Though hypocrisy may awhile conceal my guilt, at

length it will be known, and public shame and ruin
must ensue. In the meantime, what must be my life?   10
Ever to speak a language foreign to my heart, hourly
to add to the number of my crimes in order to
conceal 'em. Sure such was the condition of the
Grand Apostate[7] when first he lost his purity. Like
me disconsolate he wandered and while yet in   15
heaven bore all his future hell about him.

Enter Trueman.

TRUEMAN.

Barnwell! Oh how I rejoice to see you safe! So will
our master and his gentle daughter, who during
your absence often inquired after you.

BARNWELL. (*Aside.*)

Would he were gone; his officious love will pry   20
into the secrets of my soul.

TRUEMAN.

Unless you knew the pain the whole family* has
felt on your account, you can't conceive how much
you are beloved. But why thus cold and silent?
When my heart is full of joy for your return, why   25
do you turn away? Why thus avoid me? What have
I done? How am I altered since you saw me last?
Or rather, what have you done? And why are you
thus changed? For I am still the same.

BARNWELL. (*Aside.*)

What have I done indeed?   30

TRUEMAN.

Not speak nor look upon me!

BARNWELL. (*Aside.*)

By my face he will discover all I would conceal.
Methinks already I begin to hate him.

TRUEMAN.

I cannot bear this usage from a friend, one whom till
now I ever found so loving, whom yet I love, though   35
this unkindness strikes at the root of friendship and
might destroy it in any breast but mine.

BARNWELL.

I am not well. (*Turning to him.*) Sleep has been a
stranger to these eyes since you beheld them last.

TRUEMAN.

Heavy they look indeed, and swollen with tears;   40
now they overflow. Rightly did my sympathizing

---

7 Grand Apostate] Lucifer or Satan

heart forbode last night, when thou wast absent, something fatal to our peace.

BARNWELL.

Your friendship engages you too far. My troubles, whate'er they are, are mine alone. You have no 45 interest in them, nor ought your concern for me give you a moment's pain.

TRUEMAN.

You speak as if you knew of friendship nothing but the name. Before I saw your grief I felt it. Since we parted last I have slept no more than you, but 50 pensive in my chamber sat alone and spent the tedious night in wishes for your safety and return. E'en now, though ignorant of the cause, your sorrow wounds me to the heart.

BARNWELL.

'Twill not always be thus. Friendship and all 55 engagements cease as circumstances and occasions vary, and since you once may hate me, perhaps it might be better for us both that now you loved me less.

TRUEMAN.

Sure I but dream! Without a cause would Barnwell 60 use me thus? Ungenerous and ungrateful youth, farewell. (*Going.*) I shall endeavor to follow your advice. [*Aside.*] Yet stay: perhaps I am too rash and angry when the cause demands compassion. Some unforeseen calamity may have befallen him too 65 great to bear.

BARNWELL.

What part am I reduced to act? 'Tis vile and base to move his temper thus, the best of friends and men.

TRUEMAN.

I am to blame; prithee forgive me, Barnwell. Try to compose your ruffled mind, and let me know 70 the cause that thus transports you from yourself. My friendly counsel may restore your peace.

BARNWELL.

All that is possible for man to do for man, your generous friendship may effect. But here even that's in vain. 75

TRUEMAN.

Something dreadful is laboring in your breast. Oh, give it vent and let me share your grief. 'Twill ease your pain, should it admit no cure, and make it lighter by the part I bear.

BARNWELL.

Vain supposition! My woes increase by being 80 observed; should the cause be known they would exceed all bounds.

TRUEMAN.

So well I know thy honest heart, guilt cannot harbor there.

BARNWELL. (*Aside.*)

Oh torture insupportable! 85

TRUEMAN.

Then why am I excluded? Have I a thought I would conceal from you?

BARNWELL.

If still you urge me on this hated subject, I'll never enter more beneath this roof nor see your face again. 90

TRUEMAN.

'Tis strange. But I have done; say but you hate me not.

BARNWELL.

Hate you! I am not that monster yet.

TRUEMAN.

Shall our friendship still continue?

BARNWELL.

It's a blessing I never was worthy of yet now must 95 stand on terms and but upon conditions can confirm it.

TRUEMAN.

What are they?

BARNWELL.

Never hereafter, though you should wonder at my conduct, desire to know more than I am willing 100 to reveal.

TRUEMAN.

'Tis hard, but upon any conditions I must be your friend.

BARNWELL.

Then, as much as one lost to himself can be another's, I am yours. (*Embracing.*) 105

TRUEMAN.

Be ever so, and may Heaven restore your peace.

BARNWELL.

Will yesterday return? We have heard the glorious sun that, till then incessant rolled, once stopped his rapid course and once went back. The dead have risen, and parched rocks poured forth a liquid 110 stream to quench a people's thirst. The sea divided and formed walls of water while a whole nation passed in safety through its sandy bosom. Hungry lions have refused their prey, and men unhurt have walked amidst consuming flames.[8] But never yet did time, once past, return.

TRUEMAN.

Though the continued chain of time has never once been broke, nor ever will, but uninterrupted must keep on its course till, lost in eternity, it ends there where it first begun, yet as Heaven can repair whatever evils time can bring upon us, we[d] ought never to despair. But business requires our attendance: business, the youth's best preservative from ill, as idleness his worst of snares. Will you go with me?

BARNWELL.

I'll take a little time to reflect on what has passed, and follow you.

Exit Trueman.

I might have trusted Trueman and engaged him to apply to my uncle to repair the wrong I have done my master, but what of Millwood? Must I expose her too? Ungenerous and base! Then Heaven requires it not. But Heaven requires that I forsake her. What! Never see her more! Does Heaven require that? I hope I may see her, and Heaven not be offended. Presumptuous hope. Dearly already have I proved my frailty. Should I once more tempt Heaven, I may be left to fall never to rise again. Yet shall I leave her, forever leave her, and not let her know the cause? She who loves me with such a boundless passion! Can cruelty be duty? I judge of what she then must feel by what I now endure. The love of life and fear of shame, opposed by inclination strong as death or shame, like wind and tide in raging conflict met when neither can prevail, keep me in doubt. How then can I determine?

Enter Thorowgood.

THOROWGOOD.

Without a cause assigned or notice given, to absent yourself last night was a fault, young man, and I came to chide you for it, but hope I am prevented.* That modest blush, the confusion so visible in your face, speak grief and shame. When we have offended Heaven, it requires no more, and shall man, who needs himself to be forgiven, be harder to appease? If my pardon or love be of moment to your peace, look up secure of both.

BARNWELL. (*Aside.*)

This goodness has o'ercome me.—Oh sir! You know not the nature and extent of my offense, and I should abuse your mistaken bounty to receive 'em. Though I had rather die than speak my shame, though racks could not have forced the guilty secret from my breast, your kindness has.

THOROWGOOD.

Enough, enough, whate'er it be, this concern shows you're convinced, and I am satisfied. (*Aside.*) How painful is the sense of guilt to an ingenuous mind—some youthful folly, which it were prudent not to inquire into. When we consider the frail condition of humanity, it may raise our pity, not our wonder, that youth should go astray when reason, weak at the best when opposed to inclination, scarce formed and wholly unassisted by experience, faintly contends or willingly becomes the slave of sense. The state of youth is much to be deplored, and the more so because they see it not, being then to danger most exposed when they are least prepared for their defense.

BARNWELL.

It will be known, and you recall your pardon and abhor me.

THOROWGOOD.

I never will.[e] Yet be upon your guard in this gay, thoughtless season of your life. When the sense of pleasure's quick and passion high, the voluptuous appetites, raging and fierce, demand the strongest curb. Take heed of a relapse. When vice becomes habitual, the very power of leaving it is lost.

BARNWELL.

Hear me on my knees confess.

THOROWGOOD.

Not a syllable more upon this subject. It were not mercy but cruelty to hear what must give you such torment to reveal.

---

8 sun … flames] biblical allusions to the stories of Joshua, Lazarus and Jesus, Moses, Daniel, and Shadrach, Meshach and Abednego.

BARNWELL.

This generosity amazes and distracts me.

THOROWGOOD.

This remorse makes thee dearer to me than if thou hadst never offended. Whatever is your fault, of this I'm certain, 'twas harder for you to offend than me to pardon. (*Exit.*) 190

BARNWELL.

Villain, villain, villain! basely to wrong so excellent a man. Should I again return to folly—detested thought! But what of Millwood then? Why, I renounce her, I give her up, the struggle's over, and virtue has prevailed. Reason may convince, but 195 gratitude compels. This unlooked for generosity has saved me from destruction. (*Going.*)

Enter a footman.

FOOTMAN.

 Sir, two ladies from your uncle in the country desire to see you.

BARNWELL. (*Aside.*)

Who should they be?—Tell them I'll wait upon 200 'em.

Exit footman.

Methinks I dread to see 'em. Now everything alarms me. Guilt, what a coward hast thou made me.

[*Exit.*]

Scene ii. Another room in Thorowgood's house.

Millwood and Lucy discovered. * Enter footman.*

FOOTMAN.

Ladies, he'll wait upon you immediately.

MILLWOOD.

'Tis very well. I thank you.

Exit footman. Enter Barnwell.

BARNWELL.

Confusion! Millwood!

MILLWOOD.

That angry look tells me that here I'm an unwelcome guest. I feared as much; the unhappy 5 are so everywhere.

BARNWELL.

Will nothing but my utter ruin content you?

MILLWOOD.

Unkind and cruel! Lost myself, your happiness is now my only care.

BARNWELL.

How did you gain admission? 10

MILLWOOD.

Saying we were desired by your uncle to visit and deliver a message to you, we were received by the family* without suspicion and with much respect conducted here.

BARNWELL.

Why did you come at all? 15

MILLWOOD.

I never shall trouble you more. I'm come to take my leave forever. Such is the malice of my fate. I go hopeless, despairing ever to return. This hour is all I have left me. One short hour is all I have to bestow on love and you, for whom I thought 20 the longest life too short.

BARNWELL.

Then we are met to part forever?

MILLWOOD.

It must be so. Yet think not that time or absence shall ever put a period to my grief or make me love you less. Though I must leave you, yet condemn 25 me not.

BARNWELL.

Condemn you? No, I approve your resolution and rejoice to hear it. 'Tis just, 'tis necessary; I have well weighed and found it so.

LUCY. (*Aside.*)

I'm afraid the young man has more sense than she 30 thought he had.

BARNWELL.

Before you came I had determined never to see you more.

MILLWOOD. (*Aside.*)

Confusion!

LUCY. (*Aside.*)

Aye! We are all out. This is a turn so unexpected 35 that I shall make nothing of my part. They must e'en play the scene betwixt themselves.

MILLWOOD.

'Twas some relief to think, though absent, you would love me still. But to find though Fortune had been indulgent that you, more cruel and 40

inconstant, had resolved to cast me off, this, as I
never could expect, I have not learned to bear.

BARNWELL.

I am sorry to hear you blame in me a resolution
that so well becomes us both.

MILLWOOD.

I have reason for what I do, but you have none. 45

BARNWELL.

Can we want* a reason for parting who have so
many to wish we never had met?

MILLWOOD.

Look on me, Barnwell. Am I deformed or old, that
satiety so soon succeeds enjoyment? Nay, look
again. Am I not she whom yesterday you thought 50
the fairest and the kindest of her sex? Whose hand,
trembling with ecstasy, you pressed and molded
thus, while on my eyes you gazed with such delight
as if desire increased by being fed?

BARNWELL.

No more. Let me repent my former follies, if 55
possible, without remembering what they were.

MILLWOOD.

Why?

BARNWELL.

Such is my frailty that 'tis dangerous.

MILLWOOD.

Where is the danger, since we are to part?

BARNWELL.

The thought of that already is too painful. 60

MILLWOOD.

If it be painful to part, then I may hope at least
you do not hate me?

BARNWELL.

No, no, I never said I did.—Oh my heart!

MILLWOOD.

Perhaps you pity me?

BARNWELL.

I do, I do, indeed I do. 65

MILLWOOD.

You'll think upon me?

BARNWELL.

Doubt it not while I can think at all.

MILLWOOD.

You may judge an embrace at parting too great a
favor, though it would be the last? (*He draws back.*)
A look shall then suffice. Farewell forever. 70

Exeunt Millwood and Lucy.

BARNWELL.

If to resolve to suffer be to conquer, I have
conquered. Painful victory!

Re-enter Millwood and Lucy.

MILLWOOD.

One thing I had forgot: I never must return to my
own house again. This I thought proper to let you
know, lest your mind should change and you 75
should seek in vain to find me there. Forgive me
this second intrusion. I only came to give you this
caution, and that perhaps was needless.

BARNWELL.

I hope it was, yet it is kind, and I must thank you
for it. 80

MILLWOOD. (*To Lucy.*)

My friend, your arm.—Now I am gone forever.
(*Going.*)

BARNWELL.

One thing more: sure there's no danger in my
knowing where you go? If you think otherwise—

MILLWOOD.

Alas! (*Weeping.*) 85

LUCY. (*Aside.*)

We are right I find; that's my cue.—Ah, dear sir, she's
going she knows not whither, but go she must.

BARNWELL.

Humanity obliges me to wish you well. Why will
you thus expose yourself to needless troubles?

LUCY.

Nay, there's no help for it. She must quit the 90
Town* immediately, and the kingdom as soon as
possible. It was no small matter, you may be sure,
that could make her resolve to leave you.

MILLWOOD.

No more, my friend. Since he for whose dear sake
alone I suffer, and am content to suffer, is kind and 95
pities me. Whene'er I wander through wilds and
deserts, benighted and forlorn, that thought shall
give me comfort.

BARNWELL.

For my sake! Oh tell me how? Which way am I
so cursed as to bring such ruin on thee? 100

MILLWOOD.

No matter, I am contented with my lot.

BARNWELL.

Leave me not in this incertainty.

MILLWOOD.

I have said too much.

BARNWELL.

How, how am I the cause of your undoing?

MILLWOOD.

To know it will but increase your troubles.   105

BARNWELL.

My troubles can't be greater than they are.

LUCY.

Well, well, sir, if she won't satisfy you, I will.

BARNWELL.

I am bound to you beyond expression.

MILLWOOD.

Remember, sir, that I desired you not to hear it.

BARNWELL.

Begin, and ease my racking expectation.   110

LUCY.

Why, you must know, my lady here was an only child, but her parents, dying while she was young, left her and her fortune—no inconsiderable one, I assure you—to the care of a gentleman who has a good estate of his own.   115

MILLWOOD.

Aye, aye, the barbarous man is rich enough, but what are riches when compared to love?

LUCY.

For a while he performed the office of a faithful guardian, settled her in a house, hired her servants—but you have seen in what manner she   120 lived, so I need say no more of that.

MILLWOOD.

How I shall live hereafter, Heaven knows.

LUCY.

All things went on as one could wish till, some time ago, his wife dying, he fell violently in love with his charge and would fain have married her. Now the   125 man is neither old nor ugly but a good personable sort of a man, but I don't know how it was, she could never endure him. In short, her ill usage so provoked him that he brought in an account of his executorship, wherein he makes her debtor to him.   130

MILLWOOD.

A trifle in itself but more than enough to ruin me, whom, by his unjust account, he had stripped of all before.

LUCY.

Now she having neither money nor friend except me, who am as unfortunate as herself, he   135 compelled her to pass his account and give bond for the sum he demanded, but still provided handsomely for her and continued his courtship. Till, being informed by his spies—truly I suspect some in her own family*—that you were   140 entertained* at her house and stayed with her all night, he came this morning raving and storming like a madman, talks no more of marriage—so there's no hopes of making up matters that way— but vows her ruin unless she'll allow him the same   145 favor that he supposes she granted you.

BARNWELL.

Must she be ruined or find her refuge in another's arms?

MILLWOOD.

He gave me but an hour to resolve in. That's happily spent with you, and now I go.   150

BARNWELL.

To be exposed to all the rigors of the various seasons, the summer's parching heat and winter's cold, unhoused to wander friendless through the unhospitable world in misery and want, attended with fear and danger and pursued by malice and   155 revenge—would'st thou endure all this for me, and can I do nothing, nothing to prevent it?

LUCY.

'Tis really a pity there can be no way found out.

BARNWELL.

Oh where are all my resolutions now? Like early vapors or the morning dew chased by the sun's   160 warm beams, they're vanished and lost as though they had never been.

LUCY.

Now I advised her, sir, to comply with the gentleman. That would not only put an end to her troubles but make her fortune at once.   165

BARNWELL.

Tormenting fiend, away. I had rather perish, nay, see her perish, than have her saved by him. I will myself prevent her ruin though with my own. A moment's patience; I'll return immediately. (*Exit.*)

LUCY.

'Twas well you came, or by what I can perceive,   170 you had lost him.

MILLWOOD.

That, I must confess, was a danger I did not foresee. I was only afraid he should have come without money. You know a house of entertainment, like mine, is not kept without expense.   175

LUCY.

That's very true. But then you should be reasonable in your demands. 'Tis pity to discourage a young man.

MILLWOOD.

Leave that to me.

Re-enter Barnwell with a bag of money.

BARNWELL.

What am I about to do! Now you, who boast your   180
reason all sufficient, suppose yourselves in my condition and determine for me whether it's right to let her suffer for my faults or, by this small addition to my guilt, prevent the ill effects of what is past.

LUCY. (*Aside.*)

These young sinners think everything in the ways of   185
wickedness so strange. But I could tell him that this is nothing but what's very common, for one vice as naturally begets another as a father a son. But he'll find out that himself, if he lives long enough.

BARNWELL.

Here, take this, and with it purchase your   190
deliverance. Return to your house and live in peace and safety.

MILLWOOD.

So I may hope to see you there again.

BARNWELL.

Answer me not, but fly, lest in the agonies of my remorse I take again what is not mine to give and   195
abandon thee to want and misery.

MILLWOOD.

Say but you'll come.

BARNWELL.

You are my fate, my heaven or my hell. Only leave me now, dispose of me hereafter as you please.

Exeunt Millwood and Lucy.

BARNWELL.

What have I done? Were my resolutions founded on   200
reason and sincerely made, why then has Heaven suffered me to fall? I sought not the occasion and, if my heart deceives me not, compassion and generosity were my motives. Is virtue inconsistent with itself, or are vice and virtue only empty names?   205
Or do they depend on accidents beyond our power to produce or to prevent, wherein we have no part and yet must be determined by the event? But why should I attempt to reason? All is confusion, horror, and remorse. I find I am lost, cast down from all my   210
late erected hopes and plunged again in guilt, yet scarce know how or why.
Such undistinguished horrors make my brain,
Like hell, the seat of darkness and of pain.

Exit.

Act III, scene i. A room in Thorowgood's house.

Enter Thorowgood and Trueman.

THOROWGOOD.

Methinks I would not have you only learn the method of merchandise and practice it hereafter merely as a means of getting wealth. 'Twill be well worth your pains to study it as a science, to see how it is founded in reason and the nature of things, how   5
it promotes humanity as it has opened and yet keeps up an intercourse between nations far remote from one another in situation, customs, and religion, promoting arts, industry, peace, and plenty, by mutual benefits diffusing mutual love from pole to pole.   10

TRUEMAN.

Something of this I have considered and hope, by your assistance, to extend my thoughts much farther. I have observed those countries where trade is promoted and encouraged do not make discoveries to destroy but to improve mankind, by love and   15
friendship to tame the fierce and polish the most savage, to teach them the advantages of honest traffic by taking from them, with their own consent, their useless superfluities and giving them in return what, from their ignorance in manual arts, their situation,   20
or some other accident, they stand in need of.

THOROWGOOD.

'Tis justly observed. The populous East, luxuriant, abounds with glittering gems, bright pearls, aromatic spices, and health-restoring drugs. The late found western world's rich earth glows with   25
unnumbered veins of gold and silver ore. On every

climate and on every country Heaven has bestowed some good peculiar to itself. It is the industrious merchant's business to collect the various blessings of each soil and climate and, with the product of the whole, to enrich his native country. Well! I have examined your accounts. They are not only just, as I have always found them, but regularly kept and fairly entered. I commend your diligence. Method in business is the surest guide. He who neglects it frequently stumbles and always wanders perplexed, uncertain, and in danger. Are Barnwell's accounts ready for my inspection? He does not use to be the last on these occasions.

TRUEMAN.

Upon receiving your orders he retired, I thought in some confusion. If you please, I'll go and hasten him. I hope he hasn't been guilty of any neglect.

THOROWGOOD.

I'm now going to the Exchange.[9] Let him know, at my return, I expect to find him ready.

Exeunt. Enter Maria with a book, sits and reads.

MARIA.

How forcible is truth! The weakest mind, inspired with love of that, fixed and collected in itself, with indifference beholds the united force of earth and hell opposing. Such souls are raised above the sense of pain or so supported that they regard it not. The martyr cheaply purchases his heaven: small are his sufferings, great is his reward. Not so the wretch who combats love with duty when the mind, weakened and dissolved by the soft passion, feeble and hopeless opposes its own desires. What is an hour, a day, a year of pain to a whole life of tortures such as these?

Enter Trueman.

TRUEMAN.

Oh, Barnwell! Oh, my friend, how art thou fallen?

MARIA.

Hah! Barnwell! What of him? Speak, say what of Barnwell.

TRUEMAN.

'Tis not to be concealed. I've news to tell of him

___

9 Exchange] the Royal Exchange built in 1566 and so named by Queen Elizabeth, a central meeting place for business and financial transactions

that will afflict your generous father, yourself, and all who knew him.

MARIA.

Defend us, Heaven!

TRUEMAN.

I cannot speak it. See there. (*Gives a letter.*)

MARIA. (*Reads.*)

"Trueman, I know my absence will surprise my honored master and yourself, and the more when you shall understand that the reason of my withdrawing is my having embezzled part of the cash with which I was entrusted. After this, 'tis needless to inform you that I intend never to return again. Though this might have been known by examining my accounts, yet to prevent that unnecessary trouble and to cut off all fruitless expectations of my return I have left this from the lost George Barnwell."

TRUEMAN.

Lost indeed! Yet how he should be guilty of what he there charges himself withal raises my wonder equal to my grief. Never had youth a higher sense of virtue. Justly he thought, and as he thought he practiced. Never was life more regular than his: an understanding uncommon at his years, an open, generous, manliness of temper, his manners easy, unaffected, and engaging.

MARIA.

This and much more you might have said with truth. He was the delight of every eye and joy of every heart that knew him.

TRUEMAN.

Since such he was, and was my friend, can I support his loss? See, the fairest and happiest maid this wealthy City* boasts kindly condescends to weep for thy unhappy fate, poor, ruined Barnwell!

MARIA.

Trueman, do you think a soul so delicate as his, so sensible of shame, can e'er submit to live a slave to vice?

TRUEMAN.

Never, never. So well I know him, I'm sure this act of his, so contrary to his nature, must have been caused by some unavoidable necessity.

MARIA.

Is there no means yet to preserve him?

TRUEMAN.

Oh! that there were. But few men recover
reputation lost, a merchant never. Nor would he,
I fear, though I should find him, ever be brought
to look his injured master in the face.   100

MARIA.

I fear as much, and therefore would never have my
father know it.

TRUEMAN.

That's impossible.

MARIA.

What's the sum?

TRUEMAN.

'Tis considerable. I've marked it here to show it   105
with the letter to your father at his return.

MARIA.

If I should supply the money, could you so dispose
of that and the account as to conceal this unhappy
mismanagement from my father?

TRUEMAN.

Nothing more easy. But can you intend it? Will   110
you save a helpless wretch from ruin? Oh! 'twere
an act worthy such exalted virtue as Maria's. Sure
Heaven, in mercy to my friend, inspired the
generous thought.

MARIA.

Doubt not but I would purchase so great a   115
happiness at a much dearer price. But how shall
he be found?

TRUEMAN.

Trust to my diligence for that. In the meantime
I'll conceal his absence from your father or find
such excuses for it that the real cause shall never   120
be suspected.

MARIA.

In attempting to save from shame one whom we
hope may yet return to virtue, to Heaven and you,
the only witnesses of this action, I appeal whether
I do anything misbecoming my sex and character.   125

TRUEMAN.

Earth must approve the deed, and Heaven, I doubt
not, will reward it.

MARIA.

If Heaven succeeds it, I am well rewarded. A
virgin's fame is sullied by suspicion's lightest breath,
and therefore as this must be a secret from my   130

father and the world, for Barnwell's sake, for mine,
let it be so to him.

Exeunt.

Scene ii. A room in Millwood's house.

Enter Lucy and Blunt.

LUCY.

Well! What do you think of Millwood's conduct
now!

BLUNT.

I own it is surprising. I don't know which to admire
most, her feigned or his real passion, though I have
sometimes been afraid that her avarice would   5
discover* her. But his youth and want* of experience
make it the easier to impose on him.

LUCY.

No, it is his love. To do him justice, notwithstanding
his youth, he don't want understanding. But you
men are much easier imposed on in these affairs   10
than your vanity will allow you to believe. Let me see
the wisest of you all as much in love with me as
Barnwell is with Millwood, and I'll engage to make
as great a fool of him.

BLUNT.

And all circumstances considered, to make as   15
much money of him, too?

LUCY.

I can't answer for that. Her artifice in making him
rob his master at first, and the various stratagems
by which she has obliged him to continue that
course, astonish even me who know her so well.   20

BLUNT.

But then you are to consider that the money was
his master's.

LUCY.

There was the difficulty of it. Had it been his own,
it had been nothing. Were the world his, she might
have it for a smile. But those golden days are done;   25
he's ruined, and Millwood's hopes of farther profits
there are at an end.

BLUNT.

That's no more than we all expected.

LUCY.

Being called by his master to make up his accounts,
he was forced to quit his house and service and   30
wisely flies to Millwood for relief and entertainment.

BLUNT.

I have not heard of this before! How did she receive
him?

LUCY.

As you would expect: she wondered what he
meant, was astonished at his impudence, and, with   35
an air of modesty peculiar to herself, swore so
heartily that she never saw him before that she put
me out of countenance.

BLUNT.

That's much indeed! But how did Barnwell
behave?   40

LUCY.

He grieved and, at length enraged at this barbarous
treatment, was preparing to be gone, when,
making toward the door, he showed a sum of
money which he had brought[f] from his master's—
the last he's ever like to have from thence.   45

BLUNT.

But then Millwood?

LUCY.

Aye, she with her usual address returned to her old
arts of lying, swearing, and dissembling, hung on
his neck and wept and swore 'twas meant in jest,
till the amorous youth[g] melted into tears, threw   50
the money into her lap, and swore he had rather
die than think her false.

BLUNT.

Strange infatuation!

LUCY.

But what followed was stranger still. As doubts and
fears, followed by reconcilement, ever increase love   55
where the passion is sincere, so in him it caused
so wild a transport of excessive fondness, such joy,
such grief, such pleasure, and such anguish, that
nature in him seemed sinking with the weight and
the charmed soul disposed to quit his breast for   60
hers. Just then, when every passion with lawless
anarchy prevailed and reason was in the raging
tempest lost, the cruel, artful Millwood prevailed
upon the wretched youth to promise—what I
tremble but to think on.   65

BLUNT.

I am amazed! What can it be?

LUCY.

You will be more so to hear it is to attempt the
life of his nearest relation and best benefactor—

BLUNT.

His uncle, whom we have often heard him speak
of as a gentleman of a large estate and fair character   70
in the country, where he lives.

LUCY.

The same. She was no sooner possessed of the last,
dear purchase of his ruin, but her avarice, insatiate
as the grave, demanded this horrid sacrifice.
Barnwell's near relation and unsuspected virtue   75
must give too easy means to seize the good man's
treasure, whose blood must seal the dreadful secret
and prevent the terrors of her guilty fears.

BLUNT.

Is it possible she could persuade him to do an act like
that! He is by nature honest, grateful, com-   80
passionate, and generous. And though his love and
her artful persuasions have wrought him to practice
what he most abhors, yet we all can witness for him
with what reluctance he has still complied! So many
tears he shed o'er each offense as might, if possible,   85
sanctify theft and make a merit of a crime.

LUCY.

'Tis true, at the naming the murder of his uncle
he started into rage and, breaking from her arms
where she till then had held him with well-
dissembled love and false endearments, called her   90
cruel monster, devil, and told her she was born for
his destruction. She thought it not for her purpose
to meet his rage with rage but affected a most
passionate fit of grief, railed at her fate, and cursed
her wayward stars that still her wants* should force   95
her to press him to act such deeds as she must
needs abhor as well as he, but told him necessity
had no law and love no bounds, that therefore he
never truly loved but meant in her necessity to
forsake her. Then kneeled and swore that since, by   100
his refusal, he had given her cause to doubt his
love, she never would see him more unless, to
prove it true, he robbed his uncle to supply her
wants and murdered him to keep it from discovery.

BLUNT.

I am astonished! What said he?   105

LUCY.

Speechless he stood, but in his face you might have
read that various passions tore his very soul. Oft
he in anguish threw his eyes towards heaven and

then as often bent their beams on her, then wept and groaned and beat his troubled breast. At length, with horror not to be expressed, he cried, "Thou cursed fair! Have I not given dreadful proofs of love! What drew me from my youthful innocence to stain my then unspotted soul, but love? What caused me to rob my worthy gentle master, but cursed love? What makes me now a fugitive from his service, loathed by myself and scorned by all the world, but love? What fills my eyes with tears, my soul with torture never felt on this side death before? Why love, love, love. And why, above all, do I resolve"—for, tearing his hair, he cried, "I do resolve"—"to kill my uncle?"

BLUNT.
Was she not moved? It makes me weep to hear the sad relation.

LUCY.
Yes, with joy that she had gained her point. She gave him no time to cool but urged him to attempt it instantly. He's now gone. If he performs it and escapes, there's more money for her. If not, he'll ne'er return, and then she's fairly rid of him.

BLUNT.
'Tis time the world was rid of such a monster.

LUCY.
If we don't do our endeavors to prevent this murder, we are as bad as she.

BLUNT.
I'm afraid it is too late.

LUCY.
Perhaps not. Her barbarity to Barnwell makes me hate her. We have run too great a length with her already. I did not think her or myself so wicked as I find upon reflection we are.

BLUNT.
'Tis true we have all been too much so. But there is something so horrid in murder that all other crimes seem nothing when compared to that. I would not be involved in the guilt of that for all the world.

LUCY.
Nor I, Heaven knows. Therefore let us clear ourselves by doing all that is in our power to prevent it. I have just thought of a way that to me seems probable. Will you join with me to detect this cursed design?

BLUNT.
With all my heart.[h] He who knows of a murder intended to be committed and does not discover* it, in the eye of the law and reason, is a murderer.

LUCY.
Let us lose no time. I'll acquaint you with the particulars as we go.

Exeunt.

Scene iii. A walk at some distance
from a country seat.[10]

Enter Barnwell.

BARNWELL.
A dismal gloom obscures the face of day. Either the sun has slipped behind a cloud or journeys down the west of heaven with more than common speed to avoid the sight of what I'm doomed to act. Since I set forth on this accursed design, where'er I tread, methinks, the solid earth trembles beneath my feet. Yonder limpid stream, whose hoary fall has made a natural cascade, as I passed by in doleful accents seemed to murmur, "Murder." The earth, the air, and water seemed concerned, but that's not strange. The world is punished and Nature feels a shock when Providence permits a good man's fall. Just Heaven! Then what should I be! For him that was my father's only brother and since his death has been to me a father, who took me up an infant and an orphan, reared me with tenderest care and still indulged me with most paternal fondness. Yet here I stand avowed his destined murderer. I stiffen with horror at my own impiety. 'Tis yet unperformed. What if I quit my bloody purpose and fly the place! (*Going, then stops.*) But whither, oh whither, shall I fly! My master's once friendly doors are ever shut against me, and without money Millwood will never see me more, and life is not to be endured without her. She's got such firm possession of my heart and governs there with such despotic sway. Aye, there's the cause of all my sin and sorrow. 'Tis more than love: 'tis the fever of the soul and madness of desire. In vain does nature, reason, conscience, all oppose it.

---

10 country seat] the residence of a country gentleman, a country house

The impetuous passion bears down all before it and 30
drives me on to lust, to theft, and murder. Oh
conscience! feeble guide to virtue, who only shows
us when we go astray but wants* the power to stop
us in our course. Hah! in yonder shady walk I see my
uncle. He's alone. Now for my disguise. (*Plucks out* 35
a vizor.) This is his hour of private meditation. Thus
daily he prepares his soul for heaven whilst I—but
what have I to do with heaven! Hah! No struggles,
conscience—
Hence! hence remorse and every thought that's 40
good;
The storm that lust began must end in blood.

Puts on the vizor and draws a pistol. Exit.

Scene iv. A close walk in a wood.

Enter Uncle.

UNCLE.

If I was superstitious I should fear some danger
lurked unseen, or death were nigh. A heavy
melancholy clouds my spirits. My imagination is
filled with gashly[11] forms of dreary graves and
bodies changed by death, when the pale, lengthened 5
visage attracts each weeping eye and fills the musing
soul at once with grief and horror, pity and aversion.
I will indulge the thought. The wise man prepares
himself for death by making it familiar to his mind.
When strong reflections hold the mirror near, and 10
the living in the dead behold their future selves, how
does each inordinate passion and desire cease or
sicken at the view! The mind scarce moves. The
blood, curdling and chilled, creeps slowly through
the veins. Fixed, still, and motionless we stand, so 15
like the solemn object of our thoughts we are almost
at present what we must be hereafter, till curiosity
awakes the soul and sets it on inquiry.

Enter George Barnwell at a distance.

Oh Death, thou strange, mysterious power, seen
everyday yet never understood but by the 20
incommunicative dead, what art thou? The
extensive mind of man—that with a thought
circles the earth's vast globe, sinks to the center or

---

11 gashly] ghastly

ascends above the stars, that worlds exotic finds or
thinks it finds—thy thick clouds attempts to pass 25
in vain, lost and bewildered in the horrid gloom.
Defeated she returns more doubtful than before,
of nothing certain but of labor lost.

*During this speech Barnwell sometimes presents the
pistol and draws it back again.*

BARNWELL.
Oh, 'tis impossible!

*He throws down the pistol. His uncle starts and
attempts to draw his sword.*

UNCLE.
A man so near me, armed and masked! 30
BARNWELL.
Nay, then there's no retreat. (*Plucks a poniard from
his bosom and stabs him.*)
UNCLE.
Oh! I am slain! All-gracious Heaven regard the
prayer of thy dying servant. Bless with thy choicest
blessings my dearest nephew. Forgive my murderer
and take my fleeting soul to endless mercy. 35

*Barnwell throws off his mask, runs to him, and,
kneeling by him, raises and chafes him.*

BARNWELL.
Expiring saint! Oh murdered, martyred uncle! Lift
up your dying eyes and view your nephew in your
murderer. Oh do not look so tenderly upon me.
Let indignation lighten from your eyes and blast
me ere you die. By Heaven, he weeps in pity of 40
my woes. Tears, tears, for blood. The murdered in
the agonies of death weeps for his murderer. Oh
speak your pious purpose, pronounce my pardon
then, and take me with you. He would, but
cannot. Oh why, with such fond affection do you 45
press my murdering hand! What! will you kiss me!

Barnwell kisses his uncle, who groans and dies.

Life, that hovered on his lips till he had sealed my
pardon, in that kiss expired. He's gone forever, and
oh! I follow. (*Swoons away upon his uncle's dead
body.*) Do I still live to press the suffering bosom 50
of the earth? Do I still breathe and taint with my
infectious breath the wholesome air! Let Heaven

from its high throne, in justice or in mercy, now look down on that dear, murdered saint, and me the murderer. And if his vengeance spares, let pity strike and end my wretched being. Murder the worst of crimes and parricide the worst of murders, and this the worst of parricides. Cain, who stands on record from the birth of time and must to its last, final period as accursed, slew a brother favored above him. Detested Nero, by another's hand, dispatched a mother that he feared and hated. But I, with my own hand, have murdered a brother, mother, father, and a friend most loving and beloved. This execrable act of mine's without a parallel. Oh may it ever stand alone, the last of murders as it is the worst.

The rich man thus, in torment and despair,
Preferred[12] his vain but charitable prayer.
The fool, his own soul lost, would fain be wise
For others' good, but Heaven his suit denies.[13]
By laws and means well-known we stand or fall,
And one eternal rule remains for all.

[Scene closes on Barnwell and the body of his uncle.]

Act IV, scene i. A room in Thorowgood's house.

Enter Maria.

MARIA.

How falsely do they judge who censure or applaud as we're afflicted or rewarded here. I know I am unhappy yet cannot charge myself with any crime more than the common frailties of our kind that should provoke just Heaven to mark me out for sufferings so uncommon and severe. Falsely to accuse ourselves Heaven must abhor. Then it is just and right that innocence should suffer, for Heaven must be just in all its ways. Perhaps by that they are kept from moral evils much worse than penal, or more improved in virtue. Or may not the lesser ills that they sustain be made the means of greater good to others? Might all the joyless days and sleepless nights that I have passed but purchase peace for thee,

Thou dear, dear cause of all my grief and pain.
Small were the loss and infinite the gain,
Though to the grave in secret love I pine,
So life and fame and happiness were thine.

Enter Trueman.

What news of Barnwell?

TRUEMAN.

None. I have sought him with the greatest diligence, but all in vain.

MARIA.

Does my father yet suspect the cause of his absence?

TRUEMAN.

All appeared so just and fair to him, it is not possible he ever should. But his absence will no longer be concealed. Your father's wise, and though he seems to hearken to the friendly excuses I would make for Barnwell, yet I am afraid he regards 'em only as such, without suffering them to influence his judgment.

MARIA.

How does the unhappy youth defeat all our designs to serve him! Yet I can never repent what we have done. Should he return, 'twill make his reconciliation with my father easier and preserve him from future reproach from a malicious, unforgiving world.

Enter Thorowgood and Lucy.

THOROWGOOD.

This woman here has given me a sad and—bating some circumstances—too probable account of Barnwell's defection.

LUCY.

I am sorry, sir, that my frank confession of my former, unhappy course of life should cause you to suspect my truth on this occasion.

THOROWGOOD.

It is not that. Your confession has in it all the appearance of truth. (*To them.*) Among many other particulars, she informs me that Barnwell has been influenced to break his trust and wrong me at several times of considerable sums of money. Now, as I know this to be false, I would fain doubt the whole of her relation, too dreadful to be willingly believed.

---

12 preferred] offered

13 rich man ... denies] See Luke 16:19-31 for the story of Dives, as the rich man was called in tradition, and Lazarus.

MARIA.

Sir, your pardon. I find myself on a sudden so 50
indisposed that I must retire. (*Aside.*) Providence
opposes all attempts to save him. Poor, ruined
Barnwell! Wretched, lost Maria! (*Exit.*)

THOROWGOOD.

How am I distressed on every side: pity for that
unhappy youth, fear for the life of a much valued 55
friend, and then my child, the only joy and hope of
my declining life. Her melancholy increases hourly
and gives me painful apprehensions of her loss.—
Oh Trueman! This person informs me that your
friend, at the instigation of an impious woman, is 60
gone to rob and murder his venerable uncle.

TRUEMAN.

Oh execrable deed! I am blasted with the horror
of the thought!

LUCY.

This delay may ruin all.

THOROWGOOD.

What to do or think I know not. That he ever 65
wronged me I know is false. The rest may be so
too. There's all my hope.

TRUEMAN.

Trust not to that. Rather suppose all true than lose
a moment's time. Even now the horrid deed may
be adoing—dreadful imagination!—or it may be 70
done, and we are vainly debating on the means to
prevent what is already past.

THOROWGOOD. [*Aside.*]

This earnestness convinces me that he knows more
than he has yet discovered.*—What ho! Without
there! Who waits? 75

Enter a servant.

Order the groom to saddle the swiftest horse and
prepare to set out with speed. An affair of life and
death demands his diligence.

Exit servant.

[*To Lucy.*] For you, whose behavior on this
occasion I have no time to commend as it deserves, 80
I must engage your farther assistance. Return and
observe this Millwood till I come. I have your
directions and will follow you as soon as possible.

Exit Lucy.

Trueman, you I am sure would not be idle on this
occasion. (*Exit.*) 85

TRUEMAN.

He only who is a friend can judge of my distress.

Exit.

Scene ii. Millwood's house.

Enter Millwood.

MILLWOOD.

I wish I knew the event of his design. The attempt,
without success, would ruin him. Well! What have
I to apprehend from that? I fear too much. The
mischief being only intended, his friends, in pity
of his youth, turn all their rage on me. I should 5
have thought of that before. Suppose the deed
done; then, and then only I shall be secure. Or
what if he returns without attempting it at all?

Enter Barnwell bloody.

But he is here, and I have done him wrong. His
bloody hands show he has done the deed, but show 10
he wants* the prudence to conceal it.

BARNWELL.

Where shall I hide me? Whither shall I fly to avoid
the swift, unerring hand of justice?

MILLWOOD.

Dismiss your fears. Though thousands had
pursued you to the door, yet being entered here 15
you are safe as innocence. I have such a cavern by
art so cunningly contrived that the piercing eyes
of jealousy and revenge may search in vain nor find
the entrance to the safe retreat. There will I hide
you if any danger's near. 20

BARNWELL.

Oh hide me from myself, if it be possible. For while
I bear my conscience in my bosom, though I were
hid where man's eye never saw nor light e'er dawned,
'twere all in vain. For oh! that inmate, that impartial
judge, will try, convict, and sentence me for murder 25
and execute me with never-ending torments. Behold
these hands all crimsoned o'er with my dear uncle's
blood! Here's a sight to make a statue start with
horror or turn a living man into a statue.

MILLWOOD.

Ridiculous! Then it seems you are afraid of your 30

own shadow or what's less than a shadow, your conscience.

BARNWELL.

Though to man unknown I did the accursed act, what can we hide from Heaven's all-seeing eye?

MILLWOOD.

No more of this stuff. What advantage have you made of his death? Or what advantage may yet be made of it? Did you secure the keys of his treasure? Those no doubt were about him? What gold, what jewels, or what else of value have you brought me?

BARNWELL.

Think you I added sacrilege to murder? Oh! had you seen him as his life flowed from him in a crimson flood and heard him praying for me by the double name of nephew and murderer (alas, alas! he knew not then that his nephew was his murderer), how would you have wished as I did, though you had a thousand years of life to come, to have given them all to have lengthened his one hour. But being dead, I fled the sight of what my hands had done. Nor could I, to have gained the empire of the world, have violated by theft his sacred corpse.

MILLWOOD.

Whining, preposterous, canting villain: to murder your uncle, rob him of life (nature's first, last, dear prerogative, after which there's no injury) then fear to take what he no longer wanted and bring to me your penury and guilt. Do you think I'll hazard my reputation, nay my life, to entertain* you?

BARNWELL.

Oh, Millwood! this from thee. But I have done. If you hate me, if you wish me dead, then are you happy. For oh! 'tis sure my grief will quickly end me.

MILLWOOD. (*Aside*.)

In his madness he will discover* all and involve me in his ruin. We are on a precipice from whence there's no retreat for both. Then, to preserve myself. (*Pauses*.) There is no other way, 'tis dreadful, but reflection comes too late when danger's pressing and there's no room for choice. It must be done. (*Rings a bell*.)

Enter a servant.

Fetch me an officer and seize this villain. He has confessed himself a murderer. Should I let him escape, I justly might be thought as bad as he.

Exit servant.

BARNWELL.

Oh Millwood! Sure you do not, cannot mean it. Stop the messenger, upon my knees I beg you, call him back. 'Tis fit I die indeed, but not by you. I will this instant deliver myself into the hands of justice, indeed I will, for death is all I wish. But thy ingratitude so tears my wounded soul, 'tis worse ten thousand times than death with torture.

MILLWOOD.

Call it what you will, I am willing to live, and live secure, which nothing but your death can warrant.

BARNWELL.

If there be a pitch of wickedness that seats the author beyond the reach of vengeance, you must be secure. But what remains for me but a dismal dungeon, hard-galling fetters, an awful* trial, and ignominious death, justly to fall unpitied and abhorred? After death to be suspended between heaven and earth, a dreadful spectacle, the warning and horror of a gaping crowd.[14] This I could bear, nay wish not to avoid, had it but come from any hand but thine.

Enter Blunt, officer and attendants.

MILLWOOD.

Heaven defend me! Conceal a murderer! Here sir, take this youth into your custody. I accuse him of murder and will appear to make good my charge.

They seize him.

BARNWELL.

To whom, of what, or how shall I complain? I'll not accuse her, the hand of Heaven is in it, and this the punishment of lust and parricide. Yet Heaven, that justly cuts me off, still suffers her to live, perhaps to punish others. Tremendous mercy! So fiends are cursed with immortality, to be the executioners of Heaven.

Be warned ye youths who see my sad despair,

---

14 After … crowd] Criminals were hanged publicly, their bodies left dangling on the gallows until collected by family or friends. The bodies of the most notorious criminals were kept to be hung up for public display on gibbets until they moldered away.

Avoid lewd women, false as they are fair;   100
By reason guided, honest joys pursue.
The fair, to honor and to virtue true,
Just to herself, will ne'er be false to you.
By my example learn to shun my fate
(How wretched is the man who's wise too late?),   105
Ere innocence and fame and life be lost;
Here purchase wisdom cheaply, at my cost.

Exeunt Barnwell, officer and attendants.

MILLWOOD.

Where's Lucy? Why is she absent at such a time?

BLUNT.

Would I had been so too. Lucy will soon be here
and, I hope, to thy confusion, thou devil!   110

MILLWOOD.

Insolent! This, to me?

BLUNT.

The worst that we know of the Devil is that he
first seduces to sin and then betrays to punishment.
(*Exit.*)

MILLWOOD.

They disapprove of my conduct, then, and mean
to take this opportunity to set up for themselves.   115
My ruin is resolved. I see my danger but scorn
both it and them. I am not born to fall by such
weak instruments. (*Going.*)

Enter Thorowgood.

THOROWGOOD.

Where is this scandal of her own sex and curse of
ours?   120

MILLWOOD.

What means this insolence? Who do you seek?

THOROWGOOD.

Millwood.

MILLWOOD.

Well, you have found her then. I am Millwood.

THOROWGOOD.

Then you are the most impious wretch that e'er
the sun beheld.   125

MILLWOOD.

From your appearance I should have expected
wisdom and moderation, but your manners belie
your aspect. What is your business here? I know
you not.

THOROWGOOD.

Hereafter you may know me better. I am   130
Barnwell's master.

MILLWOOD.

Then you are master to a villain, which, I think,
is not much to your credit.

THOROWGOOD.

Had he been as much above thy arts as my credit
is superior to thy malice, I need not have blushed   135
to own him.

MILLWOOD.

My arts? I don't understand you, sir! If he has done
amiss, what's that to me? Was he my servant, or
yours? You should have taught him better.

THOROWGOOD.

Why should I wonder to find such uncommon   140
impudence in one arrived to such a height of
wickedness? When innocence is banished, modesty
soon follows. Know, sorceress, I'm not ignorant of
any of the arts by which you first deceived the
unwary youth. I know how, step by step, you've led   145
him on—reluctant and unwilling—from crime to
crime to this last horrid act which you contrived and,
by your cursed wiles, even forced him to commit[i].

MILLWOOD. (*Aside.*)

Hah! Lucy has got the advantage and accused me
first. Unless I can turn the accusation and fix it   150
upon her and Blunt, I am lost.

THOROWGOOD.

Had I known your cruel design sooner, it had been
prevented. To see you punished as the law directs is
all that now remains. Poor satisfaction! For he,
innocent as he is compared to you, must suffer too.   155
But Heaven, who knows our frame and graciously
distinguishes between frailty and presumption, will
make a difference though man cannot, who sees not
the heart but only judges by the outward action.

MILLWOOD.

I find, sir, we are both unhappy in our servants. I   160
was surprised at such ill treatment without cause
from a gentleman of your appearance and therefore
too hastily returned it. For which I ask your
pardon. I now perceive you have been so far
imposed on as to think me engaged in a former   165
correspondence with your servant and, some way
or other, accessory to his undoing.

THOROWGOOD.

I charge you as the cause, the sole cause, of all his guilt and all his suffering, of all he now endures and must endure till a violent and shameful death 170 shall put a dreadful period to his life and miseries together.

MILLWOOD.

'Tis very strange, but who's secure from scandal and detraction? So far from contributing to his ruin, I never spoke to him till since that fatal 175 accident, which I lament as much as you. 'Tis true, I have a servant on whose account he has of late frequented my house. If she has abused my good opinion of her, am I to blame? Hasn't Barnwell done the same by you? 180

THOROWGOOD.

I hear you. Pray go on.

MILLWOOD.

I have been informed he had a violent passion for her, and she for him. But till now I always thought it innocent. I know her poor and given to expensive pleasures. Now who can tell but she may 185 have influenced the amorous youth to commit this murder to supply her extravagances; it must be so. I now recollect a thousand circumstances that confirm it. I'll have her, and a manservant that I suspect as an accomplice, secured immediately. I 190 hope, sir, you will lay aside your ill-grounded suspicions of me and join to punish the real contrivers of this bloody deed. (*Offers to go.*)

THOROWGOOD.

Madam, you pass not this way. I see your design, but shall protect them from your malice. 195

MILLWOOD.

I hope you will not use your influence and the credit of your name to screen such guilty wretches. Consider, sir, the wickedness of persuading a thoughtless youth to such a crime.

THOROWGOOD.

I do, and of betraying him when it was done. 200

MILLWOOD.

That which you call betraying him may convince you of my innocence. She who loves him, though she contrived the murder, would never have delivered him into the hands of justice as I—struck with horror at his crimes—have done. 205

THOROWGOOD. [*Aside.*]

How should an unexperienced youth escape her snares? The powerful magic of her wit and form might betray the wisest to simple dotage and fire the blood that age had froze long since. Even I, that with just prejudice came prepared, had by her artful story 210 been deceived but that my strong conviction of her guilt makes even a doubt impossible.—Those whom subtly you would accuse, you know are your accusers and—what proves unanswerably their innocence and your guilt—they accused you before 215 the deed was done and did all that was in their power to have prevented it.

MILLWOOD.

Sir, you are very hard to be convinced. But I have such a proof which, when produced, will silence all objections. (*Exit.*) 220

Enter Lucy, Trueman, Blunt, officers, etc.

LUCY.

Gentlemen, pray place yourselves some on one side of that door and some on the other. Watch her entrance, and act as your prudence shall direct you. (*To Thorowgood.*) This way and note her behavior. I have observed her; she's driven to the last 225 extremity and is forming some desperate resolution. I guess at her design.

Enter Millwood with a pistol. Trueman secures her.

TRUEMAN.

Here thy power of doing mischief ends, deceitful, cruel, bloody woman!

MILLWOOD.

Fool, hypocrite, villain—man! Thou canst not call 230 me that.

TRUEMAN.

To call thee woman were to wrong the sex, thou devil!

MILLWOOD.

That imaginary being is an emblem of thy cursed sex collected, a mirror wherein each particular man 235 may see his own likeness and that of all mankind.

THOROWGOOD.

Think not by aggravating the faults of others to extenuate thy own, of which the abuse of such uncommon perfections of mind and body is not the least. 240

MILLWOOD.

If such I had, well may I curse your barbarous sex who robbed me of 'em ere I knew their worth then left me, too late, to count their value by their loss. Another and another spoiler came, and all my gain was poverty and reproach. My soul disdained, and yet disdains, dependence and contempt. Riches, no matter by what means obtained, I saw secured the worst of men from both. I found it therefore necessary to be rich, and to that end I summoned all my arts. You call 'em wicked, be it so; they were such as my conversation* with your sex had furnished me withal.

THOROWGOOD.

Sure none but the worst of men conversed with thee.

MILLWOOD.

Men of all degrees and all professions I have known, yet found no difference but in their several capacities. All were alike wicked to the utmost of their power. In pride, contention, avarice, cruelty, and revenge, the reverend priesthood were my unerring guides. From suburb magistrates, who live by ruined reputations as the unhospitable natives of Cornwall do by shipwrecks,[15] I learned that to charge my innocent neighbors with my crimes was to merit their protection. For to screen the guilty is the less scandalous when many are suspected, and detraction, like darkness and death, blackens all objects and levels all distinction. Such are your venal magistrates, who favor none but such as by their office they are sworn to punish. With them not to be guilty is the worst of crimes, and large fees, privately paid, is every needful virtue.

THOROWGOOD.

Your practice has sufficiently discovered* your contempt of laws both human and divine. No wonder then that you should hate the officers of both.

MILLWOOD.

I know you and I hate you all. I expect no mercy and I ask for none.[j] I followed my inclinations, and that the best of you does every day. All actions seem[k] alike natural and indifferent to man and beast who devour, or are devoured, as they meet with others weaker or stronger than themselves.

THOROWGOOD.

What pity it is, a mind so comprehensive, daring, and inquisitive, should be a stranger to religion's sweet and powerful charms.

MILLWOOD.

I am not fool enough to be an atheist, though I have known enough of men's hypocrisy to make a thousand simple women so. Whatever religion is in itself, as practiced by mankind it has caused the evils you say it was designed to cure. War, plague, and famine has not destroyed so many of the human race as this pretended piety has done, and with such barbarous cruelty, as if the only way to honor Heaven were to turn the present world into Hell.

THOROWGOOD.

Truth is truth, though from an enemy and spoke in malice. You bloody, blind, and superstitious bigots, how will you answer this?

MILLWOOD.

What are your laws, of which you make your boast, but the fool's wisdom and the coward's valor, the instrument and screen of all your villainies, by which you punish in others what you act yourselves or would have acted had you been in their circumstances. The judge who condemns the poor man for being a thief had been a thief himself had he been poor. Thus you go on deceiving and being deceived, harrassing, plaguing, and destroy-ing one another, but women are your universal prey:

Women, by whom you are, the source of joy,
With cruel arts you labor to destroy.
A thousand ways our ruin you pursue,
Yet blame in us those arts first taught by you.
Oh! may from hence each violated maid
By flatt'ring, faithless, barb'rous man betrayed,
When robbed of innocence and virgin fame,
From your destruction raise a nobler name:

---

15 suburb magistrates … shipwrecks] The suburbs were the areas immediately outside the City, many of them disreputable. Magistrates lived by fees collected for administering the law, and so profited from charges and accusations. The rocky coast of Cornwall was especially dangerous to shipping, and the more so as people living there would sometimes set out false beacons so that ships might founder and their goods be retrieved as salvage.

To right their sex's wrongs devote their mind, 315
And future Millwoods prove to plague mankind.

[Exeunt.]

Act V, scene i. A room in a prison.

Enter Thorowgood, Blunt and Lucy.

THOROWGOOD.

I have recommended to Barnwell a reverend divine whose judgment and integrity I am well acquainted with. Nor has Millwood been neglected, but she, unhappy woman, still obstinate, refuses his assistance. 5

LUCY.

This pious charity to the afflicted well becomes your character. Yet pardon me, sir, if I wonder you were not at their trial.

THOROWGOOD.

I knew it was impossible to save him, and I and my family* bear so great a part in his distress that 10 to have been present would have aggravated our sorrows without relieving his.

BLUNT.

It was mournful indeed. Barnwell's youth and modest deportment as he passed drew tears from every eye. When placed at the bar and arraigned 15 before the reverend judges, with many tears and interrupting sobs he confessed and aggravated his offenses without accusing or once reflecting on Millwood, the shameless author of his ruin, who dauntless and unconcerned stood by his side 20 viewing with visible pride and contempt the vast assembly, who all with sympathizing sorrow wept for the wretched youth. Millwood, when called upon to answer, loudly insisted upon her innocence and made an artful and a bold defense. 25 But finding all in vain, the impartial jury and the learned bench concurring to find her guilty, how did she curse herself, poor Barnwell, us, her judges, all mankind! But what could that avail? She was condemned and is this day to suffer with him. 30

THOROWGOOD.

The time draws on. I am going to visit Barnwell, as you are Millwood.

LUCY.

We have not wronged her, yet I dread this interview. She's proud, impatient, wrathful, and unforgiving. To be the branded instruments of 35 vengeance, to suffer in her shame and sympathize with her in all she suffers is the tribute we must pay for our former, ill-spent lives and long confederacy with her in wickedness.

THOROWGOOD.

Happy for you it ended when it did. What you have 40 done against Millwood I know proceeded from a just abhorrence of her crimes, free from interest, malice, or revenge. Proselytes to virtue should be encouraged. Pursue your purposed reformation, and know me hereafter for your friend. 45

LUCY.

This is a blessing as unhoped for as unmerited, but Heaven that snatched us from impending ruin sure intends you as its instrument to secure us from apostasy.

THOROWGOOD.

With gratitude to impute your deliverance to 50 Heaven is just. Many, less virtuously disposed than Barnwell was, have never fallen in the manner he has done. May not such owe their safety rather to Providence than to themselves? With pity and compassion let us judge him. Great were his faults, 55 but strong was the temptation. Let his ruin learn us diffidence, humanity, and circumspection. For we who wonder at his fate, perhaps had we like him been tried, like him we had fallen too.

[Exeunt.]

Scene ii. A dungeon, a table and lamp.

Barnwell reading. Enter Thorowgood at a distance.

THOROWGOOD.

There see the bitter fruits of passion's detested reign and sensual appetite indulged: severe reflections, penitence, and tears.

BARNWELL.

My honored, injured master, whose goodness has covered me a thousand times with shame, forgive 5 this last, unwilling disrespect. Indeed I saw you not.

THOROWGOOD.

'Tis well. I hope you were better employed in viewing of yourself. Your journey's long, your time for preparation almost spent. I sent a reverend divine to teach you to improve it and should be glad to hear of his success.

BARNWELL.

The Word of Truth, which he recommended for my constant companion in this my sad retirement, has at length removed the doubts I labored under. From thence I've learned the infinite extent of heavenly mercy, that my offences though great are not unpardonable, and that 'tis not my interest only but my duty to believe and to rejoice in that hope. So shall Heaven receive the glory and future penitents the profit of my example.

THOROWGOOD.

Proceed.[1]

BARNWELL.

'Tis wonderful that words should charm despair, speak peace and pardon to a murderer's conscience. But truth and mercy flow in every sentence, attended with force and energy divine. How shall I describe my present state of mind? I hope in doubt, and trembling I rejoice. I feel my grief increase even as my fears give way. Joy and gratitude now supply more tears than horror and anguish of despair before.

THOROWGOOD.

These are the genuine signs of true repentance, the only preparatory, the certain way to everlasting peace. Oh the joy it gives to see a soul formed and prepared for heaven! For this the faithful minister devotes himself to meditation, abstinence, and prayer, shunning the vain delights of sensual joys, and daily dies that others may live forever. For this he turns the sacred volumes o'er and spends his life in painful search of truth. The love of riches and the lust of power he looks on with just contempt and detestation, who only counts for wealth the souls he wins and whose highest ambition is to serve mankind. If the reward of all his pains be to preserve one soul from wandering or turn one from the error of his ways, how does he then rejoice and own his little labors overpaid.

BARNWELL.

What do I owe for all your generous kindness! But though I cannot, Heaven can and will reward you.

THOROWGOOD.

To see thee thus is joy too great for words. Farewell. Heaven strengthen thee. Farewell.

BARNWELL.

Oh! Sir, there's something I would say if my sad, swelling heart would give me leave.

THOROWGOOD.

Give it vent awhile, and try.

BARNWELL.

I had a friend. 'Tis true I am unworthy, yet methinks your generous example might persuade. Could I not see him once before I go from whence there's no return?

THOROWGOOD.

He's coming, and as much thy friend as ever. (*Aside.*) But I'll not anticipate his sorrow. Too soon he'll see the sad effect of his contagious ruin. This torrent of domestic misery bears too hard upon me. I must retire to indulge a weakness I find impossible to overcome.——Much loved and much lamented youth, farewell. Heaven strengthen thee. Eternally farewell.

BARNWELL.

The best of masters and of men, farewell. While I live, let me not want* your prayers.

THOROWGOOD.

Thou shalt not. Thy peace being made with Heaven, death's already vanquished. Bear a little longer the pains that attend this transitory life, and cease from pain forever. (*Exit.*)

BARNWELL.

Perhaps I shall. I find a power within that bears my soul above the fears of death and, spite of conscious shame and guilt, gives me a taste of pleasure more than mortal.

Enter Trueman and keeper.

KEEPER.

Sir, there's the prisoner. (*Exit.*)

BARNWELL.

Trueman! My friend, whom I so wished to see, yet now he's here I dare not look upon him. (*Weeps.*)

TRUEMAN.

Oh Barnwell! Barnwell!

BARNWELL.

Mercy! Mercy, gracious Heaven! For death, but not for this was I prepared.

TRUEMAN.

What have I suffered since I saw you last? What

pain has absence given me? But oh! to see thee thus!

BARNWELL.

I know it is dreadful! I feel the anguish of thy generous soul. But I was born to murder all who love me. 85

Both weep.

TRUEMAN.

I came not to reproach you. I thought to bring you comfort, but I'm deceived, for I have none to give. I came to share thy sorrow, but cannot bear my own. 90

BARNWELL.

My sense of guilt indeed you cannot know. 'Tis what the good and innocent, like you, can ne'er conceive. But other griefs at present I have none but what I feel for you. In your sorrow I read you love me still, but yet methinks 'tis strange when I consider what I am. 95

TRUEMAN.

No more of that. I can remember nothing but thy virtues, thy honest, tender friendship, our former happy state and present misery. Oh had you trusted me when first the fair seducer tempted you, all might have been prevented. 100

BARNWELL.

Alas, thou knowest not what a wretch I've been! Breach of friendship was my first and least offence. So far was I lost to goodness, so devoted to the author of my ruin that, had she insisted on my murdering thee, I think I should have done it. 105

TRUEMAN.

Prithee aggravate thy faults no more.

BARNWELL.

I think I should! Thus good and generous as you are, I should have murdered you! 110

TRUEMAN.

We have not yet embraced and may be interrupted. Come to my arms.

BARNWELL.

Never, never will I taste such joys on earth. Never will I so soothe my just remorse. Are those honest arms and faithful bosom fit to embrace and to support a murderer? These iron fetters only shall clasp, and flinty pavement bear me (*Throwing* 115

himself on the ground.), even these too good for such a bloody monster.

TRUEMAN.

Shall fortune sever those whom friendship joined! Thy miseries cannot lay thee so low but love will find thee.[m] Here will we offer to stern calamity, this place[n] the altar and ourselves the sacrifice. Our mutual groans shall echo to each other through the dreary vault. Our sighs shall number the moments as they pass, and mingling tears communicate such anguish as words were never made to express. 120

BARNWELL.

Then be it so. (*Rising.*) Since you propose an intercourse of woe, pour all your griefs into my breast and in exchange take mine. (*Embracing.*) Where's now the anguish that you promised? You've taken mine and make me no return. Sure peace and comfort dwell within these arms, and sorrow can't approach me while I'm here! This, too, is the work of Heaven which, having before spoke peace and pardon to me, now sends thee to confirm it. Oh take, take some of the joy that overflows my breast! 130 135

TRUEMAN.

I do, I do. Almighty Power, how have you made us capable to bear at once the extremes of pleasure and of pain? 140

Enter keeper.

KEEPER.

Sir.

TRUEMAN.

I come.

Exit keeper.

BARNWELL.

Must you leave me! Death would soon have parted us forever.

TRUEMAN.

Oh my Barnwell, there's yet another task behind. Again your heart must bleed for others' woes. 145

BARNWELL.

To meet and part with you I thought was all I had to do on earth! What is there more for me to do or suffer?

TRUEMAN.

I dread to tell thee, yet it must be known. Maria. 150

BARNWELL.

Our master's fair and virtuous daughter!

TRUEMAN.

The same.

BARNWELL.

No misfortune, I hope, has reached that lovely maid! Preserve her, Heaven, from every ill to show mankind that goodness is your care. 155

TRUEMAN.

Thy, thy misfortunes, my unhappy friend, have reached her. Whatever you and I have felt and more, if more be possible, she feels for you.

BARNWELL. (*Aside.*)

I know he doth abhor a lie and would not trifle with his dying friend. This is, indeed, the bitterness 160 of death!

TRUEMAN.

You must remember, for we all observed it, for some time past a heavy melancholy weighed her down. Disconsolate she seemed, and pined and languished from a cause unknown till, hearing of 165 your dreadful fate, the long-stifled flame blazed out. She wept, she wrung her hands and tore her hair, and in the transport of her grief discovered* her own lost state whilst she lamented yours.

BARNWELL.

Will all the pain I feel restore thy ease, lovely, 170 unhappy maid? (*Weeping.*) Why did not you let me die and never know it?

TRUEMAN.

It was impossible. She makes no secret of her passion for you and is determined to see you ere you die. She waits for me to introduce her. (*Exit.*) 175

BARNWELL.

Vain, busy thoughts be still! What avails it to think on what I might have been? I now am—what I've made myself.

Enter Trueman and Maria.

TRUEMAN.

Madam, reluctant I lead you to this dismal scene. This is the seat of misery and guilt. Here awful* 180 justice reserves her public victims. This is the entrance to shameful death.

MARIA.

To this sad place then no improper guest, the abandoned, lost Maria brings despair. And see the subject and cause of all this world of woe: silent 185 and motionless he stands, as if his soul had quitted her abode and the lifeless form alone was left behind. Yet that so perfect that beauty and death, ever at enmity, now seem united there.

BARNWELL.

I groan but murmur not. Just Heaven, I am your 190 own. Do with me what you please.

MARIA.

Why are your streaming eyes still fixed below? As though thou'dst give the greedy earth thy sorrows and rob me of my due. Were happiness within your power, you should bestow it where you pleased, but 195 in your misery I must and will partake.

BARNWELL.

Oh! say not so, but fly, abhor, and leave me to my fate. Consider what you are, how vast your fortune and how bright your fame. Have pity on your youth, your beauty, and unequalled virtue, for which so 200 many noble peers have sighed in vain. Bless with your charms some honorable lord. Adorn with your beauty and by your example improve the English court, that justly claims such merit. So shall I quickly be to you as though I had never been. 205

MARIA.

When I forget you, I must be so indeed. Reason, choice, virtue, all forbid it. Let women like Millwood, if there be more such women, smile in prosperity and in adversity forsake. Be it the pride of virtue to repair, or to partake, the ruin such have 210 made.

TRUEMAN.

Lovely, ill-fated maid! Was there ever such generous distress before? How must this pierce his grateful heart and aggravate his woes?

BARNWELL.

Ere I knew guilt or shame, when Fortune smiled 215 and when my youthful hopes were at the highest, if then to have raised my thoughts to you had been presumption in me never to have been pardoned, think how much beneath yourself you condescend to regard me now. 220

MARIA.

Let her blush who, professing love, invades the freedom of your sex's choice and meanly sues in hopes of a return. Your inevitable fate hath rendered hope impossible as vain. Then why should I fear to avow a passion so just and so disinterested?   225

TRUEMAN.

If any should take occasion from Millwood's crimes to libel the best and fairest part of the creation, here let them see their error. The most distant hopes of such a tender passion from so bright a maid might add to the happiness of the   230
most happy and make the greatest proud. Yet here 'tis lavished in vain. Though by the rich present the generous donor is undone, he on whom it is bestowed receives no benefit.   235

BARNWELL.

So the aromatic spices of the East, which all the living covet and esteem, are with unavailing kindness wasted on the dead.

MARIA.

Yes, fruitless is my love and unavailing all my sighs and tears. Can they save thee from approaching   240
death? From such a death? Oh terrible idea! What is her misery and distress who sees the first, last object of her love, for whom alone she'd live, for whom she'd die a thousand, thousand deaths if it were possible, expiring in her arms? Yet she is happy when   245
compared to me. Were millions of worlds mine, I'd gladly give them in exchange for her condition. The most consummate woe is light to mine. The last of curses to other miserable maids is all I ask for my relief, and that's denied me.   250

TRUEMAN.

Time and reflection cure all ills.

MARIA.

All but this. His dreadful catastrophe virtue herself abhors: to give a holiday to suburb slaves and passing entertain the savage herd who, elbowing each other for a sight, pursue and press upon him   255
like his fate.[16] A mind with piety and resolution

---

[16] to give … fate] "Passing" means more than dying. Condemned criminals were carried in carts to the place of execution, which could be miles away from the jail, in processions that typically attracted large crowds of spectators. These were often in a celebratory mood, there more for entertainment than edification.

armed may smile on death. But public ignominy, everlasting shame—shame, the death of souls—to die a thousand times and yet survive even death itself in never dying infamy, is this to be endured?   260
Can I who live in him and must, each hour of my devoted life, feel all these woes renewed, can I endure this!

TRUEMAN.

Grief has so impaired her spirits, she pants as in the agonies of death.   265

BARNWELL.

Preserve her, Heaven, and restore her peace. Nor let her death be added to my crimes.

Bell tolls.

I am summoned to my fate.

Enter keeper and officers.

KEEPER.

Sir, the officers attend you. Millwood is already summoned.   270

BARNWELL.

Tell 'em I'm ready. And now, my friend, farewell. (*Embracing.*) Support and comfort the best you can this mourning fair. No more. Forget not to pray for me. (*Turning to Maria.*) Would you, bright excellence, permit me the honor of a chaste embrace, the   275
last happiness this world could give were mine.

She inclines towards him; they embrace.

Exalted goodness! Oh turn your eyes from earth, and me, to heaven, where virtue like yours is ever heard. Pray for the peace of my departing soul. Early my race of wickedness began and soon I   280
reached the summit. Ere nature has finished her work and stamped me man, just at the time that others begin to stray, my course is finished. Though short my span of life and few my days, yet count my crimes for years and I have lived   285
whole ages. Thus justice in compassion to mankind cuts off a wretch like me, by one such example to secure thousands from future ruin. Justice and mercy are in Heaven the same. Its utmost severity is mercy to the whole, thereby to   290
cure man's folly and presumption which else would render even infinite mercy vain and ineffectual.

If any youth, like you, in future times
Shall mourn my fate though he abhor my crimes,
Or tender maid, like you, my tale shall hear   295
And to my sorrows give a pitying tear,
To each such melting eye and throbbing heart
Would gracious Heaven this benefit impart:
Never to know my guilt nor feel my pain.
Then must you own you ought not to complain,   300
Since you nor weep, nor shall I die in vain.

Exeunt Barnwell and officers. Enter Blunt, and Lucy.

LUCY.
Heartbreaking sight. Oh wretched, wretched
Millwood!

TRUEMAN.
You came from her, then. How is she disposed to
meet her fate?   305

BLUNT.
Who can describe unutterable woe?

LUCY.
She goes to death encompassed with horror,
loathing life and yet afraid to die. No tongue can
tell her anguish and despair.

TRUEMAN.
Heaven be better to her than her fears. May she   310
prove a warning to others, a monument of mercy
in herself.

LUCY.
Oh sorrow insupportable! Break, break my heart.

TRUEMAN.
In vain
With bleeding hearts and weeping eyes we show   315
A human, gen'rous sense of others' woe,
Unless we mark what drew their ruin on
And, by avoiding that, prevent our own.

FINIS.

Appendix.

The fifth edition (misnamed the sixth) introduced a
new final scene in 1735. This begins immediately after what had been until then Barnwell's last exit, with
the officers in V.ii. Trueman must now also exit at that
point, in order to re-enter at the end of the newly
added dialogue and so conclude the play in conversation with Lucy and Blunt, as he does in earlier ver-

sions. Maria, with no lines at all in this new scene,
would also appear to have exited with Trueman,
Barnwell, and the others. As the new scene was not
regularly presented on stage,[17] it has been printed here
as an appendix.

Scene the last. The place of execution. The gallows
and ladders[18] at the farther end of the stage.

A crowd of spectators. Blunt and Lucy.

LUCY.
Heavens! What a throng!

BLUNT.
How terrible is death when thus prepared!

LUCY.
Support them, Heaven. Thou only canst support
them. All other help is vain.

OFFICER. (*Within.*)
Make way there, make way, and give the prisoners   5
room.

LUCY.
They are here. Observe them well. How humble
and composed young Barnwell seems! But
Millwood looks wild, ruffled with passion,   10
confounded and amazed.

Enter Barnwell, Millwood, officers and executioner.

BARNWELL.
See, Millwood, see, our journey's at an end. Life,
like a tale that's told, is passed away. That short

---

17 The whole scene, for instance, is among those "lines distinguished by inverted commas" and "omitted in the
representation" in *George Barnwell .... Adapted for Theatrical Representation, as Performed at the Theatres-Royal,
Drury-Lane and Covent-Garden. Regulated from the
Prompt-Books* in *Bell's British Theatre* (London, 1791-
93). It is omitted entirely from the "10th" edition of the
play (London, 1760), "as it is acted at the Theatre-Royal
in Drury Lane."

18 gallows and ladders] Gallows were typically a stout bar
or bars supported by equally stout posts, to which the
hangman's rope could be attached. The condemned,
nooses around their necks, were compelled to climb up
ladders to a sufficient height before being "turned off"
with a push or by having the ladders knocked out from
under them.

but dark and unknown passage, death, is all the space 'tween us and endless joys or woes eternal. 15

MILLWOOD.

Is this the end of all my flattering hopes? Were youth and beauty given me for a curse and wisdom only to insure my ruin? They were, they were. Heaven, thou hast done thy worst. Or if thou hast in store some untried plague, somewhat that's 20 worse than shame, despair, and death, unpitied death, confirmed despair, and soul-confounding shame—something that men and angels can't describe and only fiends who bear it can conceive—now, pour it now on this devoted[19] 25 head that I may feel the worst thou canst inflict and bid defiance to thy utmost power.

BARNWELL.

Yet ere we pass the dreadful gulf of death, yet ere you're plunged in everlasting woe, oh bend your stubborn knees and harder heart humbly to 30 deprecate the wrath divine. Who knows but Heaven in your dying moments may bestow that grace and mercy which your life despised.

MILLWOOD.

Why name you mercy to a wretch like me? Mercy's beyond my hope, almost beyond my wish. I can't 35 repent nor ask to be forgiven.

BARNWELL.

Oh think what 'tis to be forever, ever miserable, nor with vain pride oppose a Power that's able to destroy you.

MILLWOOD.

That will destroy me. I feel it will. A deluge of 40 wrath is pouring on my soul. Chains, darkness, wheels, racks, sharp-stinging scorpions, molten lead, and seas of sulpher are light to what I feel.

BARNWELL.

Oh! add not to your vast account despair, a sin more injurious to Heaven than all you've yet 45 committed.

MILLWOOD.

Oh! I have sinned beyond the reach of mercy.

BARNWELL.

Oh say not so. 'Tis blasphemy to think it. As yon

bright roof is higher than the earth, so and much more does Heaven's goodness pass our appre- 50 hension. Oh, what created being shall presume to circumscribe mercy that knows no bounds?

MILLWOOD.

This yields no hope. Though mercy may be boundless, yet 'tis free. And I was doomed before the world began to endless pains and thou to joys 55 eternal.[20]

BARNWELL.

Oh! gracious Heaven! Extend thy pity to her. Let thy rich mercy flow in plenteous streams to chase her fears and heal her wounded soul.

MILLWOOD.

It will not be. Your prayers are lost in air or else 60 returned perhaps with double blessing to your bosom, but me they help not.

BARNWELL.

Yet hear me, Millwood!

MILLWOOD.

Away, I will not hear thee. I tell thee, youth, I am by Heaven devoted a dreadful instance of its power 65 to punish.

Barnwell seems to pray.

If thou wilt pray, pray for thyself not me.—How doth his fervent soul mount with his words, and both ascend to heaven! That heaven, whose gates are shut with adamantine bars against my prayers, 70 had I the will to pray. I cannot bear it. Sure 'tis the worst of torments to behold others enjoy that bliss that we must never taste.

OFFICER.

The utmost limit of your time's expired.

MILLWOOD.

Encompassed with horror, whither must I go? I 75 would not live, nor die. That I could cease to be! Or ne'er had been!

BARNWELL.

Since peace and comfort are denied her here, may

---

[19] devoted] formally consigned to evil or destruction, doomed

[20] doomed … eternal] Millwood here invokes the doctrines of foredestination and predestination, which assert that most people are damned but some few are destined to be saved even before they are born, indeed from the beginning of time.

she find mercy where she least expects it, and this be all her hell. From our example may all be taught to fly the first approach of vice, but if o'ertaken
By strong temptation, weakness, or surprise,
Lament their guilt and by repentance rise.
Th'impenitent alone die unforgiven;
To sin's like man, and to forgive like Heaven. 85

Enter Trueman.

[the scene then continues from
"LUCY. Heartbreaking sight. ..."
and omitting the first sentence of
Trueman's subsequent speech]

80

Textual Notes

a The copy text is the third edition "revised," a 1731 duodecimo (D1), adopted here because it includes substantive changes with authority, including new stage directions. Also consulted were the first edition, a 1731 octavo (O1); modern editions of 1939, revised 1969, based on the fifth edition (Nettleton, Case, and Stone—NCS); of 1965 based on the first edition (McBurney); and of 1993 based on the first edition (Steffenson).

b courtiers may] D1, NCS, Steffenson; courtiers, though they should deny us citizens politeness, may O1, McBurney

c put him out of countenance] D1, NCS, Steffenson; shock him O1, McBurney

d we] D1, NCS, Steffenson; he who trusts heaven O1, McBurney

e will] D1, NCS, Steffenson; will; so heaven confirm to me the pardon of my offenses O1, McBurney

f brought] D1, NCS, Steffenson; stolen O1, McBurney

g amorous youth] D1, NCS, Steffenson; easy fool O1, McBurney

h heart.] D1, NCS, Steffenson; heart. How else shall I clear myself? O1, McBurney

i commit] D1, NCS, Steffenson; commit, and then betrayed him O1, McBurney

j I know ... none.] D1, NCS, Steffenson; I hate you all. I know you and expect no mercy. Nay, I ask for none. I have done nothing I am sorry for. O1, McBurney

k seem] D1, NCS, Steffenson; are O1, McBurney

l Proceed.] D1, NCS, Steffenson; Go on. How happy am I who live to see this? O1, McBurney

m thee.] D1, NCS, Steffenson; thee. [*Lies down by him.*] Upon this rugged couch then let us lie, for well it suits our most deplorable condition. O1, McBurney

n place] D1, NCS, Steffenson; earth O1, McBurney

Tragicomic Romance

Tragicomic romance features lost heirs, lost lovers, lost rulers found again at last. It features protagonists gone on quests, often into dark and foreign lands, to retrieve some treasure, some beloved, some cultural talisman. Protagonists have brushes with death, but only villains die. The forces of evil are some dark version of the self, one's culture's greatest fear: incest, fratricide, parricide. This is the world of Shakespeare's and John Fletcher's early English baroque tragicomedies. The Restoration's great achievement in the genre is the split-plot play, juxtaposing heroic with comic plots, the conclusion of which is to compound idealistic with pragmatic rationales for societal order. The Revolution's achievement was twofold: injecting real tragedy into the genre to produce, so to speak, comitragic romance, where one of the plots ends tragically, with the death or exile of one or more of the good guys; injecting tragicomedy into the world of comedy, making it more somber, more serious, and producing novelistic melodrama, a genre which exalts the importance of the bourgeois self—and preoccupies us with that self rather than the world and its discontents.

Marriage à la Mode[a]

by John Dryden (1631-1700)

edited by Brian Corman

Marriage à la Mode is the quintessential Restoration split-plot tragicomedy. The form gained popularity in England in Shakespeare's time; *Much Ado About Nothing* is the best known example. The Restoration version of the form, perfected by Dryden, juxtaposes a comic plot of courtship and/or adultery with a heroic romance plot of love and/or courtship. The comic plot is one of private life, the heroic of the public world of politics and statecraft.

In this case, the Sicilian setting, conventionally associated with the idealized pastoral world of characters like Leonidas and Palmyra, was especially useful for distancing a play dealing with the always touchy subject of usurpation from the world of late Stuart England. That distancing is carefully balanced by the comic plot with its frequent allusions to post-Restoration London and to the English social hierarchy from the Court to its adjacent fashionable Town to the unfashionable, financial City, to the equally if not even more unfashionable Country. The relationship between two apparently dissonant plots marks the special feature of split-plot tragicomedy. No other aspect of the play has so caught the attention of critics since the initial production. Split-plot tragicomedy remains a self-consciously artificial form, and Dryden exploits its artificiality throughout with his scrupulous attention to such devices as symmetries, formal correspondences and linguistic echoes. Careful attention to detail characterizes the construction of the play throughout, leading to a whole that differs from and is greater than the sum of its parts.

Marriage à la Mode was first published in 1673, well after its initial performance. The precise date of that first performance remains uncertain, but the evidence points to late November, 1671. Like most of Dryden's plays, it was written for the King's Company, of which he was both principal playwright and shareholder. Some of the strongest actors in the company were cast in the comic plot, Charles Hart and Michael Mohun as Palamede and Rhodophil, Rebecca Marshall and Elizabeth Boutell as Doralice and Melantha (though the equally strong Edward Kynaston played Leonidas, the hero of the heroic plot). This highlighting of the comic plot no doubt reflected Dryden's own sense of where his play was strongest. *Marriage à la Mode* was a success, and it was performed and reprinted throughout Dryden's lifetime. By century's end, however, it met the fate of aristocratic tragicomic romance: neglect. The form went out of fashion, never to be revived. *Marriage à la Mode* had something of a performance afterlife in Colley Cibber's *The Comical Lovers; or, Marriage A-la-Mode* (1707), an amalgam of the comic plots of *Marriage à la Mode* and *Secret Love*, another of Dryden's tragicomedies. Cibber's play was a tribute to the staying power of Dryden's comic plot—and the absence of a similar staying power in his heroic plot.

DRAMATIS PERSONAE

MEN

    Polydamas, Usurper of Sicily.
    Leonidas, the rightful prince, unknown.
    Argaleon, favorite to Polydamas.
    Hermogenes, foster father to Leonidas.
    Eubulus, his friend and companion.
    Rhodophil, Captain of the Guards.
    Palamede, a courtier.
    [Straton, servant to Palamede.]

WOMEN

    Palmyra, daughter to the usurper.
    Amalthea, sister to Argaleon.
    Doralice, wife to Rhodophil.
    Melantha, an affected lady.
    Philotis, woman* to Melantha.
    Beliza, woman* to Doralice.
    Artemis, a court lady.

SCENE: SICILY.

Marriage à la Mode.

> *Quicquid sum ego, quamvis*
> *Infra Lucilli censum ingeniumque, tamen me*
> *Cum magnis vixisse, invita fatebitur usque*
> *Invidia, etc. fragili quaerens illidere dentem*
> *Offendet solido.* Horat. *Serm.*[1]

Act I, scene i. Walks near the court.

Enter Doralice and Beliza.

DORALICE.

Beliza, bring the lute into this arbor, the walks are
empty: I would try the song the Princess Amalthea
bade me learn.

They go in, and sing.

            1.

Why should a foolish marriage vow,
   Which long ago was made,   5

---

[1] *Quicquid ... Serm.*] Horace, *Satires* 2.1.74-79: "Such as I
am, however far beneath Lucillius in rank and native gifts,
yet Envy, in spite of herself, will ever admit that I have lived
with the great, and, while trying to strike her tooth on
something soft, will dash upon what is solid" (Loeb).

Oblige us to each other now
   When passion is decayed?
We loved and we loved as long as we could,
   Till our love was loved out in us both.
But our marriage is dead, when the pleasure is fled; 10
   'Twas pleasure first made it an oath.

            2.

If I have pleasures for a friend
   And farther love in store,
What wrong has he whose joys did end
   And who could give no more?   15

'Tis a madness that he
Should be jealous of me
Or that I should bar him of another.
For all we can gain
Is to give ourselves pain   20
When neither can hinder the other.

Enter Palamede, in riding habit, and hears the song.
Re-enter Doralice and Beliza.

BELIZA.

Madam, a stranger.

DORALICE.

I did not think to have had witnesses of my bad
singing.

PALAMEDE.

If I have erred, madam, I hope you'll pardon the 25
curiosity of a stranger, for I may well call myself
so after five years' absence from the court. But you
have freed me from one error.

DORALICE.

What's that, I beseech you?

PALAMEDE.

I thought good voices and ill faces had been 30
inseparable and that to be fair and sing well had
been only the privilege of angels.

DORALICE.

And how many more of these fine things can you
say to me?

PALAMEDE.

Very few, madam, for if I should continue to see 35
you some hours longer, you look so killingly that
I should be mute with wonder.

DORALICE.

This will not give you the reputation of a wit with

me. You traveling monsieurs live upon the stock
you have got abroad for the first day or two; to   40
repeat with a good memory and apply with a good
grace is all your wit. And commonly your gullets
are sewed up like cormorants:[2] when you have
regorged what you have taken in, you are the
leanest things in nature.   45

PALAMEDE.

Then madam, I think you had best make that use of
me. Let me wait on you for two or three days
together, and you shall hear all I have learnt of
extraordinary in other countries. And one thing
which I never saw till I came home, that is, a lady of 50
a better voice, better face, and better wit, than any
I have seen abroad. And after this, if I should not
declare myself most passionately in love with you, I
should have less wit than yet you think I have.

DORALICE.

A very plain and pithy declaration. I see, sir, you   55
have been traveling in Spain or Italy or some of
the hot countries where men come to the point
immediately. But are you sure these are not words
of course? For I would not give my poor heart an
occasion of complaint against me that I engaged   60
it too rashly and then could not bring it off.

PALAMEDE.

Your heart may trust itself with me safely: I shall
use it very civilly while it stays and never turn it
away without fair warning to provide for itself.

DORALICE.

First then, I do receive your passion with as little   65
consideration on my part as ever you gave it me
on yours. And now see what a miserable wretch
you have made yourself.

PALAMEDE.

Who, I miserable? Thank you for that. Give me
love enough and life enough, and I defy Fortune.   70

DORALICE.

Know then, thou man of vain imagination, know
to thy utter confusion, that I am virtuous.

PALAMEDE.

Such another word and I give up the ghost.

---

[2] cormorants] When used for fishing, cormorants' lower
necks were tied to prevent them from swallowing.

DORALICE.

Then, to strike you quite dead, know that I am
married, too.   75

PALAMEDE.

Art thou married? Oh thou damnable virtuous
woman!

DORALICE.

Yes, married to a gentleman, young, handsome,
rich, valiant, and with all the good qualities that
will make you despair and hang yourself.   80

PALAMEDE.

Well, in spite of all that, I'll love you. Fortune has
cut us out for one another, for I am to be married
within these three days. Married past redemption
to a young, fair, rich, and virtuous lady. And it
shall go hard, but I will love my wife as little as I   85
perceive you do your husband.

DORALICE.

Remember, I invade no propriety.[3] My servant*
you are only till you are married.

PALAMEDE.

In the meantime, you are to forget you have a
husband.   90

DORALICE.

And you, that you are to have a wife.

BELIZA. (*Aside to her lady.*)

Oh madam, my lord's just at the end of the walks
and, if you make not haste, will discover you.

DORALICE.

Some other time, new servant, we'll talk further
of the premises; in the meanwhile, break not my   95
first commandment, that is, not to follow me.

PALAMEDE.

But where, then, shall I find you again?

DORALICE.

At court. Yours for two days, sir.

PALAMEDE.

And nights, I beseech you, madam.

Exeunt Doralice and Beliza.

PALAMEDE.

Well, I'll say that for thee, thou art a very dexterous   100
executioner; thou hast done my business at one
stroke. Yet I must marry another—and yet I must

---

[3] propriety] property

love this. And if it lead me into some little
inconveniencies, as jealousies and duels and death
and so forth, yet while sweet love is in the case, 105
Fortune do thy worst, and avaunt, mortality.

Enter Rhodophil, who seems speaking to one within.

RHODOPHIL.

Leave 'em with my lieutenant while I fetch new
orders from the King. (*Sees Palamede.*) How?
Palamede!

PALAMEDE.

Rhodophil! 110

RHODOPHIL.

Who thought to have seen you in Sicily?

PALAMEDE.

Who thought to have found the court so far from
Syracuse?

RHODOPHIL.

The King best knows the reason of the progress.
But answer me, I beseech you, what brought you 115
home from travel?

PALAMEDE.

The commands of an old, rich father.

RHODOPHIL.

And the hopes of burying him?

PALAMEDE.

Both together, as you see, have prevailed on my
good nature. In few words, my old man has already 120
married me, for he has agreed with another old
man, as rich and as covetous as himself: the articles
are drawn, and I have given my consent for fear
of being disinherited and yet know not what kind
of woman I am to marry. 125

RHODOPHIL.

Sure your father intends you some very ugly wife
and has a mind to keep you in ignorance till you
have shot the gulf.

PALAMEDE.

I know not that, but obey I will and must.

RHODOPHIL.

Then I cannot choose but grieve for all the good 130
girls[4] and courtesans of France and Italy. They have
lost the most kind-hearted, doting, prodigal,
humble servant* in Europe.

PALAMEDE.

All I could do in these three years I stayed behind
you was to comfort the poor creatures for the loss 135
of you. But what's the reason that in all this time
a friend could never hear from you?

RHODOPHIL.

Alas dear Palamede, I have had no joy to write nor
indeed to do anything in the world to please me.
The greatest misfortune imaginable is fallen upon 140
me.

PALAMEDE.

Prithee, what's the matter?

RHODOPHIL.

In one word, I am married, wretchedly married,
and have been above these two years. Yes faith, the
Devil has had power over me in spite of my vows 145
and resolutions to the contrary.

PALAMEDE.

I find you have sold yourself for filthy lucre: she's
old or ill-conditioned.

RHODOPHIL.

No, none of these. I'm sure she's young, and for
her humor,* she laughs, sings, and dances eternally. 150
And which is more, we never quarrel about it, for
I do the same.

PALAMEDE.

You're very unfortunate indeed. Then the case is
plain: she is not handsome.

RHODOPHIL.

A great beauty, too, as people say. 155

PALAMEDE.

As people say? Why, you should know that best
yourself.

RHODOPHIL.

Ask those who have smelled to a strong perfume
two years together what's the scent.

PALAMEDE.

But here are good qualities enough for one woman. 160

RHODOPHIL.

Aye, too many, Palamede. If I could put 'em into
three or four women, I should be content.

PALAMEDE.

Oh, now I have found it: you dislike her for no
other reason but because she's your wife.

RHODOPHIL.

And is not that enough? All that I know of her 165

---

4 good girls] wanton wenches (Partridge)

perfections now is only by memory; I remember, indeed, that about two years ago I loved her passionately. But those golden days are gone, Palamede. Yet I loved her a whole half year, double the natural term of any mistress, and think in my conscience I could have held out another quarter. But then the world began to laugh at me, and a certain shame of being out of fashion seized me. At last, we arrived at that point that there was nothing left in us to make us new to one another. Yet still I set a good face upon the matter and am infinite fond of her before company. But when we are alone, we walk like lions in a room, she one way and I another. And we lie with our backs to each other so far distant as if the fashion of great beds[5] was only invented to keep husband and wife sufficiently asunder.

PALAMEDE.

The truth is, your disease is very desperate, but though you cannot be cured, you may be patched up a little. You must get you a mistress, Rhodophil. That, indeed, is living upon cordials, but as fast as one fails, you must supply it with another. You're like a gamester who has lost his estate, yet in doing that you have learned the advantages of play and can arrive to live upon't.

RHODOPHIL.

Truth is, I have been thinking on't and have just resolved to take your counsel. And faith, considering the damned disadvantages of a married man, I have provided well enough for a poor humble sinner that is not ambitious of great matters.

PALAMEDE.

What is she, for a woman?

RHODOPHIL.

One of the stars of Syracuse, I assure you: young enough, fair enough, and, but for one quality, just such a woman as I would wish.

PALAMEDE.

Oh friend, this is not an age to be critical in beauty. When we had good store of handsome women and but few chapmen,[6] you might have been more curious* in your choice. But now the price is

enhanced upon us, and all mankind set up for mistresses, so that poor little creatures, without beauty, birth, or breeding but only impudence, go off at unreasonable rates. And a man in these hard times snaps at 'em as he does at broad-gold,[7] never examines the weight, but takes light or heavy[8] as he can get it.

RHODOPHIL.

But my mistress has one fault that's almost unpardonable: for, being a town lady,[9] without any relation to the court, yet she thinks herself undone if she be not seen there three or four times a day with the Princess Amalthea. And for the King, she haunts and watches him so narrowly in a morning that she prevents* even the chemists* who beset his chamber to turn their mercury[10] into his gold.

PALAMEDE.

Yet hitherto, methinks, you are no very unhappy man.

RHODOPHIL.

With all this, she's the greatest gossip in nature, for besides the court, she's the most eternal visitor of the town and yet manages her time so well that she seems ubiquitary.[11] For my part, I can compare her to nothing but the sun, for like him, she takes no rest nor ever sets in one place but to rise in another.

PALAMEDE.

I confess she had need be handsome with these qualities.

RHODOPHIL.

No lady can be so curious of a new fashion as she is of a new French word. She's the very mint of the nation and, as fast as any bullion comes out of France, coins it immediately into our language.

PALAMEDE.

And her name is——?

---

7 broad-gold] or broad-piece (twenty shillings), so called to distinguish it from the guinea (introduced 1663), which was worth one shilling more

8 light or heavy] Broad-pieces, having smooth edges (as opposed to the milled edges of the guineas) could be clipped or mutilated.

9 town lady] a member of fashionable society

10 mercury] common treatment for syphilis

11 ubiquitary] ubiquitous

---

5 great beds] double beds came into fashion after the Restoration

6 chapmen] traders, with a secondary meaning of consumers

RHODOPHIL.

No naming, that's not like a cavalier. Find her if you can by my description, and I am not so ill a painter that I need write the name beneath the picture.   235

PALAMEDE.

Well then, how far have you proceeded in your love?

RHODOPHIL.

'Tis yet in the bud, and what fruit it may bear I cannot tell. For this insufferable humor* of haunting the court is so predominant that she has hitherto broken all her assignations with me for   240
fear of missing her visits there.

PALAMEDE.

That's the hardest part of your adventure. But for aught I see, Fortune has used us both alike: I have a strange kind of mistress too in court, besides her I am to marry.   245

RHODOPHIL.

You have made haste to be in love then, for if I am not mistaken, you are but this day arrived.

PALAMEDE.

That's all one, I have seen the lady already who has charmed me, seen her in these walks, courted her, and received for the first time an answer that does   250
not put me into despair.

To them, Argaleon, Amalthea, Artemis.

I'll tell you at more leisure my adventures. The walks fill apace, I see. Stay, is not that the young Lord Argaleon, the King's favorite?

RHODOPHIL.

Yes, and as proud as ever, as ambitious, and as   255
revengeful.

PALAMEDE.

How keeps he the King's favor with these qualities?

RHODOPHIL.

Argaleon's father helped him to the crown. Besides, he gilds over all his vices to the King and, standing in the dark to him, sees all his inclinations,   260
interests, and humors, which he so times and soothes that, in effect, he reigns.

PALAMEDE.

His sister Amalthea, who, I guess, stands by him, seems not to be of his temper.

RHODOPHIL.

Oh, she's all goodness and generosity.   265

ARGALEON.

Rhodophil, the King expects you earnestly.

RHODOPHIL.

'Tis done, my lord, what he commanded. I only waited his return from hunting. Shall I attend your lordship to him?

ARGALEON.

No, I go first another way. (*Exit hastily.*)   270

PALAMEDE.

He seems in haste and discomposed.

AMALTHEA. (*To Rhodophil after a short whisper.*)

Your friend? Then he must needs be of much merit.

RHODOPHIL.

When he has kissed the King's hand, I know he'll beg the honor to kiss yours. Come, Palamede.   275

Exeunt Rhodophil and Palamede bowing to Amalthea.

ARTEMIS.

Madam, you tell me most surprising news.

AMALTHEA.

The fear of it, you see,
Has discomposed my brother, but to me
All that can bring my country good is welcome.

ARTEMIS.

It seems incredible that this old King,   280
Whom all the world thought childless,
Should come to search the farthest parts of Sicily
In hope to find an heir.

AMALTHEA.

To lessen your astonishment I will
Unfold some private passages of state   285
Of which you yet are ignorant. Know first,
That this Polydamas, who reigns, unjustly
Gained the crown.

ARTEMIS.

Somewhat of this I have confus'dly heard.

AMALTHEA.

I'll tell you all in brief: Theagenes,   290
Our last great King,
Had by his queen one only son, an infant
Of three years old, called, after him, Theagenes.
The general, this Polydamas, then married,
The public feasts for which were scarcely past   295
When a rebellion in the heart of Sicily
Called out the King to arms.

ARTEMIS.
                    Polydamas
  Had then a just excuse to stay behind.
AMALTHEA.
  His temper was too warlike to accept it.   300
  He left his bride and the new joys of marriage
  And followed to the field. In short, they fought,
  The rebels were o'ercome, but in the fight
  The too bold King received a mortal wound.
  When he perceived his end approaching near,   305
  He called the general, to whose care he left
  His widow queen and orphan son, then died.
ARTEMIS.
  Then false Polydamas betrayed his trust?
AMALTHEA.
  He did. And with my father's help, for which
  Heav'n pardon him, so gained the soldiers' hearts   310
  That in few days he was saluted King.
  And when his crimes had impudence enough
  To bear the eye of day,
  He marched his army back to Syracuse.
  But see how Heav'n can punish wicked men   315
  In granting their desires: the news was brought him
  That day he was to enter it that Eubulus,
  Whom his dead master had left governor,
  Was fled and with him bore away the Queen
  And royal orphan. But what more amazed him,   320
  His wife, now big with child and much detesting
  Her husband's practices, had willingly
  Accompanied their flight.
ARTEMIS.
  How I admire her virtue!
AMALTHEA.
                    What became   325
  Of her and them since that was never known.
  Only some few days since, a famous robber
  Was taken with some jewels of vast price,
  Which, when they were delivered to the King,
  He knew had been his wife's; with these, a letter,   330
  Much torn and sullied, but which yet he knew
  To be her writing.
ARTEMIS.
                    Sure from hence he learned
  He had a son.
AMALTHEA.
                    It was not left so plain.   335

  The paper only said she died in childbed.
  But when it should have mentioned son or daughter,
  Just there it was torn off.
ARTEMIS.
                    Madam, the King.

To them, Polydamas, Argaleon, guard, and attendants.

ARGALEON.
  The robber, though thrice racked, confessed no more   340
  But that he took those jewels near this place.
POLYDAMAS.
  But yet the circumstances strongly argue
  That those for whom I search are not far off.
ARGALEON.
  I cannot easily believe it.
ARTEMIS. (*Aside.*)
                    No,   345
  You would not have it so.
POLYDAMAS.
  Those I employed have in the neighboring hamlet
  Amongst the fishers' cabins made discovery
  Of some young persons whose uncommon beauty
  And graceful carriage make it seem suspicious   350
  They are not what they seem. I therefore sent
  The captain of my guards this morning early
  With orders to secure and bring 'em to me.

Enter Rhodophil and Palamede.

  Oh here he is.——Have you performed my will?
RHODOPHIL.
  Sir, those whom you commanded me to bring   355
  Are waiting in the walks.
POLYDAMAS.
                    Conduct 'em hither.
RHODOPHIL.
  First, give me leave
  To beg your notice of this gentleman.
POLYDAMAS.
  He seems to merit it. His name and quality?*   360
RHODOPHIL.
  Palamede, son to Lord Cleodemus of Palermo,
  And new returned from travel.

Palamede approaches, and kneels to kiss the King's hand.

POLYDAMAS.
                    You're welcome.

I knew your father well. He was both brave
And honest; we two once were fellow soldiers 365
In the last civil wars.

PALAMEDE.

I bring the same unquestioned honesty
And zeal to serve your Majesty; the courage
You were pleased to praise in him
Your royal prudence and your people's love 370
Will never give me leave to try like him
In civil wars. I hope it may in foreign.

POLYDAMAS.

Attend the court, and it shall be my care
To find out some employment worthy you.
Go, Rhodophil, and bring in those without. 375

*Exeunt. Rhodophil and Palamede. Rhodophil returns
again immediately, and with him enter Hermogenes,
Leonidas, and Palmyra.*

(*Looking earnestly on Leonidas and Palmyra.*)
Behold two miracles!
Of different sexes but of equal form.
So matchless both that my divided soul
Can scarcely ask the gods a son or daughter
For fear of losing one. If from your hands, 380
You Powers, I shall this day receive a daughter,
Argaleon, she is yours. But if a son,
Then Amalthea's love shall make him happy.

ARGALEON.

Grant, Heav'n, this admirable nymph may prove
That issue which he seeks. 385

AMALTHEA.

Venus Urania,[12] if thou art a goddess,
Grant that sweet youth may prove the Prince of
   Sicily.

POLYDAMAS. (*To Hermogenes.*)
Tell me, old man, and tell me true, from whence
Had you that youth and maid?

HERMOGENES.

From whence you had 390
Your scepter, sir: I had 'em from the gods.

POLYDAMAS.

The gods then have not such another gift.
Say who their parents were.

---

12 Venus Urania] heavenly Venus, i.e. epithet for Venus as
   goddess of the heavens

HERMOGENES.

My wife and I.

ARGALEON.

It is not likely a virgin of so excellent a beauty 395
Should come from such a stock.

AMALTHEA.

Much less, that such a youth, so sweet, so graceful,
Should be produced from peasants.

HERMOGENES.

Why, Nature is the same in villages
And much more fit to form a noble issue 400
Where it is least corrupted.

POLYDAMAS.

He talks too like a man that knew the world
To have been long a peasant. But the rack
Will teach him other language. Hence with him.

As the guard are carrying him away, his peruke falls off.

Sure I have seen that face before. Hermogenes! 405
'Tis he, 'tis he who fled away with Eubulus,
And with my dear Eudoxia.

HERMOGENES.

Yes sir, I am Hermogenes.
And if to have been loyal be a crime,
I stand prepared to suffer. 410

POLYDAMAS.

If thou wouldst live, speak quickly.
What is become of my Eudoxia?
Where is the queen and young Theagenes?
Where Eubulus? And which of these is mine?
   (*Pointing to Leonidas and Palmyra*).

HERMOGENES.

Eudoxia is dead, so is the queen, 415
The infant King her son, and Eubulus.

POLYDAMAS.

Traitor, 'tis false: produce 'em, or—

HERMOGENES.

Once more
I tell you, they are dead. But leave to threaten,
For you shall know no further. 420

POLYDAMAS.

Then prove indulgent to my hopes and be
My friend forever. Tell me, good Hermogenes,
Whose son is that brave* youth?

HERMOGENES.

Sir, he is yours.

POLYDAMAS.

    Fool that I am, thou see'st that so I wish it,   425

    And so thou flatter'st me.

HERMOGENES.

                  By all that's holy.

POLYDAMAS.

    Again. Thou canst not swear too deeply.

    Yet hold, I will believe thee—yet I doubt.

HERMOGENES.

    You need not, sir.   430

ARGALEON.

    Believe him not: he sees you credulous

    And would impose his own base issue on you

    And fix it to your crown.

AMALTHEA.

    Behold his goodly shape and feature, sir.

    Methinks he much resembles you.   435

ARGALEON.

    I say, if you have any issue here,

    It must be that fair creature;

    By all my hopes I think so.

AMALTHEA.

    Yes brother, I believe you by your hopes,

    For they are all for her.   440

POLYDAMAS.

                 Call the youth nearer.

HERMOGENES.

    Leonidas, the King would speak with you.

POLYDAMAS.

    Come near and be not dazzled with the splendor

    And greatness of a court.

LEONIDAS.

    I need not this encouragement.   445

    I can fear nothing but the gods.

    And for this glory, after I have seen

    The canopy of state spread wide above

    In the abyss of heaven, the court of stars,

    The blushing morning, and the rising sun,   450

    What greater can I see?

POLYDAMAS. (*Embracing him.*)

    This speaks thee born a prince: thou art thyself

    That rising sun and shalt not see on earth

    A brighter than thyself.—All of you witness

    That for my son I here receive this youth,   455

    This brave,* this—but I must not praise him further

    Because he now is mine.

LEONIDAS. (*Kneeling.*)

    I wonnot, sir, believe

    That I am made your sport,

    For I find nothing in myself but what   460

    Is much above a scorn. I dare give credit

    To whatsoe'er a king, like you, can tell me.

    Either I am or will deserve to be your son.

ARGALEON.

    I yet maintain it is impossible

    This young man should be yours, for if he were,   465

    Why should Hermogenes so long conceal him

    When he might gain so much by his discovery?*

HERMOGENES. (*To the King.*)

    I stayed a while to make him worthy, sir, of you.

    But in that time I found

    Somewhat within him which so moved my love   470

    I never could resolve to part with him.

LEONIDAS. (*To Argaleon.*)

    You ask too many questions and are

    Too saucy for a subject.

ARGALEON.

    You rather overact your part and are

    Too soon a prince.   475

LEONIDAS.

               Too soon you'll find me one.

POLYDAMAS.

    Enough, Argaleon,

    I have declared him mine. And you, Leonidas,

    Live well with him I love.

ARGALEON.

    Sir, if he be your son, I may have leave   480

    To think your queen had twins. Look on this virgin.

    Hermogenes would enviously deprive you

    Of half your treasure.

HERMOGENES.

               Sir, she is my daughter.

    I could, perhaps, thus aided by this lord,   485

    Prefer her to be yours, but truth forbid

    I should procure her greatness by a lie.

POLYDAMAS.

    Come hither, beauteous maid. Are you not sorry

    Your father will not let you pass for mine?

PALMYRA.

    I am content to be what Heav'n has made me.   490

POLYDAMAS.

    Could you not wish yourself a princess then?

PALMYRA.

Not to be sister to Leonidas.

POLYDAMAS.

Why, my sweet maid?

PALMYRA.

Indeed I cannot tell,

But I could be content to be his handmaid.   495

ARGALEON. (*Aside*.)

I wish I had not seen her.

PALMYRA. (*To Leonidas*.)

I must weep for your good fortune.

Pray pardon me, indeed I cannot help it.

Leonidas (alas, I had forgot,

Now I must call you Prince), but must I leave you?   500

LEONIDAS. (*Aside*.)

I dare not speak to her, for if I should,

I must weep too.

POLYDAMAS.

No, you shall live at court, sweet innocence,

And see him there.—Hermogenes,

Though you intended not to make me happy,   505

Yet you shall be rewarded for th'event.

—Come my Leonidas, let's thank the gods:

Thou for a father, I for such a son.

Exeunt all but Leonidas and Palmyra.

LEONIDAS.

My dear Palmyra, many eyes observe me,

And I have thoughts so tender that I cannot   510

In public speak 'em to you. Some hours hence

I shall shake off these crowds of fawning courtiers,

And then— (*Exit*.)

PALMYRA.

Fly swift, you hours. You measure

time for me in vain

Till you bring back Leonidas again.   515

Be shorter now, and to redeem that wrong,

When he and I are met, be twice as long.

Exit.

Act II, scene i.

Melantha and Philotis.

PHILOTIS.

Count Rhodophil's a fine gentleman indeed,

madam, and I think deserves your affection.

MELANTHA.

Let me die but he's a fine man: he sings and dances

en français[13] and writes the *billets-doux* to a

miracle.   5

PHILOTIS.

And those are no small talents to a lady that

understands and values the French air, as your

ladyship does.

MELANTHA.

How charming is the French air! and what an *étourdi

bête*[14] is one of our untraveled islanders! When he   10

would make his court to me, let me die, but he is just

Aesop's ass,[15] that would imitate the courtly French

in his addresses but, instead of those, comes pawing

upon me and doing all things so *mal a droitly*.

PHILOTIS.

'Tis great pity Rhodophil's a married man, that you   15

may not have an honorable intrigue with him.

MELANTHA.

Intrigue, Philotis! that's an old phrase. I have laid

that word by: *amour* sounds better. But thou art

heir to all my cast* words, as thou art to my old

wardrobe. Oh Count Rhodophil! Ah *mon cher*! I   20

could live and die with him.

Enter Palamede and a servant.

SERVANT.

Sir, this is my lady.

PALAMEDE.

Then this is she that is to be divine and nymph

and goddess and with whom I am to be desperately

in love.   25

(*Bows to her, delivering a letter.*) This letter, madam,

which I present you from your father, has given

me both the happy opportunity and the boldness

to kiss the fairest hands in Sicily.

---

13 *en français*] Melantha obviously laces her discourse with
   French phrases (and Frenchified English)—here, as in
   the original, italicized (although there are other words
   that obviously should be spoken with a French accent,
   as suggested by the spelling or by Palamede's responses
   to her); those whose meaning seems obvious are
   unglossed.

14 *étourdi bête*] thoughtless beast

15 Aesop's ass] the ass who imitated the fawning of his master's lapdog

MELANTHA.

Came you lately from Palermo, sir?   30

PALAMEDE.

But yesterday, madam.

MELANTHA. (*Reading the letter.*)

"Daughter, receive the bearer of this letter as a
gentleman whom I have chosen to make you
happy." (Oh Venus, a new servant* sent me! And let
me die but he has the air of a gallant *homme*). "His   35
father is the rich Lord Cleodemus, our neighbor. I
suppose you'll find nothing disagree-able in his
person or his converse, both which he has improved
by travel. The treaty is already concluded, and I shall
be in town within these three days, so that you have   40
nothing to do but to obey your careful father." (*To
Palamede.*) Sir, my father, for whom I have a blind
obedience, has commanded me to receive your
passionate addresses. But you must also give me
leave to avow that I cannot merit 'em from so   45
accomplished a cavalier.

PALAMEDE.

I want* many things, madam, to render me
accomplished, and the first and greatest of 'em is
your favor.

MELANTHA. [*Aside to Philotis.*]

Let me die, Philotis, but this is extremely French. But   50
yet, Count Rhodophil.—A gentleman, sir, that
understands the *grand monde* so well, who has haunted the best conversations, and who (in short) has
voyaged, may pretend to the good graces of any lady.

PALAMEDE. (*Aside.*)

Hey day! *Grand monde*! *conversation*! *voyaged*! and   55
good graces! I find my mistress is one of those that
run mad in new French words.

MELANTHA.

I suppose, sir, you have made the *tour* of *France*
and, having seen all that's fine there, will make a
considerable reformation in the rudeness of our   60
court. For let me die, but an unfashioned,
untraveled, mere Sicilian is a *bête* and has nothing
in the world of an *honnête homme*.[16]

PALAMEDE.

I must confess, madam, that—

MELANTHA.

And what new *menuets* have you brought over with   65
you? Their *menuets* are to a miracle! And our
Sicilian jigs are so dull and fade to 'em!

PALAMEDE.

For *menuets*, madam—

MELANTHA.

And what new plays are there in vogue? And who
danced best in the last grand ballet? Come, sweet   70
servant, you shall tell me all.

PALAMEDE. (*Aside.*)

Tell her all? Why, she asks all and will hear
nothing.—To answer in order, madam, to your
demands—

MELANTHA.

I am thinking what a happy couple we shall be! For   75
you shall keep up your correspondence abroad, and
everything that's new writ in *France* and fine, I mean
all that's delicate and *bien tourné*,[17] we will have first.

PALAMEDE.

But madam, our fortune—

MELANTHA.

I understand you, sir; you'll leave that to me. For   80
the ménage of a family,* I know it better than any
lady in Sicily.

PALAMEDE.

Alas madam, we—

MELANTHA.

Then, we will never make visits together nor see a
play but always apart; you shall be every day at the   85
King's *levee*, and I at the Queen's,[18] and we will
never meet but in the Drawing Room.*

PHILOTIS.

Madam, the new prince is just passed by the end
of the walk.

MELANTHA.

The new prince, say'st thou? Adieu, dear servant;   90
I have not made my court to him these two long
hours. Oh, 'tis the sweetest prince! So obligeant,
charmant, ravissant, that—well, I'll make haste to
kiss his hands and then make half a score visits
more and be with you again in a twinkling.   95

Exit, running, with Philotis.

---

16 *honnête homme*] gentleman

17 *bien tourné*] neatly turned; well expressed
18 Queen's] Polydamas is a widower.

PALAMEDE.

Now Heaven, of thy mercy, bless me from this tongue; it may keep the field against a whole army of lawyers, and that in their own language, French gibberish.[19] 'Tis true, in the daytime 'tis tolerable, when a man has field-room to run from it. But to be shut up in a bed with her, like two cocks in a pit—humanity cannot support it. I must kiss all night, in my own defense, and hold her down like a boy at cuffs, nay, and give her the rising blow[20] every time she begins to speak.

Enter Rhodophil.

But here comes Rhodophil. 'Tis pretty odd that my mistress should so much resemble his: the same newsmonger, the same passionate lover of a court, the same— But *basta*,[21] since I must marry her, I'll say nothing, because he shall not laugh at my misfortune.

RHODOPHIL.

Well Palamede, how go the affairs of love? You've seen your mistress?

PALAMEDE.

I have so.

RHODOPHIL.

And how, and how? has the old Cupid, your father, chosen well for you? Is he a good woodman?[22]

PALAMEDE.

She's much handsomer than I could have imagined. In short, I love her and will marry her.

RHODOPHIL.

Then you are quite off from your other mistress?

PALAMEDE.

You are mistaken. I intend to love 'em both, as a reasonable man ought to do. For, since all women have their faults and imperfections, 'tis fit that one of 'em should help out t'other.

RHODOPHIL.

This were a blessed doctrine, indeed, if our wives would hear it, but they're their own enemies. If they would suffer us but now and then to make excursions, the benefit of our variety would be theirs. Instead of one, continued, lazy, tired love, they would in their turns have twenty vigorous, fresh, and active loves.

PALAMEDE.

And I would ask any of 'em whether a poor narrow brook, half dry the best part of the year and running ever one way, be compared to a lusty stream that has ebbs and flows?

RHODOPHIL.

Aye, or is half so profitable for navigation?

Enter Doralice walking by and reading.

PALAMEDE.

'Od's* my life, Rhodophil, will you keep my counsel?

RHODOPHIL.

Yes. Where's the secret.

PALAMEDE. (*Showing Doralice.*)

There 'tis. I may tell you as my friend, *sub sigillo*,[23] etcetera, this is that very numerical[24] lady with whom I am in love.

RHODOPHIL. (*Aside.*)

By all that's virtuous, my wife!

PALAMEDE.

You look strangely. How do you like her? Is she not very handsome?

RHODOPHIL. (*Aside.*)

Sure he abuses me.—Why the devil do you ask my judgment?

PALAMEDE.

You are so dogged now, you think no man's mistress handsome but your own. Come, you shall hear her talk too; she has wit, I assure you.

RHODOPHIL. (*Going back.*)

This is too much, Palamede.

PALAMEDE. (*Pulling him forward.*)

Prithee do not hang back so. Of an old, tried lover, thou art the most bashful fellow!

DORALICE. (*Looking up.*)

Were you so near and would not speak, dear husband?

---

19 French gibberish] legal French, a mixture of French, Latin, and English used in English law until the eighteenth century

20 rising blow] literally, an upper cut in a fight (cuffs)

21 *basta*] enough (It. and Sp.)

22 woodman] hunter

23 *sub sigillo*] under seal; in confidence (Lat.)

24 numerical] identical

PALAMEDE. (*Aside.*)

Husband, quotha! I have cut out a fine piece of 155
work for myself.

RHODOPHIL.

Pray Spouse, how long have you been acquainted
with this gentleman?

DORALICE.

Who, I acquainted with this stranger? To my best
knowledge, I never saw him before. 160

Enter Melantha at the other end.

PALAMEDE. (*Aside.*)

Thanks, Fortune, thou hast helped me.

RHODOPHIL.

Palamede, this must not pass so. I must know your
mistress a little better.

PALAMEDE.

It shall be your own fault else. Come, I'll introduce
you. 165

RHODOPHIL.

Introduce me! Where?

PALAMEDE. (*Pointing to Melantha, who swiftly
passes over the stage.*)

There. To my mistress.

RHODOPHIL.

Who? Melantha! Oh heavens, I did not see her.

PALAMEDE.

But I did. I am an eagle where I love; I have seen
her this half hour. 170

DORALICE. (*Aside.*)

I find he has wit, he has got off so readily. But it
would anger me if he should love Melantha.

RHODOPHIL. (*Aside.*)

Now I could e'en wish it were my wife he loved; I
find he's to be married to my mistress.

PALAMEDE.

Shall I run after and fetch her back again to present 175
you to her?

RHODOPHIL.

No, you need not, I have the honor to have some
small acquaintance with her.

PALAMEDE. (*Aside.*)

Oh Jupiter! What a blockhead was I not to find it
out! My wife that must be is his mistress. I did a little 180
suspect it before. Well, I must marry her, because
she's handsome and because I hate to be disinherited

for a younger brother, which I am sure I shall be if
I disobey. And yet I must keep in with Rhodophil,
because I love his wife. (*To Rhodophil.*) I must desire 185
you to make my excuse to your lady, if I have been
so unfortunate to cause any mistake, and withal, to
beg the honor of being known to her.

RHODOPHIL.

Oh, that's but reason. Hark you, Spouse, pray look
upon this gentleman as my friend, whom, to my 190
knowledge, you have never seen before this hour.

DORALICE.

I'm so obedient a wife, sir, that my husband's
commands shall ever be a law to me.

*Enter Melantha again, hastily, and runs to embrace
Doralice.*

MELANTHA.

Oh my dear, I was just going to pay my devoirs
to you; I had not time this morning, for making 195
my court to the King and our new Prince. Well
never nation was so happy, and all that, in a young
prince, and he's the kindest person in the world
to me, let me die if he is not.

DORALICE.

He has been bred up far from court, and 200
therefore—

MELANTHA.

That imports not. Though he has not seen the
grand monde, and all that, let me die but he has
the air of the court, most absolutely.

PALAMEDE.

But yet, madam, he— 205

MELANTHA.

Oh servant, you can testify that I am in his good
graces. Well, I cannot stay long with you, because
I have promised him this afternoon to— But hark
you, my dear, I'll tell you a secret. (*Whispers to
Doralice.*) 210

RHODOPHIL. (*Aside.*)

The Devil's in me, that I must love this woman.

PALAMEDE. (*Aside.*)

The Devil's in me, that I must marry this woman.

MELANTHA. (*Raising her Voice.*)

So the Prince and I— But you must make a secret
of this, my dear, for I would not for the world your
husband should hear it, or my tyrant there that 215
must be.

PALAMEDE. (*Aside.*)

Well, fair impertinent, your whisper is not lost, we hear you.

DORALICE.

I understand then, that—

MELANTHA.

I'll tell you, my dear, the Prince took me by the hand 220
and pressed it *à la dérobé*,[25] because the King was near, made the *doux yeux* to me,[26] and *ensuite*,[27] said a thousand gallantries, or let me die, my dear.

DORALICE.

Then I am sure you—

MELANTHA.

You are mistaken, my dear. 225

DORALICE.

What, before I speak?

MELANTHA.

But I know your meaning; you think, my dear, that I assumed something of *fierté*[28] into my countenance to *rebute*[29] him, but quite contrary, I regarded him, I know not how to express it in 230
our dull Sicilian language, *d'un air enjoué*,[30] and said nothing but *à d'autre, à d'autre*,[31] and that it was all *grimace*[32] and would not pass upon me.

Enter Artemis: Melantha sees her and runs away from Doralice.

(*To Artemis.*)

My dear, I must beg your pardon. I was just making a loose from Doralice to pay my respects 235
to you. Let me die if I ever pass time so agreeably as in your company and if I would leave it for any lady's in Sicily.

ARTEMIS.

The Princess Amalthea is coming this way.

Enter Amalthea: Melantha runs to her.

---

25 *à la dérobé*] secretly; on the sly
26 made the *doux yeux* to me] made eyes at me
27 *ensuite*] then
28 *fierté*] pride, haughtiness
29 *rebute*] discourage
30 *d'un air enjoué*] in a sprightly manner
31 *à d'autre, à d'autre*] Tell it to someone else.
32 *grimace*] affectation

MELANTHA.

Oh dear madam! I have been at your lodgings in 240
my new *calèche* so often to tell you of a new *amour* betwixt two persons whom you would little suspect for it, that, let me die if one of my coach horses be not dead and another quite tired and sunk under the *fatigue*. 245

AMALTHEA.

Oh Melantha, I can tell you news. The Prince is coming this way.

MELANTHA.

The Prince! Oh sweet Prince! He and I are to— and I forgot it. Your pardon, sweet madam, for my abruptness. Adieu, my dears. Servant, Rhodophil; 250
servant, servant, servant all. (*Exit running.*)

AMALTHEA.

Rhodophil, a word with you. (*Whispers.*)

DORALICE. (*To Palamede.*)

Why do you not follow your mistress, sir?

PALAMEDE.

Follow her? Why, at this rate she'll be at the Indies within this half hour.

DORALICE.

However, if you can't follow her all day, you'll meet 255
her at night, I hope?

PALAMEDE.

But can you in charity suffer me to be so mortified without affording me some relief? If it be but to punish that sign of a husband there, that lazy matrimony, that dull insipid taste, who leaves such 260
delicious fare at home to dine abroad on worse meat and to pay dear for't into the bargain.

DORALICE.

All this is in vain. Assure yourself, I will never admit of any visit from you in private.

PALAMEDE.

That is to tell me, in other words, my condition 265
is desperate.

DORALICE.

I think you in so ill a condition that I am resolved to pray for you this very evening in the close walk behind the terrace, for that's a private place, and there I am sure nobody will disturb my devotions. 270
And so, goodnight, sir. (*Exit.*)

PALAMEDE.

This is the newest way of making an appointment

I ever heard of. Let women alone to contrive the means; I find we are but dunces to 'em. Well, I will not be so profane a wretch as to interrupt her devotions, but to make 'em more effectual, I'll down upon my knees and endeavor to join my own with 'em. (*Exit.*) 275

AMALTHEA. (*To Rhodophil.*)

    I know already they do not love each other and that my brother acts but a forced obedience to the King's commands, so that if a quarrel* should arise betwixt the Prince and him, I were most miserable on both sides. 280

RHODOPHIL.

    There shall be nothing wanting* in me, madam, to prevent so sad a consequence. 285

Enter the King, Leonidas; the King whispers to Amalthea.

(*To himself.*)

    I begin to hate this Palamede, because he is to marry my mistress, yet break with him I dare not for fear of being quite excluded from her company. 'Tis a hard case when a man must go by his rival to his mistress, but 'tis at worst but using him like a pair of heavy boots in a dirty journey. After I have fouled him all day, I'll throw him off at night. (*Exit.*) 290

AMALTHEA. (*To the King.*)

    This honor is too great for me to hope.

POLYDAMAS.

    You shall this hour have the assurance of it.
Leonidas, come hither: you have heard, 295
I doubt not, that the father of this Princess
Was my most faithful friend while I was yet
A private man, and when I did assume
This crown, he served me in that high attempt.
You see, then, to what gratitude obliges me: 300
Make your addresses to her.

LEONIDAS.

    Sir, I am yet too young to be a courtier;
I should too much betray my ignorance
And want* of breeding to so fair a lady.

AMALTHEA. 305

    Your language speaks you not bred up in deserts
But in the softness of some Asian court,
Where luxury and ease invent kind words
To cozen tender virgins of their hearts.

POLYDAMAS.

    You need not doubt 310
But in what words soe'er a prince can offer
His crown and person, they will be received.
You know my pleasure, and you know your duty.

LEONIDAS.

    Yes sir, I shall obey in what I can.

POLYDAMAS.

    In what you can, Leonidas? Consider, 315
He's both your king and father who commands you.
Besides, what is there hard in my injunction?

LEONIDAS.

    'Tis hard to have my inclination forced.
I would not marry, sir, and when I do,
I hope you'll give me freedom in my choice. 320

POLYDAMAS.

    View well this lady,
Whose mind as much transcends her beauteous face
As that excels all others.

AMALTHEA.

    My beauty, as it ne'er could merit love,
So neither can it beg. And sir, you may 325
Believe that what the King has offered you,
I should refuse, did I not value more
Your person then your crown.

LEONIDAS.

                Think it not pride
Or my new fortunes swell me to contemn you; 330
Think less that I want* eyes to see your beauty;
And least of all think duty wanting* in me
T'obey a father's will. But—

POLYDAMAS.

                But what, Leonidas?
For I must know your reason. And be sure 335
It be convincing too.

LEONIDAS.

            Sir, ask the stars,
Which have imposed love on us like a fate,
Why minds are bent to one and fly another?
Ask why all beauties cannot move all hearts? 340
For though there may
Be made a rule for color or for feature,
There can be none for liking.

POLYDAMAS.

    Leonidas, you owe me more
Than to oppose your liking to my pleasure. 345

LEONIDAS.

I owe you all things, sir, but something too
I owe myself.

POLYDAMAS.

You shall dispute no more: I am a king,
And I will be obeyed.

LEONIDAS.

You are a king, sir, but you are no god,   350
Or if you were, you could not force my will.

POLYDAMAS. (*Aside.*)

But you are just, you gods, oh you are just
In punishing the crimes of my rebellion
With a rebellious son!
Yet I can punish him, as you do me.   355
—Leonidas, there's no jesting with
My will. I ne'er had done so much to gain
A crown, but to be absolute in all things.

AMALTHEA.

Oh sir, be not so much a king as to
Forget you are a father. Soft indulgence   360
Becomes that name. Though Nature gives you pow'r
To bind his duty, 'tis with silken bonds.
Command him, then, as you command yourself.
He is as much a part of you as are
Your appetite and will, and those you force not   365
But gently bend and make 'em pliant to your reason.

POLYDAMAS.

It may be I have used too rough a way.
Forgive me, my Leonidas. I know
I lie as open to the gusts of passion
As the bare shore to every beating surge.   370
I will not force thee now. But I entreat thee,
Absolve[33] a father's vow to this fair virgin,
A vow which hopes of having such a son
First caused.

LEONIDAS.

Show not my disobedience by your prayers,   375
For I must still deny you, though I now
Appear more guilty to myself than you.
I have some reasons, which I cannot utter,
That force my disobedience, yet I mourn
To death that the first thing you e'er enjoined me 380
Should be that only one command in nature
Which I could not obey.

---

33 absolve] discharge

POLYDAMAS. [*Aside.*]

I did descend too much below myself
When I entreated him.—Hence, to thy desert.
Thou'rt not my son or art not fit to be.   385

AMALTHEA. (*Kneeling.*)

Great sir, I humbly beg you, make not me
The cause of your displeasure. I absolve
Your vow. Far, far from me be such designs,
So wretched a desire of being great
By making him unhappy. You may see   390
Something so noble in the Prince his* nature
As grieves him more not to obey than you
That are not obeyed.

POLYDAMAS.

Then, for your sake,
I'll give him one day longer, to consider,[b]   395
Not to deny, for my resolves are firm
As Fate, that cannot change.

Exeunt King and Amalthea.

LEONIDAS.

And so are mine.
This beauteous Princess, charming as she is,
Could never make me happy. I must first   400
Be false to my Palmyra, and then wretched.
But then, a father's anger!
Suppose he should recede from his own vow.
He never would permit me to keep mine.

Enter Palmyra; Argaleon following her, a little after.

See, she appears!
I'll think no more of anything but her.   405
Yet I have one hour good ere I am wretched.
But oh! Argaleon follows her! So night
Treads on the footsteps of a winter's sun
And stalks all black behind him.

PALMYRA.

Oh Leonidas   410
(For I must call you still by that dear name),
Free me from this bad man.

LEONIDAS.

I hope he dares not be injurious to you.

ARGALEON.

I rather was injurious to myself,
Than her.   415

LEONIDAS.

That must be judged when I hear what you said.

ARGALEON.

    I think you need not give yourself that trouble.

    It concerned us alone.

LEONIDAS.

    You answer saucily and indirectly.

    What interest can you pretend in her?   420

ARGALEON.

    It may be, sir, I made her some expressions

    Which I would not repeat, because they were

    Below my rank, to one of hers.

LEONIDAS.

    What did he say, Palmyra?

PALMYRA.

    I'll tell you all. First, he began to look,   425

    And then he sighed, and then he looked again;

    At last, he said my eyes wounded his heart.

    And after that, he talked of flames and fires

    And such strange words that I believed he conjured.

LEONIDAS.

    Oh my heart! Leave me, Argaleon.   430

ARGALEON.

    Come, sweet Palmyra,

    I will instruct you better in my meaning.

    You see he would be private.

LEONIDAS.

                    Go yourself,

    And leave her here.   435

ARGALEON.

               Alas, she's ignorant

    And is not fit to entertain a prince.

LEONIDAS.

    First learn what's fit for you: that's to obey.

ARGALEON.

    I know my duty is to wait on you.

    A great king's son, like you, ought to forget   440

    Such mean converse.

LEONIDAS.

               What? A disputing subject?

    Hence, or my sword shall do me justice on thee.

ARGALEON.

    Yet I may find a time. (*Going.*)

LEONIDAS. (*Going after him.*)

              What's that you mutter,   445

    To find a time?

ARGALEON.

            To wait on you again.

(*Softly.*)

    In the meanwhile I'll watch you. (*Exit, and

        watches during the scene.*)

LEONIDAS.

    How precious are the hours of love in courts!   450

    In cottages, where love has all the day

    Full and at ease, he throws it half away.

    Time gives himself and is not valued there

    But sells at mighty rates each minute here.

    There, he is lazy, unemployed, and slow;   455

    Here, he's more swift and yet has more to do:

    So many of his hours in public move,

    That few are left for privacy and love.

PALMYRA.

    The sun, methinks, shines faint and dimly here;

    Light is not half so long nor half so clear.   460

    But oh! when every day was yours and mine,

    How early up! What haste he made to shine!

LEONIDAS.

    Such golden days no prince must hope to see,

    Whose ev'ry subject is more blessed than he.

PALMYRA.

    Do you remember, when their tasks were done,   465

    How all the youth did to our cottage run?

    While winter winds were whistling loud without,

    Our cheerful hearth was circled round about.

    With strokes in ashes maids their lovers drew,[34]

    And still* you fell to me, and I to you.   470

LEONIDAS.

    When love did of my heart possession take,

    I was so young my soul was scarce awake.

    I cannot tell when first I thought you fair,

    But sucked in love insensibly as air.

PALMYRA.

    I know too well when first my love began,   475

    When at our wake[35] you for the chaplet ran.

    Then I was made the lady of the May[36]

    And with the garland at the goal did stay.

    Still,* as you ran, I kept you full in view.

    I hoped and wished and ran, methought, for you.   480

    As you came near, I hastily did rise

---

34 drew] represented

35 wake] an annual English parish festival held in honor
    of the church's patron saint

36 lady of the May] queen of the games on May Day

And stretched my arm outright that held the prize.
The custom was to kiss whom I should crown.
You kneeled and, in my lap, your head laid down.
I blushed and blushed and did the kiss delay.   485
At last my subjects forced me to obey.
But when I gave the crown and then the kiss,
I scarce had breath to say, take that—and this.

LEONIDAS.

I felt the while a pleasing kind of smart;
The kiss went tingling to my very heart.   490
When it was gone, the sense of it did stay;
The sweetness clinged upon my lips all day
Like drops of honey loath to fall away.

PALMYRA.

Life, like a prodigal, gave all his store
To my first youth and now can give no more.   495
You are a prince and in that high degree
No longer must converse with humble me.

LEONIDAS.

'Twas to my loss the gods that title gave;
A tyrant's son is doubly born a slave.
He gives a crown but, to prevent my life   500
From being happy, loads it with a wife.

PALMYRA.

Speak quickly: What have you resolved to do?

LEONIDAS.

To keep my faith inviolate to you.
He threatens me with exile and with shame,
To lose my birthright and a prince his* name.   505
But there's a blessing which he did not mean,
To send me back to love and you again.

PALMYRA.

Why was not I a princess for your sake?
But Heav'n no more such miracles can make,
And since that cannot, this must never be: 510
You shall not lose a crown for love of me.
Live happy and a nobler choice pursue;
I shall complain of Fate but not of you.

LEONIDAS.

Can you so easily without me live?
Or could you take the counsel which you give?   515
Were you a princess, would you not be true?

PALMYRA.

I would but cannot merit it from you.

LEONIDAS.

Did you not merit, as you do, my heart?

Love gives esteem and then it gives desert.
But if I basely could forget my vow,   520
Poor helpless innocence, what would you do?

PALMYRA.

In woods and plains where first my love began,
There would I live retired from faithless man:
I'd sit all day within some lonely shade
Or that close arbor which your hands have made;   525
I'd search the groves and ev'ry tree to find
Where you had carved our names upon the rind.
Your hook, your scrip, all that was yours, I'd keep
And lay 'em by me when I went to sleep.
Thus would I live, and maidens, when I die,   530
Upon my hearse white true love knots should tie.
And thus my tomb should be inscribed above,
"Here the forsaken virgin rests from love."

LEONIDAS.

Think not that time or fate shall e'er divide
Those hearts, which love and mutual vows have   535
      tied.[37]
But we must part: farewell, my love.

PALMYRA.

                                        Till when?

LEONIDAS.

Till the next age of hours we meet again.
Meantime—we may,
When near each other we in public stand,   540
Contrive to catch a look or steal a hand.
Fancy will every touch and glance improve
And draw the most spirituous parts of love.
Our souls sit close and silently within
And their own web from their own entrails spin.   545
And when eyes meet far off, our sense is such
That, spider-like, we feel the tender'st touch.

Exeunt.

Act III, scene i.

Enter Rhodophil, meeting Doralice and Artemis.
Rhodophil and Doralice embrace.

RHODOPHIL.

My own dear heart!

---

37 mutual vows have tied] Mutual vows, even unwitnessed,
    were as legally binding as public marriage ceremonies
    in Restoration England.

DORALICE.

My own true love! (*She starts back.*) I had forgot
myself to be so kind;* indeed, I am very angry with
you, dear: you are come home an hour after you
appointed. If you had stayed a minute longer, I was   5
just considering whether I should stab, hang, or
drown myself. (*Embracing him.*)

RHODOPHIL.

Nothing but the King's business could have
hindered me, and I was so vexed that I was just
laying down my commission rather than have   10
failed my dear. (*Kissing her hand.*)

ARTEMIS.

Why, this is love as it should be betwixt man and
wife. Such another couple would bring marriage
into fashion again. But is it always thus betwixt you?

RHODOPHIL.

Always thus! This is nothing. I tell you there is not   15
such a pair of turtles* in all Sicily. There is such
an eternal cooing and kissing betwixt us that
indeed it is scandalous before civil company.

DORALICE.

Well, if I had imagined I should have been this fond
fool, I would never have married the man I loved. I   20
married to be happy and have made myself
miserable by over-loving. Nay, and now my case is
desperate, for I have been married above these two
years and find myself every day worse and worse in
love. Nothing but madness can be the end on't.   25

ARTEMIS.

Dote on to the extremity, and you are happy.

DORALICE.

He deserves so infinitely much that, the truth is,
there can be no doting in the matter. But to love
well, I confess, is a work that pays itself: 'tis telling
gold and, after, taking it for one's pains.   30

RHODOPHIL.

By that I should be a very covetous person, for I
am ever pulling out my money and putting it into
my pocket again.

Embracing each other.

DORALICE.

Oh dear Rhodophil!

RHODOPHIL.

Oh sweet Doralice!   35

ARTEMIS. (*Aside.*)

Nay, I am resolved I'll never interrupt lovers. I'll
leave 'em as happy as I found 'em. (*Steals away.*)

RHODOPHIL. (*Looking up.*)

What, is she gone?

DORALICE.

Yes, and without taking leave.   40

RHODOPHIL. (*Parting from her.*)

Then there's enough for this time.

DORALICE.

Yes, sure the scene's done, I take it.

*They walk contrary ways on the stage: he with his
hands in his pocket, whistling; she singing a dull
melancholy tune.*

RHODOPHIL.

Pox o'your dull tune, a man can't think for you.

DORALICE.

Pox o'your damned whistling: you can neither be
company to me yourself nor leave me to the   45
freedom of my own fancy.

RHODOPHIL.

Well, thou art the most provoking wife!

DORALICE.

Well, thou art the dullest husband. Thou art never
to be provoked.

RHODOPHIL.

I was never thought dull till I married thee. And   50
now thou hast made an old knife of me. Thou hast
whetted me so long, till I have no edge left.

DORALICE.

I see you are in the husband's fashion: you reserve
all your good humors for your mistresses and keep
your ill for your wives.   55

RHODOPHIL.

Prithee, leave me to my own cogitations; I am
thinking over all my sins, to find for which of them
it was I married thee.

DORALICE.

Whatever your sin was, mine's the punishment.

RHODOPHIL.

My comfort is thou art not immortal, and when   60
that blessed, that divine day comes of thy
departure, I'm resolved I'll make one holy day
more in the almanac for thy sake.

DORALICE.

Aye, you had need make a holy day for me, for I am sure you have made me a martyr. 65

RHODOPHIL.

Then, setting my victorious foot upon thy head, in the first hour of thy silence (that is, the first hour thou art dead, for I despair of it before), I will swear by thy ghost an oath, as terrible to me as Styx is to the Gods, never more to be in danger 70 of the banes[38] of matrimony.

DORALICE.

And I am resolved to marry the very same day thou die'st, if it be but to show how little I'm concerned for thee.

RHODOPHIL.

Prithee Doralice, why do we quarrel thus a-days? 75 Hah? This is but a kind of heathenish life and does not answer the ends of marriage. If I have erred, propound what reasonable atonement may be made before we sleep, and I shall not be refractory. But withal consider I have been married these three 80 years, and be not too tyrannical.

DORALICE.

What should you talk of a peace abed, when you can give no security for performance of articles?

RHODOPHIL.

Then, since we must live together and both of us stand upon our terms as to matter of dying first, 85 let us make ourselves as merry as we can with our misfortunes. Why there's the devil on't! If thou couldst make my enjoying thee but a little less easy or a little more unlawful, thou shouldst see what a termagant lover I would prove. I have taken such 90 pains to enjoy thee, Doralice, that I have fancied thee all the fine women in the town to help me out. But now there's none left for me to think on, my imagination is quite jaded. Thou art a wife, and thou wilt be a wife, and I can make thee 95 another no longer. (*Exit.*)

DORALICE.

Well, since thou art a husband and wilt be a husband, I'll try if I can find out another! 'Tis a

pretty time we women have on't, to be made widows while we are married. Our husbands think it reason- 100 able to complain that we are the same, and the same to them, when we have more reason to complain that they are not the same to us. Because they cannot feed on one dish, therefore we must be starved. 'Tis enough that they have a sufficient ordinary provided 105 and a table ready spread for 'em. If they cannot fall to and eat heartily, the fault is theirs, and 'tis pity, methinks, that the good creature should be lost when many a poor sinner would be glad on't.

Enter Melantha and Artemis to her.

MELANTHA.

Dear, my dear, pity me, I am so chagrin today and 110 have had the most signal affront at court! I went this afternoon to do my devoir to Princess Amalthea, found her, conversed with her, and helped to make her court some half an hour, after which she went to take the air, chose out two ladies 115 to go with her that came in after me, and left me most barbarously behind her.

ARTEMIS.

You are the less to be pitied, Melantha, because you subject yourself to these affronts by coming perpetually to court, where you have no business 120 nor employment.

MELANTHA.

I declare, I had rather of the two, be *raillied*,[39] nay, *mal traitée* at court, than be deified in the town. For assuredly, nothing can be so *ridicule*, as a mere town lady. 125

DORALICE.

Especially at court. How I have seen 'em crowd and sweat in the Drawing Room* on a holiday night! For that's their time to swarm and invade the presence. Oh, how they catch at a bow or any little salute* from a courtier to make show of their acquaintance! 130 And rather than be thought to be quite unknown, they curtsy to one another. But they take true pains to come near the circle and press and peep upon the Princess, to write letters into the country how she was dressed, while the ladies that stand about make 135 their court to her with abusing them.

---

38 banes] obsolete spelling of banns, the public announce-
ment of a proposed marriage, but also a pun on the
modern meanings, poison, death, destruction

39 *raillied*] mocked (Frenglish)

ARTEMIS.

These are sad truths, Melantha. And therefore I would e'en advise you to quit the court and live either wholly in the town or, if you like not that, in the country. 140

DORALICE.

In the country! Nay, that's to fall beneath the town, for they live there upon our offals here. Their entertainment of wit is only the remembrance of what they had when they were last in town. They live this year upon the last year's knowledge, as 145 their cattle do all night by chewing the cud of what they ate in the afternoon.

MELANTHA.

And they tell, for news, such unlikely stories. A letter from one of us is such a present to 'em that the poor souls wait for the carrier's day with such 150 devotion that they cannot sleep the night before.

ARTEMIS.

No more than I can the night before I am to go a journey.

DORALICE.

Or I, before I am to try on a new gown.

MELANTHA.

A song that's stale here will be new there a 155 twelvemonth hence, and if a man of the town by chance come amongst 'em, he's reverenced for teaching 'em the tune.

DORALICE.

A friend of mine, who makes songs sometimes, came lately out of the west and vowed he was so 160 put out of countenance with a song of his, for at the first country gentleman's he visited, he saw three tailors crosslegged upon the table in the hall, who were tearing as loud as ever they could sing, "After the pangs of a desperate lover,"[40] etcetera, 165 and all the day heard nothing else but the daughters of the house and the maids humming it over in every corner and the father whistling it.

ARTEMIS.

Indeed, I have observed of myself that when I am out of town but a fortnight, I am so humble that I 170 would receive a letter from my tailor or mercer for a favor.

MELANTHA.

When I have been at grass in the summer and am new come up again, methinks I'm to be turned into *ridicule* by all that see me. But when I have 175 been once or twice at court, I begin to value myself again and to despise my country acquaintance.

ARTEMIS.

There are places where all people may be adored, and we ought to know ourselves so well as to choose 'em. 180

DORALICE.

That's very true. Your little courtier's wife, who speaks to the King but once a month, need but go to a town lady and there she may vapor and cry, "The King and I," at every word. Your town lady, who is laughed at in the circle, takes her coach 185 into the city, and there she's called "your honor" and has a banquet from the merchant's wife, whom she laughs at for her kindness. And, as for my finical cit,* she removes but to her country house and there insults over the country gentlewoman 190 that never comes up, who treats her with frumenty and custard and opens her dear bottle of *mirabilis*[41] beside for a gill glass of it at parting.

ARTEMIS.

At last, I see, we shall leave Melantha where we found her, for by your description of the town and country 195 they are become more dreadful to her than the court where she was affronted. But you forget we are to wait on the Princess Amalthea. Come, Doralice.

DORALICE.

Farewell, Melantha.

MELANTHA.

Adieu, my dear. 200

ARTEMIS.

You are out of charity with her, and therefore I shall not give your service.

MELANTHA.

Do not omit it, I beseech you, for I have such a tender for the court that I love it even from the Drawing Room to the lobby and can never be 205 *rebutée* by any usage. But hark you, my dears, one thing I had forgot of great concernment.

---

40 After ... lover] a song from Dryden's play *An Evening's Love* (1668)

41 *mirabilis*] *aqua mirabilis*, a cordial distilled from wine and spices

DORALICE.

Quickly then, we are in haste.

MELANTHA.

Do not call it my "service," that's too vulgar, but
do my *baisemains*[42] to the Princess Amalthea; that   210
is *spirituelle*.[43]

DORALICE.

To do you service then, we will *prendre* the
carosse[44] to Court, and do your *baisemains* to the
Princess Amalthea, in your phrase *spirituelle*.

*Exeunt Artemis and Doralice. Enter Philotis, with a
paper in her hand.*

MELANTHA.

Oh are you there, minion? And well, are you not a   215
most precious* damsel to retard all my visits for want*
of language when you know you are paid so well for
furnishing me with new words for my daily conversation? Let me die if I have not run the risk already to
speak like one of the vulgar. And if I have one phrase   220
left in all my store that is not threadbare and *usé* and
fit for nothing but to be thrown to peasants.

PHILOTIS.

Indeed madam, I have been very diligent in my
vocation, but you have so drained all the French
plays and romances that they are not able to supply   225
you with words for your daily expenses.

MELANTHA.

Drained! what a word's there! *Épuisée*, you sot*
you. Come, produce your morning's work.

PHILOTIS. (*Shows the paper.*)

'Tis here, madam.

MELANTHA.

Oh my Venus! Fourteen or fifteen words to serve   230
me a whole day! Let me die, at this rate I cannot
last till night. Come, read your works. Twenty to
one, half of 'em will not pass muster neither.

PHILOTIS. (*Reads.*)

Sottises.[45]

MELANTHA.

Sottises: *bon*. That's an excellent word to begin   235

withal; as for example, he or she said a thousand
sottises to me. Proceed.

PHILOTIS.

Figure; as what a figure of a man is there! *Naïve*,
and *Naïveté*.   240

MELANTHA.

Naïve! As how?

PHILOTIS.

Speaking of a thing that was naturally said. It was
so *naïve*: or such an innocent piece of simplicity;
'twas such a *naïveté*.

MELANTHA.

Truce with your interpretations; make haste.   245

PHILOTIS.

*Foible, chagrin, grimace, embarrassé, double entendre,
équivoque, éclaircissement, suite, bévue,*[46] *façon,
penchant, coup d'étourdi,*[47] and *ridicule.*

MELANTHA.

Hold, hold, how did they begin?

PHILOTIS.

They began at *sottises* and ended *en ridicule.*   250

MELANTHA.

Now give me your paper in my hand and hold you
my glass* while I practice my postures for the day.
(*Melantha laughs in the glass.*) How does that laugh
become my face?

PHILOTIS.

Sovereignly well, madam.   255

MELANTHA.

Sovereignly! Let me die, that's not amiss. That word
shall not be yours. I'll invent it and bring it up
myself. My new point gorget[48] shall be yours
upon't. Not a word of the word, I charge you.

PHILOTIS.

I am dumb, madam.   260

MELANTHA. (*Looking in the glass again.*)

That glance, how suits it with my face?

PHILOTIS.

'Tis so *languissant*.

MELANTHA.

Languissant! That word shall be mine too, and my

---

42 do my *baisemains*] kiss the hands of; pay my regards to

43 *spirituelle*] witty

44 *prendre* the *carosse*] take the carriage

45 *sottises*] silly things

46 *bévue*] blunder

47 *coup d'étourdi*] thoughtless act

48 point gorget] lace wimple, a covering for the neck and
breast

last Indian gown[49] thine for it. (*Looks again.*) That sigh?   265

PHILOTIS.

'Twill make many a man sigh, madam. 'Tis a mere* *incendiaire*.

MELANTHA.

Take my gimp petticoat for that truth. If thou hast more of these phrases, let me die but I could give away all my wardrobe and go naked for 'em.   270

PHILOTIS.

Go naked? Then you would be a Venus, madam. Oh Jupiter! What had I forgot? This paper was given me by Rhodophil's page.

MELANTHA. (*Reading the letter.*)

"Beg the favor from you—gratify my passion—so far—assignation—in the grotto—behind the terrace   275
clock this evening." Well, for the *billets doux* there's no man in Sicily must dispute with Rhodophil. They are so French, so *galant*, and so *tendre*, that I cannot resist the temptation of the assignation. Now go you away, Philotis; it imports me to practice what I shall   280
say to my servant* when I meet him.

Exit Philotis.

"Rhodophil, you'll wonder at my assurance to meet you here; let me die, I am so out of breath with coming that I can render you no reason of it." Then he will make this *repartee*. "Madam, I have   285
no reason to accuse you for that which is so great a favor to me." Then I reply, "But why have you drawn me to this solitary place? Let me die but I am apprehensive of some violence from you." Then, says he, "Solitude, madam, is most fit for   290
lovers, but by this fair hand—" "Nay, now I vow you're rude, sir. Oh fie, fie, fie. I hope you'll be honorable?" "You'd laugh at me if I should, madam—" "What do you mean to throw me down thus? Ah me! ah, ah, ah."   295

Enter Polydamas, Leonidas, and guards.

Oh Venus! The King and court. Let me die, but I fear they have found my *foible*, and will turn me into *ridicule*. (*Exit running.*)

---

49 Indian gown] dressing gown made of Indian fabric

LEONIDAS.

Sir, I beseech you.

POLYDAMAS.

Do not urge my patience.   300

LEONIDAS.

I'll not deny
But what your spies informed you of is true:
I love the fair Palmyra. But I loved her
Before I knew your title to my blood.

Enter Palmyra, guarded.

See, here she comes and looks, amidst her guards,   305
Like a weak dove under the falcon's grip.
Oh Heav'n, I cannot bear it.

POLYDAMAS.

Maid, come hither.
Have you presumed so far as to receive
My son's affection?   310

PALMYRA. [*Aside.*]

Alas, what shall I answer? To confess it
Will raise a blush upon a virgin's face.
Yet I was ever taught 'twas base to lie.

POLYDAMAS.

You've been too bold, and you must love no more.

PALMYRA.

Indeed I must; I cannot help my love.   315
I was so tender when I took the bent
That now I grow that way.

POLYDAMAS.

He is a prince, and you are meanly born.

LEONIDAS.

Love either finds equality or makes it.
Like death, he knows no difference in degrees   320
But planes and levels all.

PALMYRA.

Alas, I had not rendered up my heart
Had he not loved me first. But he preferred me
Above the maidens of my age and rank,
Still* shunned their company, and still* sought mine.   325
I was not won by gifts, yet still* he gave.
And all his gifts, though small, yet spoke his love.
He picked the earliest strawberries in woods,
The clustered filberts, and the purple grapes.
He taught a prating stare[50] to speak my name.   330

---

50 stare] starling

And when he found a nest of nightingales,
Or callow linnets, he would show 'em me,
And let me take 'em out.

POLYDAMAS.

This is a little mistress, meanly born,
Fit only for a prince's vacant hours,   335
And then, to laugh at her simplicity,
Not fix a passion there. Now hear my sentence.

LEONIDAS.

Remember ere you give it, 'tis pronounced
Against us both.

POLYDAMAS.

First, in her hand   340
There shall be placed a player's painted scepter
And on her head a gilded pageant crown.
Thus shall she go,
With all the boys attending on her triumph.
That done, be put alone into a boat   345
With bread and water only for three days.
So on the sea she shall be set adrift,
And who relieves her, dies.

PALMYRA.

I only beg that you would execute
The last part first. Let me be put to sea.   350
The bread and water for my three days' life
I give you back; I would not live so long.
But let me 'scape the shame.

LEONIDAS.

Look to me, Piety, and you, oh gods, look to my
  piety:
Keep me from saying that which misbecomes a son,   355
But let me die before I see this done.

POLYDAMAS.

If you forever will abjure her sight,
I can be yet a father; she shall live.

LEONIDAS.

Hear, oh you Pow'rs, is this to be a father?
I see 'tis all my happiness and quiet   360
You aim at, sir. And take 'em.
I will not save ev'n my Palmyra's life
At that ignoble price. But I'll die with her.

PALMYRA.

So had I done by you
Had Fate made me a princess. Death, methinks,   365
Is not a terror now;
He is not fierce or grim but fawns and soothes me

And slides along, like Cleopatra's aspic,
Off'ring his service to my troubled breast.

LEONIDAS.

Begin what you have purposed when you please.   370
Lead her to scorn, your triumph shall be doubled.
As holy priests
In pity go with dying malefactors,
So will I share her shame.

POLYDAMAS.

You shall not have your will so much.—First part   375
  'em,
Then execute your office.

LEONIDAS. (*Draws his sword.*)

                              No, I'll die
In her defense.

PALMYRA.

                   Ah hold, and pull not on
A curse to make me worthy of my death.   380
Do not by lawless force oppose your father,
Whom you have too much disobeyed for me.

LEONIDAS. (*Presenting his sword to his father upon
  his knees.*)

Here, take it, sir, and with it, pierce my heart.
You have done more in taking my Palmyra.
You are my father, therefore I submit.   385

POLYDAMAS.

Keep him from anything he may design
Against his life, whilst the first fury lasts,
And now perform what I commanded you.

LEONIDAS.

In vain: if sword and poison be denied me,
I'll hold my breath and die.   390

PALMYRA.

Farewell, my last Leonidas. Yet live,
I charge you live till you believe me dead.
I cannot die in peace if you die first.
If life's a blessing, you shall have it last.

POLYDAMAS.

Go on with her, and lead him after me.   395

Enter Argaleon hastily, with Hermogenes.

ARGALEON.

I bring you, sir, such news as must amaze you
And such as will prevent you from an action
Which would have rendered all your life unhappy.

Hermogenes kneels.

POLYDAMAS.

    Hermogenes, you bend your knees in vain,   400

    My doom's already passed.

HERMOGENES.

    I kneel not for Palmyra, for I know

    She will not need my pray'rs, but for myself:

    With a feigned tale I have abused your ears

    And therefore merit death. But since, unforced,   405

    I first accuse myself, I hope your mercy.

POLYDAMAS.

    Haste to explain your meaning.

HERMOGENES.

    Then in few words, Palmyra is your daughter.

POLYDAMAS.

    How can I give belief to this impostor?

    He who has once abused me, often may.   410

    I'll hear no more.

ARGALEON.

              For your own sake, you must.

HERMOGENES.

    A parent's love (for I confess my crime)

    Moved me to say Leonidas was yours,

    But when I heard Palmyra was to die,   415

    The fear of guiltless blood so stung my conscience

    That I resolved, ev'n with my shame, to save

    Your daughter's life.

POLYDAMAS.

    But how can I be certain but that interest,

    Which moved you first to say your son was mine,   420

    Does not now move you too to save your daughter?

HERMOGENES.

    You had but then my word; I bring you now

    Authentic testimonies. Sir, in short,

    (*Delivers on his knees a jewel, and a letter.*)

    If this will not convince you, let me suffer.   425

POLYDAMAS. (*Looking first on the jewel.*)

    I know this jewel well, 'twas once my mother's,

    Which, marrying, I presented to my wife.

    And this, oh this is my Eudocia's hand.

    (*Reads.*)

    "This was the pledge of love given to Eudocia,

    Who, dying, to her young Palmyra leaves it.   430

    And this when you, my dearest lord, receive,

    Own her, and think on me, dying Eudocia."

    (*To Argaleon.*)

    Take it; 'tis well there is no more to read,

My eyes grow full and swim in their own light.

    (*He embraces Palmyra.*)

PALMYRA.

    I fear, sir, this is your intended pageant.   435

    You sport yourself at poor Palmyra's cost.

    But if you think to make me proud,

    Indeed I cannot be so: I was born

    With humble thoughts and lowly, like my birth.

    A real fortune could not make me haughty,   440

    Much less a feigned.

POLYDAMAS.

               This was her mother's temper.

    I have too much deserved thou shouldst suspect

    That I am not thy father, but my love

    Shall henceforth show I am. Behold my eyes,   445

    And see a father there begin to flow:

    This is not feigned, Palmyra.

PALMYRA.

    I doubt no longer, sir. You are a king

    And cannot lie. Falsehood's a vice too base

    To find a room in any royal breast.   450

    I know, in spite of my unworthiness,

    I am your child, for when you would have killed me,

    Methought I loved you then.

ARGALEON.

    Sir, we forget the Prince Leonidas,

    His greatness should not stand neglected thus.   455

POLYDAMAS.

    Guards, you may now retire. Give him his sword

    And leave him free.

LEONIDAS.

    Then the first use I make of liberty

    Shall be, with your permission, mighty sir,

    To pay that reverence to which nature binds me.   460

    (*Kneels to Hermogenes.*)

ARGALEON.

    Sure you forget your birth thus to misplace

    This act of your obedience; you should kneel

    To nothing but to Heav'n and to a king.

LEONIDAS.

    I never shall forget what nature owes

    Nor be ashamed to pay it. Though my father   465

    Be not a king, I know him brave and honest

    And well deserving of a worthier son.

POLYDAMAS.

    He bears it gallantly.

LEONIDAS. (*To Hermogenes.*)
Why would you not instruct me, sir, before
Where I should place my duty? 470
From which, if ignorance have made me swerve,
I beg your pardon for an erring son.

PALMYRA.
I almost grieve I am a princess, since
It makes him lose a crown.

LEONIDAS.
And next, to you, my King, thus low I kneel 475
T'implore your mercy. If in that small time
I had the honor to be thought your son
I paid not strict obedience to your will,
I thought, indeed, I should not be compelled,
But thought it as your son; so what I took 480
In duty from you I restored in courage
Because your son should not be forced.

POLYDAMAS.
You have my pardon for it.

LEONIDAS.
To you, fair Princess, I congratulate
Your birth, of which ever I thought you worthy. 485
And give me leave to add that I am proud
The gods have picked me out to be the man
By whose dejected fate yours is to rise,
Because no man could more desire your fortune
Or franklier part with his to make you great. 490

PALMYRA.
I know the King, though you are not his son,
Will still regard you as my foster-brother
And so conduct you downward from a throne
By slow degrees, so unperceived and soft
That it may seem no fall, or if it be, 495
May Fortune lay a bed of down beneath you.

POLYDAMAS.
He shall be ranked with my nobility
And kept from scorn by a large pension giv'n him.

LEONIDAS. (*Bowing.*)
You are all great and royal in your gifts,
But at the donor's feet I lay 'em down. 500
Should I take riches from you, it would seem
As I did want a soul to bear that poverty
To which the gods designed my humble birth.
And should I take your honors without merit,
It would appear I wanted* manly courage 505
To hope 'em, in your service, from my sword.

POLYDAMAS.
Still brave and like yourself.
The court shall shine this night in full splendor
And celebrate this new discovery.*
—Argaleon, lead my daughter. As we go 510
I shall have time to give her my commands,
In which you are concerned.

Exeunt all but Leonidas.

LEONIDAS.
Methinks I do not want
That huge long train of fawning followers
That swept a furlong after me. 515
'Tis true, I am alone.
So was the Godhead ere he made the world
And better served Himself than served by Nature.
And yet I have a soul
Above this humble fate. I could command, 520
Love to do good, give largely to true merit,
All that a king should do. But though these are not
My province, I have seen enough within
To exercise my virtue.
All that a heart so fixed as mine can move 525
Is that my niggard fortune starves my love.

Exit.

Scene ii.

*Palamede and Doralice meet: she with a book in her
hand, seems to start at sight of him.*

DORALICE.
'Tis a strange thing that no warning will serve your
turn and that no retirement will secure me from
your impertinent addresses! Did not I tell you that
I was to be private here at my devotions?

PALAMEDE.
Yes, and you see I have observed my cue exactly. I 5
am come to relieve you from them. Come, shut
up, shut up your book; the man's come who is to
supply all your necessities.

DORALICE.
Then it seems you are so impudent to think it was
an assignation? This, I warrant, was your lewd 10
interpretation of my innocent meaning.

PALAMEDE.
Venus forbid that I should harbor so unreasonable

a thought of a fair young lady that you should lead me hither into temptation. I confess I might think indeed it was a kind of honorable challenge to meet privately without seconds and decide the difference betwixt the two sexes. But Heaven forgive me if I thought amiss.

DORALICE.

You thought too, I'll lay my life on't, that you might as well make love* to me, as my husband does to your mistress.

PALAMEDE.

I was so unreasonable to think so too.

DORALICE.

And then you wickedly inferred that there was some justice in the revenge of it, or at least but little injury for a man to endeavor to enjoy that which he accounts a blessing and which is not valued as it ought by the dull possessor. Confess your wickedness, did you not think so?

PALAMEDE.

I confess I was thinking so, as fast as I could, but you think so much before me that you will let me think nothing.

DORALICE.

'Tis the very thing that I designed. I have forestalled all your arguments and left you without a word more to plead for mercy. If you have anything farther to offer ere sentence pass— Poor animal, I brought you hither only for my diversion.

PALAMEDE.

That you may have if you'll make use of me the right way. But I tell thee, woman, I am now past talking.

DORALICE.

But it may be I came hither to hear what fine things you could say for yourself.

PALAMEDE.

You would be very angry, to my knowledge, if I should lose so much time to say many of 'em. By this hand you would—

DORALICE.

Fie Palamede, I am a woman of honor.

PALAMEDE.

I see you are: you have kept touch with your assignation. And before we part, you shall find that I am a man of honor. Yet I have one scruple of conscience—

DORALICE.

I warrant you will not want* some naughty argument or other to satisfy yourself. I hope you are afraid of betraying your friend?

PALAMEDE.

Of betraying my friend! I am more afraid of being betrayed by you to my friend. You women now are got into the way of telling first yourselves. A man who has any care of his reputation will be loath to trust it with you.

DORALICE.

Oh, you charge your faults upon our sex. You men are like cocks: you never make love* but you clap your wings and crow when you have done.

PALAMEDE.

Nay, rather you women are like hens: you never lay but you cackle an hour after to discover* your nest. But I'll venture it for once.

DORALICE.

To convince you that you are in the wrong, I'll retire into the dark grotto to my devotion and make so little noise that it shall be impossible for you to find me.

PALAMEDE.

But if I find you—

DORALICE.

Aye, if you find me— But I'll put you to search in more corners than you imagine.

She runs in, and he after her. Enter Rhodophil and Melantha.

MELANTHA.

Let me die but this solitude and that grotto are scandalous. I'll go no further; besides, you have a sweet lady of your own.

RHODOPHIL.

But a sweet mistress, now and then, makes my sweet lady so much more sweet.

MELANTHA.

I hope you will not force me?

RHODOPHIL.

But I will, if you desire it.

PALAMEDE. (*Within.*)

Where the devil are you, madam? S'death,* I begin to be weary of this hide and seek. If you stay a little longer till the fit's over, I'll hide in my turn and put you to the finding me. (*He enters, and sees Rhodophil and Melantha.*)

How! Rhodophil and my mistress!

MELANTHA. [*Aside.*]

My servant* to apprehend me! This is *surprenant au dernier.*[51]

RHODOPHIL. [*Aside.*]

I must on; there's nothing but impudence can help 85
me out.

PALAMEDE.

Rhodophil, how came you hither in so good
company?

RHODOPHIL.

As you see, Palamede, an effect of pure friendship:
I was not able to live without you. 90

PALAMEDE.

But what makes my mistress with you?

RHODOPHIL.

Why, I heard you were here alone and could not
in civility but bring her to you.

MELANTHA.

You'll pardon the effects of a passion which I may
now avow for you, if it transported me beyond the 95
rules of *bienséance.*[52]

PALAMEDE.

But who told you I was here? They that told you
that may tell you more, for aught I know.

RHODOPHIL.

Oh for that matter, we had intelligence.

PALAMEDE.

But let me tell you, we came hither so very 100
privately that you could not trace us.

RHODOPHIL.

Us? What us? You are alone.

PALAMEDE. [*Aside.*]

Us! the devil's in me for mistaking.—Me, I meant.
Or us. That is, you are me, or I you, as we are
friends. That's us. 105

DORALICE. (*Within.*)

Palamede, Palamede.

RHODOPHIL.

I should know that voice? Who's within there that
calls you?

PALAMEDE.

Faith, I can't imagine; I believe the place is
haunted. 110

DORALICE. (*Within.*)

Palamede, Palamede, all cocks hidden.[53]

PALAMEDE.

Lord, Lord, what shall I do? Well, dear friend, to let
you see I scorn to be jealous and that I dare trust my
mistress with you, take her back, for I would not
willingly have her frighted, and I am resolved to see 115
who's there. I'll not be daunted with a bugbear, that's
certain. Prithee, dispute it not. It shall be so. Nay, do
not put me to swear, but go quickly. There's an effect
of pure friendship for you now.

Enter Doralice, and looks amazed, seeing them.

RHODOPHIL.

Doralice! I am thunderstruck to see you here. 120

PALAMEDE.

So am I! Quite thunderstruck. Was it you that
called me within? [*Aside.*] I must be impudent.

RHODOPHIL.

How came you hither, Spouse?

PALAMEDE.

Aye, how came you hither? And what is more, how
could you be here without my knowledge? 125

DORALICE.

(*To her husband.*) Oh gentleman, have I caught
you, i'faith? Have I broke forth in ambush upon
you? I thought my suspicions would prove true.

RHODOPHIL.

Suspicions! This is very fine, Spouse! Prithee, what
suspicions? 130

DORALICE.

Oh, you feign ignorance. Why, of you and
Melantha. Here have I stayed these two hours,
waiting with all the rage of a passionate, loving
wife, but infinitely jealous, to take you two in the
manner, for hither I was certain you would come. 135

RHODOPHIL.

But you are mistaken, Spouse, in the occasion, for
we came hither on purpose to find Palamede, on
intelligence he was gone before.

---

51 *surprenant au dernier*] surprising to the extreme
52 *bienséance*] decorum

53 all cocks hidden] variant of "all hid" in hide and seek,
with bawdy connotations

PALAMEDE.

I'll be hanged then if the same party who gave you
intelligence I was here did not tell your wife you 140
would come hither. Now I smell the malice on't
on both sides.

DORALICE.

Was it so, think you? Nay then, I'll confess my part
of the malice too. As soon as ever I spied my
husband and Melantha come together, I had a 145
strange temptation to make him jealous in revenge.
And that made me call "Palamede, Palamede," as
though there had been an intrigue between us.

MELANTHA.

Nay, I avow there was an appearance of an intrigue
between us too. 150

PALAMEDE.

To see how things will come about!

RHODOPHIL. (*Embraces.*)

And was it only thus, my dear Doralice?

DORALICE. (*Embracing him.*)

And did I wrong nown* Rhodophil with a false
suspicion?

PALAMEDE. (*Aside.*)

Now am I confident we had all four the same design. 155
'Tis a pretty odd kind of game this, where each of us
plays for double stakes. This is just thrust and parry
with the same motion: I am to get his wife and yet
to guard my own mistress. But I am vilely suspicious
that while I conquer in the right wing, I shall be 160
routed in the left. For both our women will certainly
betray their party, because they are each of them for
gaining of two, as well as we and I much fear,
If their necessities and ours were known,
They have more need of two than we of one. 165

Exeunt, embracing one another.

Act IV, scene i.

Enter Leonidas, musing, Amalthea following him.

AMALTHEA.

Yonder he is, and I must speak or die.
And yet 'tis death to speak, yet he must know
I have a passion for him and may know it
With a less blush, because to offer it
To his low fortunes shows I loved before 5
His person, not his greatness.

LEONIDAS.

First scorned and now commanded from the court!
The King is good, but he is wrought to this
By proud Argaleon's malice.
What more disgrace can Love and Fortune join 10
T'inflict upon one man? I cannot now
Behold my dear Palmyra. She, perhaps, too
Is grown ashamed of a mean,* ill-placed love.

AMALTHEA. (*Aside.*)

Assist me, Venus, for I tremble when
I am to speak, but I must force myself. 15
—Sir, I would crave but one short minute with you
And some few words.

LEONIDAS. (*Aside.*)

                    The proud Argaleon's sister!

AMALTHEA. (*Aside.*)

Alas, it will not out; shame stops my mouth.
—Pardon my error, sir, I was mistaken 20
And took you for another.

LEONIDAS. (*Aside.*)

In spite of all his guards, I'll see Palmyra.
Though meanly born, I have a kingly soul yet.

AMALTHEA. (*Aside.*)

I stand upon a precipice, where fain
I would retire, but love still thrusts me on. 25
Now I grow bolder and will speak to him.
—Sir, 'tis indeed to you that I would speak,
And if—

LEONIDAS.

Oh, you are sent to scorn my fortunes.
Your sex and beauty are your privilege, 30
But should your brother—

AMALTHEA. [*Aside.*]

Now he looks angry, and I dare not speak.
—I had some business with you, sir,
But 'tis not worth your knowledge.

LEONIDAS.

Then 'twill be charity to let me mourn 35
My griefs alone, for I am much disordered.

AMALTHEA.

'Twill be more charity to mourn 'em with you.
Heav'n knows I pity you.

LEONIDAS.

                    Your pity, madam,
Is generous, but 'tis unavailable.54 40

---

54 unavailable] of no avail

AMALTHEA.

You know not till 'tis tried.
Your sorrows are no secret: you have lost
A crown and mistress.

LEONIDAS.

               Are not these enough?
Hang two such weights on any other soul   45
And see if it can bear 'em.

AMALTHEA.

More: you are banished by my brother's means
And ne'er must hope again to see your princess,
Except as pris'ners view fair walks and streets
And careless passengers[55] going by their grates   50
To make 'em feel the want* of liberty.
But worse than all,
The King this morning has enjoined his daughter
T'accept my brother's love.

LEONIDAS.

               Is this your pity?   55
You aggravate my griefs and print 'em deeper
In new and heavier stamps.

AMALTHEA.

'Tis as physicians show the desperate ill
T'endear their art by mitigating pains
They cannot wholly cure. When you despair   60
Of all you wish, some part of it, because
Unhoped for, may be grateful, and some other—

LEONIDAS.

What other?

AMALTHEA.

Some other may—
(Aside.)
My shame again has seized me, and I can go   65
No farther—

LEONIDAS.

These often failings, sighs, and interruptions
Make me imagine you have grief like mine.
Have you ne'er loved?

AMALTHEA.

          I? Never. (Aside.) 'Tis in vain;   70
I must despair in silence.

LEONIDAS.

You come as I suspected then: to mock,
At least observe my griefs. Take it not ill

_____
55 passengers] passersby

That I must leave you. (Is going.)

AMALTHEA.

You must not go with these unjust opinions.   75
Command my life and fortunes. You are wise:
Think, and think well, what I can do to serve you.

LEONIDAS.

I have but one thing in my thoughts and wishes.
If by your means I can obtain the sight
Of my adored Palmyra or, what's harder,   80
One minute's time to tell her I die hers.
She starts back.
I see I am not to expect it from you
Nor could, indeed, with reason.

AMALTHEA.

Name any other thing. Is Amalthea   85
So despicable she can serve your wishes
In this alone?

LEONIDAS.

           If I should ask of Heav'n,
I have no other suit.

AMALTHEA.

To show you, then, I can deny you nothing,   90
Though 'tis more hard to me than any other,
Yet I will do't for you.

LEONIDAS.

Name quickly, name the means, speak, my good
    angel.

AMALTHEA.

Be not so much o'erjoyed, for if you are,   95
I'll rather die than do it. This night the court
Will be in masquerade.
You shall attend on me; in that disguise
You may both see and speak to her,
If you dare venture it.   100

LEONIDAS.

Yes, were a god her guardian
And bore in each hand thunder, I would venture.

AMALTHEA.

Farewell then. Two hours hence I will expect you.
[Aside.]
My heart's so full that I can stay no longer. (Exit.)

LEONIDAS.

Already it grows dusky; I'll prepare   105
With haste for my disguise. But who are these?

Enter Hermogenes and Eubulus.

HERMOGENES.

'Tis he, we need not fear to speak to him.

EUBULUS.

Leonidas.

LEONIDAS.

　　　　　Sure I have known that voice.

HERMOGENES.

You have some reason, sir, 'tis Eubulus,　　110
Who bred you with the Princess and, departing,
Bequeathed you to my care.

LEONIDAS. (*Kneeling.*)

My foster father! Let my knees express
My joys for your return!

EUBULUS.

Rise, sir, you must not kneel.　　115

LEONIDAS.

　　　　　　　E'er since you left me,
I have been wand'ring in a maze of fate,
Led by false fires of a fantastic glory
And the vain luster of imagined crowns.
But ah! Why would you leave me? Or how could you　120
Absent yourself so long?

EUBULUS.

I'll give you a most just account of both,
And something more I have to tell you which
I know must cause your wonder. But this place,
Though almost hid in darkness, is not safe.　　125

Torches appear.

Already I discern some coming towards us
With lights who may discover me.—Hermogenes,
Your lodgings are hard by and much more private.

HERMOGENES.

There you may freely speak.

LEONIDAS.

　　　　　　　Let us make haste,　　130
For some affairs and of no small importance
Call me another way.

Exeunt. Enter Palamede and Rhodophil, with visor masks in their hands and torches before 'em.

PALAMEDE.

We shall have noble sport tonight, Rhodophil: this masquerading is a most glorious invention.

RHODOPHIL.

I believe it was invented first by some jealous lover　135

to discover the haunts of his jilting mistress or perhaps by some distressed servant* to gain an opportunity with a jealous man's wife.

PALAMEDE.

No, it must be the invention of a woman: it has so much of subtlety and love in it.　　140

RHODOPHIL.

I am sure 'tis extremely pleasant, for to go unknown is the next degree to going invisible.

PALAMEDE.

What with our antique[56] habits and feigned voices, do you know me? and I know you? Methinks we move and talk just like so many　145
overgrown puppets.

RHODOPHIL.

Masquerade is only visor-mask improved, a heightening of the same fashion.

PALAMEDE.

No: masquerade is visor-mask in debauch, and I like it the better for't. For with a visor-mask, we fool　150
ourselves into courtship for the sake of an eye that glanced or a hand that stole itself out of the glove sometimes to give us a sample of the skin. But in masquerade there is nothing to be known; she's all terra incognita, and the bold discoverer leaps ashore　155
and takes his lot among the wild Indians and savages without the vile consideration of safety to his person or of beauty or wholesomeness in his mistress.

Enter Beliza.

RHODOPHIL.

Beliza, what make you here?

BELIZA.

Sir, my lady sent me after you to let you know she　160
finds herself a little indisposed so that she cannot be at court but is retired to rest in her own apartment where she shall want* the happiness of your dear embraces tonight.

RHODOPHIL.

A very fine phrase, Beliza, to let me know my wife　165
desires to lie alone.

PALAMEDE.

I doubt,* Rhodophil, you take the pains sometimes to instruct your wife's woman in these elegancies.

---

56 antique] from earlier times, but also possibly antic

RHODOPHIL.

Tell my dear lady that since I must be so unhappy as
not to wait on her tonight, I will lament bitterly for 170
her absence. 'Tis true, I shall be at court, but I will
take no divertissement there. And when I return to
my solitary bed, if I am so forgetful of my passion as
to sleep, I will dream of her and betwixt sleep and
waking put out my foot towards her side for 175
midnight consolation and, not finding her, I will
sigh and imagine myself a most desolate widower.

BELIZA.

I shall do your commands, sir. (*Exit.*)

RHODOPHIL. (*Aside.*)

She's sick as aptly for my purpose as if she had
contrived it so. Well, if ever woman was a helpmeet 180
for man, my spouse is so, for within this hour I
received a note from Melantha that she would
meet me this evening in masquerade in boy's habit
to rejoice with me before she entered into fetters.
For I find she loves me better than Palamede only 185
because he's to be her husband. There's something
of antipathy in the word "marriage" to the nature
of love; marriage is the mere ladle of affection that
cools it when 'tis never* so fiercely boiling over.

PALAMEDE.

Dear Rhodophil, I must needs beg your pardon; 190
there is an occasion fallen out which I had forgot.
I cannot be at court tonight.

RHODOPHIL.

Dear Palamede, I am sorry we shall not have one
course together at the herd. But I find your game
lies single. Good fortune to you with your mistress. 195
(*Exit.*)

PALAMEDE.

He has wished me good fortune with his wife.
There's no sin in this then; there's fair leave given.
Well, I must go visit the sick; I cannot resist the
temptations of my charity. Oh what a difference will
she find betwixt a dull, resty* husband and a quick,* 200
vigorous lover! He sets out like a carrier's horse,
plodding on because he knows he must, with the
bells of matrimony chiming so melancholy about his
neck, in pain till he's at his journey's end. And
despairing to get thither, he is fain to fortify imagin- 205
ation with the thoughts of another woman. I take
heat after heat, like a well-breathed courser, and—

(*Clashing of swords within.*) But hark, what noise is
that? Swords! Nay then, have with you. (*Exit.*)

*Reenter Palamede, with Rhodophil, and Doralice in
man's habit.*

RHODOPHIL.

Friend, your relief was very timely; otherwise, I had 210
been oppressed.

PALAMEDE.

What was the quarrel?*

RHODOPHIL.

What I did was in rescue of this youth.

PALAMEDE.

What cause could he give 'em?

DORALICE.

The cause was nothing but only the common cause 215
of fighting in masquerades: they were drunk, and
I was sober.

RHODOPHIL.

Have they not hurt you?

DORALICE.

No, but I am exceeding ill with the fright on't.

PALAMEDE.

Let's lead him to some place where he may refresh 220
himself.

RHODOPHIL.

Do you conduct him then.

PALAMEDE. (*Aside.*)

How cross this happens to my design of going to
Doralice! For I am confident she was sick on
purpose that I should visit her.—Hark you, 225
Rhodophil, could not you take care of the
stripling? I am partly engaged tonight.

RHODOPHIL.

You know I have business.—But come, youth, if
it must be so.

DORALICE. (*To Rhodophil.*)

No, good sir, do not give yourself that trouble; I shall 230
be safer and better pleased with your friend here.

RHODOPHIL.

Farewell then, once more I wish you a good
adventure.

PALAMEDE.

Damn this kindness! Now must I be troubled with
this young rogue and miss my opportunity with 235
Doralice.

Exeunt Rhodophil alone, Palamede with Doralice.

Scene ii.

Enter Polydamas.

POLYDAMAS.
  Argaleon counseled well to banish him.
  He has I know not what
  Of greatness in his looks and of high fate
  That almost awes me. But I fear my daughter,
  Who hourly moves me for him, and I marked   5
  She sighed when I but named Argaleon to her.
  But see, the maskers. Hence, my cares: this night
  At least take truce and find me on my pillow.

*Enter the Princess in masquerade, with ladies. At the
other end, Argaleon and gentlemen in masquerade,
then Leonidas leading Amalthea. The King sits. A
dance. After the dance.*

AMALTHEA. (*To Leonidas.*)
  That's the Princess;
  I saw the habit ere she put it on.   10

LEONIDAS.
  I know her by a thousand other signs;
  She cannot hide so much divinity.
  Disguised and silent, yet some graceful motion
  Breaks from her and shines round her like a glory.
    (*Goes to Palmyra.*)

AMALTHEA.
  Thus she reveals herself and knows it not.   15
  Like love's dark lantern, I direct his steps,
  And yet he sees not that which gives him light.

PALMYRA. (*To Leonidas.*)
  I know you. But alas, Leonidas,
  Why should you tempt this danger on yourself?

LEONIDAS.
  Madam, you know me not, if you believe   20
  I would not hazard greater for your sake.
  But you, I fear, are changed.

PALMYRA.
  No, I am still the same.
  But there are many things became Palmyra
  Which ill become the Princess.   25

LEONIDAS.
                        I ask nothing
  Which honor will not give you leave to grant.
  One hour's short audience at my father's house
  You cannot sure refuse me.

PALMYRA.
  Perhaps I should, did I consult strict virtue.   30
  But something must be given to love and you.
  When would you I should come?

LEONIDAS.
  This evening, with the speediest opportunity.
  I have a secret to discover* to you
  Which will surprise and please you.   35

PALMYRA.
                          'Tis enough.
  Go now, for we may be observed and known.
  I trust your honor; give me not occasion
  To blame myself or you.

LEONIDAS.
  You never shall repent your good opinion. (*Kisses 40
    her hand, and exit.*)

ARGALEON.
  I cannot be deceived: that is the Princess.
  One of her maids betrayed the habit to me.
  But who was he with whom she held discourse?
  'Tis one she favors, for he kissed her hand.   45
  Our shapes are like, our habits near the same.
  She may mistake and speak to me for him.
  I am resolved I'll satisfy my doubts
  Though to be more tormented. (*Exit.*)
                      Song.
                        I.
  Whilst Alexis lay pressed   50
  In her arms he loved best,
  With his hands round her neck
  And his head on her breast,
  He found the fierce pleasure too hasty to stay,
  And his soul in the tempest just flying away.   55
                        2.
  When Celia saw this,
  With a sigh and a kiss
  She cried, "Oh my dear, I am robbed of my bliss;
  'Tis unkind to your love and unfaithfully done
  To leave me behind you and die* all alone."   60
                        3.
  The youth, though in haste
  And breathing his last,
  In pity died slowly, while she died more fast;
  Till at length she cried, "Now my dear, now let us
    go,
  Now die, my Alexis, and I will die too."   65

4.

Thus entranced they did lie,
Till Alexis did try
To recover new breath that again he might die.
Then often they died, but the more they did so,
The nymph died more quick and the shepherd   70
     more slow.

*Another dance. After it, Argaleon reenters and stands
by the Princess.*

PALMYRA. (*To Argaleon.*)
     Leonidas, what means this quick return?
ARGALEON. (*Aside.*)
     Oh Heav'n! 'Tis what I feared.
PALMYRA.
     Is aught of moment happened since you went?
ARGALEON.
     No madam, but I understood not fully
     Your last commands.   75
PALMYRA.
                    And yet you answered to 'em.
     Retire, you are too indiscreet a lover.
     I'll meet you where I promised. (*Exit.*)
ARGALEON.
     Oh my curst fortune! What have I discovered?
     But I will be revenged. (*Whispers to the King.*) 80
POLYDAMAS.
     But are you certain you are not deceived?
ARGALEON.
     Upon my life.
POLYDAMAS.
                    Her honor is concerned.
     Somewhat I'll do, but I am yet distracted
     And I know not where to fix. I wished a child, 85
     And Heav'n, in anger, granted my request.
     So blind we are, our wishes are so vain,
     That what we most desire proves most our pain.

Exeunt omnes.

          Scene iii. An eating house.

*Bottles of wine on the table. Palamede, and Doralice in
man's habit.*

DORALICE. (*Aside.*)
     Now cannot I find in my heart to discover* myself,
     though I long he should know me.

PALAMEDE.
     I tell thee, boy, now I have seen thee safe, I must
     be gone. I have no leisure to throw away on thy
     raw conversation. I am a person that understand   5
     better things, I.
DORALICE.
     Were I a woman, oh how you'd admire me! Cry
     up every word I said and screw your face into a
     submissive smile, as I have seen a dull gallant act
     wit and counterfeit pleasantness when he whispers 10
     to a great person in a playhouse, smile and look
     briskly when the other answers, as if something of
     extraordinary had passed betwixt 'em, when,
     heaven knows, there was nothing else but, "What
     o'clock does your lordship think it is?" and my   15
     lord's repartee is, "'Tis almost parktime,"[57] or, at
     most, "Shall we out of the pit and go behind the
     scenes for an act or two?" And yet such fine things
     as these would be wit in a mistress's mouth.
PALAMEDE.
     Aye boy, there's Dame Nature in the case. He who 20
     cannot find wit in a mistress deserves to find
     nothing else, boy. But these are riddles to thee,
     child, and I have not leisure to instruct thee; I have
     affairs to dispatch, great affairs. I am a man of
     business.   25
DORALICE.
     Come, you shall not go. You have no affairs but
     what you may dispatch here, to my knowledge.
PALAMEDE.
     I find now thou art a boy of more understanding
     than I thought thee, a very lewd wicked boy. O'my
     conscience thou wouldst debauch me and hast   30
     some evil designs upon my person.
DORALICE.
     You are mistaken, sir. I would only have you show
     me a more lawful reason why you would leave me
     than I can why you should not, and I'll not stay
     you. For I am not so young but I understand the   35
     necessities of flesh and blood and the pressing
     occasions of mankind as well as you.
PALAMEDE.
     A very forward and understanding boy! Thou art
     in great danger of a page's wit, to be brisk at

---

57 parktime] the fashionable time to be in the park

fourteen and dull at twenty. But I'll give thee no 40
further account; I must and will go.
DORALICE.
My life on't, your mistress is not at home.
PALAMEDE. [*Aside.*]
This imp will make me very angry.—I tell thee,
young sir, she is at home and at home for me, and
what is more, she is abed for me and sick for me. 45
DORALICE.
For you only?
PALAMEDE.
Aye, for me only.
DORALICE.
But how do you know she's sick abed?
PALAMEDE.
She sent her husband word so.
DORALICE.
And are you such a novice in love, to believe a 50
wife's message to her husband?
PALAMEDE.
Why, what the devil should be her meaning else?
DORALICE.
It may be to go in masquerade as well as you, to
observe your haunts and keep you company
without your knowledge. 55
PALAMEDE.
Nay, I'll trust her for that. She loves me too well
to disguise herself from me.
DORALICE.
If I were she, I would disguise on purpose to try
your wit and come to my servant* like a riddle:
"Read me and take me." 60
PALAMEDE.
I could know her in any shape. My good genius*
would prompt me to find out a handsome woman.
There's something in her that would attract me to
her without my knowledge.
DORALICE.
Then you make a loadstone of your mistress? 65
PALAMEDE.
Yes, and I carry steel about me which has been so
often touched that it never fails to point to the
north pole.
DORALICE.
Yet still my mind gives me that you have met her
disguised tonight and have not known her. 70

PALAMEDE.
[*Aside.*] This is the most pragmatical,[58] conceited
little fellow. He will needs understand my business
better then myself.—I tell thee once more, thou
dost not know my mistress.
DORALICE.
And I tell you once more that I know her better 75
than you do.
PALAMEDE. [*Aside.*]
The boy's resolved to have the last word. I find I
must go without reply. (*Exit.*)
DORALICE.
Ah mischief, I have lost him with my fooling.
Palamede, Palamede. 80

*He returns. She plucks off her peruke, and puts it on
again when he knows her.*

PALAMEDE.
Oh heavens! Is it you, madam?
DORALICE.
Now, where was your good genius that would
prompt you to find me out?
PALAMEDE.
Why, you see I was not deceived; you, yourself,
were my good genius. 85
DORALICE.
But where was the steel that knew the loadstone,
hah?
PALAMEDE.
The truth is, madam, the steel has lost its virtue,
and therefore, if you please, we'll new touch it.

*Enter Rhodophil, and Melantha in boy's habit.
Rhodophil sees Palamede kissing Doralice's hand.*

RHODOPHIL.
Palamede again! Am I fallen into your quarters? 90
What? Engaging with a boy? Is all honorable?
PALAMEDE.
Oh, very honorable on my side. I was just
chastising this young villain. He was running away
without paying his share of the reckoning.
RHODOPHIL.
Then I find I was deceived in him. 95

---

58 pragmatical] officious

PALAMEDE.

Yes, you are deceived in him. 'Tis the archest rogue if you did but know him.

MELANTHA.

Good Rhodophil, let us get off *à la dérobée*[59] for fear I should be discovered.

RHODOPHIL. [*To Melantha.*]

There's no retiring now; I warrant you for   100
discovery. Now have I the oddest thought: to entertain you before your servant's* face and he never the wiser. 'Twill be the prettiest juggling trick to cheat him when he looks upon us.

MELANTHA.

This is the strangest *caprice* in you.   105

PALAMEDE. (*To Doralice.*)

This Rhodophil's the unluckiest fellow to me! This is now the second time he has barred the dice when we were just ready to have nicked him, but if ever I get the box again—

DORALICE. [*To Palamede.*]

Do you think he will not know me? Am I like   110
myself?

PALAMEDE. [*To Doralice.*]

No more than a picture in the hangings.

DORALICE. [*To Palamede.*]

Nay, then he can never discover me now the wrong side of the arras is turned towards him.

PALAMEDE. [*To Doralice.*]

At least 'twill be some pleasure to me to enjoy what   115
freedom I can while he looks on; I will storm the outworks of matrimony even before his face.

RHODOPHIL.

What wine have you there, Palamede?

PALAMEDE.

Old Chios,[60] or the rogue's damned that drew it.

RHODOPHIL.

Come: to the most constant of mistresses; that I   120
believe is yours, Palamede.

DORALICE.

Pray spare your seconds, for my part I am but a weak brother.

PALAMEDE.

Now, to the truest of turtles.* That is your wife,

Rhodophil, that lies sick at home in the bed of   125
honor.

RHODOPHIL.

Now let's have one common health and so have done.

DORALICE.

Then for once I'll begin it. Here's to him that has the fairest lady of Sicily in masquerade tonight.   130

PALAMEDE.

This is such an obliging health, I'll kiss thee, dear rogue, for thy invention. (*Kisses her.*)

RHODOPHIL.

He who has this lady is a happy man, without dispute. (*Aside.*) I'm most concerned in this, I am sure.   135

PALAMEDE.

Was it not well found out, Rhodophil?

MELANTHA.

Aye, this was *bien trouvé*[61] indeed.

DORALICE. (*To Melantha.*)

I suppose I shall do you a kindness to inquire if you have not been in France, sir?

MELANTHA.

To do you service, sir.   140

DORALICE.

Oh monsieur, *votre valet bien humble.* (*Saluting* her.*)

MELANTHA.

Votre esclave, monsieur, de tout mon coeur. (*Returning the salute.*)

DORALICE.

I suppose, sweet sir, you are the hope and joy of some thriving citizen who has pinched himself at home to breed you abroad, where you have learnt   145
your exercises, as it appears, most awkwardly and are returned with the addition of a new-laced bosom and a clap to your good old father, who looks at you with his mouth while you spout French with your man monsieur.   150

PALAMEDE.

Let me kiss thee again for that, dear rogue.

MELANTHA.

And you, I imagine, are my young master whom your mother durst not trust upon salt water but left you to be your own tutor at fourteen, to be

59 *à la dérobée*] secretly
60 Old Chios] wine from the Greek island of Chios
61 *bien trouvé*] well put

very brisk and *entreprenant*, to endeavor to be   155
debauched ere you have learnt the knack on't, to
value yourself upon a clap before you can get it,
and to make it the height of your ambition to get
a player for your mistress.

RHODOPHIL. (*Embracing Melantha.*)
Oh dear young bully, thou hast tickled him with   160
a repartee, i'faith.

MELANTHA.
You are one of those that applaud our country
plays where drums and trumpets and blood and
wounds are wit.

RHODOPHIL.
Again, my boy? let me kiss thee most abundantly.   165

DORALICE.
You are an admirer of the dull French poetry,
which is so thin that it is the very leaf-gold of wit,
the very wafers and whipped cream of sense, for
which a man opens his mouth and gapes to
swallow nothing. And to be an admirer of such   170
profound dullness, one must be endowed with a
great perfection of impudence and ignorance.

PALAMEDE.
Let me embrace thee most vehemently.

MELANTHA. (*Advancing.*)
I'll sacrifice my life for French poetry.

DORALICE.
I'll die upon the spot for our country wit.   175

RHODOPHIL. (*To Melantha.*)
Hold, hold, young Mars. Palamede, draw back
your hero.

PALAMEDE.
'Tis time; I shall be drawn in for a second else at
the wrong weapon.

MELANTHA.
Oh that I were a man for thy sake!   180

DORALICE.
You'll be a man as soon as I shall.

Enter a messenger to Rhodophil.

MESSENGER.
Sir, the King has instant business with you. I saw
the guard drawn up by your lieutenant before the
palace gate, ready to march.

RHODOPHIL.
'Tis somewhat sudden. Say that I am coming.   185

Exit Messenger.

Now Palamede, what think you of this sport?
This is some sudden tumult. Will you along?

PALAMEDE.
Yes, yes, I will go but the devil take me if ever I
was less in humor. Why the pox could they not
have stayed their tumult till tomorrow? Then I had   190
done my business and been ready for 'em. Truth
is, I had a little transitory crime to have committed
first, and I am the worst man in the world at
repenting till a sin be thoroughly done. But what
shall we do with the two boys?   195

RHODOPHIL.
Let them take a lodging in the house till the
business be over.

DORALICE.
What, lie with a boy? For my part, I own it, I
cannot endure to lie with a boy.

PALAMEDE.
The more's my sorrow. I cannot accommodate you   200
with a better bedfellow.

MELANTHA.
Let me die if I enter into a pair of sheets with him
that hates the French.

DORALICE.
Pish, take no care for us but leave us in the streets.
I warrant you, as late as it is I'll find my lodging   205
as well as any drunken bully of 'em all.

RHODOPHIL. (*Aside.*)
I'll fight in mere* revenge and wreak my passion
On all that spoil this hopeful assignation.

PALAMEDE.
I'm sure we fight in a good quarrel.*
Rogues may pretend religion and the laws,   210
But a kind* mistress is the Good Old Cause.*

Exeunt.

Scene iv.

Enter Palmyra, Eubulus, Hermogenes.

PALMYRA.
You tell me wonders, that Leonidas
Is Prince Theagenes, the late King's son.

EUBULUS.
It seemed as strange to him as now to you
Before I had convinced him. But besides

His great resemblance to the King his father,   5
The Queen his mother lives, secured by me
In a religious house, to whom each year
I brought the news of his increasing virtues.
My last long absence from you both was caused
By wounds which in my journey I received   10
When set upon by thieves; I lost those jewels
And letters which your dying mother left.

HERMOGENES.

The same he means, which, since brought to the
    King,
Made him first know he had a child alive.
'Twas then my care of Prince Leonidas   15
Caused me to say he was th'usurper's son
Till, after forced by your apparent danger,
I made the true discovery* of your birth
And once more hid my Prince's.

Enter Leonidas.

LEONIDAS.

Hermogenes and Eubulus, retire.   20
Those of our party whom I left without
Expect your aid and counsel.

Exeunt Hermogenes and Eubulus.

PALMYRA.

I should, Leonidas, congratulate
This happy change of your exalted fate,
But as my joy, so you my wonder move: 25
Your looks have more of business than of love,
And your last words some great design did show.

LEONIDAS.

I frame not any to be hid from you.
You in my love all my designs may see.
But what have love and you designed for me?   30
Fortune, once more, has set the balance right:
First equaled us in lowness then in height.
Both of us have so long like gamesters thrown,
Till Fate comes round and gives to each his own.
As Fate is equal, so may Love appear: 35
Tell me, at least, what I must hope or fear.

PALMYRA.

After so many proofs, how can you call
My love in doubt? Fear nothing and hope all.
Think what a prince, with honor, may receive
Or I may give without a parent's leave.   40

LEONIDAS.

You give and then restrain the grace you show,
As ostentatious priests when souls they woo:
Promise their Heav'n to all but grant to few.
But do for me what I have dared for you:
I did no argument from duty bring;   45
Duty's a name, and love's a real thing.

PALMYRA.

Man's love may, like wild torrents, overflow;
Woman's as deep, but in its banks must go.
My love is mine and that I can impart
But cannot give my person with my heart.   50

LEONIDAS.

Your love is then no gift:
For when the person it does not convey,
'Tis to give gold and not to give the key.

PALMYRA.

Then ask my father.

LEONIDAS.

                    He detains my throne.   55
Who holds back mine will hardly give his own.

PALMYRA.

What then remains?

LEONIDAS.

                    That I must have recourse
To arms and take my love and crown by force.
Hermogenes is forming the design,   60
And with him all the brave and loyal join.

PALMYRA.

And is it thus you court Palmyra's bed?
Can she the murd'rer of her parent wed?
Desist from force: so much you well may give
To love and me, to let my father live.   65

LEONIDAS.

Each act of mine my love to you has shown,
But you who tax my want* of it have none.
You bid me part with you and let him live,
But they should nothing ask who nothing give.

PALMYRA.

I give what virtue and what duty can   70
In vowing ne'er to wed another man.

LEONIDAS.

You will be forced to be Argaleon's wife.

PALMYRA.

I'll keep my promise though I lose my life.

LEONIDAS.

    Then you lose love, for which we both contend.

    For life is but the means, but love's the end.   75

PALMYRA.

    Our souls shall love hereafter.

LEONIDAS.

                        I much fear

    That soul which could deny the body here

    To taste of love would be a niggard there.

PALMYRA.

    Then 'tis past hope: our cruel fate, I see,   80

    Will make a sad divorce 'twixt you and me.

    For if you force employ, by Heav'n I swear

    And all blessed beings—

LEONIDAS.

                  Your rash oath forbear.

PALMYRA.

    I never—   85

LEONIDAS.

          Hold once more. But yet, as he

    Who 'scapes a dang'rous leap looks back to see,

    So I desire, now I am past my fear,

    To know what was that oath you meant to swear.

PALMYRA.

    I meant that, if you hazarded your life   90

    Or sought my father's, ne'er to be your wife.

LEONIDAS.

    See now, Palmyra, how unkind you prove!

    Could you with so much ease forswear my love?

PALMYRA.

    You force me with your ruinous design.

LEONIDAS.

    Your father's life is more your care than mine.   95

PALMYRA.

    You wrong me: 'tis not, though it ought to be;

    You are my care, Heav'n knows, as well as he.

LEONIDAS.

    If now the execution I delay,

    My honor and my subjects I betray.

    All is prepared for the just enterprise,   100

    And the whole city will tomorrow rise.

    The leaders of the party are within,

    And Eubulus has sworn that he will bring

    To head their arms the person of their King.

PALMYRA.

    In telling this, you make me guilty too;   105

    I therefore must discover* what I know.

    What honor bids you do, nature bids me prevent.

    But kill me first and then pursue your black intent.

LEONIDAS.

    Palmyra, no, you shall not need to die,

    Yet I'll not trust so strict a piety.   110

    —Within there.

Enter Eubulus.

                  Eubulus, a guard prepare.

    Here, I commit this pris'ner to your care.

Kisses Palmyra's hand, then gives it to Eubulus.

PALMYRA.

    Leonidas, I never thought these bands

    Could e'er be giv'n me by a lover's hands.   115

LEONIDAS. (*Kneeling.*)

    Palmyra, thus your judge himself arraigns;

    He who imposed these bonds, still wears your chains.

    When you to love or duty false must be,

    Or to your father guilty or to me,

    These chains alone remain to set you free.   120

Noise of swords clashing.

POLYDAMAS. (*Within.*)

    Secure these first, then search the inner room.

LEONIDAS.

    From whence do these tumultuous clamors come?

Enter Hermogenes, hastily.

HERMOGENES.

    We are betrayed, and there remains alone

    This comfort, that your person is not known.

Enter the King, Argaleon, Rhodophil, Palamede,
guards; some like citizens as prisoners.

POLYDAMAS.

    What mean these midnight consultations here,   125

    Where I, like an unsummoned guest, appear?

LEONIDAS.

    Sir—

ARGALEON.

          There needs no excuse, 'tis understood:

    You were all watching for your prince's good.

POLYDAMAS.

    My reverend city friends, you are well met!   130

On what great work were your grave wisdoms set?
Which of my actions were you scanning here?
What French invasion have you found to fear?[62]

LEONIDAS.

They are my friends and come, sir, with intent
To take their leaves before my banishment. 135

POLYDAMAS. (*Seeing Palmyra.*)

Your exile in both sexes friends can find:
I see the ladies, like the men, are kind.

PALMYRA. (*Kneeling.*)

Alas, I came but—

POLYDAMAS.

Add not to your crime
A lie. I'll hear you speak some other time. 140
How? Eubulus! Nor time, nor thy disguise
Can keep thee undiscovered from my eyes.
—A guard there, seize 'em all.

RHODOPHIL.

Yield, sir, what use of valor can be shown?

PALAMEDE.

One and unarmed against a multitude! 145

LEONIDAS.[c]

Oh for a sword!

*He reaches at one of the guard's halberds and is seized
behind.*

I wonnot lose my breath
In fruitless prayers but beg a speedy death.

PALMYRA.

Oh spare Leonidas and punish me.

POLYDAMAS.

Mean* girl, thou want'st* an advocate for thee. 150
Now the mysterious knot will be untied:
Whether the young King lives or where he died.
Tomorrow's dawn shall the dark riddle clear,
Crown all my joys, and dissipate my fear.

Exeunt omnes.

Act V, scene i.

Palamede, Straton. Palamede with a letter in his hand.

PALAMEDE.

This evening, sayest thou? will they both be here?

---

62 reverend city friends...fear] alludes to opposition in the
City of London to Charles II's policy of seeking an alliance with France and Louis XIV

STRATON.

Yes, sir, both my old master and your mistress's
father. The old gentlemen ride hard this journey.
They say it shall be the last time they will see the
town, and both of 'em are so pleased with this 5
marriage which they have concluded for you that
I am afraid they will live some years longer to
trouble you with the joy of it.

PALAMEDE.

But this is such an unreasonable thing, to impose
upon me to be married tomorrow. 'Tis hurrying a 10
man to execution without giving him time to say
his prayers.

STRATON.

Yet if I might advise you, sir, you should not delay it,
for your younger brother comes up with 'em and is
got already into their favors. He has gained much 15
upon my old master by finding fault with innkeeper's bills and by starving us and our horses to show
his frugality. And he is very well with your mistress's
father by giving him receipts* for the spleen, gout,
and scurvy and other infirmities of old age. 20

PALAMEDE.

I'll rout him and his country education. Pox on
him, I remember him before I traveled. He had
nothing in him but mere jockey,[63] used to talk
loud and make matches and was all for the crack
of the field.[64] Sense and wit were as much 25
banished from his discourse as they are when the
court goes out of town to a horse race. Go now
and provide your master's lodgings.

STRATON.

I go, sir. (*Exit.*)

PALAMEDE.

It vexes me to the heart to leave all my designs with 30
Doralice unfinished, to have flown her so often to
a mark and still to be bobbed at retrieve.[65] If I had
but once enjoyed her, though I could not have
satisfied my stomach with the feast, at least I
should have relished my mouth a little. But now— 35

---

63 jockey] horsemanship; also shrewd dealing with a suggestion of fraud
64 crack of the field] favorite
65 to have flown ... bobbed at retrieve] like a bird of prey
disappointed at the last moment of its quarry

Enter Philotis.

PHILOTIS.

Oh sir, you are happily met; I was coming to find
you.

PALAMEDE.

From your lady, I hope.

PHILOTIS.

Partly from her, but more especially from myself.
She has just now received a letter from her father   40
with an absolute command to dispose herself to
marry you tomorrow.

PALAMEDE.

And she takes it to the death?

PHILOTIS.

Quite contrary: the letter could never have come
in a more lucky minute, for it found her in an ill   45
humor with a rival of yours, that shall be nameless,
about the pronunciation of a French word.

PALAMEDE.

Count Rhodophil, never disguise it, I know the
amour. But I hope you took the occasion to strike
in for me?   50

PHILOTIS.

It was my good fortune to do you some small
service in it. For your sake I discommended him
all over: clothes, person, humor,* behavior,
everything. And to sum up all, told her it was
impossible to find a married man that was   55
otherwise, for they were all so mortified at home
with their wives' ill humors that they could never
recover themselves to be company abroad.

PALAMEDE.

Most divinely urged!

PHILOTIS.

Then I took occasion to commend your good   60
qualities: as the sweetness of your humor,* the
comeliness of your person, your good mien, your
valor, but above all your liberality.

PALAMEDE.

I vow to Gad I had like to have forgot that good
quality in myself, if thou hadst not remembered   65
me on't. Here are five pieces for thee.

PHILOTIS.

Lord, you have the softest hand, sir! It would do a
woman good to touch it. Count Rhodophil's is not

half so soft, for I remember I felt it once when he
gave me ten pieces for my New Year's gift.   70

PALAMEDE.

Oh, I understand you, madam. You shall find my
hand as soft again as Count Rhodophil's. There are
twenty pieces for you. The former was but a
retaining fee; now I hope you'll plead for me.

PHILOTIS.

Your own merits speak enough. Be sure only to ply   75
her with French words, and I'll warrant you'll do
your business. Here are a list of her phrases for this
day. Use 'em to her upon all occasions and foil her
at her own weapon. For she's like one of the old
Amazons, she'll never marry, except it be the man   80
who has first conquered her.

PALAMEDE.

I'll be sure to follow your advice, but you'll forget
to further my design.

PHILOTIS.

What, do you think I'll be ungrateful? But
however, if you distrust my memory, put some   85
token on my finger to remember it by. That
diamond there would do admirably.

PALAMEDE.

There 'tis and I ask your pardon heartily for calling
your memory into question. I assure you I'll trust
it another time without putting you to the trouble   90
of another token.

Enter Palmyra and Artemis.

ARTEMIS.

Madam, this way the prisoners are to pass;
Here you may see Leonidas.

PALMYRA.

Then here I'll stay and follow him to death.

Enter Melantha hastily.

MELANTHA.

Oh, here's her Highness! Now is my time to   95
introduce myself and to make my court to her in
my new French phrases. Stay, let me read my
catalog: *suite, figure, chagrin, naïveté,* and "let me
die" for the parenthesis of all.

PALAMEDE. (*Aside.*)

Do, persecute her, and I'll persecute thee as fast   100
in thy own dialect.

MELANTHA.

Madam, the Princess! Let me die but this is a most horrid spectacle, to see a person who makes so grand a figure in the court without the *suite* of a princess and entertaining your *chagrin* all alone. 105 [*Aside.*] *Naïveté* should have been there, but the disobedient word would not come in.

PALMYRA.

What is she, Artemis?

ARTEMIS.

An impertinent lady, madam, very ambitious of being known to your highness. 110

PALAMEDE. (*To Melantha.*)

Let me die, madam, if I have not waited you here these two long hours without so much as the *suite* of a single servant to attend me, entertaining myself with my own *chagrin* till I had the honor to see your ladyship, who are a person that makes 115 so considerable a figure in the court.

MELANTHA.

Truce with your *douceurs*, good servant;* you see I am addressing to the Princess. Pray do not *embarrass* me—*Embarrass* me! What a delicious French word do you make me lose upon you too! (*To the Princess.*) 120 Your Highness, madam, will please to pardon the *bévue* which I made in not sooner finding you out to be a princess. But let me die if this *éclaircissement* which is made this day of your quality* does not ravish me, and give me leave to tell you— 125

PALAMEDE.

But first give me leave to tell you, madam, that I have so great a tender for your person and such a *penchant* to do you service, that—

MELANTHA.

What, must I still be troubled with your *sottises*? [*Aside.*] There's another word lost that I meant for 130 the Princess, with a mischief to you.—But your Highness, madam—

PALAMEDE.

But your ladyship, madam—

Enter Leonidas guarded and led over the stage.

MELANTHA.

Out upon him, how he looks, madam! Now he's found no prince, he is the strangest figure of a 135 man. How could I make that *coup d'étourdi* to think him one?

PALMYRA.

Away, impertinent.—My dear Leonidas!

LEONIDAS.

My dear Palmyra!

PALMYRA.

Death shall never part us. 140 My destiny is yours.

He is led off; she follows.

MELANTHA.

Impertinent! Oh, I am the most unfortunate person this day breathing, that the Princess should thus *rompre en visière*[66] without occasion. Let me die but I'll follow her to death till I make my 145 peace.

PALAMEDE. (*Holding her.*)

And let me die, but I'll follow you to the infernals till you pity me.

MELANTHA. (*Turning towards him angrily.*)

Aye, 'tis long of you that this *malheur*[67] is fallen upon me; your impertinence has put me out of the 150 good graces of the Princess, and all that, which has ruined me, and all that, and, therefore, let me die, but I'll be revenged, and all that.

PALAMEDE.

Façon, façon,[68] you must and shall love me, and all that, for my old man is coming up, and all that, 155 and I am *désespéré au dernier*[69] and will not be disinherited, and all that.

MELANTHA.

How durst you interrupt me so *mal à propos* when you knew I was addressing to the Princess?

PALAMEDE.

But why would you address yourself so much *à* 160 *contretemps* then?

MELANTHA.

Ah, *mal peste!*

PALAMEDE.

Ah *j'enrage!*

PHILOTIS.

Radoucissez vous, de grâce, madame; vous êtes bien

---

66 *rompre en visière*] quarrel with openly
67 *malheur*] misfortune
68 *façon*] affectation
69 *désespéré au dernier*] desperate to the last extreme

en colère pour peu de chose. Vous n'entendez pas la 165
raillerie galante.[70]

MELANTHA.

À d'autres, à d'autres. He mocks himself of me; he
abuses me. Ah me unfortunate! (*Cries!*)

PHILOTIS.

You mistake him, madam. He does but
accommodate his phrase to your refined language. 170
Ah, qu'il est un cavalier accompli! (*To him.*) Pursue
your point, sir.

PALAMEDE. (*Singing.*)

Ah, qu'il fait beau dans ces boccages;
Ah que le ciel donne un beau jour![71]

There I was with you, with a *menuet*. 175

MELANTHA. (*Laughs.*)

Let me die now, but this singing is fine and
extremely French in him. (*Crying.*) But then, that
he should use my own words as it were in
contempt of me, I cannot bear it.

PALAMEDE. (*Singing.*)

Ces beaux séjours, ces doux ramages— 180

MELANTHA. (*Singing after him.*)

Ces beaux séjours, ces doux ramages,
Ces beaux séjours, nous invitent à l'amour![72]
(*Laughing.*)

Let me die, but he sings *en cavalier*, and so
humors the cadence.

PALAMEDE. (*Singing again.*)

Vois, ma Climène, vois sous ce chêne, 185
S'entrebaiser ces oiseaux amoreux![73]

Let me die now, but that was fine. Ah, now for three
or four brisk Frenchmen, to be put into masking
habits and to sing it on a theater, how witty it would
be! and then to dance helter skelter to a *chanson à* 190

---

[70] *Radoucissez ... galante*] Please calm yourself, madam;
you've worked yourself into a rage over nothing. You
don't understand gallant raillery.

[71] *Ah, qu'il...beau jour!*] Ah, how lovely the weather in these
thickets: Heaven grants a beautiful day (a song from
Molière's *Le Bourgeois gentilhomme*).

[72] *Ces beaux ... l'amour*] These beautiful abodes, these gentle birdsongs, these sweet abodes invite us both to love
(same song from Molière).

[73] *Vois ... amoreux*] See, my Climene, see under the oak
the amorous birds coupling (another song from the same
play).

boire: toute la terre, toute la terre est a moi![74] What's
matter though it were made and sung two or three
years ago in cabarets. How it would attract the
admiration, especially of every one that's an *éveillé.*[75]

MELANTHA.

Well I begin to have a tender for you, but yet upon 195
condition that—when we are married, you—

PHILOTIS. [*To Palamede.*]

You must drown her voice. If she makes her French
conditions, you are a slave forever.

Palamede sings, while she speaks.

MELANTHA.

First you will engage that—

PALAMEDE. (*Louder.*)

Fa, la, la, la, etc. 200

MELANTHA.

Will you hear the conditions?

PALAMEDE.

No, I will hear no conditions! I am resolved to win
you *en français:* to be very airy, with abundance of
noise and no sense. *Fa, la, la, la,* etc.

MELANTHA.

Hold, hold. I am vanquished with your *gaieté* 205
d'esprit. I am yours and will be yours *sans nulle*
réservé, ni condition. And let me die, if I do not
think myself the happiest nymph in Sicily. My dear
French dear, stay but a *minute*, till I *raccommode*
myself with the Princess, and then I am yours 210
jusqu'à la mort.—Allons donc.[76]

Exeunt Melantha, Philotis.

PALAMEDE. (*Fanning himself with his hat.*)

I never thought before that wooing was so laborious
an exercise. If she were worth a million, I have
deserved her. And now, methinks too, with taking
all this pains for her I begin to like her. 'Tis so. I have 215
known many who never cared for hare nor partridge
but those they caught themselves would eat heartily.
The pains, the story a man tells of the taking of 'em,
makes the meat go down more pleasantly. Besides,
last night I had a sweet dream of her, and Gad, she 220

---

[74] *Chanson ... moi*] a drinking song: All of the earth, all
of the earth is mine.

[75] *éveillé*] sharp, bright, alert person

[76] *jusqu'à ... donc*] until death.—Let's go, then

I have once dreamed of I am stark mad till I enjoy her, let her be never* so ugly.

Enter Doralice.

DORALICE.

Who's that you are so mad to enjoy, Palamede?

PALAMEDE.

You may easily imagine that, sweet Doralice.

DORALICE.

More easily than you think I can. I met just now with a certain man who came to you with letters from a certain old gentleman, yclept your father, whereby I am given to understand that tomorrow you are to take an oath in the church to be grave henceforward, to go ill-dressed and slovenly, to get heirs for your estate, and to dandle 'em for your diversion, and in short, that love and courtship are to be no more. 230

PALAMEDE.

Now have I so much shame to be thus appre-hended in the manner that I can neither speak nor look upon you. I have abundance of grace in me, that I find. But if you have any spark of true friendship in you, retire a little with me to the next room that has a couch or bed in't and bestow your charity upon a poor dying man. A little comfort from a mistress before a man is going to give himself in marriage is as good as a lusty dose of strong water to a dying malefactor: it takes away the sense of hell and hanging from him. 240

DORALICE.

No good Palamede, I must not be so injurious to your bride. 'Tis ill drawing from the bank today when all your ready money is payable tomorrow. 245

PALAMEDE.

A wife is only to have the ripe fruit that falls of itself, but a wise man will always preserve a shaking for a mistress.

DORALICE.

But a wife for the first quarter is a mistress. 250

PALAMEDE.

But when the second comes—

DORALICE.

When it does come, you are so given to variety that you would make a wife of me in another quarter.

PALAMEDE.

No, never, except I were married to you. Married people can never oblige one another, for all they do is duty, and consequently there can be no thanks. But love is more frank and generous than he is honest. He's a liberal giver, but a cursèd paymaster. 255

DORALICE.

I declare I will have no gallant. But if I would, he should never be a married man. A married man is but a mistress's half-servant as a clergyman is but the King's half-subject. For a man to come to me that smells o'th'wife! 'Slife,* I would as soon wear her old gown after her as her husband. 260

PALAMEDE.

Yet 'tis a kind of fashion to wear a princess's cast* shoes. You see the country ladies buy 'em to be fine in them. 265

DORALICE.

Yes, a princess's shoes may be worn after her because they keep their fashion by being so little used. But generally a married man is the creature of the world the most out of fashion. His behavior is dumpish, his discourse his wife and family, his habit so much neglected it looks as if that were married too. His hat is married, his peruke is married, his breeches are married, and if we could look within his breeches, we should find him married there too. 270 275

PALAMEDE.

Am I then to be discarded forever? Pray do but mark how terrible that word sounds. Forever! It has a very damned sound, Doralice.

DORALICE.

Aye, forever! It sounds as hellishly to me as it can do to you, but there's no help for't. 280

PALAMEDE.

Yet if we had but once enjoyed one another—but then once only is worse than not at all. It leaves a man with such a lingering after it.

DORALICE.

For aught I know 'tis better that we have not. We might upon trial have liked each other less, as many a man and woman that have loved as desperately as we and yet, when they came to possession, have sighed and cried to themselves "Is this all?" 285

PALAMEDE.

That is only if the servant* were not found a man of this world. But if upon trial we had not liked each other, we had certainly left loving, and faith, that's the greater happiness of the two. 290

DORALICE.

'Tis better as 'tis. We have drawn off already as much of our love as would run clear; after possessing, the rest is but jealousies and disquiets and quarreling and piecing.[77]

PALAMEDE.

Nay, after one great quarrel there's never any sound piecing; the love is apt to break in the same place again.

DORALICE.

I declare I would never renew a love; that's like him who trims an old coach for ten years together. He might buy a new one better cheap.

PALAMEDE.

Well madam, I am convinced that 'tis best for us not to have enjoyed. But Gad, the strongest reason is because I can't help it.

DORALICE.

The only way to keep us new to one another is never to enjoy, as they keep grapes by hanging 'em upon a line. They must touch nothing if you would preserve 'em fresh.

PALAMEDE.

But then they wither and grow dry in the very keeping. However, I shall have a warmth for you and an eagerness every time I see you, and if I chance to outlive Melantha—

DORALICE.

And if I chance to outlive Rhodophil—

PALAMEDE.

Well, I'll cherish my body as much as I can upon that hope. 'Tis true, I would not directly murder the wife of my bosom, but to kill her civilly, by the way of kindness,* I'll put[78] as fair as another man. I'll begin tomorrow night and be very wrathful with her, that's resolved on.

DORALICE.

Well Palamede, here's my hand: I'll venture to be your second wife for all your threatenings.

PALAMEDE.

In the meantime I'll watch you hourly, as I would the ripeness of a melon, and I hope you'll give me leave now and then to look on you and to see if you are not ready to be cut yet.

DORALICE.

No, no, that must not be, Palamede, for fear the gardener should come and catch you taking up the glass.[79]

Enter Rhodophil.

RHODOPHIL. (*Aside.*)

Billing so sweetly! Now I am confirmed in my suspicions. I must put an end to this, ere it go further. (*Aside to Doralice.*) Cry you mercy, Spouse, I fear I have interrupted your recreations.

DORALICE.

What recreations?

RHODOPHIL.

Nay, no excuses, good Spouse. I saw fair hand conveyed to lip and pressed, as though you had been squeezing soft wax together for an indenture. Palamede, you and I must clear this reckoning. Why would you have seduced my wife?

PALAMEDE.

Why would you have debauched my mistress?

RHODOPHIL.

What do you think of that civil couple that played at a game called "Hide and Seek" last evening in the grotto?

PALAMEDE.

What do you think of that innocent pair who made it their pretense to seek for others but came, indeed, to hide themselves there?

RHODOPHIL.

All things considered, I begin vehemently to suspect that the young gentleman I found in your company last night was a certain youth of my acquaintance.

PALAMEDE.

And I have an odd imagination that you could never have suspected my small gallant if your little villainous Frenchman had not been a false brother.

RHODOPHIL.

Farther arguments are needless. Draw off, I shall speak to you now by the way of Bilbo. (*Claps his hand to his sword.*)

PALAMEDE.

And I shall answer you by the way of Dangerfield.[80] (*Claps his hand on his.*)

---

[77] piecing] making up, making peace
[78] put] exert myself, thrust (as a weapon)

[79] glass] a protective covering for a young plant
[80] Dangerfield] a sword-carrying bully

DORALICE.

Hold, hold, are not you two a couple of mad, fighting fools to cut one another's throats for nothing?

PALAMEDE.

How, for nothing? He courts the woman I must 360
marry.

RHODOPHIL.

And he courts you whom I have married.

DORALICE.

But you can neither of you be jealous of what you love not.

RHODOPHIL.

Faith I am jealous, and that makes me partly suspect that I love you better then I thought. 365

DORALICE.

Pish! a mere jealousy of honor.

RHODOPHIL.

Gad I am afraid there's something else in't, for Palamede has wit, and if he loves you, there's something more in ye than I have found, some rich mine, for aught I know, that I have not yet discovered. 370

PALAMEDE.

'Slife,* what's this? Here's an argument for me to love Melantha, for he has loved her, and he has wit too, and for aught I know, there may be a mine. But if there be, I am resolved I'll dig for't.

DORALICE. (*To Rhodophil.*)

Then I have found my account in raising your 375
jealousy. Oh! 'Tis the most delicate sharp sauce to a cloyed stomach; it will give you a new edge, Rhodophil.

RHODOPHIL.

And a new point too, Doralice, if I could be sure thou art honest.* 380

DORALICE.

If you are wise, believe me for your own sake. Love and religion have but one thing to trust to: that's a good sound faith. Consider, if I have played false, you can never find it out by any experiment you can make upon me. 385

RHODOPHIL.

No? Why, suppose I had a delicate screwed gun. If I left her clean and found her foul, I should discover to my cost she had been shot in.

DORALICE.

But if you left her clean and found her only rusty,

you would discover to your shame she was only 390
so for want* of shooting.

PALAMEDE.

Rhodophil, you know me too well to imagine I speak for fear, and therefore, in consideration of our past friendship, I will tell you and bind it by all things holy that Doralice is innocent. 395

RHODOPHIL.

Friend, I will believe you and vow the same for your Melantha. But the devil on't is, how we shall keep 'em so.

PALAMEDE.

What dost think of a blessed community betwixt us four for the solace of the women and relief of 400
the men? Methinks it would be a pleasant kind of life: wife and husband for the standing dish and mistress and gallant for the dessert.

RHODOPHIL.

But suppose the wife and the mistress should both long for the standing dish? How should they be 405
satisfied together?

PALAMEDE.

In such a case they must draw lots. And yet that would not do neither, for they would both be wishing for the longest cut.d

RHODOPHIL.

Then I think, Palamede, we had as good make a 410
firm league not to invade each others' propriety.

PALAMEDE.

Content, say I. From henceforth let all acts of hostility cease betwixt us, and that in the usual form of treaties, as well by sea as by land, and in all fresh waters. 415

DORALICE.

I will add but one proviso: that whoever breaks the league, either by war abroad or by neglect at home, both the women shall revenge themselves by the help of the other party.

RHODOPHIL.

That's but reasonable. Come away, Doralice, I have 420
a great temptation to be sealing articles in private.

PALAMEDE. (*Claps him on the shoulder.*)

Hast thou so? Fall on Macduff, And curst be he that first cries, "Hold, enough."81

---

81 Fall on ... enough] slight misquotation of Macbeth's challenge in Act 5 of Shakespeare's *Macbeth*

Enter Polydamas, Palmyra, Artemis, Argaleon; after
them Eubulus and Hermogenes, guarded.

PALMYRA.
  Sir, on my knees I beg you.
POLYDAMAS.
  Away, I'll hear no more.   425
PALMYRA.
  For my dead mother's sake; you say you loved her,
  And tell me I resemble her. Thus she
  Had begged.
POLYDAMAS.
            And thus had I denied her.
PALMYRA.
  You must be merciful.   430
ARGALEON.
                You must be constant.
POLYDAMAS.
  Go, bear 'em to the torture.—You have boasted
  You have a king to head you. I would know
  To whom I must resign.
EUBULUS.
              This is our recompense   435
  For serving thy dead queen.
HERMOGENES.
                    And education
  Of thy daughter.
ARGALEON.
  You are too modest in not naming all
  His obligations to you. Why did you   440
  Omit his son, the Prince Leonidas?
POLYDAMAS.
  That imposture
  I had forgot; their tortures shall be doubled.
HERMOGENES.
  You please me; I shall die the sooner.
EUBULUS.
  No, could I live an age and still be racked,   445
  I still would keep the secret.

As they are going off, enter Leonidas, guarded.

LEONIDAS.
  Oh whither do you hurry innocence?
  If you have any justice, spare their lives,
  Or if I cannot make you just, at least
  I'll teach you to more purpose to be cruel.   450

PALMYRA.
  Alas, what does he seek!
LEONIDAS.
  Make me the object of your hate and vengeance!
  Are these decrepit bodies, worn to ruin,
  Just ready of themselves to fall asunder
  And to let drop the soul,   455
  Are these fit subjects for a rack and tortures?
  Where would you fasten any hold upon 'em?
  Place pains on me, united fix 'em here.
  I have both youth and strength and soul to bear 'em.
  And if they merit death, then I much more,   460
  Since 'tis for me they suffer.
HERMOGENES.
                    Heav'n forbid
  We should redeem our pains or worthless lives
  By our exposing yours.
EUBULUS.
  Away with us.—Farewell, sir.   465
  I only suffer in my fears for you.
ARGALEON. (*Aside.*)
  So much concerned for him? Then my
  Suspicion's true. (*Whispers the King.*)
PALMYRA.
  Hear yet my last request for poor Leonidas,
  Or take my life with his.   470
ARGALEON. (*To the King.*)
  Rest satisfied: Leonidas is he.
POLYDAMAS.
  I am amazed. What must be done?
ARGALEON.
  Command his execution instantly;
  Give him not leisure to discover* it;
  He may corrupt the soldiers.   475
POLYDAMAS.
  Hence with that traitor, bear him to his death.
  Haste there, and see my will performed.
LEONIDAS.
  Nay, then I'll die like him the gods have made me.
  Hold, gentlemen, I am— (*Argaleon stops his mouth.*)
ARGALEON.
  Thou art a traitor; 'tis not fit to hear thee.   480
LEONIDAS. (*Getting loose a little.*)
  I say I am the—
ARGALEON. (*Again stopping his mouth.*)
  So, gag him, and lead him off.

Leonidas, Hermogenes, Eubulus, led off. Polydamas and Argaleon follow.

PALMYRA.

Duty and love by turns possess my soul
And struggle for a fatal victory.
I will discover* he's the King. Ah no,   485
That will perhaps save him,
But then I am guilty of a father's ruin.
What shall I do or not do? Either way
I must destroy a parent or a lover.
Break, heart, for that's the least of ills to me,   490
And death the only cure. (*Swoons.*)

ARTEMIS.

Help, help the Princess.

RHODOPHIL.

Bear her gently hence where she may
Have more succor.

She is born off, Artemis follows her. Shouts within, and clashing of swords.

PALAMEDE.

What noise is that?   495

Enter Amalthea, running.

AMALTHEA.

Oh gentlemen, if you have loyalty
Or courage, show it now. Leonidas
Broke on the sudden from his guards and, snatching
A sword from one, his back against the scaffold,
Bravely defends himself and owns aloud   500
He is our long lost King, found for this moment
But, if your valors help not, lost forever.
Two of his guards, moved by the sense of virtue,
Are turned for him, and there they stand at bay
Against an host of foes.   505

RHODOPHIL.

                                 Madam, no more,
We lose time. My command or my example
May move the soldiers to the better cause.
(*To Palamede.*) You'll second me?

PALAMEDE.

Or die with you. No subject e'er can meet   510
A nobler fate than at his sovereign's feet.

Exeunt. Clashing of swords within, and shouts. Enter Leonidas, Rhodophil, Palamede, Eubulus, Hermogenes, and their party, victorious; Polydamas and Argaleon, disarmed.

LEONIDAS.

That I survive the dangers of this day,
Next to the gods, brave friends, be yours the honor.
And let Heav'n witness for me that my joy
Is not more great for this my right restored   515
Than 'tis that I have power to recompense
Your loyalty and valor. Let mean* princes
Of abject souls fear to reward great actions;
I mean to show,
That whatsoe'er subjects like you dare merit,   520
A king, like me, dares give.

RHODOPHIL.

You make us blush; we have deserved so little.

PALAMEDE.

And yet instruct us how to merit more.

LEONIDAS.

And as I would be just in my rewards,
So should I in my punishments: these two,   525
This the usurper of my crown, the other
Of my Palmyra's love, deserve that death
Which both designed for me.

POLYDAMAS.

                                           And we expect it.

ARGALEON.

I have too long been happy to live wretched.   530

POLYDAMAS.

And I too long have governed to desire
A life without an empire.

LEONIDAS.

You are Palmyra's father and as such,
Though not a king, shall have obedience paid
From him who is one. Father: in that name   535
All injuries forgot and duty owned. (*Embraces him.*)

POLYDAMAS.

Oh, had I known you could have been this King,
Thus godlike, great, and good, I should have wished
T'have been dethroned before. 'Tis now I live
And more than reign; now all my joys flow pure, 540
Unmixed with cares and undisturbed by conscience.

Enter Palmyra, Amalthea, Artemis, Doralice, and Melantha.

LEONIDAS.

See, my Palmyra comes, the frighted blood
Scarce yet recalled to her pale cheeks,
Like the first streaks of light broke loose from
    darkness

And dawning into blushes. (*To Polydamas.*) Sir, you said   545

Your joys were full. Oh, would you make mine so!

I am but half restored without this blessing.

POLYDAMAS.

The gods, and my Palmyra, make you happy,

As you make me. (*Gives her hand to Leonidas.*)

PALMYRA.

         Now all my prayers are heard: 550

I may be dutiful and yet may love.

Virtue and patience have at length unraveled

The knots which Fortune tied.

MELANTHA.

Let me die but I'll congratulate his majesty. How admirably well his royalty becomes him! Becomes!   555
That is, *lui sied*,[82] but our damned language expresses nothing.

PALAMEDE.

How? Does it become him already? 'Twas but just now you said he was such a figure of a man.

MELANTHA.

True, my dear, when he was a private man, he was   560
a figure, but since he is a king, methinks he has assumed another figure: he looks so grand and so august. (*Going to the King.*)

PALAMEDE.

Stay, stay, I'll present you when it is more convenient. [*Aside.*] I find I must get her a place   565
at court, and when she is once there, she can be no longer ridiculous. For she is young enough and pretty enough and fool enough and French enough to bring up a fashion there to be affected.

LEONIDAS. (*To Rhodophil.*)

Did she then lead you to this brave attempt?   570
(*To Amalthea.*)

To you, fair Amalthea, what I am,

And what all these, from me, we jointly owe.

First, therefore, to your great desert, we give

Your brother's life but keep him under guard   575

Till our new power be settled. What more grace

He may receive shall from his future carriage

Be given, as he deserves.

ARGALEON.

I neither now desire nor will deserve it.

My loss is such as cannot be repaired,   580

And to the wretched, life can be no mercy.

LEONIDAS.

Then be a prisoner always. Thy ill fate

And pride will have it so. But since in this I cannot,

Instruct me, generous* Amalthea, how

A king may serve you.   585

AMALTHEA.

         I have all I hope

And all I now must wish: I see you happy.

Those hours I have to live, which Heav'n in pity

Will make but few, I vow to spend with vestals:

The greatest part in pray'rs for you; the rest   590

In mourning my unworthiness.

Press me not farther to explain myself;

'Twill not become me and may cause you trouble.

LEONIDAS. (*Aside.*)

Too well I understand her secret grief

But dare not seem to know it. (*To Palmyra.*)   595

    Come my fairest,

Beyond my crown I have one joy in store:

To give that crown to her whom I adore.

Exeunt omnes.

FINIS.

Textual Notes

a Copytext is the first edition, a 1673 quarto (Q1). Also consulted: the second edition, a 1684 quarto (Q2); the third edition, a 1691 quarto (Q3); the fourth edition, a 1698 edition (Q4); the first collected edition in 1701 (C1); the second collected edition (Congreve's—C2); and modern editions of 1967 (Beaurline and Bowers—BB), of 1981 (Auburn), and of 1978 (California Edition—CE).

b consider,] C1, BB, Auburn; consider Q1-4, C2, CE

c LEONIDAS] C1, BB, Auburn, CE; *om.* Q1-4, C2

d cut] C1, BB, Auburn, CE; out Q1-4, C2

---

82 *lui sied*] It becomes him.

Oroonoko[a]

by Thomas Southerne (1660-1746)

edited by Joyce Green MacDonald

Thomas Southerne's *Oroonoko* (1695) is a dramatization of Aphra Behn's 1688 novella of the same name. Just as his play capitalized on the popularity of Behn's prose, so too did later playwrights return to Southerne's comic drama: John Hawkesworth, Francis Gentleman, John Ferriar and anonymous others all produced their own adaptations of Southerne's work. In one form or another, *Oroonoko* appeared on London stages throughout the first three-quarters of the eighteenth century.

And yet the *Oroonoko*s other playwrights modeled on Southerne's work markedly differed from it, just as his play altered Behn's powerful story of a pair of enslaved African lovers' rebellion and death in a New World jungle. Southerne paired the serious matter he borrowed from Behn with a comic plot of his own invention, in which the impecunious Welldon sisters have journeyed out from London to find rich husbands in colonial Suriname. Hawkesworth, Gentleman and the rest eliminated the Welldon sisters' plot from their adaptations of Southerne, while retaining and heightening the sentimental pathos with which he presents the doom of Oroonoko and his pregnant bride Imoinda. Southerne's adapters also retain the striking alteration he makes—without comment—in Behn: where Behn's tragic heroine is a black-skinned beauty, Southerne's is white.

Oroonoko is Southerne's second adaptation of Behn (the first was 1694's *The Fatal Marriage*). Besides Behn, his work also looks backward to the pathos of such Restoration heroic tragedies as Otway's *Venice Preserv'd*. The tone of the play's declamatory speeches about the plight of its tragic lovers and much of its language for describing Oroonoko's blackness hearken back even farther, to Shakespeare's *Othello*; Shakespearean echoes can be heard throughout the serious drama of the Restoration.

But if *Oroonoko* is thus grounded in traditional dramatic elements, it was also felt by its first audiences to be a strikingly contemporary play. Premiering near the beginnings of the development of a mercantile colonialism supported by slavery, Southerne's *Oroonoko* and its revisions increasingly came to be regarded as important documents in the eighteenth-century abolitionist movement. The play's attention to the roles of women in slavery and in slave societies perhaps offered additional interest to women in the Restoration audience. Not only were women to become notably active in English abolition, but the play also offers the comic pleasure of watching the Welldon sisters learning to negotiate the hazards of an unscrupulous sexual marketplace. As the celebrated actress Mrs. Verbruggen, who played Charlotte Welldon in the original production, declared in the epilogue:

> Men show their valor and women their discretion;
> To lands of monsters, and fierce beasts they go:
> We, to those islands, where rich husbands grow.

The clever Charlotte and the sensual Lucy can be seen as female versions of the familiar Restoration rake-hero, and as such, their success proclaims the ability of the exceptional character to recognize the essential hypocrisy and corruption of the social order, and yet to achieve romantic, social, and fiscal satisfaction within its constraints.

from Epistle Dedicatory
To his Grace, William, duke of Devonshire[1]

… I stand engaged to Mrs. Behn[2] for the occasion of a most passionate distress in my last play,[3] and in a conscience that I had not made her a sufficient acknowledgement, I have run further into her debt for *Oroonoko*, with a design to oblige me to be honest; and that everyone may find me out for ingratitude when I don't say all that's fit for me upon that subject. She had a great command of the stage, and I have often wondered that she would bury her favorite hero in a *novel*, when she might have revived him in the *scene*. She thought either that no actor could represent him, or she could not bear him represented. And I believe the last, when I remember what I have heard from a friend of hers, that she always told his story more feelingly than she writ it. Whatever happened to him in *Suriname*, he has mended his condition in *England*. He was born here under your Grace's influence, and that has carried his fortune farther into the world than all the poetical stars that I could have solicited for his success.

DRAMATIS PERSONAE

MEN

Oroonoko.
Aboan.
Lieutenant Governor of Suriname.
Blanford.
Stanmore.
Jack Stanmore.
Captain Driver.

Daniel, son to Widow Lackitt.
Hottman.
Planters, Indians, Negroes, Men, Women, and Children.

WOMEN

Imoinda.
Widow Lackitt.
Charlotte Welldon, in man's clothes.
Lucy Welldon, her sister.

THE SCENE: SURINAME,[4] A COLONY IN THE WEST INDIES AT THE TIME OF THE ACTION OF THE TRAGEDY IN POSSESSION OF THE ENGLISH.

Oroonoko.
Quo fata trahunt, virtus secura sequetur. Lucan.[5]
Virtus recludens immeritis mori
Coelum, negata tentat iter via. Hor. *Od.* 2. lib. 3.[6]

Act I, scene i. [The Welldons' house.]

Enter Welldon following Lucia.

LUCIA.
What will this come to? What can it end in? You have persuaded me to leave dear England and dearer London, the place of the world most worth living in, to follow you a-husband-hunting into America. I thought husbands grew in these plantations.

WELLDON.
Why so they do, as thick as oranges, ripening one under another. Week after week they drop into some woman's mouth. 'Tis but a little patience, spreading your apron in expectation, and one of 'em will fall into your lap at last.

LUCIA.
Aye, so you say indeed.

---

1 William, duke of Devonshire] William Cavendish (1641-1707), first duke of Devonshire, was a prominent Whig politician and opponent of James, duke of York, from the Exclusion Crisis through the Glorious Revolution.

2 Mrs. Behn] Aphra Behn (c. 1640-1689), author of the novella *Oroonoko* (1688), the source of this play, lived for almost a year in Suriname.

3 last play] *The Fatal Marriage* (1694) part of which was adapted from *The History of the Nun; or, The Fair Vow Breaker* (1689).

4 Suriname] Actually on the northern coast of South America; an English colony was founded there in 1651 and ceded to the Dutch in 1667.

5 *Quo … Lucan.*] Lucan, *Pharsalia* ii.287: "Virtue will follow fearless wherever destiny summons her" (Loeb).

6 *Virtus … 3*] Horace, *Odes* 3.2: "True worth, opening Heaven wide for those deserving not to die, essays its course by a path denied to others" (Loeb).

WELLDON.

But you have left dear London, you say. Pray what have you left in London that was very dear to you that had not left you before? 15

LUCIA.

Speak for yourself, sister.

WELLDON.

Nay, I'll keep you in countenance. The young fellows, you know, the dearest part of the Town* and without whom London had been a wilderness to you and me, had forsaken us a great while. 20

LUCIA.

Forsaken us! I don't know that they ever had us.

WELLDON.

Forsaken us the worst way, child;* that is, did not think us worth having. They neglected us, no longer designed upon us, they were tired of us. Women in London are like the rich silks: they are 25 out of fashion a great while before they wear out.

LUCIA.

The Devil take the fashion, I say.

WELLDON.

You may tumble 'em over and over at their first coming up and never disparage their price, but they fall upon wearing immediately lower and 30 lower in their value, till they come to the broker at last.

LUCIA.

Aye, aye, that's the merchant they deal with. The men would have us at their own scandalous rates. Their plenty makes 'em wanton, and in a little 35 time, I suppose, they won't know what they would have of the women themselves.

WELLDON.

Oh yes, they know what they would have. They would have a woman give the Town a pattern of her person and beauty and not stay in it so long to have 40 the whole piece worn out. They would have the good face only discovered and not the folly that commonly goes along with it. They say there is a vast stock of beauty in the Nation, but a great part of it lies in unprofitable hands. Therefore, for the good of 45 the public they would have a draught made once a quarter, send the decaying beauties for breeders into the country to make room for new faces to appear, to countenance the pleasures of the Town.

LUCIA.

'Tis very hard. The men must be young as long as 50 they live, and poor women be thought decaying and unfit for the Town at one or two and twenty. I'm sure we were not seven years in London.

WELLDON.

Not half the time taken notice of, sister. The two or three last years we could make nothing of it, even in 55 a vizard-mask: not in a vizard-mask, that has cheated many a man into an old acquaintance. Our faces began to be as familiar to the men of intrigue as their duns, and as much avoided. We durst not appear in public places and were almost grudged a gallery in 60 the churches.[7] Even there they had their jests upon us and cried, "She's in the right on't, good gentlewoman; since no man considers her body, she does very well indeed to take care of her soul."

LUCIA.

Such unmannerly fellows there will always be. 65

WELLDON.

Then, you may remember, we were reduced to the last necessity, the necessity of making silly visits to our civil acquaintance to bring us into tolerable company. Nay, the young Inns of Court* beaus of but one term's standing in the fashion, who knew 70 nobody but as they were shown 'em by the orange-women,* had nicknames for us. How often have they laughed out, "There goes my landlady. Is not she come to let lodgings yet?"[8]

LUCIA.

Young coxcombs that knew no better. 75

WELLDON.

And that we must have come to. For your part, what trade could you set up in? You would never arrive at the trust and credit of a guinea-bawd;[9] you would have too much business of your own, ever to mind other peoples'. 80

---

[7] gallery in the churches] Like a playhouse box, a gallery, or side balcony, in a London church was regarded as a place for fashionable self-display.

[8] landlady…lodgings] "landlady" could mean mistress (*OED*); to "let lodgings" implies setting up as a common prostitute.

[9] guinea-bawd] A guinea was a common fee or tip for services rendered, in this instance by the madam of a brothel.

LUCIA.

That is true indeed.

WELLDON.

Then, as a certain sign that there was nothing more
to be hoped for, the maids at the chocolate houses
found us out and laughed at us. Our *billets-doux*
lay there neglected for waste-paper; we were cried   85
down so low we could not pass upon the City* and
became so notorious in our galloping way, from
one end of the Town to the other, that at last we
could hardly compass a competent change of
petticoats to disguise us to the hackney coachmen.   90
And then it was near walking afoot indeed.

LUCIA.

Nay, that I began to be afraid of.

WELLDON.

To prevent which, with what youth and beauty was
left, some experience, and the small remainder of
fifteen hundred pounds apiece, which amounted   95
to bare two hundred between us both, I persuaded
you to bring your person for a venture to the
Indies. Everything has succeeded in our voyage: I
pass for your brother; one of the richest planters
here happening to die just as we landed, I have   100
claimed kindred with him. So, without making his
will, he has left us the credit of his relation to trade
upon. We pass for his cousins, coming here to
Suriname chiefly upon his invitation. We live in
reputation, have the best acquaintance of the place,   105
and we shall see our account in't, I warrant you.

LUCIA.

I must rely upon you.

Enter Widow Lackitt.

WIDOW.

Mr. Welldon, your servant. Your servant, Mrs.
Lucy. I am an ill visitor, but 'tis not too late, I hope,
to bid you welcome to this side of the world.   110
(*Salutes* Lucy.)

WELLDON.

Gad so, I beg your pardon, Widow. I should have
done the civilities of my house before, but as you
say, 'tis not too late, I hope. (*Going to kiss her.*)

WIDOW.

What! You think now this was a civil way of
begging a kiss, and by my troth, if it were, I see   115

no harm in't; 'tis a pitiful favor indeed that is not
worth asking for, though I have known a woman
speak plainer before now and not understood
neither.

WELLDON.

Not under my roof. Have at you, Widow.   120

WIDOW.

Why, that's well said, spoke like a younger brother
that deserves to have a widow.

He kisses her.

You're a younger brother, I know, by your kissing.

WELLDON.

How so, pray?

WIDOW.

Why, you kiss as if you expect to be paid for't. You   125
have birdlime upon your lips. You stick so close,
there's no getting rid of you.

WELLDON.

I am akin to a younger brother.

WIDOW.

So much the better. We widows are commonly the
better for younger brothers.   130

LUCIA. (*Aside.*)

Better, or worse, most of you. But you won't be
much better for him, I can tell you.

WELLDON.

I was a younger brother, but an uncle of my
mother's has maliciously left me an estate and, I'm
afraid, spoiled my fortune.   135

WIDOW.

No, no, an estate will never spoil your fortune. I
have a good estate myself, thank Heaven, and a
kind husband that left it behind him.

WELLDON.

Thank Heaven, that took him away from it,
Widow, and left you behind him.   140

WIDOW.

Nay, Heaven's will must be done; he's in a better
place.

WELLDON.

A better place for you, no doubt on't. Now you
may look about you. Choose for yourself, Mrs.
Lackitt, that's your business, for I know you design   145
to marry again.

WIDOW.

Oh dear! Not I, I protest and swear; I don't design

it. But I won't swear neither; one does not know what may happen to tempt one.

WELLDON.

Why, a lusty young fellow may happen to tempt you.   150

WIDOW.

Nay, I'll do nothing rashly; I'll resolve against nothing. The Devil, they say, is very busy upon these occasions, especially with the widows. But if I am to be tempted, it must be with a young man,   155
I promise you.—Mrs. Lucy, your brother is a very pleasant gentleman. I came about business to him, but he turns everything into merriment.

WELLDON.

Business, Mrs. Lackitt. Then I know you would have me to yourself. Pray leave us together, sister.   160

Exit Lucy.

(*Aside.*) What am I drawing upon myself here?

WIDOW.

You have taken a very pretty house here, everything so neat about you already. I hear you are laying out for a plantation.

WELLDON.

Why yes, truly, I like the country and would buy   165
a plantation if I could, reasonably.

WIDOW.

Oh! by all means, reasonably.

WELLDON.

If I could have one to my mind, I would think of settling among you.

WIDOW.

Oh! you can't do better. Indeed we can't pretend   170
to have so good company for you as you had in England, but we shall make very much of you. For my own part, I assure you, I shall think myself very happy to be more particularly known to you.

WELLDON.

Dear Mrs. Lackitt, you do me too much honor.   175

WIDOW.

Then as to a plantation, Mr. Welldon, you know I have several to dispose of. Mr. Lackitt, I thank him, has left me, though I say it, the richest widow upon the place; therefore, I may afford to use you better than other people can. You shall have one   180
upon any reasonable terms.

WELLDON.

That's a fair offer indeed.

WIDOW.

You shall find me as easy as anybody you can have to do with, I assure you. Pray try me, I would have you try me, Mr. Welldon. Well, I like that name   185
of yours exceedingly, Mr. Welldon.

WELLDON.

My name!

WIDOW.

Oh, exceedingly! If anything could persuade me to alter my own name, I verily believe nothing in the world would do it so soon as to be called Mrs.   190
Welldon.

WELLDON.

Why, indeed, Welldon does sound something better than Lackitt.

WIDOW.

Oh! a great deal better. Not that there is so much in a name neither. But I don't know, there is   195
something: I should like mightily to be called Mrs. Welldon.

WELLDON.

I'm glad you like my name.

WIDOW.

Of all things. But then there's the misfortune: one can't change one's name without changing one's   200
condition.

WELLDON.

You'll hardly think it worth that, I believe.

WIDOW.

Think it worth what, sir? Changing my condition? Indeed sir, I think it worth everything. But alas! Mr. Welldon, I have been a widow but six weeks;[b]   205
'tis too soon to think of changing one's condition yet, indeed it is. Pray don't desire it of me. Not but that you may persuade me to anything, sooner than any person in the world.

WELLDON.

Who, I, Mrs. Lackitt?   210

WIDOW.

Indeed you may, Mr. Welldon, sooner than any man living. Lord, there's a great deal in saving a decency; I never minded it before. Well, I'm glad you spoke first to excuse my modesty. But what, modesty means nothing and is the virtue of a girl   215 that does not know what she would be at; a widow should be wiser. Now I will own to you, but I won't confess neither, I have had a great respect for you a great while. I beg your pardon, sir, and I must declare to you, indeed I must, if you desire 220 to dispose of all I have in the world in an honorable way, which I don't pretend to be any way deserving your consideration, my fortune and person, if you won't understand me without telling you so, are both at your service. Gad so! another 225 time—

Stanmore enters to them.

STANMORE.

So, Mrs. Lackitt, your widowhood is waning apace. I see which way 'tis going. Welldon, you're a happy man. The women and their favors come home to you. 230

WIDOW.

A fiddle of favor, Mr. Stanmore. I am a lone woman, you know it, left in a great deal of business, and business must be followed or lost. I have several stocks and plantations upon my hands, and other things to dispose of, which Mr. 235 Welldon may have occasion for.

WELLDON.

We were just upon the brink of a bargain as you came in.

STANMORE.

Let me drive it on for you.

WELLDON.

So you must, I believe, you or somebody for me. 240

STANMORE.

I'll stand by you. I understand more of this business than you can pretend to.

WELLDON.

I don't pretend to't; 'tis quite out of my way indeed.

STANMORE.

If the widow gets you to herself, she will certainly be too hard for you. I know her of old. She has 245 no conscience in a corner, a very Jew in a bargain, and would circumcise you to get more of you.

WELLDON.

Is this true, Widow?

WIDOW.

Speak as you find, Mr. Welldon. I have offered you

very fair. Think upon't, and let me hear of you. The 250 sooner the better, Mr. Welldon. (*Exit.*)

STANMORE.

I assure you, my friend, she'll cheat you if she can.

WELLDON.

I don't know that, but I can cheat her, if I will.

STANMORE.

Cheat her? How?

WELLDON.

I can marry her. And then I'm sure I have it in 255 my power to cheat her.

STANMORE.

Can you marry her?

WELLDON.

Yes, faith, so she says. Her pretty person and fortune (which, one with the other, you know, are not contemptible) are both at my service. 260

STANMORE.

Contemptible! very considerable, egad; very desirable. Why, she's worth ten thousand pounds, man, a clear estate: no charge upon it but a boobily son. He indeed was to have half, but his father begot him and she breeds him up not to know or 265 have more than she has a mind to. And she has a mind to something else, it seems.

WELLDON. (*Musing.*)

There's a great deal to be made of this.

STANMORE.

A handsome fortune may be made on't, and I advise you to't, by all means. 270

WELLDON.

To marry her! an old, wanton witch! I hate her.

STANMORE.

No matter for that. Let her go to the devil for you. She'll cheat her son of a good estate for you. That's a perquisite of a widow's portion always.

WELLDON.

I have a design and will follow her at least till I 275 have a pennyworth of the plantation.*

STANMORE.

I speak as a friend, when I advise you to marry her. For 'tis directly against the interest of my own family. My cousin Jack has belabored her a good while that way. 280

WELLDON.

What! Honest Jack! I'll not hinder him. I'll give

over the thoughts of her.

STANMORE.

He'll make nothing on't; she does not care for him.
I'm glad you have her in your power.

WELLDON.

I may be able to serve him.   285

STANMORE.

Here's a ship come into the river; I was in hopes
it had been from England.

WELLDON.

From England!

STANMORE.

No, I was disappointed. I long to see this
handsome cousin of yours; the picture you gave   290
me of her has charmed me.

WELLDON.

You'll see whether it has flattered her or no, in a
little time. If she recovered of that illness that was
the reason of her staying behind us, I know she
will come with the first opportunity. We shall see   295
her, or hear of her death.

STANMORE.

We'll hope the best. The ships from England are
expected every day.

WELLDON.

What ship is this?

STANMORE.

A rover, a buccaneer, a trader in slaves: that's the   300
commodity we deal in, you know. If you have a
curiosity to see our manner of marketing, I'll wait
upon you.

WELLDON.

We'll take my sister with us.

Exeunt.

Scene ii. An open place.

Enter Lieutenant Governor and Blanford.

LIEUTENANT GOVERNOR.

There's no resisting your fortune, Blanford; you
draw all the prizes.

BLANFORD.

I draw for our Lord Governor, you know; his
fortune favors me.

LIEUTENANT GOVERNOR.

I grudge him nothing this time, but if fortune had   5

favored me in the last sale, the fair slave[10] had been
mine, Clemene had been mine.

BLANFORD.

Are you still in love with her?

LIEUTENANT GOVERNOR.

Every day more in love with her.

*Enter Captain Driver, teased and pulled about by
Widow Lackitt and several planters. Enter at another
door Welldon, Lucia, Stanmore.*

WIDOW.

Here have I six slaves in my lot, and not a man   10
among 'em; all women and children.[11] What can
I do with 'em, Captain? Pray consider, I am a
woman myself and can't get my own slaves, as
some of my neighbors do.

FIRST PLANTER.

I have all men in mine. Pray Captain, let the men   15
and women be mingled together for procreation's
sake and the good of the plantation.*

SECOND PLANTER.

Aye, aye, a man and a woman, Captain, for the
good of the plantation.

CAPTAIN.

Let 'em mingle together and be damned, what care   20
I? Would you have me pimp for the good of the
plantation?

FIRST PLANTER.

I am a constant customer, Captain.

WIDOW.

I am always ready money to you, Captain.

FIRST PLANTER.

For that matter, Mistress, my money is as ready as   25
yours.

WIDOW.

Pray hear me, Captain.

CAPTAIN.

Look you, I have done my part by you; I have
brought the number of slaves you bargained for.

---

10 fair slave] perhaps "white-skinned" as well as the commoner meaning, "beautiful"

11 all women and children] A lot was a previously-con-
tracted-for number of slaves. In her novel Behn writes
that whatever the gender mix in your lot, you are obliged
to take it as it is.

If your lots have not pleased you, you must draw 30
again among yourselves.

THIRD PLANTER.

I am contented with my lot.

FOURTH PLANTER.

I am very well satisfied.

THIRD PLANTER.

We'll have no drawing again.

CAPTAIN.

Do you hear, Mistress? You may hold your tongue. 35
For my part, I expect my money.

WIDOW.

Captain, nobody questions or scruples the
payment. But I won't hold my tongue; 'tis too
much to pray and pay too. One may speak for
one's own, I hope. 40

CAPTAIN.

Well, what would you say?

WIDOW.

I say no more than I can make out.

CAPTAIN.

Out with it, then.

WIDOW.

I say, things have not been so fair carried as they
might have been. How do I know how you have 45
juggled together in my absence? You drew the lots
before I came, I'm sure.

CAPTAIN.

That's your own fault, Mistress; you might have
come sooner.

WIDOW.

Then here's a prince, as they say, among the slaves, 50
and you set him down to go as a common man.

CAPTAIN.

Have you a mind to try what a man he is? You'll find
him no more than a common man at your business.

WIDOW.

Sir, you're a scurvy fellow to talk at this rate to me.
If my husband were alive, Gadsbodikins, you 55
would not use me so.

CAPTAIN.

Right, Mistress, I would not use you at all.

WIDOW.

Not use me! Your betters every inch of you, I
would have you to know, would be glad to use me,
sirrah. Marry* come up here, who are you, I trow? 60

You begin to think yourself a captain, forsooth,
because we call you so. You forget yourself as fast
as you can, but I remember you. I know you for a
pitiful paltry fellow, as you are, an upstart to prosperity, one that is but just come acquainted with 65
cleanliness and that never saw five shillings of your
own without deserving to be hanged for 'em.

LIEUTENANT GOVERNOR.

She has given you a broadside, Captain. You'll
stand up to her.

CAPTAIN.

Hang her, stinkpot, I'll come no nearer. 70

WIDOW.

By this good light, it would make a woman do a
thing she never designed—marry again, though she
were sure to repent it, to be revenged of such a—

JACK STANMORE.

What's the matter, Mrs. Lackitt? Can I serve you?

WIDOW.

No, no, you can't serve me. You are for serving 75
yourself, I'm sure. Pray go about your business, I
have none for you. You know I have told you so.
Lord! how can you be so troublesome? nay, so
unconscionable, to think that every rich widow
must throw herself away upon a young fellow that 80
has nothing?

STANMORE.

Jack, you are answered, I suppose.

JACK STANMORE.

I'll have another pluck at her.

WIDOW.

Mr. Welldon, I am a little out of order, but pray
bring your sister to dine with me. Gad's my life, 85
I'm out of all patience with that pitiful fellow. My
flesh rises at him. I can't stay in the place where
he is. (*Exit.*)

BLANFORD.

Captain, you have used the widow very familiarly.

CAPTAIN.

This is my way; I have no design and therefore am 90
not over-civil. If she had ever a handsome daughter
to wheedle her out of, or if I could make anything
of her booby son——

WELLDON. (*Aside.*)

I may improve that hint and make something of
him. 95

LIEUTENANT GOVERNOR.

She's very rich.

CAPTAIN.

I'm rich myself. She has nothing that I want; I have no leaks to stop. Old women are fortune-menders. I have made a good voyage and would reap the fruits of my labor. We plow the deep, my masters, but our harvest is on shore. I'm for a young woman.

STANMORE.

Look about, Captain, there's one ripe and ready for the sickle.

CAPTAIN.

A woman indeed! I will be acquainted with her. Who is she?

WELLDON.

My sister, sir.

CAPTAIN.

Would I were akin to her. If she were my sister, she should never go out of the family. What say you, mistress? You expect I should marry you, I suppose.

LUCIA. (*Turning away.*)

I shan't be disappointed, if you don't.

WELLDON.

She won't break her heart, sir.

CAPTAIN. (*Following her.*)

But I mean—

WELLDON.

And I mean (*Going between him and Lucia*) that you must not think of her without marrying.

CAPTAIN.

I mean so too.

WELLDON.

Why, then, your meaning's out.

CAPTAIN.

You're very short.[12]

WELLDON.

I will grow and be taller for you.

CAPTAIN.

I shall grow angry and swear.

WELLDON.

You'll catch no fish then.[13]

CAPTAIN.

I don't well know whether he designs to affront me or no.

STANMORE.

No, no, he's a little familiar, 'tis his way.

CAPTAIN.

Say you so? Nay, I can be as familiar as he, if that be it. Well sir, look upon me full. What say you? How do you like me for a brother-in-law?

WELLDON.

Why yes, faith, you'll do my business (*Turning him about.*), if we can agree about my sister's.

CAPTAIN.

I don't know whether your sister will like me or not. I can't say much to her. But I have money enough, and if you are her brother, as you seem to be akin to her, I know that will recommend me to you.

WELLDON.

This is your* market for slaves. My sister is a free woman and must not be disposed of in public. You shall be welcome to my house, if you please. And upon better acquaintance, if my sister likes you, and I like your offers—

CAPTAIN.

Very well, sir, I'll come and see her.

LIEUTENANT GOVERNOR.

Where are the slaves, Captain? They are long a-coming.

BLANFORD.

And who is this prince that's fallen to my lot for the Lord Governor? Let me know something of him, that I may treat him accordingly. Who is he?

CAPTAIN.

He's the devil of a fellow, I can tell you. A prince every inch of him. You have paid dear enough for him for all the good he'll do you. I was forced to clap him in irons and did not think the ship safe, neither. You are in hostility with the Indians, they say; they threaten you daily. You had best have an eye upon him.

---

12 short] abrupt, but also perhaps a punning reference to the stature of Susannah Verbruggen, the actress who first played Charlotte Welldon (Jordan and Love)

13 no fish then] "If you swear, you'll catch no fish": proverbial.

BLANFORD.

But who is he?

LIEUTENANT GOVERNOR.

And how do you know him to be a prince?

CAPTAIN.

He is son and heir to the great King of Angola, a 155
mischievous monarch in those parts, who, by his
good will, would never let any of his neighbors be in
quiet. This son was his general, a plaguy fighting
fellow. I have formerly had dealings with him for
slaves, which he took prisoners, and have got pretty 160
roundly by him. But the wars being at an end and
nothing more to be got by the trade of that country,
I made bold to bring the prince along with me.

LIEUTENANT GOVERNOR.

How could you do that?

BLANFORD.

What? steal a prince out of his own country? 165
Impossible!

CAPTAIN.

'Twas hard indeed, but I did it. You must know,
this Oroonoko——

BLANFORD.

Is that his name?

CAPTAIN.

Aye, Oroonoko. 170

LIEUTENANT GOVERNOR.

Oroonoko.

CAPTAIN.

——is naturally inquisitive about the men and
manners of the white nations. Because I could give
him some account of the other parts of the world,
I grew very much into his favor. In return of so 175
great an honor, you know I could do no less upon
my coming away than invite him on board me.
Never having been in a ship, he appointed his
time, and I prepared my entertainment. He came
the next evening as privately as he could with 180
about some twenty along with him. The punch
went round, and as many of his attendants as
would be dangerous I sent dead drunk on shore;
the rest we secured. And so you have the Prince
Oroonoko. 185

FIRST PLANTER.

Gad-a-mercy, Captain, there you were with him,
i'faith.

SECOND PLANTER.

Such men as you are fit to be employed in public
affairs. The plantation* will thrive by you.

THIRD PLANTER.

Industry should be encouraged. 190

CAPTAIN.

There's nothing done without it, boys. I have made
my fortune this way.

BLANFORD.

Unheard-of villainy!

STANMORE.

Barbarous treachery!

BLANFORD.

They applaud him for't. 195

LIEUTENANT GOVERNOR.

But Captain, methinks you have taken a great deal
of pains for this Prince Oroonoko. Why did you
part with him at the common rate of slaves?

CAPTAIN.

Why, Lieutenant Governor, I'll tell you. I did design
to carry him to England to have showed him 200
there,[14] but I found him troublesome upon my
hands, and I'm glad I'm rid of him.—Oh ho, here
they come.

*Black slaves—men, women, and children—pass across
the stage by two and two; Aboan and others of Oroonoko's
attendants two and two; Oroonoko last of all in chains.*

LUCIA.

Are all these wretches slaves?

STANMORE.

All sold, they and their posterity all slaves. 205

LUCIA.

Oh miserable fortune!

BLANFORD.

Most of 'em know no better: they were born so
and only change their masters. But a prince, born
only to command, betrayed and sold! My heart
drops blood for him. 210

CAPTAIN.

Now Governor, here he comes, pray observe him.

---

14 showed him there] Possibly in the manner of a public
curiosity, as American Indians were displayed in England in the sixteenth and seventeenth centuries; cf.
Shakespeare's *The Tempest*.

OROONOKO.

So sir, you have kept your word with me.

CAPTAIN.

I am a better Christian, I thank you, than to keep it with a heathen.

OROONOKO.

You are a Christian, be a Christian still: 215
If you have any god that teaches you
To break your word, I need not curse you more;
Let him cheat you, as you are false to me.
You faithful followers of my better fortune!
We have been fellow soldiers in the field; 220
Now we are fellow slaves. This last farewell.
(*Embracing his friends.*)
Be sure of one thing that will comfort us:
Whatever world we next are thrown upon
Cannot be worse than this.

All slaves go off but Oroonoko.

CAPTAIN.

You see what a bloody pagan he is, Governor, but 225
I took care that none of his followers should be in the same lot with him for fear they should undertake some desperate action to the danger of the colony.

OROONOKO.

Live still in fear, it is the villain's curse 230
And will revenge my chains. Fear even me,
Who have no pow'r to hurt thee. Nature abhors
And drives thee out from the society
And commerce of mankind for breach of faith.
Men live and prosper but in mutual trust, 235
A confidence of one another's truth.
That thou hast violated. I have done.
I know my fortune, and submit to it.

LIEUTENANT GOVERNOR.

Sir, I am sorry for your fortune and would help it, if I could. 240

BLANFORD.

Take off his chains. (*Applying to him.*) You know your condition, but you are fallen into honorable hands. You are the Lord Governor's slave, who will use you nobly. In his absence it shall be my care to serve you. 245

OROONOKO.

I hear you, but I can believe no more.

LIEUTENANT GOVERNOR.

Captain, I'm afraid the world won't speak so honorably of this action of yours, as you would have 'em.

CAPTAIN.

I have the money. Let the world speak and be 250
damned, I care not.

OROONOKO. (*To Blanford.*)

I would forget myself. Be satisfied
I am above the rank of common slaves.
Let that content you. The Christian there, that knows me,
For his own sake will not discover* more. 255

CAPTAIN.

I have other matters to mind. You have him, and much good may do you with your prince. (*Exit.*)

The Planters pulling and staring at Oroonoko.

BLANFORD.

What would you have there? You stare as if you never saw a man before. Stand further off. (*Turns them away.*)

OROONOKO.

Let 'em stare on. 260
I am unfortunate, but not ashamed
Of being so. No, let the guilty blush,
The white man that betray'd me. Honest black
Disdains to change its color. I am ready.
Where must I go? Dispose me as you please. 265
I am not well acquainted with my fortune,
But must learn to know it better. So
I know you say: Degrees make all things easy.ᶜ

BLANFORD.

All things shall be easy.

OROONOKO.

Tear off this pomp, and let me know myself. 270
The slavish habit best becomes me now.
Hard fare and whips and chains may overpow'r
The frailer flesh and bow my body down,
But there's another, nobler part of me,
Out of your reach, which you can never tame. 275

BLANFORD.

You shall find nothing of this wretchedness
You apprehend. We are not monsters all.
You seem unwilling to disclose yourself;
Therefore, for fear the mentioning your name

Should give you new disquiets, I presume 280
To call you Caesar.[15]

OROONOKO.

I am myself, but call me what you please.

STANMORE.

A very good name, Caesar.

LIEUTENANT GOVERNOR.

And very fit for his great character.

OROONOKO.

Was Caesar then a slave? 285

LIEUTENANT GOVERNOR.

I think he was; to pirates too.[16] He was a great
conqueror, but unfortunate in his friends.

OROONOKO.

His friends were Christians?

BLANFORD.

No.

OROONOKO.

No! that's strange. 290

LIEUTENANT GOVERNOR.

And murdered by 'em.

OROONOKO.

I would be Caesar there. Yet I will live.

BLANFORD.

Live to be happier.

OROONOKO.

Do what you will with me.

BLANFORD.

I'll wait upon you, attend, and serve you. 295

Exit with Oroonoko.

LUCIA.

Well, if the captain had brought this prince's
country along with him and would make me
queen of it, I would not have him, after doing so
base a thing.

WELLDON.

He's a man to thrive in the world, sister. He'll make 300
you the better jointure.

_____

15 Caesar] It was standard procedure to give slaves European names, particularly Roman.

16 to pirates too] According to legend, Julius Caesar was
   captured by Mediterranean pirates but later escaped,
   captured his former captors, and crucified them (Novak
   and Rodes).

LUCIA.

Hang him, nothing can prosper with him.

STANMORE.

Inquire into the great estates, and you will find
most of 'em depend upon the same title of honesty.
The men who raise 'em first are much of the 305
captain's principles.

WELLDON.

Ay, ay, as you say. Let him be damned for the good
of his family.——Come sister, we are invited to
dinner.

LIEUTENANT GOVERNOR.

Stanmore, you dine with me. 310

Exeunt omnes.

Act II, scene i. Widow Lackitt's house.

Widow Lackitt, Welldon.

WELLDON.

This is so great a favor, I don't know how to receive
it.

WIDOW.

Oh dear sir! you know how to receive and how to
return a favor as well as anybody, I don't doubt it.
'Tis not the first you have had from our sex, I 5
suppose.

WELLDON.

But this is so unexpected.

WIDOW.

Lord, how can you say so, Mr. Welldon? I won't
believe you. Don't I know you handsome
gentlemen expect everything that a woman can do 10
for you? And by my troth, you're in the right on't.
I think one can't do too much for a handsome
gentleman, and so you shall find it.

WELLDON.

I shall never have such an offer again, that's certain.
(*Pretending a concern.*) What shall I do? I am 15
mightily divided.

WIDOW.

Divided! Oh dear, I hope not so, sir. If I marry,
truly I expect to have you to myself.

WELLDON.

There's no danger of that, Mrs. Lackitt. I am
divided in my thoughts. My father upon his 20
deathbed obliged me to see my sister disposed of,

before I married myself. 'Tis that sticks upon me. They say, indeed, promises are to be broken or kept, and I know 'tis a foolish thing to be tied to a promise, but I can't help it. I don't know how to get rid of it.

WIDOW.

Is that all?

WELLDON.

All in all to me. The commands of a dying father, you know, ought to be obeyed.

WIDOW.

And so they may.

WELLDON.

Impossible, to do me any good.

WIDOW.

They shan't be your hindrance. You would have a husband for your sister, you say. He must be very well to pass too in the world, I suppose?

WELLDON.

I would not throw her away.

WIDOW.

Then marry her out of hand to the sea captain you were speaking of.

WELLDON.

I was thinking of him, but 'tis to no purpose. She hates him.

WIDOW.

Does she hate him? Nay, 'tis no matter, an impudent rascal as he is, I would not advise her to marry him.

WELLDON.

Can you think of nobody else?

WIDOW.

Let me see.

WELLDON.

Aye, pray do. I should be loath to part with my good fortune in you for so small a matter as a sister. But you find how it is with me.

WIDOW.

Well remembered, i'faith. Well, if I thought you would like of it, I have a husband for her. What do you think of my son?

WELLDON.

You don't think of it yourself.

WIDOW.

I protest but I do. I am in earnest, if you are. He shall marry her within this half hour, if you'll give your consent to it.

WELLDON.

I give my consent! I'll answer for my sister. She shall have him. You may be sure I shall be glad to get over the difficulty.

WIDOW.

No more to be said then, that difficulty is over. But I vow and swear you frightened me, Mr. Welldon. If I had not had a son now for your sister, what must I have done, do you think? Were not you an ill-natured thing to boggle at a promise? I could break twenty for you.

WELLDON.

I am the more obliged to you. But this son will save all.

WIDOW.

He's in the house; I'll go and bring him myself. (*Going.*) You would do well to break the business to your sister. She's within, I'll send her to you.

WELLDON.

Pray do.

WIDOW. (*Going again, comes back.*)

But do you hear? Perhaps she may stand upon her maidenly behavior and blush and play the fool and delay. But don't be answered so. What! she is not a girl at these years. Show your authority and tell her roundly, she must be married immediately. I'll manage my son, I warrant you. (*Goes out in haste.*)

WELLDON.

The widow's in haste, I see. I thought I had laid a rub in the road about my sister. But she has stepped over that. She's making way for herself as fast as she can, but little thinks where she is going. I could tell her she is going to play the fool, but people don't love to hear of their faults. Besides, that is not my business at present.

Enter Lucia.

So, sister, I have a husband for you.

LUCIA.

With all my heart. I don't know what confinement marriage may be to the men, but I'm sure the women have no liberty without it. I am for anything that will deliver me from the care of a reputation, which I begin to find impossible to preserve.

WELLDON.

I'll ease you of that care. You must be married 90
immediately.

LUCIA.

The sooner the better, for I am quite tired of
setting up for a husband. The widow's foolish son
is the man, I suppose.

WELLDON.

I considered your constitution, sister, and, finding 95
you would have occasion for a fool, I have
provided accordingly.

LUCIA.

I don't know what occasion I may have for a fool
when I'm married. But I find none but fools have
occasion to marry. 100

WELLDON.

Since he is to be a fool, then, I thought it better
for you to have one of his mother's making than
your own. 'Twill save you the trouble.

LUCIA.

I thank you; you take a great deal of pains for me.
But pray tell me, what are you doing for yourself 105
all this while?

WELLDON.

You were never true to your own secrets, and
therefore I won't trust you with mine. Only
remember this: I am your elder sister and
consequently, laying my breeches aside, have as 110
much occasion for a husband as you can have. I
have a man in my eye, be satisfied.

Enter Widow Lackitt with her son Daniel.

WIDOW.

Come Daniel, hold up thy head, child. Look like
a man. You must not take it as you have done.
Gad's my life! there's nothing to be done with 115
twirling your hat, man.

DANIEL.

Why Mother, what's to be done, then?

WIDOW.

Why, look me in the face and mind what I say to
you.

DANIEL.

Marry,* who's the fool, then? what shall I get by 120
minding what you say to me?

WIDOW. (*Going between Lucia and Daniel.*)

Mrs. Lucy, the boy is bashful, don't discourage him.
Pray come a little forward and let him salute* you.

LUCIA. (*To Welldon.*)

A fine husband I am to have, truly. 125

WIDOW.

Come Daniel, you must be acquainted with this
gentlewoman.

DANIEL.

Nay, I'm not proud, that is not my fault. I am
perfectly acquainted when I know the company,
but this gentlewoman is a stranger to me. 130

WIDOW.

She is your mistress. I have spoke a good word for
you. Make her a bow and go kiss her.

DANIEL.

Kiss her! Have a care what you say; I warrant she
scorns your words. Such fine folk are not used to
be stopped and kissed. Do you think I don't know 135
that, Mother?

WIDOW.

Try her, try her, man.

Daniel bows, she thrusts him forward.

Why, that's well done; go nearer her.

DANIEL.

Is the devil in the woman? (*To his mother.*) Why,
so I can go nearer her, if you would let a body 140
alone. (*To Lucia.*) Cry you mercy, forsooth. My
mother is always shaming one before company. She
would have me as unmannerly as herself and offer
to kiss you.

WELLDON.

Why, won't you kiss her? 145

DANIEL.

Why, pray, may I?

WELLDON.

Kiss her, kiss her, man.

DANIEL.

Marry,* and I will. (*Kisses her.*) Gadsooks! she kisses
rarely! An* please you, mistress, and seeing my
mother will have it so, I don't much care if I kiss 150
you again, forsooth. (*Kisses her again.*)

LUCIA.

Well, how do you like me now?

DANIEL.

Like you! marry,* I don't know. You have
bewitched me, I think. I was never so in my born
days before.   155

WIDOW.

You must marry this fine woman, Daniel.

DANIEL.

Hey day! Marry her! I was never married in all my
life. What must I do with her then, Mother?

WIDOW.

You must live with her, eat and drink with her, go
to bed with her, and sleep with her.   160

DANIEL.

Nay, marry,* if I must go to bed with her, I shall
never sleep, that's certain. She'll break me of my
rest, quite and clean, I tell you beforehand. As for
eating and drinking with her, why I have a good
stomach and can play my part in any company.   165
But how do you think I can go to bed to a woman
I don't know?

WELLDON.

You shall know her better.

DANIEL.

Say you so, sir?

WELLDON.

Kiss her again.   170

DANIEL. (Kisses Lucy.)

Nay, kissing I find will make us presently*
acquainted. We'll steal into a corner to practice a
little, and then I shall be able to do anything.

WELLDON.

The young man mends apace.

WIDOW.

Pray don't balk him.   175

DANIEL.

Mother, Mother, if you'll stay in the room by me
and promise not to leave me, I don't care for once
if I venture to go to bed with her.

WIDOW.

There's a good child. Go in and put on thy best
clothes; pluck up a spirit. I'll stay in the room by   180
thee. She won't hurt thee, I warrant thee.

DANIEL.

Nay, as to that matter, I'm not afraid of her. I'll
give her as good as she brings. I have a Rowland
for her Oliver,* and so you may tell her. (Exit.)

WIDOW.

Mrs. Lucy, we shan't stay for you. You are in a   185
readiness, I suppose.

WELLDON.

She's always ready to do what I would have her, I
must say that for my sister.

WIDOW.

'Twill be her own another day. Mr. Welldon, we'll
marry 'em out of hand, and then—   190

WELLDON.

And then, Mrs. Lackitt, look to yourself.

Exeunt.

Scene ii.

Oroonoko and Blanford.

OROONOKO.

You grant I have good reason to suspect
All the professions you can make to me.

BLANFORD.

Indeed you have.

OROONOKO.

The dog that sold me did profess as much
As you can do. But yet I know not why—   5
Whether it is because I'm fall'n so low
And have no more to fear—that is not it,
I am a slave no longer than I please.
'Tis something nobler. Being just myself,
I am inclining to think others so.   10
'Tis that prevails upon me to believe you.

BLANFORD.

You may believe me.

OROONOKO.

I do believe you.
From what I know of you, you are no fool.
Fools only are the knaves, and live by tricks;   15
Wise men may thrive without 'em and be honest.

BLANFORD. (Aside.)

They won't all take your counsel.

OROONOKO.

You know my story, and you say you are
A friend to my misfortunes; that's a name
Will teach you what you owe yourself and me.   20

BLANFORD.

I'll study to deserve to be your friend.
When once our noble governor arrives,

With him you will not need my interest.
He is too generous not to feel your wrongs.
But be assured I will employ my pow'r   25
And find the means to send you home again.

OROONOKO.

I thank you, sir. My honest, wretched friends!
     (*Sighing.*)
Their chains are heavy. They have hardly found
So kind a master. May I ask you, sir,
What is become of 'em? Perhaps I should not.   30
You will forgive a stranger.

BLANFORD.

                              I'll inquire
And use my best endeavors where they are
To have 'em gently used.

OROONOKO.

                              Once more I thank you.   35
You offer every cordial that can keep
My hopes alive to wait a better day.
What friendly care can do, you have applied.
But oh! I have a grief admits no cure.

BLANFORD.

You do not know, sir——   40

OROONOKO.

                              Can you raise the dead?
Pursue and overtake the wings of time?
And bring about again the hours, the days,
The years that made me happy?

BLANFORD.

                              That is not to be done.   45

OROONOKO.

No, there is nothing to be done for me.(*Kneeling
     and kissing the earth.*)
Thou god adored! Thou ever-glorious sun!
If she be yet on earth, send me a beam
Of thy all-seeing power to light me to her.
Or if thy sister-goddess has preferred   50
Her beauty to the skies to be a star,
Oh tell me where she shines, that I may stand
Whole nights and gaze upon her.

BLANFORD.

I am rude and interrupt you.

OROONOKO.

                              I am troublesome.   55
But pray give me your pardon. My swoll'n heart
Bursts out its passage, and I must complain.

Oh! Can you think of nothing dearer to me?
Dearer than liberty, my country, friends,
Much dearer than my life? That I have lost.   60
The tend'rest, best beloved, and loving wife.

BLANFORD.

Alas! I pity you.

OROONOKO.

                              Do, pity me.
Pity's akin to love, and every thought
Of that soft kind is welcome to my soul.   65
I would be pitied here.

BLANFORD.

I dare not ask more than you please to tell me,
But if you think it convenient to let me know
Your story, I dare promise you to bear
A part in your distress, if not assist you.   70

OROONOKO.

Thou honest-hearted man! I wanted such,
Just such a friend as thou art, that would sit
Still as the night and let me talk whole days
Of my Imoinda. Oh! I'll tell thee all
From first to last, and pray observe me well.   75

BLANFORD.

I will most heedfully.

OROONOKO.

There was a stranger in my father's court,
Valued and honored much. He was a white,
The first I ever saw of your complexion.
He changed his gods for ours and so grew great;   80
Of many virtues, and so famed in arms
He still* commanded all my father's wars.
I was bred under him. One fatal day,
The armies joining, he before me stepped,
Receiving in his breast a poisoned dart   85
Leveled at me; he died within my arms.
I've tired you already.

BLANFORD.

                              Pray go on.

OROONOKO.

He left an only daughter, whom he brought
An infant to Angola. When I came   90
Back to the court, a happy conqueror,
Humanity obliged me to condole
With this sad virgin for a father's loss,
Lost for my safety. I presented her
With all the slaves of battle to atone   95

Her father's ghost. But when I saw her face
And heard her speak, I offered up myself
To be the sacrifice. She bowed and blushed;
I wondered and adored. The sacred pow'r
That had subdued me then inspired my tongue,   100
Inclined her heart, and all our talk was love.

BLANFORD.
Then you were happy.

OROONOKO.
                        Oh! I was too happy.
I married her. And though my country's custom
Indulged the privilege of many wives,   105
I swore myself never to know but her.
She grew with child, and I grew happier still.
Oh my Imoinda! But it could not last.
Her fatal beauty reached my father's ears;
He sent for her to court, where, cursèd court!   110
No woman comes but for his amorous use.
He raging to possess her, she was forced
To own herself my wife. The furious king
Started at incest, but grown desperate,
Not daring to enjoy what he desired,   115
In mad revenge, which I could never learn,
He poisoned her, or sent her far, far off,
Far from my hopes ever to see her more.

BLANFORD.
Most barbarous of fathers! the sad tale
Has struck me dumb with wonder.   120

OROONOKO.
                                I have done.
I'll trouble you no farther; now and then
A sigh will have its way; that shall be all.

Enter Stanmore.

STANMORE.
Blanford, the Lieutenant Governor is gone to your
plantation. He desires you would bring the royal   125
slave with you. The sight of his fair mistress, he
says, is an entertainment for a Prince; he would
have his opinion of her.

OROONOKO.
Is he a lover?

BLANFORD.
So he says himself. He flatters a beautiful slave that   130
I have and calls her mistress.

OROONOKO.
Must he then flatter her to call her mistress?
I pity the proud man who thinks himself
Above being in love. What though she be a slave,
She may deserve him.   135

BLANFORD.
You shall judge of that when you see her, sir.

OROONOKO.
I go with you.

Exeunt.

                    Scene iii. A plantation.

Lieutenant Governor following Imoinda.

LIEUTENANT GOVERNOR.
I have disturbed you, I confess my fault,
My fair Clemene, but begin again
And I will listen to your mournful song,
Sweet as the soft complaining nightingales,
While every note calls out my trembling soul   5
And leaves me silent as the midnight groves,
Only to shelter you. Sing, sing again,
And let me wonder at the many ways
You have to ravish me.

IMOINDA.
                    Oh! I can weep   10
Enough for you and me, if that will please you.

LIEUTENANT GOVERNOR.
You must not weep. I come to dry your tears
And raise you from your sorrow. Look upon me.
Look with the eyes of kind indulging love,
That I may have full cause for what I say: 15
I come to offer you your liberty
And be myself the slave. You turn away (*Following
her.*),
But everything becomes you. I may take
This pretty hand. I know your modesty
Would draw it back, but you would take it ill   20
If I should let it go, I know you would.
You shall be gently forced to please yourself;
That you will thank me for.

*She struggles and gets her hand from him, then he
offers to kiss her.*

Nay, if you struggle with me, I must take—

IMOINDA.

You may, my life, that I can part with freely. (*Exit.*) 25

Enter Blanford, Stanmore, Oroonoko to him.

BLANFORD.

So, Governor, we don't disturb you, I hope. Your
mistress has left you; you were making love.* She's
thankful for the honor, I suppose.

LIEUTENANT GOVERNOR.

Quite insensible to all I say
And do. When I speak to her, she sighs or weeps, 30
But never answers me as I would have her.

STANMORE.

There's something nearer than her slavery that
touches her.

BLANFORD.

What do her fellow slaves say of her? Can't they
find the cause? 35

LIEUTENANT GOVERNOR.

Some of 'em, who pretend to be wiser than the
rest, and hate her, I suppose, for being used better
than they are, will needs have it that she's with
child.

BLANFORD.

Poor wretch! if it be so, I pity her. 40
She has lost a husband that perhaps was dear
To her, and then you cannot blame her.

OROONOKO. (*Sighing.*)

If it be so, indeed you cannot blame her.

LIEUTENANT GOVERNOR.

No, no, it is not so. If it be so,
I still must love her, and desiring still, 45
I must enjoy her.

BLANFORD.

Try what you can do with fair means, and
welcome.

LIEUTENANT GOVERNOR.

I'll give you ten slaves for her.

BLANFORD.

You know she is our Lord Governor's. But if I 50
could dispose of her, I would not now, especially
to you.

LIEUTENANT GOVERNOR.

Why not to me?

BLANFORD.

I mean against her will. You are in love with her.

And we all know what your desires would have: 55
Love stops at nothing but possession.
Were she within your pow'r, you do not know
How soon you would be tempted to forget
The nature of the deed and, maybe, act
A violence you after would repent. 60

OROONOKO.

'Tis godlike in you to protect the weak.

LIEUTENANT GOVERNOR.

Fie, fie, I would not force her. Though she be
A slave, her mind is free and should consent.

OROONOKO.

Such honor will engage her to consent.
And then, if you're in love, she's worth the having. 65
Shall we not see this wonder?

LIEUTENANT GOVERNOR.

Have a care:
You have a heart, and she has conquering eyes.

OROONOKO.

I have a heart, but if it could be false
To my first vows, ever to love again, 70
These honest hands should tear it from my breast
And throw the traitor from me. Oh! Imoinda!
Living or dead, I can be only thine.

BLANFORD. (*To Lieutenant Governor and
Stanmore.*)

Imoinda was his wife. She's either dead,
Or living, dead to him, forced from his arms 75
By an inhuman father. Another time
I'll tell you all.

STANMORE.

Hark! the slaves have done their work,
And now begins their evening's merriment.

BLANFORD.

The men are all in love with fair Clemene 80
As much as you are, and the women hate her
From an instinct of natural jealousy.
They sing and dance and try their little tricks
To entertain her and divert her sadness.
Maybe she is among 'em. Shall we see? 85

Exeunt.

[Scene iv.]

*The scene drawn shows the slaves—men, women, and
children—upon the ground. Some rise and dance,
others sing the following songs.*

A song.[17]

I.

A lass there lives upon the green,
  Could I her picture draw,
A brighter nymph was never seen,
That looks and reigns a little queen
  And keeps the swains in awe.   5

II.

Her eyes are Cupid's darts and wings,
  Her eyebrows are his bow,
Her silken hair the silver strings,
Which sure and swift destruction brings
  To all the vale below.   10

III.

If Pastorella's dawning light
  Can warm and wound us so,
Her noon will shine so piercing bright
Each glancing beam will kill outright
  And every swain subdue.   15

A song.[18]

I.

Bright Cynthia's pow'r divinely great,
  What heart is not obeying?
A thousand Cupids on her wait,
  And in her eyes are playing.

II.

She seems the Queen of Love to reign,   20
  For she alone dispenses
Such sweets as best can entertain
  The gust of all the senses.

III.

Her face a charming prospect brings;
  Her breath gives balmy blisses;   25

I hear an angel, when she sings,
  And taste of heaven in kisses.

IV.

Four senses thus she feasts with joy
  From Nature's richest treasure;
Let me the other sense employ   30
  And I shall die with pleasure.

During the entertainment, the [lieutenant] governor, Blanford, Stanmore, Oroonoko enter as spectators; that ended, Captain Driver, Jack Stanmore, and several planters enter with their swords drawn. A bell rings.

CAPTAIN.
  Where are you, Governor? Make what haste you can to save yourself and the whole colony. I bid 'em ring the bell.

LIEUTENANT GOVERNOR.
  What's the matter?   35

JACK STANMORE.
  The Indians are come down upon us. They have plundered some of the plantations already, and are marching this way as fast as they can.

LIEUTENANT GOVERNOR.
  What can we do against 'em?

BLANFORD.
  We shall be able to make a stand, till more planters   40
  come in to us.

JACK STANMORE.
  There are a great many more without, if you would show yourself, and put us in order.

LIEUTENANT GOVERNOR.
  There's no danger of the white slaves,[19] they'll not stir. Blanford and Stanmore come you along with   45
  me. Some of you stay here to look after the black slaves.

All go out but the captain and six planters, who all at once seize Oroonoko.

---

17 song] written by Sir Henry Sheeres (d. 1710), a minor poet, set to music by Ralph (or Raphael) Courtevill[e] (d. ca. 1735), organist at St. James' Westminster, sung by a boy who may have been Jemmy Bowen (b. c. 1685), one of the most popular child singers in the theatre of his day, and sung to Letitia Cross (d. 1737), an ingenue actress

18 song] written by a Mr. Cheek, probably Thomas Cheek, who wrote a song for Southerne's *The Wives' Excuse*, set by Courtevill[e], sung by Richard Leveridge (c. 1670-1758), a composer of theatrical music

19 white slaves] Lower-class whites (criminals, prisoners of war like the Irish) were indentured for periods of servitude in the colonies, but they were virtual slaves and were often worked to death; Imoinda is, after all, a white slave. Cf. the intended enslavement, in the West Indies, of the steward in Shadwell's *A True Widow* (included in this anthology).

FIRST PLANTER.

Aye, aye, let us alone.

CAPTAIN.

In the first place we secure you, sir, as an enemy
to the government.   50

OROONOKO.

Are you there, sir? You are my constant friend.

FIRST PLANTER.

You will be able to do a great deal of mischief.

CAPTAIN.

But we shall prevent you. Bring the irons hither.
He has the malice of a slave in him and would be
glad to be cutting his masters' throats. I know him.   55
Chain his hands and feet that he may not run over
to 'em. If they have him, they shall carry him on
their backs, that I can tell 'em.

As they are chaining him, Blanford enters, runs to them.

BLANFORD.

What are you doing there?

CAPTAIN.

Securing the main chance.* This is a bosom enemy.   60

BLANFORD.

Away, you brutes. I'll answer with my life for his
behavior; so tell the governor.

CAPTAIN, PLANTERS.

Well, sir, so we will.

Exeunt Captain and planters.

OROONOKO.

Give me a sword, and I'll deserve your trust.

*A party of Indians enter, hurrying Imoinda among the
slaves; another party of Indians sustains them retreating, followed at a distance by the [lieutenant] governor
with the planters. Blanford, Oroonoko join them.*

BLANFORD.

Hell and the Devil! They drive away our slaves   65
before our faces. Governor, can you stand tamely
by and suffer this? Clemene, sir, your mistress is
among 'em.

LIEUTENANT GOVERNOR.

We throw ourselves away in the attempt to rescue
'em.   70

OROONOKO.

A lover cannot fall more glorious

Than in the cause of love. He that deserves
His mistress' favor wonnot stay behind.
I'll lead you on: Be bold, and follow me.

*Oroonoko at the head of the planters falls upon the
Indians with a great shout and beats them off. Imoinda
enters.*

IMOINDA.

I'm tossed about by my tempestuous fate   75
And nowhere must have rest. Indians or English!
Whoever has me, I am still a slave.
No matter whose I am, since I am no more
My royal master's, since I'm his no more.
Oh! I was happy! nay, I will be happy   80
In the dear thought that I am still his wife,
Though far divided from him. (*Draws off to a
     corner of the stage.*)

*After a shout, enter the [lieutenant] governor with
Oroonoko, Blanford, Stanmore, and the planters.*

LIEUTENANT GOVERNOR.

Thou glorious man! thou something greater sure
Than Caesar ever was! That single arm
Has saved us all. Accept our general thanks.   85

All bow to Oroonoko.

And what we can do more to recompense
Such noble services, you shall command.
Clemene too shall thank you. She is safe. (*Brings
     Clemene forward, looking down on the ground.*)
Look up and bless your brave deliverer.

OROONOKO.

Bless me indeed!   90

BLANFORD.

                         You start!

OROONOKO.

                                        Oh! all you gods
Who govern this great world and bring about
Things strange and unexpected, can it be?

LIEUTENANT GOVERNOR.

What is't you stare at so?   95

OROONOKO.

Answer me some of you, you who have power
And have your senses free. Or are you all
Struck through with wonder, too? (*Looking still
     fixed on her.*)

BLANFORD.

What would you know?

OROONOKO.

My soul steals from my body through my eyes. 100
All that is left of life I'll gaze away
And die upon the pleasure.

LIEUTENANT GOVERNOR.

This is strange!

OROONOKO.

If you but mock me with her image here,
If she be not Imoinda— 105

She looks upon him and falls into a swoon; he runs to her.

Hah! She faints!
Nay, then it must be she: it is Imoinda!
My heart confesses her and leaps for joy
To welcome her to her own empire here.
I feel her all, in every part of me. 110
Oh! let me press her in my eager arms,
Wake her to life, and with this kindling kiss
Give back that soul she only lent[d] to me. (*Kisses her.*)

LIEUTENANT GOVERNOR.

I am amazed!

BLANFORD.

I am as much as you. 115

OROONOKO.

Imoinda! Oh! thy Oroonoko calls.

IMOINDA. (*Coming to life.*)

My Oroonoko! Oh! I can't believe
What any man can say. But if I am
To be deceived, there's something in that name,
That voice, that face— (*Staring on him.*) 120
Oh! If I know myself,
I cannot be mistaken. (*Runs, and embraces Oroonoko.*)

OROONOKO.

Never here
You cannot be mistaken. I am yours,
Your Oroonoko, all that you would have, 125
Your tender, loving husband.

IMOINDA.

All indeed
That I would have: my husband! Then I am
Alive and waking to the joys I feel.
They were so great, I could not think 'em true. 130

But I believe all that you say to me,
For truth itself and everlasting love
Grows in this breast, and pleasure in these arms.

OROONOKO.

Take, take me all. Inquire into my heart
(You know the way to every secret there), 135
My heart, that sacred treasury of love,
And if in absence I have misemployed
A mite from the rich store, if I have spent
A wish, a sigh, but what I sent to you,
May I be cursed to wish and sigh in vain, 140
And you not pity me.

IMOINDA.

Oh! I believe
And know you by myself. If these sad eyes,
Since last we parted, have beheld the face
Of any comfort or once wished to see 145
The light of any other heaven but you,
May I be struck this moment blind and lose
Your blessèd sight, never to find you more.

OROONOKO.

Imoinda! Oh! This separation
Has made you dearer, if it can be so, 150
Than you were ever to me. You appear
Like a kind star to my benighted steps
To guide me on my way to happiness:
I cannot miss it now.—Governor, friend,
You think me mad, but let me bless you all 155
Who, any way, have been the instruments
Of finding her again. Imoinda's found!
And everything that I would have in her.
(*Embracing her in the most passionate fondness.*)

STANMORE.

Where's your mistress now, Governor?

LIEUTENANT GOVERNOR.

Why, where most men's mistresses are forced to be 160
sometimes, with her husband it seems. (*Aside.*) But
I won't lose her so.

STANMORE.

He has fought lustily for her and deserves her, I'll
say that for him.

BLANFORD.

Sir, we congratulate your happiness. I do, most 165
heartily.

LIEUTENANT GOVERNOR.

And all of us. But how it comes to pass—

OROONOKO.

That will require more precious time than I
Can spare you now. I have a thousand things
To ask of her, and she as many more   170
To know of me. But you have made me happier,
I confess, acknowledge it, much happier,
Than I have words or pow'r to tell you.—Captain,
You, ev'n you, who most have wronged me, I
Forgive. I won't say you have betrayed me now: 175
I'll think you but the minister of Fate
To bring me to my loved Imoinda here.

IMOINDA.

How, how shall I receive you? how be worthy
Of such endearments, all this tenderness?
These are the transports of prosperity,   180
When Fortune smiles upon us.

OROONOKO.

                Let the fools
Who follow Fortune live upon her smiles.
All our prosperity is placed in love.
We have enough of that to make us happy.   185
This little spot of earth you stand upon
Is more to me than the extended plains
Of my great father's kingdom. Here I reign
In full delights, in joys to pow'r unknown:
Your love my empire, and your heart my throne.   190

Exeunt.

Act III, scene i.

Aboan with several slaves and Hottman.

HOTTMAN.

What! to be slaves to cowards! Slaves to rogues
Who can't defend themselves!

ABOAN. (*Aside to his gang.*)

Who is this fellow? He talks as if he were
acquainted with our design. Is he one of us?

SLAVE.

Not yet. But he will be glad to make one, I believe.   5

ABOAN.

He makes a mighty noise.

HOTTMAN.

Go, sneak in corners, whisper out your griefs
For fear your masters hear you. Cringe and crouch
Under the bloody whip, like beaten curs
That lick their wounds and know no other cure.   10
All, wretches all! you feel their cruelty

As much as I can feel, but dare not groan.
For my part, while I have a life and tongue,
I'll curse the authors of my slavery.

ABOAN.

Have you been long a slave?   15

HOTTMAN.

                Yes, many years.

ABOAN.

And do you only curse?

HOTTMAN.

             Curse? only curse?
I cannot conjure to raise the spirits of other men;
I am but one. Oh! for a soul of fire,   20
To warm and animate our common cause,
And make a body of us. Then I would
Do something more than curse.

ABOAN.

That body set on foot, you would be one,
A limb, to lend it motion.   25

HOTTMAN.

               I would be
The heart of it: the head, the hand, and heart.
Would I could see the day.

ABOAN.

             You will do all yourself?

HOTTMAN.

I would do more than I shall speak; but I   30
May find a time.

ABOAN.

           The time may come to you;
Be ready for't.—Methinks he talks too much.
I'll know him more, before I trust him farther.

SLAVE.

If he dares half what he says, he'll be of use to us.   35

Enter Blanford to them.

BLANFORD.

If there be anyone among you here
That did belong to Oroonoko, speak;
I come to him.

ABOAN.

          I did belong to him.
Aboan, my name.

BLANFORD.

         You are the man I want;   40
Pray, come with me.

Exeunt.

Scene ii.

Oroonoko and Imoinda.

OROONOKO.

I do not blame my father for his love
(Though that had been enough to ruin me).
'Twas Nature's fault, that made you like the sun,
The reasonable worship of mankind:
He could not help his adoration.   5
Age had not locked his senses up so close
But he had eyes that opened to his soul
And took your beauties in. He felt your pow'r,
And therefore I forgive his loving you.
But when I think on his barbarity,   10
That could expose you to so many wrongs,
Driving you out to wretched slavery
Only for being mine, then I confess
I wish I could forget the name of son,
That I might curse the tyrant.   15

IMOINDA.

                I will bless him,
For I have found you here. Heav'n only knows
What is reserved for us. But if we guess
The future by the past, our Fortune must
Be wonderful, above the common size   20
Of good or ill; it must be in extremes:
Extremely happy or extremely wretched.

OROONOKO.

'Tis in our pow'r to make it happy now.

IMOINDA.

But not to keep it so.

Enter Blanford and Aboan.

BLANFORD.

             My royal lord!   25
I have a present for you.

OROONOKO.

             Aboan!

ABOAN.

Your lowest slave.

OROONOKO.

             My tried and valued friend.
—This worthy man always prevents* my wants.   30
I only wished, and he has brought thee to me.
Thou art surprised. Carry thy duty there—

Aboan goes to Imoinda and falls at her feet.

While I acknowledge mine: (*To Blanford.*) How
shall I thank you?

BLANFORD.

Believe me honest to your interest,
And I am more than paid. I have secured   35
That all your followers shall be gently used.
This gentleman, your chiefest favorite,
Shall wait upon your person while you stay
Among us.

OROONOKO.

           I owe everything to you.   40

BLANFORD.

You must not think you are in slavery.

OROONOKO.

I do not find I am.

BLANFORD.

Kind Heaven has miraculously sent
Those comforts that may teach you to expect
Its farther care in your deliverance.   45

OROONOKO.

I sometimes think myself, Heav'n is concerned
For my deliverance.

BLANFORD.

          It will be soon:
You may expect it. Pray, in the meantime,
Appear as cheerful as you can among us.   50
You have some enemies that represent
You dangerous and would be glad to find
A reason, in your discontent, to fear:
They watch your looks. But there are honest men
Who are your friends. You are secure in them.   55

OROONOKO.

I thank you for your caution.

BLANFORD.

             I will leave you,
And be assured, I wish your liberty. (*Exit.*)

ABOAN.

He speaks you very fair.

OROONOKO.

           He means me fair.   60

ABOAN.

If he should not, my lord—

OROONOKO.

             If he should not?
I'll not suspect his truth. But if I did,
What shall I get by doubting?

ABOAN.

       You secure,   65
 Not to be disappointed. But besides,
 There's this advantage in suspecting him:
 When you put off the hopes of other men,
 You will rely upon your godlike self,
 And then you may be sure of liberty.   70

OROONOKO.

 Be sure of liberty! what dost thou mean,
 Advising to rely upon myself?
 I think I may be sure on't. We must wait.
  (*Turning to Imoinda.*)
 'Tis worth a little patience.

ABOAN.

       Oh my lord!   75

OROONOKO.

 What dost thou drive at?

ABOAN.

      Sir, another time
 You would have found it sooner. But I see
 Love has your heart and takes up all your thoughts.

OROONOKO.

 And canst thou blame me?   80

ABOAN.

      Sir, I must not blame you.
 But as our fortune stands, there is a passion
 (Your pardon, royal mistress, I must speak)
 That would become you better than your love:
 A brave* resentment, which, inspired by you,   85
 Might kindle and diffuse a generous rage
 Among the slaves to rouse and shake our chains
 And struggle to be free.

OROONOKO.

      How can we help ourselves?

ABOAN.

 I knew you when you would have found a way.   90
 How help ourselves! The very Indians teach us.
 We need but to attempt our liberty,
 And we may carry it. We have hands sufficient,
 Double the number of our masters' force,
 Ready to be employed. What hinders us   95
 To set 'em then at work? We want* but you
 To head our enterprise and bid us strike.

OROONOKO.

 What would you do?

ABOAN.

     Cut our oppressors' throats.

OROONOKO.

 And you would have me join in your design   100
 Of murder?

ABOAN.

     It deserves a better name.
 But be it what it will, 'tis justified
 By self-defense and natural liberty.

OROONOKO.

 I'll hear no more on't.   105

ABOAN.

      I am sorry for't.

OROONOKO.

 Nor shall you think of it.

ABOAN.

      Not think of it!

OROONOKO.

 No, I command you not.

ABOAN.

      Remember, sir,   110
 You are a slave yourself, and to command
 Is now another's right. Not think of it!
 Since the first moment they put on my chains,
 I've thought of nothing but the weight of 'em
 And how to throw them off. Can yours sit easy?   115

OROONOKO.

 I have a sense of my condition
 As painful and as quick* as yours can be.
 I feel for my Imoinda and myself,
 Imoinda much the tenderest part of me.
 But though I languish for my liberty,   120
 I would not buy it at the Christian price
 Of black ingratitude. They shannot say
 That we deserved our fortune by our crimes.
 Murder the innocent!

ABOAN.

      The innocent!   125

OROONOKO.

 These men are so whom you would rise against.
 If we are slaves, they did not make us slaves,
 But bought us in an honest way of trade,
 As we have done before 'em, bought and sold
 Many a wretch and never thought it wrong.   130
 They paid our price for us, and we are now
 Their property, a part of their estate,
 To manage as they please. Mistake me not,
 I do not tamely say that we should bear

All they could lay upon us. But we find 135
The load so light, so little to be felt
(Considering they have us in their power
And may inflict what grievances they please),
We ought not to complain.

ABOAN.
                          My royal lord! 140
You do not know the heavy grievances,
The toils, the labors, weary drudgeries
Which they impose: burdens more fit for beasts,
For senseless beasts, to bear than thinking men.
Then if you saw the bloody cruelties 145
They execute on every slight offense,
Nay, sometimes in their proud, insulting sport,
How worse than dogs they lash their fellow creatures,
Your heart would bleed for 'em. Oh, could you know
How many wretches lift their hands and eyes 150
To you for their relief.

OROONOKO.
                    I pity 'em
And wish I could with honesty do more.

ABOAN.
You must do more, and may, with honesty.
Oh royal sir, remember who you are, 155
A prince, born for the good of other men,
Whose godlike office is to draw the sword
Against oppression and set free mankind.
And this, I'm sure, you think oppression now.
What, though you have not felt these miseries, 160
Never believe you are obliged to them;
They have their selfish reasons, maybe, now
For using of you well, but there will come
A time when you must have your share of 'em.

OROONOKO.
You see how little cause I have to think so: 165
Favored in my own person, in my friends,
Indulged in all that can concern my care,
In my Imoinda's soft society. (*Embracing her.*)

ABOAN.
And therefore would you lie contented down
In the forgetfulness and arms of love 170
To get young princes for 'em?

OROONOKO.
                         Say'st thou! Hah!

ABOAN.
Princes, the heirs of empire, and the last

Of your illustrious lineage, to be born
To pamper up their pride and be their slaves? 175

OROONOKO.
Imoinda! Save me, save me from that thought.

IMOINDA.
There is no safety from it. I have long
Suffered it with a mother's laboring pains
And can no longer. Kill me, kill me now,
While I am blest and happy in your love, 180
Rather than let me live to see you hate me,
As you must hate me, me, the only cause,
The fountain of these flowing miseries.
Dry up this spring of life, this pois'nous spring,
That swells so fast to overwhelm us all. 185

OROONOKO.
Shall the dear babe, the eldest of my hopes,
Whom I begot a prince, be born a slave?
The treasure of this temple was designed
T'enrich a kingdom's fortune. Shall it here
Be seized upon by vile, unhallowed hands 190
To be employed in uses most profane?

ABOAN.
In most unworthy uses. Think of that,
And while you may, prevent it. Oh my lord!
Rely on nothing that they say to you.
They speak you fair, I know, and bid you wait. 195
But think what 'tis to wait on promises,
And promises of men who know no tie
Upon their words against their interest.
And where's their interest in freeing you?

IMOINDA.
Oh! Where indeed, to lose so many slaves? 200

ABOAN.
Nay, grant this man you think so much your friend
Be honest and intends all that he says.
He is but one, and in a government
Where, he confesses, you have enemies
That watch your looks. What looks can you put on 205
To please these men, who are before resolved
To read 'em their own way? Alas, my lord!
If they incline to think you dangerous,
They have their knavish arts to make you so.
And then who knows how far their cruelty 210
May carry their revenge?

IMOINDA.
                    To everything

That does belong to you: your friends, and me.
I shall be torn from you, forced away,
Helpless and miserable. Shall I live   215
To see that day again?

OROONOKO.

              That day shall never come.

ABOAN.

I know you are persuaded to believe
The Governor's arrival will prevent
These mischiefs and bestow your liberty.   220
But who is sure of that? I rather fear
More mischiefs from his coming. He is young,
Luxurious, passionate, and amorous.
Such a complexion, and made bold by power
To countenance all he is prone to do,   225
Will know no bounds, no law against his lusts.
If, in a fit of his intemperance,
With a strong hand he should resolve to seize
And force my royal mistress from your arms,
How can you help yourself?   230

OROONOKO.

              Hah! Thou hast roused
The lion in his den; he stalks abroad,
And the wide forest trembles at his roar.
I find the danger now: my spirits start
At the alarm and from all quarters come   235
To man my heart, the citadel of love.
—Is there a power on earth to force you from me?
And shall I not resist it? not strike first
To keep, to save you? to prevent that curse?
This is your cause, and shall it not prevail?   240
Oh! You were born all ways to conquer me.
—Now I am fashioned to thy purpose. Speak,
What combination, what conspiracy,
Wouldst thou engage me in? I'll undertake
All thou wouldst have me now for liberty,   245
For the great cause of Love and Liberty.

ABOAN.

Now, my great master, you appear yourself.
And since we have you joined in our design,
It cannot fail us. I have mustered up
The choicest slaves, men who are sensible   250
Of their condition and seem most resolved.
They have their several parties.

OROONOKO.

              Summon 'em,

Assemble 'em. I will come forth and show
Myself among 'em. If they are resolved,   255
I'll lead their foremost resolutions.

ABOAN.

I have provided those will follow you.

OROONOKO.

With this reserve in our proceeding still:*
The means that lead us to our liberty
Must not be bloody.   260

ABOAN.

              You command in all.
We shall expect you, sir.

OROONOKO.

              You shannot long.

*Exeunt Oroonoko and Imoinda at one door, Aboan at
another.*

              Scene iii.

Welldon coming in before Mrs. Lackitt.

WIDOW.

These unmannerly Indians were something
unseasonable to disturb us just in the nick, Mr.
Welldon, but I have the parson within call still to
do us the good turn.

WELLDON.

We had best stay a little, I think, to see things   5
settled again, had not we? Marriage is a serious
thing, you know.

WIDOW.

What do you talk of a serious thing, Mr. Welldon?
I think you have found me sufficiently serious. I
have married my son to your sister to pleasure you,   10
and now I come to claim your promise to me, you
tell me marriage is a serious thing.

WELLDON.

Why, is it not?

WIDOW.

Fiddle faddle, I know what it is. 'Tis not the first
time I have been married, I hope. But I shall begin   15
to think you don't design to do fairly by me, so I
shall.

WELLDON.

Why indeed, Mrs. Lackitt, I am afraid I can't do
as fairly as I would by you. 'Tis what you must
know, first or last, and I should be the worst man   20

in the world to conceal it any longer. Therefore, I must own to you that I am married already.

WIDOW.

Married! You don't say so, I hope! How have you the conscience to tell me such a thing to my face! Have you abused me then, fooled and cheated me? 25 What do you take me for, Mr. Welldon? do you think I am to be served at this rate? But you shan't find me the silly* creature you think me. I would have you to know, I understand better things than to ruin my son without a valuable consideration. 30 If I can't have you, I can keep my money. Your sister shan't have the catch of him she expected. I won't part with a shilling to 'em.

WELLDON.

You made the match yourself, you know: you can't blame me. 35

WIDOW.

Yes, yes, I can and do blame you. You might have told me before you were married.

WELLDON.

I would not have told you now, but you followed me so close I was forced to't. Indeed, I am married in England, but 'tis as if I were not, for I have been 40 parted from my wife a great while, and to do reason on both sides, we hate one another heartily. Now I did design and will marry you still, if you'll have a little patience.

WIDOW.

A likely business, truly. 45

WELLDON.

I have a friend in England that I will write to, to poison my wife, and then I can marry you with a good conscience if you love me as you say you do. You'll consent to that, I'm sure.

WIDOW.

And will he do it, do you think? 50

WELLDON.

At the first word, or he is not the man I take him to be.

WIDOW.

Well, you are a dear devil, Mr. Welldon. And would you poison your wife for me?

WELLDON.

I would do anything for you. 55

WIDOW.

Well, I am mightily obliged to you. But 'twill be a great while before you can have an answer of your letter.

WELLDON.

'Twill be a great while indeed.

WIDOW.

In the meantime, Mr. Welldon— 60

WELLDON.

Why in the meantime— Here's company. We'll settle that within. I'll follow you.

Exit Widow. Enter Stanmore.

STANMORE.

So sir, you carry your business swimmingly. You have stolen a wedding, I hear.

WELLDON.

Aye, my sister is married. And I am very near being 65 run away with myself.

STANMORE.

The widow will have you, then.

WELLDON.

You come very seasonably to my rescue. Jack Stanmore is to be had, I hope.

STANMORE.

At half an hour's warning. 70

WELLDON.

I must advise with you.

Exeunt.

Scene iv.

Oroonoko with Aboan, Hottman, slaves.

OROONOKO.

Impossible! nothing's impossible.
We know our strength only by being tried.
If you object the mountains, rivers, woods
Unpassable that lie before our march,
Woods we can set on fire; we swim by nature. 5
What can oppose us, then, but we may tame?
All things submit to virtuous industry.
That we can carry with us, that is ours.

SLAVE.

Great sir, we have attended all you said
With silent joy and admiration, 10
And, were we only men, would follow such,

So great a leader, through the untried world.
But oh! consider we have other names,
Husbands and fathers, and have things more dear
To us than life—our children and our wives,   15
Unfit for such an expedition.
What must become of them?
OROONOKO.

                We wonnot wrong
The virtue of our women to believe
There is a wife among 'em would refuse
To share her husband's fortune. What is hard,   20
We must make easy to 'em in our love.
While we live, and have our limbs, we can
Take care for them.
         Therefore I still propose   25
To lead our march down to the sea, and plant
A colony where, in our native innocence,
We shall live free and be able to defend
Ourselves till stress of weather or some accident
Provide a ship for us.   30
ABOAN.

           An accident!
The luckiest accident presents itself:
The very ship that brought and made us slaves
Swims in the river still. I see no cause
But we may seize on that.   35
OROONOKO.

           It shall be so.
There is a justice in it pleases me.
(*To the slaves.*) Do you agree to it?
OMNES.

              We follow you.
OROONOKO. (*To Hottman.*)
You do not relish it.   40
HOTTMAN.

        I am afraid
You'll find it difficult and dangerous.
ABOAN.

Are you the man to find the danger first?
You should have giv'n example. Dangerous!
I thought you had not understood the word: 45
You, who would be the head, the hand, and heart.
Sir, I remember you, you can talk well;
I wonnot doubt but you'll maintain your word.
OROONOKO. (*To Aboan.*)
This fellow is not right, I'll try him further.
—The danger will be certain to us all,   50

And death most certain in miscarrying.
We must expect no mercy, if we fail.
Therefore our way must be not to expect.
We'll put it out of expectation
By death upon the place or liberty.   55
There is no mean, but Death or Liberty.
There's no man here, I hope, but comes prepared
For all that can befall him. Death is all:
In most conditions of humanity
To be desired, but to be shunned in none,   60
The remedy of many, wish of some,
And certain end of all.
If there be one among us who can fear
The face of Death appearing like a friend,
As in this cause of honor Death must be,   65
How will he tremble when he sees Him dressed
In the wild fury of our enemies,
In all the terrors of their cruelty?
For now if we should fall into their hands,
Could they invent a thousand murd'ring ways   70
By racking torments, we should feel 'em all.
HOTTMAN.

What will become of us?
OROONOKO. (*To Aboan concerning Hottman.*)
Observe him now.
—I could die altogether like a man,
As you, and you, and all of us may do.   75
But who can promise for his bravery
Upon the rack? where fainting, weary life,
Hunted through every limb, is forced to feel
An agonizing death of all its parts?
Who can bear this? resolve to be impaled?   80
His skin flayed off and roasted yet alive?
The quivering flesh torn from his broken bones
By burning pincers? Who can bear these pains?
HOTTMAN. (*Discovering* all the confusion of fear.*)
They are not to be borne.
OROONOKO.

You see him now, this man of mighty words!   85
ABOAN.

How his eyes roll!
OROONOKO.

           He cannot hide his fear.
I tried him this way and have found him out.
ABOAN.

I could not have believed it. Such a blaze,
And not a spark of fire!   90

OROONOKO.

His violence

Made me suspect him first. Now I'm convinced.

ABOAN.

What shall we do with him?

OROONOKO.

He is not fit—

ABOAN.

Fit! hang him, he is only fit to be   95

Just what he is: to live and die a slave,

The base companion of his servile fears.

OROONOKO.

We are not safe with him.

ABOAN.

Do you think so?

OROONOKO.

He'll certainly betray us.   100

ABOAN.

That he shan't.

I can take care of that. I have a way

To take him off his evidence.

OROONOKO.

What way?

ABOAN.

I'll stop his mouth before you, stab him here,   105

And then let him inform. (*Going to stab Hottman,*

Oroonoko holds him.)

OROONOKO.

Thou art not mad?

ABOAN.

I would secure ourselves.

OROONOKO.

It cannot be this way, nay, cannot be.

His murder would alarm all the rest,   110

Make 'em suspect us of barbarity

And, maybe, fall away from our design.

We'll not set out in blood.—We have, my friends,

This night to furnish what we can provide

For our security and just defense.   115

If there be one among us we suspect

Of baseness or vile fear, it will become

Our common care to have our eyes on him.

I wonnot name the man.

ABOAN. (*To Hottman.*)

You guess at him.   120

OROONOKO.

Tomorrow, early as the breaking day,

We rendezvous behind the citron grove.

That ship secured, we may transport ourselves

To our respective homes. My father's kingdom

Shall open her wide arms to take you in   125

And nurse you for her own, adopt you all,

All, who will follow me.

OMNES.

All, all follow you.

OROONOKO.

There I can give you all your liberty,

Bestow its blessings, and secure 'em yours.   130

There you shall live with honor, as becomes

My fellow-sufferers and worthy friends.

This if we do succeed. But if we fall

In our attempt, 'tis nobler still to die

Than drag the galling yoke of slavery.   135

Exeunt omnes.

Act IV, scene i.

Welldon and Jack Stanmore.

WELLDON.

You see, honest Jack, I have been industrious for

you. You must take some pains now to serve

yourself.

JACK STANMORE.

Gad, Mr. Welldon, I have taken a great deal of

pains. And if the Widow speaks honestly, faith and   5

troth, she'll tell you what a pains-taker I am.

WELLDON.

Fie, fie, not me. I am her husband, you know; she

won't tell me what pains you have taken with her.

Besides, she takes you for me.

JACK STANMORE.

That's true; I'd forgot you had married her. But if   10

you knew all—

WELLDON.

'Tis no matter for my knowing all. If she does—

JACK STANMORE.

Aye, aye, she does know, and more than ever she

knew since she was a woman, for the time, I will

be bold to say. For I have done—   15

WELLDON.

The devil take you, you'll never have done.

JACK STANMORE.

As old as she is, she has a wrinkle behind more

than she had, I believe—for I have taught her what

she never knew in her life before.[20]

WELLDON.

What care I what wrinkles she has, or what you have taught her? If you'll let me advise you, you may; if not, you may prate on and ruin the whole design. 20

JACK STANMORE.

Well, well, I have done.

WELLDON.

Nobody but your cousin and you and I know anything of this matter. I have married Mrs. Lackitt and put you to bed to her, which she knows nothing of, to serve you. In two or three days, I'll bring it about so to resign up my claim, with her consent, quietly to you. 25

30

JACK STANMORE.

But how will you do it?

WELLDON.

That must be my business. In the meantime, if you should make any noise, 'twill come to her ears and be impossible to reconcile her.

JACK STANMORE.

Nay, as for that, I know the way to reconcile her, I warrant you. 35

WELLDON.

But how will you get her money? I am married to her.

JACK STANMORE.

That I don't know indeed.

WELLDON.

You must leave it to me. You find all the pains I shall put you to will be to be silent. You can hold your tongue for two or three days? 40

JACK STANMORE.

Truly, not well in a matter of this nature. I should be very unwilling to lose the reputation of this night's work, and the pleasure of telling. 45

WELLDON.

You must mortify that vanity a little. You will have time enough to brag and lie of your manhood, when you have her in a bare-faced condition to disprove you.

JACK STANMORE.

Well, I'll try what I can do. The hopes of her money must do it. 50

WELLDON.

You'll come at night again? 'tis your own business.

JACK STANMORE.

But you have the credit on't.

WELLDON.

'Twill be your own another day, as the widow says. Send your cousin to me; I want his advice. 55

JACK STANMORE.

I want to be recruited, I'm sure. A good breakfast, and to bed: she has rocked my cradle sufficiently. (*Exit.*)

WELLDON.

She would have a husband, and if all be as he says, she has no reason to complain. But there's no relying on what the men say on these occasions. They have the benefit of their bragging, by recommending their abilities to other women. Theirs is a trading estate that lives upon credit and increases by removing it out of one bank into another. Now, poor women have not these opportunities; we must keep our stocks dead by us at home to be ready for a purchase when it comes—a husband, let him be never so dear, and be glad of him. Or, venture our fortunes abroad on such rotten security that the principal and interest—nay, very often our persons—are in danger. If the women would agree (which they never will) to call home their effects,[21] how many proper gentlemen would sneak into another way of living, for want* of being responsible in this? Then husbands would be cheaper.—Here comes the widow, she'll tell truth. She'll not bear false witness against her own interest, I know. 60 65 70 75

Enter Widow Lackitt.

WELLDON.

Now, Mrs. Lackitt.

WIDOW.

Well, well, Lackitt, or what you will now, now I am married to you. I am very well pleased with what I have done, I assure you. 80

---

20 wrinkle behind…before] A new wrinkle is a new bit of knowledge or a new trick, here obviously in a sexual sense.

21 call home their effects] take themselves out of circulation

WELLDON.

And with what I have done too, I hope.

WIDOW.

Ah! Mr. Welldon! I say nothing, but you're a dear man, and I did not think it had been in you.

WELLDON.

I have more in me than you imagine. 85

WIDOW.

No, no, you can't have more than I imagine. 'Tis impossible to have more. You have enough for any woman in an honest way, that I will say for you.

WELLDON.

Then I find you are satisfied.

WIDOW.

Satisfied! no, indeed, I'm not to be satisfied, with 90 you or without you. To be satisfied is to have enough of you. Now, 'tis a folly to lie: I shall never think I can have enough of you. I shall be very fond of you. Would you have me fond of you? What do you do to me, to make me love you so 95 well?

WELLDON.

Can't you tell what?

WIDOW.

Go, there's no speaking to you. You bring all the blood of one's body into one's face, so you do. Why do you talk so? 100

WELLDON.

Why, how do I talk?

WIDOW.

You know how. But a little color becomes me, I believe. How do I look today?

WELLDON.

Oh! most lovingly, most amiably!

WIDOW.

Nay, this can't be long a secret, I find; I shall 105 discover* it by my countenance.

WELLDON.

The women will find you out, you look so cheerfully.

WIDOW.

But do I? Do I really look so cheerfully, so amiably? There's no such paint in the world as the natural 110 glowing of a complexion. Let 'em find me out, if they please, poor creatures, I pity 'em. They envy me, I'm sure, and would be glad to mend their looks upon the same occasion. The young, jill-flirting* girls, forsooth, believe nobody must have 115 a husband but themselves, but I would have 'em to know there are other things to be taken care of besides their greensickness.

WELLDON.

Aye, sure, or the physicians would have but little practice. 120

WIDOW.

Mr. Welldon, what must I call you? I must have some pretty fond name or other for you. What shall I call you?

WELLDON.

I thought you liked my own name.

WIDOW.

Yes, yes, I like it, but I must have a nickname for 125 you. Most women have nicknames for their husbands—

WELLDON.

Cuckold.

WIDOW.

No, no—but 'tis very pretty before company; it looks negligent, and is the fashion, you know. 130

WELLDON.

To be negligent of their husbands, it is indeed.

WIDOW.

Nay then, I won't be in the fashion, for I can never be negligent of dear Mr. Welldon. And to convince you, here's something to encourage you not to be negligent of me. 135

(Gives him a purse and a little casket.) Five hundred pounds in gold in this, and jewels to the value of five hundred pounds more in this.

WELLDON. (Opens the casket.)

Aye, marry,* this will encourage me indeed.

WIDOW.

There are comforts in marrying an elderly woman, 140 Mr. Welldon. Now, a young woman would have fancied she had paid you with her person, or had done you the favor.

WELLDON.

What do you talk of young women? You are as young as any of 'em in everything but their folly 145 and ignorance.

WIDOW.

And do you think me so? But I have no reason to

suspect you. Was not I seen at your house this morning, do you think?

WELLDON.

You may venture again. You'll come at night, I suppose. 150

WIDOW.

Oh dear! at night? so soon?

WELLDON.

Nay, if you think it so soon.

WIDOW.

Oh! no, it is not for that, Mr. Welldon, but—

WELLDON.

You won't come then. 155

WIDOW.

Won't! I don't say I won't. That is not a word for a wife. If you command me—

WELLDON.

To please yourself.

WIDOW.

I will come to please you.

WELLDON.

To please yourself, own it. 160

WIDOW.

Well, well, to please myself, then. You're the strangest man in the world, nothing can 'scape you. You'll to the bottom of everything.

Enter Daniel, Lucia following.

DANIEL. [*To Lucia.*]

What would you have? what do you follow me for?

LUCIA.

Why mayn't I follow you? I must follow you now all the world over. 165

DANIEL.

Hold you, hold you there. Not so far by a mile or two; I have enough of your company already, by'r Lady, and something to spare. You may go home to your brother, an* you will; I have no farther to do with you. 170

WIDOW.

Why, Daniel, child, thou art not out of thy wits sure, art thou?

DANIEL.

Nay, marry,* I don't know. But I am very near it, I believe; I am altered for the worse mightily since you saw me. And she has been the cause of it there. 175

WIDOW.

How so, child?

DANIEL.

I told you before what would come on't, of putting me to bed to a strange woman. But you would not be said nay. 180

WIDOW.

She is your wife now, child, you must love her.

DANIEL.

Why, so I did, at first.

WIDOW.

But you must love her always.

DANIEL.

Always! I loved her as long as I could, Mother, and as long as loving was good, I believe, for I find now I don't care a fig for her. 185

LUCIA.

Why, you lubberly, slovenly, misbegotten blockhead—

WIDOW.

Nay, Mistress Lucy, say anything else and spare not. But as to his begetting, that touches me. He is as honestly begotten, though I say it, that he is the worse again. 190

LUCIA.

I see all good nature is thrown away upon you.

WIDOW.

It was so with his father before him. He takes after him. 195

LUCIA.

And therefore will I use you, as you deserve, you Tony.[22]

WIDOW.

Indeed, he deserves bad enough, but don't call him out of his name; his name is Daniel, you know.

DANIEL.

She may call me hermaphrodite, if she will, for I hardly know whether I'm a boy or a girl. 200

WELLDON.

A boy, I warrant thee, as long as thou livest.

DANIEL.

Let her call me what she pleases, Mother. 'Tis not her tongue that I am afraid of.

LUCIA.

I will make such a beast of thee, such a cuckold! 205

---

22 Tony] stock name for a fool

WIDOW.

Oh pray, no, I hope. Do nothing rashly, Mrs. Lucy.

LUCIA.

Such a cuckold will I make of thee!

DANIEL.

I had rather be a cuckold than what you would make of me in a week, I'm sure. I have no more manhood left in me already than there is, saving the mark, in one of my mother's old under-petticoats here. 210

WIDOW.

Sirrah, Sirrah, meddle with your wife's petticoats, and let your mother's alone, you ungracious bird, you. (*Beats him.*)

DANIEL.

Why, is the devil in the woman? What have I said now? Do you know, if you were asked, I trow? But you are all of a bundle. Even hang together; he that unties you makes a rod for his own tail, and so he will find it that has anything to do with you. 215

WIDOW.

Aye, rogue enough, you shall find it. I have a rod for your tail still. 220

DANIEL.

No wife, and I care not.

WIDOW.

I'll swinge you into better manners, you booby.

(*Beats him off, exit.*)

WELLDON.

You have consummated our project upon him.

LUCIA.

Nay, if I have a limb of the fortune, I care not who has the whole body of the fool. 225

WELLDON.

That you shall, and a large one, I promise you.

LUCIA.

Have you heard the news? they talk of an English ship in the river.

WELLDON.

I have heard on't, and am preparing to receive it, as fast as I can. 230

LUCIA.

There's something the matter too with the slaves, some disturbance or other; I don't know what 'tis.

WELLDON.

So much the better still: we fish in troubled waters; we shall have fewer eyes upon us. Pray, go you home and be ready to assist me in your part of the design. 235

LUCIA.

I can't fail in mine. (*Exit.*)

WELLDON.

The widow has furnished me, I thank her, to carry it on. Now I have got a wife, 'tis high time to think of getting a husband. I carry my fortune about me, a thousand pounds in gold and jewels. Let me see. 'Twill be a considerable trust, and I think, I shall lay it out to advantage. 240

Enter Stanmore.

STANMORE.

So, Welldon, Jack has told me his success and his hopes of marrying the widow by your means. 245

WELLDON.

I have strained a point, Stanmore, upon your account, to be serviceable to your family.

STANMORE.

I take it upon my account, and am very much obliged to you. But here we are all in an uproar. 250

WELLDON.

So they say. What's the matter?

STANMORE.

A mutiny among the slaves. Oroonoko is at the head of 'em, our Governor is gone out with his rascally militia against 'em. What it may come to nobody knows. 255

WELLDON.

For my part, I shall do as well as the rest. But I'm concerned for my sister and cousin, whom I expect in the ship from England.

STANMORE.

There's no danger of 'em.

WELLDON.

I have a thousand pounds here, in gold and jewels, for my cousin's use that I would more particularly take care of. 'Tis too great a sum to venture at home, and I would not have her wronged of it. Therefore, to secure it I think my best way will be to put it into your keeping. 260

STANMORE.

You have a very good opinion of my honesty. (*Takes the purse and casket.*) 265

WELLDON.

    I have indeed. If anything should happen to me in this
    bustle, as nobody is secure of accidents, I know you
    will take my cousin into your protection and care.

STANMORE.

    You may be sure on't.

WELLDON.

    If you hear she is dead, as she may be, then I desire   270
    you to accept of the thousand pound as a legacy and
    token of my friendship; my sister is provided for.

STANMORE.

    Why, you amaze me. But you are never the nearer
    dying, I hope, for making your will?

WELLDON.

    Not a jot, but I love to be beforehand with   275
    Fortune. If she comes safe—this is not a place for
    a single woman, you know—pray see her married
    as soon as you can.

STANMORE.

    If she be as handsome as her picture, I can promise
    her a husband.   280

WELLDON.

    If you like her when you see her, I wish nothing
    so much as to have you marry her yourself.

STANMORE.

    From what I have heard of her, and my
    engagements to you, it must be her fault if I don't.
    I hope to have her from your own hand.   285

WELLDON.

    And I hope to give her to you, for all this.

STANMORE.

    Aye, aye, hang these melancholy reflections. Your
    generosity has engaged all my services.

WELLDON.

    I always thought you worth making a friend.

STANMORE.

    You shan't find your good opinion thrown away   290
    upon me. I am in your debt, and shall think so as
    long as I live.

Exeunt.

Scene ii.

*Enter on one side of the stage Oroonoko, Aboan, with
the slaves, Imoinda with a bow and quiver, some
women leading, others carrying their children upon
their backs.*

OROONOKO.

    The women, with their children, fall behind.
    Imoinda, you must not expose yourself.
    Retire, my love. I almost fear for you.

IMOINDA.

    I fear no danger. Life, or death, I will
    Enjoy with you.   5

OROONOKO.

               My person is your guard.

ABOAN.

    Now, sir, blame yourself. If you had not
    Prevented my cutting his throat,
    That coward there had not discovered* us.
    He comes now to upbraid you.   10

*Enter on the other side [the lieutenant] governor,
talking to Hottman, with his rabble.*

LIEUTENANT GOVERNOR.

    This is the very thing I would have wished.
    (*To Hottman.*) Your honest service to the government
    Shall be rewarded with your liberty.

ABOAN.

    His honest service! Call it what it is,
    His villainy, the service of his fear.   15
    If he pretends to honest services,
    Let him stand out and meet me like a man.
    (*Advancing.*)

OROONOKO.

    Hold, you.—And you who come against us, hold.
    I charge you in a general good to all,
    And wish I could command you, to prevent   20
    The bloody havoc of the murdering sword.
    I would not urge destruction uncompelled,
    But if you follow Fate, you find it here.
    The bounds are set, the limits of our lives;
    Between us lies the gaping gulf of Death   25
    To swallow all. Who first advances—

Enter the captain with his crew.

CAPTAIN.

    Here, here, here they are, Governor. What! seize
    upon my ship! Come boys, fall on!

Advancing first, Oroonoko kills him.

OROONOKO.

    Thou art fall'n indeed. Thy own blood be upon thee.

LIEUTENANT GOVERNOR.
    Rest it there. He did deserve his death. 30
    Take him away. (*The body removed.*)
    You see, sir, you and those mistaken men
    Must be our witnesses, we do not come
    As enemies and thirsting for your blood.
    If we desired your ruin, the revenge 35
    Of our companion's death had pushed it on.
    But that we overlook, in a regard
    To common safety and the public good.

OROONOKO.
    Regard that public good. Draw off your men
    And leave us to our fortune. We're resolved. 40

LIEUTENANT GOVERNOR.
    Resolved on what? your resolutions
    Are broken, overturned, prevented, lost:
    What fortune now can you raise out of 'em?
    Nay, grant we should draw off, what can you do?
    Where can you move? What more can you 45
        resolve,
    Unless it be to throw yourselves away?
    Famine must eat you up if you go on.
    You see, our numbers could with ease compel
    What we request. And what do we request?
    Only to save yourselves. 50

The women with their children gathering about the
men.

OROONOKO.
            I'll hear no more.

WOMEN.
    Hear him, hear him.—He takes no care of us.

LIEUTENANT GOVERNOR.
    To those poor wretches who have been seduced
    And led away, to all and every one,
    We offer a full pardon. 55

OROONOKO.
          Then fall on. (*Preparing to engage.*)

LIEUTENANT GOVERNOR.
    Lay hold upon't, before it be too late,
    Pardon and mercy.

The women clinging about the men, they leave Oroonoko
and fall upon their faces crying out for pardon.

SLAVES.
        Pardon, mercy, pardon.

OROONOKO.
    Let 'em go all.—Now, Governor, I see, 60
    I own the folly of my enterprise,
    The rashness of this action, and must blush
    Quite through this veil of night a whitely shame
    To think I could design to make those free
    Who were by nature slaves, wretches designed 65
    To be their masters' dogs and lick their feet.
    Whip, whip 'em to the knowledge of your gods,
    Your Christian gods, who suffer you to be
    Unjust, dishonest, cowardly, and base,
    And give 'em your excuse for being so. 70
    I would not live on the same earth with creatures
    That only have the faces of their kind.
    Why should they look like men, who are not so?
    When they put off their noble natures for
    The groveling qualities of downcast beasts, 75
    I wish they had their tails.

ABOAN.
              Then we should know 'em.

OROONOKO. (*To Imoinda, Aboan.*)
    We were too few before for victory.
    We're still enough to die.

Blanford enters.

LIEUTENANT GOVERNOR.
             Live, royal sir, 80
    Live and be happy long on your own terms:
    Only consent to yield, and you shall have
    What terms you can propose, for you and yours.

OROONOKO.
    Consent to yield! shall I betray myself?

LIEUTENANT GOVERNOR.
    Alas! We cannot fear that your small force— 85
    The force of two, with a weak woman's arm—
    Should conquer us. I speak in the regard
    And honor of your worth, in my desire
    And forwardness to serve so great a man.
    I would not have it lie upon my thoughts 90
    That I was the occasion of the fall
    Of such a prince, whose courage carried on
    In a more noble cause would well deserve
    The empire of the world.

OROONOKO.
             You can speak fair. 95

LIEUTENANT GOVERNOR.
    Your undertaking, though it would have brought

So great a loss to us, we must all say
Was generous and noble and shall be
Regarded only as the fire of youth,
That will break out sometimes in gallant souls;   100
We'll think it but the natural impulse,
A rash impatience of liberty:
No otherwise.

OROONOKO.
               Think it what you will.
I was not born to render an account   105
Of what I do to any but myself.

Blanford comes forward.

BLANFORD. (*To the Lieutenant Governor.*)
I'm glad you have proceeded by fair means.
I came to be a mediator.

LIEUTENANT GOVERNOR.
                  Try
What you can work upon him.   110

OROONOKO.
                      Are you come
Against me too?

BLANFORD.
      Is this to come against you? (*Offering his
      sword to Oroonoko.*)
Unarmed to put myself into your hands?
I come, I hope, to serve you.   115

OROONOKO.
                  You have served me;
I thank you for't. And I am pleased to think
You were my friend, while I had need of one.
But now 'tis past. This farewell, and be gone.
      (*Embraces him.*)

BLANFORD.
It is not past, and I must serve you still.   120
I would make up these breaches, which the sword
Will widen more, and close us all in love.

OROONOKO.
I know what I have done, and I should be
A child to think they ever can forgive.
Forgive! Were there but that, I would not live   125
To be forgiven. Is there a power on earth
That I can ever need forgiveness from?

BLANFORD.
You shannot need it.

OROONOKO.
          No, I wonnot need it.

BLANFORD.
You see he offers you your own conditions   130
For you and yours.

OROONOKO.
             I must capitulate?
Precariously compound, on stinted terms,
To save my life?

BLANFORD.
             Sir, he imposes none.   135
You make 'em for your own security.
If your great heart cannot descend to treat
In adverse fortune with an enemy,
Yet sure, your honor's safe, you may accept
Offers of peace and safety from a friend.   140

LIEUTENANT GOVERNOR. (*To Blanford.*)
He will rely on what you say to him.
Offer him what you can, I will confirm
And make all good. Be you my pledge of trust.

BLANFORD.
I'll answer with my life for all he says.

LIEUTENANT GOVERNOR. (*Aside.*)
Aye, do, and pay the forfeit if you please.   145

BLANFORD.
Consider, sir, can you consent to throw
That blessing ([*Points to*] *Imoinda.*) from you, you
    so hardly found
And so much valued once?

OROONOKO.
              Imoinda! Oh!
'Tis she that holds me on this argument   150
Of tedious life. I could resolve it soon,
Were this curst being only in debate,
But my Imoinda struggles in my soul;
She makes a coward of me. I confess
I am afraid to part with her in death   155
And more afraid of life to lose her here.

BLANFORD.
This way you must lose her. Think upon
The weakness of her sex, made yet more weak
With her condition, requiring rest
And soft indulging ease to nurse your hopes   160
And make you a glad father.

OROONOKO.
              There I feel
A father's fondness, and a husband's love.
They seize upon my heart, strain all its strings

To pull me to 'em from my stern resolve. 165
Husband and father! All the melting art
Of eloquence lives in those soft'ning names.
Methinks I see the babe with infant hands
Pleading for life and begging to be born.
Shall I forbid his birth? deny him light, 170
The heavenly comforts of all-cheering light,
And make the womb the dungeon of his death,
His bleeding mother his sad monument?
These are the calls of Nature, that call loud;
They will be heard and conquer in their cause. 175
He must not be a man who can resist 'em.
No, my Imoinda! I will venture all
To save thee and that little innocent.
The world may be a better friend to him
Than I have found it. Now I yield myself. (*Gives* 180
up his sword.)
The conflict's past, and we are in your hands.

*Several men get about Oroonoko and Aboan and seize
them.*

LIEUTENANT GOVERNOR.
So you shall find you are. Dispose of them
As I commanded you.
BLANFORD.
Good Heaven forbid! 185
You cannot mean—
LIEUTENANT GOVERNOR. (*To Blanford, who
goes to Oroonoko.*)
This is not your concern.
(*To Imoinda.*) I must take care of you.
IMOINDA.
I'm at the end
Of all my care. Here I will die with him. 190
(*Holding Oroonoko.*)
OROONOKO.
You shall not force her from me. (*He holds her.*)
LIEUTENANT GOVERNOR.
Then I must
Try other means and conquer force by force.
Break, cut off his hold, bring her away.
IMOINDA.
I do not ask to live, kill me but here. 195
OROONOKO.
Oh bloody dogs! Inhuman murderers!

*Imoinda forced out of one door by the [lieutenant]
governor and others. Oroonoko and Aboan hurried out
of another.*

Exeunt omnes.

Act V, scene i.

Enter Stanmore, Lucia, Charlotte.

STANMORE.
'Tis strange we cannot hear of him. Can nobody
give an account of him?
LUCIA.
Nay, I begin to despair; I give him for gone.
STANMORE.
Not so, I hope.
LUCIA.
There are so many disturbances in this devilish 5
country! Would we had never seen it.
STANMORE.
This is but a cold welcome for you, madam, after
so troublesome a voyage.
CHARLOTTE.
A cold welcome, indeed, sir, without my cousin
Welldon. He was the best friend I had in the world. 10
STANMORE.
He was a very good friend of yours indeed,
madam.
LUCIA.
They have made him away, murdered him for his
money, I believe. He took a considerable sum out
with him, I know; that has been his ruin. 15
STANMORE.
That has done him no injury, to my knowledge.
For this morning he put into my custody what you
speak of, I suppose a thousand pounds, for the use
of this lady.
CHARLOTTE.
I was always obliged to him, and he has shown his 20
care of me in placing my little affairs in such
honorable hands.
STANMORE.
He gave me a particular charge of you, madam,
very particular—so particular that you will be
surprised when I tell you. 25
CHARLOTTE.
What, pray sir?

STANMORE.

I am engaged to get you a husband. I promised
that before I saw you, and now I have seen you,
you must give me leave to offer you myself.

LUCIA.

Nay cousin, never be coy upon the matter. To my   30
knowledge my brother always designed you for this
gentleman.

STANMORE.

You hear madam, he has given me his interest, and
'tis the favor I would have begged of him. Lord!
you are so like him—   35

CHARLOTTE.

That you are obliged to say you like me for his sake.

STANMORE.

I should be glad to love you for your own.

CHARLOTTE.

If I should consent to the fine things you can say
to me, how would you look, at last, to find 'em
thrown away upon an old acquaintance?   40

STANMORE.

An old acquaintance!

CHARLOTTE.

Lord, how easily are you men to be imposed upon!
I am no cousin newly arrived from England, not
I, but the very Welldon you wot of.

STANMORE.

Welldon!   45

CHARLOTTE.

Not murdered, nor made away, as my sister would
have you believe, but am in very good health—
your old friend in breeches that was, and now your
humble servant in petticoats.

STANMORE.

I'm glad we have you again. But what service can   50
you do me in petticoats, pray?

CHARLOTTE.

Can't you tell what?

STANMORE.

Not I, by my troth. I have found my friend and
lost my mistress, it seems, which I did not expect
from your petticoats.   55

CHARLOTTE.

Come, come, you have had a friend of your
mistress long enough, 'tis high time now to have
a mistress of your friend.

STANMORE.

What do you say?

CHARLOTTE.

I am a woman, sir.   60

STANMORE.

A woman!

CHARLOTTE.

As arrant a woman as you would have had me. But
now, I assure you.

STANMORE.

And at my service?

CHARLOTTE.

If you have any for me in petticoats.   65

STANMORE.

Yes, yes, I shall find you employment.

CHARLOTTE.

You wonder at my proceeding, I believe.

STANMORE.

'Tis a little extraordinary, indeed.

CHARLOTTE.

I have taken some pains to come into your favor.

STANMORE.

You might have had it cheaper a great deal.   70

CHARLOTTE.

I might have married you in the person of my
English cousin, but could not consent to cheat
you, even in the thing I had a mind to.

STANMORE.

'Twas done as you do everything.

CHARLOTTE.

I need not tell you I made that little plot and   75
carried it on only for this opportunity. I was
resolved to see whether you liked me as a woman
or not. If I had found you indifferent, I would have
endeavored to have been so, too. But you say you
like me, and therefore I have ventured to discover*   80
the truth.

STANMORE.

Like you! I like you so well that I'm afraid you
won't think marriage a proof on't. Shall I give you
any other?

CHARLOTTE.

No, no, I'm inclined to believe you, and that shall   85
convince me. At more leisure I'll satisfy you how
I came to be in man's clothes—for no ill, I assure
you, though I have happened to play the rogue in

'em. They have assisted me in marrying my sister and have gone a great way in befriending your cousin Jack with the widow. Can you forgive me for pimping for your family? 90

Enter Jack Stanmore.

STANMORE.

So, Jack, what news with you?

JACK STANMORE.

I am the forepart of the widow, you know. She's coming after with the body of the family, the young squire in her hand—my son-in-law that is to be, with the help of Mr. Welldon. 95

CHARLOTTE.

Say you so, sir? (*Clapping Jack upon the back.*)

Enter Widow Lackitt with her son Daniel.

WIDOW.

So, Mrs. Lucy, I have brought him about again, I have chastised him, I have made him as supple as a glove for your wearing, to pull on or throw off at your pleasure.—Will you ever rebel again? Will you, sirrah? But come, come, down on your marrowbones and ask her forgiveness. (*Daniel kneels.*) Say after me, "Pray, forsooth, wife." 100

105

DANIEL.

Pray, forsooth, wife.

LUCIA.

Well, well, this is a day of good nature, and so I take you into favor. But first take the Oath of Allegiance. (*He kisses her hand and rises.*) If ever you do so again— 110

DANIEL.

Nay, marry,* if I do, I shall have the worst on't.

LUCIA.

Here's a stranger, forsooth, would be glad to be known to you, a sister of mine. Pray salute* her.

WIDOW. (*Starts at Charlotte.*)

Your sister! Mrs. Lucy! What do you mean? This is your brother, Mr. Welldon! Do you think I do not know Mr. Welldon? 115

LUCIA.

Have a care what you say. This gentleman's about marrying her; you may spoil all.

WIDOW.

Fiddle faddle, what! You would put a trick upon me.

CHARLOTTE.

No, faith, Widow, the trick is over, it has taken sufficiently. And now I will teach you the trick, to prevent your being cheated another time. 120

WIDOW.

How! Cheated, Mr. Welldon!

CHARLOTTE.

Why, aye, you will always take things by the wrong handle. I see you will have me Mr. Welldon. I grant you, I was Mr. Welldon a little while to please you, or so. But Mr. Stanmore here has persuaded me into a woman again. 125

WIDOW.

A woman! Pray let me speak with you. (*Drawing her aside.*) You are not in earnest, I hope? A woman! 130

CHARLOTTE.

Really a woman.

WIDOW.

Gads my life! I could not be cheated in everything. I know a man from a woman at these years, or the Devil's in't. Pray, did not you marry me? 135

CHARLOTTE.

You would have it so.

WIDOW.

And did not I give you a thousand pounds this morning?

CHARLOTTE.

Yes, indeed; 'twas more than I deserved. But you had your pennyworth for your penny, I suppose. You seemed to be pleased with your bargain. 140

WIDOW.

A rare bargain I have made on't, truly. I have laid out my money to fine purpose upon a woman.

CHARLOTTE.

You would have a husband, and I provided for you as well as I could. 145

WIDOW.

Yes, yes, you have provided for me.

CHARLOTTE.

And you have paid me very well for't, I thank you.

WIDOW.

'Tis very well. I may be with child, too, for aught I know, and may go look for the father.

CHARLOTTE.

Nay, if you think so, 'tis time to look about you 150

indeed. Even make up the matter as well as you can, I advise you as a friend, and let us live neighborly and lovingly together.

WIDOW.

I have nothing else for it, that I know now.

CHARLOTTE.

For my part, Mrs. Lackitt, your thousand pounds will engage me not to laugh at you. Then my sister is married to your son; he is to have half your estate, I know, and indeed they may live upon it very comfortably to themselves, and very creditably to you.

WIDOW.

Nay, I can blame nobody but myself.

CHARLOTTE.

You have enough for a husband still, and that you may bestow upon honest Jack Stanmore.

WIDOW.

Is he the man, then?

CHARLOTTE.

He is the man you are obliged to.

JACK STANMORE.

Yes, faith, Widow, I am the man. I have done fairly by you, you find; you know what you have to trust to beforehand.

WIDOW.

Well, well, I see you will have me, even marry me, and make an end of the business.

STANMORE.

Why, that's well said. Now we are all agreed, and all provided for.

A servant enters to Stanmore.

SERVANT.

Sir, Mr. Blanford desires you to come to him and bring as many of your friends as you can with you.

STANMORE.

I come to him.—You'll all go along with me. Come, young gentleman, marriage is the fashion, you see, you must like it now.

DANIEL.

If I don't, how shall I help myself?

LUCIA.

Nay, you may hang yourself in the noose if you please, but you'll never get out on't with struggling.

DANIEL.

Come then, let's even jog on in the old road.

Cuckold or worse, I must now be contented:
I'm not the first has married, and repented.

Exeunt.

Scene ii.

Enter [Lieutenant] Governor with Blanford and planters.

BLANFORD.

Have you no reverence of future fame?
No awe upon your actions from the tongues,
The censuring tongues of men that will be free?
If you confess humanity, believe
There is a God, or Devil, to reward   5
Our doings here, do not provoke your fate.
The hand of Heaven is armed against these crimes
With hotter thunderbolts prepared to shoot
And nail you to the earth: a sad example,
A monument of faithless infamy.   10

Enter Stanmore, Jack Stanmore, Charlotte, Lucy, Widow, and Daniel.

So, Stanmore, you I know, the women too
Will join with me. (*To the women.*) 'Tis Oroonoko's cause,
A lover's cause, a wretched woman's cause,
That will become your intercession.

FIRST PLANTER.

Never mind 'em, Governor, he ought to be made   15
an example for the good of the plantation.*

SECOND PLANTER.

Aye, aye, 'twill frighten the Negroes from attempting the like again.

FIRST PLANTER.

What, rise against their lords and masters! At this rate, no man is safe from his own slaves.   20

SECOND PLANTER.

No, no more he is. Therefore, one and all, Governor, we declare for hanging.

ALL PLANTERS.

Aye, aye, hang him, hang him.

WIDOW.

What! Hang him! Oh! forbid it, Governor!

CHARLOTTE, LUCIA.

We all petition for him.   25

JACK STANMORE.

They are for a holiday. Guilty or not,

Is not the business; hanging is their sport.

BLANFORD.

We are not sure so wretched to have these,
The rabble, judge for us, the changing crowd,
The arbitrary guard of Fortune's power,   30
Who wait to catch the sentence of her frowns
And hurry all to ruin she condemns.

STANMORE.

So far from farther wrong that 'tis a shame
He should be where he is. Good Governor,
Order his liberty. He yielded up   35
Himself, his all, at your discretion.

BLANFORD.

Discretion! no, he yielded on your word,
And I am made the cautionary pledge,
The gage and hostage of your keeping it.
Remember, sir, he yielded on your word,   40
Your word! which honest men will think should be
The last resort of truth and trust on earth.
There's no appeal beyond it but to Heaven.
An oath is a recognizance to Heaven,
Binding us over in the courts above   45
To plead to the indictment of our crimes,
That those who 'scape this world should suffer there.
But in the common intercourse of men
(Where the dread majesty is not invoked,
His honor not immediately concerned,   50
Nor made a party in our interests)
Our word is all to be relied upon.

WIDOW.

Come, come, you'll be as good as your word, we
know.

STANMORE.

He's out of all power of doing any harm now, if   55
he were disposed to it.

CHARLOTTE.

But he is not dispos'd to it.

BLANFORD.

To keep him where he is will make him soon
Find out some desperate way to liberty.
He'll hang himself or dash out his mad brains.   60

CHARLOTTE.

Pray try him by gentle means; we'll all be sureties
for him.

OMNES.

All, all.

LUCIA.

We will all answer for him now.

LIEUTENANT GOVERNOR.

Well, you will have it so, do what you please,   65
Just what you will with him. I give you leave.
(*Exit.*)

BLANFORD.

We thank you, sir. This way, pray come with me.

Exeunt.

[Scene iii.]

*The scene drawn shows Oroonoko upon his back, his
legs and arms stretched out and chained to the ground.
Enter Blanford, Stanmore, etc.*

BLANFORD.

Oh miserable sight! Help, everyone,
Assist me all to free him from his chains.

They help him up and bring him forward, looking down.

Most injured prince! how shall we clear ourselves?
We cannot hope you will vouchsafe to hear
Or credit what we say in the defense   5
And cause of our suspected innocence.

STANMORE.

We are not guilty of your injuries,
No way consenting to 'em, but abhor,
Abominate, and loathe this cruelty.

BLANFORD.

It is our curse, but make it not our crime.   10
A heavy curse upon us, that we must
Share anything in common, even the light,
The elements, and seasons, with such men,
Whose principles, like the famed dragons' teeth,[23]
Scattered and sown, would shoot a harvest up   15
Of fighting mischiefs to confound themselves
And ruin all about 'em.

---

23 dragons' teeth] The Greek hero Cadmus followed the
    Delphic oracle and went to a spring where he was told
    to make sacrifice. His companions were all killed by the
    dragon guarding the spring, and after killing the dragon,
    Cadmus obeyed the word of the goddess Athena by sow-
    ing the dragons' teeth into the ground. A tribe of armed
    men sprouted from them. Cadmus killed all except five
    survivors, and with these five founded the city of Thebes.

STANMORE.

Profligates!

Whose bold Titanian[24] impiety
Would once again pollute their Mother Earth, 20
Force her to teem with her old monstrous brood
Of giants, and forget the race* of men.

BLANFORD.

We are not so: believe us innocent.
We come prepared with all our services
To offer a redress of your base wrongs. 25
Which way shall we employ 'em?

STANMORE.

Tell us, sir,

If there is anything that can atone.
But nothing can that may be some amends—

OROONOKO.

If you would have me think you are not all 30
Confederates, all accessory to
The base injustice of your governor;
If you would have me live, as you appear
Concerned for me, if you would have me live
To thank and bless you, there is yet a way 35
To tie me ever to your honest love:
Bring my Imoinda to me. Give me her
To charm my sorrows and, if possible,
I'll sit down with my wrongs, never to rise
Against my fate or think of vengeance more. 40

BLANFORD.

Be satisfied you may depend upon us.
We'll bring her safe to you, and suddenly.

CHARLOTTE.

We wonnot leave you in so good a work.

WIDOW.

No, no, we'll go with you.

BLANFORD.

In the meantime 45
Endeavor to forget, sir, and forgive
And hope a better fortune.

Exeunt [all but Oroonoko].

OROONOKO.

Forget! forgive! I must indeed forget,
When I forgive. But while I am a man,
In flesh that bears the living mark of shame, 50

The print of his dishonorable chains,
My memory still rousing up my wrongs,
I never can forgive this governor,
This villain, the disgrace of trust and place,
Unjust[e] contempt of delegated power. 55
What shall I do? If I declare myself,
I know him, he will sneak behind his guard
Of followers and brave me in his fears.
Else, lionlike, with my devouring rage
I would rush on him, fasten on his throat, 60
Tear wide a passage to his treacherous heart,
And that way lay him open to the world.
(*Pausing.*)
If I should turn his Christian arts on him,
Promise him, speak him fair, flatter and creep
With fawning steps to get within his faith, 65
I could betray him then, as he has me.
But am I sure by that to right myself?
Lying's a certain mark of cowardice.
And when the tongue forgets its honesty,
The heart and hand may drop their functions too, 70
And nothing worthy be resolved or done.
The man must go together, bad or good:
In one part frail, he soon grows weak in all.
Honor should be concerned in honor's cause,
That is not to be cured by contraries, 75
As bodies are, whose health is often drawn
From rankest poisons. Let me but find out
An honest remedy. I have the hand,
A minist'ring hand, that will apply it home.

Exit.

Scene iv. The [lieutenant] governor's house.

Enter Lieutenant Governor.

LIEUTENANT GOVERNOR.

I would not have her tell me she consents.
In favor of the sex's modesty
That still* should be presumed, because there is
A greater impudence in owning it
Than in allowing all that we can do. 5
This truth I know, and yet against myself
(So unaccountable are lovers' ways)
I talk and lose the opportunities
Which love and she expect I should employ.
Ev'n she expects, for when a man has said 10
All that is fit to save the decency,

---

[24] Titanian] of or similar to the Titans (q.v.)

The women know the rest is to be done.
I wonnot disappoint her. (*Going.*)

Enter to him Blanford, the Stanmores, Daniel, Mrs.
Lackitt, Charlotte, and Lucy.

WIDOW.

Oh Governor! I'm glad we have lit upon you.

LIEUTENANT GOVERNOR.

Why! what's the matter?   15

CHARLOTTE.

Nay, nothing extraordinary. But one good action
draws on another. You have given the prince his
freedom; now we come a-begging for his wife. You
won't refuse us.

LIEUTENANT GOVERNOR.

Refuse you? No, no, what have I to do to refuse you?   20

WIDOW.

You won't refuse to send her to him, she means.

LIEUTENANT GOVERNOR.

I send her to him!

WIDOW.

We have promised him to bring her.

LIEUTENANT GOVERNOR.

You do very well, 'tis kindly done of you. Even
carry her to him, with all my heart.   25

LUCIA.

You must tell us where she is.

LIEUTENANT GOVERNOR.

I tell you! Why, don't you know?

BLANFORD.

Your servants say she's in the house.

LIEUTENANT GOVERNOR.

No, no. I brought her home at first indeed, but I
thought it would not look well to keep her here. I   30
removed her in the hurry, only to take care of her.
What! she belongs to you; I have nothing to do
with her.

CHARLOTTE.

But where is she now, sir?

LIEUTENANT GOVERNOR.

Why faith, I can't say certainly. You'll hear of her   35
at Parham House,25 I suppose—there, or
thereabouts. I think I sent her there.

_____

25 Parham House] the mansion of the governor of
   Suriname

BLANFORD. (*Aside.*)

I'll have an eye on him.

Exit all but the [lieutenant] governor.

LIEUTENANT GOVERNOR.

I have lied myself into a little time
And must employ it. They'll be here again,   40
But I must be before 'em. (*Going out, he meets*
   Imoinda and seizes her.)
Are you come?
I'll court no longer for a happiness
That is in mine own keeping. You may still*
Refuse to grant, so I have power to take.   45
The man that asks deserves to be denied.

She disengages one hand and draws his sword from his
side upon him. [Lieutenant] Governor starts and
retires. Blanford enters behind him.

IMOINDA.

He does, indeed, that asks unworthily.

BLANFORD.

You hear her, sir, that asks unworthily.

LIEUTENANT GOVERNOR.

You are no judge.

BLANFORD.

                         I am of my own slave.   50

LIEUTENANT GOVERNOR.

Be gone and leave us.

BLANFORD.

                         When you let her go.

LIEUTENANT GOVERNOR.

To fasten upon you.

BLANFORD.

                         I must defend myself.

IMOINDA.

Help! Murder, help!   55

Imoinda retreats towards the door, favored by Blanford.
When they are closed, she throws down the sword and
runs out. [Lieutenant] Governor takes up the sword; he
and Blanford fight, close, and fall, Blanford upon him.
Servants enter and part them.

LIEUTENANT GOVERNOR.

                         She shannot 'scape me so.
I've gone too far not to go farther. Curse
On my delay, but yet she is and shall
Be in my power.

BLANFORD.

          Nay then, it is the war   60
Of honesty. I know you and will save
You from yourself.

LIEUTENANT GOVERNOR.

  All come along with me.

Exeunt.

Scene [v].

Oroonoko enters.

OROONOKO.

To honor bound! and yet a slave to love!
I am distracted by their rival powers,
And both will be obey'd. Oh great Revenge!
Thou raiser and restorer of fall'n Fame!
Let me not be unworthy of thy aid   5
For stopping in thy course: I still am thine,
But can't forget I am Imoinda's too.
She calls me from my wrongs to rescue her.
No man condemn me, who has never felt
A woman's power or tried the force of love: 10
All tempers yield and soften in those fires.
Our honors, interests, resolving down,
Run in the gentle current of our joys,
But not to sink and drown our memory.
We mount again to action, like the sun   15
That rises from the bosom of the sea
To run his glorious race of light anew
And carry on the world. Love, love will be
My first ambition, and my fame the next.

Aboan enters bloody.

My eyes are turned against me and combine   20
With my sworn enemies to represent
This spectacle of horror.f Aboan!
My ever-faithful friend!

ABOAN.

          I have no name
That can distinguish me from the vile earth   25
To which I'm going: a poor, abject worm
That crawled awhile upon a bustling world
And now am trampled to my dust again.

OROONOKO.

I see thee gashed and mangled.

ABOAN.

             Spare my shame   30

To tell how they have used me, but believe
The hangman's hand would have been merciful.
Do not you scorn me, sir, to think I can
Intend to live under this infamy.
I do not come for pity, to complain.   35
I've spent an honorable life with you,
The earliest servant of your rising fame,
And would attend it with my latest care.
My life was yours, and so shall be my death.
You must not live—   40
Bending and sinking, I have dragged my steps
Thus far to tell you that you cannot live,
To warn you of those ignominious wrongs—
Whips, rods, and all the instruments of death—
Which I have felt and are prepared for you.   45
This was the duty that I had to pay.
'Tis done, and now I beg to be discharged.

OROONOKO.

What shall I do for thee?

ABOAN.

             My body tires
And wonnot bear me off to liberty.   50
I shall again be taken, made a slave.
A sword, a dagger yet would rescue me.
I have not strength to go to find out Death;
You must direct him to me.

OROONOKO. (*Gives him a dagger.*)

          Here he is,   55
The only present I can make thee now.
And next the honorable means of life,
I would bestow the honest means of death.

ABOAN.

I cannot stay to thank you. If there is
A being after this, I shall be yours   60
In the next world, your faithful slave again.
This is to try. (*Stabs himself.*) I had a living sense
Of all your royal favors, but this last
Strikes through my heart. I will not say farewell,
For you must follow me. (*Dies.*)

OROONOKO.

          In life and death,   65
The guardian of my honor! Follow thee!
I should have gone before thee: then perhaps
Thy fate had been prevented. All his care
Was to preserve me from the barbarous rage
That wronged him only for being mine.   70

Why, why, you gods? Why am I so accurst
That it must be a reason of your wrath,
A guilt, a crime sufficient to the fate
Of anyone, but to belong to me?
My friend has found it, and my wife will soon.   75
My wife! the very* fear's too much for life;
I can't support it. Where? Imoinda! Oh!

[He] going out, she meets him, running into his arms.

Thou bosom softness! Down of all my cares!
I could recline my thoughts upon this breast
To a forgetfulness of all my griefs   80
And yet be happy. But it wonnot be.
Thou art disordered, pale, and out of breath!
If Fate pursues thee, find a shelter here.
What is it thou wouldst tell me?

IMOINDA.
                    'Tis in vain   85
To call him villain.

OROONOKO.
              Call him Governor:
Is it not so?

IMOINDA.
            There's not another sure.

OROONOKO.
Villain's the common name of mankind here,   90
But his most properly. What? what of him?
I fear to be resolved, and must inquire.
He had thee in his power.

IMOINDA.
              I blush to think it.

OROONOKO.
Blush! to think what?   95

IMOINDA.
            That I was in his power.

OROONOKO.
He could not use it?

IMOINDA.
          What can't such men do?

OROONOKO.
But did he? durst he?

IMOINDA.
         What he could, he dared.   100

OROONOKO.
His own gods damn him, then, for ours have none,
No punishment for such unheard-of crimes.

IMOINDA.
This monster, cunning in his flatteries,
When he had wearied all his useless arts,
Leapt out, fierce as a beast of prey, to seize me.   105
I trembled, feared.

OROONOKO.
             I fear and tremble now.
What could preserve thee? what deliver thee?

IMOINDA.
That worthy man you used to call your friend—

OROONOKO.
Blanford.   110

IMOINDA.
       —Came in and saved me from his rage.

OROONOKO.
He was a friend indeed to rescue thee!
And for his sake, I'll think it possible
A Christian may yet be an honest man.

IMOINDA.
Oh! did you know what I have struggled through   115
To save me yours, sure you would promise me
Never to see me forced from you again.

OROONOKO.
To promise thee! Oh! do I need to promise?
But there is now no farther use of words.
Death is security for all our fears. (*Shows Aboan's*   120
   body on the floor.)
And yet I cannot trust him.

IMOINDA.
               Aboan!

OROONOKO.
Mangled and torn, resolved to give me time
To fit myself for what I must expect,
Groaned out a warning to me, and expired.   125

IMOINDA.
For what you must expect?

OROONOKO.
            Would that were all.

IMOINDA.
What! to be butchered thus—

OROONOKO.
            Just as thou seest.

IMOINDA.
By barbarous hands to fall at last their prey!   130

OROONOKO.
I have run the race with honor. Shall I now

Lag and be overtaken at the goal?
IMOINDA.
   No.
OROONOKO. (*Tenderly.*)
     I must look back to thee.
IMOINDA.
               You shannot need.   135
I'm always present to your purpose. Say
Which way would you dispose me?
OROONOKO.
                   Have a care.
Thou'rt on a precipice and dost not see
Whither that question leads thee. Oh! too soon 140
Thou dost inquire what the assembled gods
Have not determined and will latest doom.
Yet this I know of fate, this is most certain:
I cannot, as I would, dispose of thee,
And as I ought, I dare not. Oh Imoinda!   145
IMOINDA.
Alas! that sigh! why do you tremble so?
Nay then, 'tis bad indeed, if you can weep.
OROONOKO.
My heart runs over; if my gushing eyes
Betray a weakness which they never knew,
Believe thou, only thou, couldst cause these tears. 150
The gods themselves conspire with faithless men
To our destruction.
IMOINDA.
           Heaven and earth our foes!
OROONOKO.
It is not always granted to the great
To be most happy. If the angry pow'rs   155
Repent their favors, let 'em take 'em back.
The hopes of empire, which they gave my youth
By making me a prince, I here resign.
Let 'em quench in me all those glorious fires
Which kindled at their beams: that lust of fame, 160
That fever of ambition, restless still
And burning with the sacred thirst of sway,
Which they inspired to qualify my fate
And make me fit to govern under them,
Let 'em extinguish. I submit myself   165
To their high pleasure and devoted bow
Yet lower to continue still a slave,
Hopeless of liberty, and, if I could
Live after it, would give up honor, too,

To satisfy their vengeance, to avert   170
This only curse, the curse of losing thee.
IMOINDA.
If Heav'n could be appeased, these cruel men
Are not to be entreated or believed.
Oh! think on that and be no more deceived.
OROONOKO.
What can we do?   175
IMOINDA.
          Can I do anything?
OROONOKO.
But we were born to suffer.
IMOINDA.
               Suffer both,
Both die, and so prevent* 'em.
OROONOKO.
                 By thy death! 180
Oh! Let me hunt my traveled thoughts again,
Range the wide waste of desolate despair,
Start any hope—alas! I lose myself,
'Tis pathless, dark and barren all to me.
Thou art my only guide, my light of life, 185
And thou art leaving me. Send out thy beams
Upon the wing; let 'em fly all around,
Discover every way. Is there a dawn,
A glimmering of comfort? The great god
That rises on the world must shine on us. 190
IMOINDA.
And see us set before him.
OROONOKO.
             Thou bespeakst,
And go'st before me.
IMOINDA.
           So I would, in love:
In the dear unsuspected part of life, 195
In death for love. Alas! what hopes for me?
I was preserved but to acquit myself,
To beg to die with you.
OROONOKO.
           And canst thou ask it?
I never durst inquire into myself 200
About thy fate, and thou resolv'st it all.
IMOINDA.
Alas, my lord! my fate's resolved in yours.
OROONOKO.
Oh! Keep thee there. Let not thy virtue shrink

From my support, and I will gather strength
Fast as I can to tell thee—   205
IMOINDA.
                          I must die.
I know 'tis fit, and I can die with you.
OROONOKO.
Oh! Thou hast banished hence a thousand fears
Which sickened at my heart and quite unmanned me.
IMOINDA.
Your fear's for me. I know you feared my strength   210
And could not overcome your tenderness
To pass this sentence on me. And indeed,
There you were kind, as I have always found you,
As you have ever been. For though I am
Resigned and ready to obey my doom,   215
Methinks it should not be pronounced by you.
OROONOKO.
Oh! That was all the labor of my grief.
My heart and tongue forsook me in the strife:
I never could pronounce it.
IMOINDA.
                       I have for you,   220
For both of us.
OROONOKO.
              Alas for me! my death
I could regard as the last scene of life
And act it through with joy to have it done.
But then to part with thee—   225
IMOINDA.
                 'Tis hard to part.
But parting thus, as the most happy must,
Parting in death, makes it the easier.
You might have thrown me off, forsaken me
And my misfortunes: that had been a death   230
Indeed of terror to have trembled at.
OROONOKO.
Forsaken! thrown thee off!
IMOINDA.
                 But 'tis a pleasure
More than life can give, that with unconquered
Passion to the last you struggle still   235
And fain would hold me to you.
OROONOKO.
                   Ever, ever,
And let those stars, which are my enemies,
Witness against me in the other world

If I would leave this mansion of my bliss   240
To be the brightest ruler of their skies. (*Embracing her.*)
Oh! That we could incorporate, be one,
One body, as we have been long one mind,
That blended so, we might together mix
And, losing thus our beings to the world,   245
Be only found to one another's joys.
IMOINDA.
Is this the way to part?
OROONOKO.
                Which is the way?
IMOINDA.
The god of love is blind, and cannot find it.
But quick, make haste, our enemies have eyes   250
To find us out and show us the worst way
Of parting: think on them.
OROONOKO.
               Why dost thou wake me?
IMOINDA.
Oh! No more of love.
For if I listen to you, I shall quite   255
Forget my dangers and desire to live.
I can't live yours. (*Takes up the dagger.*)
OROONOKO.
              There all the stings of death
Are shot into my heart—what shall I do?
IMOINDA.
This dagger will instruct you. (*Gives it him.*)   260
OROONOKO.
               Hah! This dagger!
Like Fate, it points me to the horrid deed.
IMOINDA.
Strike, strike it home and bravely save us both.
There is no other safety.
OROONOKO.
                It must be.   265
But first a dying kiss— (*Kisses her.*) This last
    embrace— (*Embracing her.*)
And now—
IMOINDA.
              I'm ready.
OROONOKO.
               Oh! where shall I strike?
Is there a smallest grain of that loved body   270
That is not dearer to me than my eyes,

My bosomed heart, and all the lifeblood[h] there?
Bid me cut off these limbs, hew off these hands,
Dig out these eyes, though I would keep them last
To gaze upon thee. But to murder thee!   275
The joy and charm of every ravished sense,
My wife! Forbid it, Nature.

IMOINDA.

                       'Tis your wife
Who on her knees conjures you. Oh! in time
Prevent those mischiefs that are falling on us.   280
You may be hurried to a shameful death,
And I too dragged to the vile Governor.
Then I may cry aloud. When you are gone,
Where shall I find a friend again to save me?

OROONOKO.

It will be so. Thou unexampled virtue!   285
Thy resolution has recovered mine.
And now, prepare thee.

IMOINDA.

               Thus with open arms
I welcome you and death.

*He drops his dagger as he looks on her, and throws
himself on the ground.*

OROONOKO.

               I cannot bear it.   290
Oh, let me dash against this rock of fate,
Dig up this earth, tear, tear her bowels out
To make a grave deep as the center down
To swallow wide and bury us together.
It wonnot be. Oh! Then some pitying god   295
(If there be one a friend to innocence)
Find yet a way to lay her beauties down
Gently in death and save me from her blood.

IMOINDA.

Oh rise, 'tis more than death to see you thus.
I'll ease your love and do the deed myself.   300

*She takes up the dagger; he rises in haste to take it from
her.*

OROONOKO.

Oh! hold, I charge thee, hold!

IMOINDA.

                   Though I must own
It would be nobler for us both from you.

OROONOKO.

Oh! for a whirlwind's wing to hurry us
To yonder cliff which frowns upon the flood,   305
That in embraces locked we might plunge in,
And perish thus in one another's arms.

IMOINDA.

Alas! what shout is that?

OROONOKO.

              I see 'em coming.
They shannot overtake us. This last kiss.   310
And now, farewell.

IMOINDA.

             Farewell, farewell forever.

OROONOKO.

I'll turn my face away and do it so.
Now, are you ready?

IMOINDA.

             Now. But do not grudge me   315
The pleasure in my death of a last look.
Pray look upon me—now I'm satisfied.

OROONOKO.

So Fate must be by this.

*Going to stab her, he stops short. She lays her hands on
his in order to give the blow.*

IMOINDA.

            Nay, then, I must assist you.
And since it is the common cause of both,   320
'Tis just that both should be employed in it.
    (*Stabs herself.*)
Thus, thus 'tis finished, and I bless my fate
That where I lived, I die, in these loved arms.
    (*Dies.*)

OROONOKO.

She's gone. And now all's at an end with me.
Soft, lay her down. Oh, we will part no more.   325
    (*Throws himself by her.*)
But let me pay the tribute of my grief,
A few sad tears to thy loved memory,
And then I follow. (*Weeps over her.*) But I stay too
    long. (*A noise again.*)
The noise comes nearer. Hold, before I go,
There's something would be done. It shall be so.   330
And then, Imoinda, I'll come all to thee. (*Rises.*)

*Blanford and his party enter before the [lieutenant]
governor and his party, swords drawn on both sides.*

LIEUTENANT GOVERNOR.

   You strive in vain to save him, he shall die.

BLANFORD.

   Not while we can defend him with our lives.

LIEUTENANT GOVERNOR.

   Where is he?

OROONOKO.

         Here's the wretch whom you would have.   335

   Put up your swords and let civil broils

   Engage you in the cursèd cause of one

   Who cannot live and now entreats to die.

   This object will convince you.

BLANFORD.

               'Tis his wife!   340

They gather about the body.

   Alas! there was no other remedy.

LIEUTENANT GOVERNOR.

   Who did the bloody deed?

OROONOKO.

             The deed was mine.

   Bloody I know it is, and I expect

   Your laws should tell me so. Thus self-condemned,   345

   I do resign myself into your hands,

   The hands of justice. But I hold the sword

   For you—and for myself. (*Stabs the [lieutenant]*

      governor and himself, then throws himself by

      Imoinda's body.)

STANMORE.

   He has killed the governor and stabbed himself.

OROONOKO.

   'Tis as it should be now. I have sent his ghost   350

   To be a witness of that happiness

   In the next world which he denied us here. (*Dies.*)

BLANFORD.

   I hope there is a place of happiness

   In the next world for such exalted virtue.

   Pagan or unbeliever, yet he lived   355

   To all he knew. And if he went astray,

   There's mercy still above to set him right.

   But Christians guided by the heavenly ray

   Have no excuse if we mistake our way.

[Exeunt.]

FINIS.

Textual Notes

a Copytext is the 1696 first quarto (Q1). Other quartos have no substantive variants. Also consulted were two separate editions (a 1712 octavo [O] and a 1736 sexto [S]) and two *Collected Works* (one in 1713 [C1] and one in 1721 [C2]) that appeared during Southerne's lifetime. Consulted too were modern editions of 1976 (Novak and Rodes) and of 1988 (Jordan and Love).

b weeks] C1, C2, S, Novak and Rodes, Jordan and Love; months Qq, O

c Let … easy] Southerne's verse is not always printed as regular; here and elsewhere it is modified to be more so. Other passages printed as verse do not scan and are printed here as prose.

d lent] following a suggestion in Jordan and Love; sent Q1 and all subsequent editions.

e Unjust] And just Q1 and all subsequent editions

f horror] S, perhaps following the lead of a 1731 Dublin edition; honor Q1 and all other editions with authority

g go'st] Novak and Rodes; goes Qq; goest O, C1-2, S, Jordan and Love

h lifeblood] C1-2, S, Novak and Rodes, Jordan and Love; live-blood Qq, O

The Conscious Lovers[a]

by Richard Steele (1672-1729)
edited by Lisa A. Freeman

Students of the eighteenth century are, perhaps, better acquainted with Richard Steele as one of the editors and authors of influential periodicals such as *The Spectator*, *The Guardian*, and *The Tatler*. Yet Steele played an active role in the London theater world both as a shareholder in the patent of Drury Lane Theatre and as the author of four plays, the last of which was his masterwork, *The Conscious Lovers*.

The Conscious Lovers was first performed on November 7, 1722, at Drury Lane and was an immediate sensation, with an initial run of eighteen consecutive nights followed by eight additional performances over the course of the 1722–1723 season. This success qualified *The Conscious Lovers* as a smash hit on the London stage, and it remained a part of the repertory throughout the eighteenth century, reaching its height of popularity in the 1730s, 1740s, and 1750s. Yet the success of *The Conscious Lovers* was not without controversy. Indeed, Steele's incorporation of what he termed in his preface "a joy too exquisite for laughter" in the dramatic resolution of the forced marriage plot of the play, as well as his insistence on the primacy of filial obligation against the expression of individual passion, elicited charges that he had created a bastard breed of comedy and that he had violated all rules of probability.

Such controversy notwithstanding, *The Conscious Lovers* is generally regarded as an exemplary text in the genre called sentimental comedy. Also known as *la comédie larmoyante*, or the comedy of tears, this genre was influenced by emerging theories of sentiment and sensibility which emphasized the goodness both of human nature and of Providence. Reacting against the bawdy humor of the Restoration comedies, moreover, sentimental comedies were aimed at producing what Steele termed "innocent performance," featuring displays of moral and emotional pathos and examples of virtue rewarded. Significantly, the rise of sentiment and sensibility has been associated with the emergence of the middling classes in eighteenth-century England and with the growing influence of bourgeois moral values. In Steele's satirical portrait of the aristocratic pedant Cimberton and in the exchange between the aristocrat Sir John Bevil and the merchant Mr. Sealand, we can begin to trace one of the main projects of sentimental comedies, that of representing the middling classes as the new polite and moral gentry of their day. One might argue, in this respect, that the comedy of manners is transformed here into the comedy of good manners.

Dramatis Personae

MEN

    Sir John Bevil.

    Mr. Sealand.

    Bevil Junior, in love with Indiana.

    Myrtle, in love with Lucinda.

    Cimberton, a coxcomb.

    Humphrey, an old servant to Sir John.

    Tom, servant to Bevil Junior.

    Daniel, a country boy, servant to Indiana.

WOMEN

    Mrs. Sealand, second wife to Sealand.

    Isabella, sister to Sealand.

    Indiana, Sealand's daughter by his first wife.

    Lucinda, Sealand's daughter by his second wife.

    Phillis, maid to Lucinda.

SCENE: LONDON.

The Conscious Lovers.

Illud Genus Narrationis, quod in Personis positum est, debet habere Sermonis Festivitatem, Animorum Dissimilitudinem, Gravitatem, Lenitatem, Spem, Metum, Suspicionem, Desiderium, Dissimulationem, Misericordiam, Rerum Varietates, Fortunae Commutationem, Insperatum Incommodum, Subitam Letitiam, Jucundum Exitum Rerum.

           Cic. Rhetor. ad Herenn. Lib. I.[1]

Act I, scene i. Sir John Bevil's house.

Enter Sir John Bevil and Humphrey.

SIR JOHN BEVIL.

Have you ordered that I should not be interrupted while I am dressing?

HUMPHREY.

Yes sir. I believed you had something of moment to say to me.

---

1 *Illud … Lib I] Rhetorica ad Herennium* (no longer attributed to Cicero) I.viii: A narrative based on the persons should present a lively style and diverse traits of character, such as austerity and gentleness, hope and fear, distrust and desire, hypocrisy and compassion, and the vicissitudes of life, such as reversal of fortune, unexpected disaster, sudden joys and a happy outcome.

SIR JOHN BEVIL.

Let me see, Humphrey: I think it is now full forty years since I first took thee to be about myself.

HUMPHREY.

I thank you, sir. It has been an easy forty years, and I have passed 'em without much sickness, care, or labor.

SIR JOHN BEVIL.

Thou hast a brave* constitution; you are a year or two older than I am, sirrah.

HUMPHREY.

You have ever been of that mind, sir.

SIR JOHN BEVIL.

You knave, you know it; I took thee for thy gravity and sobriety in my wild years.

HUMPHREY.

Ah sir! Our manners were formed from our different fortunes, not our different age. Wealth gave a loose to your youth, and poverty put a restraint upon mine.

SIR JOHN BEVIL.

Well Humphrey, you know I have been a kind master to you; I have used you, for the ingenuous nature I observed in you from the beginning, more like an humble friend than a servant.

HUMPHREY.

I humbly beg you'll be so tender of me as to explain your commands, sir, without any farther preparation.

SIR JOHN BEVIL.

I'll tell thee then. In the first place, this wedding of my son's, in all probability—shut the door—will never be at all.

HUMPHREY.

How sir! Not be at all? For what reason is it carried on in appearance?

SIR JOHN BEVIL.

Honest Humphrey, have patience, and I'll tell thee all in order. I have myself, in some part of my life, lived, indeed, with freedom, but, I hope, without reproach. Now, I thought liberty would be as little injurious to my son; therefore, as soon as he grew towards man, I indulged him in living after his own manner. I knew not how, otherwise, to judge of his inclination. For what can be concluded from a behavior under restraint and fear? But what

charms me above all expression is that my son has 40
never in the least action, the most distant hint or
word, valued himself upon that great estate of his
mother's, which, according to our marriage
settlement, he has had ever since he came to age.

HUMPHREY.

No sir, on the contrary, he seems afraid of 45
appearing to enjoy it before you or any belonging
to you. He is as dependent and resigned to your
will, as if he had not a farthing but what must
come from your immediate bounty. You have ever
acted like a good and generous father, and he like 50
an obedient and grateful son.

SIR JOHN BEVIL.

Nay, his carriage is so easy to all with whom he
converses that he is never assuming, never prefers
himself to others, nor ever is guilty of that rough
sincerity which a man is not called to, and certainly 55
disobliges most of his acquaintance. To be short,
Humphrey, his reputation was so fair in the world
that old Sealand, the great India[2] merchant, has
offered his only daughter, and sole heiress to that
vast estate of his, as a wife for him. You may be 60
sure I made no difficulties, the match was agreed
on, and this very day named for the wedding.

HUMPHREY.

What hinders the proceeding?

SIR JOHN BEVIL.

Don't interrupt me. You know, I was last Thursday
at the masquerade; my son, you may remember, 65
soon found us out. He knew his grandfather's
habit, which I then wore, and though it was the
mode in the last age, yet the maskers, you know,
followed us as if we had been the most monstrous
figures in that whole assembly. 70

HUMPHREY.

I remember indeed a young man of quality* in the
habit of a clown* that was particularly
troublesome.

SIR JOHN BEVIL.

Right. He was too much what he seemed to be.
You remember how impertinently he followed and 75
teased us and would know who we were.

HUMPHREY. (*Aside.*)

I know he has a mind to come into that particular.

SIR JOHN BEVIL.

Aye, he followed us, till the gentleman who led the
lady in the Indian mantle presented the gay creature
to the rustic and bid him, like Cymon in the fable,[3] 80
grow polite by falling in love and let that worthy old
gentleman alone, meaning me. The clown was not
reformed, but rudely persisted and offered* to force
off my mask; with that the gentleman, throwing off
his own, appeared to be my son, and in his concern 85
for me, tore off that of the nobleman. At this they
seized each other, the company called the guards,
and in the surprise, the lady swooned away. Upon
which my son quitted his adversary and had now no
care but of the lady, when raising her in his arms, 90
"Art thou gone," cried he, "forever—forbid it
Heaven!" She revives at his known voice, and with
the most familiar though modest gesture hangs in
safety over his shoulder weeping, but wept as in the
arms of one before whom she could give herself a 95
loose, were she not under observation. While she
hides her face in his neck, he carefully conveys her
from the company.

HUMPHREY.

I have observed this accident has dwelt upon you
very strongly. 100

SIR JOHN BEVIL.

Her uncommon air, her noble modesty, the dignity
of her person, and the occasion itself, drew the
whole assembly together, and I soon heard it
buzzed about, she was the adopted daughter of a
famous sea-officer, who had served in France. Now 105
this unexpected and public discovery* of my son's
so deep concern for her—

HUMPHREY.

Was what I suppose alarmed Mr. Sealand, in behalf
of his daughter, to break off the match.

---

2 India] not necessarily the Asian subcontinent but possibly the Indies, East or West

3 Cymon in the fable] In Boccaccio's fable of Cymon and
   Iphigenia (translated in John Dryden's *Fables*), Cymon
   was a fair youth, who, because of his dull, brutish mind
   was exiled to the country by his father; there he encountered and fell in love with Iphigenia and was inspired
   by his love to cultivate his mind and acquire the civilities of life.

SIR JOHN BEVIL.

You are right. He came to me yesterday and said 110
he thought himself disengaged from the bargain,
being credibly informed my son was already
married, or worse, to the lady at the masquerade.
I palliated matters and insisted on our agreement,
but we parted with little less than a direct breach 115
between us.

HUMPHREY.

Well sir, and what notice have you taken of all this
to my young master?

SIR JOHN BEVIL.

That's what I wanted to debate with you. I have
said nothing to him yet. But look you, Humphrey, 120
if there is so much in this amour of his that he
denies upon my summons to marry, I have cause
enough to be offended, and then by my insisting
upon his marrying today, I shall know how far he
is engaged to this lady in masquerade and from 125
thence only shall be able to take my measures. In
the meantime I would have you find out how far
that rogue his man is let into his secret. He, I
know, will play tricks as much to cross me as to
serve his master. 130

HUMPHREY.

Why do you think so of him, sir? I believe he is
no worse than I was for you, at your son's age.

SIR JOHN BEVIL.

I see it in the rascal's looks. But I have dwelt on
these things too long; I'll go to my son
immediately, and while I'm gone, your part is to 135
convince his rogue Tom that I am in earnest. I'll
leave him to you. (*Exit.*)

HUMPHREY.

Well, though this father and son live as well
together as possible, yet their fear of giving each
other pain is attended with constant mutual 140
uneasiness. I'm sure I have enough to do to be
honest and yet keep well with them both. But they
know I love 'em, and that makes the task less
painful however.—Oh, here's the prince of poor
coxcombs, the representative of all the better fed 145
than taught. Ho! ho! Tom, whither so gay and so
airy this morning?

Enter Tom, singing.

TOM.

Sir, we servants of single gentlemen are another kind
of people than you domestic ordinary drudges that
do business. We are raised above you. The pleasures 150
of board-wages,[4] tavern-dinners, and many a clear
gain; vails,[5] alas, you never heard or dreamt of.

HUMPHREY.

Thou hast follies and vices enough for a man of
ten thousand a year, though 'tis but as t'other day
that I sent for you to Town* to put you into Mr. 155
Sealand's family,* that you might learn a little
before I put you to my young master, who is too
gentle for training such a rude thing as you were
into proper obedience. You then pulled off your
hat to everyone you met in the street, like a 160
bashful, great, awkward cub as you were. But your
great oaken cudgel when you were a booby became
you much better than that dangling stick at your
button[6] now you are a fop. That's fit for nothing,
except it hangs there to be ready for your master's 165
hand when you are impertinent.

TOM.

Uncle Humphrey, you know my master scorns to
strike his servants. You talk as if the world was now
just as it was when my old master and you were
in your youth, when you went to dinner because 170
it was so much o'clock, when the great blow was
given in the hall at the pantry-door and all the
family* came out of their holes in such strange
dresses and formal faces as you see in the pictures
in our long gallery in the country. 175

HUMPHREY.

Why, you wild rogue!

TOM.

You could not fall to your dinner till a formal
fellow in a black gown said something over the
meat, as if the cook had not made it ready enough.

HUMPHREY.

Sirrah, who do you prate after? Despising men of 180
sacred characters! I hope you never heard my good
young master talk so like a profligate?

---

4 board-wages] allowances paid to cover food expenses
5 vails] gratuities
6 stick ... button] cane suspended from a large button on
a coat

TOM.

Sir, I say you put upon me, when I first came to Town, about being orderly and the doctrine of wearing shams[7] to make linen last clean a fortnight, keeping my clothes fresh, and wearing a frock within doors.

HUMPHREY.

Sirrah, I gave you those lessons, because I supposed at that time your master and you might have dined at home everyday and cost you nothing; then you might have made a good family servant. But the gang you have frequented since at chocolate houses and taverns in a continual round of noise and extravagance—

TOM.

I don't know what you heavy inmates call noise and extravagance, but we gentlemen, who are well fed and cut a figure, sir, think it a fine life and that we must be very pretty fellows who are kept only to be looked at.

HUMPHREY.

Very well, sir, I hope the fashion of being lewd and extravagant, despising of decency and order, is almost at an end, since it is arrived at persons of your quality.

TOM.

Master Humphrey, ha, ha, you were an unhappy lad to be sent up to Town in such queer days as you were. Why now sir, the lackeys are the men of pleasure of the age; the top-gamesters and many a laced coat about Town have had their education in our parti-colored regiment.[8] We are false lovers, have a taste of music, poetry, billets-doux, dress, politics; ruin damsels; and when we are weary of this lewd town and have a mind to take up,[9] whip into our masters wigs and linen and marry fortunes.

HUMPHREY.

Hey-day!

TOM.

Nay sir, our order is carried up to the highest dignities and distinctions: step but into the Painted Chamber,[10] and by our titles you'd take us all for men of quality.* Then again, come down to the Court of Requests,[11] and you see us all laying our broken heads together[12] for the good of the Nation. And though we never carry a question *nemine contradicente*,[13] yet this I can say with a safe conscience—and I wish every gentleman of our cloth could lay his hand upon his heart and say the same—that I never took so much as a single mug of beer for my vote in all my life.

HUMPHREY.

Sirrah, there is no enduring your extravagance; I'll hear you prate no longer. I wanted to see you to inquire how things go with your master, as far as you understand them. I suppose he knows he is to be married today.

TOM.

Aye sir, he knows it and is dressed as gay as the sun, but between you and I, my dear, he has a very heavy heart under all that gaiety. As soon as he was dressed, I retired, but overheard him sigh in the most heavy manner. He walked thoughtfully to and fro in the room, then went into his closet;* when he came out, he gave me this for his mistress, whose maid you know—

HUMPHREY.

Is passionately fond of your fine person.

TOM.

The poor fool is so tender and loves to hear me talk of the world and the plays, operas, and ridottos, for the winter; the parks and Belsize,[14] for our summer diversions; and "Lard!" says she, "you are so wild—but you have a world of humor."

HUMPHREY.

Coxcomb! Well, but why don't you run with your master's letter to Mrs.* Lucinda, as he ordered you?

---

7 shams] false fronts
8 parti-colored regiment] servants in livery
9 to take up] to settle down
10 Painted Chamber] a chamber in the old Palace of West

minster in which Parliament met in early times; in the eighteenth century servants would wait for Members here and address each other by the names of their masters
11 Court of Requests] the building where the House of Lords met
12 laying … together] coming to blows
13 *Nemine Contradicente*] unanimously (literally, no man speaking against—Lat.)
14 Belsize] suburban field outside London used for summer entertainments

TOM.

Because Mrs. Lucinda is not so easily come at as you think for.

HUMPHREY.

Not easily come at? Why sirrah, are not her father and my old master agreed that she and Mr. Bevil are to be one flesh before tomorrow morning? 250

TOM.

It's no matter for that; her mother, it seems, Mrs. Sealand, has not agreed to it. And you must know, Mr. Humphrey, that in that family the gray mare is the better horse. 255

HUMPHREY.

What dost thou mean?

TOM.

In one word, Mrs. Sealand pretends to have a will of her own and has provided a relation of hers, a stiff, starched philosopher and a wise fool, for her daughter; for which reason, for these ten days past, 260 she has suffered no message nor letter from my master to come near her.

HUMPHREY.

And where had you this intelligence?

TOM.

From a foolish, fond soul that can keep nothing from me. One that will deliver this letter too, if 265 she is rightly managed.

HUMPHREY.

What! Her pretty handmaid, Mrs.* Phillis?

TOM.

Even she, sir; this is the very hour, you know, she usually comes hither under a pretence of a visit to your housekeeper forsooth, but in reality to have a 270 glance at—

HUMPHREY.

Your sweet face, I warrant you.

TOM.

Nothing else in nature. You must know, I love to fret and play with the little wanton—

HUMPHREY.

Play with the little wanton! What will this world 275 come to!

TOM.

I met her, this morning, in a new manteau and petticoat,[15] not a bit the worse for her lady's

---

15 manteau and petticoat] a loose gown, the skirt of which split in a triangle to reveal the underskirt

wearing, and she has always new thoughts and new airs with new clothes. Then she never fails to steal 280 some glance or gesture from every visitant at their house and is indeed the whole Town of coquettes at second hand.—But here she comes; in one motion she speaks and describes herself better than all the words in the world can. 285

HUMPHREY.

Then I hope, dear sir, when your own affair is over, you will be so good as to mind your master's with her.

TOM.

Dear Humphrey, you know my master is my friend, and those are people I never forget. 290

HUMPHREY.

Sauciness itself! But I'll leave you to do your best for him. (*Exit.*)

Enter Phillis.

PHILLIS.

Oh Mr. Thomas, is Mrs. Sugar-key at home? Lard, one is almost ashamed to pass along the streets. The Town is quite empty, and nobody of fashion left in 295 it, and the ordinary people do so stare to see anything dressed like a woman of condition, as it were on the same floor with them, pass by. Alas! Alas! It is a sad thing to walk. Oh Fortune! Fortune!

TOM.

What! A sad thing to walk? Why, Madam Phillis, 300 do you wish your self lame?

PHILLIS.

No Mr. Tom, but I wish I were generally carried in a coach or chair* and of a fortune neither to stand nor go, but to totter or slide, to be short-sighted or stare, to fleer in the face, to look distant, 305 to observe, to overlook, yet all become me. And if I was rich, I could twire* and loll as well as the best of them. Oh Tom! Tom! Is it not a pity that you should be so great a coxcomb and I so great a coquette, and yet be such poor devils as we are? 310

TOM.

Mrs.* Phillis, I am your humble servant for that—

PHILLIS.

Yes Mr. Thomas, I know how much you are my humble servant and know what you said to Mrs.* Judy upon seeing her in one of her lady's cast

manteaus, that any one would have thought her
the lady and that she had ordered the other to wear
it till it sat easy, for now only it was becoming: to
my lady it was only a covering, to Mrs. Judy it was
a habit. This you said, after somebody or other.
Oh Tom! Tom! Thou art as false and as base as the
best gentleman of them all. But you wretch, talk
to me no more on the old odious subject. Don't,
I say.

TOM. (*In a submissive tone, retiring.*)

I know not how to resist your commands, madam.

PHILLIS.

Commands about parting are grown mighty easy
to you of late.

TOM. (*Aside.*)

Oh, I have her: I have nettled and put her into
the right temper to be wrought upon and set a
prating. —Why truly, to be plain with you, Mrs.
Phillis, I can take little comfort of late in
frequenting your house.

PHILLIS.

Pray Mr. Thomas, what is it all of a sudden offends
your nicety at our house?

TOM.

I don't care to speak particulars, but I dislike the
whole.

PHILLIS.

I thank you, sir, I am a part of that whole.

TOM.

Mistake me not, good Phillis.

PHILLIS.

Good Phillis! Saucy enough. But however—

TOM.

I say, it is that thou art a part, which gives me pain
for the disposition of the whole. You must know,
madam, to be serious, I am a man, at the bottom,
of prodigious nice* honor. You are too much
exposed to company at your house. To be plain, I
don't like so many that would be your mistress's
lovers whispering to you.

PHILLIS.

Don't think to put that upon me. You say this,
because I wrung you to the heart when I touched
your guilty conscience about Judy.

TOM.

Ah Phillis! Phillis! If you but knew my heart!

PHILLIS.

I know too much on't.

TOM.

Nay then, poor Crispo's fate and mine are one.[16]
Therefore give me leave to say, or sing at least, as
he does upon the same occasion—

Sings "Se vedette," etc.[17]

PHILLIS.

What, do you think I'm to be fobbed off with a
song? I don't question but you have sung the same
to Mrs. Judy too.

TOM.

Don't disparage your charms, good Phillis, with
jealousy of so worthless an object; besides, she is a
poor hussy, and if you doubt the sincerity of my
love, you will allow me true to my interest. You
are a fortune, Phillis—

PHILLIS.

What would the fop be at now?—In good time
indeed, you shall be setting up for a fortune!

TOM.

Dear Mrs. Phillis, you have such a spirit that we
shall never be dull in marriage when we come
together. But I tell you, you are a fortune, and you
have an estate in my hands. *He pulls out a purse;
she eyes it.*

PHILLIS.

What pretence have I to what is in your hands,
Mr. Tom?

TOM.

As thus: there are hours, you know, when a lady
is neither pleased or displeased, neither sick or well,
when she lolls or loiters, when she's without

---

16 Crispo's fate] Crispo was the hero of *Crispus*, a recently
performed Italian Opera by Paolo Rolli and Giovanni
Bononcini; at one point Crispo is falsely accused of
making advances on his mother-in-law, the wife of the
emperor, and is condemned to death. Crispo was played
on the London stage by the famous castrato Senesino.

17 "Se vedette"] Crispo sings this aria just after he has been
condemned, trans. in the English edition of 1721: "If
you see / My Thoughts, / Ye just Gods, defend / The
Innocence of my Heart. / No one hears me, / And you
are silent: / Wicked Malice / Condemns me, and / Deceives my Father."

desires, from having more of everything than she
knows what to do with.   375

PHILLIS.

Well, what then?

TOM.

When she has not life enough to keep her bright
eyes quite open to look at her own dear image in
the glass.*

PHILLIS.

Explain thyself, and don't be so fond of thy own   380
prating.

TOM.

There are also prosperous and good-natured
moments, as when a knot or a patch is happily
fixed, when the complexion particularly flourishes.

PHILLIS.

Well, what then? I have not patience!   385

TOM.

Why then, or on the like occasions, we servants, who
have skill to know how to time business, see when
such a pretty folded thing as this (*Shows the letter.*)
may be presented, laid, or dropped, as best suits the
present humor. And madam, because it is a long,   390
wearisome journey to run through all the several
stages of a lady's temper, my master, who is the most
reasonable man in the world, presents you this to
bear your charges on the road. (*Gives her the purse.*)

PHILLIS.

Now you think me a corrupt hussy.   395

TOM.

Oh fie, I only think you'll take the letter.

PHILLIS.

Nay, I know you do, but I know my own
innocence; I take it for my mistress's sake.

TOM.

I know it, my pretty one, I know it.

PHILLIS.

Yes, I say I do it because I would not have my   400
mistress deluded by one who gives no proof of his
passion. But I'll talk more of this, as you see me
on my way home.—No Tom, I assure thee, I take
this trash of thy master's, not for the value of the
thing, but as it convinces me he has a true respect 405
for my mistress. I remember a verse to the purpose.
They may be false who languish and complain,
But they who part with money never feign.

Exeunt.

Scene ii. Bevil Junior's lodgings.

Bevil Junior, reading.

BEVIL JUNIOR.

These moral writers practice virtue after death.
This charming Vision of Mirza![18] Such an author
consulted in a morning sets the spirit for the
vicissitudes of the day better than the glass* does
a man's person. But what a day have I to go   5
through! To put on an easy look with an aching
heart. If this lady my father urges me to marry
should not refuse me, my dilemma is
insupportable. But why should I fear it? Is not she
in equal distress with me? Has not the letter I have 10
sent her this morning confessed my inclination to
another? Nay, have I not moral assurances of her
engagements too, to my friend Myrtle. It's
impossible but she must give in to it. For sure, to
be denied is a favor any man may pretend to. It   15
must be so. Well then, with the assurance of being
rejected, I think I may confidently say to my father,
I am ready to marry her. Then let me resolve upon
what I am not very good at, though it is an honest
dissimulation.   20

Enter Tom.

TOM.

Sir John Bevil, sir, is in the next room.

BEVIL JUNIOR.

Dunce! Why did not you bring him in?

TOM.

I told him, sir, you were in your closet.*

BEVIL JUNIOR.

I thought you had known, sir, it was my duty to
see my father anywhere. (*Going himself to the door.*) 25

TOM. (*Aside.*)

The devil's in my master! He has always more wit
than I have.

Bevil Junior introducing Sir John.

18 after death … Vision of Mirza] an allegorical anecdote,
    presented by Addison (d. 1719) in *Spectator #159* as an
    oriental tale in which the protagonist, Mirzah, contem-
    plates the vanity of human wishes and is treated to a
    vision both of human folly and the eternal reward that
    awaits those who strive to be worthy

BEVIL JUNIOR.

Sir, you are the most gallant, the most complaisant of all parents. Sure 'tis not a compliment to say these lodgings are yours. Why would you not walk in, sir? 30

SIR JOHN BEVIL.

I was loath to interrupt you unseasonably on your wedding day.

BEVIL JUNIOR.

One to whom I am beholden for my birthday might have used less ceremony.

SIR JOHN BEVIL.

Well son, I have intelligence you have writ to your 35 mistress this morning. It would please my curiosity to know the contents of a wedding-day letter, for courtship must then be over.

BEVIL JUNIOR.

I assure you, sir, there was no insolence in it upon the prospect of such a vast fortune's being added 40 to our family, but much acknowledgment of the lady's greater desert.

SIR JOHN BEVIL.

But dear Jack, are you in earnest in all this? And will you really marry her?

BEVIL JUNIOR.

Did I ever disobey any command of yours, sir? 45 Nay, any inclination that I saw you bent upon?

SIR JOHN BEVIL.

Why, I can't say you have, son, but methinks in this whole business you have not been so warm as I could have wished you. You have visited her, it's true, but you have not been particular. Everyone 50 knows you can say and do as handsome things as any man, but you have done nothing but lived in the general, been complaisant only.

BEVIL JUNIOR.

As I am ever prepared to marry if you bid me, so I am ready to let it alone if you will have me. 55

Humphrey enters unobserved.

SIR JOHN BEVIL.

Look you there now! Why what am I to think of this so absolute and so indifferent a resignation?

BEVIL JUNIOR.

Think? That I am still* your son, sir.—Sir—you have been married, and I have not. And you have, sir, found the inconvenience there is when a man 60

weds with too much love in his head. I have been told, sir, that at the time you married, you made a mighty bustle on the occasion. There was challenging and fighting, scaling walls, locking up the lady, and the gallant under an arrest for fear of 65 killing all his rivals. Now sir, I suppose you having found the ill consequences of these strong passions and prejudices, in preference of one woman to another, in case of a man's becoming a widower—

SIR JOHN BEVIL.

How is this! 70

BEVIL JUNIOR.

I say, sir, experience has made you wiser in your care of me. For sir, since you lost my dear mother, your time has been so heavy, so lonely, and so tasteless, that you are so good as to guard me against the like unhappiness by marrying me 75 prudentially by way of bargain and sale. For as you well judge, a woman that is espoused for a fortune is yet a better bargain if she dies, for then a man still enjoys what he did marry, the money, and is disencumbered of what he did not marry, the 80 woman.

SIR JOHN BEVIL.

But pray sir, do you think Lucinda then a woman of such little merit?

BEVIL JUNIOR.

Pardon me, sir, I don't carry it so far neither; I am rather afraid I shall like her too well: she has, for 85 one of her fortune, a great many needless and superfluous good qualities.

SIR JOHN BEVIL.

I am afraid, son, there's something I don't see yet, something that's smothered under all this raillery.

BEVIL JUNIOR.

Not in the least, sir. If the lady is dressed and ready, 90 you see I am. I suppose the lawyers are ready too.

HUMPHREY.(*Aside.*)

This may grow warm, if I don't interpose.—Sir, Mr. Sealand is at the coffee house and has sent to speak with you.

SIR JOHN BEVIL.

Oh! That's well! Then I warrant the lawyers are 95 ready.—Son, you'll be in the way, you say—

BEVIL JUNIOR.

If you please, sir, I'll take a chair* and go to Mr.

Sealand's, where the young lady and I will wait
your leisure.

SIR JOHN BEVIL.

By no means. The old fellow will be so vain, if he   100
sees—

BEVIL JUNIOR.

Aye, but the young lady, sir, will think me so
indifferent—

HUMPHREY. (*Aside to Bevil Junior.*)

Aye, there you are right. Press your readiness to go
to the bride. He won't let you.   105

BEVIL JUNIOR. (*Aside to Humphrey.*)

Are you sure of that?

HUMPHREY. (*Aside.*)

How he likes being prevented.

SIR JOHN BEVIL. (*Looking on his watch.*)

No, no. You are an hour or two too early.

BEVIL JUNIOR.

You'll allow me, sir, to think it too late to visit a
beautiful, virtuous young woman, in the pride and   110
bloom of life, ready to give herself to my arms, and to
place her happiness or misery for the future in being
agreeable or displeasing to me, is a—Call a chair.

SIR JOHN BEVIL.

No, no, no, dear Jack, this Sealand is a moody old
fellow. There's no dealing with some people, but   115
by managing with indifference. We must leave to
him the conduct of this day. It is the last of his
commanding his daughter.

BEVIL JUNIOR.

Sir, he can't take it ill that I am impatient to be
hers.   120

SIR JOHN BEVIL.

Pray let me govern in this matter. You can't tell how
humoursome old fellows are. There's no offering
reason to some of 'em, especially when they are
rich. (*Aside.*) If my son should see him before I've
brought old Sealand into better temper, the match   125
would be impracticable.

HUMPHREY. (*Aside to Sir John.*)

Pray sir, let me beg you to let Mr. Bevil go. See,
whether he will or not. (*To Bevil Junior.*) Pray sir,
command yourself; since you see my master is
positive, it is better you should not go.   130

BEVIL JUNIOR.

My father commands me as to the object of my

affections, but I hope he will not as to the warmth
and height of them.

SIR JOHN BEVIL.

So! I must even leave things as I found them. And
in the meantime, at least, keep old Sealand out of   135
his sight.—Well son, I'll go myself and take orders
in your affair. You'll be in the way, I suppose, if I
send to you. I'll leave your old friend with you.—
Humphrey, don't let him stir, d'ye hear?—Your
servant, your servant. (*Exit.*)   140

HUMPHREY.

I have a sad time on't, sir, between you and my
master. I see you are unwilling, and I know his
violent inclinations for the match.—I must betray
neither and yet deceive you both for your common
good.—Heaven grant a good end of this matter.   145
But there is a lady, sir, that gives your father much
trouble and sorrow—you'll pardon me.

BEVIL JUNIOR.

Humphrey, I know thou art a friend to both, and
in that confidence, I dare tell thee—that lady—is
a woman of honor and virtue. You may assure   150
yourself, I never will marry without my father's
consent. But give me leave to say too, this
declaration does not come up to a promise that I
will take whomsoever he pleases.

HUMPHREY.

Come sir, I wholly understand you. You would   155
engage my services to free you from this woman
whom my master intends you, to make way in
time for the woman you have really a mind to.

BEVIL JUNIOR.

Honest Humphrey, you have always been an useful
friend to my father and myself. I beg you continue   160
your good offices and don't let us come to the
necessity of a dispute, for if we should dispute, I
must either part with more than life or lose the
best of fathers.

HUMPHREY.

My dear master, were I but worthy to know this   165
secret that so near concerns you, my life, my all
should be engaged to serve you. This, sir, I dare
promise: that I am sure I will and can be secret.
Your trust, at worst, but leaves you where you were,
and if I cannot serve you, I will at once be plain   170
and tell you so.

BEVIL JUNIOR.

That's all I ask. Thou hast made it now my interest to trust thee. Be patient, then, and hear the story of my heart.

HUMPHREY.

I am all attention, sir.   175

BEVIL JUNIOR.

You may remember, Humphrey, that in my last travels my father grew uneasy at my making so long a stay at Toulon.

HUMPHREY.

I remember it; he was apprehensive some woman had laid hold of you.   180

BEVIL JUNIOR.

His fears were just, for there I first saw this lady. She is of English birth: her father's name was Danvers, a younger brother of an ancient family and originally an eminent merchant of Bristol, who upon repeated misfortunes was reduced to go privately to the Indies.   185 In this retreat Providence again grew favorable to his industry and in six years time restored him to his former fortunes. On this he sent directions over that his wife and little family should follow him to the Indies. His wife, impatient to obey such welcome   190 orders, would not wait the leisure of a convoy but took the first occasion of a single ship, and with her husband's sister only and this daughter, then scarce seven years old, undertook the fatal voyage. For here, poor creature, she lost her liberty and life. She and   195 her family, with all they had, were unfortunately taken by a privateer from Toulon. Being thus made a prisoner, though as such not ill treated, yet the fright, the shock, and cruel disappointment seized with such violence upon her unhealthy frame, she   200 sickened, pined, and died at sea.

HUMPHREY.

Poor soul! Oh, the helpless infant!

BEVIL JUNIOR.

Her sister yet survived and had the care of her. The captain too proved to have humanity and became a father to her, for having himself married an   205 English woman, and being childless, he brought home into Toulon this her little countrywoman, presenting her, with all her dead mother's moveables of value, to his wife to be educated as his own adopted daughter.   210

HUMPHREY.

Fortune here seemed, again, to smile on her.

BEVIL JUNIOR.

Only to make her frowns more terrible. For in his height of fortune, this captain too, her benefactor, unfortunately was killed at sea, and dying intestate, his estate fell wholly to an advocate his brother, who   215 coming soon to take possession, there found, among his other riches, this blooming virgin at his mercy.

HUMPHREY.

He durst not, sure, abuse his power!

BEVIL JUNIOR.

No wonder if his pampered blood was fired at the sight of her—in short, he loved. But when all arts   220 and gentle means had failed to move, he offered too his menaces in vain, denouncing vengeance on her cruelty, demanding her to account for all her maintenance from her childhood, seized on her little fortune as his own inheritance, and was   225 dragging her by violence to prison when Providence at the instant interposed and sent me, by miracle, to relieve her.

HUMPHREY.

'Twas Providence indeed. But pray sir, after all this trouble, how came this lady at last to England?   230

BEVIL JUNIOR.

The disappointed advocate, finding she had so unexpected a support, on cooler thoughts, descended to a composition, which I, without her knowledge, secretly discharged.

HUMPHREY.

That generous concealment made the obligation   235 double.

BEVIL JUNIOR.

Having thus obtained her liberty, I prevailed, not without some difficulty, to see her safe to England, where no sooner arrived, but my father, jealous of my being imprudently engaged, immediately   240 proposed this other, fatal match that hangs upon my quiet.

HUMPHREY.

I find, sir, you are irrecoverably fixed upon this lady.

BEVIL JUNIOR.

As my vital life dwells in my heart. And yet you   245 see what I do to please my father: walk in this pageantry of dress, this splendid covering of sorrow. But, Humphrey, you have your lesson.

HUMPHREY.

Now sir, I have but one material question.

BEVIL JUNIOR.

Ask it freely.   250

HUMPHREY.

Is it, then, your own passion for this secret lady or hers for you that gives you this aversion to the match your father has proposed you?

BEVIL JUNIOR.

I shall appear, Humphrey, more romantic in my answer than in all the rest of my story. For though   255
I dote on her to death and have no little reason to believe she has the same thoughts for me, yet in all my acquaintance and utmost privacies with her, I never once directly told her that I loved.

HUMPHREY.

How was it possible to avoid it?   260

BEVIL JUNIOR.

My tender obligations to my father have laid so inviolable a restraint upon my conduct that, till I have his consent to speak, I am determined on that subject to be dumb forever.

HUMPHREY.

Well sir, to your praise be it spoken, you are   265
certainly the most unfashionable lover in Great Britain.

Enter Tom.

TOM.

Sir, Mr. Myrtle's at the next door and, if you are at leisure, will be glad to wait on you.

BEVIL JUNIOR.

Whenever he pleases—hold, Tom! Did you receive   270
no answer to my letter?

TOM.

Sir, I was desired to call again, for I was told her mother would not let her be out of her sight. But about an hour hence, Mrs. Phillis[b] said I should certainly have one.   275

BEVIL JUNIOR.

Very well.

Exit Tom.[c]

HUMPHREY.

Sir, I will take another opportunity. In the meantime, I only think it proper to tell you that from a secret I know, you may appear to your father as forward as you please to marry Lucinda,   280
without the least hazard of its coming to a conclusion—sir, your most obedient servant.

BEVIL JUNIOR.

Honest Humphrey, continue but my friend in this exigence and you shall always find me yours.

Exit Humphrey.

I long to hear how my letter has succeeded with   285
Lucinda, but I think it cannot fail. For at worst, were it possible she could take it ill, her resentment of my indifference may as probably occasion a delay as her taking it right.—Poor Myrtle, what terrors must he be in all this while? Since he knows   290
she is offered to me and refused to him, there is no conversing or taking any measures with him for his own service. But I ought to bear with my friend and use him as one in adversity:

All his disquiets by my own I prove,   295
The greatest grief's perplexity in love.

Exit.

Act II, scene i. The scene continues.

Enter Bevil Junior and Tom.

TOM.

Sir, Mr. Myrtle.

BEVIL JUNIOR.

Very well, do you step again and wait for an answer to my letter.

[Exit Tom.] Enter Myrtle.

BEVIL JUNIOR.

Well Charles, why so much care in thy countenance? Is there anything in this world deserves it? You, who   5
used to be so gay, so open, so vacant!

MYRTLE.

I think we have of late changed complexions. You, who used to be much the graver man, are now all air in your behavior. But the cause of my concern may, for aught I know, be the same object that   10
gives you all this satisfaction. In a word, I am told that you are this very day, and your dress confirms me in it, to be married to Lucinda.

BEVIL JUNIOR.

You are not misinformed. Nay, put not on the terrors of a rival till you hear me out. I shall disoblige the best of fathers, if I don't seem ready to marry Lucinda. And you know I have ever told you, you might make use of my secret resolution never to marry her for your own service, as you please. But I am now driven to the extremity of immediately refusing or complying, unless you help me to escape the match.

MYRTLE.

Escape? Sir, neither her merit or her fortune are below your acceptance. Escaping, do you call it!

BEVIL JUNIOR.

Dear sir, do you wish I should desire the match?

MYRTLE.

No, but such is my humorous* and sickly state of mind, since it has been able to relish nothing but Lucinda, that though I must owe my happiness to your aversion to this marriage, I can't bear to hear her spoken of with levity or unconcern.

BEVIL JUNIOR.

Pardon me, sir, I shall transgress that way no more. She has understanding, beauty, shape, complexion, wit—

MYRTLE.

Nay dear Bevil, don't speak of her as if you loved her, neither.

BEVIL JUNIOR.

Why then, to give you ease at once, though I allow Lucinda to have good sense, wit, beauty, and virtue, I know another in whom these qualities appear to me more amiable than in her.

MYRTLE.

There you spoke like a reasonable and good-natured friend. When you acknowledge her merit and own your prepossession for another at once, you gratify my fondness and cure my jealousy.

BEVIL JUNIOR.

But all this while you take no notice, you have no apprehension of another man that has twice the fortune of either of us.

MYRTLE.

Cimberton! Hang him, a formal, philosophical, pedantic coxcomb! For the sot,* with all these crude notions of diverse things, under the direction of great vanity and very little judgment, shows his strongest bias is avarice, which is so predominant in him that he will examine the limbs of his mistress with the caution of a jockey and pays no more compliment to her personal charms than if she were a mere breeding animal.

BEVIL JUNIOR.

Are you sure that is not affected? I have known some women sooner set on fire by that sort of negligence than by—

MYRTLE.

No, no, hang him, the rogue has no art; it is pure simple insolence and stupidity.

BEVIL JUNIOR.

Yet with all this, I don't take him for a fool.

MYRTLE.

I own the man is not a natural;* he has a very quick sense, though very slow understanding. He says indeed many things that want* only the circumstances of time and place to be very just and agreeable.

BEVIL JUNIOR.

Well, you may be sure of me, if you can dissapoint him, but my intelligence says the mother has actually sent for the conveyancer to draw articles for his marriage with Lucinda, though those for mine with her are, by her father's order, ready for signing. But it seems she has not thought fit to consult either him or his daughter in the matter.

MYRTLE.

Pshaw! A poor, troublesome woman. Neither Lucinda nor her father will ever be brought to comply with it. Besides, I am sure Cimberton can make no settlement upon her without the concurrence of his great uncle Sir Geoffry in the West.

BEVIL JUNIOR.

Well sir, and I can tell you, that's the very point that is now laid before her counsel: to know whether a firm settlement can be made without his uncle's actual joining in it. Now pray consider, sir, when my affair with Lucinda comes, as it soon must, to an open rupture, how are you sure that Cimberton's fortune may not then tempt her father too to hear his proposals?

MYRTLE.

There you are right indeed. That must be provided against. Do you know who are her counsel?

BEVIL JUNIOR.

Yes, for your service I have found out that too: they are Serjeant[19] Bramble and old Target. By the way, they are neither of 'em known in the family; now I was thinking why you might not put a couple of false counsel upon her to delay and confound matters a little. Besides, it may probably let you into the bottom of her whole design against you.

MYRTLE.

As how, pray?

BEVIL JUNIOR.

Why, can't you slip on a black wig and a gown and be old Bramble yourself?

MYRTLE.

Hah! I don't dislike it. But what shall I do for a brother in the case?

BEVIL JUNIOR.

What think you of my fellow, Tom? The rogue's intelligent and is a good mimic; all his part will be but to stutter heartily, for that's old Target's case. Nay, it would be an immoral thing to mock him, were it not that his impertinence is the occasion of its breaking out to that degree. The conduct of the scene will chiefly lie upon you.

MYRTLE.

I like it of all things. If you'll send Tom to my chambers, I will give him full instructions. This will certainly give me occasion to raise difficulties, to puzzle, or confound her project for a while at least.

BEVIL JUNIOR.

I'll warrant you success. So far we are right then. And now, Charles, your apprehension of my marrying her is all you have to get over.

MYRTLE.

Dear Bevil! Though I know you are my friend, yet when I abstract myself from my own interest in the thing, I know no objection she can make to you or you to her and therefore hope——

BEVIL JUNIOR.

Dear Myrtle, I am as much obliged to you for the cause of your suspicion as I am offended at the effect. But be assured, I am taking measures for your certain security and that all things with regard to me will end in your entire satisfaction.

19 Serjeant] serjeant-at-law (q.v.)

MYRTLE.

Well, I'll promise you to be as easy and as confident as I can, though I cannot but remember that I have more than life at stake on your fidelity. (*Going.*)

BEVIL JUNIOR.

Then depend upon it, you have no chance against you.

MYRTLE.

Nay no ceremony, you know I must be going. (*Exit.*)

BEVIL JUNIOR.

Well! This is another instance of the perplexities which arise too in faithful friendship. We must often in this life go on in our good offices, even under the displeasure of those to whom we do them, in compassion to their weaknesses and mistakes.—But all this while poor Indiana is tortured with the doubt of me! She has no support or comfort but in my fidelity yet sees me daily pressed to marriage with another! How painful in such a crisis must be every hour she thinks on me? I'll let her see at least my conduct to her is not changed. I'll take this opportunity to visit her, for though the religious vow I have made to my father restrains me from ever marrying without his approbation, yet that confines me not from seeing a virtuous woman that is the pure delight of my eyes and the guiltless joy of my heart. But the best condition of human life is but a gentler misery.
To hope for perfect happiness is vain,
And love has ever its alloys of pain.

Exit.

[Scene ii. Indiana's lodgings.]

Enter Isabella and Indiana.

ISABELLA.

Yes, I say 'tis artifice, dear child; I say to thee again and again, 'tis all skill and management.

INDIANA.

Will you persuade me there can be an ill design in supporting me in the condition of a woman of quality?* Attended, dressed, and lodged like one in my appearance abroad and my furniture at home, every way in the most sumptuous manner, and he that does it has an artifice, a design in it?

ISABELLA.

Yes, yes.

INDIANA.

And all this without so much as explaining to me 10
that all about me comes from him!

ISABELLA.

Aye, aye, the more for that. That keeps the title
to all you have the more in him.

INDIANA.

The more in him! He scorns the thought—

ISABELLA.

Then he—he—he— 15

INDIANA.

Well, be not so eager. If he is an ill man, let us look
into his stratagems. Here is another of them.
(*Showing a letter.*) Here's two hundred and fifty
pound in bank notes, with these words, "To pay for
the set of dressing-plate,[20] which will be brought 20
home tomorrow." Why dear aunt, now here's
another piece of skill for you, which I own I cannot
comprehend. And it is with a bleeding heart I hear
you say anything to the disadvantage of Mr. Bevil.
When he is present, I look upon him as one to 25
whom I owe my life and the support of it. Then
again, as the man who loves me with sincerity and
honor. When his eyes are cast another way and I
dare survey him, my heart is painfully divided
between shame and love. Oh, could I tell you— 30

ISABELLA.

Ah, you need not. I imagine all this for you.

INDIANA.

This is my state of mind in his presence, and when
he is absent, you are ever dinning my ears with
notions of the arts of men: that his hidden bounty,
his respectful conduct, his careful provision for me, 35
after his preserving me from utmost misery, are
certain signs he means nothing but to make I
know not what of me.

ISABELLA.

Oh! You have a sweet opinion of him, truly.

INDIANA.

I have when I am with him ten thousand things 40
besides my sex's natural decency and shame to
suppress my heart that yearns to thank, to praise,

_____

20 dressing-plate] silver-covered articles for the toilet*

to say it loves him. I say, thus it is with me while
I see him, and in his absence I am entertained with
nothing but your endeavors to tear this amiable 45
image from my heart and in its stead to place a
base dissembler, an artful invader of my happiness,
my innocence, my honor.

ISABELLA.

Ah poor soul! Has not his plot taken? Don't you
die for him? Has not the way he has taken been 50
the most proper with you? Oh ho! He has sense
and has judged the thing right.

INDIANA.

Go on then, since nothing can answer you; say
what you will of him. Heigh ho!

ISABELLA.

Heigh ho, indeed! It is better to say so, as you are 55
now, than as many others are. There are among the
destroyers of women the gentle,* the generous,* the
mild, the affable, the humble, who all, soon after
their success in their designs, turn to the contrary of
those characters. I will own to you, Mr. Bevil carries 60
his hypocrisy the best of any man living, but still he
is a man, and therefore a hypocrite. They have
usurped an exemption from shame for any baseness,
any cruelty towards us. They embrace without love;
they make vows without conscience of obligation; 65
they are partners, nay, seducers to the crime wherein
they pretend to be less guilty.

INDIANA. (*Aside.*)

That's truly observed.—But what's all this to Bevil?

ISABELLA.

This it is to Bevil and all mankind: trust not those
who will think the worse of you for your 70
confidence in them. Serpents who lie in wait for
doves. Won't you be on your guard against those
who would betray you? Won't you doubt those
who would condemn you for believing 'em? Take
it from me, fair and natural dealing is to invite 75
injuries; 'tis bleating to escape wolves who would
devour you! Such is the world. (*Aside.*) And such
(since behavior of one man to myself) have I
believed all the rest of the sex.

INDIANA.

I will not doubt* the truth of Bevil; I will not 80
doubt it. He has not spoke it by an organ that is
given to lying. His eyes are all that have ever told

me that he was mine. I know his virtue, I know his filial piety, and ought to trust his management with a father to whom he has uncommon 85 obligations. What have I to be concerned for? My lesson is very short. If he takes me forever, my purpose of life is only to please him. If he leaves me, which Heaven avert, I know he'll do it nobly, and I shall have nothing to do but to learn to die 90 after worse than death has happened to me.

ISABELLA.

Aye, do, persist in your credulity! Flatter yourself that a man of his figure and fortune will make himself the jest of the Town* and marry a handsome beggar for love. 95

INDIANA.

The Town! I must tell you, madam, the fools that laugh at Mr. Bevil will but make themselves more ridiculous; his actions are the result of thinking, and he has sense enough to make even virtue fashionable. 100

ISABELLA.

Oh my conscience, he has turned her head. Come, come, if he were the honest* fool you take him for, why has he kept you here these three weeks without sending you to Bristol in search of your father, your family, and your relations? 105

INDIANA.

I am convinced he still designs it and that nothing keeps him here but the necessity of not coming to a breach with his father in regard to the match he has proposed him. Beside, has he not writ to Bristol? And has not he advice that my father has 110 not been heard of there almost these twenty years?

ISABELLA.

All sham, mere evasion; he is afraid if he should carry you thither, your honest relations may take you out of his hands and so blow up all his wicked hopes at once. 115

INDIANA.

Wicked hopes! Did I ever give him any such?

ISABELLA.

Has he ever given you any honest* ones? Can you say, in your conscience, he has ever once offered to marry you?

INDIANA.

No! But by his behavior I am convinced he will offer 120

it the moment 'tis in his power or consistent with his honor to make such a promise good to me.

ISABELLA.

His honor!

INDIANA.

I will rely upon it, therefore desire you will not make my life uneasy by these ungrateful jealousies 125 of one to whom I am and wish to be obliged. For from his integrity alone, I have resolved to hope for happiness.

ISABELLA.

Nay, I have done my duty; if you won't see, at your peril be it— 130

INDIANA.

Let it be. This is his hour of visiting me.

ISABELLA. (*Apart.*)

Oh, to be sure, keep up your form, don't see him in a bedchamber. This is pure prudence, when she is liable, wherever he meets her, to be conveyed where'er he pleases. 135

INDIANA.

All the rest of my life is but waiting till he comes. I live only when I'm with him. (*Exit.*)

ISABELLA.

Well, go thy ways, thou willful innocent! I once had almost as much love for a man who poorly left me to marry an estate. And I am now, against 140 my will, what they call an old maid. But I will not let the peevishness of that condition grow upon me, only keep up the suspicion of it to prevent this creature's being any other than a virgin, except upon proper terms. (*Exit.*) 145

Re-enter Indiana, speaking to a servant.

INDIANA.

Desire Mr. Bevil to walk in.—Design! Impossible! A base designing mind could never think of what he hourly puts in practice. And yet, since the late rumor of his marriage, he seems more reserved than former- ly. He sends in too, before he sees me, to know if I am 150 at leisure. Such new respect may cover coldness in the heart. It certainly makes me thoughtful. I'll know the worst at once; I'll lay such fair occasions in his way that it shall be impossible to avoid an explanation. For these doubts are insupportable!—But see! he 155 comes, and clears them all.

Enter Bevil Junior

BEVIL JUNIOR.

Madam, your most obedient. I am afraid I broke in upon your rest last night. 'Twas very late before we parted, but 'twas your own fault. I never saw you in such agreeable humor. 160

INDIANA.

I am extremely glad we were both pleased, for I thought I never saw you better company.

BEVIL JUNIOR.

Me, madam! You rally; I said very little.

INDIANA.

But I am afraid you heard me say a great deal, and when a woman is in the talking vein, the most 165 agreeable thing a man can do, you know, is to have patience to hear her.

BEVIL JUNIOR.

Then it's pity, madam, you should ever be silent, that we might be always agreeable to one another.

INDIANA.

If I had your talent or power to make my actions 170 speak for me, I might indeed be silent and yet pretend to something more than the agreeable.

BEVIL JUNIOR.

If I might be vain of anything in my power, madam, 'tis that my understanding from all your sex has marked you out as the most deserving 175 object of my esteem.

INDIANA.

Should I think I deserve this, 'twere enough to make my vanity forfeit the very esteem you offer me.

BEVIL JUNIOR.

How so, madam? 180

INDIANA.

Because esteem is the result of reason, and to deserve it from good sense, the height of human glory. Nay, I had rather a man of honor should pay me that than all the homage of a sincere and humble love. 185

BEVIL JUNIOR.

You certainly distinguish right, madam; love often kindles from external merit only—

INDIANA.

But esteem arises from a higher source, the merit of the soul—

BEVIL JUNIOR.

True. And great souls only can deserve it. (*Bowing* 190 *respectfully.*)

INDIANA.

Now, I think, they are greater still that can so charitably part with it.

BEVIL JUNIOR.

Now madam, you make me vain, since the utmost pride and pleasure of my life is that I esteem you— as I ought. 195

INDIANA. (*Aside.*)

As he ought! Still more perplexing! He neither saves nor kills my hope.

BEVIL JUNIOR.

But madam, we grow grave methinks. Let's find some other subject.—Pray how did you like the opera last night? 200

INDIANA.

First give me leave to thank you for my tickets.

BEVIL JUNIOR.

Oh your servant, madam. But pray tell me, you now, who are never partial to the fashion, I fancy must be the properest judge of a mighty dispute among the ladies, that is, whether *Crispo* or 205 *Griselda*[21] is the more agreeable entertainment.

INDIANA.

With submission now, I cannot be a proper judge of this question.

BEVIL JUNIOR.

How so, madam?

INDIANA.

Because I find I have a partiality for one of them. 210

BEVIL JUNIOR.

Pray which is that?

INDIANA.

I do not know. There's something in that rural cottage of Griselda, her forlorn condition, her poverty, her solitude, her resignation, her innocent slumbers, and that lulling "Dolce Sogno"[22] that's 215 sung over her; it had an effect upon me that—in

---

21 *Griselda*] the patient wife portrayed in another recent popular Italian Opera by Bononcini and Rolli, based on a story by both Boccaccio and Chaucer recounting her trials at the hands of a cruel husband

22 "Dolce Sogno"] "Sweet Dream" (It.)

short I never was so well deceived at any of them.

BEVIL JUNIOR.

Oh! Now then, I can account for the dispute: *Griselda*, it seems, is the distress of an injured innocent woman; *Crispo* that only of a man in the 220 same condition. Therefore the men are mostly concerned for *Crispo*, and, by a natural indulgence, both sexes for *Griselda*.

INDIANA.

So that judgment, you think, ought to be for one, though fancy and complaisance have got ground 225 for the other. Well! I believe you will never give me leave to dispute with you on any subject, for I own *Crispo* has its charms for me too. Though in the main, all the pleasure the best opera gives us is but mere sensation. Methinks it's pity the mind 230 can't have a little more share in the entertainment. The music's certainly fine, but in my thoughts there's none of your* composers come up to old Shakespeare and Otway.

BEVIL JUNIOR.

How, madam! Why if a woman of your sense were 235 to say this in the Drawing Room*—

Enter a servant.

SERVANT.

Sir, here's Signior Carbonelli says he waits your commands in the next room.

BEVIL JUNIOR.

Apropos! You were saying yesterday, madam, you had a mind to hear him. Will you give him leave 240 to entertain you now?

INDIANA.

By all means.—Desire the gentleman to walk in.
Exit servant.

BEVIL JUNIOR.

I fancy you will find something in this hand that is uncommon.

INDIANA.

You are always finding ways, Mr. Bevil, to make 245 life seem less tedious to me.

Enter music master.

When the Gentleman pleases.

After a sonata is played, Bevil waits on the master to the door, etc.

BEVIL JUNIOR.

You smile, madam, to see me so complaisant to one whom I pay for his visit. Now, I own I think it is not enough barely to pay those whose talents 250 are superior to our own—I mean such talents as would become our condition, if we had them. Methinks we ought to do something more than barely gratify them for what they do at our command only because their fortune is below us. 255

INDIANA.

You say I smile. I assure you it was a smile of approbation, for indeed I cannot but think it the distinguishing part of a gentleman to make his superiority of fortune as easy to his inferiors as he can. (*Aside.*) Now once more to try him.—I was 260 saying just now, I believed you would never let me dispute with you, and I dare say it will always be so. However I must have your opinion upon a subject which created a debate between my aunt and me just before you came hither. She would needs have 265 it that no man ever does any extra-ordinary kindness or service for a woman but for his own sake.

BEVIL JUNIOR.

Well, madam! Indeed I can't but be of her mind.

INDIANA.

What, though he should maintain and support her without demanding anything of her on her part? 270

BEVIL JUNIOR.

Why madam, is making an expense in the service of a valuable woman, for such I must suppose her, though she should never do him any favor, nay, though she should never know who did her such service, such a mighty heroic business? 275

INDIANA.

Certainly! I should think he must be a man of an uncommon mold.

BEVIL JUNIOR.

Dear madam, why so? 'Tis but, at best, a better taste in expense. To bestow upon one whom he may think one of the ornaments of the whole 280 creation, to be conscious that from his superfluity an innocent, a virtuous spirit is supported above the temptations and sorrows of life! That he sees satisfaction, health, and gladness in her countenance while he enjoys the happiness of 285 seeing her, as that I will suppose too, or he must be too abstracted, too insensible. I say, if he is allowed to delight in that prospect, alas, what mighty matter is there in all this?

INDIANA.

No mighty matter in so disinterested a friendship! 290

BEVIL JUNIOR.

Disinterested! I can't think him so. Your hero, madam, is no more than what every gentleman ought to be, and I believe very many are. He is only one who takes more delight in reflections than in sensations. He is more pleased with thinking 295 than eating. That's the utmost you can say of him. Why madam, a greater expense than all this men lay out upon an unnecessary stable of horses.

INDIANA.

Can you be sincere in what you say?

BEVIL JUNIOR.

You may depend upon it. If you know any such 300 man, he does not love dogs inordinately.

INDIANA.

No, that he does not.

BEVIL JUNIOR.

Nor cards, nor dice.

INDIANA.

No.

BEVIL JUNIOR.

Nor bottle companions. 305

INDIANA.

No.

BEVIL JUNIOR.

Nor loose women.

INDIANA.

No, I'm sure he does not.

BEVIL JUNIOR.

Take my word then, if your admired hero is not liable to any of these kind of demands, there's no 310 such preeminence in this as you imagine. Nay, this way of expense you speak of is what exalts and raises him that has a taste for it. And at the same time, his delight is incapable of satiety, disgust, or penitence.

INDIANA.

But still I insist his having no private interest in 315 the action makes it prodigious, almost incredible.

BEVIL JUNIOR.

Dear madam, I never knew you more mistaken. Why, who can be more an usurer than he who lays out his money in such valuable purchases? If pleasure be worth purchasing, how great a pleasure 320 is it to him, who has a true taste of life, to ease an aching heart, to see the human countenance lighted up into smiles of joy on the receipt of a bit of ore which is superfluous and otherwise useless in a man's own pocket? What could a man do better 325 with his cash? This is the effect of an humane disposition, where there is only a general tie of nature and common necessity. What then must it be when we serve an object of merit, of admiration!

INDIANA.

Well! The more you argue against it, the more I 330 shall admire the generosity.

BEVIL JUNIOR.

Nay, nay. Then madam, 'tis time to fly after a declaration that my opinion strengthens my adversary's argument. I had best hasten to my appointment with Mr. Myrtle and be gone while 335 we are friends and—before things are brought to an extremity— (*Exit carelessly.*)

Enter Isabella.

ISABELLA.

Well madam, what think you of him now pray?

INDIANA.

I protest I begin to fear he is wholly disinterested in what he does for me. On my heart, he has no 340 other view but the mere pleasure of doing it and has neither good or bad designs upon me.

ISABELLA.

Ah dear niece! Don't be in fear of both! I'll warrant you, you will know time enough that he is not indifferent. 345

INDIANA.

You please me when you tell me so. For if he has any wishes towards me, I know he will not pursue them but with honor.

ISABELLA.

I wish I were as confident of one as t'other. I saw the respectful downcast of his eye when you caught 350 him gazing at you during the music. He, I warrant, was surprised, as if he had been taken stealing your watch. Oh, the undissembled guilty look.

INDIANA.

But did you observe any such thing, really? I thought he looked most charmingly graceful! How 355 engaging is modesty in a man when one knows there is a great mind within. So tender a confusion! And yet, in other respects, so much himself, so collected, so dauntless, so determined!

ISABELLA.

Ah niece! There is a sort of bashfulness, which is the best engine* to carry on a shameless purpose. Some men's modesty serves their wickedness, as hypocrisy gains the respect due to piety. But I will own to you, there is one hopeful symptom, if there could be such a thing as a disinterested lover. But it's all a perplexity, till—till—till— 365

INDIANA.

Till what?

ISABELLA.

Till I know whether Mr. Myrtle and Mr. Bevil are really friends or foes. And that I will be convinced of before I sleep, for you shall not be deceived. 370

INDIANA.

I'm sure I never shall, if your fears can guard me. In the meantime, I'll wrap myself up in the integrity of my own heart, nor dare to doubt of his.

As conscious honor all his actions steers, 375
So conscious innocence dispels my fears.

Exeunt.

Act III. Sealand's house.

Enter Tom meeting Phillis.

TOM.

Well Phillis, what, with a face as if you had never seen me before. (*Aside.*) What a work have I to do now? She has seen some new visitant at their house whose airs she has caught and is resolved to practice them upon me. Numberless are the 5 changes she'll dance through before she'll answer this plain question, videlicet, have you delivered my master's letter to your lady? Nay, I know her too well to ask an account of it in an ordinary way; I'll be in my airs as well as she.—Well madam, as 10 unhappy as you are at present pleased to make me, I would not, in the general, be any other than what I am. I would not be a bit wiser, a bit richer, a bit taller, a bit shorter than I am at this instant. (*Looking steadfastly at her.*)

PHILLIS.

Did ever anybody doubt, Master Thomas, but that 15 you were extremely satisfied with your sweet self?

TOM.

I am indeed. The thing I have least reason to be satisfied with is my fortune, and I am glad of my poverty. Perhaps if I were rich, I should overlook the finest woman in the world that wants* nothing 20 but riches to be thought so.

PHILLIS. (*Aside.*)

How prettily was that said? But, I'll have a great deal more before I'll say one word.

TOM.

I should, perhaps, have been stupidly above her had I not been her equal and, by not being her 25 equal, never had opportunity of being her slave. I am my master's servant for hire; I am my mistress's from choice, would she but approve my passion.

PHILLIS.

I think it's the first time I ever heard you speak of it with any sense of the anguish, if you really do 30 suffer any.

TOM.

Ah Phillis, can you doubt after what you have seen?

PHILLIS.

I know not what I have seen, nor what I have heard. But since I'm at leisure, you may tell me when you 35 fell in love with me, how you fell in love with me, and what you have suffered or are ready to suffer for me.

TOM. (*Aside.*)

Oh the unmerciful jade! When I'm in haste about my master's letter. But I must go through it.—Ah, too well I remember when and how and on what 40 occasion I was first surprised. It was on the first of April, one thousand seven hundred and fifteen, I came into Mr. Sealand's service. I was then a hobbledehoy and you a pretty little tight girl, a favorite handmaid of the housekeeper. At that 45 time, we neither of us knew what was in us. I remember I was ordered to get out of the window, one pair of stairs,[23] to rub the sashes clean. The person employed on the innerside was your charming self, whom I had never seen before. 50

23 one pair of stairs] one flight up

PHILLIS.

I think I remember the silly accident. What made ye, you oaf, ready to fall down into the street?

TOM.

You know not, I warrant you. You could not guess what surprised me. You took no delight when you immediately grew wanton in your conquest and put your lips close and breathed upon the glass, and when my lips approached, a dirty cloth you rubbed against my face and hid your beauteous form. When I again drew near, you spit and rubbed and smiled at my undoing.

PHILLIS.

What silly thoughts you men have!

TOM.

We were Pyramus and Thisbe, but ten times harder was my fate. Pyramus could peep only through a wall; I saw her, saw my Thisbe in all her beauty but as much kept from her as if a hundred walls between, for there was more, there was her will against me. Would she but yet relent! Oh Phillis! Phillis! Shorten my torment and declare you pity me.

PHILLIS.

I believe it's very sufferable; the pain is not so exquisite but that you may bear it a little longer.

TOM.

Oh my charming Phillis, if all depended on my fair one's will, I could with glory suffer. But dearest creature, consider our miserable state.

PHILLIS.

How! Miserable!

TOM.

We are miserable to be in love and under the command of others than those we love. With that generous passion in the heart, to be sent to and fro on errands, called, checked, and rated for the meanest trifles. Oh Phillis! You don't know how many china cups and glasses my passion for you has made me break. You have broke my fortune as well as my heart.

PHILLIS.

Well Mr. Thomas, I cannot but own to you that I believe your master writes and you speak the best of any men of the world. Never was woman so well pleased with a letter, as my young lady was with his, and this is an answer to it. (*Gives him a letter.*)

TOM.

This was well done, my dearest. Consider we must strike out some pretty livelihood for ourselves by closing their affairs. It will be nothing for them to give us a little being of our own, some small tenement out of their large possessions. Whatever they give us, 'twill be more than what they keep for themselves. One acre, with Phillis, would be worth a whole county without her.

PHILLIS.

Oh, could I but believe you!

TOM.

If not the utterance, believe the touch of my lips. (*Kisses her.*)

PHILLIS.

There's no contradicting you. How closely you argue, Tom!

TOM.

And will closer, in due time. But I must hasten with this letter, to hasten towards the possession of you. Then Phillis, consider how I must be revenged, look to it, of all your skittishness, shy looks, and at best but coy compliances.

PHILLIS.

Oh Tom, you grow wanton and sensual, as my lady calls it. I must not endure it. Oh! Faugh! You are a man, an odious filthy male creature; you should behave, if you had a right sense or were a man of sense like Mr. Cimberton, with distance and indifference or, let me see some other becoming hard word, with seeming in- in- inadvertency, and not rush on one as if you were seizing a prey. But hush—the ladies are coming. Good[d] Tom, don't kiss me above once and be gone. Lard, we have been fooling and toying and not considered the main business of our masters and mistresses.

TOM.

Why, their business is to be fooling and toying as soon as the parchments are ready.

PHILLIS.

Well remembered—parchments—my lady, to my knowledge, is preparing writings between her coxcomb cousin Cimberton and my mistress, though my master has an eye to the parchments already prepared between your master Mr. Bevil and my mistress, and I believe my mistress herself

has signed and sealed, in her heart, to Mr. 125
Myrtle.—Did I not bid you kiss me but once and
be gone? But I know you won't be satisfied.

TOM.

No, you smooth creature, how should I! (*Kissing
her hand.*)

PHILLIS.

Well, since you are so humble, or so cool, as to
ravish my hand only, I'll take my leave of you like 130
a great lady and you a man of quality.* (*They
salute* formally.*)

TOM.

Pox of all this state. (*Offers to kiss her more closely.*)

PHILLIS.

No, prithee, Tom, mind your business. We must
follow that interest which will take, but endeavor
at that which will be most for us and we like 135
most.—Oh here's my young mistress!

Tom taps her neck behind and kisses his fingers.

Go, ye lickerish fool.

Exit Tom. Enter Lucinda.

LUCINDA.

Who was that you was hurrying away?

PHILLIS.

One that I had no mind to part with.

LUCINDA.

Why did you turn him away then? 140

PHILLIS.

For your ladyship's service, to carry your ladyship's
letter to his master. I could hardly get the rogue
away.

LUCINDA.

Why, has he so little love for his master?

PHILLIS.

No, but he has so much love for his mistress. 145

LUCINDA.

But I thought I heard him kiss you. Why do you
suffer that?

PHILLIS.

Why madam, we vulgar take it to be a sign of love.
We servants, we poor people that have nothing but
our persons to bestow or treat for are forced to deal 150
and bargain by way of sample. And therefore, as
we have no parchments or wax necessary in our
agreements, we squeeze with our hands and seal

with our lips to ratify vows and promises.

LUCINDA.

But can't you trust one another without such 155
earnest down?

PHILLIS.

We don't think it safe, any more than you gentry,
to come together without deeds executed.

LUCINDA.

Thou art a pert, merry hussy.

PHILLIS.

I wish, madam, your lover and you were as happy 160
as Tom and your servant are.

LUCINDA.

You grow impertinent.

PHILLIS.

I have done, madam, and I won't ask you what you
intend to do with Mr. Myrtle, what your father
will do with Mr. Bevil, nor what you all, especially 165
my lady, mean by admitting Mr. Cimberton as
particularly here as if he were married to you
already. Nay, you are married actually as far as
people of quality* are.

LUCINDA.

How's that? 170

PHILLIS.

You have different beds in the same house.

LUCINDA.

Pshaw! I have a very great value for Mr. Bevil, but
have absolutely put an end to his pretensions in
the letter I gave you for him. But my father, in his
heart, still has a mind to him, were it not for this 175
woman they talk of, and I am apt to imagine he
is married to her, or never designs to marry at all.

PHILLIS.

Then Mr. Myrtle—

LUCINDA.

He had my parents' leave to apply to me and by
that has won me and my affections. Who is to have 180
this body of mine without 'em, it seems, is nothing
to me. My mother says it's indecent for me to let
my thoughts stray about the person of my
husband. Nay, she says a maid rigidly virtuous,
though she may have been where her lover was a 185
thousand times, should not have made
observations enough to know him from another
man when she sees him in a third place.

PHILLIS.

That is more than the severity of a nun, for not to see, when one may, is hardly possible; not to see when one can't, is very easy. At this rate, madam, there are a great many whom you have not seen who— 190

LUCINDA.

Mamma says the first time you see your husband should be at that instant he is made so, when your father, with the help of the minister, gives you to him. Then you are to see him, then you are to observe and take notice of him, because then you are to obey him. 195

PHILLIS.

But does not my lady remember you are to love as well as obey? 200

LUCINDA.

To love is a passion, 'tis a desire, and we must have no desires. Oh! I cannot endure the reflection! With what insensibility on my part, with what more than patience, have I been exposed and offered to some awkward booby or other in every county of Great Britain? 205

PHILLIS.

Indeed madam, I wonder I never heard you speak of it before with this indignation.

LUCINDA.

Every corner of the land has presented me with a wealthy coxcomb. As fast as one treaty has gone off, another has come on, till my name and person have been the tittle-tattle of the whole Town. What is this world come to! No shame left! To be bartered for like the beasts of the fields, and that in such an instance as coming together to an entire familiarity and union of soul and body. Oh! And this without being so much as well-wishers to each other, but for increase of fortune. 210

215

PHILLIS.

But madam, all these vexations will end very soon in one for all. Mr. Cimberton is your mother's kinsman, and three hundred years an older gentleman than any lover you ever had, for which reason, with that of his prodigious large estate, she is resolved on him and has sent to consult the lawyers accordingly. Nay, has, whether you know it or no, been in treaty with Sir Geoffry, who, to join 220

225

in the settlement, has accepted of a sum to do it and is every moment expected in Town for that purpose.

LUCINDA.

How do you get all this intelligence? 230

PHILLIS.

By an art I have, I thank my stars, beyond all the waiting maids in Great Britain, the art of list'ning, madam, for your ladyship's service.

LUCINDA.

I shall soon know as much as you do. Leave me, leave me, Phillis, be gone. Here, here, I'll turn you out. My mother says I must not converse with my servants, though I must converse with no one else. 235

Exit Phillis.

How unhappy are we who are born to great fortunes! No one looks at us with indifference or acts toward us on the foot of plain dealing. Yet by all I have been heretofore offered to or treated for, I have been used with the most agreeable of all abuses, flattery. But now, by this phlegmatic fool, I am used as nothing or a mere thing. He, forsooth, is too wise, too learned to have any regard to desires, and I know not what the learned oaf calls sentiments of love and passion.—Here he comes with my mother. It's much if he looks at me or, if he does, takes no more notice of me than of any other moveable in the room. 240

245

250

Enter Mrs. Sealand and Mr. Cimberton.

MRS. SEALAND.

How do I admire this noble, this learned taste of yours, and the worthy regard you have to our own ancient and honorable house in consulting a means to keep the blood as pure and as regularly descended as may be. 255

CIMBERTON.

Why really madam, the young women of this age are treated with discourses of such a tendency, and their imaginations so bewildered in flesh and blood, that a man of reason can't talk to be understood. They have no ideas of happiness, but what are more gross than the gratification of hunger and thirst. 260

LUCINDA. (*Aside.*)

With how much reflection he is a coxcomb?

CIMBERTON.

And in truth, madam, I have considered it as a most brutal custom that persons of the first 265 character in the world should go as ordinarily, and with as little shame, to bed, as to dinner with one another. They proceed to the propagation of the species as openly as to the preservation of the individual. 270

LUCINDA. (*Aside.*)

She that willingly goes to bed to thee must have no shame, I'm sure.

MRS. SEALAND.

Oh Cousin Cimberton! Cousin Cimberton! How abstracted, how refined is your sense of things! But indeed, it is too true, there is nothing so ordinary 275 as to say in the best governed families, "My master and lady are gone to bed." One does not know but it might have been said of one's self. (*Hiding her face with her fan.*)

CIMBERTON.

Lycurgus, madam, instituted otherwise. Among 280 the Lacedaemonians, the whole female world was pregnant, but none but the mothers themselves knew by whom. Their meetings were secret, and the amorous congress always by stealth, and no such professed doings between the sexes as are 285 tolerated among us under the audacious word, marriage.

MRS. SEALAND.

Oh, had I lived in those days and been a matron of Sparta, one might with less indecency have had ten children according to that modest institution 290 than one under the confusion of our modern, barefaced manner.

LUCINDA. (*Aside.*)

And yet, poor woman, she has gone through the whole ceremony, and here I stand a melancholy proof of it. 295

MRS. SEALAND.

We will talk then of business. That girl walking about the room there is to be your wife. She has, I confess, no ideas, no sentiments, that speak her born of a thinking mother.

CIMBERTON.

I have observed her; her lively look, free air, and 300 disengaged countenance speak her very—

LUCINDA.

Very what?

CIMBERTON.

If you please, madam, to set her a little that way.

MRS. SEALAND.

Lucinda, say nothing to him; you are not a match for him. When you are married, you may speak 305 to such a husband when you're spoken to. But I am disposing of you above yourself every way.

CIMBERTON.

Madam, you cannot but observe the inconveniences I expose myself to in hopes that your ladyship will be the consort of my better part. 310 As for the young woman, she is rather an impediment than a help to a man of letters and speculation.[24] Madam, there is no reflection, no philosophy, can at all times subdue the sensitive[25] life, but the animal shall sometimes carry away the 315 man. Hah! Ay, the vermilion of her lips.

LUCINDA.

Pray, don't talk of me thus.

CIMBERTON.

The pretty enough—pant of her bosom.

LUCINDA.

Sir! Madam, don't you hear him?

CIMBERTON.

Her forward chest. 320

LUCINDA.

Intolerable!

CIMBERTON.

High health.

LUCINDA.

The grave, easy impudence of him!

CIMBERTON.

Proud heart.

LUCINDA.

Stupid coxcomb! 325

CIMBERTON.

I say, madam, her impatience while we are looking at her throws out all attractions—her arms—her neck—what a spring in her step!

LUCINDA.

Don't you run me over thus, you strange unaccountable! 330

---

24 speculation] intellectual interests
25 sensitive] based upon the five senses

CIMBERTON.

What an elasticity in her veins and arteries!

LUCINDA.

I have no veins, no arteries.

MRS. SEALAND.

Oh child, hear him, he talks finely, he's a scholar, he knows what you have.

CIMBERTON.

The speaking invitation of her shape, the gathering 335 of herself up, and the indignation you see in the pretty little thing—now, I am considering her, on this occasion, but as one that is to be pregnant.

LUCINDA. (*Aside.*)

The familiar, learned, unseasonable puppy!*

CIMBERTON.

And pregnant undoubtedly she will be yearly. I fear 340 I shan't for many years have discretion enough to give her one fallow season.

LUCINDA.

Monster! There's no bearing it. The hideous sot!* There's no enduring it, to be thus surveyed like a steed at sale. 345

CIMBERTON.

At sale! She's very illiterate. But she's very well limbed too. Turn her in.26 I see what she is.

Exit Lucinda in a rage.

MRS. SEALAND.

Go, you creature, I am ashamed of you.

CIMBERTON.

No harm done. You know, madam, the better sort of people, as I observed to you, treat by their lawyers of 350 weddings (*Adjusting himself at the glass.**) and the woman in the bargain, like the mansion house in the sale of the estate, is thrown in, and what that is, whether good or bad, is not at all considered.

MRS. SEALAND.

I grant it, and therefore make no demand for her 355 youth and beauty and every other accomplishment, as the common world think 'em, because she is not polite.

CIMBERTON.

Madam, I know your exalted understanding, abstracted as it is from vulgar prejudices, will not 360

be offended when I declare to you I marry to have an heir to my estate and not to beget a colony or a plantation.* This young woman's beauty and constitution will demand provision27 for a tenth child at least. 365

MRS. SEALAND. (*Aside.*)

With all that wit and learning, how considerate! What an economist!—Sir, I cannot make her any other than she is or say she is much better than the other young women of this age or fit for much besides being a mother, but I have given directions 370 for the marriage settlements, and Sir Geoffrey Cimberton's counsel is to meet ours here at this hour concerning his joining in the deed, which when executed, makes you capable of settling what is due to Lucinda's fortune. Herself, as I told you, 375 I say nothing of.

CIMBERTON.

No, no, no, indeed, madam, it is not usual, and I must depend upon my own reflection and philosophy not to overstock my family.

MRS. SEALAND.

I cannot help her, Cousin Cimberton, but she is, 380 for aught I see, as well as the daughter of anybody else.

CIMBERTON.

That is very true, madam.

Enter a servant, who whispers Mrs. Sealand.

MRS. SEALAND.

The lawyers are come, and now we are to hear what they have resolved as to the point whether 385 it's necessary that Sir Geoffry should join in the settlement, as being what they call in the remainder. But good cousin, you must have patience with 'em. These lawyers, I am told, are of a different kind. One is what they call a 390 chamber-counsel,28 the other a pleader. The conveyancer is slow, from an imperfection in his speech, and therefore shunned the bar, but

---

26 Turn her in] keep her from leaving (equestrian phrase)

27 provision] a clause in a marriage contract providing for a monetary settlement to be made in anticipation of future offspring

28 chamber-counsel] a lawyer who offers opinions in private not in court

extremely passionate and impatient of contradiction. The other is as warm as he, but has a tongue so voluble and head so conceited, he will suffer nobody to speak but himself. 395

CIMBERTON.

You mean old Serjeant Target and Counsellor Bramble? I have heard of 'em.

MRS. SEALAND.

The same.—Show in the gentlemen. 400

Exit servant. Re-enter servant, introducing Myrtle and Tom, disguised as Bramble and Target.

MRS. SEALAND.

Gentlemen, this is the party concerned, Mr. Cimberton, and I hope you have considered of the matter.

TOM.

Yes madam, we have agreed that it must be by indent—dent—dent—dent— 405

MYRTLE.

Yes madam, Mr. Serjeant and myself have agreed, as he is pleased to inform you, that it must be an indenture[29] tripartite, and tripartite let it be, for Sir Geoffry must needs be a party. Old Cimberton, in the year 1619, says in that ancient roll in Mr. Serjeant's hands, "as recourse thereto being had, will more at large appear—" 410

TOM.

Yes and by the deeds in your hands it appears, that—

MYRTLE.

Mr. Serjeant, I beg of you to make no inferences upon what is in our custody, but speak to the titles in your own deeds. I shall not show that deed till my client is in Town. 415

CIMBERTON.

You know best your own methods.

MRS. SEALAND.

The single question is whether the entail is such that my cousin Sir Geoffry is necessary in this affair? 420

MYRTLE.

Yes, as to the lordship of Tretriplet, but not as to the messuage of Grimgribber.

---

29 indenture] a deed or sealed agreement between two or more parties

TOM.

I say that Gr—gr— that Gr—gr—Grimgribber, Grimgribber is in us. That is to say the remainder thereof, as well as that of Tr—tr—Triplet. 425

MYRTLE.

You go upon the deed of Sir Ralph, made in the middle of the last century, precedent to that in which old Cimberton made over the remainder and made it pass to the heirs general, by which your client comes in, and I question whether the remainder even of Tretriplet is in him. But we are willing to wave that and give him a valuable consideration. But we shall not purchase what is in us for ever, as Grimgribber is, at the rate as we guard against the contingent of Mr. Cimberton having no son. Then we know Sir Geoffry is the first of the collateral male line in this family. Yet— 430 435

TOM.

Sir, Gr—gr—ber is—

MYRTLE.

I apprehend you very well, and your argument might be of force, and we would be inclined to hear that in all its parts. But sir, I see very plainly what you are going into. I tell you, it is as probable a contingent that Sir Geoffry may die before Mr. Cimberton, as that he may outlive him. 440 445

TOM.

Sir, we are not ripe for that yet, but I must say—

MYRTLE.

Sir, I allow you the whole extent of that argument, but that will go no farther than as to the claimants under old Cimberton. I am of opinion that according to the instruction of Sir Ralph, he could not dock the entail and then create a new estate for the heirs general. 450

TOM.

Sir, I have not patience to be told that, when Gr—gr—ber—

MYRTLE.

I will allow it you, Mr. Serjeant, but there must be the word "heirs forever" to make such an estate as you pretend. 455

CIMBERTON.

I must be impartial, though you are counsel for my side of the question. Were it not that you are so good as to allow him what he has not said, I 460 should think it very hard you should answer him without hearing him. But gentlemen, I believe you have both considered this matter and are firm in your different opinions. 'Twere better therefore you proceeded according to the particular sense of each of you and gave your thoughts distinctly in writing. And do you see, sirs, pray let me have a copy of what you say, in English.

MYRTLE.

Why, what is all we have been saying? In English! Oh, but I forgot myself, you're a wit. But however, to please you, sir, you shall have it in as plain terms as the law will admit of.

CIMBERTON.

But I would have it, sir, without delay.

MYRTLE.

That, sir, the law will not admit of. The courts are sitting at Westminster,[30] and I am this moment obliged to be at every one of them, and 'twould be wrong if I should not be in the hall to attend one of 'em at least; the rest would take it ill else. Therefore, I must leave what I have said to Mr. Serjeant's consideration, and I will digest his arguments on my part, and you shall hear from me again, sir. (*Exit.*)

TOM.

Agreed, agreed.

CIMBERTON.

Mr. Bramble is very quick. He parted a little abruptly.

TOM.

He could not bear my argument; I pinched him to the quick about that Gr—gr—ber.

MRS. SEALAND.

I saw that, for he durst not so much as hear you. I shall send to you, Mr. Serjeant, as soon as Sir Geoffry comes to Town, and then I hope all may be adjusted.

TOM.

I shall be at my chambers at my usual hours. (*Exit.*)

CIMBERTON.

Madam, if you please, I'll now attend you to the tea table, where I shall hear from your ladyship reason and good sense, after all this law and gibberish.

MRS. SEALAND.

'Tis a wonderful[31] thing, sir, that men of professions do not study to talk the substance of what they have to say in the language of the rest of the world. Sure they'd find their account in it.

CIMBERTON.

They might perhaps, madam, with people of your good sense but with the generality 'twould never do. The vulgar would have no respect for truth and knowledge if they were exposed to naked view.
Truth is too simple, of all art* bereaved:
Since the world will—why, let it be deceived.

Exeunt.

Act IV, scene i. Bevil Junior's lodgings.

Bevil Junior with a letter in his hand, followed by Tom.

TOM.

Upon my life, sir, I know nothing of the matter. I never opened my lips to Mr. Myrtle about anything of your honor's letter to Madam Lucinda.

BEVIL JUNIOR. (*Aside.*)

What's the fool in such a fright for?—I don't suppose you did. What I would know is whether Mr. Myrtle showed any suspicion or asked you any questions to lead you to say casually that you had carried any such letter for me this morning.

TOM.

Why sir, if he did ask me any questions, how could I help it?

BEVIL JUNIOR.

I don't say you could, oaf! I am not questioning you but him. What did he say to you?

TOM.

Why sir, when I came to his chambers to be dressed for the lawyer's part your honor was pleased to put me upon, he asked me if I had been at Mr. Sealand's this morning. So I told him, sir, I often went thither, because, sir, if I had not said that, he might have thought there was something more in my going now than at another time.

BEVIL JUNIOR.

Very well! (*Aside.*) The fellow's caution, I find, has

---

[30] Westminster] Westminster Hall*

[31] wonderful] odd, perplexing

given him this jealousy.—Did he ask you no other questions?

TOM.

Yes sir, now I remember, as we came away in the hackney coach from Mr. Sealand's, "Tom," says he, "as I came in to your master this morning, he bad you go for an answer to a letter he had sent. Pray did you bring him any?" says he. "Ah!" says I, "Sir, your honor is pleased to joke with me; you have a mind to know whether I can keep a secret or no."

BEVIL JUNIOR.

And so, by showing him you could, you told him you had one?

TOM. (*Confused.*)

Sir—

BEVIL JUNIOR. (*Aside.*)

What mean* actions does jealousy make a man stoop to? How poorly has he used art* with a servant to make him betray his master.—Well! And when did he give you this letter for me?

TOM.

Sir, he writ it before he pulled off his lawyer's gown at his own chambers.

BEVIL JUNIOR.

Very well, and what did he say when you brought him my answer to it?

TOM.

He looked a little out of humor, sir, and said it was very well.

BEVIL JUNIOR.

I knew he would be grave upon't. Wait without.

TOM.

Humh! 'Gad, I don't like this; I am afraid we are all in the wrong box here. (*Exit.*)

BEVIL JUNIOR.

I put on a serenity while my fellow was present. But I have never been more thoroughly disturbed. This hot man! To write me a challenge on supposed artificial dealing, when I professed myself his friend! I can live contented without glory, but I cannot suffer shame. What's to be done? But first, let me consider Lucinda's letter again. (*Reads.*) "Sir, I hope it is consistent with the laws a woman ought to impose upon herself to acknowledge that your manner of declining a treaty of marriage in our family and desiring the refusal may come from

hence has something more engaging in it than the courtship of him, who, I fear, will fall to my lot, except your friend exerts himself for our common safety and happiness. I have reasons for desiring Mr. Myrtle may not know of this letter till hereafter and am your most obliged humble servant, Lucinda Sealand." Well, but the postscript. (*Reads.*) "I won't, upon second thoughts, hide anything from you. But my reason for concealing this is that Mr. Myrtle has a jealousy in his temper which gives me some terrors. But my esteem for him inclines me to hope that only an ill effect, which sometimes accompanies a tender love, and what may be cured by a careful and unblameable conduct." Thus has this lady made me her friend and confidant and put herself, in a kind, under my protection. I cannot tell him immediately the purport of her letter, except I could cure him of the violent and untractable passion of jealousy and so serve him and her by disobeying her in the article of secrecy more than I should by complying with her directions. But then this dueling, which custom has imposed upon every man who would live with reputation and honor in the world: How must I preserve myself from imputations there? He'll, forsooth, call it or think it fear, if I explain without fighting. But his letter, I'll read it again. (*Reads.*) "Sir, you have used me basely in corresponding and carrying on a treaty where you told me you were indifferent. I have changed my sword since I saw you, which advertisement[32] I thought proper to send you against the next meeting between you and the injured, Charles Myrtle."

Enter Tom.

TOM.

Mr. Myrtle, sir. Would your honor please to see him?

BEVIL JUNIOR.

Why you stupid creature! Let Mr. Myrtle wait at my lodgings! Show him up.

Exit Tom.

Well! I am resolved upon my carriage to him. He is in love and in every circumstance of life a little distrustful, which I must allow for. But here he is.

---

32 advertisement] warning

Enter Tom introducing Myrtle.

Sir, I am extremely obliged to you for this honor.—But sir, you, with your very discerning face, leave the room. 100

Exit Tom.

Well Mr. Myrtle, your commands with me?

MYRTLE.

The time, the place, our long acquaintance, and many other circumstances which affect me on this occasion oblige me without farther ceremony or conference to desire you would not only, as you 105 already have, acknowledge the receipt of my letter but also comply with the request in it. I must have farther notice taken of my message than these half lines, "I have yours, I shall be at home."

BEVIL JUNIOR.

Sir, I own I have received a letter from you in a 110 very unusual style. But as I design everything in this matter shall be your own action, your own seeking, I shall understand nothing but what you are pleased to confirm face to face, and I have already forgot the contents of your epistle. 115

MYRTLE.

This cool manner is very agreeable to the abuse you have already made of my simplicity and frankness, and I see your moderation tends to your own advantage and not mine, to your own safety, not consideration of your friend. 120

BEVIL JUNIOR.

My own safety, Mr. Myrtle!

MYRTLE.

Your own safety, Mr. Bevil.

BEVIL JUNIOR.

Look you, Mr. Myrtle, there's no disguising that I understand what you would be at. But sir, you know I have often dared to disapprove of the 125 decisions a tyrant custom has introduced to the breach of all laws, both divine and human.

MYRTLE.

Mr. Bevil, Mr. Bevil, it would be a good first principle in those who have so tender a conscience that way to have as much abhorrence of doing 130 injuries as—

BEVIL JUNIOR.

As what?

MYRTLE.

As fear of answering for 'em.

BEVIL JUNIOR.

As fear of answering for 'em! But that apprehension is just or blameable according to the object 135 of that fear. I have often told you in confidence of heart, I abhorred the daring to offend the Author of life and rushing into His presence, I say, by the very same act to commit the crime against Him and immediately to urge on to His tribunal. 140

MYRTLE.

Mr. Bevil, I must tell you this coolness, this gravity, this show of conscience, shall never cheat me of my mistress. You have, indeed, the best excuse for life, the hopes of possessing Lucinda. But consider, sir, I have as much reason to be weary of it, if I 145 am to lose her, and my first attempt to recover her shall be to let her see the dauntless man who is to be her guardian and protector.

BEVIL JUNIOR.

Sir, show me but the least glimpse of argument that I am authorized by my own hand to vindicate 150 any lawless insult of this nature, and I will show thee, to chastise thee hardly deserves the name of courage—slight, inconsiderate man! There is, Mr. Myrtle, no such terror in quick anger, and you shall, you know not why, be cool, as you have, you 155 know not why, been warm.

MYRTLE.

Is the woman one loves so little an occasion of anger? You perhaps, who know not what it is to love, who have your ready, your commodious, your foreign trinket for your loose hours and from your 160 fortune, your specious outward carriage, and other lucky circumstances as easy a way to the possession of a woman of honor. You know nothing of what it is to be alarmed, to be distracted with anxiety and terror of losing more than life. Your marriage, 165 happy man, goes on like common business, and in the interim, you have your rambling captive, your Indian princess, for your soft moments of dalliance, your convenient, your ready Indiana.

BEVIL JUNIOR.

You have touched me beyond the patience of a 170 man, and I'm excusable, in the guard of innocence or from the infirmity of human nature which can bear no more, to accept your invitation and observe your letter. Sir, I'll attend you.

Enter Tom.

TOM.

Did you call, sir? I thought you did; I heard you speak aloud. 175

BEVIL JUNIOR.

Yes, go call a coach.

TOM.

Sir—Master—Mr. Myrtle—Friends—Gentlemen—what d'ye mean? I am but a servant, or—

BEVIL JUNIOR.

Call a coach. 180

Exit Tom. A long pause, walking sullenly by each other.
(*Aside.*) Shall I, though provoked to the uttermost, recover myself at the entrance of a third person, and that my servant too, and not have respect enough to all I have ever been receiving from infancy, the obligation to the best of fathers, to an 185 unhappy virgin too, whose life depends on mine. (*Shutting the door.*) —I have, thank Heaven, had time to recollect myself and shall not, for fear of what such a rash man as you think of me, keep longer unexplained the false appearances under 190 which your infirmity of temper makes you suffer, when, perhaps, too much regard to a false point of honor makes me prolong that suffering.

MYRTLE.

I am sure Mr. Bevil cannot doubt* but I had rather have satisfaction from his innocence than his 195 sword.

BEVIL JUNIOR.

Why then would you ask it first that way?

MYRTLE.

Consider, you kept your temper yourself no longer than till I spoke to the disadvantage of her you loved. 200

BEVIL JUNIOR.

True. But let me tell you, I have saved you from the most exquisite distress, even though you had succeeded in the dispute. I know you so well that I am sure to have found this letter about a man you had killed would have been worse than death to 205 yourself. Read it. (*Aside.*) When he is thoroughly mortified and shame has got the better of jealousy, when he has seen himself thoroughly, he will deserve to be assisted towards obtaining Lucinda.

MYRTLE. (*Aside.*)

With what a superiority has he turned the injury 210 on me as the aggressor! I begin to fear I have been too far transported. "A treaty in our family!" Is not that saying too much? I shall relapse. But I find, on the postscript, "something like jealousy." With what face can I see my benefactor? My advocate? 215 Whom I have treated like a betrayer.—Oh Bevil, with what words shall I—

BEVIL JUNIOR.

There needs none; to convince is much more than to conquer.

MYRTLE.

But can you— 220

BEVIL JUNIOR.

You have o'erpaid the inquietude you gave me in the change I see in you towards me. Alas! What machines are we! Thy face is altered to that of another man, to that of my companion, my friend.

MYRTLE.

That I could be such a precipitant wretch! 225

BEVIL JUNIOR.

Pray, no more.

MYRTLE.

Let me reflect how many friends have died by the hands of friends for want of temper, and you must give me leave to say again and again how much I am beholden to that superior spirit you have 230 subdued me with. What had become of one of us, or perhaps both, had you been as weak as I was and as incapable of reason?

BEVIL JUNIOR.

I congratulate to us both the escape from ourselves and hope the memory of it will make us dearer 235 friends than ever.

MYRTLE.

Dear Bevil, your friendly conduct has convinced me that there is nothing manly but what is conducted by reason and agreeable to the practice of virtue and justice. And yet how many have been 240 sacrificed to that idol, the unreasonable opinion of men! Nay, they are so ridiculous in it that they often use their swords against each other with dissembled anger and real fear.

Betrayed by honor and compelled by shame,   245
They hazard being to preserve a name,
Nor dare inquire into the dread mistake
Till plunged in sad eternity they wake.

Exeunt.

Scene [ii]. St. James's Park.*

Enter Sir John Bevil and Mr. Sealand.

SIR JOHN BEVIL.

Give me leave however, Mr. Sealand, as we are
upon a treaty for uniting our families, to mention
only the business of an ancient house: genealogy
and descent are to be of some consideration in an
affair of this sort—   5

MR. SEALAND.

Genealogy and descent! Sir, there has been in our
family a very large one. There was Galfrid the
father of Edward, the father of Ptolomey, the father
of Crassus, the father of Earl Richard, the father
of Henry the Marquis, the father of Duke John—   10

SIR JOHN BEVIL.

What, do you rave, Mr. Sealand? All these great
names in your family?

MR. SEALAND.

These? Yes sir, I have heard my father name 'em
all and more.

SIR JOHN BEVIL.

Aye sir? And did he say they were all in your   15
family?

MR. SEALAND.

Yes sir, he kept 'em all. He was the greatest cocker
in England. He said Duke John won him many
battles and never lost one.

SIR JOHN BEVIL.

Oh sir, your servant, you are laughing at my laying   20
any stress upon descent. But I must tell you, sir, I
never knew anyone but he that wanted* that
advantage turn it into ridicule.

MR. SEALAND.

And I never knew anyone who had many better
advantages put that into his account. But Sir John,   25
value yourself as you please upon your ancient
house, I am to talk freely of everything you are
pleased to put into your bill of rates[33] on this

---

[33] bill of rates] charges, in this case used to indicate considerations for calculating marriage contract settlements

occasion. Yet sir, I have made no objections to your
son's family. 'Tis his morals that I doubt.   30

SIR JOHN BEVIL.

Sir, I can't help saying that what might injure a citizen's* credit may be no stain to a gentleman's honor.

MR. SEALAND.

Sir John, the honor of a gentleman is liable to be
tainted by as small a matter as the credit of a trader.
We are talking of a marriage, and in such a case   35
the father of a young woman will not think it an
addition to the honor or credit of her lover—that
he is a keeper*—

SIR JOHN BEVIL.

Mr. Sealand, don't take upon you to spoil my son's
marriage with any woman else.   40

MR. SEALAND.

Sir John, let him apply to any woman else and
have as many mistresses as he pleases—

SIR JOHN BEVIL.

My son, sir, is a discreet and sober gentleman—

MR. SEALAND.

Sir, I never saw a man that wenched soberly and
discreetly that ever left it off. The decency observed   45
in the practice hides even from the sinner the
iniquity of it. They pursue it not that their
appetites hurry 'em away but, I warrant you,
because 'tis their opinion they may do it

SIR JOHN BEVIL.

Were what you suspect a truth, do you design to   50
keep your daughter a virgin till you find a man
unblemished that way?

MR. SEALAND.

Sir, as much a cit* as you take me for, I know the
Town* and the world. And give me leave to say that
we merchants are a species of gentry that have grown   55
into the world this last century and are as honorable,
and almost as useful, as you landed folks that have
always thought yourselves so much above us. For
your trading, forsooth, is extended no farther than
a load of hay or a fat ox. You are pleasant people,   60
indeed, because you are generally bred up to be lazy;
therefore, I warrant you, industry is dishonorable.

SIR JOHN BEVIL.

Be not offended, sir; let us go back to our point.

MR. SEALAND.

Oh, not at all offended, but I don't love to leave

---

any part of the account unclosed. Look you, Sir 65
John, comparisons are odious, and more
particularly so on occasions of this kind, when we
are projecting races* that are to be made out of
both sides of the comparisons.

SIR JOHN BEVIL.

But my son, sir, is, in the eye of the world, a 70
gentleman of merit.

MR. SEALAND.

I own to you, I think him so. But Sir John, I am
a man exercised and experienced in chances and
disasters. I lost in my earlier years a very fine wife 75
and with her a poor little infant; this makes me,
perhaps, over-cautious to preserve the second
bounty of Providence to me and be as careful as I
can of this child. You'll pardon me, my poor girl,
sir, is as valuable to me as your boasted son to you. 80

SIR JOHN BEVIL.

Why, that's one very good reason, Mr. Sealand,
why I wish my son had her.

MR. SEALAND.

There is nothing but this strange lady here, this
incognita, that can be objected to him. Here and
there a man falls in love with an artful creature and 85
gives up all the motives of life to that one passion.

SIR JOHN BEVIL.

A man of my son's understanding cannot be
supposed to be one of them.

MR. SEALAND.

Very wise men have been so enslaved, and when a
man marries with one of them upon his hands, 90
whether moved from the demand of the world or
slighter reasons, such a husband soils³⁴ with his
wife for a month perhaps, then good b'w'y'³⁵
madam, the show's over. Ah! John Dryden points
out such a husband to a hair, where he says, 95
And while abroad so prodigal the dolt is,
Poor spouse at home as ragged as a colt is.³⁶
Now in plain terms, sir, I shall not care to have
my poor girl turned a-grazing, and that must be
the case when— 100

---

³⁴ soils] cohabits

³⁵ b'w'y'] goodbye, from "God be with ye"

³⁶ And … is] from Dryden's epilogue to Sir John
Vanbrugh's adaptation of John Fletcher's *The Pilgrim*
(1700), slightly misquoted

SIR JOHN BEVIL.

But pray consider, sir, my son—

MR. SEALAND.

Look you, sir, I'll make the matter short. This
unknown lady, as I told you, is all the objection I
have to him. But one way or other he is or has
been certainly engaged to her. I am therefore 105
resolved this very afternoon to visit her. Now from
her behavior or appearance I shall soon be let into
what I may fear or hope for.

SIR JOHN BEVIL.

Sir, I am very confident there can be nothing
inquired into relating to my son that will not, 110
upon being understood, turn to his advantage.

MR. SEALAND.

I hope that as sincerely as you believe it. Sir John
Bevil, when I am satisfied in this great point, if
your son's conduct answers the character you give
him, I shall wish your alliance more than that of 115
any gentleman in Great Britain, and so your
servant. (*Exit.*)

SIR JOHN BEVIL.

He is gone in a way but barely civil, but his great
wealth and the merit of his only child, the heiress
of it, are not to be lost for a little peevishness. 120

Enter Humphrey.

Oh Humphrey, you are come in a seasonable
minute. I want to talk to thee and to tell thee that
my head and heart are on the rack about my son.

HUMPHREY.

Sir, you may trust his discretion, I am sure you
may. 125

SIR JOHN BEVIL.

Why, I do believe I may, and yet I'm in a thousand
fears when I lay this vast wealth before me. When
I consider his prepossessions, either generous to a
folly in an honorable love or abandoned past
redemption in a vicious one, and, from the one 130
or the other, his insensibility to the fairest prospect
towards doubling our estate, a father who knows
how useful wealth is and how necessary even to
those who despise it, I say a father, Humphrey, a
father cannot bear it. 135

HUMPHREY.

Be not transported, sir; you will grow incapable of
taking any resolution in your perplexity.

SIR JOHN BEVIL.

Yet as angry as I am with him, I would not have him surprised in anything. This mercantile, rough man may go grossly into the examination of this matter and talk to the gentlewoman so as to— 140

HUMPHREY.

No, I hope, not in an abrupt manner.

SIR JOHN BEVIL.

No, I hope not! Why, dost thou know anything of her or of him or of anything of it or all of it?

HUMPHREY.

My dear master, I know so much that I told him 145 this very day you had reason to be secretly out of humor about her.

SIR JOHN BEVIL.

Did you go so far? Well, what said he to that?

HUMPHREY.

His words were, looking upon me steadfastly: "Humphrey," says he, "that woman is a woman of 150 honor."

SIR JOHN BEVIL.

How! Do you think he is married to her or designs to marry her?

HUMPHREY.

I can say nothing to the latter. But he says he can marry no one without your consent while you are 155 living.

SIR JOHN BEVIL.

If he said so much, I know he scorns to break his word with me.

HUMPHREY.

I am sure of that.

SIR JOHN BEVIL.

You are sure of that. Well, that's some comfort. 160 Then I have nothing to do but to see the bottom of this matter during this present ruffle. Oh Humphrey—

HUMPHREY.

You are not ill, I hope, sir.

SIR JOHN BEVIL.

Yes, a man is very ill that's in a very ill humor. To 165 be a father is to be in care for one whom you oftener disoblige than please by that very care. Oh! That sons could know the duty to a father before they themselves are fathers. But perhaps, you'll say now that I am one of the happiest fathers in the 170 world. But I assure you that of the very happiest is not a condition to be envied.

HUMPHREY.

Sir, your pain arises not from the thing itself but your particular sense of it. You are overfond, nay, give me leave to say, you are unjustly apprehensive 175 from your fondness. My Master Bevil never disobliged you, and he will, I know he will, do everything you ought to expect.

SIR JOHN BEVIL.

He won't take all this money with this girl. For aught I know, he will, forsooth, have so much 180 moderation as to think he ought not to force his liking for any consideration.

HUMPHREY.

He is to marry her, not you; he is to live with her, not you, sir.

SIR JOHN BEVIL.

I know not what to think. But I know nothing can 185 be more miserable than to be in this doubt. Follow me; I must come to some resolution.

Exeunt.

Scene [iii]. Bevil Junior's lodgings.

Enter Tom and Phillis.

TOM.

Well madam, if you must speak with Mr. Myrtle, you shall; he is now with my master in the library.

PHILLIS.

But you must leave me alone with him, for he can't make me a present nor I so handsomely take anything from him before you; it would not be 5 decent.

TOM.

It will be very decent, indeed, for me to retire and leave my mistress with another man.

PHILLIS.

He is a gentleman and will treat one properly—

TOM.

I believe so. But however, I won't be far off and 10 therefore will venture to trust you. I'll call him to you. (*Exit.*)

PHILLIS.

What a deal of pother and sputter here is between my mistress and Mr. Myrtle from mere punctilio?

I could any hour of the day get her to her lover 15
and would do it. But she, forsooth, will allow no
plot to get him. But if he can come to her, I know
she would be glad of it. I must therefore do her
an acceptable violence and surprise her into his
arms. I am sure I go by the best rule imaginable: 20
if she were my maid, I should think her the best
servant in the world for doing so by me.

Enter Myrtle and Tom.

Oh sir, you and Mr. Bevil are fine gentlemen to
let a lady remain under such difficulties as my poor
mistress and no attempt to set her at liberty or 25
release her from the danger of being instantly
married to Cimberton.

MYRTLE.

Tom has been telling. But what is to be done?

PHILLIS.

What is to be done—when a man can't come at his
mistress! Why, can't you fire our house or the next 30
house to us, to make us run out and you take us?

MYRTLE.

How, Mrs. Phillis—

PHILLIS.

Aye, let me see that rogue deny to fire a house,
make a riot, or any other little thing, when there
were no other way to come at me. 35

TOM.

I am obliged to you, madam.

PHILLIS.

Why, don't we hear everyday of people's hanging
themselves for love, and won't they venture the
hazard of being hanged for love? Oh! Were I a
man— 40

MYRTLE.

What manly thing would you have me undertake,
according to your ladyship's notion of a man?

PHILLIS.

Only be at once what, one time or other, you may
be and wish to be or must be.

MYRTLE.

Dear girl, talk plainly to me and consider, I in my 45
condition can't be in very good humor. You say,
to be at once what I must be.

PHILLIS.

Aye, aye. I mean no more than to be an old man;

I saw you do it very well at the masquerade. In a
word, old Sir Geoffry Cimberton is every hour 50
expected in Town to join in the deeds and
settlements for marrying Mr. Cimberton. He is
half blind, half lame, half deaf, half dumb; though
as to his passions and desires, he is as warm and
ridiculous as when in the heat of youth— 55

TOM.

Come to the business and don't keep the
gentleman in suspense for the pleasure of being
courted, as you serve me.

PHILLIS.

I saw you at the masquerade act such a one to
perfection. Go and put on that very habit and come 60
to our house as Sir Geoffry. There is not one there
but myself knows his person. I was born in the
parish where he is lord of the manor. I have seen
him often and often at church in the country. Do
not hesitate, but come thither. They will think you 65
bring a certain security against Mr. Myrtle, and you
bring Mr. Myrtle. Leave the rest to me. I leave this
with you and expect. They don't, I told you, know
you. They think you out of town, which you had
as good be forever if you lose this opportunity. I 70
must be gone; I know I am wanted at home.

MYRTLE.

My dear Phillis! (*Catches and kisses her, and gives
her money.*)

PHILLIS.

Oh fie! My kisses are not my own; you have
committed violence. But I'll carry 'em to the right
owner. (*Tom kisses her.*) —Come, see me 75
downstairs and leave the lover to think of his last
game for the prize.

Exeunt Tom and Phillis.

MYRTLE.

I think I will instantly attempt this wild expedient.
The extravagance of it will make me less suspected,
and it will give me opportunity to assert my own 80
right to Lucinda, without whom I cannot live. But
I am so mortified at this conduct of mine towards
poor Bevil. He must think meanly of me. I know
not how to reassume myself and be in spirit
enough for such an adventure as this. Yet I must 85
attempt it, if it be only to be near Lucinda, under

her present perplexities. And sure—
The next delight to transport with the fair
Is to relieve her in her hours of care.

Exit.

Act V, scene i. Sealand's house.

Enter Phillis, with lights, before Myrtle, disguised like old Sir Geoffry, supported by Mrs. Sealand, Lucinda, and Cimberton.

MRS. SEALAND.

Now I have seen you thus far, Sir Geoffry, will you excuse me a moment, while I give my necessary orders for your accommodation? (*Exit.*)

MYRTLE.

I have not seen you, Cousin Cimberton, since you were ten years old, and as it is incumbent on you 5 to keep up our name and family, I shall, upon very reasonable terms, join with you in a settlement to that purpose. Though I must tell you, Cousin, this is the first merchant that has married into our house. 10

LUCINDA. (*Aside.*)

Deuce on 'em! Am I a merchant because my father is?

MYRTLE.

But is he directly a trader at this time?

CIMBERTON.

There's no hiding the disgrace, sir: he trades to all parts of the world. 15

MYRTLE.

We never had one of our family before who descended from persons that did anything.

CIMBERTON.

Sir, since it is a girl that they have, I am, for the honor of my family, willing to take it in again and to sink her into our name and no harm done. 20

MYRTLE.

'Tis prudently and generously resolved. Is this the young thing?

CIMBERTON.

Yes sir.

PHILLIS. (*Aside to Lucinda.*)

Good madam, don't be out of humor, but let them run to the utmost of their extravagance. Hear them 25 out.

MYRTLE.

Can't I see her nearer? My eyes are but weak.

PHILLIS. (*Aside to Lucinda.*)

Beside, I am sure the uncle has something worth your notice. I'll take care to get off the young one and leave you to observe what may be wrought out 30 of the old one for your good. (*Exit.*)

CIMBERTON.

Madam, this old gentleman, your great uncle, desires to be introduced to you and to see you nearer.—Approach, sir.

MYRTLE.

By your leave, young lady. (*Puts on spectacles.*) — 35 Cousin Cimberton! She has exactly that sort of neck and bosom for which my sister Gertrude was so much admired in the year sixty one, before the French dresses first discovered* anything in women below the chin. 40

LUCINDA. (*Aside.*)

What a very odd situation am I in. Though I cannot but be diverted at the extravagance of their humors,* equally unsuitable to their age.—"Chin," quotha! I don't believe my passionate lover there knows whether I have one or not. Ha! Ha! 45

MYRTLE.

Madam, I would not willingly offend, but I have a better glass— (*Pulls out a large one.*)

Enter Phillis to Cimberton.

PHILLIS.

Sir, my lady desires to show the apartment to you that she intends for Sir Geoffry.

CIMBERTON.

Well sir, by that time you have sufficiently gazed 50 and sunned yourself in the beauties of my spouse there, I will wait on you again.

Exeunt Cimberton and Phillis.

MYRTLE.

Were it not, madam, that I might be troublesome, there is something of importance, though we are alone, which I would say more safe from being 55 heard.

LUCINDA. (*Aside.*)

There is something in this old fellow, methinks, that raises my curiosity.

MYRTLE.

To be free, madam, I as heartily contemn this kinsman of mine as you do and am sorry to see 60 so much beauty and merit devoted by your parents to so insensible a possessor.

LUCINDA. [Aside.]

Surprising!—I hope then, sir, you will not contribute to the wrong you are so generous as to pity, whatever may be the interest of your family. 65

MYRTLE.

This hand of mine shall never be employed to sign anything against your good and happiness.

LUCINDA.

I am sorry, sir, it is not in my power to make you proper acknowledgments, but there is a gentleman in the world whose gratitude will, I am sure, be 70 worthy of the favor.

MYRTLE.

All the thanks I desire, madam, are in your power to give.

LUCINDA.

Name them, and command them.

MYRTLE.

Only, madam, that the first time you are alone with 75 your lover, you will with open arms receive him.

LUCINDA.

As willingly as his heart could wish it.

MYRTLE.

Thus then he claims your promise! Oh Lucinda!

LUCINDA.

Oh! A cheat! A cheat! A cheat!

MYRTLE.

Hush! 'Tis I, 'tis I, your lover, Myrtle himself, 80 madam.

LUCINDA.

Oh bless me! What a rashness and folly to surprise me so.—But hush, my mother—

Enter Mrs. Sealand, Cimberton, and Phillis.

MRS. SEALAND.

How now! What's the matter?

LUCINDA.

Oh madam! As soon as you left the room, my 85 uncle fell into a sudden fit, and—and—so I cried out for help to support him and conduct him to his chamber.

MRS. SEALAND.

That was kindly done. Alas sir, how do you find yourself? 90

MYRTLE.

Never was taken in so odd a way in my life. Pray lead me. Oh! I was talking here—pray carry me— to my Cousin Cimberton's young lady—

MRS. SEALAND. (Aside.)

My Cousin Cimberton's young lady! How zealous he is, even in his extremity, for the match! A right 95 Cimberton.

Cimberton and Lucinda lead him, as one in pain, etc.

CIMBERTON.

Pox! Uncle, you will pull my ear off.

LUCINDA.

Pray Uncle! You will squeeze me to death.

MRS. SEALAND.

No matter, no matter. He knows not what he does.—Come sir, shall I help you out? 100

MYRTLE.

By no means; I'll trouble nobody but my young cousins here.

They lead him off.

PHILLIS.

But pray, madam, does your ladyship intend that Mr. Cimberton shall really marry my young mistress at last? I don't think he likes her. 105

MRS. SEALAND.

That's not material. Men of his speculation are above desires. But be it as it may, now I have given old Sir Geoffry the trouble of coming up to sign and seal, with what countenance can I be off?

PHILLIS.

As well as with twenty others, madam. It is the 110 glory and honor of a great fortune to live in continual treaties and still to break off. It looks great, madam.

MRS. SEALAND.

True, Phillis. Yet to return our blood again into the Cimberton's is an honor not to be rejected. But 115 were not you saying that Sir John Bevil's creature Humphrey has been with Mr. Sealand?

PHILLIS.

Yes madam, I overheard them agree that Mr.

Sealand should go himself and visit this unknown lady that Mr. Bevil is so great with. And if he found nothing there to fright him, that Mr. Bevil should still marry my young mistress. 120

MRS. SEALAND.

How! Nay then, he shall find she is my daughter as well as his. I'll follow him this instant and take the whole family* along with me. The disputed power of disposing of my own daughter shall be at an end this very night. I'll live no longer in anxiety for a little hussy that hurts my appearance wherever I carry her and for whose sake I seem to be not^e at all regarded, and that in the best of my days. 125 130

PHILLIS.

Indeed, madam, if she were married, your ladyship might very well be taken for Mr. Sealand's daughter.

MRS. SEALAND.

Nay, when the chit has not been with me, I have heard the men say as much. I'll no longer cut off the greatest pleasure of a woman's life—the shining in assemblies—by her forward anticipation of the respect that's due to her superior. She shall down to Cimberton Hall—she shall—she shall. 135 140

PHILLIS.

I hope, madam, I shall stay with your ladyship.

MRS. SEALAND.

Thou shalt, Phillis, and I'll place thee then more about me. But order chairs* immediately; I'll be gone this minute.

Exeunt.

Scene [ii]. Charing Cross.[37]

Enter Mr. Sealand and Humphrey.

MR. SEALAND.

I am very glad, Mr. Humphrey, that you agree with me that it is for our common good I should look thoroughly into this matter.

HUMPHREY.

I am, indeed, of that opinion, for there is no artifice, nothing concealed, in our family, which 5

37 Charing Cross] crossroads in Westminster (from *cering*, bend, either of the Thames or of the Roman road running west out of London); after the Restoration, the site of executions of rebels; a fashionable area of the Town*

ought in justice to be known. I need not desire you, sir, to treat the lady with care and respect.

MR. SEALAND.

Master Humphrey, I shall not be rude, though I design to be a little abrupt and come into the matter at once, to see how she will bear upon a surprise. 10

HUMPHREY.

That's the door, sir; I wish you success.

While Humphrey speaks, Sealand consults his table-book.[38] *(Aside.)* I am less concerned what happens there, because I hear Mr. Myrtle is well-lodged as old Sir Geoffry. So I am willing to let this gentleman employ himself here to give them time at home, for I am sure 'tis necessary for the quiet of our family Lucinda were disposed of out of it, since Mr. Bevil's inclination is so much otherwise engaged. *(Exit.)* 15 20

MR. SEALAND.

I think this is the door. *(Knocks.)* I'll carry this matter with an air of authority to inquire, though I make an errand to begin discourse.

Knocks again, and enter Daniel, a foot-boy.

So young man, is your lady within?

DANIEL.

Alack sir, I am but a country boy. I dan't know whether she is or noa, but an* you'll stay a bit, I'll goa and ask the gentlewoman that's with her. 25

MR. SEALAND.

Why sirrah, though you are a country boy, you can see, can't you? You know whether she is at home when you see her, don't you? 30

DANIEL.

Nay, nay, I'm not such a country lad neither, master, to think she's at home because I see her. I have been in Town but a month, and I lost one place already for believing my own eyes.

MR. SEALAND.

Why sirrah, have you learnt to lie already? 35

DANIEL.

Ah Master, things that are lies in the country are not lies at London. I begin to know my business a little better than so. But an you please to walk in, I'll call a gentlewoman to you that can tell you for certain. She can make bold to ask my lady herself. 40

38 table-book] notebook

MR. SEALAND.

Oh! Then she is within, I find, though you dare not say so.

DANIEL.

Nay, nay! That's neither here, nor there. What's matter whether she is within or no, if she has not a mind to see anybody. 45

MR. SEALAND.

I can't tell, sirrah, whether you are arch or simple, but however, get me a direct answer and here's a shilling for you.

DANIEL.

Will you please to walk in; I'll see what I can do for you. 50

MR. SEALAND.

I see you will be fit for your business in time, child. But I expect to meet with nothing but extra-ordinaries[39] in such a house.

DANIEL.

Such a house! Sir, you han't seen it yet. Pray walk in. 55

MR. SEALAND.

Sir, I'll wait upon you.

Exeunt.

Scene [iii.] Indiana's house.

Enter Isabella.

ISABELLA.

What anxiety do I feel for this poor creature! What will be the end of her? Such a languishing, unreserved passion for a man that at last must certainly leave or ruin her, and perhaps both! Then the aggravation of the distress is that she does not 5 believe he will. Not but I must own, if they are both what they would seem, they are made for one another as much as Adam and Eve were, for there is no other of their kind but themselves.

Enter Daniel.

So Daniel, what news with you? 10

DANIEL.

Madam, there's a gentleman below would speak with my lady.

---

[39] extraordinaries] unusual, fantastic, irrational, or extravagant doings

ISABELLA.

Sirrah! Don't you know Mr. Bevil yet?

DANIEL.

Madam, 'tis not the gentleman who comes 15 everyday and asks for you and won't go till he knows whether you are with her or no.

ISABELLA. (*Aside.*)

Hah! That's a particular I did not know before.— Well, be it who it will, let him come up to me.

Exit Daniel, and re-enters with Mr. Sealand. Isabella looks amazed.

MR. SEALAND.

Madam, I can't blame your being a little surprised 20 to see a perfect stranger make a visit, and—

ISABELLA.

I am indeed surprised! (*Aside.*) I see he does not know me.

MR. SEALAND.

You are very prettily lodged here, madam. In troth, you seem to have everything in plenty. (*Aside, and* 25 *looking about.*) A thousand a year, I warrant you, upon this pretty nest of rooms and the dainty one within them.

ISABELLA. (*Apart.*)

Twenty years, it seems, have less effect in the alteration of a man of thirty than of a girl of 30 fourteen. He's almost still the same, but alas, I find by other men, as well as himself, I am not what I was. As soon as he spoke, I was convinced 'twas he. How shall I contain my surprise and satisfaction? He must not know me yet. 35

MR. SEALAND.

Madam, I hope I don't give you any disturbance. But there is a young lady here with whom I have a particular business to discourse, and I hope she will admit me to that favor.

ISABELLA.

Why sir, have you had any notice concerning her? 40 I wonder who could give it you.

MR. SEALAND.

That, madam, is fit only to be communicated to herself.

ISABELLA.

Well sir, you shall see her. (*Aside.*) I find he knows nothing yet, nor shall from me. I am resolved I will 45 observe this interlude, this sport of nature and of fortune.—You shall see her presently, sir. For now I am as a mother and will trust her with you. (*Exit.*)

MR. SEALAND.

As a mother![40] Right, that's the old phrase for one of those commode[41] ladies who lend out beauty 50 for hire to young gentlemen that have pressing occasions.—But here comes the precious lady herself. In troth a very sightly woman—

Enter Indiana.

INDIANA.

I am told, sir, you have some affair that requires your speaking with me. 55

MR. SEALAND.

Yes, madam. There came to my hands a bill* drawn by Mr. Bevil which is payable tomorrow, and he, in the intercourse of business, sent it to me, who have cash of his, and desired me to send a servant with it. But I have made bold to bring 60 you the money myself.

INDIANA.

Sir! Was that necessary?

MR. SEALAND.

No madam, but to be free with you, the fame of your beauty and the regard which Mr. Bevil is a little too well known to have for you excited my 65 curiosity.

INDIANA.

Too well known to have for me! Your sober appearance, sir, which my friend described, made me expect no rudeness or absurdity at least.— Who's there?—Sir, if you pay the money to a 70 servant, 'twill be as well.

MR. SEALAND.

Pray madam, be not offended. I came hither on an innocent, nay a virtuous design, and if you will have patience to hear me, it may be as useful to you, as you are in a friendship with Mr. Bevil, as to my only 75 daughter, whom I was this day disposing of.

INDIANA.

You make me hope, sir, I have mistaken you. I am

_____

40 mother] procuress
41 commode] accommodating

composed again. Be free, say on— (*Aside.*) what I am afraid to hear—

MR. SEALAND.

I feared, indeed, an unwarranted passion here, but 80 I did not think it was in abuse of so worthy an object, so accomplished a lady, as your sense and mien bespeak. But the youth of our age care not what merit and virtue they bring to shame, so they gratify— 85

INDIANA.

Sir, you are going into very great errors. But as you are pleased to say you see something in me that has changed at least the color of your suspicions, so has your appearance altered mine and made me earnestly attentive to what has any way concerned 90 you to inquire into my affairs and character.

MR. SEALAND. (*Aside.*)

How sensibly, with what an air she talks!

INDIANA.

Good sir, be seated and tell me tenderly—keep all your suspicions concerning me alive that you may, in a proper and prepared way, acquaint me why the care 95 of your daughter obliges a person of your seeming worth and fortune to be thus inquisitive about a wretched, helpless, friendless— (*Weeping.*) But I beg your pardon. Though I am an orphan, your child is not, and your concern for her, it seems, has brought 100 you hither. I'll be composed. Pray go on, sir.

MR. SEALAND.

How could Mr. Bevil be such a monster to injure such a woman?

INDIANA.

No, sir, you wrong him. He has not injured me. My support is from his bounty. 105

MR. SEALAND.

Bounty! When gluttons give high prices for delicates, they are prodigious bountiful.

INDIANA.

Still, still you will persist in that error. But my own fears tell me all. You are the gentleman, I suppose, for whose happy daughter he is designed a 110 husband by his good father, and he has, perhaps, consented to the overture. He was here this morning, dressed beyond his usual plainness, nay most sumptuously, and he is to be, perhaps, this night a bridegroom. 115

MR. SEALAND.

I own he was intended such. But madam, on your
account I have determined to defer my daughter's
marriage till I am satisfied from your own mouth
of what nature are the obligations you are under
to him.   120

INDIANA.

His actions, sir, his eyes have only made me think he
designed to make me the partner of his heart. The
goodness and gentleness of his demeanor made me
misinterpret all. 'Twas my own hope, my own
passion, that deluded me. He never made one
amorous advance to me. His large heart and   125
bestowing hand have only helped the miserable. Nor
know I why, but from his mere* delight in virtue,
that I have been his care, the object on which to
indulge and please himself with pouring favors.

MR. SEALAND.

Madam, I know not why it is, but I, as well as you,   130
am methinks afraid of entering into the matter I
came about. But 'tis the same thing, as if we had
talked never so distinctly—he ne'er shall have a
daughter of mine.

INDIANA.

If you say this from what you think of me, you   135
wrong yourself and him. Let not me, miserable
though I may be, do injury to my benefactor. No
sir, my treatment ought rather to reconcile you to
his virtues. If to bestow without prospect of return;
if to delight in supporting what might, perhaps,   140
be thought an object of desire with no other view
than to be her guard against those who would not
be so disinterested; if these actions, sir, can in a
careful parent's eye commend him to a daughter,
give yours, sir, give her to my honest, generous   145
Bevil. What have I to do but sigh and weep, to
rave, run wild, a lunatic in chains, or, hid in
darkness, mutter in distracted starts and broken
accents my strange, strange story!

MR. SEALAND.

Take comfort, madam.   150

INDIANA.

All my comfort must be to expostulate in madness,
to relieve with frenzy my despair, and shrieking to
demand of fate: Why, why was I born to such
variety of sorrows?

MR. SEALAND.

If I have been the least occasion—   155

INDIANA.

No, 'twas Heaven's high will I should be such: to
be plundered in my cradle! Tossed on the seas! And
even there, an infant captive! To lose my mother,
hear but of my father! To be adopted! Lose my
adopter! Then plunged again in worse calamities!   160

MR. SEALAND.

An infant captive!

INDIANA.

Yet then, to find the most charming of mankind
once more to set me free from what I thought the last
distress; to load me with his services, his bounties,
and his favors; to support my very life in a way that   165
stole, at the same time, my very soul itself from me.

MR. SEALAND.

And has young Bevil been this worthy man?

INDIANA.

Yet, then again, this very man to take another!
Without leaving me the right, the pretence of
easing my fond heart with tears! For oh, I can't   170
reproach him, though the same hand that raised
me to this height now throws me down the
precipice.

MR. SEALAND.

Dear lady! Oh, yet one moment's patience. My
heart grows full with your affliction. But yet, there's   175
something in your story that—

INDIANA.

My portion here is bitterness and sorrow.

MR. SEALAND.

Do not think so. Pray answer me, does Bevil know
your name and family?

INDIANA.

Alas! Too well! Oh, could I be any other thing than   180
what I am. I'll tear away all traces of my former
self, my little ornaments, the remains of my first
state, the hints of what I ought to have been—

*In her disorder, she throws away a bracelet, which
Sealand takes up and looks earnestly on.*

MR. SEALAND.

Hah! What's this? My eyes are not deceived? It is,
it is the same! The very bracelet which I   185
bequeathed my wife at our last mournful parting.

INDIANA.

What said you, sir! Your wife! Whither does my fancy carry me? What means this unfelt motion at my heart? And yet again my fortune but deludes me, for if I err not, sir, your name is Sealand. But my lost father's name was— 190

MR. SEALAND.

Danvers! Was it not?

INDIANA.

What new amazement! That is indeed my family.

MR. SEALAND.

Know then, when my misfortunes drove me to the Indies, for reasons too tedious now to mention, I changed my name of Danvers into Sealand. 195

Enter Isabella.

ISABELLA.

If yet there wants* an explanation of your wonder, examine well this face—yours, sir, I well remember—gaze on, and read in me your sister Isabella!

MR. SEALAND.

My sister! 200

ISABELLA.

But here's a claim more tender yet: your Indiana, sir, your long lost daughter.

MR. SEALAND.

Oh, my child! My child!

INDIANA.

All-gracious Heaven! Is it possible! Do I embrace my father! 205

MR. SEALAND.

And do I hold thee? These passions are too strong for utterance. Rise, rise, my child, and give my tears their way.—Oh, my sister! (*Embracing her.*)

ISABELLA.

Now dearest niece, my groundless fears, my painful cares no more shall vex thee. If I have wronged thy 210 noble lover with too hard suspicions, my just concern for thee, I hope, will plead my pardon.

MR. SEALAND.

Oh, make him then the full amends and be yourself the messenger of joy. Fly this instant! Tell him all these wondrous turns of Providence in his 215 favor! Tell him I have now a daughter to bestow which he no longer will decline, that this day he still shall be a bridegroom, nor shall a fortune, the

merit which his father seeks, be wanting.* Tell him the reward of all his virtues waits on his acceptance. 220

Exit Isabella.

My dearest Indiana! (*Turns, and embraces her.*)

INDIANA.

Have I then at last a father's sanction on my love! His bounteous hand to give and make my heart a present worthy of Bevil's generosity?

MR. SEALAND.

Oh my child! How are our sorrows past o'erpaid 225 by such a meeting! Though I have lost so many years of soft, paternal dalliance with thee, yet in one day to find thee thus and thus bestow thee in such perfect happiness is ample, ample reparation! And yet, again the merit of thy lover? 230

INDIANA.

Oh, had I spirits left to tell you of his actions! How strongly filial duty has suppressed his love and how concealment still* has doubled all his obligations, the pride, the joy of his alliance, sir, would warm your heart, as he has conquered mine. 235

MR. SEALAND.

How laudable is love when born of virtue! I burn to embrace him—

INDIANA.

See, sir, my aunt already has succeeded and brought him to your wishes.

Enter Isabella, with Sir John Bevil, Bevil Junior, Mrs. Sealand, Cimberton, Myrtle [as Sir Geoffry], and Lucinda.

SIR JOHN BEVIL. (*Entering.*)

Where! Where's this scene of wonder! Mr. Sealand, 240 I congratulate, on this occasion, our mutual happiness. Your good sister, sir, has, with the story of your daughter's fortune, filled us with surprise and joy! Now all exceptions are removed; my son has now avowed his love and turned all former 245 jealousies and doubts to approbation, and, I am told, your goodness has consented to reward him.

MR. SEALAND.

If, sir, a fortune equal to his father's hopes can make this object worthy his acceptance.

BEVIL JUNIOR.

I hear your mention, sir, of fortune with pleasure 250

only, as it may prove the means to reconcile the best of fathers to my love. Let him be provident, but let me be happy.—My ever-destined, my acknowledged wife! (*Embracing Indiana.*)

INDIANA.

Wife! Oh, my ever loved! My lord! My master! 255

SIR JOHN BEVIL.

I congratulate myself, as well as you, that I had a son who could, under such disadvantages, discover your great merit.

MR. SEALAND.

Oh Sir John! How vain, how weak is human prudence? What care, what foresight, what 260 imagination could contrive such blest events to make our children happy, as Providence in one short hour has laid before us?

CIMBERTON. (*To Mrs. Sealand.*)

I am afraid, madam, Mr. Sealand is a little too busy for our affair. If you please we'll take another 265 opportunity.

MRS. SEALAND.

Let us have patience, sir.

During this, Bevil Junior presents Lucinda to Indiana.

CIMBERTON.

But we make Sir Geoffry wait, madam.

MYRTLE.

Oh sir! I am not in haste.

MR. SEALAND.

But here! Here's our general benefactor! Excellent 270 young man that could be, at once, a lover to her beauty and a parent to her virtue.

BEVIL JUNIOR.

If you think that an obligation, sir, give me leave to overpay myself in the only instance that can now add to my felicity, by begging you to bestow 275 this lady on Mr. Myrtle.

MR. SEALAND.

She is his without reserve. I beg he may be sent for.—Mr. Cimberton, notwithstanding you never had my consent, yet there is, since I last saw you, another objection to your marriage with my 280 daughter.

CIMBERTON.

I hope, sir, your lady has concealed nothing from me?

MR. SEALAND.

Troth sir, nothing but what was concealed from myself: another daughter, who has an undoubted 285 title to half my estate.

CIMBERTON.

How Mr. Sealand! Why then if half Mrs.* Lucinda's fortune is gone, you can't say that any of my estate is settled upon her. I was in treaty for the whole, but if that is not to be come at, to be sure there can be 290 no bargain. Sir, I have nothing to do but to take my leave of your good lady, my cousin, and beg pardon for the trouble I have given this old gentleman.

MYRTLE.

That you have, Mr. Cimberton, with all my heart. *Discovers* himself.

OMNES.

Mr. Myrtle! 295

MYRTLE.

And I beg pardon of the whole company that I assumed the person of Sir Geoffry only to be present at the danger of this lady's being diposed of and in her utmost exigence to assert my right to her, which if her parents will ratify, as they once 300 favored my pretensions, no abatement of fortune shall lessen her value to me.

LUCINDA.

Generous* man!

MR. SEALAND.

If, sir, you can overlook the injury of being in treaty with one who as meanly left her as you have 305 generously asserted your right in her, she is yours.

LUCINDA.

Mr. Myrtle, though you have ever had my heart, yet now I find I love you more, because I bring you less.

MYRTLE.

We have much more than we want,* and I am glad 310 any event has contributed to the discovery* of our real inclinations to each other.

MRS. SEALAND. (*Aside.*)

Well! However, I'm glad the girl's disposed of any way.

BEVIL JUNIOR.

Myrtle! No longer rivals now, but brothers. 315

MYRTLE.

Dear Bevil! You are born to triumph over me! But

now our competition ceases, I rejoice in the
preeminence of your virtue, and your alliance adds
charms to Lucinda.
SIR JOHN BEVIL.

Now ladies and gentlemen, you have set the world   320
a fair example. Your happiness is owing to your
constancy and merit, and the several difficulties
you have struggled with evidently show
Whate'er the generous* mind itself denies,
The secret care of Providence supplies.   325

Exeunt.

FINIS.

Textual Notes

[a] Copytext is the first edition corrected, a 1723 octavo
(O1c). Also consulted: the uncorrected first edition (O1)
and the second edition (O2), both of which were also
published in 1723; modern editions of 1939 by
Nettleton and Case, revised by Stone in 1969 (NCS)
and of 1971 (Kenny).

[b] Phillis] Kenny; Lettice O1, O1c, O2, NCS

[c] *Exit Tom*] Kenny; *om.* O1, O1c, O2, NCS

[d] Good] O2, NCS, Kenny; God O1, O1c

[e] not] NCS, Kenny (following the 1722 Dublin edition);
om. O1, O1c, O2

Social Comedy

S ocial comedy socializes threats against hegemonic culture either by disciplining upstarts (cits and commonwealthsmen, Puritans and parvenus, rich country boobies and scientific experimenters) or by marrying rebellious youth, within their own class, for the perpetuation of the estate economy. English baroque comedy still owes a great deal to the Roman comedies of Plautus and Terence for precisely these preoccupations. In the Restoration, sometimes that estate economy is enriched by union with wealthy cits and the ideology stretched to accommodate them. More often, cits are severely disciplined by the seduction of their wives and daughters by the "naturally" superior Cavaliers. A great contribution of this comedy is the development of the "gay couple" foreshadowed in, for example, Shakespeare's Beatrice and Benedick. Post-Revolution comedy continues to put the right couple to bed, but the male has been deprived of much of his libertine sting, and it is the female coquette who must be socialized into marriage. Good nature and generosity replace wit and energy as the supreme values, as comedy becomes more a matter of feelings, more sentimental—even as bourgeois morality becomes an ethic of sentiment, of benevolence, providing the rationale for patronizing the less fortunate, less civilized.

The Committee[a]

by Sir Robert Howard (1626-1698)

edited by Cheryl L. Nixon

A statesman, poet, and dramatist, Sir Robert Howard is most often remembered for his preface to *Four New Plays* (1665), which contains the first printing of *The Committee*. The preface argues for the use of blank verse in tragedy and occasioned a famous debate with Dryden, who responded in his *Essay of Dramatic Poesy*. While the preface is remembered, *The Committee* is often overlooked. And yet, *The Committee* is Restoration social comedy at its best: the play uses the expected plot structure of loving couples overcoming obstacles to provide a biting critique of Puritan political, religious, and economic practices during the Civil Wars. As depicted by the play, the Puritan state's religious fervor is a mere premise for its larger land-grabbing desire to turn the class system upside down. The play's two Cavalier couples must not only find true love, but must outwit the Puritans who have sequestered their land and, in effect, return society to its rightful—or aristocratic and Stuart—order. The primary obstacle to the lovers' happiness proves to be the Puritan Parliament itself, as represented by the Committee of Sequestrations, which gives the play its title.[1]

The Committee was sure to please Restoration theater-goers, who would have first seen the play around 1662. With Charles II securely on the throne, the audience would have delighted in the play's depiction of the Puritan Day family, whose evil actions include the use of guardianship to seize land, the confiscation of estates from infants and widows, an attempt at forcing an unequal marriage, the forgery of a letter from the King, and the trading of the Committee's preferential treatment for goods and money. In contrast, *The Committee*'s heroes are two rakish Cavalier soldiers who refuse to trade their political and religious principles for land, reflecting Howard's career as a Royalist soldier during the Civil Wars (he was knighted for valor in 1644 and imprisoned during the Commonwealth) and his later success as a statesman loyal to the crown (he served as a member of Parliament, an appointee to the Privy Council, and a military commander). Notably, however, it is Ruth and Arbella, the play's lively and outspoken Cavalier women, who have the intelligence to manipulate the Puritan Committee to save the men's and their own estates. The play's comic relief is supplied by Teague, a good-hearted but perpetually confused Irish servant; a model for future comic Irish characters, Teague be-

---

[1] Committee of Sequestrations] a Parliament-ordered committee which confiscated Royalist estates in order to sell them to supporters of the Puritan state or seized the estates in order to re-sell them to the owners, as a means of levying a fine for the estate-owner's rebellion against the Roundheads.

Parliament published *Instructions agreed upon by a Committee of the Lords and Commons for the Committee for Sequestration of Delinquents Estates* on April 11, 1643, in the form of an eight-page pamphlet and one-page broadsheet to be distributed to locally-formed Committees. The instructions list thirteen guidelines, which, for example, order the Committee to seize "two parts [2/3] of the estates real and personal of all papists" and the

"whole estates of all other sorts of delinquents"; to "restrain tenants from paying rents to delinquents" and let the land to new tenants to increase the estate's income; to seize the delinquent's goods and chattels, and inventory, appraise, and sell them "at as great rates as you can." The instructions explain that the Committee must keep a "schedule" and "books and registers" of this income and, after giving themselves an allowance out of the income, must "convey safely" the remaining money to Parliament for the "subsistence of the army raised by Parliament."

comes the play's most famous character and was acted by the great comic actor John Lacy.

These sharply drawn characters act against a backdrop of the Civil Wars' real concerns. In 1643, the Puritan Parliament created local Committees of Sequestrations to seize the land of Royalists, suspected Papists, and critics of the Puritan state. Once their land was seized, estate-owners would have to "compound" for it, paying the Committee up to two-thirds the estate's value to reclaim it. As *The Committee* makes clear, this compounding process became particularly noxious when it demanded that estate-owners prove their loyalty to the Puritan state by swearing to the *Solemn League and Covenant* of 1643.[2] A Covenant-taker signed a parliamentary "roll" or record, pledging to support and further the reformed Protestant religion and seek out and put on trial any non-supporter. *The Committee*'s brilliance comes not from its recognition of these factual situations, but from its use of them to heighten the plot's conflicts, develop its characters, and raise larger moral questions concerning the state's coercion of economic structure and religious principle.

─────────

2 *Solemn League and Covenant* of 1643] *A Solemn League and Covenant for Reformation and Defence of Religion* records a Parliamentary order of September 25, 1643 and was published on September 29 in an eight-page pamphlet for widespread distribution. This formal agreement created an alliance between the Scottish Presbyterians and the English Puritans against Charles I and his attempt to impose Episcopalianism; the Presbyterians and Puritans were temporarily united by this desire to purge any trace of Roman Catholicism from their national religion. The Solemn League and Covenant demanded that the people of Scotland and England uphold the "true" Protestant faith, as defined by the Kirk of Scotland and reformed Church of England. The Scots won religious concessions from the Puritans, who allowed the promotion of Presbyterianism, in exchange for their assistance against Charles. The Parliamentary alliance with the Scots led to a decisive victory over Royalist forces at Naseby in June 1645, during the first Civil War (August 1642-April 1646). In 1646, Charles sur-

rendered to the Scots, expecting compassion, but they handed him over to Oliver Cromwell (1599-1658).

As the Parliamentary cause became more radically Puritan in 1646-7, this Scottish-English agreement fell apart and the Presbyterian Scots switched alliances and backed Charles against Cromwell's Independents. The brief second Civil War (February-August 1648) ended with Cromwell's defeat of the Scottish army in 1648. Presbyterians were purged from Parliament during "Prides Purge" in December of 1648, immediately preceding Charles' execution on January 30, 1649. The Scots recognized Charles I's son, Charles II, as King and fought unsuccessfully against Cromwell on his behalf in the failed Battle of Dunbar (1650) and Battle of Worcester (1651).

Dramatis Personae

[MEN]

Colonel Careless.
Colonel Blunt.
Lieutenant Story.
Nehemiah Catch,
Joseph Blemish,
Jonathan Headstrong,
Ezekiel Scrape, Committee-men.
Mr. Day, the Chairman to the Committee.
Abel, son to Mr. Day.
Obadiah, clerk to the Committee.
[Teague.]
Drawer.
Bayliffs.
Soldiers.
Two chairmen.*
Gaol-keeper.
Servant to Mr. Day.
A stagecoach man.
Bookseller.
[Porter.]
[Jack, a prentice.]

WOMEN

Mrs.* Arbella.
Mrs. Day.
Mrs.* Ruth.
Mrs. Chat.

Scene: London.

The Committee.

Act I, scene i. [A street near the Days' house.]

Enter Mrs. Arbella, Mrs. Ruth, Colonel Blunt, and a [stage]coach man. Mrs. Day enters, brushing her hoods and scarves.

MRS. DAY.

Now out upon't, how dusty 'tis. All things considered, 'tis better traveling in the winter, especially for us of the better sort, that ride in coaches. And yet, to say truth, warm weather is both pleasant and comfortable; 'tis a thousand pities that fair weather should do any hurt.—Well said, honest coachman, thou hast done thy part. My son Abel paid for my place at Reading, did he not?

COACHMAN.

Yes, an't* please you.   10

MRS. DAY.

Well, there's something extraordinary to make thee drink.

COACHMAN. (*Aside.*)

By my whip, 'tis a groat of more than ordinary thinness. Plague on this new gentry, how liberal they are.—Farewell, young mistress; farewell,   15
gentlemen. Pray when you come by Reading, let Toby carry you. (*Exit.*)

MRS. DAY.

Why how now, Mrs. Arbella? What, sad? Why what's the matter?

ARBELLA.

I am not very sad.   20

MRS. DAY.

Nay, by my honor, you need not, if you knew as much as I. Well, I'll tell you one thing, you are well enough, you need not fear, whoever does; say I told you so, if you do not hurt yourself. For as cunning as he is, and let him be as cunning as he   25
will, I can see with half an eye, that my son Abel means to take care of you in your composition[3] and will needs have you his guest. Ruth and you

_____

[3] composition] compounding for an estate

shall be bedfellows. I warrant that same Abel many and many a time will wish his sister's place, or else   30
his father ne'er got him. Though I say it that should not say it, yet I do say it—'tis a notable fellow.

ARBELLA. (*Aside.*)

I am fallen into strange hands, if they prove as busy as her tongue.   35

MRS. DAY.

And now you talk of this same Abel, I tell you but one thing, I wonder that neither he nor my husband's honor's chief clerk Obadiah is not here ready to attend me. I dare warrant my son Abel has been here two hours before us. 'Tis the veriest   40
princox; he will ever be a-galloping, and yet he is not full one and twenty, for all his appearances. He never stole this trick of galloping; his father was just such another before him and would gallop with the best of 'em. He and Mistress Busie's   45
husband were counted the best horsemen in Reading, aye, and Berkshire to boot. I have rode formerly behind Mr. Busie, but in truth I cannot now endure to travel but in a coach. My own was at present in disorder, and so I was fain to shift in   50
this. But I warrant you, if his honor, Mr. Day, chairman of the honorable Committee of Sequestrations, should know that his wife rode in a stagecoach, he would make the house too hot for some. (*To Colonel Blunt.*) Why, how is't with you,   55
sir? What, weary of your journey?

COLONEL BLUNT.

(*Aside.*)

Her tongue will never tire.—So many, mistress, riding in the coach has a little distempered me with heat.

MRS. DAY.

So many, sir? Why, there was but six. What would   60
you say if I should tell you that I was one of the eleven that traveled at one time in one coach?

COLONEL BLUNT.

(*Aside.*)

Oh the devil! I have given her a new theme.

MRS. DAY.

Why, I'll tell you. Can you guess how 'twas?   65

COLONEL BLUNT.

Not I, truly. But 'tis no matter, I do believe it.

MRS. DAY.

Look you, thus 'twas: there was, in the first place, myself, and my husband (I should have said first, but his honor would have pardoned me, if he had heard me); Mr. Busie that I told you of and his wife; the Mayor of Reading and his wife; and this Ruth that you see there, in one of our laps. But now, where do you think the rest were? 70

COLONEL BLUNT.

Atop o'th'coach, sure.

MRS. DAY.

Nay, I durst swear you would never guess. Why, would you think it? I had two growing in my belly, Mrs. Busie one in hers, and Mrs. Mayoress of Reading, a chopping boy, as it proved afterwards, in hers. As like the father as if it had been spit out of his mouth, and if he had come out of his mouth, he had come out of as honest a man's mouth as any in forty miles of the head of him. For would you think of it? At the very same time, when this same Ruth was sick, it being the first time the girl was ever coached, the good man (Mr. Mayor, I mean, that I spoke of) held his hat for the girl to ease her stomach in. 75 80 85

Enter Abel and Obadiah.

—Oh, are you come? Long looked for comes at last. What, you have a slow set pace, as well as your hasty scribble sometimes. Did you not think it fit that I should have found attendance ready for me when I alighted? 90

OBADIAH.

I ask your honor's pardon, for I do profess unto your ladyship I had attended sooner but that his young honor, Mr. Abel, demurred me by his delays. 95

MRS. DAY.

Well son Abel, you must be obeyed, and I partly, if not, guess your business: providing for the entertainment of one I have in my eye. Read her and take her. Ah, is't not so? 100

ABEL.

I have not been deficient in my care, forsooth.

MRS. DAY.

Will you never leave your "forsooths"? Art thou not ashamed to let the clerk carry himself better and show more breeding than his master's son?

ABEL.

If it please your honor, I have some business for your more private ear. 105

MRS. DAY.

Very well.

RUTH.

What a lamentable condition has that gentleman been in? Faith, I pity him.

ARBELLA.

Are you so apt to pity men? 110

RUTH.

Yes, men that are humorsome,* as I would children that are froward; I would not make them cry a purpose.

ARBELLA.

Well, I like his humor.* I dare swear he's plain and honest. 115

RUTH.

Plain enough, of all conscience. Faith, I'll speak to him.

ARBELLA.

Nay, prithee don't. He'll think thee rude.

RUTH.

Why, then I'll think him an ass.—How is't after your journey, sir? 120

COLONEL BLUNT.

Why, I am worse after it.

RUTH.

Do you love riding in a coach, sir?

COLONEL BLUNT.

No forsooth, nor talking after riding in a coach.

RUTH.

I should be loath to interrupt you meditations, sir; we may have the fruits hereafter. 125

COLONEL BLUNT. (*Aside.*)

If you have, they shall break loose spite of my teeth.* This spawn is as bad as the great pike.

ARBELLA.

Prithee peace, sir. We wish you all happiness.

COLONEL BLUNT.

And quiet, good sweet ladies. [*Aside.*] I like her well enough. Now would not I have her say anymore, for fear she should jeer, too, and spoil my good opinion. If 'twere possible, I would think well of one woman. 130

MRS. DAY.

Come, Mrs. Arbella. 'Tis as I told you, Abel has

done it; say no more.—Take her by the hand Abel. I profess she may venture to take thee for better, for worse. Come, mistress, the honorable Committee will sit suddenly.* Come, let's along. Farewell, sir.

Exeunt. Manet Colonel Blunt.

COLONEL BLUNT.

How, the Committee ready to sit? Plague on their honors; for so my honored lady, that was one of the eleven, was pleased to call 'em. I had like to have come a day after the fair. 'Tis pretty, that such as I have been, must compound for their having been rascals. Well, I must go look a lodging and a solicitor. I'll find the arrantest rogue I can too, for according to the old saying, set a thief to catch a thief.

Enter Colonel Careless and Lieutenant Story.

COLONEL CARELESS.

Dear Blunt, well met. When came you, man?

COLONEL BLUNT.

Dear Careless, I did not think to have met thee so suddenly.*—Lieutenant, your servant.—I am landed just now, man.

COLONEL CARELESS.

Thou speakest as if thou hadst been at sea.

COLONEL BLUNT.

It's pretty well guessed. I have been in a storm.

COLONEL CARELESS.

What business brought thee?

COLONEL BLUNT.

May be the same with yours: I am come to compound with their honors.

COLONEL CARELESS.

That's my business, too. Why, the Committee sits suddenly?

COLONEL BLUNT.

Yes, I know it. I heard so in the storm I told thee of.

COLONEL CARELESS.

What storm, man?

COLONEL BLUNT.

Why, a tempest as high as ever blew from woman's breath. I have rode in a stagecoach, wedged in with half a dozen; one of them was a Committeeman's wife. His name is Day, and she accordingly will be called "your honor" and "your ladyship," with a tongue that wags as much faster than all other women's, as in the several motions of a watch the hand of the minute moves faster than that of the hours. There was her daughter, too, but a bastard, without question, for she had no resemblance to the rest of the notched[4] rascals, and very pretty, and had wit enough to jeer a man in prosperity to death. There was another gentlewoman, and she was handsome, nay very handsome, but I kept her from being as sad as the rest.

COLONEL CARELESS.

Prithee, how man?

COLONEL BLUNT.

Why, she began with two or three good words, and I desired her she would be quiet while she was well.

COLONEL CARELESS.

Thou wert not so mad?

COLONEL BLUNT.

I had been mad if I had not. But when we came to our journey's end, there met us two such formal and stately rascals that yet pretended religion and open rebellion ever painted. It was the hopes and guide of the honorable family, videlicit the eldest son and the chiefest clerk, rogues. And hereby hangs a tale. This gentlewoman I told thee I kept civil by desiring her to say nothing is a rich heir of one that died in the King's service and left his estate under sequestration. This young chicken has this kite snatched up, and designs her for this, her eldest rascal.

COLONEL CARELESS.

What a dull fellow wert thou not to make love* and rescue her!

COLONEL BLUNT.

I'll woo no woman.

COLONEL CARELESS.

Wouldst thou have them court thee? A soldier, and not love a siege!

Enter Teague.

—How now, who art thou?

---

4 notched] term of contempt for the Puritans or Round-heads, referring to their close-cropped hair

TEAGUE.

A poor Irishman, and Christ save me and save you
all. I prithee give me six pence, gad mastero.[5]   200

COLONEL CARELESS.

Six pence? I see thou wouldst not lose anything
for want* of asking. Here, I am pretty near: there's
a groat for thy confidence.

TEAGUE.

By my troth, it is too little.

COLONEL CARELESS.

Troth, like enough. How long hast thou been in   205
England?

TEAGUE.

Ever since I came hither, i'faith.

COLONEL CARELESS.

That's true. What hast thou done since thou
camest into England?

TEAGUE.

Served God and St. Patrick, and my good sweet   210
King, and my good sweet master, yes indeed.

COLONEL CARELESS.

And what dost thou do now?

TEAGUE.

Cry for them every day, upon my soul.

COLONEL CARELESS.

Why, where's thy master?

TEAGUE.

He's dead, mastero, and left poor Teague. Upon   215
my soul, he never served poor Teague so before.

COLONEL CARELESS.

Who was thy master?

TEAGUE.

E'en the good Colonel Danger.

COLONEL CARELESS.

He was my dear and noble friend.

TEAGUE.

Yes, that he was, and poor Teague's, too, i'faith   220
now.

COLONEL CARELESS.

What dost thou mean to do?

TEAGUE.

I will get a good master, if any good master would
get me. I cannot tell what to do else, by my soul,
that I cannot, for I have went and gone to one   225

Lilly's.* He lives at that house, at the end of
another house, by the maypole house,[6] and tells
everybody by one star and t'other star what good
luck they shall have. But he could not tell nothing
for poor Teague.   230

COLONEL CARELESS.

Why, man?

TEAGUE.

Why 'tis done by the stars, and he told me there
were no stars for Irishmen. I told him he told two
or three lies, upon my soul. There were as many
stars in Ireland as in England, and more too, that   235
there are. And if a good master cannot get me, I
will run into Ireland and see if the stars be not
there still. And if they be, I will come back, i'faith,
and beat his pate if he will not then tell me some
good luck and some stars.   240

COLONEL CARELESS. [Aside.]

Poor fellow, I pity him. I fancy he's simply[7]
honest.—Hast thou any trade?

TEAGUE.

Bo, bub bub bo, a trade, a trade! An Irishman, a
trade! An Irishman scorns a trade, that he does; I
will run for thee forty miles, but I scorn t'have a   245
trade.

COLONEL BLUNT.

Alas, poor simple fellow.

COLONEL CARELESS.

I pity him, nor can I endure to see any miserable
that can weep for my Prince[8] and friend.—Well
Teague, what sayest thou if I will take thee?   250

TEAGUE.

Why, I will say thou wilt do very well then.

COLONEL CARELESS.

Thy master was my dear friend. Wert thou with
him when he was killed?

TEAGUE.

Yes, upon my soul, that I was, and I did howl over

---

[5] gad mastero] good master

---

[6] maypole house] The Puritan Parliament forbade maypoles (q.v.) in 1644, but a famous maypole was erected
after the Restoration in the Strand* (cf. *The Old Troop*)
at the present Saint-Mary's-in-the-Strand; perhaps Lilly's
house was nearby (bating the anachronism).

[7] simply] naively

[8] Prince] Charles II

him, and I asked him why he would leave poor 255
Teague. And i'faith, I stayed kissing his sweet face till
the rogues came upon me and took away all from
me. And I was naked till I got this mantle, that I was.
I have never any victuals neither, but a little snuff.

COLONEL CARELESS.
Come, thou shalt live with me; love me as thou 260
didst thy master.

TEAGUE.
That I will, i'faith, if thou wouldst be good too.

COLONEL CARELESS.
Now to our business, for I came but last night
myself, and the Lieutenant and I were just going
to seek a solicitor. 265

COLONEL BLUNT.
One may serve us all. What say you, Lieutenant,
can you furnish us?

LIEUTENANT STORY.
Yes, I think I can help you to plough with a heifer
of their own.

COLONEL CARELESS.
Now think on't, Blunt, why didst not thou begin 270
with the Committeeman's cow?

COLONEL BLUNT.
Plague on her, she lowbelled me so that I thought
of nothing but stood shrinking like dead lark.[9]

LIEUTENANT STORY.
But hark you, gentlemen, there's an ill-tasting dose
to be swallowed first: there's a covenant to be taken. 275

TEAGUE.
Well, what is that covenant? By my soul, I would
take it for my new master. If I could, that I would.

COLONEL CARELESS.
Thank thee, Teague.—A covenant, sayest thou?

TEAGUE.
Well, where is that covenant?

COLONEL CARELESS.
We'll not swear, Lieutenant. 280

LIEUTENANT STORY.
You must have no land then.

COLONEL BLUNT.
Then farewell acres, and may the dirt choke them.

_____
9 lowbelled...lark] a practice of hunting at night with
   torches and low-toned bells, which supposedly paralyzed
   the birds with fear and allowed them to be easily trapped

COLONEL CARELESS.
'Tis but being reduced to Teague's equipage; 'twas
a lucky thing to have a fellow that can teach one
this cheap diet of snuff. 285

LIEUTENANT STORY.
Come gentlemen, we must lose no more time. I'll
carry you to my poor house, where you shall lodge.
For know, I am married to a most illustrious
person that had a kindness* for me.

COLONEL CARELESS.
Prithee, how didst thou light upon this good 290
fortune?

LIEUTENANT STORY.
Why, you see there are stars in England, though
none in Ireland. Come gentleman, time calls us;
you shall have my story hereafter.

COLONEL BLUNT.
Plague on this covenant. 295

LIEUTENANT STORY.
Curse it not, 'twill prosper then.

COLONEL CARELESS.
Come Teague, however I have a suit of clothes for
thee; thou shalt lay by thy blanket for some time.
It may be thee and I may be reduced together to
thy country fashion. 300

TEAGUE.
Upon my soul, joy,* for I will carry thee then into
my country too.

COLONEL CARELESS.
Why, there's the worst on't. The best will help itself.

Exeunt.

[Scene ii. The Days' house.]

Enter Mr. Day and Mrs. Day

MR. DAY.
Welcome, sweet duck. I profess thou hast brought
home good company, indeed: money and money's
worth. If we can but now make sure of this heir,
Mrs. Arbella, for our son Abel.

MRS. DAY.
If we can? You are ever at your "ifs." You're afraid 5
of your own shadow. I can tell you one "if" more,
that is, "if" I did not bear you up, your heart[10]

_____
10 heart] the seat of courage

would be down in your breeches at every turn. Well, if I were gone—there's another "if" for you.

MR. DAY.

I profess thou sayest true, I should not know what to do indeed. I am beholding to thy good counsel for many good thing. I had ne'er got Ruth nor her estate into my fingers else.

MRS. DAY.

Nay, in that business, too, you were at your "ifs." Now, you see she goes currently for our own daughter, and this Arbella shall be our daughter too, or she shall have no estate.

MR. DAY.

If we could but do that, wife.

MRS. DAY.

Yet again at your "ifs"!

MR. DAY.

I have done, I have done. Your counsel, good duck, you know I depend upon that.

MRS. DAY.

You may well enough, you find the sweet on't. And to say truth, 'tis known too well that you relied upon it. In truth, they are ready to call me the Committee-man. They well perceive the weight that lies upon me, husband.

MR. DAY.

Nay good duck, no chiding now, but to your counsel.

MRS. DAY.

In the first place (observe how I lay a design in politics) d'ye mark, counterfeit me a letter from the King, where he shall offer you great matters to serve him and his interest underhand, very good. And in it let him remember his kind love and service to me. This will make them look about 'em and think you somebody. Then promise them, if they'll be true friends to you, to live and die with them and refuse all great offers. Then whilst 'tis warm, get the composition of Arbella's estate into your power, upon your design of marrying her to Abel.

MR. DAY.

Excellent.

MRS. DAY.

Mark the luck on't too, their names sound alike: Abel and Arbella. They are the same to a trifle. It seemeth a providence.

MR. DAY.

Thou observest right, duck. Thou canst see as far into a millstone* as another.

MRS. DAY.

Pish, do not interrupt me.

MR. DAY.

I do not, good duck, I do not.

MRS. DAY.

You do not, and yet you do. You put me off from the concatenation of my discourse.—Then, as I was saying, you may intimate to your honorable fellows that one good turn deserves another. That language is understood amongst you, I take it? Hah!

MR. DAY.

Yes, yes, we use those items often.

MRS. DAY.

Well, interrupt me not.

MR. DAY.

I do not, good wife.

MRS. DAY.

You do not, and yet you do.—By this means get her composition put wholly into your hands, and then, no Abel, no land.[11] But in the meantime, I would have Abel do his part, too.

MR. DAY.

Aye, aye, there's a want,* I found it.

MRS. DAY.

Yes, when I told you so before.

MR. DAY.

Why, that's true, duck. He is too backward. If I were in his place, and as young as I have been—

MRS. DAY.

Oh, you'd do wonders. But now I think on't, there may be some use made of Ruth; 'tis a notable witty harlotry.—You were so, when I told you I had thought on't first.—Let me see, it shall be so: we'll set her to instruct Abel in the first place and then to incline Arbella. They are hand and glove, and women can do much with one another.

MR. DAY.

Thou hast hit upon my own thoughts.

---

11 no Abel, no land] Arbella will be informed that she can gain access to her estate only by marrying Abel. Securing Arbella's estate through marriage would protect the Days from legal claims (from Arbella or her relatives) that might result from a simple seizure of the estate.

MRS. DAY.

Pray call her in. You thought of that too, did you
not? 75

MR. DAY.

I will, duck.—Ruth, why, Ruth!

Enter Ruth.

RUTH.

Your pleasure, sir.

MR. DAY.

Nay, 'tis my wife's desire that—

MRS. DAY.

Well, if it be your wife's, she can best tell it herself,
I suppose. D'ye hear Ruth, you may do a business 80
that may not be the worse for you. You know I
use but few words.

RUTH. (*Aside.*)

What does she call a few?

MRS. DAY.

Look you now, as I said, to be short and to the
matter, my husband and I do design this Mrs. 85
Arbella for our son Abel, and the young fellow is
not forward enough, you conceive. Prithee give
him a little instructions how to demean* himself
and in what manner to speak, which we call
address, to her, for women best know what will 90
please women. Then, work on Arbella on the other
side. Work, I say, my good girl, no more but so;
you know my custom is to use but few words.
Much may be said in a little. You shan't repent it.

MR. DAY.

And I say something too, Ruth. 95

MRS. DAY.

What need you? Do you not see it all said already
to your hand?—What sayest thou, girl?

RUTH.

I shall do my best. (*Aside.*) I would not use lose
the sport for more than I speak of.

MRS. DAY.

Go call Abel, good girl. 100

Exit Ruth.

By bringing this to pass, husband, we shall secure
ourselves if the King should come;[12] you'll be
hanged else.

_____

[12] King should come] The time setting of the play is un-

MR. DAY.

Oh good wife, let's secure ourselves by all means.
There's a wise saying: 'tis good to have a shelter 105
against every storm. I remember that.

MRS. DAY.

You may well, when you hear me say it so often.

Enter Ruth with Abel.

MR. DAY.

Oh son Abel, d'ye hear?

MRS. DAY.

Pray hold your peace and give everybody leave to
tell their own tale.—D'hear son Abel, I have 110
formerly told you that Arbella would be a good
wife for you. A word's enough to the wise: some
endeavors must be used, and you must not be
deficient. I have spoken to your sister Ruth to
instruct you what to say and how to carry your self; 115
observe her directions, as you'll answer the
contrary. Be confident, and put home. Hah boy,
hadst thou but thy mother's pate! Well, 'tis but a
folly to talk of that that cannot be. Be sure you
follow your sister's directions. 120

MR. DAY.

Be sure, boy.—Well said, duck, I say.

Exeunt [Mr. and Mrs. Day].

RUTH.

Now, brother Abel.

ABEL.

Now, sister Ruth?

RUTH. (*Aside.*)

Hitherto he observes me punctually.—Have you
a month's mind* to this gentlewoman, mistress 125
Arbella?

ABEL.

I have not known her a week yet.

RUTH.

Oh cry you mercy, good brother Abel. Well, to
begin then, you must alter your posture and by

_____

certain, so the anticipated King can be either Charles I
(in the 1640s) or Charles II (in the 1650s), although
the latter's coming would be foremost in the minds of
a Restoration audience. The earlier reference to the
King's letters is equally ambiguous.

your grave and high demeanor make your self 130
appear a hole[13] above Obadiah, lest your mistress
should take you for such another scribble-
scrabble[14] as he is. And always hold up your head
as if it were bolstered up with high matters, your
hands joined flat together, projecting a little 135
beyond the rest of your body, as ready to separate
when you begin to open.

ABEL.

Must I go apace or softly?

RUTH.

Oh gravely, by all means, as if you were loaded
with weighty considerations so.—Very well. Now 140
to apply our prescription. Suppose now that I were
your mistress Arbella and meet you by accident.
Keep your posture so, and when you come just to
me, start like a horse that has spied something on
one side of him and give a little gird out of the 145
way on a sudden, declaring that you did not see
her before by reason of your deep contemplations.
Then you must speak. Let's hear.

ABEL.

God save you, mistress.

RUTH.

Oh fie man, you should begin thus: "Pardon, 150
mistress, my profound contemplations, in which
I was so buried that I did not see you." And then,
as she answers, proceed. I know what she'll say, I
am so used to her.

ABEL.

This will do well, if I forget it not. 155

RUTH.

Well, try once.

ABEL.

Pardon, mistress, my profound contemplations, in
which I was so hid that you could not see me.

RUTH. (*Aside.*)

Better sport than I expected.—Very well done;
you're perfect. Then she will answer: "Sir, I suppose 160
you are so busied with state affairs that it may well
hinder you from taking notice of anything below
them."

ABEL.

No forsooth, I have some profound contemplations, but no state affairs. 165

RUTH.

Oh fie man, you must confess that the weighty
affairs of state lie heavy upon you, but 'tis a burden
you must bear, and then shrug your shoulders.

ABEL.

Must I say so? I am afraid my mother will be angry,
for she takes all the state matters upon herself. 170

RUTH.

Pish, did not she charge you to be ruled by me? Why
man, Arbella will never have you if she be not made
believe you can do great matters with Parliament-
men and Committee-men. How should she hope
for any good by you else in her composition? 175

ABEL.

I apprehend you now. I shall observe.

RUTH.

'Tis well at this time, I'll say no more. Put yourself
in your posture so. Now go look your mistress. I'll
warrant you the town's our own.

ABEL.

I go. (*Exit.*) 180

RUTH.

Now I have fixed him not to go off till he discharges
on his mistress. I could burst with laughing.

Enter Arbella.

ARBELLA.

What dost thou laugh at, Ruth?

RUTH.

Didst thou meet my brother Abel?

ARBELLA.

No. 185

RUTH.

If thou hadst met him right, he had played at hard
head[15] with thee.

ARBELLA.

What dost thou mean?

RUTH.

Why, I have been teaching him to woo, by
command of my superiors, and have instructed 190

---

13 a hole] a position, as on a board of pegs and holes
14 scribble-scrabble] scrawler, scratcher; a disparaging label
   for Obadiah's position as a clerk

15 played at hard head] knocked heads, or been hard-
   headed or block-headed

him to hold up his head so high, that of necessity
he must run against everything that comes in his
way.

ARBELLA.

Who is he to woo?

RUTH.

Even thy own sweet self. 195

ARBELLA.

Out upon him.

RUTH.

Nay, thou wilt be rarely courted. I'll not spoil the
sport by telling thee anything beforehand. They
have sent to Lilly,* and, his learning being built
upon knowing what most people would have him 200
say, he has told them for a certain that Abel shall
have a rich heir, and that must be you.

ARBELLA.

Must be.

RUTH.

Yes, Committee-men can compel more than stars.

ARBELLA.

I fear this too late. You are their daughter, Ruth? 205

RUTH.

I deny that.

ARBELLA.

How?

RUTH.

Wonder not that I begin thus freely with you, 'tis
to invite your confidence in me.

ARBELLA.

You amaze me. 210

RUTH.

Pray, do not wonder nor suspect.—When my
father, Sir Basil Throughgood, died, I was very
young, not above two years old. 'Tis too long to
tell you how this rascal, being a trustee, catched
me and my estate, being the sole heir unto my 215
father, into his gripes, and now, for some years, has
confirmed his unjust power by the unlawful power
of the times. I fear they have designs as bad as this
on you. You see, I have no reserve and endeavor
to be thought worthy of your friendship. 220

ARBELLA.

I embrace it with as much clearness. Let us love
and assist one another.—Would they marry me to
this, their firstborn puppy?

RUTH.

No doubt, or keep your composition from you.

ARBELLA.

'Twas my ill fortune to fall into such hands, 225
foolishly enticed by fair words and large promises
of assistance.

RUTH.

Peace.

Enter Obadiah.

OBADIAH.

Mrs. Ruth, my master is demanding your company,
together, and not singly, with Mrs. Arbella; you will 230
find them in the parlor. The Committee, being
ready to sit, calls upon my care and circumspection
to set in order the weighty matters of state for their
wise and honorable inspection.

RUTH.

We come. 235

Exit Obadiah.

Come dear Arbella, never be perplexed. Cheerful
spirits are the best bladders[16] to swim with; if thou
art sad, the weight will sink thee. Be secret, and
still know me for no other than what I seem to
be, their daughter. Another time thou shalt know 240
all particulars of my strange story.

ARBELLA.

Come wench, they cannot bring us to compound
for our humors;* they shall be free still.*

Exeunt.

Act II, scene i. [A street.]

Enter Teague.

TEAGUE.

I'faith my sweet master has sent me to a rascal,
now that he has; I will go tell him so, too. He
asked me why he could not send one that could
speak English. Upon my soul I was going to give
him an Irish knock. The Devil's in them all; they 5
will not talk with me. I will go near to knock this
man's pate, and that man Lilly's pate, too, that I
will. I will make them prate to me, that I will.

One cries "Books" within.

---

16 bladders] inflated sacs, buoyant supports

How now, what noises are that?

Enter Bookseller.

BOOKSELLER.

New books, new books! A desperate plot and 10
engagement of the bloody Cavaliers. Mr.
Saltmarsh's alarm to the Nation, after having been
three days dead.[17] *Mercurius Britanicus,*[18] etcetera.

TEAGUE.

How's that? Now, they cannot live in Ireland after
they are dead three days! 15

BOOKSELLER.

Mercurius Britanicus, or *The Weekly Post,*[19] or, *The
Solemn League and Covenant.*[20]

TEAGUE.

What is that you say? Is it the covenant? Have you
that?

BOOKSELLER.

Yes, what then, sir? 20

TEAGUE.

Which is that covenant?

BOOKSELLER.

Why, this is the *Covenant.*

TEAGUE.

Well, I must take that covenant.

BOOKSELLER.

You take my commodities?

TEAGUE.

I must take that covenant, upon my soul now, that 25
I must.

BOOKSELLER.

Stand off, sir, or I'll set you further.

TEAGUE.

Well, upon my soul now, I will take that covenant
for my master.

BOOKSELLER.

Your master must pay me for't then? 30

TEAGUE.

I'faith now, they will make him pay for't after I
have taken it for him.

BOOKSELLER.

What a devil does the fellow mean?

TEAGUE.

You will make me stay too long, that you will.
Look you now, I will knock you down upon the 35
ground if you will not let me take it.

BOOKSELLER.

Stand off, sirrah.

TEAGUE.

I'faith I will take it now. (*He throws the fellow down
and takes away the paper and runs out.*)

BOOKSELLER.

What a devil ails this fellow? He did not come to rob 40
me, certainly, for he has not taken above two
penniworth of lamentable ware away. But I feel the
rascal's fingers. I may light upon my wild Irish again,
and if I do, I will fix him with some catchpoles that
shall be worse than his own country bogs. 45

[Exit.]

[Scene ii. Another street.]

*Enter Colonel Careless, Colonel Blunt, and Lieutenant
Story.*

LIEUTENANT STORY.

And what say you, noble Colonels? How and how
d'ye like my lady? I gave her the title of illustrious
from those illustrious commodities which she deals
in: hot water and tobacco.[21]

---

17 Mr. Saltmarsh...dead] John Saltmarsh (d. 1647) a prolific writer who ardently supported church reform during the Civil Wars. This reference is most probably to a
posthumously published work, edited by his widow
Mary, titled *England's Friend, raised from the grave, giving seasonable advice to the lord generall, lieutenant
generall, and councell of warre, being the true copies of three
letters written by Mr. John Saltmash a little before his death*
(London, 1649). The reference could possibly be to either of two works by Samuel Gorton (1592/3-1677),
Saltmarsh returned from the Dead (London 1655) or *An
Antidote against the Common Plague of the World—
intitled Saltmarsh returned from the dead* (London, 1659).
18 *Mercurius Britanicus*] a periodical of the Civil Wars published in London by G. Bishop and R. White from August 1643 to May 1646; several pamphlets from the
1640s share this main title (having separate subtitles).
19 *The Weekly Post*] a Commonwealth periodical published
from 1654 through September 1655
20 *The Solemn League and Covenant*] a printed copy of the
"Solemn League and Covenant" of 1643; see headnote

---

21 hot water and tobacco] distilled alcoholic liquor and
smoking tobacco; Story's wife runs a tavern serving these
commodities.

COLONEL CARELESS.

Prithee how comest thou to think of marrying? 5

LIEUTENANT STORY.

Why, that which hinders men from those venereal conditions prompted me to matrimony: hunger and cold, Colonel.

COLONEL CARELESS.

Which you destroyed with a fat woman, strong water, and stinking tobacco. 10

LIEUTENANT STORY.

No, faith, the woman conduced but little, but the rest could not be purchased without.

COLONEL CARELESS.

She's beholding to you.

LIEUTENANT STORY.

For all your mocking, she had been ruined if it had not been for me. 15

COLONEL CARELESS.

Prithee, make but that good.

LIEUTENANT STORY.

With ease, sir. Why look you, you must know she was always a most violent Cavalier and of a most ready and large faith. Abundance of rascals had found her soft place and perpetually would bring 20 her news, news of all prizes.[22] They would tell her news from half a crown to a gill of hot water, or a pipe of the worst mundungo.[23] I have observed their usual rates: they would borrow half a crown upon a story of five thousand men up in the north; 25 a shilling upon a town's revolting; six pence upon a small castle; and consume hot water and tobacco whilst they were telling news of arms conveyed into several parts and ammunition hid in cellars. That at the last, if I had not married and blown off these 30 flies, she had been absolutely consumed.

COLONEL CARELESS.

Well Lieutenant, we are beholding to you for these hints. We may be reduced to as bad.—See where Teague comes. Goodness, how he smiles.

Enter Teague, smiling.

Why so merry, Teague? 35

TEAGUE.

I have done one thing for thee now, that I have indeed.

COLONEL CARELESS.

What hast thou done, man?

TEAGUE.

I have taken the covenant for thee, that I have, upon my soul. 40

COLONEL CARELESS.

Where hadst it thou?

TEAGUE.

Hadst it thou? I threw a fellow down, that I did, and took it away for thy sweet sake. Here it is now.

COLONEL CARELESS.

Was there ever such a fancy?—Why, didst thou think this was the way to take the covenant? 45

TEAGUE.

Aye, upon my soul, that it is. Look you there now. Have I not taken it? Is not this the covenant? Tell me that then, I prithee.

COLONEL BLUNT.

I am pleased, yet, with the poor fellow's mistaken kindness. I dare warrant him honest to the best of 50 his understanding.

COLONEL CARELESS.

This fellow, I prophesy, will bring me into many troubles by his mistakes. I must send him on no errand but "how d'ye" and to such as I would have no answer from again. Yet his simple honesty 55 prevails with me; I cannot part with him.

LIEUTENANT STORY.

Come gentlemen, some calls. How now, who's this?

Enter Obadiah, with four persons more, with papers.

COLONEL CARELESS.

I am a rogue if I have not seen a picture in hangings walk as fast.

COLONEL BLUNT.

'Slife* man, this is that good of the Committee 60 family that I told thee of, the very clerk. How the rogue's loaded with papers; those are the winding sheets to many a poor gentleman's estate. 'Twere a good deed to burn them all.

COLONEL CARELESS.

Why, thou art not mad, art?—Well met, sir. Pray do 65 not you belong to the Committee of Sequestrations?

---

22 prizes] values

23 mundungo] bad-smelling tobacco

OBADIAH.

I do belong to that honorable Committee, who are now ready to sit for the bringing on the work.

COLONEL BLUNT.

Oh plague, what work, ras—

COLONEL CARELESS.

Prithee, be quiet man.—Are they ready to sit presently?* 70

OBADIAH.

As soon as I can get ready, my presence being material. (*Exit.*)

COLONEL CARELESS.

What, wert thou mad? Wouldst thou have beaten the clerk when thou wert going to compound with 75 the rascals, his masters?

COLONEL BLUNT.

The sight of any of the villains stirs me.

LIEUTENANT STORY.

Come colonels, there's no trifling. Let's make haste and prepare your business; let's not lose this sitting. Come along, along. 80

Exeunt.

[Scene iii. Days' house.]

Enter Arbella at one door, Abel at another, as if he saw her not, and starts when he comes to her, as Ruth has taught him.

ARBELLA.

What's the meaning of this? I'll try to steal by him.

ABEL.

Pardon, mistress, my profound contemplations, in which I was so hid that you could not see me.

ARBELLA. (*Aside.*)

This is a set form; they allow it in everything but their prayers.²⁴ 5

ABEL.

Now you should speak forsooth.

ARBELLA. (*Aside.*)

Ruth, I have found you, but I'll spoil the dialogue.—What should I say, sir?

ABEL.

What you please, forsooth.

---

24 set form...prayers] Puritans encouraged personal prayer, unprescribed by the Church of England.

ARBELLA.

Why truly sir, 'tis as you say. I did not see you. 10

Enter Ruth, as overhearing them, and peeps.

RUTH.

This is lucky.

ABEL.

No forsooth, 'twas I that was not to see you.

ARBELLA.

Why sir, would your mother be angry if you should?

ABEL.

No, no, quite contrary. I'll tell you that presently. 15 But first, I must say that the weighty affairs lie heavy upon my neck and shoulders. (*Shrugs.*)

ARBELLA. (*Aside.*)

Would he were tied neck and heels! This is a notable wench. Look where the rascal peeps, too. If I should beckon to her, she'd take no notice; she's 20 resolved not to relieve me.

ABEL.

Something I can do and that with some body; that is, with those that are somebodies.

ARBELLA. (*Beckons to Ruth, and Ruth shakes her head.*)

Whist, whist! Prithee, have some pity. Oh unmerciful girl. 25

ABEL.

I know Parliament-men and sequestrators; I know Committee-men, and Committee-men know me.

ARBELLA.

You have great acquaintance, sir?

ABEL.

Yes, they ask my opinions sometimes.

ARBELLA.

What weather 'twill be? Have you any skill, sir? 30

ABEL.

When the weather is not good, we hold a fast.

ARBELLA.

And then it alters?

ABEL.

Assuredly.

ARBELLA.

In good time.—No mercy, wench?

ABEL.

Our profound contemplations are caused by the 35

conservation of our spirits for the Nation's good.
We are in labor.

ARBELLA. [*Aside.*]

And I want a deliverance.—Hark ye, Ruth: take
off your dog, or I'll turn bear indeed.[25]

RUTH.

I dare not. My mother will be angry.   40

ARBELLA.

Oh, hang you.

ABEL.

You shall perceive that I have some power, if you
please to.

ARBELLA.

Oh, I am pleased, sir, that you should have power!
I must look out my hoods and scarves, sir, 'tis   45
a'most time to go.

ABEL.

If it were not for the weighty matters of state which
lie upon my shoulders, myself would look them.

ARBELLA.

Oh, by no means, sir, 'tis below your greatness.

Enter Mrs. Day.

[*Aside.*] Some luck yet; she never came seasonably   50
before.

MRS. DAY.

Why, how now? Abel got so close to Mrs. Arbella,
so close indeed. Nay, then I smell something.—
Well, Mr. Abel, you have been so used to secrecy
in council and weighty matters that you have it at   55
your fingers' ends.—Nay, look ye mistress, look ye,
look ye; mark Abel's eyes. Ah, there be looks.—
Ruth, thou art a good girl. I find Abel has got
ground.

RUTH.

I forbore to come in till I saw your honor first   60
enter, but I have o'erheard all.

MRS. DAY.

And how has Abel behaved himself, wench, hah?

RUTH.[b]

Oh, beyond expectation. If it were lawful, I'd
undertake he'd make nothing to get as many
women's good wills as he speaks to. He'll not need   65
much teaching. You may turn him loose.

_____

[25] dog ... bear] reference to bearbaiting (q.v.)

ARBELLA. [*Aside.*]

Oh, this plaguey wench!

MRS. DAY.

Sayest thou so, girl? It shall be something in thy
way: a new gown, or so, it may be a better
penny.—Well said, Abel, I say. I did think thou   70
wouldst come out with a piece of thy mother's at
last. But I had forgot, the Committee are near
upon sitting. [*To Arbella.*] Hah, mistress, you are
crafty; you have made your composition
beforehand. Ah, this Abel's as bad as a whole   75
committee, take that item from me.—Come,
make haste. Call the coach, Abel. Well said, Abel,
I say.

ARBELLA.

We'll fetch our things and follow you.

Exeunt Mrs. Day and Abel.

Now wench, canst thou ever hope to be forgiven?   80

RUTH.

Why, what's the matter?

ARBELLA.

The matter! Couldst thou be so unmerciful to see
me practiced on and pelted at by a blunderbuss
charged with nothing but proofs, weighty affairs,
spirit, profound contemplation, and suchlike?   85

RUTH.

Why, I was afraid to interrupt you. I thought it
convenient to give you what time I could to make
his young honor your friend.

ARBELLA.

I am beholding to you; I may cry quittance.

RUTH.

But did you mark Abel's eyes? Ah, there were looks!   90

ARBELLA.

Nay, prithee give off. My hour's approaching, and
I can't be heartily merry till it be past. Come, let's
fetch our things. Her ladyship's honor will stay for
us.

RUTH.

I'll warrant ye my brethren, Abel is not in order   95
yet. He's brushing a hat almost a quarter of an
hour and as long a-driving the lint from his black
clothes with his wet thumb.

ARBELLA.

Come prithee, hold thy peace. I shall laugh in's face

else when I see him come along. Now for an old 100
shoe.[26]

Exeunt.

[Scene iv. The Committee Room.]

*A table is set out. Enter the Committee, as to sit, and
Obadiah, ordering books and paper.*

OBADIAH.
Shall I read your honors' last order and give you
the account of what you last debated?

MR. DAY.
I first crave your favors to communicate an
important matter to this honorable board, in
which I shall discover* unto you my own sincerity 5
and zeal to the good Cause.*

FIRST COMMITTEE-MAN.
Proceed sir.

MR. DAY.
The business is contained in this letter, 'tis from
no less a man than the King, and 'tis to me, as
simple as I sit here. Is it your pleasures that our 10
clerk should read it?

NEHEMIAH CATCH.
Yes, pray give it to him.

OBADIAH. (*Reads.*)
"Mr. Day, We have received good intelligence of
your great worth and ability, especially in state
matters, and therefore thought fit to offer you any 15
preferment or honor that you shall desire if you
will become my entire friend. Pray, remember my
love and service to your discreet wife and acquaint
her with this, whose wisdom I hear is great. So
recommending this to her and your wise 20
consideration, I remain, Your friend, C.K."

NEHEMIAH CATCH.
C.K.?

MR. DAY.
Aye, that's for the King.

NEHEMIAH CATCH.
I suspect: Who brought you this letter?[c]

MR. DAY. [*Aside.*]
Oh fie upon't, my wife forgot that particular.— 25

Why, a fellow left it for me and shrunk away when
he had done. I warrant you he was afraid I should
have laid hold on him. You see, brethren, what I
reject. But I doubt not but to receive my reward,
and I have now a business to offer, which in some 30
measure may afford you an occasion.

NEHEMIAH CATCH. [*Aside.*]
This letter was counterfeited, certainly.

MR. DAY.
But first be pleased to read your last order.

NEHEMIAH CATCH.[d] [*Aside.*]
What, does he mean that[27] concerns me?

OBADIAH.
The order is, that the composition arising out of 35
Mr. Lashley's estate be, and hereby is, invested and
allowed to the honorable Mr. Nehemiah Catch, for
and in respect of his sufferings and good service.

MR. DAY.
It is meet, very meet; we are bound in duty to
strengthen ourselves against the day of trouble 40
when the common enemy shall endeavor to raise
commotions in the land and disturb out new-built
Zion.

NEHEMIAH CATCH. [*Aside.*]
Then I'll say nothing, but close with him; we must
wink at one another.—I receive your sense of my 45
services with a zealous kindness. Now Mr. Day, I
pray you propose your business.

MR. DAY.
I desire this honorable board to understand that
my wife being at Reading, and to come up in the
stagecoach, it happened that one Mrs. Arbella, a 50
rich heir of one of the Cavalier party, came up
also in the same coach. Her father being newly
dead and her estate before being under sequestration, my wife, who has a notable pate of her own,
you all know her, presently* cast about to get her 55
for my son Abel and accordingly invited her to
my house, where, though time was but short, yet
my son Abel made use of it. They are without, as
I suppose, but before we call them in, pray let us
handle such other matters as are before us. 60

FIRST COMMITTEE-MAN.
Let us hear, then, what estates besides lies before

---

26 now...shoe] a popular phrase meaning "now to get our
things on"

27 that] that which

us, that we may see how large a field we have to walk in.

NEHEMIAH CATCH.

Read.

OBADIAH.

One of your last debates was upon the plea of an 65
infant, whose estate is under sequestration.

MR. DAY.

And fit to be kept so till he comes of age and may
answer for himself, that he may not be in
possession of the land till he can promise he will
not turn to the enemy. 70

OBADIAH.

Here is another of almost the like nature: an estate
before your honors under sequestration. The plea
is that the party died without any _____*e for
taking up arms, but in his opinion for the King.
He has left his widow with child, which will be 75
the heir, and his trustees complain of wrong, and
claim the estate.28

NEHEMIAH CATCH.

Well, the father in his opinion was a Cavalier?

OBADIAH.

So it is given in.

NEHEMIAH CATCH.

Nay, 'twas so, I warrant you, and there's a young 80
Cavalier in his widow's belly. I warrant you that too,
for the perverse generations increaseth. I move,
therefore, that their two estates may remain in the
hands of our brethren here and fellow laborers, Mr.
Joseph Blemish, and Mr. Jonathan Headstrong, and 85
Mr. Ezekiel Scrape, and they to be accountable at
our pleasures, whereby they may have a godly
opportunity of doing good for themselves.

MR. DAY.

Order it, order it.

THIRD COMMITTEE-MAN.

Since it is your pleasures, we are content to take the 90
burthen upon us and be stewards to the Nation.

---

28 The plea...estate] This seizure violates one of the Parliamentary instructions given to Committees of Sequestration that a person must have been "willingly drawn"
or "consented to the drawing in" of the King's Army
before he can be labeled an "delinquent" or "malignant"
and have his land seized.

NEHEMIAH CATCH.

Now verily it seemeth to me that the work goeth
forward, when brethren hold together in unity.

MR. DAY.

Well, if we have now finished, give me leave to tell
you, my wife is without, together with the 95
gentlewoman that is to compound. She will needs
have a finger in the pie.

THIRD COMMITTEE-MAN.

I profess we are to blame to let Mrs. Day wait so
long.

MR. DAY.

We may not neglect the public for private respects. 100
I hope, brethren, that you please to cast the favor
of your countenances upon Abel.

NEHEMIAH CATCH, THIRD COMMITTEE-
MAN.

You wrong us to doubt it, Brother Day. Call in the
compounders.

*Enter Mrs. Day, Abel, Arbella, Ruth, and after them
the Colonels and Teague. They give the doorkeeper
something, who seems to scrape.*

MR. DAY.

Come duck, I have told the honorable Committee 105
that you are one that will needs endeavor to do
good for this gentlewoman.

NEHEMIAH CATCH.

We are glad, Mrs. Day, that any occasion brings
you hither.

MRS. DAY.

I thank your honors. I am desirous of doing good, 110
which I know is always acceptable in your eyes.

MR. DAY.

Come on, son Abel, what have you to say?

ABEL.

I come unto your honors, full of profound
contemplations for this gentlewoman.

ARBELLA.

'Slife,* he's at's lesson, wench. 115

RUTH.

Peace. Which whelp opens next? Oh, the wolf is
going to bark.

MRS. DAY.

May it please your honors, I shall presume to
inform you that my son Abel has settled his

affections on this gentlewoman and desires your 120
honors' favor to be shown unto him in her
composition.

NEHEMIAH CATCH.

Say you so, Mrs. Day? Why the Committee have
taken it into their serious and pious consideration,
together with Mr. Day's good service, upon some 125
knowledge that is not fit to communicate.

MRS. DAY. (*Aside.*)

That was the letter I invented.

NEHEMIAH CATCH.

And the composition of this gentlewoman is
consigned to Mr. Day, that is, I suppose, to Mr.
Abel, and so consequently to the gentlewoman.— 130
You may be thankful, mistress, for such good
fortune. Your estate's discharged; Mr. Day shall
have the discharge.

COLONEL BLUNT. [*Aside.*]

Oh, damn the vultures!

COLONEL CARELESS. [*Aside.*]

Peace, man. 135

ARBELLA.

I am willing to be thankful when I understand the
benefit. I have no reason to compound for what's
my own, but if I must, if a woman can be a
delinquent,[29] I desire to know my public censure,
not be left in private hands. 140

NEHEMIAH CATCH.

Be contented, gentlewoman. The Committee does
this in favor of you. We understand how easily you
can satisfy Mr. Abel; you may, if you please, be[f]
Mrs. Day.

RUTH. (*Aside.*)

And then, good night to all. 145

ARBELLA.

How, gentlemen? Are you private marriage jobbers?
D'ye make markets for one another?

NEHEMIAH CATCH.

How's this, gentlewoman?

---

29 delinquent] The April 1, 1643 ordinance of Parliament
commands, "that the estates of such notorious delinquents, as have been the causes or instruments of the
public calamities ... should be converted and applied
towards the supportation of the great changes of the
Commonwealth."

COLONEL BLUNT. [*Aside.*]

A brave,* noble creature.

COLONEL CARELESS. [*Aside.*]

Thou are smitten, Blunt. That other female, too, 150
methinks shoots fire this way.

MRS. DAY.

I desire your honors to pardon her incessant words.
Perhaps she doth not imagine the good that is
intended her?

NEHEMIAH CATCH.

Gentlewoman, the Committee, for Mrs. Day's 155
sake, passes by your expressions. You may spare
your pains. You have the Committee's resolution;
you may be your own enemy if you will.

ARBELLA.

My own enemy?

RUTH.

Prithee, peace. 'Tis no purpose to wrangle here. We 160
must use other ways.

NEHEMIAH CATCH.

Come on, gentlemen: What's your case?

RUTH.

Arbella, there's the downright Cavalier that came
up in the coach with us. [*Aside.*] On my life, there's
a sprightly gentleman with him. 165

COLONEL CARELESS.

Our business is to compound for our estates.

*While they speak, the Colonels pull the papers out and
deliver them.*

Of which, here are the particulars, which will agree
with your own survey.

OBADIAH.

The particulars are right.

MR. DAY.

Well gentlemen, the rule is two years' purchase, the 170
first payment down, the other at six month's end,
and the estate to secure it[30].

COLONEL CARELESS.

Can you afford it no cheaper?

NEHEMIAH CATCH.

'Tis our rule.

---

30 rule...it] The financial details of settling the estate seem
to demand two years' worth of mortgage and/or income
payments made in two lump sums, with the estate itself being used as collateral.

COLONEL CARELESS.

Very well, 'tis but selling the rest to pay this,[31] and 175
our more lawful debts.

NEHEMIAH CATCH.

But gentlemen, before you are admitted, you are
to take the covenant. You have not taken it yet,
have you?

COLONEL CARELESS.

No. 180

TEAGUE.

Upon my soul, but he has now. I took it for him,
and he has taken it from me, that he has.

RUTH.

What sport are we now like to have?

NEHEMIAH CATCH.

What fellow's that?

COLONEL CARELESS.

A poor, simple fellow that serves me.—Peace, 185
Teague.

TEAGUE.

Let them not prate so, then.

NEHEMIAH CATCH.

Well gentlemen, it remains whether you'll take the
covenant.

COLONEL CARELESS.

This is strange and differs from your own 190
principle, to impose on other men's consciences.

MR. DAY.

Pish, we are not here to dispute. We act according
to our own instructions, and we cannot admit any
to compound without taking it. Therefore, your
answer. 195

TEAGUE.

Why, was it for no matter then that I have taken
the covenant? You there, Mr. Committee, do you
hear that now?

COLONEL CARELESS.

No, we will not take it. Much good may it do
them that have swallows large enough; 'twill work 200
one day in their stomachs.

COLONEL BLUNT.

The day may come when those that suffer for their
consciences and honor may be rewarded.

MR. DAY.

Aye, aye, you make an idol of that honor.

COLONEL BLUNT.

Our worships, then, are different. You make that 205
your idol which brings your interest. We can obey
that which bids us lose it.

ARBELLA.

Brave* gentlemen.

RUTH.

I stare at 'em till my eyes ache.

NEHEMIAH CATCH.

Gentlemen, you are men of dangerous spirits. 210
Know, we must keep our rules and instructions,
lest we lose what Providence hath put into our
hands.

COLONEL CARELESS.

Providence, such as thieves rob by?

NEHEMIAH CATCH.

What's that, sir? Sir, you are too bold. 215

COLONEL CARELESS.

Why in good sooth, you may give losers leave to
speak. I hope your honors, out of your bowels of
compassion, will permit us to talk over our
departing acres.

MR. DAY.

It is well you are so merry. 220

COLONEL CARELESS.

Oh, ever whilst you live, clear souls make light
hearts. Faith, would I might ask one question?

NEHEMIAH CATCH.

Swear not, then.

COLONEL CARELESS.

Thou shalt not covet thy neighbor's goods. There's
a Rowland for your Oliver.* My question is only, 225
which of all you is to have our estates, or will you
make traitors of them, draw 'em and quarter
them?

NEHEMIAH CATCH.

You grow abusive.

COLONEL BLUNT.

No, no, 'tis only to entreat the honorable persons 230
that will be pleased to be our housekeepers to keep
them in good reparations. We may take possession
again without the help of the covenant.

NEHEMIAH CATCH.

You will think better on't and take this covenant.

---

31 selling ... this] Some of the estate must be sold in order
to raise the money needed to reclaim it.

COLONEL CARELESS.

We will be as rotten first as their hearts that invented it. 235

RUTH.

'Slife* Arbella, we'll have these two men. There are not two such again to be had for love nor money.

MR. DAY.

Well gentleman, your follies light upon your own heads. We have no more to say. 240

COLONEL CARELESS.

Why then, hoist sails for a new world.— D'hear, Blunt, what gentlewoman is that?

COLONEL BLUNT.

'Tis their witty daughter I told thee of.

COLONEL CARELESS.

I'll go speak to 'em. I'd fain convert that pretty covenanter. 245

COLONEL BLUNT.

Nay prithee, let's go.

COLONEL CARELESS. [To Arbella.]

Lady, I hope you'll have that good fortune not to be troubled with the covenant.

ARBELLA.

If they do, I'll not take it.

COLONEL BLUNT.

[Aside.]

Brave lady, I must love her against my will. 250

COLONEL CARELESS. [To Ruth.]

For you, pretty one, I hope your portion will be enlarged by our misfortunes; remember your benefactors.

RUTH.

If I had all your estates, I could afford you as good a thing. 255

COLONEL CARELESS.

Without taking the covenant?

RUTH.

Yes, but I would invent another oath.

COLONEL CARELESS.

Upon your lips.

RUTH.

Nay, I am not bound to discover.*

COLONEL BLUNT.

Prithee, come, is this a time to spend in fooling? 260

COLONEL CARELESS.

Now have I forgot everything.

COLONEL BLUNT.

Come, let's go.

NEHEMIAH CATCH.

Gentleman, void the room.

COLONEL CARELESS.

Sure, 'tis impossible that kite should get that pretty merlin. 265

COLONEL BLUNT.

Come, prithee let's go. These muck-worms[32] will have earth enough to stop their mouths with one day.

COLONEL CARELESS.

Pray use our estates husband*-like. And so, our most honorable bailiffs, farewell. 270

MR. DAY.

You are rude. Doorkeeper, put 'em forth there.

KEEPER.

Come forth, ye there. This is not a place for such as you.

TEAGUE.

Ye are a rascal, that you are now.

KEEPER.

An't* please your honors, this profane Irishman 275 swore an oath at the door, even now, when I would have put him out.

NEHEMIAH CATCH.

Let him pay for't.

KEEPER.

Here, you must pay, or lie by the heels.*

TEAGUE.

What, must I pay by the heels? I will not pay by 280 the heels, that I will not, upon my soul.

COLONEL CARELESS.

Here, here's a shilling for thee. Be quiet.

Exeunt Colonel Careless and Colonel Blunt.

TEAGUE.

Well, I have not cursed you now, that I have not. What if I had cursed, then?

KEEPER.

That had been sixpence. 285

TEAGUE.

Upon my soul now, I have but one sixpence, that

---

32 muck-worms] beetle larvae, often found under dung; the term was applied to misers.

I have not. Here though, I will give it thee for a
curse.—There, Mr. Committee, now there is
sixpence for the curse beforehand, Mr. Committee.
And a plague take you all! (*Runs out.*)   290

RUTH.

Hark ye, Arbella, 'twere a sin not to love these
men.

ARBELLA.

I am not guilty, Ruth.

MRS. DAY.

Has this honorable board any other command?

NEHEMIAH CATCH.

Nothing farther, good Mrs. Day.—Gentlewoman,   295
you have nothing to care for, but be grateful and
kind to Mr. Abel.

ARBELLA.

I desire to know what I must directly trust to, or
I will complain.

MRS. DAY.

The gentlewoman needeth not doubt. She shall   300
suddenly perceive the good that is intended her,
if she does not interpose in her own light.

MR. DAY.

I pray withdraw; the Committee has passed their
order, and they must now be private.

NEHEMIAH CATCH.

Nay, pray mistress, withdraw.   305

[Exeunt Mrs. Day, Arbella, Ruth.]

So brethren, we have finished this day's work. And
let us always keep the bonds of unity unbroken,
walking hand in hand, and scattering the enemy.

MR. DAY.

You may perceive they have spirits never to be
reconciled. They walk according to nature and are   310
full of inward darkness.[33]

NEHEMIAH CATCH.

It is well truly for the good people that they are so
obstinate, whereby their estates may of right fall into
the hands of the chosen, which truly is a mercy.

MR. DAY.

I think there remaineth nothing farther but to   315
adjourn till Monday.—Take up the papers there

---

33 walk … darkness] Puritan cant: they have not the light
of grace but exist in the natural fallen state of sin.

and bring home to me their honor's order for Mrs.
Arbella's estate.—So brethren, we separate ourselves
to our particular endeavors, till we join in public
on Monday, two of the clock. And so peace remain   320
with you.

Exeunt.

Act III, scene i. [A street.]

*Enter Colonel Careless, Colonel Blunt, and Lieutenant
Story.*

LIEUTENANT STORY.

By my faith, a sad story. I did apprehend this
covenant would be the trap.

COLONEL CARELESS.

Never did any rebels fish with such cormorants:
no stoppage about their throats,[34] the rascals are
all swallow.   5

COLONEL BLUNT.

Now I am ready for any plot. I'll go find some of
these agitants and fill up a blank commission with
my name.[35] And if I can but find two or three
gathered together, they are sure of me. I will please
myself, however, with endeavoring to cut their   10
throats.

COLONEL CARELESS.

Or do something to make them hang us, that we
may but part on any terms. Nothing angered me
but that my old kitchen-stuff-acquaintance looked
another way and seemed not to know me.   15

COLONEL BLUNT.

How, kitchen-stuff-acquaintance!

COLONEL CARELESS.

Yes, Mrs. Day, that commanded the party in the
hackney coach, was my father's kitchen maid and
in time of yore called Gillian.

Enter Teague.

How now, Teague? What says the learned?   20

---

34 stoppage … throat] By tying a strap around its throat,
one can use a cormorant to catch a fish but not swallow it.

35 agitants...name] Blunt is ready to join the forces actively
conspiring against the Roundheads and will even sign
his name to one of the blank arrest warrants made up
for their capture.

TEAGUE.

Well then, upon my soul, the man in the great cloak, with the long sleeves, is mad, that he is.

COLONEL CARELESS.

Mad, Teague!

TEAGUE.

Yes, i'faith is he; he bid me be gone and said I was sent to mock him.   25

COLONEL CARELESS.

Why, what didst thou say to him?

TEAGUE.

Well now, I did ask him if he would take any counsel.

COLONEL CARELESS.

'Slife,* he might well enough think thou mock'st him. Why, thou shouldst have asked him when we   30
might have come for counsel.

TEAGUE.

Well, that is all one, is it not? If he would take any counsel, or you would take any counsel, is not that all one, then?

COLONEL CARELESS.

Was there ever such a mistake?   35

COLONEL BLUNT.

Prithee, ne'er be troubled at this. We are past counsel. If we had but a friend amongst them that could but slide us by this covenant.

LIEUTENANT STORY.

Hark ye, Colonel: What if you did visit this translated kitchen maid?   40

TEAGUE.

Well, how is that? A kitchen maid? Where is she now?

COLONEL BLUNT.

The lieutenant advises well.

COLONEL CARELESS.

Nay, stay, stay. In the first place, I'll send Teague to her to tell her I have a little business with her   45
and desire to know when I may have leave to wait on her.

COLONEL BLUNT.

We shall have Teague mistake again.

TEAGUE.

How is that so? I will not mistake that kitchen maid. Whither must I go now, to mistake that   50
kitchen maid?

COLONEL CARELESS.

But, d'hear Teague? You must take no notice of that, upon thy life. But on the contrary, at every word, you must say "your ladyship" and "your honor." As for example, when you have made a leg,   55
you must begin thus: "My master presents his service to your ladyship and, having some business with your honor, desires to know when he may have leave to wait upon your ladyship."

TEAGUE.

Well, that I will do. But was she your father's   60
kitchen maid?

COLONEL CARELESS.

Why, what then?

TEAGUE.

Upon my soul, I shall laugh upon her face, for all I would not have a mind to do it.

COLONEL CARELESS.

Not for a hundred pounds, Teague. You must be   65
sure to set your countenance and look very soberly before you begin.

TEAGUE.

If I should think then of any kettles or spits or anything that will put a mind into my head of a kitchen, I should laugh then, should I not?   70

COLONEL CARELESS.

Not for a thousand pounds, Teague. Thou mayst undo us all.

TEAGUE.

Well, I will hope I will not laugh then. I will keep my mouth, if I can, that I will, from running to one side and t'other side. Well now, where does   75
this Mrs. Tay live?

LIEUTENANT STORY.

Come Teague, I'll walk along with thee and show thee the house, that thou mayst not mistake that, however.

COLONEL CARELESS.

Prithee do, Lieutenant.—Have a care, Teague.   80
Thou shalt find us in the Temple.*

Exeunt Lieutenant Story and Teague.

Now Blunt, have I another design.

COLONEL BLUNT.

What further design canst thou have?

COLONEL CARELESS.

Why, by this means, I may chance see these women again and get into their acquaintance. 85

COLONEL BLUNT.

With both, man?

COLONEL CARELESS.

'Slife,* thou art jealous. Dost love either of 'em?

COLONEL BLUNT.

Nay, I can't tell; all is not as 'twas.

COLONEL CARELESS.

Like a man that is not well and yet knows not what ails him. 90

COLONEL BLUNT.

Thou art something near the matter, but I'll cure myself with considering that no woman can ever care for me.

COLONEL CARELESS.

And why, prithee?

COLONEL BLUNT.

Because I can say nothing to them. 95

COLONEL CARELESS.

The less thou canst say, they'll like thee the better; she'll think 'tis love that has hamstringed thy tongue. Besides man, a woman can't abide that anything in the house should talk but she and her parrot. What, 'tis the Cavalier girl thou lik'st? 100

COLONEL BLUNT.

Canst thou love any of the other breed?

COLONEL CARELESS.

Not honestly. Yet I confess that ill-begotten pretty rascal never looked towards me but she scattered sparks as fast as kindling charcoal; thine's grown already to an honest flame. Come Blunt, when 105 Teague comes, we will resolve on something.

Exeunt.

[Scene ii. The Days' house.]

Enter Arbella and Ruth.

ARBELLA.

Come now, a word of our own matters. How dost thou hope to get thy estate again?

RUTH.

You shall drink first. I was just going to ask you how you would get yours again. You are as fast as if you were under covert-baron.[36] 5

ARBELLA.

But I have more hopes than thou hast.

RUTH.

Not a scruple more, if there were but scales that could weigh hopes, for these rascals must be hanged before either of us shall get our own. You may eat and drink out of yours, as I do, and be a 10 sojourner with Abel.

ARBELLA.

I am hampered, but I'll not[h] entangle myself with Mr. Abel's conjugal cords. Nay, I am more hampered than thou thinkest, for if thou art in as bad case as I (you understand me), hold up thy finger. 15

RUTH. (*Holds up her finger.*)

Behold. Nay, I'll ne'er forsake thee. If I were not smitten, I would persuade myself to be in love if 'twere but to bear thee company.

ARBELLA.

Dear girl. Hark ye Ruth, the composition day made an end of all; all's ago. 20

RUTH.

Nay, that fatal day put me into the condition of a compounder, too; there was my heart brought under sequestration.

ARBELLA.

That day, wench?

RUTH.

Yes, that very day, with two or three forcible looks, 25 'twas driven an inch at least out of its old place. Sense or reason can't find the way to't now.

ARBELLA.

That day, that very day? If you and I should like the same man—

RUTH.

Fie upon't, as I live thou mak'st me start. Now dare 30 not I ask which thou lik'st.

ARBELLA.

Would they were now to come in that we might watch one another's eyes and discover by signs. I am not able to ask thee, neither.

---

36 covert-baron] the legal condition of a married woman, "covered" or under the complete, or "fast," control of her husband

RUTH.

Nor I tell thee. Shall we go ask Lilly* which 'tis? 35

ARBELLA.

Out upon him. Nay, there's no need of stars. We know ourselves, if we durst speak.

RUTH.

Pish, I'll speak. If it be the same, we'll draw cuts.[i]

ARBELLA.

No, hark ye Ruth, do you act them both, for you saw their several humors, and then watch my eyes 40 where I appear most concerned. I cannot dissemble for my heart.

RUTH.

I dare swear that will hinder thee to dissemble indeed. Come, have at you then. I'll speak as if I were before the honorable rascals. And first, for my 45 brave* Blunt colonel, who hating to take the oath, cried out with a brave* scorn ([*Aside.*] such as made thee in love, I hope), "Hang yourselves, rascals, the time will come when those that dare be honest shall be rewarded." Don't I act him bravely,* don't 50 I act him bravely?

ARBELLA.

Oh admirably well, dear wench; do it once more.

RUTH.

Nay, nay, I must do t'other now.

ARBELLA.

No, no, this once more, dear girl, and I'll act t'other for thee. 55

RUTH.

No, forsooth, I'll spare your pains. We are right; no need of cuts. Send thee good luck with him I acted, and wish me well with my merry Colonel, that shall act his own part.

ARBELLA.

And a thousand good lucks attend thee. We have 60 saved our blushes admirably well and relieved our hearts from hard duty.—But mum, see where the mother comes and with her, her son, a true exemplification or duplicate of the original Day. Now for a charge. 65

Enter Mrs. Day and Abel.

RUTH.

Stand fair, the enemy draws up.

MRS. DAY.

Well, Mrs. Arbella, I hope you have considered enough by this time. You need not use so much consideration for your own good. You may have your estate and you may have Abel, and you may 70 be worse offered.—Abel, tell her your mind; ne'er stand shall I, shall I.[37]—Ruth, does she incline, or is she willful?

RUTH.

I was just about the point when your honor interrupted us. One word in your ladyship's ear. 75

ABEL.

You see, forsooth, that I am somebody, though you make nobody of me. You see I can prevail. Therefore, pray say what I shall trust to, for I must not stand shall I, shall I.

ARBELLA.

You are hasty, sir. 80

ABEL.

I am called upon by important affairs, and therefore I must be bold, in a fair way, to tell you that it lies upon my spirit exceedingly.

ARBELLA.

Saffron posset drink is very good against the heaviness of the spirit. 85

ABEL.

Nay forsooth, you do not understand my meaning.

ARBELLA.

You do, I hope, sir. And 'tis no matter, sir, if one of us know it.

Enter Teague.

TEAGUE.

Well now, who are all you?

ARBELLA.

What's here, an Irish elder come to examine us all? 90

TEAGUE.

Well now, what is your names, everyone?

RUTH.

Arbella, this is a servant to one of the colonels; upon my life, 'tis the Irishman that took the covenant the right way.

ARBELLA.

Peace, what should it mean? 95

---

37 shall I, shall I] shilly-shally (q.v.)

TEAGUE.

Well, cannot some of you all say nothing?

MRS. DAY.

Why, how now, sauce box? What would you have?
What, have you left your manners without? Go out
and fetch 'em in.

TEAGUE.

What should I fetch now? 100

MRS. DAY.

Do you know who you speak to, sirrah?

TEAGUE.

Well, what are you then? Upon my soul, in my
own country, they can tell who I am.

ABEL.

You must not be so saucy unto her honor.

TEAGUE.

Well, I will knock you, if you be saucy with me 105
then.

RUTH.

This is miraculous.

TEAGUE.

Is there none of you that I must speak to now?

ARBELLA. (*Aside.*)

Now wench, if he should be sent to us.

TEAGUE.

Well, I would have one Mrs. Tay speak unto me. 110

MRS. DAY.

Well sirrah, I am she. What's your business?

TEAGUE.

Oh so then, are you Mrs. Tay? [*Aside.*] Well, I will
look well first, and I will set my face in some
worship; yes indeed, that I will. And I will tell her
then what I will speak to her. 115

RUTH.

How the fellow begins to mold himself.

ARBELLA.

And tempers his chops like a hound that has
lapped before his meat was cold enough.

RUTH.

He looks as if he had some gifts to pour forth.
Those are Mr. Day's own white eyes before he 120
begins to say grace. Now for a speech rattling in
his kecher,[38] as if his words stumbled in their way.

---

38 kecher] throat, from either the verb "keck," to cough
or gag, or a shortened use of "keckhorn" or windpipe

TEAGUE.

Well, now I will tell thee. I'faith my master, the
good Colonel Careless, bid me ask thy good
ladyship— [*Aside.*] Upon my soul, now the laugh 125
will come upon me.

MRS. DAY.

Sirrah, sirrah, what, were you sent to abuse me?

RUTH. (*Aside.*)

As sure as can be.

TEAGUE. (*He laughs always when he says "ladyship"
or "honor".*)

I'faith now, I do not abuse thy good hon—[*Aside.*]
I cannot help my laugh now; I will try again now; 130
I will not think of a kitchen then.—My master
would know of your ladyship—

MRS. DAY.

Did your master send you to abuse me, you rascal?
By my honor, sirrah?

TEAGUE.

Why, dost thou mock thy self now, joy?* 135

MRS. DAY.

How sirrah, do I mock myself? This is some Irish
traitor.

TEAGUE.

I am no traitor, that I am not. I am an Irish
rebel[39]. You are cozened now.

MRS. DAY.

Sirrah, sirrah, I will make you know who I am. An 140
impudent Irish rascal.

ABEL.

He seemeth a dangerous fellow and of a bold and
seditious spirit.

MRS. DAY.

You are a bloody rascal, I warrant ye.

TEAGUE.

You are a foolish brable-brible[40] woman, that you 145
are.

ABEL.

Sirrah, we that are at the head of affairs must
punish your sauciness.

---

39 traitor ... rebel] The Irish rebeled against England in the
early 1640s and were brutally subdued by Cromwell in
the late 1640s.

40 brable-brible] usually "bribble-brabble," meaning babbling or chattering

TEAGUE.

You shall take a knock upon your pate, if you are saucy with me, that I shall, you son of a Round-head, you.

MRS. DAY.

Ye rascally varlet, get you out of my doors.

TEAGUE.

Will not I give you my message then?

MRS. DAY.

Get you out, rascal!

TEAGUE.

I prithee, let me tell thee my message.

MRS. DAY.

Get you out, I say.

TEAGUE.

Well then, I care not neither. The Devil take your ladyship and honorship and kitchenship too. There now. (*Exit.*)

ARBELLA.

Was there ever such a scene? 'Tis impossible to guess anything.

RUTH.

Our colonels have done't, as sure as thou livest, to make themselves sport, being all the revenge that is in their power.—Look, look, how her honor trots about, like a beast stung with flies.

MRS. DAY.

How the villain has distempered me! [*To Abel.*] Out upon't too, that I have let the rascal go unpunished and you can stand by like a sheep. Run after him, then, and stop him. I'll have him laid by the heels* and make him confess who sent him to abuse me. Call help as you go; make haste, I say.

Exit Abel.

RUTH.

'Slid* Arbella, run after him and save the poor fellow for sake's sake. Stop Abel by any means, that he may 'scape.

ARBELLA.

Keep his dam off, and let me alone with the puppy. (*Exit.*)

RUTH.

Fear not.

MRS. DAY.

'Uds* my life, the rascal has heated me. Now I

think on't, I'll go myself and see it done: a saucy villain.*

RUTH.

But I must needs acquaint your honor with one thing first concerning Mrs. Arbella.

MRS. DAY.

As soon as ever I have done. Is't good news wench?

RUTH.

Most excellent. If you go out, you may spoil all. Such a discovery I have made, that you will bless the accident that angered you.

MRS. DAY.

Quickly then, girl.

RUTH.

When you sent Abel after the Irishman, Mrs. Arbella's color came and went in her face, and at last, not able to stay, slunck away after him for fear the Irishman should hurt him. She stole way and blushed the prettiest.

MRS. DAY.

I protest he may be hurt indeed. I'll run myself, too.

RUTH.

By no means, forsooth. Nor is there any need on't. For she resolved to stop him before he could get near the Irishman; she has done it, upon my life. And if you should go out, you might spoil the kindest* encounter that the loving Abel is ever like to have.

MRS. DAY.

Art sure of this?

RUTH.

If you do not find she has stopped him, let me ever have your hatred. Pray credit me.

MRS. DAY.

I do, I do believe thee. Come we'll go in where I use to read. There thou shalt tell me all the particulars and the manner of it. I warrant 'twas pretty to observe.

RUTH.

Oh, 'twas a thousand pities you did not see't. When Abel walked away so bravely and foolishly after this wild Irishman, she stole such kind looks from her own eyes and, having robbed herself, sent them after her own Abel, and then—

MRS. DAY.

Come, good wench, I'll go in and hear it all at

large. It shall be the best tale thou hast told these two days. Come, come, I long to hear all. Abel, for his part, needs no news by this time. Come, good wench. (*Exit.*)   215

RUTH.

So far, I am right. Fortune take care for future things.

[Exit.]

[Scene iii. A street.]

Enter Colonel Blunt, as taken by bailiffs.

COLONEL BLUNT.

At whose suit, rascals?

FIRST BAILIFF.

You shall know that time enough.

COLONEL BLUNT.

Time enough, dogs! Must I wait your leisures?

FIRST BAILIFF.

Oh, you are a dangerous man. 'Tis such traitors as you that disturb the peace of the Nation.   5

COLONEL BLUNT.

Take that, rascal. If I had anything at liberty besides my foot, I would bestow it on you.

FIRST BAILIFF.

You shall pay dearly for this kick before you are let loose and give good special bail. Mark that, my surly companion; we have you fast.   10

COLONEL BLUNT.

'Tis well, rogues, you caught me conveniently. Had I been aware, I would have made some of your scurvy souls my special bail.

FIRST BAILIFF.

Oh, 'tis a bloody-minded man. I'll warrant ye this vile Cavalier has eat many a child.[41]   15

COLONEL BLUNT.

I could gnaw a piece or two of you rascals.

Enter Colonel Careless.

COLONEL CARELESS.

How is this! Blunt in hold! You catchpole, let go your prey, or——

Draws, and Blunt in the scuffle throws up one of their heels, and gets a sword, and helps drive them off.

FIRST BAILIFF.

Murder, murder!

[Exeunt Bailiffs.]

COLONEL BLUNT.

Faith, Careless, this was worth thanks. I was fairly going.   20

COLONEL CARELESS.

What was the matter, man?

COLONEL BLUNT.

Why, an action or two for free quarter, now made trover and conversion.[42] Nay, I believe we shall be sued with an action of trespass for every field we   25 have marched over and be indicted for riots for going at unseasonable hours above two in company.

Enter Teague, running.

COLONEL CARELESS.

Well come, let's away.

TEAGUE.

Now upon my soul, run as I do. The men in red   30 coats are running too, that they are, and they cry "Murder, murder." I never heard such a noise in Ireland, that's true, too.

COLONEL CARELESS.

'Slife,* we must shift several ways. Farewell. If we 'scape, we meet at night. I shall take heed now.   35

TEAGUE.

Shall I tell of Mrs. Tay now?

COLONEL CARELESS.

Oh good Teague, no time for messages.

Exeunt several ways. A noise within. Enter bailiffs and soldiers.

---

41 eat many a child] a repeated slander; see *The Old Troop*, III.ii

42 an action ... conversion] Blunt was arrested for unpaid lodging expenses, which should have been waived as "free-quarter" but are now being labeled as a good whose value must be compensated for and can be recovered through "trover and conversion," a legal action which seeks to recover the value of personal property wrongly converted by another to his own use.

FIRST BAILIFF.

This way, this way. Oh villains, my neighbor Swash is hurt dangerously. Some good soldiers, follow, follow.   40

Enter Colonel Careless and Teague again.

COLONEL CARELESS.

I am quite out of breath, and the blood hounds are in full cry upon a burning scent. Plague on 'em, what a noise the kennels make.—What door's this that graciously stands a little open? What an ass am I to ask!—Teague, scout abroad. If anything   45
happens extraordinary, observe this door; there you shall find me. Be careful.—Now by your favor, landlord, as unknown.

Exeunt severally.

[Scene iv. The Days' house.]

Enter Mrs. Day and Obadiah.

MRS. DAY.

It was well observed, Obadiah, to bring the parties to me first. 'Tis your master's will that I should, as I may say, prepare matters for him. In truth, in truth, I have too great a burthen upon me. Yet for the public good I am content to undergo it.   5

OBADIAH.

I shall with sincere care present unto your honor, from time to time, such negotiations as I may discreetly presume may be material for your honor's inspection.

MRS. DAY.

It will become you so to do. You have the present   10
that came last?

OBADIAH.

Yes, an't* please your honor. The gentleman, concerning her brother's release, hath also sent in a piece of plate.*

MRS. DAY.

It's very well.   15

OBADIAH.

But the man without, about a bargain of the King's land, is come empty.

MRS. DAY.

Bid him be gone; I'll not speak with him. He does not understand himself.

OBADIAH.

I shall intimate so much to him.   20

As Obadiah goes out, Colonel Careless meets him and tumbles him back.

MRS. DAY.

Why, how now? What rude companion's this? What would you have? What's your business? What's the matter? Who sent you? Who d'you belong to? Who—

COLONEL CARELESS.

Hold, hold, if you mean to be answered to all these   25
interrogatories. You see I resolve to be your companion; I am a man; there's no great matter; nobody sent me; nor I belong to nobody. I think I have answered to the chief heads.

MRS. DAY.

Thou hast committed murder, for ought I know.—   30
How is't Obadiah?

COLONEL CARELESS. [*Aside.*]

Hah, what luck have I to fall into the territories of my old kitchen acquaintance. I'll proceed upon the strength of Teague's message, though I had no answer.   35

MRS. DAY.

How is't man?

OBADIAH.

Truly he came forcibly upon me, and I fear has bruised some intellectuals within my stomach.

MRS. DAY.

Go in and take some Irish slat[43] by way of prevention and keep yourself warm.   40

[Exit Obadiah.]

Now sir, have you any business, you that came in so rudely as if you did not know who you came to? How came you in, Sir Royster? Was not the porter at the gate?

COLONEL CARELESS.

No, truly, the gate kept itself and stood gaping as   45
if it had a mind to speak and say, "I pray come in."

---

43 Irish slat] or slate; a medicine made of powdered alum slate

MRS. DAY.

Did it so, sir? And what have you to say?

COLONEL CARELESS. [*Aside.*]

Aye, there's the point, either she does not or will
not know me. What should I say? How dull am I! 50
Pox on't, this wit is like a common friend: when
one has need on him, he won't come near one.

MRS. DAY.

Sir, are you studying for an invention? For aught
I know, you have done some mischief, and 'twere
fit to secure you. 55

COLONEL CARELESS. [*Aside.*]

So that's well. 'Twas pretty to fall into the head
quarter of the enemy.

MRS. DAY.

Nay, 'tis e'en so. I'll fetch those that shall examine
you.

COLONEL CARELESS.

Stay, thou mighty stateswoman; I did but give you 60
time to see if your memory would but be so honest
as to tell you who I am.

MRS. DAY.

What d'you mean, saucebox?

COLONEL CARELESS.

There's a word yet of thy former employments,
that "sauce." You and I have been acquainted. 65

MRS. DAY.

I do not use to have acquaintance with Cavaliers.

COLONEL CARELESS.

Nor I with Committee-men's utensils. But in *diebus
illis*,[44] you were not honorable, nor I a Malignant.[45]
Lord, Lord, you are horrible forgetful; pride comes
with godliness and good clothes. What, you think I 70
should not know you because you are disguised with
curled hair and white gloves? Alas, I know you as
well as if you were in your Sabbath-day's cinnamon
waistcoat with a silver edging 'round the skirt.

MRS. DAY.

How, sirrah? 75

COLONEL CARELESS.

And with your fair hands bathed in lather or with
your fragrant breath driving the fleeting amber

grease off from the waving kitchenstuff.

MRS. DAY.

Oh, you are an impudent Cavalier! I remember
you now, indeed, but I'll— 80

COLONEL CARELESS.

Nay, but hark you the now honorable, *non
abstante*[46] past conditions. Did not I sent my fool
man, an Irish man, with a civil message to you?
Why all this strangeness, then?

MRS. DAY.

How, how, how's this? Was you that sent that rascal 85
to abuse me, was't so?

COLONEL CARELESS.

How now! What, matters grow worse and worse?

MRS. DAY.

I'll teach you to abuse those that are in
authority.—Within there, who's within?

COLONEL CARELESS.

'Slife, I'll stop your mouth, if you raise an alarum. 90

MRS. DAY.

Stop my mouth, sirrah? Whoo, whoo, ho! (*Cries
out and Careless stops her mouth.*)

COLONEL CARELESS.

Yes, stop your mouth. What are you good at a
who-bub,[47] hah?

Enter Ruth.

RUTH.

What's the matter, forsooth?

MRS. DAY.

The matter? Why, here's a rude Cavalier has broke 95
into my house; 'twas he too that sent the Irish
rascal to abuse me too within my own walls. Call
your father that he may grant his order to secure
him. 'Tis a dangerous fellow.

COLONEL CARELESS.

Nay, good pretty gentlewoman, spare your motion. 100
[*Aside.*] What must become of me? Teague has
made some strange mistake.

RUTH. (*Aside.*)

'Tis he. What shall I do? Now, invention be equal
to my love.—Why, your ladyship will spoil all! I
sent for this gentleman and enjoined him secrecy, 105

---

44 *diebus illis*] in those (former) days (Lat.)

45 malignant] a term of Puritan opprobrium applied to
    Cavaliers and Royalists

46 *non abstante*] yet still relevant (Lat.: literally, not aloof)

47 who-bub] hubbub, outcry

even to you yourself, till I had made his way. Oh
fie upon't, I am to blame, but in truth, I did not
think he would have come these two hours.
COLONEL CARELESS. [*Aside.*]
  I dare swear she did not. I might very probably not
  have come at all.   110
RUTH.
  How came you so soon, sir? 'Twas three hours
  before you appointed.
COLONEL CARELESS. [*Aside.*]
  Hey day, I shall be made believe I came hither on
  purpose, presently.
RUTH.
  'Twas upon a message of his to me, an't* please your   115
  honor, to make his desires known to your ladyship,
  that he had considered on't and was resolved to take
  the covenant and give you five hundred pound to
  make his peace and bring his business about again,
  that he may be admitted in his first condition.[48]   120
COLONEL CARELESS.
  What's this? D'hear pretty gentlewoman?
RUTH.
  Well, well, I know your mind; I have done your
  business.
MRS. DAY.
  Oh, his stomach's come down!
RUTH. (*Whispers.*)
  Sweeten him again and leave him to me. I warrant   125
  you the five hundred pound and—
COLONEL CARELESS. [*Aside.*]
  Now I have found it: this pretty wench has a mind
  to be left alone with me at her peril.
MRS. DAY.
  I understand thee.—Well sir, I can pass by rude-
  ness when I am informed there was no intention   130
  of it. I leave you and my daughter to beget a right
  understanding. [*Exit.*]
COLONEL CARELESS. [*Aside.*]
  We should beget sons and daughters sooner. What
  does all this mean?
RUTH.
  I am sorry, sir, that your love for me should make   135
  you thus rash.

---

48 in ... condition] on the earlier conditions set forth in
    the meeting with the Committee

COLONEL CARELESS.
  That's more than you know, but you had a mind
  to be left alone with me, that's certain.
RUTH.
  'Tis too plain, sir, you'd ne'er have run yourself into
  this danger else.   140
COLONEL CARELESS.
  Nay, now you're out: the danger run after me.
RUTH.
  You may dissemble.
COLONEL CARELESS.
  Why, 'tis the proper business here. But we lose
  time; you and I are left to beget right under-   145
  standing. Come, which way?
RUTH.
  Whither?
COLONEL CARELESS.
  To your chamber or closet?*
RUTH.
  But I am engaged: you shall take the covenant.
COLONEL CARELESS.
  No, I never swear when I am bid.   150
RUTH.
  But you would do as bad?
COLONEL CARELESS.
  That's not against my principles.
RUTH.
  Thank you for your fair opinion, good Signor
  Principle. There lies your way, sir. However, I will
  own so much kindness for you, that I repent not   155
  the civility I have done to free you from the trouble
  you were like to fall into. Make me a leg, if you
  please, and cry "thank you." And so, the
  gentlewoman that desired to be left alone with you,
  desires to be left alone with herself, she being   160
  taught a right understanding of you.
COLONEL CARELESS.
  No, I am riveted, nor shall you march off thus with
  flying colors. My pretty commander in chief, let us
  parley a little further and but lay down ingenuously
  the true state of our treaty. The business in short is 165
  this: we differ seemingly upon two evils, and mine
  the least and therefore to be chosen. You had better
  take me than I take the covenant.
RUTH.
  We'll excuse one another.

COLONEL CARELESS.

You would not have me take the covenant, then?　170

RUTH.

No, I did but try you. I forgive your idle looseness; for that firm virtue be constant to your fair principles in spite of fortune.

COLONEL CARELESS.

What's this got into petticoats?—But, d'hear, I'll not excuse you from my proposition, 　175 notwithstanding my release. Come, we are half way to a right understanding. Nay, I do love thee.

RUTH.

Love virtue: you have but here and there a patch of it; y'are ragged still.

COLONEL CARELESS.

Are not you the Committee Day's daughter?　180

RUTH.

Yes, what then?

COLONEL CARELESS.

Then I am thankful. I had no defense against thee and matrimony, but thy own father and mother, which are a perfect Committee to my nature.

RUTH.

Why, are you sure I would have matched with a 　185 Malignant, not a compounder neither?

COLONEL CARELESS.

Nay, I have made thee a jointure against my will. Methinks it were as reasonable that I should do something for my jointure, but by the way of matrimony honestly to increase your generation— 　190 'tis to tell you, truth is, against my conscience.

RUTH.

Yet you would beget right understandings?

COLONEL CARELESS.

Yes, I would have 'em all bastards.

RUTH.

And me a whore.

COLONEL CARELESS.

That's a coarse name, but 'tis not fit a Committee- 　195 man's daughter should be too honest, to the reproach of her father and mother.

RUTH.

When the quarrel* of the Nation is reconciled, you and I shall agree. Till when, sir—

Enter Teague.

TEAGUE.

Are you here, then? Upon my soul, the good 　200 Colonel Blunt is overtaken again now and carried to the Devil. That he is, i'faith now.

COLONEL CARELESS.

How, taken and carried to the Devil!

TEAGUE.

He desired to go to the Devil, that he did; I wonder of my soul he was not afraid of that. 　205

COLONEL CARELESS.

I understand it now. What mischief's this?

RUTH.

You seem troubled, sir.

COLONEL CARELESS.

I have but a life to lose, that I am weary of. Come, Teague.

RUTH.

Hold, you shan't go before I know the business. 　210 What d'ye talk of?

COLONEL CARELESS.

My friend, my dearest friend, is caught up by the rascally bailiffs and carried to the Devil Tavern.[49] Pray, let me go.

RUTH.

Stay but a minute, if you have any kindness for 　215 me.

COLONEL CARELESS.

Yes, I do love you.

RUTH.

Perhaps I may serve your friend.

Enter Arbella.

Oh Arbella, I was going to seek you.

ARBELLA.

What's the matter?　220

RUTH.

The colonel which thou lik'st is taken by bailiffs. There's his friend, too, almost distracted. You know the mercy of these times.

ARBELLA.

What dost thou tell me? I am ready to sink down!

49　the Devil Tavern] a London inn situated on Fleet Street, opposite the Church of St. Dunstan. The tavern's name reflects a legend that, at this location, St. Dunstan seized the Devil by the nose with a pair of pincers.

RUTH.

Compose yourself and help him nobly. You have no way but to smile upon Abel and get him to bail him. 225

Enter Abel and Obadiah.

ARBELLA.

Look where he and Obadiah comes; should either by Providence—— Oh Mr. Abel, where have you been this long time? Can you find of your heart to keep thus out of my sight? 230

ABEL.

Assuredly some important affairs constrained my absence, as Obadiah can testify, *bona fide.*[50]

OBADIAH.

I can do so verily, myself being a material party.

COLONEL CARELESS. [*Aside.*]

Pox on 'em. How slow they speak. 235

ARBELLA.

Well, well, you shall go no more out of my sight; I'll not be satisfied with your *bona fides.* I have some occasions which call me to go a little way; you shall e'en go with me, and good Obadiah, too. You shall not deny me anything. 240

ABEL.

Is it not meet I should? I am exceedingly exalted.—Obadiah, thou shalt have the best bargain of all my tenants.

OBADIAH.

I am thankful.

COLONEL CARELESS. (*Aside.*)

What may this mean? 245

ARBELLA.

Ruth, how shall we do to keep thy swift mother from pursuing us?

RUTH.

Let me alone. As I go by the parlor where she sits, big with expectation, I'll give her a whisper that we are going to fetch the very five hundred pound. 250

ARBELLA.

How can that be?

RUTH.

No question now.—Will you march, sir?

---

[50] *bona fide*] in good faith (Lat.)

COLONEL CARELESS.

Whither?

RUTH.

Lord, how dull these men in love are! Why, to your friend. No more words. 255

COLONEL CARELESS.

I will stare upon thee, though.

Exeunt.

Act IV, scene i. [The Devil Tavern.]

Colonel Blunt brought in by Bailiffs.

FIRST BAILIFF.

Aye, aye, we thought how well you'd get bail.

COLONEL BLUNT.

Why you unconscionable rascals, are you angry that I am unlucky, or do you want some fees? I'll perish in a dungeon before I'll consume with throwing sops to such curs. 5

FIRST BAILIFF.

Choose, choose.—Come along with him.

COLONEL BLUNT.

I'll not go your pace neither, rascals. I'll go softly, if it be but to hinder you from taking up some other honest gentleman.

FIRST BAILIFF.

Very well, surly sir. We will carry you where you shall not be troubled what pace to walk. You'll find a large bell.* Blood is dear. Not yours is it? A farthing a pint were very dear* for the best urine you have. 10

Enter Arbella, Ruth, Abel, Colonel Careless, and Obadiah.

How now, are these any of your friends? 15

COLONEL BLUNT.

Never, if you see women; that's a rule.

ARBELLA. [*To Abel.*]

Nay, you need have no scruple, 'tis a near kinsman of mine. You do not think, I hope, that I would let you suffer—you—that must be nearer than a kinsman to me. 20

ABEL.

But my mother doth not know it.

ARBELLA.

If that be all, leave it to me and Ruth; we'll save

you harmless. Besides, I cannot marry if my kinsman be in prison. He must convey my estate as you appoint, for 'tis all in him. We must please him.

ABEL.

The consideration of that doth convince me.— Obadiah, 'tis necessary for us to set at liberty this gentleman, being a trustee for Mrs. Arbella's estate. Tell 'em therefore that you and I will bail this gentleman—and—d'hear, tell them who I am.

OBADIAH.

I shall.—Gentlemen, this is the honorable Mr. Abel Day, the firstborn of the honorable Mr. Day, Chairman of the Committee of Sequestrations, and I myself by name of Obadiah and clerk to the said honorable Committee.

FIRST BAILIFF.

Well sir, we know Mr. Day and Mr. Abel.

ABEL.

Yes, that's I, and I will bail this gentleman. I believe you dare not except against the bail. Nay, you shall have Obadiah's too, one that the state trusts.

FIRST BAILIFF.

With all our hearts, sir. But there are charges to be paid.

ARBELLA.

Here Obadiah, take this purse and discharge them, and give the bailiffs twenty shillings to drink.

COLONEL BLUNT.

This is miraculous.

FIRST BAILIFF.

A brave* lady. I'faith, mistress, we'll drink your health.

ABEL.

She's to be my wife, as sure as you are here. What say you to that now?

FIRST BAILIFF. [Aside.]

That's impossible; here's something more in this.— Honorable Mr. Abel, the sheriff's deputy is hard by in another room; if you please to go thither and give your bail, sir.

ABEL.

Well, show us the way, and let him know who I am.

Exeunt Abel, Obadiah and Bailiffs.

COLONEL CARELESS.

Hark ye, pretty Mrs. Ruth, if you were not a Committee-man's daughter and so consequently against monarchy, two princes[51] should have you and that gentlewoman.

RUTH.

No, no, you'll serve my turn; I am not ambitious.

COLONEL CARELESS.

Do but swear then that thou art not the issue of Mr. Day, and though I know 'tis a lie, I'll be content to be cozened and believe.

RUTH.

Fie, fie, you can't abide taking of oaths. Look, look how your friend and mine take aim at one another. Is he smitten?

COLONEL CARELESS.

Cupid has not such another wounded subject, nay, and is vexed he is in love, too. Troth, 'tis partly my own case.

RUTH.

Peace, she begins as need requires.

ARBELLA.

You are free, sir.

COLONEL BLUNT.

Not so free as you think.

ARBELLA.

What hinders it?

COLONEL BLUNT.

Nothing but I'll tell you.

ARBELLA.

Why, sir?

COLONEL BLUNT.

You'll laugh at me.

ARBELLA.

Have you perceived me apt to commit such a rudeness? Pray let me know it.

COLONEL BLUNT.

Upon two conditions you shall know it.

ARBELLA.

Well, make your own laws.

COLONEL BLUNT.

First, I thank you, y'have freed me nobly. Pray believe it, you have this acknowledgment from an

---

51 two princes] Charles and James Stuart

honest heart, one that would crack a string[52] for you. That's one thing.

ARBELLA.

Well, the other? 85

COLONEL BLUNT.

The other is only that I may stand so ready that I may be gone just as I have told it you, together with your promise not to call me back. And upon these terms, I give you leave to laugh when I am gone.—Careless, come stand ready, that at the sign 90 given, we may vanish together.

RUTH.

If you please, sir, when you are ready to start, I'll cry, "One, two, three, and away."

COLONEL BLUNT.

Be pleased to forbear, good smart gentlewoman, you have leave to jeer when I am gone and am just 95 going. By your spleens, leave a little patience.

ARBELLA.

Prithee, peace.

RUTH.

I shall contain, sir.

COLONEL BLUNT.

That's much for a woman to do.

ARBELLA.

Now sir, perform your promise. 100

COLONEL BLUNT.

Careless, have you done with your woman?

COLONEL CARELESS.

Madam—

COLONEL BLUNT.

Nay, I have thanked her already; prithee no more of that dull way of gratitude. Stand ready, man, yet nearer to the door. [*To Arbella*.] So now my 105 misfortune that I promised to discover* is—that I love you above my sense or reason. So farewell, and laugh.—Come, Careless.

COLONEL CARELESS.

Ladies, our lives are yours; be but so kind as to believe it, till you have something to command. 110

Exeunt [Colonel Blunt and Colonel Careless].

---

52 string] according to old notions of anatomy, the tendons or nerves that brace and sustain the heart within the body; a string would crack, or break, due to intense feelings of the heart.

RUTH.

Was there ever such humor?*

ARBELLA.

As I live, his confession shows nobly.

RUTH.

It shows madly, I am sure. An ill-bred fellow, not endure a woman to laugh at him!

ARBELLA.

He's honest, I dare swear. 115

RUTH.

That's more then I dare swear for my colonel.

ARBELLA.

Out upon him.

RUTH.

Nay, 'tis but for want* of a good example; I'll make him so.

ARBELLA.

But d'hear, Ruth, we were horribly to blame that 120 we did not inquire where they lodged, under pretense of sending to them about their own business.

RUTH.

Why, thy whimsical colonel discharged himself off like a gun. There was no time between the flashing 125 in the pan and the going off to ask a question. But hark ye, I have an invention upon the old account of the five hundred pound, which shall make Abel send his pursuivant Obadiah to look 'em.

ARBELLA.

Excellent! The trout Abel will bite immediately at 130 that bait. The message shall be as from his master, Day Senior, to come and speak with him; they'll think presently* 'tis about their composition and come certainly. In the meantime, we'll prepare them with counter-expectations. 135

RUTH.

You have it.

Enter Abel and Obadiah.

Peace, see where Abel and the gentle squire of low degree,[53] Obadiah, approaches, having newly entered themselves into bonds.

---

53 gentle ... degree] A common phrase, its source is a medieval poem, "The Squyer of Lo Degree."

ARBELLA.

Which I'll be sure to tell his mother, if he be ever   140
more troublesome.

RUTH.

And that he's turned an arrant Cavalier, by bailing
one of the brood.

ABEL.

I have, according to your desires, given freedom
to your kinsman and trustee. I suppose he doth   145
perceive that you may have power in right of me.

ARBELLA.

Good Mr. Abel, I am sincerely beholding to you
and your authority.

RUTH.

Oh fie upon't brother, I did forget to acquaint you
with a business before the gentlemen went. Oh me,   150
what a sieve-like memory have I. 'Twas an
important affair, too.

ABEL.

If you discover* it to me, I shall render you my
opinion upon the whole.

RUTH.

The two gentleman have repented of their   155
obstinacy and would now present five hundred
pound to your good honorable mother to stand
their friend that they may be permitted to take the
covenant. And we, negligent we, have let them go
before we knew where to send to them.   160

ABEL.

That was the want* of being used to important
affairs. It is ill to neglect the accepting of their
conversion together with their money.

RUTH.

Well, there is but one way: do you send Obadiah
in your father's name to desire them both to come   165
to his house about some business that will be for
their good, but no more. For then they'll take it
ill, for they enjoined us secrecy. And when they
come, let us alone. Obadiah may inquire them out
at some tavern.   170

OBADIAH.

The bailiffs did say they were gone to the Devil-
Tavern to pay a reckoning.

ABEL.

Hasten thither, good, good Obadiah, as if you had
met my honorable father, and desire them to come

unto his house about an important affair that is   175
for their good.

OBADIAH.

I shall use expedition. (*Exit.*)

ABEL.

And we shall hasten home, lest the gentleman
should be before us and not know how to address
their offers. And then we will hasten our being   180
united in the bonds of matrimony.

ARBELLA.

Soft and fair goes far.

Exeunt.

[Scene ii.] At the tavern.

Enter Colonel Careless, Colonel Blunt and Teague.

COLONEL CARELESS.

Did ever man get away so craftily from the thing
he liked? Terrible business, afraid to tell a woman
what she desired to hear. I pray heartily that the
boys do not come to the knowledge of thy famous
retreat. We shall be followed by those small birds,   5
as you have seen an owl pursued.

COLONEL BLUNT.

I shall break some of their wings then.

COLONEL CARELESS.

To leave a handsome woman, a woman that came
to be bound body for body for thee, one that does
that which no woman will hardly do again.   10

COLONEL BLUNT.

What's that?

COLONEL CARELESS.

Love thee and thy blunt humor.* A mere* chance,
man, a thing besides all the venerate stars.

COLONEL BLUNT.

You practice your wit to no purpose. I am not to
be persuaded to lie still, like a jack-a-lent[54] to be   15
cast at. I had rather be a wisp hung up for a
woman to scold at than a fixed lover for 'em to
point at. Your squib began to hiss.

----

54 jack-a-lent] figure of a man, set up to be pelted: an ancient form of the sport of "Aunt Sally," practised during Lent; hence figuratively, a butt for every one to
throw at (*OED*); as opposed to the following "wisp": a
twist or figure of straw for a scold to rail at (*OED*)

Enter Obadiah.

COLONEL CARELESS.

Peace, man, here's Jupiter's Mercury. Is his message
to us, trow? 20

OBADIAH.

Gentlemen, you are opportunely overtaken and
found out.

COLONEL BLUNT.

How's this?

OBADIAH.

I come unto you in the name of the honorable Mr.
Day, who desires to speak with you both about 25
some important affair, which is conducing for your
good.

COLONEL BLUNT.

What train is this?

COLONEL CARELESS.

Peace, let us not be rash.—Teague?

TEAGUE.

Well then. 30

COLONEL CARELESS.

Were it not possible that you could entertain this
fellow in the next room till he were pretty drunk?

TEAGUE.

I warrant you that now, I will make him and my
self, too, drunk for thy sweet sake.

COLONEL CARELESS.

Be sure, Teague.—Some business, sir, that will take 35
us up a very little time to finish, make us desire
your patience till we dispatch it. In the meantime,
sir, do us the favor as to call for a glass of sack.*
In the next room, Teague shall wait upon you and
drink your master's health. 40

OBADIAH.

It needeth not, nor do I use to drink healths.

COLONEL CARELESS.

None but your master's, sir, and that by way of
remembrance.

OBADIAH.

We that have the affairs of state under our tuition
cannot long delay. My presence may be required 45
for the carrying on the work.

COLONEL CARELESS.

Nay sir, it shall not exceed above a quarter of an
hour. Perhaps we'll wait upon you to Mr. Day

presently.* Pray sir, drink but one glass or two. We
would wait upon you ourselves, but that would 50
hinder us from going with you.

OBADIAH.

Upon that consideration, I shall attend a little.

COLONEL CARELESS.

Go wait upon him.—Now, Teague, or never.

TEAGUE.

I will make him so drunk as can be upon my soul.

Exeunt [Teague and Obadiah].

COLONEL BLUNT.

What a devil should this message mean? 55

COLONEL CARELESS.

'Tis too plain! This cream of Committee rascals,
who's better intelligence than a state secretary, has
heard of his son Abel's being hampered in the cause
of the wicked and in revenge would entice us into
perdition. 60

COLONEL BLUNT.

If Teague could be so fortunate as to make him
drunk, we might know all.

COLONEL CARELESS.

If the close-hearted rogue will not be open-
mouthed, we'll leave him pawned for all our scores
and stuff his pockets with blank commissions[55]. 65

COLONEL BLUNT.

Only fill up one with his master's name.

COLONEL CARELESS.

And another with his wife's name for adjutant
general, together with a bill of ammunition hid
under Day's house, and make it be digged down
with scandal of delinquency. A rascal to think to 70
invite us into Newgate!

COLONEL BLUNT.

Well, we must resolve what to do.

COLONEL CARELESS.

I have a fancy come into my head that may
produce an admirable scene.

COLONEL BLUNT.

Come, let's hear. 75

COLONEL CARELESS.

'Tis upon supposition that Teague makes him

---

[55] blank commissions] blank military orders and legal
documents

drunk, and by the way, 'tis a good omen that we have no sober apparition in that wavering posture of frailty. We'll send him home in a sedan and cause him to be delivered in that good-natured 80 condition to the ill-natured rascal, his master.

COLONEL BLUNT.

It will be excellent. How I pray for Teague to be victorious!

Enter musician.

MUSICIAN.

Gentlemen, will you have any music?

COLONEL CARELESS.

Prithee, no, we are out of tune. 85

COLONEL BLUNT.

Pish, we never will be out of humor. Dost hear, canst sing us a Malignant sonnet?

MUSICIAN.

I can sing many songs. You seem honest gentlemen.

COLONEL CARELESS.

Cavaliers, thou mean'st. Sing without any apprehension. 90

Song.

Now the veil is pulled off, and this pitiful Nation
Too late see the gull of a Kirk reformation,
How all things that should be
Are turned topsey turvey: 95
The freedom we have,
Our Prince[56] made a slave,
And the masters must now turn the waiters;
The great ones obey,
While the rascals do sway, 100
And the loyal to rebels are traitors.

The pulpits are crowded with tongues of their own,
And the preacher, spiritual Committee-men grown,
To denounce sequestration
On souls of old fashion; 105
They rail and they pray,
Till they quite preach away
The wealth that was once the wise City's.

---

56 Prince] either Charles I or Charles II, although it was the former who was held captive, except briefly, from 1647 to his execution in 1649

The courts in the Hall
Where the lawyers did bawl 110
Are turned into pious committees.

COLONEL CARELESS.

This song has raised my spirits. Here, sing always for the King. I would have every man in his way do something for him; I would have fiddlers sing for him, parsons pray for him, men fight for him, 115 women scold for him, and children cry for him, and according to this rule, Teague is drinking for him.

Enter Teague and Obadiah, drunk.

But see! See and rejoice where Teague with laurel comes. 120

COLONEL BLUNT.

And the vanquished Obadiah with nothing fixed about him but his eyes.

COLONEL CARELESS.

Stay, sing another song in the behalf of compounders if thou canst, that the vapors of the wine may have full power to ascend up to the firmament 125 of his truly reformed coxcomb.

Song.

Come drawer, some wine.
Let it sparkle and shine
And make its own drops fall abounding;
Like the hearts it makes light, 130
Let it flow pure and right,
And a plague take all kind of compounding.

We'll not be too wise
Nor try to advise
How to suffer and gravely despair: 135
For wisdom and parts*
Sit brooding on hearts,
And there they catch nothing but care.

Not a thought shall come in
But what brings our king; 140
Let committees be damned with their gain.
We'll send by this stealth
To our hearts our king's health,
And there in despite he shall reign.

Obadiah repeating with him.

COLONEL CARELESS.

This is sport beyond modest hopes. How I will 145
adore sack* that can force this fellow to religion.
The rogue is full of worship.

TEAGUE.

Well now, upon my soul, Mr. Obed Commit sings
as well as the man now. Come then, will you sing
an Irish song after me? 150

OBADIAH.

I will sing Irish for the King now.

TEAGUE.

I will sing for the King as well as you. Hark you
now.

Sings an Irish song, and Obadiah tries.

OBADIAH.

That is too hard stuff; I cannot do these and these
material matters. 155

TEAGUE.

Here now, we will take some snuff for the King.
So, there lay it upon your hand, put one of your
noses to it now, so snuff now. Upon my soul, Mr.
Obed Commit will make a brave* Irish man.

OBADIAH.

I will snuff for the King no more. Good Mr. 160
Teague, give me some more sack, and sing English
for my money.

TEAGUE.

I will tell you that Irish is as good and better too.
Come now, we will dance. Can you play an Irish
tune? Can you play this now? 165

MUSICIAN.

No sir, but I can play an excellent Irish jig.

They dance.

COLONEL CARELESS.

This is beyond thought. So this motion, like a
tumbled barrel, has set the liquor a-working again.
Now for a chair.*

Enter drawer.

COLONEL BLUNT.

Drawer, who waits there? 170

DRAWER.

What d'you want, gentlemen?

COLONEL BLUNT.

Call a chair presently* and bring their chair into
this room. Here's a friend of ours overtaken.

DRAWER.

I go, sir. (*Exit.*)

COLONEL CARELESS.

Teague, thou hast done miracles. Thou art a good 175
omen and hast vanquished the cause in this
overthrow of this counterfeit rascal, its true
epitome. And now Teague, according to the words
of condemnation, we'll send him to the place from
whence he came. 180

TEAGUE.

Upon my soul, he's dead now. Shall I howl as we
do in Ireland?

COLONEL CARELESS.

How's that, Teague?

TEAGUE. (*Howls.*)

Yo, yo.

COLONEL CARELESS.

No more, good Teague, lest you give an alarm to 185
the enemy.

Enter sedan.

Welcome, honest fellow; by your looks you seem so.

FIRST CHAIRMAN.

How Colonel, have you forgot your poor soldier
Ned?

COLONEL CARELESS.

Why, this is a miraculous pursuit of good fortune. 190
Honest Ned. What, turned chairman?

FIRST CHAIRMAN.

Anything for bread and beer. Noble Colonel, shall
I have the honor to carry you?

COLONEL CARELESS.

No, Ned. Is thy fellow honest?

FIRST CHAIRMAN.

Or I'd be hanged before I carry a chair an inch 195
with him.

COLONEL CARELESS.

'Tis well. Look you Ned, that fellow is Mr. Day
the Committee-man's clerk, whom with wonderful
industry we have made drunk. Just as he is, pack
him up in thy chair and immediately transport 200
him to his master Day's house and in the very hall
turn him out. There's half a crown for thy pains.

FIRST CHAIRMAN.

If I fail, say Ned's a coward. Come, shall we put your short-winged[57] worship into your mew? Come along.   205

They put him in and exeunt.

COLONEL CARELESS.

Farewell Ned.—Teague, come, you must carry some money to one or two confident friends of mine. We'll pay our reckoning at the bar, then go home and laugh. And if you will plot some way to see our enchanting females once more: they   210 make me so long—

Exeunt.

[Scene iii. The Days' house.]

Enter Mr. Day and Mrs. Day.

MRS. DAY.

Dispatch quickly, I say, and say I said it. Many things fall between the lip and the cup.

MR. DAY.

Nay duck, let thee alone for counsel. Ah, if thou hadst been a man.

MRS. DAY.

Why, then you would have wanted* a woman, and   5 a helper too.

MR. DAY.

I profess so I should. And a notable one, too, though I say't before thy face, and that's no ill one.

MRS. DAY.

Come, come, you are wandering from the matter. Dispatch the marriage, I say, whilst she is thus   10 taken with our Abel. Women are uncertain.

MR. DAY.

How, if she should be coy?*

MRS. DAY.

You are at your "ifs" again; if she be foolish, tell her plainly what she must trust to: no Abel, no land. Plain dealing's a jewel. Have you the writings   15 drawn as I advised you, which she must sign?

MR. DAY.

Aye, I warrant you, duck. Here, here they be. Oh, she has a brave* estate.

_____
57 short-winged] in falconry, less valuable hawks

MRS. DAY.

What news you have.

MR. DAY.

Look you, wife. (*Pulls out writings and lays out his*   20 *keys.*)

MRS. DAY.

Pish, teach your granam to spin. Let me see.

Enter servant.

SERVANT.

May it please your honor, your good neighbor Zechariah is departing this troublesome life. He has made your honor his executor but cannot   25 depart till he has seen your honors.

MR. DAY.

Alas, alas, a good man will leave us. Come good duck, let us hasten. Where is Obadiah to usher you?

MRS. DAY.

Why, Obadiah, a varlet to be out of the way at such a time; truly, he moveth my wrath. Come   30 husband, along. I'll take Abel in his place.

[Exeunt Mr. Day, Mrs. Day, and servant.] Enter Ruth and Arbella.

RUTH.

What's the meaning of this alarm? There's some carrion discovered; the crows are all gone upon a sudden.

ARBELLA.

The she-Day called most fiercely for Obadiah.   35 Look here, Ruth, what have they left behind?

RUTH.

As I live, it is the Day's bunch of keys, which he always keeps so closely. Well—if thou hast any mettle, now's the time.

ARBELLA.

To do what?   40

RUTH.

To fly out of Egypt.

Enter Abel.

ARBELLA.

Peace, we are betrayed else, as sure as can be, wench. He's come back for the keys.

RUTH.

We'll forswear 'em in confident words and no less confident countenances.   45

ABEL.

> An important affair hath called my honorable
> father and mother forth, and in the absence of
> Obadiah, I am enforced to attend their honors.
> And therefore, I conceived it right and meet to
> acquaint you with it, lest in my absence you might 50
> have apprehended that some mischance has
> befallen my person. Therefore, I desire you to
> receive consolation, and so I bid you heartily
> farewell. (*Exit.*)

ARBELLA.

> Given from his mouth this tenth of April. He put 55
> me in a cruel fright.

RUTH.

> As I live, I am all over in such a dew as hangs about
> a still when 'tis first set a-going. But this is better
> and better: there was never such an opportunity
> to break prison. I know the very places, holes in 60
> his closet,* where the composition of your estate
> lies and where the deeds of my own estate lies. I
> have cast my eye upon them often when I have
> gone up to him in errands and to call him to
> dinner. If I miss, hang me. 65

ARBELLA.

> But whither shall we go?

RUTH.

> To a friend of mine and of my father's that lives
> near the Temple* and will harbor us. Fear not, and
> so set up for ourselves and get our colonels.

ARBELLA.

> Nay, the mischief that I have done and the 70
> condition we are in makes me ready as thou art.
> Come, let's about it.

RUTH.

> Stay, do you stand sentinel here; that's the closet
> window. I'll call for thee if I need thee. And be
> sure to give notice of any news of the enemy. 75
> (*Exit.*)

ARBELLA.

> I warrant thee, may but this departing brother have
> so much string of life[58] left him as may tie this
> expecting Day to his bedside till we have

committed this honest robbery.—Hark! What's
that? This apprehension can make a noise when 80
there is none.

RUTH. (*Above.*)

> I have 'em, I have 'em. Nay, the whole covey and
> his seal at arms bearing a dog's leg.[59]

ARBELLA.

> Come, make haste then.

RUTH.

> As I live, here's a letter counterfeited from[k] the 85
> King to the rascal, his rebellious subject Day, with
> a remembrance to his discreet wife. Nay, what dost
> thou think these are? I'll but cast my eye upon
> these papers that were schismatically[60] and lay in
> separation. What dost think they are? 90

ARBELLA.

> I can't tell. Nay prithee, come away.

RUTH.

> Out upon the precise[61] baboon. They are letters
> from two wenches: one from an increase of salary
> to maintain his unlawful issue; another from a
> wench that had more conscience than he and 95
> refused to take the physic that he prescribed to take
> away a natural tympany.

ARBELLA.

> Nay prithee, dispatch.

RUTH.

> Here be abundance more. Come, run up and help
> me carry 'em. We'll take the whole index of his 100
> rogueries. We shall be furnished with such arms
> offensive and defensive that we shall never need sue
> to him for a league. Come, make haste.

ARBELLA.

> I come.

[Exit Arbella below, Ruth above.] Enter [chairmen]
with [Obadiah in] the sedan.*

FIRST CHAIRMAN.

> Come, open his portable tomb. 'Slife,* here's 105

---

58 string of life] as spun by the Fates (q.v.), who spin a person's thread of life and then cut the thread when the person dies

59 dog's leg] a heraldic baton perhaps suggesting illegiti-
macy like the traditional bar sinister

60 schismatically] set apart, separate, with the connotation
of heresy

61 precise] a contemptuous term applied to Puritan for
their supposed exactitude and righteousness

nothing in it. Ferret him or he'll never bolt. It looks as if we had brought a basket hare, to be set down and hunted.

SECOND CHAIRMAN.

He's dead.

FIRST CHAIRMAN.

Dead drunk, thou mean'st. Turn up the chair and   110
turn him out as they do badgers caught in a sack.
Shake, man. So, now he sallies.

Obadiah tumbles out of the chair and sings, as at the
tavern, of the song. Enter Arbella and Ruth from
robbing the closet.**

ARBELLA.

What's this? We are undone.

OBADIAH.

Mr. Teague, will you dance, Mr. Teague?

RUTH.

Put a good face on't or give me the van. Oh, 'tis   115
Obadiah fallen.

ARBELLA.

Nay, and cannot rise neither.—D'hear, honest
friends, was this zealous gentleman your freight?

FIRST CHAIRMAN.

Yes, mistress. Two honest gentlemen took care of
him, seeing him thus devoutly overtaken.   120

ARBELLA.

It was our colonels that thought Day sent him to
trepan them, as sure as can be.

RUTH.

No doubt on't. How unmerciful they are, Arbella,
every minute to do something or other to increase
our whimsy.—Are you paid?   125

FIRST CHAIRMAN.

Yes, mistress.—'Slife,* we shall be paid double.

RUTH.

Stay. Where did you leave the two careful-minded
gentlemen?

FIRST CHAIRMAN.

Why do you ask, mistress?

RUTH.

For no hurt. Can'st carry us near the place?   130

FIRST CHAIRMAN.

Yes, mistress.—Sure there's no danger in women.

ARBELLA. [*To Ruth.*]

What dost mean?

RUTH.

The same that thou dost: to see 'em if I can.—Is't
near Temple Bar?[62]

Obadiah sings.

FIRST CHAIRMAN.

Hard by, mistress.   135

RUTH.

Come in, there's my friend lives hard by. Fear not,
we can never fly so concealed.—May that nightingale continue his note till the owl* Day returns
to hear him.—Come honest fellow, stay over
against the place where you left the gentlemen. We   140
have some business with them. We'll pay you, and
they'll thank you. So, good night, Mr. Day.

FIRST CHAIRMAN.

I warrant you, mistress. Come along, Tom.

*Exeunt; manet Obadiah. Enter as returned, Mr. Day,
Mrs. Day, and Abel.*

MR. DAY.

He made a good end and departed as unto sleep.

MRS. DAY.

I'll assure you his wife took on grievously. I do not   145
believe she'll marry this half year.

MR. DAY.

He died full of exhortation. Hah, duck, shouldst
be sorry to lose me?

MRS. DAY.

Lose you? I warrant you, you'll live as long as a
better thing.   150

Obadiah sings.

Ah Lord, what's that?

MR. DAY.

How now! What's this? How! Obadiah? And in a
drunken distemper assuredly!

MRS. DAY.

Oh fie upon't, who would have believed that he
should have lived to have seen Obadiah overcome   155
with the creature? Where have you been, sirrah?

OBADIAH.

D—d—drinking the Ki—Ki—King's health.

MR. DAY.

Oh terrible. Some disgrace put upon us and shame

---

62 Temple Bar] the western limit of the City of London

brought within our walls. I'll go lock up my neighbor's will and come down and show him a reproof. How—how— (*Feels in his pocket and leaps up.*) I cannot feel my keys—nor—hear 'em jingle. Didst thou see my keys, duck? 160

MRS. DAY.

Duck me no ducks. I see your keys? See a fool's head of your own. Had I kept them, I warrant they had been forthcoming. You are so slappish, you throw 'em up and down at your tail.[63] Why don't you go look if you have not left them at the door? 165

MR. DAY.

I go, I go, duck. (*Exit.*) 170

MRS. DAY.

Here Abel, take up this fallen creature, who has left his uprightness, carry him to bed, and when he is returned to himself, I will exhort him.

ABEL.

He is exceedingly overwhelmed. (*Goes to lift him.*)

OBADIAH.

Stand away, I say, and give me some sack,* that I may drink a health to the King and let committees be damned with their gain. (*Sings.*) Where's Mr. Teague? 175

Enter Mr. Day.[l]

MR. DAY.

Undone, undone! Robbed, robbed! The door's left open and all my writings, papers stolen. Undone, undone!—Ruth, Ruth! 180

MRS. DAY.

Why, Ruth, I say! Thieves, thieves!

Enter servant.

SERVANT.

What's the matter, forsooth? Here has been no thieves. I have not been a minute out of the house.

MRS. DAY.

Where's Ruth and Mrs. Arbella? 185

SERVANT.

I have not seen them a pretty while.

---

63 slappish...tale] Mr. Day is given to slapping his hands, and his keys, at his coat-tails as he walks.

MR. DAY.

'Tis they have robbed me and taken way the writings of both their estates. Undone, undone!

MRS. DAY.

This came with staying for you, coxcomb. We had come back sooner else. Yes, slow drone, we must be undone for your dullness. 190

OBADIAH.

Be not in wrath.

MRS. DAY.

I'll wrath you, ye rascal you, teaching you, drunken rascal, and you, sober dullman.

OBADIAH.

Your feet are swift and violent; their motion will make them fume. 195

MRS. DAY.

D'ye lie, too, ye drunken rascal?

MR. DAY.

Nay, patience, good duck, and let's lay out for these women. They are the thieves.

MRS. DAY.

'Twas you that left your keys upon the table to tempt them. Ye need cry "good duck be patient." [*To Abel.*] Bring in the drunken rascal, ye booby; when he is sober, he may discover* something. Come, take him up. I'll have 'em hunted. 200

Exeunt [Mr. Day and Mrs. Day].

ABEL.

I rejoice yet, in the midst of my sufferings, that my mistress saw not my rebukes.—Come Obadiah, I pray raise yourself upon your feet and walk. 205

OBADIAH.

Have you taken the covenant? That's the question.

ABEL.

Yea.

OBADIAH.

And will you drink a health to the King? That's t'other question. 210

ABEL.

Make not thyself a scorn.

OBADIAH.

Scorn in thy face. Void, young Satan.

ABEL.

I pray you walk in. I shall be assisting. 215

OBADIAH.

Stand off, and you shall perceive by my steadfast going that I am not drunk. Look ye now.—So, softly, softly, gently, good Obadiah, gently and steadily, for fear it should be said that thou art in drink; so, gently and uprightly, Obadiah. (*He moves his legs, but stands still.*) 220

ABEL.

You do not move.

OBADIAH.

Then do I stand still, as fast as you go.

Enter Mrs. Day.

MRS. DAY.

What, stay all day? [*Slaps Abel.*] There's for you, sir. You are a sweet youth to leave in trust. [*To Obadiah.*] Along, you drunken rascal. I'll set you both forward. 225

OBADIAH.

The Philistines are upon us and Day is broke loose from darkness, with keeping has made her fierce.

MRS. DAY.

(*She beats them off.*) Out you drunken rascal; I'll make you move, you beast. 230

Exeunt.

Act V, scene i. [A street.]

Enter bookseller and bailiffs, having laid hold on Teague.

BOOKSELLER.

Come along, sir, I'll teach you to take covenants.

TEAGUE.

Will you teach me then? Did I not take it then? Why will you teach me now?

BOOKSELLER.

You shall pay dearly for the blows you struck me, my wild Irish, by St. Patrick you shall. 5

TEAGUE.

What have you now to do with St. Patrick? He will scorn your covenant.

BOOKSELLER.

I'll put you, sir, where you shall have worse liquor than your bonnyclabber.

TEAGUE.

Bonnyclabber? By my gossip's hand, now you are a rascal if you do not love bonnyclabber. And I will 10

break your pate if you will not let me go to my master.

BOOKSELLER.

Oh, you are an impudent rascal.—Come, away with him. 15

Enter Colonel Careless.

COLONEL CARELESS.

How now? Hold, my friend. Whither do you carry my servant?

BOOKSELLER.

I have arrested him, sir, for striking me and taking away my books.

COLONEL CARELESS.

What has he taken away? 20

BOOKSELLER.

Nay, the value of the thing is not much. 'Twas *The Covenant*, sir.

TEAGUE.

Well, I did take the covenant, and my master took it from me, and we have taken the covenant then, have we not? 25

COLONEL CARELESS.

Here, honest fellow, here's more than thy covenant's worth. Here bailiffs, here's for you to drink.

BOOKSELLER.

Well sir, you seem an honest gentleman; for your sake, and in hopes of your custom, I release him.

FIRST BAILIFF.

Thank ye, noble sir. 30

COLONEL CARELESS.

Farewell, my noble friends.

Exeunt bookseller and bailiffs.

So, d'hear, Teague? Pray, take no more covenants. Have you paid the money I sent you with?

TEAGUE.

Yes, but I will carry no more, look you there now.

COLONEL CARELESS.

Why, Teague? 35

TEAGUE.

God sa' my soul now, I shall run away with it.

COLONEL CARELESS.

Pish, thou art too honest.

TEAGUE.

That I am too, upon my soul now. But the Devil

is not honest, that he is not. He would not let me
alone when I was going, but he made go to this 40
little long place and t'other little long place, and,
upon my soul, was carrying me to Ireland, for he
made me go by dirty place like a lough now, and
therefore, I know now, it was the way to Ireland.
Then I would stand still, and then he would make 45
me go on, and then I would go to one side, and
he would make me go to t'other side. And then I
got a little farther and did run then, and upon my
soul, the Devil could not catch me. And then I did
pay the money. But I will carry no more money, 50
now, that I will not.

COLONEL CARELESS.

But thou shalt, Teague, when I have more to send.
Thou art proof now against temptations.

TEAGUE.

Well then, if you send me with money again, and
if I do not come to thee upon the time, the Devil 55
will make me be gone then with the money. Here
is a paper for thee; 'tis a quit way, indeed.

COLONEL CARELESS.

That's well said, Teague. (*Reads.*)

Enter Mr. Day, Obadiah, and soldiers.

OBADIAH.

See, sir, providence hath directed us. There is one
of them that clothed me with shame, and the most 60
malignant among the wicked.

MR. DAY.

Soldiers, seize him. I charge him with treason.
Here's a warrant to the keeper, as I told you.

FIRST SOLDIER.

Nay, no resistance now. 65

COLONEL CARELESS.

What's the matter, rascals?

MR. DAY.

You shall know that to your cost hereafter. Away
with him.

COLONEL CARELESS.

Teague, tell 'em I shall not come home tonight, I
am engaged. 70

TEAGUE.

I prithee, ben't engaged.

COLONEL CARELESS.

Gentlemen, I am guilty of nothing that I know of.

MR. DAY.

That will appear, sir. Away with him.

TEAGUE.

What will you do with my master now?

MR. DAY.

Be quiet, sir, or you shall go with him. 75

TEAGUE.

That I will, for all you now.

COLONEL CARELESS. (*Whispers.*)

Teague, come hither.

TEAGUE.

Must not I go with you then?

COLONEL CARELESS.

No, no, be sure to do as I tell you.

MR. DAY.

Away with him. We will be avenged on the scorner. 80
And I'll go home and tell my duck this part of my
good fortune.

Exeunt. Enter sedan. Ruth and Arbella come out.

RUTH.

So far, we are right.—Now honest fellow, step over
and tell the two gentlemen that we two women
desire to speak with them. 85

Enter Colonel Blunt, Lieutenant Story.

FIRST CHAIRMAN.

See, mistress, here's one of them.

RUTH.

That's thy colonel, Arbella; catch him quickly or
he'll fly again.

ARBELLA.

What should I do?

RUTH.

Put forth some good words, as they use to shake 90
oats when they go to catch a skittish jade. Advance.

ARBELLA.

Sir.

COLONEL BLUNT.

Lady.—'Tis she.

ARBELLA.

I wish, sir, that my friend and I had some
conveniency of speaking with you. We now want 95
the assistance of some noble friend.

COLONEL BLUNT.

Then I am happy. Bring me but to do something

for you; I would have my actions talk, not I. My
friend will be here immediately; I dare speak for
him, too. Pardon my last confusion, but what I   100
told you was as true as if I had stayed—

RUTH.

To make affidavit of it.

COLONEL BLUNT.

Good overcharged gentlewoman, spare me but a
little.

ARBELLA.

Prithee peace. Canst thou be merry, and we in this   105
condition?—Sir, I do believe you noble, truly
worthy. If we might withdraw any whither out of
sight, I would acquaint you with the business.

LIEUTENANT STORY.

My house, ladies, is at that door where both the
colonels lodge. Pray command it. Colonel Careless   110
will immediately be here.

Enter Teague.

TEAGUE.

Well now, my good master will not come. That
Commit rogue Day has got him with men in red
coats, and he is gone to prison here below this
street. He would not let me go with him, i'faith,   115
but made me come tell thee now.

RUTH.

Oh my heart. Tears, by your leave a while. (*Wipes
her eyes.*) D'hear, Arbella? Here, take all the
trinkets, only the bait that I'll use. Accept of this
house. [*Hands her some of the papers.*] Here let me   120
find thee. I'll try my skill. Nay, talk not. (*Exit.*)

COLONEL BLUNT.

Careless in prison! Pardon me, madam, I must
leave you for a little while. Pray be confident; this
honest friend of mine will use you with all respects
till I return.   125

ARBELLA.

What do you mean to do, sir?

COLONEL BLUNT.

I cannot tell, yet I must attempt something. You
shall have a sudden* account of all things. You say
you dare believe; pray be as good as your word,
and whatever accident befalls me, know I love you   130
dearly. Why do you weep?

ARBELLA.

Do not run yourself into a needless danger.

COLONEL BLUNT.

How, d'you weep for me? Pray let me see. Never
woman did so before, that I know of, which I am
ravished with it. The round gaping earth ne'er   135
sucked showers so greedily as my heart drinks
these. Pray, if you love me, be but so good and
kind as to confess it.

ARBELLA.

Do not ask what you may tell yourself.

COLONEL BLUNT.

I must go; honor and friendship call me.—Here,   140
dear Lieutenant, I never had a jewel but this. Use it
as right ones should be used; do not breathe upon,
but gaze as I do. Hold, one word more. The soldier
that you often talked of to me, is still honest?

LIEUTENANT STORY.

Most perfectly.   145

COLONEL BLUNT.

And I may trust him?

LIEUTENANT STORY.

With your life.

COLONEL BLUNT.

Enough.—Pray let me leave my last looks fixed
upon you. So, I love you, and am honest.*—Be   150
careful, good Lieutenant, of this treasure.—She
weeps still. I cannot go. I must. (*Exit.*)

LIEUTENANT STORY.

Madam, pray let my house be honored with you.
Be confident of all respect and faith.

ARBELLA.

What uncertainties pursue my love and fortune.   155

Exeunt.

[Scene ii. A prison.]

Enter Ruth with a soldier.

RUTH.

Come, give me the bundle, now the habit. 'Tis
well, there's for your pains. Be secret and wait
where I appointed you.

SOLDIER.

If I fail, may I die in a ditch and there lie and out-
stink it. (*Exit.*)   5

RUTH.

Now for my wild colonel. First, here's a note, with my lady Day's seal to it for his release. If that fails (as they that will shoot at these rascals must have two strings to his bow), then here's my redcoat's skin to disguise him and a string to draw up a ladder of cords, which I have prepared against it grows dark. One of them will hit sure. I must have him out, and I must have him when he is out: I have no patience to expect. Within there—ho. 10

Enter keeper.

RUTH.

You have not a prisoner, sir, in your custody, one Colonel Careless? 15

KEEPER.

Yes, mistress, and committed by your father, Mr. Day.

RUTH.

I know it, but there is a mistake in it. Here's a warrant for his delivery, under his hand and seal. 20

KEEPER.

I would willingly obey it, mistress, but there's a general order come from above that all the King's party should be kept close and none released but by the State's order.

RUTH. [*Aside.*]

This goes ill.—May I speak with him, sir? 25

KEEPER.

Very freely, mistress. There's no order to forbid any to come to him. To say truth, 'tis most pleasantest gentleman. I'll call him forth. (*Exit.*)

RUTH.

O'my conscience, everything must be in love with him. Now for my last hopes; if this fail, I'll use the ropes myself. 30

Enter keeper and Colonel Careless.

COLONEL CARELESS.

Mr. Day's daughter speak with me?

KEEPER.

Aye sir, there she is. (*Exit.*)

RUTH.

Oh sir, does the name of Mr. Day's daughter trouble you? You love the gentlewoman, but hate his daughter. 35

COLONEL CARELESS.

Yes, I do love that gentlewoman you speak of most exceedingly.

RUTH.

And the gentlewoman loves you. But what luck this is, that Day's daughter should ever be with her to spoil all! 40

COLONEL CARELESS.

Not a whit one way. I have a pretty room within, dark and convenient.

RUTH.

For what?

COLONEL CARELESS.

For you and I to give counter-security for our kindness to one another. 45

RUTH.

But Mr. Day's daughter will be there too?

COLONEL CARELESS.

'Tis dark; we'll ne'er see her.

RUTH.

You care not who you are wicked with; methinks a prison should tame you. 50

COLONEL CARELESS.

Why, d'you think a prison takes away blood and fight? As long as I am so qualified, I am touchwood, and whenever you bring fire, I shall fall a-burning.

RUTH.

And you would quench it.

COLONEL CARELESS.

And you shall kindle it again. 55

RUTH.

No, you will be burnt out at last, burnt to a coal, black as dishonest love.

COLONEL CARELESS.

Is this your business? Did you come to disturb my contemplations with a sermon? Is this all?

RUTH.

One thing more: I love you, it's true, but I love you honestly.* If you know how to love me virtuously, I'll free you from prison and run all fortunes with you. 60

COLONEL CARELESS.

Yes, I could love thee all manner of ways. If I could not, freedom were no bait, were it from death. I should despise your offer to bargain for a lie. But— 65

RUTH. [*Aside.*]

Oh noble.—But what?

COLONEL CARELESS.

The name of that rascal that got thee. Yet, I lie too:
he ne'er got a limb of thee. Pox on't, thy mother was
as unlucky to bear thee. But how shall we salve that? 70
Take off these incumbrances, and I'll purchase thee
in thy smock. But to have such a flaw in my title—

RUTH.

Can I help nature?

COLONEL CARELESS.

Or I honor? Why, hark you now, do but swear me
into a pretence, do but betray me with an oath, 75
that thou wert not begot on the body of Gillian,
my father's kitchen maid.

RUTH.

Who's that?

COLONEL CARELESS.

Why, the honorable Mrs. Day that now is.

RUTH.

Will you believe me if I swear? 80

COLONEL CARELESS.

Aye, that I will, though I know all the while 'tis
not true.

RUTH.

I swear then, by all that's good, I am not their
daughter.

COLONEL CARELESS.

Poor, kind, perjured pretty one, I am beholding 85
to thee. Wouldst damn thy self for me?

RUTH.

You are mistaken. I have tried you fully; you are
noble and I hope you love me. Be ever firm to
virtuous principles. My name is not so godly a one
as Ruth, but plain Anne, and a daughter to Sir Basil 90
Throughgood, one perhaps that you have heard of,
since in the world he has still* had so loud and fair
a character. 'Tis too long to tell you how this Day
got me, an infant, and my estate into his power and
made me pass for his own daughter, my father dying 95
when I was but two years old. This I knew but lately
by an unexpected meeting of an ancient servant of
my father's. But two hours since, Arbella and I
found an opportunity of stealing away all the
writings that belonged to my estate and her 100
composition. In our flight, we met your friend, with

whom I left her as soon as I had intelligence of your
misfortune, to try to get your liberty—which if I can
do, you have an estate, for I have mine.

COLONEL CARELESS.

Thou more than— 105

RUTH.

No, no, no raptures at this time. Here's your
disguise, purchased from a true-hearted redcoat.
Here's a bundle; let this line down when 'tis almost
dark and you shall draw up a ladder of ropes. If the
ladder of ropes be done sooner, I'll send them by a 110
soldier that I dare trust. And you may, your
window's large enough, as soon as you receive it,
come down. If not, when 'tis dusk, let down your
line. And at the bottom of the window, you shall
find yours, more than her own, not Ruth, but Anne. 115

COLONEL CARELESS.

I'll leap into thy arms.

RUTH.

So you may break your neck; if you do, I'll jump
too. But time steals on our words. Observe all I
have told you. So farewell.

COLONEL CARELESS.

Nay, as the good fellows use to say, let us not part 120
with dry lips. One kiss.

RUTH.

Not a bit of me till I am all yours.

COLONEL CARELESS.

Your hand, then, to show I am grown reasonable.
A poor compounder.

RUTH.

Pish, there's a dirty glove upon't. 125

COLONEL CARELESS.

Give me but any naked part, and I'll kiss it as a
snail creeps and leave sign where my lips slid along.

RUTH.

Good snail, get out of your hole first. Think of
your business. So fare—

COLONEL CARELESS.

Nay, prithee be not ashamed that thou art loath 130
to leave me. 'Slid,* I am a man, but I'm as arrant
a rogue as thy quondam father Day, if I could not
cry to leave thee a brace of minutes.

RUTH.

Away. We grow foolish. Farewell, yet be careful.
Nay, go in. 135

COLONEL CARELESS.

Do you go first.

RUTH.

Nay, fie, go in.

COLONEL CARELESS.

We'll fairly then divide the victory and draw off together. So, I will have the last look.

Exeunt severally, looking at one another.

[Scene iii. A street near the prison.]

Enter Colonel Blunt and soldier.

COLONEL BLUNT.

No more words. I do believe, nay, I know thou art honest. I may live to thank thee better.

SOLDIER.

I scorn any encouragement to love my King or those that serve him. I took pay under these people with a design to do him service; the Lieutenant knows it.   5

COLONEL BLUNT.

He has told me so. No more words, thou art a noble fellow. Thou art sure his window's large enough?

SOLDIER.

Fear it not.   10

COLONEL BLUNT.

Here then, carry him this ladder of ropes. So now give me the coat. Say not a word to him, but bid him dispatch when he sees the coast clear. He shall be waited for at the bottom of his window. Give him thy sword too, if he desires it.   15

SOLDIER.

I'll dispatch it instantly; therefore, get to your place.

COLONEL BLUNT.

I warrant ye.

Exit soldier. Enter Teague.

TEAGUE.

Have you done everything then? By my soul now, yonder is the man with the hard name. That man   20 now that I made drunk for thee, Mr. Tay's rascal. He is coming along there behind, now upon my soul, that he is.

COLONEL BLUNT.

The rascal comes for some mischief. Teague, now or never play the man.   25

TEAGUE.

How should I be a man, then?

COLONEL BLUNT.

Thy master is never to be got out if this rogue gets hither. Meet him therefore, Teague, in the most winning manner thou canst and make him once more drunk, and it shall be called the second   30 edition of Obadiah, put forth with Irish notes upon him. And if he will not go drink with thee—

TEAGUE.

I will carry him upon my backside if he will not go. And if he will not be drunk, I will cut his throat then, that I will, for my sweet master now,   35 that I will.

COLONEL BLUNT.

Dispatch, good Teague, and dispatch him too, if he will not be conformable. And if thou canst but once more be victorious, bring him in triumph to Lieutenant Story's; there shall be the general   40 rendezvous. Now or never, Teague.

TEAGUE.

I warrant you, I will get drink into his pate, or I will break it for him, that I will, I warrant you. He shall not come after you now.

COLONEL BLUNT.

Good luck go with thee.—The fellow's faithful and   45 stout. That fear's over; now to my station.

Exeunt.

[Scene iv. The prison.]

Colonel Careless.

COLONEL CARELESS.

The time's almost come; how slow it flutters. My desires are better winged. How I long to counterfeit a faintness when I come to the bottom and sink into the arms of this dear witty fair!— Hah, who's this?   5

Enter soldier.

SOLDIER.

Here sir, here's a ladder of ropes. Fasten it to your window and descend. You shall be waited for.

COLONEL CARELESS.

The careful her-creature has sent it.—But d'hear
sir, could you not spare that implement by your
side? It might serve to keep off small curs. 10

SOLDIER.

You'll have no need on't, but there 'tis. Make haste.
The coast is clear. (*Exit.*)

COLONEL CARELESS.

Oh, this pretty she-captain, general over my soul
and body. The thought of her musters every faculty
I have. She has sent the ropes and stays for me. No 15
danger of the ropes, ever slide down with that
swiftness (of desire, of haste) that I will make to thee.

Exit.

[Scene v. Below the prison window.]

Enter Blunt, in his soldier's coat.

COLONEL BLUNT.

All's quiet and the coast clear. So far it goes well.
That is the window; in this nook I'll stand, till I
see him coming down. (*Steps in.*)

*Colonel Careless, above, in his soldier's habit. He lets
down the ladder of ropes and speaks.*

COLONEL CARELESS.

I cannot see my north star that I must sail by, 'tis
clouded; only she stands close, perhaps in some 5
corner. I'll not trifle time, all's clear. Fortune,
forbear thy tricks but for this small occasion.

Enter Blunt.

COLONEL BLUNT.

What's this, a soldier in the place? Careless, I am
betrayed, but I'll end this rascal's duty.

COLONEL CARELESS.

How, a soldier! Betrayed! This rascal shan't laugh 10
at me.

COLONEL BLUNT.

Dog.

COLONEL CARELESS.

How, Blunt!

COLONEL BLUNT.

Careless!

COLONEL CARELESS.

You guess shrewdly. Plague, what contrivance hath 15
set you and I a-tilting at one another?

COLONEL BLUNT.

How the devil got you a soldier's habit?

COLONEL CARELESS.

The same friend for ought I know that furnished
you. This kind gentlewoman is Ruth still. Hah,
here she is; I was just ready to be suspicious. 20

Enter Ruth, with a ladder of ropes.

RUTH.

Who's there?

COLONEL CARELESS.

Two notable charging redcoats.

RUTH.

As I live, my heart is at my mouth.

COLONEL CARELESS.

Prithee, let it come to thy lips that I may kiss it.
What have you in your lap? 25

RUTH.

The ladder of ropes. How a-God's name got you
hither?

COLONEL CARELESS.

Why, I had the ladder of ropes and came down
by it.

COLONEL BLUNT.

Then the mistake is plainer; 'twas I that sent the 30
soldier with the ropes.

RUTH.

What an escape was this! Come, let's lose no time;
here's no place to explain matters in.

COLONEL CARELESS.

I will stay to tell thee, I shall never deserve thee.

RUTH.

Tell me so when you have had me a little while. 35
Come follow me, put on your plainest garb, not
like a dancing master, with your toes out. (*Pulls
their hats over their eyes.*) Come along, hang down
your head as if you wanted pay. So.

Exeunt.

[Scene vi. The Days' house.]

Enter Mr. Day, Mrs. Day, Abel, and Mrs. Chat.

MRS. DAY.

Are you sure of this, neighbor Chat?

MRS. CHAT.

I'm as sure of it as I am that I have a nose to my face.

MRS. DAY.

Is my—you may give one leave methinks to ask out one question—is my daughter Ruth with her?

MRS. CHAT.

She was not when I saw Mrs. Arbella last. I have not been so often at your honor's house but that I know Mrs. Arbella, the rich heir that Mr. Abel was to have had, good gentleman, if he has his due. They never suspected me for I used[m] to buy things of my neighbor Story, before she married the Lieutenant. And stepping in to see Mrs. Story that now is, my neighbor Wish-well that was, I saw, as I told you, this very Mrs. Arbella. And I warrant Mrs. Ruth is not far off.

MRS. DAY.

Let me advise then, husband.

MR. DAY.

Do, good duck, I'll warrant 'em.

MRS. DAY.

You'll warrant when I have done the business.

MR. DAY.

I mean so, duck.

MRS. DAY.

Well, pray spare your meaning, too. First, then, we'll go ourselves in person to this Story's house and, in the meantime, send Abel for soldiers. And when he has brought the soldiers, let them stay at the door and come up himself. And then, if fair means will not do, foul shall.

MR. DAY.

Excellent. Well advised, sweet duck. Ah, let thee alone.—Be gone, Abel, and observe thy mother's directions. Remember the place. We'll be revenged for robbing us and for all their tricks.

ABEL.

I shall perform it.

MRS. DAY.

Come along neighbor and show us the best way. And by and by, we shall have news from Obadiah, who is gone to give the t'other colonel's gaoler a double charge to keep the wild youth close. Come husband, let's hasten. Mrs. Chat, the State shall know what good service you have done.

MRS. CHAT.

I thank your honor.

Exeunt.

[Scene vii. The Storys' house.]

Enter Arbella and Lieutenant Story.

LIEUTENANT STORY.

Pray madam, weep no more. Spare your tears till you know they have miscarried.

ARBELLA.

'Tis a woman, sir, that weeps. We want* men's reasons and their courage to practice with.

LIEUTENANT STORY.

Look up, madam, and meet your unexpected joys.

Enter Ruth, Colonel Careless, and Colonel Blunt.

ARBELLA.

Oh, my dear friend, my dear, dear Ruth.

COLONEL CARELESS.

Pray, none of these phlegmatic hugs. There, take your colonel. My captain and I can hug afresh every minute.

RUTH.

When did we hug last, good soldier?

COLONEL CARELESS.

I have done nothing but hugged thy infancy ever since you, Ruth, turned Annice.

ARBELLA.

You are welcome, sir. I cannot deny I shared in all your danger.

LIEUTENANT STORY.

If she had denied it, Colonel, I would have betrayed her.

COLONEL BLUNT.

I know not what to say nor how to tell how dearly, how well—I love you.

ARBELLA. [*To Ruth.*]

Now can't I say I love him. Yet, I have a mind to tell him too.

RUTH.

Keep't in and choke yourself or get the rising of the lights.[64]

ARBELLA.

What shall I say?

RUTH.

Say something, or he'll vanish.

---

64 get...lights] a fullness of the throat characterized by oppressed breathing, a hysteria-like reaction

COLONEL BLUNT.

D'ye not believe I love you? Or can't you love me? 25
Not a word. Could you—but—

ARBELLA.

No more, I'll save you the labor of courtship,
which should be too tedious to all plain and honest
natures. It is enough I know you love me.

COLONEL BLUNT.

Or I may perish whilst I am swearing it. 30

Enter Jack.

LIEUTENANT STORY.

How now, Jack!

JACK.

Oh master, undone! Here's Mr. Day, the
Committee-man, and his fierce wife come into the
shop. Mrs. Chat brought them in, and they say
they will come up. They know that Mrs. Arbella 35
and their daughter Ruth is here. Deny 'em if you
dare, they say.

LIEUTENANT STORY.

Go down boy and tell 'em I'm coming to 'em.—
This pure jade, my neighbor Chat, has betrayed
us. What shall I do? I warrant the rascal has 40
soldiers at his heels. I think I could help the
colonels out at a back door.

COLONEL BLUNT.

I'll die, rather, by my Arbella. Now you shall see I
love you.

COLONEL CARELESS.

Nor will I, Charles, forsake you, Annice. 45

RUTH.

Come, be cheerful. I'll defend you all against the
assaults of Captain Day and Major General Day,
his new drawn-up wife. Give me my ammunition:
the papers, woman. So, if I do not rout 'em, fall
on; let's all die together and make no more graves 50
but one.

COLONEL BLUNT.

'Slife,* I love her now for all she has jeered me so.

RUTH.

Go fetch 'em in, Lieutenant.

Exit Lieutenant Story.

Stand you all drawn up as my reserve. So, I for
the forlorn hope. 55

COLONEL CARELESS.

That we had Teague here to quarrel with the
female triumphing Day, whilst I threw the male
Day out of the window. Hark, I hear the troop
marching. I know the she-Day stamp among the
tramples of a regiment. 60

ARBELLA.

They come, wench. Charge 'em bravely. I'll second
thee with a volley.

RUTH.

They'll not stand the first charge. Fear not. Now
the Day breaks.

COLONEL CARELESS.

Would 'twere his neck were broke. 65

Enter Mr. and Mrs. Day.

MRS. DAY.

Aha, my fine runaways, have I found you? What,
you think my husband's honor lives without
intelligence? Marry,* come up.

MR. DAY.

My duck tells you how 'tis. We—

MRS. DAY.

Why then, let your duck tell 'em how 'tis.—Yet 70
as I was saying, you shall perceive we abound in
intelligence, else 'twere not for us to go about to
keep the Nation quiet. But if you, Mrs. Arbella,
will deliver up what you have stolen and submit
and return with us and this ungracious Ruth— 75

RUTH.

Anne, if you please.

MRS. DAY.

Who gave you that name, pray?

RUTH.

My godfathers and godmothers in baptism. On—
for, sir, I can answer a leaf further.

MR. DAY.

Duck, good duck, a word. I do not like this name 80
Annice.

MRS. DAY.

You are ever in a fright, with a shriveled heart of
your own.—Well gentlewomen, you are merry.

ARBELLA.

As newly come out of our wardships. I hope Mr.
Abel is well. 85

MRS. DAY.

Yes, he is well. You shall see him presently;* yes, you shall see him.

COLONEL CARELESS.

That is, with myrmidons. Come good Anne, no more delay, fall on.

RUTH.

Then, before the furious Abel approaches with his redcoats, who perhaps are now marching under the conduct of that expert captain in weighty matters, know the articles of our treaty are only these: this Arbella will keep her estate and not marry Abel, but this gentleman, and I, Anne, daughter to Sir Basil Throughgood, and not Ruth as has been thought, have taken my own estate, together with this gentleman, for better for worse. We were modest, though thieves, only plundered our own.

MRS. DAY.

Yes gentlewoman, you took something else, and that my husband can prove. It may cost you your necks if you do not submit.

RUTH.

Truth on't is, we did take something else.

MRS. DAY.

Oh, did you so.

RUTH.

Pray give me leave to speak one word in private with my father Day.

MRS. DAY.

Do so, do so. Are you going to compound? Oh, 'tis father Day now.

RUTH. (*Takes him aside.*)

D'hear sir, how long is't since you have practiced physic?

MR. DAY.

Physic? What d'ye mean?

RUTH.

I mean physic. Look ye, here's a small prescription of yours: D'ye know this handwriting?

MR. DAY.

I am undone.

RUTH.

Here's another upon the same subject. This young one I believe came into this wicked world for want of your preventing dose. It will not be taken now neither; it seems your wenches are willful. Nay, I

do not wonder to see 'em have more conscience than you have.

MR. DAY.

Peace, good Mrs. Anne, I am undone if you betray me.

Enter Abel, goes to his father.

ABEL.

The soldiers are come.

MR. DAY.

Go and send 'em away, Abel. Here's no need, no need now.

MRS. DAY.

Are the soldiers come, Abel?

ABEL.

Yes, but my father biddeth me send 'em away.

MR. DAY.

No, not without your opinion, duck. But since they have but their own, I think, duck, if we were all friends——

MRS. DAY.

Oh, are you at your "ifs" again? D'you think they shall make a fool of me, though they make an ass of you? Call 'em up, Abel, if they will not submit. Call up the soldiers, Abel.

RUTH.

Why your fierce honor shall know the business that makes the wise Mr. Day inclinable to friendship.

MR. DAY.

Nay, good sweetheart, come, I pray, let us be friends.

MRS. DAY.

How's this? What, am not I fit to be trusted now? Have you built your credit and reputation upon my counsel and labors, and am not I fit now to be trusted?

MR. DAY.

Nay, good sweet duck, I confess I owe all to thy wisdom.—Good gentlemen, persuade my duck that we may be all friends.

COLONEL CARELESS.

Hark you, good Gillian Day, be not so fierce upon the husband of thy bosom. 'Twas but a small start of frailty: Say it were a wench or so?

RUTH. (*Aside.*)

As I live, he has hit upon't by chance. Now we shall 150
have sport.

MRS. DAY.

How, a wench, a wench! Out upon the hypocrite.
A wench! Was not I sufficient? A wench! I'll be
revenged. Let him be ashamed if he will. Call the
soldiers, Abel. 155

COLONEL CARELESS.

Haste, good Abel, march not off so hastily.

ARBELLA.

Soft, gentle Abel, or I'll discover you are in bonds.
You shall never be released if you move a step.

RUTH.

D'hear, Mrs. Day, be not so furious; hold your
peace. You may divulge your husband's shame, if 160
you are so simple, and cast him out of authority,
nay, and have him tried for his life. Read this.
Remember too, I know of your bribery and
cheating, and something else. You guess. Be friends
and forgive one another. Here's a letter counter- 165
feited from the King to bestow preferment upon
Mr. Day, if he would turn honest, by which means
I suppose you cozened your brother cheats, in
which he was to remember his service to you. I believe 'twas your indicting: you are the Committee- 170
man, 'tis your best way. Nay, never demure. So, kiss
and be friends. Now if you can contrive handsomely to cozen those that cozen all the world and
get these gentlemen to come by their estates easily
and without taking the covenant, the old sum of 175
five hundred pound that I used to talk of shall be
yours yet.

MRS. DAY.

We will endeavor.

RUTH.

Come Mrs. Arbella, pray let's all be friends.

ARBELLA.

With all my heart. 180

RUTH.

Brethren Abel, the bird is flown, but you shall be
released from your bonds.

ABEL.

I bear my afflictions as I may.

*Enter Teague, leading Obadiah in a halter, and
musician.*

TEAGUE.

What is this now? Who are you? Well, are you not
Mrs. Tay? Well, I will tell her what I should say 185
now. Shall I then? I will try if I cannot laugh too,
as I did, that I will.

COLONEL CARELESS.

No, good Teague, there's no need of thy message
now. But why dost thou lead Obadiah thus?

TEAGUE.

Well, I will hang him presently,* that I will.—Look 190
you here, Mrs. Tay, here's your man Obadiah. Do
you see that now? He would not let me make him
drunk no more, that he would not. So, I did take
him in this string and I did tell him if he did make
noises, I would put the knife into him, that I 195
would, upon my soul.

COLONEL BLUNT.

Honest Teague, thy master is beholding to thee in
some measure for his liberty.

COLONEL CARELESS.

Teague, I shall requite thy honesty.

TEAGUE.

Well, shall I hang him then? It is a rogue, now, 200
who would not be drunk, that he would not.

OBADIAH.

I do beseech you gentlemen, let me not be brought
unto death.

COLONEL CARELESS.

No, poor Teague, 'tis enough we are all friends.
Come, let him go. 205

TEAGUE.

Well, he shall go then.—But you shall love the
King, or I will hang you another time, that I will
by my soul. Well, look you here now, here is the
man that sung you the song, that he is. I met him
as I came and I bid him come hither and sing for 210
the King, that I did.

COLONEL CARELESS.

D'hear, my friends?—Is any of your companions
with you?

MUSICIAN.

Yes sir.

COLONEL CARELESS.

As I live, we'll all dance. It shall be the celebration of 215
our weddings.—Nay Mr. Day, as we hope to con-
tinue friends, you and your duck shall trip it, too.

TEAGUE.

Aye, by my soul will we. Obadiah shall be my
woman, too.—And you shall dance for the King,
that you shall.

COLONEL CARELESS.

Go and strike up then.—No chiding now, Mrs.
Day, come, you must not be refractory for once.

MRS. DAY.

Well husband, since these gentleman will have it
so, and that they perceive we are friends, dance.

COLONEL BLUNT.

Now Mr. Day, to your business. Get it done as
soon as you will; the five hundred pound shall be
ready.

COLONEL CARELESS.

So friends, thank honest Teague.—Thou shalt
flourish in a new livery for this.—Now Mrs.
Annice, I hope you and I may agree about kissing
and compound every way.—Now Mr. Day,
If you will have good luck in everything,
Turn Cavalier and cry, "God bless the King."

Exeunt.

FINIS.

Textual Notes

a The copytext is the first edition, a 1665 quarto (Q1),
printed in *Four New Plays*. Also consulted: the second
edition, a 1692 quarto (Q2), printed in *Five New Plays*;
the third edition, a 1710 quarto (Q3); and a modern
edition of 1921 (Thurber).

b RUTH] Q2, Q3, Thurber; *om.* Q1

c suspect—Who … letter?] Thurber; suspect who … letter. Q1-3

d NEHEMIAH CATCH] 2 Q1-3; the name is inferred
from the subsequent identification and regularized according to the Dramatis Personae. We have not substi-
tuted other names from the DP.

e _____ for] _____ for Q1-3; offer of
Thurber; the blank is inexplicable, and Thurber's conjecture as good, perhaps, as any (order, indictment, evidence, etc.)

f be] by Q1-3, Thurber

g talk] Thurber; take Q1-3 (though our copytext looks like
it might read takle, with the k and l very close together)

h not] Thurber; *om.* Q1-3

i I'll speak. If it be the same, we'll draw cuts] Thurber;
I'le speak if it be the same, we'l draw cuts Q1-3

j except] accept Q1-3, Thurber

k from] from Q3, Thurber; to Q1, Q2

l Mr. Day] Q3, Thurber; Teg Q1, Q2

m I used] —— Q1-3, Thurber

The Man of Mode; or, Sir Fopling Flutter[a]

by George Etherege (1636-1692)

edited by John H. O'Neill

Etherege's third and last comedy, *The Man of Mode*, debuted on March 11, 1676 at the Duke's Theatre in Dorset Garden, with King Charles II in attendance. According to *Roscius Anglicanus*, the memoirs of John Downes, the prompter of the Duke's Company, the cast for the performance included the following major company actors: Thomas Betterton as Dorimant; Henry Harris as Medley; William Smith as Sir Fopling Flutter; and Anthony Leigh as Old Bellair. Elizabeth Barry, fledgling starlet, apparently played Mrs. Loveit. It is unfortunate that Downes did not remember, or neglected to note, the actress who created the role of Harriet, one of the wittiest parts on the Restoration stage.

The Man of Mode took part in the 1670s' vogue for sexually explicit comedies, such as Betterton's *The Amorous Widow*, Dryden's *Marriage à la Mode* and *Mr. Limberham*, and Wycherley's *The Country Wife*. Early authorities agree that Etherege's comedy, with its accomplished actors and with splendid costumes, was highly successful in its first run—a contemporary letter says that "the entire court went three or four times to see *The Man of Mode*" (*London Stage*)—and that it remained popular with Restoration audiences well after the death of its author. It sustained its popularity on the English stage until the second half of the eighteenth century, when changing tastes made its sexual frankness seem objectionable. After a performance on October 31, 1755, Richard Cross wrote in his diary that the play was "Much dislik'd & Hiss'd" (*London Stage*). Soon thereafter, it was dropped from the repertory. There is no record of its being performed in the nineteenth century. But in the twentieth century it has been the focus of extensive critical interest. Together with Wycherley's *The Country Wife*

and Congreve's *The Way of the World*, it is among the best-known comedies of the period.

Although we know that contemporary audiences loved the play, we cannot be sure how they interpreted it. Did they see it as an elegant description of the contemporary beau monde? As a picture of vice and degeneracy? As fantasy and farce? As satire? As social comedy?

The prologue and epilogue to *The Man of Mode* provide significant critical commentary on the play's meaning for contemporaries. In the prologue, the actor warns the gallants in the audience, using the familiar metaphor of satire as a mirror, that the comedy they will see presents a reflection of their own follies. The metaphor is twice repeated in the body of the play—first in Act II, scene i, which opens with Mrs. Loveit looking into her pocket glass and complaining to Pert, "I hate myself, I look so ill today," and second in Act IV, Scene ii, where Fopling asks Dorimant why he does not have a mirror hung up in his chamber so that he can "entertain himself."

The epilogue discusses the artistic problems posed by the creation of the fool character on stage. Many productions present "monstrous fools," which seem completely unreal and are appropriate only to farce. "A substantial ass" must be a realistic fool, incorporating "something of man," so that the character may resemble the gallants in the audience. The character of Sir Fopling, the epilogue continues, is difficult to distinguish from that of a wit, combining as it does elements of nature and artifice. This critical comment reinforces Medley's observation about Fopling in Act I: "Many a fool had been lost to the world, had their indulgent parents wisely bestowed neither learning nor good breeding upon 'em."

The epilogue ends by returning to the idea that the play presents its audience with a perspective on themselves, but now the metaphor is changed. Sir Fopling is a composite figure, comprising details drawn from a variety of individuals, representing the audience as a member of Parliament represents his constituents—"He's knight o' the shire and represents ye all." The prologue and epilogue, then, stress the play's satirical caricatures. The ending of the play, however, promises to put the most energetic young people to bed together, the typical ending of comedy.

PROLOGUE[1]

Like dancers on the ropes poor poets fare:
Most perish young, the rest in danger are.
This, one would think, should make our authors
    wary,
But gamester-like, the giddy fools miscarry;
A lucky hand or two so tempts 'em on,   5
They cannot leave off play till they're undone.
With modest fears a muse does first begin,
Like a young wench newly enticed to sin,
But tickled once with praise, by her good will
The wanton fool would never more lie still.   10
'Tis an old mistress you'll meet here tonight,
Whose charms you once have looked on with
    delight.
But now, of late, such dirty drabs have known ye,
A muse o'th'better sort's ashamed to own ye.
Nature well-drawn and wit must now give place   15
To gaudy nonsense and to dull grimace,
Nor is it strange that you should like so much
That kind of wit, for most of yours is such.
But I'm afraid that, while to France we go

To bring you home fine dresses, dance, and show,[2]   20
The stage, like you, will but more foppish grow.
Of foreign wares why should we fetch the scum,
When we can be so richly served at home?
For Heav'n be thanked, 'tis not so wise an age
But your own follies may supply the stage.   25
Though often plowed, there's no great fear the soil
Should barren grow by the too-frequent toil,
While at your doors are to be daily found
Such loads of dunghill to manure the ground.
'Tis by your follies that we players thrive,   30
As the physicians by diseases live,
And as each year some new distemper reigns,
Whose friendly poison helps t'increase their gains,
So among you there starts up every day
Some new, unheard-of fool for us to play.   35
Then, for your own sakes, be not too severe,
Nor what you all admire at home damn here.
Since each is fond of his own ugly face,
Why should you, when we hold it, break the glass?*

DRAMATIS PERSONAE

GENTLEMEN
    Mr. Dorimant.
    Mr. Medley.
    Old Bellair.
    Young Bellair.
    Sir Fopling Flutter.
    [Other men]
    A shoemaker.
    Four slovenly bullies.
    Two chairmen.*
    Mr. Smirk, a parson.
    Handy, a valet de chambre.
    Pages, footmen, etc.
GENTLEWOMEN
    Lady Townley.
    Emilia.
    Mrs.* Loveit.
    Bellinda.

---

1 Prologue] probably spoken by Thomas Betterton, the actor who created the role of Dorimant (see lines 19-21, below, and note); written by "Sir Car Scroope, Baronet": Scroope (1649-1680), like Etherege, was a member of the Rochester-Buckingham circle of Whig wits in 1676.

2 to France ... show] Betterton had been sent to France as an official agent of King Charles II to study the French theater and to develop ideas for improving the quality of spectacle—costumes, sets, and machinery—on the English stage.

Lady Woodvill.
Harriet, her daughter.
Waiting women
Pert.
Busy.
[Other women]
An orange-woman.*

The Man of Mode; or, Sir Fopling Flutter.

Act I, scene i. A dressing room.
A table covered with a toilet;[3] clothes laid ready.

Enter Dorimant in his gown and slippers, with a note in his hand made up,[4] repeating verses.

DORIMANT.
"Now, for some ages, had the pride of Spain
Made the sun shine on half the world in vain."[5]
(*Then looking on the note.*) "For Mrs. Loveit." What a dull, insipid thing is a billet-doux written in cold blood, after the heat of the business is over! It is a 5 tax upon good nature which I have here been laboring to pay, and have done it, but with as much regret as ever fanatic[6] paid the Royal Aid[7] or church duties.[8] 'Twill have the same fate, I know, that all my notes to her have had of late: 10 'twill not be thought kind enough. Faith, women are i'the right when they jealously examine our letters, for in them we always first discover* our decay of passion.—Hey! Who waits?

Enter Handy.

HANDY.
Sir— 15

---

3 toilet] a richly decorated cloth used as a cover for a dressing table
4 made up] written and folded
5 "Now … vain"] Waller, "Of a War with Spain, and a Fight at Sea," 1-2
6 fanatic] an epithet applied to Dissenters, those who as a matter of conscience rejected the authority of the Crown and the Church of England
7 Royal Aid] "An extraordinary subsidy or tax made by Parliament for the King" (Barnard)
8 Church duties] local taxes charged for services of the parish church

DORIMANT.
Call a footman.
HANDY.
None of 'em are come yet.
DORIMANT.
Dogs! Will they ever lie snoring abed till noon?
HANDY.
'Tis all one, sir: if they're up, you indulge 'em so, they're ever poaching after whores all the morning. 20
DORIMANT.
Take notice henceforward who's wanting* in his duty; the next clap he gets, he shall rot for an example. What vermin are those chattering without?
HANDY.
Foggy[9] Nan, the orange-woman, and swearing 25 Tom, the shoemaker.
DORIMANT.
Go, call in that overgrown jade with the flasket[10] of guts before her. Fruit is refreshing in a morning.

Exit Handy.

"It is not that I love you less,
Than when before your feet I lay—"[11]

Enter [Handy with] orange-woman.

How now, double tripe, what news do you bring? 30
ORANGE-WOMAN.
News! Here's the best fruit has come to Town* t' year. Gad, I was up before four o'clock this morning and bought all the choice i'the market.
DORIMANT.
The nasty refuse of your shop.
ORANGE-WOMAN.
You need not make mouths at it. I assure you, 'tis 35 all culled ware.
DORIMANT.
The citizens* buy better on a holiday in their walk to Tottenham.[12]

---

9   foggy] flabby, puffy
10 flasket] a long, shallow basket
11 "It is … lay"] Waller, "The Self-Banished," 1-2
12 Tottenham] village about 8 miles north of the City of London, now part of metropolitan London

ORANGE-WOMAN.

Good or bad, 'tis all one; I never knew you commend anything. Lord, would the ladies had 40 heard you talk of 'em as I have done. Here— (*Sets down the fruit.*) Bid your man give me an angel.*

DORIMANT.

Give the bawd her fruit again.

ORANGE-WOMAN.

Well, on my conscience, there never was the like of you.—God's my life, I had almost forgot to tell 45 you, there is a young gentlewoman, lately come to Town with her mother, that is so taken with you.

DORIMANT.

Is she handsome?

ORANGE-WOMAN.

Nay,[13] gad, there are few finer women, I tell you but so, and a hugeous fortune, they say. Here, eat 50 this peach, it comes from the stone;[14] 'tis better than any Newington[15] y'ave tasted.

DORIMANT. (*Taking the peach.*)

This fine woman, I'll lay my life, is some awkward, ill-fashioned country toad, who, not having above four dozen of black hairs on her head, has adorned 55 her baldness with a large white fruz,[16] that she may look sparkishly in the forefront of the King's box at an old play.

ORANGE-WOMAN.

Gad, you'd change your note quickly if you did but see her! 60

DORIMANT.

How came she to know me?

ORANGE-WOMAN.

She saw you yesterday at the Change.* She told me you came and fooled with the woman at the next shop.

DORIMANT.

I remember, there was a mask* observed me, 65 indeed. "Fooled," did she say?

ORANGE-WOMAN.

Aye, I vow she told me twenty things you said, too,

and acted with her head[b] and with her body so like you—

Enter Medley.

MEDLEY.

Dorimant, my life, my joy, my darling sin! How 70 dost thou?

ORANGE-WOMAN.

Lord, what a filthy trick these men have got of kissing one another! (*She spits.*)

MEDLEY.

Why do you suffer this cartload of scandal to come near you and make your neighbors think you so 75 improvident to need a bawd?

ORANGE-WOMAN.

Good—now we shall have it! You did but want* him to help you. Come, pay me for my fruit.

MEDLEY.

Make us thankful[17] for it, huswife. Bawds are as much out of fashion as gentlemen-ushers;[18] none 80 but old formal ladies use the one, and none but foppish old stagers employ the other. Go, you are an insignificant brandy bottle.

DORIMANT.

Nay, there you wrong her. Three quarts of canary is her business. 85

ORANGE-WOMAN.

What you please, gentlemen.

DORIMANT.

To him! Give him as good as he brings.

ORANGE-WOMAN.

Hang him, there is not such another heathen in the Town again, except it be the shoemaker without. 90

MEDLEY.

I shall see you hold up your hand at the bar next sessions for murder, huswife. That shoemaker can take his oath you are in fee with the doctors to sell green fruit to the gentry, that the crudities[19] may breed diseases. 95

---

13 Nay] used as an interjection; does not mean "no"
14 comes from the stone] a freestone peach, one in which the fruit does not cling to the stone, or pit
15 Newington] a peach from the southeast of England
16 fruz] a frizzy, rumpled, and uneven wig

17 Make us thankful] "God make us thankful," here said ironically
18 gentlemen-ushers] door-keepers or male attendants on a lady
19 crudities] indigestible matter

ORANGE-WOMAN.

Pray give me my money.

DORIMANT.

Not a penny! When you bring the gentlewoman hither you spoke of, you shall be paid.

ORANGE-WOMAN.

The gentlewoman! The gentlewoman may be as honest* as your sisters, for aught as I know. Pray pay me, Mr. Dorimant, and do not abuse me so. I have an honester way of living; you know it. 100

MEDLEY.

Was there ever such a resty* bawd?

DORIMANT.

Some jade's tricks she has, but she makes amends when she's in good humor.—Come, tell me the lady's name, and Handy shall pay you. 105

ORANGE-WOMAN.

I must not; she forbid me.

DORIMANT.

That's a sure sign she would have you.

MEDLEY.

Where does she live?

ORANGE-WOMAN.

They lodge at my house. 110

MEDLEY.

Nay, then she's in a hopeful way.[20]

ORANGE-WOMAN.

Good Mr. Medley, say your pleasure of me, but take heed how you affront my house. God's my life, in a hopeful way!

DORIMANT.

Prithee, peace. What kind of woman's the mother? 115

ORANGE-WOMAN.

A goodly, grave gentlewoman. Lord, how she talks against the wild young men o'the Town! As for your part, she thinks you an arrant devil: should she see you, on my conscience she would look if you had not a cloven foot. 120

DORIMANT.

Does she know me?

ORANGE-WOMAN.

Only by hearsay. A thousand horrid stories have been told her of you, and she believes 'em all.

MEDLEY.

By the character,* this should be the famous Lady Woodvill and her daughter Harriet. 125

ORANGE-WOMAN. [Aside.]

The devil's in him for guessing, I think.

DORIMANT.

Do you know 'em?

MEDLEY.

Both very well. The mother's a great admirer of the forms and civility of the last age.[21]

DORIMANT.

An antiquated beauty may be allowed to be out of 130 humor at the freedoms of the present. This is a good account of the mother. Pray, what is the daughter?

MEDLEY.

Why first, she's an heiress, vastly rich.

DORIMANT.

And handsome?

MEDLEY.

What alteration a twelvemonth may have bred in 135 her, I know not, but a year ago she was the beautifullest creature I ever saw: a fine, easy, clean shape; light brown hair in abundance; her features regular; her complexion clear and lively; large, wanton eyes; but above all, a mouth that has made 140 me kiss it a thousand times in imagination—teeth white and even, and pretty, pouting lips, with a little moisture ever hanging on them, that look like the Provins rose[22] fresh on the bush ere the morning sun has quite drawn up the dew. 145

DORIMANT.

Rapture, mere* rapture!

ORANGE-WOMAN.

Nay, gad, he tells you true. She's a delicate creature.

DORIMANT.

Has she wit?

MEDLEY.

More than is usual in her sex, and as much malice. Then, she's as wild as you would wish her and has 150 a demureness in her looks that makes it so surprising.

---

20 in a hopeful way] in a situation to give hope of success (presumably, of seduction)

21 forms and civility of the last age] the formal manners of the reign of King Charles I, which ended in 1649

22 Provins rose] *Rosa gallica,* formerly known as *Rosa provinciallis,* that is, Provence Rose

DORIMANT.

Flesh and blood cannot hear this and not long to know her.

MEDLEY.

I wonder what makes her mother bring her up to Town? An old, doting keeper* cannot be more jealous of his mistress.

ORANGE-WOMAN.

She made me laugh yesterday. There was a judge came to visit 'em, and the old man, she told me, did so stare upon her and, when he saluted* her, smacked so heartily—who would think it of 'em?

MEDLEY.

God-a-mercy, Judge!

DORIMANT.

Do 'em right, the gentlemen of the long robe[23] have not been wanting* by their good examples to countenance the crying sin o'the nation.

MEDLEY.

Come, on with your trappings; 'tis later than you imagine.

DORIMANT.

Call in the shoemaker, Handy.

ORANGE-WOMAN.

Good Mr. Dorimant, pay me. Gad, I had rather give you my fruit than stay to be abused by that foul-mouthed rogue. What you gentlemen say, it matters not much, but such a dirty fellow does one more disgrace.

DORIMANT. [To Handy.]

Give her ten shillings. [To orange-woman.] And be sure you tell the young gentlewoman I must be acquainted with her.

ORANGE-WOMAN.

Now do you long to be tempting this pretty creature. Well, heavens mend you!

MEDLEY.

Farewell, bog[24]—

Exeunt orange-woman and Handy.

Dorimant, when did you see your *pis aller*, as you call her, Mrs. Loveit?

---

23 gentlemen of the long robe] lawyers and judges, the legal profession

24 bog] term for a fat person

DORIMANT.

Not these two days.

MEDLEY.

And how stand affairs between you?

DORIMANT.

There has been great patching of late, much ado; we make a shift to hang together.

MEDLEY.

I wonder how her mighty spirit bears it?

DORIMANT.

Ill enough, on all conscience. I never knew so violent a creature.

MEDLEY.

She's the most passionate in her love and the most extravagant in her jealousy of any woman I ever heard of. What note is that?

DORIMANT.

An excuse I am going to send her for the neglect I am guilty of.

MEDLEY.

Prithee, read it.

DORIMANT.

No, but if you will take the pains, you may.

MEDLEY. (*Reads.*)

"I never was a lover of business, but now I have a just reason to hate it, since it has kept me these two days from seeing you. I intend to wait upon you in the afternoon, and in the pleasure of your conversation* forget all I have suffered during this tedious absence."—This business of yours, Dorimant, has been with a vizard* at the playhouse; I have had an eye on you. If some malicious body should betray you, this kind note would hardly make your peace with her.

DORIMANT.

I desire no better.

MEDLEY.

Why, would her knowledge of it oblige you?

DORIMANT.

Most infinitely: next to the coming to a good understanding with a new mistress, I love a quarrel with an old one. But the devil's in't, there has been such a calm in my affairs of late, I have not had the pleasure of making a woman so much as break her fan, to be sullen, or forswear herself these three days.

MEDLEY.

A very great misfortune! Let me see, I love mischief 215
well enough to forward this business myself. I'll
about it presently,* and though I know the truth
of what y'ave done will set her a-raving, I'll height-
en it a little with invention, leave her in a fit o'the
mother,* and be here again before y'are ready. 220

DORIMANT.

Pray stay, you may spare yourself the labor. The
business is undertaken already by one who will
manage it with as much address and, I think, with
a little more malice than you can.

MEDLEY.

Who i'the devil's name can this be? 225

DORIMANT.

Why, the vizard, that very vizard you saw me with.

MEDLEY.

Does she love mischief so well as to betray herself
to spite another?

DORIMANT.

Not so, neither, Medley; I will make you comprehend the mystery. This mask,* for a farther confirma- 230
tion of what I have been these two days swearing to
her, made me yesterday at the playhouse make her a
promise before her face utterly to break off with
Loveit and, because she tenders my reputation and
would not have me do a barbarous thing, has 235
contrived a way to give me a handsome occasion.

MEDLEY.

Very good.

DORIMANT.

She intends, about an hour before me this
afternoon, to make Loveit a visit, and (having the
privilege by reason of a professed friendship 240
between 'em to talk of her concerns)—

MEDLEY.

Is she a friend?

DORIMANT.

Oh, an intimate friend!

MEDLEY.

Better and better! Pray proceed.

DORIMANT.

She means insensibly25 to insinuate a discourse of 245

me and artificially26 raise her jealousy to such a
height that, transported with the first motions of
her passion, she shall fly upon me with all the fury
imaginable as soon as ever I enter. The quarrel
being thus happily begun, I am to play my part: 250
confess and justify all my roguery, swear her
impertinence and ill humor makes her intolerable,
tax her with the next fop that comes into my head,
and in a huff march away, slight her, and leave her
to be taken by whosoever thinks it worth his time 255
to lie down before her.

MEDLEY.

This vizard is a spark and has a genius that makes
her worthy of yourself, Dorimant.

Enter Handy, shoemaker, and footman.

DORIMANT. [*To footman.*]

You rogue there, who sneak like a dog that has
flung down a dish! If you do not mend your 260
waiting, I'll uncase you27 and turn you loose to
the wheel of fortune.—Handy, seal this and let
him run with it presently.*

*Exeunt Handy and footman[; Handy returns after a
moment].*

MEDLEY.

Since y'are resolved on a quarrel, why do you send
her this kind note? 265

DORIMANT.

To keep her at home in order to the business. (*To
the shoemaker.*) How now, you drunken sot?

SHOEMAKER.

'Sbud,* you have no reason to talk. I have not had
a bottle of sack* of yours in my belly this fortnight.

MEDLEY.

The orange-woman says your neighbors take 270
notice what a heathen you are and design to
inform the bishop and have you burned for an
atheist.

SHOEMAKER.

Damn her, dunghill! If her husband does not
remove her, she stinks so, the parish intend to 275
indict him for a nuisance.

---

25 insensibly] gradually, imperceptibly

26 artificially] cunningly
27 uncase you] strip you of your livery, fire you

MEDLEY.

I advise you like a friend, reform your life. You have brought the envy of the world upon you by living above yourself. Whoring and swearing are vices too genteel for a shoemaker.   280

SHOEMAKER.

'Sbud, I think you men of quality* will grow as unreasonable as the women; you would engross the sins o'the nation. Poor folks can no sooner be wicked but th'are railed at by their betters.

DORIMANT.

Sirrah, I'll have you stand i'the pillory for this libel.   285

SHOEMAKER.

Some of you deserve it, I'm sure. There are so many of 'em that our journeymen nowadays, instead of harmless ballads, sing nothing but your damned lampoons.

DORIMANT.

Our lampoons, you rogue?   290

SHOEMAKER.

Nay, good master, why should not you write your own commentaries as well as Caesar?[28]

MEDLEY.

The rascal's read, I perceive.

SHOEMAKER.

You know the old proverb, ale and history.[29]

DORIMANT.

Draw on my shoes, sirrah.   295

SHOEMAKER.

Here's a shoe—

DORIMANT.

Sits with more wrinkles than there are in an angry bully's forehead.

SHOEMAKER.

'Sbud, as smooth as your mistress's skin does upon her. So, strike your foot in home. 'Sbud, if e'er a   300 monsieur of 'em all make more fashionable ware, I'll be content to have my ears whipped off with my own paring knife.

MEDLEY.

And served up in a ragout, instead of coxcombs, to a company of French shoemakers for a collation.   305

SHOEMAKER.

Hold, hold! Damn 'em, caterpillars! Let 'em feed upon cabbage!—Come master, your health this morning next my heart now.[30]

DORIMANT.

Go, get you home, and govern your family better! Do not let your wife follow you to the alehouse,   310 beat your whore, and lead you home in triumph.

SHOEMAKER.

'Sbud, there's never a man i'the Town lives more like a gentleman with his wife than I do. I never mind her motions; she never inquires into mine. We speak to one another civilly, hate one another   315 heartily, and because 'tis vulgar to lie and soak[31] together, we have each of us our several settle-bed.

DORIMANT. [*To Handy.*]

Give him half a crown.

MEDLEY.

Not without he will promise to be bloody drunk.

SHOEMAKER. [*Taking the coin.*]

Tope's the word i'the eye of the world, for my   320 master's honor, Robin!

DORIMANT.

Do not debauch my servants, sirrah.

SHOEMAKER.

I only tip him the wink; he knows an alehouse from a hovel.

Exit Shoemaker.

DORIMANT. [*To Handy.*]

My clothes, quickly!   325

MEDLEY.

Where shall we dine today?

Enter Young Bellair.

DORIMANT.

Where you will. Here comes a good third man.

YOUNG BELLAIR.

Your servant, gentlemen.

MEDLEY.

Gentle* sir, how will you answer this visit to your honorable mistress? 'Tis not her interest you should   330

---

28 commentaries ... Caesar] memoirs, as Caesar's *Gallic Wars*

29 ale and history] "Truth is in ale as in history" (proverbial).

30 your health ... now] The shoemaker asks for money to drink to Dorimant's health.

31 soak] drink

keep company with men of sense, who will be talking reason.

YOUNG BELLAIR.

I do not fear her pardon, do you but grant me yours for my neglect of late.

MEDLEY.

Though y'ave made us miserable by the want* of 335 your good company, to show you I am free from all resentment, may the beautiful cause of our misfortune give you all the joys happy lovers have shared ever since the world began.

YOUNG BELLAIR.

You wish me in heaven, but you believe me on my 340 journey to hell.

MEDLEY.

You have a good strong faith, and that may contribute much towards your salvation. I confess I am but of an untoward constitution, apt to have doubts and scruples, and in love they are no less 345 distracting than in religion. Were I so near marriage, I should cry out by fits as I ride in my coach, "Cuckold, cuckold!" with no less fury than the mad fanatic does "Glory!" in Bethlem.[32]

YOUNG BELLAIR.

Because religion makes some run mad, must I live 350 an atheist?

MEDLEY.

Is it not great indiscretion for a man of credit, who may have money enough on his word, to go and deal with Jews, who for little sums make men enter into bonds and give judgments?[33] 355

YOUNG BELLAIR.

Preach no more on this text; I am determined, and there is no hope of my conversion.

DORIMANT. (*To Handy, who is fiddling about him.*)

Leave your unnecessary fiddling. A wasp that's buzzing about a man's nose at dinner is not more troublesome than thou art. 360

HANDY.

You love to have your clothes hang just, sir.

DORIMANT.

I love to be well-dressed, sir, and think it no scandal to my understanding.

HANDY.

Will you use the essence or orange-flower water?

DORIMANT.

I will smell as I do today, no offense to the ladies' 365 noses.

HANDY.

Your pleasure, sir. [*Exit.*]

DORIMANT.

That a man's excellency should lie in neatly tying of a ribbon or a cravat! How careful's Nature in furnishing the world with necessary coxcombs! 370

YOUNG BELLAIR.

That's a mighty pretty suit of yours, Dorimant.

DORIMANT.

I am glad 't has your approbation.

YOUNG BELLAIR.

No man in Town has a better fancy in his clothes than you have.

DORIMANT.

You will make me have an opinion of my genius. 375

MEDLEY.

There is a great critic, I hear, in these matters lately arrived piping hot from Paris.

YOUNG BELLAIR.

Sir Fopling Flutter, you mean.

MEDLEY.

The same.

YOUNG BELLAIR.

He thinks himself the pattern of modern gallantry. 380

DORIMANT.

He is indeed the pattern of modern foppery.

MEDLEY.

He was yesterday at the play, with a pair of gloves up to his elbows and a periwig more exactly curled than a lady's head newly dressed for a ball.

YOUNG BELLAIR.

What a pretty lisp he has! 385

DORIMANT.

Ho, that he affects in imitation of the people of quality* of France.

MEDLEY.

His head stands for the most part on one side, and

---

32 mad fanatic ... Bethlem] Bethlehem Hospital, commonly known as Bedlam, the mental hospital in London. The "mad fanatic," formerly porter to Oliver Cromwell, was a patient in the hospital (Brett-Smith).

33 enter ... judgments] give security for a loan

his looks are more languishing than a lady's when she lolls at stretch in her coach or leans her head carelessly against the side of a box i'the playhouse. 390

DORIMANT.

He is a person indeed of great acquired follies.

MEDLEY.

He is, like many others, beholding to his education for making him so eminent a coxcomb. Many a fool had been lost to the world, had their indulgent 395 parents wisely bestowed neither learning nor good breeding on 'em.

YOUNG BELLAIR.

He has been, as the sparkish word is, brisk upon the ladies already. He was yesterday at my Aunt Townley's and gave Mrs. Loveit a catalogue of his 400 good qualities under the character* of a complete gentleman, who, according to Sir Fopling, ought to dress well, dance well, fence well, have a genius for love letters, an agreeable voice for a chamber, be very amorous, something discreet, but not overconstant. 405

MEDLEY.

Pretty ingredients to make an accomplished person!

DORIMANT.

I am glad he pitched upon Loveit.

YOUNG BELLAIR.

How so?

DORIMANT.

I wanted a fop to lay to her charge, and this is as 410 pat as may be.

YOUNG BELLAIR.

I am confident she loves no man but you.

DORIMANT.

The good fortune were enough to make me vain but that I am in my nature modest.

YOUNG BELLAIR.

Hark you, Dorimant.—With your leave, Mr. 415 Medley, 'tis only a secret concerning a fair lady.

MEDLEY.

Your good breeding, sir, gives you too much trouble. You might have whispered without all this ceremony.

YOUNG BELLAIR. (*To Dorimant.*)

How stand your affairs with Bellinda of late? 420

DORIMANT.

She's a little jilting baggage.

YOUNG BELLAIR.

Nay, I believe her false enough, but she's ne'er the worse for your purpose. She was with you yesterday in disguise at the play.

DORIMANT.

There we fell out and resolved never to speak to 425 one another more.

YOUNG BELLAIR.

The occasion?

DORIMANT.

Want* of courage to meet me at the place appointed. These young women apprehend loving as much as the young men do fighting at first, but 430 once entered, like them too, they all turn bullies straight.

Enter Handy.

HANDY. (*To Young Bellair.*)

Sir, your man without desires to speak with you.

YOUNG BELLAIR.

Gentlemen, I'll return immediately. (*Exit.*)

MEDLEY.

A very pretty fellow, this. 435

DORIMANT.

He's handsome, well-bred, and by much the most tolerable of all the young men that do not abound in wit.

MEDLEY.

Ever well-dressed, always complaisant, and seldom impertinent; you and he are grown very intimate, 440 I see.

DORIMANT.

It is our mutual interest to be so. It makes the women think the better of his understanding and judge more favorably of my reputation; it makes him pass upon some for a man of very good sense, 445 and I upon others for a very civil person.

MEDLEY.

What was that whisper?

DORIMANT.

A thing which he would fain have known, but I did not think it fit to tell him. It might have frighted him from his honorable intentions of 450 marrying.

MEDLEY.

Emilia, give her her due, has the best reputation

of any young woman about the Town who has beauty enough to provoke detraction. Her carriage is unaffected, her discourse modest—not at all censorious nor pretending, like the counterfeits of the age. 455

DORIMANT.

She's a discreet maid, and I believe nothing can corrupt her but a husband.

MEDLEY.

A husband? 460

DORIMANT.

Yes, a husband. I have known many women make a difficulty of losing a maidenhead, who have afterwards made none of making a cuckold.

MEDLEY.

This prudent consideration, I am apt to think, has made you confirm poor Bellair in the desperate 465 resolution he has taken.

DORIMANT.

Indeed, the little hope I found there was of her, in the state she was in, has made me by my advice contribute something towards the changing of her condition.

Enter Young Bellair.

Dear Bellair, by heavens, I thought we had lost 470 thee! Men in love are never to be reckoned on when we would form a company.

YOUNG BELLAIR.

Dorimant, I am undone. My man has brought the most surprising news i'the world.

DORIMANT.

Some strange misfortune is befallen your love? 475

YOUNG BELLAIR.

My father came to Town last night and lodges i'the very house where Emilia lies.

MEDLEY.

Does he know it is with her you are in love?

YOUNG BELLAIR.

He knows I love, but knows not whom, without some officious sot* has betrayed me. 480

DORIMANT.

Your Aunt Townley is your confidante and favors the business.

YOUNG BELLAIR.

I do not apprehend any ill office from her. I have received a letter, in which I am commanded by my father to meet him at my aunt's this afternoon. He 485 tells me farther he has made a match for me and bids me resolve to be obedient to his will or expect to be disinherited.

MEDLEY.

Now's your time, Bellair. Never had lover such an opportunity of giving a generous proof of his passion. 490

YOUNG BELLAIR.

As how, I pray?

MEDLEY.

Why, hang an estate, marry Emilia out of hand, and provoke your father to do what he threatens. 'Tis but despising a coach, humbling yourself to a pair of galoshes,[34] being out of countenance when 495 you meet your friends, pointed at and pitied wherever you go by all the amorous fops that know you, and your fame will be immortal.

YOUNG BELLAIR.

I could find it in my heart to resolve not to marry at all.

DORIMANT. 500

Fie, fie! That would spoil a good jest and disappoint the well-natured Town of an occasion of laughing at you.

YOUNG BELLAIR.

The storm I have so long expected hangs o'er my head and begins to pour down upon me. I am on 505 the rack and can have no rest till I'm satisfied in what I fear. Where do you dine?

DORIMANT.

At Long's or Locket's.*

MEDLEY.

At Long's let it be.

YOUNG BELLAIR.

I'll run and see Emilia and inform myself how 510 matters stand. If my misfortunes are not so great as to make me unfit for company, I'll be with you. (*Exit.*)

Enter a footman, with a letter.

FOOTMAN. (*To Dorimant.*)

Here's a letter, sir.

---

34 galoshes] pattens or clogs, wooden attachments to the shoe to raise the walker out of the mud and filth of the street

DORIMANT.

The superscription's right: "For Mr. Dorimant."

MEDLEY.

Let's see—the very scrawl and spelling of a true-bred whore.

DORIMANT.

I know the hand. The style is admirable, I assure you.

MEDLEY.

Prithee, read it.

DORIMANT. (Reads.)

"I told a you you dud not love me, if you dud, you would have seen me again ere now. I have no money and am very mallicolly. Pray send me a guynie to see the operies. Your servant to command, Molly."

MEDLEY.

Pray let the whore have a favorable answer, that she may spark it[35] in a box and do honor to her profession.

DORIMANT.

She shall, and perk up i'the face of quality.* [*To Handy*.] Is the coach at door?

HANDY.

You did not bid me send for it.

DORIMANT.

Eternal blockhead!

Handy offers to go out.

Hey, sot!*

HANDY.

Did you call me, sir?

DORIMANT.

I hope you have no just exception to the name, sir?

HANDY.

I have sense, sir.

DORIMANT.

Not so much as a fly in winter.—How did you come, Medley?

MEDLEY.

In a chair.*

FOOTMAN.

You may have a hackney coach if you please, sir.

DORIMANT.

I may ride the elephant if I please, sir. Call another chair and let my coach follow to Long's.

"Be calm, ye great parents, [of the floods and the springs,

While each Nereid and Triton plays, revels, and sings"]36

Exeunt singing.

Act II, scene i. [Lady Townley's house.]

Enter my Lady Townley and Emilia.

LADY TOWNLEY.

I was afraid, Emilia, all had been discovered.*

EMILIA.

I tremble with the apprehension still.

LADY TOWNLEY.

That my brother should take lodgings i'the very house where you lie!

EMILIA.

'Twas lucky we had timely notice to warn the people37 to be secret. He seems to be a mighty good-humored old man.

LADY TOWNLEY.

He ever had a notable smirking way with him.

EMILIA.

He calls me rogue, tells me he can't abide me, and does so bepat me.

LADY TOWNLEY.

On my word, you are much in his favor, then.

EMILIA.

He has been very inquisitive, I am told, about my family, my reputation, and my fortune.

LADY TOWNLEY.

I am confident he does not i'the least suspect you are the woman his son's in love with.

EMILIA.

What should make him then inform himself so particularly of me?

LADY TOWNLEY.

He was always of a very loving temper himself. It may be he has a doting fit upon him, who knows?

---

35 spark it] show off, look fashionable

36 "Be calm … sings"] from Shadwell's adaptation of *The Tempest* (Act V)

37 the people] the servants

EMILIA.

It cannot be.   20

Enter Young Bellair.

LADY TOWNLEY.

Here comes my nephew.—Where did you leave
your father?

YOUNG BELLAIR.

Writing a note within.—Emilia, this early visit
looks as if some kind jealousy would not let you
rest at home.   25

EMILIA.

The knowledge I have of my rival gives me a little
cause to fear your constancy.

YOUNG BELLAIR.

My constancy! I vow—

EMILIA.

Do not vow—Our love is frail as is our life, and
full as little in our power, and are you sure you   30
shall outlive this day?

YOUNG BELLAIR.

I am not, but when we are in perfect health, 'twere
an idle thing to fright ourselves with the thoughts
of sudden death.

LADY TOWNLEY.

Pray, what has passed between you and your father   35
i'the garden?

YOUNG BELLAIR.

He's firm in his resolution, tells me I must marry
Mrs.* Harriet, or swears he'll marry himself and
disinherit me. When I saw I could not prevail with
him to be more indulgent, I dissembled an   40
obedience to his will, which has composed his
passion and will give us time—and, I hope,
opportunity—to deceive him.

Enter Old Bellair, with a note in his hand.

LADY TOWNLEY.

Peace, here he comes.

OLD BELLAIR.

Harry, take this and let your man carry it for me   45
to Mr. Fourbe's[38] chamber—my lawyer, i'the
Temple.*

---

38 Fourbe] The French word *fourbe* means a cheat or "con
artist" or "scam."

[Exit Young Bellair.]

(*To Emilia.*) Neighbor, adod[39] I am glad to see
thee here.—Make much of her, sister. She's one of
the best of your acquaintance. I like her counte-   50
nance and her behavior well; she has a modesty
that is not common i'this age, adod she has.

LADY TOWNLEY.

I know her value, brother, and esteem her
accordingly.

OLD BELLAIR.

Advise her to wear a little more mirth in her face;   55
adod, she's too serious.

LADY TOWNLEY.

The fault is very excusable in a young woman.

OLD BELLAIR.

Nay, adod, I like her ne'er the worse; a melancholy
beauty has her charms. I love a pretty sadness in a
face which varies now and then, like changeable   60
colors, into a smile.

LADY TOWNLEY.

Methinks you speak very feelingly, brother.

OLD BELLAIR.

I am but five-and-fifty, sister, you know—an age
not altogether unsensible! (*To Emilia.*) Cheer up,
sweetheart; I have a secret to tell thee may chance   65
to make thee merry. We three will make collation
together anon. I'the meantime, mum, I can't abide
you; go, I can't abide you—

Enter Young Bellair.

Harry! Come, you must along with me to my Lady
Woodvill's.—I am going to slip the boy at a   70
mistress.

YOUNG BELLAIR.

At a wife, sir, you would say.

OLD BELLAIR.

You need not look so glum, sir. A wife is no curse
when she brings the blessing of a good estate with
her. But an idle Town flirt, with a painted face, a   75
rotten reputation, and a crazy fortune, adod, is the
devil and all—and such a one I hear you are in
league with.

---

39 adod] mild oath

YOUNG BELLAIR.

I cannot help detraction, sir.

OLD BELLAIR.

Out, a pize* o'their breeches, there are keeping* 80
fools enough for such flaunting baggages, and they
are e'en too good for 'em. (*To Emilia.*) Remember
night. Go, y'are a rogue, y'are a rogue. Fare you
well, fare you well.—Come, come, come along, sir.

Exeunt Old and Young Bellair.

LADY TOWNLEY.

On my word, the old man comes on apace. I'll lay 85
my life he's smitten.

EMILIA.

This is nothing but the pleasantness of his humor.*

LADY TOWNLEY.

I know him better than you; let it work. It may
prove lucky.

Enter a page.

PAGE.

Madam, Mr. Medley has sent to know whether a 90
visit will not be troublesome this afternoon.

LADY TOWNLEY.

Send him word his visits never are so.

[Exit page.]

EMILIA.

He's a very pleasant man.

LADY TOWNLEY.

He's a very necessary man among us women. He's 95
not scandalous i'the least, perpetually contriving to
bring good company together, and always ready to
stop up a gap at ombre. Then, he knows all the
little news o'the Town.

EMILIA.

I love to hear him talk o'the intrigues. Let 'em be 100
never so dull in themselves, he'll make 'em pleasant
i'the relation.

LADY TOWNLEY.

But he improves things so much one can take no
measure of the truth from him. Mr. Dorimant
swears a flea or a maggot is not made more 105
monstrous by a magnifying glass than a story is by
his telling it.

Enter Medley.

EMILIA.

Hold, here he comes.

LADY TOWNLEY.

Mr. Medley.

MEDLEY.

Your servant, madam. 110

LADY TOWNLEY.

You have made yourself a stranger of late.

EMILIA.

I believe you took a surfeit of ombre last time you
were here.

MEDLEY.

Indeed I had my bellyful of that termagant, Lady
Dealer. There never was so insatiable a carder; an 115
old gleeker[40] never loved to sit to't like her. I have
played with her now at least a dozen times, till she's
worn out all her fine complexion and her tour[41]
would keep in curl no longer.

LADY TOWNLEY.

Blame her not, poor woman. She loves nothing so 120
well as a black ace.

MEDLEY.

The pleasure I have seen her in when she has had
hope in drawing for a matadore![42]

EMILIA.

'Tis as pretty sport to her as persuading masks off
is to you, to make discoveries. 125

LADY TOWNLEY.

Pray, where's your friend Mr. Dorimant?

MEDLEY.

Soliciting his affairs. He's a man of great employment—has more mistresses now depending than
the most eminent lawyer in England has causes.

EMILIA.

Here has been Mrs. Loveit so uneasy and out of 130
humor these two days.

---

40 gleeker] one who plays gleek, a card game

41 tour] from the French expression *tour de cheveaux*, "a
tress or border of hair, going round the head, which mingled dextrously with the natural hair, lengthens and
thickens it" (*OED*)

42 matadore] in ombre, the three highest cards are called
the matadores, including the two black aces and a trump
card.

LADY TOWNLEY.

How strangely love and jealousy rage in that poor woman!

MEDLEY.

She could not have picked out a devil upon earth so proper to torment her. He's made her break a dozen or two of fans already, tear half a score points in pieces, and destroy hoods and knots without number. 135

LADY TOWNLEY.

We heard of a pleasant serenade he gave her t'other night. 140

MEDLEY.

A Danish serenade, with kettledrums and trumpets.

EMILIA.

Oh, barbarous!

MEDLEY.

What, you are of the number of the ladies whose ears are grown so delicate since our operas, you can be charmed with nothing but *flûtes douces*[43] and French hautboys? 145

EMILIA.

Leave your raillery and tell us, is there any new wit come forth, songs or novels?

MEDLEY.

A very pretty piece of gallantry, by an eminent author, called the *Diversions of Brussels*,[44] very necessary to be read by all old ladies who are desirous to improve themselves at Questions and Commands, Blindman's Buff, and the like fashionable recreations. 150 155

EMILIA.

Oh, ridiculous!

MEDLEY.

Then there is *The Art of Affectation*,[45] written by a late beauty of quality,* teaching you how to draw up your breasts, stretch up your neck, to thrust out your breech, to play with your head, to toss up your nose, to bite your lips, to turn up your eyes, to speak in a silly soft tone of a voice, and use all the foolish French words that will infallibly make your person and conversation charming, with a short apology at the latter end, in the behalf of young ladies who notoriously wash and paint,[46] though they have naturally good complexions. 160 165

EMILIA.

What a deal of stuff you tell us!

MEDLEY.

Such as the Town affords, madam. The Russians, hearing the great respect we have for foreign dancing, have lately sent over some of their best balladines,[47] who are now practicing a famous ballet which will be suddenly* danced at the Bear Garden.* 170

LADY TOWNLEY.

Pray forbear your idle stories and give us an account of the state of love as it now stands. 175

MEDLEY.

Truly there has been some revolutions in those affairs: great chopping and changing[48] among the old, and some new lovers, whom malice, indiscretion, and misfortune have luckily brought into play.

LADY TOWNLEY.

What think you of walking into the next room and sitting down before you engage in this business? 180

MEDLEY.

I wait upon you, and I hope (though women are commonly unreasonable) by the plenty of scandal I shall discover,* to give you very good content, ladies.

Exeunt.

Scene ii. [Mrs. Loveit's lodgings.]

Enter Mrs. Loveit and Pert, Mrs. Loveit putting up a letter, then pulling out her pocket glass and looking in it.*

MRS. LOVEIT.

Pert.

---

43 *flûtes douces*] "sweet flutes" or recorders (Fr.)— like the Italian opera, a recent import to England in the mid-1670's

44 *Diversions of Brussels*] identified as *A Treatise of the Sports of Wit*, published in 1675 by Richard Flecknoe

45 *The Art of Affectation*] a parodic reference to *The Gentlewoman's Companion* (1675), by Hannah Woolley (Conaghan)

46 wash and paint] use cosmetics

47 balladines] theatrical dancers

48 chopping and changing] originally terms of trade (selling and exchanging), here obviously metaphorical

PERT.

Madam?

MRS. LOVEIT.

I hate myself, I look so ill today.

PERT.

Hate the wicked cause on't, that base man Mr. Dorimant, who makes you torment and vex yourself continually.

MRS. LOVEIT.

He is to blame, indeed.

PERT.

To blame to be two days without sending, writing, or coming near you, contrary to his oath and covenant! 'Twas to much purpose to make him swear! I'll lay my life there's not an article but he has broken: talked to the vizards* i'the pit, waited upon the ladies from the boxes to their coaches, gone behind the scenes and fawned upon those little insignificant creatures, the players. 'Tis impossible for a man of his inconstant temper to forbear, I'm sure.

MRS. LOVEIT.

I know he is a devil, but he has something of the angel yet undefaced in him, which makes him so charming and agreeable that I must love him, be he never so wicked.

PERT.

I little thought, madam, to see your spirit tamed to this degree, who banished poor Mr. Lackwit but for taking up another lady's fan in your presence.

MRS. LOVEIT.

My knowing of such odious fools contributes to the making of me love Dorimant the better.

PERT.

Your knowing of Mr. Dorimant, in my mind, should rather make you hate all mankind.

MRS. LOVEIT.

So it does, besides himself.

PERT.

Pray, what excuse does he make in his letter?

MRS. LOVEIT.

He has had business.

PERT.

Business in general terms would not have been a current excuse for another. A modish man is always very busy when he is in pursuit of a new mistress.

MRS. LOVEIT.

Some fop has bribed you to rail at him. He had business; I will believe it and will forgive him.

PERT.

You may forgive him anything, but I shall never forgive him his turning me into ridicule, as I hear he does.

MRS. LOVEIT.

I perceive you are of the number of those fools his wit had made his enemies.

PERT.

I am of the number of those he's pleased to rally, madam, and if we may believe Mr. Wagfan and Mr. Caperwell, he sometimes makes merry with yourself, too, among his laughing companions.

MRS. LOVEIT.

Blockheads are as malicious to witty men as ugly women are to the handsome; 'tis their interest, and they make it their business to defame 'em.

PERT.

I wish Mr. Dorimant would not make it his business to defame you.

MRS. LOVEIT.

Should he, I had rather be made infamous by him than owe my reputation to the dull discretion of those fops you talk of.

Enter Bellinda.

(*Running to her.*) Bellinda!

BELLINDA.

My dear!

MRS. LOVEIT.

You have been unkind of late.

BELLINDA.

Do not say unkind, say unhappy!

MRS. LOVEIT.

I could chide you. Where have you been these two days?

BELLINDA.

Pity me rather, my dear, where I have been so tired with two or three country gentlewomen, whose conversation has been more insufferable than a country fiddle.

MRS. LOVEIT.

Are they relations?

BELLINDA.

No, Welsh acquaintance I made when I was last

year at St. Winifred's.[49] They have asked me a thousand questions of the modes and intrigues of the Town, and I have told 'em almost as many things for news that hardly were so when their gowns were in fashion. 70

MRS. LOVEIT.

Provoking creatures, how could you endure 'em?

BELLINDA. (*Aside.*)

Now to carry on my plot; nothing but love could make me capable of so much falsehood. 'Tis time to begin, lest Dorimant should come before her jealousy has stung her. (*Laughs and then speaks on.*) 75 I was yesterday at a play with 'em, where I was fain to show 'em the living, as the man at Westminster does the dead. That is Mrs.* Such-a-one, admired for her beauty; this is Mr. Such-a-one, cried up for a wit; that is sparkish Mr. Such-a-one, who keeps* 80 reverend Mrs. Such-a-one; and there sits fine Mrs. Such-a-one, who was lately cast off by my Lord Such-a-one.

MRS. LOVEIT.

Did you see Dorimant there?

BELLINDA.

I did, and imagine you were there with him and 85 have no mind to own it.

MRS. LOVEIT.

What should make you think so?

BELLINDA.

A lady masked, in a pretty dishabille, whom Dorimant entertained with more respect than the gallants do a common vizard.* 90

MRS. LOVEIT. (*Aside.*)

Dorimant at the play entertaining a mask!* Oh, heavens!

BELLINDA. (*Aside.*)

Good!

MRS. LOVEIT.

Did he stay all the while?

BELLINDA.

Till the play was done, and then led her out, which 95 confirms me it was you.

MRS. LOVEIT.

Traitor!

PERT.

Now you may believe he had business, and you may forgive him too.

MRS. LOVEIT.

Ungrateful, perjured man! 100

BELLINDA.

You seem so much concerned, my dear, I fear I have told you unawares what I had better have concealed for your quiet.

MRS. LOVEIT.

What manner of shape had she?

BELLINDA.

Tall and slender. Her motions were very genteel. 105 Certainly she must be some person of condition.

MRS. LOVEIT.

Shame and confusion be ever in her face when she shows it!

BELLINDA.

I should blame your discretion for loving that wild man, my dear, but they say he has a way so 110 bewitching that few can defend their hearts who know him.

MRS. LOVEIT.

I will tear him from mine, or die i'the attempt!

BELLINDA.

Be more moderate.

MRS. LOVEIT.

Would I had daggers, darts, or poisoned arrows in 115 my breast, so I could but remove the thoughts of him from thence!

BELLINDA.

Fie, fie, your transports are too violent, my dear. This may be but an accidental gallantry, and 'tis likely ended at her coach. 120

PERT.

Should it proceed farther, let your comfort be, the conduct Mr. Dorimant affects will quickly make you know your rival, ten to one let you see her ruined, her reputation exposed to the Town—a happiness none will envy her but yourself, madam. 125

MRS. LOVEIT.

Whoe'er she be, all the harm I wish her is, may she love him as well as I do, and may he give her as much cause to hate him!

PERT.

Never doubt the latter end of your curse, madam!

---

49 St. Winifred's] St. Winifred's Well, at Holywell, Wales

MRS. LOVEIT.

May all the passions that are raised by neglected 130
love—jealousy, indignation, spite, and thirst of
revenge—eternally rage in her soul, as they do now
in mine! (*Walks up and down with a distracted air.*)

Enter a page.

PAGE.

Madam, Mr. Dorimant—

MRS. LOVEIT.

I will not see him. 135

PAGE.

I told him you were within, madam.

MRS. LOVEIT.

Say you lied, say I'm busy—shut the door—say
anything!

PAGE.

He's here, madam. [*Exit.*]

Enter Dorimant.

DORIMANT.

"They taste of death who do at heaven arrive; 140
But we this paradise approach alive."[50]
(*To Mrs. Loveit.*) What, dancing the galloping nag[51]
without a fiddle? (*Offers to catch her by the hand; she
flings away and walks on.*) I fear this restlessness of
the body, madam, (*Pursuing her.*) proceeds from an 145
unquietness of the mind. What unlucky accident
puts you out of humor? A point ill-washed? Knots
spoiled i'the making up? Hair shaded awry? Or some
other little mistake in setting you in order?

PERT.

A trifle in my opinion, sir, more inconsiderable 150
than any you mention.

DORIMANT.

Oh, Mrs.* Pert! I never knew you sullen enough
to be silent. Come, let me know the business.

PERT.

The business, sir, is the business that has taken you
up these two days. How have I seen you laugh at 155
men of business, and now to become a man of
business yourself!

DORIMANT.

We are not masters of our own affections; our
inclinations daily alter. Now we love pleasure, and
anon we shall dote on business. Human frailty will
have it so, and who can help it? 160

MRS. LOVEIT.

Faithless, inhuman, barbarous man—

DORIMANT. [*Aside.*]

Good, now the alarm strikes—

MRS. LOVEIT.

Without sense of love, of honor, or of gratitude!
Tell me, for I will know, what devil masked she
was, you were with at the play yesterday. 165

DORIMANT.

Faith, I resolved as much as you, but the devil was
obstinate and would not tell me.

MRS. LOVEIT.

False in this as in your vows to me! You do know!

DORIMANT.

The truth is, I did all I could to know.

MRS. LOVEIT.

And dare you own it to my face? Hell and Furies! 170
(*Tears her fan in pieces.*)

DORIMANT.

Spare your fan, madam. You are growing hot and
will want it to cool you.

MRS. LOVEIT.

Horror and distraction seize you! Sorrow and
remorse gnaw your soul and punish all your
perjuries to me! (*Weeps.*) 175

DORIMANT. (*Turning to Bellinda.*)

"So thunder breaks the cloud in twain,
And makes a passage for the rain."[52]
(*To Bellinda.*) Bellinda, you are the devil that have
raised this storm. You were at the play yesterday
and have been making discoveries* to your dear. 180

BELLINDA.

Y'are the most mistaken man i'the world.

DORIMANT.

It must be so, and here I vow revenge—resolve to
pursue and persecute you more impertinently than
ever any loving fop did his mistress, hunt you i'the

---

50 "They … alive] Waller, "Of her Chamber," 1-2 (slightly
    misquoted)

51 galloping nag] a country dance

52 "So … rain"] Matthew Roydon, "An Elegie, or Friend's
    Passion, for his Astrophill [Sir Philip Sidney]" 34-35
    (slightly misquoted)

Park,* trace you i' the Mall,* dog you in every visit you make, haunt you at the plays and i'the Drawing Room,* hang my nose in your neck and talk to you whether you will or no, and ever look upon you with such dying eyes till your friends grow jealous of me, send you out of Town, and the world suspect your reputation. (*He looks kindly on Bellinda. In a lower voice.*) At my Lady Townley's when we go from hence.

BELLINDA.

I'll meet you there.

DORIMANT.

Enough.

MRS. LOVEIT. (*Pushing Dorimant away.*)

Stand off! You shannot stare upon her so.

DORIMANT.

Good! There's one made jealous already.

MRS. LOVEIT.

Is this the constancy you vowed?

DORIMANT.

Constancy at my years? 'Tis not a virtue in season; you might as well expect the fruit the autumn ripens i'the spring.

MRS. LOVEIT.

Monstrous principle!

DORIMANT.

Youth has a long journey to go, madam. Should I have set up my rest at the first inn I lodged at, I should never have arrived at the happiness I now enjoy.

MRS. LOVEIT.

Dissembler, damned dissembler!

DORIMANT.

I am so, I confess. Good nature and good manners corrupt me. I am honest in my inclinations and would not, were't not to avoid offense, make a lady a little in years believe I think her young, wilfully mistake art for nature, and seem as fond of a thing I am weary of as when I doted on't in earnest.

MRS. LOVEIT.

False man!

DORIMANT.

True woman.

MRS. LOVEIT.

Now you begin to show yourself!

DORIMANT.

Love gilds us over and makes us show fine things

to one another for a time, but soon the gold wears off, and then again the native brass appears.

MRS. LOVEIT.

Think on your oaths, your vows, and protestations, perjured man!

DORIMANT.

I made 'em when I was in love.

MRS. LOVEIT.

And therefore ought they not to bind? Oh, impious!

DORIMANT.

What we swear at such a time may be a certain proof of a present passion, but to say truth, in love there is no security to be given for the future.

MRS. LOVEIT.

Horrid and ungrateful, be gone! And never see me more!

DORIMANT.

I am not one of those troublesome coxcombs who, because they were once well-received, take the privi-lege to plague a woman with their love ever after. I shall obey you, madam, though I do myself some violence. (*He offers to go, and Mrs. Loveit pulls him back.*)

MRS. LOVEIT.

Come back, you shannot go! Could you have the ill nature to offer it?

DORIMANT.

When love grows diseased, the best thing we can do is to put it to a violent death. I cannot endure the torture of a lingering and consumptive passion.

MRS. LOVEIT.

Can you think mine sickly?

DORIMANT.

Oh, 'tis desperately ill! What worse symptoms are there than your being always uneasy when I visit you, your picking quarrels with me on slight occasions, and in my absence kindly listening to the impert-inences of every fashionable fool that talks to you?

MRS. LOVEIT.

What fashionable fool can you lay to my charge?

DORIMANT.

Why, the very cock-fool of all those fools, Sir Fopling Flutter.

MRS. LOVEIT.

I never saw him in my life but once.

DORIMANT.

The worse woman you, at first sight to put on all 250
your charms, to entertain him with that softness
in your voice and all that wanton kindness in your
eyes you so notoriously affect when you design a
conquest.

MRS. LOVEIT.

So damned a lie did never malice yet invent! Who 255
told you this?

DORIMANT.

No matter. That ever I should love a woman that
can dote on a senseless caper, a tawdry French
ribbon, and a formal cravat!

MRS. LOVEIT.

You make me mad! 260

DORIMANT.

A guilty conscience may do much. Go on, be the
game-mistress o'the Town and enter⁵³ all our
young fops, as fast as they come from travel.

MRS. LOVEIT.

Base and scurrilous!

DORIMANT.

A fine mortifying reputation 'twill be for a woman 265
of your pride, wit, and quality!*

MRS. LOVEIT.

This jealousy's a mere pretense, a cursed trick of
your own devising. I know you.

DORIMANT.

Believe it and all the ill of me you can. I would
not have a woman have the least good thought of 270
me that can think well of Fopling. Farewell. Fall
to, and much good may do you with your
coxcomb.

MRS. LOVEIT.

Stay! Oh stay, and I will tell you all!

DORIMANT.

I have been told too much already. (*Exit.*) 275

MRS. LOVEIT.

Call him again!

PERT.

E'en let him go, a fair riddance!

MRS. LOVEIT.

Run, I say, call him again. I will have him called!

---

⁵³ enter] instruct, initiate, train

PERT.

The Devil should carry him away first, were it my
concern. (*Exit.*) 280

BELLINDA.

He's frighted me from the very thoughts of loving
men. For Heaven's sake, my dear, do not discover*
what I told you. I dread his tongue as much as you
ought to have done his friendship.

Enter Pert.

PERT.

He's gone, madam. 285

MRS. LOVEIT.

Lightning blast him!

PERT.

When I told him you desired him to come back,
he smiled, made a mouth at me, flung into his
coach, and said—

MRS. LOVEIT.

What did he say? 290

PERT.

"Drive away," and then repeated verses.

MRS. LOVEIT.

Would I had made a contract to be a witch when
first I entertained* this greater devil. Monster,
barbarian! I could tear myself in pieces. Revenge,
nothing but revenge can ease me. Plague, war, 295
famine, fire, all that can bring universal ruin and
misery on mankind—with joy I'd perish to have
you in my power but this moment! (*Exit.*)

PERT.

Follow, madam. Leave her not in this outrageous
passion. (*Gathers up the things.*) 300

BELLINDA.

He's given me the proof which I desired of his love,
but 'tis a proof of his ill nature too. I wish I had
not seen him use her so.
I sigh to think that Dorimant may be
One day as faithless and unkind to me. 305

Exeunt.

Act III, scene i. Lady Woodvill's lodgings.

Enter Harriet and Busy, her woman.

BUSY.

Dear madam, let me set that curl in order!

HARRIET.

Let me alone! I will shake 'em all out of order!

BUSY.

Will you never leave this wildness?

HARRIET.

Torment me not!

BUSY.

Look, there's a knot falling off.   5

HARRIET.

Let it drop!

BUSY.

But one pin, dear madam.

HARRIET.

How do I daily suffer under thy officious fingers!

BUSY.

Ah, the difference that is between you and my
Lady Dapper: how uneasy she is if the least thing   10
be amiss about her.

HARRIET.

She is indeed most exact! Nothing is ever wanting*
to make her ugliness remarkable!

BUSY.

Jeering people say so.

HARRIET.

Her powdering, painting, and her patching54 never   15
fail in public to draw the tongues and eyes of all
the men upon her.

BUSY.

She is indeed a little too pretending.

HARRIET.

That women should set up for beauty as much in
spite of nature as some men have done for wit!   20

BUSY.

I hope without offense one may endeavor to make
one's self agreeable.

HARRIET.

Not when 'tis impossible. Women then ought to
be no more fond of dressing than fools should be
of talking. Hoods and modesty, masks and silence,   25
things that shadow and conceal—they should
think of nothing else.

BUSY.

Jesu! Madam, what will your mother think is
become of you? For Heaven's sake, go in again.

HARRIET.

I won't!   30

BUSY.

This is the extravagant'st thing that ever you did
in your life, to leave her and a gentleman who is
to be your husband.

HARRIET.

My husband! Hast thou so little wit to think I
spoke what I meant when I overjoyed her in the   35
country with a low curtsy and "What you please,
madam; I shall ever be obedient"?

BUSY.

Nay, I know not; you have so many fetches.

HARRIET.

And this was one, to get her up to London.
Nothing else, I assure thee.   40

BUSY.

Well, the man, in my mind, is a fine man.

HARRIET.

The man indeed wears his clothes fashionably and
has a pretty, negligent way with him, very courtly
and much affected. He bows, and talks, and smiles
so agreeably as he thinks.   45

BUSY.

I never saw anything so genteel.

HARRIET.

Varnished over with good breeding, many a
blockhead makes a tolerable show.

BUSY.

I wonder you do not like him.

HARRIET.

I think I might be brought to endure him, and that   50
is all a reasonable woman should expect in a
husband, but there is duty i'the case, and like the
haughty Merab, I

   "Find much aversion in my stubborn mind,"
whichc

   "is bred by being promised and designed."55   55

BUSY.

I wish you do not design your own ruin! I partly

_____

54 patching] applying artificial beauty marks, small pieces
   of black silk, to set off the complexion

_____

55 haughty Merab … designed] Merab, promised by her
   father Saul to David after his victory over Goliath but
   given instead to someone else (I Samuel 18:17-19), was
   portrayed by Cowley in *Davideis* as haughty; the lines
   from Cowley (Bk. III), slightly misquoted, reveal why.

guess your inclinations, madam—that Mr.
Dorimant—

HARRIET.
Leave your prating and sing some foolish song or
other.

BUSY.
I will—the song you love so well ever since you
saw Mr. Dorimant.

Song.

When first Amintas charmed my heart,
    My heedless sheep began to stray;
The wolves soon stole the greatest part,
    And all will now be made a prey.

Ah, let not love your thoughts possess,
    'Tis fatal to a shepherdess;
The dang'rous passion you must shun,
    Or else like me be quite undone.

HARRIET.
Shall I be paid down by a covetous parent for a
purchase? I need no land. No, I'll lay myself out
all in love. It is decreed—

Enter Young Bellair.

YOUNG BELLAIR.
What generous resolution are you making,
madam?

HARRIET.
Only to be disobedient, sir.

YOUNG BELLAIR.
Let me join hands with you in that—

HARRIET.
With all my heart. I never thought I should have
given you mine so willingly. Here I, Harriet—

YOUNG BELLAIR.
And I, Harry—

HARRIET.
Do solemnly protest—

YOUNG BELLAIR.
And vow—

HARRIET.
That I with you—

YOUNG BELLAIR.
And I with you—

BOTH.
Will never marry—

HARRIET.
A match!

YOUNG BELLAIR.
And no match! How do you like this indifference
now?

HARRIET.
You expect I should take it ill, I see.

YOUNG BELLAIR.
'Tis not unnatural for you women to be a little
angry, you miss a conquest—though you would
slight the poor man were he in your power.

HARRIET.
There are some, it may be, have an eye like
Bartholomew, big enough for the whole fair, but
I am not of the number, and you may keep your
gingerbread.[56] 'Twill be more acceptable to the
lady whose dear image it wears, sir.

YOUNG BELLAIR.
I must confess, madam, you came a day after the
fair.

HARRIET.
You own then you are in love?

YOUNG BELLAIR.
I do.

HARRIET.
The confidence is generous, and in return I could
almost find in my heart to let you know my
inclinations.

YOUNG BELLAIR.
Are you in love?

HARRIET.
Yes—with this dear Town, to that degree I can
scarce endure the country in landscapes and in
hangings.

YOUNG BELLAIR.
What a dreadful thing 'twould be to be hurried
back to Hampshire!

HARRIET.
Ah—name it not!

YOUNG BELLAIR.
As for us, I find we shall agree well enough. Would
we could do something to deceive the grave people!

---

56 There are … gingerbread] Bartholomew Cokes in Ben
Jonson's *Bartholomew Fair* (1614) is tempted to buy everything for sale at the fair, including gingerbread.

HARRIET.

Could we delay their quick proceeding, 'twere well. 115
A reprieve is a good step towards the getting of a
pardon.

YOUNG BELLAIR.

If we give over the game, we are undone. What
think you of playing it on booty?[57]

HARRIET.

What do you mean? 120

YOUNG BELLAIR.

Pretend to be in love with one another! 'Twill make
some dilatory excuses we may feign pass the better.

HARRIET.

Let us do't, if it be but for the dear pleasure of
dissembling.

YOUNG BELLAIR.

Can you play your part? 125

HARRIET.

I know not what it is to love, but I have made
pretty remarks[58] by being now and then where
lovers meet. Where did you leave their Gravities?

YOUNG BELLAIR.

I'th'next room. Your mother was censuring our
modern gallant. 130

Enter Old Bellair and Lady Woodvill.

HARRIET.

Peace! Here they come. I will lean against this wall
and look bashfully down upon my fan while you,
like an amorous spark, modishly entertain me.

LADY WOODVILL.

Never go about to excuse 'em. Come, come, it was
not so when I was a young woman. 135

OLD BELLAIR.

Adod, they're something disrespectful—

LADY WOODVILL.

Quality* was then considered and not rallied by
every fleering fellow.

OLD BELLAIR.

Youth will have its jest, adod it will.

LADY WOODVILL.

'Tis good breeding now to be civil to none but 140

players and Exchange* women. They are treated
by 'em as much above their condition as others are
below theirs.

OLD BELLAIR.

Out, a pize on 'em! Talk no more; the rogues ha'
got an ill habit of preferring beauty, no matter 145
where they find it.

LADY WOODVILL.

See your son and my daughter. They have improved
their acquaintance since they were within.

OLD BELLAIR.

Adod, methinks they have! Let's keep back and
observe. 150

YOUNG BELLAIR.

Now for a look and gestures that may persuade 'em
I am saying all the passionate things imaginable—

HARRIET.

Your head a little more on one side, ease yourself
on your left leg and play with your right hand.

YOUNG BELLAIR.

Thus, is it not? 155

HARRIET.

Now set your right leg firm on the ground, adjust
your belt, then look about you.

YOUNG BELLAIR.

A little exercising will make me perfect.

HARRIET.

Smile, and turn to me again very sparkish.

YOUNG BELLAIR.

Will you take your turn and be instructed? 160

HARRIET.

With all my heart.

YOUNG BELLAIR.

At one motion play your fan, roll your eyes, and
then settle a kind* look upon me.

HARRIET.

So.

YOUNG BELLAIR.

Now spread your fan, look down upon it, and tell 165
the sticks with a finger.

HARRIET.

Very modish.

YOUNG BELLAIR.

Clap your hand up to your bosom, hold down your
gown. Shrug a little, draw up your breasts and let
'em fall again, gently, with a sigh or two, etcetera. 170

---

57 playing it on booty] having one player lose intention-
    ally in order to draw in others

58 remarks] observations

HARRIET.

By the good instructions you give, I suspect you for one of those malicious observers who watch people's eyes and from innocent looks make scandalous conclusions.

YOUNG BELLAIR.

I know some, indeed, who out of mere* love to   175
mischief are as vigilant as jealousy itself and will give you an account of every glance that passes at a play and i'th'Circle!⁵⁹

HARRIET.

'Twill not be amiss now to seem a little pleasant.

YOUNG BELLAIR.

Clap your fan then in both your hands, snatch it   180
to your mouth, smile, and with a lively motion fling your body a little forwards. So—now spread it, fall back on the sudden, cover your face with it, and break out into a loud laughter—take up! Look grave and fall a-fanning of yourself.   185
Admirably well acted!

HARRIET.

I think I am pretty apt at these matters!

OLD BELLAIR.

Adod, I like this well.

LADY WOODVILL.

This promises something.

OLD BELLAIR.

Come, there is love i'th'case, adod there is, or will   190
be.—What say you, young lady?

HARRIET.

All in good time, sir. You expect we should fall to and love as gamecocks fight, as soon as we are set together. Adod, y'are unreasonable!

OLD BELLAIR.

Adod, sirrah, I like thy wit well.   195

Enter a servant.

SERVANT.

The coach is at the door, madam.

OLD BELLAIR.

Go, get you and take the air together.

LADY WOODVILL.

Will not you go with us?

OLD BELLAIR.

Out a pize! Adod, I ha' business and cannot. We shall meet at night at my sister Townley's.   200

YOUNG BELLAIR. (*Aside.*)

He's going to Emilia. I overheard him talk of a collation.

Exeunt.

Scene ii. [Lady Townley's house.]

Enter Lady Townley, Emilia, and Medley.

LADY TOWNLEY.

I pity the young lovers we last talked of, though to say truth, their conduct has been so indiscreet, they deserve to be unfortunate.

MEDLEY.

Y'ave had an exact account, from the great lady i'th'box down to the little orange-wench.   5

EMILIA.

Y'are a living libel, a breathing lampoon. I wonder you are not torn in pieces.

MEDLEY.

What think you of setting up an office of intelligence for these matters? The project may get money.   10

LADY TOWNLEY.

You would have great dealings with country ladies.

MEDLEY.

More than Muddiman⁶⁰ has with their husbands!

Enter Bellinda.

LADY TOWNLEY.

Bellinda, what has been become of you? We have not seen you here of late with your friend Mrs. Loveit.   15

BELLINDA.

Dear creature, I left her but now so sadly afflicted.

LADY TOWNLEY.

With her old distemper, jealousy?

MEDLEY.

Dorimant has played her some new prank.

---

⁵⁹ the Circle] perhaps the Ring,* perhaps the assembly of courtiers and hangers-on at Court

⁶⁰ Muddiman] Henry Muddiman (1629-92), editor of a newsletter of public affairs sent weekly from London to over 140 subscribers in the country

BELLINDA.

Well, that Dorimant is certainly the worst man
breathing.   20

EMILIA.

I once thought so.

BELLINDA.

And do you not think so still?

EMILIA.

No, indeed!

BELLINDA.

Oh, Jesu!

EMILIA.

The Town does him a great deal of injury, and I   25
will never believe what it says of a man I do not
know again, for his sake.

BELLINDA.

You make me wonder!

LADY TOWNLEY.

He's a very well-bred man.

BELLINDA.

But strangely ill-natured.   30

EMILIA.

Then he's a very witty man.

BELLINDA.

But a man of no principles.

MEDLEY.

Your man of principles is a very fine thing, indeed!

BELLINDA.

To be preferred to men of parts* by women who
have regard to their reputation and quiet. Well,   35
were I minded to play the fool, he should be the
last man I'd think of.

MEDLEY.

He has been the first in many ladies' favors, though
you are so severe, madam.

LADY TOWNLEY.

What he may be for a lover, I know not, but he's   40
a very pleasant acquaintance, I am sure.

BELLINDA.

Had you seen him use Mrs. Loveit as I have done,
you would never endure him more—

EMILIA.

What! he has quarreled with her again?

BELLINDA.

Upon the slightest occasion. He's jealous of Sir   45
Fopling.

LADY TOWNLEY.

She never saw him in her life but yesterday, and
that was here.

EMILIA.

On my conscience, he's the only man in Town
that's her aversion. How horribly out of humor she   50
was all the while he talked to her!

BELLINDA.

And somebody has wickedly told him—

Enter Dorimant.

EMILIA.

Here he comes.

MEDLEY.

Dorimant, you are luckily come to justify yourself.
Here's a lady—   55

BELLINDA.

Has a word or two to say to you from a
disconsolate person.

DORIMANT.

You tender your reputation too much, I know,
madam, to whisper with me before this good
company.   60

BELLINDA.

To serve Mrs. Loveit, I'll make a bold venture.

DORIMANT.

Here's Medley, the very spirit of scandal.

BELLINDA.

No matter!

EMILIA.

'Tis something you are unwilling to hear, Mr.
Dorimant.   65

LADY TOWNLEY.

Tell him, Bellinda, whether he will or no!

BELLINDA. (*Aloud.*)

Mrs. Loveit—

DORIMANT.

Softly, these are laughers; you do not know 'em.

BELLINDA. (*To Dorimant, apart.*)

In a word, y'ave made me hate you, which I
thought you never could have done.   70

DORIMANT.

In obeying your commands?

BELLINDA.

'Twas a cruel part you played! How could you act it?

DORIMANT.

Nothing is cruel to a man who could kill himself

to please you. Remember, five o'clock tomorrow
morning.   75

BELLINDA.
I tremble when you name it.

DORIMANT.
Be sure you come.

BELLINDA.
I shannot.

DORIMANT.
Swear you will.

BELLINDA.
I dare not.   80

DORIMANT.
Swear, I say.

BELLINDA.
By my life! by all the happiness I hope for—

DORIMANT.
You will.

BELLINDA.
I will.

DORIMANT.
Kind.   85

BELLINDA.
I am glad I've sworn. I vow I think I should ha'
failed you else.

DORIMANT.
Surprisingly kind! In what temper did you leave
Loveit?

BELLINDA.
Her raving was prettily[61] over, and she began to   90
be in a brave way of defying you and all your
works. Where have you been since you went from
thence?

DORIMANT.
I looked in at the play.

BELLINDA.
I have promised and must return to her again.   95

DORIMANT.
Persuade her to walk in the Mall* this evening.

BELLINDA.
She hates the place and will not come.

DORIMANT.
Do all you can to prevail with her.

BELLINDA.
For what purpose?

DORIMANT.
Sir Fopling will be here anon. I'll prepare him to   100
set upon her there before me.

BELLINDA.
You persecute her too much. But I'll do all you'll
ha' me.

DORIMANT. (Aloud.)
Tell her plainly, 'tis grown so dull a business I can
drudge on no longer.   105

EMILIA.
There are afflictions in love, Mr. Dorimant.

DORIMANT.
You women make 'em, who are commonly as
unreasonable in that as you are at play: without
the advantage be on your side, a man can never
quietly give over when he's weary.   110

MEDLEY.
If you would play without being obliged to
complaisance, Dorimant, you should play in
public places.

DORIMANT.
Ordinaries were a very good thing for that, but
gentlemen do not of late frequent 'em. The deep   115
play is now in private houses.

Bellinda offering to steal away.

LADY TOWNLEY.
Bellinda, are you leaving us so soon?

BELLINDA.
I am to go to the Park* with Mrs. Loveit,
madam—(*Exit.*)

LADY TOWNLEY.
This confidence[62] will go nigh to spoil this young   120
creature.

MEDLEY.
'Twill do her good, madam. Young men who are
brought up under practicing lawyers prove the
abler counsel when they come to be called to the
bar themselves—   125

DORIMANT.
The Town has been very favorable to you this
afternoon, my Lady Townley. You use to have an

---

61 prettily] mostly

62 confidence] intimate friendship

embarras[63] of chairs* and coaches at your door, an uproar of footmen in your hall, and a noise of fools above here. 130

LADY TOWNLEY.

Indeed, my house is the general rendezvous and, next to the playhouse, is the common refuge of all the young idle people.

EMILIA.

Company is a very good thing, madam, but I wonder you do not love it a little more chosen. 135

LADY TOWNLEY.

'Tis good to have an universal taste. We should love wit, but for variety be able to divert ourselves with the extravagancies of those who want* it.

MEDLEY.

Fools will make you laugh.

EMILIA.

For once or twice, but the repetition of their folly 140
after a visit or two grows tedious and insufferable.

LADY TOWNLEY.

You are a little too delicate, Emilia.

Enter a page.

PAGE.

Sir Fopling Flutter, madam, desires to know if you are to be seen.

LADY TOWNLEY.

Here's the freshest fool in Town, and one who has 145
not cloyed you yet.—Page!

PAGE.

Madam?

LADY TOWNLEY.

Desire him to walk up.

[Exit Page.]

DORIMANT.

Do not you fall on him, Medley, and snub him. Soothe him up in his extravagance. He will show 150
the better.

MEDLEY.

You know I have a natural indulgence for fools and need not this caution, sir.

Enter Sir Fopling Flutter, with his page after him.

---

63 *embarras*] congestion (Fr.)

SIR FOPLING.

Page! Wait without.

[Exit Page.]

(*To Lady Townley.*) Madam, I kiss your hands. I see yesterday was nothing of chance: the *belles* 155
assemblées[64] form themselves here every day. (*To Emilia.*) Lady, your servant.—Dorimant, let me embrace thee. Without lying, I have not met with any of my acquaintance who retain so much of Paris as thou dost—the very air thou hadst when 160
the marquise mistook thee i'th'Tuileries[65] and cried "Hey, chevalier!" and then begged thy pardon.

DORIMANT.

I would fain wear in fashion as long as I can, sir. 'Tis a thing to be valued in men as well as baubles.

SIR FOPLING.

Thou art a man of wit and understands the Town. 165
Prithee let thee and I be intimate. There is no living without making some good man the confidant of our pleasures.

DORIMANT.

'Tis true! But there is no man so improper for such a business as I am. 170

SIR FOPLING.

Prithee, why hast thou so modest an opinion of thyself?

DORIMANT.

Why first, I could never keep a secret in my life, and then, there is no charm so infallibly makes me fall in love with a woman as my knowing a friend 175
loves her. I deal honestly with you.

SIR FOPLING.

Thy humor's* very gallant, or let me perish. I knew a French count so like thee.

LADY TOWNLEY.

Wit, I perceive, has more power over you than beauty, Sir Fopling, else you would not have let 180
this lady stand so long neglected.

SIR FOPLING. (*To Emilia.*)

A thousand pardons, madam. Some civility's due of course upon the meeting a long absent friend.

---

64 *belles assemblées*] fashionable gatherings (Fr.)
65 Tuileries] palace in Paris, or the gardens adjacent to it

The éclat of so much beauty, I confess, ought to
have charmed me sooner.   185

EMILIA.

The *brilliant*[66] of so much good language, sir, has
much more power than the little beauty I can
boast.

SIR FOPLING.

I never saw anything prettier than this high work[67]
on your *point d'Espagne*—   190

EMILIA.

'Tis not so rich as *point de Venise*[68] —

SIR FOPLING.

Not altogether, but looks cooler and is more proper
for the season.—Dorimant, is not that Medley?

DORIMANT.

The same, sir.

SIR FOPLING.

Forgive me, sir: in this *embarras* of civilities I could   195
not come to have you in my arms sooner. You
understand an equipage the best of any man in
Town, I hear.

MEDLEY.

By my own you would not guess it.

SIR FOPLING.

There are critics who do not write, sir.   200

MEDLEY.

Our peevish poets will scarce allow it.

SIR FOPLING.

Damn 'em, they'll allow no man wit who does not
play the fool like themselves and show it! Have you
taken notice of the calash I brought over?

MEDLEY.

Oh, yes! 'T has quite another air than th'English   205
makes.

SIR FOPLING.

'Tis as easily known from an English tumbrel as
an Inns of Court* man is from one of us.

DORIMANT.

Truly there is a *bel air*[69] in calashes as well as men.

MEDLEY.

But there are few so delicate to observe it.   210

SIR FOPLING.

The world is generally very *grossier*[70] here, indeed.

LADY TOWNLEY. [*To Emilia.*]

He's very fine.

EMILIA.

Extreme proper.

SIR FOPLING.

A slight suit I made to appear in at my first arrival,
not worthy your consideration, ladies.   215

DORIMANT.

The pantaloon is very well mounted.

SIR FOPLING.

The tassels are new and pretty.

MEDLEY.

I never saw a coat better cut.

SIR FOPLING.

It makes me show long-waisted, and I think
slender.   220

DORIMANT.

That's the shape our ladies dote on.

MEDLEY.

Your breech, though, is a handful too high, in my
eye, Sir Fopling.

SIR FOPLING.

Peace, Medley, I have wished it lower a thousand
times, but a pox on't, 'twill not be!   225

LADY TOWNLEY.

His gloves are well fringed, large and graceful.

SIR FOPLING.

I was always eminent for being *bien ganté*.[71]

EMILIA.

He wears nothing but what are originals of the
most famous hands in Paris.

SIR FOPLING.

You are in the right, madam.   230

LADY TOWNLEY.

The suit?

SIR FOPLING.

Barroy.

EMILIA.

The garniture?

SIR FOPLING.

Le Gras—

---

66 *brilliant*] sparkle (Fr.)
67 high work] raised needlework
68 *point d'Espagne … Venise*] Spanish and Venetian lace (Fr.)
69 *bel air*] grace, poise, style (Fr.)

70 *grossier*] coarse, uncouth (Fr.)
71 *bien ganté*] well-gloved (Fr.)

MEDLEY.

The shoes? 235

SIR FOPLING.

Piccar!

DORIMANT.

The periwig?

SIR FOPLING.

Chedreux.[72]

LADY TOWNLEY, EMILIA.

The gloves?

SIR FOPLING.

Orangerie![73] You know the smell, ladies!— 240
Dorimant, I could find in my heart for an amusement to have a gallantry with some of our English
ladies.

DORIMANT.

'Tis a thing no less necessary to confirm the
reputation of your wit than a duel will be to satisfy 245
the Town of your courage.

SIR FOPLING.

Here was a woman yesterday—

DORIMANT.

Mistress Loveit.

SIR FOPLING.

You have named her!

DORIMANT.

You cannot pitch on a better for your purpose. 250

SIR FOPLING.

Prithee, what is she?

DORIMANT.

A person of quality,* and one who has a rest of
reputation enough to make the conquest
considerable. Besides, I hear she likes you, too!

SIR FOPLING.

Methought she seemed, though, very reserved and 255
uneasy all the time I entertained her.

DORIMANT.

Grimace and affectation! You will see her i'th'Mall
tonight.

SIR FOPLING.

Prithee, let thee and I take the air together.

DORIMANT.

I am engaged to Medley, but I'll meet you at Saint 260
James's* and give you some information, upon the
which you may regulate your proceedings.

SIR FOPLING.

All the world will be in the Park* tonight.—Ladies,
'twere pity to keep so much beauty longer within
doors and rob the Ring of all those charms that 265
should adorn it.—Hey, page!

Enter page.

See that all my people be ready.

[Page] goes out again.

Dorimant, au revoir. [*Exit.*]

MEDLEY.

A fine-mettled coxcomb.

DORIMANT.

Brisk and insipid— 270

MEDLEY.

Pert and dull.

EMILIA.

However you despise him, gentlemen, I'll lay my
life he passes for a wit with many.

DORIMANT.

That may very well be. Nature has her cheats,
stums* a brain, and puts sophisticate* dullness 275
often on the tasteless multitude for true wit and
good humor.—Medley, come.

MEDLEY.

I must go a little way; I will meet you i'the Mall.

DORIMANT.

I'll walk through the garden thither. (*To the
women.*) We shall meet anon and bow. 280

LADY TOWNLEY.

Not tonight! We are engaged about a business, the
knowledge of which may make you laugh
hereafter.

MEDLEY.

Your servant, ladies.

DORIMANT.

Au revoir, as Sir Fopling says. 285

Exeunt Medley and Dorimant.

LADY TOWNLEY.

The old man will be here immediately.

---

72 most famous hands in Paris … Chedreux] Presumably
the names are those of Parisian artisans, but of these only
Chedreux* has been identified.

73 Orangerie] a scent made from orange-blossoms

EMILIA.

Let's expect him i'th'garden—

LADY TOWNLEY.

Go, you are a rogue!

EMILIA.

I can't abide you!

Exeunt.

Scene iii. The Mall.

Enter Harriet and Young Bellair, she pulling him.

HARRIET.

Come along!

YOUNG BELLAIR.

And leave your mother?

HARRIET.

Busy will be sent with a hue and cry after us, but that's no matter.

YOUNG BELLAIR.

'Twill look strangely in me.   5

HARRIET.

She'll believe it a freak of mine and never blame your manners.

YOUNG BELLAIR.

What reverend acquaintance is that she has met?

HARRIET.

A fellow beauty of the last king's time, though by the ruins you would hardly guess it.   10

Exeunt. Enter Dorimant and crosses the stage. Enter Young Bellair and Harriet.

YOUNG BELLAIR.

By this time your mother is in a fine taking.[74]

HARRIET.

If your friend Mr. Dorimant were but here now, that she might find me talking with him!

YOUNG BELLAIR.

She does not know him but dreads him, I hear, of all mankind.   15

HARRIET.

She concludes if he does but speak to a woman, she's undone—is on her knees every day to pray Heaven defend me from him.

YOUNG BELLAIR.

You do not apprehend him so much as she does.

HARRIET.

I never saw anything in him that was frightful.   20

YOUNG BELLAIR.

On the contrary, have you not observed something extreme delightful in his wit and person?

HARRIET.

He's agreeable and pleasant, I must own, but he does so much affect being so, he displeases me.

YOUNG BELLAIR.

Lord madam, all he does and says is so easy and   25
so natural.

HARRIET.

Some men's verses seem so to the unskillful, but labor i'the one and affectation i'the other to the judicious plainly appear.

YOUNG BELLAIR.

I never heard him accused of affectation before.   30

Enter Dorimant and stares upon her.

HARRIET.

It passes on the easy Town, who are favorably pleased in him to call it humor.*

Exeunt Young Bellair and Harriet.

DORIMANT.

'Tis she! It must be she—that lovely hair, that easy shape, those wanton eyes, and all those melting charms about her mouth which Medley spoke of.   35
I'll follow the lottery and put in for a prize with my friend Bellair.

Exit Dorimant, repeating:

"In love the victors from the vanquished fly;
They fly that wound, and they pursue that die."[75]

Enter Young Bellair and Harriet, and after them Dorimant, standing at a distance.

YOUNG BELLAIR.

Most people prefer Hyde Park* to this place.   40

HARRIET.

It has the better reputation, I confess, but I

---

74 a fine taking] a disturbed or agitated state of mind

75 "In love … that die."] Waller, "To a Friend, of the Different Success of their Loves," 27-28

abominate the dull diversions there—the formal
bows, the affected smiles, the silly by-words and
amorous tweers[76] in passing. Here one meets with
a little conversation now and then.   45

YOUNG BELLAIR.
These conversations* have been fatal to some of
your sex, madam.

HARRIET.
It may be so. Because some who want temper have
been undone by gaming, must others who have it
wholly deny themselves the pleasure of play?   50

DORIMANT. (*Coming up gently and bowing to her.*)
Trust me, it were unreasonable, madam.

She starts and looks grave.

HARRIET.
Lord! who's this?

YOUNG BELLAIR.
Dorimant.

DORIMANT. [*To Young Bellair.*]
Is this the woman your father would have you
marry?   55

YOUNG BELLAIR.
It is.

DORIMANT.
Her name?

YOUNG BELLAIR.
Harriet.

DORIMANT.
I am not mistaken; she's handsome.

YOUNG BELLAIR.
Talk to her; her wit is better than her face. We were   60
wishing for you but now.

DORIMANT. (*To Harriet.*)
Overcast with seriousness o'the sudden! A thousand
smiles were shining in that face but now. I never
saw so quick a change of weather.

HARRIET. (*Aside.*)
I feel as great a change within, but he shall never   65
know it.

DORIMANT.
You were talking of play, madam. Pray, what may
be your stint?

---

76 tweers] glances, leers

HARRIET.
A little harmless discourse in public walks, or at
most an appointment in a box, barefaced, at the   70
playhouse. You are for masks and private meetings,
where women engage for all they are worth, I hear.

DORIMANT.
I have been used to deep play, but I can make one
at small game when I like my gamester well.

HARRIET.
And be so unconcerned you'll ha' no pleasure in't.   75

DORIMANT.
Where there is a considerable sum to be won, the
hope of drawing people in makes every trifle
considerable.

HARRIET.
The sordidness of men's natures, I know, makes
'em willing to flatter and comply with the rich,   80
though they are sure never to be the better for 'em.

DORIMANT.
'Tis in their power to do us good, and we despair
not but at some time or other they may be willing.

HARRIET.
To men who have fared in this Town like you,
'twould be a great mortification to live on hope.   85
Could you keep a Lent for a mistress?

DORIMANT.
In expectation of a happy Easter, and though time
be very precious, think forty days well lost to gain
your favor.

HARRIET.
Mr. Bellair! Let us walk, 'tis time to leave him. Men   90
grow dull when they begin to be particular.

DORIMANT.
Y'are mistaken: flattery will not ensue, though I
know y'are greedy of the praises of the whole Mall.

HARRIET.
You do me wrong.

DORIMANT.
I do not. As I followed you, I observed how you   95
were pleased when the fops cried, "She's handsome,
very handsome, by God she is!" and whispered
aloud your name—the thousand several forms you
put your face into; then, to make yourself more
agreeable, how wantonly you played with your   100
head, flung back your locks, and looked smilingly
over your shoulder at 'em.

HARRIET.

I do not go begging the men's, as you do the ladies', good liking, with a sly softness in your looks and a gentle slowness in your bows as you pass by 'em— as thus, sir—(*Acts him.*) Is not this like you? 105

Enter Lady Woodvill and Busy.

YOUNG BELLAIR.

Your mother, madam! (*Pulls Harriet. She composes herself.*)

LADY WOODVILL.

Ah, my dear child Harriet!

BUSY.

Now is she so pleased with finding her again, she cannot chide her. 110

LADY WOODVILL.

Come away!

DORIMANT.

'Tis now but high Mall, madam—the most entertaining time of all the evening.

HARRIET.

I would fain see that Dorimant, Mother, you so cry out of for a monster. He's in the Mall, I hear. 115

LADY WOODVILL.

Come away, then! The plague is here, and you should dread the infection.

YOUNG BELLAIR.

You may be misinformed of the gentleman.

LADY WOODVILL.

Oh, no! I hope you do not know him. He is the prince of all the devils in the Town—delights in nothing but in rapes and riots. 120

DORIMANT.

If you did but hear him speak, madam—

LADY WOODVILL.

Oh! he has a tongue, they say, would tempt the angels to a second fall!

Enter Sir Fopling with his equipage, six footmen and a page.

SIR FOPLING.

Hey, Champagne, Norman, La Rose, La Fleur, La Tour, La Verdure!—Dorimant! 125

LADY WOODVILL.

Here, here he is among this rout! He names him! Come away, Harriet, come away!

Exeunt Lady Woodvill, Harriet, Busy, and Young Bellair.

DORIMANT.

This fool's coming has spoiled all: she's gone. But she has left a pleasing image of herself behind that wanders in my soul. It must not settle there. 130

SIR FOPLING.

What reverie is this? Speak, man!

DORIMANT.

"Snatched from myself, how far behind
Already I behold the shore!"[77]

Enter Medley.

MEDLEY.

Dorimant, a discovery! I met with Bellair— 135

DORIMANT.

You can tell me no news, sir. I know all.

MEDLEY.

How do you like the daughter?

DORIMANT.

You never came so near truth in your life as you did in her description.

MEDLEY.

What think you of the mother? 140

DORIMANT.

Whatever I think of her, she thinks very well of me, I find.

MEDLEY.

Did she know you?

DORIMANT.

She did not. Whether she does now or no, I know not. Here was a pleasant scene towards, when in 145 came Sir Fopling, mustering up his equipage, and at the latter end named me and frighted her away.

MEDLEY.

Loveit and Bellinda are not far off. I saw 'em alight at St. James's.*

DORIMANT.

Sir Fopling, hark you, a word or two. (*Whispers.*) 150 Look you do not want* assurance.

SIR FOPLING.

I never do on these occasions.

---

77 "Snatched … shore!" Waller, "Of Loving at First Sight," 3-4

DORIMANT.

Walk on; we must not be seen together. Make your advantage of what I have told you. The next turn you will meet the lady. 155

SIR FOPLING.

Hey! Follow me all. (*Exit with equipage.*)

DORIMANT.

Medley, you shall see good sport anon between Loveit and this Fopling.

MEDLEY.

I thought there was something toward, by that whisper. 160

DORIMANT.

You know a worthy principle of hers?

MEDLEY.

Not to be so much as civil to a man who speaks to her in the presence of him she professes to love.

DORIMANT.

I have encouraged Fopling to talk to her tonight.

MEDLEY.

Now you are here, she will go nigh to beat him. 165

DORIMANT.

In the humor she's in, her love will make her do some very extravagant thing, doubtless.

MEDLEY.

What was Bellinda's business with you at my Lady Townley's?

DORIMANT.

To get me to meet Loveit here in order to an éclaircissement. I made some difficulty of it and have prepared this rencounter to make good my jealousy. 170

Enter Mrs. Loveit, Bellinda, and Pert.

MEDLEY.

Here they come!

DORIMANT.

I'll meet her and provoke her with a deal of dumb civility in passing by, then turn short and be behind her when Sir Fopling sets upon her. 175

[*Bows to Mrs. Loveit.*]

"See how unregarded now
That piece of beauty passes."[78]

---

[78] "See ... passes."] a paraphrase of Suckling, *Sonnets*, I, 1–2

Exeunt Dorimant and Medley.

BELLINDA.

How wonderful respectfully he bowed! 180

PERT.

He's always over-mannerly when he has done a mischief.

BELLINDA.

Methought indeed, at the same time he had a strange, despising countenance.

PERT.

The unlucky look he thinks becomes him. 185

BELLINDA.

I was afraid you would have spoke to him, my dear.

MRS. LOVEIT.

I would have died first. He shall no more find me the loving fool he has done.

BELLINDA.

You love him still!

MRS. LOVEIT.

No. 190

PERT.

I wish you did not.

MRS. LOVEIT.

I do not, and I will have you think so!—What made you hale me to this odious place, Bellinda?

BELLINDA.

I hate to be hulched[79] up in a coach. Walking is much better. 195

MRS. LOVEIT.

Would we could meet Sir Fopling now!

BELLINDA.

Lord! would you not avoid him?

MRS. LOVEIT.

I would make him all the advances that may be.

BELLINDA.

That would confirm Dorimant's suspicion, my dear. 200

MRS. LOVEIT.

He is not jealous, but I will make him so and be revenged a way he little thinks on.

BELLINDA. (*Aside.*)

If she should make him jealous, that may make him fond of her again. I must dissuade her from

---

[79] hulched up] bundled up, bent like a hunchback

it.—Lord! My dear, this will certainly make him 205
hate you.

MRS. LOVEIT.

'Twill make him uneasy, though he does not care
for me. I know the effects of jealousy on men of
his proud temper.

BELLINDA.

'Tis a fantastic remedy: its operations are dangerous 210
and uncertain.

MRS. LOVEIT.

'Tis the strongest cordial we can give to dying love.
It often brings it back when there's no sign of life
remaining. But I design not so much the reviving
his, as my revenge. 215

Enter Sir Fopling and his equipage.

SIR FOPLING.

Hey! Bid the coachman send home four of his
horses and bring the coach to Whitehall.* I'll walk
over the Park.* [*To Mrs. Loveit.*] Madam, the honor
of kissing your fair hands is a happiness I missed
this afternoon at my Lady Townley's. 220

MRS. LOVEIT.

You were very obliging, Sir Fopling, the last time
I saw you there.

SIR FOPLING.

The preference was due to your wit and beauty.
[*To Bellinda.*] Madam, your servant. There never
was so sweet an evening. 225

BELLINDA.

'T has drawn all the rabble of the Town hither.

SIR FOPLING.

'Tis pity there's not an order made that none but
the beau monde should walk here.

MRS. LOVEIT.

'Twould add much to the beauty of the place. See
what a sort of nasty fellows are coming! 230

Enter four ill-fashioned fellows singing,

"'Tis not for kisses alone,
[So long I have made my address.]"

MRS. LOVEIT.

Faugh! Their periwigs are scented with tobacco so
strong—

SIR FOPLING.

It overcomes our pulvillio.* Methinks I smell the 235
coffeehouse they come from.

FIRST MAN.

Dorimant's convenient,[80] Madam Loveit.

SECOND MAN.

I like the oily _____* buttock with her.

THIRD MAN.

What spruce prig is that?

FIRST MAN.

A caravan,[81] lately come from Paris. 240

SECOND MAN.

Peace, they smoke!

All of them coughing, exeunt singing,

"There's something else to be done,
[Which you cannot choose but guess]."[82]

Enter Dorimant and Medley.

DORIMANT.

They're engaged—

MEDLEY.

She entertains him as if she liked him. 245

DORIMANT.

Let us go forward—seem earnest in discourse and
show ourselves. Then you shall see how she'll use
him.

BELLINDA.

Yonder's Dorimant, my dear.

MRS. LOVEIT.

I see him. (*Aside.*) He comes insulting, but I will 250
disappoint him in his expectation. (*To Sir Fopling.*)
I like this pretty, nice* humor* of yours, Sir
Fopling.—With what a loathing eye he looked
upon those fellows!

SIR FOPLING.

I sat near one of 'em at a play today and was almost 255
poisoned with a pair of cordovan gloves he wears—

MRS. LOVEIT.

Oh, filthy cordovan! How I hate the smell! (*Laughs
in a loud, affected way.*)

---

80 convenient] mistress or whore

81 caravan] a prospective victim of plunder, evidenced by
his equipage

82 "'Tis not for kisses … [choose but guess]."] lines from
a popular song, first published in 1676, beginning "Tell
me no more you love, / Unless you will grant my desire."

SIR FOPLING.

Did you observe, madam, how their cravats hung loose an inch from their neck, and what a frightful air it gave 'em?   260

MRS. LOVEIT.

Oh! I took particular notice of one that is always spruced up with a deal of dirty, sky-colored ribbon.

BELLINDA.

That's one of the walking flageolets[83] who haunt the Mall o'nights—

MRS. LOVEIT.

Oh! I remember him! H'as a hollow tooth, enough   265
to spoil the sweetness of an evening.

SIR FOPLING.

I have seen the tallest walk the streets with a dainty pair of boxes,[84] neatly buckled on.

MRS. LOVEIT.

And a little footboy at his heels, pocket-high, with a flat cap,[85] a dirty face—   270

SIR FOPLING.

And a snotty nose—

MRS. LOVEIT.

Oh—odious! There's many of my own sex with that Holborn[86] equipage trig[87] to Gray's Inn Walks, and now and then travel hither on a Sunday.

MEDLEY. [*To Dorimant.*]

She takes no notice of you.   275

DORIMANT.

Damn her! I am jealous of a counterplot!

MRS. LOVEIT.

Your liveries are the finest, Sir Fopling—Oh, that page! That page is the prettily'st dressed—they are all Frenchmen?

SIR FOPLING.

There's one damned English blockhead among   280
'em. You may know him by his mien.

---

83 flageolet] a small wind instrument similar to a recorder
84 boxes] probably galoshes again, platform shoes
85 flat cap] a round cap with a low, flat crown, worn in the 16th-17th c. by London citizens, particularly apprentices
86 Holborn] a borough in the commercial district of London, which includes several of the Inns of Court, including Gray's Inn
87 trig] walk briskly, trip

MRS. LOVEIT.

Oh, that's he, that's he! What do you call him?

SIR FOPLING.

Hey—I know not what to call him—

MRS. LOVEIT.

What's your name?

FOOTMAN.

John Trott, madam.   285

SIR FOPLING.

Oh, insufferable! Trott, Trott, Trott! There's nothing so barbarous as the names of our English servants. What countryman are you, sirrah?

FOOTMAN.

Hampshire, sir.

SIR FOPLING.

Then Hampshire be your name. Hey, Hampshire!   290

MRS. LOVEIT.

Oh, that sound! That sound becomes the mouth of a man of quality!*

MEDLEY.

Dorimant, you look a little bashful on the matter!

DORIMANT.

She dissembles better than I thought she could have done.   295

MEDLEY.

You have tempted her with too luscious a bait. She bites at the coxcomb.

DORIMANT.

She cannot fall from loving me to that?

MEDLEY.

You begin to be jealous in earnest.

DORIMANT.

Of one I do not love—   300

MEDLEY.

You did love her.

DORIMANT.

The fit has long been over—

MEDLEY.

But I have known men fall into dangerous relapses when they have found a woman inclining to another.   305

DORIMANT (*To himself.*)

He guesses the secret of my heart! I am concerned but dare not show it, lest Bellinda should mistrust all I have done to gain her.

BELLINDA. (*Aside.*)

I have watched his look and find no alteration there. Did he love her, some signs of jealousy would have appeared. 310

DORIMANT. [*To Mrs. Loveit.*]

I hope this happy evening, madam, has reconciled you to the scandalous Mall. We shall have you now hankering[88] here again.

MRS. LOVEIT.

Sir Fopling, will you walk? 315

SIR FOPLING.

I am all obedience, madam—

MRS. LOVEIT.

Come along, then—and let's agree to be malicious on all the ill-fashioned things we meet.

SIR FOPLING.

We'll make a critique on the whole Mall, madam.

MRS. LOVEIT.

Bellinda, you shall engage— 320

BELLINDA.

To the reserve of our friends, my dear.

MRS. LOVEIT.

No! No exceptions—

SIR FOPLING.

We'll sacrifice all to our diversion—

MRS. LOVEIT.

All—all—

SIR FOPLING.

All! 325

BELLINDA.

All? Then let it be.

Exeunt Sir Fopling, Mrs. Loveit, Bellinda, and Pert, laughing.

MEDLEY.

Would you had brought some more of your friends, Dorimant, to have been witnesses of Sir Fopling's disgrace and your triumph!

DORIMANT.

'Twere unreasonable to desire you not to laugh at me, but pray do not expose me to the Town this day or two. 330

MEDLEY.

By that time you hope to have regained your credit.

---

88 hankering] loitering, "hanging out"

DORIMANT.

I know she hates Fopling and only makes use of him in hope to work me on again. Had it not been for some powerful considerations which will be removed tomorrow morning, I had made her pluck off this mask and show the passion that lies panting under. 335

Enter a footman.

MEDLEY.

Here comes a man from Bellair, with news of your last adventure. 340

DORIMANT.

I am glad he sent him. I long to know the consequence of our parting.

FOOTMAN.

Sir, my master desires you to come to my Lady Townley's presently and bring Mr. Medley with you. My Lady Woodvill and her daughter are there. 345

MEDLEY.

Then all's well, Dorimant.

FOOTMAN.

They have sent for the fiddles and mean to dance. He bid me tell you, sir, the old lady does not know you, and would have you own yourself to be Mr. Courtage. They are all prepared to receive you by that name. 350

DORIMANT.

That foppish admirer of quality,* who flatters the very meat at honorable tables and never offers love to a woman below a lady-grandmother! 355

MEDLEY.

You know the character you are to act, I see.

DORIMANT.

This is Harriet's contrivance—wild, witty, lovesome, beautiful and young!—Come along, Medley.

MEDLEY.

This new woman would well supply the loss of Loveit. 360

DORIMANT.

That business must not end so. Before tomorrow sun is set, I will revenge and clear it.

And you and Loveit, to her cost, shall find
I fathom all the depths of womankind. 365

Exeunt.

Act IV, scene i. [Lady Townley's house.]

The scene opens with the fiddles playing a country dance. Enter Dorimant [and] Lady Woodvill, Young Bellair and Mrs. Harriet, Old Bellair and Emilia, Mr. Medley and Lady Townley, as having just ended the dance.

OLD BELLAIR.

So, so, so! A smart bout, a very smart bout, adod!

LADY TOWNLEY.

How do you like Emilia's dancing, brother?

OLD BELLAIR.

Not at all, not at all!

LADY TOWNLEY.

You speak not what you think, I am sure.   5

OLD BELLAIR.

No matter for that—go, bid her dance no more. It don't become her, it don't become her. Tell her I say so. (*Aside.*) Adod, I love her.

DORIMANT. (*To Lady Woodvill.*)

All people mingle nowadays, madam. And in public places women of quality* have the least   10 respect showed 'em.

LADY WOODVILL.

I protest you say the truth, Mr. Courtage.

DORIMANT.

Forms and ceremonies, the only things that uphold quality* and greatness, are now shamefully laid aside and neglected.   15

LADY WOODVILL.

Well, this is not the women's age, let 'em think what they will. Lewdness is the business now; love was the business in my time.

DORIMANT.

The women, indeed, are little beholding to the young men of this age. They're generally only dull   20 admirers of themselves and make their court to nothing but their periwigs and their cravats—and would be more concerned for the disordering of 'em, though on a good occasion, than a young maid would be for the tumbling of her head or   25 handkercher.[89]

---

89 head ... handkercher] hairdo and a kerchief worn as a head-covering

LADY WOODVILL.

I protest you hit 'em.

DORIMANT.

They are very assiduous to show themselves at Court, well-dressed, to the women of quality,* but their business is with the stale mistresses of the   30 Town, who are prepared to receive their lazy addresses by industrious old lovers who have cast 'em off and made 'em easy.

HARRIET.

He fits my mother's humor* so well, a little more and she'll dance a kissing dance[90] with him anon.   35

MEDLEY.

Dutifully observed, madam.

DORIMANT.

They pretend to be great critics in beauty: by their talk you would think they liked no face—and yet can dote on an ill one if it belongs to a laundress or a tailor's daughter. They cry a woman's past her   40 prime at twenty, decayed at four-and-twenty, old and insufferable at thirty.

LADY WOODVILL.

Insufferable at thirty! That they are in the wrong, Mr. Courtage. At five-and-thirty there are living proofs enough to convince 'em.   45

DORIMANT.

Aye, madam! there's Mrs. Setlooks, Mrs. Droplip, and my Lady Lowd! Show me among all our opening buds a face that promises so much beauty as the remains of theirs.

LADY WOODVILL.

The depraved appetite of this vicious age tastes   50 nothing but green fruit and loathes it when 'tis kindly[91] ripened.

DORIMANT.

Else so many deserving women, madam, would not be so untimely neglected.

LADY WOODVILL.

I protest, Mr. Courtage, a dozen such good men as   55 you would be enough to atone for that wicked Dorimant and all the under-debauchees of the Town.

---

90 kissing dance] cushion dance, a round dance, formerly danced at weddings, in which the women and men alternately knelt on a cushion to be kissed (*OED*)

91 kindly] naturally

Harriet, Emilia, Young Bellair, Medley, and Lady Townley break out into a laughter.

What's the matter there?

MEDLEY.

A pleasant mistake, madam, that a lady has made occasions a little laughter.   60

OLD BELLAIR.

Come, come, you keep 'em idle! They are impatient till the fiddles play again.

DORIMANT.

You are not weary, madam?

LADY WOODVILL.

One dance more! I cannot refuse you, Mr. Courtage.   65

They dance. After the dance, Old Bellair singing and dancing up to Emilia.

EMILIA.

You are very active, sir.

OLD BELLAIR.

Adod, sirrah, when I was a young fellow, I could ha' capered up to my woman's gorget.

DORIMANT. [*To Lady Woodvill.*]

You are willing to rest yourself, madam?

LADY TOWNLEY.

We'll walk into my chamber and sit down.   70

MEDLEY.

Leave us Mr. Courtage: he's a dancer, and the young ladies are not weary yet.

LADY WOODVILL.

We'll send him out again.

HARRIET.

If you do not quickly, I know where to send for Mr. Dorimant.   75

LADY WOODVILL.

This girl's head, Mr. Courtage, is ever running on that wild fellow.

DORIMANT.

'Tis well you have got her a good husband, madam. That will settle it.

Exeunt Lady Townley, Lady Woodvill, and Dorimant.

OLD BELLAIR (*To Emilia.*)

Adod, sweetheart, be advised and do not throw   80
thyself away on a young, idle fellow.

EMILIA.

I have no such intention, sir.

OLD BELLAIR.

Have a little patience! Thou shalt have the man I spake of. Adod, he loves thee and will make a good husband. But no words—   85

EMILIA.

But sir—

OLD BELLAIR.

No answer—out a pize! Peace! and think on't.

Enter Dorimant.

DORIMANT.

Your company is desired within, sir.

OLD BELLAIR.

I go, I go, good Mr. Courtage. (*To Emilia.*) Fare you well. Go, I'll see you no more!   90

EMILIA.

What have I done, sir?

OLD BELLAIR.

You are ugly, you are ugly!—Is she not, Mr. Courtage?

EMILIA.

Better words, or I shan't abide you!

OLD BELLAIR.

Out a pize! Adod, what does she say?—Hit her a   95
pat for me there. (*Exit.*)

MEDLEY. [*To Emilia.*]

You have charms for the whole family.

DORIMANT.

You'll spoil all with some unseasonable jest, Medley.

MEDLEY.

You see I confine my tongue and am content to   100
be a bare spectator, much contrary to my nature.

EMILIA.

Methinks, Mr. Dorimant, my Lady Woodvill is a little fond of you.

DORIMANT.

Would her daughter were.

MEDLEY.

It may be you may find her so. Try her. You have 105
an opportunity.

DORIMANT.

And I will not lose it.—Bellair, here's a lady has something to say to you.

YOUNG BELLAIR.

I wait upon her.—Mr. Medley, we have both business with you. 110

DORIMANT.

Get you all together, then.

[He approaches Harriet and bows; she curtsies.]

(*To Harriet.*) That demure curtsy is not amiss in jest, but do not think in earnest it becomes you.

HARRIET.

Affectation is catching, I find; from your grave bow I got it. 115

DORIMANT.

Where had you all that scorn and coldness in your look?

HARRIET.

From nature, sir; pardon my want* of art. I have not learnt those softnesses and languishings which now in faces are so much in fashion. 120

DORIMANT.

You need 'em not. You have a sweetness of your own, if you would but calm your frowns and let it settle.

HARRIET.

My eyes are wild and wandering like my passions and cannot yet be tied to rules of charming. 125

DORIMANT.

Women, indeed, have commonly a method of managing those messengers of love. Now they will look as if they would kill, and anon they will look as if they were dying. They point and rebate their glances, the better to invite us. 130

HARRIET.

I like this variety well enough, but hate the set face that always looks as it would say, "Come love me"— a woman who at plays makes the *doux yeux*[92] to a whole audience and at home cannot forbear 'em to her monkey. 135

DORIMANT.

Put on a gentle smile and let me see how well it will become you.

HARRIET.

I am sorry my face does not please you as it is, but I shall not be complaisant and change it.

---

92 *doux yeux*] flirtatious glances (Fr.)

DORIMANT.

Though you are obstinate, I know 'tis capable of 140 improvement and shall do you justice, madam, if I chance to be at Court when the critics of the Circle pass their judgment, for thither you must come.

HARRIET.

And expect to be taken in pieces, have all my features examined, every motion censured, and on 145 the whole be condemned to be but pretty, or a beauty of the lowest rate. What think you?

DORIMANT.

The women—nay, the very lovers who belong to the Drawing Room*—will maliciously allow you more than that. They always grant what is 150 apparent, that they may the better be believed when they name concealed faults they cannot easily be disproved in.

HARRIET.

Beauty runs as great a risk exposed at Court as wit does on the stage, where the ugly and the foolish 155 are all free to censure.

DORIMANT (*Aside.*)

I love her and dare not let her know it. I fear sh'as an ascendant o'er me and may revenge the wrongs I have done her sex. (*To her.*) Think of making a party, madam; love will engage. 160

HARRIET.

You make me start! I did not think to have heard of love from you.

DORIMANT.

I never knew what 'twas to have a settled ague yet, but now and then have had irregular fits.

HARRIET.

Take heed—sickness after long health is commonly 165 more violent and dangerous.

DORIMANT. (*Aside.*)

I have took the infection from her and feel the disease now spreading in me. (*To her.*) Is the name of love so frightful that you dare not stand it?

HARRIET.

'Twill do little execution out of your mouth on me, 170 I am sure.

DORIMANT.

It has been fatal—

HARRIET.

To some easy women, but we are not all born to

one destiny. I was informed you use to laugh at
love, and not make it.*   175

DORIMANT.
The time has been, but now I must speak—

HARRIET.
If it be on that idle subject, I will put on my
serious look, turn my head carelessly from you,
drop my lip, let my eyelids fall and hang half o'er
my eyes—thus—while you buzz a speech of an   180
hour long in my ear and I answer never a word.
Why do you not begin?

DORIMANT.
That the company may take notice how
passionately I make advances of love and how
disdainfully you receive 'em.   185

HARRIET.
When your love's grown strong enough to make
you bear being laughed at, I'll give you leave to
trouble me with it. Till when, pray forbear, sir.

Enter Sir Fopling and others in masks.

DORIMANT.
What's here, masquerades?

HARRIET.
I thought that foppery had been left off, and   190
people might have been in private with a fiddle.

DORIMANT.
'Tis endeavored to be kept on foot still by some
who find themselves the more acceptable, the less
they are known.

YOUNG BELLAIR.
This must be Sir Fopling.   195

MEDLEY.
That extraordinary habit shows it.

YOUNG BELLAIR.
What are the rest?

MEDLEY.
A company of French rascals whom he picked up
in Paris and has brought over to be his dancing
equipage on these occasions. Make him own   200
himself; a fool is very troublesome when he
presumes he is incognito.

SIR FOPLING. (*To Harriet.*)
Do you know me?

HARRIET.
Ten to one but I guess at you.

SIR FOPLING.
Are you women as fond of a vizard as we men are?   205

HARRIET.
I am very fond of a vizard that covers a face I do
not like, sir.

YOUNG BELLAIR.
Here are no masks, you see, sir, but those which
came with you. This was intended a private
meeting, but because you look like a gentleman,   210
if you will discover* yourself and we know you to
be such, you shall be welcome.

SIR FOPLING. (*Pulling off his mask.*)
Dear Bellair.

MEDLEY.
Sir Fopling! How came you hither?

SIR FOPLING.
Faith, as I was coming late from Whitehall,* after   215
the King's *couchée*,93 one of my people told me he
had heard fiddles at my Lady Townley's, and—

DORIMANT.
You need not say any more, sir.

SIR FOPLING.
Dorimant, let me kiss thee.

DORIMANT.
Hark you, Sir Fopling—(*Whispers.*)   220

SIR FOPLING.
Enough, enough, Courtage. [*Indicates Harriet.*] A
pretty kind of young woman that, Medley. I
observed her in the Mall, more *éveillée*94 than our
English women commonly are. Prithee, what is
she?   225

MEDLEY.
The most noted coquette in Town; beware of her.

SIR FOPLING.
Let her be what she will, I know how to take my
measures. In Paris the mode is to flatter the *prude*,
laugh at the *faux-prude*, make serious love to the
demi-prude, and only rally with the coquette.   230
Medley, what think you?

MEDLEY.
That for all this smattering of the mathematics,
you may be out in your judgment at tennis.

---

93 *couchée*] the formal ceremony accompanying the king's
    going to bed (Fr.)
94 *eveillée*] lively, sprightly, intelligent (Fr.)

SIR FOPLING.

What *coq-à-l'âne*[95] is this? I talk of women and thou answer'st tennis.   235

MEDLEY.

Mistakes will be, for want of apprehension.

SIR FOPLING.

I am very glad of the acquaintance I have with this family.

MEDLEY.

My lady truly is a good woman.

SIR FOPLING.

Ah, Dorimant—Courtage, I would say—would   240
thou hadst spent the last winter in Paris with me. When thou wert there, La Corneus and Sallyes[96] were the only habitudes we had; a comedian would have been a *bonne fortune*. No stranger ever passed his time so well as I did some months before I   245
came over. I was well received in a dozen families, where all the women of quality* used to visit. I have intrigues to tell thee more pleasant than ever thou read'st in a novel.

HARRIET.

Write 'em, sir, and oblige us women. Our language   250
wants* such little stories.

SIR FOPLING.

Writing, madam, 's a mechanic part of wit. A gentleman should never go beyond a song or a *billet*.

HARRIET.

Bussy was a gentleman.

SIR FOPLING.

Who, d'Ambois?[97]   255

MEDLEY. [*Aside*.]

Was there ever such a brisk blockhead?

HARRIET.

Not d'Ambois, sir, but Rabutin.[98] He who writ the *Loves of France*.

---

95 *coq-à-l'âne*] cock-and-bull story, nonsense (Fr.)

96 Corneus and Sallyes] Mmes. Corneul and Selles, keepers of Parisian salons (Verity)

97 d'Ambois] Bussy d'Ambois, hero and title character of the 1604 tragedy by the English playwright George Chapman, seen in revival on the Restoration stage

98 Rabutin] Roger de Rabutin, Comte de Bussy (1618-1693), author of the *Histoire Amoureuse des Gaules*, whose title Harriet translates into English in this sentence.

SIR FOPLING.

That may be, madam! many gentlemen do things that are below 'em.—Damn your authors,   260
Courtage, women are the prettiest things we can fool away our time with.

HARRIET.

I hope ye have wearied yourself tonight at Court, sir, and will not think of fooling with anybody here.   265

SIR FOPLING.

I cannot complain of my fortune there, madam.—Dorimant—

DORIMANT.

Again!

SIR FOPLING.

Courtage, a pox on't! I have something to tell thee. When I had made my court within, I came out   270
and flung myself upon the mat under the state[99] i'th'outward room, i'th'midst of half a dozen beauties who were withdrawn to jeer among themselves, as they called it.

DORIMANT.

Did you know 'em?   275

SIR FOPLING.

Not one of 'em, by heavens! not I. But they were all your friends.

DORIMANT.

How are you sure of that?

SIR FOPLING.

Why, we laughed at all the Town—spared nobody but yourself. They found me a man for their   280
purpose.

DORIMANT.

I know you are malicious to your power.

SIR FOPLING.

And faith, I had occasion to show it, for I never saw more gaping fools at a ball or on a birthday.*

DORIMANT.

You learned who the women were?   285

SIR FOPLING.

No matter! they frequent the Drawing Room.*

DORIMANT.

And entertain themselves pleasantly at the expense of all the fops who come there.

---

99 state] ceremonial canopy

SIR FOPLING.

That's their business. Faith, I sifted 'em and find they have a sort of wit among them——(*Pinches a tallow candle.*) Ah, filthy! 290

DORIMANT.

Look, he has been pinching the tallow candle.

SIR FOPLING.

How can you breathe in a room where there's grease frying? Dorimant, thou art intimate with my lady; advise her, for her own sake and the good company that comes hither, to burn wax lights. 295

HARRIET.

What are these masquerades who stand so obsequiously at a distance?

SIR FOPLING.

A set of balladines, whom I picked out of the best in France and brought over with a *flûte douce* or two, my servants. They shall entertain you. 300

HARRIET.

I had rather see you dance yourself, Sir Fopling.

SIR FOPLING.

And I had rather do it——all the company knows it——but, madam——

MEDLEY.

Come, come! No excuses, Sir Fopling. 305

SIR FOPLING.

By heavens, Medley——

MEDLEY.

Like a woman, I find, you must be struggled with before one brings you to[d] what you desire.

HARRIET. (*Aside.*)

Can he dance?

EMILIA.

And fence and sing too, if you'll believe him. 310

DORIMANT.

He has no more excellence in his heels than in his head. He went to Paris a plain, bashful English blockhead and is returned a fine, undertaking[100] French fop.

MEDLEY.

I cannot prevail. 315

SIR FOPLING.

Do not think it want* of complaisance, madam.

HARRIET.

You are too well-bred to want that, Sir Fopling. I believe it want of power.

SIR FOPLING.

By heavens, and so it is! I have sat up so damned late and drunk so cursed hard since I came to this lewd Town that I am fit for nothing but low dancing now——a *courante*, a *bourrée*, or a *menuet*.[101] But St. André[102] tells me, if I will but be regular, in one month I shall rise again. (*Endeavors at a caper.*) Pox on this debauchery! 320 325

EMILIA.

I have heard your dancing much commended.

SIR FOPLING.

It had the good fortune to please in Paris. I was judged to rise within an inch as high as the Basque[103] in an entry[104] I danced there.

HARRIET. [*To Emilia.*]

I am mightily taken with this fool. Let us sit.—— Here's a seat, Sir Fopling. 330

SIR FOPLING.

At your feet, madam. I can be nowhere so much at ease. By your leave, gown. [*Sits.*]

HARRIET, EMILIA.

Ah, you'll spoil it!

SIR FOPLING.

No matter, my clothes are my creatures. I make 'em to make my court to you ladies.——Hey, *qu'on commence*![105] 335

Dance. [Sir Fopling points] to an English dancer.[e]

English motions! I was forced to entertain* this fellow, one of my set miscarrying.——Oh, horrid! Leave your damned manner of dancing and put on the French air. Have you not a pattern before you?——Pretty well! Imitation in time may bring him to something. 340

___

100 undertaking] enterprising

101 low dancing … *menuet*] Fopling calls such dances "low" because they do not require capers.

102 St. André] a well-known French dancing master and choreographer for the English stage

103 the Basque] probably "le Basque sauter," a French dancer (Barnard)

104 entry] a dance performed as an interlude in an entertainment

105 *qu'on commence*] begin! (Fr.)

After the dance, enter Old Bellair, Lady Woodvill, and Lady Townley.

OLD BELLAIR.
  Hey, adod, what have we here? A mumming?
LADY WOODVILL.
  Where's my daughter? Harriet!   345
DORIMANT.
  Here, here, madam! I know not but under these
  disguises there may be dangerous sparks. I gave the
  young lady warning.
LADY WOODVILL.
  Lord! I am so obliged to you, Mr. Courtage.
HARRIET.
  Lord! How you admire this man!   350
LADY WOODVILL.
  What have you to except against him?
HARRIET.
  He's a fop.
LADY WOODVILL.
  He's not a Dorimant, a wild, extravagant fellow of
  the times.
HARRIET.
  He's a man made up of forms and commonplaces,   355
  sucked out of the remaining lees of the last age.
LADY WOODVILL.
  He's so good a man that were you not engaged—
LADY TOWNLEY.
  You'll have but little night to sleep in.
LADY WOODVILL.
  Lord, 'tis perfect day!
DORIMANT. (*Aside.*)
  The hour is almost come I appointed Bellinda, and   360
  I am not so foppishly in love here to forget. I am
  flesh and blood yet.
LADY TOWNLEY.
  I am very sensible, madam.
LADY WOODVILL.
  Lord, madam—
HARRIET.
  Look, in what a struggle is my poor mother   365
  yonder!
YOUNG BELLAIR.
  She has much ado to bring out the compliment.
DORIMANT.
  She strains hard for it.

HARRIET.
  See, see! her head tottering, her eyes staring, and
  her underlip trembling—   370
DORIMANT.
  Now, now she's in the very convulsions of her
  civility. (*Aside.*) 'Sdeath, I shall lose Bellinda! I must
  fright her hence. She'll be an hour in this fit of
  good manners else. (*To Lady Woodvill.*) Do you not
  know Sir Fopling, madam?   375
LADY WOODVILL.
  I have seen that face—Oh Heaven, 'tis the same
  we met in the Mall! How came he here?
DORIMANT.
  A fiddle in this Town is a kind of fop-call. No
  sooner it strikes up, but the house is besieged with
  an army of masquerades straight.   380
LADY WOODVILL.
  Lord, I tremble, Mr. Courtage. For certain
  Dorimant is in the company.
DORIMANT.
  I cannot confidently say he is not. You had best
  be gone. I will wait upon you. Your daughter is in
  the hands of Mr. Bellair.   385
LADY WOODVILL.
  I'll see her before me.—Harriet, come away!
YOUNG BELLAIR. [*Calling to servants offstage.*]
  Lights, lights!
LADY TOWNLEY.
  Light, down there!
OLD BELLAIR.
  Adod, it needs not—
DORIMANT.
  Call my Lady Woodvill's coach to the door quickly!   390

*[Exeunt Emilia, Young Bellair, Lady Woodvill,
Harriet, Lady Townley, and Dorimant.]*

OLD BELLAIR.
  Stay, Mr. Medley; let the young fellows do that
  duty. We will drink a glass of wine together. 'Tis
  good after dancing. What mumming spark is that?
MEDLEY.
  He is not to be comprehended in few words.
SIR FOPLING.
  Hey, La Tour!   395
MEDLEY.
  Whither away, Sir Fopling?

SIR FOPLING.

I have business with Courtage.

MEDLEY.

He'll but put the ladies into their coach and come up again.

OLD BELLAIR.

In the meantime I'll call for a bottle. (*Exit.*) 400

Enter Young Bellair.

MEDLEY.

Where's Dorimant?

YOUNG BELLAIR.

Stol'n home. He has had business waiting for him there all this night, I believe, by an impatience I observed in him.

MEDLEY.

Very likely. 'Tis but dissembling drunkenness, 405 railing at his friends, and the kind* soul will embrace the blessing and forget the tedious expectation.

SIR FOPLING.

I must speak with him before I sleep.

YOUNG BELLAIR. [*To Medley.*]

Emilia and I are resolved on that business.

MEDLEY.

Peace, here's your father. 410

Enter Old Bellair and butler with a bottle of wine.

OLD BELLAIR.

The women are all gone to bed.—Fill, boy!—Mr. Medley, begin a health.

MEDLEY.

To Emilia.

OLD BELLAIR.

Out a pize! She's a rogue, and I'll not pledge you.

MEDLEY. (*Whispers.*)

I know you will.f 415

OLD BELLAIR.

Adod, drink it, then!

SIR FOPLING.

Let us have the new *bachique.*

OLD BELLAIR.

Adod, that is a hard word! What does it mean, sir?

MEDLEY.

A catch or drinking song.

OLD BELLAIR.

Let us have it, then. 420

SIR FOPLING.

Fill the glasses round and draw up in a body.— Hey! music!

They sing.

The pleasures of love and the joys of good wine,
To perfect our happiness wisely we join.
We to beauty all day 425
Give the sovereign sway
And her favorite nymphs devoutly obey.
At the plays we are constantly making our court,
And when they are ended, we follow the sport
To the Mall* and the Park,* 430
Where we love till 'tis dark;
Then sparkling champagne
Puts an end to their reign;
It quickly recovers
Poor languishing lovers, 435
Makes us frolic and gay, and drowns all our sorrow;
But alas! we relapse again on the morrow.
     Let every man stand
     With his glass in his hand,
And briskly discharge at the word of command. 440
     Here's a health to all those
     Whom tonight we depose.
Wine and beauty by turns great souls should inspire;
Present all together; and now, boys, give fire!

OLD BELLAIR.

Adod, a pretty business and very merry! 445

SIR FOPLING.

Hark you, Medley, let you and I take the fiddles and go waken Dorimant.

MEDLEY.

We shall do him a courtesy, if it be as I guess. For after the fatigue of this night, he'll quickly have his belly full and be glad of an occasion to cry, 450 "Take away, Handy!"

YOUNG BELLAIR.

I'll go with you, and there we'll consult about affairs, Medley.

OLD BELLAIR. (*Looks on his watch.*)

Adod, 'tis six o'clock!

SIR FOPLING.

Let's away, then. 455

OLD BELLAIR.

Mr. Medley, my sister tells me you are an honest

man. And adod, I love you. Few words and hearty,
that's the way with old Harry, old Harry.

SIR FOPLING.

Light your flambeaux! Hey!

OLD BELLAIR.

What does the man mean?   460

MEDLEY.

'Tis day, Sir Fopling.

SIR FOPLING.

No matter. Our serenade will look the greater.

Exeunt omnes.

Scene ii. Dorimant's lodging, a table,
a candle, a toilet, etc.

Handy tying up linen. Enter Dorimant in his gown,
and Bellinda.

DORIMANT.

Why will you be gone so soon?

BELLINDA.

Why did you stay out so late?

DORIMANT.

Call a chair,* Handy!

[Exit Handy.]

What makes you tremble so?

BELLINDA.

I have a thousand fears about me. Have I not been   5
seen, think you?

DORIMANT.

By nobody but myself and trusty Handy.

BELLINDA.

Where are all your people?

DORIMANT.

I have dispersed 'em on sleeveless[106] errands. What
does that sigh mean?   10

BELLINDA.

Can you be so unkind to ask me?—Well—(*Sighs.*)
were it to do again—

DORIMANT.

We should do it, should we not?

BELLINDA.

I think we should: the wickeder man you, to make
me love so well. Will you be discreet now?   15

_____
106 sleeveless] useless

DORIMANT.

I will—

BELLINDA.

You cannot.

DORIMANT.

Never doubt it.

BELLINDA.

I will not expect it.

DORIMANT.

You do me wrong.   20

BELLINDA.

You have no more power to keep the secret than I
had not to trust you with it.

DORIMANT.

By all the joys I have had and those you keep in
store—

BELLINDA.

You'll do for my sake what you never did before—   25

DORIMANT.

By that truth thou hast spoken, a wife shall sooner
betray herself to her husband—

BELLINDA.

Yet I had rather you should be false in this than
in another thing you promised me.

DORIMANT.

What's that?   30

BELLINDA.

That you would never see Loveit more but in
public places—in the Park,* at Court and plays.

DORIMANT.

'Tis not likely a man should be fond of seeing a
damned old play when there is a new one acted.

BELLINDA.

I dare not trust your promise.   35

DORIMANT.

You may—

BELLINDA.

This does not satisfy me. You shall swear you never
will see her more.

DORIMANT.

I will! a thousand oaths—by all—

BELLINDA.

Hold—you shall not, now I think on't better.   40

DORIMANT.

I will swear—

BELLINDA.

I shall grow jealous of the oath and think I owe your truth to that, not to your love.

DORIMANT.

Then, by my love! No other oath I'll swear.

(Enter Handy.)

HANDY.

Here's a chair.

BELLINDA.

Let me go.

DORIMANT.

I cannot.

BELLINDA.

Too willingly, I fear.

DORIMANT.

Too unkindly feared. When will you promise me again?

BELLINDA.

Not this fortnight.

DORIMANT.

You will be better than your word.

BELLINDA.

I think I shall. Will it not make you love me less?

Fiddles without.

(Starting.) Hark! what fiddles are these?

DORIMANT.

Look out, Handy.

Exit Handy and returns.

HANDY.

Mr. Medley, Mr. Bellair, and Sir Fopling. They are coming up.

DORIMANT.

How got they in?

HANDY.

The door was open for the chair.

BELLINDA.

Lord! let me fly!

DORIMANT.

Here, here—down the back stairs. I'll see you into your chair.

BELLINDA.

No, no! stay and receive 'em. And be sure you keep your word and never see Loveit more. Let it be a proof of your kindness.*

DORIMANT.

It shall.—Handy, direct her. (*Kissing her hand.*) Everlasting love go along with thee.

Exeunt Bellinda and Handy. Enter Young Bellair, Medley, and Sir Fopling.

YOUNG BELLAIR.

Not abed yet?

MEDLEY.

You have had an irregular fit, Dorimant.

DORIMANT.

I have.

YOUNG BELLAIR.

And is it off already?

DORIMANT.

Nature has done her part, gentlemen. When she falls kindly to work, great cures are effected in little time, you know.

SIR FOPLING.

We thought there was a wench in the case, by the chair that waited. Prithee, make us a *confidence.*

DORIMANT.

Excuse me.

SIR FOPLING.

Le sage[107] Dorimant—was she pretty?

DORIMANT.

So pretty she may come to keep her coach and pay parish duties, if the good humor of the age continue.

MEDLEY.

And be of the number of the ladies kept by public-spirited men for the good of the whole Town.

SIR FOPLING.

Well said, Medley. (*Dancing by himself.*)

YOUNG BELLAIR.

See Sir Fopling dancing.

DORIMANT.

You are practicing and have a mind to recover, I see.

SIR FOPLING.

Prithee, Dorimant, why hast not thou a glass* hung up here? A room is the dullest thing without one!

YOUNG BELLAIR.

Here is company to entertain you.

45

50

55

60

65

70

75

80

85

90

---

107 *sage*] wise, discreet (Fr.)

SIR FOPLING.

But I mean in case of being alone. In a glass a man may entertain himself—

DORIMANT.

The shadow of himself, indeed.

SIR FOPLING.

Correct the errors of his motions and his dress.

MEDLEY.

I find, Sir Fopling, in your solitude you remember   95
the saying of the wise man, and study yourself.

SIR FOPLING.

'Tis the best diversion in our retirements. Dorimant, thou art a pretty fellow and wear'st thy clothes well, but I never saw thee have a handsome cravat. Were they made up like mine, they'd give   100
another air to thy face. Prithee, let me send my man to dress thee but one day. By heavens, an Englishman cannot tie a ribbon!

DORIMANT.

They are something clumsy-fisted—

SIR FOPLING.

I have brought over the prettiest fellow that ever   105
spread a toilet. He served some time under Merrille, the greatest *génie* in the world for a valet de chambre.

DORIMANT.

What, he who formerly belonged to the duke of Candale?[108]   110

SIR FOPLING.

The same, and got him his immortal reputation.

DORIMANT.

Y'ave a very fine brandenburgh[109] on, Sir Fopling.

SIR FOPLING.

It serves to wrap me up, after the fatigue of a ball.

MEDLEY.

I see you often in it, with your periwig tied up.

SIR FOPLING.

We should not always be in a set dress. 'Tis more   115
en cavalier to appear now and then in a dishabille.

MEDLEY.

Pray, how goes your business with Loveit?

SIR FOPLING.

You might have answered yourself in the Mall last night.—Dorimant! did you not see the advances she made me? I have been endeavoring at a song!   120

DORIMANT.

Already!

SIR FOPLING.

'Tis my *coup d'essai*[110] in English. I would fain have thy opinion of it.

DORIMANT.

Let's see it.

SIR FOPLING.

Hey, page, give me my song.—Bellair, here. Thou   125
hast a pretty voice: sing it.

YOUNG BELLAIR.

Sing it yourself, Sir Fopling.

SIR FOPLING.

Excuse me.

YOUNG BELLAIR.

You learnt to sing in Paris.

SIR FOPLING.

I did—of Lambert,[111] the greatest master in the   130
world. But I have his own fault, a weak voice, and care not to sing out of a *ruelle*.[112]

DORIMANT.

A *ruelle* is a pretty cage for a singing fop, indeed.

Young Bellair reads the song.

How charming Phillis is, how fair!
    Ah, that she were as willing   135
To ease my wounded heart of care
    And make her eyes less killing.
I sigh! I sigh! I languish now,
    And love will not let me rest;
I drive about the Park* and bow   140
    Still as I meet my dearest.

SIR FOPLING.

Sing it, sing it, man! It goes to a pretty new tune which I am confident was made by Baptiste.[113]

---

108 the Duke of Candale] Louis-Charles Gaston de Nogaret de Foix, Duc de Candale (1627-58), a French general admired for his elegance of dress

109 brandenburgh] woolen morning gown

110 *coup d'essai*] first attempt (Fr.)

111 Lambert] Michel Lambert (1610-96), French lutenist and singer

112 *ruelle*] a space in a bedchamber, where fashionable visitors attended women of quality at their levees

113 Baptiste] probably Jean-Baptiste Lully (1632-87),

MEDLEY.

Sing it yourself, Sir Fopling. He does not know the
tune.

SIR FOPLING.

I'll venture. (*Sings.*)

DORIMANT.

Aye, marry,* now 'tis something. I shall not flatter
you, Sir Fopling; there is not much thought in't.
But 'tis passionate and well-turned.

MEDLEY.

After the French way. 150

SIR FOPLING.

That I aimed at—does it not give you a lively
image of the thing? Slap, down goes the glass,[114]
and thus we are at it.

DORIMANT.

It does indeed. I perceive, Sir Fopling, you'll be the
very head of the sparks who are lucky in 155
compositions of this nature.

Enter Sir Fopling's footman.

SIR FOPLING.

La Tour, is the bath ready?

FOOTMAN.

Yes, sir.

SIR FOPLING.

Adieu donc, mes chers.[115]

Exeunt Sir Fopling and footman.

MEDLEY.

When have you your revenge on Loveit, Dorimant? 160

DORIMANT.

I will but change my linen and about it.

MEDLEY.

The powerful considerations which hindered have
been removed, then?

DORIMANT.

Most luckily, this morning. You must along with
me; my reputation lies at stake there. 165

MEDLEY.

I am engaged to Bellair.

DORIMANT.

What's your business?

MEDLEY.

Ma-tri-mony, an't* like you.

DORIMANT.

It does not, sir.

YOUNG BELLAIR.

It may in time, Dorimant. What think you of Mrs. 170
Harriet?

DORIMANT.

What does she think of me?

YOUNG BELLAIR.

I am confident she loves you.

DORIMANT.

How does it appear?

YOUNG BELLAIR.

Why, she's never well but when she's talking of you, 175
but then she finds all the faults in you she can. She
laughs at all who commend you, but then she
speaks ill of all who do not.

DORIMANT.

Women of her temper betray themselves by their
over-cunning. I had once a growing love with a 180
lady who would always quarrel with me when I
came to see her and yet was never quiet if I stayed
a day from her.

YOUNG BELLAIR.

My father is in love with Emilia.

DORIMANT.

That is a good warrant for your proceedings. Go 185
on and prosper; I must to Loveit.—Medley, I am
sorry you cannot be a witness.

MEDLEY.

Make her meet Sir Fopling again in the same place
and use him ill before me.

DORIMANT.

That may be brought about, I think.—I'll be at 190
your aunt's anon and give you joy, Mr. Bellair.

YOUNG BELLAIR.

You had not best think of Mrs. Harriet too much.
Without church security, there's no taking up there.

---

master of court music to Louis XIV; possibly Giovanni
Battista Draghi (c. 1640-1710), Italian harpsichordist
and composer living in England and writing for the
stage

114 down goes the glass] perhaps a window glass, perhaps
a wine glass, perhaps a mirror—in that order of probability

115 *Adieu donc, mes chers*] Good-bye, then, my dears (Fr.)

DORIMANT.

I may fall into the snare, too. But—
The wise will find a difference in our fate: 195
You wed a woman, I a good estate.

Exeunt.

Scene iii. [The Mall.]

Enter the chair with Bellinda; the men set it down
and open it. Bellinda starting.*

BELLINDA. (*Surprised.*)

Lord! where am I? In the Mall! Whither have you
brought me?

FIRST CHAIRMAN.

You gave us no directions, madam.

BELLINDA. (*Aside.*)

The fright I was in made me forget it.

FIRST CHAIRMAN.

We use to carry a lady from the squire's hither.   5

BELLINDA. (*Aside.*)

This is Loveit! I am undone if she sees me.—
Quickly, carry me away!

FIRST CHAIRMAN.

Whither, an't* like your honor?

BELLINDA.

Ask no questions—

Enter Mrs. Loveit's footman.

FOOTMAN.

Have you seen my lady, madam?   10

BELLINDA.

I am just come to wait upon her.

FOOTMAN.

She will be glad to see you, madam. She sent me
to you this morning to desire your company, and
I was told you went out by five o'clock.

BELLINDA. (*Aside.*)

More and more unlucky!   15

FOOTMAN.

Will you walk in, madam?

BELLINDA.

I'll discharge my chair and follow. Tell your
mistress I am here.

Exit footman. [Bellinda] gives the chairmen money.

Take this, and if ever you should be examined, be
sure you say you took me up in the Strand,* over   20

against the Exchange,* as you will answer it to Mr.
Dorimant.

CHAIRMEN.

We will, an't like your honor.

Exeunt chairmen.

BELLINDA.

Now to come off, I must on—
In confidence and lies some hope is left;   25
'Twere hard to be found out in the first theft.

Exit.

Act V, scene i. [*Mrs. Loveit's lodgings.*]

Enter Mrs. Loveit and Pert.

PERT.

Well! In my eyes, Sir Fopling is no such despicable
person.

MRS. LOVEIT.

You are an excellent judge.

PERT.

He's as handsome a man as Mr. Dorimant, and as
great a gallant.   5

MRS. LOVEIT.

Intolerable! Is't not enough I submit to his impertinences, but must I be plagued with yours, too?

PERT.

Indeed, madam—

MRS. LOVEIT.

'Tis false, mercenary malice—

Enter her footman.

FOOTMAN.

Mrs.* Bellinda, madam—   10

MRS. LOVEIT.

What of her?

FOOTMAN.

She's below.

MRS. LOVEIT.

How came she?

FOOTMAN.

In a chair; ambling Harry brought her.

MRS. LOVEIT.

He bring her! His chair stands near Dorimant's   15
door and always brings me from thence—run and
ask him where he took her up. Go!

[Exit footman.]

There is no truth in friendship neither. Women as well as men, all are false, or all are so to me, at least.

PERT.

You are jealous of her, too?

MRS. LOVEIT.

You had best tell her I am. 'Twill become the liberty you take of late. This fellow's bringing of her, her going out by five o'clock—I know not what to think.

Enter Bellinda.

Bellinda, you are grown an early riser, I hear.

BELLINDA.

Do you not wonder, my dear, what made me abroad so soon?

MRS. LOVEIT.

You do not use to be so.

BELLINDA.

The country gentlewomen I told you of (Lord! They have the oddest diversions!) would never let me rest till I promised to go with them to the markets this morning to eat fruit and buy nosegays.

MRS. LOVEIT.

Are they so fond of a filthy nosegay?

BELLINDA.

They complain of the stinks of the Town and are never well but when they have their noses in one.

MRS. LOVEIT.

There are essences and sweet waters.

BELLINDA.

Oh, they cry out upon perfumes, they are unwholesome. One of 'em was falling into a fit with the smell of these neroli.

MRS. LOVEIT.

Methinks in complaisance you should have had a nosegay too.

BELLINDA.

Do you think, my dear, I could be so loathsome to trick myself up with carnations and stock-gillyflowers?[116] I begged their pardon and told

them I never wore anything but orange-flowers and tuberose. That which made me willing to go was a strange desire I had to eat some fresh nectarines.

MRS. LOVEIT.

And had you any?

BELLINDA.

The best I ever tasted.

MRS. LOVEIT.

Whence came you now?

BELLINDA.

From their lodgings, where I crowded out of a coach and took a chair* to come and see you, my dear.

MRS. LOVEIT.

Whither did you send for that chair?

BELLINDA.

'Twas going by empty.

MRS. LOVEIT.

Where do these country gentlewomen lodge, I pray?

BELLINDA.

In the Strand,* over against the Exchange.*

PERT.

That place is never without a nest of 'em. They are always, as one goes by, fleering in balconies or staring out of windows.

Enter footman.

MRS. LOVEIT. (*To the Footman.*)

Come hither. (*Whispers.*)

BELLINDA. (*Aside.*)

This fellow by her order has been questioning the chairmen! I threatened 'em with the name of Dorimant. If they should have told truth, I am lost forever.

MRS. LOVEIT.

In the Strand, said you?

FOOTMAN.

Yes, madam, over against the Exchange. (*Exit.*)

MRS. LOVEIT. [*Aside.*]

She's innocent, and I am much to blame.

BELLINDA. (*Aside.*)

I am so frighted, my countenance will betray me.

MRS. LOVEIT.

Bellinda! what makes you look so pale?

---

116 stock-gillyflowers] a kind of carnation: The plant *Matthiola incana*; so called as having a woody stem, in distinction from clove-gillyflower (*OED*)

BELLINDA.

Want* of my usual rest and jolting up and down so long in an odious hackney.

Footman returns.

FOOTMAN.

Madam, Mr. Dorimant.

MRS. LOVEIT.

What makes him here?

BELLINDA. (*Aside.*)

Then I am betrayed indeed. He's broke his word, and I love a man that does not care for me.   80

MRS. LOVEIT.

Lord, you faint, Bellinda!

BELLINDA.

I think I shall! Such an oppression here on the sudden.

PERT.

She has eaten too much fruit, I warrant you.   85

MRS. LOVEIT.

Not unlikely.

PERT.

'Tis that lies heavy on her stomach.

MRS. LOVEIT.

Have her into my chamber, give her some surfeit-water, and let her lie down a little.

PERT.

Come, madam. I was a strange devourer of fruit when I was young—so ravenous.   90

Exeunt Bellinda and Pert, leading her off.

MRS. LOVEIT.

Oh, that my love would be but calm awhile, that I might receive this man with all the scorn and indignation he deserves!

Enter Dorimant.

DORIMANT.

Now for a touch of Sir Fopling to begin with.   95
Hey—page— Give positive order than none of my people stir—Let the canaille wait, as they should do.
—Since noise and nonsense have such pow'rful charms,
"I, that I may successful prove,
Transform myself to what you love."117   100

---

117 "I … love"] Waller, "To the Mutable Fair," 5-6 (slightly altered)

MRS. LOVEIT.

If that would do, you need not change from what you are; you can be vain and loud enough.

DORIMANT.

But not with so good a grace as Sir Fopling.—Hey, Hampshire!—Oh, that sound! That sound becomes the mouth of a man of quality.*   105

MRS. LOVEIT.

Is there a thing so hateful as a senseless mimic?

DORIMANT.

He's a great grievance, indeed, to all who, like yourself, madam, love to play the fool in quiet.

MRS. LOVEIT.

A ridiculous animal, who has more of the ape than the ape has of the man in him.   110

DORIMANT.

I have as mean an opinion of a sheer mimic as yourself, yet were he all ape, I should prefer him to the gay, the giddy, brisk, insipid, noisy fool you dote on.

MRS. LOVEIT.

Those noisy fools, however you despise 'em, have good qualities which weigh more (or ought, at   115
least) with us women than all the pernicious wit you have to boast of.

DORIMANT.

That I may hereafter have a just value for their merit, pray do me the favor to name 'em.

MRS. LOVEIT.

You'll despise 'em as the dull effects of ignorance and   120
vanity, yet I care not if I mention some. First, they really admire us, while you at best but flatter us well.

DORIMANT.

Take heed! fools can dissemble, too—

MRS. LOVEIT.

They may, but not so artificially as you—there is no fear they should deceive us. Then, they are   125
assiduous, sir. They are ever offering us their service and always waiting on our will.

DORIMANT.

You owe that to their excessive idleness. They know not how to entertain themselves at home, and find so little welcome abroad, they are fain to fly to you   130
who countenance 'em as a refuge against the solitude they would be otherwise condemned to.

MRS. LOVEIT.

Their conversation,* too, diverts us better.

DORIMANT.

Playing with your fan, smelling to your gloves, commending your hair, and taking notice how 'tis 135 cut and shaded after the new way—

MRS. LOVEIT.

Were it sillier than you can make it, you must allow 'tis pleasanter to laugh at others than to be laughed at ourselves, though never so wittily. Then, though they want* skill to flatter us, they flatter 140 themselves so well, they save us the labor. We need not take that care and pains to satisfy 'em of our love, which we so often lose on you.

DORIMANT.

They commonly, indeed, believe too well of themselves and always better of you than you 145 deserve.

MRS. LOVEIT.

You are in the right. They have an implicit faith in us, which keeps 'em from prying narrowly into our secrets and saves us the vexatious trouble of clearing doubts which your subtle and causeless 150 jealousies every moment raise.

DORIMANT.

There is an inbred falsehood in women which inclines 'em still* to them whom they may most easily deceive.

MRS. LOVEIT.

The man who loves above his quality* does not 155 suffer more from the insolent impertinence of his mistress than the woman who loves above her understanding does from the arrogant presumptions of her friend.

DORIMANT.

You mistake the use of fools: they are designed for 160 properties and not for friends. You have an indifferent stock of reputation left yet. Lose it all like a frank gamester on the square. 'Twill then be time enough to turn rook* and cheat it up again on a good, substantial bubble.* 165

MRS. LOVEIT.

The old and the ill-favored are only fit for properties, indeed, but young and handsome fools have met with kinder fortunes.

DORIMANT.

They have, to the shame of your sex be it spoken. 'Twas this, the thought of this, made me by a 170

timely jealousy endeavor to prevent the good fortune you are providing for Sir Fopling—but against a woman's frailty all our care is vain.

MRS. LOVEIT.

Had I not with a dear experience bought the knowledge of your falsehood, you might have fooled 175 me yet. This is not the first jealousy you have feigned to make a quarrel with me and get a week to throw away on some such unknown, inconsiderable slut as you have been lately lurking with at plays.

DORIMANT.

Women, when they would break off with a man, 180 never want* th'address to turn the fault on him.

MRS. LOVEIT.

You take a pride of late in using of me ill, that the Town may know the power you have over me, which now (as unreasonably as yourself) expects that I (do me all the injuries you can) must love you still. 185

DORIMANT.

I am so far from expecting that you should, I begin to think you never did love me.

MRS. LOVEIT.

Would the memory of it were so wholly worn out in me that I did doubt it too! What made you come to disturb my growing quiet? 190

DORIMANT.

To give you joy of your growing infamy.

MRS. LOVEIT.

Insupportable! Insulting devil! This from you, the only author of my shame! This from another had been but justice, but from you, 'tis a hellish and inhuman outrage. What have I done? 195

DORIMANT.

A thing that puts you below my scorn and makes my anger as ridiculous as you have made my love.

MRS. LOVEIT.

I walked last night with Sir Fopling.

DORIMANT.

You did, madam, and you talked and laughed aloud—Ha, ha, ha—Oh, that laugh, that laugh 200 becomes the confidence of a woman of quality.*

MRS. LOVEIT.

You, who have more pleasure in the ruin of a woman's reputation than in the endearments of her love, reproach me not with yourself and I defy you to name the man can lay a blemish on my fame. 205

DORIMANT.

To be seen publicly so transported with the vain
follies of that notorious fop to me is an infamy
below the sin of prostitution with another man.

MRS. LOVEIT.

Rail on! I am satisfied in the justice of what I did;
you had provoked me to't.   210

DORIMANT.

What I did was the effect of a passion whose
extravagancies you have been willing to forgive.

MRS. LOVEIT.

And what I did was the effect of a passion you may
forgive if you think fit.

DORIMANT.

Are you so indifferent grown?   215

MRS. LOVEIT.

I am.

DORIMANT.

Nay, then 'tis time to part. I'll send you back your
letters you have so often asked for. I have two or
three of 'em about me.

MRS. LOVEIT.

Give 'em me.   220

DORIMANT.

You snatch as if you thought I would not—there—
and may the perjuries in 'em be mine if e'er I see
you more. (Offers to go; she catches him.)

MRS. LOVEIT.

Stay!

DORIMANT.

I will not.   225

MRS. LOVEIT.

You shall!

DORIMANT.

What have you to say?

MRS. LOVEIT.

I cannot speak it yet.

DORIMANT.

Something more in commendation of the fool.
Death! I want* patience! Let me go.   230

MRS. LOVEIT.

I cannot. (Aside.) I can sooner part with the limbs
that hold him.—I hate that nauseous fool, you
know I do.

DORIMANT.

Was it the scandal you were fond of, then?

MRS. LOVEIT.

Y'ad raised my anger equal to my love, a thing you   235
ne'er could do before, and in revenge I did—I
know not what I did. Would you would not think
on't any more.

DORIMANT.

Should I be willing to forget it, I shall be daily
minded of it. 'Twill be a commonplace for all the   240
Town to laugh at me, and Medley, when he is
rhetorically drunk, will ever be declaiming it on
my ears.

MRS. LOVEIT.

'Twill be believed a jealous spite. Come, forget it.

DORIMANT.

Let me consult my reputation; you are too careless   245
of it. (Pauses.) You shall meet Sir Fopling in the
Mall again tonight.

MRS. LOVEIT.

What mean you?

DORIMANT.

I have thought on it, and you must. 'Tis necessary
to justify my love to the world. You can handle a   250
coxcomb as he deserves when you are not out of
humor, madam.

MRS. LOVEIT.

Public satisfaction for the wrong I have done you?
This is some new device to make me more
ridiculous!   255

DORIMANT.

Hear me!

MRS. LOVEIT.

I will not.

DORIMANT.

You will be persuaded.

MRS. LOVEIT.

Never.

DORIMANT.

Are you so obstinate?   260

MRS. LOVEIT.

Are you so base?

DORIMANT.

You will not satisfy my love?

MRS. LOVEIT.

I would die to satisfy that, but I will not, to save
you from a thousand racks, do a shameless thing
to please your vanity.   265

DORIMANT.

Farewell, false woman.

MRS. LOVEIT.

Do! Go!

DORIMANT.

You will call me back again.

MRS. LOVEIT.

Exquisite fiend! I knew you came but to torment me.   270

Enter Bellinda and Pert.

DORIMANT. (*Surprised.*)

Bellinda here!

BELLINDA. (*Aside.*)

He starts and looks pale! The sight of me has touched his guilty soul.

PERT.

'Twas but a qualm, as I said, a little indigestion. The surfeit-water did it, madam, mixed with a   275
little mirabilis.[118]

DORIMANT. [*Aside*].

I am confounded and cannot guess how she came hither!

MRS. LOVEIT.

'Tis your fortune, Bellinda, ever to be here when I am abused by this prodigy of ill nature.   280

BELLINDA.

I am amazed to find him here! How has he the face to come near you?

DORIMANT. (*Aside.*)

Here is fine work towards! I never was at such a loss before.

BELLINDA.

One who makes a public profession of breach of   285
faith and ingratitude! I loathe the sight of him.

DORIMANT. [*Aside*].

There is no remedy. I must submit to their tongues now and some other time bring myself off as well as I can.

---

118 mirabilis] *aqua mirabilis*, literally, wonderful water (Latin), a medicinal potion, "prepared of cloves, galangals, cubebs, mace, cardomums, nutmegs, ginger, and spirit of wine, digested twenty-four hours, then distilled" (Johnson's *Dictionary*)

BELLINDA.

Other men are wicked, but then they have some   290
sense of shame! He is never well but when he triumphs—nay, glories—to a woman's face in his villainies.

MRS. LOVEIT.

You are in the right, Bellinda, but methinks your kindness for me makes you concern yourself too   295
much with him.

BELLINDA.

It does indeed, my dear. His barbarous carriage to you yesterday made me hope you ne'er would see him more, and the very next day to find him here again provokes me strangely. But because I know   300
you love him, I have done.

DORIMANT.

You have reproached me handsomely, and I deserve it for coming hither, but—

PERT.

You must expect it, sir. All women will hate you for my lady's sake!   305

DORIMANT.

Nay, if she begins too, 'tis time to fly. I shall be scolded to death, else. (*Aside to Bellinda.*) I am to blame in some circumstances, I confess, but as to the main, I am not so guilty as you imagine.—I shall seek a more convenient time to clear myself.   310

MRS. LOVEIT.

Do it now! What impediments are here?

DORIMANT.

I want* time, and you want* temper.

MRS. LOVEIT.

These are weak pretenses.

DORIMANT.

You were never more mistaken in your life—and so farewell. (*Flings off.*)   315

MRS. LOVEIT.

Call a footman, Pert! Quickly! I will have him dogged.

PERT.

I wish you would not, for my quiet and your own.

MRS. LOVEIT.

I'll find out the infamous cause of all our quarrels, pluck her mask off, and expose her bare-faced to   320
the world!

BELLINDA. (*Aside.*)

Let me but escape this time, I'll never venture more.

MRS. LOVEIT.

Bellinda, you shall go with me.

BELLINDA.

I have such a heaviness hangs on me with what I did this morning, I would fain go home and sleep, my dear.

MRS. LOVEIT.

Death and eternal darkness! I shall never sleep again. Raging fevers seize the world and make mankind as restless all as I am! (*Exit.*)

BELLINDA.

I knew him false and helped to make him so. Was not her ruin enough to fright me from the danger? It should have been, but love can take no warning.

Exit.

Scene ii. Lady Townley's house.

Enter Medley, Young Bellair, Lady Townley, Emilia, and chaplain [Mr. Smirk].

MEDLEY.

Bear up, Bellair, and do not let us see that repentance in thine we daily do in married faces.

LADY TOWNLEY.

This wedding will strangely surprise my brother when he knows it.

MEDLEY.

Your nephew ought to conceal it for a time, madam. Since marriage has lost its good name, prudent men seldom expose their own reputations till 'tis convenient to justify their wives'.

OLD BELLAIR. (*Without.*)

Where are you all there? Out, adod, will nobody hear?

LADY TOWNLEY.

My brother! Quickly, Mr. Smirk, into this closet.* You must not be seen yet.

[Smirk] goes into the closet. Enter Old Bellair and Lady Townley's page.

OLD BELLAIR. [*To page.*]

Desire Mr. Fourbe to walk into the lower parlor. I will be with him presently.

[Exit Page.]

(*To Young Bellair.*) Where have you been, sir, you could not wait on me today?

YOUNG BELLAIR.

About a business.

OLD BELLAIR.

Are you so good at business? Adod, I have a business too, you shall dispatch out of hand, sir.— Send for a parson, sister. My Lady Woodvill and her daughter are coming.

LADY TOWNLEY.

What need you huddle up things thus?

OLD BELLAIR.

Out a pize! Youth is apt to play the fool, and 'tis not good it should be in their power.

LADY TOWNLEY.

You need not fear your son.

OLD BELLAIR.

He's been idling this morning, and adod, I do not like him. (*To Emilia.*) How dost thou do, sweetheart?

EMILIA.

You are very severe, sir. Married in such haste!

OLD BELLAIR.

Go to,* thou'rt a rogue, and I will talk with thee anon.

Enter Lady Woodvill, Harriet, and Busy.

Here's my Lady Woodvill come.—Welcome, madam. Mr. Fourbe's below with the writings.[119]

LADY WOODVILL.

Let us down and make an end, then.

OLD BELLAIR.

Sister, show the way. (*To Young Bellair, who is talking to Harriet.*) Harry, your business lies not there yet!—Excuse him till we have done, lady, and then, adod, he shall be for thee.—Mr. Medley, we must trouble you to be a witness.

MEDLEY.

I luckily came for that purpose, sir.

Exeunt Old Bellair, Medley, Young Bellair, Lady Townley, and Lady Woodvill.

BUSY.

What will you do, madam?

---

119 writings] the contracts and documents of the marriage settlement

HARRIET.
Be carried back and mewed up in the country again, run away here—anything rather than be married to a man I do not care for.—Dear Emilia, do thou advise me!

EMILIA.
Mr. Bellair is engaged, you know.

HARRIET.
I do, but know not what the fear of losing an estate may fright him to.

EMILIA.
In the desperate condition you are in, you should consult with some judicious man. What think you of Mr. Dorimant?

HARRIET.
I do not think of him at all.

BUSY. [Aside.]
She thinks of nothing else, I am sure—

EMILIA.
How fond your mother was of Mr. Courtage!

HARRIET.
Because I contrived the mistake to make a little mirth, you believe I like the man.

EMILIA.
Mr. Bellair believes you love him.

HARRIET.
Men are seldom in the right when they guess at a woman's mind. Would she whom he loves loved him no better!

BUSY. (Aside.)
That's e'en well enough, on all conscience.

EMILIA.
Mr. Dorimant has a great deal of wit.

HARRIET.
And takes a great deal of pains to show it.

EMILIA.
He's extremely well fashioned.

HARRIET.
Affectedly grave, or ridiculously wild and apish.

BUSY.
You defend him still* against your mother.

HARRIET.
I would not, were he justly rallied, but I cannot hear anyone undeservedly railed at.

EMILIA.
Has your woman learnt the song you were so taken with?

HARRIET.
I was fond of a new thing. 'Tis dull at second hearing.

EMILIA.
Mr. Dorimant made it.

BUSY.
She knows it, madam, and has made me sing it at least a dozen times this morning.

HARRIET.
Thy tongue is as impertinent as thy fingers.

EMILIA. [To Busy.]
You have provoked her.

BUSY.
'Tis but singing the song and I shall appease her.

EMILIA.
Prithee, do.

HARRIET.
She has a voice will grate your ears worse than a catcall and dresses so ill she's scarce fit to trick up a yeoman's daughter on a holiday.

Busy sings.

Song.[120]

As Amoret with Phillis sat
    One evening on the plain,
And saw the charming Strephon wait
    To tell the nymph his pain,

The threat'ning danger to remove,
    She whispered in her ear,
"Ah, Phillis, if you would not love,
    This shepherd do not hear.

None ever had so strange an art,
    His passion to convey
Into a list'ning virgin's heart
    And steal her soul away.

Fly, fly betimes, for fear you give
    Occasion for your fate."
"In vain," said she, "in vain I strive,
    Alas! 'tis now too late."

---

120 Song] author identified in the text as "Sir C. S.," probably Sir Car Scroope again

Enter Dorimant.

DORIMANT.

"Music so softens and disarms the mind—"

HARRIET.

"That not one arrow does resistance find."[121]

DORIMANT.

Let us make use of the lucky minute, then.   100

HARRIET. (*Aside, turning from Dorimant.*)

My love springs with my blood into my face. I dare
not look upon him yet.

DORIMANT.

What have we here, the picture of celebrated
Beauty giving audience in public to a declared
Lover?   105

HARRIET.

Play the dying Fop and make the piece complete, sir.

DORIMANT.

What think you if the hint were well improved?
The whole mystery of making love pleasantly
designed and wrought in a suite of hangings?

HARRIET.

'Twere needless to execute fools in effigy who suffer   110
daily in their own persons.

DORIMANT. (*To Emilia, aside.*)

Mrs. Bride, for such I know this happy day has
made you—

EMILIA.

Defer the formal joy you are to give me, and mind
your business with her. (*Aloud.*) Here are the   115
dreadful preparations, Mr. Dorimant—writings
sealing, and a parson sent for—

DORIMANT.

To marry this lady—

BUSY.

Condemned she is, and what will become of her I
know not, without you generously engage in a   120
rescue.

DORIMANT.

In this sad condition, madam, I can do no less
than offer you my service.

HARRIET.

The obligation is not great; you are the common

sanctuary for all young women who run from their   125
relations.

DORIMANT.

I have always my arms open to receive the
distressed. But I will open my heart and receive
you where none yet did ever enter. You have filled
it with a secret, might I but let you know it—   130

HARRIET.

Do not speak it if you would have me believe it.
Your tongue is so famed for falsehood, 'twill do the
truth an injury. (*Turns away her head.*)

DORIMANT.

Turn not away, then, but look on me and guess
it.   135

HARRIET.

Did you not tell me there was no credit to be given
to faces? That women nowadays have their passions
as much at will as they have their complexions and
put on joy and sadness, scorn and kindness with
the same ease they do their paint and patches—   140
Are they the only counterfeits?

DORIMANT.

You wrong your own while you suspect my eyes.
By all the hope I have in you, the inimitable color
in your cheeks is not more free from art than are
the sighs I offer.   145

HARRIET.

In men who have been long hardened in sin, we
have reason to mistrust the first signs of
repentance.

DORIMANT.

The prospect of such a heaven will make me
persevere and give you marks that are infallible.   150

HARRIET.

What are those?

DORIMANT.

I will renounce all the joys I have in friendship and
in wine, sacrifice to you all the interest I have in
other women—

HARRIET.

Hold! Though I wish you devout, I would not   155
have you turn fanatic. Could you neglect these a
while and make a journey into the country?

DORIMANT.

To be with you, I could live there and never send
one thought to London.

---

121 "Music ... find"] Waller, "Of my Lady Isabella, Playing on the Lute," 11-12 (slightly misquoted)

HARRIET.

Whate'er you say, I know all beyond Hyde Park's a desert to you, and that no gallantry can draw you farther.

160

DORIMANT.

That has been the utmost limit of my love—but now my passion knows no bounds, and there's no measure to be taken of what I'll do for you from anything I ever did before.

165

HARRIET.

When I hear you talk thus in Hampshire, I shall begin to think there may be some little truth enlarged upon.

DORIMANT.

Is this all? Will you not promise me—

170

HARRIET.

I hate to promise. What we do then is expected from us and wants* much of the welcome it finds when it surprises.

DORIMANT.

May I not hope?

HARRIET.

That depends on you and not on me, and 'tis to no purpose to forbid it. (*Turns to Busy.*)

175

BUSY.

Faith, madam, now I perceive the gentleman loves you, too, e'en let him know your mind and torment yourselves no longer.

HARRIET.

Dost think I have no sense of modesty?

180

BUSY.

Think, if you lose this, you may never have another opportunity.

HARRIET.

May he hate me (a curse that frights me when I speak it!) if ever I do a thing against the rules of decency and honor.

185

DORIMANT. (*To Emilia.*)

I am beholding to you for your good intentions, madam.

EMILIA.

I thought the concealing of our marriage from her might have done you better service.

DORIMANT.

Try her again.

190

EMILIA.

What have you resolved, madam? The time draws near.

HARRIET.

To be obstinate and protest against this marriage.

Enter Lady Townley in haste.

LADY TOWNLEY. (*To Emilia.*)

Quickly, quickly, let Mr. Smirk out of the closet!

Smirk comes out of the closet.

HARRIET.

A parson! Had you laid him in here?

195

DORIMANT.

I knew nothing of him.

HARRIET.

Should it appear you did, your opinion of my easiness may cost you dear.

Enter Old Bellair, Young Bellair, Medley, and Lady Woodvill.

OLD BELLAIR.

Out a pize, the canonical hour* is almost past! Sister, is the man of God come?

200

LADY TOWNLEY.

He waits your leisure.

OLD BELLAIR.

By your favor, sir.—Adod, a pretty spruce fellow! What may we call him?

LADY TOWNLEY.

Mr. Smirk, my Lady Biggot's chaplain.

OLD BELLAIR.

A wise woman, adod she is. The man will serve for the flesh as well as the spirit.—Please you, sir, to commission a young couple to go to bed together a God's name?—Harry!

205

YOUNG BELLAIR.

Here, sir—

OLD BELLAIR.

Out a pize! Without your mistress in your hand?

210

SMIRK.

Is this the gentleman?

OLD BELLAIR.

Yes, sir.

SMIRK.

Are you not mistaken, sir?

OLD BELLAIR.

Adod, I think not, sir!

SMIRK.

Sure you are, sir.   215

OLD BELLAIR.

You look as if you would forbid the banns, Mr.
Smirk. I hope you have no pretension to the lady.

SMIRK.

Wish him joy, sir! I have done him the good office
today already.

OLD BELLAIR.

Out a pize! What do I hear?   220

LADY TOWNLEY.

Never storm, brother. The truth is out.

OLD BELLAIR.

How say you, sir? Is this your wedding day?

YOUNG BELLAIR.

It is, sir.

OLD BELLAIR.

And adod, it shall be mine, too! (*To Emilia.*) Give
me thy hand, sweetheart. [*She declines to give her*   225
hand.] What dost thou mean? Give me thy hand,
I say!

Emilia kneels and Young Bellair.

LADY TOWNLEY.

Come, come, give her your blessing. This is the
woman your son loved and is married to.

OLD BELLAIR.

Hah! Cheated! Cozened! And by your contrivance,   230
sister!

LADY TOWNLEY.

What would you do with her? She's a rogue, and
you can't abide her.

MEDLEY.

Shall I hit her a pat for you, sir?

OLD BELLAIR.

Adod, you are all rogues, and I never will forgive   235
you.

LADY TOWNLEY.

Whither? Whither away?

MEDLEY.

Let him go and cool awhile.

LADY WOODVILL. (*To Dorimant.*)

Here's a business broke out now, Mr. Courtage. I
am made a fine fool of.   240

DORIMANT.

You see the old gentleman knew nothing of it.

LADY WOODVILL.

I find he did not. I shall have some trick put upon
me, if I stay in this wicked Town any longer.—
Harriet! Dear child, where art thou? I'll into the
country straight.   245

OLD BELLAIR.

Adod, madam, you shall hear me first.

Enter Mrs. Loveit and Bellinda.

MRS. LOVEIT.

Hither my man dogged him.

BELLINDA.

Yonder he stands, my dear.

MRS. LOVEIT.

I see him—(*Aside.*) and with him the face that has
undone me! Oh, that I were but where I might   250
throw out the anguish of my heart! Here it must
rage within and break it.

LADY TOWNLEY.

Mrs. Loveit! Are you afraid to come forward?

MRS. LOVEIT.

I was amazed to see so much company here in a
morning. The occasion sure is extraordinary.   255

DORIMANT. (*Aside.*)

Loveit and Bellinda! The Devil owes me a shame
today and I think never will have done paying it.

MRS. LOVEIT.

Married! Dear Emilia! How am I transported with
the news!

HARRIET. (*To Dorimant.*)

I little thought Emilia was the woman Mr. Bellair   260
was in love with. I'll chide her for not trusting me
with the secret.

DORIMANT.

How do you like Mrs. Loveit?

HARRIET.

She's a famed mistress of yours, I hear.

DORIMANT.

She has been, on occasion.   265

OLD BELLAIR. (*To Lady Woodvill.*)

Adod, madam, I cannot help it.

LADY WOODVILL.

You need make no more apologies, sir.

EMILIA. (*To Mrs. Loveit.*)

The old gentleman's excusing himself to my Lady Woodvill.

MRS. LOVEIT.

Ha, ha, ha! I never heard of anything so pleasant. 270

HARRIET. (*To Dorimant.*)

She's extremely overjoyed at something.

DORIMANT.

At nothing. She is one of those hoiting[122] ladies who gaily fling themselves about and force a laugh when their aching hearts are full of discontent and malice. 275

MRS. LOVEIT.

Oh Heaven, I was never so near killing myself with laughing.—Mr. Dorimant! are you a brideman?

LADY WOODVILL.

Mr. Dorimant! Is this Mr. Dorimant, madam?

MRS. LOVEIT.

If you doubt it, your daughter can resolve you, I suppose. 280

LADY WOODVILL.

I am cheated, too, basely cheated!

OLD BELLAIR.

Out a pize, what's here? More knavery yet?

LADY WOODVILL.

Harriet! On my blessing, come away, I charge you.

HARRIET.

Dear mother, do but stay and hear me.

LADY WOODVILL.

I am betrayed, and thou art undone, I fear. 285

HARRIET.

Do not fear it. I have not, nor never will, do anything against my duty. Believe me, dear mother, do!

DORIMANT. (*To Mrs. Loveit.*)

I had trusted you with this secret but that I knew the violence of your nature would ruin my 290 fortune—as now unluckily it has. I thank you, madam.

MRS. LOVEIT.

She's an heiress, I know, and very rich.

DORIMANT.

To satisfy you, I must give up my interest wholly to my love. Had you been a reasonable woman, I 295 might have secured 'em both and been happy.

---

122 hoiting] given to noisy and silly mirth

MRS. LOVEIT.

You might have trusted me with anything of this kind; you know you might. Why did you go under a wrong name?

DORIMANT.

The story is too long to tell you now. Be satisfied— 300 this is the business; this is the mask* has kept me from you.

BELLINDA. (*Aside.*)

He's tender of my honor, though he's cruel to my love.

MRS. LOVEIT.

Was it no idle mistress, then? 305

DORIMANT.

Believe me, a wife, to repair the ruins of my estate that needs it.

MRS. LOVEIT.

The knowledge of this makes my grief hang lighter on my soul, but I shall never more be happy.

DORIMANT.

Bellinda— 310

BELLINDA.

Do not think of clearing yourself with me. It is impossible—Do all men break their words thus?

DORIMANT.

Th'extravagant words they speak in love. 'Tis as unreasonable to expect we should perform all we promise then, as do all we threaten when we are 315 angry. When I see you next—

BELLINDA.

Take no notice of me, and I shall not hate you.

DORIMANT.

How came you to Mrs. Loveit?

BELLINDA.

By a mistake the chairmen* made for want* of my giving them directions. 320

DORIMANT.

'Twas a pleasant one. We must meet again.

BELLINDA.

Never.

DORIMANT.

Never?

BELLINDA.

When we do, may I be as infamous as you are false.

LADY TOWNLEY.

Men of Mr. Dorimant's character always suffer in 325 the general opinion of the world.

MEDLEY.

You can make no judgment of a witty man from common fame, considering the prevailing faction, madam.

OLD BELLAIR.

Adod, he's in the right. 330

MEDLEY.

Besides, 'tis a common error among women to believe too well of them they know and too ill of them they don't.

OLD BELLAIR.

Adod, he observes well.

LADY TOWNLEY.

Believe me, madam, you will find Mr. Dorimant 335 as civil a gentleman as you thought Mr. Courtage.

HARRIET.

If you would but know him better—

LADY WOODVILL.

You have a mind to know him better? Come away—You shall never see him more.

HARRIET.

Dear mother, stay! 340

LADY WOODVILL.

I wonnot be consenting to your ruin.

HARRIET.

Were my fortune in your power—

LADY WOODVILL.

Your person is.

HARRIET.

Could I be disobedient, I might take it out of yours and put it into his. 345

LADY WOODVILL.

'Tis that you would be at: you would marry this Dorimant.

HARRIET.

I cannot deny it! I would, and never will marry any other man.

LADY WOODVILL.

Is this the duty that you promised? 350

HARRIET.

But I will never marry him against your will.

LADY WOODVILL. (*Aside.*)

She knows the way to melt my heart. (*To Harriet.*) Upon yourself light your undoing.

MEDLEY. (*To Old Bellair.*)

Come sir, you have not the heart any longer to refuse your blessing. 355

OLD BELLAIR.

Adod, I ha' not.—Rise, and God bless you both. Make much of her, Harry; she deserves thy kindness.* (*To Emilia.*) Adod sirrah, I did not think it had been in thee.

Enter Sir Fopling and his page.

SIR FOPLING.

'Tis a damned windy day! Hey, page! Is my periwig 360 right?

PAGE.

A little out of order, sir.

SIR FOPLING.

Pox o'this apartment! It wants* an antechamber to adjust oneself in. (*To Mrs. Loveit.*) Madam, I came from your house, and your servants directed me 365 hither.

MRS. LOVEIT.

I will give order hereafter they shall direct you better.

SIR FOPLING.

The great satisfaction I had in the Mall last night has given me much disquiet since. 370

MRS. LOVEIT.

'Tis likely to give me more than I desire.

SIR FOPLING. [*Aside.*]

What the devil makes her so reserved?—Am I guilty of an indiscretion, madam?

MRS. LOVEIT.

You will be of a great one, if you continue your mistake, sir. 375

SIR FOPLING.

Something puts you out of humor.

MRS. LOVEIT.

The most foolish, inconsiderable thing that ever did.

SIR FOPLING.

Is it in my power?

MRS. LOVEIT.

To hang or drown it. Do one of 'em, and trouble me no more. 380

SIR FOPLING.

So *fière? Serviteur*, madam.[123]—Medley, where's Dorimant?

---

[123] So *fière? Serviteur*, madam] So haughty? Your servant, madam (Fr.)

MEDLEY.

Methinks the lady has not made you those advances today she did last night, Sir Fopling.

SIR FOPLING.

Prithee, do not talk of her.   385

MEDLEY.

She would be a *bonne fortune.*

SIR FOPLING.

Not to me at present.

MEDLEY.

How so?

SIR FOPLING.

An intrigue now would be but a temptation to me to throw away that vigor on one which I mean   390 shall shortly make my court to the whole sex in a ballet.

MEDLEY.

Wisely considered, Sir Fopling.

SIR FOPLING.

No one woman is worth the loss of a cut* in a caper.   395

MEDLEY.

Not when 'tis so universally designed.

LADY WOODVILL.

Mr. Dorimant, everyone has spoke so much in your behalf that I can no longer doubt but I was in the wrong.

MRS. LOVEIT.

There's nothing but falsehood and impertinence in   400 this world! All men are villains or fools. Take example from my misfortunes. Bellinda, if thou wouldst be happy, give thyself wholly up to goodness.

HARRIET. (*To Mrs. Loveit.*)

Mr. Dorimant has been your God almighty long   405 enough. 'Tis time to think of another.

MRS. LOVEIT.

Jeered by her! I will lock myself up in my house and never see the world again.

HARRIET.

A nunnery is the more fashionable place for such a retreat and has been the fatal consequence of   410 many a *belle passion.*

MRS. LOVEIT.

Hold, heart, till I get home! Should I answer, 'twould make her triumph greater. (*Going out.*)

DORIMANT.

Your hand, Sir Fopling—

SIR FOPLING.

Shall I wait upon you, madam?   415

MRS. LOVEIT.

Legion of fools,[124] as many devils take thee! (*Exit.*)

MEDLEY.

Dorimant, I pronounce thy reputation clear—and henceforward, when I would know anything of woman, I will consult no other oracle.

SIR FOPLING.

Stark mad, by all that's handsome!—Dorimant,   420 thou hast engaged me in a pretty business.

DORIMANT.

I have not leisure now to talk about it.

OLD BELLAIR.

Out a pize, what does this man of mode do here again?

LADY TOWNLEY.

He'll be an excellent entertainment within, brother,   425 and is luckily come to raise the mirth of the company.

LADY WOODVILL.

Madam, I take my leave of you.

LADY TOWNLEY.

What do you mean, madam?

LADY WOODVILL.

To go this afternoon part of my way to   430 Hartly—[125]

OLD BELLAIR.

Adod, you shall stay and dine first! Come, we will all be good friends, and you shall give Mr. Dorimant leave to wait upon you and your daughter in the country.   435

LADY WOODVILL.

If his occasions bring him that way, I have now so good an opinion of him, he shall be welcome.

HARRIET.

To a great, rambling, lone house that looks as it were not inhabited, the family's* so small. There

---

124 legion] a multitude, with an allusion to the devils exorcised by Jesus in Mark 5:9: "My name is Legion: for we are many."

125 Hartly] "Hartley Row, Hampshire, about half-way between London and Salisbury" (NCS)

you'll find my mother, an old lame aunt, and 440
myself, sir, perched up on chairs at a distance in a
large parlor, sitting moping like three or four
melancholy birds in a spacious volary—[126] Does
not this stagger your resolution?

DORIMANT.

Not at all, madam! The first time I saw you, you 445
left me with the pangs of love upon me, and this
day my soul has quite given up her liberty.

HARRIET.

This is more dismal than the country!—Emilia,
pity me, who am going to that sad place. Methinks
I hear the hateful noise of rooks already—kaw, 450
kaw, kaw!—There's music in the worst cry in
London: "My dill and cucumbers to pickle."

OLD BELLAIR.

Sister, knowing of this matter, I hope you have
provided us some good cheer.

LADY TOWNLEY.

I have, brother, and the fiddles too— 455

OLD BELLAIR.

Let 'em strike up, then. The young lady shall have
a dance before she departs.

Dance.

(*After the dance.*) So now we'll in, and make this
an arrant wedding day. (*To the pit.**)
And if these honest gentlemen rejoice, 460
Adod, the boy has made a happy choice.

Exeunt omnes.

EPILOGUE[127]

Most modern wits such monstrous fools have
   shown,
They seemed not of Heav'n's making, but their
   own.
Those nauseous harlequins in farce may pass,
But there goes more to a substantial ass!
Something of man must be exposed to view, 5
That, gallants, they may more resemble you.
Sir Fopling is a fool so nicely* writ,

---

126 volary] a large bird-cage or aviary
127 Epilogue] written by Dryden, spoken by William
   Smith, who played Sir Fopling

The ladies would mistake him for a wit
And (when he sings, talks loud, and cocks) would
   cry:
"I vow, methinks he's pretty company— 10
So brisk, so gay, so traveled, so refined,
As he took pains to graft upon his kind."[128]
True fops help Nature's work, and go to school
To file and finish God a'mighty's fool.
Yet none Sir Fopling him, or him, can call; 15
He's knight o'th'shire[129] and represents ye all.
From each he meets, he culls whate'er he can;
Legion's his name, a people in a man.
His bulky folly gathers as it goes,
And, rolling o'er you, like a snowball grows. 20
His various modes from various fathers follow:
One taught the toss,[130] and one the new French
   wallow.[131]
His sword-knot,[132] this; his cravat, this designed;
And this, the yard-long snake[133] he twirls behind.
From one, the sacred periwig he gained, 25
Which wind ne'er blew, nor touch of hat
   profaned;
Another's diving bow he did adore,
Which with a shog[134] casts all the hair before,
Till he with full decorum brings it back
And rises with a water spaniel shake. 30
As for his songs (the ladies' dear delight),
Those sure he took from most of you who write.
Yet every man is safe from what he feared,
For no one fool is hunted from the herd.

FINIS.

---

128 graft upon his kind] to improve his natural qualities
129 knight o'th'shire] local representative in Parliament
130 toss] toss of the head
131 wallow] rolling walk or gait
132 sword-knot] a ribbon or tassel tied to the hilt of a sword
   for ornament
133 snake] a long curl or tail attached to a wig
134 shog] shake, jerk

ᵃ Copytext is the first edition, the 1676 quarto (Q1), incorporating stop-press corrections. Also consulted were the 1684 quarto edition (Q2) and the modern editions of 1888 (Verity); 1927 (Brett-Smith); 1939, revised 1969 (Nettleton, Case, and Stone—NCS); 1953 (Harris); 1959 (Wilson); 1966 (Carnochan); 1973 (Conaghan); 1979 (Barnard); 1982 (Cordner); and 1994 (Lawrence). For readings in the posthumous early editions, including the 1693 quarto edition (Q3), the 1704 *Works of Sir George Etherege* (W), the 1711 *Collection of the Best English Plays* (CBEP), and the 1711 octavo edition (O), I have used the tables of variants printed in some of the modern editions listed above.

ᵇ with her head] W, Verity, Brett-Smith, NCS, Wilson, Carnochan, Barnard, Lawrence; with head Q1, Q2, Q3, Harris, Conaghan, Cordner

ᶜ which] In Q1, printed as the catchword at the bottom of p. 32 but not in the text. In Q2, Q3, W, Verity, and Lawrence it is added to the succeeding line. Except for Lawrence, editors since Brett-Smith have printed the word as Harriet's link between the two lines, as here.

ᵈ you to what] W, Verity, Brett-Smith, NCS, Harris, Wilson, Carnochan, Conaghan, Barnard, Cordner, Lawrence; you what Q1, Q2, Q3

ᵉ *to an English dancer* (s.d.)] Conaghan, Barnard; *om.* Q1 (uncorrected); to an English dancer (text) Q1 (corrected), Q2, Verity, Brett-Smith, NCS, Harris, Wilson, Carnochan, Cordner, Lawrence

ᶠ will] CBEP, Verity, Brett-Smith, NCS, Harris, Wilson, Carnochan, Barnard, Lawrence; well Q1, Q2, Q3, W, O, Conaghan, Cordner

The Rover; or, The Banished Cavaliers[a]

by Aphra Behn (1640?-1689)

edited by Anne Russell

Almost nothing is known with certainty of Aphra Behn's early life. From 1671 until her death in 1689, Behn earned her living as a prolific playwright, translator, editor, poet, and novelist. Behn's plays were a significant part of the theatrical repertoire until the middle of the eighteenth century.

The Rover, or The Banish'd Cavaliers (1677) was one of Behn's most popular plays. Like many of her contemporaries, Behn adapted an earlier play, Thomas Killigrew's *Thomaso, or The Wanderer*. In *The Rover*, Behn examines contemporary issues such as forced marriage and double sexual standards with particular focus on the perspectives of women characters. The complex plot, relying on disguise and mistaken identity, includes many parallels of character and situation. The virginal sisters Hellena and Florinda complain that their brother has arranged Florinda's marriage to an old man and Hellena's admission to a nunnery. In another plot the courtesan Angellica Bianca argues that wives and prostitutes are treated similarly as commodities. Her thoughtful analysis points to a recurring plot motif— the male characters' difficulty in distinguishing "a maid of quality" from a "harlot."

The Rover is set during the Commonwealth, when Parliament under Oliver Cromwell ruled England and many of the supporters of the monarchy lived in exile; it was performed, however, after the restoration of the monarchy. The Rover of the title, the aptly named Willmore, is a rake and libertine. He and other "Banish'd Cavaliers" arrive in Naples during carnival, eager to take advantage of the sexual opportunities allowed by the temporary freedom of masks and disguises. In a long scene, Willmore and Angellica Bianca debate the relations between love and money. Succumbing to Willmore's argument that love ought to be given rather than sold, she gives her love and her money to Willmore, who immediately shifts his attention to the pursuit of the witty Hellena, who is in carnival disguise.

Other characters include Willmore's friend Belvile, who is in love with Florinda. Blunt, a dim-witted comic butt during most of the play, is attracted to a prostitute he thinks to be a young wife; however, she and her pimp rob and humiliate him. Blunt's desire to take revenge by beating and raping other women endangers Florinda, and also moves the many plots towards closure.

As this brief summary suggests, there are many inconsistencies of tone in this comedy. The plot includes duels, robberies, and rape attempts; many characters make casual anti-semitic and anti-catholic slurs. Women characters complain about their subjection to male control, yet seem indulgently tolerant of the men who threaten them. Sexual double standards are criticized in the early parts of the play but deflected in the conclusion. The eloquent Angellica Bianca is silenced; Willmore, the proselytizer of free love, accepts marriage (which conveniently comes with Hellena's fortune); and the attempted rapes by Willmore, Blunt and others are instantly forgiven and forgotten.

Critics are divided on how to interpret the conventional round of marriages and forgiveness with which *The Rover* ends. Does the conclusion portray imperfect, but pragmatic, strategies needed for survival in a violent and ruthless society? Or do the final scenes endorse a return to the socio-economic order, socializing the great sexual energy of its lead character? Behn did not let the question settle. The character of Willmore was so popular that she wrote a sequel in 1681. As it opens, Willmore offhandedly notes that Hellena has died and that he has spent her money. He then proceeds to pursue free love, as he had done in *The Rover*.

DRAMATIS PERSONAE

[MEN]

Don Antonio, the Viceroy's son.

Don Pedro, a noble Spaniard, his friend.

Belvile, an English colonel in love with
    Florinda.

Willmore, the Rover.[1]

Frederick, an English gentleman and friend to
    Belvile and Blunt.[b]

Blunt, an English country gentleman.

Stephano, servant to Don Pedro.

Phillippo, Lucetta's gallant.

Sancho, pimp to Lucetta.

Biskey, and Sebastian, two bravoes[2] to
    Angellica.

Officers and Soldiers.

[Diego,] Page to Don Antonio.

Boy.

WOMEN.

Florinda, sister to Don Pedro.

Hellena, a gay young woman designed for a
    nun, and sister to Florinda.

Valeria, a kinswoman to Florinda.

Angellica Bianca, a famous courtesan.

Moretta, her woman.

Callis, governess to Florinda and Hellena.

Lucetta, a jilting wench.

Servants, other masqueraders, men and women.

THE SCENE: NAPLES, IN CARNIVAL TIME.

The Rover; or, The Banished Cavaliers.[3]

Act I, scene i. A chamber.

Enter Florinda and Hellena.

FLORINDA.

What an impertinent thing is a young girl bred in
a nunnery! How full of questions! Prithee no more
Hellena; I have told thee more than thou
understand'st already.

---

1 Rover] wanderer; also pirate

2 bravoes] hired soldiers; bodyguards

3 *Cavaliers*] Supporters of the English monarchy during
the English Civil War; many cavaliers left England after the execution of King Charles I in 1649.

HELLENA.

The more's my grief. I would fain know as much   5
as you, which makes me so inquisitive; nor is't
enough I know you're a lover, unless you tell me
too, who 'tis you sigh for.

FLORINDA.

When you're a lover, I'll think you fit for a secret
of that nature.   10

HELLENA.

'Tis true, I never was a lover yet, but I begin to
have a shrewd guess what it is to be so and fancy
it very pretty to sigh, and sing, and blush, and
wish, and dream, and wish, and long and wish to
see the man, and when I do, look pale and tremble;   15
just as you did when my brother brought home
the fine English colonel to see you. What do you
call him, Don Belvile?

FLORINDA.

Fie, Hellena.

HELLENA.

That blush betrays you. I am sure 'tis so—or is it   20
Don Antonio the viceroy's son? or perhaps the rich
old Don Vincentio whom my father designs you
for a husband? Why do you blush again?

FLORINDA.

With indignation, and how near soever my father
thinks I am to marrying that hated object, I shall   25
let him see I understand better what's due to my
beauty, birth and fortune, and more to my soul,
than to obey those unjust commands.

HELLENA.

Now hang me if I don't love thee for that dear
disobedience. I love mischief strangely, as most of   30
our sex do, who are come to love nothing else. But
tell me dear Florinda, don't you love that fine
Anglese?[4] For I vow, next to loving him myself,
'twill please me most that you do so, for he is so
gay and so handsome.   35

FLORINDA.

Hellena, a maid designed for a nun ought not to
be so curious in a discourse of love.

HELLENA.

And dost thou think that ever I'll be a nun? or at
least till I'm so old, I'm fit for nothing else? Faith

---

4 *Anglese*] Englishman (It.)

no, sister. And that which makes me long to know 40
whether you love Belvile is because I hope he has
some mad companion or other that will spoil my
devotion. Nay, I'm resolved to provide myself this
carnival, if there be e'er a handsome proper fellow
of my humor* above ground, though I ask first. 45

FLORINDA.

Prithee, be not so wild.

HELLENA.

Now you have provided yourself of a man, you take
no care for poor me. Prithee, tell me, what dost thou
see about me that is unfit for love? Have I not a
world of youth? a humor* gay? a beauty passable? a 50
vigor desirable? well shaped? clean limbed? sweet
breathed? and sense enough to know how all these
ought to be employed to the best advantage? Yes, I
do and will; therefore, lay aside your hopes of my
fortune by my being a devote,[5] and tell me how you 55
came acquainted with this Belvile, for I perceive you
knew him before he came to Naples.

FLORINDA.

Yes, I knew him at the siege of Pamplona.[6] He was
then a colonel of French horse, who when the
town was ransacked, nobly treated my brother and 60
myself, preserving us from all insolences, and I
must own (besides great obligations) I have I know
not what that pleads kindly for him about my
heart, and will suffer no other to enter.—But see,
my brother. 65

*Enter Don Pedro, Stephano with a masquing habit,[7]
and Callis.*

PEDRO.

Good morrow, sister. Pray, when saw you your
lover Don Vincentio?

FLORINDA.

I know not, sir. Callis, when was he here? For I
consider it so little, I know not when it was.

PEDRO.

I have a command from my father here to tell you, 70
you ought not to despise him, a man of so vast a

fortune, and such a passion for you.—Stephano,
my things.

Puts on his masquing habit.

FLORINDA.

A passion for me, 'tis more than e'er I saw, or he
had a desire should be known. I hate Vincentio, 75
sir, and I would not have a man so dear to me as
my brother follow the ill customs of our country
and make a slave of his sister. And sir, my father's
will I'm sure you may divert.

PEDRO.

I know not how dear I am to you, but I wish only 80
to be ranked in your esteem equal with the English
Colonel Belvile. Why do you frown and blush? Is
there any guilt belongs to the name of that cavalier?

FLORINDA.

I'll not deny I value Belvile. When I was exposed
to such dangers as the licensed lust of common 85
soldiers threatened, when rage and conquest flew
through the city, then Belvile, this criminal for my
sake, threw himself into all dangers to save my
honor. And will you not allow him my esteem?

PEDRO.

Yes, pay him what you will in honor, but you must 90
consider Don Vincentio's fortune and the jointure
he'll make you.

FLORINDA.

Let him consider my youth, beauty and fortune,
which ought not to be thrown away on his age and
jointure. 95

PEDRO.

'Tis true, he's not so young and fine a gentleman
as that Belvile, but what jewels will that cavalier
present you with? those of his eyes and heart?

HELLENA.

And are not those better than any Don Vincentio
has brought from the Indies? 100

PEDRO.

Why, how now! Has your nunnery breeding taught
you to understand the value of hearts and eyes?

HELLENA.

Better than to believe Vincentio's deserve value
from any woman. He may perhaps increase her
bags,[8] but not her family. 105

---

5 devote] a nun or religious person, devotee
6 Pamplona] a fortified town in Navarre in the north of
Spain, disputed by France
7 *masquing habit*] costume worn at carnival

8 bags] wealth

PEDRO.

This is fine. Go—up to your devotion; you are not designed for the conversation* of lovers.

HELLENA. (*Aside.*)

Nor saints yet a while, I hope. Is't not enough you make a nun of me, but you must cast my sister away too, exposing her to a worse confinement ₁₁₀ than a religious life?

PEDRO.

The girl's mad! It is a confinement to be carried into the country, to an ancient villa belonging to the family of the Vincentios these five hundred years, and have no other prospect than that ₁₁₅ pleasing one of seeing all her own that meets her eyes—a fine air, large fields and gardens, where she may walk and gather flowers.

HELLENA.

When, by moonlight? For I am sure she dares not encounter with the heat of the sun; that were a task ₁₂₀ only for Don Vincentio and his Indian breeding,[9] who loves it in the dog days. And if these be her daily divertissements, what are those of the night, to lie in a wide moth-eaten bed chamber, with furniture in fashion in the reign of King Sancho ₁₂₅ the First;[10] the bed, that which his forefathers lived and died in.

PEDRO.

Very well.

HELLENA.

This apartment (new furbished and fitted out for the young wife) he (out of freedom) makes his ₁₃₀ dressing room, and being a frugal and jealous coxcomb, instead of a valet to uncase his feeble carcass, he desires you to do that office—signs of favor I'll assure you, and such as you must not hope for, unless your woman be out of the way. ₁₃₅

PEDRO.

Have you done yet?

HELLENA.

That honor being past, the giant stretches itself, yawns and sighs a belch or two, loud as a musket, throws himself into bed, and expects you in his foul sheets, and ere you can get yourself undressed, ₁₄₀ calls you with a snore or two. And are not these fine blessings to a young lady?

PEDRO.

Have you done yet?

HELLENA.

And this man you must kiss, nay you must kiss none but him, too, and nuzzle through his beard ₁₄₅ to find his lips. And this you must submit to for threescore years, and all for a jointure.

PEDRO.

For all your character* of Don Vincentio, she is as like to marry him as she was before.

HELLENA.

Marry Don Vincentio! Hang me, such a wedlock ₁₅₀ would be worse than adultery with another man. I had rather see her in the Hotel de Dieu,[11] to waste her youth there in vows and be a handmaid to lazars and cripples, than to lose it in such a marriage.

PEDRO.

You have considered, sister, that Belvile has no ₁₅₅ fortune to bring you to—banished his country, despised at home, and pitied abroad.

HELLENA.

What then? The viceroy's son is better than that old Sir Fifty. Don Vincentio! Don Indian! He thinks he's trading to Gambo[12] still and would ₁₆₀ barter himself (that bell and bauble[13]) for your youth and fortune.

PEDRO.

Callis, take her hence, and lock her up all this Carnival, and at Lent she shall begin her everlasting penance in a monastery. ₁₆₅

HELLENA.

I care not; I had rather be a nun than be obliged to marry as you would have me, if I were designed for't.

PEDRO.

Do not fear the blessing of that choice. You shall be a nun. ₁₇₀

---

9 Indian breeding] presumably Don Vincentio was raised in the Indies

10 King Sancho the First] a king from long ago

11 Hotel de Dieu] hospital run by nuns for the care of the destitute and outcast

12 Gambo] Gambia, on the Slave Coast of Africa

13 bell and bauble] trifles, but also the signs of a professional fool

HELLENA.

Shall I so? You may chance to be mistaken in my way of devotion. A nun! Yes, I am like to make a fine nun! I have an excellent humor* for a grate.[14] (*Aside.*) No, I'll have a saint of my own to pray to shortly, if I like any that dares venture on me. 175

PEDRO.

Callis, make it your business to watch this wild cat. As for you, Florinda, I've only tried you all this while and urged my father's will; but mine is that you would love Antonio. He is brave and young, and all that can complete the happiness of a gallant 180 maid. This absence of my father will give us opportunity to free you from Vincentio by marrying here, which you must do tomorrow.

FLORINDA.

Tomorrow!

PEDRO.

Tomorrow, or 'twill be too late. 'Tis not my 185 friendship to Antonio which makes me urge this, but love to thee and hatred to Vincentio. Therefore, resolve upon tomorrow.

FLORINDA.

Sir, I shall strive to do as shall become your sister.

PEDRO.

I'll both believe and trust you. Adieu. 190

Exeunt Pedro and Stephano.

HELLENA.

As becomes his sister! That is to be as resolved your way, as he is his—(*Hellena goes to Callis.*)

FLORINDA.

I ne'er till now perceived my ruin near.
I've no defense against Antonio's love,
For he has all the advantages of nature, 195
The moving arguments of youth and fortune.

HELLENA.

But hark you, Callis, you will not be so cruel to lock me up indeed, will you?

CALLIS.

I must obey the commands I have. Besides, do you consider what a life you are going to lead? 200

HELLENA.

Yes, Callis, that of a nun; and till then I'll be

---

14 grate] bars in the door of a convent, marking the separation of the nun from the world

indebted a world of prayers to you if you'll let me now see what I never did, the divertissements of a carnival.

CALLIS.

What, go in masquerade? 'Twill be a fine farewell 205 to the world, I take it. Pray, what would you do there?

HELLENA.

That which all the world does, as I am told: be as mad as the rest and take all innocent freedoms. Sister, you'll go too, will you not? Come, prithee 210 be not sad. We'll outwit twenty brothers if you'll be ruled by me. Come, put off this dull humor* with your clothes and assume one as gay and as fantastic, as the dress my cousin Valeria and I have provided, and let's ramble. 215

FLORINDA.

Callis, will you give us leave to go?

CALLIS. (*Aside.*)

I have a youthful itch of going myself.—Madam, if I thought your brother might not know it, and I might wait on you; for by my troth I'll not trust young girls alone. 220

FLORINDA.

Thou seest my brother's gone already, and thou shalt attend and watch us.

Enter Stephano.

STEPHANO.

Madam, the habits are come, and your cousin Valeria is dressed and stays for you.

FLORINDA.

'Tis well. I'll write a note, and if I chance to see Belvile 225 and want an opportunity to speak to him, that shall let him know what I've resolved in favor of him.

HELLENA.

Come, let's in and dress us.

Exeunt.

Scene ii. A long street.

Enter Belvile melancholy, Blunt and Frederick.

FREDERICK.

Why, what the devil ails the colonel? In a time when all the world is gay, to look like mere* Lent thus? Had'st thou been long enough in Naples to have been in love, I should have sworn some such judgment had befallen thee.

BELVILE.

No, I have made no new amours since I came to Naples.

FREDERICK.

You have left none behind you in Paris?

BELVILE.

Neither.

FREDERICK.

I cannot divine the cause, then, unless the old cause, the want of money.

BLUNT.

And another old cause, the want of a wench. Would not that revive you?

BELVILE.

You are mistaken, Ned.

BLUNT.

Nay, 'sheartlikins,[15] then thou'rt past cure.

FREDERICK.

I have found it out; thou hast renewed thy acquaintance with the lady that cost thee so many sighs at the siege of Pamplona—pox on't, what d'ye call her—her brother's a noble Spaniard—nephew to the dead general—Florinda—ay Florinda—and will nothing serve thy turn but that damned virtuous woman? whom on my conscience thou lovest in spite too, because thou seest little or no possibility of gaining her.

BELVILE.

Thou art mistaken. I have int'rest enough in that lovely virgin's heart to make me proud and vain, were it not abated by the severity of a brother, who perceiving my happiness—

FREDERICK.

Has civilly forbid thee the house?

BELVILE.

'Tis so; to make way for a powerful rival, the viceroy's son, who has the advantage of me in being a man of fortune, a Spaniard, and her brother's friend; which gives him liberty to make his court, whilst I have recourse only to letters and distant looks from her window, which are as soft and kind as those which Heaven sends down on penitents.

BLUNT.

Heyday! 'Sheartlikins, simile! By this light, the man is quite spoiled. Fred, what the devil are we made of that we cannot be thus concerned for a wench? 'Sheartlikins, our cupids are like the cooks of the camp, they can roast or boil a woman, but they have none of the fine tricks to set 'em off, no hogoes* to make the sauce pleasant and the stomach sharp.

FREDERICK.

I dare swear I have had a hundred as young, kind and handsome as this Florinda, and dogs eat me, if they were not as troublesome to me i'the morning as they were welcome o'er night.

BLUNT.

And yet I warrant he would not touch another woman if he might have her for nothing.

BELVILE.

That's thy joy, a cheap whore.

BLUNT.

Why, ay, 'sheartlikins, I love a frank soul. When did you ever hear of an honest woman that took a man's money? I warrant 'em good ones. But gentlemen, you may be free, you have been kept so poor with Parliaments and Protectors,[16] that the little stock you have is not worth preserving. But I thank my stars, I had more grace than to forfeit my estate by cavaliering.[17]

BELVILE.

Methinks only following the Court[18] should be sufficient to entitle 'em to that.

BLUNT.

'Sheartlikins, they know I follow it to do it no good, unless they pick a hole in my coat for

---

15 'sheartlikins] God's little heart; a "minced oath" combining "God's heart" and "bodikin." Also "heartikin," "adsheartlikins."

16 Protectors] During the period of Parliamentary rule, Oliver Cromwell used the title of Protector of England.

17 cavaliering] During the protectorate, cavaliers who left England could have their estates confiscated. Blunt boasts that he has managed to travel overseas without identifying himself, or being identified, as a cavalier, and hence is not liable to lose his property. There is the connotation that Blunt refused to fight as well.

18 Court] retinue of the exiled Charles II

lending you money now and then, which is a greater crime to my conscience, gentlemen, than to the Commonwealth.[19]

Enter Willmore.

WILLMORE.
Hah! Dear Belvile! Noble colonel!

BELVILE.
Willmore! Welcome ashore, my dear rover! What happy wind blew us this good fortune?

WILLMORE.
Let me salute* my dear Frederick and then command me. How is't, honest lad?

FREDERICK.
Faith, sir, the old compliment, infinitely the better to see my dear mad Willmore again. Prithee, why camest thou ashore? And where's the Prince?[20]

WILLMORE.
He's well, and reigns still lord of the watery element. I must aboard again within a day or two, and my business ashore was only to enjoy myself a little this carnival.

BELVILE.
Pray, know our new friend, sir; he's but bashful, a raw traveller, but honest, stout and one of us.

WILLMORE. (*Embraces Blunt.*)
That you esteem him gives him an int'rest here.

BLUNT.
Your servant, sir.

WILLMORE.
But well—faith, I'm glad to meet you again in a warm climate, where the kind sun has its god-like power still over the wine and women. Love and mirth are my business in Naples, and if I mistake not the place, here's an excellent market for chapmen of my humor*.

BELVILE.
See, here be those kind merchants of love you look for.

Enter several men in masquing habits, some playing on music, others dancing after; women dressed like courtesans, with papers pinned on their breasts, and baskets of flowers in their hands.

BLUNT.
'Sheartlikins, what have we here?

FREDERICK.
Now the game begins.

WILLMORE.
Fine pretty creatures! May a stranger have leave to look and love? What's here? (*Reads the papers.*) "Roses for every month"?

BLUNT.
Roses for every month? What means that?

BELVILE.
They are, or would have you think, they're courtesans, who here in Naples, are to be hired by the month.

WILLMORE.
Kind and obliging to inform us. Pray, where do these roses grow? I would fain plant some of 'em in a bed of mine.

WOMEN.
Beware such roses, sir.

WILLMORE.
A pox of fear: I'll be baked with thee between a pair of sheets, and that's thy proper still;[21] so I might but strew such roses over me, and under me.—Fair one, would you would give me leave to gather at your bush this idle month; I would go near to make some body smell of it all the year after.

BELVILE.
And thou hast need of such a remedy, for thou stink'st of tar and rope's ends, like a dock or pest-house.[22]

The woman puts herself into the hands of a man and exeunt.

WILLMORE.
Nay, nay, you shall not leave me so.

BELVILE.
By all means use no violence here.

---

19 Commonwealth] name for England during Parliamentary rule
20 Prince] Charles II

21 baked ... still] Willmore's double entendre refers to the process by which rose petals are distilled to make rosewater.
22 pest-house] hospital for plague victims

WILLMORE.

Death! Just as I was going to be damnably in love, 115
to have her led off! I could pluck that rose out of
his hand, and even kiss the bed the bush grew in.

FREDERICK.

No friend to love like a long voyage at sea.

BLUNT.

Except a nunnery, Frederick.

WILLMORE.

Death! But will they not be kind? quickly be kind? 120
Thou know'st I'm no tame fighter, but a rampant
lion of the forest.

*Advance from the farther end of the scenes two men
dressed all over with horns* of several sorts, making
grimaces at one another, with papers pinned on their
backs.*

BELVILE.

Oh the fantastical rogues, how they're dressed! 'Tis
a satire against the whole sex.

WILLMORE.

Is this a fruit that grows in this warm country? 125

BELVILE.

Yes, 'tis pretty to see these Italians start, swell and
stab at the word "cuckold," and yet stumble at
horns on every threshold.

WILLMORE.

See what's on their back. (*Reads.*) "Flowers of every
night." Ah, rogue! and more sweet than roses of 130
every month! This is a gardener of Adam's own
breeding.

They dance.

BELVILE.

What think you of those grave people? Is a wake
in Essex half so mad or extravagant?

WILLMORE.

I like their sober grave way; 'tis a kind of legal author- 135
ized fornication, where the men are not chid for't, nor
the women despised, as amongst our dull English
even the monsieurs want that part of good manners.

BELVILE.

But here in Italy a monsieur is the humblest, best-
bred gentleman; duels are so baffled by bravoes, that 140
an age shows not one but between a Frenchman and
a hangman, who is as much too hard for him on the
piazza, as they are for a Dutchman on the New
Bridge.[23]—But see, another crew.

*Enter Florinda, Hellena and Valeria, dressed like
gypsies; Callis and Stephano; Lucetta, Phillipo and
Sancho in masquerade.*

HELLENA.

Sister, there's your Englishman, and with him a 145
handsome proper fellow. I'll to him, and instead
of telling him his fortune, try my own.

WILLMORE.

Gypsies, on my life. Sure these will prattle if a man
cross their hands.[24] (*Goes to Hellena.*) Dear, pretty
(and I hope) young devil, will you tell an amorous 150
stranger what luck he's like to have?

HELLENA.

Have a care how you venture with me, sir, lest I pick
your pocket, which will more vex your English
humor* than an Italian fortune will please you.

WILLMORE.

How the devil cam'st thou to know my country 155
and humor*?

HELLENA.

The first I guess by a certain forward impudence,
which does not displease me at this time; and the
loss of your money will vex you because I hope you
have but very little to lose. 160

WILLMORE.

Egad, child, thou'rt i'th' right; it is so little, I dare
not offer it thee for a kindness. But cannot you
divine what other things of more value I have
about me, that I would more willingly part with?

HELLENA.

Indeed no, that's the business of a witch, and I am 165
but a Gypsy yet. Yet without looking in your hand,
I have a parlous guess 'tis some foolish heart you
mean, an inconstant English heart, as little worth
stealing as your purse.

WILLMORE.

Nay, then thou dost deal with the devil, that's 170

---

23 Dutchman on the New Bridge] an anachronistic reference to the French defeat of the Dutch at Niuewerbrug
in 1673.

24 cross their hands] with silver, as payment for telling a
fortune

certain. Thou hast guessed as right as if thou had'st
been one of that number it has languished for. I
find you'll be better acquainted with it, nor can
you take it in a better time; for I am come from
the sea, child, and Venus not being propitious to 175
me in her own element,[25] I have a world of love
in store. Would you would be good-natured and
take some on't off my hands.

HELLENA.

Why, I could be inclined that way, but for a foolish
vow I am going to make—to die a maid. 180

WILLMORE.

Then thou art damned without redemption, and
as I am a good Christian, I ought in charity to
divert so wicked a design; therefore prithee, dear
creature, let me know quickly when and where I
shall begin to set a helping hand to so good a work. 185

HELLENA.

If you should prevail with my tender heart (as I
begin to fear you will, for you have horrible loving
eyes), there will be difficulty in't, that you'll hardly
undergo for my sake.

WILLMORE.

Faith, child, I have been bred in dangers and wear a 190
sword that has been employed in a worse cause than
for a handsome kind woman. Name the danger. Let
it be anything but a long siege, and I'll undertake it.

HELLENA.

Can you storm?

WILLMORE.

Oh most furiously. 195

HELLENA.

What think you of a nunnery wall? For he that
wins me must gain that first.

WILLMORE.

A nun! Oh how I love thee for't! There's no sinner
like a young saint. Nay, now there's no denying
me, the old law[26] had no curse (to a woman) like 200
dying a maid; witness Jepthah's daughter.[27]

---

25 Venus ... element] Venus, goddess of love, emerged from
the sea.

26 old law] Old Testament law

27 Jephthah's daughter] Jephthah delayed the sacrifice of his
virginal daughter for two months while she "bewailed
her virginity"; see Judges 11: 30-40.

HELLENA.

A very good text this, if well handled, and I
perceive, Father Captain, you would impose no
severe penance on her who were inclined to
console herself, before she took orders. 205

WILLMORE.

If she be young and handsome.

HELLENA.

Ay, there's it. But if she be not—

WILLMORE.

By this hand, child, I have an implicit faith, and
dare venture on thee with all faults. Besides, 'tis
more meritorious to leave the world when thou 210
hast tasted and proved the pleasure on't. Then,
'twill be a virtue in thee, which now will be pure
ignorance.

HELLENA.

I perceive, good Father Captain, you design only
to make me fit for heaven, but if on the contrary, 215
you should quite divert me from it and bring me
back to the world again, I should have a new man
to seek, I find; and what a grief that will be, for
when I begin, I fancy I shall love like anything. I
never tried yet. 220

WILLMORE.

Egad and that's kind.—Prithee, dear creature, give
me credit for a heart, for faith, I'm a very honest
fellow. Oh, I long to come first to the banquet of
love! And such a swingeing appetite I bring—oh,
I'm impatient—thy lodging, sweetheart, thy 225
lodging, or I'm a dead man!

HELLENA.

Why must we be either guilty of fornication or
murder if we converse with you men? And is there
no difference between leave to love me, and leave
to lie with me? 230

WILLMORE.

Faith, child, they were made to go together.

LUCETTA.

Are you sure this is the man? (*Pointing to Blunt.*)

SANCHO.

When did I mistake your game?

LUCETTA.

This is a stranger, I know by his gazing; if he be
brisk, he'll venture to follow me, and then, if I 235
understand my trade, he's mine. He's English too,

and they say that's a sort of good-natured loving people, and have generally so kind an opinion of themselves, that a woman of any wit may flatter 'em into any sort of fool she pleases.   240

She often passes by Blunt and gazes on him; he struts and cocks, and walks and gazes on her.

BLUNT. [*Aside.*]

'Tis so. She is taken. I have beauties which my false glass* at home did not discover.

FLORINDA. [*Aside.*]

This woman watches me so, I shall get no opportunity to discover myself to him and so miss the intent of my coming.—But as I was saying, sir   245 (*Looking in his hand.*), by this line you should be a lover.

BELVILE.

I thought how right you guessed, all men are in love, or pretend to be so. Come, let me go, I'm weary of this fooling.   250

[*He] walks away. She holds him, he strives to get from her.*

FLORINDA.

I will not, till you have confessed whether the passion that you have vowed Florinda be true or false.

BELVILE. (*Turns quick towards her.*)

Florinda!

FLORINDA.

Softly.   255

BELVILE.

Thou hast named one will fix me here for ever.

FLORINDA.

She'll be disappointed, then, who expects you this night at the garden gate, and if you fail not, as— let me see the other hand—you will go near to do, she vows to die or make you happy. (*Looks on   260 Callis, who observes 'em.*)

BELVILE.

What canst thou mean?

FLORINDA.

That which I say. Farewell. (*Offers to go.*)

BELVILE.

Oh charming sibyl, stay, complete that joy which as it is will turn into distraction! Where must I be?   265

At the garden gate? I know it. At night you say? I'll sooner forfeit heaven than disobey.

Enter Don Pedro and other masquers, and pass over the stage.

CALLIS.

Madam, your brother's here.

FLORINDA.

Take this to instruct you farther. (*Gives him a letter and goes off.*)

FREDERICK.

Have a care, sir, what you promise; this may be a   270 trap laid by her brother to ruin you.

BELVILE.

Do not disturb my happiness with doubts. (*Opens the letter.*)

WILLMORE.

My dear pretty creature, a thousand blessings on thee! Still in this habit, you say? and after dinner   275 at this place?

HELLENA.

Yes, if you will swear to keep your heart and not bestow it between this and that.

WILLMORE.

By all the little gods of love, I swear I'll leave it with you, and if you run away with it, those deities   280 of justice will revenge me.

Exeunt all the women.

FREDERICK.

Do you know the hand?

BELVILE.

'Tis Florinda's.

All blessings fall upon the virtuous maid.

FREDERICK.

Nay, no idolatry; a sober sacrifice I'll allow you.   285

BELVILE.

Oh friends, the welcom'st news! the softest letter! Nay, you shall all see it! And could you now be serious, I might be made the happiest man the sun shines on!

WILLMORE.

The reason of this mighty joy?   290

BELVILE.

See how kindly she invites me to deliver her from the threatened violence of her brother. Will you not assist me?

WILLMORE.

I know not what thou mean'st, but I'll make one at any mischief where a woman's concerned. But she'll be grateful to us for the favor, will she not?

BELVILE.

How mean you?

WILLMORE.

How should I mean? Thou know'st there's but one way for a woman to oblige me.

BELVILE.

Do not profane. The maid is nicely virtuous.

WILLMORE.

Whoo, pox, then she's fit for nothing but a husband; let her e'en go, Colonel.

FREDERICK.

Peace, she's the colonel's mistress, sir.

WILLMORE.

Let her be the devil; if she be thy mistress, I'll serve her. Name the way.

BELVILE.

Read here this postscript. (*Gives him a letter.*)

WILLMORE. (*Reads.*)

"At ten at night—at the garden gate—of which, if I cannot get the key, I will contrive a way over the wall—come attended with a friend or two." Kind heart, if we three cannot weave a string to let her down a garden wall, 'twere pity but the hangman wove one for us all.

FREDERICK.

Let her alone for that. Your woman's wit, your fair kind woman, will out-trick a broker or a Jew, and contrive like a Jesuit in chains.—But see, Ned Blunt is stolen out after the lure of a damsel.

Exeunt Blunt and Lucetta.

BELVILE.

So he'll scarce find his way home again, unless we get him cried by the bellman in the market-place, and 'twould sound prettily——a lost English boy of thirty.

FREDERICK.

I hope 'tis some common crafty sinner, one that will fit* him; it may be she'll sell him for Peru;[28] the rogue's sturdy and would work well in a mine; at least I hope she'll dress him for our mirth, cheat

him of all, then have him well-favoredly hanged and turned out naked at midnight.

WILLMORE.

Prithee, what humor* is he of that you wish him so well?

BELVILE.

Why of an English elder brother's humor*, educated in a nursery, with a maid to tend him till fifteen, and lies with his grandmother till he's of age: one that knows no pleasure beyond riding to the next fair, or going up to London with his right worshipful father in Parliament-time, wearing gay clothes, or making honorable love to his lady mother's laundry-maid; gets drunk at a hunting-match, and ten to one then gives some proofs of his prowess. A pox upon him, he's our banker and has all our cash about him, and if he fail, we are all broke.

FREDERICK.

Oh let him alone for that matter, he's of a damned stingy quality that will secure our stock. I know not in what danger it were indeed if the jilt should pretend she's in love with him, for 'tis a kind believing coxcomb; otherwise, if he part with more than a piece of eight—geld[29] him: for which offer he may chance to be beaten, if she be a whore of the first rank.

BELVILE.

Nay, the rogue will not be easily beaten, he's stout enough. Perhaps if they talk beyond his capacity, he may chance to exercise his courage upon some of them; else I'm sure they'll find it as difficult to beat as to please him.

WILLMORE.

'Tis a lucky devil to light upon so kind a wench!

FREDERICK.

Thou had'st a great deal of talk with thy little Gypsy; could'st thou do any good upon her? For mine was hard-hearted.

---

28 Peru] known for its many mines using slave labor

29 geld] Behn (whose spelling is "gueld") puns on near homynyms: geld] to castrate; gild] to overlay with gold. The second is latent because Frederick has just referred to pieces of eight. There is a third possible pun in the archaic sense of gild] to make bloody. Both the second and third meanings seem picked up in Frederick's subsequent "beaten."

WILLMORE.

Hang her, she was some damned honest person of quality,* I'm sure, she was so very free and witty. If her face be but answerable to her wit and humor*, I would be bound to constancy this month to gain her. In the meantime, have you made no kind acquaintance since you came to town? You do not use to be honest so long, gentlemen.   360

FREDERICK.

Faith, love has kept us honest; we have been all fired with a beauty newly come to town, the famous Paduana,[30] Angellica Bianca.   365

WILLMORE.

What, the mistress of the dead Spanish general?

BELVILE.

Yes, she's now the only adored beauty of all the youth in Naples, who put on all their charms to appear lovely in her sight, their coaches, liveries, and themselves, all gay as on a monarch's birthday, to   370 attract the eyes of this fair charmer, while she has the pleasure to behold all languish for her that see her.

FREDERICK.

'Tis pretty to see with how much love the men regard her, and how much envy the women.

WILLMORE.

What gallant has she?   375

BELVILE.

None, she's exposed to sale, and four days in the week she's yours—for so much a month.

WILLMORE.

The very thought of it quenches all manner of fire in me. Yet prithee, let's see her.

BELVILE.

Let's first to dinner, and after that we'll pass the   380 day as you please. But at night ye must all be at my devotion.

WILLMORE.

I will not fail you.

Act II, scene i. The long street.

Enter Belvile and Frederick in masquing habits, and Willmore in his own clothes, with a vizard in his hand.

WILLMORE.

But why thus disguised and muzzled?

---

30 Paduana] a woman from Padua

BELVILE.

Because whatever extravagances we commit in these faces, our own may not be obliged to answer 'em.

WILLMORE.

I should have changed my eternal buff too; but no   5 matter, my little Gypsy would not have found me out then, for if she should change hers, it is impossible I should know her, unless I should hear her prattle. A pox on't, I cannot get her out of my head. Pray Heaven, if ever I do see her again, she   10 prove damnably ugly, that I may fortify myself against her tongue.

BELVILE.

Have a care of love, for o'my conscience, she was not of a quality to give thee any hopes.

WILLMORE.

Pox on 'em, why do they draw a man in then? She   15 has played with my heart so, that 'twill never lie still till I have met with some kind wench that will play the game out with me. Oh, for my arms full of soft, white, kind—woman! such as I fancy Angellica.   20

BELVILE.

This is her house, if you were but in stock[31] to get admittance. They have not dined yet; I perceive the picture is not out.

Enter Blunt.

WILLMORE.

I long to see the shadow of the fair substance; a man may gaze on that for nothing.   25

BLUNT.

Colonel, thy hand—and thine, Fred. I have been an ass, a deluded fool, a very coxcomb from my birth till this hour, and heartily repent my little faith.

BELVILE.

What the devil's the matter with thee, Ned?

BLUNT.

Oh such a mistress, Fred, such a girl!   30

WILLMORE.

Ha! where?

FREDERICK.

Ay, where!

---

31 in stock] supplied with funds

BLUNT.

So fond, so amorous, so toying and so fine! and all for sheer love, ye rogue! Oh how she looked and kissed! and soothed my heart from my bosom. I cannot think I was awake, and yet methinks I see and feel her charms still. Fred, try if she have not left the taste of her balmy kisses upon my lips. (*Kisses him.*)

BELVILE.

Ha! Ha! Ha!

WILLMORE.

Death, man, where is she?

BLUNT.

What a dog was I to stay in dull England so long. How have I laughed at the colonel when he sighed for love! But now the little archer[32] has revenged him! And by this one dart, I can guess at all his joys, which then I took for fancies, mere dreams and fables. Well, I'm resolved to sell all in Essex, and plant here for ever.

BELVILE.

What a blessing 'tis thou hast a mistress thou dar'st boast of, for I know thy humor* is rather to have a proclaimed clap than a secret amour.

WILLMORE.

Dost know her name?

BLUNT.

Her name? No, 'sheartlikins, what care I for names? She's fair! young! brisk and kind! even to ravishment! And what a pox care I for knowing her by any other title?

WILLMORE.

Didst give her anything?

BLUNT.

Give her! Ha, ha, ha! Why she's a person of quality.* That's a good one, give her! 'Sheartlikins, dost think such creatures are to be bought? Or are we provided for such a purchase? Give her, quoth ye? Why, she presented me with this bracelet for the toy of a diamond I used to wear. No, gentlemen, Ned Blunt is not everybody. She expects me again tonight.

WILLMORE.

Egad, that's well; we'll all go.

BLUNT.

Not a soul. No, gentlemen, you are wits; I am a dull country rogue, I.

FREDERICK.

Well, sir, for all your person of quality, I shall be very glad to understand your purse be secure; 'tis our whole estate at present, which we are loath to hazard in one bottom. Come, sir, unlade.

BLUNT.

Take the necessary trifle, useless now to me that am beloved by such a gentlewoman. 'Sheartlikins, money! Here, take mine too.

FREDERICK.

No, keep that to be cozened, that we may laugh.

WILLMORE.

Cozened! Death! Would I could meet with one that would cozen me of all the love I could spare tonight.

FREDERICK.

Pox, 'tis some common whore, upon my life.

BLUNT.

A whore! Yes, with such clothes! such jewels! such a house! such furniture, and so attended! A whore!

BELVILE.

Why yes, sir, they are whores, though they'll neither entertain you with drinking, swearing, or bawdry; are whores in all those gay clothes and right jewels; are whores with those great houses richly furnished with velvet beds, store of plate, handsome attendance and fine coaches; are whores, and arrant ones.

WILLMORE.

Pox on't, where do these fine whores live?

BELVILE.

Where no rogues in office yclept constables dare give 'em laws, nor the wine-inspired bullies of the town break their windows; yet they are whores, though this Essex calf[33] believe 'em persons of quality.

BLUNT.

'Sheartlikins, y'are all fools; there are things about this Essex calf that shall take with the ladies, beyond all your wit and parts. This shape and size,

---

32 little archer] Cupid

33 Essex calf] fool; a native of Essex. Blunt's home county of Essex was famous for its calves.

gentlemen, are not to be despised—my waist too, tolerably long, with other inviting signs, that shall be nameless.

WILLMORE.

Egad, I believe he may have met with some person of quality that may be kind to him.

BELVILE.

Dost thou perceive any such tempting things about him that should make a fine woman, and of quality, pick him out from all mankind to throw away her youth and beauty upon, nay and her dear heart too! No, no, Angellica has raised the price too high.

WILLMORE.

May she languish for mankind till she die, and be damned for that one sin alone.

Enter two bravoes, and hang up a great picture of Angellica's against the balcony, and two little ones at each side of the door.

BELVILE.

See there, the fair sign to the inn where a man may lodge that's fool enough to give her price.

Willmore gazes on the picture.

BLUNT.

'Sheartlikins, gentlemen, what's this!

BELVILE.

A famous courtesan, that's to be sold.

BLUNT.

How? To be sold! Nay then, I have nothing to say to her. Sold! What impudence is practiced in this country? With what order and decency whoring's established here by virtue of the Inquisition. Come, let's be gone, I'm sure we're no chapmen for this commodity.

FREDERICK.

Thou art none, I'm sure, unless thou could'st have her in thy bed at a price of a coach in the street.

WILLMORE.

How wondrous fair she is. A thousand crowns a month! By heaven, as many kingdoms were too little. A plague of this poverty—of which I ne'er complain but when it hinders my approach to beauty which virtue ne'er could purchase. (*Turns from the picture.*)

BLUNT.

What's this? (*Reads.*) "A thousand crowns a month"!—'Sheartlikins, here's a sum! Sure 'tis a mistake.—Hark you friend, does she take or give so much by the month?

FREDERICK.

A thousand crowns! Why 'tis a portion for the Infanta.

BLUNT.

Hark ye, friends, won't she trust?

BRAVO.

This is a trade, sir, that cannot live by credit.

Enter Don Pedro in masquerade, followed by Stephano.

BELVILE.

See, here's more company. Let's walk off a while.

Exeunt English. Pedro reads. Enter Angellica and Moretta in the balcony, and draw a silk curtain.

PEDRO.

Fetch me a thousand crowns, I never wished to buy this beauty at an easier rate. (*Passes off.*)

ANGELLICA.

Prithee, what said those fellows to thee?

BRAVO.

Madam, the first were admirers of beauty only, but no purchasers; they were merry with your price and picture, laughed at the sum, and so passed off.

ANGELLICA.

No matter, I'm not displeased with their rallying; their wonder feeds my vanity, and he that wishes but to buy gives me more pride than he that gives my price can make my pleasure.

BRAVO.

Madam, the last I knew through all his disguises to be Don Pedro, nephew to the general, and who was with him in Pamplona.

ANGELLICA.

Don Pedro! My old gallant's nephew. When his uncle died he left him a vast sum of money; it is he who was so in love with me at Padua, and who used to make the general so jealous.

MORETTA.

Is this he that used to prance before our window and take such care to show himself an amorous ass? If I am not mistaken, he is the likeliest man to give your price.

ANGELLICA.

The man is brave and generous, but of an humor*
so uneasy and inconstant, that the victory over his   160
heart is as soon lost as won, a slave that can add little
to the triumph of the conqueror. But inconstancy's
the sin of all mankind; therefore, I'm resolved that
nothing but gold shall charm my heart.

MORETTA.

I'm glad on't; 'tis only interest that women of our   165
profession ought to consider, though I wonder
what has kept you from that general disease of our
sex so long, I mean that of being in love.

ANGELLICA.

A kind but sullen star under which I had the
happiness to be born. Yet I have had no time for   170
love; the bravest and noblest of mankind have
purchased my favors at so dear a rate as if no coin
but gold were current with our trade.—But here's
Don Pedro again, fetch me my lute, for 'tis for him
or Don Antonio the viceroy's son that I have   175
spread my nets.

*Enter at one door Don Pedro, Stephano; Don Antonio
and Diego [Page] at the other door, with people
following him in masquerade, antically attired, some
with music; they both go up to the picture.*

ANTONIO.

A thousand crowns! Had not the painter flattered
her, I should not think it dear.

PEDRO.

Flattered her! By Heav'n, he cannot; I have seen
the original, nor is there one charm here more than   180
adorns her face and eyes; all this soft and sweet,
with a certain languishing air, that no artist can
represent.

ANTONIO.

What I heard of her beauty before had fired my
soul, but this confirmation of it has blown it to a   185
flame.

PEDRO.

Hah!

PAGE.

Sir, I have known you throw away a thousand
crowns on a worse face, and though y'are near your
marriage, you may venture a little love here.   190
Florinda will not miss it.

PEDRO. (*Aside.*)

Hah! Florinda! Sure 'tis Antonio.

ANTONIO.

Florinda! Name not those distant joys; there's not
one thought of her will check my passion here.

PEDRO.

Florinda scorned! (*A noise of a lute above.*) and all   195
my hopes defeated of the possession of Angellica.
(*Antonio gazes up.*) Her injuries, by Heaven, he
shall not boast of.

    Song (*to a lute above.*)
    When Damon first began to love
    He languished in a soft desire,   200
    And knew not how the gods to move,
    To lessen or increase his fire.
    For Caelia in her charming eyes
Wore all love's sweets, and all his cruelties.

    II.
    But as beneath a shade he lay,   205
    Weaving of flow'rs for Caelia's hair,
    She chanced to lead her flock that way,
    And saw the am'rous shepherd there.
    She gazed around upon the place,
    And saw the grove (resembling night)   210
To all the joys of love invite,
Whilst guilty smiles and blushes dressed her face.
At this the bashful youth all transport grew,
And with kind force he taught the virgin how
To yield what all his sighs could never do.   215

*Angellica throws open the curtains and bows to
Antonio, who pulls off his vizard and bows and blows
up kisses. Pedro unseen looks in's face.*

ANTONIO.

By Heav'n, she's charming fair!

PEDRO.

'Tis he; the false Antonio!

ANTONIO. (*To the bravo.*)

Friend, where must I pay my offering of love?
My thousand crowns I mean.

PEDRO.

That offering I have designed to make.   220
And yours will come too late.

ANTONIO.

Prithee, be gone, I shall grow angry else.
And then thou art not safe.

PEDRO.

My anger may be fatal, sir, as yours,
And he that enters here may prove this truth.   225

ANTONIO.

I know not who thou art, but I am sure thou'rt
worth my killing, for aiming at Angellica.

*They draw and fight. Enter Willmore and Blunt who
draw and part 'em.*

BLUNT.

'Sheartlikins, here's fine doings.

WILLMORE.

Tilting for the wench, I'm sure. Nay, gad, if that
would win her, I have as good a sword as the best   230
of ye. Put up—put up, and take another time and
place, for this is designed for lovers only.

They all put up.

PEDRO.

We are prevented; dare you meet me tomorrow
on the Molo?[34]
For I've a title to a better quarrel,*   235
That of Florinda, in whose credulous heart
Thou'st made an int'rest and destroyed my hopes.

ANTONIO.

Dare!
I'll meet thee there as early as the day.

PEDRO.

We will come thus disguised that whosoever   240
chance to get the better, he may escape unknown.

ANTONIO.

It shall be so.

Exeunt Pedro and Stephano.

Who should this rival be? unless the English
colonel, of whom I've often heard Don Pedro
speak; it must be he, and time he were removed,   245
who lays claim to all my happiness.

*Willmore having gazed all this while on the picture,
pulls down a little one.*

WILLMORE.

This posture's loose and negligent,
The sight on't would beget a warm desire

---

34 the Molo] pier; from French *môle*

In souls whom impotence and age had chilled.
—This must along with me.   250

BRAVO.

What means this rudeness, sir? Restore the picture.

ANTONIO.

Hah! Rudeness committed to the fair Angellica!
Restore the picture, sir—

WILLMORE.

Indeed I will not, sir.

ANTONIO.

By Heaven, but you shall.   255

WILLMORE.

Nay, do not show your sword; if you do, by this
dear beauty—I will show mine too.

ANTONIO.

What right can you pretend to't?

WILLMORE.

That of possession, which I will maintain. You
perhaps have a thousand crowns to give for the   260
original.

ANTONIO.

No matter, sir, you shall restore the picture.

Angellica and Moretta above.

ANGELLICA.

Oh Moretta! What's the matter?

ANTONIO.

Or leave your life behind.

WILLMORE.

Death! You lie. I will do neither.   265

*They fight; the Spaniards join with Antonio; Blunt
laying on like mad.*

ANGELLICA.

Hold, I command you, if for me you fight.

They leave off and bow.

WILLMORE.

How heavenly fair she is! Ah, plague of her price.

ANGELLICA.

You sir, in buff, you that appear a soldier, that first
began this insolence—

WILLMORE.

'Tis true, I did so, if you call it insolence for a man   270
to preserve himself. I saw your charming picture and
was wounded; quite through my soul each pointed

beauty ran, and wanting a thousand crowns to
procure my remedy, I laid this little picture to my
bosom—which if you cannot allow me, I'll resign. 275

ANGELLICA.

No, you may keep the trifle.

ANTONIO.

You shall first ask me leave, and this. (*Fight again*
as before.)

Enter Belvile and Frederick who join with the English.

ANGELLICA.

Hold! Will you ruin me? Biskey—Sebastian—part
'em.

The Spaniards are beaten off.

MORETTA.

Oh madam, we're undone. A pox upon that rude   280
fellow, he's set on to ruin us. We shall never see
good days till all these fighting poor rogues are sent
to the galleys.

Enter Belvile, Blunt, Frederick, and Willmore with's
shirt bloody.

BLUNT.

'Sheartlikins, beat me at this sport, and I'll ne'er
wear sword more.   285

BELVILE.

The devil's in thee for a mad fellow; thou art
always one at an unlucky adventure. Come, let's
be gone whilst we're safe, and remember these are
Spaniards, a sort of people that know how to
revenge an affront.   290

FREDERICK. (*To Willmore.*)

You bleed! I hope you are not wounded.

WILLMORE.

Not much. A plague on your dons; if they fight
no better, they'll ne'er recover Flanders.* What the
devil was't to them that I took down the picture?

BLUNT.

Took it! 'Sheartlikins, we'll have the great one too;   295
'tis ours by conquest. Prithee, help me up and I'll
pull it down—

ANGELLICA.

Stay, sir, and ere you affront me farther, let me
know how you durst commit this outrage. To you
I speak, sir, for you appear a gentleman.   300

WILLMORE.

To me, madam?—Gentlemen, your servant.

Belvile stays him.

BELVILE.

Is the devil in thee? Dost know the danger of
entering the house of an incensed courtesan?

WILLMORE.

I thank you for your care, but there are other
matters in hand, there are, though we have no   305
great temptation.—Death! Let me go.

FREDERICK.

Yes, to your lodging if you will, but not in here.—
Damn these gay harlots. By this hand I'll have as
sound and handsome a whore for a patacoon.[35]—
Death, man, she'll murder thee.   310

WILLMORE.

Oh! Fear me not. Shall I not venture where a
beauty calls? a lovely, charming beauty! for fear of
danger! when, by Heaven, there's none so great as
to long for her whilst I want money to purchase
her.   315

FREDERICK.

Therefore, 'tis loss of time unless you had the
thousand crowns to pay.

WILLMORE.

It may be she may give a favor; at least I shall have
the pleasure of saluting her when I enter, and when
I depart.   320

BELVILE.

Pox, she'll as soon lie with thee as kiss thee, and
sooner stab than do either. You shall not go.

ANGELLICA.

Fear not, sir, all I have to wound with is my eyes.

BLUNT.

Let him go. 'Sheartlikins, I believe the gentlewoman means well.   325

BELVILE.

Well, take thy fortune; we'll expect you in the next
street. Farewell, fool—farewell—

WILLMORE.

Bye, Colonel. (*Goes in.*)

---

35 patacoon] Spanish coin; value in seventeenth century,
ca. one fourth of an English pound

FREDERICK.

The rogue's stark mad for a wench.

Exeunt.

Scene ii. A fine chamber.

Enter Willmore, Angellica and Moretta.

ANGELLICA.

Insolent sir, how durst you pull down my picture?

WILLMORE.

Rather, how durst you set it up, to tempt poor
amorous mortals with so much excellence, which I
find you have but too well consulted by the
unmerciful price you set upon't? Is all this heaven of 5
beauty shown to move despair in those that cannot
buy? And can you think th'effects of that despair
should be less extravagant than I have shown?

ANGELLICA.

I sent for you to ask my pardon, sir, not to
aggravate your crime. I thought I should have seen 10
you at my feet imploring it.

WILLMORE.

You are deceived; I came to rail at you, and rail
such truths too, as shall let you see the vanity of
that pride which taught you how to set such price
on sin. For such it is, whilst that which is love's 15
due is meanly bartered for.

ANGELLICA.

Ha! ha! ha! Alas, good captain, what pity 'tis your
edifying doctrine will do no good upon me.—
Moretta! Fetch the gentleman a glass, and let him
survey himself, to see what charms he has—(*Aside* 20
in a soft tone.) and guess my business.

MORETTA.

He knows himself of old; I believe those breeches
and he have been acquainted ever since he was
beaten at Worcester.[36]

ANGELLICA.

Nay, do not abuse the poor creature— 25

MORETTA.

Good weather-beaten corporal, will you march off?
We have no need of your doctrine, though you

have of our charity, but at present we have no
scraps, we can afford no kindness for God's sake.
In fine, sirrah, the price is too high i'th'mouth[37] 30
for you; therefore, troop, I say.

WILLMORE.

Here, good forewoman of the shop, serve me, and
I'll be gone.

MORETTA.

Keep it to pay your laundress, your linen stinks of
the gunroom, for here's no selling by retail. 35

WILLMORE.

Thou hast sold plenty of thy stale ware at a cheap
rate.

MORETTA.

Ay, the more silly,* kind heart I, but this is an age
wherein beauty is at higher rates. In fine, you know
the price of this. 40

WILLMORE.

I grant you 'tis here set down, a thousand crowns
a month. Pray, how much may come to my share
for a pistole? Bawd, take your black lead and sum
it up, that I may have a pistole's worth of this vain
gay thing, and I'll trouble you no more. 45

MORETTA.

Pox on him, he'll fret me to death.—Abominable
fellow, I tell thee, we only sell by the whole piece.

WILLMORE.

'Tis very hard, the whole cargo or nothing. Faith,
madam, my stock will not reach it; I cannot be
your chapman. Yet I have countrymen in town, 50
merchants of love like me; I'll see if they'll put in
for a share. We cannot lose much by it, and what
we have no use for, we'll sell upon the Friday's mart
at "Who gives more?"—I am studying, madam,
how to purchase you, though at present I am 55
unprovided of money.

ANGELLICA. [*Aside.*]

Sure, this from any other man would anger me,
nor shall he know the conquest he has made.—
Poor angry man, how I despise this railing.

WILLMORE.

Yes, I am poor—but I'm a gentleman, 60
And one that scorns this baseness which you practice;
Poor as I am, I would not sell myself,

---

36 Worcester] The Battle of Worcester (1651) was the final defeat of Charles II by the Parliamentary forces, after which he fled to the continent.

37 high i'th'mouth] elevated

No, not to gain your charming, high-prized person.
Though I admire you strangely for your beauty,
Yet I contemn your mind.— 65
And yet I would at any rate enjoy you
At your own rate—but cannot. See here
The only sum I can command on earth;
I know not where to eat when this is gone.
Yet such a slave I am to love and beauty 70
This last reserve I'll sacrifice to enjoy you.
—Nay, do not frown, I know you're to be bought,
And would be bought by me, by me,
For a mean trifling sum if I could pay it down;
Which happy knowledge I will still repeat, 75
And lay it to my heart; it has a virtue in't,
And soon will cure those wounds your eyes have
    made.
—And yet—there's something so divinely
    powerful there—
Nay, I will gaze—to let you see my strength.

Holds her, looks on her, and pauses and sighs.

By Heav'n, bright creature—I would not for the 80
    world
Thy fame were half so fair as is thy face.

Turns her away from him.

ANGELLICA. (*Aside.*)
His words go through me to the very soul.
—If you have nothing else to say to me—
WILLMORE.
Yes, you shall hear how infamous you are—
For which I do not hate thee— 85
But that secures my heart, and all the flames it feels
Are but so many lusts—
I know it by their sudden bold intrusion.
The fire's impatient and betrays, 'tis false—
For had it been the purer flame of love, 90
I should have pined and languished at your feet,
Ere found the impudence to have discovered it.
I now dare stand your scorn, and your denial.
MORETTA.
Sure she's bewitched, that she can stand thus
tamely and hear his saucy railing.—Sirrah, will you 95
be gone?
ANGELLICA. (*To Moretta.*)
How dare you take this liberty? Withdraw.—Pray

tell me, sir, are not you guilty of the same
mercenary crime? When a lady is proposed to you
for a wife, you never ask how fair, discreet, or 100
virtuous she is, but what's her fortune—which if
but small, you cry, "She will not do my business"
and basely leave her, though she languish for you.
Say, is not this as poor?
WILLMORE.
It is a barbarous custom, which I will scorn to 105
defend in our sex, and do despise in yours.
ANGELLICA.
Thou'rt a brave fellow! Put up thy gold, and know,
That were thy fortune large as is thy soul,
Thou should'st not buy my love.
Couldst thou forget those mean effects of vanity 110
Which set me out to sale, and, as a lover, prize my
    yielding joys?
Canst thou believe they'll be entirely thine,
Without considering they were mercenary?
WILLMORE.
I cannot tell, I must bethink me first. (*Aside.*) Hah!
Death, I'm going to believe her. 115
ANGELLICA.
Prithee, confirm that faith—or if thou canst not—
flatter me a little, 'twill please me from thy mouth.
WILLMORE. (*Aside.*)
Curse on thy charming tongue!—Dost thou return
My feigned contempt with so much subtlety?
Thou'st found the easiest way into my heart, 120
Though I yet know that all thou say'st is false.

Turning from her in rage.

ANGELLICA.
By all that's good, 'tis real;
I never loved before, though oft a mistress.
Shall my first vows be slighted?
WILLMORE. (*Aside.*)
What can she mean? 125
ANGELLICA. (*In an angry tone.*)
I find you cannot credit me.
WILLMORE.
I know you take me for an arrant ass,
An ass that may be soothed into belief
And then be used at pleasure—
But madam, I have been so often cheated 130
By perjured, soft, deluding hypocrites,

That I've no faith left for the cozening sex;
Especially for women of your trade.
ANGELLICA.
The low esteem you have of me, perhaps
May bring my heart again—   135
For I have pride that yet surmounts my love.

She turns with pride; he holds her.

WILLMORE.
Throw off this pride, this enemy to bliss,
And show the pow'r of love; 'tis with those arms
I can be only vanquished, made a slave.
ANGELLICA.
Is all my mighty expectation vanished?   140
—No, I will not hear thee talk. Thou hast a charm
In every word that draws my heart away.
And all the thousand trophies I designed
Thou hast undone—Why art thou soft?
Thy looks are bravely rough, and meant for war.   145
Could'st thou not storm on still?
I then perhaps had been as free as thou.
WILLMORE. (*Aside.*)
Death, how she throws her fire about my soul!
—Take heed, fair creature, how you raise my hope,
Which, once assumed, pretends to all dominion.   150
There's not a joy thou hast in store,
I shall not then command—
For which I'll pay thee back my soul! my life!
—Come, let's begin th'account this happy minute!
ANGELLICA.
And will you pay me then the price I ask?   155
WILLMORE.
Oh, why dost thou draw me from an awful worship,
By showing thou art no divinity?
Conceal the fiend, and show me all the angel!
Keep me but ignorant, and I'll be devout
And pay my vows forever at this shrine.   160

Kneels and kisses her hand.

ANGELLICA.
The pay I mean is but thy love for mine.
Can you give that?—
WILLMORE.
Entirely. Come, let's withdraw! where I'll renew my
vows—and breathe 'em with such ardor thou shalt   165
not doubt my zeal.

ANGELLICA.
Thou hast a pow'r too strong to be resisted.

Exeunt Willmore and Angellica.

MORETTA.
Now my curse go with you. Is all our project fallen
to this? to love the only enemy to our trade? Nay, to
love such a shameroon,[38] a very beggar, nay a pirate   170
beggar, whose business is to rifle, and be gone, a no-
purchase, no-pay tatterdemalion and English
picaroon, a rogue that fights for daily drink and
takes a pride in being loyally lousy. Oh, I could curse
now, if I durst. This is the fate of most whores.   175
Trophies, which from believing fops we win,
Are spoils to those who cozen us again.

Act III, scene i. A street.

*Enter Florinda, Valeria, Hellena, in antic different
dresses from what they were in before. Callis attending.*

FLORINDA.
I wonder what should make my brother in so ill a
humor*? I hope he has not found out our ramble
this morning.
HELLENA.
No, if he had, we should have heard on't at both
ears, and have been mewed up this afternoon,   5
which I would not for the world should have
happened.—Hey ho, I'm as sad as a lover's lute.
VALERIA.
Well, methinks we have learnt this trade of gypsies
as readily as if we have been bred upon the road
to Loretto,[39] and yet I did so fumble when I told   10
the stranger his fortune that I was afraid I should
have told my own and yours by mistake. But
methinks Hellena has been very serious ever since.
FLORINDA.
I would give my garters she were in love to be
revenged upon her for abusing me.—How is't,   15
Hellena?
HELLENA.
Ah—would I had never seen my mad monsieur—
and yet for all your laughing, I am not in love—

---

38 shameroon] one who deceives or uses false pretenses
39 Loretto] a city in Italy famous as a place of pilgrimage

and yet this small acquaintance, o'my conscience, will never out of my head. 20

VALERIA.

Ha, ha, ha! I laugh to think how thou art fitted with a lover, a fellow that I warrant loves every new face he sees.

HELLENA.

Hum—he has not kept his word with me here— and may be taken up. That thought is not very 25 pleasant to me. What the deuce should this be, now, that I feel?

VALERIA.

What is't like?

HELLENA.

Nay, the lord knows. But if I should be hanged, I cannot choose but be angry and afraid when I 30 think that mad fellow should be in love with anybody but me. What to think of myself, I know not. Would I could meet with some true damned Gypsy, that I might know my fortune.

VALERIA.

Know it! Why there's nothing so easy; thou wilt 35 love this wandering inconstant till thou find'st thyself hanged about his neck, and then be as mad to get free again.

FLORINDA.

Yes, Valeria, we shall see her bestride his baggage horse, and follow him to the campaign. 40

HELLENA.

So, so, now you are provided for, there's no care taken of poor me. But since you have set my heart a-wishing, I am resolved to know for what. I will not die of the pip, so I will not.

FLORINDA.

Art thou mad to talk so? Who will like thee well 45 enough to have thee that hears what a mad wench thou art?

HELLENA.

Like me! I don't intend every he that likes me shall have me, but he that I like; I should have stayed in the nunnery still, if I had liked my lady Abbess 50 as well as she liked me. No, I came thence not (as my wise brother imagines) to take an eternal farewell of the world, but to love and to be beloved, and I will be beloved, or I'll get one of your men, so I will. 55

VALERIA.

Am I put into the number of lovers?

HELLENA.

You? Why, coz, I know thou'rt too good-natured to leave us in any design; thou wouldst venture a cast, though thou comest off a loser, especially with such a gamester. I observe your man and your 60 willing ear incline that way; and if you are not a lover, 'tis an art soon learnt, that I find. (*Sighs.*)

FLORINDA.

I wonder how you learnt to love so easily; I had a thousand charms to meet my eyes and ears ere I could yield, and 'twas the knowledge of Belvile's 65 merit, not the surprising person, took my soul. Thou art too rash to give a heart at first sight.

HELLENA.

Hang your considering lover; I never thought beyond the fancy that 'twas a very pretty, idle, silly kind of pleasure to pass one's time with, to write 70 little soft nonsensical billets, and with great difficulty and danger receive answers in which I shall have my beauty praised, my wit admired (though little or none), and have the vanity and power to know I am desirable; then I have the 75 more inclination that way, because I am to be a nun, and so shall not be suspected to have any such earthly thoughts about me. But when I walk thus—and sigh thus—they'll think my mind's upon my monastery and cry how happy 'tis she's 80 so resolved. But not a word of man.

FLORINDA.

What a mad creature's this?

HELLENA.

I'll warrant, if my brother hears either of you sigh, he cries (gravely), "I fear you have the indiscretion to be in love, but take heed of the honor of our 85 house, and your own unspotted fame," and so he conjures on till he has laid the soft-winged god in your hearts, or broke the bird's nest.—But see, here comes your lover, but where's my inconstant? Let's step aside, and we may learn something. (*Go aside.*) 90

Enter Belvile, Frederick and Blunt.

BELVILE.

What means this! The picture's taken in.

BLUNT.

It may be the wench is good-natured and will be kind gratis. Your friend's a proper handsome fellow.

BELVILE.

I rather think she has cut his throat and is fled: I am mad he should throw himself into dangers. Pox on't, I shall want him too at night. Let's knock and ask for him. 95

HELLENA.

My heart goes a-pit a-pat, for fear 'tis my man they talk of.

Knock; Moretta above.

MORETTA.

What would you have! 100

BELVILE.

Tell the stranger that entered here about two hours ago that his friends stay here for him.

MORETTA.

A curse upon him for Moretta; would he were at the devil. But he's coming to you.

Enter Willmore.

HELLENA.

Aye, aye, 'tis he! Oh how this vexes me. 105

BELVILE.

And how and how dear lad, has fortune smiled? Are we to break her windows? Or raise up altars to her, hah?

WILLMORE.

Does not my fortune sit triumphant on my brow? Dost not see the little wanton god there all gay and 110 smiling? Have I not an air about my face and eyes that distinguish me from the crowd of common lovers? By Heaven, Cupid's quiver has not half so many darts as her eyes! Oh, such a bona roba*! To sleep in her arms is lying in fresco,⁴⁰ all perfumed 115 air about me.

HELLENA. (*Aside.*)

Here's fine encouragement for me to fool on.

WILLMORE.

Hark ye, where didst thou purchase that rich canary we drank today! Tell me, that I may adore the spigot and sacrifice to the butt! The juice was 120

----

40 in fresco] alfresco

divine! into which I must dip my rosary and then bless all things that I would have bold or fortunate.

BELVILE.

Well, sir, let's go take a bottle and hear the story of your success.

FREDERICK.

Would not French wine do better? 125

WILLMORE.

Damn the hungry balderdash,⁴¹ cheerful sack* has a generous virtue in't inspiring a successful confidence, gives eloquence to the tongue, and vigor to the soul, and has in a few hours completed all my hopes and wishes! There's nothing left to 130 raise a new desire in me. Come, let's be gay and wanton—and gentlemen, study, study what you want, for here [*Jingles a purse.*] are friends that will supply, gentlemen. Hark! What a charming sound they make—'tis he and she gold whilst here, and 135 shall beget new pleasures every moment.

BLUNT.

But hark ye sir, you are not married, are you?

WILLMORE.

All the honey of matrimony, but none of the sting, friend.

BLUNT.

'Sheartlikins, thou'rt a fortunate rogue! 140

WILLMORE.

I am so, sir, let these [*Jingles again.*] inform you! Hah, how sweetly they chime! Pox of poverty, it makes a man a slave, makes wit and honor sneak. My soul grew lean and rusty for want of credit.

BLUNT.

'Sheartlikins, this I like well, it looks like my lucky 145 bargain! Oh how I long for the approach of my squire that is to conduct me to her house again. Why, here's two provided for.

FREDERICK.

By this light, y'are happy men.

BLUNT.

Fortune is pleased to smile on us, gentlemen——to 150 smile on us.

Enter Sancho and pulls down Blunt by the sleeve.

----

41 balderdash] a mixture of alcoholic drinks

SANCHO.

Sir, my lady expects you— (*They go aside.*) She has removed all that might oppose your will and pleasure—and is impatient till you come.

BLUNT.

Sir, I'll attend you.—Oh, the happiest rogue! I'll take no leave, lest they either dog me, or stay me.   155

Exit with Sancho.

BELVILE.

But then the little Gypsy is forgot?

WILLMORE.

A mischief on thee for putting her into my thoughts. I had quite forgot her else, and this night's debauch had drunk her quite down.   160

HELLENA.

Had it so, good captain! (*Claps him on the back.*)

WILLMORE. (*Aside.*)

Hah! I hope she did not hear me.

HELLENA.

What, afraid of such a champion?

WILLMORE.

Oh! You're a fine lady of your word, are you not? To make a man languish a whole day—   165

HELLENA.

In tedious search of me.

WILLMORE.

Egad child, thou'rt in the right; had'st thou seen what a melancholy dog I have been ever since I was a lover, how I have walked the streets like a Capuchin with my hands in my sleeves, faith,   170
sweetheart, thou wouldst pity me.

HELLENA. [*Aside.*]

Now if I should be hanged I can't be angry with him, he dissembles so heartily.—Alas, good captain, what pains you have taken. Now were I ungrateful not to reward so true a servant.   175

WILLMORE.

Poor soul! That's kindly said; I see thou bearest a conscience. Come then, for a beginning show me thy dear face.

HELLENA.

I'm afraid, my small acquaintance, you have been staying that swingeing stomach you boasted this   180
morning; I then remember my little collation would

have gone down with you, without the sauce of a handsome face. Is your stomach so queasy now?

WILLMORE.

Faith, long fasting, child, spoils a man's appetite— yet if you durst treat, I could so lay about me still—   185

HELLENA.

And would you fall to, before a priest says grace?

WILLMORE.

Oh fie, fie, what an old, out of fashioned thing hast thou named? Thou couldst not dash me more out of countenance shouldst thou show me an ugly face.

Whilst he is seemingly courting Hellena, enter Angellica, Moretta, Biskey and Sebastian, all in masquerade; Angellica sees Willmore and stares.

ANGELLICA.

Heavens, 'tis he! and passionately fond to see   190
another woman.

MORETTA.

What could you less expect from such a swaggerer?

ANGELLICA.

Expect! As much as I paid him, a heart entire
Which I had pride enough to think when ere I gave,
It would have raised the man above the vulgar,   195
Made him all soul! and that all soft and constant.

HELLENA.

You see, Captain, how willing I am to be friends with you, till time and ill luck make us lovers, and ask you the question first, rather than put your modesty to the blush by asking me (for alas!) I   200
know you captains are such strict men and such severe observers of your vows to chastity, that 'twill be hard to prevail with your tender conscience to marry a young willing maid.

WILLMORE.

Do not abuse me, for fear I should take thee at   205
thy word, and marry thee indeed, which I'm sure will be revenge sufficient.

HELLENA.

O' my conscience, that will be our destiny, because we are both of one humor*; I am as inconstant as you, for I have considered, Captain, that a   210
handsome woman has a great deal to do whilst her face is good, for then is our harvest-time to gather friends; and should I in these days of my youth catch a fit of foolish constancy, I were undone; 'tis

loitering by daylight in our great journey. 215
Therefore, I declare I'll allow but one year for love,
one year for indifference, and one year for hate—
and then—go hang yourself! For I profess myself
the gay, the kind, and the inconstant. The devil's
in't if this won't please you. 220

WILLMORE.
Oh most damnably! I have a heart with a hole
quite through it too: no prison mine to keep a
mistress in.

ANGELLICA. (*Aside.*)
Perjured man! How I believe thee now.

HELLENA.
Well, I see our business as well as humors* are 225
alike; yours to cozen as many maids as will trust
you, and I as many men as have faith. See if I have
not as desperate a lying look as you can have for
the heart of you. (*Pulls off her vizard: he starts.*)
How do you like it, captain? 230

WILLMORE.
Like it! By Heaven, I never saw so much beauty!
Oh the charms of those sprightly black eyes! that
strangely fair face, full of smiles and dimples! those
soft round melting cherry lips! and small even
white teeth! not to be expressed, but silently 235
adored! Oh, one look more! and strike me dumb,
or I shall repeat nothing else till I'm mad.

He seems to court her to pull off her vizard: she refuses.

ANGELLICA.
I can endure no more, nor is it fit to interrupt him,
for if I do, my jealousy has so destroyed my reason,
I shall undo him; therefore, I'll retire. (*To one of* 240
her bravoes.) And you, Sebastian, follow that
woman and learn who 'tis, (*To the other bravo.*)
while you tell the fugitive, I would speak to him
instantly.

*Exit. This while Florinda is talking to Belvile, who
stands sullenly. Frederick courting Valeria.*

VALERIA. [*To Belvile.*]
Prithee, dear stranger, be not so sullen, for though 245
you have lost your love, you see my friend frankly
offers you hers to play with in the meantime.

BELVILE.
Faith, madam, I am sorry I can't play at her game.

FREDERICK.
Pray, leave your intercession and mind your own
affair. They'll better agree apart; he's a modest sigher 250
in company, but alone no woman scapes him.

FLORINDA.
[*Aside.*] Sure he does but rally, yet if it should be
true—I'll tempt him farther.—Believe me, noble
stranger, I'm no common mistress, and for a little
proof on't, wear this jewel—nay, take it, sir, 'tis 255
right, and bills of exchange may sometimes
miscarry.

BELVILE.
Madam, why am I chose out of all mankind to be
the object of your bounty?

VALERIA.
There's another civil question asked. 260

FREDERICK.
Pox of's modesty, it spoils his own markets and
hinders mine.

FLORINDA.
Sir, from my window, I have often seen you, and
women of my quality have so few opportunities
for love that we ought to lose none. 265

FREDERICK.
Aye, this is something! Here's a woman! When
shall I be blessed with so much kindness from your
fair mouth?
(*Aside to Belvile.*)—Take the jewel, fool.

BELVILE.
You tempt me strangely, madam, every way— 270

FLORINDA. (*Aside.*)
So, if I find him false, my whole repose is gone.

BELVILE.
And but for a vow I've made to a very fair^d lady,
this goodness had subdued me.

FREDERICK.
Pox on't, be kind, in pity to me be kind, for I am
to thrive here but as you treat her friend. 275

HELLENA.
Tell me what you did in yonder house, and I'll
unmask.

WILLMORE.
Yonder house—oh—I went to—a—to—why,
there's a friend of mine lives there.

HELLENA.
What, a she, or a he friend? 280

WILLMORE.

A man, upon honor! a man. A she friend? No, no, madam, you have done my business, I thank you.

HELLENA.

And was't your man friend that had more darts in's eyes than Cupid carries in's whole budget of arrows?

WILLMORE.

So—   285

HELLENA.

Ah, such a bona roba*! to be in her arms is lying alfresco, all perfumed air about me—was this your man friend too?

WILLMORE.

So—

HELLENA.

That gave you the he and the she gold that begets   290
young pleasures?

WILLMORE.

Well, well, madam, then you see there are ladies in the world that will not be cruel—there are, madam, there are—

HELLENA.

And there be men too, as fine, wild, inconstant   295
fellows as yourself, there be, Captain, there be, if you go to that now. Therefore, I'm resolved—

WILLMORE.

Oh!

HELLENA.

To see your face no more—

WILLMORE.

Oh!   300

HELLENA.

Till tomorrow.

WILLMORE.

Egad, you frighted me.

HELLENA.

Nor then neither, unless you'll swear never to see that lady more.

WILLMORE.

See her! Why, never to think of womankind again.   305

HELLENA.

Kneel—and swear—

Kneels, she gives him her hand.

WILLMORE.

I do, never to think—to see—to love—nor lie—with any but thy self.

HELLENA.

Kiss the book.

WILLMORE.

Oh, most religiously. (*Kisses her hand.*)   310

HELLENA.

Now what a wicked creature am I, to damn a proper fellow.

CALLIS. (*To Florinda.*)

Madam, I'll stay no longer, 'tis e'en dark.

FLORINDA.

However, sir, I'll leave this with you—that when I'm gone, you may repent the opportunity you   315
have lost by your modesty.

Gives him the jewel which is her picture, and exits. He gazes after her.

WILLMORE.

'Twill be an age till tomorrow—and till then I will most impatiently expect you. Adieu, my dear pretty angel.

Exeunt all the women.

BELVILE.

Hah! Florinda's picture—'twas she herself—what   320
a dull dog was I! I would have given the world for one minute's discourse with her.

FREDERICK.

This comes of your modesty! Ah, pox o' your vow, 'twas ten to one, but we had lost the jewel by't.

BELVILE.

Willmore! The blessed'st opportunity lost!   325
Florinda! Friends! Florinda!

WILLMORE.

Ah rogue! such black eyes! such a face! such a mouth! such teeth! and so much wit!

BELVILE.

All, all, and a thousand charms besides.

WILLMORE.

Why, dost thou know her?   330

BELVILE.

Know her! Aye, aye, and a pox take me with all my heart for being modest.

WILLMORE.

But hark ye, friend of mine, are you my rival? And have I been only beating the bush all this while?

BELVILE.

I understand thee not. I'm mad. See here— (*Shows* 335
the picture.)

WILLMORE.

Hah! Whose picture's this? 'Tis a fine wench!

FREDERICK.

The colonel's mistress, sir.

WILLMORE.

Oh, oh, here—I thought't had been another prize.
Come, come, a bottle will set thee right again.
(*Gives the picture back.*)

BELVILE.

I am content to try, and by that time 'twill be late 340
enough for our design.

WILLMORE.

Agreed.
Love does all day the soul's great empire keep,
But wine at night lulls the soft god asleep.

Exeunt.

Scene ii. Lucetta's house.

Enter Blunt and Lucetta with a light.

LUCETTA.

Now we are safe and free; no fears of the coming
home of my old jealous husband, which made me
a little thoughtful when you came in first. But now
love is all the business of my soul.

BLUNT. (*Aside.*)

I am transported! Pox on't, that I had but some fine 5
things to say to her, such as lovers use. I was a fool
not to learn of Frederick a little by heart before I
came. Something I must say.—'Sheartlikins, sweet
soul! I am not used to compliment, but I'm an
honest gentleman, and thy humble servant. 10

LUCETTA.

I have nothing to pay for so great a favor, but such
a love as cannot but be great, since at first sight of
that sweet face and shape, it made me your
absolute captive.

BLUNT.

Kind heart! (*Aside.*) How prettily she talks! Egad, 15
I'll show her husband a Spanish trick: send him
out of the world and marry her. She's damnably
in love with me and will ne'er mind settlements,
and so there's that saved.

LUCETTA.

Well, sir, I'll go and undress me and be with you 20
instantly.

BLUNT.

Make haste, then, for 'sheartlikins, dear soul, thou
canst not guess at the pain of a longing lover, when
his joys are drawn within the compass of a few
minutes. 25

LUCETTA.

You speak my sense, and I'll make haste to prove
it.

Exit.

BLUNT.

'Tis a rare girl! And this one night's enjoyment with
her will be worth all the days I ever passed in Essex.
Would she would go with me into England; 30
though to say truth, there's plenty of whores
already. But a pox on 'em, they are such mercenary,
prodigal whores, that they want such a one as this
that's free and generous to give 'em good examples.
Why, what a house she has, how rich and fine! 35

Enter Sancho.

SANCHO.

Sir, my lady has sent me to conduct you to her
chamber.

BLUNT.

Sir, I shall be proud to follow.—Here's one of her
servants too! 'Sheartlikins, by this garb and gravity,
he might be a justice of peace in Essex and is but 40
a pimp here.

Exeunt.

Scene iii.

*The scene changes to a chamber with an alcove bed in't,
a table, etc. Lucetta in bed. Enter Sancho and Blunt,
who takes the candle of Sancho at the door.*

SANCHO.

Sir, my commission reaches no farther.

BLUNT.

Sir, I'll excuse your compliment.

[*Exit Sancho.*]

What, in bed my sweet mistress?

LUCETTA.

You see, I still outdo you in kindness.

BLUNT.

And thou shalt see what haste I'll make to quit scores. —Oh, the luckiest rogue! (*He undresses himself.*)

LUCETTA.

Should you be false or cruel now!

BLUNT.

False! 'Sheartlikins, what dost thou take me for? a Jew? an insensible heathen? A pox of thy old jealous husband; an he were dead, egad, sweet soul, it should be none of my fault if I did not marry thee.

LUCETTA.

It never should be mine.

BLUNT.

Good soul! [*Aside.*] I'm the fortunatest dog!

LUCETTA.

Are you not undressed yet?

BLUNT.

As much as my impatience will permit.

Goes toward the bed in his shirt, drawers, etc.

LUCETTA.

Hold, sir, put out the light, it may betray us else.

BLUNT.

Anything, I need no other light but that of thine eyes! —'Sheartlikins, there I think I had it.

Puts out the candle; the bed descends [presumably through a trap door]; he gropes about to find it.

Why—why—where am I got? What, not yet? Where are you sweetest?Ah, the rogue's silent now—a pretty love-trick this. How she'll laugh at me anon!—You need not, my dear rogue! You need not! I'm all on fire already. Come, come, now call me in pity.—Sure I'm enchanted! I have been round the chamber and can find neither woman nor bed. I locked the door. I'm sure she cannot go that way, or if she could, the bed could not.— Enough, enough, my pretty wanton, do not carry the jest too far— (*Lights on a trap and is let down.*) Hah, betrayed! Dogs! Rogues! Pimps! Help! Help!

Enter Lucetta, Phillippo, and Sancho with a light.

PHILLIPPO.

Ha, ha, ha, he's dispatched finely.

LUCETTA.

Now, sir, had I been coy, we had missed of this booty.

PHILLIPPO.

Nay, when I saw't was a substantial fool, I was mollified; but when you dote upon a serenading coxcomb, upon a face, fine clothes, and a lute, it makes me rage.

LUCETTA.

You know I was never guilty of that folly, my dear Phillippo, but with yourself. But come, let's see what we have got by this.

PHILLIPPO.

A rich coat! Sword and hat—these breeches, too, are well lined. See here, a gold watch! a purse— hah! Gold! at least two hundred pistoles! a bunch of diamond rings! and one with the family arms! a gold box—with a medal of his king! and his lady mother's picture! These were sacred relics, believe me. See, the waistband of his breeches have a mine of gold! Old Queen Bess's,[42] we have a quarrel* to her ever since eighty-eight,[43] and may therefore justify the theft; the Inquisition might have committed it.

LUCETTA.

See, a bracelet of bowed[44] gold! These his sisters tied about his arm at parting. But well—for all this, I fear his being a stranger may make a noise and hinder our trade with them hereafter.

PHILLIPPO.

That's our security; he is not only a stranger to us, but to the country too. The common shore* into which he is descended, thou knowst conducts him into another street, which this light will hinder him from ever finding again. He knows neither your name, nor that of the street where your house is, nay, nor the way to his own lodgings.

---

42 old Queen Bess] Queen Elizabeth I, who reigned from 1558-1603

43 eighty-eight] 1588, year of the defeat of the Spanish Armada

44 bowed] bent, braided

LUCETTA.

And art not thou an unmerciful rogue! not to afford him one night for all this? I should not have been such a Jew. 65

PHILLIPPO.

Blame me not, Lucetta, to keep as much of thee as I can to myself. Come, that thought makes me wanton! Let's to bed!—Sancho, lock up these.
This is the fleece which fools do bear, 70
Designed for witty men to shear.

Exeunt.

Scene iv

The scene changes and discovers Blunt, creeping out of a common shore, his face, etc. all dirty.

BLUNT.

Oh lord! (*Climbing up.*) I am got out at last, and (which is a miracle) without a clue—and now to damning and cursing—but if that would ease me, where shall I begin? With my fortune, myself, or the quean that cozened me? What a dog was I to believe 5 in woman! Oh coxcomb! Ignorant conceited coxcomb! To fancy she could be enamoured with my person! At first sight enamoured! Oh, I'm a cursed puppy! 'Tis plain, "fool" was writ upon my forehead! She perceived it—saw the Essex calf there—for what 10 allurements could there be in this countenance, which I can endure, because I'm acquainted with it—oh, dull, silly dog! To be thus soothed into a cozening! Had I been drunk, I might fondly have credited the young quean! But as I was in my right 15 wits, to be thus cheated confirms it I am a dull, believing, English country fop—but my comrades! Death and the devil! There's the worst of all—then a ballad will be sung tomorrow on the *prado*,[45] to a lousy tune of "The Enchanted 'Squire, and the 20 Annihilated Damsel"—but Frederick, that rogue, and the colonel, will abuse me beyond all Christian patience—had she left me my clothes, I have a bill of exchange at home would have saved my credit— but now all hope is taken from me—well, I'll home 25 (if I can find the way) with this consolation, that I am not the first kind, believing coxcomb; but there

_____
45 *prado*] field, lawn, meadow (Sp.)

are, gallants, many such good natures amongst ye. And though you've better arts to hide your follies, Adsheartlikins y'are all as arrant cullies. 30

Exit.

Scene v. The garden in the night.

Enter Florinda in an undress, with a key and a little box.

FLORINDA.

Well, thus far I'm on my way to happiness. I have got myself free from Callis; my brother, too, I find by yonder light, is got into his cabinet and thinks not of me; I have by good fortune got the key of the garden back door. I'll open it to prevent 5 Belvile's knocking—a little noise will now alarm my brother. Now am I as fearful as a young thief. (*Unlocks the door.*) Hark—what noise is that? Oh, 'twas the wind that played amongst the boughs.— Belvile stays long, methinks—it's time—stay—for 10 fear of a surprise, I'll hide these jewels in yonder jessamine. (*She goes to lay down the box.*)

Enter Willmore drunk.

WILLMORE.

What the devil is become of these fellows, Belvile and Frederick? They promised to stay at the next corner for me, but who the devil knows the corner 15 of a full moon? Now, whereabouts am I? Hah— what have we here? a garden! a very convenient place to sleep in. Hah—what has God sent us here? a female! by this light, a woman! I'm a dog if it be not a very wench! 20

FLORINDA.

He's come! Hah—who's there?

WILLMORE.

Sweet soul! Let me salute* thy shoestring.

FLORINDA.

'Tis not my Belvile. Good heavens! I know him not.—Who are you, and from whence come you?

WILLMORE.

Prithee, prithee child—not so many questions. Let 25 it suffice I am here, child. Come, come kiss me.

FLORINDA.

Good gods! what luck is mine?

WILLMORE.

Only good luck, child, parlous good luck. Come hither. —'Tis a delicate, shining wench—by this hand she's perfumed and smells like any nosegay.—Prithee, dear soul, let's not play the fool and lose time, precious time, for as Gad shall save me, I'm as honest a fellow as breathes, though I'm a little disguised* at present. Come, I say. Why, thou may'st be free with me, I'll be very secret. I'll not boast who 'twas obliged me, not I—for hang me if I know thy name.

FLORINDA.

Heavens! What a filthy beast is this?

WILLMORE.

I am so, and thou ought'st the sooner to lie with me for that reason—for look you child, there will be no sin in't, because 'twas neither designed nor premeditated. 'Tis pure accident on both sides—that's a certain thing now. Indeed, should I make love to you, and to°you vow fidelity—and swear and lie till you believed and yielded—that were to make it wilful fornication, the crying sin of the nation. Thou art therefore (as thou art a good Christian) obliged in conscience to deny me nothing. Now—come be kind without any more idle prating.

FLORINDA.

Oh I am ruined.—Wicked man, unhand me.

WILLMORE.

Wicked! Egad child, a judge, were he young and vigorous and saw those eyes of thine, would know 'twas they gave the first blow—the first provocation. Come prithee, let's lose no time, I say—this is a fine convenient place.

FLORINDA.

Sir, let me go, I conjure you, or I'll call out.

WILLMORE.

Aye, aye, you were best to call witness to see how finely you treat me—do—

FLORINDA.

I'll cry murder! rape! or anything! if you do not instantly let me go.

WILLMORE.

A rape! Come, come, you lie, you baggage, you lie. What, I'll warrant you would fain have the world believe now that you are not so forward as I. No,

not you. Why, at this time of night, was your cobweb door set open, dear spider—but to catch flies? Hah—come—or I shall be damnably angry. Why, what a coil is here—

FLORINDA.

Sir, can you think—

WILLMORE.

That you would do't for nothing—oh, oh, I find what you would be at—look, here's a pistole for you—here's a work indeed—here—take it I say—

FLORINDA.

For Heaven's sake, sir, as you're a gentleman—

WILLMORE.

So—now—now—she would be wheedling me for more—what, you will not take it then—you are resolved you will not? Come, come take it or I'll put it up again—for look ye, I never give more. Why how now, mistress, are you so high i'th'mouth a pistole won't down with you? Hah—why, what a work's here—in good time—come, no struggling to be gone—but an y'are good at a dumb wrestle I'm for ye—look ye—I'm for ye— (*She struggles with him.*)

Enter Belvile and Frederick.

BELVILE.

The door is open. A pox of this mad fellow; I'm angry that we've lost him; I durst have sworn he had followed us.

FREDERICK.

But you were so hasty, Colonel, to be gone.

FLORINDA.

Help! Help! Murder! Help—oh, I am ruined.

BELVILE.

Hah! Sure that's Florinda's voice. (*Comes up to them.*) A man!—Villain, let go that lady!

Willmore turns and draws, Frederick interposes.

FLORINDA.

Belvile! (*A noise.*) Heavens! My brother too is coming, and 'twill be impossible to escape.—Belvile, I conjure you to walk under my chamber window, from whence I'll give you some instructions what to do. This rude man has undone us.

Exit.

WILLMORE.

Belvile!

Enter Pedro, Stephano, and other servants with lights.

PEDRO.

I'm betrayed! Run, Stephano, and see if Florinda
be safe.

Exit Stephano.

So, whoe'er they be, all is not well. I'll to Florinda's
chamber.   100

*They fight and Pedro's party beats 'em out. Going out,
meets Stephano.*

STEPHANO.

You need not, sir; the poor lady's fast asleep and
thinks no harm. I would not awake her, sir, for fear
of frighting her with your danger.

PEDRO.

I'm glad she's there.—Rascals, how came the
garden door open?   105

STEPHANO.

That question comes too late, sir; some of my
fellow servants masquerading, I'll warrant.

PEDRO.

Masquerading! a lewd custom to debauch our
youth. There's something more in this than I
imagine.   110

Exeunt.

Scene vi. Scene changes to the street.

*Enter Belvile in rage, Frederick holding him, and
Willmore melancholy.*

WILLMORE.

Why, how the devil should I know Florinda?

BELVILE.

A plague of your ignorance! If it had not been
Florinda, must you be a beast? a brute? a senseless
swine?

WILLMORE.

Well, sir, you see I am endued with patience—I can   5
bear—though egad, y'are very free with me, methinks. I was in good hopes the quarrel* would have
been on my side, for so uncivilly interrupting me.

BELVILE.

Peace, brute! whilst thou'rt safe.—Oh, I'm
distracted.   10

WILLMORE.

Nay, nay, I'm an unlucky dog, that's certain.

BELVILE.

Ah, curse upon the star that ruled my birth! or
whatsoever other influence that makes me still* so
wretched.

WILLMORE.

Thou break'st my heart with these complaints.   15
There is no star in fault, no influence but sack,*
the cursed sack I drunk.

FREDERICK.

Why, how the devil came you so drunk?

WILLMORE.

Why, how the devil came you so sober?

BELVILE.

A curse upon his thin skull, he was always   20
beforehand that way.

FREDERICK.

Prithee, dear Colonel, forgive him, he's sorry for
his fault.

BELVILE.

He's always so after he has done a mischief—a
plague on all such brutes.   25

WILLMORE.

By this light, I took her for an arrant harlot.

BELVILE.

Damn your debauched opinion! Tell me sot, had'st
thou so much sense and light about thee to
distinguish her woman, and could'st not see
something about her face and person to strike an   30
awful reverence into thy soul?

WILLMORE.

Faith no, I considered her as mere* a woman as I
could wish.

BELVILE.

'Sdeath,* I have no patience.—Draw, or I'll kill
you.   35

WILLMORE.

Let that alone till tomorrow, and if I set not all
right again, use your pleasure.

BELVILE.

Tomorrow! Damn it.
The spiteful light will lead me to no happiness.

Tomorrow is Antonio's and perhaps
Guides him to my undoing. Oh, that I could meet
This rival! This pow'rful fortunate! 40

WILLMORE.
What then?

BELVILE.
Let thy own reason, or my rage, instruct thee.

WILLMORE.
I shall be finely informed, then, no doubt. Hear 45
me, Colonel—hear me—show me the man and I'll
do his business.

BELVILE.
I know him no more than thou, or if I did, I
should not need thy aid.

WILLMORE.
This, you say, is Angellica's house. I promised the 50
kind baggage to lie with her tonight. (*Offers* to go in.)

*Enter Antonio and his page. Antonio knocks on the hilt
of's sword.*

ANTONIO.
You paid the thousand crowns I directed?

PAGE.
To the lady's old woman, sir, I did.

WILLMORE.
Who the devil have we here!

BELVILE.
I'll now plant myself under Florinda's window, and 55
if I find no comfort there, I'll die.

Exeunt Belvile and Frederick. Enter Moretta.

MORETTA.
Page!

PAGE.
Here's my lord.

WILLMORE.
How is this! a picaroon going to board my frigate?
Here's one chase gun[46] for you. 60

*Drawing his sword, jostles Antonio who turns and
draws. They fight, Antonio falls.*

MORETTA.
Oh bless us! We're all undone! (*Runs in and shuts
the door.*)

---

[46] chase gun] swivel gun on bow or stern used in pursuit

PAGE.
Help! Murder!

Belvile returns at the noise of the fighting.

BELVILE.
Hah! The mad rogue's engaged in some unlucky
adventure again.

Enter two or three masqueraders.

MASQUERADERS.
Hah! A man killed! 65

WILLMORE.
How! a man killed! Then I'll go home to sleep.

Puts up and reels out. Exeunt masqueraders another way.

BELVILE.
Who should it be! Pray Heaven the rogue is safe,
for all my quarrel* to him.

*As Belvile is groping about, enter an officer and six
soldiers.*

SOLDIER.
Who's there?

OFFICER.
So here's one dispatched.—Secure the murderer. 70

Soldiers seize on Belvile.

BELVILE.
Do not mistake my charity for murder!
I came to his assistance.

OFFICER.
That shall be tried, sir.—St. Jago,[47] swords drawn
in Carnival time! (*Goes to Antonio.*)

ANTONIO.
Thy hand, prithee. 75

OFFICER.
Hah! Don Antonio!—Look well to the villain
there.—How is it, sir?

ANTONIO.
I'm hurt.

BELVILE.
Has my humanity made me a criminal?

OFFICER.
Away with him. 80

---

[47] St. Jago] Santiago (St. James the Apostle), patron saint
of Spain

BELVILE.

What a cursed chance is this!

Exeunt soldiers with Belvile.

ANTONIO.

This is the man that has set upon me twice.—(*To the officer.*) Carry him to my apartment, till you have farther orders from me.

Exit Antonio led.

Act IV, scene i. A fine room.

Discovers Belvile as by dark alone.

BELVILE.

When shall I be weary of railing on Fortune, who is resolved never to turn with smiles upon me? Two such defeats in one night none but the devil and that mad rogue could have contrived to have plagued me with. I am here a prisoner—but where, 5 Heaven knows—and if there be murder done, I can soon decide[48] the fate of a stranger in a nation without mercy. Yet this is nothing to the torture my soul bows with when I think of losing my fair, my dear, Florinda.—Hark, my door opens—a 10 light—a man—and seems of quality*—armed too! Now shall I die like a dog without defense.

Enter Antonio in a nightgown with a light; his arm in a scarf, and a sword under his arm. He sets the candle on the table.*

ANTONIO.

Sir, I come to know what injuries I have done you that could provoke you to so mean an action as to attack me basely, without allowing time for my 15 defense?

BELVILE.

Sir, for a man in my circumstances to plead innocence would look like fear, but view me well, and you will find no marks of coward on me, nor anything that betrays that brutality you accuse me with. 20

ANTONIO.

In vain, sir, you impose upon my sense.
You are not only he who drew on me last night,
But yesterday before the same house, that of
     Angellica.

_____
[48] decide] determine

Yet there is something in your face and mien
That makes me wish I were mistaken. 25

BELVILE.

I own I fought today in the defense of a friend of
mine with whom you (if you're the same) and your
party were first engaged.
Perhaps you think this crime enough to kill me,
But if you do, I cannot fear you'll do it basely. 30

ANTONIO.

No, sir, I'll make you fit for a defense with this.
(*Gives him the sword.*)

BELVILE.

This gallantry surprises me—nor know I how to
use this present, sir, against a man so brave.

ANTONIO.

You shall not need.
For know, I come to snatch you from a danger 35
That is decreed against you:
Perhaps your life or long imprisonment;
And 'twas with so much courage you offended,
I cannot see you punished.

BELVILE.

How shall I pay this generosity? 40

ANTONIO.

It had been safer to have killed another
Than have attempted me.
To show your danger, sir, I'll let you know my
     quality;
And 'tis the viceroy's son whom you have wounded.

BELVILE.

The viceroy's son! (*Aside.*) 45
Death and confusion! Was this plague reserved
To complete all the rest? Obliged by him!
The man of all the world I would destroy.

ANTONIO.

You seem disordered, sir.

BELVILE.

Yes, trust me, sir, I am, and 'tis with pain 50
That man receives such bounties
Who wants the pow'r to pay 'em back again.

ANTONIO.

To gallant spirits 'tis indeed uneasy;
But you may quickly overpay me, sir.

BELVILE. (*Aside.*)

Then I am well.—Kind Heav'n, but set us even, 55
That I may fight with him and keep my honor safe.

—Oh, I'm impatient, sir, to be discounting
The mighty debt I owe you. Command me
  quickly—

ANTONIO.

I have a quarrel* with a rival, sir,
About the maid we love.   60

BELVILE. (*Aside.*)

Death, 'tis Florinda he means—
That thought destroys my reason,
And I shall kill him—

ANTONIO.

                 My rival, sir,
Is one has all the virtues man can boast of.   65

BELVILE. (*Aside.*)

Death! Who should this be?

ANTONIO.

He challenged me to meet him on the Molo
As soon as day appeared; but last night's quarrel*
Has made my arm unfit to guide a sword.

BELVILE.

I apprehend you, sir; you'd have me kill the man   70
That lays a claim to the maid you speak of.
I'll do't—I'll fly to do't!

ANTONIO.

Sir, do you know her?

BELVILE.

No, sir, but 'tis enough she is admired by you.

ANTONIO.

Sir, I shall rob you of the glory on't,   75
For you must fight under my name and dress.

BELVILE.

That opinion must be strangely obliging that makes
You think I can personate the brave Antonio,
Whom I can but strive to imitate.

ANTONIO.

You say too much to my advantage.   80
Come, sir, the day appears that calls you forth.
Within, sir, is the habit.

Exit Antonio.

BELVILE.

Fantastic Fortune, thou deceitful light,
That cheats the wearied traveller by night,
Though on a precipice each step you tread,   85
I am resolved to follow where you lead.

Exit.

Scene ii. The Molo.

Enter Florinda and Callis in masks with Stephano.

FLORINDA. (*Aside.*)

I'm dying with my fears; Belvile's not coming as I
expected under my window makes me believe that
all those fears are true.—
Canst thou not tell with whom my brother fights?

STEPHANO.

No, madam, they were both in masquerade. I was   5
by when they challenged one another, and they
had decided the quarrel* then, but were prevented
by some cavaliers, which made 'em put it off till
now—but I am sure 'tis about you they fight.

FLORINDA. (*Aside.*)

Nay, then 'tis with Belvile, for what other lover   10
have I that dares fight for me, except Antonio? And
he is too much in favor with my brother. If it be
he, for whom shall I direct my prayers to heaven?

STEPHANO.

Madam, I must leave you, for if my master see me,
I shall be hanged for being your conductor. I   15
escaped narrowly for the excuse I made for you last
night i'th'garden.

FLORINDA.

And I'll reward thee for't. Prithee no more.

Exit Stephano. Enter Don Pedro in his masquing habit.

PEDRO.

Antonio's late today; the place will fill, and we may
be prevented. (*Walks about.*)   20

FLORINDA. (*Aside.*)

"Antonio"—sure I heard amiss.

PEDRO.

But who will not excuse a happy lover
When soft fair arms confine the yielding neck,
And the kind whisper languishingly breathes,
"Must you be gone so soon?"   25
Sure I had dwelt for ever on her bosom.
But stay, he's here.

Enter Belvile dressed in Antonio's clothes.

FLORINDA.

'Tis not Belvile; half my fears are vanished.

PEDRO.

Antonio!

BELVILE. (*Aside.*)

This must be he.—You're early, sir. I do not use 30
to be outdone this way.

PEDRO.

The wretched, sir, are watchful, and 'tis enough
You've the advantage of me in Angellica.

BELVILE. (*Aside.*)

Angellica! Or I've mistook my man or else Antonio.
Can he forget his int'rest in Florinda, 35
And fight for common prize?

PEDRO.

Come, sir, you know our terms—

BELVILE. (*Aside.*)

By Heav'n not I.—
No talking, I am ready, sir. (*Offers to fight,
Florinda runs in.*)

FLORINDA. (*To Belvile.*)

Oh hold! Whoe'er you be, I do conjure you hold! 40
If you strike here—I die.

PEDRO.

Florinda!

BELVILE. [*Aside.*]

Florinda imploring for my rival!

PEDRO.

Away, this kindness is unseasonable.

*Puts her by; they fight; she runs in just as Belvile
disarms Pedro.*

FLORINDA.

Who are you, sir, that dares deny my prayers? 45

BELVILE.

Thy prayers destroy him; if thou would'st preserve
him,
Do that thou'rt unacquainted with and curse him.

She holds him.

FLORINDA.

By all you hold most dear, by her you love,
I do conjure you, touch him not.

BELVILE.

By her I love!
See—I obey—and at your feet resign 50
The useless trophy of my victory.

Lays his sword at her feet.

PEDRO.

Antonio, you've done enough to prove you love
Florinda.

BELVILE.

Love Florinda! Does Heav'n love adoration, prayer 55
or penitence! Love her! Here, sir—your sword
again. (*Snatches up the sword and gives it him.*)
Upon this truth I'll fight my life away.

PEDRO.

No, you've redeemed my sister, and my friendship!

*He gives him Florinda and pulls off his vizard to show
his face and puts it on again.*

BELVILE.

Don Pedro! 60

PEDRO.

Can you resign your claims to other women,
And give your heart entirely to Florinda?

BELVILE.

Entire! as dying saints' confessions are!
I can delay my happiness no longer.
This minute let me make Florinda mine! 65

PEDRO.

This minute let it be—no time so proper.
This night my father will arrive from Rome
And possibly may hinder what we purpose!

FLORINDA.

Oh heavens! this minute!

Enter masqueraders and pass over.

BELVILE.

Oh, do not ruin me! 70

PEDRO.

The place begins to fill, and that we may not be
observed, do you walk off to St. Peter's Church,
where I will meet you and conclude your happiness.

BELVILE.

I'll meet you there—(*Aside.*) if there be no more
saints' churches in Naples. 75

FLORINDA.

Oh, stay sir, and recall your hasty doom!
Alas, I have not yet prepared my heart
To entertain* so strange a guest.

PEDRO.

Away, this silly* modesty is assumed too late.
(*Pedro talks to Callis this while.*)

BELVILE.

Heaven, madam! What do you do?   80

FLORINDA.

Do! Despise the man that lays a tyrant's claim
To what he ought to conquer by submission.

BELVILE.

You do not know me. Move a little this way.
   (*Draws her aside.*)

FLORINDA.

Yes, you may force me even to the altar,
But not the holy man that offers there   85
Shall force me to be thine.

BELVILE.

Oh do not lose so blest an opportunity—
See—'tis your Belvile—not Antonio,
Whom your mistaken scorn and anger ruins.
   (*Pulls off his vizard.*)

FLORINDA.

Belvile!   90
Where was my soul it could not meet thy voice
And take this knowledge in?

*As they are talking, enter Willmore, finely dressed, and
Frederick.*

WILLMORE.

No intelligence, no news of Belvile yet! Well, I am
the most unlucky rascal in nature. Hah—am I
deceived? or is it he? Look, Fred—'tis he—my dear   95
Belvile!

*Runs and embraces him. Belvile's vizard falls out on's
hand.*

BELVILE.

Hell and confusion seize thee!

PEDRO.

Hah! Belvile! I beg your pardon sir.

Takes Florinda from him.

BELVILE.

Nay, touch her not. She's mine by conquest, sir;
I won her by my sword.   100

WILLMORE.

Didst thou so! And egad, child, we'll keep her by
   the sword.

Draws on Pedro. Belvile goes between.

BELVILE.

Stand off!
Thou'rt so profanely lewd, so curst by Heaven,
All quarrels* thou espousest must be fatal.

WILLMORE.

Nay, an you be so hot, my valor's coy, and shall   105
be courted when you want it next. (*Puts up his
sword.*)

BELVILE. (*To Pedro.*)

You know I ought to claim a victor's right.
But you're the brother to divine Florinda,
To whom I'm such a slave—to purchase her,
I durst not hurt the man she holds so dear.   110

PEDRO.

'Twas by Antonio's, not by Belvile's sword
This question should have been decided, sir.
I must confess, much to your bravery's due,
Both now, and when I met you last in arms.
But I am nicely punctual in my word,   115
As men of honor ought, and beg your pardon.
For this mistake another time shall clear.
(*Aside to Florinda as they are going out.*)
This was some plot between you and Belvile.
But I'll prevent you.

*Belvile looks after her and begins to walk up and down
in rage.*

WILLMORE.

Do not be modest now and lose the woman, but   120
if we shall fetch her back so—

BELVILE.

Do not speak to me—

WILLMORE.

Not speak to you? Egad, I'll speak to you, and will
be answered, too.

BELVILE.

Will you, sir—   125

WILLMORE.

I know I've done some mischief, but I'm so dull a
puppy, that I'm the son of a whore if I know how,
or where—prithee inform my understanding—

BELVILE.

Leave me, I say, and leave me instantly.

WILLMORE.

I will not leave you in this humor*, nor till I know 130
my crime.

BELVILE.

Death, I'll tell you sir—

Draws and runs at Willmore. He runs out, Belvile after him; Frederick interposes. Enter Angellica, Moretta and Sebastian.

ANGELLICA.

Hah—Sebastian—

Is not that Willmore? Haste—haste and bring
    him back.   135

FREDERICK.

The colonel's mad—I never saw him thus before.
I'll after 'em lest he do some mischief, for I am
sure Willmore will not draw on him.

Exit.

ANGELLICA.

I am all rage! my first desires defeated!
For one for aught he knows that has no   140
Other merit than her quality,
Her being Don Pedro's sister—he loves her!
I know 'tis so—dull, dull, insensible—
He will not see me now though oft invited,
And broke his word last night—false perjured man!   145
He that but yesterday fought for my favors
And would have made his life a sacrifice
To've gained one night with me
Must now be hired and courted to my arms.

MORETTA.

I told you what would come on't, but Moretta's an   150
old doting fool. Why did you give him five
hundred crowns, but to set himself out for other
lovers! You should have kept him poor if you had
meant to have had any good from him.

ANGELLICA.

Oh, name not such mean trifles; had I given him all   155
My youth has earned from sin,
I had not lost a thought, nor sigh upon't.
But I have given him my eternal rest,
My whole repose, my future joys, my heart!
My virgin heart, Moretta! Oh, 'tis gone!   160

MORETTA.

Curse on him, here he comes; how fine she has
made him too.

Enter Willmore and Sebastian; Angellica turns and walks away.

WILLMORE.

How now, turned shadow!
Fly when I pursue and follow when I fly! (*Sings.*)
Stay, gentle shadow of my dove   165
And tell me ere I go,
Whether the substance may not prove
A fleeting thing like you.

As she turns she looks on him.

There's a soft kind look remaining yet.

ANGELLICA.

Well sir, you may be gay; all happiness, all joys,   170
pursue you still. Fortune's your slave and gives you
every hour choice of new hearts and beauties, till
you are cloyed with the repeated bliss which others
vainly languish for. (*Turns away in rage.*) But know,
false man, that I shall be revenged.   175

WILLMORE.

So, gad, there are of those faint-hearted lovers whom
such a sharp lesson next their hearts would make as
impotent as fourscore. Pox o' this whining. My
business is to laugh and love. A pox on't, I hate your
sullen lover. A man shall lose as much time to put you 180
in humor now, as would serve to gain a new woman.

ANGELLICA.

I scorn to cool that fire I cannot raise,
Or do the drudgery of your virtuous mistress.

WILLMORE.

A virtuous mistress! Death, what a thing thou hast
found out for me! Why, what the devil should I do   185
with a virtuous woman? a sort of ill-natured
creatures, that take a pride to torment a lover. Virtue
is but an infirmity in woman, a disease that renders
even the handsome ungrateful; whilst the ill-favored,
for want of solicitations and address, only fancy   190
themselves so. I have lain with a woman of quality,*
who has all the while been railing at whores.

ANGELLICA.

I will not answer for your mistress's virtue,
Though she be young enough to know no guilt;
And I could wish you would persuade my heart   195
'Twas the two hundred thousand crowns you
    courted.

WILLMORE.

Two hundred thousand crowns! What story's this?
What trick? What woman? Hah!

ANGELLICA.

How strange you make it; have you forgot the 200
creature you entertained on the piazza last night?

WILLMORE. (*Aside.*)

Hah! My Gypsy worth two hundred thousand
crowns! Oh, how I long to be with her. Pox, I
knew she was of quality.*

ANGELLICA.

False man! I see my ruin in thy face. 205
How many vows you breathed upon my bosom,
Never to be unjust—have you forgot so soon?

WILLMORE.

Faith no, I was just coming to repeat 'em—but
here's a humor indeed would make a man a saint.
(*Aside.*) Would she would be angry enough to leave 210
me and command me not to wait on her.

Enter Hellena dressed in man's clothes.

HELLENA.

This must be Angellica! I know it by her
mumping* matron here. Aye, aye, 'tis she! My mad
captain's with her too, for all his swearing—how
this unconstant humor* makes me love him!— 215
Pray, good grave gentlewoman, is not this
Angellica?

MORETTA.

My too young sir, it is.—I hope 'tis one from Don
Antonio. (*Goes to Angellica.*)

HELLENA. (*Aside.*)

Well, something I'll do to vex him for this. 220

ANGELLICA.

I will not speak with him; am I in humor to receive
a lover?

WILLMORE.

Not speak with him! Why, I'll be gone and wait
your idler minutes. Can I show less obedience to
the thing I love so fondly? (*Offers to go.*) 225

ANGELLICA.

A fine excuse this! Stay—

WILLMORE.

And hinder your advantage! Should I repay your
bounties so ungratefully?

ANGELLICA.

Come hither, boy—that I may let you see
How much above the advantages you name 230
I prize one minute's joy with you.

WILLMORE.

Oh, you destroy me with this endearment.
(*Impatient to be gone.*) Death! How shall I get
away?—Madam, 'twill not be fit I should be seen
with you; besides, it will not be convenient—and 235
I've a friend—that's dangerously sick.

ANGELLICA.

I see you're impatient—yet you shall stay.

WILLMORE. (*Aside, and walks about impatiently.*)

And miss my assignation with my Gypsy.

*Moretta brings Hellena, who addresses herself to
Angellica.*

HELLENA.

Madam, you'll hardly pardon my intrusion
When you shall know my business, 240
And I'm too young to tell my tale with art;
But there must be a wondrous store of goodness,
Where so much beauty dwells.

ANGELLICA.

A pretty advocate, whoever sent thee.
Prithee proceed—(*To Willmore, who is stealing* 245
off.) Nay, sir, you shall not go.

WILLMORE. (*Aside.*)

Then I shall lose my dear Gypsy for ever. Pox on't,
she stays me out of spite.

HELLENA.

I am related to a lady, madam,
Young, rich, and nobly born, but has the fate
To be in love with a young English gentleman. 250
Strangely she loves him, at first sight she loved him,
But did adore him when she heard him speak;
For he, she said, had charms in every word,
That failed not to surprise, to wound and conquer.

WILLMORE. (*Aside.*)

Hah! Egad, I hope this concerns me. 255

ANGELLICA. [*Aside.*]

'Tis my false man, he means—would he were gone.
This praise will raise his pride and ruin me— (*To
Willmore.*) Well
Since you are so impatient to be gone,
I will release you, sir.

WILLMORE. (*Aside.*)

Nay, then, I'm sure 'twas me he spoke of; this 260
cannot be the effects of kindness in her.—No,
madam, I've considered better on't and will not
give you cause of jealousy.

ANGELLICA.

But, sir, I've—business, that—

WILLMORE.

This shall not do; I know 'tis but to try me. 265

ANGELLICA.

Well, to your story, boy— (*Aside.*) though 'twill
  undo me.

HELLENA.

With this addition to his other beauties,
He won her unresisting tender heart.
He vowed, and sighed, and swore he loved her dearly;
And she believed the cunning flatterer 270
And thought herself the happiest maid alive.
Today was the appointed time by both
To consummate their bliss,
The virgin, altar, and the priest were dressed
And whilst she languished for th'expected 275
  bridegroom,
She heard he paid his broken vows to you.

WILLMORE.

So, this is some dear rogue that's in love with me
and this way lets me know it, or if it be not me,
he means someone whose place I may supply.

ANGELLICA.

Now I perceive 280
The cause of thy impatience to be gone
And all the business of this glorious dress.

WILLMORE.

Damn the young prater, I know not what he means.

HELLENA.

Madam,
In your fair eyes I read too much concern 285
To tell my farther business.

ANGELLICA.

Prithee, sweet youth, talk on, thou mayest perhaps
Raise here a storm that may undo my passion,
And then I'll grant thee anything.

HELLENA.

Madam, 'tis to entreat you (oh unreasonable) 290
You would not see this stranger;
For if you do, she vows you are undone,
Though nature never made a man so excellent,
And sure he'd been a god, but for inconstancy.

WILLMORE. (*Aside.*)

Ah, rogue, how finely he's instructed! 'Tis plain; 295
some woman that has seen me *en passant*.

ANGELLICA.

Oh, I shall burst with jealousy! Do you know the
man you speak of?

HELLENA.

Yes, madam, he used to be in buff and scarlet. 300

ANGELLICA. (*To Willmore.*)

Thou, false as hell, what canst thou say to this?

WILLMORE.

By Heaven— (*He walks about, they follow.*)

ANGELLICA.

Hold, do not damn thyself—

HELLENA.

Nor hope to be believed.

ANGELLICA.

Oh perjured man! 305
Is't thus you pay my generous passion back?

HELLENA.

Why would you, sir, abuse my lady's faith?

ANGELLICA.

And use me so unhumanely.

HELLENA.

A maid so young, so innocent—

WILLMORE.

Ah, young devil. 310

ANGELLICA.

Dost thou know thy life is in my power?

HELLENA.

Or think my lady cannot be revenged?

WILLMORE. (*Aside.*)

So, so, the storm comes finely on.

ANGELLICA.

Now thou art silent, guilt has struck thee dumb.
Oh, hadst thou still been so, I'd lived in safety. 315
  (*She turns away and weeps.*)

WILLMORE. (*Aside to Hellena; looks toward
  Angellica to watch her turning and as she comes
  towards them he meets her.*)

Sweetheart, the lady's name and house—quickly,
I'm impatient to be with her.

HELLENA. (*Aside.*)

So, now is he for another woman.

WILLMORE.

The impudent'st young thing in nature,
I cannot persuade him out of his error, madam. 320

ANGELLICA.

I know he's in the right—yet thou'st a tongue

That would persuade him to deny his faith. (*In rage walks away.*)

WILLMORE.

Her name, her name, dear boy— (*Said softly to Hellena.*)

HELLENA.

Have you forgot it, sir?

WILLMORE. (*Aside.*)

Oh, I perceive he's not to know I am a stranger to this lady.—Yes, yes, I do know—but I have forgot the—

Angellica turns.

—By heaven such early confidence I never saw.

ANGELLICA.

Did I not charge you with this mistress, sir? Which you denied, though I beheld your perjury. This little generosity of thine has rendered back my heart. (*Walks away.*)

WILLMORE.

So, you have made sweet work here, my little mischief; look your lady be kind and good-natured now, or I shall have but a cursed bargain on't.

Angellica turns toward them.

—The rogue's bred up to mischief; Art thou so great a fool to credit him?

ANGELLICA.

Yes, I do, and you in vain impose upon me. —Come hither, boy. Is not this he you spake of?

HELLENA.

I think—it is; I cannot swear, but I vow he has just such another lying lover's look. (*Hellena looks in his face, he gazes on her.*)

WILLMORE. (*Aside.*)

Hah! Do not I know that face? By Heaven, my little Gypsy! what a dull dog was I! Had I but looked that way I'd known her. Are all my hopes of a new woman banished?—Egad, if I do not fit thee for this, hang me.— Madam, I have found out the plot.

HELLENA. [*Aside.*]

Oh lord, what does he say? Am I discovered now?

WILLMORE.

Do you see this young spark here?

HELLENA. [*Aside.*]

He'll tell her who I am.

WILLMORE.

Who do you think this is?

HELLENA. [*Aside.*]

Aye, aye, he does know me.—Nay, dear Captain! I am undone if you discover me.

WILLMORE.

Nay, nay, no cogging; she shall know what a precious* mistress I have.

HELLENA.

Will you be such a devil?

WILLMORE.

Nay, nay, I'll teach you to spoil sport you will not make.—This small ambassador comes not from a person of quality,* as you imagine and he says, but from a very arrant Gypsy, the talkingest, pratingest, cantingest little animal thou ever saw'st.

ANGELLICA.

What news you tell me, that's the thing I mean.

HELLENA. (*Aside.*)

Would I were well off the place; if ever I go a captain-hunting again—

WILLMORE.

Mean that thing? that Gypsy thing? Thou may'st as well be jealous of thy monkey or parrot, as of her; a German motion* were worth a dozen of her, and a dream were a better enjoyment, a creature of a constitution fitter for heaven than man.

HELLENA. (*Aside.*)

Though I'm sure he lies, yet this vexes me.

ANGELLICA.

You are mistaken, she's a Spanish woman Made up of no such dull materials.

WILLMORE.

Materials, egad, an she be made of any that will either dispense or admit of love, I'll be bound to continence.

HELLENA. (*Aside to him.*)

Unreasonable man, do you think so?

WILLMORE.

You may return, my little brazen head,[49] and tell your lady that till she be handsome enough to be beloved, or I dull enough to be religious, there will be small hopes of me.

---

49 brazen head] a brazen (brass) head which can speak or prophesy

ANGELLICA.

Did you not promise then to marry her?   380

WILLMORE.

Not I, by Heaven.

ANGELLICA.

You cannot undeceive my fears and torments till
you have vowed you will not marry her.

HELLENA. (*Aside.*)

If he swears that, he'll be revenged on me indeed
for all my rogueries.   385

ANGELLICA.

I know what arguments you'll bring up against
me—fortune, and honor—

WILLMORE.

Honor, I tell you, I hate it in your sex, and those that
fancy themselves possessed of that foppery are the
most impertinently troublesome of all womankind   390
and will transgress nine commandments to keep
one, and to satisfy your jealousy, I swear—

HELLENA. (*Aside to him.*)

Oh, no swearing, dear Captain.

WILLMORE.

If it were possible I should ever be inclined to
marry, it should be some kind young sinner, one   395
that has generosity enough to give a favor
handsomely to one that can ask it discreetly, one
that has wit enough to manage an intrigue of
love—oh, how civil such a wench is, to a man that
does her the honor to marry her.   400

ANGELLICA.

By Heaven, there's no faith in anything he says.

Enter Sebastian.

SEBASTIAN.

Madam, Don Antonio—

ANGELLICA.

Come hither.

HELLENA. [*Aside.*]

Hah! Antonio! He may be coming hither, and he'll
certainly discover me. I'll therefore retire without   405
a ceremony.

Exit Hellena.

ANGELLICA.

I'll see him; get my coach ready.

SEBASTIAN.

It waits you, madam.

WILLMORE.

This is lucky.—What, madam, now I may be gone
and leave you to the enjoyment of my rival?   410

ANGELLICA.

Dull man, that canst not see how ill, how poor,
That false dissimulation looks. Be gone,
And never let me see thy cozening face again,
Lest I relapse and kill thee.

WILLMORE.

Yes, you can spare me now— Farewell, till you're   415
in better humor.—I'm glad of this release—
Now for my Gypsy:
For though to worse we change, yet still we find
New joys, new charms, in a new miss that's kind.

Exit Willmore.

ANGELLICA.

He's gone, and in this ague of my soul,   420
The shivering fit returns;
Oh, with what willing haste he took his leave,
As if the longed-for minute were arrived
Of some blest assignation.
In vain I have consulted all my charms,   425
In vain this beauty prized, in vain believed
My eyes could kindle any lasting fires.
I had forgot my name, my infamy,
And the reproach that honor lays on those
That dare pretend a sober passion here.   430
Nice* reputation, though it leave behind
More virtues than inhabit where that dwells,
Yet that once gone, those virtues shine no more.
Then since I am not fit to be beloved,
I am resolved to think on a revenge   435
On him that soothed me thus to my undoing.

Exeunt.

                    Scene iii. A street.

*Enter Florinda and Valeria in habits different from
what they have been seen in.*

FLORINDA.

We're happily escaped, and yet I tremble still.

VALERIA.

A lover and fear! Why, I am but half an one, and

yet I have courage for any attempt. Would Hellena were here, I would fain have had her as deep in this mischief as we; she'll fare but ill else, I doubt.

FLORINDA.

She pretended a visit to the Augustine nuns, but I believe some other design carried her out. Pray Heaven we light on her. Prithee, what didst do with Callis?

VALERIA.

When I saw no reason would do good on her, I followed her into the wardrobe, and as she was looking for something in a great chest, I toppled her in by the heels, snatched the key of the apartment where you were confined, locked her in, and left her bawling for help.

FLORINDA.

'Tis well you resolve to follow my fortunes, for thou darest never appear at home again after such an action.

VALERIA.

That's according as the young stranger and I shall agree. But to our business: I delivered your letter, your note to Belvile, when I got out under pretence of going to mass. I found him at his lodging, and believe me it came seasonably, for never was a man in so desperate a condition. I told him of your resolution of making your escape today if your brother would be absent long enough to permit you; if not, to die rather than be Antonio's.

FLORINDA.

Thou shouldst have told him I was confined to my chamber upon my brother's suspicion that the business on the Molo was a plot laid between him and I.

VALERIA.

I said all this, and told him your brother was now gone to his devotion, and he resolves to visit every church till he find him and not only undeceive him in that, but caress him so as shall delay his return home.

FLORINDA.

Oh heavens! He's here, and Belvile with him too.

They put on their vizards. Enter Don Pedro, Belvile, Willmore; Belvile and Don Pedro seeming in serious discourse.

VALERIA.

Walk boldly by them, and I'll come at distance, lest he suspect us. (*She walks by them, and looks back on them.*)

WILLMORE.

Hah! A woman, and of an excellent mien.

PEDRO.

She throws a kind look back on you.

WILLMORE.

Death, 'tis a likely wench, and that kind look shall not be cast away—I'll follow her.

BELVILE.

Prithee do not.

WILLMORE.

Do not? By heavens, to the antipodes with such an invitation.

She goes out, and Willmore follows her.

BELVILE.

'Tis a mad fellow for a wench.

Enter Frederick.

FREDERICK.

Oh Colonel, such news!

BELVILE.

Prithee what?

FREDERICK.

News that will make you laugh in spite of Fortune.

BELVILE.

What, Blunt has had some damned trick put upon him: Cheated, banged or clapped?[50]

FREDERICK.

Cheated sir, rarely cheated of all but his shirt and drawers. The unconscionable whore, too, turned him out before consummation, so that traversing the streets at midnight, the watch found him in this fresco, and conducted him home. By Heaven, 'tis such a sight, and yet I durst as well been hanged as laugh at him or pity him; he beats all that do but ask him a question, and is in such an humor.

PEDRO.

Who is't has met with this ill usage, sir?

---

50 clapped] hit, struck; also, to get the clap (venereal disease)

BELVILE.

A friend of ours whom you must see for mirth's
sake. (*Aside.*) I'll employ him to give Florinda time
for an escape.   65

PEDRO.

What is he?

BELVILE.

A young countryman of ours, one that has been
educated at so plentiful a rate, he yet ne'er knew
the want of money, and 'twill be a great jest to see
how simply he'll look without it. For my part, I'll   70
lend him none, an the rogue know not how to put
on a borrowing face and ask first; I'll let him see
how good 'tis to play our parts whilst I play his.—
Prithee Frederick, do you go home and keep him
in that posture till we come.   75

*Exeunt. Enter Florinda from the farther end of the
scene, looking behind her.*

FLORINDA.

I am followed still— Hah! my brother too,
advancing this way. Good heavens, defend me
from being seen by him.

*She goes off. Enter Willmore, and after him Valeria, at
a little distance.*

WILLMORE.

Ah! There she sails; she looks back as she were
willing to be boarded. I'll warrant her prize.[51]   80

*He goes out, Valeria following. Enter Hellena, just as
he goes out, with a page.*

HELLENA.

Hah, is not that my captain that has a woman in
chase? 'Tis not Angellica. Boy, follow those people
at a distance, and bring me an account where they
go in.—I'll find his haunts and plague him
everywhere.—Hah, my brother—   85

*Exit page; Belvile, Willmore, Pedro cross the stage;
Hellena runs off.*

---

51 sails ... boarded ... prize] In sea battles and piracy, captured ships, called prizes, were seized as the property of
those who boarded them.

Scene iv. Scene changes to another street.

Enter Florinda.

FLORINDA.

What shall I do, my brother now pursues me.
Will no kind pow'r protect me from his tyranny?
Hah, here's a door open; I'll venture in, since
nothing can be worse than to fall into his hands.
My life and honor are at stake, and my necessity   5
has no choice.

*She goes in. Enter Valeria and Hellena's page peeping
after Florinda.*

PAGE.

Here she went in; I shall remember this house.

Exit Boy.

VALERIA.

This is Belvile's lodging; she's gone in as readily as
if she knew it.—Hah! here's that mad fellow again.
I dare not venture in. I'll watch my opportunity.   10

Goes aside. Enter Willmore, gazing about him.

WILLMORE.

I have lost her hereabouts. Pox on't, she must not
scape me so. (*Goes out.*)

Scene v. Blunt's chamber.

*Blunt discovered sitting on a couch in his shirt and
drawers, reading.*

BLUNT.

So, now my mind's a little at peace, since I have
resolved revenge. A pox on this tailor though, for
not bringing home the clothes I bespoke. And a
pox of all poor cavaliers, a man can never keep a
spare suit for 'em, and I shall have these rogues   5
come in and find me naked. And then I'm undone.
But I'm resolved to arm myself—the rascals shall
not insult over me too much. (*Puts on an old rusty
sword and buff belt.*) Now, how like a morris dancer
I am equipped. A fine lady-like whore to cheat me   10
thus, without affording me a kindness for my
money. A pox light on her, I shall never be
reconciled to the sex more; she has made me as
faithless as a physician, as uncharitable as a

churchman, and as ill-natured as a poet. Oh, how 15
I'll use all womankind hereafter! What would I
give to have one of 'em within my reach now! Any
mortal thing in petticoats, kind Fortune, send me,
and I'll forgive thy last night's malice. Here's a
cursed book too (a warning to all young travellers) 20
that can instruct me how to prevent such mischiefs
now 'tis too late; well, 'tis a rare convenient thing
to read a little now and then, as well as hawk and
hunt. (*Sits down again and reads.*)

Enter to him Florinda.

FLORINDA.
This house is haunted sure; 'tis well furnished and 25
no living thing inhabits it.—Hah, a man! Heavens,
how he's attired! Sure 'tis some ropedancer or
fencing master;[52] I tremble now for fear, and yet
I must venture now to speak to him.—Sir, if I may
not interrupt your meditations— 30

He starts up and gazes.

BLUNT.
Hah, what's here! Are my wishes granted? and is
not that a she creature? 'Sheartlikins, 'tis! What
wretched thing art thou——hah!

FLORINDA.
Charitable sir, you've told yourself already what I
am, a very wretched maid, forced by a strange 35
unlucky accident to seek safety here,
And must be ruined, if you do not grant it.

BLUNT.
Ruined! Is there any ruin so inevitable as that
which now threatens thee? Dost thou know,
miserable woman, into what den of mischiefs thou 40
art fallen? what abyss of confusion—hah! Dost not
see something in my looks that frights thy guilty
soul and makes thee wish to change that shape of
woman for any humble animal or devil? For those
were safer for thee, and less mischievous. 45

FLORINDA.
Alas, what mean you, sir? I must confess, your
looks have something in 'em makes me fear, but I

---

52 ropedancer or fencing-master] like a morris dancer, a
ropedancer or fencing master would wear loose, light
clothing.

beseech you, as you seem a gentleman, pity a
harmless virgin that takes your house for sanctuary.

BLUNT.
Talk on, talk on, and weep too, till my faith return. 50
Do, flatter me out of my senses again—a harmless
virgin with a pox, as much one as t'other,
'sheartlikins. Why, what the devil, can I not be safe
in my house for you, not in my chamber, nay, even
being naked too cannot secure me; this is an 55
impudence greater than has invaded me yet. (*Pulls
her rudely.*) Come, no resistance.

FLORINDA.
Dare you be so cruel?

BLUNT.
Cruel? 'Sheartlikins, as a galley slave, or a Spanish
whore. Cruel? Yes, I will kiss and beat thee all over, 60
kiss and see thee all over; thou shalt lie with me
too, not that I care for the enjoyment, but to let
thee see I have ta'en deliberated malice to thee and
will be revenged on one whore for the sins of
another. I will smile and deceive thee, flatter thee, 65
and beat thee, kiss and swear and lie to thee,
embrace thee and rob thee, as she did me; fawn
on thee and strip thee stark naked; then hang thee
out at my window by the heels, with a paper of
scurvy verses fastened to thy breast, in praise of 70
damnable women. Come, come along.

FLORINDA.
Alas, sir, must I be sacrificed for the crimes of the
most infamous of my sex? I never understood the
sins you name.

BLUNT.
Do, persuade the fool you love him, or that one 75
of you can be just or honest; tell me I was not an
easy coxcomb, or any strange impossible tale. It
will be believed sooner than thy false showers or
protestations. A generation of damned hypocrites
to flatter my very clothes from my back! 80
Dissembling witches! Are these the returns you
make an honest gentleman, that trusts, believes,
and loves you? But if I be not even with you—
(*Pulls her again.*) Come along—or I shall—

Enter Frederick.

FREDERICK.
Hah! What's here to do? 85

BLUNT.

'Sheartlikins, Fred. I am glad thou art come to be a witness of my dire revenge.

FREDERICK.

What's this, a person of quality* too, who is upon the ramble to supply the defects of some grave impotent husband? 90

BLUNT.

No, this has another pretence; some very unfortunate accident brought her hither to save a life pursued by I know not who, or why, and forced to take sanctuary here at Fool's Haven. 'Sheartlikins, to me of all mankind for protection? 95 Is the ass to be cajoled again, think ye? No, young one, no prayers or tears shall mitigate my rage; therefore, prepare for both my pleasures of enjoyment and revenge, for I am resolved to make up my loss here on thy body; I'll take it out in 100 kindness and in beating.

FREDERICK.

Now, mistress of mine, what do you think of this?

FLORINDA.

I think he will not—dares not—be so barbarous.

FREDERICK.

Have a care, Blunt, she fetched a deep sigh; she is enamored with thy shirt and drawers. She'll strip 105 thee even of that. There are of her calling such unconscionable baggages, and such dextrous thieves, they'll flay a man and he shall ne'er miss his skin till he feels the cold. There was a countryman of ours robbed of a row of teeth whilst 110 he was a-sleeping, which the jilt made him buy again when he waked. You see, lady, how little reason we have to trust you.

BLUNT.

'Sheartlikins, why this is most abominable.

FLORINDA.

Some such devils there may be, but by all that's 115 holy, I am none such; I entered here to save a life in danger.

BLUNT.

For no goodness, I'll warrant her.

FREDERICK.

Faith, damsel, you had e'en confessed the plain truth, for we are fellows not to be caught twice in the 120 same trap. Look on that wreck, a tight vessel when

he set out of haven, well trimmed and laden, and see how a female picaroon of this island of rogues has shattered him, and canst thou hope for any mercy?

BLUNT.

No, no, gentlewoman, come along; 'sheartlikins, 125 we must be better acquainted.—We'll both lie with her, and then let me alone to bang her.

FREDERICK.

I'm ready to serve you in matters of revenge that has a double pleasure in't.

BLUNT.

Well said. You hear, little one, how you are 130 condemned by public vote to the bed within. (*Pulls her.*) There's no resisting your destiny, sweetheart.

FLORINDA.

Stay, sir, I have seen you with Belvile, an English cavalier; for his sake use me kindly. You know him, sir.

BLUNT.

Belvile, why yes, sweeting, we do know Belvile, and 135 wish he were with us now; he's a cormorant at whore and bacon; he'd have a limb or two of thee, my virgin pullet, but 'tis no matter, we'll leave him the bones to pick.

FLORINDA.

Sir, if you have any esteem for that Belvile, I 140 conjure you to treat me with more gentleness; he'll thank you for the justice.

FREDERICK.

Hark ye, Blunt, I doubt we are mistaken in this matter.

FLORINDA.

Sir, if you find me not worth Belvile's care, use me 145 as you please, and that you may think I merit better treatment than you threaten—pray take this present—

Gives him a ring; he looks on it.

BLUNT.

Hum—a diamond! Why, 'tis a wonderful virtue now that lies in this ring, a mollifying virtue; 150 'sheartlikins, there's more persuasive rhetoric in't than all her sex can utter.

FREDERICK.

I begin to suspect something; and 'twould anger us vilely to be trussed up for a rape upon a maid of quality,* when we only believe we ruffle a harlot. 155

BLUNT.

Thou art a credulous fellow, but 'sheartlikins, I have
no faith yet. Why, my saint prattled as parlously as
this does, she gave me a bracelet too, a devil on her,
but I sent my man to sell it today for necessaries, and
it proved as counterfeit as her vows of love.   160

FREDERICK.

However, let it reprieve her till we see Belvile.

BLUNT.

That's hard, yet I will grant it.

Enter a servant.

SERVANT.

Oh, sir, the colonel is just come in with his new
friend and a Spaniard of quality, and talks of
having you to dinner with 'em.   165

BLUNT.

'Sheartlikins, I'm undone—I would not see 'em for
the world. Hark ye, Fred, lock up the wench in
your chamber.

FREDERICK.

Fear nothing, madam; whate'er he threatens, you
are safe whilst in my hands.   170

Exeunt Frederick and Florinda.

BLUNT.

And, sirrah, upon your life, say—I am not at
home—or that I'm asleep—or—or anything—
away—I'll prevent their coming this way.

Locks the door and exeunt.

Act V, scene i. Blunt's Chamber.

*After a great knocking as at his chamber door, enter
Blunt softly crossing the stage, in his shirt and drawers
as before.*

[VOICES.] (*Call and knocking within.*)

Ned, Ned Blunt, Ned Blunt.

BLUNT.

The rogues are up in arms. 'Sheartlikins, this
villainous Frederick has betrayed me; they have
heard of my blessed fortune—

[VOICES.]

Ned Blunt, Ned, Ned—   5

BELVILE. [*Within.*]

Why, he's dead, sir, without dispute dead, he has

not been seen today; let's break open the door—
here—boy—

BLUNT.

Hah, break open the door! 'Sheartlikins, that mad
fellow will be as good as his word.   10

BELVILE. [*Within.*]

Boy, bring something to force the door.

A great noise within, at the door again.

BLUNT.

So, now must I speak in my own defense; I'll try
what rhetoric will do.—Hold, hold, what do you
mean gentlemen, what do you mean?

BELVILE. (*Within.*)

Oh rogue, art alive? Prithee, open the door and   15
convince us.

BLUNT.

Yes, I am alive gentlemen—but at present a little
busy.

BELVILE. (*Within.*)

How, Blunt grown a man of business? Come,
come, open and let's see this miracle.   20

BLUNT.

No, no, no, no, gentlemen, 'tis no great business—
but—I am—at—my devotion—'sheartlikins, will
you not allow a man time to pray?

BELVILE. (*Within.*)

Turned religious! a greater wonder than the first!
Therefore, open quickly, or we shall unhinge, we   25
shall.

BLUNT.

This won't do—why hark ye, Colonel, to tell you
the plain truth, I am about a necessary affair of
life—I have a wench with me—you apprehend
me?—The devil's in't if they be so uncivil as to   30
disturb me now.

WILLMORE. [*Within.*]

How, a wench! Nay then, we must enter and
partake. No resistance—unless it be your lady of
quality,* and then we'll keep our distance.

BLUNT.

So, the business is out.   35

WILLMORE. [*Within.*]

Come, come, lend's more hands to the door—now
heave altogether—so, well done, my boys—
(*Breaks open the door.*)

Enter Belvile, Willmore, Frederick, Pedro [and Boy].
Blunt looks simply, they all laugh at him, he lays his
hand on his sword, and comes up to Willmore.

BLUNT.

Hark ye sir, laugh out your laugh quickly, d'ye
hear, and be gone. I shall spoil your sport else,
'sheartlikins sir, I shall—the jest has been carried   40
on too long. (*Aside.*) A plague upon my tailor.

WILLMORE.

'Sdeath,* how the whore has dressed him. Faith,
sir, I'm sorry.

BLUNT.

Are you so, sir; keep't to yourself then, sir, I advise
you, d'ye hear, for I can as little endure your pity   45
as his mirth. (*Lays his hand on's sword.*)

BELVILE.

Indeed, Willmore, thou wert a little too rough with
Ned Blunt's mistress. Call a person of quality*
whore? and one so young, so handsome, and so
eloquent—ha, ha, he—   50

BLUNT.

Hark ye sir, you know me, and know I can be
angry; have a care—for, 'sheartlikins, I can fight
too—I can, sir—do you mark me? No more—

BELVILE.

Why so peevish, good Ned? Some disappointments
I'll warrant. What, did the jealous count her   55
husband return just in the nick?

BLUNT.

Or the devil, sir. (*They laugh.*) D'ye laugh? Look
ye settle me a good sober countenance, and that
quickly too, or you shall know Ned Blunt is not—

BELVILE.

Not everybody, we know that.   60

BLUNT.

Not an ass to be laughed at, sir.

WILLMORE.

Unconscionable sinner, to bring a lover so near his
happiness, a vigorous, passionate lover, and then
not only cheat him of his movables, but his very
desires too.   65

BELVILE.

Ah! Sir, a mistress is a trifle with Blunt. He'll have
a dozen the next time he looks abroad. His eyes
have charms not to be resisted; there needs no

more than to expose that taking person to the view
of the fair, and he leads 'em all in triumph.   70

PEDRO.

Sir, though I'm a stranger to you, I am ashamed at
the rudeness of my nation and, could you learn who
did it, would assist you to make an example of 'em.

BLUNT.

Why, aye, there's one speaks sense now, and
han'somely; and let me tell you, gentlemen, I   75
should not have showed myself like a Jack
Pudding,[53] thus to have made you mirth, but that
I have revenge within my power. For know, I have
got into my possession a female who had better
have fallen under any curse than the ruin I design   80
her; 'sheartlikins, she assaulted me here in my own
lodgings, and had doubtless committed a rape
upon me, had not this sword defended me.

FREDERICK.

I know not that, but o'my conscience, thou had
ravished her, had she not redeemed herself with a   85
ring. Let's see't, Blunt. (*Blunt shows the ring.*)

BELVILE. [*Aside.*]

Hah, the ring I gave Florinda, when we exchanged
our vows!—Hark ye Blunt— (*Goes to whisper to*
him.)

WILLMORE.

No whispering, good Colonel, there's a woman in
the case; no whispering.   90

BELVILE.

Hark ye fool, be advised, and conceal both the ring
and the story for your reputation's sake. Do not
let people know what despised cullies we English
are, to be cheated and abused by one whore, and
another rather bribe thee than be kind to thee, is   95
an infamy to our nation.

WILLMORE.

Come, come, where's the wench? We'll see her, let
her be what she will; we'll see her.

PEDRO.

Aye, aye, let us see her. I can soon discover whether
she be of quality,* or for your diversion.   100

BLUNT.

She's in Fred's custody.

---

53 Jack Pudding] a clown or buffoon; clowning assistant
to a mountebank or street performer

WILLMORE.

Come, come, the key. (*To Frederick who gives him the key; they are going.*)

BELVILE.

Death, what shall I do?—Stay gentlemen.—Yet if I hinder 'em, I shall discover* all.—Hold, let's go at once. Give me the key.   105

WILLMORE.

Nay, hold there, Colonel. I'll go first.

FREDERICK.

Nay, no dispute, Ned and I have the propriety of her.

WILLMORE.

Damn propriety. Then we'll draw cuts. (*Belvile goes to whisper Willmore.*) Nay, no corruption, good   110 Colonel. Come, the longest sword carries her—

They all draw, forgetting Don Pedro, being as a Spaniard, had the longest.

BLUNT.

I yield up my interest to you, gentlemen, and that will be revenge sufficient.

WILLMORE. (*To Pedro.*)

The wench is yours— [*Aside.*] Pox of his Toledo,* I had forgot that.   115

FREDERICK.

Come sir, I'll conduct you to the lady.

Exeunt Frederick and Pedro.

BELVILE. (*Aside.*)

To hinder him will certainly discover* her.—Dost know, dull beast, what mischief thou hast done?

Willmore walking up and down out of humor.

WILLMORE.

Aye, aye, to trust our fortune to lots, a devil on't; 'twas madness, that's the truth on't.   120

BELVILE.

Oh intolerable sot—

Enter Florinda running masked, Pedro after her; Willmore gazing round her.

FLORINDA. (*Aside.*)

Good Heaven, defend me from discovery.

PEDRO.

'Tis but in vain to fly me, you're fallen to my lot.

BELVILE.

Sure she's undiscovered yet, but now I fear there is no way to bring her off.   125

WILLMORE.

Why, what a pox; is not this my woman, the same I followed but now?

Pedro talking to Florinda, who walks up and down.

PEDRO.

As if I did not know ye, and your business here.

FLORINDA. (*Aside.*)

Good Heaven, I fear he does indeed—

PEDRO.

Come, pray be kind; I know you meant to be so   130 when you entered here, for these are proper gentlemen.

WILLMORE.

But sir—perhaps the lady will not be imposed upon. She'll choose her man.

PEDRO.

I am better bred, than not to leave her choice free.   135

Enter Valeria, and is surprised at sight of Don Pedro.

VALERIA. (*Aside.*)

Don Pedro here! There's no avoiding him.

FLORINDA. (*Aside.*)

Valeria! Then I'm undone—

VALERIA. (*To Pedro, running to him.*)

Oh! Have I found you, sir. The strangest accident—if I had breath—to tell it.

PEDRO.

Speak: Is Florinda safe? Hellena well?   140

VALERIA.

Aye, aye, sir—Florinda—is safe—from any fears of you.

PEDRO.

Why, where's Florinda? Speak—

VALERIA.

Ay, where indeed, sir, I wish I could inform you— but to hold you no longer in doubt—   145

FLORINDA. (*Aside.*)

Oh, what will she say—

VALERIA.

She's fled away in the habit—of one of her pages, sir—but Callis thinks you may retrieve her yet. If you make haste away, she'll tell you, sir, the rest—

(*Aside.*) if you can find her out.   150

PEDRO.

Dishonorable girl, she has undone my aim.—Sir, you see my necessity of leaving you, and I hope you'll pardon it; my sister, I know, will make her flight to you; and if she do, I shall expect she should be rendered back.   155

BELVILE.

I shall consult my love and honor, sir.

Exit Pedro.

FLORINDA. (*To Valeria.*)

My dear preserver, let me embrace thee.

WILLMORE.

What the devil's all this?

BLUNT.

Mystery by this light.

VALERIA.

Come, come, make haste and get yourselves   160
married quickly, for your brother will return again.

BELVILE.

I'm so surprised with fears and joys, so amazed to find you here in safety, I can scarce persuade my heart into a faith of what I see.

WILLMORE.

Hark ye, Colonel, is this that mistress who has cost   165
you so many sighs, and me so many quarrels* with you?

BELVILE.

It is— (*To Florinda.*) Pray give him the honor of your hand.

WILLMORE.

Thus it must be received then. (*Kneels and kisses*   170
her hand.)
And with it give your pardon, too.

FLORINDA.

The friend to Belvile may command me anything.

WILLMORE. (*Aside.*)

Death, would I might; 'tis a surprising beauty.

BELVILE.

Boy, run and fetch a father instantly.

Exit Boy.

FREDERICK.

So, now do I stand like a dog and have not a   175
syllable to plead my own cause with. By this hand,

madam, I was never thoroughly confounded before, nor shall I ever more dare look up with confidence, till you are pleased to pardon me.

FLORINDA.

Sir, I'll be reconciled to you on one condition, that   180
you'll follow the example of your friend, in marrying a maid that does not hate you and whose fortune (I believe) will not be unwelcome to you.

FREDERICK.

Madam, had I no inclinations that way, I should obey your kind commands.   185

BELVILE.

Who, Frederick marry? He has so few inclinations for womankind, that had he been possessed of paradise he might have continued there to this day, if no crime but love could have disinherited him.

FREDERICK.

Oh, I do not use to boast of my intrigues.   190

BELVILE.

Boast, why thou dost nothing but boast; and I dare swear, wert thou as innocent from the sin of the grape, as thou art from the apple, thou might'st yet claim that right in Eden which our first parents lost by too much loving.   195

FREDERICK.

I wish this lady would think me so modest a man.

VALERIA.

She would be sorry, then, and not like you half so well, and I should be loath to break my word with you, which was, that if your friend and mine agreed, it should be a match between you and I.   200
(*She gives him her hand.*)

FREDERICK.

Bear witness, Colonel, 'tis a bargain. (*Kisses her hand.*)

BLUNT. (*To Florinda.*)

I have a pardon to beg too, but 'sheartlikins, I am so out of countenance that I'm a dog if I can say anything to purpose.

FLORINDA.

Sir, I heartily forgive you all.   205

BLUNT.

That's nobly said, sweet lady.—Belvile, prithee present her her ring again; for I find I have not courage to approach her myself.

Gives him the ring; he gives it to Florinda. Enter Boy.

BOY.

Sir, I have brought the father that you sent for. [*Exit.*]

BELVILE.

'Tis well, and now my dear Florinda, let's fly to 210 complete that mighty joy we have so long wished and sighed for.—Come, Fred—you'll follow?

FREDERICK.

Your example, sir, 'twas ever my ambition in war, and must be so in love.

WILLMORE.

And must not I see this juggling* knot tied? 215

BELVILE.

No, thou shalt do us better service, and be our guard, lest Don Pedro's sudden return interrupt the ceremony.

WILLMORE.

Content. I'll secure this pass.

Exeunt Belvile, Florinda, Frederick and Valeria. Enter Boy.

BOY. (*To Willmore.*)

Sir, there's a lady without would speak to you. 220

WILLMORE.

Conduct her in, I dare not quit my post.

BOY.

And sir, your tailor waits you in your chamber.

BLUNT.

Some comfort yet, I shall not dance naked at the wedding.

Exeunt Blunt and Boy. Enter again the Boy, conducting in Angellica in a masquing habit and a vizard. Willmore runs to her.

WILLMORE.

This can be none but my pretty Gypsy.—Oh, I 225 see you can follow as well as fly. Come, confess thyself the most malicious devil in nature; you think you have done my business with Angellica—

ANGELLICA.

Stand off, base villain— (*She draws a pistol, and holds it to his breast.*)

WILLMORE.

Hah, 'tis not she.—Who art thou? and what's thy 230 business?

ANGELLICA.

One thou hast injured and who comes to kill thee for't.

WILLMORE.

What the devil canst thou mean?

ANGELLICA.

By all my hopes to kill thee— (*Holds still the pistol* 235 *to his breast, he going back, she following still.*)

WILLMORE.

Prithee, on what acquaintance? For I know thee not.

ANGELLICA.

Behold this face—so lost to thy remembrance, And then call all thy sins about thy soul, (*Pulls off her vizard.*) And let 'em die with thee. 240

WILLMORE.

Angellica!

ANGELLICA.

Yes, traitor, Does not thy guilty blood run shivering through thy veins? Hast thou no horror at this sight that tells thee Thou hast not long to boast thy shameful conquest? 245

WILLMORE.

Faith, no, child, my blood keeps its old ebbs and flows still and that usual heat too that could oblige thee with a kindness, had I but opportunity.

ANGELLICA.

Devil! Dost wanton with my pain? Have at thy heart. 250

WILLMORE.

Hold, dear virago! Hold thy hand a little; I am not now at leisure to be killed—hold and hear me— (*Aside.*) Death, I think she's in earnest.

ANGELLICA. (*Aside, turning from him.*)

Oh, if I take not heed, My coward heart will leave me to his mercy. 255 —What have you, sir, to say? But should I hear thee, Thou'dst talk away all that is brave about me: (*Follows him with the pistol to his breast.*) And I have vowed thy death, by all that's sacred.

WILLMORE.

Why, then there's an end of a proper handsome fellow, That might 'a lived to have done good service yet; 260 That's all I can say to't.

ANGELLICA. (*Pausingly.*)

Yet—I would give thee—time for—penitence.

WILLMORE.

Faith child, I thank God I have ever took

Care to lead a good, sober, hopeful life, and am of

   a religion

That teaches me to believe I shall depart in peace. 265

ANGELLICA.

So will the devil! Tell me,

How many poor believing fools thou hast undone?

How many hearts thou hast betrayed to ruin?

Yet these are little mischiefs to the ills

Thou'st taught mine to commit: thou'st taught it 270

   love.

WILLMORE.

Egad, 'twas shrewdly hurt the while.

ANGELLICA.

Love, that has robbed it of its unconcern,

Of all that pride that taught me how to value it.

And in its room

A mean submissive passion was conveyed, 275

That made me humbly bow, which I ne'er did

To any thing but Heaven.

Thou, perjured man, didst this, and with thy oaths,

Which on thy knees, thou didst devoutly make,

Softened my yielding heart—and then, I was a 280

   slave—

Yet still had been content to've worn my chains,

Worn 'em with vanity and joy forever,

Hadst thou not broke those vows that put them on.

'Twas then I was undone. (*All this while follows*

   him with the pistol to his breast.)

WILLMORE.

Broke my vows! Why, where hast thou lived? 285

Amongst the gods? For I never heard of mortal man

That has not broke a thousand vows.

ANGELLICA.

Oh impudence!

WILLMORE.

Angellica! That beauty has been too long tempting

Not to have made a thousand lovers languish, 290

Who in the amorous fever[f] no doubt have sworn

Like me. Did they all die in that faith? still

   adoring?

I do not think they did.

ANGELLICA.

No, faithless man; had I repaid their vows, as I

   did thine,

I would have killed the ingrateful that had 295

   abandoned me.

WILLMORE.

This old general has quite spoiled thee; nothing makes a woman so vain as being flattered. Your old lover ever supplies the defects of age, with intolerable dotage, vast charge, and that which you call constancy; and attributing this to your own 300 merits, you domineer, and throw your favors in's teeth, upbraiding him still with the defects of age, and cuckold him as often as he deceives your expectations. But the gay, young, brisk lover that brings his equal fires, and can give you dart for 305 dart, will be as nice as you sometimes.

ANGELLICA.

All this thou'st made me know, for which I hate

   thee.

Had I remained in innocent security,

I should have thought all men were born my slaves,

And worn my pow'r like lightning in my eyes, 310

To have destroyed at pleasure when offended.

But when love held the mirror, the undeceiving

   glass

Reflected all the weakness of my soul, and made

   me know

My richest treasure being lost, my honor,

All the remaining spoil could not be worth 315

The conqueror's care or value.

Oh how I fell, like a long worshipped idol

Discovering all the cheat.

Would not the incense and rich sacrifice,

Which blind devotion offered at my altars, 320

Have fall'n to thee?

Why wouldst thou then destroy my fancied pow'r?

WILLMORE.

By Heaven, thou'rt brave, and I admire thee

   strangely.

I wish I were that dull, that constant thing

Which thou wouldst have and nature never meant 325

   me.

I must, like cheerful birds, sing in all groves

And perch on every bough,

Billing the next kind she that flies to meet me;

Yet after all could build my nest with thee,

Thither repairing when I'd loved my round, 330

And still reserve a tributary flame.

To gain your credit, I'll pay you back your charity
And be obliged for nothing but for love. (*Offers
her a purse of gold.*)

ANGELLICA.

Oh that thou wert in earnest!
So mean a thought of me   335
Would turn my rage to scorn, and I should pity thee
And give thee leave to live;
Which for the public safety of our sex
And my own private injuries I dare not do.
Prepare— (*Follows still, as before.*)   340
I will no more be tempted with replies.

WILLMORE.

Sure—

ANGELLICA.

Another word will damn thee! I've heard thee talk
too long.

*She follows him with the pistol ready to shoot; he retires
still amazed. Enter Don Antonio, his arm in a scarf,
and lays hold on the pistol.*

ANTONIO.

Hah! Angellica!

ANGELLICA.

Antonio! What devil brought thee hither?   345

ANTONIO.

Love and curiosity, seeing your coach at door.
Let me disarm you of this unbecoming instrument
of death—
(*Takes away the pistol.*) Amongst the number of
your slaves, was there not one worthy the honor   350
to have fought your quarrel*?
—Who are you, sir, that are so very wretched
To merit death from her?

WILLMORE.

One, sir, that could have made a better end of an
amorous quarrel without you than with you.   355

ANTONIO.

Sure 'tis some rival. Hah, the very man took down
her picture yesterday, the very same that set on me
last night. Blest opportunity— (*Offers to shoot
him.*)

ANGELLICA.

Hold, you're mistaken sir.

ANTONIO.

By Heaven, the very same!   360

—Sir, what pretensions have you to this lady?

WILLMORE.

Sir, I do not use to be examined and am ill at all
disputes but this— (*Draws; Antonio offers to shoot.*)

ANGELLICA. (*To Willmore.*)

Oh hold! You see he's armed with certain death.
—And you Antonio, I command you hold,   365
By all the passion you've so lately vowed me.

Enter Don Pedro, sees Antonio and stays.

PEDRO. (*Aside.*)

Hah, Antonio! and Angellica!

ANTONIO.

When I refuse obedience to your will,
May you destroy me with your mortal hate.
By all that's holy I adore you so,   370
That even my rival, who has charms enough
To make him fall a victim to my jealousy,
Shall live, nay and have leave to love on still.

PEDRO. (*Aside.*)

What's this I hear?

ANGELLICA. (*Pointing to Willmore.*)

Ah thus! 'Twas thus he talked, and I believed.   375
—Antonio, yesterday,
I'd not have sold my interest in his heart
For all the sword has won and lost in battle.
—But now to show my utmost of contempt,
I give thee life, which if thou wouldst preserve,   380
Live where my eyes may never see thee more,
Live to undo someone whose soul may prove
So bravely constant to revenge my love.

Goes out, Antonio follows, but Pedro pulls him back.

PEDRO.

Antonio—stay.

ANTONIO.

Don Pedro—   385

PEDRO.

What coward fear was that prevented thee
From meeting me this morning on the Molo?

ANTONIO.

Meet thee?

PEDRO.

Yes me; I was the man that dared thee to't.

ANTONIO.

Hast thou so often seen me fight in war   390

To find no better cause to excuse my absence?
I sent my sword and one to do thee right,
Finding myself uncapable to use a sword.

PEDRO.

But 'twas Florinda's quarrel* we fought,
And you, to show how little you esteemed her,   395
Sent me your rival, giving him your interest.
But I have found the cause of this affront,
And when I meet you fit for the dispute,
I'll tell you my resentment.

ANTONIO.

I shall be ready, sir, ere long, to do you reason.   400

Exit Antonio.

PEDRO.

If I could find Florinda now whilst my anger's
high, I think I should be kind and give her to
Belvile in revenge.

WILLMORE.

Faith, sir, I know not what you would do, but I
believe the priest within has been so kind.   405

PEDRO.

How! My sister married?

WILLMORE.

I hope by this time he is, and bedded too, or he
has not my longings about him.

PEDRO.

Dares he do this! Does he not fear my power?

WILLMORE.

Faith, not at all. If you will go in, and thank him   410
for the favor he has done your sister, so; if not, sir,
my power's greater in this house than yours. I have
a damned surly crew here, that will keep you till
the next tide, and then clap you on board for
prize;§ my ship lies but a league off the Molo, and   415
we shall show your donship a damned tramontane
rover's trick.

Enter Belvile.

BELVILE.

This rogue's in some new mischief—hah, Pedro
returned!

PEDRO.

Colonel Belvile, I hear you have married my sister?   420

BELVILE.

You have heard the truth then, sir.

PEDRO.

Have I so; then, sir, I wish you joy.

BELVILE.

How!

PEDRO.

By this embrace I do, and I am glad on't.

BELVILE.

Are you in earnest?   425

PEDRO.

By our long friendship and my obligations to
     thee, I am,
The sudden change I'll give you reasons for anon.
Come lead me to my sister,
That she may know I now approve her choice.

*Exeunt Belvile with Pedro. Willmore goes to follow
them. Enter Hellena as before in boy's clothes, and pulls
him back.*

WILLMORE.

Hah! My Gypsy!—Now a thousand blessings on   430
thee for this kindness. Egad child, I was e'en in
despair of ever seeing thee again; my friends are
all provided for within, each man his kind woman.

HELLENA.

Hah! I thought they had served me some such
trick!   435

WILLMORE.

And I was e'en resolved to go aboard and condemn
myself to my lone cabin and the thoughts of thee.

HELLENA.

And could you have left me behind, would you
have been so ill natured?

WILLMORE.

Why, 'twould have broke my heart, child. But since   440
we are met again, I defy foul weather to part us.

HELLENA.

And would you be a faithful friend now, if a maid
should trust you?

WILLMORE.

For a friend I cannot promise; thou art of a form
so excellent, a face and humor* too good for cold   445
dull friendship. I am parlously afraid of being in
love, child, and you have not forgot how severely
you have used me?

HELLENA.

That's all one; such usage you must still look for,

to find out all your haunts, to rail at you to all that love you, till I have made you love only me in your own defense, because nobody else will love you.

WILLMORE.

But hast thou no better quality to recommend thyself by?

HELLENA.

Faith, none, Captain. Why, 'twill be the greater charity to take me for thy mistress. I am a lone child, a kind of orphan lover, and why I should die a maid, and in a captain's hands too, I do not understand.

WILLMORE.

Egad, I was never clawed away with broadsides from any female before. Thou hast one virtue I adore, good nature. I hate a coy, demure mistress, she's as troublesome as a colt; I'll break none. No, give me a mad mistress when mewed and, in flying, one I dare trust upon the wing, that whilst she's kind will come to the lure.

HELLENA.

Nay, as kind as you will, good Captain, whilst it lasts, but let's lose no time.

WILLMORE.

My time's as precious to me as thine can be; therefore, dear creature, since we are so well agreed, let's retire to my chamber, and if ever thou wert treated with such savory love—Come, my bed's prepared for such a guest, all clean and sweet as thy fair self. I love to steal a dish and a bottle with a friend, and hate long graces. Come let's retire and fall to.

HELLENA.

'Tis but getting my consent, and the business is soon done. Let but old gaffer Hymen and his priest say amen to't, and I dare lay my mother's daughter by as proper a fellow as your father's son, without fear or blushing.

WILLMORE.

Hold, hold, no bug* words, child. Priest and Hymen! Prithee, add a hangman to 'em to make up the consort. No, no, we'll have no vows but love, child, nor witness but the lover; the kind deity enjoins naught but love and enjoy! Hymen and priest wait still upon portion and jointure; love and beauty have their own ceremonies. Marriage is as certain a bane to love as lending money is to

friendship. I'll neither ask nor give a vow—though I could be content to turn Gypsy, and become a left-handed bridegroom[54] to have the pleasure of working that great miracle of making a maid a mother, if you durst venture; 'tis upse[55] Gypsy that, and if I miss, I'll lose my labor.

HELLENA.

And if you do not lose, what shall I get? a cradle full of noise and mischief, with a pack of repentance at my back? Can you teach me to weave inkle to pass my time with? 'Tis upse Gypsy that too.

WILLMORE.

I can teach thee to weave a true love's knot better.

HELLENA.

So can my dog.

WILLMORE.

Well, I see we are both upon our guards, and I see there's no way to conquer good nature, but by yielding—here—give me thy hand—one kiss and I am thine—

HELLENA.

One kiss! How like my page he speaks; I am resolved you shall have none, for asking such a sneaking sum. He that will be satisfied with one kiss, will never die of that longing. Good friend single kiss, is all your talking come to this? a kiss, a caudle! Farewell, captain single kiss. (*Going out; he stays her.*)

WILLMORE.

Nay, if we part so, let me die like a bird upon a bough, at the sheriff's charge.[56] By Heaven, both the Indies shall not buy thee from me. I adore thy humor* and will marry thee, and we are so of one humor*, it must be a bargain. Give me thy hand— (*Kisses her hand.*) And now let the blind ones (Love and Fortune) do their worst.

HELLENA.

Why, God-a-mercy, Captain!

WILLMORE.

But hark ye, the bargain is now made, but is it not

---

54 left-handed bridegroom] one married in a morganatic ceremony, leading to no inheritance
55 upse] in the manner or fashion of
56 let me ... at the sheriff's charge] let me be hanged (Spencer)

fit we should know each other's names, that when
we have reason to curse one another hereafter (and
people ask me who 'tis I give to the devil) I may
at least be able to tell what family you came of.

HELLENA.

Good reason, Captain; and where I have cause (as   525
I doubt not but I shall have plentiful) that I may
know at whom to throw my—blessings—I beseech
ye your name.

WILLMORE.

I am called Robert the Constant.

HELLENA.

A very fine name; pray was it your falconer or   530
butler that christened you? Do they not use to
whistle when they call you?

WILLMORE.

I hope you have a better, that a man may name
without crossing himself, you are so merry with
mine.   535

HELLENA.

I am called Hellena the Inconstant.

Enter Pedro, Belvile, Florinda, Frederick, Valeria.

PEDRO. [*Aside.*]

Hah! Hellena!

FLORINDA.

Hellena!

HELLENA.

The very same.—Hah, my brother!—Now Captain,
show your love and courage; stand to your arms, and   540
defend me bravely, or I am lost forever.

PEDRO.

What's this I hear! False girl, how came you hither
and what's your business? Speak. (*Goes roughly to
her.*)

WILLMORE.

Hold off, sir, you have leave to parley only. (*Puts
himself between.*)

HELLENA.

I had e'en as good tell it, as you guess it; faith,   545
brother, my business is the same with all living
creatures of my age, to love, and be beloved, and
here's the man.

PEDRO.

Perfidious maid, hast thou deceived me too?
deceived thyself and Heaven?   550

HELLENA.

'Tis time enough to make my peace with that.
Be you but kind; let me alone with Heaven.

PEDRO.

Belvile, I did not expect this false play from you.
Was't not enough you'd gain Florinda (which I
pardoned) but your lewd friends too must be   555
enriched with the spoils of a noble family?

BELVILE.

Faith, sir, I am as much surprised at this as you
can be. Yet sir, my friends are gentlemen, and
ought to be esteemed for their misfortunes, since
they have the glory to suffer with the best of men   560
and kings; 'tis true, he's a rover of fortune, yet a
prince aboard his little wooden world.

PEDRO.

What's this to the maintenance of a woman of her
birth and quality?*

WILLMORE.

Faith, sir, I can boast of nothing but a sword which   565
does me right where'er I come and has defended
a worse cause than a woman's; and since I loved
her before I either knew her birth or name, I must
pursue my resolution and marry her.

PEDRO.

And is all your holy intent of becoming a nun   570
debauched into a desire of man?

HELLENA.

Why, I have considered the matter, brother, and
find the three hundred thousand crowns my uncle
left me (and you cannot keep from me) will be
better laid out in love than in religion, and turn   575
to as good an account. Let most voices carry it,
for Heaven or the captain?

ALL CRY.

A captain! A captain!

HELLENA.

Look ye, sir, 'tis a clear case.

PEDRO. (*Aside.*)

Oh I am mad. If I refuse, my life's in danger.—   580
Come. There's one motive induces me. Take her.
I shall now be free from fears of her honor. Guard
it you now, if you can; I have been a slave to't long
enough. (*Gives her to him.*)

WILLMORE.

Faith, sir, I am of a nation that are of opinion a   585

woman's honor is not worth guarding when she
has a mind to part with it.

HELLENA.

Well said, Captain.

PEDRO. (*To Valeria.*)

This was your plot, mistress, but I hope you have   590
married one that will revenge my quarrel to you—

VALERIA.

There's no altering destiny, sir.

PEDRO.

Sooner than a woman's will. Therefore, I forgive
you all—and wish you may get my father's pardon
as easily, which I fear.   595

*Enter Blunt dressed in a Spanish habit, looking very
ridiculously; his man adjusting his band.*

MAN.

'Tis very well, sir—

BLUNT.

Well sir, 'sheartlikins, I tell you 'tis damnable ill,
sir—a Spanish habit, good lord! Could the devil
and my tailor devise no other punishment for me,
but the mode of a nation I abominate?   600

BELVILE.

What's the matter, Ned?

BLUNT.

Pray view me round, and judge— (*Turns round.*)

BELVILE.

I must confess thou art a kind of an odd figure.

BLUNT.

In a Spanish habit with a vengeance! I had rather
be in the Inquisition for Judaism, than in this   605
doublet and breeches; a pillory were an easy collar
to this, three handfuls high; and these shoes too,
are worse than the stocks, with the sole an inch
shorter than my foot. In fine, gentlemen, methinks
I look altogether like a bag of bays[57] stuffed full   610
of fool's flesh.

BELVILE.

Methinks 'tis well, and makes thee look *en
cavalier.** Come, sir, settle your face and salute* our
friends.—Lady—

BLUNT.

Hah! Say'st thou so, my little rover— (*To Hellena.*)   615

---

57 bag of bays] a bag of bay leaves used in cooking

Lady (if you be one), give me leave to kiss your hand,
and tell you, 'sheartlikins, for all I look so, I am your
humble servant.—A pox of my Spanish habit.

Music is heard to play. Enter Boy.

WILLMORE.

Hark—what's this?

BOY.

Sir, as the custom is, the gay people in masquerade   620
who make every man's house their own are coming
up.

*Enter several men and women in masquing habits with
music; they put themselves in order and dance.*

BLUNT.

'Sheartlikins, would 'twere lawful to pull off their
false faces, that I might see if my doxy were not
among'st 'em.   625

BELVILE. (*To the masquers.*)

Ladies and gentlemen, since you are come so
apropos, you must take a small collation with us.

WILLMORE.

Whilst we'll to the good man within, who stays
to give us a cast of his office. (*To Hellena.*) Have
you no trembling at the near approach?   630

HELLENA.

No more than you have in an engagement or a
tempest.

WILLMORE.

Egad thou'rt a brave girl, and I admire thy love
and courage.

Lead on, no other dangers they can dread,
Who venture in the storms o'th' marriage bed.

Exeunt.

THE END.

^a The copytext is the first edition, a 1667 quarto (Q1), which exists in three issues. Although the title pages of the first two issues do not name the author, the "Prologue" of all three issues refers to the author as "he." The third issue, however, adds "written by Mrs. A. Behn" to the title page. In some copies of the second issue, and in the third issue, the author's "Postscript" is printed with the addition of the phrase "especially of our sex," an acknowledgment that the author is a woman.

Other editions consulted include quartos from 1697 (Q2) and 1709 (Q3); collections of Behn's works published in 1702 (A) and 1724 (B); and modern editions of 1915 (Summers); 1967 (Link); 1995 (Spencer); and 1995 (Todd).

^b Blunt] Q2, A, B, Summers, Link, Spencer; Fred. Q1, Q3, Todd

^c Why] The first edition reads "whe," an exclamation used for emphasis or to demand attention; variant of archaic "we" (OED). Since there is no satisfactory modern equivalent for this now-archaic expression, I have followed the examples of previous editors and changed "whe" to "why" throughout.

^d fair] Q3, Link, Spencer, Todd; *om.* Q2, A, and some copies of Q1; fine B, Summers

^e to] *om.* Q1, Q2, Q3, A, B, Summers, Link; vow you Spencer, Todd

^f fever] Q3, Link, Spencer, Todd; favour Q1, Q2, A, B, Summers

^g for prize] Q3, Link, Spencer; for prise Q1, Todd; my prize Q2, A, B, Summers

City Politics[a]

by John Crowne (ca. 1640-1712)

edited by Kirk Combe

John Crowne wrote at least sixteen plays in a variety of genres between the years 1671 and 1698. He met with his greatest theatrical accomplishments, however, in the early to mid 1680s with two comedies produced under the good graces of Charles II, with whom Crowne was on familiar terms. The first of these comedies was *City Politics*, produced at the Theatre Royal in Drury Lane on January 19, 1683 and published in February that same year. The performance of the play was delayed for some six months due to censorship issues that are not entirely clear to us today. When *City Politics* finally came to the stage, it played with good success, having the best actors of the United Company at its disposal (especially Tony Leigh as Bartoline), became well known to playgoers of the era, and enjoyed occasional revivals until 1717.

City Politics combines farce with political satire. As a farce, the play is filled with fools and knaves, schemes, sexual intrigue in the form of two cuckolding plots leading to discovery scenes, mistaken identities, disguises, beatings, and the like. Characters are well drawn and the situations into which they are placed are entertainingly absurd. At this level, *City Politics* reads well (and would stage well) even today. As political satire, the play is more difficult, of course, for modern readers to understand. Local allusions to actual people and events are numerous and often not easy to sort out. However, this politicality makes Crowne's play significant to the history of the emerging modern state.

City Politics is a pro-royalist, Tory satire against the Whigs. In it, issues and incidents from the Popish Plot and the Exclusion Crisis figure prominently, as do the political players involved in those recent troubling events. Whig notables such as the earl of Shaftesbury, the duke of Buckingham, Titus Oates, Stephen College, Slingsby Bethel, and others are personated by Crowne's farcical characters. Crowne's play might well be considered as part of the so-called "Stuart Revenge" against the Whig faction after Charles II turned the political tide against them.

Interestingly, in a preface to the play Crowne claims that he writes generalized satire against social vices of the times, not particularized political commentary aimed at real persons. In a (intentionally?) weak effort to distance the play from English political reality, Crowne sets his farce in pre-1620 Naples. He also avoids any reference in the play to the duke of Monmouth, still a favorite of Charles in 1683. Nonetheless, Crowne was roughed up in an alleyway by an unknown assailant a week after *City Politics* was staged. Apparently, someone took exception to what was seen as an unflattering portrayal of the late, celebrated (and Whiggish) libertine John Wilmot, the earl of Rochester, in the character of Artall. Thus, despite Crowne's protests of satiric innocence, contemporary audiences readily saw through the thin disguises of his characters. His play unabashedly celebrates Tories triumphant—for the moment—over the Whigs.

DRAMATIS PERSONAE

[MEN]

Florio, a debauch who pretends to be dying of the diseases his vices brought upon him and penitent, in love with Rosaura.

[Pietro, his servant.]

Artall, a debauch that follows the Court, in love with Lucinda.

Paulo Camillo,[1] a factious, proud, busy, credulous, foolish, rich Citizen, chosen Chief Magistrate or Lord Podesta of Naples.

Craffy, his son, an impudent, amorous, pragmatical fop, that pretends to wit and poetry, in love with his father's wife.

A Bricklayer,[2] a bold, saucy, factious fellow, that governs the Podesta

Doctor Sanchy,[b3] an ignorant, railing fellow that pretends to learning.

Bartoline,[4] an old, corrupt lawyer.

The Governor of the City,* a man of honor and worth.

[Two] foolish mistaking Irish witness[es] suborned by Bartoline.

[WOMEN]

Rosaura, a wanton, beautiful woman, married to the Podesta, and in love with Florio.

[Maria, her maid.]

Lucinda, an ignorant, wanton country girl, married to Bartoline.

[Clerk, citizens, soldiers, servants, waiting women, boys, beggars, and porter.]

SCENE: NAPLES.[5]

City Politics.

Act I, scene i. A bedchamber [in the Podesta's house].

Enter Florio in his nightgown. Enter Pietro.

FLORIO.
Pietro.
PIETRO.
Sir.
FLORIO.
What news, Pietro? Has the worthy citizen,* whom I have elected to be my cuckold, attained the other dignity of Podesta of Naples yet? 5
PIETRO.
Not yet, sir, but he will attain it very speedily. All his party are hard at work, voices and elbows at it, and they exceed the other forty for one.[6]

---

1 Paulo Camillo] probably is a composite of various Whig politicians: Slingsby Bethel, sheriff of London; Sir Thomas Player, chamberlain of London and a powerful merchant; Sir Robert Clayton, lord mayor of London, 1679-1680; Sir Patience Ward, lord mayor, 1680-1681; and Sir Robert Peyton, one of the Whig founders of the Green Ribbon Club. However, Bethel seems to figure most in the Podesta.

2 Bricklayer] a portrait of Stephen College, who was known as "the Protestant Joiner." A Whig citizen of London, College was put on trial for seditious words and actions in the wake of the Popish Plot. He was executed in 1681 and became the first martyr of the Whig cause. In his characterization of College, Crowne emphasizes such traits as rudeness to superiors, being argumentative, claiming to know Latin and the law, and writing treasonable songs and libels.

3 Sanchy] suggestive of Sancho Panza, Don Quixote's foolish squire, but more importantly, Doctor Sanchy represents the nefarious Titus Oates of Popish Plot infamy. Along with being accused of fabricating the plot and contriving testimony for it, Oates was also reputed to use constant lewd oaths and offensive name-calling in his conversation.

4 Bartoline] another composite satiric target for Crowne, this time that of a Whig lawyer. Various critics have suggested candidates for whom Bartoline might represent: Sir William Jones, Aaron Smith, Sir John Maynard,

William Williams, Robert West, Richard Goodenough, Edward Whitacre. All performed legal work for the Whig cause and were well-known.

5 Naples] Perhaps as a way to disclaim any local applications of his satire, and thereby serve as a precaution against Whig reprisals, Crowne sets his play in Naples, a volatile kingdom ruled by Spain through a viceroy. The action seems to take place during the Duke of Ossuna's vice-regency from 1616-1620; however, there is a reference to Masaniello's rebellion in 1647.

6 party ... one] The allegory of Whig versus Tory is blatant throughout.

FLORIO.

I am glad of it, Pietro, for when he is Chief
Magistrate of Naples, I shall be _____* of his   10
wife, dispatch his domestic affairs, and receive all
the fees of that sweet office.

PIETRO.

In troth you deserve it, sir, for you buy the place
dear.

FLORIO.

Indeed, I give a great deal for it, Pietro. I give some   15
scores of ready mistresses I have in bank for
the reversion of one, which perhaps I may never
enjoy.

PIETRO.

A great price, sir.

FLORIO.

'Tis so, Pietro. I give away a hundred other   20
pleasures into the bargain, as drunkenness, a sweet
sin, Pietro. Wine is as necessary to a man as a
navigable river to a city. It conveys to him many
pleasant commodities; without it, he must depend
upon his own growth.   25

PIETRO.

'Tis true, sir.

FLORIO.

Then I part with all the society of my witty lewd
friends, to keep company with dull lewd Saints.*

PIETRO.

Not Saints, sir, but Whigs.

FLORIO.

That's as bad, and so lose the reputation of my   30
loyalty and good affection to my Prince.[7]

PIETRO.

You also part with the reputation of being sound,*
sir, and of your affection to women. In short sir,
you pass for a poor, rotten, dying Saint.

FLORIO.

A dead Saint, Pietro, at least a dead sinner, for I   35
appear the ghost of what I was, all my vices
mortified, and I am in a world very different from
that I used to live in: I talk godly, a strange language
to me, Pietro. I pray, hear sermons, live soberly,
abstain from wine, women, and wits—a strange life   40
to me. But this new world is a dismal Purgatory, for

as yet I have not attained my Heaven, my Rosaura!
If I should never attain her, Pietro—

PIETRO.

'Twill not be her fault, sir.

FLORIO.

That's true, Pietro.

PIETRO.

I suppose sir, she is not frightened by the ghost
you appear to be.

FLORIO.

No Pietro, she knows me to be flesh and blood,
sound* flesh and blood, whose only disease is a
troublesome, watchful cuckold. If I can be cured   50
of him, she'll venture on me.

PIETRO.

If you never attain her, sir, Heaven be praised, you
won't lose your sufferings. You will attain the
statesman's mistress, Popularity.

FLORIO.

Popularity! Damn her! A lewd, inconstant, common   55
prostitute, so old she's blind and cannot distinguish
an honest man from a knave. Though she has a
hundred pair of spectacles put on her nose that show
the knave never so clear, she cries, "I can't see him."
Ignoramus, Ignoramus,[8] that's all the sense she has.   60

PIETRO.

It may be not, sir: she sees well enough, but is too
cunning to lay open the blemishes of her stallion.[9]

FLORIO.

It may be so, but were she fairer than the most
doting old statesman thinks her, she is not so
charming as a hundred beautiful women which I   65
lose for her.

PIETRO.

That's true, sir.

FLORIO.

Do not the ladies give me for gone?

PIETRO.

For a dead man, sir.

---

7 Prince] in the English political allegory, Charles II

8 *Ignoramus*] literally "we take no notice of it," the Latin
legal term by which a grand jury of Whigs rejected an
indictment of the earl of Shaftesbury for treason brought
against him by the Tories in 1681

9 stallion] probably Shaftesbury, who courted popularity
(especially in Tory propaganda)

FLORIO.

And do they lament me? 70

PIETRO.

All, all, sir. The virtuous ladies sigh and cry, "'Tis pity," the other run distracted, the very common whores abstain from plays, and bawds neglect their brandy bottles.

FLORIO.

You see what it is, Pietro, to do good in a man's 75 generation. Hark!

A shout, "Paulo! Paulo!" Pietro goes out and presently* re-enters.

The news, Pietro?

PIETRO.

Your friend is chosen, sir.

FLORIO.

Is he? Then shall I enter into my employment speedily; now he is filled with authority, he will 80 be drunk with pride to th'end of his year, and I can make him reel whither and when I please. Hark! Somebody comes—

Pietro looks out.

PIETRO.

Esquire Artall, sir.

FLORIO.

That rogue! My patch upon my nose,* my pillow 85 and sick equipage quickly.

Enter Artall.

ARTALL.

Where's this damned, confounded hypocrite? this religious, factious, dying Saint? I come to give you thanks for the legacy you leave the nation, a sweet rogue you have helped into power; we shall have 90 a fine time on't.

FLORIO.

Sir, if I have committed any crime in't, let the law punish me, but do not murder me with all this noise. I have mortal distempers enough upon me; I need not your bawling. 95

ARTALL.

That you have not one sound part in your soul or body I firmly believe; that the greatest part of your body comes out of shops, and every night goes not into bed but boxes, I know; but that your soul and body, although they have used one another, are 100 upon parting, I no more believe than that your soul and your vices are parted.

FLORIO.

I value not what you believe, sir, but why should it be incredible a man should part with anything that uses him ill? Say my vices had not murdered 105 me, 'tis sufficient they fooled and enslaved me.

ARTALL.

Ah, poor man!

FLORIO.

I was a common bellman with my rhymes to chime fools asleep in their sins, a beadle to whip out of the parish impudent beggars, and such we 110 esteem all church creeds and principles.

ARTALL.

So you do still, sir, and are as little charitable to 'em, whatever you pretend, as to any other kind of beggars, for you will give good words to any handsome beggar you hope to make a whore of. 115 And you have a worse design on religion, to make her a bawd to carry on some lewd project.

FLORIO.

Rail on, or laugh on, or both, I care not. You and the rest of my atheistical companions were Heaven-threatening, which stood long between me and the 120 church, and though I dwelt among you, I confess, to my shame, I was afraid of you. But now (Heaven be praised) I have traveled beyond you and shall never look back on those horrors and precipices more.

ARTALL.

And are now got within a day's journey of heaven. 125 Are you not, sir?

FLORIO.

What is that to you, sir? Get you about your business; do not disturb me and make me waste^c my spirits to no purpose.

ARTALL.

I would only take my leave, wish you a good 130 journey, and ask you when we shall see you again, for you will not stay long in heaven I know; there's no company that you will like, sir.

FLORIO.

None that I like so ill as yours, sir. (*Aside.*) This fellow vexes me so, I almost faint. 135

ARTALL.

There are none of your Club,[10] sir, wits that
believe one _____ *[11] divine before all the twelve
Apostles, sir—

FLORIO.

I am quite fainting.

ARTALL.

That count his story true, and all theirs a sham,   140
sir.

FLORIO.

This fellow babbles me out of my senses.

ARTALL.

You would babble and scribble us out of our
estates.

FLORIO.

Quite babbled me dead. I faint! Give me a cordial!   145
If ever you let him in again—I'll—Pooh—I can
hardly speak—give me that cordial quickly.
(*Drinks.*)

ARTALL.

A plague on you.

FLORIO.

Oh! He has startled me with his frightful curse!   150
Made me spill my cordial, slabber myself, and
almost choke myself. Bless me! What works here
with this fellow?

ARTALL.

Have I almost choked thee with a cordial? Then
thou art no right Saint, for I have seen one of those   155
they call the true Protestants swallow another man's
whole estate for a cordial and never choke
himself.[12] Choke thee? damn thee!

FLORIO.

Mercy on me! What a cursing and swearing the

wretch keeps. To what purpose is all this, thou silly   160
fellow? I warrant thou thinkest those fine-mouthed
jewels become thee and art as proud of them as a
cannibal of a ring in his nose. If to be one of the
Devil's knights, called an atheist, be a fine thing,
prithee wear a better badge of thy order than an   165
oath or a curse, for those are porterly badges.[13]

ARTALL.

Confound thee, sink thee.

FLORIO.

Take me away, take me away, I am not able to bear
this! (*Exit, led out by his servants.*)

ARTALL.

Ha, ha, ha! The dissimulation of these fellows is   170
pleasant, but a pox on't, we pay too dear for these
jests: they cost us confusion and also ruin. These
fellows so love division, every one of 'em has two
parties in himself.
There is in every true Protestant breast   175
A *Heraclitus ridens*[14] his* contest:
A knave in earnest, and a saint in jest.
The saint looks up to heaven, the knave that while
Your pocket picks and at the cheat does smile.
Catch him, he, like a hedgehog, scrapes your fury   180
Under the prickles of a sturdy jury;
Then, looking out, he does the hunters brave,
For squinting vilely between Saint and knave,
He looks ten ways at once, so they that watch him,
Cannot tell which he'll take and never catch him.   185
    (*Exit.*)

Enter Pietro peeping.

PIETRO.

Sir, he's gone.

Enter Florio.

FLORIO.

Is he? That's well.

---

10 Club] Artall probably means the Whig political group
the Green Ribbon Club.
11 _____] *Stet* Q1, Q2. The word "stet" is a proofread-
er's term meaning "let it stand." It appears in this speech
probably because of an objection to an inflammatory adjective, such as "false" or "damned," that would have
caused the play further trouble. Apparently, the com-
positor accidentally printed the term instead of the word
Crowne wanted to remain.
12 one … himself] Artall refers to Cromwell's seizure of
Royalist property during the Civil War and Commonwealth era.

13 porterly badges] Badges identified porters who could be
hired to carry parcels or messages; hence, Artall's
"badge"—his vulgar language—is common.
14 *Heraclitus ridens*] Latin for "Heraclitus laughing," a para-
dox, since Heraclitus traditionally was the *weeping* philosopher; John Flatman's *Heraclitus Ridens; or a Discourse
between Jest and Earnest* was a Tory periodical that ran
from 1 February 1681 to 22 August 1682 (Wilson).

Enter a servant.

SERVANT.

Sir, here's the new Lord Podesta's son, Mr. Craffy.

FLORIO.

Oh! My friend's son! You must let him come in, though he be a very troublesome coxcomb.   190

Enter Craffy.

CRAFFY.

Oh friend Florio, are you here?

FLORIO.

Aye, sir, thanks to my distemper that keeps me prisoner.

CRAFFY.

Whoo! But aren't you wi'my father yonder?

FLORIO.

No, I profess I am here, sir.   195

CRAFFY.

How are you able to be here?

FLORIO.

I am not able to be anywhere else, I'm so ill.

CRAFFY.

Ill? You are dull, man, for if you were not dull, you would go to my father's election; if you were giving up the ghost, 'tis better than a thousand   200 bearbaitings. Stay, "A Camillo! A Camillo! A Camillo!" say our party. "What, do you keep such a bawling for such a fellow?" says one of theirs. "Such a fellow!" say our party and set up a-laughing and hissing, and a-hissing and a-laughing.   205 "For all your laughing and hissing I'll speak my mind," says the man. "Will ye so?" says one of our party and gives him a thump with his elbow under the small guts. "Now will you speak your mind?" says our man. The man is speechless.[15]   210

FLORIO.

A good way of silencing a man.

CRAFFY.

The best we have. So upon that some of their party

---

15 thump … speechless] Physical violence could be part of the political process. For example, at the election of Slingsby Bethel and Henry Cornish, both Whigs, as sheriffs of London in the summer of 1680, one of the outgoing sheriffs was both throttled and punched (Wilson).

began to bear up, but we never gave over till we had quite hissed 'em and hooted 'em and rogued 'em and Toried 'em[16] out of the hall.   215

FLORIO.

I am glad of it.

CRAFFY.

But who do you think was the captain of all our party? to lead 'em on wherever he saw an enemy? and, I believe, discharged "Rogue, rogue" forty times for any man's once?   220

FLORIO.

Who?

CRAFFY.

Your chaplain, Doctor Sanchy.

FLORIO.

Oh! He is a zealous man. Where is he? For I want to go to my prayers.

CRAFFY.

Pray? He can't speak he's so hoarse; he's gone to   225 drink a glass of sack* to clear his pipes. The truth is, I had as lieve he should pray for me as any body.

FLORIO.

Why so?

CRAFFY.

Because no saint in heaven dare deny him anything, for if he should, he'd call him rogue and   230 rascal. Well, but this is not the business I come to thee about. What dost think it is?

FLORIO.

I cannot guess.

CRAFFY.

Guess! No, I'll give thee a thousand guesses to guess it. I will give thee ten thousand; come, I'll   235 give till this time twelve-month, and thou shalt think of nothing else.

FLORIO.

Really, I have a little other business to employ my thoughts about.

CRAFFY.

Well, I'll put thee out of thy pain and tell thee the   240 oddest thing that ever thou heardest in thy life. Thou knowest my father has lately married the most delicate, luscious—luscious—lus—didst ever see such a woman in thy life?

---

16 Toried 'em] called them Tories

FLORIO.

I can't tell; I am past those studies now. The young 245
lady no doubt is handsome enough. But what o'that?

CRAFFY.

I'm stark mad in love with her.

FLORIO.

In love with your father's wife?

CRAFFY.

Aye, so mad for her, that I am quite out o'my wits;
nay, I ha'not only lost my wits, but my stomach. 250

FLORIO.

The greater loss of the two.

CRAFFY.

I can't eat nor drink; I can't sleep neither. I was
once a rare sleeper: constantly after supper my eyes
used to call for their evening's draught, and I was
no sooner in bed, but they would tope off fourteen 255
hours at one go-down. Now I tumble and toss like
a child that has the worms. Love and poetry are
continually biting me. I can't pray neither when I
fall to my beads; instead of crying "Ave Maria" I
cry "Ave mother-in-law." I have given over all sorts 260
of pleasures; I read no news, go to no coffee-
house,[17] frequent no club, and take no snuff.

FLORIO.

Why, you are come to a sad pass.

CRAFFY.

In troth I am. Thou wouldst say so if thou knewest
all, and I come to thee, to beg of thee, as ever thou 265
wouldst save the life of an honest young fellow of
thy own party, and a true Whig as I hope to be
saved, to lend me a little of thy assistance, for thou
art a rare fellow at wenching, knowest all the tricks
of women, and hast great power over my mother. 270

FLORIO.

And so I must procure her for you, sir?

CRAFFY.

Aye, prithee do now, prithee dear rogue, do now.
Brother Whig, brother Whig, prithee dear brother
Whig, do now.

---

17 coffeehouse] a new type of establishment in London at
the time, site for informal but intense political debate.
Coffee drinking was associated with the Whigs, while
pubs and spirits drinking were associated with the Tories.

FLORIO.

Brother Whig! Thou horrid wretch, brother to the 275
Devil, art thou in earnest?

CRAFFY.

Why thou horrid fool, brother to a changeling,
dost think I come to hear myself prate?

FLORIO.

Then wouldst thou cuckold thy father, thou
monster? 280

CRAFFY.

Would I not, if I could, thou monster? Would
anything refuse to lie with such a sweet creature
but a monster?

FLORIO.

Would anything but the horrid'st villain upon
earth endeavor to dishonor his father's bed? 285

CRAFFY.

Would anything but the horrid'st ass upon earth
say a lusty young fellow shall not honor his father's
bed more than an old fumbler that disgraces it!

FLORIO.

Then 'tis a thing of reputation with thee to commit
incest? 290

CRAFFY.

Incest? Prithee don't trouble me with hard names.
I don't think it is any more incest to lie with the
same woman my father does than to drink in the
same glass or sit in the same pew at church.

FLORIO.

Is there no difference between your father's wife 295
and his pew?

CRAFFY.

He makes none, for they only both lay him to
sleep. I would make a difference, I confess, in the
sweet use. Not that I think his wife more sacred
than his pew, for the locking of a man to a woman 300
in marriage, or in a pew in a church, are only a
couple of church-tricks to get money, one for the
priest, and t'other for the sexton—that's all.

FLORIO.

You are a fine fellow.

CRAFFY.

I would I were so fine a fellow as to please my 305
mother-in-law, and I would not change to be thee
if thou wert at thy best. And I do all I can to be a
fine fellow. It costs me the Lord knows what in one

beauty-water or another to mend my face, and a pox on't, I'm never the handsomer. Prithee hast e'er a looking glass to see how I look? 310

FLORIO.

Why, if thou look'st never so well, dost thou think thou couldst charm thy mother into an incestuous strumpet?

CRAFFY.

What a robust word is there? Look thee, I understand trap[18] and so does she. I kissed her behind t'other day, that is, I came behind and kissed her, pretending I took her for the waiting woman, and she let me, pretending she took me for my father. A rank sham o'both sides: we had both a mind to kiss, and there's an end. And I swear she let me rumple those sweet lips of hers as patiently as a mercer will let a good customer do his silks in hopes to put 'em off.[19] 315 320

FLORIO.

Hah! I'm glad you tell me this, sir; since she is so weak a piece, I'll fortify her. 325

CRAFFY.

With godly counsels! Putting forces into her head will never fortify her tail. What signifies fortifying the capital city when the remote provinces rebel?

FLORIO.

I shall bring down the prince of the country, your father, sir, upon you, who if he cannot quell the rebellion, shall deal with you. 330

CRAFFY.

Why, thou wouldst not betray me, wouldst thou? I never knew a religious fool that was not a rogue in my life. I tell thee what, if thou dost tell my father I would lie with his wife, egad I'll swear to him thou dost lie with her, and I'll bring a hundred witnesses to confirm it, besides corroborators. 335

FLORIO.

How!

CRAFFY.

Yes, that I will. I'll teach you to play the knave, you stinking, damned fellow you. I'm going now by my father's order to search the cathedral for arms to af-front the clergy and make 'em suspected for plotters; 340

now, instead of arms, I'll search for swearers, and if they catch you by the back, they'll shake you worse than an ague and be harder to cure than the pox, sir. 345

FLORIO.

There is a way to be cured, sir.

CRAFFY.

Aye, twelve Protestant consciences cleanly picked,[20] not one of[d] t'other side amongst 'em, are as certain a cure of an evidence* as Jesuit's Powder* of an ague: *probatum est*.[21] (*Going off.*) 350

FLORIO.

Come back. Thou art such a villain, I know not what to do with thee.

CRAFFY.

And thou art such a knave, I know not what to do with thee. Pox on me for trusting thee. 355

FLORIO.

If I should conceal thy wickedness, thou wouldst proceed in it.

CRAFFY.

I will proceed, whether thou concealest it or no.

FLORIO.

And ruin thy soul.

CRAFFY.

I don't know whether I have a soul or no. 360

FLORIO.

If I tell thy father—

CRAFFY.

Then I'll forswear it.

FLORIO.

And hide your roguery with perjury?

CRAFFY.

Aye, and be a true Protestant for all that.

FLORIO.

And break your father's heart? 365

CRAFFY.

I'll come the sooner to his estate, and the easier to his wife.

FLORIO.

Oh, fine fellow! Well sir, out of love to your good father, whose heart this news would break, and out of love to the City, whose safety depends much 370

---

18 understand trap] to know one's own interest (*OED*)
19 put 'em off] sell them

20 twelve … picked] a jury packed with Whigs
21 *probatum est*] Latin for "it has been proved," meaning tried and true

upon your wise father's conduct, I will conceal this.
But I'll watch you.

CRAFFY.

Watch and be hanged. I would watch thee for my
mother, but that she knows thou art such a foul,
rusty gun, if she should discharge thee, thou   375
wouldst fly in pieces and hazard her life too.

FLORIO.

Away, you monster.

CRAFFY.

Away, you godly, false puppy.* (*Exit.*)

FLORIO.

I am glad the fool gave me this notice. I do not know
But my fair love, like an o'er-fertile field,   380
May breed rank weeds, if she be idly tilled.
Lest love for fools should in her bosom live,
She shall have all the tillage I can give. (*Exit.*)

Scene ii. The street.

Enter the Governor of the City, Artall, and guard.

GOVERNOR.

This foolish, headstrong City will choose that
factious, troublesome coxcomb Paulo Camillo for
their Podesta.

*A shout, "A Paulo, a Paulo!" Enter Podesta, Citizens,
Bricklayer.*

BRICKLAYER.

A brave Paulo, we ha' carried thee, boy!

GOVERNOR.

Is this gentleman elected?   5

BRICKLAYER.

Yes, that he is, for all the tricks that were used to
hinder it.

GOVERNOR.

I thought his Excellency the Viceroy[22] had given
you intimation another person would be more
pleasing to him and, in this juncture, more fitting 10
for the office.

PODESTA. (*Aside.*)

Another man more fit to be Podesta than me?

Then I shall think another man more fit to be
Viceroy than he, and so I'll make bold humbly to
acquaint his Majesty.[23]   15

BRICKLAYER.

Are we to follow the Viceroy's pleasure or our own
consciences?

ARTALL.

Here's a saucy rogue.

GOVERNOR.

What are you, sir, that undertake thus impudently
for all the rest?   20

BRICKLAYER.

'Tis well known what I am. I am a freeman of
Naples, a bricklayer by trade.

GOVERNOR.

Oh, I have heard of a busy, pragmatical fellow that
calls himself the Catholic Bricklayer. Are you he, sir?

BRICKLAYER.

I am not bound by law to give an account what I   25
am; if anyone has anything to say to me, let him
deal with me according to law.

GOVERNOR.

But sir, you might be so civil as to make me an
answer.

BRICKLAYER.

I'll do nothing for no man, but according to law. 30

PODESTA.

My lord, the man as to his occupation is but a
mean man, but as to his abilities, he makes a very
considerable figure.

ARTALL.

He is a pretty figure indeed.

BRICKLAYER.

We have a Charter for the free election of our   35
magistrate, and what we have done, our Charter
will justify.[24]

---

22 Viceroy] Don Pedro, duke of Ossuna, representing
    Charles II and perhaps to some extent his brother, James,
    duke of York, as well

23 Majesty] the king of Spain.

24 Charter … justify] The city charter of London was a
    hotly contested issue between Charles II and the Whigs.
    Under the ancient city charter, London citizens claimed
    the right, among other things, to exist as their own po-
    litical corporation and to elect their own city officials,
    particularly sheriffs. Part of Charles' "Stuart Revenge"
    after the Exclusion Crisis was to revoke that original
    charter and replace it with a new one under royal con-
    trol. The king accomplished this in October of 1683.

GOVERNOR.

Have you a charter to be saucy, sir?

BRICKLAYER.

What I speak is according to law, and I may speak law in defense of our proceedings. 40

PODESTA.

Come, pray be silent; 'tis according to law also for me to speak. His Excellence the Viceroy has been pleased to oppose my election, stimulated thereunto by evil men, enemies to the City and Nation. They would betray and sell us to the French,[25] and 45 they're angry so active a man as I am put over the City to prevent their wicked^e machinations. For that reason I will be ten times more active.

ARTALL. (*Aside.*)

A pox of an active rogue.

GOVERNOR.

Who are these evil men you speak of? Indict 'em 50 and prove 'em guilty, and I'll engage the Viceroy will severely punish 'em.

PODESTA.

I don't know who they are. All's one for that; I'm sure there are such traitors, though I don't know who they are, and Frenchmen, though I don't 55 know where they are, and plots, though I don't know what they are, and I'll make work.

GOVERNOR.

May not you be deceived?

PODESTA.

No, I'm never deceived. For the preservation therefore of the Town,* I will have four regiments 60 of the train bands be upon the guard during my whole year, and I, or my officers, will every four and twenty hours search every house in the City.[26]

GOVERNOR.

At this rate you will not let people be quiet in their houses. 65

---

25 French] To the Whigs, and to most English of the era, the French under Louis XIV represented the double nemesis of absolutism and Catholicism.

26 train bands … City] During the late 1670s and early 1680s, London Whig officials were frequently agitated with rumors of Papist plots to massacre Protestants. The "train band" here refers to trained bands of militia that patrolled London.

PODESTA.

No, nor out of their houses neither. I will have no ranting, reveling, gaming, drinking, no, nor eating immoderately. I will have all persons eat and drink according to law, and I will have all men's tables examined to see if there be no letters conveyed into 70 their dishes from the French, and if I find but the least cause of suspicion, I'll take their dinners into custody. I will have all persons be in bed at the ringing of the nine o'clock bell, and I, or my officers, will see 'em in bed, and see who they have abed with 'em too. 75

ARTALL.

Here's a fine business. Pox o'thee and thy officers! Shall we neither eat, drink, nor lie abed in quiet, for thee and thy officers?

PODESTA.

Pox o'me and my officers? Pox o'your wenches, sir. I'll make you know I am a magistrate. Seize him! 80

GOVERNOR.

And have I no authority, that you offer to seize him in my presence?

BRICKLAYER.

Yes, we know your authority, know you are Military Governor of the City, Captain of the Viceroy's Guards, a lord, nay more than all this, a 85 Justice of Peace, and twenty things more. What do we care for all that? We are in the City liberties, and what we do is according to law.

GOVERNOR.

Hold your prating, sirrah.

PODESTA.

He says truth. 90

GOVERNOR.

It may be according to law, but 'tis unmannerly.

BRICKLAYER.

All's one, 'tis according to law.

GOVERNOR.

But sir, this gentleman is an officer under me, and you have not power over him; therefore, I advise you not to meddle with him. 95

BRICKLAYER.

Have a care what you do. Do nothing but according to law.

PODESTA.

Have you a care of advising me. I know what I do. I'll do nothing but according to law.

GOVERNOR.

Nor I neither, for I have authority by law to protect 100
my officer by force, if you use force. But because
I'll make no disturbance, let him alone, and I'll
pass my word for him.

BRICKLAYER.

If the law will let him alone, do, otherwise not.

GOVERNOR.

Will you not take my word? 105

BRICKLAYER.

Advise with counsel.

PODESTA.

Advise me again! I know what I do. I will advise
with counsel.

GOVERNOR.

Advise with counsel whether my word's to be taken
or no? Guards, force Artall out of their hands and 110
take that rascally Bricklayer into custody, and let
me see who dares resist. (*Bricklayer is seized.*) Now
sirrah, though I could punish you by law for your
insolence, since you are a freeman, I will not
disturb the City Festival[27] with the punishment 115
o'the least o'their members, though they deserve it
not; therefore sirrah, if any of your great friends
here will be bound for your good behavior, I'll
release you.

PODESTA.

'Tis beneath my dignity, though I respect the man. 120

GOVERNOR.

Who else will be bound for him? Nobody? You see,
sirrah, for what special friends you leave your trade
and venture your neck.

BRICKLAYER.

Hang 'em, I knew the rogues were of untempered
mortar. A word with you, sir, in private.—Procure 125
me a pension, I'll come over to your party.

GOVERNOR.

A pension! a whip, you rascal. Go, sirrah, I give
you liberty. Follow your trade and mind all of you
your own matters. Leave state affairs to your
governors. We have more to lose than any of you. 130

PODESTA.

I don't know but[f] I have a hundred thousand
pound to lose, and that's enough for one man; but
however, my lord, if you please to introduce me
to his Excellence the Viceroy—

GOVERNOR.

What, to be—? I understand you, my lord. 135

PODESTA. [*Aside.*]

How the devil came he to understand my mind
so well?

GOVERNOR.

Truly my lord, I must tell you plainly, I don't care
to do so ungrateful an office to his Excellency, for
I know his mind very well. I know, till you have a 140
better introducer than myself, I mean your good
management of affairs, you will not be very
welcome to him, nor receive any honor from
him.[28] And so farewell my lord.

Exeunt Governor, Artall, and guards.

PODESTA.

Say ye so, shall I not be welcome to him? Then 145
he sha' not be welcome to me. And since he'll do
me no honor, I'll do his government no honor. My
wife, for want* of this knighthood, will lead me
an ill life, and I for want of it will lead him an ill
life. Since he is so huffy and stormy, I'll be a storm. 150

CITIZENS.

Do, my lord.

PODESTA.

A whirlwind, that shall rumble and roar over his
head, tear open doors by day and by night, toss
his friends out of their coaches and beds into gaols;
nor shall all the preachings and pulpit-charms of 155
their priests
Dispossess me or fright me in the least:
A Whig's a devil that can cast out a priest.

Exeunt.

---

27 City Festival] Lord Mayor's Day in London was celebrated October 29 and ended with a great banquet in
the Guildhall, the seat of London's government.

28 nor … him] In 1680, Charles in fact went against custom and refused to meet with the two new London sheriffs, Bethel and Cornish, when they were presented by
the lord mayor to be knighted.

Act II, scene i. The Podesta's house.

Enter Podesta, Citizens.

PODESTA.

Not knight me? When he knew I was a proud man, a very proud man, opposed him out o'pride, and a knighthood might ha' bought me. He shall repent it.

Enter Rosaura attended.

ROSAURA.

Welcome home, my lord. I wish you joy of your   5
new honor.

PODESTA.

Thank you, sweetheart. I am glad I'm in a capacity to do my country service, but I'm sorry I can't do you the service you affect.

ROSAURA.

What's that, my lord?   10

PODESTA.

Give you lasting honor. The title I shall bestow on you will live no longer than a grasshopper or a silkworm; 'twill die at the end of the year. Your present title of ladyship will then die into an alderman's wife, for I am not knighted.   15

ROSAURA.

Not knighted?

PODESTA.

Not knighted.

ROSAURA.

How dare they use you thus?

PODESTA.

They are desperate.

ROSAURA.

I'm troubled.   20

PODESTA.

I know it.

ROSAURA.

I was born well, and I affect honor.

PODESTA.

I know it. I know your spirit better than you do yourself and am pleased with your affection[29] to honor, for honor is an excellent guard to virtue. I   25
know you are punctually just to me.

ROSAURA.

Am I? I think I am.

PODESTA.

Out of a point of honor I know it, scorning to appear what you are not; not out of dulness and want* of gaiety you affect pleasures and follow 'em.   30

ROSAURA.

I do.

PODESTA.

Out of a point of honor, to appear what you are, I know you, know your temper perfectly.

ROSAURA.

So perfectly you amaze me.

PODESTA.

Oh! I have a penetrating judgment, know your   35
passion for honor, highly commend it, and would gratify it if I could, but since I cannot, I will give you a kind of honor, revenge. The methods you must leave to me.

ROSAURA.

Give me greatness, and do you keep policy.

PODESTA.

Well carved.   40

ROSAURA. (*Aside.*)

So, I have nursed the wen of his vanity, till it has blinded his eyes and made him mistake his affectation for mine; what I really affect, he is never like to see, and that's only my dear Florio.

Enter the Bricklayer.

BRICKLAYER.

Your servant, sir. I am much beholding to you and the   45
rest of my brethren of the City for the kindness you showed me today in refusing to be bound for me.

PODESTA.

I'll answer you, sir. We resolved to go prudently to work. We did not know but they might have laid treason to your charge, so we resolved to see   50
whether they durst have tried you, and if they had tried you, whether they durst have brought you in guilty, and if they had brought you in guilty, whether they durst have hanged you, and if they hanged you[30]—then let 'em look to themselves.   55

---

29 affection] propensity or disposition

30 hanged you] Stephen College was hanged on 31 August 1681.

BRICKLAYER.

And who should ha' looked to me then? A very fine business. Come, come, this was scurvy, but I'll stick to the Cause* whilst I have a drop of blood.

Enter Craffy.

CRAFFY.

Hah! There's my delicate mother-in-law. That ever such a curious appendix should be bound up with such a volume of nonsense covered with calves leather,[31] as that old fellow is. I will tear her from him. I'll be hanged if she loves him, and as for marriage promises, they are but church-mouth-glue. They won't hold a couple together three days.

PODESTA.

Oh, are you come, sir? Well, what ha' you done, sir?

CRAFFY. (*Aside.*)

A delicate woman!

PODESTA.

Sir? Are you asleep, sir?

CRAFFY.

No, nor abed, sir. (*Aside.*) Would I were wi' your wife, sir.

PODESTA.

What are you staring on, sir? Why don't you give me an account of what I sent you about? Did not I send you to search the cathedral for arms, sir?

CRAFFY.

Yes sir.

PODESTA.

And what ha' you done, sir?

CRAFFY.

Sir, I have been searching—searching—searching—sir—that mother-in-law—

PODESTA.

Searching your mother-in-law, sir?

CRAFFY.

The cathedral, the cathedral I mean, sir.

PODESTA.

Sirrah, you said mother-in-law.

CRAFFY.

Why, is not a cathedral a mother-church, sir?

PODESTA.

Sirrah, you said mother-in-law.

CRAFFY.

Why, is not a cathedral according to law, sir? I spoke jeeringly, and you know we use to jeer the church, sir.

PODESTA.

That's true.

CRAFFY.

Lord, sir, must I teach you the language of your own family?

PODESTA.

Well, did the priests let you come in patiently?

CRAFFY.

Aye, aye. (*Aside.*) Fiddle—faddle—a delicate woman!

PODESTA.

That's very strange. Then they are not afraid o'me?

BRICKLAYER.[g]

I hope shortly to leave never a priest in Christendom. They call themselves the pillars o'truth; they are rather the whipping-posts o'truth and sign-posts of faction.

PODESTA.

I'll handle greater people than they.

CRAFFY. (*Aside.*)

I must have this woman; if courtship won't do, love-powder shall.

PODESTA.

Come sir, I'll try your understanding.

CRAFFY. (*Aside.*)

I am resolved upon love-powder.

PODESTA.

I can put the City in arms, upon pretense of a French invasion, but when they see no invasion, and the fright is over, how shall I keep up that army?

CRAFFY.

The best way will be by love-powder.

PODESTA.

How! Keep up an army by love-powder? You impudent, ill-mannered, unnatural rascal, you. Do you jeer your father?

CRAFFY.

Sir, I don't jeer you.

PODESTA.

Sirrah, you either jeer me, or, which is almost as saucy, did not attend to what I said.

---

31 calves leather] Crowne may have complicated this extended metaphor by alluding to Bethel's membership in the Leather Sellers Company; Wilson thinks so.

CRAFFY.

Well, I confess my wits were a-wool-gathering, and I beg your pardon, sir.

PODESTA.

A-wool-gathering? A-whore-gathering by your story of love-powder, you saucy, debauched fop, you. When your father condescends to talk wisely to you of state affairs, must your brains be rambling after wenches? 115

CRAFFY.

Wenches are fitter for me than state affairs, sir. What a deuce should such a young fellow as I trouble himself with state affairs for? 120

PODESTA.

Who used to trouble themselves, and others too, about state affairs more than you, sir? Were you not such a tempestuous disputer in coffeehouses that as soon as ever you appeared in one, both sides would run away, our friends out of envy, and our enemies out of fear? 125

BRICKLAYER.

'Tis my case; no man will sit by me in a coffeehouse.

PODESTA.

Were not your writings like so many firedrakes? No printer would meddle with 'em, no person come near 'em. 130

BRICKLAYER.

His things are very near my style, and I am forced to print all my things at my own charge.[32]

PODESTA.

And now, sirrah, all o'the sudden, you are unfit for state affairs. Come, come, sirrah, you are a villain, have turned cat in pan,[33] and are a Tory. 135

CRAFFY.

A Tory? That's a good one, when I'm now writing an answer to *Absalom and Achitophel*.[34]

---

[32] print … charge] At his trial, College was accused of publishing an abundance of political songs, libels, and ballads for the Whig cause. His most famous was *The Raree-Show*. (Wilson)

[33] turned cat in pan] turned coat

[34] *Absalom and Achitophel*] John Dryden's famous allegorical satire against the Whigs, published in 1681 and responded to in kind.

PODESTA.

How! 140

ROSAURA.

'Tis true indeed, he read part of it to my maid last night.

MARIA.

He did indeed, madam, and 'tis very fine.

BRICKLAYER.

May be that puzzles his head then.

PODESTA.

Nay, if it be so, I shall not be angry with him, for o'my word, a good answer to that would do us service. 145

BRICKLAYER.

And 'twill require pains.

PODESTA.

It will do so. If he employs his time and thoughts so well as that,[h] I shall be very well satisfied. What do you call this poem? 150

CRAFFY.

Azariah and Hushai.[35]

PODESTA.

A very good subject.

BRICKLAYER.

Well chosen.

CRAFFY.

Is not this a strange thing, now, that you, who are no poet nor understand poetry no more than a cat, should lie insulting o'er a man o'sense, when he is breaking his brains for the service and honor of you and your party? 155

PODESTA.

Well, well, Craffy, I did not know it, I did not know it. 160

CRAFFY.

Not know it? Then you should not meddle with that you do not understand. I must break my sleep and spoil my stomach in studying to do you service, and be called a villain and a Tory? 165

---

[35] *Azariah and Hushai*] an anti-Tory satire attributed to Samuel Pordage and published in 1682 that attempts to answer Dryden's damaging portraits of Shaftesbury and Monmouth in *Absalom and Achitophel*; "Monmouth is represented as Azariah, David's obedient son, and Shaftesbury as Hushai, a wise and loyal counselor" (Wilson).

PODESTA.

Well, well, child, I am sorry, I am sorry.

CRAFFY.

Sorry? What does you sorriness signify? Suppose your vexing me should make me write but a sorry poem, as twenty to one but it will, and so I'll go burn what I ha' done, and there's an end. 170

PODESTA.

Nay, prithee, child.

CRAFFY.

I will.

PODESTA.

Prithee, dear child.

CRAFFY.

I say I will.

PODESTA.

No, prithee child, let me see what thou hast done, 175
and finish the remainder.

CRAFFY.

I won't.

PODESTA.

Prithee, do now, 'twill joy my heart.

CRAFFY.

I say I won't.

PODESTA.

This it is to breed our sons wiser than ourselves; 180
we are despised for our pains.

BRICKLAYER.

Look, if he has not made his good father weep. Are not you a cross-grained, ill-natured fellow to make your old father weep? What if he be not so good a poet and scholar as you, he has as good natural 185
parts,* and better.

PODESTA.

He is ungrateful to me, for what learning he has, my purse paid for. But I always find overmuch wit and learning make people insolent, and when all's done, a fool's a better comfort to his parents than 190
one of these great wits.

BRICKLAYER.

Go fetch the poem, and be whipped to you.[36]

ROSAURA.

Do, Mr. Craffy, 'twill oblige your father and me both.

_____

36 be whipped to you] be quick about it

CRAFFY.

Will it oblige your la'ship, madam? To do that I'll 195
run a thousand miles upon my bare head, madam.
(*Exit.*)

PODESTA.

I'm glad he pays so much respect to you, sweetheart, though he will pay none to me.

ROSAURA.

Yes, yes, he will, but great wits are humorsome.[37]

PODESTA.

Nay, the boy has excellent parts, that's certain, but 200
when all's done, 'tis but a folly to breed boys up to this height, for it does but spoil them and all business, for they will be a-top o'business, riding upon old men's backs, and so the old men go lamely, and the boys ride madly, and the business 205
goes awkwardly.

ROSAURA. (*Aside.*)

Now shall I be wedged in between the old fool and the young by the heavy beetle[38] of this poem and have no opportunity with my charming Florio. When he comes, I'll lay away the beetle.—Maria. 210

MARIA.

Madam.

ROSAURA.

Did not you say Craffy fell asleep last night in reading his own verses and, when he waked, forgot 'em in your chamber?

MARIA.

Yes, madam. 215

ROSAURA.

Run quickly and bring 'em to me.

Exit Maria. Enter Florio wrapped in his cloak.

PODESTA.

Oh! How do you, good Mr. Florio?

FLORIO.

Thank you, good my lord, the better to see things go so well that you are chosen.

PODESTA.

Oh! We carried clearly. 220

FLORIO.

Aye, so my chaplain Dr. Sanchy said, who I think labored for my lord.

_____

37 humorsome] whimsical, moody
38 beetle] a heavy ram for driving wedges

BRICKLAYER.

Aye indeed, he took great pains; there was scarce a man appeared 'gainst my lord that he did not call rogue and rascal a hundred times. 225

FLORIO.

He is a zealous man, and so seldom calls any man by his Christian name, that he is suspected to be an Anabaptist and against christening.—Oh! Dear madam, is your ladyship here? When I came into the room, I saw a lady and turned my head aside, 230 as my usual manner is when I see women, for they ha' been no good friends o'mine, and so I did not mind your ladyship. I beg your pardon.

ROSAURA.

Oh! It needs not, sir. I am very glad to see you look so well. 235

PODESTA.

Aye truly, Mr. Florio looks very fine and fresh, ruddy and plump; methinks I have hopes of him. What say your doctors, sir?

FLORIO.

Alas! My lord, they have given me over long since; all my trust is in an incomparable nurse. 240

PODESTA.

Pray, who is she?

FLORIO.

As you came along, my lord, you might ha' seen her tied by a rope to my door.

PODESTA.

Tied with a rope? What, is she a madwoman?

FLORIO.

No, no, my lord, a cow, my lord, a cow. 245

PODESTA.

A cow?

FLORIO.

Aye, my lord. Ha' not I managed myself well to bring myself from one of those they call[i] the wits of the kingdom to be one of the calves and live upon the breasts of a poor beast, for thence I have 250 all my subsistence.

PODESTA.

Alack! Yet your face says you are as well as ever you were in your life; I protest it does.

FLORIO.

My face is as false as ever my heart was. It might have more innocence, for it is scarce two months 255 old, I mean the flesh of it.

PODESTA.

Is it possible? I warrant if you were to begin the world again, you would have none of the mad frolics you had.

FLORIO.

I think I should not. I laughed once at mad fellows 260 that in drunken frolics eat fire, but was not I more mad to belch fire at Heaven itself, as I have often done in my abominable talk?[39] But what did I get by it? He threw it all back again in my face, and almost consumed me. Man is a shallow[j] animal, 265 can bear no excess: too much wit makes him as mad as too much wine, and a little oversets him, yet he thinks his silly skull contains all things, rules all things, and Omnipotence itself is afraid of that pitiful engine.* 270

PODESTA.

Very well.

FLORIO.

When all that the most hot-brained fellow in the world can do is to make a smoke to darken things, he can't strike fire enough out of himself to light him into the nature of a fly. But 'tis time we went 275 to prayers.—Doctor Sanchy.

Enter Doctor Sanchy.

SANCHY.

I'm a-coming.

FLORIO.

Good Doctor, give us a few prayers.

SANCHY.

Aye, if you will.

FLORIO.

My lord being a magistrate, I think, Doctor, you 280 must read the prayers of the church.

SANCHY.

I'll see 'em burnt first, and all priests hanged, before I read any of their prayers.[40]

---

39 abominable talk] perhaps a jibe at the duke of Buckingham, famous for his obscene mock sermons (Wilson)

40 prayers of the church … their prayers] Florio insists that, according to the Test Act, which mandated all officials swear allegiance to the Church of England, Sanchy must read prayers in the household of the newly elected Podesta out of the Anglican Book of Common Prayer;

FLORIO.

  The law commands it.

SANCHY.

  Therefore I won't do it. I'll be commanded by   285
nothing, and do nothing I'm commanded.

BRICKLAYER.

  For matter o'law, we can easily come off; nobody
dare indict us.

FLORIO.

  But for matter o'conscience.

SANCHY.

  Hang conscience. I do it out o'matter of honor and   290
matter of revenge. The priests are rascals and slight
me, and I'll slight their prayers.

FLORIO.

  We should not be humoursome in our prayers,
Doctor.

SANCHY.

  I'll do what I please, or I'll do nothing.   295

PODESTA.

  Pray, let him, for we are all obliged to the Doctor
for the assistance he gave my election.

SANCHY.

  He had need of it: there was a damned company
o'rogues appeared against you. I hope to see 'em
all hanged.   300

BRICKLAYER.

  There was one great man.[41]

SANCHY.

  A great rogue; he deserves to be burnt.

PODESTA.

  There was a great lady[42] very busy.

SANCHY.

  A great whore; she deserves to be whipped. I hope
to see all such rogues and whores whipped out of   305
the kingdom. But come, let us go to prayers.

Enter Craffy.

Sanchy, a stand-in for Titus Oates, whose antipathy for
the Church of England was infamous, refuses.

41 great man] possibly Sir George Jeffreys, Recorder of London, who opposed the election of Bethel and Cornish
in 1680 (Wilson)

42 great lady] possibly Louise Kéroualle, duchess of Portsmouth, a Catholic and the King's mistress (Wilson)

CRAFFY.

  Oh, the Devil, the Devil!

PODESTA.

  What's the matter?

CRAFFY.

  I ha' lost my *Hushai*; I can't find it high nor low.
Who saw my *Hushai*?   310

SANCHY.

  What, the poem that you read to me that was an
answer to *Absalom*?

CRAFFY.

  Aye.

SANCHY.

  I had rather ha' lost ten pounds out o'my own
pocket.   315

PODESTA.

  Then do you like it, Doctor?

SANCHY.

  'Twas an admirable thing! 'Twould ha' made the
rogue that writ *Absalom* hang himself. Look about
for this *Hushai*.

FLORIO.

  Won't you go to prayers first, Doctor?   320

SANCHY.

  Hang prayers! This is a thing of forty times the
consequence. We may pray at any time, or if we
never pray at all, 'tis no great matter: it is but a
thing of form to please the people. Look for this
Hushai. I'll look for't myself. (*Exit.*)   325

CRAFFY.

  Who the devil has got my *Hushai*?

Enter a vintner's boy.

BOY.

  Is Mr. Craffy here?

CRAFFY.

  Well sir, what would you have?

BOY.

  I come from the Club; they stay for you, sir.

CRAFFY.

  The Club be damned. I can't come; I ha' lost my   330
Hushai.

[Exit boy.]

PODESTA.

  What club is it?

CRAFFY.

The club o'young politic Whigs, you know 'em.

PODESTA.

Oh, Craffy, you must go to 'em; they are all persons of quality.*   335

CRAFFY.

What care I for their quality? They are but a company o'young coxcombs. I won't lose my *Hushai* for 'em.

PODESTA.

Sirrah, you are a saucy fellow to call young men o'their parts and quality coxcombs. They are   340 admitted into better company than yours, sir.

CRAFFY.

Aye, to help to pay reckonings, flatter an old knave's vanity, and give a guinea to the burning of a Pope.[43]

PODESTA.

Sir, some of 'em have had the honor to sit in great   345 cabals.

CRAFFY.

I wonder they could.

PODESTA.

Why so, sir?

CRAFFY.

Because some of 'em were so lately whipped at school for blockheads, I wonder they could sit   350 anywhere; they have the marks of fools both before and behind, and if ever they speak, the mark's in their mouths.

BRICKLAYER.

I don't like this fellow.

PODESTA.

Sirrah, I now begin to suspect you again for a Tory.   355 And get you to 'em, or I'll not only cudgel you, but disinherit you.

CRAFFY.

Take notice if I go to 'em, I shall be very drunk.

PODESTA.

I care not, if you be in such company as they are.

CRAFFY. (*Aside.*)

Your wife's honesty may pay for't, for I shall be very   360 impudent when I am drunk.—Look all for my *Hushai*. (*Exit.*)

BRICKLAYER.

What else!

ROSAURA. (*Aside.*)

So, we are rid of one fool, could we have as good luck with the rest!   365

Enter Doctor Sanchy.

SANCHY.

What is become of this *Hushai*? Some concealed rogue has burnt it out of envy.

Enter a coffee boy.

COFFEE BOY.

Doctor, you must come to the coffeehouse.

SANCHY.

Must come?

COFFEE BOY.

Aye, to a person of quality.*   370

SANCHY.

That person of quality is a coxcomb, and you are a saucy rascal. Must come?

COFFEE BOY.

'Tis the lame lord.[44]

SANCHY.

He is a rascal.

COFFEE BOY.

Your friend.   375

SANCHY.

Oh! Then I'll come, but look all about for this *Hushai*.

PODESTA.

Do so, and let me have an account of it when I come home.

Exeunt Sanchy and boy.

ROSAURA.

Are you a-going abroad, my lord?   380

---

43 reckonings] tavern bills; the "old knave" probably refers to Shaftesbury. From 1679 to 1681, Queen Elizabeth's birthday (17 November) was observed in London with massive parades and a "pope burning," that is, the burning of an effigy of the Catholic leader. Green Ribbon Club members were said to contribute a guinea apiece to help fund these festivities (Wilson).

44 lame lord] probably Shaftesbury, who suffered from the gout (Wilson).

PODESTA.

Yes, sweetheart, and shall not come home these three hours. Mr. Florio, you'll excuse me, I leave you.

FLORIO.

Oh! Good my lord!

Exeunt Podesta, Bricklayer, and Citizens.

Hah! Rid of all my diseases at once! I mean my   385
fools, and left alone with my health! My Rosaura!

ROSAURA.

My life! My Florio!

FLORIO.

My Rosaura! (*They embrace.*)

Enter Podesta and Bricklayer.

ROSAURA.

My husband! Faint, faint in my arms.—Help, help, help!   390

PODESTA.

What's the matter?

ROSAURA.

Mr. Florio is fallen into an apoplectic fit and dies in my arms.

PODESTA.

Alas, poor gentleman! Who's there?

Enter Pietro.

Help in with your master and call a doctor. I'm   395
cruelly afraid he'll go away in one of these fits.

Exit Pietro, Rosaura, and Florio. Enter a servant.

SERVANT.

My lord, here's an old counselor, Bartoline, lighted at your door and is coming up to speak with your lordship.

PODESTA.

This old lawyer is a strange fellow. He is very old   400
and very rich, and yet follows the term[45] as if he were to begin the world.

BRICKLAYER.

He has lost all his teeth that he can hardly speak,

and he will be pleading for his fee, but he's of our side, and so we must not speak against him.   405

Enter Bartoline, Lucinda, and (at a distance) Artall.

ARTALL. [*Aside.*]

What pretty country creature's this! I cannot but venture in after her; the Podesta's house is public, and so I shall not be taken notice of.

BARTOLINE.[46]

Where's my Lord Podesta? Hah! Where ish he?

PODESTA.

Here, here, old friend, do not you see me?   410

BARTOLINE.

No faid, my eysh are none of the besht.

PODESTA.

You follow the term still?

BARTOLINE.

Aye, and will ash long ash I live; yersh no caush wi'out me.

BRICKLAYER.

How can you follow all causes?   415

BARTOLINE.

Yey follow me, yey will ha' me.

PODESTA.

What young gentlewoman ha' you brought with you here?

BARTOLINE.

One I may be ashamed on—shesh my folly, yat ish cho shay, my wife—I ha' played ye fool and   420
married a young garl.

ARTALL. (*Aside.*)

Thy wife? If thou beest her husband, thou shalt be my cuckold.

---

45 follows the term] Bartoline attends the four sessions of the law courts: Easter, Trinity, Michaelmas, and Hilary terms.

46 BARTOLINE] Aged and toothless, Bartoline lisps and slurs words. He is intentionally not easy to understand, and this no doubt is part of Crowne's satire both upon lawyers in general and Whig lawyers in particular. Representing Bartoline's strange speech habits in print, however, is a problem. In his preface to the published play, Crowne goes into some detail about how to read the lawyer's lines. Thus, *th* becomes *y* (as in "yat" for "that," "yosh" for "those"); sometimes a *t* is left out ("houshand" for "thousand"); *s* becomes *sh* ("shir" for "sir," "musht" for "must"); *t* becomes *ch* ("chrue" for "true," "chreason" for "treason," "cho" for "to"); and *ch* is only to be pronounced as in "child," never as a *k*.

PODESTA.

  Welcome to Town,* madam.

BRICKLAYER.

  Welcome, mistress.   425

BARTOLINE.

  Ish she not pritchy? You shee I have a shweet chooth in my head shtill.

PODESTA.

  Sweet tooth? You ha' never a tooth in your head.

BARTOLINE.

  Yatsh chrue, but I'll bite for all yat wi' my wit.

PODESTA.

  Why would you marry such a young thing as this?   430

BRICKLAYER.

  A man of fourscore be so fond?* Fie, fie.

BARTOLINE.

  A man of foashco—yersh no shuch thing, ye are boysh of foashco—if you will, after hreeshco we ought cho go in long coash, for breechesh are imposhchuresh and prechend cho what yey ha'   435 not. I believe, my Lord Podesta, you are behind-hand wi' your wife ash well ash I, I believe sho. Hah!

PODESTA.

  Though I be, I shall suffer no disgrace.

BARTOLINE.

  How do you know yat?   440

PODESTA.

  Because I married a virtuous woman.

BARTOLINE.

  A vartuoush woman? Why sho did I for ought I know, but we may be bo'h mishchaken.

PODESTA.

  No, I am never mistaken.

BARTOLINE.

  Oh, you're a happy man. I ha' no shuch   445 confidentsh in a woman; I declare it before my girlesh faish, I'll wash her wachersh.*

PODESTA.

  Do, if you please.

BARTOLINE.

  And for yat reashon I have brought her hither, deshire you cho let her be in your housh; yoursh   450 is a shivil family, and here she'll have a great yeal of good company yat will chake off her fanchy from going abroad and playing ye fool.

ARTALL. (*Aside.*)

  So, now I shall know where to find her.

PODESTA.

  What, would you ha' me keep a boarding house?   455

BARTOLINE.

  What do you shtand upon sheremonyesh with an old friend for? You and I have known one anoyer fortchy years, and when y'are in bed with your wife, yersh shomehing about you dosh confesh you cho be old. Come, if you'll let me be here, I'll give your wife   460 a jewel, and you a peish o'plate,* and I'll pay a good rate beshidesh. What chay you cho yish now, huh?

PODESTA.

  With all my heart.

BARTOLINE.

  Will my lady conshent? For I believe de mare'sh de letcher[k] hoish.[47]   465

PODESTA.

  My will is hers.

BARTOLINE.

  I would know yat of her.

PODESTA.

  She is busied now in a work of charity, about a poor gentleman that's fallen in an apoplectic fit. I don't know whether he'll recover it. If he does, he   470 can't live long; he's in a deep consumption. I should be sorry to lose him, though in point o'money I should be a gainer by his death, for he will leave us a very good legacy.

BARTOLINE.

  A legashy? Huh!   475

PODESTA.

  Yes, for he's a rich bachelor.

BARTOLINE.

  What, a kinshman?

PODESTA.

  No kin at all, but he has a great friendship for us because we are a strict sober family, and he is a mighty religious gentleman.   480

ARTALL. (*Aside.*)

  Oh! I know this religious rogue; 'tis Florio.

---

47 maresh … hoish] "the mare is the better horse," a prov-
    erb meaning that the wife is the master; Bartoline's slip
    further reveals his misogynistic insecurity.

BARTOLINE.

Will he leave you money becaush you are shober?
Huh!

PODESTA.

You must know he was a great follower of naughty
women, and now he feels the sad consequence and   485
has a great value for virtue, and I believe will leave
my wife a great part of his estate, because she is a
virtuous woman.

BARTOLINE.

Do you hear, girl? You are fallen incho a brave*
housh, where you may get money by vartshow and   490
shobrietchy. Come, my lord, what will you have;
I'll pay you any rate. Come.

PODESTA.

You and I will not fall out.

ARTALL. [Aside.]

Hah! Is he a-providing a Florio for his wife? I'll
provide him a Florio. By good luck I have an   495
Indian gown and cap[48] at the door, just new out
of the shop. (Exit.)

BARTOLINE.

What ish yish gentleman'sh name?

PODESTA.

Florio.

BARTOLINE.

Oh! Yere ish shuch a man. I never shaw him, but   500
I have heard of him. A great debosh, wash he not?
And a good witshy fellow.

PODESTA.

Oh! A very witty man, and a wicked man too once,
but now the most penitent creature in the world,
and he had need be so: he is going out of it; he   505
cannot live many months.

BARTOLINE.

Alash, poor man, and when he diesh he'll leave all
hish money to vartuoush people, will he? Huh.

PODESTA.

Yes, he says 'tis sowing seed in good ground. Well,
I ha' some occasions call me away. You may be here   510
if you will, old acquaintance.

BRICKLAYER.

Aye, let him, let him, and come away about your

_____

48 Indian gown and cap] "a dressing gown and nightcap
made of Indian silk or cotton" (Wilson)

business.

Exeunt Podesta and Bricklayer.

BARTOLINE.

Hark you, hark you! Sho, yish wash very lucky.
Girl, you mush make it your buishnesh cho get   515
incho yish genkleman'sh favor by your shobriechy,
and you may mump[49] my Lady Poshta of hish
eschate for oughtch I know.

*Enter Artall in a nightgown and cap, a patch on his
nose, led by two servants.*

ARTALL.

I grow weaker and weaker every day, my time
draws on. Heaven prepare me for my change, yet   520
I'll use the means to live. Give me my milk.

BARTOLINE.

I' my consciensh, yish ish de genkleman!

ARTALL.

Give me my milk I say, you rascals. What have I
said? Indeed I should not call anything out of its
name; I ask your pardon for it.   525

FIRST SERVANT.

Ah, sir! Ask your poor servant's pardon?

ARTALL.

Aye, and thank you too, if you will give it me. I
was so accustomed in the days of my wickedness
to libel everything, I cannot leave the ill habit still.

BARTOLINE.

Aye, yish ish he, yish ish he sharchainly.   530

ARTALL.

Truth is, atheism is nothing else but a libel on the
whole creation, calling it the offspring of paltry
Chance, when 'tis the child of Heaven, that I ought
to ask pardon of every dog for detracting from his
descent. But give me my milk and set me a chair   535
to repose myself, for I am very weak.[50]

BARTOLINE.

Alack! Alack! Yish ish de poor genkleman. But

_____

49 mump] cheat (*OED*)
50 rascals … weak] In his sudden kind treatment of his
  servants, his denunciation of atheism, and his laments
  for squandering his youth in the libertine lifestyle, Artall
  here duplicates the supposed miraculous conversion of
  John Wilmot, earl of Rochester during his dying days.

what a hing it ish yat yish young fellow should bring himshelush incho shuch a shad condition. Let me shee how he looksh! 540

Puts on his spectacles and looks on Artall, whilst Artall holds the pot to his nose.

LUCINDA.

Certainly this handsome sick gentleman is the fine unhappy Mr. Florio I have heard so much talk of. A thousand pities such a delicate gentleman should bring himself to this!

BARTOLINE.

He looksh very white—odsha' me—'twash the 545 white potch—aye, 'twash the potch, and he looks very rudgy, but men in yat giet[51] will do sho, aye, yey will do sho.

ARTALL.

Oh, Florio, Florio!

BARTOLINE.

Oh! Now I am shachishfied 'tish he. 550

ARTALL.

How hast thou brought on this youth all the infirmities of age? My eyes are dim, my breath is short, my limbs are weak. Limbs, did I say? I have none, at least of Heaven's making. I have embezzled all the furniture of my soul and body 555 in vice; though Heaven gave me an excellent housekeeper to look to it all, a careful wakeful creature, called a conscience, which never slept, never let me sleep in ill, but I abused her, fought to turn her out of doors, nay, murder her, but 560 could not.

BARTOLINE.

I prochesht, yish ish very shad.

LUCINDA.

Exceeding pitiful.

ARTALL.

Ashamed of her I was and to all my atheistical companions denied her, at the same time she stared 565 me in the face. 'Tis the atheist's trick to hide his conscience, as the tradesman does his wench, for fear of spoiling his credit and losing his traffic with those ill people who will not come near him if he owns so scandalous a thing as a conscience. 570

LUCINDA.

I swear he almost makes me weep.

BARTOLINE.

Why chruly I am chroubled, and I don't ushe cho be sho.

ARTALL.

But alas! Let him hide her for a time; when diseases and death come and shake the building in pieces, 575 as now they do mine, the poor foul conscience will appear through all the rubbish and call out, "Mercy, mercy!" when it may be 'tis too late. Thank Heaven for the fair warning I have had. Is my coffin ready? 580

SECOND SERVANT.

Dear sir, why does your honor think of a coffin? 'Tis time enough to talk of that forty years hence.

ARTALL.

Oh! Prithee don't flatter my crazed body. I cannot live; I hang on the eaves of life like a trembling drop, ready every minute to fall and be seen no 585 more.

BARTOLINE.

Alash, alash.

FIRST SERVANT.

Oh, dear! And please your honor, here is company; I doubt your honor entrenches on a gentleman's chamber? 590

ARTALL.

Heaven forbid! Where is the gentleman?—I beg your pardon, sir, a thousand times. My good friend the new Lord Podesta, you know, sir, is a sober, discreet, frugal person, hates the vanity and prodigality of splendid housekeeping,[52] and so I 595 suppose may content himself with a part of this house and oblige a friend with the remainder. If you be the friend, I beg your pardon, sir. I would ha' gone up higher, but truly I wanted* breath.

BARTOLINE.

Why chruly, you shay chrue, shir, my lord yosh 600

---

51 white potch … giet] "White potch" is "pox," meaning venereal disease. "Rudgy" is "ruddy," meaning the flush of fever. "Giet" is "diet," meaning Artall's milk diet, which was a common treatment for venereal disease (Wilson).

52 hates … housekeeping] a taunt at Sheriff Bethel, who was notorious for being cheap in his domestic affairs

oblige me with part of hish housh, which part, or the whole housh, if it were mine, should be at your shervish, good Mr. Florio.

ARTALL.

Do you know me, sir?

BARTOLINE.

No, shir, but I have heard mush of your great partsh, and my Lord Poshta chellsh me what a good man you are, and I have heard it choo wi' my own earsh.

ARTALL.

May I crave you name, sir?

BARTOLINE.

I am called Barcholine, shir. I am a fellow pritchy well known among lawyersh.

ARTALL.

The famous counselor Bartoline?

BARTOLINE.

I have some repuchation in yat way, shir.

ARTALL.

I am glad to know you, sir. I think I see a young woman there, very young—is she your grandchild, sir?

BARTOLINE.

Why, chruly, shir, I am almosht ashamed cho chell you she is my wife.

ARTALL.

Oh, dear! Would you marry one so young, sir?

BARTOLINE.

I wanched* a comfort for my age, shir.

ARTALL.

And she wants a comfort for her youth. Heaven, that made both sexes, would have both provided for. Can you provide for hers?

BARTOLINE.

Whatch I want in provisionsh I make up in a heartchy welcome. Hah!

ARTALL.

But will that suffice her?

BARTOLINE.

It may in chime; cushtom ish a great matcher. I have obsherved lushty so'diers by custom got cho dine and shup very comforchably on a pipe o' chobacco.

ARTALL.

But they steal many a good bit that nobody knows of.

BARTOLINE.

Why chruly she may, shir, but not if she be honesht.*

ARTALL.

Many an honest parishioner follows private meetings[53] because he finds no comfort from the parson of the parish. But she seems a virtuous, modest young lady, and I would pay my respects to her in a salute,* but I fear my breath may offend her. Pray excuse me to her, sir.

BARTOLINE.

Oh, good shir! Well, shir, she and I are sho chaken with the discourshesh we have heard fall from you yat we are exshtremely deshiroush to be frequently wi' you, shir.

ARTALL.

Alas, sir! I am unfit for company. My good Lady Podesta indeed will sit by me half a day here, as by a murmuring brook that slides fast away and soon will be dried up forever, and she is content to hear my little purlings.

BARTOLINE.

Aye, yey are very well ingeed, shir, very well, and you would much obligsh ush. My wife wantsh* shuch good company; she'sh a young creature yat never in Chown* before, and yosh not know the world, shir.

ARTALL.

Is it possible! Sweet madam, you are sailed into a dangerous gulf which few young ladies pass without casting away their reputations, or honesties, or both; I have been an admiral here, and you see to what I am brought!

BARTOLINE.

Well, shir, affairsh call me away; I'll make bold cho leave you chogether, shir.

ARTALL.

She will be weary of me, sir, for I am weary of myself.

BARTOLINE.

No ingeed, shir, she chaksh great gelight in your dishcoursh; pray letch her have it, shir. I'll rechurn presently.—Wheegle him, d'ee hear? Wheegle him, you may get a good legashy. (*Exit.*)

_____

53 private meetings] secret services of religious dissenters, conventicles

ARTALL.

Is he gone? 665

FIRST SERVANT.

He's gone, sir.

ARTALL.

My periwig and love equipage, quickly.

LUCINDA.

How now! What's this?

ARTALL.

An adorer of yours, fair creature: no unsound, false, wicked Florio, but a sound, young, vigorous, 670 passionate lover. If you will not believe my tongue, believe my nose: the patch covers wholesome flesh. Believe my legs, which leap, vault, and run, except from you, sweet creature.

LUCINDA.

I am betrayed! Drawn into a snare. (*Aside.*) But 'tis 675 a sweet one.—Help, help, help!

ARTALL.

I need no help, my dear.

LUCINDA.

But I do. Help, help, help! (*Aside.*) Oh, 'tis a lovely gentleman!—Help, help! (*Aside.*) 'Tis a delicate gentleman!—Help, help! 680

ARTALL.

Why do you call so loud? I can help you to what you want.

LUCINDA.

Help, help! Will you force me? (*Aside.*) I can't resist him.—Help, help!

ARTALL.

All this is to no purpose. 685

LUCINDA.

Oh, fie upon you, what a man you are! (*Aside.*) A handsome man, I mean.—I am out of breath with striving. Help, help! Oh, my heart pants! Help, help, help!

Artall carries her off.

Act III, scene i. The scene continues.

Enter Artall and Lucinda.

LUCINDA.

Oh! Fie upon you! Fie upon you! Was ever virtuous gentlewoman served such a trick before?

ARTALL.

Oh, frequently! Scores of 'em are served so every Easter Term.[54]

LUCINDA.

What, women that are as virtuous as myself? 5

ARTALL.

Aye, full as virtuous.

LUCINDA.

Oh, Lord bless us! What a place is this! I did not think there had been such a place, nor such a man as you in the world. I shall never endure to see you more.

ARTALL.

Do not say so. 10

LUCINDA.

No, never, as long as I live.

ARTALL.

You'll change your mind.

LUCINDA.

Never whilst I breathe.

ARTALL.

Yes, when I come next. Meanwhile, I am your humble servant. 15

LUCINDA.

Your servant, dear sir.

ARTALL.

When shall I wait on you again, madam?

LUCINDA.

When you please, sir. I shall at all times be glad of your good company.

ARTALL.

Your servant, dear madam. 20

LUCINDA.

Your servant, dear sir.

Exit Artall. Enter Bartoline and his clerk with papers.

BARTOLINE.

Wher'sh my wife and poo Mishte Florio? Huh! Where are yey?

LUCINDA.

Here's your wife, but poor Mr. Florio is gone away very ill. 25

---

54 Easter Term] began shortly after Easter and lasted about a month; many country gentlemen brought their wives to Town during the terms for a little society while they conducted legal business.

BARTOLINE.

Were you not weary of him? Huh!

LUCINDA.

No indeed, I could have been with him all day and all night.

BARTOLINE.

I doubt* you dishemble.

LUCINDA.

Indeed I do not.   30

BARTOLINE.

I doubch you had rather been at a play or shome other diverchishment.

LUCINDA.

I swear I had more pleasure from him than ever I had from any divertissement in my life.

BARTOLINE.

Well, be good whilsht I live; 'twill be the betcher   35
for you when I die. Then I shall leave you rich
enough cho chake your choish of young,
handshome coxshcombs.

LUCINDA.

Do not tell me of young, handsome coxcombs.

BARTOLINE.

You won't marry, I warrant, when I am gead? No,   40
not you? A housand to one you will be married
before. Nay, I dare hold chen pound you are
conchracted now?

LUCINDA.

How!

BARTOLINE.

Nay, not by a priesh, but by looksh and shmirksh,   45
echshechera,[l] twisching of eyebeamsh, and making
a wedging-ring of the fine round mouh——and
yush, I believe you have promished yourshelf cho
a housand foolsh.

LUCINDA.

You wrong me extremely.   50

BARTOLINE.

All ye betcher. I'm shure I shall disherve your
kindness, for I am labring cho make you a rich
widgow; the term won't lasht a month, and I ha'
more breviatsh[55] and papersh putch incho my
hand shince I went out yan I can read in hree   55
monhsh, I'm shure on't.

_____

55 breviatsh] legal briefs

LUCINDA.

And what must become o'your clients' causes?

BARTOLINE.

I yon't care; I know what will become o'yeir money.
I'll lock it up preshently,* all for you.—Gi' me my
papersh, come, let me shee now——let me shee——   60
whatsh here cho do? (*Reads his papers.*) Oh! Among
other hingsh, here'sh a buishnesh in which my
brother'sh neck'sh consherned. He ish hirchy years
younger yan I am, yet he ish old enough cho be
wiser. He hath played de fool and killg a man, and   65
ye widow bringsh an appeal,[56] in which it sheemsh
yere arishesh matcher of law—my brother shendsh
me chen poun cho rechain me; ye widow shendsh
me twenchy, sho I follow ye poor widyow'sh
buishnesh. I am for ye poor widow, I.   70

LUCINDA.

Will you hang your brother for ten pound?

BARTOLINE.

You should ashk me if I would hang him for chen
shillingsh, yen I might conshiger it. But chen poun
ish a great yeal o'money, tish a great yeal of money.
(*Reads.*) Come let me shee.   75

LUCINDA.

Methinks 'tis a little against the law of nature.

BARTOLINE.

Ye law of natchure belongsh cho pchivilians,
woman; we common lawyersh yon't studgy ye law
of natchure, 'tish none of our shtudgy—no—no.
But come, let me shee—whatsh here now? Come.   80

*Exit Lucinda. Bartoline reads, drums beat without;
enter Podesta, Bricklayer, and a gentleman.*

GENTLEMAN.

My lord.

PODESTA.

What's your business, sir?

GENTLEMAN.

I have a message to your lordship from his
Highness the Viceroy.

PODESTA.

Very well, sir, I attend.   85

_____

56 appeal] to support conviction of her husband's murderer,
Bartoline's brother

GENTLEMAN.

His Highness desires your lordship not to disturb and frighten the City by raising the Town forces[57] to no purpose.

PODESTA.

He is of opinion 'tis to no purpose, is he?

GENTLEMAN.

Yes, my lord.   90

PODESTA.

I am of a contrary opinion, and I am seldom mistaken.

GENTLEMAN.

His Highness bid me tell you, that for the bare satisfaction of the people (though danger requires it not), he is willing you should keep up half you   95 do.

PODESTA.

He would have me keep but half?

GENTLEMAN.

Yes,[m] my lord.

PODESTA.

Then I will keep as many more.

GENTLEMAN.

Is that your answer?   100

BRICKLAYER.

Yes, and we will justify it by law.

GENTLEMAN.

Well-bred, good-humored gentlemen these, and fine subjects. (*Exit.*)

PODESTA.

He shall shortly hear from us things that will vex him worse than this, articles that may cost him his   105 employment. We'll not only humbly address to his Majesty, but impeach him;[58] I'll teach him not to knight me.

---

57 City … forces] The Viceroy warns the Podesta against raising the militia unnecessarily; here the strict analogy between Naples and London breaks down: the train bands the Lord Mayor might raise would not be the forces of the Town, Westminster, seat of the Court.

58 articles … impeach him] suggesting the Exclusion Bill against James, duke of York; the "him" refers not to His Majesty, the King of Spain (it would be an audacious threat, indeed, to impeach him) but rather to the Viceroy, who may allegorically stand for James.

BRICKLAYER.

Here is Counselor Bartoline, the greatest lawyer in the kingdom, and one of our own party; you can't   110 possibly advise with a better man about 'em. Give him the hundred pound fee the City allows you to retain some eminent lawyer.

PODESTA.

I will.—Counselor Bartoline, I must speak a word wi' you.   115

BARTOLINE.

I'm not at leishure; I have caushesh cho look over yat are cho come on chomorrow.

PODESTA.

But we have a cause in which the whole City's concerned.

BARTOLINE.

You must defer it yen, for if I yon't appear in yish   120 cause chomorrow, 'twill be losht. It wholly dependsh upon me, and I cannot but in conshiensh atchend it; I have a fiftshy pound fee.

PODESTA.

We'll give you a hundred pound, mun.

BARTOLINE.

How? A hundgerd poun? Huh?   125

PODESTA.

Aye, there 'tis.

BARTOLINE. (*To his clerk.*)

Here, lay ashide yesh papers.—Well, what'sh your buishnesh now—come—huh?

BRICKLAYER.

We are drawing up articles against the Man of the Castle.   130

BARTOLINE.

Ye Man at ye Cashtle, wosh yat?

PODESTA.

He means the Viceroy.

BARTOLINE.

Archiclsh against the Vicehroy—huh?

PODESTA.

Aye.

BARTOLINE.

Gi' me ye papersh again; I won't meggle in't.   135

BRICKLAYER.

How! Not meddle?

BARTOLINE.

No, I won't meggle, I won't meggle.

BRICKLAYER.

Your reason?

BARTOLINE.

I may losh my head, mun. I won't meggle, no, no. (*Reads his papers again.*) Come, let me shee.   140

BRICKLAYER.

No matter if you do lose your head, if you have no more honesty nor love for your country than to refuse to do your country's business, when you have received your country's money.

BARTOLINE.

I yon't care whosh money 'tish, let it be ye Devil'sh   145 money, I'll keep it, now I have it, but I won't meggle in the buishnesh—no—no. (*Reads.*) Come—come.

BRICKLAYER.

Keep our money? and not do our business?

BARTOLINE.

'Tish our way. 'Tish our way.

PODESTA.

Sir, by your favor, either do our business or pay   150 back our fee.

BARTOLINE.

Pay back your fee! 'Twash never known, mun, and I won't shet an ill pregident; no, no, 'tish shufficient I won't be against you, yat'sh enough.— Come, let me shee.   155

BRICKLAYER.

Did one ever know such a knave? What shall we do? For you and I must account for this money.

PODESTA.

Let me alone with him; I understand mankind.— Counselor Bartoline, do not play the fool wi' yourself and lose a thousand pound, which you   160 may get by this cause.

BARTOLINE.

A houshand pound? Huh!

PODESTA.

Yes, this is a great cause, and the City will go through with it, whatever it costs 'em.

BARTOLINE.

Come, I'll underchake ye buishnesh—come.   165

PODESTA.

Did not I tell you I understand mankind?

BARTOLINE.

But I won't appea publicly—d'ee hear—I won't appea.

BRICKLAYER.

Give us counsels will do the Man at the Castle's business, and we don't care.   170

BARTOLINE.

Let me alone.[59]

Enter a second gentleman.

SECOND GENTLEMAN.

Counselor Bartoline, a word wi' you.

BARTOLINE.

Your buishnesh.

SECOND GENTLEMAN.

I am sent to you by his Highness the Viceroy.

BARTOLINE.

Hish Highnesh the Vishroy? Shpeak shoftly.   175

SECOND GENTLEMAN.

His Highness is informed you are here, and very great[60] with these men.

BARTOLINE.

I great with yesh men? 'Tish falsh, they're knavsh, I haitch 'em, I haitch 'em.

SECOND GENTLEMAN.

Nay, he believes you only assist 'em as a lawyer for   180 your fees. You have too much wisdom and law to engage in their ill and dangerous designs.

BARTOLINE.

Hang 'em, hang 'em.

SECOND GENTLEMAN.

And such they have, his Highness is well assured.

BARTOLINE.

No doubch on't, mosht sherchain.   185

SECOND GENTLEMAN.

And therefore he's resolved to punish 'em.

BARTOLINE.

He musht do't! He musht.

SECOND GENTLEMAN.

To that end he intends to indict 'em of several crimes.

BARTOLINE.

I am glad of it.   190

SECOND GENTLEMAN.

How far they will extend in law he knows not.

BARTOLINE.

Very probable.

---

59 Let me alone] to do it; trust me
60 very great] thick, in cahoots

SECOND GENTLEMAN.

Therefore he sends you by me a hundred pieces[61]—

BARTOLINE.

He doesh very well—very well—he'sh a wysh man.   195

SECOND GENTLEMAN.

For your advice.

BARTOLINE.

I'll give it him, but not publicly—I won't appea, but I'll give him shuch advysh ash shall do yeir buyshnesh.

SECOND GENTLEMAN.

I'll tell it him.   200

BARTOLINE.

If he hash a fanshy cho hang 'em, he shall.

SECOND GENTLEMAN.

I'll tell him. (*Exit.*)

BRICKLAYER.

Well, you'll undertake our business?

BARTOLINE.

Let me alone. Give me your articlesh.—Come, now I'll go studgy, come along.   205

Exeunt Bartoline and clerk.

BRICKLAYER.

So, this is a notable old fellow; if he undertakes the business, he'll do't.

PODESTA.

You need not inform me in mankind.

Enter Florio wrapped in a cloak, leaning on a staff, led by Pietro.

FLORIO.

Where's my—where's my—every little thing puts me so out of breath—where's my Lord Podesta?   210

PODESTA.

Here, Mr. Florio.

FLORIO.

I have great—pooh! (*Blows.*) I am so faint with every little motion and little talk—I have great news for you.

PODESTA.

Great news and I not know it? There is seldom anything to be known that I don't know.   215

FLORIO.

I'll tell it you, but I must open a vein[62] first that I may breathe.—Fetch a surgeon.

[Exit Pietro.]

I played the fool—uh! as I came—uh! along. I saw a young woman with naked—pooh!—breasts—going I'm certain—pooh!—to be naught.* So I reproved her, but she was very angry and said she was an honest* woman; then I said she was to blame to let those two breasts come abroad, like two domestic intelligences[63] to slander her; so she said she did it to please her—pooh!—her husband; so I said her husband was a wise man to make his wife show her—pooh!—her breasts in such a town as this; such treasure would invite pickpockets enough to rob him of it. And thus with this wanton woman I wasted my—pooh!—my spirits.   220   225   230

PODESTA.

So you have done now more than needs; you might have told us the news in the time you have told the story.

FLORIO.

'Tis true indeed—well, I'll tell you the news. You may see how things go; for my part I am glad I have not long to live, to see the Nation ruined.   235

BRICKLAYER.

Why, what's the business?

FLORIO.

There's a French fleet upon the coast, and six of the principal commanders lurk in the disguise of pilgrims about Mount Vesuvio, to burn the town by night and let in their friends.[64]   240

---

61 pieces] guineas, probably; a hundred would be worth slightly more than a hundred pounds but nowhere near a thousand; Bartoline intends to keep both retainers, however, and two birds in the hand are worth more than a thousand in the bush.

62 open a vein] have blood let from him, a medical procedure

63 domestic intelligences] household spies, with perhaps an allusion to *The True Domestic Intelligence*, an anti-Whig periodical

64 French … friends] In December 1678 the false rumor spread through London that a great number of French troops had landed in Dorsetshire. Also, one of the stories circulated by the Whigs was that an Irish army disguised as pilgrims was to land at Milford Haven (Wilson).

PODESTA.

    I knew all this several hours ago.

FLORIO.

    Is it possible, my lord? You have excellent
intelligence.   245

PODESTA.

    So I have.

FLORIO. (*Aside.*)

    I'm sure 'tis not half an hour since I invented it.

PODESTA.

    What do you think made me raise the militia?

BRICKLAYER.

    Was it for that?

PODESTA.

    Do you think I raised 'em for nothing? I never do   250
a foolish thing.

BRICKLAYER.

    And why would you not tell me?

PODESTA.

    I had some reasons of state.

FLORIO.

    And what will your lordship do in it?

PODESTA.

    What else, but seize 'em?   255

BRICKLAYER.

    We must do it very privately, lest they ha' notice,
for they have friends in town.

PODESTA.

    You need not teach me my business, nor that they
have friends in town. What meant the order to put
down two regiments o'the militia?   260

FLORIO.

    Was there such an order?

BRICKLAYER.

    I was an ear-witness.

PODESTA.

    You may see how things go; whereupon I smartly
replied, "Would they have two down?" said I,
"Then I will have four more up," said I, smartly.   265

FLORIO.

    That was very well.

BRICKLAYER.

    As well as I could have advised.

PODESTA.

    Sir, I know what I do.

BRICKLAYER.

    I protest I thought you had done it only to cross 'em.

PODESTA.

    Sir, I have deeper fetches in things than you are   270
aware of.

BRICKLAYER.

    I see you have.

PODESTA.

    Now you shall see how I'll manage this business.
I will leave my hat, gown, and periwig here, put
on your hat, coat, and periwig, Bricklayer, and go   275
out so disguised that my own family shall not
know what is become of me.

FLORIO.

    That will do very well.

BRICKLAYER.

    I cannot advise better.

PODESTA.

    Then I'll go to your house, Bricklayer, and there send   280
for twenty men such as I can trust and arm them,
and when that's done I won't trust them neither, but
take 'em along, and they themselves shall not know
whither they go. What say you to this?

FLORIO.

    Incomparable.   285

BRICKLAYER.

    Very well. But why would you not do this before,
since you had intelligence of these men?

PODESTA.

    For good reasons, you may be sure; I never do a
foolish thing. Come, give me your things.

BRICKLAYER.

    What shall I wear myself?   290

PODESTA. (*Disguising himself.*)

    Any porter's so far as your house. (*Armed with a
blunderbuss at his back.*) Now will not this deal
with pilgrims? Mr. Florio, have you strength to go
with us?

FLORIO.

    To Mount Vesuvio? I may as well hope to carry   295
the mountain on my back, but if I had strength I
durst not venture.

BRICKLAYER.

    Why, what are you afraid of?

FLORIO.

    Pride, pride, I am mighty apt to be vain. Formerly

a little success in a jest or a song or libel would 300
ha' made me a notorious ass. Imagine, then, if
when I come from this great expedition, I should
see my name in every intelligence, my picture on
every wall, what an insufferable, haughty coxcomb
I should be? Lord, Lord, I should be so proud! 305

BRICKLAYER.

For my part now, I go o'purpose for these things and
intend to sit for my picture as soon as ever I come
home. I was bid money for my face yesterday.

FLORIO.

You who have but one infirmity need not fear it.
But my vices, like Tories,[65] ride in troops, and if 310
one gets into me, a hundred will follow. If, now I
am sick, I should love your praises, when I am well,
I shall love your wives.

PODESTA.

He speaks a great deal of reason; we'll go without
him. 315

BRICKLAYER.

But who shall guide us?

FLORIO.

My lord needs no guide.

PODESTA.

No, I know where they are to a hair's breadth. Here
comes my wife; don't let her know who I am.

Enter Rosaura.

I remember I read in Plutarch that Brutus would 320
not trust his wife Portia with affairs of state; I'll
imitate his politics.

ROSAURA.

No news o'my lord?

FLORIO.

I suppose, madam, he's busied about some great
affair. 325

ROSAURA.

Mr. Florio, I have an humble address to make to
you.

FLORIO.

What is it, good madam?

ROSAURA.

I am a woman more nice* and careful of my honor

---

65 Tories] here not primarily the opponents of the Whigs
but literally Irish bandits

than any other woman is of her face or skin; in 330
my husband's presence I am secure from malice,
but in his absence I can never open my doors but
Slander will enter. Even your religion and virtue,
sir, cannot hinder her from following you in and
fastening on us both. 335

FLORIO.

Slander will have lean food in me, madam.

ROSAURA.

All's one, sir, 'tis best to avoid her. I would therefore
humbly beg you at all times of my husband's
absence to bestow your excellent conversation*
elsewhere. 340

FLORIO.

'Twill be very prudent, madam.

ROSAURA.

I hope you'll not take it ill, sir.

FLORIO.

By no means, madam. (*Aside.*) Do you hear what
an excellent wife you have?

PODESTA.

I know her, sir. 345

FLORIO.

An admirable woman!

PODESTA.

Sir, you need not inform me.

ROSAURA.

Who ha' you got wi' you there?

FLORIO.

A very honest man, madam.

ROSAURA.

Are you sure o'that? 'Cause these are dark times; a 350
knave will shine in 'em like rotten wood by night.
And that man has a notable outside; he resembles
much my husband, who is one of the wisest men
in this age.

FLORIO.

Do you hear? 355

PODESTA.

Sir, she is a woman of vast parts.*

ROSAURA.

I have a great fancy to secure him.

BRICKLAYER.

Pshaw, we shall have a fiddle faddle with her and
spoil our business.—Get you gone, go.

Exit Podesta.

ROSAURA.

How, does he fly? That's suspicious. Seize him.   360

BRICKLAYER.

Away, away man, I'll follow you. (*Exit.*)

FLORIO.

No, good madam, I'll be bound for him.—Ha!
Ha! What a coxcomb is this? Now is he gone he
knows not whither to catch he knows not whom.

ROSAURA.

What an excellent thing and how useful in the   365
world is credulity.

FLORIO.

'Tis so to many excellent trades. To the sparkish
fop, the shopkeeper's large faith swells his feather
and garniture. To the politician, the believing,
empty-headed rabble are his bladders. But oh, 'tis   370
of excellent use to a lover.

ROSAURA.

And to a trade you ha' not named—a swearer.

FLORIO.

A lover is a swearer, a private one; he is not a public
evidence,* a swearer-general.

ROSAURA.

You were once swearer-general to our whole sex.   375

FLORIO.

But I recant and now will I kiss no book but these
sweet lips.

ROSAURA.

Hold! Not so fast.

FLORIO.

Why, what's to do?

ROSAURA.

I must blush awhile.   380

FLORIO.

Blushes are for the morning of love. We have
traveled many tedious hours since that and without
any refreshment except baiting now and then at a
kiss. Those lips are delightful places, but not the
end of the journey.   385

ROSAURA.

You say you have traveled in love. You say true:
you have passed through many hearts, and I fear
have wasted all your love by the way.

FLORIO.

I have only trifled away some unnecessary traveling
expenses; here will I lay out my whole heart.   390

ROSAURA.

A mortgaged heart!

FLORIO.

Indeed, it is not.

ROSAURA.

What security will you give me?

FLORIO.

Have I not pawned a kingdom to you? I was king
of libertines, and I have left my dominions and all   395
my fair female subjects to be a slave to you and a
fool to the priests.

Knocks.

Knocking! We're undone! Have talked away our
precious minutes. Heaven grant it be not the old
coxcomb.   400

ROSAURA.

Whoever it be, we are in an ill condition to be thus
locked up together.

Louder knocking.

FLORIO.

Venture to ask who 'tis.

ROSAURA.

Who's there?

CRAFFY. (*Within.*)

'Tis I, madam.   405

ROSAURA.

'Tis the fool, Craffy.

FLORIO.

What shall we do with him?

CRAFFY. (*Within.*)

Madam, I must speak with your ladyship.

ROSAURA.

Come some other time, I'm very busy now.

CRAFFY. (*Within.*)

This business must be done now, madam.   410

ROSAURA.

Dispatch it where you are, then.

CRAFFY. (*Within.*)

I cannot, this is private business, madam.

ROSAURA.

Then you must let it alone, for I neither can nor
will speak wi' you.

CRAFFY. [*Within.*]

You must and shall speak with me, since you go   415

to that, and if you won't let me in at the door, I'll climb in at the window.

ROSAURA.

You are saucy, sirrah.

CRAFFY. [*Within.*]

There is no business to be done without sauciness.

FLORIO.

What shall we do with this fellow?   420

ROSAURA.

Put on my husband's gown, hat, and periwig and lie upon the couch as if you slept.

CRAFFY. [*Within.*]

Will you let me in or no?

ROSAURA.

You are in great haste, sir.

CRAFFY. [*Within.*]

Yes, that I am, my business is earnest.   425

Florio is disguised and lies down. Rosaura opens the door. Enter Craffy drunk.

CRAFFY.

So, she's all alone, as I hope to be saved!

ROSAURA.

Well, what's your business, sir?

CRAFFY.

I have sweet business! Delicate business, and I'll do't I'll warrant me! (*Aside.*) Drunkenness has given me wit and impudence. If it don't disfigure me, I   430 don't care. I am cursedly afraid 'twill put my features out of rank and file; they won't march even and gracefully and in battalia.

ROSAURA.

Well, hast thou given me all this trouble and now hast nothing to say?   435

CRAFFY.

Yes, I have something to say, and now it shall out. I come—I come—most sweet—

ROSAURA.

Speak softly, for your father's asleep on the couch.

CRAFFY. [*Aside.*]

My father there! The Devil take him for his pains. That blockhead never did me any good, nor ever   440 will; now he lies like a great boom to hinder my vessel from coming into the harbor when the wind is fair. 'Od,* I could find in my heart to cut him!

ROSAURA.

Well sir, you ha' no business, it seems?

CRAFFY. [*Aside.*]

'Od, I'll do my business, and let the old fool   445 dispose his greasy bags[66] as he has a mind; I care not, I'll pass the Rubicon and be *aut Caesar, aut nullus*.[67]—I come, then, to tell thee such a story as no age nor history can do the like.

ROSAURA.

Ay, prithee let me hear that.   450

CRAFFY.

Ay, prithee let me hear that—with a smile! many a Roman general has fought a battle upon the encouragement of birds[68] that have not chirped half so prettily. Prithee let me hear that. And thou, sweet rogue, thou sha't—   455

ROSAURA.

The brute is drunk, and I never discerned it.

CRAFFY.

Then, thou delicate creature, I come to tell thee I love and adore thee!

ROSAURA.

Love and adore me? What does the coxcomb mean? But why should I consider the meaning of   460 a fool in drink?

CRAFFY.

Nay, my news does come wet out o'the press, that's certain. 'Tis delicate news, is't not? What sayst thou? Have I no darts nor arrows in my eye? Prithee look upon me—nay, look if this fantastic woman will look   465 upon me? Prithee look upon me. I'm newly shaved, and a man looks like a notable smirk[69] rogue when he's shaved; his face is like a bowl new wiped. He may kiss the mistress if he has any skill, and I'll try.

ROSAURA.

Sirrah, attempt any rudeness to me, and I'll waken   470 your father and ruin ye. I am amazed he should sleep thus!

---

66 bags] stomach, entrails (*OED*)

67 Rubicon ... *nullus*] The Latin means "Either Caesar or nobody"; the historical allusion to the Rubicon had become proverbial for going beyond a point of no return.

68 Roman ... birds] Romans watched the flight of birds as omens.

69 smirk] smiling

CRAFFY.

I believe there is a proclamation come out against sleeping, and the rogue takes a nap to affront the government, for nothing else could make a Whig quiet so long, that's certain. 475

ROSAURA.

So, sir, you are a ranting Tory. Begone, you had best, before I waken your father, and you who are now so full o'wine be turned out o'doors and want* bread. Consider that, sir. 480

CRAFFY.

How! When I have thee before my eyes, dost thou think I can consider a crust? What a pitiful hungry thought was there?

ROSAURA.

Disinheriting, then, and starving are nothing to thee. 485

CRAFFY.

I starve now. Love has disinherited my stomach, which, before I fell in love with thee, had as good a title to meat as any stomach in Christendom, that is, if meat be made for stomachs. And now if I were to go to law with a chicken for crumbs, he'd cast[70] me. I should ha' nothing to show for 'em, so that I must enjoy thee that I may eat again. 490

ROSAURA.

Enjoy me, sirrah! Do you know who I am, you dare mention such a word before me?

CRAFFY.

Know thee! Aye, well enough. 495

ROSAURA.

Am not I your father's wife, sir?

CRAFFY.

And what of all that?

ROSAURA.

What of all that?

CRAFFY.

Thou thinkst, I warrant, I'll be frightened with incest? With fee, fa, fum? I am not a child to be scared from a sack* posset with a white sheet. If we must meddle with nothing that is akin to us, we must not eat or drink, for we are all near akin to our victuals. But thou art no kin to me. Thou art only tacked to my father's side by a priest and art no more my mother than his backsword is, for that's buckled 500 505

to his side sometimes. Besides, I don't know whether he be my father or no; I'm sure he is not fit for't.

ROSAURA.

Whatever I am to him or thee, 'tis sufficient I am nearly related to virtue and honor, and do not dare, sirrah, so much as to talk indecently before me. 510

CRAFFY.

Why dost thou talk indecently before me?

ROSAURA.

Who, I?

CRAFFY.

Yes, thy eyes talk bawdy, thou hast the wantonest eyes that ever I saw in my life. Gi' me a kiss, gi' me a kiss, I say—the best you have in the house, won't you? I'll come to the vessel myself, then. 515

ROSAURA.

Bless me! Husband! Husband!

CRAFFY.

Let him wake if he dares.

ROSAURA.

Oh, Lord! What shall I do? 520

Craffy chases her around chairs. Florio snorts.

CRAFFY.

Hah! Does he snort? Let him snort again; he has neither powder nor shot in his nose.

Knocking at the door; Craffy starts. Rosaura opens it. Enter Pietro.

PIETRO.

Oh, madam! Your husband and the bricklayer.

ROSAURA.

How! Where are they?

PIETRO.

Just coming into this room. 525

ROSAURA.

Cannot your master possibly get by?

PIETRO.

Not possibly.

ROSAURA.

Oh, misery! Shame! Death! What shall I do?

CRAFFY.

What's the matter, madam?

ROSAURA. (*Aside.*)

Hah! What comes into my head? I'll make this fool beat his father out.—Oh, your father will be murdered and I abused. Here are villains got into 530

---

[70] cast] defeat in a lawsuit or action (*OED*)

the house in arms. One of them, they say, has a design upon my person.

CRAFFY.

Your person? 535

ROSAURA.

Aye, help us for Heaven's sake!

CRAFFY.

Where are they?

ROSAURA.

Just coming into this room. Beat 'em out o'the house, as you value your father's life and my honor.

CRAFFY.

I'll do't. 540

ROSAURA.

Here they come.

Enter Podesta and Bricklayer, with muskets and blunder-busses at their backs, their waists stuck around with pistols.[71] Craffy knocks his father down; Pietro gets down the bricklayer. Whilst they are scuffling, Rosaura conveys Florio away and lays the hat, gown, and periwig upon the couch, as if one slept under 'em. After some rolling upon the stage, Podesta gets Craffy undermost.

PODESTA.

Someone help me to kill this unnatural rogue.

BRICKLAYER.

No, take him alive, I charge you, that we may know who put him upon this horrible, damnable plot, for this is as horrible a plot as has been these 545 thousand years.

PODESTA.

Sirrah, who put you upon this horrible wickedness?

CRAFFY.

Sirrah, who put you upon the horrible wickedness of attempting this sweet lady? Not nature, for nature and you have parted these twenty years.[n] 550

PODESTA.

This fellow's drunk.

ROSAURA.

As drunk as he is, he asks no impertinent questions, nor has he committed any great error in the ill-favored entertainment he has given you for entering my husband's house in this armed 555

posture, in these dangerous times, without giving me any notice. What he has done, he did by my command, and I'll justify it.

PODESTA.

This is a wise woman.

BRICKLAYER.

The woman could not act wiser if she were my 560 own wife.

PODESTA.

I'll reveal myself to her.—Sweetheart, I am your husband.

ROSAURA.

Come, sir, lay aside your unseasonable and unmannerly mirth; these are no rallying times, or if they 565 were, you are not my equal at repartee with me. But now I think on't, see what's become of my husband, somebody. He has slept these two hours upon that couch, and this rude scuffle has frighted him away.

PIETRO.

Indeed, madam, I fancy this is my lord. 570

PODESTA.

Sweetheart, upon my honor, I left my gown, hat, and periwig upon that couch, and there's no difference between the Lord Podesta and me but a gown.

CRAFFY.

Then there is roguery, for there lay a fellow under that gown; I'll swear I heard his nose go. 575

ROSAURA.

He says true.

PODESTA.

Bless me! Here's a plot.

ROSAURA.

Some of the French pilgrims to murder you and burn your house.

PODESTA.

Most certain. Fetch a regiment of the militia. I'll 580 have a sentry at every door in my house, two at every post of my bed, and one under my bolster.

BRICKLAYER.

Search all the tubs, pots, bottles, and vessels in your house for gunpowder.[72]

---

71 muskets … pistols] possibly a wry allusion to the Whigs who came heavily armed to the Oxford Parliament in 1681 (Wilson)

72 Search … gunpowder] In October 1680, the Whig lords commissioned College to search for gunpowder beneath the Houses of Parliament (Wilson). Crowne's audience would remember the infamous Gunpowder Plot to blow up Parliament in 1605; the allusion is ironic, for it associates the Whigs with Catholic conspirators.

PODESTA.

Yes, and I'll unpave the streets to see if the stones 585
be not hand granados.

ROSAURA.

'Tis necessary, and I hope your lordship will not
blame me for defending your house, though you
suffered something by it.

PODESTA.

'Twas admirably done. 590

BRICKLAYER.

Wisely, very wisely.

PODESTA.

Like a woman that knows mankind.

CRAFFY.

Well, and shall I no praises have that beat the
knave?

PODESTA.

Oh, 'twas very well done, Craffy. 595

BRICKLAYER.

Very well indeed.

PODESTA.

But are not these unhappy times,
That I can take no joy
In such a wife and great estate—

CRAFFY.

And such a son as I? 600

Exeunt.

Act IV, scene i. A garden.

*Enter Podesta, Bricklayer, Captain of the Militia, and
two soldiers.*

PODESTA.

Come Captain, place those two soldiers behind
those two doors, and then my house will be too
hot for a knave.

BRICKLAYER.

For the justification of our proceedings, we will
print a narrative of "The Pilgrim under the 5
Gown." As paper in Holland passes for money,
pamphlets with us pass for religion and policy. A
bit of paper in Holland, from a man of credit,
takes up goods here, pays debts there; so a
pamphlet will take up fools here, make fools there. 10
A pamphleteer is the best fool-maker in the nation.
And this story well improved—

PODESTA.

The story's well enough. What need we lie to no
purpose?

BRICKLAYER.

By your favor, 'twill be to good purpose; a lie will 15
give it the stamp of our party. Lies are the supporters
of our arms and the Great Seal[73] of our corporation.

PODESTA.

If a lie will do the Nation any service, I shall not
scruple.

BRICKLAYER.

You would ha' no reason, for that lie that does as 20
much good as truth is as good as true; ergo, 'tis
true. *Quicquid est idem, est idem*[74] is a rule in logic,
but you know no logic.

PODESTA.

But I know a rule in divinity that says you are not
to do evil that good may come thereby.[75] 25

BRICKLAYER.

Aye, that good may come and not come. But the
evil that does good is a good evil; but no evil is
good; ergo, 'tis no evil at all. But there's no talking
logic to you; you don't understand it.

Enter a man with prisoners' basket and beggars.

PODESTA.

How now, what would you have? 30

MAN.

May it please you honor, my lord—

BRICKLAYER.

Speak to me, I am my lord; that is, I manage all.

MAN.

It has always been a custom for the new Lord
Podesta to send poor prisoners some relief.

BRICKLAYER.

It has been a custom, you say? 35

---

73 arms ... Great Seal] as if the Whig party would have a
coat of arms and a great seal, the sign of the monarch's
sovereignty

74 *Quicquid ... idem*] "That which is the same is the same"
(Latin), the definition of tautology

75 rule ... thereby] alluding to St. Paul's defense of the
Christians against the slander that they are motivated
by the rationale "Let us do evil that good may come"
(Rom 3.8)

MAN.

Yes, master.

BRICKLAYER.

Is there any law for it?

MAN.

Law, master?

BRICKLAYER.

Aye, for we will do nothing but according to law.

MAN.

You would not have poor prisoners starve, master? 40

BRICKLAYER.

Sir, if they starve according to law, nobody has anything to say.

MAN.

That's hard, master.

BRICKLAYER.

Go, get you about your business.

MAN.

Pray, master. 45

SECOND BEGGAR.

I hope, master, you will be kinder to us, master.

BRICKLAYER.

Why, what are you?

SECOND BEGGAR.

Honest poor people, master, that always used to have some broken meats from my Lord Podesta's table, and now we ha' not had one bit. 50

BRICKLAYER.

Is there any law for it?

FIRST BEGGAR.

Law, master?

BRICKLAYER.

Aye, for in plain terms, we will do nothing for anybody that is not of our party but what we are forced to by law. 55

FIRST BEGGAR.

We are all o'your party, master.

BEGGARS AND MAN.

Aye, master, we are all Whigs, master, we are all Whigs.

SECOND BEGGAR.

Master, I polled for you.

THIRD BEGGAR.

I polled three times over for my lord; came in three 60 several coats and passed for three men.

PODESTA.

Say you so? Who employed you?

THIRD BEGGAR.

The Doctor, master.

MAN.

And several of our prisoners polled for my lord, master. 65

PODESTA.

Well, give 'em halfpence apiece.

OMNES.

Halfpence! My lord—halfpence!

PODESTA.

Well, when my year's out, I'll consider farther.

FIRST BEGGAR.

We shall starve in that time, master.

PODESTA.

Go, go, begone, the bricklayer and I are consulting 70 about affairs of state for the good of you all, how to secure your religion and property.

SECOND BEGGAR.

Our property, master?

BRICKLAYER.

Go, go, you ha' no property, nor, I think, religion; you are idle knaves—begone.[76] 75

FIRST BEGGAR. (*Aside.*)

The Devil take you—a halfpenny lord. Is the Podesta's place worth but a halfpenny?

SECOND BEGGAR. (*Aside.*)

Plague rot you—a halfpenny lord. I'd ha' seen the Devil have you before I'd ha' chose you, if I had known. 80

ALL.

A halfpenny lord—confound 'em damned rebel rogues, I hope to see 'em hanged.

Exeunt beggars and man.

BRICKLAYER.

Now let us to Counselor Bartoline's chamber to know his opinion concerning our arming and fortifying. 85

---

[76] relief … begone] In *The Observator* of 28 September 1681, Roger L'Estrange reported that supposedly Sheriff Bethel had ignored custom and sent no relief to distressed prisoners (Wilson); Crowne compounds the offense.

PODESTA.

One lawyer is positive against us.

BRICKLAYER.

That's a Tory fellow. I don't mind Tory law.

PODESTA.

But he spoke a great deal of reason.

BRICKLAYER.

I care not a farthing for reason, law, nor scripture if they side with the Tories. I prefer Whig nonsense before Tory reason. But come. 90

Exeunt. Enter a gentleman, Bartoline and his clerk at a little distance after.

GENTLEMAN.

Nobody in the house here? Oh, sir, you are the man I desire to speak with. I suppose you remember me?

BARTOLINE.

I remember you? How should I remember all the people yat come cho me? 95

GENTLEMAN.

'Tis strange you should forget me; 'tis not long since I put just such another fee into your hand as this.

BARTOLINE.

'Od sha' me! Now you putch it incho my headg, I do remember you; you come from ye Vishroy. 100

GENTLEMAN.

I do so.

BARTOLINE.

He ish a worhy genkleman; I shall be glad to sherve him.

GENTLEMAN.

The business is, my Lord Podesta fortifies without his leave. 105

BARTOLINE.

Doesh he? Yen he'sh a yebel; shay I shay it.

GENTLEMAN.

But is there no clause in their Charter will bear 'em out?

BARTOLINE.

Shir, if yere be shuch a claush, 'twill overthrow yeir Charcher; 'twill argue the King was desheived, so his grant will be void. 'Tish against ye Peyogative,[77] ash 110

---

77 Peyogative] Prerogative, the discretionary power seated in the British monarch

I'll prove outch common law and clea shatchute law, and if I yon't hrow 'em on yeir backsh, I'll hang for't. Sho chell ye Vishroy—but I'll be privatsh. 115

GENTLEMAN.

I'll tell him.

Exit. Enter Podesta and Bricklayer.

PODESTA.

Oh, here he is! Come, counselor, we must speak with you.

BARTOLINE.

You musht not, for I am very buishy.

BRICKLAYER.

But these ten pieces must and shall speak with you. 120

BARTOLINE.

Why, chruly, I have a great yeal o'buishnesh, but I have alsho a great kindnesh for boh you, for I hink you are very honesht men and wish well to ye Nation and have very good yeshignsh. And I will do you what kindnesh I can, I will ingeed. 125 Well come, your buishnesh—huh?

BRICKLAYER.

May the subject—subject? I don't love that word subject. But come, may the subject fortify by law without leave?

BARTOLINE.

May he wear a shword by hish shide without leave? 130 A shimple shtory.

PODESTA.

But a lawyer told me the contrary.

BARTOLINE.

'Twash not ye lawyer, 'twash hish fee, and fees will shay anyhing.

PODESTA.

He said 'twas against clear statutes. 135

BARTOLINE.

Yer'sh no shuch hing ash a clea shtachute. Han't we lawyersh the penning of 'em, and do you hink we won't make work for ourshelvsh? We hate a clea shtachute as a housebreaker yoesh a clea night. I shpeak against my own profession, for I'm an 140 honesht fellow; I am worth but shix housand a year, and I mightch ha' been worth twenchy if I would ha' been a knave. But I love cho make a consciensh of what I shay and do, I do ingeed, ingeed I do. 145

BRICKLAYER.

But we are told that 'tis so against law that, if there should be any such power in our Charter, 'twould argue the King was deceived and overthrow the Charter.

BARTOLINE.

If such a power in your Charcher should overthrow 150 it, 'twould argue the King had yesheived you, mun, and who dares shay yat? Yer'sh a chrick for you. Yey chalk like foolsh and knavsh; yey don't know what yey shay. Let me alone wi' you buishnesh, d'ee hea? But privately, very privately.—Come 155 along, come.

Exit Bartoline and his clerk.

PODESTA.

This is a notable old fellow.

BRICKLAYER.

I was of his opinion.

Enter Rosaura.

ROSAURA.

My lord, will you continue those guards and sentries about your house? 160

PODESTA.

Sweetheart, to ask my wisdom questions is to question my wisdom.

ROSAURA.

I confess, you have reason to stand upon your guard; 'twere well the people knew it, and your son Craffy has a pen fit for the purpose. 165

PODESTA.

He shall meddle no more with his pen; it has almost moped him. I would give five hundred pound he had never seen a pen in's life, but I will take him from it before he's too far gone and enter him into business. 170

Enter Craffy.

Here he is powdered, a feather in's cap, and catechizing his face in a glass,* but it does not make him one wise answer. The boy is spoiled.

CRAFFY.

Aye, this will do—this will do—nature writ no good hand when she penned me, because she 175 wrote after a damned copy, the fool my father, but

this will mend some letters. This will take my mother.—

PODESTA.

Craffy.

CRAFFY.

Drunkenness, like a hog in a garden, rooted up my 180 flowers, but now the tulips in my face begin to lift up their heads.

PODESTA.

Craffy.

CRAFFY.

They do, i'faith.

BRICKLAYER.

Why don't you come? 185

PODESTA.

Let him alone. All this is not his folly, but mine, who have let him take more poetry than his brains would bear and have ruined my child—and though I say it, a delicate young fellow.

BRICKLAYER.

I fancy he's turned amorous fop, for he's broke out 190 into a feather and all those fooleries that trouble lovesick people.

ROSAURA.

Indeed, his feather says some such thing.

BRICKLAYER.

And I'll take the feather's word.

PODESTA.

Before mine? Do not you teach me to know my 195 own boy, nor anything. I'd give you a hundred pound I were an ass—

ROSAURA. (*Aside.*)

You may have it cheaper.

PODESTA.

I mean in this, that I mistook the boy's distemper. Lord, that I should let him spoil himself! 200

ROSAURA.

I have a mind to know his contemplations. I'll go towards him.

CRAFFY.

Hah, my delicate mother-in-law? I'm ready for her; I'll charge her with smiles, wit, impudence, modesty, humility, all sorts of weapons. First, with 205 humility upon my knees.—Most sweet, dear— [*Aside.*] Hah! My father behind! That old fool is always in my way! How shall I get from my knees

again? The Devil take him!—Most sweet, dear
madam, pray to Heaven to bless me.—Pray, my   210
lord, pray to Heaven to bless me.

PODESTA.

Bless thee?

CRAFFY.

Aye, to bless me.

PODESTA.

What, o'this time o'day?

CRAFFY.

A blessing will do a man no hurt at any time o'day.   215

PODESTA.

Well, the Lord bless thee and deliver thee from
poetry, say I; it has utterly spoiled thee. That ever
I should let this fellow tamper with poetry. I could
ha' made him—I don't know what—I could ha'
made him such a statesman as these times could   220
not ha' produced. These times? Pitiful fellows! The
statesmen o'these times were all starved at nurse.
Some of 'em were foundlings; one found under a
Rump, another was a maggot in English Noll's
nose.[78] A pack of strange fellows they are all. In   225
short, Craffy—

CRAFFY. (Aside.)

Most sweet woman.

PODESTA.

You shall never write nor read more, but be a man
of business.

CRAFFY.

Yes, madam.   230

PODESTA.

Madam?

CRAFFY.

Yes, my lord, I mean—

PODESTA.

Did you mind what I said to you?

CRAFFY.

No, madam—yes, madam—aye, my lord, I mean.

PODESTA.

Yes, madam—aye, my lord—sirrah, where are your   235

brains?

CRAFFY.

Brains, madam?—my lord, I mean.

PODESTA.

In your inkpot, sirrah?

CRAFFY.

I'm now answering *The Medal*.[79]

PODESTA.

I thought as much. The Devil take thy poetry.   240
Sirrah, meddle with pen and ink more if you dare.

CRAFFY.

Who must answer these things then? There's ne'er
a man o'wit of our party but myself, and my things
are discommended. I know several people don't
like my *Hushai*, that I intend to call my poem *The*   245
Medal Reversed, written by him who was not the
author of *Hushai*, nor of any pen writ of our
side.[80]

PODESTA.

Come, poetry be hanged, and prose too.

BRICKLAYER.

Come, come, my answer will be the best.   250

PODESTA.

What's that?

BRICKLAYER.

A flail—if I meet with the author in a convenient
place, I'll give him an answer.[81]

PODESTA.

Yes.—And sirrah, you shall never meddle with pen,
ink, nor book more, but be a man o'business.   255

---

[78] Rump … nose] the Rump Parliament, with which
Bethel himself was associated; Noll refers to Oliver
Cromwell, to whom Shaftesbury, among many such
pinworms, had been a trusted friend and advisor from
1650-1654.

[79] *The Medal*] In November 1681 a Whig grand jury returned a verdict of *ignoramus* on charges of treason
against Shaftesbury. Upon his release an ornamental
medal was issued by the Whigs to celebrate the occasion. In March 1682 Dryden published a political satire entitled *The Medal* condemning these events.

[80] *The Medal Reversed … Hushai*] published in 1682 and
subtitled *A Satire against Persecution*, this answer to
Dryden's poem was identified on the title page as having been written *By the Author of Azariah and Hushai*.

[81] flail … answer] Supposedly College invented "the Protestant flail," a pocket weapon of lead-weighted wood
(Wilson). As seen with Crowne himself, authors being
physically assaulted for their writings was a possibility.
Dryden had been roughed up in Rose Alley in 1679.

CRAFFY.

I shall be a pretty man o'business, never write nor read.

PODESTA.

Sir, the greatest politicians of our times never write nor read, as you may see by their speeches. Come sirrah, you have wit enough and courage too, and we have business and enemies to employ both, insomuch I shall not dare to go to bed tonight. 260

CRAFFY. (*Aside.*)

Sha'nt you? Then I'll dare to go thither in your stead. I have showed my mother my wit; I never showed her my skin yet. I'll tempt her with that. 265

PODESTA.

I'll have you, in the head of a party, go to Mount Vesuvio.

CRAFFY. (*Aside.*)

I'm resolved to steal to her when she's abed.

PODESTA.

Get a-horseback presently,* d'ee hear?

CRAFFY.

Aye, my lord—in a rich nightgown, *point de Venice*82 shirt, and velvet slippers. 270

PODESTA.

How, a-horseback in this equipage? Do you know I bid you get your horse?

CRAFFY.

Aye, my lord—washed from head to foot in rose water. 275

PODESTA.

This is mockery; give me a cane.

CRAFFY.

Oh, good my lord!

BRICKLAYER.

Come, let him alone.

PODESTA.

I will not.

CRAFFY.

What's the matter? What's the matter? 280

PODESTA.

What's the matter wi' your brains, sirrah? For when I come to one side of your head, they shift o't'other, that you never mind what I say. Get you gone, you rascal you.

---

82 *point de Venice*] Venetian lace

CRAFFY. (*Aside.*)

Sweet rogue, I'll be with thee at night. (*Exit.*) 285

PODESTA.

Would the Devil had had this fellow's poetry. A gentleman may carry a little of it for an ornament and pleasure, as a lady carries an orange in her hand, but to have a fool carry a great basket on his head, like a costard-monger, and break his brains— 290

Enter Florio panting, Pietro leading him.

FLORIO.

Clambering up these stairs has almost spent me; I'm ready to tumble down dead.

PODESTA.

Poor man, how bad he is!

ROSAURA.

I wonder he's come abroad! 295

BRICKLAYER.

'Tis pity, he's a pretty fellow.

FLORIO.

My good lord, I beg your pardon a thousand times for the liberty and confidence83 I take in your house.

PODESTA.

You are very welcome, good Mr. Florio. 300

ROSAURA.

You may believe my lord, sir; he's your very humble servant.

FLORIO.

Your servant, good madam. Why truly, we sick people take upon us a strange authority, I know not by what commission. I think 'tis because sickness is Heaven's messenger, and when a man is upon the road in a messenger's hands,84 all people give way; and I am riding post. 305

Enter Doctor Sanchy.

SANCHY.

Where are you all? Where are you all?

PODESTA.

What's the matter? 310

---

83 confidence] assumption of a relationship of trust
84 in a messenger's hands] in the custody of a court officer

SANCHY.

Who says there are no plots?

BRICKLAYER.

He that has a mind to be hanged.

PODESTA.

As he shall be. He that will not believe in the Doctor must expect no salvation in this life.

ROSAURA.

What's the plot, good Doctor? 315

SANCHY.

Only to cut your husband's throat, and all our throats, that's all.

ROSAURA.

Oh, you ha' struck me dead! Some help! I faint!

PODESTA.

Good creature, she's swooning.—Who's there?

Enter women.

WOMEN.

My lord. 320

PODESTA.

Your lady swoons.

SANCHY.

Carry her away; don't let us be troubled with women.

PODESTA.

Take her into the fresh air and give her some strong water—and, do you hear?—bring me some 325 privately.85

Exeunt women with Rosaura.

BRICKLAYER.

Come, the plot.

SANCHY.

What do you think the Tory rogues have done? They have met with our Paper of Association.86

BRICKLAYER.

What care we for that? 330

SANCHY.

Aye, but they have drawn up one among themselves, in imitation of ours, cast one in our own mold, taken our own words, and discharge 'em upon us.

BRICKLAYER.

The Devil!

SANCHY.

As you shall hear. [*Reads.*] "We, the loyal, *etcetera*, 335 finding, to the grief of° our hearts, a certain sort of people, consisting of Hobbists, Atheists, Fanatics, and Republicans, have, for several years last past, pursued a pernicious plot to root out the true religion, subvert our laws and liberties, and 340 set up arbitrary power"—

BRICKLAYER.

Well, and what of all this?

FLORIO.

Pray hear.

SANCHY.

"And it being notorious that they have been highly encouraged by the countenance and protection 345 given 'em by the rabble and by their expectations of the said rabble coming to the government, it appears also to us that for these designs *ignoramus* garrisons have been established among us, by whose assistance these men have laid a blockade 350 before the Crown itself, denying it all relief unless 'twill own itself a dependence upon them"87—

BRICKLAYER.

All this is true, and we are not ashamed of it.

PODESTA.

Go on.

SANCHY.

"And we considering with heavy hearts how greatly 355 the reputation and honesty of the kingdom hath been wasted in maintaining the said garrisons, and finding the same counsels, after exemplary justice upon some of the conspirators, to be still pursued with the utmost devilish malice and desire of 360 revenge, whereby his Majesty is in continual hazard to be destroyed to make way for the said rabble's advancement to the Crown"—

---

85 strong water … privately] an alcoholic beverage, like aqua vitae, used for medicinal purposes; "Bethel was said to be a teetotaler" (Wilson).

86 Paper of Association] a burlesque of a document found among Shaftesbury's papers when he was arrested for treason in July 1681 (Wilson); Crowne here imagines that document as a kind of Whig manifesto that the Tories now imitate with one of their own.

87 denying … them] "The Whig-controlled House of Commons refused to vote appropriations to the king until the Exclusion Bill was approved" (Wilson). But such a maneuver was typical of Parliament throughout its struggle with the Stuarts.

BRICKLAYER.

Well, and what of all this?

PODESTA.

Have patience. 365

SANCHY.

"the whole kingdom in such case, being destitute of all security of their religion, laws, estates, and liberties; sad experience in the case—the Rump Committee of Safety, Noll and Dick in England, and Masaniello here[88]—having proved the wisest 370 laws to be of little force to keep out tyranny under no prince, or no lawful prince"—

BRICKLAYER.

I would we had 'em.

SANCHY.

"we have, therefore, several times endeavored in a legal way, by indictments, to bring the said 375 criminals to condign punishment, but being utterly rejected and brought almost to despair, we bind ourselves one to another, jointly and severally, in the bond of one firm and loyal society and association, and do solemnly vow, promise, and 380 protest to demolish the said *ignoramus* garrisons, which are kept up in and about this city, to the great terror and amazement of all the good people in the land"—

BRICKLAYER.

And shall be in spite of 'em. 385

SANCHY.

"and utterly destroy all that shall seek to set up the said rabble's pretended title, or shall raise any war, tumult, or sedition in his behalf or by his command, as public enemies to our laws, King, religion, and country, and this on penalty of being 390 esteemed such ourselves. Witness our hands"—

PODESTA.

Are there any names to it?

SANCHY.

Only nicknames to know one another by, as "Loyal Domestic, Absalom and Achitophel, Tory Coffee House, Towzer,[89] Heraclitus," and such names— 395 forty thousand.

BRICKLAYER.

Oh, we have six times their number.

SANCHY.

Pray hear the postscript: "Persons to be destroyed, *imprimis*, the Podesta"[90]—

PODESTA.

Am I to me murdered *imprimis*? Bloody rogues. 400

SANCHY.

"Then the Doctor"—And why after him? Unmannerly rascals.

PODESTA.

Why after me? Sure, good Doctor, you won't dispute precedency with me.

SANCHY.

But I will, good Podesta, with you or any man in 405 Christendom. What the Devil are you?

PODESTA.

What am I?

SANCHY.

Aye, if you compare yourself with me, you are a fop.

PODESTA.

Fop! You are an unmannerly fellow. 410

SANCHY.

How!—Ho! Call one of my men, somebody.

Enter a servant.

SERVANT.

Sir.

SANCHY.

Go bid the Archbishop of Naples come to me; I'll make his fortunes.

[Exit Servant.]

<hr/>

88 Rump ... Masaniello] the Committee of Safety perhaps means the Rump Parliament's Council of State of 1649. Both "Rump" and "Committee" recall anti-Commonwealth plays of those titles in the 60s (and included in this anthology); "Noll and Dick" are Oliver Cromwell and his son, Richard; "Masaniello" is Tommaso Aniello, who led a Neapolitan revolt against the Spanish in 1647.

89 Towzer] typically a name for a dog, with reference to the Whig nickname for Sir Roger L'Estrange, a Tory pamphleteer (Wilson)

90 Persons ... *imprimis*] The postscript parodies Shaftesbury's proscription list, beginning with (*imprimis*) the Podesta—as well, perhaps, as the most famous such proscription list, that of Octavius and Mark Antony, beginning with Cicero.

BRICKLAYER.

Nay, nay, Doctor, Doctor.   415

PODESTA.

He means, bid the archbishoprick of Naples come
to him, but it won't come, Doctor.[91]

SANCHY.

You are a rascal.

PODESTA.

Call a constable.

FLORIO.

Gentlemen, gentlemen, are you out of your wits   420
to quarrel who should be murdered first? I need
care for it as little as you; I shall lose as few days.
For shame, reconcile, pray reconcile.

SANCHY.

Then let him not play the coxcomb. If the Pope
disparage me, I'd say he were a rascal.   425

BRICKLAYER.

Well, well, the Podesta respects you, Doctor; give
him your hand.

SANCHY.

Give him my hand first? I'd scorn to do't if he were
a prince.

BRICKLAYER.

Then give him your hand, Podesta.   430

PODESTA.

Well come, Mr. Sanchy.

SANCHY.

Mr. Sanchy?

PODESTA.

Doctor, I mean; come, Doctor.

SANCHY.

Then come, Podesta.

FLORIO.

So, this is well; now let us know whose throat is   435
to be cut next.

SANCHY.

The bricklayer's and yours, "*cum multis aliis quae
nunc praescribere longum est.*"[92]

FLORIO.

Will they cut mine? They may spare their pains.
Well, we had more need go to prayers than quarrel.   440
Pray Doctor.

SANCHY.

Pray, fool's head? What should we pray for? That's
like your papists, who think to keep off devils with
holy water, as if a devil were like a cat: he could
not endure to wet his foot. These devils are best   445
driven away with firelocks.

BRICKLAYER.

You are in the right, Doctor.

FLORIO.

I'm sure our Cause* is in the right.

BRICKLAYER.

We have a hundred thousand men, and they are
always in the right. Set me in the head of such a   450
general counsel, and I'll be pope, the only infallible
judge.

PODESTA.

Aye, and have what forms of worship you will.
When a cannon's[93] the preacher, who dare shut up
the conventicle? And nothing opens and divides a   455
text like gunpowder.

FLORIO.

Heaven turn these wicked men; I love their souls.

BRICKLAYER.

Heaven turn 'em out of the kingdom, for I love
their lands; that's my way of turning my
adversaries, and I'll set 'em part o'their way tonight.   460
I'll shove the whole town against 'em; that shall
be my business. (*Exit.*)

PODESTA.

I'll go arm myself, and then watch upon the
battlements.

SANCHY.

I'll go with you.   465

Exeunt Podesta, Doctor Sanchy, Captain of the Militia.

FLORIO.

I'll to my devotions.—That is, to your wife, if I
knew where she was.

---

91 archbishoprick] "Oates hoped someday to be made a
    bishop, and in later years he claimed that he had been
    offered the bishopric of Chichester" (Wilson).

92 *cum … est*] "with many others whom to list would take
    too much time" (Latin)

93 cannon] Modernizing the spelling here erases the dou-
    ble pun on *canon*, a minor clergyman and/or established
    religious texts.

Enter Rosaura.

ROSAURA.

Not far off.

FLORIO.

I might ha' guessed it by the sudden gaiety of all things; the whole face of nature smiled on her sweet favorite. 470

ROSAURA.

Upon the ridiculous cuckold and his wise companions, which you have finely fooled. For was not this paper yours, sir?

FLORIO.

It was. 475

ROSAURA.

What a ghost every shadow appears to a guilty conscience. Therefore I had not best consent to your murder of my honesty, for I shall never sleep for fear of the discovery, and you men commonly boast of those murders and cast a brazen image of 480 the dead creature in an impudent libel.

FLORIO.

If this be not privately buried, it shall be your own fault.

ROSAURA.

It shall be yours, for I have provided a chapel fit for the work, this garden house. 485

FLORIO.

Then will I be a second Nero; I have put all my city in a flame.

And now, with harp in hand, I will survey

My burning Rome, and whilst it burns I'll play.

ROSAURA.

Then, Nero, take thy harp into thy hand,

The tuneful strings will follow thy command. 490

Now equal Orpheus in thy art divine,

Make all things round thee dance, with one sweet touch of thine.

Exeunt.

Scene ii. Scene continues.

Enter Bartoline with Artall.

BARTOLINE.

Come, pray come in, shir, ingeed I love your company mighchily. Come, how ish't wi'you, shir?

ARTALL.

Better and better, sir; that is to say, worse and worse, nearer my end, which I hope will be the better for me. 5

BARTOLINE.

Aye, yer'sh no doubt on't, shir, you're a very good young genkleman.

ARTALL.

Not so good as I ha' been bad, sir.

BARTOLINE.

'Tish no great matcher, shir, we have all been bad one chime or anoyer. 10

ARTALL.

Not so bad as I, sir; the Devil is not, cannot be so bad as I. He cannot drink, can he, sir?

BARTOLINE.

Why chruly, shir, I believe notch; I yon't know what he can goo; I yon't chrouble myself much wid him. 15

ARTALL.

I was one of the Devil's low countries, always under a flood. The Devil cannot whore, sir, neither, can he?

BARTOLINE.

I yon't know, shir, in chroth, but I believe in general he ish a great rashcal. 20

ARTALL.

I have not only debauched women, but the whole age, poisoned all its morals, murdered thousands o'young consciences, sung others asleep, pumped others with drunkenness; sin I honored and privileged as a peer to the Devil; Heaven I 25 affronted, libeled His Court, and in my drunken altitudes have endeavored to scour the whole creation of souls and spirits. Now is it fit I should be saved?[94]

---

94 debauched ... saved] In this speech Crowne aptly characterizes Rochester's popular legacy as an aristocratic libertine. In a letter to a friend, Rochester confesses that for a five-year period he was nearly continually drunk. He was a notorious womanizer. He wrote bawdy songs and biting satires flouting the moral, religious, and intellectual status quo. Rochester died from his extreme lifestyle at the age of thirty-three. In Rochester's funeral sermon, the Wilmot family chaplain remarked of the iconoclastic earl that he had died "a Martyr for Sin."

BARTOLINE.

Aye, why not, shir? Yon't chrouble yourshelf wi' 30
yosh mattchersh.

ARTALL.

I doubt I trouble you, sir, with my tedious
discourses?

BARTOLINE.

Oh, no, shir, yey are ve'y goodg ingeed; I never
heardg a parshon chalk sho well in a pulpit, and I 35
hear 'em shomechimes.

ARTALL.

Don't you go always to church, sir?

BARTOLINE.

Yesh, shir, but we lawyersh are sho employed all
th'week yat we may be excused if we chake a nap
a Shunday at a shermon. 40

ARTALL.

You should not neglect the business of your soul,
sir.

BARTOLINE.

No chruly, shir, but we have a great yeal of
business, a great yeal of business.

ARTALL.

I do believe so, sir; therefore, I don't know how I 45
can with any confidence beg the favor of you to
be one of my executors.

BARTOLINE.

Oh, yesh shir, I'll find a chime for yat, I wayant
you; pray employ me, shir.

ARTALL.

Thank you, good sir; I will endeavor to reward 50
your trouble.

BARTOLINE.

Oh, good shir, what you pleash; I shall be glad of
any choken of you love.

ARTALL.

I have drawn up some heads of a will.

BARTOLINE.

You have yone mighchy wishely, shir. 55

ARTALL.

Will you please to look over it, sir, as also some
deeds of my estate, whilst I lay me down? For I
am very faint. Shall I borrow your bed, sir?

BARTOLINE.

Aye, with all my heart, shir.—Lushenda, girl!

Enter Lucinda.

LUCINDA.

Husband. 60

BARTOLINE. (*Aside.*)

Why gee come wi'out a godly book in your hand,
when you know how he'sh inclined?

LUCINDA.

I ha' none; you must lend me one out of your
study.

BARTOLINE. (*Aside [to Lucinda].*)

I ha' none in my shtudy, neve hadg one in my life; 65
we lawyersh yead no yivinichy. Buy one.—Come,
chake yish poo genkleman and lay him upon our
bedg and cover him warm and shit by him. (*Aside
[to Lucinda].*) And, gee hear, chalk goly to him;
he'sh making his will; you yon't know how you 70
may win upon him.—Pray, shir, go in, and I'll go
cho my shtudy and come chee in a minute.

ARTALL. (*Aside.*)

Pox o'thy haste.—I'm in no haste, sir, take your time.

BARTOLINE.

No, no, I won't shtay, shir, but pray let me lead
you, for you are very weak. 75

ARTALL.

Oh, no, sir.

BARTOLINE.

Pray, shir, let me.

Exit Artall, led by Bartoline and Lucinda.

Scene iii. Scene continues.

Enter Craffy.

CRAFFY.

What new 'larum's this? And I'm enquired after to
be made an ass on and sent on some silly errand
and so shan't come at my mother tonight. Pox, I'll
ha' none o'these foolish doings. I'll get out o'the
way, and now I think on't, I'll hide myself in this 5
room. How now, the door's shut; there's somebody
in the room sure. I'll peep. (*Throws himself down
and raves.*) I'm shot! I'm shot! I'm shot!

*Enter Podesta, Doctor Sanchy, Captain of the Militia,
soldiers, Bricklayer first.*

BRICKLAYER.

What's the matter? What's the matter? What's the
news? 10

CRAFFY.

I'm shot, I'm shot, I'm shot.

BRICKLAYER.

Guard, guard, guard! Trainbands! Podesta, Podesta! Come hither all quickly.

PODESTA.

Bless us, what's the matter?

BRICKLAYER.

Your son's killed! 15

PODESTA.

My son killed?

CRAFFY.

I'm shot—I'm shot—I'm shot.

PODESTA.

Oh, where, where, where? Poor child—poor boy.

CRAFFY.

To the very soul, to the very soul.

PODESTA.

Oh, my poor boy, my poor boy! Who shot thee, 20 and where are the murderers?

SANCHY.

Who should, but the associating bully Tories.

CRAFFY.

Aye, aye, associators, associators.

PODESTA. SANCHY. BRICKLAYER.

Oh, rogues, villains!

CRAFFY.

A whore and a rascal are associated in that room. 25 I mean your wife and Florio are there joined in one close abominable bond of lewdness and cuckold you, as if they were to be hanged if they did not dispatch it in a minute. The sight has shot me to my soul, my soul. 30

PODESTA.

How, sirrah, have you invented such a notorious sham as this to set me at variance with my wife and my friend? And to buzz me wi'domestic confusions that I might not ha' my brains at liberty for the public? Is it possible? 35

SANCHY.

Sirrah, you are a traitorly rogue.

CRAFFY.

I'll call you as much out of your name, sirrah; you are a doctor of divinity.

BRICKLAYER.

Sirrah, you are an associating Tory.

CRAFFY.

Sirrah, you are an hermaphrodite, compounded of 40 two sexes, verse and prose, and engender with neither.

BRICKLAYER.

Sirrah, I make better verses than yourself, and verses is all that you are good for. I make officers and jurymen and evidences and pictures and 45 poppets,[95] and as good verses as you into the bargain. I made your father what he is. That you are an ungrateful fellow to be thus saucy with me.

PODESTA.

Come, sirrah, you are a notorious parricide and plot with traitors against your own father. 50

CRAFFY.

Father, you are an abominable cuckold and plot with him that makes you one against your own son. I will swear Florio is in that room aboard your vessel and stealing all your customs. And here you stand upon[96] the key and let him. 55

PODESTA.

I will break open the door to show thou art a rascal.

BRICKLAYER.

Are you mad? Is not this a plain sham plot? Here are either traitors or treasonable papers, and they will be found and laid to your charge. 60

PODESTA.

You speak with a great deal of prudence. And I'll guard the door with my life, for my honor is concerned.

CRAFFY.

Your honor is concerned, for you're made a cuckold.

PODESTA.

The honor of my loyalty is concerned, for sirrah, 65 you would make a traitor of me that you might hang me and get my estate.

CRAFFY.

I will call a guard, break open the door, and show

---

95 pictures and poppets] College illustrated some of his libels with caricatures of his victims. It is also likely that he carved the heads of some of the puppet (poppet) popes used in the "pope-burning" processions (Wilson).

96 stand upon] to argue or to quibble about as well as to withhold

that you are a cuckold, the Doctor, Bricklayer, a couple of pimps. And I see a guard go by. Guard, guard, guard! Treason, treason, treason!

PODESTA.

Nay then. Militia, militia, militia! Keep this door here. Treason, treason!

CRAFFY.

Why, who the devil's able to bear this? Give me a pike. I'll force my way in.

PODESTA.

Nay then, give me a pike.

CRAFFY.

Oh, cuckold, cuckold! Wittol, wittol!

PODESTA.

Oh, unnatural monster!

SANCHY.

Villain!

BRICKLAYER.

Tory!

PODESTA.

Hold, gentlemen, I have considered of it. Because this fellow is so insolent and positive and may report to the world I hinder truth from coming to light, to clear the honor of myself, my wife, and my friend, I will open the door in the presence of you all, and you shall see what's there. And so, gentlemen, all bear witness.

BRICKLAYER.

You shall not open the door.

PODESTA.

I will.

BRICKLAYER.

You shall not.

SANCHY.

He shall.—Break open the door.

PODESTA.

Break open the door.

Enter Bartoline.

BARTOLINE.

What, are you all madg? Are we in Beglam here? You a magishchrate and shuffer shuch dishorgersh as yesh in you housh? You may be ashamed! If you ha' no yegard cho your own cregit, ha' shome pitchy on a poo genkleman almost murgered by the noish you make, your own friend, Mishte Florio.

PODESTA.

Florio! Why, where is he?

BARTOLINE.

Upon my bedg, giving up the ghosht.

SANCHY.

So, sirrah, and you say he is in this room.

CRAFFY.

Giving up the ghost upon that old fellow's bed?

BRICKLAYER.P

Now the sham plot's plain.

CRAFFY.

Then he has given up the ghost, and I saw his ghost in this room.

PODESTA.

And has Wife given up the ghost too, sir?

CRAFFY.

I don't know, but if they were ghosts, they were the lewdest ghosts that ever I saw.

BRICKLAYER.

Come, sirrah, confess your rogueries.

CRAFFY.

What rogueries? Is it treason to be mad? If he be there, my wits are not here; I'm cracked, and there's an end.

BARTOLINE.

Sho, shcolding again? I shuppose he'll conshiger your shivilitiesh in hish will, which he's now a-making. (*Exit.*)

PODESTA.

So sir, we shall lose all our legacies through your roguery; come ask him pardon on your knees.

BRICKLAYER.

I'm cruel afraid he'll die before we come; let's go quickly, quickly.

Exeunt omnes. Florio and Rosaura coming out of the room where they were hid.

FLORIO.

Hah! Gone! This was good fortune; away to thy chamber, my dear.

ROSAURA.

And do you go home.

Exeunt. Enter Artall.

ARTALL.

Pox on't, my pretty opportunity is cast away in a

storm; I must make t'other voyage. I venture boldly into the dominion of these arbitrary rogues, who have a strange, absolute authority over their own consciences in lying and swearing. But love, love, love! (*Exit.*)

Enter Podesta, Bricklayer, Doctor Sanchy, Craffy, Bartoline, Lucinda, militia.

BARTOLINE.
Gone away in dishconchent?

LUCINDA.
No, but in great pain; he said his head was torn in pieces.

BARTOLINE.
Well, I shall be no losher; he knowsh 'twash not my fault. Come away, girl.

Exeunt Bartoline and Lucinda.

BRICKLAYER.
Now I'll see what's in this house. Fellow soldiers, guard me in and have a care o'me.

Exeunt Bricklayer and soldiers. Enter waiting woman.

WOMAN.
My lord, my lady's extremely discomposed with the fright she had about your lordship and begs there may not be so much noise; it almost kills her.

PODESTA.
Poor kind heart, where is she?

WOMAN.
In her chamber upon her bed.

PODESTA.
So, sir, and you said she was in this room.

CRAFFY.
Well, I'm mad, and there's an end.

PODESTA.
Tell her there shall be no noise made.

[Exit waiting woman.] Enter Bricklayer and soldiers.

BRICKLAYER.
There's nothing in this room.

PODESTA.
Nothing?

BRICKLAYER.
Nothing.

SANCHY.
What do you say to this, sirrah?

CRAFFY.
That thou art an ass to talk to a madman, for my wits ha' given me the slip all o'th'sudden; I don't know how nor which way.

PODESTA.
Truly I'm convinced he says true, and my heart's ready to break.

BRICKLAYER.
I am partly o'that mind, for in the room is no sign of a sham plot.

SANCHY.
He does look wildly, that's the truth on't.

PODESTA.
He's mad, he's mad, and I ha' lost my child, my dear child, my poor child.

CRAFFY.
Well, well, poor father, don't take on so, my wits are not gone far. They'll come again, I warrant 'em, for I don't know who the devil will entertain* 'em; they were mad sort o' wits, and they are as mad that entertain a poet's wits.

PODESTA.
Oh curse, curse on poetry, that ever I should let thee meddle with it, my poor boy.

CRAFFY.
Nay, prithee father, don't take on thus; thou'lt make me cry too.

PODESTA.
I am so grieved that I will eat and drink and sleep and never mind what becomes o'the world.

BRICKLAYER.
Fie, fie, you won't be so wicked as that.

PODESTA.
Wherefore should I trouble myself, when I have nobody to inherit my labors?

BRICKLAYER.
You ha' friends enow, the Doctor, and I another.

PODESTA.
Puh, a child's above all. Don't we see old politicians venture their necks for half a child, a changeling?[97] And I have lost a boy worth millions, millions; and so I'll enjoy myself 'till my heart breaks, and there's an end.

97 old politicians ... changeling] a jibe at Shaftesbury, whose son was handsome but lacked the intelligence and ingenuity of his father

BRICKLAYER.

Come, come, leave off this.

PODESTA.

No, I remember a saying of a wise man:
Who plays the knave t'enrich his son, a fool,   180
Is like a fox that ventures for a prey
To bury it in some poor dirty hole
And feed an idle dog that trots that way:
The beast is torn with fruitless pain and care
And hanged at last to make his foe his heir.   185
I shall play the knave and be hanged for a mad
son and so have a Tory beg my estate.[98] No, no,
no! (*Exit.*)

BRICKLAYER.

Let's after him and get him out of this humor.

Exeunt.

Act V, scene i. The [Podesta's] house.

Enter Artall.

ARTALL.

I am strangely taken with this sweet young
creature; 'tis so pleasant to drink at such a fresh
spring, which never brute defiled or muddied. This
old fellow is but a withered tree that shades it. 'Tis
so much wholesomer to love than the sophisticated   5
beauties o'this town, which sicken and kill an
intrigue in a few days. Hah! Where's my gown and
cap? I came in such amorous haste I forgot my sick
dress, and I shall never be able to act my sick part
without it. But I ha' no patience to go back for't   10
now. Here she comes! (*Enter Lucinda.*) My dear!
Where's the old devil that would hinder our
happiness? Old tempter I will not call him.

LUCINDA.

I will not tell you.

ARTALL.

But you do.   15

LUCINDA.

What?

ARTALL.

That he's abroad, your smiles say it; those birds

would be gone if that winter were here. They say
he won't come home a great while.

LUCINDA.

You are a witch, I think.   20

ARTALL.

We'll lose no time.

LUCINDA.

Fie! Fie! You must not do such things as these.

Enter Bartoline and his clerk.

CLERK.

Oh, sir! Here's a gentleman kissing my mistress.

BARTOLINE.

How?

LUCINDA.

Oh dear, my husband!   25

ARTALL.

Sirrah, you lie! Unsay't again, or you are a dead
rogue!

CLERK.

No, no, sir, you did not indeed.—Sir, I mistook;
this is the sick gentleman, Mr. Florio.

BARTOLINE.

How? A shick man kish my wife?   30

ARTALL.

No, no, I am not the sick man.

BARTOLINE.

What are you, yen?—Call shomebody cho sheize
the rogue.

ARTALL.

Yes, yes, I am the sick man.—I don't know what I
am, a pox.   35

BARTOLINE.

Yesh, yesh, I know what you are, a raschcal, and you
choo have abused me, a yamned rogue and shlut.

ARTALL.

No, no, sir—

BARTOLINE.

Why do you geny yourshelf yen?

ARTALL.

Sir, I was afraid you might be jealous because I was   40
whispering in your lady's ear, my lungs being weak.

BARTOLINE.

Your lungsh weak, and huff and rant like a bully?
Ah! You are rogue.

ARTALL.

That was only a sudden blast of zeal for your good

---

98 Tory ... estate] a Tory will inherit his estate by begging
      for it from the king after it has been forfeited for trea-
      son.

lady's reputation and mine; 'twill shorten my days. 45
I han't above a month to live, and I have spent a
fortnight's breath beforehand.

BARTOLINE.

Oh, you rashcal! Have I catched you in your
chricksh? Ha' you sherved me shush?

ARTALL.

Why do you censure so rashly? I appeal to your lady. 50

BARTOLINE.

Make a partchy judge? No, you have put choo
goodg a fee in you hand cho let her bechray your
caush.

LUCINDA.

You wrong me extremely.

BARTOLINE.

I wronged myshelf cho entcher incho bondsh of 55
marriage and could not perform covenantsh.99 I
might well hink you would chake the forfeychure
of the bond, and I never found equichy in a bedg
in my life. But I'll trounce you boh. I have paved
jailsh wi'the bonesh of honester people yen you are, 60
yat neve' did me nor any man any wrong, but had
law o'yeir shidsh and right o' yeir shidsh, but cause
yey had not me o' yeir shidsh, I ha' beggared 'em,
hrown 'em in jailsh and got yeir eshchatsh for my
clientsh, yat had no more chitle to 'em yen dogsh. 65

ARTALL.

And were you a good man in that?

BARTOLINE.

I wash a good lawyer, and sho you shall find cho
your cosht wi''in yish twelvemonth you shall not
be worth a groatch.

ARTALL.

Oh, I have too good a title to what I have. 70

BARTOLINE.

Chitle? I value not your chitle; beggarsh ha' not sho
many chricksh cho make shorsh in yeir bodyesh ash
we have cho make 'em in chitlesh. But I'll chell you
what, I'll draw you up an exshellent chitle cho the
jail, and if you have any children, I'll shettle it upon 75
you and your heirsh forever; a jail shall be the sheat
of your family. (*Aside.*) 'Od sha' me, if any brishk
rogue would cut hish hroat neatly and privately, yat

---

99 perform covenantsh] fulfill agreements; in this case,
sexually consummate their union

nothing might appear against him but shircum-
shansesh, I'd bring him off, proviged it be not a 80
shimple rogue yat wantsh money.

ARTALL.

At this rate, your wife shall be never the better for
the settlement you have made upon her.

BARTOLINE.

No, no more than I am the betcher for the
shettlement the priesht hash made of her upon me, 85
the devil chake him for hish painsh, would I could
find a flaw in't.

ARTALL.

Now thou makest me angry, thou ungrateful
knave. Suppose she and I have sinned, hast thou
got an estate in the Devil's service, and wouldst 90
thou hinder his work—

BARTOLINE.

Oh! You impugent whoremashcher!

ARTALL.

Sirrah, you have made more whores than ever I
did.

BARTOLINE.

I make whorsh? 95

ARTALL.

Yes, thou hast debauched whole families by
beggaring 'em, made fathers and mothers bawds
to their own daughters to earn that bread thou hast
cheated 'em of.

BARTOLINE.

You lie, you lie. But if I have, I only followed my 100
chrade.

ARTALL.

Well, and it may be my trade is whoring, and I'll
follow that.

BARTOLINE.

Follow it wi'your own commoditchiesh then, and
don't meggle wi'mine. 105

ARTALL.

No more I ha' not. Your clerk is a lying fellow, and
your lady a virtuous young woman and my near
kinswoman, and since you abuse her, I'll take her
into my protection.—Come, cousin—

BARTOLINE.

Oh, brave* rogue! He chaksh away my wife before 110
my faish. Shirrah, I'll ha' forty actionsh on you
back preshently.*

ARTALL.

Then in a little time will I have forty swords at
your throat, French swords.[100] I'll let in the enemy
and cut the throats of such rogues as you, who   115
abuse your trade, and like so many padders* make
all people deliver their purse that ride in the road
of justice. Better be ruled by the swords of gallant
men than the mercenary tongues of such rascals
as you are.   120

BARTOLINE.

Bear witnesh! Chreashon, chreashon, horrible
chreashon!

ARTALL.

I defy thee, do thy worst. I am Florio, Prince of
Whigs, never without a chosen lifeguard of jurymen
with brazen consciences, proof against oaths, like   125
bucklers against arrows.—So, come away, cousin.
[Aside.] Now will this rogue fall on Florio.

Exeunt Artall and Lucinda.

BARTOLINE.

Oh, impugent yamned rogue!—Shirrah, be sure
you yemember all yish chreashon. Ha' you a good
memory?   130

CLERK.

Yes, sir.

BARTOLINE.

I mean a ferchile memory. Will a hing grow in it?

CLERK.

I'll remember enough to hang Florio; I'll warrant
him I'll remember all he said.

BARTOLINE.

And more choo. And becaush the rogue runsh   135
away wi'my wife, he'll shay I proshecute him out
o'malish; sho if nobody swearesh against him but
you and I, the rashcal may come off; yerefore, we
musht look out for an evidensh or choo more. Go
cho shome able atchurney; they are acquainched   140

---

100 French swords] The unholy, backstairs alliance between
the Stuarts and the Catholic French, long suspected by
Parliamentarians, was made manifest when news of
French subsidies, negotiated in the infamous Treaty of
Dover between Charles II and Louis XIV in 1670,
leaked out during the Exclusion Crisis. The threat of
French military aid is incredibly impudent.

with 'em all; I'll look out for shome myshelf. And
run for myᴿ Lord Chief Jushchish'sh warrant cho
apprehend yish rashcal. Go quickly, quickly.

Exeunt Bartoline and clerk.

Scene ii. Scene continues.

*Enter Podesta, Rosaura, Florio, Doctor Sanchy,
Bricklayer.*

ROSAURA.

Impudent, lying, perjured villain, accuse me of
being a secret strumpet?

FLORIO.

And me of being your gallant? I'm in a fine
condition to be a gallant to a fair lady.

ROSAURA.

All's one. Malice will believe it, and I, though   5
innocent, shall live in reproach.

FLORIO.

Not long, madam, not above a week. My doctor
has confessed to me I shall die someday next week,
and then I suppose this story will die too.

PODESTA.

How! Are you to die next week?   10

FLORIO.

Yes, a great lady will call for me, the only lady in
the world I have an intrigue withal.

PODESTA.

What lady?

FLORIO.

The moon, my lord, the moon: she has an intrigue
with my body and never puts on new clothes but   15
at my cost. She means to be very fine about
Thursday come sennight, that is to say, in the full,
and then the world will see if my bankrupt body
be able to carry on such a trade.

ROSAURA.

All's one, sir: if you were dead, malice would live   20
and entertain* censure.

PODESTA.

Well sweetheart, as long as I don't entertain it, you
need not be troubled.

ROSAURA.

I confess, if I have the comfort of your love—

BRICKLAYER.

You have, you have, woman. Don't make more   25

fiddle faddle than needs and hinder us from business of consequence.

PODESTA.

Sweetheart, nobody takes a degree in my university but they perform their exercises, which you two have done. I have had experience of your virtues and pronounce you both innocent. All the shame and grief is mine that my only son, the pillar of my family, is cracked or rotten, mad or a knave. I say he is mad. 30

SANCHY.

I say he is a suborned rascal.

BRICKLAYER.

I'm o'the doctor's mind. 35

PODESTA.

I'll give you an unanswerable reason to the contrary.

SANCHY.

What's that?

PODESTA.

I never discovered it, not so much as in the boy's face, and I'll see through such a boy as he as plain 40 as through a new-laid egg. The oldest face shall no more cheat me than old coin does an antiquary.

SANCHY.

And what am I? An owl?*

PODESTA.

I don't say you are.

BRICKLAYER.

You two will kindle again. 45

PODESTA.

No, the boy shall decide the difference. I ha' sent for him; here he comes.

Enter servants with Craffy.

CRAFFY. (*Aside.*)

This woman is a whore, and I was in the right.

PODESTA.

What say you now? Does not the madman peep through all his looks and gestures? 50

SANCHY.

I'll examine him.—Sirrah.

CRAFFY.

Hold your prating. (*Aside.*) Damned whore.

PODESTA.

D'ee see? Stark mad.

SANCHY.

Who suborned you to accuse your mother of being prostitute to Florio? 55

CRAFFY.

Who suborned you to accuse the title of Doctor of Divinity of being a prostitute to such an ignorant ass?

SANCHY.

Sirrah, I am a scholar, and you are an ignorant, saucy, pragmatical rascal. 60

CRAFFY.

Nay, if rogue and rascal be Latin and Greek, thou art the best scholar in Christendom, for no man living is so versed in those languages.

SANCHY.

When I use those languages, I, like Adam, give every beast its proper name. 65

CRAFFY.

And when I call thee ignorant coxcomb, I give thee no other name than thy own sermons do. That thou art an insolent fool is the only true doctrine thou preachest.

PODESTA.

Is he mad or no? 70

BRICKLAYER.

He is more knave than fool.—Sirrah, don't you abuse the doctor.

CRAFFY.

How do I know he's a doctor? We have only his word for it, nor that neither when he preaches.

SANCHY.

Sirrah, I'll hang you. 75

CRAFFY.

Aye, thou art a doctor at that.

SANCHY.

Aye, and of divinity too, you impudent rascal.

CRAFFY.

Where did you take your degree in, Bear Garden?*

SANCHY.

In a learned university,[101] sir.

CRAFFY.

Aye, the university of coffeehouses, the university 80 of lies, where if anyone speaks truth the university

---

101 learned university] Oates claimed a doctorate in divinity from the University of Salamanca in Spain.

forfeits its charter. There thou'rt a doctor and the
bricklayer principal fellow of a college.

BRICKLAYER.

Don't you meddle wi'me, you malapert boy you.
The greatest lords and politicians of the kingdom   85
of our party won't be so saucy wi'me as you are,
but court me and are proud o'me and depend upon
my counsel and countenance.

CRAFFY.

Depend on thy countenance! They have a foolish
dependence. (*Aside.*) Damned confounded   90
woman! Great with a rascal gnawed with diseases
till he's as venomous as a chawed bullet,[102] and
refuse me! Jilt, I'll make her great with me.

PODESTA.

You see what sallies o'madness he has.—Craffy!—
But to what purpose should I speak to him?—   95
Craffy, if you have any understanding, say whether
you saw your mother in the garden house wi'Florio
or not?

CRAFFY.

Why, I will swear that—

PODESTA.

Look upon her.   100

CRAFFY.

She's the handsomest woman in the world. What
breasts she has!

PODESTA.

The handsomest woman? What's that to the
business?—Is not this distraction, gentlemen?—
Answer to the question. Did you see her in the   105
garden house with Florio?

CRAFFY. (*Aside.*)

I'll see her there with me or I'll— (*Aside [to
Rosaura].*) Hark you, gentlewoman, you know I
saw you there. I have three witnesses to swear it;
meet me there, I'll bring you off.   110

ROSAURA. [*To Craffy.*]

Your witnesses are perjured rascals, and you are an
ass, who abuse me just now I'm coming to have
more inclination for you than my conscience will
admit of.

CRAFFY. (*Aside [to Rosaura].*)

Sayest thou so?—I did not see her there, I did not.   115

_____

[102] chawed bullet] chewed lead ball, thus more destructive

PODESTA.

Then thou art mad.

CRAFFY. (*Aside [to Rosaura].*)

Will you meet me there?

ROSAURA. [*To Craffy.*]

Perhaps I may, if you'll be civil.

CRAFFY. (*Aside.*)

Delicate rogue.—Now I swear I did not see her
there, but that damned rascal I did see there; an   120
impudent, rotten fellow that has never a sound*
bit about him of his own, but is inlaid like a
cabinet. That he should dare to kiss and embrace
such a delicate woman as my mother, there!

PODESTA.

Why, did he?   125

CRAFFY.

Did he? Aye, a hundred times; I saw him, a rascal.

PODESTA.

And yet just now you said she was not there.

ROSAURA.

How now? Was I there?

CRAFFY. (*Aside.*)

I forget myself.—No, faith, she was not there.

PODESTA.

How could he embrace her then?   130

CRAFFY.

In his fancy, I saw her in his fancy, as plain as could
be; he has a huge fancy for her.

PODESTA.

Fancy! Lord help thee, boy, thou hast strange
fancies.—Take him away, he's a sad sight; take him
away, or he'll break my heart. Lock him up.   135

CRAFFY. [*Aside.*]

Lock me up? How shall I come at my mother
then? Pox take it.[r] Now I think on't, I have a
picklock in my pocket.[s]

Exeunt servants with Craffy.

FLORIO.

He's far gone.

PODESTA.

I think my judgment is to be relied upon.   140

FLORIO.

I wish in his madness he had not torn my good
reputation, the only image of a man we ought to
venerate.

BRICKLAYER.

I would have nobody's picture preserved but the doctor's. 145

FLORIO.

Nor I. Well, I have news to tell you from another world; the very devils have more care of us than our pretended friends have.ᵗ A spirit appeared to a country maid and told her Naples would be burned on this night if care was not taken.103 150

PODESTA.

Is it possible! Where is the maid?

FLORIO.

In the country. She was coming to town, fell ill by the way, so she has sent the story to the Viceroy by the post.

PODESTA.

And what says he? 155

FLORIO.

He laughs at it.

SANCHY.

He's a fine fellow.

BRICKLAYER.

He's in the right. Why the devil would not the spirit come post himself, but deliver a message of this consequence to a silly* country gossip? The 160 Devil never employs any but fops of spirits; he's not fit to be a devil. I'll justify it.

PODESTA.

How do you know 'twas a devil? Maybe 'twas the soul of some of our friends.

BRICKLAYER.

Let it be whose soul it will, I say the soul was a 165 fop. I think people when they are dead turn tonies;* they never say one wise word nor ever come into any wise company.

SANCHY.

The Viceroy is a pure canary bird;104 I'll have him turned out of his place. I'll prove he is a 170

Muhammedan; he was circumcised at Bar—bar—badoes.

PODESTA.

I believe you mean Barbary, Doctor.

SANCHY.

Why, aye, Barbadoes is the Latin name for Barbary. I love to swear like a scholar and a doctor, 175 as I am.ᵘ

BRICKLAYER.

Well, I'll go put all the town in arms. (*Exit.*)

SANCHY.

I'll go wi'you; I dare not stay in any house. (*Exit.*)

PODESTA.

I dare not stir out o'mine.

*Enter a servant conducting Pietro, who is disguised like a Spaniard of quality.**

SERVANT.

My lord, here is a great gentleman says he must 180 needs speak with your lordship presently about affairs that concern yourself.

PODESTA.

Look to me, for I know not what he is.

PIETRO.

My lord, I must beg leave to whisper you.

PODESTA.

You may, sir, but I must also beg leave to use 185 caution. These are dangerous times; some men ha' been almost whispered out o'their necks.

PIETRO.

I come from the Viceroy; he is sensible of your great parts* and interest and desires to speak wi'you presently.* And if you will be his friend, he offers 190 you your own terms for honor, profit, and greatness.

PODESTA.

Hah! Is it come to this? I like this.—Sir, I'll go.

PIETRO.

A chair* waits for you at the door. He desires this intrigue may be managed with all secrecy till 'tis settled. 195

PODESTA.

'Twill be best; he's a wise man.—Mr. Florio, I'm called away about matters of very great importance. I must take my leave.

ROSAURA.

O'this time o'night, my lord?

---

103 A spirit ... taken] In January 1681, a strange story circulated concerning a country maid from Hatfield who claimed a spirit had appeared to her and told her to warn Charles II not to summon the Parliament at Oxford in March; if he did, he would be poisoned (Wilson).

104 pure canary bird] a veritable rogue (*OED*)

PODESTA.

It must be. 200

ROSAURA.

Would the nation were settled once, that we might enjoy one another.

PODESTA.

It may be very speedily. Good night.

FLORIO.

Good night, madam.

PODESTA.

You going too, Mr. Florio? Are you well enough? 205

FLORIO.

All's one, my lord: my good name is the child of a sick man, seldom sound, never thought to be so. I must be tender of it.—Good night, madam.— Come, my lord, I'll see you in your chair.

PODESTA.

No, no, I cannot stay for your dreaming pace; I'm 210 in haste.

FLORIO.

Pray, my lord.

PODESTA.

I cannot stay, I cannot stay; good night, good night.

Exeunt Podesta, Pietro, [and servant].

FLORIO.

Ha, ha, ha! How greedily this fool swallows the 215 bait. Is the room that must pass with him for the Court, and secure him till his horns* be grown, so dressed he cannot know it to be one in his own house?

ROSAURA.

That was my care. 220

FLORIO.

You see my man's new furniture* has cheated him.

ROSAURA.

So shall the room.

FLORIO.

Then we may securely hoist sail for the haven of love. All the mud that barred it up we have conveyed away, and I will come ashore on these 225 white cliffs, and plant my heart there forever.

ROSAURA.

Do so, and I'll promise thee the happiness and wealth I gain by the residence of my prince shall

not make me ungratefully factious. Be true to me, and I'll be most loyal to thee. 230

FLORIO.

Then we'll be the happiest pair in the whole world.

Exeunt.

Scene iii. [Another room in the Podesta's house.]

Enter Pietro conducting the Podesta with ceremony.

PIETRO.

My lord, you are very welcome to Court.

PODESTA.

Your most humble servant, sir.

PIETRO.

Take not your private reception ill, for few or none are entrusted with this intrigue. 'Tis a great state secret, and great honors, to my knowledge, are 5 designed you, no less than the high office of Lord Treasurer.[105]

PODESTA.

Lord Treasurer?

PIETRO.

Sir, I speak what I know. 'Twill be some time before you come to it, and the Viceroy will expect 10 you sacrifice to him the doctor, bricklayer, Florio—

PODESTA.

Aye, and my father too, if he were alive; he should hang 'em all. Lord Treasurer!

PIETRO.

I hope, my lord, you won't refuse some oaths and—

PODESTA.

Nothing, I'll refuse nothing, sir, for such honor as 15 this. Lord Treasurer!

PIETRO.

I'll acquaint his Highness with your arrival. You must be willing to suffer some attendance, the common affliction of all courtiers.

PODESTA.

I'll do or suffer anything for so much glory as this. 20 Lord Treasurer!

PIETRO.

Your humble servant, my lord. (*Exit.*)

---

105 Lord Treasurer] Sir Robert Clayton, the Whig Lord Mayor of London from 1679-1680, was rumored to be seeking appointment to this high office (Wilson).

PODESTA.

Your most humble servant, sir.—Lord Treasurer!
To what grandeur am I rising? Some of the Court
are coming.   25

A noise of picking the lock, and enter Craffy.

CRAFFY.

So, I ha' got out o'my prison.

PODESTA.

Craffy in Court!

CRAFFY.

So, I have shut back the lock admirably and got
out of prison. My father! But why should I be
afraid of him? He thinks me mad and will be afraid   30
o'me.

PODESTA.

What a notable boy is this? I thought he was mad,
and he has more wit than myself, has climbed to
preferment before me. I always said this boy had
nimble parts.—Son.   35

CRAFFY.

My lord.

PODESTA.

You are surprised to see me in Court.

CRAFFY.

In Court!

PODESTA.

I am as much surprised to see your wit, which so
subtly disguised your policy under pretended   40
madness.

CRAFFY.

Policy! Am I grown from a madman to a
politician?

PODESTA.

Well, I am proud o'thee. Father and son, both
favorites! O'my word, we shall be a great family.   45
Well—what says the Viceroy to thee o'me?

CRAFFY.

Viceroy!

PODESTA.

Aye, and how art thou in with the Vice-Queen?

CRAFFY.

Vice-Queen?

PODESTA.

Aye, for women have great power in all courts.   50
Didst now come out of the Vice-Queen's side?

CRAFFY.

Out of her side!

PODESTA.

Her side. That is, her part o'th'Court? Her
apartments. Thou thinkst I'm a raw courtier? No,
sir, I know Court phrases.   55

CRAFFY.

My dirty hole the Vice-Queen's apartment!

PODESTA.

Why art so shy to thy brother courtier? I'm thy
brother courtier now.

CRAFFY. [*Aside.*]

Now would I give ten pound to know which of
us two is mad. If I were sure he were mad, I'd run   60
and beg him presently;* but the danger is lest I be
begged myself.[106]

PODESTA.

Thou art close wi'me, but I'll be open with thee. I
have sold all the Whigs and myself into the
bargain. And what dost think the Court gave me?   65

CRAFFY.

I don't know.

PODESTA.

The Lord Treasurer's place; I am to be Lord
Treasurer, boy! So the Whigs are all to go to pot
and the Court to win the game, boy, which they
had done long since if they had put one black rook   70
into the bag where they put me, but the game's
their own in getting me; they'll pick up t'other
men apace. The doctor's a desperate black knight,
skips over rooks, bishops, nay, the queen herself,
and checks the king, but he'll be snapped.   75

CRAFFY.

Why do you call the doctor a knight?

PODESTA.

Because a knight's notched in the crown, and the
doctor's a little cracked there.[107] But he and all the

---

106 If … myself] If his father is insane, Craffy can beg to
be appointed guardian of his estate, but if not, then
Craffy risks being beggared out of his inheritance.

107 black rook … cracked there] If the Tories had granted
the Podesta his wish to be knighted, they would have
ended the political game of chess earlier, but now they
have him and will snap up the rest of the pieces, notwithstanding Sanchy's antics as leaping black knight,
cracked in the head as knight pieces were notched.

Whigs will be snapped. "And hey then up go   80
we."108

*Sings and dances.*ᵛ

CRAFFY.

Father!

PODESTA.

Child!

CRAFFY.

The Lord bless thee and deliver thee from poetry,
for thou art a sad sight.

PODESTA.

Hah! A noise! The Court assaulted! I am cruel afraid   85
the Whigs ha' made some attempt upon the Court
and got the better; then will they catch me in court
and hang me for a turncoat.—Hide, boy, hide.

CRAFFY.

Yet cannot I tell which of us is mad, or where I am.

Exeunt Podesta and Craffy. Enter Governor, a guard,
Doctor Sanchy and Bricklayer prisoners, porter of the
Podesta's house.

GOVERNOR.

Friend, you were best confess where your lord is   90
before I break open any more doors, for if I find
him in the house, after your denial of him, I shall
punish you.

PORTER.

Indeed, if it please your Highness, he never came
home since he went abroad with a strange   95
gentleman.

GOVERNOR.

Your lady you say's abed and will not be disturbed?

PORTER.

I must disturb her, if it be your pleasure, but she
has forbid any person coming near her chamber.

Enter Podesta and Craffy peeping.

PODESTA.

The Governor o'th'City here? Then the Whigs are   100
worsted, and I'll show myself.

CRAFFY.

The governor here! Then this is the Court.

---

108 "And … we"] refrain of a popular Whig song of
   wish fulfillment

PODESTA.

My lord.

GOVERNOR.

D'ee see, sirrah? Your master's in the first room I
come in.   105

PORTER.

I did not know it, indeed, my lord.

GOVERNOR.

Secure the Podesta.

PODESTA.

Secure me!

GOVERNOR.

Aye, the Viceroy will endure your intolerable
disorders no longer: arm the city at midnight and   110
send your agitators abroad to disperse new minted
lies among 'em, the coin wherewithᵂ you pay all
your forces. I have order to secure you all.

SANCHY.

I fear you not.

BRICKLAYER.

I demand my habeas corpus.109   115

CRAFFY.

How now, brother courtier! Is this your greatness?

PODESTA.

Hah! Am I trepanned? Was this fair o'th'Viceroy
to entice me to court with promises of honors and
preferments and then secure me?

GOVERNOR.

The Viceroy entice you to court with promises?   120

PODESTA.

Yes, you had not seen me in court else.

GOVERNOR.

Why, when did I see you in court?

PODESTA.

When! That's a strange question. Where am I now?

GOVERNOR.

That's a stranger question. Do you not know where
you are? Do you not know your own home?   125

PODESTA.

My own home! Why, am I at home?

GOVERNOR.

The man's mad.

---

109 habeas corpus] The threat of illegal imprisonment was
    conspicuous at this time. Many people were imprisoned
    without due process of law, which the right of habeas
    corpus was supposed to prevent.

CRAFFY.

Then the dispute's at an end? My lord, I beg to be his guardian.

PODESTA.

If I be at home, I have had a fine trick played me, 130 and by this gentleman. (*Enter Pietro.*) I am glad I have you, sir.—Pray, let him be secured and examined, sir.—Where am I?

PIETRO.

At home, sir.

PODESTA.

At home! And wherefore did you entice me out 135 o'my house and, after you had danced me to and fro, bring me home again, pretending you brought me to court?

GOVERNOR.

Confess, sir.

CRAFFY.

His periwig and false beard confess 'twas that his 140 master might make my Lord Treasurer a cuckold— for this is Florio's man.

PODESTA.

Florio's man! Then his master is an impostor, my wife a slut, and I'm a fool.

SANCHY.

And a knave, for I believe you went abroad with 145 designs to betray us.[110]

PODESTA.

I shan't inform you, sir.

BRICKLAYER.

There's not an honest man in the world.

CRAFFY.

Now am I to be believed or no? Sirrah, you pimp, where ha' you pimped this couple together? 150

PIETRO.

In the next room.

GOVERNOR.

Force open the door.

The scene is drawn; Florio and Rosaura are discovered* sitting arm in arm. They offer to fly and are catched.

---

110 In November 1679, Sir Robert Peyton was discovered holding secret correspondence with James, the duke of York. Peyton was accused of betraying his party (Wilson).

CRAFFY. (*Draws.*)

You villain!

GOVERNOR.

Disarm the fellow.

PODESTA.

You strumpet! 155

CRAFFY.

You jilt!

SANCHY.

You rogue!

BRICKLAYER.

Tory in masquerade!

GOVERNOR.

Are you sick, sir? I'll know the state of your body.

PODESTA.

My wife can tell. 160

GOVERNOR.

There's another lady[111] shall enquire a rack.

FLORIO.

That lady's a scurvy bedfellow; I'll spare her pains.

PODESTA.

Are you to die a-Thursday come sennight?

FLORIO.

I believe 'twill be put off a little longer now.

CRAFFY.

So, you are a healthy rascal, are you? 165

FLORIO.

Why truly I find myself very finely well, I thank Heaven, very well.

BRICKLAYER.

Oh, you shamming rascal!

ROSAURA.

How! Ha' you abused me thus? And are you an impostor? 170

PODESTA.

And would you abuse us, madam? And cheat us into a belief you did not know it?

ROSAURA.

Do you believe I did?

PODESTA.

Did not all our eyes see you arm in arm?

ROSAURA.

What o'that? I invoke Heaven to witness— 175

---

111 another lady] iron maiden, a torture device that will rack Florio

PODESTA.

Away, you strumpet.

ROSAURA.

Is it possible—

PODESTA.

Never come near my bed or sight more.

ROSAURA.

I invoke Heaven to witness—

PODESTA.

What? 180

ROSAURA.

That thou shalt never come near my bed or sight more.

PODESTA.

Oh, impudences!

ROSAURA.

The impudence is yours. I modestly concealed your shame and mine, and you would force me 185 impudently to confess.

PODESTA.

Is it my shame that you are a strumpet?

FLORIO.

Yes, she is a true Whig and has revolted from you because you did not pay her nightly pension well.

PODESTA.

I hope you have, sir. 190

FLORIO.

I wonnot say whether I have or no.

PODESTA.

But I will say thou art a rascal.

FLORIO.

I'm an honester man than yourself and truer to my principles; you would have left 'em for preferment. I retain 'em. Our principles are: he is not to be 195 regarded who has a right to govern, but he who can best serve the ends of government.[112] I can better serve the ends of your lady than you can, so I lay claim to your lady.

ROSAURA.

And you have my consent. 200

FLORIO.

So, I have the voice o'the subject too; then you are my wife and I'll keep you.

PODESTA.

Oh brave!*—Sir, must this be?

GOVERNOR.

Ask the law, I must do all things according to law.

CRAFFY.

Your servant, my Lord Treasurer.—These are a fine 205 crew, sir. Here's the bricklayer, sir, a fine privy counselor, is he not? He expects also every day to be a colonel; he is already a colonel presumptive.[113]

BRICKLAYER.

Very well.

CRAFFY.

Here's the doctor too, a fine divine, sir. 210

SANCHY.

Sirrah, don't meddle with me.

CRAFFY.

He applies himself very much to the Bible, I mean to kiss it. He prays much, so help him the contents o'th'Book, and they have helped him to many a pound,[114] though they and he scarce ever saw one 215 another. The Bible is the only benefice he has, sir.

SANCHY.

Sirrah, I'll have your ears.*

CRAFFY.

Never when you preach, Doctor.—They are all very good men, never take Heaven's name in vain—that is, swear and get nothing by it—but to 220 get your estate or command they'll swear your head off.

GOVERNOR.

That I believe.

CRAFFY.

They are moderate drinkers o'wine, but will carouse water abundantly, for they'll drink your 225 rivers, fish and all, and put your land into it for a toast, if you'll let 'em. And yet sometimes they have very narrow swallows; they cannot down with a

---

112 Our principles ... government] standard Republican political theory

113 colonel presumptive] During his trial in August 1681, College was accused of, among many other things, boasting that very soon he was to be made a colonel (Wilson).

114 contents ... pound] For his services for being an informer and for testifying under oath (kissing the book) during the Popish Plot, Oates received about £1,800 in pension payments, plus lodgings in Whitehall Palace.

little church ceremony, but they'll swallow church 230
lands, hedges and ditches.

GOVERNOR.

Well, my Lord Podesta, your office the Viceroy and
the Council will order be managed by a wiser man.

PODESTA.

I wonnot part wi'my office but by law. I have done
nothing but by the advice of able counsel. Here
he comes. 235

GOVERNOR.

That knave!

Enter Bartoline and two witnesses.

PODESTA.

Counselor Bartoline, will our Charter justify us?

BARTOLINE.

In what? Keeping a bawdy housh? Your housh hash
been made a bawdy housh, notch by me, but by
Florio, your shick Shaint,* a yamned rascal. 240

PODESTA.

I know it to my sorrow. But the question I ask is
will our Charter justify our arming without the
Viceroy's leave?

BARTOLINE.

I have chold you it will a hundred chimsh, and let
the Vishroy do hish worsht. 245

GOVERNOR.

How! Bring that knave to me.

GENTLEMAN.

Sir, the Governor o'th'City commands you to come
to him.

BARTOLINE.

The governor here? 'Od sha' me, yen I'm ruined,
I'm ruined. 250

GOVERNOR.

Sir, did not the Viceroy retain you for his lawyer,
and did not you send him the direct contrary
opinion?

BARTOLINE.

Yesh, and pleash you lordship, and I sent his
Highnesh chrue law. I only shcatchered chaff 255
among these fellowsh cho catch 'em, caush I found
'em arrant rashcalsh, and cho show my loyalchy I
have drawn up Articlsh of High Chreason against
'em, and you may hang 'em all.

SANCHY.

What a rogue's here! 260

BRICKLAYER.

This was you that understood mankind.

PODESTA.

I'll never pretend to it more.

BARTOLINE.

There yey are, shir.

GOVERNOR. [*Reads.*]

"Articles of High Treason, with other high crimes
and misdemeanors, against Don Pedro, duke of 265
Ossuna, Viceroy of Naples."—How! Articles of
Treason against the Viceroy?

BARTOLINE.

Oh, my lord, my lord, I ha' given you the wrong
paper; yat wash a paper I drew to delude yesh
rogush. Pray don't chake advanchage of an old 270
fumbling fellow.

GOVERNOR.

An old bloodhound.

BARTOLINE.

I beg your lordship's pardon on my kneesh.

GOVERNOR.

Oh, sir, if the Viceroy were at a bar,[115] you'd bring
him upon his knees. 275

BARTOLINE.

Ingeed I am loyal, shir. I have discovered a horrible
plotch; one Florio has plotched cho open the
gatesh and letch in the French.

FLORIO.

How?

GOVERNOR.

What, Florio? 280

BARTOLINE.

A debaushed fellow yat prechends to be shick and
godly, preachesh up and down for a benefish, yat
ish, any man'sh wife he likesh.

GOVERNOR.

Here's the man you speak of.

BARTOLINE.

Then I desire he may be apprehenged for high 285
chreason. I have choo witneshesh will shwear all
yish upon him.

_____

[115] at a bar] at the bar of justice

[V.iii]

FLORIO.

What means the rascal?

BARTOLINE.

Yesh are the men.

GOVERNOR.

What countrymen are they?   290

FIRST WITNESS.

I am an Irishman;[116] I'm not ashamed o'my country.

GOVERNOR.

What religion are you of?

FIRST WITNESS.

Hubbubbow! Ask an Irishman what religion he is of? Shertainly if I be an Irishman, I'm a good   295 Catholic.

GOVERNOR.

Well, and what can you swear against Florio?

FIRST WITNESS.

I'll shwear hesh a knave and a rascal and a traitor, and hash been in a plot.

FLORIO.

What plot?   300

FIRST WITNESS.

To kill all the town and let in the French, yesh indeed.

FLORIO.

Kill all the town by myself.

FIRST WITNESS.

No, I wash to have a toushand cobs to help tee.

FLORIO.

Cobs! What are those?   305

FIRST WITNESS.

Pieshes of eight, and I wash to have ten hundred of 'em.

FLORIO.

To do what?

---

116 Irishman] In 1680 as part of their efforts to exclude James, duke of York, from succession, Shaftesbury and the Whigs brought to light the "Irish Plot," an alleged plan of Catholic uprising and takeover in Ireland. Shaftesbury had shipped over to London some fourteen Irish witnesses to testify to the existence of the conspiracy. During the Popish Plot, many Irish witnesses also had been produced to corroborate the testimony of Oates and others. In the following passages these "Irish testimonies" are satirized as mere perjury.

[FIRST] WITNESS.

To let in the French and make a fire in the town and cut all our troatsh, yesh indeed.   310

FLORIO.

All our troatsh? Wast thou to cut thy own throat?

SANCHY.

Sir, we won't have our evidence* baffled. He means all our throats.—Dost not?

[FIRST] WITNESS.

Yesh indeed—all our throatsh.

FLORIO.

I'll swear I never saw this fellow's face before in my 315 life.

[FIRST] WITNESS.

Hubbubbow, tou hasht drunk above a tousand times ushquebaugh wi'me, to de carrying on of tish plot.

FLORIO.

Ushquebaugh! What's that?   320

SECOND WITNESS.

A brave* liquor tat we have in Ireland. Tersh no such here; I never shaw any here.

FLORIO.

How could I drink it then?

[FIRST] WITNESS.

I don't know how tou couldst drink it, but tou hash drunk it above a toushand times, and a   325 toushand.

GOVERNOR.

Come, come, sirrah, I doubt* you are a villain.

[FIRST] WITNESS.

Hubbubbow! Tou talkst like an English *ignoramus* juryman. Wilt tou be an English heretic and not believe an Irishman?   330

SANCHY.

Come, come, the fellow's an honest, simple fellow.

[FIRST] WITNESS.

Aye, by Shaint Patrick am I.

SANCHY.

He's discovered a horrible plot, only wants expression.—Is it possible, you rogue you? Was this the meaning of all your canting and deluding us, 335 to lull us asleep whilst our throats are cut?

PODESTA.

Thou monster! Not only cuckold me, but cut my throat.

706   JOHN CROWNE

FLORIO.

'Tis false.

SANCHY.

'Tis true.

FLORIO.

I never saw the fellow before.

SANCHY.

I'll swear I have seen him with thee above forty times.

CRAFFY.

And so have I too. (*Aside.*) I'll teach the rogue to lie with my mistress; I'll hang him if I can.

BRICKLAYER.

So the plot's proved, plainly proved.

FLORIO.

A plot to murder me is proved, but sure such a rascal as this who has sworn contradictions shall not be believed.

SANCHY.

He is a rogue and a traitor that does not believe every word he says.

Enter the clerk and officers, with Artall and Lucinda.

CLERK.

Sir, I have catched Mr. Florio here.

BARTOLINE.

What Florio? Art out of thy witsh?

CLERK.

The Florio that was to let in the French and run away with my mistress. I ha' catched 'em together and brought 'em.

BARTOLINE.

Thou art mad. Our evigensh has shworn againsht anoyer man.

CLERK.

Then your evidence* is mad and don't know what they swear.

[SECOND] WITNESS.

Sir, I know what I swear as well as you do and know Mr. Florio as well as any man. I have known him this seven years and know this man to be the true Florio and a traitor that plotted to let in the French.

CLERK.

Then thou art a rascal and bought off, for this is the true Florio and the traitor that plotted to let in the French.

GOVERNOR.

Then thou art a rascal and hired to be one, for I and all the town can swear his name is Artall.

CRAFFY.

Oh, the devil! All our plot's confounded.

GOVERNOR.

You Irishman, which do you say is the true Florio?

[FIRST] WITNESS.

Tish ish de man I wash bid to shwear againsht.

GOVERNOR.

Bid to swear against? Who bid you? Confess, or the rack shall make you.

[FIRST] WITNESS.

Oh! Preedee do not wrack me, and I will confess. Tish knave and I had shome acquaintansh, and sho I had shome occasionsh for money, and I borrowed shome of him, and he had shome occasionsh for teshtimony, and sho I tought I wash obliged in shivility to lend him shome teshtimony, and sho he bid me shwear againsht one Florio and shaid tish was de man, but if tou wilt forgive me, I'll shwear him off again.

GOVERNOR.

So, sirrah, and who put you upon this?

[SECOND] WITNESS.

An attorney, sir, employed, I suppose, by this counselor.

SANCHY.

Oh, notorious mercenary rogues! Who'll believe such rogues as they are?

BRICKLAYER.

None but rogues.

GOVERNOR.

Just now you said he was a rogue that would not believe 'em.

SANCHY.

Aye, when they said the same things that I did. What I said was confirmed by Craffy, a considerable young man, heir to a great estate, and of a spotless reputation. No man can say the least against him.

GOVERNOR.

And what say you, Craffy? Speak truth, if you mean to have any ears.

PODESTA.

Or any part o'my estate.

GOVERNOR.

Did you ever see this Irishman with Florio?   400

CRAFFY.

I only spoke in a little passion. I have some of the doctor's infirmities—I'm passionate, and apt to swear in my passion.

FLORIO.

Be perjured in a passion?

SANCHY.

This fellow's the lyingest rogue in the nation and   405
has been so from his craddle.

GOVERNOR.

Just now you said no man could say the least against him.

BRICKLAYER.

Sham upon sham.

ARTALL.

My lord, I'll clear all. This young woman is my   410
kinswoman. I hearing she was married to that old man, brought to town, and lodged in a house which Florio frequented; she not knowing me; I took upon me Florio's name and made addresses to her, partly to divertise[117] myself, but chiefly to   415
make trial of her virtue. The old man catched me in the act of courtship, grew jealous, and would have abused his wife, which, to prevent, I took her from him. He, to be revenged, hired witnesses to hang me for treason.   420

BARTOLINE.

I'll shwear he shpoke creashon, but 'tish to no purpose, for now 'twill appear malish.

GOVERNOR.

To prison with 'em all.

ARTALL.

I beg your lordship to intercede with the Viceroy for the old man for my cousin's sake and command   425
him to use her kindly.

GOVERNOR.

I shall consider of it.

BARTOLINE.

I hank you lordship, but my heart'sh broken.

BRICKLAYER.

Hang me, if you will. I'll swear I'm murdered by suborners and sham-plotters.   430

_____
117 divertise] amuse

SANCHY.

And traitorly rogues.

ARTALL.

Well said, Doctor; thou wilt give titles in the last day of thy reign.

GOVERNOR.

The last day it shall be. The Viceroy and all of us will put an end to his absolute negative voice, his   435
great power of degrading lords and dukes into rogues and rascals, if they will not purchase of him the confirmation of their titles by capping[118] to him—nay, of deposing kings if they slight his counsels. We will also dissolve all his privy council.   440
And so, gentlemen, henceforward be wise, leave off the new trade you have taken up of managing state affairs, and betake yourselves to the callings you were bred to and understand. Be honest; meddle not with other men's matters, especially with   445
government; 'tis none of your right. In short, trouble not yourselves more than needs:
Chiefly you married men, for all allow
You married men have private plagues enow.

[Exeunt.]

FINIS.

_____
118 capping] doffing their hats

a Copytext is the first quarto in 1683 (Q1). Also consulted: a second quarto in 1688 (Q2); a modern edition in 1967 (Wilson).

b Sanchy] used interchangeably with Panchy throughout Q1-2

c waste] Q1; spend Q2

d one of] Wilson; one or Q1, Q2

e wicked] Q1, Wilson; *om.* Q2

f but] Q2, Wilson; that Q1

g BRICKLAYER] CRAFFY Q1, Q2, Wilson (who suggests but does not make the emendation)

h a good answer to . . . so well as that] Q1; *om.* Q2.

i call] Q2, Wilson; call one of Q1

j shallow] Q1; shadow Q2

k letcher] Q1, Q2; betcher Wilson, whose emendation brings us closer to the proverb—but loses Bartoline's slip of the tongue.

l echshechera] *&c.* Q1, Q2, Wilson

m Yes] Wilson; No Q1, Q2

n Not … years.] Q2, Wilson; *om.* Q1

o of] Wilson (a silent emendation); *om.* Q1, Q2

p BRICKLAYER] Wilson; *Bar.* (for BARTOLINE) Q1, Q2

q for my] my for Q1; for Q2, Wilson

r Pox take it.] Q1, Wilson; *om.* Q2

s Now … pocket.] Q2, Wilson; *om.* Q1

t have] Q2, Wilson; *om.* Q1

u The Viceroy ,… I am.] Q1, Wilson; *om.* Q2

v So the Whigs … *dances.*] Q2, Wilson; *om.* Q1

w pay] Q1, Wilson; raise Q2

Love's Last Shift; or, The Fool in Fashion[a]

by Colley Cibber (1671-1757)

edited by Gary A. Richardson

Whatever notoriety may have subsequently attached to Colley Cibber as the "hero" of the later version of Alexander Pope's *The Dunciad* (1742-43), his fame as a playwright stems almost exclusively from his remarkable first play. An enticing blend of both the theatrically old and the culturally nascent, *Love's Last Shift* and his acting in it established Cibber as a major comedian and a significant playwright at the same time that it hinted at a potential response to continuing critiques of the ribaldry and license of the stage that was to reach a kind of culmination in the so-called Collier controversy two years after the play's opening.

Having languished for several years as a minor actor in the Drury Lane company, Cibber took the occasion of the particularly competitive climate of the 1695-96 season to advance his career in new directions. The longstanding financial difficulties of the combined company, exacerbated by the oppressive management of Christopher Rich, finally precipitated a rebellion that again introduced competition to the London theatrical scene when Thomas Betterton and several other actors secured a royal license to establish a new theater in Lincolns Inn Fields. The contest for audiences was intense, and into that breach stepped Cibber. Repeating a practice well-established by compatriots such as Betterton, William Mountfort, and George Powell, Cibber penned a play designed to highlight his acting talents, in the process adding parts for his wife and his musician brother-in-law. When the play was produced at the Theatre Royal in January 1696, Cibber was triumphant as the fool of the subtitle, Sir Novelty Fashion. Despite its importance to Cibber's theatrical career, the play's significance today resides primarily as a marker of the shifting theatrical tastes of the era and as a harbinger of the coming ascendancy of middle-class sensibilities within the theater.

Conceived and produced in the wake of the Glorious Revolution of 1688 and in a time of Jacobite intrigues and ongoing political instability, *Love's Last Shift* examines the fates of three couples, each of which is grappling with the establishment or re-establishment of a private polity in the form of marriage. While much of the fare features conventional witty young rakes and coquettes attempting to pair off in spite of the interference of inept rivals and crotchety authority figures of the older generation, Cibber's play treats marriage with a seriousness rarely seen in the era and introduces two characters that set the play apart, his beau extraordinaire, Sir Novelty, and Amanda, a long-suffering wife, intent upon reclaiming her wastrel and lecherous husband. In the action surrounding Amanda, Cibber tapped an emotional wellspring that nourished the emergence of the sentimental as a significant style in English drama.

The exact length of the play's initial, apparently very successful, run is uncertain. What is known is that the play quickly became a part of the Drury Lane repertoire and was produced more than two hundred times in the next seventy-seven years. Its popularity is also evidenced by the eight editions published during Cibber's life as well as Sir John Vanbrugh's response, *The Relapse*.

DRAMATIS PERSONAE

MEN

Sir William Wisewoud, a rich old gentleman
that fancies himself a great master of his
passion, which he only is in trivial matters.

Loveless, of a debauched life, grew weary of his
wife in six months; left her, and the Town,* for
debts he did not care to pay; and having spent
the last part of his estate beyond sea, returns to
England in a very mean* condition.

Sir Novelty Fashion, a coxcomb that loves to be
the first in all foppery.

Elder Worthy, a sober gentleman of a fair estate
in love with Hillaria.

Young Worthy, his brother, of a looser temper,
lover to Narcissa.

Snap, servant to Loveless.

Sly, servant to Young Worthy.

A lawyer.

WOMEN

Amanda, a woman of strict virtue, married to
Loveless very young and forsaken by him.

Narcissa, daughter to Sir William Wisewoud, a
fortune.

Hillaria, his niece.

Flareit, a kept* mistress of Sir Novelty's.

Woman* to Amanda.

Maid to Flareit.

THE SCENE: LONDON

Love's Last Shift; or, The Fool in Fashion.

Act I, scene i. The Park.*

Enter Loveless and Snap.

LOVELESS.

Sirrah! Leave your preaching. Your counsel's like
an ill clock, either stands still or goes too slow. You
ne'er thought my extravagancies amiss while you
had your share of 'em, and now I want* money
to make myself drunk, you advise me to live sober, 5
you dog. They that will hunt pleasure as I ha' done,
rascal, must never give over in a fair chase.

SNAP.

Nay, I knew you would never rest till you had tired

your dogs. Ah sir! What a fine pack of guineas have
you had! And yet you would make them run till 10
they were quite spent. Would I were fairly turned
out of your service. Here we have been three days
in Town,* and I can safely swear I have lived upon
picking a hollow tooth ever since.

LOVELESS.

Why don't you eat then, sirrah? 15

SNAP.

Even because I don't know where, sir.

LOVELESS.

Then stay till I eat, hangdog! Ungrateful rogue! to
murmur at a little fasting with me when thou hast
been an equal partner of my good fortune.

SNAP.

Fortune! It makes me weep to think what you have 20
brought yourself and me to! How well might you
have lived, sir, had you been a sober man. Let me
see, I ha' been in your service just ten years: in the
first you married and grew weary of your wife; in
the second you whored, drank, gamed, run in 25
debt, mortgaged your estate, and was forced to
leave the kingdom; in the third, fourth, fifth, sixth,
and seventh you made the tour of Europe with the
state and equipage of a French court favorite, while
your poor wife at home broke her heart for the loss 30
of you; in the eighth and ninth you grew poor and
little the wiser; and now in the tenth you are
resolved I shall starve with you.

LOVELESS.

Despicable rogue! Canst thou not bear the frowns
of a common strumpet, Fortune? 35

SNAP.

S'bud,* I never think of the pearl necklace you
gave that damned Venetian strumpet but I wish
her hanged in't!

LOVELESS.

Why, sirrah! I knew I could not have her without
it, and I had a night's enjoyment of her was worth 40
a pope's revenue for't.

SNAP.

Ah! You had better ha' laid out your money here in
London. I'll undertake you might have had the
whole Town over and over for half the price. Beside
sir, what a delicate creature was your wife! She was 45
the only celebrated beauty in Town. I'll undertake

there were more fops and fools run mad for her—
'Od*'sbud* she was more plagued with 'em, and
more talked of than a good actress with a maidenhead! Why the devil could not she content you?   50

LOVELESS.

No sirrah, the world to me is a garden stocked with
all sorts of fruit, where the greatest pleasure we can
take is in the variety of taste. But a wife is an
eternal apple tree. After a pull or two, you are sure
to set your teeth on edge.   55

SNAP.

And yet I warrant you grudged another man a bit
of her, though you valued her no more than you
would a half-eaten pippin that had lain a week a-
sunning in a parlor window.—But see, sir, who's
this? For methinks I long to meet with an old   60
acquaintance!

LOVELESS.

Hah! Egad, he looks like one, and may be
necessary, as the case stands with me.

SNAP.

Pray Heaven he do but invite us to dinner!

Enter Young Worthy.

LOVELESS.

Dear Worthy! let me embrace thee. The sight of   65
an old friend warms me beyond that of a new
mistress.

YOUNG WORTHY.

S'death,* what bully's this?—Sir, your pardon, I
don't know you!

LOVELESS.

Faith Will, I am a little out of repairs at present.   70
But I am all that's left of honest Ned Loveless.

YOUNG WORTHY.

Loveless! I am amazed! What means this
metamorphosis? Faith Ned, I am glad to find thee
amongst the living, however. How long hast thou
been in Town?   75

LOVELESS.

About three days. But prithee Will, how goes the
world?

YOUNG WORTHY.

Why like a bowl, it runs on at the old rate. Interest
is still the jack it aims at, and while it rolls, you
know, it must of necessity be often turned upside   80

down. But I doubt,* friend, you have bowled out
of the green, have lived a little too fast, (*Surveying
his dress.*) like one that has lost all his ready money,
and are forced to be an idle spectator. Prithee, what
brought thee at last to England?   85

LOVELESS.

Why, my last hopes, faith, which were to persuade
Sir William Wisewoud (if he be alive), to whom I
mortgaged my estate, to let me have five hundred
pound more upon it, or else get some honest friend
to redeem the mortgage and share the over-plus!   90
Beside, I thought that London might now be a place
of uninterrupted pleasure, for I hear my wife is dead.
And to tell you the truth, 'twas the staleness of her
love was the main cause of my going over.

YOUNG WORTHY. (*Aside.*)

His wife dead! Hah! I'm glad he knows no other.   95
I won't undeceive him, lest the rogue should go
and rifle her of what she has.—Yes faith, I was at
her burial and saw her take posession of her long
home and am sorry to tell you, Ned, she died with
grief. Your wild courses broke her heart.   100

LOVELESS.

Why faith! she was a good-natured fool, that's the
truth on't. Well! rest her soul.

SNAP.

Now sir, you are a single man indeed, for you have
neither wife nor estate.

YOUNG WORTHY.

But how hast thou improved thy money beyond   105
sea? What hast thou brought over?

LOVELESS.

Oh, a great deal of experience.

YOUNG WORTHY.

And no money?

SNAP.

Not a sou, faith, sir, as my belly can testify.

LOVELESS.

But I have a great deal more wit than I had!   110

SNAP.

Not enough to get your estate again, or to know
where we shall dine today. (*Aside.*) Oh Lord, he
don't ask us yet!

YOUNG WORTHY.

Why, your rogue's witty, Ned. Where didst thou
pick him up?   115

LOVELESS.

Don't you remember Snap, formerly your pimp in
ordinary? But he is much improved in his calling,
I assure you, sir.

YOUNG WORTHY.

I don't doubt it, considering who has been his master.

SNAP.

Yes sir, I was an humble servant of yours and am   120
still, sir, and should be glad to stand behind your
chair at dinner, sir. (*Bows.*)

YOUNG WORTHY.

Oh sir! that you may do another time, but today
I am engaged upon business; however, there's a
meal's meat for you. (*Throws him a guinea.*)   125

SNAP.

Bless my eyesight! a guinea! Sir, is there e'er a whore
you would have kicked? Any old bawd's windows
you would have broken? Shall I beat your tailor for
disappointing you? Or your surgeon that would be
paid for a clap of two years standing? If you have   130
occasion, you may command your humble servant.

YOUNG WORTHY.

Sweet sir, I am obliged to you! But at present am
so happy as to have no occasion for your
assistance.—But hark you Ned, prithee, what hast
thou done with thy estate?   135

LOVELESS.

I pawned it to buy pleasure, that is old wine, young
whores, and the conversation of brave* fellows as
mad as myself. Pox! If a man has appetites, they
are torments if not indulged! I shall never complain
as long as I have health and vigor. And as for my   140
poverty, why the devil should I be ashamed of that,
since a rich man won't blush at his knavery?

YOUNG WORTHY.

Faith Ned, I am as much in love with wickedness
as thou canst be, but I'm for having it at a cheaper
rate than my ruin! Don't it grate you a little to see   145
your friends blush for you?

LOVELESS.

'Tis very odd that people should be more ashamed
of others' faults than their own. I never yet could
meet with a man that offered me counsel but had
more occasion for it himself.   150

YOUNG WORTHY.

So far you may be in the right: For indeed, good

counsel is like a home jest, which every busy fool
is offering to his fellow and yet won't take himself.

LOVELESS.

Right. Thus have I known a jolly, red-nosed parson
at three o'clock in the morning belch out invectives   155
against late hours and hard drinking and a canting
hypocritical sinner protest against fornication when
the rogue was himself just crawling out of a flux.[1]

YOUNG WORTHY.

Though these are truths, friend, yet I don't see any
advantage you can draw from them. Prithee, how   160
will you live now all your money's gone?

LOVELESS.

Live! How dost thou live? thou are but a younger
brother, I take it.

YOUNG WORTHY.

Oh very well, sir, though faith, my father left me
but three thousand pound, one of which I gave for   165
a place at court that I still enjoy; the other two are
gone after pleasure, as thou say'st. But beside this,
I am supplied by the continual bounty of an
indulgent brother. Now I am loath to load his
good nature too much and therefore have e'en   170
thought fit, like the rest of my raking brotherhood,
to purge out my wild humors* with matrimony.
By the way, I have taken care to see the dose well
sweetened with a swingeing portion.

LOVELESS.

Ah Will, you'll find marrying to cure lewdness is   175
like surfeiting to cure hunger. For all the
consequence is, you loath what you surfeit on and
are only chaste to her you marry. But prithee,
friend, what is thy wife that must be?

YOUNG WORTHY.

Why faith, since I believe the matter is too far gone   180
for any man to postpone me (at least, I am sure
thou wilt not do me an injury to do thy self no
good) I'll tell thee. You must know, my mistress is
the daughter of that very knight to whom you
mortgaged your estate, Sir William Wisewoud.   185

LOVELESS.

Why, she's an heiress and has a thousand pound a
year in her own hands, if she be of age. But I
suppose the old man knows nothing of your

---

[1] flux] a purge to cure venereal disease

intentions. Therefore, prithee, how have you had opportunities of promoting your love? 190

YOUNG WORTHY.

Why thus: you must know, Sir William (being very well acquainted with the largeness of my brother's estate) designs his daughter for him and to encourage his passion offers him out of his own pocket the additional blessing of five thousand 195 pound. This offer my brother, knowing my inclinations, seems to embrace but at the same time is really in love with his niece, who lives with him in the same house. And therefore, to hide my design from the old gentleman, I pretend visits to 200 his daughter as an intercessor for my brother only. And thus he has given me daily opportunities of advancing my own interest. Nay, and I have so contrived it that I design to have the five thousand pound too. 205

LOVELESS.

How is that possible, since I see no hopes of the old man's consent for you?

YOUNG WORTHY.

Have a day's patience, and you'll see the effects on't. In a word, 'tis so sure that nothing but delays can hinder my success; therefore, I am very earnest 210 with my mistress that tomorrow may be the day. But a pox on't, I have two women to prevail with, for my brother quarrels every other day with his mistress, and while I am reconciling him, I lose ground in my own amour. 215

LOVELESS.

Why, has not your mistress told you her mind yet?

YOUNG WORTHY.

She will, I suppose, as soon as she knows it herself, for within this week she has changed it as often as her linen and keeps it as secret too, for she would no more own her love before my face than she 220 would shift herself before my face.

LOVELESS.

Pshaw! she shows it the more by striving to conceal it.

YOUNG WORTHY.

Nay, she does give me some proofs indeed, for she will suffer nobody but herself to speak ill of me, is 225 always uneasy till I am sent for, never pleased when I am with her, and still jealous when I leave her.

LOVELESS.

Well! Success to thee, Will. I will send the fiddles to release you from your first night's labor.

YOUNG WORTHY.

But hark you, have a care of disobliging the bride, 230 though.—Hah! yonder goes my brother! I am afraid his walking so early proceeds from some disturbance in his love. I must after him and set him right. Dear Ned, you'll excuse me. Shall I see you at the Blue Posts[2] between five and six this 235 afternoon?

LOVELESS.

With all my heart. But d'ye hear, canst not thou lend me the fellow to that same guinea you gave my man? I'll give you my bond, if you mistrust me.

YOUNG WORTHY.

Oh sir, your necessity is obligation enough. There 240 'tis, and all I have, faith. When I see you at night, you may command me farther. Adieu. At six at farthest. (*Exit.*)

LOVELESS.

Without fail.—So! Now rascal, you are an hungry, are you! Thou deserv'st never to eat again. Rogue! 245 Grumble before Fortune had quite forsaken us!

SNAP.

Ah dear sir, the thoughts of eating again have so transported me, I am resolved to live and die with you.

LOVELESS.

Look ye, sirrah, here's that will provide us of a 250 dinner and a brace of whores into the bargain, at least as guineas and whores go now.

SNAP.

Ah good sir! no whores before dinner, I beseech you.

LOVELESS.

Well, for once I'll take your advice, for to say truth, 255 a man is as unfit to follow love with an empty stomach as business with an empty head. Therefore I think a bit and a bottle won't be amiss first.

The gods of wine and love were ever friends,
For by the help of wine, Love gains his ends. 260

Exeunt. Enter Elder Worthy with a letter.

---

2 Blue Posts] name of a couple of popular taverns

ELDER WORTHY.

How hard is it to find that happiness which our shortsighted passions hope from woman! 'Tis not their cold disdain or cruelty should make a faithful lover curse his stars. That is but reasonable. 'Tis the shadow in our pleasure's picture! Without it, love could ne'er be heightned! No, 'tis their pride and vain desire of many lovers that robs our hope of its imagined rapture. The blind are only happy! For if we look through reason's never-erring perspective,* we then survey their souls and view the rubbish we were chaffering for. And such I find Hillaria's mind is made of. This letter is an order for the knocking off my fetters, and I'll send it her immediately.

Enter to him Young Worthy.

YOUNG WORTHY.

Morrow, brother. (*Seeing the letter.*) What! is your fit returned again? What beau's box has Hillaria taken snuff from? What fool has led her from the box to her coach? What fop has she suffered to read a play or novel to her? Or whose money has she indiscreetly won at basset?* Come, let's see the ghastly wound she has made in your quiet that I may know how much claret to prescribe you.

ELDER WORTHY.

I have my wound and cure from the same person, I'll assure you: the one from Hillaria's wit and beauty, the other from her pride and vanity.

YOUNG WORTHY.

That's what I could ne'er yet find her guilty of. Are you angry at her loving you?

ELDER WORTHY.

I am angry at myself for believing she e'er did.

YOUNG WORTHY.

Have her actions spoke the contrary? Come, you know she loves.

ELDER WORTHY.

Indeed she gave a great proof on't last night here in the Park* by fastening upon a fool and caressing him before my face, when she might have so easily avoided him.

YOUNG WORTHY.

What! And I warrant, interrupted you in the middle of your sermon, for I don't question but

you were preaching to her. But prithee, who was the fool she fastened upon?

ELDER WORTHY.

One that Heaven intended for a man, but the whole business of his life is to make the world believe he is of another species. A thing that affects mightily to ridicule himself only to give others a kind of necessity of praising him. I can't say he's a slave to every new fashion, for he pretends to be the master of it and is ever reviving some old or advancing some new piece of foppery. And though it don't take, is still as well pleased because it then obliges the Town to take the more notice of him. He's so fond of a public reputation that he is more extravagant in his attempts to gain it than the fool that fired Diana's temple[3] to immortalize his name.

YOUNG WORTHY.

You have said enough to tell me his name is Sir Novelty Fashion.

ELDER WORTHY.

The same. But that which most concerns me is that he has the impudence to address to Hillaria and she vanity enough not[b] to discard him.

YOUNG WORTHY.

Is this all? Why, thou art as hard to please in a wife as thy mistress in a new gown. How many women have you took in hand and yet can't please yourself at last?

ELDER WORTHY.

I had need to have the best goods when I offer so great a price as marriage for them. Hillaria has some good qualities but not enough to make a wife of.

YOUNG WORTHY.

She has beauty!

ELDER WORTHY.

Granted.

YOUNG WORTHY.

And money.

ELDER WORTHY.

Too much. Enough to supply her vanity.

---

3 fired Diana's temple] In 356 BCE, Herostratus set fire to the Temple of Diana in an attempt to guarantee the immortality of his name. Ancient tradition had it that the fire occurred the very night Alexander the Great was born.

YOUNG WORTHY.

She has sense.

ELDER WORTHY.

Not enough to believe I am no fool.

YOUNG WORTHY.

She has wit. 330

ELDER WORTHY.

Not enough to deceive me.

YOUNG WORTHY.

Why then you are happy if she can't deceive you.

ELDER WORTHY.

Yet she has folly enough to endeavor it. I'll see her no more, and this shall tell her so.

YOUNG WORTHY.

Which in an hour's time you'll repent, as much as 335 ever.

ELDER WORTHY.

As ever I should marrying her.

YOUNG WORTHY.

You'll have a damned meaking[4] look when you are forced to ask her pardon for your ungenerous suspicion and lay the fault upon excess of love. 340

ELDER WORTHY.

I am not so much in love as you imagine.

YOUNG WORTHY.

Indeed sir, you are in love, and that letter tells her so.

ELDER WORTHY.

Read it, you'll find the contrary.

YOUNG WORTHY.

Prithee, I know what's in't better than thou dost: 345 You say 'tis to take your leave of her, but I say 'tis in hopes of a kind, excusive answer. But faith, you mistake her and yourself too. She is too high-spirited not to take you at your word, and you are too much in love not to ask her pardon. 350

ELDER WORTHY.

Well then, I'll not be too rash but will show my resentment in forbearing my visits.

YOUNG WORTHY.

Your visits! Come, I shall soon try what a man of resolution you are—for yonder she comes. Now, let's see if you have power to move. 355

---

4 meaking] submissive, sheepishly meek

ELDER WORTHY.

I'll soon convince you of that. Farewell. (*Exit.*)

YOUNG WORTHY.

Hah! Gone! I don't like that! I am sorry to find him so resolute. But I hope Hillaria has taken too fast hold of his heart to let this fit shake him off. I must to her and make up this breach, for while 360 his amour stands still, I have no hopes of advancing my own. (*Exit.*)

Enter Hillaria, Narcissa, and Amanda in mourning.

HILLARIA.

Well dear Amanda, thou art the most constant wife I ever heard of: not to shake off the memory of an ill husband after eight or ten years absence, nay 365 to mourn, for aught you know, for the living too, and such an husband that, though he were alive, would never thank you for't. Why d'ye persist in such a hopeless grief?

AMANDA.

Because 'tis hopeless! For if he be alive, he is dead 370 to me. His dead affections not virtue's self can e'er retrieve. Would I were with him, though in his grave!

HILLARIA.

In my mind you are much better where you are! The grave! Young widows use to have warmer 375 wishes. But methinks, the death of a rich old uncle should be a cordial to your sorrows.

AMANDA.

That adds to 'em, for he was the only relation I had left and was as tender of me as the nearest! He was a father to me. 380

HILLARIA.

He was better than some fathers to you, for he died just when you had occasion for his estate.

NARCISSA.

I have an old father, and the deuce take me, I think he only lives to hinder me of my occasions. But Lord bless me, madam, how can you be unhappy 385 with two thousand pound a year in your own possession?

HILLARIA.

For my part, the greatest reason I think you have to grieve is that you are not sure your husband's dead, for were that confirmed, then indeed there 390 were hopes that one poison might drive out another. You might marry again.

AMANDA.

All the comfort of my life is that I can tell my conscience I have been true to virtue.

HILLARIA.

And to an extravagant husband that cares not a farthing for you. But come, let's leave this unseasonable talk and, pray, give me a little of your advice. What shall I do with this Mr. Worthy? Would you advise me to make a husband of him? 395

AMANDA.

I am but an ill judge of men. The only one I thought myself secure of most cruelly deceived me. 400

HILLARIA.

A losing gamester is fittest to give counsel. What d'ye think of him?

AMANDA.

Better than of any man I know. I read nothing in him but what is some part of a good man's character.* 405

HILLARIA.

He's jealous.

AMANDA.

He's a lover.

HILLARIA.

He taxes me with a fool!

AMANDA.

He would preserve your reputation, and a fool's love ends only in the ruin of it. 410

HILLARIA.

Methinks he's not handsome.

AMANDA.

He's a man, madam.

HILLARIA.

Why then e'en let him make a woman of me.

NARCISSA.

Pray madam, what d'ye think of his brother? (Smiling.) 415

AMANDA.

I would not think of him.

NARCISSA.

Oh dear, why, pray?

AMANDA.

He puts me in mind of a man too like him, one that had beauty, wit, and falsehood!

NARCISSA.

You have hit some part of his character, I must confess, madam, but as to his truth, I'm sure he loves only me. 420

AMANDA.

I don't doubt but he tells you so, nay, and swears it too.

NARCISSA.

Oh Lord, madam, I hope I may without vanity believe him. 425

AMANDA.

But you will hardly without magic secure him.

NARCISSA.

I shall use no spells or charms but this poor face, madam.

AMANDA.

And your fortune, madam. 430

NARCISSA. (Aside.)

Senseless malice!—I know he'd marry me without a groat.

AMANDA.

Then he's not the man I take him for.

NARCISSA.

Why pray, what do you take him for?

AMANDA.

A wild young fellow that loves everything he sees. 435

NARCISSA. (Peevishly.)

He never loved you yet.

AMANDA.

I hope, madam, he never saw anything in me to encourage him.

NARCISSA.

In my conscience you are in the right on't, madam. I dare swear he never did nor e'er would though he gazed till doomsday. 440

AMANDA.

I hope, madam, your charms will prevent his putting himself to the trial, and I wish he may never—

NARCISSA.

Nay dear madam, no more railing at him, unless you would have me believe you love him. 445

HILLARIA.

Indeed ladies, you are both in the wrong: you, cousin, in being angry at what you desired, her opinion of your lover; and you, madam, for speaking truth against the man she resolves to love. 450

NARCISSA.

Love him! Prithee cousin, no more of that old stuff.

HILLARIA.

Stuff! Why, don't you own you are to marry him this week?—Here he comes. I suppose you'll tell him another thing in his ear.

Enter Young Worthy.

HILLARIA.

Mr. Worthy, your servant! You look with the face   455
of business. What's the news, pray?

YOUNG WORTHY.

Faith madam, I have news for you all, and private news too, but that of the greatest consequence is with this lady. Your pardon, ladies. I'll whisper with you all one after another.   460

NARCISSA.

Come cousin, will you walk? The gentleman has business; we shall interrupt him.

HILLARIA.

Why really, cousin, I don't say positively you love Mr. Worthy, but I vow this looks very like jealousy.

NARCISSA.

Pish! Lord! Hillaria, you are in a very odd humor   465
today. But to let you see I have no such weak thoughts about me, I'll wait as unconcerned as your self. (*Aside.*) I'll rattle him.

AMANDA.

Not unpleasing, say you? Pray sir, unfold yourself, for I have long despaired of welcome news.   470

YOUNG WORTHY.

Then in a word, madam, your husband, Mr. Loveless, is in Town and has been these three days. I parted with him not an hour ago.

AMANDA.

In Town! you amaze me! For Heaven's sake go on.

YOUNG WORTHY.

Faith madam, considering Italy and those parts have   475
furnished him with nothing but an improvement of that lewdness he carried over, I can't properly give you joy of his arrival. Besides, he is so very poor that you would take him for an inhabitant of that country. And when I confirmed your being dead, he   480
only shook his head and called you good-natured fool, or to that effect, nay, though I told him his unkindness broke your heart.

AMANDA.

Barbarous man! not shed a tear upon my grave? But why did you tell him I was dead?   485

YOUNG WORTHY.

Because madam, I thought you had no mind to have your house plundered. And for another reason, which if you dare listen to me, perhaps you'll not dislike. In a word, 'tis such a stratagem that will either make him ashamed of his folly or   490
in love with your virtue.

AMANDA.

Can there be a hope, when even my death could not move him to a relenting sigh? Yet pray, instruct me, sir.

YOUNG WORTHY.

You know, madam, 'twas not above four or five   495
months after you were married but (as most young husbands do) he grew weary of you. Now, I am confident 'twas more an affectation of being fashionably vicious than any reasonable dislike he could either find in your mind or person.   500
Therefore, could you, by some artifice, pass upon him as a new mistress, I am apt to believe you would find none of the wonted coldness in his love but a younger heat and fierce desire.

AMANDA.

Suppose this done. What would be the conse-   505
quence?

YOUNG WORTHY.

Oh, your having then a just occasion to reproach him with his broken vows and to let him see the weakness of his deluded fancy, which even in a wife, while unknown, could find those real charms   510
which his blind, ungrateful lewdness would ne'er allow her to be mistress of. After this, I'd have you seem freely to resign him to those fancied raptures which he denied were in a virtuous woman. Who knows but this with a little submissive eloquence   515
may strike him with so great a^c sense of shame as may reform his thoughts and fix him yours?

AMANDA.

You have revived me, sir. But how can I assure myself he'll like me as a mistress?

YOUNG WORTHY.

From your being a new one. Leave the manage-   520
ment of all to me. I have a trick shall draw him to

your bed, and when he's there, faith, e'en let him cuckold himself. I'll engage he likes you as a mistress, though he could not as a wife. (*Aside*.) At least, she'll have the pleasure of knowing the difference between a husband and a lover without the scandal of the former.

AMANDA.

You have obliged me, sir. If I succeed, the glory shall be yours.

YOUNG WORTHY.

I'll wait on you at your lodging and consult how I may be farther serviceable to you. But you must put this in a speedy execution, lest he should hear of you and prevent your designs. In the meantime, 'tis a secret to all the world but yourself and me.

AMANDA.

I'll study to be grateful, sir.

YOUNG WORTHY. (*To Hillaria.*)

Now for you, madam.

NARCISSA. (*Aside*.)

So! I am to be last served. Very well!

YOUNG WORTHY.

My brother, madam, confesses he scattered some rough words last night. And I have taken the liberty to tell you, you gave him some provocation.

HILLARIA.

That may be, but I'm resolved to be mistress of my actions before marriage, and no man shall usurp a power over me till I give it him.

YOUNG WORTHY.

At least, madam, consider what he said as the effects of an impatient passion and give him leave this afternoon to set all right again.

HILLARIA.

Well, if I don't find myself out of order after dinner, perhaps I may step into the garden. But I won't promise you neither.

YOUNG WORTHY.

I dare believe you without it. (*To Narcissa.*) Now madam, I am your humble servant.

NARCISSA.

And everybody's humble servant. (*Walks off.*)

YOUNG WORTHY.

Why madam, I am come to tell you—

NARCISSA.

What success you have had with that lady, I suppose. I don't mind intrigues, sir.

YOUNG WORTHY. [*Aside.*]

I like this jealousy, however, though I scarce know how to appease it.—'Tis business of moment, madam, and may be done in a moment.

NARCISSA.

Yours is done with me, sir, but my business is not so soon done as you imagine.

YOUNG WORTHY.

In a word, I have very near reconciled my brother and your cousin, and I don't doubt but tomorrow will be the day, if I were but as well assured of your consent for my happiness too!

NARCISSA.

First tell me your discourse with that lady and afterwards, if you can, look me in the face. Oh, are you studying, sir?

YOUNG WORTHY. [*Aside.*]

S'death!* I must not trust her with it; she'll tell it the whole Town for a secret. Pox! ne'er a lie!

NARCISSA.

You said it was of the greatest consequence too!

YOUNG WORTHY. (*Aside.*)

A good hint, faith.—Why madam, since you will needs force it from me, 'twas to desire her to advance my interest with you. But all my entreaties could not prevail, for she told me I was unworthy of you. Was not this of consequence, madam?

NARCISSA.

Nay, now I must believe you, Mr. Worthy, and I ask your pardon, for she was just railing against you for a husband before you came.

YOUNG WORTHY.

Oh! Madam, a favored lover, like a good poem, for the malice of some few makes the generous temper more admire it.

NARCISSA.

Nay, what she said, I must confess, had much the same effect as the coffee-critics ridiculing *Prince Arthur*,5 for I found a pleasing disappointment in

---

5 coffee-critics … *Prince Arthur*] Sir Richard Blackmore, personal physician to Charles II and amateur poet, used the preface to his epic, *Prince Arthur* (1695), to criticize the stage for immorality. In retaliation, wits who frequented the fashionable coffee houses subjected his poetry to brutal attack.

my reading you. And till I see your beauties equaled, I shan't dislike you for a few faults. 585

YOUNG WORTHY.

Then madam, since you have blest me with your good opinion, let me beg of you before these ladies to complete my happiness tomorrow. Let this be the last night of your lying alone. 590

NARCISSA.

What d'ye mean?

YOUNG WORTHY.

To marry you tomorrow, madam.

NARCISSA.

Marry me! Who put that in your head?

YOUNG WORTHY.

Some small encouragement which my hopes have formed, madam. 595

NARCISSA.

Hopes! Oh, insolence! If it once comes to that I don't question but you have been familiar with me in your imagination. Marry you! What, lie in a naked bed with you! Trembling by your side, like a tame lamb for sacrifice![d] D'ye think I can be moved to love a man, to kiss him, toy with him, and so forth! 600

YOUNG WORTHY. (*Aside.*)

Egad, I find nothing but downright impudence will do with her.—No madam, 'tis the man must kiss and toy with you, and so forth! Come my dear angel, pronounce the joyful word and draw the scene of my eternal happiness. Ah! methinks I'm there already, eager and impatient of approaching bliss! Just laid within the bridal bed, our friends retired, the curtains close drawn around us, no light but Celia's eyes, no noise but her soft trembling words and broken sighs that plead in vain for mercy. And now a trickling tear steals down her glowing cheek, which tells the rushing lover at length she yields—yet vows she'd rather die. But still submits to the unexperienced joy. (*Embracing her.*) 605 610 615

HILLARIA.

What raptures, Mr. Worthy?

YOUNG WORTHY.

Only the force of love in imagination, madam.

NARCISSA.

Oh Lord! Dear cousin! and madam! Let's be gone. 620

I vow he grows rude! Oh, for Heaven's sake! I shan't shake off my fright these ten days. Oh Lord! I will not stay.—Be gone! For I declare I loathe the sight of you. (*Exit.*)

YOUNG WORTHY.

I hope you'll stand my friend, madam. 625

HILLARIA.

I'll get her into the garden after dinner.

Exeunt [Hillaria and Amanda].

YOUNG WORTHY.

I find there's nothing to be done with my lady before company; 'tis a strange affected piece. But there's no fault in her thousand pound a year, and that's the lodestone that attracts my heart. The wise and grave may tell us of strange chimeras called virtues in a woman and that they alone are the best dowry, but faith, we younger brothers are of another mind. 630

Women are changed from what they were of old; 635
Therefore, let lovers still* this maxim hold:
She's only worth that brings her weight in gold.

Exit.

Act II, scene i. A garden belonging
to Sir William Wisewoud's house.

Enter Narcissa, Hillaria, and Sir Novelty Fashion.

HILLARIA.

Oh for Heaven's sake! No more of this gallantry, Sir Novelty, for I know you say the same to every woman you see.

SIR NOVELTY.

Everyone that sees you, madam, must say the same. Your beauty, like the rack, forces every beholder to confess his crime—of daring to adore you. 5

NARCISSA. [*Aside.*]

Oh! I han't patience to hear all this! If he be blind, I'll open his eyes.—I vow, Sir Novelty, you men of amour are strange creatures. You think no woman worth your while unless you walk over a rival's ruin to her heart. I know nothing has encouraged your passion to my cousin more than her engagement to Mr. Worthy. 10

HILLARIA. (*Aside.*)

Poor creature, now is she angry she han't the 15
address of a fop I nauseate!

SIR NOVELTY.

Oh madam, as to that, I hope the lady will easily
distinguish the sincerity of her adorers. Though I
must allow Mr. Worthy is infinitely the handsomer
person! 20

NARCISSA.

Oh! fie Sir Novelty, make not such a preposterous
comparison!

SIR NOVELTY.

Oh Ged, madam, there is no comparison!

NARCISSA.

Pardon me, sir, he's an unpolished animal!

SIR NOVELTY.

Why, does your ladyship really think me tolerable? 25

HILLARIA. (*Aside.*)

So! she has snapped his heart already.

SIR NOVELTY.

Pray madam, how do I look today? What, cursedly,
I'll warrant, with a more hellish complexion than a
stale actress at a rehearsal.ᵉ I don't know, madam.
'Tis true: the Town* does talk of me, indeed. But the 30
devil take me, in my mind I am a very ugly fellow!

NARCISSA.

Now you are too severe, Sir Novelty!

SIR NOVELTY.

Not I, burn me. For Heaven's sake, deal freely with
me, madam, and if you can, tell me—one tolerable
thing about me. 35

HILLARIA. (*Aside.*)

'Twould pose me, I'm sure.

NARCISSA.

Oh! Sir Novelty, this is unanswerable. 'Tis hard to
know the brightest part of a diamond.

SIR NOVELTY.

You'll make me blush, stop my vitals, madam.
(*Aside.*) Egad, I always said she was a woman of 40
sense. Strike me dumb, I am in love with her. I'll
try her farther.—But madam, is it possible I may
vie with Mr. Worthy? Not that he is any rival of
mine, madam, for I can assure you my inclinations
lie where, perhaps, your ladyship little thinks. 45

HILLARIA. (*Aside.*)

So! now I am rid of him.

SIR NOVELTY.

But pray tell me, madam, for I really love a severe
critic, I am sure you must believe he has a more
happy genius in dress. For my part, I am but a
sloven. 50

NARCISSA.

He a genius! Unsufferable! Why he dresses worse
than a captain of the militia. But you, Sir Novelty,
are a true original, the very pink of fashion. I'll
warrant there's not a milliner in Town but has got
an estate by you. 55

SIR NOVELTY.

I must confess, madam, I am for doing good to
my country. For you see this suit, madam. I
suppose you are not ignorant what a hard time the
ribbon-weavers have had since the late mourning.⁶
Now my design is to set the poor rogues up again 60
by recommending this sort of trimming. The fancy
is pretty well for second mourning.⁷ By the way,
madam, I had fifteen hundred guineas laid in my
hand as a gratuity to encourage it, but egad, I
refused them, being too well acquainted with the 65
consequence of taking a bribe in a national
concern!

HILLARIA.

A very charitable fashion, indeed, Sir Novelty! But
how if it should not take?

NARCISSA.

Ridiculous! Take! I warrant you in a week the 70
whole Town will have it, though perhaps Mr.
Worthy will be one of the last of 'em. He's a mere
valet de chambre to all fashion and never is in any
till his betters have left them off.

SIR NOVELTY.

Nay Ged, now I must laugh, for the devil take me 75
if I did not meet him not above a fortnight ago in
a coat with buttons no bigger than nutmegs.

HILLARIA.

There, I must confess, you outdo him, Sir Novelty.

SIR NOVELTY.

Oh dear madam, why, mine are not above three
inches diameter. 80

---

6 mourning] following the death of Queen Mary in 1694
7 second mourning] After full mourning, some color was
allowed.

HILLARIA.

But methinks, Sir Novelty, your sleeve is a little too extravagant.

SIR NOVELTY.

Nay madam, there you wrong me. Mine does but just reach my knuckles, but my Lord Overdo's covers his diamond ring.   85

HILLARIA.

Nay I confess, the fashion may be very useful to you gentlemen that make campaigns, for should you unfortunately lose an arm or so that sleeve might be very convenient to hide the defect on't.

SIR NOVELTY. (*Hiding his hand in his sleeve.*)

Hah! I think your ladyship's in the right on't, madam.   90

NARCISSA.

Oh, such an air! So becoming a negligence! Upon my soul, Sir Novelty, you'll be the envy of the beau monde!

HILLARIA.

Mr. Worthy! A good fancy were thrown away upon   95
him! But you, sir, are an ornament to your clothes.

SIR NOVELTY.

Then your ladyship really thinks they are—*bien entendus*!8

HILLARIA.

À mervielle, monsieur!

SIR NOVELTY. [*Aside.*]

She has almost as much wit as her cousin.—I must   100
confess, madam, this coat has had a universal approbation. For this morning I had all the eminent tailors about Town at my levee earnestly petitioning for the first measure of it. Now madam, if you thought 'twould oblige Mr. Worthy,   105
I would let his tailor have it before any of 'em.

NARCISSA.

See here he comes, and the deuce take me, I think 'twould be a great piece of good nature, for I declare he looks as rough as a Dutch corporal.9 Prithee Sir Novelty, let's laugh at him!   110

---

8 *bien entendus*] in good taste
9 rough as a Dutch corporal] The English often stereo-
    typed the Dutch as unkempt, a portrait that here takes
    on connotations of resentment, for William III had
    brought soldiers with him from his native Netherlands.

SIR NOVELTY.

Oh Ged no, madam, that were too cruel. Why you know he can't help it. Let's take no notice of him.

HILLARIA. (*Aside.*)

Wretched coxcomb.

Enter Elder Worthy.

ELDER WORTHY. [*Aside.*]

I find my resolution is but vain. My feet have brought me hither 'gainst my will. But sure I can   115
command my tongue, which I'll bite off ere it shall seek a reconciliation. Still so familiar there! But 'tis no matter. I'll try if I can wear indifference and seem as careless in my love as she is of her honor, which she can never truly know the worth of while   120
she persists to let a fool thus play with it.—Ladies, your humble servant.

HILLARIA. (*Aside.*)

Now can't I forbear fretting his spleen a little.— Oh Mr. Worthy, we are admiring Sir Novelty and his new suit. Did you ever see so sweet a fancy?   125
He is as full of variety as a good play.

ELDER WORTHY.

He's a very pleasant comedy indeed, madam, and dressed with a great deal of good satire and no doubt may oblige both the stage and the Town, especially the ladies.   130

HILLARIA. (*Aside.*)

So! There's for me.

SIR NOVELTY.

Oh Ged! Nay prithee, Tom, you know my humor.* Ladies! Stop my vitals! I don't believe there are five hundred in Town that ever took any notice of me.

ELDER WORTHY.

Oh sir, there are some that take so much notice   135
of you that the Town takes notice of them for't.

HILLARIA. (*Aside.*)

It works rarely.

SIR NOVELTY.

How, of them, Tom, upon my account? Oh Ged, I would not be the ruin of any lady's reputation for the world. Stop my vitals, I am very sorry for't.   140
Prithee, name but one that has a favorable thought of me, and to convince you that I have no design upon her I'll instantly visit her in an unpowdered periwig.

ELDER WORTHY.

Nay, she I mean is a woman of sense too.   145

SIR NOVELTY.

Faugh! Prithee, pox, don't banter me! 'Tis
impossible! What can she see in me?

ELDER WORTHY.

Oh, a thousand taking qualities! This lady will
inform you. (*Pulls him.*) Come, I'll introduce you.

SIR NOVELTY.

Oh Ged, no! Prithee! Hark you in your ear! I am off   150
of her! Damn me, if I be not! I am, stop my vitals!

ELDER WORTHY. (*Aside.*)

Wretched rogue!—Pshaw! no matter, I'll reconcile
you.—Come, come, madam.

HILLARIA.

Sir!

ELDER WORTHY.

This gentleman humbly begs to kiss your hands.   155

HILLARIA.

He needs not your recommendation, sir.

ELDER WORTHY.

True! A fool recommends himself to your sex, and
that's the reason men of common sense live
unmarried.

HILLARIA.

A fool without jealousy is better than a wit with   160
ill nature.

ELDER WORTHY.

A friendly office, seeing your fault is ill nature.

HILLARIA.

Believing more than we have is pitiful.—You know
I hate this wretch, loathe, and scorn him.

ELDER WORTHY.

Fools have a secret art of pleasing women. If he   165
did not delight you, you would not hazard your
reputation by encouraging his love.

HILLARIA.

Dares he wrong my reputation?

ELDER WORTHY.

He need not. The world will do it for him while
you keep him company.   170

HILLARIA.

I dare answer it to the world.

ELDER WORTHY.

Then why not to me?

HILLARIA.

To satisfy you were a fondness* I never should
forgive myself.

ELDER WORTHY.

To persist in it is what I'll ne'er forgive.   175

HILLARIA.

Insolence! Is it come to this? Never see me more.

ELDER WORTHY. (*As Hillaria is going off.*)

I have lost the sight of you already. There hangs a
cloud of folly between you and the woman I once
thought you.

Enter Young Worthy.

YOUNG WORTHY.

What to ourselves in passion we propose,   180
   The passion ceasing, does the purpose lose.
Madam, therefore, pray let me engage you to stay
a little till your fury^f is over, that you may see
whether you have reason to be angry or no.

SIR NOVELTY. (*To Narcissa.*)

Pray madam, who is that gentleman?   185

NARCISSA.

Mr. Worthy's brother, sir, a gentleman of no mean
parts,* I can assure you.

SIR NOVELTY.

I don't doubt it, madam. He has a very good
walk.[10]

[Narcissa and Sir Novelty go off.]

HILLARIA.

To be jealous of me with a fool is an affront to   190
my understanding.

YOUNG WORTHY.

Tamely to resign your reputation to the merciless
vanity of a fool were no proof of his love.

HILLARIA.

'Tis questioning my conduct.

YOUNG WORTHY.

Why, you let him kiss your hand last night before   195
his face.

HILLARIA.

The fool diverted me, and I gave him my hand as

---

10 The 1721 edition changes "walk" to "periwig," reflecting, perhaps, Cibber's sense of how closely Sir Novelty
had come to be associated with his trademark hairpiece.

I would lend my money, fan, or handkerchief to a
legerdemain that I might see him play all his tricks
over.   200

YOUNG WORTHY.

Oh madam, no juggler is so deceitful as a fop, for
while you look his folly in the face, he steals away
your reputation with more ease than the other
picks your pocket.

HILLARIA.

Some fools indeed are dangerous.   205

YOUNG WORTHY.

I grant you your design is only to laugh at him.
But that's more than he finds out. Therefore, you
must expect he will tell the world another story,
and 'tis ten to one but the consequence makes you
repent of your curiosity.   210

HILLARIA.

You speak like an oracle. I tremble at the thoughts
on't.

YOUNG WORTHY.

Here's one shall reconcile your fears.—Brother, I
have done your business. Hillaria is convinced of
her indiscretion and has a pardon ready for your   215
asking it.

ELDER WORTHY.

She's the criminal. I have no occasion for it.

YOUNG WORTHY.

See, she comes toward you. Give her a civil word
at least.

HILLARIA.

Mr. Worthy, I'll not be behindhand in the acknow-   220
ledgment I owe you. I freely confess my folly and
forgive your harsh construction of it. Nay, I'll not
condemn your want* of good nature in not
endeavoring (as your brother has done) by mild
arguments to convince me of my error.   225

ELDER WORTHY.

Now you vanquish me! I blush to be outdone in
generous love! I am your slave, dispose of me as
you please.

HILLARIA.

No more. From this hour be you the master of my
actions and my heart.   230

ELDER WORTHY.

This goodness gives you the power, and I obey
with pleasure.

YOUNG WORTHY.

So! I find I han't preached to no purpose! Well,
madam, if you find him guilty of love, e'en let
tomorrow be his execution day. Make a husband   235
of him, and there's the extent of Love's law.

ELDER WORTHY.

Brother, I am indebted to you.

YOUNG WORTHY.

Well, I'll give you a discharge, if you will but leave
me but half an hour in private with that lady.

HILLARIA.

How will you get rid of Sir Novelty?   240

YOUNG WORTHY.

I'll warrant you, leave him to me.

HILLARIA.

Come Mr. Worthy, as we walk, I'll inform you how
I intend to sacrifice that wretch to your laughter.

ELDER WORTHY.

Not, madam, that I want revenge on so
contemptible a creature. But I think you owe this   245
justice to yourself, to let him see (if possible) you
never took him for any other than what he really
is.

YOUNG WORTHY.

Well! Pox of your politicks. Prithee consult of 'em
within.   250

HILLARIA.

We'll obey you, sir.

Exeunt Elder Worthy and Hillaria.

YOUNG WORTHY.

Pray madam, give me leave to beg a word in
private with you. (*To Sir Novelty, who is taking
snuff.*) Sir, if you please—

SIR NOVELTY. (*Offering his box.*)

Aye sir, with all my heart.   255

YOUNG WORTHY.

Sir—

SIR NOVELTY.

Nay, 'tis right, I'll assure you.

YOUNG WORTHY.

Aye, sir. But now the lady would be alone.

SIR NOVELTY.

Sir!

YOUNG WORTHY.

The lady would be alone, sir.   260

SIR NOVELTY.

I don't hear her say any such thing.

YOUNG WORTHY.

Then I tell you so, and I would advise you to believe me.

SIR NOVELTY.

I shall not take your advice, sir. But if you really think the lady would be alone, why—you had best leave her. 265

YOUNG WORTHY.

In short, sir, your company is very unseasonable at present.

SIR NOVELTY.

I can tell you, sir, if you have no more wit than manners, the lady will be but scurvily entertained. 270

NARCISSA.

Oh fie, gentlemen, no quarreling before a woman, I beseech you. Pray let me know the business.

SIR NOVELTY.

My business is love, madam.

NARCISSA.

And yours, sir?

YOUNG WORTHY.

What I hope you are no stranger to, madam. As for that spark, you need take no care of him, for if he stays much longer, I will do his business myself. 275

NARCISSA. [Aside.]

Well I vow, love's a pleasant thing when the men come to cutting of throats once. Oh Gad! I'd fain have them fight a little. Methinks, Narcissa would sound so great in an expiring lover's mouth. Well, I am resolved Sir Novelty shall not go yet, for I will have the pleasure of hearing myself praised a little, though I don't marry this month for't.— Come gentlemen, since you both say love's your business, e'en plead for yourselves, and he that speaks the greater passion shall have the fairest return. 280 285

YOUNG WORTHY. [Aside.]

Oh the devil! Now is she rapt with the hopes of a little flattery. There's no remedy but patience. S'death,* what a piece have I to work upon! 290

NARCISSA.

Come, gentlemen, one at a time. Sir Novelty, what have you to say to me?

SIR NOVELTY.

In the first place, madam, I was the first person in England that was complimented with the name of Beau which is a title I prefer before Right Honourable, for that may be inherited, but this I extorted from the whole nation by my surprising mien and unexampled gallantry. 295 300

NARCISSA.

So, sir!

SIR NOVELTY.

Then another thing, madam. It has been observed that I have been eminently successful in those fashions I have recommended to the Town, and I don't question but this very suit will raise as many ribbon-weavers as ever the clipping* or melting trade did goldsmiths. 305

NARCISSA. [Aside.]

Pish! What does the fool mean? He says nothing of me yet.

SIR NOVELTY.

In short, madam, the cravat-string, the garter, the sword knot, the centurine, the bardash,[11] the steenkirk,* the large button, the long sleeve, the plume, and full peruke were all created, cried down, or revived by me. In a word, madam, there has never been anything particularly taking or agreeable for these ten years past, but your humble servant was the author of it. 310 315

YOUNG WORTHY. [Aside.]

Where the devil will this end?

NARCISSA.

This is all extravagant, Sir Novelty, but what have you to say to me, sir? 320

SIR NOVELTY.

I'll come to you presently, madam, I have just done. Then you must know, my coach and equipage are as well known as myself. And since the conveniency of two playhouses,[12] I have a better opportunity of showing them. For between every act—whisk—I am gone from one to th'other. 325

---

11 centurine … bardash] belt and fringed sash, respectively
12 two playhouses] Drury Lane had served as London's only theater from 1682 to 1695 when a second company opened Lincoln's Inn Fields under the management of Thomas Betterton.

Oh! what pleasure 'tis at a good play to go out before half an act's done!

NARCISSA.

Why at a good play?

SIR NOVELTY.

Oh madam, it looks particular and gives the whole audience an opportunity of turning upon me at once. Then do they conclude I have some extraordinary business or a fine woman to go to at least. And then again, it shows my contempt of what the dull Town think their chiefest diversion. But if I do stay a play out, I always set with my back to the stage.

NARCISSA.

Why so, sir?

SIR NOVELTY.

Then everybody will imagine I have been tired with it before or that I am jealous who talks to who in the King's box. And thus, madam, do I take more pains to preserve a public reputation than ever any lady took after the smallpox to recover her complexion.

NARCISSA.

Well, but to the point. What have you to say to me, Sir Novelty?

YOUNG WORTHY. [Aside.]

Now does she expect some compliment shall outflatter her glass.*

SIR NOVELTY.

To you, madam? Why, I have been saying all this to you.

NARCISSA.

To what end, sir?

SIR NOVELTY.

Why, all this have I done for your sake.

NARCISSA.

What kindness is it to me?

SIR NOVELTY.

Why madam, don't you think it more glory to be beloved by one eminently particular person whom all the Town knows and talks of than to be adored by five hundred dull souls that have lived incognito?

NARCISSA.

That, I must confess, is a prevailing argument, but still you han't told me why you love me.

YOUNG WORTHY.

That's a task he has left for me, madam.

SIR NOVELTY.

'Tis a province I never undertake, I must confess. I think 'tis sufficient, if I tell a lady why she should love me.

NARCISSA. [Aside.]

Hang him! He's too conceited. He's so in love with himself, he won't allow a woman the bare comfort of a cold compliment.—Well, Mr. Worthy.

YOUNG WORTHY.

Why madam, I have observed several particular qualities in your ladyship that I have perfectly adored you for: (*What he speaks, she imitates in dumb show.*) as, the majestic toss of your head, your obliging bowed curtsy, your satirical smile, your blushing laugh, your demure look, the careless tie of your hood, the genteel flirt of your fan, the designed accident in your letting fall, and your agreeable manner of receiving it from him that takes it up.

They both offer to take up her fan and in striving, Young Worthy pushes Sir Novelty on his back.

SIR NOVELTY. (*Adjusting himself.*)

I hope your ladyship will excuse my disorder, madam.

Enter a footman to Sir Novelty.

How now!

FOOTMAN.

Oh sir! Mrs.* Flareit—

SIR NOVELTY.

Hah! Speak lower. What of her?

FOOTMAN.

By some unlucky accident has discovered your being here and raves like a madwoman. She's at your lodging, sir, and had broke you above forty pounds worth of china before I came away; she talked of following hither; and if you don't make haste, I'm afraid will be here before you can get through the house, sir.

SIR NOVELTY. [Aside.]

This woman is certainly the Devil. Her jealousy is implacable. I must get rid of her, though I give her more for a separate maintenance than her conscience demanded for a settlement before enjoyment.—See the coach ready, and if you meet her, be sure you stop her with some pretended business till I am got away from hence.—Madam, I ask your ladyship ten thousand pardons. There's a person of quality* expects me at my lodging upon extraordinary business.

NARCISSA.

What, will you leave us, Sir Novelty?

SIR NOVELTY.

As unwillingly as the soul the body. But this is an irresistable occasion! Madam, your most devoted slave.—Sir, your most humble servant.—Madam, I kiss your hands.

Young Worthy sees him to the door.

Oh Ged, no farther, dear sir, upon my soul I won't stir if you do. (*Exit.*)

YOUNG WORTHY.

Nay then, sir, your humble servant. So, this was a lucky deliverance.

NARCISSA.

I overheard the business. You see, Mr. Worthy, a man must be a slave to a mistress sometimes as well as a wife. Yet all can't persuade your sex to a favorable opinion of poor marriage.

YOUNG WORTHY.

I long, madam, for an opportunity to convince you of your error. And therefore, give me leave to hope tomorrow you will free me from the pain of farther expectation and make an husband of me. Come, I'll spare your blushes and believe I have already named the day.

NARCISSA.

Had not we better consider a little?

YOUNG WORTHY.

No, let's avoid consideration. 'Tis an enemy both to love and courage. They that consider much live to be old bachelors and young fighters. No! no! we shall have time enough to consider after marriage. But why are you so serious, madam?

NARCISSA.

Not but I do consent tomorrow shall be the day, Mr. Worthy, but I'm afraid you have not loved me long enough to make our marriage be the Town talk. For 'tis the fashion now to be the Town talk,

and you know one had as good be out of the world as out of the fashion.

YOUNG WORTHY.

I don't know, madam, what you call Town talk, but it has been in the newsletters above a fortnight ago that we were already married. Beside, the last song I made of you has been sung at the music-meeting, and you may imagine, madam, I took no little care to let the ladies and the beaux know who 'twas made on.

NARCISSA.

Well, and what said the ladies?

YOUNG WORTHY.

What was most observable, madam, was that, while it was singing, my Lady Manlove went out in a great passion.

NARCISSA.

Poor jealous animal! On my conscience that charitable creature has such a fund of kind compliance for all young fellows whose love lies dead upon their hands that she has been as great a hindrance to us virtuous women as ever the Bank of England was to the City* goldsmiths.[13]

YOUNG WORTHY.

The reason of that is, madam, because you virtuous ladies pay no interest. I must confess the principal, our health, a little securer with you.

NARCISSA.

Well. And is not that advantage worth entering into bonds for? Not but I vow we virtuous devils do love to insult a little, and to say truth, it looks too credulous and easy in a woman to encourage a man before he has sighed himself to a skeleton.

YOUNG WORTHY.

But Heaven be thanked, we are pretty even with you in the end, for the longer you hold us off before marriage the sooner we fall off after it.

NARCISSA.

What, then you take marriage to be a kind of Jesuit's powder* that infallibly cures the fever of love?

---

13 Bank of England ... goldsmiths] The Bank of England, established in 1694, competed with private firms, frequently headed by goldsmiths, in the exchange of money and credit.

YOUNG WORTHY.

'Tis indeed a Jesuit's powder, for the priests first
invented it and only abstained from it because they
knew it had a bitter taste, then gilded it over with
a pretended blessing and so palmed it upon the 465
unthinking laity.

NARCISSA.

Prithee, don't screw your wit beyond the compass
of good manners. D'ye think I shall be tuned to
matrimony by your railing against it? If you have
so little stomach to it, I'll ev'n make you fast a 470
week longer.

YOUNG WORTHY.

Aye, but let me tell you, madam, 'tis no policy to
keep a lover at a thin diet in hopes to raise his
appetite on the wedding night, for then

> We come like starving beggars to a feast, 475
> Where, unconfined, we feed with eager haste,
> Till each repeated morsel palls the taste.

> Marriage gives prodigals a boundless treasure,
> Who squander that which might be lasting
>   pleasure,
> And women think they ne'er have over measure. 480

[Exeunt.]

Act III, [scene i]. Sir William Wisewoud's house.

Enter Amanda and Hillaria, meeting.

AMANDA.

My dear, I have news for you.

HILLARIA.

I guess at it and would be fain satisfied of the
particulars. Your husband is returned and, I hear,
knows nothing of your being alive. Young Worthy
has told me of your design upon him. 5

AMANDA.

'Tis that I wanted your advice in. What think you
of it?

HILLARIA.

Oh, I admire it. Next to forgetting your husband,
'tis the best counsel was ever given you, for under
the disguise of mistress you may now take a fair 10
advantage of indulging your love. And the little
experience you have had of it already has been just
enough not to let you be afraid of a man.

AMANDA.

Will you never leave your mad humor?*

HILLARIA.

Not till my youth leaves me. Why should women 15
affect ignorance among themselves? When we
converse* with men, indeed, modesty and good
breeding oblige us not to understand what
sometimes we can't help thinking of.

AMANDA.

Nay, I don't think the worse of you for what you 20
say. For 'tis observed that a bragging lover and an
over shy lady are the farthest from what they would
seem: the one is as seldom known to receive a favor
as the other to resist an opportunity.

HILLARIA.

Most women have a wrong sense of modesty, as 25
some men of courage. If you don't fight with all
you meet or run from all you see, you are
presently* thought a coward or an ill woman.

AMANDA.

You say true, and 'tis as hard a matter nowadays
for a woman to know how to converse with men 30
as for a man to know when to draw his sword. For
many times both sexes are apt to overact their
parts. To me the rules of virtue have been ever
sacred, and I am loath to break 'em by an
unadvised understanding.ᵍ Therefore dear Hillaria, 35
help me, for I am at a loss. Can I justify, think you,
my intended design upon my husband?

HILLARIA.

As how, prithee?

AMANDA.

Why, if I court and conquer him as a mistress, am
not I accessary to his violating the bonds of 40
marriage? For though I am his wife, yet while he
loves me not as such, I encourage an unlawful
passion. And though the act be safe, yet his intent
is criminal. How can I answer this?

HILLARIA.

Very easily, for if he don't intrigue with you, he will 45
with somebody else in the meantime, and I think
you have as much right to his remains as any one.

AMANDA.

Aye, but I am assured the love he will pretend to
me is vicious. And 'tis uncertain that I shall prevent
his doing worse elsewhere. 50

HILLARIA.

'Tis true, a certain ill ought not to be done for an uncertain good. But then again, of two evils, choose the least. And sure 'tis less criminal to let him love you as a mistress than to let him hate you as a wife. If you succeed, I suppose you will easily 55 forgive your guilt in the undertaking.

AMANDA.

To say truth, I find no argument yet strong enough to conquer my inclination to it. But is there no danger, think you, of his knowing me?

HILLARIA.

Not the least, in my opinion. In the first place, he 60 confidently believes you are dead. Then he has not seen you these eight or ten years. Besides, you were not above sixteen when he left you. This, with the alteration the smallpox have made in you (though not for the worse), I think are sufficient disguises 65 to secure you from his knowledge.

AMANDA.

Nay, and to this I may add the considerable amendment of my fortune, for when he left me, I had only my bare jointure for a subsistence. Beside my strange manner of receiving him. 70

HILLARIA.

That's what I would fain be acquainted with.

AMANDA.

I expect further instructions from Young Worthy every moment. Then you shall know all, my dear.

HILLARIA.

Nay, he will do you no small service. For a thief is the best thief-catcher. 75

Enter a servant to Amanda.

SERVANT.

Madam, your servant is below, who says Young Mr. Worthy's man waits at your lodgings with earnest business from his master.

AMANDA.

'Tis well.

[Exit servant.]

Come my dear, I must have your assistance too. 80

HILLARIA.

With all my heart. I love to be at the bottom of a secret. For they say the confidant of any amour has sometimes more pleasure in the observation than the parties concerned in the enjoyment. But methinks you don't look with a good heart upon 85 the business.

AMANDA.

I can't help a little concern in a business of such moment. For though my reason tells me my design must prosper, yet my fears say 'twere happiness too great. Oh! to reclaim the man I'm bound by 90 Heaven to love, to expose the folly of a roving mind in pleasing him with what he seemed to loathe were such a sweet revenge for slighted love, so vast a triumph of rewarded constancy, as might persuade the looser part of womankind ev'n to 95 forsake themselves and fall in love with virtue.

Re-enter the servant to Hillaria.

SERVANT.

Sir Novelty Fashion is below in his coach, madam, and enquires for your ladyship or Madam Narcissa.

HILLARIA.

You know my cousin is gone out with my Lady Tattle-tongue. I hope you did not tell him I was 100 within!

SERVANT.

No madam, I did not know if your ladyship would be spoke with and therefore came to see.

HILLARIA.

Then tell him I went with her.

SERVANT.

I shall, madam. (*Exit.*) 105

HILLARIA.

You must know, my dear, I have sent to that fury, Mrs. Flareit, whom this Sir Novelty keeps,* and have stung her to some purpose with an account of his passion for my cousin. I owed him a quarrel for that he made between Mr. Worthy and me, and 110 I hope her jealousy will severely revenge it. Therefore, I sent my cousin out of the way because, unknown to her, her name is at the bottom of my design. Here he comes. Prithee my dear, let's go down the back stairs and take coach 115 from the garden.

Exeunt Amanda and Hillaria. Re-enter the servant conducting Sir Novelty.

SIR NOVELTY.

Both the ladies abroad, say you? Is Sir William within?

SERVANT.

Yes sir. If you please to walk in, I'll acquaint him that you expect him here.

SIR NOVELTY.

Do so, prithee.

[Exit servant.]

And in the meantime let me consider what I have to say to him. Hold! In the first place, his daughter is in love with me! Would I marry her? Noh! Demmit, 'tis mechanical to marry the woman you love. Men of quality* should always marry those they never saw. But I hear Young Worthy marries her tomorrow, which if I prevent not, will spoil my design upon her. Let me see—I have it! I'll persuade the old fellow that I would marry her myself, upon which he immediately rejects Young Worthy and gives me free access to her! Good! What follows upon that? Opportunity, importunity. Resistance, force, entreaty, persisting! Doubting, swearing, lying. Blushes, yielding, victory, pleasure!—indifference.—Oh, here he comes *in ordine ad*—14

Enter Sir William Wisewoud.

SIR WILLIAM.

Sir Novelty, your servant. Have you any commands for me, sir?

SIR NOVELTY.

I have some proposals to make, sir, concerning your happiness and my own, which perhaps will surprise you. In a word, sir, I am upon the very brink of matrimony.

SIR WILLIAM.

'Tis the best thing you can pursue, sir, considering you have a good estate.

SIR NOVELTY.

But whom do you think I intend to marry?

SIR WILLIAM.

I can't imagine. Dear sir, be brief, lest your delay

---

14 *in ordine ad*] perhaps short for, as MJ suggests, *in ordinem adducere*, to reduce to order

transport me into a crime I would avoid, which is impatience. Sir, pray go on.

SIR NOVELTY.

In fine, sir, 'tis to your very daughter, the fair Narcissa.

SIR WILLIAM.

Humph! Pray sir, how long have you had this in your head?

SIR NOVELTY.

Above these two hours, sir.

SIR WILLIAM.

Very good! then you han't slept upon't?

SIR NOVELTY.

No! nor shan't sleep for thinking on't. Did not I tell you I would surprise you?

SIR WILLIAM.

Oh, you have indeed, sir. I am amazed! I am amazed!

SIR NOVELTY.

Well sir, and what think you of my proposal?

SIR WILLIAM.

Why truly sir, I like it not. But if I did, 'tis now too late. My daughter is disposed of to a gentleman that she and I like very well. At present, sir, I have a little business. If this be all, your humble servant, I am in haste.

SIR NOVELTY. *[Aside.]*

Demme! What an insensible blockhead's this?— Hold, sir, d'ye hear? Is this all the acknowledgment you make for the honor I designed you?

SIR WILLIAM.

Why truly sir, 'tis an honor that I am not ambitious of. In plain terms, I do not like you for a son-in-law.

SIR NOVELTY.

Now you speak to the purpose, sir. But prithee, what are thy exceptions to me?

SIR WILLIAM.

Why, in the first place, sir, you have too great a passion for your own person to have any for your wife's. In the next place, you take such an extravagant care in the clothing your body that your understanding goes naked for't. Had I a son so dressed, I should take the liberty to call him an egregious fop.

SIR NOVELTY.

Egad, thou art a comical old gentleman, and I'll

tell thee a secret. Understand then, sir, from me, that all young fellows hate the name of fop as women do the name of whore. But egad, they both love the pleasure of being so. Nay faith, and 'tis as hard a matter for some men to be fops, as you call 'em, as 'tis for some women to be whores. 185

SIR WILLIAM.

That's pleasant, in faith. Can't any man be a fop or any woman be a whore that has a mind to't?

SIR NOVELTY.

No faith, sir. For let me tell you, 'tis not the coldness of my Lady Freelove's inclination but her age and wrinkles that won't let her cuckold her husband. 190 And again, 'tis not Sir John Wouldlook's aversion to dress but his want* of a fertile genius that won't let him look like a gentleman. Therefore, in vindication of all well-dressed gentlemen, I intend to write a play 195 where my chiefest character shall be a downright English booby that affects to be a beau without either genius or foreign education and to call it, in imitation of another famous comedy, *He Would if He Could*.[15] And now, I think, you are answered, sir. 200 Have you any exceptions to my birth or family, pray sir?

SIR WILLIAM.

Yes sir, I have. You seem to me the offspring of more than one man's labor. For certainly no less than a dancing, singing, and fencing-master with 205 a tailor, milliner, perfumer, peruke-maker, and a French valet de chambre could be at the begetting of you.

SIR NOVELTY.

All these have been at the finishing of me since I was made. 210

SIR WILLIAM.

That is, Heaven made you a man, and they have made a monster of you. And so, farewell to ye! (*Is going.*)

SIR NOVELTY.

Hark ye, sir, am I to expect no farther satisfaction in the proposals I made you? 215

SIR WILLIAM.

Sir, nothing makes a man lose himself like passion.

Now I presume you are young and consequently rash upon a disappointment. Therefore, to prevent any difference that may arise by repeating my refusal of your suit, I do not think it convenient 220 to hold any farther discourse with you.

SIR NOVELTY.

Nay faith, thou shall stay to hear a little more of my mind first.

SIR WILLIAM.

Since you press me, sir, I will rather bear than resist you. 225

SIR NOVELTY.

I doubt,* old gentleman, you have such a torrent of philosophy running through your pericranium that it has washed your brains away.

SIR WILLIAM.

Pray sir, why do you think so?

SIR NOVELTY.

Because you choose a beggarly, unaccountable sort 230 of younger brotherish rakehell for your son-in-law before a man of quality,* estate, good parts,* and breeding, demme.

SIR WILLIAM.

Truly sir, I know neither of the persons to whom these characters* belong. If you please to write their 235 names under 'em, perhaps I may tell you if they be like or no.

SIR NOVELTY.

Why then, in short, I would have been your son-in-law and you, it seems, prefer Young Worthy before me. Now are your eyes open? 240

SIR WILLIAM.

Had I been blind, sir, you might have been my son-in-law. And if you were not blind, you would not think that I design my daughter for Young Worthy. His brother, I think, may deserve her.

SIR NOVELTY.

Then you are not jealous of Young Worthy? Humph! 245

SIR WILLIAM.

No really, sir, nor of you neither.

SIR NOVELTY.

Give me thy hand. Thou art very happy, stop my vitals, for thou does not see that thou art blind. Not jealous of Young Worthy? Ha! Ha! How now!

Enter Sir Novelty's servant with a porter.

---

15 *He Would if He Could*] Sir Novelty's model is Sir George Etherege's *She Would if She Could* (1668).

SERVANT.

Sir, here's a porter with a letter for your honor.   250

PORTER.

I was ordered to give it into your own hands, sir,
and expect an answer.

SIR NOVELTY. (*Reads [aside]*.)

"Excuse, my dear Sir Novelty, the forced
indifference I have shown you and let me recompense your past sufferings with an hour's conversa-   255
tion, after the play, at Rosamond's Pond,[16] where
you will find an hearty welcome to the arms of your
Narcissa!" Unexpected happiness! The arms of your
Narcissa! Egad, and when I am there, I'll make
myself welcome. Faith, I did not think she was so far   260
gone neither! But I don't question, there are five
hundred more in her condition. I have a good mind
not to go, faith! Yet hang it, I will, though only to be
revenged of this old fellow! Nay, I'll have the
pleasure of making it public too. For I will give her   265
the music and draw all the Town to be witness of my
triumph! (*To the Porter.*) Where is the lady?

PORTER.

In a hackney coach at the corner of the street.

SIR NOVELTY.

Enough. Tell her I will certainly be there.

Exit Porter.

Well old gentleman, then you are resolved I shall   270
be no kin to you? Your daughter is disposed of.
Humph!

SIR WILLIAM.

You have your answer, sir. You shall be no kin to
me.

SIR NOVELTY.

Farewell, old philosophy. And d'ye hear, I would   275
advise you to study nothing but the art of patience.
You may have an unexpected occasion for it. Hark
you! Would not it nettle you damnably to hear my
son call you grandfather?

SIR WILLIAM.

Sir, notwithstanding this provocation, I am calm,   280
but were I like other men, a slave to passion, I
should not forbear calling you impertinent! How

---

[16] Rosamond's Pond] a pond in St. James's Park* named
after Henry II's mistress, Rosamond Clifford

I swell with rising vexation! (*Angrily.*) Leave me,
leave me, go, sir, go, get you out of my house.

SIR NOVELTY.

Oh, have a care of passion, dear Diogenes. Ha! ha!   285
ha! he!

SIR WILLIAM. (*Sighing.*)

So! At last I have conquered it.—Pray sir, oblige me
with your absence, (*Taking off his hat.*) I protest I am
tired with you. (*Submissively.*) Pray leave my house.

SIR NOVELTY.

Damn your house, your family, your ancestors,   290
your generation, and your eternal posterity. (*Exit.*)

SIR WILLIAM.

Ah! A fair riddance. How I bless myself that it was
not in this fool's power to provoke me beyond that
serenity of temper which a wise man ought to be
master of. How near are men to brutes when their   295
unruly passions break the bounds of reason. And
of all passions, anger is the most violent, which
often puts me in mind that admirable saying,
    He that strives not to stem his anger's tide
    Does a mad horse without a bridle ride.   300

Scene [ii]. St. James's Park.*

*Enter Young Worthy and Loveless as from the tavern,
Snap following.*

YOUNG WORTHY.

What a sweet evening 'tis.—Prithee Ned, let's walk
a little. Look how lovingly the trees are joined since
thou wert here, as if nature had designed this walk
for the private shelter of forbidden love.

Several crossing the stage.

Look, here are some for making use of the   5
conveniency.

LOVELESS.

But hark ye, friend, are the women as tame and
civil as they were before I left the Town? Can they
endure the smell of tobacco or vouchsafe a man a
word with a dirty cravat on?   10

YOUNG WORTHY.

Aye, that they will, for keeping* is almost out of
fashion. So that now an honest fellow with a
promising back need not fear a night's lodging for
bare good fellowship.

LOVELESS.

If whoring be so poorly encouraged, methinks the   15
women should turn honest* in their own defense.

YOUNG WORTHY.

Faith, I don't find there's a whore the less for it.
The pleasure of fornication is still the same. All the
difference is, lewdness is not so barefaced as
heretofore. Virtue is as much debased as our   20
money, for maidenheads are as scarce as our milled
half crowns and, faith, *Dei Gratia*[17] is as hard to
be found in a girl of sixteen as round the brims of
an old shilling.

LOVELESS.

Well I find, in spite of law and duty, the flesh will   25
get the better of the spirit. But I see no game yet.
Prithee Will, let's go and take t'other bumper to
enliven assurance that we may come downright to
the business.

YOUNG WORTHY.

No, no, what we have in our bellies already, by the   30
help of a little fresh air, will soon be in our
pericraniums and work us to a right pitch to taste
the pleasures of the night.

LOVELESS.

The day, thou mean'st. My day always breaks at
sunset. We wise fellows, that know the use of life,   35
know too that the moon lights men to more
pleasures than the sun. The Sun was meant for dull
souls of business and poor rogues that have a mind
to save candles.

YOUNG WORTHY.

Nay, the night was always a friend to pleasure, and   40
that made Diana run a-whoring by the light of her
own horns.[18]

LOVELESS.

Right. And prithee, what made Daphne run away
from Apollo, but that he wore so much daylight
about his ears?   45

YOUNG WORTHY.

Hah! Look out, Ned, there's the enemy before you!

---

17 *Dei Gratia*] "By the grace of God," inscribed after the
soverign's name on English coins

18 Diana run … horns] A reference to the Greek legend
of Endymion's seduction by Selene, goddess of the
moon, with which Diana was also associated; "horns"
are the ends of the crescent moon.

LOVELESS.

Why then, as Caesar said, Come follow me. (*Exit.*)

YOUNG WORTHY.

I hope 'tis his wife whom I desired to meet me here
that she might take a view of her soldier before she
new-mounted him. (*Exit.*)   50

Enter Mrs. Flareit and her maid.

MAID.

I wonder, madam, Sir Novelty don't come yet. I
am so afraid he should see Narcissa and find out
the trick of your letter.

MRS. FLAREIT.

No, no, Narcissa is out of the way. I am sure he
won't be long, for I heard the hautbois, as they   55
passed by me, mention his name. I suppose to
make the intrigue more fashionable he intends to
give me the music.

MAID.

Suppose he take you for Narcissa, what advantage
do you propose by it?   60

MRS. FLAREIT.

I shall then have a just occasion to quarrel with
him for his perfidiousness and so force his pocket
to make his peace with me. Beside, my jealousy
will not let me rest till I am revenged.

MAID.

Jealousy! why, I have often heard you say you   65
loathed him.

MRS. FLAREIT.

'Tis my pride, not love, that makes me jealous. For
though I don't love him, yet I am incensed to think
he dares love another.

MAID.

See madam, here he is and the music with him.   70

MRS. FLAREIT.

Put on your mask and leave me.

They mask. Enter Sir Novelty with the music.

SIR NOVELTY.

Here gentlemen, place yourselves on this spot and
pray oblige me with a trumpet sonata.

The music prepare to play.

This taking a man at his first word is a very new   75
way of preserving reputation, stop my vitals, nay

and a^h secure one too, for now may we enjoy and grow weary of one another before the Town can take any notice of us.

Flareit making towards him.

Hah! this must be she.—I suppose, madam, you are no stranger to the contents of this letter.

MRS. FLAREIT.

Dear sir, this place is too public for my acknowledgment. If you please to withdraw to a more private conveniency.

Exeunt [Sir Novelty, Mrs. Flareit, and maid]. The music prepare to play, and all sorts of people gather about it. Enter at one door Narcissa, Hillaria, Amanda, Elder Worthy, and Young Worthy; at another, Loveless and Snap, talking to masks. *

ELDER WORTHY.

What say you, ladies, shall we walk homewards? It begins to be dark.

YOUNG WORTHY.

Prithee don't be so impatient, it's light enough to hear the music, I'll warrant ye.

AMANDA.

Mr. Worthy, you promised me a sight I long for. Is Mr. Loveless among all those?

YOUNG WORTHY.

That's he, madam, a-surveying that masked lady.

AMANDA.

Hah! Is't possible! Methinks I read his vices in his person! Can he be insensible ev'n to the smart of pinching poverty? Pray sir, your hand. I find myself disordered. It troubles me to think I dare not speak to him after so long an absence.

YOUNG WORTHY.

Madam, your staying here may be dangerous. Therefore, let me advise you to go home and get all things in order to receive him. About an hour hence will be a convenient time to set my design a-going. Till when, let me beg you to have a little patience. Give me leave, madam, to see you to your coach.

AMANDA.

I'll not trouble you, sir. Yonder's my cousin Welbred. I'll beg his protection. (*Exit.*)

The music plays, after which Narcissa speaks.

NARCISSA.

I vow it's very fine, considering what dull souls our nation are. I find 'tis an harder matter to reform their manners than their government or religion.

ELDER WORTHY.

Since the one has been so happily accomplished, I know no reason why we should despair of the other. I hope in a little time to see our youth return from travel big with praises of their own country. But come, ladies, the music's done, I suppose. Shall we walk?

NARCISSA.

Time enough. Why, you have no taste of the true pleasure of the Park. I'll warrant you hate as much to ridicule others as to hear yourself praised. For my part, I think a little harmless railing's half the pleasure of one's life.

ELDER WORTHY.

I don't love to create myself enemies by observing the weakness of other people. I have more faults of my own than I know how to mend.

NARCISSA.

Protect me! How can you see such a medley of human stuffs as here is without venting your spleen? Why, look there now. Is not it comical to see that wretched creature there with her autumnal face, dressed in all the colors of the spring?

ELDER WORTHY.

Pray, who is she, madam?

NARCISSA.

A thing that won't believe herself out of date, though she was a known woman at the Restoration.

YOUNG WORTHY.

Oh! I know her. 'Tis Mrs.* Holdout, one that is proud of being an original of fashionable fornication and values herself mightily for being one of the first mistresses that ever kept her coach publicly in England.

HILLARIA.

Pray who's that impudent young fellow there?

ELDER WORTHY.

Oh, that's an eternal fan-tearer and a constant persecutor of womankind. He had a great misfortune lately.

NARCISSA.

Pray, what was it?

ELDER WORTHY.

Why, impudently presuming to cuckold a Dutch 140
officer, he had his fore-teeth kicked out.

OMNES.

Ha, ha, ha!

NARCISSA.

There's another too, Mr. Worthy. Do you know
him?

YOUNG WORTHY.

That's Beau Noisy, one that brags of favors from 145
my lady, though refused by her woman;* that sups
with my lord and borrows his club of his footman;
that beats the watch and is kicked by his
companions; that is one day at court and the next
in jail; that goes to church without religion, is 150
valiant without courage, witty without sense, and
drunk without measure.

ELDER WORTHY.

A very complete gentleman.

HILLARIA.

Prithee cousin, who's that over shy lady there that
won't seem to understand what that brisk young 155
fellow says to her?

NARCISSA.

Why, that's my Lady Slylove; that other
ceremonious gentleman is her lover. She is so over
modest that she makes a scruple of shifting herself
before her woman* but afterwards makes none of 160
doing it before her gallant.

YOUNG WORTHY.

Hang her, she's a jest to the whole Town, for
though she has been the mother of two by-blows,
endeavors to appear as ignorant in all company as
if she did not know the distinction of sexes. 165

NARCISSA.

Look, look! Mr. Worthy, I vow, there's the
Countess of Incog out of her dishabille, in a high
head, I protest!

YOUNG WORTHY.

'Tis as great a wonder to see her out of an hackney
coach as out of debt or— 170

NARCISSA.

Or out of countenance.

YOUNG WORTHY.

That, indeed, she seldom changes, for she is never
out of a mask and is so well known in't that when
she has a mind to be private she goes barefaced.

NARCISSA.

But come, cousin, now let's see what monsters the 175
next walk affords.

ELDER WORTHY.

With all my heart, 'tis in our way home.

YOUNG WORTHY.

Ladies, I must beg your pardon for a moment.
Yonder comes one I have a little business with. I'll
dispatch it immediately and follow you. 180

HILLARIA.

No, no, we'll stay for you.

NARCISSA.

You may if you please, cousin, but I suppose he
will hardly thank you for't.

HILLARIA.

What, then you conclude 'tis a woman's business
by his promising a quick dispatch? 185

YOUNG WORTHY.

Madam, in three minutes you shall know the
business. If it displease you, condemn me to an
eternal absence.

ELDER WORTHY.

Come madam, let me be his security.

NARCISSA.

I dare take your word, sir. 190

*Exeunt Elder Worthy, Hillaria, and Narcissa. Enter
Sly, servant to Young Worthy.*

YOUNG WORTHY.

Well! how go matters? Is she in a readiness to
receive him.

SLY.

To an hair, sir. Every servant has his cue and all
are impatient till the comedy begins.

YOUNG WORTHY.

Stand aside a little and let us watch our 195
opportunity.

SNAP. (*To a mask.*)

Enquire about half an hour hence for number two
at the Gridiron.[19]

MASK.

Tomorrow with all my heart, but tonight I am
engaged to the chaplain of Colonel Thunder's 200
regiment.

---

19 Gridiron] presumably an inn

SNAP.

What, will you leave me for a mutton chop? For
that's all he'll give you, I'm sure.

MASK.

You are mistaken, faith, he keeps* me.

SNAP.

Not to himself, I'll engage him. Yet he may too if   205
nobody likes you no better than I do. Hark you,
child, prithee, when was your smock washed?

MASK.

Why, dost thou pretend to fresh linen that never
wore a clean shirt but of thy mother's own
washing? (*Goes from him.*)   210

LOVELESS.

What, no adventure, no game, Snap?

SNAP.

None, none, sir. I can't prevail with any from the
point headcloths to the horse-guard whore.

LOVELESS.

What a pox! Sure the whores can't smell an empty
pocket.   215

SNAP.

No, no, that's certain, sir; they must see it in our
faces.

SLY. (*To Loveless.*)

My dear boy, how is't? Egad, I am glad thou art come
to Town. My lady expected you above an hour ago,
and I am overjoyed I ha' found thee. Come, come,   220
come along, she's impatient till she sees you.

SNAP.

'Odsbud,* sir, follow him, he takes you for another.

LOVELESS.

Egad, it looks with the face of an intrigue. I'll
humor him.—Well, what, shall we go now?

SLY.

Aye, aye, now it's pure and dark, you may go   225
undiscovered.

LOVELESS.

That's what I would do.

SLY.

'Odsheart,* she longs to see thee, and she is a
curious* fine creature, ye rogue! such eyes! such
lips! and such a tongue between 'em! Ah, the tip   230
of it will set a man's soul on fire!

LOVELESS. (*Aside.*)

The rogue makes[i] me impatient!

SLY.

Come, come, the key, the key, the key, you dear
rogue!

SNAP. (*Aside.*)

Oh Lord! the key, the key!   235

LOVELESS.

The key. Why sh-sh-sh-should yo-yo-you have it?

SLY.

Aye, aye! Quickly, give 's it!

LOVELESS.

Why, what the devil, sure I han't lost it. Oh no!
Gad, it is not there. What shall we do?

SLY.

'Oons,* ne'er stand fumbling. If you have lost it,   240
we must shoot the lock, I think.

LOVELESS.

Egad, and so we must, for I han't it.

SLY.

Come, come along, follow me.

LOVELESS.

Snap, stand by me, you dog.

SNAP.

Aye, aye, sir.   245

Exeunt Sly, Loveless, and Snap.

YOUNG WORTHY.

Ha! ha! The rogue managed him most dexterously.
How greedily he chopped at the bait? What the
event will be, Heaven knows! But thus far 'tis
pleasant. And since he is safe, I'll venture to divert
my company with the story. Poor Amanda, thou   250
well deservest a better husband. Thou wert never
wanting* in thy endeavors to reclaim him. And
faith, considering how a long despair has worn
thee,

'Twere pity now thy hopes should not succeed;   255
This new attempt is love's last shift indeed.

[*Exeunt.*]

Act IV, scene [i]. Continues.

*Enter two bullies and Sir William Wisewould
observing them.*

FIRST BULLY.

Damme Jack, let's after him, and fight him; 'tis not
to be put up.

SECOND BULLY.

No! Damn him! Nobody saw the affront, and what need we take notice of it?

FIRST BULLY.

Why that's true! But damme! I have much ado to forebear cutting his throat. 5

SIR WILLIAM.

Pray gentlemen, what's the matter? Why are you in such passion?

FIRST BULLY.

What's that to you, sir? What would you have?

SIR WILLIAM.

I hope, sir, a man may ask a civil question. 10

FIRST BULLY.

Damme, sir, we are men of honor. We dare answer any man.

SIR WILLIAM.

But why are you angry, gentlemen? Have you received any wrong?

SECOND BULLY.

We have been called rascals, sir, have had the lie* given and had like to have been kicked! 15

SIR WILLIAM.

But I hope you were not kicked, gentlemen.

SECOND BULLY.

How, sir! we kicked!

SIR WILLIAM.

Nor do I presume that you are rascals!

FIRST BULLY.

Blood and thunder! Sir, let any man say it that wears an head! We rascals! 20

SIR WILLIAM.

Very good! Since then you are not rascals, he rather was one who maliciously called you so. Pray take my advice, gentlemen. Never disturb yourselves for any ill your enemy says of you, for from an enemy the world will not believe it. Now you must know, gentlemen, that a flea bite is to me more offensive than the severest affront any man can offer me! 25

FIRST BULLY.

What, and so you would have us put it up! Damme, sir, don't preach cowardice to us. We are men of valor. You won't find us cowards, sir. 30

SECOND BULLY.

No, sir! We are no cowards, though you are.

FIRST BULLY.

Hang him. Let him alone. I see a coward in his face. 35

SIR WILLIAM.

If my face make any reflection, sir, 'tis against my will.

SECOND BULLY.

Prithee Tom, let's affront him and raise his spleen a little.

SIR WILLIAM.

Raise my spleen? That's more than any man could ever boast of. 40

FIRST BULLY.

You lie.*

SIR WILLIAM.

I am not angry yet; therefore, I do not lie, sir. Now one of us must lie. I do not lie. Ergo—

FIRST BULLY.

Damme, sir, have a care! Don't give me the lie. I shan't take it, sir. 45

SIR WILLIAM.

I need not, sir! You give it yourself.

FIRST BULLY.

Well sir, what then? If I make bold with myself, every old puppy shall not pretend to do it.

SIR WILLIAM.

Ha! ha! ha! ha! ha! 50

FIRST BULLY.

Damme, sir, what do you laugh at?

SIR WILLIAM.

To let you see that I am no puppy, sir, for puppies are brutes. Now brutes have not risibility. But I laugh; therefore, I am no puppy, ha! ha!

FIRST BULLY.

Blood and thunder, sir! Dare you fight? 55

SIR WILLIAM.

Not in cool blood, sir, and I confess 'tis impossible to make me angry.

SECOND BULLY.

I'll try that! Hark ye, don't you know you are a sniveling old cuckold?

SIR WILLIAM.

No, really, sir. 60

SECOND BULLY.

Why then I know you to be one.

SIR WILLIAM.

Look you, sir, my reason weighs this injury which is so light it will not raise my anger in the other scale.

FIRST BULLY.

'Oons!* What a tame old prig's this? I'll give you better weight then. I know who got all your children. 65

SIR WILLIAM.

Not so well as my wife, I presume. Now she tells me 'twas myself, and I believe her too.

FIRST BULLY.

She tells you so because the poor rogue that got 'em is not able to keep* 'em. 70

SIR WILLIAM.

Then my keeping them is charity.

FIRST BULLY.

Blood and thunder, sir, this is an affront to us, not to be angry after all these provocations. (*As they lay hold on him.*) Damme Jack, let's souse him in the canal. 75

Enter Elder Worthy, Young Worthy, Narcissa, and Hillaria.

YOUNG WORTHY.

S'death,* what's here? Sir William in the rogues hands that affronted the ladies.—Oh, forbear, forbear— (*Strikes them.*)

ELDER WORTHY.

So gentlemen, I thought you had fair warning before. Now you shall pay for't. 80

Enter three or four sentinels.

Hark you, honest soldiers, pray do me the favor to wash these rascals in the canal, and there's a guinea for your trouble.

BULLIES.

Damme, sir! We shall expect satisfaction.

Exeunt [sentinels] dragging the bullies.

SIR WILLIAM.

Oh dear gentlemen, I am obliged to you, for I was just going to the canal myself if you had not come as you did. 85

ELDER WORTHY.

Pray sir, what had you done to 'em?

SIR WILLIAM.

Why, hearing the music from my parlor window and being invited by the sweetness of the evening, I ev'n took a walk to see if I could meet with you, when the first objects that presented themselves were these bullies threatening to cut somebody's throat. Now I, endeavoring to allay their fury, occasioned their giving me scurrilous language. And finding they could not make me as angry as themselves, they offered* to fling me into the water. 90 95

ELDER WORTHY.

I am glad we stepped to your deliverance.

SIR WILLIAM.

Oh I thank you, gentlemen. I'll e'en go home and recover my fright. Good night, good night to you all. (*Exit.*) 100

ELDER WORTHY. (*To his servant.*)

Harry, see Sir William safe to his lodging.ʲ—Well ladies, I believe it's time for us to be walking too.

HILLARIA.

No, pray let me engage you to stay a little longer. Yonder comes Sir Novelty and his mistress in pursuance of the design I told you of. Pray have a little patience, and you will see the effect on't. 105

ELDER WORTHY.

With all my heart, madam.

They stand aside. Enter Sir Novelty, embracing Flareit, masked.

SIR NOVELTY.

Generous creature! This is an unexampled condescension to meet my passion with such early kindness.* Thus let me pay my soft acknowledgments. (*Kisses her hand.*) 110

HILLARIA.

You must know, he has mistaken her for another.

MRS. FLAREIT.

For Heaven's sake let me go. If Hillaria should be at home before me, I am ruined forever. 115

NARCISSA.

Hillaria! What does she mean?

SIR NOVELTY.

Narcissa's reputation shall be ever safe while my life and fortune can protect it.

NARCISSA.

Oh Gad, let me go. Does the impudent creature take my name upon her? I'll pull off her headcloths. 120

HILLARIA.

Oh fie! Cousin, what an ungenteel revenge would that be! Have a little patience.

NARCISSA.

Oh! I am in a flame. (*Throwing back her hoods.*)

MRS. FLAREIT.

But will you never see that common creature 125
Flareit more?

SIR NOVELTY.

Never! Never! Feed on such homely fare after so rich a banquet?

MRS. FLAREIT.

Nay, but you must hate her too.

SIR NOVELTY.

That I did long ago for her stinking breath.[k] 'Tis 130
true, I have been led away, but I detest a strumpet.
I am informed she keeps* a fellow under my nose,
and for that reason I would not make the
settlement I lately gave her some hopes of. But
e'en let her please herself, for now I am wholly 135
yours.

MRS. FLAREIT.

Oh, now you charm me, but will you love me ever?

SIR NOVELTY.

Will you be ever kind?*

MRS. FLAREIT.

Be sure you never see Flareit more.

SIR NOVELTY.

When I do, may this soft hand revenge my perjury. 140

MRS. FLAREIT.

So it shall, villain! (*Strikes him a box on the ear and unmasks.*)

OMNES.

Ha! ha! ha!

SIR NOVELTY.

Flareit, the devil!

MRS. FLAREIT.

What, will nothing but a maidenhead[l] go down
with you? Thou miserable, conceited wretch. 145
Faugh! My breath stinks, does it?[m] I'm a homely
puss! A strumpet, not worth your notice! Devil, I'll
be revenged.

SIR NOVELTY. (*Holding his cheek.*)

Damn your revenge, I'm sure I feel it.

NARCISSA.

Really Sir Novelty, I am obliged to you for your 150

kind thoughts of me and your extraordinary care
of my reputation.

SIR NOVELTY. [*Aside.*]

S'death,* she here! Exposed to half the Town! Well,
I must brazen it out however! (*Walks unconcerned.*)

MRS. FLAREIT.

What! No pretence! No evasion now! 155

SIR NOVELTY.

There's no occasion for any, madam.

MRS. FLAREIT.

Come, come, swear you knew me all this while.

SIR NOVELTY.

No faith, madam, I did not know you. For if I had,
you would not have found me so furious a lover.

MRS. FLAREIT.

Furies and hell! Dares the monster own his guilt? 160
This is beyond all sufferance! Thou wretch, thou
thing, thou animal, that I (to the everlasting
forfeiture of my sense and understanding) have
made a man. For till thou knewest me, 'twas
doubted if thou were of humankind. And dost 165
thou think I'll suffer such a worm as thee to turn
against me? No! When I do, may I be cursed to
thy embraces all my life and never know a joy
beyond thee.

SIR NOVELTY.

Why-wh-wh-what will your ladyship's fury do, 170
madam? (*Smiling.*)

MRS. FLAREIT.

Only change my lodging, sir.

SIR NOVELTY.

I shall keep mine, madam, that you may know
where to find me when your fury is over. You see
I am good-natured. (*Walks by her.*) 175

MRS. FLAREIT. (*Aside.*)

This bravery's affected: I know he loves me, and
I'll pierce him to the quick. I have yet a surer way
to fool him.

HILLARIA.

Methinks the knight bears it bravely.

NARCISSA.

I protest the lady weeps. 180

YOUNG WORTHY.

She knows what she does, I'll warrant you.

ELDER WORTHY.

Aye, aye, the fox is a better politician than the lion.

MRS. FLAREIT. (*Aside.*)

Now, woman. (*With tears in her eyes.*) Sir Novelty, pray sir, let me speak with you.

SIR NOVELTY.

Aye, madam.   185

MRS. FLAREIT.

Before we part (for I find I have irrecoverably lost your love), let me beg of you that from this hour you ne'er will see me more or make any new attempts to deceive my easy temper. For I find my nature's such, I shall believe you, though to my   190 utter ruin.

SIR NOVELTY. (*Aside.*)

Pray Heaven she be in earnest.

MRS. FLAREIT.

One thing more, sir. Since our first acquaintance you have received several letters from me. I hope you will be so much a gentleman as to let me have   195 'em again. Those I have of yours shall be returned tomorrow morning. And now sir, wishing you as much happiness in her you love as you once pretended I could give you, I take of you my everlasting leave. (*Is going.*) Farewell, and may your   200 next mistress love you till I hate you.

SIR NOVELTY. [*Aside.*]

So! Now must I seem to persuade her.—Nay, prithee my dear! Why do you struggle so? Whither would you go?

MRS. FLAREIT. (*Crying.*)

Pray sir, give me leave to pass, I can't bear to stay.   205

SIR NOVELTY.

What is't that frightens you?

MRS. FLAREIT.

Your barbarous usage. Pray let me go.

SIR NOVELTY.

Nay, if you are resolved, madam, I won't press you against your will. Your humble servant (*Leaves her.*) and a happy riddance, stop my vitals!   210

MRS. FLAREIT. (*Looking back.*)

Hah! not move to call me back! So unconcerned! Oh, I could tear my flesh, stab every feature in this dull, decaying face that wants* a charm to hold him! Damn him! I loathe him too! But shall my pride now fall from such an height and bear the   215 torture unrevenged? No, my very soul's on fire, and nothing but the villain's blood shall quench it.

(*Snatches Young Worthy's sword and runs at him.*)

Devil, have at thee.

YOUNG WORTHY.

Have a care, sir.   220

SIR NOVELTY. (*Draws and stands upon his guard.*)

Let her alone, gentlemen, I'll warrant you.

Young Worthy takes the sword from her and holds her.

MRS. FLAREIT.

Prevented. Oh! I shall choke with boiling gall. Oh! oh! uumh! Let me go. (*Raving.*) I'll have his blood, his blood, his blood!

SIR NOVELTY.

Let her come, let her come, gentlemen.   225

MRS. FLAREIT.

Death and vengeance, am I become his sport! He's pleased and smiles to see me rage the more! But he shall find no fiend in hell can match the fury of a disappointed woman! Scorned, slighted, dismissed without a parting pang! Oh torturing   230 thought! May all the racks mankind e'er gave our easy sex, neglected love, decaying beauty, and hot raging lust[n] light on me, if e'er I cease to be the eternal plague of his remaining life, nay after death,

When his, his black soul lies howling in   235
    despair,

I'd plunge to hell and be his torment there.

(*Exit in a fury.*)

ELDER WORTHY.

Sure Sir Novelty, you never loved this lady if you are so indifferent at parting.

SIR NOVELTY.

Why faith, Tom, to tell you the truth, her jealousy has been so very troublesome and expensive to me   240 of late that I have these three months sought an opportunity to leave her. But faith, I had always more respect to my life than to let her know it before.

HILLARIA.

Methinks, Sir Novelty, you had very little respect   245 to her life when you drew upon her.

SIR NOVELTY.

Why, what would you have had me done, madam? Complimented her with my naked bosom? No! no! Look ye, madam, if she had made any advances, I could have disarmed her in second at the very first   250

pass. But come, ladies, as we walk, I'll beg your
judgments in a particular nice* fancy that I intend
to appear in the very first week the court is quite
out of mourning.

ELDER WORTHY.

With all my heart, Sir Novelty.—Come, ladies, 255
considering how little rest you'll have tomorrow
night,° I think it were charity not to keep you up
any longer.

YOUNG WORTHY.

Nay as for that matter, the night before a wedding
is an unfit to sleep in, as the night following. 260
Imagination's a very troublesome bedfellow.—Your
pardon, ladies. I only speak for myself.P

ELDER WORTHY. (*To his servant.*)

See the coaches at St. James's Gate.

Exeunt.

Scene [ii]. Amanda's house.

Enter two servants.

FIRST SERVANT.

Come, come make haste. Is the supper and the
music ready?

SECOND SERVANT.

It is, it is. Well, is he come?

FIRST SERVANT.

Aye, aye, I came before to tell my lady the news.
That rogue Sly managed him rarely. He has been 5
this half hour pretending to pick the lock of the
garden door. Well, poor lady! I wish her good luck
with him, for she's certainly the best mistress living.
Hark ye, is the wine strong, as she ordered it? Be
sure you ply him home, for he must have two or 10
three bumpers to qualify him for her design. See
here he comes. Away to your post.

*Exeunt. Enter Loveless, conducted by Sly, Snap stealing
after them.*

LOVELESS.

Where the devil will this fellow lead me? Nothing
but silence and darkness! Sure the house is
haunted, and he has brought me to face the spirit 15
at his wonted hour!

SLY.

There, there, in, in. Slip on your nightgown* and

refresh yourself. In the meantime I'll acquaint my
lady that you are here. (*Exit.*)

LOVELESS.

Snap. 20

SNAP.

Aye, aye, sir, I'll warrant you.

Exeunt.

Scene [iii]. An antechamber, a table, light, a
nightgown,* and a periwig lying by.

They re-enter.

LOVELESS.

Hah, what sweet lodgings are here! Where can this
end?

SNAP.

Egad sir, I long to know. Pray Heaven we are not
deluded hither to be starved. Methinks I wish I
had brought the remnants of my dinner with me. 5

LOVELESS.

Hark, I hear somebody coming! Hide yourself,
rascal. I would not have you seen.

SNAP.

Well sir, I'll line this trench in case of your being
in danger. (*Gets under the table.*)

LOVELESS.

Hah! this nightgown and peruke don't lie here for 10
nothing. I'll make myself agreeable. I have balked
many a woman in my time for want* of a clean
shirt. (*Puts 'em on.*)

*Enter servants with a supper [and exeunt]; after them a
woman.*

LOVELESS.

Hah, a supper! Heaven send it be no vision! If the
meat be that real, I shall believe the lady may prove 15
flesh and blood. Now am I damnably puzzled to
know whether this be she or not. Madam—
(*Bows.*)

WOMAN.

Sir, my lady begs your pardon for a moment.

LOVELESS.

Humph! Her lady! Good! 20

WOMAN.

She's unfortunately detained by some female visitors,
which she will dispatch with all the haste imaginable.

In the meantime, be pleased to refresh yourself with what the house affords. Pray sir, sit down.

LOVELESS.

Not alone. Madam, you must bear me company.   25

WOMAN.

To oblige you, sir, I'll exceed my commission.

SNAP. (*Under the table.*)

Was there ever so unfortunate a dog! What the devil put it in my head to hide myself before supper? Why this is worse than being locked into a closet* while another man's abed with my wife!   30 I suppose my master will take as much care of me too, as I should of him if I were in his place.

WOMAN.

Sir, my humble service to you. (*Drinks.*)

LOVELESS.

Madam, your humble servant. I'll pledge you. (*Aside to Snap.*) Snap, when there's any danger, I'll   35 call you. In the meantime lie still, d'ye hear?

SNAP.

Egad, I'll shift for myself then. (*Snatches a flask unseen.*) So, now I am armed, defiance to all danger.

LOVELESS.

Madam, your lady's health.   40

SNAP.

Aye, aye, let it go round, I say. (*Drinks.*)

WOMAN.

Well really, sir, my lady's very happy that she has got loose from her relations. For they were always teasing her about you. But she defies them all now. Come sir, success to both your wishes. (*Drinks.*)   45

LOVELESS.

Give me a glass. Methinks this health inspires me. My heart grows lighter for the weight of wine.— Here madam, prosperity to the man that ventures most to please her.

WOMAN.

What think you of a song to support this gaiety?   50

LOVELESS.

With all my Heart.

A song here.

LOVELESS.

You have obliged me, madam. [*Aside.*] Egad, I like this girl! She takes off her glass so feelingly I am

half persuaded she's of a thirsty love. If her lady don't make a little haste, I find I shall present my   55 humble service to her.

Enter a servant, who whispers Amanda's woman.

WOMAN.

Sir, I ask your pardon. My lady has some commands for me. I will return immediately. [*Exit.*]

LOVELESS.

Your servant.—Methinks this is a very new method of intriguing!   60

SNAP.

Pray Heaven it be new! For the old way commonly ended in a good beating. But a pox of danger, I say, and so here's good luck to you, sir.

LOVELESS.

Take heed, rogue, you don't get drunk and discover* yourself.   65

SNAP.

It must be with a fresh flask then, for this is expired, *supernaculum*.[20]

LOVELESS.

Lie close, you dog. I hear somebody coming. I am impatient till I see this creature. This wine has armed me against all thoughts of danger! Pray   70 Heaven she be young, for then she can't want* beauty. Hah! here she comes! Now, never-failing impudence assist me.

Enter Amanda loosely dressed.

AMANDA.

Where's my love? Oh, let me fly into his arms and live forever there.   75

LOVELESS.

My life, my soul! (*Runs and embraces her.*) By Heaven, a tempting creature! Melting, soft, and warm—as my desire.—Oh, that I could hide my face forever thus, that, undiscovered, I might reap the harvest of a ripe desire without the lingering   80 pains of growing love. (*Kisses her hand.*)

---

20 *supernaculum*] "Used in reference to the practice of turning up the emptied cup or glass on one's left thumbnail, to show that all the liquor has been drunk; hence to the last drop, to the bottom" (*OED*).

AMANDA.

Look up, my lord, and bless me with a tender look and let my talking eyes inform thee how I have languished for thy absence.

LOVELESS.

Let's retire and chase away our fleeting cares with 85 the raptures of untired love.

AMANDA.

Bless me! Your voice is strangely altered! Hah, defend me! Who's this? Help! help! Within there.

LOVELESS.

So! I am discovered! A pox on my tattling! That I could not hold my tongue till I got to her 90 bedchamber.

Enter Sly and other servants.

SLY.

Did your ladyship call help, madam? What's the matter?

AMANDA.

Villain! Slave! Who's this? What ruffian have you brought me here. Dog, I'll have you murdered. 95

Sly looks in his face.

SLY.

Bless me! Oh Lord! Dear madam, I beg your pardon. As I hope to be saved, madam, 'tis a mistake: I took him for Mr.——

AMANDA.

Be dumb, eternal blockhead.—Here! take this fellow, toss him in a blanket,21 and let him be 100 turned out of my doors immediately.

SLY.

Oh pray! Dear madam, for Heaven's sake, I am a ruined man.

SNAP.

Ah Snap, what will become of thee? Thou art fallen into the hands of a tigress that has lost her whelp. 105 I have no hopes but in my master's impudence! Heaven strengthen it!

AMANDA.

I'll hear no more! Away with him!

---

21 toss … blanket] a form of vigilante discipline, often dangerous, consisting of tossing the offender's body high in the air off a blanket repeatedly

Exeunt the servants with Sly.

Now sir, for you. I expected—

LOVELESS.

A man, madam, did you not? 110

AMANDA.

Not a stranger, sir. But one that has a right and title to that welcome which by mistake has been given to you.

LOVELESS.

Not an husband, I presume? He would not have been so privately conducted to your chamber and 115 in the dark too!

AMANDA.

Whoever it was, sir, is not your business to examine. But if you would have civil usage, pray be gone.

LOVELESS.

To be used civilly, I must stay, madam. There can 120 be no danger with so fair a creature!

AMANDA.

I doubt* you are mad, sir.

LOVELESS.

While my senses have such luscious food before 'em, no wonder if they are in some confusion, each striving to be foremost at the banquet. 125 (*Approaching her.*) And sure my greedy eyes will starve the rest.

AMANDA.

Pray sir, keep your distance, lest your feeling too be gratified.

SNAP.

Oh Lord! Would I were hundred leagues off at sea! 130

LOVELESS.

Then briefly thus, madam. Know, I like and love you. Now if you have so much generosity as to let me know what title my pretended rival has to your person or your inclinations, perhaps the little hopes I then may have of supplanting him may make me 135 leave your house. If not, my love shall still pursue you, though to the hazard of my life, which I shall not easily resign while this sword can guard it, madam.

AMANDA. (*Aside.*)

Oh, were this courage shown but in a better cause, how worthy were the man that owned it!—What 140 is it, sir, that you propose by this unnecessary trifling? Know then, that I did expect a lover, a man, perhaps, more brave than you. One, that if present, would have given you a shorter answer to your question. 145

LOVELESS.

I am glad to hear he's brave, however. It betrays no weakness in your choice. But if you'd still preserve or raise the joys of love, remove him from your thoughts a moment and in his room receive a warmer heart, a heart that must admire you more 150 than he because my passion's of a fresher date.

AMANDA.

What d'ye take me for?

LOVELESS.

A woman, and the most charming of your sex. One whose pointed eyes declare you formed for love. And though your words are flinty, your every 155 look and motion all confess there's a secret fire within you, which must sparkle when the steel of love provokes it. Come, now pull away your hand and make me hold it faster.

AMANDA.

Nay, now you are rude, sir. 160

LOVELESS.

If love be rudeness, let me be impudent. When we are familiar, rudeness will be love. No woman ever thought a lover rude after she had once granted him the favor.

AMANDA.

Pray sir, forbear. 165

LOVELESS.

How can I when my desire's so violent. Oh, let me snatch the rosy dew from those distilling lips, and as you see your power to charm, so chide me with your pity. Why do you thus cruelly turn away your face? I own the blessing's worth an age's expectation, but 170 if refused till merited, 'tis esteemed a debt. Would you oblige your lover, let loose your early kindness.*

AMANDA.

I shall not take your counsel, sir, while I know a woman's early kindness is as little sign of her generosity as her generosity is a sign of her discretion. 175 Nor would I have you believe I am so ill provided for that I need listen to any man's first addresses.

LOVELESS.

Why madam, would not you drink the first time you had a thirst?

AMANDA.

Yes, but not before I had. 180

LOVELESS.

If you can't drink, yet you may kiss the cup, and that may give you inclination.

AMANDA.

Your pardon, sir. I drink out of nobody's glass but my own. As the man I love confines himself to me, so my inclination keeps me true to him. 185

LOVELESS.

That's a cheat imposed upon you by your own vanity. For when your back's turned, your very chambermaid sips of your leavings and becomes your rival. Constancy in love is all a cheat. Women of your understanding know it. The joys of love 190 are only great when they are new, and to make 'em lasting, we must often change.

AMANDA.

Suppose 'twere a fresh lover I now expected?

LOVELESS.

Why then, madam, your expectation's answered. For I must confess, I don't take you for an old 195 acquaintance, though somewhere I have seen a face not much unlike you. Come, your arguments are vain, for they are so charmingly delivered, they but inspire me the more, as blows in battle raise the brave man's courage. Come, everything pleads for 200 me: your beauty, wit, time, place, opportunity, and my own excess of raging passion.

AMANDA.

Stand off, distant as the globes of heaven and earth, that like a falling star I may shoot with greater force into your arms, and think it heaven to lie 205 expiring there. (*Runs into his arms.*)

SNAP.

Ah! ah! ah! Rogue, the day's our own.

LOVELESS.

Thou sweetest, softest creature Heav'n e'er formed. Thus let me twine myself about thy beauteous limbs till, struggling with the pangs of painful bliss, 210 motionless and mute, we yield to conquering love, both vanquished and both victors.

AMANDA. (*Aside.*)

Can all this heat be real? Oh, why has hateful vice such power to charm, while poor abandoned virtue lies neglected? 215

LOVELESS.

Come, let us surfeit on our new-born raptures. Let's waken sleeping nature with delight, till we may justly say, now! now! we live!

AMANDA.

Come on, let's indulge the transports of our present bliss and bid defiance to our future change 220 of fate.—Who waits there?

Enter Amanda's woman.

AMANDA.

Bring me word immediately if my apartment's ready as I ordered it.

[Exit woman.]

Oh, I am charmed, I have found the man to please me now. One that can and dares maintain the 225 noble rapture of a lawless love. I own myself a libertine, a mortal foe to that dull thing called virtue, that mere disease of sickly nature. Pleasure's the end of life, and while I'm mistress of myself and Fortune, I will enjoy it to the height. Speak 230 freely then (not that I love, like other women, the nauseous pleasure of a little flattery) but answer me like a man that scorns a lie. Does my face invite you, sir? May I from what you see of me propose a pleasure to myself in pleasing you? 235

LOVELESS.

By Heaven you may. I have seen all beauties that the sun shines on but never saw the sun outshined before. I have measured half the world in search of pleasure but, not returning home, had ne'er been happy. 240

AMANDA.

Spoken like the man I wish might love me. (*Aside.*) Pray Heaven his words prove true.—Be sure you never flatter me and, when my person tires you, confess it freely. For change whene'er you will, I'll change as soon. But while we chance to meet, still* 245 let it be with raging fire. No matter how soon it dies, provided the small time it lasts it burn the fiercer.

LOVELESS.

Oh! would the blinded world, like us, agree to change, how lasting might the joys of love be? For 250 thus beauty, though stale to one, might somewhere else be new, and while this man were blest in leaving what he loathed, another were new-ravished in receiving what he ne'er enjoyed.

Re-enter Amanda's woman.

WOMAN.

Madam, everything is according to your order. 255

LOVELESS.

Oh! lead me to the scene of unsupportable delight, rack me with pleasures never known before, till I lie gasping with convulsive passion. This night let us be lavish to our unbounded wishes,

Give all our stock at once to raise the fire, 260
And revel to the height of loose desire.

Exeunt [Loveless and Amanda].

WOMAN.

Ah! what an happy creature's my lady now! There's many an unsatisfied wife about Town would be glad to have her husband as wicked as my master upon the same terms my lady has him. Few 265 women, I'm afraid, would grudge an husband the laying out his stock of love that could receive such considerable interest for it! Well! Now shan't I take one wink of sleep for thinking how they'll employ their time tonight. Faith I must listen, if I were to 270 be hanged for it. (*Listens at the door.*)

SNAP.

So! my master's provided for; therefore, 'tis time for me to take care of myself. I have no mind to be locked out of my lodging. I fancy there's room for two in the maid's bed, as well as my lady's. This same 275 flask was plaguy strong wine. I find I shall storm if she don't surrender fairly.—By your leave, damsel.

WOMAN.

Bless me! who's this? Oh Lord, what would you have? Who are you?

SNAP.

One that has a right and title to your body, my 280 master having already taken possession of your lady's.

WOMAN.

Let me go, or I'll cry out.

SNAP.

Ye lie, ye dare not disturb your lady. But the better to secure you, thus I stop your mouth. (*Kisses her.*) 285

WOMAN.

Umh! Lord bless me, is the Devil in you, tearing one's things!

SNAP.

Then show me your bedchamber.

WOMAN.

The Devil shall have you first. 290

SNAP.

A* shall have us both together then. Here will I fix, (*Takes her about the neck.*) just in this posture till tomorrow morning. In the meantime, when you find your inclination stirring, prithee give me a call, for at present I am very sleepy. (*Seems to* 295 *sleep.*)

WOMAN.

Faugh! how he stinks.

*He belches.*q

Ah! what a whiff was there. The rogue's as drunk as a sailor with a twelve-months' arrears in his pocket or a Jacobite upon a day of ill news. I'll ha' nothing to say to him. Let me see, how shall I get 300 rid of him? Oh, I have it! I'll soon make him sober, I'll warrant him.—So ho! Mr. What-do-ye-call-'um. Where do you intend to lie tonight?

SNAP.

Humph! Why, where you lay last night, unless you change your lodging. 305

WOMAN.

Well, for once I'll take pity of you. Make no noise but put out the candles and follow me softly for fear of disturbing my lady.

SNAP.

I'll warrant ye, there's no fear of spoiling her music, while we are playing the same tune. 310

[Exeunt.]

Scene [iv]. A dark entry.

They re-enter.

WOMAN.

Where are you? Lend me your hand.

SNAP.

Here! here! Make haste, my dear concupiscence.

WOMAN.

Hold! stand there a little, while I open the door gently without waking the footmen. (*She feels about and opens a trapdoor.*) Come along softly this way! 5

SNAP.

Whereabouts are you?

WOMAN.

Here, here, come straight forward.

He goes forward and falls into the cellar.

SNAP.

Oh Lord! Oh Lord! I have broke my neck.

WOMAN.

I am glad to hear him say so, howeverʳ I should be loath to be hanged for him.—How d'ye, sir? 10

SNAP.

D'ye, sir! I am a league underground.

WOMAN.

Whereabouts are you?

SNAP.

In hell, I think.

WOMAN.

No! no! you are but in the road to it, I dare say. Ah, dear! why will you follow lewd women at this 15 rate when they lead you to the very gulf of destruction? I knew you would be swallowed up at last. Ha! ha! ha! ha!

SNAP.

Ah, ye sneering whore!

WOMAN.

Shall I fetch you a prayer book, sir, to arm you 20 against the temptations of the flesh?

SNAP.

No! you need but show your own damned ugly face to do that. Hark ye, either help me out, or I'll hang myself and swear you murdered me.

WOMAN.

Nay, if you are so bloody-minded, good night to 25 ye, sir.

She offers to shut the door over him, and he catches hold on her.

SNAP.

Ah! ah! ah! have I caught you? Egad, we'll pig together now.

WOMAN.

Oh Lord! pray let me go, and I'll do anything.

SNAP.

And so you shall, before I part with you. (*Pulls her* 30
in to him.) And now, master, my humble service
to you.

He pulls the door over them.

Act V, scene [i]. Sir William Wisewoud's house.

*Enter Elder Worthy, Young Worthy, and a lawyer with
writing.*

ELDER WORTHY.

Are the ladies ready?

YOUNG WORTHY.

Hillaria is just gone up to hasten her cousin, and
Sir William will be here immediately.

ELDER WORTHY.

But hark you, brother! I have considered of it, and
pray let me oblige you not to pursue your design 5
upon his five thousand pound. For in short, 'tis
no better than a cheat and what a gentleman
should scorn to be guilty of. Is not it sufficient that
I consent to your wronging him of his daughter?

YOUNG WORTHY.

Your pardon, brother, I can't allow that a wrong. For 10
his daughter loves me; her fortune, you know, he has
nothing to do with; and it's a hard case a young
woman shall not have the disposal of her heart.
Love's a fever of the mind, which nothing but our
own wishes can assuage, and I don't question but we 15
shall find marriage a very cooling cordial. And as to
the five thousand pound, 'tis no more than what he
has endeavored to cheat his niece of.

ELDER WORTHY.

What d'ye mean? I take him for an honest man!

YOUNG WORTHY.

Oh! very honest! As honest as an old agent to a 20
new-raised regiment. No faith, I'll say that for him,
he will not do an ill thing unless he gets by it. In
a word, this so very honest Sir William, as you take
him to be, has offered me the refusal of your
mistress, and upon condition I will secure him five 25
thousand pound upon my day of marriage with
her, he will secure me her person and ten thousand
pound, the remaining part of her fortune! There's
a guardian for ye! What think ye now, sir?

ELDER WORTHY.

Why, I think he deserves to be served in the same 30
kind! I find age and avarice are inseparable!
Therefore, ev'n make what you can of him, and I
will stand by you.—But hark you, Mr. Forge, are
you sure it will stand good in law if Sir William
signs the bond? 35

LAWYER.

In any court in England, sir.

ELDER WORTHY.

Then there's your fifty pieces, and if it succeeds,
here are as many more in the same pocket to
answer 'em. But mum—here comes Sir William
and the ladies. 40

*Enter Sir William Wisewoud, Hillaria, and Narcissa
[and servant].*

SIR WILLIAM.

Good morrow, gentlemen! Mr. Worthy, give you
joy! 'Odso,* if my heels were as light as my heart,
I should ha' much ado to forbear dancing. Here,
here, take her, man, (*Gives him Narcissa's hand.*)
she's yours, and so is her thousand pound a year, 45
and my five thousand pound shall be yours too.

YOUNG WORTHY. (*Aside.*)

You must ask me leave, first.

SIR WILLIAM.

Odso! Is the lawyer come?

ELDER WORTHY.

He is, and all the writings are ready, sir.

SIR WILLIAM.

Come, come, let's see, man! What's this? 'Odd!*
This law is a plaguy troublesome thing, for 50
nowadays it won't let a man give away his own
without repeating the particulars five hundred
times over, when in former times a man might
have held his title to twenty thousand pound a year
in the compass of an hornbook. 55

LAWYER.

That is, sir, because there are more knaves
nowadays, and this age is more treacherous and
distrustful than heretofore.

SIR WILLIAM.

That is, sir, because there are more lawyers than
heretofore. But come, what's this, prithee? 60

LAWYER.

These are the old writings of your daughter's fortune; this is Mr. Worthy's settlement upon her; and this, sir, is your bond for five thousand pound to him. There wants nothing but filling up the blanks with the parties' names. If you please, sir, I'll do't immediately.   65

SIR WILLIAM.

Do so.

LAWYER.

May I crave your daughter's Christian name? The rest I know, sir.

SIR WILLIAM.

Narcissa. Prithee make haste.   70

YOUNG WORTHY. (*Aside to the lawyer.*)

You know your business.

LAWYER.

I'll warrant you, sir. (*Sits to write.*)

SIR WILLIAM.

Mr. Worthy, methinks your brother does not relish your happiness as he should do. Poor man! I'll warrant he wishes himself in his brother's   75
condition!

YOUNG WORTHY.

Not I, I'll assure you, sir.

SIR WILLIAM.

Niece! Niece! Have you no pity? Prithee look upon him a little! 'Odd! He's a pretty young fellow. I am sure he loves you, or he would not have frequented   80
my house so often! D'ye think his brother could not tell my daughter his own story without his assistance? Pshaw! waw! I tell you, you were the beauty that made him so assiduous. Come, come, give him your hand, and he'll soon creep into your   85
heart, I'll warrant you. Come, say the word and make him happy.

HILLARIA.

What, to make myself miserable, sir! Marry a man without an estate!

SIR WILLIAM.

Hang an estate! True love's beyond all riches! 'Tis   90
all dirt—mere dirt! Beside, han't you fifteen thousand pound to your portion?

HILLARIA.

I doubt,* sir, you would be loath to give him your daughter, though her fortune's larger.

SIR WILLIAM.

'Odd, if he loved her but half so well as he loves   95
you, he should have her for a word speaking.

HILLARIA.

But sir, this asks some consideration.

NARCISSA.

You see, Mr. Worthy, what an extraordinary kindness my father has for you!

YOUNG WORTHY.

Aye madam, and for your cousin too. But I hope,   100
with a little of your assistance, we shall be both able very shortly to return it.

NARCISSA.

Nay, I was always ready to serve Hillaria. For Heaven knows, I only marry to revenge her quarrel to my father. I cannot forgive his offering to sell her.   105

YOUNG WORTHY.

Oh, you need not take such pains, madam, to conceal your passion for me. You may own it without a blush upon your wedding day.

NARCISSA.

My passion! When did you hear me acknowledge any? If I thought you could believe me guilty of   110
such a weakness, though after I had married you, I would never look you in the face.

YOUNG WORTHY. (*Aside.*)

A very pretty humor this, faith! What a world of unnecessary sins have we two to answer for! For she has told more lies to conceal her love than I   115
have sworn false oaths to promote it.—Well madam, at present I'll content myself with your giving me leave to love.

NARCISSA.

Which if I don't give, you'll take, I suppose.

HILLARIA.

Well Uncle, I won't promise you, but I'll go to   120
church and see them married; when we come back, 'tis ten to one but I surprise you where you least think on.

SIR WILLIAM.

Why, that's well said!—Mr. Worthy, now, now's your time. 'Odd! I have so fired her, 'tis not in her   125
power to deny you, man. To her! to her! I warrant her thy own, boy! You'll keep your word, five thousand pound upon the day of marriage?

YOUNG WORTHY.

I'll give you my bond upon demand, sir.

SIR WILLIAM.

Oh! I dare take your word, sir.—Come lawyer, have you done? Is all ready? 130

LAWYER.

All, sir! This is your bond to Mr. Worthy. Will you be pleased to sign that first, sir?

SIR WILLIAM.

Aye, aye, let's see. (*Reads.*) "The condition of this obligation—" hum, um.—Come, lend me the pen. There.—Mr. Worthy, I deliver this as my act and deed to you, and Heaven send you a good bargain.—Niece, will you witness it? (*Which she does.*) Come lawyer, your fist too. 135

Lawyer witnesses it.

LAWYER.

Now sir, if you please to sign the jointure. 140

ELDER WORTHY.

Come on.—Sir William, I deliver this to you for the use of your daughter. Madam, will you give yourself the trouble once more?

Hillaria sets her hand.

Come sir—

The lawyer does the same.

So, now let a coach be called as soon as you please, sir. 145

SIR WILLIAM.

You may save that charge. I saw your own at the door.

ELDER WORTHY.

Your pardon, sir, that would make our business too public. For which reason, Sir William, I hope you will excuse our not taking you along with us. 150

Exit a servant.

SIR WILLIAM.

Aye, aye, with all my heart. The more privacy, the less expense. But pray, what time may I expect you back again? For Amanda has sent to me for the writings of her husband's estate. I suppose she intends to redeem the mortgage, and I am afraid she will keep me there till dinnertime. 155

YOUNG WORTHY.

Why, about that time she has obliged me to bring some of her nearest friends to be witnesses of her good or evil fortune with her husband. Methinks I long to know her success. If you please, Sir William, we'll meet you there. 160

SIR WILLIAM.

With all my heart.

Enter a Servant.

Well, is the coach come?

SERVANT.

It is at the door, sir. [*Exit.*] 165

SIR WILLIAM.

Come gentlemen, no ceremony; your time's short.

ELDER WORTHY.

Your servant, Sir William.

Exeunt Elder Worthy, Young Worthy, Narcissa, and Hillaria.

SIR WILLIAM.

So! here's five thousand pounds got with a wet finger! This 'tis to read mankind! I knew a young lover would never think he gave too much for his mistress! Well, if I don't suddenly meet with some misfortune, I shall never be able to bear this tranquility of mind. 170

Exit.

Scene [ii]. Amanda's house.

Enter Amanda sola.

AMANDA.

Thus far my hopes have all been answered, and my disguise of vicious love has charmed him ev'n to a madness of impure desire. But now I tremble to pull off the mask lest barefaced virtue should fright him from my arms forever. Yet sure, there are charms in virtue, nay, stronger and more pleasing far than hateful vice can boast of, else why have holy martyrs perished for its sake? While lewdness ever gives severe repentance and unwilling death. Good Heaven, inspire my heart and hang upon my tongue the force of truth and eloquence, that I may lure this wandering falcon back to love and virtue.—He comes, and now my dreaded task begins! 5 10

Enter Loveless in new clothes.

AMANDA.

How fare you, sir? D'ye not already think yourself confined? Are you not tired with my easy love? 15

LOVELESS.

Oh, never! never! You have so filled my thoughts with pleasures past, that but to reflect on 'em is still* new rapture to my soul, and the bliss must last while I have life or memory.

AMANDA.

No flattery, sir! I loved you for your plain-dealing 20 and to preserve my good opinion, tell me, what think you of the grape's persuading juice? Come, speak freely, would not the next tavern bush put all this out of your head?

LOVELESS.

Faith madam, to be free with you, I am apt to 25 think you are in the right on't. For though love and wine are two very fine tunes, yet they make no music if you play them both together; separately, they ravish us. Thus the mistress ought to make room for the bottle, the bottle for the mistress, and 30 both to wait the call of inclination.

AMANDA.

That's generously spoken. I have observed, sir, in all your discourse you confess something of a man that has thoroughly known the world. Pray give me leave to ask you, of what condition you are and 35 whence you came?

LOVELESS.

Why, in the first place, madam, by birth I am a gentleman; by ill friends, good wine, and false dice, almost a beggar; but by your servant's mistaking me, the happiest man that ever love and beauty 40 smiled on.

AMANDA.

One thing more, sir! Are you married? *(Aside.)* Now my fears.

LOVELESS.

I was, but very young.

AMANDA.

What was your wife? 45

LOVELESS.

A foolish, loving thing that built castles in the air and thought it impossible for a man to forswear himself when he made love.

AMANDA.

Was she not virtuous?

LOVELESS.

Uumh! Yes faith, I believe she might. I was ne'er jealous of her. 50

AMANDA.

Did you ne'er love her?

LOVELESS.

Ah, most damnably at first, for she was within two women of my maidenhead.

AMANDA.

What's become of her?

LOVELESS.

Why, after I had been from her beyond sea about 55 seven or eight years, like a very loving fool she died of the pip and civilly left me the world free to range in.

AMANDA.

Why did you leave her?

LOVELESS.

Because she grew stale, and I could not whore in quiet for her. Besides, she was always exclaiming 60 against my extravagancies, particularly my gaming, which she so violently opposed that I fancied a pleasure in it which since I never found, for in one month I lost between eight and ten thousand pound, which I had just before called in to pay my 65 debts. This misfortune made my creditors come so thick upon me that I was forced to mortgage the remaining part of my estate to purchase new pleasure, which I knew I could not do on this side the water amidst the clamors of insatiate duns and 70 the more hateful noise of a complaining wife.

AMANDA.

Don't you wish you had taken her counsel, though?

LOVELESS.

Not I, faith, madam.

AMANDA.

Why so?

LOVELESS.

Because 'tis to no purpose. I am master of more 75 philosophy than to be concerned at what I can't help. But now, madam, pray give me leave to inform myself as far in your condition.

AMANDA.

In a word, sir, till you know me thoroughly, I must own myself a perfect riddle to you. 80

LOVELESS.

Nay, nay, I know you are a woman. But in what circumstances, wife or widow?

AMANDA.

A wife, sir, a true, a faithful, and a virtuous wife.

LOVELESS.

Humph! Truly madam, your story begins something like a riddle. A virtuous wife, say you? 85 What, and was you never false to your husband?

AMANDA.

I never was, by Heaven! For him, and only him, I still love above the world.

LOVELESS.

Good again! Pray madam, don't your memory fail you sometimes? Because I fancy you don't 90 remember what you do overnight!

AMANDA.

I told you, sir, I should appear a riddle to you. But if my heart will give me leave, I'll now unloose your fettered apprehension. But I must first amaze you more. Pray sir, satisfy me in one particular. 'Tis 95 this: What are your undissembled thoughts of virtue? Now, if you can, shake off your loose, unthinking part and summon all your force of manly reason to resolve me.

LOVELESS.

Faith madam, methinks this is a very odd question 100 for a woman of your character. I must confess you have amazed me.

AMANDA.

It ought not to amaze you! Why should you think I make a mock of virtue? But last night you allowed my understanding greater than is usual in 105 our sex. If so, can you believe I have no farther sense of happiness than what this empty, dark, and barren world can yield me? No, I have yet a prospect of a sublimer bliss, an hope that carries me to the bright regions of eternal day. 110

LOVELESS. [Aside.]

Humph! I thought her last night's humor was too good to hold. I suppose, by and by she will ask me to go to church with her.—Faith madam, in my mind this discourse is a little out of the way. You told me I should be acquainted with your 115 condition, and at present that's what I had rather be informed of.

AMANDA.

Sir, you shall. But first, this question must be answered: Your thoughts of virtue, sir? By all my hopes of bliss hereafter, your answering this 120 pronounces half my good or evil fate forever. But on my knees I beg you, do not speak till you have weighed it well. Answer me with the same truth and sincerity as you would answer Heaven at your latest hour. 125

LOVELESS.

Your words confound me, madam. Some wondrous secret sure lies ripened in your breast and seems to struggle for its fatal birth! What is it I must answer you?

AMANDA.

Give me your real thoughts of virtue, sir: Can you 130 believe there ever was a woman truly mistress of it, or is it only notion?

LOVELESS.

Let me consider, madam. (Aside.) What can this mean? Why is she so earnest in her demands and begs me to be serious, as if her life depended on 135 my answer? I will resolve her as I ought, as truth and reason and the strange occasion seems to press me.—Most of your sex confound the very name of virtue, for they would seem to live without desires, which, could they do, that were not virtue 140 but the defect of unperforming nature and no praise to them. For who can boast a victory when they have no foe to conquer? Now, she alone gives the fairest proofs of virtue whose conscience and whose force of reason can curb her warm desires 145 when opportunity would raise 'em. That such a woman may be found, I dare believe.

AMANDA.

May I believe that from your soul you speak this undissembled truth?

LOVELESS.

Madam, you may. But still you rack me with 150 amazement! Why am I asked so strange a question?

AMANDA.

I'll give you ease immediately. Since then you have allowed a woman may be virtuous, how will you excuse the man who leaves the bosom of a wife so qualified for the abandoned pleasures of deceitful 155 prostitutes? Ruins her fortune! Contemns her counsel! Loathes her bed and leaves her to the lingering miseries of despair and love. While in return of all these wrongs, she, his poor forsaken wife, meditates no revenge but what her piercing tears and secret vows to Heaven for his conversion yield her. Yet still loves on, is constant and unshaken to the last! Can you believe that such a man can live without the stings of conscience and yet be master of his senses? Conscience! Did you ne'er feel the checks of it? Did it never, never tell you of your broken vows?

LOVELESS.

That you should ask me this confounds my reason. And yet your words are uttered with such a powerful accent, they have awaked my soul and strike my thoughts with horror and remorse. (*Stands in a fixed posture.*)

AMANDA.

Then let me strike you nearer, deeper yet. But arm your mind with gentle pity first, or I am lost forever.

LOVELESS.

I am all pity, all faith, expectation, and confused amazement. Be kind, be quick, and ease my wonder.

AMANDA.

Look on me well. Revive your dead remembrance. And oh! for pity's sake, (*Kneels.*) hate me not for loving long. Faithfully forgive this innocent attempt of a despairing passion, and I shall die in quiet.

LOVELESS. (*Amazed.*)

Hah! Speak on!

AMANDA.

It will not be!⁵ The word's too weighty for my faltering tongue, and my soul sinks beneath the fatal burden. Oh! (*Falls on the ground.*)

LOVELESS.

Hah! She faints! Look up, fair creature! Behold a heart that bleeds for your distress and fain would share the weight of your oppressing sorrows! Oh! thou hast raised a thought within me that shocks my soul.

AMANDA.

'Tis done! (*Rising.*) The conflict's past, and Heaven bids me speak undaunted. Know then, ev'n all the boasted raptures of your last night's love you found in your Amanda's arms. I am your wife.

LOVELESS.

Hah!

AMANDA.

Forever blest or miserable as your next breath shall sentence me.

LOVELESS.

My wife! Impossible! Is she not dead? How shall I believe thee?

AMANDA.

How time and my afflictions may have altered me I know not. But here's an indelible confirmation. (*Bares her arm.*) These speaking characters, which in their cheerful bloom our early passions mutually recorded.

LOVELESS.

Hah! 'Tis here. 'Tis no illusion, but my real name, which seems to upbraid me as a witness of my perjured love. Oh, I am confounded with my guilt and tremble to behold thee. Pray give me leave to think. (*Turns from her.*)

AMANDA.

I will. (*Kneels.*) But you must look upon me. For only eyes can hear the language of the eyes, and mine have sure the tenderest tale of love to tell that ever misery at the dawn of rising hope could utter.

LOVELESS.

I have wronged you. Oh! rise! basely wronged you! And can I see your face?

AMANDA.

One kind, one pitying look cancels those wrongs forever. And oh! forgive my fond presuming passion, for from my soul I pardon and forgive you all. All, all but this, the greatest, your unkind delay of love.

LOVELESS.

Oh! seal my pardon with thy trembling lips, while with this tender grasp of fond reviving love I seize my bliss and stifle all thy wrongs forever. (*Embraces her.*)

AMANDA.

No more. I'll wash away their memory in tears of flowing joy.

LOVELESS.

Oh! thou hast roused me from my deep lethargy of vice! For hitherto my soul has been enslaved to loose

desires, to vain deluding follies and shadows of 230
substantial bliss. But now I wake with joy to find my
rapture real. Thus let me kneel and pay my thanks to
her whose conquering virtue has at last subdued me.
Here will I fix, thus prostrate, sigh my shame, and
wash my crimes in never-ceasing tears of penitence. 235

AMANDA.

Oh rise! This posture heaps new guilt on me! Now
you overpay me.

LOVELESS.

Have I not used thee like a villain? For almost ten
long years deprived thee of my love and ruined all
thy fortune? But I will labor, dig, beg, or starve to 240
give new proofs of my unfeigned affection.

AMANDA.

Forbear this tenderness, lest I repent of having
moved your soul so far. You shall not need to beg.
Heaven has provided for us beyond its common
care. 'Tis now near two years since my uncle Sir 245
William Wealthy sent you the news of my
pretended death. Knowing the extravagance of
your temper, he thought it fit you should believe
no other of me, and about a month after he had
sent you that advice, poor man, he died and left 250
me in full possession of two thousand pounds a
year, which I now cannot offer as a gift because
my duty and your lawful right makes you the
undisputed master of it.

LOVELESS.

How have I labored for my own undoing, while 255
in despite of all my follies, kind Heaven resolved
my happiness!

Enter a servant to Amanda.

SERVANT.

Madam, Sir William Wisewoud has sent your
ladyship the writings you desired him and says he'll
wait upon you immediately. 260

AMANDA.

Now sir, if you please to withdraw a while, you may
inform yourself how fair a fortune you are master of.

LOVELESS.

None, none that can outweigh a virtuous mind.
While in my arms I thus can circle thee, I grasp
more treasure than in a day the posting sun can 265
travel o'er. Oh! why have I so long been blind to

the perfections of thy mind and person? Not
knowing thee a wife, I found thee charming
beyond the wishes of luxurious love. Is it then a
name, a word shall rob thee of thy worth? Can 270
fancy be a surer guide to happiness than reason?
Oh! I have wandered like a benighted wretch and
lost myself in life's unpleasing journey.

'Twas heedless fancy first that made me stray,
But reason now breaks forth and lights me on 275
my way.

Exeunt.

Scene [iii]. An entry.

Enter three or four servants.

FIRST SERVANT.

Prithee Tom, make haste below there. My lady has
ordered dinner at half an hour after one precisely.
Look out some of the red that came in last.

*Two of the servants haul Snap and Amanda's woman
out of the cellar.*

SECOND SERVANT.

Come sir, come out here and show your face.

WOMAN.

Oh, I am undone, ruined! 5

SECOND SERVANT.

Pray sir, who are you, and what was your business,
and how in the devil's name came you in here?

SNAP.

Why truly, sir, the flesh led me to the cellar door,
but I believe the Devil pushed me in. That
gentlewoman can inform you better. 10

THIRD SERVANT.

Pray Mrs.* Anne, how came you two together in
the cellar?

WOMAN. (*Sobbing.*)

Why, he—he—pu—pu—pulled me in.

THIRD SERVANT.

But how the devil came he in?

WOMAN.

He fe—fe—fe—fell in. 15

SECOND SERVANT.

How came he into the house?

WOMAN.

I don—do—don't know.

SECOND SERVANT.

Ah! you are a crocodile. I thought what was the reason I could never get a good word from you! What, in a cellar too! But come, sir, we will take care of you, however. Bring him along. We will first carry him before my lady and then toss him in a blanket.   20

SNAP.

Nay, but gentlemen! Dear gentlemen.

Exeunt.

[Scene iv. An interior room of Amanda's house.]

Enter Loveless, Amanda, Elder Worthy, Young Worthy, Narcissa, and Hillaria.

ELDER WORTHY.

This is indeed a joyful day. We must all congratulate your happiness.

AMANDA.

Which while our lives permit us to enjoy, we must still* reflect with gratitude on the generous author of it. Sir, we owe you more than words can pay you.   5

LOVELESS.

Words are indeed too weak. Therefore, let my gratitude be dumb till it can speak in actions.

YOUNG WORTHY.

The success of the design I thought on sufficiently rewards me.

HILLARIA.

When I reflect upon Amanda's past afflictions, I could almost weep to think of her^t unexpected change of fortune.   10

ELDER WORTHY.

Methinks her fair example should persuade all constant wives ne'er to repine at unrewarded virtue. Nay, ev'n my brother being the first promoter of it has atoned for all the looseness of his character.   15

LOVELESS.

I never can return his kindness.

NARCISSA.

In a short time, sir, I suppose you'll meet with an opportunity, if you can find a receipt* to preserve love after his honeymoon's over.   20

LOVELESS.

The receipt is easily found, madam. Love's a tender plant which can't live out of a warm bed. You must take care with undissembled kindness* to keep him from the northern blast of jealousy.   25

NARCISSA.

But I have heard your* experienced lovers make use of coldness, and that's more agreeable to my inclination.

LOVELESS.

Coldness, madam, before marriage, like throwing a little water upon a clear fire, makes it burn the fiercer, but after marriage, you must still* take care to lay on fresh fuel.   30

NARCISSA.

Oh fie, sir! How many examples have we of men's hating their wives for being too fond of 'em?

LOVELESS.

No wonder, madam. You may stifle a flame by heaping on too great a load.   35

NARCISSA.

Nay sir, if there be no other way of destroying his passion, for me he may love till doomsday.

ELDER WORTHY.

Humph! Don't you smell powder, gentlemen? Sir Novelty is not far off.   40

LOVELESS.

What, not our fellow collegian, I hope, that was expelled the university for beating the proctor?

ELDER WORTHY.

The same.

LOVELESS.

Does that weed grow still?

ELDER WORTHY.

Aye faith, and as rank as ever, as you shall see, for here he comes.   45

Enter Sir Novelty.

SIR NOVELTY.

Ladies, your humble servant.—Dear Loveless, let me embrace thee. I am o'erjoyed at thy good fortune, stop my vitals. The whole Town rings of it already. My Lady Tattletongue has tired a pair of horses in spreading the news about. Hearing, gentlemen, that you were all met upon an extraordinary good occasion, I could not resist this opportunity of joining my joy with yours: For you must know I am—   55

NARCISSA.

Married, sir!

SIR NOVELTY.

To my liberty, madam! I am just parted from my mistress.

NARCISSA.

And pray, sir, how do you find yourself after it?

SIR NOVELTY.

The happiest man alive, madam. Pleasant, easy, 60
gay, light, and free as air. Hah. (*Capers.*) I beg your ladyship's pardon, madam, but upon my soul, I cannot confine my rapture.

NARCISSA.

Are you so indifferent, sir?

SIR NOVELTY.

Oh madam, she's engaged already to a Temple* 65
beau! I saw 'em in a coach together, so fond, and bore it with as unmoved countenance as Tom Worthy does a thundering jest in a comedy, when the whole house roars at it.

YOUNG WORTHY.

Pray sir, what occasioned your separation? 70

SIR NOVELTY.

Why this, sir: you must know, she being still possessed with a brace of implacable devils, called revenge and jealousy, dogged me this morning to the chocolate house,[22] where I was obliged to leave a letter for a young, foolish girl that— (You will 75
excuse me, sir.) Which I had no sooner delivered to the maid of the house, but whip, she snatches it out of her hand, flew at her like a dragon, tore off her headcloths, flung down three or four sets of lemonade glasses, dashed my Lord Whiffle's 80
chocolate in his face, cut him over the nose, and had like to have strangled me in my own steenkirk.

LOVELESS.

Pray sir, how did this end?

SIR NOVELTY.

Comically, stop my vitals, for in the cloud of powder that she had battered out of the beaux' 85
periwigs, I stole away. After which, I sent a friend

---

22 chocolate house] A meeting place of the fashionably wealthy after 1657 when a French expatriate opened the first chocolate house in London; the expense of the beverage put it beyond the means of most Londoners.

to her with an offer, which she readily accepted: three hundred pound a year during life, provided she would renounce all claims to me and resign my person to my own disposal. 90

ELDER WORTHY.

Methinks, Sir Novelty, you were a little too extravagant in your settlement, considering how the price of women is fallen.

SIR NOVELTY.

Therefore I did it—to be the first man should raise their price. For the devil take me, but the women 95
of the Town now come down so low that my very footman, while he kept my place t'other day at the playhouse, carried a mask* out of the side box with him and, stop my vitals, the rogue is now taking physic for't. 100

Enter the servants with Snap.

FIRST SERVANT.

Come, bring him along there.

LOVELESS.

How now! hah! Snap in hold? Pray let's know the business.—Release him, gentlemen.

FIRST SERVANT.

Why, an't* please you, sir, this fellow was taken in the cellar with my lady's woman. She says he kept 105
her in by force and was rude to her. She stands crying here without and begs her ladyship to do her justice.

AMANDA.

Mr. Loveless, we are both the occasion of this misfortune, and for the poor girl's reputation's sake, 110
something should be done.

LOVELESS.

Snap, answer me directly, have you lain with this poor girl?

SNAP.

Why truly, sir, imagining you were doing little less with my lady, I must confess I did commit 115
familiarity with her, or so, sir.

LOVELESS.

Then you shall marry her, sir! No reply, unless it be your promise.

SNAP.

Marry her! Oh Lord, sir, after I have lain with her? Why, sir! how the devil can you think a man can 120 have any stomach to his dinner after he has had three or four slices off of the spit?

LOVELESS.

Well sirrah, to renew your appetite, and because thou hast been my old acquaintance, I'll give thee an hundred pound with her and thirty pound a year during life to set you up in some honest employment. 125

SNAP.

Ah sir, now I understand you. Heaven reward you! Well sir, I partly find that the genteel scenes of our lives are pretty well over, and I thank Heaven that I have so much grace left that I can repent when I have no more opportunities of being wicked.— Come, spouse. 130

She enters.

Here's my hand, the rest of my body shall be forthcoming. Ah! little did my master and I think last night that we were robbing our own orchards. 135

Exeunt Snap and woman.

ELDER WORTHY.

Brother, stand upon your guard. Here comes Sir William.

Enter Sir William Wisewoud.

SIR WILLIAM.

Joy, joy to you all! Madam, I congratulate your good fortune.—Well, my dear rogue, must not I give thee joy too? hah! 140

YOUNG WORTHY.

If you please, sir. But I confess I have more than I deserve already.

SIR WILLIAM.

And art thou married?

YOUNG WORTHY.

Yes sir, I am married. 145

SIR WILLIAM.

'Odso,* I am glad on't. I dare swear thou dost not grudge me the five thousand pound.

YOUNG WORTHY.

Not I, really sir. You have given me all my soul could wish for—but the addition of a father's blessing. (*Kneels with Narcissa.*) 150

SIR WILLIAM.

Humph! What dost thou mean? I am none of thy father.

YOUNG WORTHY.

This lady is your daughter, sir, I hope.

SIR WILLIAM.

Prithee get up! Prithee get up! Thou art stark mad! True, I believe she may be my daughter. Well, and so, sir! 155

YOUNG WORTHY.

If she be not, I'm certain she's my wife, sir.

SIR WILLIAM.

Humph! Mr. Worthy, pray sir, do me the favor to help me to understand your brother a little. Do you know anything of his being married? 160

ELDER WORTHY.

Then, without any abuse, Sir William, he married your daughter this very morning, not an hour ago, sir.

SIR WILLIAM.

Pray sir, whose consent had you? Who advised you to it? 165

YOUNG WORTHY.

Our mutual love and your consent, sir, which these writings, entitling her to a thousand pound a year, and this bond, whereby you have obliged yourself to pay me five thousand pound upon our day of marriage, are sufficient proofs of. 170

SIR WILLIAM.

He, he! I gave your brother such a bond, sir?

YOUNG WORTHY.

You did so, but the obligation is to me. Look there, sir.

SIR WILLIAM.

Very good! this is my hand, I must confess, sir. And what then? 175

YOUNG WORTHY.

Why then, I expect my five thousand pound, sir. Pray sir, do you know my name?

SIR WILLIAM.

I am not drunk, sir. I am sure it was Worthy and Jack, or Tom, or Dick, or something.

YOUNG WORTHY.

No sir, I'll show you. 'Tis William. Look you there, sir. You should have taken more care of the lawyer, sir, that filled up the blank. 180

ELDER WORTHY.

So, now his eyes are open.

SIR WILLIAM.

And have you married my daughter against my consent and tricked me out of five thousand pound, sir? 185

HILLARIA.

His brother, sir, has married me too with my consent, and I am not tricked out of five thousand pound.

SIR WILLIAM.

Insulting witch! Look ye, sir, I never had a 190 substantial cause to be angry in my life before, but now I have reason on my side. I will indulge my indignation most immoderately. I must confess, I have not patience to wait the slow redress of a tedious lawsuit, therefore am resolved to right 195 myself the nearest way. Draw, draw, sir. You must not enjoy my five thousand pound, though I fling as much more after it, in procuring a pardon for killing you. (*They hold him.*) Let me come at him! I'll murder him! I'll cut him! I'll tear him, I'll broil 200 him and eat him! a rogue! a dog! a cursed dog! a cut-throat, murdering dog!

ELDER WORTHY.

Oh fie, Sir William, how monstrous is this passion.

SIR WILLIAM.

You have disarmed me, but I shall find a time to poison him. 205

LOVELESS.

Think better on't, Sir William, your daughter has married a gentleman and one whose love entitles him to her person.

SIR WILLIAM.

Aye, but the five thousand pound, sir! Why the very report of his having such a fortune will ruin 210 him. I warrant you, within this week he will have more duns at his chamber in a morning than a gaming lord after a good night at the groom-porter's* or a poet upon the fourth day of his new play.[23] I shall never be pleased with paying it 215 against my own consent, sir.

---

[23] fourth day ... play] Playwrights received the profits of the third night, if their new plays survived till then.

HILLARIA.

Yet you would have had me done it, Sir William. But however, I heartily wish you would as freely forgive Mr. Worthy, as I do you, sir.

SIR WILLIAM.

I must confess, this girl's good nature makes me 220 ashamed of what I have offered. But Mr. Worthy, I did not expect such usage from a man of your character. I always took you for a gentleman.

ELDER WORTHY.

You shall find me no other, sir.—Brother, a word with you. 225

LOVELESS.

Sir William, I have some obligations to this gentleman, and have so great a confidence in your daughter's merit and his love that I here promise to return you your five thousand pound, if after the expiration of one year, you are then dissatisfied 230 in his being your son-in-law.

YOUNG WORTHY.

But see, brother, he has forestalled your purpose.

ELDER WORTHY.

Mr. Loveless, you have been beforehand with me, but you must give me leave to offer Sir William my joint security for what you have promised him. 235

LOVELESS.

With all my heart, sir. Dare you take our bonds, Sir William?

YOUNG WORTHY.

Hold, gentlemen! I should blush to be obliged to that degree. Therefore, Sir William, as the first proof of that respect and duty I owe a father I here, 240 unasked, return your bond and will henceforth expect nothing from you but as my conduct shall deserve it.

AMANDA.

This is indeed a generous act. Methinks 'twere pity it should go unrewarded. 245

SIR WILLIAM.

Nay, now you vanquish me. After this, I can't suspect your future conduct. There, sir, 'tis yours, I acknowledge the bond and wish you all the happiness of a bridal bed. Heaven's blessing on you both. Now rise my boy and let the world know 250 'twas I set you upon your legs again.

YOUNG WORTHY.

I'll study to deserve your bounty, sir.

LOVELESS.

Now Sir William, you have shown yourself a father. This prudent action has secured your daughter from the usual consequence of a stolen marriage, a parent's curse. Now she must be happy in her love, while you have such a tender care on't. 255

AMANDA.

This is indeed a happy meeting. We all of us have drawn our several prizes in the lottery of human life. Therefore, I beg our joys may be united. Not one of us must part this day. The ladies I'll entreat my guests. 260

LOVELESS.

The rest are mine, and I hope will often be so.

AMANDA.

'Tis yet too soon to dine; therefore, to divert us in the meantime, what think you of a little music, the subject perhaps not improper to the occasion. 265

ELDER WORTHY.

T'will oblige us, madam, we are all lovers of it.

The scene draws and discovers Love seated on a throne attended with a chorus.*

FAME.

Hail! Hail! Victorious Love,
To whom all hearts below
With no less pleasure bow 270
Than to the thund'ring Jove
The happy souls above.

CHORUS.

Hail, etc.

Enter Reason.

REASON.

Cease, cease, fond fools, your empty noise,
And follow not such fleeting toys[u]: 275
Love gives you but a short-lived bliss,
But I bestow immortal happiness.

LOVE.

Rebellious Reason, talk no more;
Of all my slaves, I thee abhor.
But thou, alas! dost strive in vain 280
To free the lover from a pleasing chain;
In spite of Reason, Love shall live and reign.

CHORUS.

In spite, etc.
A martial symphony.

Enter Honor.

HONOR.

What wretch would follow Love's alarms, 285
When Honor's trumpet sounds to arms!
Hark! how the warlike notes inspire
In ev'ry breast a glowing fire!

LOVE.

Hark! how it swells with love and soft desire!

HONOR.

Behold, behold the married state, 290
By thee too soon betrayed,
Repenting now too late.

Enter Marriage with his yoke.

MARRIAGE.

Oh! tell me cruel god of love,
Why didst thou my thoughts possess
With an eternal round of happiness? 295
And yet alas! I lead a wretched life,
Doomed to this galling yoke—the emblem of a wife!

LOVE.

Ungrateful wretch! how dar'st thou Love upbraid?
I gave thee raptures in the bridal bed.

MARRIAGE.

Long since, alas! the airy vision's fled, 300
And I, with wand'ring flames, my passion feed.
Oh! tell me, pow'rful God,
Where I shall find
My former peace of mind?

LOVE.

Where first I promised thee a happy life, 305
There thou shalt find it in a virtuous wife.

LOVE, FAME.

Go home, unhappy wretch, and mourn
For all thy guilty passion past;
There thou shalt those joys return,
Which shall forever, ever last. 310

End with the first chorus.

LOVELESS.

'Twas generously designed, and all my life to come shall show how I approve the moral. Oh Amanda! once more receive me to thy arms, and while I am there, let all the world confess my happiness. By my example taught, let every man whose fate has 315

bound him to a married life beware of letting loose
his wild desires. For if experience may be allowed
to judge, I must proclaim the folly of a wandering
passion. The greatest happiness we can hope on
earth,   320

And sure the nearest to the joys above,
Is the chaste rapture of a virtuous love.

[Exeunt.]

FINIS.

Textual Notes

a Copytext is the first edition, a 1696 quarto (Q1). Also
consulted: the second edition, a 1702 quarto (Q2); a
1721 collected edition of Cibber's *Plays* (P); and modern editions of 1939 (Macmillan and Jones—MJ) and
of 1973 (Sullivan). Sullivan chose P as her copytext, an
edition Cibber considerably bowdlerized. Only the most
humorous of these changes have been cited.

b not] P, Sullivan; *om.* Q1-2, MJ
c a] P, Sullivan; *om.* Q1-2, MJ
d If … sacrifice!] Q1-2, MJ; *om.* P, Sullivan
e at a rehearsal] Q1-2, MJ; in a morning P, Sullivan
f fury] Q1-2, MJ; resentment P, Sullivan
g understanding] Q1-2, MJ; undertaking P, Sullivan
h a] P, Sullivan; *om.* Q1-2, MJ
i rogue makes] P, Sullivan; rogues make Q1-2, MJ
j *Enter two bullies … his lodging*] Q1-2, MJ; *om.* P,
Sullivan
k for her stinking breath] Q1-2, MJ; *om.* P, Sullivan
l maidenhead] Q1-2, MJ; maid P, Sullivan
m My … it?] Q1-2, MJ; *om.* P, Sullivan
n hot raging lust] Q1-2, MJ; all the dotage of undone desire P, Sullivan
o considering … night] Q1-2, MJ; *om.*P, Sullivan
p YOUNG WORTHY… . myself.] Q1-2, MJ; *om.* P,
Sullivan
q *He belches*] Q1-2, MJ; *om.* P, Sullivan
r so, however] so, however; Q2; so however, D3-7
s It will not] P, Sullivan; I wonot Q1-2; I would not MJ
t her] P, MJ, Sullivan; his Q1-2
u such fleeting toys] such joys Q2; such idle joys P,
Sullivan

The Way of the World[a]

by William Congreve (1670-1729)
edited by Richard Kroll

Though William Congreve was to remain active into the eighteenth century, *The Way of the World*, performed in 1700 and considered in subsequent theater history to be a jewel of great comedy, marked the end of a brief but brilliant stage career. The commonly held view that *The Way of the World* was a flop is mistaken, though that may reflect the notorious difficulty—for critics and audiences alike—of disentangling the complex web of social relations in the play. The central action of the play, however, can be understood by the following question: How can Mirabell successfully court Millamant, a vastly rich heiress, yet secure her entire fortune of 12,000 pounds, which depends on her marrying with her aunt and guardian Lady Wishfort's consent?

Though performed in 1700, this play is often thought of as one of the last true Restoration comedies, bearing close affinities in theme and style to some of the great comedies of the 1670s. It is important to see how this play both follows and differs from plays like Etherege's *The Man of Mode* (1676). Both plays bring witty rakes into proximate union with heiresses. Yet Congreve was writing in a new social atmosphere that seems to have emerged after 1688. This change of opinion is epitomized, both in theater histories and in Congreve's own references in the play itself, by Jeremy Collier's misleadingly titled *A Short View of the Immorality and Profaneness of the English Stage, Together with the Sense of Antiquity upon this Argument* (1698). In this tract, which follows a long line of seventeenth-century attacks on the stage (and which Congreve also places satirically as reading matter in Lady Wishfort's closet*), Collier vents his fury against what he sees as the excesses of the comedies of the 1670s, in particular plays like Wycherley's *The Country Wife* (1675). At one level Congreve rebuffs

Collier by writing a play which, in its broad outline and in its language, echoes those of his distinguished forerunners, but at another level, Congreve massages the plot in such a way as to avoid any further attacks like Collier's. It is true that Dorimant (Etherege's hero) and Mirabell (Congreve's) are cousins, but there are important differences. Whereas we are allowed to witness the messy consequences of Dorimant's various affairs in *The Man of Mode*, the entire plot of *The Way of the World* hinges on the fact that Mirabell is a reformed rake, having arranged that his former lover marry Fainall, while at the same time arranging for her future security by holding her money in trust, so that Fainall cannot do what he attempts, which is to seize her assets for his own purposes.

Finally, the play echoes its era by being a play very much about the difficulties and dangers of women in the sexual marketplace, seen from their own perspective. Millamant is a splendid creation who lives with the consciousness that she will grow older and perhaps as desperate as Lady Wishfort, who will not commit Mrs. Fainall's mistake, and who cannot allow herself to be governed by vengeful jealousies like Mrs. Marwood. All round her are warnings of the dangers in her situation, in which she must delay marriage so that she can choose well, while marriage itself remains inescapable. The inevitability of marriage for a woman, with the hope that some of its otherwise draconian consequences can be mitigated by negotiation, is the moral framework for the proviso scene, in which Mirabell and Millamant debate the circumstances of their intended union. Some critics have pointed out that this scene—the most famous one in Restoration comedy after the china scene in *The Country Wife*—shows Congreve's approval of the Glorious Revolution because Mirabell's and

Millamant's compact echoes the terms of Locke's second *Treatise of Government*, which had been published five years before. For Congreve, apparently, the "way of the world" involves the need to forge workable political compromises.

DRAMATIS PERSONAE

MEN

Fainall, in love with Mrs.* Marwood.
Mirabell, in love with Mrs.* Millamant.
Witwoud,
Petulant, followers of Mrs. Millamant.
Sir Wilfull Witwoud, half–brother to Witwoud and nephew to Lady Wishfort.
Waitwell, servant to Mirabell.

WOMEN

Lady Wishfort, enemy to Mirabell for having falsely pretended love to her.
Mrs.* Millamant, a fine lady, niece to Lady Wishfort and loves Mirabell.
Mrs.* Marwood, friend to Mr. Fainall, and likes Mirabell.
Mrs. Fainall, daughter to Lady Wishfort and wife to Fainall, formerly friend to Mirabell.
Foible, woman* to Lady Wishfort.
Mincing, woman* to Mrs. Millamant.
Dancers, footmen, and attendants.

SCENE: LONDON. THE TIME EQUAL TO
THAT OF THE PRESENT ACTION.

The Way of the World.

Audire est Operae pretium, procedere recte
Qui moechis non voltis … Hor. Sat. 2.1.1
… Metuat, doti deprensa. … Ibid.[1]

---

[1] *Audire … Ibid.*] Horace, *Satire* 1.2.37 ff, 131. Congreve expects his audience to remember the rest of the opening sentence: "*ut omni parte laborent, / utque illis multo corrupta dolore voluptas / atque haec rara cadat dura inter saepe pericla*": "It is worth your while, ye who would have disaster wait on adulterers, to hear how on every side they fare ill, and how for them pleasure is marred by much pain, and, rare as it is, comes oft amid cruel perils" (Loeb); "She fears being deprived of her dowry" (ed.).

Act I. A chocolate house.

Mirabell and Fainall rising from cards, Betty waiting.

MIRABELL.
You are a fortunate man, Mr. Fainall.
FAINALL.
Have we done?
MIRABELL.
What you please. I'll play on to entertain you.
FAINALL.
No, I'll give you your revenge another time, when you are not so indifferent; you are thinking of 5 something else now, and play too negligently. The coldness of a losing gamester lessens the pleasure of the winner. I'd no more play with a man that slighted his ill fortune, than I'd make love* to a woman who undervalued the loss of her 10 reputation.
MIRABELL.
You have a taste extremely delicate and are for refining on your pleasures.
FAINALL.
Prithee, why so reserved? Something has put you out of humor. 15
MIRABELL.
Not at all. I happen to be grave today, and you are gay. That's all.
FAINALL.
Confess, Millamant and you quarrelled last night after I left you. My fair cousin has some humors* that would tempt the patience of a Stoic. What, 20 some coxcomb came in and was well received by her while you were by.
MIRABELL.
Witwoud and Petulant. And what was worse, her aunt, your wife's mother, my evil genius,* or to sum up all in her own name, my old Lady 25 Wishfort came in.
FAINALL.
Oh there it is then. She has a lasting passion for you, and with reason. What, then my wife was there?
MIRABELL.
Yes, and Mrs.* Marwood and three or four more, 30 whom I never saw before. Seeing me, they all put on their grave faces, whispered one another, then

complained aloud of the vapors, and after fell into a profound silence.

FAINALL.

They had a mind to be rid of you. 35

MIRABELL.

For which reason I resolved not to stir. At last the good old lady broke through her painful taciturnity with an invective against long visits. I would not have understood her, but Millamant joining in the argument, I rose and with a constrained smile told 40 her I thought nothing was so easy as to know when a visit began to be troublesome; she reddened and I withdrew, without expecting her reply.

FAINALL.

You were to blame to resent what she spoke only in compliance with her aunt. 45

MIRABELL.

She is more mistress of herself than to be under the necessity of such a resignation.

FAINALL.

What? Though half her fortune depends upon her marrying with my lady's approbation?

MIRABELL.

I was then in such a humor that I should have been 50 better pleased if she had been less discreet.

FAINALL.

Now I remember, I wonder not that they were weary of you. Last night was one of their cabal nights; they have 'em three times a week and meet by turns at one another's apartments, where they 55 come together like the coroner's inquest, to sit upon the murdered reputations of the week. You and I are excluded, and it was once proposed that all the male sex should be excepted, but somebody moved that to avoid scandal there might be one 60 man of the community, upon which motion Witwoud and Petulant were enrolled members.

MIRABELL.

And who may have been the foundress of this sect? My Lady Wishfort, I warrant, who publishes her detestation of mankind and, full of the vigor of 65 fifty-five, declares for a friend and ratafia, and let posterity shift for itself, she'll breed no more.

FAINALL.

The discovery of your sham addresses to her, to conceal your love to her niece, has provoked this separation. Had you dissembled better, things 70 might have continued in the state of nature.

MIRABELL.

I did as much as man could with any reasonable conscience: I proceeded to the very last act of flattery with her and was guilty of a song in her commendation. Nay, I got a friend to put her into 75 a lampoon and complement her with the imputation of an affair with a young fellow, which I carried so far that I told her the malicious Town took notice that she was grown fat of a sudden and, when she lay in of a dropsy, persuaded her she was 80 reported to be in labor. The devil's in't if an old woman is to be flattered further, unless a man should endeavor downright personally to debauch her, and that my virtue forbade me. But for the discovery* of that amour, I am indebted to your 85 friend, or your wife's friend, Mrs. Marwood.

FAINALL.

What should provoke her to be your enemy, without she has made you advances which you have slighted? Women do not easily forgive omissions of that nature. 90

MIRABELL.

She was always civil to me, till of late. I confess I am not one of those coxcombs who are apt to interpret a woman's good manners to her prejudice and think that she who does not refuse 'em everything can refuse 'em nothing. 95

FAINALL.

You are a gallant man, Mirabell, and though you may have cruelty enough not to satisfy a lady's longing, you have too much generosity not to be tender of her honor. Yet you speak with an indifference which seems to be affected and 100 confesses you are conscious of a negligence.

MIRABELL.

You pursue the argument with a distrust that seems to be unaffected and confesses you are conscious of a concern for which the lady is more indebted to you than your wife. 105

FAINALL.

Fie, fie, friend, if you grow censorious, I must leave you; I'll look upon the gamesters in the next room.

MIRABELL.

Who are they?

FAINALL.

Petulant and Witwoud. [*To Betty.*] Bring me some 110
chocolate. (*Exit.*)

MIRABELL.

Betty, what says your clock?

BETTY.

Turned of the last canonical hour, sir.* (*Exit.*)

MIRABELL.

How pertinently the jade answers me! (*Looking on
his watch.*) Hah? Almost one o'clock! 115

Enter a servant.

Oh, you are come. Well, is the grand affair over?
You have been something tedious.

SERVANT.

Sir, there's such coupling at Pancras[2] that they
stand behind one another as 'twere in a country
dance. Ours was the last couple to lead up, and 120
no hopes appearing of despatch; besides, the
parson growing hoarse, we were afraid his lungs
would have failed before it came to our turn, so
we drove round to Duke's Place,[3] and there they
were riveted in a trice. 125

MIRABELL.

So, so, you are sure they are married.

SERVANT.

Married and bedded, sir, I am witness.

MIRABELL.

Have you the certificate?

SERVANT.

Here it is, sir.

MIRABELL.

Has the tailor brought Waitwell's clothes home and 130
the new liveries?

SERVANT.

Yes sir.

MIRABELL.

That's well. Do you go home again, d'ye hear, and
adjourn the consummation till farther order. Bid

---

2 Pancras] At the time, St. Pancras was outside City jurisdiction and so marriages could be performed for a fee
on demand.

3 Dukes' Place] St. James's church, Duke's Place, Aldgate,
notorious for irregular marriages

Waitwell shake his ears and Dame Partlet[4] rustle 135
up her feathers and meet me at one o'clock by
Rosamond's Pond* that I may see her before she
returns to her lady. And as you tender your ears,
be secret.

Exit servant. Reenter Fainall [and Betty].

FAINALL.

Joy of your success, Mirabell; you look pleased. 140

MIRABELL.

Aye, I have been engaged in a matter of some sort
of mirth, which is not ripe for discovery.* I am glad
this is not a cabal night. I wonder, Fainall, that you
who are married, and of consequence should be
discreet, will suffer your wife to be of such a party. 145

FAINALL.

Faith, I am not jealous. Besides, most who are
engaged are women and relations, and for the men,
they are of a kind too contemptible to give scandal.

MIRABELL.

I am of another opinion. The greater the coxcomb,
always the more the scandal: for a woman who is 150
not a fool can have but one reason for associating
with a man that is.

FAINALL.

Are you jealous as often as you see Witwoud
entertained by Millamant?

MIRABELL.

Of her understanding I am, if not of her person. 155

FAINALL.

You do her wrong, for to give her her due, she has
wit.

MIRABELL.

She has beauty enough to make any man think so
and complaisance enough not to contradict him
who shall tell her so. 160

FAINALL.

For a passionate lover, methinks you are a man
somewhat too discerning in the failings of your
mistress.

MIRABELL.

And for a discerning man, somewhat too
passionate a lover, for I like her with all her faults, 165

---

4 Dame Partlet] wife of Chanticleer in Chaucer's fable (the
Nun's Priest's Tale)

nay, like her for her faults. Her follies are so natural or so artful that they become her, and those affectations which in another woman would be odious serve but to make her more agreeable. I'll tell thee, Fainall, she once used me with that 170 insolence, that in revenge I took her to pieces, sifted her and separated her failings; I studied 'em and got 'em by rote. The catalogue was so large, that I was not without hopes one day or other to hate her heartily: to which end I so used myself 175 to think of 'em, that at length, contrary to my design and expectation, they gave me every hour less and less disturbance, till in a few days it became habitual to me to remember 'em without being displeased. They are now grown as familiar 180 to me as my own frailties, and in all probability in a little time longer I shall like 'em as well.

FAINALL.

Marry her, marry her. Be half as well acquainted with her charms as you are with her defects, and my life on't, you are your own man again. 185

MIRABELL.

Say you so?

FAINALL.

Aye, aye, I have experience: I have a wife, and so forth.

Enter messenger.

MESSENGER.

Is one Squire Witwoud here?

BETTY.

Yes, what's your business? 190

MESSENGER.

I have a letter for him, from his brother Sir Wilfull, which I am charged to deliver into his own hands.

BETTY.

He's in the next room, friend—that way.

Exit messenger.

MIRABELL.

What, is the chief of that noble family in Town, Sir Wilfull Witwoud? 195

FAINALL.

He is expected today. Do you know him?

MIRABELL.

I have seen him. He promises to be an extraordinary person. I think you have the honor to be related to him.

FAINALL.

Yes, he is half-brother to this Witwoud by a former 200 wife, who was sister to my Lady Wishfort, my wife's mother. If you marry Millamant, you must call cousins too.

MIRABELL.

I had rather be his relation than his acquaintance.

FAINALL.

He comes to Town in order to equip himself for 205 travel.

MIRABELL.

For travel? Why the man that I mean is above forty.

FAINALL.

No matter for that; 'tis for the honor of England that all Europe should know that we have 210 blockheads of all ages.

MIRABELL.

I wonder there is not an act of Parliament to save the credit of the Nation and prohibit the exportation of fools.

FAINALL.

By no means, 'tis better as 'tis; 'tis better to trade 215 with a little loss than to be quite eaten up with being overstocked.

MIRABELL.

Pray, are the follies of this knight-errant, and those of the squire his brother, anything related?

FAINALL.

Not at all. Witwoud grows by the knight, like a 220 medlar grafted on a crab. One will melt in your mouth, and t'other set your teeth on edge; one is all pulp, and the other all core.

MIRABELL.

So one will be rotten before he be ripe, and the other will be rotten without ever being ripe at all. 225

FAINALL.

Sir Wilfull is an odd mixture of bashfulness and obstinacy. But when he's drunk, he's as loving as the monster in *The Tempest*[5] and after much the same manner. To give t'other his due, he has

---

5 *Tempest*] an allusion to Caliban in Dryden's and Davenant's version of Shakespeare's play

something of good nature and does not always 230
want* wit.

MIRABELL.

Not always, but as often as his memory fails him
and his commonplace of comparisons. He is a fool
with a good memory and some few scraps of other
folks' wit. He is one whose conversation can never 235
been approved, yet it is now and then to be
endured. He has indeed one good quality: he is not
exceptious, for he so passionately affects the
reputation of understanding raillery that he will
construe an affront into a jest and call downright 240
rudeness and ill language satire and fire.

FAINALL.

If you have a mind to finish his picture, you have
an opportunity to do it at full length. Behold the
original.

Enter Witwoud.

WITWOUD.

Afford me your compassion, my dears, pity me, 245
Fainall, Mirabell, pity me.

MIRABELL.

I do from my soul.

FAINALL.

Why, what's the matter?

WITWOUD.

No letters for me, Betty?

BETTY.

Did not the messenger bring you one but now, sir? 250

WITWOUD.

Aye, but no other?

BETTY.

No sir.

WITWOUD.

That's hard, that's very hard. A messenger, a mule, a
beast of burden, he has brought me a letter from the
fool my brother as heavy as a panegyric in a funeral 255
sermon or a copy of commendatory verses from one
poet to another. And what's worse, 'tis as sure a
forerunner of the author as an epistle dedicatory.

MIRABELL.

A fool, and your brother, Witwoud!

WITWOUD.

Aye, aye, my half-brother. My half-brother he is, 260
no nearer, upon honor.

MIRABELL.

Then 'tis possible he may be but half a fool.

WITWOUD.

Good, good Mirabell, *le drôle*! Good, good, hang
him, don't let's talk of him.—Fainall, how does
your lady? Gad, I say anything in the world to get 265
this fellow out of my head. I beg pardon that I
should ask a man of pleasure and the Town a
question at once so foreign and domestic. But I
talk like an old maid at a marriage, I don't know
what I say, but she's the best woman in the world. 270

FAINALL.

'Tis well you don't know what you say, or else your
commendation would go near to make me either
vain or jealous.

WITWOUD.

No man in Town lives well with a wife but
Fainall.—Your judgment, Mirabell? 275

MIRABELL.

You had better step and ask his wife if you would
be credibly informed.

WITWOUD.

Mirabell.

MIRABELL.

Aye.

WITWOUD.

My dear, I ask ten thousand pardons—Gad I have 280
forgot what I was going to say to you.

MIRABELL.

I thank you heartily, heartily.

WITWOUD.

No, but prithee excuse me—my memory is such
a memory.

MIRABELL.

Have a care of such apologies, Witwoud, for I 285
never knew a fool but he affected to complain
either of the spleen or his memory.

FAINALL.

What have you done with Petulant?

WITWOUD.

He's reckoning his money—my money it was. I
have no luck today. 290

FAINALL.

You may allow him to win of you at play, for you
are sure to be too hard for him at repartee. Since
you monopolize the wit that is between you, the
fortune must be his of course.

MIRABELL.

I don't find that Petulant confesses the superiority 295
of wit to be your talent, Witwoud.

WITWOUD.

Come, come, you are malicious now and would
breed debates. Petulant's my friend and a very
honest fellow and a very pretty fellow and has a
smattering, faith and troth, a pretty deal of an odd 300
sort of a small wit. Nay, I'll do him justice. I'm
his friend, I won't wrong him neither. And if he
had but any judgment in the world, he would not
be altogether contemptible. Come, come, don't
detract from the merits of my friend. 305

FAINALL.

You don't take your friend to be over-nicely* bred.

WITWOUD.

No, no, hang him, the rogue has no manners at
all, that I must own. No more breeding than a
bum-baily,6 that I grant you. 'Tis pity, faith, the
fellow has fire and life. 310

MIRABELL.

What, courage?

WITWOUD.

Hum, faith I don't know as to that—I can't say as
to that— Yes faith, in a controversy he'll contradict
anybody.

MIRABELL.

Though 'twere a man whom he feared or a woman 315
whom he loved?

WITWOUD.

Well, well, he does not always think before he
speaks. We have all our failings. You're too hard
upon him, you are faith. Let me excuse him. I can
defend most of his faults except one or two; one 320
he has, that's the truth on't, if he were my brother,
I could not acquit him, that indeed I could wish
were otherwise.

MIRABELL.

Aye marry,* what's that, Witwoud?

WITWOUD.

Oh pardon me—expose the infirmities of my 325
friend—no, my dear, excuse me there.

---

6 bum-baily] the lowest kind of bailiff, involved in enforc-
ing arrests

FAINALL.

What, I warrant he's unsincere, or 'tis some such
trifle.

WITWOUD.

No, no, what if he be? 'Tis no matter for that, his
wit will excuse that: a wit should no more be 330
sincere than a woman constant; one argues a decay
of parts,* as t'other of beauty.

MIRABELL.

Maybe you think him too positive?

WITWOUD.

No, no, his being positive is an incentive to
argument and keeps up conversation. 335

FAINALL.

Too illiterate!

WITWOUD.

That! That's his happiness. His want* of learning
gives him more opportunities to show his natural
parts.*

MIRABELL.

He wants* words? 340

WITWOUD.

Aye, but I like him for that now, for his want* of
words gives me the pleasure very often to explain
his meaning.

FAINALL.

He's impudent?

WITWOUD.

No, that's not it. 345

MIRABELL.

Vain?

WITWOUD.

No.

MIRABELL.

What! He speaks unseasonable truths sometimes,
because he has not wit enough to invent an
evasion. 350

WITWOUD.

Truths! Ha, ha, ha! No, no, since you will have it—
I mean he never speaks truth at all, that's all. He
will lie like a chambermaid or a woman of
quality's* porter. Now that is a fault.

Enter coachman.

COACHMAN.

Is Master Petulant here, mistress? 355

BETTY.

Yes.

COACHMAN.

Three gentlewomen in the coach would speak with him.

FAINALL.

Oh brave* Petulant, three!

BETTY.

I'll tell him.

COACHMAN.

You must bring two dishes of chocolate and a glass of cinnamon-water.

Exeunt Coachman [and Betty].

WITWOUD.

That should be for two fasting strumpets and a bawd troubled with wind. Now you may know what the three are.

MIRABELL.

You are very free with your friend's acquaintance.

WITWOUD.

Aye, aye, friendship without freedom is as dull as love without enjoyment or wine without toasting. But to tell you a secret, these are trulls that he allows coach-hire, and something more by the week, to call on him once a day at public places.

MIRABELL.

How!

WITWOUD.

You shall see that he won't go to 'em because there's no more company here to take notice of him. Why, this is nothing to what he used to do. Before he found out this way, I have known him call for himself.

FAINALL.

Call for himself? What dost thou mean?

WITWOUD.

Mean? Why he would slip you out of this chocolate house, just when you had been talking to him. As soon as your back was turned, whip he was gone, then trip to his lodging, clap on a hood and scarf and mask, slap into a hackney-coach, and drive hither to the door again in a trice, where he would send in for himself, that I mean, call for himself, wait for himself, nay and what's more, not finding himself, sometimes leave a letter for himself.

MIRABELL.

I confess this is something extraordinary. I believe he waits for himself now, he is so long a-coming. Oh, I ask his pardon.

Enter Petulant.

BETTY.

Sir, the coach stays.

PETULANT.

Well, well, I come. 'Sbud,* a man had as good be a professed midwife as a professed whoremaster, at this rate: to be knocked up and raised at all hours and in all places. Pox on 'em, I won't come, d'ye hear, tell 'em I won't come. Let 'em snivel and cry their hearts out.

FAINALL.

You are very cruel, Petulant.

PETULANT.

All's one, let it pass. I have a humor to be cruel.

MIRABELL.

I hope they are not persons of condition that you use at this rate.

PETULANT.

Condition! Condition's a dried fig, if I am not in humor. By this hand, if they were your—a—a—your* what-d'ye-call-'ems themselves, they must wait or rub off, if I want* appetite.

MIRABELL.

What-d'ye-call-'ems! What are they, Witwoud?

WITWOUD.

Empresses, my dear, by your what-d'ye-call-'ems he means sultana queens.

PETULANT.

Aye, Roxolanas.[7]

MIRABELL.

Cry you mercy.

FAINALL.

Witwoud says they are—

PETULANT.

What does he say th'are?

WITWOUD.

I? Fine ladies, I say.

---

7 Roxolanas] ironically named after the Sultana in Davenant's *Siege of Rhodes*

PETULANT.

Pass on Witwoud.—Harkee by this light, his relations: two coheiresses, his cousins, and an old aunt that loves caterwauling better than a conventicle.

WITWOUD.

Ha, ha, ha, I had a mind to see how the rogue would come off. Ha, ha, ha, Gad, I can't be angry with him if he said they were my mother and my sisters.

MIRABELL.

No!

WITWOUD.

No, the rogue's wit and readiness of invention charm me. Dear Petulant.

BETTY.

They are gone, sir, in great anger.

PETULANT.

Enough, let 'em trundle. Anger helps complexion, saves paint.

FAINALL.

This continence is all dissembled; this is in order to have something to brag of the next time he makes court to Millamant and swear he has abandoned the whole sex for her sake.

MIRABELL.

Have you not left off your impudent pretensions there yet? I shall cut your throat sometime or other, Petulant, about that business.

PETULANT.

Aye, aye, let that pass, there are other throats to be cut—

MIRABELL.

Meaning mine, sir?

PETULANT.

Not I—I mean nobody—I know nothing—but there are uncles and nephews in the world—and they may be rivals—what then? All's one for that—

MIRABELL.

How! Harkee Petulant, come hither. Explain, or I shall call your interpreter.

PETULANT.

Explain? I know nothing. Why you have an uncle, have you not, lately come to Town and lodges by my Lady Wishfort's?

MIRABELL.

True.

PETULANT.

Why that's enough. You and he are not friends, and if he should marry and have a child, you may be disinherited, hah?

MIRABELL.

Where hast thou stumbled upon all this truth?

PETULANT.

All's one for that. Why, then say I know something.

MIRABELL.

Come, thou art an honest fellow, Petulant, and shalt make love* to my mistress, thou sha't, faith. What hast thou heard of my uncle?

PETULANT.

I? Nothing I. If throats are to be cut, let swords clash. Snug's the word, I shrug and am silent.

MIRABELL.

Oh raillery, raillery. Come, I know thou art in the women's secrets. What, you're a cabalist. I know you stayed at Millamant's last night after I went. Was there any mention made of my uncle or me? Tell me. If thou hadst but good nature equal to thy wit, Petulant, Tony Witwoud, who is now thy competitor in fame, would show as dim by thee as a dead whiting's eye by a pearl of orient; he would no more be seen by thee than Mercury is by the sun. Come, I'm sure thou wouldst tell me.

PETULANT.

If I do, will you grant me common sense, then, for the future?

MIRABELL.

Faith, I'll do what I can for thee, and I'll pray that Heaven may grant it thee in the meantime.

PETULANT.

Well, harkee.

FAINALL.

Petulant and you both will find Mirabell as warm a rival as a lover.

WITWOUD.

Pshaw, pshaw, that she laughs at Petulant is plain. And for my part, but that it is almost a fashion to admire her, I should— Harkee, to tell you a secret, but let it go no further, between friends, I shall never break my heart for her.

FAINALL.

How!

WITWOUD.

She's handsome, but she's sort of an uncertain woman. 480

FAINALL.

I thought you had died for her.

WITWOUD.

Umh—no—

FAINALL.

She has wit.

WITWOUD.

'Tis what she will hardly allow anybody else. Now 485 demme, I should hate that if she were as handsome as Cleopatra. Mirabell is not so sure of her as he thinks for.

FAINALL.

Why do you think so?

WITWOUD.

We stayed pretty late there last night and heard 490 something of an uncle to Mirabell who is lately come to Town and is between him and the best part of his estate. Mirabell and he are at some distance, as my Lady Wishfort has been told, and you know she hates Mirabell worse than a Quaker 495 hates a parrot or than a fishmonger hates a hard frost. Whether this uncle has seen Mrs.* Millamant or not I cannot say, but there were items of such a treaty being in embryo, and if it should come to life, poor Mirabell would be in some sort 500 unfortunately fobbed, i'faith.

FAINALL.

'Tis impossible Millamant should hearken to it.

WITWOUD.

Faith my dear, I can't tell; she's a woman and a kind of humorist.

MIRABELL.

And this is the sum of what you could collect last 505 night?

PETULANT.

The quintessence. Maybe Witwoud knows more: he stayed longer. Besides, they never mind him; they say anything before him.

MIRABELL.

I thought you had been the greatest favorite. 510

PETULANT.

Aye, tête-a-tête, but not in public, because I make remarks.

MIRABELL.

Do you?

PETULANT.

Aye, aye, pox I'm malicious, man. Now he's soft you know, they are not in awe of him. The fellow's 515 well bred, he's what you call a—what-d'ye-call-'em, a fine gentleman, but he's silly withal.

MIRABELL.

I thank you, I know as much as my curiosity requires.—Fainall, are you for the Mall?*

FAINALL.

Aye, I'll take a turn before dinner. 520

WITWOUD.

Aye, we'll all walk in the Park.* The ladies talked of being there.

MIRABELL.

I thought you were obliged to watch for your brother Sir Wilfull's arrival.

WITWOUD.

No, no, he comes to his aunt's, my Lady Wishfort. 525 Pox on him, I shall be troubled with him too. What shall I do with the fool?

PETULANT.

Beg him for his estate, that I may beg you afterwards and so have but one trouble with you both.

WITWOUD.

Oh rare Petulant, thou art as quick as a fire in a 530 frosty morning; thou shalt to the Mall with us, and we'll be very severe.

PETULANT.

Enough, I'm in a humor to be severe.

MIRABELL.

Are you? Pray then walk by yourselves. Let us not be accessory to your putting the ladies out of 535 countenance with your senseless ribaldry, which you roar out aloud as often as they pass by you, and when you have made a handsome woman blush, then you think you have been severe.

PETULANT.

What, what? Then let 'em either show their 540 innocence by not understanding what they hear or else show their discretion by not hearing what they would not be thought to understand.

MIRABELL.

But hast not thou then sense enough to know that thou ought'st to be most ashamed thyself when 545 thou hast put another out of countenance.

PETULANT.

Not I, by this hand, I always take blushing either for a sign of guilt or ill breeding.

MIRABELL.

I confess you ought to think so. You are in the right, that you may plead the error of your   550
judgment in defence of your practice.
Where modesty's ill manners, 'tis but fit
That impudence and malice pass for wit.

Exeunt.

Act II. St. James's Park.*

Enter Mrs. Fainall and Mrs. Marwood.

MRS. FAINALL.

Aye, aye, dear Marwood, if we will be happy, we must find the means in ourselves and among ourselves. Men are ever in extremes, either doting or averse. While they are lovers, if they have fire and sense, their jealousies are insupportable. And   5
when they cease to love (we ought to think at least), they loathe; they look upon us with horror and distaste; they meet us like the ghosts of what we were and as such fly from us.

MRS. MARWOOD.

True, 'tis an unhappy circumstance of life that love   10
should ever die before us and that the man so often should outlive the lover. But say what you will, 'tis better to be left than never to have been loved. To pass our youth in dull indifference, to refuse the sweets of life because they once must leave us, is   15
as preposterous as to wish to have been born old because we one day must be old. For my part, my youth may wear and waste, but it shall never rust in my possession.

MRS. FAINALL.

Then it seems you dissemble an aversion to   20
mankind only in compliance with my mother's humor.

MRS. MARWOOD.

Certainly. To be free, I have no taste of those insipid dry discourses with which our sex of force must entertain themselves apart from men. We may affect   25
endearments to each other, profess eternal friendships, and seem to dote like lovers, but 'tis not in our natures long to persevere. Love will resume

his empire in our breasts, and every heart, or soon or late, receive and readmit him as its lawful tyrant.   30

MRS. FAINALL.

Bless me, how have I been deceived! Why you profess a libertine.

MRS. MARWOOD.

You see my friendship by my freedom. Come, be as sincere, acknowledge that your sentiments agree with mine.   35

MRS. FAINALL.

Never.

MRS. MARWOOD.

You hate mankind.

MRS. FAINALL.

Heartily, inveterately.

MRS. MARWOOD.

Your husband?

MRS. FAINALL.

Most transcendently, aye, though I say it,   40
meritoriously.

MRS. MARWOOD.

Give me your hand upon it.

MRS. FAINALL.

There.

MRS. MARWOOD.

I join with you. What I have said has been to try you.   45

MRS. FAINALL.

Is it possible? Dost thou hate those vipers, men?

MRS. MARWOOD.

I have done hating 'em and am now come to despise 'em; the next thing I have to do is eternally to forget 'em.

MRS. FAINALL.

There spoke the spirit of an Amazon, a   50
Penthesilea.[8]

MRS. MARWOOD.

And yet I am thinking sometimes to carry my aversion further.

MRS. FAINALL.

How?

MRS. MARWOOD.

Faith, by marrying. If I could but find one that   55
loved me very well and would be thoroughly

---

8 Penthesilea] a queen of the Amazons

sensible of ill usage, I think I should do myself the
violence of undergoing the ceremony.

MRS. FAINALL.

You would not make him a cuckold?

MRS. MARWOOD.

No, but I'd make him believe I did, and that's as 60
bad.

MRS. FAINALL.

Why, had you as good do it?

MRS. MARWOOD.

Oh if he should ever discover it, he would then
know the worst and be out of his pain, but I would
have him ever to continue upon the rack of fear 65
and jealousy.

MRS. FAINALL.

Ingenious mischief! Would thou wert married to
Mirabell.

MRS. MARWOOD.

Would I were.

MRS. FAINALL.

You change color. 70

MRS. MARWOOD.

Because I hate him.

MRS. FAINALL.

So do I, but I can hear him named. But what
reason have you to hate him in particular?

MRS. MARWOOD.

I never loved him. He is and always was
insufferably proud. 75

MRS. FAINALL.

By the reason you gave for your aversion, one
would think it dissembled, for you have laid a fault
to his charge of which his enemies must acquit
him.

MRS. MARWOOD.

Oh, then it seems you are one of his favorable 80
enemies. Methinks you look a little pale, and now
you flush again.

MRS. FAINALL.

Do I? I think I am a little sick o'the sudden.

MRS. MARWOOD.

What ails you?

MRS. FAINALL.

My husband. Don't you see him? He turned short 85
upon me unawares and has almost overcome me.

Enter Fainall and Mirabell.

MRS. MARWOOD.

Ha, ha, ha, he comes opportunely for you.

MRS. FAINALL.

For you, for he has brought Mirabell with him.

FAINALL.

My dear.

MRS. FAINALL.

My soul. 90

FAINALL.

You don't look well today, child.*

MRS. FAINALL.

D'ye think so?

MIRABELL.

He is the only man that does, madam.

MRS. FAINALL.

The only man that would tell me so at least, and
the only man from whom I could hear it without 95
mortification.

FAINALL.

Oh my dear, I am satsified of your tenderness; I
know you cannot resent anything from me,
especially what is an effect of your concern.

MRS. FAINALL.

Mr. Mirabell, my mother interrupted you in a 100
pleasant relation last night. I would fain hear it out.

MIRABELL.

The persons concerned in that affair have yet a
tolerable reputation. I am afraid Mr. Fainall will
be censorious.

MRS. FAINALL.

He has a humor* more prevailing than his curiosity 105
and will willingly dispense with the hearing of one
scandalous story to avoid giving an occasion to
make another by being seen to walk with his wife.
This way, Mr. Mirabell, and I dare promise you
will oblige us both. 110

Exeunt Mrs. Fainall and Mirabell.

FAINALL.

Excellent creature! Well, sure if I should live to be
rid of my wife, I should be a miserable man.

MRS. MARWOOD.

Aye!

FAINALL.

For having only that one hope, the accomplishment
of it of consequence must put an end to all my 115

hopes. And what a wretch is he who must survive his hopes! Nothing remains when that day comes but to sit down and weep like Alexander[9] when he wanted other worlds to conquer.

MRS. MARWOOD.

Will you not follow 'em?   120

FAINALL.

Faith, I think not.

MRS. MARWOOD.

Pray let us; I have a reason.

FAINALL.

You are not jealous?

MRS. MARWOOD.

Of whom?

FAINALL.

Of Mirabell.   125

MRS. MARWOOD.

If I am, is it inconsistent with my love to you that I am tender of your honor?

FAINALL.

You would intimate, then, as if there were a fellow-feeling between my wife and him.

MRS. MARWOOD.

I think she does not hate him to that degree she   130
would be thought.

FAINALL.

But he, I fear, is too insensible.

MRS. MARWOOD.

It may be you are deceived.

FAINALL.

It may be so. I do now begin to apprehend it.

MRS. MARWOOD.

What?   135

FAINALL.

That I have been deceived madam, and you are false.

MRS. MARWOOD.

That I am false! What mean you?

FAINALL.

To let you know I see through all your little arts. Come, you both love him, and both have equally   140
dissembled your aversion. Your mutual jealousies of one another have made you clash till you have both struck fire. I have seen the warm confession redden-

---

9 Alexander] the Great.

ing on your cheeks and sparkling from your eyes.

MRS. MARWOOD.

You do me wrong.   145

FAINALL.

I do not. 'Twas for my ease to oversee and wilfully neglect the gross advances made him by my wife, that by permitting her to be engaged, I might continue unsuspected in my pleasures and take you   150
oftener to my arms in full security. But could you think because the nodding husband would not wake, that e'er the watchful lover slept?

MRS. MARWOOD.

And wherewithal can you reproach me?

FAINALL.

With infidelity, with loving of another, with love   155
of Mirabell.

MRS. MARWOOD.

'Tis false. I challenge you to show an instance that can confirm your groundless accusation. I hate him.

FAINALL.

And wherefore do you hate him? He is insensible, and your resentment follows his neglect. An   160
instance? The injuries you have done him are a proof: your interposing in his love. What cause had you to make discoveries* of his pretended passion? To undeceive the credulous aunt and be the officious obstacle of his match with Millamant.

MRS. MARWOOD.

My obligations to my lady urged me. I had   165
professed a friendship to her and could not see her easy nature so abused by that dissembler.

FAINALL.

What, was it conscience then? Professed a friendship! Oh the pious friendships of the female sex!   170

MRS. MARWOOD.

More tender, more sincere, and more enduring than all the vain and empty vows of men, whether professing love to us or mutual faith to one another.

FAINALL.

Ha, ha, ha, you are my wife's friend too.   175

MRS. MARWOOD.

Shame and ingratitude! Do you reproach me? You, you upbraid me! Have I been false to her through strict fidelity to you and sacrificed my friendship

to keep my love inviolate, and have you the
baseness to charge me with the guilt, unmindful 180
of the merit? To you it should be meritorious that
I have been vicious. And do you reflect that guilt
upon me which should lie buried in your bosom?

FAINALL.

You misinterpret my reproof. I meant but to
remind you of the slight account you once could 185
make of strictest ties when set in competition with
your love to me.

MRS. MARWOOD.

'Tis false, you urged it with deliberate malice.
'Twas spoke in scorn, and I never will forgive it.

FAINALL.

Your guilt, not your resentment, begets your rage. 190
If yet you loved, you could forgive a jealousy, but
you are stung to find you are discovered.

MRS. MARWOOD.

It shall be all discovered.* You too shall be
discovered,* be sure you shall. I can but be
exposed. If I do it myself, I shall prevent* your 195
baseness.

FAINALL.

Why, what will you do?

MRS. MARWOOD.

Disclose it to your wife, own what has passed
between us.

FAINALL.

Frenzy! 200

MRS. MARWOOD.

By all my wrongs, I'll do't, I'll publish to the world
the injuries you have done me both in my fame
and fortune. With both I trusted you, you
bankrupt in honor as indigent of wealth.

FAINALL.

Your fame I have preserved. Your fortune has been 205
bestowed as the prodigality of your love would have
it, in pleasures which we both have shared. Yet had
not you been false, I had ere this repaid it. 'Tis true,
had you permitted Mirabell with Millamant to have
stolen their marriage, my lady had been incensed 210
beyond all means of reconcilement: Millamant had
forfeited the moiety of her fortune, which then
would have descended to my wife. And wherefore
did I marry but to make lawful prize of a rich
widow's wealth and squander it on love and you? 215

MRS. MARWOOD.

Deceit and frivolous pretence.

FAINALL.

Death, am I not married? What's pretence? Am I not
imprisoned, fettered? Have I not a wife? Nay a wife
that was a widow, a young widow, a handsome
widow, and would be again a widow but that I have 220
a heart of proof and something of a constitution to
bustle through the ways of wedlock and this world.
Will you yet be reconciled to truth and me?

MRS. MARWOOD.

Impossible. Truth and you are inconsistent. I hate
you, and shall forever. 225

FAINALL.

For loving you?

MRS. MARWOOD.

I loathe the name of love after such usage, and next
to the guilt with which you would asperse me, I
scorn you most. Farewell.

FAINALL.

Nay, we must not part thus. 230

MRS. MARWOOD.

Let me go.

FAINALL.

Come, I'm sorry.

MRS. MARWOOD.

I care not. Let me go. Break my hands, do, I'd leave
'em to get loose.

FAINALL.

I would not hurt you for the world. Have I no 235
other hold to keep you here?

MRS. MARWOOD.

Well, I have deserved it all.

FAINALL.

You know I love you.

MRS. MARWOOD.

Poor dissembling! Oh that— Well, it is not yet—

FAINALL.

What? What is it not? What is it not yet? It is not 240
yet too late?

MRS. MARWOOD.

No, it is not yet too late, I have that comfort.

FAINALL.

It is to love another.

MRS. MARWOOD.

But not to loathe, detest, abhor mankind, myself,
and the whole treacherous world. 245

FAINALL.

Nay, this is extravagance. Come, I ask your pardon. No tears. I was to blame. I could not love you and be easy in my doubts.* Pray forbear. I believe you. I'm convinced I've done you wrong and any way, every way will make amends. I'll hate my wife yet more. Damn her, I'll part with her, rob her of all she's worth, and will retire somewhere, anywhere to another world. I'll marry thee. Be pacified.— 'Sdeath,* they come. Hide your face, your tears. You have a mask, wear it a moment. This way, this way, be persuaded. 255

Exeunt. Enter Mirabell and Mrs. Fainall.

MRS. FAINALL.

They are here yet.

MIRABELL.

They are turning into the other walk.

MRS. FAINALL.

While I only hated my husband, I could bear to see him, but since I have despised him, he's too 260 offensive.

MIRABELL.

Oh, you should hate with prudence.

MRS. FAINALL.

Yes, for I have loved with indiscretion.

MIRABELL.

You should have just so much disgust for your husband as may be sufficient to make you relish 265 your lover.

MRS. FAINALL.

You have been the cause that I have loved without bounds, and would you set limits to that aversion of which you have been the occasion? Why did you make me marry this man? 270

MIRABELL.

Why do we daily commit disagreeable and dangerous actions? To save that idol reputation. If the familiarities of our loves had produced that consequence of which you were apprehensive, where could you have fixed a father's name with 275 credit but on a husband? I knew Fainall to be a man lavish of his morals, an interested and professing friend, a false and designing lover, yet one whose wit and outward fair behavior have gained a reputation with the Town, enough to 280

make that woman stand excused who has suffered herself to be won by his addresses. A better man ought not to have been sacrificed to the occasion; a worse had not answered to the purpose. When you are weary of him, you know your remedy. 285

MRS. FAINALL.

I ought to stand in some degree of credit with you, Mirabell.

MIRABELL.

In justice to you I have made you privy to my whole design and put it in your power to ruin or advance my fortune. 290

MRS. FAINALL.

Whom have you instructed to represent your pretended uncle?

MIRABELL.

Waitwell, my servant.

MRS. FAINALL.

He is an humble servant to Foible my mother's woman* and may win her to your interest. 295

MIRABELL.

Care is taken for that: she is won and worn by this time. They were married this morning.

MRS. FAINALL.

Who?

MIRABELL.

Waitwell and Foible. I would not tempt my servant to betray me by trusting him too far. If your 300 mother, in hopes to ruin me, should consent to marry my pretended uncle, he might, like Mosca in *The Fox*,[10] stand upon terms; so I made him sure beforehand.

MRS. FAINALL.

So, if my poor mother is caught in a contract, you 305 will discover* the imposture betimes and release her by producing a certificate of her gallant's former marriage.

MIRABELL.

Yes, upon condition she consent to my marriage with her niece and surrender the moiety of her 310 fortune in her possession.

---

10 Mosca in *The Fox*] the tricky servant who betrays his master, the title character in Ben Jonson's Jacobean comedy, *Volpone*

MRS. FAINALL.

She talked last night of endeavoring at a match between Millamant and your uncle.

MIRABELL.

That was by Foible's direction and my instruction, that she might seem to carry it more privately.   315

MRS. FAINALL.

Well, I have an opinion of your success, for I believe my lady will do anything to get a husband, and when she has this, which you have provided for her, I suppose she will submit to anything to get rid of him.   320

MIRABELL.

Yes, I think the good lady would marry anything that resembled a man, though 'twere no more than what a butler could pinch out of a napkin.

MRS. FAINALL.

Female frailty! We must all come to it if we live to be old and feel the craving of a false appetite   325
when the true is decayed.

MIRABELL.

An old woman's appetite is depraved like that of a girl: 'tis the green sickness of a second childhood and, like the faint offer of a latter spring, serves but to usher in the fall and withers in an affected bloom.   330

MRS. FAINALL.

Here's your mistress.

Enter Mrs. Millamant, Witwoud, and Mincing.*

MIRABELL.

Here she comes i'faith full sail, with her fan spread and her streamers out and a shoal of fools for tenders. Hah, no, I cry her mercy.

MRS. FAINALL.

I see but one poor empty sculler, and he tows her   335
woman* after him.

MIRABELL.

You seem to be unattended, madam. You used to have the beau monde throng after you, and a flock of gay fine perrukes hovering round you.

WITWOUD.

Like moths about a candle. I had like to have lost   340
my comparison for want of breath.

MILLAMANT.

Oh I have denied myself airs today. I have walked as fast through the crowd—

WITWOUD.

As a favorite in disgrace, and with as few followers.

MILLAMANT.

Dear Mr. Witwoud, truce with your similitudes,   345
for I am as sick of 'em—

WITWOUD.

As a physician of a good air. I cannot help it madam, though 'tis against myself.

MILLAMANT.

Yet again! Mincing, stand between me and his wit.

WITWOUD.

Do Mrs.* Mincing, like a screen before a great fire.   350
I confess I do blaze today, I am too bright.

MRS. FAINALL.

But dear Millamant, why were you so long?

MILLAMANT.

Long! Lord, have I not made violent haste? I have asked every living thing I met for you; I have enquired after you as after a new fashion.   355

WITWOUD.

Madam, truce with your similitudes. No, you met her husband and did not ask him for her.

MIRABELL.

By your leave, Witwoud, that were like enquiring after an old fashion, to ask a husband for his wife.

WITWOUD.

Hum, a hit, a hit, a palpable hit, I confess it.   360

MRS. FAINALL.

You were dressed before I came abroad.

MILLAMANT.

Aye, that's true. Oh, but then I had—Mincing, what had I? Why was I so long?

MINCING.

Oh mem, your la'ship stayed to peruse a packet of letters.   365

MILLAMANT.

Oh aye, letters—I had letters—I am persecuted with letters—I hate letters—nobody knows how to write letters, and yet one has 'em, one does not know why. They serve one to pin up one's hair.

WITWOUD.

Is that the way? Pray madam, do you pin up   370
your hair with all your letters? I find I must keep copies.

MILLAMANT.

Only with those in verse, Mr. Witwoud. I never

pin up my hair with prose. I fancy one's hair would not curl if it were pinned up with prose.[b] I think I tried once, Mincing. 375

MINCING.

Oh mem, I shall never forget it.

MILLAMANT.

Aye, poor Mincing tiffed[11] and tiffed all the morning.

MINCING.

'Till I had the cremp in my fingers, I'll vow mem. And all to no purpose. But when your la'ship pins it up with poetry, it sits so pleasant the next day as anything, and is so pure and so crips. 380

WITWOUD.

Indeed, so crips?

MINCING.

You are such a critic, Mr. Witwoud. 385

MILLAMANT.

Mirabell, did not you take exceptions last night? Oh aye, and went away. Now I think on't, I'm angry—No, now I think on't, I'm pleased. For I believe I gave you some pain.

MIRABELL.

Does that please you? 390

MILLAMANT.

Infinitely. I love to give pain.

MIRABELL.

You would affect a cruelty which is not in your nature; your true vanity is in the power of pleasing.

MILLAMANT.

Oh I ask your pardon for that. One's cruelty is one's power, and when one parts with one's cruelty, one parts with one's power, and when one has parted with that, I fancy one's old and ugly. 395

MIRABELL.

Aye, aye, suffer your cruelty to ruin the object of your power, to destroy your lover. And then how vain, how lost a thing you'll be! Nay, 'tis true: you are no longer handsome when you've lost your lover; your beauty dies upon the instant, for beauty is the lover's gift. 'Tis he bestows your charms; your glass* is all a cheat. The ugly and the old, whom the looking glass mortifies, yet after commendation can be flattered by it and discover beauties in it, 400 405

for that reflects our praises rather than your face.

MILLAMANT.

Oh the vanity of these men! Fainall, d'ye hear him? If they did not commend us, we were not handsome! Now you must know they could not commend one if one was not handsome. Beauty the lover's gift! Lord, what is a lover, that it can give? Why, one makes lovers as fast as one pleases, and they live as long as one pleases, and they die as soon as one pleases, and then if one pleases, one makes more. 410 415

WITWOUD.

Very pretty. Why, you make no more of making of lovers, madam, than of making so many card-matches.[12]

MILLAMANT.

One no more owes one's beauty to a lover than one's wit to an echo. They can but reflect what we look and say: vain empty things if we are silent or unseen, and want* a being. 420

MIRABELL.

Yet to those two vain empty things, you owe two the greatest pleasures of your life.

MILLAMANT.

How so? 425

MIRABELL.

To your lover you owe the pleasure of hearing yourselves praised, and to an echo the pleasure of hearing yourselves talk.

WITWOUD.

But I know a lady that loves talking so incessantly she won't give an echo fair play; she has that everlasting rotation of tongue, that an echo must wait till she dies before it can catch her last words. 430

MILLAMANT.

Oh fiction. Fainall, let us leave these men.

MIRABELL. (*Aside to Mrs. Fainall.*)

Draw off Witwoud.

MRS. FAINALL.

Immediately.—I have a word or two for Mr. Witwoud. 435

MIRABELL.

I would beg a little private audience too.

Exeunt Witwoud and Mrs. Fainall.

---

11 tiffed] arranged, decked out

12 card-matches] matches made of cardboard

You had the tyranny to deny me last night, though you knew I came to impart a secret to you that concerned my love.

MILLAMANT.

You saw I was engaged.

MIRABELL.

Unkind. You had the leisure to entertain a herd of fools, things who visit you from their excessive idleness, bestowing on your easiness that time which is the encumbrance of their lives. How can you find delight in such society? It is impossible they should admire you; they are not capable, or if they were, it should be to you as a mortification, for sure to please a fool is some degree of folly.

MILLAMANT.

I please myself. Besides, sometimes to converse with fools is for my health.

MIRABELL.

Your health? Is there a worse disease than the conversation of fools?

MILLAMANT.

Yes, the vapors; fools are physic for it, next to asafoetida.

MIRABELL.

You are not in a course of fools?

MILLAMANT.

Mirabell, if you persist in this offensive freedom, you'll displease me. I think I must resolve after all not to have you. We shan't agree.

MIRABELL.

Not in our physic it may be.

MILLAMANT.

And yet our distemper in all likelihood will be the same, for we shall be sick of one another. I shan't endure to be reprimanded nor instructed. 'Tis so dull to act always by advice and so tedious to be told of one's faults. I can't bear it. Well, I won't have you Mirabell—I'm resolved—I think—you may go—ha, ha, ha. What would you give that you could help loving me?

MIRABELL.

I would give something that you did not know I could not help it.

MILLAMANT.

Come, don't look grave then. Well, what do you say to me?

MIRABELL.

I say that a man may as soon make a friend by his wit or a fortune by his honesty as win a woman with plain dealing and sincerity.

MILLAMANT.

Sententious Mirabell! Prithee don't look with that violent and inflexible wise face, like Solomon at the dividing of the child in an old tapestry-hanging.[13]

MIRABELL.

You are merry, madam, but I would persuade you for one moment to be serious.

MILLAMANT.

What, with that face? No, if you keep your countenance, 'tis impossible I should hold mine. Well, after all, there is something very moving in a love-sick face. Ha, ha, ha! Well I won't laugh, don't be peevish. Heigho! Now I'll be melancholy, as melancholy as a watch-light.[14] Well Mirabell, if ever you will win me, woo me now. Nay, if you are so tedious, fare you well.—I see they are walking away.

MIRABELL.

Can you not find in the variety of your disposition one moment—

MILLAMANT.

To hear you tell me that Foible's married and your plot like to speed? No.

MIRABELL.

But how you came to know it—

MILLAMANT.

Unless by the help of the devil, you can't imagine. Unless she should tell me herself. Which of the two it may have been, I will leave you to consider, and when you have done thinking of that, think of me. (*Exit*.)

MIRABELL.

I have something more— Gone. Think of you! To think of a whirlwind, though 'twere in a whirlwind, were a case of more steady contemplation, a very tranquility of mind and mansion.

---

13 Solomon … tapestry-hanging] a portrayal of Solomon's clever decision concerning the parentage of a child; see 1 Kings 3:16-28.

14 watch-light] night-light, hence dim, dark

A fellow that lives in a windmill has not a more 505
whimsical dwelling than the heart of a man that
is lodged in a woman. There is no point of the
compass to which they cannot turn and by which
they are not turned and by one as well as another,
for motion not method is their occupation. To 510
know this and yet continue to be in love is to be
made wise from the dictates of reason and yet
persevere to play the fool by the force of instinct.—
Oh, here come my pair of turtles.*

Enter Waitwell and Foible.

What, billing so sweetly! Is not Valentine's Day 515
over with you yet? Sirrah Waitwell, why sure you
think you were married for your own recreation
and not for my conveniency.

WAITWELL.
Your pardon, sir. With submission, we have indeed
been solacing in lawful delights, but still with an eye 520
to business, sir. I have instructed her as well as I
could. If she can take your directions as readily as my
instructions, sir, your affairs are in a prosperous way.

MIRABELL.
Give you joy, Mrs. Foible.

FOIBLE.
Oh las sir, I am so ashamed. I'm afraid my lady 525
has been in a thousand inquietudes for me. But I
protest, sir, I made as much haste as I could.

WAITWELL.
That she did indeed, sir. It was my fault that she
did not make more.

MIRABELL.
That I believe. 530

FOIBLE.
But I told my lady as you instructed me, sir: that
I had a prospect of seeing Sir Rowland, your uncle,
and that I would put her ladyship's picture in my
pocket to show him, which I'll be sure to say has
made him so enamored of her beauty that he burns 535
with impatience to lie at her ladyship's feet and
worship the original.

MIRABELL.
Excellent Foible! Matrimony has made you
eloquent in love.

WAITWELL.
I think she has profited, sir. I think so. 540

FOIBLE.
You have seen madam Millamant, sir?

MIRABELL.
Yes.

FOIBLE.
I told her, sir, because I did not know that you
might find an opportunity. She had so much
company last night. 545

MIRABELL. (*Gives money.*)
Your diligence will merit more. In the
meantime—

FOIBLE.
Oh dear sir, your humble servant.

WAITWELL.
Spouse.

MIRABELL.
Stand off sir, not a penny.—Go on and prosper, 550
Foible. The lease shall be made good and the farm
stocked, if we succeed.

FOIBLE.
I don't question your generosity, sir, and you need
not doubt of success. If you have no more
commands, sir, I'll be gone. I'm sure my lady is at her 555
toilet* and can't dress till I come. (*Looking out.*) Oh
dear, I'm sure that was Mrs. Marwood that went by
in a mask. If she has seen me with you, I'm sure she'll
tell my lady. I'll make haste home and prevent* her.
Your servant, sir. B'w'y, Waitwell. (*Exit.*) 560

WAITWELL.
Sir Rowland, if you please.—The jade's so pert
upon her preferment, she forgets herself.

MIRABELL.
Come sir, will you endeavor to forget yourself and
transform into Sir Rowland?

WAITWELL.
Why sir, it will be impossible I should remember 565
myself: married, knighted, and attended all in one
day! 'Tis enough to make any man forget himself.
The difficulty will be how to recover my
acquaintance and familiarity with my former self
and fall from my transformation to a reformation 570
into Waitwell. Nay, I shan't be quite the same
Waitwell neither. For now I remember me, I am
married and can't be my own man again.
Aye, there's the grief; that's the sad change of life:
To lose my title and yet keep my wife. 575

Exeunt.

Act III. A room in Lady Wishfort's house.

Lady Wishfort at her toilet,* Peg waiting.

LADY WISHFORT.

Merciful, no news of Foible yet?

PEG.

No madam.

LADY WISHFORT.

I have no more patience. If I have not fretted myself till I am pale again, there's no veracity in me. Fetch me the red. The red, do you hear, sweetheart? An arrant ash color, as I'm a person. Look you how this wench stirs! Why dost thou not fetch me a little red? Didst thou not hear me, Mopus?[15]

PEG.

The red ratafia does your ladyship mean or the cherry brandy?

LADY WISHFORT.

Ratafia, fool? No, fool. Not the ratafia, fool. Grant me patience! I mean the Spanish paper,[16] idiot. Complexion darling. Paint, paint, paint, dost thou understand that, changeling, dangling thy hands like bobbins before thee. Why dost thou not stir, puppet? Thou wooden thing upon wires.

PEG.

Lord madam, your ladyship is so impatient. I cannot come at the paint, madam; Mrs. Foible has locked it up and carried the key with her.

LADY WISHFORT.

A pox take you both. Fetch me the cherry brandy then.

Exit Peg.

I'm as pale and as faint, I look like Mrs. Qualmsick the curate's wife that's always breeding.—Wench, come, come, wench. What art thou doing? Sipping? Tasting? Save thee, dost thou not know the bottle?

Enter Peg with a bottle and china cup.

PEG.

Madam, I was looking for a cup.

LADY WISHFORT.

A cup, save thee, and what a cup hast thou brought! Dost thou take me for a fairy, to drink out of an acorn? Why didst thou not bring thy thimble? Hast thou ne'er a brass thimble clinking in thy pocket with a bit of nutmeg?[17] I warrant thee. Come, fill, fill. So. Again.

One knocks.

See who that is. Set down the bottle first. Here, here, under the table. What, wouldst thou go with the bottle in thy hand like a tapster? As I'm a person, this wench has lived in an inn upon the road before she came to me, like Maritornes the Asturian in *Don Quixote*. No Foible yet?

PEG.

No madam, Mrs. Marwood.

LADY WISHFORT.

Oh Marwood, let her come in. Come in good Marwood.

Enter Mrs. Marwood.

MRS. MARWOOD.

I'm surprised to find your Ladyship in deshabille at this time of day.

LADY WISHFORT.

Foible's a lost thing, has been abroad since morning and never heard of since.

MRS. MARWOOD.

I saw her but now as I came masked through the Park,* in conference with Mirabell.

LADY WISHFORT.

With Mirabell! You call my blood into my face with mentioning that traitor. She durst not have the confidence. I sent her to negotiate an affair, in which if I'm detected I'm undone. If that wheedling villain has wrought upon Foible to detect me, I'm ruined. Oh my dear friend, I'm a wretch of wretches if I'm detected.

MRS. MARWOOD.

Oh madam, you cannot suspect Mrs. Foible's integrity.

LADY WISHFORT.

Oh, he carries poison in his tongue that would corrupt integrity itself. If she has given him an

---

15 Mopus] a stupid person

16 Spanish paper] either a kind of rouge or a method of applying it

17 thimble ... nutmeg] used as good-luck charms

opportunity, she has as good put her integrity into his hands. Ah dear Marwood, what's integrity to an opportunity? Hark! I hear her.——Go, you thing, and send her in. 60

Exit Peg.

Dear friend, retire into my closet* that I may examine her with more freedom. You'll pardon me, dear friend, I can make bold with you. There are books over the chimney—Quarles and Prynne, and the *Short View of the Stage*, with Bunyan's works—to entertain you.[18] 65

Exit Marwood. Enter Foible.

Oh Foible, where hast thou been? What hast thou been doing? 70

FOIBLE.
Madam, I have seen the party.

LADY WISHFORT.
But what hast thou done?

FOIBLE.
Nay, 'tis your ladyship has done, and are to do; I have only promised. But a man so enamored, so transported! Well, here it is, all that is left, all that is not kissed away.[c] Well, if worshipping of pictures be a sin, poor Sir Rowland, I say. 75

LADY WISHFORT.
The miniature has been counted like. But hast thou not betrayed me, Foible? Hast thou not detected me to that faithless Mirabell? What hadst thou to do with him in the Park? Answer me, has he got nothing out of thee? 80

FOIBLE. [*Aside.*]
So, the devil has been beforehand with me. What shall I say?—Alas madam, could I help it if I met that confident thing? Was I in fault? If you had heard how he used me, and all upon your ladyship's account, I'm sure you would not suspect my fidelity. Nay, if that had been the worst, I could have borne, but he had a fling at your Ladyship too, and then I could not hold. But i'faith, I gave him his own. 85 90

18 Quarles … Bunyan] Francis Quarles and John Bunyan wrote devotional works; William Prynne and Jeremy Collier, author of the *Short View*, wrote tracts against the stage.

LADY WISHFORT.
Me? What did the filthy fellow say?

FOIBLE.
Oh madam, 'tis a shame to say what he said, with his taunts and his fleers, tossing up his nose. "Humph," says he, "what, you are a-hatching some plot," says he, "you are so early abroad, or catering," says he, "ferreting for some disbanded officer, I warrant. Half pay is but thin subsistence," says he, "well, what pension does your lady propose? Let me see," says he, "what, she must come down pretty deep now she's superannuated," says he, "and"— 95 100

LADY WISHFORT.
'Odds* my life, I'll have him, I'll have him murdered. I'll have him poisoned. Where does he eat? I'll marry a drawer to have him poisoned in his wine. I'll send for Robin from Locket's* immediately. 105

FOIBLE.
Poison him? Poisoning's too good for him. Starve him, madam, starve him: marry Sir Rowland and get him disinherited. Oh you would bless yourself to hear what he said. 110

LADY WISHFORT.
A villain. Superannuated!

FOIBLE.
"Humph," says he, "I hear you are laying designs against me too," says he, "and Mrs.* Millamant is to marry my uncle." (He does not suspect a word of your ladyship.) "But," says he, "I'll fit you for that, I warrant you," says he, "I'll hamper you for that," says he, "you and your old frippery too," says he, "I'll handle you"— 115

LADY WISHFORT.
Audacious villain! Handle me, would he durst. Frippery? Old frippery! Was there ever such a foul-mouthed fellow? I'll be married tomorrow; I'll be contracted tonight. 120

FOIBLE.
The sooner the better, madam.

LADY WISHFORT.
Will Sir Rowland be here, say'st thou? When, Foible? 125

FOIBLE.
Incontinently, madam. No new sheriff's wife expects

the return of her husband after knighthood with that impatience in which Sir Rowland burns for the dear hour of kissing your ladyship's hands after dinner. 130

LADY WISHFORT.

Frippery? Superannuated frippery! I'll frippery the villain; I'll reduce him to frippery and rags. A tatterdemalion! I hope to see him hung with tatters, like a Long Lane penthouse[19] or a gibbet-thief. A slander-mouthed railer. I warrant the 135 spendthrift prodigal's in debt as much as the million lottery[20] or the whole court upon a birthday. I'll spoil his credit with his tailor. Yes, he shall have my niece with her fortune, he shall.

FOIBLE.

He! I hope to see him lodge in Ludgate[21] first and 140 angle into Blackfriars[22] for brass farthings with an old mitten.

LADY WISHFORT.

Aye, dear Foible. Thank thee for that, dear Foible. He has put me out of all patience. I shall never recompose my features to receive Sir Rowland with 145 any economy of face. This wretch has fretted me that I am absolutely decayed. Look Foible.

FOIBLE.

Your ladyship has frowned a little too rashly, indeed, madam. There are some cracks discernible in the white varnish. 150

LADY WISHFORT.

Let me see the glass.* Cracks, say'st thou? Why, I'm arrantly flayed; I look like an old peeled wall. Thou must repair me, Foible, before Sir Rowland comes, or I shall never keep up to my picture.

FOIBLE.

I warrant you, madam, a little art once made your 155 picture like you, and now a little of the same art must make you like your picture. Your picture must sit for you, madam.

---

19 Long Lane penthouse] Long Lane is where the rag trade flourished.

20 million lottery] possibly referring to the government lottery of 1694, which attempted to raise 1,000,000 pounds

21 Ludgate] prison near the west gate of the City of London

22 Blackfriars] residential district of the City on the Thames

LADY WISHFORT.

But art thou sure Sir Rowland will not fail to come? Or will a* not fail when he does come? Will 160 he be importunate, Foible, and push? For if he should not be importunate, I shall never break decorums. I shall die with confusion if I am forced to advance. Oh no, I can never advance; I shall swoon if he should expect advances. No, I hope 165 Sir Rowland is better bred than to put a lady to the necessity of breaking her forms. I won't be too coy neither. I won't give him despair. But a little disdain is not amiss; a little scorn is alluring.

FOIBLE.

A little scorn becomes your ladyship. 170

LADY WISHFORT.

Yes, but tenderness becomes me best, a sort of a-dyingness. You see that picture has a sort of a—hah, Foible? A swimmingness in the eyes. Yes, I'll look so. My niece affects it, but she wants* features. Is Sir Rowland handsome? Let my toilet* be 175 removed. I'll dress above. I'll receive Sir Rowland here. Is he handsome? Don't answer me. I won't know; I'll be surprised. I'll be taken by surprise.

FOIBLE.

By storm, madam. Sir Rowland's a brisk man.

LADY WISHFORT.

Is he? Oh then he'll importune, if he's a brisk man. 180 I shall save decorums if Sir Rowland importunes. I have a mortal terror at the apprehension of offending against decorums. Nothing but importunity can surmount decorums.[d] Oh I'm glad he's a brisk man. Let my things be removed, 185 good Foible. (*Exit.*)

Enter Mrs. Fainall.

MRS. FAINALL.

Oh Foible, I have been in a fright lest I should come too late. That devil Marwood saw you in the Park with Mirabell, and I'm afraid will discover* it to my lady. 190

FOIBLE.

Discover what, madam?

MRS. FAINALL.

Nay, nay, put not on that strange face. I am privy to the whole design and know what Waitwell, to whom thou wert this morning married, is to personate Mirabell's uncle, and as such winning my lady, to involve her in those difficulties from which Mirabell only must release her by his making his conditions to have my cousin and her fortune left to her own disposal.

FOIBLE.

Oh dear madam, I beg your pardon. It was not my confidence in your ladyship that was deficient, but I thought the former good correspondence between your ladyship and Mr. Mirabell might have hindered his communicating this secret.

MRS. FAINALL.

Dear Foible, forget that.

FOIBLE.

Oh dear madam, Mr. Mirabell is such a sweet winning gentleman—but your ladyship is the pattern of generosity, sweet lady, to be so good! Mr. Mirabell cannot choose but be grateful. I find your ladyship has his heart still. Now madam, I can safely tell your ladyship our success. Mrs. Marwood had told my lady, but I warrant, I managed myself. I turned it all for the better. I told my lady that Mr. Mirabell railed at her. I laid horrid things to his charge, I'll vow, and my lady is so incensed that she'll be contracted to Sir Rowland tonight, she says. I warrant, I worked her up, that he may have her for asking for, as they say of a Welsh maidenhead.

MRS. FAINALL.

Oh rare Foible!

FOIBLE.

Madam, I beg your ladyship to acquaint Mr. Mirabell of his success. I would be seen as little as possible to speak to him; besides, I believe Madam Marwood watches me. She has a month's mind,* but I know Mr. Mirabell can't abide her.

Enter Footman.

John, remove my lady's toilet.*—Madam, your servant. My lady is so impatient, I fear she'll come for me if I stay.

MRS. FAINALL.

I'll go with you up the back stairs, lest I should meet her.

Exeunt. Enter Mrs. Marwood.

MRS. MARWOOD.

Indeed Mrs. Engine,* is it thus with you? Are you become a go-between of this importance? Yes, I shall watch you. Why, this wench is the passe-partout, a very master-key to everybody's strongbox. My friend Fainall, have you carried it so swimmingly? I thought there was something in it, but it seems it's over with you. Your loathing is not from a want* of appetite, then, but from a surfeit. Else you could never be so cool to fall from a principal to be an assistant, to procure for him! A pattern of generosity, that I confess. Well, Mr. Fainall, you have met with your match. Oh man, man! Woman, woman! The devil's an ass. If I were a painter, I would draw him like an idiot, a driveler, with a bib and bells. Man should have his head and horns,* and woman the rest of him. Poor simple fiend! Madam Marwood has a month's mind, but he can't abide her. 'Twere better for him you had not been his confessor in that affair without you had kept his counsel closer. I shall not prove another pattern of generosity and stalk for him till he takes his stand to aim at a fortune.ᵉ He has not obliged me to that with those excesses of himself. And now I'll have none of him.—Here comes the good lady, panting ripe, with a heart full of hope and a head full of care, like any chemist* upon the day of projection.

Enter Lady Wishfort.

LADY WISHFORT.

Oh dear Marwood, what shall I say for this rude forgetfulness? But my dear friend is all goodness.

MRS. MARWOOD.

No apologies, dear madam. I have been very well entertained.

LADY WISHFORT.

As I'm a person, I am in a very chaos to think I should so forget myself. But I have such an olio of affairs, really I know not what to do. (*Calls.*) Foible. —I expect my nephew Sir Wilfull every moment too.—Why Foible.—He means to travel for improvement.

MRS. MARWOOD.

Methinks Sir Wilfull should rather think of marrying than travelling at his years. I hear he is turned of forty.

LADY WISHFORT.

Oh he's in less danger of being spoiled by his travels. I am against my nephew's marrying too young. It will be time enough when he comes back and has acquired discretion to choose for himself. 270

MRS. MARWOOD.

Methinks Mrs. Millamant and he would make a very fit match. He may travel afterwards. 'Tis a thing very usual with young gentlemen. 275

LADY WISHFORT.

I promise you I have thought on't. And since 'tis your judgment, I'll think on't again. I assure you I will; I value your judgment extremely. On my word I'll propose it. 280

Enter Foible.

Come, come Foible, I had forgot my nephew will be here before dinner. I must make haste.

FOIBLE.

Mr. Witwoud and Mr. Petulant are come to dine with your ladyship.

LADY WISHFORT.

Oh dear, I can't appear till I'm dressed. Dear Marwood, shall I be free with you again and beg you to entertain 'em? I'll make all imaginable haste. Dear friend excuse me. 285

Exeunt Lady Wishfort and Foible. Enter Mrs. Millamant and Mincing.

MILLAMANT.

Sure never anything was so unbred as that odious man.—Marwood, your servant. 290

MRS. MARWOOD.

You have a color. What's the matter?

MILLAMANT.

That horrid fellow Petulant has provoked me into a flame. I have broke my fan.—Mincing, lend me yours.—Is not all the powder out of my hair?

MRS. MARWOOD.

No. What has he done? 295

MILLAMANT.

Nay, he has done nothing; he has only talked. Nay, he has said nothing neither, but he has contradicted everything that has been said. For my part, I thought Witwoud and he would have quarrelled.* 300

MINCING.

I vow mem, I thought once they would have fit.

MILLAMANT.

Well, 'tis a lamentable thing, I'll swear, that one has not the liberty of choosing one's acquaintance as one does one's clothes.

MRS. MARWOOD.

If we had the liberty, we should be as weary of one set of acquaintance, though never so good, as we are of one suit, though never so fine. A fool and a doily stuff[23] would now and then find days of grace and be worn for variety. 305

MILLAMANT.

I could consent to wear 'em if they would wear alike, but fools never wear out. They are such drap-du-Berry[24] things without one could give 'em to one's chambermaid after a day or two. 310

MRS. MARWOOD.

'Twere better so indeed. Or what think you of the playhouse? A fine, gay, glossy fool should be given there, like a new masking habit after the masquerade is over and we have done with the disguise. For a fool's visit is always a disguise and never admitted by a woman of wit but to blind her affair with a lover of sense. If you would but appear bare-faced now and own Mirabell, you might as easily put off Petulant and Witwoud as your hood and scarf. And indeed 'tis time, for the Town has found it: the secret is grown too big for the pretence. 'Tis like Mrs. Primly's great belly: she may lace it down before, but it burnishes on her hips. Indeed Millamant, you can no more conceal it than my Lady Strammel can her face, that goodly face, which, in defiance of her Rhenish-wine tea,[25] will not be comprehended in a mask. 315 320 325 330

MILLAMANT.

I'll take my death, Marwood, you are more censorious than a decayed beauty or a discarded toast.—Mincing, tell the men they may come up. My aunt is not dressing.

Exit Mincing.

---

23 doily stuff] light, cheap woollen material

24 Drap-du-Berry] woollen cloth from Berry, France

25 Rhenish-wine-tea] Rhine wines were thought to be slimming.

Their folly is less provoking than your malice; the Town has found it. What has it found? That Mirabell loves me is no more a secret than it is a secret that you discovered* it to my aunt or than the reason why you discovered it is a secret.

MRS. MARWOOD.

You are nettled.

MILLAMANT.

You're mistaken. Ridiculous!

MRS. MARWOOD.

Indeed my dear, you'll tear another fan if you don't mitigate those violent airs.

MILLAMANT.

Oh silly! Ha, ha, ha. I could laugh immoderately. Poor Mirabell! His constancy to me has quite destroyed his complaisance for all the world beside. I swear, I never enjoined it him to be so coy. If I had the vanity to think he would obey me, I would command him to show more gallantry. 'Tis hardly well bred to be so particular on one hand and so insensible on the other. But I despair to prevail and so let him follow his own way. Ha, ha, ha. Pardon me, dear creature, I must laugh, ha, ha, ha, though I grant you 'tis a little barbarous, ha, ha, ha.

MRS. MARWOOD.

What pity 'tis, so much fine raillery, and delivered with so significant gesture, should be so unhappily directed to miscarry.

MILLAMANT.

Hah? Dear creature, I ask your pardon. I swear, I did not mind you.

MRS. MARWOOD.

Mr. Mirabell and you both may think it a thing impossible, when I shall tell him, by telling you—

MILLAMANT.

Oh dear, what? For it is the same thing, if I hear it—ha, ha, ha.

MRS. MARWOOD.

That I detest him, hate him, madam.

MILLAMANT.

Oh madam, why so do I. And yet the creature loves me, ha, ha, ha. How can one forbear laughing to think of it. I am a sibyl if I am not amazed to think what he can see in me. I'll take my death, I think you are handsomer. And within a year or two as young. If you could but stay for me, I should

overtake you. But that cannot be. Well, that thought makes me melancholy. Now I'll be sad.

MRS. MARWOOD.

Your merry note may be changed sooner than you think.

MILLAMANT.

D'ye say so? Then I'm resolved I'll have a song to keep up my spirits.

Enter Mincing.

MINCING.

The gentlemen stay but to comb, madam, and will wait on you.

MILLAMANT.

Desire Mrs. ____* that is in the next room to sing the song I would have learned yesterday.—You shall hear it madam. Not that there's any great matter in it. But 'tis agreeable to my humor.

Song.26

I.
Love's but the frailty of the mind
    When 'tis not with ambition joined,
A sickly flame, which if not fed expires,
And feeding, wastes in self-consuming fires.

II.
'Tis not to wound a wanton boy
    Or am'rous youth that gives the joy,
But 'tis the glory to have pierced a swain,
For whom inferior beauties sighed in vain.

III.
Then I alone the conquest prize
    When I insult a rival's eyes;
If there's delight in love, 'tis when I see
The heart which others bleed for, bleed for me.

Enter Petulant and Witwoud.

MILLAMANT.

Is your animosity composed, gentlemen?

WITWOUD.

Raillery, raillery, madam. We have no animosity. We hit off a little wit now and then, but no animosity. The falling out of wits is like the falling out of lovers. We agree in the main,27 like treble and bass. Hah, Petulant?

---

26 Song] composed by John Eccles and sung by a "Mrs. Hodgson"

27 main] the middle or tenor part

PETULANT.

Aye in the main, but when I have a humor to
contradict—

WITWOUD.

Aye, when he has a humor to contradict, then I
contradict too. What, I know my cue. Then we
contradict one another like two battledores, for   405
contradictions beget one another like Jews.

PETULANT.

If he says black's black—if I have a humor to say
'tis blue—let that pass—all's one for that. If I have
a humor to prove it, it must be granted.

WITWOUD.

Not positively must, but it may, it may.   410

PETULANT.

Yes, it positively must, upon proof positive.

WITWOUD.

Aye, upon proof positive it must, but upon proof
presumptive it only may. That's a logical
distinction now, madam.

MRS. MARWOOD.

I perceive your debates are of importance and very   415
learnedly handled.

PETULANT.

Importance is one thing, and learning's another,
but a debate's a debate, that I assert.

WITWOUD.

Petulant's an enemy to learning; he relies altogether
on his parts.*   420

PETULANT.

No, I'm no enemy to learning; it hurts not me.

MRS. MARWOOD.

That's a sign indeed it's no enemy to you.

PETULANT.

No, no, it's no enemy to anybody but them that
have it.

MILLAMANT.

Well, an illiterate man's my aversion. I wonder at   425
the impudence of any illiterate man to offer to
make love.*

WITWOUD.

That I confess I wonder at too.

MILLAMANT.

Ah! To marry an ignorant that can hardly read or
write!   430

PETULANT.

Why should a man be ever the further from being
married though he can't read any more than he is
from being hanged? The ordinary's[28] paid for
setting the psalm, and the parish priest for reading
the ceremony. And for the rest which is to follow   435
in both cases, a man may do it without book. So
all's one for that.

MILLAMANT.

D'ye hear that creature? Lord, here's company. I'll
be gone.

Exeunt Millamant and Mincing.

WITWOUD.

In the name of Bartlemew and his fair,[29] what have   440
we here?

MRS. MARWOOD.

'Tis your brother, I fancy. Don't you know him?

WITWOUD.

Not I—yes, I think it is he—I've almost forgotten
him; I have not seen him since the Revolution.[30]

*Enter Sir Wilfull Witwoud in a country riding habit,
and servant to Lady Wishfort.*

SERVANT.

Sir, my lady's dressing. Here's company, if you   445
please to walk in, in the mean time.

SIR WILFULL.

Dressing! What, it's but morning here I warrant
with you in London; we should count it towards
afternoon in our parts, down in Shropshire. Why
then belike my aunt han't dined yet, hah friend?   450

SERVANT.

Your aunt, sir?

SIR WILFULL.

My aunt sir, yes my aunt sir, and your lady sir. Your
lady is my aunt, sir. Why, what, dost thou not

---

28 being hanged … ordinary] Prisoners who could read
(usually a psalm chosen by the ordinary or prison chaplain) were saved from being hanged "by benefit of
clergy."

29 Bartlemew] Bartholemew Fair occurred at Smithfield on
August 24 (St. Bartholemew's Day); it was the site of
many curiosities.

30 Revolution] the Revolution of 1688, or "Glorious"
Revolution

know me, friend? Why then send somebody here that does. How long hast thou lived with thy lady, fellow, hah? 455

SERVANT.

A week, sir, longer than anybody in the house, except my lady's woman.*

SIR WILFULL.

Why then belike thou dost not know thy lady if thou see'st her, hah friend? 460

SERVANT.

Why truly sir, I cannot safely swear to her face in a morning before she is dressed. 'Tis like I may give a shrewd guess at her by this time.

SIR WILFULL.

Well prithee try what thou canst do. If thou canst not guess, enquire her out, dost hear fellow? And tell 465 her, her nephew Sir Wilfull Witwoud is in the house.

SERVANT.

I shall, sir.

SIR WILFULL.

Hold ye, hear me friend. A word with you in your ear. Prithee who are these gallants?

SERVANT.

Really sir, I can't tell; here come so many here, 'tis 470 hard to know 'em all. (*Exit.*)

SIR WILFULL.

'Oons,* this fellow knows less than a starling; I don't think a* knows his own name.

MRS. MARWOOD.

Mr. Witwoud, your brother is not behindhand in forgetfulness. I fancy he has forgot you too. 475

WITWOUD.

I hope so. The devil take him that remembers first, I say.

SIR WILFULL.

Save you gentlemen and lady.

MRS. MARWOOD.

For shame Mr. Witwoud. Why won't you speak to him?—And you, sir. 480

WITWOUD.

Petulant, speak.

PETULANT.

And you, sir.

SIR WILFULL.

No offence, I hope. (*Salutes* Marwood.*)

MRS. MARWOOD.

No sure, sir.

WITWOUD.

This is a vile dog, I see that already. No offence! 485 Ha, ha, ha, to him, to him Petulant. Smoke him.

PETULANT. (*Surveying him round.*)

It seems as if you had come a journey, sir, hem, hem.

SIR WILFULL.

Very likely, sir, that it may seem so.

PETULANT.

No offence, I hope, sir. 490

WITWOUD.

Smoke the boots, the boots, Petulant, the boots, ha, ha, ha.

SIR WILFULL.

Maybe not, sir; thereafter as 'tis meant, sir.

PETULANT.

Sir, I presume upon the information of your boots.

SIR WILFULL.

Why 'tis like you may, sir. If you are not satisfied 495 with the information of my boots, sir, if you will step to the stable, you may enquire further of my horse, sir.

PETULANT.

Your horse, sir! Your horse is an ass, sir!

SIR WILFULL.

Do you speak by way of offence, sir? 500

MRS. MARWOOD.

The gentleman's merry, that's all, sir.—S'life,* we shall have a quarrel betwixt an horse and an ass before they find one another out.—You must not take anything amiss from your friends, sir. You are among your friends here, though it may be you 505 don't know it. If I am not mistaken, you are Sir Wilfull Witwoud.

SIR WILFULL.

Right lady, I am Sir Wilfull Witwoud, so I write myself—no offence to anybody, I hope—and nephew to the Lady Wishfort of this mansion. 510

MRS. MARWOOD.

Don't you know this gentleman, sir?

SIR WILFULL.

Hum! What, sure 'tis not—yea by'r lady, but 'tis— 'sheart* I know not whether 'tis or no—yea but 'tis, by the Wrekin.[31] Brother Anthony! What, Tony

---

[31] Wrekin] an important hill in Shropshire

i'faith! What, dost thou not know me? By'r lady, nor 515
I thee, thou art so becravatted and beperriwigged.
'Sheart, why dost not speak? Art thou o'erjoyed?

WITWOUD.

'Odso* brother, is it you? Your servant, brother.

SIR WILFULL.

Your servant! Why yours, sir. Your servant again.
'Sheart, and your friend and servant to that—and 520
a—(*Puff.*) and a flap-dragon[32] for your service, sir.
And a hare's foot and a hare's scut for your service,
sir, an* you be so cold and so courtly!

WITWOUD.

No offence, I hope, brother.

SIR WILFULL.

'Sheart, sir, but there is, and much offence. A pox, 525
is this your Inns o'Court* breeding not to know
your friends and your relations, your elders and
your betters.

WITWOUD.

Why, brother Wilfull of Salop, you may be as short
as a Shrewsbury cake,[33] if you please. But I tell 530
you, 'tis not modish to know relations in Town.
You think you're in the country, where great
lubberly brothers slabber and kiss one another
when they meet, like a call of serjeants.[34] 'Tis not
the fashion here, 'tis not indeed, dear brother. 535

SIR WILFULL.

The fashion's a fool, and you're a fop, dear brother.
'Sheart, I've suspected this. By'r lady, I conjectured
you were a fop since you began to change the style
of your letters and write in a scrap of paper gilt
round the edges no broader than a subpoena. I 540
might expect this, when you left off "honored
brother" and "hoping you are in good health," and
so forth, to begin with a "Rat* me, knight, I am
so sick of last night's debauch," 'Od's* heart, and
then tell a familiar tale of a cock and a bull and a 545
whore and a bottle and so conclude. You could
write news before you were out of your time,[35]

---

32 flap-dragon] raisin snatched from burning brandy and
   popped into the mouth, hence insignificant thing
33 Shrewsbury cake] a flat cake associated with the chief
   market town in Shropshire.
34 call of serjeants] a group called to the bar at the same time
35 out of your time] while you were still indentured to a
   lawyer

---

when you lived with honest Pimple Nose the
attorney of Furnival's Inn.[36] You could entreat to
be remembered then to your friends round the 550
Wrekin. We could have gazettes then, and *Dawks's
Letter*,[37] and the weekly bill,* till of late days.

PETULANT.

'Slife,* Witwoud, were you ever an attorney's clerk?
Of the family of the Furnivals? Ha, ha, ha.

WITWOUD.

Aye, aye, but that was for a while. Not long, not 555
long. Pshaw, I was not in my own power then. An
orphan, and this fellow was my guardian. Aye, aye,
I was glad to consent to that man to come to
London. He had the disposal of me then. If I had
not agreed to that, I might have been bound 560
prentice to a felt-maker in Shrewsbury. This fellow
would have bound me to a maker of felts.

SIR WILFULL.

'Sheart, and better than to be bound to a maker
of fops, where, I suppose, you have served your
time, and now you may set up for yourself. 565

MRS. MARWOOD.

You intend to travel, sir, as I'm informed.

SIR WILFULL.

Belike I may, madam. I may chance to sail upon
the salt seas, if my mind hold.

PETULANT.

And the wind serve.

SIR WILFULL.

Serve or not serve, I shan't ask licence of you, sir, 570
nor the weathercock your companion. I direct my
discourse to the lady, sir.—'Tis like my aunt may
have told you, madam. Yes, I have settled my
concerns, I may say now, and am minded to see
foreign parts. If and how that the peace[38] holds, 575
whereby, that is, taxes abate.

MRS. MARWOOD.

I thought you had designed for France at all
adventures.

SIR WILFULL.

I can't tell that. 'Tis like I may, and 'tis like I may

---

36 Furnival's Inn] associated with the major Inns of Court*
37 Dawks's Letter] a contemporary newspaper
38 peace] the Peace of Ryswick (1697), creating a lull in
   William III's wars with France

not. I am somewhat dainty in making a resolution, because when I make it, I keep it. I don't stand shilly-shally, then. If I say't, I'll do't. But I have thoughts to tarry a small matter in Town, to learn somewhat of your lingo first before I cross the seas. I'd gladly have a spice of your French, as they say, whereby to hold discourse in foreign countries. 580 585

MRS. MARWOOD.

Here is an academy in Town for that use.

SIR WILFULL.

There is? 'Tis like there may.

MRS. MARWOOD.

No doubt you will return very much improved.

WITWOUD.

Yes, refined, like a Dutch skipper from a whale-fishing. 590

Enter Lady Wishfort and Fainall.

LADY WISHFORT.

Nephew, you are welcome.

SIR WILFULL.

Aunt, your servant.

FAINALL.

Sir Wilfull, your most faithful servant.

SIR WILFULL.

Cousin Fainall, give me your hand. 595

LADY WISHFORT.

Cousin Witwoud, your servant. Mr. Petulant, your servant. Nephew, you are welcome again. Will you drink anything after your journey, Nephew, before you eat? Dinner's almost ready.

SIR WILFULL.

I'm very well, I thank you, Aunt. However, I thank you for your courteous offer. 'Sheart, I was afraid you would have been in the fashion too and have remembered to have forgot your relations. Here's your cousin Tony. Belike I mayn't call him brother for fear of offence. 600 605

LADY WISHFORT.

Oh, he's a railer, Nephew. My cousin's a wit. And your wits always rally their best friends to choose. When you have been abroad, Nephew, you'll understand raillery better.

Fainall and Mrs. Marwood talk apart.

SIR WILFULL.

Why then, let him hold his tongue in the meantime and rail when that day comes. 610

Enter Mincing.

MINCING.

Mem, I come to acquaint your la'ship that dinner is impatient.

SIR WILFULL.

Impatient? Why then belike it won't stay till I pull off my boots. Sweetheart, can you help me to a pair of slippers? My man's with his horses, I warrant. 615

LADY WISHFORT.

Fie, fie, Nephew, you would not pull off your boots here. Go down into the hall. Dinner shall stay for you.—My nephew's a little unbred; you'll pardon him, madam. Gentlemen will you walk? Marwood— 620

MRS. MARWOOD.

I'll follow you, madam, before Sir Wilfull is ready.

[Exeunt all but] Mrs. Marwood and Fainall.

FAINALL.

Why then, Foible's a bawd, an arrant, rank, match-making bawd. And I it seems am a husband, a rank husband, and my wife a very arrant, rank wife—all in the way of the world. 'Sdeath,* to be an anticipated cuckold, a cuckold in embryo! Sure I was born with budding antlers like a young satyr or a citizen's child.[39] 'Sdeath, to be outwitted, to be out-jilted, out-matrimonied. If I had kept my speed like a stag, 'twere somewhat, but to crawl after with my horns* like a snail and outstripped by my wife, 'tis scurvy wedlock. 625 630

MRS. MARWOOD.

Then shake it off. You have often wished for an opportunity to part, and now you have it. But first, prevent their plot. The half of Millamant's fortune is too considerable to be parted with to a foe, to Mirabell. 635

FAINALL.

Damn him, that had been mine, had you not made that fond* discovery*. That had been forfeited, had they been married. My wife had added luster to my 640

---

[39] citizen's child] Citizens or burghers were conventionally cuckolded by fine gentlemen or courtiers.

horns by that increase of fortune: I could have worn
'em tipped with gold, though my forehead had been
furnished like a deputy-lieutenant's hall.

MRS. MARWOOD.

They may prove a cap of maintenance[40] to you
still, if you can away with your wife. And she's no 645
worse than when you had her. I dare swear she had
given up her game before she was married.

FAINALL.

Hum! That may be. She might throw up her cards,
but I'll be hanged if she did not put Pam[41] in her
pocket.[f] 650

MRS. MARWOOD.

You married her to keep* you, and if you can
contrive to have her keep* you better than you
expected, why should you not keep her longer than
you intended?

FAINALL.

The means, the means? 655

MRS. MARWOOD.

Discover* to my lady your wife's conduct. Threaten
to part with her. My lady loves her and will come
to any composition to save her reputation. Take
the opportunity of breaking it just upon the
discovery* of this imposture. My lady will be 660
enraged beyond bounds and sacrifice niece and
fortune and all at that conjuncture. And let me
alone to keep her warm. If she should flag in her
part, I will not fail to prompt her.

FAINALL.

Faith, this has an appearance. 665

MRS. MARWOOD.

I'm sorry I hinted to my lady to endeavor a match
between Millamant and Sir Wilfull. That may be
an obstacle.

FAINALL.

Oh for that matter, leave me to manage him. I'll
disable him for that; he will drink like a Dane. 670
After dinner, I'll set his hand in.

MRS. MARWOOD.

Well, how do you stand affected towards your lady?

---

40 cap of maintenance] cap with two points like horns behind, and a feature in some families' coats of arms
41 Pam] The Jack of Clubs was highest trumps in the game
of loo.

FAINALL.

Why faith, I'm thinking of it. Let me see. I am
married already, so that's over. My wife has played the
jade with me. Well, that's over too. I never loved her, 675
or if I had, why, that would have been over too by this
time. Jealous of her I cannot be, for I am certain; so
there's an end of jealousy. Weary of her I am and shall
be. No, there's no end of that; no, no, that were too
much to hope. Thus far concerning my repose. Now 680
for my reputation. As to my own, I married not for
it, so that's out of the question. And as to my part in
my wife's, why, she had parted with hers before. So,
bringing none to me, she can take none from me.
'Tis against all rule of play that I should lose to one 685
who has not wherewithal to stake.

MRS. MARWOOD.

Besides, you forget, marriage is honorable.

FAINALL.

Hum! Faith, and that's well thought on. Marriage
is honorable, as you say, and if so, wherefore
should cuckoldom be a discredit, being derived 690
from so honorable a root?

MRS. MARWOOD.

Nay, I know not. If the root be honorable, why
not the branches?

FAINALL.

So, so, why this point's clear. Well, how do we
proceed? 695

MRS. MARWOOD.

I will contrive a letter which shall be delivered to my
lady at the time when the rascal who is to act Sir
Rowland is with her. It shall come as from an
unknown hand, for the less I appear to know of the
truth, the better I can play the incendiary. Besides, 700
I would not have Foible provoked if I could help it,
because, you know, she knows some passages. Nay,
I expect all will come out, but let the mine be sprung
first, and then I care not if I'm discovered.

FAINALL.

If the worst come to the worst, I'll turn my wife 705
to grass. I have already a deed of settlement of the
best part of her estate, which I wheedled out of
her, and that you shall partake at least.

MRS. MARWOOD.

I hope you are convinced that I hate Mirabell.
Now you'll be no more jealous. 710

FAINALL.

Jealous, no, by this kiss. Let husbands be jealous, but let the lover still* believe. Or if he doubt, let it be only to endear his pleasure and prepare the joy that follows when he proves his mistress true. But let husbands' doubts convert to endless jealousy, or if 715 they have belief, let it corrupt to superstition and blind credulity. I am single and will herd no more with 'em. True, I wear the badge, but I'll disown the order. And since I take my leave of 'em, I care not if I leave 'em a common motto, to their common crest: 720

　　All husbands must or pain or shame endure;
　　The wise too jealous are, fools too secure.

Exeunt.

Act IV. [Scene continues.]

Enter Lady Wishfort and Foible.

LADY WISHFORT.

Is Sir Rowland coming, say'st thou, Foible? And are things in order?

FOIBLE.

Yes, madam. I have put wax lights in the sconces and placed the footmen in a row in the hall in their best liveries, with the coachman and postilion to 5 fill up the equipage.

LADY WISHFORT.

Have you pullvilled the coachman and postilion that they may not stink of the stable when Sir Rowland comes by?

FOIBLE.

Yes, madam. 10

LADY WISHFORT.

And are the dancers and the music ready, that he may be entertained in all points with correspondence to his passion?

FOIBLE.

All is ready, madam.

LADY WISHFORT.

And—well—and how do I look, Foible? 15

FOIBLE.

Most killing well, madam.

LADY WISHFORT.

Well, and how shall I receive him? In what figure shall I give his heart the first impression? There is a great deal in the first impression. Shall I sit? No I

won't sit. I'll walk. Aye, I'll walk from the door upon 20 his entrance, and then turn full upon him. No, that will be too sudden. I'll lie—aye, I'll lie down. I'll receive him in my little dressing room: there's a couch. Yes, yes, I'll give the first impression on a couch. I won't lie neither but loll and lean upon one 25 elbow with one foot a little dangling off, jogging in a thoughtful way. Yes. And then as soon as he appears, start, aye, start and be surprised, and rise to meet him in a pretty disorder. Yes. Oh, nothing is more alluring than a levee from a couch in some 30 confusion. It shows the foot to advantage and furnishes with blushes and recomposing airs beyond comparison. Hark! There's a coach.

FOIBLE.

'Tis he, madam.

LADY WISHFORT.

Oh dear, has my nephew made his addresses to 35 Millamant? I ordered him.

FOIBLE.

Sir Wilfull is set into drinking, madam, in the parlor.

LADY WISHFORT.

'Od's* my life, I'll send him to her. Call her down, Foible, bring her hither. I'll send him as I go. 40 When they are together, then come to me, Foible, that I may not be too long alone with Sir Rowland. (*Exit.*)

Enter Mrs. Millamant and Mrs. Fainall.

FOIBLE.

Madam, I stayed here to tell your ladyship that Mr. Mirabell has waited this half hour for an 45 opportunity to talk with you, though my lady's orders were to leave you and Sir Wilfull together. Shall I tell Mr. Mirabell that you are at leisure?

MILLAMANT.

No. What would the dear man have? I am thoughtful and would amuse myself. Bid him 50 come another time. (*Repeating and walking about.*)
　　"There never yet was woman made
　　　　Nor shall but to be cursed."42

That's hard!

---

42 "There ... cursed"] the opening lines of a lyric by Sir John Suckling (1609-42)

MRS. FAINALL.

You are very fond of Sir John Suckling today, 55
Millamant, and the poets.

MILLAMANT.

He? Aye, and filthy verses. So I am.

FOIBLE.

Sir Wilfull is coming, madam. Shall I send Mr.
Mirabell away?

MILLAMANT.

Aye, if you please, Foible, send him away, or send 60
him hither. Just as you will, dear Foible. I think
I'll see him. Shall I? Aye, let the wretch come.
(*Repeating.*)
        "Thyrsis a youth of the inspired train"—[43]
Dear Fainall, entertain Sir Wilfull. Thou hast phil- 65
osophy to undergo a fool; thou art married and hast
patience. I would confer with my own thoughts.

MRS. FAINALL.

I am obliged to you that you would make me your
proxy in this affair, but I have business of my own.

Enter Sir Wilfull.

Oh Sir Wilfull, you are come at the critical instant. 70
There's your mistress up to the ears in love and
contemplation. Pursue your point, now or never.

SIR WILFULL. (*This while Millamant walks about
repeating to herself.*)

Yes, my aunt would have it so. I would gladly have
been encouraged with a bottle or two, because I'm
somewhat wary at first before I am acquainted. But 75
I hope after a time I shall break my mind, that is,
upon further acquaintance. So for the present,
cousin, I'll take my leave. If so be you'll be so kind
to make my excuse, I'll return to my company.

MRS. FAINALL.

Oh fie, Sir Wilfull! What, you must not be 80
daunted.

SIR WILFULL.

Daunted? No, that's not it; it is not so much for
that, for if so be that I set on't, I'll do't. But only
for the present. 'Tis sufficient till further
acquaintance. That's all. Your servant. 85

MRS. FAINALL.

Nay, I'll swear you shall never lose so favorable an
opportunity, if I can help it. I'll leave you together
and lock the door. (*Exit.*)

SIR WILFULL.

Nay, nay, cousin, I have forgot my gloves. What
d'ye do? 'Sheart,* a* has locked the door indeed, 90
I think. Nay, cousin Fainall, open the door. Pshaw,
what a vixen trick is this? Nay, now a* has seen
me too.—Cousin, I made bold to pass through as
it were. I think this door's enchanted.

MILLAMANT. (*Repeating.*)

"I prithee spare me gentle boy, 95
Press me no more for that slight toy."[44]

SIR WILFULL.

Anon? Cousin, your servant.

MILLAMANT.

"That foolish trifle of a heart."—Sir Wilfull!

SIR WILFULL.

Yes, your servant. No offence I hope, cousin.

MILLAMANT. (*Repeating.*)

"I swear it will not do its part, 100
Though thou dost thine, employ'st thy power and
art."

Natural, easy Suckling!

SIR WILFULL.

Anon? Suckling! No such suckling neither, cousin,
nor stripling. I thank heaven, I'm no minor.

MILLAMANT.

Ah rustic! Ruder than Gothic. 105

SIR WILFULL.

Well, well, I shall understand your lingo one of
these days, cousin. In the meanwhile, I must
answer in plain English.

MILLAMANT.

Have you any business with me, Sir Wilfull?

SIR WILFULL.

Not at present, cousin. Yes, I made bold to see, to 110
come and know if that how you were disposed to
fetch a walk this evening. If so be that I might not be
troublesome, I would have sought a walk with you.

MILLAMANT.

A walk? What then?

---

43 "Thyrsis … train"] opening line of "The Story of
Phoebus and Daphne, Applied," by Edmund Waller
(1606–87)

---

44 "I … toy"] Millmant continues to quote Suckling.

SIR WILFULL.

Nay, nothing. Only for the walk's sake, that's all. 115

MILLAMANT.

I nauseate walking. 'Tis a country diversion. I loathe the country and everything that relates to it.

SIR WILFULL.

Indeed! Hah! Look ye, look ye, you do? Nay, 'tis like you may. Here are choice of pastimes here in Town, as plays and the like; that must be confessed 120 indeed.

MILLAMANT.

Ah *l'etourdi!*45 I hate the Town too.

SIR WILFULL.

Dear heart, that's much. Hah! That you should hate 'em both! Hah! 'Tis like you may. There are some can't relish the Town, and others can't away 125 with the country. 'Tis like you may be one of those, cousin.

MILLAMANT.

Ha, ha, ha. Yes, 'tis like I may. You have nothing further to say to me?

SIR WILFULL.

Not at present, cousin. 'Tis like when I have an 130 opportunity to be more private, I may break my mind in some measure. I conjecture you partly guess. However that's as time shall try, but spare to speak and spare to speed, as they say.

MILLAMANT.

If it is of no great importance, Sir Wilfull, you will 135 oblige me to leave me. I have just now a little business.

SIR WILFULL.

Enough, enough, cousin. Yes, yes, all a case. When you're disposed, when you're disposed. Now's as well as another time, and another time as well as 140 now. All's one for that. Yes, yes, if your concerns call you, there's no haste. It will keep cold as they say. Cousin, your servant. I think this door's locked.

MILLAMANT.

You may go this way, sir. 145

SIR WILFULL.

Your servant, then. With your leave, I'll return to my company. (*Exit.*)

_____
45 *l'etourdi*] scatterbrain

MILLAMANT.

Aye, aye, ha, ha, ha.

"Like Phoebus sung the no less am'rous boy"—

Enter Mirabell.

MIRABELL.

"Like Daphne she as lovely and as coy."46 150

Do you lock your self up from me to make my search more curious?* Or is this pretty artifice contrived to signify that here the chase must end and my pursuit be crowned, for you can fly no further. 155

MILLAMANT.

Vanity! No. I'll fly and be followed to the last moment, though I am upon the very verge of matrimony. I expect you should solicit me as much as if I were wavering at the grate of a monastery with one foot over the threshold. I'll be solicited 160 to the very last, nay and afterwards.

MIRABELL.

What, after the last?

MILLAMANT.

Oh, I should think I was poor and had nothing to bestow if I were reduced to an inglorious ease and freed from the agreeable fatigues of 165 solicitation.

MIRABELL.

But do not you know that, when favors are conferred upon instant and tedious solicitation, that they diminish in their value, and that both the giver loses the grace and the receiver lessens his pleasure? 170

MILLAMANT.

It may be in things of common application, but never sure in love. Oh, I hate a lover that can dare to think he draws a moment's air independent on the bounty of his mistress. There is not so impudent thing in nature as the saucy look of an 175 assured man, confident of success. The pedantic arrogance of a very* husband has not so pragmatical an air. Ah! I'll never marry unless I am first made sure of my will and pleasure.

MIRABELL.

Would you have 'em both before marriage? Or will 180

_____
46 Like Phoebus ... coy] a couplet from Waller's "Story of Phoebus and Daphne"

you be contented with the first now and stay for the other till after grace?[47]

MILLAMANT.

Ah, don't be impertinent.—My dear liberty, shall I leave thee? My faithful solitude, my darling contemplation, must I bid you then adieu? Ayy, adieu my morning thoughts, agreeable wakings, indolent slumbers, all ye *douceurs*, ye *sommeils du matin*,[48] adieu. I can't do't. 'Tis more than impossible. Positively, Mirabell, I'll lie a bed in a morning as long as I please.

MIRABELL.

Then I'll get up in a morning as early as I please.

MILLAMANT.

Ah! Idle creature, get up when you will. And d'ye hear, I won't be called names after I'm married. Positively, I won't be called names.

MIRABELL.

Names?

MILLAMANT.

Aye, as wife, spouse, my dear, joy, jewel, love, sweetheart and the rest of that nauseous cant in which men and their wives are so fulsomely familiar. I shall never bear that. Good Mirabell, don't let us be familiar or fond nor kiss before folks, like my Lady Fadler[49] and Sir Francis, nor go to Hyde Park* together the first Sunday in a new chariot* to provoke eyes and whispers and then never to be seen there together again, as if we were proud of one another the first week and ashamed of one another forever after. Let us never visit together nor go to a play together, but let us be very strange and well bred. Let us be as strange as if we had been married a great while and as well bred as if we were not married at all.

MIRABELL.

Have you any more conditions to offer? Hitherto your demands are pretty reasonable.

MILLAMANT.

Trifles: as liberty to pay and receive visits to and from whom I please; to write and receive letters without interrogatories or wry faces on your part; to wear what I please and choose conversation* with regard only to my own taste; to have no obligation upon me to converse with wits that I don't like because they are your acquaintance or to be intimate with fools because they may be your relations. Come to dinner when I please. Dine in my dressing room when I'm out of humor without giving a reason. To have my closet* inviolate. To be sole empress of my tea table, which you must never presume to approach without first asking leave. And lastly, wherever I am, you shall always knock at the door before you come in. These articles subscribed, if I continue to endure you a little longer, I may by degrees dwindle into a wife.

MIRABELL.

Your bill of fare is something advanced in this latter account. Well, have I liberty to offer conditions, that when you are dwindled into a wife, I may not be beyond measure enlarged into a husband?

MILLAMANT.

You have free leave. Propose your utmost. Speak and spare not.

MIRABELL.

I thank you. Imprimis, then, I covenant that your acquaintance be general; that you admit no sworn confidante or intimate of your own sex; no she friend to screen her affairs under your countenance and tempt you to make trial of a mutual secrecy. No decoy-duck to wheedle you a fop, scrambling to the play in a mask, then bring you home in a pretended fright, when you think you shall be found out, and rail at me for missing the play and disappointing the frolic which you had, to pick me up and prove my constancy.

MILLAMANT.

Detestable imprimis! I go to the play in a mask!

MIRABELL.

Item, I article that you continue to like your own face as long as I shall and, while it passes current with me, that you endeavor not to new coin it. To which end, together with all vizards for the day, I prohibit all masks for the night made of oiled skins and I know not what: hog's bones, hare's gall, pig water, and the marrow of a roasted cat. In short, I forbid all commerce with the gentlewoman in what-d'ye-call-it court. Item, I shut my doors

---

47 grace] the prayer concluding the marriage ceremony
48 *douceurs ... matin*] sweetnesses ... morning slumbers
49 Fadler] To "faddle" is to fondle.

against all bawds with baskets and pennyworths of muslin, china, fans, atlases,[50] etcetera. Item, when you shall be breeding—

MILLAMANT.

Ah! Name it not.

MIRABELL.

Which may be presumed, with a blessing on our endeavors—

MILLAMANT.

Odious endeavors!

MIRABELL.

I denounce against all strait-lacing, squeezing for a shape, till you mold my boy's head like a sugarloaf and, instead of a man-child, make me the father to a crooked billet. Lastly, to the dominion of the tea table I submit. But with proviso that you exceed not in your province but restrain yourself to native and simple tea-table drinks, as tea, chocolate, and coffee. As likewise to genuine and authorized tea-table talk, such as mending of fashions, spoiling reputations, railing at absent friends, and so forth, but that on no account you encroach upon the men's prerogative and presume to drink healths or toast fellows. For prevention of which, I banish all foreign forces, all auxiliaries to the tea table, as orange-brandy, all aniseed, cinnamon, citron, and Barbados-Waters, together with ratafia and the most noble spirit of clary.[51] But for cowslip-wine, poppy-water, and all dormatives,[52] those I allow. These provisos admitted, in other things I may prove a tractable and complying husband.

MILLAMANT.

Oh horrid provisos! Filthy strong waters! I toast fellows, odious men! I hate your odious provisos.

MIRABELL.

Then we're agreed. Shall I kiss your hand upon the contract? And here comes one to be a witness to the sealing of the deed.

Enter Mrs. Fainall.

---

50 atlas] silk-satin manufactured in the orient
51 orange-brandy … clary] strong fortified drinks
52 dormatives] sleeping-draughts

MILLAMANT.

Fainall, what shall I do? Shall I have him? I think I must have him.

MRS. FAINALL.

Aye, aye, take him, take him. What should you do?

MILLAMANT.

Well then. I'll take my death: I'm in a horrid fright. Fainall, I shall never say it. Well—I think—I'll endure you.

MRS. FAINALL.

Fie, fie, have him, have him, and tell him so in plain terms, for I am sure you have a mind to him.

MILLAMANT.

Are you? I think I have—and the horrid man looks as if he thought so too.—Well, you ridiculous thing you, I'll have you. I won't be kissed, nor I won't be thanked. Here, kiss my hand though. So, hold your tongue now, and don't say a word.

MRS. FAINALL.

Mirabell, there's a necessity for your obedience. You have neither time to talk nor stay. My mother is coming and, in my conscience, if she should see you, would fall into fits and maybe not recover time enough to return to Sir Rowland, who as Foible tells me is in a fair way to succeed. Therefore, spare your extasies for another occasion and slip down the back stairs, where Foible waits to consult you.

MILLAMANT.

Aye, go, go. In the meantime, I suppose you have said something to please me.

MIRABELL.

I am all obedience. (*Exit.*)

MRS. FAINALL.

Yonder Sir Wilfull's drunk and so noisy that my mother has been forced to leave Sir Rowland to appease him, but he answers her only with singing and drinking. What they have done by this time, I know not. But Petulant and he were upon quarrelling* as I came by.

MILLAMANT.

Well, if Mirabell should not make a good husband, I am a lost thing, for I find I love him violently.

MRS. FAINALL.

So it seems, when you mind not what's said to you. If you doubt him, you had best take up with Sir Wilfull.

MILLAMANT.

How can you name that superannuated lubber? 325
Faugh!

Enter Witwoud from drinking.

MRS. FAINALL.

So, is the fray made up, that you have left 'em?

WITWOUD.

Left 'em? I could stay no longer. I have laughed
like ten christenings—I am tipsy with laughing. If
I had stayed any longer I should have burst; I must 330
have been let out and pieced in the sides like an
unsized camlet. Yes, yes, the fray is composed. My
lady came in like a nolle prosequi and stopped
their proceedings.

MILLAMANT.

What was the dispute? 335

WITWOUD.

That's the jest. There was no dispute. They could
neither of 'em speak for rage and so fell a-
sputtering at one another like two roasting apples.

Enter Petulant drunk.

Now Petulant, all's over, all's well. Gad, my head
begins to whim it about. Why dost thou not speak? 340
Thou art both as drunk and as mute as a fish.

PETULANT.

Look you, Mrs.* Millamant, if you can love me,
dear nymph, say it, and that's the conclusion. Pass
on or pass off. That's all.

WITWOUD.

Thou hast uttered volumes, folios, in less than 345
decimo sexto,[53] my dear Lacedaemonian. Sirrah
Petulant, thou art an epitomizer of words.

PETULANT.

Witwoud, you are an annihilator of sense.

WITWOUD.

Thou art a retailer of phrases and dost deal in
remnants of remnants, like a maker of pincushions. 350
Thou art in truth (metaphorically speaking) a
speaker of shorthand.

PETULANT.

Thou art (without a figure) just one half of an ass,

and Baldwin[54] yonder, thy half-brother, is the rest.
A gemini of asses split would make just four of you. 355

WITWOUD.

Thou dost bite, my dear mustard seed. Kiss me for
that.

PETULANT.

Stand off. I'll kiss no more males. I have kissed
your twin yonder in a humor of reconciliation till
he (*Hiccup.*) rises upon my stomach like a radish. 360

MILLAMANT.

Eh! Filthy creature. What was the quarrel?

PETULANT.

There was no quarrel. There might have been a
quarrel.

WITWOUD.

If there had been words enow between 'em to have
expressed provocation, they had gone together by 365
the ears like a pair of castanets.

PETULANT.

You were the quarrel.

WITWOUD.

Me?

PETULANT.

If I had a humor to quarrel, I can make less matters
conclude premises. If you are not handsome, what 370
then, if I have a humor to prove it? If I shall have
my reward, say so; if not, fight for your face the
next time yourself. I'll go sleep.

WITWOUD.

Do, wrap thyself up like a wood louse and dream
revenge. And hear me, if thou canst learn to write 375
by tomorrow morning, pen me a challenge. I'll
carry it for thee.

PETULANT.

Carry your mistress's monkey a spider. Go flay
dogs and read romances. I'll go to bed to my maid.
(*Exit.*) 380

MRS. FAINALL.

He's horridly drunk. How came you all in this
pickle?

WITWOUD.

A plot, a plot to get rid of the knight. Your
husband's advice, but he sneaked off.

---

53 *decimo sexto*] a very small book, about 1/8 the size of a
    folio (a large book)

54 Baldwin] an ass in the beast epic, *Reynard the Fox.*

Enter Lady Wishfort and Sir Wilfull drunk.

LADY WISHFORT.

Out upon't, out upon't, at years of discretion and   385
comport yourself at this rantipole[55] rate.

SIR WILFULL.

No offence, Aunt.

LADY WISHFORT.

Offence? As I'm a person, I'm ashamed of you.
Faugh! How you stink of wine! D'ye think my
niece will ever endure such a borachio?[56] You're an   390
absolute borachio.

SIR WILFULL.

Borachio?

LADY WISHFORT.

At a time when you should commence an amour
and put your best foot foremost.

SIR WILFULL.

'Sheart,* an* you grudge me your liquor, make a   395
bill. Give me more drink and take my purse.
(*Sings.*)

> Prithee fill me the glass
> Till it laugh in my face,
> With ale that is potent and mellow;   400
> He that whines for a lass
> Is an ignorant ass,
> For a bumper has not its fellow.

But if you would have me marry my cousin, say
the word, and I'll do't. Wilfull will do't, that's the   405
word. Wilfull will do't, that's my crest. My motto
I have forgot.

LADY WISHFORT.

My nephew's a little overtaken, cousin. But 'tis
with drinking your health. O'my word, you are
obliged to him.   410

SIR WILFULL.

In vino veritas, Aunt.—If I drunk your health
today, cousin, I am a borachio. But if you have a
mind to be married, say the word and send for the
piper: Wilfull will do't. If not, dust it away, and
let's have t'other round.—Tony, 'Odd's* heart,   415
where's Tony? Tony's an honest fellow, but he spits
after a bumper, and that's a fault. (*Sings.*)

> We'll drink and we'll never have done, boys,
> Put the glass then around with the sun, boys.
> Let Apollo's example invite us;   420
> For he's drunk every night,
> And that makes him so bright,
> That he's able next morning to light us.

The sun's a good pimple,[57] an honest soaker: he
has a cellar at your antipodes. If I travel, Aunt, I   425
touch at your* antipodes. Your antipodes are a
good rascally sort of topsy-turvy fellows. If I had
a bumper, I'd stand upon my head and drink a
health to 'em.—A match or no match, cousin with
the hard name.—Aunt, Wilfull will do't. If she has   430
her maidenhead, let her look to't. If she has not,
let her keep her own counsel in the meantime and
cry out at the nine months' end.

MILLAMANT.

Your pardon madam, I can stay no longer. Sir
Wilfull grows very powerful. Egh! How he smells!   435
I shall be overcome if I stay.—Come, cousin.

Exeunt Millamant and Mrs. Fainall.

LADY WISHFORT.

Smells! He would poison a tallow chandler and his
family. Beastly creature, I know not what to do with
him. Travel, quotha. Aye travel, travel. Get thee
gone, get thee but far enough, to the Saracens or the   440
Tartars or the Turks, for thou art not fit to live in a
Christian commonwealth, thou beastly pagan.

SIR WILFULL.

Turks, no. No Turks, Aunt. Your* Turks are infidels
and believe not in the grape. Your* Mahometan,
your Mussulman is a dry stinkard. No offence,   445
Aunt. My map says that your* Turk is not so
honest a man as your* Christian. I cannot find by
the map that your* mufti is orthodox, whereby it
is a plain case, that orthodox is a hard word, Aunt,
and (*Hiccup.*) Greek for claret. (*Sings.*)   450

> To drink is a Christian diversion,
> Unknown to the Turk and the Persian:
>   Let Mahometan fools
>   Live by heathenish rules,
> And be damned over teacups and coffee.   455

---

[55] rantipole] unmannerly
[56] borachio] drunkard

[57] pimple] boon companion

But let British lads sing,
Crown a health to the King,
And a fig for your sultan and sophy.
Ah, Tony!

Enter Foible and whispers Lady Wishfort.

LADY WISHFORT.

Sir Rowland impatient? Good lack! What shall I do   460
with this beastly tumbrel?—Go lie down and sleep,
you sot, or, as I'm a person, I'll have you bastinadoed
with broomsticks.—Call up the wenches.

Exit Foible.

SIR WILFULL.

Ahey! Wenches, where are the wenches?

LADY WISHFORT.

Dear cousin Witwoud, get him away and you will   465
bind me to you inviolably. I have an affair of
moment that invades with some precipitation.
You will oblige me to all futurity.

WITWOUD.

Come, knight.—Pox on him, I don't know what
to say to him.—Will you go to a cock-match?   470

SIR WILFULL.

With a wench, Tony? Is she a shake-bag,[58] sirrah?
Let me bite your cheek for that.

WITWOUD.

Horrible! He has a breath like a bagpipe.—Aye,
aye, come, will you march, my Salopian?

SIR WILFULL.

Lead on, little Tony. I'll follow thee, my Anthony,   475
my Tantony. Sirrah, thou shalt be my Tantony, and
I'll be thy pig.[59]
And a fig for your sultan and sophy. (*Exit singing
with Witwoud.*)

LADY WISHFORT.

This will never do. It will never make a match at   480
least before he has been abroad.

Enter Waitwell, disguised as Sir Rowland.

Dear Sir Rowland, I am confounded with
confusion at the retrospection of my own rudeness.

---

58 shake-bag] a large fowl
59 Anthony ... pig] St. Anthony was often shown accom-
    panied by a pig.

I have more pardons to ask than the Pope
distributes in the year of jubilee. But I hope where   485
there is likely to be so near an alliance, we may
unbend the severity of decorum and dispense with
a little ceremony.

WAITWELL.

My impatience, madam, is the effect of my
transport, and till I have possession of your   490
adorable person, I am tantalized on a rack and do
but hang, madam, on the tenter of expectation.

LADY WISHFORT.

You have excess of gallantry, Sir Rowland, and
press things to a conclusion with the most
prevailing vehemence. But a day or two for   495
decency of marriage—

WAITWELL.

For decency of funeral, madam. The delay will
break my heart, or if that should fail, I shall be
poisoned. My nephew will get an inkling of my
designs and poison me, and I would willingly   500
starve him before I die. I would gladly go out of
the world with that satisfaction. That would be
some comfort to me, if I could but live so long as
to be revenged on that unnatural viper.

LADY WISHFORT.

Is he so unnatural, say you? Truly, I would   505
contribute much both to the saving of your life
and the accomplishment of your revenge. Not that
I respect myself, though he has been a perfidious
wretch to me.

WAITWELL.

Perfidious to you!   510

LADY WISHFORT.

Oh Sir Rowland, the hours that he has died away
at my feet, the tears that he has shed, the oaths
that he has sworn, the palpitations that he has felt.
The trances and the tremblings, the ardors and the
extacies, the keelings and the risings, the heart-   515
heavings and the hand-grippings, the pangs and
the pathetic regards of his protesting eyes! Oh no
memory can register.

WAITWELL.

What, my rival? Is the rebel my rival? A* dies.

LADY WISHFORT.

No, don't kill him at once, Sir Rowland; starve him   520
gradually inch by inch.

WAITWELL.

I'll do't. In three weeks he shall be barefoot, in a month out at knees with begging an alms. He shall starve upward and upward, till he has nothing living but his head and then go out in a stink like a candle's end upon a save-all. 525

LADY WISHFORT.

Well Sir Rowland, you have the way. You are no novice in the labyrinth of love: you have the clue. But as I am a person, Sir Rowland, you must not attribute my yielding to any sinister appetite or indigestion of widowhood nor impute my complacency to any lethargy of continence. I hope you do not think me prone to any iteration of nuptials. 530

WAITWELL.

Far be it from me—

LADY WISHFORT.

If you do, I protest I must recede—or think that I have made a prostitution of decorums, but in the vehemence of compassion and to save the life of a person of so much importance. 535

WAITWELL.

I esteem it so.

LADY WISHFORT.

Or else you wrong my condescension— 540

WAITWELL.

I do not, I do not—

LADY WISHFORT.

Indeed you do.

WAITWELL.

I do not, fair shrine of virtue.

LADY WISHFORT.

If you think the least scruple of carnality was an ingredient— 545

WAITWELL.

Dear madam, no. You are all camphor[60] and frankincense, all chastity and odor.

LADY WISHFORT.

Or that—

Enter Foible.

FOIBLE.

Madam, the dancers are ready, and there's one with a letter, who must deliver it into your own hands. 550

---

60 camphor] thought to modify sexual desire

LADY WISHFORT.

Sir Rowland, will you give me leave? Think favorably, judge candidly, and conclude you have found a person who would suffer racks in honor's cause, dear Sir Rowland, and will wait on you incessantly. (*Exit.*) 555

WAITWELL.

Fie, fie! What a slavery have I undergone. Spouse, hast thou any cordial? I want spirits.

FOIBLE.

What a washy rogue art thou to pant thus for a quarter of an hour's lying and swearing to a fine lady.

WAITWELL.

Oh, she is the antidote to desire. Spouse, thou wilt fare the worse for't. I shall have no appetite to iteration of nuptials this eight and forty hours. By this hand I had rather be a chairman* in the dog days than act Sir Rowland till this time tomorrow. 560

Enter Lady Wishfort with a letter.

LADY WISHFORT.

Call in the dancers.—Sir Rowland, we'll sit if you please, and see the entertainment. 565

Dance.

Now with your permission, Sir Rowland, I will peruse my letter. I would open it in your presence, because I would not make you uneasy. If it should make you uneasy, I would burn it. Speak if it does. But you may see by the superscription it is like a woman's hand. 570

FOIBLE. [*Aside.*]

By Heaven! Mrs.* Marwood's. I know it. My heart aches. (*To Waitwell.*) Get it from her.

WAITWELL.

A woman's hand? No madam, that's no woman's hand. I see that already. That's somebody whose throat must be cut. 575

LADY WISHFORT.

Nay Sir Rowland, since you give me a proof of your passion by your jealousy, I'll promise you I'll make you a return by a frank communication. You shall see it. We'll open it together. Look you here. (*Reads.*) "Madam, though unknown to you"— Look you there, 'tis from nobody that I know. "I have that honor for your character, that I think myself obliged to let you know you are abused. He 580 585 who pretends to be Sir Rowland is a cheat and a rascal"— Oh heavens! What's this?

FOIBLE. [*Aside.*]

Unfortunate, all's ruined.

WAITWELL.

How, how, let me see, let me see. (*Reading.*) "A rascal, and disguised and suborned for that imposture"— Oh villainy, oh villainy! "by the contrivance of"—

LADY WISHFORT.

I shall faint, I shall die, I shall die, oh!

FOIBLE. (*To Waitwell.*)

Say 'tis your nephew's hand. Quickly, his plot, swear, swear it.

WAITWELL.

Here's a villain! Madam, don't you perceive it, don't you see it?

LADY WISHFORT.

Too well, too well. I have seen too much.

WAITWELL.

I told you at first I knew the hand. A woman's hand? The rascal writes a sort of a large hand, your Roman[61] hand. I saw there was a throat to be cut presently. If he were my son as he is my nephew, I'd pistol him.

FOIBLE.

Oh treachery! But are you sure, Sir Rowland, it is his writing?

WAITWELL.

Sure? Am I here? Do I live? Do I love this pearl of India? I have twenty letters in my pocket from him in the same character.

LADY WISHFORT.

How!

FOIBLE.

Oh what luck it is, Sir Rowland, that you were present at this juncture! This was the business that brought Mr. Mirabell disguised to Madam Millamant this afternoon. I thought something was contriving when he stole by me and would have hid his face.

LADY WISHFORT.

How, how! I heard the villain was in the house indeed, and now I remember, my niece went away

abruptly when Sir Wilfull was to have made his addresses.

FOIBLE.

Then, then madam, Mr. Mirabell waited for her in her chamber, but I would not tell your ladyship to discompose you when you were to receive Sir Rowland.

WAITWELL.

Enough, his date is short.

FOIBLE.

No, good Sir Rowland, don't incur the law.

WAITWELL.

Law? I care not for law. I can but die, and 'tis in a good cause. My lady shall be satisfied of my truth and innocence, though it cost me my life.

LADY WISHFORT.

No, dear Sir Rowland, don't fight. If you should be killed, I must never show my face—or hanged. Oh consider my reputation, Sir Rowland. No, you shan't fight. I'll go in and examine my niece. I'll make her confess. I conjure you, Sir Rowland, by all your love not to fight.

WAITWELL.

I am charmed madam, I obey. But some proof you must let me give you. I'll go for a black box, which contains the writings of my whole estate, and deliver that into your hands.

LADY WISHFORT.

Aye, dear Sir Rowland, that will be some comfort. Bring the black box.

WAITWELL.

And may I presume to bring a contract to be signed this night? May I hope so far?

LADY WISHFORT.

Bring what you will but come alive, pray come alive. Oh this is a happy discovery.

WAITWELL.

Dead or alive, I'll come, and married we will be in spite of treachery, aye, and get an heir that shall defeat the last remaining glimpse of hope in my abandoned nephew. Come, my buxom widow.
Ere long you shall substantial proof receive
That I'm an errant knight—

FOIBLE.

      Or arrant knave.

Exeunt.

---

61 Roman] round and bold

Act V. Scene continues.

Lady Wishfort and Foible.

LADY WISHFORT.

Out of my house, out of my house, thou viper, thou serpent that I have fostered, thou bosom traitress that I raised from nothing. Be gone, be gone, be gone, go, go, that I took from washing of old gauze and weaving of dead hair, with a bleak, blue nose, over a chafing dish of starved embers and dining behind a traverse rag in a shop no bigger than a bird cage. Go, go, starve again, do, do.

FOIBLE.

Dear madam, I'll beg pardon on my knees.

LADY WISHFORT.

Away, out, out, go set up for yourself again. Do, drive a trade, do, with your threepenny-worth of small ware, flaunting upon a packthread, under a brandy-seller's bulk,[62] or against a dead wall by a ballad-monger. Go hang out an old frisoneer-gorget,[63] with a yard of yellow colberteen[64] again, do, an old gnawed mask, two rows of pins and a child's fiddle, a glass necklace with the beads broken, and a quilted nightcap with one ear. Go, go, drive a trade: these were your commodities, you treacherous trull, this was your merchandise you dealt in when I took you into my house, placed you next myself, and made you governante of my whole family. You have forgot this, have you? Now you have feathered your nest.

FOIBLE.

No, no, dear madam. Do but hear me, have but a moment's patience. I'll confess all. Mr. Mirabell seduced me. I am not the first that he has wheedled with his dissembling tongue. Your ladyship's own wisdom has been deluded by him. Then how should I, a poor ignorant, defend myself? Oh madam, if you knew but what he promised me and how he assured me your Ladyship should come to no damage, or else the wealth of the Indies should not have bribed me to conspire against so good, so sweet, so kind a lady as you have been to me.

LADY WISHFORT.

No damage? What, to betray me, to marry me to a cast* serving man, to make me a receptacle and hospital for a decayed pimp? No damage? Oh thou frontless impudence, more than a big-bellied actress.

FOIBLE.

Pray, do but hear me, madam: he could not marry your ladyship, madam. No indeed, his marriage was to have been void in law, for he was married to me first to secure your ladyship. He could not have bedded your ladyship, for if he had consummated with your ladyship, he must have run the risk of the law and been put upon his clergy.[65] Yes indeed, I enquired of the law in that case before I would meddle or make.

LADY WISHFORT.

What, then I have been your property, have I? I have been convenient to you it seems. While you were catering for Mirabell, I have been broker for you? What, have you made a passive bawd of me? This exceeds all precedent. I am brought to fine uses, to become a botcher of second-hand marriages between Abigails and Andrews! I'll couple you. Yes, I'll baste you together, you and your Philander. I'll Duke's Place you, as I'm a person. Your turtle* is in custody already; you shall coo in the same cage, if there be constable or warrant in the parish. (*Exit.*)

FOIBLE.

Oh that ever I was born. Oh that I was ever married. A bride, aye I shall be a Bridewell bride. Oh!

Enter Mrs. Fainall.

MRS. FAINALL.

Poor Foible, what's the matter?

FOIBLE.

Oh madam, my lady's gone for a constable. I shall be had to a justice and put to Bridewell to beat hemp. Poor Waitwell's gone to prison already.

---

62 bulk] stall
63 frisoneer-gorget] woolen covering for the neck
64 colberteen] cheap lace

65 risk … clergy] of being potentially hanged for bigamy, from which he could escape through benefit of clergy

MRS. FAINALL.

Have a good heart, Foible, Mirabell's gone to give 70
security for him. This is all Marwood's and my
husband's doing.

FOIBLE.

Yes, yes, I know it madam. She was in my lady's
closet* and overheard all that you said to me before
dinner. She sent the letter to my lady, and that miss- 75
ing effect, Mr. Fainall laid this plot to arrest Waitwell,
when he pretended to go for the papers, and in the
meantime, Mrs. Marwood declared all to my lady.

MRS. FAINALL.

Was there no mention made of me in the letter?
My mother does not suspect my being in the 80
confederacy? I fancy Marwood has not told her,
though she has told my husband.

FOIBLE.

Yes madam, but my lady did not see that part: we
stifled the letter before she read so far. Has that
mischievous devil told Mr. Fainall of your ladyship 85
then?

MRS. FAINALL.

Aye, all's out: my affair with Mirabell, everything
discovered.* This is the last day of our living
together, that's my comfort.

FOIBLE.

Indeed madam, and so 'tis a comfort if you knew 90
all. He has been even with your ladyship, which I
could have told you long enough since, but I love
to keep peace and quietness by my goodwill. I had
rather bring friends together than set 'em at
distance. But Mrs. Marwood and he are nearer 95
related than ever their parents thought for.

MRS. FAINALL.

Say'st thou so, Foible? Canst thou prove this?

FOIBLE.

I can take my oath of it, madam. So can Mrs.
Mincing. We have had many a fair word from
Madam Marwood to conceal something that 100
passed in our chamber one evening when you were
at Hyde Park* and we were thought to have gone
a-walking. But we went up unawares, though we
were sworn to secrecy too. Madam Marwood took
a book and swore us upon it, but it was but a book 105
of verses and poems. So long as it was not a Bible
oath, we may break it with a safe conscience.

MRS. FAINALL.

This discovery* is the most opportune thing I
could wish.—Now Mincing?

Enter Mincing.

MINCING.

My lady would speak with Mrs. Foible, mem. Mr. 110
Mirabell is with her. He has set your spouse at
liberty, Mrs. Foible, and would have you hide
yourself in my lady's closet,* till my old lady's anger
is abated. Oh, my old lady is in a perilous passion
at something Mr. Fainall has said. He swears, and 115
my old Lady cries. There's a fearful hurricane, I
vow. He says, mem, how that he'll have my lady's
fortune made over to him or he'll be divorced.

MRS. FAINALL.

Does your lady and Mirabell know that?

MINCING.

Yes mem, they have sent me to see if Sir Wilfull 120
be sober and to bring him to them. My lady is
resolved to have him, I think, rather than lose such
a vast sum as six thousand pound.—Oh come,
Mrs. Foible, I hear my old lady.

MRS. FAINALL.

Foible, you must tell Mincing that she must 125
prepare to vouch when I call her.

FOIBLE.

Yes, yes madam.

MINCING.

Oh yes, mem, I'll vouch anything for your
ladyship's service, be what it will.

*Exeunt Mincing and Foible. Enter Lady Wishfort and
Marwood.*

LADY WISHFORT.

Oh my dear friend, how can I enumerate the 130
benefits that I have received from your goodness?
To you I owe the timely discovery* of the false
vows of Mirabell, to you the detection of the
impostor Sir Rowland. And now you are become
an intercessor with my son-in-law to save the 135
honor of my house and compound for the frailties
of my daughter. Well friend, you are enough to
reconcile me to the bad world, or else I would
retire to deserts and solitudes and feed harmless
sheep by groves and purling streams. Dear 140

Marwood, let us leave the world and retire by ourselves and be shepherdesses.

MRS. MARWOOD.

Let us first despatch the affair in hand, madam. We shall have leisure to think of retirement afterwards. Here is one who is concerned in the treaty. 145

LADY WISHFORT.

Oh daughter, daughter, is it possible thou shouldst be my child, bone of my bone and flesh of my flesh, and as I may say, another me, and yet transgress the most minute particle of severe virtue? Is it possible you should lean aside to iniquity who have been cast 150 in the direct mold of virtue? I have not only been a mold but a pattern for you and a model for you after you were brought into the world.

MRS. FAINALL.

I don't understand your ladyship.

LADY WISHFORT.

Not understand? Why, have you not been naught?* 155 Have you not been sophisticated?* Not understand? Here I am ruined to compound for your caprices and your cuckoldoms. I must pawn my plate* and my jewels and ruin my niece, and all little enough— 160

MRS. FAINALL.

I am wronged and abused, and so are you. 'Tis a false accusation, as false as hell, as false as your friend there, aye, or your friend's friend, my false husband.

MRS. MARWOOD.

My friend, Mrs. Fainall? Your husband my friend? 165 What do you mean?

MRS. FAINALL.

I know what I mean, madam, and so do you, and so shall the world at a time convenient.

MRS. MARWOOD.

I am sorry to see you so passionate, madam. More temper would look more like innocence. But I 170 have done.—I am sorry my zeal to serve your ladyship and family should admit of misconstruction or make me liable to affronts. You will pardon me, madam, if I meddle no more with an affair in which I am not personally concerned. 175

LADY WISHFORT.

Oh dear friend, I am so ashamed that you should meet with such returns.—You ought to ask pardon on your knees, ungrateful creature: she deserves more from you than all your life can accomplish.— Oh don't leave me destitute in this perplexity. No, 180 stick to me, my good genius.*

MRS. FAINALL.

I tell you, madam, you're abused. Stick to you? Aye, like a leech, to suck your best blood. She'll drop off when she's full. Madam, you shan't pawn a bodkin nor part with a brass counter in 185 composition for me. I defy 'em all. Let 'em prove their aspersions. I know my own innocence and dare stand a trial.ᵍ (*Exit.*)

LADY WISHFORT.

Why, if she should be innocent, if she should be wronged after all, hah? I don't know what to think, 190 and I promise you, her education has been unexceptionable. I may say it, for I chiefly made it my own care to initiate her very infancy in the rudiments of virtue and to impress upon her tender years a young odium and aversion to the 195 very sight of men. Aye friend, she would ha' shrieked if she had but seen a man till she was in her teens. As I am a person, 'tis true. She was never suffered to play with a male child, though but in coats;⁶⁶ nay, her very babies* were of the feminine 200 gender. Oh, she never looked a man in the face but her own father or the chaplain, and him we made a shift to put upon her for a woman by the help of his long garments and his sleek face till she was going in her fifteen. 205

MRS. MARWOOD.

'Twas much she should be deceived so long.

LADY WISHFORT.

I warrant you, or she would never have borne to have been catechised by him and have heard his long lectures against singing and dancing and such debaucheries and going to filthy plays and profane 210 music-meetings, where the lewd trebles squeak nothing but bawdy and the basses roar blasphemy. Oh, she would have swooned at the sight or name of an obscene playbook. And can I think after all this that my daughter can be naught?* What, a 215

---

66 male … coats] Young males were dressed in (petti)coats, not breeches.

whore? And thought it excommunication to set her foot within the door of a playhouse. Oh my dear friend, I can't believe it. No, no, as she says, let him prove it, let him prove it.

MRS. MARWOOD.

Prove it, madam? What, and have your name 220 prostituted in a public court, yours and your daughter's reputation worried at the bar by a pack of bawling lawyers? To be ushered in by an oyez of scandal and have your case opened by an old fumbling lecher in a coif like a man midwife to 225 bring your daughter's infamy to light, to be a theme for legal punsters and quibblers by the statute and become a jest, against a rule of court, where there is no precedent for a jest in any record, not even in Domesday Book. To discompose the 230 gravity of the bench and provoke naughty interrogatories in more naughty law-Latin, while the good judge, tickled with the proceeding, simpers under a gray beard and fidges off and on his cushion as if he had swallowed cantharides, or 235 sat upon cow-itch.[67]

LADY WISHFORT.

Oh, 'tis very hard.

MRS. MARWOOD.

And then to have my young revellers of the Temple* take notes like prentices at a conventicle and, after, talk it all over again in commons or 240 before drawers in an eating house.

LADY WISHFORT.

Worse and worse.

MRS. MARWOOD.

Nay, this is nothing; if it would end here, 'twere well. But it must after this be consigned by the shorthand writers to the public press and from 245 thence be transferred to the hands, nay, into the throats and lungs of hawkers with voices more licentious than the loud flounder-man's or the woman that cries "gray peas."[h] And this you must hear till you are stunned; nay, you must hear 250 nothing else for some days.

LADY WISHFORT.

Oh, 'tis insupportable. No, no, dear friend, make it up, make it up. Aye, aye, I'll compound. I'll give

---

[67] cow-itch] stinging plant

up all, myself and my all, my niece and her all— anything, everything for composition. 255

MRS. MARWOOD.

Nay madam, I advise nothing. I only lay before you as a friend the inconveniencies which perhaps you have overseen. Here comes Mr. Fainall. If he will be satisfied to huddle up all in silence, I shall be glad. You must think I would rather 260 congratulate than condole with you.

Enter Fainall.

LADY WISHFORT.

Aye, aye, I do not doubt it, dear Marwood. No, no, I do not doubt it.

FAINALL.

Well madam, I have suffered myself to be overcome by the importunity of this lady your 265 friend and am content you shall enjoy your own proper estate during life, on condition you oblige yourself never to marry, under such penalty as I think convenient.

LADY WISHFORT.

Never to marry? 270

FAINALL.

No more Sir Rowlands. The next imposture may not be so timely detected.

MRS. MARWOOD.

That condition, I dare answer, my lady will consent to without difficulty. She has already but too much experienced the perfidiousness of men. 275 Besides, madam, when we retire to our pastoral solitude, we shall bid adieu to all other thoughts.

LADY WISHFORT.

Aye, that's true, but in case of necessity, as of health or some such emergency—

FAINALL.

Oh, if you are prescribed marriage, you shall be 280 considered. I will only reserve to myself the power to choose for you. If your physic be wholesome, it matters not who is your apothecary. Next, my wife shall settle on me the remainder of her fortune not made over already and for her maintenance 285 depend entirely on my discretion.

LADY WISHFORT.

This is most inhumanly savage, exceeding the barbarity of a Muscovite husband.

FAINALL.

I learned it from his Czarish majesty's retinue[68] in a winter evening's conference over brandy and pepper, amongst other secrets of matrimony and policy as they are at present practiced in the northern hemisphere. But this must be agreed unto and that positively. Lastly, I will be endowed in right of my wife with that six thousand pound which is the moiety of Mrs.* Millamant's fortune in your possession and which she has forfeited (as will appear by the last will and testament of your deceased husband, Sir Jonathan Wishfort) by her disobedience in contracting herself against your consent or knowledge and by refusing the offered match with Sir Wilfull Witwoud, which you like a careful aunt had provided for her.

LADY WISHFORT.

My nephew was *non compos*[69] and could not make his addresses.

FAINALL.

I come to make demands. I'll hear no objections.

LADY WISHFORT.

You will grant me time to consider.

FAINALL.

Yes, while the instrument is drawing, to which you must set your hand till more sufficient deeds can be perfected, which I will take care shall be done with all possible speed. In the meanwhile, I will go for the said instrument, and till my return you may balance this matter in your own discretion. (*Exit.*)

LADY WISHFORT.

This insolence is beyond all precedent, all parallel. Must I be subject to this merciless villain?

MRS. MARWOOD.

'Tis severe indeed, madam, that you should smart for your daughter's wantonness.

LADY WISHFORT.

'Twas against my consent that she married this barbarian, but she would have him, though her year[70] was not out. Ah! Her first husband, my son

Languish, would not have carried it thus. Well, that was my choice; this is hers. She is matched now, with a witness. I shall be mad, dear friend. Is there no comfort for me? Must I live to be confiscated at this rebel-rate? Here come two more of my Egyptian plagues[71] too.

Enter Millamant and Sir Wilfull.

SIR WILFULL.

Aunt, your servant.

LADY WISHFORT.

Out caterpillar, call not me aunt. I know thee not.

WILFULL.

I confess I have been a little in disguise* as they say. S'heart!* And I am sorry for't. What would you have? I hope I committed no offence, Aunt, and if I did, I am willing to make satisfaction. And what can a man say fairer? If I have broke anything, I'll pay for't, an* it cost a pound. And so let that content for what's past, and make no more words. For what's to come, to pleasure you I'm willing to marry my cousin. So pray, let's all be friends. She and I are agreed on the matter before a witness.

LADY WISHFORT.

How's this, dear niece? Have I any comfort? Can this be true?

MILLAMANT.

I am content to be a sacrifice to your repose, madam, and to convince you that I had no hand in the plot, as you were misinformed, I have laid my commands on Mirabell to come in person and be a witness that I give my hand to this flower of knighthood. And for the contract that passed between Mirabell and me, I have obliged him to make a resignation of it in your ladyship's presence. He is without and waits your leave for admittance.

LADY WISHFORT.

Well, I'll swear I am something revived at this testimony of your obedience, but I cannot admit that traitor. I fear I cannot fortify myself to support his apprearance. He is as terrible to me as a Gorgon; if I see him, I fear I shall turn to stone, petrify incessantly.[72]

---

68 Czarish … retinue] Peter the Great had visited London in the mid 1690s.
69 *non compos*] not in his right mind
70 her year] conventional period of mourning after the death of an husband

71 Egyptian plagues] those visited on Egypt by Moses (Exodus 7-11)
72 incessantly] immediately

MILLAMANT.

If you disoblige him, he may resent your refusal and insist upon the contract still. Then, 'tis the last time he will be offensive to you.

LADY WISHFORT.

Are you sure it will be the last time? If I were sure of that—shall I never see him again? 360

MILLAMANT.

Sir Wilfull, you and he are to travel together, are you not?

SIR WILFULL.

'Sheart,* the gentleman's a civil gentleman. Aunt, let him come in. Why, we are sworn brothers and fellow travelers. We are to be Pylades and Orestes,[73] 365 he and I; he is to be my interpreter in foreign parts. He has been overseas once already and, with proviso that I marry my cousin, will cross 'em once again only to bear me company. 'Sheart, I'll call him in. An* I set on't once, he shall come in, and see who'll 370 hinder him. (Exit.)

MRS. MARWOOD. [Aside.]

This is precious fooling, if it would pass, but I'll know the bottom of it.

LADY WISHFORT.

Oh dear Marwood, you are not going?

MRS. MARWOOD.

Not far madam; I'll return immediately. (Exit.) 375

Reenter Sir Wilfull and Mirabell.

SIR WILFULL.

Look up man, I'll stand by you; 'sbud,* an* she do frown, she can't kill you. Besides, hearkee, she dare not frown desperately, because her face is none of her own. 'Sheart, an she should, her forehead would wrinkle like the coat of a cream cheese, but 380 mum for that, fellow traveler.

MIRABELL.

If a deep sense of the many injuries I have offered to so good a lady, with a sincere remorse and a hearty contrition, can but obtain the least glance of compassion, I am too happy. Ah madam, there was 385 a time—but let it be forgotten. I confess I have deservedly forfeited the high place I once held of sighing at your feet. Nay, kill me not by turning from

me in disdain. I come not to plead for favor, nay not for pardon; I am a suppliant only for your pity. I am 390 going where I never shall behold you more—

SIR WILFULL.

How, fellow traveler! You shall go by yourself, then.

MIRABELL.

Let me be pitied first and afterwards forgotten. I ask no more.

SIR WILFULL.

By'r lady, a very reasonable request and will cost you 395 nothing, Aunt. Come, come, forgive and forget, Aunt. Why, you must an* you are a Christian.

MIRABELL.

Consider madam, in reality you could not receive much prejudice. It was an innocent device; though I confess it had a face of guiltiness, it was at most 400 an artifice which love contrived, and errors which love produces have ever been accounted venial. At least think it is punishment enough that I have lost what in my heart I hold most dear; that to your cruel indignation I have offered up this beauty and 405 with her my peace and quiet, nay, all my hopes of future comfort.

SIR WILFULL.

An* he does not move me, would I might never be o'the quorum.[74] An* it were not as good a deed as to drink to give her to him again, I would I 410 might never take shipping. Aunt, if you don't forgive quickly, I shall melt, I can tell you that. My contract went no further than a little mouth glue, and that's hardly dry. One doleful sigh more from my fellow traveller and 'tis dissolved. 415

LADY WISHFORT.

Well Nephew, upon your account—ah, he has a false insinuating tongue.—Well sir, I will stifle my just resentment at my nephew's request. I will endeavor what I can to forget but on proviso that you resign the contract with my niece immediately. 420

MIRABELL.

It is in writing and with papers of concern, but I have sent my servant for it, and will deliver it to you with all acknowledgments for your transcendant goodness.

---

73 Pylades and Orestes] classical emblem of friendship

74 o'the quorum] a justice of the peace or county magistrate

LADY WISHFORT. (*Apart.*)

Oh, he has witchcraft in his eyes and tongue. When 425
I did not see him, I could have bribed a villain to his
assassination, but his appearance rakes the embers
which have so long lain smothered in my breast.

Enter Fainall and Mrs. Marwood.

FAINALL.

Your date of deliberation, madam, is expired. Here
is the instrument. Are you prepared to sign? 430

LADY WISHFORT.

If I were prepared, I am not empowered. My niece
exerts a lawful claim, having matched herself by
my direction to Sir Wilfull.

FAINALL.

That sham is too gross to pass on me, though 'tis
imposed on you, madam. 435

MILLAMANT.

Sir, I have given my consent.

MIRABELL.

And sir, I have resigned my pretensions.

SIR WILFULL.

And sir, I assert my right and will maintain it in
defiance of you, sir, and of your instrument.
S'heart,* an* you talk of an instrument, sir, I have 440
an old fox by my thigh shall hack your instrument
of ram vellum to shreds, sir. It shall not be
sufficient for a mittimus or a tailor's measure.[75]
Therefore, withdraw your instrument, sir, or by'r
lady, I shall draw mine. 445

LADY WISHFORT.

Hold, Nephew, hold.

MILLAMANT.

Good Sir Wilfull, respite your valor.

FAINALL.

Indeed? Are you provided of a guard, with your
single beefeater there? But I'm prepared for you
and insist on my first proposal. You shall submit 450
your own estate to my management and absolutely
make over my wife's to my sole use, as pursuant
to the purport and tenor of this other covenant.—
I suppose, madam, your consent is not requisite
in this case, nor, Mr. Mirabell, your resignation, 455

---

[75] tailor's measure] tape measure, often made from a strip
of parchment

nor, Sir Wilfull, your right. You may draw your
fox if you please, sir, and make a Bear Garden*
flourish somewhere else, for here it will not avail.
This, my Lady Wishfort, must be subscribed, or
your darling daughter's turned adrift like a leaky 460
hulk to sink or swim as she and the current of this
lewd Town can agree.

LADY WISHFORT.

Is there no means, no remedy, to stop my ruin?
Ungrateful wretch! Dost thou not owe thy being,
thy subsistence to my daughter's fortune? 465

FAINALL.

I'll answer you when I have the rest of it in my
possession.

MIRABELL.

But that you would not accept of a remedy from
my hands— I own I have not deserved you should
owe any obligation to me, or else perhaps I could 470
advise—

LADY WISHFORT.

Oh what? What? To save me and my child from
ruin, from want,* I'll forgive all that's past. Nay,
I'll consent to anything to come, to be delivered
from this tyranny. 475

MIRABELL.

Aye madam, but that is too late: my reward is
intercepted. You have disposed of her who only
could have made me a compensation for all my
services. But be it as it may, I am resolved I'll serve
you. You shall not be wronged in this savage manner. 480

LADY WISHFORT.

How! Dear Mr. Mirabell, can you be so generous
at last? But it is not possible. Hearkee, I'll break
my nephew's match: you shall have my niece yet
and all her fortune, if you can but save me from
this imminent danger. 485

MIRABELL.

Will you? I take you at your word. I ask no more.
I must have leave for two criminals to appear.

LADY WISHFORT.

Aye, aye, anybody, anybody.

MIRABELL.

Foible is one, and a penitent.

*Enter Mrs. Fainall, Foible, and Mincing. Mirabell
and Lady Wishfort go to Mrs. Fainall and Foible.*

MRS. MARWOOD. (*To Fainall.*)

Oh my shame! These corrupt things are bought 490
and brought hither to expose me.

FAINALL.

If it must all come out, why, let 'em know it. 'Tis
but the way of the world. That shall not urge me
to relinquish or abate one tittle of my terms. No,
I will insist the more. 495

FOIBLE.

Yes indeed madam, I'll take my Bible oath of it.

MINCING.

And so will I, mem.

LADY WISHFORT.

Oh Marwood, Marwood, art thou false? My friend
deceive me? Hast thou been a wicked accomplice
with that profligate man? 500

MRS. MARWOOD.

Have you so much ingratitude and injustice to give
credit against your friend to the aspersions of two
such mercenary trulls?

MINCING.

Mercenary, mem? I scorn your words. 'Tis true we
found you and Mr. Fainall in the blue garret. By 505
the same token, you swore us to secrecy upon
Messalina's poems. Mercenary? No, if we would
have been mercenary, we should have held our
tongues. You would have bribed us sufficiently.

FAINALL.

Go, you are an insignificant thing. Well, what are 510
you the better for this? Is this Mr. Mirabell's
expedient? I'll be put off no longer. You thing that
was a wife shall smart for this. I will not leave thee
wherewithal to hide thy shame; your body shall be
naked as your reputation. 515

MRS. FAINALL.

I despise you and defy your malice. You have
aspersed me wrongfully. I have proved your
falsehood. Go you and your treacherous—I will
not name it—but starve together, perish.

FAINALL.

Not while you are worth a groat, indeed, my 520
dear.—Madam, I'll be fooled no longer.

LADY WISHFORT.

Ah Mr. Mirabell, this is small comfort, the
detection of this affair.

MIRABELL.

Oh in good time. Your leave for the other offender
and penitent to appear, madam. 525

Enter Waitwell with a box of writings.

LADY WISHFORT.

Oh Sir Rowland— Well, rascal?

WAITWELL.

What your ladyship pleases. I have brought the
black box at last, madam.

MIRABELL.

Give it me.—Madam, you remember your
promise? 530

LADY WISHFORT.

Aye, dear sir!

MIRABELL.

Where are the gentlemen?

WAITWELL.

At hand, sir, rubbing their eyes, just risen from
sleep.

FAINALL.

S'death,* what's this to me? I'll not wait your 535
private concerns.

Enter Petulant and Witwoud.

PETULANT.

How now? What's the matter? Whose hand's out?

WITWOUD.

Hey day! What, are you all got together like players
at the end of the last act?

MIRABELL.

You may remember, gentlemen, I once requested 540
your hands as witnesses to a certain parchment.

WITWOUD.

Aye, I do, my hand I remember. Petulant set his
mark.

MIRABELL.

You wrong him; his name is fairly written, as shall
appear. (*Undoing the box.*) You do not remember, 545
gentlemen, anything of what that parchment
contained?

WITWOUD.

No.

PETULANT.

Not I. I writ. I read nothing.

MIRABELL.

Very well, now you shall know.——Madam, your 550
promise.

LADY WISHFORT.

Aye, aye, sir, upon my honor.

MIRABELL.

Mr. Fainall, it is now time that you should know
that your lady, while she was at her own disposal
and before you had by your insinuations wheedled 555
her out of a pretended settlement of the greatest
part of her fortune—

FAINALL.

Sir! Pretended?

MIRABELL.

Yes sir. I say that this lady, while a widow, having,
it seems, received some cautions respecting your 560
inconstancy and tyranny of temper, which from
her own partial opinion and fondness of you she
could never have suspected, she did, I say, by the
wholesome advice of friends and of sages learned
in the laws of this land, deliver this same as her 565
act and deed to me in trust and to the uses within
mentioned. (*Holding out the parchment.*) You may
read if you please, though perhaps what is
inscribed on the back may serve your occasions.

FAINALL.

Very likely sir. What's here? Damnation! (*Reads.*) 570
"A deed of conveyance of the whole estate real of
Arabella Languish, widow, in trust to Edward
Mirabell." Confusion!

MIRABELL.

Even so, sir, 'tis the way of the world, sir, of the
widows of the world. I suppose this deed may bear 575
an elder date than what you have obtained from
your lady.

FAINALL.

Perfidious fiend! Then thus I'll be revenged—
(*Offers* to run at Mrs. Fainall.*)

SIR WILFULL.

Hold sir. Now you may make your Bear Garden 580
flourish somewhere else, sir.

FAINALL.

Mirabell, you shall hear of this, sir, be sure you
shall.—Let me pass, oaf. (*Exit.*)

MRS. FAINALL.

Madam, you seem to stifle your resentment. You
had better give it vent. 585

MRS. MARWOOD.

Yes, it shall have vent—and to your confusion, or
I'll perish in the attempt. (*Exit.*)

LADY WISHFORT.

Oh daughter, daughter, 'tis plain thou hast
inherited thy mother's prudence.

MRS. FAINALL.

Thank Mr. Mirabell, a cautious friend, to whose 590
advice all is owing.

LADY WISHFORT.

Well Mr. Mirabell, you have kept your promise,
and I must perform mine. First, I pardon for your
sake Sir Rowland there and Foible. The next thing
is to break the matter to my nephew. And how to 595
do that—

MIRABELL.

For that, madam, give yourself no trouble. Let me
have your consent. Sir Wilfull is my friend; he has
had compassion upon lovers and generously
engaged a volunteer in this action for our service 600
and now designs to prosecute his travels.

SIR WILFULL.

S'heart,* Aunt, I have no mind to marry. My cousin's
a fine lady, and the gentleman loves her and she loves
him, and they deserve one another. My resolution is
to see foreign parts. I have set on't, and when I'm set 605
on't, I must do't. And if these two gentlemen would
travel too, I think they may be spared.

PETULANT.

For my part, I say little. I think things are best off
or on.

WITWOUD.

Egad, I understand nothing of the matter. I'm in 610
a maze yet, like a dog in a dancing school.

LADY WISHFORT.

Well sir, take her, and with her all the joy I can
give you.

MILLAMANT.

Why does not the man take me? Would you have
me give myself to you over again? 615

MIRABELL. (*Kisses her hand.*)

Aye, and over and over again, for I would have you
as often as possibly I can. Well, Heaven grant I love
you not too well; that's all my fear.

SIR WILFULL.

S'heart, you'll have him time enough to toy after

you're married, or if you will, toy now. Let us have   620
a dance in the meantime, that we who are not
lovers may have some other employment besides
looking on.

MIRABELL.

With all my heart, dear Sir Wilfull. What shall we
do for music?   625

FOIBLE.

Oh sir, some that were provided for Sir Rowland's
entertainment are yet within call.

A dance.

LADY WISHFORT.

As I am a person, I can hold out no longer. I have
wasted my spirits so today already, that I am ready
to sink under the fatigue, and I cannot but have   630
some fears upon me yet that my son Fainall will
pursue some desperate course.

MIRABELL.

Madam, disquiet not yourself on that account. To
my knowledge his circumstances are such he must of
force comply. For my part, I will contribute all that   635
in me lies to a reunion. (*To Mrs. Fainall.*) In the
meantime, madam, let me before these witnesses
restore to you this deed of trust. It may be a means,
well managed, to make you live easily together.

From hence let those be warned who mean to wed,   640
Lest mutual falsehood stain the bridal bed,
For each deceiver to his cost may find
That marriage frauds too oft are paid in kind.

Exeunt omnes.

FINIS.

Textual Notes

ª Copytext is the first edition, a 1700 quarto (Q1). Also
consulted, the second quarto of 1706 (Q2) and editions
of the collected works in 1710 (W1) and 1719 (W2);
the definitive modern edition of 1967 (Davis). The
omitting of certain phrases, marked below, indicate a ti-
dying up of indecorums as the Revolutionary reform
movement wore on.

ᵇ I fancy … prose] Q1, Davis; *om.* Q2, Ww

ᶜ Well … away] Q1, Davis; *om.* Q2, Ww

ᵈ Nothing … decorums] Q1, Davis; *om.* Q2, Ww

ᵉ and … fortune] Q1, Davis; *om.* Q2, Ww

ᶠ She … pocket] Q1, Davis; *om.* Q2, Ww

ᵍ a trial] Q2, W1, W2, Davis; by a trial Q1

ʰ or … peas] Q1, Davis; *om.* Q2, Ww

The Beau Defeated; or, The Lucky Younger Brother[a]

by Mary Pix (1666-1709?)

edited by Elizabeth Kubek

Mary Pix, the daughter of an Oxfordshire vicar with connections amongst the gentry, was married to a well-to-do merchant tailor and living at least part of the year in London when she began to write plays and novels. She thus represents the emergence of a middle-class female voice in the London literary scene—one that achieved sufficient critical and financial success for Pix to be satirized, along with Delarivier Manley and Catharine Trotter, in the caustic play *The Female Wits*. Like the Tory satirist Manley, Pix also participated in the political discourse of her day. A supporter of William of Orange, and later of the Hanoverians (as was her friend and mentor, Congreve), Mary Pix displays in her work a cluster of "progressive" attitudes typical of Whig playwrights: contempt for the laws of primogeniture, respect for the merchant classes, and the conviction that women's marital choices were significant socially as well as personally.

The political situation subtly addressed in Pix's plays involved marital and political choices at no less an elevation than that of the English throne. In 1688, the unpopular Catholic Stuart King James II, faced with the threat of civil rebellion, fled London. His opponents, declaring this an abdication, promptly offered the crown to James' daughter Mary and her husband William of Orange, both Protestants. One of William's conditions for assisting in this "Glorious Revolution" was that he be made king in his own right rather than merely as Mary's consort.

Ten years later, when Pix was enjoying theatrical success, William was a widower whose claim to the throne was under renewed scrutiny. England had endured a decade of costly and painful wars. William himself had survived an assassination plot, ongoing diplomatic and military struggle with the Catholic Louis XIV (a Stuart ally), and popular criticism of his imperialist policies and his wealthy favorites. In early 1699, William considered abdicating, so unsure was he of Parliamentary and ministerial support.

But to his supporters, "Dutch William" represented a future in which manly worth was more valued than aristocratic birth. These progressive values appear in the serious romantic plot of *The Beau Defeated*: the virtuous younger brother Clerimont, impoverished by traditional patterns of inheritance, is rescued by the love of the significantly-named Lady Landsworth. Simultaneously, the comic heroine, Mrs. Rich, learns to value her own middle-class status and wealth over the trappings of "quality," a message underlined by Mr. Rich's final speech praising the imperial power of London's emerging capitalist class. In both cases, the heroine emulates the Whig image of Queen Mary: by choosing good men she benefits society. The implied argument—that women's choices deserve respect and that virtue entails economic success—subtly promotes both William's continued claim to power and the agenda of the Whig politicians. Pix's comedy speaks to the private concerns of middle-class men and women while also showing them the importance of their overall place in English society and politics.

DRAMATIS PERSONAE

MEN

    Sir John Roverhead, a beau.

    Elder Clerimont, a country squire.

    Younger Clerimont.

    Belvoir, his friend.

    Mr. Rich, a citizen.*

    Chris, servant to Sir John.

    Toby and Jack, servants to the two Clerimonts.

    [Vermin, a footman.]

WOMEN

    Lady Landsworth, a rich widow of the North.

    Mrs. Rich, a fantastic City* widow.

    Mrs.* Clerimont.

    Lucinda, [daughter to Mr. Rich], niece to the
        widow Rich.

    Her governess.

    Lady la Basset* and Mrs.* Trickwell, gamesters.

    Mrs. Fidget, landlady to younger Clerimont.

    Betty, Mrs. Rich's maid.

    [Lucetta, Mrs. Clerimont's maid.]

[SCENE: LONDON.]

The Beau Defeated; or, The Lucky Younger Brother.

Act I, scene i.

[Mrs. Rich's house in Covent Garden.*]

Enter Mrs. Rich with Betty, her maid.

BETTY.

What's the matter, madam? What has happened
to you? What has anybody done to you?

MRS. RICH.

An affront—ah! I die. An affront—I faint, I cannot
speak. A chair, quickly.

BETTY. (*Giving a chair.*)

An affront! To you, madam, an affront! Is it   5
possible!

MRS. RICH.

But too true, my poor Betty. Oh! I shall die. To
disrespect me in the open street! What insolence!

BETTY.

How, madam! Not to show respect to such a
person as you? Madam Rich, the widow of an   10
honest banker, who got two hundred thousand

pounds in the King's service? Pray madam, who
has been thus insolent?

MRS. RICH.

A duchess, who had the confidence to thrust my
coach from the wall, and make it run back above   15
twenty yards.

BETTY.

A very impertinent duchess. What! Madam, your
person shining all o'er with jewels, your new gilt
coach, your dappled Flanders* with long tails, your
coachman with cocking whiskers like a Swiss   20
Guard,[1] your six footmen covered with lace, more
than any on a Lord Mayor's Day?[2] I say, could not
all this imprint some respect in the duchess?

MRS. RICH.

Not at all. And this beggarly duchess, at the end
of an old coach drawn by two miserable starved   25
jades, made her tattered footmen insult me.

BETTY.

S'life!* Where was Betty. I'd have told her what she
was.

MRS. RICH.

I spoke to her with a mien and tone pro-
portionable to my equipage, but she with a   30
scornful smile cried, "Hold thy peace, citizen,"*
struck me quite dumb.

BETTY.

Citizen! Citizen! To a lady in a gilt coach, lined with
crimson velvet, and hung round with a gold fringe?

MRS. RICH.

I swear to thee that I had not the force to answer   35
to this deadly injury, but ordered my coachman
to turn and drive me home a-full gallop.

BETTY.

But madam, pray consider things rightly and take
this as it was intended, for I conceive it was not
against your person but your name that this affront   40
was designed. And why do you not make haste to
change it?

MRS. RICH.

That I have resolved, but I quarrel daily with my
destiny, that I was not at first a woman of quality.*

---

1 Swiss Guard] Pope's ceremonial guard

2 Lord Mayor's Day] important City holiday, especially for
   London's upper middle class

BETTY.

Well, well, madam, you have no great reason to complain, and though you are not as yet a woman of quality, you are at least very rich, and you know that with money you may buy quality, but birth very often brings no estate. 45

MRS. RICH.

That's nothing; there is something very charming in quality and a great name. 50

BETTY.

Yet sure you'd think yourself in a worse condition, madam, were you as many great ladies in the world are who want* everything and in spite of their great name are known but by the great number of creditors that are bawling at their doors from morning till night. 55

MRS. RICH.

That's the modish air, 'tis that distinguishes the people of quality.

BETTY.

Methinks madam, 'tis a great satisfaction to dare to go out at the great gate without being in danger of having your coach and horses seized by a troop of sergeants. What would you say if you were obliged to return home in a filthy hack, as several of quality have done? 60

MRS. RICH.

Ah! Would to heavens that had happened to me and that I were a countess.

BETTY.

But madam, you don't imagine—

MRS. RICH.

Yes, yes, I do imagine, and I had rather be the beggarliest countess in the Town* than the widow of the richest banker in Europe. Well, I am resolved, and I will be a countess, cost what it will, and to that intent I'll absolutely break all commerce with those little cits* by whose alliance I am debased, and first I'll begin with Mr. Rich. 70

BETTY.

Mr. Rich, madam, your brother-in-law? 75

MRS. RICH.

My brother-in-law! My brother-in-law! Thou simple wench! Prithee know better!

BETTY.

Pardon me, madam, I thought he had been your brother-in-law, because he was brother to your deceased husband. 80

MRS. RICH.

That's true, my husband's brother, but my husband being dead, fool, Mr. Rich is now no more kin to me than my footman. Nevertheless the fellow thinks himself of importance and is continually a-censuring my conduct and controlling my actions; nay, even the little minx his daughter, when we go in my coach together, places herself at the end[3] by my side. 85

BETTY.

Little ridiculous creature! 90

MRS. RICH.

But that which angers me the most is that with her little smiling, mimicking behavior, she attracts the eyes of the whole Town, and I have not so much as a glance.

BETTY.

What a foolish Town is this! Because she's young and pretty, they take more notice of her than you. 95

MRS. RICH.

It shall be otherwise, or I'll see her no more.

BETTY.

Nay, your ladyship will humble her, for of late you rarely suffer her to come near you.

MRS. RICH.

Well, I will have a title and a name, that's resolved, a name that shall fill the mouth. 100

BETTY.

Ah! Madam, a great name will become you extremely, but a name is not sufficient; I believe you must have a husband, too, and you ought to take care what choice you make. 105

MRS. RICH.

I know the world well enough and have in my eye one of the most accomplished gentlemen in the Town.

BETTY.

How madam, already made your choice and I know nothing? 110

MRS. RICH.

Sir John would not let me tell thee.

---

[3] at the end] facing forward (the most comfortable seat, and therefore a sign of rank)

BETTY.

What, Sir John? Sir John Roverhead, of Roverhead Castle?

MRS. RICH.

He himself.

BETTY.

Why madam, speak seriously: Is it Sir John 115
Roverhead you design to marry?

MRS. RICH.

Prithee where's the wonder?

BETTY.

Why pray consider, madam, Sir John is not worth
a groat.

MRS. RICH.

I have sufficient for us both, and there is justice 120
in what I design. Mr. Rich did not get his estate
too honestly, and 'tis some kind of restitution to
raise up, with what he has left me, one of the
ancients' families in the North.[4]

BETTY.

Oh! Since 'tis a marriage of conscience, I have no 125
more to say.

MRS. RICH.

Betty.

BETTY.

Madam?

MRS. RICH.

Prithee, what's thy surname?

BETTY.

Has your ladyship forgot?

MRS. RICH.

Dost imagine it worth a place in my memory? 130

BETTY.

Cork, madam.

MRS. RICH.

Oh, filthy! From henceforth let me call thee de la
Bett; that has an air French and agreeable.

BETTY.

What you please, madam.

MRS. RICH.

De la Bett, whatever bills the mechanical fellows, 135

little trades people, bring ye, let 'em wait, let 'em
walk for't, and watch my levee. But if Monsieur
comes that brought the prohibited gloves, l'eau de
fleur d'orange, and the complexion,[5] you understand me, give him his price and ready money. 140

BETTY.

Yes, madam.

MRS. RICH.

And do ye hear, put a hundred guineas in the
embroidered purse for basset.*

BETTY.

Bless me, madam! Have you lost all that I put in
yesterday morning? 145

MRS. RICH.

Impertinence! I am sufficiently recompensed in
learning the game, and the honorable company I
am admitted into.

BETTY.

Indeed madam, the footmen say Mrs.* Trickwell
is a perfect female rook, lives upon gaming, nay, 150
and keeps* out on't, they say, and they can tell.

MRS. RICH.

Hold your tongue. She is a woman of quality,*
knows everybody at Court, all their intrigues, is
as deep in affairs and keeps as many secrets as
Maintenon,[6] I'll be sworn, ma foie.[7] What a word 155
was there! But as I was saying, she has told me and
half a dozen ladies more secrets six hours together
and such secrets, de la Bett, let me die, were we
not women of discretion, might reach the lives of,[b]
or eternally disgrace, some that shall be nameless. 160

BETTY.

They are very happy, if they are in her power.

MRS. RICH.

Peace. Has nobody sent a How-de-ye yet?

BETTY.

No.

---

4 restitution … ancients' families] Possibly a reference to
  the forced redistribution of Royalist estates, many in the
  north of England, during the Commonwealth to
  Cromwell's London supporters.

5 prohibited gloves … complexion] illegal French imports,
  including perfume and rouge

6 Maintenon] Madame de Maintenon, favorite of, and secretly married to, the French King Louis XIV

7 ma foie] literally, my liver (Fr.); Pix gives us a visual joke,
  for Mrs. Rich has ignorantly mouthed an affected
  French exclamation, ma foi ("by my faith").

MRS. RICH.

'Tis my horrid custom of getting up so early in a
morning.   165

BETTY.

Madam, 'tis past twelve.

MRS. RICH.

And I dressed and have been abroad. Abominable!
I charge ye, tomorrow don't bring my clothes till
past two, if I am so mad to call for 'em.

BETTY.

Won't your ladyship inquire after my Lady   170
Landsworth's health? Methinks you neglect her,
though she is rich, gay, and beautiful and honors
your house with her choice of it whilst she's in Town.

MRS. RICH.

Honors! Who art thou speaking to, sweetheart? I
do not like her, she won't play, nay, will sit ye two   175
hours together and speak ill of nobody; she is not
fit for the conversation of quality.*

Enter a boy.

BOY.

Madam, Mrs. Trickwell and another lady is come to
teach your ladyship shombring, I think they call it.

MRS. RICH.

Ombre, sot.* I shall be rid of thee, thou fragment   180
of the shop. De la Bett, I'll go to them. If Sir John
comes, call me, not else.

Exit Mrs. Rich and boy. Enter Lady Landsworth.

LADY LANDSWORTH.

My dear Mrs.* Betty, I'm glad to find thee alone.

BETTY.

Your ladyship does me too much honor.

LADY LANDSWORTH.

Thou art so discreet and obliging, I cannot love   185
thee too well. Where's thy impertinent mistress?

BETTY.

Gone to learn ombre, with a hundred guineas in
her pocket.

LADY LANDSWORTH.

Ha, ha, ha! Her pride, ill nature, and self-opinion
makes her follies unpitied. I'd fain be rid of the   190
nauseous conversation this house abounds with.

BETTY.

Indeed, my City lady, turning courtier, has a
hopeful stock of teachers: mistresses grown old and

then forsaken, who in the tatters of their prosperity
pass upon her for decayed quality; female   195
gamesters; and fools in abundance.

LADY LANDSWORTH.

They are affected without beauty or good clothes,
though that alone's enough to spoil one that had
both; their mirth is insipid, and their raillery
abusive and yet not poignant. For my part, I've   200
almost lost my gay humor* for fear of being like
'em. If I continue here for one week longer, I shall
e'en exchange the Town, where I expected such
pleasure, for my old Yorkshire retirement.

BETTY.

Could you but get Mrs. Clerimont to ye, madam,   205
she'd immediately introduce you to the beau
monde, where wit, gallantry, and good breeding
are emulators. You say she's a relation.

LADY LANDSWORTH.

She is so at a distance, but you see all my sending
will not prevail with her to come at me nor   210
appoint a time when I shall wait upon her. What
can be the reason?

BETTY.

I know not, unless 'tis being here, for truly I fancy,
though my mistress is fled to Covent Garden, she is
as much despised by the real quality as she is cajoled   215
by the pretenders to it. You say you are not acquainted with Mrs. Clerimont, though related to her; so
perhaps she guesses you of our stamp and avoids ye.
For Heaven's sake, madam, how came ye hither?

LADY LANDSWORTH.

Why, I'll tell thee, Betty: I was married a mere   220
baby to a very old man, who, in his youth having
been a debauchee and dealing only with the worst
of our sex, had an ill opinion of all, kept me like
a nun, broke off all commerce to London, or
indeed with anybody, not excepting relations.   225

BETTY.

And could you endure this?

LADY LANDSWORTH.

Most patiently: never found fault with his woolen
shirts or nightcaps, lay all night to the music of
his cough or the rattling of his ptisick,[8] writ

---

8 ptisick] phthisic (tuberculosis), here merely phlegm in
the throat

nothing but receipts,* scarce ever opened my
mouth but out came, "How do ye do, my dear,
did the syrup I made last please ye?"

BETTY.

Your ladyship was a miracle.

LADY LANDSWORTH.

And what do you think I got by doing this?

BETTY.

I don't know, but I'm sure you deserved a great deal.

LADY LANDSWORTH.

Even three thousand pounds a year, besides money,
plate, and jewels. This Mrs. Rich's husband was my
old man's banker, and once I saw her in the
country; besides, she had money of mine in her
hands. So to her and this dear Town I came,
resolving to participate all the innocent liberty my
youth, my wealth, and sex desires.

BETTY.

Ah, madam! Had our sex but your forbearance,
they might all be happy.

LADY LANDSWORTH.

I am of the mind that Fortune offers every mortal
their share of satisfaction, but if they pluck the green
fruit, forestall her purpose, or miss the ripened
moment, they rarely have another prospect.

BETTY.

Right, madam, and is it not the same in love? If a
lady refuses the man she likes, all her adventures
in that kind prove awkward and unlucky after it.

LADY LANDSWORTH.

Say'st thou so, Mrs. Betty? Well, I am resolved to
indulge my inclinations and, rather than not
obtain the person I like, invert the order of nature
and pursue, though he flies.

BETTY.

Impossible: one glance of yours subdues the
proudest love-defier of them all.

LADY LANDSWORTH.

Pho, you flatter. But seriously, my dear confidante,
being once condemned to matrimony without ever
asking my consent, now I have the freedom to
make my own choice and the whole world the
mart—I have the oddest whimsies.

BETTY.

Then your ladyship intends to venture on a second
marriage?

LADY LANDSWORTH.

Truly Mrs. Betty, I believe so. Why should we
dissemble when we are alone? But such a husband
I would have.

BETTY.

What sort of a husband? Let's hear the marks, that
I may try to find the man.

LADY LANDSWORTH.

He should be genteel, yet not a beau; witty, yet no
debauchee; susceptible of love, yet abhorring lewd
women; learned, poetical, musical without one
dram of vanity. In fine, very meritorious, yet very
modest, generous* to the last degree and master
of no estate, mightily in love with me and not so
much as know I am worth the clothes I wear.

BETTY.

Ha, ha, ha! To your romances again, lady fair, 'tis
only there you can converse with those heroes; this
Town affords no such, I can assure you. Modest,
meritorious, and genteel, ha, ha, ha! Your pardon,
madam, why, such a wight would not get his daily
bread, not rags to cover his nakedness. 'Tis
frontless impudence makes the grand appearance
and carries the world before it.

LADY LANDSWORTH.

I suppose I shall increase your laughter when I tell
you I fancy I have found the man.

BETTY.

Madam.

LADY LANDSWORTH.

You know, throughly tired with the impertinence
within and not being fitted to give or receive visits,
I have often rambled with my woman*
incognito—and have done the strangest things.

BETTY.

What, for heaven's sake?

LADY LANDSWORTH.

Even lost my heart: in love, Mrs. Betty, desperately
in love.

BETTY.

With whom, dear madam?

LADY LANDSWORTH.

Oh, a pretty gentleman, who has all those
accomplishments I desire writ in his face, as plain
as—

BETTY.

The nose in't, I warrant.

LADY LANDSWORTH.

Yes truly, for all your jesting: I sate by him in the 300
playhouse and discovered his sense as taking as his
figure.

BETTY.

But where was his modesty, when he attacked a
mask?*

LADY LANDSWORTH.

That's your mistake, 'twas I gave the onset; nay, 305
went farther: appointed him a meeting there again,
enjoined him not to dog me, nor endeavor to learn
who I was, which he punctually obeyed.

BETTY.

And you performed your assignation?

LADY LANDSWORTH.

Yes indeed, last night, and to try his generosity, 310
when the doorkeeper came into the side box for
money,[9] I seemed in a great fright, and said I had
left my purse at home. He immediately offered me
a guinea, which though I accepted, by the
melancholy air of his face I guessed it had not a 315
twin brother.

BETTY.

Bless me, madam! That pretense, and taking his
money, made you look like a woman of the
Town.[10]

LADY LANDSWORTH.

So I designed. I forced him to tell me his name 320
and lodging ere I'd accept the favor, and now I
have a game to play, wherein you must assist me.

BETTY.

In whatever you desire. Oh! Madam, Sir John
Roverhead is just upon us.

LADY LANDSWORTH.

What luck is this! Is there no avoiding the fop? 325

Enter Sir John Roverhead and Chris, his man.

SIR JOHN.

Hah, Chris! The beautiful wealthy widow of the
North.

CHRIS.

Why sir, she is not Mrs. Rich.

SIR JOHN.

Sagely discovered, but she's better, Mr. Wisdom,
more desirable, and deeper in my affections. 330

CHRIS.

Your pardon, sir, I have done.

SIR JOHN. (*Adjusting himself to Chris.*)

Stand back.

LADY LANDSWORTH.

What postures the thing uses to make it more
ridiculous than Nature first designed it.

SIR JOHN. (*To Chris.*)

Now to be florid.—Sure some auspicious planet 335
ruled today, for every star is witness how often,
when I have made my visit here, I have sighed to
see your ladyship—

LADY LANDSWORTH.

Still* taking coach or chair.* Have I not helped you
out, sir? 340

SIR JOHN.

Lord madam, such beauty, wit, and dress what
man can bear?

LADY LANDSWORTH.

Such affectation, folly, and nonsense what woman
can endure? (*Exit.*)

SIR JOHN.

Aye, hey, Mrs.—Betty, what's the meaning of this? 345

BETTY.

The effect of her country ignorance.

SIR JOHN.

It must be so, for I think, Chris, I am nicely*
dressed today.

CHRIS.

Aye, but perhaps she likes the inward man.[11]

SIR JOHN.

She's a fool, that's certain. But Mrs. Betty, I hope 350
my affairs stand well with your lady; this was but
a trifle whom I addressed too with my universal
gallantry, which had she received, I should have
laughed at. My valet knows 'tis my way to all who
make an appearance. 355

---

9 money] Theater patrons often paid admission after the
first act.

10 woman of the Town] prostitute or kept mistress

---

11 inward man] a Quaker expression, meaning to value the
spirit over the flesh

CHRIS.

Under fifty.

SIR JOHN.

Or above, if they make an appearance.

BETTY.

Aye Sir John, 'tis you alone have the bewitching way, court all the world, and catch my unwary mistress by the by, because 'tis like quality.* 360

SIR JOHN.

Like! That's degrading. I'd be an original, like nothing.

BETTY.

Nothing, sure, can be like you.

SIR JOHN.

A witty baggage, this; we must engage her.

CHRIS.

With all my heart; secure you the mistress, and let me alone for the maid. 365

SIR JOHN.

Well, but Mrs. Betty, after this idle chat shall we crave leave to see your mistress.

BETTY.

You may, and you only; she's at cards.

SIR JOHN.

I profess thou art charmingly dressed and pretty, I vow. What design have you today? 370

BETTY.

Is it to me you speak, sir?

SIR JOHN.

To whom else?

BETTY.

I thought, like a poet, you were repeating and designed the compliment for the next of quality you met. 375

SIR JOHN.

Fie, fie, let me die if you are not the prettiest amiable creature I know. Prithee, who makes thy mantuas? How modestly the little creature dresses her head, too! 380

BETTY.

Ha, ha, ha, this is excess of French breeding. But Sir John, you forget my lady expects you.

SIR JOHN.

I shall ever forget her when I look upon thee, my life, my soul.

(Sings.)

She threw by her knotting[12] in haste— 385
Ho, ho, ho, come along Chris, I've shot her flying.
(Sings.)
And caught me about my well-shaped waist—
Ho, ho, ho. (Exit, singing, [Chris with him].)

BETTY.

So, this is the high, top fool in my lady's equipage, the favored fool, and she has enough in her train 390 to give a man of sense the spleen but to hear her catalog. Well, since Fortune has thrown me into this chambermaid station, I'll revenge her cruelty and plague her favorites.

No fool by me shall e'er successful prove; 395
My plots shall help the man of sense in love.

[Exit.]

Act II, [scene i. Younger Clerimont's lodgings.]

Enter Belvoir meeting Jack.

BELVOIR.

How now Jack, is thy master within?

JACK.

No sir.

BELVOIR.

"No sir." Let me come morning, noon, or night, still* I am answered, "No sir." 'Twas by accident I found his lodgings, and I plainly perceive he is 5 denied; this is most injurious to our former friendship, quite contrary to the contract made when we were fellow students, when I was only Clerimont's, and Clerimont Belvoir's.

JACK.

Aye sir, my master's strangely altered, but I dare 10 not tell.

BELVOIR.

Come, for once I'll tempt thee to a breach of trust. I may do him service; I hear his father's dead.

JACK.

Ah, sir! That's his grief, the very fountain of his discontentment. 15

BELVOIR.

Trust me, Jack, few young gentlemen use to break their hearts for such a loss.

---

12 knotting] form of needlework

JACK.

Yes, if they are younger brothers and left not worth a groat, 'twill go a great way with them, a great way indeed, sir.

BELVOIR.

But he was the old lord's favorite, who had land enough without entail to make my Clerimont happy.

JACK.

Alas! Mr. Belvoir, I find you know not our story.

BELVOIR.

Not the particulars, only what I've heard from fame; if thou believest me thy master's friend, hide nothing from me.

JACK.

I do, so notwithstanding his commands you shall hear our misfortunes. You know my master's elder brother is a perfect squire, on my conscience the product of two virginities;[13] such an unaccountable blockhead, that though he gave the assured proof of spending his father's estate and did it so ungenteelly that he was despised by men of sense, shunned by all but the unthinking rabble, ridiculous even below lampooning—

BELVOIR.

Why Jack, the Town* improves thee beyond the university: thou growest witty.

JACK.

No, 'tis the approach of poverty whets my spleen; egad, if I am reduced to rags I'll spare ne'er an elder brother of them all, though he were a prince.

BELVOIR.

A-well-a-day,[14] for the poor gentlemen in gilt coaches. But proceed to the matter, good friend John.

JACK.

Why this dunce, I think I called him before, shatter-brains—

BELVOIR.

Hold.

JACK.

Whose whole delight lay in his kindred hounds, who for his hunting companions entertained* all the lubbers of the four adjacent parishes, till the country was going to petition the Parliament for laborers;[15] this monster of the woods, this—

BELVOIR.

Well, what of him?

JACK.

Has got every penny of my old lord's estate, whilst my master, the most deserving of his race* (though I say it that should not), is left to starve, rob, drown, or what he pleases.

BELVOIR.

But how came this to pass, Jack, hah?

JACK.

Why, that damned jilt Fortune, or her left-handed daughter,[16] as blind as she, Chance.

BELVOIR.

A mischance, upon my word.

JACK.

A confounded one. My old lord lay long bedrid of the gout, and the wight I have described lived in an estate some few miles distant. One day, hunting that way, he bethought himself and made his sick father a visit, but knowing he could not sit a moment without talking to his beloved Jowler, Ringwood, etcetera, takes the whole kennel along with him into the chamber, whilst t'other kennel below (I mean the peasants) were so sharp-set, they scarce left my lord an unmauled dish to come to his table.

BELVOIR.

Horrid, filthy brutes!

JACK.

In fine, this so exasperated the old man that in a rage he burnt his will, designing to leave my master whatever was in his power, but the malicious Fates decreed it otherwise, for that very night the angered father died suddenly, and all his wealth fell to that soft-headed fool in one swoop, and the Deel,* I say, do him good with it.

---

13 product …virginities] child of two virgins, proverbially naïve and simple

14 A-well-a-day] exclamation of sorrow (like alas)

15 country … laborers] If Elder Clerimont depopulated the labor force of the region, it could petition Parliament to relocate the poor from other parishes.

16 left-handed daughter] offspring from a morganatic (q.v.) union

BELVOIR.

Pho, there must be application made to him, Jack; this must not be suffered.

JACK.

To his huntsman apply then, for he's his only oracle.

BELVOIR.

There's Mrs. Clerimont in Town, his first cousin, 85 a vast fortune,[17] and one who has a larger share of wit and goodness; she shall be consulted. What, a young gentleman shall never droop for missing a paltry fortune.

JACK.

Dear sir, do your best. But now I beg of you to be 90 gone; I hear him coming, and he will be in such a passion if he discover I have been talking to you or told he was at home, for 'tis his humor to hide from all his friends.

BELVOIR.

Well, I'll not cross him now but certainly find out 95 some way to assist him. Farewell, honest Jack, be sure you prove faithful and kind to him.

JACK.

Upon my veracity, to my uttermost. I only wish to serve him.

Exit Belvoir. Jack stands out of sight. Enter Clerimont, in mourning.

CLERIMONT.

Mine's not the mourning of an heir. Oh! my noble 100 father, sure I should have grieved enough for thee, for thy unspeakable loss, without additional calamities. What will become of me? Must I wait at proud men's doors and cringe for an admittance? Can I flatter the puffed-up lord and fawn for a vile office? 105 Debase my immortal soul to feed this molding clay? 'Tis impossible, 'tis more than man can bear!

JACK.

Sir.

CLERIMONT.

What?

JACK.

I thought you called.

---

17 a vast fortune] heiress to a large estate

CLERIMONT.

Thou art too officious. I have advised thee oft to leave me and seek thy fortune where the goddess 110 smiles. I am a wretch that now is sinking lower than his own despairing thoughts can frame.

JACK.

Lord sir, is this all the philosophy you have learned? I think I am the best proficient: starving frights not me half so much as parting; faith, 115 though the world is crowded with knaves that an honest gentleman can scarce breathe, I'll jostle stoutly but you shall have elbow room.

CLERIMONT.

Poor fellow! Thou differest from the common tribe of servants; they fly poverty worse than infection 120 or else with saucy impudence insult.

Enter a coachman with a letter.

COACHMAN.

Is this Mr. Clerimont's lodging?

JACK.

Well, and what then, how came you here without calling me? What's your name, and what's your business? 125

COACHMAN.

Not with you, sauce-box.

JACK.

How, sirrah!

CLERIMONT.

Peace. My name is Clerimont.

COACHMAN.

Then sir, there's a lady in my coach has sent you this; she says it requires no answer. (*Gives a letter* 130 *and goes off.*)

CLERIMONT.

Hah, gold! Fly, Jack, call him back.

JACK. (*Pulling in the coachman.*)

Hark ye, you sneak-nose, hound's-face, you have affronted my master.

COACHMAN.

Why fool, I brought him money. 135

JACK.

I thought so, ye pimp; he scorns it.

CLERIMONT.

Here, return this back. Tell the lady she mistakes the man, and I'll wait upon her where she appoints and convince her that she does.

COACHMAN.

Gad, a notable mistake. 140

CLERIMONT.

Rascal, no fingering. [*To Jack.*] Follow, you, and take the number of his coach.—If you are not honest, sirrah, I shall find a time to cut your ears* off.

JACK.

I'll watch him, I warrant. Bring money to my master! Sirrah, get you gone. 145

COACHMAN.

Sure they are all distracted!

(Exit Jack and coachman.)

CLERIMONT.

From my mask* in the play-house: by my life, a very* harlot. How few in my circumstances would refuse these offers, but my nature's quite otherwise. I cannot be obliged where I contemn nor live so 150 vile a way. Not but the temptation's doubly baited, profit and pleasure. For though the baggage is loose as the wanton winds, yet she is witty beyond her sex. What a medley's here. (*Reads.*) "When I tell ye I am in love, by that modest air and downcast 155 look of yours I guess you'll think me mad and expect (according to the damsels in romance) I should have a fit of sickness, been at the point of death, ere made the discovery;* but women of my character are not so nice.* I am a mistress, have 160 abundance of money, if you have but little. A wise man may pick comfort out of this. I send you a token, as an earnest of my future favors. Agreeable to your wonted obedience, come not to the coach, but meet me at four in the Park,* and thank me 165 with your acceptance." Ha, ha, ha, ha, I see the Devil's not wanting* on his part: he'd have me a greater sinner ere I come to despair. The postscript is the same mad stuff. "You shall know me by an affected motion in my walk and a belle toss with 170 my head, humph!"18

Enter Jack.

JACK.

The lady's gone, sir, and the money too. Gad sir,

---

18 humph] an affected sniff of disdain that accompanies the "belle toss" of her head

though to please you I was in a passion, yet my mouth watered plaguily at the gold.

CLERIMONT.

What said the creature? 175

JACK.

The creature! Gad, she was an angel. She pulled off her mask, I believe to laugh freely, for she burst out vehemently, and when the man said you'd have none on't, she gave herself a swing, and cried, "The more fool he. Drive on, coachman." 180

CLERIMONT.

So merry! But 'tis her time whilst youth and beauty last; she'll have years enough of sorrow.

JACK.

Sir, my landlady's a-coming; you have used her so to sack* and chocolate in a morning that she'll ne'er fail you. 185

CLERIMONT.

Pish, I am sick of her impertinence.

Enter Mrs. Fidget.

MRS. FIDGET.

Good morrow, Mr. Clerimont. Good lord, still walking with that melancholy air! Well, well, were I such a pretty gentleman, I'd defy Fortune.

CLERIMONT.

Prithee landlady, what would you have me do? If 190 you think the ladies will like me so well, take my picture and hang it out at your balcony; e'en make your best of me, if that will content ye.

MRS. FIDGET.

Fie, fie, you might have private chamber-practice enough, if you'd give your mind to't. 'Ud's* my life, 195 if the young handsome fellows were like you, there would never have come so many of them to their coach and six. Let me tell ye, Mr. Clerimont, if I had thought you had been of this reserved humor,* I'd not have let my lodgings to you. I used to have 200 women of quality* to my fine gentlemen, and suppers dressed in my house have lasted my family a week, besides that put into my hand that shall be nameless, else I had never lived in the credit you see me in these twenty years in the parish— 205

CLERIMONT.

Good Mrs. Fidget—

MRS. FIDGET.

Nay, you shall hear me. Brought up my daughters as I have done: as fine women, though I say it, as any that adorn Covent Garden* Church.

CLERIMONT.

Church! I should rather have thought they'd adorn 210
the playhouse.

MRS. FIDGET.

Now, out upon you, Mr. Clerimont, my daughters are never seen at the playhouse; I bring them up in the fear of Heaven.

JACK.

Yes, and they are both married in the fear of 215
Heaven too: for neither of them troubled the Church in that affair, as I have been told.

MRS. FIDGET.

Well, saucy-face.—But Mr. Clerimont, what I have said is all for your good, and I hope you do take it into your consideration, for truly today there 220
came a very pretty lady, and notwithstanding your order, I sent up the coachman. I am willing to bring you to preferment.

CLERIMONT.

Bring me to the pox and the Devil—

MRS. FIDGET.

Marry gap,[19] is this my thanks! 225

CLERIMONT.

I tell ye, I am tired of these morning lectures, and if my lodgings cannot be free from noise and impertinence, I must quit them.—Follow me, Jack, I'll take the air.

Exeunt [Clerimont and Jack.]

MRS. FIDGET.

So, out of sorts, and gone without giving me my 230
morning's draught.—Why, Master John, Master John, give me the key of the closet; I must rummage it for a dram of the bottle. 'Ud's flesh, I shan't be in humor again this half-hour. The man's a fool, I think. When beauty courts, the charming pleasures shun; 235
Be virtuous, though he's sure to be undone;
He's mad, 'Ud's flesh! I'd sooner turn a nun.

Exit.

---

[19] Marry gap] corruption of "marry* go up," an archaic exclamation

---

[Scene ii. Mrs. Rich's house.]

Scene draws and discovers Mrs. Rich, Mrs. Trickwell, and Lady La Basset, rising from play.*

MRS. TRICKWELL. (*To Mrs. Rich.*)

I protest, your ladyship plays to a miracle, but I would not have had you venture money yet.

MRS. RICH.

Oh pardon me, madam, I should not have minded it else. But do you think I shall ever be capable?

LADY LA BASSET.

Why, you are perfect already, a wonderful 5
apprehension.

MRS. RICH.

Oh fie! my Lady La Basset, you compliment. In reality, may I hope to play at Court? I have a great ambition to play at Court. Oh my stars! I should torment our City* ladies to death to talk of honors 10
done me at Court.

LADY LA BASSET.

Yes, yes, you shall be introduced and honored at Court, I'll promise ye, or my interest fails me, and for setting it out, let me alone,[20] I'll make their ears tingle, i'faith. 15

MRS. RICH.

Oh my dear, dear Lady La Basset, let me embrace ye. The very conception on't is felicity to the highest degree. *Mon Dieu!* How we'll tease the little City creatures.

Enter Mrs. Betty.

BETTY.

Madam, Sir John Roverhead is come to wait on 20
you and has got some music to entertain your ladyships. (*Exit.*)

MRS. RICH.

Oh heavens! That master of accomplishments! Instruct me, dear ladies, how to receive him.

LADY LA BASSET.

Seem in a cabal, then burst out a-laughing, and 25
let fall some mysterious words that tend towards scandal.

MRS. RICH.

Good! [*Raising her voice.*] Ridiculous to the highest

---

[20] setting… alone] for making it public, leave it to me

degree that ever a woman of her quality* should make such a faux pas; the Town will ring on't. Oh my stars! 'Tis something so odd, ha, ha, ha, ha. 30

MRS. TRICKWELL.

Transportingly foolish! Yet it makes me laugh, ha, ha, ha, ha.

LADY LA BASSET.

Who can forbear, ha, ha, ha.

Enter Sir John.

SIR JOHN.

Pardon, ladies, the interruption. May I participate? 35 I die to laugh in consort with women of your wit and merit.

MRS. RICH.

Oh fie! Sir John, 'tis a secret, upon my word. We must be tender of our own sex. You are but too well acquainted with our weakness. Scandal of an hour 40 old is as much out of date with you as a gazette in the afternoon to the sots that hunt foreign news.[21]

SIR JOHN.

News! Gad madam, there's no such thing. There's nothing new under the sun; the world is a continual round of nauseous repetition. In the last 45 generation and this, young girls were mad for husbands, then mad to get rid of 'em; sharpers had their cullies; gamesters, their fools; physicians killed their patients and were paid for't; lawyers got estates, and their clients were undone with suing 50 for 'em; courtiers' promises and bullies' oaths ever made a great noise and signified nothing.

MRS. RICH.

Satirical, I vow! Why, you are in a mortifying way, Sir John.

SIR JOHN.

Indeed, scarce fit to appear before your ladyship. 55 I have had a billet-doux from a woman of sixty, which has given me the spleen to that degree, I could outrail a hypocritical fanatic.

MRS. RICH.

Sixty! Pleasant, I protest.

SIR JOHN.

She's a walking memento mori. I have suffered 60 some time under the persecution, and in bitterness and gall instead of ink have wrote a stanza to show how awkwardly an old woman makes advances.

MRS. RICH.

Oh dear Sir John, let us have it.

LADY LA BASSET.

We are all petitioners. 65

SIR JOHN.

You shall command me, ladies.

Song by Sir John.

Delia tired Strephon[22] with her flame,
    While languishing she viewed him.
The well-dressed youth despised the dame,
    But still old Puss pursued him. 70

"Some pity on a wretch bestow
    That lies at your devotion."
"Perhaps near fifty years ago,
    Some might have liked the motion."

"No heart like mine did ever burn. 75
    I'm rich too, I'll assure ye."c
"And I must tell you in return,
    You're uglier than a Fury."

"If you, proud youth, my flame despise,
    I'll hang me in my garters." 80
"Why then, make haste to win the prize
    Among Love's foolish martyrs."

"Can you see Delia brought so low
    And make her no requitals?"
"Delia may to the Devil go 85
    For Strephon, stop my vitals."

"I'll be as constant as a dove,
    And always we'll be billing."

---

21 gazette ... news] early newspapers, which contained a great deal of gossip and trivia as well as domestic and international news, which latter dealt currently with ne- gotiations that would help determine the commercial and colonial future of England's relations with the Con- tinent.

---

22 Delia and Strephon] Traditional names for lovers in pas- toral romantic poetry; at this point, they were cliches.

"No more damned stories of your love!
    Your very breath is killing." 90

"These eyes for you shall learn to shine,
    That twinkle in their sockets."
"I'll never in a cellar dine
    When I may go to Locket's."*

"What in my charms and youth I want,* 95
    I'll make it up in duty."
"Prithee leave off this foolish cant.
    I'll stoop to naught but beauty."

MRS. TRICKWELL. (*To Mrs. Rich, aside.*)
    Did you observe how my Lady La Basset eyed Sir
    John? 100

MRS. RICH.
    Yes and am pleased with it: I would not have a
    fellow pretend to me that all the fine women in
    Town are not fond of. (*To Sir John*) Our thanks
    in abundance. 'Tis wonderful pretty.

SIR JOHN.
    Your pardon, harsh and untunable, like the subject. 105

Enter Mrs. Betty

BETTY. (*To Mrs. Rich, aside.*)
    Mr. Rich will not be answered, madam. I had
    much ado to keep him out here.

MRS. RICH.
    Ladies, let me beg you would take Sir John into
    the drawing room and entertain him a moment.
    A hideous citizen will tease me about a little 110
    business, but I'll dispatch him in the third part of
    a minute and rejoin the agreeable conversation.

SIR JOHN.
    We shall wait with impatience, madam.

*Exeunt severally. Enter Mr. Rich, meeting Mrs. Rich
and Betty.*[23]

BETTY.
    There he walks, madam. He would stay in spite
    of me. 115

---

[23] Enter … Betty] As later stage directions make clear, the
inner stage here closes again, and Mr. Rich and Mrs.
Rich encounter each other towards the front of the stage,
probably before a sliding backdrop meant to represent
an anteroom.

MRS. RICH.
    Ah Mr. Rich! What design brings you hither? Your
    absence this day would have been very obliging,
    but since you are here, let's finish, pray, as soon as
    you can. Well, what's the business?

MR. RICH.
    Hey-day! What's this? Good madam Rich, my 120
    sister-in-law, how despisingly you talk! Hark ye,
    hark ye, this behavior does not become ye, and
    without telling you what relates to me, you'll one
    day repent of your ridiculous way of living and
    carriage. 125

MRS. RICH.
    An elbow-chair,[24] Betty. I foresee Mr. Rich intends
    to talk me to sleep.

MR. RICH.
    No madam, on the contrary, for were you in your
    right senses, what I have to say would most terribly
    keep you awake. 130

MRS. RICH.
    You strangely concern yourself with my conduct.

MR. RICH.
    And who will concern himself if I don't? You are
    my daughter's aunt, widow of Paul Rich my
    brother, and I will not have it said upon the
    Exchange* that my brother's widow and daughter's 135
    aunt is run stark mad.

MRS. RICH.
    How, mad! You lose all respect, Mr. Rich, but I
    shall find a way to get rid of you, that I may hear
    no more such sottish unmannerly language, to
    which I scorn to answer. 140

MR. RICH.
    Oh! 'Slife,* Madam Rich, you ought to get rid of
    all your ridiculous airs of quality* and greatness,
    that you may receive no more affronts equal to this
    day's.

MRS. RICH.
    You ought not, Mr. Rich, to reproach me of that 145
    where I am only exposed because I'm thought your
    sister-in-law. But there's an end of that, Mr. Rich.
    I'll have it published in the Gazette that since my
    widowhood I am no more your sister, and so I

---

[24] elbow-chair] armchair

renounce you for my brother-in-law, Mr. Rich,[25] 150
and since hitherto my expenses, my noble manner
of living, and what I every day practice, could
never correct the fault of having once been a
citizen's wife, I do now pretend–

MR. RICH.

Zooks, Madam Rich, 'tis the best part of your 155
history, that name of Rich, and had it not been
for the good conduct of the poor deceased, you
had not been in a condition for so much pomp
and greatness. I would fain know—

MRS. RICH.

Courage, courage, Mr. Rich, you do well. Talk on, 160
talk on, 'tis your last time.

MR. RICH.

I would fain know, let me tell you, if it would not
be more decent for you to have a good grave coach
lined with an olive-colored cloth, a lean coachman
in a dark brown coat, a little modest boy with short 165
hair to open the door, and a pair of gentle geldings,
than all this sumptuous equipage that makes
people inquire who you are; these modish prancing
Flanders,* that dash the industrious people that
walk, and all that useless numerous train, which 170
makes you despised by the people of quality,*
envied by your equals, and cursed by the mob. You
ought, Mrs. Rich, to retrench all this greatness and
folly with which you are surrounded.

BETTY.

But Sir— (*To Mrs. Rich, who coughs and spits.*) 175
What's the matter with you, madam?

MRS. RICH.

I take breath, Betty. Is not Mr. Rich come to his
second point?[26]

MR. RICH.

No, good Mrs. Rich, and I return still to the
equipage. 180

MRS. RICH.

Oh, the long-winded, tiresome man!

MR. RICH.

Among the rest, what d'ye do with that huge bulky
coachman, with his curling whiskers like a Dutch
mastiff's tail? 'Sbud,* he looks as if he belonged
to the Czar of Muscovy. 185

BETTY.

But sir, would you have my lady turn barber and
shave her coachman?

MR. RICH.

No, but she may turn him away and take another.

MRS. RICH.

Well sir, one word's as good as a thousand: I pretend
to live as I please and will have none of your counsel. 190
I laugh at you and all your reproofs. I am a widow
and depend on nobody but myself. You come here
and control me, as if you had an absolute authority
over me. Oh my stars! What rudeness are you guilty
of? But it is your City* breeding. 195

MR. RICH.

Still abusing the City. 'Tis a shame, Mrs. Rich, a
burning shame. I tell thee, thou proud vain thing,
thou gilt gingerbread:[27] the City is famous for men
substantial in their persons, their purses, their
credits, when your Limberhamed,[28] this-end-of- 200
the-Town beaux are the half product of Nature,
wretchedly pieced up by Art, weak in their bodies,
their brains, their everything. And 'Uds* bones!
they have no more credit than they have religion,
whilst as I said before the City is famous for— 205

MRS. RICH.

Cuckolds. Good Mr. Rich, take my advice and
take breath; you have outdone one of our holders-
forth, upon my word ye have.

MR. RICH. (*Mimicking her.*)

Upon my word ye have. What an affected tone's
there! Gadzooks, my brother Rich was a fool. 210

MRS. RICH.

That's no wonder; most citizens are.

MR. RICH.

Yes, to their wives, ungrateful cockatrice, and he,

25 published ... Mr. Rich] The *London Gazette* and similar periodicals published announcements of individuals'
financial status, including statements by husbands that
they would no longer be held responsible for debts incurred by estranged wives; thus a sort of economic divorce.

26 *coughs and spits ... second point*] It was conventional
in sermons to pause between sections, thus allowing the
audience to make noise.

27 gilt gingerbread] a showy treat, often sold at fairs

28 Limberhamed] effete; resembling Limberham, a foolish
dupe from John Dryden's *The Kind Keeper* (1678)

blind, credulous man, to pretend to leave my daughter a fortune to your management, forsooth. Gadzooks, I had rather he had left her never a groat. 215

MRS. RICH.

So had I. There we agree once.—Put it down, Betty, for a miracle.—Oh! Is it done? Have ye said all? Will you go out of my house, or must I go? Upon my word, I have company waits for me that are a thousand and a thousand times more 220 engaging. Will ye believe me or no, Mr. Rich?

MR. RICH.

What company? Fools, I warrant 'em.

MRS. RICH.

He must be convinced. Perhaps, Betty, that will drive him hence: open the door.

Scene draws and discovers Sir John, Lady La Basset, Mrs. Trickwell, and Vermin, a footman.

Oh! I am just suffocated with impertinence, 225 expiring under the heavy load of nonsense. Dear Lady La Basset, revenge me, ridicule that lump of the City till he frets himself into shape. I'll introduce ye.—Look ye, sir, this is the Honorable Lady La Basset, this is the ingenious Mrs. 230 Trickwell; the gentleman I leave to speak for himself.

SIR JOHN.

I am, sir—

MR. RICH. (*Roughly.*)

And what are you, sir?

SIR JOHN.

Why, your humble servant, sir, that's all, sir.

LADY LA BASSET.

I vow he nods like the statue in *Don John*,[29] ha, 235 ha, he, he.

MRS. TRICKWELL.

And looks like—

MRS. RICH.

A citizen, and that's ridiculous enough, of all conscience, he, he.

MR. RICH. (*Mimicking.*)

Good lack, he, he, he. Gadzooks, you are a parcel 240 of tawdry, insignificant butterflies; if ye provoke me, I'll draw your pictures with a vengeance.

SIR JOHN.

Dawley[30] has done mine at length already, much more to my satisfaction; it hangs at Court in a duchess's bedchamber, Cit. 245

MR. RICH.

The devil it does! The mop that cleans it, set upright, and good drapery, would be a better figure.

LADY LA BASSET.

Filthy simile!

MRS. TRICKWELL.

Why *m'amie*, this is the reverse of Sir Courtly; a second Surly,[31] I protest. 250

MR. RICH.

Thou wretched woman, whom I justly shame to call sister, these are things that live on thee, prey on thy very substance, and have no more worth or real quality than the ornament of pageants. Look, here's the equipage of one. (*Pulls Vermin* 255 *forward.*) Those lank cheeks are to be filled out at thy table, and thy pocket rooked at games thou dost not understand, for rigging.

LADY LA BASSET.

Now, out upon ye! Stand back, Vermin. See if the ill-natured man has not quite dashed the boy. 'Tis 260 the filthy tailor's fault.

MR. RICH.

What, he'll trust[32] no longer?

SIR JOHN.

Fie Mr. Rich, this is prodigiously abusive, upon my honor. I presume you've never been at the Court.

MR. RICH.

Nor you at the camp, which now's the only way 265 to make a perfect courtier.[33] I tell thee, fop, if thou art known there, 'tis only for thy folly; thy

---

29 Don John] In the classic Spanish tale, which had recently been dramatized by both Molière and Shadwell, Don Juan is turned over to the devil by the avenging statue of a man he has killed.

30 Dawley] unidentified

31 Sir Courtly … Surly] characters from John Crowne's 1685 comedy *Sir Courtly Nice*: a fop and a cynic, respectively

32 trust] give credit

33 camp … courtier] William III's military policies favored courtiers with camp experience.

reputation lies in ruining others, which thou dost infallibly by being once in their company; and thy chiefest accomplishment is taking snuff with a belle air, patching, painting, powdering like a woman and squeaking like a eunuch, Gadzooks! 270

SIR JOHN.

Sir!

MR. RICH.

Look ye, if you are offended, or think the ladies so, as much a citizen as I am, I wear a sword, and follow me, ye caper-cutter, if ye dare. 275

SIR JOHN.

Some colonel of the trainbands, I warrant. I'll not disorder my dress. I am weary of this fulsome stuff. —To the Park,* my angels, and let's breathe a little.

ALL.

Aye, aye, to the Park, to the Park. 280

MRS. RICH.

With all my heart, to the Park.—Lackeys, is my coach there? [*To Mr. Rich.*] But my house is at your service.—Cool yourself, sweet Sir John, whilst we laugh at this adventure.—Shall we not, Lady La Basset? 285

LADY LA BASSET.

I cannot help it.

SIR JOHN.

Nor I, upon my honor.

Exeunt, laughing; manent Mr. Rich and Betty.

MR. RICH.

Why what the devil's here to do, Betty?

BETTY.

My mistress is run stark staring mad, but I humor her distraction till we can find a way to cure it. 290

MR. RICH.

Prithee let's in and consult; I placed thee here for that purpose and trust in thee.

BETTY.

I will ever prove faithful, sir.

MR. RICH.

Two powerful fiends, lust and ambition, reign
In this rich, buxom widow's sickly brain; 295
To lay them both, a husband must be had,
Beauish and young, with sounding titles clad,
But that shall be your care and mine, egad.

Act III, [scene i. Mrs. Clerimont's house.]

Enter Mrs. Clerimont and Belvoir.

MRS. CLERIMONT.

This is strange news you tell me of my cousin. I heard indeed the unhappy accident of his father's sudden death but thought he had been still in the country.

BELVOIR.

No, he lives in Town retired, shuns all his 5 acquaintance; his noble mind surmounts his fortunes and he disdains to be obliged. It affects me strongly, for I loved him with such a passion, loved him that I thought, till I beheld your beauteous self, it could never have been exceeded. 10

MRS. CLERIMONT.

When I reflect how cold our present friendships are, I needs must own 'tis nobly generous in you to seek and serve him in this distress, nor shall my assistance any way be wanting,* let us but find the means.

BELVOIR.

First we must endeavor to see him, reconcile him 15 to the world, and try to cure his melancholy.

Enter Lucetta.

LUCETTA.

Madam, there's a gentleman below who says his name is Clerimont.

BELVOIR.

Clerimont!

LUCETTA.

He seems of some far country by his dress and 20 attendance.

MRS. CLERIMONT.

On my life, the elder brother. This may prove lucky.—Bring him up.

[*Exit Lucetta.*]

Come sir, we will have some contrivance how to make the younger easy. 25

BELVOIR.

Such goodness and ingenuity as yours cannot fail when 'tis employed for merit.

Enter the Elder Clerimont and Lucetta, followed by Toby leading two hounds coupled.

ELDER CLERIMONT. (*Speaks entering.*)

Nay sweetheart, dan't fear your rooms. My dogs have been in ladies' chambers afore now; my lady mother would let 'em lie on her bed rather than cross me. Love me, love my dog, as the saying is.— Come along, Toby. 30

MRS. CLERIMONT.

What a scene is here!

BELVOIR.

Exactly as Jack described him.

ELDER CLERIMONT.

Servant, Cuz. Do ye see, I am come to Lounnon. 35 Hey, 'tis no matter for ceremony; I ha' just now been bussing Jewel. Might-hap you dan't care to be kissed after the dog.

MRS. CLERIMONT.

You are in the right on't; 'tis not material.

ELDER CLERIMONT.

I have a free way, Cuz; you must excuse me. 40

MRS. CLERIMONT.

Oh, you are very welcome.

ELDER CLERIMONT.

No, for matter o'that I shan't trouble you; I shall lie in my inn. Here's Toby, my huntsman, he'd a main mind to see Lounnon, so I did it to please the booby.—Hah, Toby? 45

TOBY.

Nay, nay, master, dan't lay it awl upon me, an* any bad chance should happen. You were as forward as I, else we'd ne'er a-come; you are a little too stubborn, by the Mess.[34]

BELVOIR.

Well said, Toby.—Toby has a free way too, I 50 perceive, sir.

ELDER CLERIMONT.

Yes marry,* I allow it him: he is a rare huntsman. Show thy parts,* Toby; hallo, hallo, Toby.

TOBY.

Holla, holla, holla (etc.)!

MRS. CLERIMONT.

Oh! 'Tis mighty well. But, good Cousin, it goes 55 quite through my head.

ELDER CLERIMONT.

Might hap so; you are used not to it.—Hah, boys! He'll make the woods ring, i'faith.

BELVOIR.

'Tis much better there, I believe.

ELDER CLERIMONT.

Good Lord! It offends your tender ears, does it? I 60 warrant you are one of the zilken sparks[35] a rough wind would blow to pieces.—Pardon me, Cuz, I must be merry.

MRS. CLERIMONT.

Oh, the gentleman will take nothing ill from a relation of mine. 65

ELDER CLERIMONT.

Midhap he is your husband, or midhap he is your sweetheart, for he creeps main close to ye.

BELVOIR.

I am the humblest of the lady's servants.

ELDER CLERIMONT.

Oh ho! Her humble servant, that's all one. In our country they call 'em sweethearts or suitors; 'tis 70 e'en all one.

MRS. CLERIMONT.

Pray Cousin, give me leave to ask you if you are married yet or not.

ELDER CLERIMONT.

No, by my fackings,* I ha' e'en more wit than that comes to; I learned so much by my dogs. 75

MRS. CLERIMONT.

By your dogs?

ELDER CLERIMONT.

Aye, by my dogs. See this couple now, how they leer, how spitefully they look at one another. I tell thee, Cuz, this is Jewel, and this is Beauty; the bitch is Beauty, do ye mark me, Cuz. There was 80 not two dogs in the whole pack loved like these two; they played together like two kittens. Nay, for all they are hounds, one would not eat without t'other, and now they are joined, their hate is the same: one snarls, t'other bites; one pulls this way, 85 t'other that. Gadzooks! They'd either venture hanging to be parted; therefore, no coupling for me, I say. Ha, ha, ha, ha, Cuz.

MRS. CLERIMONT.

Ha, ha, ha, ha, ha.

---

34 by the Mess] by the Mass (Catholic ritual); a rural oath

35 zilken sparks] silken men of fashion; in Elder Clerimont's dialect, some "s" sounds become "z."

TOBY.

Nay, by the Mess this is true master has spoken 90
all at once; master's a shrewd man, foth and troth.

ELDER CLERIMONT.

Well, but Cuz, I come to Lounnon a'purpose to
see sports we han't i'the country and to spend my
money, d'ye see.

MRS. CLERIMONT.

What diversions are you for? 95

ELDER CLERIMONT.

Why look ye, I'd vain[36] see a good bear-baiting,
and I'd see the tiger.[37] Ah! That's a parlous beast;
we will see the tiger, shan't we Toby?

TOBY.

Aye, 'Uds* lid, though I shall be a little avraid.

BELVOIR.

You would not have the lady carry you to those 100
places, I hope?

ELDER CLERIMONT.

Aye, why not sir? They'll see I'm a country man,
and that wan't disgrace her; besides, I have four
thousand pounds a year, for all I wear my own hair,
Monsieur Perriwig. 105

BELVOIR.

The more's the pity.

MRS. CLERIMONT.

Peace, Mr. Belvoir; we shall lose our design else.—
Cousin, 'tis impossible for me to go to the Bear
Garden.* If you'll oblige me, you shall spend this
day with me and participate of the pleasures I take; 110
tomorrow some fitter companion shall show you
what you like better.

ELDER CLERIMONT.

A match! I dan't pass upon't, if I do throw away a
day with you.

MRS. CLERIMONT.

We'll first to the Park,* and then in the afternoon 115
to the play.

TOBY.

Aye, d'ye, master, do ye. 'Uds lid, I ha' longed to
zee a play e'er since I zaw the poppet show at our
vair.

ELDER CLERIMONT.

Come, my poor dogs! Evads, Cuz, you'll scarce 120
think it, I'd as liev kiss this poor creature as e'er a
lady in Christendom. I'm sure her breath's as sweet.
They'll not like Lounnon; we must hasten down[38]
again, Toby.

TOBY.

Aye master, when we've zeen a little; here's rare vine 125
voke!

MRS. CLERIMONT.

Lead, Mr. Belvoir.

BELVOIR.

We shall be the sport of the Park.

MRS. CLERIMONT.

No matter. My cousin shall gallant me.

ELDER CLERIMONT.

Come on, i'faith! Follow, Toby! 130

Scene [ii.] The Park.

Enter Lady Landsworth and Mrs. Betty.

LADY LANDSWORTH.

He refused it, my best confidante! Nobly despised
the shining gold! By all my amorous stars, he has
bravely won my heart! Panting and warm I feel
him there! Oh! The dear god of my desire.

BETTY.

In raptures? Nay, then you are lost indeed!—Hah! 5
Here comes my lady and her worthy train!

Enter Mrs. Rich, Sir John, et al.

MRS. RICH.

My Lady Landsworth! Let us only make our
honours en passant. (*Curtsies to Lady Landsworth,
with ridiculous airs. Lady Landsworth mimics her.*)
Mon Dieu! I did not think it had been in her—I 10
protest, to a miracle!

SIR JOHN.

Shall we not address?

MRS. RICH.

No, no, no, no. Away to the Mall.*

SIR JOHN. (*Looking amorously on Lady Landsworth.*)
Ah me!

[Exeunt Mrs. Rich, Sir John, and their party.]

LADY LANDSWORTH.

There's a foil to my hero! What a languishing air the 15
fop put on! When such stuff as that enters into my
thoughts, I shall turn girl again and play with babies.*

BETTY.

See who walks there in mourning!

LADY LANDSWORTH.

Bless me! You made me start. 'Tis he! Yes, that's
the shape where manly majesty's triumphant! Who 20
would not be in love with sorrow, when they see
it in that face? Who would not long to remove the
cause and dress it up in charming smiles? Forgive
me, Virtue! Forgive me, Love, if I a little farther
make the trial. Now to disguise my face and heart. 25
(*Claps on her mask and walks carelessly off.*)

Enter Clerimont and Jack.

JACK.

Do you think ye shall know her, sir?

CLERIMONT.

Know her! 'Tis impossible to mistake! Gay as the
gaudy sun or distant flowery fields! She moves like
air and throws her charms around. But be not 30
caught, my soul! She is what I would still* abhor:
a name, would blacken her lillied bosom and
wither all the roses that spread that face of beauty!

JACK.

But sir! If she has a world of money, sir—

CLERIMONT.

Peace, fool! 35

JACK.

I ha' done, sir! But abundance of money covers a
multitude of faults, that's all, sir!

CLERIMONT.

Blockhead!—Why so fast, fair lady? At this rate,
by that time a man has overtaken ye, he'll have lost
the breath he should employ in saying fine things. 40
Will ye not stay?

LADY LANDSWORTH.

Not stay! Yes, stay an age; fixed, never to remove;
an everlasting monument of love. I know you dote
upon *héroique*:[39] I have been reading three

whining plays this morning, that I may love in 45
your strain.

CLERIMONT.

For Heaven's sake, tell me truly what thou art, for sure
there's something in thee I so love and hate[40] that,
were my Fortune kind, I shall ne'er be happy more.

LADY LANDSWORTH.

I'll tell ye with a truth equal to the freedom I use (for 50
sincerity is all the virtue I pretend to): it was my first
fate to be kept* by an alderman, but he was formal,
stiff, and too suspicious for my humor;* so I fled
from him into the arms of a brisk, airy young
colonel; then the days were spent in revels. When he 55
went to Flanders,* I campaigned it too, but ah! as I
had dressed my fluttering hero up like any
bridegroom, a saucy bullet came and spoiled the
work of tailors, milliners, and fifty trades besides:
down dropped the beau. 60

CLERIMONT.

You speak this without any concern.

LADY LANDSWORTH.

Alas! Grieving for the dead would spoil us for the
living. Now I am a perquisite of a country
gentleman, a man of gravity, and one of the pious
senators,[41] a great stickler against wenching and 65
profaneness. He allows me wealth enough and
liberty enough. Besides him, I have two or three
interlopers, each fancying himself my particular,
when for my part I care not a straw for any of 'em.
But ah! amongst my numerous lovers, I know not 70
how, Myrtillo[42] has crept too near my heart—
that's meaning you, sir.

CLERIMONT.

This relation freezes up my youthful blood and
checks desire with horror! Does none tell thee what
a wretch thou art? 75

LADY LANDSWORTH.

None. They call me goddess, angel, and court me
with unbated fires. The first, the very earliest
product of the year, dainties fit for queens' tables,
still* load the board; far-fetched wines, such as

---

39 *héroique*] heroic poetry, such as employed in the serious plays of both France and England in the mid- to
late seventeenth century

40 love and hate] from the Latin love poet Catullus' famous
"*Odi et amo*"

41 senators] members of the House of Commons

42 Myrtillo] a stock pastoral name for a fawning lover

unbend the soul from cares and lock up every
thought that would disturb us. Yet amidst this
flowing plenty, amidst this crowd of flatterers, my
awkward fancy sickens at their offered loves,
loathes their soft endearments, and builds its sole
happiness in manly roughness like yours.

CLERIMONT.

Thou art one of Nature's favorites, formed when
she was gay and decked in her own smiles. Yet me
you cannot charm. There's a rustic, out-of-fashion
grace, a modest innocence, which only takes my
soul, nor can I value favors that may be bought
with any other price than love.

LADY LANDSWORTH. (*Aside.*)

He speaks as my own heart had coined the words.
I would not be too credulous.—Believe me, sir, I
am not used to woo or be refused, but I perceive
when once we love, we quit our pride. I can bear
reproof from you and, rather than not see ye, see
you still to chide me.

CLERIMONT.

No, I must fly if I'd be safe. I cannot boast a virtue
stoical enough to behold you with indifference.
Those eyes were made to conquer! Oh pity, that
they scatter contagion only! I could crawl low as
the earth to touch that beauteous hand, but when
I reflect that a senseless fop, for some vain present,
may rifle all those sweets, then I could eat my lips
ere join 'em to infection. Farewell.

LADY LANDSWORTH.

Stay but some moments longer; I have a few things
more to offer. Hear 'em. Perhaps I ne'er may
trouble you again.

CLERIMONT.

I shall be fooled at last, believe her love, trust her,
and be undone!—What would ye say?

LADY LANDSWORTH.

Come this way, lest we are observed.

They walk backward. Jack and Betty come forward.

JACK.

Is thy lady so plaguey rich, say'st thou, damsel?

BETTY.

Rich! Why, she values a hundred pounds no more
than I do a brass farthing. She makes nothing to
present a man she likes with a coach and six. And

your master here, with his puling modesty, will stand
preaching morals till he has balked her fancy, and
then 'twill be in vain to cry peccavi; for she, like
Opportunity, when once she turns her back leaves no
grasping hold.[43]

JACK.

Hark ye, my dear, can ye keep a secret?

BETTY.

As well as any of my sex: according as the nature
of the secret is. If 'twill make no mischief; take
away nobody's fame; in short, if 'twill do rather
good than harm to divulge it, ten to one but it goes
no farther for me.

JACK.

Well, that's ingenious, and I'll trust thee. This
master of mine is the veriest* libertine the whole
Town affords, has tired Vice in every one of her
shapes, and now, forsooth, for variety turns
hypocrite, that he may find their pleasures out.

BETTY.

Hah! Is't possible?

JACK.

True, upon my honor, though he'd kill me should
he know I discovered* it and deny all with a face
as grave as a fanatic. Oh! he's a rare mimic.

BETTY.

But how shall my lady be convinced he is such a
rake, if he'll deny't?

JACK.

Our landlady sells china.[44] Bring her thither; my
master will never know. She'll tell you as much.
(*Aside.*) I can make my landlady say what I will.
Well Jack, thy brain shall still secure this cargo.

BETTY.

If she thinks it worth her while to inquire, I'll tell
her.—Look, they are parting.

JACK.

'Udso, so they are indeed. I must after. Ply him,
my dear—and I'll ply thee.

---

43 Opportunity … hold] This Classical goddess (Occasio)
has only a forelock, which if one does not grasp, one
cannot do so once she has passed.

44 sells china] a fad item in the period; "selling china" in
fiction often implies that the seller uses this trade as a
cover for arranging sexual trysts for profit.

Exeunt Clerimont and Jack.

LADY LANDSWORTH.

Oh my dear Betty! How shall I express my joys! Sure such a man no age produced before! He's the phoenix of his kind!

BETTY.

I wish he prove so.

LADY LANDSWORTH.

Why?   150

BETTY.

Hush! Here comes Mrs. Clerimont you have so often sent to.

LADY LANDSWORTH.

Hah! Dear Betty, tell her who I am.—Now for an air of gravity and quite another humor* than what I have shown to her namesake, lest they should   155 find me out by description.

Enter Elder Clerimont, Belvoir, and Mrs. Clerimont. Betty whispers to Mrs. Clerimont.

MRS. CLERIMONT.

Is it?—Cousin, your most humble servant. I ask your pardon a thousand times for my neglect to wait on you. I have designed it every day, but—

LADY LANDSWORTH.

No excuse, good madam. Ladies in this Town have   160 too much business on their hands to throw an hour upon a thing so insignificant as a country relation, one so remote, too, that only claims that honor by marriage.

MRS. CLERIMONT.

Nay, madam—   165

LADY LANDSWORTH.

Besides, had you given yourself the trouble, 'twould have been but one, I am sure, for my conversation is only praises of the country; raving at every diversion here, because I understand it not; my discourse leaping perpetually into Yorkshire and talking   170 forever of my turkeys, my dairy, and so forth.

BETTY. (*Aside.*)

Hey! What maggot's this? Then am I the most deceived in the appearance of a woman that ever I was in my life.

ELDER CLERIMONT.

A shrewd gentlewoman this! I like her mainly.—   175

Pray, mistress, what made you come to Lounnon then?

LADY LANDSWORTH.

Truly sir, 'twas business, monies left in banker's hands by my dear husband deceased—oh!

ELDER CLERIMONT.

Good soul! She weeps! So young, and weep for a   180 dead husband? Good soul!

MRS. CLERIMONT.

Melancholy suits ill with such charming youth. Cousin, you have been unfortunately by your affairs driven into a house, the rendezvous of fops and senseless coquettes, who have entertained you with   185 pleasures so insipid, they have given you a disgust to those more refined that will reconcile you to the pretty epitome of our English world, the Town.

ELDER CLERIMONT.

Marry gap! Dan't spoil the gentlewoman, Cuz. Mayhaps she likes the country best. Why so do I.   190 No offense, I hope, Cuz.

BELVOIR.

We must not suffer so fair an enemy. The playhouse, Hyde Park,* everything shall contribute to force a kinder opinion from you.

LADY LANDSWORTH.

I have seen it all and despise it: at the theatre am   195 tired with the double-acted farce on the stage and in the side boxes; the noisy nonsense of the pit, the impudence of the orange women,* renders the whole entertainment to me a disagreeable medley. Then for Hyde Park, that's madness in perfection, and the   200 poor lunatic that runs an eternal circle in his Bedlam apartment has, in my judgment, equal pleasure.

MRS. CLERIMONT.

Oh fie my Lady Landsworth, this cannot be your real thoughts.

LADY LANDSWORTH.

To a tittle, I assure ye.   205

ELDER CLERIMONT.

I'fackings, the young woman speaks rarely. Why Toby, she has run down the Lounnoners.—Toby! Ah Lard! Where is Toby and the two dogs? So ho, so ho!

MRS. CLERIMONT.

Peace, good cousin; I believe they are at the park   210 gate.

ELDER CLERIMONT.

Oh, my man! My dogs! Where are they? I shall run mad! So ho, Toby!

LADY LANDSWORTH.

Mrs. Betty, let's steal off; I think I have dissembled enough for one day.   215

BETTY. [Aside.]

And I hear you have been met with,[45] too.—I follow, madam.

Exeunt Lady Landsworth and Betty.

ELDER CLERIMONT.

Why Toby! I say Toby! Speak to thy nown* master, Toby!

BELVOIR.

Come sir, we shall find 'em out.   220

ELDER CLERIMONT.

Ah, never, I fear. Toby, Toby!

Enter Toby, with his head broken.

TOBY.

What ails ye to bawl so? D'ye zee how I have been served? I went to come in with my hounds, and an ugly fellow in red[46] knocked me down and took the poor curs from me.   225

ELDER CLERIMONT.

Ay, ye coward! Where was the quarterstaff?

TOBY.

Why, he had a sword. Zee how my head's broke.

ELDER CLERIMONT.

I had rather thy neck were broke than my dogs lost.

TOBY.

Zome wiser than some. Zo had not I. Goa out   230
yonder, and ha'um in again for a tester.

ELDER CLERIMONT.

Go then!—Farewal, Cuz; you'll ne'er bring me hither again, I's warrant.

Exeunt Elder Clerimont and Toby.

MRS. CLERIMONT.

Let's after, we must not part thus. And as we go, I'll tell ye my opinion of my Lady Landsworth.   235

---

45 been met with] met your match
46 fellow in red] a red-coated Royal Guardsman

BELVOIR.[d]

I confess she is past my apprehension.

Exeunt Mrs. Clerimont and Belvoir. Enter Sir John Roverhead and Chris.

SIR JOHN.

With much ado I have broke from the widow. I appointed to meet here the prettiest rosebud; if her fortune equals the widow, she secures me.

CHRIS.

Ah sir! I wish the common fortune hunter's fate   240
be not yours: to take the worst at last.

SIR JOHN.

Fool! That genius* that raised me to this will no doubt preserve me conspicuous, the ornament of the Town and idol of the ladies. You must know, dunce, I love the young creature I am to meet now,   245
and I'd marry the widow.

CHRIS.

Why then I should think you liked her.

SIR JOHN.

Incorrigible sot!* I hate her as the devil. But has she not five thousand a year? Let that, forever, stop thy mouth.   250

CHRIS.

Then 'tis the five thousand a year you'd marry— I ha' done, sir, I ha' done.

SIR JOHN.

She comes. Remember, I am the lord. The title will strike an awe into her and make her refuse me nothing.   255

Enter Lucinda and her governess.

LUCINDA.

But d'ye think he'll come, Governess?

GOVERNESS.

I hope his lordship will.

LUCINDA.

His lordship! That sounds purely.[47] I vow my aunt will love me, when I am a great lady.—Look, here he is, Governess. Oh jiminy!* 'Tis a dear man.   260

SIR JOHN.

My little angel! This was kind! The place appeared gloomy as shades beneath till your bright eyes, exceeding the stars, created a double day.

---

47 purely] good, pleasing

LUCINDA.

Oh, la! What fine words he has!—Sir—my lord, I mean—I am a foolish girl and know not how to answer, but I am young and not unapt to learn. 265

GOVERNESS.

Nay, I'll say that for miss, she was ever as forward as the best of 'em.

SIR JOHN.

Pretty innocence! She shall not want instructions. Modeled by me, the world will own her perfect. 270

GOVERNESS.

And truly, my lord, she has enough to pay her teacher.

SIR JOHN.

Hold, hold! Name not wealth; 'tis a dross I despise.

LUCINDA.

Fie, Governess! Do you think his lordship values money?

SIR JOHN.

Not I, upon my honor. (*Aside, to Chris.*) Get it out 275 of the old one what she's worth, lest it prove not worth my while to follow her any longer.

CHRIS.

Yes sir, yes.

LUCINDA.

Now my lord, the reason why I have a mind to be married is because I may have a little more 280 freedom. I never go anywhere now but that old woman's at my heels, and I have heard 'em say wives go where they will and do what they will.

SIR JOHN.

So sha't thou, my dear miss. (*Aside.*) Marry,* quotha, more words than one to that bargain.⁴⁸ 285

LUCINDA.

But when will you meet me here again then and run away with me? For I was told I should be run away with; they say most fortunes are.

CHRIS. (*To Sir John.*)

Sir, twenty thousand pounds when she is at age.

SIR JOHN. (*Aside.*)

Very well! Gad, I'll marry her; by that time I shall 290 have spent it, broke her heart, and be ready for another.—My dear blossom, how happy am I to have gained your affections! Though 'tis no wonder, for the universality of women die for me.

_____

48 more … bargain] That goes both ways.

LUCINDA.

For my part, you spoke to me; for that I like ye. 295 Else, truly, Mr.—pish, my lord—I see as fine things walk here as you.

SIR JOHN.

Oh fie!

CHRIS.

This is true nature, a baby indeed; she has not yet learnt to dissemble. 300

SIR JOHN.

Can you get out in a morning, my dear?

LUCINDA.

Yes, anytime. I am left wholly to my governess, and you won her heart t'other morning with some sack.* Promise her some more and she'll bring me, I warrant. 305

SIR JOHN.

There's that will buy sack. Will ye bring Miss tomorrow by five o'clock?

GOVERNESS.

Yes, yes, she shall wait on your honor. Nobody minds us at home, but we'll serve 'em a trick.

CHRIS.

Sir, Sir, Mrs. Rich and the company you left are 310 just coming into this walk.

SIR JOHN.

My dear, dear, farewell! One of my relations that I dare not see. Farewell this instant. Keep these verses to remember me, and tomorrow—

LUCINDA.

Oh jiminy! If I forget, I'll be hanged. I shan't sleep 315 all night for thinking on't. Goodbye.

Exeunt Sir John and Chris.

Is he not a pure man, nurse?

GOVERNESS.

Aye marry,* is he. They shan't think to thrust us up in a garret. We'll ha' money and good things, as well as your proud aunt and her folks. 320

LUCINDA.

Oh la, mum! Here's my aunt and all they upon our backs. What shall we say now?

Enter Mrs. Rich, Lady La Basset, and Mrs. Trickwell.

MRS. RICH.

This was furiously odd, to desert us only with the whim to show us airs in bowing when we meet.

LUCINDA.

Oh la! "Furiously": there's a hard word! I'll learn 325
my aunt's words that I may appear agreeable to my
lord. "Furiously." Remember, Governess!

MRS. RICH.

Mrs. Trickwell, I am sick of the park; here's neither
the beaux nor the belle monde. Really, when Sir
John's gone, we search in vain for gallantry or a 330
good appearance.

LADY LA BASSET.

I wonder how he durst quit the place when I was
here.

MRS. RICH.

You!

MRS. TRICKWELL.

Upon my life, madam, the ladies are all mad for 335
this miracle of a knight. I wish your ladyship had
him fixed in the matrimonial noose, that the rest
might burst with envy.

MRS. RICH.

Fear not, Mrs. Trickwell, I have him with a double
chain: love and interest— Hah! This impertinent 340
girl here!

LUCINDA.

Pray don't be angry, Aunt.

MRS. RICH.

In the first place, leave off that word "aunt" and
make use of "madam," or stay at home with your
father. 345

LUCINDA.

But Aunt, since you are my aunt, why may I not
call you aunt?

MRS. RICH.

Why, I being a woman of quality* and you but a
citizen's daughter, I cannot in decency be your aunt
without degrading myself in some measure. 350

LUCINDA.

Oh good Aunt, let that not concern you, for I shall
be a woman of quality too in a little time.

MRS. RICH.

What says the girl?

LUCINDA.

'Tis in my power to be as great a lady as you, Aunt,
at least. 355

MRS. RICH.

Child!

LUCINDA.

I am acquainted with a lord, the handsomest and
most obliging in the world. I have met him several
times in the park, and he'll marry me when I
please. Therefore never trouble yourself, Aunt, 360
about my quality.

MRS. RICH.

And what's this lord's name?

LUCINDA.

They call him my Lord Fourbind;[49] he's very rich
and of great quality, for he told me so.

MRS. RICH.

Truly niece, I am very well pleased that, 365
notwithstanding the mean education your father
bestowed on you, you have thoughts worthy the
honor I do you of suffering you to be my niece, and
you are obliged to me and my conversation* for this.

LUCINDA.

I have another obligation to desire, Aunt. 370

MRS. RICH.

What is that?

LUCINDA.

To marry as soon as 'tis possible, if you please
Aunt, the gentleman you love, that it may
countenance my marriage with him I love; that
when my father would chide me I may answer 375
him, I have not done worse than my aunt.

MRS. TRICKWELL.

You're in the right. (Aside.) What a terrible thing
is example.

LUCINDA.

But my aunt must make what haste she can. My
Lord Fourbind, my lover, is most furiously 380
impatient.

MRS. RICH.

Ah! Mrs. Trickwell! Now can I be revenged of Mr.
Rich! His daughter is in love with a courtier and
a courtier with her, and she's distracted to be
married to him. If the father and mother would 385
but die with vexation, I should be rid of
troublesome creatures.

MRS. TRICKWELL.

But madam, are you resolved to assist your niece
in her design?

_____

49 Fourbind] a play off *fourbe*, tricky, deceitful

MRS. RICH.

Certainly. And I would not for a thousand pound 390
lose this excellent occasion of sending Mr. Rich to
Bedlam.

MRS. TRICKWELL.

That is very charitable, truly.

MRS. RICH.

Come ladies, let's home to dinner; this news has
pleased me.

My niece and I will the example lead, 395
Teach City* dames the way to mend their breed:
Choose for ourselves. Let our dull parents pray,
Devoutly cheat, each other's lives betray,
And whilst they drudge, we'll briskly throw away.

Act IV, [scene i. Younger Clerimont's lodgings.]

Enter Younger Clerimont.

CLERIMONT.

What a wretch am I! Forsook by Fate, abandoned to
want* and misery, my soul denied to use her faculty,
no generous power to help the afflicted, and as if this
were not enough, my virtue too, the last stake that
I could boast of, is going! I love this vicious creature; 5
in spite of all her crimes, her charms have won my
heart. Be gone, thou soft intruder, thou effeminate
passion, only fit for lazy minds. Have I not wracks
without thee to keep me waking? 'Sdeath!* What a
dog I am! Going to be kept* by a vile prostitute! Her 10
drudge; unkenneled for a fop, lord, or some wealthy
fool; sent to my post of watching! Confusion! I'll not
endure it! (*Walks about distracted.*)

Enter Belvoir, Mrs. Clerimont, and Jack.

JACK.

There he is; I must not be seen.

BELVOIR.

My dearest friend! My Clerimont! What have I 15
done to merit this unkindness? Why dost thou
shun those friends who fondly love thee? This lady,
your relation, begs to serve ye.

CLERIMONT.

Alas! I am infectious! The detested plague Poverty's
upon me! The meager fiend approaches fast with 20
her attendants, Starving and Rags! She'll render me
so odious I shall fly, if possible, myself.

MRS. CLERIMONT.

Better fortune waits to crown your virtues. Believe
me, Cousin, it does. Your brother's in Town, at my
house; send to him. 25

CLERIMONT.

What, to be answered as I was last: if I would be
his bailiff, I might eat. Curses, I'd sooner feed on
my own flesh! Sue to him, who never knew
humanity!

BELVOIR.

Well, grant him a churl, there are a thousand ways 30
besides to advance your fortune.

CLERIMONT.

None but such as I despise.

MRS. CLERIMONT.

Allow me one request: give me your company this
day and submit to my contrivance. I have thoughts
at work that may produce your future peace. 35

BELVOIR.

My friend, I am sure, used to have more
compliance than to deny a lady.

CLERIMONT.

I am at your dispose, but remember, madam,
nothing shall tempt me for bread to do an ill thing.

MRS. CLERIMONT.

Nor would I offer it. 40

BELVOIR.

Come with us, then, and shake off these
melancholy looks.

CLERIMONT.

Impossible.—Jack!

JACK.

Sir?

CLERIMONT.

Stay you at home, and d'ye hear, if any messages 45
come— (*Whispers.*)

JACK.

I shall, sir.

MRS. CLERIMONT.

Come sir, uncloud that brow. We won't leave you
in despair, though we found you so.

CLERIMONT.

Your kindness comes too late. 50
For if ye could the weight of Fate remove,
I'm dashed again and cursed with guilty love.

Exeunt [Belvoir, Clerimont, and Mrs. Clerimont].

JACK.

Landlady! Landlady!

Enter Mrs. Fidget.

MRS. FIDGET.

Why how now, Impudence! D'ye think you are in
an alehouse? 55

JACK.

I humbly beg your pardon, sweet Madam Fidget.

MRS. FIDGET.

Well, 'tis your ignorance; I excuse it. What humor's
your hopeful master in now?

JACK.

Oh, these were his relations; I hope all will be
amended. But landlady, humph, madam, there's a 60
plot you and I must carry on for his good.

MRS. FIDGET.

With all my heart. I love a plot extremely. I was
ever good at plotting. But dear brother plotter, let
us do nothing rashly.

JACK.

What, a glass of sack first? Ye shall have it, ye shall 65
have it.

MRS. FIDGET.

Truly, it helpeth invention.

JACK.

Come, here's prosperity to our honest endeavors.

MRS. FIDGET.

With all my spirit.

JACK.

T'other glass to the success. 70

MRS. FIDGET.

Agreed. Now let me know it.

JACK.

There's a lady in love with my master.

MRS. FIDGET.

What, she that called in the coach?

JACK.

The same.

MRS. FIDGET.

By my troth, a lovely woman! That there may 75
come no worse news to England, fill my glass,
sirrah.

JACK.

Now this lady is not a whore, nor a married
woman, nor a widow, nor a maid—

MRS. FIDGET.

I understand ye. 80

JACK.

D'ye, faith, why, what is she, say you?

MRS. FIDGET.

A kept* mistress, fool.

JACK.

Right, egad! Well, these Londoners are plaguey
sharp; we should ne'er have guessed in the country.
This damsel is worth thousands, and she'd fain 85
throw some away upon my master; he, modest fool
(begging his pardon), he'll none on't, forsooth. So I,
being cunning, have found out her humor* by her
appurtenance, her waiting gentlewoman, and lied
my master into her good graces: told her he was a 90
mere debauchee. She partly believed me but comes
to you to be confirmed, if you can lie, landlady.

MRS. FIDGET.

Mistrust me not, Jack, I warrant ye. But if he won't
stand to it, what signifies our promises?

JACK.

Oh, 'twill create a longer acquaintance, and truly 95
I'll get some money out of her if he won't. We
must not perish, nor will I forsake him.

MRS. FIDGET.

Well, I'll do my best, in an honest way.

JACK.

Hark, a coach stops. Bring 'em up to show your
china, and I'll be there to confirm what you say. 100

MRS. FIDGET.

I run. (*Exit.*)

JACK.

'Tis a delicate age, by jingo, when the rake is the
fine gentleman, and the fine gentleman is the lady's
favorite, egad. Mum, she comes.

*Re-enter Mrs. Fidget, with Lady Landsworth and Mrs.
Betty.*

LADY LANDSWORTH.

Where d'ye lead me, madam? 105

MRS. FIDGET.

Oh, I always keep my best china in my chambers.

LADY LANDSWORTH.

This looks like a gentleman's lodging.

MRS. FIDGET.

'Tis so, but he's very rarely in 'em. He lay abroad

last night, and sent word that he should not be home till twelve this night. I have a sad hand with him. Here's his man at home, if any of your* misses should send to him. He has forty ladies, I think, after him. I must give him warning, my house will be scandalous else, though 'tis a good natured wretch and can look as demure, I warrant, when a body chides him, as any saint. Nay, to some he'll carry himself like one too. 110 115

LADY LANDSWORTH. (*Aside to Betty.*)
Oh horrid! Let us be gone; my ears are blasted!

BETTY.
I could have told you as much, but durst not; you seemed to be well assured. 120

LADY LANDSWORTH.
Dissembling wretch! Yet I will see him once again, then in my own freedom be safe, innocent, and, far from this bewitching Town, pass my days serenely, nor think of false mankind, nor trust, and therefore be deceived no more. (*To Jack.*) Well, then there's no probability of seeing your hopeful master today. 125

JACK.
Yes, yes, madam, I can find him in a minute when the summons is to a fair lady.

LADY LANDSWORTH.
That's well; thou art a diligent servant. 130

JACK.
Aye madam, though I say it, I am fit to be e'er a gentleman's pimp in England, and that's a bold word, now.

LADY LANDSWORTH.
Excellent office! Pray, Mr. Pimp, then do me the favor to tell your master I'll be here at five o'clock to look on some china. 135

JACK.
It shall be done, madam.

MRS. FIDGET.
If he forgets, fear not, madam, I'll remember.

LADY LANDSWORTH.
No doubt on't. You have a noble vocation too, I suppose, though it has but a coarse name.—Come Betty.—Farewell, at night I'll choose some china. 140

MRS. FIDGET.
You are very welcome, madam.

Exeunt Lady Landsworth [and Betty].

JACK.
What think ye now, Madam Fidget?

MRS. FIDGET.
Faith, I know not what to think; her looks were cold and scornful. 145

JACK.
Pho, pho, she's as wanton and warm as e'er a one of your daughters after a zealous fit of devotion.

MRS. FIDGET.
Impudence! How dare you mention my daughters so irreverently?

JACK.
Nay, nay, no harm. Come, let's in and take a glass to clear our understanding and ripen our plot. 150

MRS. FIDGET.
You are an unlucky dog, I see it in your face, and will never bring it to anything.

JACK.
Thou art old enough to be a prophetess, only truth and you were at mortal odds ever since you eat[50] chalk and tobacco pipes.[51] 155

MRS. FIDGET.
Thou art a rogue, but sack* shall atone.

JACK.
Come then.

Exeunt.

Scene [ii.] Mrs. Rich's house.

Enter Mrs. Rich [and her servants], Lady La Basset, and Mrs. Trickwell.

MRS. RICH. [*To her servants.*]
Here, fellows, stand at all your several posts, and let the world know I am at home: I will appear in state.

MRS. TRICKWELL.
Why does not your ladyship establish your visiting days?[52] 5

---

50 eat] archaic form of "ate," pronounced "et"

51 ever … pipes] Eating types of earth (here chalk and clay pipes) is a symptom of a form of anemia, in early modern England called "greensickness" (q.v.) and attributed to young girls' sexual longings.

52 visiting days] Women of rank and fashion were officially "at home" to be called upon on certain days.

MRS. RICH.

I have, Mrs. Trickwell, and the rude Town takes no notice of 'em. Would you believe it? I have sat ye five, six hours, and not a soul but an ill-bred citizen's wife, whose unconscionable visit lasted the whole time and her whole discourse, let me die, of the awkward brutes her children. O'my soul they were begot by her husband, the things were so ungenteel.

MRS. TRICKWELL.

Ha, ha, ha, ha! What a prodigious deal of wit your ladyship has.

MRS. RICH.

So amongst ourselves I think too. Yet would you believe that ill-mannered oaf my husband's brother had the confidence to tell me the envious world said I was a fool, my Lady La Basset, a fool. Would you believe it, I say, that parts* and sheer wit could be so maligned?

LADY LA BASSET.

'Tis a censorious world. (*Aside.*) I begin to hate her, though I win her money, now she's likely to get Sir John from me.

Enter Lucinda.

LUCINDA.

Oh ma'am, your la'ship's humble servant.

MRS. RICH.

So, that's pretty well. Give yourself airs, child, when I admit ye into my company: humph! Pluck up53 your head. What! No motion with your fan? Ah, 'tis awkward, but sure by my example she'll learn.

MRS. TRICKWELL. (*Aside.*)

To be ridiculous.—Mind your aunt, miss, if you'd be the emblem of perfection.

MRS. RICH.

Fie, fie, Mrs. Trickwell, you flatter me.

LUCINDA.

Oh la, I can't make my fan do like my aunt's.

MRS. RICH.

Oh my stars! She'll make a horrid person of quality.* But prithee, niece, how dost thou know this lord loves thee, hey?

LUCINDA.

Oh ma'am, he has told me so, and my governess says 'tis unmannerly not to believe a lord. Besides, he makes verses on me.

MRS. RICH.

Verses? Oh my stars! What a theme he has chose. Let's see 'em.

LUCINDA.

Here, Aunt, they be pure verses; there's a hugeous deal of love in 'em.

MRS. RICH. (*Reads.*)

"I love you, charming fair one, more
Than ever mortal loved before.
And though, to my surprising joy,
The little wanton beardless boy54
Has heard my prayers and made you feel
The amorous sharpness of his steel,
Confusion seize me if my heart
Don't with a mightier passion smart."

LADY LA BASSET. (*Aside.*)

What do I hear!—And have you the impudence to say this poetry was designed for you!

LUCINDA.

Ma'am!

MRS. RICH.

Monkey! The girl has stolen 'em out of my cabinet.

LUCINDA.

Aunt—

MRS. RICH.

Hold your peace, be gone, and never let me see that young bewitching face again.

LADY LA BASSET.

I can hold no longer; the verses belong to me.

LUCINDA.

The verses belong to you! That's furiously impossible, as my aunt says. How should my lord know you to make verses of you? You may look high indeed, but not so high as a lord, sure.

MRS. RICH.

By my stars, that's well enough. Have I not bid you go, ye little impertinence; there must be some mistake.

---

53 Pluck up] toss (as in Act II, with "humph" as a sound effect)

54 beardless boy] Cupid

LUCINDA.

There must so, ma'am, I warrant your lover has begged 'em of my lord and given 'em you.

MRS. RICH.

Unlucky creature, will ye go?

LUCINDA.

Yes. I'll find my dear lord and ask him; not that I care for the verses, so I have the man. (*Exit.*) 70

MRS. RICH.

What a confusion I am in. If I break with Lady La Basset, she may expose my foibles to the whole Town, and to brook a rival— (*Walks disturbed.*)

MRS. TRICKWELL. [*To Lady La Basset.*]

Observe how Mrs. Rich is disturbed. Here we shall 75
lose a bubble* for your foolish love affair.

LADY LA BASSET.

Confound her! Have I kept* Sir John and run all the risks in the universe to maintain his port, and shall he dare address without my leave.

MRS. TRICKWELL.

'Twas ever so, Lady La Basset. We little ones dote 80
upon the handsome footman first, make a hard shift to equip him, then some topping dame swoops the dressed-up fellow, and he forgets his original.

LADY LA BASSET.

I'll lower his topsail and make him know he's mine, and only mine. 85

MRS. RICH.

Is it any happy thing we know, my lady, that has the honor to be yours, and only yours?

LADY LA BASSET.

Yes verily, a thing you are fond of, and to convince ye how vain all your hopes are, know he sacrifices all his fools to me! Here's a list of 'em. Chaw upon't 90
and farewell! (*Exit.*)

MRS. RICH.

Mon Dieu! She has won three hundred pound of my money and now she picks a quarrel with me. Civil, I protest.

MRS. TRICKWELL.

Ungrateful wretch! Should I forsake my friend! 95

MRS. RICH.

Never, whilst they have three hundred pound left! 'Tis against the rule of prudence.

MRS. TRICKWELL.

Alas madam, what d'ye mean?

MRS. RICH.

Your pardon, Mrs. Trickwell! I mean nothing. I am angry with the whole world, will indulge my ill 100
nature, and never bless 'em with a smile again.

MRS. TRICKWELL.

I thought your ladyship would have allowed your lover to have been beloved.

MRS. RICH.

But not to love; there's the distinction. To increase my spleen, let's see what this Fury has left! (*Reads.*) "A 105
list of the fools that dote on my proper person." So. "Dorimene the Backbiter, at the Gilt Post in Twatling Square." Very well. "The rich amorous banker's widow, removed from behind the Exchange* at the Citizen's Folly into Covent Garden.*" Oh! How I 110
hate myself for having loved him. "Miranda the Jilt in Scotland Yard. Arabella the Affected, in Pride Lane at the Dressing Box. The Lady Hazard, under the doctor's care in Covent Garden at the Magdalen." He's a monster. "The fat marchioness, with her 115
shining face, near the Red House in Plaster Street." Villain! I'll see him no more.—Betty!

BETTY.

Madam.

MRS. RICH.

'Tis resolved on: I'll see Sir John no more.

BETTY.

I believe I hear him. 120

MRS. RICH.

Whither do you go?

BETTY.

I'm going to meet him, madam, to tell him you'll see him no more.

MRS. RICH.

No, no, Betty, let him come in. I will confound him, and see with what impudence he'll justify this 125
list.

BETTY.

Here he is, madam.

Enter Sir John.

SIR JOHN.

Ah, are you there madam? You cannot imagine my impatience till I see you!

MRS. RICH.

From what quarter of the Town come you, sir? 130

From Twatling Square? Or Covent Garden? Or is it the rich amorous banker you left last?

SIR JOHN.

I know not what you mean, madam!

MRS. RICH.

Not what I mean, perfidious man?

SIR JOHN.

Upon my honor, madam, I do not understand you.   135

MRS. RICH.

See the obliging list of your fools, sir.

SIR JOHN.

Ha, ha, ha, and has this discomposed your la'ship? Only a frolic at my Lady Jeerwell's: we were all set[55] to abuse our friends. A lady put down her   140 list and writ me the leading coxcomb, at which we laughed for half an hour. I never knew your ladyship so out in[56] the practice of quality* in my whole life. Why, the wit of the age lies in abuses. I warrant ye, there's my Lady Tossbum did a   145 thousand ridiculous things and at last cried for very* vexation that none of the scribblers would put her in rhyme doggerel.

MRS. RICH.

I fear I'm in the wrong, Mrs. Trickwell.

MRS. TRICKWELL.

I fear so too. Sir John is nice* at these things,   150 extremely nice.

MRS. RICH.

Aye, but the verses, Mrs. Trickwell.

MRS. TRICKWELL.

The verses, Sir John, the verses.

SIR JOHN.

Why, that was the very adventure I was coming to laugh with your ladyship about. I must confess,   155 I was indiscreet enough to communicate. My heart and tongue being full of my passion, I went, madam, to the chocolate house, where I met with five or six wits. Yes madam, five or six, and let that not astonish you, for we live in a very fertile age   160 for wits.

MRS. RICH.

And what then, sir?

SIR JOHN.

What then, madam? Why, they told me how that my Lord Fourbind had given these verses to a citizen's young daughter; that Mr. Flutter had sent   165 them to a she-friend of his; that Sir Richard Welbred had obtained favors from his mistress by these verses, ha, ha, ha, ha. Is not this diverting, madam?

MRS. RICH.

So, I suppose you are extremely vain and pleased to see your works thus universal.   170

MRS. TRICKWELL.

As we are, madam, we leaders of the Town and fronters of the boxes, when we find a fashion begun by us awkwardly aimed at by all the little pretenders to dress.

SIR JOHN.

When alas, borrowed wit, like borrowed clothes,   175 fits none but the owners. To you, and you alone, the song is apropos.

My heart is only sensible of so much fire,
Your eyes have only power thus to inspire.

MRS. TRICKWELL.

How full of tenderness is all Sir John says. (Aside.)   180 I shall deserve the five hundred pounds, Sir John.

MRS. RICH.

I grant his expressions are full of douceurs,[57] but then he wants* sincerity and truth, Mrs. Trickwell.

MRS. TRICKWELL.

Truth in a compliment or courtier? Oh fie, madam! 'Tis against the nature of the thing.   185

MRS. RICH.

Why, de la Bett, how charmingly contrary is this to my City* education. But canst thou believe Sir John's in love with aught but that dear shadow of his, which he's caressing so passionately in the glass?*

BETTY.

I dare swear that's his idol, but your ladyship will   190 not hear me.

MRS. RICH. [Aside, to Betty.]

Yes Betty, I shall take a time, for I am vexed but scorn to show it.

BETTY.

Madam—

---

55 set] instructed, assigned
56 out in] unaware of

57 douceurs] sweet things

MRS. RICH.

Peace, see and admit 'em. 195

Exit Betty.

SIR JOHN. (*Setting his wig in the glass.*)

Pax of this ill-favored curl, how many hairs it exceeds his fellows. This Monsieur Cheuruex[58] is a booby, demme.

MRS. RICH.

How concerned Sir John is in his justification, madam. 200

MRS. TRICKWELL. (*Aside.*)

This fool will lose his opportunity, and I my money.—The glass robs us of your conversation, Sir John.

SIR JOHN.

No, 'tis the lady robs me of myself; I am perpetually studying new airs only to please her. 205

Enter Betty.

BETTY.

Madam, Mrs. Clerimont and a world of company to wait on you.

MRS. RICH.

Oh my stars, and are the Indian curtains drawn, the wax candles ready, the keys with the gold strings in the cabinet doors? 210

Enter footmen.

BETTY.

Yes madam, all is in order.

MRS. RICH.

Why, Tom, Ralph, Waitwell.

BETTY. (*Aside.*)

So, the fit of vanity returns.—They are, madam, where you commanded 'em.

MRS. RICH.

Oh heavens! Now Sir John should be caught saying 215 fine things to me, and he's practicing grimaces in the glass.

MRS. TRICKWELL.

Sir John, here's visitors to the lady.

SIR JOHN.

Hah! Where? Be near me, Chris. We will receive 'em. 220

MRS. RICH.

Shall I be laughing or in a passion or how, dear Mrs. Trickwell? Quick, quick, your instructions. Some say I become a passion rarely.

MRS. TRICKWELL.

In no passion, I beseech you, madam, but that of joy to see your friends: look, they are here. 225

MRS. RICH.

Well, I'll be advised, but my City neighbors said I chid my maids with such a grace, they'd have given all the world to have done like me.

Enter Belvoir, Elder Clerimont, Mrs. Clerimont, and Toby.

ELDER CLERIMONT.

A neat place this, Toby, but our house i'th'country was nigh as handsome till the hounds and my 230 hunts-folk tore it about.

TOBY.

Aye master, but ye had not near so much earthenware, that ye had not. 'Od,* our Mopsa would make rare work wi'it, 'Uds* nigs[59] she would. 235

MRS. CLERIMONT.

Why Mr. Belvoir, I am balked in the design of my visit: I intended to have brought the younger Clerimont and the Lady Landsworth to an interview, and his man has whisked him away just as we came out of the coach. 240

BELVOIR.

We must on now, there's no retreating; they look as if they had been setting themselves this hour.

MRS. CLERIMONT.

I have a sudden whim. Prithee assist.

BELVOIR.

What is't?

MRS. CLERIMONT.

I'll make my lubberly cousin pass upon that 245 fantastic creature for a beau in disguise.

---

58 Monsieur Cheuruex] presumably Sir John's wigmaker, perhaps the famous M. Chedreux,* but his fractured French garbles the name and confuses *cheveux* (hair) with *chevreaux* (goatlings, kids)

59 nigs] nicks, wounds

BELVOIR.

That's an odd fancy indeed; surely 'tis impossible.

MRS. RICH.

Sir John! Is this the mode of the wits, to come into one's house and find all the discourse among themselves? 250

SIR JOHN.

I am in a maze, madam! Let us accost 'em.

MRS. RICH.

If you please, give me leave, Sir John.—What honors are these ye heap upon me, ma'am. To receive a visit from the charming Mrs. Clerimont!

MRS. CLERIMONT.

Charms and perfections lose their signification 255 when applied to any, where Mrs. Rich is by.

MRS. RICH.

Oh madam—

ELDER CLERIMONT.

Aye Toby, here's words. I brought thee in to learn a little.

TOBY.

'Uds nigs, 'tis rare, master. 260

SIR JOHN.

Mr. Belvoir, I cast me at your feet.

BELVOIR.

Sir John, I kiss your hands.

SIR JOHN. (*To [Elder] Clerimont.*)

Sir, I am yours.

TOBY.

Nouns, what's he a-going to do, unbuckle master's shoe? 265

ELDER CLERIMONT.

What a plague, ye have run your mop into my face and e'en choked me with your powder.

SIR JOHN.

Ah hey! The meaning of this, my dear Belvoir?

BELVOIR.

An uncommon fancy, Sir John, you cannot find out, I perceive. 270

SIR JOHN.

Poison me, 'twas the oddest reception! For Pluto's sake, what is he?

TOBY.

What is he? Why, he is my master, 'Uds nigs! Dan't provoke'n; he'll have a game at fisticuffs wi'ye as well as e'er a man in vorty mile on him. 275

ELDER CLERIMONT.

Let'n alone, Toby, 'tis another o'th'libken[60] souls a high wind or a shower frights into fits of the mother.* I despise'n.

MRS. RICH.

Oh my stars! Who has your ladyship got with ye?

MRS. CLERIMONT.

Let me beg your private ear: that man is the 280 greatest, nicest* beau in Christendom.

MRS. RICH.

Ye amaze me, madam.

MRS. CLERIMONT.

Very true, upon my word. That fellow there that looks so like a John-a-Nokes[61] is the jemmiest[62] valet; a countess has been in love with him. 285

MRS. RICH.

Oh my stars, can I believe you?

MRS. CLERIMONT.

You may. No creature knows it but myself. I beg ye keep it a secret, especially from Sir John, or murder will ensue.

MRS. RICH.

I engage. Oh, I love a secret extremely. But what 290 could be the occasion?

MRS. CLERIMONT.

A lady affronted him, and he swore never to address again but in this strange disguise, because his mistress chose his rival only for having his wig better powdered; he'll not alter this behavior, nor 295 dress, till some other lady makes him amends. He's my relation; I wonder you can't perceive some airs of greatness through those clouds.

MRS. RICH.

Not I, I protest, but the more naturally he does it, he shows his parts* the more. 300

MRS. CLERIMONT.

He calls his gentleman Toby. Could you think one bred a page had power to put on such a shuffling gait?

---

60 libken] Somewhat obscure; probably a dialect version of "libben," meaning castrated.

61 John-a-Nokes] the equivalent of "John Doe" in a legal case; a nobody

62 jemmiest] neatest and most stylish

MRS. RICH.

'Tis a diverting whimsy now one knows it, he, he, he!

SIR JOHN.

Won't you give me leave to laugh with ye, ladies, 305
at those strange figures? I beg it of ye, for I am
ready to burst.

MRS. RICH.

It may be dangerous, Sir John, and I advise you
to keep your countenance.—How pretty 'tis to
know a thing the rest of the company does not! 310

ELDER CLERIMONT.

Come Cuz, what must we do next? We ha' stared
about us long enough, madam. Ha' ye ne'er a
smoking room and a cup of hearty March,[63] hah?

TOBY.

Aye fackings, had master and I been at e'er a
gentleman's house i'th'country, by this time we had 315
been half-seas-over,* 'Uds nigs.

MRS. RICH.

Rarely performed, I vow.

MRS. CLERIMONT.

Now must I keep up the humor* and pretend to
direct him.—Fie Cousin, talk of drinking before
ladies. You should entertain them with fine 320
conversation and songs.

ELDER CLERIMONT.

I dan't pass and I do gi' ye a song; come, a hunting
song. [Sings.]

SIR JOHN.

Ridiculous.

MRS. RICH.

Better and better, by my stars. 325

SIR JOHN. (To Mrs. Trickwell.)

She seems pleased.

MRS. TRICKWELL.

I am in the dark.

MRS. RICH.

Excellent.

SIR JOHN.

Excellent! Abominable.

MRS. CLERIMONT.

Now, if you please, madam, we'll pay a visit to my 330
Lady Landsworth; my cousin said he would return.

MRS. RICH.

With all my heart. [Aside.] I believe she's not at
home, but the opportunity will show my
apartments.

SIR JOHN.

Madam, my hand. 335

MRS. RICH.

Your pardon, Sir John. This gentleman's a stranger.

SIR JOHN.

Preferred to me!

ELDER CLERIMONT.

Stand by, musk-cat.[64] You see the gentlewoman
likes ye not.

TOBY.

Well done, master. Egad, he'll put by a hundred 340
such Limberhamed beaus as you, egad; he'll cram
'em in a mouse hole, i'fackings.

MRS. CLERIMONT.

Ah, poor Sir John, e'en take that tattered frigate,
and be content.

MRS. TRICKWELL.

Let's follow and find out the meaning. 345

SIR JOHN.

Ye gods and goddesses, hell, devils, and furies, I'll
be revenged.

TOBY.

Ha, ha, ha, what strange oaths he has!

Exeunt.

Scene [iii.] Younger Clerimont's lodgings.

Enter Clerimont and Jack.

CLERIMONT.

Where is she? How my desires are changed!
Triumphant Love prevails. A thousand fires shot
from those fair eyes have warmed me; a thousand
arguments, pleading all for pleasure, lead me on.
The lord within plants[65] and heaves my bosom, 5
whilst circling tides roll round apace and give
tumultuous joys.

---

63 March] March ale, a strong beer

64 musk-cat] civet cat (q.v.)

65 lord within plants] The trope of Love as an armed victor planting his flag is common in early modern English poetry.

JACK.

Aye marry,* sir, now you look and breathe another man. Good Fortune is your slave; she always waits upon the bold. 10

CLERIMONT.

And what know I but the coy* dame, who hides her face at the least word awry and blushes to be gazed on, has in her heart looser fires than my gay mistress? How many an honest wretch, that asked would swear his arms enfolded a Lucrece,* yet truly 15 hugs in the dissembled saint a vile jilt?

JACK.

Right sir, right. Oh, I could burn my cap for joy to see you thus.

CLERIMONT.

She's coming and seems in busy talk. Let us not disturb her. 20

Enter Lady Landsworth and Betty.

BETTY.

As soon as ever my lady was engaged, I fled to overtake ye, madam.

LADY LANDSWORTH.

'Twas kindly done.—Yonder he stands. Methinks I hate him, now he has lost that modest sweetness which caught my unwary soul; his looks are wild 25 and lewd, and all I ever feared in men appears in that deceitful face. I would I were away.

BETTY.

Nay madam, make this last trial since you have gone so far.

CLERIMONT.

May I yet approach? 30

LADY LANDSWORTH.

You may. I do remember when we parted last, 'twas on odd terms. Nature seemed reversed: you fled and I pursued in vain, I practiced all my charms and tried my utmost art in vain; your virtue like the mountain snow, the nearer I advanced, 35 congealed the more, and in the bloom of youth, rigid and cold as frozen age, you awed me with severity. Are ye still thus resolved?

CLERIMONT.

Oh no, I am altered quite; my very soul's on fire. Do not my eyes speak for me? I languish, burn, 40 and die.

LADY LANDSWORTH.

Then we have conquered, and like libertines we'll rove, tire every pleasure, tread rounds of joy the insipid world shall wonder at but never know to taste.

JACK. [*To Betty.*]

Nay, we shall live a delicious life, that's certain, hah, 45 my dear damsel.

BETTY.

Peace, and mind your betters.

CLERIMONT.

What music's in that voice; it dances through my ears and puts my heart in tune. Not painted cherubs, not the first dawn of cheerful day or 50 opening spring is half so pleasing. Oh, thou art rapture all and all divine; down at thy loved sight each sense drinks deep draughts of joy.

LADY LANDSWORTH.

Throw off these mourning weeds and let me dress thee extravagant as my desires, like a queen's 55 favorite, for I would be profuse.

JACK.

Lard, Lard, how fine we shall be.

CLERIMONT.

If there must be profusion, let it be in love; there lay out all thy stock. Let days and nights and years serve only to count the acts of love. 60

LADY LANDSWORTH.

Yes, and teach us to deceive my keeper:* his purse must help our riots, his credulity supply our mirth.

CLERIMONT.

Ah, why hast dashed my rising ecstasies with the detested thought that thou art shared? But in thy arms I'll lose the goading torment; in those blissful 65 moments I'm sure thou art only mine, my life, my all! (*Embraces her.*)

LADY LANDSWORTH.

Stand off, thou monster, viler, worse than man; let thy contagious breath infect at distance. I will remove thee from my sight and from my soul, as 70 far as thou art gone from honor, truth, and honesty.

JACK.

Here's a turn, ye gods. Why what's the matter now?

CLERIMONT.

Madam—

LADY LANDSWORTH.

Speak not, nor dare to stay me, for I'll leave thee 75
like thy good genius* in thy distressful hours, never
to return. Oh, I could curse myself, my follies, to
believe there was virtue in thy sex, thou vile
dissembler. May it return upon thee: dissembled
be thy joys; dissembled be thy friends; above all 80
may thy mistress prove the abstract of
dissimulation.

CLERIMONT.

Hear me but speak.

LADY LANDSWORTH.

No, haste thee to some mart of luxury and shame;
preach there, but defile my ears no more.—Away, 85
my friends, away:
Let's fly that wretch, fly him and all mankind,
Nor° for the curst pursuer leave a track behind.

Exeunt Lady Landsworth and Betty.

CLERIMONT.

What's the meaning of all this?

JACK.

Mad, sir, raving mad. 90

CLERIMONT.

Can she be honest?*

JACK.

Impossible: had she the roguish leer, the tip,⁶⁶ the
wink, the everything.

CLERIMONT.

Peace, rascal. She is, and not the world shall hide
her from me. 95

JACK.

Now must we go upon knight-errantry. May
Heaven be praised, we are as poor as knights-errant
already.

CLERIMONT.

Fly, search, inquire.
She cannot, must not long remain unknown; 100
She'll be discovered* by her charms alone.
I'll find, I'll claim, I'll seize her for my own,
Breathe at her feet my vows, nor thence remove,
Till I am blessed with her returning love.

---

66 tip] a light touch or tap in passing, often used by prostitutes to attract attention

Act V, [scene i: Clerimont's lodgings.]

Enter Clerimont, Mrs. Fidget, and Jack.

CLERIMONT.

Sure 'twas all a dream; I neither saw, nor liked, nor
loved; it was a dream. The gaudy vision's vanished,
and I am waked again to my calamities. Or grant
it real, what had I to do with Love? Love's the gay
banquet of luxurious hours; he shakes his golden 5
wings and flies detested poverty:
To downy couches under gilded roofs he flies,
There lays his wanton head, there revels in the fair
one's eyes.

JACK.

Sir, sir.

CLERIMONT.

When the poor join, they hardly taste a night of 10
peace: Strife traces Hymen's steps so close, the
haggard thrusts between at bed, at board, and
drives the gentle god away. Oh, my distracted
thoughts!—Why do ye follow me? Is misery
denied the privilege to be alone? 15

MRS. FIDGET.

Ah sir, 'tis that unlucky dog your man has done
this.

JACK.

Hist!

MRS. FIDGET.

Nay, it shall out.

CLERIMONT.

What has he done? Speak! 20

MRS. FIDGET.

Why, sir—

JACK.

Peace, I say, ye ungrateful cockatrice, now will not
all the sack* I have rammed down that
unconscionable throat keep this poor secret in?
Though upon my word, I meant it for the best: 25
believe that, I beseech you, sir.

CLERIMONT.

What's the matter? What have ye said?

MRS. FIDGET.

Aye, said, there ye have hit it: he has said enough,
by my troth.

JACK.

I am sure you always say too much. 30

MRS. FIDGET.

Say ye so, sirrah? Know then, sir, that hopeful rogue gave ye such a character* to the young gentlewoman, 'twould have frighted the Devil.

JACK.

And what said you, Mrs. Delilah?

MRS. FIDGET.

Even the same, by thy instigation, thou tempter. 35

JACK.

Keep that name to yourself, it belongs to you, woman.—I thought, sir, she loved nothing but a rake, a madman. I did all for the best, indeed I did, sir.

CLERIMONT.

No matter, 'tis the malice of my fate, which would 40 have found an instrument hadst thou been silent.

MRS. FIDGET.

Come, hang melancholy and cast away care. My mind gives me this damsel will wheel about again: I never yet knew man or woman weary of an intrigue when 't has gone no further than yours 45 has done.

JACK.

Right: there ye are in the right, i'faith, Landlady.

MRS. FIDGET.

Well, sauce, you'll never leave your impudence. "Landlady"! Blockhead!

JACK.

Thank ye, madam. 50

Enter Belvoir.

BELVOIR.

Still with folded arms and looks of sorrow? I come to cheer thee, my friend, to make thee laugh, to give thee lasting joy.

CLERIMONT.

Impossible!

BELVOIR.

Thy brother is fallen in love with the fantastical 55 Widow Rich; her wealth and beauty has charmed him. Ye know that he is possessed of a great estate. He never had management enough to be master of money, and hearing the widow has so much, he is distracted for't, whilst she takes him for a beau 60 in masquerade, is wonderfully pleased, and, I believe, will be a match.

CLERIMONT.

And what's all this to me?

BELVOIR.

Oh, much to your advantage, for he has promised Mrs. Clerimont, if she can bring this marriage to 65 pass, he will resign that part of the estate to you your father in his lifetime had designed ye.

CLERIMONT.

There thou speakest comfort that suits my wishes, for I would fain travel but want* the means.

BELVOIR.

Travel! 70

CLERIMONT.

My friend, 'tis not wealth can make me happy now.

JACK.

Ah sir, but wealth's a good stroke: I see Providence has not quite forgot us.

BELVOIR.

Whatever you have resolved, I beg ye to go this moment with me to Mrs. Clerimont's: a busy 75 minute now is worth a lazy year.

CLERIMONT.

Do even what you please with me.

BELVOIR.

Come on, then.

MRS. FIDGET.

Good luck attend ye.

Exeunt.

Scene [ii.] Mrs. Rich's house.

Enter Mrs. Rich and two footmen.

MRS. RICH.

I design a ball tonight, sots, and would have, if possible, you rascals clean, and you, d'ye hear—

Enter Lady La Basset, [armed with sword and pistol,] and Vermin.

LADY LA BASSET.

I'll fright this little pretender to quality* till she either quits Sir John or buys him of me at a good round rate. He has made many a penny of me; 5 now 'tis time to retaliate.—Madam, send off your footmen; I would speak with ye alone.

MRS. RICH.

Madam!

LADY LA BASSET.

Be gone, scoundrels, or I shall drive ye hence.

MRS. RICH.

Fellows, be near me; I know not what her design 10
is.

LADY LA BASSET.

My design is honorable.

MRS. RICH.

Heavens! What can she mean?

LADY LA BASSET.

Base coward, are ye afraid?

MRS. RICH.

Afraid, madam? I! I— 15

LADY LA BASSET.

Come, no dallying. You have robbed me of Sir
John: I demand satisfaction.

MRS. RICH.

Oh my stars! This is extravagant to the last degree.
Alas madam, what satisfaction can a lady give to
a lady? 20

LADY LA BASSET.

I'd have thee fight. Dare you set up for quality and
dare not fight, pitiful citizen? 'Tis for thy honor;
'tis modish too, extremely French and agreeable to
thy own phrase. I'll have thee fight, I say.

MRS. RICH.

What need I, when I have conquered already? Can 25
I help the power of my eyes or Sir John's sensibility?
My stars, this is prodigious! What weapon must we
use in this unusual combat, hey, madam?

LADY LA BASSET.

D'ye make a jest on't? Sword and pistol, madam.

MRS. RICH.

Oh heavens! I swoon at the sight of either. 30

LADY LA BASSET.

Thou art the offspring of an alderman, I of quality:
I can fight, ride, play, equal the men in any virtue
or vice. Thou little creature, yield, or sa, sa—Thus
for Sir John: sa, sa.[67]

MRS. RICH.

The woman's mad. Will ye come in my house and 35
murder me?

LADY LA BASSET.

Look, is this a jest? (*Draws a pistol.*)

---

67 sa, sa] sounds that in fencing accompany cuts with a foil

MRS. RICH.

Murder! Murder! Jack! Jeffery! George! Help! Help!

Enter Mr. Rich.

MR. RICH.

Heyday! What's the house turned into a perfect
Bedlam? Learning to fence, Madam Whimsical? 40

MRS. RICH.

Oh brother, save me from that furious woman, and
I'll submit for the future to your conduct.

LADY LA BASSET. (*Aside.*)

Curse on him, this is a sensible fellow, and my
design's lost.

MR. RICH.

And what are you, a lady errant, and this the squire 45
of the body? He looks as if he had lived upon
adventures, indeed.

LADY LA BASSET.

No matter what I am. I am mad.

MR. RICH.

I believe so.

MRS. RICH.

I shan't recover the fright this twelvemonth. 50

LADY LA BASSET.

She would be a woman of quality, and dares not
fight. By the honor of my ancestors, I'll go find
out Sir John, and if he does not change his
resolution, he and I shall dispute it. Come along,
Vermin. (*Exeunt Lady La Basset and Vermin.*) 55

MR. RICH.

Ha, ha, that would be a pretty combat, in troth;
he dares not fight a man; this woman will be an
excellent match for him. Dost thou yet see thy
folly, thy own and thy instructor's folly? These
things teach thee to appear like the truly great? 60
Alas, mistaken wretch, they are as far from noble
natures as light from darkness.

MRS. RICH.

I do begin to find my error and am mending my
conversation,* yet think not, though ye have
humbled me, you shall e'er bring me back to the 65
City again. No, I have still spirit enough to defy
the City and all its works.[68] By my stars, I'll never

---

68 defy … works] parody of the baptismal phrase, "defy
Satan and all his works"

endure a greasy City feast;[69] a set custard is my aversion of all aversions, as Olivia[70] has it.

MR. RICH.

'Tis impossible to turn the current of a woman's will, though it perpetually runs the wrong way. 70

Enter Mrs. Betty.

BETTY.

Oh madam, such a piece of treachery, such perfidiousness, have I discovered.

MRS. RICH.

In whom? My stars, this is a day of wonders!

BETTY.

Even Sir John, going from your ladyship in a huff 75 because you smiled upon the worthy gentleman in disguise, met your niece; she flew upon him with a violent exclamation, "My Lord Fourbind, yours entirely!" He answered in a passionate tone, "Ah, *mon cher*,[71] I die for ye." 80

MR. RICH.

My daughter!

BETTY.

Yes, your daughter, and together they whisked cross the gallery to miss's apartment. I left 'em there and came to inform your ladyship.

MRS. RICH.

'Tis all confusion and amazement! 85

MR. RICH.

I am distracted! My daughter! I'll kick him, burn his flaxen wig, dirty his white coat, knock out his butter-teeth,[72] wring off his nose, and spoil him for being a beau forever.

MRS. RICH.

Whilst I conceal myself in one of the closets.* If 90 this be true, Betty, I have such a revenge shall make the Town ring on't.

BETTY.

Do, madam. (*Aside to Mr. Rich.*) Now sir, now's the time to clear the house of the locusts, these swarm of fools. 95

---

69 City feast] London merchants and members of the City's government held official feasts famous for their luxury.

70 Olivia] character in William Wycherley's 1676 comedy *The Plain-Dealer*

71 *mon cher*] fractured French for *ma cherie* (my dear)

72 butter-teeth] front teeth

MR. RICH.

Set all thy wits at work, my good girl. Come, show me this happy couple; I shall spoil their mirth, egad.

Exeunt.

[Scene iii. Lucinda's apartment.]

Enter Sir John, Lucinda, Chris, and governess.

SIR JOHN.

Beyond my wish! Mrs. Rich's niece. The world shall applaud my revenge.—But my dear, are you sure none of the family will interrupt us?

LUCINDA.

No, no, they mew me here eternally with that old woman. My aunt hates a younger face than her 5 own should appear where she is: I am not such a child but I can find that. Come, hasten, Governess, pack up all my jewels; we'll steal out at the back door. Bid adieu to my sweet aunt, till my dear lord and I visit her in a coach and six. 10

SIR JOHN.

That's my cherubim.—Help, Chris, help, I long to be gone.

CHRIS.

My lord, we'll ha' down in a twinkling.

LUCINDA.

But look you, my lord, I must tell you my mind in two or three words before we go, what you must 15 trust to. Do you see, I am not furiously in love, as my aunt says; I run away only for more pleasure, more liberty, etcetera. I will go every day to the play or else to the park, and every time I go to the park, to the Lodge, to Chelsea:[73] in fine, where I please. 20 Or as I run away with you, I'll run away from you, sue for my own fortune again, and live as I please: what I have heard how ladies with fortunes do.

SIR JOHN. (*Aside.*)

A young Gypsy this. Who'd have thought it had been in her?—*Mon cher amie*,[74] you shall have 25 your will.

---

73 Lodge … Chelsea] public resorts; the public gardens of Chelsea, south of Hyde Park and close to the Thames, had a somewhat shady reputation in this period.

74 *Mon cher amie*] *ma chère amie* (my dear friend, Fr.)

LUCINDA.

That you must expect, my dear lord, for had I loved obedience, I had still* obeyed my father, and she that begins with her father generally makes an end with her husband. But that's furiously modish 30 and therefore so much the better. Quick, quick, good Governess, and then a-hey for disobedience.

Enter Mr. Rich and Betty.

MR. RICH.

And then a-hey for disobedience. Who is this, my daughter, with her a-hey for disobedience?

LUCINDA.

Oh jiminy,* my father! What shall I do now? Well, 35 I'll even turn sides, take my father's part if he's uppermost, and rail at my lord furiously.

MR. RICH.

Art thou the staring fop my hopeful sister's fond on, descended from thy duchess's bedchamber to steal my daughter? 40

SIR JOHN.

I am a gentleman, sir, and expect to be used like one.

MR. RICH.

'Tis false, thou art not. I have traced thy original and found thou art none.

LUCINDA.

Oh la! Not a gentleman? Why, he swore to me he 45 was a lord. Out upon him.

SIR JOHN.

Well said, miss. I find we may e'en be marching for any friends we have here.—Thou unpolished thing, I answer thy affront with my mien, my dress, my air: all show the gentleman and give the 50 lie to thy ill-mannered malice.

MR. RICH.

Defy me, thou thing equipped! Canst thou justify the worst of thefts, stealing my child? Draw.

SIR JOHN.

Your pardon, sir, not before the lady. I may discompose her; perhaps the sight of a sword may 55 fright her into a fit.

LUCINDA.

Oh la, don't let me hinder ye.

MR. RICH.

Art thou not a fool?

SIR JOHN.

A fool à la mode, sir.

MR. RICH.

A coward. 60

SIR JOHN.

I am a beau, sir.

MR. RICH.

All sound and no sense.

SIR JOHN.

I sing tolerably well. [*Sings.*] For who would in a cellar dine, when he may go to Locket's.*

MR. RICH.

Thou trifling coxcomb, all wig and no brains, be gone 65 this very instant, or I'll lead thee thus by the nose. I'll lead thee to a she-fop of thy acquaintance, coxcomb, I will. Therefore make use of thy heels.

SIR JOHN.

Egad, this is very uncivil.

MR. RICH.

I meant it so. 70

SIR JOHN.

I'll lampoon thee till your friends shall fly ye, your neighbors despise ye, and the world laugh at ye.

MR. RICH.

I believe your wit's as dangerous as your courage. Be gone, insect.

LUCINDA.

Pretend to be a lord, and balk a young woman's 75 expectation!

BETTY.

Ah, poor Sir John, ha, ha.

SIR JOHN.

Has she been a spectator? I shall be jeered to death.—I will study a revenge shall make you tremble, I will, thou barbarous cit.* 80

MR. RICH.

Go set your perriwig to rights, fop, ha, ha.

SIR JOHN.

Curses, curses, ah, I shall choke! (*Exit.*)

MR. RICH.

Farewell, fool.—You, madam, I shall find a time to discourse with.—Dear Mrs. Betty, take her into your care whilst I turn this old limb of iniquity 85 out of doors. [*To governess.*] Here, you had a mind to run away; now I desire you to walk about your business. Be gone, thou unnecessary evil.

LUCINDA.

Let her go, I say, she seduced me I'm sure.

GOVERNESS.

Oh fie, fie, miss. [*Exit.*]   90

MR. RICH.

Be gone! 'Twas her canting deceived me. What care
we ought to take whom we set over our children!

Enter Mrs. Rich.

So madam, are you satisfied?

MRS. RICH.

Rage, spite, shame, and resentment at once
torment me. So base a coward! My stars, I shall   95
go mad.

MR. RICH.

Dear sister, let your stars alone and learn to shun
folly wheresoe'er you find it.

MRS. RICH.

Then I must shun you, myself, and all the world.
You have a set and formal folly, I a vain and airy   100
folly, but he the basest, most betraying folly.

MR. RICH.

Then redeem your judgment and stop censorious
mouths by accepting Mrs. Clerimont's kinsman,
whom your woman tells me has a plentiful estate.
This will turn the laughter of the Town* upon Sir   105
John and leave you in happy circumstances.

MRS. RICH.

I will do something, something to plague that
fellow.

BETTY.

Here comes the lady, I believe to plead in her
friend's behalf.   110

Enter Lady Landsworth and Mrs. Clerimont.

MRS. CLERIMONT.

Ah madam, such a misfortune.

MRS. RICH.

The whole deceitful world, by my stars, I think is
full of nothing else.

MRS. CLERIMONT.

But this, madam, your bright eyes create.

MRS. RICH.

I? My eyes? that's pleasant.   115

MRS. CLERIMONT.

The strictness of his vow racks him, for he knows

a lady thus accomplished can never like him as he
appears.

LADY LANDSWORTH.

Indeed, I pity him.

MR. RICH.

Pray ladies, what's the case?   120

MRS. CLERIMONT.

Alas sir, a cousin of mine, who wants* not the
goods of fortune but lies under an obligation to
seem the greatest clown* in the universe, till Fate
has made him reparation for the affront he received
when all his study was dress and conversation.   125

MRS. RICH.

And has he a good estate?

MRS. CLERIMONT.

Four thousand a year, I assure ye.

MR. RICH.

Gadzooks, what matter is it whether^f he is dressed,
as ye call it, again or no.

MRS. RICH.

Yes, yes, that is material, upon my word, Mr. Rich. 130

MRS. CLERIMONT.

Would you consent to marry him? For so far his
oath extends. Believe me, madam, he'd soon break
forth to your amazement.

MRS. RICH.

I profess, ladies, you give me such an air of blushing
when I reflect on what ye are tempting me to.   135

MRS. CLERIMONT.

I profess, ma'am, 'tis a very becoming air.

MRS. RICH.

My stars! 'Twill sound so odd.

MRS. CLERIMONT.

'Twill surprise the Town so prettily.

MR. RICH.

Zooks, 'tis the best thing to piece up your
fantastical character;* 'twill surprise the world   140
indeed to see you do a wise thing.

MRS. RICH.

Speak not you, sir, for I yield only to the ladies.—
Well, where is the gentleman?

MRS. CLERIMONT.

Languishing within, madam, condemned to
silence lest his rough-hewn expressions should   145
offend.

MRS. RICH.

De la Bett, a pen and ink. Perhaps I may expose the knight and satisfy your friend. Your pardon for some moments.——Come with me, niece.

LUCINDA.

Yes madam, pray let us be revenged on this sham 150
lord; you can't think what a liar he is.

MRS. RICH.

Your servant.

MRS. CLERIMONT.

Yours.

Exeunt Mrs. Rich and Lucinda.

LADY LANDSWORTH.

Follow, dear De la Bett, as thy lady has it, and now
show thy masterpiece. 155

BETTY.

I lay my life 'tis done; I see it in her eyes.

MR. RICH.

In hopes on't, I'll get a parson. This widow married, my affairs are prosperous, and my daughter and her fortune return to me.

MRS. CLERIMONT.

Hasten, good sir, for this fair lady and I have a little 160
business of our own.

MR. RICH.

More weddings, I hope; then we'll have dancing in abundance.——Come, honest De la Bett; I promise thee a new portion to thy new name.

BETTY.

I'll endeavor to deserve it, sir. 165

Exeunt Mr. Rich and Betty.

MRS. CLERIMONT.

My charming cousin, have not I found a pretty employment, to turn general matchmaker? But for the younger Clerimont I own I could do anything.

LADY LANDSWORTH.

I should dissemble worse than I thought he did, not to say I'm pleased to find his character what I 170
so heartily wished it.

MRS. CLERIMONT.

To convince ye thoroughly, I have sent for his landlady, whose odd account of him must proceed from folly or malice. Oh, here she comes!

Enter Mrs. Fidget.

MRS. CLERIMONT.

Your servant, madam. 'Twas not for goods, as I 175
pretended, I gave you this trouble, but to ask after the deportment of my relation Mr. Clerimont, your lodger.

LADY LANDSWORTH.

The wild, mad spark that scarce ever lies at home. You know me, madam, I suppose? 180

MRS. FIDGET.

Yes, yes, madam, in verity I must beg your pardon. I did belie the gentleman, abominably belie him.

LADY LANDSWORTH.

What provoked you to it?

MRS. FIDGET.

Truly, John and^g I contrived it, thinking it would please your ladyship. 185

LADY LANDSWORTH.

John? Pray, who is John?

MRS. FIDGET.

My friend, and his footman.

MRS. CLERIMONT.

My cousin, I am sure, was always accounted a very modest, sober gentleman.

MRS. FIDGET.

Modest! 'Uds flesh, he has not his peer in the 190
whole Town. By my fackings, he's a little too modest; that's his fault.

MRS. CLERIMONT.

I dare affirm he's truly noble; not in these straits of fortune would he quit his honor to be great or his integrity to be rich. 195

MRS. FIDGET.

Or his religion to be thought a wit.

LADY LANDSWORTH.

Enough, ladies, I am fully satisfied; only, to his love, if I have made any impression.

MRS. CLERIMONT.

That this moment you yourself shall be judge of. He's coming. If you please to retire, you shall 200
overhear me sound his inclinations.

MRS. FIDGET.

Aye, there he is. Heaven bless him, he's a sweet young man.

LADY LANDSWORTH.

Come with me, Mrs. Fidget.——Now, Clerimont,
If thy heart does with generous passion burn, 205
Then I with joy will love for love return.

Exeunt Lady Landsworth and Mrs. Fidget. Enter the Younger Clerimont, Belvoir, and Jack.

BELVOIR.

I have brought him, madam, but I am ashamed to say with what reluctancy; he flies even you, you the fair contriver of his auspicious fortunes.

CLERIMONT.

I am sure I am ashamed to see you take such pains   210
about a thing not worth your care.

MRS. CLERIMONT.

When the good suffer, the virtuous part of human-kind are all concerned. When we suffer by our fate and not our faults, Heaven always makes the trial short and shows an easy way for our deliverance.   215

CLERIMONT.

In vain you soothe me with your friendship. Did you fully know me, you would know there scarce is left a room for hope.

MRS. CLERIMONT.

Suppose there is a lady in love with you, surrounded thus as you are with your misfortunes;   220
suppose her chaste and rich and fair, who, though her eyes never yet encountered yours, by my description dotes upon a character* so singular and different from your wild sex.

CLERIMONT.

Were she as fair as women would be thought; as   225
virtuous as they were of old, ere 'twas fashionable to be false; had she wealth would satisfy the vain, the miser, the ambitious; so far am I from once consent-ing to what your kindness has proposed, I would not to rid me of half my sorrows so much as see her.   230

BELVOIR.

Ah, my friend! This must be some prepossession; you already are in love.

CLERIMONT.

It is enough to say I am a fool must search the world and know it better ere I pretend to speak my thoughts.—If, madam, from my brother ye can   235
procure my father's first design, I shall own myself eternally obliged and trouble ye no more.

MRS. CLERIMONT.

I sigh to say it is not in my power, since you refuse the advantageous offers of the lady's love.

CLERIMONT.

Then all I beg is that ye would inquire for me no   240
more. There is no warding the blows of Fate; the wretch that's doomed unfortunate no arm of power can save.

BELVOIR.

But you look through despair. Believe me, friend, 'tis a false glass. Fortune has a fairer face to show   245
you.

MRS. CLERIMONT.

That pleasing task be mine.

Re-enter Lady Landsworth and Mrs. Fidget.

Madam, you hear the gentleman is obstinate.—But now, sir, if you are not charmed with this appearance, you have a relish different from the universal world.   250

CLERIMONT.

Hah! 'Tis she! 'Tis she! Here let me fix, thus let me clasp my bliss, thus forever secure my only valued treasure!

JACK.

Aye, 'tis she, 'tis she, egad, and my landlady too!

MRS. FIDGET.

Yes, Manners, your landlady too.   255

LADY LANDSWORTH.

And dare you venture upon me after the alderman, the colonel, and the senator?

CLERIMONT.

My eyes should have contradicted all other senses: sweet innocence is writ in that dear face, and virtue in her brightest characters.   260

MRS. CLERIMONT.

Virtuous—and great: the charming widow of Sir John Landsworth; her husband formerly I believe you have seen. What could you ask of Fate more than to love and be beloved by her?

CLERIMONT.

And have I been repining, when the bounteous   265
heavens were pouring such lavish blessings down? Oh, my ravished soul! My first, my only dear!

LADY LANDSWORTH.

'Tis wondrous pretty when love's soft passion first invades our breast; it brings a thousand charms, a thousand joys, unknown before. But ah! too often,   270
in your sex, rolling time or some newer face puts out the kindly flame, and the forsaken fair is left to live

and languish on the kind words which she will hear
no more. What can secure me from such a fate? Not
even your present thoughts, for they may change. 275

CLERIMONT.

Never, my charmer, never! To look on thee secures
a heart like mine from roving; to hear thee talk will
fix me forever in the chains of love. But oh! To
have thee all: there words cannot aim, there breath
is lost in ecstasy. 280

MRS. CLERIMONT.

Here's a world of fine things, though I am a little
of the lady's mind, 'twill scarce hold out seven
years.

BELVOIR.

So, there's two in perfect happiness. I hope,
madam, you that were so compassionate to others 285
will not yourself be cruel but reward my constant
vows nor let me longer sigh in vain.

MRS. CLERIMONT.

Mr. Belvoir, I have allowed you too long a favored
lover in honor to go back; we are as good as
married already. 290

BELVOIR.

No, my dear angel, the greatest sweet's to come!

MRS. CLERIMONT.

Aye, and the sour too, that's the worst on't. Look,
here's another happy couple.

*Enter Elder Clerimont, Mrs. Rich, Mr. Rich, Lucinda,
Betty, and Toby.*

MRS. RICH.

Well, ladies, what d'ye think I have been doing
since I went out? By my stars! A world of business, 295
and that's a thing I hate: writ a billet-doux to the
beau in appearance; married the beau in a disguise;
given occasion for forty stories and fifty lampoons,
ha, ha, ha! I have done it all in a humor, by my
stars! 300

MRS. CLERIMONT.

E'en carry it on, madam, never have a grave fit and
repent, I say.

ELDER CLERIMONT.

Yes faith, I'm sped, and all o'th' sudden. She's
handsomer, trath, than our Sh'riff's daughter.—
How they'll stare, Toby, when she shows her paces 305

through our alley to the great pew.[75]—Brother
Charles, how came you here? Well, I've gi'n the
writings into Cousin's hands. 'Uds lids, does that
pretty lady belong to you? Why, this is a rare place
for handsome women, by my troth. 310

MRS. RICH.

Come sir, the transformation has been comical
enough, but now I beg you to reassume your
former mien and dress, and let me make as great
a sacrifice to you as the lady made of you.

MRS. CLERIMONT.

Oh, dear Belvoir, say something to keep in my 315
laugh, or I'm undone.

BELVOIR.

I dare not lift up my eyes, nor scarce open my lips
to let my words out.

MR. RICH.

I confess my gravity is put to the test now.

MRS. RICH.

Come Mr. Clerimont, will ye hasten? Pray dress 320
immediately, because I expect Sir John this moment.

ELDER CLERIMONT.

Yes, 'fags,* I'll dress as soon as I can get my clothes
made, and since I'm wed, I'll bestow more money
than I thought by five pound.

MRS. RICH.

Nay, now the humor's* tiresome; here's only 325
friends.

BETTY.

Oh madam, I shall break my lace.[76]

CLERIMONT.

What's the meaning of all this?

LADY LANDSWORTH.

The tittering damsel behind ye can tell.

MRS. RICH.

Come, I would not for a thousand pound Sir John 330
should find you thus; this is carrying the jest too
far.—Speak to him, madam.

MRS. CLERIMONT.

Indeed madam, I fear it must go a little farther,
for to tell ye the plain truth, he has the estate I

---

75 alley … great pew] The "great pew" is the estate's special pew, while the "alley" is probably a lane lined with
trees leading to the churchyard.

76 lace] used to tie a corset

mentioned and is my relation, but for the accomplishments you expect, they are yet to learn, upon my word. 335

MRS. RICH.

How! I'm undone! What, no conversation, no judgment in dress, no mien, no airs?

ELDER CLERIMONT.

Prithee Cuz, what is that same airs, d'ye see? I'd willingly please her now I have her, d'ye see. 340

MRS. CLERIMONT.

Airs? Why, 'tis a foolish word, used by those that do understand it and those that do not: 'tis what's pretty when Nature gives it, and what, when affected, spoils all that Nature gives beside. 345

MRS. RICH.

Oh! I shall go mad. Is that an object fit to please a woman nice* as I am?

MR. RICH.

Come sister, a long perriwig, an à la mode steen-kirk,* etcetera, has made a worse face a perfect beau ere now. Consider, he has some thousands a year. 350

ELDER CLERIMONT.

Aye marry,* have I; nay, 'Uds lid, I have a title too. I value no more, d'ye see, killing a man than I do killing a mouse; for I'd take up my patent,[77] be a lord, and be tried by my peers.

BELVOIR.

Thy peers! Where would'st find them? 355

MRS. RICH.

Oh my cursed stars! First a citizen's and then a country squire's wife. Ah! I shall never endure him, that's certain.

ELDER CLERIMONT.

Midhap so, and midhap ye may. I shan't cross ye mich. All the hunting season I'll be in the country, and you shall hunt pleasures here in Town.* Gi' me a little of your money to pay my debt, and I won't trouble you, d'ye see. 360

---

[77] patent] letter from a sovereign conferring a title, in this case the right to the title Elder Clerimont stands to inherit from his deceased father, which right he has not yet exercised, thereby remaining temporarily the "country squire" of the dramatis personae and Mrs. Rich's momentary comment

LADY LANDSWORTH.

Well said, Mr. Bridegroom. Come madam, few beaux would be more complaisant. 365

BETTY.

Madam, Sir John—

MRS. RICH.

Mountains cover my shame! What shall I say now?

LADY LANDSWORTH.

Say! Laugh at him, as all the world ought.

MRS. CLERIMONT.

Believe me, madam, ye have made the better choice. 370

MR. RICH.

A thousand times.

Enter Sir John and Mrs. Trickwell.

MRS. TRICKWELL.

You bring me here to see you triumph. I can never believe it; you have some trick put upon you, Sir John.

SIR JOHN.

Have I not her own note, that spite of her jealousies and her brother's tyranny she will this day be married? 375

MRS. TRICKWELL.

She does not say to you. Hah! What a world of company is here?

SIR JOHN.

The brother, and the young Gypsy his daughter: I'll be gone. 380

BELVOIR.

Nay no retreating, Sir John; you must at least wish the lady joy.

MRS. RICH.

Pshaw, my design's broke, my plots spoiled. Can I triumph at his defeat and show that awkward figure? 385

SIR JOHN.

Madam, your summons brought me hither, I hoped to joys.

MRS. RICH.

I hate you and all mankind.

LUCINDA.

So do I, ye sham lord, ye brag, ye bounce, ye— 390

BELVOIR.

Enough, good miss.—Sir John, I perceive you

must search for new gallantries; here the ladies are provided for, except this little one, who seems to have no inclination.

SIR JOHN.

Pax take ye all; they were fond,* I'm sure.   395

MR. RICH.

Come ye young coquette, your education shall be altered, I assure ye; 'tis e'en high time.

MRS. TRICKWELL.

Well, I believe my booty with yonder fantastical lady is at an end, so I'll steal off unobserved. (*Exit.*)

Enter Lady La Basset.

LADY LA BASSET.

Where is this villain, this false, ungrateful villain?   400

SIR JOHN.

So, another outcry?

LADY LA BASSET.

Yes traitor, and a just one: know all, this was but a servant in Sir John Roverhead's family; I dressed him in these borrowed honors, knowing Sir John never came to Town. I taught him the modes and   405
manners here, and he has rewarded me with inconstancy.

SIR JOHN.

Hold, hold, not so fast. How came you to be the Honorable the Lady La Basset? I think 'twas I dubbed ye. As I take it, ye were but the cast*   410
mistress of Sir Francis Basset when I found ye.

MR. RICH.

See sister, how the quality* you were fond of expose one another.

MRS. CLERIMONT.

And seeing this, be reconciled to your new spouse, who is of a noble family, and I promise to   415
introduce ye to persons of merit and honor.

LADY LANDSWORTH.

We shall all be fond of ye, for of yourself you are charming and sensible; 'tis only these wretches have rendered ye ridiculous.

MR. RICH.

Come, give him your hand. 'Tis a gentle   420
punishment for so much vanity.

MRS. RICH.

Well, since my malicious stars have thus decreed

it. But d'ye hear, I expect to have your estate in my power and that same title you talked of looked into.   425

ELDER CLERIMONT.

I'fackings, and so you shall, but must not I have your fine person in my power too? Hah!

MRS. RICH.

Has the thing sense enough to be in love?

CLERIMONT.

Now, I hope, all's well, and I have prevailed with my landlady to give ye a song.   430

LADY LANDSWORTH.

Do, good Mrs. Fidget.

MRS. FIDGET.

Anything to divert ye.

TOBY.

And adod, after that I'll give 'em a donce.

BELVOIR.

Well said, honest Toby.

MRS. RICH.

Sir John, will ye participate our diversion, or   435
employ your time in reconciling yourself to this enraged lady?

SIR JOHN.

Shame, disappointment, and disreputation light upon you all. Would all the whole sex were upon Salisbury Plain and their rigging on fire about their   440
ears. (*Exit.*)

MRS. CLERIMONT.

And that's the dreadful curse of a defeated beau.—
Follow, madam, and put him in a better humor.

LADY LA BASSET.

Hang him, as I would myself, you, and all the world. (*Exit.*)   445

BETTY.

A fair riddance.

CLERIMONT.

Now the song, and then the dance.

MR. RICH.

Now sister and daughter, to you I chiefly speak.
Let this day's adventure make ye forever cautious of your conversation.* Ye see how near these   450
pretenders to quality had brought you to ruin: the truly great are of a quite different character.
The glory of the world our British nobles are,
The ladies too, renowned and chaste and fair,

But to our citizens, Augusta's[78] sons,   455
The conquering wealth of both the Indias[79] runs.
Though less in name, of greater power by far;
Honors alone but empty scutcheons are.
Mixed with their coin, the title sweetly sounds;
No such alloy as twenty thousand pounds.   460

[Exeunt.]

THE END.

Textual Notes

a Copytext the first and only edition, a 1700 quarto (Q1).
  Also consulted, a modern edition of 1991 (Lyons and
  Morgan—LM).

b lives of] lives, or eternally disgrace, of Q1, LM

c Ye] you Q1, LM

d Belvoir] LM; Betty Q1

e Nor] Now Q1, LM

f whether] where ever Q1; wherever LM

g John and I] Ian, I Q1; Ian LM. However, this is almost
  certainly a corruption for "J. and I"; there are no italics, as there are everywhere else in the text where a name
  is mentioned. The copytext is corrupt at Mrs. Fidget's
  line (see textual note); Lady Landsworth's line following is actually "Ian? Pray, who is Ian?" Ian is, of course,
  the same name as John (given name for Jack), which
  Mrs. Fidget uses in Act II. Mrs. Fidget may simply be
  saying Ian, especially since in this period J and I were
  interchangeable; however, this would confuse an audience. Furthermore, Mrs. Fidget has no reason to invent
  an "Ian" here, since Lady Landsworth has actually spoken to Jack in Act IV. For this reason, and also because
  of similar errors in Act V (i.e. "Jan" for "John"), and the
  lack of customary italics for character names in these
  lines, "Ian" is here treated as a typesetter's error.

---

78 Augusta] allegorical figure representing London as an
   Imperial Roman goddess.

79 both the Indias] More often called the East and West
   Indies; respectively, India and Southeast Asia, and the
   Caribbean islands: important colonial trade areas, and
   the source of much of London's mercantile wealth in the
   early modern period

Love at a Loss; or, Most Votes Carry It[a]

by Catharine Trotter (1679—1749)

edited by Roxanne M. Kent-Drury

Catharine Trotter's career as a playwright began in 1696 when she was only seventeen and ended in 1708, when she married Patrick Cockburn, a Scottish clergyman. She was best known by contemporaries as a writer of moral tragedies and philosophical essays, for which she earned the respect and friendship of such important figures as playwrights William Wycherley and William Congreve and philosophers John Locke and Gottfried Wilhelm Leibnitz. Her social comedy *Love at a Loss; or, Most Votes Carry It* premiered at Drury Lane Theater on 23 November 1700, the only performance listed in *The London Stage*. Trotter later updated the play as *The Honourable Deceivers; or, All Right at the Last*, though no copy of the later version survives.

Although it was not a successful play when performed, *Love at a Loss* is important today for its uncharacteristic exploration of social comedy's familiar marriage plot from the perspective of the play's female characters. Like most contemporary social comedy, *Love at a Loss* examines the interactions of betrothed couples as they encounter and resolve impediments to marriage. Trotter does use several conventional plot devices, such as intercepted letters, overheard conversations, and the intervention of witty servants to resolve conflicts. Many of the central characters are also stock types and were played by actors Drury Lane audiences expected to see in those roles. Beaumine was acted by Robert Wilks, who usually played fine gentlemen. Cleon, a "vain and affected fellow," was played by the famous actor Colley Cibber, who often portrayed fops. The role of Bonsot, the play's most foolish character, may have been written for William Pinkethman, who was notorious for his clowning and impromptu adlibbing to the audience. Anne Oldfield,

who as one of the theater's most famous actresses later portrayed sophisticated heroines opposite Wilks, was only beginning her career when cast as Lucilia.

Despite its reliance on stock characters and plot devices, however, *Love at a Loss* avoids the usual trajectory of social comedy, which tacitly approves both trickster men who marry for land and money and the women who marry them over the objections of their obstructing guardians. Although they are mentioned, marriage settlements are of secondary importance to issues of affection and choice, and the only obstructing guardian is the one Beaumine fabricates to postpone his marriage to Lesbia. Instead, the play analyzes the institution of marriage itself and the infrequency of happy marriage, especially for women. Even though Miranda loves Constant, she puts off their marriage and flirts with Beaumine because she equates marriage to subjection and tyranny. The libertine Beaumine avoids marrying his Lesbia, whom he has seduced, because marriage to him involves loss of freedom and novelty. Although the play ends predictably with a series of marriages, Lesbia's lack of agency is demonstrated when her future partner is chosen, not by her, but by a vote of the other characters. Lesbia complacently accepts the result because honor demands that she fulfill her contractual obligations to Beaumine, even though she loves Grandfoy and faces the probability of an unhappy marriage to a philanderer who has already tired of the relationship. The result is a play that upsets the conventional endings of social comedy, thereby offering a critique of the institutional basis of marriage and its restrictive effects on women. In this sense, it contrasts sharply with many of the social comedies written by Trotter's contemporaries.

DRAMATIS PERSONAE

MEN

Beaumine, a gay, roving spark.

Phillabell, in love with Lucilia.

Constant, contracted to Miranda.

Grandfoy, in love with Lesbia.

Cleon, a vain, affected fellow.

Bonsot, a good-natured, officious fool.

WOMEN

Lesbia, contracted to Beaumine.

Miranda, a gay coquette.

[Her woman.*]

Lucilia, in love with Phillabell.

Lysetta, her governess.

[Young woman, servant of Lucilia's, niece to
Lysetta.]

Servants.

Love at a Loss; or, Most Votes Carry It.

Act I, scene i. [Lucilia's lodging.]

Enter Lucilia and Lysetta.

LUCILIA.

Does the fool think to threaten me into love?
Hearts must be won a softer way.

LYSETTA.

Aye madam, but our fear often does the men's
business as well as our inclinations. More women
have sacrificed their virtue to reputation than ever 5
love has ruined, and if they can but make us kind,*
what need they care why we are so?

LUCILIA.

Cleon seems indeed to be of that opinion.

LYSETTA.

Every man is that would be master of his pleasure.

LUCILIA.

Phillabell has told me a thousand times he should 10
not think me his unless my inclination gave me
to him.

LYSETTA.

Because he finds that his best friend. If he would
refuse you from any other, it does not much
recommend his love. 15

LUCILIA.

That's your notion, but ever since I have begun to

know myself, your maxims are not oracles with me.
You shall no more debauch my reason.

LYSETTA.

Why madam, what false maxims did I ever give you?

LUCILIA.

Should you not have warned me of the deceit and 20
treachery of men? Instead of that, what did you
entertain me with but tales of happy or unhappy
lovers? All to insinuate the violence of Cleon's
passion. How did you represent him to my vanity,
adoring, dying for me. I thought it a fine thing to 25
be courted in rhymes and ecstasies, though even
in that distinguishing age he never pleased me,
which you knew, and therefore to move my pity,
made my credulous ignorance believe that if I
would not give him some hopes, he must infallibly 30
die for me. The poor innocent thought she was
obliged in conscience to save a man's life!

LYSETTA.

Lord madam, what ado is here about nothing!
Where was the harm of writing a few kind letters
to a man? Is there ever a lady in Paris that has not 35
done more for half a dozen before she can resolve
to marry one? And a wise husband would no more
repine at that than he would that his clothes does
not come directly to him from the weavers. All the
little gallantries do but fashion her for his wearing. 40

LUCILIA.

Phillabell loves too nicely* not to grudge the least
kind thought for any other man, and should this
Cleon expose your letters (for so I must call 'em,
since I was but the scribe of what you dictated),
I'm utterly undone, my reputation ruined, and 45
what is worse, Phillabell lost forever.

LYSETTA.

That would be a base balk to a young lady just
upon the point of yielding to her wishes.
Tomorrow is to be the happy day.

LUCILIA.

Was to be, but Cleon's resolute to hinder it. Can 50
you invent a way to countermine him? You have
been cunning to undo me. Employ your art for
once to save me.

LYSETTA.

Madam, whatever the event has been, my aim was
never to undo, but serve you. If I had known that 55

you could never have loved Cleon or foreseen your passion for Phillabell, I had not engaged you so far, but since 'tis past recalling, we should only think of preventing future mischiefs. But all my counsels will be suspected. 60

LUCILIA.

Indeed I believe you wish me well. Prithee advise me.

LYSETTA.

You must by no means undeceive Cleon till you are married. Persuade him that you love him still and only marry Phillabell in obedience to your father. Give him some hopes of making him happy 65 afterwards.

LUCILIA.

Well, and what will this do?

LYSETTA.

Do? Is there any man that would not rather have another man's wife than make her his own? 'Twill do all that you would have it, make him as eager 70 for the match as you are yourself, instead of preventing it, as his letter threatens.

LUCILIA.

But can I endure he should imagine I would wrong Phillabell so basely?

LYSETTA.

What are you the worse for his imaginations? 75 Besides, you can easily dispossess him of 'em when you have once secured your husband.

LUCILIA.

Methinks 'tis so dishonorable a deceit I can't relish it.

LYSETTA.

Nay, if you scruple the cheat, you may keep your word with him. 80

LUCILIA.

Prithee be serious.

LYSETTA.

Well madam, this is certain: unless you give him hopes false or true, he will not fail to expose all your letters to Phillabell. I need not make you apprehend the consequence. 85

LUCILIA.

'Tis such a fatal one, I would not at any rate[1] prevent it. But you know he's not allowed to visit

---

[1] not at any rate] the negative is an intensifier: at any cost whatsoever

me. 'Tis impossible for me to see him today in private, and to write a letter after the manner proposed, you would be putting it more in his 90 power to ruin me than I have ever done before.

LYSETTA.

Aye, but at the same time you give him the power, you show him that 'tis against his own interest to use it. And when you are once believed (which his vanity will help you in) and have gained a little 95 time, twenty wiles may be thought of to get the letters out of his hands.

LUCILIA.

My case is desperate, and therefore the remedy must be so. Once more I will be governed by you. He sends me word he shall be in the walks this 100 evening. You shall carry the letter thither to him.

Enter Lesbia.

LESBIA.

'Tis seasonable to wish you joy today, Lucilia; tomorrow Phillabell will give it you, and then my wishes would be needless.

LUCILIA.

He is indeed a man to make a woman happy. 105

LESBIA.

Ha, ha, ha! Are you practising the decent gravities of a bride against tomorrow? Prithee, away with that sullen look, or I shall think you are angry with this impertinent day for stepping between you and the wedding one. 110

LUCILIA.

You are not so much in haste I find. But my dear, what if you should marry Beaumine tomorrow? 'Twould be friendly to keep me in countenance.

LESBIA.

No, no, I won't lose the pleasure of making observations upon you. 115

LUCILIA.

But tell me seriously why you delay your marriage so long.

LESBIA.

Faugh, I came to divert myself with talking of your wedding, and you would make me dull with the thoughts of my own. 120

LUCILIA.

Believe me, Lesbia, if I did not love you, I would

not urge you farther, but I am vexed to hear some malicious reflections that are whispered of you and must ask you why you give the occasion.

LESBIA.

Some fitter time I'll tell you.   125

LUCILIA.

Lysetta, we would be private.

Exit Lysetta.

Now be free with me.

LESBIA.

Well, if I must lay aside my mirth awhile to tell you a sad tale: you have often heard me speak of one Grandfoy, whom I loved before I knew Beaumine.   130

LUCILIA.

You have told me he was false.

LESBIA.

I thought him so, but he has since convinced me that I wronged him, though my suspicions were, you know, well grounded. He's still the man which he appeared at first, all truth and goodness, and   135 loves me more than I can now deserve.

LUCILIA.

I shall think you deserve a great deal of him, an* if you decline so considerable a match as Beaumine for his sake.

LESBIA.

When you know my story, I fear you'll say he   140 ought to despise me.

LUCILIA.

That's impossible, but pray, my dear, go on.

LESBIA.

Just in the height of my resentment against Grandfoy, Beaumine first saw and loved me. He addressed to my mother, who easily gave her   145 consent, his fortune being very considerable. To be short, her commands were sacred to me, and I believed it would be some revenge upon Grandfoy, which was the chief motive of my resolving to marry Beaumine. He proposed to have it secret whilst his   150 mother lived, because she designed him for another. No priest would marry us without her consent.[2] He

told me then it was the tie of hearts that made a marriage, but fearing mine should change, to make me sure, he writ a contract, which we both signed   155 with our blood. And to confirm it, he led me to the holy altar, where he vowed to take me for his wife— I don't know how to tell you the rest.

LUCILIA.

You e'en took him for a husband,[3] is it not so?

LESBIA.

He often importuned me to live with him as such   160 and at my refusal lost all the natural gaiety of his temper and much avoided seeing me. My mother dying, he came to condole with me. I saw myself unguarded, and willing to engage him in my interests, I flattered him with all the artful   165 tenderness I could affect. This made him press me more eagerly than ever. Agreeable as he is, I never loved him much, and yet I don't know how he found the yielding minute. Betwixt you and I, Lucilia, is not there one of which we are not master?   170

LUCILIA.

I will believe so for your sake, though I think it would be always in my power to refuse a man anything that is not fit for him to ask. But how did Beaumine behave himself afterwards?

LESBIA.

Very fond at first, but now grows careless and   175 sometimes insolent. Still* he let me hope that he would marry me after his mother's death, which satisfied till Grandfoy assured me she died just after mine, though he conceals it from me.

LUCILIA.

That does not look as if he meant you fairly, but   180 your contract will oblige him to do you justice.

LESBIA.

If it could, I would not marry him against his inclination.

LUCILIA.

What do you resolve on then?

---

2 No … consent] Beaumine may have been underage (21) and therefore, according to the canons of 1604, could not marry legally without parental consent.

3 You … husband] They were solemnly betrothed, pre-contracted. At this time, such promises were binding and, even though absent church ceremony with a priest, sufficient to constitute an actual marriage under the law if the marriage was subsequently consummated.

LESBIA.

I must first know certainly what he intends.   185

LUCILIA.

His intentions seem so indifferent to you, that I must believe yours are more for Grandfoy.

LESBIA.

Indeed he shows so generous an affection for me, it claims all my gratitude. And since I find my suspicions of him were unjust, did not my honor   190 oppose it, I confess I could love him more than ever.

LUCILIA.

Does he know of your affair with Beaumine?

LESBIA.

He does and made me promise that, if upon the trial I found Beaumine unfaithful, I would be governed by him. To confirm my word I gave him   195 a ring, which was Beaumine's first gift to me. You have seen me wear it.

LUCILIA.

Did not Beaumine miss it?

LESBIA.

I told him I had lost it, which he easily believed, not having ever heard that I loved another, and I   200 have taken care as far as art would go to persuade him that I love him, for that I thought both my interest and duty.

LUCILIA.

I wish you may not find yourself abused. The world is much mistaken in him if he has any thoughts of marriage but to rail or make his jest   205 of it.

LESBIA.

A man of this age must no more speak well of it than of religion, and yet perhaps there are as few marriage haters as atheists.

LUCILIA.

What then can put the men upon professing it?   210 One would think it can be neither much for their honor or interest.

LESBIA.

At first to gain the reputation of wit by affecting a singularity in their notions. And since that by imitation or humor* they are become the common   215 topics of raillery, many take up with it for want* of resolution to bear with their being the ridicule of their companions.

LUCILIA.

And is this your opinion of Beaumine?

LESBIA.

I believe there's more humor* and affectation than   220 any serious reflection in it and have less reason to fear his love of liberty than some other chains.

LUCILIA.

Why, are you jealous of him?

LESBIA.

Only of his rambling temper; he takes care to give me no particular aim.   225

LUCILIA.

He seems indeed to make love* to every woman and mean it to none.

LESBIA.

Miranda and he were mightily pleased with one another t'other day. She happened to come in when he was with me. She gave him leave to visit her and   230 talks of him perpetually ever since. He does not seem to think much of her, or I should apprehend her a dangerous rival, she's so much of his own humor.*

LUCILIA.

But she's engaged to another too.

LESBIA.

Aye, and says she loves him.   235

LUCILIA.

'Tis strange she should; there can't be two more opposite tempers than Constant's and hers.

LESBIA.

And what pleasure she takes in teasing and tormenting his gravity.

LUCILIA.

And in pleasing every man else.   240

LESBIA.

Well, coquette as she is, I should not be pleased to have Beaumine pursue the acquaintance.

LUCILIA.

Then he has not made her a visit yet.

LESBIA.

He does not own it to me.   245

LUCILIA.

I shall see her today, and if I hear anything of him, you shall be sure to know it, for if he is not sincere, the sooner you are undeceived, the better. My dear, will you go to my closet* with me? I have a letter to write in haste. 'Twill be quickly done; you'll   250 excuse me for a minute.

LESBIA.

I expect to see Grandfoy immediately and must take my leave of you.

LUCILIA.

May all you undertake succeed to your own wishes.

LESBIA.

I scarce know what I wish, only all happiness to you. 255

Exeunt severally.

Scene [ii]. Phillabell's lodgings.

Enter Beaumine and a servant.

BEAUMINE.

Is your master busy?

SERVANT.

He'll be at leisure to see you, sir, I am sure.

BEAUMINE.

Tell him I'm here.

Exit servant.

Egad, I pity this poor fellow. He might have been a fit companion for us men of spirit and pleasure but for this damned, dull matrimony. 5

Enter Phillabell.

PHILLABELL.

Beaumine! What sudden dearth of wine or kind women has reduced thee to thinking?

BEAUMINE.

Only a sense of my friend's misfortune. I came to condole with you. Faith Phillabell, I am heartily sorry for thee. 10

PHILLABELL.

For me! Why, what's the matter? I know no cause you have. I was never so satisfied, so easy, so full of joy, as in this minute.

BEAUMINE.

Why, is your marriage broke off? 15

PHILLABELL.

Broke! Heaven forbid! You would have reason to condole with me then indeed.

BEAUMINE.

And are you certainly to be married tomorrow?

PHILLABELL.

I hope so.

BEAUMINE.

Strange! But he's mad, poor man. 20

PHILLABELL.

Why, did you hear anything to the contrary?

BEAUMINE.

No, and therefore am amazed to hear such agreeable words—satisfied, easy, full of joy—out of the mouth of a condemned man, if thou art in thy senses.

PHILLABELL.

Oh, a satire upon marriage. Is that your intent? 25

BEAUMINE.

Faith, I would willingly reclaim thee if thou art not too far gone to hear reason.

PHILLABELL.

I could never find any reason why a man should be uneasy in the possession of a woman that he loves only because he enjoys her without breaking human or divine laws. 30

BEAUMINE.

What are laws but chains to our wills, our inclinations? Destroyers of liberty, the dear prerogative of Nature.

PHILLABELL.

But libertinism is not a privilege to be very fond of, and that's all we are denied. 35

BEAUMINE.

'Tis better to be lost with pleasure than preserved in pain.

PHILLABELL.

The pain of being always my Lucilia's won't much employ my philosophy to support it. 40

BEAUMINE.

And are you sure you will be always of this mind? Do you imagine she will be always young, always handsome, and that you shall always love her?

PHILLABELL.

I am sure she will always have wit, good humor, and virtue and, by consequence, that I shall always love her. 45

BEAUMINE.

But what if all that you call good humor should prove affectation, nothing else, and virtue but the art of well dissembling?

PHILLABELL.

To dissemble well is virtue, or what we can't distinguish from it. 50

BEAUMINE.

Aye, aye, but the disguise is always laid aside when

there's no farther need of it. When you are entered into bonds, 'twon't be worth her pains; the fear of losing a lover only can make 'em careful to please. If you but saw the fond, endearing Lesbia, what arts she uses to engage me, how well she thinks 'em all returned by one kind word or look, and then the tender niceness of her passion: she lost a ring the other day which I had given her. Never was anything so moving as her complaints; I told her she should have one twice the value, but that would not appease her. She said 'twas the first present I had made her, and she feared the loss, a sad presage that she should lose my heart. Nothing could comfort her but my repeated vows of never changing. Are there such tender sentiments in marriage? You'll find a cold civility the best part of their entertainment after a month's enjoyment.

PHILLABELL.

I should expect no better if I had chose an unthinking coquette or one whose broken fortune might make her snatch at the first hope of repairing it, but Lucilia is reserved and prudent. Her fortune equals mine, she has refused many considerable matches, and I have reason to think myself the only man that has found the way to her heart. I know she hates Cleon and treats with scorn or coldness the rest that languish for her. In fine, I have all the security for a lasting love and happiness that reason can desire or give.

BEAUMINE.

Lasting! Why, thou hast named the very bane of love and happiness. What that's old can charm to ecstasy? Or not be dull with being oft repeated?

PHILLABELL.

And what that's new can be relied upon? Or how can you enjoy a happiness that you are always in danger of losing?

BEAUMINE.

Relied on? Oh most firmly, Phil. (*Sings.*) "They still* are constant whilst possessed and can do more for no man——"[4] And faith, fickle as they are, they must be plaguey quick to make me complain of losing them. But if any of 'em should run out

of my arms to another's (for then she is sure to have the start of me), I have always one in hand that supplies the vacancy.

PHILLABELL.

Nay, that's the way indeed not to be much grieved at their loss, for betwixt two, you can't be very fond of either.

BEAUMINE.

You're mistaken man; it makes me very fond of both. If they knew nature, a woman would never fear losing a man so much as when the coyness* or jealousy of one has vexed him. He flies to another that with kindness* restores his good humor, and when her over-fondness has cloyed him, he returns to the first for fresh appetite, for by one of these extremes the women always lose us. They are either so capricious, they grow troublesome, or so tender, they grow dull. But tempered thus, they give the relish to each other.

PHILLABELL.

If you could convince the women of this doctrine, you might both have your ends by it. But whilst they are of another opinion, whatever advantage it may be to them you'll hardly find your account in it. He that pursues two hares will catch neither.

BEAUMINE.

Still he has the greater pleasure in the chase, to observe their different crossings, windings, and little arts. Sometimes their very fear, you know, makes 'em run full into the hound's mouth. But if you do not give over too soon, there's none of them but may be wearied out. Then seize the panting quarry, and she's yours.

PHILLABELL.

Well, give me the woman that resigns herself upon deliberation and solid reason that, as it makes the gift more valuable, so more secure.

BEAUMINE.

That is, more insipid.

PHILLABELL.

There's no disputing tastes. The very trouble of continual fresh pursuits would make variety disgustful to me.

BEAUMINE.

Which gives me the highest relish. But I need not endeavor to convince thee; thy wife will do it

---

4 "They … man—"] unidentified, as are most of the song snatches

effectually, since thou art resolved to purchase wisdom at the dearest rate, experience. What a lamentable figure thou'lt make, preaching it to others, as a fellow at the gallows does honesty when 'tis too late to make use of it himself. But I'll leave you to prepare for your solid blessing. Will you meet me in the walk this evening? 135

PHILLABELL.

If I have nothing else to do, perhaps I may.

BEAUMINE.

Egad, I beg thy pardon. I forgot thou'rt a man of business.[5] Honest matrimony. Adieu. 140

PHILLABELL.

Well, well, laugh on. I am contented you should have your jest, so I secure my happiness, With a chaste wife, like my Lucilia, true.

BEAUMINE.

I, with a mistress, ever gay and new.

Exeunt severally.

Act II, scene [i]. Lesbia's lodgings.

Enter Lesbia and Grandfoy.

GRANDFOY.

I would not appear in your defense till you have tried Beaumine to the utmost, that he may have no pretence against you.

LESBIA.

I never gave him any yet, nor can he find an excuse now for deferring our marriage, since the only obstacle he pretended is removed by his mother's death. 5

GRANDFOY.

But I advise you not to take notice of your knowing it nor show any distrust of him. If he has the least honor, the confidence you seem to have in him will be a stronger[b] engagement. 10

LESBIA.

But should he still refuse me?

GRANDFOY.

You promise then to be disposed by me; I wear the pledge of your fidelity.

LESBIA.

Won't it be a bold venture to put myself in the power of a man I have injured? 15

GRANDFOY.

Unless in your unjust suspicions of me, you only have been injured. Your misfortune with Beaumine has a thousand excuses on your part, as unhappy as it makes me. Oh Lesbia, that I should ever think it reasonable to wish you another's! To force a man 20 to deprive me of all I value!

LESBIA.

'Tis scarce reasonable indeed to value me now so much as to care whose I am.

GRANDFOY.

I have such an opinion of your sincerity and virtue that even now, would you consent to be mine, I 25 should receive you as the greatest earthly blessing, but that you have refused me unless Beaumine, by a declared infidelity, entirely release you.

LESBIA.

Imagine with what difficulty I do it whilst I receive such proofs of love from you, whom I have had 30 too much kindness for ever to be indifferent to or equally to value any other.

GRANDFOY.

Curse on that fate that forced me from you so abruptly to make me lose that kindness by seeming false then when I loved you most, and ever must, 35 though now your heart's another's.

LESBIA.

I fear, Grandfoy, you are still but too dear to it.

GRANDFOY.

Yet you refuse the offer I have made to marry you.

LESBIA.

'Tis the only return I can make to so generous an offer. If my own honor did not oblige me to it, I 40 owe it to your love and good opinion, for 'tis the only way I can deserve 'em.

GRANDFOY.

How little does Beaumine deserve this treasure that values it so lightly! I must approve the virtue that undoes me. And to preserve it as free from suspicion 45 as it is of guilt, I'll leave you, since you expect Beaumine. For your sake I would not have him know me, unless he force me to revenge your wrongs.

LESBIA.

You are in all things noble.

GRANDFOY.

If you are for the walks this evening, I shall see you 50

---

[5] man of business] like a cit*

again. Cleon sent this morning to desire I would meet him there. He has something to ask my advice in, I suppose some love adventure, for that's his only business.

LESBIA.

His only discourse indeed, but the great talkers of 55 intrigues, as of religion, have usually the least of either. And indeed, whatever a man studiously affects to seem, 'tis a shrewd sign he's conscious of not being it in reality.

GRANDFOY.

But the reality of intrigues are generally private and 60 only to be known by talking of 'em, which, believe me, is the chief part of the pleasure of many of our sex.

LESBIA.

I fancy only to those that are allowed no other part, but they who are truly well received among us, if not 65 in gratitude to those who have obliged 'em, will be cautious to secure their designs upon others. Love is not to be raised like valor, by emulation.

GRANDFOY.

I don't know what it may do towards kindling a flame, but I am sure 'twill increase it. Many a 70 woman from a little liking to a man has become passionately in love, only upon finding another was pleased with him.

LESBIA.

Then she must know it by her rival's indiscretion and not his vanity, for that only shows his 75 weakness, but the other the force of his merit. But indeed, if Cleon should rely upon that, his mistress would scarce find any occasion of jealousy. His vanity appears too grossly; the good-natured fool his brother is the more supportable. 80

GRANDFOY.

Poor Bonsot. He always means well but unluckily makes more mischief by officiously endeavoring to prevent it and pretending to know everybody's business.

LESBIA.

Then his bulls[6] are diverting enough, they fall so 85 naturally from him.

---

6 bulls] verbal blunders

GRANDFOY.

As near relations, I must bear with and would hide their follies. But we shall forget ourselves, till we give Beaumine occasion of jealousy, which, though sometimes our sex find their ends in, 'tis always a 90 dangerous expedient for yours, for what you gain in inclination, you lose in our esteem.
Fear of a rival will enflame desire,
But distrust of her soon quench the fire.

LESBIA.

That way leads to the back door. You'll be secure 95 from meeting him.

Exit Grandfoy.

Few men would use as Grandfoy does such a confidence as I have had in him. But sure never any woman made the experiment before me. If the lover can but be kept ignorant, no matter what he 100 discover when secured a husband—I must own those women have more courage than I. Cheating in all other cases may be only playing the knave, but any deceit in marriage must be egregiously playing the fool, when the very injury we do gives 105 the power of revenging it.

Enter Beaumine.

BEAUMINE. [*Aside.*]

Aye, at home you're as sure of finding an old mistress as a creditor that expects you to pay him an old debt, in good humor too, I warrant.—I was afraid, madam, you had not come home yet. 110

LESBIA.

How could you imagine that, when I had hopes of seeing you?

BEAUMINE. [*Aside.*]

Ay, I thought so; well, this is the devil.—Faith Lesbia, I do what I can to be very fond of you, but you will take pains to hinder it. I cannot help it. 115

LESBIA.

I don't know that I have done anything to displease you.

BEAUMINE.

Why, there's it. You should do something to displease me:
Love is an active, restless fire 120
That without agitation must expire.

LESBIA.

I thought a constant fuel of lasting worth and kindness would preserve it.

BEAUMINE.

It may keep it in, but 'twill burn very dimly without blowing, Lesbia. 125

LESBIA.

I wish I knew the art of doing it.

BEAUMINE.

Why, you should go abroad when you're sure I shall come to see you; look angry or cold upon me without telling me why when I would caress you; and when I expect you should be fond of me, 130 make me suspect you are thinking of another. In short, vex, perplex, and disquiet me, that supplying me always with something to employ my thoughts on, they may have no leisure to wander.

LESBIA.

I rather take care by the regularity of my conduct to 135 show you what you may always expect from me. For though these arts may be agreeable in a mistress, you would scarce be pleased with 'em in a wife.

BEAUMINE.

Nay, thou hast thought of a way now to put a man out of his humor with a vengeance by[c] the worst 140 contrivance to raise an appetite you could have found out. You have all of a wife but the name. The want* of that flatters me with an imagined liberty, and you must bring it in to spoil a man's fancy.

LESBIA.

I like your raillery, Beaumine, since I don't doubt 145 but your serious thoughts are to make me that in earnest, which the name of serves you for a jest.

BEAUMINE.

Aye, aye, there will be a time for serious thoughts, respect, and reverence, which wives should have, and that, you know, is paid to antiquity, Lesbia, 150 but love and raptures, for the young and free.

LESBIA.

Thus I can never be satisfied or angry with this man. Is it impossible for you ever to answer seriously and directly, Beaumine?

BEAUMINE.

Why truly, if you would have my thoughts, I 155 would counsel you against the most unaccountable extravagance you are designing.

LESBIA.

What's that?

BEAUMINE.

You have now a great deal of my love; 'tis certain marriage won't add one jot to it, and very possible 160 it may extremely lessen it. Now would anyone in their senses that were in possession of a good estate, without any prospect of bettering it, put it to the chance of a die whether they should keep it or lose it? I am thy own, and keep me as thou hast me. 165 (*Sings.*) "Thus ever frolic, ever gay."[7]

LESBIA.

Thou art the most agreeable, tormenting devil. But prithee, tell me what I am to expect.

BEAUMINE.

Expect! Why, that the old woman will die, and that— 170

LESBIA.

But will the old woman ever die, Beaumine?

BEAUMINE.

Humph! pugh, what's age and death to us, my love? They are melancholy thoughts. We've life and youth and liberty, my Lesbia. (*Sings.*) "And live a thousand years a day." 175

LESBIA. [*Aside.*]

Thus may this gay humor fool me on forever. I must try him farther.—Well, thou art the maddest fellow. Sure there is not your peer in France, unless Miranda. 'Tis pity Fate has not joined you. What did you think of her? 180

BEAUMINE.

I thought very well of her whilst I saw her but have not thought at all of her since. She's a very* coquette, pleased with every man and pleases all whilst with 'em, but no sooner out of sight than she forgets and is as easily forgot. 185

LESBIA.

She has not forgot you so soon, I assure you. But have not you refreshed her memory?

BEAUMINE.

Not I, upon honor.

---

7 "Ever frolic, ever gay"] probably from a drinking song; cf. Sir Fopling's song in Etherege's *Man of Mode* (IV.ii) praising champagne as that which "Makes us frolic and gay, and drowns all our sorrow."

LESBIA.

I'm glad of it.

BEAUMINE.

Why? You would not have been jealous.   190

LESBIA.

No, but I think 'twill be better you should not visit her at all, for I know she likes you.

BEAUMINE.

Not visit her because she likes me! Now hang me if I can find that out to be a good reason.

LESBIA.

It might be dangerous to fan a fire that's yet but   195
kindled.

BEAUMINE.

Nay, I have no design to see her, but what whim of yours is this? She likes anything for her diversion.

LESBIA.

But talks of you in heroics.

BEAUMINE.

A new humor.   200

LESBIA.

And is very importunate to know if there's any amour betwixt you and me.

BEAUMINE.

Curiosity, I hope, did not satisfy her.

LESBIA.

She seemed so much concerned I could not deny her positively but betwixt raillery and earnest left   205
her in doubt, which made her so uneasy she said she would soon see me again and hoped I would be more sincere with her.

BEAUMINE.

By no means, I charge you. Women of her humor* are always prying into the intrigues of their   210
companions by gaining their confidence or raising their jealousy to make 'em the jest of the next company. Never trust any of your own sex, especially such a giddy thing as Miranda.

LESBIA.

Since you desire it, you may be sure I'll be   215
cautious, though I know she was serious.

BEAUMINE.

I suppose you can't think you have any reason to fear her.

LESBIA.

If I had distrusted you, I would not have told you

of such an agreeable rival, and I expect, in return   220
of the confidence I have in you, you should avoid a woman that I believe loves you.

BEAUMINE.

Egad, a very nice* piece of honor. I must have no mind to a handsome woman because you have let me know she has a mind to me. Well, as far as flesh   225
and blood can reach it, I'll act this romantic lover.

LESBIA.

Then you won't visit Miranda.

BEAUMINE.

No, since you would not have me, not that I think there's any danger in it, but I'm very indifferent in the matter. If she happen to fall in my way and mischief   230
should ensue—remember you were my tempter.

LESBIA.

I dare trust you.

BEAUMINE.

Well then, to put my virtue to the proof. (*Going.*)

LESBIA.

Where are you going?

BEAUMINE.

To Miranda.   235

LESBIA.

Pshaw, you're always fooling, but I have business.

BEAUMINE.

So have I, but what's yours about?

LESBIA.

Our marriage.

BEAUMINE.

And mine is love. I cannot think of two things at once so directly opposite. So first for that of   240
greatest moment. (*Going.*)

LESBIA.

But will you tell me—

BEAUMINE.

How Miranda receives me, what favors she refuses, what she grants. All, all.

LESBIA.

But Beaumine.   245

BEAUMINE.

But Miranda.

LESBIA.

Pugh, that's a jest.

BEAUMINE.

Then you don't believe I'm going to her.

LESBIA.

No, I'm sure you won't.

BEAUMINE. [*Aside.*]

Now the De—il take her for not being jealous, that 250
I might have a right to deceive her, for I'm afraid
I cannot forbear. But 'tis no matter; there's no truth
in these cases, and since

We all are false alike in love, 'tis clear,

He that dissembles best is most sincere. (*Exit.*) 255

LESBIA.

Thou maggoty, barbarous, good-humored, ill-
natured toad. He is gone as fleet as winds, but I
as fast shall fly,

Since, whilst a stale, tried lover I pursue,

If he escape me, I secure a new. 260

Exit.

Scene [ii]. Miranda's lodgings.

Enter Lucilia and Miranda.

LUCILIA.

Nay I protest you're to blame, Miranda, to use a
man thus that dotes upon you.

MIRANDA.

If he does not like the humor,* what makes him dote
on me? We're both pleased with one another, only
have different ways of showing it. He's fond of my 5
gaiety, I laugh at his gravity. He whines, I sing. He
takes care to show his fidelity, I to make him jealous.
That's his way, this is mine. We take several roads,
but I fear both lead to the same dreadful end. We
shall e'en meet at last in matrimony, though I am for 10
going the farthest way about.

LUCILIA.

Since you are resolved to go through the journey,
'tis the wisest way to make it as short as possible
for fear you should spend too much of your stock
of love or be robbed of it by another upon the road 15
and not have enough to subsist on when your
travels are over.

MIRANDA.

I'm not so extravagant in my expenses of it, and
for robbers there's more danger of them in our
place of rest. For though matrimony is too strong 20
an edifice to be demolished, its guards and
enclosures are weak and easily broke through. And

love is a treasure not to be confined; it slips like
water from the hand that would restrain it. If you
would secure it, leave it loose and free. 25

LUCILIA.

But 'tis impossible you can love Constant and not
have a mind to marry him.

MIRANDA.

Indeed I don't love him so well but that I had
rather torment him than he should torment me,
rather have variety of diversions lie heavy upon my 30
hands than the affairs of my family. I like the
squeaking of a fiddle better than the squalling of
brats, and an obsequious humble servant better
than a surly lord and master.

LUCILIA.

I fancy 'tis some other humble servant you like 35
better; this Beaumine you were talking of runs
mightily in your head.

MIRANDA.

In my head! In my heart, in my sleep. I dream of
him, sigh for him, die for him. Oh 'tis the easiest,
gayest, wildest, most engaging, everything that 40
suits my humor.* I long for him again. If he likes
me well enough to visit me, I shall grow so fond
of him.

LUCILIA.

Why, you can't love 'em both.

MIRANDA.

I'll swear, I do extremely. I love Constant best at a 45
distance, Beaumine when he's with me: to think
of one, laugh with t'other. He diverts me, t'other
improves me. One will make the better husband,
t'other the more agreeable gallant.

LUCILIA.

Well, wildly as you talk, I don't doubt but you'll 50
make a very good wife.

MIRANDA.

I don't doubt but he'll make me so, take a full
revenge of my tyranny when he has got the power
in his hands; therefore, I resolve to reign as long
as I can. 55

Enter Constant.

But here comes my sovereign elect.—I thought, sir,
you had business with my uncle and therefore left
you without hopes of this happiness so soon.

CONSTANT.

I thought, madam, you had business, that you ran from me so abruptly when I was talking to you of what concerns me nearest, but it seems 'twas only to be rid of me. I'm sorry my company is so displeasing.

MIRANDA.

'Tis a strange lover that won't give his mistress leave to think of him; I came but to sigh for you in secret.

CONSTANT.

Sigh in secret, when we may smile together? Oh Miranda, sure you but abuse my doting heart and make my love your sport.

MIRANDA.

Why, what's love or anything else good for, unless to divert us?

CONSTANT.

I might have thought, indeed, your sprightly temper could not long brook my heavy, sullen nature, but tell me freely I am troublesome, and as I never asked your uncle his consent till you permitted me, so will I not now use his authority but leave you free to choose a humor* that may suit you better.

MIRANDA.

Don't disturb yourself about that. I shall quickly be as sullen as you when we're married, no doubt.

CONSTANT.

That would but hinder our resemblance then, for sure that happy day that calls you mine will quite dissolve the earthly part of me, refine this mass, and make me spirit all.

MIRANDA.

Leave you the ghost of your departed love
And me to mourn in tears my wretched fate:
That yours expired too soon, mine lived too late.
There's rapture for your rapture, Constant.

CONSTANT.

Well dear tormenter, don't weary out my love then ere you use it, but cherish it whilst young and vigorous, and it will be immortal.

MIRANDA.

Then I must keep it in its native air, for they say marriage is a very cold climate.

LUCILIA.

I believe indeed it kills the hottest hasty plants but

preserves and often produces such solid fruits as are most fit for constant nourishment and bears sweets of its own growth too, Miranda.

MIRANDA.

Well seriously Lucilia, I have been trying this month to compose my face for the wedding day, for I fancy if one has not a most reverend countenance, one will never be thought in earnest at so unreasonable a thing as taking for better, for worse. It looks so like a jest or stark madness.

CONSTANT.

Keep your mad countenance, then, and do it in jest.

MIRANDA.

Aye, but that surly one of yours, Constant, has such a husbandly air 'twill spoil the jest. I never look upon it but I'm afraid I'm married already.

CONSTANT.

I'll endeavor to put on a more agreeable one, turn merry-andrew, anything to please you.

MIRANDA.

Then 'tis resolved we will be kings no more?

CONSTANT.

Oh when, my life? My joy, now I am gay as thou art.

MIRANDA.

Nay that has undone all again. Those laughing eyes bring to my thoughts that charming fellow that danced and sung himself into my heart; I must have some time to drive him out again, and then Constant—

CONSTANT.

Who? What is it you talk of?

MIRANDA.

Oh such a grace, such an air, such a humor;* if you knew him you must be fond of him for love of me. He's just my counterpart.

CONSTANT. [Aside.]

I know she rallies, yet it tortures me.

MIRANDA.

What, in the dumps! Nay, don't be jealous.

CONSTANT.

No, no, but 'tis intolerable cruelty to make your sport of what my life depends on.

MIRANDA.

'Tis in concern for your life I would delay this marriage, for if in the height of my passion the tempter should come in my way, he makes an attack, duty opposes, inclination assists him, prohibition strengthens it, nature prevails, runs away with me, you pursue and cut his throat, I break my heart. You can do no less than stab yourself to complete the tragedy and prevent this mischief.

CONSTANT.

We'll take care to avoid the tempter.

MIRANDA.

That can't be done without having him always in my thoughts. No, no, Constant, you have a better way of curing a woman's love: being perpetually with her. And since you have found it so effectual an experiment, I'm resolved to try it upon my new inclination till he has said all the fine things he can, showed all his humors,* played over all his tricks, left nothing farther for imagination to work on, but grown as dull to me as a book I have just read.

CONSTANT.

Or as I am to you now.

MIRANDA.

Then you'll be new again, like one that has been long out of print, and I am always fond of the second edition, revised, corrected, and amended. But be sure you take care never to let me peruse it through. Reserve something for my curiosity, Constant, for you know the best books, when we have studied 'em perfectly, are thrown aside or only kept for show, and any trifling novel that we never met with before entertains us better.

CONSTANT.

Thou art never to be thoroughly known; the more I study thee, the more I am perplexed: find something clear enough to engage my search, but still too doubtful to determine on. Would you provoke me first to break a contract you repent? Or is't to try my constancy you thus torment me? Are you not satisfied? What fool but I could have endured so much? But madam, I'm not made to bear forever.

MIRANDA.

What, is it nangry[8] now? And what would it do? Can it break its cage? Flutter about, tire itself, and hurt its wings? And to what purpose?

CONSTANT.

I am thy slave, Miranda, but 'tis the more ungenerous to use a creature in thy power so inhumanly. I dote upon thee, dote on that very humor* that distracts me. Be serious once to free me from the fear of losing thee, and ever after I would have thee gay as nature formed thee.

MIRANDA.

Forever after, I am sure, be dull enough and therefore now indulge my natural gaiety. But let me see what time of the moon is it; about the full, I may be disposed.

CONSTANT.

Still in raillery. I beg thee. I conjure thee.

MIRANDA.

Well, I am good-natured, and since you are so impatient—

CONSTANT.

Oh speak.

MIRANDA.

I am resolved—

CONSTANT.

When, when, my charmer?

MIRANDA.

As soon as possible to engage my charmer, grow weary of him as fast as I can, return to you with new pleasure, then here's my hand on't.

CONSTANT.

Oh torture, torture. 'Tis too much, Miranda. You may find, fond of my prison as I am, I'm not so strongly chained as you imagine.

MIRANDA.

Alas, and will you leave me?

CONSTANT.

Well madam, you shall no more insult. (*Exit.*)

MIRANDA.

Not these two hours, I'll engage.

LUCILIA.

Nay, he can never return after this.

MIRANDA.

Only half a dozen times a day he makes and breaks these noble resolutions.

LUCILIA.

I'm sure you deserve to lose his love, and for my part, I'm amazed it has subsisted so long with such ill usage.

---

8 nangry] Rendered babytalk often adds an *n* to the beginning of a word (as in *nown**).

MIRANDA.

Oh! The men's love is not so easily starved as surfeited; 'twill live upon the lightest airy hope, though soon destroyed with fondness. We lose lovers by overcare than neglect, Lucilia. 195

LUCILIA.

You would make 'em very ungenerous creatures, but I believe gratitude is as strong a tie to them as to us. 200

MIRANDA.

Just as strong indeed, and if you would speak your heart as freely as I do, you would own we take most pains to appear agreeable to a new acquaintance, put on our best looks, show all our wit, all our good humor, everything that may engage, whilst a lover we have well enough secured not to fear losing is received and entertained as negligently as a cousin-german. 205

LUCILIA.

On the contrary, if I would use any arts, it should be to please a man who by proofs of a lasting affection had engaged mine, and I could never think it returned with sufficient tenderness. 210

MIRANDA.

Think! But I speak of what we do without thinking, the natural effect of such a composition as mankind are of. Vanity is inconstancy. 215

Enter Beaumine.

LUCILIA. (*Aside.*)

Of which behold the very abstract! Lesbia must know this.

MIRANDA.

This wild creature here! And who the deuce expected him. 220

LUCILIA.

There was no need of expectation to make the blessing dear.

MIRANDA.

Psha, because I jested. Would he were hanged for coming.

LUCILIA.

Nay, now I shall believe you love him in earnest. 225

MIRANDA. (*Aside.*)

I'll swear, so shall I too. I was never so confounded in my life.—Love him, aye, I love him well

enough—anywhere else—but methinks here—I don't know—I wish he had not come.

LUCILIA.

Well, I'll leave you, for I believe he wishes so too, finding me here. [*Exit.*] 230

BEAUMINE. [*Aside.*]

A very odd reception. Maybe she does not know me again, but I'm sure Lucilia does, and this goes to Lesbia immediately. But no matter: I know how to make peace with her when I have settled my new conquest. 235

MIRANDA. (*Aside.*)

Wish she had not seen him here? What can that mean? Is she my rival too?

BEAUMINE.

I fear I am unwelcome, madam, though I had not ventured without your permission. 240

MIRANDA.

Pardon me, sir, I was persuading the lady to stay, the more to oblige you in return of this favor.

BEAUMINE.

The lady knew better how to oblige me.

MIRANDA.

I don't doubt but she knows much better how to please you. 245

BEAUMINE.

She has only put me in the way of being pleased. But that depends upon the fair Miranda, which if she design, she need only be herself again; indeed, that gravity is no more becoming than natural to you.

MIRANDA.

Why d'ye think I affect it? 250

BEAUMINE.

That I can't tell: whether you are displeased with seeing me or mightily pleased and have no mind to show it, those eyes must better inform me.

MIRANDA.

Whatever they say, I find you can make a favorable interpretation of it. 255

BEAUMINE.

I confess, madam, I love to be easy and to give everything the most advantageous sense it will bear. If it ben't the way to the truth, I am sure it is to happiness.

MIRANDA.

Giving yourself false hopes is the sure way to meet with disappointments. 260

BEAUMINE.

Not at all. Vanity gives a man confidence, and that's successful with the fair as well as the great.

MIRANDA.

Why, do you believe any woman ever loved a man because he had the vanity to fancy she did? 265

BEAUMINE.

At least it gives him a chance for being beloved, which he can never have without the courage to attempt. For example, madam, had I modestly said to myself, "Beaumine, thou'rt a very disagreeable fellow. Miranda can never like thee; 270 'tis in vain to hope it," I had certainly not come near you; you had thought of me no more; or I had lost the advantage of your thoughts, however favorable.

MIRANDA.

And you have the impudence to tell me you believe 275 I shall like you.

BEAUMINE.

And does not every man that tells you he likes you mean the same thing? But I beg your pardon, madam, I confess 'twas very indecent, so unmodish a thing as speaking truth to a lady. 280

MIRANDA.

Which is so far from offending me, you could not have obliged me more than by telling me your thoughts to give me the pleasure of disappointing you. And to show you how vain, how mistaken you are, how little an opinion I have of you, I 285 must tell you when you came in, I was thinking you the most fickle, inconstant, falsest thing in nature.

BEAUMINE.

Now cannot I help thinking you would not have troubled your head whether I was false or not, if 290 you had not been concerned in it.

MIRANDA.

And do you imagine I can like a man I have such an opinion of?

BEAUMINE.

We are naturally fond of our own resemblance, and by that rule, to gain Miranda's good graces, I can't 295 be too false or too *volage.*[9] (*Sings.*)

When present we'll love, when absent agree,
I think not of Iris, nor Iris of me.[10]

MIRANDA.

Nay, now you have vanquished. There's no resisting that, the very image of my own heart. I can make 300 the exchange without missing it. But not a word of sighing, dying, fidelity, constancy, or any of that dull form, for 'twill immediately be sensible of being out of its element and return upon the wing.

BEAUMINE.

And upon peril of losing mine, let me never hear 305 you have the least remembrance of me when I am from you; not a word of me in heroics to Lesbia.

MIRANDA.

For fear of spoiling your amour with her.

BEAUMINE.

What, jealous? That's against the very end of our agreement. But I don't care if we do clear accounts 310 to this day and begin upon a new score of roving.

MIRANDA.

In which we'll strive to outdo one another in extravagance. But first, how far you are engaged with Lesbia?

BEAUMINE.

That you may be judge yourself, whether she can 315 have any concern in me: know, she told me you had a penchant for my person.

MIRANDA.

By which I conclude she was jealous.

BEAUMINE.

And do you think then she would have ventured to let me know of so dangerous a rival? 320

MIRANDA.

'Twas in raillery no doubt.

BEAUMINE.

Aye indeed, she did rally enough upon it, that the gay, the free Miranda should be caught at last. Therefore, not only for fear I should suspect you of constancy, but if you would not be subject of her 325 mirth, speak of me for the future with more caution.

MIRANDA.

And Lesbia's jest, I suppose, has occasioned me this favor.

---

[9] *volage*] flighty or fickle (Fr.)

[10] When … me] from Mercury's song to Phaedra in Dryden's *Amphitryon* IV.490-91

BEAUMINE.

Why really, madam, I might protest and lie and swear I could neither eat nor rest since I saw you. 330 But if you'd have the truth, I have always found, among all other attractions, kindness* only has resistless charms, and by the means you've gained, secure your conquest.

MIRANDA.

A way by which most of your sex are lost. But why 335 may not you be as particular as I am? This plain dealing of yours has charmed me beyond all things, and sure 'tis as much out of the road for a woman's affection to be engaged by sincerity as a man's to be secured by kindness.* 340

BEAUMINE.

Aye indeed, you are seldom to be satisfied unless we engage for as much more love than we have as we are willing to release you from paying. But I am no dissembler, madam, and must confess my love for you is none of those violent passions that 345 will of course abate. 'Tis in so moderate a degree that even your fondness could not lessen it.

MIRANDA.

And mine so indifferent your sincerity can't disturb me. So without scruple, confess what interest Lucilia has in you. 350

BEAUMINE.

Really madam, she's at present very indifferent to me, but I believe I shall shortly have a violent passion for her. She's going to ruin an honest friend of mine, and I shall hate her heartily for it.

MIRANDA.

How will she ruin him? 355

BEAUMINE.

Marry him. How can a woman ruin a man else?

MIRANDA.

Oh mischievous! But to show you that I know she is not indifferent to you, she said herself you would wish she had not been here at your coming.

BEAUMINE. (*Aside.*)

And thereby hangs a tale.—Faith madam, she was 360 in the right on't. I had much rather have had you alone; she knew my thoughts and complied with 'em. I thank her, the first favor she ever did me or I ever wished from her. So now, I hope all past accounts are cleared. 365

MIRANDA.

And for the future. Beaumine,
(Sings.)
We'll neither believe what either can say,
So neither believing, can neither betray.[11]

BEAUMINE.

And at this rate our loves must be eternal; there's no danger of quarrels or satiety. 370

MIRANDA.

Aye, if all lovers had followed our example, we had not heard so many complaints of faithless nymphs and perjured swains.

BEAUMINE.

But they must be perpetually dangling at one another's elbows and, the little time they are 375 parted, inquiring after every action or step they take for fear they should go astray.

MIRANDA.

So tire one another when together and torment themselves asunder. And no wonder: they soon break a knot that with drawing too straight sits 380 uneasy upon them and is the weaker itself. It bursts upon the least irregular motion.

BEAUMINE.

Well madam, that we may profit by others' follies, I believe it's time to part before we are weary of one another. 385

MIRANDA.

For now we have told all our thoughts, we are in great danger of growing dull. Next time we meet, ten to one, but we shall be quite of another mind and so new again. In order to it, I'll give you a song made by a heroic lover of mine. Perhaps it may 390 infect you with sighing, whining, dying love.— Who's there? Desire the gentlewoman in the next room to walk in.

[Enter gentlewoman.]

You'll oblige us, madam, with the song I gave you last to learn. *Song.* 395
Well Beaumine, how does that affect you?

---

11 We'll … betray] from the same song in *Amphitryon* (IV.486-87)

BEAUMINE.

I melt, I languish, am all transport now, (*Sings a line of the song.*) "What shall I say to work upon thy soul!"

MIRANDA.

Oh most apish! How ridiculous a man appears 400 when he would cross nature! He may as well expect to be finely shaped by putting on another man's clothes because they fit well upon him they were made for, as to please by affecting the most agreeable humor* in another. It hangs as 405 awkwardly upon him and is as easily perceived not to be his own.

BEAUMINE.

Then I must e'en stay from you till I am so much forgot my own will be new again.

MIRANDA.

Which need not be long, I assure you: out of sight, 410 out of mind.

BEAUMINE.

A pleasant way of inviting me to return soon.
Thus whilst the artful sex in words deny,
The secret sense and their kind* looks comply.
    (*Exit.*)

MIRANDA.

Thus we gain lovers and secure our fame: 415
We promise nothing, and they nought can claim;
They fancy pleasures, when we speak of pain,
And hopes enough, their passion to maintain.

Exit.

Act III, scene i. The Public Walks.

Enter Lesbia and Lucilia.

LESBIA.

By his manner of speaking I could not imagine he would visit her; this is a new way to deceive by speaking truth.

LUCILIA.

A sure one: 'tis so little expected from a lover.

LESBIA.

I'll never forgive it him. What pretence can he have 5 to excuse this?

LUCILIA.

If he get off now, 'twill be a masterpiece of his art indeed.

LESBIA.

Impossible. I wish we may see Grandfoy here tonight; he said he was to meet Cleon in the walks, 10 and I would willingly have his advice how to behave myself now, before I see Beaumine.

LUCILIA.

I'm mistaken if that is not Beaumine coming this way with Phillabell.

LESBIA.

The very same, and gay as innocence itself. 15

LUCILIA.

There's no avoiding 'em now. They're so near, they see us.

LESBIA.

Well, I won't disappoint you, for I know you would be so peevish all this evening; if you should not speak to him now, there would be no enduring 20 you, though he was with you so lately.

LUCILIA.

You're mistaken. Though I never think I see him too often, I could have spared it now. Since Cleon is to be here, their meeting might prove of ill consequence, considering that coxcomb's design I 25 told you of. 'Tis not yet the time he appointed me to send my answer, but we'll go off soon and oblige them to go with us, if we can.

Enter Beaumine and Phillabell.

BEAUMINE.

So the friends are together, and all's out. Well, I must take the old way of complaining first when 30 we know ourselves in fault.

PHILLABELL.

I'm pleased at this unexpected good fortune. Madam, the sight of you gives me soft pleasures that compose my soul transported, now my happiness approaches, with my impatience of one 35 day's delay and joy to think it is but one.

BEAUMINE.

Indeed Lesbia, I did not imagine you had so much indiscretion, but women can no more forbear talking of their amours than an ill poet of his verses, though they equally expose their folly by 40 what they design to gratify their vanity with and usually prove as tiresome to their hearers, unless such as have ill nature enough to divert themselves with everything that's ridiculous in another.

LESBIA.

I don't know what you aim at, but I think indeed 45
women deserve to be laughed at that boast of any
kind thoughts for such faithless things as men are.

BEAUMINE.

You'll guess what I mean when I tell you I have
seen Miranda and know all you said to her.

LESBIA.

You'll know what I mean when I tell you I heard 50
that before and guess what you said to her.

BEAUMINE.

Really madam, so you may. You gave me cause
enough to suspect you had let her know of our
engagement, and I resolved to see her to find out
how far you had discovered.* I was never so out 55
of countenance in my life.

LESBIA.

'Twould have been a wonder to have seen that
indeed, for I'll swear you have an extraordinary
assurance.

BEAUMINE.

To be so laughed at, to hear you so ridiculed for 60
being overreached by a creature that professes
abusing everybody; you would have been ashamed
to have seen yourself so described, so mimicked,
so—I did not know what to say for myself or you.

LESBIA.

She abused you if she told you I said anything 65
positive.

BEAUMINE.

Positive! but such signs, such things— Oh Lesbia,
Lesbia, that you could be caught by such a shallow
artifice.

LESBIA.

I'm sorry, sir— 70

BEAUMINE.

Well, you know I love you and can easily forgive
you anything, but I hope you'll be more cautious
hereafter.

LESBIA.

I think, Beaumine, 'tis time our engagement were
made known to everybody. 75

BEAUMINE.

Aye, Aye,
We'll write each other's name on every bark;
The winds shall bear our vows to distant climes,
And Echo every tender word rebound.

LESBIA.

Good romantic sir, will you condescend for once 80
to answer directly a little intelligible sense?

BEAUMINE.

Oh! That were to wrong my love! A lover and
speak sense! To answer in cross purposes, in broken
murmurs, and disjointed words expresses passion.

LESBIA.

Do you think I'll be always put off with this 85
trifling, Beaumine?

BEAUMINE.

Oh! Mighty things have been produced from
trifles. The cackling of geese* once saved the
capitol. Men's promises have gained many a fair
one, and women's favors lost 'em many lovers. 90
Trifles, trifles all, but great effects.

LESBIA.

Is not that to tell me I have lost you by what you
think a trifle?

BEAUMINE.

No, to show you I don't think your favors a trifle
and have no mind you should lose me, I would 95
have 'em still* favors, the more to engage me and
not turn all to duty.

LESBIA.

Had you talked thus to me at first, Beaumine—

BEAUMINE.

You had lost a great deal of pleasure, Lesbia, and
laughed at me for a fool. 100

LESBIA.

Which is something better than a knave.

BEAUMINE.

Good words, good words, madam. Knaves are
precise, protesting, plotting, thinking creatures, but
you'll find this mad, maggoty fellow a very honest
fellow at last. 105

LESBIA.

At last.

BEAUMINE.

Well, if you'll have me marry you just now, I'll run
and fetch a priest immediately. (*Going.*)

LESBIA.

I think you're mad in earnest. Why Beaumine!

BEAUMINE.

Oh gad, I forgot. The canonical hour* is over. 110
(Sings.) "But if I ever play the fool, dear Cloris, I
am thine."

(*Turning to Phillabell [and Lucilia].*) Well, what can you have to say to one another all this while? You are agreed upon the premises, are convinced of that mutual affection, and to answer for the future can only serve to call the sincerity of the present in question.

LUCILIA.

Why so, sir? I think 'tis rather a proof of the present, a sign we find it so great we believe it will always last.

BEAUMINE.

Aye madam, but if I hear a man swear to a thing done out of his sight, though it may happen to be true, I shall think he has a large conscience and scarce believe him in what he might know. And indeed, we may as well swear to anything done in Japan; as for our future inclinations, they are no less out of our knowledge or power.

PHILLABELL.

I think a man that knows himself not to be of a wavering temper, if he has well considered the merit of his choice, may venture to promise for his constancy without prejudice to his honor.

BEAUMINE.

But to what end should he promise? Will it secure his inclination one minute the longer? Oh, but it secures the woman he would engage.—Madam, my friend's a very honest fellow; I believe he thinks what he says, but 'tis your fault if you take his word for what he cannot know. We had rather you should rely upon the power of your charms, and if the ladies will force us to add perjury to our natural levity, the sin must lie at their door.

LESBIA.

'Tis a folly indeed to rely upon their word for future inclinations, since few of 'em can answer for their future actions.

BEAUMINE.

Really madam, our actions are generally guided by our inclinations; this is not an age of much mortification. But are not you for walking, ladies?

LUCILIA.

I'm a little tired. What think you of going off, Lesbia?

LESBIA.

I'll wait upon you, madam.

PHILLABELL.

We'll attend to your coach, ladies.

LUCILIA.

Maybe you would not leave the walks so soon.

PHILLABELL.

Well, come back and take another turn or two. Tomorrow early as the day I'll visit you and hope your wishes, my fair bride, will meet me.

LUCILIA.

You never yet could come too early for 'em.

BEAUMINE.

What a deal of tenderness are they going tomorrow to destroy! (*Sings.*)

Would you, would you love the nymph forever,
Never, never, never, never, never let her be your wife.

Exeunt.

[Scene ii. The same.]

Enter Grandfoy, Cleon, and Bonsot.

CLEON.

Let me expire. My false nymph, going off with her lover! Before my face! In the very place where I sent her word I would be tonight! The inexpressible confidence of a faithless woman!

BONSOT.

Nay Brother, don't be angry. I dare say she meant no affront to you, only to make him believe she don't care for you.

CLEON.

Then she's the greater jilt, Brother.

BONSOT.

Humph, pugh, Lord, you will think the worst of everything! Do but look how loath she is to leave you; she stands still all the while she goes.

GRANDFOY.

That's an extraordinary art indeed.

CLEON.

I don't doubt her affection. But the fellow's rich, if she consulted her honor or happiness. Is such a *grossier*[12] as Phillabell to be preferred to me? I protest, I almost pity her.

GRANDFOY.

Aye, Aye, e'en let the weakness of her choice be her punishment. 'Tis below your resentment.

---

12 *grossier*] coarse, crude fellow (Fr.)

CLEON.

Nay, 'tis not that I value the creature, but then to disappoint my rival will be a good revenge for his presuming to hope where I had once made my pretensions; therefore, he shall see all her letters. I can't but think how sillily the fellow will look. Ha, ha, ha.

GRANDFOY.

But you don't consider what a kindness you'll do your rival in preventing his marriage with such an undistinguishing coquette; I fancy they'll better revenge you upon one another.

CLEON.

Egad, thou art in the right, Coz.

BONSOT.

Aye faith, that's well said. I hate mischief. And then you know, Brother, 'twould vex you more if she should refuse you after you had shown so much concern for her.

CLEON.

Impertinent suppositions! To show you the impossibility of it, I'm now positively resolved to pursue my design.

BONSOT.

Hey, why, I meant, in case, d'ye see— Pugh, Brother, you are so hasty. I would have said, psha, do not be so ill-natured. But I mean, that if, suppose, he should be very fond of the honor of being your rival—aye, d'ye mind that now? and so force her willingly to marry him.

CLEON.

Then would I, after they are married, expose her letters to the whole tawn; that will be an immoderate pleasure, rat[13] me.

BONSOT.

That might breed quarrels now between a man and his wife.

CLEON.

She'll be the more sensible of the ill judgment of her choice.

BONSOT.

Faugh.

GRANDFOY.

Oh but that is not *en cavalier,** 'twill be looked upon as vanity.

BONSOT.

Aye this will do—but now I think on't better, I don't believe he'll be angry. Being a very humble sort of a man, he's likely to be proud that you should be vain of his wife's letters.

CLEON.

Vain! No, no, the town know well enough, if I would boast, there are ladies of more wit and better judgment than Lucilia that have afforded me *de quoi*.[14]

BONSOT.

Aye Brother, the lady, you know, that never worked in her life and made you a cravat all with her own hands.

GRANDFOY.

What, she drew the picture of his cravat?

CLEON.

Oh no, she really made the very lace I have on. Now you know women of a great deal of wit never work, but as love once raised a blacksmith to a painter,[15] so it made her descend from her nicer* speculations to this mechanic employment, that I might wear the product of her fingers.

GRANDFOY.

Oh wonderful effect of passion, I confess.

Beaumine and Phillabell enter unseen.

CLEON.

Aye, if you consider the elegancy of the work.

GRANDFOY.

Oh extremely elegant.

CLEON.

That's a very fine ring. I never saw thee wear it before. Some lady's favor* undeniably. Come, confess, confess.

---

13 tawn … rat] town, rot; Cibber's characters often speak with open o's, represented by a's (cf. *The Relapse* below).

14 *de quoi*] of what [shall go unspoken] (Fr.); a euphemism for sexual favors

15 blacksmith … painter] Quentin Massys (c. 1465-1530), Flemish landscape and portrait painter, who worked as a blacksmith but became an artist after he fell in love with an artist's daughter

GRANDFOY.

Why, yes faith, 'twas a lady's favor.

CLEON.

She must be of quality* by the value of the present.

GRANDFOY.

'Twas given her by another lover, his first present too. 80

CLEON.

Oh most obliging! But how did he bear it?

[Beaumine] sees the ring.

BONSOT.

Aye, if he should hear of it now, what a deal of mischief might come on't.

GRANDFOY.

I laughed heartily at the pains he took and the presents he made, that she might be the less 85 afflicted at the loss.

CLEON.

Kind cully! So, she pretended she had lost it?

GRANDFOY.

Aye, the jest is— (*Seeing Beaumine.*) Prithee Cleon, turn this way.

CLEON.

This is the place I appointed to send the answer 90 of my letter.

GRANDFOY.

Damn your letter, prithee come.

Exit Cleon and Grandfoy in confusion.

BONSOT.

Hey day, what vagary's this? He's afraid of somebody, I think.

BEAUMINE.

Hah! This confirms me. Damned jilt.

BONSOT. 95

And this gentleman seems angry. I have a good mind to stay and hear what he says that I may prevent their quarrelling* together whilst they're asunder.

PHILLABELL.

How now, Beaumine! What's the matter?

BEAUMINE.

Did you know him that turned off just now? 100

PHILLABELL.

Very well. 'Tis my coxcombly rival, Cleon. Don't you know him?

BEAUMINE.

Pox of your rival. T'other, he with the ring I'd know.

BONSOT.

Aye, 'tis so. 105

PHILLABELL.

But why so fretful?

BEAUMINE.

Plague! Do you know him? Can't you answer?

PHILLABELL.

Why, I do not know him, but what if I did?

BEAUMINE.

Oh dissembling witch!

PHILLABELL.

What's this passion for? Who has offended you? 110

BONSOT.

I hope, sir, you are not angry with the gentleman you inquire after; he's a relation of mine, sir, and a very honest gentleman. I dare say, if he offends anybody willfully, it must be without his knowledge.

BEAUMINE.

Then you may give him the knowledge, sir, that 115 he willfully wears a ring I may make bold to take from him, sir.

BONSOT.

Oh Lord, sir, as for that, if you have a mind for the ring, I'll engage 'twill be at your service. My cousin's a generous person that does not value such 120 a trifle nor the person he had it from, in comparison of your friendship, I dare say, sir.

BEAUMINE.

Why, do you know the person he had it from, sir?

BONSOT.

Aye sir, anybody may know her: a mere common creature. She's kept* indeed by a coxcomb, a soft- 125 headed cully.

BEAUMINE.

You know him too, sir, I suppose.

BONSOT.

A fellow not worth knowing—but the wench is very fond of my cousin, and a man does not know how to deny a woman. 130

BEAUMINE.

Very well, sir—

BONSOT.

I tell you the plain truth to show you that you need

not quarrel* with my cousin about the ring, for he does not care this _____* for it, nor the lady neither. You may have them both, if you please, sir. 135

BEAUMINE.

You are very impertinently civil, sir.

BONSOT.

Oh Lord, sir, nay I must say that for myself. I am a very civil, good-natured fellow. I can't abide to see people when they are at quiet and in good humor quarrelling with one another. 140

PHILLABELL.

That's a strange sight indeed, sir.

BONSOT.

Aye sir, I hope you'll persuade your friend not to be in a passion for nothing, about something of a ring and a lady, a jilt not worth his concern, sir.

BEAUMINE.

That I am very well convinced of, sir. Your cousin 145 and the lady and the ring may go to the Devil for me, as they please, sir.

BONSOT.

Oh sir, your very humble servant. That's all I desire, that they may have leave to go to the Devil in quiet, sir, I have no more to say, sir. I'll be sure 150 to tell him how civil a person you are, and I don't doubt he'll have the same complaisance for you, begin your journey when you will. He's none of the hottest choleric fellows; whenever he's in a heat against any, 'tis in cold blood. Your very humble 155 servant, sir. I'm extremely obliged to you indeed, sir. (*Exit.*)

PHILLABELL.

What a soft officious fool this is! But prithee, what concern have you in the ring you talked of?

BEAUMINE.

By Heaven, the very same I gave to Lesbia. 160

PHILLABELL.

Ha, ha, ha, ha, ha! Why, thou can'st not be jealous, what of Lesbia! The fear of losing thee, you know, will keep her faithful.

BEAUMINE.

Who could have suspected?

PHILLABELL.

Oh never think it: she that valued not the loss but 165 as a sad presage thy dearer heart would follow. Ha, ha, ha!

BEAUMINE.

Prithee leave thy fooling.

PHILLABELL.

Were she a wife, indeed. But Lesbia, she whom nothing could console but thy repeated vows of 170 never changing. Ha, ha, ha!

BEAUMINE.

Lesbia false! Where shall we look for truth?

PHILLABELL.

Not in a woman that has sacrificed her honor, but such a one as my Lucilia. Oh what a treasure! This makes me more impatient to be master of it; 'tis an 175 age till tomorrow. Would she this night were mine.

BEAUMINE.

Why, truly when a man is to be hanged, a night's reprieve gives him but so much time to torment himself with the apprehension. Oh I could curse the whole jilting, hypocritical sex. 180

PHILLABELL.

They are all Lesbias, but thou mayst rail. Thy malice cannot reach Lucilia, the abstract of all goodness, so true, so innocent. I had much ado to persuade her t'other day that any woman could be false to her husband or even pretend to love 185 where she did not.

BEAUMINE.

And you believe her? Is there any of 'em that cannot talk of sincerity?

PHILLABELL.

Oh! 'Tis stamped on all her actions. Then she's so reserved, she hated Cleon for his impudence. He has 190 made her blush a thousand times with the liberty of his discourse and actions.—Is not that her governess?

BEAUMINE.

I think so.

Enter Lysetta with a letter, which, going to hide as she sees Phillabell, she lets fall accidentally.

LYSETTA.

This is the place, but I see Phillabell here! Then I must not stay for Cleon. (*Exit.*) 195

BEAUMINE.

She's in mighty haste. What have we here? A billet-doux!

PHILLABELL.

I believe 'tis Lysetta's. You had best call after her.

BEAUMINE.

The direction gives me a curiosity to open it. (*Reads it to himself.*) Nay now, Phillabell, I'm made 200 a convert to marriage.

PHILLABELL.

What can have wrought such a miracle!

BEAUMINE.

Why a proof of thy Lucilia's virtue and sincerity. Do you know her hand?

PHILLABELL.

Perfectly. 205

BEAUMINE.

Is this like it?

PHILLABELL.

The same, to Cleon. Some severe repulse I suppose.

BEAUMINE.

Aye really, 'tis pity to use the poor man so severely.

PHILLABELL.

She never thinks she can use him ill, or me well 210 enough. (*Reads.*) "You are ignorant what force the first engagements have, and you as little know my heart, when you imagine it capable of loving anything—but you." Am I awake! "If I marry Phillabell, 'tis to obey a cruel father, who will 215 sacrifice me to his interest—" The rest is yet more baseness. It can't be Lucilia's.

BEAUMINE.

No, no, Lucilia's! You know she hates the impudent fellow, for making her blush so often.

PHILLABELL.

I can scarce credit my own eyes. 220

BEAUMINE.

Oh! Why should you against so much sincerity? 'Tis stamped on all her actions—I dare swear 'tis in this—she can't think it possible for a woman to be false to her husband or pretend to love where she does not. There's a treasure! 'Tis an age till 225 tomorrow; shan't we have a wedding tonight, Phil?

PHILLABELL.

I'll not believe it.

BEAUMINE.

Never, never: were she a woman that had sacrificed her honor, indeed. But one so reserved as thy Lucilia. Ha, ha, ha! Prithee let's have the wedding 230 tonight, Phil. Come, hang delays.

PHILLABELL.

Torment me. Am I thus paid for all my doting love and generous trust?

BEAUMINE.

The sure reward of trusting. What should hinder people from being false, when they are certain not 235 to be suspected?

PHILLABELL.

'Tis a base principle.

BEAUMINE.

A woman's principle.

PHILLABELL.

Nay, I can join with thee now in railing.

BEAUMINE.

Let's bid defiance together to the whole ensnaring, 240 damned, lying sex.

PHILLABELL.

Agreed, and yet there was such pleasure in believing, I could almost wish I had not been undeceived; had she but truth, she were an angel.

BEAUMINE.

Maybe so, for I am sure she could not be a woman. 245 Betwixt you and I, what a couple of coxcombs we are to dote upon what we despise! I see you love this Lucilia still, and to confess the truth (now neither of us can laugh at t'other) I find Lesbia's infidelity strikes deeper at my heart than I thought 250 any of her sex could reach. She has in gaining and losing spoiled more of my good humor than the whole kind could be worth in exchange.

BEAUMINE.

Oh! A mere liking only. She is young and airy.[d]

PHILLABELL.

And new. 255

BEAUMINE.

Aye, if you could add kind.* I do not know but those two monosyllables might have more force to make me bear Lesbia's inconstancy than all Seneca's morals.[16] But there is an old mistress of mine that still rivals them all, the faithful bottle. Shall we try it? 260

PHILLABELL.

I care not if I do, for I fear I shall never forget Lucilia but when I forget myself.

---

16 Seneca's morals] L. Annæus Seneca (d. 65 CE), stoic philosopher and dramatist famous for his moralizing

BEAUMINE.

Come along then, this is a mistress we can both
enjoy without being jealous of one another.
Love's niggard spirit must the bliss engross;   265
Companions would the happiness destroy.
But wine does all its charming pleasure lose,
Unless we generously share the joy.

Exeunt.

[Scene iii. The same.]

Enter Lucilia and Lysetta.

LYSETTA.

Aye, this is the unlucky place.

LUCILIA.

There's no hopes of finding it. I am undone. I shall
be exposed to the whole town; nay, for ought I
know, Phillabell himself may have found it.

LYSETTA.

This comes of a woman's taking pains to do good,   5
laboring out of her own vocation.—Oh! Madam,
there's Cleon coming this way. Now you may e'en
carry your message yourself, that it may be sure not
to fail.

LUCILIA.

'Twill be the likelier to fail. I cannot speak such   10
things as you made me write, or if I should,
'twould be with so much constraint, he must
perceive it false. You know I can't dissemble.

LYSETTA.

I know you have practiced it as little as any
woman, but trust nature, madam, trust nature and   15
consider, a young husband will do you a great deal
of good. Your sincerity? e'en have none at all. 'Tis
not a virtue for this designing world. Nay on my
conscience, I don't know why it should not be
thought as much a vice to prostitute our minds to   20
every fool as our bodies. Truth is the chastity of
the soul and should not be exposed to any man
that would put it to the proof.—Here he is. Have
a care of your metaphorical chastity, or you may
be forced to keep the real one for Philabell. And   25
if that does not frighten you—

LUCILIA.

Peace, fool.

Enter Cleon.

CLEON.

I hope I have not missed the letter, for I cannot
positively determine whether I shall condescend to
hinder her marriage or not till I know how she   30
expresses herself. Here in person! This is excess of
civility indeed. I always thought her well bred.—
This unexpected favor, madam—

LUCILIA.

And undesigned, sir, I assure you.

LYSETTA.

Oh sir, the most unfortunate accident. My lady   35
sent me with a letter to you, but meeting with one
here I was afraid should see me, I dropped it in
my surprise. My lady, in a fright, came hither to
look for it, but in vain. 'Twas gone, and nobody
knows what mischief may be done with it.   40

CLEON.

Was the subject of it dangerous?

LUCILIA.

Indeed it was.

LYSETTA.

It complained of your injustice in suspecting my
lady's love, because she was forced to marry
another, and said such kind things of hereafter.   45

CLEON.

Was there a superscription?

LYSETTA.

Aye, aye, your name was upon it.

CLEON.

Oh very well. That will be an excuse for what it
contains to those that know me.

LUCILIA. [*Aside.*]

Ridiculous vanity! There need not much pains, I   50
find, to persuade this thing he is beloved.

CLEON.

So madam, you marry Phillabell to express your
aversion very emphatically! But how do you show
your affection for me?

LUCILIA.

By not marrying you.   55

CLEON.

That is a favor I confess, but methinks not very
particular. I've a world of rivals in it.

LUCILIA.

Oh that can't be avoided, but you are the only
person I particularly resolve never to marry.

CLEON.

As a proof of your fondness.

LYSETTA.

Aye sir, my lady fears she should have such a world of rivals, she could never be easy with you.

CLEON.

Oh Lard, madam, there's no danger. But really I think, when a man is singularly eminent, he should never marry, for he injures the person he bestows himself upon, by exposing her to the envy of your sex, and the rest by giving 'em despair. It was worth the care of the government in this scarcity of persons of merit to forbid monopolizing 'em.

LUCILIA.

Indeed I would not injure my sex so much as to monopolize such an extraordinary person as Cleon. (*Aside.*) This fool can't be flattered too grossly.

CLEON.

Well madam, since you are pleased to prefer me to Phillabell in your esteem, I won't disturb his imaginary felicity. But I was thinking it might not be amiss to show some of your obliging letters to my friends, that it might justify to the world (who might judge you by your choice in a husband) the niceness* of your wit and judgment.

LUCILIA.

Oh by no means, sir. They'll conclude you would not have done it but by my consent and take it as an effect of my vanity.

CLEON.

You are in the right, madam. There may be cause to suspect it, and vanity is of all follies the most odious.

LUCILIA. [*Aside.*]

And yet he thinks himself agreeable!—Nay really I think vanity a very harmless thing; it does nobody any hurt. Those it deceives are the better for it, having no other quality to make 'em satisfied with 'emselves. The rest of the world know, that like all other artificial lights, 'tis only to supply the defect of the natural, and as they burn the brighter in the darkest nights, so it appears most where there's least merit.

CLEON.

Justly observed, madam. Vanity is a very charitable flatterer. I have known it encourage an unbred, ill-dressed fellow to make love* to a lady that everybody knew I was well with.

LUCILIA.

That might make him despair of pleasing her indeed, but I hope the lady judged better of your merits.

CLEON.

Yes faith, madam, she judged him blockhead enough for that dull animal a husband, avoided me to secure her virtue, and carried him out of town to show she was ashamed of him. And if that did not mortify his vanity—

LUCILIA.

And secure him from jealousy, it showed her discretion as great as her judgment.

CLEON.

No, strike me dead, it had been wiser to have stayed and given him a cause of jealousy. The only excuse a woman can have for marrying a man she does not love is to secure her pleasure with the man she does. 'Tis a way among the women of condition to contrive for their interest before they marry, and their inclination after. But the rustic had infected her with his stupid society. 'Twas only want* of modish conversation, a finished good breeding.

LUCILIA.

Well, to show you I am better bred and not to be spoiled by the stupid conversation of a husband, I'll always have it with the ceremony of a new and the coldness of an old acquaintance, never have the same diversions, and seldom the same bed.

CLEON.

Very courtly, upon honor. Then for your lover, madam, he must make one in all your avowed pleasures for a blind to the secret stolen ones, be always with you at cards, hand you to your coach from the play, be very free together in public to appear more innocent. Then he must be very intimate with your husband to make him the more secure of you—and the town the more suspicious.

LUCILIA.

I don't doubt but with your instructions to prove as modish a mistress as a wife. I promise never to avoid you to secure my virtue.

CLEON.

Then I have no obstacle to fear, for all the women

I have addressed to would never see me again, 135
knowing the only way to conquer was to fly. I shall
certainly attack, madam, and then you will not
find your virtue in danger—but no virtue at all, I
am positive.

LUCILIA.

Indeed, I positively believe there will be no virtue 140
at all in the case. I shall not once struggle with my
inclinations to resist you.

CLEON.

Ah, ah, it would be in vain, but a little for
decorum.—The poor thing is strangely fond.—
Well madam, that I may be happy hereafter, I will 145
be secret now and, if you please, appear at your
wedding more gay than the bridegroom.

LUCILIA.

You'll be a welcome guest. But I dare stay no
longer. Live upon hopes.—Substantial food
enough for thee: 150
Vain, empty things, more solid could not bear;
Who're nothing else themselves must live on air.
(*Exit.*)

CLEON.

Well I profess this is a very generous age. These
married men are at the expense of what we don't
care to do, and we in return do for them what they 155
never could do.
In mutual charities we pass our lives:
They keep* our mistresses, we please their wives!

Act IV, scene [i]. Miranda's lodgings.

Enter Miranda and her woman. *

MIRANDA.

Oh aye, I'm within to her. Desire her to walk up.

Exit woman.

This is a very quick return of my visit. How fond
Lesbia and I grow of late; there are not such dear
friends and constant companions in the world as
women that are jealous of one another. 5

Enter Lesbia.

Oh my dear, this is so obliging.

LESBIA.

I could not deny myself the satisfaction any longer,

and I hope you'll take it kindly, for there's nobody I
desire more to be believed a friend to than Miranda.

MIRANDA.

And nobody, I assure you, desires more to be yours. 10
But how can I think you mine when you are not free
with me? You always speak with so much reserve.

LESBIA.

Indeed, if I had any secret to impart, I should do
it freely, but since Beaumine has been to visit you,
no doubt he has convinced you, you had no reason 15
to think there was anything between us. You may
engage with him as you think fit, without any
injury to me.

MIRANDA.

I engage with him! Lord, I but jested. Sure you did
not think me serious. I had a curiosity indeed to 20
know your amour, but did you imagine I could
have any design upon such a vain, pert,
unaccountable creature?

LESBIA. (*Aside.*)

This is certainly affected. I'll be hanged if the traitor
has not cautioned her too against trusting me.—You 25
gave him much better epithets once, Miranda, but
instead of thinking him that charming fellow, I find
now you extremely dislike him.

MIRANDA.

No extremes indeed; he's perfectly indifferent to
me. 30

LESBIA.

'Tis true, that's all he deserves to be. I see nothing
extraordinary in him.

MIRANDA.

You thought much better of him once too, Lesbia.
(*Aside.*) Now have I a shrewd suspicion this
faithless swain has made us distrust one another 35
that he might the better deceive us both. Well, if
it is so, I'm resolved to torment her and be
revenged of him.—Well my dear, since you assure
me you have no concern in him, I'll confess my
weakness that 'twas with all the difficulty 40
imaginable I constrained myself for your sake not
to make a return to such tender, engaging things
as I thought him uncapable of saying.

LESBIA. [*Aside.*]

Oh villain!—No doubt he can say what he pleases,
madam. 45

MIRANDA.

Oh, but in a manner so persuading— And yet, till you confirmed it, I would not believe him, though he vowed he had no love for you and told me all you said to him of me.

LESBIA. [*Aside.*]

Traitor!—As a friend, Miranda, I advise you not 50 to rely too much upon what he tells you, for to my knowledge, you are not the only person he makes addresses to.

MIRANDA.

Nor is he the only I'll receive addresses from. (*Sings.*) "He's fickle and false, and there we 55 agree."17 We shall have the more adventures to entertain one another with, so be diverting always, always new, and I'll engage to secure him the more by not endeavoring to confine him.

LESBIA.

Secure him! Sure you forget you're engaged to 60 Constant.

MIRANDA.

No, but I'm in hopes very soon to torment him out of his love or his senses, that I may have my liberty.

LESBIA.

Faugh, now I find you jest indeed.

MIRANDA.

The D—'s in me, I think, I'm so possessed with 65 this giddy humor. It gives a tincture to my most weighty affairs. But if I could look languishing, and sigh, "Oh the dear charming man! There are no joys, no life without him!" 'twould not half express my heart now I have found he's not insensible. And 70 then you know his fortune's very considerable; I can't see how I can do better.

LESBIA.

Whether you are in earnest or no, Miranda, I must tell you seriously it won't be for your reputation to receive from a man of his wild character. 75

MIRANDA.

Really! I'll swear I should not have thought so, having met him at your lodgings.

LESBIA.

I intend to get rid of him as soon as I can.

---

17 He's … agree] Mercury's song to Phaedra, *Amphitryon* IV.484 (slightly modified)

MIRANDA.

Oh! If everybody throws him off, I'm resolved to receive him, for by being so scandalously general, 80 he'll be forced to be particular, and 'tis many a pious man's case, who would never have been honest if he had not lost his credit, never virtuous if his appetites had not decayed. 'Tis the best thing you can do for his reformation and my happiness. 85

LESBIA.

Well, well, madam, however you flatter yourself, I don't doubt but you'll find yourself as unhappy with him as he has made others. So, your servant madam. I shan't trouble you more with my counsel, but you'll repent— 90

MIRANDA.

What? Nay Lesbia, I can't let you go now. 'Tis so obliging to be moved at this rate for your friend's good. Come, come, had not you better confess what this concern enough discovers.* If you would be sincere with me, I could tell you a secret worth 95 two of yours and would give you more satisfaction than all your own art or resentment ever can.

LESBIA.

Perhaps I could tell you something, too, that would undeceive you, but I have no great encouragement from the use you made of what I 100 hinted before for your advantage, repeating it to Beaumine, and ridiculing me for it.

MIRANDA.

The lying toad! May I never have a secret of my own worth keeping or of another's worth telling if I said one word of it. But 'twas a wonder I did 105 not, for if I discover anything of myself that can make a jest, out it comes at all adventures. But when I am thoroughly trusted, though with a jest, I can keep it without bursting and faithfully will, I promise you. 110

LESBIA.

Then I will own to you, Beaumine and I are so solemnly engaged that if he has made you any proposal, he's the most perfidious man on earth.

MIRANDA.

Nay, then 'tis past jesting, and I must tell you, what I said was only to try you. All his discourse to me 115 was a mere gallantry and with his usual gaiety and humor. Yet by the care I find he has taken to hinder us from confiding in one another, I apprehend he may have some farther design.

LESBIA.

Then if you've none upon him, you may assist me in one I have of consequence. 120

MIRANDA.

With all my heart, for whatever little inclinations I may have, they only amuse me for the present but the more endear Constant to my serious thought, whose plain dealing and true affection I find nowhere equaled and will get the better of my fickleness at last. 125

LESBIA.

But that I desire you to disguise from Beaumine and to pretend you are dissatisfied with your uncle's choice, which will encourage him to declare himself if he has any serious designs, and you carry it on handsomely. 130

MIRANDA.

Let me alone for that. I have acted an indifference for Constant long enough to be perfect in't.

Enter Miranda's woman.

WOMAN.

A gentleman, madam, that calls himself Bonsot, inquires if you are here. 135

MIRANDA.

Oh, by all means let him come.

[Exit woman.]

That creature can never be unentertaining; if we can furnish no occasion for his good nature to do mischief in, the elegancy of his bulls must divert us. 140

Enter Bonsot.

BONSOT.

Since you command me to do myself this honor, I hope, madam, you'll forgive my intruding without your leave, where I have no business, being 'tis a concern of consequence brings me.

MIRANDA.

Then it seems, sir, you have business here. 145

BONSOT.

Aye, with this lady, madam. I was to wait on you at your lodgings and was told you were at Miranda's, so having something to say to you, I came to let you know it because I can't inform you of it there.ᵉ

MIRANDA.

Pray use your liberty, sir. 150

BONSOT.

Your very humble servant. Why look you, madam, my brother sending me, I came of my own accord to desire you will tell your friend Lucilia that he don't know but he's very certain Phillabell found the last letter she writ to him. For I saw him just in the place where it was lost, mightily concerned at a paper he had in his hand. I knew by his voice he was in a passion, but he was not within hearing. 155

LESBIA.

I thought you heard his voice.

BONSOT.

Aye madam, but I could not tell what he said, for though I was pretty near, 'twas at a good distance. 160

LESBIA.

Well sir, I'll be sure to tell her what you don't know, but are very certain of.

BONSOT.

That will be very kind, madam, but if I could meet with him, I warrant I'd appease him. 165

Enter woman.

WOMAN.

A gentleman below, madam, desires to wait on you.

MIRANDA.

Who is it?

WOMAN.

The young brisk gentleman that I told your ladyship would make a rare gallant for you when you are married, but he looks sullen enough now for a husband. 170

MIRANDA.

Beaumine, on my life. Let him come up.

Exit woman.

Now if you'll step into that closet,* you may be witness of the whole scene. 175

LESBIA.

With all my heart. This is lucky, but should not Bonsot retire too?

MIRANDA.

No, he may stay if he'll be sure not to discover* your being here.

BONSOT.

You need not fear me, madam. I never discover a   180
secret, unless it should happen to be something I
don't know.

MIRANDA.

In! In! He's coming!

Enter Beaumine.

BEAUMINE.

I was told, madam, Lesbia was here.

MIRANDA.

She's just gone.   185

BEAUMINE.

Do you know whither, madam?

BONSOT.

No sir, I can assure you she does not know.

MIRANDA.

Now, do you think to make me jealous, or is it to
make yourself new? It is indeed extremely new but
no very taking way of addressing to a woman by   190
showing a concern for another.

BEAUMINE.

Faith madam, the concern I have for her at present
need disturb nobody but myself, for I do hate her
heartily.

MIRANDA.

Which would not disturb you, if you had not   195
rather love her heartily.

BONSOT.

Nay, why so madam? I don't believe the gentleman
had rather love her, but a man may love a woman
that he hates, whether he will or not, and then 'tis
not his fault.   200

MIRANDA.

So you have mended the matter.

BEAUMINE.

A man can't bear to be imposed upon.

MIRANDA.

And now, can a woman impose upon a man when
they have no interest in one another, as you would
have me believe?   205

BEAUMINE.

Damn her, I shall be an extravagant lover indeed
to lose a new mistress for grief that I have lost an
old one.

BONSOT.

There you are too hard again, madam. Mayn't a
woman impose upon a man, merely out of a jilting   210
nature, though she have no interest at all in it?
Especially if she finds him fond and credulous.

BEAUMINE.

I have a rare advocate.—Well madam, in anger as
well as in wine there is truth. I confess, Lesbia once
had such an interest in me as would have cost the   215
best part of my possessions to satisfy. But thanks
to the virtue of her sex, she has forfeited.

MIRANDA.

What, a debt upon your estate?

BEAUMINE.

Upon my liberty, the most unreasonable of debts.
But I'm released and——seized again by another. But   220
there's no more bond and judgments against me.
I shall only be your prisoner at large; you may call
me in when you please, Miranda.

MIRANDA.

How can I trust you when Lesbia, that had so fast
confined, could not secure you? Come Beaumine,   225
honestly own you broke loose from her to give
yourself to me. 'Twill be far the better compliment,
and more generous to her than to wrong her every
way.

BONSOT.

Really, the gentleman seems to me a very honest   230
gentleman, that would not wrong any lady unless
it were in a just cause. I warrant if he had not been
in love with you or somebody else, he would never
have forsaken her, but when a greater merit claims
his heart, d'ye see, a man has right on his side to   235
do wrong to the less worthy.

MIRANDA.

Most solidly and eloquently argued.

BEAUMINE.

'Tis such a well-meaning blunderer.—I'm
extremely obliged to you, sir.

BONSOT.

Not at all, sir, I always endeavor to make a right   240
understanding between any persons that I am
acquainted with, though they are absolute strangers
to me.

BEAUMINE.

Ha, ha, ha! Very charitably done indeed, sir.—But

madam, on my honor I have not injured Lesbia. 245
Hah, I feel my liberty: "Lighter by what I've lost,
I tread on air." Have a care of yourself, Miranda:
she has left a plaguy deal of love upon my hands,
and if you should be forced to bear it all—

MIRANDA.

I dare undertake it, like Æsop's choice of the bread: 250
though the heaviest burden at first, being our
constant subsistence, 'twill waste every day, and
soon be light enough.[18]

BEAUMINE.

Then you must resolve to have no other subsistence.

MIRANDA.

Oh such a dry diet! a little variety to make it relish 255
the better. But if you are for devouring it so fast,
let's e'en make but one meal on't: marry, and there's
an end. What think you of that, Beaumine?

BEAUMINE.

Think? Aye faith, we must e'en do it without
thinking, or we shall never have the courage. 260

MIRANDA.

Nay, but I'm serious.

BEAUMINE.

What, before we're married? Time enough after.
This is a time for gaiety and joy. Hah, my fair
bride, here let me plight my vows on this soft
hand. 265

Constant enters here unseen.

CONSTANT.

So close!

BEAUMINE.

But now I think on't, there's a matrimonial rival
in the case. He'll certainly forbid the banns.

MIRANDA.

Ah, name him not. I am so sick of his fulsome,
whining stuff. 270

BEAUMINE.

I'm afraid there's more love than you'll confess, by
what I have heard of the matter.

---

18 Æsop's ... enough] In this popular story, Aesop goes on
a journey with fellow slaves, who make fun of him for
choosing to carry a heavy load of bread. He proves wisest, however, because his load becomes lighter each time
they stop to eat.

MIRANDA.

They talk of putting us together indeed, but sure
you're more a man of this age than to think love a
consequence of marriage. 275

BONSOT.

Aye pox, love is never any part of the concern in
marriage. Some indeed marry only for love, but
then—

BEAUMINE.

Aye madam, 'tis sometimes the cause of it. Love
has many extravagant effects. 280

MIRANDA.

His love may be the cause of it, for it makes him
so indefatigable a tormentor that, if you have not
courage enough to free me, I must marry him at
last, for that's a sure way to be rid of him.

CONSTANT.

Fortune has found you out a quicker way. My 285
passion now no longer shall torment you, nor I be
more the subject of your mirth.

MIRANDA. [*Aside.*]

What must I say now! If I undeceive him, it will
discover* Lesbia's secret; besides, I lose the dear
pleasure of teasing him. 290

BONSOT.

What can I contrive now!

CONSTANT.

Is there excuse for this ungenerous usage? Had I
by violent means or indirect pursued you— But
how oft, Miranda, with bleeding heart and gushing
eyes have I sworn rather to place you in another's 295
arms than fetter you in mine against your will?
Why then, if I were so uneasy to you, could you
not rid yourself with honor of me? Why this unfair
proceeding?

BONSOT.

Nay sir, I must needs say, the whole fault was partly 300
mine, of their being so good friends, for when they
first met, this lady was jealous of another, and he
was in an anger. They seemed to have very little
kind thoughts for one another, but you must
know, I, sir— 305

CONSTANT.

Have very well reconciled 'em since, I see sir—so
far engaged anger and jealousy between 'em. Oh
faithless woman! What pretence.

MIRANDA.

Well, who can tell when to believe these lovers? 'Twas but yesterday he swore I was too great a good to be engrossed. Nature designed me an universal blessing. And now I must make nobody happy but himself. 310

CONSTANT.

Miranda, you're a woman.—Sir, this is no proper place for our dispute. (*Going.*) 315

BEAUMINE.

Now must I fight with him for having taken his mistress from him and with her relations for not taking her.

BONSOT.

Oh madam—pray sir, hear me, for you must know, I was with them all the time they were alone, though somebody, that shall be nameless, would have had me go, but I assured her, I could keep a secret. 320

CONSTANT.

You would have obliged her more in giving her a privater opportunity, no doubt. (*Aside.*) Oh torture! 325

BONSOT.

Pugh, that was as I told you, a person that must be nameless.

CONSTANT.

Sir, I am not in a humor to be fooled with. (*Going.*)

BONSOT.

Fooled, sir! 330

MIRANDA.

This is carrying the jest a little too far, though. Constant—

CONSTANT.

Madam.

MIRANDA.

I would fain know upon what terms we part, before you go. 335

CONSTANT.

Terms of never meeting. I know no other can be made between us. (*Going.*)

MIRANDA.

But one thing more: I am considering which of us must wear the willow.* Can you resolve me?

CONSTANT.

Am I your jest? 340

MIRANDA.

Well, but in earnest now, stay but a minute.

CONSTANT.

What to be more abused? I have been fooled enough.

As he is going, Lesbia comes out of the closet and stops him.

LESBIA.

Stay to be disabused.

CONSTANT.

I know enough.

BEAUMINE.

Lesbia here! Then I am afraid, 'tis I have been fooled. 345

BONSOT.

Lord, that she should discover* herself! But do what she will, I'm resolved not to betray my trust.

LESBIA.

Nay, you shall stay and know the truth. 350

BEAUMINE.

I know, madam, that you are a very virtuous, generous person.

LESBIA.

Thou the basest of men, but I have not leisure to upbraid thee till I have justified my friend.

BONSOT.

So, more mischief forwards. I must not betray my trust. 355

LESBIA.

I dare affirm she had not now a thought of wronging you, for 'twas at my request, to try Beaumine's truth, she gave him this obliging reception. Bonsot can witness— 360

BONSOT.

I scorn to betray my trust, madam.—As for me, sir, I can't say Lesbia was here before, but I can affirm this to my knowledge, that Miranda had no design of quarrelling with you. But you not being here, d'ye see, and this gentleman a very engaging person, she could not be so hard-hearted, you must think, to put him quite in despair. 365

CONSTANT.

Do you insult me, sir?

BONSOT.

Sir—

MIRANDA.

He does not know his humor.* 370

BONSOT.

Why should you be so peevish, sir? What if she had sent him away in despair, and he had gone and hanged himself?

CONSTANT.

Then you might have hanged with him for company, sir. 375

BONSOT.

Oh, oh, oh, to do you service, sir.

LESBIA.

An officious coxcomb not worth your anger, but what I have asserted—

CONSTANT.

You'll pardon me if I believe herself. She has not offered to deny but justifies her infidelity. 380

LESBIA.

That was, I suppose, her too scrupulous care to conceal what I entrusted her with. But I saw there could be no other proof of her innocence but my appearing, which must convince you 'twas a plot between us. What else could I be hid for? You need 385 not conceal it now, Bonsot.

BONSOT.

Nay, nay, don't think to draw me in so. I know better things. (*To Beaumine.*) This is all to make a difference betwixt you and Miranda. Now I see the drift on't. But don't mind her. 390

CONSTANT.

Your witness is not well enough instructed.

BONSOT. (*To Constant.*)

Oh, as to that I know all, and if you will have it, Lesbia did hide herself indeed. Not that there was any plot against Beaumine, but Miranda having a desire to be alone with him— Not that she 395 designed to injure you, sir, intending you should know all— (*To Beaumine.*) Not that she would have betrayed you, sir, but for fear he should discover it— (*To Constant.*) Though there was no harm, but you might have been jealous, and made a fighting 400 business on't— (*To Beaumine.*) So you might have been killed, sir— (*To Constant.*) And your life in danger, sir— (*To Beaumine.*) But the lady having a great value for you, sir— (*To Constant.*) And fearing to lose you, sir— And as I was saying— Ay pox, I'd 405

fain have you both satisfied.

CONSTANT.

What impertinence is this?

BEAUMINE.

Is it not my turn to complain now, madam? Well, there is no confiding in you women. Your vanity or jealousy is sure to betray us. But if ever I trust two 410 that know one another with the same secret again— You are the strangest incontinent creatures.

MIRANDA.

And have you the impudence to complain of us that you were endeavoring to deceive!

BEAUMINE.

Why, have you not both deceived me? 415

MIRANDA.

Hang me, if I could not be fond of him again for this humor.—But you, I hope, Constant, are now convinced.

CONSTANT.

Yes madam, though I took pains to cheat myself, now every act of your disdain and coldness upbraids 420 the folly of my blinded passion that would believe they rise from any cause but strong aversion.

MIRANDA.

One would think a woman of my fortune need not be so desperate at these years to bestow herself upon one that is her aversion. 425

CONSTANT.

You knew my credulous nature fit to work on, and now I should deserve to be so used, be made the tool you meant me for, if I again believed. But no, Miranda, I've broke my chain, and here I throw it from me. Thus, from my injured heart, I'll throw 430 you too forever. (*Going.*)

MIRANDA.

Oh come back, I beg you.

CONSTANT.

Never.

MIRANDA.

Then he is lost indeed, and I am wretched.

BONSOT.

But sir, pray consider, as the lady was saying, she's 435 a young lady, and a rich lady, and might have anybody she pleases. I would marry her with all my heart, myself, though I'm resolved never to marry, so what need can she have—

CONSTANT.

None of me, sir, so pray give me leave. 440

BONSOT.

Nor of any man for a tool, sir, for this I can say, she had no design to have a gallant, for as soon as the gentleman talked of love to her, she proposed marriage.

CONSTANT.

She was very forward it seems. I must be gone, sir. 445

As Constant offers to go, Bonsot still* stops him.

BONSOT.

Forward, sir? Oh, I suppose that. Nay hear me, sir.

CONSTANT.

Provoking coxcomb.

LESBIA.

This is barbarous. For shame, Constant, you won't leave her thus in tears.

CONSTANT.

Tears? Come madam, you need not hide your 450 mirth. I can laugh with you now. (*He takes her handkerchief from her face.*) Hah! She weeps indeed! Oh let those precious drops fall on this bosom, soften this stubborn heart, that would contend against thy virtue and its own persuasion. 455

BONSOT.

Aye, I knew I should reconcile 'em at last.

MIRANDA.

Why, will you believe? These tears may be dissembled.

CONSTANT.

No, thou art truth itself, and my proud heart wanted* but this excuse for its submission. Can 460 you forgive me?

MIRANDA.

Indeed you were unkind, though you had reason, for, I confess, I have not used you well.

CONSTANT.

Do you confess it? 'Tis too large atonement. Oh that in this soft minute I could hear my charmer speak me 465 happy. Tell me, Miranda, when will you be mine?

MIRANDA.

Indeed the apprehension of losing you was so dreadful to me, that now, methinks, I can't be secure of you too soon.

CONSTANT.

Shall it be tomorrow then? 470

MIRANDA.

You dispose of me.

CONSTANT.

Tomorrow then, Miranda, makes us one. Oh my transported soul leaps at the thought as if it would break forth to speak its joy! It will not stay but flies to meet with thine through this loved bosom and 475 take an earnest of our coming bliss. Tomorrow, my Miranda, oh my love!

LESBIA.

I wish you would take an earnest large enough to subsist on a day or two longer. I shall be at a loss else how to divide myself betwixt you and Lucilia. 480

BEAUMINE.

You may engage yourself here, if you please, madam, for I believe Lucilia will have no great occasion for you tomorrow unless it be to condole with her.

LESBIA.

Condole with her! For what?

[BEAUMINE.]

Only for being disappointed of a good-natured 485 cuckold, madam, that's all.

BONSOT.

That is pity!

LESBIA.

Scandalous! You are such an enemy to virtue. None that profess it can 'scape your censure. What is't you mean by these accusations? 490

BEAUMINE.

Why, I mean that a very civil letter which she designed for her gallant fell by chance into Phillabell's hands at the very same time that the ring you had given yours happened into the sight of your humble servant. 495

LESBIA.

I suppose you both wanted* an excuse[19] for your constancy and so fell upon this invention.

BONSOT.

No indeed, madam, 'tis not his invention. The thing is true, only 'tis a mistake. A ring there was, but you know sir, I told you 'twas given by a 500 wench, a very jilt.

BEAUMINE.

I believe you, sir, indeed.

---

[19] wanted an excuse for] lacked the means to escape

CONSTANT.

As you have been an instrument in this division,
I hope, Miranda, it will be your care to reconcile
these lovers. I must leave you to give some orders   505
for tomorrow's happy business. [*Exit.*]

MIRANDA.

Come, what say you to it? Will you accept of me
for arbitrator? I'll be a very impartial judge.

BEAUMINE.

Lesbia, I have still some regard for your honor and
would be loath to publish your baseness.   510

MIRANDA.

Will you, Beaumine, do her justice, if she is
innocent and can clear herself?

BEAUMINE.

Aye, aye, if the sky fall, madam.

LESBIA.

I don't doubt my justification, but that must be
deferred.   515

BEAUMINE. [*Aside.*]

Venus forbid! Upon the assurance that was
impossible, I was just going to make her the
promise.

LESBIA.

Methinks, Beaumine, it would become you at this
time to answer Miranda's question in a more   520
serious manner.

BONSOT.

Seriously then, be it known, Lesbia, there is a law
that excludes anyone from witnessing in their own
cause.[20]

BONSOT.

That's a very silly law though, for does not one   525
know their own cause best and are most concerned
to clear themselves, right or wrong?

BEAUMINE.

Therefore, sir—

LESBIA.

But if I should bring proofs?

BEAUMINE.

Aye, aye, there are proofs that the earth moves, and   530
that it does not move. Everything can be proved,
but where we are concerned, the strongest
argument is always on the side our inclinations are
for. So, first make me sensible you were innocent.

LESBIA.

Are you resolved then?   535

BEAUMINE.

Never resolve anything. I did resolve to believe you
faithful; you resolved to deceive me. Both have
been disappointed. Little said's soon amended.
Words are but wind. All promises are either broke
or kept. Proverbs flow against you.   540

LESBIA.

Intolerable trifler, Beaumine, I shall find a way to
force a juster answer from you.

BEAUMINE. (*Sings.*)

"Women's rage like shallow waters."[21]

BONSOT.

Egad, I love to see people merry. Come madam,
never spoil company. You see this gentleman's   545
pleased; here's nobody out of humor now but you.

LESBIA.

Here nobody has cause but I.

BONSOT.

Pugh, not a whit. I'll engage Beaumine will never
give you any farther trouble.

LESBIA.

Prithee Bonsot, I'm not in a humor now to be   550
pleased with your good-natured impertinence.

BONSOT.

Ay, ay, this is always my reward for taking pains
to do good. When people are in a peevish mood,
presently* I'm impertinent.

MIRANDA.

Come, come. A truce with your anger till a better   555
opportunity of clearing the debate.

LESBIA. (*Aside.*)

I had almost forgot Lucilia. She must know of the
letter he talks of.—Adieu, my dear, 'tis late and
time to leave you. (*Exit.*)

BONSOT.

I must follow her, for I never leave people till I   560
have argued or teased 'em out of their anger.—And
sir, if you don't find her as fond of you as ever she

---

20 witnessing ... cause] Not strictly accurate: defendants
could testify, but could not be compelled to do so after
the Interregnum.

21 "Women's rage like shallow waters."] from Thomas
Durfey's *Don Quixote* (2.III.i.99-100)

was in her life next time you meet, say I'm an officious, impertinent, insignificant fellow. (*Exit.*)

BEAUMINE.

That will be an extraordinary obligation indeed, sir. 565

MIRANDA.

Well, Beaumine, you must consider too it grows late, and that I must begin to think of the virtues of a wife's discretion and obedience.

BEAUMINE.

Ah! That's a virtue I must have too, but mightily against my will when you command me to leave 570 you. This has been a very tragical day to lovers: Phillabell his* mistress false; Lesbia lost a believing coxcomb, I my hopes of the most agreeable woman in France; and she I'm afraid will find herself in a greater distress than any of us, for faith, Miranda, 575 whatever the inexperienced may fancy of marriage, As those who furrowed fields at distance view May think 'em smooth and flowery as they shew, But he that enters, curses what they praise, Finds 'em deceitful, toilsome, rugged ways. 580

Act V, scene i. The Walks.

Enter Bonsot with Grandfoy.

BONSOT.

Cousin, I say, trouble yourself no more about this matter. Beaumine is thoroughly satisfied, for you must know, I told him the person you had the ring from was a common jilt, a wench you had no value for, and he presently* believed me. 5

GRANDFOY.

Thy folly's so ridiculous it mocks my anger. Would thou couldst at once be sensible how unluckily thou ever toil'st against thy own designs, thy good nature then would surely silence thee. To be always meddling where you have nothing to do in things 10 you know nothing of!

BONSOT.

Ay, ay, I know nothing. I don't know that he was in such a passion with you. If I had not hindered him, he'd have cut your throat before now, without giving you time to say your prayers. 15

GRANDFOY.

Better he had than she had been abused, the woman in the world whose honors I am most concerned to vindicate and most to him.

BONSOT.

Why, her honor's ne'er the worse for what I said of her. But to please you now, I'll go to him again 20 and tell him I was mistaken, that the lady never had a kindness for any man but you—

GRANDFOY.

That will mend the matter indeed.

BONSOT. (*Going.*)

Well, then you shall see how I'll manage it.

GRANDFOY.

Prithee Bonsot be quiet. All the kindness I ask of 25 thee is never to intend me any.

BONSOT.

But would not you have me do justice to a lady you say I have wronged?

GRANDFOY.

No, no, I am just going to Beaumine, where I have appointed him to meet me, and shall find a way 30 to do her justice myself.

BONSOT.

Oh ho, then I'll go with you.

GRANDFOY.

Indeed you shan't, sir.

BONSOT.

Try me but once, if I don't make all well again—

GRANDFOY.

Pray, hold your tongue, sir. 35

BONSOT.

Well, I will hold my tongue, then, if you'll let me go, for I know you'll begin a quarrel* now and put Beaumine out of his good humor, and then he'll never let you go to the devil in quiet, cousin.— Oh there's my brother's rival. I must talk with him. 40 Stay for me but a little while now.

Enter Phillabell.

GRANDFOY.

Little enough, I promise you—a lucky deliverance. (*Exit.*)

BONSOT.

Sir, your humble servant. Happening to see you take up a letter in the walks, I imagine it might be one my brother expected there because he did 45 not receive it.

PHILLABELL.

If he would know what it contained, no doubt the
lady that sent it will inform him.

BONSOT.

Aye sir, but that is not the thing now. I can tell
you more, because you have reason to take it ill, 50
to show you have no reason, sir.

PHILLABELL.

No reason, sir?

BONSOT.

Not a dram, sir, upon my word, for you must
know all the kind* things in it were only to pacify
my brother for fear he should show you the rest 55
of her fond letters, not but she really designed to
marry you.

PHILLABELL.

I don't question it, upon my word, sir.

BONSOT.

Aye sir, to be sure she was in earnest with you. She
admitted you to the house, when he could only 60
see her by stealth.

PHILLABELL.

Confound 'em.

BONSOT.

And then, you have a much better estate than he,
sir.

PHILLABELL.

I believe she was sincere with that, sir. 65

BONSOT.

So I hope, sir, I have satisfied you, and since you
know she designed you her sober choice and only
to play the fool a little with him, you won't be
angry if he shows you her letters, and I may have
leave to wish you joy, sir. 70

PHILLABELL.

Joy sir! Thou busy trifler, hence and don't provoke
my rage. What devil sent thee, when I am going
to Lucilia, whom I would meet as calmly as if I
were not injured?

BONSOT.

Injured? Why don't I tell you, sir, I'm certain she 75
designs to marry you.

PHILLABELL.

Thy folly gives thee a privilege to abuse men safely;
there's no way to resent it but by flying from
impertinence. (*Exit.*)

BONSOT.

Psha, psha. As I was saying, sir— Faugh, why so fast 80
sir— That men should be such enemies to truth
they don't care to hear it, though for their good!
Everybody runs away from me when I would tell it
'em as if I were a monster. Oh yonder's Beaumine.
I'll go satisfy him, and then to see what humor 85
Lesbia's in, and then to my cousin, and my brother's.
I'll go to 'em all round. I do take a deal of pains, and
do a world of good—to no purpose. (*Exit.*)

[Scene ii. Lucilia's lodgings.]

Enter Lucilia and Lysetta.

LUCILIA.

This comes of taking your pernicious counsels.
They have always been fatal to me.

LYSETTA.

I'm sure I meant well, though it falls out so
unluckily. Who could dream of such an accident?

LUCILIA.

Dream! For aught I know the fool hired you to 5
betray the letter to Phillabell.

LYSETTA.

Nay madam, I know you can't suspect my fidelity
to you.

LUCILIA.

How dare you talk to me? Get you out of my sight.

LYSETTA.

Dear madam, have patience. If you'll be advised, 10
all may be well yet.

LUCILIA.

You're very free of your wise counsels indeed, but
I'll hear no more of 'em.

LYSETTA.

Nay good madam, be pacified. I know I have been
the cause of this misfortune, and therefore I would 15
fain do you some service that may recompense it.

LUCILIA.

What recompense? What service can you pretend
to do me? Has he not seen the letter under my own
hand?

LYSETTA.

If you can but deny it confidently enough, I don't 20
doubt your coming off, for all that.

LUCILIA.

Deny it! What, when he has the proof in his possession? What could that signify, unless to show him I had joined impudence to infidelity?

LYSETTA.

Nay, it must be managed artfully. You must seem angry with him as if you suspected a forgery. You know I can counterfeit that hand. Insinuate that to him cunningly. Do you observe me, madam?

LUCILIA.

Well, what does all this tend to?

LYSETTA.

'Tis a nice* business and will require no little artifice, but let all your care be very slyly to give him a suspicion of me.

LUCILIA.

Do you think he'll be imposed upon so? It can but make him doubt at most.

LYSETTA.

Aye, but I have a further plot. We may be thankful for this time to be prepared for him before he comes, instead of repining at the accident. How lucky it was that Lesbia should hear of it and that you were not at home when Phillabell came last night before she had given you notice of it.

LUCILIA.

I shall be little the better for it, I'm afraid.

LYSETTA.

Look you, madam, take my advice. He's a lover and by consequence credulous. That will make him believe you enough to have a mind to examine me, and being jealous, he'll probably doubt you enough to do it immediately, that we mayn't have time to lay our heads together. 'Tis very likely he'll come directly from you to look for me; then let him alone for the rest of the project. I engage to return him to you the most satisfied, humble thing, begging pardon, calling himself a jealous pated coxcomb and you the most innocent injured—

Enter a young woman, servant of Lucilia's, niece to Lysetta.

YOUNG WOMAN.

Madam, here's Phillabell coming up.

LYSETTA.

Dear madam, will you follow my directions?

LUCILIA.

Well, well, be gone, I hear him.

LYSETTA.

Niece, come with me hussy. I have business with you. Quick. Quick.

Exit Lysetta and niece.

LUCILIA.

I hate deceit, but sure 'tis of all others the most innocent to cheat a man to a belief of truth. How my heart trembles.

Enter Phillabell.

You seem disturbed. Can there be any cause of sadness on this day?

PHILLABELL.

Why, madam, not on this?

LUCILIA.

Does Phillabell ask why! He who so often swore this day would pay the sum of all his wishes!

PHILLABELL.

Alas there's nothing man so much deceives himself in as the means to his own happiness. I thought to make you mine the certain way, but unless your heart could be secured, all other ties is wretched slavery.

LUCILIA.

That you need not doubt, for whom I've laid aside my virgin modesty to confess I loved you.

PHILLABELL.

You have told me so indeed, but are you sure th'obedience of a daughter has not swayed you against your inclination?

LUCILIA.

Heaven can witness that you are much less my father's choice than mine.

PHILLABELL.

Have a care, madam, what you call Heaven to attest, and deal with me sincerely, for I am come as one that truly loves you, to offer you my service in whatever way can best conduce to make you happy.

LUCILIA.

Your service! Can anything in nature make me happy but your love?

PHILLABELL.

I would not have you made a sacrifice, and if you fear t'offend your father in refusing me, confess it generously.* I'll take it upon me, seem to fall off, and whatever his resentment may proceed to, I promise you to bear it all, rather than expose you to it.

LUCILIA.

I don't know what you mean. This is strange 90
language to me.

PHILLABELL.

Does this speak plain enough? (*Gives her a letter, and whilst she reads, says [aside.]*) So unmoved! She must be practiced sure in falsehood.

LUCILIA.

What's the design of all this? 95

PHILLABELL.

You best know that, madam.

LUCILIA.

I know it! What, to disguise your own inconstancy must you tax me with such baseness?

PHILLABELL.

Why, you won't pretend to deny your own
handwriting, I hope. 100

LUCILIA.

My writing! Who dares say I writ it?

PHILLABELL.

Oh woman! woman!

LUCILIA.

This is a masterpiece of villainy indeed!

PHILLABELL. [*Aside.*]

I was not prepared for this turn, I confess, but who
can reach the depths of woman's artifice? 105

LUCILIA.

'Twill be enough to wrong my love by your infidelity without this forgery to injure my reputation. This from a man whom I despised all others for!

PHILLABELL.

I forge it! I have not the art of counterfeiting so 110
well as you, madam, but I may learn in time of so
perfect a mistress.

LUCILIA.

You have found a much better for your purpose, I
assure you.

PHILLABELL.

That would be a prodigy indeed. 115

LUCILIA.

There's few can exceed my sweet governess, who I
don't doubt was employed in this contrivance.

PHILLABELL.

Employed by whom? For what?

LUCILIA.

To sacrifice my honor for your base ends.

PHILLABELL.

Oh madam, you need not distrust her. 'Twas not 120
she betrayed you. Fortune was my only friend in
this matter.

LUCILIA.

Indeed, I shall hardly take your word for it.
Perhaps you imagine I don't know her skill in
counterfeiting my hand, though she might have 125
told you I did.

PHILLABELL. [*Aside.*]

Is it possible there can be a deceit in this? If my reason would be as soon convinced as my fond heart, I could not think her false one minute. Lysetta counterfeit her hand? To what end? And 130
yet I can see nothing of that confusion or disorder in her looks which guilt would naturally have upon so unexpected a discovery.* What can resolve me in this hell of doubts?

LUCILIA. (*Aside.*)

So there's some hopes. It begins to work.—I see 135
you are surprised to find your accomplice so soon
suspected.

PHILLABELL.

Madam, I thought you had known me too well to believe me capable of such a villainy. If you are innocent, we are both abused. 140

LUCILIA.

I thought too my virtue had been better known, and I will clear it. If my false governess dare deny it, there may be ways to force the truth from you and her.

PHILLABELL.

There may be ways too, madam, to make her own
whatever you please. 145

LUCILIA.

You may prevent that if you please, but I suppose you'll be loath to lose so good a pretence for denying my innocence, if I should make it appear.

PHILLABELL.

Oh could you look into my heart, Lucilia, it would tell you that with the forfeiture of half my reason 150
I would believe you're wronged, so much I wish it. But though I should be easily convinced, yet

for your sake, that there may be no room left for malice, I'll tax your governess before you see her with this forgery, as if I knew it hers. That perhaps may induce her to confess it.   155

LUCILIA.

You may do as you think fit.

PHILLABELL.

Till then believe I suffer more than you. What different effects does passionate love produce:
Fearful to lose, we quickly jealous grow,   160
And wishing to be loved, soon think we're so. (*Exit*.)

LUCILIA.

Now, if Lysetta play her part as well, who can condemn this harmless artifice? The main points, that I love Phillabell and despise Cleon, are truths. Where then would be the virtue or wisdom to let   165
him know some disagreeable circumstances which would make us both really uneasy, though there were only an imaginary reason for it? But happy are those who have ruled their lives with so much prudence that every action may appear barefaced,   170
for to be forced to the least disguise is some violence to an honest nature, and though 'tis not disused to injure others, 'tis a corruption, at least a blemish, to do injury to itself. Yet would the men dissemble no otherwise with us, we could easily   175
forgive 'em, but they with baser arts,
All their past faults with impudence reveal,
And only those which they intend conceal.

Exit.

Scene [iii]. The Walks.

Enter Beaumine and Grandfoy.

GRANDFOY.

Thus sir, lest my sword should fail to do her justice, I have endeavored to convince you how little Lesbia has deserved such unhandsome usage from you and am ready to confirm the truth of what I have said with the hazard of my life. We need go no farther,   5
sir. This place is private and convenient—

BEAUMINE.

To give me satisfaction, sir, for you have done me such an injury.

GRANDFOY.

I thought, sir, what I have told you with so much

frankness and Lesbia's letters, which you saw,   10
refusing the offer I had made to marry her and mentioning on what account the ring was given me were proofs that we never injured you.

BEAUMINE.

Why, that's the mischief on't. You have convinced me she has been so honorable that I must be   15
married, the greatest misfortune you could have drawn me into that I know of, indeed, sir.

GRANDFOY.

Then it seems you don't love her, sir.

BEAUMINE.

Because I have no mind to marry her? Then no man ever did love, for no man ever had or can have   20
a mind absolutely to marry any woman.

GRANDFOY.

Why, has not many a man married merely* for love?

BEAUMINE.

Aye sir, and many a man has taken a house he liked, with a considerable fine upon it, because he   25
knew it would not be let otherwise, but I'll be hanged if any man had not rather have it without.

GRANDFOY.

And be the more unwilling to pay it after he has been long in possession.

BEAUMINE.

But rather than forfeit his word or his house, for   30
I find there's love as well as honor in the case.

GRANDFOY.

Well sir, if you resolve to do her justice upon any motive, 'tis all that Lesbia can require of you. But since we both have a claim to her, nothing but our swords can decide it.   35

BEAUMINE.

Oh yes, sir, she can do it much better, for though it's true, women are seldom favorable to merit, we must own they are better judges than the most judicious sword in Europe; the advantage is, the person she rejects will be in a better condition than   40
may be his chance if we fall to cutting of throats. For him she chooses, I can't promise it, indeed.

GRANDFOY.

You talk very little like a lover. I wish her choice were placed where 'twould be welcomer, but I prefer Lesbia's satisfaction to my own and therefore   45
am content to submit to her sentence.

BEAUMINE.

Wisely resolved, sir. A man of honor should not decline fighting upon any reasonable occasion but where it can answer the end. If it be for revenge, stabbing a man is a very substantial one, but for a mistress, how the devil does my sword know her inclinations? If it happen to dispatch the man she likes, I am sure to be hated the more for it; if a man she dislikes, there was no danger in him. So it can never be to any purpose. Come sir, let us try other means. Capitulate with the lady: Women by force of arms can ne'er be won, Unless the guards within betray the town. Sound a parley, ye fair, and surrender.

Exit singing with Grandfoy.

Scene [iv]. Lesbia's Lodgings.

Enter Lesbia and Lucilia [and Bonsot].

LUCILIA.

You see how dear* this foolish gallantry had like to have cost me, if your timely notice had not put me upon my guard.

LESBIA.

This comes of being so hasty to run into an amour. Before the heart engages, we must retreat and know not how to do it with honor, but when love leads us on, however dangerous the consequences are, it makes 'em easy to us.

LUCILIA.

But 'tis indeed a strange folly to hazard our reputation only for the vanity of securing a conquest. The prize is so little worth in respect of the venture.

LESBIA.

What think you of the contrary fault, affecting an indifference for those we really love?

LUCILIA.

That's as much a greater folly, as our own happiness is of more consequence to us than other people's opinion.

LESBIA.

How blind we are to our own faults! Now don't you see that what you have been condemning you are at this instant guilty of: flying Phillabell when you most wish to meet him and seeming angry with him when you know he's in the right?

LUCILIA.f

But 'twould not be wise to know it, as our affairs stand, and I have ordered Lysetta to tell Phillabell I am at your lodgings. If he comes here I can't avoid him and so give him an opportunity of reconciling himself without seeming to desire it.

BONSOT.

I'll engage, madam, he'll come. I'm sure I said enough in your defense to satisfy any reasonable man.

LESBIA.

No doubt a little harmless artifice is sometimes necessary, and for a young beginner, you have performed pretty well, but Lysetta's part was managed with wonderful dexterity.

LUCILIA.

The design indeed was cunningly laid and happily effected.

LESBIA.

Hold. Is not that Phillabell's voice below?

Enter Phillabell and Lysetta.

LUCILIA.

I think it is. Now for my last deceit.—Madam, I'll take my leave of you.

LESBIA.

Nay, now indeed you shan't.

PHILLABELL.

Be so just to hear what I have to say before you condemn me, madam.

LUCILIA.

I have heard you say too much.

BONSOT.

Now what can she be angry at?

PHILLABELL.

But hear Lysetta, madam.—Come, you must speak the truth.

LYSETTA.

I beg your pardon, madam, I did not think any harm would come on't, but truly I did write some letters in your name to Cleon. Indeed I did not intend to do you any injury by it.

LUCILIA.

No injury! What else could induce you to it? Who set you on?

LYSETTA.

Nobody set me on, but Cleon took care to pay me

so well for deceiving him, that I thought it worth
my pains.

LUCILIA.

It seems, Phillabel, you have great power with her
to make her confess all this.   55

BONSOT.

What, is she jealous of her?—Oh, madam, there's
nothing in that but money too. He has only given
her money enough, take my word for it.

LUCILIA.

So I imagine, sir.

BONSOT.

Psha, you think 'twas upon some slippery account   60
now, but 'twas only to make her own this cheat. I
can answer for him.

PHILLABELL.

Prithee give me leave to vindicate myself, Bonsot.

BONSOT.

With all my heart, sir, now I have satisfied her as
to the main point.   65

LESBIA.

Aye, like all other universal friends, commendingg
everyone alike, their praises always injure.

PHILLABELL.

I took her in the very fact, madam: my good
genius* led me thither just as she was writing and
so intent upon her treachery, I came into the   70
chamber unperceived, heard her admiring with her
niece her skill in counterfeiting your hand so
perfectly. When I had heard enough, I snatched
the paper, which was to the same effect of that I
showed you. It having miscarried, she was writing   75
it again, which left her no room to deny her guilt,
nor me to doubt your innocence.

LUCILIA.

'Twas happy, since it proves a means of putting an
end to this cheat and gives us power to punish the
author of it, which she shall find severely.   80

PHILLABELL.

But first, Lucilia, let us think of our own happiness
that no new chance may cross it.

LUCILIA.

'Tis not enough that you believe me innocent.
Since Cleon and perhaps, by his vanity, many
others suspect me of infidelity, I must not let you   85
share in my dishonor.

BONSOT.

Why madam, 'twill make your part the less.

LYSETTA.

If I might hope for pardon of my fault by making
some kind of reparation, I would tell Cleon how
I have all this while abused him.   90

BONSOT.

And let me alone to appease him. I'll tell him 'tis
all but a sham, to a certain purpose.

LUCILIA.

I hope he knows his brother well enough to esteem
what he says as it deserves.

LESBIA.

Upon those terms I must become her intercessor.   95

PHILLABELL.

And I have reason to join with you.

LUCILIA.

You have too much power with me to be refused
anything you desire.

PHILLABELL.

Then you are mine again. At your feet receive my
thanks, and let this hand give me possession.   100

As he kneels, Beaumine, Grandfoy, and Cleon enter.

BONSOT.

See now how good friends I have made you, and
here comes my cousin and Beaumine together. I
thought I had made up matters between them too.

BEAUMINE.

So this is the way on't. When the women have
played us false, we must submit and beg pardon   105
for having the impudence to see it.

PHILLABELL.

Oh Beaumine, my Lucilia's innocent.

BEAUMINE.

Aye, aye, so they are all, if they have but cunning
enough.

PHILLABELL.

Thou'rt a mere* infidel.   110

BEAUMINE.

No faith, Phillabell, no offense to thee. I'm e'en
as credulous a coxcomb as thyself. Prithee don't
laugh at me. There are two evils you know that
go by destiny.

PHILLABELL.

Of which I should least expect marriage to be   115
thine, indeed.

GRANDFOY.

My cousin Cleon, madam, met us as we were coming hither and would needs have me bring him to wait on you.

LESBIA.

Being your relation, he must be welcome to me, but I'm sorry it happens at a time when things are in such a posture that I cannot be so easy, so much at liberty as I should to be entertained by so extraordinary a person.   120

CLEON. (*Aside.*)

That is, she would be alone with me.—Oh madam, I shall find a happier opportunity, but since I cannot enjoy it now, I'm extremely pleased to meet such good company here.—I have a great respect for these lovers, and wish you joy with all my heart, upon my word, sir.   125

PHILLABELL.

Oh I thank you, sir, but must desire another favor of you: you received some letters in this lady's name, which I expect you should return.   130

CLEON.

In that lady's name, sir? Then it seems she is not ashamed of her name, that she has told you where to find it. I protest, I resolved to conceal 'em, but if you have a mind to have 'em published, madam, I can put 'em in the press. They will be a very extraordinary epithalamium.   135

LUCILIA.

Sir, you have been deceived. Those letters never expressed my thoughts.   140

CLEON.

Very probable. Women's words seldom express their thoughts. I did not doubt but you had more kindness* for me than they expressed.

LYSETTA.

Ah sir, my lady never thought one word of what was writ. 'Twas all of my contrivance. I confess, sir, I was loath to let you despair.   145

BONSOT.

Hark you, Brother, this is only a plot to make you part with your mistress the more easily, but don't you seem to know it, and yet don't be angry neither.   150

CLEON.

But seem as good-natured a fool as you. Brother,

you had the best contrivance last night in the walks to keep me from despair.—But not one word of your lady's thoughts?

LUCILIA.

I'll be sworn I spoke truth, but abusing a man is complimenting him when vanity's the interpreter.   155

LYSETTA.

Well sir, since the deceit is discovered,* I suppose you won't think my letters worth keeping.

CLEON.

Her letters— *Madame la Gouvernante,*[22] when you grant me the favor, I desire it may be in the same shape you made me the promise in last night.   160

LYSETTA.

Aye, aye, sir. This shape is only put on, that we may keep it with the more security.

CLEON.

Oh, I apprehend.

PHILLABELL.

I hope, sir, you believe Lucilia had no hand in deceiving you?   165

CLEON.

Pasitively, I assure you, sir.

PHILLABELL.

And be so ungenerous to refuse the letters.

CLEON.

Sir, I happen to have 'em all about me; I had some thoughts you might have a curiosity to know how well she could write before you married her. They're at your service, sir, if you please to peruse 'em. (*Gives the letters.*)   170

PHILLABELL.

I have not the curiosity indeed, sir.—Here Lysetta. (*Gives 'em her.*)   175

CLEON. [*Aside.*]

The best bred husband in the world, rat me.

BONSOT.

I told you I should satisfy him, sir. Now you must know he thinks the letters were Lucilia's, for all this.

PHILLABELL.

Does he so, sir? I shall find a way then to convince him they are not.   180

---

22 *Gouvernante*] governess (Fr.)

BONSOT.

Hey, why are you angry at that? Nay, rather than you should quarrel,* I'll tell him myself that she only ordered Lysetta to write 'em.

PHILLABELL.

What you say is of so little consequence, I care not what you tell him.   185

BONSOT.

Ay, ay. This is always my reward, but for all that, I shall never give over—

PHILLABELL.

Being impertinent, I dare engage for thee. 'Tis the happiest, though the most incurable distemper a   190
man can have, and both for the same reason: he can never be made sensible of it.

BEAUMINE.

Among the many interposers in affairs they have nothing to do with, who, when they laugh at this officious meddler, will consider him as their own   195
picture?

LUCILIA. [Aside.]

Well, I am happily come off, but through such dangers, such anxieties, as might warn all our sex against those little gallantries with which they only think to amuse themselves but, though innocent,   200
too often gain 'em such a character* of lightness as their future conduct never can efface. Nay, though I have succeeded better, I find within all is not as it should be: a secret check, that so entire a confidence as Phillabell has in me is not returned with that   205
plain, open, artless dealing it deserves. That will be the lasting punishment of my childish fault.

LESBIA.

Grandfoy tells me, Beaumine, you will both submit to my choice between you.

BEAUMINE.

So we agreed, madam. I'm impatient to know   210
which blessing I must lose, you or my liberty.

Enter Constant and Miranda.

LESBIA.

Miranda! And married I'll engage, by that affected gravity.

LUCILIA.

Miranda married at last!

LESBIA.

I hope, sir, I may give you joy?   215

MIRANDA.

Aye, you may give him joy, for 'tis the first day of his reign.

CONSTANT.

Of my happiness indeed, but 'twould be ungrateful to use it to the prejudice of your power, from whom I have received it.   220

MIRANDA.

I begin to be terribly afraid I shall certainly love you, and you have loved me so fast, you must be near the end of the race before I am set out.

CONSTANT.

Oh! 'Tis an endless race; endeavor but to overtake me.   225

BEAUMINE.

This is a dreadful omen to me, madam; there was so much sympathy between us, I'm afraid it reaches to our destinies too.

MIRANDA.

Do the planets incline to conjunction then? I could not forbear coming to inquire how your affairs   230
went?

BEAUMINE.

Very ill indeed, madam: there is but a woman's inclinations betwixt me and ruin, which would certainly give her to that gentleman, if I were as fond of marrying her as he is. But your sex's   235
darling, contradiction, I fear will carry it.

MIRANDA.

What, Lesbia in profound meditation?

LESBIA.

Advise me, Miranda: I'm a little puzzled in this affair.

MIRANDA.

Divided betwixt love and honor?   240

BONSOT.

Now, I advise you, madam, in this case—

LESBIA.

What, without knowing it?

BONSOT.

Let it be what it will, I am never of honor's side. It's good for nothing but to make people uneasy, and I would have everybody please themselves,   245
whether they can or no.

LESBIA.

You must teach 'em the art then.—But prithee should I, out of a foolish scruple, tie myself to Beaumine when we are weary of one another—

MIRANDA.

Or lay the yoke upon a fresh lover that will hold out longer— 250

LESBIA.

And bear it easier? How shall I resolve? I think they had best throw dice for me.

MIRANDA.

E'en put it to the vote.

LESBIA.

With all my heart. 255

MIRANDA.

What say you, gentlemen? Lesbia is so unwilling to disoblige either of you, she's resolved to be his that has most voices for him.

BEAUMINE.

What she pleases.

GRANDFOY.

I shall never dispute her will. 260

CLEON.

This is extremely new. But I don't know why it should not be brought into a custom to marry as well as to divorce by vote,[23] unless indeed, that getting rid of our wives will be more for the general good.

MIRANDA.

Well sir, which are you for? 265

CLEON.

Since there is so good a relief, for him that will soonest be weary of her.

GRANDFOY.

That I grant is on Beaumine's side.

MIRANDA.

What say you, Constant?

CONSTANT.

I am for him that loves her best. 270

GRANDFOY.

That favors me.

BONSOT.

I am for him that won't quarrel with her.

BEAUMINE.

That's likely to be me, for I shall be least with her.

LUCILIA.

I am for him that can plead most right in her.

BEAUMINE.

Ah the devil! That's me again. 275

PHILLABELL.

I am for him that she loves best.

MIRANDA.

And I for him that she loves least.

BEAUMINE.

That's undone me; 'twas pure malice, Miranda.

LESBIA.

The odds are on Beaumine's side: whether I declare I love him least or best, there's a vote for him; his 280 right is indisputable; he says he shan't quarrel with me; and he's weary of me already. So there can be but two against him.

BEAUMINE.

You'll find hereafter there were more: my late suspicion of you gave me such disquiets as showed 285 me how dear you are to me, and the proofs of your innocence confirm my love with my esteem.

LESBIA.

Which to preserve, and for all our quiets, I propose that for the future Grandfoy be a stranger to us.

BONSOT.

Oh! That's cruel. Sir, my cousin has a great kindness 290 for you and your lady. I'll engage he'll do her no harm.

BEAUMINE.

Oh, no sir.

GRANDFOY.

I must submit but may have still, I hope, some pretence to your friendship.

BEAUMINE.

You have deserved it, sir, and are welcome to share 295 with us this day's diversions.

CONSTANT.

I have ordered some music. With your leave, madam, we'll employ 'em.

A dance.

PHILLABELL.

'Tis time now to think upon the ceremony that yet remains to make us master of our wishes. 300

---

23 marry … vote] Since only Parliament had the authority to dissolve marriages at this time, divorces were, in a sense, subject to a vote.

BEAUMINE.

Which performed, I resolve to show those married
men whom I have laughed out of their fondness
or civility for their wives that I have learned by
their weakness how to avoid giving 'em a revenge
and will so shamelessly boast of loving mine that   305
'twill put raillery out of countenance and, by
preserving my complaisance for her, show I know
how to value myself.

For treating them with rudeness or neglect
Does most dishonor on ourselves reflect;   310
If that respect which their own merit drew
We think by their becoming ours less due,
And as in choosing we their worth approve,
We tax our judgment when we cease to love.

[Exeunt.]

FINIS.

Textual Notes

a Copytext is the corrected state of the first edition, a 1701
  quarto (Qc). Also consulted were the uncorrected state
  (Qu), and a modern edition of 1988 (Kendall).
b stronger] stranger Qc, Qu, Kendall
c by] but Qc, Qu, Kendall
d exchange. BEAUMINE. Oh! … airy.] Qc, Qu; exchange. Oh! … airy. Kendall [Obviously a speech by
  Phillabell inquiring about Miranda has been omitted.]
e there] here, Qc, Qu, Kendall
f LUCILIA.] Kendall; LES. Qc, Qu
g commending] commanding Qc, Qu, Kendall

A Bold Stroke for a Wife[a]

by Susanna Centlivre (1669?-1723)

edited by Nancy Copeland

Susanna Centlivre was one of the most important comic playwrights of the first part of the eighteenth century. She was also the most successful female dramatist between 1660 and 1800, in terms of the number of her plays that were produced and the number of years some of them, including *A Bold Stroke for a Wife*, remained in the repertoire. *A Bold Stroke* typifies her comic style in its combination of an intricate love intrigue, humours comedy (in the characterization of the guardians), and the outrageous situations and physical comedy of farce. In its emphasis on action and situation rather than wit, its mild satire, and the honest, straightforward relationship of its lovers, it exemplifies the kind of play that Shirley Strum Kenny terms "humane comedy."

First performed on 3 February 1718 at Lincoln's Inn Fields, *A Bold Stroke* was well suited to the resources of the company, which featured established comic performers such as William Bullock (Tradelove) and George Pack (Prim). Fainwell was a vehicle for Christopher Bullock, son of William, who was also co-manager of the theater during this season, while his wife, Jane, played Anne Lovely. Some of the play's features recall the harlequinades that were a mainstay of the company's repertoire. Such entertainments, not yet called pantomimes, are particularly evoked by the play's fairy-tale plot; by the centrality of transformation; and by some of the more extravagant farce, notably the scene in act three in which Fainwell convinces Periwinkle that he can make himself invisible by sinking through the stage's trapdoor.

The play portrays the mercantile culture of early-Georgian London, most explicitly in the scene inside Jonathan's Coffee-house (IV.i), but also through its characters. The guardians represent a range of propertied urban types, and Fainwell's plotting is well suited to his capitalist milieu. Like a tradesman who suits his manner to his customers, Fainwell adopts characters that flatter the prejudices of each of the guardians to get the better of them in a bargain for Anne Lovely, a bargain which is confirmed by a written contract. Anne's position within these transactions is that of a commodity, coveted by Fainwell and traded by her guardians. Her largely passive role is characteristic of the developing position of the genteel middle-class woman within capitalism, and she struggles against the Prims to exercise her right to be an idle consumer of luxury goods. The guardians too, despite their differences, all participate in the pervasive commercial culture, either as producers or consumers.

Centlivre was unequivocally Whig in her politics, and *A Bold Stroke* is permeated by Whig principles. The play constructs an implicit, Whiggish argument that the propertied interests represented by the guardians, both "trading" and "landed," should cooperate with one another and unite behind the army through supporting Colonel Fainwell, one of Centlivre's many soldier heroes. The concept of liberty, fundamental to Whig ideology, connects Centlivre's political views to her feminism: Anne Lovely, for example, speaks of the "tyranny" of her guardians in the language of political liberty.

The play was successful from its first production and became one of Centlivre's most-performed plays. Thanks to the opportunities Fainwell offers to the virtuoso comic actor, the play continued to be frequently performed throughout the eighteenth century and well into the nineteenth.

DRAMATIS PERSONAE

MEN

Sir Philip Modelove, an old beau.

Periwinkle, a kind of a silly virtuoso.[1]

Tradelove, a changebroker.[2]

Obadiah Prim, a Quaker.

Colonel Fainwell, in love with Mrs.* Lovely.

Freeman, his friend, a merchant.

Simon Pure, a Quaking preacher.

Mr. Sackbut,[3] a tavern-keeper.

WOMEN

Mrs. Lovely, a fortune of thirty thousand pound.

Mrs. Prim, wife to Prim the hosier.[4]

Betty, servant to Mrs. Lovely.

Footmen, drawers, etc.

A Bold Stroke for a Wife.

Omnia vincit amor.[5]

Act I, scene i. A tavern.

Colonel Fainwell and Freeman over a bottle.

FREEMAN.

Come, Colonel, His Majesty's health. You are as melancholy as if you were in love; I wish some of the beauties at Bath[6] ha'n't snapped your heart.

COLONEL.

Why, faith, Freeman, there is something in't; I have seen a lady at Bath who has kindled such a flame in me that all the waters there can't quench. 5

---

1 virtuoso] a collector of antiquities and natural curiosities

2 changebroker] an exchange broker, a middleman in the exchange of bills of credit

3 Sackbut] a compound: sack, white wine imported from Spain or the Canary Islands; butt, a wine cask

4 hosier] a dealer in stockings and knitted underclothes

5 *Omnia … amor.*] Virgil, *Eclogues* X: Love conquers all (Lat.).

6 Bath] In the eighteenth century Bath, with its medicinal springs and baths, became a fashionable summer resort for the titled and the wealthy.

FREEMAN.

Women, like some poisonous animals, carry their antidote about 'em. Is she not to be had, Colonel?

COLONEL.

That's a difficult question to answer; however, I resolve to try. Perhaps you may be able to serve me; 10 you merchants know one another. The lady told me herself she was under the charge of four persons.

FREEMAN.

Odso! 'Tis Mrs. Anne Lovely.

COLONEL.

The same. Do you know her? 15

FREEMAN.

Know her! Aye—Faith, Colonel, your condition is more desperate than you imagine; why she is the talk and pity of the whole town; and it is the opinion of the learned that she must die a maid.

COLONEL.

Say you so? That's somewhat odd, in this charitable 20 city. She's a woman, I hope.

FREEMAN.

For aught I know; but it had been as well for her had nature made her any other part of the creation. The man which keeps this house served her father; he is a very honest fellow and may be of use to 25 you; we'll send for him to take a glass with us; he'll give you the whole history, and 'tis worth your hearing.

COLONEL.

But may one trust him?

FREEMAN.

With your life; I have obligations enough upon 30 him to make him do anything; I serve him with wine. (*Knocks.*)

COLONEL.

Nay, I know him pretty well myself; I once used to frequent a club that was kept here.

Enter drawer.

DRAWER.

Gentlemen, d'you call? 35

FREEMAN.

Aye, send up your master.

DRAWER.

Yes, sir. (*Exit.*)

COLONEL.

Do you know any of this lady's guardians, Freeman?

FREEMAN.

Yes, I know two of them very well. 40

COLONEL.

What are they?

Enter Sackbut.

FREEMAN.

Here comes one will give you an account of them all.—Mr. Sackbut, we sent for you to take a glass with us. 'Tis a maxim among the friends of the bottle, that as long as the master is in company 45 one may be sure of good wine.

SACKBUT.

Sir, you shall be sure to have as good wine as you send in.—Colonel, your most humble servant; you are welcome to town.

COLONEL.

I thank you, Mr. Sackbut. 50

SACKBUT.

I am as glad to see you as I should a hundred tun of French claret custom-free. My service to you, sir. (*Drinks.*) You don't look so merry as you used to do. Are you not well, Colonel?

FREEMAN.

He has got a woman in his head, landlord, can you 55 help him?

SACKBUT.

If 'tis in my power, I shan't scruple to serve my friend.

COLONEL.

'Tis one perquisite of your calling.

SACKBUT.

Aye, at t'other end of the town,[7] where you officers 60 use, women are good forcers of trade; a well-customed house, a handsome bar-keeper, with clean, obliging drawers, soon gets the master an estate; but our citizens* seldom do anything but

cheat within the walls. But as to the lady, Colonel: 65 Point you at particulars, or have you a good champagne[8] stomach? Are you in full pay or reduced, Colonel?

COLONEL.

Reduced, reduced, landlord.

FREEMAN.

To the miserable condition of a lover! 70

SACKBUT.

Pish! That's preferable to half pay; a woman's resolution may break before the peace;[9] push her home, Colonel, there's no parleying with that sex.

COLONEL.

Were the lady her own mistress, I have some reasons to believe I should soon command in chief. 75

FREEMAN.

You know Mrs. Lovely, Mr. Sackbut.

SACKBUT.

Know her! Aye, poor Nancy;[10] I have carried her to school many a frosty morning. Alas! If she's the woman, I pity you, Colonel. Her father, my old master, was the most whimsical, out-of-the-way 80 tempered man I ever heard of, as you will guess by his last will and testament. This was his only child: I have heard him wish her dead a thousand times.

COLONEL.

Why so?

SACKBUT.

He hated posterity, you must know, and wished 85 the world were to expire with himself. He used to swear if she had been a boy, he would have qualified him for the opera.[11]

FREEMAN.

'Tis a very unnatural resolution in a father.

SACKBUT.

He died worth thirty thousand pounds, which he 90 left to this daughter, provided she married with the

---

7 t'other ... town] the West End, the fashionable part of London, which Sackbut contrasts with the City.* Women in West End establishments would draw in customers with the prospect of sex, to the profit of the tavern owners; city cheaters were not, according to Sackbut, so enterprising.

8 champagne] probably in two senses: an open field and a military campaign

9 the peace] the Peace of Utrecht (1713) led to officers being reduced to half pay; it was unpopular with many Whigs, including Centlivre.

10 Nancy] diminutive of Anne

11 qualified ... opera] castrated him, as were the *castrati* who sang male soprano roles in Italian opera

consent of her guardians. But that she might be
sure never to do so, he left her in the care of four
men as opposite to each other as light and
darkness. Each has his quarterly rule, and three   95
months in a year she is obliged to be subject to
each of their humours, and they are pretty
different, I assure you. She is just come from Bath.

COLONEL.

'Twas there I saw her.

SACKBUT.

Aye, sir, the last quarter was her beau-guardian's.   100
She appears in all public places during his reign.

COLONEL.

She visted a lady who boarded in the same house
with me. I liked her person,* and found an
opportunity to tell her so. She replied, she had no
objection to mine; but if I could not reconcile   105
contradictions, I must not think of her, for that
she was condemned to the caprice of four persons
who never yet agreed in any one thing, and she
was obliged to please them all.

SACKBUT.

'Tis most true, sir; I'll give you a short description   110
of the men and leave you to judge of the poor
lady's condition. One is a kind of a virtuoso, a silly,
half-witted fellow, but positive and surly; fond of
nothing but what is antique and foreign, and wears
his clothes of the fashion of the last century; dotes   115
upon travelers and believes Sir John Mandeville[12]
more than the Bible.

COLONEL.

That must be a rare old fellow!

SACKBUT.

Another is a changebroker; a fellow that will out-lie
the devil for the advantage of stock and cheat his   120
father that got him in a bargain. He is a great stickler
for trade and hates everything that wears a sword.

FREEMAN.

He is a great admirer of the Dutch management[13]

---

12 Sir John Mandeville] (fl. 1356) the ostensible author of
a collection of travelers' tales, who by the eighteenth century was regarded as a great liar
13 Dutch management] The Dutch provided the English
with models for advanced trade and financial practices,
including the national debt and the stock market.

and swears they understand trade better than any
nation under the sun.   125

SACKBUT.

The third is an old beau that has May in his fancy
and dress, but December in his face and his heels;
he admires nothing but new fashions, and those
must be French; loves operas, balls, masquerades,
and is always the most tawdry of the whole   130
company on a birthday.*

COLONEL.

These are pretty opposite to one another, truly!
And the fourth, what is he, landlord?

SACKBUT.

A very rigid Quaker, whose quarter begun this day.
I saw Mrs. Lovely go in not above two hours ago.   135
Sir Philip set her down. What think you now,
Colonel, is not the poor lady to be pitied?

COLONEL.

Aye, and rescued too, landlord.

FREEMAN.

In my opinion, that's impossible.

COLONEL.

There is nothing impossible to a lover. What   140
would not a man attempt for a fine woman and
thirty thousand pounds? Besides, my honor is at
stake; I promised to deliver her—and she bade me
win her and take her.

SACKBUT.

That's fair, faith.   145

FREEMAN.

If it depended upon knight-errantry, I should not
doubt your setting free the damsel; but to have
avarice, impertinence, hypocrisy, and pride at once
to deal with, requires more cunning than generally
attends a man of honor.   150

COLONEL.

My fancy tells me I shall come off with glory; I
resolve to try, however.—Do you know all the
guardians, Mr. Sackbut?

SACKBUT.

Very well, sir, they all use my house.

COLONEL.

And will you assist me, if occasion be?   155

SACKBUT.

In everything I can, Colonel.

FREEMAN.

I'll answer for him; and whatever I can serve you in, you may depend on. I know Mr. Periwinkle and Mr. Tradelove; the latter has a very great opinion of my interest abroad. I happened to have a letter from a correspondent two hours before the news arrived of the French king's death;[14] I communicated it to him; upon which he bought up all the stock he could, and what with that and some wagers he laid, he told me, he had got to the tune of five hundred pounds; so that I am much in his good graces.

COLONEL.

I don't know but you may be of service to me, Freeman.

FREEMAN.

If I can, command me, Colonel.

COLONEL.

Is it not possible to find a suit of clothes ready-made at some of these sale shops,[15] fit to rig out a beau, think you, Mr. Sackbut?

SACKBUT.

Oh, hang 'em. No, Colonel, they keep nothing ready-made that a gentleman would be seen in. But I can fit you with a suit of clothes, if you'd make a figure—velvet and gold brocade—they were pawned to me by a French Count, who had been stripped at play and wanted money to carry him home; he promised to send for them, but I have heard nothing from him.

FREEMAN.

He has not fed upon frogs long enough yet to recover his loss! Ha, ha.

COLONEL.

Ha, ha. Well, those clothes will do, Mr. Sackbut—though we must have three or four fellows in tawdry liveries; those can be procured, I hope.

FREEMAN.

Egad, I have a brother come from the West Indies that can match you; and, for expedition sake, you shall have his servants; there's a black, a tawny-moor,[16] and a Frenchman; they don't speak one word of English, so can make no mistake.

COLONEL.

Excellent. Egad, I shall look like an Indian prince. First I'll attack my beau-guardian. Where lives he?

SACKBUT.

Faith, somewhere about St. James's;* though to say in what street, I cannot; but any chairman* will tell you where Sir Philip Modelove lives.

FREEMAN.

Oh! You'll find him in the Park* at eleven every day; at least I never passed through at that hour without seeing him there. But what do you intend?

COLONEL.

To address him in his own way, and find what he designs to do with the lady.

FREEMAN.

And what then?

COLONEL.

Nay, that I can't tell, but I shall take my measures accordingly.

SACKBUT.

Well, 'tis a mad undertaking, in my mind; but here's to your success, Colonel. (*Drinks.*)

COLONEL.

'Tis something out of the way, I confess; but Fortune may chance to smile, and I succeed. Come, landlord, let me see those clothes. Freeman, I shall expect you'll leave word with Mr. Sackbut where one may find you upon occasion; and send my equipage of India immediately, do you hear?

FREEMAN.

Immediately. (*Exit.*)

COLONEL.

Bold was the man who ventured first to sea,
But the first vent'ring lovers bolder were:
The path of love's a dark and dangerous way,
Without a landmark, or one friendly star,
And he that runs the risk, deserves the fair. (*Exit.*)

---

14 French king's death] Louis XIV died September 1, 1715; this prevented France from carrying out plans to support the Jacobite rebellion in England and was therefore good for trade.

15 sale shops] shops specializing in inferior, ready-made clothing

16 tawny-moor] brown-skinned foreigner, originally referring to North Africans

Scene ii. Prim's House.
Enter Mrs. Lovely and her maid Betty.

BETTY.

Bless me, madam! Why do you fret and tease
yourself so? This is giving them the advantage with
a witness.

MRS. LOVELY.

Must I be condemned all my life to the
preposterous humours of other people and pointed   5
at by every boy in town? Oh! I could tear my flesh
and curse the hour I was born. Is it not
monstrously ridiculous that they should desire to
impose their Quaking dress[17] upon me at these
years? When I was a child, no matter what they   10
made me wear; but now—

BETTY.

I would resolve against it, madam; I'd see 'em
hanged before I'd put on the pinched[18] cap again.

MRS. LOVELY.

Then I must never expect one moment's ease; she has
rung such a peal in my ears already that I shan't have   15
the right use of them this month. What can I do?

BETTY.

What can you not do, if you will but give your
mind to it? Marry, madam.

MRS. LOVELY.

What! and have my fortune go to build churches
and hospitals?   20

BETTY.

Why, let it go. If the Colonel loves you, as he
pretends, he'll marry you without a fortune,
madam; and I assure you, a colonel's lady is no
despicable thing; a colonel's post will maintain you
like a gentlewoman, madam.   25

MRS. LOVELY.

So you would advise me to give up my own
fortune and throw myself upon the colonel's.

BETTY.

I would advise you to make yourself easy, madam.

MRS. LOVELY.

That's not the way, I am sure. No, no, girl, there
are certain ingredients to be mingled with   30

matrimony without which I may as well change
for the worse as for the better. When the woman
has fortune enough to make the man happy, if he
has either honor or good manners, he'll make her
easy. Love makes but a slovenly figure in that house   35
where poverty keeps the door.

BETTY.

And so you resolve to die a maid, do you, madam?

MRS. LOVELY.

Or have it in my power to make the man I love
master of my fortune.

BETTY.

Then you don't like the colonel so well as I thought   40
you did, madam, or you would not take such a
resolution.

MRS. LOVELY.

It is because I do like him, Betty, that I take such
a resolution.

BETTY.

Why, do you expect, madam, the colonel can work   45
miracles? Is it possible for him to marry you with
the consent of all your guardians?

MRS. LOVELY.

Or he must not marry me at all, and so I told him;
and he did not seem displeased with the news. He
promised to set me free, and I, on that condition,   50
promised to make him master of that freedom.

BETTY.

Well! I have read of enchanted castles, ladies
delivered from the chains of magic, giants killed,
and monsters overcome; so that I shall be the less
surprised if the colonel should conjure you out of   55
the power of your guardians. If he does, I am sure
he deserves your fortune.

MRS. LOVELY.

And shall have it, girl, if it were ten times as much.
For I'll ingenuously confess to thee, that I do like
the colonel above all men I ever saw. There's   60
something so *jantée*[19] in a soldier, a kind of a je
ne sais quoi air that makes 'em more agreeable than
the rest of mankind. They command regard, as
who should say, "We are your defenders, we
preserve your beauties from the insults of rude,   65
unpolished foes," and ought to be preferred before

---

17 Quaking dress] the very plain, old-fashioned, and concealing style of dress worn by Quaker women
18 pinched] pleated

19 *jantée*] dashing (Fr.)

those lazy, indolent mortals, who, by dropping into their father's estate, set up their coaches and think to rattle themselves into our affections.

BETTY.

Nay, madam, I confess that the army has engrossed all the prettiest fellows. A laced coat and feather have irresistible charms. 70

MRS. LOVELY.

But the colonel has all the beauties of the mind, as well as person. Oh all ye powers that favor happy lovers, grant he may be mine! Thou God of Love, if thou be'st ought but name, assist my Fainwell. Point all thy darts to aid my love's design, And make his plots as prevalent as thine. 75

Act II, scene i. The park.

Enter Colonel finely dressed, three footmen after him.

COLONEL.

So, now if I can but meet this beau. Egad, methinks I cut a smart figure, and have as much of the tawdry air as any Italian count or French marquis of 'em all. Sure I shall know this knight again.—Hah! Yonder he sits, making love* to a mask,* i'faith. I'll walk up the Mall,* and come down by him. (*Exit.*) 5

Scene draws and discovers Sir Philip upon a bench with a woman, masked.*

SIR PHILIP.

Well, but, my dear, are you really constant to your keeper*?

WOMAN.

Yes, really, sir.—Hey day! Who comes yonder? He cuts a mighty figure. 10

SIR PHILIP.

Hah! A stranger, by his equipage keeping so close at his heels. He has the appearance of a man of quality.* Positively French by his dancing air.

WOMAN.

He crosses, as if he meant to sit down here. 15

SIR PHILIP.

He has a mind to make love to thee, child.

Enter Colonel and seats himself upon the bench by Sir Philip.

WOMAN.

It will be to no purpose if he does.

SIR PHILIP.

Are you resolved to be cruel then?

COLONEL.

You must be very cruel, indeed, if you can deny anything to so fine a gentleman, madam. (*Takes out his watch.*) 20

WOMAN.

I never mind the outside of a man.

COLONEL.

And I'm afraid thou art no judge of the inside.

SIR PHILIP.

I am, positively, of your mind, sir. For creatures of her function seldom penetrate beyond the pocket. 25

WOMAN. (*Aside.*)

Creatures of your composition have, indeed, generally more in their pockets than in their heads.

SIR PHILIP.

Pray what says your watch? Mine is down. (*Pulling out his watch.*) 30

COLONEL.

I want* thirty-six minutes of twelve, sir. (*Puts up his watch and takes out his snuffbox.*)

SIR PHILIP.

May I presume, sir?

COLONEL.

Sir, you honor me. (*Presenting the box.*)

SIR PHILIP. [*Aside.*]

He speaks good English, though he must be a foreigner.—This snuff is extremely good and the box prodigious fine; the work is French, I presume, sir. 35

COLONEL.

I bought it in Paris, sir. I do think the workmanship pretty neat. 40

SIR PHILIP.

Neat, 'tis exquisitely fine, sir; pray, sir, if I may take the liberty of inquiring—what country is so happy to claim the birth of the finest gentleman in the universe? France, I presume.

COLONEL.

Then you don't think me an Englishman? 45

SIR PHILIP.

No, upon my soul don't I.

COLONEL.

I am sorry for't.

SIR PHILIP.

Impossible you should wish to be an Englishman. Pardon me, sir, this island could not produce a person of such alertness. 50

COLONEL.

As this mirror shows you, sir. (*Puts up a pocket-glass to Sir Philip's face.*)

WOMAN. [*Aside.*]

Coxcombs, I'm sick to hear 'em praise one another; one seldom gets anything by such animals, not even a dinner, unless one can dine upon soup and 55 celery. (*Exit.*)

SIR PHILIP.

Oh Ged, sir!—Will you leave us, madam? Ha, ha.

COLONEL.

She fears 'twill be only losing time to stay here, ha, ha. I know not how to distinguish you, sir, but your mien and address speak you Right Honorable.[20] 60

SIR PHILIP.

Thus great souls judge of others by themselves. I am only adorned with knighthood, that's all, I assure you, sir; my name is Sir Philip Modelove.

COLONEL.

Of French extraction?

SIR PHILIP.

My father was French. 65

COLONEL.

One may plainly perceive it—there is a certain gaiety peculiar to my nation (for I will own myself a Frenchman), which distinguishes us everywhere. A person of your figure would be a vast addition to a coronet. 70

SIR PHILIP.

I must own, I had the offer of a barony about five years ago,[21] but I abhorred the fatigue which must have attended it. I could never yet bring myself to join with either party.

COLONEL.

You are perfectly in the right, Sir Philip. A fine 75

person should not embark himself in the slovenly concern of politics; dress and pleasure are objects proper for the soul of a fine gentleman.

SIR PHILIP.

And love—

COLONEL.

Oh! That's included under the article of pleasure. 80

SIR PHILIP.

Parbleu, il est un homme d'esprit.[22]—I must embrace you. (*Rises and embraces.*) Your sentiments are so agreeable to mine that we appear to have but one soul, for our ideas and conceptions are the same. 85

COLONEL. (*Aside.*)

I should be sorry for that.—You do me too much honor, Sir Philip.

SIR PHILIP.

Your vivacity and *jantée* mien assured me at first sight there was nothing of this foggy island in your composition. May I crave your name, sir? 90

COLONEL.

My name is La Fainwell, sir, at your service.

SIR PHILIP.

The La Fainwells are French, I know; though the name is become very numerous in Great Britain of late years. I was sure you was French the moment I laid my eyes upon you; I could not come into the 95 supposition of your being an Englishman; this island produces few such ornaments.

COLONEL.

Pardon me, Sir Philip, this island has two things superior to all nations under the sun.

SIR PHILIP.

Aye! What are they? 100

COLONEL.

The ladies and the laws.

SIR PHILIP.

The laws indeed do claim a preference of other nations, but by my soul there are fine women everywhere. I must own I have felt their power in all countries. 105

COLONEL.

There are some finished beauties, I confess, in France, Italy, Germany, nay, even in Holland; *mais*

---

20 Right Honorable] i.e. a member of the nobility

21 offer ... ago] a reference to Queen Anne's creation of twelve new Tory peers in 1712 to ensure that the Treaty of Utrecht would pass the House of Lords

22 *Parbleu ... d'esprit*] Good Lord, he is a man of wit. (Fr.)

sont bien rares.[23] But *les belles Anglaises!*[24] Oh, Sir Philip, where find we such women! such symmetry of shape! such elegancy of dress! such regularity of features! such sweetness of temper! such commanding eyes! and such bewitching smiles?

SIR PHILIP.

Ah! *Parbleu, vous êtes attrapé.*[25]

COLONEL.

Non, je vous assure, chevalier[26]—but I declare there is no amusement so agreeable to my *goût,*[27] as the conversation* of a fine woman. I could never be prevailed upon to enter into what the vulgar calls the pleasure of the bottle.

SIR PHILIP.

My own taste, *positivement.* A ball or a masquerade is certainly preferable to all the productions of the vineyard.

COLONEL.

Infinitely! I hope the people of quality in England will support that branch of pleasure which was imported with their peace[28] and since naturalized by the ingenious Mr. Heidegger.[29]

SIR PHILIP.

The ladies assure me it will become part of the constitution, upon which I subscribed an hundred guineas. It will be of great service to the public, at least to the Company of Surgeons[30] and the City in general.

COLONEL.

Ha, ha, it may help to ennoble the blood of the City.[31] Are you married, Sir Philip?

SIR PHILIP.

No, nor do I believe I ever shall enter into that honorable state; I have an absolute tender for the whole sex.

COLONEL. (*Aside.*)

That's more than they have for you I dare swear.

SIR PHILIP.

And I have the honor to be very well with the ladies, I can assure you, sir, and I won't affront a million of fine women to make one happy.

COLONEL.

Nay, marriage is really reducing a man's taste to a kind of half-pleasure, but then it carries the blessing of peace along with it; one goes to sleep without fear and wakes without pain.

SIR PHILIP.

There is something of that in't; a wife is a very good dish for an English stomach, but gross feeding for nicer* palates, ha, ha, ha!

COLONEL.

I find I was very much mistaken—I imagined you had been married to that young lady which I saw in the chariot* with you this morning in Gracechurch Street.[32]

SIR PHILIP.

Who, Nancy Lovely? I am a piece of a guardian to that lady, you must know; her father, I thank him, joined me with three of the most preposterous old fellows—that upon my soul I'm in pain for the poor girl—she must certainly lead apes,[33] as the saying is, ha, ha.

COLONEL.

That's pity. Sir Philip, if the lady would give me leave, I would endeavor to avert that curse.

SIR PHILIP.

As to the lady, she'd gladly be rid of us at any rate, I believe; but here's the mischief, he who marries

---

23 *mais ... rares*] but they are very rare (Fr.)

24 *les ... Anglaises*] the English beauties (Fr.)

25 *Parbleu ... attrapé.*] Good Lord, you are caught. (Fr.)

26 *Non ... chevalier*] No, I assure you, knight. (Fr.)

27 *goût*] taste (Fr.)

28 branch ... peace] The French ambassador to England, the Duc D'Aumont, held some of the earliest masked balls in London in 1713, after the Peace of Utrecht.

29 Mr. Heidegger] John James ("Count") Heidegger (1659?-1749), the manager of the Haymarket Theater, who began presenting public masquerades there in 1717

30 Company of Surgeons] the doctors' guild, the members of which will be paid for cures for venereal disease

31 ennoble ... City] Masquerades were condemned for promoting immorality and the indiscriminate mingling of

classes (thanks to the leveling anonymity of masquerade costume which fostered sexual liasions across class boundaries).

32 Gracechurch Street] in the City, running from London Bridge and the Monument to Cornhill; nearby was the oldest Quaker meeting-house in London.

33 lead apes] proverbial: old maids lead apes in hell as punishment for not marrying while they could.

Miss Lovely, must have the consent of us all four, or not a penny of her portion. For my part, I shall never approve of any but a man of figure, and the rest are not only averse to cleanliness, but have each a peculiar taste to gratify. For my part, I declare, I would prefer you to all men I ever saw—— 165

COLONEL.

And I her to all women——

SIR PHILIP.

I assure you, Mr. Fainwell, I am for marrying her, for I hate the trouble of a guardian, especially among such wretches; but resolve never to agree to the choice of any one of them, and I fancy they'll be even with me, for they never came into any proposal of mine yet. 170

COLONEL.

I wish I had your leave to try them, Sir Philip.

SIR PHILIP.

With all my soul, sir, I can refuse a person of your appearance nothing. 175

COLONEL.

Sir, I am infinitely obliged to you.

SIR PHILIP.

But do you really like matrimony?

COLONEL.

I believe I could with that lady, sir.

SIR PHILIP.

The only point in which we differ—but you are master of so many qualifications that I can excuse one fault, for I must think it a fault in a fine gentleman; and that you are such, I'll give it under my hand. 180

COLONEL.

I wish you'd give me your consent to marry Mrs. Lovely under your hand, Sir Philip. 185

SIR PHILIP.

I'll do't, if you'll step into St. James's Coffee-house,[34] where we may have pen and ink. Though I can't forsee what advantage my consent will be to you without you could find a way to get the rest of the guardians'. But I'll introduce you, however; she is now at a Quaker's, where I carried her this morning, when you saw us in Gracechurch 190

Street. I assure you she has an odd *ragoût* of guardians, as you will find when you hear the characters,* which I'll endeavor to give you as we go along.—— Hey! Pierre, Jacques, Renault—where are you all, scoundrels? Order the chariot to St. James's Coffee-house. 195

COLONEL.

Le noir, le brun, le blanc—mortbleu, où sont ces coquins-là? Allons, monsieur le chevalier.[35] 200

SIR PHILIP.

Ah! *Pardonnez moi, monsieur.*

COLONEL.

Not one step, upon my soul, Sir Philip.

SIR PHILIP.

The best-bred man in Europe, positively.

Exeunt.

Scene ii. Obadiah Prim's house.

Enter Mrs. Lovely followed by Mrs. Prim.

MRS. PRIM.

Then thou[36] wilt not obey me; and thou dost really think those fal-lals becometh thee?

MRS. LOVELY.

I do, indeed.

MRS. PRIM.

Now will I be judged by all sober people, if I don't look more like a modest woman than thou dost, Anne. 5

MRS. LOVELY.

More like a hypocrite, you mean, Mrs. Prim.

MRS. PRIM.

Ah! Anne, Anne, that wicked Philip Modelove will undo thee. Satan so fills thy heart with pride during the three months of his guardianship, that thou becomest a stumbling block to the upright. 10

MRS. LOVELY.

Pray, who are they? Are the pinched cap and formal

---

34 St. James's Coffee-house] on St. James's Street, a Whig establishment, patronized by Steele and Addison

35 *Le noir ... chevalier.*] The black, the brown, the white—zounds, where are these rascals? Let us go, sir knight. (Fr.)

36 thou] the use of "thee" and "thou" was one of the Quaker "public testimonies" of conversion; it was intended to reproduce biblical language and to eliminate one of the designations of rank, since inferiors were expected to use "you" to their superiors.

hood the emblems of sanctity? Does your virtue consist in your dress, Mrs. Prim?

MRS. PRIM.

It doth not consist in cut hair, spotted face,[37] and bare necks. Oh, the wickedness of this generation! The primitive women[38] knew not the abomination of hooped petticoats. 15

MRS. LOVELY.

No, nor the abomination of cant neither. Don't tell me, Mrs. Prim, don't. I know you have as much pride, vanity, self-conceit, and ambition among you, couched under that formal habit and sanctified countenance, as the proudest of us all; but the world begins to see your prudery. 20

MRS. PRIM.

Prudery! What! Do they invent new words[39] as well as new fashions? Ah! Poor, fantastic age, I pity thee. Poor deluded Anne, which dost thou think most resemblest the saint and which the sinner, thy dress or mine? Thy naked bosom allureth the eye of the bystander, encourageth the frailty of human nature, and corrupteth the soul with evil longings. 25 30

MRS. LOVELY.

And pray who corrupted your son Tobias with evil longings? Your maid Tabitha wore a handkerchief,[40] and yet he made the Saint* a sinner. 35

MRS. PRIM.

Well, well, spit thy malice. I confess Satan did buffet my son Tobias and my servant Tabitha; the evil spirit was at that time too strong and they both became subject to its workings—not from any outward provocation—but from an inward call; he was not tainted with the rottenness of the fashions, nor did his eyes take in the drunkenness of beauty. 40

---

37 cut hair, spotted face] hair trimmed to frame the face, rather than being pulled straight back; face fashionably decorated with patches made of silk or velvet

38 primitive women] women of the earliest Christian church

39 Prudery ... new words] prudishness; originally a French word; the first recorded English usage occurs in *The Tatler*, No. 126 (1709).

40 handkerchief] scarf draped around the neck to conceal a low neckline

MRS. LOVELY.

No! That's plainly to be seen.

MRS. PRIM.

Tabitha is one of the faithful, he fell not with a stranger. 45

MRS. LOVELY.

So! Then you hold wenching no crime, provided it be within the pale of your own tribe. You are an excellent casuist, truly.

Enter Obadiah Prim.

OBADIAH PRIM.

Not stripped of thy vanity yet, Anne? Why dost not thou make her put it off, Sarah? 50

MRS. PRIM.

She will not do it.

OBADIAH PRIM.

Verily, thy naked breasts troubleth my outward man; I pray thee hide 'em, Anne; put on a handkerchief, Anne Lovely.

MRS. LOVELY.

I hate handkerchiefs when 'tis not cold weather, Mr. Prim. 55

MRS. PRIM.

I have seen thee wear a handkerchief; nay, and a mask to boot, in the middle of July.

MRS. LOVELY.

Aye, to keep the sun from scorching me.

OBADIAH PRIM.

If thou couldst not bear the sunbeams, how dost thou think man should bear thy beams? Those breasts inflame desire; let them be hid, I say. 60

MRS. LOVELY.

Let me be quiet, I say. Must I be tormented thus forever? Sure no woman's condition ever equalled mine; foppery, folly, avarice, and hypocrisy are by turns my constant companions, and I must vary shapes as often as a player. I cannot think my father meant this tyranny! No; you usurp an authority which he never intended you should take. 65

OBADIAH PRIM.

Hark thee, dost thou call good counsel tyranny? Do I, or my wife, tyrannize when we desire thee in all love to put off thy tempting attire and veil thy provokers to sin? 70

MRS. LOVELY.

Deliver me, good Heaven! Or I shall go distracted. (*Walks about.*)

MRS. PRIM.

So! Now thy pinners are tossed and thy breasts pulled up; verily they were seen enough before; fie upon the filthy tailor who made them stays.

MRS. LOVELY.

I wish I were in my grave! Kill me rather than treat me thus.

OBADIAH PRIM.

Kill thee! Ha, ha; thou think'st thou art acting some lewd play sure; kill thee! Art thou prepared for death, Anne Lovely? No, no, thou wouldst rather have a husband, Anne. Thou wantest a gilt coach with six lazy fellows behind to flaunt it in the ring of vanity among the princes and rulers of the land, who pamper themselves with the fatness thereof; but I will take care that none shall squander away thy father's estate; thou shalt marry none such, Anne.

MRS. LOVELY.

Would you marry me to one of your own canting sect?[b]

OBADIAH PRIM.

Yea, verily, none else shall ever get my consent, I do assure thee, Anne.

MRS. LOVELY.

And I do assure thee, Obadiah, that I will as soon turn papist and die in a convent.

MRS. PRIM.

Oh wickedness!

MRS. LOVELY.

Oh stupidity!

OBADIAH PRIM.

Oh blindness of heart!

MRS. LOVELY. [*Aside to Prim.*]

Thou blinder of the world, don't provoke me, lest I betray your sanctity and leave your wife to judge of your purity. What were the emotions of your spirit when you squeezed Mary by the hand last night in the pantry, when she told you, you bussed so filthily? Ah! You had no aversion to naked bosoms when you begged her to show you a little, little, little bit of her delicious bubby. Don't you remember those words, Mr. Prim?

MRS. PRIM.

What does she say, Obadiah?

OBADIAH PRIM.

She talketh unintelligibly, Sarah. (*Aside.*) Which way did she hear this? This should not have reached the ears of the wicked ones; verily, it troubleth me.

Enter servant.

SERVANT.

Philip Modelove, whom they call Sir Philip,[41] is below, and such another with him; shall I send them up?

OBADIAH PRIM.

Yea. (*Exit [servant].*)

Enter Sir Philip and Colonel.

SIR PHILIP.

How dost thou do, Friend Prim. Odso! My she-Friend here too! What, you are documenting[42] Miss Nancy, reading her a lecture upon the pinched coif, I warrant ye.

MRS. PRIM.

I am sure thou never readest her any lecture that was good.—My flesh riseth so at these wicked ones that prudence adviseth me to withdraw from their sight. (*Exit.*)

COLONEL. (*Aside.*)

Oh! That I could find means to speak to her! How charming she appears! I wish I could get this letter into her hand.

SIR PHILIP.

Well, Miss Cocky,[43] I hope thou hast got the better of them.

MRS. LOVELY.

The difficulties of my life are not to be surmounted, Sir Philip. (*Aside.*) I hate the impertinence of him as much as the stupidity of the other.

OBADIAH PRIM.

Verily, Philip, thou wilt spoil this maiden.

---

41 Philip … Sir Philip] the refusal to use honorific titles was another Quaker public testimony.

42 documenting] admonishing in an authoritative or imperious manner

43 Miss Cocky] a term of endearment

SIR PHILIP.

I find we still differ in opinion; but that we may none of us spoil her, prithee, Prim, let us consent to marry her. I have sent for our brother guardians to meet me here about that very thing.—Madam, will you give me leave to recommend a husband to you? Here's a gentleman which, in my mind, you can have no objection to. (*Presents the Colonel to her; she looks another way.*) 135

MRS. LOVELY. (*Aside.*)

Heaven deliver me from the formal and the fantastic fool.

COLONEL.

A fine woman, a fine horse, and fine equipage are the finest things in the universe. And if I am so happy to possess you, madam, I shall become the envy of mankind, as much as you outshine your whole sex. (*As he takes her hand to kiss it, he endeavors to put a letter into it; she lets it drop; Prim takes it up.*) 145

MRS. LOVELY. (*Turning from him.*)

I have no ambition to appear conspicuously ridiculous, sir.

COLONEL.

So fall^c the hopes of Fainwell.

MRS. LOVELY. (*Aside.*)

Hah! Fainwell! 'Tis he! What have I done? Prim has the letter and all will be discovered. 155

OBADIAH PRIM.

Friend, I know not thy name, so cannot call thee by it, but thou seest thy letter is unwelcome to the maiden; she will not read it.

MRS. LOVELY.

Nor shall you. (*Snatches the letter.*) I'll tear it in a thousand pieces and scatter it, as I will the hopes of all those that any of you shall recommend to me. (*Tears the letter.*) 160

SIR PHILIP.

Hah! Right woman, faith!

COLONEL. (*Aside.*)

Excellent woman.

OBADIAH PRIM.

Friend, thy garb favoreth too much of the vanity of the age for my approbation; nothing that resembleth Philip Modelove shall I love, mark that; therefore, Friend Philip, bring no more of thy own apes under my roof. 165

SIR PHILIP.

I am so entirely a stranger to the monsters of thy breed that I shall bring none of them, I am sure. 170

COLONEL. (*Aside.*)

I am likely to have a pretty task by that time I have gone through them all; but she's a city worth taking and egad I'll carry on the siege. If I can but blow up the outworks, I fancy I am pretty secure of the town. 175

Enter servant.

SERVANT. (*To Sir Philip.*)

Toby Periwinkle and Thomas Tradelove demandeth to see thee.

SIR PHILIP.

Bid them come up.

MRS. LOVELY.

Deliver me from such an inundation of noise and nonsense. [*Aside.*] Oh Fainwell! Whatever thy contrivance is, prosper it Heaven; but oh, I fear thou never canst redeem me. (*Exit.*) 180

SIR PHILIP.

Sic transit gloria mundi.

Enter Mr. Periwinkle and Tradelove.

(*Aside to the Colonel.*) These are my brother guardians, Mr. Fainwell; prithee observe the creatures. 185

TRADELOVE.

Well, Sir Philip, I obey your summons.

PERIWINKLE.

Pray, what have you to offer for the good of Mrs. Lovely, Sir Philip?

SIR PHILIP.

First, I desire to know what you intend to do with that lady. Must she be sent to the Indies for a venture,^44 or live to be an old maid and then entered amongst your curiosities and shown for a monster,^45 Mr. Periwinkle? 190

---

44 sent ... venture] sent to the colonies in one of Tradelove's enterprises, here perhaps securing a marriage to a wealthy planter

45 live ... monster] old maids were considered unnatural in the sense that their reproductive capacities were not turned to account; as a virtuoso, Periwinkle collects such oddities ("curiosities").

COLONEL. (*Aside*.)

Humph, curiosities! That must be the virtuoso. 195

PERIWINKLE.

Why, what would you do with her?

SIR PHILIP.

I would recommend this gentleman to her for a husband, sir—a person whom I have picked out from the whole race of mankind.

OBADIAH PRIM.

I would advise thee to shuffle him again with the 200
rest of mankind, for I like him not.

COLONEL.

Pray, sir, without offence to your formality, what may be your objections?

OBADIAH PRIM.

Thy person; thy manners; thy dress; thy acquaintance; thy everything, Friend. 205

SIR PHILIP.

You are most particulary obliging, Friend, ha, ha.

TRADELOVE.

What business do you follow, pray, sir?

COLONEL. (*Aside*.)

Humph, by that question he must be the broker.—Business, sir! The business of a gentleman.

TRADELOVE.

That is as much to say, you dress fine, feed high, 210
lie with every woman you like, and pay your surgeon's bills[46] better than your tailor's or your butcher's.

COLONEL.

The Court is much obliged to you, sir, for your character* of a gentleman. 215

TRADELOVE.

The Court, sir! What would the Court do without us citizens?

SIR PHILIP.

Without your wives and daughters, you mean, Mr. Tradelove?

PERIWINKLE.

Have you ever traveled, sir? 220

COLONEL. [*Aside*.]

That question must not be answered now.—In books I have, sir.

PERIWINKLE.

In books? That's fine traveling indeed!—Sir Philip, when you present a person I like, he shall have my consent to marry Mrs. Lovely—till when, your 225
servant. (*Exit*.)

COLONEL. (*Aside*.)

I'll make you like me before I have done with you, or I am mistaken.

TRADELOVE.

And when you can convince me that a beau is more useful to my country than a merchant, you 230
shall have mine—till then, you must excuse me. (*Exit*.)

COLONEL. (*Aside*.)

So much for trade. I'll fit* you too.

SIR PHILIP.

In my opinion, this is very inhumane treatment as to the lady, Mr. Prim. 235

OBADIAH PRIM.

Thy opinion and mine happens to differ as much as our occupations, Friend; business requireth my presence and folly thine, and so I must bid thee farewell. (*Exit*.)

SIR PHILIP.

Here's breeding for you, Mr. Fainwell! Gad take 240
me, I'd give half my estate to see these rascals bit.*

COLONEL. (*Aside*.)

I hope to bite you all, if my plots hit.

Act III, scene i. The tavern.

Sackbut and the Colonel in an Egyptian dress.[47]

SACKBUT.

A lucky beginning, Colonel—you have got the old beau's consent.

COLONEL.

Aye, he's a reasonable creature, but the other three will require some pains. Shall I pass upon him, think you? Egad, in my mind, I look as antique 5
as if I had been preserved in the ark.

SACKBUT.

Pass upon him! Aye, aye, as roundly as white wine

---

46 pay ... bills] payment for cures for venereal disease

47 *an Egyptian dress*] probably the conventional theatrical costume for Middle-Eastern characters: a long robe, baggy breeches, and a turban

dashed with sack does for mountain[48] and sherry, if you have but assurance enough.

COLONEL.

I have no apprehension from that quarter; 10
assurance is the cockade of a soldier.

SACKBUT.

Aye, but the assurance of a soldier differs much from
that of a traveler. Can you lie with a good grace?

COLONEL.

As heartily, when my mistress is the prize, as I would
meet the foe when my country called and king 15
commanded; so don't you fear that part; if he don't
know me again, I'm safe. I hope he'll come.

SACKBUT.

I wish all my debts would come as sure. I told him
you had been a great traveler, had many valuable
curiosities, and was a person of a most singular 20
taste; he seemed transported and begged me to
keep you till he came.

COLONEL.

Aye, aye, he need not fear my running away. Let's
have a bottle of sack, landlord, our ancestors drank
sack. 25

SACKBUT.

You shall have it.

COLONEL.

And whereabouts is the trap door you mentioned?

SACKBUT.

There's the conveyance, sir. (*Exit.*)

COLONEL.

Now if I should cheat all these roguish guardians
and carry off my mistress in triumph, it would be 30
what the French call a *grand coup d'éclat*.[49] Odso!
Here comes Periwinkle. Ah! Deuce take this beard;
pray Jupiter it does not give me the slip and spoil all.

Enter Sackbut with wine and Periwinkle following.

SACKBUT.

Sir, this gentleman, hearing you have been a great
traveler and a person of fine speculation,[50] begs 35
leave to take a glass with you; he is a man of
curious taste himself.

COLONEL.

The gentleman has it in his face and garb: sir, you
are welcome.

PERIWINKLE.

Sir, I honor a traveler and men of your inquiring 40
disposition. The oddness of your habit pleases me
extremely; 'tis very antique, and for that I like it.

COLONEL.

It is very antique, sir. This habit once belonged to
the famous Claudius Ptolemeus,[51] who lived in the
year a hundred and thirty five. 45

SACKBUT. (*Aside.*)

If he keeps up to the sample, he shall lie with the
devil for a bean-stack and win it every straw.[52]

PERIWINKLE.

A hundred and thirty-five! Why, that's prodigious
now. Well, certainly 'tis the finest thing in the
world to be a traveler. 50

COLONEL.

For my part, I value none of the modern fashions
of[53] a fig-leaf.

PERIWINKLE.

No more do I, sir; I had rather be the jest of a fool,
than his favorite. I am laughed at here for my
singularity. This coat, you must know, sir, was 55
formerly worn by that ingenious and very learned
person, John Tradescant.[54]

COLONEL.

John Tradescant! Let me embrace you, sir. John
Tradescant was my uncle, by mother-side; and I
thank you for the honor you do his memory; he 60
was a very curious man indeed.

PERIWINKLE.

Your uncle, sir! Nay then, 'tis no wonder that your
taste is so refined; why, you have it in your blood.

---

48 mountain] a variety of Malaga white wine made from
grapes grown in the mountains

49 *grand ... d'éclat*] great, dazzling feat (Fr.)

50 speculation] profound, conjectural reasoning

51 Claudius Ptolemeus] famous Greek astronomer, math-
ematician, and geographer of Alexandria, also known as
Ptolemy

52 lie ... straw] In a lying contest with the devil for a stack
of recently harvested beans, the Colonel would win it
down to the last straw.

53 of] at

54 John Tradsescant] (1608-1662) traveler, naturalist, and
gardener; his collection of natural curiosities was famous
and became the basis of the Ashmolean Museum.

My humble service to you, sir, to the immortal
memory of John Tradescant, your never-to-be-
forgotten uncle. (*Drinks.*)

COLONEL.

Give me a glass, landlord.

PERIWINKLE.

I find you are primitive even in your wine; canary
was the drink of our wise forefathers; 'tis balsamic
and saves the charge of apothecaries' cordials. Oh!
that I had lived in your uncle's days! Or rather, that
he were now alive. Oh! How proud he'd be of such
a nephew!

SACKBUT. (*Aside.*)

Oh pox! That would have spoiled the jest.

PERIWINKLE.

A person of your curiosity must have collected
many rarities.

COLONEL.

I have some, sir, which are not yet come ashore,
as an Egyptian's idol.

PERIWINKLE.

Pray, what might that be?

COLONEL.

It is, sir, a kind of an ape, which they formerly
worshipped in that country; I took it from the
breast of a female mummy.

PERIWINKLE.

Ha, ha! Our women retain part of their idolatry
to this day, for many an ape lies on a lady's breast,
ha, ha—

SACKBUT. (*Aside.*)

A smart old thief.

COLONEL.

Two tusks of an hippopotamus, two pair of
Chinese nutcrackers, and one Egyptian mummy.

PERIWINKLE.

Pray, sir, have you never a crocodile?

COLONEL.

Humph! The boatswain brought one with design to
show it, but touching at Rotterdam and hearing it
was no rarity in England, he sold it to a Dutch poet.

SACKBUT.

The devil's in that nation, it rivals us in everything.

PERIWINKLE.

I should have been very glad to have seen a living
crocodile.

COLONEL.

My genius led me to things more worthy of my
regard. Sir, I have seen the utmost limits of this
globular world; I have seen the sun rise and set;
know in what degree of heat he is at noon to the
breadth of a hair and what quantity of
combustibles he burns in a day, how much of it
turns to ashes and how much to cinders.

PERIWINKLE.

To cinders? You amaze me, sir; I never heard that
the sun consumed anything. Descartes[55] tells us—

COLONEL.

Descartes, with the rest of his brethren both
ancient and modern, knew nothing of the matter.
I tell you, sir, that nature admits an annual decay,
though imperceptible to vulgar eyes. Sometimes
his rays destroy below, sometimes above. You have
heard of blazing comets, I suppose?

PERIWINKLE.

Yes, yes, I remember to have seen one and our
astrologers tell us of another which shall happen
very quickly.[56]

COLONEL.

Those comets are little islands bordering on the sun,
which at certain times are set on fire by that
luminous body's moving over them perpendicular,
which will one day occasion a general conflagration.

SACKBUT. (*Aside.*)

One need not scruple the colonel's capacity, faith.

PERIWINKLE.

This is marvellous strange! These cinders are what
I never read of in any of our learned dissertations.

COLONEL. (*Aside.*)

I don't know how the devil you should.

SACKBUT. (*Aside.*)

He has it at his fingers' ends; one would swear he
had learned to lie at school, he does it so cleverly.

PERIWINKLE.

Well, you travelers see strange things! Pray, sir, have
you any of those cinders?

---

55 Descartes] René Descartes (1596-1650) wrote about sun
spots in his unfinished scientific work, *The World*.

56 astrologers … quickly] "astrologers" for "astronomers";
in 1705 Edmund Halley predicted the return of the
comet he had observed in 1682.

COLONEL.

I have, among my other curiosities.

PERIWINKLE.

Oh, what have I lost for want of traveling! Pray, what have you else?

COLONEL.

Several things worth your attention. I have a muff made of the feathers of those geese* that saved the 130 Roman Capitol.

PERIWINKLE.

Is't possible?

SACKBUT. (Aside.)

Yes, if you are such a goose to believe him.

COLONEL.

I have an Indian leaf, which open will cover an acre of land, yet folds up into so little a compass,* you 135 may put it into your snuffbox.

SACKBUT. (Aside.)

Humph! That's a thunderer.

PERIWINKLE.

Amazing!

COLONEL.

Ah! Mine is but a little one; I have seen some of them that would cover one of the Caribbean 140 islands.

PERIWINKLE.

Well, if I don't travel before I die, I shan't rest in my grave. Pray, what do the Indians with them?

COLONEL.

Sir, they use them in their wars for tents, the old women for riding hoods, the young for fans and 145 umbrellas.

SACKBUT. (Aside.)

He has a fruitful invention.

PERIWINKLE.

I admire our East India Company[57] imports none of them; they would certainly find their account in them. 150

COLONEL. (Aside.)

Right, if they could find the leaves.—Look ye, sir, do you see this little vial?

PERIWINKLE.

Pray you, what is it?

COLONEL.

This is called *poluflosboio*.[58]

PERIWINKLE.

Poluflosboio! It has a rumbling sound. 155

COLONEL.

Right, sir, it proceeds from a rumbling nature. This water was part of those waves which bore Cleopatra's vessel when she sailed to meet Anthony.

PERIWINKLE.

Well, of all that ever traveled, none had a taste like you. 160

COLONEL.

But here's the wonder of the world. This, sir, is called, *zona*[59] or *moros musphonon*,[60] the virtues of this is inestimable.

PERIWINKLE.

Moros musphonon! What in the name of wisdom can that be? To me it seems a plain belt. 165

COLONEL.

This girdle has carried me all the world over.

PERIWINKLE.

You have carried it, you mean.

COLONEL.

I mean as I say, sir. Whenever I am girded with this, I am invisible; and by turning this little screw can be in the court of the Great Mogul, the Grand 170 Seignior,[61] and King George in as little time as your cook can poach an egg.

PERIWINKLE.

You must pardon me, sir, I can't believe it.

COLONEL.

If my landlord pleases, he shall try the experiment immediately. 175

SACKBUT.

I thank you kindly, sir, but I have no inclination to ride post to the devil.

---

57 East India Company] joint-stock trading company with the monopoly on trade with India and Asia

58 *poluflosboio*] [*poluphloisboio*] loud-roaring (as of the sea—Greek)

59 *zona*] Latin form of the Greek word *zone*, a sash wrapped about the waist, usually having magical properties, often called in earlier periods a girdle

60 *moros musphonon*] fanciful Greek: "mousetrap for a fool" (Stathas)

61 Grand Seignior] the Sultan of Turkey

COLONEL.

No, no, you shan't stir a foot; I'll only make you invisible.

SACKBUT.

But if you could not make me visible again? 180

PERIWINKLE.

Come try it upon me, sir, I am not afraid of the devil nor all his tricks. 'Zbud,* I'll stand 'em all.

COLONEL.

There, sir, put it on. Come, landlord, you and I must face the east. (*They turn about.*) Is it on, sir?

PERIWINKLE.

'Tis on. (*They turn about again.*) 185

SACKBUT.

Heaven protect me! Where is he?

PERIWINKLE.

Why here, just where I was.

SACKBUT.

Where, where, in the name of virtue? Ah, poor Mr. Periwinkle! Egad, look to't, you had best, sir, and let him be seen again, or I shall have you burnt for a wizard. 190

COLONEL.

Have patience, good landlord.

PERIWINKLE.

But really, don't you see me now?

SACKBUT.

No more than I see my grandmother that died forty years ago. 195

PERIWINKLE.

Are you sure you don't lie? Methinks I stand just where I did and see you as plain as I did before.

SACKBUT.

Ah! I wish I could see you once again.

COLONEL.

Take off the girdle, sir. (*He takes it off.*)

SACKBUT.

Ah, sir, I am glad to see you with all my heart. (*Embraces him.*) 200

PERIWINKLE.

This is very odd; certainly, there must be some trick in't.—Pray, sir, will you do me the favor to put it on yourself?

COLONEL.

With all my heart. 205

PERIWINKLE.

But first I'll secure the door.

COLONEL.

You know how to turn the screw, Mr. Sackbut.

SACKBUT.

Yes, yes.—Come, Mr. Periwinkle, we must turn full east.

They turn; the Colonel sinks down a trapdoor.

COLONEL.

'Tis done; now turn. 210

They turn.

PERIWINKLE.

Hah! Mercy upon me! My flesh creeps upon my bones.—This must be a conjurer, Mr. Sackbut.

SACKBUT.

He is the devil, I think.

PERIWINKLE.

Oh! Mr. Sackbut, why do you name the devil when perhaps he may be at your elbow. 215

SACKBUT.

At my elbow! Marry, Heaven forbid.

COLONEL.

(*Below.*) Are you satisfied, sir?

PERIWINKLE.

Yes, sir, yes.—How hollow his voice sounds!

SACKBUT.

Yours seemed just the same. Faith, I wish this girdle were mine, I'd sell wine no more. Hark ye, Mr. Periwinkle (*takes him aside till the Colonel rises again*), if he would sell this girdle, you might travel with great expedition. 220

COLONEL.

But it is not to be parted with for money.

PERIWINKLE.

I am sorry for't, sir, because I think it the greatest curiosity I ever heard of. 225

COLONEL.

By the advice of a learned physiognomist in Grand Cairo, who consulted the lines in my face, I returned to England, where he told me I should find a rarity in the keeping of four men, which I was born to possess for the benefit of mankind, and the first of the four that gave me his consent, I should present him with this girdle. Till I have found this jewel, I shall not part with the girdle. 230

PERIWINKLE.

What can that rarity be? Did he not name it to you? 235

COLONEL.

Yes, sir; he called it a chaste, beautiful, unaffected woman.

PERIWINKLE.

Pish! Women are no rarities. I never had any great taste that way. I married, indeed, to please a father and I got a girl to please my wife; but she and the child (thank Heaven) died together. Women are the very gewgaws of the creation; playthings for boys, which, when they write man, they ought to throw aside.

SACKBUT. (*Aside.*)

A fine lecture to be read to a circle of ladies!

PERIWINKLE.

What woman is there, dressed in all the pride and foppery of the times, can boast of such a foretop[62] as the cockatoo?

COLONEL.

(*Aside.*) I must humor him.—Such a skin as the lizard?

PERIWINKLE.

Such a shining breast as the hummingbird?

COLONEL.

Such a shape as the antelope?

PERIWINKLE.

Or, in all the artful mixture of their various dresses, have they half the beauty of one box of butterflies?

COLONEL.

No, that must be allowed. For my part, if it were not for the benefit of mankind, I'd have nothing to do with them, for they are as indifferent to me as a sparrow or a flesh fly.

PERIWINKLE.

Pray, sir, what benefit is the world to reap from this lady?

COLONEL.

Why, sir, she is to bear me a son, who shall restore the art of embalming and the old Roman manner of burying their dead, and, for the benefit of posterity, he is to discover the longitude,[63] so long sought for in vain.

---

62 foretop] a nautical term, applied to hair arranged on the forehead; by analogy, the cockatoo's crest

63 discover the longitude] In 1714 Parliament had passed a bill offering a prize of £20,000 for the first person to develop an accurate way of finding the longitude at sea.

PERIWINKLE.

Od! These are very valuable things, Mr. Sackbut.

SACKBUT. (*Aside.*)

He hits it off admirably and t'other swallows it like sack* and sugar.—Certainly this lady must be your ward, Mr. Periwinkle, by her being under the care of four persons.

PERIWINKLE.

By the description it should. (*Aside.*) Egad, if I could get that girdle, I'd ride with the sun and make the tour of the whole world in four-and-twenty hours.—And are you to give that girdle to the first of the four guardians that shall give his consent to marry that lady, say you, sir?

COLONEL.

I am so ordered, when I can find him.

PERIWINKLE.

I fancy I know the very woman—her name is Anne Lovely.

COLONEL.

Excellent! He said, indeed, that the first letter of her name was *L*.

PERIWINKLE.

Did he really? Well, that's prodigiously amazing, that a person in Grand Cairo should know anything of my ward.

COLONEL.

Your ward?

PERIWINKLE.

To be plain with you, sir, I am one of those four guardians.

COLONEL.

Are you indeed, sir? I am transported to find the man who is to possess[d] this *moros musphonon* is a person of so curious a taste. Here is a writing drawn up by that famous Egyptian, which, if you will please to sign, you must turn your face full north, and the girdle is yours.

PERIWINKLE.

If I live till this boy is born, I'll be embalmed and sent to the Royal Society[64] when I die.

COLONEL.

That you shall most certainly.

---

64 Royal Society] scientific society founded by Royal Charter in 1662; by 1718 it was the butt of many a joke.

Enter drawer.

DRAWER.

Here's Mr. Staytape the tailor, inquires for you, Colonel.

SACKBUT.

Who do you speak to, you son of a whore?

PERIWINKLE. (*Aside.*)

Hah! Colonel!

COLONEL. (*Aside.*)

Confound the blundering dog!   300

DRAWER.

Why, to Colonel—

SACKBUT.

Get you out, you rascal. (*Kicks him out and exit after him.*)

DRAWER. [*As he exits.*]

What the devil is the matter?

COLONEL.(*Aside.*)

This dog has ruined all my scheme, I see by   305
Periwinkle's looks.

PERIWINKLE.

How finely I should have been choused.—Colonel, you'll pardon me that I did not give you your title before; it was pure ignorance, faith it was. Pray—hem, hem—pray, Colonel, what post had this   310
learned Egyptian in your regiment?

COLONEL. (*Aside.*)

A pox of your sneer.—I don't understand you, sir.

PERIWINKLE.

No? That's strange! I understand you, Colonel. An Egyptian of Grand Cairo! Ha, ha, ha. I am sorry such a well-invented tale should do you no more   315
service. We old fellows can see as far into a millstone* as him that picks it. I am not to be tricked out of my trust, mark that.

COLONEL. (*Aside.*)

The devil! I must carry it off; I wish I were fairly out.—Look ye, sir, you may make what jest you   320
please, but the stars will be obeyed, sir, and, depend upon it, I shall have the lady and you none of the girdle. (*Aside.*) Now for Freeman's part of the plot. (*Exit.*)

PERIWINKLE.

The stars! Ha, ha. No star has favored you, it   325
seems. The girdle! Ha, ha, ha, none of your legerdemain tricks can pass upon me. Why, what

a pack of trumpery has this rogue picked up? His *pagod*,[65] *poluflosboios*, his *zonas*, *moros musphonons*, and the devil knows what. But I'll take care—Hah! Gone? Aye, 'twas time to sneak off.—Soho!   330
the house! (*Enter Sackbut.*) Where is this trickster? Send for a constable, I'll have this rascal before the Lord Mayor; I'll Grand Cairo him, with a pox to him. I believe you had a hand in putting this imposture upon me, Sackbut.   335

SACKBUT.

Who, I, Mr. Periwinkle? I scorn it; I perceived he was a cheat and left the room on purpose to send for a constable to apprehend him, and endeavored to stop him when he went out, but the rogue made but one step from the stairs to the door, called a coach,   340
leapt into it, and drove away like the devil, as Mr. Freeman can witness, who is at the bar and desires to speak with you; he is this minute come to town.

PERIWINKLE.

Send him in. (*Exit Sackbut.*) What a scheme this rogue had laid! How I should have been laughed at,   345
had it succeeded! (*Enter Freeman booted and spurred.*) Mr. Freeman, your dress commands your welcome to town. What will you drink? I had like to have been imposed upon here by the veriest rascal—

FREEMAN.

I am sorry to hear it. The dog flew for't—he had   350
not 'scaped me if I had been aware of him; Sackbut struck at him, but missed his blow, or he had done his business for him.

PERIWINKLE.

I believe you never heard of such a contrivance, Mr. Freeman, as this fellow had found out.   355

FREEMAN.

Mr. Sackbut has told me the whole story, Mr. Periwinkle, but now I have something to tell you of much more importance to yourself. I happened to lie one night at Coventry, and knowing your uncle, Sir Toby Periwinkle, I paid him a visit and   360
to my great surprise found him dying.

PERIWINKLE.

Dying!

FREEMAN.

Dying, in all appearance; the servants weeping, the

---

65 *pagod*] an Eastern idol

room in darkness; the apothecary, shaking his head, told me the doctors had given him over, and then there is small hopes, you know. 365

PERIWINKLE.

I hope he has made his will. He always told me he would make me his heir.

FREEMAN.

I have heard you say as much and therefore resolved to give you notice. I should think it would not be amiss if you went down tomorrow morning. 370

PERIWINKLE.

It is a long journey, and the roads very bad.

FREEMAN.

But he has a great estate, and the land very good. Think upon that.

PERIWINKLE.

Why, that's true, as you say; I'll think upon it. In the meantime, I give you many thanks for your civility, Mr. Freeman, and should be glad of your company to dine with me. 375

FREEMAN.

I am obliged to be at Jonathan's Coffee-house[66] at two, and it is now half-an-hour after one; if I dispatch my business, I'll wait on you; I know your hour. 380

PERIWINKLE.

You shall be very welcome, Mr. Freeman; and so, your humble servant. (*Exit.*)

Re-enter Colonel and Sackbut.

FREEMAN.

Ha, ha, ha! I have done your business, Colonel; he has swallowed the bait. 385

COLONEL.

I overheard all, though I am a little in the dark. I am to personate a highwayman, I suppose. That's a project I am not fond of; for though I may fright him out of his consent, he may fright me out of my life[67] when he discovers me, as he certainly must in the end. 390

FREEMAN.

No, no, I have a plot for you without danger, but first we must manage Tradelove. Has the tailor brought your clothes? 395

SACKBUT.

Yes, pox take the thief.

COLONEL.

Pox take your drawer for a jolt-headed rogue.

FREEMAN.

Well, well, no matter, I warrant we have him yet. But now you must put on the Dutch merchant.

COLONEL.

The deuce of this trading-plot. I wish he had been an old soldier, that I might have attacked him in my own way, heard him fight over all the battles of the Civil War—but for trade, by Jupiter, I shall never do it. 400

SACKBUT.

Never fear, Colonel, Mr. Freeman will instruct you. 405

FREEMAN.

You'll see what others do, the coffee-house will instruct you.

COLONEL.

I must venture, however. But I have a farther plot in my head upon Tradelove, which you must assist me in, Freeman; you are in credit with him, I heard you say. 410

FREEMAN.

I am, and will scruple nothing to serve you, Colonel.

COLONEL.

Come along then. Now for the Dutchman. Honest Ptolemy, by your leave, 415

Now must bob wig[68] and business come in play,
And a fair thirty-thousand-pounder leads the way.

Act IV, scene i. Jonathan's Coffee-house in Exchange Alley.

Crowd of people with rolls of paper and parchment[69] in their hands; a bar, and coffee-boys waiting. Enter Tradelove and stockjobbers with rolls of paper and parchment.

---

66 Jonathan's Coffee-house] in Exchange Alley near the Royal Exchange; center for speculators; the forerunner of the Stock Exchange

67 fright ... life] because highway robbery was punishable by death

68 bob wig] a simple, undress wig

69 *rolls ... parchment*] for recording stock transactions

FIRST STOCKJOBBER.

South Sea at seven-eighths![70] Who buys?

SECOND STOCKJOBBER.

South Sea bonds due at Michaelmas,[71] 1718. Class lottery tickets.[72]

THIRD STOCKJOBBER.

East India bonds?

FOURTH STOCKJOBBER.

What, all sellers and no buyers? Gentlemen, I'll buy a thousand pound for Tuesday next at three-fourths.

COFFEE-BOY.

Fresh coffee, gentlemen, fresh coffee?

TRADELOVE.

Hark ye, Gabriel, you'll pay the difference of that stock we transacted for t'other day.

GABRIEL.

Aye, Mr. Tradelove, here's a note for the money upon the Sword Blade Company.[73] (*Gives him a note.*)

COFFEE-BOY.

Bohea tea, gentlemen?

Enter a Man.

MAN.

Is Mr. Smuggle here?

FIRST COFFEE-BOY.

Mr. Smuggle's not here, sir, you'll find him at the books.

SECOND STOCKJOBBER.

Ho! Here come^e two sparks from the other end of the town. What news bring they?

Enter Two Gentlemen.

TRADELOVE.

I would fain bite that spark in the brown coat: he comes very often into the Alley, but never employs a broker.

Enter Colonel and Freeman.

SECOND STOCKJOBBER.

Who does anything in the Civil List lottery?[74] Or cacao? Zounds, where are all the Jews[75] this afternoon? Are you a bull or a bear today, Abraham?

THIRD STOCKJOBBER.

A bull, faith, but I have a good put for next week.

TRADELOVE.

Mr. Freeman, your servant! Who is that gentleman?

FREEMAN.

A Dutch merchant, just come to England. But hark ye, Mr. Tradelove, I have a piece of news will get you as much as the French king's death did, if you are expeditious.

TRADELOVE.

Say you so, sir! Pray, what is it?

FREEMAN. (*Showing him a letter.*)

Read there, I received it just now from one that belongs to the Emperor's[76] minister.

TRADELOVE. (*Reads.*)

"Sir, As I have many obligations to you, I cannot miss any opportunity to show my gratitude; this moment my lord has received a private express that the Spaniards have raised their siege from before Cagliari;[77] if this prove any advantage to you, it will answer both the ends and wishes of, sir, your most obliged humble servant, Henricus

---

70 South Sea at seven-eighths] stock in the South Sea Company, a chartered joint-stock trading company, with the monopoly on English trade with South America and the Pacific; founded in 1711, mainly to fund the national debt. Stock prices were conventionally quoted in eighths; only the final fraction is quoted.

71 Michaelmas] Feast of St. Michael, 29 September; one of the four quarter days of the business year, on which financial transactions were completed

72 Class lottery tickets] one of the lotteries run by the government to fund the national debt; tickets were divided into classes with different prizes for each.

73 Sword Blade Company] the major stock brokerage firm of the time and banker for the South Sea Company

74 Civil … lottery] a government lottery (1713) to discharge the debts of the royal household

75 Jews] many jobbers and brokers were Jews, but prejudice reinforced the association between Jews and the market

76 Emperor's] Charles VI, Emperor of Austria

77 siege … Cagliari] Cagliari is the capital of Sardinia, at this time part of the Austrian empire; Spain had invaded Sardinia in August 1717, provoking a crisis in the Mediterranean.

Dusseldorp. Postscript, In two or three hours the news will be public." (*Aside to Freeman*.) May one depend upon this, Mr. Freeman?

FREEMAN.

You may. I never knew this person send me a false piece of news in my life.

TRADELOVE.

Sir, I am much obliged to you. Egad, 'tis rare news.—Who sells South Sea[78] for next week?

STOCKJOBBERS. (*All together*.)

I sell; I, I, I, I, I sell.

FIRST STOCKJOBBER.

I'll sell five thousand pounds for next week at five-eighths.

SECOND STOCKJOBBER.

I'll sell ten thousand at five-eighths for the same time.

TRADELOVE.

Nay, nay, hold, hold, not all together, gentlemen, I'll be no bull, I'll buy no more than I can take. Will you sell ten thousand pound at a half for any day next week, except Saturday?

FIRST STOCKJOBBER.

I'll sell it you, Mr. Tradelove.

Freeman whispers to one of the gentlemen.

GENTLEMAN. (*Aloud*.)

The Spaniards raised the siege of Cagliari! I don't believe one word of it.

SECOND GENTLEMAN.

Raised the siege! As much as you have raised the Monument.[79]

FREEMAN.

'Tis raised, I assure you, sir.

SECOND GENTLEMAN.

What will you lay on't?

FREEMAN.

What you please.

FIRST GENTLEMAN.

Why, I have a brother upon the spot in the Emperor's service; I am certain if there were any such thing, I should have had a letter.

A STOCKJOBBER.

How's this? The siege of Cagliari raised; I wish it may be true, 'twill make business stir and stocks rise.

FIRST STOCKJOBBER.

Tradelove's a cunning fat bear; if this news proves true, I shall repent I sold him the five thousand pounds.[80]—Pray, sir, what assurance have you that the siege is raised?

FREEMAN.

There is come an express to the Emperor's minister.

SECOND STOCKJOBBER.

I'll know that presently. (*Exit*.)

FIRST GENTLEMAN.

Let it come where it will, I'll hold you fifty pounds 'tis false.

FREEMAN.

'Tis done.

SECOND GENTLEMAN.

I'll lay you a brace of hundreds upon the same.

FREEMAN.

I'll take you.

FOURTH STOCKJOBBER.

Egad, I'll hold twenty pieces 'tis not raised, sir.

FREEMAN.

Done with you too.

TRADELOVE.

I'll lay any man a brace of thousands the siege is raised.

FREEMAN. (*Aside to Tradelove*.)

The Dutch merchant is your man to take in.

TRADELOVE.

Does not he know the news?

FREEMAN. (*To Tradelove*.)

Not a syllable; if he did, he would bet a hundred thousand pound as soon as one penny; he's plaguy rich, and a mighty man at wagers.

TRADELOVE.

Say you so.—Egad, I'll bite him if possible.—Are you from Holland, sir?

COLONEL.

Ya, mynheer.

---

78 South Sea] The South Sea Company traded with the Spanish empire, whose military fortunes would affect stock prices.

79 Monument] a column designed by Christopher Wren commemorating the Great Fire of 1666

80 five thousand pounds] ten thousand according to the first stockjobber's revised offer to Tradelove

TRADELOVE.

Had you the news before you came away?

COLONEL.

Wat believe you, mynheer?

TRADELOVE.

What do I believe? Why, I believe that the Spaniards have actually raised the siege of Cagliari.

COLONEL.

Wat duyvels niews is dat? 'Tis niet waer, 100
mynheer,—'tis no true, sir.

TRADELOVE.

'Tis so true, mynheer, that I'll lay you two thousand pounds upon it.—You are sure the letter may be depended upon, Mr. Freeman?

FREEMAN. (*Aside to Tradelove.*)

Do you think I would venture my money if I were 105
not sure of the truth of it?

COLONEL.

Two duysend pond, mynheer, 'tis gedaen—dis gentleman sal hold de gelt.^{f} (*Gives Freeman money.*)

TRADELOVE.

With all my heart—this binds the wager. You have certainly lost, mynheer, the siege is raised indeed. 110

COLONEL.

Ik gelove't niet, Mynheer Freeman, ik sal ye dubbled houden, if you please.

FREEMAN.

I am let into the secret, therefore won't win your money.

TRADELOVE.

Ha, ha, ha! I have snapped the Dutchman, faith, 115
ha, ha! This is no ill day's work.—Pray, may I crave your name, mynheer?

COLONEL.

Myn naem, mynheer! Myn naem is Jan Van Timtamtirelireletta Heer Van Fainwell.

TRADELOVE.

Zounds, 'tis a damned long name, I shall never 120
remember it: Mynheer Van Tim, Tim, Tim— What the devil is it?

FREEMAN.

Oh! Never heed, I know the gentleman and will pass my word for twice the sum.

TRADELOVE.

That's enough. 125

COLONEL. (*Aside.*)

You'll hear of me sooner than you'll wish, old gentleman, I fancy.—You'll come to Sackbut's, Freeman? (*Exit.*)

FREEMAN. (*Aside to the Colonel.*)

Immediately.

FIRST MAN.

Humphrey Hump here? 130

SECOND COFFEE-BOY.

Mr. Humphrey Hump is not here; you'll find him upon the Dutch walk.^{81}

TRADELOVE.

Mr. Freeman, I give you many thanks for your kindness.

FREEMAN. (*Aside.*)

I fear you'll repent when you know all. 135

TRADELOVE.

Will you dine with me?

FREEMAN.

I am engaged at Sackbut's; adieu. (*Exit.*)

TRADELOVE.

Sir, your humble servant. Now I'll see what I can do upon Change with my news. (*Exit.*)

Scene ii. The tavern.

Enter Freeman and Colonel.

FREEMAN.

Ha, ha, ha! The old fellow swallowed the bait as greedily as a gudgeon.

COLONEL.

I have him, faith, ha, ha, ha. His two thousand pound's secure—if he would keep his money, he must part with the lady, ha, ha. What came of your 5
two friends? They performed their part very well; you should have brought 'em to take a glass with us.

FREEMAN.

No matter, we'll drink a bottle together another time. I did not care to bring them hither; there's no necessity to trust them with the main secret, 10
you know, Colonel.

COLONEL.

Nay, that's right, Freeman.

---

81 Dutch walk] meeting place for Dutch merchants in the courtyard of the Royal Exchange

Enter Sackbut.

SACKBUT.

Joy, joy, Colonel, the luckiest accident in the world!

COLONEL.

What say'st thou?

SACKBUT.

This letter does your business. 15

COLONEL. (*Reads.*)

"To Obadiah Prim, hosier, near the building called the Monument, in London."

FREEMAN.

A letter to Prim; how came you by it?

SACKBUT.

Looking over the letters our post-woman brought, as I always do, to see what letters are directed to 20 my house (for she can't read, you must know), I spied this to Prim, so paid for't[82] among the rest; I have given the old jade a pint of wine on purpose to delay time, till you see if the letter will be of any service; then I'll seal it up again and tell her I 25 took it by mistake; I have read it and fancy you'll like the project—read, read, Colonel.

COLONEL. (*Reads.*)

"Friend Prim, There is arrived from Pennsylvania one Simon Pure, a leader of the faithful, who hath sojourned with us eleven days and hath been of 30 great comfort to the brethren. He intendeth for the quarterly meeting in London; I have recommended him to thy house; I pray thee intreat him kindly and let thy wife cherish him, for he's of weakly constitution. He will depart from us the 35 third day;[83] which is all from thy Friend in the faith, Aminidab Holdfast." Ha, ha! Excellent! I understand you, landlord, I am to personate this Simon Pure, am I not?

SACKBUT.

Don't you like the hint?

COLONEL. 40

Admirably well!

FREEMAN.

'Tis the best contrivance in the world, if the right Simon gets not there before you.

COLONEL.

No, no, the Quakers never ride post; he can't be here before tomorrow at soonest. Do you send and 45 buy me a Quaker's dress, Mr. Sackbut; and suppose, Freeman, you should wait at the Bristol coach, that if you see any such person, you might contrive to give me notice.

FREEMAN.

I will.—The country dress and boots, are they 50 ready?

SACKBUT.

Yes, yes, everything, sir.

FREEMAN.

Bring 'em in then. (*Exit Sackbut.*) Thou must dispatch Periwinkle first. Remember his uncle, Sir Toby Periwinkle, is an old bachelor of seventy-five; that he 55 has seven hundred a year, most in abbey land;[84] that he was once in love with your mother, and shrewdly suspected by some to be your father; that you have been thirty years his steward, and ten years his gentleman—remember to improve these hints. 60

COLONEL.

Never fear, let me alone for that—but what's the steward's name?

FREEMAN.

His name is Pillage.

COLONEL.

Enough. (*Enter Sackbut with clothes.*) Now for the country put.[85] (*Dresses.*) 65

FREEMAN.

Egad, landlord, thou deservest to have the first night's lodging with the lady for thy fidelity. What say you, Colonel, shall we settle a club here, you'll make one?

COLONEL.

Make one? I'll bring a set of honest officers that 70 will spend their money as freely to their King's health as they would their blood in his service.

---

82 paid for't] Postage at the time was paid by the recipient.

83 third day] Tuesday; Quakers designated the days of the week in this way to avoid the conventional designations derived from the names of the pagan gods.

84 abbey land] part of the estate of an abbey before the dissolution of the monasteries at the Reformation

85 country put] bumpkin

SACKBUT.

I thank you, Colonel. (*Bell rings.*) Here, here. (*Exit Sackbut.*)

COLONEL.

So now for my boots. (*Puts on boots.*) Shall I find 75
you here, Freeman, when I come back?

FREEMAN.

Yes, or I'll leave word with Sackbut where he may
send for me. Have you the writings? the will, and
everything?

COLONEL.

All, all! 80

Enter Sackbut.

SACKBUT.

Zounds! Mr. Freeman! Yonder is Tradelove in the
damnedest passion in the world. He swears you are
in the house—he says you told him you was to
dine here.

FREEMAN.

I did so. Ha, ha, ha! He has found himself bit 85
already.

COLONEL.

The devil! He must not see me in this dress.

SACKBUT.

I told him I expected you here, but you were not
come yet.

FREEMAN.

Very well.—Make you haste out, Colonel, and let 90
me alone to deal with him. Where is he?

SACKBUT.

In the King's Head.

COLONEL.

You remember what I told you?

FREEMAN.

Aye, aye, very well.—Landlord, let him know I am
come in.—And now, Mr. Pillage, success attend you. 95

Exit Sackbut.

COLONEL.

Mr. Proteus, rather.
From changing shape and imitating Jove,
I draw the happy omens of my love.
I'm not the first young brother of the blade
Who made his fortune in a masquerade. (*Exit* 100
Colonel.)

Enter Tradelove.

FREEMAN.

Zounds! Mr. Tradelove, we're bit it seems.

TRADELOVE.

Bit do you call it, Mr. Freeman, I am ruined. Pox
on your news.

FREEMAN.

Pox on the rascal that sent it me.

TRADELOVE.

Sent it you! Why Gabriel Skinflint has been at the 105
minister's and spoke with him, and he has assured
him 'tis every syllable false; he received no such
express.

FREEMAN.

I know it. I this minute parted with my friend,
who protested he never sent me any such letter. 110
Some roguish stockjobber has done it on purpose
to make me lose my money, that's certain. I wish
I knew who he was, I'd make him repent it—I
have lost three hundred pounds by it.

TRADELOVE.

What signifies your three hundred pounds to what 115
I have lost? There's two thousand pounds to that
Dutchman with the cursed long name, besides the
stock I bought. The devil! I could tear my flesh. I
must never show my face upon Change more, for,
by my soul, I can't pay it. 120

FREEMAN.

I am heartily sorry for't! What can I serve you in?
Shall I speak to the Dutch merchant and try to
get you time for the payment?

TRADELOVE.

Time! Adsheart! I shall never be able to look up
again. 125

FREEMAN.

I am very much concerned that I was the occasion
and wish I could be an instrument of retrieving
your misfortune; for my own, I value it not.—
Adso! A thought comes into my head, that well
improved, may be of service. 130

TRADELOVE.

Ah! There's no thought can be of any service to
me, without paying the money or running away.

FREEMAN.

How do you know? What do you think of my
proposing Mrs. Lovely to him? He is a single man,

and I heard him say he had a mind to marry an English woman. Nay, more than that, he said somebody told him, you had a pretty ward. He wished you had bet her instead of your money.

TRADELOVE.

Aye, but he'd be hanged before he'd take her instead of the money: the Dutch are too covetous for that. Besides, he did not know that there were three more of us, I suppose.

FREEMAN.

So much the better; you may venture to give him your consent, if he'll but forgive you the wager. It is not your business to tell him that your consent will signify nothing.

TRADELOVE.

That's right, as you say, but will he do it, think you?

FREEMAN.

I can't tell that, but I'll try what I can do with him. He has promised me to meet me here an hour hence; I'll feel his pulse and let you know. If I find it feasible, I'll send for you; if not, you are at liberty to take what measures you please.

TRADELOVE.

You must extol her beauty, double her portion, and tell him I have the entire disposal of her and that she can't marry without my consent and that I am a covetous rogue and will never part with her without a valuable consideration.

FREEMAN.

Aye, aye, let me alone for a lie at a pinch.

TRADELOVE.

Egad, if you can bring this to bear, Mr. Freeman, I'll make you whole again; I'll pay the three hundred pounds you lost, with all my soul.

FREEMAN.

Well, I'll use my best endeavors. Where will you be?

TRADELOVE.

At home. Pray Heaven you prosper. If I were but the sole trustee now, I should not fear it. Who the devil would be a guardian,
If when cash runs low, our coffers t'enlarge,
We can't, like other stocks, transfer our charge?
     (*Exit.*)

FREEMAN.

Ha, ha, ha! He has it. (*Exit.*)

Scene iii. Periwinkle's house.

Enter Periwinkle on one side and footman on the other.

FOOTMAN.

A gentleman from Coventry inquires for you, sir.

PERIWINKLE.

From my uncle, I warrant you, bring him up. [*Exit footman.*] This will save me the trouble, as well as the expenses of a journey.

Enter Colonel.

COLONEL.

Is your name Periwinkle, sir?

PERIWINKLE.

It is, sir.

COLONEL.

I am sorry for the message I bring. My old master, whom I served these forty years, claims the sorrow due from a faithful servant to an indulgent master. (*Weeps.*)

PERIWINKLE.

By this I understand, sir, my uncle, Sir Toby Periwinkle, is dead.

COLONEL.

He is, sir, and he has left you heir to seven hundred a year in as good abbey land as ever paid Peter's pence to Rome. I wish you long to enjoy it, but my tears will flow when I think of my benefactor. (*Weeps.*) Ah! He was a good man—he has not left many of his fellows—the poor laments him sorely.

PERIWINKLE.

I pray, sir, what office bore you?

COLONEL.

I was his steward, sir.

PERIWINKLE.

I have heard him mention you with much respect; your name is—

COLONEL.

Pillage, sir.

PERIWINKLE.

Aye, Pillage! I do remember he called you Pillage. Pray, Mr. Pillage, when did my uncle die?

COLONEL.

Monday last, at four in the morning. About two he signed this will and gave it into my hands and strictly charged me to leave Coventry the moment

he expired and deliver it to you with what speed I 30
could. I have obeyed him, sir, and there is the will.
(*Gives it to Periwinkle.*)

PERIWINKLE.

'Tis very well, I'll lodge it in the Commons.*

COLONEL.

There are two things which he forgot to insert, but
charged me to tell you that he desired you'd 35
perform them as readily as if you had found them
written in the will, which is to remove his corpse
and bury him by his father in St. Paul, Covent
Garden,* and to give all his servants mourning.

PERIWINKLE. (*Aside.*)

That will be a considerable charge; a pox of all 40
modern fashions.—Well! It shall be done, Mr.
Pillage; I will agree with one of death's fashion-
mongers, called an undertaker, to go down and
bring up the body.

COLONEL.

I hope, sir, I shall have the honor to serve you in the 45
same station I did your worthy uncle; I have not
many years to stay behind him and would gladly
spend them in the family where I was brought up.
(*Weeps.*) He was a kind and tender master to me.

PERIWINKLE.

Pray don't grieve, Mr. Pillage; you shall hold your 50
place and everything else which you held under my
uncle. You make me weep to see you so concerned.
(*Weeps.*) He lived to a good old age—and we are
all mortal.

COLONEL.

We are so, sir, and therefore I must beg you to sign 55
this lease. You'll find Sir Toby has ta'en particular
notice of it in his will. I could not get it time
enough from the lawyer, or he had signed it before
he died. (*Gives him a paper.*)

PERIWINKLE.

A lease for what? 60

COLONEL.

I rented a hundred a year of Sir Toby upon lease,
which lease expires at Lady Day next, and I desire
to renew it for twenty years—that's all, sir.

PERIWINKLE.

Let me see. (*Looks over the lease.*)

COLONEL. (*Aside.*)

Matters go swimmingly, if nothing intervene. 65

PERIWINKLE.

Very well. Let's see what he says in his will about
it. (*Lays the lease upon the table and looks on the
will.*)

COLONEL. (*Aside.*)

He's very wary, yet I fancy I shall be too cunning
for him. 70

PERIWINKLE.

Ho, here it is. "—The farm lying—now in
possession of Samuel Pillage—suffer him to renew
his lease—at the same rent."—Very well, Mr.
Pillage, I see my uncle does mention it, and I'll
perform his will. Give me the lease. (*Colonel gives* 75
it him; he looks upon it and lays it upon the table.)
Pray you step to the door and call for a pen and
ink, Mr. Pillage.

COLONEL.

I have pen and ink in my pocket, sir. (*Pulls out an
inkhorn.*) I never go without that. 80

PERIWINKLE.

I think it belongs to your profession. (*He looks upon
the pen while the Colonel changes the lease and lays
down the contract.*) I doubt this is but a sorry pen,
though it may serve to write my name. (*Writes.*)

COLONEL. (*Aside.*)

Little does he think what he signs. 85

PERIWINKLE.

There is your lease, Mr. Pillage. (*Gives him the
paper.*) Now I must desire you to make what haste
you can down to Coventry and take care of
everything, and I'll send down the undertaker for
the body; do you attend it up, and whatever charge 90
you are at, I will repay you.

COLONEL. (*Aside.*)

You have paid me already, I thank you, sir.

PERIWINKLE.

Will you dine with me?

COLONEL.

I would rather not; there are some of my neighbors
which I met as I came along, who leaves the town 95
this afternoon, they told me, and I should be glad
of their company down.

PERIWINKLE.

Well, well, I won't detain you.

COLONEL. (*Aside.*)

I don't care how soon I am out.

PERIWINKLE.

I will give orders about mourning.   100

COLONEL. [*Aside*.]

You will have cause to mourn, when you know
your estate imaginary only.
You'll find your hopes and cares alike are vain,
In spite of all the caution you have ta'en,
Fortune rewards the faithful lover's pain. (*Exit*.)   105

PERIWINKLE.

Seven hundred a year! I wish he had died seventeen
years ago. What a valuable collection of rarities
might I have had by this time? I might have traveled
over all the known parts of the globe and made my
own closet rival the Vatican at Rome. Odso, I have   110
a good mind to begin my travels now—let me see—
I am but sixty! My father, grandfather, and great-
grandfather reached ninety-odd; I have almost forty
years good. Let me consider! What will seven
hundred a year amount to—in—aye! in thirty years,   115
I'll say but thirty—thirty times seven, is seven times
thirty—that is—just twenty-one thousand
pound—'tis a great deal of money—I may very well
reserve sixteen hundred of it for a collection of such
rarities as will make my name famous to posterity. I   120
would not die like other mortals, forgotten in a year
or two, as my uncle will be. No.
With nature's curious works I'll raise my fame,
That men, till doomsday, may repeat my name.
(*Exit*.)

Scene iv. A tavern.

Freeman and Tradelove over a bottle.

TRADELOVE.

Come, Mr. Freeman, here's Mynheer Jan Van Tim,
Tam, Tam—I shall never think of that Dutchman's
name.

FREEMAN.

Mynheer Jan Van Timtamtirelireletta Heer Van
Fainwell.   5

TRADELOVE.

Aye, Heer Van Fainwell, I never heard such a
confounded name in life—here's his health, I say.
(*Drinks*.)

FREEMAN.

With all my heart.

TRADELOVE.

Faith, I never expected to have found so generous   10
a thing in a Dutchman.

FREEMAN.

Oh, he has nothing of the Hollander in his
temper—except an antipathy to monarchy.[86] As
soon as I told him your circumstances, he replied he
would not be the ruin of any man for the world and   15
immediately made this proposal himself. Let him
take what time he will for the payment, said he, or
if he'll give me his ward, I'll forgive him the debt.

TRADELOVE.

Well, Mr. Freeman, I can but thank you. Egad, you
have made a man of me again, and if ever I lay a   20
wager more, may I rot in a gaol.

FREEMAN.

I assure you, Mr. Tradelove, I was very much
concerned because I was the occasion—though
very innocently, I protest.

TRADELOVE.

I dare swear you was, Mr. Freeman.   25

Enter a fiddler.

FIDDLER.

Please to have a lesson of music or a song,
gentlemen?

FREEMAN.

A song, aye, with all our hearts. Have you ever a
merry one?

FIDDLER.

Yes, sir, my wife and I can give you a merry   30
dialogue.

Here is the song.

TRADELOVE.

'Tis very pretty, faith.

FREEMAN.

There's something for you to drink, friend; go, lose
no time.

FIDDLER.

I thank you, sir. (*Exit*.)   35

*Enter drawer and Colonel, dressed for the Dutch
merchant.*

---

86 antipathy to monarchy] Holland was a republic.

COLONEL.

Hah, Mynheer Tradelove, Ik ben sorry voor your troubles, maer Ik sal you easie maeken, Ik wil de gelt niet hebben.

TRADELOVE.

I shall forever acknowledge the obligation, sir.

FREEMAN.

But you understand upon what condition, Mr. 40 Tradelove: Mrs. Lovely.

COLONEL.

Ya, de juffrow sal al te regt setten, mynheer.

TRADELOVE.

With all my heart, mynheer, you shall have my consent to marry her freely.

FREEMAN.

Well then, as I am a party concerned between you, 45 Mynheer Jan Van Timtamtirelireletta Heer Van Fainwell shall give you a discharge of your wager under his own hand, and you shall give him your consent to marry Mrs. Lovely under yours; that is the way to avoid all manner of disputes hereafter. 50

COLONEL.

Ya, waeragtig.

TRADELOVE.

Aye, aye, so it is, Mr. Freeman, I'll give it under mine this minute. (*Sits down to write.*)

COLONEL.

And so sal Ik. (*Sits down to write.*)

FREEMAN.

So, ho, the house. (*Enter drawer.*) Bid your master 55 come up. [*Exit drawer.*] (*Aside.*) I'll see there be witnesses enough to the bargain.

Enter Sackbut.

SACKBUT.

Do you call, gentlemen?

FREEMAN.

Aye, Mr. Sackbut, we shall want your hand here.

TRADELOVE.

There, mynheer, there's my consent as amply as 60 you can desire, but you must insert your own name, for I know not how to spell it; I have left a blank for it. (*Gives the Colonel a paper.*)

COLONEL.

Ya, Ik sal dat well doen.

FREEMAN.

Now, Mr. Sackbut, you and I will witness it. (*They* 65 *write.*)

COLONEL.

Daer, Mynheer Tradelove, is your discharge. (*Gives him a paper.*)

TRADELOVE.

Be pleased to witness this receipt too, gentlemen.

Freeman and Sackbut put their hands.

FREEMAN.

Aye, aye, that we will. 70

COLONEL.

Well, mynheer, ye most meer doen, ye most myn voorspraek to de juffrow syn.

FREEMAN.

He means you must recommend him to the lady.

TRADELOVE.

That I will, and to the rest of my brother guardians. 75

COLONEL.

Wat, voor den duyvel, heb you meer guardians?

TRADELOVE.

Only three, mynheer.

COLONEL.

Wat donder heb ye myn betrocken, mynheer? Had Ik that gewoeten, Ik soude eaven met you geweest syn. 80

SACKBUT.

But Mr. Tradelove is the principal, and he can do a great deal with the rest, sir.

FREEMAN.

And he shall use his interest I promise you, mynheer.

TRADELOVE.

I will say all that ever I can think on to recommend 85 you, mynheer, and if you please, I'll introduce you to the lady.

COLONEL.

Well, dat is waer. Maer ye must first spreken of myn to de juffrow and to de oudere gentlemen.

FREEMAN.

Aye, that's the best way, and then I and the Heer 90 Van Fainwell will meet you there.

TRADELOVE.

I will go this moment, upon honor. Your most

obedient humble servant.—My speaking will do you little good, mynheer, ha, ha. We have bit you, faith, ha, ha. My debt's discharged, and for the man, 95 He's my consent—to get her if he can. (*Exit.*)

COLONEL.

Ha, ha, ha, this was a masterpiece of contrivance, Freeman.

FREEMAN.

He hugs himself with his supposed good fortune and little thinks the luck's of our side, but come, 100 pursue the fickle goddess while she's in the mood. Now for the Quaker.

COLONEL.

That's the hardest task. Of all the counterfeits performed by man, A soldier makes the simplest Puritan. (*Exit.*) 105

Act V, scene i. Prim's house.

Enter Mrs. Prim and Mrs. Lovely in Quaker's dress, meeting.

MRS. PRIM.

So, now I like thee, Anne. Art thou not better without thy monstrous hoop coat[87] and patches! If Heaven should make thee so many black spots upon thy face, would it not fright thee, Anne?

MRS. LOVELY.

If it should turn your inside outward and show all 5 the spots of your hypocrisy, 'twould fright me worse.

MRS. PRIM.

My hypocrisy! I scorn thy words, Anne. I lay no baits.

MRS. LOVELY.

If you did, you'd catch no fish. 10

MRS. PRIM.

Well, well, make thy jests, but I'd have thee to know, Anne, that I could have catched as many fish (as thou call'st them) in my time, as ever thou didst with all thy fool-traps about thee. If admirers be thy aim, thou wilt have more of them in this dress than thy 15 other. The men, take my word for't, are most desirous to see what we are most careful to conceal.

---

87 hoop coat] hooped petticoat

MRS. LOVELY.

Is that the reason for your formality, Mrs. Prim? Truth will out. I ever thought, indeed, there was more design than godliness in the pinched cap. 20

MRS. PRIM.

Go, thou art corrupted with reading lewd plays and filthy romances, good for nothing but to lead youth into the high road of fornication. Ah! I wish thou art not already too familiar with the wicked ones.

MRS. LOVELY.

Too familiar with the wicked ones! Pray, no more 25 of those freedoms, madam. I am familiar with none so wicked as yourself. How dare you talk thus to me! You, you, you unworthy woman you. (*Bursts into tears.*)

Enter Tradelove.

TRADELOVE.

What, in tears, Nancy? What have you done to her, 30 Mrs. Prim, to make her weep?

MRS. LOVELY.

Done to me! I admire I keep my senses among you. But I will rid myself of your tyranny, if there be either law or justice to be had; I'll force you to give me up my liberty. 35

MRS. PRIM.

Thou hast more need to weep for thy sins, Anne— yea, for thy manifold sins.

MRS. LOVELY.

Don't think that I'll be still the fool which you have made me. No, I'll wear what I please, go when and where I please, and keep what company I think 40 fit and not what you shall direct—I will.

TRADELOVE.

For my part, I do think all this very reasonable, Mrs. Lovely—'tis fit you should have your liberty, and for that very purpose I am come.

Enter Mr. Periwinkle and Obadiah Prim, with a letter in his hand.

PERIWINKLE.

I have bought some black stockings of your 45 husband, Mrs. Prim, but he tells me the glover's trade belongs to you; therefore, I pray you look me out five or six dozen of mourning gloves, such as are given at funerals, and send them to my house.

OBADIAH PRIM.

My friend Periwinkle has got a good windfall 50
today—seven hundred a year.

MRS. PRIM.

I wish thee joy of it, neighbor.

TRADELOVE.

What, is Sir Toby dead then?

PERIWINKLE.

He is!—You'll take care, Mrs. Prim?

MRS. PRIM.

Yea, I will, neighbor. 55

OBADIAH PRIM.

This letter recommendeth a speaker,[88] 'tis from
Aminidab Holdfast of Bristol. Peradventure, he
will be here this night; therefore, Sarah, do thou
take care for his reception. (*Gives her the letter.*)

MRS. PRIM.

I will obey thee. (*Exit.*) 60

OBADIAH PRIM.

What art thou in the dumps for, Anne?

TRADELOVE.

We must marry her, Mr. Prim.

OBADIAH PRIM.

Why truly, if we could find a husband worth
having, I should be as glad to see her married as
thou wouldst, neighbor. 65

PERIWINKLE.

Well said, there are but few worth having.

TRADELOVE.

I can recommend you a man now, that I think you
can none of you have an objection to!

Enter Sir Philip Modelove.

PERIWINKLE.

You recommend! Nay, whenever she marries, I'll
recommend the husband. 70

SIR PHILIP.

What, must it be a whale or a rhinoceros, Mr.
Periwinkle? Ha, ha, ha!—Mr. Tradelove, I have a
bill* upon you (*Gives him a paper.*) and have been
seeking for you all over the town.

TRADELOVE.

I'll accept it, Sir Philip, and pay it when due. 75

---

88 speaker] minister

PERIWINKLE.

He shall be none of the fops at your end of the
town, with full perukes and empty skulls, nor yet
none of your trading gentry, who puzzle the
heralds to find arms for their coaches. No, he shall
be a man famous for travels, solidity, and curiosity, 80
one who has searched into the profundity of
nature. When Heaven shall direct such a one, he
shall have my consent, because it may turn to the
benefit of mankind.

MRS. LOVELY.

The benefit of mankind! What, would you 85
anatomize me?

SIR PHILIP.

Aye, aye, madam, he would dissect you.

TRADELOVE.

Or pore over you through a microscope to see how
your blood circulates from the crown of your head to
the sole of your foot, ha, ha! But I have a husband for 90
you, a man that knows how to improve your fortune,
one that trades to the four corners of the globe.

MRS. LOVELY.

And would send me for a venture perhaps.

TRADELOVE.

One that will dress you in all the pride of Europe,
Asia, Africa, and America—a Dutch merchant, my 95
girl!

SIR PHILIP.

A Dutchman! Ha, ha, there's a husband for a fine
lady — Ya, juffrow, will you met myn slapen? Ha,
ha! He'll learn you to talk the language of the hogs,
madam, ha, ha. 100

TRADELOVE.

He'll learn you that one merchant is of more
service to a nation than fifty coxcombs. The Dutch
know the trading interest to be of more benefit to
the state than the landed.

SIR PHILIP.

But what is either interest to a lady? 105

TRADELOVE.

'Tis the merchant makes the belle. How would the
ladies sparkle in the box without the merchant? The
Indian diamonds! The French brocade! The Italian
fan! The Flanders* lace! The fine Dutch holland!
How would they vent their scandal over their tea 110
tables? And where would you beaus have champagne
to toast your mistresses, were it not for the merchant?

OBADIAH PRIM.

Verily, neighbor Tradelove, thou dost waste thy breath about nothing. All that thou hast said tendeth only to debauch youth and fill their heads with the pride and luxury of this world. The merchant is a very great friend to Satan and sendeth as many to his dominions as the pope. 115

PERIWINKLE.

Right, I say knowledge makes the man.

OBADIAH PRIM.

Yea, but not thy kind of knowledge—it is the knowledge of Truth. Search thou for the light within and not for baubles, Friend. 120

MRS. LOVELY.

Ah, study your country's good, Mr. Periwinkle, and not her insects. Rid you of your homebred monsters before you fetch any from abroad. I dare swear you have maggots enough in your own brain to stock all the virtuosos in Europe with butterflies. 125

SIR PHILIP.

By my soul, Miss Nancy's a wit.

OBADIAH PRIM.

That is more than she can say by thee, Friend. Look ye, it is in vain to talk; when I meet a man worthy of her, she shall have my leave to marry him. 130

MRS. LOVELY.

Provided he be one of the faithful. (*Aside.*) Was there ever such a swarm of caterpillars to blast the hopes of a woman!—Know this, that you contend in vain: I'll have no husband of your choosing, nor shall you lord it over me long. I'll try the power of an English senate. Orphans have been redressed and wills set aside, and none did ever deserve their pity more.—Oh Fainwell! Where are thy promises to free me from these vermin? Alas! The task was more difficult than he imagined! 135

A harder task than what the poets tell
Of yore, the fair Andromeda befell;
She but one monster feared, I've four to fear,
And see no Perseus, no deliv'rer near. (*Exit.*) 145

Enter servant and whispers to Prim.

SERVANT.

One Simon Pure inquireth for thee.

PERIWINKLE.

The woman is mad. (*Exit.*)

SIR PHILIP.

So are you all, in my opinion. (*Exit.*)

OBADIAH PRIM.

Friend Tradelove, business requireth my presence.

TRADELOVE.

Oh, I shan't trouble you.—Pox take him for an unmannerly dog.—However, I have kept my word with my Dutchman, and will introduce him too for all you. (*Exit.*) 150

Enter Colonel in a Quaker's habit.

OBADIAH PRIM.

Friend Pure, thou art welcome. How is it with Friend Holdfast and all Friends in Bristol? Timothy Littlewit, John Slenderbrain, and Christopher Keepfaith? 155

COLONEL. (*Aside.*)

A goodly company!—They are all in health, I thank thee for them.

OBADIAH PRIM.

Friend Holdfast writes me word that thou camest lately from Pennsylvania. How do all Friends there? 160

COLONEL. (*Aside.*)

What the devil shall I say? I know just as much of Pennsylvania as I do of Bristol.

OBADIAH PRIM.

Do they thrive?

COLONEL.

Yea, Friend, the blessing of their good works fall upon them. 165

Enter Mrs. Prim and Mrs. Lovely.

OBADIAH PRIM.

Sarah, know our Friend Pure.

MRS. PRIM.

Thou art welcome.

He salutes* her.

COLONEL. (*Aside.*)

Here comes the sum of all my wishes. How charming she appears, even in that disguise. 170

OBADIAH PRIM.

Why dost thou consider the maiden so intentively,[89] Friend?

---

89 intentively] earnestly, intently

COLONEL.

I will tell thee. About four days ago I saw a vision—this very maiden, but in vain attire, standing on a precipice—and heard a voice, which 175 called me by my name and bade me put forth my hand and save her from the pit. I did so, and methought the damsel grew to my side.

MRS. PRIM.

What can that portend?

OBADIAH PRIM.

The damsel's conversion, I am persuaded. 180

MRS. LOVELY. (*Aside.*)

That's false, I'm sure.

OBADIAH PRIM.

Wilt thou use the means, Friend Pure?

COLONEL.

Means! What means? Is she not thy daughter and already one of the faithful?

MRS. PRIM.

No, alas! She's one of the ungodly. 185

OBADIAH PRIM.

Pray thee mind what this good man will say unto thee; he will teach thee the way that thou shouldst walk, Anne.

MRS. LOVELY.

I know my way without his instructions. I hoped to have been quiet, when once I had put on your 190 odious formality here.

COLONEL.

Then thou wearest it out of compulsion, not choice, Friend?

MRS. LOVELY.

Thou art in the right of it, Friend.

MRS. PRIM.

Art not thou ashamed to mimic the good man? 195 Ah! Thou art a stubborn girl.

COLONEL.

Mind her not; she hurteth not me. If thou wilt leave her alone with me, I will discuss some few points with her that may, perchance, soften her stubborness and melt her into compliance. 200

OBADIAH PRIM.

Content, I pray thee put it home to her. Come, Sarah, let us leave the good man with her.

MRS. LOVELY. (*Catching hold of Prim; he breaks loose and exits [with Mrs. Prim].*)

What do you mean—to leave me with this old enthusiastical[90] canter? Don't think, because I complied with your formality, to impose your 205 ridiculous doctrine upon me.

COLONEL.

I pray thee, young woman, moderate thy passion.

MRS. LOVELY.

I pray thee, walk after thy leader; you will but lose your labor upon me.—These wretches will certainly make me mad. 210

COLONEL.

I am of another opinion; the spirit telleth me that I shall convert thee, Anne.

MRS. LOVELY.

'Tis a lying spirit; don't believe it.

COLONEL.

Say'st thou so? Why then thou shalt convert me, my angel. (*Catching her in his arms.*) 215

MRS. LOVELY. (*Shrieks.*)

Ah! Monster, hold off, or I'll tear thy eyes out.

COLONEL.

Hush! For Heaven's sake—dost thou know me? I am Fainwell.

MRS. LOVELY.

Fainwell! (*Enter old Prim. [Mrs. Lovely says] aside.*) Oh I'm undone, Prim here. I wish with all my soul 220 I had been dumb.

OBADIAH PRIM.

What is the matter? Why didst thou shriek out, Anne?

MRS. LOVELY.

Shriek out! I'll shriek and shriek again, cry murder, thieves, or anything to drown the noise of that 225 eternal babbler, if you leave me with him any longer.

OBADIAH PRIM.

Was that all? Fie, fie, Anne.

COLONEL.

No matter, I'll bring down her stomach, I'll warrant thee—leave us, I pray thee. 230

OBADIAH PRIM.

Fare thee well. (*Exit.*)

COLONEL. (*Embraces her.*)

My charming, lovely woman.

90 enthusiastical] having the quality of religious fanaticism

MRS. LOVELY.

What means thou by this disguise, Fainwell?

COLONEL.

To set thee free, if thou wilt perform thy promise.

MRS. LOVELY.

Make me mistress of my fortune and make thy 235
own conditions.

COLONEL.

This night shall answer all thy wishes. See here, I
have the consent of three of thy guardians already
and doubt not but Prim shall make the fourth.

Prim listening.

OBADIAH PRIM. (*Aside.*)

I would gladly hear what argument the good man 240
useth to bend her.

MRS. LOVELY.

Thy words give me new life, methinks.

OBADIAH PRIM.

What do I hear?

MRS. LOVELY.

Thou best of men, Heaven meant to bless me sure,
when first I saw thee. 245

OBADIAH PRIM.

He hath mollified her. Oh wonderful conversion!

COLONEL.

Hah! Prim listening.—No more, my love, we are
observed; seem to be edified and give 'em hopes
that thou wilt turn Quaker, and leave the rest to
me. (*Aloud.*) I am glad to find that thou art 250
touched with what I said unto thee, Anne; another
time I will explain the other article to thee; in the
meanwhile, be thou dutiful to our Friend Prim.

MRS. LOVELY.

I shall obey thee in everything.

Enter old Prim.

OBADIAH PRIM.

Oh what a prodigious change is here! Thou hast 255
wrought a miracle, Friend! Anne, how dost thou
like the doctrine he hath preached?

MRS. LOVELY.

So well, that I could talk to him forever, methinks.
I am ashamed of my former folly and ask your
pardon, Mr. Prim. 260

COLONEL.

Enough, enough that thou art sorry; he is no pope,
Anne.

OBADIAH PRIM.

Verily, thou dost rejoice me exceedingly, Friend. Will
it please thee to walk into the next room and refresh
thyself? Come, take the maiden by the hand. 265

COLONEL.

We will follow thee.

Enter servant.

SERVANT.

There is another Simon Pure inquireth for thee,
master.

COLONEL. (*Aside.*)

The devil there is.

OBADIAH PRIM.

Another Simon Pure? I do not know him. Is he 270
any relation of thine?

COLONEL.

No, Friend, I know him not. (*Aside.*) Pox take him,
I wish he were in Pennsylvania again, with all my
blood.

MRS. LOVELY. (*Aside.*)

What shall I do? 275

OBADIAH PRIM.

Bring him up.

COLONEL. [*Aside.*]

Humph! Then one of us must go down, that's
certain. Now Impudence assist me.

Enter Simon Pure.

OBADIAH PRIM.

What is thy will with me, Friend?

SIMON PURE.

Didst thou not receive a letter from Aminidab 280
Holdfast of Bristol concerning one Simon Pure?

OBADIAH PRIM.

Yea, and Simon Pure is already here, Friend.

COLONEL. (*Aside.*)

And Simon Pure will stay here, Friend, if possible.

SIMON PURE.

That's an untruth, for I am he.

COLONEL.

Take thou heed, Friend, what thou dost say; I do 285
affirm that I am Simon Pure.

SIMON PURE.

Thy name may be Pure, Friend, but not that Pure.

COLONEL.

Yea, that Pure which my good Friend Aminidab
Holdfast wrote to my Friend Prim about, the same
Simon Pure that came from Pennsylvania and   290
sojourned in Bristol eleven days. Thou wouldst not
take my name from me, wouldst thou? (*Aside.*) Till
I have done with it.

SIMON PURE.

Thy name! I am astonished.

COLONEL.

At what? at thy own assurance? (*Going up to him;*   295
Simon Pure starts back.)

SIMON PURE.

Avaunt, Sathan, approach me not; I defy thee and
all thy works.[91]

MRS. LOVELY. (*Aside.*)

Oh, he'll outcant him. Undone, undone forever.

COLONEL.

Hark thee, Friend, thy sham will not take. Don't   300
exert thy voice; thou art too well acquainted with
Sathan to start at him, thou wicked reprobate.
What can thy design be here?

Enter servant and gives Prim a letter.

OBADIAH PRIM.

One of these must be a counterfeit, but which I
cannot say.   305

COLONEL. (*Aside.*)

What can that letter be?

SIMON PURE.

Thou must be the devil, Friend, that's certain, for
no human power can stock so great a falsehood.

OBADIAH PRIM.

This letter sayeth that thou art better acquainted
with that prince of darkness than any here. Read   310
that, I pray thee, Simon. (*Gives it the Colonel.*)

COLONEL. [*Aside.*]

'Tis Freeman's hand. (*Reads.*) "There is a design
formed to rob your house this night and cut your
throat, and for that purpose there is a man
disguised like a Quaker, who is to pass for one   315

---

91 *Sathan ... works*] formulaic rejection of Satan, using an
   archaic spelling

Simon Pure; the gang whereof I am one, though
now resolved to rob no more, has been at Bristol;
one of them came up in the coach with the
Quaker, whose name he hath taken, and from
what he gathered from him, formed that design,
and did not doubt but he should impose so far
upon you as to make you turn out the real Simon   320
Pure and keep him with you. Make the right use
of this. Adieu." (*Aside.*) Excellent well!

OBADIAH PRIM. (*To Simon Pure.*)

Dost thou hear this?

SIMON PURE.

Yea, but it moveth me not; that, doubtless, is the
impostor. (*Pointing at the Colonel.*)   325

COLONEL.

Ah! Thou wicked one—now I consider thy face I
remember thou didst come up in the leathern
convenience[92] with me—thou hadst a black bob
wig on, and a brown camblet[93] coat with brass
buttons. Canst thou deny it, hah?   330

SIMON PURE.

Yea, I can, and with a safe conscience too, Friend.

OBADIAH PRIM.

Verily, Friend, thou art the most impudent villain
I ever saw.

MRS. LOVELY. (*Aside.*)

Nay then, I'll have a fling at him too.—I remember
the face of this fellow at Bath. Aye, this is he that   335
picked my Lady Raffle's pocket upon the Grove.[94]
Don't you remember that the mob pumped[95] you,
Friend? This is the most notorious rogue.

SIMON PURE.

What doth provoke thee to seek my life? Thou wilt
not hang me, wilt thou, wrongfully?   340

OBADIAH PRIM.

She will do thee no hurt, nor thou shalt do me
none; therefore, get thee about thy business,
Friend, and leave thy wicked course of life, or thou
may'st not come off so favorably everywhere.

---

92 leathern convenience] Quaker for coach
93 camblet] a light cloth of mixed silk and wool
94 the Grove] the Orange Grove, a public walk planted
   with trees named for a column honoring William of
   Orange
95 pumped] put under a stream of water from a pump, for
   punishment

COLONEL.

Go, Friend, I would advise thee, and tempt thy fate no more.

SIMON PURE.

Yea, I will go, but it shall be to thy confusion; for I shall clear myself. I will return with some proofs that shall convince thee, Obadiah, that thou art highly imposed upon. (*Exit.*)

COLONEL. (*Aside.*)

Then here will be no staying for me, that's certain. What the devil shall I do?

OBADIAH PRIM.

What monstrous works of iniquity are there in this world, Simon!

COLONEL.

Yea, the age is full of vice. (*Aside.*) Z'death, I am so confounded, I know not what to say.

OBADIAH PRIM.

Thou art disordered, Friend—art thou not well?

COLONEL.

My spirit is greatly troubled, and something telleth me, that though I have wrought a good work in converting this maiden, this tender maiden, yet my labor will be in vain; for the evil spirit fighteth against her, and I see, yea I see with the eyes of my inward man, that Sathan will rebuffet her again, whenever I withdraw myself from her, and she will, yea this very damsel will return again to that abomination from whence I have retrieved her, as if it were, yea, as if it were out of the jaws of the Fiend—hum—

OBADIAH PRIM.

Good lack! Thinkest thou so?

MRS. LOVELY. (*Aside.*)

I must second him.—What meaneth this struggling within me? I feel the spirit resisting the vanities of this world, but the flesh is rebellious, yea the flesh—I greatly fear the flesh and the weakness thereof—hum—

OBADIAH PRIM.

The maid is inspired.

COLONEL.

Behold, her light begins to shine forth. (*Aside.*) Excellent woman!

MRS. LOVELY.

This good man hath spoken comfort unto me, yea comfort, I say; because the words which he hath breathed into my outward ears are gone through and fixed in mine heart, yea verily in mine heart, I say—and I feel the spirit doth love him exceedingly, hum—

COLONEL. (*Aside.*)

She acts it to the life.

OBADIAH PRIM.

Prodigious! The damsel is filled with the spirit, Sarah!

Enter Mrs. Prim.

MRS. PRIM.

I am greatly rejoiced to see such a change in our beloved Anne. I came to tell thee that supper stayeth for thee.

COLONEL.

I am not disposed for thy food—my spirit longeth for more delicious meat; fain would I redeem this maiden from the tribe of sinners and break those cords asunder wherewith she is bound—hum—

MRS. LOVELY.

Something whispers in my ears, methinks, that I must be subject to the will of this good man and from him only must hope for consolation—hum—it also telleth me that I am a chosen vessel to raise up seed to the faithful and that thou must consent that we two be one flesh according to the Word—hum—

OBADIAH PRIM.

What a Revelation is here? This is certainly part of thy vision, Friend, this is the maiden's growing to thy side. Ah! With what willingness should I give thee my consent, could I give thee her fortune too, but thou wilt never get the consent of the wicked ones.

COLONEL. (*Aside.*)

I wish I was as sure of yours.

OBADIAH PRIM.

My soul rejoiceth, yea, it rejoiceth, I say, to find the spirit within thee; for lo, it moveth thee with natural agitation—yea, with natural agitation, I say again, and stirreth up the seeds of thy virgin inclination towards this good man—yea, it stirreth, as one may say—yea verily, I say it stirreth up thy inclination—yea, as one would stir a pudding.

MRS. LOVELY.

I see, I see! The spirit guiding of thy hand, good 415
Obadiah Prim, and now behold thou art signing thy
consent, and now I see myself within thy arms, my
Friend and Brother, yea, I am become bone of thy
bone and flesh of thy flesh. (*Embraces him.*) Hum—

COLONEL. (*Aside.*)

Admirably performed.—And I will take thee in all 420
spiritual love for an helpmeet, yea, for the wife of my
bosom—and now, methinks—I feel a longing—
yea, a longing, I say, for the consummation of thy
love, hum—yea, I do long exceedingly.

MRS. LOVELY.

And verily, verily my spirit feeleth the same 425
longing.

MRS. PRIM.

The spirit hath greatly moved them both. Friend
Prim, thou must consent; there is no resisting of
the spirit.

OBADIAH PRIM.

Yea, the light within showeth me that I shall fight 430
a good fight—and wrestle through those reprobate
fiends, thy other guardians—yea, I perceive the
spirit will hedge thee into the flock of the
righteous—Thou art a chosen Lamb—yea, a
chosen Lamb, and I will not push thee back—no, 435
I will not, I say—no, thou shalt leap-a, and frisk-
a, and skip-a, and bound, and bound, I say—yea,
bound within the fold of the righteous—yea, even
within thy fold, my Brother. Fetch me the pen and
ink, Sarah—and my hand shall confess its 440
obedience to the spirit. [*Exit Mrs. Prim.*]

COLONEL. [*Aside.*]

I wish it were over.

Enter Mrs. Prim with pen and ink.

MRS. LOVELY. (*Aside.*)

I tremble lest this quaking rogue should return and
spoil all.

OBADIAH PRIM.

Here, Friend, do thou write what the spirit 445
prompteth, and I will sign it.

Colonel sits down [and writes].

MRS. PRIM.

Verily, Anne, it greatly rejoiceth me, to see thee

reformed from that original wickedness wherein I
found thee.

MRS. LOVELY.

I do believe thou art, and I thank thee. 450

COLONEL. (*Reads.*)

"This is to certify all whom it may concern, that I
do freely give up all my right and title in Anne
Lovely to Simon Pure, and my full consent that
she shall become his wife according to the form
of marriage. Witness my hand." 455

OBADIAH PRIM.

That is enough—give me the pen. (*Signs it.*)

Enter Betty running to Mrs. Lovely.

BETTY.

Oh! Madam, madam, here's the Quaking man
again; he has brought a coachman and two or three
more.

MRS. LOVELY. (*Aside to Colonel.*)

Ruined past redemption. 460

COLONEL. [*Aside to her.*]

No, no, one minute sooner had spoiled all, but
now—(*Going up to Prim hastily.*) Here is company
coming, Friend, give me the paper.

OBADIAH PRIM.

Here it is, Simon, and I wish thee happy with the
maiden. 465

MRS. LOVELY.

'Tis done, and now, devil do thy worst.

Enter Simon Pure and coachman, etc.

SIMON PURE.

Look thee, Friend, I have brought these people to
satisfy thee that I am not that impostor which thou
didst take me for; this is the man which did drive
the leathern conveniency that brought me from 470
Bristol, and this is—

COLONEL.

Look ye, Friend, to save the Court the trouble of
examining witnesses, I plead guilty, ha, ha!

OBADIAH PRIM.

How's this? Is not thy name Pure, then?

COLONEL.

No really, sir, I only made bold with this 475
gentleman's name, but I here give it up safe and
sound; it has done the business which I had

occasion for, and now I intend to wear my own, which shall be at his service upon the same occasion at any time, ha, ha, ha!

SIMON PURE.

Oh! The wickedness of this age.

COACHMAN.

Then you have no farther need of us, sir. (*Exit.*)

COLONEL.

No, honest man, you may go about your business.

OBADIAH PRIM.

I am struck dumb with thy impudence, Anne; thou hast deceived me and perchance undone thyself.

MRS. PRIM.

Thou art a dissembling baggage, and shame will overtake thee. (*Exit.*)

SIMON PURE.

I am grieved to see thy wife so much troubled; I will follow and console her. (*Exit.*)

Enter servant.

SERVANT.

Thy brother guardians inquireth for thee; there is another man with them.

MRS. LOVELY. (*To the Colonel.*)

Who can that other man be?

COLONEL.

'Tis one Freeman, a friend of mine, whom I ordered to bring the rest of thy guardians here.

Enter Sir Philip, Tradelove, Periwinkle, and Freeman.

FREEMAN. (*To the Colonel.*)

Is all safe? Did my letter do you service?

COLONEL. (*Aside [to Freeman].*)

All! All's safe; ample service.

SIR PHILIP.

Miss Nancy, how dost do, child?

MRS. LOVELY.

Don't call me miss, Friend Philip, my name is Anne, thou knowest.

SIR PHILIP.

What, is the girl metamorphosed?

MRS. LOVELY.

I wish thou wert so metamorphosed. Ah! Philip, throw off that gaudy attire and wear the clothes becoming of thy age.

OBADIAH PRIM. (*Aside.*)

I am ashamed to see these men.

SIR PHILIP.

My age! The woman is possessed.

COLONEL.

No, thou art possessed rather, friend.

TRADELOVE.

Hark ye, Mrs. Lovely, one word with you. (*Takes hold of her hand.*)

COLONEL.

This maiden is my wife, thanks to Friend Prim, and thou hast no business with her. (*Takes her from him.*)

TRADELOVE.

His wife! Hark ye, Mr. Freeman—

PERIWINKLE.

Why, you have made a very fine piece of work of it, Mr. Prim.

SIR PHILIP.

Married to a Quaker! Thou art a fine fellow to be left guardian to an orphan, truly—there's a husband for a young lady!

COLONEL.

When I have put on my beau clothes, Sir Philip, you'll like me better.

SIR PHILIP.

Thou wilt make a very scurvy beau, Friend.

COLONEL.

I believe I can prove it under your hand that you thought me a very fine gentleman in the park today, about thirty-six minutes after eleven; will you take a pinch, Sir Philip—out of the finest snuffbox you ever saw. (*Offers him snuff.*)

SIR PHILIP.

Ha, ha, ha! I am overjoyed, faith I am, if thou be'st that gentleman. I own I did give my consent to the gentleman I brought here today, but if this is he I can't be positive.

OBADIAH PRIM.

Canst thou not. Now I think thou art a fine fellow to be left guardian to an orphan. Thou shallow-brained shuttlecock, he may be a pickpocket for aught thou dost know.

PERIWINKLE.

You would have been two rare fellows to have been trusted with the sole management of her fortune, would ye not, think ye? But Mr. Tradelove and myself shall take care of her portion.

TRADELOVE.

Aye, aye, so we will. Did not you tell me the Dutch merchant desired me to meet him here, Mr. Freeman?

FREEMAN.

I did so, and I am sure he will be here, if you have a little patience. 540

COLONEL.

What, is Mr. Tradelove impatient? Nay then, ik ben gereet veor you, heb ye Jan Van Timtam-tirelireletta Heer Van Fainwell vergeeten?

TRADELOVE.

Oh! Pox of the name! What, have you tricked me too, Mr. Freeman? 545

COLONEL.

Tricked, Mr. Tradelove! Did I not give you two thousand pound for your consent fairly? And now do you tell a gentleman that he has tricked you?

PERIWINKLE.

So, so, you are a pretty guardian, faith, sell your charge. What, did you look upon her as part of your stock? 550

OBADIAH PRIM.

Ha, ha, ha! I am glad thy knavery is found out however. I confess the maiden overeached me, and no sinister end at all. 555

PERIWINKLE.

Aye, aye, one thing or another overreached you all, but I'll take care he shall never finger a penny of her money, I warrant you. Overreached, quoth'a? Why I might have been overreached too, if I had had no more wit. I don't know but this very fellow 560 may be him that was directed to me from Grand Cairo today. Ha, ha, ha.

COLONEL.

The very same, sir.

PERIWINKLE.

Are you so, sir, but your trick would not pass upon me. 565

COLONEL.

No, as you say, at that time it did not, that was not my lucky hour, but hark ye, sir, I must let you into one secret—you may keep honest John Tradescant's coat on, for your uncle, Sir Toby Periwinkle, is not dead—so the charge of mourning will be saved, ha, 570 ha! Don't you remember Mr. Pillage, your uncle's steward, ha, ha, ha?

PERIWINKLE.

Not dead! I begin to fear I am tricked too.

COLONEL.

Don't you remember the signing of a lease, Mr. Periwinkle? 575

PERIWINKLE.

Well, and what signifies that lease, if my uncle is not dead? Hah! I am sure it was a lease I signed.

COLONEL.

Aye, but it was a lease for life, sir, and of this beautiful tenement, I thank you. (*Taking hold of Mrs. Lovely.*) 580

OMNES.

Ha, ha, ha, neighbor's fare![96]

FREEMAN.

So then, I find you are all tricked, ha, ha!

PERIWINKLE.

I am certain I read as plain a lease as ever I read in my life.

COLONEL.

You read a lease I grant you, but you signed this 585 contract. (*Showing a paper.*)

PERIWINKLE.

How durst you put this trick upon me, Mr. Freeman, did not you tell me my uncle was dying?

FREEMAN.

And would tell you twice as much to serve my friend, ha, ha. 590

SIR PHILIP.

What, the learned, famous Mr. Periwinkle choused too? Ha, ha, ha! I shall die with laughing, ha, ha, ha.

OBADIAH PRIM.

It had been well if her father had left her to wiser heads than thine and mine, Friend, ha, ha.

TRADELOVE.

Well, since you have outwitted us all, pray you, 595 what and who are you, sir?

SIR PHILIP.

Sir, the gentleman is a fine gentleman. I am glad you have got a person, madam, who understands dress and good breeding. I was resolved she should have a husband of my choosing. 600

OBADIAH PRIM.

I am sorry the maiden is fallen into such hands.

---

96 neighbor's fare] same fate or luck

TRADELOVE.

A beau! Nay then, she is finely helped up.

MRS. LOVELY.

Why, beaus are great encouragers of trade, sir, ha, ha!

COLONEL.

Look ye, gentlemen, I am the person who can give 605
the best account of myself, and I must beg Sir
Philip's pardon, when I tell him that I have as
much aversion to what he calls dress and breeding
as I have to the enemies of my religion. I have had
the honor to serve his Majesty and headed a 610
regiment of the bravest fellows that ever pushed
bayonet in the throat of a Frenchman, and
notwithstanding the fortune this lady brings me,
whenever my country wants my aid, this sword
and arm are at her service. 615

And now, my fair, if you'll but deign to smile,
I meet a recompense for all my toil:
Love and religion ne'er admit restraint,
Force makes many a sinner, not one saint;
Still free as air the active mind does rove, 620
And searches proper objects for its love,
But that once fixed, 'tis past the power of art
To chase the dear ideas from the heart:
'Tis liberty of choice that sweetens life,
Makes the glad husband and the happy wife. 625

[Exeunt.]

FINIS.

Textual Notes

[a] The copytext is the 1718 duodecimo, which exists in
two states, with a copy in the British Library containing three press variants. This issue is designated D1a,
the others D1b. When all three copies of the first edition agree, they are referred to as D1. There was another
duocecimo edition (D2) in 1724, of doubtful authority. Also consulted are modern editions by Stathis (1968)
and Rogers (1994).

[b] sect] Sex D1, D2

[c] fall] D2; falls D1

[d] possess] D2; profess D1

[e] come] D2; comes D1

[f] gelt] D2; Celt D1

Subversive Comedy

Subversive comedy reveals fissures under the smooth surface of official ideology, even as the plays end in ritual celebration of society's centripetal power—usually a marriage. These fissures sometimes include sympathetic glimpses of the oppressed or cracks in ruling-class solidarity or threats to the genealogical system for the transmission of power and property. Jacobean city comedy is full of such fissures. In the Restoration, folk energy disrupts officialdom; aristocratic friends turn on one another, often seducing each other's wife; witty women get away with sexual promiscuity. Post-Revolution subversive comedy features women who even more thoroughly threaten: not just the order controlling sex through monogamy but that controlling gender difference and class difference. And it presents the new tricksters on the horizon as not sexual but economic. The omnivorous predation of capitalism gapes so widely in a few plays that the endings barely paper over its abyss as the audience takes refuge in the fantasy of art.

The Old Troop; or, Monsieur Raggou[a]

by John Lacy (?-1681)

edited by Maja-Lisa von Sneidern

John Lacy was apprenticed to John Ogilby, a dancing master and theater owner (later made notorious by Dryden in "MacFlecknoe" and Pope in the *Dunciad*), in 1631. During the Civil War, Lacy served as a lieutenant and quartermaster for the royalist cause. After 1660, Lacy acted and wrote for the King's Company, and his performances were much admired by diarists John Evelyn and Samuel Pepys. Lacy's reputation as a comedian was well established by such roles as Scruple in *The Cheats*, Teague in *The Committee*, Bayes in *The Rehearsal*, and Raggou in his own play *The Old Troop*.

The play was first performed in 1664, some eight years prior to the publication of the first quarto, and was revived frequently over the next half century. Its debut was after Cromwell's body was exhumed, hanged and mutilated, after the frequent and barbarous executions of the regicides, and after the purge of Commonwealth's men (supporters of "The Good Old Cause" or "Saints" as the experiment in republicanism and its adherents were sarcastically called), but before the sobering events—the plague and fire of London—of 1665–66.

The Old Troop is particularly interesting because it worries less over Roundhead hypocrisy than Cavalier excess. It stages and then manages the most egregious accusations against the royalists. Rumor, as reported in lampoons, had it that some of Charles I's officials were overly fond of eating children. Act III proposes that, while originating in necessity, the threatened cannibalism was mere "mirth" that no reasonable person could take seriously; however, enemies of the king would "noise" the rumor as fact.

The problems of provisioning and quartering armies most central to the play are not so facilely resolved. The third amendment to the U. S. Constitution guarantees only that property owners must consent to quartering soldiers "in time of peace." As in Lacy's play, at war we can only trust that the "timbers" of state "would rather have" our "hearts than money."

The Old Troop is a farce, and students need to interpolate the slapstick and accept the crudity of the humor as they might a contemporary comedian-actor—the frequently bigoted, potty-mouthed, coarse buffoon, without apparent taste or values. In *The Old Troop*, the "serious" business, including the restoration of the King and the romantic interest, is thin at best. Raggou and most of "the old troop" wallow in their ill-gotten gains "like de dog dat tumbla in de carrion." But it is worthwhile to remember that the theater audience both reviled and admired the Reformation of the church, French savoir faire and cuisine, Dutch economic and political successes, and the events that restored Charles II to his throne. Lacy toys with stereotypes and these ambivalent attitudes to entertain his audience by making them feel more secure in their faith, their taste, their economy, their monarchy, and their King.

DRAMATIS PERSONAE

Captain [Honor]
Lieutenant
Cornet
Tom Tell-troth.
} of the Troop.

Raggou.[1]
Flea-flint, Plunder-master General.
Captain Ferret-farm.
Quartermaster Burndorp.
Biddy, the Cornet's Boy.
Dol Troop.
Troopers.
Constables.
[Watch.]
[Marshal.]
Painter.
Carpenter.
Servants.
Women and Children in abundance.
Roundheads:
Governor of a Garrison.
Captain Holdforth.
Captain Tubtext, and his two holy sisters.

The[b] Old Troop; or, Monsieur Raggou

Act I. [The camp of the Cavalier troop.]

Tell-troth and Dol Troop.

DOL.

I have heard your story and much pity you, but in truth, I am a wicked, very wicked woman, for I never did one good deed in all my life, and I doubt* you're unlucky that your fate directs you to me.

TELL-TROTH.

I find you have opportunity to do good and will 5 to serve me. And for reward, if that—

DOL.

Nay, y'are liberal enough, you understand the world, for money creates good and evil. And I, that never thought of doing good, will now heartily endeavor it. Go to my quarters, for I have a great 10 deal of roguery to act for myself, besides the good I am to do for you.

---

1 Raggou] or ragout, from the French for a highly seasoned stew

TELL-TROTH.

Inquire all you can into the last thing you spoke of, for I confess that troubles me. If she proves but honest,* I'll forgive her wildness. 15

DOL.

I'll do it with all the craft I can.

Exeunt.

Enter Lieutenant, Flea-flint, Ferret-farm, and Burndorp.

FLEA-FLINT.

Good morrow, good morrow, Lieutenant.

LIEUTENANT.

Precious rogues! What brave honors and titles you have arrived at in the wars, rascals! Plunder-master General Flea-flint! What Prince can give thee so 20 great a title? a great credit for my colonel, rogue. Then here's Captain Ferret-farm, an honorable gentleman: for always when we are fighting, you are ferreting the farms and searching the women for letters of intelligence, you damned rogue. 25 Then, here's the quartermaster Burndorp, a rogue that, when we have brave* large quarters assigned, you sell half of 'em, and then truss us up nine or ten in one house together. A pox on you, rascal!

BURNDORP.

But why are you thus cruel, Lieutenant? 30

LIEUTENANT.

Hang you, dogs. Did not I know you at first to be three tattered musketeers, and by plundering a malt-mill of three blind horses, you then turned dragooners, and so, quartering in a farm where a good team was, you changed your blind horses for 35 better, and then you commenced troopers at Oxford, and when you had plundered yourselves into good clothes, you impudently called yourselves Major and Captain and Quartermaster, and then you ran away from your own troop, and 40 I entertained* you for reformado-officers?[2] You

---

2 Musketeers … reformado officers] musketeer: foot soldier; dragoon: infantryman on horseback; trooper: cavalryman; reformado officer: officer removed from command, but retaining rank and sometimes pay. Oxford, about midway between London and Bristol, was traditionally a royalist stronghold.

know I know this, and yet, you dull, ungrateful rascals, you will not know why I am angry.

FERRET-FARM.

Why are you angry?

FLEA-FLINT.

Why? I'll tell thee why. He wants* twenty pounds 45
and a good gelding, coxcomb. He must have it, too; I know him well enough.

BURNDORP.

Is that it? He shall have it, and thank him, too.
Pray, accept of this twenty pound, Lieutenant.

FERRET-FARM.

And we have a good gelding for you, Lieutenant, 50
as ever you laid leg over.

LIEUTENANT.

Why so? Why will you put me to't to give you ill language? Cannot you understand me without scurvy usage?

FERRET-FARM.

I did not understand you, by my troth, Lieutenant. 55

LIEUTENANT.

Pray, understand me hereafter. Now are you three as honest, harmless fellows! How dost thou do?
Who dares say that thou wilt flea a flint?[3] or he search for letters in a wench's placket? or the quartermaster burn a town? I'll set 'em by the heels 60
that say it. Honest Robin, Tom, and Dick, when shall we drink a tub of ale together?

BURNDORP.

When you please, worthy Lieutenant.

LIEUTENANT.

Get a tub at one of your quarters, and I'll come to you. And pray, understand me thoroughly hereafter. 65
I believe I shall be very angry within this week again;
therefore, pray, take care to prevent it. (*Exit.*)

FLEA-FLINT.

It were a good deed ne'er to plunder more.

BURNDORP.

Why, prithee?

FLEA-FLINT.

No thriving on't for these damned officers. To put 70
excise and custom upon plundering! to put toll upon fleaing a flint! I hold my own quarters to be my

lawful inheritance as much as any man's land or office that is held by old custom and time out of mind.

FERRET-FARM.

Nay, I hold my quarters to be so much my own, 75
that the wife, the daughter and maidservants ought to be in my occupation.

BURNDORP.

I deny that, for the man of the house ought to have his wife himself, in case he have a daughter to furnish you. Nay, the strictness of the statute of 80
plundering says, that in case he has but barely a maidservant, you ought not to meddle with his wife, or indeed his daughter.

FLEA-FLINT.

I am of the opinion of the gentleman that spoke last, for I am (in my own quarter) lord of the 85
manor, and all wefts[4] and strays are mine.

BURNDORP.

I'll say that for thee, a maid cannot go a-milking but thou mak'st a weft or stray of her.

Enter Cornet.

CORNET.

Here's the faithful fraternity, a league of knaves that's never to be broke. It is a joyful thing when 90
brethren plunder together in unity. How d'ye, Plunder-master General?

FLEA-FLINT.

We have all arrived at excellent nicknames, to say truth, according to our several degrees and ways of plundering. But you, Cornet, have a name that's 95
proper for all cornets to be called by, for they are all beardless boys in our army.[5] For the most part of our horse were raised thus: The honest country gentleman raises the troop at his own charge, then he gets a low-country lieutenant[6] to fight his troop 100
safely, then sends for his son from school to be his cornet, and he puts off his child's coat to put on a

---

3 flea a flint] flay or skin a flint, to obtain money in any cruel or hardhearted way, as in modern "skinflint"

4 weft] waif

5 cornet] (1) lowest ranking cavalry officer, (2) immature grain, without a "beard."

6 low-country lieutenant] The sense is a professional soldier, but there is a possible allusion to Prince Rupert from Germany, who led Royalist troops for his uncle Charles I.

buff coat; and this is the constitution of our army. So I salute you, Cornet Beardless.—Thou art called Ferret-farm because thou are so terrible valiant amongst the country bumpkins, and Aspen because thou shakest and tremblest in a day of battle. 105

FERRET-FARM.

Whoo, pox, this is absolute malice.

CORNET.

There thou art out, for this is neither malice nor anger, but downright truth. 110

FLEA-FLINT.

You abuse him, i'faith. I have seen him up to the chin in blood.

CORNET.

'Twas in a saw-pit,[7] then. Yet, when the armies meet (I'll say that for him) he will draw up as confidently as if he would take a general by the 115 beard. And he will as confidently ride out of the army before the battle joins, and if any man ask him whither he goes, he says he is sent for orders. So you hear of him no more, and the next day you find him as sure in a saw-pit. 120

FERRET-FARM.

Pray let the saw-pit alone and provoke me not. Good men have done the like; therefore, be not too bold with your betters.

FLEA-FLINT.

Provoke him not, for he's a devil at a sword though he tremble at a gun. 125

FERRET-FARM.

A gun, I confess, is as terrible to me as thunder and lightning; they're out of my element. Well, but leave this discourse, and, so you do not laugh at me, I'll tell you a story.

FLEA-FLINT.

What is't? 130

FERRET-FARM.

Why, faith, our Dol's with child and lays it to me.

BURNDORP.

Pox on her, she was with me this morning, and I compounded with her for five pound.

FERRET-FARM.

The whore had seven of me, by this light.

CORNET.

An excellent cunning quean! She knows the family 135 of the Flea-flints are ever the moneyed men of the troop. I'll make use of my time too; give me ten pound to keep counsel, or I'll make you the laughingstock o'th' army.

FLEA-FLINT.

Thou wilt not turn treacherous rogue now, sure? 140

CORNET.

'Tis no treachery. Show me a soldier that will not take advantage.

FLEA-FLINT.

Aye, of the enemy.

CORNET.

For ten pound any man's my enemy or friend. There's another principle for you, and very fit for 145 the Flea-flints to make use of.

BURNDORP.

We scorn to compound, but we will lend you so much money if you will mortgage[8] the next fresh quarters.

CORNET.

I'll do't. 150

BURNDORP.

Then there's your ten pound.

CORNET.

Now are you men of inheritance. Now you have a good title to every man's goods and chattels, and for ten pound more I'll help you to a lawyer shall plead it and make it good to you and your heirs forever.[9] 155

Enter Tell-troth.

TELL-TROTH.

God give you good morn, sirs. I pray you, which of you is the Captain Commander?

FLEA-FLINT.

Why, friend, we have ne'er a captain here. He lies leiger[10] at Oxford to give the King intelligence when his troop beats or is beaten. 160

---

7 saw-pit] a pit over which timber is sawed by two men, one above and one below, hence a safe hole for hiding

8 mortgage] promise

9 men of inheritance … forever] The cornet implies that the cash loan can be converted into "real" property; until 1867 only male landowners deriving income from real estate could vote.

10 leiger] permanently

CORNET.

There y'are a scandalous rascal. Some captains, I confess, have that trick, but our captain always fights his troop himself. But we have a good lieutenant here, if that will serve your turn.

BURNDORP.

Aye, he's too good for us; I would the devil had 165 him.

CORNET.

What's thy business?

TELL-TROTH.

I'd be a trooper.

FERRET-FARM.

And canst thou fight?

TELL-TROTH.

Wilt thou try? 170

FERRET-FARM.

No, faith friend, I believe thee. Wast ever a soldier?

TELL-TROTH.

Aye, a Parliament one.

FLEA-FLINT.

What, and didst thou run away?

TELL-TROTH.

No, I walked this pace; I scorn to run.

BURNDORP.

I believe this fellow's a spy. 175

TELL-TROTH.

You lie;* I am very honest. Now, dare you fight?

BURNDORP.

No, by my troth, not with thee.

TELL-TROTH.

Then remember, if anybody want the lie, you had it last.

FLEA-FLINT. [*Aside.*]

This is such a fellow as I never met with.—Yet why 180 didst thou leave the Parliament?

TELL-TROTH.

For the same cause that I believe I shall leave you.

FLEA-FLINT.

What's that?

TELL-TROTH.

Because I liked 'em not.

FERRET-FARM.

Who was thy captain? 185

TELL-TROTH.

One Captain Verily Rett.

FERRET-FARM.

Of what profession was he?

TELL-TROTH.

Of everyone's profession, I think.

FERRET-FARM.

What's that?

TELL-TROTH.

An hypocrite.

BURNDORP. 190

And dost thou come out of love to the King?

TELL-TROTH.

No. I come to see fashions.

BURNDORP.

But why didst thou leave thy captain?

TELL-TROTH.

Because he is a hypocrite, a yea-and-nay knave. He cannot endure to plunder, but (in a godly manner) 195 he will take all he can lay his hands on.

CORNET.

But wilt thou fight for the King out of stark love and kindness?

TELL-TROTH.

No; I'll fight for him as all men fight for kings, partly for love, partly for my own ends. I'll fight 200 bravely for a battle or two, then beg an old house to make a garrison of, grow rich, consequently a coward, and then let the dog bite the bear, or the bear the dog,[11] I'll make my own peace, I warrant you. And, in short, this is my business hither. 205

Enter Lieutenant.

LIEUTENANT.

Where are you, sirs? The captain has brought orders to march, but whither I know not. And, better news than that, he has brought pay, boys.

FLEA-FLINT.

I hope you are not angry, Lieutenant?

LIEUTENANT.

I am not yet, but I shall be very suddenly; 210 therefore, provide against it. The next fresh quarter you will have advantage enough. I hope we understand of all hands?

---

11 dog bite … the dog] The outcome is irrelevant; a reference to bear-baiting, a popular entertainment.

FLEA-FLINT.

'Tis sufficient, Lieutenant.

CORNET.

But here's the strangest fellow come to be a trooper. 215

LIEUTENANT.

He's welcome.—Hast thou a good horse, friend?

TELL-TROTH.

No, but I've a bridle, and if you'll entertain* me, I shall quickly have a horse. Are you the captain?

LIEUTENANT.

I am but lieutenant, friend.

TELL-TROTH.

Ho, I thought you had all been captains. I'm sure 220 you are all called so.

Enter Captain.

LIEUTENANT.

But here comes one that is so; this is a very* captain.

TELL-TROTH.

I tell thee that's very much. What's his name?

LIEUTENANT.

Captain Honor. 225

TELL-TROTH.

Aye? Have you such a thing as honor amongst you?

CAPTAIN.

Lieutenant, get your corporals together and give 'em orders to make ready for a march, and be sure you charge 'em to see every horse in their squadron's shod; otherwise, we shall have 'em lie behind 230 drinking and plundering and then pretend they stay to shoe their horses. Let me hear no more on't.

TELL-TROTH.

'Tis possible a very captain may be honest.

LIEUTENANT.

But, sir, before you do anything, talk with this fellow; he would fain be a trooper. 235

CAPTAIN.

Now, friend, wouldst thou be a soldier?

TELL-TROTH.

Yes, if I could light of a good side: a right cause and good men to manage it.

CAPTAIN.

On my word, that's shrewdly put. Well, I'll promise thee a good cause and some good men; 240 in multitudes all are not virtuous, nor valiant.

TELL-TROTH.

That's well said; I think I shall begin to take a liking to you. But, Captain, I hear a man may learn to flea a flint amongst you, to drink and plunder.

CAPTAIN.

D'ye hear that, rascals?—But where didst thou 245 hear this report of us?

TELL-TROTH.

In a London pulpit. But another sort of people told me; they preached interest more than Gospel, so that a man knows not which side to take.

CAPTAIN.

Nay, upon my word, thou art come to the right side. 250

TELL-TROTH.

I guess as much, for you talk worse than you do, and they do worse than they talk.

CAPTAIN.

This is an odd kind of fellow, and I believe a dangerous.—Friend, withdraw while I read my orders to my officers. 255

TELL-TROTH.

A word in your ear first: Are you wonderful honest?

CAPTAIN.

Thou art a strange, blunt fellow. Yes, I am honest.

TELL-TROTH.

But are you wise too? For else the want* of wit to manage your honesty may make you a knave. I 260 know 'tis some men's cases.

CAPTAIN.

Thou dost surprise me. Sure thou hast more business than to be a trooper?

TELL-TROTH.

I have so, but I must ask you another question ere you know it. Are you staunch enough to keep a 265 secret? Be not angry. Many of your party cannot hold, for tell you news and you fly like lightning to the next man to disgorge it, and so it goes round till it comes to the enemy, and thus you betray your business and intend it not neither. 270

CAPTAIN.

I have not heard so dangerous a man.—Pray, friend, think me worthy to know your business.

TELL-TROTH.

You shall. And to show you that I have business, I know what your orders are.

CAPTAIN.

Why, 'tis impossible. 275

TELL-TROTH.

Nothing impossible, you are to remove your troop to Cilstow, there quarter till further orders, but not to go to bed, for you are within three miles of a little house called Thievesden Garrison, and you are to expect a company of foot to quarter with 280 you. Is that your orders?

CAPTAIN.

You amaze me! How came you by this intelligence?

TELL-TROTH.

It came to Thievesden house this morning and so to me. I am their confidant and would fain be yours. 285

CAPTAIN.

Do you not know who sent it?

TELL-TROTH.

No, nor they neither. There's the subtle carriage of the thing.

CAPTAIN.

But pray, sir, let me ask you who you are?

TELL-TROTH.

I am a plain, honest-meaning man, a neighbor to 290 that garrison of Thievesden, and one that has dived into the bottom of both your parties and find that you have faults, but the other great wickedness.

FLEA-FLINT.

I do not like this fellow; he had a fling against drink. 295

FERRET-FARM.

And plundering, but twenty to one he hath paid for't.

FLEA-FLINT.

He had a plaguy jerk* at flaying of flints too.

CAPTAIN.

What if you went to Oxford with me?

TELL-TROTH.

So I may be hanged when I come home again? for 300 they will know it as sure. Pray let me eat and refresh myself, and then conclude of something.

Exeunt.

Enter Dol, and calls Lieutenant back.

DOL.

Lieutenant, I'd speak with you.

LIEUTENANT.

Dol, I'll come to thee presently. (*Exit.*)

DOL.

I cannot say I am with child, but with children, 305 for here has been all nations and all languages to boot. If the several tongues should work upwards now, and I speak all languages? Why, I am not the first learned woman, but I believe the first that ever came by her learning that way. If I should have for 310 every man that has been dealing here a child, and if the children should be born with every one a back and breast12 on, as they were got? Bless me, what hard labor should I have! But, for all this, I hope I do not go with above a squadron of 315 children. But to my business. I mean to lay this great belly to every man that has but touched my apron strings. I thank the law, 'tis very favorable in this point, for when I have played the whore, the law gives me leave to play the rogue, and lay 320 it to whom I will.13

Enter Lieutenant.

LIEUTENANT.

Why, how now, Dol? How go matters with you, good Dol?

DOL.

I desire you stand my friend, sir. You see my condition. 325

LIEUTENANT.

Thou wilt not lay thy child to my charge, I hope?

DOL.

No, sir, I have more wit; my drift is to lay it to more than one man or one squadron. Sir, I understand there's a month's pay in your hands, and I am resolved to lay this great belly to every man round 330 the troop. Some I have struck already, and they have very fairly compounded with me; some, I suppose, may bustle and stand out, but if you will counte-nance me, then they must compound at our rates.

---

12 back and breast] backplate and breastplate, armor parts
13 law … will] Prior to 1754 an unmarried pregnant woman would be brought before a Justice of the Peace by parish officials to name the father, who would then be arrested and offered the choice of on the spot mar-riage or prison.

LIEUTENANT.

But, Dol, what benefit is this to me? For I profess no friendship but follow the general principle of mankind, Dol, which is to pick the money out of thy pocket to put it into mine. So, Dol, in plain terms, what will you give me? 335

DOL.

Why, Lieutenant, you shall go snips.[14] 340

LIEUTENANT.

Why, Dol, we are agreed. But after we have struck the troop round, who dost thou pitch upon to father it?

DOL.

Why, faith, I did design to marry Monsieur Raggou, the French cook that rides in your troop. 345

LIEUTENANT.

Thou wilt never endure to live with him, 'tis such a nasty slovenly rogue.

DOL.

'Tis no matter for living with him, I want* a husband.

LIEUTENANT.

He stinks above ground. He has not had a shirt on's back time out of mind. 350

DOL.

That makes it a fit match, for by my troth, I do not deserve a man that's worth a shirt.

LIEUTENANT.

Well, Dol, upon the aforesaid terms you're sure of me; play your game with all confidence. 355

DOL.

Well, I'll to work amongst 'em presently,* or if I might gain you to advance my greater desires, which is my cornet's boy that waits on him. I am foolish, for I love him strangely, desperately. A hundred pounds, in plain terms, make him mine. 360

LIEUTENANT.

But, Dol, where is this hundred pound?

DOL.

I have sharked these four years and made a shift to scrape four hundred pounds together.

LIEUTENANT.

Still, I say, you're sure of me with ready money.

Enter Monsieur Raggou and his landlady.

---

14 go snips] have a share

Well, Dol, away; here comes Monsieur Raggou. Step aside. 365

DOL.

Oh, let him have his money. If our cornet's boy fail, I'll have him, or he shall certainly keep* the child. (*Exit.*)

RAGGOU.

Landlady, come, take-a my pistol and lock in your trunk very safe. 370

LANDLADY.

Yes, sir.

RAGGOU.

Take heed, for begar* you will be hang if my pistol run away.

LANDLADY.

Oh Lord, I'll take no charge on't! 375

RAGGOU.

You roundhead whore, lock it up, or me will kill you, begar.

LANDLADY.

I'll take all care I can on't, sir. (*Exit.*)

RAGGOU.

So, me will steal my pistol from her trunk, and say she carry it to de enemy, and den me will so plundra de dam whore. 380

Enter bumpkin.

Stand; who are you for, Bumpkin?

BUMPKIN.

Oh Lord, sir, I am for nobody.

RAGGOU.

You dog, be you for de King or de Parliamenta?

BUMPKIN.

Why, I am for—pray, sir, who are you for? 385

RAGGOU.

Tank you for dat. Begar, you be very full wid cunning. You will be of my-a side if me name myself first. Speak, you dam dog. Who be you for?

BUMPKIN.

In truth it is not good manners to say who I am for; your worship ought to speak first. 390

RAGGOU.

Pox take you, me be for de Parliament, you dog.

BUMPKIN.

Oh, the Lord bless your worship, I am for the good Parliament, too.

RAGGOU.

Jernie,* I am for de King, you roundhead dog. Begar, me will plundra you, soul and body. 395

BUMPKIN.

Oh, good sir, spare me; I am for the King.

RAGGOU.

Diable, me will plundra you for being Jack[15] of both sides. [*Aside.*] Diantie,[16] he have but one silling about his soul and bodee.—Get you gone, you dog. 400

Exit bumpkin.

Begar, me have no luck. Zoun, me plundra every day dis tre years, and begar me never get but one silling or one sixpenne, begar. Hah! Monsieur Lieutenant, me hear very brave* ting of you.

LIEUTENANT.

What's that? 405

RAGGOU.

Me hear you have some largion[17] for Monsieur la Soldier. Pray, how much will come to Monsieur Moy?

LIEUTENANT.

Faith, monsieur, some three pounds.

RAGGOU.

How, tre pone? Whar be de tre pone? How much be tre pone? 410

LIEUTENANT.

Why, here 'tis, Monsieur, so much as you see.

RAGGOU.

Begar, sure you mock-a de moy; begar, me never see so much money togeder in my life. Me will lie down and tumble in my money like de dog dat tumbla in 415 de carrion, it is so sweet. Oh brave Capitain, oh brave Lieutenant, Gad-a bless de King of England, and de King of France, too, when he give me tre pone. Lieutenant, be to be mad a dangerous ting?

LIEUTENANT.

Oh, very dangerous. 420

RAGGOU.

Begar, dere be your tre pone again. It will make-a me tark-a mad; me no know vat me sall do with all dis money. Begar, me admire tre pone of all ting in dis varle; it vill make de great Turk de Christian, or de Christian de Turk, better den all de argument 425 in de varle. Pray, Lieutenant, keep dis money for me, one, two, tre year, till me take counsel of all my friend in France vat me sall do wid dat.

LIEUTENANT.

Go to Oxford and buy some necessaries with it; you are so nasty, nobody is able to come near you. 430 Buy some shirts, to keep you sweet and clean.

RAGGOU.

Buy some shart? Me love you very vell, Lieutenant, but you no understand. For vat sall me have some shart?

LIEUTENANT.

To keep yourself sweet and from being lousy.* 435

RAGGOU.

Who can see my shart? Here be my doublet come close, my coat come over all dat, den who de devil see my shart? For vat sall me have a shart, when nobody see my shart?

LIEUTENANT.

But then you want* stockings and twenty 440 necessaries.

RAGGOU.

Me pull up my boot, who see me have a stockin? You vill have a little English tricka and never understand. For vat vill you have more ting about you den vat vill make a show in de varle and 445 everybody can see? Pray, let me lay out my money to please my own fancee.

LIEUTENANT.

With all my heart.

RAGGOU.

Den me will lay it out for my honor, and for de honor of de King and my Lieutenant. So adieu. 450 Buy shart? Who see my shart? (*Exit.*)

Enter Dol.

DOL.

Faith, Lieutenant, I'll at him and some of the rest presently;* therefore, leave me to work. I am ashamed; I am such a fool to dote on a boy, but 455 no remedy. Remember, therefore, and about it.

---

15 Jack] a knave, a nickname usually indicating a youthful or impish miscreant, not a dangerous felon

16 Diantie] probably a corruption of *Diantre*, a mild French oath perhaps best translated as "the dickens"

17 largion] *l'argent*, money

LIEUTENANT.

Do you remember the hundred pound; I'll work him, fear not.

Exeunt severally.

Act II, scene i. [The troop's camp.]

Enter Dol Troop.

DOL.

Now to my business. My Flintflayer compounded with me very civilly, that I did fear would have outwitted me. I am afraid of nothing but an impudent rogue that has no shame in him, that will father the child rather than part with his money, and 5 so spoil my compounding with the rest of the troop. I'll be as wise as I can, so have among 'em.

Enter a trooper.

TROOPER.

What a pox makes she here?

DOL.

How d'ye, Mr. William? I'm come to tell you I am gone half my time, that you may provide, for I am 10 quick.*

TROOPER.

Art thou? Faith, I'll be as quick as thou art, for I'll be in Holland (if the wind serve) tomorrow. (*Exit.*)

DOL.

'Slife, if they should all boggle thus, I should make a thin troop on't. 15

Enter Raggou.

RAGGOU.

Oh, Madam Dol! Ow dee? Ow dee?

DOL.

You see how I do. I am near my time; I desire you to provide. You swore a thousand oaths to me you would keep* the child.

RAGGOU.

But me did but swear in French, Madam Dol, and 20 dat vill no stand good in English law, Madam Dol.

DOL.

Come, sir, come, I'll make you father my child, or I'll make you do worse. Will you compound?

RAGGOU.

Me scorn to compone and scorn to fader your shild. You be a dam whore, Madam Dol. 25

DOL.

You are a rascal, Mr. Monsieur, and I'll make you father the child in spite of your French teeth.*

RAGGOU.

Begar, Madam Dol, you be de great whore de Babylon.* Begar, me vill make appear noting can get you wid shild but de maypole in de Strana,[18] 30 and den me can make appear by good vitteness dat me have no maypole abouta me. So adieu, Madam Babylon. Pox take you, me fader your dam son of a whore shild! (*Exit.*)

DOL.

You fickle Frenchman, I shall be revenged on thee. 35 I'll marry thee, but I'll be revenged on thee.

Enter Cornet, Lieutenant, and Biddy.

But here comes my cornet and his boy, and the lieutenant. I see he is mindful of my business. (*Exit.*)

LIEUTENANT.

Cornet, I have an earnest and (by my troth) a most pleasant suit to you. 40

CORNET.

You cannot miss the grant of it. What is't?

LIEUTENANT.

But first, do you love money?

CORNET.

By my troth, I know not, for I never had a sum worth loving in my life yet.

LIEUTENANT.

Will fifty pound do any hurt? 45

CORNET.

But what must I do for it? betray the troop to the enemy, or some garrison? For under that I cannot deserve fifty pound.

LIEUTENANT.

Towns are not so cheap yet. Though treason be plentiful, 'tis not grown a drug. But to my suit, 50 you are to know that our Dol is desperately in love and with whom.

CORNET.

Not with me? I find I must earn this fifty pound.

LIEUTENANT.

No such matter; you have too great a conceit of your good face. 55

---

[18] de Strana] the Strand*

BIDDY. (*Aside.*)

Indeed you lie, Lieutenant, for he can never think too well of that face.

CORNET.

Who is it she is in love with?

LIEUTENANT.

By my troth, with thy boy here, desperately in love with thy boy. 60

BIDDY. (*Aside.*)

The devil take her for her pains. But why do I curse her, that am so desperately in love myself?

CORNET.

Why, this story is very pleasant, if you knew all.

BIDDY.

Oh Lord, you will not tell him what I am, I hope?

CORNET.

Lieutenant, I must deny your suit, for it must not 65 be a match, for the boy is, in plain terms, a girl.

BIDDY.

The devil take you for telling him.

CORNET.

Why so? My lieutenant's very faithful.

LIEUTENANT.

A girl? Let me see your face.

BIDDY.

Oh, you unworthy man!—Good sir, forgive me, 70 for I am even ready to scold.

LIEUTENANT.

This is the pretty young daughter that belonged to your winter quarters, and so came away for love?

BIDDY.

Yes, sir, but if your cornet had been true, I had been past love by this time. I had been married. 75

LIEUTENANT.

Why, are all married people past love?

BIDDY.

Yes, sir, of the men's side especially, but sir, I am naturally very merry, and shall be, if you will but do me the favor to think me very honest.*

LIEUTENANT.

I shall do you a great favor if I do, for I never thought 80 anybody so yet. But if it please you, I'll try your honesty, and then I'll give you my opinion.

BIDDY.

Be not rude when you try me. If you be, you were better venture on a maiden cat at midnight, for I

shall scratch worse and so mark you, not for my 85 humble servant, but my humble caterwauler.

LIEUTENANT.

I could meet such a creature o'th'housetop at any hour, and scratch and squeak, and tumble down together, and get the prettiest kitlings as we fall.

BIDDY.

I am glad to see you merry, sir, for merry people 90 are likely honest.

LIEUTENANT.

Well, we'll try, but if you love mirth, consent to marry with this Dol. There's money for us all. (*Exit.*)

BIDDY.

Content, i'faith. 'Twill be excellent sport to marry her, for I love roguery well enough, but the devil's 95 in't; she'll know me to be a girl.

Enter Dol aloof.[19]

CORNET.

No, no. She shall not come near you, nor touch you, till she's brought to bed. Then two to one but the troop marches away and leaves her behind. Then I'm sure the country bumpkins will knock 100 her o'th'head.[20]

DOL. [*Aside.*]

There's a cornet in grain, i'faith.

BIDDY.

Troth, you are very charitable. Well, since my hand's in at wearing breeches, I'll do all the offices of a man. I would I had wherewithal to perform, 105 for by my troth, I am weary of our own sex.

DOL. [*Aside.*]

She cries, i'faith; I like that well.

CORNET.

You little fool, you do not cry, I hope?

BIDDY.

No, faith, that was but a tear by chance. You made me leave my friends, you know, when you talked 110 of marriage to me, but not one word on't now you have made me your be-de-boy.[21]

---

19 aloof] at a distance, i.e., unseen by Biddy and the Cornet.

20 knock her o'th'head] bludgeon her to death

21 be-de-boy] bidding boy, an ad hoc servant who attends to light, ephemeral tasks; the character name, "Biddy," emphasizing the function

DOL. [*Aside.*]

I know not what to say to that.

CORNET.

We'll talk of those things when we are settled.

BIDDY.

By my troth, you have put me in such a gog* of 115
marriage that it will not out of my head, and yet
I scorn to ask you to marry me, and I scorn to
crack a commandment with you. Was not that
basely done of you to tempt me? But I shall scold,
which is a thing I hate. Oh base fellow! You would 120
be going o'th'score[22] with me for my virginity?
Faith sir, I'd have you know 'tis worth ready money
at any time, and, faith, I'll swear it shall ne'er go
under matrimony.

DOL. [*Aside.*]

She is honest,* i'faith. I love a virtuous woman, 125
though I am none myself, like him that loved the
sound of Greek though he understood it not. She
is right honest, i'faith.

BIDDY.

Marry me, and then halloo, dog, for thy silver
collar, but till then I'll gnaw my under-sheet to the 130
bedcord before you shall have your will of me. I
am sometimes mad when I think how I left my
friends. Sometimes I could scold, and sometimes
I could cry, and the devil take that good face of
yours, I can do neither for it. 135

CORNET.

Come, come, you trust your person with me, and
why not your virginity? How long do you think
you can hold out at this staunch rate?

BIDDY.

Faith sir, I can hold out till it's fit for nobody, till
I'm past the use of man, before thou shalt have it, 140
shameless wretch.

DOL. [*Aside.*]

She is certainly honest, and that's half our work
done.

CORNET.

Come, prithee let's think of our mock-marriage
with Dol, and after we'll be serious. 145

BIDDY.

Why, I'm for that too. But yet I cannot choose but

cry to see how false you are, and how they talk at
home of me, "She's run away with a soldier, and
that rascal will not marry her." Oh, the devil take
you; I shall never recover that credit again! 150

CORNET.

Come, we'll cozen 'em all at last.

BIDDY.

Nay, I believe thou'lt cozen more than me, for what
woman can forbear running away with thee, that
sees those leering eyes, thou bewitching devil, thou!

CORNET.

Oh, remember you hate scolding, Biddy. 155

BIDDY.

I had forgot that, indeed.

CORNET.

Nay, prithee, no more of this story.

BIDDY.

Well, I will not, but truly I grow weary of your
unkindness, and I am served well enough for
scorning a man that doted on me. 160

DOL. [*Aside.*]

Aha! Aye, marry,* that's somewhat, indeed.

BIDDY.

But I see, a cornet with his flying colors and his
word, "Have at all," goes a great way with a virgin.
Who can resist it?

Exeunt.

[Scene ii. The troop's headquarters.]

Enter Captain, Lieutenant, and Tell-troth.

CAPTAIN.

Lieutenant, stay and receive orders. But, sir, how
many companies are there in Thievesden Garrison?

TELL-TROTH.

Ne'er a company, for not one of 'em will be called
captain of a company, but captain of a congregation.
One is called Captain Holdforth; another Captain 5
Tubtext, rogues marked at the font[23] for rebellion.

CAPTAIN.

Rebellion is the first point of Reformation always.

TELL-TROTH.

They are formed to a new stamp of villainy, the
last impression——that which put the devil into a

---

22 o'th'score] cross the line

23 at the font] at baptism, since birth

cold sweat.[24] Take the wickedest and worst reputed 10
men you have and turn 'em loose to plunder, and
I defy 'em to make the tithe o'th'spoil these
hypocrites have done!

CAPTAIN.

You are very bitter.

TELL-TROTH.

Malice cannot lay 'em open. They lecture[25] it 15
thrice a week, and summon the country to come
in. They that refuse, they take their goods and
leave 'em ne'er a groat. And then they say they
took but their own, for the good creature is the
inheritance of the people of God. 20

CAPTAIN.

It seems every captain is a teacher, and his own
company is his congregation, so that they hang and
draw religion among themselves. No doubt most
blasphemous villains.

TELL-TROTH.

Well sir, I'll home tonight. March your troop to 25
Lavel tomorrow; stay till I come to you. So fare
you well, and I wish a blessing upon your good
meaning. (*Exit.*)

CAPTAIN.

Lieutenant, be careful how you march tomorrow,
and take heed I hear no complaint. I'll to Oxford 30
in the morning to give an account of this fellow.

LIEUTENANT.

I hope you'll allow us our old harmless drolleries.

CAPTAIN.

Aye, most freely. (*Exit.*)

Enter Cornet.

CORNET.

Lieutenant, half the troop will be gone. Dol has laid
her child to 'em all, and they're for horse and away. 35

LIEUTENANT.

What shall we do?

---

24 last impression … cold sweat] the image stamped would
be of Armageddon prophesied in Revelations; hence the
defeat of the devil.

25 lecture] preach. After the Restoration, dissenters often
privately hired lecturers or speakers to address congregations and supplement or counteract the teachings of
the official Anglican church.

CORNET.

Endeavor to prevent it, that is all that's to be said.

Exeunt.

*Enter a trooper with his arms, and Monsieur Raggou
meets him.*

RAGGOU.

Ow dee, ow dee, Monsieur Lancashire?[26] Vat make
you have your arms so late at night? Is dere alarm?
Be de enemy in de quarteer? 40

FIRST TROOPER.

Worse than the enemy, the devil's in the quarter.
Our Dol is with child and would lay it to me, but
I'll lay down my arms and go home.

RAGGOU.

Begar, me vil lay down my arms and go home too.
Hah! Begar, now I tink, me have no home. (*Exit.*) 45

FIRST TROOPER.

Captain! Captain!

[VOICE.] (*Within.*)

Who's there? What's the matter?

FIRST TROOPER.

Thomas, 'tis I, the old mutineer. Tell the Captain
I must speak with him.

[VOICE.] (*Within.*)

He is but just laid down on the bed to sleep a little. 50
Come i'th'morning!

FIRST TROOPER.

Flesh and blood, I will speak with him.

[Enter] Captain above.

CAPTAIN.

What's the matter? an alarm?

FIRST TROOPER.

Aye, marry is there, Captain; there will be a whole
squadron upon you presently. 55

CAPTAIN.

'Sdeath,* my horse presently.*

FIRST TROOPER.

The enemy, Dol, is fallen into our Lancashire
quarters and has laid her child to our squadron.
So here is your back and your breast, Captain, and
I'll go home. 60

---

26 Lancashire] at the time a very rural northwestern county
in England

Enter four troopers and Raggou.

SECOND TROOPER.

Flesh! We'll father no child, not we.

RAGGOU.

Begar, me vil fader no shild too.—Hey, Monsieur Captain, here be your one pistol.

THIRD TROOPER.

Captain, we have brought you some Lancashire arms; here is some ten or eleven sowze kidgiors[27] for you.

CAPTAIN. (*Above.*)

What the devil ails the fellows?

RAGGOU.

Begar, Capitain, me vil keep* no shild; your dam madam Dol have get us all with a shild.

CAPTAIN.

Run for the quean to come to me. I shall have all my troop forsake me. Stay, sirs, I'll come to you.— I must as well humor 'em as be severe, or else no soldiers. (*Exit from above.*)

RAGGOU.

Vell, me do know very well how it sall be my shild or no.

FOURTH TROOPER.

Well monsieur, and I have a mark to know whether it be mine or no as well as you.

SECOND TROOPER.

And so we have all.

Enter Captain and Cornet.

CAPTAIN.

My masters, you might have had so much manners to have held your complaints till morning. But, however, I have sent for Dol, and I'll do you justice before I stir now. How now, Raggou? What are thy sleeves stuffed withal so?

RAGGOU.

Begar, dis sleeve be my stabla: dere be good oata for mine arse. And dis sleeve be my kitchin: dere be meat for myself. Vill you eat dis morning, Capitain?

CAPTAIN.

Faugh! Your sleeves stink abominably.

RAGGOU.

Zoun, do you call dat a stinka? 'Tis true, it have a little hogoe.* Begar, dis sleeve keep your troop alive; dis sleeve is de physician to all de troop. When any man be sick, me set on some hot vatera, dere let my sleeve boil one hour in it, and dat make de comfortable pottage in de varle. Have not me cure you all?

FOURTH TROOPER.

Yes, indeed, Captain, he has cured us twenty times.

RAGGOU.

Begar, Capitain, me have cure that dam whore Madam Dol, and yet for all dat she lay her shild a top upon me.

Enter Dol.

CAPTAIN.

Oh, here she is. Now, you audacious quean, what makes you alarm these people thus? Who got you with child? Speak, and speak truth, I charge you.

DOL.

Why, then, I will speak truth an't* please you. Good Captain, do not fright me.

CAPTAIN.

Well, then, is it his child? Did he get it?

DOL.

I cannot say absolutely 'tis his, Captain.

CAPTAIN.

Why, is it this fellow's?

DOL.

I cannot say directly 'tis his neither.

CAPTAIN.

Is it Monsieur Raggou's?

DOL.

I cannot say, to speak truth, 'tis his in particular.

CAPTAIN.

Death, you abominable quean, say whose 'tis, or I'll slit your nose.[28]

----

27 sowse kidgiors] probably pig prods, useful for plundering

28 slit your nose] Mutilating (branding) petty criminals to identify them as such was part of the official criminal code, particularly in the military, until the mid-19th century. Nose-slitting, cutting the nostril up as far as the bridge, appears to be a practice of hooliganism or vigilantism.

DOL.

Why, truly, I cannot lay it to any one man, but, Gad is my judge, 'tis the troop's child, Captain.

CAPTAIN.

Was ever such a slut heard of!

DOL.

I desire your worship to believe me in one thing. Truly, Captain, and, as Gad's my comfort, I have been as true and faithful a woman to the troop as ever wife was to a husband, Captain.

RAGGOU.

Oh ho! Are you so? Me tink now, Madam Dol, you are de whore de Babylon, for one whole troop may make a maypole.

CAPTAIN.

Why, this is some honesty yet, that she is true to the troop.

RAGGOU.

Ould, Capitain! For oughta me see, dis shild be your shild.

CAPTAIN.

How prove you that, sir?

RAGGOU.

Begar, she say de shild belong to de troop, and you say de troop belong to you; derefore, de shild is your shild, begar.

CAPTAIN.

But I'll make some of you father it. There is none of you but have some private mark to know it to be your own by.

FOURTH TROOPER.

Faith, Captain, if it be born with a gauntlet and a headpiece[29] on, I'll own it.

SECOND TROOPER.

Troth, Captain, if it be born with a bridle in its hand and boots and spurs on, I'll own it.

FIRST TROOPER.

Troth, Captain, I ne'er touched her. I was about it once, but the jade laid herself so like a constable tied neck and heels together, that I went to plunder her, and she up and beat me like a dog.

THIRD TROOPER.

And by my troth, if it be born leading a horse into the world, 'tis my child, Captain.

---

29 headpiece] helmet

RAGGOU.

Ould, you every one have a mark to know your shild. Madam Dol, before my Capitain, if your shild be born wid never a shart, den it be my shild, for me have had no shart dis forty week.

Enter Ferret-farm.

FERRET-FARM.

By your leave, Captain.

CAPTAIN.

What want you, Aspen?

FERRET-FARM.

I come to free all these men and to own the child, Captain.

DOL.

How, own my child? The rogue never touched me in his life, Captain.

FERRET-FARM.

Hah, Dol! Confess, confess! Will you have the truth, Captain?

CAPTAIN.

Aye, prithee, with all my heart.

FERRET-FARM.

Why, then, I must confess she goes with two children; one I got on the great trunk's end and the other on a staircase, by my life, Captain.

CAPTAIN.

I never heard of staircase children before.

RAGGOU.

But vat if de shild be born wid no shart? You sall be hang before you fader my shild.

DOL.

Captain, if I were to die tomorrow, the rogue never touched me.

FERRET-FARM.

I'll cudgel the rogue to death, Captain.

CAPTAIN.

Hold! Hold!

RAGGOU.

Let him come, Captain! Me vill kill him, begar! (*Draws and throws off his coat.*)

CAPTAIN.

Hold, Dol.—I charge you to put up, monsieur.

RAGGOU.

Me vill put up, den.

CAPTAIN.

Not one word more, I charge you, but all to your

---

quarters. Be gone!—Cornet, 'tis time to sound to 170
horse, and take heed I hear of no complaints.

RAGGOU.

Begar, me never see all dat before. Diable, me be
Monsieur Raggou indeed. Me vill put on my coat
presan,* for, begar, if Monsieur Dunghill-raker see
me, begar he vill put me in his sack. 175

Exeunt.

[Scene iii. The troop's camp.]

Enter twelve troopers at six doors, two at a door.

FIRST TROOPER.

Pox of this French fool. What, does he mean to
give us all ribbons? We do but laugh at him.

THIRD TROOPER.

His business is to be admired. I admire he has
bought him ne'er a shirt.

SECOND TROOPER.

He is like the hypocrites that will not sing psalms 5
because they've ne'er a room to the street, they
cannot be heard.

FOURTH TROOPER.

And so he'll have ne'er a shirt because it cannot
be seen.

Enter Lieutenant, Flea-flint, Ferret-farm, and Burndorp.

LIEUTENANT.

Come, to horse, to horse. 10

FLEA-FLINT.

Lieutenant, pray let Monsieur Raggou ride before
and make the quarters tonight.

FERRET-FARM.

Pray do, sir, for every fresh quarter we know you
expect, and therefore you must wink.

LIEUTENANT.

But, sirs, I dare not own you, for my captain is so 15
severe that I protest he'll hang any man that
plunders, especially you flint-flayers that he has
forgiven so often.

BURNDORP.

Why, sir, we'll venture that, for we have a way to
come off. 20

LIEUTENANT.

Pray, how? For if the country complain (and they
discover you) the world cannot save you.

FLEA-FLINT.

Why, sir, you know Monsieur Raggou has a
remarkable coat with one sleeve always full of meat
for himself and the other full of oats for his horse. 25

LIEUTENANT.

Well, what then?

FLEA-FLINT.

Why, I have such a coat, and I will stuff up the
sleeves and rob like him. I can spatter French and
have everything so like him that yourself cannot
distinguish. 30

LIEUTENANT.

Well, and how rob the rest?

FERRET-FARM.

To satisfy you, in such disguises as the devil cannot
find us out in.

LIEUTENANT.

You'll do well to keep in those disguises still,* for,
i'faith, he'll find you at the long run else. Well, if 35
you will venture, do; I'll aid you in what I can.

BURNDORP.

If the country complain, they come directly to you,
Lieutenant.

FERRET-FARM.

Then you bid 'em describe the men, and without
peradventure they fall upon the Frenchman with 40
his remarkable sleeves.

LIEUTENANT.

But suppose he stand it out and make it out where
he was in the time of plundering?

FLEA-FLINT.

That's shrewd, I confess.

LIEUTENANT.

Come, I'll help you. If the countrymen come in 45
and describe him, I'll go directly to him and tell
him I have orders to seize him, for my captain is
resolved to hang him. So, out of my kindness to
him, I'll let him make his escape, and I'll warrant
he'll away as if the devil drove him. 50

FERRET-FARM.

But suppose he will not go at that neither? For he's
impudent enough.

LIEUTENANT.

Hah! If he will not (let me see) I'll write a letter and
have it ready in my hand, and we'll pretend to search
him for letters of intelligence, and so clap the letter 55

into his pocket and pull it out again, which shall be
as if it came from the enemy, and that, according to
his promise, they hope he will betray the troop.

FERRET-FARM.

Aye, marry, this is something. Needs must he go
that the devil drives.   60

FLEA-FLINT.

Then much more must he go that the Lieutenant
drives. I warrant he goes to some purpose.

FERRET-FARM.

Good, and when he is gone and fled for't—

LIEUTENANT.

The case is plain, he's guilty. None but he could
do it.   65

BURNDORP.

Why, this is plot and intrigue, Lieutenant, bravely*
laid, i'faith.

FLEA-FLINT.

Why then, *Esperanza*,[30] Flea-flint.

FERRET-FARM.

What work we'll make!

Enter Raggou and his landlady.

LIEUTENANT.

Here comes the poor rogue and his landlady. He   70
little thinks of our tragical design against him. I'll
step aside and see what work he'll make.

Exeunt.

RAGGOU.

Come, Landlady, bring me my pistol, me must
march.

LANDLADY.

Aye, sir, I'll fetch it you; 'tis safe enough. (*Exit.*)   75

RAGGOU.

Begar, me have steal my pistol. Me vill make her
believe she vill be hang, and den she vill endure
plundering de betra. But, pox take her, me have
search, and she have noting to plundra.

Enter Landlady.

LANDLADY.

Oh Lord! What shall I do, Monsieur? Your pistol's   80
gone.

RAGGOU.

Hah!

LANDLADY.

It is gone; it is stolen.

RAGGOU.

Hah! You have carry my pistol to de enemy, you
dam whore. Begar, you sall hang tre pair of stair   85
higher den Haman.

LANDLADY.

Truly, I know not what's become on't. I hope you
have it yourself.

RAGGOU.

Oh, you dam whore, me vill plundra your house
for slander a moy.   90

LANDLADY.

Good sir, I have nothing worth plundering but a
great cheese.

RAGGOU.

Give me your sheese, you devil you.

LANDLADY.

Here it is, sir, and all I have in the world.

RAGGOU.

Pox take you, give me one silling for my sheese.   95

LANDLADY.

With all my heart. Truly it's all the money I have.

RAGGOU.

Now give me my sheese agen, you dam whore.—
Vat sall me do wid dis sheese? It vill not go into
my kitchin sleeve.—Begar, for one shilling more
you sall have the sheese indeed.   100

LANDLADY.

You'll plunder it again?

RAGGOU.

Begar, it go agen my conscience to take your
sheese, because it vill no go in my kitchin sleeve.

LANDLADY.

I have not a penny to save my life.

RAGGOU.

Begar, me sell it to your neighbor.   105

Enter Neighbor.

Vat vill you give me for my sheese?

LANDLADY.

It's my cheese.

RAGGOU.

Begar, she lie. Me plunder it very fair from her.

NEIGHBOR.

Then I hope I may buy plundered goods as well
as other people. What's your price?   110

RAGGOU.

Begar, dog-sheap: one silling.

NEIGHBOR.

There's your money.

LANDLADY.

Will you offer to buy my cheese?

NEIGHBOR.

'Tis my cheese.

LANDLADY.

I'll try that.   115

Fight and exeunt [neighbor and landlady].

RAGGOU.

Begar, fight till de devil part you.

Enter Lieutenant and all the troopers.

Oh, Monsieur Lieutenant!

LIEUTENANT.

What dost with that cheese?

RAGGOU.

My landlady love me vera dear, and she give me
dis sheese as a token to wear for her sake.   120

LIEUTENANT.

Raggou, you must needs go make the quarters for
the troop.

RAGGOU.

Wid all min heart! But, Lieutenant, dere be a
favor* for you. (*Gives him a knot of ribbon.*)

LIEUTENANT.

But what is the meaning of this?   125

RAGGOU.

Begar, it be for my honer; me have lay out all my
tre pone in ribbon and give all de troop my favor
to wear in de hat.

LIEUTENANT.

What, and is all thy three pound gone in ribbon,
and bought never a shirt? 'Tis very fine.   130

RAGGOU.

Begar, and so it be very fine. As me tell you before,
who de devil see my shart? All de varle see Monsieur
Raggou in de hat; every man vill admire, and ask,
"Who gave all that favor to de troop?" Den dey cry,
"Monsieur Raggou, de French cook." Begar, dat sall   135

be more honer for me den ever you sall get by your
shart.

LIEUTENANT.

Thou art a right Frenchman.—My horse there,
groom. Let's march away.

Exeunt.

Act III, scene i.
[Various locations near the troop's camp.]

Enter Flea-flint, Ferret-farm, and Burndorp.

FLEA-FLINT.

Is not this like him as can be?

BURNDORP.

'Tis like enough to delude the people with.

FLEA-FLINT.

I'll rant and tear the ground, boys. I will so plundra
all de dam bumpkin dog.

FERRET-FARM.

That will pass; that's his word; 'tis like him.   5

FLEA-FLINT.

Be you pretty modest, sirs, and let me play the devil
among 'em. I will so terrify 'em with French gibberish that you shall appear nobody amongst 'em.

BURNDORP.

Good, for the more active and terrible thou art,
they will the more remember thee when they come   10
to complain, and so we shall be sure to 'scape.

FLEA-FLINT.

Come away, sirs; we must be quick and ride hard
for't.

Exeunt.

Enter Raggou, like Flea-flint.

RAGGOU.

Begar, me have maka myself like Flea-flint, and me
vill burn one, two town as me go to make-a de   15
quarter, and me vill speak English, and me vill call
myself Flea-flint. Let me see.—Come, where is this
constable? Where are all these damn'd, dery[31]
damned, rogues and whores? I'll flay your very
souls, you beastly bawds.—Begar, all dat be very   20
good English, and it be very much like Monsieur

---

31 dery] direly

Flea-flint, and begar, me hope he vill be taken and
hang for dat, for begar me vill plundra de devel if
me catch him. (*Exit.*)

Enter Cornet and Biddy.

CORNET.

Come, let me see, Biddy, how finely you'll court   25
your mistress, now.

BIDDY.

I can court her as all men court women. You shall
lend me two or three hundred oaths, your
dissembling tongue, and your false heart, and then
I cannot miss the right way of wooing her.   30

CORNET.

This comes very near scolding, Biddy. (*Takes her
by the chin.*)

BIDDY.

You make me forget myself. Look you now, would
any honest man take a maid so kindly by the chin
and yet not mean to marry her?   35

CORNET.

Thou little fool, at that rate every man i'th'kingdom
would have ten thousand wives. If you'll part with
your maidenhead, have at you, Biddy. Come, come,
you loving worm, I know I shall have it at last.

BIDDY.

Nay, o'my conscience, I believe thee, yet I have   40
held fast hitherto.

CORNET.

I am glad to hear that, i'faith.

BIDDY.

But I find I must look no more on those eyes; if I
do, i'faith, I shall flutter so long about the candle
that I shall singe my virgin wings at last. I will   45
therefore now conclude I am a man and must go
court my mistress.

Enter Lieutenant and Dol.

CORNET.

Here's the lieutenant and Dol; now behave yourself
like a man.

BIDDY.

Could you show me how to behave myself like an   50
honest man? That's out of your way, I doubt.*

DOL. [*Aside.*]

Still better and better! This confirms me.

BIDDY.

Well, give me thy hand. I'm resolved to be very
vir-tuous and very merry and never think more of
thee.   55

CORNET.

Well, Mrs.* Dol, here's one has consented in part
to marry you.

DOL.

Pretty creature!

BIDDY. (*Aside.*)

Ugly toad.

DOL.

Well, and will you be content to ride before me   60
lovingly a days?

LIEUTENANT.

Aye, and behind thee, too; ride thee all points
o'th'compass, wench, fear not.

BIDDY.

Oh Lord! But is there so many ways of riding,
Lieutenant?   65

LIEUTENANT.

Hast thou lived to these years and not known that
yet?

CORNET.

Well, but when will you marry?

BIDDY.

Nay, by my faith, let us woo first and then marry,
because I believe there is more pleasure in wooing   70
than in the effects of it.

CORNET.

Why do not you begin and court her then?

BIDDY.

Nay, by my faith, let her begin first.

LIEUTENANT.

That's not the mode for the woman to woo the
man.   75

BIDDY.

That is, if the man love the woman, but that's not
my case, for 'tis she loves me, not I her.

LIEUTENANT.

Oh, but in complaisance you must begin. It is not
civil to put a woman to't.

BIDDY.

Not I, faith. Pray, forsooth, do you begin.   80

DOL.

Indeed it shall be yours.

BIDDY.

I protest it shall be yours; therefore, begin or I vow I'll break off the match.

DOL.

Nay, rather than so, I'll begin. Sweet sir, I am much and greatly ashamed. 85

BIDDY.

Were you ever so before, mistress?

DOL.

Yes, truly, I have been ashamed, but it is so long since—

BIDDY.

That you have forgot it, I suppose. But I disturb you, forsooth. 90

DOL.

No disturbance, sweet sir; I want* fine words to express my love in. I am sorry that the cart-wheel of Fortune should drive me into the coach-box[32] of your affection.

BIDDY.

Fortune will take it scurvily to call her wheel a 95 cartwheel. Besides, coach-box and cartwheel did never agree in this world yet.

DOL.

I am not able to express my love as it deserves, but I have four hundred pound in gold, if that will do it.

BIDDY.

By my faith, you express yourself very well, and I 100 will woo you heartily for it. Madam, you have struck me with such a desperate dart from those fair somewhat or other that you have about you.— Are you sure you have the gold you spoke of?

DOL.

Yes, my dear heart, very sure. 105

BIDDY.

Then if I do not love you above all womankind, perish me, and sink me, refuse me, rot me, and renounce me.

CORNET.

Hold, hold, hold! Do you call this wooing?

BIDDY.

Yes, faith, I had a sister cast away with the very 110 same speech; therefore, do not interrupt me, for I know all mankind woos thus.—And as I was

_____
32 coach-box] tool box carried along to repair the coach

swearing, madam, the devil take—

LIEUTENANT.

Enough, enough, enough, enough!

BIDDY.

But, madam, are you satisfied? 115

DOL.

I am, to the full, and do believe you.

BIDDY.

But if you please, madam, now my hand is in, to accept of a hundred or two of oaths more.

DOL.

No, no, no, by no means. I believe you without 'em, and I am yours. 120

BIDDY.

I have not sworn out half my alphabet yet.

DOL.

You have done sufficiently, indeed.

BIDDY.

Well, give me your hand, then. You are the first woman, certainly, that was ever gained with so little swearing. 125

CORNET.

Thou hast wooed her and won her most bravely.*

BIDDY.

Have I? Why, then, I'm thine. But hark you, Lieutenant and Cornet, we will be married privately and in the dark, because her face shall not turn my stomach.—Madam, I have one ill-humor: 130 I cannot abide a woman with a bare face. Therefore, if I could buy you a mask that would stick to your face and never come off, I believe I should love you very well.

DOL.

I have a mask, or what you please, my dear.— 135 Next bout, I hope, will be my turn to jeer.

LIEUTENANT.

Come, let's in, and visit our new quarters.

Exeunt.

[Scene ii. In a nearby village.]

Enter Raggou making quarters, constables and neighbors.

FIRST NEIGHBOR.

I beseech your worship do not quarter so many upon me; I'm but a poor man.

SECOND NEIGHBOR.

Alas, poor man! You have overcharged him. Rogue, he has more money than half the town.

RAGGOU.

You be a dam dog to betray your neighbor. Who would tink to find de devel in a country bumpkin! Begar, me vill make use of your develry.

FIRST NEIGHBOR.

I pray your worship, take four horse from me.

RAGGOU.

You be a dam rich dog; begar, you sall have a squadron upon you if you no understand me.

FIRST NEIGHBOR.

How should I understand you?

RAGGOU.

You be a dam dog; begar, me vill put twenty horse upon your back till you understand a moy. Vat vill you give me if I take all de horse from you?

FIRST NEIGHBOR.

Indeed, I'll pray for your worship.

RAGGOU.

Oh ho! Be dat all? Do you understand noting but prayer? Divel, you fool, vat be prayer to de quarteermaster? But can you pray in French?

FIRST NEIGHBOR.

Alas! Not I, an't* please you.

RAGGOU.

Den, begar, your English prayer will no save a Frenchman; you sall have ten arse more fo dat.

SECOND NEIGHBOR.

An't please you, monsieur, I understand you. [*Puts money in his pocket.*]

RAGGOU.

You sall have no arse upon you.

THIRD NEIGHBOR.

And I understand you very well, sir. [*Puts money in his pocket.*]

RAGGOU.

Begar, you have very mush, a great deal of understanding.

THIRD NEIGHBOR.

Here are more of our neighbors that understand you, sir.

RAGGOU.

Begar, den me understand too. Get all your money togedra, and put in my pocket yourself, den me can

swear, begar, me never take no penny of you, aha!

THIRD NEIGHBOR.

We will do it gladly, sir, and pray for you too.

RAGGOU.

Begar, me no care for dat.——But you dam dog that no understan a moy sall quarteer all de troop, and den look to your wife, for, begar, Flea-flint vill so get your shild for you.

Exeunt.

Enter Flea-flint, Ferret-farm, Burndorp, Lieutenant, Cornet, Raggou, and Dol.

BURNDORP.

Lieutenant, we have done the work.

FERRET-FARM.

We have burnt seven towns.

FLEA-FLINT.

We have raised fourscore pound.

LIEUTENANT. (*Aside.*)

Y'are dexterous at your trade. You have made quick dispatch; but peace, we'll share anon.——Now you're welcome. Come, where's the boors o'th'house? We'll see what my quarters can afford. Where are you all? What house here, ho?

Enter woman and maid.

WOMAN.

What want you, sir?

LIEUTENANT.

Art thou the woman o'th'house?

WOMAN.

Yes, sir, a poor woman.

LIEUTENANT.

Art thou poor? What a pox do I in such a quarter? Why, Quartermaster Raggou, is this the best house in the village?

RAGGOU.

Zoun, hang 'em, they're very rich dog, but you sall have no meat for yourself, no oat for your arses, but her dam husband vill feast you all wid pray for you.

LIEUTENANT.

Diable, you Rotterdam[33] whore, I'll make you

———

33 Rotterdam] rich Dutch seaport. The Dutch republic was anathema to royalists.

bring out your things. Where's your cows, your
calves, and your sheep?

WOMAN.

Alas! We have none, sir.   60

CORNET.

Hast thou any drink, good woman?

WOMAN.

No, truly, we have none.

FLEA-FLINT.

Nor hast thou no wine nor strong water, good
woman?

WOMAN.

No, indeed, we have none.   65

RAGGOU.

Why, den, a pox take you, good woman.

LIEUTENANT.

No hens, nor turkeys, nor swine, nor nothing?

RAGGOU.

Hang her, begar, she hide everyting when dey hear
me come to make-a de quarteer.

FERRET-FARM.

Send to the market town and buy provision, and   70
be hanged, or I'll set fire o'your house, you
damned, dery damned, whore.

RAGGOU. [*Aside*.]

Zoun, dis dam coward, how he domineer over de
bumpkin woman.

WOMAN.

Alas, we have no money, sir, not we.   75

FERRET-FARM.

What dost thou tremble and shake so for? What
a pox ails thee?

CORNET. [*To the Troop.*]

What shall we do? Threatening will not serve the
turn.

LIEUTENANT. [*To the Troop.*]

Do but second me, and I'll make 'em bring out   80
all they have, I warrant you. Do but talk as if we
used to eat children.

FERRET-FARM. [*To the Troop.*]

'Tis enough!

LIEUTENANT.

Why, look you, good woman, we do believe you
are poor, so we'll make a shift with our old diet.   85
You have children i'th'town?

WOMAN.

Why do you ask, sir?

LIEUTENANT.

Only toc have two or three to supper.—Flea-flint,
you have the best way of cooking children.

FLEA-FLINT.

I can powder 'em³⁴ to make you taste your liquor.   90
I'm never without a dried child's tongue or ham.

WOMAN.

Oh, bless me!

FLEA-FLINT.

Mine's but the ordinary way, but Ferret-farm is the
man; he makes you the savoriest pie of a child's
chaldron³⁵ that ever was eat!   95

LIEUTENANT.

A pox, all the world cannot cook a child like
Monsieur Raggou.

RAGGOU.

Begar, me tink so. For vat was me bred in de King
of Mogul's kitchin for? Tere ve kill twenty shild of
a day. Take you one shild by both his two heels   100
and put his head between your two leg, den take
your great knife and slice off all de buttack, so
fashion; begar, dat make a de best Scots'³⁶ collop
in de varle.

LIEUTENANT.

Ah! He makes the best pottage of a child's head   105
and purtenance! But you must boil it with bacon.
Woman, you must get bacon.

FERRET-FARM.

And then it must be very young.

LIEUTENANT.

Yes, yes. Good woman, it must be a fine squab
child of half a year old: a man-child. Dost hear?   110

WOMAN.

Oh Lord! Yes, sir.

RAGGOU.

Do you hear? Get me one she-shild, a little whore-
shild, and save me all de lamb-stone³⁷ and
sweetbread, and all de pig-petty-toe of de shild. Do
you hear, you Roundhead whore?   115

---

34 powder 'em] reducing human parts for medicinal purposes
35 chaldron] entrails
36 Scots'] proverbially, Scots were cannibals.
37 lamb-stone] testicles, here a non-sequitur

WOMAN.

Aye, sir, aye.—Oh, that ever I should live to see such men! (*Exit.*)

LIEUTENANT.

I warrant you it works. If there be provision in the country, we shall have it.

FLEA-FLINT.

How the whore trembled for fear! 120

CORNET.

We shall have all the women in the village about our ears, hide-bound whores! It's a question whether they'll part with their meat or their children first.

LIEUTENANT.

This foolery will be noised about the country, and 125 then the odium will never be taken off.[38]

CORNET.

Why, what can they make on't? All understanding people will know it to be mirth.

LIEUTENANT.

I know they will, but the envious priests will make fine talk on't, and make a great advantage on't too. 130 Though they know it to be nothing but mirth, they'll preach their parishioners into a real belief of it,[39] on purpose to make us odious. They'll preach against anything. I heard a scandalous sermon of two hours long against Prince Rupert's dog.[40] 135

CORNET.

Come, 'tis no matter what hypocrites preach. Let us see what the event will be.

Exeunt.

---

38 odium … off] According to Sir Walter Scott, Sir Thomas Lunsford was rumored to have a taste for broiled child steaks, and when he fell at the Siege of Bristol in 1643 that he "had child's hand in his pocket."

39 They'll preach … of it] probably a reference to John Lilburne, a vocal enemy of Thomas Lunsford during the Civil War

40 Prince Rupert's dog] Nephew of Charles I, Prince Rupert was a staunch and effective Royalist commander during the English Civil War and, after the restoration of Charles II, against the Dutch. Republican factions tarred him with flamboyancy and affectation so permanent that even the 1970 film, *Cromwell*, depicts him cuddling his lapdog on the field of battle.

[Scene iii. A neighborhood in the village.]

Enter women in a fright, alarmed by their neighbor.

WOMAN.

Look to your children! If ever you mean to see your children alive, hide your children; they'll eat your children.

FIRST NEIGHBOR.

Woe is me! What's the matter, neighbor?

WOMAN.

I say, hide your children. 5

SECOND NEIGHBOR.

Ah! Good neighbor, what's the matter?

WOMAN.

Why, run away with your children.

THIRD NEIGHBOR.

Why, that ever we were born! What's the matter?

WOMAN.

They will eat your children.

FOURTH NEIGHBOR.

Oh, these bloody Cavaliers! How, eat our children? 10

WOMAN.

They talk of boiling your children.

ALL.

Oh, mercy on us!

WOMAN.

And roasting your children.

ALL.

Oh, bloody villains!

WOMAN.

And baking your children. 15

FIRST NEIGHBOR.

Oh, hellish cavaliering devils!

WOMAN.

There's nothing to be thought of but hiding your children.

FIRST NEIGHBOR.

I would mine were in my belly again.

WOMAN.

That's not safe. They'll search there in the first 20 place, to be sure.

SECOND NEIGHBOR.

I'll hide mine in the straw.

WOMAN.

And so we shall have one of 'em lay you down atop of it and smother one child whilst he is getting another. I say, run away with your children. 25

THIRD NEIGHBOR.

Oh, bloody wretches! I have heard much of their getting children, but never of their eating children before.

FOURTH NEIGHBOR.

Neighbor, their getting of children might be borne with, but eating 'em was never heard of. 30

WOMAN.

They have got a cook from the Great Mogul on purpose to kill children, and they talk of roasting their haunches, and baking the chaldron and broiling the chine.

MAID.

And making pottage of the child's head and 35 purtenance.

ALL.

Oh, deliver our poor children.

WOMAN.

Do you stand whining and crying? Fetch out your sheep, and your calves, your hens, your pigs, and your geese, and your bacon, for there's no other 40 way to save your children.

ALL.

Aye, with all our hearts.

FIRST NEIGHBOR.

I'll bring two fat sheep.

SECOND NEIGHBOR.

I'll bring turkeys and hens.

THIRD NEIGHBOR.

I have a brave* fat calf, worth eleven nobles; by 45 my troth, I had as leave part with one of my children.

WOMAN.

Oh, you uncharitable beast! Go fetch your calf. Run, everybody, and bring your things to my house as fast as you can drive. 50

Exeunt.

[Scene iv. With the troop.]

Enter Lieutenant, Cornet, Flea-flint, Ferret-farm, Burndorp, and Raggou.

LIEUTENANT.

Meat or children to supper, for a wager, gentlemen?

CORNET.

Meat, for a wager, if they have it.

LIEUTENANT.

Aye, without doubt, for never was women and children so alarmed in this world.

FLEA-FLINT.

When they were got together and told their 5 children would be eaten, they set up their throats and made a more horrid noise than a Welsh hubbub or an Irish dirge.

Enter nurse with two children.

FERRET-FARM.

How now! What think you if we be put to eat children indeed? By this light, here's a woman with 10 two children.

LIEUTENANT.

We shall be crossbit* with these country whores. What shall we do?

RAGGOU.

Begar, me vill help you off; you sall eat no shildren.

NURSE.

By your leaves, your good worships, I make bold 15 to bring you in some provisions.

FERRET-FARM.

Provisions! Where, where is thy provisions?

NURSE.

Here, an't* please you. I have brought you a couple of fine fleshy children.

CORNET.

Was ever such a horrid whore! What shall we do? 20

NURSE.

Truly, gentlemen, they're as fine squab children— shall I turn 'em up? They have the bravest brawny buttocks!

LIEUTENANT.

No, no. But, woman, art thou not troubled to part with thy children? 25

NURSE.

Alas, they are none of mine, sir. They are but nurse-children.[41]

RAGGOU.

Dere be a dam whore for you.

LIEUTENANT.

What a beast is this! Whose children are they?

---

41 nurse-children] babies turned over to wet-nurses until weaned

NURSE.

A Londoner's, that owes me for a year's nursing. I 30
hope they'll prove excellent meat. They're twins, too.

RAGGOU.

Aha! But, begar, we never eat no twin-shild; de
law[42] forbid dat. But, hark you, have any woman
with shild in de town?

NURSE.

Yes, half a dozen. 35

RAGGOU.

Lieutenant, it be de best meat in de varle. Begar,
a woman with shild is better meat den one hen
with egg at Shrovetide.

Enter Landlady and women with provision.

LIEUTENANT.

How now, what news, Landlady?

WOMAN.

Here is a great many poor women that have brought 40
in provisions in hope you'll spare their children.

FIRST NEIGHBOR.

We beseech your worships, spare our poor
children, and you shall want for nothing our
country can afford.

LIEUTENANT.

Good woman, we are content to spare your 45
children, but you must get us some strong drink.

SECOND NEIGHBOR.

Aye, aye, we'll get you everything you want.

LIEUTENANT.

Why, then, go all home and be contented, for we
promise you, if we eat any children, it shall be the
two nurse-children. 50

ALL.

Ah—preserve you all, gentlemen.

RAGGOU.

Take some comfort, for if we should eat your
shildren you sall no be a loser by dat. For look you,
good woman, how many shildren we eat in a
parish so many shild we are bound to get before 55
we leave it. Dat is very fair.

Exeunt women.

LIEUTENANT.

Why, is not this better than fasting?

_____
42 de law] a parody of biblical dietary restrictions

FLEA-FLINT.

Well, and what harm is there in all this?

CORNET.

None i'th'world. Come, let's in and dress our
supper. 60

RAGGOU.

Me will go eat at my own quarteer. It be a brave*
ting to be in office. Begar, de clowns* worship me
as if me were dere great god Bumpkin.

Exeunt.

Act IV, scene i. [Outside Raggou's quarters.]

Lieutenant, Flea-flint, Ferret-farm, and Burndorp.

FLEA-FLINT.

Lieutenant, here's all our country crew that we
plundered yesterday.

FERRET-FARM.

But our comfort is they know us not, but cry out
of a Frenchman, with two coat sleeves stuffed like
two country bag-puddings. 5

LIEUTENANT.

This cunning rogue has crossbit* you all. He has
been plundering as he went to make his quarters,
and in a buff coat, too, for here is a dozen fellows
at my quarter, and they all describe a rogue so like
thee that I protest thou wilt suffer for it. Nay, the 10
rogue called himself Flea-flint, too.

FLEA-FLINT.

Ouns! What shall we do, sir?

LIEUTENANT.

Upon my word, this is no jesting business.

FERRET-FARM.

'Sheart,* overreached thus!

LIEUTENANT.

You must e'en think of overreaching him again. 15
You must first think of stopping the clamor of the
bumpkins; that's your first point of security.

FLEA-FLINT.

But, Lieutenant, how should we do't? Faith, you
must try your wits and stick to us.

LIEUTENANT.

I knew you would venture so far 'twould come to 20
my turn to fetch you off at last, rogues.

FLEA-FLINT.

Why, sir, my man and his both shall swear Raggou
borrowed a buff coat of them.

LIEUTENANT.

Let him be gone first, and then you may swear anything. One of you go, tell the bumpkins I am searching for the rogue; the rest go with me to Raggou.

Exit Ferret-farm.

BURNDORP.

This is his quarter.

LIEUTENANT.

This? Knock. It seems to be the best house i'th'town. (*Knocks.*)

MAID. (*Within.*)

Who would you speak with?

LIEUTENANT.

With Monsieur Raggou.

MAID. [*Opening the door.*]

Sir, he gave us strict charge to let nobody speak with him.

LIEUTENANT.

But I must and will speak with him.

MAID.

Indeed, sir, he charged us, upon pain of his displeasure, not to disturb him.

LIEUTENANT.

Pain of his displeasure? What an impudent rogue's this! Show us, show us.

[*The scene draws.*] Raggou *is discovered* in a taffeta bed, with a back, breast, and headpiece on.*

How now!—what, in taffeta curtains? The impudent rogue makes me laugh. You rascal, Raggou. Look, in his headpiece, too!

RAGGOU.

Who de devel disturb me? You dam whore, you know vat me do to you last night?

LIEUTENANT.

Why, what was that you did to her last night?

RAGGOU.

Begar, me lie with her at three motion, as de musketeer shoot off his gun—make ready, present, and give fire.

LIEUTENANT.

O'my word, that's good discipline.

RAGGOU.

Begar, she sall make ready for you, if you will present and give fire.

LIEUTENANT.

But how came it that I had not this good quarter?

RAGGOU.

Because me knew me should make-a de quarter but one night, and so, begar, me make-a de best use of my time, as all the whole varle do too.

LIEUTENANT.

But what a rogue art thou. Why dost thou lie in such a bed in thy arms?

RAGGOU.

For two gran reason, sir. First, because my French louse sall go great way about before he come to de clean sheet, next, because-a de dam English flea shall not bite-a my sweet French body.

LIEUTENANT.

Well, maid, go down; I must speak with him.

Exit maid.

RAGGOU.

Vat you have wid me, Lieutenant?

LIEUTENANT.

Faith, out of my love, I would save thee from hanging.

RAGGOU.

Hang! For vat? Begar, hang me if me deserve, so you hang all dat deserve-a de hang. Begar, dat is de whole troop—Lieutenant and all.

LIEUTENANT.

Here you plunder in one shape, and there in another—sometimes, like Flea-flint, in buff; sometimes like yourself—that here is all the country come in with such horrid complaints. Nay, they say you ravish women too.

RAGGOU.

Lieutenant, begar, me never ravish but one old woman, and she give me five shilling for my pain.

LIEUTENANT.

Nay, here is worse than all that. My captain has intelligence you're a dangerous man and hold correspondence with the enemy.

RAGGOU.

Me sall be hang, Lieutenant, if you tink so.

LIEUTENANT.

Nay, 'tis so; I have orders to search you. (*Aside.*) Put that in his pocket and pull it out again.

RAGGOU.

Ah, begar, me have no long life before me be hang.

BURNDORP.

Oh, sir! Are you good at that?—He was going to convey letters out on's pocket.

RAGGOU.

Begar, he lie, Lieutenant; me have no lettra. Begar, 85
hang-a me if me can write an read. De hornbook be de Hebrew to me, begar.

LIEUTENANT.

Search him, search him.

*Search, and pulls a letter out and an engine.**

BURNDORP.

Here's a letter, Lieutenant, and an engine, I think.

FLEA-FLINT.

What's this? 90

LIEUTENANT.

Oh, you need not write and read if you have this. I'll be hanged if this be not the key of his character he writes to the enemy with.

RAGGOU.

Dat make-a de French pie, and make-a de garniture for de dish; dat be all. 95

LIEUTENANT.

Let's see. The case is plain; he sent his intelligence in characters of paste. This very thing will hang him. But let's read the letter.

RAGGOU.

Begar, me have no lettra. De devil send it in my pocket. 100

LIEUTENANT. (*Reads.*)

"Monsieur Raggou, in hope that under this poor disguise of a French cook you will show a rich faith"—

RAGGOU.

Vat he mean by fait? Begar, me have no fait.

LIEUTENANT. (*Reads.*)

"And when you have delivered up your troop to 105
us, the Parliament will own you as yourself, and give you the respects due to your great and honorable family."

RAGGOU.

Devel, me have no honorable, nor family neider, begar. 110

FLEA-FLINT.

The case is plain; you are of some great family.

RAGGOU.

Lieutenant, me confess me come of de King of France kitchin, of de honorable family of de Turnspit. Begar, me tell you true, dere be all my family, and my honorable too. 115

BURNDORP.

Oh, sir, 'tis a very cunning fellow. My captain sends word he used to be conversant with the Roundheads and pray with them.

RAGGOU.

The devel take-a me, me never pray in my life. Me swear altogedra in de King of France kitchin! 120

LIEUTENANT.

I love you so well that I'd be loath to hang you, monsieur; therefore, I'm content to let you 'scape. But be sure you be not taken.

RAGGOU.

Begar, den hang a moy, for my arse vill no go very far. 125

LIEUTENANT.

Well, pray be gone and say you found a friend.

RAGGOU.

Gad-a bless you, Lieutenant. Ven me come in France, zoun, me vill so pray for you.

FLEA-FLINT.

And yet you say you never prayed in your life.

RAGGOU.

Begar, me tank Gad me never have occasion to 130
pray till just now. Adieu, adieu-a.—Who send me dat dam lettra in my pocket? (*Exit.*)

LIEUTENANT.

Well, now we must keep the bumpkins here till he is gone and give 'em orders to search the countries for him. 135

BURNDORP.

And that will whidle[43] them as well as if you had given them their money again.

Exeunt.

[Scene ii. Thievesden Garrison.]

Enter Governor, Captain Holdforth, Mr. Tell-troth, and Captain Tubtext.

HOLDFORTH.

In truth, drinking is a harmless recreation, so we proceed not to drunkenness.

_____

43 whidle] quiet

TUBTEXT.

Pray, how far forth may we proceed in drink? For I would take no more than is fit to be taken with a safe conscience.   5

TELL-TROTH.

Why, Captain Tubtext, if thy belly were as large as thy conscience, by that computation the great tun at Heidelberg[44] would be just thy morning's draught.

TUBTEXT.

Here is old Tom Tell-troth. Ha, ha, ha!

HOLDFORTH.

In truth, if he were not very faithful, we should   10
never away with his boldness.

TUBTEXT.

Well said, Captain Holdforth, but to the question. How far may we proceed in drink?

GOVERNOR.

As far as the innocent recreation of knocking one another down with cushions come to. It is the   15
exercise of our superior officers.

HOLDFORTH.

I have observed, indeed, they do three things together: they drink, then practice pulpit faces—

TELL-TROTH.

To cheat the people with.

TUBTEXT.

Ha, ha, ha! In truth, you hit so home.   20

HOLDFORTH.

And the third is throwing of cushions. The practicing and dissembling of holy looks is of great use and design.

TUBTEXT.

And drinking and throwing cushions, a great refreshing to the body.   25

GOVERNOR.

As, for example. (*Throws a cushion.*)

HOLDFORTH.

Ha, ha, ha! I have seen our grandee throw a cushion at the man with the great thumb, and say, "Colonel, wilt thou be a cobbler again?" (*Throws a cushion.*)   30

ALL.

Ha, ha, ha!

---

44 great tun at Heidelberg] a cask of legendary capacity in Germany

TUBTEXT.

Come, here's to you, Governor,—You, Colonel Goldsmith, with a conscience as dirty as a blacksmith, will you sell thimbles again? (*Throws a cushion.*)   35

ALL.

Ha, ha, ha!

HOLDFORTH.

Noble Colonel, wilt thou brew ale again? (*Throws a cushion, etc.*) What an everlasting cheat is Reformation and false doctrine! It has raised us from cobblers to commanders.[45]   40

TUBTEXT.

There is no other way to raise rebellion but by religion.

ALL.

Ha, ha, ha!

GOVERNOR.

I never knew the use of religion before.

TUBTEXT.

The women tickle like trouts* at it. Ha, ha, ha!   45

All laugh.

TELL-TROTH.

I believe the country will find it so, for I hear of twenty wenches with child.

GOVERNOR.

In truth, I wonder at the witchcraft of it, for, notwithstanding the people have been bit through the chine-bone with it, yet, for all that, before the   50
old wound is healed, they are ready to run after the lanthorn of new lights again. Ha, ha, ha!

TELL-TROTH.

Well, sirs, since you are in such an ingenious way of confessing, tell me one thing: Do not you wish your garrison afire, so you were at home with all   55
the wealth you've got?

---

45 cobblers to commanders] from tradesmen to politically influential people, a recurring Cavalier grouse about a changing social order. The former cobbler is probably George Fox (1624-91), founder of the Quakers, targets for ridicule in many English plays during the period. John Lilburne, a member of the gentry but apprenticed to a London cloth merchant, was a spokesman for the Levellers, a group with radically democratic notions.

TUBTEXT.

Thought's free.[46] But talk no more of that; these are both treacherous rogues; I dare not trust 'em.

TELL-TROTH.

Well, you are merry, sirs. But faith, be plain, sirs, what says my seeming Saint* that drinks by the conscience? Dost not wish thyself at home wallowing in thy plunder? 60

HOLDFORTH.

You might find a better name for it. Hark in your ear:——We are all such treacherous rogues, we dare not trust one another, but we'll talk in private. 65

GOVERNOR.

But our contribution women will come in anon.

HOLDFORTH.

Ha, ha, ha! In truth, they edify as one would have 'em.

TELL-TROTH.

Well, now you ought to be serious and consider the enemy's[d] approaching. 70

TUBTEXT.

In truth, a good occasion to fetch in all the goods and chattels of the country upon pretence of securing them, and so make conditions with the enemy to march away with them. I see we shall be rascals to the last gasp. 75

HOLDFORTH.

And so we shall have provisions for a long siege.

GOVERNOR. [Aside.]

I'll make your siege short enough.

Exit Governor and one captain.

TUBTEXT.

You are faithful; they are rogues. Read that, and tell me whether you will undertake or no. (*Gives Tell-troth a letter, and exit.*) 80

TELL-TROTH.

How! Very good. Is't possible? This is a greater rogue in his own nature than the devil's invention can make him. He would not only betray his trust, but deliver up all the rest of the garrison to mercy, conditionally that he may have all their wealth and safe convoy to his own house. I need lay no plot; 85

'tis done to my hand. I love the King well, yet my own ends are mingled because I have a mistress among 'em and cannot have her but by serving the King. And I believe most men have their reasons for their loyalty as well as I, so that, good King, wheresoe'er you see me, trust to yourself. Yet I will do something. What if I betrayed this rogue and his letter to the governor to secure myself? But then, if they have a mind to deliver up the garrison, 'twill make 'em shy of me. I find I have a hard task on't. 90 95

Enter Governor.

GOVERNOR.

Oh, Tell-troth, I came to ask thee a question, and what thinkst thou?

TELL-TROTH.

Troth, I know not. 100

GOVERNOR.

To know whether thou lov'st me truly or no.

TELL-TROTH.

If you be serious, I could be angry with you for raising such a doubt. To show you that I love you (I do not say your cause, but you) read there. Look you, one of your captain rogues gave me that letter, and the other gave me a whisper to the same purpose, too. 105

GOVERNOR.

Is't possible? What's to be done with these villains?

TELL-TROTH.

Something must be done; they'll betray you else.

GOVERNOR.

I thank thy honesty; I find it so. 110

TELL-TROTH.

Shall I speak boldly? Serve 'em in their own kind.

GOVERNOR.

In troth, I had it in my head before to betray 'em, for the rogues are rich.

TELL-TROTH.

Come, let not you and I be shy of one another. Do it yet. 115

GOVERNOR.

Art thou in earnest?

TELL-TROTH.

By my life, and I will put you in a way, too.

---

46 Thought's free] here probably an allusion to "free thinking" or heretical, dissident religious notions

GOVERNOR.

Let's in, and consider how. Had we best secure 'em?

TELL-TROTH.

No. First command their two companies out, then draw 'em into several parties, and then with your own company disarm 'em, and so clap them up and their officers; then show 'em the reason, this letter. When that's done, send the letter to the Parliament and write how you have secured 'em, which will so ingratiate you with them that you'll never be suspected for betraying on't yourself.

GOVERNOR.

My worthy friend, shall I fall on my knees and worship thee?

TELL-TROTH.

Let's be wise and about our business.

Exeunt.

[Scene iii. The troop's camp.]

Enter Cornet and two troopers.

CORNET.

Where have you been, sirs?

FIRST TROOPER.

Why, we have been to take Flea-flint. My captain is resolved to hang him.

CORNET.

For what?

SECOND TROOPER.

For plundering, and so forth. But the rogue has intelligence of it and is gone, but he is in as bad a case as Raggou, for we must send hue and cry after him.

Exeunt.

[Scene iv. At some distance from the camp.]

Enter Raggou.

RAGGOU.

Ah, *jan povera de moy.* May arse can no carry me from de danger of de hang-a de moy, and yet me have spur two such great hole in his rib dat you may creep quite trow him. Me must go change mine coat and mine hat; begar, me sall be known by dat. Vat come here now?

Enter Frenchman with a show.[47]

What come?

FRENCHMAN.

Come, who see my fine shite,[48] my rare shite? Who see my fine shite, my rare shite?

RAGGOU.

Monsieur, where you go wid your shite?

FRENCHMAN.

To de Bristol Fair,[49] monsieur.

RAGGOU.

Dis Frenchman look as if he will be hang. Begar, me vill put a de sheat of de hang upon him! Monsieur, begar, me have de very fine shite too, and it vill come de Bristol Fair too. It be de great vonder of de varle; it be de great fat dromedary.[50] You hear of dat?

FRENCHMAN.

Wee, wee; all de varle know de fat dromedary.

RAGGOU.

Begar, you and me vill join partiner in de fair, because you be my countryman.

FRENCHMAN.

Aye, monsieur, and tank you too.

RAGGOU.

We vill give out in de bill of de two famous Frenchman; one inventra de show of all trade, and de oder make-a de invent of de fat dromedary.

FRENCHMAN.

Monsieur, wid all my heart!

---

47 show] a pushcart that opened up to reveal a puppet theater. Puppeteers enacted a range of stories, from the biblical to the pornographic.

48 shite] since the puppet master of ceremonies is later called "Monsieur Puppey," perhaps a corruption of *chiot*, French for puppy; if so, Lacy wants the English pun; *puppy*, however, is derivative from Middle French *poupée*, doll or toy.

49 Bristol] the major seaport in western England some sixty miles from Oxford, important for trans-Atlantic trade and a Royalist stronghold during the Civil War. The Bristol Fair would have been a major event in the region.

50 fat dromedary] exotic animals were major news and attractions throughout England

RAGGOU.

Vera good. You sall go take-a de best house in de town. Dere be two piece, two jacoby[51] for you; get some vera good dinner. You shall take-a my coat and de hat, and leave your show wid me, for my waggon will come wid my dromedary presan. 30

FRENCHMAN. (*Aside.*)

I had good luck to light o'this Frenchman.

RAGGOU. [*Aside.*]

Begar, me have betra luck to light o'dis Frenchman.—So, help me wid your waistcoat. Vera good. So, now make all de haste in de varle. Adieu, adieu! 35

Exit Frenchman.

So now, begar, me be very safe. But how de devil sall me show mine shite? Begar, me forget to ask vat language all de puppet in de show speak. *Parla françois, Monsieur Puppey?* Owieda.* Aha! very good.

Enter constables.

FIRST CONSTABLE.

Sure we shall catch this fellow at last, for we hear of him everywhere. 40

SECOND CONSTABLE.

Aye, his two sleeves stuffed and his French hat edged with ribbons will discover* him.

RAGGOU.

Diable, dere be de constable and Mr. Hue-Cry come to catch-a me.—Who see my shite, my rare shite, my fine shite?—Begar, me sall shite myself indeed. 45

FIRST CONSTABLE.

What a pox does he mean?

SECOND CONSTABLE.

He would have you see his show.

FIRST CONSTABLE.

Come, faith, let us. You, fellow, come, let's see your show. 50

RAGGOU. [*Aside.*]

How sall me do now? Begar, me must show it as well as me can.

SECOND CONSTABLE.

Sirrah, did not you see a Frenchman pass by?

RAGGOU.

Frenchman? Vat have he upon him? 55

FIRST CONSTABLE.

Why, he has a greasy coat with the sleeves stuffed out.

RAGGOU.

A pox take him! Begar, he rob me just now of two piece, all me have in de varle. Dat make-a me cry.

SECOND CONSTABLE.

Oh rogue, rascal! Alas today! Give him a crown, churchwarden; we are at the parish charge.[52] 60

FIRST CONSTABLE.

Come, do not cry, poor fellow. Let's see thy shite. There's a crown for thee.

RAGGOU.

A Gad bless you. Here be de brave* shite of de varle. Here be de King of Spain play on de bagpipe to his Privy Council. Dat's a very good jest. Den dere be de King of Solomon; he give judgment upon de vise child. Dere is de first act. Now, put on your hat and look upon all de lady. 65

Plays and sings.

"Jam more cum povera bla cum povera, 70
Jam, jam, jam, jam tomba nette,
Jam, jang tombe nette equbla."[53]
Now, here be de Queen of Swiveland.[54] She sit in great majesty; her leg hang over de chair, vera full of temptation—make your chops watra. Vera good 75
jest. Den dere be de whore of Babylon; she make great love to de Maypole in de Stran. Second act. "Jam more cum povera," etc. (*Plays and sings.*) Dere be de King of Denmarks and Norvay learning to juggle of de Bishop of Munsera.[55] Dat's 80
a very good jest. Dere be de silent ministra; he

---

51 jacoby] jacobus, gold coin valued a little over a pound.

52 parish charge] public expense

53 Jam … equbla] This fractured French means roughly "I am in love with a poor woman, a poor woman; I love to fall flat; I go down for everyone."

54 Swiveland] the land of sexual intercourse; perhaps an allusion to Queen Christine of Sweden, philosophical libertine who had abdicated in 1654

55 King … Munsera] a fractured version of seventeenth-century religious warfare probably alluding to the king of Denmark and Norway, Christian IV, negotiating for

make-a de long preach in de playhouse.[56] Dere is tre act; dat is all.

SECOND CONSTABLE.

I thought your plays had always had five acts.

RAGGOU.

Dey be de great puppet have five act; de little puppet have but tre. Vill you go catch dis dam dog for me and get-a my money for me agen, my two jacoby? Begar, me be undone if you no catch dis dam dog for me!

FIRST CONSTABLE.

We'll away. We'll have him, I warrant thee.

Exeunt.

RAGGOU.

Begar, me be very fine sheat, if it vill hold out. But hold-a—vat if dey catch my coat? Begar, den dey vill hang-a my coat. But dam dog vill confess me have his show, den. Begar, me sall be hang wid mine coat. Begar, me vill put away mine show.

Enter Flea-flint, with hue and cry after him.

Who de devil is dat?

FLEA-FLINT. [*Aside.*]

A pox on 't, I must be robbing alone, and without my lieutenant's advice. I must be careful or suffer for it. The rogues follow me with hue and cry; I am not able to go further; I must change my clothes. How now? What fellow's this? 'Sheart, would I could persuade him out of his show and take my cloak for it.

RAGGOU. [*Aside.*]

Begar, would me could persuade him to take my show and give me de cloak for dat!

FLEA-FLINT.

Come hither, honest fellow.

RAGGOU. [*Aside.*]

Devil, it is Flea-flint. Hah, me be povera de moy; begar, me be half hang already. Me vill no speak

French, begar, den he vill know me; me vill belch Dutch at him.—*Yaw, min heer.*

FLEA-FLINT.

Come hither, honest man. What's that? A show?

RAGGOU.

Yaw, min heer.—Begar, me vill slit my mouth from one ear to de odra to speak good Dutch; and den when me speak French, begar, me vill sew it up again.[57] Dere's a vera good trick to save-a my life.

FLEA-FLINT.

Fellow, wilt thou sell thy show?

RAGGOU.

Yaw, min heer.—Begar, dis Dutch make me vera sick. Look! Begar, every time me cry *Yaw, min heer,* dere come up a pickle herring with it. *Yaw*—look, dere it go.

FLEA-FLINT.

Art thou a Dutchman?

RAGGOU.

Yaw, verathticke.

FLEA-FLINT.

Where hab you de neder lands go weston?

RAGGOU. [*Aside.*]

Diable, vat sall me say? Begar, me have no more Dutch!

FLEA-FLINT.

Hab you de neder lands go west, lanceman?

RAGGOU.

Ick haben de hoigh Dutch lander goe weston, lanceman.

FLEA-FLINT. [*Aside.*]

Nay, it may be what Dutch it will, for I can speak no more.

RAGGOU.

Ick maken weel vander slapan can helder hought.

FLEA-FLINT.

But wilt thou sell thy show?

RAGGOU.

Yaw, yaw, ick vill van hundred gilder haben.[58]

---

peace with both Sweden and France, perhaps (anachronistically) learning to "juggle" or play both sides from the famous warlike Bishop of Münster, Bernhard von Galen, erstwhile unreliable ally of England against the Dutch.

56 silent ministra … playhouse] perhaps an allusion to William Prynne, famous Puritan who attacked the English stage and who had his ears cropped for sedition

57 slit my mouth] The English actor's parody of Dutch or German emphasizes open and guttural sounds, of French closed and labial; thus, "sew it up again".

58 *Yaw … haben*] nonsense Dutch, though some words are recognizable, the most important of which is *gilder,* Dutch coins

FLEA-FLINT.

That's ten pound; that's too much.—I would I had it at any rate.

RAGGOU. [*Aside*.]

Begar, never fear, you sall have it.

FLEA-FLINT.

Wilt thou take five pound?

RAGGOU.

Neave ick; ick maken de show myself, and ick maken 135
dat better as dis, and dat's better as dat, and dat's
better as all, begott.

FLEA-FLINT. [*Aside*.]

I hear 'em coming.—Here's ten pound for thee, and I'll give thee my cloak to boot, and hat.

RAGGOU.

Dere be my show and my cap. Me tank you, 140
lanceman.—So, dis dam rogue never do no good in all his life before; and me hope, begar, he vill be hang for dat. (*Exit*.)

FLEA-FLINT.

Now, what shall I do with this show? for I cannot show it. Why, if anybody would see it, I must say 145 it's locked up, the key is gone before to Bristol Fair; that's all I have for't.

Enter constables looking for Flea-flint.

FOURTH CONSTABLE.

Come sirs, we shall have him at last.

THIRD CONSTABLE.

Stay sirs. What fellow's this? Who are you, sir?

FLEA-FLINT.

A poor man, master, going with my show to the 150 fair to get a penny, and a rogue has robbed me of all I have, almost ten pound.

FOURTH CONSTABLE.

Oh damned rogue! Had he not a gray cloak and hat?

FLEA-FLINT.

Aye (wicked villain!) the same, master.

THIRD CONSTABLE.

It's the same rogue we are looking for; we shall have 155 him i'th'fair, I warrant you. Let's away.

Exeunt constables.

FLEA-FLINT.

This rogue thinks himself so safe now, and he'll be hanged sure enough if they catch him.

Enter the first constables with him that had Raggou's clothes.

FIRST CONSTABLE.

Look you, there's the notorious rogue with the show. Take him. 160

FLEA-FLINT.

What would you have with me, gentlemen?

FRENCHMAN.

Begar, me vill have my show from you.

FLEA-FLINT.

Pox take you and your show! A damned rogue that had it has robbed me of ten pound and my hat and cloak. 165

FIRST CONSTABLE.

Come, these are both rogues; bring 'em away.

FIRST WATCH.

Hold, it will do us no good to have them hanged. What if we plunder them as they use to do us?

CONSTABLE.

'Tis a very good notion.—Do you hear? We are to ask you a question. Will you be hanged or be 170 plundered?

FLEA-FLINT.

I'll be hanged before I part with my money.

SECOND WATCH.

Then let's hang him; we can take his money when he is dead.

CONSTABLE.

Then do you hang him. 175

Enter bumpkin, passing over the stage.

FIRST WATCH.

Not I; I know not how to hang him.

SECOND WATCH.

Troth, hang him yourself, if you'll have him hanged.

CONSTABLE. (*Calls to the bumpkin*.)

Dost hear, brother bumpkin? I'll give thee an angel,* and hang this fellow. 180

BUMPKIN.

It is not worthwhile for one, but I'll take angels apiece to hang you all.

CONSTABLE.

Hang you, rascal.—Come there, fall on boys and plunder him.

Plunder Flea-flint.

FLEA-FLINT.

Pray you, gentlemen, give me some money again 185
to bear my charges home.

CONSTABLE.

There's a crown for thee, and farewell.

Exeunt all but bumpkin.

BUMPKIN.

Hey day! This will prove a very wonder,
That Bumpkin should a soldier plunder.

Act V, scene i. [Pre-dawn in a village street.]

*Enter a joiner, servant, and a painter at one door, and
Raggou at another.*

SERVANT.

Joiner, make haste, and set your t'other post up,
and painter, fetch your colors, your pots, and
pipkins, and paint this post in the meantime. It
must be dispatched before the people are stirring.

PAINTER.

My things are all ready, sir, at the next house. We 5
can scarce see to work yet.

SERVANT.

And be hanged, then. Go, get some ale to clear
your eyesight; I'll warrant you'll see the bottom of
the pot well enough without daylight.

JOINER.

Make what haste you can. I'll bring my post as 10
soon as you'll be ready to paint it. (*Exit.*)

PAINTER.

I'd laugh at that, i'faith. But friend, what noise was
this all night? I think the watch was searching for
somebody.

SERVANT.

Aye, aye, hark, you may hear 'em searching still. 15
Why, it seems 'tis a kind of outlandish Frenchman
that they look for; he has a gray hat and a gray
cloak. But come, let us mind our business and
make haste.

Exeunt.

RAGGOU.

Dat be me. Dey slandra a moy; me be no outlandish 20
Frenchman. Begar, me be a French Frenchman.

Hark, dey come. Vat sall me do? Begar, me vill stand
for de odra post till de dam bumpkin be gone. A pox
take 'em! De devel could not hue and cry me so
close. How sall me do to be like a dat post? Hark,
dey come now. (*Raggou gets upon the post and sits in* 25
the posture of the other post.)

Enter constable and watch.

CONSTABLE.

Pox o' this outlandish French fellow for me. I'm
as dry as a dog.

FIRST WATCH.

So we are all; let's go and knock 'em up at an
alehouse and eat and drink a little. 30

SECOND WATCH.

With all our hearts.

Enter painter.

Honest painter, canst tell where we may have a
little ale?

PAINTER.

Aye, sure; two or three doors off you'll find 'em
up and a good fire, where you may toast your 35
noses, boys.

CONSTABLE.

Thou didst not see an outlandish Frenchman this
way?

PAINTER.

No, I saw no Frenchman.

Exeunt constables and watch.

Why, what a devil. This joiner has been here and 40
set up his post before I came. How time slips away
at an alehouse!

RAGGOU. [*Aside.*]

Begar, would a good rope would slip away you too.

PAINTER.

Now to work. (*Whistles and paints him.*)

RAGGOU. [*Aside.*]

He vill paint-a me; vat sall me do? 45

As he stoops, Raggou throws a stone at him.

PAINTER.

A pox o'these roguing prentices! Sirrah, I'll have
you by the ears. A company of rogues, a man
cannot work for you! If you serve me such another
trick, I'll break all your windows.

RAGGOU. [*Aside.*]

De pox break all your neck. (*Throws the pipkin at him as he stoops.*) 50

PAINTER.

Why, you damned rogue, you have broke my head. 'Sheart, I'll complain to your master. Spoiled all my colors, too! I'll not endure it; I'll be revenged, whatsoe'er it cost me. (*Exit.*) 55

RAGGOU.

A pox dis rogue, he murder mine face wid his dam paint. Now de coast be clear, me vill take-a de coat of Monsieur Jack Painter and go, for begar, dere be no stay in dis town for moy.

Enter joiner with his post.

Hark! Dere be someting; me must be de post agen. 60 A pox on dat! (*He stands up for a post again.*)

JOINER.

Why, how now? What a devil, another post, and none of my work? 'Sheart, do you employ two men at once? I'll not be used thus; I'll be paid for my work, and then let the devil set up your posts. (*Exit.*) 65

RAGGOU.

So, now, begar, me vill take de coat of de Jack Paintra, and de post of de Jack Joiner, den no man will suspect a moy. (*Offers to lift a post.*) Diable, it is too much heavy for moy; begar, me betra be hang den have all dis dam joiner sit upon me. 70 Diable, and vould me vere in bed wid all de king of France army, begar, me vould fain see vat dam English bumpkin, Mr. Hue-Cry, come fetch me from dem. (*Exit.*)

Enter servant, painter, and joiner.

SERVANT.

Why, what a foolish fellow art thou to be so angry. 75 I employed no joiner but thyself.

JOINER.

'Sheart, there was two carved posts up, and I'm sure I brought the third.

SERVANT.

Thou art mad, and so is this fool, too, to complain of throwing stones at thee, when we have ne'er a 80 prentice, nor none within six doors of us.

PAINTER.

I'm sure my pipkin's broke, and my head too; pray, look here.

SERVANT.

Why, what's here? Here's a broken pipkin indeed, but where's the three carved posts? 85

JOINER.

There was two stood up when I came to the house, and I set the third down here. Ouns, my post and my tools and all's gone.

SERVANT.

I believe you are both drunk.

PAINTER.

Heart, man, I painted the post that stood there. 90

JOINER.

Well, and heart, man, I brought the t'other, an* you call it heart, man, and all's gone, you see.

SERVANT.

My masters, go look after your things and make an end of your work.

PAINTER.

Let's go search for this fellow that stole our goods 95 here.

Exeunt.

[Scene ii. At the camp.]

Enter Tell-troth and Dol.

TELL-TROTH.

Oh, Dol, d'ye hear? Put her off till your friend come as before you pretended and say you'll marry when the garrison is delivered up.

DOL.

The lieutenant and cornet are very eager to have it dispatched, that they may have the money I prom- 5 ised, and then they are resolved to laugh me to death.

TELL-TROTH.

Well, but you know it will be our turn to laugh at them, if all be right you have told me.

DOL.

Upon my life, I have been faithful in all points, and I find I shall take pride in doing good since I 10 have prospered so well in serving you.

TELL-TROTH.

Your reward shall answer your service. I must to the captain and give him an account of all I undertook, which will meet his expectation.

DOL.

Let me alone to manage my undertakings. 15

Enter Captain and Lieutenant.

TELL-TROTH.

Here's the captain. Be you gone, therefore; I would not be seen with you till I make him acquainted with everything.

Exeunt [Tell-troth and Dol].

LIEUTENANT.

But pray, sir, why are you thus severe now to banish the flint-flayers? 20

CAPTAIN.

The King's honor and interest is so abused with these scandalous fellows that I'm resolved to cashier 'em.

Enter Tell-troth.

Oh, friend Tell-troth! Look you, Lieutenant, my opinion seldom fails me. 25

TELL-TROTH.

So, you had some dispute, then, concerning me? Look you, sir, it's now in my power to do more than e'er I hoped for. You have a foot company?

CAPTAIN.

Yes; they are now marching into th'quarter.— Lieutenant, see they march fair and do no wrong. 30

Exit Lieutenant.

TELL-TROTH.

Read that. Upon my life there is but three companies and two of 'em are disarmed and prisoners, officers and all. I laid no plot to do it. I found 'em all ready to betray one another to get the wealth; the manner how, hereafter. The 35 governor has commissioned me to make his conditions, which must be a convoy with all his wealth to his own home. The country bring in their plate and goods to secure 'em from your party, and he'll make conditions with you to march 40 away with 'em and so cheat the people (precious rogues!), besides what they preach the women out of.

CAPTAIN.

That must not be, for the King has intelligence that they have great treasure there. 45

TELL-TROTH.

Does he know how they came by it?

CAPTAIN.

Yes, very well, with the cheat of preaching. (I mean tub-preaching[59] and lectures.) The lectures your wives read you never awed you so.

TELL-TROTH.

But faith, sir, give him his conditions. 50

CAPTAIN.

I'll storm it first.

TELL-TROTH.

I intend not to have you keep conditions when you have made 'em.

CAPTAIN.

That's base. I scorn that; my honor is at stake.

TELL-TROTH.

What, for breaking articles with a rebel? Had it been 55 a fair enemy, I grant you. Suppose you storm it, and be beaten off? The King would give you little thanks for the punctilio of your own private honor. Let your lieutenant do it; the captain may with his honor break the conditions that his lieutenant makes. 60

CAPTAIN.

I may approve of that; I would not have my own hand appear against me. But I am glad to see you thus earnest for the King. Sure you have some design?

TELL-TROTH.

By my troth, I have, but so small a one it is not worth this labor; you shall know it, for you must 65 assist me.

CAPTAIN.

With all faithfulness.

TELL-TROTH.

Come, then, let's sign articles. So, march and take possession.

Exeunt.

Enter Raggou like an old woman.

RAGGOU.

Me vill make-a me nose of wax like de old woman 70 and vill go to Madame Dol and tell her me come from Monsieur Raggou. Vera good. And if she vill beg his pardon of de capitain, he vill come and marry her, although her shild be born wid a shart, and back and breast too; for begar, me find in mine conscience 75 me had betra marry a dam whore dan be hang. (*Exit.*)

---

59 tub-preaching] ad hoc pulpit, dissenters' sermons

Enter Tell-troth, Captain, Lieutenant, Cornet, etc.,
with the Governor prisoner.

TELL-TROTH.

Now sir, are you satisfied in my faith?

CAPTAIN.

I am so, and I have found you a worthy person.
Command me to anything.

TELL-TROTH.

Then I'll make you merry till I go about my design. 80
Captain Tubtext, that got the two sisters with child,
is now in bed with them eating a sack* posset, and
that we may both shame and fright 'em, there are
bears i'th'town and other shows that are going to
Bristol Fair. Now, I'll speak to the bearward to 85
muzzle a bear and turn him loose into the room, and
I'll bring you where you shall see the sight.

CAPTAIN.

Content, for I am a great lover of sports.[60] Let not
the shows go away, for I mean to celebrate Dol's
wedding. 90

LIEUTENANT.

That's kindly done. You'll need no other sport than
to see Dol rant and tear when she finds she has
married a girl.

CAPTAIN.

But the sport will be when you and the cornet
receive your fifty pound apiece you told me of. 95

LIEUTENANT.

Yes, faith, we shall have it sure enough.

CAPTAIN.

Yes, for 'tis deposited in my hands.

CORNET.

Never was jade so deeply in love! But the jest is,
the girl has made conditions with Dol to put on a
mask when she is marrying, for her face is so bad 100
she cannot away with it.

CAPTAIN.

Give all the troop favors;* let 'em dispatch, and
bring them in to the baiting of the sack posset, and
let the country be summoned in.

Exeunt.

---

60 sports] games, and gaming occasions like bear-baiting,
often played on Sundays and suppressed during the interregnum

[Scene iii.] Tubtext and his Sisters
are discovered* in bed eating a sack posset.

Enter Captain, Lieutenant, Cornet, and Ferret-farm above.

TUBTEXT.

Here is this spoonful in remembrance of our sweet
sister's precious fruit she goes with. (*He puts a*
spoonful in each of their mouths.)

FIRST SISTER.

My tender and most shame-faced thanks be
returned to you. 5

TUBTEXT.

Now, here is to the maiden-fruits of this our weeping
sister. Wipe your tears. If they were cavaliering
burthens you went with, your case were mournful,
but as they are my offspring, repent not, for your
infants, be assured, will be babes of grace.[61] 10

CAPTAIN.

What a damned rogue is this!

FIRST SISTER.

Why, then, it seems we religious lambs may play
with one another without sinning?

CAPTAIN.

Was ever such blasphemous rogues and whores! I
tremble to hear 'em! Let in the bear upon 'em. 15

FIRST SISTER.

Here is to this our sweet comforting man.

SECOND SISTER.

I am overjoyed to hear that religious lambs may
play and yet not sin. (*Put their spoons in his mouth.*)

Enter bear.

TUBTEXT.

What's here, a bear? Mercy upon us!

ALL.

Help, help, help, help! 20

TUBTEXT.

Shift for yourselves, sweet sisters.

CAPTAIN.

Now bear! Now Saint*!

LIEUTENANT.

Halloo, Saint! Halloo, bear! I'll hold a—

---

61 babes of grace] a parody of the Calvinist notion of the
elect. Some sects, notably the Ranters, held that they
answered only to God and were not subject to civil,
criminal, or ecclesiastical laws.

CORNET.

Hundred pound of the bear, thou boy bear.

LIEUTENANT.

A hundred pound of the Saint. So now, take off[62] 25
your bear.

FERRET-FARM.

By my faith, we must stave and tail[63] him off for
aught I see, Captain. I have been at many a bear-
baiting, but never at a Saint-bear-baiting before.

Exit bear, etc.

CAPTAIN.

Now, sir, is your name Tubtext? 30

TUBTEXT.

Yea.

CAPTAIN.

And do you think your two whores are with child
with two babes of grace?

TUBTEXT.

Yea, foul mouth.

CAPTAIN.

What an audacious rogue is this!—And dost thou 35
really believe thyself in such a degree of perfection
that thou canst not sin, and so need no repentance?

TUBTEXT.

Yea, sure, we are past repentance.

CAPTAIN.

Thou damned villain, I believe thee. Blasphemous
rogue! How many poor souls hast thou deluded? 40
Sirrah, it were just to make thee marry these two
women, and then hang thee for having two wives.[64]

Enter Ferret-farm.

FERRET-FARM.

Sir, our wedding folks are coming and are so merry
and so pleased that, if their joy continue, the
example will make us all marry. 45

*Enter Biddy as bridegroom, Tell-troth in her hand
dressed in Dol's clothes, and Dol in other clothes, and
Raggou dressed like an old woman with a muffler.*

Look you, here they are, pleased as you see.

---

62 take off] close the wager, (your bet is covered)
63 stave and tail] in bear-baiting, to check the bear with a
    staff and hold back the dog by the tail
64 hang … two wives] Bigamy was a felony, and techni-
    cally all felonies were capital crimes.

DOL.

Now stand you here till I beg your pardon of my
captain.

BIDDY.

By your leave, Captain, I have made bold to espouse
your old handmaid, Dol. And give us leave to laugh, 50
for faith, my lieutenant and cornet has cheated her,
Captain, for they have matched her to a girl. I am a
very* girl, and yet I have not wronged you, for I told
you before I could not get your children.

TELL-TROTH.

And we laugh to think how we have cheated you. 55
For though you cannot get my children, if I can
get yours we shall do well enough.

BIDDY.

Oh Lord, what's that? That is not Dol's voice.

DOL.

Y'are i'th'right; it is not Dol's voice, nor Dol that
has married you,—Keep the money, Captain.— 60
But your old love Tell-troth. Pray have your
money, Lieutenant, before you laugh me to death.

BIDDY.

What? My old lover, Tell-troth!

TELL-TROTH.

Now the laugh is on our side, gentlemen.—Come,
be not troubled, for I am the same honest lover 65
that e'er I was.

BIDDY.

Nay, I'll swear thou deservest me; thou art a desperate
lover to venture on a wench that has trooped so long
under such a handsome cornet. But he's a fool too,
for if he had followed his blow close at one time, he 70
had had all that I could have given him.

TELL-TROTH.

I had spies upon you and am well assured of your
honesty.* Ask Dol.

DOL.

Yes, faith, I watched your water* at every turn. Do
you remember he would have gone o'th'score for 75
your maidenhead? But you cried 'twas worth ready
money at any time; but marry me, and then halloo
dog for thy silver collar. You remember this?

BIDDY.

Aye, to my shame I do.

TELL-TROTH.

What, are you ashamed that you are honest? 80

BIDDY.

No, but I'm ashamed that I lost so much time, for
I'm sure thou wouldst ha' had me honest or not
honest.

TELL-TROTH.

Come, be not troubled; I pass by all.

BIDDY.

I love thee for thy confidence; give me thy hand.   85
By my life, I'm very honest, but I have had as
much ado to keep myself so as ever poor wench
i'th'world had.

CORNET.

But I hope, Biddy, you and I shall not lose our
acquaintance?   90

BIDDY.

If my husband will have it so, I cannot help it. But
I hope he has more wit than ever to let me see you
again.—If you have not, husband, in good faith,
at your own peril.

TELL-TROTH.

I'll have wit enough; fear not.   95

Enter Ferret-farm.

FERRET-FARM.

Sir, here's the country gentlemen come.

CAPTAIN.

Pray, let 'em come in.

Enter country gentlemen.

Gentlemen, 'tis not unknown how publicly you
have appeared against your Prince and how secure
you thought yourselves under the protection of   100
these hypocrites. But, to show you what rogues
they are, all the wealth that you brought hither to
be secured from us, they would have made
conditions to have marched away with and so
cheated the whole country. Look you, there's their   105
articles. There's Reformation for you.

FIRST GENTLEMAN.

We are deceived indeed in them. To have used us
thus!

CAPTAIN.

You must own, gentlemen, that all the wealth that's
here is justly forfeited to the King.   110

SECOND GENTLEMAN.

We grant it, worthy Captain, and our lives to boot.

CAPTAIN.

Although the wealth that's here be great and the
King's wants require it, yet, to show that he had rather have his subjects' hearts than money, he has
commissioned me to return every man his own again.   115

FIRST GENTLEMAN.

Sir, this gracious act of the King, and your
readiness to perform it, shall turn us all faithful
subjects to the extent of our lives and fortunes.

CAPTAIN.

Now, you deserve his mercy.

DOL.

Sir, will you grant me a request? Poor Raggou has   120
sent me word, if I can beg his pardon of you, he'll
marry me.

CAPTAIN.

Dol, you have been instrumental to our friend Tell-
troth; I must grant you anything.

DOL.

Then pray, sir, let's make a little sport with him.   125
Who do you think that old woman is?

CAPTAIN.

I know not.

DOL.

'Tis Raggou himself. Pray, fright him a little before
you seal his pardon.

CAPTAIN.

What a devil has he done to his face?   130

DOL.

I know not. I believe he has clapped wax upon't.

CAPTAIN.

Now, good woman, what wouldst thou have?

RAGGOU.

Me come in de crowd, in hope to see a soldier
hang. It would be great satisfaction to de country,
truly.   135

CAPTAIN.

Well, good woman, where dost thou dwell?

RAGGOU. [*Aside.*]

Begar, me have no dwell; vat sall me say to him?—
I live at Bristol town's end, an't* please your
worship.

CAPTAIN.

But woman, if thou wouldst tell me where to find   140
a plundering Frenchman called Raggou, the
country should hang him with all my heart, for

that's a notorious rogue, and he shall be hanged if he live above ground.

RAGGOU. (*Aside.*)

Begar, he serve-a me vera well to hang me. Vat a 145 devil make-a me come here? Dis be my vit. A pox on mine French wit.

CAPTAIN.

Woman, find out that rascal for me. Here is ten shillings in earnest, and when thou takest him, I'll make it ten pound. 150

RAGGOU.

But will your worship secure me that I shall have no harm if I find him?

CAPTAIN.

Aye, upon my honor, before all this company, thou shalt have no harm.

RAGGOU.

Bear witness, gentlemen. Now give me ten pound, 155 for begar, me be de man; me be Monsieur Raggou.

ALL.

How! Monsieur Raggou!

RAGGOU.

Wie, mafoy,65 ha, ha! Me have sheat-a my capitain of ten pound, and save-a my life too. Dere be de French vit! Begar, me honor my vit very much for dat. 160

CAPTAIN.

Call the marshal. Take him, and hang him upon the next tree.

RAGGOU.

Hang a moy! Did not you before vitness engage your honor dat me sall have no harm? Begar, you vill do me great deal wrong if you hang me now. 165

CAPTAIN.

I promised, indeed, that the old woman should have no harm, but Raggou shall certainly be hanged.

RAGGOU.

Aha! Dere be a dam English trick vill hang a Frenchman. But hold, hold. If you hang Raggou, how can you save de old woman? Dere be law case 170 for you! Let me have fair play for my life.

CAPTAIN.

Take the old woman's garments and lay them up safe, and then they have no harm, then my honor is clear, and here is Raggou fairly to be hanged.

_____
65 mafoy] my faith

MARSHAL.

Come, come away. 'Tis a plain case; you must hang 175 for't.

DOL.

Why were you such a fool as to come hither?

RAGGOU.

For the love of you, you dam whore, you.

DOL.

Why would you betray yourself for ten pound?

RAGGOU.

Dat be my cunning. De hangman sall have de ten 180 pound because he sall no hurt66 a me when he hang me. But, Capitain, begar you can no hang me in justice, for de old woman is Raggou, and Raggou is de old woman, and de devil can no part us. So, if you hang Raggou, you hang de old 185 woman, and you hang your own honor too, begar.

CAPTAIN.

Well sir, you have pleaded so well for yourself that, conditionally you will marry Dol, I'll pardon you.

RAGGOU.

If you tink it better to marry den to be hang, Capitain, me leave all to your judgment. 190

CAPTAIN.

Why, then marry her.

RAGGOU.

But who sall keep* de shild?

CAPTAIN.

The troop shall keep it.

RAGGOU.

Why may not de troop as vell marry her, and me vill make one? Dat's very fair, me tinks. 195

CAPTAIN.

Nay, you may be hanged yet if you will.

[Raggou] takes the woman in one hand, and the halter in the other.

RAGGOU.

Let-a me see. Here be whore, and here be halter— vera fine shoice, begar! Me can no tell which to shuse; but me vill e'en stan to mine fortune, and cross and pile67 for it. 200

_____
66 no hurt] tipping the executioner was proverbial practice
67 cross and pile] flip a coin; cross (heads) generally had a human figure with a cross, pile (tails) generally a building.

CAPTAIN.

By my troth, it shall be so! And take your choice—
cross or pile?

LIEUTENANT.

Why, cross he shall be hanged, and pile he shall
be married.

RAGGOU.

No, begar. It sall be cross if me be married, and   205
pile if me be hang.

LIEUTENANT.

Now, it's an even lay whether this farce be a
comedy or a tragedy.

CORNET.

Come, gentlemen, whore or halter for a wager?

LIEUTENANT.

Whore, for a wager.   210

CORNET.

Halter, for a wager.

RAGGOU.

Hold, hold, vat if it be nedra cross nor pile?

CAPTAIN.

If it be neither cross nor pile, thou shalt neither
be married nor hanged, upon my honor. Come,
here is your fortune for you. [*Flips coin.*] I'faith,   215
'tis cross. Thou art to be married.

RAGGOU.

Den dere be your halter again, and me tank you.

CAPTAIN.

Come, take your beloved wife and strike a match.

RAGGOU.

Den let her take me and de devil in hell give her
good of me.   220

CAPTAIN.

Then you have my pardon and all is well.

Enter Ferret-farm.

FERRET-FARM.

Sir, here are two of Queen Elizabeth's tilters, going
to Bristol Fair, desire to dance before you.

CAPTAIN.

With all my heart, call 'em in.

A dance of two hobbyhorses in armor, and a jig.

You have done well. Where's my man? Give 'em   225
half a piece. You have done prettily indeed.
Lieutenant, cashier the flint-flayers. As for these
hypocrites, I'll keep them prisoners till the King
dispose of 'em, which will be but too mercifully,
I'm sure.   230

CORNET.

I suppose, Governor, the Parliament will reward
you with some Bishops' lands for being so
honorably pulled by the ears out of your garrison?

CAPTAIN.

Come, upbraid 'em not; I hate that. Tomorrow,
sirs, summon in the country and every man shall   235
have his right.

ALL.

God bless the King and all his good soldiers!

CAPTAIN.

You see, Lieutenant, how with good usage the
people return to their loyalty. I know you are a
brave fellow, but you have been to blame in the   240
country, and that disserves your Prince more than
your courage can recompense.

LIEUTENANT.

Sir, you shall never have occasion to say this again.

CAPTAIN.

I believe you, and I wish that the great timber, the
pieces of state, that lie betwixt the King and   245
subjects—
I wish that they would take a hint from hence,
To keep the people's hearts close to their Prince.

Exeunt omnes.

FINIS.

Textual Notes

a The copytext is the 1672 first quarto (Q1), which exists in both uncorrected and corrected states. Also consulted are the 1698 second quarto (Q2) and an 1885 edition of the works (Maidmont and Logan—ML).

b *The*] *An* Q1, ML

c to] *om.* Q1, Q2, ML

d enemy's] ML; enemies Q1, Q2

The Careless Lovers[a]

by Edward Ravenscroft
edited by Elizabeth Kraft

Edward Ravenscroft's *The Careless Lovers* was performed at the Duke's Theater on 12 March 1673. It was Ravenscroft's second play and followed the success of his first, *Mamamouchi; or, The Citizen Turn'd Gentleman*, which had been performed the preceding year by some of the company's leading actors. *The Careless Lovers*, though, was a Lenten play, written for and performed by the "young" actors of the company—that is the nonshareholders, some of them not young at all—during the season when the theaters were normally dark. Ravenscroft had been asked by these actors to write this play; by his own admission, he did it hurriedly, in the span of one week. Yet, he claims, it is all his own, not derived, as was his first play, from the plots of French playwright Molière.

Actually, that is not quite accurate, for the scene in Act IV in which the "wenches of the Town" confront De Boastado with children they assert to be his bastard offspring is drawn from Molière's *M. de Pourceaugnac* (Act II, scenes vii and viii). Further, the second-act duet between Lovell and Toby in which they complain about Jacinta and Beatrice is indebted to the same playwright's *Le Bourgeois gentilhomme* (Act III, scenes x–xii). In his own time, Ravenscroft was taken to task for this "plagiarism," but the fact of the matter is that Molière was a common source of inspiration (and plot) for many Restoration playwrights, including William Wycherley and Ravenscroft's good friend Aphra Behn.

Echoes of French comedy notwithstanding, *The Careless Lovers* is, as Ravenscroft asserted, primarily his own and is distinguished by its contribution to the conventions of English Restoration comedy. Most significant, perhaps, is the gay couple at the center of the play—the witty lovers, Careless and Hillaria (prototype of Etherege's Harriet and Behn's Hellena), characterized like all such couples in Restoration comedy by their cavalier perspective and their sparkling repartee. The proviso scene between this pair that concludes the play is also a staple of Restoration comedy. Dryden had employed it before in benign fashion, but Ravenscroft follows more malicious twists in plays by Buckingham and James Howard to produce his careless lovers' bold contract centered on the mutual right to pursue other lovers after marriage.

Another convention of Restoration comedy well-exploited is the farcical treatment of satiric butts. De Boastado combines the swagger of the alazon of classical comedy and the silliness of the fop more familiar to the Restoration, for which he must be disciplined. His manipulation by other stock characters, clever servants, leads to an unearned happy fate, but the generosity with which his story is resolved is typical of Ravenscroft's genial dramatic vision.

A gentleman and a lawyer by profession, Edward Ravenscroft would be known in the Restoration dramatic world for a theatrical skirmish with John Dryden, for his friendship (perhaps more?) with Aphra Behn, and for writing plays that pleased the Town.

DRAMATIS PERSONAE

[MEN]

Mr. Muchworth, an old alderman.
Mr. Lovell, a well-bred gentleman.
Mr. Careless, a Town* gallant.
De Boastado, a conceited lord and traveler.
Toby, a servant to Mr. Lovell.

WOMEN

Jacinta, daughter to Mr. Muchworth.
Hillaria.
Beatrice, their maid.
Mrs. Clappam and Mrs. Breedwell, two
wenches of the Town.
A parson, a tailor, ghosts, fiddlers, drawers.

THE SCENE: COVENT GARDEN.*

The Careless Lovers.

Act I. [Street before Muchworth's
house in Covent Garden.]

Enter Lovell and Careless.

CARELESS.

Come back! Prithee Lovell, come back, and let's
to the tavern.

LOVELL.

Unconscionable man! I tell thee I am going to see
my mistress.

CARELESS.

Pox o'thy mistress; if thou wert going to a wench,   5
I would excuse thee, but I should think myself
damned should I consent to thy going to solicit
any woman in the way of matrimony.

LOVELL.

Wilt thou never leave this lewd, wild humor*?

CARELESS.

Not upon the score of matrimony. Why, Jack Lovell,   10
I'll tell thee I am now like a colt in the fens, that
straggles everywhere, and feed where I like best, but
should I marry, I should be tethered to one spot of
ground—at best, confined to an enclosure.[1]

---

[1] enclosure] an area of land protected by boundaries and
owned by an individual as opposed to open public fields
available to any farmer in the community for grazing
livestock

LOVELL.

But the horse that is loose often falls into a foul   15
ditch[2] or is put in the pound for straying into his
neighbor's ground. Marriage is honest and safe.

CARELESS.

Yes, if all wives were honest, I'll undertake a miss
shall love thee twice as long as any wife thou canst
find; nothing chokes love like the surety of   20
possession. Love is an excellent meat, but marriage
is an ill sauce, and believe me, it is the worst estate
of mankind. If I was going to Tyburn,* I would
cry, "Drive on carman," and choose to sing my
penitential psalms at the gallows, rather than   25
return to say, "For better for worse."[3]

LOVELL.

Atheists in love, like them in religion, are not to
be reclaimed by argument yet now and then are
converted by some accident or other. Thou may'st
one day see a beauty that like a burning-glass[4] shall   30
draw all thy loose flames within a narrow compass.

CARELESS.

Beauty is more brittle than the glass thou talk'st
of, and man's estimation of it less durable. I may
perchance love only one at once, but not that one
always, and whilst I am in my right wits, I will not   35
leave delightful variety for the unsavory insipid bits
of constancy.

LOVELL.

Well, Jacinta has a kinswoman for her companion,
so beautiful, her eyes would fix thy wandering
thoughts and make thee abandon all women for   40
her sake.

CARELESS.

So thinks the devout young novice newly entered

---

[2] ditch] a pun: ditch was slang for female genitalia.

[3] Drive ... worse] The ritual of hanging included the procession to the gallows of the cart bearing the condemned
and an attendant clergyman who prayed for and often
received evidence of the criminal's repentance moments
before the noose was slipped over his head by the hangman. "For better for worse" is, of course, from the marriage ceremony in the Book of Common Prayer.

[4] burning-glass] a lens, by which the rays of the sun may
be concentrated on an object, so as to burn it if com-
bustible (*OED*)

into his cloister; he has no sooner forsaken the world, the flesh, and the devil,[5] but imagines he is able to persuade the greatest debauchee, to make himself a fool in the like manner.

LOVELL.
I have not seen my mistress these three days, and my mind is not composed enough to return an answer to everything you urge. But venture thy body within these doors, and if ever thou return'st the same man—

CARELESS.
I know myself so well grounded in sin and have tasted so much the sweets of wickedness that I dare venture myself into any temptations to the contrary. And for this once, I will suffer myself to be seduced by thee into civil company, and if they do debauch me—

LOVELL.
Come then.

CARELESS.
But I know not how I shall forgive myself the sin of forsaking wine, women, and dice, for the conversation* of damned virtuous women.

Enter De Boastado and his man, combing his wig, and adjusting his garniture.

LOVELL.
Careless, we are undone!

CARELESS.
What fantastic is this?

LOVELL.
It is the vain, idle, simple, conceited, impertinent, talking, traveling Lord De Boastado (as he calls himself).

CARELESS.
He looks like a good subject for mirth; let's hear his character* more at large.

LOVELL.
I ne'er saw him but twice in my life, but once is enough to know what he is, for like a word writ in text, you may read him at first sight.

CARELESS.
So—

LOVELL.
He much values himself upon his traveling; many countries have taken notice of him, and he of a few. He passed them o'er as some men do a great library of books who read the title-page then turn to *Finis*. He carried more money out with him than he brought wit home. His observations are of modes, fashions, and women. He speaks some few words in most languages but sense in none. He has baptized himself with the honorable titles of most countries; his name is as long as a coach and six horses.

CARELESS.
Let's fall upon him.

LOVELL.
Shun him as you would the plague.

CARELESS.
Thou shalt stay, he makes full at us.

LOVELL.
He, he has pruned himself and comes with a full swoop.

DE BOASTADO.
Mr. Lovell, good morrow to you.

LOVELL.
Good morrow to your lordship.

DE BOASTADO.
What gentleman is this?

LOVELL.
A worthy friend of mine.

CARELESS.
One that has the ill fortune to be unknown to your lordship.

DE BOASTADO.
My friend's friend must not be a stranger. I am covetous of your better acquaintance.

CARELESS.
Pray do me the honor to let me know to whom my services are owing.

DE BOASTADO.
My name is *Monsieur Heiro Signioro Countalto Donno D'Boastado*.

CARELESS.
Bless me! *De Boastado*, what arms bears that family?

---

5 world … devil] Those entering religious life give up material things (the world), sensual pleasure (the flesh) and evil (the devil).

DE BOASTADO.

Sir, they are very famous and thus blazoned, but first imagine the escutcheon in a frame of beaten gold, richly enameled, set with pearls, rubies, diamonds, and other precious stones of great value and number incredible, for such an one have I hangs up in my diningroom against my embroidered hangings, that were presented me by the emperor; betwixt a golden watch in a rich case, given me by the king of Spain, and a great medal, with the pope's image on't. And underneath all this hangs the golden armor I won in France at the head of fourscore thousand men. I must confess there was not anyone could do the like, though they all tried one by one. But no matter for that, let that pass.

LOVELL.

I have heard much of your fame, but as to your heraldry—

CARELESS.

You do well to put him in mind of his text, for he was run too far from it to come to't again under the turning of an hourglass.

DE BOASTADO.

Well, now as to my arms. The supporters of this frame are the griffin and the tiger *couchant*, for on their two backs it is born up at each corner, in the middle, by the flower *de less crescent*; on each side, guarded by the dromedary and elephant *rampant*, which stand upon a castle *guardant*; on the top of the frame, is the helmet *militant*, held up in the talons of an eagle *volant*, bearing a crown upon her head *triumphant*.[6]

CARELESS.

The flourish of all Christendom!

LOVELL.

This is a strain beyond what I ever heard yet.

CARELESS.

His heraldry has run him out of breath.

DE BOASTADO.

Then gallants, in the escutcheon, is only a man with a spade *fodant* in a field *gules*.[7]

CARELESS.

A silver brim to a wooden dish.

LOVELL.

Or a leek enchased in gold.

CARELESS.

That would be a fit arms for him, for by the length of his name, he should be a Welshman.[8]—But my lord, these may be said the arms of Adam.

DE BOASTADO.

They are so; ours is a very ancient family, and we are lineally descended from him, and our motto is *Dii Vendent Omnia Laboribus*. In Italian, *Ciascunno è figliolo del sue operè*. In English, *Without Pains, no Gains*.[9]

CARELESS.

We have trespassed on your lordship's patience.

LOVELL.

We beg your pardon and take our leaves.

DE BOASTADO.

I hope your friend's better acquaintance.

CARELESS.

You honor me much.

DE BOASTADO.

How far walk you this way?

CARELESS.

No farther than this house.

DE BOASTADO.

Thither I am going too.

LOVELL.

Are you acquainted with Mr. Muchworth?

DE BOASTADO.

His daughter will be a great fortune, and I am in treaty with him about a marriage.

---

6 griffin ... *triumphant*] These grotesque arms violate the conventions of heraldry; viz. the coat of arms should have two supporters, De Boastado's has seven; the castle is described inaccurately as "guardant," a term which in heraldry can apply only to beasts as it signifies the direct gaze of the eyes; the helmet is described as "militant," another term used inaccurately as it should be applied only to the standard; the flower de less (fleur de lis) is upside down (Henry).

7 *fodant ... gules*] digging on a field of red

8 leek ... Welshman] the leek is the national symbol of Wales, where people have names that seem long and strange to non-Celts.

9 *Dii ... Gains*] The English proverb does not really translate the Latin ("The gods sell all to those who labor") or the Italian ("Each is the son of his works").

LOVELL.

About marriage!

DE BOASTADO.

Great persons of mean estates choose wives out of the City;* they are covetous of honor, and we of money. And here comes the alderman. 160

Enter Muchworth.

MUCHWORTH.

Good morrow to your lordship.

DE BOASTADO.

How does your fair daughter?

MUCHWORTH.

You honor me with inquiring after her.—Oh Mr. Lovell, a word with you in private. Sir, you have for some time made addresses to my Jacinta, but 165 for the future I desire you would be a stranger to her. To me you shall be always welcome, but she is otherwise engaged.

LOVELL.

It is less in my power not to love her than to hate you, though she should follow your example and 170 turn me off too.

MUCHWORTH.

You know my mind, and shortly she'll let you know hers. Your servant.—My lord, I'll wait you in. My daughter and my niece are but gone to buy a few trifles at the Exchange;* they'll be back soon. 175

DE BOASTADO.

Gentlemen, your servant.

Exeunt Muchworth and De Boastado.

LOVELL.

Jacinta engaged! False, faithless woman.

CARELESS.

Prithee think no more of her. Come now, go with me and be merry; we'll have women in abundance.

LOVELL.

Hang 'em, jilts. 180

CARELESS.

No, such women as your mistress is are more like jilts. These are good conscionable girls, that will not let you spend your money for nothing; with the others you waste your gold and time, and at last, like young heifers when they come to be milked, they 185 spurn at you in defiance and away they frisk.

LOVELL.

Ah Jacinta! Hast thou forgot my vows? Unhappy lover.

CARELESS.

Damn this pining, whining, puling, peaking, sneaking, sniveling love. I'll carry thee where thou 190 shalt see merry, gay, jocund, sprightly love. Thou shalt have it in armfuls, and dilate thyself in pleasure.

LOVELL.

My soul is out of tune!

Enter Toby.

TOBY.

Sir, master, sir, Madam Jacinta and her cousin Hillaria are just turned the corner of this street; I 195 suppose they are coming home.

LOVELL.

I'll meet her and tax her with her inconstancy.

TOBY.

They have both their masks on, but you'll know 'em by Beatrice, my sweet Beatrice.

Enter Jacinta, Hillaria, Beatrice.

CARELESS.

These are they. Lovell, accost thy own natural,[10] 200 and leave me to manage the other impertinent.

LOVELL.

My heart's my guide. Jacinta stay, stay Jacinta; speak, though but one word, and tell me the cause of this sudden alteration. Pull off your mask, and let me see if your face is altered as much as I hear 205 your heart is. Unkind woman, dost thou fly me! I'll pursue thee as a ghost does the guilty murderer.

TOBY.

Now you and I, like squire and damsel, will follow, Beatrice; if thou hast lost thy tongue too, you and your mistress are a blessed pair, for were it not for 210 your tongues, you women would all be angels.

BEATRICE.

Da, da, da.

Exeunt Jacinta, Lovell, Beatrice, [Toby].

---

10 natural] one without the ability to reason or a half-wit; in certain contexts, mistress. Here either meaning could apply.

CARELESS.

Nay, nay, madam! You are not to pass so.

HILLARIA.

What would the man be at?

CARELESS.

The man's at what he would be; he's at you. 215

HILLARIA.

What do you mean?

CARELESS.

Faith, I can't resolve you till I see your face; pull off your mask, and then I'll tell you what I mean.

HILLARIA.

Suppose I won't.

CARELESS.

Nay, if you are good at suppositions, suppose I am 220 resolved to see it off.

HILLARIA.

Then I should suppose you very rude.

CARELESS.

And if you don't, I shall suppose you very ugly, for I never knew a woman that had a handsome face could endure to hide it. 225

HILLARIA.

Yes, if she like not her company.

CARELESS.

Yet, she'd have her company like her; I trust more to a woman's pride than her love or good nature. For though they are ugly, they think themselves handsome and would be thought so by others. 230

HILLARIA.

Why then do they maintain the humor* of vizard-masks?

CARELESS.

Because under them they sin concealed. I'll engage vizard-masks ruin more women's virtues than all the bawds in town. 235

HILLARIA.

Your reason for that.

CARELESS.

Under the vizard the wife goes to the play, ball, or masquerade undiscovered to her husband; the maid unknown to her mistress; the daughter or niece unperceived by her relations. The mask 240 invites the gallants, and though at first you come but out of curiosity to hear what men will say, our alamode repartees, our genteel bawdry and brisk raillery tickles your ears; your bodies are buxom, your bloods grow wanton, your fancies strike 245 firmly on some man or other; the gallant grows importunate, and you are conquered.

HILLARIA.

Do you find women then so frail?

CARELESS.

A woman's ear is the outwork to her chastity; get but there, and the fort is more than half taken. 250 When once a woman hears what you say, she'll soon do what you'd have her.

HILLARIA.

Then you take a parley for a surrender.

CARELESS.

No, but after a parley they soon yield.

HILLARIA.

Now have I a mind to stay and talk with you but 255 must be forced to leave you to avoid your ill opinion.

CARELESS.

Nay, if you have a mind to't, you'll do't; let me think what I will. And if you won't pull off your mask, I'll e'en be gone and leave you. Fare you well.

HILLARIA.

And fare you well. 260

Turn from each other and look back over their shoulders.

CARELESS.

Nay, if you look o'er shoulder after me, I'll turn again, for you have no mind I should be gone, I am sure.

HILLARIA.

Why did you look back at me?

CARELESS.

To see— 265

HILLARIA.

If I would look at you, and so we e'en caught one another. And what can you say to me of that which I can't retort on you again?

CARELESS.

But I'll be judged by yourself if I have not more reason to think you desire my stay than I yours: 270 you have a full sight of me and see what I am and know whether you like me or not; you are all vizard, long scarf, and petticoat. For ought I know, you may want* a nose, a set of teeth, be squint-eyed or blobber-lipped. 275

HILLARIA.

You'll make me as ugly as the devil. Am I not cloven-footed think you?

CARELESS.

I'll tell you that presently.* (*Offers to look on her legs.*)

HILLARIA.

Nay.

CARELESS.

A handsome leg and a foot I'll be sworn, and here's a well shaped hand and arm, and what breasts are here? How round and plump?

HILLARIA.

Hands off, your inquiry begins to grow troublesome.

CARELESS.

If you have a face and features answerable to your limbs, you're a prime piece of woman's flesh.

HILLARIA.

Do you think I have?

CARELESS.

Gad, do I.

HILLARIA.

Then to keep you in your good opinion, I'll be gone, and you shan't see't. Nay, nay, no attempts, hands off.

CARELESS.

I have sworn to see't.

HILLARIA.

And I have sworn you shall, but stand at greater distance. Farther, farther yet—See—

Hillaria gets her back close to her uncle's door, pulls off her mask, steps in, and shuts it.

CARELESS.

Excellent creature!

HILLARIA.

Fare you well.

CARELESS.

Hah! are you so cunning? She has locked the door against me.

Enter Toby.

TOBY.

My master, sir, is gone out the back way and sent me to give you notice.

CARELESS.

I'll be with him presently.

Exit Toby.

By her wit, I did not judge she had so good a face, for wit and beauty seldom go together in a woman. She has a large stock of both, and I could wish myself in bed with her, but the thoughts of her are momentary.

I'll keep my soul free as the bird that flies i'th'air.

I'll ne'er love one, till I of all besides despair.

Exit.

Act II. [The same.]

Enter Lovell and Toby, Beatrice meeting them.

BEATRICE.

Most luckily met. I am sent ambassadress of good news and was just coming—

LOVELL.

Return, and attempt not to deceive me with fair words. Return, I bid thee, and tell thy faithless mistress her unhappy lover will not long be the subject of her scorn. Bid her practice her deceit elsewhere.

BEATRICE.

My sweet face, tell me, what humor is this has possessed thy master?

TOBY.

Your sweet face, you impertinent. Go, do as you're bidden. Be gone, go.

BEATRICE.

Hey! Are you in the same tone?

TOBY.

Be gone, baggage. Speak not a word more for your life.

BEATRICE.

What a vengeance ails you both? Well, I'll go inform my mistress how squares go.[11] (*Exit.*)

LOVELL.

Thus to treat a lover, and one that was the most passionate and most faithful of all lovers.

TOBY.

'Tis strange to me they should treat us so.

---

[11] how squares go] how matters stand

LOVELL.

I have showed the greatest love and tenderness for her that can be imagined. I loved nothing in the world but her, thought of nothing but her, and sleeping, dreamt of nothing but her. She was all my desire, all my joy; I spoke not of anything but her. And is such a love thus rewarded! These three days I have not seen her seemed so many ages to me. And am I in three days forsaken and forgotten? I meet her, and she will not speak to me, not look at me, but shuns me as a thing she hates.

TOBY.

Ah sir, I may say the same, for Beatrice will follow her mistress, honey or t____* as she is.

LOVELL.

Can Jacinta be matched for ingratitude?

TOBY.

Or that baggage Beatrice?

LOVELL.

To forsake me after so many sighs and vows which I have offered to her charms.

TOBY.

To leave me after so many good offices and daily services I have done for her.

LOVELL.

After so many tears shed at her feet.

TOBY.

After so many pails of water lugged up stairs for her to wash her rooms.

LOVELL.

After I had expressed so ardent an affection and so gen'rous a flame for her.

TOBY.

After I have so often kindled a fire for her in her mistress's chamber and scorched myself with taking her heaters[12] for her out of the fire.

LOVELL.

Does she after all this, refuse to speak to me?

TOBY.

Does she for all this turn cat in pan?[13]

LOVELL.

And fly from my sight.

TOBY.

And turn her backside with a pox to me.

LOVELL.

Her unkindness deserves my severest resentments.

TOBY.

Her pettishness merits a hundred kicks i'th'breech.

LOVELL.

I charge thee never to speak to me of her, nor for her.

TOBY.

I, sir! not I, by my grandsire's beard.

LOVELL.

Never attempt to excuse her infidelity.

TOBY.

Never fear't.

LOVELL.

I'll be deaf to all you can say in her behalf.

TOBY.

I think not anything of't.

LOVELL.

I will cherish my anger and break off all intimacy with her.

TOBY.

Agreed. And I'll break off my intrigue.

LOVELL.

Perhaps she's taken with this foolish lord and puffed up with hopes of being a lady. Ambition is the vice of her sex, but she shall not boast an absolute glory, for I'll abandon her as she does me.

TOBY.

I much approve your resolution.

LOVELL.

Do thou lend it aid against all that love can urge to the contrary; I conjure thee, find all the faults in her thou canst and lampoon her to me in a description.

TOBY.

Shaw waugh—You may find a thousand prettier women than she. In the first place, her hair inclines to yellow.

LOVELL.

That's but the luster of her hair.

TOBY.

Her forehead's low.

LOVELL.

But smooth and delicate.

---

12 heaters] "Irons made hot, and put into a box-iron, to smooth and plait linen" (Johnson's *Dictionary*, 1755)

13 turn cat in pan] to become the opposite of what she was or seemed originally to be

TOBY.

Her nose is too big.

LOVELL.

But well shaped.

TOBY.

When she speaks, she draws her mouth from ear to ear.

LOVELL.

Which discovers such a fine set of teeth, so white and even, and her lips so red. 80

TOBY.

And keeps her teeth close, which makes such a jarring in her speech.

LOVELL.

That breaks the fullness of the voice and makes a pretty kind of harmony. 85

TOBY.

Her face is a white clumsy big-face.

LOVELL.

But every feature is so excellent, the greatest critic in beauty knows not where to take away or what to add.

TOBY.

Then she has a peaking way of holding down her head. 90

LOVELL.

But at the same time, appears such a pattern of modesty and innocence.

TOBY.

Her breasts are too big.

LOVELL.

But are firm and white, and such delicate blue veins, their bigness seems graceful. 95

TOBY.

She's lank buttocked.

LOVELL.

Finely turned about the hips.

TOBY.

Her stature is low.

LOVELL.

Augh! of a fine middle size; not so tall to o'ertop a man, nor so low as to be o'erlooked. 100

TOBY.

She's of too dull and serious a humor.*

LOVELL.

That which you call dullness is her modesty, and her seriousness is the effect of her sage discreet behavior.

TOBY.

But she's very pettish. 105

LOVELL.

Which shows she has a spirit. But in the fair nothing seems amiss, and in them we easily pass o'er small faults.

TOBY.

Lord sir! She's a book without an errata; never did such a perfect impression come from the press of 110 Nature. I see how things will go. Whom we excuse, we love.

LOVELL.

Love her! I'll rather die. I'll more disesteem her than ever I prized her.

TOBY.

This is not the right course you take. 115

LOVELL.

In this my revenge will show itself; the more full of charms she appears, the more glorious will the conquest be when from my heart I drive the sentiments of love and plant in their room contempt and disdain. 120

Enter Jacinta and Beatrice.

TOBY.

Here she comes; now stand your ground.

BEATRICE.

His behavior madam was such, I have nothing to say in his excuse.

JACINTA.

He's here.

LOVELL.

I'll not so much as speak to her. 125

TOBY.

I'll follow your example.

JACINTA.

What makes you so strange?

BEATRICE.

Why stand you at so great a distance?

JACINTA.

What disturbs your mind?

BEATRICE.

What a murrain ails you? 130

LOVELL.

Perfidious woman.

TOBY.

Hah! Mrs.* Judas.

JACINTA.

I see my company is troublesome to you. Was my
silence this morning the ground of your anger?

LOVELL.

Let me tell you, you shall not triumph in your   135
infidelity; I will banish the love I have for you from
my heart and leave in it no impression your eyes
have made.

TOBY.

No, nor I neither.

JACINTA.

I will acquaint you with the cause why I held not   140
discourse with you this morning.

LOVELL.

I'll hear nothing.

BEATRICE.

I'll tell you why we were mum.

TOBY.

I am deaf.

JACINTA.

My father—   145

LOVELL.

I care not.

BEATRICE.

My mistress—

TOBY.

My master.

JACINTA.

Hear me!

LOVELL.

No.   150

BEATRICE.

Hark you—

TOBY.

No, hark you.

JACINTA.

Mr. Lovell—

LOVELL.

Mrs.* Jacinta.

BEATRICE.

Dear Toby—   155

TOBY.

Sweet Beatrice.

JACINTA.

Stay.

LOVELL.

Not I.

BEATRICE.

Come back.

TOBY.

I won't.   160

JACINTA.

Pray hear me.

LOVELL.

Excuse me.

BEATRICE.

One word—

TOBY.

Not a syllable.

JACINTA.

You'll be gone?   165

LOVELL.

Yes.

BEATRICE.

You won't stay?

TOBY.

No.

JACINTA.

Well, since you will not hear me speak, remain in
your ignorance and do as you please.   170

BEATRICE.

Since you are so frumpish, a pin for you.

TOBY.

And a fart for you, Mrs. Turd-pie.

LOVELL.

Well then, say what you would say.

JACINTA.

My mind is altered now.

TOBY.

Come tell your tale.   175

BEATRICE.

No matter now.

LOVELL.

What was it?

JACINTA.

Nothing.

TOBY.

Begin.

BEATRICE.

I have done.   180

LOVELL.

Pray speak.

JACINTA.

    Excuse me.

TOBY.

    Come out with it.

BEATRICE.

    Let me alone.

LOVELL.

    I entreat.   185

JACINTA.

    In vain.

TOBY.

    I petition.

BEATRICE.

    To no purpose.

LOVELL.

    I conjure you.

JACINTA.

    Pray go.   190

TOBY.

    In the name of Jupiter, speak.

BEATRICE.

    Be gone.

LOVELL.

    Jacinta.

JACINTA.

    Lovell.

TOBY.

    Beatrice.   195

BEATRICE.

    Toby.

LOVELL.

    You're resolved.

JACINTA.

    I am.

TOBY.

    You'll be obstinate.

BEATRICE.

    Yes.   200

LOVELL.

    Lay aside your anger.

JACINTA.

    Never.

TOBY.

    Let your gizzard leave grumbling.

BEATRICE.

    I'll have nothing to do with you.

LOVELL.

    Since you are so averse to let me know the cause   205
    why you treated me so ill and proved so false to
    your faith, this is the last time you shall ever see
    me, for I will turn wanderer and spend my days
    in travel.

TOBY.

    Aye, and so will I.   210

JACINTA.

    But Lovell—

LOVELL.

    Your pleasure.

BEATRICE.

    But Toby—

TOBY.

    Say you.

JACINTA.

    What are your intentions?   215

LOVELL.

    To banish myself from my country.

BEATRICE.

    What mean you?

TOBY.

    To turn vagabond.

JACINTA.

    You must not go.

LOVELL.

    Your unkindness drives me hence.   220

BEATRICE.

    You shan't be gone.

TOBY.

    You're grown so turdy the devil would not endure
    your company.

JACINTA.

    Lovell, 'tis you are unkind to condemn me
    unheard.   225

LOVELL.

    You refused to speak for yourself.

JACINTA.

    It was not then convenient. My father both this
    morning and e'er since I saw you last charged me
    never to admit you more in conversation,* nor to
    see you (Could I help it?) and says his curses shall   230
    be my portion if I disobey him.

LOVELL.

    Will you be so unjust?

JACINTA.

Never, though you should prove so to me!

LOVELL.

By your father's words, I understood you were as
willing to retreat from my love as he to have you.   235

JACINTA.

I saw, e'er since that foppish lord made his
pretensions to me, that my father was resolved to
put a stop to our proceedings. I seemingly
complied, for had I urged his anger with my
denials, he would not only have banished you from   240
his house, but have immured me in my chamber
till I had been disposed of; then I should have lost
the satisfaction of seeing you, which I now may
have if things be managed discreetly.

LOVELL.

You acted prudently.   245

JACINTA.

I durst not speak to you this morning. When I
returned, I spied my father at the window.

BEATRICE.

Look you now, the secret is out.

TOBY.

'Twas e'en so, I verily believe.

LOVELL.

Ah Jacinta! See what power you have o'er me, that   250
can with one word appease all the mutinies in my
mind, and with what facility we let ourselves be
persuaded by them we love.

TOBY.

Ah these white devils[14] have as great power over
their servants, as the black devil over sinners.   255

BEATRICE.

Madam, the door begins to open.

JACINTA.

Be gone, sir. I fear it is my father.

LOVELL.

Adieu.

Exeunt Lovell, Toby. Enter Hillaria.

HILLARIA.

Ha, ha, ha!

JACINTA.

You have a happy time on't cousin, you are always   260
merry!

---

14 white devils] fair but evil beings

HILLARIA.

I vow, Coz, I have so laughed at his lordship.

JACINTA.

How canst thou laugh at such a fool?

HILLARIA.

He's one of the most pleasant comedies Nature
ever brought into the world.   265

JACINTA.

He's but a mere farce!

HILLARIA.

His tailor is come after him with a new suit but
of the oddest fashion. He is putting it on and will
soon be here to show it you; he says 'tis of his own
invention.   270

JACINTA.

I wish thee in my place; you would know how to
manage him.

HILLARIA.

I would my uncle had ordained him for my lover.

JACINTA.

And do you wish he were to be your husband too?

BEATRICE.

There's a certain reason, madam, why a woman   275
should wish to have a fool for her husband.

HILLARIA.

Yes, Beatrice, but I don't; he's not fool enough for
that!

BEATRICE.

For my part I believe it to be a vulgar error.

HILLARIA.

Some are so skillful as to judge of those matters   280
from the features, but experience is the best
mistress.

BEATRICE.

Aye madam! from thence comes the most certain
knowledge.

JACINTA.

You talk so I don't know what you mean.   285

HILLARIA.

Alas poor innocent!

BEATRICE.

Why madam, we may talk or mean what we will;
we are alone.

JACINTA.

I blush at your answer.

HILLARIA.

Dear coz, you are a very wag at your heart, or you'd 290
not blush at what she said.

JACINTA.

Here comes your animal.

Enter De Boastado in his new suit, and a tailor.

TAILOR.

Never let me have your custom if it be not exactly
to your description!

DE BOASTADO.

I think it is. Madam Jacinta, I come to show you 295
my gallantry. 'Tis an odd fancy but new; 'tis my
own invention. How does it please you?

JACINTA.

Wonderfully well.

HILLARIA.

It is well quartered.

JACINTA.

We want a herald to blazon it. 300

BEATRICE.

I never liked suit better.

DE BOASTADO.

I am glad you all like it, for I would not let my tailor
go till I had got your approbation.—Hark you! How
many artists sat in consultation about it?

TAILOR.

According to your lordship's appointment, twelve. 305

JACINTA.

A jury of tailors to make up one fool.

DE BOASTADO.

How make you up the number?

TAILOR.

Four French tailors.

HILLARIA.

Why four French?

DE BOASTADO.

Because they are the best mathematicians at cutting 310
out. Go on.

TAILOR.

Three Spanish.

JACINTA.

Why Spanish?

DE BOASTADO.

Auh! Their deliberation in proceeding does much.
They set not a stitch without thought, and their 315

gravity is a good allay for the French mercury.[15]
It gives fixation to their volatile spirits. Proceed.

TAILOR.

Two Italians, one German, and one Polander.

BEATRICE.

And why those, my lord?

DE BOASTADO.

Because I passed through their countries in my 320
travels and have here something of the best of all
their garbs.

HILLARIA.

Good.

DE BOASTADO.

In this suit, ladies, you may read all the countries
of my travels; I designed it on purpose to give the 325
world intelligence where I have been.

HILLARIA.

I vow 'twas a pretty contrivance.

JACINTA.

Yes, very ingenious.

TAILOR.

And to make the number, the twelfth was an
Englishman, and that myself. 330

DE BOASTADO.

Go thy ways and carry thy bill to my steward and
bid him pay thee thy money.

TAILOR.

I thank your lordship. (*Exit.*)

JACINTA.

Now do I wish to be well quit of him.

HILLARIA.

Go you in, and I'll endeavor to detain him. 335

DE BOASTADO.

Going away? 'Tis unkind not to take me with you.

JACINTA.

I am going about a small affair my maid tells me of.

HILLARIA.

Accept of my company till she returns.

Exeunt Jacinta and Beatrice.

DE BOASTADO.

Oh madam, 'tis most agreeable.

---

15 French mercury] liveliness, but also an allusion to the
French malady—syphilis—the common treatment for
which was mercury

HILLARIA.

I would it were, my lord. (*Sighs.*)   340

DE BOASTADO.

Why sigh you, madam?

HILLARIA.

Would I was as handsome as my cousin.

DE BOASTADO.

You are, lady.

HILLARIA.

And as good a fortune too.

DE BOASTADO.

Your fortune is large, your uncle tells me.   345

HILLARIA.

But not answerable to hers. I would it was.

DE BOASTADO.

Repine not, fair one.

HILLARIA.

Hi ho!

DE BOASTADO.

Pray why sigh you so?

HILLARIA.

I wish, my lord—   350

DE BOASTADO.

What, pretty one?

HILLARIA.

That you had never seen my cousin.

DE BOASTADO.

Why?

HILLARIA.

Because I think she'll love you.

DE BOASTADO.

And I'll love her.   355

HILLARIA.

But I wish you'd love somebody else.

DE BOASTADO.

And why do you wish it?

HILLARIA.

Because a friend of mine loves you.

DE BOASTADO.

You mock me. Ha, ha, ha.

HILLARIA.

No my lord, 'tis too true. That you may know I   360
do not, I could tell you of more than one that loves
you passionately.

DE BOASTADO.

I must confess it has been my fortune to be beloved

by considerable persons, in all places wherever I have
traveled. At Rome the Pope's niece fell in love with   365
me and sent me her picture richly set in jewels. In
Tuscany the Grand Duke's sister. I could tell you
something of an intrigue with the Sultana, when I
was at Constantinople, but it is something incredible.

HILLARIA.

Nay, I have reason to believe it, for no woman sees   370
you without some concern; even in this very street
lies a young lady that has forty thousand pounds
to her portion, and she but saw you pass along the
street once or twice, as you came hither, and is
fallen in love with you and, hearing of your   375
pretensions here, is since fallen sick and has kept
her bed these two days.

DE BOASTADO.

I protest I am sorry, but is she so great a fortune?

HILLARIA.

My uncle knows her and all her concerns as to
those things.   380

DE BOASTADO.

Humh—

HILLARIA.

I could tell you of somebody else too. But 'tis not
convenient.

DE BOASTADO. [*Aside.*]

That's herself; this may be worth inquiry.

Enter Muchworth.

MUCHWORTH.

My lord, my lawyer's within; if you please, we will   385
look o'er some particulars of your estate that we
may forward the settlement of a jointure for my
daughter.

DE BOASTADO.

I have some reason to think she and I may not
disagree. Your servant, lady.   390

Exeunt Muchworth and De Boastado. Enter Jacinta.

JACINTA.

I had not returned to you but that I saw my father
come this way.

HILLARIA.

You missed the relation of his foreign amours. But
I have persuaded his lordship that you and I are
in love with him and that a great fortune has kept   395
her bed this two days hearing he pretends to you.

JACINTA.

And is sick for love of him.

HILLARIA.

Yes! he believes it.

JACINTA.

He's a most credulous coxcomb. But should he find you out to be a liar.   400

HILLARIA.

Not a greater than himself, he cannot I am sure!

JACINTA.

How canst thou in conscience make such a fool of him.

HILLARIA.

Heaven ordained everything for some use or another, and he can serve for no other than our pastime.   405

Enter Careless.

CARELESS.

Hah! these are they!

JACINTA.

Here comes Mr. Lovell's friend.

CARELESS.

Now which of 'em is she that I am in love with?

JACINTA.

He's at a stand.[16]

HILLARIA.

He'd fain know me again, but prithee take up a   410
brisk humor, and let's try to puzzle him.

JACINTA.

No! Prithee let's go in.

CARELESS.

What, are you upon this wing? Do you come out a grazing like rabbits just at the burrow's mouth, that as soon as anybody comes, you may pop into   415
your holes again?

HILLARIA.

We had need be watchful, when such poachers as you are abroad.

CARELESS.

Your watchfulness signifies little. I come now like a ferret to creep into your holes and scare you out   420
of your burrows.

_____

16 at a stand] A state of checked or arrested movement; a standstill; spec., the rigid attitude assumed by a dog on finding game (*OED*)

JACINTA.

But if instead of a burrow, you should run into a warrener's trap?

HILLARIA.

And that you may easily do, for we are no outlying coneys,[17] we keep within heart of the warren.   425

CARELESS.

Aye, but I know your mews, your inlets and outlets, and wherever the rabbits pass, the ferret or weasel may venture. You see I come just to the same place; 'twas here you popped in from me before, but now I am got between you and the hedge.   430

JACINTA.

But how do you know that we are the same pair?

HILLARIA.

And which of us is it that was too nimble for you?

JACINTA.

You had best have a care on which you adventure, for in such cases you ought not to spoil your friend's game.   435

CARELESS.

'Tis one of you!

HILLARIA.

I see you are no good hound. You can't follow the scent well.

CARELESS.

Many a good-nosed dog is at a loss when the scent is crossed, but if I catch one, and my friend   440
another, if we are mistaken, let him say which is his, and we'll make a change.

JACINTA.

But which of us two, do you think, would fall to your share?

CARELESS.

Egad, I don't know.   445

HILLARIA.

Don't you know a woman's face when you see't a second time?

CARELESS.

She showed it with such a legerdemain; her mask was no sooner off than on again, and she was gone.

JACINTA.

Observe us well.   450

_____

17 coneys] rabbits; also bawdy slang for young women

CARELESS.

Let me see—faith not I—if you had your masks on, I should know her from a thousand; at the very sight of her vizard, my heart would go pittypat.

HILLARIA.

If you are so in love with the complexion of velvet, you should have a Negra for your mistress.   455

CARELESS.

There is beauty in black. Why else do ladies put on patches? And some love black hair better than light, and why not black faces as well?

JACINTA.

But you'd be for a white one at this time, if you knew but which was under the vizard.   460

HILLARIA.

'Tis well for us he does not, for then he'd pretend love to one of us.

CARELESS.

Gad, but I would not to you, nor ne'er a woman in the world.

JACINTA.

I dare swear you would.   465

CARELESS.

Perhaps I might make you believe I was in love with you.

HILLARIA.

No, that you could ne'er do.

CARELESS.

Why, don't you think yourselves handsome enough to be loved?   470

JACINTA.

Yes, but we think you have more wit.

CARELESS.

What, than to love one of you?

HILLARIA.

Yes, or anybody else that is never like to love you again.

CARELESS.   475

Are you an enemy to me or to love?

HILLARIA.

To love. I think it is a very foolish thing.

CARELESS.

But 'tis marriage makes it so. Give me love as Nature made it, free and unconfined. Observe but mistress and gallant. How brisk, how gay, how fierce they are in their amours! Whilst marriage-   480

love comes like a slave loaden with fetters, dull and out of humor.

HILLARIA.

For my part, I am rather for a gallant than a husband.

JACINTA.

So am I, clearly.   485

CARELESS.

'Tis well dissembled on one side; one of you, I am sure, speaks against her conscience, but if you are as you say, you're girls for me.

JACINTA.

What, both?

CARELESS.

Both, egad both.   490

HILLARIA.

Hold, one's enough, and if you'll be a gallant to one of us, we expect you should be constant.

CARELESS.

That circumstance makes it too like marriage.

HILLARIA.

The constancy is while you pretend; not but that either mistress or gallant may choose elsewhere, but they must love but one at once.   495

JACINTA.

But which of us will you choose?

CARELESS.

Faith, I'll be for her I talked to in the mask.

Enter Beatrice.

BEATRICE.

Madam! Dinner's on the table.

JACINTA.

Already?   500

BEATRICE.

My master has called for't, he's in haste to go out. (*Exit.*)

HILLARIA.

We come. Well sir, when you find which of us two is she, claim her for your mistress.

CARELESS.

Adieu.   505

HILLARIA.

Come, Hillaria.

Exeunt Jacinta, Hillaria.

CARELESS.

Hah! Hillaria, i'faith, that's she. But they are gone. Jacinta, I remember, is the name of Lovell's mistress; till now I fancied the other was she, because she was more brisk and airy. Well, I'll find out my friend, and we'll give a visit in the afternoon.

If for a wife my liberty I'd lose,
One of these two should catch me in a noose.

Exit.

Act III. [Hall in Muchworth's house.]

Enter Muchworth, Jacinta, Hillaria.

MUCHWORTH.

Your jointure is agreed on, and directions are given for the drawing of the writings; therefore, put things in readiness and dispose yourself for marriage, for it must be within a day or two.

JACINTA.

Sure sir, if you loved me, you'd not be so hasty to be rid of me.

MUCHWORTH.

It is the great care and love I have for thee makes me solicitous to see thee well-disposed. My lord is a person of worth and honor, and thou wilt be happy in his love; Jacinta, thou'lt be a lady.*

JACINTA.

My lord merits, I question not, a wife much above me in desert, but how do you think I can on the sudden resolve to leave the family of him that got me, bred me, and brought me up to what I am.

MUCHWORTH.

Your mother did the same before you, and for this thou hast had all thy education. This is the last great act a father can do for his child; in this his care ends, and when we give a daughter in marriage, 'tis supposed, we give her to more than a father, for such is a husband; husband and wife are one.

HILLARIA.

That rule, uncle, won't hold in arithmetic, for according to the first principle, one and one make two.

MUCHWORTH.

Mad-cap niece, meddle with your own matters. Let me see——

HILLARIA.

Nay uncle, ne'er put on your considering-cap for an answer. What I say is true, and I'll give you a further demonstration that man and wife are not one. For in this age they are seldom, or never together; the man's in one place, and the wife in another, as far asunder as ever they can get. And you know it is impossible for one and the same thing to be at the same time in several places.

MUCHWORTH.

She has a very unhappy wit. I am glad, daughter, that you are going from her, for she's enough to spoil all the young women she meets with, but I hope she'll have a husband will meet with her.

HILLARIA.

Never of your choosing, uncle.

MUCHWORTH.

Likely so, for you're hair-brained enough to do things of your own head. But your father, when he died, left you to my care and bid that you should be ruled by me, and if you are not, your disobedience will come home to you one day or other.

HILLARIA.

This is but talk. Do you think, uncle, I han't as much wit to choose a husband as you?

MUCHWORTH.

Well, well, follow your own course, but I hope you'll get a husband one day will cudgel your bones for you.

HILLARIA.

But uncle, it is not now as it was in your young days; women then were poor sneaking sheepish creatures. But in this age, we know our own strength and have wit enough to make use of our talents. If I meet with a husband makes my heart ache, I'll make his head ache,[18] I'll warrant him.

MUCHWORTH.

Nay, I am apt enough to believe one house will be too hot to hold you long. I doubt not but your husband (whoe'er has the ill fortune to be so) will in a short time be as weary of you as I am.

---

18 head ache] because of the protruding horns of the cuck-old

HILLARIA.

If he should prove but half so ill-natured as you 60
are (which certainly no young man can), I'd swear
myself a virgin and, consequently, sue a divorce
against him for impotency.

MUCHWORTH.

I must be gone. This wench will never hold her
prattle; she'd out-talk 'em at a bake-house. (*Exit*.) 65

JACINTA.

Well, thou'rt a mad wench to talk so.

HILLARIA.

Pish! I'll have women say and do what they will.
Have not we rational souls as well as men. What
made women mopes in former ages, but being
ruled by a company of old men and women? 70
Dotage then was counted wisdom and formerly
called gravity and good behavior.

JACINTA.

What canst thou advise me to in this extremity? I
hate this foolish lord.

HILLARIA.

Let him know your mind, and if he won't believe 75
you, tell him he's an unmannerly fool.

JACINTA.

If I break with him, my father will conclude I
affect Mr. Lovell, and to cross me, never consent
I should have him. And he's the only man I can
love. 80

HILLARIA.

See! he's here, and our gallant with him; we'll
conspute[19] the business with them.

Enter Lovell, Careless.

JACINTA.

Mr. Lovell, how durst you venture here?

LOVELL.

This gentleman told me your father was to go
abroad this afternoon, and by his persuasion and 85
my own inclinations, we adventured to wait on
you, and just as we came into the street, my lord
and he passed by us in a coach.

HILLARIA.

And who sent for you, gallant?

_____

[19] conspute] dispute together

CARELESS.

I hope, madam, you'll allow a man to look after 90
his heart when 'tis gone astray.

HILLARIA.

You could not find it the last time you were here.

CARELESS.

You conspired to juggle me on't, but I know well
enough which of you had it.

JACINTA.

You are beholding to Mr. Lovell for your 95
knowledge.

LOVELL.

No, madam, upon my word, but he has told me
his adventures.

CARELESS.

Well, madam, I hope you'll stand to your bargain.

HILLARIA.

We are no flinchers; we'll not be worse than our 100
words.

CARELESS.

Well then (*Takes Jacinta by the hand.*), you I
challenge for my mistress; you were the lady I
talked to in the mask.

JACINTA.

I am not her, I'll assure you. 105

CARELESS.

I am well assured it could be none but you; I knew
it when I was here before, though I did not then
own it.

JACINTA.

Take my word, sir.

CARELESS.

Lord, that you should think to deceive me. Why, 110
all the while I was in the company before, my heart
beat all on that side you stood, and my cheek next
you burnt and glowed.

HILLARIA.

Ha, ha, 'slife,* he has not found it out yet.

CARELESS.

Hah! 115

LOVELL.

No, I'll be sworn, Careless, han't you.

CARELESS.

I'll be sworn madam, Hillaria was the person.

HILLARIA.

Ha, ha, ha! But that's my cousin Jacinta.

CARELESS.

No, no, no, did not you call her Hillaria as you
went in? 120

HILLARIA, JACINTA.

Ha, ha, ha!

HILLARIA.

I thought how well you knew and did that on
purpose to try you.

CARELESS.

Bah—

LOVELL.

Now, Careless, thou art caught. 125

CARELESS. [*Aside*.]

What would I give now to come handsomely off!
I must be impudent.—Well, madam, to let you see
that I did, go both of you out of the room and
come in masked, and if I don't choose the right,
I'll be content to resign the hopes of a mistress. 130

JACINTA.

There is but right and wrong.

CARELESS.

To give you a greater proof on't, I'll make my
choice blindfold.

HILLARIA.

'Twill still be an even wager that you hit on the
right. 135

LOVELL.

Careless, thou art outwitted, i'faith.

HILLARIA.

Servant, our covenant is void for nonperformance
of the conditions.

CARELESS.

But calling of me servant after the condition is
broken is a confirmation and will make it stand 140
good in law.

LOVELL.

No, Careless, that quirk won't do neither.

CARELESS.

But madam, I hope you'll give a man leave to retreat,
when he finds his error. Yourself occasioned the
mistake. 'Twas an error of my hand, not of my heart, 145
for at the same time I told you Hillaria was she and
you are Hillaria; therefore, 'twas you I meant.

HILLARIA.

Yes, yes, 'twas me you meant when your cheek
glowed and your heart beat on the left side!

HILLARIA, JACINTA.

Ha, ha, ha. 150

JACINTA.

Cousin, you are too great a tyrant.

LOVELL.

You pursue your victory too severely; 'tis generous
to give the vanquished quarter.

HILLARIA.

I do more; I give him liberty to make his retreat.

Enter Beatrice.

BEATRICE.

Ah madam, your father has met with his lawyer's 155
clerk, who told him his master was not at home,
and he's returned already.

JACINTA.

Convey Mr. Lovell out quickly, sir.—Will you go
with him?

BEATRICE.

'Tis not possible, madam, he's just coming into the 160
room.

JACINTA.

What shall we do?

Enter Muchworth.

MUCHWORTH.

Hah! Mr. Lovell!—Daughter, I see you observe my
commands well. Sir, I beseech you, what makes
you here? 165

LOVELL.

Sir, I come to wait on my friend.

CARELESS.

Yes sir, I had much ado to persuade him, but
considering the business I came about required
somebody to give you an account of me, which
none could do better than he, he did adventure 170
to trespass on you to serve me.

MUCHWORTH.

What business, pray sir!

HILLARIA.

Aye, what indeed?

CARELESS.

It was my fortune twice or thrice to have a sight
of your fair niece as she went abroad. 175

JACINTA. [*Aside*.]

Sure he's not so mad to tell him.

CARELESS.

To whom, sir, I took so great a liking that day nor night I could not rest till I had found who she was and where she lived—which I had no sooner done but engaged him to come along with me to acquaint you who I am and what my fortunes are, hoping to gain your leave to make my addresses to this fair lady. 180

LOVELL.

This I hope, sir, will gain me your pardon.

MUCHWORTH.

Do you, sir, know this gentleman?

LOVELL.

Yes, his name is Careless; I believe, sir, you might know his father. 185

MUCHWORTH.

I did so, he was a worthy gentleman; 'tis now some eight years since he died.

CARELESS.

'Tis so long; peace be with him.

MUCHWORTH.

He left some twelve hundred a year[20] to his son, then not at age. 190

LOVELL.

This gentleman is that son.

MUCHWORTH.

But has he that estate?

CARELESS.

Every acre, sir.

MUCHWORTH.

I heard you were a little wild. 195

CARELESS.

I have my frolics as most young men have, but I keep my estate out of the devil's clutches; I have yet not sold one foot of land or cut down one stick of wood.

MUCHWORTH.

Nay sir, if you were as wild as wild could be, you'd meet with your match there; my niece is as wild as you can be: she's vain, idle, careless, and talkative. 200

HILLARIA.

Uncle, you should do in driving bargains for marriage as they do in selling of horses: tell their good qualities, and leave it to 'em to find out the ill. 205

MUCHWORTH.

These are faults will be discovered in you at first sight.

HILLARIA.

Sir, I hope you'll like me ne'er the worse for what he says.

MUCHWORTH.

Instead of his getting you for a wife, you intend to get him for a husband. 210

HILLARIA.

It is more to the humor of the age. If you won't commend me, I'll commend myself. And if I thought but half so well of him as I do of myself, we'd soon shake hands for to have and to hold without your leave. 215

MUCHWORTH.

You see her humor,* sir. If after this you dare venture on her, I shall not counsel her against you, provided what Mr. Lovell and yourself say be confirmed by good authors,[21] for I wish her well married. 220

HILLARIA.

Stay uncle, now I think on't, you may take him with you. Marriage is quite out of fashion, and I hate to be out of it as much as you do to be in't. If he had ten or twelve thousand a year, would keep me a coach and six horses and all things suitable to that grandeur, I might admit him as a gallant, and all that. 225

MUCHWORTH.

I'll leave you to her; at this mad rate she talks all the year round. (*Exit.*) 230

LOVELL.

I did not think, Careless, thou hadst had a lie so much at command.

CARELESS.

It was to serve my friend and these ladies.

HILLARIA.

But the jest would be if your lie should prove true and you should play such a simple trick as to fall in love with me indeed and indeed. 235

CARELESS.

Make your own words true and accept me for a gallant, I know not what may follow.

---

20 twelve ... year] that is, an estate that generates such an amount per year in revenues

21 authors] those who can avouch on good authority

HILLARIA.

But you know what you must have first—a huge
estate. But because you brought us so handsomely
off, there's my hand to kiss, and I confer on you
the title of my servant.

JACINTA.

He cured a present evil. I wish he could as easily
divert what I fear will follow.

CARELESS.

Madam, we must court Fortune as we do a
mistress; never leave her when she's in a good
humor. Let's hear your grievance.

JACINTA.

'Tis the match my father drives on so eagerly with
that lord.

CARELESS.

Will he not be satisfied if you tell him you can't
love him?

HILLARIA.

He'll not take that answer from her nor ne'er a
woman alive.

JACINTA.

He thinks we are both in love with him.

HILLARIA.

Since dinner I writ a love letter to him; I have
made him believe, too, that the rich heiress that
lodges in this street languishes for him.

JACINTA.

And he pities her extremely.

CARELESS.

Hark you, Lovell, let's put him upon courting this
great fortune.

LOVELL.

But it may be he'll not quit his hold here.

CARELESS.

For so great an advantage he may. And it must be
your parts, ladies, to give him sufficient grounds
to conclude that neither of you love him.

HILLARIA.

Let us alone to give him proof of that.

CARELESS.

Then we will contrive to bring him in disgrace
with your father. Lady of the bedchamber, you
must act a part in our comedy. Attend us to the
door; you shall receive instructions as we go.

*Exeunt Careless, Lovell, Beatrice. Enter Muchworth,
De Boastado.*

JACINTA.

Here's my father; let us retreat and consult about
our affairs.

DE BOASTADO.

You know this lady, I suppose.

MUCHWORTH.

I have seen her, but I am very well acquainted with
her uncle.

DE BOASTADO.

And has she so great a fortune?

MUCHWORTH.

Yes, it lies in the three bankers' hands we were but
now speaking of.

DE BOASTADO.

I know it does, for when I parted with you, I made
inquiry, and they confirmed it. She lodges in the
middle of this street. Mrs. Rich is her name.

MUCHWORTH.

Right. But my lord, do you think she has so great
a kindness* for you?

DE BOASTADO.

I speak not without good reason, and were I not
engaged by love and honor to your daughter, I
would make an attempt.

MUCHWORTH.

Her uncle trusts her not out of his sight.

DE BOASTADO.

I could find ways to speak to her, but I prize Mrs.
Jacinta above all women. Though there are others
have no small kindness* for my person,* and one
you know, too, but she shall be nameless. Yet I'll
show you what a passionate letter she sent me. You
shall hear it. (*Reads.*) "My lord: Your person* is so
taking and your obligements so conquering, that no
woman living, and you beholding, can resist loving.
Therefore, since of this you are knowing, I doubt
not your pardoning her, that with blushing tells you
her ailing—the joy of whose being, is, when you she
is seeing. Yours remaining for everlasting."

MUCHWORTH.

This is a very odd strain.

DE BOASTADO.

Ah, 'tis very amorous, and I pity the lady for your
sake.

MUCHWORTH.

Is she related to me!

DE BOASTADO.

The first letter of her name is Hillaria.

MUCHWORTH. [*Aside.*]

My niece. This is some trick of hers, but I dare
not tell him he's abused, lest he should take it ill   305
and think my daughter had a hand in't.—But of
all that love you, your lordship can have but one.

DE BOASTADO.

True. Yet 'twould vex a man to discard trumps, but
'tis a forced put.[22] This I tell you to give you a
proof of my love for your daughter. I know, poor   310
thing, she loves me.

Hillaria and Jacinta appear.

JACINTA.

My lord! You're a happy man, we have overheard
your amours.

DE BOASTADO.

I did not think you had been so nigh.

JACINTA.

Without doubt, you were wrapped in your   315
mother's smock.[23]

HILLARIA.

Hey ho!

DE BOASTADO. [*Aside.*]

Observe that sigh, and how she eyes me.—Lady,
you're melancholy.

HILLARIA.

You called my thoughts from a pleasing   320
contemplation. I was thinking—

DE BOASTADO.

Of what madam?

HILLARIA.

Of you, my lord.

DE BOASTADO.

I saw you look wishly[24] on me.

HILLARIA.

I was thinking what good eyes your lordship has.   325

---

22 forced put] an unavoidable action
23 wrapped … smock] a catch-phrase used for men, meaning "born lucky," with particular reference to sexual success
24 wishly] intently, steadfastly

JACINTA.

Oh fine eyes! if they stood but more out and were
not sunk in's head, like candle-snuffs[25] in their
sockets.

HILLARIA.

And did not squint so much.

DE BOASTADO.

Mine, mine, ladies.   330

MUCHWORTH.

Why, baggages—

JACINTA.

He has a handsome nose, too.

HILLARIA.

Was it not an inch too short.

JACINTA.

And turned up at the end with the air of a French   335
dog.

DE BOASTADO.

How's this?

MUCHWORTH.

Why girls, what mean you?

HILLARIA.

Pretty good cheeks—were they not so lean and pale!

JACINTA.

And fallen in for want of side-teeth.   340

MUCHWORTH.

The devil's in 'em both.

JACINTA.

A handsome mouth, were it not so wide.

HILLARIA.

And his lips not so thin and bluish.

DE BOASTADO.

I am abused.

MUCHWORTH.

Have done, or I'll lay my staff about your ears.   345

JACINTA.

His gums not so worn away.

HILLARIA.

And his teeth not so rotten.

JACINTA.

His mouth not so furred.[26]

HILLARIA.

His breath not so scented with the French hogoe.*

---

25 candle-snuffs] the burnt wicks of candles
26 furred] encrusted, coated with morbid matter

DE BOASTADO.

Disgrace to my dignity. 350

MUCHWORTH.

They are mad, distracted. They know not what they do.

HILLARIA.

He's leather-jawed—chapfallen.

JACINTA.

And has a swarthy, tawny, tallow complexion.

MUCHWORTH.

Peace and have done, in the devil's name. 355

JACINTA.

In fine, was your lordship but ten times as handsome, you'd be a pretty well-favored man.

HILLARIA.

And fit to be loved, by a woman of sixty and upwards.

DE BOASTADO.

Intolerable, insufferable, insupportable! 360

MUCHWORTH.

Ho! Within there!

Enter Beatrice.

BEATRICE.

What's the matter?

MUCHWORTH.

You huswifes[27] you, say you are mad, say you are drunk, or anything, or I'll swinge you.

HILLARIA.

No, no, uncle, we are neither mad nor drunk. 365

MUCHWORTH.

Hussy, your reason for this.

JACINTA.

Why does he make his brags that we are in love with him and so fond of his company?

HILLARIA.

We have given him proofs of our kindness.* In love with him! 370

MUCHWORTH.

Get you up to your chambers, go! Husbands? halters you deserve.

Exeunt Hillaria, Jacinta, [Beatrice].

---

27 huswifes] used so in the 17th century, a term denoting not housewives but impertinent girls; hussy for short

Have patience, be pacified, the baggages shall down on their knees to you.

DE BOASTADO.

Ha, ha, ha! This is only to blind you. Ha, ha, ha, 375 'twas your niece's frolic; they love me as they love their own eyes. And because I told you on't—ha, ha, ha—see what tricks they play to cozen you, ha, ha, ha.

MUCHWORTH.

I'll instantly know the truth on't or— (*Exit.*) 380

DE BOASTADO.

Henceforward, I will hate their whole sex for their sakes. I will defame the living, revile the dead, and leave a curse to the generation of females to come.

Enter Beatrice.

BEATRICE.

My lord, my lord—

DE BOASTADO.

Avoid, thou she-devil; thou art a Satan in 385 petticoats.

BEATRICE.

Ah my lord, if you knew my errand, you'd say I was an angel, I have such news for your lordship.

DE BOASTADO.

News! What is't?

BEATRICE.

If a woman might but trust your lordship with her 390 secrets.

DE BOASTADO. [*Aside.*]

I hope she's in love with me; she's a bit will serve to stay a man's stomach when he's hungry.—What secrets, pretty Beatrice? Dost thou love me?

BEATRICE.

Ah dearly, dearly, my lord, but— 395

DE BOASTADO.

But you are ashamed to tell me your mind.

BEATRICE.

I am afraid—

DE BOASTADO.

Thou shouldst have a great belly.

BEATRICE.

No, my lord, that you should tell—

DE BOASTADO.

No, I'll tell nobody; go, go up to your chamber, 400 and I'll steal after you.

BEATRICE.

No my lord, I can do the business here.

DE BOASTADO.

Art thou a virgin?

BEATRICE.

As to deeds, a very innocent, but in words and
thoughts, I have been a little waggish.   405

DE BOASTADO.

Come into the next room.

BEATRICE.

No, no, I am only to tell you—

DE BOASTADO.

No matter for telling, we will talk afterwards.

BEATRICE.

See this gold, my lord, here are twenty pieces.

DE BOASTADO.

And you would have as much more.   410

BEATRICE.

I shall deserve it.

DE BOASTADO.

Wilt thou go then? go.

BEATRICE.

This gold, my lord, was given me.

DE BOASTADO.

For that, that thou hast more mind I should have.

BEATRICE.

No, my lord, it was given me to betray my mistress.   415

DE BOASTADO.

Hau—Who has plots upon her body?

BEATRICE.

Nobody; it was given me to deprive her of you,
my lord.

DE BOASTADO.

What mean'st thou?

BEATRICE.

To tell your lordship that—But I am so afraid, you   420
should tell again.

DE BOASTADO.

I'll be secret, on my honor.

BEATRICE.

That there is a rich heiress not far off in love with
your lordship.

DE BOASTADO.

Humh—And is not this a plot laid—   425

BEATRICE.

Yes, my lord, 'tis a plot laid.

DE BOASTADO.

To betray me?

BEATRICE.

Yes, my lord.

DE BOASTADO.

And you'll discover* it.

BEATRICE.

To none but your lordship: It is to betray you— But   430
will your lordship be sure not to speak on't again?

DE BOASTADO.

I will not.

BEATRICE.

To betray your lordship into a marriage with this
great fortune.

DE BOASTADO.

How!   435

BEATRICE.

I am to tell her name, too, and how you shall come
to see her, for all the dragon her uncle, and how
you shall steal a marriage and all.

DE BOASTADO.

What say'st thou, Beatrice?

BEATRICE.

Nothing but truth: Her name is Mrs. Rich, she   440
lives in this street and is sick in bed for love of you.
She sent for me and gave me this gold, with
promise of much more, if I would be true to her
and acquaint you with her condition and be
instrumental in helping her to see you.   445

DE BOASTADO.

How, Beatrice, may I come to the sight of her?

BEATRICE.

She has bribed her physician to join in the
conspiracy; he will pretend to bring an able doctor
of his acquaintance to see her, that with him he
may consult of her disease and cure. You are to be   450
this physician, and the parson[b] in the habit of an
apothecary—which you are to provide, for we
know none.

DE BOASTADO.

Let me alone for that!

BEATRICE.

Then if your lordship like her, you may there   455
marry her.

DE BOASTADO.

A very neat invention! Oh subtle woman!

BEATRICE.

    This, my lord, was my plot.

DE BOASTADO.

    'Tis well laid.

BEATRICE.

    She has promised I shall live with her when I am   460
married.

DE BOASTADO.

    Thou shalt. But Beatrice, thou'lt keep thy
maiden[28] for me, wilt thou not?

BEATRICE.

    If I find you can keep secrets, I will trust your
lordship with anything.   465

DE BOASTADO.

    I knew thou didst love me better than thy mistress
or her flirting cousin. Well, were it not for what
thou hast told me, their affronts would drive me
to my country house, where I'd live like a hermit
and leave half the Town languishing.   470

BEATRICE.

    You would leave many a lady bleeding. But I hope
your lordship is better natured and more just than
to revenge the faults of a few upon the whole sex.
I'll go put my affairs in a posture for my getting
abroad to wait on your lordship.   475

DE BOASTADO.

    And I the meantime will disengage myself from all
concerns here and to Jacinta's father resign the
interest he gave me in her.

BEATRICE. [*Aside.*]

    Go thy ways, Lord Credulous. How greedily he
swallows the bait with which he was caught before.   480
A fool will often run into the snare,
But once escaped, the wise man does beware.

Exeunt.

    Act IV, scene i. Hall continues.

Enter De Boastado, Muchworth, Jacinta.

MUCHWORTH.

    Come huswife, ask forgiveness. (*Threatens Jacinta
with his cane.*)

JACINTA.

    I have, sir.

---

28 maiden] maidenhead; virginity

MUCHWORTH.

    But on your knees.

JACINTA.

    Sir.   5

MUCHWORTH.

    Quickly down, down on your knees, baggage.

Enter Hillaria with a cane in her hand.

HILLARIA.

    Courage, cousin Jacinta, I am come to your aid.
Look you uncle, I have got as tough a cane as
yours.

MUCHWORTH.

    Get you out of my doors, huswife.—So, down,   10
down on your knees.

JACINTA.

    I do, sir. (*Kneels.*)

HILLARIA.

    Down, my lord, come you must down too.

DE BOASTADO.

    Hold! hold! hold!

MUCHWORTH.

    Why niece—   15

HILLARIA.

    Nay, 'tis very true uncle, if you lay't on there, I'll
lay't on here with a vengeance. Down on your
marrowbones.

DE BOASTADO.

    Why look you, lady, to serve you— (*Kneels.*)

MUCHWORTH.

    Get you out of my doors; get you out of my house.   20

HILLARIA.

    Nay uncle, keep off, I am resolved to stand upon
my guard.

MUCHWORTH.

    Get you gone, I say, and never come near me more.

HILLARIA.

    But don't you think to domineer when I am gone.
If I hear you do, I'll have a bout too with you   25
uncle, as old a cock of the game as you are, I'll
have a sparring blow too with you.

*Enter Beatrice and Toby following in a disguise, a suit
of four quarters, representing the four parts of the
world, with his head habited[c] like a Spaniard.*

BEATRICE.

Here's a stranger inquires for you, my lord.

HILLARIA.

Here's a cavalier to defend us; cudgel, lie thou there. 30

TOBY.

I am your humble, my lord.

DE BOASTADO.

Sir, I am yours.

TOBY.

I have had the honor to see your lordship in many countries abroad, and you appeared so pleasing to me, that returning from travel, I could not but take 35 England in my way (though I had formerly lived here six years) that I might receive the honor of kissing your hand and making myself familiar in your lordship's acquaintance.

DE BOASTADO.

Which I covet abundantly. A traveler cannot but 40 be worthy my knowledge. I venerate a pilgrim's shoe as much as they do saints, whose shrines they go to visit, because it hath trod the dust of many countries. Shall I beg cognizance of your name, *Signior*. 45

TOBY.

My name is *Signior Simplaio, Folio del no no, Witesso At-Allo*.

MUCHWORTH.

Bless me!

HILLARIA.

The count's name is but monosyllable to this.

DE BOASTADO.

This is a noble family, as I take it. 50

JACINTA. [*Aside*.]

And you are a great fool for your pains.

TOBY.

'Tis a very noble one in Spain. I was born at Castile, christened at Rome, educated in Paris, returned to Italy, left my virginity at Venice, sailed from thence to Constantinople, traveled to 55 Jerusalem, and there I first shaved my beard.

HILLARIA.

Uncle, he may well have a long name that went as far as Rome to be christened.

MUCHWORTH.

He appears to be a great traveler.

JACINTA.

His face shows it. 60

HILLARIA.

He has indeed a right olive complexion, which is a sign he has been much in the sun.

TOBY.

My lord, I hope you'll command my pardon for this gentleman and these ladies if my respects to your lordship makes me appear uncivil to them. 65

MUCHWORTH.

Not in the least. My lord merits all.

TOBY.

My lord, don't you remember to have seen me in your travels?

DE BOASTADO.

I begin to call you to mind: as I take it, I saw you in the court of Spain. 70

TOBY.

Right, you did so; I was then playing a game at chess with the king!

DE BOASTADO.

And at Vienna, the Emperor's court.

TOBY.

The Emperor and I, the first morning I saw you there, were at tennis. I remember I lost a set for a 75 thousand pistoles to satisfy my curiosity of looking upon your lordship; that was the second time I had the honor to see you.

MUCHWORTH.

This is a great person; behave yourselves with respect. 80

DE BOASTADO.

And as I take it, I saw you as I accompanied Cardinal Palavincina, the pope's nephew, to the consistory; I was at that time in his coach.

TOBY.

I think you were, and I well remember, I rid with His Holiness in his. And your lordship gave me 85 the grace of a bow, which I returned your lordship with so great obeisance that, had not His Holiness caught hold on me behind, I had tumbled out o'er the boot of the coach.

DE BOASTADO.

You did much honor my civilities. 90

TOBY.

Now we have increased our acquaintance, I'll

obtrude the trouble on you to go with me to Court
some day and present me to the king that I may
have the honor to kiss his hand.

DE BOASTADO.

I swell with the ambition of waiting on so noble a   95
cavaliero; now I perfectly remember you.

Enter Lovell.

LOVELL.

I beg your pardon.

DE BOASTADO.

Sir, pray advance, here's only a noble stranger, one
that's a great traveler and of my former acquaintance; he's worth your knowledge. Oh Sir *Cavaliero*,   100
pray receive this gentleman into your arms.

LOVELL.

Hah! sure I know that habit—hah—sirrah—you
rogue, what make you here?

DE BOASTADO.

Sir! Your language is too bold.

MUCHWORTH.

You take too great a liberty to affront any man in   105
my house; besides, he's a man of quality.*

LOVELL.

I'll fetch his qualities out of him, with a pox to
him. (*Beats Toby.*)

TOBY.

Ah good sir, hold sir, or you'll make a discovery.*

LOVELL.

Ah sir, I'll make you discover what tricks you are   110
playing here. (*Strikes him.*)

DE BOASTADO, MUCHWORTH.

Hold, hold, sir, hold—

TOBY.

Ah, ah, good sir—nay sir—good sir—pray, good
master.

DE BOASTADO, MUCHWORTH.

How!   115

JACINTA, HILLARIA, BEATRICE.

Ha, ha, ha, he!

TOBY.

Ah sir, I ask you forgiveness on my knees.

LOVELL.

Sirrah, what makes you loitering here, when I send
you about business?

TOBY.

Ah Lord, sir, I only put on your masquerading suit   120
to come to Mrs.* Beatrice in, to see if she could
know me!

HILLARIA, JACINTA, BEATRICE.

Ha, ha, ha, he! Toby! Ha, ha, ha, ha.

LOVELL.

I thought I should find you here. Go, get you
home, you rogue, go.   125

DE BOASTADO. [*Aside.*]

Would I was gone too.

WOMEN.

Ha, ha, ha!

HILLARIA.

My lord, won't you follow and wait on your
cavaliero to kiss the king's hand? Ha, ha, ha.

DE BOASTADO. (*A forced laugh.*)

Ha, ha, ha, ha.   130

JACINTA.

Your lordship saw him in Spain, Germany and
Rome. Ha, ha, ha.

HILLARIA.

And bowed to him out of the cardinal's coach. Ha,
ha, ha.

DE BOASTADO.

Ha, ha, ha.   135

MUCHWORTH.

I am amazed. Ha, ha, ha.

LOVELL.

What mean you, ladies?

DE BOASTADO.

Ladies, gentlemen: a good jest—ha, ha, ha—laugh
at it, ha, ha—laugh heartily, ha, ha, ha.

JACINTA, BEATRICE.

Ha, ha, ha.   140

DE BOASTADO.

He's a witty knave, ha, ha, ha, my sides will burst
with laughing. Ha, ha, ha.

LOVELL.

I am afraid the rogue has played some unlucky
trick.

DE BOASTADO.

No, no—ha, ha, ha, a jest, a very good jest, ha,   145
ha, ha. I protest my laughing has made me sick.
I'll take my leave, sir.

MUCHWORTH.

Beatrice, fetch in a bottle of sack.* My lord, pray drink a glass of sack if you're not well.

[Exit Beatrice.]

DE BOASTADO.

No matter.   150

MUCHWORTH.

Oh, by all means! My lord, how came you to be so mistaken in him?

DE BOASTADO.

There was a noble cavalier, that I often met in my travels, sir, like this knave, ha, ha, ha. I protest, I thought it had been he. Well sir, your man's a witty   155 knave.

LOVELL.

I am glad he has made you all merry; I was afraid he had played the rogue, for which, I would have so beat him. My lord, your servant; your servant, sir; ladies, your servant. (*Exit.*)   160

Knocking within. Enter Beatrice.

MUCHWORTH.

Come Beatrice, fill my lord a glass of sack. See who knocks at the door, Beatrice.

De Boastado drinks.

BEATRICE. (*Goes to the door.*)

Here's a woman would speak with my lord.

MUCHWORTH.

Bid her come in.

Enter Mrs. Breedwell [and] Jenny, Sarah, two children.

BREEDWELL.

Hah! Have I found you at last? Are you come   165 again, after so many years' absence? Could you, wicked man, think to forsake me forever?

DE BOASTADO.

What means the woman!

BREEDWELL.

Ah, hard-hearted lord, you know well enough what I mean! Can you see me and not blush? Was it for   170 this that you pretended love to me and caused my poor parents to break off my marriage with the vicar's son? And did you marry me yourself only to leave me and make me wretched?

MUCHWORTH.

How's this?   175

JACINTA, HILLARIA.

Married!

DE BOASTADO.

Woman! What in the devil's name dost thou mean?

BREEDWELL.

I mean your going away and leaving of me after you had married me: as soon as you saw me with child, you pretended business to London. You left me   180 money to keep me six months, but before the time expired, you ran beyond sea without letting me know whither you were gone, not sending me anything to maintain me in that condition. And to increase my misfortunes, I had two children at a birth.   185

MUCHWORTH.

Does not your lordship know her?

DE BOASTADO.

An impudent quean! I never saw her before. I know her not.

BREEDWELL.

Not know your own wife! Shameless lord! You are a dishonor to the womb that bare you. Have my   190 cares and miseries this seven years so altered me, that you don't know me? Yes, you know me, but you won't. Ah that I had never known you, then I should not have known sorrow. You were in hopes it would break my heart, but I live to plague you.   195

JACINTA.

Alas, poor woman!

BREEDWELL.

Heaven help us poor wretches, if we must have such hard fortune! To be forsaken by our husbands and left without money in our pocket, clothes to the back, and meat or drink for the belly.   200

DE BOASTADO.

The woman's distracted; send her to Bedlam.

MUCHWORTH.

The woman talks sensibly.

BREEDWELL.

Ah! How dost think I have maintained myself and these two poor children these six years and more. E'en with the work of my own hands, God help   205 me. (*Cries.*)

HILLARIA.

Alas, poor woman!

JACINTA.

It grieves me to see her weep.

MUCHWORTH.

What should this mean?

HILLARIA.

It appears by the story that she's his wife! 210

DE BOASTADO.

Not my wife, I protest.

Knocking at door.

BEATRICE.

Here's another woman with child inquires for my lord.

Enter Clappam [and] Tommie, a child, as out of breath.

CLAPPAM.

Let me come in—hau, hau—I am almost dead; I am out of breath—oh wicked man, it is after you 215 that I run thus up and down, hau, hau, hau. But now I have found you, you shall not escape me.

DE BOASTADO.

What mean'st thou now?

CLAPPAM.

I mean to cross your marriage; you thought I was dead or far enough from England ne'er to trouble 220 you more, did you?

MUCHWORTH.

What's your business?

CLAPPAM.

Ah, that wretch of a husband there, that unnatural wretch: he sold his own wife, sold his child, sold his own flesh and blood. 225

MUCHWORTH.

This is some mistake.

HILLARIA.

Are you his wife?

CLAPPAM.

Yes, madam, he married me and carried me from my friends; he carried me with him beyond sea, and when he got me there and I began to grow 230 big with child, he pretended to send me by sea to England to live with my friends till he returned. But instead of that, I was carried to Japan; he had sold me to the master of the ship, who was a Dutchman. He sold me, and this poor child that 235 was in my belly, to slavery and bondage.

BREEDWELL.

Which do you say is your husband?

CLAPPAM.

E'en this; this is he, let him deny't if he can.

BREEDWELL.

No, 'tis I am his wife.

CLAPPAM.

You his wife too! What, has the wretch two wives? 240 That will hang him.

BREEDWELL.

Hang him? no, you're none of his wife.

CLAPPAM.

Yes, he is my husband.

BREEDWELL.

I say, he is my husband, and I can prove it.

DE BOASTADO.

Are ye both possessed? I am husband to neither 245 of ye.

BREEDWELL.

We have been married this seven years.

CLAPPAM.

It is six, since he married me.

BREEDWELL.

Is this true, you wicked lord?

DE BOASTADO.

Yes, yes, one's as true as the other. 250

BREEDWELL.

Ah shameless man! Dost thou confess thou hast two wives? Come hither, little Jenny, come hither, Sarah. Look you, these are the fruits of our marriage.

CLAPPAM.

And here's my child too.

BREEDWELL.

Look here upon these two sweet babies. 255

CLAPPAM.

And look here too: here's thy own flesh and blood which thou didst so barbarously sell.

DE BOASTADO.

Never were two such impudent carrions seen.

HILLARIA.

They are as like you, my lord—

BREEDWELL.

Yes, lady, and so they are. 260

JACINTA.

This has the very eyes and mouth of him; he is so like his lordship.

MUCHWORTH.

They are sweet children indeed.

DE BOASTADO.

Ye all dream; they are neither like me, nor pretty, nor nothing. 265

BREEDWELL.

Kneel, Jenny, kneel down, little Sarah, and ask father blessing, and let's see if he can be so unnatural to disown you.

CLAPPAM.

And do you kneel, Tommie, ask blessing; 'tis thy own daddy. 270

THREE CHILDREN.

Father, father, father.

DE BOASTADO.

The devil take you for whore's-birds.

THREE CHILDREN.

Father, father, father.

BREEDWELL.

Don't you think to be gone and leave them; I'll follow you and proclaim it to all the world. 275

CLAPPAM.

And I'll haunt you where'er you go; I'll be satisfied, if she is your wife too, and if I find it true, I'll have recourse to justice; you shall be hanged, if all the law in England will hang you, for having two wives.

THREE CHILDREN.

Father, father. 280

BREEDWELL, CLAPPAM.

Justice, justice, justice, etc.

THREE CHILDREN.d

Father, father, father, etc.

BEATRICE. [Aside.]

Now must I bestir myself.

De Boastado, Clappam, three children, Beatrice run out.

MUCHWORTH.

I am so amazed, I know not what to think of all that we have seen and heard. 285

JACINTA.

They are both his wives for certain.

HILLARIA.

This would have been a fine husband for my cousin. Now uncle, are you beholden to Fortune, or your wisdom, for her deliverance? Cousin, let me choose a husband for you the next time. 290

MUCHWORTH.

Jacinta, be not ruled by her nor hearken to her counsel but on all occasions show all ready compliance to my commands. For you, niece, you may stay in my house. I forgive you.

HILLARIA.

Ah uncle, and I pardon you. Come old man, let's 295 shake hands; you see I am good-natured. So now we are all friends.

MUCHWORTH.

Well, I must be gone abroad.

HILLARIA.

Fare you well, uncle.

Exit Muchworth.

Now he's gone, we'll be gone too. Come cousin, 300 we'll spend this afternoon in a frolic: we'll go see a play at the Nursery;[29] I'll put on the boy's habit I made for a masquerading suit.

JACINTA.

Let's go in our scarves, vizards, and masks.

HILLARIA.

You shall, but I'll have my own humor: I'll cock 305 and strut and so hector the young cits,* if they come to disturb us with their impertinences—

Exeunt Hillaria, Jacinta.

Scene ii. [Street in front of a
tavern in]e Covent Garden.

Enter Careless and Lovell, meeting.

LOVELL.

You come luckily; our plot succeeds rarely.

CARELESS.

Have we routed the enemy?

LOVELL.

Horse and foot; he'll ne'er be able to appear in the field again.

CARELESS.

Our new alderman Rich and his niece are ready 5 to receive 'em if he comes.

LOVELL.

His wives followed him so close, I am afraid they have scared his lordship out of Town, if not out of's wits.

29 Nursery] a training house for actors

CARELESS.

　　We must find out Beatrice and recover him, for 10
all things are so well prepared—

LOVELL.

　　She's after him where'er he is. But by what means
have you compassed the business we last spoke of?

CARELESS.

　　I sent a letter, as from an unknown friend, to the
alderman to let him know there was an appointment 15
made by his niece and some gallants to steal her
away tonight; this he easily believed, because 'tis but
what he always fears and is jealous of. He presently
out of pretense to carry her abroad in's coach to take
the air has conveyed her to his country house, which 20
is but eight miles from London.

LOVELL.

　　Good.

CARELESS.

　　This the landlady told me, for she's my friend, and
I have feed her to let a lady of my acquaintance
have the command of the lodging for this night, 25
and thither I have conveyed our counterfeit heiress.

LOVELL.

　　And Toby is now a grave alderman.

CARELESS.

　　I sent him one of her uncle's old suits, which I
borrowed of the landlady.

LOVELL.

　　He's at the tavern here waiting for orders. 30

Enter Beatrice.

　　Here's Beatrice now.

CARELESS.

　　But where's my lord?

BEATRICE.

　　In my pursuit I saw him give his pursuers the dodge.
I gave 'em the sign to make a fault; he turned clear
back this way, and they keep at a distance, and I am 35
come a nearer way to meet him here.

LOVELL.

　　We are ready to receive him.

Enter De Boastado.

BEATRICE.

　　That's well. Here he comes. Let's slip in there that
he may not see us together. (*They retire.*)

DE BOASTADO.

　　With much ado I have at length got clear of 'em. 40
The jades and their bawling bastards—father,
father, father—I have run myself almost out of
breath.

Beatrice appears.

BEATRICE.

　　I am glad I have found you, my lord; I have run
myself almost off my legs to o'ertake ye. 45

DE BOASTADO.

　　Pox o'th'whores, my shirt sticks to my back.

BEATRICE.

　　But my lord, are you married to any of 'em?

DE BOASTADO.

　　Oh the devil! Not I.

BEATRICE.

　　Nor promised 'em marriage neither?

DE BOASTADO.

　　Not I. 50

BEATRICE.

　　If it should appear so hereafter, it would be an
injury to the lady, and I would not have a hand
in doing her any wrong for the world. I love her
as my life!

DE BOASTADO.

　　I never saw either of 'em before. Upon my honor, 55
I did not.

BEATRICE.

　　Now I believe your lordship, but if anything of this
should come to the lady's ear, it would ruin our
design.

DE BOASTADO.

　　But I hope she'll not hear't so soon. 60

BEATRICE.

　　We must outfly report. Come my lord, let's
instantly about it to prevent danger—

DE BOASTADO.

　　But I have got no parson yet.

BEATRICE.

　　It can't be helped. I hear her uncle will be abroad
all this afternoon, and we'll persuade her to 65
counterfeit a fit of illness, and the doctor shall tell
the landlady and the servants that she must
presently take the air, or she'll die; that she has an
oppression of spirits about her heart; and that the

jogging of a coach will relieve her. And when we   70
get her abroad, we know what to do.

DE BOASTADO.

Yet I wish we had a parson ready, for fear her uncle
should be at home or come in by accident; then
we might do't, and he in the house.

BEATRICE.

At worst, you may contract, and break a piece of   75
gold betwixt you.[30]

THREE CHILDREN. (*Within.*)

Father, father, father.

DE BOASTADO.

Hark! The beagles follow us; they have taken the
scent afresh and come with a full cry.

THREE CHILDREN. (*Within.*)

Father, father, father.   80

BEATRICE.

The cry comes this way. Follow me with all the haste
you can, that they not come within view of us.

*Exeunt De Boastado, Beatrice. Enter Mrs. Breedwell
and Clappam.*

BREEDWELL.

So, now the children are sent home, let's to the
place of rendezvous.

CLAPPAM.

Here's the tavern, enter.   85

Exeunt to the tavern. Lovell and Careless appear.

CARELESS.

Come Lovell, they are gone to the tavern to look
for us.

LOVELL.

I am the worst man i'th'world to converse with this
sort of cattle.

CARELESS.

Thou ought'st to be civil to 'em upon account of   90
the kindness they have done for thee at my request.

LOVELL.

Will not my money excuse my company?

CARELESS.

Did not I condescend to visit a pair of honest
women at your request? Aye, and visit them a

second time? and can you in conscience refuse to   95
accompany me now?

LOVELL.

Your first visit was made by my persuasions, but
the second was the effect of your own inclinations.

CARELESS.

Well, but come along, if you like not your
company, be gone as soon as you will.   100

Exeunt Lovell, Careless. Enter Hillaria and Jacinta.

HILLARIA.

'Tis e'en so: your lover and my gallant are gone in
after 'em. We'll put off our frolic of going to the
Nursery, and I'll adventure into the tavern to see
after what manner they treat 'em.

JACINTA.

But should they know you—   105

HILLARIA.

They know me? they can't in this disguise, but if
they do, 'twill pass for a frolic.

Exeunt.

Scene iii. [A tavern.]

Enter Mrs. Breedwell, Clappam, drawer.

DRAWER.

What wine do you please to drink, ladies?

BREEDWELL.

Sack and claret. Is it good?

DRAWER.

We have as good as any is in England.

CLAPPAM.

But you son of a whore, shall we have any of it?

DRAWER.

I'll bring you that shall please you. (*Exit.*)   5

*Breedwell and Clappam both sing and dance about.
Enter Lovell and Careless, singing.*

Song.

I found a thief a managing
My natural* on a chair,
I pulled out Focus[31] speedily—

CARELESS.

Hah! Merry lasses!

---

30 break ... you] a folk custom signifying betrothal

31 Focus] name for a sword, with bawdy connotations

CLAPPAM.

    As merry as birds in a fair morning.   10

BREEDWELL.

    Or crickets in a warm chimney.

LOVELL.

    Fill some wine boy.—This will increase your mirth.
    (*Drinks.*)

BREEDWELL.

    Here, Careless, you son of a whore, here's to you.

CARELESS.

    I thank you Mrs. Breedwell.   15

LOVELL.

    Lady, my service to you—

CLAPPAM.

    Damn your compliment. "My service to you"—
    you'd have said as much as that to an honest woman.

LOVELL.

    Ladies, I can't talk at your rate,[32] but if you are
    for downright drinking, have at you.   20

CLAPPAM.

    Here, Careless, you damned, confounded dog, give
    me your hand.

BREEDWELL.

    Pray mind your own intrigue; we are agreed.

CLAPPAM.

    Mrs. Breedwell, what right have you to choose
    your man before me?   25

BREEDWELL.

    I have been acquainted with him longer than you.

CLAPPAM.

    Mr. Careless, do you like a woman e'er the better
    for being an old acquaintance?

BREEDWELL.

    He chose me, and that's a sign he likes me better
    than you.   30

CARELESS.

    I took the first that came to my hand.

CLAPPAM.

    Yes, she's so forward.

LOVELL.

    I am then shut out for a wrangler.

BREEDWELL.

    Rot your humor!* That you'll be so disobliging to
    any gentleman.   35

---

32 rate] in your idiom

CLAPPAM.

    He's as dull as an alderman.

Enter drawer.

DRAWER.

    Madam! There's a young gentleman at the door
    desires to speak with you.

Clappam goes to door.

CARELESS.

    Come Lovell, here's both their healths to you.

[Enter Hillaria.]

HILLARIA.

    Madam, I had a sight of you as you came upstairs   40
    and was extremely taken with you. Pray oblige me
    so far as to own me for your acquaintance and
    introduce me into the company, which I much
    desire, for your sake.

CLAPPAM.

    Sir, you may command me.—Lord 'tis the prettiest   45
    man.—Nay sir, you shall come in. Here are none
    but friends.

LOVELL.

    Sir, you must not refuse a lady's invitation.

HILLARIA.

    I fear I shall be uncivil.

CARELESS.

    That you can hardly be in our company.   50

LOVELL.

    Sir, these ladies' healths to you.

HILLARIA.

    Come on, sir; ladies, to your good healths.

BREEDWELL.

    And here's Mr. Lovell's health.

CLAPPAM.

    I am ready to pledge it.

LOVELL.

    And to make it go down the pleasanter, there's that   55
    to sweeten your wine and yours. (*Puts four or five*
    guineas into the glass.)

CLAPPAM.

    Were we but sure such sand lay at the bottom of
    the sea, we'd drink the ocean off.

BREEDWELL.

    Look you, sir.   60

LOVELL.

And now ladies, I thank you for the good service
you have done for me.

BREEDWELL.

Will you leave us then?

LOVELL.

My absence is no injury now you have got another
man.   65

CLAPPAM.

But sir—

LOVELL.

And I have a little business.

HILLARIA.

Damn business, when wine and women are in the
case.

LOVELL.

It is of great concern.   70

HILLARIA.

Sir, can there be affairs of greater importance than
drinking and wenching?

CARELESS.

To tell you true, sir, he's going to see a lady that
he's in love with.

HILLARIA.

What sots love makes of men.   75

LOVELL.

Your servant, gallants. (*Exit.*)

BREEDWELL, CLAPPAM.

Your servant.

HILLARIA.

I hope he'll find compunction of heart e'er he gets
there, repent of's sin, and so come back again.

BREEDWELL. [*Aside.*]

As I live, this is the prettiest youth.—Come, let's   80
be freely merry.

HILLARIA.

I love freedom in my mirth. Come sir, will you
pledge me on that lady's lips? Ten go downs upon
reputation.

CARELESS.

Sir! I'll pledge you here, and there, and everywhere.   85

*Kiss each other's woman, and then change and kiss
their own. Music plays.*

HILLARIA.

I hear music. Come, you sons of melody.

BREEDWELL.

Come, my little squire of the body, you and I will
have a dance together.

CLAPPAM.

Nay, keep to your own man.

BREEDWELL.

I have as much reason to dance with him as you.   90

CLAPPAM.

You lie—and you take tobacco, and I am satisfied.

BREEDWELL.

What interest have you in him, I wonder?

CLAPPAM.

To beat you with your own cudgel: know that I
am his old acquaintance, and he chose me.

BREEDWELL.

That was because he thought I had been engaged   95
elsewhere.

CARELESS. [*Aside.*]

So, now they quarrel for him, and I am in the
condition my friend was just now.

HILLARIA.

Ladies, I am ready to serve you in any kind, but
then you must take me by turns.   100

CARELESS.

I'll ease you of half your burden; Mrs. Breedwell,
you and I won't part so.

HILLARIA.

Strike up, you rogues.

A dance here of four.

BREEDWELL.

Now sir, let me oblige you to dance a jig.

CLAPPAM.

Lord, Mrs. Breedwell, you are so forward. I can   105
oblige him to't as well as you.

CARELESS. [*Aside.*]

They are at it again. A pox of this smock-faced[33]
rogue. I must be forced to kick this fellow out of
company.—Some wine, boy. Mrs. Clappam, you
are not so obliging today as you used to be.   110

CLAPPAM.

Not I, sir, I swear, I beg your pardon. I'll pledge
you, sir.

---

33 smock-faced] smooth-faced, effeminate

BREEDWELL.

How your dancing has made you sweat. Let me wipe your face. How long, sir, have you known that lady? 115

HILLARIA.

Some few days.

BREEDWELL.

Have you ever been concerned with her?

HILLARIA.

No, but 'tis my present business.

BREEDWELL.

Have a care how you venture: I would not say so much but that I have a kindness* for you. 120

HILLARIA.

Is she not well?

BREEDWELL.

Pretty well again now, but she's not quite out of the surgeon's hands[34] yet.

HILLARIA.

I am just now in the humor, but I had rather have your company. 125

BREEDWELL.

Take your leave, and I'll follow you to the next tavern.

CARELESS.

You must pledge me now.

HILLARIA.

That they may not suspect, go you first.

CLAPPAM.

That's not fair play, Mrs. Breedwell. 130

BREEDWELL.

If you are jealous, wipe his face yourself.—Some wine, boy.—To your good thoughts.

CLAPPAM.

How do you like Mrs. Breedwell?

HILLARIA.

Well enough.

CLAPPAM.

On my word, you'll not find a finer woman in 135 Town of her age. How old do you think she is?

HILLARIA.

Eighteen.

CLAPPAM.

Jiminy!* I am as much.

---

[34] surgeon's hands] for treatment of venereal disease

HILLARIA.

I may be mistaken.

CLAPPAM.

Why, she lay in a year ago of her fifth child, and 140 were't not for some defect in her teeth which taints her breath a little, she's not to be disliked.

HILLARIA. [Aside.]

How malicious are women against one another! Let us alone to discover* each other's faults.

CLAPPAM.

Has she not acquainted you with her lodging? 145

HILLARIA.

You need not be jealous, let me but know where yours is.

CLAPPAM.

Hark you, sir.

CARELESS.

I must be forced to kick these two out of the room; I hate whispering, it spoils good company. 150

HILLARIA.

Enough.—We have done, sir.—Slip from the company and go home. I'll come to you.

BREEDWELL.

Again.

Enter second drawer.

CLAPPAM.

What are you for?

SECOND DRAWER.

There are a couple of seamen in the next room 155 desires to entertain you with a dance.

HILLARIA.

Bid 'em come in.—Play away.

CARELESS.

Give 'em what wine they'll drink, and clap't to our reckoning.

[Exit second drawer.] The dance of seamen.

HILLARIA.

One of you two ladies I hope will entertain us with 160 a song.

CARELESS.

Mrs. Clappam, you have a good voice.

HILLARIA.

Before you hear't, I'll lay a wager 'tis either a drinking or a bawdy song.

CARELESS.

Is there not Phillis[35] in't? 165

CLAPPAM.

No.

CARELESS.

Then it may not be bawdy. Come, let's hear your old out-of-fashion song.

CLAPPAM.

'Tis called "The Agreement."

BREEDWELL.

Now I'll steal away. (*Exit.*) 170

CLAPPAM. (*Sings.*)

Come peevish lovers, hear and see
How my love and I agree:
We are in sweet embraces twined;
I am constant, and she is kind.

Enter second drawer with a letter and gives it Careless.

SECOND DRAWER.

Sir, a porter has brought this letter for you and 175
stays for an answer.

CLAPPAM.

I'll take this occasion to slip away. (*Exit.*)

HILLARIA.

I'll o'ertake you.

CARELESS. (*Reads.*)

"Gallant, I know not what's the cause, but I am very
melancholy. Pray come and spend the rest of this 180
afternoon with me, for I find an inclination to your
company; perhaps the sight of you may cure me.
Hillaria." This 'tis to have the acquaintance of
honest* women, they presently grow troublesome.

HILLARIA.

Why, sir? 185

CARELESS.

Why, if they be of the dull sober sort, a man can
hardly get acquainted with them, but they fall flat
in love with him. If they be of a sprightly gay
humor,* they presently grow impertinent: they will
ever be sending such notes as these to a man or 190
running after him.

HILLARIA.

But is she handsome that sends you this invitation?

---

35 Phillis] stereotypical woman's name in Restoration lyrics, often employing pastoral motifs erotically

CARELESS.

Yes, hang her, she's well enough.

HILLARIA.

Then you should tak't for a kindness.

CARELESS.

Yes, just as a husband does when his wife jogs him 195
by the elbow and asks him the question. I wonder
women han't wit enough to know when a man
cares for their love or their company. To be sure,
when he has a mind to either, he'll be coming or
sending to them. 200

HILLARIA.

But won't you go?

CARELESS.

Dost think I'll leave good sociable company to go
to a dull honest wench?

HILLARIA.

She'll take it ill.

CARELESS.

I have a better opinion of her wit than to think 205
she'd desire me if she knew how the case stands.
It would be as unreasonable in her as to invite a
hungry man from a well-furnished table to go and
look upon the picture of a banquet where he can
only feast his eye but never allay his appetite.— 210
Boy, bid the porter tell her he can't find me.—I'll
make such visits when I can have no better
company.

[Exit second drawer.]

HILLARIA.

But where are our women?

DRAWER.

One of 'em went out just before the song and bid 215
me tell you— (*Whispers with Hillaria.*)

CARELESS.

Speak out, you rogue.

DRAWER.

That she was gone to th'place appointed.

CARELESS.

Young squire, you don't play me square play. You
ought not to take up another man's dice. 220

Enter second drawer.

And where's she that sung?—Do you know where
the lady is that was here but e'en now?

SECOND DRAWER.

She's gone, sir. (*Offers to whisper Hillaria.*)

CARELESS.

Whither? Are you going to whisper too? Speak out.

SECOND DRAWER.

I suppose that gentleman knows. She sent to desire 225
him to make haste.

CARELESS.

Get you both down; we'll pay at the bar.

Exeunt drawers.

Sir, you make too bold with me: to take one
mistress from me was ill manners; to rob me of
both, malice and ill nature! 230

HILLARIA.

I do't by way of reprisal; you have took one from
me, and I have got two from you.

CARELESS.

I take one from you!

HILLARIA.

Yes, I have had a long intrigue with the lady named
Hillaria, and I hear you are become her servant. 235

CARELESS.

Hillaria!

HILLARIA.

Yes.

CARELESS.

I was ignorant of any such pretensions.

HILLARIA.

I shall spoil your markets there too: I shall tell her
that she's impertinent to send after you, and all 240
that, and when you can find no better company,
you'll come to her, and all that.

CARELESS.

Nay then, I'll take another course with you. Come,
sir. (*Draws.*)

HILLARIA.

Surely, you'll not be so mad to fight for one you 245
don't love?

CARELESS.

Look you, sir, though I scorn to tell her so, or any
of her sex, yet I do love her, will love her, and must
love her: and nobody else shall love her.

HILLARIA.

But I do, shall, and will love her—better than you. 250

CARELESS.

Come, give me a proof on't then. Draw.

HILLARIA.

Yes sir, I will give you a proof of't. (*Discovers*
herself.*) Ha, ha, ha.

CARELESS.

Hillaria!

HILLARIA.

Alas, poor gallant—ha, ha, ha—observe, now you 255
are cheated of three mistresses. Ha, ha, ha—fare
you well, gallant.

CARELESS.

Hark you, stay.

HILLARIA.

No, women are so impertinent, men will come
after them, when they love them. Adieu. (*Exit.*) 260

CARELESS.

Gad, she's too unconscionable to deprive me of
two mistresses and then to run away herself, and
now she knows I love her, she'll insult o'er me. And
those damned whores to serve me such a dog trick.
I thought they had some honor in them, 265
But I find that women are by nature guilty,
For be they whores or no whores, they will jilt ye.

Exit.

Act V, scene i. Covent Garden.

*Enter De Boastado in the habit of a physician, Toby
like an old, rich alderman.*

TOBY.

Mr. Doctor, I desire no more of your consultations
with my niece. I say no more but I smell a fox.

DE BOASTADO.

What do you mean, sir?

TOBY.

I say no more but some wiser than some.

DE BOASTADO.

That, sir, was the very reason why the doctor 5
brought me with him, thinking I might observe
some circumstances which might discover* the
nature of your niece's disease, of which he yet
remains doubtful.

TOBY.

And you discovered that it was good for her to go 10
abroad in a coach, to take the air.

DE BOASTADO.

Yes sir, and I'll give you a reason for't: for want of

exercise the blood grows thick and corrupts in the veins, which are the channels nature has designed for it. Sir, does it not stand to reason that motion and exercise, which opens the veins, rarefies the blood, and gives it a free passage, should not in some measure work its effects on your niece. 15

TOBY.

Well, sir, I say no more but that some are fools and some are physicians. 20

DE BOASTADO.

I will maintain it against the learnedest professors in Town,* that it will do your niece more good to jolt about one hour in a coach every morning and evening for a month than to take ten purges a day.

TOBY.

I am much of your mind, Mr. Doctor, and I say no more but that it is not good for sick folks to go abroad in the air. 25

DE BOASTADO.

Her sickness is for want of air.

TOBY.

And I say no more but that some people's reasons for her going abroad is that she's an heiress. 30

DE BOASTADO.

I hope you don't think that I am an instrument in any design.

TOBY.

I say no more but that there are blades upon the randan[36] that would feel her pulse and stir her blood to some purpose, and that's one reason why 'tis not good for her to go abroad. 35

DE BOASTADO.

I beg your pardon, sir, I spoke as a physician in consideration of her health, and Mr. Doctor within was partly of my mind.

TOBY.

He was of the mind, too, that my cookmaid would not die yesterday, and I say no more but that she died within two hours after. 40

DE BOASTADO.

Physicians sometimes say what they think will best please their patients.

TOBY.

And you thought 'twould please her best to be 45

---

36 blades … randan] gallants on a spree

gadding abroad; I say no more but that if her blood want stirring, I'll get her a husband.

DE BOASTADO.

Yes, sir, that will do best of all.

TOBY.

Sir, then we agree at last, and I say no more but that his lordship shall go without her. 50

DE BOASTADO.

What lord, sir?

TOBY.

A friend, a neighbor of mine, sends me word that she's in love with a foolish fantastic lord.

DE BOASTADO.

What is this lord?

TOBY.

I say no more but that he has been a traveler, is 55 very conceited, and very ridiculous.

DE BOASTADO.

What is his name?

TOBY.

You may as soon call o'er a troop of horse as name him; I know no more but that he has two wives already, that he is a very great fool, and I say no 60 more but that I'll have my niece into the country tomorrow. (*Exit.*)

Enter Beatrice.

DE BOASTADO.

Let me tell you, Beatrice, this alderman is an old rook;* he smells powder[37] a great way off.

BEATRICE.

Does he suspect you? 65

DE BOASTADO.

He suspects everybody: he has heard the whole story of her being in love with me.

BEATRICE.

It comes from our house, I warrant you. But was it not very unfortunate for us that he should come home just as we had convinced the landlady and 70 servants that it was necessary for the lady to go abroad?

DE BOASTADO.

The coach sent for and all.

---

37 smells powder] a cheat, who like a crow (also called a rook) can smell gunpowder from afar

BEATRICE.

And when he came, he was so earnest for you to
be gone, being a stranger, and kept such a fiddling 75
about his niece that you could not break a piece
of gold, as we designed, and make a contract.

DE BOASTADO.

Fate was indeed very malicious.

BEATRICE.

But how does your lordship like her?

DE BOASTADO.

She's a miracle! I protest I saw not so great a rarity 80
in all my travels.

BEATRICE.

What a pretty mouth she has, so little, and her
nether lip so cherry-like, and then she's such a
pattern of modesty and innocence, one would
wonder how she got the confidence to be in love. 85

DE BOASTADO.

She's a rare creature!

BEATRICE.

She loves the very ground you go on.

DE BOASTADO.

Oh Beatrice, if I had her—

BEATRICE.

She's resolved by some stratagem or another to get
to you tonight; therefore, be sure you be not out 90
of the way.

DE BOASTADO.

I'll go directly to my lodgings.

BEATRICE.

Be careful you are not seen i'th'streets, for if those
two women once get sight of you, their tongues
will blow up your credit. 95

DE BOASTADO.

I'll be gone, lest they should come and find me
here. (*Exit.*)

[Toby] peeps at the door.

BEATRICE.

You may venture forth; he's gone.

Enter Toby.

TOBY.

'Twas damned ill luck that we had ne'er a parson
here; the business had been done. 100

BEATRICE.

He failed of bringing one with him, and if we had

provided a parson, our forwardness might have
given him cause of suspicion, but disappointment
does make men more eager.

TOBY.

So much for that now, Beatrice; being at leisure, let 105
us examine how matters stand 'twixt you and me.

BEATRICE.

Just as they did, on my part.

TOBY.

But methinks now you have seen how well I acted
the gentleman, traveler, and the old alderman, you
should love me much better for my ingenuity. 110

BEATRICE.

In the first shape, you appeared so much like a
gentleman, and in this, so like an old, rich
alderman that I shall never endure to see you your
own man again.

TOBY.

When I am neither gentleman nor alderman, I 115
shall be Toby still, and I am no more now.

BEATRICE.

But if we two should marry, how should we do to
live?

TOBY.

Live? Well enough: we'll live by our wits.

BEATRICE.

Then I must maintain you and myself too. 120

TOBY.

Why, Beatrice? Dost think I have not so much wit
as thee?

BEATRICE.

No, marry, han't you.

TOBY.

This day I have given the world sufficient proofs
of my wit. 125

BEATRICE.

I doubt not but ere night to give you a better proof
of mine than any you have or can give of yours.

TOBY.

Pshaw, pshaw.—Yonder's my master, go and
acquaint him how matters succeed. (*Exit.*)

Enter Lovell and Careless.

LOVELL.

The truth is, she played the tyrant with thee, but 130
you deserved that and more.

CARELESS.

Well, were not the use and conversation* of women absolutely necessary for man, I would forswear the whole sex.

LOVELL.

I know by the constitution of your body that you'd 135
not be able to keep that oath, but I advise you to forswear all but one.

CARELESS.

That is, you'd have me marry.

LOVELL.

Yes, you'll find more comfort in a wife than in ten mistresses. 140

CARELESS.

If what you say be true, why do most husbands in this age (which I take to be wiser than any that's past) turn away their wives and keep* wenches? At least, those that are so civil to keep a wife, they keep a mistress besides. 145

LOVELL.

And if it be not true, why do the great wenchers at last forsake all their mistresses for a wife? For we find most of them marry at the long run; nay, generally they prove the best husbands. And the reason is, they have experimented the folly of that 150
lewd course of life.

CARELESS.

I have never so good an opinion of marriage as now, for this dog-trick that these two jilting jades showed me in leaving me so in the lurch has lessened 'em in my esteem to the degree of honest 155
women. And now the scales are equal, the first of either party that obliges me draws it down on that side.

LOVELL.

Then I hope Hillaria will turn the balance.

CARELESS.

If the devil is minded to lose a gamester, let him 160
venture to make her and me friends.

BEATRICE.

Sir, we are still successful in our designs. It is drawing to a conclusion; therefore, be in a posture to receive us.f

LOVELL. (To Careless.)

I'll give 'em notice within. You'll take care of the 165
rest?

CARELESS.

The parson and the fiddlers, I believe, are drunk together and fallen asleep in the tavern, but I'll marshal 'em presently.*

BEATRICE.

And I'll back to my employment. 170

Exeunt Lovell, Beatrice severally. Enter Hillaria.§

HILLARIA.

How now, gallant.

CARELESS.

Oh, madam. (Sings, and walks about.)

HILLARIA.

You are very merry, gallant.

CARELESS.

I have no reason to be otherwise.

Sings and walks about two or three times, and [they] jostle one another.

Why do you jostle me? 175

HILLARIA.

And why do you jostle me?

CARELESS.

You walk in my way.

HILLARIA.

'Tis you walk in my way.

CARELESS.

Get farther off.

HILLARIA.

Go you farther off. 180

CARELESS.

I was here first.

HILLARIA.

Then you may be gone first.

CARELESS.

I have business here.

HILLARIA.

What, to see me?

CARELESS.

No. (Sings and walks about carelessly.) 185

HILLARIA.

Yes, in my conscience, you was coming to see me.

CARELESS.

Now I think on't, so I was, on purpose to let you see that I am alive, for I believe you thought I had either hanged myself (for the trick you put on me today) or had broke my heart with sighing for your absence, with whom I am too desperately in love, but believe me, I have not yet broke so much as a button, and may I break my neck when I do, either for love or you or any woman alive.

HILLARIA.

Yet you love me.

CARELESS.

'Tis true, I love you well enough, because you are unlucky, and was not honesty* in the case, I should love you better, but as it is, you are in a desperate condition.

HILLARIA.

Must I then despair?

CARELESS.

You are for matrimony, and that I hate; I can no more endure a wife than a standing dish of meat.

HILLARIA.

You think, then, I am in love with you.

CARELESS.

Think it, ha, ha, ha—As though I did not know that by your following me up and down. What came you to the tavern for after me? And for what came you hither now, if you an't in love with me? And what made you seduce the ladies from me but that you had a mind to have me all yourself?

HILLARIA.

I vow, now you put me in mind on't, I may be in love with you. But you say my case is desperate; then desperate must be the cure, and I must e'en resolve to be your mistress or wench or what you will.

CARELESS.

That's your only remedy. I am a bird of prey and fly at all.

HILLARIA.

Nay, then, I'm a dead woman still, for you'll soon take a flight from me to another.

CARELESS.

But when I have catched my prey, I take my belly full of it; I never leave it till I am gorged.

HILLARIA.

And will your stomach come to you again?

CARELESS.

Yes, sometimes, but generally some ravenous fowl or another picks up my leavings and flies away with't.

HILLARIA.

But would you have no more care of me?

CARELESS.

My care would signify but little, for a man seldom finds either money or a woman in the same place he left 'em.

HILLARIA.

But they say 'tis a rule amongst you men not to leave the women you debauch but, if they prove constant, to provide for 'em.

CARELESS.

Provide for 'em! Is it not enough we teach 'em a trade by which they may get their livings? But you will not want providing for, you have a good portion. But if I would, you yourself in a short time would be for change.

HILLARIA.

Well, Careless, we'll do nothing rashly; I'll in and consider on't, and some other time I'll tell you more of my mind.

CARELESS.

But let me give you this caution: be not deceived with the vain considerations of virtue, modesty, honor, chastity, reputation, and the like; these are bug* words that awed the women in former ages and still fool a great many in this, and if once these idle notions get into your thoughts, I shall give you over for a lost woman.

HILLARIA.

The common practice of my sex may prevail much; evil example makes twenty sinners to the devil's one. Adieu.

CARELESS.

Adieu.

Exeunt Careless and Hillaria, severally. Enter De Boastado in masquerade, reading a letter.

DE BOASTADO. (*Reads.*)

"My lord, This night is to be the burial of one of my uncle's maids, who died yesterday morning; put yourself in masquerade and stand over against Mr. Muchworth's house, for near to that is the churchyard. When you see the corpse pass that way, sing these words (*Hums to himself.*); then whatsoever you see, be not startled, for it is all but design to affright the people and make 'em run away. Come you to the coffin, and instead of a corpse, you shall find her that for love of you attempts thus to make an escape." This is notably contrived. What a witty wife shall I have! [*Reads.*] "I am informed by Beatrice that there will be dancing at Mr. Muchworth's; we will venture in amongst them as masqueraders, and she has promised there shall be a parson ready to marry us, and then in spite of my uncle, I shall forever be—Yours, Grace Rich." Here comes company; I will retire till they are gone past. (*Exit.*) 260 265

Enter Careless, leading in Mrs. Breedwell and Clappam, musicians playing before them.

CARELESS.
Now ladies, you may pull off your masks; you're no strangers to one another. 270

Clappam, Breedwell pull of their masks.

BREEDWELL.
Mrs. Clappam.

CLAPPAM.
Mrs. Breedwell.

CARELESS.
I know you wonder to see one another here, but both of you came to th'tavern on the same account.

BREEDWELL.
On what account. 275

CARELESS.
To see what was become of the young gentleman.

BREEDWELL.
I love you for that.

CARELESS.
Nay, Mrs. Breedwell, I was behind you when you asked the drawer what was become of him; it seems he failed you both of your assignation. 280

CLAPPAM.
'Slife!* Did she dare to have an intrigue with my man?

BREEDWELL.
Your man!

CLAPPAM.
Yes, my man, you impudent hussy. I'll scratch your eyes out. 285

BREEDWELL.
Touch me if you dare.

CLAPPAM.
If I dare?

Breedwell, Clappam fight and tear one another about.

CARELESS.
So, so; enough, enough; brave girls both——

CLAPPAM.
Dare me!

BREEDWELL.
You, what are you? 290

CLAPPAM.
A degree above you, I think.

BREEDWELL.
Yes, so you are, for I am not whore and bawd too, as you are.

CLAPPAM.
You han't wit enough to be a bawd, and scarce beauty enough to drive on the vocation of whoring. And let me advise you to make much of those clothes you have on, for that face will not be able to bring you a new gown again. 295

BREEDWELL.
And do you make much of the embroidered bodices you use to run to plays in the last summer; neither your beauty nor your wit will ever bring you such another pair. You may speak French long enough before you get such again. 300

CLAPPAM.
My back is not my wardrobe, as yours is; I had a new gown but a month ago. 305

BREEDWELL.
What, the mourning gown you bought at second hand? A woman of the Town needs no curses when she once comes to a black cloth gown and plain linen; that is their last refuge in point of clothes, and when that's worn out, she must on with the striped semar and turn bulker[38]—at which trade I hope to see you suddenly.* 310

CLAPPAM.
And I as suddenly* expect to see you so miserable as to abuse charity to relieve your own necessities and go up and down with a purse to all your 315

---

38 semar ... bulker] a plain loose coat worn by a common prostitute, streetwalker

acquaintance to gather relief for some pretended poor woman that is sick or in prison.

CARELESS.

Enough, enough. Bravely performed on both sides: you fought well, and you scold well.

CLAPPAM.

If you had not^h been here, I would have so tewed^39 that spawn of a sempstress— 320

BREEDWELL.

And I would so have clawed off that shoemaker's daughter that she should have thought it worse than her last child or her last clap or the scuffle she had with the sedan men when they tore the 325 clothes off her back for four shillings which she owed 'em at least half a year.

CLAPPAM.

And you should have 'scaped no better than you did when the coachman met you at the New Exchange* that you bilked of his fare after five 330 hours' ramble.

CARELESS.

No more, come a truce, a truce. You served one another no more than you both served me. I have reason to be angry with you on account of your leaving my company for that fair, smooth, chitty-faced^40 stranger that neither of you ever saw before. 335

CLAPPAM.

Ah, he was such a pretty gentleman and had such a boon mien—

CARELESS.

But the devil a penny of money in his pocket. I paid the whole reckoning. I had a good mind to 340 have sent him to you in revenge, that he might have bilked you both, for his jilting me.

BREEDWELL.

And bilking is so used nowadays that 'tis not more hard for a man to find a woman with whom he may safely venture than 'tis for a woman to meet 345 with a man who, the next morning or as soon as she has been kind to him, will not say, "Egad, madam, I have got no money about me, I had damned ill luck at play, but I am going to receive some this afternoon, and if you'll let me know 350

---

39 tewed] beaten
40 chitty-faced] baby-faced

where I shall be so happy as to meet you anon in the evening, you shall find none more a gentleman."

CLAPPAM.

And if you make an appointment, he meets you no more than he goes to pay off his tailor's bill at 355 the day promised. Hang me if I was not served so three times the last week.

BREEDWELL.

Men are grown so base that 'tis enough to make any woman forswear keeping company, but if that young gentleman had served me so, I vow I should 360 not have been vexed.

CLAPPAM.

And I had rather he should have served me so than failed of coming as he promised.

CARELESS.

I find both of you have a kindness* for him, but I am persuaded, when you see him again, that you 365 will not be so fond of him. Come shake hands and be friends, and I will carry you to him; he shall have his choice, and I'll be content with the other.

CLAPPAM.

Mrs. Breedwell, come kiss and be friends.

BREEDWELL.

With all my heart. 370

CARELESS.

Now put on your masks, and in here with me.

Exit Careless, Breedwell, and Clappam. Enter De Boastado.

DE BOASTADO.

So, they are gone, and in good time. Here comes the burial. I'll stand close.

[Enter] Toby in the habit of a bearer; four bearers with a coffin on a bier; four maids in white bearing up the four corners of the sheet; they walk round the stage, set down the corpse as to rest themselves; attended with some few followers.

TOBY.

Come, let's rest a little.

FIRST BEARER.

Ay, set down, set down. 375

Set down the corpse.

FIRST MAID.
  Ah, poor Betty.
SECOND MAID.
  Ay, she was as good a natured maid—
THIRD MAID.
  And as pretty a servant as ever lived in the parish.
FOURTH MAID.
  She's in heaven, I hope, poor wench.
DE BOASTADO. (Sings.)
  Wake all the dead, what ho, what ho—   380
TOBY AND ALL THE BEARERS.
  Hark.
BEATRICE. (In the coffin speaks with a mournful
    voice.)
  Who's there?
FOUR MAIDS.
  Hark, hark.
DE BOASTADO. (Sings.)
  The windows are oped, the doors unbarred, come
  from the church, and the churchyard.   385
SECOND BEARER.
  The voice is this way.
BEATRICE. (In the coffin.)
  Who's there?
FIRST BEARER.
  No, 'tis in the coffin, in the coffin, neighbor.

Enter four ghosts, two men and two women, the
women in long winding-sheets, the men with mufflers,
caps, white clothes, waistcoats, drawers, breeches,
stockings and pumps.

FOUR GHOSTS.
  Make room, make room.
DE BOASTADO.
  The world's at an end.   390
FOUR GHOSTS, BEATRICE.
  And we come, we come.

Beatrice rises upright in the coffin in a winding-sheet.

TOBY AND ALL THE BEARERS.
  Look, look, look.

[Toby], bearers, maids, and followers, all run out
speaking.

ALL FOUR MAIDS.
  Ah, ah, ah, ah, ah, ah.

De Boastado helps Beatrice down and carries her into
Muchworth's house.

FOUR GHOSTS.
  Away, away, lovers away.

Exeunt.

          Scene ii. A room in Muchworth's house.

Enter Lovell and Jacinta.

LOVELL.
  Why Jacinta, do you fear your love will wrong your
  duty?
JACINTA.
  You know my father's command; if I marry you, I
  disobey him.
LOVELL.
  And if you do not, you're unjust to love.   5
JACINTA.
  I will still be true to love: I will never marry any
  other man, for your sake.
LOVELL.
  But if your father command, will you not obey?
JACINTA.
  Never.
LOVELL.
  Not to obey his commands in marrying will have   10
  the same event as to disobey him now in marrying
  me.
JACINTA.
  'Twill not then be disobedience, though parents
  have power to command us not to marry.
LOVELL.
  Ah Jacinta, was your love like mine, you would not   15
  stand upon such niceties; a perfect love inspires
  those minds with courage where it inhabits.
JACINTA.
  I love you so well, I will not make you unhappy.
  Till I can bring a portion with me, I will not be
  your wife.   20
LOVELL.
  I was discarded to make room for that pretender,
  whom we have now defeated; he being removed,
  your father will soon be reconciled.
JACINTA.
  Endeavor then to get his consent.

LOVELL.

'Twill be a greater expense of time and labor to get 25
his consent before marriage than to reconcile him
after. When all things are once done and not to
be recalled, men are soon pacified.

JACINTA.

It may be more easy, but not so secure; old age is
very exceptious,[41] wherefore excuse me if I dare 30
not venture to disoblige a father, whose love may
be considerable and an advantage to me.

Enter Hillaria.

HILLARIA.

Come leave off your sneaking, pitiful love. My
gallant has brought some company, let's dance and
be merry. Here they come, strike up music. 35

Flourish below. Enter Careless, Clappam, and Breedwell.

LOVELL.

But we want* men.

CARELESS.

You'll have more company presently; the parson is
doing execution in the next room.

Enter Muchworth.

HILLARIA.

Here's my uncle; we'll have him in. Come uncle,
will you make one in a country dance? 40

MUCHWORTH.

What's the matter here? What are you doing here?
What, are candles lighted in every room? And what
does music here?

HILLARIA.

I believe you are fuddled, uncle, you are so full of
questions. 45

MUCHWORTH.

I say, what is all this for?

LOVELL.

Give me leave, Jacinta, to pretend this our wedding
night and that all this is on that account.

JACINTA.

If he resents it ill, I shall soon undeceive him.

MUCHWORTH.

What, will nobody speak? Daughter, what's the 50
occasion of all this?

---

41 exceptious] cranky, obdurate

LOVELL.

The occasion, sir, is such that she is afraid to tell
you, and I should be loath to let you know it but
that we hope your pardon, without which we
cannot be truly merry. 55

MUCHWORTH.

What's the matter, Mr. Lovell?

Lovell and Jacinta kneel.

LOVELL.

From this posture you may guess.

MUCHWORTH.

What mean you by it?

LOVELL.

To beg at once your pardon and your blessing.

MUCHWORTH.

Hah! Is it so? 60

HILLARIA.

It will be otherwise with 'em anon, uncle.

MUCHWORTH.

You are married then?

CARELESS.

It was their fate, sir; the business is done.

HILLARIA.

Now do I hope my uncle will take pet at the
marriage and give me all his estate when he dies 65
to vex his daughter.

MUCHWORTH.

Rather than you shall see a groat on't, I would give
it to hospitals, which is the worst use a man can
put his money to, because the poor are always
cheated on't.—Mr. Lovell, rise. If you do well and 70
prove a good husband, I have all I can desire,
which is to see my daughter well disposed of, and
I shall do well by you. If you prove an ill husband,
she may thank herself, and her disobedience will
be punished in the event. 75

HILLARIA.

Lord, uncle, that you should do this on purpose
to spite me.

MUCHWORTH.

I believe you was an instrument in the design.

HILLARIA.

Nay, uncle, I must confess you have over-reached
me clearly. 80

CARELESS.

But, sir, my being here is on another account. I come to desire you to use your authority with your niece and keep her at home, for I can be nowhere, either about business or taking my recreation, but she presently* comes and disturbs me, insomuch 85 that, if you don't take some speedy order with her, I must be forced to leave the Town to avoid her company.

MUCHWORTH.

Pray take her along with you, and you'll free me of a greater trouble, for she's my vexation all the 90 day long.

HILLARIA.

'Tis true, uncle, that gentleman and I have been a little troublesome to one another. For you know, he came to solicit me in the way of matrimony, which I don't much approve of, for it makes folks 95 fall out: the first day of marriage is the last day of love. I liked him well enough for a gallant, and if he would accept of me for a mistress or so? But he had a foolish scruple of conscience, nothing would serve him but marriage, and so away came 100 I. This is all, uncle.

MUCHWORTH.

If you will have my opinion in the case, you were cut out one for the other, and 'tis pity two houses should part you; therefore, if she'll agree to your desires or you conform to hers, 'tis all one to me, 105 you have my consent to either. All that I desire is that you'll make an end quickly, that I may be clear of her company.

HILLARIA.

Then sir, you may either go into the country or stay in Town, if you please, with danger of being 110 troubled with me, for I absolutely declare against marriage, and if nothing else will serve your turn, you may go where you will and do what you please, I'll have nothing to do with such an unreasonable man as you are. 115

CARELESS.

To convince you, Mr. Muchworth, that what she says is not true, but that,[i] on the contrary, I am for having her for a mistress, and she is for being my wife, here are a couple of ladies, to whom, on or off, I have been gallant this seven or eight years, 120

and they can witness I have continually railed against marrying. Mrs. Clappam, Mrs. Breedwell, what say you?

BREEDWELL.

Yes, sir.

CLAPPAM.

Yes. 125

CARELESS.

Now lady, if you are not for what I proposed, you may e'en keep your maidenhead till it stinks and is not fit for man to meddle with.

HILLARIA.

I except against your witnesses, they are bribed, and rather than such a lying man as you shall have 130 it, I'll keep it still.*

Enter De Boastado, Beatrice like a ghost.

MUCHWORTH.

What new masque is this?

LOVELL.

Some masquers, hearing the music as they were passing by, are come in to dance with us.

DE BOASTADO. (*To Jacinta in a squeaking voice.*)

Do you know me? 135

JACINTA.

Not I, sir.

BEATRICE. (*To Careless.*)

Do you know me?

CARELESS.

You should be a cat, by your little squeaking voice.

LOVELL.

Jacinta, let us take this occasion to slip into the next room to the parson; now with security we 140 may perfect our desires.

[*Exeunt.*]

DE BOASTADO. (*To Muchworth.*)

Do you know me?

MUCHWORTH.

When I see your face, I'll tell you.

DE BOASTADO.

Look you, sir.

MUCHWORTH.

Is't your lordship? 145

HILLARIA.

My lord!

CARELESS.

Has your lordship (out of a frolic) robbed the churchyard for a companion? If so, you'll have but a cold bedfellow.

DE BOASTADO.

No, feel here, she's warm flesh and blood.   150

CARELESS.

Marry sir, she relishes well in the hand.

HILLARIA.

Pray my lord, who is she?

DE BOASTADO.

She is my wife, lady, my wife. I have married a lady, a lady, that has some forty or fifty thousand pounds to her portion. I took her by way of cordial   155 to revive my spirits, much weakened by the grief I had for losing your daughter.

Enter Toby, alderman-like, three bearers, one having Toby's habit in his hand.

TOBY.

Neighbors, here, here she is. Aye, here she is.

MUCHWORTH.

Who are these?

CARELESS.

You'll see anon.   160

DE BOASTADO.

Keep off the ministers of death, this is a living body.

TOBY.

She is my maid, I'll have her again, she shall serve her year out.[42]

DE BOASTADO.

Good Mr. Alderman, you are deceived, this is your 165 niece.

TOBY.

My niece is at home in chamber.

DE BOASTADO.

No, sir, but your maid is at home and as dead as a herring; it was not a corpse, but a quick* body that came out of your house in the coffin. It was not your 170 maid you suppose but your niece. And now, I think, my wit hath been too quick for you all.

---

[42] maid … out] finish her contracted time, typically a year (breaching her contract would be a criminal offense).

TOBY.

Niece, come away from him.

DE BOASTADO.

You cannot have her, she is my wife.

TOBY.

Are you married then already?   175

DE BOASTADO.

Yes, sir.

TOBY.

For certain?

DE BOASTADO.

The parson is still in the house.

TOBY.

Then, sir, see your alderman, your fellow-traveler, and Toby, all in one.   180

DE BOASTADO.

Hah!

HILLARIA, CARELESS.

Toby!

MUCHWORTH.

This's some new trick.

TOBY.

And now, I think, our wits have been too quick for your lordship.   185

DE BOASTADO.j

Who have I married here? I would fain see, but I dare not.

CARELESS.

I will inform your lordship who your wife is, as yet I know her better than your lordship. I had here in Town three mistresses, of which one of 'em 190 was very young and very pretty and but newly debauched. I thought it great pity she should drive that trade and therefore advised her to get her a husband before she had quite ruined her credit. To advance her design, she took the name of 195 Alderman Rich's niece and this morning took the same lodging too, and by the story, I guess this must be she you have married.

MUCHWORTH.

The alderman and his niece went this morning out of Town.   200

DE BOASTADO.

Oh! I am undone.

HILLARIA.

Ha, ha, ha! If your lordship has any grief at your

heart, go to bed and take a sup of your cordial, ha, ha, ha.

CARELESS.

Since your lordship has been so kind to take one of 205
my mistresses off of my hand, I'll make you some
requital in releasing you of your wives. See, my lord,
these are my other two; they shall never trouble your
lordship more upon the account of marriage.

BREEDWELL.

All the right of a husband that I have in you I 210
resign to that lady.

CLAPPAM.

I do the same.

CARELESS.

Now, my lord, you have got one wife, and lost two.

Enter Lovell and Jacinta.

LOVELL.

Now marriage has made us one, our wishes are
complete. 215

HILLARIA.

My lord, now you have drawn your lot, see
whether Fortune has sent you a blank or a prize.

TOBY.

Aye, aye, come, Mrs. Grace, you may e'en show
your face.

DE BOASTADO.

Married to a wench. I am abused, cheated. 220

BEATRICE. (*Beatrice discovers* herself.*)

Yes, my lord, and so they are all.

OMNES.

Beatrice!

TOBY.

How, Mrs. Beatrice!

BEATRICE.

Beatrice I am, but not your Beatrice now.

TOBY.

Art thou married then? 225

BEATRICE.

Yes, to a lord. Who has most wit now, Toby?

TOBY.

Am I then forsaken? Oh! That the fates would be
so kind to lend a dagger or a knife to an incensed
lover.

BEATRICE.

What would you do? 230

TOBY.

I would kill myself to be revenged on thee.

BEATRICE.

There are knives enough for that execution in the
table-basket that stands i'th'hall.

TOBY.

Are there? (*Toby runs out.*)

LOVELL.

But how came you to surprise us with this new 235
turn?

BEATRICE.

Out of pure kindness* to his lordship; rather than he
should marry a wench, I cast myself away upon him.

CARELESS.

My lord, comfort yourself with the old rule: Since
'tis no better, it's well it is no worse. 240

HILLARIA.

Take her to you, my lord. Had she not been your
friend, you had been in a much worse condition.

MUCHWORTH.

Though my daughter's servant, she is a good
gentlewoman born and near related to us.

JACINTA.

'Tis well your lordship has lighted on^k an honest* 245
woman.

BEATRICE.

One proof of my honesty is, I promised your
lordship my maidenhead, and now 'tis at your
service.

Enter Toby.

TOBY.

Look, look here, ungrateful Beatrice, look how I^l 250
on my breast thy perfidiousness revenge.

BEATRICE.

Aye, I see.

TOBY.

Then, Toby, die, die the death of a faithful lover.

Toby strikes himself on the breast and falls down.

BEATRICE, JACINTA, HILLARIA.

Ay.

BEATRICE.

Ay, Toby, what hast thou done? 255

Beatrice looks on his breast and takes up a great candle.

Ha, ha, ha, ha, ha, ha, ha.

HILLARIA.

What dost laugh at?

BEATRICE.

Look here, he has mistaken a great candle for a case knife.

OMNES.

Ha, ha, ha, ha, ha.   260

BEATRICE.

He scared me: it gave way, and I thought verily I had seen it run into his body.

LOVELL.

Rise, Toby, you have only greased your doublet.

TOBY.

I durst have sworn I had left a knife in my heart.

BEATRICE.

If you go to the basket again, be sure you bring a   265
knife with you.

TOBY.

No, methought self-murder was a great sin, and now I have considered on't a little, I'm glad to see myself alive again. And now, rather than kill myself for you or any woman breathing, I would first see   270
the souls of a hundred thousand of 'em rammed into a mortar piece and shot into a Dutch fire-ship. And so I leave you to his lordship, and to let you see I am my own man again, I and my friends will dance at your wedding. Come give me my habit.   275

(*Puts on a bearer's habit.*)

BEATRICE.

My lord, you see I did not anything for want of an husband; what I have done was purely out of kindness* to your lordship.

DE BOASTADO.

Beatrice, I have considered on't, and I will own   280
thee for my wife. And as my wife thou art a lady and know your state and take the upper hand of your two mistresses: 'tis some revenge to see thee take place of those two proud minxes.

CARELESS.

Come, play away for the dance.   285

All the company seat themselves; Beatrice takes place of all the women. A dance. Toby in the habit of a bearer and the three bearers dance with the four maids.

MUCHWORTH.

So, Mr. Lovell and daughter, I wish you much joy

together: the match is of your own making, and when either of you repent it, you must blame yourselves.

LOVELL.

That marriage can hardly know repentance in   290
which both parties had their choice.

MUCHWORTH.

My lord, I entreat you, let my house have the honor to treat you tonight.

DE BOASTADO.

I embrace your kindness.—Give me your hand, now no more Beatrice but my lady. We will   295
suddenly* down to my country house and there fix ourselves and visit London but seldom; the Town is not a place for wives to live in that bring no portions.

BEATRICE.

I shall like a country life very well, if I have but the honor of your lordship's good company, and I   300
doubt not but in few years to raise a portion out of my good huswifery.[43]

MUCHWORTH.

Come, I'll lead you the way to a better room. Mr. Careless, ladies, and all, pray follow.

HILLARIA.

Hold, hold, uncle, 'slife,* you are for rising from   305
table before dinner's done; the third course is yet to come up.

CARELESS.

Pray, lead on, sir, I beseech you, lead on, sir.

HILLARIA.

Come, come, Careless, ne'er halt before a cripple.

CARELESS.

Good madam, you are sharp set, I dare not trust   310
myself with you unless they will all stay.

MUCHWORTH.

Niece, what say you to me?

HILLARIA.

It come just now in my mind that I have lost my bedfellow, and now my cousin is gone, I know not what I shall do, for I vow, I dare not lie alone.   315

CARELESS.

Oh no, 'tis dangerous, for after seeing marriages and new married folks put to bed together, as strange dreams and fancies will be apt to run in

_____

43 huswifery] thrifty management of household affairs

your mind as after seeing bloody executions and
dead people at the gallows, and who knows what
a taking you may be in i'th'night and what strange
fits you may have.

HILLARIA.

Aye, some e'en rave upon the like occasions and
bite and gnaw and tear the very sheets in pieces.

CARELESS.

Oh madam, aye, so they do.

HILLARIA.

Well uncle, you may go; I'll e'en send for one of
the neighbor's daughters from the next door to lie
with me.

CARELESS.

Oh madam, 'tis a hundred to one but she may fall
into the same fits and fancies too, and that will be
more dangerous still, to have two mad folks in a
bed and neither able to allay the other's fury.

HILLARIA.

Oh sir, do you begin to come about, would you
beat off others that you may be my bedfellow
yourself? I perceive that you are for having a wife.

CARELESS.

I for a wife?

HILLARIA.

Nay, nay, 'tis so, ne'er deny't. Well sir, give me your
hand. Rather then lie alone tonight I'll do
anything.

CARELESS.

I knew 'twould come to this.

HILLARIA.

I will be your wife, and since I can't have a gallant
before marriage, I'll do like other wives and have
one after. And now I think on't too, a husband is
very necessary, if it is only to save the trouble of
being asked questions o'er and o'er, as who's the
father? who got it? And besides, what children the
gallant gets, the husband must keep.

CARELESS.

I can be even with you there, for you can bring
me none to keep but what are your own at least,
and if you expect I should be father to all your
children, I expect you should be a nurse to all
mine, and I may have 'em brought home to me
on all sides, from twenty several women, for I
intend to be a great getter and father of many.

HILLARIA.

Well, I have but this thing more to say to you:
whosoever I choose for my gallant, you are not to
quarrel or fall out with him but, on the contrary,
to make him your particular intimate friend, to be
always inviting him home to dinner, and the like.

CARELESS.

And also, whosoever I like for a mistress, be she
maid, wife, or widow, you are to get acquainted
with her, to visit her often, to speak in my praise,
and tell my good qualities, to commend my
abilities, and in fine, to use the utmost of your
power to bring us together, gain us an opportunity,
and if need be, to watch at the stair head, and in
case of necessity, to hold the door.

HILLARIA.

In company, you shall never call me wife or dear
or sweetheart but madam.

CARELESS.

In company, you shall never call me husband or
by my Christian name but Mr. Careless.

HILLARIA.

In none of these particulars will I ever offend, Mr.
Careless.

CARELESS.

In none of these particulars will I ever offend you,
madam.

HILLARIA.

This 'tis for folks to meet that understand
themselves; marriage with these circumstances I
like well enough and must certainly be very
pleasant and delightful.

CARELESS.

Sir, I beg your pardon, for detaining you and the
company so long, but you'll excuse it, being a
business of concern, and each party ought to
understand the other before they set their hands
and seals to the engagement.

HILLARIA.

Uncle, pray, con o'er the articles, for you are to be
summoned for a witness upon occasion.

MUCHWORTH.

It is like to be a fine marriage.

LOVELL.

Yes, if it go on according to agreement.

CARELESS.

You shall see our marriage (which you think is clapped up out of a frolic) go on more cheerfully than yours, made out of stark love and desperate affection. We, like two birds (though we roost together at night), will have our freedom all day and fly chirping about, whilst you like two domestic animals, tied too close together in a string, shall still* be snarling and biting one another.

HILLARIA.

And we have the trouble every now and then to part you, mark the event on't.

CARELESS.

Mrs. Clappam and Mrs. Breedwell, you must not think you have quite lost me because I am married, and so pray tell the rest of my acquaintance I am entered into matrimony but not into bondage.

HILLARIA.

He has, as it were, but one mistress the more. Lead away, uncle.
Whilst other wives and husbands scold and rant,
We two will live like mistress and gallant.

[Exeunt.]

FINIS.

Textual Notes

a Copytext is the 1673 quarto (Q1), corrected according to an errata sheet (some stage directions are obviously from a prompt book and are included only if they are considered substantial, following Henry [1987]).

b parson] Person Q1, Henry

c habited] Q1; *om.* errata, Henry

d THREE CHILDREN] D. Boast Q1, Henry

e Street in front of a tavern in] Muchworth's House, Q1, Henry

f BEATRICE ... us] Q1, Henry; *om.* errata

g Enter Hillaria] Q1 has an impertinent s.d. for her entrance earlier, which we have removed; Henry interprets that impertinent s.d. as meant for Beatrice, whom he removes from the stage when Toby tells her to go to Lovell and Careless, who are just entering, and inform them the state of their plot. But Q1's s.d. at that point says only "Toby Ex:"

h not] Henry; *om.* Q1

i that] Henry; what Q1

j DE BOASTADO] Henry; Q1 runs on with Toby's previous speech

k lighted on] light of Q1, Henry

l I] *om.* Q1, Henry

The Country Wife[a]

by William Wycherley (1641-1715)

edited by Peggy Thompson

William Wycherley was an aspiring courtier, occasional soldier, and Shropshire heir, whose long life was marred by illness, debt, litigation, and two controversial marriages. At the time he wrote *The Country Wife* (1675), however, he enjoyed the friendship of the Court wits, the admiration of the Court ladies, and the fondness of the King himself. The third of Wycherley's four comedies for the stage, *The Country Wife* was first performed by the King's Company at the Theatre Royal, Drury Lane, probably on January 12, 1675. It featured several original members of the company, including Charles Hart as the deceptive, self-serving Horner, a role that contrasted ironically with the many heroic and tragic parts Hart had previously played. Elizabeth Boutell played Margery Pinchwife, one of the breeches roles for which she was famous and which, with the introduction of actresses after the Restoration, had assumed new significance by publicly exposing the shape of a woman's legs.

The importance of *The Country Wife* in the history of dramatic literature is suggested by both the extensive praise it received for its wit and the increasing censure it incurred for its licentiousness. The play was moderately successful on the stage through the mid-eighteenth century. But it was controversial almost immediately, as evidenced by Wycherley's next play, *The Plain Dealer* (1676), which features a discussion of the offending "china scene." In 1753, *The Country Wife* disappeared from the stage, replaced a few years later by two radical adaptations which claimed to have excised the impropriety of the original: a two-act afterpiece by John Lee (1765) and a full-length play, *The Country Girl*, by David Garrick (1766). Both eliminated what scholars have long seen as the vital center of the play, Horner's character and the Fidget-Squeamish plot of lust and deception. Although Wycherley's own comedy did not reappear on the English stage until 1924; *The Country Wife*, together with *The Plain Dealer*, eventually secured his reputation as a powerful comedic and satiric dramatist.

DRAMATIS PERSONAE

[MEN]

    Mr. Horner.
    Mr. Harcourt.
    Mr. Dorilant.
    Mr. Pinchwife.
    Mr. Sparkish.
    Sir Jaspar Fidget.
    A boy.
    [Dr.] Quack.
    [Clasp, a bookseller.]
    [A parson.]
    Waiters, servants, and attendants.

[WOMEN]

    Mrs. Margery Pinchwife.
    Mrs.* Alithea.
    My Lady Fidget.
    Mrs.* Dainty Fidget.
    Mrs.* Squeamish.
    Old Lady Squeamish.
    Lucy, Alithea's maid.

THE SCENE: LONDON.

The Country Wife.

Indignor quicquam reprehendi, non quia crasse
Compositum illepideve putetur, sed quia nuper,
Nec veniam antiquis, sed honorem et praemia posci.
Horat.[1]

Act I, scene i. [Horner's lodging.]

Enter Horner and Quack following him at a distance.

HORNER. (*Aside.*)

A quack is as fit for a pimp as a midwife for a
bawd; they are still but in their way both helpers
of nature.—Well my dear doctor, hast thou done
what I desired?

QUACK.

I have undone you forever with the women and   5
reported you throughout the whole Town* as bad
as an eunuch with as much trouble as if I had
made you one in earnest.

HORNER.

But have you told all the midwives you know, the
orange wenches* at the playhouses, the City*   10
husbands, and old fumbling keepers* of this end of
the Town? For they'll be the readiest to report it.

QUACK.

I have told all the chambermaids, waiting women,
tirewomen,[2] and old women of my acquaintance,
nay, and whispered it as a secret to 'em and to the   15
whisperers of Whitehall,* so that you need not
doubt 'twill spread, and you will be as odious to
the handsome young women as—

HORNER.

As the small pox. Well—

QUACK.

And to the married women of this end of the Town   20
as—

HORNER.

As the great ones,[3] nay, as their own husbands.

QUACK.

And to the City dames as Aniseed Robin[4] of filthy
and contemptible memory, and they will frighten
their children with your name, especially their   25
females.

HORNER.

And cry, "Horner's coming to carry you away!" I
am only afraid 'twill not be believed. You told 'em
'twas by an English-French disaster and an English-
French chirurgeon,[5] who has given me at once, not   30
only a cure, but an antidote for the future against
that damned malady and that worse distemper,
love, and all other women's evils.

QUACK.

Your late journey into France has made it the more

---

1 *Indignor … Horat.*] Horace, *Epistles* II.i.76-78: "I am
impatient that any work is censured, not because it is
thought to be coarse or inelegant in style, but because
it is modern, and that what is claimed for the ancients
should be, not indulgence, but honour and rewards"
(Loeb).

2 tirewomen] ladies' maids in charge of attire

3 the great ones] the great (or French) pox, i.e., syphilis

4 Aniseed Robin] a notorious hermaphrodite

5 English-French disaster … English-French chirurgeon]
a French pox caught by an Englishman, treated by an
English doctor practicing in France

credible, and your being here a fortnight before 35
you appeared in public looks as if you apprehended
the shame, which I wonder you do not. Well, I
have been hired by young gallants to belie 'em
t'other way, but you are the first would be thought
a man unfit for women. 40

HORNER.

Dear Mr. Doctor, let vain rogues be contented only
to be thought abler men than they are; generally 'tis
all the pleasure they have, but mine lies another way.

QUACK.

You take, methinks, a very preposterous way to it
and as ridiculous as if we operators in physic 45
should put forth bills to disparage our
medicaments with hopes to gain customers.

HORNER.

Doctor, there are quacks in love as well as physic
who get but the fewer and worse patients for their
boasting; a good name is seldom got by giving it 50
one's self, and women no more than honor are
compassed by bragging. Come, come, doctor, the
wisest lawyer never discovers* the merits of his
cause till the trial; the wealthiest man conceals his
riches, and the cunning gamester his play; shy 55
husbands and keepers,* like old rooks,* are not to
be cheated but by a new unpracticed trick: false
friendship will pass now no more than false dice
upon 'em, no, not in the City.

Enter boy.

BOY.

There are two ladies and a gentleman coming up. 60

HORNER.

A pox! some unbelieving sisters of my former
acquaintance, who, I am afraid, expect their sense
should be satisfied of the falsity of the report.

Enter Sir Jaspar Fidget, Lady Fidget, and Dainty.

No—this formal fool and women!

QUACK.

His wife and sister. 65

SIR JASPAR.

My coach breaking just now before your door, sir,
I look upon as an occasional⁶ reprimand to me,
sir, for not kissing your hands, sir, since your

coming out of France, sir, and so my disaster, sir,
has been my good fortune, sir, and this is my wife 70
and sister, sir.

HORNER.

What then, sir?

SIR JASPAR.

My lady and sister, sir.—Wife, this is Master
Horner.

LADY FIDGET.

Master Horner, husband! 75

SIR JASPAR.

My lady, my Lady Fidget, sir.

HORNER.

So, sir.

SIR JASPAR.

Won't you be acquainted with her, sir? (*Aside.*) So
the report is true, I find by his coldness or aversion
to the sex, but I'll play the wag with him.—Pray 80
salute* my wife, my lady, sir.

HORNER.

I will kiss no man's wife, sir, for him, sir; I have
taken my eternal leave, sir, of the sex already, sir.

SIR JASPAR. (*Aside.*)

Ha, ha, ha, I'll plague him yet.—Not know my
wife, sir? 85

HORNER.

I do know your wife, sir: she's a woman, sir, and
consequently a monster, sir, a greater monster than
a husband, sir.

SIR JASPAR.

A husband! How, sir?

HORNER. (*Makes horns.*)

So, sir. But I make no more cuckholds, sir. 90

SIR JASPAR.

Ha, ha, ha, Mercury, Mercury.⁷

LADY FIDGET.

Pray Sir Jaspar, let us be gone from this rude fellow.

DAINTY.

Who, by his breeding, would think he had ever
been in France?

LADY FIDGET.

Faugh, he's but too much a French fellow, such as 95

---

⁶ occasional] timely, arising from the occasion

⁷ Mercury] god associated with wit (who wears a hat with
wings resembling cuckold's horns); also, substance used
to treat venereal disease

hate women of quality* and virtue for their love to their husbands, Sir Jaspar; a woman is hated by 'em as much for loving her husband as for loving their money. But pray, let's be gone.

HORNER.

You do well, madam, for I have nothing that you 100 came for. I have brought over not so much as a bawdy picture, new postures,* nor the second part of the *Ecole des filles*,[8] nor——

QUACK. (*Apart to Horner.*)

Hold for shame, sir. What d'ye mean? You'll ruin yourself forever with the sex. 105

SIR JASPAR.

Ha, ha, ha, he hates women perfectly, I find.

DAINTY.

What pity 'tis he should.

LADY FIDGET.

Aye, he's a base rude fellow for it, but affectation makes not a woman more odious to them than virtue. 110

HORNER.

Because your virtue is your greatest affectation, madam.

LADY FIDGET.

How, you saucy fellow, would you wrong my honor?

HORNER.

If I could. 115

LADY FIDGET.

How d'ye mean, sir?

SIR JASPAR.

Ha, ha, ha, no, he can't wrong your ladyship's honor, upon my honor; he, poor man—hark you in your ear—a mere eunuch.

LADY FIDGET.

Oh filthy French beast! Faugh, faugh! Why do we 120 stay? Let's be gone; I can't endure the sight of him.

SIR JASPAR.

Stay but till the chairs* come; they'll be here presently.

LADY FIDGET.

No, no.

---

8 *Ecole des filles*] notoriously bawdy dialogues by Michel Millot (1655); the "second part," like the "new postures," was nonexistent

SIR JASPAR.

Nor can I stay longer: 'tis—let me see, a quarter 125 and a half quarter of a minute past eleven; the Council[9] will be sat; I must away. Business must be preferred always before love and ceremony with the wise, Mr. Horner.

HORNER.

And the impotent, Sir Jaspar. 130

SIR JASPAR.

Aye, aye, the impotent Master Horner, ha, ha, ha!

LADY FIDGET.

What, leave us with a filthy man alone in his lodgings?

SIR JASPAR.

He's an innocent man now, you know. Pray stay, I'll hasten the chairs to you.—Mr. Horner, your servant. 135 I should be glad to see you at my house. Pray, come and dine with me and play at cards with my wife after dinner; you are fit for women at that game yet, ha, ha! (*Aside.*) 'Tis as much a husband's prudence to provide innocent diversion for a wife as to hinder 140 her unlawful pleasures, and he had better employ her than let her employ herself.—Farewell. (*Exit.*)

HORNER.

Your servant, Sir Jaspar.

LADY FIDGET.

I will not stay with him, faugh!

HORNER.

Nay madam, I beseech you stay, if it be but to see 145 I can be as civil to ladies yet as they would desire.

LADY FIDGET.

No, no, faugh, you cannot be civil to ladies.

DAINTY.

You as civil as ladies would desire!

LADY FIDGET.

No, no, no, faugh, faugh, faugh!

Exeunt Lady Fidget and Dainty.

QUACK.

Now I think, I, or you yourself rather, have done 150 your business with the women.

HORNER.

Thou art an ass. Don't you see already upon the

---

9 Council] the Privy Council, the King's advisory body

report and my carriage, this grave man of business
leaves his wife in my lodgings, invites me to his
house and wife, who before would not be   155
acquainted with me out of jealousy?

QUACK.

Nay, by this means you may be the more acquainted
with the husbands, but the less with the wives.

HORNER.

Let me alone; if I can but abuse the husbands, I'll
soon disabuse the wives. Stay—I'll reckon you up   160
the advantages I am like to have by my strategem:
first, I shall be rid of all my old acquaintances, the
most insatiable sorts of duns that invade our
lodgings in a morning. And next to the pleasure
of making a new mistress is that of being rid of   165
an old one and of all old debts: love, when it comes
to be so, is paid the most unwillingly.

QUACK.

Well, you may be so rid of your old acquaintances,
but how will you get any new ones?

HORNER.

Doctor, thou wilt never make a good chemist,[10]   170
thou art so incredulous and impatient. Ask but all
the young fellows of the Town if they do not lose
more time, like huntsmen, in starting the game than
in running it down; one knows not where to find
'em, who will or will not. Women of quality* are so   175
civil, you can hardly distinguish love from good
breeding, and a man is often mistaken. But now I
can be sure, she that shows an aversion to me loves
the sport, as those women that are gone, whom I
warrant to be right. And then the next thing is,   180
your* women of honor, as you call 'em, are only
chary of their reputations, not their persons, and 'tis
scandal they would avoid, not men. Now may I have
by the reputation of an eunuch the privileges of one
and be seen in a lady's chamber in a morning as early 185
as her husband, kiss virgins before their parents or
lovers, and may be, in short, the passe-partout of the
Town. Now, doctor.

QUACK.

Nay, now you shall be the doctor, and your process
is so new that we do not know but it may succeed.   190

---

[10] chemist] alchemist, who needs both credulity and patience to see his projection through

HORNER.

Not so new neither: *probatum est*,* doctor.

QUACK.

Well, I wish you luck and many patients whilst I
go to mine. (*Exit.*)

Enter Harcourt and Dorilant to Horner.

HARCOURT.

Come, your appearance at the play yesterday has,
I hope, hardened you for the future against the   195
women's contempt and the men's raillery, and now
you'll abroad as you were wont.

HORNER.

Did I not bear it bravely?*

DORILANT.

With a most theatrical impudence, nay, more than
the orange wenches show there or a drunken vizard   200
mask* or a great bellied actress, nay, or the most
impudent of creatures, an ill poet, or what is yet
more impudent, a second-hand critic.

HORNER.

But what say the ladies? Have they no pity?

HARCOURT.

What ladies? The vizard masks, you know, never   205
pity a man when all's gone though in their service.

DORILANT.

And for the women in the boxes, you'd never pity
them when 'twas in your power.

HARCOURT.

They say 'tis pity, but all that deal with common
women should be served so.   210

DORILANT.

Nay I dare swear, they won't admit you to play at
cards with them, go to plays with 'em, or do the
little duties which other shadows of men are wont
to do for 'em.

HORNER.

Who do you call shadows of men?   215

DORILANT.

Half men.

HORNER.

What, boys?

DORILANT.

Aye, your old boys, old *beaux garçons*,[11] who like

---

[11] *beaux garçons*] fops (literally, pretty boys [Fr.])

superannuated stallions are suffered to run, feed, 220
and whinny with the mares as long as they live,
though they can do nothing else.

HORNER.

Well, a pox on love and wenching; women serve
but to keep a man from better company. Though
I can't enjoy them, I shall you the more. Good 225
fellowship and friendship are lasting, rational, and
manly pleasures.

HARCOURT.

For all that, give me some of those pleasures you
call effeminate, too; they help to relish one another.

HORNER.

They disturb one another. 230

HARCOURT.

No, mistresses are like books: if you pore upon
them too much, they doze you and make you unfit
for company, but if used discreetly, you are the
fitter for conversation by 'em.

DORILANT.

A mistress should be like a little country retreat 235
near the Town, not to dwell in constantly but only
for a night and away, to taste the Town the better
when a man returns.

HORNER.

I tell you, 'tis as hard to be a good fellow, a good
friend, and a lover of women as 'tis to be a good 240
fellow, a good friend, and a lover of money. You
cannot follow both; then choose your side. Wine
gives you liberty; love takes it away.

DORILANT.

Gad, he's in the right on't.

HORNER.

Wine gives you joy; love, grief and tortures, besides 245
the chirurgeon's. Wine makes us witty; love, only
sots. Wine makes us sleep; love breaks it.

DORILANT.

By the world, he has reason, Harcourt.

HORNER.

Wine makes—

DORILANT.

Aye, wine makes us—makes us princes; love makes 250
us beggars, poor rogues, egad—and wine—

HORNER.

So, there's one converted.—No, no, love and wine,
oil and vinegar.

HARCOURT.

I grant it: love will still* be uppermost.

HORNER.

Come, for my part I will have only those glorious 255
manly pleasures of being very drunk and very
slovenly.

Enter boy.

BOY.

Mr. Sparkish is below, sir.

HARCOURT.

What, my dear friend! a rogue that is fond of me
only, I think, for abusing him. 260

DORILANT.

No, he can no more think the men laugh at him
than that women jilt him, his opinion of himself
is so good.

HORNER.

Well, there's another pleasure by drinking, I
thought not of: I shall lose his acquaintance 265
because he cannot drink, and you know 'tis a very
hard thing to be rid of him, for he's one of those
nauseous offerers at wit who, like the worst
fiddlers, run themselves into all companies.

HARCOURT.

One that by being in the company of men of sense 270
would pass for one.

HORNER.

And may so to the short-sighted world, as a false
jewel amongst true ones is not discerned at a
distance; his company is as troublesome to us as a
cuckold's when you have a mind to his wife's. 275

HARCOURT.

No, the rogue will not let us enjoy one another,
but ravishes our conversation, though he signifies
no more to't than Sir Martin Mar-all's[12] gaping
and awkward thrumming upon the lute does to his
man's voice and music. 280

DORILANT.

And to pass for a wit in Town shows himself a fool
every night to us that are guilty of the plot.

---

12 Sir Martin Mar-all] foolish hero of Dryden's play of that
name (1667), who mimes a serenade to his mistress even
after his hidden servant has stopped singing and playing his lute

HORNER.

Such wits as he are, to a company of reasonable men, like rooks[13] to the gamesters, who only fill a room at the table but are so far from contributing to the play that they only serve to spoil the fancy of those that do.

DORILANT.

Nay, they are used like rooks, too—snubbed, checked, and abused—yet the rogues will hang on.

HORNER.

A pox on 'em and all that force Nature and would be still what she forbids 'em; affectation is her greatest monster.

HARCOURT.

Most men are the contraries to that they would seem: your bully, you see, is a coward with a long sword; the little humbly fawning physician with his ebony cane is he that destroys men.

DORILANT.

The usurer, a poor rogue possessed of moldy bonds and mortgages, and we they call spendthrifts are only wealthy who lay out his money upon daily new purchases of pleasure.

HORNER.

Aye, your arrantest cheat is your trustee or executor; your jealous man, the greatest cuckold; your churchman, the greatest atheist; and your noisy pert rogue of a wit, the greatest fop, dullest ass, and worst company, as you shall see. For here he comes.

Enter Sparkish to them.

SPARKISH.

How is't, sparks, how is't? Well faith, Harry, I must rally thee a little, ha, ha, ha, upon the report in Town of thee, ha, ha, ha. I can't hold i'faith. Shall I speak?

HORNER.

Yes, but you'll be so bitter then.

SPARKISH.

Honest Dick and Frank here shall answer for me; I will not be extreme bitter, by the universe.

HARCOURT.

We will be bound in ten thousand pound bond, he shall not be bitter at all.

DORILANT.

Nor sharp, nor sweet.

HORNER.

What, not downright insipid?

SPARKISH.

Nay then, since you are so brisk and provoke me, take what follows: you must know, I was discoursing and rallying with some ladies yesterday, and they happened to talk of the fine new signs in Town.

HORNER.

Very fine ladies, I believe.

SPARKISH.

Said I, "I know where the best new sign is." "Where?" says one of the ladies. "In Covent Garden,*" I replied. Said another, "In what street?" "In Russell Street," answered I. "Lord," says another, "I'm sure there was ne'er a fine new sign there yesterday." "Yes, but there was," said I again, "and it came out of France and has been there a fortnight."

DORILANT.

A pox, I can hear no more, prithee.

HORNER.

No, hear him out; let him tune his crowd* a while.

HARCOURT.

The worst music, the greatest preparation.

SPARKISH.

Nay faith, I'll make you laugh. "It cannot be," says a third lady. "Yes, yes," quoth I again. Says a fourth lady—

HORNER.

Look to't, we'll have no more ladies.

SPARKISH.

No? Then mark, mark, now. Said I to the fourth, "Did you never see Mr. Horner? He lodges in Russell Street, and he's a sign of a man, you know, since he came out of France." He, ha, he!

HORNER.

But the devil take me if thine be the sign of a jest.

SPARKISH.

With that they all fell a-laughing till they bepissed themselves. What, but it does not move you, methinks? Well, I see one had as good go to law without a witness as break a jest without a laugher on one's side.—Come, come, sparks, but where do we dine? I have left at Whitehall an earl to dine with you.

---

13 rooks] here gulls or foolish victims, rather than the more common meaning, tricksters or cheaters

DORILANT.

Why, I thought thou hadst loved a man with a title better than a suit with a French trimming to't.

HARCOURT.

Go, to him again.

SPARKISH.

No sir, a wit to me is the greatest title in the world. 350

HORNER.

But go dine with your earl, sir; he may be exceptious. We are your friends and will not take it ill to be left, I do assure you.

HARCOURT.

Nay, faith he shall go to him.

SPARKISH.

Nay, pray gentlemen. 355

DORILANT.

We'll thrust you out if you wonnot. What, disappoint anybody for us?

SPARKISH.

Nay, dear gentlemen, hear me.

HORNER.

No, no, sir, by no means; pray go, sir.

SPARKISH.

Why, dear rogues— 360

DORILANT.

No, no.

They all thrust him out of the room.

ALL.

Ha, ha, ha.

Sparkish returns.

SPARKISH.

But sparks, pray hear me. What, d'ye think I'll eat then with gay shallow fops and silent coxcombs? I think wit as necessary at dinner as a glass of good 365 wine, and that's the reason I never have any stomach when I eat alone. Come, but where do we dine?

HORNER.

Ev'n where you will.

SPARKISH.

At Chateline's.[14] 370

_____

[14] Chateline's] fashionable French restaurant in Covent Garden*

DORILANT.

Yes, if you will.

SPARKISH.

Or at the Cock.[15]

DORILANT.

Yes, if you please.

SPARKISH.

Or at the Dog and Partridge.[16]

HORNER.

Aye, if you have a mind to't, for we shall dine at 375 neither.

SPARKISH.

Pshaw, with your fooling we shall lose the new play, and I would no more miss seeing a new play the first day than I would miss sitting in the wits' row[17]; therefore, I'll go fetch my mistress and 380 away. (*Exit.*)

Enter Pinchwife.

HORNER.

Who have we here, Pinchwife?

PINCHWIFE.

Gentlemen, your humble servant.

HORNER.

Well Jack, by thy long absence from the Town, the grumness[18] of thy countenance, and the 385 slovenliness of thy habit, I should give thee joy, should I not, of marriage?

PINCHWIFE. (*Aside.*)

Death, does he know I'm married, too? I thought to have concealed it from him at least.—My long stay in the country will excuse my dress, and I have a suit 390 of law that brings me up to Town that puts me out of humor; besides, I must give Sparkish tomorrow five thousand pound to lie with my sister.

HORNER.

Nay, you country gentlemen, rather than not purchase, will buy anything, and he is a cracked 395

_____

[15] the Cock] Out of many taverns by that name, this probably refers to a less fashionable one in Bow Street, Covent Garden, frequented by Wycherley.

[16] the Dog and Partridge] an unfashionable tavern in Fleet Street

[17] wits' row] near the front of the theater pit

[18] grumness] moroseness, gloominess

title,[19] if we may quibble. Well, but am I to give thee joy? I heard thou wert married.

PINCHWIFE.

What then?

HORNER.

Why, the next thing that is to be heard is thou'rt a cuckold.   400

PINCHWIFE. (*Aside.*)

Insupportable name.

HORNER.

But I did not expect marriage from such a whoremaster as you: one that knew the Town so much and women so well.

PINCHWIFE.

Why, I have married no London wife.   405

HORNER.

Pshaw, that's all one: that grave circumspection in marrying a country wife is like refusing a deceitful pampered Smithfield[20] jade to go and be cheated by a friend in the country.

PINCHWIFE. (*Aside.*)

A pox on him and his simile.—At least we are a   410
little surer of the breed there, know what her keeping has been, whether foiled[21] or unsound.*

HORNER.

Come, come, I have known a clap gotten in Wales, and there are cozens,[22] justices, clerks, and chaplains in the country; I won't say coachmen.   415
But she's handsome and young?

PINCHWIFE. (*Aside.*)

I'll answer as I should do.—No, no, she has no beauty but her youth, no attraction but her modesty: wholesome, homely, and housewifely, that's all.

DORILANT.

He talks as like a grazier as he looks.   420

PINCHWIFE.

She's too awkward, ill-favored, and silly* to bring to Town.

---

19 cracked title] Either Sparkish's patrimony or his genealogy is of questionable value.

20 Smithfield] suburban market, known for its sharp practice

21 foiled] injured (of a horse), deflowered (of a woman)

22 cozens] a variant of "cozeners" (q.v.) or possibly an alternate spelling of "cousins"

HARCOURT.

Then methinks you should bring her to be taught breeding.

PINCHWIFE.

To be taught! No sir, I thank you, good wives and   425
private soldiers should be ignorant. [*Aside.*] I'll keep her from your instructions, I warrant you.

HARCOURT. (*Aside.*)

The rogue is as jealous as if his wife were not ignorant.

HORNER.

Why, if she be ill-favored, there will be less danger   430
here for you than by leaving her in the country: we have such variety of dainties that we are seldom hungry.

DORILANT.

But they have always coarse, constant, swingeing stomachs in the country.   435

HARCOURT.

Foul feeders indeed.

DORILANT.

And your hospitality is great there.

HARCOURT.

Open house, every man's welcome.

PINCHWIFE.

So, so, gentlemen.

HORNER.

But prithee, why wouldst thou marry her? If she   440
be ugly, ill-bred, and silly, she must be rich then.

PINCHWIFE.

As rich as if she brought me twenty thousand pound out of this Town, for she'll be as sure not to spend her moderate portion as a London baggage would be to spend hers, let it be what it would; so 'tis all one. Then   445
because she's ugly, she's the likelier to be my own, and being ill-bred, she'll hate conversation and, since silly and innocent, will not know the difference betwixt a man of one-and-twenty and one of forty.

HORNER.

Nine—to my knowledge. But if she be silly, she'll   450
expect as much from a man of forty-nine as from him of one-and-twenty. But methinks wit is more necessary than beauty, and I think no young woman ugly that has it and no handsome woman agreeable without it.   455

PINCHWIFE.

'Tis my maxim: he's a fool that marries, but he's a

greater that does not marry a fool. What is wit in a wife good for but to make a man a cuckold?

PINCHWIFE.

Well gentlemen, you may laugh at me, but you shall never lie with my wife. I know the Town.   490

HORNER.

Yes, to keep it from his knowledge.

HORNER.

But prithee, was not the way you were in better? Is not keeping* better than marriage?

PINCHWIFE.

A fool cannot contrive to make her husband a   460
cuckold.

PINCHWIFE.

A pox on't, the jades would jilt me; I could never keep a whore to myself.

HORNER.

No, but she'll club with a man that can, and what is worse, if she cannot make her husband a cuckold, she'll make him jealous and pass for one, and then 'tis all one.   465

HORNER.

So then you only married to keep a whore to   495
yourself. Well but let me tell you, women, as you say, are, like soldiers, made constant and loyal by good pay rather than by oaths and covenants. Therefore, I'd advise my friends to keep rather than marry since, too, I find by your example it does   500
not serve one's turn, for I saw you yesterday in the eighteen-penny place[24] with a pretty country wench.

PINCHWIFE.

Well, well, I'll take care for one: my wife shall make me no cuckold though she had your help, Mr. Horner. I understand the Town, sir.

DORILANT. (Aside.)

His help!

PINCHWIFE. (Aside.)

How the devil! Did he see my wife then? I sat there that she might not be seen, but she shall never go   505
to a play again.

HARCOURT. (Aside.)

He's come newly to Town, it seems, and has not   470
heard how things are with him.

HORNER.

What, dost thou blush at nine-and-forty for having been seen with a wench?

HORNER.

But tell me, has marriage cured thee of whoring, which it seldom does?

DORILANT.

No faith, I warrant 'twas his wife, which he seated there out of sight, for he's a cunning rogue and   510
understands the Town.

HARCOURT.

'Tis more than age can do.

HARCOURT.

He blushes; then 'twas his wife, for men are now more ashamed to be seen with them in public than with a wench.

HORNER.

No, the word is, "I'll marry and live honest.*" But   475
a marriage vow is like a penitent gamester's oath and entering into bonds and penalties to stint himself to such a particular small sum at play for the future, which makes him but the more eager, and not being able to hold out, loses his money   480
again and his forfeit to boot.

PINCHWIFE. (Aside.)

Hell and damnation! I'm undone since Horner has   515
seen her and they know 'twas she.

DORILANT.

Aye, aye, a gamester will be a gamester whilst his money lasts, and a whoremaster, whilst his vigor.

HORNER.

But prithee, was it thy wife? She was exceedingly pretty. I was in love with her at that distance.

PINCHWIFE.

You are like never to be nearer to her. Your servant, gentlemen. (Offers* to go.)   520

HARCOURT.

Nay, I have known 'em, when they are broke and can lose no more, keep a-fumbling with the box[23]   485
in their hands to fool with only and hinder other gamesters.

DORILANT.

That had wherewithal to make lusty stakes.

---

23 box] dice cup, with bawdy suggestion

---

24 the eighteen-penny place] the middle gallery in the theater, away from the gallants in the pit and boxes

HORNER.

Nay, prithee stay.

PINCHWIFE.

I cannot; I will not.

HORNER.

Come, you shall dine with us.

PINCHWIFE.

I have dined already.

HORNER.

Come, I know thou hast not. I'll treat thee, dear   525
rogue; thou shalt spend none of thy Hampshire
money today.

PINCHWIFE. (Aside.)

Treat me! So he uses me already like his cuckold.

HORNER.

Nay, you shall not go.

PINCHWIFE.

I must I have business at home. (Exit.)   530

HARCOURT.

To beat his wife: he's as jealous of her as a
Cheapside* husband of a Covent Garden* wife.

HORNER.

Why, 'tis as hard to find an old whoremaster
without jealousy and the gout as a young one
without fear or the pox.   535
As gout in age from pox in youth proceeds,
So wenching past, then jealousy succeeds:
The worst disease that love and wenching breeds.

[Exeunt.]

Act II, scene i. [Pinchwife's lodging.]

*Margery Pinchwife and Alithea, Pinchwife peeping
behind at the door.*

MARGERY.

Pray sister, where are the best fields and woods to
walk in in London?

ALITHEA.

A pretty question. Why sister, Mulberry Garden[25]
and St. James's Park* and, for close walks, the New
Exchange.*   5

_____

25 Mulberry Garden] a fashionable promenade within St.
James's Park,* at the site of the current Buckingham
Palace

MARGERY.

Pray sister, tell my why my husband looks so grum
here in Town and keeps me up so close and will
not let me go a-walking nor let me wear my best
gown yesterday?

ALITHEA.

Oh, he's jealous, sister.   10

MARGERY.

Jealous, what's that?

ALITHEA.

He's afraid you should love another man.

MARGERY.

How should he be afraid of my loving another
man when he will not let me see any but himself?

ALITHEA.

Did he not carry you yesterday to a play?   15

MARGERY.

Aye, but we sat amongst ugly people; he would not
let me come near the gentry, who sat under us, so
that I could not see 'em. He told me none but
naughty women sat there, whom they toused and
moused, but I would have ventured for all that.   20

ALITHEA.

But how did you like the play?

MARGERY.

Indeed I was aweary of the play, but I liked
hugeously the actors; they are the goodliest,
properest men, sister.

ALITHEA.

Oh, but you must not like the actors, sister.   25

MARGERY.

Ay, how should I help it, sister? Pray sister, when
my husband comes in, will you ask leave for me
to go a-walking?

ALITHEA. (Aside.)

A-walking, ha, ha! Lord, a country gentlewoman's
leisure is the drudgery of a foot post, and she   30
requires as much airing as her husband's horses.

Enter Pinchwife.

But here comes your husband; I'll ask, though I'm
sure he'll not grant it.

MARGERY.

He says he won't let me go abroad for fear of
catching the pox.   35

ALITHEA.

Fie, the small pox you should say.

MARGERY.

Oh my dear, dear bud, welcome home. Why dost thou look so froppish?[26] Who has nangered[27] thee?

PINCHWIFE.

You're a fool. 40

Margery goes aside and cries.

ALITHEA.

Faith so she is, for crying for no fault, poor, tender creature!

PINCHWIFE.

What, you would have her as impudent as yourself, as arrant a jill-flirt,* a gadder, a magpie, and, to say all, a mere* notorious Town woman? 45

ALITHEA.

Brother, you are my only censurer, and the honor of your family shall sooner suffer in your wife there than in me, though I take the innocent liberty of the Town.

PINCHWIFE.

Hark you, mistress, do not talk so before my wife. 50 The innocent liberty of the Town!

ALITHEA.

Why pray, who boasts of any intrigue with me? What lampoon has made my name notorious? What ill women frequent my lodgings? I keep no company with any women of scandalous 55 reputations.

PINCHWIFE.

No, you keep the men of scandalous reputations company.

ALITHEA.

Where? Would you not have me civil? answer 'em in a box at the plays? in the Drawing Room* at White- 60 hall?* in St. James's Park? Mulberry Garden? or—

PINCHWIFE.

Hold, hold, do not teach my wife where the men are to be found; I believe she's the worse for your Town documents[28] already. I bid you keep her in ignorance as I do. 65

---

26 froppish] fretful, peevish

27 nangered] angered; Margery tacks on the *n* in her characteristic babytalk with her *bud*.

28 documents] lessons

MARGERY.

Indeed, be not angry with her, bud; she will tell me nothing of the Town, though I ask her a thousand times a day.

PINCHWIFE.

Then you are very inquisitive to know, I find?

MARGERY.

Not I, indeed, dear. I hate London. Our place- 70 house[29] in the country is worth a thousand of 't. Would I were there again!

PINCHWIFE.

So you shall, I warrant, but were you not talking of plays and players when I came in?—You are her encourager in such discourses. 75

MARGERY.

No indeed, dear, she chid me just now for liking the playermen.

PINCHWIFE. (Aside.)

Nay, if she be so innocent as to own to me her liking them, there is no hurt in't.—Come my poor rogue, but thou lik'st none better than me? 80

MARGERY.

Yes indeed, but I do: the playermen are finer folks.

PINCHWIFE.

But you love none better then me?

MARGERY.

You are mine own dear bud, and I know you; I hate a stranger.

PINCHWIFE.

Aye my dear, you must love me only and not be 85 like the naughty Town women, who only hate their husbands and love every man else, love plays, visits, fine coaches, fine clothes, fiddles, balls, treats, and so lead a wicked Town life.

MARGERY.

Nay, if to enjoy all these things be a Town life, 90 London is not so bad a place, dear.

PINCHWIFE.

How! If you love me, you must hate London.

ALITHEA. [Aside.]

The fool has forbid me discovering* to her the pleasures of the Town, and he is now setting her agog upon them himself. 95

---

29 place-house] chief residence of an estate

MARGERY.

But husband, do the Town women love the playermen, too?

PINCHWIFE.

Yes, I warrant you.

MARGERY.

Ay, I warrant you.

PINCHWIFE.

Why, you do not, I hope?   100

MARGERY.

No, no, bud, but why have we no playermen in the country?

PINCHWIFE.

Hah! Mrs. Minx, ask me no more to go to a play.

MARGERY.

Nay, why, love? I did not care for going, but when you forbid me, you make me, as't were, desire it.   105

ALITHEA. (Aside.)

So 'twill be in other things, I warrant.

MARGERY.

Pray, let me go to a play, dear.

PINCHWIFE.

Hold your peace; I wonnot.

MARGERY.

Why, love?

PINCHWIFE.

Why, I'll tell you.

ALITHEA. (Aside.)   110

Nay, if he tell her, she'll give him more cause to forbid her that place.

MARGERY.

Pray, why, dear?

PINCHWIFE.

First, you like the actors, and the gallants may like you.   115

MARGERY.

What, a homely country girl? No, bud, nobody will like me.

PINCHWIFE.

I tell you, yes, they may.

MARGERY.

No, no, you jest. I won't believe you; I will go.

PINCHWIFE.

I tell you then that one of the lewdest fellows in   120
Town, who saw you there, told me he was in love with you.

MARGERY.

Indeed! Who, who, pray, who was't?

PINCHWIFE. (Aside.)

I've gone too far and slipped before I was aware. How overjoyed she is!   125

MARGERY.

Was it any Hampshire gallant, any of our neighbors? I promise you, I am beholding to him.

PINCHWIFE.

I promise you, you lie, for he would but ruin you as he has done hundreds. He has no other love for women but that. Such as he look upon women like   130
basilisks, but to destroy 'em.

MARGERY.

Ay, but if he loves me, why should he ruin me? Answer me to that. Methinks he should not; I would do him no harm.

ALITHEA.

Ha, ha, ha.   135

PINCHWIFE.

'Tis very well, but I'll keep him from doing you any harm, or me either.

Enter Sparkish and Harcourt.

But here comes company. Get you in, get you in.

MARGERY.

But pray, husband, is he a pretty gentleman that loves me?   140

PINCHWIFE.

In baggage, in. (*Thrusts her in; shuts the door.*)
What, all the lewd libertines of the Town brought to my lodging by this easy coxcomb! S'death,* I'll not suffer it.

SPARKISH.

Here Harcourt, do you approve my choice?—Dear   145
little rogue, I told you I'd bring you acquainted with all my friends, the wits, and—

Harcourt salutes her.*

PINCHWIFE.

Aye, they shall know her as well as you yourself will, I warrant you.

SPARKISH.

This is one of those, my pretty rogue, that are to   150
dance at your wedding tomorrow, and him you must bid welcome ever to what you and I have.

PINCHWIFE. (*Aside.*)

Monstrous!

SPARKISH.

Harcourt, how dost thou like her, faith?—Nay dear, do not look down; I should hate to have a 155 wife of mine out of countenance at any thing.

PINCHWIFE.

Wonderful!

SPARKISH.

Tell me, I say, Harcourt, how dost thou like her? Thou hast stared upon her enough to resolve me.

HARCOURT.

So infinitely well that I could wish I had a mistress, 160 too, that might differ from her in nothing but her love and engagement to you.

ALITHEA.

Sir, Master Sparkish has often told me that his acquaintance were all wits and railleurs,[30] and now I find it. 165

SPARKISH.

No, by the universe, madam, he does not rally now; you may believe him. I do assure you, he is the honestest, worthiest, true-hearted gentleman— a man of such perfect honor, he would say nothing to a lady he does not mean. 170

PINCHWIFE. [*Aside.*]

Praising another man to his mistress!

HARCOURT.

Sir, you are so beyond expectation obliging, that—

SPARKISH.

Nay, egad, I am sure you do admire her extremely; I see't in your eyes.—He does admire you, madam.—By the world, don't you? 175

HARCOURT.

Yes, above the world or the most glorious part of it, her whole sex, and till now I never thought I should have envied you, or any man about to marry, but you have the best excuse for marriage I ever knew.

ALITHEA.

Nay, now, sir, I'm satisfied you are of the society of 180 the wits and railleurs since you cannot spare your friend, even when he is but too civil to you, but the surest sign is since you are an enemy to marriage, for that I hear you hate as much as business or bad wine.

HARCOURT.

Truly madam, I never was an enemy to marriage 185 till now because marriage was never an enemy to me before.

ALITHEA.

But why, sir, is marriage an enemy to you now? because it robs you of your friend here? For you look upon a friend married as one gone into a 190 monastery, that is, dead to the world.

HARCOURT.

'Tis indeed because you marry him. I see, madam, you can guess my meaning. I do confess heartily and openly I wish it were in my power to break the match. By heavens, I would! 195

SPARKISH.

Poor Frank!

ALITHEA.

Would you be so unkind to me?

HARCOURT.

No, no, 'tis not because I would be unkind to you.

SPARKISH.

Poor Frank! No, gad, 'tis only his kindness to me.

PINCHWIFE. (*Aside.*)

Great kindness to you, indeed. Insensible fop, let 200 a man make love* to his wife to his face!

SPARKISH.

Come, dear Frank, for all my wife there that shall be, thou shalt enjoy me sometimes, dear rogue. By my honor, we men of wit condole for our deceased brother in marriage as much as for one dead in earnest. 205 I think that was prettily said of me, hah, Harcourt? But come, Frank, be not melancholy for me.

HARCOURT.

No, I assure you I am not melancholy for you.

SPARKISH.

Prithee Frank, dost think my wife that shall be there a fine person? 210

HARCOURT.

I could gaze upon her till I became as blind as you are.

SPARKISH.

How, as I am! How?

HARCOURT.

Because you are a lover, and true lovers are blind, stock-blind.[31] 215

---

30 railleurs] those who banter or mock; a fashionable French word appealing to Sparkish

31 stock-blind] blind as a stock, or log, purblind (cf. stock-still)

SPARKISH.

True, true, but by the world, she has wit, too, as
well as beauty. Go, go with her into a corner and
try if she has wit; talk to her anything; she's bashful
before me.

HARCOURT.

Indeed, if a woman wants* wit in a corner, she has   220
it nowhere.

ALITHEA. (*Aside to Sparkish.*)

Sir, you dispose of me a little before your time.

SPARKISH.

Nay, nay, madam, let me have an earnest of your
obedience, or— Go, go, madam

Harcourt courts Alithea aside.

PINCHWIFE.

How, sir! if you are not concerned for the honor   225
of a wife, I am for that of a sister. He shall not
debauch her. Be a pander to your own wife, bring
men to her, let 'em make love* before your face,
thrust 'em into a corner together, then leave 'em
in private! Is this your Town wit and conduct?   230

SPARKISH.

Ha, ha, ha, a silly* wise rogue would make one
laugh more than a stark fool, ha, ha! I shall burst.
Nay, you shall not disturb 'em. I'll vex thee, by the
world. (*Struggles with Pinchwife to keep him from
Harcourt and Alithea.*)   235

ALITHEA.

The writings are drawn, sir, settlements made; 'tis
too late, sir, and past all revocation.

HARCOURT.

Then so is my death.

ALITHEA.

I would not be unjust to him.

HARCOURT.

Then why to me so?   240

ALITHEA.

I have no obligation to you.

HARCOURT.

My love.

ALITHEA.

I had his before.

HARCOURT.

You never had it: he wants,* you see, jealousy, the
only infallible sign of it.   245

ALITHEA.

Love proceeds from esteem; he cannot distrust my
virtue. Besides, he loves me, or he would not marry
me.

HARCOURT.

Marrying you is no more sign of his love than
bribing your woman, that he may marry you, is a   250
sign of his generosity. Marriage is rather a sign of
interest than love, and he that marries a fortune,
covets a mistress, not loves her. But if you take marriage for a sign of love, take it from me immediately.

ALITHEA.

No, now you have put a scruple in my head. But   255
in short, sir, to end our dispute, I must marry him:
my reputation would suffer in the world else.

HARCOURT.

No, if you do marry him, with your pardon,
madam, your reputation suffers in the world, and
you would be thought in necessity for a cloak.   260

ALITHEA.

Nay, now you are rude, sir.—Mr. Sparkish, pray
come hither; your friend here is very troublesome
and very loving.

HARCOURT. (*Aside to Alithea.*)

Hold, hold—

PINCHWIFE.

D'ye hear that?   265

SPARKISH.

Why, d'ye think I'll seem to be jealous, like a
country bumpkin?

PINCHWIFE.

No, rather be a cuckold, like a credulous cit.*

HARCOURT.

Madam, you would not have been so little
generous* as to have told him.   270

ALITHEA.

Yes, since you could be so little generous* as to
wrong him.

HARCOURT.

Wrong him! No man can do't; he's beneath an
injury: a bubble,* a coward, a senseless idiot, a
wretch so contemptible to all the world but you   275
that—

ALITHEA.

Hold, do not rail at him, for since he is like to be
my husband, I am resolved to like him. Nay, I

think I am obliged to tell him you are not his friend.—Master Sparkish, Master Sparkish. 280

SPARKISH.

What, what? Now, dear rogue, has not she wit?

HARCOURT. (*Speaks surlily.*)

Not so much as I thought and hoped she had.

ALITHEA.

Mr. Sparkish, do you bring people to rail at you?

HARCOURT.

Madam—

SPARKISH.

How! No, but if he does rail at me, 'tis but in jest, 285 I warrant, what we wits do for one another and never take any notice of it.

ALITHEA.

He spoke so scurrilously of you I had no patience to hear him; besides, he has been making love* to me. 290

HARCOURT. (*Aside.*)

True, damned, tell-tale woman.

SPARKISH.

Pshaw, to show his parts.* We wits rail and make love often but to show our parts; as we have no affections, so we have no malice, we—

ALITHEA.

He said you were a wretch, below an injury. 295

SPARKISH.

Pshaw.

HARCOURT. [*Aside.*]

Damned, senseless, impudent, virtuous jade! Well, since she won't let me have her, she'll do as good: she'll make me hate her.

ALITHEA.

A common bubble.* 300

SPARKISH.

Pshaw.

ALITHEA.

A coward.

SPARKISH.

Pshaw, pshaw.

ALITHEA.

A senseless, driveling idiot.

SPARKISH.

How! Did he disparage my parts?* Nay, then my 305 honor's concerned. I can't put up that, sir.—By the world, brother, help me to kill him. (*Aside.*) I may

draw now, since we have the odds of him; 'tis a good occasion, too, before my mistress. (*Offers* to draw.*) 310

ALITHEA.

Hold, hold!

SPARKISH.

What, what?

ALITHEA. (*Aside.*)

I must not let 'em kill the gentleman neither, for his kindness* to me. I am so far from hating him that I wish my gallant had his person and 315 understanding. Nay, if my honor—

SPARKISH.

I'll be thy death.

ALITHEA.

Hold, hold! Indeed, to tell the truth, the gentleman said after all that what he spoke was but out of friendship to you. 320

SPARKISH.

How! Say I am, I am a fool, that is, no wit, out of friendship to me?

ALITHEA.

Yes, to try whether I was concerned enough for you, and made love* to me only to be satisfied of my virtue, for your sake. 325

HARCOURT. (*Aside.*)

Kind however—

SPARKISH.

Nay, if it were so, my dear rogue, I ask thee pardon, but why would not you tell me so, faith?

HARCOURT.

Because I did not think on't, faith.

SPARKISH.

Come, Horner does not come, Harcourt, let's be 330 gone to the new play.—Come, madam.

ALITHEA.

I will not go if you intend to leave me alone in the box and run into the pit, as you use to do.

SPARKISH.

Pshaw, I'll leave Harcourt with you in the box to entertain you, and that's as good. If I sat in the 335 box, I should be thought no judge but of trimmings.—Come away, Harcourt, lead her down.

Exeunt Sparkish, Harcourt, and Alithea.

PINCHWIFE.

Well, go thy ways, for the flower of the true Town fops, such as spend their estates before they come to 'em and are cuckolds before they're married. But let me go look to my own freehold.—How— 340

Enter My Lady Fidget, Dainty, and Mistress Squeamish.

LADY FIDGET.

Your servant, sir. Where is your lady? We are come to wait upon her to the new play.

PINCHWIFE.

New play! 345

LADY FIDGET.

And my husband will wait upon you presently.

PINCHWIFE. (*Aside.*)

Damn your civility.—Madam, by no means, I will not see Sir Jaspar here till I have waited upon him at home, nor shall my wife see you till she has waited upon your ladyship at your lodgings. 350

LADY FIDGET.

Now we are here, sir—

PINCHWIFE.

No, madam.

DAINTY.

Pray, let us see her.

MRS. SQUEAMISH.

We will not stir till we see her.

PINCHWIFE. (*Aside.*)

A pox on you all. (*Goes to the door and returns.*) 355
She has locked the door and is gone abroad.

LADY FIDGET.

No, you have locked the door, and she's within.

DAINTY.

They told us below she was here.

PINCHWIFE. [*Aside.*]

Will nothing do?—Well it must out then: to tell you the truth, ladies, which I was afraid to let you 360 know before lest it might endanger your lives, my wife has just now the small pox come out upon her. Do not be frightened, but pray, be gone ladies. You shall not stay here in danger of your lives. Pray get you gone, ladies. 365

LADY FIDGET.

No, no, we have all had 'em.

MRS. SQUEAMISH.

Alack, alack.

DAINTY.

Come, come, we must see how it goes with her. I understand the disease.

LADY FIDGET.

Come. 370

PINCHWIFE. (*Aside.*)

Well, there is no being too hard for women at their own weapon, lying; therefore, I'll quit the field. (*Exit.*)

MRS. SQUEAMISH.

Here's an example of jealousy.

LADY FIDGET.

Indeed, as the world goes, I wonder there are no 375 more jealous, since wives are so neglected.

DAINTY.

Pshaw, as the world goes, to what end should they be jealous?

LADY FIDGET.

Faugh, 'tis a nasty world.

MRS. SQUEAMISH.

That men of parts,* great acquaintance, and 380 quality* should take up with and spend themselves and fortunes in keeping* little playhouse creatures, faugh!

LADY FIDGET.

Nay, that women of understanding, great acquaintance, and good quality should fall a- 385 keeping, too, of little creatures, faugh!

MRS. SQUEAMISH.

Why, 'tis the men of quality's fault: they never visit women of honor and reputation as they used to do and have not so much as common civility for ladies of our rank but use us with the same indifference 390 and ill breeding as if we were all married to 'em.

LADY FIDGET.

She says true. 'Tis an arrant shame women of quality should be so slighted; methinks birth, birth, should go for something. I have known men admired, courted, and followed for their titles only. 395

MRS. SQUEAMISH.

Aye, one would think men of honor should not love, no more than marry, out of their own rank.

DAINTY.

Fie, fie upon 'em, they are come to think crossbreeding for themselves best, as well as for their dogs and horses. 400

LADY FIDGET.

They are dogs and horses for't.

MRS. SQUEAMISH.

One would think if not for love, for vanity a little.

DAINTY.

Nay, they do satisfy their vanity upon us sometimes and are kind* to us in their report, tell all the world they lie with us. 405

LADY FIDGET.

Damned rascals, that we should be only wronged by 'em! To report a man has had a person, when he has not had a person, is the greatest wrong in the whole world that can be done to a person.

MRS. SQUEAMISH.

Well, 'tis an arrant shame noble persons should be so wronged and neglected. 410

LADY FIDGET.

But still 'tis an arranter shame for a noble person to neglect her own honor and defame her own noble person with little inconsiderable fellows, faugh!

DAINTY.

I suppose the crime against our honor is the same with a man of quality as with another. 415

LADY FIDGET.

How! No, sure the man of quality is likest one's husband, and therefore, the fault should be the less.

DAINTY.

But then the pleasure should be the less. 420

LADY FIDGET.

Fie, fie, fie, for shame sister! Whither shall we ramble? Be continent in your discourse, or I shall hate you.

DAINTY.

Besides, an intrigue is so much the more notorious for the man's quality. 425

MRS. SQUEAMISH.

'Tis true, nobody takes notice of a private man, and therefore, with him 'tis more secret, and the crime's the less when 'tis not known.

LADY FIDGET.

You say true. I'faith, I think you are in the right on't. 'Tis not an injury to a husband till it be an injury to our honors, so that a woman of honor loses no honor with a private person, and to say truth— 430

DAINTY. (*Apart to Mrs. Squeamish.*)

So the little fellow is grown a private person—with her— 435

LADY FIDGET.

But still my dear, dear honor.

Enter Sir Jaspar, Horner, Dorilant.

SIR JASPAR.

Aye, my dear, dear of honor, thou hast still so much honor in thy mouth—

HORNER. (*Aside.*)

That she has none elsewhere—

LADY FIDGET.

Oh, what d'ye mean to bring in these upon us? 440

DAINTY.

Faugh, these are as bad as wits!

MRS. SQUEAMISH.

Faugh!

LADY FIDGET.

Let us leave the room.

SIR JASPAR.

Stay, stay, faith, to tell you the naked truth.

LADY FIDGET.

Fie, Sir Jaspar, do not use that word "naked." 445

SIR JASPAR.

Well, well, in short, I have business at Whitehall* and cannot go to the play with you; therefore, would have you go—

LADY FIDGET.

With those two to a play?

SIR JASPAR.

No, not with t'other, but with Mr. Horner; there can be no more scandal to go with him than with Mr. Tattle or Master Limberham.³² 450

LADY FIDGET.

With that nasty fellow! No—no.

SIR JASPAR.

Nay prithee dear, hear me. (*Whispers to Lady Fidget.*) 455

Horner, Dorilant drawing near Squeamish and Dainty.

---

32 Mr. Tattle or Master Limberham] obviously, by their names, unthreatening as companions: Tattle is self-explanatory; Limberham implies loose-limbed (we might say "weak-kneed")

HORNER.

Ladies.

DAINTY.

Stand off.

MRS. SQUEAMISH.

Do not approach us.

DAINTY.

You herd with the wits; you are obscenity all over.

MRS. SQUEAMISH.

And I would as soon look upon a picture of Adam   460
and Eve without fig leaves as any of you, if I could
help it; therefore, keep off and do not make us sick.

DORILANT.

What a devil are these?

HORNER.

Why, these are pretenders to honor, as critics to wit,
only by censuring others, and as every raw, peevish,   465
out-of-humored, affected, dull, tea-drinking,
arithmetical[33] fop sets up for a wit by railing at men
of sense, so these for honor, by railing at the Court
and ladies of as great honor as quality.*

SIR JASPAR.

Come Mr. Horner, I must desire you to go with   470
these ladies to the play, sir.

HORNER.

I, sir!

SIR JASPAR.

Aye, aye, come, sir.

HORNER.

I must beg your pardon, sir, and theirs. I will not
be seen in women's company in public again for   475
the world.

SIR JASPAR.

Ha, ha, strange aversion!

MRS. SQUEAMISH.

No, he's for women's company in private.

SIR JASPAR.

He—poor man—he! Ha, ha, ha.

DAINTY.

'Tis a greater shame amongst lewd fellows to be   480
seen in virtuous women's company than for the
women to be seen with them.

HORNER.

Indeed madam, the time was I only hated virtuous

_____

33 arithmetical] precise

women, but now I hate the other, too. I beg your
pardon, ladies.   485

LADY FIDGET.

You are very obliging, sir, because we would not
be troubled with you.

SIR JASPAR.

In sober sadness he shall go.

DORILANT.

Nay, if he wonnot, I am ready to wait upon the
ladies, and I think I am the fitter man.   490

SIR JASPAR.

You, sir! no, I thank you for that. Master Horner
is a privileged man amongst the virtuous ladies;
'twill be a great while before you are so. He, he,
he, he's my wife's gallant, he, he, he. No, pray
withdraw, sir, for as I take it, the virtuous ladies   495
have no business with you.

DORILANT.

And I am sure, he can have none with them. 'Tis
strange a man can't come amongst virtuous women
now but upon the same terms as men are admitted
into the Great Turk's seraglio, but heavens keep me   500
from being an ombre player with 'em. But where
is Pinchwife? (*Exit.*)

SIR JASPAR.

Come, come, man. What, avoid the sweet society of
womankind? that sweet, soft, gentle, tame, noble
creature woman, made for man's companion—   505

HORNER.

So is that soft, gentle, tame, and more noble
creature a spaniel, and has all their tricks: can fawn,
lie down, suffer beating, and fawn the more, barks
at your friends when they come to see you, makes
your bed hard, gives you fleas and the mange   510
sometimes, and all the difference is, the spaniel's
the more faithful animal and fawns but upon one
master.

SIR JASPAR.

He, he, he.

MRS. SQUEAMISH.

Oh, the rude beast!   515

DAINTY.

Insolent brute!

LADY FIDGET.

Brute! Stinking, mortified, rotten French wether,
to dare—

SIR JASPAR.

Hold, an't* please your ladyship.—For shame, Master Horner, your mother was a woman. (*Aside.*) 520 Now shall I never reconcile 'em.—Hark you, madam, take my advice in your anger: you know you often want* one to make up your drolling pack of ombre players, and you may cheat him easily, for he's an ill gamester and consequently 525 loves play. Besides, you know, you have but two old civil gentlemen (with stinking breaths, too) to wait upon you abroad. Take in the third into your service. The other are but crazy, and a lady should have a supernumerary gentleman-usher, as a 530 supernumerary coach-horse, lest sometimes you should be forced to stay at home.

LADY FIDGET.

But are you sure he loves play and has money?

SIR JASPAR.

He loves play as much as you and has money as much as I. 535

LADY FIDGET.

Then I am contented to make him pay for his scurrility; money makes up in a measure all other wants* in men. (*Aside.*) Those whom we cannot make hold for gallants, we make fine.[34]

SIR JASPAR. (*Aside.*)

So, so, now to mollify, to wheedle him.—Master 540 Horner, will you never keep civil company? Methinks 'tis time now, since you are only fit for them. Come, come, man, you must e'en fall to visiting our wives, eating at our tables, drinking tea with our virtuous relations after dinner, dealing cards 545 to 'em, reading plays and gazettes to 'em, picking fleas out of their shocks* for 'em, collecting receipts,* new songs, women, pages, and footmen for 'em.

HORNER.

I hope they'll afford me better employment, sir.

SIR JASPAR.

He, he, he! 'Tis fit you know your work before you 550 come into your place, and since you are unprovided of a lady to flatter and a good house to eat at, pray frequent mine and call my wife "mistress," and she shall call you "gallant," according to the custom. 555

---

34 fine] pay a penalty

HORNER.

Who, I?

SIR JASPAR.

Faith, thou shalt for my sake; come, for my sake only.

HORNER.

For your sake—

SIR JASPAR.

Come, come, here's a gamester for you; let him be a little familiar sometimes. Nay, what if a little rude? 560 Gamesters may be rude with ladies, you know.

LADY FIDGET.

Yes, losing gamesters have a privilege with women.

HORNER.

I always thought the contrary, that the winning gamester had most privilege with women, for when you have lost your money to a man, you'll lose 565 anything you have, all you have, they say, and he may use you as he pleases.

SIR JASPAR.

He, he, he! Well, win or lose, you shall have your liberty with her.

LADY FIDGET.

As he behaves himself and for your sake, I'll give 570 him admittance and freedom.

HORNER.

All sorts of freedom, madam?

SIR JASPAR.

Aye, aye, aye, all sorts of freedom thou canst take, and so go to her; begin thy new employment. Wheedle her, jest with her, and be better 575 acquainted one with another.

HORNER. (*Aside.*)

I think I know her already, therefore, may venture with her, my secret for hers.

Horner and Lady Fidget whisper.

SIR JASPAR.

Sister, cuz, I have provided an innocent playfellow for you there. 580

DAINTY.

Who, he!

MRS. SQUEAMISH.

There's a playfellow indeed.

SIR JASPAR.

Yes, sure. What, he is good enough to play at cards, blindman's buff, or the fool with sometimes.

MRS. SQUEAMISH.

    Faugh, we'll have no such playfellows.   585

DAINTY.

    No sir, you shan't choose playfellows for us, we
thank you.

SIR JASPAR.

    Nay, pray hear me. (*Whispering to them.*)

LADY FIDGET. [*Aside to Horner.*]

    But poor gentleman, could you be so generous?*
so truly a man of honor, as for the sakes of us   590
women of honor, to cause your self to be reported
no man? no man! and to suffer your self the
greatest shame that could fall upon a man, that
none might fall upon us women by your
conversation.* But indeed, sir, as perfectly,   595
perfectly the same man as before your going into
France, sir, as perfectly, perfectly, sir?

HORNER.

    As perfectly, perfectly, madam. Nay, I scorn you
should take my word; I desire to be tried only,
madam.   600

LADY FIDGET.

    Well, that's spoken again like a man of honor; all
men of honor desire to come to the test. But
indeed, generally you men report such things of
yourselves one does not know how or whom to
believe, and it is come to that pass, we dare not   605
take your words, no more than your tailors,[35]
without some staid servant of yours be bound with
you. But I have so strong a faith in your honor,
dear, dear, noble sir, that I'd forfeit mine for yours
at any time, dear sir.   610

HORNER.

    No madam, you should not need to forfeit it for
me: I have given you security already to save you
harmless, my late reputation being so well known
in the world, madam.

LADY FIDGET.

    But if upon any future falling out or upon a   615
suspicion of my taking the trust out of your hands
to employ some other, you yourself should betray

---

35 tailors] Unpunctuated in the original, "tailors" has three
    grammatical possibilities: nominative plural, possessive
    plural, and possessive singular—each with different in-
    terpretive possibilities.

your trust, dear sir? I mean, if you'll give me leave
to speak obscenely, you might tell, dear sir.

HORNER.

    If I did, nobody would believe me: the reputation   620
of impotency is as hardly recovered again in the
world as that of cowardice, dear madam.

LADY FIDGET.

    Nay then, as one may say, you may do your worst,
dear, dear, sir.

SIR JASPAR.

    Come, is your ladyship reconciled to him yet?   625
Have you agreed on matters? For I must be gone
to Whitehall.

LADY FIDGET.

    Why indeed, Sir Jaspar, Master Horner is a
thousand, thousand times a better man than I
thought him.—Cousin Squeamish, Sister Dainty,   630
I can name him now. Truly not long ago, you
know, I thought his very name obscenity, and I
would as soon have lain with him as have named
him.

SIR JASPAR.

    Very likely, poor madam.   635

DAINTY.

    I believe it.

MRS. SQUEAMISH.

    No doubt on't.

SIR JASPAR.

    Well, well, that your ladyship is as virtuous as any
she, I know, and him all the Town knows, he, he,
he. Therefore, now you like him, get you gone to   640
your business together. Go, go, to your business,
I say, pleasure, whilst I go to my pleasure, business.

LADY FIDGET.

    Come then, dear gallant.

HORNER.

    Come away, my dearest mistress.

SIR JASPAR.

    So, so, why 'tis as I'd have it. (*Exit.*)   645

HORNER.

    And as I'd have it.

LADY FIDGET.

    Who for his business from his wife will run
    Takes the best care to have her business done.

Exeunt.

Act III, scene i. [Pinchwife's lodging.]

Alithea and Margery.

ALITHEA.

Sister, what ails you, you are grown melancholy?

MARGERY.

Would it not make anyone melancholy to see you go every day fluttering about abroad, whilst I must stay at home like a poor lonely, sullen bird in a cage?

ALITHEA.

Aye sister, but you came young and just from the nest to your cage, so that I thought you liked it and could be as cheerful in't as others that took their flight themselves early and are hopping abroad in the open air.

MARGERY.

Nay, I confess I was quiet enough till my husband told me what pure[36] lives the London ladies live abroad, with their dancing, meetings, and junketings, and dressed every day in their best gowns, and I warrant you, play at ninepins every day of the week, so they do.

Enter Pinchwife.

PINCHWIFE.

Come, what's here to do? You are putting the Town pleasures in her head and setting her a-longing.

ALITHEA.

Yes, after ninepins! You suffer none to give her those longings, you mean, but yourself.

PINCHWIFE.

I tell her of the vanities of the Town like a confessor.

ALITHEA.

A confessor! just such a confessor as he that by forbidding a silly* ostler to grease the horses' teeth,[37] taught him to do't.

PINCHWIFE.

Come Mistress Flippant, good precepts are lost when bad examples are still* before us: the liberty you take abroad makes her hanker after it and out of humor at home, poor wretch! She desired not to come to London; I would bring her.

---

36 pure] fine, wonderful; a ruralism
37 grease the horses's teeth] a ruse so that the horses cannot eat what the owner has paid for

ALITHEA.

Very well.   30

PINCHWIFE.

She has been this week in Town and never desired, till this afternoon, to go abroad.

ALITHEA.

Was she not at a play yesterday?

PINCHWIFE.

Yes, but she ne'er asked me; I was myself the cause of her going.   35

ALITHEA.

Then if she ask you again, you are the cause of her asking, and not my example.

PINCHWIFE.

Well, tomorrow night I shall be rid of you, and the next day before 'tis light, she and I'll be rid of the Town and my dreadful apprehensions.—   40 Come, be not melancholy, for thou shalt go into the country after tomorrow, dearest.

ALITHEA.

Great comfort.

MARGERY.

Pish, what d'ye tell me of the country for?

PINCHWIFE.

How's this! What, pish at the country?   45

MARGERY.

Let me alone; I am not well.

PINCHWIFE.

Oh, if that be all—what ails my dearest?

MARGERY.

Truly I don't know, but I have not been well since you told me there was a gallant at the play in love with me.   50

PINCHWIFE.

Hah—

ALITHEA.

That's by my example too.

PINCHWIFE.

Nay, if you are not well but are so concerned because a lewd fellow chanced to lie and say he liked you, you'll make me sick, too.   55

MARGERY.

Of what sickness?

PINCHWIFE.

Oh, of that which is worse than the plague, jealousy.

MARGERY.

Pish, you jeer. I'm sure there's no such disease in our receipt-book* at home. 60

PINCHWIFE.

No, thou never met'st with it, poor innocent. (*Aside.*) Well, if thou cuckold me, 'twill be my own fault, for cuckolds and bastards are generally makers of their own fortune.

MARGERY.

Well but pray, bud, let's go to a play tonight. 65

PINCHWIFE.

'Tis just done; she comes from it.—But why are you so eager to see a play?

MARGERY.

Faith dear, not that I care one pin for their talk there, but I like to look upon the playermen and would see, if I could, the gallant you say loves me; 70 that's all, dear bud.

PINCHWIFE.

Is that all, dear bud?

ALITHEA.

This proceeds from my example.

MARGERY.

But if the play be done, let's go abroad, however, dear bud. 75

PINCHWIFE.

Come, have a little patience, and thou shalt go into the country on Friday.

MARGERY.

Therefore, I would see first some sights to tell my neighbors of. Nay, I will go abroad, that's once.[38]

ALITHEA.

I'm the cause of this desire, too. 80

PINCHWIFE.

But now I think on't, who was the cause of Horner's coming to my lodging today? That was you.

ALITHEA.

No, you, because you would not let him see your handsome wife out of your lodging. 85

MARGERY.

Why, oh Lord! Did the gentleman come hither to see me indeed?

PINCHWIFE.

No, no.—You are not cause of that damned question, too, Mistress Alithea? (*Aside.*) Well, she's in the right of it: he is in love with my wife—and comes 90 after her. 'Tis so. But I'll nip his love in the bud, lest he should follow us into the country and break his chariot* wheel near our house on purpose for an excuse to come to't. But I think I know the Town.

MARGERY.

Come, pray bud, let's go abroad before 'tis late, for 95 I will go, that's flat and plain.

PINCHWIFE. (*Aside.*)

So! The obstinacy already of a Town wife, and I must, whilst she's here, humor her like one.— Sister, how shall we do, that she may not be seen or known? 100

ALITHEA.

Let her put on her mask.

PINCHWIFE.

Pshaw, a mask makes people but the more inquisitive and is as ridiculous a disguise as a stage beard; her shape, stature, habit will be known, and if we should meet with Horner, he would be sure 105 to take acquaintance with us, must wish her joy, kiss her, talk to her, leer upon her, and the devil and all. No, I'll not use her to a mask; 'tis dangerous, for masks have made more cuckolds than the best faces that ever were known. 110

ALITHEA.

How will you do then?

MARGERY.

Nay, shall we go? The Exchange* will be shut, and I have a mind to see that.

PINCHWIFE.

So—I have it. I'll dress her up in the suit we are to carry down to her brother, little Sir James; nay, I 115 understand the Town tricks. Come, let's go dress her. A mask! No—a woman masked, like a covered dish, gives a man curiosity and appetite, when, it may be, uncovered, 'twould turn his stomach. No, no.

ALITHEA.

Indeed, your comparison is something a greasy 120 one. But I had a gentle gallant used to say, a beauty masked, like the sun in eclipse, gathers together more gazers than if it shined out.

Exeunt.

---

38 that's once] that's final, or positive; once and for all

Act III, scene ii. The New Exchange.*

Enter Horner, Harcourt, Dorilant; [Clasp at his booth].

DORILANT.

Engaged to women, and not sup with us?

HORNER.

Aye, a pox on 'em all.

HARCOURT.

You were much a more reasonable man in the
morning and had as noble resolutions against 'em
as a widower of a week's liberty.   5

DORILANT.

Did I ever think to see you keep company with
women in vain?

HORNER.

In vain! No, 'tis since I can't love 'em, to be
revenged on 'em.

HARCOURT.

Now your sting is gone, you looked in the box   10
amongst all those women like a drone in the hive:
all upon you, shoved and ill-used by 'em all, and
thrust from one side to t'other.

DORILANT.

Yet he must be buzzing amongst 'em still, like
other old beetle-headed, lickerish drones. Avoid   15
'em and hate 'em as they hate you.

HORNER.

Because I do hate 'em and would hate 'em yet
more, I'll frequent 'em. You may see by marriage,
nothing makes a man hate a woman more than
her constant conversation.* In short, I converse   20
with 'em, as you do with rich fools, to laugh at
'em and use 'em ill.

DORILANT.

But I would no more sup with women unless I
could lie with 'em, than sup with a rich coxcomb
unless I could cheat him.   25

HORNER.

Yes, I have known thee sup with a fool for his
drinking; if he could set out your hand[39] that way
only, you were satisfied, and if he were a wine-
swallowing mouth, 'twas enough.

HARCOURT.

Yes, a man drinks often with a fool, as he tosses   30

with a marker, only to keep his hand in ure.[40] But
do the ladies drink?

HORNER.

Yes sir, and I shall have the pleasure at least of
laying 'em flat with a bottle and bring as much
scandal that way upon 'em as formerly t'other.   35

HARCOURT.

Perhaps you may prove as weak a brother amongst
'em that way as t'other.

DORILANT.

Faugh, drinking with women is as unnatural as
scolding with 'em, but 'tis a pleasure of decayed
fornicators and the basest way of quenching love.   40

HARCOURT.

Nay, 'tis drowning love instead of quenching it.
But leave us for civil women, too!

DORILANT.

Aye, when he can't be the better for 'em. We hardly
pardon a man that leaves his friend for a wench,
and that's a pretty lawful call.   45

HORNER.

Faith, I would not leave you for 'em if they would
not drink.

DORILANT.

Who would disappoint his company at Lewis's[41]
for a gossiping?

HARCOURT.

Faugh, wine and women good apart, together as   50
nauseous as sack* and sugar. But hark you, sir,
before you go, a little of your advice; an old
maimed general, when unfit for action, is fittest
for counsel. I have other designs upon women than
eating and drinking with them. I am in love with   55
Sparkish's mistress, whom he is to marry tomorrow.
Now how shall I get her?

Enter Sparkish, looking about.

HORNER.

Why, here comes one will help you to her.

HARCOURT.

He! He, I tell you, is my rival and will hinder my
love.   60

---

39 set out your hand] furnish you

40 tosses … ure] throws dice with a scorekeeper (i.e. one
who doesn't play for money) only to keep in practice

41 Lewis's] presumably, a tavern or eating house, though
not positively identified

HORNER.

No, a foolish rival and a jealous husband assist their rivals' designs, for they are sure to make their women hate them, which is the first step to their love for another man.

HARCOURT.

But I cannot come near his mistress but in his company. 65

HORNER.

Still the better for you, for fools are most easily cheated when they themselves are accessories, and he is to be bubbled* of his mistress, as of his money, the common mistress, by keeping him company. 70

SPARKISH.

Who is that, that is to be bubbled? Faith, let me snack;[42] I han't met with a bubble since Christmas. Gad, I think bubbles are like their brother woodcocks, go out with the cold weather.

HARCOURT. (*Apart to Horner.*)

A pox! He did not hear all, I hope. 75

SPARKISH.

Come, you bubbling rogues, you. Where do we sup?—Oh Harcourt, my mistress tells me you have been making fierce love* to her all the play long, ha, ha—but I—

HARCOURT.

I make love to her? 80

SPARKISH.

Nay, I forgive thee, for I think I know thee, and I know her, but I am sure I know myself.

HARCOURT.

Did she tell you so? I see all women are like these of the Exchange, who, to enhance the price of their commodities, report to their fond* customers 85 offers which were never made 'em.

HORNER.

Aye, women are as apt to tell before the intrigue as men after it and so show themselves the vainer sex. But hast thou a mistress, Sparkish? 'Tis as hard for me to believe it as that thou ever hadst a 90 bubble, as you bragged just now.

SPARKISH.

Oh your servant, sir. Are you at your raillery, sir? But we were some of us beforehand with you today

at the play. The wits were something bold with you, sir. Did you not hear us laugh? 95

HARCOURT.

Yes, but I thought you had gone to plays to laugh at the poet's wit, not at your own.

SPARKISH.

Your servant, sir. No, I thank you. Gad, I go to a play as to a country treat: I carry my own wine to one and my own wit to t'other, or else I'm sure I 100 should not be merry at either, and the reason why we are so often louder than the players is because we think we speak more wit and so become the poet's rivals in his audience. For to tell you the truth, we hate the silly rogues, nay, so much that 105 we find fault even with their bawdy upon the stage whilst we talk nothing else in the pit as loud.

HORNER.

But why shouldst thou hate the silly poets? Thou hast too much wit to be one, and they, like whores, are only hated by each other, and thou dost scorn 110 writing, I'm sure.

SPARKISH.

Yes, I'd have you to know, I scorn writing, but women, women, that make men do all foolish things, make 'em write songs, too; everybody does it. 'Tis e'en as common with lovers as playing with 115 fans, and you can no more help rhyming to your Phyllis than drinking to your Phyllis.

HARCOURT.

Nay, poetry in love is no more to be avoided than jealousy.

DORILANT.

But the poets damned your songs, did they? 120

SPARKISH.

Damn the poets! They turned 'em into burlesque, as they call it; that burlesque is a hocus-pocus trick they have got, which by the virtue of "*hictius doctius,* topsey turvey," they make a wise and witty man in the world a fool upon the stage, you know not how, 125 and 'tis, therefore, I hate 'em too, for I know not but it may be my own case, for they'll put a man into a play for looking asquint. Their predecessors were contented to make serving men only their stage fools, but these rogues must have gentlemen, with a 130 pox to 'em, nay, knights. And indeed, you shall hardly see a fool upon the stage but he's a knight,

---

42 snack] share, take part

and to tell you the truth, they have kept me these six years from being a knight in earnest, for fear of being knighted in a play and dubbed a fool.   135

DORILANT.

Blame 'em not; they must follow their copy, the age.

HARCOURT.

But why shouldst thou be afraid of being in a play, who expose yourself everyday in the playhouses and as public places?

HORNER.

'Tis but being on the stage instead of standing on   140
a bench in the pit.

DORILANT.

Don't you give money to painters to draw you like? And are you afraid of your pictures at length in a playhouse where all your mistresses may see you?

SPARKISH.

A pox! Painters don't draw the small pox or   145
pimples in one's face. Come, damn all your silly authors whatever, all books and booksellers, by the world, and all readers, courteous or uncourteous.

HARCOURT.

But who comes here, Sparkish?

Enter Pinchwife and his wife in man's clothes; Alithea; Lucy, her maid.

SPARKISH.

Oh hide me! There's my mistress, too. (*Hides*   150
himself behind Harcourt.)

HARCOURT.

She sees you.

SPARKISH.

But I will not see her; 'tis time to go to Whitehall,* and I must not fail the Drawing Room.*

HARCOURT.

Pray, first carry me and reconcile me to her.   155

SPARKISH.

Another time, faith, the King will have supped.

HARCOURT.

Not with the worse stomach for thy absence. Thou art one of those fools that think their attendance at the King's meals as necessary as his physicians', when you are more troublesome to him than his   160
doctors or his dogs.

SPARKISH.

Pshaw, I know my interest, sir. Prithee hide me.

HORNER.

Your servant, Pinchwife.—What, he knows us not!

PINCHWIFE. (*To his wife aside.*)

Come along.

MARGERY.

Pray, have you any ballads? Give me six-penny   165
worth.

CLASP.

We have no ballads.

MARGERY.

Then give me *Covent Garden Drollery*,[43] and a play or two.—Oh here's *Tarugo's Wiles* and *The Slighted Maiden*.[44] I'll have them.   170

PINCHWIFE. (*Apart to her.*)

No, plays are not for your reading. Come along. Will you discover* yourself?

HORNER.

Who is that pretty youth with him, Sparkish?

SPARKISH.

I believe his wife's brother, because he's something like her, but I never saw her but once.   175

HORNER.

Extremely handsome. I have seen a face like it, too. Let us follow 'em.

Exeunt Pinchwife, Margery; Alithea, Lucy, Horner, Dorilant following them.

HARCOURT.

Come Sparkish, your mistress saw you and will be angry you go not to her; besides, I would fain be reconciled to her, which none but you can do, dear   180
friend.

SPARKISH.

Well that's a better reason, dear friend. I would not go near her now for hers or my own sake, but I can deny you nothing, for though I have known thee a great while, never go,[45] if I do not love thee   185
as well as a new acquaintance.

---

43 *Covent Garden Drollery*] a miscellany of songs, poems, prologues and epilogues by various writers, including Wycherley, published in 1672

44 *Tarugo's Wiles* and *The Slighted Maiden*] a comedy by Sir Thomas St. Serfe (1668) and a tragicomedy by Sir Robert Staplyton (1663)

45 never go] like "never stir" below, a phrase of reassurance meaning roughly "don't worry"

HARCOURT.

I am obliged to you indeed, dear friend. I would
be well with her only to be well with thee still, for
these ties to wives usually dissolve all ties to friends.
I would be contented she should enjoy you a-   190
nights, but I would have you to my self a-days, as
I have had, dear friend.

SPARKISH.

And thou shalt enjoy me a-days, dear, dear friend,
never stir, and I'll be divorced from her sooner than
from thee. Come along.   195

HARCOURT. (*Aside.*)

So we are hard put to't when we make our rival our
procurer, but neither she nor her brother would let
me come near her now. When all's done, a rival is the
best cloak to steal to a mistress under without
suspicion, and when we have once got to her as we   200
desire, we throw him off like other cloaks.

*Exit Sparkish, Harcourt following him. Re-enter
Pinchwife, Margery in man's clothes.*

PINCHWIFE. (*To Alithea [offstage].*)

Sister, if you will not go, we must leave you.
(*Aside.*) The fool, her gallant, and she will muster
up all the young saunterers of this place, and they
will leave their dear seamstresses to follow us. What   205
a swarm of cuckolds and cuckold-makers are
here?—Come let's be gone, Mistress Margery.

MARGERY.

Don't you believe that, I han't half my belly full
of sights yet.

PINCHWIFE.

Then walk this way.   210

MARGERY.

Lord, what a power of brave* signs are here! Stay—
the Bull's Head, the Ram's Head, and the Stag's
Head, dear—

PINCHWIFE.

Nay, if every husband's proper sign here were
visible, they would be all alike.   215

MARGERY.

What d'ye mean by that, bud?

PINCHWIFE.

'Tis no matter—no matter, bud.

MARGERY.

Pray tell me, nay, I will know.

PINCHWIFE.

They would be all bulls', stags', and rams' heads.

*Exeunt Pinchwife, Margery. Re-enter Sparkish,
Harcourt, Alithea, Lucy at t'other door.*

SPARKISH.

Come dear madam, for my sake, you shall be   220
reconciled to him.

ALITHEA.

For your sake, I hate him.

HARCOURT.

That's something too cruel, madam, to hate me for
his sake.

SPARKISH.

Aye indeed, madam, too, too cruel to me to hate   225
my friend for my sake.

ALITHEA.

I hate him because he is your enemy, and you
ought to hate him, too, for making love* to me,
if you love me.

SPARKISH.

That's a good one! I hate a man for loving you! If he   230
did love you, 'tis but what he can't help, and 'tis your
fault not his, if he admires you. I hate a man for
being of my opinion! I'll ne'er do't, by the world.

ALITHEA.

Is it for your honor or mine to suffer a man to
make love to me, who am to marry you tomorrow?   235

SPARKISH.

Is it for your honor or mine to have me jealous?
That he makes love to you is a sign you are
handsome, and that I am not jealous is a sign you
are virtuous. That, I think, is for your honor.

ALITHEA.

But 'tis your honor, too, I am concerned for.   240

HARCOURT.

But why, dearest madam, will you be more
concerned for his honor than he is himself? Let his
honor alone for my sake and his. He, he, has no
honor—

SPARKISH.

How's that?   245

HARCOURT.

But what my dear friend can guard himself.

SPARKISH.

Oh ho—that's right again.

HARCOURT.

Your care of his honor argues his neglect of it, which is no honor to my dear friend here; therefore, once more, let his honor go which way 250 it will, dear madam.

SPARKISH.

Aye, aye, were it for my honor to marry a woman whose virtue I suspected and could not trust her in a friend's hands?

ALITHEA.

Are you not afraid to lose me? 255

HARCOURT.

He afraid to lose you, madam! No, no— you may see how the most estimable and most glorious creature in the world is valued by him. Will you not see it?

SPARKISH.

Right, honest Frank, I have that noble value for 260 her that I cannot be jealous of her.

ALITHEA.

You mistake him: he means you care not for me nor who has me.

SPARKISH.

Lord madam, I see you are jealous. Will you wrest a poor man's meaning from his words? 265

ALITHEA.

You astonish me, sir, with your want* of jealousy.

SPARKISH.

And you make me giddy, madam, with your jealousy and fears and virtue and honor; gad, I see virtue makes a woman as troublesome as a little reading or learning. 270

ALITHEA.

Monstrous!

LUCY. (*Behind.*)

Well, to see what easy husbands these women of quality* can meet with! A poor chambermaid can never have such ladylike luck. Besides, he's thrown away upon her; she'll make no use of her fortune, 275 her blessing. None to a gentleman for a pure cuckold, for it requires good breeding to be a cuckold.

ALITHEA.

I tell you then plainly: he pursues me to marry me.

SPARKISH.

Pshaw— 280

HARCOURT.

Come madam, you see you strive in vain to make him jealous of me; my dear friend is the kindest creature in the world to me.

SPARKISH.

Poor fellow.

HARCOURT.

But his kindness only is not enough for me, 285 without your favor; your good opinion, dear madam, 'tis that must perfect my happiness. Good gentleman, he believes all I say; would you would do so. Jealous of me! I would not wrong him nor you for the world. 290

Alithea walks carelessly to and fro.

SPARKISH.

Look you there, hear him, hear him, and do not walk away so.

HARCOURT.

I love you, madam, so—

SPARKISH.

How's that! Nay—now you begin to go too far indeed. 295

HARCOURT.

So much, I confess, I say I love you, that I would not have you miserable and cast yourself away upon so unworthy and inconsiderable a thing as what you see here. (*Clapping his hand on his breast, points at Sparkish.*) 300

SPARKISH.

No, faith, I believe thou wouldst not, now his meaning is plain. But I knew before thou wouldst not wrong me nor her.

HARCOURT.

No, no, heavens forbid the glory of her sex should fall so low as into the embraces of such a 305 contemptible wretch, the last of mankind—my dear friend here—I injure him. (*Embracing Sparkish.*)

ALITHEA.

Very well.

SPARKISH.

No, no, dear friend, I knew it.—Madam, you see he will rather wrong himself than me in giving 310 himself such names.

ALITHEA.

Do not you understand him yet?

SPARKISH.

Yes, how modestly he speaks of himself, poor fellow.

ALITHEA.

Methinks he speaks impudently of yourself, 315
since—before yourself, too, insomuch that I can
no longer suffer his scurrilous abusiveness to you,
no more than his love to me. (*Offers* to go.*)

SPARKISH.

Nay, nay, madam, pray stay. His love to you! Lord
madam, has he not spoke yet plain enough? 320

ALITHEA.

Yes indeed, I should think so.

SPARKISH.

Well then, by the world, a man can't speak civilly to
a woman now but presently* she says he makes love
to her. Nay madam, you shall stay, with your
pardon, since you have not yet understood him, till 325
he has made an éclaircissement of his love to you,
that is, what kind of love it is.—Answer to thy
catechism. Friend, do you love my mistress here?

HARCOURT.

Yes, I wish she would not doubt it.

SPARKISH.

But how do you love her? 330

HARCOURT.

With all my soul.

ALITHEA.

I thank him, methinks he speaks plain enough
now.

SPARKISH.

(*To Alithea.*)
You are out[46] still.—But with what kind of love, 335
Harcourt?

HARCOURT.

With the best and truest love in the world.

SPARKISH.

Look you there then: that is with no matrimonial
love, I'm sure.

ALITHEA.

How's that, do you say matrimonial love is not 340
best?

SPARKISH. [*Aside.*]

Gad, I went too far ere I was aware.—But speak

---

46 out] mistaken

for thyself, Harcourt: you said you would not
wrong me nor her.

HARCOURT.

No, no, madam, e'en take him for Heaven's sake— 345

SPARKISH.

Look you there, madam.

HARCOURT.

Who should in all justice be yours, he that loves
you most. (*Claps his hand on his breast.*)

ALITHEA.

Look you there, Mr. Sparkish. Who's that?

SPARKISH.

Who should it be? Go on, Harcourt. 350

HARCOURT.

Who loves you more than women, titles, or
fortune fools. (*Points at Sparkish.*)

SPARKISH.

Look you there: he means me still, for he points
at me.

ALITHEA.

Ridiculous! 355

HARCOURT.

Who can only match your faith and constancy in
love.

SPARKISH.

Aye.

HARCOURT.

Who knows, if it be possible, how to value so
much beauty and virtue. 360

SPARKISH.

Aye.

HARCOURT.

Whose love can no more be equaled in the world
than that heavenly form of yours.

SPARKISH.

No—

HARCOURT.

Who could no more suffer a rival than your 365
absence and yet could no more suspect your virtue
than his own constancy in his love to you.

SPARKISH.

No—

HARCOURT.

Who, in fine, loves you better than his eyes that
first made him love you. 370

SPARKISH.

Aye.—Nay madam, faith you shan't go till—

ALITHEA.

Have a care lest you make me stay too long—

SPARKISH.

But till he has saluted* you, that I may be assured you are friends after his honest advice and declaration. Come pray, madam, be friends with him. 375

Enter Pinchwife, Margery.

ALITHEA.

You must pardon me, sir, that I am not yet so obedient to you.

PINCHWIFE.

What, invite your wife to kiss men? Monstrous! Are you not ashamed? I will never forgive you.

SPARKISH.

Are you not ashamed that I should have more 380 confidence in the chastity of your family than you have? You must not teach me: I am a man of honor, sir, though I am frank and free. I am frank, sir—

PINCHWIFE.

Very frank, sir, to share your wife with your friends. 385

SPARKISH.

He is an humble, menial friend, such as reconciles the differences of the marriage bed. You know man and wife do not always agree. I design him for that use, therefore, would have him well with my wife.

PINCHWIFE.

A menial friend—you will get a great many menial 390 friends by showing your wife as you do.

SPARKISH.

What then, it may be I have a pleasure in't, as I have to show fine clothes at a playhouse the first day and count money before poor rogues.

PINCHWIFE.

He that shows his wife or money will be in danger 395 of having them borrowed sometimes.

SPARKISH.

I love to be envied and would not marry a wife that I alone could love; loving alone is as dull as eating alone. Is it not a frank age, and I am a frank person? And to tell you the truth, it may be I love to have 400 rivals in a wife: they make her seem to a man still* but as a kept* mistress, and so good night, for I must to Whitehall.—Madam, I hope you are now reconciled to my friend, and so I wish you a good

night, madam, and sleep if you can, for tomorrow 405 you know I must visit you early with a canonical gentleman.—Good night, dear Harcourt. (*Exit.*)

HARCOURT.

Madam, I hope you will not refuse my visit tomorrow, if it should be earlier, with a canonical gentleman, than Mr. Sparkish's. 410

PINCHWIFE. (*Coming between Alithea and Harcourt.*)

This gentlewoman is yet under my care; therefore, you must yet forbear your freedom with her, sir.

HARCOURT.

Must, sir—

PINCHWIFE.

Yes, sir, she is my sister.

HARCOURT.

'Tis well she is, sir—for I must be her servant, 415 sir.—Madam—

PINCHWIFE.

Come away, sister. We had been gone if it had not been for you and so avoided these lewd rakehells who seem to haunt us.

Enter Horner, Dorilant to them.

HORNER.

How now, Pinchwife? 420

PINCHWIFE.

Your servant.

HORNER.

What, I see a little time in the country makes a man turn wild and unsociable and only fit to converse with his horses, dogs, and his herds.

PINCHWIFE.

I have business, sir, and must mind it. Your 425 business is pleasure; therefore, you and I must go different ways.

HORNER.

Well, you may go on, but this pretty young gentleman— (*Takes hold of Margery.*)

HARCOURT.

The lady— 430

DORILANT.

And the maid—

HORNER.

Shall stay with us, for I suppose their business is the same with ours, pleasure.

PINCHWIFE. (*Aside.*)

'Sdeath,* he knows her, she carries it so sillily,* yet if he does not, I should be more silly to discover* it 435 first.

ALITHEA.

Pray let us go, sir.

PINCHWIFE.

Come, come—

HORNER. (*To Margery.*)

Had you not rather stay with us?—Prithee Pinchwife, who is this pretty young gentleman? 440

PINCHWIFE.

One to whom I'm a guardian. (*Aside.*) I wish I could keep her out of your hands—

HORNER.

Who is he? I never saw any thing so pretty in all my life.

PINCHWIFE.

Pshaw, do not look upon him so much. He's a poor 445 bashful youth; you'll put him out of countenance. Come away, brother. (*Offers* to take her away.*)

HORNER.

Oh your brother!

PINCHWIFE.

Yes, my wife's brother.—Come, come, she'll stay supper for us. 450

HORNER.

I thought so, for he is very like her I saw you at the play with, whom I told you I was in love with.

MARGERY. (*Aside.*)

Oh jiminy!* Is this he that was in love with me? I am glad on't, I vow, for he's a curious fine gentleman, and I love him already, too. (*To Mr.* 455 *Pinchwife.*) Is this he, bud?

PINCHWIFE. (*To his wife.*)

Come away, come away.

HORNER.

Why, what haste are you in? Why won't you let me talk with him?

PINCHWIFE.

Because you'll debauch him. He's yet young and 460 innocent, and I would not have him debauched for anything in the world. (*Aside.*) How she gazes on him! The devil—

HORNER.

Harcourt, Dorilant, look you here: this is the

likeness of that dowdy he told us of, his wife. Did 465 you ever see a lovelier creature? The rogue has reason to be jealous of his wife, since she is like him, for she would make all that see her in love with her.

HARCOURT.

And as I remember now, she is as like him here as 470 can be.

DORILANT.

She is indeed very pretty, if she be like him.

HORNER.

Very pretty? a very pretty commendation! She is a glorious creature, beautiful beyond all things I ever beheld. 475

PINCHWIFE.

So, so.

HARCOURT.

More beautiful than a poet's first mistress of imagination.

HORNER.

Or another man's last mistress of flesh and blood.

MARGERY.

Nay, now you jeer, sir. Pray don't jeer me— 480

PINCHWIFE.

Come, come. (*Aside.*) By heavens, she'll discover* herself!

HORNER.

I speak of your sister, sir.

PINCHWIFE.

Aye, but saying she was handsome, if like him, made him blush. (*Aside.*) I am upon a rack— 485

HORNER.

Methinks he is so handsome, he should not be a man.

PINCHWIFE. [*Aside.*]

Oh there 'tis out! He has discovered her! I am not able to suffer any longer. (*To his wife.*) Come, come away, I say— 490

HORNER.

Nay by your leave, sir, he shall not go yet.— Harcourt, Dorilant, let us torment this jealous rogue a little.

HARCOURT AND DORILANT.

How?

HORNER.

I'll show you. 495

PINCHWIFE.

Come, pray let him go. I cannot stay fooling any longer. I tell you his sister stays supper for us.

HORNER.

Does she? Come then we'll all go sup with her and thee.

PINCHWIFE.

No, now I think on't, having stayed so long for us, I warrant she's gone to bed. (*Aside.*) I wish she and I were well out of their hands.—Come, I must rise early tomorrow, come.

HORNER.

Well then, if she be gone to bed, I wish her and you a good night.—But pray, young gentleman, present my humble service to her.

MARGERY.

Thank you heartily, sir.

PINCHWIFE. (*Aside.*)

S'death,* she will discover* herself yet in spite of me.—He is something more civil to you, for your kindness to his sister, than I am, it seems.

HORNER.

Tell her, dear sweet little gentleman, for all your brother there, that you have revived the love I had for her at first sight in the playhouse.

MARGERY.

But did you love her indeed and indeed?

PINCHWIFE. (*Aside.*)

So, so.—Away, I say.

HORNER.

Nay, stay. Yes, indeed and indeed, pray do you tell her so and give her this kiss from me. (*Kisses her.*)

PINCHWIFE. (*Aside.*)

Oh heavens! What do I suffer! Now 'tis too plain he knows her and yet—

HORNER.

And this and this— (*Kisses her again.*)

MARGERY.

What do you kiss me for? I am no woman.

PINCHWIFE. (*Aside.*)

So—there 'tis out.—Come, I cannot, nor will stay any longer.

HORNER.

Nay, they shall send your lady a kiss, too. Here Harcourt, Dorilant, will you not?

They kiss her.

PINCHWIFE. (*Aside.*)

How! Do I suffer this? Was I not accusing another just now for this rascally patience in permitting his wife to be kissed before his face? Ten thousand ulcers gnaw away their lips.—Come, come.

HORNER.

Good night, dear little gentleman.—Madam, good night.—Farewell, Pinchwife. (*Apart to Harcourt and Dorilant.*) Did not I tell you I would raise his jealous gall?

Exeunt Horner, Harcourt, and Dorilant.

PINCHWIFE.

So they are gone at last.—Stay, let me see first if the coach be at this door. (*Exit.*)

Horner, Harcourt, Dorilant return.

HORNER.

What, not gone yet? Will you be sure to do as I desired you, sweet sir?

MARGERY.

Sweet sir, but what will you give me then?

HORNER.

Anything. Come away into the next walk.

Exit Horner, haling away Margery.

ALITHEA.

Hold, hold, what d'ye do?

LUCY.

Stay, stay, hold—

Alithea, Lucy struggling with Harcourt and Dorilant.

HARCOURT.

Hold, madam, hold. Let him present[47] him; he'll come presently. Nay, I will never let you go till you answer my question.

LUCY.

For God's sake, sir, I must follow 'em.

DORILANT.

No, I have something to present you with, too. You shan't follow them.

Pinchwife returns.

PINCHWIFE.

Where? how? what's become of—? Gone! Whither?

---

47 present] give him a present

LUCY.

He's only gone with the gentleman, who will give
him something, an't* please your worship.   550

PINCHWIFE.

Something—give him something, with a pox!
Where are they?

ALITHEA.

In the next walk only, brother.

PINCHWIFE.

Only! Only! Where? Where? (*Exit and returns
presently,* then goes out again.*)   555

HARCOURT.

What's the matter with him? Why so much
concerned?—But dearest madam—

ALITHEA.

Pray let me go, sir. I have said and suffered enough
already.

HARCOURT.

Then you will not look upon nor pity my   560
sufferings?

ALITHEA.

To look upon 'em, when I cannot help 'em, were
cruelty, not pity; therefore, I will never see you
more.

HARCOURT.

Let me then, madam, have my privilege of a   565
banished lover: complaining or railing and giving
you but a farewell reason why, if you cannot
condescend to marry me, you should not take that
wretch my rival.

ALITHEA.

He only, not you, since my honor is engaged so   570
far to him, can give me a reason why I should not
marry him, but if he be true and what I think him
to me, I must be so to him. Your servant, sir.

HARCOURT.

Have women only constancy when 'tis a vice and,
like Fortune, only true to fools?   575

DORILANT. (*To Lucy, who struggles to get from him.*)

Thou shalt not stir, thou robust creature. You see
I can deal with you; therefore, you should stay the
rather and be kind.*

Enter Pinchwife.

PINCHWIFE.

Gone, gone, not to be found! quite gone! Ten thousand plagues go with 'em! Which way went they?   580

ALITHEA.

But into t'other walk, brother.

LUCY.

Their business will be done presently sure, an't*
please your worship; it can't be long in doing, I'm
sure on't.

ALITHEA.

Are they not there?   585

PINCHWIFE.

No, you know where they are, you infamous wretch,
eternal shame of your family, which you do not
dishonor enough yourself, you think, but you must
help her to do it, too, thou legion of bawds!

ALITHEA.

Good brother!   590

PINCHWIFE.

Damned, damned sister!

ALITHEA.

Look you here, she's coming.

*Enter Margery in man's clothes, running with her hat
under her arm, full of oranges and dried fruit, Horner
following.*

MARGERY.

Oh dear bud, look you here what I have got! See.

PINCHWIFE. (*Aside, rubbing his forehead.*)

And what I have got here, too, which you can't see.

MARGERY.

The fine gentleman has given me better things yet. 595

PINCHWIFE.

Has he so? (*Aside.*) Out of breath and colored—I
must hold yet.

HORNER.

I have only given your little brother an orange, sir.

PINCHWIFE. (*To Horner.*)

Thank you, sir. (*Aside.*) You have only squeezed my
orange, I suppose, and given it me again, yet I   600
must have a City* patience. (*To his wife.*) Come,
come away.

MARGERY.

Stay, till I have put up my fine things, bud.

Enter Sir Jaspar Fidget.

SIR JASPAR.

Oh, Master Horner, come, come, the ladies stay
for you. Your mistress, my wife, wonders you make 605
not more haste to her.

HORNER.

I have stayed this half hour for you here, and 'tis your fault I am not now with your wife.

SIR JASPAR.

But pray, don't let her know so much; the truth on't is I was advancing a certain project to his 610 Majesty about—I'll tell you.

HORNER.

No, let's go and hear it at your house.—Good night, sweet little gentleman. One kiss more.(*Kisses her.*) You'll remember me now, I hope.

DORILANT.

What, Sir Jaspar, will you separate friends? He 615 promised to sup with us, and if you take him to your house, you'll be in danger of our company, too.

SIR JASPAR.

Alas gentlemen, my house is not fit for you: there are none but civil women there, which are not for your turn. He, you know, can bear with the society 620 of civil women, now, ha, ha, ha. Besides he's one of my family;* he's—he, he, he.

DORILANT.

What is he?

SIR JASPAR.

Faith my eunuch, since you'll have it, he, he, he.

Exit Sir Jaspar Fidget and Horner.

DORILANT.

I rather wish thou wert his, or my cuckold.— 625 Harcourt, what a good cuckold is lost there for want of a man to make him one; thee and I cannot have Horner's privilege, who can make use of it.

HARCOURT.

Aye, to poor Horner 'tis like coming to an estate at threescore, when a man can't be the better for't. 630

PINCHWIFE.

Come.

MARGERY.

Presently, bud.

DORILANT.

Come, let us go, too. (*To Alithea.*) Madam, your servant. (*To Lucy.*) Good night, strapper.

HARCOURT.

Madam, though you will not let me have a good 635 day or night, I wish you one, but dare not name the other half of my wish.

ALITHEA.

Good night, sir, forever.

MARGERY.

I don't know where to put this. Here, dear bud, you shall eat it. Nay, you shall have part of the fine 640 gentleman's good things, or treat as you call it, when we come home.

PINCHWIFE.

Indeed I deserve it, since I furnished the best part of it. (*Strikes away the orange.*)

The gallant treats, presents, and gives the ball, 645
But 'tis the absent cuckold pays for all.

Act IV, scene i. Pinchwife's house in the morning.

Lucy, Alithea dressed in new clothes.

LUCY.

Well madam, now have I dressed you and set you out with so many ornaments and spent upon you ounces of essence and pulvillio,* and all this for no other purpose but as people adorn and perfume a corpse for a stinking second-hand grave, such or 5 as bad I think Master Sparkish's bed.

ALITHEA.

Hold your peace.

LUCY.

Nay madam, I will ask you the reason why you would banish poor Master Harcourt forever from your sight? How could you be so hard-hearted? 10

ALITHEA.

'Twas because I was not hard-hearted.

LUCY.

No, no, 'twas stark love and kindness, I warrant.

ALITHEA.

It was so: I would see him no more because I love him.

LUCY.

Hey day, a very pretty reason. 15

ALITHEA.

You do not understand me.

LUCY.

I wish you may yourself.

ALITHEA.

I was engaged to marry, you see, another man, whom my justice will not suffer me to deceive or injure. 20

LUCY.

Can there be a greater cheat or wrong done to a man than to give him your person without your heart? I should make a conscience of it.

ALITHEA.

I'll retrieve it for him after I am married awhile.

LUCY.

The woman that marries to love better will be as much mistaken as the wencher that marries to live better. No madam, marrying to increase love is like gaming to become rich: alas, you only lose what little stock you had before.

ALITHEA.

I find by your rhetoric you have been bribed to betray me.

LUCY.

Only by his merit that has bribed your heart, you see, against your word and rigid honor. But what a devil is this honor? 'Tis sure a disease in the head, like the megrim or falling sickness,[48] that always hurries people away to do themselves mischief. Men lose their lives by it; women, what's dearer to 'em, their love, the life of life.

ALITHEA.

Come, pray talk you no more of honor nor Master Harcourt. I wish the other would come to secure my fidelity to him and his right in me.

LUCY.

You will marry him then?

ALITHEA.

Certainly, I have given him already my word and will my hand, too, to make it good when he comes.

LUCY.

Well, I wish I may never stick pin more, if he be not an arrant natural* to t'other fine gentleman.

ALITHEA.

I own he wants* the wit of Harcourt, which I will dispense withal for another want he has, which is want of jealousy, which men of wit seldom want.

LUCY.

Lord madam, what should you do with a fool to your husband? You intend to be honest,* don't you? Then that husbandly virtue, credulity, is thrown away upon you.

ALITHEA.

He only that could suspect my virtue should have cause to do it; 'tis Sparkish's confidence in my truth that obliges me to be so faithful to him.

LUCY.

You are not sure his opinion may last.

ALITHEA.

I am satisfied 'tis impossible for him to be jealous after the proofs I have had of him. Jealousy in a husband, Heaven defend me from it! It begets a thousand plagues to a poor woman: the loss of her honor, her quiet, and her—

LUCY.

And her pleasure.

ALITHEA.

What d'ye mean, impertinent?

LUCY.

Liberty is a great pleasure, madam.

ALITHEA.

I say loss of her honor, her quiet, nay, her life sometimes, and what's as bad almost, the loss of this Town; that is, she is sent into the country, which is the last ill usage of a husband to a wife, I think.

LUCY. (Aside.)

Oh does the wind lie there?—Then of necessity, madam, you think a man must carry his wife into the country if he be wise. The country is as terrible I find to our young English ladies as a monastery to those abroad. And on my virginity, I think they would rather marry a London gaoler than a high sheriff of a county, since neither can stir from his employment. Formerly women of wit married fools for a great estate, a fine seat, or the like, but now 'tis for a pretty seat only in Lincoln's Inn Fields, St. James's Fields, or the Pall Mall.[49]

Enter to them Sparkish and Harcourt dressed like a parson.

SPARKISH.

Madam, your humble servant, a happy day to you and to us all.

HARCOURT.

Amen.

---

48 falling sickness] epilepsy

49 Lincoln's Inns Fields, St. James's Fields, … the Pall Mall] fashionable places to live in London

ALITHEA.

Who have we here?

SPARKISH.

My chaplain, faith. Oh madam, poor Harcourt 85
remembers his humble service to you and, in
obedience to your last commands, refrains coming
into your sight.

ALITHEA.

Is not that he?

SPARKISH.

No, fie, no, but to show that he ne'er intended to 90
hinder our match, has sent his brother here to join
our hands. When I get me a wife, I must get her
a chaplain, according to the custom; this is his
brother and my chaplain.

ALITHEA.

His brother? 95

LUCY. (*Aside.*)

And your chaplain, to preach in your pulpit then.

ALITHEA.

His brother!

SPARKISH.

Nay, I knew you would not believe it.—I told you,
sir, she would take you for your brother Frank.

ALITHEA.

Believe it! 100

LUCY. (*Aside.*)

His brother! Ha, ha, he, he has a trick left still it
seems.

SPARKISH.

Come my dearest, pray let us go to church before
the canonical hour* is past.

ALITHEA.

For shame! You are abused still. 105

SPARKISH.

By the world, 'tis strange now you are so
incredulous.

ALITHEA.

'Tis strange you are so credulous.

SPARKISH.

Dearest of my life, hear me: I tell you this is Ned
Harcourt of Cambridge; by the world, you see he 110
has a sneaking college look. 'Tis true he's something
like his brother Frank, and they differ from each
other no more than in their age, for they were twins.

LUCY.

Ha, ha, he.

ALITHEA.

Your servant, sir. I cannot be so deceived, though 115
you are. But come let's hear, how do you know
what you affirm so confidently?

SPARKISH.

Why, I'll tell you all. Frank Harcourt coming to
me this morning to wish me joy and present his
service to you, I asked him if he could help me to 120
a parson, whereupon he told me he had a brother
in Town who was in orders, and he went straight
away and sent him you see there to me.

ALITHEA.

Yes, Frank goes, and puts on a black coat, then tells
you he is Ned; that's all you have for't. 125

SPARKISH.

Pshaw, pshaw, I tell you by the same token, the
midwife put her garter about Frank's neck to know
'em asunder, they were so like.

ALITHEA.

Frank tells you this, too.

SPARKISH.

Aye, and Ned there too; nay, they are both in a 130
story.

ALITHEA.

So, so, very foolish.

SPARKISH.

Lord, if you won't believe one, you had best try
him by your chambermaid there, for chambermaids must needs know chaplains from other men, 135
they are so used to 'em.[50]

LUCY.

Let's see: nay, I'll be sworn he has the canonical
smirk and the filthy, clammy palm of a chaplain.

ALITHEA.

Well, most reverend doctor, pray let us make an
end of this fooling. 140

HARCOURT.

With all my soul, divine, heavenly creature, when
you please.

ALITHEA.

He speaks like a chaplain indeed.

---

50 chambermaids … used to 'em] Alleged promiscuity between chambermaids and the clergy was a standard joke
of the time.

SPARKISH.

Why, was there not, "soul," "divine," "heavenly," in what he said? 145

ALITHEA.

Once more, most impertinent blackcoat, cease your persecution and let us have a conclusion of this ridiculous love.

HARCOURT. (*Aside.*)

I had forgot, I must suit my style to my coat, or I wear it in vain. 150

ALITHEA.

I have no more patience left; let us make once an end of this troublesome love, I say.

HARCOURT.

So be it, seraphic lady, when your honor shall think it meet and convenient so to do.

SPARKISH.

Gad, I'm sure none but a chaplain could speak so, 155 I think.

ALITHEA.

Let me tell you, sir, this dull trick will not serve your turn. Though you delay our marriage, you shall not hinder it.

HARCOURT.

Far be it from me, munificent patroness, to delay 160 your marriage. I desire nothing more than to marry you presently,* which I might do, if you yourself would, for my noble, good-natured, and thrice generous patron here would not hinder it.

SPARKISH.

No, poor man, not I, faith. 165

HARCOURT.

And now, madam, let me tell you plainly, nobody else shall marry you, by heavens. I'll die first, for I'm sure I should die* after it.

LUCY. [*Aside.*]

How his love has made him forget his function, as I have seen it in real parsons. 170

ALITHEA.

That was spoken like a chaplain, too! Now you understand him, I hope.

SPARKISH.

Poor man, he takes it heinously to be refused. I can't blame him; 'tis putting an indignity upon him not to be suffered. But you'll pardon me, madam, it shan't 175 be; he shall marry us. Come away, pray madam.

LUCY.

Ha, ha, he, more ado! 'Tis late.

ALITHEA.

Invincible stupidity, I tell you he would marry me as your rival, not as your chaplain.

SPARKISH. (*Pulling her away.*)

Come, come, madam. 180

LUCY.

I pray, madam, do not refuse this reverend divine the honor and satisfaction of marrying you, for I dare say, he has set his heart upon't, good doctor.

ALITHEA.

What can you hope or design by this?

HARCOURT. [*Aside.*]

I could answer her, a reprieve for a day only often 185 revokes a hasty doom; at worst, if she will not take mercy on me and let me marry her, I have at least the lover's second pleasure, hindering my rival's enjoyment, though but for a time.

SPARKISH.

Come, madam, 'tis e'en twelve o'clock, and my 190 mother charged me never to be married out of the canonical hours. Come, come. Lord, here's such a deal of modesty, I warrant, the first day.

LUCY.

Yes, an't* please your worship, married women show all their modesty the first day, because 195 married men show all their love the first day.

Exeunt.

Scene [ii]. A bedchamber.

Pinchwife, Margery.

PINCHWIFE.

Come tell me, I say.

MARGERY.

Lord, han't I told it an hundred times over?

PINCHWIFE. (*Aside.*)

I would try, if in the repetition of the ungrateful tale, I could find her altering it in the least circumstance, for if her story be false, she is so too.—Come how was't, baggage? 5

MARGERY.

Lord, what pleasure you take to hear it, sure!

PINCHWIFE.

No, you take more in telling it, I find, but speak. How was't?

MARGERY.

He carried me up into the house next to the Exchange. 10

PINCHWIFE.

So, and you two were only in the room.

MARGERY.

Yes, for he sent away a youth that was there, for some dried fruit and China oranges.*

PINCHWIFE.

Did he so? Damn him for it—and for—

MARGERY.

But presently* came up the gentlewoman of the 15 house.

PINCHWIFE.

Oh 'twas well she did. But what did he do whilst the fruit came?

MARGERY.

He kissed me an hundred times and told me he fancied he kissed my fine sister, meaning me, you 20 know, whom he said he loved with all his soul and bid me be sure to tell her so and to desire her to be at her window by eleven of the clock this morning, and he would walk under it at that time.

PINCHWIFE. (*Aside.*)

And he was as good as his word, very punctual. A 25 pox reward him for't.

MARGERY.

Well, and he said if you were not within, he would come up to her, meaning me, you know, bud, still.

PINCHWIFE. (*Aside.*)

So—he knew her certainly, but for this confession I am obliged to her simplicity.—But what, you 30 stood very still when he kissed you?

MARGERY.

Yes, I warrant you. Would you have had me discovered* myself?

PINCHWIFE.

But you told me he did some beastliness to you, as you called it. What was't? 35

MARGERY.

Why, he put—

PINCHWIFE.

What?

MARGERY.

Why he put the tip of his tongue between my lips and so muzzled[51] me—and I said I'd bite it.

PINCHWIFE.

An eternal canker seize it, for a dog! 40

MARGERY.

Nay, you need not be so angry with him neither, for to say truth, he has the sweetest breath I ever knew.

PINCHWIFE.

The devil—you were satisfied with it then and would do it again.

MARGERY.

Not unless he should force me. 45

PINCHWIFE.

Force you, changeling! I tell you no woman can be forced.

MARGERY.

Yes, but she may sure, by such a one as he, for he's a proper, goodly strong man; 'tis hard, let me tell you, to resist him. 50

PINCHWIFE. [*Aside.*]

So, 'tis plain she loves him, yet she has not love enough to make her conceal it from me, but the sight of him will increase her aversion for me and love for him, and that love instruct her how to deceive me and satisfy him, all idiot as she is. Love, 'twas he gave 55 women first their craft, their art of deluding; out of Nature's hands they came plain, open, silly,* and fit for slaves, as she and Heaven intended 'em, but damned Love—well—I must strangle that little monster whilst I can deal with him.—Go fetch pen, 60 ink, and paper out of the next room.

MARGERY.

Yes bud. (*Exit.*)

PINCHWIFE.

Why should women have more invention in love than men? It can only be because they have more desires, more soliciting passions, more lust, and 65 more of the Devil.

Margery returns.

Come minx, sit down and write.

MARGERY.

Aye, dear bud, but I can't do't very well.

PINCHWIFE.

I wish you could not at all.

---

51 muzzled] "to fondle with the mouth close" (Johnson's *Dictionary*); to French kiss

MARGERY.

But what should I write for? 70

PINCHWIFE.

I'll have you write a letter to your lover.

MARGERY.

Oh Lord, to the fine gentleman a letter!

PINCHWIFE.

Yes, to the fine gentleman.

MARGERY.

Lord, you do but jeer; sure you jest.

PINCHWIFE.

I am not so merry. Come write as I bid you. 75

MARGERY.

What, do you think I am a fool?

PINCHWIFE. [Aside.]

She's afraid I would not dictate any love to him; therefore, she's unwilling.—But you had best begin.

MARGERY.

Indeed and indeed, but I won't, so I won't. 80

PINCHWIFE.

Why?

MARGERY.

Because he's in Town; you may send for him if you will.

PINCHWIFE.

Very well, you would have him brought to you. Is it come to this? I say take the pen and write, or 85 you'll provoke me.

MARGERY.

Lord, what d'ye make a fool of me for? Don't I know that letters are never writ but from the country to London and from London into the country? Now he's in Town, and I am in Town, 90 too; therefore, I can't write to him, you know.

PINCHWIFE. (Aside.)

So, I am glad it is no worse; she is innocent enough yet.—Yes, you may when your husband bids you write letters to people that are in Town.

MARGERY.

Oh may I so! Then I'm satisfied. 95

PINCHWIFE.

Come begin. (Dictates.) "Sir"—

MARGERY.

Shan't I say, "Dear Sir"? You know one says always something more than bare "Sir."

PINCHWIFE.

Write as I bid you, or I will write whore with this penknife in your face. 100

MARGERY.

Nay, good bud. (She writes.) "Sir"—

PINCHWIFE.

"Though I suffered last night your nauseous, loathed kisses and embraces"—Write.

MARGERY.

Nay, why should I say so? You know I told you he had a sweet breath. 105

PINCHWIFE.

Write!

MARGERY.

Let me but put out "loathed."

PINCHWIFE.

Write I say!

MARGERY.

Well then. (Writes.)

PINCHWIFE.

Let's see what have you writ. (Takes the paper and 110 reads.) "Though I suffered last night your kisses and embraces"—Thou impudent creature! Where is "nauseous" and "loathed"?

MARGERY.

I can't abide to write such filthy words.

PINCHWIFE. (Holds up penknife.)

Once more, write as I'd have you and question it 115 not, or I will spoil thy writing with this. I will stab out those eyes that cause my mischief.

MARGERY.

Oh Lord, I will! [Writes.]

PINCHWIFE.

So—so—let's see now! (Reads.) "Though I suffered last night your nauseous, loathed kisses, and 120 embraces." Go on: "Yet I would not have you presume that you shall ever repeat them." So—

She writes.

MARGERY.

I have writ it.

PINCHWIFE.

On then: "I then concealed myself from your knowledge to avoid your insolencies." 125

She writes.

MARGERY.

So—

PINCHWIFE.

"The same reason now I am out of your hands"—

She writes.

MARGERY.

So—

PINCHWIFE.

"Makes me own to you my unfortunate though innocent frolic of being in man's clothes"— 130

She writes.

MARGERY.

So—

PINCHWIFE.

"That you may forever more cease to pursue her who hates and detests you"—

She writes on.

MARGERY.

So—h— (*Sighs.*)

PINCHWIFE.

What, do you sigh?—"detests you—as much as she 135 loves her husband and her honor."

MARGERY.

I vow, husband, he'll ne'er believe I should write such a letter.

PINCHWIFE.

What, he'd expect a kinder from you? Come now, your name only. 140

MARGERY.

What, shan't I say "Your most faithful, humble servant till death"?

PINCHWIFE.

No, tormenting fiend. (*Aside.*) Her style, I find, would be very soft.—Come wrap it up now whilst I go fetch wax and a candle and write on the back 145 side "For Mr. Horner." (*Exit.*)

MARGERY.

"For Mr. Horner." So, I am glad he has told me his name. Dear Mr. Horner, but why should I send thee such a letter that will vex thee and make thee angry with me?—Well, I will not send it.—Aye, 150 but then my husband will kill me, for I see plainly he won't let me love Mr. Horner.—But what care I for my husband?—I won't so, I won't send poor

Mr. Horner such a letter.—But then my husband— But oh, what if I writ at bottom, "My 155 husband made me write it"?—Aye, but then my husband would see't.—Can one have no shift? Ah, a London woman would have had a hundred presently.* Stay—what if I should write a letter and wrap it up like this and write upon't, too?—Aye, 160 but then my husband would see't.—I don't know what to do.—But yet y'vads[52] I'll try, so I will, for I will not send this letter to poor Mr. Horner, come what will on't. (*She writes and repeats what she hath writ.*) "Dear, sweet Mr. Horner"—so— 165 "My husband would have me send you a base, rude, unmannerly letter, but I won't,"—so—"and would have me forbid you loving me, but I won't,"—so—"and would have me say to you, I hate you, poor Mr. Horner, but I won't tell a lie 170 for him,"—there—"for I'm sure if you and I were in the country at cards together,"—so—"I could not help treading on your toe under the table"— so—"or rubbing knees with you and staring in your face till you saw me"—very well—"and then 175 looking down and blushing for an hour together."—so—"But I must make haste before my husband come, and now he has taught me to write letters, you shall have longer ones from me who am, dear, dear, poor dear Mr. Horner, your 180 most humble friend and servant to command till death, Margery Pinchwife." Stay, I must give him a hint at bottom—so—now wrap it up just like t'other—so—now write "For Mr. Horner."—But oh now what shall I do with it? For here comes 185 my husband.

Enter Pinchwife.

PINCHWIFE. (*Aside.*)

I have been detained by a sparkish coxcomb who pretended a visit to me, but I fear 'twas to my wife.—What, have you done?

MARGERY.

Aye, aye, bud, just now. 190

PINCHWIFE.

Let's see't. What d'ye tremble for? What, you would not have it go?

---

52 y'vads] in faith; a rustic expression

MARGERY.

Here. (*Aside.*) No, I must not give him that; so I
had been served if I had given him this.

He opens and reads the first letter.

PINCHWIFE.

Come, where's the wax and seal?   195

MARGERY. (*Aside.*)

Lord, what shall I do now? Nay, then I have it.—
Pray let me see't. Lord, you think me so arrant a
fool, I cannot seal a letter? I will do't, so I will.
(*Snatches the letter from him, changes it for the other,
seals it, and delivers it to him.*)   200

PINCHWIFE.

Nay, I believe you will learn that and other things,
too, which I would not have you.

MARGERY.

So, han't I done it curiously?[53] (*Aside.*) I think I
have: there's my letter going to Mr. Horner, since
he'll needs have me send letters to folks.   205

PINCHWIFE.

'Tis very well, but I warrant, you would not have
it go now?

MARGERY.

Yes indeed, but I would, bud, now.

PINCHWIFE.

Well, you are a good girl then. Come let me lock
you up in your chamber till I come back, and be   210
sure you come not within three strides of the
window when I am gone, for I have a spy in the
street.

Exit Margery. Pinchwife locks the door.

At least 'tis fit she think so. If we do not cheat
women, they'll cheat us, and fraud may be justly   215
used with secret enemies, of which a wife is the
most dangerous. And he that has a handsome one
to keep, and a frontier town, must provide against
treachery rather than open force. Now I have
secured all within, I'll deal with the foe without 220
with false intelligence.

Holds up the letter and exits.

---

53 curiously] skillfully

Scene [iii]. Horner's lodging.

Quack and Horner.

QUACK.

Well sir, how fadges[54] the new design? Have you
not the luck of all your brother projectors,* to
deceive only yourself at last?

HORNER.

No, good domine[55] doctor, I deceive you, it seems,
and others too, for the grave matrons and old rigid 5
husbands think me as unfit for love as they are.
But their wives, sisters, and daughters know, some
of 'em, better things already.

QUACK.

Already!

HORNER.

Already, I say. Last night I was drunk with half a 10
dozen of your* civil persons, as you call 'em, and
people of honor and so was made free of their society
and dressing rooms forever hereafter and am already
come to the privileges of sleeping upon their pallets,
warming smocks, tying shoes and garters, and the   15
like, doctor, already, already, doctor.

QUACK.

You have made use of your time, sir.

HORNER.

I tell thee, I am now no more interruption to 'em
when they sing or talk bawdy than a little, squab,
French page who speaks no English.   20

QUACK.

But do civil persons and women of honor drink
and sing bawdy songs?

HORNER.

Oh amongst friends, amongst friends. For your
bigots in honor are just like those in religion: they
fear the eye of the world more than the eye of Heaven 25
and think there is no virtue but railing at vice and no
sin but giving scandal. They rail at a poor, little, kept*
player and keep themselves some young, modest
pulpit comedian to be privy to their sins in their
closets,* not to tell 'em of them in their chapels. 30

QUACK.

Nay, the truth on't is, priests amongst the women

---

54 fadges] prospers
55 domine] master (of a profession)

now have quite got the better of us lay confessors, physicians.

HORNER.

And they are rather their patients, but—

Enter Lady Fidget, looking about her.

Now we talk of women of honor, here comes one. 35 Step behind the screen there and but observe if I have not particular privileges with the women of reputation already, doctor, already.

LADY FIDGET.

Well Horner, am not I a woman of honor? You see I'm as good as my word. 40

HORNER.

And you shall see, madam, I'll not be behindhand with you in honor, and I'll be as good as my word, too, if you please but to withdraw into the next room.

LADY FIDGET.

But first, my dear sir, you must promise to have a 45 care of my dear honor.

HORNER.

If you talk a word more of your honor, you'll make me incapable to wrong it. To talk of honor in the mysteries of love is like talking of Heaven or the Deity in an operation of witchcraft: just when you 50 are employing the Devil, it makes the charm impotent.

LADY FIDGET.

Nay, fie, let us not be smutty! But you talk of mysteries and bewitching to me; I don't understand you. 55

HORNER.

I tell you, madam, the word "money" in a mistress's mouth at such a nick of time is not a more disheartening sound to a younger brother than that of "honor" to an eager lover like myself.

LADY FIDGET.

But you can't blame a lady of my reputation to be 60 chary.

HORNER.

Chary! I have been chary of it already by the report I have caused of myself.

LADY FIDGET.

Aye, but if you should ever let other women know that dear secret, it would come out. Nay, you must 65

have a great care of your conduct, for my acquaintance are so censorious (oh 'tis a wicked censorious world, Mr. Horner), I say, are so censorious and detracting that perhaps they'll talk to the prejudice of my honor, though you should 70 not let them know the dear secret.

HORNER.

Nay madam, rather than they shall prejudice your honor, I'll prejudice theirs, and to serve you, I'll lie with 'em all, make the secret their own, and then they'll keep it. I am a Machiavel* in love, madam. 75

LADY FIDGET.

Oh no, sir, not that way.

HORNER.

Nay, the devil take me if censorious women are to be silenced any other way.

LADY FIDGET.

A secret is better kept, I hope, by a single person than a multitude; therefore, pray do not trust 80 anybody else with it, dear, dear Mr. Horner. (*Embracing him.*)

Enter Sir Jaspar Fidget.

SIR JASPAR.

How now!

LADY FIDGET. (*Aside.*)

Oh my husband—prevented—and what's almost as bad, found with my arms about another man. 85 That will appear too much. What shall I say?— Sir Jaspar, come hither. I am trying if Mr. Horner were ticklish, and he's as ticklish as can be. I love to torment the confounded toad. Let you and I tickle him. 90

SIR JASPAR.

No, your ladyship will tickle him better without me, I suppose. But is this your buying china? I thought you had been at the china house?

HORNER. (*Aside.*)

China house, that's my cue; I must take it.—A pox, can't you keep your impertinent wives at 95 home? Some men are troubled with the husbands, but I with the wives. But I'd have you to know, since I cannot be your journeyman by night, I will not be your drudge by day, to squire your wife about and be your man of straw, or scarecrow, only 100 to pies and jays that would be nibbling at your

forbidden fruit. I shall be shortly the hackney
gentleman-usher of the Town.

SIR JASPAR. (*Aside.*)

He, he, he, poor fellow, he's in the right on't, faith:
to squire women about for other folks is as   105
ungrateful an employment as to tell money for
other folks.—He, he, he, ben't angry, Horner—

LADY FIDGET.

No, 'tis I have more reason to be angry, who am
left by you to go abroad indecently alone or, what
is more indecent, to pin myself upon such ill-bred   110
people of your acquaintance, as this is.

SIR JASPAR.

Nay prithee, what has he done?

LADY FIDGET.

Nay, he has done nothing.

SIR JASPAR.

But what d'ye take ill if he has done nothing?

LADY FIDGET.

Ha, ha, ha! Faith, I can't but laugh, however. Why,   115
d'ye think, the unmannerly toad would not come
down to me to the coach. I was fain to come up
to fetch him or go without him, which I was
resolved not to do, for he knows china very well
and has himself very good, but will not let me see   120
it, lest I should beg some. But I will find it out
and have what I came for yet.

*Exit Lady Fidget, and locks the door, followed by
Horner to the door.*

HORNER. (*Apart to Lady Fidget.*)

Lock the door, madam.— So, she has got into my
chamber and locked me out. Oh the impertinency
of womankind! Well Sir Jaspar, plain dealing is a   125
jewel: if ever you suffer your wife to trouble me
again here, she shall carry you home a pair of
horns,* by my Lord Mayor she shall; though I
cannot furnish you myself, you are sure yet I'll find
a way.   130

SIR JASPAR. (*Aside.*)

Ha, ha, he, at my first coming in and finding her
arms about him, tickling him it seems, I was half
jealous, but now I see my folly.—He, he, he, poor
Horner.

HORNER.

Nay, though you laugh now, 'twill be my turn ere   135

long. Oh women, more impertinent, more cunning,
and more mischievous than their monkeys and to
me almost as ugly.—Now is she throwing my things
about and rifling all I have, but I'll get into her the
back way and so rifle her for it.   140

SIR JASPAR.

Ha, ha, ha, poor angry Horner.

HORNER.

Stay here a little. I'll ferret her out to you presently,
I warrant. (*Exit at t'other door.*)

SIR JASPAR.

Wife, my Lady Fidget, wife, he is coming into you
the back way.   145

*Sir Jaspar calls through the door to his wife; she
answers from within.*

LADY FIDGET.

Let him come, and welcome, which way he will.

SIR JASPAR.

He'll catch you and use you roughly and be too
strong for you.

LADY FIDGET.

Don't you trouble yourself; let him if he can.

QUACK. (*Behind.*)

This indeed I could not have believed from him   150
nor any but my own eyes.

Enter Mistress Squeamish.

MRS. SQUEAMISH.

Where's this woman-hater, this toad, this ugly,
greasy, dirty sloven?

SIR JASPAR. [*Aside.*]

So the women all will have him ugly. Methinks he
is a comely person, but his wants* make his form   155
contemptible to 'em, and 'tis e'en as my wife said
yesterday, talking of him, that a proper handsome
eunuch was as ridiculous a thing as a gigantic
coward.

MRS. SQUEAMISH.

Sir Jaspar, your servant. Where is the odious beast? 160

SIR JASPAR.

He's within in his chamber with my wife; she's
playing the wag with him.

MRS. SQUEAMISH.

Is she so? And he's a clownish* beast: he'll give her
no quarter; he'll play the wag with her again, let

me tell you. Come, let's go help her. What, the 165
door's locked?

SIR JASPAR.

Aye, my wife locked it.

MRS. SQUEAMISH.

Did she so? Let us break it open then.

SIR JASPAR.

No, no, he'll do her no hurt.

MRS. SQUEAMISH.

No. (*Aside.*) But is there no other way to get into 170
'em? Whither goes this? I will disturb 'em.

*Exit Squeamish at another door. Enter Old Lady
Squeamish.*

OLD LADY SQUEAMISH.

Where is this harlotry, this impudent baggage, this
rambling tomrig?[56]—Oh Sir Jaspar, I'm glad to see
you here. Did you not see my vild[57] grandchild
come in hither just now? 175

SIR JASPAR.

Yes.

OLD LADY SQUEAMISH.

Aye, but where is she then? Where is she? Lord,
Sir Jaspar, I have e'en rattled myself to pieces in
pursuit of her. But can you tell what she makes
here? They say below, no woman lodges here. 180

SIR JASPAR.

No.

OLD LADY SQUEAMISH.

No—what does she here then? Say if it be not a
woman's lodging, what makes she here? But are
you sure no woman lodges here?

SIR JASPAR.

No, nor no man neither: this is Mr. Horner's 185
lodging.

OLD LADY SQUEAMISH.

Is it so? Are you sure?

SIR JASPAR.

Yes, yes.

OLD LADY SQUEAMISH.

So then there's no hurt in't, I hope. But where is he?

---

56 tomrig] "a strumpet, a romping girl, a tomboy" (*OED*)
57 vild] archaic (as suits Old Lady Squeamish) form of
"vile"

SIR JASPAR.

He's in the next room with my wife. 190

OLD LADY SQUEAMISH.

Nay, if you trust him with your wife, I may with
my Biddy. They say he's a merry, harmless man
now, e'en as harmless a man as ever came out of
Italy with a good voice and as pretty harmless
company for a lady as a snake without his teeth. 195

SIR JASPAR.

Aye, aye, poor man.

Enter Mrs. Squeamish.

MRS. SQUEAMISH.

I can't find 'em.—Oh are you here, Grandmother?
I followed, you must know, my Lady Fidget hither;
'tis the prettiest lodging, and I have been staring
on the prettiest pictures. 200

*Enter Lady Fidget with a piece of china in her hand
and Horner following.*

LADY FIDGET.

And I have been toiling and moiling for the
prettiest piece of china, my dear.

HORNER.

Nay, she has been too hard for me, do what I could.

MRS. SQUEAMISH.

Oh Lord, I'll have some china, too. Good Mr.
Horner, don't think to give other people china and 205
me none. Come in with me, too.

HORNER.

Upon my honor I have none left now.

MRS. SQUEAMISH.

Nay, nay, I have known you deny your china
before now, but you shan't put me off so. Come—

HORNER.

This lady had the last there. 210

LADY FIDGET.

Yes indeed, madam, to my certain knowledge he
has no more left.

MRS. SQUEAMISH.

Oh but it may be he may have some you could
not find.

LADY FIDGET.

What, d'ye think if he had had any left, I would 215
not have had it too? For we women of quality*
never think we have china enough.

HORNER.

Do not take it ill. I cannot make china for you all, but I will have a roll-waggon[58] for you, too, another time.   220

MRS. SQUEAMISH.

Thank you, dear toad.

LADY FIDGET. (*To Horner, aside.*)

What do you mean by that promise?

HORNER. (*Apart to Lady Fidget.*)

Alas, she has an innocent, literal understanding.

OLD LADY SQUEAMISH.

Poor Mr. Horner. He has enough to do to please you all, I see.   225

HORNER.

Aye madam, you see how they use me.

OLD LADY SQUEAMISH.

Poor gentleman, I pity you.

HORNER.

I thank you, madam. I could never find pity but from such reverend ladies as you are; the young ones will never spare a man.   230

MRS. SQUEAMISH.

Come, come, beast, and go dine with us, for we shall want a man at ombre after dinner.

HORNER.

That's all their use of me, madam, you see.

MRS. SQUEAMISH.

Come sloven, I'll lead you to be sure of you. (*Pulls him by the cravat.*)   235

OLD LADY SQUEAMISH.

Alas, poor man, how she tugs him. Kiss, kiss her! That's the way to make such nice* women quiet.

HORNER.

No madam, that remedy is worse than the torment; they know I dare suffer anything rather than do it.

OLD LADY SQUEAMISH.

Prithee, kiss her, and I'll give you her picture in   240 little[59] that you admired so last night, prithee do.

HORNER.

Well, nothing but that could bribe me. I love a woman only in effigy and good painting as much as I hate them. I'll do't, for I could adore the Devil well painted. (*Kisses Mrs. Squeamish.*)   245

58 roll-waggon] a cylindrically shaped Chinese vase
59 picture in little] miniature

MRS. SQUEAMISH.

Faugh, you filthy toad! Nay, now I've done jesting.

OLD LADY SQUEAMISH.

Ha, ha, ha, I told you so.

MRS. SQUEAMISH.

Faugh, a kiss of his—

SIR JASPAR.

Has no more hurt in't than one of my spaniel's.

MRS. SQUEAMISH.

Nor no more good neither.   250

QUACK. (*Behind.*)

I will now believe anything he tells me.

Enter Pinchwife.

LADY FIDGET.

Oh Lord, here's a man, Sir Jaspar! My mask, my mask. I would not be seen here for the world.

SIR JASPAR.

What, not when I am with you?

LADY FIDGET.

No, no, my honor—let's be gone.   255

MRS. SQUEAMISH.

Oh Grandmother, let us be gone. Make haste, make haste. I know not how he may censure us.

LADY FIDGET.

Be found in the lodging of anything like a man? Away.

Exeunt Sir Jaspar, Lady Fidget, Old Lady Squeamish, Mrs. Squeamish.

QUACK. (*Behind.*)

What's here, another cuckold? He looks like one,   260 and none else sure have any business with him.

HORNER.

Well, what brings my dear friend hither?

PINCHWIFE.

Your impertinency.

HORNER.

My impertinency! Why, you gentlemen that have got handsome wives think you have a privilege of   265 saying anything to your friends and are as brutish as if you were our creditors.

PINCHWIFE.

No sir, I'll ne'er trust you anyway.

HORNER.

But why not, dear Jack? Why diffide in[60] me thou knowst so well? 270

PINCHWIFE.

Because I do know you so well.

HORNER.

Han't I been always thy friend, honest Jack, always ready to serve thee, in love or battle, before thou wert married and am so still?

PINCHWIFE.

I believe so; you would be my second now indeed. 275

HORNER.

Well then, dear Jack, why so unkind, so grum, so strange to me? Come, prithee kiss me, dear rogue. Gad, I was always, I say, and am still as much thy servant as—

PINCHWIFE.

As I am yours, sir. What, you would send a kiss 280 to my wife, is that it?

HORNER.

So there 'tis. A man can't show his friendship to a married man but presently* he talks of his wife to you. Prithee, let thy wife alone and let thee and I be all one, as we were wont. What, thou art as shy 285 of my kindness as a Lombard Street[61] alderman of a courtier's civility at Locket's.*

PINCHWIFE.

But you are over-kind to me, as kind as if I were your cuckold already, yet I must confess you ought to be kind and civil to me since I am so kind, so 290 civil to you as to bring you this. Look you there, sir. (*Delivers him a letter.*)

HORNER.

What is't?

PINCHWIFE.

Only a love letter, sir.

HORNER.

From whom? (*Reads.*) 295

How, this is from your wife!—hum—and hum—

PINCHWIFE.

Even from my wife, sir. Am I not wondrous kind and civil to you now, too? (*Aside.*) But you'll not think her so.

HORNER. (*Aside.*)

Hah, is this a trick of his or hers? 300

PINCHWIFE.

The gentleman's surprised, I find. What, you expected a kinder letter?

HORNER.

No faith, not I. How could I?

PINCHWIFE.

Yes, yes, I'm sure you did. A man so well made as you are must needs be disappointed if the women 305 declare not their passion at first sight or opportunity.

HORNER. [*Aside.*]

But what should this mean? Stay, the postscript: "Be sure you love me whatsoever my husband says to the contrary, and let him not see this, lest he should come home and pinch me or kill my squirrel." It 310 seems he knows not what the letter contains.

PINCHWIFE.

Come, ne'er wonder at it so much.

HORNER.

Faith, I can't help it.

PINCHWIFE.

Now I think I have deserved your infinite friendship and kindness and have showed myself sufficiently an 315 obliging kind friend and husband. Am I not so, to bring a letter from my wife to her gallant?

HORNER.

Aye, the devil take me, art thou the most obliging, kind friend and husband in the world, ha, ha.

PINCHWIFE.

Well, you may be merry, sir, but in short I must 320 tell you, sir, my honor will suffer no jesting.

HORNER.

What dost thou mean?

PINCHWIFE.

Does the letter want a comment? Then know, sir, though I have been so civil a husband as to bring you a letter from my wife, to let you kiss and court her 325 to my face, I will not be a cuckold, sir, I will not.

HORNER.

Thou art mad with jealousy. I never saw thy wife in my life but at the play yesterday, and I know not if it were she or no. I court her, kiss her!

PINCHWIFE.

I will not be a cuckold, I say; there will be danger 330 in making me a cuckold.

---

60 diffide in] distrust
61 Lombard Street] in the City

HORNER.

Why, wert thou not well cured of thy last clap?

PINCHWIFE.

I wear a sword.

HORNER.

It should be taken from thee lest thou shouldst do thyself a mischief with it. Thou art mad, man. 335

PINCHWIFE.

As mad as I am and as merry as you are, I must have more reason from you ere we part, I say again, though you kissed and courted last night my wife in man's clothes, as she confesses in her letter.

HORNER. (*Aside*.)

Hah! 340

PINCHWIFE.

Both she and I say you must not design it again, for you have mistaken your woman, as you have done your man.

HORNER. (*Aside*.)

Oh I understand something now.—Was that thy wife? Why wouldst thou not tell me 'twas she? Faith, 345 my freedom with her was your fault, not mine.

PINCHWIFE. (*Aside*.)

Faith, so 'twas.

HORNER.

Fie, I'd never do't to a woman before her husband's face, sure.

PINCHWIFE.

But I had rather you should do't to my wife before 350 my face than behind my back, and that you shall never do.

HORNER.

No, you will hinder me.

PINCHWIFE.

If I would not hinder you, you see by her letter, she would. 355

HORNER.

Well, I must e'en acquiesce then and be contented with what she writes.

PINCHWIFE.

I'll assure you 'twas voluntarily writ; I had no hand in't, you may believe me.

HORNER.

I do believe thee, faith. 360

PINCHWIFE.

And believe her too, for she's an innocent creature, has no dissembling in her, and so fare you well, sir.

HORNER.

Pray however, present my humble service to her and tell her I will obey her letter to a tittle and 365 fulfill her desires be what they will or with what difficulty soever I do't, and you shall be no more jealous of me, I warrant her, and you—

PINCHWIFE.

Well then, fare you well, and play with any man's honor but mine, kiss any man's wife but mine, and 370 welcome. (*Exit*.)

HORNER.

Ha, ha, ha, doctor.

QUACK.

It seems he has not heard the report of you or does not believe it.

HORNER.

Ha, ha, now doctor, what think you? 375

QUACK.

Pray let's see the letter. (*Reads*.) Hum—"for"— "dear"—"love you"—

HORNER.

I wonder how she could contrive it! What say'st thou to't? 'Tis an original.

QUACK.

So are your cuckolds, too, originals, for they are 380 like no other common cuckolds, and I will henceforth believe it not impossible for you to cuckold the Grand Signior[62] amidst his guards of eunuchs, that I say.

HORNER.

And I say for the letter, 'tis the first love letter that 385 ever was without flames, darts, fates, destinies, lying, and dissembling in't.

Enter Sparkish pulling in Pinchwife.

SPARKISH.

Come back! You are a pretty brother-in-law, neither go to church nor to dinner with your sister bride. 390

PINCHWIFE.

My sister denies her marriage and you see is gone away from you dissatisfied.

---

62 Grand Signior] the Sultan of Turkey

SPARKISH.

Pshaw, upon a foolish scruple that our parson was not in lawful orders and did not say all the Common Prayer,63 but 'tis her modesty only, I believe. But let women be never so modest the first day, they'll be sure to come to themselves by night, and I shall have enough of her then. In the meantime, Harry Horner, you must dine with me; I keep my wedding at my aunt's in the Piazza.64 400

HORNER.

Thy wedding! What stale maid has lived to despair of a husband, or what young one of a gallant?

SPARKISH.

Oh your servant, sir. This gentleman's sister then— no stale maid.

HORNER.

I'm sorry for't. 405

PINCHWIFE. (*Aside.*)

How comes he so concerned for her?

SPARKISH.

You sorry for't! Why, do you know any ill by her?

HORNER.

No, I know none but by thee; 'tis for her sake, not yours, and another man's sake that might have hoped, I thought— 410

SPARKISH.

Another man, another man, what is his name?

HORNER.

Nay, since 'tis past, he shall be nameless. (*Aside.*) Poor Harcourt, I am sorry thou hast missed her.

PINCHWIFE. (*Aside.*)

He seems to be much troubled at the match.

SPARKISH.

Prithee, tell me.—Nay, you shan't go, brother. 415

PINCHWIFE.

I must of necessity, but I'll come to you to dinner. (*Exit.*)

SPARKISH.

But Harry, what, have I a rival in my wife already? But with all my heart, for he may be of use to me hereafter, for though my hunger is now my sauce 420 and I can fall on heartily without. But the time will come, when a rival will be as good sauce for a married man to a wife as an orange to veal.

HORNER.

Oh thou damned rogue, thou hast set my teeth on edge with thy orange. 425

SPARKISH.

Then let's to dinner. There I was with you again. Come.

HORNER.

But who dines with thee?

SPARKISH.

My friends and relations, my brother Pinchwife, you see, of your acquaintance. 430

HORNER.

And his wife?

SPARKISH.

No, gad, he'll ne'er let her come amongst us good fellows. Your stingy country coxcomb keeps his wife from his friends as he does his little firkin of ale for his own drinking, and a gentleman can't get 435 a smack on't. But his servants, when his back is turned, broach it at their pleasure and dust it away, ha, ha, ha. Gad, I am witty, I think, considering I was married today, by the world, but come—

HORNER.

No, I will not dine with you unless you can fetch 440 her, too.

SPARKISH.

Pshaw, what pleasure canst thou have with women now, Harry?

HORNER.

My eyes are not gone. I love a good prospect yet and will not dine with you unless she does too. Go 445 fetch her, therefore, but do not tell her husband 'tis for my sake.

SPARKISH.

Well, I'll go try what I can do. In the meantime, come away to my aunt's lodging; 'tis in the way to Pinchwife's. 450

HORNER. [*Apart to Quack.*]

The poor woman has called for aid and stretched forth her hand, doctor; I cannot but help her over the pale out of the briars.

Exeunt.

---

63 Common Prayer] the marriage service within the Anglican *Book of Common Prayer*

64 Piazza] arcade around two sides of Covent Garden*

Scene [iv]. Pinchwife's house.

Margery alone leaning on her elbow. A table, pen, ink, and paper.

MARGERY.

Well 'tis e'en so: I have got the London disease they
call love; I am sick of my husband and for my
gallant. I have heard this distemper called a fever,
but methinks 'tis liker an ague, for when I think
of my husband, I tremble and am in a cold sweat   5
and have inclinations to vomit, but when I think
of my gallant, dear Mr. Horner, my hot fit comes,
and I am all in a fever indeed, and as in other
fevers, my own chamber is tedious to me, and I
would fain be removed to his, and then methinks   10
I should be well. Ah poor Mr. Horner! Well, I
cannot, will not stay here; therefore, I'll make an
end of my letter to him, which shall be a finer
letter than my last, because I have studied it like
anything. Oh sick! sick! (*Takes the pen and writes.*)   15

*Enter Mr. Pinchwife, who, seeing her writing, steals
softly behind her and looking over her shoulder,
snatches the paper from her.*

PINCHWIFE.

What, writing more letters?

MARGERY.

Oh Lord, bud, why d'ye fright me so?

She offers to run out; he stops her and reads.

PINCHWIFE.

How's this! Nay, you shall not stir, madam. "Dear,
dear, dear, Mr. Horner"—very well—I have taught
you to write letters to good purpose, but let's see't.   20
"First I am to beg your pardon for my boldness
in writing to you, which I'd have you to know I
would not have done, had not you said first you
loved me so extremely, which if you do, you will
never suffer me to lie in the arms of another man,   25
whom I loathe, nauseate, and detest." Now you
can write these filthy words! But what follows?
"Therefore, I hope you will speedily find some way
to free me from this unfortunate match, which was
never, I assure you, of my choice, but I'm afraid   30
'tis already too far gone; however, if you love me,
as I do you, you will try what you can do, but you

must help me away before tomorrow, or else, alas,
I shall be forever out of your reach for I can defer
no longer our—" (*The letter concludes.*) "Our"?   35
What is to follow "our"? Speak! What? Our
journey into the country, I suppose. Oh woman,
damned woman! And Love, damned Love, their
old tempter! For this is one of his miracles: in a
moment he can make those blind that could see   40
and those see that were blind, those dumb that
could speak and those prattle who were dumb
before, nay, what is more than all, make these
dough-baked,[65] senseless, indocile animals,
women, too hard for us, their politic lords and   45
rulers, in a moment. But make an end of your
letter, and then I'll make an end of you thus and
all my plagues together. (*Draws his sword.*)

MARGERY.

Oh Lord, oh Lord, you are such a passionate man,
bud!   50

Enter Sparkish.

SPARKISH.

How now, what's here to do?

PINCHWIFE.

This fool here now!

SPARKISH.

What, drawn upon your wife? You should never do
that but at night in the dark when you can't hurt her.
This is my sister-in-law, is it not? (*Pulls aside her*   55
handkerchief.) Aye faith, e'en our country Margery,
one may know her. Come, she and you must go dine
with me; dinner's ready, come. But where's my wife?
Is she not come home yet? Where is she?

PINCHWIFE.

Making you a cuckold. 'Tis that they all do as soon   60
as they can.

SPARKISH.

What, the wedding day? No, a wife that designs
to make a cully of her husband will be sure to let
him win the first stake of love, by the world. But
come, they stay dinner for us; come, I'll lead down,   65
our Margery.

MARGERY.

No sir, go, we'll follow you.

---

65 dough-baked] half-baked, foolish

SPARKISH.

I will not wag without you.

PINCHWIFE.

This coxcomb is a sensible torment to me amidst
the greatest in the world.   70

SPARKISH.

Come, come, Madam Margery.

PINCHWIFE.

No, I'll lead her my way. What, would you treat
your friends with mine, for want* of your own
wife? (*Leads her to t'other door and locks her in and
returns. Aside.*) I am contented my rage should take   75
breath.

SPARKISH.

I told Horner this.

PINCHWIFE.

Come now.

SPARKISH.

Lord, how shy you are of your wife, but let me tell
you, brother, we men of wit have amongst us a   80
saying that cuckolding, like the small pox, comes
with a fear, and you may keep your wife as much
as you will out of danger of infection, but if her
constitution incline her to't, she'll have it sooner
or later, by the world, say they.   85

PINCHWIFE. (*Aside.*)

What a thing is a cuckold, that every fool can
make him ridiculous.—Well sir, but let me advise
you, now you are come to be concerned because
you suspect the danger, not to neglect the means
to prevent it, especially when the greatest share of   90
the malady will light upon your own head, for
Hows'e'er the kind wife's belly comes to swell,
The husband breeds[66] for her and first is ill.

Act V, scene i. Pinchwife's house.

Enter Pinchwife and Margery. A table and candle.

PINCHWIFE.

Come, take the pen and make an end of the letter,
just as you intended. If you are false in a tittle, I
shall soon perceive it and punish you with this as
you deserve. (*Lays his hand on his sword.*)

_____

66 breeds] grows the cuckold's horns

Write what was to follow. Let's see. "You must   5
make haste and help me away before tomorrow,
or else I shall be forever out of your reach, for I
can defer no longer our—" What follows "our"?

MARGERY.

Must all out then, bud? (*Margery takes the pen and
writes.*) Look you there then.   10

PINCHWIFE.

Let's see. "For I can defer no longer our—wedding.
Your slighted Alithea." What's the meaning of this,
my sister's name to't? Speak, unriddle!

MARGERY.

Yes indeed, bud.

PINCHWIFE.

But why her name to't? Speak—speak, I say!   15

MARGERY.

Aye, but you'll tell her then again. If you would
not tell her again—

PINCHWIFE.

I will not. I am stunned; my head turns round.
Speak.

MARGERY.

Won't you tell her indeed and indeed?   20

PINCHWIFE.

No. Speak, I say.

MARGERY.

She'll be angry with me, but I had rather she
should be angry with me than you, bud, and to
tell you the truth, 'twas she made me write the
letter and taught me what I should write.   25

PINCHWIFE. [*Aside.*]

Hah! I thought the style was somewhat better than
her own.—But how could she come to you to
teach you, since I had locked you up alone?

MARGERY.

Oh, through the keyhole, bud.

PINCHWIFE.

But why should she make you write a letter for her   30
to him, since she can write herself?

MARGERY.

Why, she said because—for I was unwilling to do it.

PINCHWIFE.

Because what? Because?

MARGERY.

Because lest Mr. Horner should be cruel and refuse
her, or vain afterwards and show the letter, she   35
might disown it, the hand not being hers.

PINCHWIFE. (*Aside.*)

How's this? Hah! Then I think I shall come to myself again. This changeling could not invent this lie. But if she could, why should she? She might think I should soon discover it. Stay—now I think 40 on't, too, Horner said he was sorry she had married Sparkish, and her disowning her marriage to me makes me think she has evaded it for Horner's sake. Yet why should she take this course? But men in love are fools; women may well be so.—But 45 hark you, madam, your sister went out in the morning and I have not seen her within since.

MARGERY.

Alackaday, she has been crying all day above, it seems, in a corner.

PINCHWIFE.

Where is she? Let me speak with her. 50

MARGERY. (*Aside.*)

Oh Lord, then he'll discover all.—Pray hold, bud. What, d'ye mean to discover* me? She'll know I have told you then. Pray bud, let me talk with her first.

PINCHWIFE.

I must speak with her to know whether Horner ever made her any promise and whether she be 55 married to Sparkish or no.

MARGERY.

Pray dear bud, don't till I have spoken with her and told her that I have told you all, for she'll kill me else.

PINCHWIFE.

Go then, and bid her come out to me. 60

MARGERY.

Yes, yes, bud.

PINCHWIFE.

Let me see—

MARGERY. [*Aside.*]

I'll go, but she is not within to come to him. I have just got time to know of Lucy, her maid, who first set me on work, what lie I shall tell next, for I am 65 e'en at my wit's end. (*Exit.*)

PINCHWIFE.

Well, I resolve it: Horner shall have her. I'd rather give him my sister than lend him my wife, and such an alliance will prevent his pretensions to my wife, sure. I'll make him of kin to her, and then 70 he won't care for her.

Margery returns.

MARGERY.

Oh Lord, bud, I told you what anger you would make me with my sister.

PINCHWIFE.

Won't she come hither?

MARGERY.

No no, alackaday, she's ashamed to look you in the 75 face, and she says if you go in to her, she'll run away downstairs and shamefully go herself to Mr. Horner, who has promised her marriage, she says, and she will have no other, so she won't—

PINCHWIFE.

Did he so—promise her marriage? Then she shall 80 have no other. Go tell her so, and if she will come and discourse with me a little concerning the means, I will about it immediately. Go.

Exit Margery.

His estate is equal to Sparkish's, and his extraction as much better than his as his parts* are, but my 85 chief reason is I'd rather be of kin to him by the name of brother-in-law than that of cuckold.

Enter Margery.

Well, what says she now?

MARGERY.

Why, she says she would only have you lead her to Horner's lodging—with whom she first will 90 discourse the matter before she talk with you, which yet she cannot do, for, alack poor creature, she says she can't so much as look you in the face; therefore, she'll come to you in a mask, and you must excuse her if she make you no answer to any 95 question of yours till you have brought her to Mr. Horner, and if you will not chide her nor question her, she'll come out to you immediately.

PINCHWIFE.

Let her come. I will not speak a word to her nor require a word from her. 100

MARGERY.

Oh, I forgot: besides, she says, she cannot look you in the face though through a mask; therefore, would desire you to put out the candle.

PINCHWIFE.

I agree to all; let her make haste.

Exit Margery; [Pinchwife] puts out the candle.

There, 'tis out. My case is something better: I'd 105
rather fight with Horner for not lying with my
sister than for lying with my wife, and of the two,
I had rather find my sister too forward than my
wife. I expected no other from her free education,
as she calls it, and her passion for the Town. Well, 110
wife and sister are names which make us expect
love and duty, pleasure and comfort, but we find
'em plagues and torments and are equally, though
differently, troublesome to their keeper, for we have
as much ado to get people to lie with our sisters 115
as to keep 'em from lying with our wives.

Enter Margery masked and in hoods and scarves and a
nightgown* and petticoat of Alithea's, in the dark.

What, are you come, sister? Let us go then, but
first let me lock up my wife. Mistress Margery,
where are you?

MARGERY.
Here, bud.

PINCHWIFE. 120
Come hither, that I may lock you up.

Margery gives him her hand, but when he lets her go,
she steals softly on t'other side of him.

Get you in. (*Locks the door.*) Come, sister, where
are you now?

[She] is led away by him for his sister Alithea.

Scene [ii]. Horner's lodging.

Quack, Horner.

QUACK.
What, all alone, not so much as one of your cuckolds
here nor one of their wives? They use to take their
turns with you as if they were to watch you.

HORNER.
Yes, it often happens that a cuckold is but his wife's
spy and is more upon family duty when he is with 5
her gallant abroad hindering his pleasure than when
he is at home with her playing the gallant. But the
hardest duty a married woman imposes upon a lover
is keeping her husband company always.

QUACK.
And his fondness wearies you almost as soon as 10
hers.

HORNER.
A pox, keeping a cuckold company after you have
had his wife is as tiresome as the company of a
country squire to a witty fellow of the Town when
he has got all his money. 15

QUACK.
And as at first a man makes a friend of the
husband to get the wife, so at last you are fain to
fall out with the wife to be rid of the husband.

HORNER.
Aye, most cuckold-makers are true courtiers: when
once a poor man has cracked his credit for 'em, 20
they can't abide to come near him.

QUACK.
But at first to draw him in, are so sweet, so kind,
so dear, just as you are to Pinchwife. But what
becomes of that intrigue with his wife?

HORNER.
A pox, he's as surly as an alderman that has been 25
bit,* and since he's so coy, his wife's kindness* is
in vain, for she's a silly* innocent.

QUACK.
Did she not send you a letter by him?

HORNER.
Yes, but that's a riddle I have not yet solved. Allow
the poor creature to be willing, she is silly, too, and 30
he keeps her up so close—

QUACK.
Yes, so close that he makes her but the more
willing and adds but revenge to her love, which
two, when met, seldom fail of satisfying each other
one way or other. 35

HORNER.
What, here's the man we are talking of, I think.

Enter Pinchwife leading in his wife masked, muffled,
and in her sister's gown.

HORNER.
Pshaw.

QUACK.
Bringing his wife to you is the next thing to
bringing a love letter from her.

HORNER.
What means this? 40

PINCHWIFE.
The last time, you know, sir, I brought you a love

letter; now you see a mistress. I think you'll say I am a civil man to you.

PINCHWIFE.

Do you speak to her; she would never be ruled by me.

HORNER.

Aye, the devil take me, will I say thou art the civilest man I ever met with, and I have known some. I fancy I understand thee now better than I did the letter, but hark thee in thy ear— 45

HORNER.

Madam—

PINCHWIFE.

What?

Margery whispers to Horner.

HORNER.

Nothing but the usual question, man. Is she sound,* on thy word? 50

She says she must speak with me in private. Withdraw, prithee. 75

PINCHWIFE.

PINCHWIFE. (*Aside.*)

What, you take her for a wench and me for a pimp?

She's unwilling, it seems, I should know all her undecent conduct in this business.—Well then, I'll leave you together and hope when I am gone you'll agree; if not, you and I shan't agree, sir.

HORNER.

Pshaw, wench and pimp, paw[67] words. I know thou art an honest fellow and hast a great acquaintance among the ladies and perhaps hast made love* for me rather than let me make love to thy wife— 55

HORNER. [*Aside.*]

What means the fool?—If she and I agree, 'tis no matter what you and I do. 80

PINCHWIFE.

Whispers to Margery, who makes signs with her hand for [Pinchwife] to be gone.

Come sir, in short, I am for no fooling.

HORNER.

PINCHWIFE.

Nor I neither. Therefore, prithee, let's see her face presently;* make her show, man. Art thou sure I don't know her? 60

In the meantime, I'll fetch a parson and find out Sparkish and disabuse him. You would have me fetch a parson, would you not? [*Aside.*] Well then, now I think I am rid of her and shall have no more trouble with her. Our sisters and daughters, like usurers' money, are safest when put out, but our wives, like their writings, never safe but in our closets* under lock and key. (*Exit.*) 85

PINCHWIFE.

I am sure you do know her.

HORNER.

A pox, why dost thou bring her to me then?

PINCHWIFE.

Because she's a relation of mine.

HORNER.

Enter Boy.

Is she, faith, man? Then thou art still more civil and obliging, dear rogue. 65

BOY.

Sir Jaspar Fidget, sir, is coming up. 90

PINCHWIFE.

HORNER. [*Aside to Quack.*]

Who desired me to bring her to you.

HORNER.

Here's the trouble of a cuckold now we are talking of. A pox on him! Has he not enough to do to hinder his wife's sport, but he must other women's, too?—Step in here, madam.

Then she is obliging, dear rogue.

PINCHWIFE.

You'll make her welcome, for my sake, I hope.

HORNER.

Exit Margery. Enter Sir Jaspar.

I hope she is handsome enough to make herself welcome. Prithee, let her unmask. 70

SIR JASPAR.

My best and dearest friend. 95

HORNER. [*Aside to Quack.*]

The old style, doctor.—Well, be short, for I am busy. What would your impertinent wife have now?

---

67 paw] "improper, naughty, obscene" (*OED*)

SIR JASPAR.

Well guessed i'faith, for I do come from her.

HORNER.

To invite me to supper. Tell her I can't come. Go. 100

SIR JASPAR.

Nay, now you are out, faith, for my lady and the whole knot of the virtuous gang, as they call themselves, are resolved upon a frolic of coming to you tonight in a masquerade and are all dressed already.

HORNER.

I shan't be at home. 105

SIR JASPAR.

Lord, how churlish he is to women! Nay, prithee don't disappoint 'em; they'll think 'tis my fault. Prithee, don't. I'll send in the banquet and the fiddles, but make no noise on't, for the poor virtuous rogues would not have it known for the 110 world that they go a-masquerading, and they would come to no man's ball but yours.

HORNER.

Well, well—get you gone and tell 'em if they come, 'twill be at the peril of their honor and yours.

SIR JASPAR.

He, he, he—we'll trust you for that. Farewell. 115 (Exit.)

HORNER.

Doctor, anon you too shall be my guest,
But now I'm going to a private feast.

[Exeunt.]

Scene [iii]. The Piazza of Covent Garden.

Sparkish, Pinchwife.

SPARKISH. (The letter in his hand.)

But who would have thought a woman could have been false to me? By the world, I could not have thought it.

PINCHWIFE.

You were for giving and taking liberty; she has taken it only, sir, now you find in that letter. You 5 are a frank person, and so is she, you see there.

SPARKISH.

Nay, if this be her hand, for I never saw it.

PINCHWIFE.

'Tis no matter whether that be her hand or no. I am sure this hand, at her desire, led her to Mr. Horner, with whom I left her just now to go fetch a parson 10 to 'em at their desire, too, to deprive you of her forever, for it seems yours was but a mock marriage.

SPARKISH.

Indeed, she would needs have it that 'twas Harcourt himself in a parson's habit that married us, but I'm sure he told me 'twas his brother Ned. 15

PINCHWIFE.

Oh there 'tis out, and you were deceived, not she, for you are such a frank person. But I must be gone. You'll find her at Mr. Horner's; go and believe your eyes. (Exit.)

SPARKISH.

Nay, I'll to her and call her as many crocodiles, 20 sirens, harpies, and other heathenish names as a poet would do a mistress who had refused to hear his suit, nay more, his verses on her. But stay, is not that she following a torch at t'other end of the Piazza, and from Horner's certainly? 'Tis so. 25

Enter Alithea following a torch and Lucy behind.

You are well met, madam, though you don't think so. What, you have made a short visit to Mr. Horner, but I suppose you'll return to him presently; by that time the parson can be with him.

ALITHEA.

Mr. Horner and the parson, sir! 30

SPARKISH.

Come madam, no more dissembling, no more jilting, for I am no more a frank person.

ALITHEA.

How's this?

LUCY. (Aside.)

So 'twill work, I see.

SPARKISH.

Could you find out no easy country fool to abuse? 35 None but me, a gentleman of wit and pleasure about the Town? But it was your pride to be too hard for a man of parts,* unworthy, false woman, false as a friend that lends a man money to lose, false as dice, who undo those that trust all they have to 'em. 40

LUCY. (Aside.)

He has been a great bubble* by his similes, as they say.

ALITHEA.

You have been too merry, sir, at your wedding dinner, sure.

SPARKISH.

What, d'ye mock me too?

ALITHEA.

Or you have been deluded. 45

SPARKISH.

By you.

ALITHEA.

Let me understand you.

SPARKISH.

Have you the confidence—I should call it something else, since you know your guilt—to stand my just reproaches? You did not write an 50 impudent letter to Mr. Horner, who I find now has clubbed with you in deluding me with his aversion for women, that I might not, forsooth, suspect him for my rival?

LUCY. (*Aside.*)

D'ye think the gentleman can be jealous now, 55 madam?

ALITHEA.

I write a letter to Mr. Horner!

SPARKISH.

Nay madam, do not deny it; your brother showed it me just now and told me likewise he left you at Horner's lodging to fetch a parson to marry you 60 to him, and I wish you joy, madam, joy, joy, and to him, too, much joy and to myself, more joy for not marrying you.

ALITHEA. (*Aside.*)

So I find my brother would break off the match, and I can consent to't, since I see this gentleman 65 can be made jealous.—Oh Lucy, by his rude usage and jealousy, he makes me almost afraid I am married to him. Art thou sure 'twas Harcourt himself and no parson that married us?

SPARKISH.

No madam, I thank you. I suppose that was a 70 contrivance too of Mr. Horner's and yours to make Harcourt play the parson, but I would as little as you have him one now, no, not for the world, for shall I tell you another truth? I never had any passion for you till now, for now I hate you. 'Tis 75 true I might have married your portion, as other men of parts* of the Town do sometimes, and so, your servant, and to show my unconcernedness, I'll come to your wedding and resign you with as

much joy as I would a stale wench to a new cully, 80 nay, with as much joy as I would after the first night, if I had been married to you. There's for you, and so, your servant, servant. (*Exit.*)

ALITHEA.

How was I deceived in a man!

LUCY.

You'll believe, then, a fool may be made jealous 85 now? For that easiness in him that suffers him to be led by a wife will likewise permit him to be persuaded against her by others.

ALITHEA.

But marry Mr. Horner? My brother does not intend it, sure. If I thought he did, I would take 90 thy advice and Mr. Harcourt for my husband, and now I wish that if there be any over-wise woman of the Town, who, like me, would marry a fool for fortune, liberty, or title: first, that her husband may love play and be a cully to all the Town but her 95 and suffer none but Fortune to be mistress of his purse; then, if for liberty, that he may send her into the country under the conduct of some housewifely mother-in-law; and if for title, may the world give 'em none but that of cuckold. 100

LUCY.

And for her greater curse, madam, may he not deserve it.

ALITHEA.

Away, impertinent!—Is not this my old Lady Lanterlu's?[68]

LUCY.

Yes, madam. (*Aside.*) And here I hope we shall find 105 Mr. Harcourt.

Exeunt.

Scene [iv]. Horner's lodging.

Horner, Lady Fidget, Dainty, Mrs. Squeamish. A table, banquet, and bottles.

HORNER. (*Aside.*)

A pox, they are come too soon—before I have sent back my new mistress! All I have now to do is to lock her in that they may not see her.

---

68 Lady Lanterlu's] lanterloo, or loo, a popular card game; from *lanturelu*, French for twaddle

LADY FIDGET.

That we may be sure of our welcome, we have brought our entertainment with us and are resolved to treat thee, dear toad— 5

DAINTY.

And that we may be merry to purpose, have left Sir Jaspar and my old Lady Squeamish quarreling at home at backgammon.

MRS. SQUEAMISH.

Therefore, let us make use of our time, lest they should chance to interrupt us. 10

LADY FIDGET.

Let us sit then.

HORNER.

First that you may be private, let me lock this door and that, and I'll wait upon you presently.

LADY FIDGET.

No sir, shut 'em only and your lips forever, for we 15 must trust you as much as our women.*

HORNER.

You know all vanity's killed in me; I have no occasion for talking.

LADY FIDGET.

Now ladies, supposing we had drank each of us our two bottles, let us speak the truth of our hearts. 20

DAINTY AND MRS. SQUEAMISH.

Agreed.

LADY FIDGET.

By this brimmer, for truth is nowhere else to be found. (*Aside to Horner.*) Not in thy heart, false man.

HORNER. (*Aside to Lady Fidget.*)

You have found me a true man, I'm sure. 25

LADY FIDGET. (*Aside to Horner.*)

Not every way.—But let us sit and be merry. (*Sings.*)

I.

Why should our damned tyrants oblige us to live
On the pittance of pleasure which they only give?
    We must not rejoice 30
    With wine and with noise.
In vain we must wake in a dull bed alone,
Whilst to our warm rival the bottle they're gone.
    Then lay aside charms
    And take up these arms.* 35

(**The glasses.*)

II.

'Tis wine only gives 'em their courage and wit;
Because we live sober to men, we submit.
    If for beauties you'd pass,
    Take a lick of the glass;
'Twill mend your complexions, and when they are 40 gone,
The best red we have is the red of the grape.
    Then sisters lay't on
    And damn a good shape.

DAINTY.

Dear brimmer! Well, in token of our openness and plain dealing, let us throw our masks over our 45 heads.

HORNER.

So 'twill come to the glasses anon.

MRS. SQUEAMISH.

Lovely brimmer! Let me enjoy him first.

LADY FIDGET.

No, I never part with a gallant till I've tried him. Dear brimmer that mak'st our husbands short- 50 sighted—

DAINTY.

And our bashful gallants bold—

MRS. SQUEAMISH.

And for want* of a gallant, the butler lovely in our eyes. Drink, eunuch.

LADY FIDGET.

Drink, thou representative of a husband. Damn a 55 husband—

DAINTY.

And as it were a husband, an old keeper*—

MRS. SQUEAMISH.

And an old grandmother—

HORNER.

And an English bawd and a French chirurgeon.

LADY FIDGET.

Aye, we have all reason to curse 'em. 60

HORNER.

For my sake, ladies.

LADY FIDGET.

No, for our own, for the first spoils all young gallant's industry—

DAINTY.

And the other's art makes 'em bold only with common women— 65

MRS. SQUEAMISH.

And rather run the hazard of the vile distemper amongst them than of a denial amongst us.

DAINTY.

The filthy toads choose mistresses now as they do stuffs, for having been fancied and worn by others— 70

MRS. SQUEAMISH.

For being common and cheap—

LADY FIDGET.

Whilst women of quality,* like the richest stuffs, lie untumbled and unasked for.

HORNER.

Aye, neat and cheap and new often they think best.

DAINTY.

No sir, the beasts will be known by a mistress 75 longer than by a suit—

MRS. SQUEAMISH.

And 'tis not for cheapness neither—

LADY FIDGET.

No, for the vain fops will take up druggets and embroider 'em. But I wonder at the depraved appetites of witty men; they used to be out of the common 80 road and hate imitation. Pray tell me, beast, when you were a man, why you rather chose to club with a multitude in a common house for an entertainment than to be the only guest at a good table.

HORNER.

Why faith, ceremony and expectation are 85 unsufferable to those that are sharp bent;[69] people always eat with the best stomach at an ordinary, where every man is snatching for the best bit—

LADY FIDGET.

Though he get a cut over the fingers. But I have heard people eat most heartily of another man's 90 meat, that is, what they do not pay for.

HORNER.

When they are sure of their welcome and freedom, for ceremony in love and eating is as ridiculous as in fighting: falling on briskly is all should be done in those occasions. 95

LADY FIDGET.

Well then, let me tell you, sir, there is nowhere more freedom than in our houses, and we take

freedom from a young person as a sign of good breeding, and a person may be as free as he pleases with us, as frolic, as gamesome, as wild as he will. 100

HORNER.

Han't I heard you all declaim against wild men?

LADY FIDGET.

Yes, but for all that, we think wildness in a man as desirable a quality as in a duck or rabbit. A tame man, faugh!

HORNER.

I know not, but your reputations frightened me 105 as much as your faces invited me.

LADY FIDGET.

Our reputation! Lord, why should you not think that we women make use of our reputation as you men of yours, only to deceive the world with less suspicion? Our virtue is like the stateman's religion, 110 the Quaker's word,[70] the gamester's oath, and the great man's honor: but to cheat those that trust us.

MRS. SQUEAMISH.

And that demureness, coyness, and modesty that you see in our faces in the boxes at plays is as much a sign of a kind* woman as a vizard-mask* in the 115 pit.

DAINTY.

For I assure you, women are least masked when they have the velvet vizard on.

LADY FIDGET.

You would have found us modest women in our denials only— 120

MRS. SQUEAMISH.

Our bashfulness is only the reflection of the men's—

DAINTY.

We blush when they are shame-faced.

HORNER.

I beg your pardon, ladies, I was deceived in you devilishly. But why that mighty pretense to honor? 125

LADY FIDGET.

We have told you, but sometimes 'twas for the same reason you men pretend business often: to avoid ill company, to enjoy the better and more privately those you love.

---

[69] sharp bent] hungry

[70] Quaker's word] Quakers do not take oaths.

HORNER.

But why would you ne'er give a friend a wink then? 130

LADY FIDGET.

Faith, your reputation frightened us as much as ours did you, you were so notoriously lewd—

HORNER.

And you so seemingly honest.*

LADY FIDGET.

Was that all that deterred you?

HORNER.

And so expensive— (You allow freedom, you say?) 135

LADY FIDGET.

Aye, aye.

HORNER.

That I was afraid of losing my little money, as well as my little time, both which my other pleasures required.

LADY FIDGET.

Money, faugh! You talk like a little fellow now. Do 140 such as we expect money?

HORNER.

I beg your pardon, madam, I must confess I have heard that great ladies, like great merchants, set but the higher prices upon what they have because they are not in necessity of taking the first offer. 145

DAINTY.

Such as we make sale of our hearts?

MRS. SQUEAMISH.

We bribed for our love? Faugh!

HORNER.

With your pardon, ladies, I know, like great men in offices, you seem to exact flattery and attendance only from your followers, but you have 150 receivers[71] about you and such fees to pay, a man is afraid to pass your grants;[72] besides, we must let you win at cards, or we lose your hearts, and if you make an assignation, 'tis at a goldsmith's, jeweler's, or china house, where for your honor you 155 deposit to him, he must pawn his to the punctual cit,* and so paying for what you take up, pays for what he takes up.

---

71 receivers] servants who must be paid for cooperation and silence

72 pass your grants] accept your favors

DAINTY.

Would you not have us assured of our gallant's love? 160

MRS. SQUEAMISH.

For love is better known by liberality than by jealousy—

LADY FIDGET.

For one may be dissembled, the other not. (*Aside.*) But my jealousy can be no longer dissembled, and they are telling-ripe.—Come, here's to our gallants 165 in waiting, whom we must name, and I'll begin: this is my false rogue. (*Claps him on the back.*)

MRS. SQUEAMISH.

How!

HORNER.

So all will out now—

MRS. SQUEAMISH. (*Aside to Horner.*)

Did you not tell me 'twas for my sake only you 170 reported yourself no man?

DAINTY. (*Aside.*)

Oh wretch! Did you not swear to me 'twas for my love and honor you passed for that thing you do?

HORNER.

So, so.

LADY FIDGET.

Come, speak ladies. This is my false villain.* 175

MRS. SQUEAMISH.

And mine too.

DAINTY.

And mine.

HORNER.

Well then, you are all three my false rogues too, and there's an end on't.

LADY FIDGET.

Well then, there's no remedy, sister sharers. Let us 180 not fall out but have a care of our honor. Though we get no presents, no jewels of him, we are savers of our honor, the jewel of most value and use, which shines yet to the world unsuspected, though it be counterfeit. 185

HORNER.

Nay and is e'en as good as if it were true, provided the world think so, for honor, like beauty now, only depends on the opinion of others.

LADY FIDGET.

Well Harry Common, I hope you can be true to

three. Swear. But 'tis no purpose to require your 190
oath, for you are as often forsworn as you swear
to new women.

HORNER.

Come, faith madam, let us e'en pardon one
another, for all the difference I find betwixt we
men and you women, we forswear ourselves at the 195
beginning of an amour, you, as long as it lasts.

Enter Sir Jaspar Fidget and Old Lady Squeamish.

SIR JASPAR.

Oh my Lady Fidget, was this your cunning, to
come to Mr. Horner without me? But you have
been no where else, I hope?

LADY FIDGET.

No, Sir Jaspar. 200

OLD LADY SQUEAMISH.

And you came straight hither, Biddy?

MRS. SQUEAMISH.

Yes indeed, Lady Grandmother.

SIR JASPAR.

'Tis well, 'tis well. I knew when once they were
thoroughly acquainted with poor Horner, they'd
ne'er be from him. You may let her masquerade it 205
with my wife and Horner, and I warrant her
reputation safe.

Enter boy.

BOY.

Oh sir, here's the gentleman come whom you bid
me not suffer to come up without giving you
notice, with a lady, too, and other gentlemen. 210

HORNER.

Do you all go in there, whilst I send 'em away.—
And boy, do you desire 'em to stay below till I
come, which shall be immediately.

*Exeunt Sir Jaspar, [Old] Lady Squeamish, Lady
Fidget, Dainty, Mrs. Squeamish.*

BOY.

Yes sir. (*Exit.*)

Exit Horner at t'other door, and returns with Margery.

HORNER.

You would not take my advice to be gone home 215
before your husband came back. He'll now

discover all, yet pray, my dearest, be persuaded to
go home and leave the rest to my management;
I'll let you down the back way.

MARGERY.

I don't know the way home, so I don't. 220

HORNER.

My man shall wait upon you.

MARGERY.

No, don't you believe that I'll go at all. What, are
you weary of me already?

HORNER.

No my life, 'tis that I may love you long, 'tis to
secure my love and your reputation with your 225
husband; he'll never receive you again else.

MARGERY.

What care I? D'ye think to frighten me with that?
I don't intend to go to him again; you shall be my
husband now.

HORNER.

I cannot be your husband, dearest, since you are 230
married to him.

MARGERY.

Oh, would you make me believe that? Don't I see
every day at London here, women leave their first
husbands and go and live with other men as their
wives? Pish, pshaw, you'd make me angry, but that 235
I love you so mainly.

HORNER.

So, they are coming up. In again, in, I hear 'em.

Exit Margery.

Well, a silly mistress is like a weak place, soon got,
soon lost; a man has scarce time for plunder. She
betrays her husband first to her gallant and then 240
her gallant to her husband.

*Enter Pinchwife, Alithea, Harcourt, Sparkish, Lucy,
and a parson.*

PINCHWIFE.

Come madam, 'tis not the sudden change of your
dress, the confidence of your asseverations, and
your false witness there shall persuade me I did not
bring you hither just now; here's my witness, who 245
cannot deny it, since you must be confronted.—
Mr. Horner, did not I bring this lady to you just
now?

HORNER. (*Aside.*)

Now must I wrong one woman for another's sake, but that's no new thing with me, for in these cases 250 I am still on the criminal's side against the innocent.

ALITHEA.

Pray speak, sir.

HORNER. (*Aside.*)

It must be so. I must be impudent and try my luck; impudence uses to be too hard for truth. 255

PINCHWIFE.

What, you are studying an evasion or excuse for her. Speak, sir.

HORNER.

No, faith, I am something backward only to speak in women's affairs or disputes.

PINCHWIFE.

She bids you speak. 260

ALITHEA.

Aye, pray sir, do, pray satisfy him.

HORNER.

Then truly, you did bring that lady to me just now.

PINCHWIFE.

Oh ho!

ALITHEA.

How, sir!

HARCOURT.

How, Horner! 265

ALITHEA.

What mean you, sir? I always took you for a man of honor.

HORNER. (*Aside.*)

Aye, so much a man of honor that I must save my mistress, I thank you, come what will on't.

SPARKISH.

So if I had had her, she'd have made me believe, 270 the moon had been made of a Christmas pie.

LUCY. (*Aside.*)

Now could I speak, if I durst, and solve the riddle, who am the author of it.

ALITHEA.

Oh unfortunate woman! [*To Harcourt.*] A combination against my honor, which most 275 concerns me now, because you share in my disgrace, sir, and it is your censure, which I must now suffer, that troubles me, not theirs.

HARCOURT.

Madam, then have no trouble; you shall now see 'tis possible for me to love, too, without being 280 jealous. I will not only believe your innocence myself, but make all the world believe it. (*Apart to Horner.*) Horner, I must now be concerned for this lady's honor.

HORNER.

And I must be concerned for a lady's honor, too. 285

HARCOURT.

This lady has her honor, and I will protect it.

HORNER.

My lady has not her honor, but has given it me to keep, and I will preserve it.

HARCOURT.

I understand you not.

HORNER.

I would not have you. 290

MARGERY. (*Peeping in behind.*)

What's the matter with 'em all?

PINCHWIFE.

Come, come, Mr. Horner, no more disputing. Here's the parson; I brought him not in vain.

HARCOURT.

No sir, I'll employ him, if this lady please.

PINCHWIFE.

How, what d'ye mean? 295

SPARKISH.

Aye, what does he mean?

HORNER.

Why, I have resigned your sister to him; he has my consent.

PINCHWIFE.

But he has not mine, sir. A woman's injured honor, no more than a man's, can be repaired or satisfied 300 by any but him that first wronged it, and you shall marry her presently,* or— (*Lays his hand on his sword.*)

Enter Margery.

MARGERY.

Oh Lord, they'll kill poor Mr. Horner! Besides, he shan't marry her whilst I stand by and look on; I'll 305 not lose my second husband so.

PINCHWIFE.

What do I see?

ALITHEA.

My sister in my clothes!

SPARKISH.

Hah!

MARGERY. (*To Pinchwife.*)

Nay, pray now don't quarrel* about finding work 310
for the parson; he shall marry me to Mr. Horner,
for now I believe you have enough of me.

HORNER.

Damned, damned, loving changeling.

MARGERY.

Pray sister, pardon me for telling so many lies of you.

HARCOURT.

I suppose the riddle is plain now. 315

LUCY.

No, that must be my work, good sir, hear me.
Kneels to Pinchwife, who stands doggedly, with his
hat over his eyes.

PINCHWIFE.

I will never hear woman again, but make 'em all
silent thus— (*Offers* to draw upon his wife.*) 320

HORNER.

No, that must not be.

PINCHWIFE.

You then shall go first; 'tis all one to me. (*Offers**
to draw on Horner, stopped by Harcourt.)

HARCOURT.

Hold—

Enter Sir Jaspar Fidget, Lady Fidget, Old Lady
Squeamish, Dainty, Mrs. Squeamish.

SIR JASPAR.

What's the matter, what's the matter, pray what's 325
the matter, sir? I beseech you communicate, sir.

PINCHWIFE.

Why, my wife has communicated, sir, as your wife
may have done, too, sir, if she knows him, sir.

SIR JASPAR.

Pshaw, with him, ha, ha, he!

PINCHWIFE.

D'ye mock me, sir? A cuckold is a kind of wild 330
beast, have a care, sir.

SIR JASPAR.

No, sure you mock me, sir. He cuckold you! It
can't be, ha, ha, he. Why, I'll tell you, sir. (*Offers*
to whisper.)

PINCHWIFE.

I tell you again, he has whored my wife and yours, 335
too, if he knows her, and all the women he comes
near. 'Tis not his dissembling, his hypocrisy can
wheedle me.

SIR JASPAR.

How! Does he dissemble? Is he a hypocrite? Nay,
then—how—wife—sister, is he a hypocrite? 340

OLD LADY SQUEAMISH.

A hypocrite! A dissembler! Speak, young harlotry,
speak. How!

SIR JASPAR.

Nay, then—oh my head too—oh thou libidinous
lady!

OLD LADY SQUEAMISH.

Oh thou harloting harlotry, hast thou done't then? 345

SIR JASPAR.

Speak, good Horner. Art thou a dissembler, a
rogue? Hast thou—

HORNER.

Soh—

LUCY. (*Apart to Horner.*)

I'll fetch you off and her too, if she will but hold
her tongue. 350

HORNER. (*Apart to Lucy.*)

Canst thou? I'll give thee—

LUCY. (*To Mr. Pinchwife.*)

Pray have but patience to hear me, sir, who am the
unfortunate cause of all this confusion. Your wife
is innocent, I only culpable, for I put her upon
telling you all these lies concerning my mistress in 355
order to the breaking off the match between Mr.
Sparkish and her to make way for Mr. Harcourt.

SPARKISH.

Did you so, eternal rotten tooth? Then it seems
my mistress was not false to me; I was only
deceived by you.—Brother that should have been, 360
now, man of conduct, who is a frank person now?
To bring your wife to her lover—hah!

LUCY.

I assure you, sir, she came not to Mr. Horner out
of love, for she loves him no more—

MARGERY.

Hold! I told lies for you, but you shall tell none 365
for me, for I do love Mr. Horner with all my soul,
and nobody shall say me nay. Pray don't you go

to make poor Mr. Horner believe to the contrary.
'Tis spitefully done of you, I'm sure.

HORNER. (*Aside to Margery.*)

Peace, dear idiot. 370

MARGERY.

Nay, I will not peace.

PINCHWIFE.

Not till I make you.

Enter Dorilant, Quack.

DORILANT.

Horner, your servant. I am the doctor's guest; he
must excuse our intrusion.

QUACK.

But what's the matter, gentlemen? For Heaven's 375
sake, what's the matter?

HORNER.

Oh 'tis well you are come. 'Tis a censorious world
we live in. You may have brought me a reprieve,
or else I had died for a crime I never committed,
and these innocent ladies had suffered with me; 380
therefore, pray satisfy these worthy, honorable,
jealous gentlemen that—(*Whispers.*)

QUACK.

Oh I understand you. Is that all?—Sir Jasper, by
heavens and upon the word of a physician, sir,—
(*Whispers to Sir Jaspar.*) 385

SIR JASPAR.

Nay, I do believe you truly.—Pardon me, my
virtuous lady and dear of honor.

OLD LADY SQUEAMISH.

What, then all's right again.

SIR JASPAR.

Aye, aye, and now let us satisfy him, too.

They whisper with Pinchwife.

PINCHWIFE.

An eunuch! Pray no fooling with me. 390

QUACK.

I'll bring half the chirurgeons in Town to swear it.

PINCHWIFE.

They! They'll swear a man that bled to death
through his wounds died of an apoplexy.

QUACK.

Pray hear me, sir. Why, all the Town has heard the
report of him. 395

PINCHWIFE.

But does all the Town believe it?

QUACK.

Pray inquire a little and first of all these.

PINCHWIFE.

I'm sure when I left the Town he was the lewdest
fellow in't.

QUACK.

I tell you, sir, he has been in France since. Pray 400
ask but these ladies and gentlemen, your friend Mr.
Dorilant.—Gentlemen and ladies, han't you all
heard the late sad report of poor Mr. Horner?

ALL LADIES.

Aye, aye, aye.

DORILANT.

Why, thou jealous fool, dost thou doubt it? He's 405
an arrant French capon.

MARGERY.

'Tis false, sir, you shall not disparage poor Mr.
Horner, for to my certain knowledge—

LUCY.

Oh hold!

MRS. SQUEAMISH. (*Aside to Lucy.*)

Stop her mouth! 410

LADY FIDGET. (*To Pinchwife.*)

Upon my honor, sir, 'tis as true—

DAINTY.

D'ye think we would have been seen in his
company—

MRS. SQUEAMISH.

Trust our unspotted reputations with him?

LADY FIDGET. (*Aside to Horner.*)

This you get and we, too, by trusting your secret 415
to a fool.

HORNER.

Peace, madam. (*Aside to Quack.*) Well Doctor, is
not this a good design that carries a man on
unsuspected and brings him off safe?

PINCHWIFE. (*Aside.*)

Well, if this were true, but my wife— 420

Dorilant whispers with Margery.

ALITHEA.

Come brother, your wife is yet innocent, you see,
but have a care of too strong an imagination, lest
like an over-concerned, timorous gamester, by

fancying an unlucky cast, it should come. Women
and Fortune are truest still* to those that trust 'em. 425
LUCY.
And any wild thing grows but the more fierce and
hungry for being kept up and more dangerous to
the keeper.
ALITHEA.
There's doctrine for all husbands, Mr. Harcourt.
HARCOURT.
And I edify, madam, so much that I am impatient 430
till I am one.
DORILANT.
And I edify so much by example I will never be one.
SPARKISH.
And because I will not disparage my parts,* I'll
ne'er be one.
HORNER.
And I, alas, can't be one. 435
PINCHWIFE.
But I must be one against my will, to a country
wife, with a country murrain to me.
MARGERY. (Aside.)
And I must be a country wife still, too, I find, for
I can't, like a City* one, be rid of my musty
husband and do what I list. 440
HORNER.
Now sir, I must pronounce your wife innocent,
though I blush whilst I do it, and I am the only
man by her now exposed to shame, which I will
straight drown in wine, as you shall your suspicion,
and the ladies' troubles we'll divert with a ballet.— 445
Doctor, where are your maskers?

LUCY.
Indeed, she's innocent, sir. I am her witness, and
her end of coming out was but to see her sister's
wedding, and what she has said to your face of her
love to Mr. Horner was but the usual innocent 450
revenge on a husband's jealousy, was it not?
Madam, speak.
MARGERY. (Aside to Lucy and Horner.)
Since you'll have me tell more lies.—Yes indeed,
bud.
PINCHWIFE.
For my own sake, fain I would all believe: 455
Cuckolds, like lovers, should themselves deceive.
But— (Sighs.)
His honor is least safe (too late I find)
Who trusts it with a foolish wife or friend.

A dance of cuckolds.

HORNER.
Vain fops but court and dress and keep a pother 460
To pass for women's men with one another,
But he who aims by women to be prized,
First by the men, you see, must be despised.

[Exeunt.]

FINIS.

Textual Notes

[a] Copytext is the first edition, a 1675 quarto (Q1). Also
consulted: modern editions of 1924 (Summers), 1967
(Weales), 1975 (Cook and Swannell), 1979 (Friedman),
1981 (Holland), 1991 (Ogden), and 1996 (Dixon).

Friendship in Fashion[a]

by Thomas Otway (1652-1685)

edited by Melissa Mowry

Friendship in Fashion was Thomas Otway's first effort at comedy. It played at the Duke's Theater in Dorset Garden in April 1678. The Duke's lead actor, Thomas Betterton, played the role of Goodvile opposite the brilliant and rising young talent, Elizabeth Barry, playing the role of Mrs. Goodvile. A Mrs. Guin is listed as playing Lady Squeamish. This is not Nell Gwynn but Anne Marshall Quin, grande dame of the Restoration actresses. Three of the Restoration's greatest comic actors were featured: Cave Underhill as Sir Noble Clumsy, Thomas Jevon as Caper, and, most notably, Anthony Leigh as Malagene.

Montague Summers, one of Otway's early twentieth-century editors, notes that Charles II attended the play twice, once on April 5 and again on April 25, but the play was never popular, and when an attempt was made to revive it in 1750, cultural taste had changed so drastically that the play was booed off the stage and never performed again.

Friendship in Fashion portrays not only the ongoing struggle for political power between the English aristocracy, represented here by the Town wits, and the citizenry of London, or "Cits," represented by Sir Noble, son of an alderman, and by other parvenus. It also portrays conflict within the ruling class itself. Indeed, Otway's "Epistle Dedicatory" indicates that Otway's handling of the play's class distinctions almost cost him the Earl of Dorset's patronage, who suspected that the aristocracy itself might be the object of Otway's jibes. But Otway could take refuge in the supposed distinction between upper aristocracy and the gentry: although wealthy enough to own both a country and a city residence, the Goodviles are untitled, excluding them from the nobility. Only Sir Noble and Lady Squeamish have titles. We know almost nothing about Lady Squeamish's title, which may have come to her by marriage or by birth. But we know at least that Sir Noble, as the son of an Alderman, probably purchased his, making him still a "Cit." The only other character in the play who claims a connection with the aristocratic world of the court is Malagene, whom Otway portrays as such a buffoon that his claims to frequent aristocratic circles are highly suspicious. Nevertheless, a good deal of Otway's satire is directed at the gentry and, by implication, at the entire ruling class.

Modern readers should also be aware that, in addition to the class satire advanced by *Friendship in Fashion*, Otway's play calls upon the tradition of gender satires like *Now or Never: Or a New Parliament of Women* (1656) that were royalist stock in trade from the 1640s to the 1680s. Among the most subversive features of *Friendship in Fashion* is the relationship between Mrs. Goodvile and Victoria. The coalition between the two women to punish Goodvile would certainly have sounded a cautionary note with citizen and aristocratic audience members alike. For, however justified Goodvile's punishment is, the women usurp the moral authority in the play and thus challenge the patriarchal order of the culture as a whole.

[I]

DRAMATIS PERSONAE

[MEN]

    Goodvile.
    Truman.
    Valentine.
    Sir Noble Clumsy.
    Malagene.[1]
    Caper.
    Saunter.
    [Goodvile's boy.]
    [Caper's boy.]
    [Mrs. Goodvile's page.]
    [Truman's servant.]
    [Servants, footmen.]

WOMEN

    Mrs. Goodvile.
    Victoria.
    Camilla.
    Lady Squemish.
    Lettice[, Mrs. Goodvile's maid].
    Bridget[, Lady Squeamish's maid].

Friendship in Fashion.

Archilochum Rabies armavit Iambo.[2]

Act I. The Mall.*

Truman reading a billet, and [his] servant.

TRUMAN.

In a visor say you?

[TRUMAN'S] SERVANT.

Yes, sir, and as soon as she had delivered it, without anything more, gave the word to the coachman, drew up the tin lattice, and away she hurried. [*Exit.*] 5

TRUMAN.

The meaning of a billet of this nature without a name is a riddle to me. (*Reads.*) "You know me and see me often. I wish I may never see you more, except you knew better where to place your love,

---

1 Malagene] etymologically, ill-born

2 *Archilochum … Iambo*] Horace, *Ars poetica*: Fierceness armed Archilochus with iambics (literally, an iamb: the metric form of his satires).

or I were abler to govern mine. As you are a 10 gentleman, burn this so soon as it comes to your hands. Adieu." Well, this can be no other than some staunch virtue of thirty-five that is just now fallen under the temptation or, what is as bad, one of those cautious dealers that never venture but in 15 masquerade, where they are sure to be wondrous kind,* though they discover* no more to the lover than he has just occasion to make use of.

Enter Goodvile and Valentine.

VALENTINE.

Truman, good morrow. Just out of your lodging? 20 But that I know thee better, I should swear thou hadst resolved to spend this day in humiliation and repentance for the sins of the last.

GOODVILE.

I beg your pardon! Some lady has taken up your time. Thou canst no more rise in a morning without 25 a wench than thou canst go to bed at night without a bottle. Truman, wilt thou never leave whoring?

TRUMAN.

Peace, matrimony, peace. Speak more reverently of your dearly beloved whoring.—Valentine, he is the mere* spirit of hypocrisy. He'd hardly been married 30 ten days, but he left his wife to go home from the play alone in her coach whilst he debauched me with two visors* in a hackney to supper.

VALENTINE.

Truly Goodvile, that was very civil and may come to something. But gentlemen, it begins to grow 35 late. Where shall we dine?

TRUMAN.

Where you will, I am indifferent.

GOODVILE.

And I.

VALENTINE.

I had appointed to meet at Chateline's,* but—

TRUMAN.

With whom? 40

VALENTINE.

Why, your cousin Malagene, Goodvile.

GOODVILE.

Valentine, thou art too much with that fellow. 'Tis true, indeed, he is some relation to me, but 'tis such a lying varlet, there is no enduring of him.

VALENTINE.

But rogues and fools are so very plenty 'tis hard always to escape 'em. 45

TRUMAN.

Besides, he dares be no more a friend than a foe. He never spoke well of any man behind his back nor ill before his face. He is a general disperser of nauseous scandal, though it be of his own mother 50 or sister. Prithee, let's avoid him if we can today.

GOODVILE.

'Twill be almost impossible, for he is as impudent as he is troublesome; as there is no company so ill but he'll keep, so there is none so good but he'll pretend to. If he has ever seen you once, he'll be 55 sure of you. And if he knows where you are, he's no more to be kept out of your room than you can keep him out of your debt.

VALENTINE.

He came where I was last night, roaring drunk. Swore, damn him, he had been with my lord such 60 a one and had swallowed three quarts of champagne for his share, said he had much ado to get away, but came then particularly to drink a bottle with me. I was forced to promise him I would meet him today to get rid of him. 65

GOODVILE.

Faith gentlemen, let us all go dine at my house. I have snubbed him of late, and he'll hardly venture that way so soon again. At night I'll promise you good company. My wife (for I allow her for my own sake what freedom she pleases) has sent for 70 the fiddles to come.

TRUMAN.

Goodvile, if there be any such thing as ease in matrimony, thou hast it. But methinks there's, as it were, a mark upon married men that makes them as distinguishable from one of us as your 75 Jews are from the rest of mankind.

GOODVILE.

Oh, there are pleasures you dream not of. He is only confined by it that will be so. A man may make his condition as easy as he pleases. Mine is such a fond, wanton ape, I never come home, but 80 she entertains* me with fresh kindness* and, Jack, when I have been hunting for game with you and missed of an opportunity, stops a gap well enough.

TRUMAN.

There's no condition so wretched but has its reserve. Your spaniel turned out of doors goes 85 contentedly to his kennel. Your beggar, when he can get no better lodging, knows his old warm bush, and your married whore-master that misses of his wench, goes honestly home, and there's madam wife. But Goodvile, who are to be the 90 company at night?

GOODVILE.

In the first place, my cousin Victoria, your idol, Jack Truman; then Mr. Valentine, there will be the charming Camilla, and another that never fails upon such an occasion, the inimitable Lady Squeamish. 95

TRUMAN.

That, indeed, is a worthy person, a great critic, forsooth, one that censures plays and takes it very ill she has none dedicated to her yet, a constant frequenter of all masquerades and public meetings, a perfect coquette, very affected, and something old. 100

VALENTINE.

Discourses readily of all the love intrigues of the Court and Town,* a strange admirer of accomplishments and good breeding as she calls it, a restless dancer, one that by her own good will would never be out of motion. 105

TRUMAN.

How Valentine! You were once a great admirer there. Have a care how you speak too harshly of your mistress, though the business be over. You stand well with the ladies yet and are held a man of principles. 110

GOODVILE.

That, indeed, is a fine creature. Your old harassed stager has always some such resty* whore-master or another whom she makes the best of her despair withal and, after being forsaken by half the Town besides, comforts herself in her man of principles. 115 But now I think on't, we delay too long. I'll go before and prepare. Gentlemen, you'll be sure to follow?

TRUMAN.

Sir, we'll not fail to wait on you.

Exit Goodvile.

Boy! is the coach ready?—Valentine! I have had the oddest adventure this morning—hah—Malagene! 120

Enter Malagene.

How came he hither?

MALAGENE.

Jack Truman, Monsieur Valentine, bon jour—was not that Goodvile I met coming in—hah?

VALENTINE.

Yes, he parted hence but now.

MALAGENE.

Faith, I'll tell you what gentlemen, Goodvile's a 125 very honest fellow as can be, but he and I are fallen out of late, though, faith, 'twas none of my seeking.

TRUMAN.

No, I'll be sworn for thee, thou lov'st thyself better.

VALENTINE.

Pray, what was the matter, Malagene?

MALAGENE.

Why, I was advising him to look after things better 130 at home. The fellow has married a young wife, and there he lets her make balls and give entertainments. I was very free with him and told him of it to the purpose. For, faith, I should be sorry to see any ill come on't, very sorry. 135

TRUMAN.

But hark ye, Malagene, Goodvile's a sort of surly companion and apt to have so good an opinion of himself that he is able to manage affairs without your advice. He might have been very severe with you upon this occasion. 140

MALAGENE.

Severe with me! I thank you for that with all my heart. That had been the way to have made a fine piece of work on't, indeed! Hark ye (under the rose*), he's sweetly fitted with my cousin, though.

VALENTINE.

Pray sir, speak with more respect. We are his 145 friends and not prepared to relish any of your satire at present.

MALAGENE.

Oh Lord, sir! I beg your pardon, you are a new acquaintance there, I remember, and may design an interest. Faith Ned, if thou dost, I'll ne'er be 150 thy hindrance, for all she's my kinswoman.

TRUMAN.

The rascal, if he had an opportunity, would pimp for his sister, though but for the bare pleasure of telling it himself.

MALAGENE.

Now when he comes home, will she be hanging about his neck, with, "Oh Lord, Dear! where have 155 you been this morning? I can't abide you should go abroad so soon, that I can't. You are never well,[3] but when you are with that wicked, lewd Truman and his debauched companion young Valentine. But that I know you are a good Dear, I should be 160 apt to be jealous of you, that I should." Ha, ha.

TRUMAN.

Sir, you are very bold with our characters, methinks.

MALAGENE.

I, pshaw! your servant. Sure, we that know one another may be free. You may say as much of me, if you please. But no matter for that, did you hear 165 nothing of my business last night, hah?

TRUMAN.

Not a word I assure you, sir. Pray how was it?— Prithee, let him alone a little, Valentine.

MALAGENE.

Why, coming out of Chatoline's last night (where it had cost me a guinea-club, with a right honorable[4] 170 or two of this kingdom which shall be nameless), just as I was getting into the coach, who should come by but a blustering fellow with a woman in his hand and swore, damn him, the coach was for him. We had some words, and he drew. With that, I put 175 by his pass, closed with him, and threw up his heels, took away Toledo,* gave him two or three good cuts over the face, seized upon damsel, carried her away with me to my chamber, managed her all night, and just now sent her off. Faith, amongst friends, she was 180 a person of quality,* I'll tell you that.

TRUMAN.

What! a person of quality at that time o'th'night and on foot too?

MALAGENE.

Aye, and one that you both know very well. But take no notice on't. 185

VALENTINE.

Oh, sir, you may be sure we shall be very cautious of spreading any secrets of yours of this nature.— Lying rakehell, the highest he ever arrived at was

---

3 well] in a good mood
4 guinea-club … honorable] coins of relatively high value

a bawd, and she too banished him at last because 190
he boasted of her favors.

MALAGENE.

Nay, not that I care very much neither, you may tell
it if you will, for I think it was no more than anyone
would have done upon the same occasion, hah?

TRUMAN.

Doubtless, sir, you were much in the right. But Valentine, we shall stay too long. 'Tis time we were going. 195

MALAGENE.

What, to dinner? I'll make a third man. Where
shall it be?

TRUMAN.

Sir, I am sorry, we must beg your excuse this time,
for we are both engaged.

MALAGENE.

Whoo! prithee, that's all one, I am sure I know the 200
company. I'll go along at a venture.

VALENTINE.

No, but Malagene! to make short of the business,
we are going into company that are not very good
friends of yours and will be very uneasy if you be
there. 205

MALAGENE.

What's that to the purpose? I care as little for them
as they do for me. Though on my word, sparks!
of honest fellows, you keep the oddest company
sometimes that ever I knew!

TRUMAN.

But, sir, we are resolved to reform it, and in order 210
thereunto desire you would leave us to ourselves
today.

MALAGENE.

No—but I'll tell you, go along with me, I have
discovered a treasure of pale wine—I'll assure you
'tis the same the King drinks of—what say you, 215
Jack? I am but for one bottle or two, for faith, I
have resolved to live sober for a week.

TRUMAN.

Prithee, tormentor, leave us! Do not I know the
wine thou drink'st is as base as the company thou
keep'st? To be plain with you, we will not go with 220
you, nor must you go with us.

MALAGENE.

Why, if one should ask the question now, whither
are you going, hah?

VALENTINE.

How comes it, Malagene, you are not with your
two friends, Caper and Saunter? You may be sure 225
of them; they'll eat and drink and go all over the
world with you.

MALAGENE.

How canst thou think that I would keep such
loathsome company? A brace of silly, talking,
dancing, singing rascals. 'Tis true, I contracted an 230
acquaintance with 'em, I know not how, and, now
and then when I am out of humor, love to laugh at
and abuse 'em for an hour or two. But come what
will on't, I am resolved to go along with you today.

TRUMAN.

Upon my word, sir, you cannot. Why should you 235
make so many difficulties with your friends?

MALAGENE.

Whoo! prithee leave fooling. You would shake me
off now, would you? But I know better things. The
sham won't pass upon me, sir, it won't, look you.

TRUMAN.

Death, we must use him ill, or there is no getting 240
rid of him.—Not pass, sir?

MALAGENE.

No, sir!

TRUMAN.

Pray, sir, leave us.

MALAGENE.

I shan't do it, sir.

TRUMAN.

But you must, sir. 245

MALAGENE.

Maybe not, sir.

TRUMAN.

I am going this way. (*Walking off.*)

MALAGENE.

So am I.

TRUMAN.

But, sir, I must stay here a little longer.

MALAGENE.

With all my heart! 'tis the same thing, I am not in 250
haste.

VALENTINE.

Have a care, Malagene, how you provoke Truman.
You'll run the hazard of a scurvy beating, my
friend, if you do.

MALAGENE.

Beating! I am sorry, sir, you know no better. Pox, 255
I am used to serve him so, man. Let me alone, you
shall see how I'll tease him.—Hark you, Jack.

TRUMAN.

Sir, you are an impudent, troublesome coxcomb.

MALAGENE.

No matter for that, I shan't leave you.

TRUMAN.

Sir, I shall pull you by the nose then. 260

MALAGENE.

'Tis all one to me, do your worst.

TRUMAN.

Take that then, sir. (*Tweaks him by the nose.*) Now,
d'ye hear—go about your business.

MALAGENE.

Nay, faith, Jack, now you drive the jest too far.
What a pox, I know you are not in earnest. Prithee 265
let's go.

TRUMAN.

Death, sir, you lie. Not in earnest! Let this
convince you. (*Kicks him.*) How like you the jest
now, sir?

MALAGENE.

Hark you, Truman, we shan't dine together then, 270
shall we?

VALENTINE.

Faith, to tell you the truth of the matter, Truman
had a quarrel last night, and we are just now going
to make an end on't. 'Tis that makes him so surly.
Nevertheless, now I think on't better, if you'll go, you 275
shall: perhaps we may have occasion for a third man.

MALAGENE.

No, no, if that be the business, I'll say no more.
Puh—I hate to press into any man's company
against his inclination. Truman! Upon my
reputation, you are very uncivil now, that you are. 280
But hark you, I ran to the groom-porter's* last
night and lost my money—prithee, lend me two
guineas till next time I see thee, child.*

TRUMAN.

With all my heart, sir, I was sure 'twould come to
this at last. 'Tis here, you may command what you 285
please from your servant. Malagene, good morrow.

Enter Caper and Saunter.

MALAGENE.

Dear Jack Truman, your humble—

Exit Truman.

VALENTINE.

Won't you go along with us then, Malagene?

MALAGENE.

No, here are two silly fellows coming. I'll go and
divert myself a little with them at present. 290

VALENTINE.

Why, those are the very people you railed at so but
now. You will not leave us for them? at a time
when you may be so serviceable?

MALAGENE.

Hang't, you'll have no occasion for me, man. Say 295
no more on't, but take my advice. Be sure you
stand fast, don't give ground, d'ye hear, push
briskly, and I'll warrant you do your business.

VALENTINE.

Sir, I thank you for your counsel and am sorry we
can't have your company. But you are engaged? 300

MALAGENE.

Are you sure, though, it will come to fighting? I
have no mind to leave your company, methinks.

VALENTINE.

Nay, nothing so certain as that we shall fight. I
wish you would go, for I fancy there will be three
in the field. 305

MALAGENE.

A pox on't, now I remember. I promised to meet
these people here and can't avoid 'em now. I'd go
with you else with all my heart, faith and troth.
But if you'd have me send a guard, I'll do it.

VALENTINE.

No, sir, there's no danger. [*Aside.*] Nothing but the 310
rogue's cowardice could have rid us of him. (*Exit.*)

MALAGENE.

How now, bullies, whither so fast this morning? I
parted just now with Jack Truman and Ned Valentine. They would fain have had me to dinner with
'em, but I was not in humor of drinking, and to speak 315
the truth on't, you are better company ten to one.
They engross still all the discourse to them-selves,
and a man can never be free with them neither.

CAPER.

Oh Lord, Malagene! We met the delicatest creature

but now as we came round. I am a rascal if I don't think her one of the finest women in the world. I shan't get her out of my mind this month.

SAUNTER.

'Twas Victoria, my Lady Fairfield's daughter that came to Town last summer when Goodvile was married. (*Sings.*) He in love with her, poor soul! I shall beg his pardon there as I take it.

MALAGENE.

That's Truman's blowing.⁵ She's always lingering after him here and at the playhouse. She heats herself here every morning against the general course at night, where she comes as constantly as my Lady Squeamish herself.

SAUNTER.

I vow, that's a fine person too. Don't you think she has an abundance of wit, Malagene? She and I did so rally Caper t'other day.

CAPER.

Aye, it may be so.

SAUNTER.

But did you never hear her sing? She made me sit with her till two o'clock t'other morning to teach her an Italian song. I have, and I vow she sings it wonderfully.

MALAGENE.

Damn her, she's the most affected, amorous jilt and loves young fellows more than an old kite does young chicken. There is not a coxcomb of eighteen in Town can escape her. We shall have her draw one of you into matrimony within this fortnight.

CAPER.

Malagene, thou art the most satirical thief breathing. I'd give anything thou didst but love dancing, that I might have thee on my side sometimes.

SAUNTER.

Well Malagene, I hope to see thee so in love one day, as to leave off drinking as I have done and set up for a shape and a face. Or what is all one, write amorous sonnets and fight duels with all that do but look like rivals. I would not be in love for all the world, I vow and swear. (*Walks up and down with an affected motion.*)

CAPER.

Nor I. (*Sings.*)
Ah Phyllis, if you would not love
The shepherd, etc.
But d'ye hear, Malagene, they say Goodvile gives a ball tonight. Is it true?

MALAGENE.

Yes, I intend to be there, if I do not go to Court.

CAPER.

I am glad of it with all my heart.—Saunter, there's my Lady. To be sure, she'll not fail.

SAUNTER.

But will you go, Malagene? Goodvile and you are at a distance.

MALAGENE.

Whoo! pox that's nothing. I'll go for all that. But faith, I should meet my Lord _____* at Court tonight. Besides, I han't been in the Drawing Room* these three days; the company will wonder what's become of me.

Enter Lady Squeamish.

She here! Nay then—

CAPER.

Madam, your ladyship's most humble servant. (*Congees⁶ affectedly.*)

LADY SQUEAMISH.

Mr. Caper! Your most devoted.—Oh dear Mr. Saunter! a thousand thanks to you for my song.

SAUNTER.

Your ladyship does your servant too much honor. (*Sings, As Cloe full of, etc.*)

LADY SQUEAMISH.

Mr. Caper, you are a stranger, indeed. I have not seen you this two days. Lord, where d'ye live?

CAPER.

I should have waited on your ladyship but was so tired at the masquerade at my Lord Flutter's t'other night. (*Dances and capers.*)

SAUNTER.

Madam, madam, Mr. Goodvile gives a ball tonight. Will your ladyship be there?

LADY SQUEAMISH.

Yes, I heard of it this morning. Victoria sent me word.

---

⁵ blowing] mistress

⁶ Congees] bows

CAPER.

Oh madam, d'ye hear the news? Goodvile makes 385
a ball tonight. I hope I shall have honor of your
ladyship's company.

LADY SQUEAMISH.

Oh, by all means. Mr. Caper, pray don't you fail
us.—Oh Lord, Mr. Malagene, I beg your pardon.
Upon my honor I did not see you, I was so 390
engaged in the civilities of these gentlemen.

MALAGENE.

Your wit and beauty, Madam, must command the
honor and admiration of all the world. But when
did your ladyship see Mr. Valentine?

LADY SQUEAMISH.

Oh, name him not, Mr. Malagene. He's the 395
unworthiest, basest fellow—besides he has no
principles nor breeding. I wonder you gentlemen
will keep him company. I'll swear he's enough to
bring an odium on the whole sex.

MALAGENE.

The truth on't is, madam, I do drink with him now 400
and then, because the fellow has some wit, but it is
when better company is out of the way, and faith,
he's always very civil to me as can be. I can rule him.

LADY SQUEAMISH.

Oh Lord, 'tis impossible. Wit! Why, he was abroad
but two years and all that time too in an academy. 405
He knows nothing of the intrigues of the French
Court and has the worst mien in the world. He
has a sort of an ill-natured way of talking, indeed,
and they say makes bold with me sometimes. But
I'll assure you, I scorn him. 410

MALAGENE.

Truly, he has made very bold with you, or he is
foully belied. Ha, ha, ha.

LADY SQUEAMISH.

They say he's grown a great admirer of Madam
Camilla of late, who passes for a wit, forsooth. 'Tis
true, she's well enough, but I suppose is not the 415
first that has been troubled with his impertinent
addresses.

MALAGENE.

Indeed, he would not let me alone till I brought
him acquainted there. He owes that happiness to
me. But methinks your ladyship speaks with 420
something of heat.—By Heaven, she's jealous!

LADY SQUEAMISH.

No, I assure you, sir, I am not concerned at it in
the least. But did you ever hear 'em discourse
anything of me?

MALAGENE.

Never any ill, madam, only a little idle raillery now 425
and then. But Truman and he are wont to be
something lavish when they have been drunk in
my company.—'Twill work.

LADY SQUEAMISH.

Nay, I know he has spoken dishonorably of me
behind my back, because he failed in his filthy 430
designs. Madam Camilla may deserve better of
him, I doubt not. (*Aside.*) But if I am not revenged
on his falsehood— Mr. Caper.

CAPER, SAUNTER.

Madam.

LADY SQUEAMISH.

Where do you go today? 435

CAPER.

Will your ladyship be at the new play?

LADY SQUEAMISH.

No, I saw it the first day and don't like it.

MALAGENE.

Madam, it has no ill character about the Town.

LADY SQUEAMISH.

Oh Lord, sir, the Town is no judge. 'Tis a tragedy,
and I'll assure you there's nothing in it that's 440
moving. I love a tragedy that moves mightily.

SAUNTER.

Does your ladyship know who writ it?

LADY SQUEAMISH.

Yes, the poet came and read it to me at my
lodgings. He is but a young man, and I suppose
he has not been a writer long. Besides, he has had 445
little or no conversation with the Court, which has
been the reason he has committed a great many
indecorums in the conduct of it.

SAUNTER.

I did not like it neither for my part. There was
never a song in it, hah! 450

CAPER.

No, nor so much as a dance.

MALAGENE.

Oh, it's impossible it should take if there were
neither song nor dance in it.

LADY SQUEAMISH.

And then their comedies nowadays are the filthiest things, full of bawdy and nauseous doings which they mistake for raillery and intrigue. Besides, they have no wit in 'em neither, for all their gentlemen and men of wit, as they style 'em, are either silly, conceited, impudent coxcombs or else rude, ill-mannerly, drunken fellows—faugh—I am ashamed anyone should pretend to write a comedy that does not know the nicer rules of the Court and all the intrigues and gallantries that pass, I vow. 455 460

MALAGENE.

Who would improve in those things, must consult with your ladyship. 465

LADY SQUEAMISH.

I swear, Mr. Malagene, you are an obliging person. I wonder the world should be so malicious to give you so undeserving a character* as they do. I always found you extremely generous and a person of worth.

MALAGENE.

In troth, madam, your ladyship and myself are the subjects of abundance of envy. For I love to be malicious now and then and, faith, am the very scourge of the Court. They all stand in awe of me, for I must speak what I know, though sometimes I am used a little scurvily for it. But faith, I can't help it, 'tis my way. 470 475

LADY SQUEAMISH.

Ha, ha, ha, really I love scandal extremely too sometimes, so it be decently managed. But, as I was saying, there is not a person in the world understands the intrigues of the Court better than myself. I am the general confidante of the Drawing Room and know the loves of all the people of quality* in Town. 480

CAPER.

Dear Madam, how stands the affair between my Lord Supple and Madam Lofty?

LADY SQUEAMISH.

Worse than ever. 'Tis very provoking to see how she uses the poor creature. But the truth is, she can never be at rest for him. He's more troublesome than an old husband, continually whispering his softnesses and making his vows, till at last she is forced to fly to me for shelter, and then we do so laugh—which the good-natured creature takes so patiently, I swear I pity him. 485 490

SAUNTER.

But my Lady Colt, they say, is kinder* to the sparkish Mr. Pruneit.

LADY SQUEAMISH.

Oh Lord, Mr. Saunter, that you should understand no better. To my knowledge, it is all false. I know all that intrigue from the beginning to the ending. It has been off this month. Besides, he keeps* a player again-.-Oh, Mr. Saunter! whatever you do, never concern yourself with those players. 495 500

SAUNTER.

Madam, I have left the folly long since. When first I came to Town, I must confess I had a gallantry there. But since I have been acquainted with your ladyship's wit and beauty, I have learned to lay out my heart to better advantage.—I think that was finely said! 505

LADY SQUEAMISH.

I'll swear, Mr. Saunter, you have the most court-like way of expressing yourself—

SAUNTER.

Oh Lord, Madam! (*Bows and cringes.*)

LADY SQUEAMISH.

Mr. Malagene, these are both my intimate acquaintance, and I'll swear I am proud of them. Here is Mr. Saunter sings the French manner better than ever I heard any English gentleman in my life. Besides, he pronounces his English in singing with a French kind of a tone or accent, that gives it a strange beauty.— Sweet sir, do me the favor of the last new song. 510 515

SAUNTER.

Let me die! your ladyship obliges me beyond expression.—Malagene, thou shalt hear me. (*Sings a song in a French tone.*)

MALAGENE.

What a devil was this. I understand not a word on it. 520

SAUNTER.

Hah, Malagene, hah?

LADY SQUEAMISH.

Did you ever hear anything so fine?

MALAGENE.

Never, madam, never. I swear, your ladyship is a great judge.

LADY SQUEAMISH.

But how plain and distinctly too every word was pronounced! 525

MALAGENE.

Oh, to admiration, to admiration. (*Makes mouths aside.*)

LADY SQUEAMISH.

Well, Mr. Saunter, you are a charming creature. Oh sad, Mr. Caper, I long till night comes. I'll dance 530 with nobody but you tonight, for I swear I believe I shall be out of humor.

MALAGENE. [*Aside.*]

That's more than she ever was in her life, so long as she had a fool or a fiddle in her company.

LADY SQUEAMISH.

Though, really, I love dancing immoderately. But 535 now you talk of intrigues, I am mistaken if you don't see something where we are going tonight.

MALAGENE.

What, Goodvile is to commence cuckold, is it not so?

LADY SQUEAMISH.

Oh, fie, Mr. Malagene, fie. I vow you'll make me hate you, if you talk so strangely. But let me die, I 540 can't but laugh, ha, ha, ha.—Well, gentlemen, you shall dine with me today.—What say you, Mr. Malagene, will you go?

MALAGENE.

Your ladyship may be sure of me, I hate to break good company. 545

LADY SQUEAMISH.

And pray, now let us be very severe and talk maliciously of all the Town.—Mr. Caper, your hand.— Oh, dear Mr. Saunter, how shall I divide myself. I'll swear, I am strangely at a loss.—Mr. Malagene, you must be Mr. Saunter's mistress I think at present. 550

MALAGENE.

With all my heart, madam.—Sweet Mr. Saunter, your hand. I swear you are a charming creature, and your courtship is as extraordinary as your voice. Let me die, and I vow I must have t'other song after dinner, for I am very humorsome and 555 very whimsical I think. Ha, ha, ha.

Exeunt omnes.

Act II. [Goodvile's Town* house above an] ordinary.

Enter Mrs. Goodvile and Lettice.

MRS. GOODVILE.

Did you deliver the billet?

LETTICE.

Yes, madam, faithfully.

MRS. GOODVILE.

But are you sure you did?

LETTICE.

Can your ladyship think I would be guilty of the least neglect in a concern of such moment? 5

MRS. GOODVILE.

And are you sure he dines here today?

LETTICE.

Madam, they are now at dinner below. Mr. Valentine's there too. Oh, I'll swear he's a fine man, the most courteous person!

MRS. GOODVILE.

What, because he hunts and kisses you when he's 10 drunk? No, Lettice. Truman, Truman, oh that Truman!

LETTICE.

I wonder your ladyship should be so taken with him. Were I to choose, I should think my master the more agreeable man. 15

MRS. GOODVILE.

And you may take him if you will. He is as much a husband as one would wish. I have not seen him this fortnight. He never comes home till four in the morning, and then he sneaks to his separate bed, where he lies till afternoon, then rises and out 20 again upon his parole.* Flesh and blood can't endure it.

LETTICE.

But he always visits your ladyship first.

MRS. GOODVILE.

That's his policy, as great debtors are always very respectful and acknowledging where they never 25 mean to pay. 'Tis true, he gives me what freedom I can desire, but God knows that's all.

LETTICE.

And where's the pleasure of going abroad and getting a stomach to return and starve at home?

MRS. GOODVILE.

I laugh, though, to think what an easy fool he 30 believes me. He thinks me the most contented, innocent, harmless turtle* breathing, the very pattern of patience.

LETTICE.

A jewel of a wife.

MRS. GOODVILE.

And as blind with love as his own good opinion 35
of himself has made him.

LETTICE.

And can you find in your heart to wrong so good
a natured, complete, well-meaning harmless
husband that has so good an opinion of you?

MRS. GOODVILE.

Hah, wrong him! what you say, Lettice! I wrong 40
my husband! Such another word forfeits my good
opinion of thee forever.

LETTICE.

What meant the billet to Mr. Truman, then, this
morning?

MRS. GOODVILE.

To make him my friend perhaps and discover, if I 45
can, who it is that wrongs me in my husband's
affection. For I am sure I have a rival. And I am
apt to believe Victoria deserves no better than
ordinary of me, if the truth were known.

LETTICE.

Why, she is his near kinswoman and lives here in 50
the house with you. Besides, he would never
dishonor his own family, surely.

MRS. GOODVILE.

You are a fool, Lettice: the nearness of blood is the
least thing considered. Besides, as I have heard, 'tis
almost the only way relations care to be kind* to 55
one another nowadays.

LETTICE.

Yet, madam, you never meet but you are as kind
and fond of him as if you had all the joys of love
about you. Lord! How can you dissemble with him
so? Besides, Mr. Truman, madam, you know is his 60
friend.

MRS. GOODVILE.

Oh, if I would ever consent to wrong my husband
(which Heaven forbid, Lettice!) it should be to
choose with his friend. For such a one has a double
obligation to secrecy, as well for his own honor as 65
mine. But I'll swear, Lettice, you are an idle girl
for talking so much of this, that you are. 'Tis
enough to put ill thoughts into one's head, which
I am the most averse to of all things in the world.

LETTICE.

But, madam, thoughts are free, and it is as hard not 70

to think a little idly sometimes, as it is to be always
in good humor. But it would make anyone laugh to
think Mr. Truman should be in love with Madam
Victoria, if all be real which your ladyship suspects.

MRS. GOODVILE.

Aye, and with a design of marriage too. But a 75
ranging gallant thinks he fathoms all and counts
it as much beneath his experience to doubt his
security in a wife as success in a mistress.

LETTICE.

Besides, after a little time, he is so very industrious
in cuckolding others that he never dreams how 80
swimmingly his own affairs are managed at home.

Enter Victoria.

MRS. GOODVILE.

But hush—she's here.

VICTORIA.

A happy day to you, madam.

MRS. GOODVILE.

Dear Cousin, your humble servant. Have you
heard who are below? 85

VICTORIA.

Yes, young Truman and his inseparable
companion, Valentine.

MRS. GOODVILE.

Well, what will you do, Cousin? Truman comes
resolved on conquest. For with the advantages he
has in your heart already, 'tis impossible you should 90
be able to hold out against him.

VICTORIA.

Yes, powerful champagne, as they call it, may do
much. A spark can no more refrain running into
love after a bottle than a drunken country vicar can
avoid disputing of religion when his patron's ale 95
grows stronger than his reason.

MRS. GOODVILE.

Come, come, dissemble your inclinations as
artfully as you please, I am sure they are not so
indifferent but they may be easily discerned.

VICTORIA.

Truly, madam, you may be mistaken in your guess. 100

MRS. GOODVILE.

How! I doubt it is some other man then has caused
this alteration in you.—Lord, Lettice, is she not
extremely altered?

VICTORIA.

Altered, madam, what do you mean?

MRS. GOODVILE.

Nay, Lettice, fetch a glass* and let her see herself.— 105
Lord, you are paler than you use to be.

LETTICE.

Aye, and then that blueness under the eyes.[7]

MRS. GOODVILE.

Besides, you are not so lively as I have known you.
Pardon me, Cousin.

LETTICE.

Well, if there be a fault, marriage will cure all. 110

VICTORIA.

I'll assure you, I have none that I know of stands
in need of so desperate a remedy. Marriage! Fault!
What can all this tend to?

Enter Page.

MRS. GOODVILE.

Well, what now?

PAGE.

Madam Camilla is coming to wait upon your 115
ladyship.

MRS. GOODVILE.

Hah, Camilla! Tell her I'll attend her. Won't you
go with me, Victoria?

VICTORIA.

I'll but step into my chamber and follow you
instantly. 120

Exeunt Mrs. Goodvile and Page.

Whither can all this drive? Surely, she has
discovered something of Goodvile's love and mine.
If she has, I am ruined.

Enter Goodvile.

GOODVILE.

Victoria! your cousin is not here, is she? What, in
clouds? I stole this minute from my friends on 125
purpose to see thee, and must not I have a look?
not a word?

VICTORIA.

Oh, I am ruined and lost forever. I fear your wife

has had some knowledge of our loves. And if it be
so, what will then become of me? 130

GOODVILE.

Prithee, no more. My wife! she has too good an
opinion of herself to have any ill one of me and
would as soon believe her glass* could flatter her
as I be false to her. My wife!—ha, ha.

VICTORIA.

Yes, I am sure it must be so. It can be no otherwise. 135
But you are satisfied and now have nothing more
to do but to leave me to be miserable.

GOODVILE.

Leave thee! By Heaven, I'd sooner renounce my
family and own myself the bastard of a rascal.
Come, quiet thy doubts. Truman is here, and take 140
my love for thy security, he shall be thine tonight.

VICTORIA.

I have great reason to expect it, indeed, that you
would hazard your interest in so good a friend for
the reparation of my honor, that so little concerns
you and which you have already made your best of. 145

GOODVILE.

No more of that. Love's my province. And thine is
too dear to me to be neglected. 'Tis true, I have
made him my friend, and I hope he will deserve it by
doing thee that justice which I am incapable of.

VICTORIA.

You can promise easily. 150

GOODVILE.

Aye, and as resolutely perform. When I have
heated him with wine, prepare to receive him.

Enter Mrs. Goodvile.

Hah, she here!

MRS. GOODVILE.

So, so, Mr. Goodvile, are you there indeed? I
thought I should catch you. 155

GOODVILE.

Faith, my dear, I have been speaking a good word
for Jack Truman. My cousin Victoria's too cruel.

MRS. GOODVILE.

Oh, fie, Victoria! Can you be so hard-hearted to
deny anything when Mr. Goodvile is an advocate?

VICTORIA.

I must confess it is with some difficulty. But should 160
I too easily comply upon Mr. Goodvile's

---

7 blueness under the eyes] according to Summers, "supposed to be a sign of pregnancy"

intercession, who knows but your ladyship might be jealous? For he that can prevail for another may presume there's hopes for himself.

MRS. GOODVILE.

Aye, but Cousin, I know you are my friend and would not, though but in regard of that, do me such injury. Besides, Mr. Goodvile knows I dare trust him.—Don't you, love? 165

GOODVILE.

Trust me! yes, for if you don't, 'tis all one— (*Aside.*) Credulous innocence!—Alas, my dear, were I as false as thou art good, thy generous confidence would shame me into honesty. 170

Enter Camilla running and squeaking. Truman and Valentine after her.

CAMILLA.

For Heaven's sake, madam, save me!—Mr. Goodvile, 'tis safer travelling through the deserts of Arabia than entering your house. Had I not ran hard for it, I had been devoured, that's certain. 175

VALENTINE.

Oh, madam, are you herded? It will be to little purpose. I am staunch and never change my game.

CAMILLA.

But when you have lost it, if fresh start up, you can be as fully satisfied, who hunt more for the love of the sport than for the sake of prey. 180

VALENTINE.

But, madam, should you chance to be taken, look to it. For I shall touse and worry you most unmercifully, till I have revenged myself severely for the pains you cost me catching. 185

CAMILLA.

Therefore, I am resolved to keep out of your reach. Lord! what would become of such a poor little creature as I am in the paws of so ravenous an animal?

TRUMAN.

But are you too, lady, so wild, as Mrs. Camilla?

VICTORIA.

Oh, sir, to the full! But I hope you are not so unmerciful as Mr. Valentine. 190

TRUMAN.

No, madam, quite on the contrary, as soft and pliant as your pillow. You may mold me to your own ease and pleasure, which way you will.

VICTORIA.

'Tis strange two of such different tempers should so well agree. Methinks you look like two as roaring, ranting, tory rory* sparks as one would wish to meet withal. 195

VALENTINE.

Yes, madam, at the playhouse in a visor, when you come dressed and prepared for the encounter. There, indeed, we can be as unanimously modish and impertinent as the pertest coxcombs of 'em all, till like them too, we lose our hearts, and never know what becomes of 'em. 200

CAMILLA.

But the comfort is, you are sure to find 'em again in the next bottle. 205

MRS. GOODVILE.

Then drink 'em down to the ladies' healths, and they are as well at ease as ever they were.

TRUMAN.

Why, you would not be so unconscionable as to have us two such whining crop-sick[8] lovers as sigh away their hours and write lamentable ditties to be sung about the Town by fools and bullies in taverns. 210

GOODVILE.

Till some Smithfield[9] doggerel, taking the hint, swells the sonnet to a ballad, and Chloris dwindles to a kitchen wench. 215

VICTORIA.

'Tis presumed then you are of that familiar tribe that never make love but by contraries and rally our faults when you pretend to admire our perfections.

CAMILLA.

As if the only way to raise a good opinion of your-selves were to let us know how ill a one you have of us. 220

TRUMAN.

Faith, madam, 'tis a hard world, and when beauty is held at so dear* a rate, 'tis the best way to beat down the market as much as we can.

VALENTINE.

But you shall find, ladies, we'll bid like chapmen for all that. 225

---

8 crop-sick] starving (from crop or craw)
9 Smithfield] entertainment area of low repute in the northwest suburbs of London

VICTORIA.

You had best have a care, though, lest you overreach yourselves and repent of your purchase when 'tis too late.

CAMILLA.

Besides, I hate a Dutch bargain[10] that's made in 230 heat of wine. For the love it raises is generally like the courage it gives, very extraordinary, but very short lived.

GOODVILE.

How, Madam! have a care what you say. Wine is the prince of love, and all ladies that speak against 235 it forfeit their charter. I must not have my favorite traduced.—Boy, bring some wine.—You shall prove its good effects and then acknowledge it your friend. We'll drink—

CAMILLA.

Till your brains are afloat and all the rest sink. 240

VALENTINE.

I find then, ladies, you have the like opinion of our heads as you have of our hearts.

CAMILLA.

Really sir, you are much in the right.

TRUMAN.

But if your ladyship should be in the wrong—Though love like wine be a good refresher, yet 'tis 245 much more dangerous to be too busy withal. And though now and then I may overheat my head with drinking, yet, confound me, I think I shall have a care never to break my heart with loving.

MRS. GOODVILE.

But sir, if all men were of your cruel temper, what 250 would become of those tender-hearted creatures that cannot forbear saluting* ye with a billet in the morning, though it comes without a name and makes you as unsatisfied as they, poor creatures, are themselves?

TRUMAN. [Aside.]

Hah, this concerns me! Blockhead, dull, leaden 255 sot* that I was not to be sensible it must be she and none but she could send mine this morning. Well, poor Jack Truman, look to thyself, snares are laid for thee. But the virtuous must suffer temptation. And Heaven knows all flesh is frail. 260

---

10 Dutch bargain] an agreement negotiated in a state of inebriation

Enter [Goodvile's] boy with wine.

GOODVILE.

Now boy, fill the glasses.

[Goodvile's boy fills and exits.]

But before we proceed, one thing is to be considered. My dear, you and I are to be no man and wife for this day but be as indifferent and take as little notice one of another as we may chance 265 to do seven years hence. But at night—

VALENTINE.

A very fair proposal.

MRS. GOODVILE.

Agreed, sir, if you will have it so.

GOODVILE.

The wine—now each man to his post.

They separate, Goodvile to Camilla, Valentine to Victoria, Truman to Mrs. Goodvile. All take glasses.

The word? 270

TRUMAN.

Love and wine.

GOODVILE.

Pass. (They drink.)

Enter Lettice.

Now that nothing may be wanting, Lettice you must sing the song I brought home the other morning, for music is as great an encouragement 275 to drinking as fighting.

LETTICE. (Sings.)

Song.

How blessed he appears,
That revels and loves out his happy years,
That fiercely spurs on till he finish his race:
    And knowing life's short, chooses living apace. 280
To cares we were born, 'twere a folly to doubt it,
Then love and rejoice, there's no living without it.

2.

    Each day we grow older,
But as fate approaches, the brave still are bolder.
    The joys of love with our youth slide away, 285
    But yet there are pleasures that never decay:
When beauty grows dull, and our passions grow cold,
Wine still keeps its charms, and we drink when we're old.

GOODVILE.

So, now show me an enemy to divine, harmonious drinking!

[Enter Goodvile's boy.]

[GOODVILE'S] BOY.

Sir, my Lady Squeamish is below, just alighted out of her coach.

GOODVILE.

Nay, then drinking will have the major vote against it. She is the most exact observer of decorums and decency alive.—But she is not alone, I hope?

[GOODVILE'S] BOY.

No, sir, there is Mr. Malagene with her and three more gentlemen. One they call Sir Noble Clumsy, a full portly gentleman. *[Exit.]*

TRUMAN.

That's a hopeful animal, an elder brother of a fair estate and her kinsman, newly come to Town, whom her ladyship has undertaken to polish and make a fine gentleman.

VALENTINE.

'Tis such a fulsome, overgrown rogue yet hopes to be a fine spark and a very courtly youth. He has been this half year endeavoring at a shape, which he loves eating and drinking too well ever to attain to. The other, I'll warrant you, are the nimble Mr. Caper and his polite companion, Mr. Saunter.

GOODVILE.

She's never without a kennel of fools at her heels, and we may know as well when she is near by the noise her coxcombs make, as we know when a certain spark of this Town is at hand by the new fangled jingle of his coach. She comes—and woe be to the wretch whom she first lights upon.

Enter Lady Squeamish, Sir Noble Clumsy, Malagene, Caper and Saunter.

LADY SQUEAMISH.

Dear Madam Goodvile, ten thousand happinesses wait on you.—Fair Madam Victoria, sweet charming Camilla, which way shall I express my service to you?—Cousin, your honor, your honor to the ladies.

SIR NOBLE.

Ladies, as low as knee can bend, or head can bow, I salute* you all.—And gallants, I am your most humble, most obliged, and most devoted servant. *[Aside.]* That I learned at the end of an epistle dedicatory.

GOODVILE.

Sir Noble Clumsy is too great a courtier.

SIR NOBLE.

Yes, sir, I can compliment upon an occasion. My Lady knows I am a pretty apt scholar.

LADY SQUEAMISH.

Gallants, you must pardon my cousin here, he is but as it were a novice yet and has had little conversation* but what I have had the honor to instruct him in.

MALAGENE.

But let me tell you, he is a man of parts* and one that I respect and honor. Pray gentlemen, know my friend.

VALENTINE.

Hark you Malagene, how durst you venture hither, knowing that Goodvile and Truman care so little for your company?

MALAGENE.

Oh, sir, your servant, your servant, sir. I guessed this was the duel you were going about. I should not have left you else, faith Ned, I should not.

GOODVILE.

But, madam, can the worthy knight your kinsman drink?—What think you, Sir Noble, of the ladies' healths?

SIR NOBLE.

In a glass of small beer, if you please.

LADY SQUEAMISH.

Oh sweet Mr. Goodvile, don't tempt him to drink, don't! I'll swear, I am so afraid he should spoil himself with drinking. Lord, how I should loath a fellow with a red nose!

VALENTINE.

See, Truman, the two coxcombs are already boarding our mistresses.

TRUMAN.

Oh, 'twere a pity to interrupt 'em. A woman loves to play and fondle with a coxcomb sometimes as naturally as with a lapdog, and I could no more be jealous of one than the other.

VALENTINE.

I am not of your opinion. They are too apt to love anything that but makes 'em sport. And the familiarity of fools proceeds often times from a privilege we are not aware of. For my part, I shall make bold to divert.—Mr. Saunter, a word: Have you any pretenses with that lady? hah? 355

SAUNTER.

Some small encouragement I have had, sir, but I never make my boast of those favors, never.

VALENTINE.

No, sir, 'twere not your best course. 360

SAUNTER.

Oh Lord, you are pleased to be merry.—Sure he takes me for a fool, but no matter for that. (*Sings, Would Phyllis be mine, and for, etc.*)

Enter [Goodvile's] boy.

[GOODVILE'S] BOY.

Madam, the fiddles are below. Shall I call 'em up?

MRS. GOODVILE.

No, let 'em stay a little, we'll dance below. 365

[Exit Goodvile's boy.]

CAPER.

Hah, the fiddles! (*Caper capers.*) Boy, where are you?

[Enter Caper's boy.]

[CAPER'S] BOY.

Here, sir.

CAPER.

Have you brought my dancing shoes?

[CAPER'S] BOY.

No, sir, you gave me no order. But your fiddle is below under the seat of the coach. 370

CAPER.

Rascal, dog, fool. When did you ever know me go abroad without my dancing shoes? Sirrah, run home and fetch 'em quickly, or I'll cut off both your ears and have 'em fastened to the heels of those I have on. 375

[Exit Caper's boy.]

TRUMAN.

It is an unpardonable fault, sir, that your boy should forget your dancing shoes.

CAPER.

Aye, hang him, blockhead. He has no sense. I must get rid of him as soon as I can. I would no more

dance in a pair of shoes that we commonly wear 380 than I would ride a race in a pair of gambados.

LADY SQUEAMISH.

Mr. Valentine I hope is a better bred gentleman than to leave his mistress for wine. (*To Valentine.*) I hear, sir, there is a love between you and Madam Camilla. [*Aside.*] Thou monster of perjury. 385

VALENTINE.

Faith, madam, you are very much in the right. There is abundance of love on my side, but I can find very little on hers. If your ladyship would but stand my friend on this occasion.—I think this is civil.

LADY SQUEAMISH.

I'll swear, sir, you are a most obliging person.— 390 Ladies and gallants, poor Mr. Valentine here is fallen in love and has desired me to be his advocate. Who could withstand that eye, that lip, that shape and mien. Besides a thousand graces in everything he does?—Oh lovely Camilla! guard, 395 guard your heart. But I'll swear, if it were my own case, I doubt I should not—ha, ha, ha.

VALENTINE.

Madam? what means all this?

GOODVILE.

Poor Ned Valentine!

TRUMAN.

'Tis but what I told him he must look for. But stay, 400 there is more yet coming.

LADY SQUEAMISH.

Nay, this is not half of what thou art to expect. I'll haunt thee worse than thy ill genius, take all opportunities to expose thy folly and falsehood everywhere, till I have made thee as ridiculous to 405 our whole sex as thou art odious to me.

VALENTINE. (*Approaches.*)

But has your ladyship no mercy? Will nothing but my ruin appease you? Why should you choose by your malice to expose your decay of years and lay open your poor lovers' follies to all because you 410 could improve 'em to your own use no longer?

LADY SQUEAMISH.

Come not near me, traitor.—Lord, Madam Camilla, how can you be so cruel? See, see, how wildly he looks. For Heaven's sake have a care of him. I fear he is distempered in his mind. What pity 'tis so hopeful 415 a gentleman should run mad for love—ha, ha, ha.

MRS. GOODVILE.

Dear madam, how can you use Mr. Valentine so? 'Tis enough to put him out of humor and spoil him for being good company all the day after it.

LADY SQUEAMISH.

Oh Lord, madam, 'tis the greatest pleasure to me 420 in the world. Let me die, but I love to rally a bashful young lover and put him out of countenance, at my heart.

SAUNTER.

Ha, ha, ha, and I'll swear the devil and all's in her wit when she sets on't. Poor Ned Valentine! Lord, 425 how sillily he looks!

CAPER.

Aye, and would fain be angry if he knew but how.

VALENTINE.

Hark you, coxcomb, I can be angry, very angry, d'ye mark me?

SIR NOBLE.

No, but sir, don't be in a passion, my lady will have 430 her humor.* But she's a very good woman at the bottom.

VALENTINE.

Very likely, sir.

MRS. GOODVILE.

Now, madam, if your ladyship thinks fit, we'll withdraw and leave the gentlemen to themselves 435 a little. Only Mr. Caper and Mr. Saunter must do us the honor of their company.

SAUNTER.

Say you so, madam? In faith, and you shall have it.—Come Caper, we are the men for the ladies, I see that.—Hey boys! 440

LADY SQUEAMISH.

Oh, dear and sweet Mr. Saunter shall oblige us with a song.

SAUNTER.

Oh madam, ten thousand, ten thousand if you please. I'll swear, I believe I could sing all day and all night and never be weary. (*Sings.*) 445
When Phyllis watched her harmless sheep,
Not one poor lamb, etc.

Exeunt Saunter, Caper, ladies.

GOODVILE.

A happy riddance this. Now, gentlemen, for one

bottle to entertain* our noble friend and now acquaintance, Sir Noble Clumsy. 450

SIR NOBLE.

Really gallants, I must beg your pardon. I dare not drink, for I have but a very weak brain, sir, and my head won't bear it.

TRUMAN.

Oh, surely that honorable bulk could never be maintained with thin regular diet and small beer. 455

SIR NOBLE.

I must confess, sir, I am something plump, but a little fat is comely. I would not be too lean.

MALAGENE.

No, by no means, my dear, thou hast an heroic face which well becomes the noble port and fullness of thy body. 460

VALENTINE.

Goodvile, we have a suit to you. Here is Malagene has been sometime in a cloud. For this once, receive him into good grace and favor again.

MALAGENE.

Faith, Goodvile do, for without any more words, I love thee with all my heart—faith and troth— 465 give me thy hand.

GOODVILE.

But, sir, should I allow you my countenance, you would be very drunk, very rude, and very unmannerly, I fear.

MALAGENE.

Drunk, sir? I scorn your words, I'd have you know 470 I han't been drunk this week. No, I am the son of a whore if I won't be very sober. This noble knight shall be security for my good behavior.—Wilt thou not, knight?

SIR NOBLE.

Sir, you are a person altogether a stranger to me. 475 And I have sworn never to be bound for any man.

TRUMAN.

Oh, but Sir Noble, you are obliged in honor to serve a gentleman and your friend.

SIR NOBLE.

Say you so, sir? Obliged in honor? I am satisfied. Sir, this gentleman is my friend and acquaintance, 480 and whatsoever he says I'll stand to.

MALAGENE.

Hark thee, son of Mars, thou art a knight already.

I'll marry thee to a lady of my acquaintance and
have thee made a lord.

GOODVILE.

Boy, the wine.   485

[Enter Goodvile's boy.]

Give Sir Noble his glass.—Gentlemen, Sir Noble's
lady's health.

SIR NOBLE.

Od's* my life, I'll drink that, though I die for't.
Gallants, I have a lady in this head of mine and
that you shall find anon. By my troth, I think this   490
be a glass of good wine!

VALENTINE.

Say you so? Take the other glass then, Sir Noble.

SIR NOBLE.

'Fore George[11] and so I will. Pox on't, let it be a
brimmer. Gentlemen, God save the King.

MALAGENE.

Well said, my lovely man of might. His worship   495
grows good company.

TRUMAN.

Sir Noble, you are a great acquaintance with Mr.
Caper and Mr. Saunter. They are men of pretty
parts.*

SIR NOBLE.

Oh sir, the finest persons—the most obliging, well-   500
bred, complaisant, modish gentlemen. They are
acquainted with all the ladies in Town and are men
of fine estates.

TRUMAN.

This rogue is one of the earthy mongrels that
knows the value of nothing but a good estate and   505
loves a fellow with a great deal of land and a title,
though his grandfather were a blacksmith.

SIR NOBLE.

How say you, sir, a good estate? Od's heart, give me
the other glass, I have two thousand pounds a year.[12]

MALAGENE.

Sayst thou so?—Boy, bring more wine. Wine in   510
abundance, sirrah, d'ye hear?—Frank Goodvile,

---

[11] 'Fore George] a mild oath by St. George, patron saint
of England

[12] two thousand pounds a year] that is, an estate that generates so much revenue p.a.

thou see'st I am free. For faith, I hate ceremony
and would fain make the knight merry.

GOODVILE.

Malagene, it shall be your task. Drink him up
lustily, and when that's done, we'll bring him to   515
my lady his cousin. It may make some sport.

VALENTINE.

A very good proposal.

MALAGENE.

Say no more. Thy word's a law, and it shall be
done.—Come, bear up, my lusty limb of honor,
and hang sobriety.   520

SIR NOBLE.

Aye, so say I, hang sobriety—drink, whore, rant,
roar, swear, make a noise, and all that. But be
honest, dost hear, be honest.

TRUMAN. *[Aside.]*

I would very fain be so if I could. But the damned
billet this morning won't out of my head. Well,   525
Madam Goodvile, if any mischief comes on't, 'tis
your own fault, not mine. I did not strike first, and
there's an end on't.

Music within. Enter Lettice.

LETTICE.

Sir, the fiddles are ready, and the ladies desire your
company.—Mr. Truman, my lady wants you.   530

TRUMAN.

Say'st thou so? I thank thee for thy news with all
my heart. *[Aside.]* The devil, I see, will get the
better on't, and there is no resisting.

LETTICE.

Sir Noble, my Lady Squeamish sent me to tell you,
she wants your company to dance.   535

SIR NOBLE.

Tell her I am busy about a grand affair of the Nation
and cannot come.—Dance? I look like a dancer
indeed! but these women will be always putting us
on more than we can do.—Boy, give me more wine.

GOODVILE.

Malagene, remember, and use expedition.   540

Exeunt Goodvile, Truman, Valentine, Lettice.

SIR NOBLE.

Sirrah, do you know me? I am a knight. And here's
a health to all the whores in Christendom.

MALAGENE.

Not forgetting all the ladies within. (*Drinks.*) Now we are alone, I may talk.

SIR NOBLE. (*Breaks a glass.*)

So, there's for you, do you see? Sirrah, don't you look scurvily. I have money in my pocket, you must know that.—Bring us more wine.—Malagene, thou art a pretty fellow. Dost thou love me? Give me thy hand. I will salute* thy under lip. (*Staggers.*)

MALAGENE.

Hah, what's the meaning of this? I doubt I shall almost be drunk as soon as the knight. Sir Noble, canst thou whore?

SIR NOBLE.

How, whore! what a question's there? Thou shalt be my pimp, and I'll prefer* thee.

MALAGENE.

What a rascal this knight is? I have known as worthy a person as himself a pimp and one that thought it no blemish to his honor neither.

Enter Lady Squeamish at the door.

SIR NOBLE.

Hah, my lady cousin?—Faith, madam, you see I am at it.

MALAGENE.

The devil's in't, I think we could no sooner talk of whores, but she must come in with a pox to her.—Madam, your ladyship's most humble servant.

LADY SQUEAMISH.

Oh, odious! insufferable! Who would have thought, Cousin, you would have served me so.—Faugh, how he stinks of wine, I can smell him hither.—How have you patience to hear the noise of fiddles and spend your time in nasty drinking?

SIR NOBLE.

Hum! 'Tis a good creature. Lovely lady, thou shalt take thy glass.

LADY SQUEAMISH.

Uh gud, murder, I had rather you offered me a toad.

SIR NOBLE.

Then Valentine, here's a health to my lady cousin's Pelion upon Ossa.[13] (*Drinks and breaks glass.*)

LADY SQUEAMISH.

Lord, dear Mr. Malagene, what's that?

MALAGENE.

A certain place, Madam, in Greece, much talked of by the ancients. The noble gentleman is well-read.

LADY SQUEAMISH.

Nay, he is an ingenious person, I'll assure you.

SIR NOBLE.

Now lady bright, I am wholly thy slave. Give me thy hand. I'll go straight and begin my grandmother's kissing dance.[14] But first design me the private honor of thy lip.

LADY SQUEAMISH.

Nay, fie Sir Noble! How I hate you now! For shame, be not so rude. I'll swear you are quite spoiled. Get you gone, you good-natured toad you.

Exeunt omnes.

Act III. [Garden adjacent to Goodville's Town house.]

Enter Goodvile a little heated.

GOODVILE.

What a damned chicken-brained fellow am I grown? If I but dip my bill, I am giddy. Now, am I as hot-headed with my bare two bottles as a drunken prentice on a holiday.[15] Truman marries Victoria, that's resolved on, and so one care is over. But then Camilla! how I shall get possession of her. Well, my mind misgives me, I shall do something may call my discretion in question, and yet I can't avoid it. Camilla I do love and must have her, come what will on't. And no time so fit to begin the enterprise as this. She may make a good wife for Valentine for all that.

Enter Truman, Valentine. Music.

---

13 Pelion upon Ossa] two mountains in Greece, perhaps a bawdy joke

14 kissing dance] According to Summers, "A round dance, formerly very popular at weddings, in which the women and the men alternately knelt upon a cushion to be kissed"

15 drunken … holiday] Traditionally, apprentices were given four holidays a year from their work, during which they were notoriously drunk and disorderly.

Fie, gentlemen, without the ladies! Did you quit champagne for this? Faith, I begin to despair of you and doubt you are grown as weak lovers as drinkers.

TRUMAN.

Goodvile, thou hast no conscience. A decayed cavalier captain that drinks journeywork under a deputy lieutenant in the country[16] is not able to keep thee company. Two bottles, as I take it, is no such trifling matter.

GOODVILE.

Oh, but I hate to be balked, and a friend that leaves me at two bottles is as unkind as a mistress that jilts me when I thought I had made sure of the business. But gallants, how stand the affairs of love? Truman, is Victoria kind?* I question not your friendship in the matter but trust the honor of my family in your hands.

VALENTINE. (Aside.)

He little thinks Truman is informed of all and no longer a stranger on what score he is so wondrous civil. But I am mistaken if he be behind with him in kindness long.

TRUMAN.

A pox on it. I am afraid this marriage will never agree with me. Methinks the very thought on't goes a little against my stomach. Like a young thief, though I have some itching to be at it, yet I am loathe to venture what may follow.

GOODVILE.

Well, I'll go in and better prepare Victoria. In the meantime, believe it only my ambition to be as well allied in blood as friendship to so good and generous a person as Truman. [Exit.]

TRUMAN.

What a damned creature man is!—Valentine, did'st thou believe this fellow could be a villain?

VALENTINE.

I must confess, it something surprises me. He might have found out a fitter person to put his mistress upon than his friend. But how the devil got you the knowledge of it?

TRUMAN.

Faith, I'll tell thee, for I think I am no way obliged

to conceal it: his wife, even his very wife told me all.

VALENTINE.

I begin to suspect that Mrs. Goodvile has no ill opinion of you. I observed something but now very obliging towards you. Besides, when a woman begins to betray her husband's secrets, 'tis a certain sign she has a mind to communicate very important ones of her own.

TRUMAN.

Valentine, no more of that, though it would be a rare revenge to make a cuckold of this smiling rogue.

VALENTINE.

'Tis fifty times better than cutting his throat; that were to do him more honor than he deserves.

Enter Malagene.

MALAGENE.

Ha, ha, ha, the rarest sport—Jack Truman, Ned Valentine.

TRUMAN.

Why, what's the matter? Where?

MALAGENE.

Yonder's my rogue of a knight as drunk as a porter, and faith Jack, I am but little better.

VALENTINE.

Dear sir, and what of all this?

MALAGENE.

Why with a bottle under his arm and a beer glass in his hand, I set him full drive at my Lady Squeamish for nothing else but to make mischief, Ned—nothing else in the world. For everybody knows I am the worst-natured fellow breathing. 'Tis my way of wit.

VALENTINE.

Do you love nobody, then?

MALAGENE.

No, not I. Yes, a pox on it, I love you well enough, because ye are a rogue I have known a good while. Though should I take the least prejudice against you, I could not afford you a good word behind your back for my heart.

TRUMAN.

Sir, we are much obliged to you.—'Tis a sign the rogue is drunk that he speaks truth.

MALAGENE.

I tell you what I did t'other day. Faith, 'tis as good a jest as ever you heard.

---

16 decayed … country] The sense is that such a down-and-out officer in such a terrible post would drink mightily.

VALENTINE.

Pray sir, do. 80

MALAGENE.

Why walking along, a lame fellow followed me and asked my charity, which, by the way, was a pretty proposition to me. Being in one of my witty, merry fits, I asked him how long he had been in that condition? The poor fellow shook his head and told 85 me he was born so. But how d'ye think I served him?

VALENTINE.

Nay, the devil knows.

MALAGENE.

I showed my parts,* I think, for I tripped up both his wooden legs and walked off gravely about my business. 90

TRUMAN.

And this, you say, is your way of wit.

MALAGENE.

Aye, altogether this and mimicry. I am a very good mimic. I can act Punchinello, Scaramouchio, Harlequin, Prince Prettyman,[17] or anything. I can act the rumbling of a wheelbarrow. 95

VALENTINE.

The rumbling of a wheelbarrow!

MALAGENE.

Aye, the rumbling of a wheelbarrow, so I say. Nay, more than that, I can act a sow and pigs, sausages a-broiling, a shoulder of mutton a-roasting. I can act a fly in a honey pot. 100

TRUMAN.

That, indeed, must be the effect of very curious* observation.

MALAGENE.

No, hang it, I never make it my business to observe anything that is mechanic.[18] But all this I do, you shall see me if you will. But here comes her 105 ladyship and Sir Noble.

Enter Lady Squeamish and Sir Noble.

LADY SQUEAMISH.

Oh dear Mr. Truman, rescue me.—Nay, Sir Noble, for Heaven's sake.

---

17 Punchinello ... Prettyman] comic characters, generally buffoons, mostly from the Italian Commedia dell'Arte.
18 mechanic] lifeless, unanimated

SIR NOBLE.

I tell thee lady, I must embrace thy lovely body.— Sir, do you know me? I am Sir Noble Clumsy. I 110 am a rogue of an estate, and live I— Do you want any money? I have fifty pound.

VALENTINE.

Nay, good Sir Noble, none of your generosity we beseech you. The lady, the lady Sir Noble.

SIR NOBLE.

Nay, 'tis all one to me if you won't take it, there it 115 is. Hang money, my father was an alderman.

MALAGENE.

'Tis pity good guineas should be spoiled. Sir Noble, by your leave. (*Picks them up.*)

SIR NOBLE.

But sir, you will not keep my money?

MALAGENE.

Oh, hang money, sir, your father was an alderman. 120

SIR NOBLE.

Well, get thee gone for an arch-wag. I do but sham all this while. But by dod, he's pure company.

TRUMAN.

Was there ever such a blockhead! Now, has he nevertheless a mighty opinion of himself and thinks all this wit and pretty discourse. 125

SIR NOBLE.

Lady, once more I say be civil and come kiss me. I shall ravish else. I shall ravish mightily.

VALENTINE.

Well done, Sir Noble. To her, never spare.

LADY SQUEAMISH.

I may be even with you, though, for all this, Mr. Valentine.—Nay, dear Sir Noble.—Mr. Truman, 130 I'll swear he'll put me into fits.

SIR NOBLE.

No, but let me salute* the hem of thy garment. (*Kneels.*) Wilt thou marry me?

MALAGENE.

Faith, madam, do. Let me make the match.

LADY SQUEAMISH.

Let me die, Mr. Malagene. You are a strange man 135 and, I'll swear, have a great deal of wit. Lord, why don't you write?

MALAGENE.

Write? I thank your ladyship for that with all my heart. No, I have a finger in a lampoon or so sometimes, that's all. 140

TRUMAN.

But he can act.

LADY SQUEAMISH.

I'll swear, and so he does better than anyone upon
our theaters. I have seen him. Oh, the English
comedians are nothing, not comparable to the
French or Italian. Besides, we want* poets.   145

SIR NOBLE.

Poets! why I am a poet. I have written three acts
of a play and have named it already. 'Tis to be a
tragedy.

LADY SQUEAMISH.

Oh, Cousin, if you undertake to write a tragedy,
take my counsel. Be sure to say soft, melting,   150
tender things in it that may be moving, and make
your ladies' characters virtuous, whate'er you do.

SIR NOBLE.

Moving? Why, I can never read it myself but it
makes me laugh. Well, 'tis the prettiest plot and
so full of waggery.   155

LADY SQUEAMISH.

Oh ridiculous!

MALAGENE.

But knight, the title, knight, the title.

SIR NOBLE.

Why let me see, 'tis to be called *The Merry Conceits
of Love; or, The Life and Death of the Emperor Charles
the Fifth, with the Humours of his Dog Bobadillo.*   160

MALAGENE.

Ha, ha, ha.

VALENTINE.

But Sir Noble, this sounds more like a comedy.

SIR NOBLE.

Oh, but I have resolved it shall be a tragedy, because
Bobadillo's to be killed in the play. Comedy! no, I
scorn to write comedy. I know several that can squirt   165
comedy. I'll tell you more of this when I am sober.

LADY SQUEAMISH.

But dear Mr. Malagene, won't you let us see you
act a little something of Harlequin? I'll swear you
do it so naturally, it makes me think I am at the
Louvre[19] or Whitehall* all the time.   170

Malagene acts.

---

19 Louvre] at this time the French royal palace

Oh Lord, don't, don't neither. I'll swear you'll make
me burst. Was there every anything so pleasant?

TRUMAN. [*Aside.*]

Was ever anything so affected and ridiculous? Her
whole life surely is a continued scene of
impertinence. What a damned creature is a   175
decayed woman with all the exquisite silliness and
vanity of her sex, yet none of the charms.

Malagene speaks in Punchinello's voice.

LADY SQUEAMISH.

Oh Lord, that, that, that, is a pleasure intolerable.
Well, let me die if I can hold out any longer. Pray
Mr. Malagene, how long have you been in love   180
with Mrs. Tawdry the actress?

MALAGENE. (*In his own voice aloud.*)

Ever since your ladyship has been off from the
hooks with Mr. Valentine.

LADY SQUEAMISH.

Uh gud! I always thought Mr. Malagene had been
better bred than to upbraid me with any such base   185
thing to my face, whatever he might say of me
behind my back. But there is no honor, no civility
in the world. That I am satisfied of.

VALENTINE.

Can your ladyship take anything ill from Mr.
Malagene? A woman should bear with the unlucky   190
jerks* of her buffoon or coxcomb, as well as with the
ill manners of her monkey sometimes. The fools and
rascals your sex delights in ought to have the privilege
of saying as well as they have of doing anything.

LADY SQUEAMISH.

Which you men of wit (as you think yourselves!)   195
are very angry you should be debarred of. Lord,
what pity 'tis your good parts* should be your
misfortune.

VALENTINE.

Ay madam, I feel the curse of it. I who had just
sense enough to fall in love with so much beauty   200
and merit yet could not be able to keep the
paradise I was so happily possessed of.

LADY SQUEAMISH.

This malice and ill-nature shall not serve your turn.
I shall know all your proceedings and intrigues with
Camilla and be revenged on your love to her, for all   205
the affronts and injuries you have done to mine.

Enter Caper and Saunter.

CAPER.

Oh dear madam, we're utterly undone for want of your ladyship's company, I'll vow. Madam Goodvile is coming with the fiddles to wait on you here. (*Cuts* [a caper] backward.*)   210

SIR NOBLE.

Sir, are you a dancing master? You are very nimble, methinks.

CAPER.

Aye sir, I hate to stand still. But Sir Noble, I thought you had known me. I doubt you may be a little overtaken. Faith, dear heart, I am glad to   215
see thee so merry.

SIR NOBLE.

Yes, I do love dearly to be drunk once a year or so, 'tis good for my bodily health. But do you never drink?

CAPER.

No, Sir Noble, that is not my province, you know.   220
I mind dancing altogether.

SIR NOBLE.

Nor you? Can't you drink, hah?

SAUNTER.

No, I make love and sing to ladies.

SIR NOBLE.

Whores, to my knowledge, arrant, rank, common whores. A pox on your woman of quality* that you   225
carried me to in the Mall.*

TRUMAN.

Why, what was the matter, Sir Noble?

SIR NOBLE.

By yea and by nay, a foul overgrown strumpet, with a running bawd instead of waiting woman, a great deal of paint, variety of old clothes, and nothing to eat.   230

LADY SQUEAMISH.

Oh dear, let me die, if that was not extravagantly pleasant.

TRUMAN.

I believe Sir Noble is much in the right, for I never came near these giddy intriguing blockheads but they were talking of love and ladies, nor ever met with a   235
hackney, stripping[20] whore that did not know 'em.

CAPER.

Ned Valentine, I have a kindness to beg of you.

VALENTINE.

Sir, you may command me anything.

CAPER.

Why, you must know I am in love with Camilla.

VALENTINE.

Very good.   240

CAPER.

Now, I would have you speak to Frank Goodvile not to make love to her as he does. I'faith, I can't bear it. For to tell you the truth on't, I intend to marry her. I catched him at it but now. Faith, it made my heart ache, never stir if it did not.   245

Ex[eunt Lady Squeamish, Caper, Saunter, Sir Noble].

VALENTINE.

In troth sir, 'tis very uncivil.—Truman, this Goodvile has a mind to oblige us both. He's providing a wife for me too as fast as he can. Camilla's his quarry now, I understand, and by that time he has played as fair a game with her as he   250
has done with your mistress Victoria, I may stand fair to put in for the rubbers.[21]

TRUMAN.

Valentine, thou art upon too sure grounds for him there. Camilla has both too much wit and virtue and each with as little affectation as the other.   255

VALENTINE.

Jack, after this, I cannot but be very free with you. I know there is some love hatching between you and his wife. Both our revenge lies in thy hands, and if thou dost not thyself and me justice, I'll disown thee forever.   260

TRUMAN.

See where he comes with a heart as gay and light, as if there was nothing but honesty in it.

Enter Goodvile.

GOODVILE. (*Sings.*)

When beauty can't move, and our passions grow cold,
Wine still keeps its charms, and we drink when
    we're old.

---

20 hackney, stripping] common, thieving

21 rubbers] seconds (from an extra match to determine the winner)

Jack Truman, yonder have I and Victoria been 265
laughing at thee till we were weary. She swears thou
art so very modest, she would not for all the world
marry thee for fear of spoiling that virtue.

TRUMAN.

Nay, then I doubt I have lost her forever. For if
she complains of my modesty, she has found a fault 270
which I never thought I had been guilty of before.

GOODVILE.

But that is a quality which, though they hate never
so much in a gallant, they are apt for many reasons
to value in a husband. Fear not, dissimulation is
the natural adjunct of their sex, and I would no 275
more despair of a woman, though she swore she
hated me, than I would believe her, though she
swore she loved me.

*Enter Lady Squeamish and the rest of the company
with the fiddles.*

LADY SQUEAMISH.

Oh, a country dance, a country dance! Mr. Caper
where are you? You shall dance with Madam 280
Camilla. Mr. Saunter wait on Victoria. Mr.
Goodvile, your humble servant. Dear Mr. Truman,
won't you oblige me? Madam Goodvile—ha, ha,
ha. I'll swear I'd utterly forgotten Mr. Valentine.

VALENTINE.

Your ladyship knows me to be a civil person. If you 285
please, I'll keep good orders.

All take out the women.

MALAGENE.

Faith, Ned do, and I'll keep the music in tune.
Away with it. (*Music plays.*) Hold, hold—what
insufferable rascals are these? Why ye scurvy,
thrashing, scraping mongrels, ye make a worse 290
noise than cramped hedgehogs. An old gouty
dancing master that teaches to dance with his
spectacles on makes better music on his cracked
kit. 'Sdeath,* ye dogs, can't you play now as a
gentleman sings? Hah— 295

GOODVILE.

Sir, will you never leave this nauseous humor* of
yours? I can never be with you, but I must be
forced to use you ill or endure the perpetual
torment of your impertinence.

MALAGENE.

Well sir, I ha' done, sir, I ha' done. But 'tis very hard 300
a man can't be permitted to show his parts.* 'Sdeath
Frank, dost thou think thou understand'st music?

GOODVILE.

Sir, I understand it so well that I won't have it
interrupted in my company by you.

MALAGENE.

I am glad on't with all my heart. I never thought 305
you had understood anything before. I think there
I was pretty even with you.

GOODVILE.

Sauciness and ill manners are so much your
province that nothing but kicking is fit for you.

MALAGENE.

Sir, you may use your pleasure. But I care no more 310
for being kicked than you do for kicking. But
prithee Frank, why should you be out of humor
so? The devil take me, if I shall not give thee such
a jerk* presently will make thee angry indeed.

LADY SQUEAMISH.

Lord, Mr. Goodvile, how can you be so ill- 315
natured? I'll swear, Mr. Malagene is in the right.
These people have no manners in the least, play
not at all to dancing. But I vow he himself sings a
tune extreme prettily.

GOODVILE. [*Aside.*]

Death, hell, and the devil, how am I teased? I shall 320
have no opportunity to pursue my business with
Camilla. I must remove this troublesome coxcomb,
and that perhaps may put stop at least to her
impertinence.

LADY SQUEAMISH.

Mr. Truman, Mr. Goodvile, and ladies, I beseech 325
you, do me the favor to hear Mr. Malagene sing a
Scotch song. I'll swear, I am a strange admirer of
Scotch songs. They are the prettiest, soft, melting,
gentle, harmless things—

SAUNTER.

By dod, and so they are. (*Sings, In January last—*) 330

VALENTINE.

Deliver us! A Scotch song! I hate it worse than a
Scotch bagpipe, which even the bears are grown
weary of and have better music. I wish I could see
her ladyship dance a Scotch jig to one of 'em.

MALAGENE.

I must needs beg your ladyship's pardon, I have 335
forgotten the last new Scotch song. But if you
please, I'll entertain you with one of another
nature, which I am apt to believe will be as
pleasant.

LADY SQUEAMISH.

Let me die, Mr. Malagene, you are eternally 340
obliging me.

Malagene sings an Irish cronon.[22]

MALAGENE.

Well, madam, how like you it, madam, hah?

LADY SQUEAMISH.

Really, it is very pretty now—the prettiest odd out
of the way notes. Don't you admire it strangely?

MALAGENE.

I'll assure your ladyship I learned it of an Irish 345
musician that's lately come over and intend to
present it to an author of my acquaintance to put
it in his next play.

LADY SQUEAMISH.

Ha, ha, Mr. Valentine, I would have you learn it
for a serenade to your mistress, ha, ha, ha. 350

VALENTINE.

My page, madam, is docible[23] and has a pretty
voice. He shall learn it if you please, and if your
ladyship has any further service for him—

LADY SQUEAMISH.

Ah Lord, wit, wit, wit, as I live! Come let's dance.

TRUMAN.

Valentine, thou art something too rough. I am afraid 355
her ladyship will be revenged. I see mischief in her
eyes. 'Tis safer provoking a Lancashire witch[24] than
an old mistress and she as violent in her malice too.

GOODVILE.

Malagene, a word with you— (*Goes to the door.*)
hark ye, come hither. 360

MALAGENE.

Well Frank, what's the business now? I am clearly

---

22 cronon] a monotonous chant
23 docible] teachable
24 Lancashire witch] northwest county of England famous
for witches, as reflected in the title of Shadwell's *Lancashire Witches*

for mischief. Shall I break the fiddles and turn the
rascals out of doors?

GOODVILE.

No, sir. But I'll be so civil to turn you out of doors.
Nay, sir, no struggling, I have footmen within. 365

MALAGENE.

Whoo, prithee, what's all this for? What a pox, I
know my lady well enough for a silly, affected,
fantastical gypsy. I did all this but on purpose to
show her—let me alone, I'll abuse her worse.

GOODVILE.

No, sir. But I'll take more care of your reputation 370
and turn you out to learn better manners. No
resistance, as you tender your ears, but be gone.

Exit [Malagene].

GOODVILE.

So, he's gone, and now, I hope I may have some
little time to myself. Fiddles strike up.

Dance.

TRUMAN.

Thus madam, you freely enjoy all the pleasures of a 375
single life and ease yourself of that wretched formal
austerity which commonly attends a married one.

MRS. GOODVILE.

Who would not hate to be one of those simpering
saints that enter into marriage as they would go
into a nunnery, where they keep very strict to their 380
devotion for a while but at last turn arrant sinners
as e'er they were.

TRUMAN.

Marriages, indeed, should be repaired to as
commonly as nunneries are, for handsome retreats
and conveniences, not for prisons, where those that 385
cannot live without 'em may be safe yet sometimes
venture too abroad a little.

MRS. GOODVILE.

But never, sir, without a lady abbess or a confessor
at least.

TRUMAN.

Might I, madam, have the honor to be your 390
confessor. I should be very indulgent and lavish of
absolution to so pretty a sinner.

MRS. GOODVILE.

See, Mr. Goodvile and Madam Camilla I believe
are at shrift already.

TRUMAN.

And poor Ned Valentine looks as pensively as if 395
all the sins of the company were his own.

MRS. GOODVILE.

See, Mr. Caper, your mistress.

CAPER.

Hah Camilla!—Sir, your servant, may I have the
honor to lead this lady in a coranto?

GOODVILE.

No, sir.—Death! surely I have fools that rest and 400
harbor in my house, and they are a worse plague
than bugs and moths. Shall I never be quiet?

VALENTINE.

Sir Noble, Sir Noble, have a care of your mistress!
Do you see there?

SIR NOBLE. (*Wakes and rises.*)

Hum—hah—where? oh— 405

SAUNTER.

Nay, faith madam, Harry Caper's as pretty a fellow!
'Tis the wittiest rogue. He and I laugh at all the
Town.—Harry, I shall marry her.

SIR NOBLE.

Marry, sir! Whom will you marry, sir? You lie.—
Sweetheart, come along with me. I'll marry thee 410
myself presently.

VICTORIA.

You, Sir Noble! (*She squeaks.*) what do you mean?

SIR NOBLE.

Mean! honorably, honorably, I mean honorably.
These are rogues, my dear, arrant rogues. Come
along— 415

Exeunt Sir Noble, Victoria.

CAPER.

Hah, Saunter—

SAUNTER.

Aye Caper, hah! let us follow this drunken knight.

CAPER.

I'faith and so I will—I don't value him this!
(*Cuts.**)

Exeunt Caper and Saunter.

LADY SQUEAMISH.

Ha, ha, ha! Well, I'll swear my cousin Sir Noble is 420
a strange pleasant creature.—Dear madam, let us
follow and see the sport.—Mr. Truman, will you
walk? Oh dear, 'tis violent hot.

Exeunt [Lady Squeamish, Mrs. Goodvile, and Truman].

VALENTINE.

I'll withdraw too and at some distance observe how
matters are carried between Goodvile and Camilla. 425
(*Exit.*)

GOODVILE.

Are you then, madam, resolved to ruin me? Why
should all that stock of beauty be thrown away on
one that can never be able to deserve the gleanings
of it? I love you— 430

CAMILLA.

And all the sex besides. That ever any man should
take such pains to forswear himself to no purpose!

GOODVILE.

Nay, then there's hope yet. If you pretend to doubt
the truth of my love, 'tis a sign you have some
inclinations at least that are my friends. 435

CAMILLA. [*Aside.*]

This Goodvile, I see, is one of those spruce polished
fools, who have so good an opinion of themselves
that they think no woman can resist 'em nor man of
better sense despise 'em. I'll seem at present to
comply and try how far 'twill pass upon him. 440

GOODVILE.

Well madam, have you considered on't? Will the
stone in your heart give way?

CAMILLA.

No, sir. 'Tis full as firm and hard as ever 'twas.

GOODVILE.

And I may then go hang, or drown, or do what I
will with myself, hah? 445

CAMILLA.

At your own discretion, sir, though I should be
loath to see so proper a handsome gentleman come
to an ill end.

GOODVILE.

Good charitable creature! But madam, know I can
be revenged on you for this, and my revenge shall be 450
to love you still, gloat on and loll after you where'er
I see you, in all public meetings haunt and vex you,
write lamentable sonnets on you and so plain that
every fop that sings 'em shall know 'tis you I mean.

CAMILLA.

So sir, this is something. Could not you as well have 455
told me you had been very ill-natured at first? You
did not know how far it might have wrought upon

me. Besides, 'tis a thousand times better than vowing and bowing and making a deal of love and noise, and all to as little purpose as anything you say else.

GOODVILE.

Right exquisite tyrant! I'll set a watch and guard 460 so strict upon you, you shall not entertain* a well-dressed fool in private, but I'll know it, then in a lewd lampoon publish it to the Town till you shall repent and curse the hour you ever saw me.

CAMILLA.

Ah, would I could, ill-natured cruel man! 465

GOODVILE.

Hah, how's that? Am I then mistaken? and have I wronged you all this while? I ask ten thousand pardons. Cursed, damned sot* that I was! I have ruined myself now forever.

CAMILLA.

Well sir, should I now forgive you all, could you 470 consent to wrong your lady so far? You have not yet been married a full year. How must I then suspect your love to me that can so soon forget your faith to her?

GOODVILE.

Oh madam, what do you do? The name of a wife 475 to a man in love is worse than cold water in a fever. 'Tis enough to strike the distemper to my heart and kill me quite, my lady, quotha!

CAMILLA.

Besides, Valentine you know is your friend.

GOODVILE.

I grant it, he is so: a friend is a thing I love to eat 480 and drink and laugh withal. Nay more, I would on a good occasion lose my life for my friend, but not my pleasure. Say where and when it shall be.

CAMILLA.

Never, I dare not.

GOODVILE.

You must by and by when 'tis a little darker, in the 485 left hand walk in the lowest garden.

CAMILLA.

I won't promise you. Can't you trust my good nature?

GOODVILE.

Charming creature! I do. [Aside.] Now, if I can but make up the match between Truman and Victoria, 490 my hopes are completed.

CAMILLA.

Haste! haste! away sir. I see Valentine coming.

Exit Goodvile. Enter Valentine.

VALENTINE.

Madam, you are extremely merry. I am glad Mr. Goodvile has left you in so good a humor.

CAMILLA.

Aye sir, and what may please you more, he is parted 495 hence in as good a humor as he has left me here.

Enter Lady Squeamish, Bridget at the door.

LADY SQUEAMISH.

Valentine and Camilla alone together! Now, for an opportunity to be revenged! Ah, how I love malice!

VALENTINE.

Ungratefullest of women!

CAMILLA.

Foolishest of men! Can you be so very silly to be 500 jealous? For I find you are so. What have you ever observed since first your knowledge of me that might persuade you I should ever grow fond of a man as notoriously false to all women as you are unworthy of me? 505

LADY SQUEAMISH. (*Aside.*)

Has Valentine been false to her too? Nay, then there is some pleasure left yet, to think I am not the only woman that has suffered by his baseness.

VALENTINE.

What then, I'll warrant you were alone together half an hour only for a little harmless raillery or 510 so, an honor I could never obtain without hard suit and humble supplication.

CAMILLA.

Alas! how very politic you are grown! you would pretend displeasure to try your power. No—I shall henceforth think you never had a good opinion of 515 me but that your love was at first as ill-grounded as your fantastical jealousy is now.

VALENTINE.

What specious pretence can you urge? (I know a woman can never be without one.) Come, I am easy and good-natured, willing to believe and be 520 deceived. What, not a word?

CAMILLA.

Though I can hardly descend to satisfy your

distrust, for which I hardly value you and almost hate you, yet to torment you farther, know I did discourse with him and of love too. Nay more, granted him an appointment, but one I never meant to keep and promised it only to get rid of him. This is more than I am obliged to tell you but that I wanted such an opportunity as this to check your pretenses, which I found grew too unruly to be kept at a distance.

VALENTINE.

Though I had some reason to be in doubt, yet this true resentment and just proceeding has convinced me. For Goodvile is a man I have little reason to trust, as will appear hereafter, and 'twas my knowledge of his baseness made them run into so mean a distrust of you. But forgive me this, and when I fail again, discard me forever.

CAMILLA.

Yes. But the next time I shall happen to discourse with a gentleman in private, I shall have you listening at the door or eavesdropping under the window. What, distrust your friend the honorable, worthy Mr. Goodvile! Fie, how can you be so ungenerous?

VALENTINE.

There is not such another hypocrite in the world. He never made love but to delude, nor friendship but for his ends. Even his own kinswoman and charge, Victoria, he has long since corrupted and now would put her on his best friend Truman for a wife.

CAMILLA.

I cannot but laugh to think how easily he swallowed the cheat. He could not be more transported at possession than he was with expectation, and he went away in a greater triumph than if he had conquered the Indies.

VALENTINE.

Where did you promise him?

CAMILLA.

In the left hand walk in the lower garden.

LADY SQUEAMISH. (*Aside.*)

So, in the left hand walk in the lower garden. I heard that. But Mr. Valentine, you may chance to meet another there. Let me die, this is pleasant.

VALENTINE.

And when?

CAMILLA.

Anon, when it begins to grow dark.

LADY SQUEAMISH. [*Aside.*]

Enough, I know the time and place, and Madam Camilla, I shall make bold to cheat you of your lover tonight. Alas, poor inconsiderable creature, how this makes me loathe her!

CAMILLA.

Now, would this news be more welcome to her ladyship Madam Squeamish than a new fashion, a new dance, or a new song. How many visits would she make on the occasion! Not a family in Town would be at rest for her, till she had made it a jest, from the mother of the maids to the attorney's wife in Holborn.[25]

VALENTINE.

But for some private reasons, I would have kept it from her and from Madam Goodvile too. There are affairs to be carried on tonight, which the least accident may interrupt. Besides, I have thought upon't and will so contrive the matter that Goodvile shall keep his assignation and her ladyship herself supply the place of the much expected charming Camilla.

CAMILLA.

But would you, sir, do me such an injury as to make me break my word with Mr. Goodvile? That were inhuman.

VALENTINE.

Good, conscionable creature, have patience and don't you think of paying debts too fast. There's an account yet between you and I which must be made even, and I think I had best secure it now I have you in my custody.

CAMILLA.

Aye, but sir, if I part with anything, I shall expect to have something to show for it.

VALENTINE.

Nay, if I don't offer as lusty security and conditions as any man, let me lose all I lay claim to. That's fair.

Exeunt [Valentine and Camilla].

LADY SQUEAMISH.

So, are they gone? Now, let me but live if this

25 mother … Holborn] from the Court to the City

intrigue be not extremely surprising.—Bridget, go home and fetch me the morning gown[26] I had last made in imitation of Camilla's, for perhaps I shall go a-masquerading tonight, or it may be not, but fetch it nevertheless.

BRIDGET.

Madam, won't the other serve? You may remember you left it at my Lady Foplove's t'other night. That's nearer.

LADY SQUEAMISH.

Impertinent creature! and wouldst thou have me appear in it twice? Do as I bid you, I say. And d'ye hear, bring me a mask with an amber-bead, for I fear I may have fits tonight.[27]

BRIDGET.

I never knew her without fantastical ones, I am sure, for they cost me many a weary errand. (*Exit.*)

Enter Victoria.

LADY SQUEAMISH.

Oh my dear Victoria! the most unlooked for happiness! the pleasantest accident! the strangest discovery! the very thought of it were enough to cure melancholy. Valentine and Camilla, Camilla and Valentine, ha, ha, ha.

VICTORIA.

Dear madam, what is it so transports you?

LADY SQUEAMISH.

Nay, 'tis too precious to be communicated. Hold me, hold me, or I shall die with laughter—ha, ha, ha, Camilla and Valentine, Valentine and Camilla—ha, ha, ha. Oh dear, my heart's broke.

VICTORIA.

Good madam, refrain your mirth a little, and let me know the story that I may have a share in it.

LADY SQUEAMISH.

An assignation! an assignation tonight in the lower garden. By strong good fortune, I overheard it all just now. But to think on the pleasant consequence that will happen drives me into an excess of joy beyond all sufferance.

---

26 morning gown] a dress worn abroad during the day, as opposed to an evening gown

27 amber-bead … fits tonight] amber was used to attract romantic partners; like other isoprenoids, it was thought to have medicinal qualities, as well.

VICTORIA.

Madam, in all probability the pleasantest consequence is like to be theirs if anybody's, and I cannot guess how it should touch your ladyship in the least.

LADY SQUEAMISH.

Oh Lord, how can you be so dull? Why, at the very hour and place appointed will I meet Valentine in Camilla's stead, before she can be there herself. Then when she comes, expose her infamy to all the world, till I have thoroughly revenged myself for all the base injuries her lover has done to me.

VICTORIA.

But madam, can you endure to be so malicious?

LADY SQUEAMISH.

That, that's the dear pleasure of the thing. For I vow, I'd sooner die ten thousand deaths if I thought I should hazard the least temptation to the prejudice of my honor.

VICTORIA.

But why should your ladyship run into the mouth of danger? Who knows what scurvy, lurking devil may stand in readiness and seize your virtue before you are aware of him?

LADY SQUEAMISH.

Temptation? No, I'd have you know I scorn temptation. I durst trust myself in a convent amongst a kennel of crammed friars. Besides, that ungrateful ill-bred fellow Valentine is my mortal aversion: more odious to me than foul weather on a May Day or ill smell in a morning.

VICTORIA.

Nay, now madam, you are too violent.

LADY SQUEAMISH.

Too violent! I would not keep a waiting-woman that should commend any one thing about him. Dear Victoria, urge nothing in his behalf. For if you do, you lose my friendship forever, though I swear he was a fine person once, before he was spoiled.

VICTORIA. (*Aside.*)

I am sure your ladyship had the best share in his spoiling then.

LADY SQUEAMISH.

No, were I inclined to entertain* addresses, I assure I need not want for servants. For I swear I am so perplexed with billet doux every day, I know not which way to turn myself. Besides, there is no fidelity, no honor in mankind. Oh dear Victoria! whatever you do, never let love come near your heart. Though really I think true love is the greatest pleasure in the world. 665

VICTORIA. [*Aside.*]

Would I had never known love. My honor had not then lain at the mercy of so ungrateful a wretch as Goodvile, who now has certainly abandoned and forgotten me.

LADY SQUEAMISH.

Well, certainly, I am the most unsteady, restless, 670 humorsome woman breathing. Now I am so transported at the thoughts of what I have designed that I long till the hour comes with more impatience than— I'll swear I know not what to say—dear Victoria, ten thousand adieus—wish me 675 good success—yet now I think on't, I'll stay a little longer—I'll swear I must not neither—well! I'll go—no, I'll stay—well, I am resolved neither to stand still—sit still—nor lie still—nor have one thought at rest—till the business be over—I'll 680 swear I am a strange creature. (*Exit.*)

VICTORIA.

Farewell, whirligig.

Enter Goodvile.

GOODVILE.

Victoria here! To meet with an old mistress when a man is in pursuit of a fresh one is a worse omen than a hare in a journey. I'll step aside this way till she's 685 past me, so, farewell, fubb.* (*Makes mouths.*)

Exit Victoria.

Now, for the lovely, kind, yielding Camilla! How I long for the happy hour! Swelling, burning breasts, dying eyes, balmy lips, trembling joints, millions of kisses and unspeakable joys wait for me. 690

Enter Truman and Valentine.

Well, gentlemen! Now you have left the ladies, I hope there may be room near your hearts for a bottle or two.

TRUMAN.

Dear Goodvile, thou are too powerful to be denied anything. 'Tis a fine, cool evening, and a swift glass 695

or two now were seasonable and refreshing to wash away the toil and fatigue of the day.

VALENTINE.

After a man has been disturbed with the public impertinences and follies he meets withal abroad, he ought to recompense himself with a friend and 700 a bottle in private at night.

GOODVILE.

Spoken like men that deserve the life you enjoy. I'll in before and put all things in readiness. (*Exit.*)

VALENTINE.

This worthy person, for his honesty and sobriety, would have made a very good Dutch burgo- 705 master.[28] But he is as damnable an English friend and gentleman as one would wish to meet withal.

TRUMAN.

Valentine, thou art too much concerned at him. Methinks Camilla's justice and the pleasant cheat she has put upon him should rather make thee 710 despise* and laugh at him as I do.

VALENTINE.

Truman, thou indeed hast reason. And when I shall know the happy success of the revenge thou hast in store for him, I may do myself and him that justice as scorn him but am too angry yet. 715

TRUMAN.

Then to give thee ease (for I dare trust thee) know this very night I also have an assignation with his wife in the grotto at the upper end of the garden, the opposite walk to that where he expects to meet Camilla.

VALENTINE.

Then I am at rest, let's in. I have nothing else to do 720 but take care so to finish him, as that you shall fear no interruption. At least he will be so full of his expectation of Camilla, that he'll never dream in what posture his own affairs stand in another place.

TRUMAN.

Away then. And may good luck attend us. Ere yet 725 two hours are past, his wife's my own, methinks, already in that secure dark private grotto.
Close in my arms and languishing she lies,
With dying looks, short breath, and wishing eyes,
And the supine, dull cuckold nothing spies. 730

Exeunt.

---

28 Dutch burgomaster] mayor of a Dutch town

Act IV. Night [in the] garden.

Enter Goodvile at one door, Mrs. Goodvile and Lettice following her at the other.

GOODVILE.

So, I think I came off in good time. Hold! now for Camilla. By Jove, I think I am little better than drunk. Hah! Who's there? Victoria, as I live. Nay, it must be she. As I said before, the poor gypsy's jealous, has had some intimation of my appointment with Camilla. I'll luff off and observe which way she steers.

MRS. GOODVILE.

Lettice, I fear that's Mr. Goodvile's voice. Whatever you do, if any cross accident happens, be sure you call me Victoria.

GOODVILE.

Aye, aye, 'tis Victoria! Vigilant devil! but I'll take this way and wait at the lower end of the walk. [*Exit.*]

MRS. GOODVILE.

Lettice, look well 'round you that nobody see us and then follow me. [*Exeunt.*] *Enter Truman.*

TRUMAN.

Thus far all is well. How I pity poor Valentine! Yonder is he plying bumpers, as they call 'em, more furiously than a foreign minister that comes into England to drink for the honor of his country. I have waited something long, though.—Who comes here?

Enter Lettice.

LETTICE.

'Tis I, sir, your servant Lettice.

TRUMAN.

My little good-natured agent, is it you? Where's thy lady? She's too cruel to let a poor lover languish here so long in expectation. It looks as if she rather meant to make a trial of my patience than my love. Is she coming?

LETTICE.

Well I swear (as my Lady Squeamish says), you are a strange creature. But I'll go and tell her. Though I'll vow I utterly disown having any hand in this business. And if any ill comes of it, 'tis none of my fault.

TRUMAN.

No, no, not in the least, prithee dispatch.—How's this! more company! Who comes there?

Enter Valentine.

VALENTINE.

'Tis I, Jack Truman, your friend Valentine.

TRUMAN.

My dear encourager of iniquity! What news? Where's Goodvile?

VALENTINE.

No matter for Goodvile! here comes your mistress.

Enter Mrs. Goodvile, Valentine retires.

TRUMAN.

Now, now, now, what the devil ails me? How I shall quake and tremble?—Madam, dear madam, where are you?

MRS. GOODVILE.

Mr. Truman, is't your voice?—Lettice, you may go in again if you will.

Exit Lettice.

Well sir, I'll vow sir, had it not been that I hate to break my word, I would not have ventured abroad this cold, damp evening for a world.

TRUMAN.

I'll warrant you madam, whilst you are in my possession, no cold shall hurt you. Come, shall we withdraw to the grotto?

MRS. GOODVILE.

Withdraw to the grotto? Bless me, sir! What do you mean? I'll swear, you make my heart ache.

TRUMAN.

Oh madam! I have the best cure for the passion of the heart in the world. I have tried it, madam, 'tis *probatum.** Come, come, let's retire—do, make a disturbance and ruin yourself and me, do!

MRS. GOODVILE.

Nay, I'll swear, sir, you are insufferably rude. You had best make a noise and alarm my husband, you had. For hang me, I shall cry out.

TRUMAN.

No, no, I'm sure you won't complain before you are hurt, and I'll use you so gently— Hark! Don't you hear? There's somebody coming.

MRS. GOODVILE.

Where, where, where? If we are seen, we are undone forever. Well, I'll never give you such an advantage again.

TRUMAN.

I'm sure you would not, if I should let slip this. Come, come, delays are dangerous, and I can endure 'em no longer.

MRS. GOODVILE.

Ah Lord, you kill me! What will become of me— ah—

Carries her in.

VALENTINE.

Nay, faith madam, your condition is something desperate, that's certain. 'Tis a pretty employment I am like to have here, but it is for the sake of my friend and my revenge, and two dearer arguments there cannot be to persuade me to anything.

Enter Malagene at some distance.

MALAGENE.

So, Jack Truman and Madam Goodvile have ordered matters pretty well. I'll say that for my kinswoman, she lays about handsomely, but certainly I hear another voice this way. I'll withdraw once again, there may be more sport yet.

VALENTINE.

That should be Goodvile. I'll step behind this tree and see how he and her ladyship behave themselves. This is like to be a night of as civil business as I have known a great while.

Enter Goodvile.

GOODVILE.

Death and the devil, how that puny rogue Valentine has soused me! If I should have overstayed the time now and missed of my appointment with Camilla— Truman is reeled home, that's certain, and Valentine, I believe, has followed him by this time.—Camilla, dear, lovely, kind, tender, melting Camilla, where art thou?

Enter Lady Squeamish.

LADY SQUEAMISH.

That must be Valentine, nay, I am sure it is he! How sneakingly will he look when he shall find his mistake! But I'll take care, if possible, that no

such thing shall happen, so mine be the pleasure and Camilla's the scandal. I'll rush by him through the walk into the wilderness. (*Runs across the walk.*)

GOODVILE.

That must be she. How swiftly she flew along, as if she feared to be too late, loosely attired and fit for joys! Now, all the power of love and good fortune direct me. (*Exit.*)

VALENTINE.

So, thanks to our stars, he is safe. Though a pox on't, methinks this dry pimping is but a scurvy employment. Had I but a sister or kinswoman of his to keep doing withal, there were some comfort in it.—But here comes Truman and the lady. I must not be seen. (*Exit.*)

Enter Truman and Mrs. Goodvile.

TRUMAN.

You shall not go. Come but back a little, I have something more to tell you that nearly concerns us both. Besides, Mr. Goodvile's in the garden, and if he should chance to meet us, what excuse could we make to him?

MRS. GOODVILE.

But will you promise me Victoria shall never rob me of your heart? She does not deserve it, I am sure, half so well as I.

TRUMAN.

Kind, tender-hearted creature, I know it. Nor shall she ever come so near it as to know that I have one.

Noise.

Alas! we talk too long. I hear company coming. We shall be surprised and disappointed, and then I am undone.

MRS. GOODVILE.

I'll swear you make me tremble, every joint of me. What would you have me do?

TRUMAN.

See, see, who are yonder.

Exeunt Truman and Mrs. Goodvile. Enter Goodvile and Lady Squeamish.

GOODVILE.

What a feast of delight have I had! Surely, she was born only to make me happy! Her natural and

unexperienced tenderness exceeded practiced 125
charms.—Dear, blessed, lovely Camilla, oh! my joys!

LADY SQUEAMISH.

Ha, ha, ha!

GOODVILE.

How's this? My Lady Squeamish! Death and the
devil.

LADY SQUEAMISH.

Truly, sweet Mr. Valentine, the same. Now, sir, I 130
hope— Ugh gad! Mr. Goodvile!

They stare at each other.

GOODVILE.

Have I been mumbling an old kite all this while
instead of my young partridge? A pox o'my
depraved palate that could distinguish no better.

LADY SQUEAMISH.

Lord, Mr. Goodvile, what ails you! This was an 135
unexpected adventure. But let, let me die, it is very
pleasant. Ha, ha, ha.

GOODVILE.

A pox on the pleasures and you too, I say.

LADY SQUEAMISH. [*Aside.*]

This malicious devil Camilla has overreached
me.—Well Mr. Goodvile, you are the worthiest 140
person—had I an only daughter, I durst trust her
with you. You are so very civil—well, innocence
is the greatest happiness in the world.

GOODVILE.

Right madam, it is so, and you know we have been
very innocent, done no harm in the world, not we. 145

LADY SQUEAMISH.

The censorious world if they knew of this accident,
I know, would be apt enough to speak reproachfully.
But so long as I myself am satisfied in the integrity
of my honor, the world is a thing I defy and scorn.

GOODVILE.

Very philosophically spoken. But madam, so long 150
as the world is to be a stranger to our happiness,
why should we deny ourselves the second pleasure
of congratulation?

LADY SQUEAMISH.

Alas, alas, Mr. Goodvile, you cannot say that you
have had the least advantage over my frailty. Well, 155
what might have happened if the strict severity of
both our virtues had not secured us?

GOODVILE. [*Aside.*]

This affected impudence of hers is beyond all the
impertinence I ever knew her guilty of. Virtue with
a pox! I think I have reason to know her pretty 160
well, and the devil of any virtue found I about her.

LADY SQUEAMISH.

But dear sir, let us talk no more of it, though I
am extremely mistaken if I saw not Mr. Valentine
enter the garden before me and am as much
mistaken if a lady was not with him too. 165

GOODVILE.

Hell and confusion! That must be Victoria. I
thought, indeed, I saw her, but being hot-headed
and apprehending she came with a malicious
design of discovering me, avoided her. False to me
with Valentine? 170

LADY SQUEAMISH.

I'll swear Mr. Goodvile, I have long suspected an
intrigue between you and Madam Victoria, and
this jealousy has confirmed me, and I would not
for all the world but have known it. Ha, ha, ha.

GOODVILE.

Death, madam! This is beyond all sufferance.— 175
Disappointed and jilted by Camilla! abused by
Victoria! and with Valentine too, Truman's friend,
whom I thought should have married her! Shame
and infamy light upon the whole sex! May the best
of 'em be ever suspected and the most cautious
always betrayed. 180

LADY SQUEAMISH.

Dear Mr. Goodvile, be patient. Let me die, you
are enough to frighten our whole sex from ever
loving or trusting men again. Lord, I would not
be poor Madam Victoria to gain an empire. I'll
swear, if you are not more moderate, you'll 185
discompose me strangely—how my heart beats!

GOODVILE.

Patience! Preach it to a galled lion.—No, I am sure
she is not far off, and I will find her, surprise her
in the midst of her infamy and prostitution.—
S'death,* madam, let me go. 190

LADY SQUEAMISH.

I will not part with you, you ill-natured creature.
You shall not go. I vow, I'll cry rape if you offer
to stir.—Oh my heart, here's Malagene.

Enter Malagene singing, Frank, Frank, Frank, etc.

MALAGENE.

Why, how now Frank, what a pox, out of humor?—Why madam, what have you done to 195 him, what have you done to him madam? Lord, how he looks!—Why Frank, I say, prithee bear up.

GOODVILE.

Hark you, dog, fool, coxcomb, hold that impertinent, impudent tongue of yours, or I'll cut it out. 'Sdeath, you buffoon, I will. 200

MALAGENE.

No, but hark you, dear heart, good words, good words do you hear, or I shall publish, by my soul's joy, I shall.

GOODVILE.

How am I continually plagued with rogues and owls!* I'll set my house o'fire rather than have it 205 haunted and pestered by such vermin.

MALAGENE.

Faith, Frank, do. I have not seen a house o'fire this great while. It would be a pretty frolic. Prithee, let us about it presently.*

LADY SQUEAMISH.

Dear Mr. Goodvile, you shall be persuaded. Don't 210 run yourself into danger thus rashly.

GOODVILE.

Do you hear then, Monsieur Pimponio, as you expect to live a quiet hour, run in and call for some lights and return with 'em instantly.

MALAGENE.

Say no more, dear heart. I'll do't.—If mischief 215 comes not of this, the devil's in't.—But dear Frank, stay till I come again, I'll be back in a trice. Take t'other turn with her ladyship into the wilderness, or anything. (*Exit.*)

LADY SQUEAMISH.

Let me not live, this Mr. Malagene is a very 220 obliging person, and methinks, Mr. Goodvile, you use him too severely.

GOODVILE.

I wish, madam, he may deserve that character* of you. He is one of those worldlings you were speaking of that are apt to talk reproachfully and, 225 I believe, knows all that has passed between us tonight. For he has a shrewd discerning judgment in these matters.

LADY SQUEAMISH.

Lord Mr. Goodvile, what can he say of me? I defy

even envy itself to do me or my honor any 230 prejudice. Though I wish I had let this frolic alone tonight.

GOODVILE.

Frolic with a pox!—If these be her frolics, what the devil is she when she is in earnest?

[Re-enter Malagene.]

Oh, he returns with the lights.—Look, who are 235 these?

Enter Truman and Mrs. Goodvile.

By Heaven, the same.

TRUMAN.

Gently, gently madam, for fear of an ambuscade. I wonder I hear nothing from Ned Valentine since?

MRS. GOODVILE.

See, see sir, here's Mr. Goodvile. Haste, haste down 240 the other walk, or we are ruined.

TRUMAN.

Fear not, trust all to my conduct.

Exeunt [Truman and Mrs. Goodvile]. As Mrs. Goodvile is going away, Goodvile catches hold of her gown—she claps on her mask.

GOODVILE.

Stay, madam Victoria, nay, you may stay, 'tis in vain to fly. I have discovered all your falsehood, I have. Was mine a passion to be thus abused? I who have 245 given you all my heart! Perfidious false woman! Is your lover too ashamed or afraid to show himself? Where is he? Why comes he not forth?

Enter Truman.

TRUMAN.

Here I am, sir.

GOODVILE.

Hah! Truman! 250

Mrs. Goodvile gets loose and exits.

TRUMAN.

Yes sir, the same. Ready both to acknowledge and justify my being here with Victoria, which I thought, sir, might have been allowed without any offence to Mr. Goodvile. That she is innocent as to anything on my part, I am ready with my sword to 255 make good. But sir, I wear it to do my own honor justice and to demand of you on what grounds you

appear so highly concerned for a woman you were
pleased to commend to your friend for a wife?

GOODVILE.

Concerned, sir! Have I not reason to be concerned 260
for the honor of my family? For a kinswoman
under my charge to be abroad and alone with a
gentleman at this unseasonable hour might alarm
a man less tender of his reputation than I am.

TRUMAN.

Sir, this excuse won't serve my turn. Nor am I so 265
blind as not to be sensible (which I before suspected)
that Victoria has been long your mistress. A pox of
the honor of your family. You had given her all your
heart, you said, and your passion was not a thing to
be thus abused. Nor sir, is my honor. 270

GOODVILE.

No, but dear Jack Truman, thou art my friend.

TRUMAN.

You would have made me believe so, indeed. But the
daubing was too coarse, and the artificial face
appeared too plain. One would have thought, sir,
that you who keep a general decoy here for fools and 275
coxcombs, might have found one to have recompensed a cast* mistress withal and not endeavored
the betraying the honor of a gentleman and your
friend. But sir, I am glad I have heard it from your
own mouth. I hope it will not be esteemed much ill- 280
nature in me if worthy Mr. Malagene and I join
forces to publish a little, as he calls it.

MALAGENE.

Faith, Jack Truman, with all my heart.—Now I
have him on my side, I dare say anything.—Frank
Goodvile, pugh. 285

GOODVILE.

Sir, I shall require a better account of this hereafter.

LADY SQUEAMISH.

Lord, Mr. Truman, what ails Mr. Goodvile? How
happened this difference? I'll swear, I am strangely
surprised.

TRUMAN.

Your ladyship, I suppose, can best give an account 290
how matters are with him. I am apt to believe he
has been very free with you.

LADY SQUEAMISH.

Dear sir, what do you mean? I'll swear, you are a
scandalous person.

GOODVILE.

Sir, since you are so rough, be pleased not to 295
concern yourself with the honor of this lady. You
may have enough to do if you dare justify your
own tomorrow.

TRUMAN.

If I dare? Nay sir, since you question it, I'll
convince you presently.* Draw. 300

They fight. Enter Valentine.

VALENTINE.

Hold, hold, what's the matter here? Jack Truman,
Frank Goodvile, for shame put up.

Enter Mrs. Goodvile.

MRS. GOODVILE.

Where is this perfidious, false man? Where is Mr.
Goodvile? So sir, I have found now the original of
all my misfortunes. I have a rival it seems. Victoria, 305
the happy Victoria, possesses all my joys. What,
have you been fighting too for the honor of your
mistress? Here, come kill me. Would I had been
laid in my grave, ere I had known thy odious,
polluted bed. 310

GOODVILE. [*Aside.*]

'Sdeath,* I thought she had been in her chamber
this hour at least.—'Tis true, my dear, I must own
a kindness* for Victoria, as my kinswoman, but—

MRS. GOODVILE.

How! dare you own it? and to my face too?
Matchless impudence! let me come at him, that I 315
may tear out those hot, lascivious, glowing eyes
that wander after every beauty in their way. Oh!
that I could blast him with a look! Was my love
so despicable to be abandoned for Victoria's! The
thought of it makes me mad. I'll endure it no 320
longer, I will have revenge or I will die! Oh!

TRUMAN. [*Aside.*]

Delicate dissimulation! How I love her!

GOODVILE.

Dear madam, hear me speak—madam, I say
that—

MRS. GOODVILE.

I know you cannot want* an excuse. Dissimulation 325
and falsehood have been your practice. But that
you should wrong me with Victoria, a woman that

for the sake of your relation I had made my friend (for everything that was allied to you was dear to me), is an injury so great that it distracts my reason. I could pardon anything but my wronged love. Let me be gone; send me to a nunnery; confine me to a charnel house, vile ungrateful wretch, anything but thy presence I can endure.

GOODVILE.

Is there everyway so damned a creature as a wife?— Lord madam, do you know what you do?

MRS. GOODVILE.

I'll warrant it, you would persuade me I am mad. Would I had been born a fool! I might then have been happy, patiently have passed over the many tedious nights I have endured in your absence, contented myself with prayers for your safety.

MALAGENE.

Oh Lord, prayers!

MRS. GOODVILE.

When you in the very instant were languishing in the arms of a prostitute.

GOODVILE.

Lord, madam, I thought you had been in your chamber now.—Curse on her, what shall I do!

MRS. GOODVILE.

'Tis a sign you believed me safe enough. You would not certainly else have had the impudence to have brought a new mistress under my nose.—I see there how guilty she stands.—Have you a stomach so hot that it can digest carrion that has been buzzed about and blown upon by all the flies in the Town? Or was it the fantasticalness of your appetite to try how so coarse a dish would relish after being cloyed with better feeding? Nay sir, I have been informed of all.

VALENTINE. (*To Lady Squeamish.*)

Has then your virtuous ladyship been taking a little love and air with Mr. Goodvile this evening?

GOODVILE.

Well, she has dealt with the devil that's certain. A pox on't, I see there's no living for me in this side of the world.—Go, let the coach be made ready. I'll into the country.

MRS. GOODVILE.

Nay sir, I know my presence has always been uneasy to you. Day and night you are from me, or if ever you come home, 'tis with an aching head and heavy heart, which Victoria only has charms enough to cure. This in the first year of our marriage! Nay, and to own it! proclaim your own falsehood and my disgraceful injury in the face of the world, when Malagene too, the trumpet of all the scandal in town, was by to be a witness. 'Twas very discreetly done, and doubtless will be a secret long.

GOODVILE.

Whirr. Nay, since it is so, why the devil should I strive to smother my good actions?—Well, if you will have it so, madam, Victoria has been my mistress, is my mistress, and shall be my mistress, and what a pox would you have more? And so good bye to you.

Enter Sir Noble, Caper, and Saunter.

SIR NOBLE.

How's this! Who's that speaks dishonorably of my love and lady that shall be, Victoria? Before George, she's a queen, and whoever says to the contrary, I'll first make him eat my sword and then beat out his teeth with the hilt of it.

CAPER.

Oh! Dear madam, yonder's all the Town in masquerade. Won't you walk in? They'll be gone if they see no company.—Jack Truman, dear Jack, prithee go and take one frisk. As I hope to be saved, there are three or four the finest ladies, the delicatest shaped women. I am sure I know 'em all.

TRUMAN.

Sir, I wish you good fortune, but I dare not venture. You know my temper. I shall be very boisterous and mistake 'em for whores. Though if they be of your acquaintance, I know they must be of quality.*

CAPER.

Egad, and so they are, but mum for that. One of 'em is she that gave me this ring, and the other presented me with a gold enamelled watch could not cost less than thirty guineas. Trifles Jack, which I have the fortune to meet withal sometimes.

SAUNTER.

Nay sir, you must not come off so. Victoria your mistress!

GOODVILE.

Yes sir, and how are you concerned at it?

SAUNTER.

Nay sir, I can be as civil as anybody. Victoria your mistress!

GOODVILE.

'Sdeath, you coxcomb, mind your singing, do you hear? And play the fool by yourself, or— 405

SAUNTER.

Sing, sir? So I can, fa la da la la, etc. Victoria your mistress!

GOODVILE.

Yes sir, I say my mistress.

SIR NOBLE.

Ounds,* then draw.

VALENTINE.

Hold Sir Noble, you are too furious. What's the 410 matter?

CAPER.

Why, how now, Saunter? How dost do, dear heart?—Sir, this gentleman's my friend, and—

GOODVILE.

Was ever man so overwhelmed with fools and blockheads? Why, you ill-ordered, addlepated, wad- 415 dling brace of puppies.—You, fool in the first place, sing and be safe.—And you, slight grasshopper, dance and divert me. Dance sirrah, do you hear?

CAPER.

Dance sir? And so I think I can, sir, and fence, and play at tennis, and make love, and fold up a billet 420 doux, or anything better than you, sir. Dance quotha—there sir.

MRS. GOODVILE.

Nay Sir Noble, not only so, but owned and boasted of it to my face. Told me—

SIR NOBLE.

Soul of my honor, 'tis unpardonable. And I'll eat 425 his heart for it.

GOODVILE.

Dear raw head and bloody bones,[29] be patient a little.—See, see, you beagles, game for you, fresh game. That great towser has started it already, on, on, on, halloo, halloo, halloo.[30] (*Thrusts 'em at his* 430 *wife, and exits.*)

---

[29] raw ... bones] names of bugbears or bogeymen to frighten children

[30] towser ... haloo] generic name for a hunting dog, thus the hunting cry

LADY SQUEAMISH.

But dear Mr. Caper, masqueraders did you say! I'll swear, I'll among 'em. Shall I not have your company? Oh! Dear masqueraders! I'll vow I can stay no longer. (*Exit hastily.*) 435

VALENTINE.

Curse on her, she's gone and has prevented me.— Caper, Saunter, did you not hear my lady call you? She's gone to the masqueraders. For shame, follow her. She'll take it ill you did not wait on her.

SAUNTER.

Faith, Caper, and so she will. Well, I am resolved 440 to marry Victoria for fear of the worst.—Madam, your most devoted servant. I hope our difference with Mr. Goodvile tonight—

MRS. GOODVILE.

Dear sir, it needs no excuse.

CAPER.

My ressentiments, madam— 445

TRUMAN.

You are too ceremonious, gentleman, and my lady will fear she has lost you.

CAPER.

Dear Jack, as I told thee before, I must bring thee acquainted with those ladies.

SAUNTER.

Prithee, put on a mask and come among us, Jack, 450 faith do.

TRUMAN.

Sirs, I'll wait on you in a moment.

BOTH.

Dear soul, adieu. (*Embracing him. Exeunt singing and dancing.*)

TRUMAN.

These coxcombs, madam, came in a good time; 455 they were never seasonable before.

MRS. GOODVILE.

Diseases and visitations are necessary sometimes to sweep away the noisome crowds that infest and encumber the world.

MALAGENE.

As I have often said, I must publish, I must spread, 460 and so good bye to you. (*Exit.*)

Enter Lettice.

LETTICE.

Oh madam, yonder's my master raving for his

coach. Says he'll into the country presently.* Has given order to disperse the company. What will you do? 465

MRS. GOODVILE.

Let him go, 'twere pity to hinder him. Ha! ha! ha! into the country? I'd as soon believe he would turn Capuchin.

TRUMAN.

But madam, 'twas inhumanly done to come yourself upon him. One would have thought that I had used him bad enough for the wise mistake he made of Victoria. 470

MRS. GOODVILE.

I would not have missed it for the world. Now would he come on his knees for composition, and if I do not bring him to it within these four hours— 475

TRUMAN.

Why madam, what will you do?

MRS. GOODVILE.

Put on all the notorious affectations and ridiculous impertinencies that ever the most eminent of our sex have studied or the coxcombs of your sex admired, then of a sudden, seem to grow fond of both those clinquant fools, which I am sure he of all things loathes. Yet do it too so forcedly that he himself shall find it only intended to give him vexation. 480

TRUMAN.

Have you then maliciously designed, in spite of nature, to keep me constant? 485

MRS. GOODVILE.

Which you will be sure to be!

TRUMAN.

A dozen new, fresh, unseen beauties and the devil himself in the rear of 'em cannot make me otherwise. I never really loved or lived till now. There is nothing I'd not wish to be, except the very husband himself, rather than lose you. 490

Enter Valentine and Camilla.

VALENTINE.

Jack Truman!

TRUMAN.

Well, Ned, what's the matter?

VALENTINE.

Treason, Truman. Your being here with Mrs. Goodvile I fear is discovered. I heard some such thing 495

whispered among the masqueraders, and Goodvile himself seems suddenly altered. I would advise you to come and show yourself and make the best on't.

MRS. GOODVILE.

Let me alone. I'll secure all, I'll warrant you. I'm sure he can have no positive proofs. I'll instantly go and put all things in a confusion, contradict all the orders he has given for going into the country, shut up myself in my chamber, and not hear a word of him till he comes upon submission.— Lettice follow me to my chamber presently.* (*Exit.*) 500 505

TRUMAN.

Right exquisite woman and wife, good luck attend thee. (*Exit.*)

LETTICE.

Well, my lady certainly of a young lady knows her business and understands the managing of a husband the best of any woman in the world. I'll swear she is an ingenious person. Forty ladies now at such an accident would have been hurried and afraid, and the poor waiting woman must have been sent forward and backward and backward and forward to hearken and inquire, but she shows all her changes in a motion. 510 515

Enter Goodvile.

GOODVILE.

How now, Lettice? Where's your lady?

LETTICE.

Within sir, in her chamber.

GOODVILE.

Are you sure of it?

LETTICE.

Sir, she commanded me to follow her thither but now. 520

GOODVILE.

Is she alone there?

LETTICE.

Aye sir, I'll assure you, she seldom desires company. But I must hasten and follow her.

GOODVILE.

Stay a little. Are you sure she was in the house before this disturbance happened in the garden? 525

LETTICE.

Sure sir! why I myself was at the chamber window with her when first she heard you exclaim against

Madam Victoria! Poor creature, I was afraid she would have fallen down dead on the floor. I catched her in my arms, begged of her on my knees not to run out, but she would hear nothing but, spite of force, broke from me and came hither with all that impatience and rage the too sensible resentment of your unkindness had raised in her.

GOODVILE.

Get you in presently,* do you hear? And take no notice of what I have said to you, as you tender your well-being.

LETTICE.

Yes, sir.—But if I conceal a word of it, may I never serve London lady again, but be condemned to be a country chamber maid and kill fleas as long as I live. (*Exit.*)

GOODVILE.

If I should have been in the wrong all this while and mistaken my own dear wife for Victoria! Ah! Curse on this hot head of mine! Pox on't, it is impossible! Yet that mischievous rogue Malagene was all the while in the garden, and he has been at his doubts and ambiguities and maybes with me. By this light, I am a cuckold, an arrant, rank, stinking cuckold.

Enter Victoria.

VICTORIA.

What will become of me! Whither shall I fly to hide my misfortune? Oh! that I might never see the light again but be forever concealed in these shades.

GOODVILE.

Dear Victoria, is it you? Be free with me. Were you really in the garden before tonight or no?

VICTORIA.

I have not been out of the house since it was dark, till this minute, nor had I come hither now but that I am destitute where to conceal myself from the malicious eyes and tongues of those to whom your baseness has given an opportunity of triumphing over my misfortune and ruined honor.

GOODVILE.

Be not so outrageous. I'll reconcile all yet.

VICTORIA.

Which way is it possible? By tomorrow morning your very footmen will have it in their mouths.

And Malagene, that keeps an office of intelligence for all the scandal in town, will be spreading it among his coffee-house companions and at the play whisper it to the orange women,* who shall make a fulsome jest of it to the next coxcomb that comes in half drunk to loll and play and be nauseously lewd with 'em in public.

GOODVILE.

I tell thee, it shall not be. Malagene's my creature, or at least, henceforth I'll make him so. I have reasons for it, and to believe also that my wife, my own delicate damned wife, was the same I mistook for you in the garden tonight.

VICTORIA.

'Tis true, I was at the same time to see for her in her chamber, and she was not there, but cannot believe her in the least guilty of what you seem to accuse her of.

GOODVILE.

Confound her. She's an exquisite jilt, thorough paced and practiced in all the cunning arts and sleights of falsehood. 'Sdeath,* how I could mince her!—But here comes Malagene, he knows all, and I'll make him confess all, or I'll murder him.

Enter Malagene.

Well sir, what say you to this matter?

MALAGENE.

Faith bully, I think my dear kinswoman has mauled you to some purpose. I'll say this for her, she has the true blood of the Malagenes in her. To lol dara lal, etc.

GOODVILE.

What is't you mean, fool? Be plain and unfold yourself.

MALAGENE.

Why, you must know, Frank, having a particular esteem for my family (the nearest relation of which, I would go fifty miles to see hanged), I do think her as very a— But no more—mum, dear heart, mum, I say.

GOODVILE.

What's that you say, sir? What do you think my wife?

MALAGENE.

Aye, what, Frank? What now?

GOODVILE.

Nay sir, that you must resolve me.

MALAGENE.

Why then I'll tell thee, Frank. Dost thou really think I love thee?

GOODVILE.

I know you'll say so, sir, because you fear me.

MALAGENE.

Then prithee do so much as lend me ten guineas for a day or two.   605

GOODVILE.

Oh, sir, to the purpose, to the purpose. Be brief.

MALAGENE.

Nay then, mum I say again.

GOODVILE.

Will you never leave vexing me with your impertinence? Must I be always forced to use you ill to bring you to good manners?   610

MALAGENE.

Faith child,* I am loath to make mischief. I have been a very wicked, ill-natured, impudent fellow. That's the truth on't. But I find I lose myself by it. The very poets themselves, that were wont to stand in awe of   615 me, care not a louse for me now, and there's not a common whore in Town but calls me rogue and rascal to my face as impudently as if I were her pimp.

GOODVILE.

Therefore, sir, resolve to turn honest and be just to your friend.   620

MALAGENE.

The devil take me, Frank, if thou art not a very impertinent fellow. Know! Why, who should know better than yourself, hah?

GOODVILE.

Here are five guineas for you upon condition you make a full and true relation of all you have   625 discovered this night.

MALAGENE.

I'll do't. Down with your dust.

GOODVILE.

What will not this rakehell do to borrow money? I knew him make love to a chambermaid till he had borrowed five pounds of her at half a crown a time.   630

MALAGENE.

Well, Frank Goodvile, you may think as you please of me, but hang me like a dog if I am not a very

honest fellow in my heart. You would have me deal freely with you, you say, in this business?

GOODVILE.

I would so, sir, or I shall deal very roughly with   635 you.

MALAGENE.

And you lent me these five guineas to that purpose?

GOODVILE.

You are much in the right, sir.

MALAGENE.

Then to make short of the matter, thou art as   640 arrant a poor, silly cuckold as one would wish to drink withal, and confound me if I shall not be ashamed of thy company.

GOODVILE.

Confounded whore! Oh, for a legion of devils to hurry her to hell and that I had but the driving of 'em!   645

MALAGENE.

Nay, nay man, since 'tis so, never be angry for the matter. What a pox, you thought to put the mistress upon Truman! Truman has put the cuckold upon you. Valentine has been pimp in the business, and the devil take me if I don't think   650 myself the honestest fellow amongst you.

VICTORIA.

Now sir, consider what wretched thing you have made me.

GOODVILE.

No more. I'm thine, and here I seal my heart to thee forever.   655

MALAGENE.

Well Frank, can I serve thee any further in this business?

GOODVILE.

That sir, is as time shall try. And to convince you how fit I think you for my purpose, I know you are a rascal not to be trusted. Therefore, observe   660 it. If you offer to stir beyond the limits I set you, at that very instant, I'll murder you.

MALAGENE.

Prithee, talk not to me of limits and murdering. I hope you take me, sir (under the rose*), for no fool. And what a pox do you think to make of me?   665

GOODVILE.

A spaniel to hunt and set the game I mean to take.

Oh! Malagene, there will be mischief, Malagene, and new, ripe, fresh scandal to treat of. I know it is an office thou lovest and therefore do it to oblige thee.

MALAGENE.

I'faith and so I do with all my heart. But Frank, I 670 don't know how this business will be brought about well. I have promised to meet two or three hearty old souls tomorrow at dinner, to swear and drink and talk bawdy and treason together for an hour or two. They are all atheists and very honest fellows. 675

GOODVILE.

Oh sir, you may be hanged in good time. But for this present occasion, I must use you.—Victoria, do you with all your utmost art dissemble but the least knowledge of what has happened tonight.— And, sir, do you keep still that lying, sneering, ugly, 680 merry face which you always wear when you design mischief. I'll pretend this morning to pursue my design of going into the country, then, when they are in the height of their pleasures and assurance of their safety, return and surprise 'em. 685

VICTORIA.

But do you believe, sir, that you can utterly abandon all sense of your past love and tenderness for a woman who has been so dear to you? You are apt to relapse again.

GOODVILE.

I will sooner return to my vomit. I am rather glad 690 of the occasion to be rid of so troublesome, uneasy a burden. A wife, after a year, like a garment that has been worn too long, hangs loose and awkwardly on a man and grows a scandal to him that wears it. 695

VICTORIA.

But can you then resolve to quit and disown her forever?

GOODVILE.

Forever, my Victoria! No more, but straight go to thy chamber and wait for the happy issue.—You sir, keep close to me.—Quit her! as cheerfully as I 700 would a shoe that wrings me. Then how loosely shall I move,
Free and unbounded, taste the sweets of life!
Love where I please and know no more the strife
That's bred by that domestic plague called wife. 705

Exeunt.

Act V. [Opens upstage to reveal]
Victoria's chamber [in Goodvile's Town house].

Enter Victoria.

VICTORIA.

Now I am satisfied I must be wretched! Oh love! Unhappy women's curse and men's slight game to pass their idle time at. I find too in myself the common companion of infamy, malice. Has Goodvile's wife ever wronged me? Never. Why 5 then should I conspire to betray her? No, let my revenge light wholly on that false, perjured man. As he has deceived and ruined me, I'll play false with him, make myself privy to his whole design of surprising Truman and his wife together. Then 10 like a true mistress, betray his counsels to her, that she like a true wife may, spite of his teeth, deceive him quite. And so I have the pleasure of seeing him a sealed, stigmatized, fond, believing cuckold. 'Twill at least be some ease to me. Here he comes, 15 equipped and prepared for the pretended journey.

Enter Goodvile and [his] boy.

GOODVILE.

Go, bid the coachman hasten and get all things ready. I am uneasy till I am gone. 'Tis time we were set out.

[Exit Goodvile's boy.]

"The wolves have preyed, and look, the gentle Day 20
Before the wheels of Phoebus[31] all about
Dapples the drowsy east with spots of gray."[32]
Wife! Adieu, dear wife.—Ah my Victoria, up already? so diligent to wish me a happy journey? Certainly, my good angel is like thee, and 25 whenso'er I err must meet me in thy shape and with such softness smile and direct me.

VICTORIA.

As those whom will-o'-the-wisp bewitches
Through bogs, through hedges and ditches.

GOODVILE.

No. Thou hast led me out of the crooked, froward 30

---

31 wheels of Phoebus] Apollo's chariot, carrying the sun across the sky

32 "The wolves … gray."] Goodvile slightly misquotes Pedro from Shakespeare's *Much Ado about Nothing*, V.iii.

road of matrimony into the pleasant, easy path of
love, where I can never leave my way and must be
always happy. But where's Malagene?

VICTORIA.

Below with Sir Noble. Whilst the butler was asleep,
they stole the key from him. And there they are 35
with the fat, red-faced fiddler that plays upon the
base, sitting cross-legged upon the floor, stripped
to their shirts and drinking bawdy healths.

GOODVILE.

That fulsome rogue will ruin all our business. See
here what I have discovered just now in the private 40
corner of a window (a place I suppose appointed for
the purpose!). I found this billet to my sweet wife.
(*Reads.*) "If Goodvile goes out of Town this
morning, let me know it, that I may wait on you and
tell you the rest of my heart. For you do not know 45
how much I love you yet. Truman." Now, if I am not
a cuckold, let any honest wittol judge. Ha, ha, ha.
How it pleases me! Blood! Fire! and Daggers!

VICTORIA.

But sir! what do you resolve on?

GOODVILE.

As I told thee, instantly to pretend a journey out 50
of Town and return and surprise 'em. For I am sure
they'll not be long asunder when I am out of the
way. Oh! this billet is a very honest billet and, I
know, won't lie. But why should I spend my time
in talking of what but vexes me, when pleasures 55
are so near me? Come my Victoria, take me to thy
arms, a moment's joy with thee would sweeten
years of cares.—The devil—

Enter Mrs. Goodvile and Lettice.

MRS. GOODVILE.

Good morning to you, sir.

GOODVILE.

Good night to you, madam. 60

MRS. GOODVILE.

How so, sir?

GOODVILE.

Why, good night or good morrow, 'tis all one.
Ceremony is the least thing I take care of. You see
I am busy.

MRS. GOODVILE.

I must confess, considering the humble duty of a 65

wife, 'tis something rude in me to interrupt you,
but I hope when you know my intentions, you'll
pardon me. They were only to take a civil leave of
you. I find you are preparing for the country, sir.

GOODVILE.

Aye! A little air will be very seasonable at present, 70
madam. I shall grow rank else, and all the company
I keep will smell me out.

MRS. GOODVILE.

Oh, what joy will fill each neighboring village to
hear our landlord's honor is coming down! The bells
shall jangle out of tune all day. And at night the 75
curate of the hamlet comes in the name of the whole
parish to bid his patron welcome into the country
and invite himself the next Lord's Day to dinner.

GOODVILE.

I am glad to see you so pleasant, madam.

MRS. GOODVILE.

Then the next morning our tenant's dainty daughter 80
is sent with a present of pippins of the largest size,
culled by the good old drudge her mother, which she
delivers with a curtsey and blushes in expectation of
what his worship will bestow upon her.

GOODVILE.

Oh madam, let not any thoughts of that nature 85
disturb you. I shall leave my wanton inclinations
here and only please myself when I am there
sometimes to contemplate your ladyship's picture
in the gallery.

MRS. GOODVILE.

Then come the country squires and their dogs, the 90
cleanlier sort of creatures of the two. Straight, we
are invited to the noble hunt and not a deer in all
the forest's safe.

GOODVILE.

No, madam. No horned beast shall suffer for my
pleasure. I am lately grown a philosopher, madam, 95
and find we ought not hurt our fellow creatures.

MRS. GOODVILE.

What is the reason that you use me thus?

GOODVILE.

What is't I would not do to purchase quietness?
Your injurious suspicions of me were tolerable, but
the wrongs your jealousy has done Victoria— 100

MRS. GOODVILE.

I jealous of Victoria! No, though my passion last

night made me extravagant when I discovered you with that naughty Lady Squeamish, which I can easily forgive, if you'll but promise to forget her. For I am confident it was your first transgression. 105

GOODVILE.

Very quaint and pretty.

MRS. GOODVILE.

Yet I am too well satisfied of Victoria's virtue, for she's my friend, and though I should see her in your arms, I could not harbor such a thought. No, Victoria, you must love me, and I'll love you. You 110
shall call me your love, and I'll call you my dear, and we'll always go to the play together and to the park together and everywhere together. And when Mr. Goodvile's out of Town, we'll lie together.

Enter [Goodvile's boy].[b]

[GOODVILE'S BOY].

Sir, the coach is ready. [*Exit.*] 115

GOOODVILE.

You think, madam, you have a fine, easy fool to play withal, but the gayness of your face is too thin to hide the rancor of your heart, and so my dear, jocund, witty devil wife, I take my leave of you, never more from this minute to look on you. 120

MRS. GOODVILE.

Are you then inexorable? Relentless, cruel man!

GOODVILE.

Good, easy, melting, kind-hearted woman, farewell. (*Exit.*)

MRS. GOODVILE.

Ah, wretched me.

LETTICE.

My lady swoons.—Dear Madam Victoria, hasten 125
and bring my master back again. You can do anything with him.

Exit Victoria.

MRS. GOODVILE.

No, no, Lettice! Let him alone. Art thou sure he's gone?

LETTICE.

I hope so, madam. 130

MRS. GOODVILE.

Then so soon as I am returned to my chamber, be sure you go yourself to Mr. Truman and tell him if he has nothing else to do, he may come hither today.

Enter Victoria.

VICTORIA.

There is no prevailing with him. He cries aloud his house is infected and that no man that values 135
his health will stay in it. My Lady Squeamish too is arrived just as he left the door. I am sure she'll come in. Will you see her, madam?

MRS. GOODVILE.

Oh, I am sick at the very name of her. Let all the doors be barred against her, and gunpowder under 140
each threshold place,[c] ready to blow her up if she but offer an entrance.—Lettice, lend me your hand a little. I'll to my chamber instantly. Oh my head!

Exit with Lettice.

VICTORIA.

This management of hers so charms me that I can almost forget all the mischief she has done me. 'Tis 145
true she reproached me, but 'twas done so handsomely that I had doubly deserved it to have taken notice of it.

Enter Lady Squeamish.

LADY SQUEAMISH.

Oh dear Victoria, what will become of me! I am lost and undone forever. Oh I shall die, I shall die, the 150
lord of my heart, the jewel of my soul is false to me.

VICTORIA.

What ails your ladyship?—Surely, she's distracted?

LADY SQUEAMISH.

Oh Goodvile, Goodvile! the false, cruel, remorseless Goodvile! I came just as his coach was parting from the door, yet he would not speak to me, 155
would hardly see me, but away he drove and smiling mocked my sorrows.

VICTORIA.

Alas! Her ladyship is passionate, as I live, very passionate.

LADY SQUEAMISH.

So Theseus left the wretched Ariadne on the shore, 160
so fled the false Aeneas from his Dido.[33]

---

33 Theseus ... Dido] Even after she gave him the clue to the labyrinth so he could defeat the Minotaur, the Greek hero Theseus abandoned Minos's beautiful daughter, Ariadne, on an island; even though he had been her

VICTORIA.

What could you expect less of him, madam? Falsehood is his province. Your ladyship should have made choice of a civil, sober, discreet person, but Goodvile, you know, is a spark, a very* spark. 165

LADY SQUEAMISH.

That, that has been my ruin. It was therefore I adored him. What woman would dote on a dull, melancholy ass because she might be sure of him? No, a spark is my life, my darling, the joy of my soul. Oh, how I dote on a spark! I could live and die with a spark. Victoria, I make you a confidante, and you must pardon me for robbing you of Mr. Goodvile. Come, come, I know all. 170

VICTORIA.

Your ladyship knows more than all the world besides. 175

LADY SQUEAMISH.

And, as I was saying, a spark is the dearest thing to me in the world. I have had acquaintance I think with all the sparks. Well, one of 'em that you know was a sweet person. Oh, he danced and sung and dressed to a miracle, and then he spoke French 180 as if he had been bred all his lifetime at Paris and admired everything that was French. Besides, he would look so languishingly and lisp so prettily when he talked and then never wanted* discourse. I'll swear he has entertained me two hours together 185 with the description of an equipage.

VICTORIA.

That must needs be very charming.

LADY SQUEAMISH.

But Mr. Goodvile was a wit too. Oh, I never had a wit before, for to speak the truth, now I think on't better, all my lovers have been a little foolish, 190 I'll swear, ha, ha, ha.

Sir Noble and Malagene at the door drunk.

MALAGENE.

Scour, scour, scour.34

_____

lover and she offered him a share of her kingdom of Carthage, Trojan Aeneas deserted Queen Dido for his destiny in Latium, where his descendants would found Rome.

34 scour] to clear out a street or area by bullying

SIR NOBLE.

Down goes the mainmast, down, down, down.

They enter.

Malagene, roar, roar, and ravish, here are punks in beaten satin, sirrah, termagant, triumphant, first- 195 rate punks, you rogue.

VICTORIA.

How came these ruffians here?

SIR NOBLE.

Ruffians! do you know who you talk to, madam? I am a civil, sober, discreet person and come particularly to embrace thy lovely body. 200

MALAGENE.

Look you madam, make no noise about this matter. This is a person of quality* and a friend of mine; therefore, pray be civil.

LADY SQUEAMISH.

Has Mr. Goodvile left no footmen at home to cudgel such fops? Faugh—how like drunken 205 journeymen taylors they look?

MALAGENE.

Journeymen madam! hold there! none of your ladyship's journeymen, that's one comfort! woe to the poor devil that is, I say.

LADY SQUEAMISH.

Were Mr. Goodvile at home, you durst not talk 210 thus, you scandalous fellow.

MALAGENE.

Goodvile you say—hark you my dear, were he here in person, I would first of all decently kick him out of doors, then turn up thy keel and discover* here to thy kinsman what a leaky vessel thou art. 215

SIR NOBLE.

Why, what is that Goodvile? Will he wrestle? Or will he box for fifty pounds? Look you, this fellow is my pimp. 'Tis true his countenance is none of the best. But he's a neat lad and keeps good company.

MALAGENE.

Hark you, knight! You'll bear me out in this 220 business, knight? For under the rose,* I have apprehension that this carcass of mine may suffer else.

SIR NOBLE.

No more of that rogue! no more. Take notice, good people, this civil person shall marry my sister. She 225 is a pretty hopeful lady—truly, she is not full thirteen—but she has had two children already, Odd's* heart.

VICTORIA.

Ridiculous oaf!

SIR NOBLE.

Come, let us talk bawdy.   230

VICTORIA.

I'll call those shall talk with you presently.* (*Exit.*)

SIR NOBLE.

Wheugh—she's gone.

LADY SQUEAMISH.

Beast! Brute! Barbarian! Sot!

SIR NOBLE.

Oh law! my aunt! What have I done now? Madam, as I hope to be— (*Runs against her and almost beats   235 her backward.*)

LADY SQUEAMISH.

Oh help! I am murdered! Oh my head!

SIR NOBLE.

Nay lady, that was no fault of mine. You shall see I'll keep my distance, and (as I was saying) if I have offended— (*Reels against a table and throws down   240 a china jar and several little china dishes.*)

LADY SQUEAMISH.

Oh insufferable! quickly, quickly, a porter and basket to carry out this swine to a dunghill. (*Exit.*)

SIR NOBLE.

Look you madam, no harm! no harm! You shall see me behave myself notably yet—as for   245 example—suppose now—suppose this the door. (*Goes to the door.*) Very well. Thus then I move.— (*Steps forward and leaves his peruke on one of the hinges.*) Hah, who was that? Rogues! Dogs! Sons of whores!   250

Enter servants.

FIRST SERVANT.

Such as we are, sir, you shall find us at your service.

SIR NOBLE.

Murder, murder, murder—

MALAGENE.

Where there is such odds, a man may with honor retire and steal off. (*Exit.*)

Enter Caper and Saunter.

CAPER.

Where is this rascal? this coxcomb? this fop? How   255 dare you come hither, sir, to affront the ladies and persons of quality?*

SIR NOBLE.

Sir, your humble servant. Did you see my periwig?

CAPER.

Sir, you are an ass and never wore a periwig in your life. Jernie,* what bush of briars and thorns is here?   260 The mane of my Lady Squeamish's shock* is a Chedreux* to it.

SIR NOBLE.

Why, sir, I know who made it. He was an honest fellow and a barber, and one that loved music and poetry.   265

SAUNTER.

How sir!

CAPER.

But, sir, come close to the business. How durst you treat ladies so rudely as we saw you but now? Answer to that, and tell not us of music and poetry.   270

SIR NOBLE.

Why, he had all *Westminster Drollery* and *Oxford Jests* at his fingers' ends. And for the cittern, if ever Troy town were a tune, he'd master it upon that instrument;[35] when he was our butler in the country, an old maid of my grandmother's took   275 great delight in him for it.

SAUNTER.

But, sir, this is nothing to our business.

SIR NOBLE.

Business! hang business! I hate a man of business. If you'll drink or whore, break windows, or commit murder, I am for you.   280

CAPER.

Sir, will you fight?

SIR NOBLE.

Fight! with whom? for what?

CAPER.

With me.

---

35 *Westminster … instrument*] Sir Noble's barber's dubious accomplishments include quoting from collections of low-brow verse, student wit, and mastering a common ballad on his guitar.

SAUNTER.

With me.

SIR NOBLE.

Aye sir, with all my heart. I love fighting, sir. 285

SAUNTER.

But will you, sir? dare you?

CAPER.

Aye sir, will you fight? Do you think you dare fight?

SIR NOBLE.

Why, you sweet, perfumed, jessamine-knaves! You rogues in buckram! were there a dozen of you, I'd 290 beat you out of your artificial sweetness into your own natural rankness, you stinkards! Shall I draw my Cerberus36 and cut you off, you gawdy popinjays?

CAPER.

This fellow's mad, Saunter, stark mad, by Jericho! Dear knight, how long hast thou been in this 295 pickle? this condition, knight? hah?

SIR NOBLE.

What pickle? what condition, you worms?

SAUNTER.

Aye, aye, 'tis so, the poor devil must to Bedlam: Bedlam, knight, the madman's hospital.

SIR NOBLE.

What will become of you, then, you vermin? 300 There's never a hospital for fools yet. Mercy on me if there were! How many handsome fellows in this Town might be provided for?

Fiddles play within.

CAPER.

Hey day! Fiddles!

SAUNTER.

Madam Goodvile, hearing we were here, hath sent 305 for 'em on purpose to regale us.

Enter Mrs. Goodvile, Lady Squeamish, Lettice, with the fiddles playing; Saunter falls to sing the tune with 'em, and Caper dances to it.

MRS. GOODVILE.

Let my servants take care that all the doors stand open. I'll have entrance denied to no one fool in Town.

---

36 Cerberus] Sir Noble would name his sword after the famous three-headed hellhound from Greek mythology.

[Exit several servants.]

Mr. Caper and Mr. Saunter here? Then we can never want* company.—Come, madam, let us begin the 310 revels of the day. I long to enjoy the freedom I am mistress of.—Lettice, try your voice.d

LADY SQUEAMISH.

Oh madam! This gallant spirit ravishes me.—Dear Mr. Caper, you and Mr. Saunter were born to be happy! Madam Goodvile has resolved to sacrifice this 315 day to pleasure. What shall we do with ourselves?

CAPER.

Do, madam! We'll dance forever.

LADY SQUEAMISH.

Oh aye, dance.

SAUNTER.

And sing.

LADY SQUEAMISH.

And sing. 320

BOTH.

And love.

LADY SQUEAMISH.

Oh aye, love! But Madam Goodvile, have you resolved to wear the willow* and be very melancholy—ha, ha, ha.—Fiddles! Where are you? I cannot endure you out of my sight. 325

MRS. GOODVILE.

Willow! hang it. Give it to the country girls that sigh for clowns.* And melancholy's a disease for bankrupt beauty. I have yet a stock of youth and charms unsullied by the hands of age or care,
And whilst that lasts what woman would despair? 330

SIR NOBLE.

In the meantime, I'll scout out for a doxy of my acquaintance hard by, return in triumph, and let Victoria go hang and despair. (*Sings.*)
To love is a pleasure divine,
Yet I'll never sigh or be sad: 335
They are coxcombs that languish and pine,
So long as whores are to be had.—To daroll, darolla.

LADY SQUEAMISH. [*To remaining servants.*]

Oh secure that deformed monster, that rebel of mine. Fellows, take care of him and keep him up till I talk with him and make him sensible of his 340 enormities.

SIR NOBLE.

Slaves! Avaunt! if my lady will have it so, I'll walk

soberly into the garden and consider of what is past. (*[Sings,] To love is a pleasure, etc. Exit[, followed by servants].*)   345

MRS. GOODVILE.

Lettice!

LETTICE.

Madam.

MRS. GOODVILE.

Is Mr. Truman come?

LETTICE.

He'll be here presently,* madam.

Enter Page with a letter.

PAGE.

A letter for your ladyship.   350

MRS. GOODVILE.

Who brought it?

PAGE.

A porter brought it to the door, madam, but said he had no orders to stay for an answer. (*Exit.*)

MRS. GOODVILE.

A woman's hand! (*Reads.*) "Mr. Goodvile's journey out of Town is but a pretence. He is jealous of you   355 and Mr. Truman; you will find him anon returned in hopes to surprise you together. Though he has trusted me with the secret and obliged me to assist him in it, yet I would endeavor by this discovery* to persuade you that I am your real servant.   360 Victoria. Postscript: Beware of Malagene, for he's appointed the spy to betray you." This is generously done, Victoria, and I'll study to deserve it of thee. Now, if I plague not this wise jealous husband of mine, let all wives curse me and   365 cuckolds laugh at me!—Fiddles! lead in! Mr. Caper and Mr. Saunter, pray wait on my lady and entertain her a little. I'll follow you presently.

LADY SQUEAMISH.

Come Mr. Caper, will you walk?

CAPER.

A coranto, madam?   370

LADY SQUEAMISH.

Aye, ten thousand, ten thousand, Mr. Saunter. I would be always near you two! Oh, for a grove now and purling brook with that delightful charming voice of yours. Come! Let us walk and study which way to divert ourselves.   375

CAPER.

Allons![37] for love and pleasure. By these hands—

SAUNTER.

By those eyes—

LADY SQUEAMISH.

Oh no more, no more! I shall be lost in happiness!

Exeunt [all but Mrs. Goodvile and Lettice].

MRS. GOODVILE.

So, this consort of fools shall be the chorus to my farce. Now, all the malice, ill-nature, falsehood, and   380 hypocrisy of my sex inspire me.—Lettice! see Camilla be sent for instantly.

[Exit Lettice.]

She shall join with me in my revenge; she has reason. Mr. Valentine I suppose will be here with Mr. Truman.   385

Enter Mr. Truman.

TRUMAN.

And think you, madam, he durst not answer a fair lady's challenge without a second?

MRS. GOODVILE.

You would pretend, I'll warrant you, to be very stout. You hectors in love are as arrant cheats as hectors in fighting that bluster, rant, and make a noise for the   390 present, but when they come to the business, prove arrant dastards, and good for nothing.

TRUMAN.

But madam, you should find I dare do something, would you but be civil and stand your ground.

MRS. GOODVILE.

What think you, though, of a cutthroat husband   395 now behind the hangings? What would become of you then?

TRUMAN.

Whilst I have such beauty on my side, nothing can hurt me.

MRS. GOODVILE.

Then, sir, prepare yourself. Mr. Goodvile is really   400 jealous and mistrusts all or more than has passed between us. His journey out of Town was but a pretence, but we shall see him instantly in expectation to catch us together.

---

[37] Allons!] Let's go! (Fr.)

TRUMAN.

Fear him not madam, these moles that work 405
underground are as blind as they are busy. Let him
run on in his dull jealousy, whilst we still find new
windings out and lose him in the maze.

MRS. GOODVILE.

Then if you wish to preserve me yours, join with
me today in my design, which is, if possible, to 410
make him mad, work him up to the height of
furious suspicion, and at that moment when he
thinks his jealousy most just, baffle him out of it.
And let the world know how dull a tool a husband
is compared with that triumphant thing a wife and 415
her guardian angel lover.

TRUMAN.

But Mr. Goodvile, madam, has wit, and so good
an opinion of it too.

MRS. GOODVILE.

'Tis that shall be his ruin. Were he a fool, he were
not worth the trouble of deceiving. 420

TRUMAN.

Dear jewel of my soul, proceed, then, and prosper.
But what must be my part?

MRS. GOODVILE.

To secure Malagene. That ill-natured villain has
betrayed us and is appointed by Goodvile chief
instrument in his discovery. He has cowardice 425
enough to sell his soul to buy off a beating. He
never told truth enough to be believed once so
long as he lives. Get him but in your power, and
he shall own more villainies than ever were in his
thoughts to commit or the necessity of our affair 430
can invent to put upon him.

TRUMAN.

And I'll be sure of him, or may I never taste those
lips again, but be condemned to cast* mistresses
in the side-box at the playhouse or, what is worse,
take up with a sempstress and drudge[38] for cuffs 435
and cravats.

Enter Malagene.

MRS. GOODVILE.

Here he comes!

_____

38 drudge] provide sexual service

TRUMAN.

Oh Monsieur Malagene, welcome!

MALAGENE.

Jack Truman, your humble servant.

TRUMAN.

Whither so fast, I beseech you, sir! A word with 440
you, a word with you.

MALAGENE.

Why! can I do anything for thee? Hast thou any
business for me? Prithee what is it?

TRUMAN.

Sir! You must lie for me.

MALAGENE.

Ha, ha, ha. Is that all? 445

TRUMAN.

Nay sir, you must!

MALAGENE.

Anything in a civil way or so, Jack! But nothing
upon compulsion, lad! Prithee, let me do nothing
upon compulsion, prithee now!

TRUMAN.

Then sir, to be brief, this is the business: Goodvile, I 450
hear, has been informed by you of what passed in the
garden last night. How durst you be so impudent as
to pry into my secrets where I was concerned?

MALAGENE.

Why, look you, Jack, curiosity, you know, and a
natural inclination which I have— 455

TRUMAN.

To pimping.

MALAGENE.

Confound me, Jack, thou art much in the right. I
believe thou art a witch. I knew as well, man—

TRUMAN.

What did you know?

MALAGENE.

Why I knew thee to be an arch wag and an honest 460
fellow! Ah rogue, prithee kiss me!—The rogue's out
of humor.

TRUMAN.

No sir! I dare not use you so like a friend; you must
deserve it better first.

MALAGENE.

Look you Jack, the truth of the business is, I am 465
bespoke. But the love I have to see the business
go forward may persuade me to much.

TRUMAN.

Then presently* resolve entirely to disown and abjure all the intelligence you gave Goodvile, or promise to yourself that, wherever next I meet you, I'll cut your throat upon the spot. 470

MALAGENE.

But hark you, Jack, how shall I come off with the business? I shall be kicked and used very scurvily. For the truth is, I did tell—

TRUMAN.

What did you tell? 475

MALAGENE.

Why, I told him, you knave—I won't tell! you little cunning cur—I told him all, man!

TRUMAN.

All, sir!

MALAGENE.

Aye, hang me like a dog, all.—But madam, you must pardon me, there was not a word of it true. 480

TRUMAN.

And what do you think to do with yourself?

MALAGENE.

Do? why I'll deny it all again, man, every word of it, as impudently as ever I at first affirmed it. Maybe he'll kick me and beat me and use me like a dog, man—that's nothing, nothing at all, man, I do not value it this! (*Pulls out a Jews Trump and plays.*)[39] 485

TRUMAN.

And this, sir, you'll stand to.

MALAGENE.

If I do not, hang me up for a sign at a bawdy house door. In the meantime, I'll retire and pursue a young lampoon, which I am lately the happy father of. 490

TRUMAN.

Nay sir! you are not to stir from me!

Enter Lettice.

LETTICE.

Oh madam! shift for yourself. Madam Victoria sent me to tell you that my master is returned and that he pretends to come as a masquerader.

MALAGENE.

Well! since it must be so, I'll deny all indeed! What an excellent fellow might I have been? Some men 495

now with my stock of honesty, and a little more gravity, would have made a fortune. Well, I have been a lazy rogue and never knew till now that I was fit for business. 500

MRS. GOODVILE.

Mr. Goodvile in masquerade, say you?

LETTICE.

Yes madam, and two women with him, madam; they are just now alighted.

MRS. GOODVILE.

Women with him! nay then, he comes triumphantly indeed.—Mr. Truman, do you retire with Malagene. I'll stay here and receive this Machiavel* in disguise. 505

[Exeunt Truman and Malagene.]

Now, once more let me invoke all the arts of affectation, all the revenge, the counterfeit passions, pretended love, pretended jealousy, pretended rage, and in sum, the very genius of my sex to my assistance. 510

Enter Goodvile and others masked [including footmen].

So! Here they come. Now this throw for all my future peace. Who waits there?

Enter servants.

GOODVILE.

Madam! You'll excuse this freedom.

MRS. GOODVILE.

You oblige me by using it.—Let all the company know that these noble persons of quality* have honored me with their presence. Let the fiddles be ready, and see the banquet prepared, and let Mr. Truman come to me instantly, I cannot live a minute, a moment without him. 515 520

[Exeunt servants.]

GOODVILE.

Delicate devil!

MRS. GOODVILE.

Sir! let me beg your patience for a moment, whilst I go and put things in order fit for your reception. (*Exit.*)

GOODVILE.

Footmen! take care that the engines which I have ordered be ready when I call for 'em. 525

[Exeunt footmen.]

---

39 Jew's trump] Jew's harp

Truman, I see, is a man of punctual assignation, and my wife is a person very adroit at these matters. Some hotbrained, horn-mad cuckold now would be for cutting of throats. But I am resolved to turn a civil, sober, discreet person, and hate bloodshed. No. I'll manage the matter so temperately that I'll catch her in his very arms, then civilly discard her, bag and baggage, whilst you, my dainty doxies, take possession of her privileges and enter the territories with colors flying. 530 535

FIRST WOMAN.

And shall I keep my coach, Mr. Goodvile?

GOODVILE.

Aye, and six, my lovely rampant.[40] Nay, thou shalt every morning swoop the Exchange* in triumph to see what gaudy bauble thou canst first grow fond of and afternoon at the theater exalted in a box give audience to every trim, amorous, twiring[41] fop of the corner that comes thither to make a noise, hear no play, and show himself, thou shalt, my bona roba.* 540 545

SECOND WOMAN.

But Mr. Goodvile, what shall I do then?

GOODVILE.

Oh! thou! thou shalt be my more peculiar punk, my housekeeper, my necessary sin, manage all the affairs of my estate and family, ride up and down in my own coach attended by my own footmen. Nose[42] my wife where you meet, and if I had any, breed my children. Oh what a delicious life will this be! 550

Fiddles without.

FIRST WOMAN.

Hear you, sir, the fiddles? 555

GOODVILE.

Oh, the procession's coming: put on your visors and observe the ceremony.

Enter Truman, Mrs. Goodvile, Caper, Saunter, Lady Squeamish, Camilla, with fiddles, a letter.

---

40 rampant] lustful, vicious person
41 twiring] giving sly glances (Ghosh)
42 Nose] turn up your nose at

MRS. GOODVILE.

Mr. Caper, Mr. Saunter, you are the life and soul of all good company: command me anything, command my house, that and all freedom are yours. 560

CAPER.

Masks! my life, my joy, my top of happiness!—Sir, your humble servant.—By your leave, madam, shall you and I toss and tumble together in the drawing room hard by for half an hour or so, hah? (*Cuts.**) 565

SAUNTER.

Fa toldera, toldara, etc. Ah madam, what do you wear a mask for? Have you never a nose or but one eye? Let me see how you are furnished?

SECOND WOMAN.

Sir, if I want* anything, 'tis to be doubted* you cannot supply me. 570

GOODVILE.

So! sure, this must come to something anon!

MRS. GOODVILE.

Ah were but Mr. Goodvile here now, what a happy day might this be! But he is melancholy and forlorn in the country, summoning in his tenants and their rents, that shining pelf that must support me in my pleasures. 575

GOODVILE.

Is he then, madam, so kind a husband?

MRS. GOODVILE.

Oh the most indulgent creature in the world!— What husband but he, Mr. Truman, would have so seasonably withdrawn and left me mistress of such freedom? to spend my days in triumph as I do, to sacrifice myself, my soul, and all my sense to you, the lord of all my joys, my conqueror and protector? 580

CAMILLA.

Heavens madam, you'll provoke him beyond all patience. 585

MRS. GOODVILE.

Who, Mr. Goodvile! Which way shall it reach his knowledge? No, we'll be as secret—

TRUMAN.

As we are happy. So subtly lay the scene of all our joys, that envy or malice, nay the very husband himself and Malagene to boot, well-hired to the business, shall ne'er discover us. 590

MRS. GOODVILE.

Oh, discover us! a husband discover us! Were he indeed as jealous as he has reason, I could no more apprehend discovery than a kindness* from him.

GOODVILE.

This impudence is so rank that I can hold no longer.—Say you so, madam? (*Unmasks.*)

MRS. GOODVILE.

Oh a ghost! a ghost! save me, save me, Mr. Truman, see, see, Mr. Goodvile's spirit! Sure some base villain has murdered him, and his angry ghost is come to revenge it on me.

GOODVILE.

No madam, fear nothing. I am a very harmless goblin, though you are a little shocked at the sight of me.

CAPER.

Ha, ha, ha, Goodvile returned? Dear Frank!

SAUNTER.

Honest Goodvile, thou seest, dear soul, we are free here in thy absence.

GOODVILE.

I see you are, gentlemen, and shall take an opportunity to return the favor. [*calls offstage.*] Footmen, be ready.

MRS. GOODVILE.

But is it really Mr. Goodvile then? Let me receive him to my arms. Welcome ten thousand, thousand, thousand times. Dear sir, how does my picture in the gallery do?

GOODVILE.

Oh madam, it looked so very charmingly that I had no power to stay longer from the dear loving original.

MRS. GOODVILE.

So, now begins the battle.

GOODVILE.

Well madam, and for your set of fools here, to what end and purpose have you decreed them in this new model of your family? I hope you have not designed 'em for your own use?

MRS. GOODVILE.

Why sir, methinks you should not grudge me a coxcomb or two to pass away the time withal, since you had taken your dearer conversation* from me.

GOODVILE.

No madam, I understand your diet better. A fool is too squab and tender a bit for your fierce appetite. You are for a substantial dish, a man of heat and honor, such as Mr. Truman I know is, and I doubt not will do me reason.

TRUMAN.

Aye sir, whenever you'll demand it.

MRS. GOODVILE.

Nay sirs, no quarrelling,* I beseech you. What would you be at, sir?

GOODVILE.

At rest madam, like an honest snail shrink up my horns into my shell and, if possible, hold a quiet possession of it.

MRS. GOODVILE.

I hope I have done nothing that may disturb your quiet, sir.

GOODVILE.

Nothing madam, nothing in the least. How is it possible that anything should disturb me! a sot,* a beetle, a drone of a husband, a mere utensil, a block for you to fashion all your falsehood on, whilst I must still* be stupid,* bear my office, and never be disturbed, I.

MRS. GOODVILE.

So, now your heart is opening, and for your ease, I'll give it a little vent myself. You are jealous, alas, jealous of Truman, are you?

GOODVILE.

And I have no reason, madam, though I come and catch you in his arms, rolling and throwing your wanton eyes like fireballs at his heart? Oh, what an indulgent creature's Mr. Goodvile! So seasonably to withdraw and leave you mistress of such freedom. To spend your days in triumph as you do, to sacrifice yourself, your soul and sense to him, the lord of all your joys, your conqueror and protector.

MRS. GOODVILE.

I am glad to find my plot so well succeed. I knew of your jealousy last night, knew too your journey out of Town was but a pretence in hope to return and surprise me with Truman. I was informed too of your return but now, and your disguise. I knew you through it so soon as I saw you, and therefore

I acted all that fondness to Truman before your face. It was all the revenge I had within my power.

GOODVILE.

Can you deny your being with Truman in the garden last night? Were you not there so openly, that even the broad eyes of fools might see? 665

MRS. GOODVILE.

What fool? What villain have you dares accuse me?

GOODVILE.

One, who though he rarely told truth before, will be sure to do it now. Malagene, your kinsman, Malagene, a hopeful branch of your own stock. 670

TRUMAN.

The rascal dares not own it.

GOODVILE.

But he shall, sir, though you protect him.

TRUMAN.

'Twas basely done to set a spy upon your friend after the trick you had played me with Victoria. 675

GOODVILE.

Basely done!

TRUMAN.

Yes, basely, sir.

GOODVILE.

Death, you lie, sir! Why do I trifle thus when I have a sword by my side?

CAPER.

Nay, look you, Frank! You had better be patient. 680
Here shall be nothing done; therefore, pray put up.

Enter Valentine.

VALENTINE.

What, again quarrelling?* Goodvile, this must not be. Truman is my friend and, if he has done you wrong, I'll engage, shall make you satisfaction.

SAUNTER.

Aye, aye, prithee man, take some other time and 685
don't quarrel now and spoil good company.

GOODVILE.

Death! you dancing, talking, mettled,[43] frisking rogues, stand off! Oh I had forgot— Footmen, where are ye?

Enter Footmen.

_____

[43] mettled] spirited or half drunk (*OED*)

Here, take away these butterflies and do speedy 690
execution upon 'em as I ordered, do it instantly.

They seize 'em.

CAPER.

Nay, Frank! what's all this for?

SAUNTER.

Nay, Goodvile, prithee, now as I hope to live—

Enter Malagene.

GOODVILE.

Away with 'em—

Exeunt [Footmen] with Caper and Saunter.

Now, for Malagene—oh, here he comes, madam, 695
who will refresh your memory! Speak sir: As you tender life and limb, whom did you see together in the garden last night?

MALAGENE.

Hah? nobody!

GOODVILE.

Were not Truman and my wife there, to your 700
knowledge, privately?

MALAGENE.

Ha, ha, ha—child!* no.

GOODVILE.

Did you not tell me that you overheard 'em whispering in the grotto together?

MALAGENE.

No. 705

GOODVILE.

Hell and devils! This fellow has been tampered withal and instructed to abuse me. This is all contrivance, a studied scene to fool me of my reason.

Enter Footmen.

Here, take him hence and harness him with the 710
other two till he confess the truth.

MRS. GOODVILE.

He shall not go, touch him who dares. Must people then be forced and tortured to accuse me falsely? Ah Mr. Goodvile, how have I deserved this at your hands? Let not my good name be ravished 715
from me. If you have resolved to break my heart, kill me now quickly and put me out of pain.

Malagene runs away.

GOODVILE.

Nay madam, here is that shall yet convince—see here a letter from your lover left for you in a private corner. Hear me read it. And if you have modesty enough left, blush. (*Reads.*) "If Goodvile goes out of town this morning, let me know of it that I may wait on you and tell you the rest of my heart. For you do not know how much I love you yet. Truman."

MRS. GOODVILE.

Death and destruction! It was all my own contrivance. Madded with your jealousy, I sought all ways to vex you. I counterfeited it with my own hand and left it in a place where you might be sure to find it. To convince you farther, see here a caution sent me just before by one whom you have trusted and loved too much for my quiet. Peruse it, and when you have done, consider how you have used me, and how I have deserved it. Oh. (*Gives Victoria's letter.*)

GOODVILE. (*Reads.*)

"Journey out of Town—is a pretence—return and surprise—believe by this discovery—Your servant, Victoria." Victoria, has she betrayed me? Nay then, I pronounce there is no trust nor faith in the sex. By Heaven, in every condition, they are all jilts, all false from the bawd to the babe.

MRS. GOODVILE.

Now sir, I hope I may withdraw. From this minute never expect I'll see your face again. No, I'll leave you to be happy at your own choice. Love where you please and be as free as if I ne'er had had relation to you. I shall take care to trouble you no more, but wish you may be happier than ever yet I made you.

GOODVILE.

Stay, madam.

MRS. GOODVILE.

No, sir, I'll be gone. I will not stay a moment longer. Inhuman, cruel, false traitor! Wert thou now languishing on thy knees, prostrate at my feet, ready to grow mad with thy own guilt, I would not stop nor turn my face to save thee from despair.

GOODVILE.

You shall.

MRS. GOODVILE.

For what?

GOODVILE.

To let the world see how much a fool I can be. Art thou innocent?

MRS. GOODVILE.

By my love I am, I never wronged you, but you have undone me, ruined my fame and quiet. What mouth will not be full of my dishonor? Henceforth, let all my sex remember me when they'd upbraid mankind for baseness. Oh, that I could dissemble longer with you that I might to your torment persuade you still all your jealousies were just, and I as infamous as you are cruel. (*Exit in a rage.*)

GOODVILE.

Get thee in, then, and talk to me no more, there's something in thy face will make a fool of me, and there's a devil in this business, which yet I cannot discover.—Truman, if thou hast enjoyed her, I beg thee keep it close, and if it be possible, let us yet be friends.

TRUMAN.

'Tis not my fault if we be foes.

GOODVILE.

But now to my fools, bring 'em forth and let us see how their new equipage becomes 'em.—Oh dear Valentine! how does the fair Camilla?

VALENTINE.

Faith sir, she and I have been dispatching a trifling affair this morning commonly called matrimony.

GOODVILE.

Married! nay, then there is some comfort yet that thou art fallen into the snare. Valentine! Look to her, keep her as secret as thou wouldst a murder, hadst thou committed one. Trust her not with thy dearest friend. She has beauty enough to corrupt him.

Enter [footmen with] Caper and Saunter, their hands tied behind 'em, fools caps on their heads. Caper with one leg tied up and Saunter gagged.

See here these rogues how like themselves they look.—Now, you paltry vermin, you rats that run squeaking from house to house, up and down the Town, that no man can eat his bread in quiet for

you. Take warning of what you feel, and come not 790
near these doors again on peril of hanging.——Here,
discharge them of their punishment, and see 'em
forth the gates.

[Exeunt footmen with Caper and Saunter.] Enter Lady
Squeamish, Sir Noble, and Victoria.

LADY SQUEAMISH.

Oh gallants, your humble servant.——Dear Mr.
Goodvile, be pleased to give my kinsman, Sir 795
Noble, joy. He has done himself the honor to
marry your cousin Victoria, whom now I must be
proud to call my relation, since she has accepted
of the title of my Lady Clumsy.

SIR NOBLE.

Aye sir, I am married, and will be drunk again too 800
before night, as simply as I stand here.

GOODVILE.

Sir Noble married? to Victoria too? nay, then in
spite of misfortunes——

This day shall be a day of jubilee.

But first—— 805
 Good people all that my sad fortune see,
 I beg you to take warning here by me:
Marriage and hanging go by Destiny.
Especially you gay young married blades,
Beware and keep your wives from balls and 810
 masquerades.

Exeunt omnes.

FINIS.

Textual Notes

[a] Copytext is the first edition, corrected state, a 1678
quarto (Q1b). Also consulted: modern editions in 1926
(Summers), 1932 (Ghosh).

[b] Goodvile's boy] servant all editions

[c] threshold place] threshold-place Q1, Summers, Ghosh

[d] voice] Summers, Ghosh; Vow Q1

A True Widow[a]

by Thomas Shadwell (c. 1641-1692)

edited by Christopher J. Wheatley

Thomas Shadwell was the victim of one of the most effective personal attacks in the English language: John Dryden's *MacFlecknoe*. Consequently Shadwell is remembered not as his contemporaries regarded him—Rochester, for instance, paired him with Wycherley as the two writers of true comedy—but as the heir to the throne of dullness. Dryden and Shadwell's literary and political rupture was not open at the time of *A True Widow*, since Dryden contributed a prologue; that does not demonstrate that *Macflecknoe* was not in circulation yet. It is not clear when, but at some point Shadwell confronted Dryden with *MacFlecknoe*, and Dryden denied authorship. Shadwell was the most talented of the comparatively few Whig playwrights, while Dryden was only the most prominent of the numerous Tory playwrights. Shadwell succeeded Dryden as poet-laureate in 1688 after the Glorious Revolution, and there has been no shortage of critics who have made Dryden a sympathetic victim of political forces. What is more rarely mentioned is that Dryden helped to bar Shadwell from the stage from 1681 until the Glorious Revolution and that Shadwell was a supporter of parliamentary restrictions upon Stuart absolutism.

But Shadwell was also at odds with his age in that he favored instructive humors comedy over the comedy of wit (although his own conversation was highly regarded for its wit). He had engaged in a lengthy public debate with Dryden, carried on in introductions to plays, over the relative importance of wit and judgment, and was also consistently a satirist of the libertine ethos of some Restoration drama. *A True Widow*, which probably premiered on March 21,

1678, failed miserably, according to Shadwell because of "the calamity of the time, which made people not care for diversions, or through the anger of a great many, who thought themselves concerned in the satyr." In short, Shadwell's political affiliation and satirical impulses combined to doom a play of which Shadwell was justly proud.

The play itself attacks numerous social abuses. Selfish's vanity bars him from knowing himself, Gartrude's idiocy makes her prefer Selfish to the gentlemanly (albeit waspish) Stanmore, Young Maggot pretends to wit though unfitted for it, and Prig makes the recreations of a gentleman the work of his life. Above all, Lady Cheatly trades on traditional assumptions about aristocratic honor to cheat the citizens, who, because of religious hypocrisy, richly deserve it. The play within a play, a terrifically funny parody of the comic sublime in sex comedies of the late 1670s (in particular Tom Durfey's *A Fond Husband*) derides the current taste for farce, a genre that avoids the theater's obligation to hold the mirror up to social vice. Only Carlos, Isabella, and the converted Bellamour believe not everything should be for sale in a world turned upside down.

Despite the satire, *A True Widow* has a comic plenitude matched by few plays of the period, and Shadwell was justified in saying in his own defense, "till I see more variety of new humor, than I have produced in my comedies, and more naturally drawn, I shall not despair of bearing up near my contemporaries of the first rate, who write comedy, and of always surmounting the little poetasters of the fourth rate, who condemn me."

DRAMATIS PERSONAE

[MEN]

Bellamour, a gentleman of the Town,* who had retired some time into the country.

Carlos, a gentleman returned from travel, with wit enough left to love his own country.

Stanmore, a gentleman of the Town.

Selfish, a coxcomb conceited of his beauty, wit, and breeding, thinking all women in love with him, always admiring and talking of himself.

Old Maggot, an old credulous fellow, a great enemy to wit, and a great lover of business for business' sake.

Young Maggot, his nephew: an Inns of Court* man, who neglects his law and runs mad after wit, pretending much to love, and both in spite of nature, since his face makes him unfit for one and his brains for the other.

Prig, a coxcomb that never talks or thinks of anything but dogs, horses, hunting, hawking, bowls, tennis, and gaming; a rook,* a most noisy jockey.[1]

Lump, a methodical blockhead, as regular as a clock and goes as true as a pendulum, one that knows what he shall do every day of his life by his almanac, where he sets down all his actions beforehand, a mortal enemy to wit.

[WOMEN]

Lady Cheatly, the true widow, that comes to Town and makes a show of a fortune to put off herself and her two daughters.

Isabella, her eldest, a woman of wit and virtue.

Gartrude, her youngest, very foolish and whorish.

Theodosia, a young lady of wit and fortune, beloved by Carlos.[b]

Lady Busy, a woman of intrigue, very busy in love matters of all kinds, too old for love of her own, always charitably helping forward that of others, very fond of young women, very wise and discreet, half bawd, half matchmaker.

Steward to Lady Cheatly.

---

[1] jockey] cant term for one who cheats at games

Players, doorkeepers, and many other persons, the audience to the play in the play.

Scene: London.

A True Widow.

Odi profanum Vulgus & arceo.[2]

Act I, [scene i. Bellamour's chamber.]

Enter Bellamour and Stanmore.

STANMORE.

Come Bellamour, what not dressed yet? Methinks after so long a fast from wit and fine women as you have had in the country, you should be sharper set after both than to fool away a morning thus in your chamber.   5

BELLAMOUR.

There is a respect due from a country gentleman to a new suit and peruke: they must not be hastily put on. And the women of this Town, if you don't take care of your own outside, will never let you be acquainted with their insides.   10

STANMORE.

Thou art mistaken: men succeed now according to the clothes they give, not those they wear.

BELLAMOUR.

Amongst your little whores, Stanmore.

STANMORE.

And amongst your great whores too Bellamour. I knew a gentleman who was so ugly, a modish spark   15
would scarce have given him a livery, yet by a correspondence he kept with a tailor and shoemaker at Paris and two or three of that sort, got one of the finest women in England.

BELLAMOUR.

How so?   20

STANMORE.

Why she had always the fashion a month before any of the court-ladies, never wore anything made in England, scarce washed there, and had all the affected new words sent her before they were in

---

[2] *Odi … arceo*] Horace, *Odes*, 3.1.1: I hate the uninitiate crowd and keep them far away.

print, which made her pass among fops for a kind 25
of French wit.

BELLAMOUR.

But were not these French petticoats, though given
by one man, taken up by many?

STANMORE.

'Faith I think not, she considered her own vanity
above any man's address, though one lord made 30
coaches at her, another squeezed in his fat sides at
her, till he looked like a full sack; a third writ
lamentable sonnets to her; a fourth observed her
motions in the park, which, by the way is the new
method of making love.* 35

BELLAMOUR.

What, do they make love without speaking to one
another?

STANMORE.

A great many very fine gentlemen, to look at, better
than with it: your side glass[3] let down hastily, when
the party goes by, is very passionate if she side-glass 40
you again, for that's the new word. Ply her next day
with a billet-doux and you have her sure.

BELLAMOUR.

What if we chance to go the same way, or she won't
receive my billet-doux, as you call it?

STANMORE.

For the first, it must never chance; you must 45
instruct your coachman. And for the second, after
such an advance as side-glassing of you, if she
refuse your billet, she is a jilt, and you must rail
at her in all companies.

BELLAMOUR.

I am pretty good at railing, but not so good as thou 50
art, Stanmore.

STANMORE.

I had forgotten half: you must turn as she turns,
quit the Park* when she goes out, pass by her twice
or thrice between that and St. James's,* talk to her
at night in the Drawing Room*— 55

BELLAMOUR.

Before forty coxcombs, and then the business is
sufficiently proclaimed, is it not, think you?

STANMORE.

'Tis all one, it must be so, or you will pass for an

___
3 side glass] coach window, often opaque

old-fashioned lover and never succeed beyond a
chambermaid. 60

BELLAMOUR.

This is a folly of our own growth: it came not to
us out of France.

STANMORE.

That nation has at this time no folly so harmless.

BELLAMOUR.

But if there be any stirring of what kind soever,
our empty young fellows will be sure to fill 65
themselves with it and prefer it to all the sense and
good breeding of their own country. But now we
talk of France, I wonder we see not Carlos; he was
expected from thence two or three nights since.

Enter Carlos.

STANMORE.

See where he comes. Dear Carlos, I could not run 70
more hastily upon my mistress after a long absence;
thou art the delight of all thy friends, and even thy
enemies take a malignant pleasure to behold that
shape, that feature, and that mien.

CARLOS.

Hold Stanmore, I think thou takest me for a 75
mistress indeed by thy compliments, which I know
not how to return.

STANMORE.

Thou art so improved, a man must love as I do
not to envy thee.

CARLOS.

Enough Stanmore, your friendship blinds you— 80
(*Aside.*) I never knew any of these loving rogues
good for anything.—Bellamour, I am overjoyed to
see thee here! I heard thou hadst forsworn the Town.

BELLAMOUR.

Now I see Carlos here, methinks I am a perfect
man of the Town again; I only forswore it for a 85
time. 'Faith, money is a thing gotten in ill
company and spent in good; I have been laying
up.

CARLOS.

Men-of-war after a warm engagement must into
the docks to be new built for fight. 90

BELLAMOUR.

Right, but how goes matters in France? What new
foppery is turned up trump there?

CARLOS.

What with governors, ladies' eldest sons, ambassadors and envoys, you have 'em here almost as soon as the French themselves. 95

STANMORE.

No alteration since we were there?

CARLOS.

Wit and women are quite out of fashion, so are *flûtes douces*[4] and fiddlers: drums and trumpets are their only music.

BELLAMOUR.

'Tis but ill music for their neighbors. 100

CARLOS.

At home they are always roaring out *Te Deums* for stealing[5] of some town or other: war and equipage is their discourse, which by the way is so pompous, that should they conquer Europe they should scarce be savers. 105

STANMORE.

How came wit and women out of fashion?

CARLOS.

Why, in camps they learn to live without women, and for wit, great men that love to play the fool in quiet find it troublesome.

BELLAMOUR.

'Faith the latter of these is a great grievance here; 110 our great men hate wit, but love damned flattery, though never so fulsome.

CARLOS.

Pray what fools does this Town afford?

STANMORE.

Very choice ones, we'll bring you where you shall enjoy 'em. There is a widow lately come to Town who 115 sets up for a great fortune, has taken a good house, and lives very splendidly, I suppose with intention to put off herself and two daughters, who are very pretty, one of which Bellamour is in love with.

BELLAMOUR.

I make love* to her, I confess, but 'tis a harmless, 120 lambent flame and aims but at fornication. But

Stanmore is in love with the other, and Heaven knows what that may end in.

STANMORE.

I have no designs upon her fortune, I aim only at her person; I yet run at the whole herd. 125

CARLOS.

Come, you know your own tempers no more in love than in play, where those who are very stingy at first, will bleed deeply at last.

BELLAMOUR.

This widow, by name the Lady Cheatly, has made her house the rendezvouz of fools, knaves, 130 whoremasters, ladies of all sorts, and young heirs. Amongst the rest of fops, there is Young Maggot, one whom his uncle, whose heir he is, bred at the Inns of Court* and intended for the law. But he has left that and is run wit-mad, thinks of nothing, 135 endeavors at nothing but to be a wit and a lover, and both in spite of nature.

STANMORE.

And though he has made love and wit his whole business, he is gotten no further yet than to be thought a wit by the fools and an ass by the witty men. 140

CARLOS.

This is a choice spirit. Indeed, 'tis a general folly, for wit is a common idol that every coxcomb worships in his heart, though some blockheads of business dissemble it.

BELLAMOUR.

But there is another coxcomb of that extreme 145 vanity that Nature amongst all her variety of fops has not produced the like: he draws all lines of discourse to the center of his own person and never was known to speak, but "I did" or "I said" was at the beginning or end of it. 150

STANMORE.

He is lean as a skeleton and yet sets up for shape; he changed his tailor twice, because his shoulder bone sticks out.

BELLAMOUR.

He thinks all women in love with him and all men his intimate friends; he will make *doux yeux*[6] 155 to a judge upon the bench and not despair of getting a widow at her husband's funeral; thinks

---

4 *flûtes douces*] gentle or soft flutes (Fr.)

5 stealing] In the 1670s under Louis XIV, the "chamber of reunion" was established to find legal grounds for French claims on cities, which Louis would promptly annex.

6 *doux yeux*] loving glances, sheep's eyes (Fr.)

himself very well bred and welcome at all times to all people, though sober among drunkards, and without a penny in his pocket to men deep at play.

CARLOS.
Oh! I remember this coxcomb, he has no fortune, and yet is always talking of equipage and dressing: 'tis Selfish. But do any women favor that fop?

STANMORE.
Oh yes! There is no more account to be given of their love before they know man, than their longings after, but both are most commonly for nauseous, nasty things.

CARLOS.
They do most things by chance, but when they choose, 'tis ever for the worst.

Enter footman.

FOOTMAN.
Mr. Selfish is combing his peruke below stairs and will be here instantly.

BELLAMOUR.
Retire while I show him.

*[Exit footman. Carlos and Stanmore] retire. Enter Selfish, sets his peruke, and bows to the glass.**

SELFISH.
How dost thou do, Bellamour? You fat fellows have always glasses that make one look so thin.

BELLAMOUR.
You look in it much as you do out on't.

SELFISH.
Sure I am not so lean; I was told I looked pretty plump today.—Hah! My damned rogue has put me into the most bustling stuff. Bellamour, I like thy breeches well.

BELLAMOUR.
Why, you don't see 'em.

SELFISH.
Yes, I see 'em in the glass. Your tailor shall make mine! A pox on my *valet de chambre*, how he has tied my cravat up today; a man cannot get a good *valet de chambre*, French or English.

BELLAMOUR.
A French one is fittest for him, because he can fast best.

SELFISH.
I begin to belly, I think, very much: I must go into France and flux; 'twill do my complexion good as well as my shape.

BELLAMOUR.
Why, thou art fit to be hung up at Barber-Surgeons-Hall[7] for a skeleton; a woman had as good lie with a fagot.

SELFISH.
Thou art envious; the ladies are of another mind. I am sure you are above whoremasters' weight, and a woman had as good lie with a pound of candles.[8]

BELLAMOUR.
Enough of this. There is a friend of mine, one Carlos, lately come from France, that understands dressing; I must bring you together.

SELFISH.
You talk of my leanness, I had the most lucky adventure: I was happy in the conversation* of a pretty person of quality,* young and witty; I went in a coach with my hand in her neck from the Duke's Playhouse[9] to the Pall Mall,* kissing her all the way.

BELLAMOUR.
There is a thing happened to me, in which I have occasion for your assistance and advice.

SELFISH.
I have lately succeeded in the affections of so many pretty creatures, faith, I know not how to turn my hands to 'em, poor rogues. If you did but see the advances that all the ladies that come to the widow's and her daughters make to me, you would stand amazed, and so should I, but that I am used to those things.

CARLOS.
This fool is much improved since I went into France.

STANMORE.
Fools always improve in folly, as witty men in understanding.

---

7 Barber-Surgeons-Hall] home of the guild for barber-surgeons, who both cut hair and practiced a primitive form of medicine

8 candles] Inexpensive candles were made with tallow (fat).

9 Duke's Playhouse] Dorset Garden, where this play was itself produced

CARLOS.

Indeed, he has great acquired parts.*

SELFISH.

Bellamour, fare thee well, I must go home and answer two or three billet-doux from persons of quality; I have a bushel in a year. Adieu. (*Exit.*)   220

CARLOS.

A most admirable coxcomb: he is so full of himself, he ne'er minds another man and so answers quite from the purpose.

BELLAMOUR.

He never answers any man nor cares to be answered; he desires but to be heard. But come Carlos, let's take the air and while away a dining time.   225

CARLOS.

I hate a dinner: 'tis a good meal for a dull plodding fellow of business that must bait like a carrier's horse and then to plodding again, but the supper is the meal of pleasure and enjoyment.   230

STANMORE.

Supping indeed is a solemn thing and should be used but with few; every blockhead can dine.

BELLAMOUR.

That is, fill a belly, but there are few men fit to sup: there's more than eating required for that mystery; there must be wit and sense.   235

Enter Young Maggot.

YOUNG MAGGOT.

Your servant gentlemen. I see, Bellamour, you are going abroad. I only come to show you my last verses.

BELLAMOUR.

Your last verses! I would I could be so happy as to see them.   240

YOUNG MAGGOT.

You have company, and I have business; some other time.

BELLAMOUR.

What business?

YOUNG MAGGOT.

Why, wit and beauty, I know no other. I am longed for by the ladies now to give account of the play, for the poets will not write, the players act, nor the ladies censure without my judgment first.   245

BELLAMOUR.

The ladies are indeed your finger watches, that go just as you set them.   250

YOUNG MAGGOT.

Faith, that's very well imagined, well said. I think thou hast near^c as much wit as one of us writers.

CARLOS.

What is your opinion of the play?

YOUNG MAGGOT.

I saw it scene by scene and helped him in the writing. It breaks well, the *protasis* good, the *catastasis* excellent, there's no *episode*, but the *catastrophe*[10] is admirable—I lent him that and the love parts and the songs. There are a great many sublimes[11] that are very poetical.   255

STANMORE.

Poetical, in his judgment, is always fustian and nonsense in another's. I warrant 'tis some roaring, ranting play that's upon the fret all the while.   260

BELLAMOUR.

Will you carry us to a rehearsal?

YOUNG MAGGOT.

'Tis a familiarity among us writers to see one another naked. You are men of wit and desperate critics, and we poets fear you as singing birds do a hawk.   265

CARLOS.

Thank you for your hawk.

YOUNG MAGGOT.

Aye, was it not well said?

CARLOS.

But methinks fools should be your only enemies.

YOUNG MAGGOT.

They can't hurt us; besides, a dedication, writing   270

---

10 *protasis … catastrophe*] As Montague Summers suggests, Shadwell probably derives this passage from Dryden's *Of Dramatick Poesie*, where Eugenius describes the parts of a play as the "*Protasis*, or entrance, which gives light only to the characters of the persons"; the "*Epitasis*, or working up of the plot"; "the *Catastasis*, called by the Romans, *Status*, the height and full growth of the play"; and "Lastly, the *Catastrophe* . . . the discovery, or unravelling of the plot." Eugenius does not mention the *episode*, which means an incidental narration or digression.

11 sublimes] instances of elevated style, especially as recently made fashionable through Boileau's translation of Longinus's treatise *On the Sublime*

songs for their mistresses, or showing them a play before hand will take them off.

Enter footman.

FOOTMAN.

Sir, Mr. Prig is coming up. [*Exit.*]

YOUNG MAGGOT.

Now shall we be troubled with fools; a man can never enjoy thee half an hour to himself, thou art so haunted with fops. 275

BELLAMOUR.

How insupportable the rogues are to one another.

CARLOS.

What is this Prig?

STANMORE.

He is an universal gamester, an admirable horse and dog herald, knows all the remarkable ones, 280 their families, and alliances, is indeed more intimately acquainted with beasts than men, and 'tis fit he should be so.

BELLAMOUR.

He is, in short, a led-eater,[12] intelligencer, and dry-jester[13] to gaming- and jockey-lords; flatters, rooks, 285 and passes for a jolly companion amongst 'em; and makes those things which are but the recreations of men of sense his whole business.

Enter Prig.

PRIG.

Gentlemen good morrow, though I think 'tis almost noon. Where were you last night? If you 290 had been at my Lord Squanders, you had seen the best play you had seen this month. My lord lost a thousand pound, Jack Sharper won three hundred, Tom Whiskin an hundred, my Lord Whimsey lost five hundred, Sir Thomas Rantipol lost six 295 hundred, Sir Nicholas Wachum won two hundred, and the rooks were very busy.

STANMORE.

Then you were not idle?

PRIG.

No, faith. But I am come to get you to look upon the best bred horse in England. Woodcock was his 300 grandfather; he is the son of Bay-lusty and the brother of Red Rose; his sister is the white mare,

the cousin-german of Crack-a-fart, cousin once removed to Nutmeg, third cousin to my Lord Squander's colt, allied to Flea-bitten by the second 305 venter. In short he is of an excellent family, and I am going to make a civil visit to him. He's to run for the plate at Brackley, Stamford, and Newmarket,[14] and goes out of Town tomorrow.

BELLAMOUR.

We cannot see him, we're engaged. 310

PRIG.

Engaged! No, faith, let's make a match at tennis today. I was invited to dine by two or three lords, but if you will let me have pen, ink, and paper, I'll send my dispatches and disengage myself. How will that gentleman and you play with Stanmore, 315 and I keep his back hand at Gibbons'?[15]

BELLAMOUR.

I do not know his play.

PRIG.

We'll take a bisque of you.

BELLAMOUR.

No, you shan't.

PRIG.

You're half fifteen better than I to a grain.[16] 320

STANMORE.

No, that he is not.

PRIG.

I never heard the like in my life. Gad, you'll never let me make a reasonable match with you; you beat Sharper at a bisque, and he beats me. What will Stanmore and you give Maggot and me at 325 Whitehall[17] and play the best of your play? hah?

YOUNG MAGGOT.

I never play, I stay at home and write.

PRIG.

Pish, 'tis all one for that: we'll play with you at a bisque and a fault for twenty pound.

YOUNG MAGGOT.

I will not, sir. 330

---

12 led-eater] a parasite or sychophant
13 dry-jester] one whose jokes fall flat

14 Brackley … Newmarket] sites of racetracks all round England
15 Gibbons'] tennis court
16 bisque … grain] Prig seeks a handicap.
17 Whitehall] Whitehall* contained tennis courts, a cockpit, and grounds for tilting and bear-baiting.

PRIG.

Come, I'll hold you twenty pound you do not
make a fairer match. Let me see—hold—anon—
hum—hah—aye—'tis just so to a hair's breadth.
Come, we'll play it.[18]

BELLAMOUR.

I tell you I am engaged today.   335

PRIG.

We'll play or pay tomorrow at ten. Where shall we
sup?

STANMORE.

Nowhere, you cannot sup.

PRIG.

Not sup?

BELLAMOUR.

No, you are not fit to sup.   340

PRIG.

No? I am sure I have as good a stomach and will eat
two meals a day with any man that wears a head.

CARLOS.

That will not do.

PRIG.

No? I'll eat three then. What say you, Maggot, will
you play?   345

YOUNG MAGGOT.

I will never play as long as I live at that or any
thing else while I can have pen, ink, and paper.

PRIG.

Oh Lord! Oh Lord! I would not say so for all the
world.

BELLAMOUR.

A man must use exercise to keep himself down,   350
he will belly else, and the ladies will not like him.

YOUNG MAGGOT.

I have another way to bring down my belly.

STANMORE.

Another? What's that?

YOUNG MAGGOT.

Why, I study, I study and write. 'Tis exercise of
the mind does it. I have none of the worst shapes   355
or complexions. 'Tis writing and inventing does
my business.

CARLOS.

Will that do't, sir?

PRIG.

Think? What a pox should a gentleman think of
but dogs, horses, dice, tennis, bowls, races, or   360
cockfighting? The devil take me, I never think of
anything else, but now and then of a whore (when
I have a mind to her).

CARLOS.

This is strange, Mr. Maggot, and very curious.
How do you know how much you fall away in a   365
day's time?

YOUNG MAGGOT.

I have an engine* to weigh myself when I sit down
to write or think and when I unbend myself again.

PRIG.

How do you unbend?

YOUNG MAGGOT.

Why, I unbend my imagination, my intellect.   370

PRIG.

Your intellect? Pray sir, what's that? Is't a new word
for a crossbow?

YOUNG MAGGOT.

How I scorn fops! Why, I have been in love these
two months, and I have wasted above fourteen
pound. Love is a great preserver of the shape, a very 375
great one. You know my mistress, the widow's
youngest daughter.

CARLOS.

This is a curious coxcomb.

PRIG.

Love! Aye, if a man gets a clap, 'twill take him
down.   380

YOUNG MAGGOT.

May it take down your nose,* you unthinking
animal.

PRIG.

What a devil does he mean?

YOUNG MAGGOT.

Why, I weighed myself when I writ my last song,
and I wasted six ounces *aver du pois*[19] weight in   385
the writing. And I was not above twelve hours
about it.

---

18 Let … it] Unclear, but perhaps Prig is measuring
Bellamour's rooms for a tennis court; tennis was played
indoors and does not much resemble the modern game.

19 *aver du pois*] avoirdupois; the spelling indicates the Anglicization of pronunciation.

CARLOS.

I beseech you, let's hear it, sir.

YOUNG MAGGOT.

With all my heart.

Damon see how charming Chloris,   390
    Who gives love to all that see her,
Burning us yet in coldness, glories
    And is never never freer.
Though darts and flames from her eye fly, sir,
    And her breast is warm and spicy,   395
Yet there is coldness in her eye, sir,
    And her heart's all over icy.
By coldness I am more inflamed,
    As in winter is springwater;
My love by scorn cannot be tamed,   400
    But I the rather would be at her.

PRIG.

Did this make you waste six ounces? I writ a song
t'other day, and it did not make me waste at all.

BELLAMOUR.

Prithee Prig, let's hear it.

PRIG. (Sings.)

One night walking in a wood   405
    I met one was a maid as good
        As e're she could,
        But she fired my blood,
        And to her I stood.
With a hey boys, ding, ding, ding boys hey,   410
With a hey boys, ding, ding, ding.

Quoth I, my pretty buxom lass,
From me this time thou shalt not pass.
        In any case,
        For the sake of thy face!   415
        I'll lay thee on the grass.
With a hey boys, ding, etc.

YOUNG MAGGOT.

Oh what violence does he to my ears.

PRIG.

What, he does not like it? Pox! These wits like
nothing but what they do themselves. I love a   420
tavern song that will roar and make one merry. A
pox of his Strephons and Phillises.

BELLAMOUR.

What will become of you, Young Maggot? Your

Uncle Maggot, that common foe to wit, is coming
up.   425

YOUNG MAGGOT.

Hide me, gentlemen, hide me. I am undone if he
finds me in your company.

BELLAMOUR.

Step in there.

Young Maggot retires. Enter Maggot.

MAGGOT.

Gentlemen, I come to look out an ungracious
nephew of mine, who I hear by virtue of your   430
company sets up for a wit. Will any of you keep
him when you have made him good for nothing?

BELLAMOUR.

Good for nothing! Why, he is the darling of the
ladies: they dote on him for his songs and fear him
for his lampoons. And the men think no debauch   435
perfect without him.

MAGGOT.

Yes, I hear he writ a libel. I shall have him scribble
away his ears or write himself so far into the ladies'
favors to lose his nose* or be knocked o'th'head.
These are the fruits of wit.   440

CARLOS.

The disasters rather.

MAGGOT.

The world will bear with you that have estates,
though you have a little, but 'tis enough to undo
a man that is to make his fortune. My roguy
nephew must leave Cook upon Littleton for   445
Beaumont and Fletcher.[20]

STANMORE.

Poetry is an ornament to a man of any profession.

MAGGOT.

'Tis a damned weed and will let nothing good or
profitable grow by it; 'tis the language of the Devil
and begun with oracles. Where did you know a   450
wit thrive or indeed keep his own?

---

20 Cook … Fletcher] Coke upon Littleton, that is, Sir Edward Coke's (1552-1634) commentary on Sir Thomas
Littleton's (1422-1481) treatise on tenures, would have
been a law student's first book. Francis Beaumont (1584-
1616) and John Fletcher (1579-1625) collaborated on
numerous plays in the early seventeenth century.

CARLOS.

They part with their money for pleasure, and fools part with their pleasure for money; the one will make a better last will and testament, but the other lead a happier life. 455

YOUNG MAGGOT.

Profit be gone, what art thou but a breath.
I'll live proud of my infamy and shame,
Graced with the triumphs of a poet's name;
Men can but say, wit did my reason blind,
And wit's the noblest frailty of the mind. 460
Methinks it runs well thus.

MAGGOT.

What noise is that? Hah! My ungracious nephew repeating verses. Come out you rascal. Dost thou not tremble at my anger? Thou that mightest have been a judge in time, to make a wit of thyself thus! 465

BELLAMOUR.

Good sir, be patient. Did not the great pleader Cicero make verses?

MAGGOT.

And you see what came on't: he died a beggar and of a violent death.

YOUNG MAGGOT.

Sir, the verses were not my own. 470

MAGGOT.

Sir, be gone to the Temple,* and let me once more find you at wit, and I'll disinherit you.

YOUNG MAGGOT.

Good sir, hear me.

MAGGOT.

Be gone, I say.

CARLOS.

This is ridiculous enough and odd. 475

BELLAMOUR.

There is a powerful faction against wit.

STANMORE.

Come, let's take the air.

Exeunt omnes.

[Scene ii. Lady Cheatly's lodgings.]

Enter Lady Cheatly and Mr. Lump, her brother.

LUMP.

I see, lady sister, you are resolved to push on the remnant of your estate and make the snuff* of your fortune burn clearest.

LADY CHEATLY.

As my fortune was, it would do us no good. But this Town, and the way I take, may advance it, or 5 at least dispose of my own person.

LUMP.

You shall not want* my money, so long as I have deeds of trust from you; you shall have the name on't. I have helped you to sober, solid, godly men, who will help to carry on your design. 10

LADY CHEATLY.

Some cautious old fellow or other (who is wise enough to have his own wisdom contribute to the cheating of him) may snap at me, and some rash, amorous, young fellows may catch at my daughters.

LUMP.

I wish you had set up in the City* among our party 15 and gone to meetings; it might have been a great advantage. I myself have made much benefit of religion, as to my temporal concerns, and (so long as it be directed to a good end) it is a pious fraud and very lawful. 20

LADY CHEATLY.

No, brother, the godly have two qualities which would spoil my design: great covetousness (which would make 'em pry too narrowly into our fortune) and much eating (which would too soon devour what I have left). 25

LUMP.

Reproach not the godly, lady sister, I do not like it.

LADY CHEATLY.

Where is there a better market for beauty than near the Court? And who will more likely snap at the shadow of a good fortune than the gentlemen of this end of the Town, who are most of 'em in debt? 30 And I have chosen the best instrument in the world to make 'em believe me rich.

LUMP.

Who is that?

LADY CHEATLY.

A very busy old gentleman and very credulous, that loves to tell news and always magnifies a true story 35 till it becomes a lie, one Mr. Maggot.

LUMP.

I know he is a person of parts,* but he is not solid, he's hot-brained, and has not method in him. For my own part, I think not anyone wise who does

not know what he shall do this day fifty years, if 40
he lives. I for my part do.

LADY CHEATLY.

I hope 'tis dining with me, brother.

LUMP.

No, upon the one and twentieth of March I shall
fifty years hence dine with Mr. Ananias Felt, an
elder of our church, if we live and he observe his 45
method. My journal tells what I shall do each day
of my life.

LADY CHEATLY.

Can you tell what you shall do next Midsummer
Day fifty years?

LUMP.

I shall go down to my house in Kent. 50

LADY CHEATLY.

Do you never alter your day?

LUMP.

By no means: if one link of the chain be broken,
wisdom falls to the ground.

LADY CHEATLY.

What do you do upon the sixth of May come fifty
year? 55

LUMP.

This book will tell you—May—May—6th—6th.
Let me see—6th—I take physic and shave myself.

LADY CHEATLY.

What, sick or well, beard or no beard?

LUMP.

'Tis all one for that, I never break my method—
Let me see—the next day—I walk to Hampstead, 60
dine at the Queens Head, come back in my coach,
visit Sir Formal Trifle,21 and at night I do
communicate with my wife.

LADY CHEATLY.

Not fifty years hence; you'll go near to break that
method. 65

LUMP.

I never break any—no man can be wise without
this principle—but sister, I am to give you a main
caution: have a care of wits at this end of the Town;

wits are good for nothing, of no use in a
commonwealth, they understand not business. 70

LADY CHEATLY.

The better for my purpose. They value pleasure
and will bid high for't.

LUMP.

I say they are good for nothing; they are not men
of method and business.

LADY CHEATLY.

So fools say, who seem to be excellent men of 75
business, because they always make a business of
what is none and seem to be always very
industrious, because they take great pains for what
a witty man does with ease.

LUMP.

You are out, you are out. Hang 'em wits, when did 80
you see any of 'em rise?

LADY CHEATLY.

No, because the fools are so numerous and strong,
they keep 'em down, or rather, because men of wit
(that have fortunes) know what a senseless thing
the drudgery of business and authority is, and 85
those that have none, want* the impudence,
flattery, and importunity of blockheads.

LUMP.

I fear you are tainted, vilely tainted with wit. If you
had fixed in the City, you might have 'scaped the
infection; nobody would have put you in the head 90
of wit there. But hold, my hour is come: At three
a clock I will throw away a quarter of an hour
upon you. Farewell. (Exit.)

LADY CHEATLY.

Who waits there?

Enter steward.

Oh my good steward! Are the scriveners come? 95

STEWARD.

Yes, madam, your design prospers beyond our
hopes; it has taken fire like a train22 and run
through all the Town, and all believe you to be a
great fortune.

LADY CHEATLY.

I have chosen as proper an engine* for my business 100
as can be, my Lady Busy, a perpetual gossiper and

---

21 Sir Formal Trifle] an "Orator, a florid Coxcomb" in
Shadwell's *The Virtuoso*, played by Tony Leigh very suc-
cessfully just two years before this play. Did Leigh play
Lump? If so, the reflexivity is multiple.

22 train] a trail of gunpowder

visiter in all families, a very wise lady, a great tattle and newsmonger, who, being something too old for an intrigue of her own, is as good a body to help on those of others as can be and is glad to bring lovers of any kind together.

STEWARD.

Already the belief of your wealth has spread so far that I have had two of the City this morning with me (who having been shrewdly bitten* by goldsmiths) are very desirous to trust their money in your hands, hearing what mortgages you have and believing you can employ it better than anybody.

LADY CHEATLY.

You did not, sure, refuse 'em?

STEWARD.

No, I'll warrant you, madam, they will bring their money presently. Mr. Maggot too entreats me that I will be very importunate with your ladyship to employ a thousand pound of his for him.

LADY CHEATLY.

There needs no importunity, subtle rogue. He thinks to lay it here for a nest egg and that I shall lay many more to it, which he hopes he may have again together with my person.

STEWARD.

No, madam, 'tis held in mortmain, never to return again. Besides, we have presents enough to keep your house this month brought in this morning: a red deer potted, a brace of fat does, hams of Bayonne bacon, a brace of swans, potted chars, brant geese, and (besides all this) a piece[23] of the best wine in England. Here are the names of the presenters.

LADY CHEATLY.

Let me see: all well-willers to myself or daughters; cunning fools—how very politic they are! Well, policy is most commonly the foolishest thing in the world.

STEWARD.

Madam, there are a great many waiting about money-business without. Shall I call any of 'em in?

LADY CHEATLY.

By no means when I am alone. When company is

with me, they are of use and spread my fame abroad. Entertain 'em well and bid 'em hasten dinner.

Exeunt omnes.

Act II, [scene i. Lady Cheatly's lodgings.]

Enter Lady Cheatly and Lady Busy.

LADY CHEATLY.

Madam, I am so infinitely obliged to your ladyship, who can be so careful of my whole family.

LADY BUSY.

Why truly madam, I love to do good offices. We are bound in Christian charity to one another, and I wished Mr. Maggot to your ladyship, if he be not somewhat too old for the vigor of your ladyship: he is rich and is discreet, and his other defects may be supplied elsewhere.

LADY CHEATLY.

Your ladyship's very obliging.

LADY BUSY.

If not, there's Mr. Prig, an ingenious gentleman of a pretty fortune, whom I wished to you. He is in great favor with lords; I warrant you, you shall seldom take him without a lord in his mouth, they do so court him: they love him mightily.

LADY CHEATLY.

And he loves lords mightily for being so.

LADY BUSY.

Oh mightily! Well madam, your two daughters are accounted the beauties of the Drawing Room;* there's nobody while they are there[d] will vouchsafe to look upon a maid of honor, no, not they, and they are as mad at it.

LADY CHEATLY.

'Tis not the beauty of my daughters makes 'em look at 'em so, but they like an indifferent new face better than those faces they are used to every night. They are weary of 'em.

LADY BUSY.

Oh no, really, your daughters are the prettiest creatures in Town, and I would fain have 'em well settled, one way or other. I have had several offers of husbands for 'em, but I do not think I have yet met with fortunes good enough. But that great lord I told you of is very pressing to enjoy your eldest, and as I said, he offers a thousand pounds

---

23 piece] a cask of wine equivalent to the butt, holding between 108 and 140 gallons

down and three hundred per annum during life.
But that I know your ladyship is discreet and one
that has seen the world, I dared not have
propounded this to you.   35

LADY CHEATLY.

My daughters have fortunes enough to marry 'em
to good estates, but your ladyship is wise: 'tis good
to treat with all persons, and all ways, to settle a
young—girl in the world.

LADY BUSY.

Why madam, this will be a great addition to her   40
fortune, and besides, you do not know how he
may prefer her, or for ought we know, after he has
tried her, he may like her so well as to own her—
who knows? Be pleased to consider how marriage
is cried down and that there are few that are good   45
for anything will think on't nowadays; besides,
custom alters all things mightily: mothers very
frequently do this for their daughters now, and if
it be a fashion, you know—

LADY CHEATLY.

I am very much obliged to your ladyship's advice.   50
I have propounded it to my daughter, but she is
so perverse, she will not listen to me but says she
had rather marry a groom than be mistress to a
prince.

LADY BUSY.

Oh fie, she has a wrong notion of the thing. I will   55
try to advise her better.

LADY CHEATLY.

Your ladyship will do me a great favor. Here they
come both.

Enter Isabella and Gartrude.

LADY BUSY.

Ladies, your servant.

ISABELLA, GARTRUDE.

Your ladyship's most humble servant.   60

LADY BUSY.

Mrs. Isabella, I have something to advise you for
your good.

ISABELLA.

For my good, madam?

LADY BUSY.

Yes madam, and therefore be pleased to give
attention to me.   65

ISABELLA.

Good manners will make me do that.

LADY BUSY.

Why look you, you are young, I am in years, an
ancient woman, and have seen the world, as they
say.

ISABELLA.

Ancient? Your ladyship looks very youthfully.   70

LADY BUSY.

No, no, you are pleased to compliment me, but
as I said, my lady and myself have known the
world, as the saying is.

ISABELLA. (*Aside.*)

And you the flesh and the devil,[24] as the saying
is.   75

LADY BUSY.

And 'tis fit the young should submit themselves to
the gravity and discretion of the old.

ISABELLA.

Yes, where they can find it.

LADY BUSY.

Go to*—my lady is a person whose aim is to settle
you well in the world—do you conceive me—and   80
she knows what's fittest and most convenient for
you—and obedience is the best virtue.

ISABELLA.

Very well, madam.

LADY BUSY.

Now there is a certain lord, whom my lady has
mentioned to you.   85

ISABELLA.

A lord? a beast, and one that would make me as
bad as himself.

LADY CHEATLY.

Good Mrs. Pert, keep in that foolish instrument,
your tongue. A beast? There are a great many like
him.   90

LADY BUSY.

Be not so forward, all things have two faces—do
not look upon the wrong one—go to—you are a
fine young lady and are brought by your lady
mother to Town, the general mart for beauty.
Well—you would be so settled in the world, as to   95

---

24 world … devil] "The world, the flesh, and the devil"
was a common, proverbial phrase.

have a certain fund^e whereon you may rely, which
in age may secure you from contempt——good.

ISABELLA.

I hope I shall have enough to keep me honest.

LADY BUSY.

Nay, Heaven forbid I should persuade you to be
dishonest. Virtue is a rare thing, a heavenly thing.   100
But I say still, be mindful of the main:* alas, a
woman is a solitary, helpless creature without a
man, God knows——good. How may this man be
had in marriage say you? Very well if you could
get a fine gentleman with money enough, but alas!   105
those do not marry, they have left it off. The
customs of the world change in all ages.

ISABELLA.

In ours for the worse.

LADY BUSY.

Very well said, but yet the wisest must obey 'em
as they change—Do you conceive, madam?   110

ISABELLA. (*Aside.*)

Yes, I do conceive you to be doing a very reverend
office.

GARTRUDE.

Methinks her ladyship speaks a great deal of
reason; she's a fine spoken lady truly.

LADY BUSY.

Now I say, since custom has so run down wedlock,   115
what remains but that we should make use of the
next thing to it? Good. Nay, not but that virtue is
a rare thing—Heaven forbid I should detract from
that—but I say, the main* is to be respected: a
good deal of money, there's the point.   120

ISABELLA.

With little or no reputation, there's the point.

LADY CHEATLY.

Money brings reputation, fool, or at least puts one
into that condition that fellows dare not question
it.

LADY BUSY.

Nay, Heaven forbid you should lose that, but I say   125
the next thing to marriage is being kind* to a noble
lord, etcetera. And if good terms be made and you
be well settled in the world—

ISABELLA.

That would be to be settled out of the world, for
I should never dare to show my face again.   130

LADY CHEATLY.

There are as good faces as yours, and better, my
nimble chaps, that are shown everyday in the
playhouse after it and with the best quality* too.

LADY BUSY.

Yes, and in front of boxes—nay, nay, not but that
a good wealthy marriage is beyond it.   135

ISABELLA.

A very comfortable thing for a gentlewoman to
bring herself into a condition of never conversing
with a woman of quality,* who has wit and honor,
again, but must sort with those tawdry painted
things of the Town.   140

GARTRUDE.

Can't you keep company with my mother and me?

LADY BUSY.

Look you madam, you are under a great mistake,
for do not ladies of wit and honor keep daily
company with those things as you call them? But
d'ye conceive me, the finest things, the gayest   145
things, and some the richest things, I say no more,
I pray conceive me—as long as you are true to one
man, madam, you are in a manner his lady, I say
in a manner his lady; 'tis a kind of marriage, and
great persons most commonly cohabit longer with   150
mistresses than they used to do with wives.

LADY CHEATLY.

My lady says right, 'tis nowadays more like
marriage than marriage itself.

GARTRUDE.

Oh sister! Do what my lady says, she's a rare
person.   155

LADY BUSY.

A thousand pound, and three hundred pound per
annum—say we bring him to four hundred pound,
good—a great lord—that is in the way to prefer you,
very good—or maybe, may like you so well, as to
own you—best of all. Consider.—'Tis enough,   160
madam, at once. Let her ruminate upon this.

GARTRUDE.

Oh Lord, pray sister do. Why, we shall be all made,
prithee do.

ISABELLA.

Go you to your Mr. Maggot that dies and makes
songs for you.   165

GARTRUDE.

No, I'll swear he's a fine witty person, but he has

such a grievous face, I can't abide it. But there's Mr. Selfish is the most gentile, well-bred gentleman and has the finest ways among ladies. He will tell you such pretty things of himself, he talks of himself 170 always so prettily and says such neat, gentile, well-bred things to one.

Enter steward.

STEWARD.
Madam, some gentlemen are coming in.

LADY CHEATLY.
Bid the scriveners and the rest of the people come in.   175

[Exit steward.]

—Daughters go, and walk in the garden.

Exeunt daughters.

—I hope your ladyship will pardon me; this money-business must be minded.

LADY BUSY.
By all means, madam. I'll go make a visit. Your servant. (*Exit.*)   180

Enter scriveners and several others [including counsel and steward].

SCRIVENER.
I have brought the mortgage, and the mortgager is here ready to seal upon the payment of the within-named sum.

LADY CHEATLY.
Has my counsel perused it?

COUNSEL.
Yes, and find it to be very well drawn.   185

LADY CHEATLY.
Let me read it.

Enter Stanmore, Bellamour, Carlos, and Maggot.

STEWARD.
The company is come.

LADY CHEATLY.
Peace, I see 'em.

MAGGOT.
Look you, did I not tell you? she's always thus busy, I warrant upon a mortgage or a purchase. She's a 190 vast fortune. I know where her money lies and in what hands. She has a vast deal. Do not interrupt her, you shall hear.

BELLAMOUR.
Then you know all?

MAGGOT.
Know all? Aye. Why Sir William, her late husband, 195 was my intimate friend. Know? Why, I hired this house and bought all the furniture for her. Her daughters will be worth ten thousand pound apiece, at least, to my knowledge—

STANMORE.
This fellow will outlie any traveler.   200

MAGGOT.
I knew her father as well as any man in the world. Know? Why, I know all.

CARLOS.
This lady must be a cheat, by doing her business so publicly.

MAGGOT.
Mr. Carlos, I knew your father as well as any man 205 in England. Honest James, his keeper: I have had many a buck of him.

BELLAMOUR.
Did you know my father?

MAGGOT.
Did I? No flesh alive better. I did more for him than any man in England. I was a father to him.   210

BELLAMOUR.
Ay! Then you are my grandfather! But how were you a father to him?

MAGGOT.
How? Why, I gave him his second wife.

COUNSEL. (*Reads.*)
"To have and to hold."

LADY CHEATLY.
'Tis very well: five thousand pound is the sum.— 215
Steward, pay him the money and take the writings.

MAGGOT.
Look you there, did not I tell you?

FIRST CITIZEN.
Well, she's a rare woman at business.

SECOND CITIZEN.
As ever I saw.

STEWARD.
Here are the two gentlemen I spoke of, who 220 humbly desire to place some money in your ladyship's hands.

LADY CHEATLY.

I do not love to meddle with other people's money, you know; besides, I shall have no occasion. I have a great sum to be paid in within this fortnight.   225

STEWARD.

I know it, madam, but if a purchase should be offered in the mean time—

FIRST CITIZEN.

I beseech your ladyship, take our money. We have been so cheated by base goldsmiths,[25] we are afraid to trust anybody but your ladyship.   230

LADY CHEATLY.

I do not love to stand charged for other people's money.—Oh me, gentlemen! I was so busy I did not see you. You have not waited long, I hope. Pray forgive my rudeness.

BELLAMOUR.

The rudeness is on our side, to intrude into your   235
ladyship's privacies.

LADY CHEATLY.

By no means. You do me honor.

STANMORE.

Madam, we take the liberty to present Mr. Carlos, a friend of ours lately come out of France, to your ladyship.   240

LADY CHEATLY.

Sir, I have heard of your noble family, and you'll honor mine in your acquaintance with it.—Sweet Mr. Maggot, your servant.—Gentlemen, have but a little patience till I have dispatched some business, and I'll wait on you.   245

MAGGOT.

God, she's the finest person in the world and a vast fortune. I would my ungracious nephew had one of her daughters.

Enter Prig.

PRIG.

Madam, your most humble servant.

LADY CHEATLY.

Your servant, sweet Mr. Prig.   250

PRIG.

Sweet Mr. Prig! Good: matters go on well.—Come gentlemen, since my lady's busy, let's go to langtriloo[26] or ombre.

CARLOS.

Is there no way of spending our time but playing?

PRIG.

None so good. Why, what a pox should one do?   255

CARLOS.

Read, it is a manly diversion.

PRIG.

Read? So I have read *Markham, The Compleat Farrier,*[27] and two or three books about horses; a book that's written about ombre and that about piquet; and for other books, pox there's nothing   260
in 'em at all.—What think you Bellamour?

BELLAMOUR.

You are in the right.

PRIG.

Look you there, there's nothing in 'em, hah.

STANMORE.

Methinks discourse is a pretty good way of passing one's time.   265

PRIG.

Gad, so it is: I talk as much as any man in England; my tongue seldom lies still. Oh! I love discourse mightily and though I say it, I am able to run down all I meet about dogs and horses. Now I think on't, have you ever hunted with my   270
Lord Squander's fox-dogs, Bellamour?

BELLAMOUR.

No. [*Aside.*] Now he's in.

PRIG.

They are the best in England. But there is one dog we call Ranter, I christened him, I was his god-father. He was gotten upon my lord's famous bitch,   275
Lady. You remember what a bitch she was. Oh poor Lady! I was not sorrier when my sister died than when poor Lady died. But let that pass. Ranter was gotten by your father's dog, Rockwood.

BELLAMOUR.

Did you know Rockwood?   280

---

25 goldsmiths] who dominated banking in seventeenth-century London; the Bank of England was not established until 1694, and even then was primarily a source of funds for William III's continental military operations.

26 langtriloo] or lanterloo, an older form of loo (q.v.)

27 *Markham … Farrier*] two books on horses, *Markham's Masterpiece* (there was an edition in 1675) and *The English Horseman and Compleat Farrier* (1673)

PRIG.

Know him? As well as any man in the world. His father was a dog of my father's, called Jowler; his mother was my noble Lord Squander's father's famous bitch, Venus, which you have heard of.— I remember, Mr. Carlos, Venus was sister to your father's dog, Ringwood.—Rockwood? I knew him as well as I knew your father. Well, rest their souls of a dog and a man, I shall never see two better in the field than Rockwood and your father.

CARLOS.

How the rogue has coupled them.

PRIG.

Yet Ranter's an admirable dog, the best at a cold scent that ever I saw. If there be any forty couple in the field, I'll hold an hundred pound he works it out soonest and leads 'em all when he has done. I love and honor Ranter, I care not who knows it. I made a song of him and have his picture by my bed-side and some of his hair here in a crystal locket.

MAGGOT.

I beseech your ladyship, accept of my thousand pound, 'twill make up the money for that purchase, sweet madam.

LADY CHEATLY.

Well sir, since you will have it so, I'll give my bond for it.

MAGGOT.

Oh madam! I scorn it, I'll have nothing under hand for it.

LADY CHEATLY.

Then I will not take it; nay, I have sworn first.

MAGGOT.

Well, I'll go and fetch it, and your ladyship and I will agree upon that. (*Exit.*)

PRIG.

Hah! The young ladies are in the garden.

BELLAMOUR.

Say you so? Prithee, let's steal down to 'em.

PRIG.

Do, and leave me with the widow.

Exeunt Bellamour, Stanmore, Carlos.

LADY CHEATLY.

Steward, do you take care of all the rest, while I retire from (what I do not care for) business.

[Exit steward.]

—Now I am at leisure. Are the gentlemen gone?

PRIG.

They are gone but into the garden and will wait on your ladyship presently. They have left me that happy opportunity I wished for to renew the suit I have so often made to your ladyship: I beseech you, madam, be pleased to consider my passion, which is so violent to your ladyship, I cannot rest since first I saw your ladyship, for it has indeed put me besides myself. I have not the heart to ride so much as one heat at Newmarket since, and I used to go once in ten days down on purpose, nor have I been able to ride a fox chase since I have had your ladyship in chase. I shall be undone if your la'ship don't quiet my mind with some assurances: I overset[f 28] at trictrac, dealt my self ten at ombre, and all through my passion for your dear self.

LADY CHEATLY.

Sir, though I have a great esteem for your person, yet we widows that have some fortune are to consider something besides passion.

PRIG.

As I have told you before, my estate is not inconsiderable, besides the great favor I have with the gaming and jockey lords, and besides, if the king frequents Newmarket, I doubt not but in a short time to rise.

LADY CHEATLY.

But you are a gamester.

PRIG.

Aye madam, but I never play, I do but rook.

LADY CHEATLY.

Rook? What's that? Cheat?

PRIG.

No madam, I go to twelve and the better of the lay;[29] besides, I get five hundred pound a year at

---

28 overset] to not take a possible point through carelessness

29 twelve … lay] Unclear. Twelve penny ordinaries (see act V) served a complete meal for a shilling at twelve. After the meal the tables would be cleared and gambling would commence. Alternately, one ruse of rooks dealing with gulls was to bet that they could roll a seven before the gull could role a twelve; the gull would

horse races and cock matches by being in fee with
the grooms and cock keepers.[30] And madam, I play
as well at tennis, ombre, backgammon, trictrac, and
crimp,[31] as any man, which is no small addition to   345
my estate. I gave you these things in my particular,
if your ladyship please to remember.

LADY CHEATLY.

But you cannot make a jointure of these things,
and therefore, I must consider a little longer.

PRIG.

With all my heart, madam, but in the meantime   350
let you and I play a set at trictrac, and when the
rest come in, we'll make a match at ombre.

Enter steward.

STEWARD.

Madam, there are some tenants wait without to
speak with you.

LADY CHEATLY.

You'll pardon me, I must go to 'em. (*Exit.*)   355

PRIG.

Come on, Mr. Steward, what say you to a game
at backgammon?

STEWARD.

If you'll retire to my chamber, have at you.

PRIG.

With all my heart.

Exeunt.

[Scene ii. The garden at Lady Cheatly's.]

Enter Theodosia, Isabella, Bellamour, Carlos,
Stanmore.

CARLOS.

Who's there, the Lady Pleasant's daughter,
Theodosia?

BELLAMOUR.

It is: she's young and handsome, has a great deal
of wit, and a very good fortune, which makes her

set up for marriage and is impregnable to anything   5
else.

CARLOS.

She's extreme pretty; I loved her violently before I
went into France, but now she's a thousand times
more beautiful.

STANMORE.

Ladies, your humble servant.   10

BELLAMOUR.

A gentleman, a friend of ours, lately come out of
France. (*He salutes* 'em.)

CARLOS.

And glad I am so, for all that nation could not
show me so much beauty.

THEODOSIA.

I see, sir, you have not been in France for nothing;   15
you have imported French goods, I mean
compliments. They are a nation full of
complimenters.

CARLOS.

They are so, madam, and the tailor does it full as
well as the gentleman; 'tis a road of speaking which   20
all of 'em have. I was not dull enough to get it of
'em, nor would I bring so common a thing as a
compliment to you, madam.

THEODOSIA.

You can bring it to nobody that dislikes it more.

CARLOS.

Or needs it less.   25

THEODOSIA.

Thus I have heard a very rhetorical oration against
eloquence.

Enter Gartrude.

GARTRUDE.

Oh Lord, Mr. Stanmore here. (*Runs out.*)

BELLAMOUR.

Run Stanmore, your business is more than half
done; 'tis a certain sign when a woman seeks   30
corners that she means some good by it.

STANMORE.

I'll try that. (*Exit.*)

BELLAMOUR. [*To Isabella.*]

I see my friend's caught again, for all his travel. I
have a fellow-feeling of his case; let's retire and give
him opportunity.   35

___

apparently not realize how much the odds were against
him. Thus Prig would have the better part of the wager
or lay, which could also mean a trick.

30 in fee … cock keepers] Prig bribes grooms and cock
    keepers for inside information.

31 crimp] a card game

ISABELLA.

With all my heart; opportunity is safe in the beginning of an amour, though it may be dangerous afterwards.

They retire.

THEODOSIA.

I hear never a French word from you, and that's strange: for all our sparks are so refined, they scarce 40 speak a sentence without one, and though they seldom arrive at good French, yet they get enough to spoil their English.

CARLOS.

If a man means nothing, he cannot choose a better language, for it makes a pretty noise without any 45 manner of thought.

THEODOSIA.

You have scarce brought one substantial vanity over with you. What have you learnt there?

CARLOS.

To love my own country and to think that none can show us so fine women. In France they buy 50 their beauty and sell their love.

THEODOSIA.

That fashion is coming up apace here.

CARLOS.

True beauty, madam, can no more be bought than true love; in me behold the one, while I admire the other in yourself. 55

THEODOSIA.

How many French ladies have you said as much to?

CARLOS.

I went thither to be cured of love, not to make* it.

THEODOSIA.

What love?

CARLOS.

My love of you, which began so early in my heart, 60 self-love was scarce before it. When your disdain could not remove it, I tried absence but in vain too.

THEODOSIA.

'Tis impossible you could bring a heart unhurt from France.

CARLOS.

My love to you preserved me from all foreign 65 invasion.

THEODOSIA.

If you make love, you'll grow dull; it spoils a man of wit, as much as business.

CARLOS.

If love be predominant in conversation,* I confess it, but a little relish of it does well. 70

THEODOSIA.

The imitation of it may be born, but the thing itself is a dead weight upon the mind, and a man can no more please under that disadvantage, than a horse can run a race with a pair of panniers on his back. 75

CARLOS.

And yet that horse may do it, if the match be well made.

THEODOSIA.

I must have my servant all wit, all gaiety, and the ladies of the Town run mad for him. I would not only triumph over him, but over my whole sex in him. 80

CARLOS.

This is hard doctrine for a man of my sincerity and truth in love.

THEODOSIA.

Make Isabella slight Bellamour, little Gartrude sacrifice Selfish, be the third word in every lady's mouth from fifteen to five and thirty, and you shall 85 find what I'll say to you.

CARLOS.

To attempt this were great vanity and no less dishonesty to my friend Bellamour.

THEODOSIA.

If you love, you'll think anything lawful.32 This must be done: I dare not trust my own judgment; I 90 will have you in vogue, ere I favor you in the least.

CARLOS.

Well, since these ladies are your outworks, I will on, and by the force of imagination, make every one Theodosia. But if I fail, think on my constant love, which will not suffer me to use deceit. 95

THEODOSIA.

Suppose I should answer you in your whining strain, and say my love were true as yours, my flame as great, and all your wishes mine.

---

32 love … lawful] alluding to the proverb, all's fair in love and war

CARLOS.

Then were Carlos the happiest man on earth.

THEODOSIA.

No, then the game were up betwixt us and there were no more to do but pay the stakes and then to something else.

CARLOS.

We might play set after set forever.

THEODOSIA.

No, one of us would be broke. Go get you about your task, I say.

Exeunt Carlos and Theodosia. Enter Selfish and Young Maggot.

YOUNG MAGGOT.

Did you see how the ladies flocked about me at court when I made a relation of the rehearsal and afterwards when I read my song to 'em?

SELFISH.

I think I am as well with the ladies there as any man, and they like my songs too; they say they're so easy, so gentile, and well-bred and so pat to the women's understandings. The men say they're silly, but they are envious.

YOUNG MAGGOT.

I'll secure you the play takes; I have done the poet's business with the ladies, who, you know, govern the men, as the moon does the sea.

SELFISH.

There is a pretty creature not past eighteen, whom I have formerly enjoyed, has to oblige me taken upon her the figure of a procurer and is to bring me a maid-enhead anon, which fell in love with me at a play.

YOUNG MAGGOT.

But I'll show you my song.

SELFISH.

Of late I have had no leisure to make a song, I am so overrun with new acquaintances.

YOUNG MAGGOT. (*Reads.*)

"Damon see how charming Chloris, etc." How do you like it?

SELFISH.

'Tis soft and very much after my own way, and I like it well. But how like you this peruke?

YOUNG MAGGOT.

'Tis very proper.

SELFISH.

I have five as good by me; I have an hundred pound I got at ombre; Mr. Whimsey owes me two hundred; I have a pad or two, and when I get this debt in, I will buy a chariot,* and perhaps have as good equipage as any man, if I can get an hundred pound Sir Nicholas Wachum owes me. I only want* a couple of hunters for Windsor,[33] and then—

YOUNG MAGGOT.

You don't mind my song, 'tis to my mistress.

SELFISH.

Yes, but I was saying, now I am at ease in my fortune till next Michaelmas.[34]

YOUNG MAGGOT.

But to go on.

SELFISH.

I have lately got a conquest over a lady, the prettiest creature; I snatched a rose from her soft bosom. She is of quality,* all the Town were mad after her, and she threw herself into my arms, and I am the happy man.

YOUNG MAGGOT.

Well, to be in love is the greatest pleasure in the world: it makes one so sweetly melancholy and composed and so fit to write; besides, it keeps one in shape.

SELFISH.

I have not much occasion for love; the ladies follow me and love me so, I have no time for't. Why, I have had three maidenheads this week.

YOUNG MAGGOT.

I would not be without love and writing for all the world. I had a billet from the prettiest creature of sixteen today, I'll tell you.

Enter Carlos, Bellamour, Theodosia and Isabella.

YOUNG MAGGOT.

I have an amour.

SELFISH.

I—

YOUNG MAGGOT.

I—

---

33 hunters … Windsor] horses for a royal fox hunt
34 Michaelmas] September 29, one of the four quarter ending days of the English business year, when revenues—and bills—were due

SELFISH.

I—

YOUNG MAGGOT.

I—

SELFISH.

This fellow is always talking of himself; one can't 160
speak to him, but he is always at I, I. I wonder at
the impertinence of such people.

THEODOSIA.

These fools are always talking of themselves.

ISABELLA.

They are the worst things they can talk of.

CARLOS.

Or we either; therefore, madam, hear me on the 165
last subject.

THEODOSIA.

That's as bad.

BELLAMOUR.

He went a mile to put on that fair peruke for the
sake of his complexion.

THEODOSIA.

Prithee Isabella, let's find fault with 'em both and 170
break his heart.

Enter Stanmore and Gartrude.

GARTRUDE.

Fie upon you Mr. Stanmore, I'll ne'er come near
you again if you use me so. You nothing but kiss
one, and ruffle one, and spoil one's things, that you
do. 175

STANMORE.

Why are you so pretty then, to provoke a man
beyond all patience?

GARTRUDE.

Why, how do I provoke you? I have done nothing
to anger you, have I?

BELLAMOUR.

What, are you fallen out with your mistress? 180

STANMORE.

No, but since she's insensible of all I can speak to
her and yet so pretty, I cannot but love her; if
words won't move her, actions must.

SELFISH.

Oh! Here are the ladies; now you shall see what
advances they will make to me, but especially 185
Gartrude, that pretty creature.

YOUNG MAGGOT.

This is a very conceited fellow and would call a
gypsy that liked him pretty creature.

SELFISH.

Ladies, your most humble servant.—Now you shall
see Maggot.—Dear pretty creature, let me kiss that 190
nosegay. Well, 'tis a thousand times sweeter in that
pretty bosom than in its own bed, though at the sun
rising, when the morning dew is in drops upon it,
sweet madam. Let me kiss that hand that gathered it.

GARTRUDE.

Oh fine, what rare words are these! He uses me 195
like a princess. Sir, 'tis more your goodness than
my desert.—Sister, this is a rare man. Mr.
Stanmore is a wit they say, but I don't understand
him half so well. I always think they jeer one.

ISABELLA.

Indeed, 'tis a hard thing for wit to descend to your 200
capacity.

SELFISH.

I was with some ladies last night did so commend
you and said you were the most delicate creature.
They did me the favor to say your eyes were black
and sparkling like mine, and your nose very much 205
resembling mine, and that you have a pretty
pouting about the mouth like me, and fine little
blub[35]-lips. I am very well with the ladies at Court,
but I see none like you.

STANMORE.

Do you know I love that lady? 210

SELFISH.

If you do, I pity you; she is otherwise engaged, to
my knowledge.

Enter Prig.

PRIG.

Come, faith, since we are all together, let's go to
ombre, two companies, and make an afternoon on't.

YOUNG MAGGOT.

I desire you will not interrupt me; I am singing 215
the ladies a new song.

PRIG.

Song? Pish, is not gaming better than hearing of
songs? Here's such a stir with these wits.

---

35 blub] full, swelling

ISABELLA.

No, pray let's hear it.

Young Maggot sings Damon, etc.

PRIG.

I observe you wits are always making songs of the 220
love of shepherds and shepherdesses, a company
of blockheaded, clownish,* ugly, tawny, sunburnt
people. I had e'en as lief hear songs upon the love
of their sheep as their own.

CARLOS.

I see these fools need nobody to show 'em; they 225
show themselves well enough.

PRIG.

Methinks that old song is very pretty: "My Mistress
is a Tennis Ball, etc."

YOUNG MAGGOT.

This rogue has nothing but tennis courts and
bowling greens in his head. 230

BELLAMOUR.

Prithee Prig, sing one of your own making.

PRIG.

With all my heart.

Enter Lady Cheatly.

LADY CHEATLY.

Mrs. Theodosia, your humble servant.—
Gentlemen, I hope you'll pardon me, I could not
neglect business. I think one had better be poor 235
than be troubled with money thus. But if you
please to walk in, there's a small banquet waits, and
fiddles, to dance, if you please.

ISABELLA.

Pray madam, let's hear Mr. Prig's song first; 'tis his
own. 240

PRIG.

I am glad your ladyship is come to hear it. (*Sings.*)
Hey ho, hey ho,
The merry horn does blow.
'Tis broad day,
Come away. 245
Twivee, twivee, twivee, hey,
Do not stay.
Then have at the hare,
Let old puss[36] beware.

Twivee, twivee, twivee, ho, 250
The merry horn does blow.
Come away.

YOUNG MAGGOT.

What a happy thing 'tis to have wit.

PRIG.

Hang wit, give me mirth. This is a catch that I
made, and my Lord Squander and I always roar it 255
out after a fox chase. Pox, I hate your swains and
your nymphs.

SELFISH.

Do they wear breeches thus cut in France?

CARLOS.

Yes sir.

SELFISH.

What blockheads are our English tailors. I must 260
have some new clothes made immediately in this
fashion; I cannot rest till I bespeak 'em.

ISABELLA.

Pray madam, join with us, we shall have very good
sport.—Are you well, Mr. Selfish? Sure you are
not. I never saw you look so ill before. 265

THEODOSIA.

He looks extreme ill.—Your complexion seems to
have too much of the olive in it today.

SELFISH.

Pardon me, ladies, I think my complexion is well
enough, or my glass* is false: I never looked clearer.

CARLOS.

That trimming too, with your favor, is very 270
disagreeable and does not cohere with your
complexion at all.

SELFISH.

I assure you, sir, all the ladies I saw today are of
another opinion: they said my complexion was
much like pretty Mrs. Gartrude's here. 275

LADY CHEATLY.

Methinks you look mighty lean and thin. I fear
you are going into a consumption, sir.

SELFISH.

Oh no, madam! I am very plump, I am only afraid
of being too gross and bellying. I am very fat, I
assure your ladyship. Pray feel my ribs, madam. 280

PRIG.

They laugh at him. The devil take me, I never saw
a fellow so altered in my life.—Thou canst not live
long, thou smell'st of earth, faugh.

---

36 puss] the hare (baby hares and rabbits are sometimes
called kittens)

SELFISH.

You mistake, I am one of the vigorest fellows, the strongest bodies in England. I was taken for Mr. Carlos today at a little distance. 285

BELLAMOUR.

Prithee Selfish, do not play the fool with thyself. Get a physician: I never saw your complexion so sallow; thou look'st prodigiously ill.

SELFISH.

Good sir, I know what I am: my cheeks are as plump and my complexion as fresh as any here, my eyes and mouth as cheerful, and everything. 290

CARLOS.

Nothing will mortify the rogue. He thinks so well of Selfish, that he thinks Selfish can never look ill, nor be ill. I believe he thinks Selfish can never die. 295

SELFISH.

I have a face that will not alter. If I were a-dying, 'twould look well; indeed, my complexion changes sometimes, but never looks ill, I assure you.

GARTRUDE.

I wonder you should be so mistaken all. Methinks he looks very neatly. 300

BELLAMOUR.

This is a damned peruke. Why did you put it on today?

CARLOS.

But indeed that suit is an odious thing and the trimming the worst I ever saw. 'Tis your tailor's fancy; it becomes you very ill. 305

SELFISH.

Methinks it is very pretty.—I think they are all out of their wits.

LADY CHEATLY.

'Tis enough: we shall make the man hang himself.

YOUNG MAGGOT.

Do you think I'll suffer you forever to cross me with your damned insipid songs? Let me tell you, 310 it is a grand impertinence.

PRIG.

Gad, I do not know what you mean by your gibberish, but I suppose you call me impertinent, and therefore, I'll be beforehand with you: you are a son of a whore. (*Gives Young Maggot a box on* 315 *the ear. They draw, the ladies run out shrieking.*)

SELFISH.

I will wait upon the ladies.

BELLAMOUR.

Hold, hold.

CARLOS.

Let 'em alone. If you offer to part 'em, they'll hurt one another. 320

YOUNG MAGGOT.

I'll not be brutal. You shall answer for it.—Sir, you are lately come out of France and cannot deny a man of honor your assistance.

PRIG.

Prithee Stanmore, be my second. I'll wit him, with a pox to him. 325

YOUNG MAGGOT.

Tomorrow morning, done.

PRIG.

Let my second appoint the place.

YOUNG MAGGOT.

With all my heart.—Monsieur Carlos, agree with him.

STANMORE.

Come, let's in, and put it off to the ladies as if you 330 were friends.

PRIG.

Aye, with all my heart. What care I?

YOUNG MAGGOT.

Morbleu,[37] brutal.

Act III, [scene i. Lady Cheatly's lodgings.]

Enter Lady Cheatly, Carlos, Bellamour, Stanmore, Isabella, Theodosia, Gartrude, Lady Busy, Young Maggot, Selfish, Prig, Maggot, Lump.

LUMP.

Lady sister, I am much offended to see you take this course of vanity: Would any wise woman make use of fiddlers, minstrels, and singers? I am very much ashamed of it. It is folly, great folly, not becoming the blood of the Lumps. 5

ISABELLA.

Let's withdraw, we shall have a lesson from this formal uncle.

GARTRUDE.

I can't abide him.

---

37 Morbleu] French euphemism for *Mort dieu*, by God's (Christ's) death, similar to English *'sdeath*

Exeunt all but Lady Cheatly, Lump, Prig, and Old Maggot.

LUMP.

What pleasure can there be to hear fellows scrape upon cats-guts? There's nothing in't. 10

LADY CHEATLY.

'Tis the way to get credit at our end of the Town, as singing psalms and praying loud in a foreroom[38] is at yours.

LUMP.

You talk not wisely. Do not several godly men by those means and by frequenting meetings get 15 credit enough to break[39] for a hundred thousand pound and are made by it forever.

MAGGOT.

He is one of the wisest men of the Nation; he is a mighty sober, solid fellow and a rare man at business and loves business mightily. 20

LUMP.

And for the wits that come hither, I doubt not but these gentlemen are of my opinion: I say they are dangerous, scandalous, and good for nothing.

MAGGOT.

'Tis true, madam, they are a company of flashy, frothy fellows and have no solidity in them. 25

LADY CHEATLY. (*Aside.*)

I find these coxcombs mistake dullness for solidity.

PRIG.

They talk of wit and this and that and keep a coil and a pother about wit. There's nothing at all in't. What a pox is't good for? I would not give a farthing for wit. Here's Young Maggot and Selfish: 30 why they don't know how to bet at a horse race or make a good match at tennis and are cross-bitten* at bowls. Hang wit.

MAGGOT.

Wit is one of the grievances of the Nation.

LUMP.

It is, as this gentleman has wisely observed, a 35 grievance, a sore grievance, and I would have an Act of Parliament against it.

MAGGOT.

Let me take a wit at business, see how I'll handle him; I would not be a wit for all the world.

PRIG.

Nor I neither, I hate it; they are a company of 40 fleering, jeering, ill-natured fellows to boot too.

LADY CHEATLY.

Be comforted, gentlemen, you are in no danger.

LUMP.

I say they are in danger, and you too, of catching it, if you suffer them to come amongst ye. I have known solid men, by keeping that base company, become 45 witty and have ruined themselves. For my own part, I would as soon catch the plague as that disease of wit.

LADY CHEATLY.

Oh brother! You have a strong antidote against it.

LUMP.

Thanks be to Heaven, I hate wits! Out upon 'em. They write satires upon good men and will laugh 50 at wise men.

LADY CHEATLY.

Why truly, brother, sometimes wise men will provoke 'em very much.

LUMP.

You are i'th wrong.

Enter steward.

STEWARD.

Here is your scrivener, Mr. Lump, and several 55 others met upon money business.

LUMP.

I ordered mine to come to you. I have four thousand pound paid in this day, which you may use. I will leave my scrivener to take your assignments, either of bonds, judgments, or mortgages, as it shall 60 happen to be disposed by you.

LADY CHEATLY.

But will the scrivener be true and publish it to be my money?

LUMP.

I warrant you, he's a godly man, and you may trust him. He has contributed more to your fame than 65 anyone. I myself have brought in Ananias, and he will send money to you to put out[40] for him. 'Tis

---

38 foreroom] front room, nearest the street, whence such praying would be audible as desired

39 break] something like our modern sense of "spring for," here to come up with venture capital

40 put out] invest

near four, I must be gone. Though haste does not
become a wise man, yet at the present I have some
upon me.   70

LADY CHEATLY.

The haste of a fool is the slowest thing in the
world.

LUMP.

It is my hour of walking.

LADY CHEATLY.

Will you not stay and take the assignments?

LUMP.

I will not break my method for the world. I have 75
these twenty years walked through Turnstile Alley
to Holborn Fields⁴¹ at four. All the good women
observe me and set their bread into the oven by
me and by no other clock. When I go by, I hear
'em call, "Carry the bread to the oven, the old   80
gentleman is going by." I do love to be taken notice
of for my method. Farewell. (*Exit.*)

LADY CHEATLY.

Let's into the garden.

Exeunt omnes.

[Scene ii. The garden.]

Enter Bellamour and Isabella.

BELLAMOUR.

By Heaven, I love thee more than light or liberty,
joy of my heart.

ISABELLA.

Such hearts as yours are seldom near their mouths.

BELLAMOUR.

A kiss of this fair hand will bring mine thither. 'Tis
there. But if it were your lips, where would it be?   5

ISABELLA.

Raptures in love have no more meaning in 'em
than rants in poetry, mere fustian; 'tis the stum*
of love that makes it fret and fume and fly and
never good.

BELLAMOUR.

Can a young lady in so warm an age be insensible 10
of love?

ISABELLA.

A virtuous woman is ever insensible of such a love

_____

⁴¹ Holborn Fields] at this time a poor suburb of the City

as is unfit for her. But you sparks, like wolves after
many battles, by often preying on carcasses, come
at last to venture upon the living: modest or not, 15
'tis all one to you, you are so well fleshed.

BELLAMOUR.

Not so, madam. I know my duty and your worth,
and would time stand still, I could be content to
gaze upon that face and not tempt you. But our love
is frail, and we must take our pleasure while we may. 20

ISABELLA.

I must consider while I may and on the shore
think on the ruins of a shipwrecked fame.

BELLAMOUR.

We shall never reach love's Indies, if we fear
tempests already.

ISABELLA.

Think not to conquer me by dint of simile. I'll never 25
venture the pain and peril of such a bold voyage.

BELLAMOUR.

As tender barks make it daily and return home
richly fraught, keep coaches, and live splendidly
the rest of their lives.

ISABELLA.

Infamously rather.   30

BELLAMOUR.

I know not that, but they have their days of
visiting, play at ombre, make treats as high and as
often as the persons of quality,* wear as good
clothes, and want* no fashionable folly that
woman's heart can wish for. And of all such my   35
Isabella shall ride admiral.

ISABELLA.

Can you pretend to love and tempt me from my
honor? Coaches and clothes! So rogues will rob to
live like gentlemen.

BELLAMOUR.

'Tis no dishonor, custom has made it otherwise.   40

ISABELLA.

When a man of honor can turn coward, you may
prevail on me; the case is equal.

BELLAMOUR.

On the contrary, kindness* in women is like
courage in men.

ISABELLA.

Did not the general license of the time excuse you, 45
I ne'er would see you more.

BELLAMOUR.

What, will nothing down but to have and to hold? I'll marry nobody else, and when my inclination dies, leave you its wealthy widow; you may marry after it.

ISABELLA.

I'll bring no infamy where I bring my person.   50

BELLAMOUR.

This coldness inflames me more. Consent to my desires and none of all the ladies shall outshine, no equipage exceed yours.

ISABELLA.

And I the while shall be but a part of your equipage, to be kept.* What is it but to wear your   55
livery and take board-wages?

BELLAMOUR.

I love you well enough to marry you, but dare not put my self into your hands, knowing what a jade I am at a long journey.

ISABELLA.

If you ever loved, you can never hate, and I can   60
be content where I have had the best, to keep the rest, and if you love me less, shall lay the fault on Nature, not on you.

BELLAMOUR.

It goes more against a man's heart to fall in his love, than his expense, and they that do either, most   65
commonly remove for it; there is no enduring it in the same place. Think on my love, my fortune shall be yours.

ISABELLA.

I scorn a fortune with the ruin of my honor.

BELLAMOUR.

It is but heading with another sort of people,   70
leaving the melancholy hypocrites for the gay cheerful sinners, the envious for the envied.

ISABELLA.

These tales may catch unheedful silly creatures, whom nature half debauches to your hands, but for myself I swear—   75

Lady Busy appears to 'em.

LADY BUSY.

Swear not, ungracious child, I have heard all your discourse. The gentleman is a fine gentleman, and his proposals are as reasonable as any lady can wish for; every man cannot bring himself to marry and yet may love better and longer than those that do.   80

BELLAMOUR.

Right, madam.—This is an unexpected assistance.

LADY BUSY.

There's Mr. Maggot kept* Mrs. Wagtail, after the whole Town had done with her, and loves her very well still. Nay, some have not grudged to spend ten thousand pounds upon a mistress, though they   85
have starved their wives and children.

ISABELLA.

Have you feed this lady to plead for you, or is it the baseness of her own nature?

LADY BUSY.

Is my charity thus rewarded? My honor questioned? I that am companion to the ladies of   90
the best quality?* The jealousest lord thinks his lady safe in my company. My honor is dearer to me than all the world, and but for endeavoring to have you well settled in the world, as I have my daughters, do I deserve this?   95

ISABELLA.

She is as silly as she's naught.* When you see me next, bring nobler thoughts and better purposes. And so farewell. (*Exit.*)

BELLAMOUR.

What a devil shall I do? She's virtuous and fit enough for a wife. 'Ounds,* how that word makes   100
me start! But all this may be a copy of her countenance,[42] there may by huffs in virtue as well as courage.

LADY BUSY.

I hope, sir, you'll not conceive amiss for what she says.   105

BELLAMOUR.

No, madam.—Pox on this bawd, I love the treason, but I hate the traitor. (*Exit.*)

Enter Stanmore.

STANMORE.

Your humble servant, madam. Has your ladyship had the goodness to mind my affair?

LADY BUSY.

I have, sir; I see her coming. Retire and let me   110
alone.—Come, pretty Mrs. Gatty.

Exit Stanmore. Enter Mrs. Gartrude.

---

42 copy … countenance] a deceptive appearance

GARTRUDE.

Your servant, madam.

LADY BUSY.

Thou art a pretty creature! Ah, 'twould do a man good to lie by such flesh and blood as thou art. All the matter is to choose a good bedfellow, and for that trust me: there is the prettiest man and the finest gentleman not far off. 115

GARTRUDE.

Aye, so there is really. Mr. Selfish is the finest person, so civil and well-bred, and is very ingenious too. I vow 'twould do one good to have such a bedfellow. 120

LADY BUSY.

You are out: 'tis Mr. Stanmore is the man and will make a good settlement, go to,* which the other cannot.

GARTRUDE.

He is a fine gentleman indeed, but really I don't care 125 for a wit: I do not know what to say before 'em. But I can talk with Mr. Selfish all the day long. Oh, he does tell such pretty stories of himself! He is a very fair-spoken man, and I'll swear he is the purest company for a lady that ever was, and so handsome. 130

LADY BUSY.

Not comparable to Stanmore.

GARTRUDE.

Oh jiminy!* That your ladyship should say so.

LADY BUSY.

I have experience in the world. I know what I say. Your lady mother has desired me to take care to put you into the world. Youth is indiscreet and 135 unwary. Trust us, and 'twill be your own another day. I say, Mr. Stanmore will settle ten times more upon you than the other is worth.

GARTRUDE.

But really, madam, I must confess I don't love a wit. They say they are not good-natured, and they 140 don't admire one half so much as others do, neither.

LADY BUSY.

Come, come madam, if a wit will keep,* he will serve as well as a fool (let 'em say what they will), and you have a way to be too hard for the best of 145 'em for all their wits.

Enter Selfish.

GARTRUDE.

Oh Lord, here he is! I wonder you should say Mr. Stanmore is as handsome as he. Well, he's a lovely man.

SELFISH.

Ladies, I kiss both your hands. Methinks I see the 150 freshness of the spring in one, and the fruitfulness of the autumn in the other.

GARTRUDE.

Oh rare, what a saying that is, and so like a gentleman!

Stanmore enters.

STANMORE. [*Aside.*]

Now 'tis time to speak for myself: she is very pretty, 155 but why should I love a fool that loves a fool? I see I am a devilish carnal fellow and mind nothing but the body.

LADY BUSY.

I'll steal out to my lady and leave you. We have business of consequence. (*Exit.*) 160

STANMORE.

Madam, your humble servant.

SELFISH.

Mr. Stanmore, your servant. Were you not at the audience this afternoon?

STANMORE.

No, sir.

SELFISH.

Indeed, I have committed a great fault, to wait 165 upon these ladies when the Court was to appear in all the splendor it could be with all the well-dressed and well-bred men about it, and I was not there. I wish it be not taken ill.

STANMORE.

Oh vanity, vanity! 170

SELFISH.

I know I was missed and asked for there, but I can mind nothing when ladies are in the way, especially such pretty creatures as Mrs. Gatty.

GARTRUDE.

You are pleased to say so.

STANMORE.

Well, my dear little one, I am resolved to be 175 revenged upon this beauty of yours for making me so mad in love with you.

GARTRUDE.

Why, what will you do with it?

STANMORE.

I'll have no mercy on't, I'll never spare it, faith, you shan't think to make me in love with you for nothing. 180

SELFISH.

I shall have a new suit come home tomorrow morning in Mr. Carlos his* fashion, but I assure you 'tis something better fancied, both for the color and the garniture.

GARTRUDE.

Really, sir, methinks Mr. Selfish is the prettiest 185 modish person and so gentile, is not he?

STANMORE. [Aside.]

S'heart, what an entertainment is this to me that I should love such a thing?—Don't mistake him, he is an ass, I assure you.

GARTRUDE.

Oh Lord, that you should say so now! He does 190 everything so like a gentleman, as my Lady Busy says, and is so well-bred.

STANMORE.

Well-bred? Hang him, he is a finical clown,* he has not breeding enough for a valet de chambre.

GARTRUDE.

What a strange man are you! Well, you wits never 195 speak well of one another, I vow.

STANMORE.

'Ounds, what a pretty fool she is! But I am vigorous still; her folly cannot thrust me off, so much as her beauty pulls me to.

SELFISH.

I am going to buy me a pretty, convenient coach. 200 What color do you fancy, dear Mrs. Gatty? I think purple will suit best with my complexion.

GARTRUDE.

Oh yes, purple will be very pretty.

SELFISH.

Nay, I'll say that for myself, my fancy always pleases the ladies. Pretty miss, let me see that 205 delicate busk;43 I will write a distich upon it, and present it to you.

GARTRUDE.

Pray do.

SELFISH.

Let me kiss that happy busk, that goes so near your lovely body, and that delicate, sweet, white, soft hand that gave it me. 210

GARTRUDE.

Well, he's a rare man and is so full of fine courtship.

STANMORE.

Do you know that I will not suffer you to smile and cringe and play the monkey44 here?

SELFISH.

I cannot help it. If ladies will love me and be 215 affected with my person, what is it to me?

STANMORE.

Get you gone, you coxcomb, I'll endure it no longer. (He fillips him and pulls off his peruke.)

GARTRUDE.

Nay, what have you done to poor Mr. Selfish?

SELFISH.

I wonder you should have no more breeding; one 220 would have thought I might have taught you more in this time.

GARTRUDE.

Pray let me help you, I'll set it right again.

STANMORE.

Death and damnation! What's this?

SELFISH.

The devil take me, if I could not find in my heart 225 to ruffle your cravat before the lady for this outrage of yours.

STANMORE.

Do you hear, sir? Be gone and leave us, or by Heaven I will cut your throat.

SELFISH.

Well, I cannot be ill-bred, though you can, and 230 therefore I take my leave. (Exit.)

GARTRUDE.

Nay, look you now, 'udds fiddles, what have you done? You have made Mr. Selfish go away. I'll follow him, that I will.

Enter Lady Cheatly and Maggot.

---

43 busk] a corset stay

44 monkey] Monkeys had become fashionable pets among the aristocracy.

LADY CHEATLY.

Do you hear, minx? Be civiller than I hear you are 235
to Mr. Stanmore, and know, I'll turn you out of
my house, if you think on Selfish.—Sir, your
servant.

GARTRUDE.

Oh lack! What does she say?

STANMORE.

Nay, I'll follow you. 240

Exit Gartrude and Stanmore.

MAGGOT.

Catch her, man, she'll be a vast fortune: my lady
wallows in money, she knows not what to do with
it.—But good madam, let me humbly petition you
to consider my passion and have some regard to my
estate, which is a plentiful one. And then madam, 245
for business, you see a proof: Did you ever see a man
tell money better than I do? I do all the ladies'
business hereabouts, and great persons', etcetera.

LADY CHEATLY.

I must first consider of reducing my estate into
some order before I think of disposing my person. 250

MAGGOT.

If any man solicits your business like me—try me,
madam. I do everything for the ladies.

Enter steward.

STEWARD.

Madam, I have private business for your ladyship's
ear.

MAGGOT.

Your servant, madam, I will retire. Be pleased to 255
consider me. (*Exit.*)

STEWARD.

My business concerns your ladyship and myself so
nearly that you must pardon me if I urge it home.

LADY CHEATLY. (*Aside.*)

What means he?

STEWARD.

That I have served you faithfully, yourself can 260
witness.

LADY CHEATLY.

I can, and I'll reward you largely.

STEWARD.

'Tis that I ask. Think, madam, I have in your

service lost my honesty, laid by my conscience, and
while I contribute to your fraud or others, I must 265
not be deceived myself.

LADY CHEATLY. (*Aside.*)

What will he drive at?—I am sorry you ask for
what I intended to give you; I did resolve to give
you a thousand pound.

STEWARD.

Do not I know that all the bonds you have given to 270
people and the assignments and declarations of trust
to your brother are written with the ink I bought of
a great artist, and that within a month it will wear
out, and nothing will remain but blanks?

LADY CHEATLY.

What then? My husband was cheated of his estate 275
by my brother and other rascals, and 'tis fit I
should take letters of reprisal.[45]

STEWARD.

No doubt. Your bonds you have taken from others
are written with ink I had of the same man, which
(rubbed over with a spirit) makes impressions into 280
many sheets, so that you have many bonds for one;
the sums are easily altered.

LADY CHEATLY. (*Aside.*)

What would this rascal have?

STEWARD.

A thousand pound! I scorn it: I aim at higher
things; I am a gentleman by[h] birth, your equal. 285

LADY CHEATLY. [*Aside.*]

Heaven and earth! What have I brought myself
to?—When my estate is out of dispute, I will
increase your reward.

STEWARD.

No madam, I have long honored and loved your
ladyship, and nothing less than your person can 290
ever satisfy me.

LADY CHEATLY.

How sir!

STEWARD.

Hold madam, if you use me roughly, I in a
moment will blast all your fortunes, and you shall
fly from hence as naked as you came. But if you'll 295
marry me, I'll be as humble a servant as I have
been before.

---

45 letters of reprisal] letters of marque (q.v.)

LADY CHEATLY. (*Aside.*)

Insolent villain. (*To him.*) Sure thou art not in earnest.

STEWARD.

By Heaven I am, and I will perish or attain my ends. 300

LADY CHEATLY. (*Aside.*)

He may undo me. Oh that I should lay my plots so shallow! I must have a trick for the rogue.—Give me time to consider of it.

STEWARD.

I can give none, nor will.

LADY CHEATLY.

Marriage would stop my business, and I shall get 305 no more money of my brother or others.

STEWARD.

We'll keep it private.

LADY CHEATLY.

Though modesty would not let me propose it to you, and I would rather have died than done it, I must confess the thing I wished for upon earth. 310

STEWARD.

Then I am happy and will serve you 'till my death.

LADY CHEATLY.

Forgive this frailty and use me well. Shame and blushes will confound me.

STEWARD.

Dear madam! There's no shame in love and marriage. (*Aside.*) I see she loves me. 315

LADY CHEATLY.

There yet remains one difficulty: you are my main witness, and (when we are married) you can be none; therefore, if you will go to a Master[46] in Chancery and swear to all my deeds and make affidavit to my false estate, the next hour shall 320 make you master of me and mine.

STEWARD. (*Aside.*)

Hah! I may be catched, and after I have sworn to that, I have no hank upon her.—Before, madam, I never will, but after, for my own sake, I must. I'll get a parson (whom I can trust) and none shall 325 know of the marriage but himself.

LADY CHEATLY. (*Aside.*)

This will not do, I must have another trick for the

_____

46 Master] an officer of the court who acts as assistant to the judge

rascal.—You have convinced me, but I am engaged to a parson already, whom I promised that office to. I'll send for him presently.* 330

STEWARD.

I am transported with my happiness.

LADY CHEATLY.

Withdraw, sir, I'll come to you instantly.

[Exit Steward.] Enter Prig.

Hah! This fellow shall be my engine,* and I must lose no time.—I am glad you are come: I have a business to communicate to you that concerns you 335 nearly, in which you must be secret.

PRIG.

Does it concern my honor? Madam, I'll cut their throats.

LADY CHEATLY.

No sir, it concerns your love.

PRIG.

Then I'll cut their throats too. 340

LADY CHEATLY.

No, it is not come to that. But just as I was resolved (having considered your passion) to bestow myself upon you—

PRIG.

Oh dear madam! Let me kiss your fair hand.

LADY CHEATLY.

Would you believe it? This villainous steward, 345 having writings in his hands for the greatest part of my estate, is arrived to that insolence, he threatens to burn 'em unless I will instantly marry him.

PRIG.

Oh dog! Rogue! Your servant, madam: I'll cut his throat immediately. 350

LADY CHEATLY.

Hold, sir, he's an odd, humorous fellow and will not have his throat cut.

PRIG.

Will he not? Why then I won't.

LADY CHEATLY.

I have designed a better way: to put a false marriage upon him, and you shall be my chaplain. 355 You can get the habit of a parson?

PRIG.

Aye, aye, this is very pretty. I your chaplain? Ha, ha! If my face would but look solid enough for a divine.

LADY CHEATLY.

I warrant you, 'tis a very judicious face and will
be very parsonical.   360

PRIG.

Not so, a gamester's at your service.

LADY CHEATLY.

And you can read the Common Prayer,[47] that's
material, for some gentleman can scarce read
nowadays.

PRIG.

I warrant you, madam. This will be the prettiest   365
trick.

LADY CHEATLY.

When you have married him and me about an
hour hence (nobody else being by), I'll take care
to pack him far enough afterwards and thus reserve
myself for you. Get a habit quickly and lay it in   370
the closet. Here's the key, there you shall shift. I
must be gone. (*Exit.*)

PRIG.

Oh happy man! I shall never need to sneak after a
lord, to sing catches, break jests, to eat and rook
with him. Well, I'll go no more to twelve, that's   375
certain. I'll get me a pack of fox dogs, hunt every
day, and play at the groom-porter's* at night.
(*Exit.*)

[Scene iii.] In the garden.

Enter Theodosia and Isabella.

THEODOSIA.

Dear Isabella, how I love these solitary walks, free
from the noise and importunity of men.

ISABELLA.

So much the contrary, that should you hear the
rattling of a coach, you'd be ready to leap over the
wall.   5

THEODOSIA.

If it were Bellamour's.

ISABELLA.

Why Bellamour's? No, though you knew it to be
a tired hackney with six dusty passengers in't. Thou
art the giddiest creature.

---

47 Common Prayer] i.e. the marriage service in the Angli-
    can Book of Common Prayer

THEODOSIA.

I do not love to be solid as you are and fix upon   10
one man; 'tis better to like all, and love none.

ISABELLA.

Thou hypocrite; do not I know that none but
Carlos can please you? He has caught you fast.

THEODOSIA.

No, never think so. Do but hear the men talk of
another, and 'tis antidote enough against 'em. They   15
are as malicious as we women and would quarrel
as often, if it were not for fear of fighting.

ISABELLA.

Of all men I wonder Stanmore 'scapes it; he speaks
well of no man.

THEODOSIA.

'Tis fit to speak ill of fops, who were lost to the   20
world if men of wit might not show 'em.

ISABELLA.

For ought I see, laughing at them does no hurt,
for they rise and get fortunes for all that. Fools are
lawful prize, but Stanmore speaks ill of witty men.

THEODOSIA.

When the witty men fall upon one another, they   25
make sport for the fools, and so laughing goes
round, no matter how.

ISABELLA.

Stanmore says, Carlos has an ill breath and takes
physic of a French surgeon, and that Bellamour
keeps* a player and will run out his estate.   30

THEODOSIA.

And yet you see how dear they are one to another
when they meet: 'tis the fashion.

Enter Gartrude.

GARTRUDE.

Oh sister, come hither! Here are four men
measuring of swords. I believe they are going to
fight in the next field.   35

Exeunt.

[Scene iv.] In the field.

Carlos, Prig, Stanmore, and Young Maggot.

YOUNG MAGGOT.

How shall I kill this Prig? He wants* two of his
vital parts, a brain and a heart.

PRIG.

I'll spoil your writing: have at your madrigal arm,
you wit you. (*Prig disarms Young Maggot and comes
up to Carlos.*)

STANMORE.

Carlos, you see our advantage.

CARLOS.

And scorn it. Have at you first. (*Disarms Prig. To
Stanmore.*) Now, sir, for you.   5

STANMORE.

We are friends, I love thee, prithee let it alone.

CARLOS.

Not so great friends: I overheard you speaking ill   10
of me to my mistress.

STANMORE.

Prithee Carlos, that's nothing: we all speak ill of
one another, and it goes for nothing.

CARLOS.

I am not of your opinion. Have at you.

STANMORE.

At you!   15

Carlos disarms Stanmore.

Well, you have it, and I am glad I had to do with
a brave man.

CARLOS.

You are men of honor and may be trusted with
your swords. Let's in amongst the ladies, as if
nothing had passed between us.   20

PRIG. [*Aside.*]

You may do what you will, but the valiant Prig
desires his widow may hear of his prowess at least.

YOUNG MAGGOT.

That I should be worsted by an ass.

Exeunt.

[Scene v. The garden.]

The Ladies reenter.

GARTRUDE.

I am afraid Carlos has hurt honest Mr. Stanmore,
but Carlos is a fine gentleman and fights so like a
gentleman. He said the prettiest things to me in
an arbor. Mr. Selfish could not have courted me
at a higher rate. I vow I begin to like him strangely.   5
I like a wit better than I did.

ISABELLA.

Thou'lt like any body.

THEODOSIA.

Pray Heaven Carlos be not hurt.

ISABELLA.

You seem disordered.

THEODOSIA.

No, no, what makest thou think so?   10

ISABELLA.

I am confident Carlos is not hurt.

THEODOSIA.

I think not of him.

ISABELLA.

I cannot blame you. I believe he has honesty to
his wit, and honor to his courage; I never saw a
finer gentleman.   15

GARTRUDE.

He has almost as taking a way with him as Mr.
Selfish.

THEODOSIA.

I don't like his face, 'tis too serious; his mien is stiff,
and he dances ill.

ISABELLA.

You are too nice:* his looks and mien are manly,   20
and he dances like a person of quality;* you are
for a page's face and a dancing master's legs, and I
hate both.

THEODOSIA.

Nay, never let's fall out about him.

ISABELLA.

If we should, he's here to part us.   25

Enter Carlos, Prig, and Young Maggot.

THEODOSIA.

He goes on faster with his task than I'd have him.

YOUNG MAGGOT.

There is no living two hours out of the beau
monde: I am out of the lady's company like a fish
out of the water. Is not that well said, Prig?

PRIG.

Not at all, the devil take me.   30

THEODOSIA.

Not so mute as a fish, I hope.

YOUNG MAGGOT.

No, we witty men are always talking, now and
then two or three of us at a time, invention does

so flow, but I had rather say one fine thing to a lady than twenty to the best wits in Town.   35

PRIG.

Say fine things! What a pox! Don't we all speak alike? Don't we all speak English?

THEODOSIA.

Had you never a mistress that was a fool?

YOUNG MAGGOT.

None are so gross but they guess when a man says a witty thing; when I say it, I am sure.   40

PRIG.

Pox on saying, I love doing a witty thing: to win a man's money is to outwit him, I think, and I'll undertake to win yours at ten several games.

YOUNG MAGGOT.

What, cheat me?

PRIG.

No, upon the square, by mere* judgment. A wit   45
is like a running horse, good for no earthly thing beside. When did you ever know any of 'em well with a great man or so much as taken down to a lord's house a-buck-hunting? They can drink some of 'em, but then they talk of philosophy, history,   50
poetry, as if they came into company to study. This is stuff the Devil would not hear.

THEODOSIA.

What would you have 'em talk of?

PRIG.

Why dogs, hawks and horses, crimp, trictrac, and primero. Make me a match at bowls or tennis over   55
a bottle; come, even or odd for two pieces, I hate to be idle.

ISABELLA.

What an intolerable fool is this!

PRIG.

There are three matches to be run at Newmarket, I'll bet money on every one of 'em: I'll hold you six to   60
four of the gelding against the mare; gold to silver on the bay stone-horse[48] against the fleabitten; and an even fifty pound, or what you will—

YOUNG MAGGOT.

You need not run your self out of breath. I will never bet while I live.   65

---

48 stone-horse] a horse that retains its stones or testicles: a
    stallion

PRIG.

Ladies, what think you of five merry guineas? Will either of you bet?

THEODOSIA. [Aside.]

I do not like Carlos his talking so long with that fool: she is young and handsome, she has beauty enough to invite, and folly enough to grant.   70

PRIG.

I hold five pound I make a tennis ball lie upon that stand once in thrice.

ISABELLA.

This fellow has no genius but to play nor no argument but a wager.

YOUNG MAGGOT.

One that wants* wit deserves not to bear the figure   75
of a man.

THEODOSIA.

Such fellows are but ciphers to you men of wit; they make you of greater value.

YOUNG MAGGOT.

I'll swear, that's well said. I don't think I could have said better myself.   80

PRIG.

What will you give me for this ring at the day of marriage?

CARLOS. [To Gartrude.]

You are so pretty and so obliging, there's no resisting both. But will you come and see my lodgings? I have the finest French things.   85

GARTRUDE.

Really sir, you are so courteous and well-behaved, I cannot deny you coming. You put me so in mind of Mr. Selfish: you have his way with you to a hair. Do you write too? He is a very pretty poet.

CARLOS. [Aside.]

Were I not sharp set, this would turn my   90
stomach.—Selfish steals all he writes out of French poetry; he has neither wit nor money but what he borrows. Forget him, and I'll be your servant.

GARTRUDE.

You shall promise to be very civil, when I come.

CARLOS. (Aside.)

She is very easy, pray Heaven she be sound.* I'll   95
promise anything. Well, Theodosia, if I be false, 'tis your command has pushed me into temptation.

PRIG.

Come, here's ten guineas, I'll lay 'em upon my toe, and in six times kick 'em all into my mouth.

ISABELLA.

And what if you do?   100

PRIG.

Talk of wit! I'll play at prick-penny[49] for twenty pound, with anyone here.

CARLOS.

I am for you at tennis.

PRIG.

I'll give you a bisk at Longs[50] for ten pound.

THEODOSIA.

Bowling methinks is better.   105

PRIG.

I'll give him one in seven for fifty pound.[i]

CARLOS.

We had better reserve our strength; I'll hunt tomorrow.

PRIG.

With all my heart. Halloo, hey Ringwood, Rockwood Jowler, hey. Well, I'll go and play in the   110
meantime.—Pox, this is the basest company, there's no money stirring. (*Exit.*)

THEODOSIA.

What could you do with that fool all this while?

CARLOS.

In obedience to your command, I suffered her impertinence. You are a very tyrant: your beauty obliges me   115
to love none but you, and yet you'll have me make love to all. Flesh and blood is not able to bear it.

THEODOSIA.

Not so: I would have you gain their esteem and be cried up among 'em. Using us scurvily often does that. Women love the careless, insolent, and loud.   120

CARLOS.

Faith madam, I am a moral man, I do as I would be done by.

THEODOSIA.

I would not be in love with you for a million: 'twould tempt you horribly.

CARLOS.

It would tempt me to vanity, but never to   125
ingratitude.

THEODOSIA.

Vanity and ingratitude are as inseparable as old age and ugliness. They that think too well of themselves, ever think too ill of others, and I will give you no temptation of any kind.   130

CARLOS.

You are nothing but temptation: your face, your shape, your voice, nay, your very coldness is a tempter, and therefore have a care on't.

ISABELLA.

You have met with the greatest tyrant of our sex.

CARLOS.

The greatest conqueror, but she has too much   135
goodness for a tyrant; however, I'll tire her cruelty with my patience, and I'll hold her the greatest wager in the world that I get her heart at last.

THEODOSIA.

You have a pretty confidence. Pray what's your wager?   140

CARLOS.

A wedding night.

THEODOSIA.

Who shall be judge?

CARLOS.

Your friend here.

THEODOSIA.

I can't have a better. Done.

CARLOS.

Done, madam. I am sure good service and   145
perseverance will gain a reasonable woman, where there is not a downright antipathy, and I am resolved never to give you over.

THEODOSIA.

Love in this age is as well counterfeited as complexion: what with the men's lying and   150
swearing, and the women's waters and washes,[51] we know not what to make of one another.

CARLOS.

Try me with commands.

THEODOSIA.

I must have you poetical: that's a great sign of love in a man of wit. I must have songs and sonnets plenty.   155

---

49 prick-penny] a game of dice involving legerdemain
50 Longs] Summers suggests the famous ordinary (tavern with food) in the Haymarket, although another of the same name existed in Convent Garden,* and a place with a tennis court would seem to be indicated.

---

51 waters and washes] colognes and cosmetics

CARLOS.

Very well.

THEODOSIA.

I must never have you see a play but when I am there.

CARLOS.

That is, I must see none at all, for when you are there, I can see nothing but yourself.   160

THEODOSIA.

Then upon no pretence whatsoever must you go behind the scenes.

CARLOS.

That's grown the sign of a fop, and for my own sake I'll avoid it.

THEODOSIA.

But the women have beauty and wit enough to   165
hearken to a keeper.

CARLOS.

Some of 'em are so far from having wit of their own that they spoil that little the poets put into 'em by base utterance, and for beauty they lay it on so, that 'tis much alike from fifteen to five and   170
forty.

THEODOSIA.

Item, you must not talk with visors* in the pit,* though they look never* so like women of quality* and are never* so coming.

CARLOS.

Be it so. I never knew any good come of that way   175
of fooling yet, for if they were afraid of me, I was ever more afraid of them. But how shall I arrive at the general fame and reputation you spoke of, with these restraints? The men in vogue forbear none of all these things; they dive like ducks at one   180
end of the pit and rise at the other, then whisk into the whore-boxes, then into the scenes, and always hurry up and down.[52] The devils in an opera are not so busy.[53]

THEODOSIA.

You must take other courses.   185

---

52 scenes … down] Rakehells were notorious for actually going on stage during a performance.
53 devils … busy] a reference to Shadwell's 1674 operatic version of Dryden and Davenant's revision of Shakespeare's *Tempest*

CARLOS.

I have bespoken a play for you and all the good company of this house; when the other is done, I hope, madam, you will honor it with your presence.

THEODOSIA.

I'll do as the rest do.   190

ISABELLA.

This is a new piece of gallantry, Theodosia.

THEODOSIA.

The invitation's general.

GARTRUDE. [*Aside.*]

How mad would they be, if they knew this were meant to me?

Enter Maggot, unseen by the rest.

YOUNG MAGGOT.

Now pretty Mrs. Gartrude and the rest of the good   195
company, I have the poem about me which I told you I writ upon beauty. 'Tis elaborate. I kept my chamber about it as long as a spark does of a clap or a lady of a child; I purged and bled and entered into a diet about it, and that made me have so clear   200
a complexion and write so well, and brought down my belly too.

MAGGOT.

How now, wit! Let me see that damned poem you lay in of so long when you should have studied the law.   205

YOUNG MAGGOT.

Oh Heaven! I am undone.

MAGGOT.

I shall spoil that month's work.

YOUNG MAGGOT.

Ladies, pray intercede for me and save my poem.

THEODOSIA.

Hold sir, reprieve it.

YOUNG MAGGOT.

'Tis not mine, 'tis a friend's of mine.   210

MAGGOT.

Ah graceless fool! The worst friend thou hast: thyself thou meanest. (*He tears it and scatters it.*)

YOUNG MAGGOT.

Save this, and I will never be witty again.

MAGGOT.

No sir, there, there, so, 'tis done.

Young Maggot goes to gather up the pieces.

By Heaven, touch a piece on't, and I'll disinherit   215
you.

CARLOS.

Let me intercede for him. He'll mend, and be less
witty everyday.

YOUNG MAGGOT.

Forgive me once, and I'll mend and be as dull as
an old fat alderman that sleeps over justice at the   220
Old Bailey.54

MAGGOT.

At your simile's again? Oh you incorrigible wit! Let
me see what poetry you have about you.

YOUNG MAGGOT.

Ladies, for Heaven's sake, plead for me, or I am
utterly ruined.—Sir, will you disgrace me before   225
my mistress Gartrude?

MAGGOT.

Hang you, coxcomb. She hates wit, because she's
a fool, as I do, because I am wise. Stand still. (*He
pulls out bundles of papers.*)

YOUNG MAGGOT.

Mercy upon me! What will become of me?   230

ISABELLA.

Good Mr. Maggot, be more merciful.

MAGGOT.

What's here? A poem called, "A Posy for the Ladies'
Delight." A second, "The Flower of Love's
Constancy." An "Answer" to it. "Distichs to Write
upon Lady's Busks." "Epigram Written in a Lady's   235
Bible in Covent-Garden-Church." Oh wicked wit!
"Posies for Wedding Rings." Oh idle rakehell! I
shall have you come to write to tobacco boxes and
swordblades and knives and to all the ironwork at
Sheffield: all these go to it.   240

YOUNG MAGGOT.

Hold good sir, hold, upon my knees I beg you'll
hold. Here cut off this joint, this, this, any joint
about me, so you'll spare my poetry.

THEODOSIA.

Have pity on the poor gentleman.

GARTRUDE.

Oh pray, give me those upon the busks.   245

---

54 Old Bailey] central criminal court, beside Newgate
prison

MAGGOT.

Not one shall live to make him infamous.j Must
you needs be a wit to the dishonor of your family
and the disturbance of your good old father's ashes?
I never knew one of our family a witk before. I'll
alter my will instantly. (*Exit.*)   250

YOUNG MAGGOT.

Nay, now you may hang me an* you will, now you
have torn my poetry. I have never a copy of any
of 'em. I will go hide my self in a hole and never
show my head again. (*Exit.*)

CARLOS.

Come ladies, shall we prepare for the play after this   255
farce?

ISABELLA.

With all our hearts.

Act IV, [scene i]. The playhouse.

*Enter Carlos, Theodosia, Prig, Lady Cheatly, Maggot,
Lady Busy, Bellamour, Isabella, Stanmore, Gartrude,
Young Maggot, and Selfish and others coming into the
playhouse, seating themselves.*

ISABELLA.

By being masked, I shall observe Bellamour's actions.

GARTRUDE.

Now nobody will know me; they'll take me for you
in this petticoat.

ISABELLA.

If you hold your tongue, sister. But that makes a
great difference betwixt us.   5

GARTRUDE.

Aye, but I'll whisper, and they shall not know my
voice.

ISABELLA.

But they'll soon discover your sense.

CARLOS.

My dear mistress, since you accept my service, I
am resolved to ply you so that I must win at last.   10

THEODOSIA.

You are very resolute and shall find me so. You
think to go on like the French king: we shall have
you do as he does by a town in Flanders,* set a
day when you will take me.l

CARLOS.

I hope to corrupt you within with love and make   15
my conquest easier.

BELLAMOUR.

I wonder Isabella is not here, Stanmore. I am so damnably in love, I am afraid thou'lt never own me; I am a very recreant.

STANMORE.

My mistress is not here neither. Her folly has a little cooled my love, but I have a most abominable lust to her, the wiser passion of the two, and no despair: though that rogue Selfish has her mind, I do not doubt but to get her body, which is worth two of it for my use.

YOUNG MAGGOT.

I wonder pretty Mrs. Gartrude is not here.

SELFISH.

I am amazed at it, for she knew I was to come.

A great knocking at the door. Enter doorkeeper.

CARLOS.

How now! What means that knocking?

DOORKEEPER.

Sir, ladies and several gentlemen knock to get in.

CARLOS.

Let the ladies in for nothing, but make the men pay.

Exit doorkeeper.

PRIG.

Had you ever such a chaplain? I was so disguised, he could not suspect me; methinks I dispatched the business as well as if I had been used to be married myself.

LADY CHEATLY.

'Twas very well. I have since gotten my deeds from him, and because he was a main witness to many of my bonds and mortgages, I have made him swear to 'em all before a Master in Chancery, upon pretence that when it should be known he was my husband, his testimony would not be good.

PRIG.

Ha! Ha! Ha! This was the prettiest invention and will make well for us. But where is the fool?

LADY CHEATLY.

There is a kinsman of mine going for the Indies: I sent him to him with an hundred pound for a venture and have taken care he shall not come back again, for he'll clap him under hatches, carry him

away, and sell him for a rogue[55] as he is. He sails this tide.

Several more come in [including several doorkeepers], women masked and men of several sorts. Several young coxcombs fool with the orange women. *

ORANGE WOMAN.

Oranges, will you have any oranges?

FIRST BULLY.

What play do they play? Some confounded play or other.

PRIG.

A pox on't, madam! What should we do at this damned playhouse? Let's send for some cards, and play at langtriloo in the box. Pox on 'em! I ne'er saw a play had anything in't; some of 'em have wit now and then, but what care I for wit?

SELFISH.

Does my cravat sit well? I take all the care I can it should. I love to appear well. What ladies are here in the boxes? Really I never come to a play, but upon account of seeing the ladies.

CARLOS.

Doorkeeper, are they ready to begin?

DOORKEEPER.

Yes, immediately.

SELFISH.

Now you shall see the ladies make up to me; where e're I am, they flock about me. I think I am one of the happiest men on earth! I thank Heaven every day for making me just as I am, Bellamour.

BELLAMOUR. [*Aside.*]

That's Isabella, I am sure, I know the petticoat; what a devil makes her talk to that rogue?

Gartrude chooses to sit by Selfish.

YOUNG MAGGOT.

You'll find it an admirable plot; there's great force and fire in the writing; so full of business and trick, and very fashionable; it passed through my hands; some of us helped him in it.

---

55 sell … rogue] criminals and the poor were often transported or "spirited" (shanghaied) to the colonies, where they were "indentured"—or virtually enslaved; the steward has been spirited but will be passed off as a transported criminal

FIRST BULLY.

Dam'me! When will these fellows begin? Plague
on't! here's a staying.   75

SECOND MAN.

Whose play is this?

THIRD MAN.

One Prickett's, poet Prickett.

FIRST MAN.

Oh hang him! Pox on him! He cannot write.
Prithee let's to Whitehall.*

YOUNG MAGGOT.

Not write, sir? I am one of his patrons. I know the   80
wits don't like him, but he shall write with any of
'em all for an hundred pound.

PRIG.

Aye that he shall. They say, he puts no wit in his
plays, but 'tis all one for that, they do the business.
He is my poet too, I hate wit.   85

Enter several ladies and several men.

DOORKEEPER.

Pray sir, pay me, my masters will make me pay it.

THIRD MAN.

Impudent rascal! Do you ask me for money? Take
that, sirrah. [*Strikes him.*]

SECOND DOORKEEPER.

Will you pay me, sir?

FOURTH MAN.

No: I don't intend to stay.   90

SECOND DOORKEEPER.

So you say every day and see two or three acts for
nothing.

FOURTH MAN.

I'll break your head, you rascal.

FIRST DOORKEEPER.

Pray sir, pay me.

THIRD MAN.

Set it down, I have no silver about me, or bid my   95
man pay you.

THEODOSIA.

What, do gentlemen run on tick for plays?

CARLOS.

As familiarly as with their tailors.

THIRD DOORKEEPER.

Pox on you, sirrah! Go and bid 'em begin quickly.

*Exit [first] doorkeeper. The [company] play[s during]
the curtain-time, then take their places.*

CARLOS.

Now they'll begin.   100

Selfish and Young Maggot go to sit down.

YOUNG MAGGOT.ᵐ

Don't come to us, let you wits sit together. [*To
Lady Cheatly.*] These fellows will be witty and
trouble us.—Go to your brother wits and make a
noise among yourselves, brother wits.

They go on the other side.

SELFISH.

I am always hated by the fools, but I think it rather   105
out of envy than malice.

BELLAMOUR.

Faith! you shan't sit by us.

STANMORE.

Gentlemen, do not mistake yourselves, for you are
no wits, though y'are poets, and we will not own
you of our party.   110

YOUNG MAGGOT.

This is mere* envy against us writers, Selfish.

SELFISH.

It is so. I for my part will throw myself at a lady's
feet, play with her fan, and fan her gently with it.

The play begins. Enter lover and wife.

LOVER.

Dear madam, let us not omit any occasion but take
every opportunity by the hand to improve those   115
amours, which have rendered us so happy to be
elevated above the reach of envy.

WIFE.

Sir, I should not entertain a thought that might
in any wise be prejudicial to our amours or the
improvement thereof, if I were not so extremely   120
obnoxious to* the great infelicity of being subject
to a husband, whose jealousy has so much the
ascendant over him that it renders him so vigilant
not seldom to interrupt our happiest hours.

LOVER.

That turbulent temper does too often disorder the   125
fair quiet of his own mind, as well as discompose
ours, and jealousy proves as often an obstruction
to his own tranquility as it does an impediment
to our fruition.

WIFE.

It is a privilege too absolutely imperious, which, by a seeming conjugal right, our husbands claim over us to make so subtle a scrutiny into all our enterprizes, since they with too great a regret entertain the least motion of ours whereby we would insinuate into their affairs.

LOVER.

But since Fortune (by so many frequent signalizations) has demonstrated how much she is a friend to us in assisting us with so many subterfuges when most we have needed them, it will be a heinous tergiversation from her to abandon that trust we formerly have reposed in her, and she may justly take a pique at our infidelity and, in that caprice, may contrive a revenge suitable to our delinquency.

WIFE.

Rather, Fortune may be apt to believe us too audacious in tempting her with so much importunity that it must needs be more vexatious than agreeable, and while we make such vigorous addresses to another deity, for ought we know, Love may wax jealous of our applications to it: for though he's blind, he can descry and will greatly resent our dereliction, and, when he is incensed, his nature is highly vindicative.

LOVER.

When Fortune takes such pains to assist us in our amours, Love will certainly be very sensible of our omission, and when he is once provoked, he seldom buries injuries in the grave of oblivion.

THEODOSIA.

This is very lewd stuff! Is this the new way of writing?

CARLOS.

A man would think these lovers in plays did not care a farthing for one another, when they find nothing to do but to be florid and talk impertinently when they are alone.

YOUNG MAGGOT.

This is a very strong, sinewy, and correct style, and yet neat, and florid.

SELFISH.

I have taught 'em all this way of writing; I always strive to write like a gentleman, so easy, and well-bred.

PRIG.

These are very good lines, faith.

YOUNG MAGGOT.

Nay, 'tis admirably worded, that's the truth on't.

FIRST MAN.

Dam'me! I don't like it.

SECOND MAN.

Pox on the coxcomb that writ it! There's nothing in't.

FIRST MAN.

God I love drums and trumpets and much ranting, roaring, huffing, and fretting and good store of noise in a play.

LOVER.

I have sufficiently confuted all your argumentation, and nothing then remains but that I should humbly petition to hold the honor of your fair embraces.

WIFE.

The motion is so civil and savors so much of a sincere affection that I can no longer resist it.

LOVER.

Let us retire.

WIFE.

Come.

Exit Lover and Wife.

BELLAMOUR.

So, now they are come to the matter in hand. But here comes the husband.

The husband knocks at the door and turns his back.
The lover kicks him several times and retires.

YOUNG MAGGOT.

Now it begins to warm; 'tis an admirable plot.

SELFISH.

Bellamour, see how kind the ladies are to me.— Pretty rogue! Let me repose my head in thy soft bosom.

BELLAMOUR.

'Sdeath!* What's this? She will not speak to me yet suffers that familiarity with that rascal as if it were on purpose to provoke me.

CARLOS.

Why does not the fool look where the blows come?

THEODOSIA.

Oh! That would spoil the plot.

HUSBAND.

This must be the Devil that strikes me. Some whoring rogue or other is gotten with my wife, and the Devil pimps for him. But I have a key to a back door and will surprise him. (*Exit.*)   195

STANMORE.

I cannot find my mistress, but I'll divert myself with a vizard* in the meantime.

FIRST MAN.

What, not a word? All over in disguise: silence for your folly and a vizard for your ill face?   200

SECOND MAN. (*To a vizard.*)

Gad! Some whore, I warrant you, or chambermaid, in her lady's old clothes. (*He sits down and lolls in the orange-wench's lap.*)

THIRD MAN.

She must be a woman of quality;* she has right point.[56]   205

FOURTH MAN.

Faith! She earns all the clothes on her back by lying on't: some punk* lately turned out of keeping,* her livery not quite worn out.

ISABELLA.

I deserve this by coming in a mask, and if I should now discover* myself, 'twould make a quarrel.*   210

PRIG.

You shall see what tricks I'll play. Faith! I love to be merry. (*Raps people on the backs and twirls their hats and then looks demurely as if he did not do it.*)

Enter two lovers, and wife.

SECOND LOVER.

Have I catcht them? I was jealous of this before, but now I will make further discovery. (*Goes under the table.*)   215

FIRST LOVER.

In verity it savors of incivility to interrupt our joys in the middle of our felicity, but since the barbarous intruder is defeated, let us embrace the present occasion, which seems to court us.   220

WIFE.

If anything which I can do can felicitate you, you may command my person.

SECOND LOVER.

Oh damned jade!

---

56 right point] genuine lace

Enter husband.

WIFE.

Oh God! My husband.   225

FIRST LOVER.

'Sdeath!* What shall we do?

YOUNG MAGGOT.

Now it thickens, an admirable plot.

HUSBAND. (*Falls over a form and breaks his shins and puts out the candle.*)

Oh my shins, my shins!

WIFE.

'Tis as we wished.

[The husband] takes up the candle and blows it in again.

YOUNG MAGGOT.

There's a turn. Who would expect that? As great a turn as can be, from darkness to light: Can anything be greater?   230

FIRST LOVER.

Now we are undone again.

HUSBAND.

Now tremble at my vengeance, thou most perfidious strumpet, for I will kill thee before thou prayest.   235

WIFE.

What means my dearest honey?

HUSBAND.

Oh thou salacious jade! Canst thou ask, when that stallion-rogue is there.

WIFE.

What rogue? Art thou mad? Here's nobody.

HUSBAND.

Nobody? Why, who's that? Thou most lascivious quean!   240

WIFE.

Where?

HUSBAND.

There.

WIFE.

I see nobody. Thou art distracted.

FIRST LOVER.

How I adore her for her wit.   245

HUSBAND.

What fellow's that, huswife?

WIFE.

Which? I see none.

HUSBAND.

But I do, and have at him first.

WIFE.

Hold, my dear, if thou seest anybody, it is the
Devil, and if thou strik'st it, it will tear thee in 250
pieces.

HUSBAND.

Are you mad? Do you see nobody there?

WIFE.

No, Heaven knows, not I. Oh Heaven! The house
is haunted. What does it look like?

HUSBAND.

Oh Lord! It looks like a man. Hah! Methinks he 255
has glaring eyes. Oh! oh! I see his cloven foot: this
is that that struck me just now. Oh, Heaven help
me!

WIFE.

Oh help! I swound, I swound.

HUSBAND.

Oh my dear wife! Oh the Devil! 260

First lover goes under the table.

SECOND LOVER.

Have I caught you, sir?

FIRST LOVER.

Since you have, for the lady's sake, don't discover*
me.

WIFE.

Oh! Is it there still, my dear?

HUSBAND.

No, I think 'tis gone. Hah! 'tis vanished. 265

YOUNG MAGGOT.

Well, it concerns me so, I am not able to bear it.

HUSBAND.

My poor dear! I have wronged thee. Prithee forgive
me.

WIFE.

I am always abused thus by you. I am too honest.*

HUSBAND.

Prithee forgive me, I will never tax thee more, but 270
I must change my house if it be thus haunted.

WIFE.

I am afraid to live here any longer. Do, my dear.

ISABELLA.

I see Bellamour minds no woman but my foolish
sister (whom, I fear, he takes for me), yet she is so

ridiculously fond of that fool that he cannot 275
reasonably imagine I would be.

SELFISH.

Do you not see how fond that pretty creature is of
me? I make no doubt but I shall enjoy her person.

BELLAMOUR.

Damnation on this rascal! Can a woman of so much
wit like him? I'll watch her. Women have odd, 280
fantastic appetites, and there's no trusting of 'em.

SECOND LOVER.

'Tis too apparent that she's false to me, and I'll
revenge it by discovering* her to her husband, for
all her trick.

FIRST LOVER.

I will cut your throat if you offer it. 285

SECOND LOVER.

Nay then, you rascal, have at you.

*They scuffle under the table, rise with it on their backs;
the table falls down; they draw their swords and fight.*

HUSBAND.

Oh villainous woman! Are these spirits? Now I am
convinced. I know one whoremaster too well to
believe it.

*Prig strikes a bully over the back; he takes it to be
another and strikes him. They fight.*

FIRST MAN.

Zounds you rogue! Do you play your tricks with me? 290

SECOND MAN.

Have at you, dog.

CARLOS.

Impudent rascals! Have at you all.

*Bellamour, Stanmore, Carlos beat the bullies out of the
house; the actors run off; ladies run out shrieking.*

SELFISH.

I will make good the ladies retreat. (*He retreats
behind the ladies, with his sword drawn.*)

BELLAMOUR.

Where is this Selfish gone? I must watch him and 295
the lady. (*Exit.*)

CARLOS.

What rascals and cowards are these bullies! Where
are the ladies? Boy, go out and bid the players go on.

Enter Theodosia and Isabella.

Oh madam! I am ashamed of this disorder.

THEODOSIA.

Are you not hurt, sir? 300

CARLOS.

Only a little in the hand.

THEODOSIA.

Come tomorrow, and my shock dog shall lick you whole. A hurt in the hand? Why, 'tis gotten with opening of oysters and cured with a cobweb.[57]

CARLOS.

If you will but pity the wounds you give yourself, 305
I'll ne'er complain to you of any other.

ISABELLA.

Theodosia may affect ill nature, which perhaps her heart is no more guilty of than mine. But I am sure I am extremely troubled at your hurt and would not have you neglect it. 310

CARLOS.

You are too obliging, 'tis slight and worth neither of your[n] cares.

GARTRUDE.

Oh Lord! Mr. Carlos is hurt, I shall swoon. Oh dear sir! My heart went pit a pat all the while you were fighting. 315

CARLOS.

That pretty heart should only leap for joy.

LADY BUSY.

Sir, pray let me be so happy as to apply my white ointment; 'tis very sovereign for a green wound.

LADY CHEATLY.

I have a balsam that never fails, and I were most unhappy if one I esteem so well should miscarry 320
for want of it.

THEODOSIA.

Here's a do about a slight hurt; a butcher at the Bear Garden* makes nothing of forty such. I would have the sun shine through my servant now and then.

CARLOS.

You would have one serve you as they do a 325
mountebank, to be run through for him.

ISABELLA.

I cannot rest till I see if Bellamour be wounded. (*Exit.*)

Enter one of the actors.

ACTOR.

Sir, we cannot go on with our play: one of our young women, being frighted with the swords, is 330
fallen into a fit and carried home sick.

CARLOS.

Boy, go and find the company. I have prepared an entertainment upon the stage: we'll have an entry, a song, or some music. There is no loss of the play. This Prickett can write none but low farce, and his 335
fools are rather odious than ridiculous.

THEODOSIA.

You are once in the right.

CARLOS.

My cruel mistress! You see I had some favor from every one but yourself.

THEODOSIA.

I believe it has cost you five pound in penny 340
gleek[58] to get the good will of the old ladies, and the hopes of marriage has prevailed upon the young ones.

CARLOS.

I was never so serious as that comes to with any but yourself. 345

THEODOSIA.

No more of this. I accept your entertainment.

[Exeunt.]

[Scene ii.] The stage and scenes
[of the play-within-the-play].

Enter Selfish and Gartrude.

SELFISH.

Now if your love has any resolution, you may enjoy me and make yourself the happiest lady in Town and please me too.

GARTRUDE.

Indeed you are so well-bred and so much a gentleman, the ladies cannot but love you. 5

SELFISH.

I have no reason to complain.

GARTRUDE.

And then you dress so finely.

---

57 cured … cobweb] traditional folk cure, but listed in Schroeder's *Compleat Chymical Dispensatory* (1669)

58 gleek] a three-handed card game played with a forty-four card deck

SELFISH.

Indeed, most young fellows when they come to Town, dress at me. But pretty creature, let us retire.

GARTRUDE.

What you please, dear sir, if you'll be civil. 10

SELFISH. [*Aside*.]

Pretty soul! How she loves me! I am a rogue to be false to these poor creatures.—While they divert themselves with the vulgar entertainments of music and dancing, I will steal the happiest minute that love and beauty can afford. 15

GARTRUDE.

You shall not need to steal; I'll give you anything. But will you make a song on me?

SELFISH.

Thou shalt be my Chloris, my Phyllis, CÆlia, my all. Let's away my dear.

Exit Selfish and Gartrude. Enter Bellamour.

BELLAMOUR.

Whither is that rascal carrying Isabella? She must 20 do this on purpose to make me mad, for I can never believe she can like Selfish. I'll follow. (*Exit*.)

Enter Stanmore and Isabella.

STANMORE.

Well, you must be my mistress: my heart beats, and I have a thousand disorders upon me which none but she can cause. 25

ISABELLA.

It beats a false alarm for once. [*Lifts and replaces mask.*] You see I am not she, but she is somewhere behind the scenes. Pray go and look after her.

Exit Stanmore. Enter Carlos and Theodosia.

THEODOSIA.

Prithee pull off thy mask and conceal thyself no longer. 30

ISABELLA.

Do not discover* me. I hear Bellamour keeps a player; I am resolved to watch him and see if I can make any discovery. [*Exit.*]

Enter Lady Cheatly, Lady Busy, Prig, Maggot, [and carpenter].

MAGGOT.

Madam, your ladyship is so pestered with this gamester Prig that I cannot have time to talk with 35 you.

LADY CHEATLY.

I am so, and I have business of great concernment to confer with you about. Would I were rid of him.

MAGGOT.

I'll have a trick for him.

PRIG.

Sirrah Maggot! I will not suffer you to talk to my 40 lady; she is mine, you old fool.

MAGGOT.

Come out, you young blockhead, and let our swords try whose she is.

PRIG.

Let's fight here. I would have my mistress see how I put in my pass and what a yerk I give it. 45

MAGGOT.

Thou o'ergrown coward!

LADY CHEATLY.

Gentlemen, I must not suffer quarreling* before me. Mr. Prig, be more temperate.

PRIG.

I will, madam, though 'tis hard when love or honor bids me draw. 50

Enter Young Maggot.

YOUNG MAGGOT.

Gentlemen, be not so much troubled that the play was interrupted by the bullies, for I have a poem about me, which I'll entertain you with, that perhaps may be more agreeable. I will read it to you. 55

CARLOS.

But first let's have a dance.

YOUNG MAGGOT.

With all my heart.

LADY CHEATLY.

Do you hear, carpenter? Can you make the machines work? I shall have use of 'em.

CARPENTER.

Yes, madam. 60

LADY CHEATLY.

Pray be ready when I give you order, do you hear? Thus. Let us all sit and see this dance.

An entry of clowns. Enter Lump.*

LADY CHEATLY.

My brother's here. What shall we do now?

LUMP.

I am ashamed, sister, of your sin and vanity and cannot in conscience let you alone in your evil ways. What makes you in this wicked place? this sink of sin? this house of abominations, where wise men and godly men are abused? It is great wickedness, and I cannot be silent; my zeal and wisdom will not let me be silent.

LADY CHEATLY.

Brother, have a little breeding, as well as zeal and wisdom, and do not disturb the gentlemen.

LUMP.

I care not for breeding. Shall zeal and wisdom give place to that? I say, 'tis not lawful, 'tis sinful, 'tis abominable, to come under the roof with these hornets. There is wit, flashy wit stirring here, and I would as soon be in a pesthouse.

LADY CHEATLY.

I must comply with those I have designs upon for my fortune's sake and for my daughters'.

LUMP.

That does something mollify the sin, but it is too great, and I cannot bear it. Cannot you take religious courses in order to your design? And then you may serve Heaven and yourself together. You are foolish, very foolish, and have no method in you.

CARLOS.

This gentleman is going to read a pious poem to us. Pray, do not interrupt him.

LUMP.

Sir, I must interrupt him, I have a call, a great call to it. All poetry is abominable, and all wit is an idol, a very* Dagon,[59] I will down with it. All the wise and godly party of the Nation hate wit.

YOUNG MAGGOT.

None but fools hate wit, and those that cannot think. For my part, I will venture my blood in defense of poetry.

LUMP.

I will preach against it while I have breath.

YOUNG MAGGOT.

Peace, fool! I will read on.

LUMP.

Sister, you shall not hear it: 'tis profane, abominable, a grace-resisting, soul-destroying, conscience-choking, most unutterably sin-nourishing thing, and I cannot bear it, I cannot suffer it.

Lady Cheatly whistles: two mock-devils descend and fly up with Lump.

Murder, murder, what dost thou do, Satan? Whither dost thou fly with me?

YOUNG MAGGOT.

This is very well. Ha! Ha! Ha! Now I may read in quiet.

PRIG.

Pray my dear, let's be going. I hate this wit. I think Mr. Lump is in the right.

LADY CHEATLY.

Sit but a while, and I'll go.

YOUNG MAGGOT. (*Reads.*)

"Beauty, thou great preserver of the world,
By which into dead lumps, quick* life is hurled—"

Prig and Young Maggot are carried up in their chairs and hang in the air.

LADY CHEATLY.

So, now I shall have time to speak with you.

Exit Maggot, Lady Cheatly, Lady Busy.

PRIG.

Hold! Hold! Murder! Murder! What a devil do you mean? My dear! Honey! Where is my lady? Madam! Madam!

YOUNG MAGGOT.

What can this mean? But hold, I'll read on, if you will. "Beauty thou great, etc."

All go out, and leave 'em hanging.

PRIG.

They are all gone. What shall I do? Pox on your wit, sirrah! This is your wit, you damned wit, you.

YOUNG MAGGOT.

You lie, fool! 'Tis a wheadle,[60] a crossbite* of the widow's.

---

59 Dagon] or Dagan, west Semitic god of fertility, particularly for the Philistines, whose temple to Dagon Samson destroyed (Judges 16)

60 wheadle] a sharper's trick using wheedling (q.v.) (Partridge)

PRIG.

Oh, you damned, scribbling, senseless, singsong wit!

YOUNG MAGGOT.

Oh you damned, gaming, jockey, hunting, tennis   120
fool.

Enter Bellamour.

BELLAMOUR.

Hell and damnation! What have I seen? A curse
on all the sex! Is this the virtue she pretended to?
To be lewd with so despicable a coxcomb as Selfish,
so nauseous a fellow! Death and Hell!   125

PRIG.

Hark you, Bellamour, prithee help me down.

YOUNG MAGGOT.

Pray let me down.

BELLAMOUR.

Pox on you both.

Enter Selfish.

SELFISH.

Ah Bellamour! I am the happiest man, I think, that
ever the sun shined on: I have enjoyed the prettiest   130
creature, just now, in a room behind the scenes. I
cannot help telling of thee because thou art my
friend. Faith! telling is half the pleasure to me, for
I confess to thee, I think, we that are happy in
ladies' affections make love as much for vanity as   135
anything else. You know the lady.

BELLAMOUR. (*Aside.*)

Damn the dog.—'Twas one of my lady Cheatly's
daughters. Which of 'em was it?

SELFISH.

Well, I can keep nothing from thee: it was one of
'em, but upon your honor, keep it secret. Guess   140
which—they are both desperately in love with me,
hah!

BELLAMOUR.

Impudent rascal and coxcomb! (*He strikes him, then
beats him with his sword.*)

SELFISH.

What ill breeding is this? Are you distracted?   145

[Enter Isabella.]

ISABELLA.

Heaven! What's the matter? Hold, hold.

BELLAMOUR.

Be gone, rascal, or I'll run you through.

SELFISH.

I will not be uncivil before a lady. Another time I
shall call you to an account.—An ill-bred fellow!
(*Exit.*)   150

ISABELLA.

What's the reason of this quarrel?*

BELLAMOUR.

Here, carpenter.

[Enter carpenter.]

CARPENTER.

Here, sir.

BELLAMOUR.

Let down those fools and dispose of 'em so they
may not trouble us.   155

Carpenter lets 'em down, and presently they sink
down and roar out.*

PRIG.

So, this is well.

YOUNG MAGGOT.

Bellamour, I thank you.

BELLAMOUR.

You know too well the occasion of the quarrel.

ISABELLA.

What do you mean?

BELLAMOUR.

Is all your pretense of virtue come to this? and   160
must my love be thus rewarded?

ISABELLA.

This rudeness of yours amazes me.

BELLAMOUR.

'Tis I have cause to be amazed: to be refused the
favor, and you grant it to that filthy fool, Selfish.
There's nothing but dissembling, treachery, and   165
ingratitude in your whole sex.

ISABELLA.

A favor to Selfish? The fool of all the world I scorn
and hate the most? But now I see you'll give me
occasion to rank you with him.

BELLAMOUR.

No, you shall never rank me with him. I scorn to   170
be obliged to one who is so free to lay out herself
upon such an ass.

ISABELLA.

Has that vain rascal lied on me? and do you believe him?

BELLAMOUR.

My eyes will not lie, madam, I will trust them. And though you have let down your skirt, I know the petticoat too well.   175

ISABELLA.

Unworthy man! I could stab thee for this affront, but that thou art not worthy of a serious thought. Is this the petticoat you mean?—What has my foolish sister done?   180

BELLAMOUR.

How? This is not the petticoat.

Enter Stanmore and Gartrude barefaced.

Heaven and earth! 'twas Gartrude I see now.

ISABELLA.

I scorn and hate thee, for thy base suspicion, more than all mankind.   185

BELLAMOUR.

Madam, I am a dog, a villain,* not fit to live. Kill me, for if you forgive me not, I'll do't myself.

ISABELLA.

I'll never see thy odious face again, do what thou wilt. Farewell, base man. (*Exit.*)

BELLAMOUR.

Hell and devils! What has my rashness brought me to? (*Exit.*)   190

STANMORE.

Pretty miss! Be not so troubled. I have used thee kindly, very kindly.

GARTRUDE.

Kindly? Oh sad! I'll tell my mother what you have done to me, so I will.   195

STANMORE.

Thou art not mad, child!* Prithee don't.

GARTRUDE.

But I was mad to let you be so uncivil, and I will tell her. Here she is.

Enter Lady Busy, Lady Cheatly, and Maggot.

STANMORE.

S'heart! What a fool she is! I'll not stand the brunt. (*Exit.*)   200

MAGGOT.

Well madam, I'll dispatch the business and wait on you again. (*Exit.*)

GARTRUDE.

Oh madam! What shall I do? What shall I do?

LADY CHEATLY.

What's the matter?

GARTRUDE.

I thought what 'twould come to: you charged me to be civil to Stanmore, and I am deflowered, so I am.   205

LADY CHEATLY.

Oh Heaven! What, did he ravish you?

GARTRUDE.

No, because you bid me be civil to him, I consented. I was afraid to anger you, madam.

LADY CHEATLY.

Civil? That was civil with a vengeance! Let me come, I'll knock her on the head, filthy creature.   210

LADY BUSY.

Hold madam, be wise and make the best on't. Let me alone to manage this affair.—Come pretty Mrs. Gartrude, has he made no settlement upon thee?

GARTRUDE.

He settled nothing but himself upon me, that I know.   215

LADY CHEATLY.

No, that's the plague: I knew there was no settlement; if that had been done, it had been somewhat.

LADY BUSY.

Go to,* be patient. Let me alone; withdraw, good madam, and trust me.   220

Exit Lady Cheatly. Enter Stanmore.

Come on, Mr. Stanmore, I must talk with you a little.

STANMORE.

Now for a wise lecture.

LADY BUSY.

Look up, pretty miss, come on.—Sir, my lady   225
Cheatly is a worthy person and of good quality*—
right. Mrs. Gartrude is a very pretty young lady—
-true. Nor is it fit my lady (who has entertained you so often and so nobly in her house) should be abused——do you conceive me? Nor is it fit that   230
this pretty young thing should be injured——you understand me?

STANMORE.

Your ladyship speaks like an oracle.

LADY BUSY.

Very good. This pretty thing, I understand, has been very kind* to you—very well—— 235

STANMORE.

Fie miss! Fie! Tell tales out of school?—If she has, I am sure I was as kind as she could be for her heart.

LADY BUSY.

Very good—-come, I understand you—-ah, what pleasure 'tis to lie by such a sweet bedfellow! such pretty little swelling breasts! such delicate, black, 240 sparkling eyes! such a fresh complexion! such red, pouting lips! and such a skin! I say no more—in short, she would make a husband very happy. Come, let it be so, and let no more words be made of this matter. 245

STANMORE.

I'll do what I can to help her to one.

LADY BUSY.

Go to—-that's well said—-yourself then be the man—-oh how the Town will envy you the enjoyment of so fine a lady!

STANMORE.

S'heart, madam, what do you take me for? If you 250 knew all, what need I marry for the matter?

LADY BUSY.

Go to, she may make as good a wife as can be for all that. Have you not many examples?

STANMORE.

No madam, I have made a vow of chastity that way, which I will never break. 255

LADY BUSY.

I would not my lady should know this for the world; she would be revenged to the last degree. Let me tell you, you have been very uncivil.

STANMORE.

Faith madam, I think not.

GARTRUDE.

Yes, but you have been uncivil though, that you 260 have.

LADY BUSY.

Go to.—-Do you mind? Do you think a family is to be dishonored? Is that like a gentleman? Nay, not but that human frailty must be passed by, for young people, when they meet, are apt and liable—-'tis 265 confessed—-but then—-Aye, what then? Why, your gentlemen and your worthy persons strive to make

it good—very well. But how is it to be made good? Hmm—-why, either by marriage or settlement.

STANMORE.

I have a private reason must keep me from doing 270 either.

LADY BUSY.

No, no, that won't pass: I know you are too much a gentleman; besides, you made me aº promise you would keep;* and let me tell you, my honor is concerned in it, and I would not have my honor 275 touched for the world.

STANMORE.

I did not promise to keep for another, as I must if I keep her.

GARTRUDE.

You do not say true then.

LADY BUSY.

Fie Mr. Stanmore, that you should say such an 280 ungenteel thing!—Come miss, bear up, and do not cry.—How can you endure to see a young lady's tears and not melt?—Come on, pretty miss, I am sure you will be kind* and constant to Mr. Stanmore, will you not? 285

GARTRUDE.

Yes, yes.

LADY BUSY.

Good.—Why look you, sir, I know you are a worthy gentleman and will consider of a settlement such as befits a gentlewoman.

STANMORE.

No, madam. Selfish, this evening, in a greenroom 290 behind the scenes, was beforehand with me. She ne'er tells of that. Can I love one that prostitutes herself to that fellow?

LADY BUSY.

How's this?

GARTRUDE.

Oh sad, that you should say such a thing! I am 295 sure he will not say so for the world. Would I might ne'er stir out of this place alive now if I did.

STANMORE.

I had it from his own mouth.

GARTRUDE.

Oh Lord, I'll be far enough,[61] if you had! I'm sure

---

[61] far enough] colloquial expression expressing absolute negation (Partridge), as in "I'll be hornswoggled"

he's too fine a gentleman and too well-bred to tell such a grievous lie of a lady. I am sure he did not say so, that he did not.

STANMORE.

How she commends him!

LADY BUSY.

You know, Selfish is the vainest fellow that ever was born. Can you believe that coxcomb? It is not generous.

STANMORE.

Shall I believe Bellamour's eyes? He saw it. Good madam, be pleased to forbear your tricks upon me. Farewell. I hate the leavings of a fool; I'll as soon eat the meat he has chewed or wear his foul linen after him. Adieu, good madam. (*Exit.*)

LADY BUSY.

Now see what your indiscretion has done. Did I not tell you Selfish would undo you?

GARTRUDE.

Oh what shall I do! What shall I do! Does your ladyship think you could not get Mr. Selfish to marry me? Oh, he's the prettiest man: I could live and die with him.

LADY BUSY.

Go to, you will utterly ruin yourself. Do you think a fellow that has been so base to boast of your kindness* will marry you? Peace, I say. I will try another: Young Maggot shall be the man.

GARTRUDE.

I can't abide him.

LADY BUSY.

I say go to——you must marry him, if he will, and be glad on't too. Stanmore has forsaken you; Selfish can't keep* you; your mother will turn you out of doors; and you will starve. Come, come along with me and be better advised.

Exeunt.

Act V. [Lady Cheatly's lodgings.]

Enter Prig and Lady Cheatly.

PRIG.

Now madam, I hope you will be persuaded to dispatch this business of wedlock this morning; 'twould be much more convenient for me than tomorrow, because I am to go to Newmarket to a cock match. I have laid fifty pound upon Jackanapes against Tom Prig's Boxen Beak; my Dun fights a battle with Tom Whiskin's Duckwing for fifty pound. 'Twill be the best sport in the world. I would fain marry today and go thither tomorrow. Will your ladyship go and see it?

LADY CHEATLY.

No, pray sir, if that be the best sport in the world, see that first and marry afterwards.

PRIG.

Newmarket's a rare place! There a man's never idle: we make visits to horses and talk with grooms, riders, and cock keepers, and saunter in the heath all the forenoon; then we dine and never talk a word but of dogs, cocks, and horses; then we saunter into the heath again; then to a cock match; then to a play in a barn; then to supper and never speak a word but of dogs, cocks, and horses again; then to the groom-porters, where you may play all night. Oh, 'tis a heavenly life! We are never idle.

LADY CHEATLY.

For ought I see, you are never otherwise.

Enter steward.

Heaven! Is this villain returned?

STEWARD.

Yes, perfidious woman! I am returned, and will make you know that I am not to be used so. What? to be clapped under hatches and carried to the Indies to be sold for a slave? A fine design, truly. But come, madam, I will make you know your lord and master.

LADY CHEATLY.

What means your impudence?

STEWARD.

Impudence! to command my wife? Know your duty.

PRIG.

Your wife? Why, you are her man, are you not?

STEWARD.

What fellow's this? I must have new orders: I must have no such customers about my house.

LADY CHEATLY.

Call a constable, the poor fellow's distracted.

STEWARD.

No, but I may make the lady so, if she persists in her impudence.

PRIG.

Thou art very saucy to thy lady and mistress.

STEWARD.

    Peace, fool! Saucy to my wife?   40

PRIG.

    Fool? Hah, fool! What a pox would you be at?

LADY CHEATLY.

    Impudent villain!* Thy wife?

STEWARD.

    Most audacious woman! Darest thou deny it? Was
I not married to you yesterday in your own
chamber by a parson of your own choosing?   45

LADY CHEATLY.

    How dar'st thou affirm so impudent a lie? Where
didst thou dream this?

PRIG.

    I have my cue: I'll have my hand in the plot. (*Exit.*)

STEWARD.

    Why, thou most infamous of women! Canst thou
deny this?   50

LADY CHEATLY.

    Yes, thou most impudent of rascals, I will deny it
to all the world, and I have taken care that thou
shalt never prove it.

STEWARD.

    Hell and devils! Is there one amongst you like this
woman?   55

LADY CHEATLY.

    Well, if you will be quiet and stir no farther in this
business, a thousand pound is yours; if not, you
never shall have me nor anything of mine. Marry
such a fellow?

STEWARD.

    No, base woman! I'll undo thee.   60

LADY CHEATLY.

    'Tis out of your power, fool: you have sworn to
all my bonds and deeds already.

STEWARD.

    Most vile of cheats! I'll find your parson, if he be
in England.

Enter Prig in the habit of a parson.

    Oh happy fortune! Here he is.   65

LADY CHEATLY. [*Aside.*]

    What means this coxcomb Prig?

STEWARD.

    Now, madam.—Did not you marry me to this
lady yesterday? Speak, upon the word of a priest.

PRIG.

    Yes, I did.

STEWARD.

    Now, what says your impudence? I thought I   70
should catch you. Were you so cunning to deny
it?—Where do you live, sir?

PRIG.

    Madam, pray help me off with my habit.

LADY CHEATLY.

    This is well enough.

STEWARD.

    Hah! What a devil's this? Were you the parson?   75

PRIG.

    Yes, good sir.

LADY CHEATLY.

    Yes, this was my chaplain, you saucy fool! Could you
think I would marry such a filthy fellow as you are?

STEWARD.

    I will give you to understand, madam, that 'tis a
good marriage.—And I'll bring you into the court   80
to swear it, sir.

PRIG.

    If you do, sir, I'll hold six to four, I forswear it,
sir.

STEWARD.

    Why, sure you dare not.

PRIG.

    By Heaven, I dare, and will forswearᴾ myself for   85
such a widow; gentlemen forswear themselves to
get whores, and make nothing on't. Be gone out
of my house, she is mine. Fellow, be gone, I say.

STEWARD.

    Curse on my shallow head! that I should be so
credulous to believe her to be true to me when I was   90
an hourly witness of her falsehood to others.—I will
have you my wife or be revenged to that degree you
shall repent this treachery your whole life. I am going
to visit all those you have had business with this
month, and I shall tell 'em such a tale. (*Exit.*)   95

PRIG.

    I'll cut his throat; say no more.

LADY CHEATLY.

    Pray hasten after this malicious, clamorous rascal
and stop him some way or other. He'll invent a
thousand lies of me. Get him arrested upon an
action of ten thousand pound at my suit.   100

PRIG.

Let me alone, I'll do as becomes a gentleman. (*Exit.*)

LADY CHEATLY.

This trouble, joined with that fool my daughter, will undo me, but I will find out Maggot, and he shall help to salve up all.

Enter Maggot.

Oh Mr. Maggot! I have business to communicate 105 to you of the greatest concernment to me that ever happened.

MAGGOT.

Gad madam, do! If any man in England understands business or loves it better than I do, I'll be burnt. 110

LADY CHEATLY.

Every man loves what he is good at. Give me a man of business for my friend. The fine gentlemen of the Town are like fiddlers, only good at idle hours.

MAGGOT.

There are no great persons at this end of the Town have any business but I do it for 'em. I am the 115 busiest man in England, and I hope, madam, you'll consider of my love to business, and to your ladyship.

LADY CHEATLY.

Why, that is part of the business I am to confer with you about. 120

Enter Lady Busy and Young Maggot.

LADY BUSY.

Madam, I beg you will retire. I have an affair with Young Mr. Maggot that concerns you and Mrs. Gartrude.

Exeunt Lady Cheatly and Maggot.

Mr. Maggot, I can never enough admire your Uncle Maggot's aversion to wit and breeding, nor 125 can I choose but pity you, who are like to be so great a sufferer for your love to both.

YOUNG MAGGOT.

I glory in my suffering for so good a cause.

LADY BUSY.

Well, many a man would be proud of such a nephew. But is it true that you are like to be 130 disinherited?

YOUNG MAGGOT.

It is as true as I myself will ever be to wit and beauty, unless I will recant my works and for the future renounce tropes, figures, similes, and all ornaments of speech. 135

LADY BUSY.

These are hard conditions.

YOUNG MAGGOT.

A man of my vigorous imagination had as good have been born dumb. I will sing, and starve to death like a grasshopper, ere I submit.

LADY BUSY.

Go to,* suppose some friend of yours, more careful 140 of you than you are of yourself, should find a way to compose this matter without prejudice to your poetry.

YOUNG MAGGOT.

That friend should be another Apollo, if a man, and a tenth muse to me, if a woman. 145

LADY BUSY.

Good. There is a woman, a pretty one, young and rich too in the case—very well. But how shall I come by this woman, say you? Go to, let me alone: a fine woman, with a good fortune, were no ill refuge from the anger of your uncle, hah? 150

YOUNG MAGGOT.

But if I should marry, what will the world say of my wit? I had rather lose my honor and starve than lose the name of a wit.

LADY BUSY.

Your reputation is established already. Go to, consider. 155

YOUNG MAGGOT.

But madam, my heart is engaged, and the poor soul loves me again to madness. I did but kiss my hand to a lady in a window t'other day, and the poor thing fell into a fit; she will never outlive such a heinous tergiversation. 160

LADY BUSY.

Come, come, you know not the world. This is some soft-hearted fool, that will be as fond of another in three days. Go to, I know the sex better than you. But such a reputation, such a face, and such a fortune! 165

YOUNG MAGGOT.

Nay, if she have a better face and reputation than

my Gartrude, I will forswear poetry and write shorthand at conventicles all the rest of my life.

LADY BUSY.

Is she the woman? My lady Cheatly looks very high for her daughter: Stanmore and several fortunes are about her. Do you conceive me?   170

YOUNG MAGGOT.

That's all one.
As for my part I have chosen one,
And I'll have my love, or I'll have none.

LADY BUSY.

Hold: a lady of fortune, beauty, and one that loves   175
you, and admires you for your wit, is not to be neglected.

YOUNG MAGGOT.

How? Then she has wit too.

LADY BUSY.

How else should she admire it in you?

YOUNG MAGGOT.

Since she has wit, I will see her, that's certain, and   180
love her, if I can; if not, I'll make her some handsome excuse for't in my next song.

Enter Gartrude.

LADY BUSY.

Well then, here she comes. It is this pretty Gartrude: Ah! what a bedfellow is this, with above ten thousand pound too.   185

YOUNG MAGGOT.

Pretty creature! Are you she?

GARTRUDE.

Yes, that I am.

YOUNG MAGGOT.

But madam, do you not think marriage will spoil my poetry?

GARTRUDE.

I would not marry you if I thought it would, for   190
I love your verses dearly.

LADY BUSY.

Stanmore and Selfish will hang themselves when they hear of your good fortune.

YOUNG MAGGOT.

Aye, so they will.

GARTRUDE.

Everybody says they love one to one's face, but you   195
said so behind my back: I heard you tell my lady

so, and I am resolved I will have you, though my mother turn me out of doors, that I will.

LADY BUSY.

Go, get you together, loving rogues, and let me alone to make your peace with my Lady Cheatly.   200

Exeunt.

[Scene ii. The same.]

Enter Selfish and Isabel.

SELFISH.

Consider my person and my breeding. Think not of Bellamour, he has two ladies with child by him, and one claims marriage.

ISABELLA.

You had best marry her for him; he'll give a good portion.   5

SELFISH.

I did not think so harsh a repartee could have come out of that pretty mouth: sure you take something ill from me; my conduct among the ladies does not please you. I confess, I have been somewhat too general in my addresses, but I am resolved to apply   10
myself to you and be less gallant hereafter.

ISABELLA.

Be less vain and less a coxcomb, and know that nothing you forbear or do can please or trouble me.

SELFISH.

Were I not skilled in the various dispositions of   15
your soft sex, these words would make me despair, but I have often known such peevishness the child of love.

ISABELLA.

Were I a man, I'd cudgel you out of this conceit of yourself, but as I am, I can only despise and   20
laugh at you.

SELFISH.

Ha! ha! ha! You are pleasant, and I am glad to find you so. I often discover ladies' affections to me that way, for I am sure they love me, when they are so familiar with me, my pretty *railleur*.62   25

ISABELLA.

Monster of vanity! be gone.

_____

62 *railleur*] joker, kidder (Fr.)

Enter Bellamour.

BELLAMOUR.

I beg upon my knees you will once more hear me.

ISABELLA.

I never will. [*Exit.*]

SELFISH.

It is in vain: Give her over, Bellamour. What would
you have her do, poor lady? she loves me. Dost   30
thou think ever to get a lady where I am? Why,
my mother has often told me I was born with a
caul[63] upon my head, and she wrapped me up in
her shift to make me lucky to ladies.

BELLAMOUR.

Impudent coxcomb! I will not disturb the house,   35
but follow me or I'll cut your throat here. You are
the occasion of this storm.

SELFISH.

With all my heart. I did intend to demand
satisfaction for your ill breeding at the playhouse,
and you shall find I can fight as well as I can make   40
love.*

BELLAMOUR.

Come on, vanity.

Exeunt.

[Scene iii. The same.]

Enter Carlos and Theodosia.

THEODOSIA.

I see you are resolved to watch me, to make me
confess love as they do witches, to make 'em own
their contracts with the Devil.

CARLOS.

If you would but look a little guiltily, I would take
you upon suspicion.   5

THEODOSIA.

And so hurry me away to execution. Alas, poor
Carlos! Don't I look as if I died for thee? Are not
my eyes languishing enough?

CARLOS.

You are pleasant, madam, as becomes a winning
gamester.   10

_____

63 caul] To be born with this membrane around the head
   was considered a good omen.

THEODOSIA.

If I should play on, luck may turn; I think 'tis best
to give over as I am.

CARLOS.

But consider how entirely I love you.

THEODOSIA.

Consider how little I care for you.

CARLOS.

The greatest beauties are not always most sincerely   15
loved.

THEODOSIA.

No, they are commonly like great places: courted
and won by vain designing knaves. And were I
such, I should be yet more suspicious.

CARLOS.

A man that's ready to die a martyr need make no   20
other professions; I should else—

THEODOSIA.

Talk like an ass of charms and tyranny of mine,
of chains and slavery of yours. A man that should
overhear you would think you had been taken by
the Turk.   25

CARLOS.

'Tis not in your power to make me leave loving
you.

THEODOSIA.

'Tis very unreasonable that my indifference should
not make you love me less.

CARLOS.

'Tis very unreasonable that my perseverance should   30
not make you love me more. But I will yet hope.

THEODOSIA.

Hope is a thin diet and may be allowed in your
feverish condition and, indeed, is the only food
that love can live on.

CARLOS.

Oh madam, marriage—   35

THEODOSIA.

Is to love as the Jesuit's powder* to an ague: it stops
the fit and in a little time wears it quite off.

Enter Isabella.

ISABELLA.

My dear, how dost thou?—Carlos, will you forgive
me? Lovers take it as ill to be parted as men of
honor.   40

CARLOS.

I was just upon the point of yielding.

THEODOSIA.

I scorn to take advantages, but I had reduced him to offer marriage.

ISABELLA.

Then it seems he is weary of being your slave and would make you his.

CARLOS.

Madam, you should be generous and take the weakest side. No, I am resolved ever to be her servant, but would be glad of a nearer employment about her person.

THEODOSIA.

Come, prithee Isabella, let's take a turn in the garden and see if we can talk of something else.

CARLOS.

Where'er I go, I shall carry my love with me, and that will not suffer me to talk or think of anything but your dear self.

Exeunt.

[Scene iv. The field.]

Enter Bellamour and Selfish.

BELLAMOUR.

Come sir, I hope you like this place. You are very nice* in choosing one.

SELFISH.

Yes, I like this, for here I ran one man through and gave another his life.

BELLAMOUR.

Let me see if you be armed or not.

SELFISH.

No, I am too well-bred for that.

BELLAMOUR.

Make ready.

SELFISH. [*Aside.*]

And yet I am damnably afraid, but if I should not fight, the ladies will not be so apt to love me as they are.

BELLAMOUR.

Come, will you never have done?

SELFISH.

Yes sir. What great haste are you in?

Beauty, what art thou? But a fading flower.

BELLAMOUR.

Beauty? What a devil hast thou to do with beauty? You are a damned ugly, ill-bred coxcomb, and the ladies care not one jot for you. Draw.

SELFISH.

Come on, I will vindicate myself and the ladies. Now for the ladies.

They fight. Bellamour throws Selfish down and takes his sword.

Do not kill me! Consider how the ladies will hate you if you should.

BELLAMOUR.

No, prithee live, and be an ass still,* but trouble me no more.

SELFISH.

Thou art a strange, rough, ill-bred fellow to fight so: to fling a man down and spoil his clothes. You have dirtied all my garniture and spoiled my cravat. Could you not have fought easily, handsomely, and like a gentleman? You were never bred in an academy: they never fight thus brutally in France.

BELLAMOUR.

This is ridiculous enough.

SELFISH.

I warrant, you have done me ten pounds worth of hurt with fighting with me. I do not know how to appear before the ladies. I can't abide such tricks.

BELLAMOUR.

Fare thee well.—If I were not extremely troubled about Isabella, I would divert myself with this coxcomb. (*Exit.*)

SELFISH.

A brutal fellow! to spoil one's things thus. But I'll go home and dress me. (*Exit.*)

[Scene v. Lady Cheatly's lodgings.]

Enter Lady Cheatly and Maggot.

LADY CHEATLY.

You see I have considered your passion and how apt you are for business. I am afraid of a suit or two in law, which I know you can manage.

MAGGOT.

As well as any man in the world.

LADY CHEATLY.

I have told you of the insolence of the steward and   5
the artifice I used to get rid of him.

MAGGOT.

That shows your ladyship understands business.
How happy shall I be! How I shall laugh at and
triumph over all my rivals!

LADY CHEATLY.

Not a word of what has passed betwixt us till a   10
fitter opportunity.

Enter Prig, with a plaster upon his face.

How now, Mr. Prig. What ails your face?

PRIG.

Be not frightened my dear, 'tis no great hurt.

MAGGOT.

My dear! Poor fool, how I pity him!

PRIG.

I went to stop that rogue, your steward, and   15
demand satisfaction, as becomes a gentleman, and
in fine, we drew, and after some two or three and
thirty passes, I found myself run into the arm, and
the face, but I worsted him. Yet when I was at a
surgeon's the rascal got away.   20

LADY CHEATLY.

I am sorry you should venture so much for me.

PRIG.

Oh, madam! 'Twas for myself, for we are to be all one
flesh, Now nothing troubles me but that this hurt
will hinder my journey to Newmarket tomorrow.

MAGGOT.

He, all one flesh with her? Poor coxcomb!   25

Enter two scriveners.

FIRST SCRIVENER.

Madam, I wonder a lady of quality* should be
guilty of such fraud and covin[64] to write bonds
with ink that will wear out in a month.

SECOND SCRIVENER.

Other ink you have, too, that with a spirit rubbed
upon the paper will make impression through a   30
whole quire.

LADY CHEATLY.

What mean these fellows? Are you mad?

---

64 covin] criminal conspiracy

FIRST SCRIVENER.

No, but this is enough to make us mad, for ourselves
and our clients to be cheated of such sums.

SECOND SCRIVENER.

Pray madam, give us security and let me renew the   35
bonds with my own ink.

LADY CHEATLY.

Go home and sleep and be sober.

MAGGOT.

What's the meaning of this? Is my lady a cheat?

PRIG.

This is the rogue, your steward's lie.

LADY CHEATLY.

Oh, gentlemen! You have been with that rascal, my   40
steward, the most impudent villain, who, having
most of the writings that concern my estate in his
hands, had the impudence to threaten to burn 'em,
unless I would marry him.

PRIG.

'Tis very true, upon my honor.   45

LADY CHEATLY.

I, by a wile, got 'em out of his hands, and he, out of
revenge for being so disappointed, has invented
these malicious lies. But I shall lay him fast enough.

Enter two citizens.

FIRST CITIZEN.

Madam, we did not think your ladyship would put
such things upon us to give us false notes for our   50
money.

SECOND CITIZEN.

Notes written with ink that will wear out: we shall
have nothing but blanks for our money.

FIRST CITIZEN.

Pray let me have my five hundred pound again.

SECOND CITIZEN.

And me, mine. You have not laid it out yet.   55

LADY CHEATLY.

What! my rogue of a steward has been with you
too, has he?

SECOND CITIZEN.

Rogue! He's an honest man to give us notice of this
deceit. Madam, I wonder your ladyship is not
ashamed.   60

PRIG.

How now, impudence! I tell you the steward is the

cheat and rogue. He has lied and abused you. My
lady is a person of honor.

MAGGOT.

Hah! There must be something in this: he would
not be so foolish to tell so silly a lie.   65

SECOND SCRIVENER.

My lady is a worthy person, and the steward has
invented these lies out of revenge because he had the
impudence to pretend* to marry my lady and would
have kept all her writings. He'd force her to do it, but
she was too hard for him. We know all.   70

SECOND CITIZEN.

This is strange.

Enter Lump.

LUMP.

Oh thou vile woman! thou reprobate! thou most
audacious, seared-conscienced creature! Could such
a wicked branch spring from our family, who are
precious, godly men and women, all but thyself?   75

LADY CHEATLY.

Are you mad, brother?

Enter steward.

LUMP.

I knew you would cheat the rest. But must you
betray me and give me false deeds? Must I have
nothing but blanks for my money?

FIRST SCRIVENER.

What ails thee?ʳ   80

FIRST CITIZEN.

How, are we cheated?

MAGGOT.

S'death! There must be some fire under all this
smoke.

LUMP.

Had it not been for this honest man, who was
troubled in conscience and could no longer conceal   85
your fraud, I had ne'er known it, but now I will
make an example of you.

FIRST CITIZEN.

How, sir? Are you a precious, godly man and knew
of a cheat and would not discover* it?

SECOND CITIZEN.

One of our own church to suffer us to be betrayed?   90

LUMP.

I had no call to it, till now I am myself concerned.

LADY CHEATLY.

Will you believe this most infamous rascal, that
would have dishonored your family and, having all
my writings, would have married me or have burnt
'em? I, by seeming to consent to his desires, got   95
'em out of his hands, made him swear to 'em
before a Master in Chancery; then I turned him
away for a villain, as he is.

LUMP.

What say you, sir?

PRIG.

Say? I'll hold six to four, he cannot say a word.   100
Upon my honor, this is all true, to my knowledge.

STEWARD.

She caused me to be clapped under hatches in a
ship going to the Indies because I knew this secret,
and I do assure you, ye are all cheated and in less
than a month will have nothing to show for all   105
your money. I cannot in conscience but reveal this.

LADY CHEATLY.

Impudent, lying varlet! How darest thou affirm so
devilish a lie?

STEWARD. (*Whispers.*)

Will you marry me yet, and I will retrieve all.

LADY CHEATLY.

Oh heaven and earth! The villain whispers me in   110
the ear now and tells me, if I will marry him, he
will deny all.

STEWARD.

Mercy upon me! Will your ladyship's conscience
give you leave to say that? Pray madam, consider
your soul.   115

FIRST CITIZEN.

Aye madam, consider your soul.

SECOND CITIZEN.

And the payment of my money.

LADY CHEATLY.

Heaven can witness what I say is true: even just
now he asked me to marry him.

LUMP.

If this be true, lady sister, I will ask your pardon. 120

STEWARD.

What need I ask that which I have already? I am
married to her.

ALL.

How!

STEWARD.

And her great anger, and the reason she would have sold me to Jamaica was because I could not in 125 conscience conceal these deceits though I might have had the benefit of 'em.

LADY CHEATLY.

This is so extravagantly ridiculous, it makes me laugh. I will not give a serious answer to it.

MAGGOT.

Hah! Married? You did not consummate, I hope. 130 Who married you?

STEWARD.

Why, the truth is, she thought to put a false marriage upon me: when she discovered my intention of making a restitution to those she had injured, she dressed that fellow Prig in the disguise 135 of a parson, and he married us in her bedchamber. But I'll make her know, 'tis a good marriage.

MAGGOT.

Did you know him in the disguise?

STEWARD.

No, till this day he appeared in it to me and then pulled it off to show me 'twas a mock marriage, as 140 they thought. But I will make 'em know otherwise.

LADY CHEATLY.

This is the most amazing impudence. Mr. Prig, declare yourself. (*Aside.*) Deny it, or we are undone.

PRIG.

Is there ever a magistrate here? I will swear that 145 there is not one word of all this true. I know not what he means. I hold gold to silver he's mad.

LADY CHEATLY.

Do you see, brother, what a rascal you have believed? and how you have injured me?

LUMP.

Why thou wicked locust! thou spawn of a serpent! 150 to invent such cursed lies. I'll lay thee within four walls.

STEWARD.

By Heaven, 'tis all true! I'll swear it; nay, I'll swear with you for a thousand pound.

MAGGOT.

Let him swear it, that we may have his ears.* 155

FIRST CITIZEN.

Madam, we ask your pardon with all our hearts.

SECOND CITIZEN.

Impudent fellow! to abuse my lady so.

STEWARD.

Let me but speak.

FIRST SCRIVENER.

No, base fellow! thou shalt not speak.

SECOND SCRIVENER.

Abuse so worthy a lady? Out, thou wicked fellow! 160

STEWARD.

'Tis very fine.

LUMP.

Lay an action of ten thousand pound upon him; see who will bail him. To my certain knowledge, she has a great estate and has been always a very conscientious woman; indeed, I was something 165 amazed at this story.

FIRST CITIZEN.

Aye sir, we believe your worship.

SECOND CITIZEN.

We know you are a precious, godly man.

STEWARD.

Are you distracted? Well, be all cheated, an* you will, I have discharged my conscience. 170

LUMP.

Conscience? thou seed of Beelzebub!

PRIG.

Conscience? An impudent rogue, that offers to forswear himself! I offered to lay him ten to one 'twas all false, and you saw he durst not bet.

FIRST SCRIVENER.

Hang him! 175

SECOND SCRIVENER.

Base, lying rogue!

Enter sergeants.

FIRST SERGEANT.

I arrest you at the suit of my Lady Cheatly, in an action of ten thousand pounds.

STEWARD.

Oh vile woman!

LADY CHEATLY.

Away with him. 180

SECOND CITIZEN.

Away with him.

ALL.

Away with the rogue.

LUMP.

I do beseech your pardon, sister: I was mistaken, which I do not use to be, yet that trick at the playhouse was base.   185

LADY CHEATLY.

I could not help it; I knew not of it.

Enter two creditors.

FIRST CREDITOR.

Madam, you have undone us: you gave us bonds for two hundred pound apiece above six weeks since, and we have nothing but the seals left.

SECOND CREDITOR.

All the ink is worn out: behold here, madam.   190
(*Shows a paper.*)

LADY CHEATLY.

Impostors! lying rogues! I owe you nothing.

LUMP.

These are instruments of this rascally steward's. How come they by the seal?

LADY CHEATLY.

From the steward.   195

FIRST CREDITOR.

Are ye all mad? We had it from you, for which you had two hundred pounds apiece from us.

PRIG.

Out, you impudent rogue! Get you gone.

FIRST CITIZEN.

Away, lying fellows!

LUMP.

Be gone, ye vipers!   200

They thrust 'em out.

LADY CHEATLY.

Now gentlemen, I desire you that remain to take part of a collation with me, and I will show all the evidences of my estate to you.

Exeunt.

[Scene vi. The garden.]

Enter Isabella and Bellamour.

ISABELLA.

There can be no defense to suspect me, and with that wretch Selfish too.

BELLAMOUR.

Jealousy, like the smallpox if it comes out kindly, is never mortal, and my love will be the stronger and the more vigorous for this short distemper.   5

ISABELLA.

It may relapse again.

BELLAMOUR.

'Tis past all danger now.

ISABELLA.

And will you still give a thousand pounds down and three hundred pounds a year for this tenement, notwithstanding the encumbrance of Selfish upon it?   10

BELLAMOUR.

When I made these offers, I did not know half your worth: I was a fair chapman for your beauty, but your virtue and other perfections are inestimable.

ISABELLA.

And shall I flaunt it in the Park* with my gray Flanders,* crowd the walk with my equipage, and   15
be the envy of all the butterflies in Town?

BELLAMOUR.

Forget that vain discourse, as I have done, and take me and all I have forever.

ISABELLA.

Sure a man of your wit will never marry. Every rich fool can get a woman that way.   20

BELLAMOUR.

Do not insult, but take me quickly to your mercy.

ISABELLA.

I'll not deceive you: whatever show my mother makes, I have no portion, nor was ever troubled at the thought of it till now.

BELLAMOUR.

I am glad of it, for now my love will be the more   25
easily believed and better taken.

ISABELLA.

No, Bellamour.

BELLAMOUR.

How, madam?

ISABELLA.

No, I say——for were I Queen of Europe, your love would be as well accepted as 'tis now.   30

BELLAMOUR.

You surprise me with an honor too great to bear.

Enter Lady Cheatly

LADY CHEATLY.

What? Are you agreed yet? She is a foolish girl, sir, and looks as high as better women.

BELLAMOUR.

She's very humble and is pleased to accept me for a husband, and there wants* only your consent and a few words from a parson to complete my happiness. 35

LADY CHEATLY.

You honor our family and cannot doubt of my consent: she is yours.

Enter Lady Busy, Young Maggot, and Gartrude.

LADY BUSY.

I present you here with a son and daughter: I saw 'em married. Give 'em your blessing. 40

LADY CHEATLY.

Heaven bless you!—Madam, I can never thank you enough; you have made me happy in removing my greatest affliction.

Enter Selfish and Stanmore.

LADY BUSY.

I love to put lovers together: virtuous actions reward themselves. 45

STANMORE.

Young Maggot married? Give you joy, sir: your love to wit and beauty is at length rewarded.

YOUNG MAGGOT.

I will now keep company with none but the top wits and write plays, songs, and lampoons in defiance of the fop, my uncle. 50

LADY BUSY.

Not so fast: get him to settle first.

LADY CHEATLY.

I'll call my brother and the rest of my company to be witnesses to my happiness. (*Exit.*)

SELFISH.

Pretty mistress! You look today like a delicate picture, and Young Maggot your foil. 55

GARTRUDE.

I vow, you court me so genteelly I shall die to part with you: I cried in the church, that I did, and had like to have spoiled all.

SELFISH.

But will you promise me a meeting.

YOUNG MAGGOT.

Stand off: she's mine. 60

SELFISH.

You are to have her ever after; methinks, you should allow her one day to take leave of her friends.

Enter Lady Cheatly, Lump, Maggot, Prig, etc.

YOUNG MAGGOT.

Uncle, your unkindness has made me look about me, and Heaven has blest my wit and poetry with a rich wife here, Mrs. Gartrude: I won her by 'em. 65

MAGGOT.

Aye boy, I know it and know her fortune as well as my own. Thou art a mettled lad, and I like thy humor* well. Give me a Phillis with ten thousand pounds, I could sing one of thy own songs myself, I am so taken with this match. 70

YOUNG MAGGOT.

I hope then you will settle your estate, as you always promised, if I married to your liking.

MAGGOT.

If I have no children by my dear wife, her mother here.

PRIG.

Lady Cheatly your wife! She has promised me 75 marriage.

MAGGOT.

Whate'er she has promised you, she has performed marriage with me this morning. Be gone, rook, they stay for thee at the twelve-penny ordinary.

PRIG.

What say you, madam? 80

LADY CHEATLY.

'Tis very true.

PRIG.

Then you are very false.

MAGGOT.

As your dice. Gamester, I'll hold you cockpit lay, ten pound to a crown, she's bone of my bone and flesh of my flesh. 85

LADY CHEATLY.

This is the gentleman I'll live and die with.

PRIG.

Death and hell! I'll declare all I know.

LADY CHEATLY. (*Aside.*)

You will declare yourself a perjured knave if you do. Hark here.

MAGGOT.

What do they whisper for? 90

LADY CHEATLY.

All the steward says is true: I am worth little or nothing; my whole fortune a cheat; this old gentleman I chose because he is governable and loves business, of which my broken fortune will give him enough.

PRIG.

What a crossbite* have I 'scaped? This sham was well carried on, madam. Did you hear, old fool?

MAGGOT.

'Ounds! I am cheated, undone, and my nephew ruined and married to a beggar.

YOUNG MAGGOT.

I must even write hard for the playhouse. I may get the reversion of the Poet Laureate's place. I thought, uncle, you had known every foot of her estate.

PRIG.

Well, I'll go to Newmarket and never have to do with a two-legged jade more. I shall rook, and go to twelve, let what will come on't.

MAGGOT.

Since she has no fortune, I shall have no business neither.

YOUNG MAGGOT.

None but that which I am afraid you can't do, uncle.

MAGGOT.

Is this a time for wit, you rascal, when we are both undone.

He beats Young Maggot's perriwig off; from under it drop several copies of verses.

STANMORE.

A muss, a muss. A copy of verses upon a flea, presented to his mistress in a gold chain. [*Reads.*]
"Oh happy Flea! that mayst both kiss and bite,
Like lovers in their height of appetite,
    Her neck so white.
Pretty black alderman, in golden chain,
Who suck'st her blood yet putt'st her to no pain,
    Whil'st I in vain."65

MAGGOT.

What would become of the writing coxcombs, if it were not for reading ones? I'll hear no more.

LADY CHEATLY.

If you will go on and maintain what I have done, I shall have a good estate yet, though it belongs of right to other people.

MAGGOT.

Right? 'Tis no matter for right: I'll show 'em law.

THEODOSIA.

The plague of marriage rages in this house; let us fly from the infection.

CARLOS.

I am so far gone, 'tis to no purpose to remove. Well, if you continue to be so unkind, you will ruin my soul, body, and estate.

THEODOSIA.

How so?

CARLOS.

Why, I can never marry any other, and in despair of you, I shall turn the most debauched whoring rogue, 'twould grieve your heart to see it. I shall never be able to sleep without my three bottles and a fresh woman every night.

ISABELLA.

'Tis an act of charity to redeem him.

THEODOSIA.

The Devil seldom loses anything by matrimony; they most commonly grow worse for't.

CARLOS.

I will lead a solid, sober, husbandly life, if you will marry me; if not, whoring and drinking will ensue.

ISABELLA.

Nay, now I must judge against you: you have lost your wager, and you must pay it; you have confessed to me you loved him infinitely.

THEODOSIA.

Believe her not, I deny it.

CARLOS.

Though I distrust myself, I must believe my fair judge: I will have a canonical bom-baily66 and arrest you upon execution.

THEODOSIA.

I will have a month's time. You shall be so long a probationer before you enter in the order.

---

65 "Oh … vain."] Maggot's poem invites comparison with John Donne's "The Flea," which would have been regarded as false wit by most Restoration poets.

66 canonical bom-baily] bumbailiff, a bailiff of the lowest kind, one employed in arrests (*OED*), here an officer of the ecclesiastical court, which would enforce the wager through marriage.

CARLOS.

In hope of your good nature, I will press no farther
at this time.—Now, you that have reached at your
Inn of Matrimony will pray for us travelers upon
the road.   155

STANMORE.

So, gentlemen, we have lost ye: ye are not men of
this world. Now make much of your matrimonial
bonds; I am glad I have done my business without
'em.

SELFISH.

Ladies are so kind to me, I need never marry one   160
for the matter. Well, I will go home and put on a
very delicate, neat, convenient suit to dance with
the brides in here.

LUMP.

I give you all joy. You see, sister, how things prosper
when godly men are the instruments. I say to all,   165
to all of you I say,
Be godly, observe method, and be wise;

CARLOS.

Most excellent means to cover cheats and lies.

[Exeunt.]

FINIS.

Textual Notes

^a Copytext is the 1679 first quarto (Q). The quarto of
1689 is in fact the 1679 printing with a new title page
etc. The 1693 *Works* of Shadwell are separate printings
of plays bound together, *A True Widow* being the "1689"
quarto. In 1720 an entirely new edition appeared in *The
Works of Thomas Shadwell, Esq.* (W). Shadwell's son John
wrote a dedication for the four volume set to George I

and may have exercised some editorial control, perhaps
working from earlier editions with corrections marked
by his father.

In 1903 George Saintsbury edited a collection of four
of Shadwell's plays including *A True Widow*, the copy
text is W and Saintsbury has introduced no new material, nor are there any useful notes. Montague Summers'
edition of Shadwell's complete works in 1927 is of interest for the lengthy introduction to the collection as a
whole and Summers' quirky notes. His text, however,
is unreliable; although it claims to be derived from Q
with few changes, it differs in numerous places.

Contrary to accepted editorial practice, I have
adopted numerous readings and a great many punctuation changes from the posthumous W. First, Shadwell
complained in a note to Q about numerous errors in
the text, particularly in the third and fourth acts, and
W corrects the errors that Shadwell specifically pointed
out, as well as other obvious misprints. Second, the
punctuation of W is closer to modern usage, particularly in the use of commas.

^b Theodosia ... Carlos] W; *om.* Q
^c near] W; ne're Q
^d they are there] W; they there Q
^e fund] W; fond Q
^f overset] W; over-see Q
^g hate] W; have Q
^h by] W; in Q
ⁱ fifty pound] W; five shilling Q
^j infamous] W; in favour Q
^k a wit] W; *om.* Q
^l me] W; it Q
^m YOUNG MAGGOT] Q, W (though the line may be
more suitable for Prig)
ⁿ your] W; our Q
^o a] W; *om.* Q
^p will forswear] W; will not forswear Q
^q of a] W; *om.* Q
^r thee] the Q; she W, Summers

Sir Anthony Love; or, The Rambling Lady[a]

by Thomas Southerne (1659-1746)
edited by Kristina Straub

Southerne is best known for *Oroonoko* (1695), a dramatic reworking of Aphra Behn's novel of the same name, which had remarkable endurance on the stage throughout the eighteenth century. Because of this play's association with Behn and its themes of race, gender, and miscegenation, Southerne has most recently received attention from feminist and postcolonial critics of the period. *Sir Anthony Love*, a comedy very unlike the tragic *Oroonoko*, initiated Southerne's return to the theater after a short-lived career in the military that ended with the Revolution of 1688–89. While the play did not have the staying power of *Oroonoko*, it was a success in its first performance in 1690. Susanna Mountfort (a skilled and popular actress) in the breeches part of Sir Anthony probably contributed to the play's success, as did the comic talents of Anthony Leigh as the abbé, Mountfort's husband as Valentine, and Anne Bracegirdle. The actor and, later, writer, theatrical manager, and Poet Laureate of England, Colley Cibber, made his debut in this performance as well.

Sir Anthony Love is probably best seen as the satirical comedy that flourished under the monarchy of Charles II (1660–1685) and during the 1690s began to give way, or at least shared the stage with, comedy that emphasized the morally sympathetic nature of characters, as well as laughing at their foibles and flaws. Southerne's later comedies tend to be more of the "mixed" sort, blending social satire with points of moral edification; *Sir Anthony Love*, with its pragmatic emphases on economic survival and sexual conquest, seems, to many critics, to resist the "mixed" classification, though I would argue that the play's interest in sympathetic, morally coherent character, if it has any, lies with its female characters, particularly the indominitable Sir Anthony/Lucia. The plot driving the marriages of Floriante and Charlott is modelled after that of Aphra Behn's novel, *The Lucky Mistake* (1689), and it shares its investment in the marital fate of deserving young women. Southerne gives Behn's love story a pragmatic spin, however, in its pessimism about the degree of happiness that is (or is not) open to women in the married state. Marriage is important to the economic survival of women and their protection against sexual exploitation, but no one in the play seems to see conjugal love as the necessary condition for personal fulfillment and happiness. Indeed, much of the play's focus is on finding pleasure within the context of economic and social survival, not always through morally conventional means.

This play calls for some discussion of the issues of sexuality and gender, in particular in relation to the cross-dressed heroine and the homosexual desire that is depicted in the character of the abbé. Of the latter, it is important to note that the scene involving the abbé's attempted seduction of Sir Anthony was cut from performance, though included in the first and subsequent printings of the play. It has been posited that the scene was cut to avoid allusion to the alleged homosexual propensities of King William, but such specific reasons are perhaps not necessary to understanding why the scene was not performed. One way to situate the abbé's desires is to see them in the context of anti-Catholic satire, a common enough pastime during a period which produced some of English history's most notable instances of anti-Catholic hysteria, such as the events of the Popish Plot. The abbé's sympathetic role in promoting the marriages of his nieces complicates this reading, however; he is less a monstrous sodomite than a likably comic uncle who sees women as people with complex lives and needs, including the sexual. The character of Sir Anthony gives us a woman of remarkable personal autonomy who is hard to reduce to the conventional breeches appeal of the actress's pretty legs. Breeches parts for attractive actresses like Mountfort were prevalent in the highly competitive London theater, but reducing their appeal to that of a girly show does little justice to the actresses' skills and the audiences' complex responses. While certainly sexy, Sir Anthony is hard to think of purely as a sexual object. Rather, she presents us with a model for female desire that subverts the moral imperative of containing women's desires within the bounds of marriage.

DRAMATIS PERSONAE

MEN

Sir Anthony Love.
Valentine.
Ilford.
Sir Gentle* Golding.
An abbé.
Count Canaille,[1] his brother.
Count Vérole.[2]
Palmer, a pilgrim.
Waitwell, Sir Anthony's governor and confidant.
Traffique, a merchant.
Cortaut, a taylor's man.
Bravos belonging to Count Vérole.
Servants.
Servant to Sir Gentle.
Servant to Ilford.

WOMEN

Floriante,
Charlott, daughters to Count Canaille.
Volante,[3] the abbé's niece and charge.

---

[1] Canaille] *Canaille* is French for scoundrel, rogue.

[2] Vérole] *La grande vérole* is French for syphilis.

[3] Volante] French for flying, on the wing

SCENE: MONTPELIER.

Sir Anthony Love; or, The Rambling Lady.

Artis severae si quis amat effectus,
Mentémque magnis applicat—
*　　—det primos versibus annos,*
Maeoniumque bibat faelici pectore fontem.
　　　　Petro. Arb. *Satyr.* pag. 3.[4]

Act I. [Sir Anthony's lodging.]

Enter Sir Anthony Love and Waitwell following him.

SIR ANTHONY.
　　Well Governor, I think I have achieved, under thy conduct, as considerable a character, in as short a time—
WAITWELL.
　　Nay, you come on amain.
SIR ANTHONY.
　　And, though I say it, have done as much—　　5
WAITWELL.
　　And suffered as much.
SIR ANTHONY.
　　For the credit of my countrymen and the reputation of a whoremaster as the arrantest rakehell of 'em all.
WAITWELL.
　　You're a pretty proficient, indeed, and so perfectly　　10 act the Cavalier that, could you put on our sex with your breeches, o'my conscience you would carry all the women before you.
SIR ANTHONY.
　　And drive all the men before me; I am for Universal Empire and would not be stinted to one　　15 province; I would be feared, as well as loved: as famous for my action with the men, as for my passion for the women.

---

[4] *Artis … 3*] Petronius, *Satyricon* 5: "If any man seeks for success in stern art and applies his mind to great tasks … let him give the years of youth to poetry, and let his fortunate soul drink of the Maeonian fount" (Loeb, which chooses *ambit* as an alternative reading for *amat*; Maeon was Homer's father).

WAITWELL.

You're in the way to it; you change your men as often as you do your women and have every day a new mistress and a new quarrel.* 20

SIR ANTHONY.

Why, 'tis only the fashion of the world that gives your sex a better title than we have to the wearing a sword; my constant exercise with my fencing master and conversation* among men, who make little of the matter, have at last not only made me adroit, but despise the danger of a quarrel* too. 25

WAITWELL.

A ladylike reputation, truly. But how preposterously Fortune places her favors, when nobody is the better for 'em. 30

SIR ANTHONY.

Why how now, Governor?

WAITWELL.

She seldom gives a man an estate who has either the conscience or youth to enjoy it—

SIR ANTHONY.

But he may leave it to one who has.

WAITWELL.

An honest man might be thankful for half your fortune with the women. But what pleasure can you find in following 'em? 35

SIR ANTHONY.

The same that some of the men find.

WAITWELL.

You can't enjoy 'em.

SIR ANTHONY.

But I may make 'em ready for those who can. 40

WAITWELL.

Are there such sportsmen?

SIR ANTHONY.

Very many, who beat about more for company than the pleasure of the sport, and if they do start anything, are better pleased with the accidents of the chase, the hedges, and ditches, than the close pursuit of the game. And these are sure never to come into the quarry. 45

WAITWELL.

This is so like you now. Why, love should be your business, and you make a business of your love. You are young and handsome, in petticoats, yet are contented to part with the pleasures of your own 50

sex to ramble into the troubles of ours. In my opinion, you might be better employed.

SIR ANTHONY.

I do it to be better employed: to recommend me to Valentine, for whose dear sake I first engaged in the adventure, robbed my keeper,* that nauseous fool Golding, of five hundred pounds, and under thy discretion come a-colonelling[5] after him here into France. 55

WAITWELL.

Why do you lose time then? Why don't you tell him so? 60

SIR ANTHONY.

Thou wouldst have had me, with the true conduct of an English mistress, upon the first inclination cloy him with my person without any assurance of his relishing me enough to raise my appetite to a second taste. No, now I am sure he likes me, and likes me so well in a man, he'll love me in a woman. And let him make the discovery if he dares. 65

WAITWELL.

Let me direct him—

SIR ANTHONY.

To the lodgings you shall; those I saw and liked: they're private and convenient. Make 'em ready. I'll tell thee all anon—and do you hear?—my female wardrobe too must be produced, my woman's equipage— 70

Waitwell going.

For as the conduct of affairs now goes, 75
I'm best disguised in my own sex and clothes.
Hey, I had forgot: bring me the fifty pieces I spoke of, the five hundred are in good health yet, Governor.

WAITWELL.

But sicken at that sound. 80

SIR ANTHONY.

Valentine and Ilford are disappointed of their bills* and in spite of their good estates want* money. Now, though I lend upon the old consideration of borrowing a greater sum, fifty pieces are convenient. 85

---

5 a-colonelling] acting like a colonel; a humorous term for gathering recruits, in this case, sexual partners

WAITWELL.

And will be welcome to 'em at this time—

SIR ANTHONY.

Most certainly. And take this along with you, Governor: you must make your conversation necessary sometimes, as well as agreeable, to preserve a friendship with an Englishman.   90

Enter Valentine and Ilford.

VALENTINE.

How's this, Sir Anthony? under the discipline of your governor and his wisdom this morning?

SIR ANTHONY.

Like a good Christian, Valentine, clearing old accounts, that I may begin a new score with a better conscience.   95

ILFORD.

Confessing and repenting past enormities—

SIR ANTHONY.

About the pitch of thy piety, Ilford: repenting only because they are past.

VALENTINE.

So far you may repent with honor.

SIR ANTHONY.

Nay, I confess myself a child of this world, for at   100
this moment I have a hint from my constitution that tells me, the pleasure of thy example—

VALENTINE.

Thou art above example or imitation—

SIR ANTHONY.

Will go near to overthrow the wisdom of his precepts: the morality of thy beard, Governor—   105

WAITWELL.

But, sir, it would be well—

SIR ANTHONY.

It would be better, sir, thou pitiful preacher, wouldst thou but follow thy pimping; 'tis a better trade and becomes thy discretion as well. You'll find me hereabouts— (*Thrusts out Waitwell.*)   110

VALENTINE.

You have compounded for whoring then, Sir Anthony?

SIR ANTHONY.

Anything but fighting. He has swinged me away for my quarrel* yesterday in the Tennis Court.

ILFORD.

You deserved to be swinged for it—   115

VALENTINE.

I should chide you too, though 'twas upon my account.

ILFORD.

To run a gentleman through the arm for not witnessing all you said in commendation of Valentine—

VALENTINE.

When he was not so much as acquainted with my   120
person—

ILFORD.

Was—

SIR ANTHONY.

Something more bold than welcome, I grant you. But I had not fought a great while, my hand was in, and I was pushing at reputation. For egad, I   125
look upon courage to proceed more from habit and practice than any virtue of the mind.

VALENTINE.

How, how, Sir Anthony? There's something in family sure—

SIR ANTHONY.

Wooden legs, in a great many, Valentine.   130

ILFORD.

Courage often runs in a blood—

SIR ANTHONY.

They say so of the pox, indeed. The sins of the fathers may run in the blood sometimes, and visit the third and fourth generation,[6] but their virtues die with the men. And if the example and custom   135
of the world (supported by good eating and drinking) had not infused a nobler spirit into the blood than any derived from the father, most men had continued like those who stay with their fathers: elder brothers all,[7] and had never offered   140

---

6 sins … generation] a common biblical prediction concerning the consequences of sin

7 elder brothers all] Primogeniture was prevalent among landed families in 17th-century England, especially after the strict Act of Settlement in 1662. Eldest sons, who inherited the bulk of the estate, were most likely to live at home with their fathers, learning the duties of the landlord before they inherited. The young sons were often educated in professions, such as the military or the clergy, which took them from their homes and could offer them more opportunities for a range of adventures, including the sexual.

at an intrigue above a red petticoat,[8] or a quarrel* above a rubber at cuffs.[9]

ILFORD.

'Tis sensibly extravagant and wild!

VALENTINE.

Inimitably new! But how do you to avoid drinking? 145

SIR ANTHONY.

Why that avoids me, thanks to the custom of the country and the better diversions of this place: not but I can arrive at a bottle too.

ILFORD.

If you were in London—

SIR ANTHONY.

There I grant you—where the young fellows begin 150 the reputation of their humor and wit in a pint glass, carrying 'em, without intermission of sense or jest, to the end of the third bottle and then through the public places and folly of the Town.*

VALENTINE.

There you would be at a loss. 155

SIR ANTHONY.

I should indeed: where they go to taverns to swallow a drunkenness and then to a play to talk over their liquor.

ILFORD.

I thought that folly fell off with their fathers[10]—

VALENTINE.

The entertainment of it did indeed. 160

ILFORD.

Who, as they began it in their frolic, supported it in their wit.

SIR ANTHONY.

And since the sons are so plainly disinherited of the sense, they have no title to the sins of their fathers.

VALENTINE.

Unless they kept 'em more in countenance. 165

ILFORD.

Yet they would do something, like their fathers.

VALENTINE.

As an ignorant player in England, who I saw undertaking to copy a master actor of his time,

began at his infirmity in his feet and, growing famous for the imitation of his gout, he could walk 170 like him, when he could do nothing else like him.[11]

SIR ANTHONY.

The gout and the pox take him for it—

ILFORD.

And all those, I say, who, only from their opinion of themselves, are encouraged to meddle in other men's matters without ever bringing anything 175 about of their own.

SIR ANTHONY.

Aye, those meddling fools, Ilford! Who are in all places yet ever out of their way—

ILFORD.

And not only out of their own way but always in other men's— 180

SIR ANTHONY.

And still as ridiculous as a fellow of thy severity and reserve would be in the fantastical figure of a lover.

ILFORD.

Whoever has the woman, you have your wit, Sir Anthony— 185

SIR ANTHONY.

They go together, sir—you'll find it so.

Enter a pilgrim.

VALENTINE.

Whom have we here!

SIR ANTHONY.

A broking[12] brother of Bethlehem[13] with all his frippery about him!

VALENTINE.

One of that traveling Tribe, without their 190 circumcision.

SIR ANTHONY.

Of Christian appellation, a pilgrim.

VALENTINE.

'Tis a senseless constitution of men!

---

8 red petticoat] a servant or peasant

9 rubber at cuffs] a fist-fight

10 their fathers] the previous generation of wits

11 ignorant player ... like him] probably a hit at the great actor Thomas Betterton's rival, George Powell, who had taken to parodying Betterton—and who was waiting offstage to enter as the pilgrim (Jordan and Love)

12 broking] bargaining, dealing, in a contemptuous sense

13 Bethlehem] London hospital for the insane

SIR ANTHONY.

Who make themselves mad to make the rest of the world fools by finding a faith for all their fopperies. 195

VALENTINE.

How can they pass upon the world?

SIR ANTHONY.

As other constitutions and orders of men as senseless pass, that are founded too in as much cozenage and roguery as this can be.

ILFORD.

You are an enemy of forms, Sir Anthony. 200

SIR ANTHONY.

Oh, sir, the virtue of the habit often covers the vices of the man: there's field enough in England to find this in, without the Abbylands, gentlemen.

ILFORD.

Weeds are the general growth of every soil.

VALENTINE.

How many fools in the State and atheists in the 205 Church carry themselves current through their congregations and clients to great employments and, being armed only with the authority and countenance of their clothing, secure themselves from the discovery and censure of the Court and 210 Town?

SIR ANTHONY.

There are disguises, I grant you, worth a sensible man's putting on, but a pilgrim's habit is as ridiculous as his pretence, and I would no more wear a fool's coat to be thought devout than be 215 devout for the sake of the livery.

ILFORD.

Fools are the guts of all churches[b] and make the bulk of every opinion.

Exit pilgrim.

VALENTINE.

Hang him, let him pass; spare him for the sake of the Church, and spare the Church for the sake of 220 our abbé.

SIR ANTHONY.

Who is, indeed, a most considerable pillar of it to his own profit and our pleasurable living in this town.

ILFORD.

He is a very pope in Montpelier, the head here— 225

SIR ANTHONY.

And a fit head he is for such sinful members as we are.

ILFORD.

We members! You are a Protestant, Sir Anthony.

SIR ANTHONY.

You may be surly enough to tell 'em you are one, but I am always of the religion of the government 230 I am in—

VALENTINE.

And of the women you converse with, knight?

SIR ANTHONY.

And when I can't convince 'em, I conform.

ILFORD.

A very civil character* of a fashionable conscience.

VALENTINE.

Of a sensible man, I think: Why must your 235 capacity be the measure of another man's understanding? and all men be in the wrong who don't dance i'th'circle of your thoughts?

SIR ANTHONY.

Every man a villain, or a fool, who does not fall into your notion of things? 240

VALENTINE.

No opinion ever sprung out of a universal consent; truth can no more be comprehended than beauty; we have our several reasons for the one and fancies for the other. And as beauty has not the same influence upon all complexions, so reason has not 245 the same force upon all understandings. We embrace what pleases us in both, secure ourselves in a probability, and guess out the rest.

SIR ANTHONY.

Ilford is one of those fellows whom, if you divide from in one thing, will never close with you in any. Though 250 the abbé and you do differ about the way to heaven, you may go to the devil together, I warrant you.

VALENTINE.

However wide we may be from his opinion of t'other world, I'm sure he joins with us in our opinion of this. 255

SIR ANTHONY.

For my part, I regard the man, not his religion, and if he does my business in this world, let him do his own in the next.

ILFORD.

Nay, gentlemen, I have as honorable an opinion
of the abbé as you can have. I know there's nothing   260
to be done without him—

SIR ANTHONY.

That the conversation* of the best families in
Montpelier runs through his reformation—

ILFORD.

That some of our fortunes—

SIR ANTHONY.

All our fortunes—   265

ILFORD.

Yours particularly with Floriante at present
depending upon his favor against the authority of
her father—

VALENTINE.

And the quality* of my rival, Count Vérole.

SIR ANTHONY.

No dancings, no balls, no masquerades in a sweet   270
circle of society, as it has been from one good
house to another, without his introduction and
gravity to qualify the scandal.

VALENTINE.

Substantial reasons for our respect.

ILFORD.

Weighty motives all for our attendance.   275

SIR ANTHONY.

Are they so, sir? No more of your Protestant, then,
if you would not be damned for a heretic by the
women in a Catholic country.

VALENTINE.

We should ha' been at our patron's levee,
gentlemen.   280

SIR ANTHONY.

He'll bate us the ceremony. You're going to visit
him?

VALENTINE.

You must along with us.

SIR ANTHONY.

I'll follow you.

VALENTINE.

You are his favorite; we are nobody without you—   285

ILFORD.

The support of our interest with him.

SIR ANTHONY.

Business, business, gentlemen.

VALENTINE.

Pox o'your business—

ILFORD.

'Twill end in that.—Prithee let him go; a whore I
warrant you—   290

SIR ANTHONY.

Money, money, sir,
More filthy and more common than a whore,
More prostituted, too, to knaves and fools:
Yet my grave friend, you'll have a share in both,
Or I mistake your nature.   295

VALENTINE.

You are answered.

ILFORD.

Indeed, my little friend is so far right:
Money and whore make one another's use;
Either is dull alone.

Enter pilgrim

VALENTINE.

This pilgrim here again!   300

SIR ANTHONY.

He follows us. What would he have?

PILGRIM.

Your charity, good gentlemen.

SIR ANTHONY.

Prithee leave us. There's charity in my advice to thee
not to lose thy labor. Besides we are Englishmen and
never think of the poor out of our own parish.   305

VALENTINE.

Nor there neither, but according to law, and when
we cannot help it.[14]

ILFORD.

Charity is a free-will offering, and we part with
nothing we can keep, I assure you—

VALENTINE.

Not so much as our sins.   310

ILFORD.

Especially at this time—

---

14 poor … help it] Poor relief was mandated within each
separate parish in England. Each parish was excusively
responsible for "its" poor, and landed gentlemen would
bear the economic burden of supporting those unable
to work, including, often, the illegitimate infants they
fathered.

SIR ANTHONY.

Unless it be to live upon 'em.

PILGRIM.

Alas! what pity 'tis, that gentlemen so much in debt—

SIR ANTHONY.

That we shall never pay—   315

PILGRIM.

To Heaven—

SIR ANTHONY.

And other creditors.

PILGRIM.

Of youth so sweet, of form so excellent—

SIR ANTHONY.

You or me, Ilford? Who does he mean?

PILGRIM. (*To Sir Anthony.*)

So finished, by the great Creator's hand,   320
I worship him in thee.

ILFORD.

As thou dost the King's picture in his coin—

VALENTINE.

In hopes of getting by it.

PILGRIM.

You are so fashioned—

SIR ANTHONY.

For a sinner.   325

PILGRIM.

And by Nature's hand designed—

SIR ANTHONY.

A whoremaster.

PILGRIM.

You can't want*—

SIR ANTHONY.

Women? No, Pilgrim, I shan't want 'em in thy acquaintance, I'm sure.   330

PILGRIM.

You can't want grace, the beauty of the soul,
The accomplishment of virtue to the work;
You can't want charity, for charity
Is called our gratitude to Heav'n—

ILFORD.

You call it so.   335

PILGRIM.

You would not be ungrateful?

SIR ANTHONY.

I would not be a fool nor imagine such an ass as

thou art could ever be commissioned, a' God's name, to collect the revenues of this world—

VALENTINE.

Nor to convert (those deodands[15] of devotion) the   340
public charitable endowments of bigotted or dying
fools to the private luxury of your own lazy tribe.

ILFORD.

We build no churches, Pilgrim, nor found
hospitals, but in our own country; nor there
neither, but to father our own bastards.   345

SIR ANTHONY.

Your mendicant women-saints, we allow of indeed:
all our charity runs through their devotion.

VALENTINE.

Soft little hands become an offering, and those we
often fill.

PILGRIM.

Are you so lost?   350

ILFORD.

To all that thou can'st say.

SIR ANTHONY.

Thy godliness may convert others, though it does
nothing upon us.

PILGRIM.

What can I do for you?

SIR ANTHONY.

Pimp for us.   355

PILGRIM.

I will pray for you.

SIR ANTHONY.

Do it in a corner alone, then. (*Thrusts him out.*)
Be as godly as thou wouldst by thyself, and leave
us to our devotions.

PILGRIM.

I may join with you in yours, before I have done;   360
the abbé won't fail me. (*Exit.*)

SIR ANTHONY.

I have my hands full, gentlemen, but my trade is
settled, my correspondence easy, my factors
employed, and my returns will be quick.

VALENTINE.

Pray make 'em so and come as soon as you can to   365
us.

_____

15 deodands] gifts devoted to religious purposes

SIR ANTHONY.

I sail with every wind, in the teeth of fortune sometimes.

VALENTINE.

Have a care of being bit,* Sir Anthony.

SIR ANTHONY.

I kiss as close as an older sinner, Valentine, I warrant you. (*Exit.*)

ILFORD.

You may venture him: he has nothing to lose, that I know of, but his youth, and that wonnot long support the expense of the life he leads.

VALENTINE.

He loses no time, indeed.

ILFORD.

But misemploys a great deal, in my opinion.

VALENTINE.

Youth will have its sallies.

ILFORD.

The sallies of his youth will sooner lead him to repentance and the pox than to his manor of Lovedale, as he calls it.

VALENTINE.

His mansion-house in Glocestershire.

ILFORD.

His castle in the air, which no man ever heard of till he was pleased to fancy and christen it for the seat of his family.

VALENTINE.

Then you don't believe him a baronet of twelve hundred pounds a year,[16] under age, and upon an allowance for his travel from his guardians?

ILFORD.

I believe he may have been some court page, spoiled first by the confidence of his lady in knowing her secrets, then coming early into the iniquity of the Town, by the merit of his person and impudence has since made a fashionable livelihood out of women and fools.

VALENTINE.

I don't know who he is or what he has: if he be no knight, he's a pretty fellow, and that's better. And if he has not twelve hundred pounds a year, he deserves it, and does not want it, which is more than you can say of most of your knights that have that estate, I'm sure.

ILFORD.

Nay, that I grant you too.

VALENTINE.

He lives as like a gentleman, has all things as well about him, is as much respected by the men, and better received by the women, than any of us.

ILFORD.

He's a pretty woman's man, indeed.

VALENTINE.

And a merry man's man too, sir, for you must own he has a great deal of wit.

ILFORD.

Pretty good natural parts,* I confess, but a fool has the keeping 'em, no judgment in the world. And what he says, comes as much by chance—

VALENTINE.

As Epicurus's world[17] did: perfect and uniform without a design.

ILFORD.

He flies too much at random to please any man of discretion.

VALENTINE.

There is indeed the quarrel of twelve years difference between thy discretion and his wit. He may live up to thy discretion, George, but we shall neither of us arrive at his wit.

ILFORD.

How long will his wit support him?

VALENTINE.

That must be his care and not our business; I never examine any man's pockets that is not troublesome to mine.

ILFORD.

If he be not troublesome, his necessities may throw him upon some scandalous action—

VALENTINE.

That may require thy bailing him?

ILFORD.

That may reflect upon us.

VALENTINE.

Oh! thou wert always tender of thy reputation

---

16 twelve … year] the fictional annual revenue of Lovedale

17 Epicurus's world] the theory that the world is created out of the random movement of atoms

when thou wert to pay for the scandal, I'll say that
for thee, Ilford. But if want* of money be a crime,
Heaven help the guilty; we are disappointed of our
bills* at present too.   430

ILFORD.
But we have letters of credit and may use 'em upon
occasion.

VALENTINE.
And he has credit without letters, which he may use
too, upon occasion, for I am so far from apprehending he may, that I am resolved he shall want*   435
nothing I can oblige him in, pocket or person.

ILFORD.
Oh sir, you need not doubt his giving you an
opportunity of showing your gallantry in that part
of your friendship; he'll borrow money of you, I
warrant you.   440

VALENTINE.
And he shall have it, though I borrow it for him.
But sir, you had not always this slight opinion of
Sir Anthony.

ILFORD.
I did not always know him. (*Walking off.*)

VALENTINE.
Nor he the abbé's niece.   445

ILFORD.
I found him out but lately.

VALENTINE.
For your rival.

ILFORD.
His vanity, extravagance, and general pretension to
women are intolerable—

VALENTINE.
Especially when the gaiety of that humor* is likely   450
to get the better of your formality in Volante's
esteem: he is your rival.

ILFORD.
My rival!

VALENTINE.
And I don't wonder, you don't like him.

ILFORD.
He's a general undertaker, indeed, and in that part   455
of his conversation* is as impertinent to the
women as in other things he is troublesome to the
men; so I think it would be our common good
fortune to get rid of him.

VALENTINE.
I am not of your mind, and here he comes to   460
convince you.

Enter Sir Anthony.

SIR ANTHONY.
Just as I left you! you scorn to stir an inch out of
your quality* to put yourselves in the way of
Fortune, though you know her to be blind.

VALENTINE.
You meet her at every turn, Sir Anthony.   465

SIR ANTHONY.
She must come home to you to be welcome.

ILFORD.
When do you bring her home?

SIR ANTHONY.
But you may be sullen and sour, domineer,
threaten your stewards, and talk loud at a
disappointment, you are in possession, gentlemen.   470

Enter Waitwell with a purse.

My guardians won't be so served; my governor
teaches me to provide against accidents: what I
want* of my age, (*Waitwell gives him the purse.*) I
must supply with my diligence.

ILFORD.
And have your labor for your pains.   475

SIR ANTHONY.
I can take pains, sir, and the profit of my pains,
sir; fifty pieces in a morning, sir, the price of my
pains, and give the lady a penniworth into the
bargain.

ILFORD.
How! Fifty pieces?   480

VALENTINE.
From a woman, Sir Anthony?

SIR ANTHONY.
Nothing, sir, a trifle.

VALENTINE.
Your mistress pays like a widow—

SIR ANTHONY.
That had lost her youth upon a husband, and the
hopes of a jointure—   485

ILFORD.
And just delivered, would redeem the folly of the
past by the enjoyment of what's to come—

VALENTINE.

In a sober resolution of making the price of her penance the purchase of her pleasure—

SIR ANTHONY.

By refunding upon a young fellow what she had wheedled from an old one. 490

ILFORD.

I warrant her old and ugly, by her pension.

SIR ANTHONY.

She's young enough to be a maid, handsome enough to be a mistress, cunning enough to be a wife, and rich enough to be a widow. 495

VALENTINE.

Faith, she comes down—

SIR ANTHONY.

Deeper than I can, I assure you.

ILFORD.

She pays well, I'll say that for her.

SIR ANTHONY.

And is well—I'll say that for her.

VALENTINE.

And does everything well. 500

SIR ANTHONY.

You would say that for her, Valentine? And she does everything well; that way she is a widow, I promise you.

ILFORD.

Take us into your assistance.

VALENTINE.

We are friends and will stand by you. 505

ILFORD.

We are out of employment that way—

VALENTINE.

And would journeywork under you.

SIR ANTHONY.

Anything to be wicked, gentlemen. But Ilford, thou art honorable in love and hast it too much in thy head to have it anywhere else. Besides, she's so much of my humor* she'll never relish thine. 510

VALENTINE.

She must not go out of our family.

SIR ANTHONY.

She's handsome and convenient, as able to answer all our wants,* as all we are to satisfy the importunity of hers. 515

VALENTINE.

Well, I am satisfied; I am her man.

SIR ANTHONY.

Or any woman's man who wants to be satisfied.

VALENTINE.

She must like me for being of her opinion in liking thee.

SIR ANTHONY.

That indeed may do something, and time may bring it about; in short, this is the English lady you have heard me speak of: I allow her the favor of my person, and she allows me the freedom of her purse. And I am glad I command it so luckily to answer the occasions of my friends. 520 ... 525

ILFORD.

You can command nothing we can have occasion for.

VALENTINE.

By your pardon, sir, you may be too proud to be obliged, but I have occasion for the money and woman too, so as you were saying, Sir Anthony—

Enter a servant, Ilford goes to him.

SIR ANTHONY.

Why, I still say a true bred Englishman is ever out of humor when he's out of pocket: he knows no more how to want* money than how to borrow it— 530

VALENTINE.

And, when he does, is as surly in borrowing as others are in lending money.

SIR ANTHONY.

'Tis almost as dangerous, too, to offer him money, as to lend money to another man, for he is as likely out of a want* of sense to suffer^c your courtesy as a stranger out of a want of honesty never to return it. 535

VALENTINE.

That way, indeed, our countrymen take care never to think themselves obliged; we can be ungrateful— 540

SIR ANTHONY.

And cheat our benefactors of their good offices by an ingratitude almost natural to us. And that makes a tolerable amends for our want of the more sublimed villainies of warmer countries.

VALENTINE.

But the lady, Sir Anthony— 545

SIR ANTHONY.

More of the lady at leisure; in the mean time, here are fifty pieces of hers to keep up your fancy: if your occasions require a greater sum, she shall supply you—

VALENTINE.

And I'll supply her. 550

SIR ANTHONY.

Upon your bond for the payment of the whole to her in England—

VALENTINE.

By all means.

SIR ANTHONY.

A blank bond, because she would not be known here. 555

VALENTINE.

With all my heart, but won't she take a gentleman's word?

SIR ANTHONY.

Oh yes, when she has his bond for the performance. When our surly friend is civil enough to be obliged, I have a twin purse at his service too. 560

VALENTINE.

You are very much out of his favor of late.

SIR ANTHONY.

So I find. What's the matter with the fool?

VALENTINE.

How have you disobliged him?

SIR ANTHONY.

But he's in love, and consequently an ass.

VALENTINE.

And I believe jealous of you. 565

SIR ANTHONY.

Faith, I'll give him cause. Volante is as fit for my purpose of tormenting him that way as I could wish. Shall we go to the abbé, gentlemen?

ILFORD.

Golding! an Englishman?

SERVANT.

So his servants tell me, sir. 570

ILFORD.

Just come to town, say'st thou?

SERVANT.

He has not peeped abroad since his coming, sir.

ILFORD.

Do you know any such gentleman, Valentine?

VALENTINE.

I did: a considerable coxcomb of that name in England, a knight, Sir Gentle Golding. Sir 575
Anthony, you may have known him too.

SIR ANTHONY.

I have heard of him. (*Aside to Waitwell.*) If this should prove my coxcomb, Governor—

VALENTINE.

But damn him, he has not courage enough to cross the Channel. 580

SIR ANTHONY.

I know he is in France, I heard of him at Paris.

SERVANT.

Faith, sir, it must be the man—

SIR ANTHONY. (*To Waitwell.*)

Whom we must manage then.

VALENTINE.

Why dost think so?

SERVANT.

Your description is so like him, sir. 585

VALENTINE.

Why, hast thou found him out?

ILFORD.

For his father's son, and his mother's fool.

SIR ANTHONY.

And our fool, gentlemen. If he be a fool, I'll have my snack[18] of him.

SERVANT.

There's enough for you all without wronging the 590
family, as he will quickly convince you. (*To Valentine.*) He knows you, sir—

VALENTINE.

Then 'tis the very fool.

SERVANT.

And designs to wait upon you.

VALENTINE.

At his peril be't: I owe him a revenge for Lucia's sake. 595

ILFORD.

Is this the spark?

VALENTINE.

That bought her of her aunt—

SIR ANTHONY. (*To Waitwell.*)

Now for my character.*

VALENTINE.

When she was yet too young to judge between the fortune and the fool. 600

SIR ANTHONY.

That's some excuse, however.

---

18 snack] a joke on someone

ILFORD.

A little time showed her her senseless bargain.

VALENTINE.

So I hear.

SIR ANTHONY.

Which, she repenting, gave you the cheaper penniworth of her person: then was the time— 605

VALENTINE.

That I was in France, out of the reach of any other pleasure, had she designed me any, than the bare news that she had found him out, loathed, and abhorred him.

ILFORD.

Loathing and abhorring are tokens of mortification 610 indeed, but penance is not enough for such a fault; 'tis generally as short lived as the sin that begot it. What marks of amendment has she since given?

SIR ANTHONY.

What marks of amendment would you have?

VALENTINE.

I know nothing of her amendment. 615

SIR ANTHONY.

Would you have her snivel like a girl, more afraid of her mother than the sin, and cry, "Forgive me this one slip, I'll do so no more—"

VALENTINE.

Repent upon the first intrigue—

SIR ANTHONY.

Turn honest and disparage the pleasure by leaving 620 the trade?

VALENTINE.

That must not be.

SIR ANTHONY.

By no means, Valentine.

VALENTINE.

Would you have her already fall off—

SIR ANTHONY.

Become a civil person— 625

VALENTINE.

And take up—

ILFORD.

With somebody that better deserves her. That way I would have her a civil person and fall off from her fool.

SIR ANTHONY.

Indeed a woman never repents of a fool so heartily 630

as in the arms of a man of sense.

VALENTINE.

How Fortune has disposed of her, I know not, but I liked her once so well, I would have her still preserve my good opinion of her conduct: if she has managed her monster, as he deserved, she has made 635 money and mirth of him, and me some amends for the loss of her, by mending her condition.

SIR ANTHONY.

If that will preserve your good opinion of her, she will continue it, for I hear she has used him as ill as you could desire from your revenge or the Town 640 expect from their hopes of a libel.

VALENTINE.

Then I honor her.

SIR ANTHONY.

She has robbed him of five hundred pounds, run away from him, and so exposed him, that he has been the common rhyming theme, the hackney 645 Pegasus for the puny poets to set out upon in their vast ambition of arriving at a lampoon.

ILFORD.

And that perhaps has sent him into France.

VALENTINE.

Well, I will have her knighted.

SIR ANTHONY.

Of what order? A Knight Errant, or an Errant[19] 650 Knight?

VALENTINE.

A Knight Errant of thy order she must be—

WAITWELL. (*Aside.*)

That she is already.

VALENTINE.

And thee a Right Honorable, for thy news.

SIR ANTHONY.

You may depend upon it. 655

VALENTINE.

If ever I light on her, I'll thank her for this justice to us all.

ILFORD.

Golding may tell us more of her.

VALENTINE.

So he may. (*To a Servant.*) You, sir, wait at our

---

19 Errant] first means "wandering," then "erring": obvious play on "arrant"

lodgings for him and direct him to the abbé's, if 660
he comes:

We'll laugh at him, if we do nothing more.

SIR ANTHONY. [*Aside.*]

But he and I must clear another score.

Exeunt.

Act II. A garden.

Count Canaille and the abbé.

CANAILLE.

Brother, you may forget yourself and your rank as
much as you please in our niece, Volante; I have
nothing to do with her but to wish her well.

ABBÉ.

'Tis very well.

CANAILLE.

You are her guardian: her person, her fortune, and 5
her conduct are in your care.

ABBÉ.

I'll take care of 'em.

CANAILLE.

You must answer for 'em.

ABBÉ.

I will answer for 'em.

CANAILLE.

But my daughters are under my government, and 10
whilst they are, they must, nay, shall do nothing
to dishonor me.

ABBÉ.

They will do nothing to dishonor you.

CANAILLE.

I'll put it out of their power, had they a mind to't.

ABBÉ.

They ha' no such mind.

CANAILLE. 15

That's more than I can tell from the liberties you
give these Englishmen in our family—

ABBÉ.

They are gentlemen.

CANAILLE.

I apprehend a danger, though you won't.

ABBÉ.

Pugh, pugh, there is no danger. 20

CANAILLE.

I'll prevent it, if there were.

ABBÉ.

All men of fortune in their country.

CANAILLE.

They are not men of quality.* (*Walking about.*)
Would Count Vérole were come.

ABBÉ.

Don't do so rash a thing. 25

CANAILLE.

I'll rid myself of all my fears at once: dispose my
youngest daughter in a nunnery and instantly
marry Floriante—

ABBÉ.

To make her more miserable.

CANAILLE.

Suitable to her birth. 30

ABBÉ.

To a fool, the worst of fools: a singular,
opinionated, obstinate, crooked-tempered, jealous-
pated fool.

CANAILLE.

If he were so, that fool's a count, and the count
makes amends for the fool. 35

ABBÉ.

Then he is welcome—

Count Vérole enters to 'em.

Virtue created first nobililty,
But in our honorable ignorance
Nobility makes virtue.

VÉROLE.

What says the abbé? 40

CANAILLE.

Sir, you are most welcome.

VÉROLE.

I shall be glad to find it from the man
I so much honor—

Exeunt Vérole and Canaille.

ABBÉ.

For his title, that's all this fellow thinks worth
honoring. Hang 'em, they make me grave—but that 45
a brother of my blood should choose a coxcomb
out—but if my brother prove a coxcomb too? That
wonder's over—then 'tis their mutual interest to
join; each likes the other to excuse himself.

Sir Anthony, Valentine and Ilford enter to him.

SIR ANTHONY.

Ah, Monsieur l'Abbé. 50

ILFORD.

You have prevented us.

VALENTINE.

We were going to visit you.

ABBÉ.

In nomine domini,[20] amen.

ILFORD.

The abbé making his will!

SIR ANTHONY.

Amen to our abbé's devotions. 55

ABBÉ.

You fall as naturally as a parish clerk into the close of a prayer.

SIR ANTHONY.

I love to bring things to a good end.

ABBÉ.

Nay, I have done, my devotion won't tire your attention. 60

SIR ANTHONY.

You are like the prelate that, being dignified for long prayers, hated them ever after.

ABBÉ.

Long prayers are for poor priests that want preferment, men of quality* rise without 'em.

VALENTINE.

In men of your rank they are pharisaical and always 65 to carry on a design.

ABBÉ.

I neither have a faith in them nor their followers, and therefore I seldom or never pray at all.

ILFORD.

How! Never pray at all?

ABBÉ.

The Church and I are agreed upon the bargain, 70 and few words are best when the parties are of a mind.

VALENTINE.

But the Church may better your bargain.

ABBÉ.

I am mortified to the dignities and designs of the Church, have laid aside the pomp and pride of my 75

profession. I am contented to sit down in a sinecure and, with the poor pittance of two thousand pistoles a year, make the most of a good conscience and good company.

ILFORD.

A good conscience is good company indeed. 80

ABBÉ.

I mean, sir, I'll make a conscience of good company—

SIR ANTHONY.

Make the best of the blessing and enjoy it as long as you can.

ABBÉ.

Ah! My little knight understands me (*To Ilford.*) 85 though you won't, sir.

VALENTINE.

You'll anger him—

ABBÉ.

He jumps into the point with me.

SIR ANTHONY.

And into the company too, dear abbé. I must make one. 90

ABBÉ.

Make one? (*Abbé wantons with Sir Anthony.*) Thou mak'st all, thou'rt all in all, the whole company thyself, thou art everything with everybody, a man among the women, and a woman among the men.

VALENTINE.

How Abbé! Sir Anthony a woman? 95

ABBÉ.

One might indeed mistake him, by his face.

ILFORD.

He would mistake him I believe.

VALENTINE.

Somewhere else.

ABBÉ.

But there's no faith in faces; the women have found him out and won't trust him. 100

SIR ANTHONY.

Aye, aye, the women, Abbé, the ladies—

ABBÉ.

As mad as ever they were, my nieces you mean!

SIR ANTHONY.

I long to be among 'em.

ABBÉ.

Nay, they long too, if that would do 'em any good. And think it long. 105

20 *In nomine domini*] "In the name of the Lord" (Latin): an opening for wills and a conclusion for prayers

SIR ANTHONY.

I have not spoke to a woman this half hour.

VALENTINE.

We are all idle without you.

ILFORD.

Sin has been as silent among us—

SIR ANTHONY.

As in the first session of a parliament in fear of a reformation.[21]   110

ABBÉ.

Ah! very well, in faith, my little man! But no, no reformation, I warrant you. Matters shall not be much mended by my management; sin must sometimes get the better of the saint.

SIR ANTHONY.

Or the Devil may still wear black, sir.   115

ABBÉ.

Let him wear what he will; we have had him in our family this morning.

VALENTINE.

What's the matter?

ABBÉ.

My brother has discovered something between you and his eldest daughter.   120

VALENTINE.

That's unlucky.

ABBÉ.

Which to prevent, he designs to marry her instantly to Count Vérole.

ILFORD.

That's bad indeed.

VALENTINE.

What is there to be done?   125

ABBÉ.

Nothing that I know of.

SIR ANTHONY.

What's to be done? Anything's to be done.

VALENTINE.

What if I run away with her?

ABBÉ.

With all my heart.

VALENTINE.

Or if I cut his throat.   130

SIR ANTHONY.

With all my heart.

VALENTINE.

Or bedrid him with a beating.

ILFORD.

With all my heart.

SIR ANTHONY.

If none of these will do, let him marry her.

VALENTINE.

I must say, with all my heart.   135

SIR ANTHONY.

If you can't make her your wife, make him your cuckold.

ABBÉ.

With all my heart.

VALENTINE.

Ah! if I durst but hope that way.

ABBÉ.

Hope, you must hope, man, and you must dare,   140
man, if you would do anything with the women.

VALENTINE.

Can you encourage me?

ABBÉ.

Why faith, whatever her father designs, she does not design to marry him, and disobedience may make way for other sins.   145

VALENTINE.

I know she hates him.

ABBÉ.

And I know she likes you. And if I have any authority from the Church—

ILFORD.

Which is not to be disputed—

ABBÉ.

Or any interest from my estate—   150

VALENTINE.

Which must be considerable—

SIR ANTHONY.

Not to be opposed—

ABBÉ.

And which must furnish the better part of her fortune, he shan't have her.

VALENTINE.

That's gaining time at least.   155

ILFORD.

He's naturally jealous.

---

[21] reformation] dissolution

SIR ANTHONY.

And has settled that nature by a Spanish education[22] they say.

ABBÉ.

He was bred in Spain indeed.

ILFORD.

A miserable woman she must be then.   160

ABBÉ.

I would not have a niece of mine married into a family or nation where, if she dislike her own man, she can have nobody else.

VALENTINE.

Our women are the happy women, sir.

ABBÉ.

Why indeed, you Englishmen are the fittest men   165
for husbands in the world! Would all my female relations were married into your country!

ILFORD.

Would they thought as well of us as you do.

ABBÉ.

There is a lady quarrels at her condition, or likes another man better than her husband, which   170
sometimes may happen you know—

VALENTINE.

Such things have happened, indeed.

ABBÉ.

There they say cuckoldom is in fashion.

SIR ANTHONY.

Nay, more than in fashion, sir, 'tis according to law: cuckoldom is the liberty, and a separate   175
maintenance* the property, of the freeborn women of England.*

ILFORD.

We give our women fair play for't.

VALENTINE.

And scorn any tie upon 'em more than their inclinations.   180

ABBÉ.

Why, what would a lady ask more in marriage? I'll maintain it, such a privilege is better than her dower and, in a prudent woman's thoughts, must take place of any other consideration.

---

22 Spanish education] Spaniards were stereotypically portrayed as irrationally jealous in English literature of the seventeenth century.

ILFORD.

'Tis as much before a dower in profit, too, as in   185
time, for a husband may cheat a wife of her dower—

SIR ANTHONY.

Or wear out her title by outliving her, and then she is bobbed of her reversion—

VALENTINE.

Or leave her so old, she may be past having any   190
good from it—

SIR ANTHONY.

Unless she lays it out in redeeming some younger brother—

ILFORD.

That had spent his annuity in a lord's company—

SIR ANTHONY.

Or in following a common whore—   195

VALENTINE.

Or in following as common a mistress, the Court—

SIR ANTHONY.

And being reduced to the last fifty, had ventured it prudently on a birthday* coat and the hopes of an employment—   200

ILFORD.

One, who in spite of having been once undone, will have no more profit from his experience than to fall into the same folly again with the same occasion.

ABBÉ.

Then hang him for a fool, enough of him. I am   205
convinced with what you say, gentlemen, and you shall have my niece. You have her consent and my consent and Sir Anthony's good word, which, I promise you, goes a great way with the women.

VALENTINE.

Your niece Volante is her confidant.   210

ABBÉ.

I'll make her your friend. (*A servant whispers the abbé.*)

SIR ANTHONY.

I'll secure her for you.

ILFORD.

Why you secure her?

SIR ANTHONY.

For such a favor, sir, I think I may.   215

ILFORD.

Your interest is mighty.

SIR ANTHONY.

So far I can engage her.

ILFORD.

You engage her!

SIR ANTHONY.

Nay, oblige her.

ILFORD.

Her friendship may oblige her, but not you.   220

ABBÉ.

Pray don't quarrel about obliging her. Volante is
my favorite, she shall please herself— [*Aside.*] and,
I believe, would please Sir Anthony.—Gentlemen,
you are three, and my nieces are three. I won't
meddle in your choice. Agree among yourselves,   225
win 'em and wear 'em. I had rather you should
have 'em than my brother dispose of 'em.

VALENTINE.

Sir, you oblige us all.

ABBÉ.

Our dinner stays for us. We'll settle those things
within. I have almost forgot the extraordinary part 230
of my entertainment: I have a pilgrim for you.

ILFORD.

We have had him already.

SIR ANTHONY.

And our share of laughing at him, too, sir.

ABBÉ.

He pretends to be a man of extraordinary sanctity.
I meddled with that as little as I could, for fear of 235
raising a spirit I could not lay; besides, I had
matters of more moment to mind then.

VALENTINE.

How did you get rid of him?

ABBÉ.

With much ado I put him and his history off,
telling him some English heretics were to dine with 240
me—

SIR ANTHONY.

We were obliged to you, sir.

ABBÉ.

And if he pleased to spare that miraculous account
(which he will be sure to give of himself) for the
conversion of the wicked, he might then have a   245
proper occasion for so great a design.

SIR ANTHONY.

I should think the worse of my constitution as long
as I lived if I should grow qualmish of anything
he could say to me.

ABBÉ.

I knew I must hear him and therefore provided   250
your conversation* to qualify his.

VALENTINE.

The novelty may divert us.

ILFORD.

He professes more charity than to force his
nonsense upon you.

ABBÉ.

That punishment I must go through, before he will 255
go away, and pay for my penance, too.

ILFORD.

At the expence of his vow of poverty.

ABBÉ.

Pray gentlemen, along with me. I don't desire you
to believe all he says. Take what you like, and laugh
at all the rest.   260

VALENTINE.

Why, there our Christian liberty's confessed.

SIR ANTHONY.

Would we had ne'er a more imposing priest.

*Exeunt [Abbé and Valentine]. Ilford pulls Sir Anthony
by the sleeve.*

ILFORD.

One word before you go.

SIR ANTHONY.

Prithee come along—no cautioning in such a slight
affair—   265

ILFORD.

I am glad you think it such a slight affair.

SIR ANTHONY.

Mere merriment.

ILFORD.

I never thought it more.

SIR ANTHONY.

Matter of mirth and jest.

ILFORD.

Nay, that's too much.   270

SIR ANTHONY.

Upon a foolish pilgrim?

ILFORD.

Upon Volante.

SIR ANTHONY.

Volante, thou talk'st of Volante, and I answer thee, the pilgrim. Why, thou art distracted, man, and I shall suspect myself to be no wiser than I should   275
be for keeping thee company.

ILFORD.

Sir, however you think to carry it, I must tell you—

SIR ANTHONY.

With a very grave face—

ILFORD.

This is no jesting time—   280

SIR ANTHONY.

Because 'tis a ridiculous subject—

ILFORD.

That I am in love—

SIR ANTHONY.

In serious sadness—

ILFORD.

With that lady—

SIR ANTHONY.

That never was sad, nor serious in her life. Prithee,   285
no more of this. Ilford in love! Thou art a very honest fellow and hast a great many good qualities, but thy talent lies quite another way.

ILFORD.

Sir, I am serious enough to be angry, if you laugh at me.   290

SIR ANTHONY.

But you are in love with her, you say. Why, everybody that sees her is in love with her, if that would do any good, but is she in love with you?

ILFORD.

I think my estate may recommend my person to a welcome, wherever I pretend.   295

SIR ANTHONY.

Does she think so?

ILFORD.

Why do you ask the question?

SIR ANTHONY.

Volante is too witty to be very wise and requires no settlement but her man.

ILFORD.

And why may not I be her man, pray?   300

SIR ANTHONY.

Fie, fie, sir, more modesty might become a man of your gravity! You her man! No, no, she's otherwise disposed of, I assure you.

ILFORD.

What, you follow her!

SIR ANTHONY.

Nay, you follow her, she does not put me to the   305
trouble.

ILFORD.

No, sir—I shall put you to more trouble if you don't quit your pretensions to her.

SIR ANTHONY.

Quit my pretensions to her!

ILFORD.

And promise me—   310

SIR ANTHONY.

I will promise you—

ILFORD.

Oh, will you so, sir?

SIR ANTHONY.

That (whatever I would have done by fair means) I will now follow her in spite of your teeth.*

ILFORD.

In spite of my teeth—   315

SIR ANTHONY.

Pursue her till she yield to my desires—

ILFORD.

The devil you will!

SIR ANTHONY.

And lie with her under your nose.

ILFORD.

You shall be damned first.

SIR ANTHONY.

Nay then, have at the lady.   320

Volante entering, sees 'em fighting, shrieks, and runs out, Sir Anthony after her, and returns with her in his hand.]

ILFORD.

This was a trick to save his cowardice.

SIR ANTHONY.

I had rather part with my pretension to a quarrel* than to my mistress at any time.

VOLANTE.

I hope you are not hurt.

ILFORD.

Sir, you assert a privilege the lady never gave you   325
of treating her at that familiar rate.

VOLANTE.

At what familiar rate?

SIR ANTHONY.

Sir, you may be respectful, look simply, and bow
at a distance in a modest despair of ever coming
nearer to please, but I am for a closer conversation*   330
when I like my company.

VOLANTE.

I am sorry, sir, my carriage gives offence, but I
must think you treat me more familiarly that
saucily should dare to censure me, limit my
actions, and prescribe me rules.   335

SIR ANTHONY.

A foolish fellow, madam, not worth your anger.
Leave him to his repentance and your scorn.

ILFORD.

I must bear it all.

VOLANTE.

But pray, how came this difference?

ILFORD.

'Twas your quarrel,* madam.   340

VOLANTE.

I am sorry for it.

SIR ANTHONY.

You may judge what a husband he'll make who
(being but a servant) dares assume an authority
over you—

VOLANTE.

Which I never gave him, that I remember.   345

SIR ANTHONY. (*To Ilford.*)

I told you you were out of the road of her favor.

VOLANTE.

The report of this quarrel and the occasion of it
will be but a scandalous addition to my fame when
it comes to be the tattle of the town.

ILFORD.

It shall go no further for me.   350

VOLANTE.

I suppose the folly on't will keep you silent. You
may be ashamed on't, indeed.

ILFORD.

I beg your pardon for it.

VOLANTE.

Beg Sir Anthony's, for till he pardons you, I am
sure I won't.   355

SIR ANTHONY.

There is no remedy, you must submit.

ILFORD.

I am a woman's fool and must obey.

They embrace.

SIR ANTHONY.

'Tis many a wise man's fortune.

ILFORD.

We are friends.

VOLANTE.

If you have favors to expect from me, deserve 'em   360
by fair means.

SIR ANTHONY.

Or come to me, and I'll speak a good word for thee
to the lady.

ILFORD.

You triumph, sir.

SIR ANTHONY.

Till when, we take our leaves. (*Leads Volante out.*)   365

ILFORD.

Pox! I deserve it all for putting it into her power
to use me so. He's ten years younger than I am
and, consequently, so much handsomer in her eye.
He prates a great deal more and better than I do,
for her purpose, and therefore lies better in her ear.   370
He has the advantage of me in every vanity that
can betray a girl. Volante's a girl, and what could
I expect for my honorable love for her when, in
the weakness of a woman's choice, she will prefer
the present laughing hour to all that can come   375
after? If this would cure me now, 'twere a lesson
well learned. I'll hear what the pilgrim can say
upon this subject. I'll listen to his lies: they are less
mischievous and may drive this woman out of my
head. (*Exit.*)   380

[A song.]d

I.

Pursuing Beauty, men descry
    The distant shore and long to prove
(Still richer in variety)
    The treasures of the land of love.
              II.

We women, like weak Indians, stand   385
    Inviting from our golden coast
The wandering rovers to our land,
    But she who trades with 'em is lost.

III.

With humble vows they first begin,
    Stealing unseen into the heart,   390
But by possession settled in,
    They quickly act another part.
           IV.
For beads and baubles we resign,
    In ignorance, our shining store,
Discover* nature's richest mine,   395
    And yet the tyrants will have more.
           V.
Be wise, be wise, and do not try
    How he can court or you be won,
For love is but discovery:
    When that is made, the pleasure's done.   400

Enter Floriante and Charlott.

FLORIANTE.

Is not that Sir Anthony?

CHARLOTT.

With my cousin Volante; we shall have 'em at the
turning of the walk.

FLORIANTE.

They are as proper counselors for our purpose of
disobedience—   405

CHARLOTT.

As we could ha' met withal.

FLORIANTE.

You'll be no nun, Sister?

CHARLOTT.

Nor you no countess?

FLORIANTE.

I would be as willingly enclosed in the walls of a
monastery as in the arms of that Count Vérole,   410
and in the arms of Death rather than in either.

CHARLOTT.

Well, I'm not so difficult: I had rather be alive
upon any terms than dead upon the best; I had
rather be a nun than be nothing at all, though
there's nothing I had not rather be than be a nun.   415

FLORIANTE.

Any man's company rather than the company of
all women.

CHARLOTT.

'Tis more to my humor,*ᵉ I confess to you, among
the rest of my venial offences. But Valentine! he is
your man, Sister. Would I had the fellow of him—   420

FLORIANTE.

For your confessor, Sister?

CHARLOTT.

I could confess something to him that would make
him enjoin me another kind of penance than my
prayers.

FLORIANTE.

What! absolve you from your devotion?   425

CHARLOTT.

And persuade him to make a sinner of me rather
than suffer my father to make me a saint so much
before my time.

FLORIANTE.

You are a mad girl. But what of Valentine?

CHARLOTT.

He should not be out of our design.   430

FLORIANTE.

I'll answer for him, he won't.

CHARLOTT.

His interest's so concerned, he should not be
wanting* in any occasion of abusing our father.

FLORIANTE.

Or of using the count as he deserves.

CHARLOTT.

They're both behind us, mum—   435

Count Canaille and Count Vérole enter.

CANAILLE.

I have prepared my daughter to receive
The honor you intend our house and her
By this alliance with us; she too well knows
What's owing to a father and herself,
To my authority and her own birth,   440
Now to dispute what I design for her.
She has my will, the rest I leave to you. (*Exit.*)

VÉROLE.

Madam, you hear your father, and I come
Through his authority to speak my love;
Though bating his authority, I must think   445
There need not many arguments to move
More than your knowing me, and what I am.

FLORIANTE.

My lord, that goes a great way with me, I assure
you.

CHARLOTT.

She knows you and your qualities, my lord, and   450

esteems 'em accordingly: I have heard her say, she was
very much obliged to you, and should be more—

FLORIANTE. (*Aside.*)

If he would hang himself—

VÉROLE.

For what, young lady?

CHARLOTT.

For your kind care of me.   455

VÉROLE.

I'm glad you're sensible I mean you well.

CHARLOTT.

Oh yes, sir, sensible! so sensible, I must be obliged
in conscience to thank you for advising my father
to send me to a nunnery. (*Aside.*) The Devil will
take you for your advice.   460

VÉROLE.

A nunnery is virtue's best retreat from a bad world.

CHARLOTT.

But if my sister's fortune, in your opinion, had not
wanted* mending more than my manners—

FLORIANTE.

Fie, Charlott, you'll tell all.

VÉROLE.

How could she guess at that?   465

CHARLOTT. [*To Floriante.*]

I might have continued in this bad world for any
advice the count would have given in his great care
of me to my father. But I'll be revenged on him—
do as much mischief as I can while I am in the
world, and repent when I am out on't and can do   470
no more.

FLORIANTE. [*To Charlott.*]

Bring Sir Anthony to my rescue, I beseech thee.

Exit Charlott.

VÉROLE.

Your sister's disobliged, but I've my ends in serving
you—

FLORIANTE.

In serving of yourself: 475
For what I get[f] by her, my father says,
You must command.

VÉROLE.

                      To make it but more yours.

FLORIANTE.

So you promise all

Before you have enclosed us but, possessed   480
Our fortunes, and our persons are your slaves,
Used like your slaves, and often both abused.

VÉROLE.

This is a common subject for your sex

Sir Anthony, Volante, and Charlott enter.

To boast the glory of your wit upon,
But I'm above the taste of common things,   485
Being born above the rank of common men.

SIR ANTHONY.

Out of the rank, he means, of common men, and
indeed, he scarcely looks of human kind.

VÉROLE.

What do I look like then?

SIR ANTHONY.

There's nothing like you, you are yourself.   490

VÉROLE.

I would be nothing else.

SIR ANTHONY.

What, not of God's creation?

VÉROLE.

I am of his creation.

SIR ANTHONY.

Of the King's you may be,
But he who makes a count ne'er made a man.   495
Remember that, and fall that mighty crest.

VÉROLE.

It seems you know me then.

SIR ANTHONY.

By that coy, cocked-up nose, that hinders you
From seeing any man that does not stand
Upon the shoulders of his ancestors   500
For long descents of far-famed heraldry.
I take you for a thing they call a count,
For had you not been a count, you had been
nothing,
At least I'm sure you had been nothing here.

VÉROLE.

I would be nothing, if I were no count.   505

CHARLOTT.

Pray, more respect.

FLORIANTE.

This is the Count Vérole—

SIR ANTHONY.

Oh, is it so?

VOLANTE.

That's to marry my cousin.

SIR ANTHONY.

I have been too bold. Pray ladies, join with me— 510

CHARLOTT.

To laugh at him—

SIR ANTHONY.

To ask his pardon.

VÉROLE.

For the future, know me, and know yourself, I ask no more.

SIR ANTHONY.

Then I am pardoned, for I know myself, and think 515
I know your Worship. Can you fight?

VÉROLE.

Hah! What do you mean?

SIR ANTHONY.

Why faith, I come but upon a surly embassy, and a finical phrase that would fit the fineness of your quality* would not become my business. 520

VÉROLE.

What does the gentleman mean?

SIR ANTHONY.

Walk but aside with me, I'll tell you what I mean.

VÉROLE.

You have no secret for me?

SIR ANTHONY.

Why then it shall be none.

VÉROLE. (Aside.)

He won't draw before the women sure. 525

SIR ANTHONY.

Since the ladies must be by, as they must be the judges at last, you must know then, I come to you from a gentleman—

VÉROLE.

Is he no more?

SIR ANTHONY.

He's everything in that, that makes a man. 530

VÉROLE.

You may go as you came for me, sir, if he be but a gentleman.

SIR ANTHONY.

His name is Valentine, your rival in that lady.

VÉROLE.

My rival is my equal; I am born
Above his rank, he cannot rival me. 535

SIR ANTHONY.

He does rival you, and will rival you.

VÉROLE.

Envy he may my fortune with that lady.

SIR ANTHONY.

Well! Envy then, if that must be the word: he envies you and only wants* an opportunity of telling you how much he envies you. 540

FLORIANTE.

A modest request truly—

CHARLOTT.

He can't deny it him—

VOLANTE.

Before his mistress too.

SIR ANTHONY.

Now sir, if you will be so courteous as by me, who am to be his second, to favor him with knowing 545
where and when he may wait upon you, you will oblige me by this civility to serve your friend, as he designs to serve you.

VÉROLE.

How may that be, pray?

SIR ANTHONY.

To cut your throat, sir. 550

VÉROLE.

Oh, sir, I'll spare his compliment.

SIR ANTHONY.

My friend's an Englishman and never loses a mistress for want* of fighting for her, I assure you; nay, I have known some of my countrymen, rather than not make a quarrel* in the families they made 555
love in, have beat their very* women into good nature and consent.

CHARLOTT.

It should be good nature for another, then—

FLORIANTE.

Such arguments would not prevail on us—

VOLANTE.

Unless to cuckold 'em. 560

SIR ANTHONY.

For one reason or another (Goes to Vérole.) there are cuckolds everywhere.

CHARLOTT.

How will our count get rid of this business?

SIR ANTHONY.

I wait your answer, sir.

VÉROLE.

My answer is, when I am as angry as your friend 565
is, which, at present, I have no reason to be, nor,
to a day, can certainly say when I shall be—

SIR ANTHONY.

You must be made angry then.

VÉROLE.

When I am under a defeat of my hopes about that
lady, as he may be, and in an absolute despair of 570
better success and have nothing else to do with
myself, I may be angry, and then I may fight with
him.

SIR ANTHONY.

Must you be angry when you fight?

VÉROLE.

Or mad, or drunk: 'tis no employment for a sober 575
man.

SIR ANTHONY.

Have you no notion of courage?

VÉROLE.

Notion indeed, young man, for courage is
No more than just such a degree of heat,
To some complexions natural, but those men 580
Who want* that heat may raise their spirits to't.

SIR ANTHONY.

Aye, marry!* there's a receipt* indeed.

VÉROLE.

Passion will fire the coldest elements;
The lees of wine ferment the dullest phlegm
To froth and vapor. 585
I've seen a drunkard in his fit attempt
Dangers to rival Caesar.
If such extravagancies make the brave,
Madmen are heroes.

SIR ANTHONY.

This won't do my business. Will you fight? 590

VÉROLE.

'Tis common soldiers' work.

SIR ANTHONY.

You must fight with him.

VÉROLE.

Not while I can hire ruffians to take the trouble
off my hands.

SIR ANTHONY.

You must expect to be used very scurvily wherever 595
he meets you.

Valentine, Ilford, with Sir Gentle Golding enter.

VÉROLE.

I shall be provided for him.

SIR ANTHONY.

Oh, here he comes himself.

VÉROLE. [*To the sisters.*]

If you're for mustering your friends, I have your
father of my party. (*Exit in disorder; women laugh* 600
at him.)

VALENTINE.

The ladies never want* an entertainment when
they have Sir Anthony to encourage the mirth.

The ladies aside with Valentine.

Pray, what particular diversion has he given you?

CHARLOTT.

Very particular indeed— 605

VOLANTE.

You were a party concerned—

FLORIANTE.

And only wanting* to make up the farce.

SIR ANTHONY. [*Aside.*]

Yes, this is he, my very, very* fool!

SIR GENTLE.

Very handsome gentlewomen indeed, all three of
'em, and that's Sir Anthony, that the abbé 610
commended so much.

ILFORD.

The very same, sir.

SIR GENTLE.

I will be acquainted with him. (*Goes to salute* Sir
Anthony.*)

ILFORD.

Sir Anthony— 615

SIR GENTLE.

Sir, your most humble servant.

SIR ANTHONY.

Do you know me, sir?

SIR GENTLE.

Not I, but I'm an Englishman and the English
always keep together abroad, they say, for fear of
being cheated. 620

ILFORD.

Of their money or manners?

SIR ANTHONY.

Of their mother tongue.

SIR GENTLE.

Of their Mother Church, their religion. Now I designing to continue, as I am—

ILFORD.

A fool.   625

SIR GENTLE.

Have a mind to spend my money among my countrymen.

SIR ANTHONY.

You're very welcome—

ILFORD.

To be cheated only by your friends.

SIR GENTLE.

There's Valentine, a very pretty fellow, but I have   630
known him a great while. I am for variety and
fresh faces. Here's honest Ilford, my very good
friend of half an hour's acquaintance, will
recommend me.

SIR ANTHONY.

You recommend yourself, sir.   635

SIR GENTLE.

Truly, I hear you are an extraordinary person, and
a knight, sir. I am a knight myself, sir!

SIR ANTHONY.

And an extraordinary person, truly. Pray of what
family, sir?

SIR GENTLE.

Of what family? of my father's family before me,   640
the family of the Goldings, of which I am your
servant and Sir Gentle Golding.

VALENTINE.

Alas, poor Count! I vow I pity him. Where's this
mad knight? Oh! (*Sees the two knights in
salutation.*) You are before me it seems, but since   645
I come too late to recommend Sir Gentle to you,
pray do you recommend him to the ladies.

SIR ANTHONY.

This is Sir Gentle Golding—

Sir Gentle salutes the women.*

SIR GENTLE.

Sir, as I may say, I may thank you for this favor.

SIR ANTHONY.

If you are for this sport, I'll find you game, sir.   650

SIR GENTLE.

Oh, of all things I love the women.

VOLANTE.

Sir Gentle declares that by his dressing.

SIR ANTHONY.

You shan't dress in vain. I'll find you employment
among 'em.

SIR GENTLE.

I'll depend upon you then, and from this time   655
forward, we must be intimate as men of the same
brotherhood and worship ought to be.

CHARLOTT.

See, see, our count has rallied again! (*Looking
[offstage]*.)

VALENTINE.

With your father in his tail, to sustain him.   660

FLORIANTE.

We must not stay till they come. At night may I
expect you?

VALENTINE.

If anything extraordinary happens—

VOLANTE.

I'll come express with the tidings.

FLORIANTE.

You shall hear from us.   665

SIR ANTHONY.

Your servant, your servant.

Exeunt women.

VALENTINE.

You see, Sir Gentle, we make a shift.

SIR ANTHONY.

Make a shift! We make a carnival, all year a
carnival: every man his woman, and a new one at
every town we come at.   670

SIR GENTLE.

Ah, would I could say so too!

VALENTINE.

You say so, Sir Gentle? Fie, fie, you don't desire to
say so, to my knowledge.

SIR GENTLE.

That's very fine, i'faith.

VALENTINE.

You only rally your countrymen.   675

SIR GENTLE.

Not I, as I hope to be saved, Val. Though I love a
joke, I never rally a friend.

VALENTINE.

You a mistress! why, you have forsworn the sex!

SIR GENTLE.

Oh Lord, oh Lord! that's a likely business indeed! I forswear the sex! I would as soon forswear my own sex, as the women's; why I have made it my endeavor, ever since I was a man of estate, to be accounted a knight of intrigue. So you never were more mistaken since you were born, sir.

VALENTINE.

Why, what a lying world we live in! I was told you were so scurvily used in England—

SIR GENTLE.

Softly, softly, man—

VALENTINE.

By Lucia—

SIR GENTLE.

A jilting jade! You knew her, not worth remembering.

VALENTINE.

That you were resolved never to venture on the sex again.

SIR GENTLE.

Prithee, dear Val, no more on't. There's some ill nature in my part of the story. I would not have it go further for my own sake.

ILFORD.

It goes no further for our hearing it.

SIR ANTHONY.

We know it already.

SIR GENTLE.

Ay, it may be so. I confess, poor creature, I gave her a jealousy of another woman.

SIR ANTHONY.

And that perhaps, in her despair of pleasing you much longer, might be a reason of doing what she did.

SIR GENTLE.

Why truly, very likely.

VALENTINE.

And therefore she robbed you?

ILFORD.

Of five hundred pounds?

SIR ANTHONY.

She might ha' showed a conscience in her cheating though! Five hundred pounds was too much in reason—

SIR GENTLE.

Sir Anthony, you are my friend upon all occasions,

but the truth is, I gave her an opportunity, left my cabinet open on purpose, and was glad to get rid of her for the money.

SIR ANTHONY. (*Aside.*)

You shall pay as round a sum for this lie before I part with your vanity.

VALENTINE.

And this is all?

SIR GENTLE.

The short and long of the story.

SIR ANTHONY.

Leave the silly creature to her garret, where she will be in a little time; she'll hang herself in her garters when the money is spent.

SIR GENTLE.

I warrant her, will she, and be glad to come off so too.

VALENTINE.

So, forgetting disasters at home, you travel—

ILFORD.

To drive an old mistress out of his head.

SIR ANTHONY.

And recover here what he had lost in England by the gallantry of a French intrigue—

SIR GENTLE.

Which I come qualified for, gentlemen, being able to bid up to the price of any of 'em.

VALENTINE.

If you show your money, we may borrow.

SIR GENTLE.

You may borrow, but I never lend. You are acquainted and have your good breeding and behavior to recommend you to the ladies.

SIR ANTHONY.

You show your wisdom in your good husbandry, Sir Gentle. You are a stranger and must be obliged to your pocket for what you must expect from 'em.

SIR GENTLE.

And therefore, Sir Anthony, I will part with my new acquaintances, my louis d'ors,[23] to none but the ladies.

SIR ANTHONY.

Money does everything with the women in France, sir.

---

23 louis d'ors] French gold coins

SIR GENTLE.

I won't spare it upon them, Sir Anthony; I rely upon you for a mistress, then.

SIR ANTHONY.

You shall see her this evening.

SIR GENTLE.

Bills* and business, gentlemen. But now we live together, no ceremony. Adieu for a moment, and dear Sir Anthony, yours. (*Exit.*)

VALENTINE.

You are in his favor.

SIR ANTHONY.

And will be in his pocket.

Abbé, Pilgrim and Waitwell enter.

Leave him to me.

ILFORD.

Our abbé and the pilgrim, again! This visit is to you.

SIR ANTHONY.

He has a mind to make a convert out of me, that's certain, but whether in the flesh or the spirit is the question.

VALENTINE.

He's for the outward man, I warrant him.

ILFORD.

And his argument's of this world, whatever the pilgrim's may be.

ABBÉ.

Ah my little man! You have lost a mighty satisfaction: the pilgrim has wrought wonders upon us all within.

VALENTINE.

Much above my expectation, indeed.

ILFORD.

His story staggers me, I confess, and has cured me of an old diffidence I had of all religious pretenders.

SIR ANTHONY.

Well, he's a rogue, and you han't found him.

ABBÉ.

You are the only infidel in the company.

SIR ANTHONY.

You dissemble a belief; 'tis necessary to the Church, and you get by the trade, but none of you remove mountains that I hear of.

ABBÉ.

Do but hear what he can say.

SIR ANTHONY.

I'll give him both my ears—

Pilgrim advances.

(*To Waitwell.*) But not a word here. I must have him to myself to discover the bottom of him.

PILGRIM.

'Tis a work of the Spirit indeed, and the Spirit works unseen of human eyes, therefore, in private would do very well.

SIR ANTHONY.

Do as I order you.

Exit Waitwell.

PILGRIM.

There is an obstinacy in sin that won't be confuted before company. Reproof may return into our own teeth* a rebuke and a reproach unto ourselves. For which reason I am assured that a privacy in communication and a retirement from the eyes of the world (when the cause is conscientious) are always necessary to a conviction and conversion of the wicked.

SIR ANTHONY.

Those necessaries thou shalt have at my lodging. I follow thee, pilgrim.—Farewell, gentlemen, if I am convinced in this point and live to set foot in England again, I shall satisfy those heretical unbelievers that I have seen one miracle in a Catholic country.

(*Exit after the pilgrim.*)

ILFORD.

Thus every man to his own interest tends:
The pilgrim makes his converts, we make friends
With the same conscience all, for our own ends.

Exeunt.

Act III, scene i. [Sir Anthony's lodging.]

Waitwell placing bottles on the table. Enter Sir Anthony and the pilgrim.

SIR ANTHONY.

This is a dry subject, Pilgrim; there's no engaging in it without a bottle.

PILGRIM.

You'll have your own ways here. (*Walks about.*)

SIR ANTHONY.

Have you infused the opiate in his wine?

WAITWELL.

I warrant him he sleeps for't; yours is half water.   5

SIR ANTHONY.

If I don't find him a knave, I'll make him a fool
for troubling me with his impertinence, but chiefly
for the dear jest of exposing his reverence to the
laughter of the profane. Have you done there?

Waitwell goes out.

Lock the door and let nobody come near us.—   10
Now Pilgrim, we are alone, and sit you down—

Pilgrim stands and crosses himself and Sir Anthony.

Nay, I will have no blessing upon our endeavors
but a bumper—this will banish crosses. Here's to
the falling of the flesh and the rising of the spirit.
(*Drinks.*)   15

PILGRIM.

'Tis a mysterious health, of sacred sense,
Ev'n to the pulling down of Satan's throne. (*Drinks.*)

SIR ANTHONY.

A little wine does well to qualify the water you
drink in your pilgrimage.

PILGRIM.

Sometimes without offence, wine may be used,   20
Though our whole life is but a pilgrimage—

Sir Anthony fills again the glasses.

SIR ANTHONY.

That's as you please to make it. Come sir, this is
the searcher of hearts. Here's to the opening of
ours—(*Drinks.*)

PILGRIM.

Hearts and eyes, that we may see our errors.   25
(*Aside.*) This wine will warm him, sure.

SIR ANTHONY.

Confession is a step to repentance, you say?

PILGRIM.

The ready road—

SIR ANTHONY.

Then drink off your glass, Pilgrim. How do you
like your wine?   30

PILGRIM.

'Tis warm, I promise you—

SIR ANTHONY.

Able to distinguish a saint from a sinner and will keep
you out of the mire better than your wooden shoes.

PILGRIM.

'Twill rather leave us there. But to our purpose
now—   35

SIR ANTHONY.

Another glass to strengthen my attention; I shall
edify the better by it. (*Fills the glass.*)

PILGRIM. (*Aside.*)

Sure he can't make me drunk.

SIR ANTHONY.

I expected you would ha' drunk to my conversion.

PILGRIM.

I should ha' began it in charity, indeed, but I'll   40
make you what reparation I may and drink a full
glass for my forgetfulness. (*Fills himself a bumper.*)

SIR ANTHONY.

I warrant him my own.

PILGRIM.

To your conversion be it. (*Drinks.*)

SIR ANTHONY.

This is the way to it, and the pleasantest road you   45
can travel in. For let me tell you, the world is bad
enough at the best; we need not take pains to make
it worse.

PILGRIM.

Too many do indeed.

Sir Anthony drinks.

SIR ANTHONY.

Such foolish apostles as thou art then. Why, I begin   50
to despair of thee. I took thee for a sanguine,
sensual sinner, a man of sense, and an hypocrite,
but I find thee a peaking penitent, and an ass.

PILGRIM.

You sit in the seat of the scorner.

SIR ANTHONY.

Though you pass upon the abbé and other fools,   55
I expected you would have opened yourself to me.
I profess myself what I thought you were under
your habit, a rogue. We might have been of use
to one another, but since you are for cheating
nobody but yourself, (*Fills again.*) I'll make an end   60
of my bottle and business and leave you to say
grace to the next courtesy I offer you. (*Drinks.*)

PILGRIM.

I must not lose this opportunity.

SIR ANTHONY.

Now I begin to believe all the silly things you have said of yourself: your being weary of and leaving 65 the world when you had a good share of it your own; your parting with the pleasures (which you call the vanities) of it, at a time when you were in a condition of enjoying 'em, by senseless resigning up your birthright— 70

PILGRIM.

My service to you. (*Drinks.*)

SIR ANTHONY.

Of a considerable quality and fortune to a younger brother, who indeed needed no other expectation for his wants* than the abundance of your folly to live upon. 75

PILGRIM.

You censure me too rashly. (*Rises.*)

SIR ANTHONY.

I speak my thoughts and am so far from imitating you any way, that when an elder brother stood between me and a good estate, I made bold to remove him— 80

PILGRIM.

By no violent means.

SIR ANTHONY.

Something before his time. I had a jointure too encumbered me, but a physician after my own heart eased me, and my good Lady-Grandmother.24

PILGRIM.

And dare you own it? 85

SIR ANTHONY.

Not at a bar of justice.

PILGRIM.

So horrid a villainy!

SIR ANTHONY.

Never troubles me. I don't proclaim it but in my cups, and where I think I'm safe to men of my own kidney— 90

PILGRIM.

You confess yourself a villain?

SIR ANTHONY.

Any kind of rogue that serves my turn, for I am of a principle that levels everything in the way of my pleasure or profit.

PILGRIM.

A worthy principle! 95

SIR ANTHONY.

I cheat the men and lie with the women, as many as I can get in my power.

PILGRIM.

Sir, I honor you. Pray, sit down again.

They sit.

SIR ANTHONY.

To hear you preach again?

PILGRIM.

And are you really this rogue you pretend to be? 100

SIR ANTHONY.

Are you the fool you pretend to be?

PILGRIM.

I must come nearer you. (*Shows a casket.*)

SIR ANTHONY.

How, jewels!

PILGRIM.

I bring my welcome with me.

SIR ANTHONY.

Enough to set up a saint. The Lady of Loretto25 105 may keep her chamber, thou hast spoiled her holy days by robbing her shrine, for thou hast robbed hers or some other, that's certain.

PILGRIM.

'Tis certain I have the jewels; how I came by 'em, and why I put on this habit— 110

SIR ANTHONY.

Then you are no pilgrim?

PILGRIM.

No more than you are a priest. I am as arrant a rogue as you can be, a shifter of shapes and names, have

---

24 jointure … Lady-Grandmother] Sir Anthony's fictional grandmother retained part of the Love estate as a jointure after the grandfather's death—a part "encumbered" to devolve upon Sir Anthony; Sir Anthony claims to have redeemed it by means of a physician.

25 Lady of Loretto] a statue of the Virgin Mary enclosed in the shrine at Loretto supposedly in Mary's own chamber transported miraculously from the Holy Land to Italy; the shrine was famous for its treasures, many of which bedecked the statue itself.

travelled through every profession and cheated in all.
So having by my industry gathered a handsome   115
fortune, I converted that into jewels and myself into
a pilgrim for the safer conveyance of both into
Spain, whither I was going till I lit upon you.

SIR ANTHONY.

I saw through your weeds and had a mind to
discover* you.   120

PILGRIM.

Well, now you have discovered me—

SIR ANTHONY.

Why, now I like you.

PILGRIM.

But are you sure you like me?

SIR ANTHONY.

Like you extremely.

PILGRIM.

If you can like me, you may love me too, for a   125
woman I know you are.

SIR ANTHONY. (*Aside.*)

Am I discovered too?

PILGRIM.

Nay, I'm resolved to like you in any sex. (*Squeezing
and kissing her hand.*) But it is impossible such
beauty should be a man's, and I will think you a   130
woman— (*Approaching nearer still.*) till you
convince me to the contrary.

SIR ANTHONY.

Have you a mistress to be convinced to the
contrary?

PILGRIM.

We were made for one another's conversation;*   135
here's that shall keep it in humor. (*Lays his hand
on the casket.*)

SIR ANTHONY.

I have heard of Mark Antony's pearl cordial.[26]

PILGRIM.

You shall drink nothing else but pearl dissolved.
Hah! What's the matter with me? (*Yawns often.*)   140

SIR ANTHONY.

Now, now my dose begins.—You grow
indifferent—

---

26 Mark Antony's pearl cordial] legendary pearl dissolved
    in wine by Cleopatra for Antony

PILGRIM.

My senses vanish all. (*Rises and struggles all he can
against it, but falls into his chair asleep.*)

SIR ANTHONY.

What, fall asleep before me?   145

PILGRIM.

By and by I'll come again to you.

SIR ANTHONY.

So, he's as safe as his casket in my custody.—
Governor, you may appear.

Enter Waitwell.

Here's an Oriental present from the Mogul, by the
hands of his ambassador there.   150

WAITWELL.

He looks as he were drunk-dead, or dead-drunk.

SIR ANTHONY.

Examine his pockets, let's see what credentials he
has for his character, though you see I have treated
him like an ambassador without 'em.

WAITWELL.

Here are tablets full of memorandums to avoid   155
such and such places where he has done his
rogueries.

SIR ANTHONY.

Very well. These, when he wakes, will make good,
if he should have the impudence to dispute my
title to the theft.   160

WAITWELL.

You won't keep all the jewels?

SIR ANTHONY.

A round ransom may redeem 'em, but him I must
expose, Governor. When I send for him, bring him
in a chair* to the abbé's.

WAITWELL.

Most carefully.   165

SIR ANTHONY.

And if Sir Gentle inquire for me, as I expect he
will, direct him thither.

WAITWELL.

I won't fail.

SIR ANTHONY.

I have a mistress for him. (*Exit.*)

The pilgrim carried off.

Scene ii. The street.

Ilford alone.

ILFORD.

Volante is so busy for another she has nothing to do for herself. So closely employed for Valentine, she has no employment for anybody, or when she has, 'tis partially designed for that boy-knight in prejudice of every man that may with more reason pretend— 5

Sir Anthony crosses the stage.

Sir Anthony—Sir Anthony—a word with you—

SIR ANTHONY.

Prithee let me go. I am big with a jest and shall certainly miscarry with the first grave word you say to me.

ILFORD.

Be delivered of your burden then, lay it at my door, 10 I'll father it for a friend. (*Bringing him back by the hand.*)

SIR ANTHONY.

As some men would a bastard, for the reputation of getting it.

ILFORD.

I have thought better of this rivaling business 15 between us; I see plainly Volante declares for you—

SIR ANTHONY.

I think the poor creature loves me indeed.

ILFORD.

And 'tis to no purpose to proceed—

SIR ANTHONY.

None in the world, sir.

ILFORD.

In the measures I had taken in making my way to 20 her; therefore, now I come, like a friend, to desire a favor of you.

SIR ANTHONY.

Now you say something, Ilford.

ILFORD.

And like a friend to advise you, you're a very pretty fellow and have a great many dancing years to trip 25 over before you come to be serious.

SIR ANTHONY.

I hope so, sir.

ILFORD.

You should ramble before you settle—

SIR ANTHONY.

For fear of rambling after—

ILFORD.

You are too great a good among the women to 30 think of being particular, a dozen years too gay for the condition—

SIR ANTHONY.

Too gay for a lover.

ILFORD.

Too gay for a husband.

SIR ANTHONY.

Aye, marry* sir, a husband! 35

ILFORD.

How sir?

SIR ANTHONY.

I make love sometimes, but do not often marry.

ILFORD.

What do you follow Volante for then?

SIR ANTHONY.

Can't you tell for what? For as good a thing you may swear, Ilford. You guess at her inclinations, 40 poor rogue, and a lady shall never lose her longing upon me. I design to lie with her.

ILFORD.

Without marrying her?

SIR ANTHONY.

Without asking any consent but her own; I am not for many words when I have a mind to be doing. 45

ILFORD.

So impudent a thing I never heard!

Enter Volante.

VOLANTE.

Quarreling again, gentlemen!

SIR ANTHONY.

Upon the old subject.

ILFORD.

I hate the employment and character of an informer, but you come so upon the scandalous 50 minute, I must tell you what that young gentleman—

VOLANTE.

Sir Anthony has no friend of you, sir.

ILFORD.

Nor you of him, madam, as you will find when you hear what he says of you. 55

VOLANTE.

Pray, what's the matter?

ILFORD.

He has the impudence not only to design it, but even to me, his rival, who love and honor you—

VOLANTE.

Your story, sir, your story!

ILFORD.

He dares notoriously tell me to my face that he never designed to marry you, but because you were in love with him, poor creature, he would do you the favor to lie with you.

SIR ANTHONY.

Madam, you know he hates me upon your account, and this is one of the poor endeavors of his malice to ruin me. You can't think I would be such a villain—

VOLANTE.

I won't think it, Sir Anthony.

SIR ANTHONY.

Such an idiot, if I could have it in my head, to declare it to my rival.

VOLANTE.

Oh no—it is not probable.

ILFORD.

By heaven and earth, he said it.

VOLANTE.

I would not believe it for earth and heaven, if he did.

ILFORD.

Nay then, 'tis labor lost.

VOLANTE.

If you'll deliver this letter to Valentine, you'll do him more service (*Gives Ilford a letter.*) than you have me with your news.—I won't leave you behind me, Sir Anthony.

SIR ANTHONY.

I'm going to the abbé's, madam.

Exeunt [Sir Anthony and Volante].

ILFORD.

Well! I could almost wish he would lie with her to convince her; though she won't believe me, she will him, and that in time will be a sufficient revenge upon her folly.

Enter Abbé and Valentine to Ilford; Count Vérole, with six bravos on the other side; they stare upon each other and pass on. Abbé, Valentine, and Ilford remain.

ABBÉ.

The count has his *gardes du corps*,[27] Valentine.

VALENTINE.

Sir Anthony has alarmed him.

ILFORD.

He is in a state of war, fit to give battle already.

VALENTINE.

What he wants* in his person* he has in his equipage, but they threaten too much to do any harm.

ABBÉ.

Do you secure your person; Volante shall secure your mistress against him, I warrant her.

ILFORD.

Here's a letter she gave me for you.

Exeunt.

Scene iii. The abbé's house.

Pilgrim brought in a chair, Sir Anthony Love after it.*

SIR ANTHONY.

Down with your burden and place him in that chair. So, this is as proper a scene to recommend our farce to the family as we can have—

Enter Waitwell.

WAITWELL.

Sir Gentle Golding is below and would speak with you.

SIR ANTHONY. (*To the chairmen who go out.*)

One of you bring him up.—Governor, he must not know you belong to me.

WAITWELL.

I know your design upon him, and I'll be gone to put things in order to receive him—

SIR ANTHONY.

To receive Valentine. He shall be welcome to me, but to deceive Sir Gentle.

WAITWELL.

You are as busy as a projector.* Some of your plots must miscarry.

---

27 *gardes du corps*] bodyguard

SIR ANTHONY.

Hah! he begins to stir. How long will the opiate hold him? 15

WAITWELL.

If he wakes before the company comes, you lose your pleasure of laughing at him.

SIR ANTHONY.

But I have a sudden thought may give us a better diversion.

Exit Waitwell.
Enter Sir Gentle Golding.

SIR GENTLE.

Sir Anthony! Your most incomparable humble 20 servant.

SIR ANTHONY.

Sir Gentle, I've done your business.

SIR GENTLE.

With the lady you promised me?

SIR ANTHONY.

With that very lady. I've secured an appointment for you, but being a woman of quality*— 25

SIR GENTLE.

There you oblige me forever.

SIR ANTHONY.

Though something decayed and fallen in her fortune—she must be humored in little things; she will have her forms.

SIR GENTLE.

I warrant her, and very fit she should. A person of 30 quality is known by her forms.

SIR ANTHONY.

They'll last but till the evening, then I'll carry you to wait on her. (*Shows the pilgrim.*) Here's a drunken pilgrim will afford you merriment enough to entertain some part of the time. 35

SIR GENTLE.

Dead drunk, as I intend to live sober.

SIR ANTHONY.

Do me the favor to stay and secure him if he should wake. I'll but bring the abbé and his family to share in abusing him and be with you again. (*Exit.*) 40

SIR GENTLE.

Why, what an unlucky, hypocritical rogue is this, to be discovered and to lie at the mercy of Sir Anthony! If he were but half as holy as he pretended, he might 'scape by a miracle, but he sleeps so sound no Revelation can wake him. 45

PILGRIM.

Boy, draw the curtain, sirrah—(*Turns in his chair and makes signs of waking.*)

SIR GENTLE.

Is the light in your eyes, sir?—What pains he takes, to come to himself! Gad, I'll play the midwife to his labor—stay, let me see, a stiff straw would do 50 rarely to probe his sobriety. If his brain be touched, he'll take up the more time in his cure, and 'tis well if ever he be his own man again. Now for the experiment. (*Tickling his nose; the pilgrim jumps up and throws Sir Gentle down,g and in his 55 thoughtfulness,[28] stumbles over him. Both amazed, raise themselves upon their bottoms, and stare at each other.*)

PILGRIM.

Hah! Am I alive? Where have I been? Where am I now? How came I here? Who are you? What 60 would you have?

SIR GENTLE.

Have! Myself in a wish to England. Would I were in my mother's belly again.

PILGRIM.

Speak, I conjure you, speak to me.

SIR GENTLE.

He's as heartily frightened as I can be; I'll pluck 65 up a spirit and speak to him.

PILGRIM.

Some ill thing has possessed me.

SIR GENTLE.

Yes, possessed thou art, by the lewd spirit of powerful wine possessed, a drunken devil.

PILGRIM.

A bottle, and Sir Anthony I remember, and the 70 discoveries* I made him.

Both rise.

SIR GENTLE.

You are discovered, and in the abbé's house—

PILGRIM.

In the abbé's house!

---

28 thoughtfulness] distracton

SIR GENTLE.

    Where now your business is to be laughed at and
exposed. And the whole family are coming to make 75
your Holiness a ridiculous visit to that purpose.

PILGRIM.

    That young rogue Sir Anthony! Has he done
nothing else to me? (*Examining his pockets.*)
Undone, undone! I'm robbed and ruined. My jewels
gone! My table book gone too! That may do me 80
more harm than the jewels can do anybody good.

SIR GENTLE.

    Have you lost your learning? How could you miss
it so soon? A table book?

PILGRIM.

    Sir, I am robbed, and I took you very suspiciously
about my pockets. You shall answer the robbery. 85

SIR GENTLE.

    Why, do I look like a pickpocket? I'd have you to
know I scorn your words, but that trick shan't serve
your turn.

PILGRIM.

    Serve my turn, sir? (*Offering to go by him.*)

SIR GENTLE.

    You must not 'scape me so. 90

PILGRIM.

    Why, sir, am I your prisoner? (*Aside.*) I must not be
found here. I have an inkhorn may frighten him.

SIR GENTLE.

    Look you, sir, here's the inside of my pockets. I
have nothing about me but bills of exchange and
this purse of Elizabeth broad gold.[29] You shall 95
search me, if you please.

PILGRIM.

    I have searched you, and found you, and must go
by you too. (*Presents an inkhorn to his breast.*)

SIR GENTLE.

    Oh Lord, sir, I don't hinder you—

PILGRIM.

    No, no, you had not best. 100

SIR GENTLE.

    Pray take it away. I have a natural aversion to the
smell of gun powder—though 'twill be difficult to
get away, for the servants are ordered to stop you.

---

29 Elizabeth broad gold] Elizabethan coins, called "broad"
because flatter than those in the Restoration

PILGRIM.

    How! to stop me!

SIR GENTLE. [*Aside.*]

    Now he won't offer to go. 105

PILGRIM.

    The servants ordered to stop me, do you say?

SIR GENTLE.

    If you be the pilgrim.

PILGRIM.

    Then I'll be the pilgrim no longer. (*Undresses
himself.*)

SIR GENTLE.

    What will you be, then, pray? 110

PILGRIM.

    Even Sir Gentle Golding. I will get off in your per-
son,* since I can't in my own. I must change outsides
with you. (*Begins to undress Sir Gentle Golding.*)

SIR GENTLE.

    Oh Lord, sir, there's no occasion for it. I know
nothing of a design upon you. 115

PILGRIM.

    That's more than I know.

SIR GENTLE.

    Faith and troth now, what I said was only to play
the rogue with you.

PILGRIM.

    And what I do is to play the fool with you. You
must strip, sir. 120

SIR GENTLE.

    Oh, but this is carrying the jest too far.

PILGRIM.

    Look you, you may keep your worship and wit for
your own wearing, but I must borrow your clothes.

SIR GENTLE.

    At any other time, and welcome, I should be pleased
with the humor on't, but this is my first day of 125
wearing 'em; besides, there's a mistress in the case—

PILGRIM.

    As long as you live, prefer a friend to a mistress,
Sir Gentle. (*Dresses himself in Sir Gentle's clothes.*)
Come, sir, a little of your assistance.

SIR GENTLE.

    But I am to see her this evening, and one would 130
be well dressed you know, the first time.

PILGRIM.

    If you must see your mistress, visit her in

masquerade: 'tis a fashionable way of beginning an intrigue—and a pilgrim's habit—is as fantastical, as you can contrive—to give a lady a curiosity— 135 of knowing more of you—and that I know is your business.

SIR GENTLE.

That is my business indeed, but if I lose my time—

PILGRIM.

Don't make a noise nor follow me if you would see her or little England again. Know your friends 140 and give thanks, sir— (*Exit.*)

SIR GENTLE.

What a pass have I brought myself to by my own policy! Why must I needs lie myself out of my clothes? If I had held my tongue or spoke but the truth, he would ha' gone about his business 145 without interrupting mine. Now here I must stay to be exposed in his room, but in a foolisher figure than ever the pilgrim made. He was only disguised, but I am stript. He was drunk indeed; would I were dead drunk, to cover my shame, any way, 150 would I had any disguise. Egad, I'll put on the pilgrim's—it can't be worse with me—besides the respect that is paid to this clothing will at least carry me safe to my lodging. (*Exit.*)

Scene iv. The street.

Pilgrim in Sir Gentle's clothes, with Monsieur Traffique.

TRAFFIQUE.

Sir, I have accepted these bills* already.

PILGRIM.

I know you have, but my occasions are falling out more extraordinary than I expected; I am forced to press you for this bill of a hundred pistoles before the day. 5

TRAFFIQUE.

I have so often suffered for those complemental payments that I have resolved against 'em. But my correspondent gives me an account of Sir Gentle Golding; you shall have what credit you please with me. 10

PILGRIM.

A hundred pistoles I have present use for.

TRAFFIQUE.

If my cashier were at home, you should have 'em along with you, but in the morning, as soon as you please—

PILGRIM.

I'll send my servant to you. Pray sir, what news 15 have you in the city?

TRAFFIQUE.

The newest, sir, is of a pilgrim that is suspected of something; I am imperfect in the particulars, but there are warrants out to apprehend him, that I know.

PILGRIM.

There's no believing outsides. Sir, your servant. 20 (*Exit.*)

TRAFFIQUE.

So I think too, and therefore I will be better informed whether you are Sir Gentle Golding or no before I leave you. (*Exit.*)

Pilgrim enters at another door.

PILGRIM.

The hundred pistoles, if I had received 'em, had 25 carried me off cleverly and for some time supported my designs in another place till an opportunity had favored me in making a handsome composition with Sir Anthony about my jewels. However, I make a pretty good figure still. Here's a good suit of clothes 30 to begin the world with again. (*Strutting and looking on his clothes.*)

Enter Cortaut, the tailor's man.

CORTAUT.

Bless your worship, Sir Gentle, long may you live to wear 'em. How do your clothes fit you, sir?

PILGRIM.

Very well, friend, very well. 35

CORTAUT.

Have you forgot me, master?

PILGRIM.

No, no, I han't forgot thee, for I never saw thee before.

CORTAUT.

I am poor Cortaut, your tailor's finisher; I brought your Honor's clothes home to you this morning— 40

PILGRIM.

Did you so, did you so?

CORTAUT.

By the same token, you said you would give me

something to drink your health, but you were
pleased to forget it.

PILGRIM.

I remember I gave thee nothing indeed, but the 45
next time—

CORTAUT.

Aye, an't* like your Honor, I am contented to stay, if
my master would, but he has beaten me black and blue
for leaving the clothes behind me without money.

PILGRIM.

Gad forgive me, that I should forget that too! But 50
come to my lodging an hour hence—

CORTAUT.

Please you, I'll wait upon you now to your lodging.

PILGRIM. [*Aside.*]

How shall I shake him off?

CORTAUT.

For I dare not go home without the money or
some part on't. 55

PILGRIM.

Here, take this purse, 'tis more than the debt, but
take the rest for thyself, now I remember thee—

Enter Traffique with a servant of Sir Gentle's.

The Elizabeth broad gold has delivered me.

SERVANT.

Yes, Master Monsieur, that is my master, Sir Gentle
Golding; you shall see me speak to him— (*Goes* 60
to the Pilgrim.)

TRAFFIQUE. (*To Courtaut.*)

Young man, a word with you.

PILGRIM.

More debts to pay! I shall fall like an executor
without assets.

SERVANT.

Sir, I have been about your business with the 65
messenger, as you ordered me—

PILGRIM. [*Aside.*]

This is one of my English servants, it seems; I'll
answer him in French to get rid of him.

SERVANT.

If you were at leisure—

PILGRIM.

Que demandez-vous? que dîtes-vous, laquais? 70
Entendez-vous le français, grand coquen?[30]

SERVANT.

How's this? I durst have sworn it had been my
master, but I am sure he has no more languages
than tongues, and that his mother give him.
Besides he's too good an Englishman to learn 75
anything in another country.

PILGRIM.

Je ne vous entends pas, je ne parle pas anglais.[31]

SERVANT.

It seems I was mistaken, sir, this is some outlandish
man; he can't speak English.

TRAFFIQUE.

How, not speak English! 80

CORTAUT.

I'm sure he paid me for the suit upon his back,
but just now, in very good English.

TRAFFIQUE.

And would have borrowed a hundred pistoles of
me in as civil English—

PILGRIM.

I can speak English, gentlemen. I spoke French 85
only to try if that fellow had learnt anything since
he came into the country.

SERVANT.

I'll have a trial with you. This is some rogue that
has murdered my master—

CORTAUT.

And stole his clothes— 90

TRAFFIQUE.

And robbed him of his bills of exchange.

SERVANT.

Murder, murder, roguery, thievery, stop him.

*Exeunt after the pilgrim. Enter Sir Anthony, Valentine,
Ilford, and Abbé.*

ILFORD.

Nay, the pilgrim was in the right in getting off
before your evidence came upon him.

ABBÉ.

I never heard of so extraordinary a rogue as he 95
confesses himself to be in these tablets.

VALENTINE.

But that our gentle knight should neither hinder him

---

30 *Que ... coquen*] What are you asking? What are you saying, lackey? Do you understand French, you big fool?

31 *Je ... anglais*] I don't understand you, I don't speak English.

from going nor be forthcoming himself makes me
believe some ridiculous accident has lit upon him.

SIR ANTHONY.

Let it be but ridiculous enough, and I may forgive   100
him.

ABBÉ.

The ports are shut, and for the pilgrim, if he be
in the city, we shall have him again.

Enter Sir Gentle in the pilgrim's habit.

ILFORD.

What's that sneaks by us so?

VALENTINE.

Our very, very* saint. (*Gathering about him.*)   105

SIR ANTHONY.

Good morrow, Pilgrim!

ABBÉ.

Won't you know your friends?

ILFORD.

We were too late for your levee, but men of your
austerity and life never indulge the flesh by
sleeping long; you are an early stirrer.   110

ABBÉ.

Pray look up. You can do nothing, sure, to cast you
down.

OMNES.

Sir Gentle Golding!

SIR GENTLE.

Even the very same.

VALENTINE.

What do you in this habit?   115

SIR GENTLE.

'Tis whimisical and odd: I had a mind to try if you
could know me in this disguise.

SIR ANTHONY.

Oh yes, we know you in any disguise.

ABBÉ.

But there's a warrant out against the pilgrim; you'll
be taken up for him.   120

SIR GENTLE.

Why? You don't take me for the pilgrim.

ILFORD.

But the government will.

SIR GENTLE.

The government, then, will take me for as very a
rascal as lives unhanged in it.

VALENTINE.

But what's become of him?   125

SIR ANTHONY.

You were last with him—

VALENTINE.

You have conveyed him away—

ILFORD.

Or murdered him—

ABBÉ.

You must answer for him, for you have his clothes.

SIR GENTLE.

Nay if it be so, I'll tell you how I came by 'em—   130

ILFORD.

The whole truth, and nothing but the truth.

SIR GENTLE.

I'll see him hanged, before I tell a lie for a rogue
that has used me so scurvily—

SIR ANTHONY.

How scurvily, dear knight?

SIR GENTLE.

Why, when you left me, you know, alone with   135
him, he took his time, when my back was turned,
and clapt a pistol to my breast.

ABBÉ.

Bless the mark! a pistol!

VALENTINE.

A pistol, Sir Gentle!

SIR GENTLE.

A double-barreled pistol.   140

SIR ANTHONY.

A brace of bullets in each, I warrant you.

SIR GENTLE.

I warrant you there were, for he swore he would
shoot me through the head—

ILFORD.

The pistol was at your breast, Sir Gentle.

SIR GENTLE.

Breast, did I say? Did I say at my breast,   145
gentlemen? But breast or head, sir—he swore he
would murder me if I did not give him my clothes
to make his escape in.

VALENTINE.

And so, you gave him your clothes?

SIR GENTLE.

No, I thank you; that were to make myself   150
accessory. I put him to the trouble of taking 'em.

ABBÉ.

And very wisely done, sir.

SIR ANTHONY.

So he stript you?

SIR GENTLE.

To my very shirt, I'll make oath on't before a magistrate.

ILFORD.

You put on his clothes, then, some may say, in your own defense?

SIR GENTLE.

You may say so indeed.

ABBÉ.

Stick there, sir, *se defendendo*[32] will bring you off.

SIR GENTLE.

I must ha' gone home naked else.

SIR ANTHONY.

And could you have passed sullenly by us and concealed such an occasion of laughing at you?

SIR GENTLE.

Prithee, Sir Anthony, no more on't.

Officers bring in the pilgrim. Monsieur Traffique, Cortaut, and Sir Golding's servant.

SERVANT.

Bring him along, bring him along—

VALENTINE.

What rabble have we here?

SERVANT.

We are enow to hang one rogue, or we deserve to beat hemp[33] for one another.

ABBÉ.

Where are you haling the gentleman?

PILGRIM.

Sir Anthony, I am in your power. Stand but my friend in this business and bring me off, you shall make your own conditions about the jewels—

He and Sir Anthony confer.

SERVANT.

I'll swear point blank my master's murder upon him.

ABBÉ.

Who is your master, friend?

SERVANT.

Sir Gentle Golding, an't[h]* like you, and I am his man.

SIR GENTLE.

Aye, 'tis my man indeed. Would I were his master again.

SERVANT.

You my master, you rascal! My master's a knight.

SIR ANTHONY.

Now, Abbé, I am even with you and your pilgrim, but since I have brought him so far into this business, 'tis a matter of conscience to bring him out again. I was provided for his impertinence, and since I could not make him drunk, I gave him an opiate to expose him as if he were. For that purpose I removed him to your house, but coming to himself before I expected, he 'scaped that design—

PILGRIM.

And finding the disgrace ready to fall on me and in your house, I made bold to change clothes with Sir Gentle Golding.

SIR GENTLE.

'Tis true indeed, gentlemen.

PILGRIM.

But since matters are brought to a clearing, I am ready to return 'em to the gentleman.

SIR ANTHONY.

As you had 'em, I hope?

PILGRIM.

Everything but his purse, which I was forced to give his tailor there to get rid of him.

ABBÉ.

Return the purse.

TRAFFIQUE. (*To Cortaut.*)

I'll see your master paid. (*To the pilgrim.*) The hundred pistoles are ready, sir.

PILGRIM.

For Sir Gentle Golding; I only hastened you.

SIR GENTLE.

Why, how did you know I wanted such a sum?

TRAFFIQUE.

It shall be paid to you or your order.

SIR GENTLE.

Pray, pay it to nobody else.

---

32 *se defendendo*] in self defense

33 beat hemp] Beating hemp was a form of hard labor given for punishment; hemp was used to make the ropes that were used for hanging.

Exeunt Traffique and Cortaut.

ABBÉ.

You've done your duty, gentlemen, 'tis very well.
Pilgrim, a word with you—(*Takes him aside.*)

VALENTINE.

How this fooling has run away with the time!   205
(*Looks on's watch.*)

SIR ANTHONY.

I'll be for you immediately. (*Takes Sir Gentle aside.*)

VALENTINE.

Within a quarter of ten already!

ILFORD.

I should ha' been glad to ha' made one, Valentine.

VALENTINE.

I thank you, but numbers may discover* us, and   210
Sir Anthony won't be out of the business.

ABBÉ.

Do me but this piece of service, and I won't only
pardon you, but reward you well when you ha'
done't. Besides, 'tis a kind of revenge upon Sir
Anthony.   215

PILGRIM.

I am at your mercy, and you shall command me
anything.

ILFORD.

Sir Gentle says, you drew a pistol upon him.

VALENTINE.

That was not according to the law of arms.

PILGRIM.

I can't tell how his fear represented it, but it was   220
an inkhorn that disarmed him.

SIR ANTHONY.

You won't fail, when I send for you?

SIR GENTLE.

I'll but change clothes with that gentleman and be
ready as soon as you please.

Exeunt Sir Gentle, Pilgrim, and servant.

SIR ANTHONY.

Now Valentine, have with you—   225

ABBÉ.

'Tis near upon your appointment with my niece;
I'll secure her father within, the better to favor her
running away from him.

ILFORD.

I wish you well, gentlemen.

*They go out several ways, Ilford and the abbé, but Sir
Anthony and Valentine together.*

Scene v. The backside of
[Count Canaille's] great house, with gardens.

Count Vérole with six bravos.

VÉROLE.

Tomorrow, let but once tomorrow come,
And she is mine, married, and wholly mine.
If then not wholly mine, 'twill be my fault.
—Gentlemen, we must be everywhere tonight:
This Englishman that dares to rival me   5
May attempt farther; if he should, I think
Floriante but too inclined to pardon him.
But we'll prevent the worst.

*Valentine and Sir Anthony make the signal (a whistle)
at the garden door, which opens upon it, [revealing
Floriante].*

Stand and observe their motions.
Nay then 'tis he, be sure you murder him.   10

*Floriante retires upon the noise of swords, crying
murder. Count Canaille, with sword in hand, runs to
assist Valentine and Sir Anthony against the bravos.*

CANAILLE.

Villains and murderers!—I hope you are not hurt.

VALENTINE.

Thank your assistance, sir.

SIR ANTHONY.

If I am not a man in this point, I'll never wear
breeches more.

VALENTINE.

I know 'twas Count Vérole.   15

CANAILLE.

He has not raised himself in my esteem by this
base action—

Enter Floriante.

What do you do out of doors?

FLORIANTE.

I could not stay within, knowing your danger.

CANAILLE.

'Tis over, now retire.   20

FLORIANTE.

Pray pardon me, if I have done any undecent thing,
my duty caused it in my fears for you. (*Exit.*)

VALENTINE.

I'm sorry I have alarmed your family.

SIR ANTHONY.

I dare swear for him he is.

CANAILLE.

So far 'tis well, sir. If you think yourself obliged   25
for what is past, show it in what's to come: forbear
my house; my daughter is disposed of. So, good
night. (*Exit.*)

SIR ANTHONY.

Very good advice, Valentine. Since you can't make
it a good night with his daughter, make it as good   30
as you can with somebody else.

VALENTINE.

Why faith, the expectation of her has raised me
into a desire of anything in petticoats.

SIR ANTHONY.

What think you of my English lady?

VALENTINE.

You owe me a favor there, Sir Anthony.   35

SIR ANTHONY.

Tonight I'll pay it then. I have an appointment
upon me now, but not being in so perfect a
condition to oblige her, you shall make an end of
my quarrel.*

VALENTINE.

With all my heart.   40

SIR ANTHONY.

I'll send my governor to conduct you.

VALENTINE.

He, like other wise men, makes no scruple of
pimping when he gets by the employment.

SIR ANTHONY.

Then you are not one of those fine gentlemen
who, because they are in love with one woman, can   45
lie with nobody else?

VALENTINE.

Not I, faith, knight, I may be a lover, but I must
be a man.

SIR ANTHONY.

When the dear days of rambling joys are o'er,
When Nature grudges to supply your whore,   50
There's love enough for marriage left in store.

Exeunt.

Act IV, scene i. [Sir Anthony's lodging.]

Waitwell disguised with Sir Gentle Golding.

WAITWELL.

Sir Anthony not being able to wait upon you in
person, as he designed, has desired me his friend—

SIR GENTLE.

Sir, your most humble servant.

WAITWELL.

To show you the way.

SIR GENTLE.

I'll show my good breeding and follow you.   5

WAITWELL.

The lady is at present in private; when she has
dispatched her own business, she'll be ready for
yours.

SIR GENTLE.

Then she's a woman of business.

WAITWELL.

And of dispatch, too, sir. If you love pictures,   10
there's a gallery will take up your thoughts till the
lady's at leisure to employ 'em better. I'll let her
know you're here. (*Exit.*)

SIR GENTLE.

How ceremony disguises anything! I can't take this
civil gentleman for a pimp, though I have occasion   15
for him, nor this house for a bawdy house, though
I have a mind to make it one. Would Sir Anthony
were here to encourage me with his impudence.
When I have company to halloo me, I can fasten like
a bull dog. But I have a villainous suspicion that,   20
when I see this lady, I shall take her for a civil
gentlewoman, abuse her a way she does not deserve,
think too well of her, and lose my labor. (*Exit.*)

Scene ii. A bedchamber.

A song.

WOMAN.

No more, sir, no more, I'll ev'n give it o'er;
    I see it is all but a cheat:
Your soft wishing eyes, your vows, and your lies,
    Which thus you so often repeat.

MAN.

'Tis you are to blame, who foolishly claim   5
    So silly* a lean sacrifice,

But lovers who pray must always obey
    And bring down their knees and their eyes.
WOMAN.
Of late you have made devotion a trade,
    In loving as well as religion,   10
But you cannot prove, thro' th'Ages of Love,
    Any worship was offered but one.
MAN.
That one let it be in which we agree;
    Leave forms to the maids who are younger:
We're both of a mind, make haste and be kind,   15
    And continue a Goddess no longer.

*Valentine following Sir Anthony Love in her woman's
clothes.*

VALENTINE.
Faith madam, your entertainment will keep you
in countenance; you may own the making of it.
SIR ANTHONY.
You'll trust your stomach with a covered dish
another time, sir?   20
VALENTINE.
You may show your face after it and expect the
thanks of the company.
SIR ANTHONY.
And disgrace the reputation I have got with you
in other things?
VALENTINE.
Nay, if you think so, I would not have you show   25
it for the world.
SIR ANTHONY.
That were to ruin the compliment you intend me.
VALENTINE.
But after all, if your face should be as delicate as
your other charms—
SIR ANTHONY.
But if it should not be as delicate—   30
VALENTINE.
Then keep it to yourself, but 'tis pity 'tis not. But
be it what it is, I will pay some part of my thanks
in advising you.
SIR ANTHONY.
You would say grace and be gone, my serious
sinner, would you?   35
VALENTINE.
Only to make sure of coming again, child,* that's all.

SIR ANTHONY.
Some of that all, I beseech you—
VALENTINE.
My doctrine will turn to thy use, child, and lead
me often to thee, if thou hast but the grace to
make the right application.   40
SIR ANTHONY.
Good Holder-Forth, bate your damned faces and
begin.
VALENTINE.
Why then, in the first place, about our friend Sir
Anthony: he's a very pretty fellow I grant you, but
he's a boy, a giddy-pated boy.   45
SIR ANTHONY.
A little too young indeed to be trusted—
VALENTINE.
In an affair of this nature, by any woman that has
a reputation to secure with her pleasure.
SIR ANTHONY.
I have been afraid of his talking indeed a great
while.   50
VALENTINE.
You must expect it, madam; he has not experience
enough to value you. All women are alike to the
young fellows, as indeed all fellows are alike to the
young women. Neither sex chooses well till they
come to an age of discretion.   55
SIR ANTHONY.
There I am with you indeed.
VALENTINE.
There is a maturity required in love, as in other
fruits, to recommend the true relish of it to the
distinguishing palate of an epicure. I am something
of a better judge of that pleasure than he can be, and   60
I think fitter a great deal for an intrigue with your
ladyship both in discretion and performance—
SIR ANTHONY.
Than Sir Anthony can be. (*Shows her face.*)
VALENTINE.
Sir Anthony in petticoats! My good friend Mrs.
Lucy!ⁱ   65
SIR ANTHONY.
But are not you a rogue, Valentine? not to receive
a courtesy from a lady by the favor of your friend,
but you must abuse your trust and supplant the
very interest that raised you to her?

VALENTINE.

I am confounded indeed! But are you Sir Anthony 70
Love?

SIR ANTHONY.

All but my petticoats.

VALENTINE.

And are you sure you're a woman?

SIR ANTHONY.

Are not you sure of that, sir?

VALENTINE.

I am, and charmed with the certainty. (*Kisses her.*) 75
Now every pleasure past comes o'er my thoughts:
How many opportunities have I lost,
That you have giv'n me, and must answer for!

SIR ANTHONY.

There are as many to come; you shall command
'em all. 80

VALENTINE.

Now I remember: you fathered a bastard for me
at Paris—

SIR ANTHONY.

I had the reputation of it, indeed, and should have
had the cow with the calf, for her father pursued
me to marry her, through all means of 85
accommodation, into the strait at last of confessing
my sex to the English ambassador—

VALENTINE.

This you never told me before.

SIR ANTHONY.

He had her punished and secured me in his family,
as long as I stayed there, for you know, he was a 90
man of honor—

VALENTINE.

And a man of gallantry, too, madam, that knew
which way to improve such a piece of good
fortune—

SIR ANTHONY.

As well as anybody, and so he did, Valentine: by his 95
generosity and good usage, he pressed me so very far
that, not being able to answer the obligations I had
to him (having you in my head at that very time), I
was forced to run away from him to get rid of him.

VALENTINE.

How could you keep this from me so long? 100

SIR ANTHONY.

Now 'tis more welcome to you?

VALENTINE.

Had I known it before, it had been in my power—

SIR ANTHONY.

Not to marry me, I hope, Valentine! But if you
could be in that mind (which I neither desire nor
deserve), I know you too well to think of securing 105
you that way.

VALENTINE.

But I would not have engaged myself anywhere
else—

SIR ANTHONY.

I know your engagements to Floriante, and you shall
marry her. That will disengage you, I warrant you. 110

VALENTINE.

You continue your opinion of marriage.

SIR ANTHONY.

Floriante, I grant you, would be a dangerous rival
in a mistress—

VALENTINE.

Nothing can rival thee.

SIR ANTHONY.

And you might linger out a long liking of her to my 115
uneasiness and your own, but matrimony, that's her
security, is mine: I can't apprehend her in a wife.

Enter Waitwell.

SIR ANTHONY.

Well, Governor, what think you of my
management?

WAITWELL.

Why, if you take but half the pains in your profit 120
that you have spent in your pleasure, I think we
may expect a very good account of the knight—

VALENTINE.

Sir Gentle Golding! He's in your debt indeed. I
had not leisure to remember him.

SIR ANTHONY.

We'll laugh at him at leisure. 125

WAITWELL.

He's in the gallery, expecting your pleasure.

SIR ANTHONY.

My pleasure is to see him. Bring him in.

Exit Waitwell.

I promised him a mistress, you must know. 'Twill
be foolish enough to observe him when he
discovers me. Pray stay and laugh with me. 130

VALENTINE.

  The interview must needs be ridiculous. (*Goes to the door.*)

Sir Gentle Golding introduced by Waitwell: he is surprised at the sight of Sir Anthony.

WAITWELL.

  My office ends where the lady begins; I'll leave you to her.

SIR GENTLE.

  Pray sir, a word with you.   135

WAITWELL.

  The fewer the better till you have saluted* her: you see she expects it.

SIR GENTLE.

  I should have saluted her, indeed, but the surprise of your beauty, madam, made me forget my compliment.   140

SIR ANTHONY.

  My face has surprised him, I believe.

SIR GENTLE.

  Pray, did I never see this gentlewoman before?

WAITWELL.

  You best can tell that, sir, but you are concerned at something.

SIR GENTLE.

  A little concerned I am, indeed, but 'tis only to   145
  know whether I know her or no.

WAITWELL.

  In your tour of France you may have seen her: she's of the country.

SIR GENTLE.

  A French woman.

WAITWELL.

  Of Languedoc.[34]   150

SIR GENTLE.

  I durst ha' sworn she was an English woman!

WAITWELL.

  Born and bred among us.

SIR GENTLE.

  I'm glad on't with all my heart. For I know a little woman, but a great devil, so like her in England—

WAITWELL.

  Very like, sir.   155

---

34 Languedoc] the province in which Montpelier was located

SIR GENTLE.

  That faith and troth, I was downright confounded at the sight of her.

WAITWELL.

  Some mistress that you have forsaken—

SIR GENTLE.

  Oh fie, sir, I never do those things.

WAITWELL.

  I warrant you, and the guilt of her ill usage haunts   160
  you up and down in her shape.

SIR GENTLE.

  Nay, I deserve it, indeed, if it should be so, for I was too barbarous to the poor devil, considering I was the first that undid her.

Sir Anthony making a curtsy, points Sir Gentle to a chair.

WAITWELL.

  See, sir, the lady would have you sit down by her.   165
  I never saw her make such advances before; you are very much in favor.

SIR GENTLE.

  Soft and fair. I must be more in your favor, before I have done with you.

WAITWELL.

  She does not speak English. But there's an universal   170
  character in love which every creature can comprehend. When she has you alone, she'll grope out your meaning, I warrant you. (*Exit.*)

SIR GENTLE.

  So, since we have nothing to say to one another, we shall lose no time in compliments. I like her   175
  exceedingly, though I never look upon her but Lucia comes in my thoughts. She's so very like that jilting jade I shall never love her heartily; a week will be the farthest I shall be constant to her. What sign shall I make to put her in mind of her bed chamber?   180
  Money speaks all languages: this purse shall be my interpreter. *Voulez-vous*[35] do me the grand favor—

SIR ANTHONY.

  But how shall we do to understand one another? You speak no French, and I speak no English; 'tis impossible to understand one another.   185

SIR GENTLE.

  Madam, you do speak English—

---

35 *Voulez-vous*] Do you wish to …

SIR ANTHONY.

I understand it a little, enough to know I resemble one, what did you call her, Lucia, aye, Lucia, a jilting jade you don't like, that for that reason you can't love me heartily nor be constant above a week—I understand so much, without speaking English, as you find to be understood. 190

SIR GENTLE.

I find I do understand you.

SIR ANTHONY.

But I'll try to speak plainer to you.

SIR GENTLE.

Nay, you speak plain enough, Mrs.* Lucy. Would I were anywhere to be rid of you. 195

SIR ANTHONY.

You see, we were not to part so. Fortune will have me obliged to you. I have almost spent the five hundred pounds I borrowed of you.

SIR GENTLE.

I'm glad I had it for you, madam. 200

SIR ANTHONY.

And faith, 'tis very kind in an old acquaintance to follow me into France to supply me again. I know you came a-purpose—

SIR GENTLE.

Not quite a-purpose—

SIR ANTHONY.

No, not quite a-purpose, some little business by the by of your own you might have, I grant you. But this purse you never designed for me— 205

SIR GENTLE.

I'll force nothing upon you, madam; you may give it me again, if you don't like it.

SIR ANTHONY.

Yes, yes, the purse is an amiable purse and very well to be liked, only the sum does not amount to my occasions. There's no retreating, Sir Gentle, you are in my power and, without a ransom, must continue my prisoner. You know I never want* a pistol upon these occasions; 'tis not the first time I have robbed you. 210 215

SIR GENTLE.

Any composition, but don't murder me. You know I hate a pistol.

SIR ANTHONY.

What have you in your pockets? Nothing but papers?

SIR GENTLE.

You have got already all the money I had about me. 220

SIR ANTHONY.

About you! with a pox to you. Must I be so answered? And why had not you more about you? Stay, here's a bill* of a hundred pistoles at present shall excuse you—

SIR GENTLE.

'Tis very well it does. 225

SIR ANTHONY.

Payable to you or your order? Who's there?

Enter Waitwell.

Run and receive this bill for the gentleman.

WAITWELL.

He should endorse it first.

SIR ANTHONY.

Come sir, you must lend me your order.

SIR GENTLE.

No borrowing among friends; I'll give it you, to Monsieur Traffique. 230

SIR ANTHONY.

Why, that's well said.

Writes and gives Sir Anthony the bill, and Sir Anthony gives it to Waitwell, who goes out.

SIR GENTLE.

You live as it were by your wits; 'tis better I should lose a little money than you should forget your trade for want* of employment. 235

SIR ANTHONY.

A great deal better, Sir Gentle! But I must lock you up till the money be paid.

SIR GENTLE.

Aye, aye, with all my heart, but he won't scruple the payment.

SIR ANTHONY.

The next time I do you this favor, take care to be better provided. Don't let me lose my labor upon you. I speak as a friend to you. 240

SIR GENTLE.

I'll take your advice.

SIR ANTHONY.

If I were not just upon my leaving the town and in very great haste, I can tell you, you should not get off so easily. 245

SIR GENTLE.

I am beholding to you, but I am sorry we lose you
so soon.

SIR ANTHONY.

You may find me again, if Christendom stands
where it does a twelve-month to an end. Let not   250
that trouble you. (*Exit after Sir Gentle. Valentine
comes forth.*)

VALENTINE.

Thus all things are provided for by Fate;
The witty man enjoys the fool's estate.
So rich and poor, let 'em compute their gains,   255
One has his lot in lands, and one in brains,
And 'tis but justice Fortune should do more
For him who, being born so, would be poor. (*Exit.*)

Scene iii. The street.

Enter Count Canaille and Abbé.

CANAILLE.

I allow all you say, and last night's action
Has not declined the Count from my esteem
More than it raises Valentine.

ABBÉ.

He'll keep your daughter more orderly than a
nunnery can. Ev'n let him marry her.   5

CANAILLE.

You know I am out of my own power and choice.

ABBÉ.

Hang your choice, you may be ashamed on't.

CANAILLE.

Indeed, I do repent it, but my word
And reputation are engaged to him.

ABBÉ.

Is that a man to make a grandfather?   10

CANAILLE.

No other shall, by Floriante, make me one:
And therefore she shall be religious,
And take the habit in her sister's room—

ABBÉ.

What, make a nun of her, against her will!

CANAILLE.

To cut off all pretenders. But to prove   15
How I regard your friend: Charlott, you know,
Inferior in nothing but her years,
If Valentine likes her, she has my leave

And shall receive his visits at the grate.
Let him but conquer her, he has gained me. (*Exit.*)   20

ABBÉ.

Let him get Floriante, and he conquers thee.

P[ilgrim] enters in another disguise [as a palmer].

Ah, my little palmer! You lie as close as a man in
a proclamation;[36] but you are a pilgrim of honor,
I find—

PILGRIM.

Where I am engaged, sir—   25

ABBÉ.

Sir Anthony can never discover thee. (*Turns him
about.*)

PILGRIM.

I warrant I do your business—

ABBÉ.

And your own business—

PILGRIM.

My own business to be sure, and Sir Anthony's,   30
too, or I shall lose my labor.

ABBÉ.

About it, about it instantly, and prosper, my little
palmer.

*Exit P[ilgrim]. Enter Valentine with Sir Anthony and
Sir Gentle.*

Valentine! I have some news for you— (*Walks off
with him.*)   35

SIR ANTHONY.

But you amaze me, Sir Gentle—

SIR GENTLE.

It would amaze one indeed, Sir Anthony.

SIR ANTHONY.

'Tis the oddest piece of roguery and impudence
that I have heard of.

SIR GENTLE.

Aye, so 'tis, 'tis pretty odd and impudent indeed.   40

SIR ANTHONY.

A cheating gypsy. I warrant she has had her eye
upon you from your first coming to town.

---

36 proclamation] The abbé presumably means a man who
    has been banned by royal or other official proclamation
    and is waiting, close at hand, in hopes of returning to
    his homeland.

SIR GENTLE.

Nay, not unlikely.

SIR ANTHONY.

I began to suspect her myself, she pressed me so
often to bring you.   45

SIR GENTLE.

Ah, if I had known that, Sir Anthony!

SIR ANTHONY.

Why, what if you had?

SIR GENTLE.

Why, I would ha' stayed away, but if you had been
with me, it had been the better for me.

SIR ANTHONY.

Much at one for that, I believe. But is she gone   50
out of town do you say? You should have
apprehended her—

SIR GENTLE.

Pugh, pugh—she's gone from her lodging; she
must not stay long in a place.

SIR ANTHONY.

'Tis very well she's gone—   55

SIR GENTLE.

Aye, so it is, and I hope I shall never see her again.
(*Exit.*)

SIR ANTHONY.

I dare swear for him, he speaks his heart.

Enter P[ilgrim as palmer] to him.

Well sir—your business with me? If it be grave or
wise, keep it for your own use; I never approve   60
discretion in any man but a pimp.

PILGRIM.

Sir, you may say what you please, or call me what
you please—

SIR ANTHONY.

Nay, sir, I honor you if you are one.

PILGRIM.

Then I am one, and one employed to you.   65

SIR ANTHONY.

Begin your employment, that I may go about mine.

PILGRIM.

Why then, sir, in a few: there's a lady dying for you.

SIR ANTHONY.

I never visit the sick. Let her die in peace, but don't
let a priest come near her. He'll ask her bawdy
questions, when she has a mind to be serious.   70

PILGRIM.

She's only dying for you, sir.

SIR ANTHONY.

Were she living for me, I could say something to
her. If she make a will, as far as the legacy goes I
may remember her.

PILGRIM.

Your mirth becomes you, sir, but the lady's in very   75
good health and, in short, only dying in love with
you—

SIR ANTHONY.

Short and sweet—

PILGRIM.

And has a mind—

SIR ANTHONY.

I know her mind, and what she has a mind to.   80

PILGRIM.

You know the world enough, sir, to excuse a lady
in love—

SIR ANTHONY.

And absolve her, too—

PILGRIM.

Though she should have a husband—

SIR ANTHONY.

For making him a cuckold—   85

PILGRIM.

Not to make a practice of it.

SIR ANTHONY.

The oftener the better.

PILGRIM.

Nay indeed, there's a great deal to be said for the
poor women. How can they help or avoid their
inclinations?   90
Men are to blame, who like young conjurers, prove
(Safe in the circle of a wedding ring)
The magic spell of wedlock upon love:
So, cuckolds make themselves by marrying.

SIR ANTHONY.

Very casuistically brought about, sir. And I am so   95
much of your opinion, that I think the lady cannot
do herself a better justice, nor me a greater favor,
than allow me to wait upon her on such an occasion.

PILGRIM.

That she does in this billet and, if you think it
worth your while to visit her, will do you richer   100
and greater favors.

SIR ANTHONY.

I am at present engaged, but in the evening—

PILGRIM.

The evening would do well. I am bade to say her husband's out of town; the rest, her note will best inform you in. (*Going.*) 105

SIR ANTHONY.

Then this shall be my guide.

PILGRIM. [*Aside.*]

I may cheat you out of your cunning before I ha' done with you. (*Exit.*)

SIR ANTHONY.

Why, what the devil am I engaging in again! I shall draw all the women in town upon me at this rate: 110 maids, wives, and widows have one curiosity or another always to be satisfied. I have a reputation among 'em, and if I don't keep it up by answering their expectations, I shall fail of mine in my frolics and be discovered, and that I have no mind to be yet 115 a while! But how the devil shall I answer their expectations? or this lady's in particular, who has bespoke me for her evening's service? If I go, I shall disappoint her more than if I stay away, and I know, good soul, she would be as much concerned for me 120 to find me no man as at another time she would be for herself to be found no maid, if she had a mind to be thought one. Oh, here comes Valentine!

Enter Valentine.

VALENTINE.

I would as soon be a lawyer as a lover at this rate. Following a mistress to no purpose is as bad as 125 trudging afoot to Westminster[37] for no fee. Can you corrupt a nunnery for me, my little knight!

SIR ANTHONY.

I will do anything for you, but first you must lend me your limbs to carry on a design—

VALENTINE.

Do what you please with me. 130

Exeunt. P[ilgrim] re-enters with the abbé.

ABBÉ.

Thou art a most incomparable fellow, Palmer: the Prince of Pimps and Pilgrims! But what! Sir

Anthony is a young, smoky[38] rogue, I warrant you: he suspected something—

PILGRIM.

Not a bit of suspicion. 135

ABBÉ.

He might scruple at it at first, you know.

PILGRIM.

First nor last, he made no scruple at all! but came into my net as fast as I could spread it for him!

ABBÉ.

But came into my net as fast as I could spread it for him! Prettily expressed upon the occasion! And 140 I shall love a setting dog as long as I live for the sake of the simile.

PILGRIM.

I'm glad it pleases you.

ABBÉ.

Pleases me! Yes, yes, it pleases me! everything pleases me. But hah! my boy! he must not get from 145 us, now we have him in the net?

PILGRIM.

'Tis our fault if he does.

ABBÉ.

Why, Sir Anthony has used thee but scurvily—

PILGRIM.

To my cost.

ABBÉ.

And revenge is very natural— 150

PILGRIM.

And very sweet—

ABBÉ.

Revenge is sweet indeed; it must be sweet, a sweet revenge, upon so sweet a boy. And take my word, I'll do you that justice upon him, for I'll tell you what I intend to do with him. 155

PILGRIM.

Aye, pray, sir.

ABBÉ.

Why in the first place I intend—not to open my lips upon that subject. But I mean—

PILGRIM.

I hope so, sir.

ABBÉ.

If I can compass my design, I mean— 160

PILGRIM.

What do you mean?

ABBÉ.

Not to explain myself, Palmer—ah rogue! But you know what I mean.

Exeunt.

Scene iv. Sir Anthony's lodging.

Enter Sir Anthony and Ilford.

SIR ANTHONY.

Why to tell you the truth, Ilford, there is a woman in the case; I expect her every minute.

ILFORD.

I fancied some such thing.

SIR ANTHONY.

She is a thing to be fancied, and you would think so if you saw her.   5

ILFORD.

Do I know her, Sir Anthony?

SIR ANTHONY.

You have seen her.

ILFORD.

What, nothing more of her?

SIR ANTHONY.

None of your peevish questions.

ILFORD.

'Tis not Volante?   10

SIR ANTHONY.

If it were, you don't come to quarrel* for her?

ILFORD.

Not I, faith, knight. I come in absolute good nature to visit you.

SIR ANTHONY.

Why indeed, I could not expect the favor at your hands as matters stand between us.   15

ILFORD.

Nothing shall stand between us. Nothing did, but a woman, and I come to strike up a friendship, offensive and defensive with you, by making a very fair offer to dispose of her.

SIR ANTHONY.

If you mean Volante, she will dispose of herself.   20

ILFORD.

I know she would dispose of herself to you, but you won't marry her, Sir Anthony. Now I am one of those foolish fellows who don't apprehend a danger till they are in't. I never think of being a cuckold. I love Volante and would marry her. Come, come,   25
there are women enow for the ill-natured purpose of your love. Quit her to me; do a generous thing to a woman that loves you and to a man who would engage you for a friend.

SIR ANTHONY.

Why faith, Ilford, I would do a great deal for you,   30
but I must do something for her.

ILFORD.

Do me a favor, and don't undo her fame.

SIR ANTHONY.

But there's the pleasure on't—

ILFORD.

To ruin the woman that loves you—

SIR ANTHONY.

Not so much out of ill nature to her, as good   35
nature to myself. Reputation must be had, and we young men generally raise ours out of the ruin of the women's.

ILFORD.

But Volante is a woman of quality* and has relations to do her right, if you don't do her reason.   40

SIR ANTHONY.

Would she had a brother to make a business on't. He could not do her so much right in fighting for her as he would do me reason in making it the talk of the town.

ILFORD.

That would set it about indeed.   45

SIR ANTHONY.

If I should say I had lain with her or endeavor to set it afoot, 'twould fall of itself.

ILFORD.

As an impotent piece of vanity or folly in a young man.

SIR ANTHONY.

But nobody dares make a doubt of a report when   50
a relation has taken an honorable care by a duel to fix the scandal in the family.

ILFORD.

Why truly, I think the men of honor are out in that business. Scandal does not fall into the hands of a surgeon like the wounds of the body for a   55
cure. Opening and probing makes the malady but

more inveterate, and the least air taints it to a mortification.

SIR ANTHONY.

It heals best of itself without a plaster.

ILFORD.

And time must finish the work. I have observed 60 some women live themselves into a second reputation—

SIR ANTHONY.

And other women who by a natural negligence, never setting up for any, from the freedom of their behavior have passed uncensured in those public 65 places and pleasures which would have undone ladies of a sprucer conversation* but to have appeared in.

ILFORD.

So that 'tis not what they do, but not doing all of a piece, that ruins their character* and undoes the 70 women—

SIR ANTHONY.

And condemns the men, too, for 'tis not any man's opinion, but his shifting it to the occasion, that makes him a rascal. As let his opinion be what it will, if he continues the same and acts upon a 75 principle, he may be an honest man. But 'tis no character I would advise a friend to.

ILFORD.

But this is from my business, Sir Anthony! And all things considered, the difficulties of getting and the danger of enjoying Volante—in my opinion, 80 her woman* would be the better intrigue.

SIR ANTHONY.

Why indeed, the woman would often be the better intrigue, were she as difficult to be compassed as her lady.

ILFORD.

It seems the danger doubles your delight. 85

SIR ANTHONY.

And we naturally covet what we are forbid, for very often 'tis the bare pleasure of breaking the commandment that makes another man's wife more desirable than his own.

ILFORD.

As at present, the bare pleasure of opposing my 90 interest has carried on yours with Volante farther than otherwise you designed.

SIR ANTHONY.

Why faith, there's something in that, too, Ilford; not but I have a very good opinion of the lady.

ILFORD.

Well Sir Anthony, I wish you would think it worth 95 your while to make a friend of me.

SIR ANTHONY.

I would make a friend of you.

ILFORD.

Resign your title then; 'tis but giving me now what in a little time you will decline of yourself. Make Volante mine, and make me yours. 100

SIR ANTHONY.

I would, with all my heart, if I could do it with honor.

ILFORD.

I warrant you, with honor.

SIR ANTHONY.

But how can I disengage myself? Matters are gone a great way between us—she's coming up to me. 105

Waitwell whispers and goes out.

Step into that closet, you will overhear what we say. I won't promise I can do you any service with her, but I'll do you all the good I can; that you may be sure of and depend upon.

ILFORD.

At least seeing her here will do some good upon 110 me. (*Goes in.*)

Enter Volante.

SIR ANTHONY.

Oh madam, you are as good as your word.

VOLANTE.

I can keep it, you see, at your cost, when I like the occasion.

SIR ANTHONY.

We men are not more punctual to an appointment 115 upon the hopes of a new mistress than you women are upon the first promise of a husband.

VOLANTE.

And it stands us upon to be diligent in both sexes. For neither the men, nor the women, continue long in the mind of allowing those favors. 120

SIR ANTHONY.

Why faith, child, the best excuse for foolish things (as marriage you allow to be one—

VOLANTE.

A convenient foolish thing)—

SIR ANTHONY.

Is the doing 'em without thinking. But what, madam, can't a man sport off a little innocent 125 gallantry with a lady without being serious a'both sides. You are in earnest, I see—

VOLANTE.

Why, there's the jest—

SIR ANTHONY.

And keep me to my word.

VOLANTE.

On my word will I.

SIR ANTHONY. 130

You take all advantages.

VOLANTE.

I may be allowed to take what advantage I can in the beginning; I shall be sure to be the loser in the end.

SIR ANTHONY.

In all plays,* one side must be the loser, but marriage is the only game where nobody can be 135 the winner.

VOLANTE.

That's making an ill bet, indeed, where we may lose and can't win. Yet I am resolved to venture.

SIR ANTHONY.

But child,* hast thou no more mercy upon my youth, my dress, my wit, and good humor than 140 to make a husband of me!

VOLANTE.

Since you could not have me on your own terms, I know you'll take me on mine.

SIR ANTHONY.

Well, there's nothing but cheating in love. Very often indeed we are beforehand with the women, 145 but when we marry 'em, I'm sure they cheat us.

VOLANTE.

And when do I cheat you, Sir Anthony?

SIR ANTHONY.

Have a care of cheating yourself, madam!

VOLANTE.

Nay, one time or other all women are to be fooled, and I had rather you should have the profit of me 150 than anybody else.

SIR ANTHONY.

And pleasure, too, I beseech you. I am now going

with Valentine to the nunnery to see his new mistress, Charlott—

VOLANTE.

And by her interest, to see his old mistress, 155 Floriante. I know the story and what the abbé designs in it.

SIR ANTHONY.

I shall be back in an hour; by that time the evening will conceal you the better. If then you are brave enough— 160

VOLANTE.

To meet you with a priest for a second.

SIR ANTHONY.

I'll have a father ready to bless our endeavors.

VOLANTE.

Let him be by to see you play me fair,
And do your worst, or best, and never spare. (*Exit.*)

SIR ANTHONY.

I warrant you, the first night for an heir. 165

Ilford coming forward to Sir Anthony.

ILFORD.

Oh sir, your servant. I see I am beholden to you.

SIR ANTHONY.

The most in the world, egad, when you know all.

ILFORD.

Know all? I know enough to convince me that you are not capable of a serious design of serving your honor or your friend— 170

SIR ANTHONY.

What's the matter now, man?

ILFORD.

And I was a coxcomb for thinking you could.

SIR ANTHONY.

Nay, you may be a coxcomb, however.

ILFORD.

What's that you say?

SIR ANTHONY.

No quarelling,* I beseech you, till you have cause. 175

ILFORD.

Till I have cause! I think you have given me sufficient cause—

SIR ANTHONY.

To thank me, I have, if you know how to be grateful.

ILFORD.

Oh I must needs be grateful and always confess the

obligation you have laid upon me in promoting   180
my interest so visibly with Volante—

SIR ANTHONY.

So opposite to my own with her.

ILFORD.

With so much diligence and good nature—

SIR ANTHONY.

Well remembered, egad.

ILFORD.

That in my hearing, and still to advance my   185
interest, you have made an appointment to marry
her.

SIR ANTHONY.

And put you to bed to her.

ILFORD.

How, how, Sir Anthony?

SIR ANTHONY.

I knew there was no other way to do you a service   190
with her; therefore, I resolved to marry her for you,
and put you to bed to her, for me.

ILFORD.

Incomparable design!

SIR ANTHONY.

A poor project* of mine, sir. If you had engaged
in't, it might ha' turned to account, but as 'tis, I   195
go as I did.

ILFORD.

But take me along with you.

SIR ANTHONY.

I never impose a courtesy upon any man, nor
quarrel,* because he is not sensible I am his friend.
When you come to yourself, you may repent—   200

ILFORD.

I do repent and confess myself—

SIR ANTHONY.

Well, what do you confess youself to be?

ILFORD.

A fool, an ass, to pretend to vie with you in
anything.

SIR ANTHONY.

And will you always keep in this humble opinion   205
of yourself? And allow me the ascendant?

ILFORD.

I shall be an ass if I don't.

SIR ANTHONY.

But you must confess yourself a coxcomb—

ILFORD.

Aye, anything.

SIR ANTHONY.

For pretending to censure before you understood   210
my design.

ILFORD.

You told me I was a coxcomb before, and now I
begin to believe it myself.

SIR ANTHONY.

Well, upon your penitence, I pardon and take you
into favor again.   215

ILFORD.

And into the design.

SIR ANTHONY.

That you must be. And to convince you that what
I do is perfectly in your interest, you shall marry
us yourself.

ILFORD.

With all my heart.   220

SIR ANTHONY.

I have a habit for you.
Thus in the world men keep a pother
And marry wives for one another,
And most, like me, in frolics woo
And, to their shame, as little do.   225
But married women know the sense
And rights of due benevolence.
I but provide for mine what she would soon,
For, first or last, that duty must be done.

Exeunt.

Act V, scene i. [Sir Anthony's lodging.]

*Ilford in a priest's habit between Sir Anthony and
Volante; Sir Anthony leads her to the door. Ilford dresses
himself in his own clothes.*

SIR ANTHONY.

Now you have done the office of a father to the
lady, you may do the office of a friend to me, and
go to bed to her. I can do no more than give you
an opportunity, but if you don't employ it to her
advantage, she'll never rely upon you to improve   5
another to your own.

ILFORD.

I never deserve another, if I don't make use of this.

SIR ANTHONY.

There's no ceremony to make the bride coy in
going to bed. She came in an undress as loose as
her wishes, and being under the impediment of   10
but two pins, I warrant she's in expectation already.

ILFORD.

She shan't expect long.

SIR ANTHONY.

There she is. Kiss my wife and welcome. She won't
cry out for her own sake, till 'tis too late to discover
it for mine.   15

ILFORD.

If she should, I think the castle's our own.

SIR ANTHONY.

I leave you to your fortune; I am going to seek
mine in another adventure. (*Exit.*)

ILFORD.

You have made my fortune here. (*Exit.*)

Scene ii. A bedchamber.

Song.

I.

In vain, Clemene, you bestow
    The promised empire of your heart
If you refuse to let me know
    The wealthy charms of every part.

II.

My passion with your kindness grew,   5
    Tho' beauty gave the first desire,
But beauty only to pursue
    Is following a wand'ring fire.[39]

III.

As hills in perspective* suppress
    The free inquiry of the sight,   10
Restraint makes every pleasure less
    And takes from love the full delight.

IV.

Faint kisses may in part supply
    Those eager longings of my soul,
But oh! I'm lost if you deny   15
    A quick possession of the whole.

Volante sola.

---

39 wand'ring fire] an ignis fatuus

VOLANTE.

Methinks my knight begins to show himself
already in a husband's indifference, making me
wait so long alone in a place where nothing but
his company can entertain me. But I have heard,   20
indeed, that she who marries a man for his
conversation or good humor takes care only to
secure the least or worst part of it to herself: so this
is but a small fault in matrimony, and ten to one,
before the year comes about, I may have a more   25
reasonable cause of repenting. I think I hear him.
Oh sir, are you come?

Enter Ilford to her.

ILFORD.

Sooner than you expected, I believe.

VOLANTE.

How! Ilford! (*Surprised, and turning away.*)

ILFORD.

I see you are surprised to see me here, and indeed the   30
occasion that brings me to you is very surprising.

VOLANTE.

What can you mean by this?

SIR ANTHONY.

A poor project of mine, sir. If you had—

VOLANTE.

You have stolen a wedding, madam, though you
think to make it a secret; you can't expect that Sir
Anthony should bring his vanity so low not to   35
make a boast of the favor he has done you.

VOLANTE.

By sending you to me?

ILFORD.

To wish you joy.

VOLANTE.

A very likely story.

ILFORD.

And give you joy, madam.   40

VOLANTE.

Would Sir Anthony would come to thank you for
your compliment.

ILFORD.

He sent me with the compliment—

VOLANTE.

He send you!

ILFORD.

To supply his place tonight. Your husband wonnot   45
come.

VOLANTE.

Not come to me?

ILFORD.

Be satisfied so far, you are abused, and to convince you, though too late, how unreasonably you have preferred that creature to everybody, he has done what nobody else could ha' done to you. 50

VOLANTE.

What has he done?

ILFORD.

Given me a fuller revenge upon your folly and scorn than I could ha' conceived for myself—

VOLANTE.

What has he done to me? 55

ILFORD.

He has married and undone you, left you—

VOLANTE.

Left me!

ILFORD.

The first night left you, left you to me. Not that I believe he designed me a favor more than he would ha' done any man else, but you had used me so 60 very ill, he imagined I was capable of any malicious design of exposing you.

VOLANTE.

Of exposing me!

ILFORD.

But that you need not apprehend from me.

VOLANTE.

I'm in your power, but pity me. My folly and my 65 fortune are too plain.

ILFORD.

Do you perceive it now?

VOLANTE.

I should ha' seen it sooner.

ILFORD.

'Tis well you find it now. However you deserve of me, I come to serve you, and since this 70 opportunity (that favors and was given me for baser ends) encourages me to nothing beyond the hope of your esteem, you must give me leave to think that, from my behavior, I deserve that honor better than my trifling rival does the title of your 75 love.

VOLANTE.

You deserve everything.

ILFORD.

I said enough to warn you of him, but you would venture.

VOLANTE.

My shame confounds me! 80

ILFORD.

You would not credit me.

VOLANTE.

I can but wish I had.

ILFORD.

Were it to do again, you would follow your inclination and do the same thing?

VOLANTE.

I hate the villain. 85

ILFORD.

In your anger?

VOLANTE.

No, to death I hate him, and were I free from him—

ILFORD.

You would not marry him!

VOLANTE.

Never. 90

ILFORD.

Then you are free from him.

VOLANTE.

How! free from him!

ILFORD.

Not married to him.

VOLANTE.

Would you could prove it, too.

ILFORD.

I'll make it plain, if you'll consent to it. 95

VOLANTE.

More willingly than I did e'er consent. Make that but plain to me, and what returns are in the poor power of one so lost—

ILFORD.

So saved, I hope.

VOLANTE.

You shall command. 100

ILFORD.

I may restore you to your liberty, but never can myself.

Exeunt.

Scene iii. The street.

Enter Sir Anthony and Valentine.

SIR ANTHONY.
    This is the time and place of appointment. What
    'twill come to, Valentine, I can't tell.
VALENTINE.
    'Tis a whimsical undertaking, methinks, to support
    another woman's intrigue at your expense—
SIR ANTHONY.
    There's no buying such a frolic too dear.   5
VALENTINE.
    And part with your lover to oblige her!
SIR ANTHONY.
    So long I can't part with you to provide for your
    pleasure as well as my own. Besides, 'tis a diverting
    piece of roguery and will be a jest as long as we
    know one another.   10

Enter P[ilgrim as palmer].

PILGRIM.
    Who's there? Sir Anthony!
SIR ANTHONY.
    The same. I am aforehand with you.
PILGRIM.
    The lady, sir, will thank you. Whom have you with
    you there?
SIR ANTHONY.
    Only a servant.   15
PILGRIM.
    You'll have no need of him, I come to serve you;
    besides, he may be seen.
SIR ANTHONY.
    I'll send him away.
PILGRIM.
    I'll but step in to make your way to the lady and
    will wait upon you again. (*Exit.*)   20
VALENTINE.
    By this fellow's advising to send away your servant,
    I fancy he may be a rogue.
SIR ANTHONY.
    If he be a rogue, I am resolved to discover the
    bottom of him, but if there be a woman in the
    case, I'll leave you to the employment—   25

Enter P[ilgrim].

PILGRIM.
    Sir.

SIR ANTHONY.
    Here.
PILGRIM.
    Are you alone?
SIR ANTHONY.
    I am.
PILGRIM.
    Follow me.   30
SIR ANTHONY.
    Follow me.

Exeunt, Valentine following Sir Anthony.

Scene iv. The inside of a house.

Enter Sir Anthony and Valentine.

VALENTINE.
    Your pimp proceeds with caution. But these dark
    deeds may require our dark lantern.
SIR ANTHONY.
    Give it me, I can manage this; you must manage
    the lady, and for once, not to make a custom of
    it, I'll hold a candle to you.   5

P[ilgrim] enters.

PILGRIM.
    Where are you, Sir Anthony?
VALENTINE.
    Here.
PILGRIM.
    I'm glad you are, and here I'll keep you—
VALENTINE.
    Hah!
PILGRIM.
    Have you forgot your friend the pilgrim? I am that   10
    lady in love with you, and now I have you to
    myself, I must come nearer to you.
VALENTINE.
    The devil you must— (*Throws P[ilgrim] down. Sir
    Anthony with his lanthorn goes to 'em.*)
SIR ANTHONY.
    Are you my friend, the pilgrim, do you say?   15
PILGRIM.
    Then I am lost again.
SIR ANTHONY.
    Why, how came I to forget you so soon? And are
    you the lady that was in love with me?

VALENTINE.

Rise, and tell all you know of this business, or it shall be the last you shall ever engage in. I know enough of you to send you to the galleys.[40]   20

PILGRIM.

Why indeed, gentlemen, I won't stand trial with you. I confess some design of my own upon Sir Anthony. But your very good friend, the abbé, first set it on foot by employing and paying me well   25 to decoy you into his power. Now sir, knowing your character,* I thought nothing would sooner spirit you anywhere than the hopes of a new woman.

SIR ANTHONY.

You see I am true to my assignation.   30

VALENTINE.

But where's the abbé all this while?

PILGRIM.

He's in the house expecting the good hour.

VALENTINE.

How shall we do with him?

PILGRIM.

To make my peace with you, I'll contribute to any design against him.   35

VALENTINE.

That must be your way.

SIR ANTHONY.

Go then, and to keep up the jest, say nothing of what is past, but bring him to me.

Exit P[ilgrim].

VALENTINE.

What do you design now?

SIR ANTHONY.

To continue the scene with him. For having, as I   40 told you, disposed of his niece Volante to our friend Ilford, I suppose they may have occasion by tomorrow for his approbation of what they are doing tonight.

VALENTINE.

That's well thought on; his consent will come the   45 easier for our having a hanck[41] upon him.

---

[40] galleys] a form of official punishment: being set to hard labor on ship

[41] hanck] check or restraint

SIR ANTHONY.

Get you gone, then, like an evidence,* behind the hangings.

Valentine retires. The abbé enters to Sir Anthony, singing, and dances round him.

A Song.[42]

ABBÉ.

Have I caught you my little Mercury! have I caught you!   50

SIR ANTHONY.

You're very nimble, sir.

ABBÉ.

Aye, aye, I have it in my head.

SIR ANTHONY.

And in your heels, too.

ABBÉ.

Upon occasion! Ah, my little man! I'm young again, when I like my company.   55

SIR ANTHONY.

But who could expect to see you here?

ABBÉ.

Why, anybody would have expected it. How could you expect otherwise? How could you think I could stay from you so long? What, you expected a woman?

SIR ANTHONY.

I did indeed.   60

ABBÉ.

Let the women expect you: there's a plentiful crop of maidenheads. If the war continues to carry off the whoremasters, some of 'em must fall of themselves without gathering. There will scarce be reapers enow for the harvest.   65

SIR ANTHONY.

There's no female famine in this year's almanack, no fear of wanting* women.

ABBÉ.

No, no, no fear of wanting women. But a good-natured, old merry fellow, as I may be, who can tittle-tattle and gossip in their families upon an   70 ancient privilege with the mothers, may do anything with the daughters. Such a man is a jewel to bring you together.

---

[42] song] lost, perhaps because this scene was suppressed in production

SIR ANTHONY.

Such a man would be a jewel indeed.

ABBÉ.

I know you, little rogue: your business is to be   75
wicked. I love to be wicked myself, too, sometimes,
as often as I can decently bring it about without
scandal. And I will be as wicked, as wicked as I
can be, for you, and with you.

SIR ANTHONY.

You can do no more than you can do, good old   80
gentleman.

ABBÉ.

Old gentleman! I won't be an old gentleman; I'm
never older than the company I am in. What! Five
and fifty does not make an old man; 'tis want* of
appetite, infirmity, and decay, not five and fifty that   85
makes a man old. Five and fifty has its pleasures.

SIR ANTHONY.

As good have none, Abbé, they are faint and feeble.

ABBÉ.

Delicate and dainty, my dear, palatable and
pleasant, and thou art mine.

SIR ANTHONY.

How shall I know that, sir?   90

ABBÉ.

Why thou shalt know, all in good time, child, but
an old fellow, you say— (*Unbuttons, and throws
down his cloak.*) What shall I do now to convince
you that I am not an old fellow? Let me see, what
shall I do for you?   95

SIR ANTHONY.

What can you do for me!

ABBÉ.

What can I do for you?

SIR ANTHONY.

To prove you are not an old fellow.

ABBÉ.

What can I? Why I can—I can part with my
money to thee.   100

SIR ANTHONY.

That's one argument indeed.

ABBÉ.

Besides I can—I won't tell you what I can, but if
you'll step into the next room with me, I have a
collation for you, and a—there you shall find what
I can do for you.   105

SIR ANTHONY.

If I should retire with you, you'll be
disappointed—

ABBÉ.

No, no, don't talk of a disappointment; I hate to
be disappointed. We're very luckily alone and
should make a good use of our time; nobody will   110
come to disturb us.

SIR ANTHONY.

But I may disappoint you myself—

ABBÉ.

You will exceedingly, if you don't go along with me.
Delays are dangerous when opportunities are
scarce, and we elderly fellows have 'em but   115
seldom—I vow I'll tease you and kiss you into
good humor, I swear I will, if you won't go.

SIR ANTHONY.

But 'tis not in my power to oblige you.

ABBÉ.

I'll put it into your power, I warrant you.

SIR ANTHONY.

But that I doubt, sir. For very unhappily for your   120
purpose, I am a—woman.

ABBÉ.

Hah! (*Drops her hand.*) How, a woman!

SIR ANTHONY.

A woman!

ABBÉ.

What the devil have I been doing all this while. A
woman! Are you sure you're a woman?   125

SIR ANTHONY.

How shall I convince you?

ABBÉ.

Nay, nay, I am easily convinced; the very name has
convinced me.

SIR ANTHONY.

But if you have a mind to be satisfied—

ABBÉ.

Thank you, madam, I am satisfied, more than I   130
desire to be satisfied, and as much satisfied as I can
be, with a woman. (*Puts on his cloak again.*)

SIR ANTHONY.

I told you I should disappoint you.

ABBÉ.

You did, indeed, and you have kept your word
with me, you have disappointed me, plaguely   135

disappointed me. But I beg your pardon, madam,
I hope there's no offense in a little waggery—

SIR ANTHONY.

None at all, sir.

ABBÉ.

I don't use to take the freedom of being so familiar
with the ladies—   140

SIR ANTHONY.

I do believe you.

ABBÉ.

Indeed I don't; I pay a greater respect to your sex,
and had I known you were a woman before, I had
kept my distance.

SIR ANTHONY.

Fie, fie, sir, ceremony among friends! Though you   145
know me now to be a woman, you need not keep a
distance. What though I have disappointed you in
your way, I may make you amends in my own—

ABBÉ.

So you may indeed, madam—

SIR ANTHONY.

You guess what I mean, Abbé?   150

ABBÉ.

If you would be but so gracious.

SIR ANTHONY.

How gracious would you have me be?

ABBÉ.

Ah! you'll never grant me the favor.

SIR ANTHONY.

What favor?

ABBÉ.

Why—to say nothing of this business.   155

SIR ANTHONY.

Is that the favor?

ABBÉ.

That's all, madam, the greatest favor you can do
me, and then you do my business.

SIR ANTHONY.

Can you part with any money now to me, now
I'm a woman?   160

ABBÉ.

Here are a hundred louis d'ors in this purse—

SIR ANTHONY.

To muzzle the scandal.

ABBÉ.

And I'll get you a husband into the bargain.

Enter Valentine and P[ilgrim as palmer].

VALENTINE.

She'll keep your counsel, Abbé.

ABBÉ.

Hem, hem, hem!   165

VALENTINE.

And in this scarcity of men, you'll do her a mighty
favor, I can tell her, to secure a husband for her.

ABBÉ.

Hold your tongue, sir. You shall have a wife, too,
if Floriante will content you. That rogue Palmer
has betrayed me.   170

VALENTINE.

Nobody shall betray you; we are all friends, but
this lady and I have a favor to beg of you.

ABBÉ.

A favor to beg of me! Anything, anything, as many
favors as you please; 'tis but asking, and having,
in the humor I am in, gentlemen.   175

SIR ANTHONY.

Our friend, Ilford, has married your niece Volante,
and you must give your consent to the wedding.

ABBÉ.

Give my consent to the wedding! Why, I'll dance
at the wedding. I'll have a fiddle, and a young
fellow to tickle me and teach me to caper. Gads   180
so, I don't know what legs I stand upon at the news
on't! I'll be as brisk as the bridegroom the first
night. But we shall neither of us hold it; 'twon't
last the year round with us. I'm an old fellow, that's
the truth on't, 'tis done with me already: I'm upon 185
my last legs. But I have Floriante and Charlott to
provide for still. Poor girls! While they are in a
nunnery, they lie upon my conscience. Let me but
bring them into the world again, and I'll be
contented to go out on't—   190

VALENTINE.

Not yet a great while, Abbé.

ABBÉ.

As soon as I can get myself in the mind.

SIR ANTHONY.

We'll keep you in another mind.

ABBÉ.

Nay, I am easily persuaded, but I have done with
you.   195

VALENTINE.

The Lady Abbess is consenting to their escape.

ABBÉ.

Being a kinswoman, she was easily persuaded to give 'em an opportunity.

VALENTINE.

'Tis near the time now. Would I had Ilford here.

SIR ANTHONY.

Why, I am here; I'll stand and fall by you.   200

VALENTINE.

I must not now expose you.

ABBÉ.

If you can but carry 'em off, the business is laid to your hands.

Exeunt [Abbé, Sir Anthony, and Valentine].

PILGRIM.

My business is over in this town, and I had best get off while I can for fear of bringing a worse   205
business upon me. (*Exit.*)

Scene v. The backside of a nunnery.

Enter Vérole and his bravos.

VÉROLE.

What Floriante means by this invitation to me, I can't tell; 'tis a favor she never vouchsafed me before. Perhaps the apprehension of taking the habit, which her father intends she shall, has wrought upon her to consent rather to marry me. But let her consent and   5
design what she please, if she puts herself in my power, as tonight she says she will, I design to let her see how very little I value that favor, for which I must be obliged more to her confinement than to her inclination or choice. Stand close, here's company.   10

Enter Valentine, Sir Anthony, and two servants.

VALENTINE.

I am as full of apprehension as an old soldier upon the guard of a counterscarp,[43] where his fears could not be more uneasy than my hopes are now.

VÉROLE.

He should be an Englishman, by the similitude,

───────────────

43 counterscarp] slope on the outside of a ditch surrounding a fortification; a dangerous place for sentry duty.

to let his friends know, from his own mouth, that   15
he has made a campaign.

SIR ANTHONY.

This is the backside of a nunnery—

VALENTINE.

And the garden door—I think I hear it open—

Charlott enters.

Oh, Floriante!

VÉROLE.

Floriante!   20

SIR ANTHONY.

Stand fast, we're set upon.

VALENTINE. (*To Sir Anthony.*)

You must not meet the danger—

VÉROLE.

Fall on, and kill the ravisher— (*Fights.*) Come my fair fugitive, you must along with me. (*Leads her out.*)

Valentine's party beats the bravos off; one wounded stays. Floriante enters as Charlott did.

FLORIANTE.

What noise was that?   25

BRAVO.

Some help I hope.

FLORIANTE.

How my sister Charlott has succeeded under my name with her count tomorrow will discover.*

BRAVO.

Hah! The count then has the wrong woman.

FLORIANTE.

Would Valentine were come.   30

BRAVO.

Oh, would he were to help me!

FLORIANTE.

Who's there? a man wounded?

BRAVO.

One of your servants, if you are Floriante.

FLORIANTE.

I am.

BRAVO.

And wounded in your cause.   35

FLORIANTE.

I'm sorry for't. Do you belong to Valentine?

BRAVO.

I do.

FLORIANTE.

Where is he?

BRAVO.

He got off safe, and if you'll lend me your charitable hand, I'll guide you to him. (*She leads him off.*) 40

Re-enter Valentine and Sir Anthony.

SIR ANTHONY.

Rogues, sons of whores, and cowards!

FLORIANTE.

Sir Anthony.

SIR ANTHONY.

Here am I.

VALENTINE.

Floriante!

FLORIANTE.

Valentine! 45

VALENTINE.

I was afraid I had lost you.

FLORIANTE.

Here's an honest man was conducting me to you, one of your friends.

VALENTINE.

One of my friends! He's one I did not reckon upon 50 if he be. This is one of Count Vérole's bravos.

BRAVO.

I am, and had not you interrupted me, I had done my master service, carried the lady to him.

FLORIANTE.

What a mischief I have 'scaped—

VALENTINE.

Thou art a gallant fellow and dost deserve a better 55 master, but thou hast done thy duty, and I will do mine. Carry him home and get a surgeon to him—

[Bravo] led off.

FLORIANTE.

Well, I run a mighty venture.

SIR ANTHONY.

Of losing a maidenhead, I grant you.

FLORIANTE.

I may repent— 60

SIR ANTHONY.

The keeping of it so long.

FLORIANTE.

I may repent at leisure.

VALENTINE.

You may indeed, if you don't make haste, for we must expect to be pursued.

SIR ANTHONY.

You and I, madam, are much about a size. What 65 if we change clothes? It may favor your escape if you come to be followed.

VALENTINE.

Admirably thought on! Madam, you need not make a scruple of shifting before Sir Anthony, whom from this time you may know to be a woman. 70

FLORIANTE.

A woman!

SIR ANTHONY.

Now for my petticoats again.

Exeunt.

Scene vi. The abbé's house.

Count Canaille, Count Vérole, Abbé and Charlott.

CANAILLE.

Sir, I must thank you for the care you have shown of my family, though I believe it has carried you farther than you are aware of: this is my daughter Charlott.

VÉROLE.

Charlott!

ABBÉ.

Charlott! 5

CHARLOTT.

The very same. But Floriante is obliged to you; you meant this favor to her. But by this time, she has put herself into the care of a gentleman who will find a kinder way of disposing her than into the hands of her father. 10

CANAILLE.

Dishonorable girl!

VÉROLE.

If it be possible, I'll recover her and yet revenge my love. (*Exit.*)

CANAILLE.

But Charlott, how came you to think of running away with Valentine, when you know I designed 15 you to marry him.

CHARLOTT.

Why, I thank you, sir, you designed very well for me, but I was too well acquainted with Valentine

and my sister's thoughts to depend over much
upon that hope. I knew there was no parting them,
therefore consented the easier to assist her in
getting out of the nunnery.

ABBÉ.

Very well.

CANAILLE.

Very well, Brother!

ABBÉ.

Let her go on.

CHARLOTT.

I began to apprehend the danger of staying behind
in a place and profession wholly disagreeable to my
humor.*

ABBÉ.

And well you might.

CHARLOTT.

I thought fit to provide for myself.

ABBÉ.

In good time you did, Niece.

CHARLOTT.

And accordingly, in my sister's name, I sent to
Count Vérole. He came at the time appointed,
expecting Floriante, but Valentine, by what accident
I know not, coming before his time, knowing
nothing of me or my plot upon the count, took me
for her, called me Floriante, upon which his bravos
fell upon Valentine. But the count, in a more
gentlemanly regard to his person, encountered me
and brought me where you find me.

ABBÉ.

But methinks the count, taking you for Floriante,
his old mistress, might ha' made another use of his
victory than to have brought you in triumph to
your father.

CHARLOTT.

I expected he would indeed, but by what he said
to me, I found he had little or no design in coming
there but to revenge himself upon my sister and
her scorn.

CANAILLE.

I'm glad he has no other design upon her.

CHARLOTT.

And so am I, indeed, sir.

ABBÉ.

Why Charlott? You are not in love with the count?

CHARLOTT.

Not so much in love with the count as I am out of
love with a nunnery: any man had been as welcome.

CANAILLE.

Well, well. If Valentine be not hurt, this matter will
clear of itself—

ABBÉ.

And so it will, I warrant you.

Exeunt.

Scene vii. The street.

Enter Sir Gentle Golding.

SIR GENTLE.

Why, how a man may be mistaken in his friends!
I could not ha' believed it (had not one of their
underling rogues told me so himself) that anyone
could ha' been so cheated as I have been by my
own countrymen. If I durst but send any of 'em a
challenge, I might get some of my money again,
but that may draw me into a worse praemunire[44]
than I have yet been in. Let me see: Can't I have a
safer revenge upon 'em? Valentine has stolen a
fortune and entrusted me to bring a father to
marry 'em. Now if I should go willfully in a
mistake to the gentlewoman's own father for a
license to marry 'em— The truth on't is, I have a
mind to forbid the banns and get her myself if I
can, for Floriante is a woman of quality.*

*Count Vérole in pursuit of [Floriante], enters with his
bravos.*

VÉROLE.

Do you know her, sir?

SIR GENTLE.

Yes sir, I think I do.

VÉROLE.

Then as you are a gentleman, assist me; thus far I
have news of her.

SIR GENTLE.

I am a gentleman, sir; you shall find me a

---

44 praemunire] a legal term signifying a severe form of punishment such as banishment or the loss of one's property that had passed into common usage with the sense
of a nasty predicament

gentleman, and I'll tell you more news of her. I'll carry you to the very place where she is, sir, and that's as much as you can expect from a gentleman, when a friend is concerned.

VÉROLE.

It is indeed, sir, more than I expected. Pray, along 25
with me.

Exeunt. Valentine with Floriante in Sir Anthony's and Sir Anthony in her clothes.

VALENTINE.

So far we are safe, ladies, and the shifting your habits will secure us so. Would Sir Gentle would come again.—You're grave at the thought of him!

FLORIANTE.

Men of your conversation* and experience in the 30
world, Valentine, seldom like the women you marry.

VALENTINE.

Because we seldom marry the women we like.

FLORIANTE.

Well, since marriage at best is a venture, I had as good make it myself as let another make it for me at my cost. 35

VALENTINE.

To let a father choose for you in love is as unlucky as, when you are in fancy at play* and pushing at a sum, to desire another to throw out your hand.

SIR ANTHONY. (*Looking out.*)

I'll be hanged if that fool Sir Gentle has not betrayed us. 40

VALENTINE.

Yonder he comes, indeed, with a rabble of rogues at his heels.

SIR ANTHONY.

There's no resisting 'em. Provide for yourselves as well as you can.

Exeunt [Valentine and Floriante].

I have yet a trick to cozen 'em. (*Exit.*) 45

Enter Sir Gentle and Vérole as before.

VÉROLE.

See, see, upon sight of us, they have quitted their prize: Is this their English gallantry? They're out of sight already. Let 'em go, the lady is our game. (*Exit with followers.*)

SIR GENTLE.

I'll make some of 'em know to their cost that by 50
using me so little like a gentleman they have taught me to do as I do and use 'em as they deserve.

Vérole returns with Sir Anthony.

VÉROLE.

Now, Floriante, you find you have thrown yourself away upon a fellow that has not the spirit to stand by you, or himself, to keep your folly in 55
countenance.

SIR ANTHONY.

Pray sir, a word with you— (*Takes him aside.*)

VÉROLE.

Well, madam, what can you say to me?

SIR ANTHONY.

Why, I say you're an ass to run about to disturb other people. I am Sir Anthony Love, not 60
Floriante. Don't discover* me for your own sake, but get you gone about your business and leave me to this Englishman.

VÉROLE.

I'll take his advice, for fear of being laughed at.— Sir, you have behaved yourself so like a man of 65
honor in this business that I must desire you to take care of the lady while I go to inform her father of what has happened.

Exit Vérole and his followers.

SIR GENTLE.

Yes, yes, I'll take care of her, I warrant you.—Why what a lucky rogue am I! Upon my first inclination 70
to play the knave, to have so good an occasion of doing it. And indeed, who would take a trust upon him but for the privilege and benefit of breaking it?—So, madam, now I have you in my care.

SIR ANTHONY.

You are a civil gentleman, I know you. 75

SIR GENTLE.

You shall know me for a civil gentleman, if you please, though I am a knight where I am not familiar.

SIR ANTHONY.

I know you are, sir; you may have pity for me.

SIR GENTLE.

Alack a day! I have indeed a heart brimful for you. 80

SIR ANTHONY.

You won't force me to marry that monster?

SIR GENTLE.

Not I, as I hope to be saved, madam, nothing against fancy.

SIR ANTHONY.

To throw away my youth, beauty, and fortune, which you know are not contemptible.   85

SIR GENTLE.

Incomparable, madam, incomparable. Your youth and beauty without your fortune—

SIR ANTHONY.

Would they were worth your asking.

SIR GENTLE.

Would I might have 'em for the asking.

SIR ANTHONY.

Valentine I despair of, but if there be an   90
Englishman, as an Englishman he must be—

SIR GENTLE.

Why, I am an Englishman, and would marry you.

SIR ANTHONY.

The sooner you secure me the better, then.

SIR GENTLE.

I think so too, madam.

*Exeunt. Canaille, Vérole, Abbé, Ilford, Volante,
Charlott enter.*

ABBÉ.

Why here's a night of action, indeed. Ilford, you   95
began the dance with Volante, and Count, I hope
you'll continue it with my niece Charlott. As for
Valentine and Floriante, they have had their frisk
in a corner by this time, or he is not the man I
take him for.   100

VÉROLE.

When you fell into my hands tonight, had I
known my good fortune, I had improved it then,
but now I have it in having you—and am^k happier
yet in having your consent.

CANAILLE.

You have my blessing both.   105

Valentine and Floriante at the door.

ABBÉ.

You may appear, we're all of a family now, cousins-
german, and friends.—Come here's a pair that
wants your blessing, too.

CANAILLE.

I can't deny it now. Rise and be happy.

ABBÉ.

I have a blessing too for you, my girls: five thousand   110
crowns a piece more than I designed you, and a
thousand extraordinary for her who brings me the
first boy. A small gratuity, gentlemen, to keep up
your fancy and encourage your pains, that you
mayn't think it unprofitable labor upon your wives.   115

CANAILLE.

But why in Sir Anthony's clothes, Floriante? Where
is this mad knight?

FLORIANTE.

Somewhere in my petticoats, but the count can
give you the best tidings of him.

VÉROLE.

I left him with one Sir Gentle Golding, one whom   120
you are beholden to, for familiarly, upon the first
word, he betrayed you and carried me to seize you.

VALENTINE.

Well, I don't doubt but she will give us a handsome
revenge upon him.

CANAILLE.

She? Who?   125

VALENTINE.

Sir Anthony, sir, for this Sir Anthony, after all, is
a woman.

OMNES.

A woman!

ABBÉ.

Aye, pox take her, she is a woman.

VOLANTE.

Then I am free indeed.   130

ILFORD.

And I am happy.

VALENTINE.

At leisure I'll tell you all her story.

Enter Sir Gentle with Sir Anthony.

SIR GENTLE.

Now, I am sufficiently revenged on Valentine and
Sir Anthony for cheating me. I think I have paid
'em in their own coin and disappointed the count,   135
too, in marrying Floriante.

OMNES.

Floriante!

SIR GENTLE.

Come father-in-law, this business will out I see. If you'll give us your blessing, so; if not, I shall begin upon your daughter without saying grace. 140

CANAILLE.

Much good may do you sir, with your bride.

VALENTINE.

Aye, aye, we must all wish you joy, sir: you have a blessing sufficient in a good wife—

SIR ANTHONY.

If you know when you're well.

SIR GENTLE.

Oh deliver me! What do I see! 145

VALENTINE.

Why, you see your old Mrs.* Lucy in your new lady*-wife. We are all witnesses of your owning your marriage.

SIR GENTLE.

I do not own it! I'll hang like a dog, drown like a blind puppy, die and be damned, but I'll be 150 divorced from her.

VALENTINE.

That's your nearest way to divorce.

ILFORD.

And will save the trouble of Doctor's Commons.*

VALENTINE.

Come, come, I'll put you in a better. There are old scores between you and Mrs. Lucy—you have 155 made her a lady indeed, which shows a grateful nature in you and will sound well in the ears of the world. But to support her quality*—

SIR GENTLE.

Her qualities will support that.

VALENTINE.

Out of your two thousand pounds a year, give her 160 a rent-charge of five hundred, and she shall never trouble you more, not so much as to be a godfather to another man's child upon her body, which may otherwise inherit your acres.

SIR GENTLE.

Why there's the devil on't again, to father another 165 man's children when one is not so much as a kin to 'em! Well, any composition to be rid of her; I find 'tis a blessing I must pay for.

VALENTINE.

Come, come, we must have a dance to all these weddings. 170

A Dance.

SIR ANTHONY.

Thus coxcombs always the best husbands prove:
When we are faulty and begin to rove,
A sep'rate maintenance* supplies our love.

SIR GENTLE.

When we have mistresses above our sense,
We must redeem our persons with our pence. 175

[Exeunt.]

FINIS.

Textual Notes

a The copytext is the first quarto printed in 1691 (Q1). Also consulted: a 1698 quarto (Q2); the first collected edition in duodecimo in 1713 (D1); the second collected duodecimo in 1721 (D2); a third collected duodecimo in 1774 (D3); and the modern edition in 1988 (Jordan and Love).

b churches] Qq, Jordan and Love; bodies Dd

c suffer] Qq; suspect Dd, Jordan and Love

d A song] printed as an appendix in all editions; placement suggested by Jordan and Love

e humor] Qq, D1, D2, Jordan and Love; honor D3

f get] Dd, Jordan and Love; got Qq

g down] Jordan and Love; along Qq, Dd

h an't] and Qq, Dd, Jordan and Love

i My good friend Mrs. Lucy!] Dd, Jordan and Love; *om.* Qq

j Who's] Dd, Jordan and Love; What's Qq

k am] Jordan and Love; *om.* Qq, Dd

The Beaux' Stratagem[a]

by George Farquhar (1677?-1707)

edited by Helen M. Burke

George Farquhar was the son of a Protestant clergyman from the north of Ireland, and as such, he was born into the Anglo-Irish colonial ruling class. Nevertheless, as a refugee of war—his family was burnt out of their estate in the 1689–91 wars—and as a penniless Anglo-Irishman living in London, Farquhar was always somewhat of an outsider in the English society of his day, and this outsider's perspective informs all his comedies, including his last work, *The Beaux' Stratagem*.

First performed on March 8, 1707, at the Queen's Theatre in the Haymarket, the play seems, on the surface, to endorse the entrepreneurial and militaristic values of the mercantile class that was then energetically supporting the long-drawn-out War of Spanish Succession. In what could be read as an allegory of the wished-for outcome of this war, the play's two heroes, Archer and Aimwell, defeat a plot by a French count and an Irish priest, and in the process, find wealth and happiness. The militaristic connotations of the beaux's names also underline the connection between their "stratagem" and the ongoing war effort.

Anticipating Gay's *The Beggar's Opera* (1728), however, *The Beaux' Stratagem* also focuses on the activities of a gang of common house-breakers and highwaymen, and by showing the overlap between their robbery plot and the beaux's plot, the play offers a subtle critique of the expansionist ethos of the new Great Britain. Fine gentlemen, like Archer and Aimwell, it suggests, are, in many ways, indistinguishable from "gentlemen of the pad" (highwaymen); money and power are the dominant values in both groups.

A similar instability marks the sexual politics of this play. Again the play pays lip service to emerging middle-class values when it ensures that Mrs. Sullen never breaks her marriage vows and when it shows Aimwell reforming under the influence of Dorinda's goodness. However, in presenting a graphic image of the horrors of a bad marriage, and in advocating divorce on the grounds of irreconcilable differences, *The Beaux' Stratagem* also advances notions that were far in advance of eighteenth-century bourgeois morality and contemporary English marital law.

It was undoubtedly this play's ability to appeal to all sides of the political, social, and sexual spectrum that explains its lasting success. During the entire eighteenth century, it was performed on the London stage every season but one, and it was equally a favorite in Dublin and in provincial theaters.

DRAMATIS PERSONAE

MEN

Aimwell and Archer, two gentlemen of broken fortunes, the first as master, and the second as servant.

Count Bellair, a French officer, prisoner at Litchfield.[1]

Sullen, a country blockhead, brutal to his wife.

Freeman, a gentleman from London.

Foigard,[2] a priest, chaplain to the French officers.

Gibbet, a highwayman.

Hounslow and Bagshot,[3] his companions.

Bonniface, landlord of the inn.

Scrub, servant to Mr. Sullen.

WOMEN

Lady Bountiful, an old, civil country gentle-woman, that cures all her neighbors of all distempers, foolishly fond of her son, Sullen.

Dorinda, Lady Bountiful's daughter.

Mrs. Sullen, her daughter-in-law.

Gipsey, maid to the ladies.

Cherry, the landlord's daughter in the inn.

SCENE: LITCHFIELD.

The Beaux' Stratagem.

Act I, scene i. An inn.

Enter Bonniface running.

BONNIFACE.

Chamberlain![4] Maid! Cherry! daughter Cherry! all asleep? all dead?

Enter Cherry running.

CHERRY.

Here, here! Why d'ye bawl so, father? D'ye think we have no ears?

---

1 Litchfield] modern Lichfield, a town in Staffordshire in central England

2 Foigard] garbled French for, ironically, guardian of the faith

3 Hounslow and Bagshot] named after two London heaths that were favorite haunts of highwaymen

4 Chamberlain] the servant in charge of the bedchambers

BONNIFACE.

You deserve to have none, you young minx! The company of the Warrington[5] coach has stood in the hall this hour and nobody to show them to their chambers. 5

CHERRY.

And let 'em wait farther![b] There's neither redcoat in the coach, nor footman behind it. 10

BONNIFACE.

But they threaten to go to another inn tonight.

CHERRY.

That they dare not, for fear the coachman should overturn them tomorrow.—Coming! coming!—Here's the London coach arrived!

Enter several people with trunks, bandboxes, and other luggage, and cross the stage.

BONNIFACE.

Welcome, ladies!

CHERRY.

Very welcome, gentlemen!—Chamberlain, show the Lion and the Rose.[6] (*Exit with the company.*) 15

Enter Aimwell in riding habit, Archer as footman carrying a portmanteau.

BONNIFACE.

This way, this way, gentlemen!

AIMWELL.

Set down the things. Go to the stable, and see my horses well rubbed. 20

ARCHER.

I shall, sir. (*Exit.*)

AIMWELL.

You're my landlord, I suppose?

BONNIFACE.

Yes sir, I'm old Will Bonniface, pretty well known upon this road, as the saying is.

AIMWELL.

Oh Mr. Bonniface, your servant! 25

BONNIFACE.

Oh sir! What will your honor please to drink, as the saying is?

---

5 Warrington] a town about sixty miles from Litchfield

6 Lion ... Rose] names of bedrooms in the inn

AIMWELL.

I have heard your town of Litchfield much famed for ale. I think I'll taste that.

BONNIFACE.

Sir, I have now in my cellar ten tun of the best ale in Staffordshire; 'tis smooth as oil, sweet as milk, clear as amber, and strong as brandy and will be just fourteen year old the fifth day of next March old style.[7]   30

AIMWELL.

You're very exact, I find, in the age of your ale.   35

BONNIFACE.

As punctual, sir, as I am in the age of my children. I'll show you such ale!—Here, tapster, broach number 1706,[8] as the saying is.—Sir, you shall taste my *Anno Domini*. I have lived in Litchfield, man and boy, above eight and fifty years and, I believe, have not consumed eight and fifty ounces of meat.   40

AIMWELL.

At a meal, you mean, if one may guess your sense by your bulk.

BONNIFACE.

Not in my life, sir; I have fed purely upon ale. I have eat my ale, drank my ale, and I always sleep upon ale.   45

Enter tapster with a bottle and glass.

Now, sir, you shall see! (*Filling it out.*) Your worship's health. Hah! delicious, delicious—fancy it burgundy, only fancy it, and 'tis worth ten shillings a quart!   50

AIMWELL. (*Drinks.*)

'Tis confounded strong!

BONNIFACE.

Strong! It must be so, or how should we be strong that drink it?

AIMWELL.

And have you lived so long upon this ale, landlord?

BONNIFACE.

Eight and fifty years, upon my credit, sir, but it killed my wife, poor woman, as the saying is.   55

AIMWELL.

How came that to pass?

BONNIFACE.

I don't know how, sir. She would not let the ale take its natural course, sir; she was for qualifying it every now and then with a dram, as the saying is, and an honest gentleman that came this way from Ireland made her a present of a dozen bottles of usquebaugh[9]—but the poor woman was never well after. But howe'er, I was obliged to the gentleman, you know.   60   65

AIMWELL.

Why, was it the usquebaugh that killed her?

BONNIFACE.

My Lady Bountiful said so. She, good lady, did what could be done: she cured her of three tympanies, but the fourth carried her off. But she's happy, and I'm contented, as the saying is.   70

AIMWELL.

Who's that Lady Bountiful, you mentioned?

BONNIFACE.

'Od's* my life, sir, we'll drink her health! (*Drinks.*) My Lady Bountiful is one of the best of women. Her last husband, Sir Charles Bountiful, left her worth a thousand pound a year, and I believe she lays out one half on't in charitable uses for the good of her neighbors. She cures rheumatisms, ruptures, and broken shins in men; greensickness, obstructions, and fits of the mother* in women; the king's evil, chincough,[10] and chilblains in children. In short, she has cured more people in and about Litchfield within ten years than the doctors have killed in twenty, and that's a bold word.   75   80

AIMWELL.

Has the lady been any other way useful in her generation?   85

BONNIFACE.

Yes, sir. She has a daughter by Sir Charles, the finest woman in all our country, and the greatest fortune.

---

7 old style] Until 1752, England used the Julian calendar which was eleven days behind the calendar used in many other parts of western Europe.

8 1706] The code number given to this ale (1706) suggests that it was brewed the previous year, not fourteen years earlier.

9 usquebaugh] whiskey; *uisce beatha*, literally "the water of life" (Irish)

10 chincough] whooping-cough

She has a son, too, by her first husband, Squire
Sullen, who married a fine lady from London t'other
day; if you please, sir, we'll drink his health.   90

AIMWELL.

What sort of a man is he?

BONNIFACE.

Why sir, the man's well enough: says little, thinks
less, and does—nothing at all, faith! But he's a man
of a great estate, and values nobody.

AIMWELL.

A sportsman, I suppose?   95

BONNIFACE.

Yes sir, he's a man of pleasure. He plays at whist
and smokes his pipe eight and forty hours together
sometimes.

AIMWELL.

And married, you say?

BONNIFACE.

Aye, and to a curious woman, sir. But he's a —he   100
wants* it, here, sir. (*Pointing to his forehead.*)

AIMWELL.

He has it there, you mean.[11]

BONNIFACE.

That's none of my business. He's my landlord, and
so a man, you know, would not—but, icod,[12] he's
no better than—sir, my humble service to you.   105
(*Drinks.*) Though I value not a farthing what he can
do to me, I pay him his rent at quarter day,[13] I have
a good running trade, I have but one daughter, and
I can give her—but no matter for that.

AIMWELL.

You're very happy, Mr. Bonniface. Pray what other   110
company have you in town?

BONNIFACE.

A power of fine ladies, and then we have the
French officers.[14]

AIMWELL.

Oh, that's right, you have a good many of those
gentlemen. Pray how do you like their company?   115

---

11 has it there] wears the horns of a cuckold

12 icod] rural variant of egad, a mild oath

13 quarter day] one of four fixed days of the year for paying rent

14 French officers] officers captured during the ongoing
War of Spanish Succession and quartered on parole in
various parts of England

BONNIFACE.

So well, as the saying is, that I could wish we had
as many more of 'em. They're full of money and
pay double for every thing they have. They know,
sir, that we paid good round taxes for the taking
of 'em, and so they are willing to reimburse us a   120
little. One of 'em lodges in my house.

Enter Archer.

ARCHER.

Landlord, there are some French gentlemen below
that ask for you.

BONNIFACE.

I'll wait on 'em. (*[Aside] to Archer.*) Does your
master stay long in town, as the saying is?   125

ARCHER.

I can't tell, as the saying is.

BONNIFACE.

Come from London?

ARCHER.

No.

BONNIFACE.

Going to London, mayhap?

ARCHER.

No.   130

BONNIFACE.

An odd fellow this!—I beg your worship's pardon.
I'll wait on you in half a minute. (*Exit.*)

AIMWELL.

The coast's clear, I see.—Now, my dear Archer,
welcome to Litchfield!

ARCHER.

I thank thee, my dear brother in iniquity.   135

AIMWELL.

Iniquity! prithee leave canting! You need not
change your style with your dress.

ARCHER.

Don't mistake me, Aimwell, for 'tis still* my maxim
that there is no scandal like rags nor any crime so
shameful as poverty.   140

AIMWELL.

The world confesses it every day in its practice,
though men won't own it for their opinion. Who
did that worthy lord, my brother, single out of the
side box to sup with him t'other night?

ARCHER.

Jack Handicraft, a handsome, well dressed, mannerly, sharping[15] rogue, who keeps the best company in town.

AIMWELL.

Right, and pray who married my Lady Manslaughter t'other day, the great fortune?

ARCHER.

Why, Nick Marrabone,* a professed pickpocket, and a good bowler, but he makes a handsome figure and rides in his coach that he formerly used to ride behind.

AIMWELL.

But did you observe poor Jack Generous* in the Park* last week?

ARCHER.

Yes, with his autumnal periwig shading his melancholy face, his coat older than anything but its fashion, with one hand idle in his pocket and with the other picking his useless teeth. And though the Mall* was crowded with company, yet was poor Jack as single and solitary as a lion in a desert.

AIMWELL.

And as much avoided for no crime upon earth but the want* of money.

ARCHER.

And that's enough. Men must not be poor; idleness is the root of all evil. The world's wide enough; let 'em bustle. Fortune has taken the weak under her protection, but men of sense are left to their industry.

AIMWELL.

Upon which topic we proceed and, I think, luckily hitherto. Would not any man swear now that I am a man of quality* and you my servant, when if our intrinsic value were known—

ARCHER.

Come, come, we are the men of intrinsic value, who can strike our fortunes out of ourselves, whose worth is independent of accidents in life or revolutions in government. We have heads to get money and hearts to spend it.

AIMWELL.

As to our hearts, I grant ye, they are as willing tits[16] as any within twenty degrees, but I can have

no great opinion of our heads from the service they have done us hitherto, unless it be that they have brought us from London hither to Litchfield, made me a lord, and you my servant.

ARCHER.

That's more than you could expect already. But what money have we left?

AIMWELL.

But two hundred pound.

ARCHER.

And our horses, clothes, rings, etcetera— Why, we have very good fortunes now for moderate people, and let me tell you, besides, that this two hundred pound, with the experience that we are now masters of, is a better estate than the ten thousand[c] we have spent. Our friends, indeed, began to suspect that our pockets were low, but we came off with flying colors, showed no signs of want* either in word or deed.

AIMWELL.

Aye, and our going to Brussels was a good pretence enough for our sudden disappearing, and, I warrant you, our friends imagine that we are gone a-volunteering.

ARCHER.

Why faith, if this prospect fails, it must e'en come to that. I am for venturing one of the hundreds, if you will, upon this knight-errantry, but in case it should fail, we'll reserve the t'other to carry us to some counter scarp, where we may die as we lived—in a blaze.

AIMWELL.

With all my heart. And we have lived justly, Archer: we can't say that we have spent our fortunes but that we have enjoyed 'em.

ARCHER.

Right! So much pleasure for so much money! We have had our pennyworths, and had I millions, I would go to the same market again. Oh London, London! Well, we have had our share, and let us be thankful. Past pleasures, for aught I know, are best, such as we are sure of; those to come may disappoint us.

AIMWELL.

It has often grieved the heart of me to see how some inhuman wretches murder their kind fortunes— those that by sacrificing all to one appetite shall

---

15 sharping] cheating
16 tits] serviceable horses

starve all the rest. You shall have some that live only
in their palates and, in their sense of tasting, shall
drown the other four. Others are only epicures in
appearances, such who shall starve their nights to   220
make a figure a-days and famish their own to feed
the eyes of others. A contrary sort confine their
pleasures to the dark and contract their spacious
acres to the circuit of a muff-string.[17]

ARCHER.

Right, but they find the Indies in the spot where   225
they consume 'em, and I think your kind keepers*
have much the best on't, for they indulge the most
senses by one expense. There's the seeing, hearing,
and feeling amply gratified, and some philosophers
will tell you that from such a commerce, there   230
arises a sixth sense that gives infinitely more
pleasure than the other five put together.

AIMWELL.

And to pass to the other extremity, of all keepers,
I think those the worst that keep their money.

ARCHER.

Those are the most miserable wights in being: they   235
destroy the rights of Nature, and disappoint the
blessings of Providence. Give me a man that keeps
his five senses keen and bright as his sword, that
has 'em always drawn out in their just order and
strength with his reason as commander at the head   240
of 'em, that detaches 'em by turns upon whatever
party of pleasure agreeably offers* and commands
'em to retreat upon the least appearance of
disadvantage or danger. For my part I can stick to
my bottle, while my wine, my company, and my   245
reason holds good. I can be charmed with Sappho's
singing without falling in love with her face; I love
hunting, but would not, like Actaeon, be eaten up
by my own dogs; I love a fine house, but let
another keep it; and just so I love a fine woman.   250

AIMWELL.

In that last particular you have the better of me.

ARCHER.

Aye, you're such an amorous puppy that I'm afraid
you'll spoil our sport: you can't counterfeit the
passion without feeling it.

AIMWELL.

Though the whining part be out-of-doors[18] in   255
Town,* 'tis still in force with the country ladies.
And let my tell you, Frank, the fool in that passion
shall outdo the knave at any time.

ARCHER.

Well, I won't dispute it now; you command for the
day, and so I submit. At Nottingham, you know,   260
I am to be master.

AIMWELL.

And at Lincoln, I again.

ARCHER.

Then at Norwich I mount, which, I think, shall be
our last stage, for if we fail there, we'll embark for
Holland, bid adieu to Venus, and welcome Mars.   265

AIMWELL.

A match!

Enter Bonniface.

Mum!

BONNIFACE.

What will your worship please to have for supper?

AIMWELL.

What have you got?

BONNIFACE.

Sir, we have a delicate piece of beef in the pot and   270
a pig at the fire.

AIMWELL.

Good supper-meat, I must confess. I can't eat beef,
landlord.

ARCHER.

And I hate pig.

AIMWELL.

Hold your prating, sirrah! Do you know who you   275
are?

BONNIFACE.

Please to bespeak something else; I have everything
in the house.

AIMWELL.

Have you any veal?

BONNIFACE.

Veal! Sir, we had a delicate loin of veal on   280
Wednesday last.

AIMWELL.

Have you got any fish or wildfowl?

---

17 muff-string] string attaching a hand-covering to a woman's neck

18 out-of-doors] unfashionable

BONNIFACE.

As for fish, truly, sir, we are an inland town and indifferently provided with fish, that's the truth on't, and then for wildfowl—we have a delicate 285 couple of rabbits.

AIMWELL.

Get me the rabbits fricasseed.

BONNIFACE.

Fricasseed! Lard, sir, they'll eat much better smothered with onions.

ARCHER.

Pshaw! Damn your onions! 290

AIMWELL.

Again, sirrah!—Well landlord, what you please. But hold, I have a small charge of money, and your house is so full of strangers that I believe it may be safer in your custody than mine, for when this fellow of mine gets drunk, he minds nothing.— 295 Here sirrah, reach me the strongbox.

ARCHER.

Yes, sir. (*Aside.*) This will give us a reputation. (*Brings the box.*)

AIMWELL.

Here, landlord. The locks are sealed down both for your security and mine. It holds somewhat above 300 two hundred pound; if you doubt it, I'll count it to you after supper. But be sure you lay it where I may have it at a minute's warning, for my affairs are a little dubious at present: perhaps I may be gone in half an hour, perhaps I may be your guest 305 till the best part of that be spent. And pray order your ostler to keep my horses always saddled. But one thing above the rest I must beg, that you would let this fellow have none of your *Anno Domini*, as you call it, for he's the most insufferable 310 sot.—Here sirrah, light me to my chamber. (*Exit, lighted by Archer.*)

BONNIFACE.

Cherry! daughter Cherry!

Enter Cherry.

CHERRY.

D'ye call, father?

BONNIFACE.

Aye, child. You must lay by this box for the 315 gentleman: 'tis full of money.

CHERRY.

Money! all that money! Why sure, father, the gentleman comes to be chosen parliament-man.[19] Who is he?

BONNIFACE.

I don't know what to make of him. He talks of 320 keeping his horses ready saddled and of going perhaps at a minute's warning or of staying perhaps till the best part of this be spent.

CHERRY.

Aye, ten to one, father, he's a highwayman.

BONNIFACE.

A highwayman! Upon my life, girl, you have hit 325 it, and this box is some new-purchased booty. Now could we find him out, the money were ours.

CHERRY.

He don't belong to our gang.

BONNIFACE.

What horses have they?

CHERRY.

The master rides upon a black. 330

BONNIFACE.

A black! Ten to one the man upon the black mare! And since he don't belong to our fraternity, we may betray him with a safe conscience. I don't think it lawful to harbor any rogues but my own. Look'ye, child, as the saying is, we must go cunningly to 335 work; proofs we must have. The gentleman's servant loves drink—I'll ply him that way—and ten to one loves a wench—you must work him t'other way.

CHERRY.

Father, would you have me give my secret for his?

BONNIFACE.

Consider, child, there's two hundred pound to 340 boot. (*Ringing without.*) Coming! coming!—Child, mind your business. [*Exit.*]

CHERRY.

What a rogue is my father! My father! I deny it— my mother was a good, generous, free-hearted woman, and I can't tell how far her good nature 345 might have extended for the good of her children. This landlord of mine, for I think I can call him no more, would betray his guest and debauch his daughter into the bargain—by a footman too!

---

19 parliament-man] Candidates for parliamentary election commonly used bribes to ensure their seats.

Enter Archer.

ARCHER.

What footman, pray mistress, is so happy as to be   350
the subject of your contemplation?

CHERRY.

Whoever he is, friend, he'll be but little the better
for't.

ARCHER.

I hope so, for I'm sure you did not think of me.

CHERRY.

Suppose I had?   355

ARCHER.

Why then, you're but even with me, for the minute
I came in, I was a-considering in what manner I
should make love* to you.

CHERRY.

Love to me, friend!

ARCHER.

Yes, child.*   360

CHERRY.

Child? Manners! If you kept a little more distance,
friend, it would become you much better.

ARCHER.

Distance! Good night, saucebox! (*Going.*)

CHERRY.

A pretty fellow! I like his pride.—Sir, pray sir, you
see, sir, (*Archer returns.*) I have the credit to be   365
entrusted with your master's fortune here, which
sets me a degree above his footman. I hope, sir, you
an't affronted.

ARCHER.

Let me look you full in the face, and I'll tell you
whether you can affront me or no.—S'death,*   370
child, you have a pair of delicate eyes, and you
don't know what to do with 'em!

CHERRY.

Why sir, don't I see everybody?

ARCHER.

Aye, but if some women had 'em, they would kill
everybody. Prithee instruct me, I would fain make   375
love to you, but I don't know what to say.

CHERRY.

Why, did you never make love to anybody before?

ARCHER.

Never to a person of your figure, I can assure you,
madam. My addresses have been always confined

to people within my own sphere; I never aspired   380
so high before. (*Sings*)

A Song.

But you look so bright,
And are dressed so tight,
That a man would swear you're right,
As arm was e'er laid over.   385
    Such an air
    You freely wear
    To ensnare
As makes each guest a lover.

Since then, my dear, I'm your guest,   390
    Prithee give me of the best
    Of what is ready dressed:
Since then, my dear, etc.[d]

CHERRY. (*Aside.*)

What can I think of this man?—Will you give me
that song, sir?   395

ARCHER.

Aye my dear, take it while 'tis warm. (*Kisses her.*)
Death and fire! her lips are honeycombs.

CHERRY.

And I wish there had been bees too, to have stung
you for your impudence.

ARCHER.

There's a swarm of Cupids, my little Venus, that   400
has done the business much better.

CHERRY. (*Aside.*)

This fellow is misbegotten as well as I.—What's
your name, sir?

ARCHER. (*Aside.*)

Name! Egad, I have forgot it!—Oh! Martin.

CHERRY.

Where were you born?   405

ARCHER.

In St. Martin's parish.

CHERRY.

What was your father?

ARCHER.

St. Martin's Parish.[20]

---

[20] Parish] an orphan raised by the parish

CHERRY.

Then, friend, good night!

ARCHER.

I hope not.   410

CHERRY.

You may depend upon't.

ARCHER.

Upon what?

CHERRY.

That you're very impudent.

ARCHER.

That you're very handsome.

CHERRY.

That you're a footman.   415

ARCHER.

That you're an angel.

CHERRY.

I shall be rude.

ARCHER.

So shall I.

CHERRY.

Let go my hand.

ARCHER.

Give me a kiss. (*Kisses her.*)   420

[BONIFACE.] (*Calls without.*)

Cherry! Cherry!

CHERRY.

I'm-m^e—my father calls. You plaguy devil, how
durst you stop my breath so? Offer* to follow me
one step, if you dare! [*Exit.*]

ARCHER.

A fair challenge, by this light! This is a pretty fair   425
opening of an adventure, but we are knight-
errants, and so Fortune be our guide.

Exit.

Act II, scene [i]. A gallery in Lady Bountiful's house.

Mrs. Sullen and Dorinda meeting.

DORINDA.

Morrow, my dear sister. Are you for church this
morning?

MRS. SULLEN.

Anywhere to pray, for Heaven alone can help me.
But I think, Dorinda, there's no form of prayer in
the liturgy against bad husbands.   5

DORINDA.

But there's a form of law in Doctors Commons,*
and I swear, sister Sullen, rather than see you thus
continually discontented, I would advise you to
apply to that. For besides the part that I bear in
your vexatious broils, as being sister to the husband   10
and friend to the wife, your example gives me such
an impression of matrimony that I shall be apt to
condemn my person to a long vacation all its life.
But supposing, madam, that you brought it to a
case of separation, what can you urge against your   15
husband? My brother is, first, the most constant
man alive.

MRS. SULLEN.

The most constant husband, I grant ye.

DORINDA.

He never sleeps from you.

MRS. SULLEN.

No, he always sleeps with me.   20

DORINDA.

He allows you a maintenance suitable to your
quality.*

MRS. SULLEN.

A maintenance! Do you take me, madam, for an
hospital child,[21] that I must sit down and bless my
benefactors for meat, drink and clothes? As I take   25
it, madam, I brought your brother ten thousand
pounds, out of which I might expect some pretty
things called pleasures.

DORINDA.

You share in all the pleasures that the country
affords.   30

MRS. SULLEN.

Country pleasures! Racks and torments! Dost
think, child,* that my limbs were made for leaping
of ditches and clambering over stiles? or that my
parents, wisely foreseeing my future happiness in
country pleasures, had early instructed me in the   35
rural accomplishments of drinking fat[22] ale,
playing at whist, and smoking tobacco with my
husband? or of spreading of plasters, brewing of
diet-drinks, and stilling rosemary-water with the
good old gentlewoman, my mother-in-law?   40

---

21 hospital child] one in a charitable institution
22 fat] full-bodied

DORINDA.

I'm sorry, madam, that it is not more in our power to divert you; I could wish, indeed, that our entertainments were a little more polite or your taste a little less refined. But pray madam, how came the poets and philosophers, that labored so much in hunting after pleasure, to place it at last in a country life? 45

MRS. SULLEN.

Because they wanted* money, child, to find out the pleasures of the Town. Did you ever see a poet or philosopher worth ten thousand pound? If you can show me such a man, I'll lay you fifty pound you'll find him somewhere within the weekly bills.* Not that I disapprove rural pleasures, as the poets have painted them! In their landscape, every Phyllis has her Corydon,²³ every murmuring stream and every flowery mead gives fresh alarms to love. Besides, you'll find that their couples were never married.— But yonder I see my Corydon, and a sweet swain it is, Heaven knows!—Come Dorinda, don't be angry, he's my husband and your brother, and between both is he not a sad brute? 60

DORINDA.

I have nothing to say to your part of him. You're the best judge.

MRS. SULLEN.

Oh sister, sister! if ever you marry, beware of a sullen, silent sot, one that's always musing but never thinks! There's some diversion in a talking blockhead, and since a woman must wear chains, I would have the pleasure of hearing 'em rattle a little. Now you shall see, but take this by the way: He came home this morning at his usual hour of four, wakened me out of a sweet dream of something else by tumbling over the tea table, which he broke all to pieces; after his man and he had rolled about the room like sick passengers in a storm, he comes flounce into bed, dead as a salmon into a fishmonger's basket, his feet cold as ice, his breath hot as a furnace, and his hands and his face as greasy as his flannel nightcap—oh, matrimony! He tosses up the clothes with a barbarous swing over his shoulders, disorders the 50 55 65 70 75

whole economy of my bed, leaves me half naked, and my whole night's comfort is the tuneable serenade of that wakeful nightingale, his nose! Oh, the pleasure of counting the melancholy clock by a snoring husband! But now, sister, you shall see how handsomely, being a well-bred man, he will beg my pardon. 80 85

Enter Sullen.

SULLEN.

My head aches consumedly.

MRS. SULLEN.

Will you be pleased, my dear, to drink tea with us this morning? It may do your head good.

SULLEN.

No. 90

DORINDA.

Coffee, brother?

SULLEN.

Pshaw!

MRS. SULLEN.

Will you please to dress and go to church with me? The air may help you.

SULLEN.

Scrub!²⁴ 95

Enter Scrub.

SCRUB.

Sir!

SULLEN.

What day o'th'week is this?

SCRUB.

Sunday, an't* please your worship.

SULLEN.

Sunday! Bring me a dram, and d'ye hear, set out the venison pasty and a tankard of strong beer upon the hall table. I'll go to breakfast. (*Going.*) 100

DORINDA.

Stay, stay, brother, you shan't get off so; you were very naught* last night and must make your wife reparation. Come, come, brother, won't you ask pardon? 105

---

23 Phyllis … Corydon] typical names for a nymph and her swain in pastoral poetry

24 Scrub] His name refers to his household function but also to his stunted growth; this role was originally played by Norris, an actor who was short in stature.

SULLEN.

For what?

DORINDA.

For being drunk last night.

SULLEN.

I can afford it, can't I?

MRS. SULLEN.

But I can't, sir.

SULLEN.

Then you may let it alone.   110

MRS. SULLEN.

But I must tell you, sir, that this is not to be borne.

SULLEN.

I'm glad on't.

MRS. SULLEN.

What is the reason, sir, that you use me thus
inhumanely?

SULLEN.

Scrub?   115

SCRUB.

Sir!

SULLEN.

Get things ready to shave my head. (*Exit [with
Scrub].*)

MRS. SULLEN.

Have a care of coming near his temples, Scrub, for
fear you meet something there that may turn the   120
edge of your razor.—Inveterate stupidity! Did you
ever know so hard, so obstinate a spleen as his! Oh,
sister, sister! I shall never ha' good of the beast till
I get him to Town: London, dear London, is the
place for managing and breaking a husband.   125

DORINDA.

And has not a husband the same opportunities
there for humbling a wife?

MRS. SULLEN.

No, no, child,* 'tis a standing maxim in conjugal
discipline that when a man would enslave his wife,
he hurries her into the country, and when a lady   130
would be arbitrary with her husband, she wheedles
her booby up to Town. A man dare not play the
tyrant in London because there are so many
examples to encourage the subject to rebel. Oh,
Dorinda! Dorinda! a fine woman may do anything   135
in London; o'my conscience, she may raise an army
of forty thousand men!

DORINDA.

I fancy, sister, you have a mind to be trying your
power that way here in Litchfield: you have drawn
the French count to your colors already.   140

MRS. SULLEN.

The French are a people that can't live without
their gallantries.

DORINDA.

And some English that I know, sister, are not averse
to such amusements.

MRS. SULLEN.

Well sister, since the truth must out, it may do as   145
well now as hereafter. I think one way to rouse my
lethargic, sottish husband is to give him a rival.
Security begets negligence in all people, and men
must be alarmed to make 'em alert in their duty.
Women are like pictures of no value in the hands   150
of a fool till he hears men of sense bid high for
the purchase.

DORINDA.

This might do, sister, if my brother's understanding
were to be convinced into a passion for you. But
I fancy there's a natural aversion of his side, and I   155
fancy, sister, that you don't come much behind
him, if you dealt fairly.

MRS. SULLEN.

I own it: we are united contradictions, fire and
water. But I could be contented, with a great many
other wives, to humor the censorious mob and give   160
the world an appearance of living well with my
husband, could I bring him but to dissemble a
little kindness to keep me in countenance.[25]

DORINDA.

But how do you know, sister, but that instead of
rousing your husband by this artifice to a   165
counterfeit kindness, he should awake in a real
fury?

MRS. SULLEN.

Let him! If I can't entice him to the one, I would
provoke him to the other.

DORINDA.

But how must I behave myself between ye?   170

MRS. SULLEN.

You must assist me.

_____

25 in countenance] so I could save face

DORINDA.

What, against my own brother!

MRS. SULLEN.

He's but half a brother, and I'm your entire friend. If I go a step beyond the bounds of honor, leave me; till then I expect you should go along with me 175 in everything. While I trust my honor in your hands, you may trust your brother's in mine.—The count is to dine here today.

DORINDA.

'Tis a strange thing, sister, that I can't like that man. 180

MRS. SULLEN.

You like nothing; your time is not come. Love and death have their fatalities and strike home one time or other. You'll pay for all one day, I warrant ye.— But come, my lady's tea is ready, and 'tis almost church time. 185

Exeunt.

Scene [ii]. The inn.

Enter Aimwell dressed, and Archer.

AIMWELL.

And was she the daughter of the house?

ARCHER.

The landlord is so blind as to think so, but I dare swear she has better blood in her veins.

AIMWELL.

Why dost think so?

ARCHER.

Because the baggage has a pert *je ne sais quoi;* she 5 reads plays, keeps a monkey, and is troubled with vapors.

AIMWELL.

By which discoveries I guess that you know more of her.

ARCHER.

Not yet, faith! The lady gives herself airs; forsooth, 10 nothing under a gentleman!

AIMWELL.

Let me take her in hand.

ARCHER.

Say one word more o'that, and I'll declare myself, spoil your sport there, and everywhere else. Look'ye, Aimwell, every man in his own sphere! 15

AIMWELL.

Right, and therefore, you must pimp for your master.

ARCHER.

In the usual forms, good sir, after I have served myself.—But to our business. You are so well dressed, Tom, and make so handsome a figure, that 20 I fancy you may do execution in a country church; the exterior part strikes first, and you're in the right to make that impression favorable.

AIMWELL.

There's something in that which may turn to advantage. The appearance of a stranger in a country 25 church draws as many gazers as a blazing star; no sooner he comes into the cathedral but a train of whispers runs buzzing round the congregation in a moment: "Who is he? Whence comes he? Do you know him?" Then I, sir, tips me the verger with half 30 a crown; he pockets the simony and inducts me into the best pew in the church; I pull out my snuffbox, turn my self round, bow to the bishop, or the dean if he be the commanding officer; single out a beauty, rivet both my eyes to hers, set my nose a-bleeding by 35 the strength of imagination, and show the whole church my concern by my endeavoring to hide it. After the sermon, the whole town gives me to her for a lover, and by persuading the lady that I am a-dying for her, the tables are turned, and she in good earnest 40 falls in love with me.

ARCHER.

There's nothing in this, Tom, without a precedent, but instead of riveting your eyes to a beauty, try to fix 'em upon a fortune; that's our business at present.

AIMWELL.

Pshaw! no woman can be a beauty without a 45 fortune. Let me alone, for I am a marksman.

ARCHER.

Tom!

AIMWELL.

Aye.

ARCHER.

When were you at church before, pray?

AIMWELL.

Um—I was there at the coronation.[26] 50

---

[26] coronation] of Queen Anne in 1702

ARCHER.

And how can you expect a blessing by going to church now?

AIMWELL.

Blessing! nay, Frank, I ask but for a wife. (*Exit.*)

ARCHER.

Truly the man is not very unreasonable in his demands. (*Exit at the opposite door.*) 55

Enter Bonniface and Cherry.

BONNIFACE.

Well, daughter, as the saying is, have you brought Martin to confess?

CHERRY.

Pray father, don't put me upon getting anything out of a man; I'm but young, you know, father, and I don't understand wheedling. 60

BONNIFACE.

Young! why, you jade, as the saying is, can any woman wheedle that is not young? Your mother was useless at five and twenty. Not wheedle! would you make your mother a whore and me a cuckold, as the saying is? I tell you his silence confesses it, 65 and his master spends his money so freely and is so much a gentleman every manner of way that he must be a highwayman.

Enter Gibbet in a cloak.

GIBBET.

Landlord, landlord, is the coast clear?

BONNIFACE.

Oh, Mr. Gibbet, what's the news? 70

GIBBET.

No matter, ask no questions, all fair and honour-able.—Here, my dear Cherry. (*Gives her a bag.*) Two hundred sterling pounds, as good as any that ever hanged or saved a rogue; lay 'em by with the rest, and here—three wedding or mourning rings,[27] 'tis much 75 the same you know. Here, two silver-hilted swords; I took those from fellows that never show any part of their swords but the hilts. Here is a diamond necklace which the lady hid in the privatest place in the coach, but I found it out. This gold watch I took 80 from a pawnbroker's wife; it was left in her hands by

---

27 mourning rings] worn by friends of the deceased

a person of quality;* there's the arms upon the case.

CHERRY.

But who had you the money from?

GIBBET.

Ah! poor woman! I pitied her—from a poor lady just eloped from her husband. She had made up her 85 cargo and was bound for Ireland as hard as she could drive; she told me of her husband's barbarous usage, and so I left her half a crown. But I had almost forgot, my dear Cherry, I have a present for you.

CHERRY.

What is't? 90

GIBBET.

A pot of ceruse, my child, that I took out of a lady's under-pocket.

CHERRY.

What, Mr. Gibbet, do you think that I paint?

GIBBET.

Why you jade, your betters do! I'm sure the lady that I took it from had a coronet upon her 95 handkerchief. Here, take my cloak and go, secure the premises.

CHERRY.

I will secure 'em. (*Exit.*)

BONNIFACE.

But hark ye, where's Hounslow and Bagshot?

GIBBET.

They'll be here tonight. 100

BONNIFACE.

D'ye know of any other gentlemen o'the pad on this road?

GIBBET.

No.

BONNIFACE.

I fancy that I have two that lodge in the house just now. 105

GIBBET.

The devil! How d'ye smoke 'em?

BONNIFACE.

Why, the one is gone to church.

GIBBET.

That's suspicious, I must confess.

BONNIFACE.

And the other is now in his master's chamber; he pretends to be servant to the other. We'll call him 110 out and pump him a little.

GIBBET.

With all my heart.

BONNIFACE.

Mr. Martin! Mr. Martin!

Enter Archer combing a periwig and singing.

GIBBET.

The roads are consumed deep; I'm as dirty as old Brentford at Christmas.[28]—A good pretty fellow that.—Whose servant are you, friend? 115

ARCHER.

My master's.

GIBBET.

Really?

ARCHER.

Really.

GIBBET.

That's much.—The fellow has been at the bar by his evasions!—But pray sir, what is your master's name? 120

ARCHER. (*Sings and combs the periwig.*)

Tall, all dall! This is the most obstinate curl—

GIBBET.

I ask you his name?

ARCHER.

Name, sir?—*Tall, all dall!*—I never asked him his name in my life. *Tall, all dall!* 125

BONNIFACE. [*Aside to Gibbet.*]

What think you now?

GIBBET. [*Aside to Bonniface.*]

Plain, plain: he talks now as if he were before a judge.—But pray friend, which way does your master travel?

ARCHER.

A-horseback. 130

GIBBET. [*Aside to Bonniface.*]

Very well again, an old offender, right!—But, I mean does he go upwards or downwards?

ARCHER.

Downwards, I fear, sir.—*Tall, all!*

GIBBET.

I'm afraid my fate will be a contrary way.[29]

BONNIFACE.

Ha, ha, ha! Mr. Martin, you're very arch! This gentleman is only travelling towards Chester, and would be glad of your company, that's all.—Come Captain, you'll stay tonight, I suppose? I'll show you a chamber. Come, Captain. 135

GIBBET.

Farewell, friend. (*Exit [with Bonniface].*) 140

ARCHER.

Captain, your servant.—Captain! a pretty fellow! S'death,* I wonder that the officers of the army don't conspire to beat all scoundrels in red but their own!

Enter Cherry.

CHERRY. (*Aside.*)

Gone, and Martin here! I hope he did not listen: I would have the merit of the discovery all my own, because I would oblige him to love me.—Mr. Martin, who was that man with my father? 145

ARCHER.

Some recruiting sergeant or whipped-out[30] trooper, I suppose.

CHERRY. [*Aside.*]

All's safe, I find. 150

ARCHER.

Come my dear, have you conned over the catechise[31] I taught you last night?

CHERRY.

Come, question me.

ARCHER.

What is Love?

CHERRY.

Love is I know not what, it comes I know not how, and goes I know not when. 155

ARCHER.

Very well, an apt scholar! (*Chucks her under the chin.*) Where does Love enter?

CHERRY.

Into the eyes.

ARCHER.

And where go out? 160

---

28 Brentford at Christmas] a town that was notoriously muddy in winter

29 contrary way] Gibbet fears he is going to hung up on the gallows (the fate of convicted highwaymen).

30 whipped-out] flogged out of the army

31 catechise] Mock-catechisms like the one that follows had become popular as exercises of libertine wit in the early eighteenth century.

CHERRY.

I won't tell ye.

ARCHER.

What are objects[f] of that passion?

CHERRY.

Youth, beauty, and clean linen.

ARCHER.

The reason?

CHERRY.

The two first are fashionable in Nature, and the third at Court. 165

ARCHER.

That's my dear! What are the signs and tokens of that passion?

CHERRY.

A stealing look, a stammering tongue, words improbable, designs impossible, and actions impracticable. 170

ARCHER.

That's my good child!* Kiss me.—What must a lover do to obtain his mistress?

CHERRY.

He must adore the person that disdains him, he must bribe the chambermaid that betrays him, and court the footman that laughs at him. He must, he must— 175

ARCHER.

Nay child, I must whip you if you don't mind your lesson. He must treat his—

CHERRY.

Oh, aye! He must treat his enemies with respect, his friends with indifference, and all the world with contempt; he must suffer much and fear more; he must desire much and hope little; in short, he must embrace his ruin and throw himself away. 180

ARCHER.

Had ever man so hopeful a pupil as mine? Come my dear, why is Love called a riddle? 185

CHERRY.

Because being blind, he leads those that see, and though a child, he governs a man.

ARCHER.

Mighty well!—And why is Love pictured blind?

CHERRY.

Because the painters out of the weakness or privilege of their art chose to hide those eyes that they could not draw. 190

ARCHER.

That's my dear little scholar! Kiss me again.—And why should Love, that's a child, govern a man?

CHERRY.

Because that a child is the end of Love.

ARCHER.

And so ends Love's catechism.—And now, my dear, we'll go in and make my master's bed. 195

CHERRY.

Hold, hold, Mr. Martin! You have taken a great deal of pains to instruct me, and what d'ye think I have learnt by it?

ARCHER.

What? 200

CHERRY.

That your discourse and your habit are contradictions, and it would be nonsense in me to believe you a footman any longer.

ARCHER.

'Oons,* what a witch it is!

CHERRY.

Depend upon this, sir, nothing in this garb shall ever tempt me, for though I was born to servitude, I hate it. Own your condition, swear you love me, and then— 205

ARCHER.

And then we shall go make the bed?

CHERRY.

Yes. 210

ARCHER.

You must know, then, that I am born a gentleman. My education was liberal, but I went to London a younger brother, fell into the hands of sharpers who stripped me of my money. My friends disowned me, and now my necessity brings me to what you see. 215

CHERRY.

Then take my hand—promise to marry me before you sleep, and I'll make you master of two thousand pound.

ARCHER.

How!

CHERRY.

Two thousand pound that I have this minute in my own custody; so throw off your livery this instant, and I'll go find a parson. 220

ARCHER.

What said you? A parson!

CHERRY.

What! Do you scruple?

ARCHER.

Scruple! No, no, but—two thousand pound, you 225
say?

CHERRY.

And better.

ARCHER. [*Aside.*]

S'death, what shall I do?—But hark ye, child, what
need you make me master of yourself and money,
when you may have the same pleasure out of me 230
and still keep your fortune in your hands?

CHERRY.

Then you won't marry me?

ARCHER.

I would marry you, but—

CHERRY.

Oh, sweet sir, I'm your humble servant! You're fairly
caught! Would you persuade me that any gentleman 235
who could bear the scandal of wearing livery would
refuse two thousand pound, let the condition be
what it would? No, no, sir! But I hope you'll pardon
the freedom I have taken, since it was only to inform
myself of the respect that I ought to pay you. (*Going.*) 240

ARCHER.

Fairly bit,* by Jupiter!—Hold! hold! And have you
actually two thousand pound?

CHERRY.

Sir, I have my secrets as well as you—when you
please to be more open, I shall be more free. And
be assured that I have discoveries* that will match 245
yours, be what they will. In the meanwhile, be
satisfied that no discovery I make shall ever hurt
you, but beware of my father! [*Exit.*]

ARCHER.

So! We're like to have as many adventures in our
inn as Don Quixote had in his. Let me see—two 250
thousand pound! If the wench would promise to
die when the money were spent, egad, one would
marry her, but the fortune may go off in a year or
two, and the wife may live—Lord knows how
long! Then, an innkeeper's daughter! Aye, that's the 255
devil—there my pride brings me off.

For whatsoe'er the sages charge on pride,
The angels fall, and twenty faults beside,

On earth I'm sure, 'mong us of mortal calling,
Pride saves man oft, and woman too, from falling. 260

Exit.

Act III, scene [i.
The gallery in Lady Bountiful's house].

Enter Mrs. Sullen, Dorinda.

MRS. SULLEN.

Ha, ha, ha! My dear sister, let me embrace thee!
Now we are friends indeed, for I shall have a secret
of yours as a pledge for mine—now you'll be good
for something. I shall have you conversable in the
subjects of the sex. 5

DORINDA.

But do you think that I am so weak as to fall in
love with a fellow at first sight?

MRS. SULLEN.

Pshaw! Now you spoil all! Why should not we be
as free in our friendships as the men? I warrant you
the gentleman has got to his confidant already, has 10
avowed his passion, toasted your health, called you
ten thousand angels, has run over your lips, eyes,
neck, shape, air, and everything, in a description
that warms their mirth to a second enjoyment.

DORINDA.

Your hand, sister, I an't well. 15

MRS. SULLEN.

So—she's breeding already!—Come child,* up
with it—hem a little—so—now tell me, don't you
like the gentleman that we saw at church just now?

DORINDA.

The man's well enough.

MRS. SULLEN.

Well enough! Is he not a demigod, a Narcissus, a 20
star, the man i'the moon?

DORINDA.

Oh sister, I'm extremely ill!

MRS. SULLEN.

Shall I send to your mother, child, for a little of
her cephalic plaster to put to the soles of your feet,
or shall I send to the gentleman for something for 25
you?—Come, unlace your stays, unbosom
yourself.—The man is perfectly a pretty fellow; I
saw him when he first came into church.

DORINDA.

I saw him too, sister, and with an air that shone,
methought, like rays about his person. 30

MRS. SULLEN.

Well said! Up with it!

DORINDA.

No forward coquet behavior, no airs to set him off,
no studied looks nor artful posture—but nature
did it all—

MRS. SULLEN.

Better and better!—One touch more—come!— 35

DORINDA.

But then his looks!—Did you observe his eyes?

MRS. SULLEN.

Yes, yes, I did—his eyes, well, what of his eyes?

DORINDA.

Sprightly, but not wandering; they seemed to view,
but never gazed on anything but me—and then his
looks so humble were and yet so noble, that they 40
aimed to tell me that he could with pride die at my
feet, though he scorned slavery anywhere else.

MRS. SULLEN.

The physic works purely!—How d'ye find yourself,
now, my dear?

DORINDA.

Hem! much better, my dear.—Oh, here comes our 45
Mercury!

Enter Scrub.

Well Scrub, what news of the gentleman?

SCRUB.

Madam, I have brought you a packet of news.

DORINDA.

Open it quickly, come!

SCRUB.

In the first place, I inquired who the gentleman was; 50
they told me he was a stranger. Secondly, I asked what
the gentleman was; they answered and said, that they
never saw him before. Thirdly, I inquired what
countryman he was; they replied 'twas more than
they knew. Fourthly, I demanded whence he came; 55
their answer was, they could not tell. And fifthly, I
asked whither he went, and they replied they knew
nothing of the matter—and this is all I could learn.

MRS. SULLEN.

But what do people say? Can't they guess?

SCRUB.

Why, some think he's a spy, some guess he's a 60
mountebank, some say one thing, some another—
but for my part, I believe he's a Jesuit.

DORINDA.

A Jesuit! Why a Jesuit?

SCRUB.

Because he keeps his horses always ready saddled,
and his footman talks French.[32] 65

MRS. SULLEN.

His footman!

SCRUB.

Aye, he and the count's footman were jabbering
French like two intriguing ducks in a mill pond,
and I believe they talked of me, for they laughed
consumedly. 70

DORINDA.

What sort of livery has the footman?

SCRUB.

Livery! Lord, madam, I took him for a captain, he's
so bedizened with lace, and then he has tops to
his shoes up to his mid leg, a silver headed cane
dangling at his knuckles; he carries his hands in 75
his pockets just so— (*Walks in the French air.*) and
has a long fine periwig tied up in a bag. Lord,
madam, he's clear another sort of man than I!

MRS. SULLEN.

That may easily be.—But what shall we do now,
sister? 80

DORINDA.

I have it! This fellow has a world of simplicity and
some cunning; the first hides the latter by
abundance.—Scrub!

SCRUB.

Madam!

DORINDA.

We have a great mind to know who the gentleman 85
is, only for our satisfaction.

SCRUB.

Yes madam, it would be a satisfaction, no doubt.

DORINDA.

You must go and get acquainted with his footman

---

32 Jesuit … French] Jesuits were commonly thought to be
in the secret service of the French government; they were
known to be conspirators against the English.

and invite him hither to drink a bottle of your ale,
because you're butler today.   90

SCRUB.

Yes, madam. I am butler every Sunday.

MRS. SULLEN.

Oh brave!* Sister, o'my conscience, you understand
the mathematics already—'tis the best plot in the
world! Your mother, you know, will be gone to
church, my spouse will be got to the alehouse with   95
his scoundrels, and the house will be our own—
so we drop in by accident and ask the fellow some
questions ourselves. In the country, you know, any
stranger is company, and we're glad to take up with
the butler in a country dance, and happy if he'll   100
do us the favor.

SCRUB.

Oh madam, you wrong me! I never refused your
ladyship the favor in my life.

Enter Gipsey.

GIPSEY.

Ladies, dinner's upon table.

DORINDA.

Scrub, we'll excuse your waiting. Go where we   105
ordered you.

SCRUB.

I shall.

Exeunt.

Scene [ii]. The inn.

Enter Aimwell and Archer.

ARCHER.

Well Tom, I find you're a marksman.

AIMWELL.

A marksman! who so blind could be as not discern
a swan among the ravens.

ARCHER.

Well, but hark ye, Aimwell—

AIMWELL.

Aimwell! Call me Oroondates, Cesario, Amadis[33]—   5
all that romance can in a lover paint, and then I'll
answer. Oh Archer, I read her thousands in her

looks! She looked like Ceres in her harvest: corn,
wine and oil, milk and honey, gardens, groves, and
purling streams played on her plenteous face.   10

ARCHER.

Her face! her pocket, you mean: the corn, wine and
oil lies there. In short, she has ten thousand pound;
that's the English on't.

AIMWELL.

Her eyes—

ARCHER.

Are demi-cannons, to be sure, so I won't stand   15
their battery. (*Going.*)

AIMWELL.

Pray excuse me, my passion must have vent.

ARCHER.

Passion! what a plague! D'ye think these romantic
airs will do our business? Were my temper as
extravagant as yours, my adventures have   20
something more romantic by half.

AIMWELL.

Your adventures!

ARCHER.

Yes,

The nymph that with her twice ten hundred pounds,
With brazen engine* hot and coif clear starched,   25
Can fire the guest in warming of the bed—

There's a touch of sublime Milton for you, and the
subject but an innkeeper's daughter! I can play with
a girl as an angler does with his fish; he keeps it at
the end of his line, runs it up the stream and down   30
the stream, till at last he brings it to hand, tickles
the trout,* and so whips it into his basket.

Enter Bonniface.

BONNIFACE.

Mr. Martin, as the saying is, yonder's an honest
fellow below, my Lady Bountiful's butler, who begs
the honor that you would go home with him and   35
see his cellar.

ARCHER.

Do my *baisemains*[34] to the gentleman, and tell him
I will do myself the honor to wait on him
immediately.

_____

33 Oroondates … Amadis] names of heroes in well-known
    romances

_____

34 Do my *baisemains*] Pay my respects.

Exit Bonniface.

AIMWELL.

What do I hear?
Soft Orpheus play, and fair Toftida[35] sing?   40

ARCHER.

Pshaw! damn your raptures! I tell you here's a
pump going to be put into the vessel, and the ship
will get into harbor, my life on't! You say there's
another lady very handsome there?   45

AIMWELL.

Yes, faith.

ARCHER.

I'm in love with her already.

AIMWELL.

Can't you give me a bill[36] upon Cherry in the
meantime?

ARCHER.

No, no, friend, all her corn, wine and oil is   50
engrossed to my market. And once more I warn
you to keep your anchorage clear of mine, for if
you fall foul of me, by this light, you shall go to
the bottom. What! Make prize of my little frigate
while I am upon the cruise for you! (*Exit.*)   55

Enter Bonniface.

AIMWELL.

Well, well, I won't.—Landlord, have you any
tolerable company in the house? I don't care for
dining alone.

BONNIFACE.

Yes sir, there's a captain below, as the saying is, that
arrived about an hour ago.   60

AIMWELL.

Gentlemen of his coat are welcome everywhere.
Will you make him a compliment from me, and
tell him I should be glad of his company?

BONNIFACE.

Who shall I tell him, sir, would—

AIMWELL. [*Aside.*]

Hah! that stroke was well thrown in.—I'm only a   65
traveler like himself and would be glad of his
company, that's all.

---

35 Toftida] Katherine Tofts was a well-known contemporary soprano.
36 bill] of lading

BONNIFACE.

I obey your commands, as the saying is. (*Exit.*)

Enter Archer.

ARCHER.

S'Death!* I had forgot! What title will you give
yourself?   70

AIMWELL.

My brother's, to be sure; he would never give me
anything else, so I'll make bold with his honor this
bout—you know the rest of your cue.

ARCHER.

Aye, aye. (*Exit.*)

Enter Gibbet.

GIBBET.

Sir, I'm yours.   75

AIMWELL.

'Tis more than I deserve, sir, for I don't know you.

GIBBET.

I don't wonder at that, sir, for you never saw me
before— (*Aside.*) I hope.

AIMWELL.

And pray sir, how came I by the honor of seeing
you now?   80

GIBBET.

Sir, I scorn to intrude upon any gentleman, but
my landlord—

AIMWELL.

Oh, sir, I ask your pardon! You're the captain he
told me of?

GIBBET.

At your service, sir.   85

AIMWELL.

What regiment, may I be so bold?

GIBBET.

A marching regiment, sir, an old corps.

AIMWELL. (*Aside.*)

Very old, if your coat be regimental.—You have
served abroad, sir?

GIBBET.

Yes sir, in the plantations;[37] 'twas my lot to be sent   90
into the worst service. I would have quitted it,
indeed, but a man of honor, you know—besides,

---

37 plantations] the colonies; criminals were frequently
transported to the plantations overseas.

'twas for the good of my country that I should be abroad—anything for the good of one's country—I'm a Roman for that.

AIMWELL. (*Aside.*)

One of the first,[38] I'll lay my life.—You found the West Indies very hot, sir?

GIBBET.

Aye sir, too hot for me.

AIMWELL.

Pray sir, han't I seen your face at Will's coffee-house?

GIBBET.

Yes sir, and at White's, too.[39]

AIMWELL.

And where is your company now, Captain?

GIBBET.

They an't come yet.

AIMWELL.

Why, d'ye expect 'em here?

GIBBET.

They'll be here tonight, sir.

AIMWELL.

Which way do they march?

GIBBET.

Across the country.—The devil's in't, if I han't said enough to encourage him to declare, but I'm afraid he's not right; I must tack about.

AIMWELL.

Is your company to quarter in Litchfield?

GIBBET.

In this house, sir.

AIMWELL.

What! all?

GIBBET.

My company's but thin. Ha, ha, ha! We are but three! Ha, ha, ha!

AIMWELL.

You're merry, sir.

GIBBET.

Aye sir, you must excuse me, sir; I understand the world, especially the art of travelling. I don't care, sir, for answering questions directly upon the road—for I generally ride with a charge[40] about me.

AIMWELL. (*Aside.*)

Three or four, I believe!

GIBBET.

I am credibly informed that there are highwaymen upon this quarter. Not, sir, that I could suspect a gentleman of your figure—but truly, sir, I have got such a way of evasion upon the road that I don't care for speaking truth to any man.

AIMWELL.

Your caution may be necessary.—Then I presume you're no captain?

GIBBET.

Not I, sir. Captain is a good travelling name, and so I take it; it stops a great many foolish inquiries that are generally made about gentlemen that travel. It gives a man an air of something, and makes the drawers obedient—and thus far I am a captain, and no farther.

AIMWELL.

And pray sir, what is your true profession?

GIBBET.

Oh sir, you must excuse me: upon my word, sir, I don't think it safe to tell you.

AIMWELL.

Ha, ha, ha! upon my word, I commend you.

Enter Bonniface.

Well, Mr. Bonniface, what's the news?

BONNIFACE.

There's another gentleman below, as the saying is, that hearing you were but two, would be glad to make the third man, if you would give him leave.

AIMWELL.

What is he?

BONNIFACE.

A clergyman, as the saying is.

---

38 Roman ... first] Gibbet implies that he has the Roman virtue of patriotism; besides continuing to suggest that he is old, Aimwell perhaps suggests that he is more like the rabble who settled early Rome.

39 Will's ... White's] the former was a resort of literary men; the latter was a chocolate house popular with gamblers.

40 charge] sum of money, but also, as Aimwell takes it, either multiple loads of powder for his pistols or criminal charges—or both

AIMWELL.

A clergyman! Is he really a clergyman? or is it only 145
his travelling name, as my friend the captain has it.

BONNIFACE.

Oh sir, he's a priest and a chaplain to the French
officers in town.

AIMWELL.

Is he a Frenchman?

BONNIFACE.

Yes sir, born at Brussels. 150

GIBBET.

A Frenchman and a priest! I won't be seen in his
company, sir; I have a value for my reputation, sir.

AIMWELL.

Nay but Captain, since we are by ourselves.—Can
he speak English, landlord?

BONNIFACE.

Very well, sir. You may know him, as the saying 155
is, to be a foreigner by his accent, and that's all.

AIMWELL.

Then he has been in England before?

BONNIFACE.

Never, sir, but he's a master of languages, as the
saying is. He talks Latin; it does me good to hear
him talk Latin. 160

AIMWELL.

Then you understand Latin, Mr. Bonniface?

BONNIFACE.

Not I, sir, as the saying is, but he talks it so very
fast that I'm sure it must be good.

AIMWELL.

Pray, desire him to walk up.

BONNIFACE.

Here he is, as the saying is. 165

Enter Foigard.

FOIGARD.

Save you, gentlemens, both.

AIMWELL. [*Aside.*]

A Frenchman!—Sir, your most humble servant.

FOIGARD.

Och, dear joy,* I am your most faithful shervant,
and yours alsho.[41]

GIBBET.

Doctor, you talk very good English, but you have 170
a mighty twang of the foreigner.

FOIGARD.

My English is very vel for the vords, but we
foreigners, you know, cannot bring our tongues
about the pronunciation so soon.

AIMWELL. (*Aside.*)

A foreigner! a downright Teague,* by this light!— 175
Were you born in France, Doctor?

FOIGARD.

I was educated in France, but I was borned at
Brussels. I am a subject of the King of Spain, joy.

GIBBET.

What King of Spain, sir? speak!

FOIGARD.

Upon my shoul, joy, I cannot tell you as yet.[42] 180

AIMWELL.

Nay Captain, that was too hard upon the doctor:
he's a stranger.

FOIGARD.

Oh, let him alone, dear joy! I am of a nation that
is not easily put out of countenance.

AIMWELL.

Come, gentlemen, I'll end the dispute.—Here 185
landlord, is dinner ready?

BONNIFACE.

Upon the table, as the saying is.

AIMWELL.

Gentlemen—pray—that door—

FOIGARD.

No, no, fait! the captain must lead.

AIMWELL.

No Doctor, the church is our guide. 190

GIBBET.

Aye, aye, so it is.—

Exit foremost, they follow.

---

41 Och … alsho] Foigard is speaking the exaggerated form
of Hiberno-English that was characteristically attributed
to Irish characters on the eighteenth-century English
stage.

42 King of Spain … as yet] The War of Spanish Succession, which was to determine the heir to the Spanish
throne, was still in progress.

Scene [iii]. A gallery in Lady Bountiful's house.

Enter Archer and Scrub singing and hugging one another, Scrub with a tankard in his hand, Gipsey listening at a distance.

SCRUB.

Tall, all dall.—Come my dear boy, let's have that song once more.

ARCHER.

No, no, we shall disturb the family.—But will you be sure to keep the secret?

SCRUB.

Pho! upon my honor, as I'm a gentleman!   5

ARCHER.

'Tis enough. You must know, then, that my master is the Lord Viscount Aimwell. He fought a duel t'other day in London, wounded his man so dangerously that he thinks fit to withdraw till he hears whether the gentleman's wounds be mortal   10 or not. He never was in this part of England before, so he chose to retire to this place, that's all.

GIPSEY. [*Aside.*]

And that's enough for me. (*Exit.*)

SCRUB.

And where were you when your master fought?

ARCHER.

We never know of our masters' quarrels.*   15

SCRUB.

No! If our masters in the country here receive a challenge, the first thing they do is tell their wives; the wife tells the servants, the servants alarm the tenants, and in half an hour you shall have the whole county in arms.   20

ARCHER.

To hinder two men from doing what they have no mind for.—But if you should chance to talk now of my business?

SCRUB.

Talk! aye sir, had I not learned the knack of holding my tongue, I had never lived so long in a   25 great family.

ARCHER.

Aye, aye, to be sure, there are secrets in all families.

SCRUB.

Secrets, aye! But I'll say no more. Come, sit down, we'll make an end of our tankard. Here—

ARCHER.

With all my heart! Who knows but you and I may   30 come to be better acquainted, eh? Here's your ladies' healths! You have three, I think, and to be sure there must be secrets among 'em.

SCRUB.

Secrets! Aye, friend. I wish I had a friend—

ARCHER.

Am not I your friend? Come, you and I will be   35 sworn brothers.

SCRUB.

Shall we?

ARCHER.

From this minute. Give me a kiss.—And now, brother Scrub—

SCRUB.

And now, brother Martin, I will tell you a secret   40 that will make your hair stand on end: you must know that I am consumedly in love.

ARCHER.

That's a terrible secret, that's the truth on't.

SCRUB.

That jade, Gipsey, that was with us just now in the cellar, is the arrantest whore that ever wore a   45 petticoat, and I'm dying for love of her.

ARCHER.

Ha, ha, ha! Are you in love with her person or her virtue, brother Scrub?

SCRUB.

I should like virtue best because it is more durable than beauty, for virtue holds good with some   50 women long and many a day after they have lost it.

ARCHER.

In the country, I grant ye, where no woman's virtue is lost till a bastard be found.

SCRUB.

Aye, could I bring her to a bastard, I should have   55 her all to myself, but I dare not put it upon that lay for fear of being sent for a soldier. Pray brother, how do you gentlemen in London like that same Pressing Act?[43]

---

43 Pressing Act] By a 1703-1704 law, men could be impressed into military service for various causes, among them petty offenses.

ARCHER.

Very ill, brother Scrub—'tis the worst that ever was 60
made for us. Formerly I remember the good days
when we could dun our masters for our wages, and
if they refused to pay us, we could have a warrant
to carry 'em before a justice. But now if we talk
of eating, they have a warrant for us, and carry us 65
before three justices.

SCRUB.

And to be sure we go if we talk of eating, for the
justices won't give their own servants a bad example.
Now this is my misfortune: I dare not speak in the
house while that jade Gipsey dings about like a 70
fury.—Once I had the better end of the staff.

ARCHER.

And how comes the change now?

SCRUB.

Why, the mother of all this mischief is a priest.

ARCHER.

A priest!

SCRUB.

Aye, the damned son of a whore of Babylon* that 75
came over hither to say grace to the French officers
and eat up our provisions. There's not a day goes
over his head without dinner or supper in this
house.

ARCHER.

How came he so familiar in the family? 80

SCRUB.

Because he speaks English as if he had lived here
all his life and tells lies as if he had been a traveler
from his cradle.

ARCHER.

And this priest, I'm afraid, has converted the
affections of your Gipsey. 85

SCRUB.

Converted! aye, and perverted, my dear friend, for
I'm afraid he has made her a whore and a papist.
But this is not all. There's the French count and
Mrs. Sullen. They're in the confederacy and for
some private ends of their own, to be sure. 90

ARCHER.

A very hopeful family, yours, brother Scrub! I
suppose the maiden lady has her lover too?

SCRUB.

Not that I know; she's the best on 'em, that's the

truth on't. But they take care to prevent my curiosity
by giving me so much business that I'm a perfect 95
slave. What d'ye think is my place in this family?

ARCHER.

Butler, I suppose.

SCRUB.

Ah, Lord help you! I'll tell you. Of a Monday, I drive
the coach; of a Tuesday, I drive the plough; on
Wednesday, I follow the hounds; a-Thursday, I dun 100
the tenants; on Friday, I go to market; on Saturday,
I draw warrants;[44] and a-Sunday, I draw beer.

ARCHER.

Ha, ha, ha! If variety be a pleasure in life, you have
enough on't, my dear brother.—But what ladies are
those? 105

SCRUB.

Ours, ours: that upon the right hand is Mrs.
Sullen, and the other is Mrs.* Dorinda. Don't
mind 'em; sit still, man—

Enter Mrs. Sullen and Dorinda.

MRS. SULLEN.

I have heard my brother talk of my Lord Aimwell,
but they say that his brother is the finer gentleman. 110

DORINDA.

That's impossible, sister.

MRS. SULLEN.

He's vastly rich, but very close, they say.

DORINDA.

No matter for that: if I can creep into his heart,
I'll open his breast, I warrant him. I have heard
say that people may be guessed at by the behavior 115
of their servants. I could wish we might talk to that
fellow.

MRS. SULLEN.

So do I, for I think he's a very pretty fellow. Come
this way. I'll throw out a lure for him presently.*

They walk a turn towards the opposite side of the stage.

ARCHER. [*Aside.*]

Corn, wine, and oil, indeed—but, I think, the wife 120
has the greatest plenty of flesh and blood; she
should be my choice.

---

44 warrants] for arrests: Squire Sullen is a Justice of the
Peace.

Mrs. Sullen drops her glove, Archer runs, takes it up, and gives it to her.

Aha,ᵍ say you so.—Madam, your ladyship's glove.

MRS. SULLEN.

Oh sir, I thank you! [*To Dorinda.*] What a handsome bow the fellow has!　125

DORINDA.

Bow! Why I have known several footmen come down from London, set up here for dancing masters, and carry off the best fortunes in the country.

ARCHER. (*Aside.*)

That project, for ought I know, had been better　130 than ours.—Brother Scrub, why don't you introduce me?

SCRUB.

Ladies, this is the strange gentleman's servant that you see at church today. I understood he came from London, and so I invited him to the cellar　135 that he might show me the newest flourish in whetting my knives.

DORINDA.

And I hope you have made much of him?

ARCHER.

Oh yes, madam, but the strength of your ladyship's liquor is a little too potent for the constitution of　140 your humble servant.

MRS. SULLEN.

What! then you don't usually drink ale?

ARCHER.

No madam, my constant drink is tea or a little wine and water; 'tis prescribed me by the physician for a remedy against the spleen.　145

SCRUB.

Oh la! Oh la! a footman have the spleen!

MRS. SULLEN.

I thought that distemper had been only proper to people of quality.*

ARCHER.

Madam, like all other fashions, it wears out, and so descends to their servants,⁴⁵ though in a great　150 many of us, I believe, it proceeds from some

---

45　fashions … servants] Rich people commonly gave their outmoded clothes to their servants.

melancholy particles in the blood occasioned by the stagnation of wages.

DORINDA. [*Aside.*]

How affectedly the fellow talks!—How long, pray, have you served your present master?　155

ARCHER.

Not long: my life has been mostly spent in the service of the ladies.

MRS. SULLEN.

And pray, which service do you like best?

ARCHER.

Madam, the ladies pay best. The honor of serving them is sufficient wages; there is a charm in their　160 looks that delivers a pleasure with their commands and gives our duty the wings of inclination.

MRS. SULLEN. [*Aside.*]

That flight was above the pitch of a livery.—And, sir, would not you be satisfied to serve a lady again?

ARCHER.

As a groom of the chamber, madam, but not as a　165 footman.

MRS. SULLEN.

I suppose you served as footman before?

ARCHER.

For that reason I would not serve in that post again, for my memory is too weak for the load of messages that the ladies lay upon their servants in　170 London. My Lady Howd'ye, the last mistress I served, called me up one morning and told me: "Martin, go to my Lady Allnight with my humble service; tell her I was to wait on her ladyship yesterday and left word with Mrs.* Rebecca that　175 the preliminaries of the affair she knows of are stopped till we know the concurrence of the person that I know of, for which there are circumstances wanting* which we shall accommodate at the old place, but that, in the meantime, there is a person　180 about her ladyship that, from several hints and surmises, was accessory at a certain time to the disappointments that naturally attend things, that to her knowledge are of more importance—"

MRS. SULLEN, DORINDA.

Ha, ha, ha! Where are you going, sir?　185

ARCHER.

Why I han't half done! The whole howd'ye was about half an hour long; so I happened to misplace two syllables and was turned off and rendered incapable—

DORINDA. [*Aside to Mrs. Sullen.*]

The pleasantest fellow, sister, I ever saw!—But friend, if your master be married, I presume you still serve a lady? 190

ARCHER.

No, madam, I take care never to come into a married family: the commands of the master and mistress are always so contrary that 'tis impossible to please both. 195

DORINDA. (*Aside.*)

There's a main point gained: my lord is not married, I find.

MRS. SULLEN.

But I wonder, friend, that in so many good services, you had not a better provision made for you. 200

ARCHER.

I don't know how, madam. I had a lieutenancy offered me three or four times, but that is not bread, madam. I live much better as I do.

SCRUB.

Madam, he sings rarely. I was thought to do pretty well here in the country till he came, but alack a day, I'm nothing to my brother Martin. 205

DORINDA.

Does he? Pray sir, will you oblige us with a song?

ARCHER.

Are you for passion, or humor?

SCRUB.

Oh la! He has the purest ballad about a trifle— 210

MRS. SULLEN.

A trifle! pray sir, let's have it!

ARCHER.

I'm ashamed to offer you a trifle, madam. But since you command me— (*Sings to the tune of Sir Simon the King.*[46])

A trifling song you shall hear, 215
Begun with a trifle and ended;
All trifling people draw near,
And I shall be nobly attended.

Were it not for trifles, a few,
That lately have come into play, 220
The men would want* something to do,
And the women want something to say.

What makes men trifle in dressing?
Because the ladies (they know)
Admire, by often possessing, 225
That eminent trifle, a beau.

When the lover his moments has trifled
The trifle of trifles to gain,
No sooner the virgin is rifled
But a trifle shall part 'em again. 230

What mortal man would be able
At White's half an hour to sit?
Or who could bear a tea table
Without talking of trifles for wit?

The Court is from trifles secure, 235
Gold keys are no trifles, we see;
White rods[47] are no trifles, I'm sure,
Whatever their bearers may be.

But if you will go to the place
Where trifles abundantly breed, 240
The levee will show you his grace
Makes promises trifles indeed.

A coach with six footmen behind
I count neither trifle nor sin,
But ye gods! how oft do we find 245
A scandalous trifle within?

A flask of champagne, people think it
A trifle or something as bad,
But if you'll contrive how to drink it,
You'll find it no trifle, egad! 250

A parson's a trifle at sea,
A widow's a trifle in sorrow,
A peace is a trifle today,
Who knows what may happen tomorrow?

---

46 Sir Simon the King] a popular tune, first printed in the seventeenth century

47 Gold keys … White rods] symbols of high offices

A black coat a trifle may cloak,   255
Or to hide it, the red[48] may endeavor:
But if once the army is broke,[49]
We shall have more trifles than ever.

The stage is a trifle, they say,
The reason, pray carry along,   260
Because at every new play,
The house they with trifles so throng.

But with people's malice to trifle,
And to set us all on a foot:
The author of this is a trifle,   265
And his song is a trifle to boot.[h]

MRS. SULLEN.
    Very well, sir, we're obliged to you. (*Offering him
    money.*) Something for a pair of gloves.

ARCHER.
    I humbly beg leave to be excused. My master,
    madam, pays me, nor dare I take money from any   270
    other hand without injuring his honor and
    disobeying his commands. (*Exit.*)

DORINDA.
    This is surprising! Did you ever see so pretty a well-
    bred fellow?

MRS. SULLEN.
    The devil take him for wearing that livery!   275

DORINDA.
    I fancy, sister, he may be some gentleman, a friend
    of my lord's, that his lordship has pitched upon
    for his courage, fidelity, and discretion to bear him
    company in this dress and who, ten to one, was
    his second too.   280

MRS. SULLEN.
    It is so, it must be so, and it shall be so: for I like him.

DORINDA.
    What! better than the count?

MRS. SULLEN.
    The count happened to be the most agreeable man
    upon the place, and so I chose him to serve me in
    my design upon my husband. But I should like   285
    this fellow better in a design upon myself.

---

48 black … red] the former worn by clergymen, the latter
    by soldiers
49 broke] discharged at the end of a war

DORINDA.
    But now, sister, for an interview with this lord and
    this gentleman: How shall we bring that about?

MRS. SULLEN.
    Patience! you country ladies give no quarter, if once
    you be entered.[50] Would you prevent* their desires   290
    and give the fellows no wishing-time? Look ye,
    Dorinda, if my Lord Aimwell loves you or deserves
    you, he'll find a way to see you, and there we must
    leave it. My business comes now upon the tapis.
    Have you prepared your brother?   295

DORINDA.
    Yes, yes.

MRS. SULLEN.
    And how did he relish it?

DORINDA.
    He said little, mumbled something to himself,
    promised to be guided by me. But here he comes—

Enter Sullen.

SULLEN.
    What singing was that I heard just now?   300

MRS. SULLEN.
    The singing in your head, my dear. You
    complained of it all day.

SULLEN.
    You're impertinent.

MRS. SULLEN.
    I was ever so, since I became one flesh with you.

SULLEN.
    One flesh! rather two carcasses joined unnaturally   305
    together.[51]

MRS. SULLEN.
    Or rather a living soul coupled to a dead body.

DORINDA.
    So, this is fine encouragement for me!

SULLEN.
    Yes, my wife shows you what you must do.

---

50 entered] engaged in action
51 one flesh … together] the play on the biblical descrip-
    tion of marriage ("and they shall be one flesh" [Gen.
    2:24]), plus a number of the ideas in Mrs. Sullen's sub-
    sequent speech on marriage and divorce, are borrowed
    from John Milton's *The Doctrine and Discipline of Di-
    vorce.*

MRS. SULLEN.

And my husband shows you what you must suffer. 310

SULLEN.

S'death,* why can't you be silent?

MRS. SULLEN.

S'death, why can't you talk?

SULLEN.

Do you talk to any purpose? 315

MRS. SULLEN.

Do you think to any purpose?

SULLEN.

Sister, hark ye. (*Whispers [to Dorinda, then says* 320
aloud].) I shan't be home till it be late. (*Exit.*)

MRS. SULLEN.

What did he whisper to ye?

DORINDA.

That he would go round the back way, come into
the closet,* and listen as I directed him. But let
me beg you once more, dear sister, to drop this 325
project, for as I told you before, instead of awaking
him to kindness, you may provoke him to a rage,
and then who knows how far his brutality may
carry him?

MRS. SULLEN.

I'm provided to receive him, I warrant you. But 330
here comes the count—vanish!

Exit Dorinda;[i] *enter Count Bellair.*

Don't you wonder, Monsieur le Count, that I was
not at church this afternoon?

COUNT BELLAIR.

I more wonder, madam, that you go dere at all or
how you dare lift those eyes to Heaven that are 335
guilty of so much killing.

MRS. SULLEN.

If Heaven, sir, has given to my eyes with the power
of killing the virtue of making a cure, I hope the
one may atone for the other.

COUNT BELLAIR.

Oh largely, madam, would your ladyship be as 340
ready to apply the remedy as to give the wound.
Consider, madam, I am doubly a prisoner: first to
the arms of your general, then to your more
conquering eyes. My first chains are easy—there a
ransom may redeem me—but from your fetters, I 345
never shall get free.

MRS. SULLEN.

Alas sir, why should you complain to me of your
captivity, who am in chains myself? You know, sir,
that I am bound, nay, most be-tied[j] up, in that
particular that might give you ease. I am like you, 350
a prisoner of war—of war indeed! I have given my
parole of honor. Would you break yours to gain
your liberty?

COUNT BELLAIR.

Most certainly I would, were I a prisoner among
the Turks. Dis is your case: you're a slave, madam, 355
slave to the worst of Turks, a husband.

MRS. SULLEN.

There lies my foible, I confess. No fortifications,
no courage, conduct, nor vigilancy can pretend to
defend a place where the cruelty of the governor
forces the garrison to mutiny. 360

COUNT BELLAIR.

And where de besieger is resolved to die before de
place. Here I will fix. (*Kneels.*) With tears, vows,
and prayers assault your heart, and never rise till
you surrender. Or if I must storm—Love and St.
Michael! And so I begin the attack— 365

MRS. SULLEN.

Stand-off! (*Aside.*) Sure, he hears me not! And I
could almost wish he—did not—the fellow makes
love very prettily.—But sir, why should you put
such a value upon my person, when you see it
despised by one that knows it so much better? 370

COUNT BELLAIR.

He knows it not, though he possesses it. If he but
knew the value of the jewel he is master of, he
would always wear it next his heart and sleep with
it in his arms.

MRS. SULLEN.

But since he throws me unregarded from him— 375

COUNT BELLAIR.

And one that knows your value well comes by and
takes you up, is it not justice? (*Goes to lay hold on
her.*)

Enter Sullen with his sword drawn.

SULLEN.

Hold, villain, hold!

MRS. SULLEN. (*Presenting a pistol.*)

Do you hold! 380

SULLEN.

What! murder your husband to defend your bully?52

MRS. SULLEN.

Bully! for shame, Mr. Sullen! Bullies wear long swords, the gentleman has none; he's a prisoner, you know. I was aware of your outrage and 385 prepared this to receive your violence and, if occasion were, to preserve myself against the force of this other gentleman.

COUNT BELLAIR.

Oh madam, your eyes be bettre firearms than your pistol; they nevre miss. 390

SULLEN.

What! court my wife to my face!

MRS. SULLEN.

Pray Mr. Sullen, put up. Suspend your fury for a minute.

SULLEN.

To give you time to invent an excuse!

MRS. SULLEN.

I need none. 395

SULLEN.

No, for I heard every syllable of your discourse.

COUNT BELLAIR.

Aye! and begar,* I tink de dialogue was vera pretty.

MRS. SULLEN.

Then I suppose, sir, you heard something of your own barbarity?

SULLEN.

Barbarity! 'oons,* what does the woman call 400 barbarity? Do I ever meddle with you?

MRS. SULLEN.

No.

SULLEN.

As for you, sir, I shall take another time.

COUNT BELLAIR.

Ah, begar, and so must I.

SULLEN.

Look ye, madam, don't think that my anger 405 proceeds from any concern I have for your honor but for my own, and if you can contrive any way of being a whore without making me a cuckold, do it and welcome.

_____

52 bully] here sweetheart; Mrs. Sullen takes it in the sense of ruffian as well.

MRS. SULLEN.

Sir, I thank you kindly; you would allow me the 410 sin but rob me of the pleasure. No, no, I'm resolved never to venture upon the crime without the satisfaction of seeing you punished for't.

SULLEN.

Then will you grant me this, my dear? Let anybody else do you the favor but that Frenchman, for I 415 mortally hate his whole generation. (*Exit.*)

COUNT BELLAIR.

Ah sir, that be ungrateful, for begar, I love some of yours. (*Approaching her.*) Madam—

MRS. SULLEN.

No, sir.

COUNT BELLAIR.

No, sir! Garzoon,53 madam, I am not your 420 husband!

MRS. SULLEN.

'Tis time to undeceive you, sir. I believed your addresses to me were no more than an amusement, and I hope you will think the same of my complaisance. And to convince you that you 425 ought, you must know that I brought you hither only to make you instrumental in setting me right with my husband, for he was planted to listen by my appointment.

COUNT BELLAIR.

By your appointment? 430

MRS. SULLEN.

Certainly.

COUNT BELLAIR.

And so, madam, while I was telling twenty stories to part you from your husband, begar, I was bringing you together all the while.

MRS. SULLEN.

I ask your pardon, sir, but I hope this will give you 435 a taste of the virtue of the English ladies.

COUNT BELLAIR.

Begar, madam, your virtue be vera great, but garzoon, your honeste be vera little.

Enter Dorinda.

MRS. SULLEN.

Nay, now you're angry, sir.

_____

53 Garzoon] a pseudo-French version of "God's wounds"

COUNT BELLAIR.

Angry!—"Fair Dorinda." (*Sings "Dorinda," the* 440
opera tune, and addresses to Dorinda.) Madam,
when your ladyship want a fool, send for me. "Fair
Dorinda, Revenge," etc.[54] (*Exit.*)

MRS. SULLEN.

There goes the true humor of his nation:
resentment with good manners and the height of 445
anger in a song.—Well sister, you must be judge,
for you have heard the trial.

DORINDA.

And I bring in my brother guilty.

MRS. SULLEN.

But I must bear the punishment. 'Tis hard, sister.

DORINDA.

I own it—but you must have patience. 450

MRS. SULLEN.

Patience! the cant of custom! Providence sends no
evil without a remedy: should I lie groaning under
a yoke I can shake off, I were accessory to my ruin,
and my patience were no better than self-murder.[55]

DORINDA.

But how can you shake off the yoke? Your divisions 455
don't come within the reach of the law for divorce.

MRS. SULLEN.

Law! what law can search into the remote abyss of
nature? What evidence can prove the unaccountable
disaffections of wedlock? Can a jury sum up the
endless aversions that are rooted in our souls, or can 460
a bench give judgment upon antipathies?

DORINDA.

They never pretended, sister; they never meddle
but in case of uncleanness.[56]

MRS. SULLEN.

Uncleanness! Oh sister, casual violation is a transient
injury and may possibly be repaired, but can radical 465
hatreds be ever reconciled? No, no, sister. Nature is
the first lawgiver, and when she has set tempers

opposite, not all the golden links of wedlock nor
iron manacles of law can keep 'em fast.

Wedlock we own ordained by Heaven's decree, 470
But such as Heaven ordained it first to be,
Concurring tempers in the man and wife
As mutual helps to draw the load of life.
View all the works of Providence above,
The stars with harmony and concord move; 475
View all the works of Providence below,
The fire, the water, earth, and air, we know,
All in one plant agree to make it grow.
Must man, the chiefest work of art divine,
Be doomed in endless discord to repine? 480
No, we should injure Heaven by that surmise:
Omnipotence is just, were man but wise.

[Exeunt.]

Act IV, scene [i]. Continues.

Enter Mrs. Sullen.

MRS. SULLEN.

Were I born an humble Turk, where women have
no soul nor property, there I must sit contented.
But in England, a country whose women are its
glory, must women be abused? Where women rule,
must women be enslaved? nay, cheated into slavery, 5
mocked by a promise of comfortable society into
a wilderness of solitude! I dare not keep the
thought about me.—Oh, here comes something
to divert me—

Enter a Country Woman.

WOMAN.

I come, an't* please your ladyships—you're my 10
Lady Bountiful, an't ye?

MRS. SULLEN.

Well good woman, go on.

WOMAN.

I come seventeen long mail to have a cure for my
husband's sore leg.

MRS. SULLEN.

Your husband! What, woman, cure your husband! 15

WOMAN.

Aye, poor man, for his sore leg won't let him stir
from home.

---

54 "Fair Dorinda" … etc.] The count sings snatches of two
     songs, "Fair Dorinda" and "Revenge, Revenge," from the
     opera *Camilla* (1706).
55 cant … self-murder] There are frequent echoes of
     Milton's *Doctrine and Discipline of Divorce* in this and
     the next two speeches by Mrs. Sullen.
56 uncleanness] adultery

MRS. SULLEN.

There, I confess, you have given me a reason. Well good woman, I'll tell you what you must do. You must lay your husband's leg upon a table, and with a chopping-knife you must lay it open as broad as you can; then you must take out the bone and beat the flesh soundly with a rolling pin; then take salt, pepper, cloves, mace, and ginger, some sweet herbs, and season it very well; then roll it up like brawn and put it into the oven for two hours.

WOMAN.

Heavens reward your ladyship! I have two little babies too that are piteous bad with the graips,[57] an't* please ye.

MRS. SULLEN.

Put a little pepper and salt in their bellies, good woman.

Enter Lady Bountiful.

I beg your ladyship's pardon for taking your business out of your hands; I have been a-tampering here a little with one of your patients.

LADY BOUNTIFUL.

Come good woman, don't mind this mad creature. I am the person that you want, I suppose. What would you have, woman?

MRS. SULLEN.

She wants something for her husband's sore leg.

LADY BOUNTIFUL.

What's the matter with his leg, goody?

WOMAN.

It come first, as one might say, with a sort of dizziness in his foot, then he had a kind of a laziness in his joints, and then his leg broke out, and then it swelled, and then it closed again, and then it broke out again, and then it festered, and then it grew better, and then it grew worse again.

MRS. SULLEN.

Ha, ha, ha!

LADY BOUNTIFUL.

How can you be merry with the misfortunes of other people?

MRS. SULLEN.

Because my own make me sad, madam.

_____

57 graips] gripes or colic

LADY BOUNTIFUL.

The worst reason in the world, daughter; your own misfortunes should teach you to pity others.

MRS. SULLEN.

But the woman's misfortunes and mine are nothing alike; her husband is sick, and mine, alas, is in health.

LADY BOUNTIFUL.

What! would you wish your husband sick?

MRS. SULLEN.

Not of a sore leg, of all things.

LADY BOUNTIFUL.

Well good woman, go to the pantry, get your bellyful of victuals, then I'll give you a receipt* of diet-drink for your husband. But d'ye hear, goody, you must not let your husband move too much.

WOMAN.

No, no, madam, the poor man's inclinable enough to lie still. (*Exit.*)

LADY BOUNTIFUL.

Well, daughter Sullen, though you laugh, I have done miracles about the country here with my receipts.

MRS. SULLEN.

Miracles, indeed, if they have cured anybody. But I believe, madam, the patient's faith goes farther toward the miracle than your prescription.

LADY BOUNTIFUL.

Fancy helps in some cases. But there's your husband who has as little fancy as anybody; I brought him from death's door.

MRS. SULLEN.

I suppose, madam, you made him drink plentifully of ass's milk.

Enter Dorinda, runs to Mrs. Sullen.

DORINDA.

News, dear sister! News! News!

Enter Archer running.

ARCHER.

Where, where is my Lady Bountiful? Pray, which is the old lady of you three?

LADY BOUNTIFUL.

I am.

ARCHER.

Oh madam, the fame of your ladyship's charity,

goodness, benevolence, skill, and ability have
drawn me hither to implore your ladyship's help
in behalf of my unfortunate master, who is this
moment breathing his last.   80

LADY BOUNTIFUL.

Your master! where is he?

ARCHER.

At your gate, madam. Drawn by the appearance of
your handsome house to view it nearer and walking
up the avenue within five paces of the courtyard, he
was taken ill of a sudden with a sort of I know not   85
what, but down he fell, and there he lies.

LADY BOUNTIFUL.

Here Scrub! Gipsey! all run, get my easy chair*
downstairs, put the gentleman in it, and bring him
in quickly, quickly!

ARCHER.

Heaven will reward your ladyship for this   90
charitable act.

LADY BOUNTIFUL.

Is your master used to these fits?

ARCHER.

Oh yes, madam, frequently: I have known him
have five or six of a night.

LADY BOUNTIFUL.

What's his name?   95

ARCHER.

Lord madam, he's a-dying! A minute's care or
neglect may save or destroy his life!

LADY BOUNTIFUL.

Ah, poor gentleman! come friend, show me the
way. I'll see him brought in myself. (*Exit with
Archer.*)   100

DORINDA.

Oh sister, my heart flutters about strangely! I can
hardly forbear running to his assistance.

MRS. SULLEN.

And I'll lay my life he deserves your assistance
more than he wants* it! Did not I tell you that my
lord would find a way to come at you? Love's his   105
distemper, and you must be the physician: put on
all your charms, summon all your fire into your
eyes, plant the whole artillery of your looks against
his breast, and down with him.

DORINDA.

Oh sister, I'm but a young gunner! I shall be afraid 110

to shoot for fear the piece should recoil and hurt
myself.

MRS. SULLEN.

Never fear! you shall see me shoot before you, if
you will.

DORINDA.

No, no, dear sister. You have missed your mark so   115
unfortunately that I shan't care for being instructed
by you.

Enter Aimwell in a chair, * carried by Archer and
Scrub, Lady Bountiful, Gipsey; Aimwell counterfeiting
a swoon.*

LADY BOUNTIFUL.

Here, here, let's see the hartshorn-drops.—Gipsey,
a glass of fair[58] water! His fit's very strong. Bless
me, how his hands are clinched!   120

ARCHER.

For shame, ladies, what d'ye do? Why don't you
help us? (*To Dorinda.*) Pray madam, take his hand
and open it if you can, whilst I hold his head.

DORINDA.

Poor gentleman! (*Taking his hand.*) Oh! he has got
my hand within his and squeezes it unmercifully—   125

LADY BOUNTIFUL.

'Tis the violence of his convulsion, child.

ARCHER.

Oh madam, he's perfectly possessed in these cases:
he'll bite if you don't have a care.

DORINDA.

Oh, my hand! my hand!

LADY BOUNTIFUL.

What's the matter with the foolish girl? I have got   130
this hand open, you see, with a great deal of ease.

ARCHER.

Aye, but madam, your daughter's hand is
somewhat warmer than your ladyship's, and the
heat of it draws the force of the spirits that way.

MRS. SULLEN.

I find, friend, you're very learned in these sorts of fits. 135

ARCHER.

'Tis no wonder, madam, for I'm often troubled
with them myself. I find myself extremely ill at this
minute. (*Looking hard at Mrs. Sullen.*)

---

[58] fair] pure

MRS. SULLEN. (*Aside.*)

  I fancy I could find a way to cure you.

LADY BOUNTIFUL.

  His fit holds him very long.   140

ARCHER.

  Longer than usual, madam.—Pray young lady, open his breast and give him air.

LADY BOUNTIFUL.

  Where did his illness take him first, pray?

ARCHER.

  Today at church, madam.

LADY BOUNTIFUL.

  In what manner was he taken?   145

ARCHER.

  Very strangely, my lady. He was of a sudden touched with something in his eyes, which at the first he only felt, but could not tell whether 'twas pain or pleasure.

LADY BOUNTIFUL.

  Wind, nothing but wind.

ARCHER.

  By soft degrees it grew and mounted to his brain;   150
there his fancy caught it; there formed it so beautiful and dressed it up in such gay, pleasing colors that his transported appetite seized the fair idea and straight conveyed it to his heart. That hospitable seat of life sent all its sanguine spirits forth to meet, and opened   155
all its sluicy gates to take the stranger in.

LADY BOUNTIFUL.

  Your master should never go without a bottle to smell to—oh—he recovers! The lavender water, some feathers to burn under his nose, Hungary-water[59] to rub his temples. Oh, he comes to   160
himself! Hem a little, sir, hem.—Gipsey, bring the cordial-water.

Aimwell seems to awake in amaze.

DORINDA.

  How d'ye, sir?

AIMWELL.

  Where am I? (*Rising.*)

  Sure I have passed the gulph of silent death,   165
  And now I land on the Elysian shore.

---

59 Hungary-water] a concoction of wine and rosemary flowers

Behold the goddess of those happy plains:
Fair Proserpine, let me adore thy bright divinity.

Kneels to Dorinda and kisses her hand.

MRS. SULLEN.

  So, so, so! I knew where the fit would end!

AIMWELL.

  Eurydice, perhaps—   170
  How could thy Orpheus keep his word
  And not look back upon thee?
  No treasure but thyself could sure have bribed him
  To look one minute off thee.

LADY BOUNTIFUL.

  Delirious, poor gentleman!   175

ARCHER.

  Very delirious, madam, very delirious!

AIMWELL.

  Martin's voice, I think.

ARCHER.

  Yes my lord. How does your lordship?

LADY BOUNTIFUL.

  Lord! did you mind that, girls?

AIMWELL.

  Where am I?   180

ARCHER.

  In very good hands, sir. You were taken just now with one of your old fits under the trees just by this good lady's house; her ladyship had you taken in and has miraculously brought you to yourself, as you see.

AIMWELL.

  I am so confounded with shame, madam, that I   185
can now only beg pardon—and refer my acknowledgements for your ladyship's care till an opportunity offers of making some amends. I dare be no longer troublesome.—Martin, give two guineas to the servants. (*Going.*)   190

DORINDA.

  Sir, you may catch cold by going so soon into the air. You don't look, sir, as if you were perfectly recovered.

Here Archer talks to Lady Bountiful in dumb show.

AIMWELL.

  That I shall never be, madam. My present illness is so rooted that I must expect to carry it to my grave.   195

MRS. SULLEN.

Don't despair, sir. I have known several in your distemper shake it off with a fortnight's physic.

LADY BOUNTIFUL.

Come, sir, your servant has been telling me that you're apt to relapse if you go into the air. Your good manners shan't get the better of ours: you 200 shall sit down again, sir. Come sir, we don't mind ceremonies in the country. Here sir, my service t'ye. You shall taste my water; 'tis a cordial, I can assure you, and of my own making—drink it off, sir.

Aimwell drinks.

And how d'ye find yourself now, sir? 205

AIMWELL.

Somewhat better—though very faint still.

LADY BOUNTIFUL.

Aye, aye, people are always faint after these fits.— Come girls, you shall show the gentleman the house.—'Tis but an old family building, sir, but you had better walk about and cool by degrees than 210 venture immediately into the air. You'll find some tolerable pictures.—Dorinda, show the gentleman the way. I must go to the poor woman below. (*Exit.*)

DORINDA.

This way, sir.

AIMWELL.

Ladies, shall I beg leave for my servant to wait on 215 you, for he understands pictures very well?

MRS. SULLEN.

Sir, we understand originals[60] as well as he does pictures, so he may come along.

Exit Dorinda, Mrs. Sullen, Aimwell, Archer; Aimwell leads Dorinda. Enter Foigard and Scrub, meeting.

FOIGARD.

Save you, master Scrub.

SCRUB.

Sir, I won't be saved your way: I hate a priest, I 220 abhor the French, and I defy the devil. Sir, I'm a bold Briton, and will spill the last drop of my blood to keep out popery and slavery.

FOIGARD.

Master Scrub, you would put me down in politics, and so I would be speaking with Mrs.* Shipsey. 225

---

60 originals] both paintings (not copies) and odd persons

SCRUB.

Good Mr. Priest, you can't speak with her. She's sick, sir, she's gone abroad, sir, she's—dead two months ago, sir.

Enter Gipsey.

GIPSEY.

How now, impudence! How dare you talk so saucily to the doctor?—Pray sir, don't take it ill, 230 for the common people of England are not so civil to strangers as—

SCRUB.

You lie! You lie! 'Tis the common people that are civilest to strangers.

GIPSEY.

Sirrah, I have a good mind to—get you out, I say. 235

SCRUB.

I won't.

GIPSEY.

You won't, sauce-box!—Pray Doctor, what is the captain's name that came to your inn last night?

SCRUB. [*Aside.*]

The captain! Ah the devil, there she hampers me again! The captain has me on one side, and the 240 priest on t'other, so between the gown and the sword, I have a fine time on't. But *Cedunt arma togae.*[61] (*Going.*)

GIPSEY.

What sirrah, won't you march?

SCRUB.

No my dear, I won't march—but I'll walk— 245 [*Aside.*] and I'll make bold to listen a little too.

Goes behind the side-scene and listens.

GIPSEY.

Indeed Doctor, the count has been barbarously treated, that's the truth on't.

FOIGARD.

Ah, Mrs. Gipsey, upon my shoul, now, gra,[62] his complainings would mollify the marrow in your 250 bones and move the bowels of your commiseration; he veeps, and he dances, and he fistles, and he swears, and he laughs, and he stamps, and he

---

61 *Cedunt arma togae*] Arms yield to the gown (Cicero).
62 gra] abbreviated form of "a ghra": "loved one" (Irish)

sings: in conclusion, joy, he's afflicted, *a la françois*,[63] and a stranger would not know whider   255
to cry or to laugh with him.

GIPSEY.

What would you have me do, Doctor?

FOIGARD.

Noting, joy, but only hide the count in Mrs.
Sullen's closet* when it is dark.

GIPSEY.

Nothing! Is that nothing? It would be both a sin   260
and a shame, Doctor.

FOIGARD.

Here is twenty louis d'ors, joy, for your shame, and
I will give you an absolution for the shin.

GIPSEY.

But won't that money look like a bribe?

FOIGARD.

Dat is according as you shall tauk it: if you receive   265
the money beforehand, 'twill be *logicè*[64] a bribe,
but if you stay till afterwards, 'twill be only a
gratification.

GIPSEY.

Well Doctor, I'll take it *logicè*. But what must I do
with my conscience, sir?   270

FOIGARD.

Leave dat wid me, joy; I am your priest, gra, and
your conscience is under my hands.

GIPSEY.

But should I put the count into the closet—

FOIGARD.

Vel, is dere any shin for a man's being in a closhet?
One may go to prayers in a closhet.   275

GIPSEY.

But if the lady should come into her chamber and
go to bed?

FOIGARD.

Vel, and is dere any shin in going to bed, joy?

GIPSEY.

Aye, but if the parties should meet, Doctor?

FOIGARD.

Vel den the parties must be responsible. Do you   280

---

63 *a la françois*] *a la française*: in the French manner
64 *logicè*] logically (It.); Foigard's moral hairsplitting repre-
    sents the specious casuistry supposedly practiced by the
    Jesuits.

be after putting the count in the closet and leave
the shins wid themselves. I will come with the
count to instruct you in your chamber.

GIPSEY.

Well Doctor, your religion is so pure! Methinks I'm
so easy after an absolution and can sin afresh with   285
so much security, that I'm resolved to die a martyr
to't.—Here's the key of the garden door; come in
the back way when 'tis late—I'll be ready to receive
you. But don't so much as whisper; only take hold
of my hand, I'll lead you, and do you lead the   290
count, and follow me.

Exeunt. Enter Scrub.

SCRUB.

What witchcraft now have these two imps of the
devil been a hatching here? There's twenty louis
d'ors; I heard that and saw the purse. But I must
give room to my betters. [*Exit.*]   295

Enter Aimwell, leading Dorinda and making love in
dumb show; Mrs. Sullen and Archer.*

MRS. SULLEN. (*To Archer.*)

Pray sir, how d'ye like that piece?

ARCHER.

Oh, 'tis Leda!—You find, madam, how Jupiter
comes disguised to make love—

MRS. SULLEN.

But what think you there of Alexander's battles?

ARCHER.

We want* only a Le Brun, madam, to draw greater   300
battles and a greater general of our own. The
Danube, madam, would make a greater figure in
a picture than the Granicus, and we have our
Ramillies to match their Arbela.[65]

MRS. SULLEN.

Pray sir, what head is that in the corner there.   305

---

65 Le Brun … Arbela] a French court painter who did a
    series of paintings on the battles of Alexander the Great,
    including Alexander's victories at Granicus and Arbela.
    Archer is suggesting that the recent victories of the Duke
    of Marlborough (the "greater general of our own") at
    Blenheim (1707) on the Danube and at Ramillies
    (1706) would make at least as good, if not a better, sub-
    ject for painting.

ARCHER.

Oh madam, 'tis poor Ovid in his exile.

MRS. SULLEN.

What was he banished for?

ARCHER.

His ambitious love, madam. (*Bowing.*) His misfortune touches me.

MRS. SULLEN.

Was he successful in his amours? 310

ARCHER.

There he has left us in the dark. He was too much a gentleman to tell.

MRS. SULLEN.

If he were secret, I pity him.

ARCHER.

And if he were successful, I envy him.

MRS. SULLEN.

How d'ye like that Venus over the chimney? 315

ARCHER.

Venus! I protest, madam, I took it for your picture, but now I look again, 'tis not handsome enough.

MRS. SULLEN.

Oh, what a charm is flattery! If you would see my picture, there it is, over that cabinet. How d'ye like it? 320

ARCHER.

I must admire anything, madam, that has the least resemblance of you. But methinks, madam— (*He looks at the picture and Mrs. Sullen three or four times, by turns.*) Pray madam, who drew it?

MRS. SULLEN.

A famous hand, sir. 325

Here Aimwell and Dorinda go off.

ARCHER.

A famous hand, madam! Your eyes, indeed, are featured there, but where's the sparkling moisture, shining fluid in which they swim? The picture indeed has your dimples, but where's the swarm of killing Cupids that should ambush there? The lips too are figured out, but where's the carnation dew, the pouting ripeness that tempts the taste in the original? 330

MRS. SULLEN. [*Aside.*]

Had it been my lot to have matched with such a man! 335

ARCHER.

Your breasts, too! presumptuous man! What, paint Heaven! Apropos, madam, in the very next picture is Salmoneus, that was struck dead with lightning for offering to imitate Jove's thunder; I hope you served the painter so, madam? 340

MRS. SULLEN.

Had my eyes the power of thunder, they should employ their lightning better.

ARCHER.

There's the finest bed in that room, madam. I suppose 'tis your ladyship's bedchamber?

MRS. SULLEN.

And what then, sir? 345

ARCHER.

I think the quilt is the richest that ever I saw. I can't at this distance, madam, distinguish the figures of the embroidery. Will you give me leave, madam?

MRS. SULLEN. [*Aside.*]

The devil take his impudence! Sure if I gave him an opportunity, he durst not offer* it? I have a great mind to try. (*Going; returns.*) S'death,* what am I doing? And alone too!—Sister! sister! (*Runs out.*) 350

ARCHER.

I'll follow her close—

For where a Frenchman durst attempt to storm, 355
A Briton sure may well the work perform. (*Going.*)

Enter Scrub.

SCRUB.

Martin! brother Martin!

ARCHER.

Oh brother Scrub, I beg your pardon; I was not a-going. Here's a guinea my master ordered you.

SCRUB.

A guinea! Hi, hi, hi! a guinea! eh? by this light, it is a guinea! But I suppose you expect one and twenty shillings in change? 360

ARCHER.

Not at all! I have another for Gipsey.

SCRUB.

A guinea for her! Faggot and fire for the witch! Sir, give me that guinea, and I'll discover* a plot. 365

ARCHER.

A plot!

SCRUB.

Aye sir, a plot, and a horrid plot! First, it must be a plot because there's a woman in't; secondly, it must be a plot because there's a priest in't; thirdly, it must be a plot because there's French gold in't; and fourthly it must be a plot because I don't know what to make on't.   370

ARCHER.

Nor anybody else, I'm afraid, brother Scrub.

SCRUB.

Truly, I'm afraid so too, for where there's a priest and a woman, there's always a mystery and a   375
riddle. This I know, that here has been the doctor with a temptation in one hand and an absolution in the other, and Gipsey has sold herself to the Devil. I saw the price paid down, my eyes shall take their oath on't.   380

ARCHER.

And is all this bustle about Gipsey?

SCRUB.

That's not all; I could hear but a word here and there, but I remember they mentioned a count, a closet, a back door, and a key.

ARCHER.

The count! Did you hear nothing of Mrs. Sullen?   385

SCRUB.

I did hear some word that sounded that way, but whether it was Sullen or Dorinda, I could not distiguish.

ARCHER.

You have told this matter to nobody, brother?

SCRUB.

Told! No sir, I thank you for that! I'm resolved   390
never to speak one word, pro nor con, till we have a peace.

ARCHER.

You're i'th right, brother Scrub. Here's a treaty afoot between the count and the lady; the priest and the chambermaid are the plenipotentiaries. It shall go   395
hard but I find a way to be included in the treaty. Where's the doctor now?

SCRUB.

He and Gipsey are this moment devouring my lady's marmalade in the closet.

AIMWELL. (*From without.*)

Martin! Martin!   400

ARCHER.

I come, sir! I come!

SCRUB.

But you forget the other guinea, brother Martin.

ARCHER.

Here, I give it with all my heart.

SCRUB.

And I take it with all my soul.

Exit Archer.

I'cod, I'll spoil your plotting, Mrs. Gipsey, and if   405
you should set the captain upon me, these two guineas will buy me off. (*Exit.*)

Enter Mrs. Sullen and Dorinda, meeting.

MRS. SULLEN.

Well, sister.

DORINDA.

And well, sister.

MRS. SULLEN.

What's become of my lord?   410

DORINDA.

What's become of his servant?

MRS. SULLEN.

Servant! He's a prettier fellow and a finer gentleman by fifty degrees than his master.

DORINDA.

O'my conscience, I fancy you could beg that fellow at the gallows-foot![66]   415

MRS. SULLEN.

O'my conscience, I could, provided I could put a friend of yours in his room.

DORINDA.

You desired me, sister, to leave you, when you transgressed the bounds of honor.

MRS. SULLEN.

Thou dear censorious country girl! What dost   420
mean? You can't think of the man without the bedfellow, I find.

DORINDA.

I don't find anything unnatural in that thought; while the mind is conversant with flesh and blood, it must conform to the humors* of the company.   425

---

66 beg … gallows-foot] Under an old law, a condemned criminal could be reprieved from the gallows if a respectable woman offered to marry him.

MRS. SULLEN.

How a little love and good company improves a woman! Why child,* you begin to live—you never spoke before.

DORINDA.

Because I was never spoke to. My lord has told me that I have more wit and beauty than any of my sex and, truly, I begin to think the man is sincere!

430

MRS. SULLEN.

You're in the right, Dorinda. Pride is the life of a woman, and flattery is our daily bread, and she's a fool that won't believe a man there, as much as she that believes him in anything else. But I'll lay you a guinea that I had finer things said to me than you had.

435

DORINDA.

Done! What did your fellow say to ye?

MRS. SULLEN.

My fellow took the picture of Venus for mine.

DORINDA.

But my lover took me for Venus herself.

MRS. SULLEN.

Common cant! Had my spark called me a Venus directly, I should have believed him a footman in good earnest.

440

DORINDA.

But my lover was upon his knees to me.

MRS. SULLEN.

And mine was upon his tiptoes to me.

DORINDA.

Mine vowed to die for me.

445

MRS. SULLEN.

Mine swore to die* with me.

DORINDA.

Mine spoke the softest moving things.

MRS. SULLEN.

Mine had his moving things too.

DORINDA.

Mine kissed my hand ten thousand times.

MRS. SULLEN.

Mine has all that pleasure to come.

450

DORINDA.

Mine offered marriage.

MRS. SULLEN.

O Lard! D'ye call that a moving thing?

DORINDA.

The sharpest arrow in his quiver, my dear sister!

Why, my ten thousand pounds may lie brooding here this seven years and hatch nothing at last but some ill-natured clown* like yours! Whereas if I marry my Lord Aimwell, there will be title, place and precedence, the Park,* the play, and the Drawing Room,* splendor, equipage, noise, and flambeaux: "Hey, my Lady Aimwell's servants there!—Lights, lights to the stairs!*—My Lady Aimwell's coach put forward!—Stand by, make room for her ladyship!" Are not these things moving? What! melancholy of a sudden?

455

460

MRS. SULLEN.

Happy, happy sister! Your angel has been watchful for your happiness, whilst mine has slept regardless of his charge. Long smiling years of circling joys for you, but not one hour for me! (*Weeps.*)

465

DORINDA.

Come my dear, we'll talk of something else.

MRS. SULLEN.

Oh Dorinda, I own myself a woman, full of my sex, a gentle, generous soul, easy and yielding to soft desires, a spacious heart, where Love and all his train might lodge. And must the fair apartment of my breast be made a stable for a brute to lie in?

470

DORINDA.

Meaning your husband, I suppose.

475

MRS. SULLEN.

Husband! No, even husband is too soft a name for him.—But come, I expect my brother here tonight or tomorrow. He was abroad when my father married me; perhaps he'll find a way to make me easy.

DORINDA.

Will you promise not to make yourself easy in the meantime with my lord's friend?

480

MRS. SULLEN.

You mistake me, sister. It happens with us, as among the men. The greatest talkers are the greatest cowards, and there's a reason for it: those spirits evaporate in prattle which might do more mischief if they took another course. Though to confess the truth, I do love that fellow, and if I met him dressed as he should be, and I undressed as I should be— Look ye, sister, I have no supernatural gifts; I can't swear I could resist the temptation, though I can safely promise to avoid it, and that's as much as the best of us can do.

485

490

Exeunt Mrs. Sullen and Dorinda.

[Scene ii. The inn.]

Enter Aimwell and Archer laughing.

ARCHER.
And the awkward kindness of the good motherly old gentlewoman—

AIMWELL.
And the coming easiness of the young one— s'death,* tis pity to deceive her!

ARCHER.
Nay, if you adhere to those principles, stop where you are. 5

AIMWELL.
I can't stop, for I love her to distraction.

ARCHER.
S'death, if you love her a hair's breadth beyond discretion you must go no farther.

AIMWELL.
Well, well, any thing to deliver us from sauntering 10 away our idle evenings at White's, Tom's, 67 or Will's, and be stinted to bear looking at our old acquaint- ance, the cards, because our impotent pockets can't afford us a guinea for the mercenary drabs.

ARCHER.
Or be obliged to some purse-proud coxcomb for 15 a scandalous bottle, where we must not pretend to our share of the discourse, because we can't pay our club o'th'reckoning. Damn it, I had rather sponge upon Morris,68 and sup upon a dish of bohea scored behind the door! 20

AIMWELL.
And there expose our want* of sense by talking criticisms, as we should our want of money by railing at the government.

ARCHER.
Or be obliged to sneak into the side box and between both houses steal two acts of a play,69 and 25 because we han't money to see the other three, we come away discontented and damn the whole five.

---

67 Tom's] another London coffee-house

68 Morris] owner of another coffee-shop in London

69 both houses … play] Payment was not demanded if a patron only stayed for one act of a play; by moving be- tween the two playhouses, it was possible to see two acts without paying anything.

AIMWELL.
And ten thousand such rascally tricks—had we outlived our fortunes among our acquaintance. But now— 30

ARCHER.
Aye, now is the time to prevent all this. Strike while the iron is hot.—This priest is the luckiest part of our adventure: he shall marry you, and pimp for me.

AIMWELL.
But I should not like a woman that can be so fond 35 of a Frenchman.

ARCHER.
Alas, sir! Necessity has no law. The lady may be in distress; perhaps she has a confounded husband, and her revenge may carry her farther than her love. Egad, I have so good an opinion of her, and 40 of myself, that I begin to fancy strange things, and we must say this for the honor of our women, and indeed of ourselves, that they do stick to their men, as they do to their Magna Charta. If the plot lies as I suspect, I must put on the gentleman.—But 45 here comes the doctor. I shall be ready. (*Exit.*)

Enter Foigard.

FOIGARD.
Sauve you, noble friend.

AIMWELL.
Oh sir, your servant! Pray Doctor, may I crave your name?

FOIGARD.
Fat naam is upon me? My name is Foigard, joy. 50

AIMWELL.
Foigard, a very good name for a clergyman! Pray Doctor Foigard, were you ever in Ireland?

FOIGARD.
Ireland! No, joy. Fat sort of plaace is dat saam Ireland? Dey say de people are catched dere when dey are young. 55

AIMWELL.
And some of 'em when they're old—as, for example: (*Takes Foigard by the shoulder.*) Sir, I arrest you as a traitor against the government; you're a subject of England, and this morning showed me a commission by which you served as chaplain in 60

the French army. This is death by our law, and your reverence must hang for't.[70]

FOIGARD.

Upon my shoul, noble friend, dis is strange news you tell me! Fader Foigard, a subject of England! De son of a burgomaster of Brussels a subject of England! Ubooboo——[71]

AIMWELL.

The son of a bogtrotter[72] in Ireland! Sir, your tongue will condemn you before any bench in the kingdom.

FOIGARD.

And is my tongue all your evidence, joy?

AIMWELL.

That's enough.

FOIGARD.

No, no, joy, for I vill never spake English no more.

AIMWELL.

Sir, I have other evidence.—Here Martin, you know this fellow.

Enter Archer.

ARCHER. (*In a brogue.*)

Saave you, my dear cussen, how does your health?

FOIGARD. (*Aside.*)

Ah! Upon my shoul dere is my countryman, and his brogue will hang mine.—*Mynheer, Ick wet neat watt hey zacht. Ick universton ewe neat, sacramant.*[73]

AIMWELL.

Altering your language won't do, sir. This fellow knows your person and will swear to your face.

FOIGARD.

Faace! fey, is dere a brogue upon my faash, too?

ARCHER.

Upon my soulvation dere ish, joy! But cussen Mackshane, vil you not put a remembrance upon me?

FOIGARD. (*Aside.*)

Mackshane! By St. Paatrick, dat is naame,[k] shure enough.

AIMWELL. [*Aside to Archer.*]

I fancy Archer, you have it.

FOIGARD.

The Devil hang you, joy! By fat acquaintance are you my cussen?

ARCHER.

Oh, de Devil hang yourself, joy! You know we were little boys togeder upon de school, and your foster moder's son was married upon my nurse's chister, joy, and so we are Irish cussens.[74]

FOIGARD.

De Devil taak the relation! Vel, joy, and fat school was it?

ARCHER.

I tinks it vas—aay—'twas Tipperary.

FOIGARD.

No, no, joy: it vas Kilkenny.

AIMWELL.

That's enough for us—self-confession! Come sir, we must deliver you into the hands of the next magistrate.

ARCHER.

He sends you to gaol; you're tried next assizes, and away you go swing into purgatory.

FOIGARD.

And is it so wid you, cussen?

ARCHER.

It vil be sho wid you, cussen, if you don't immediately confess the secret between you and Mrs. Gipsey.—Look ye, sir, the gallows or the secret, take your choice.

FOIGARD.

The gallows! Upon my shoul I hate that saam gallow, for it is a diseash dat is fatal to our family. Vel den, dere is nothing, shentlemens, but Mrs. Shullen would spaak wid the count in her chamber at midnight, and dere is no haarm, joy, for I am to conduct the count to the plash myshelf.

[65]

[70]

[75]

[80]

[85]

[90]

[95]

[100]

[105]

[110]

---

[70] traitor … hang for't] The Irish were subjects of the Crown at this time; therefore, by serving in the army of the enemy (the French), Foigard was committing treason. Many dispossessed Irish Catholics did serve in the French army in support of the Jacobite cause.

[71] Ubooboo] an anglicization of the Irish "ababu," an exclamation of displeasure

[72] bogtrotter] pejorative term for an Irishman

[73] *Mynheer … sacramant*] fractured Flemish: "Sir, I don't know what he says. I don't understand you, by the sacrament!"

[74] Irish cussens] Gaelic Irish families traditionally fostered out their children into other families, creating a complex kinship web that was often the subject of ridicule by English commentators.

ARCHER.

As I guessed.—Have you communicated the matter to the count?

FOIGARD.

I have not sheen him since.

ARCHER.

Right again.—Why then, Doctor, you shall 115 conduct me to the lady instead of the count.

FOIGARD.

Fat, my cussin to the lady! Upon my shoul, gra, dat is too much upon the brogue.

ARCHER.

Come, come, Doctor. Consider we have got a rope about your neck, and if you offer* to squeak, we'll 120 stop your windpipe, most certainly; we shall have another job for you in a day or two, I hope.

AIMWELL.

Here's company coming this way. Let's into my chamber and there concert our affair farther.

ARCHER.

Come, my dear cussen, come along. 125

Exeunt. Enter Bonniface, Hounslow and Bagshot at one door, Gibbet at the opposite.

GIBBET.

Well, gentlemen, 'tis a fine night for our enterprise.

HOUNSLOW.

Dark as hell.

BAGSHOT.

And blows like the devil. Our landlord here has showed us the window where we must break in and tells us the plate* stands in the wainscot 130 cupboard in the parlor.

BONNIFACE.

Aye, aye, Mr. Bagshot, as the saving is—knives and forks, and cups and cans, and tumblers and tankards. There's one tankard, as the saying is, that's near upon as big as me; it was a present to 135 the squire from his godmother and smells of nutmeg and toast like an East India ship.

HOUNSLOW.

Then you say we must divide at the stair-head?

BONNIFACE.

Yes, Mr. Hounslow, as the saying is. At one end of that gallery lies my Lady Bountiful and her daughter, 140 and at the other Mrs. Sullen. As for the squire—

GIBBET.

He's safe enough; I have fairly entered him, and he's more than half-seas-over* already. But such a parcel of scoundrels are got about him now that, egad, I was ashamed to be seen in their company! 145

BONNIFACE.

'Tis now twelve, as the saying is. Gentlemen, you must set out at one.

GIBBET.

Hounslow, do you and Bagshot see our arms fixed, and I'll come to you presently.*

HOUNSLOW, BAGSHOT.

We will. (*Exeunt.*) 150

GIBBET.

Well, my dear Bonny, you assure me that Scrub is a coward.

BONNIFACE.

A chicken, as the saying is. You'll have no creature to deal with but the ladies.

GIBBET.

And I can assure you, friend, there's a great deal 155 of address and good manners in robbing a lady; I am the most a gentleman that way that ever traveled the road. But my dear Bonny, this prize will be a galleon, a Vigo business;[75] I warrant you we shall bring off three or four thousand pound. 160

BONNIFACE.

In plate, jewels, and money, as the saying is, you may.

GIBBET.

Why then, Tyburn, I defy thee! I'll get up to Town, sell off my horse and arms, buy myself some pretty employment in the Household,[76] and be as snug and as honest as any courtier of 'um all. 165

BONNIFACE.

And what think you then of my daughter Cherry for a wife?

GIBBET.

Look ye, my dear Bonny, Cherry is the goddess I adore, as the song goes, but it is a maxim that man and wife should never have it in their power to 170 hang one another, for if they should, the Lord have mercy on 'um both.

Exeunt.

---

75 Vigo business] The English captured Spanish treasure-ships in Vigo harbor in Spain in 1702.

76 Household] dwelling of the Royals

Act V, scene [i]. Scene continues.

Knocking without. Enter Bonniface.

BONNIFACE.

Coming! coming!—A coach and six foaming horses at this time o'night! Some great man, as the saying is, for he scorns to travel with other people.

Enter Sir Charles Freeman.

SIR CHARLES.

What fellow! a public house, and abed when other people sleep! 5

BONNIFACE.

Sir, I an't abed, as the saying is.

SIR CHARLES.

Is Mr. Sullen's family abed, think ye?

BONNIFACE.

All but the squire himself, sir, as the saying is. He's in the house.

SIR CHARLES.

What company has he? 10

BONNIFACE.

Why sir, there's the constable, Mr. Gage the exciseman, the hunchbacked barber, and two or three other gentlemen.

SIR CHARLES. [*Aside.*]

I find my sister's letters gave me the true picture of her spouse. 15

Enter Sullen drunk.

BONNIFACE.

Sir, here's the squire.

SULLEN.

The puppies left me asleep.—Sir!

SIR CHARLES.

Well sir.

SULLEN.

Sir, I'm an unfortunate man: I have three thousand pound a year, and I can't get a man to drink a cup 20 of ale with me.

SIR CHARLES.

That's very hard.

SULLEN.

Aye sir. And unless you have pity upon me and smoke one pipe with me, I must e'en go home to my wife, and I had rather go to the devil by half. 25

SIR CHARLES.

But I presume, sir, you won't see your wife tonight; she'll be gone to bed. You don't use to lie with your wife in that pickle?

SULLEN.

What! not lie with my wife! Why sir, do you take me for an atheist or a rake? 30

SIR CHARLES.

If you hate her, sir, I think you had better lie from her.

SULLEN.

I think so too, friend. But I'm a justice of peace and must do nothing against the law.

SIR CHARLES.

Law! As I take it, Mr. Justice, nobody observes law for law's sake, only for the good of those for whom 35 it was made.

SULLEN.

But if the law orders me to send you to gaol, you must lie there, my friend.

SIR CHARLES.

Not unless I commit a crime to deserve it.

SULLEN.

A crime! 'Oons,* an't I married? 40

SIR CHARLES.

Nay sir, if you call marriage a crime, you must disown it for a law.

SULLEN.

Eh! I must be acquainted with you, sir. But sir, I should be very glad to know the truth of this matter. 45

SIR CHARLES.

Truth, sir, is a profound sea, and few there be that dare wade deep enough to find out the bottom on't. Besides sir, I'm afraid the line of your understanding mayn't be long enough.

SULLEN.

Look ye, sir, I have nothing to say to your sea of 50 truth, but if a good parcel of land can entitle a man to a little truth, I have as much as any he in the country.

BONNIFACE.

I never heard your worship, as the saying is, talk so much before. 55

SULLEN.

Because I never met with a man that I liked before—

BONNIFACE.

Pray sir, as the saying is, let me ask you one question: Are not man and wife one flesh?

SIR CHARLES.

You and your wife, Mr. Guts, may be one flesh, 60 because ye are nothing else—but rational creatures have minds that must be united.

SULLEN.

Minds!

SIR CHARLES.

Aye, minds, sir. Don't you think that the mind takes place of[77] the body? 65

SULLEN.

In some people.

SIR CHARLES.

Then the interest of the master must be consulted before that of his servant.

SULLEN.

Sir, you shall dine with me tomorrow. 'Oons, I always thought that we were naturally one. 70

SIR CHARLES.

Sir, I know that my two hands are naturally one, because they love one another, kiss one another, help one another in all the actions of life, but I could not say so much, if they were always at cuffs.

SULLEN.

Then 'tis plain that we are two. 75

SIR CHARLES.

Why don't you part with her, sir?

SULLEN.

Will you take her, sir?

SIR CHARLES.

With all my heart.

SULLEN.

You shall have her tomorrow morning and a venison pasty into the bargain. 80

SIR CHARLES.

You'll let me have her fortune too?

SULLEN.

Fortune! why sir, I have no quarrel at her fortune. I only hate the woman, sir, and none but the woman shall go.

SIR CHARLES.

But her fortune, sir— 85

SULLEN.

Can you play at whist, sir?

SIR CHARLES.

No, truly, sir.

SULLEN.

Nor at all-fours?[78]

SIR CHARLES.

Neither!

SULLEN. (*Aside.*)

'Oons! where was this man bred?—Burn me, sir, 90 I can't go home; 'tis but two o'clock.

SIR CHARLES.

For half an hour, sir, if you please, but you must consider 'tis late.

SULLEN.

Late! that's the reason I can't go to bed. Come, sir!

Exeunt. Enter Cherry, runs across the stage and knocks at Aimwell's chamber door. Enter Aimwell in his nightcap and gown.

AIMWELL.

What's the matter? You tremble, child,* you're 95 frighted.

CHERRY.

No wonder, sir—but in short, sir, this very minute a gang of rogues are gone to rob my Lady Bountiful's house.

AIMWELL.

How! 100

CHERRY.

I dogged 'em to the very door and left 'em breaking in.

AIMWELL.

Have you alarmed anybody else with the news?

CHERRY.

No, no, sir. I wanted to have discovered* the whole plot and twenty other things to your man Martin, 105 but I have searched the whole house and can't find him. Where is he?

AIMWELL.

No matter, child. Will you guide me immediately to the house?

CHERRY.

With all my heart, sir. My Lady Bountiful is my 110 godmother, and I love Mrs. Dorinda so well—

---

77 place of] precedence over

78 all-fours] card game, played by two

AIMWELL.

Dorinda! The name inspires me! The glory and the danger shall be all my own.—Come, my life, let me but get my sword.

Exeunt.

Scene [ii]. A bedchamber in Lady Bountiful's house.

Enter Mrs. Sullen, Dorinda undressed;[79] *a table and lights.*

DORINDA.

'Tis very late, sister. No news of your spouse yet?

MRS. SULLEN.

No, I'm condemned to be alone till towards four, and then perhaps I may be executed with his company.

DORINDA.

Well my dear, I'll leave you to your rest; you'll go 5
directly to bed, I suppose.

MRS. SULLEN.

I don't know what to do. Heigh-ho!

DORINDA.

That's a desiring sigh, sister.

MRS. SULLEN.

This is a languishing hour, sister.

DORINDA.

And might prove a critical minute, if the pretty 10
fellow were here.

MRS. SULLEN.

Here! what, in my bedchamber, at two o'clock o'th'morning, I undressed, the family asleep, my hated husband abroad, and my lovely fellow at my feet? Oh gad, sister! 15

DORINDA.

Thoughts are free, sister, and them I allow you. So my dear, good night. [*Exit.*]

MRS. SULLEN.

A good rest to my dear Dorinda.—Thoughts free! Are they so? Why then, suppose him here, dressed like a youthful, gay and burning bridegroom, (*Here* 20
Archer steals out of the closet.) with tongue enchanting, eyes bewitching, knees imploring— (*Turns a little o' one side and sees Archer in the posture she describes.*) Ah! (*Shrieks, and runs to the*

—————

79 *undressed*] in night attire

other side of the stage.) Have my thoughts raised a 25
spirit?—What are you, sir, a man or a devil?

ARCHER. (*Rising.*)

A man! a man, madam!

MRS. SULLEN.

How shall I be sure of it?

ARCHER.

Madam, I'll give you demonstration this minute. (*Takes her hand.*) 30

MRS. SULLEN.

What, sir! Do you intend to be rude?

ARCHER.

Yes madam, if you please.

MRS. SULLEN.

In the name of wonder, whence came ye?

ARCHER.

From the skies, madam: I'm a Jupiter in love, and you shall be my Alcmene. 35

MRS. SULLEN.

How came you in?

ARCHER.

I flew in at the window, madam; your cousin Cupid lent me his wings, and your sister Venus opened the casement.

MRS. SULLEN.

I'm struck dumb with admiration!* 40

ARCHER. (*Looks passionately at her.*)

And I with wonder.

MRS. SULLEN.

What will become of me?

ARCHER.

How beautiful she looks! The teeming jolly spring smiles in her blooming face, and when she was conceived, her mother smelt to roses, looked on lilies— 45

Lilies unfold their white, their fragrant charms,
When the warm sun thus darts into their arms.
    (*Runs to her.*)

MRS. SULLEN. (*Shrieks.*)

Ah!

ARCHER.

'Oons,* madam, what d'ye mean? You'll raise the house. 50

MRS. SULLEN.

Sir, I'll wake the dead before I bear this. What! approach me with the freedoms of a keeper!* I'm glad on't; your impudence has cured me.

ARCHER.

If this be impudence, (*Kneels.*) I leave to your partial self; no panting pilgrim after a tedious, painful voyage, e'er bowed before his saint with more devotion. 55

MRS. SULLEN. (*Aside*)

Now, now, I'm ruined if he kneels!—Rise thou prostrate engineer;* not all thy undermining skill shall reach my heart. Rise, and know, I am a 60 woman without my sex: I can love to all the tenderness of wishes, sighs, and tears—but go no farther. Still, to convince you that I'm more than woman, I can speak my frailty, confess my weakness even for you—but— 65

ARCHER. (*Going to lay hold on her.*)

For me!

MRS. SULLEN.

Hold, sir, build not upon that, for my most mortal hatred follows if you disobey what I command you now: Leave me this minute. (*Aside.*) If he denies, I'm lost. 70

ARCHER.

Then you'll promise—

MRS. SULLEN.

Anything another time.

ARCHER.

When shall I come?

MRS. SULLEN.

Tomorrow, when you will.

ARCHER.

Your lips must seal the promise. 75

MRS. SULLEN.

Pshaw!

ARCHER.

They must, they must! (*Kisses her.*) Raptures and paradise! And why not now, my angel? The time, the place, silence and secrecy, all conspire—and the now conscious stars have preordained this moment 80 for my happiness. (*Takes her in his arms.*)

MRS. SULLEN.

You will not! cannot, sure!

ARCHER.

If the sun rides fast and disappoints not mortals of tomorrow's dawn, this night shall crown my joys.

MRS. SULLEN.

My sex's pride assist me! 85

ARCHER.

My sex's strength help me!

MRS. SULLEN.

You shall kill me first.

ARCHER.

I'll die* with you. (*Carrying her off.*)

MRS. SULLEN.

Thieves! Thieves! Murder!

Enter Scrub in his breeches and one shoe.

SCRUB.

Thieves! Thieves! Murder! Popery! 90

ARCHER.

Hah! the very* timorous stag will kill in rutting time. (*Draws and offers* to stab Scrub.*)

SCRUB. (*Kneeling.*)

Oh, pray, sir, spare all I have and take my life.

MRS. SULLEN. (*Holding Archer's hand.*)

What does the fellow mean?

SCRUB.

Oh madam, down upon your knees, your 95 marrowbones—he's one of 'um!

ARCHER.

Of whom?

SCRUB.

One of the rogues—I beg your pardon, sir, one of the honest gentlemen that just now are broke into the house. 100

ARCHER.

How!

MRS. SULLEN.

I hope you did not come to rob me?

ARCHER.

Indeed I did, madam, but I would have taken nothing but what you might ha' spared. But your crying "Thieves" has waked this dreaming fool, 105 and so he takes 'em for granted.

SCRUB.

Granted! 'tis granted, sir, take all we have.

MRS. SULLEN.

The fellow looks as if he were broke out of Bedlam.

SCRUB.

'Oons madam, they're broke into the house with fire and sword! I saw them, heard them, they'll be 110 here this minute.

ARCHER.

What, thieves?

SCRUB.

Under favor, sir, I think so.

MRS. SULLEN.

What shall we do, sir?

ARCHER.

Madam, I wish your ladyship a good night.   115

MRS. SULLEN.

Will you leave me?

ARCHER.

Leave you! Lord madam, did not you command
me to be gone just now upon pain of your
immortal hatred?

MRS. SULLEN.

Nay, but pray sir— (*Takes hold of him.*)   120

ARCHER.

Ha, ha, ha! now comes my turn to be ravished. You
see now, madam, you must use men one way or
other. But take this by the way, good madam, that
none but a fool will give you the benefit of his
courage, unless you'll take his love along with it.—   125
How are they armed, friend?

SCRUB.

With sword and pistol, sir.

ARCHER.

Hush! I see a dark lantern coming through the
gallery.—Madam, be assured I will protect you or
lose my life.   130

MRS. SULLEN.

Your life! No, sir, they can rob me of nothing that
I value half so much; therefore, now sir, let me
entreat you to be gone.

ARCHER.

No madam, I'll consult my own safety for the sake
of yours; I'll work by stratagem. Have you courage   135
enough to stand the appearance of 'em?

MRS. SULLEN.

Yes, yes, since I have 'scaped your hands, I can face
anything.

ARCHER.

Come hither, brother Scrub. Don't you know me?

SCRUB.

Eh! My dear brother, let me kiss thee. (*Kisses   140
Archer.*)

ARCHER.

This way—here— (*Archer and Scrub hide behind
the bed.*)

*Enter Gibbet with a dark lantern in one hand and a
pistol in t'other.*

GIBBET.

Aye, aye, this is the chamber, and the lady alone.

MRS. SULLEN.

Who are you, sir? What would you have? D'ye   145
come to rob me?

GIBBET.

Rob you! Alack a day, madam, I'm only a younger
brother, madam. And so, madam, if you make a
noise, I'll shoot you through the head, but don't be
afraid, madam. (*Laying his lantern and pistol upon the*   150
table.) These rings, madam. Don't be concerned,
madam, I have a profound respect for you, madam.
Your keys, madam. (*Searching her pockets.*) Don't be
frighted, madam, I'm the most of a gentleman. This
necklace, madam. I never was rude to a lady. I have   155
a veneration—for this necklace—

*Here Archer having come round and seized the pistol
takes Gibbet by the collar, trips up his heels, and claps
the pistol to his breast.*

ARCHER.

Hold, profane villain, and take the reward of thy
sacrilege!

GIBBET.

Oh! Pray sir, don't kill me: I an't prepared.

ARCHER.

How many is there of 'em, Scrub?   160

SCRUB.

Five and forty, sir.

ARCHER.

Then I must kill the villain to have him out of the
way.

GIBBET.

Hold, hold, sir! We are but three, upon my honor!

ARCHER.

Scrub, will you undertake to secure him?   165

SCRUB.

Not I, sir! Kill him, kill him!

ARCHER.

Run to Gipsey's chamber. There you'll find the
doctor; bring him hither presently.*

Exit Scrub running.

Come rogue, if you have a short prayer, say it.

GIBBET.

Sir, I have no prayer at all; the government has 170
provided a chaplain to say prayers for us on these
occasions.

MRS. SULLEN.

Pray sir, don't kill him. You fright me as much as
him.

ARCHER.

The dog shall die, madam, for being the occasion 175
of my disappointment.—Sirrah, this moment is
your last.

GIBBET.

Sir, I'll give you two hundred pound to spare my
life.

ARCHER.

Have you no more, rascal? 180

GIBBET.

Yes sir, I can command four hundred, but I must
reserve two of 'em to save my life at the sessions.

Enter Scrub and Foigard.

ARCHER.

Here Doctor, I suppose Scrub and you between
you may manage him. Lay hold of him, Doctor.

Foigard lays hold of Gibbet.

GIBBET.

What! Turned over to the priest already!—Look ye, 185
Doctor, you come before your time: I'ant
condemned yet, I thank ye.

FOIGARD.

Come, my dear joy, I vill secure your body and
your shoul too; I vill make you a good Catholic
and give you an absolution. 190

GIBBET.

Absolution! Can you procure me a pardon,
Doctor?

FOIGARD.

No, joy.

GIBBET.

Then you and your absolution may go to the devil.

ARCHER.

Convey him into the cellar; there bind him. Take 195
the pistol, and if he offers* to resist, shoot him
through the head and come back to us with all the
speed you can.

SCRUB.

Aye, aye. Come Doctor, do you hold him fast, and
I'll guard him. 200

[Exeunt Scrub and Foigard with Gibbet.]

MRS. SULLEN.

But how came the doctor?

ARCHER.

In short, madam— (*Shrieking without.*) S'death,*
the rogues are at work with the other ladies! I'm
vexed I parted with the pistol, but I must fly to
their assistance. Will you stay here, madam, or 205
venture yourself with me?

MRS. SULLEN.

Oh, with you, dear sir, with you.

Takes him by the arm and exeunt.

Scene [iii]. Another apartment in the same house.

*Enter [Bagshot] dragging in Lady Bountiful, and
[Hounslow] hauling in Dorinda; the rogues with
swords drawn.*

HOUNSLOW.

Come, come, your jewels, mistress!

BAGSHOT.

Your keys, your keys, old gentlewoman!

Enter Aimwell and Cherry.

AIMWELL.

Turn this way, villains! I durst engage an army in
such a cause. (*He engages 'em both.*)

DORINDA.

Oh madam, had I but a sword to help the brave 5
man!

LADY BOUNTIFUL.

There's three or four hanging up in the hall, but
they won't draw. I'll go fetch one, however. (*Exit.*)

Enter Archer and Mrs. Sullen.

ARCHER.

Hold, hold, my lord! every man his bird, pray.

*They engage man to man; the rogues are thrown and
disarmed.*

CHERRY. [*Aside.*]

What! the rogues taken! Then they'll impeach my 10
father; I must give him timely notice. (*Runs out.*)

ARCHER.

Shall we kill the rogues?

AIMWELL.

No, no, we'll bind them.

ARCHER.

Aye, aye. (*To Mrs. Sullen who stands by him.*) Here madam, lend me your garter.   15

MRS. SULLEN. [*Aside.*]

The devil's in this fellow! He fights, loves, and banters, all in a breath.—Here's a cord that the rogues brought with 'em, I suppose.

ARCHER.

Right, right, the rogue's destiny, a rope to hang himself.—Come my lord, this is but a scandalous sort of   20 an office, (*Binding the rogues together.*) if our adventures should end in this sort of hangman-work. But I hope there is something in prospect that—

Enter Scrub.

Well, Scrub, have you secured your Tartar?

SCRUB.

Yes sir, I left the priest and him disputing about   25 religion.

AIMWELL.

And pray, carry these gentlemen to reap the benefit of the controversy.

Delivers the prisoners to Scrub, who leads 'em out.

MRS. SULLEN.

Pray sister, how came my lord here?

DORINDA.

And pray, how came the gentleman here?   30

MRS. SULLEN.

I'll tell you the greatest piece of villainy—

They talk in dumb show.

AIMWELL.

I fancy, Archer, you have been more successful in your adventures than the house-breakers.

ARCHER.

No matter for my adventure, yours is the principal. Press her this minute to marry you, now while she's   35 hurried between the palpitation of her fear and the joy of her deliverance, now while the tide of her spirits are at high-flood. Throw yourself at her feet, speak some romantic nonsense or other, address

her like Alexander[80] in the height of his victory,   40 confound her senses, bear down her reason, and away with her. The priest is now in the cellar and dare not refuse to do the work.

Enter Lady Bountiful.

AIMWELL.

But how shall I get off without being observed?

ARCHER.

You a lover, and not find a way to get off! Let me   45 see—

AIMWELL.

You bleed, Archer!

ARCHER.

S'death,* I'm glad on't: this wound will do the business. I'll amuse the old lady and Mrs. Sullen about dressing my wound, while you carry off   50 Dorinda.

LADY BOUNTIFUL.

Gentlemen, could we understand how you would be gratified for the services—

ARCHER.

Come, come, my lady, this is no time for compliments. I'm wounded, madam.   55

LADY BOUNTIFUL, MRS. SULLEN.

How! wounded!

DORINDA.

I hope, sir, you have received no hurt?

AIMWELL.

None but what you may cure. (*Makes love* in dumb show.*)

LADY BOUNTIFUL.

Let me see your arm, sir. I must have some   60 powder-sugar to stop the blood. Oh me! an ugly gash, upon my word! Sir, you must go into bed.

ARCHER.

Aye my lady, a bed would do very well. (*To Mrs. Sullen.*) Madam, will you do me the favor to conduct me to a chamber?   65

LADY BOUNTIFUL.

Do, do, daughter, while I get the lint and the probe and the plaster ready.

---

80 address … Alexander] In Nathaniel Lee's still popular play, *The Rival Queens* (1677), Alexander the Great uses his rhetorical skills to woo Statira.

Runs out one way; Aimwell carries off Dorinda another.

ARCHER.
  Come madam, why don't you obey your mother's
  commands?

MRS. SULLEN.
  How can you, after what is past, have the   70
  confidence to ask me?

ARCHER.
  And if you go to that, how can you, after what is
  past, have the confidence to deny me? Was not this
  blood shed in your defense and my life exposed
  for your protection? Look ye, madam, I'm none   75
  of your romantic fools that fight giants and
  monsters for nothing; my valor is downright
  Swiss;[81] I'm a soldier of fortune and must be paid.

MRS. SULLEN.
  'Tis ungenerous in you, sir, to upbraid me with
  your services.   80

ARCHER.
  'Tis ungenerous in you, madam, not to reward 'em.

MRS. SULLEN.
  How! at the expense of my honor?

ARCHER.
  Honor! Can honor consist with ingratitude? If you
  would deal like a woman of honor, do like a man of
  honor. D'ye think I would deny you in such a case? 85

Enter a servant.

SERVANT.
  Madam, my lady ordered me to tell you that your
  brother is below at the gate. [*Exit.*]

MRS. SULLEN.
  My brother! Heavens be praised!—Sir, he shall
  thank you for your services. He has it in his power.

ARCHER.
  Who is your brother, madam?   90

MRS. SULLEN.
  Sir Charles Freeman. You'll excuse me, sir; I must
  go and receive him. [*Exit.*]

ARCHER.
  Sir Charles Freeman! S'death and hell! my old
  acquaintance! Now unless Aimwell has made good

use of his time, all our fair machine goes souse into   95
the sea like the Eddystone.[82]

Exit.

  Scene [iv]. The gallery in the same house.

Enter Aimwell and Dorinda.

DORINDA.
  Well, well, my lord, you have conquered. Your late
  generous action will, I hope, plead for my easy
  yielding, though I must own your lordship had a
  friend in the fort before.

AIMWELL.
  The sweets of Hybla[83] dwell upon her tongue!   5

Enter Foigard with a book.

  Here, Doctor—

FOIGARD.
  Are you prepared boat?

DORINDA.
  I'm ready. But first, my lord, one word: I have a
  frightful example of a hasty marriage in my own
  family; when I reflect upon't, it shocks me. Pray   10
  my lord, consider a little—

AIMWELL.
  Consider! Do you doubt my honor or my love?

DORINDA.
  Neither: I do believe you equally just as brave. And
  were your whole sex drawn out for me to choose,
  I should not cast a look upon the multitude if you   15
  were absent. But my lord, I'm a woman: colors,
  concealments may hide a thousand faults in me;
  therefore, know me better first. I hardly dare affirm
  I know myself in anything except my love.

AIMWELL. (*Aside.*)
  Such goodness who could injure? I find myself   20
  unequal to the task of villain; she has gained my
  soul and made it honest like her own. I cannot,
  cannot hurt her.—Doctor, retire.

Exit Foigard.

  Madam, behold your lover and your proselyte and
  judge of my passion by my conversion: I'm all a   25

---

81 Swiss] The Swiss were renowned for being mercenary
  soldiers.

82 Eddystone] lighthouse destroyed by a great storm in
  1703
83 Hybla] mountain in Sicily known for its honey

lie, nor dare I give a fiction to your arms; I'm all counterfeit except my passion.

DORINDA.

Forbid it, Heaven! A counterfeit!

AIMWELL.

I am no lord, but a poor needy man come with a mean, a scandalous design to prey upon your fortune. But the beauties of your mind and person have so won me from myself, that like a trusty servant, I prefer the interest of my mistress to my own.

DORINDA.

Sure I have had the dream of some poor mariner, a sleepy image of a welcome port, and wake involved in storms!—Pray sir, who are you?

AIMWELL.

Brother to the man whose title I usurped, but stranger to his honor or his fortune.

DORINDA.

Matchless honesty! Once I was proud, sir, of your wealth and title but now am prouder that you want* it. Now I can show my love was justly leveled and had no aim but love.—Doctor, come in.

Enter Foigard at one door, Gipsey at another, who whispers Dorinda.

[*To Foigard.*] Your pardon, sir, we shannot want you now.¹ [*To Aimwell.*] Sir, you must excuse me, I'll wait on you presently.* (*Exit with Gipsey.*)

FOIGARD.

Upon my shoul, now, dis is foolish! (*Exit.*)

AIMWELL.

Gone! and bid the priest depart! It has an ominous look.

Enter Archer.

ARCHER.

Courage, Tom! Shall I wish you joy?

AIMWELL.

No.

ARCHER.

'Oons* man, what ha' you been doing?

AIMWELL.

Oh Archer, my honesty, I fear, has ruined me.

ARCHER.

How?

AIMWELL.

I have discovered* myself.

ARCHER.

Discovered! and without my consent? What! have I embarked my small remains in the same bottom with yours, and you dispose of all without my partnership?

AIMWELL.

Oh Archer, I own my fault!

ARCHER.

After conviction, 'tis then too late for pardon. You may remember, Mr. Aimwell, that you proposed this folly. As you begun, so end it. Henceforth I'll hunt my fortune single. So farewell!

AIMWELL.

Stay, my dear Archer, but a minute!

ARCHER.

Stay! What, to be despised, exposed and laughed at? No, I would sooner change conditions with the worst of the rogues we just now bound, than bear one scornful smile from the proud knight that once I treated as my equal.

AIMWELL.

What knight?

ARCHER.

Sir Charles Freeman, brother to the lady that I had almost—but no matter for that. 'Tis a cursed night's work, and so I leave you to make your best on't. (*Going.*)

AIMWELL.

Freeman! One word, Archer. Still I have hopes; methought she received my confession with pleasure.

ARCHER.

S'death! who doubts it?

AIMWELL.

She consented after to the match, and still I dare believe she will be just.

ARCHER.

To herself, I warrant her, as you should have been.

AIMWELL.

By all my hopes, she comes, and smiling comes!

Enter Dorinda, mighty gay.

DORINDA.

Come my dear lord, I fly with impatience to your

arms. The minutes of my absence was a tedious 85
year. Where's this tedious priest?

Enter Foigard.

ARCHER.
  'Oons, a brave* girl!

DORINDA.
  I suppose, my lord, this gentleman is privy to our
  affairs?

ARCHER.
  Yes, yes, madam. I'm to be your father. 90

DORINDA.
  Come priest, do your office.

ARCHER.
  Make haste, make haste! Couple 'em any way.
  (*Takes Aimwell's hand.*) Come madam, I'm to give
  you—

DORINDA.
  My mind's altered. I won't. 95

ARCHER.
  Eh?

AIMWELL.
  I'm confounded.

FOIGARD.
  Upon my shoul, and sho is myshelf.

ARCHER.
  What's the matter now, madam?

DORINDA.
  Look ye, sir, one generous* action deserves 100
  another: this gentleman's honor obliged him to
  hide nothing from me; my justice engages me to
  conceal nothing from him. In short, sir, you are
  the person that you thought you counterfeited: you
  are the true Lord Viscount Aimwell, and I wish 105
  your lordship joy.—Now priest, you may be gone.
  If my lord is pleased now with the match, let his
  lordship marry me in the face of the world.

AIMWELL, ARCHER.
  What does she mean?

DORINDA.
  Here's a witness for my truth. 110

Enter Sir Charles and Mrs. Sullen.

SIR CHARLES.
  My dear Lord Aimwell, I wish you joy.

AIMWELL.
  Of what?

SIR CHARLES.
  Of your honor and estate: your brother died the
  day before I left London, and all your friends have
  writ after you to Brussels; among the rest I did 115
  myself the honor.

ARCHER.
  Hark ye, Sir Knight, don't you banter now?

SIR CHARLES.
  'Tis truth upon my honor.

AIMWELL.
  Thanks to the pregnant stars that formed this
  accident! 120

ARCHER.
  Thanks to the womb of time that brought it forth!
  Away with it!

AIMWELL.
  Thanks to my guardian angel that led me to the
  prize. (*Taking Dorinda's hand.*)

ARCHER.
  And double thanks to the noble Sir Charles 125
  Freeman. My lord, I wish you joy.—My lady, I
  wish you joy.—Egad, Sir Freeman, you're the
  honestest fellow living.—S'death, I'm grown
  strange airy upon this matter!—My lord, how d'ye?
  A word, my lord: don't you remember something 130
  of a previous agreement that entitles me to the
  moiety of this lady's fortune, which, I think, will
  amount to five thousand pound?

AIMWELL.
  Not a penny, Archer! You would ha' cut my throat
  just now because I would not deceive this lady. 135

ARCHER.
  Aye, and I'll cut your throat again, if you should
  deceive her now.

AIMWELL.
  That's what I expected, and to end the dispute: the
  lady's fortune is ten thousand pound; we'll divide
  stakes. Take the ten thousand pound, or the lady. 140

DORINDA.
  How! Is your lordship so indifferent?

ARCHER.
  No, no, no, madam, his lordship knows very well
  that I'll take the money. I leave you to his lordship,
  and so we're both provided for.

Enter Count Bellair.

COUNT BELLAIR.

Mesdames and Messieurs, I am your servant trice 145
humble! I hear you be rob here.

AIMWELL.

The ladies have been in some danger, sir.

COUNT BELLAIR.

And begar,* our inn be rob too!

AIMWELL.

Our inn! By whom?

COUNT BELLAIR.

By the landlord, begar! Garzoon, he has rob 150
himself and run away!

ARCHER.

Robbed himself!

COUNT BELLAIR.

Aye, begar, and me too of a hundre pound.

ARCHER.

A hundred pound?

COUNT BELLAIR.

Yes, that I owed him. 155

AIMWELL.

Our money's gone, Frank.

ARCHER.

Rot the money! My wench is gone.—*Savez-vous
quelque chose de Mademoiselle Cherry?*[84]

Enter a fellow with a strongbox and a letter.

FELLOW.

Is there one Martin, here?

ARCHER.

Aye, aye, who wants him? 160

FELLOW.

I have a box here and letter for him.

ARCHER. (*Taking the box.*)

Ha, ha, ha! what's here? Legerdemain! By this light,
my lord, our money again! But this unfolds the
riddle. (*Opening the letter, reads.*) Hum, hum, hum.
Oh, 'tis for the public good and must be communi- 165
cated to the company. "Mr. Martin, My father being
afraid of an impeachment by the rogues that are
taken tonight is gone off, but if you can procure him
a pardon, he will make great discoveries* that may
be useful to the country. Could I have met you 170

instead of your master tonight, I would have
delivered myself into your hands with a sum that
much exceeds that in your strongbox, which I have
sent you, with an assurance to my dear Martin, that
I shall ever be his most faithful friend till death. 175
Cherry Bonniface." There's a billet-doux for you! As
for the father, I think he ought to be encouraged,
and for the daughter—pray my lord, persuade your
bride to take her into her service instead of Gipsey.

AIMWELL.

I can assure you, madam, your deliverance was 180
owing to her discovery.*

DORINDA.

Your command, my lord, will do without the
obligation. I'll take care of her.

SIR CHARLES.

This good company meets opportunely in favor of
a design I have in behalf of my unfortunate sister. 185
I intend to part her from her husband.—
Gentlemen, will you assist me?

ARCHER.

Assist you! S'death, who would not!

COUNT BELLAIR.

Assist! Garzoon, we all assest!

Enter Sullen.

SULLEN.

What's all this? They tell me, Spouse, that you had 190
like to have been robbed.

MRS. SULLEN.

Truly, Spouse, I was pretty near it, had not these
two gentlemen interposed.

SULLEN.

How came these gentlemen here?

MRS. SULLEN.

That's his way of returning thanks, you must know. 195

COUNT BELLAIR.

Garzoon, the question be apropos for all dat!

SIR CHARLES.

You promised last night, sir, that you would deliver
your lady to me this morning.

SULLEN.

Humph!

ARCHER.

Humph! What do you mean by humph? Sir, you 200
shall deliver her. In short, sir, we have saved you

---

84 *Savez-vous ... Cherry?*] "Do you know anything about
Miss Cherry?" (Fr.).

and your family, and if you are not civil, we'll unbind the rogues, join with 'um, and set fire to your house.—What does the man mean? not part with his wife! 205

COUNT BELLAIR.
Aye garzoon, de man no understand common justice.

MRS. SULLEN.
Hold gentlemen, all things here must move by consent. Compulsion would spoil us. Let my dear and I talk the matter over, and you shall judge it between us. 210

SULLEN.
Let me know first who are to be our judges.—Pray sir, who are you?

SIR CHARLES.
I am Sir Charles Freeman, come to take away your wife.

SULLEN.
And you, good sir? 215

AIMWELL.
Thomas^m Viscount Aimwell, come to take away your sister.

SULLEN.
And you pray, sir?

ARCHER.
Francis Archer, Esquire, come—

SULLEN.
To take away my mother, I hope. Gentlemen, you're 220 heartily welcome. I never met with three more obliging people since I was born.—And now, my dear, if you please, you shall have the first word.

ARCHER.
And the last for five pound.

MRS. SULLEN.
Spouse. 225

SULLEN.
Rib.*

MRS. SULLEN.
How long have we been married?

SULLEN.
By the almanac, fourteen months—but by my account, fourteen years.

MRS. SULLEN.
'Tis thereabout by my reckoning. 230

COUNT BELLAIR.
Garzoon, their account will agree.

MRS. SULLEN.
Pray Spouse, what did you marry for?

SULLEN.
To get an heir to my estate.

SIR CHARLES.
And have you succeeded?

SULLEN.
No. 235

ARCHER.
The condition fails of his side.—Pray madam, what did you marry for?

MRS. SULLEN.
To support the weakness of my sex by the strength of his, and to enjoy the pleasures of an agreeable society. 240

SIR CHARLES.
Are your expectations answered?

MRS. SULLEN.
No.

COUNT BELLAIR.
A clear case! a clear case!

SIR CHARLES.
What are the bars to your mutual contentment?

MRS. SULLEN.
In the first place I can't drink ale with him. 245

SULLEN.
Nor can I drink tea with her.

MRS. SULLEN.
I can't hunt with you.

SULLEN.
Nor can I dance with you.

MRS. SULLEN.
I hate cocking[85] and racing.

SULLEN.
And I abhor ombre and piquet. 250

MRS. SULLEN.
Your silence is intolerable.

SULLEN.
Your prating is worse.

MRS. SULLEN.
Have we not been a perpetual offence to each other—a gnawing vulture at the heart?

---

85 cocking] cock-fighting

SULLEN.

A frightful goblin to the sight?   255

MRS. SULLEN.

A porcupine to the feeling?

SULLEN.

Perpetual wormwood to the taste?

MRS. SULLEN.

Is there on earth a thing we could agree in?

SULLEN.

Yes: to part.

MRS. SULLEN.

With all my heart.   260

SULLEN.

Your hand.

MRS. SULLEN.

Here.

SULLEN.

These hands joined us, these shall part us. Away!

MRS. SULLEN.

North.

SULLEN.

South.   265

MRS. SULLEN.

East.

SULLEN.

West—far as the poles asunder.

COUNT BELLAIR.

Begar, the ceremony be vera pretty.

SIR CHARLES.

Now Mr. Sullen, there wants* only my sister's
fortune to make us easy.   270

SULLEN.

Sir Charles, you love your sister, and I love her
fortune; every one to his fancy.

ARCHER.

Then you won't refund?

SULLEN.

Not a stiver.

ARCHER.

Then I find, madam, you must e'en go to your   275
prison again.

COUNT BELLAIR.

What is the portion?

SIR CHARLES.

Ten thousand pound, sir.

COUNT BELLAIR.

Garzoon, I'll pay it, and she shall go home with me.

ARCHER.

Ha, ha, ha! French all over! Do you know, sir, what   280
ten thousand pound English is?

COUNT BELLAIR.

No begar, not *justement*.[86]

ARCHER.

Why sir, 'tis a hundred thousand livres.

COUNT BELLAIR.

A hundre tousand livres! Ah garzoon! me canno do't.
Your beauties and their fortunes are both too much   285
for me.

ARCHER.

Then I will. This night's adventure has proved
strangely lucky to us all, for Captain Gibbet in his
walk had made bold, Mr. Sullen, with your study and
escritoire, and had taken out all the writings of your   290
estate, all the articles of marriage with this[n] lady, bills,
bonds, leases, receipts to an infinite value. I took 'em
from him, and I deliver them to Sir Charles. (*Gives
him a parcel of papers and parchments.*)

SULLEN.

How, my writings! my head aches consumedly.—   295
Well gentlemen, you shall have her fortune, but I
can't talk. If you have a mind, Sir Charles, to be
merry and celebrate my sister's wedding and my
divorce,[87] you may command my house. But my
head aches consumedly.—Scrub, bring me a dram.   300

ARCHER. (*To Mrs. Sullen.*)

Madam, there's a country dance to the trifle that
I sung today; your hand, and we'll lead it up.

Here a dance.

ARCHER.

'Twould be hard to guess which of these parties is
the better pleased, the couple joined or the couple
parted: the one rejoicing in hopes of an untasted   305
happiness, and the other in their deliverance from
an experienced misery.

---

86 *justement*] exactly (Fr.)

87 divorce] Divorces were legal only by act of Parliament;
however, in the comic world of the play, the Sullens
have, in effect, been granted an annulment.

Both happy in the several states we find,
Those parted by consent, and those conjoined.
Consent, if mutual, saves the lawyer's fee,   310
Consent is law enough to set you free.

[Exeunt.]

FINIS.

Textual Notes

a The copytext is the first edition, a 1707 quarto (Q1).
  Other editions consulted include a 1708 collection of
  Farquhar's comedies (C), a 1728 edition of his works
  (W) and the modern editions of 1930 (Stonehill); of
  1939, revised 1969 (Nettleton, Case, and Stone—NCS);
  of 1977 (Fifer); and of 1988 (Kenny).

b wait farther] Q1, Stonehill, NCS, Fifer, Kenny; wait,
  father C, W

c besides, that … than the ten thousand we have spent]
  W, Stonehill, NCSS, Fifer; besides thousand, that …
  than the ten we have spent Q1, Kenny (who notes no
  textual problem); besides, that … than the ten we have
  spent (C)

d Song … etc.] W, Stonehill, NCS, Fifer, Kenny; only the
  first two lines of the song are in Q1, C

e I'm-m] NCS; I'mm Q1, Stonehill, Fifer, Kenny; I'm C,
  W

f are objects] Q1, Kenny; are the objects C, W, Stonehill,
  NCS, Fifer

g Aha] Fifer; Ah, a Q1, Stonehill, NCS, Kenny; Ay, ay
  C, W

h A trifling … boot] W (after the epilogue), Stonehill,
  NCS, Fifer, Kenny; only the first two lines are in Q1,
  C.

i *Exit Dorinda*] The remainder of this act was printed in
  italics in the 1728 *Works* (W), with a note that said that
  "the entire part of the Count was cut out by the Author, after the first Night's Representation; and where
  he should enter in the last scene of the fifth Act, it is
  added to the part of Foigard."

k dat is naame] Q1, C, Stonehill, Fifer, Kenny; dat is my
  name W, NCS

l shannot want you now. … Sir,] W, NCS, Fifer; shannot;
  won't you now, Sir? Q1, C, Stonehill; shannot want you
  now, Sir? Kenny

m Thomas] NCS, Fifer (Aimwell is called Tom in Act II,
  scene ii); Charles Q1, C, W, Stonehill, Kenny

n this] Fifer (citing a 1710 octavo); his Q1, C, W,
  Stonehill, NCS; your Kenny (citing a 1711 octavo)

The Beggar's Opera[a]

by John Gay (1685-1732)

edited by Dianne Dugaw

John Gay's *The Beggar's Opera* was arguably the most influential English drama of the eighteenth century. Staged continuously for more than a century, the play continues to be revived in our own day. With it, Gay invented the ballad opera, in which spoken dramatic parts are interspersed with songs set to well-known popular tunes, a form that presages modern musical comedy. Within a few years of the play's opening, hundreds of imitations were staged. In our own era, *The Beggar's Opera* has been reworked by three important modern playwrights: Bertolt Brecht in the 1920s, John Latouche in the 1940s, Václav Havel and Wole Soyinka in the 1970s, and Alan Ayckbourn in the 1980s.

Orphaned at an early age, Gay went to London as a young man from Devon in the west of England and after a short stint working in trade became a well-known literary figure until his death. Gay did not receive a university education, and though in time he moved in circles of the social and artistic elite, his family background was only precariously "genteel." From the beginning his writing shows an attention to rank and socio-cultural modes and mores that probably derives from his own ambiguous class background. Hinging on burlesque reversals of high and low, *The Beggar's Opera* identifies as similar the antics of beggars and thieves, on the one hand, and nobles and chief ministers, on the other. Thus the play brings us to consider power, justice, honor, and heroism in a world divided into social categories of power, wealth, and gender.

When it premiered at Lincoln's Inn Fields on 29 January 1728, *The Beggar's Opera* was immediately seen as not only a parody of the new fashion for opera in England, especially as written by G. F. Händel,[1] whom George I brought over from Germany, but also as a satire on the Whig ministry of Robert Walpole. At a deeper level, Gay satirizes the corruption, self-interest, and profiteering of the ruling political and social order of the day as the profit-driven schemes of Georgian businessmen and courtiers were establishing the mercantile capitalism that has dominated world politics and economics from that time to this. So perceptively did *The Beggar's Opera* propose the ironies, predicaments, and moral dilemmas of the new order that its satire continues to fit our post-modern era of globalization and website investment. Moreover, Gay's critique is shaped by a comic wit that reveals in the play's rascals and tarts the all-too-human sentiments and behaviors that we all share. In addition, the songs that fill the play, for all their humor, satiric bite, and confounding ironies, are not only lively, artful, and memorable, but often beautifully poignant as well. Gay's *The Beggar's Opera* introduced to the English theater an ingenious mix of social satire, comic wit, and popular musical art that continues to amuse and accuse us nearly three hundred years later.

---

[1] parody ... Händel] Although Gay certainly parodies Händelian opera, he and G. F. Händel actually traveled in the same circles, especially during the first decade of Händel's career in England. The two collaborated on an operatic masque, *Acis and Galatea*, in 1718.

DRAMATIS PERSONAE

MEN
    Peachum.[2]
    Lockit.
    Macheath.[3]
    Filch.
    Jemmy Twitcher,[4]
    Crook-fingered Jack,
    Wat Dreary,
    Robin of Bagshot,[5]
    Nimming[6] Ned,
    Harry Padington,[7]
    Matt of the Mint,[8]
    Ben Budge,[9] Macheath's gang.
    Beggar.
    Player.
    Constables, drawer, turnkey, [musicians], etc.
WOMEN
    Mrs. Peachum.
    Polly Peachum.
    Lucy Lockit.
    Diana Trapes,[10]
    Mrs.* Coaxer,
    Dolly Trull,
    Mrs.* Vixen,
    Betty Doxy,
    Jenny Diver,[11]
    Mrs.* Slammekin,[12]
    Suky Tawdry,
    Molly Brazen, women of the Town.

---

2 Peachum] peach (q.v.) 'em. Gay's characters usually have names relating to underworld activities; some are self-explanatory, some require glossing, as below.

3 Macheath] *mac* (son of); *heath* (typical setting for highway robbery)

4 Twitcher] pickpocket

5 Bagshot] name of heath notorious for highwaymen

6 Nimming] stealing

7 Padington] notorious district, housing the gallows at Tyburn* (the day of execution was referred to as Padington Fair Day)

8 Mint] formerly a sanctuary for debtors, now a refuge for various outlaws

9 Budge] clothes thief

10 Trapes] slattern

11 Diver] pickpocket

12 Slammekin] slut

INTRODUCTION.

Beggar, player.

BEGGAR.

If poverty be a title to poetry, I am sure nobody can dispute mine. I own myself of the Company of Beggars, and I make one at their weekly festivals at St. Giles's.[13] I have a small yearly salary for my catches and am welcome to a dinner there whenever I please, which is more than most poets can say.

PLAYER.

As we live by the Muses, 'tis but gratitude in us to encourage poetical merit wherever we find it. The Muses, contrary to all other ladies, pay no distinction to dress and never partially mistake the pertness of embroidery for wit, nor the modesty of want* for dullness. Be the author who he will, we push his play as far as it will go. So (though you are in want) I wish you success heartily.

BEGGAR.

This piece I own was originally writ for the celebrating the marriage of James Chanter and Moll Lay, two most excellent ballad singers.[14] I have introduced the similes that are in all your celebrated operas: the swallow, the moth, the bee, the ship, the flower, etcetera. Besides, I have a prison scene which the ladies always reckon charmingly pathetic. As to the parts, I have observed such a nice* impartiality to our two ladies that it is impossible for either of them to take offence.[15] I hope I may be forgiven that I have not made my opera throughout

---

13 St. Giles] The parish of St. Giles, Holborn, named after the patron saint of beggars and lepers, extends to the east of Charing Cross Road. The area was a crime-ridden slum in the eighteenth century.

14 Chanter … singers] The names of these singers signify their disreputable occupation. A "chanter" was a street singer; "lay" is a word for a song that also was used as a slang term for a criminal activity such as picking pockets. Ballad singers on the streets often worked together with pick-pockets.]

15 ladies … offence] This is a joking reference to Italian opera in London in the 1720s. Two rival prima donnas, Francesca Cuzzoni and Faustina Bordoni, quarreled publicly over parts and preference in 1726 and 1727, even coming to blows during a performance.

unnatural, like those in vogue, for I have no recitative. Excepting this, as I have consented to have neither prologue nor epilogue, it must be allowed an opera in all its forms. The piece indeed hath been heretofore frequently represented by ourselves in our great room at St. Giles's, so that I cannot too often acknowledge your charity in bringing it now on the stage. 30

PLAYER.

But I see 'tis time for us to withdraw; the actors are preparing to begin.—Play away the overture. 35

Exeunt.

The Beggar's Opera.

Act I, scene i. Peachum's house.

Peachum sitting at a table with a large book of accounts before him.

Air 1. "An old woman clothed in gray," etc.

[PEACHUM.]

Through all the employments of life
    Each neighbor abuses his brother;
Whore and rogue they call husband and wife:
    All professions be-rogue one another.
The priest calls the lawyer a cheat, 5
    The lawyer be-knaves the divine,
And the statesman, because he's so great,
    Thinks his trade as honest as mine.
A lawyer is an honest employment, so is mine. Like me too he acts in a double capacity, both against 10 rogues and for 'em, for 'tis fitting that we should protect and encourage cheats, since we live by them.

Air 1

Scene ii.

Peachum, Filch.

FILCH.

Sir, Black Moll hath sent word her trial comes on in the afternoon, and she hopes you will order matters so as to bring her off.

PEACHUM.

Why, she may plead her belly[16] at worst; to my knowledge she hath taken care of that security. But 5 as the wench is very active and industrious, you may satisfy her that I'll soften the evidence.*

FILCH.

Tom Gagg, sir, is found guilty.

PEACHUM.

A lazy dog! When I took him the time before, I told him what he would come to if he did not 10 mend his hand. This is death without reprieve. I may venture to book him. (*Writes.*) "For Tom Gagg, forty Pounds."[17] Let Betty Sly know that I'll save her from transportation, for I can get more by her staying in England. 15

FILCH.

Betty hath brought more goods into our lock[18] to-year than any five of the gang, and in truth, 'tis a pity to lose so good a customer.[19]

PEACHUM.

If none of the gang take her off, she may, in the common course of business, live a twelvemonth 20 longer. I love to let women 'scape. A good sportsman always lets the hen partridges fly, because the breed of the game depends upon them. Besides, here the law allows us no reward; there is nothing to be got by the death of women—except 25 our wives.

---

16 plead her belly] A pregnant woman could not be executed.

17 forty pounds] the standard government reward to an informer when the person reported on was convicted of theft

18 lock] "A cant word, signifying a warehouse where stolen goods are deposited" (Gay in a note later in the play).

19 customer] (1) a prostitute; and (2) an official who collects custom money or dues

FILCH.

Without dispute, she is a fine woman! 'Twas to her
I was obliged for my education, and (to say a bold
word) she hath trained up more young fellows to
the business than the gaming table.   30

PEACHUM.

Truly Filch, thy observation is right. We and the
surgeons are more beholden to women than all the
professions besides.[20]

Air 2. "The bonny gray-eyed morn," etc.

FILCH.

'Tis woman that seduces all mankind;   35
    By her we first were taught the wheedling arts.
Her very eyes can cheat; when most she's kind,*
    She tricks us of our money with our hearts.
For her like wolves by night we roam for prey
    And practice ev'ry fraud to bribe her charms.   40
For suits of love, like law, are won by pay,
    And beauty must be feed into our arms.

PEACHUM.

But make haste to Newgate, boy, and let my
friends know what I intend, for I love to make
them easy one way or other.   45

FILCH.

When a gentleman is long kept in suspense,
penitence may break his spirit ever after. Besides,
certainty gives a man a good air upon his trial and
makes him risk another without fear or scruple.
But I'll away, for 'tis a pleasure to be the messenger   50
of comfort to friends in affliction. [*Exit.*]

---

20 surgeons ... besides] Doctors received fees for treating
    venereal disease.

Air 2

Scene iii.

Peachum.

[PEACHUM.]

But 'tis now high time to look about me for a decent
execution against next sessions. I hate a lazy rogue,
by whom one can get nothing till he is hanged. A
register of the gang: (*Reads.*) "Crook-fingered Jack,"
a year and a half in the service. Let me see how much   5
the stock owes to his industry: one, two, three, four,
five gold watches and seven silver ones. A mighty
clean-handed fellow! Sixteen snuffboxes, five of
them of true gold. Six dozen of handkerchiefs, four
silver-hilted swords, half a dozen of shirts, three tie-   10
periwigs, and a piece of broadcloth. Considering
these are only the fruits of his leisure hours, I don't
know a prettier fellow, for no man alive hath a more
engaging presence of mind upon the road. "Wat
Dreary, alias Brown Will," an irregular dog, who   15
hath an underhand way of disposing of his goods.
I'll try him only for a sessions or two longer upon his
good behavior. "Harry Padington," a poor petty-
larceny rascal, without the least genius; that fellow,
though he were to live these six months, will never   20
come to the gallows with any credit. "Slippery Sam."
He goes off the next sessions, for the villain hath the
impudence to have views of following his trade as a
tailor, which he calls an honest employment. "Matt
of the Mint," listed not above a month ago, a   25
promising sturdy fellow and diligent in his way,
somewhat too bold and hasty, and may raise good
contributions on the public, if he does not cut
himself short by murder. "Tom Tipple," a guzzling,
soaking sot, who is always too drunk to stand   30
himself or to make others stand. A cart[21] is
absolutely necessary for him. "Robin of Bagshot,
alias Gorgon, alias Bluff Bob, alias Carbuncle, alias
Bob Booty."[22]

---

21 cart] mode of conveyance to carry condemned crimi-
    nals to the gallows
22 Robin ... Booty] This list of aliases would have been
    recognized by contemporary audiences as well-known
    insulting nicknames for the chief minister, Robert
    Walpole.

Scene iv.

Peachum, Mrs. Peachum.

MRS. PEACHUM.

What of Bob Booty, Husband? I hope nothing bad hath betided him. You know, my dear, he's a favorite customer of mine. 'Twas he made me a present of this ring.

PEACHUM.

I have set his name down in the blacklist, that's all, my dear. He spends his life among women, and as soon as his money is gone, one or other of the ladies will hang him for the reward, and there's forty pound lost to us forever.

MRS. PEACHUM.

You know, my dear, I never meddle in matters of death; I always leave those affairs to you. Women indeed are bitter bad judges in these cases, for they are so partial to the brave that they think every man handsome who is going to the camp or the gallows.

Air 3. "Cold and raw," etc.

If any wench Venus's Girdle[23] wear,
 Though she be never so ugly,
Lilies and roses will quickly appear,
 And her face look wondrous smugly.
Beneath the left ear so fit but a cord
 (A rope so charming a zone is!)
The youth in his cart hath the air of a lord,
 And we cry, "There dies an Adonis!"

But really, Husband, you should not be too hard-hearted, for you never had a finer, braver set of

---

[23] Venus's Girdle] The belt (or zone) belonging to Venus, goddess of Love, made the wearer instantly desirable.

Air 3

men than at present. We have not had a murder among them all these seven months. And truly, my dear, that is a great blessing.

PEACHUM.

What a dickens is the woman always a-whimpering about murder for? No gentleman is ever looked upon the worse for killing a man in his own defense, and if business cannot be carried on without it, what would you have a gentleman do?

MRS. PEACHUM.

If I am in the wrong, my dear, you must excuse me, for nobody can help the frailty of an over-scrupulous conscience.

PEACHUM.

Murder is as fashionable a crime as a man can be guilty of. How many fine gentlemen have we in Newgate every year, purely upon that article! If they have wherewithal to persuade the jury to bring it in manslaughter, what are they the worse for it? So, my dear, have done upon this subject. Was Captain Macheath here this morning for the banknotes he left with you last week?

MRS. PEACHUM.

Yes, my dear, and though the bank hath stopped payment, he was so cheerful and so agreeable! Sure there is not a finer gentleman upon the road[24] than the captain! If he comes from Bagshot at any reasonable hour he hath promised to make one this evening with Polly and me and Bob Booty at a party of quadrille. Pray my dear, is the Captain rich?

PEACHUM.

The Captain keeps too good company ever to grow rich. Marrabone* and the chocolate houses are his undoing. The man that proposes to get money by play should have the education of a fine gentleman and be trained up to it from his youth.

MRS. PEACHUM.

Really, I am sorry upon Polly's account the Captain hath not more discretion. What business hath he to keep company with lords and gentlemen? He should leave them to prey upon one another.

PEACHUM.

Upon Polly's account! What a plague does the woman mean, upon Polly's account?

---

[24] gentleman upon the road] euphemism for highwayman

MRS. PEACHUM.

Captain Macheath is very fond of the girl.

PEACHUM.

And what then? 65

MRS. PEACHUM.

If I have any skill in the ways of women, I am sure Polly thinks him a very pretty man.

PEACHUM.

And what then? You would not be so mad to have the wench marry him! Gamesters and highwaymen are generally very good to their whores, but they 70 are very* devils to their wives.

MRS. PEACHUM.

But if Polly should be in love, how should we help her or how can she help herself? Poor girl, I am in the utmost concern about her.

Air 4. "Why is your faithful slave disdained?" etc. 75

> If Love the virgin's heart invade,
> How, like a moth, the simple maid
> Still* plays about the flame!
> If soon she be not made a wife,
> Her honor's singed, and then for life 80
> She's—what I dare not name.

PEACHUM.

Look ye, Wife, a handsome wench in our way of business is as profitable as at the bar of a Temple* coffee house, who looks upon it as her livelihood to grant every liberty but one. You see I would indulge 85 the girl as far as prudently we can. In anything but marriage! After that, my dear, how shall we be safe? Are we not then in her husband's power? For a husband hath the absolute power over all a wife's secrets but her own. If the girl had the discretion of 90 a Court lady, who can have a dozen young fellows at her ear without complying with one, I should not matter it. But Polly is tinder, and a spark will at once

set her on a flame. Married! If the wench does not know her own profit, sure she knows her own 95 pleasure better than to make herself a property! My daughter to me should be, like a Court lady to a minister of state, a key to the whole gang. Married! If the affair is not already done, I'll terrify her from it by the example of our neighbors. 100

MRS. PEACHUM.

Mayhap, my dear, you may injure the girl. She loves to imitate the fine ladies, and she may only allow the Captain liberties in the view of interest.

PEACHUM.

But 'tis your duty, my dear, to warn the girl against her ruin and to instruct her how to make the most 105 of her beauty. I'll go to her this moment and sift her. In the meantime, Wife, rip out the coronets and marks[25] of these dozen of cambric handkerchiefs, for I can dispose of them this afternoon to a chap[26] in the City.* [*Exit.*] 110

Scene v.

Mrs. Peachum.

[MRS. PEACHUM.]

Never was a man more out of the way in an argument than my husband! Why must our Polly, forsooth, differ from her sex and love only her husband? And why must Polly's marriage, contrary to all observation, make her the less followed by 5 other men? All men are thieves in love and like a woman the better for being another's property.

Air 5. "Of all the simple things we do," etc.

---

[25] coronets and marks] embroidered insignia, the first for aristocratic members of the peerage

[26] chap] short for chapman (q.v.)

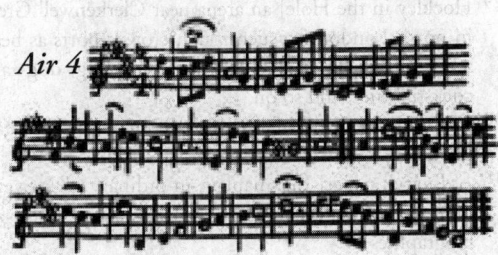

A maid is like the golden ore,
Which hath guineas intrinsical in't,
    Whose worth is never known before
It is tried and imprest in the mint.
    A wife's like a guinea in gold,
Stamped with the name of her spouse:
    Now here, now there, is bought or is sold,   15
And is current in every house.

Scene vi.

Mrs. Peachum, Filch.

MRS. PEACHUM.

Come hither, Filch. I am as fond of this child as
though my mind misgave me he were my own. He
hath as fine a hand at picking a pocket as a woman
and is as nimble-fingered as a juggler. If an unlucky
session does not cut the rope of thy life, I   5
pronounce, Boy, thou wilt be a great man* in
history. Where was your post last night, my boy?

FILCH.

I plied at the opera, madam, and considering 'twas
neither dark nor rainy, so that there was no great
hurry in getting chairs* and coaches, made a toler-   10
able hand on't. These seven handkerchiefs, madam.

MRS. PEACHUM.

Colored ones, I see. They are of sure sale from our
warehouse at Redriff[27] among the seamen.

FILCH.

And this snuffbox.

MRS. PEACHUM.

Set in gold! A pretty encouragement this to a   15
young beginner.

FILCH.

I had a fair tug at a charming gold watch. Pox take
the tailors for making the fobs so deep and narrow!
I stuck by the way, and I was forced to make my
escape under a coach. Really madam, I fear I shall
be cut off in the flower of my youth, so that every   20
now and then (since I was pumped[28]) I have

thoughts of taking up and going to sea.

MRS. PEACHUM.

You should go to Hockley in the Hole[29] and to
Marrabone,* child, to learn valor. These are the
schools that have bred so many brave men. I   25
thought, Boy, by this time thou hadst lost fear as
well as shame. Poor lad! how little does he know
as yet of the Old Bailey![30] For the first fact I'll
insure thee from being hanged, and going to sea,
Filch, will come time enough upon a sentence of   30
transportation. But now, since you have nothing
better to do, ev'n go to your book and learn your
catechism, for really a man makes but an ill figure
in the ordinary's paper[31] who cannot give a
satisfactory answer to his questions. But hark you,   35
my lad: don't tell me a lie, for you know I hate a
liar. Do you know of any thing that hath past
between Captain Macheath and our Polly?

FILCH.

I beg you, madam, don't ask me, for I must either
tell a lie to you or to Miss Polly. For I promised   40
her I would not tell.

MRS. PEACHUM.

But when the honor of our family is concerned—

FILCH.

I shall lead a sad life with Miss Polly if ever she
come to know that I told you. Besides, I would
not willingly forfeit my own honor by betraying   45
anybody.

MRS. PEACHUM.

Yonder comes my husband and Polly. Come Filch,
you shall go with me into my own room and tell
me the whole story. I'll give thee a glass of a most
delicious cordial[b] that I keep for my own drinking.   50

[Exeunt.]

---

27 Redriff] the common name for Rotherhithe, the port
    district of London on the south bank of the Thames
    about a mile down river from the Tower of London
28 pumped] Pickpockets caught in the act were often pun-
    ished as first offenders by being held under a water pump.

29 Hockley in the Hole] an arena near Clerkenwell Green
    in north London for such rough crowd sports as bear-
    and bull-baiting, sword fighting, wrestling, dog- and
    cock-fighting, and so on.
30 Old Bailey] London's criminal court near Newgate
    Prison
31 ordinary's paper] the chaplain-in-ordinary of Newgate
    often published accounts of criminals called "Newgate
    biographies."

Scene vii.

Peachum, Polly.

POLLY.

I know as well as any of the fine ladies how to make
the most of my self and of my man too. A woman
knows how to be mercenary, though she hath never
been in a court or at an assembly.[32] We have it in our
natures, Papa. If I allow Captain Macheath some   5
trifling liberties, I have this watch and other visible
marks of his favor to show for it. A girl who cannot
grant some things, and refuse what is most material,
will make but a poor hand of her beauty and soon be
thrown upon the common.

Air 6. "What shall I do to show how much I love her,"   10
etc.

Virgins are like the fair flower in its luster,
　　　Which in the garden enamels the ground;
Near it the bees in play flutter and cluster,
　　　And gaudy butterflies frolic around.
But when once plucked, 'tis no longer alluring;   15
　　　To Covent Garden* 'tis sent (as yet sweet),
There fades and shrinks and grows past all
　　enduring,
　　　Rots, stinks, and dies and is trod under feet.

PEACHUM.

You know, Polly, I am not against your toying and
trifling with a customer in the way of business or to   20
get out a secret or so. But if I find out that you have
played the fool and are married, you jade you, I'll cut
your throat, hussy. Now you know my mind.

---

32 assembly] a fashionable gathering, usually with music
　　and dancing

Scene viii.

Peachum, Polly, Mrs. Peachum.

Air 7. "Oh London is a fine town."

MRS. PEACHUM. (*In a very great Passion.*)

Our Polly is a sad slut! nor heeds what we have
　　taught her.
I wonder any man alive will ever rear a daughter!
For she must have both hoods and gowns, and
　　hoops to swell her pride,
With scarves and stays, and gloves and lace, and
　　she will have men beside.
And when she's dressed with care and cost, all   5
　　tempting, fine and gay,
As men should serve a cucumber,* she flings
　　herself away.
Our Polly is a sad slut, etc.
You baggage! you hussy! you inconsiderate jade!
Had you been hanged, it would not have vexed
me, for that might have been your misfortune, but   10
to do such a mad thing by choice! The wench is
married,[33] Husband.

PEACHUM.

Married! The Captain is a bold man and will risk
any thing for money; to be sure he believes her a
fortune.—Do you think your mother and I should   15
have lived comfortably so long together, if ever we
had been married, baggage?

MRS. PEACHUM.

I knew she was always a proud slut, and now the
wench hath played the fool and married, because
forsooth she would do like the gentry. Can you   20
support the expense of a husband, hussy, in
gaming, drinking, and whoring? have you money
enough to carry on the daily quarrels of man and
wife about who shall squander most? There are not
many husbands and wives who can bear the   25

---

33 married] Clandestine marriages were illegal but binding.

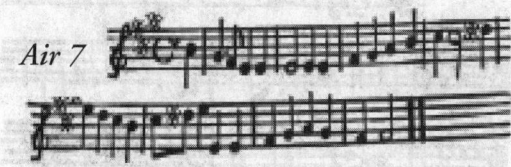

charges of plaguing one another in a handsome way. If you must be married, could you introduce nobody into our family but a highwayman? Why thou foolish jade, thou wilt be as ill-used and as much neglected as if thou hadst married a lord! 30

PEACHUM.

Let not your anger, my dear, break through the rules of decency, for the captain looks upon himself in the military capacity, as a gentleman by his profession. Besides what he hath already, I know he is in a fair way of getting or of dying, and both these ways, let 35 me tell you, are most excellent chances for a wife.— Tell me, hussy, are you ruined or no?

MRS. PEACHUM.

With Polly's fortune, she might very well have gone off to a person of distinction.—Yes, that you might, you pouting slut! 40

PEACHUM.

What, is the wench dumb? Speak or I'll make you plead by squeezing out an answer from you. Are you really bound wife to him or are you only upon liking? (*Pinches her.*)

POLLY. (*Screaming.*)

Oh! 45

MRS. PEACHUM.

How the mother is to be pitied who hath handsome daughters! Locks, bolts, bars, and lectures of morality are nothing to them, they break through them all. They have as much pleasure in cheating a father and mother as in cheating at cards. 50

PEACHUM.

Why Polly, I shall soon know if you are married by Macheath's keeping from our house.

Air 8. "Grim king of the ghosts," etc.

POLLY.

Can love be controlled by advice?
    Will Cupid our mothers obey? 55

Though my heart were as frozen as ice,
    At his flame 'twould have melted away.

When he kissed me so closely he pressed,
    'Twas so sweet that I must have complied;
So I thought it both safest and best 60
    To marry for fear you should chide.

MRS. PEACHUM.

Then all the hopes of our family are gone forever and ever!

PEACHUM.

And Macheath may hang his father and mother-in-law in hope to get into their daughter's fortune. 65

POLLY.

I did not marry him (as 'tis the fashion) coolly and deliberately for honor and money. But I love him.

MRS. PEACHUM.

Love him! worse and worse! I thought the girl had been better bred. Oh Husband, Husband! her folly makes me mad! my head swims! I'm distracted! I 70 can't support myself—oh! (*Faints.*)

PEACHUM.

See, wench, to what a condition you have reduced your poor mother! a glass of cordial, this instant.— How the poor woman takes it to heart!

Polly goes out and returns with it.

Ah hussy, now this is the only comfort your 75 mother has left!

POLLY.

Give her another glass, sir; my mama drinks double the quantity whenever she is out of order. This, you see, fetches her.

MRS. PEACHUM.

The girl shows such a readiness and so much 80 concern that I could almost find in my heart to forgive her.

Air 9. "Oh Jenny, oh Jenny, where hast thou been."

Oh Polly, you might have toyed and kissed.
By keeping men off, you keep them on. 85

POLLY.

> But he so teased me,
>> And he so pleased me,
>> What I did, you must have done.

MRS. PEACHUM.

Not with a highwayman, you sorry slut!

PEACHUM.

A word with you, Wife. 'Tis no new thing for a 90
wench to take man without consent of parents.
You know 'tis the frailty of woman, my dear.

MRS. PEACHUM.

Yes indeed, the sex is frail. But the first time a
woman is frail, she should be somewhat nice,*
methinks, for then or never is the time to make 95
her fortune. After that, she hath nothing to do but
to guard herself from being found out, and she
may do what she pleases.

PEACHUM.

Make your self a little easy; I have a thought shall
soon set all matters again to rights.—Why so 100
melancholy, Polly? Since what is done cannot be
undone, we must all endeavor to make the best of it.

MRS. PEACHUM.

Well Polly, as far as one woman can forgive
another, I forgive thee. Your father is too fond of
you, hussy. 105

POLLY.

Then all my sorrows are at an end.

MRS. PEACHUM.

A mighty likely speech, in troth, for a wench who
is just married!

Air 10. "Thomas, I cannot," etc.

POLLY.

> I, like a ship in storms, was tossed 110
> Yet afraid to put in to land,
> For seized in the port the vessel's lost,
> Whose treasure is contraband.

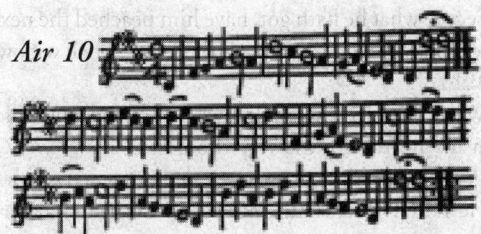

> The waves are laid,
>> My duty's paid— 115
> Oh joy beyond expression!
>> Thus, safe ashore,
>> I ask no more,
> My all is in my possession.

PEACHUM.

I hear customers in t'other room. Go talk with 'em, 120
Polly, but come to us again as soon as they are gone.
But hark ye, child, if 'tis the gentleman who was here
yesterday about the repeating-watch,[34] say you
believe we can't get intelligence of it till tomorrow.
For I lent it to Suky Straddle to make a figure with it 125
tonight at a tavern in Drury Lane. If t'other
gentleman calls for the silver-hilted sword, you know
beetle-browed Jemmy hath it on, and he doth not
come from Tunbridge till Tuesday night so that it
cannot be had till then.[35] 130

[Exit Polly.]

Scene ix.

Peachum, Mrs. Peachum.

PEACHUM.

Dear Wife, be a little pacified. Don't let your
passion run away with your senses. Polly, I grant
you, hath done a rash thing.

MRS. PEACHUM.

If she had had only an intrigue with the fellow,
why the very best families have excused and 5
huddled up a frailty of that sort. 'Tis marriage,
Husband, that makes it a blemish.

PEACHUM.

But money, Wife, is the true Fuller's Earth[36] for
reputations: there is not a spot or a stain but what
it can take out. A rich rogue nowadays is fit 10
company for any gentleman, and the world, my

---

34 repeating-watch] one that chimes

35 customers … then] Victims of theft frequently advertised
and offered a reward for return of their possessions. Fences
such as Peachum would contact them and arrange for a
recovery though perhaps, as here, not before they had been
put to some use. Drury Lane was an area of London notorious for prostitutes; Tunbridge Wells was a fashionable
resort about thirty-five miles southeast of London.

36 Fuller's Earth] a clay used to clean fabrics

dear, hath not such a contempt for roguery as you imagine. I tell you, Wife, I can make this match turn to our advantage.

MRS. PEACHUM.

I am very sensible, Husband, that Captain Macheath is worth money, but I am in doubt whether he hath not two or three wives already, and then if he should die in a session or two, Polly's dower would come into dispute.

PEACHUM.

That, indeed, is a point which ought to be considered.

Air 11. "A soldier and a sailor."

A fox may steal your hens, sir,
A whore your health and pence, sir,
Your daughter rob your chest, sir;
Your wife may steal your rest, sir,
    A thief your goods and plate.*
But this is all but picking,
With rest, pence, chest and chicken;
It ever was decreed, sir,
If lawyer's hand is feed, sir,
    He steals your whole estate.

The lawyers are bitter enemies to those in our way. They don't care that anybody should get a clandestine livelihood but themselves.

Scene x.

Mrs. Peachum, Peachum, Polly.

POLLY.

'Twas only Nimming Ned. He brought in a damask window curtain, a hoop-petticoat, a pair of silver candlesticks, a periwig, and one silk stocking from the fire that happened last night.

Air 11

PEACHUM.

There is not a fellow that is cleverer in his way and saves more goods out of the fire than Ned. But now, Polly, to your affair, for matters must not be left as they are. You are married then, it seems?

POLLY.

Yes sir.

PEACHUM.

And how do you propose to live, child?

POLLY.

Like other women, sir, upon the industry of my husband.

MRS. PEACHUM.

What, is the wench turned fool? A highwayman's wife, like a soldier's, hath as little of his pay as of his company.

PEACHUM.

And had not you the common views of a gentlewoman in your marriage, Polly?

POLLY.

I don't know what you mean, sir.

PEACHUM.

Of a jointure and of being a widow.

POLLY.

But I love him, sir: How then could I have thoughts of parting with him?

PEACHUM.

Parting with him! Why, that is the whole scheme and intention of all marriage articles. The comfortable estate of widowhood is the only hope that keeps up a wife's spirits. Where is the woman who would scruple to be a wife, if she had it in her power to be a widow whenever she pleased? If you have any views of this sort, Polly, I shall think the match not so very unreasonable.

POLLY.

How I dread to hear your advice! Yet I must beg you to explain yourself.

PEACHUM.

Secure what he hath got, have him peached the next sessions, and then at once you are made a rich widow.

POLLY.

What, murder the man I love! The blood runs cold at my heart with the very thought of it.

PEACHUM.

Fie Polly! What hath murder to do in the affair?

Since the thing sooner or later must happen, I dare say the captain himself would like that we should get the reward for his death sooner than a stranger. Why Polly, the captain knows that as 'tis his employment   40
to rob, so 'tis ours to take robbers. Every man in his business. So that there is no malice in the case.

MRS. PEACHUM.

Aye Husband, now you have nicked the matter. To have him peached is the only thing could ever make me forgive her.   45

Air 12. "Now ponder well, ye parents dear."

POLLY.

Oh, ponder well! be not severe,
     So save a wretched wife!
For on the rope that hangs my dear
     Depends poor Polly's life.   50

MRS. PEACHUM.

But your duty to your parents, hussy, obliges you to hang him. What would many a wife give for such opportunity!

POLLY.

What is a jointure, what is widowhood to me? I know my heart. I cannot survive him.   55

Air 13. "Le printemps rappelle aux armes."[37]

The turtle* thus with plaintive crying,
     Her lover dying,
The turtle thus with plaintive crying,
     Laments her dove.   60

---

37 Le printemps … armes] Springtime recalls one to arms (Fr.).

Air 12

Air 13

Down she drops quite spent with sighing,
Paired in death, as paired in love.
Thus, sir, it will happen to your poor Polly.

MRS. PEACHUM.

What is the fool in love in earnest then? I hate thee for being particular. Why, wench, thou art a shame   65
to thy very* sex.

POLLY.

But hear me, Mother. If you ever loved—

MRS. PEACHUM.

Those cursed playbooks she reads have been her ruin.—One word more, hussy, and I shall knock your brains out, if you have any.   70

PEACHUM.

Keep out of the way, Polly, for fear of mischief and consider of what is proposed to you.

MRS. PEACHUM.

Away, hussy. Hang your husband and be dutiful.

[Polly starts out.]

Scene xi.

Mrs. Peachum, Peachum, Polly listening.

MRS. PEACHUM.

The thing, Husband, must and shall be done. For the sake of intelligence[38] we must take other measures and have him peached the next session without her consent. If she will not know her duty, we know ours.

PEACHUM.

But really, my dear, it grieves one's heart to take off   5
a great man.* When I consider his personal bravery, his fine stratagem, how much we have already got by him, and how much more we may get, methinks I can't find in my heart to have a hand in his death. I wish you could have made Polly undertake it.   10

MRS. PEACHUM.

But in a case of necessity: our own lives are in danger.

PEACHUM.

Then, indeed, we must comply with the customs of the world and make gratitude give way to interest. He shall be taken off.   15

MRS. PEACHUM.

I'll undertake to manage Polly.

---

38 intelligence] information Macheath possesses

PEACHUM.

And I'll prepare matters for the Old Bailey.

[Exeunt.]

Scene xii.

Polly.

[POLLY.]

Now I'm a wretch, indeed: methinks I see him already in the cart, sweeter and more lovely than the nosegay in his hand! I hear the crowd extolling his resolution and intrepidity! What volleys of sighs are sent from the windows of Holborn,[39] that so comely a youth should be brought to disgrace! I see him at the tree! The whole circle are in tears, even butchers weep! Jack Ketch[40] himself hesitates to perform his duty and would be glad to lose his fee by a reprieve. What then will become of Polly! As yet I may inform him of their design and aid him in his escape— It shall be so— But then he flies, absents himself, and I bar myself from his dear, dear conversation!* That too will distract me— If he keep out of the way, my papa and mama may in time relent, and we may be happy— If he stays, he is hanged, and then he is lost forever! He intended to lie concealed in my room till the dusk of the evening: If they are abroad, I'll this instant let him out, lest some accident should prevent him.

Exit and returns.

Scene xiii.

Polly, Macheath.

Air 14. *"Pretty parrot, say—"*

MACHEATH.

    Pretty Polly, say,

---

39 nosegay … Holborn] Holborn street led from Newgate prison to Tyburn.* Spectators lined the streets to see about-to-be-executed criminals riding by in carts, with nooses around their necks, and frequently threw them nosegays.

40 Jack Ketch] generic name for the public hangman, after the notoriously inefficient original, who held the post from 1663 to 1686

        When I was away,
    Did your fancy never stray
        To some newer lover?

POLLY.

        Without disguise,
        Heaving sighs,
        Doting eyes,
    My constant heart discover.*
        Fondly let me loll!

MACHEATH.

        Oh pretty, pretty Poll.

POLLY.

    And are you as fond as ever, my dear?

MACHEATH.

    Suspect my honor, my courage, suspect anything but my love. May my pistols misfire and my mare slip her shoulder while I am pursued if I ever forsake thee!

POLLY.

    Nay my dear, I have no reason to doubt you, for I find in the romance you lent me, none of the great heroes were ever false in love.

Air 15. *"Pray, fair one, be kind*"—*

MACHEATH.

    My heart was so free,
    It roved like the bee,
    Till Polly my passion requited;

I sipped each flower,
I changed ev'ry hour,
But here ev'ry flower is united.   25
POLLY.
Were you sentenced to transportation, sure my dear, you could not leave me behind you—could you?
MACHEATH.
Is there any power, any force that could tear me from thee? You might sooner tear a pension out of the hands of a courtier, a fee from a lawyer, a pretty woman from a looking glass, or any woman from quadrille. But to tear me from thee is impossible!   30

Air 16. "Over the hills and far away."

Were I laid on Greenland's coast,
And in my arms embraced my lass,   35
Warm amidst eternal frost,
Too soon the half-year's night would pass.
POLLY.
Were I sold on Indian soil,
Soon as the burning day was closed,
I could mock the sultry toil,   40
When on my charmer's breast reposed.
MACHEATH.
And I would love you all the day,
POLLY.
Every night would kiss and play,
MACHEATH.
If with me you'd fondly stray—
POLLY.
Over the hills and far away.   45
Yes, I would go with thee. But oh! how shall I speak it? I must be torn from thee. We must part.
MACHEATH.
How! Part!
POLLY.
We must, we must. My papa and mama are set

against thy life. They now, even now are in search   50
after thee. They are preparing evidence against thee. Thy life depends upon a moment.

Air 17. "Gin thou wert mine awn thing"—

Oh what pain it is to part!
Can I leave thee, can I leave thee?   55
Oh what pain it is to part!
Can thy Polly ever leave thee?
But lest death my love should thwart
And bring thee to the fatal cart,
Thus I tear thee from my bleeding heart!   60
Fly hence and let me leave thee.
One kiss and then—one kiss—be gone—farewell.
MACHEATH.
My hand, my heart, my dear, is so riveted to thine that I cannot unloose my hold.
POLLY.
But my papa may intercept thee and then I should   65
lose the very glimmering of hope. A few weeks, perhaps, may reconcile us all. Shall thy Polly hear from thee?
MACHEATH.
Must I then go?
POLLY.
And will not absence change your love?   70
MACHEATH.
If you doubt* it, let me stay—and be hanged.
POLLY.
Oh how I fear! how I tremble! Go—but when safety will give you leave, you will be sure to see me again, for till then Polly is wretched.

Air 18. "Oh the broom," etc.   75

Parting, and looking back at each other with fondness; he at one door, she at the other.

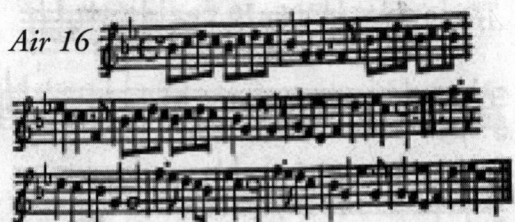

MACHEATH.

> The miser thus a shilling sees
> > Which he's obliged to pay,
> With sighs resigns it by degrees
> > And fears 'tis gone for aye.

POLLY.

> The boy thus, when his sparrow's flown,   80
> > The bird in silence eyes,
> But soon as out of sight 'tis gone,
> > Whines, whimpers, sobs, and cries.

Act II, scene i. A tavern near Newgate.

Jemmy Twitcher, Crook-fingered Jack, Wat Dreary,
Robin of Bagshot, Nimming Ned, Henry Padington,
Matt of the Mint, Ben Budge, and the rest of the gang
at the table with wine, brandy, and tobacco.

BEN.

> But prithee Matt, what is become of thy brother
> Tom? I have not seen him since my return from
> transportation.

MATT.

> Poor brother Tom had an accident this time
> twelvemonth, and so clever a made fellow he was   5
> that I could not save him from those flaying rascals
> the surgeons, and now, poor man, he is among the
> otamies at Surgeon's Hall.[41]

BEN.

> So it seems, his time was come.

JEMMY.

> But the present time is ours, and no body alive   10
> hath more. Why are the laws leveled at us? Are we

---

41 accident … Hall] Tom's "accident" was to be executed,
and he is now a skeleton (an "otamy") on display after
he was dissected by the "flaying" surgeons for an
anatomy demonstration.

more dishonest than the rest of mankind? What
we win, gentlemen, is our own by the law of arms
and the right of conquest.

CROOK-FINGERED JACK.

> Where shall we find such another set of practical   15
> philosophers, who to a man are above the fear of
> death?

WAT.

> Sound men, and true!

ROBIN.

> Of tried courage and indefatigable industry!

NED.

> Who is there here that would not die for his friend?   20

HARRY.

> Who is there here that would betray him for his
> interest?

MATT.

> Show me a gang of courtiers that can say as much.

BEN.

> We are for a just partition of the world, for every
> man hath a right to enjoy life.   25

MATT.

> We retrench the superfluities of mankind. The
> world is avaricious, and I hate avarice. A covetous
> fellow, like a jackdaw, steals what he was never
> made to enjoy for the sake of hiding it. These are
> the robbers of mankind, for money was made for   30
> the free-hearted and generous, and where is the
> injury of taking from another what he hath not
> the heart to make use of?

JEMMY.

> Our several stations for the day are fixed. Good
> luck attend us all. Fill the glasses.   35

Air 19. "Fill ev'ry glass," etc.

MATT.

> Fill ev'ry glass, for wine inspires us,
> > And fires us

With courage, love, and joy.
Women and wine should life employ.
Is there aught else on earth desirous?   40
CHORUS.
Fill ev'ry glass, etc.

Scene ii.

To them enter Macheath.

MACHEATH.
Gentlemen, well met. My heart hath been with
you this hour, but an unexpected affair hath
detained me. No ceremony, I beg you.
MATT.
We were just breaking up to go upon duty. Am I
to have the honor of taking the air with you, sir,   5
this evening upon the heath? I drink a dram now
and then with the stage-coachmen in the way of
friendship and intelligence, and I know that about
this time there will be passengers upon the Western
Road,[42] who are worth speaking with.   10
MACHEATH.
I was to have been of that party—but—
MATT.
But what sir?
MACHEATH.
Is there any man who suspects my courage?
MATT.
We have all been witnesses of it.
MACHEATH.
My honor and truth to the gang?   15
MATT.
I'll be answerable for it.
MACHEATH.
In the division of our booty, have I ever shown the
least marks of avarice or injustice?
MATT.
By these questions something seems to have ruffled
you. Are any of us suspected?   20
MACHEATH.
I have a fixed confidence, gentlemen, in you all as
men of honor, and as such I value and respect you.
Peachum is a man that is useful to us.

---

42 Western Road] the principal route from London to
    Cornwall. Macheath's men probably plan to rob travelers
    on Bagshot Heath along this route.

MATT.
Is he about to play us any foul play? I'll shoot him
through the head.   25
MACHEATH.
I beg you, gentlemen, act with conduct and
discretion. A pistol is your last resort.
MATT.
He knows nothing of this meeting.
MACHEATH.
Business cannot go on without him. He is a man
who knows the world and is a necessary agent to us.   30
We have had a slight difference, and till it is
accommodated, I shall be obliged to keep out of his
way. Any private dispute of mine shall be of no ill
consequence to my friends. You must continue to
act under his direction, for the moment we break   35
loose from him, our gang is ruined.
MATT.
As a bawd to a whore, I grant you, he is to us of
great convenience.
MACHEATH.
Make him believe I have quitted the gang, which
I can never do but with life. At our private quarters   40
I will continue to meet you. A week or so will
probably reconcile us.
MATT.
Your instructions shall be observed. 'Tis now high
time for us to repair to our several duties; so till
the evening at our quarters in Moorfields[43] we bid   45
you farewell.
MACHEATH.
I shall wish myself with you. Success attend you.
(*Sits down melancholy at the table.*)

*Air 20. "March in Rinaldo,[44] with drums and
Trumpets."*

---

43 Moorfields] a disreputable area north of the city famous
    for brandy shops and rough sports and pastimes
44 *Rinaldo*] Händel's first English opera (1711).

MATT.

Let us take the road.   50
    Hark! I hear the sound of coaches!
    The hour of attack approaches,
To your arms, brave boys, and load.
    See the ball I hold!
Let the chemists* toil like asses,   55
Our fire their fire surpasses,
    And turns all our lead to gold.

*The gang, ranged in the front of the stage, load their
pistols, and stick them under their girdles then go off
singing the first part in chorus.*

Scene iii.

Macheath.

MACHEATH.

What a fool is a fond wench! Polly is most confoundedly bit. I love the sex. And a man who loves
money might as well be contented with one guinea
as I with one woman. The Town* perhaps hath been
as much obliged to me for recruiting it with free-   5
hearted ladies as to any recruiting officer in the army.
If it were not for us and the other gentlemen of the
sword, Drury Lane would be uninhabited.

Air 21. *"Would you have a young virgin," etc.*

If the heart of a man is depressed with cares,   10
The mist is dispelled when a woman appears.
Like the notes of a fiddle, she sweetly, sweetly
Raises the spirits and charms our ears;
    Roses and lilies her cheeks disclose,
    But her ripe lips are more sweet than those.   15
      Press her,
      Caress her

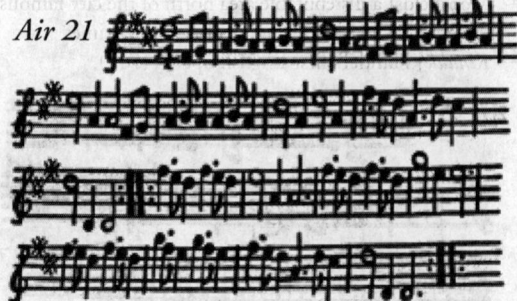

Air 21

      With blisses,
      Her kisses
Dissolve us in pleasure and soft repose.   20
I must have women. There is nothing unbends the
mind like them. Money is not so strong a cordial
for the time.—Drawer.

Enter drawer.

Is the porter gone for all the ladies, according to
my directions?   25

DRAWER.

I expect him back every minute. But you know, sir,
you sent him as far as Hockley in the Hole for three
of the ladies, for one in Vinegar Yard, and for the rest
of them somewhere about Lewkner's Lane.[45] Sure
some of them are below, for I hear the bar bell. As   30
they come I will show them up.—Coming, coming.
[*Exit.*]

Scene iv.

*Macheath, Mrs. Coaxer, Dolly Trull, Mrs. Vixen, Betty
Doxy, Jenny Diver, Mrs. Slammekin, Suky Tawdry,
and Molly Brazen.*

MACHEATH.

Dear Mrs.* Coaxer, you are welcome. You look
charmingly today. I hope you don't want the repairs
of quality,* and lay on paint.—Dolly Trull! kiss me,
you slut. Are you as amorous as ever, hussy? You are
always so taken up with stealing hearts that you   5
don't allow yourself time to steal anything else. Ah
Dolly, thou wilt ever be a coquette!—Mrs.* Vixen,
I'm yours, I always loved a woman of wit and spirit;
they make charming mistresses, but plaguy wives.—
Betty Doxy! Come hither, hussy. Do you drink as   10
hard as ever? You had better stick to good
wholesome beer, for in troth, Betty, strong waters
will in time ruin your constitution. You should leave
those to your betters.—What! and my pretty Jenny
Diver too! As prim and demure as ever! There is not   15
any prude, though ever so high bred, hath a more
sanctified look, with a more mischievous heart. Ah!

---

45 Vinegar … Lane] Vinegar Yard, properly Vine Garden
Yard, or Vineyard, was a small court just off Drury Lane.
Lewkner's Lane (now Macklin Street) is also near Drury
Lane.

thou art a dear artful hypocrite.—Mrs.* Slammekin! as careless and genteel as ever! all you fine ladies, who know your own beauty, affect an undress.—But see, here's Suky Tawdry come to contradict what I was saying. Everything she gets one way she lays out upon her back. Why Suky, you must keep* at least a dozen tallymen.—Molly Brazen!

She kisses him.

That's well done. I love a free-hearted wench. Thou hast a most agreeable assurance, girl, and art as willing as a turtle.*—But hark! I hear music. The harper is at the door. "If music be the food of love, play on."⁴⁶ Ere you seat yourselves, ladies, what think you of a dance?—Come in.

Enter harper.

Play the French tune that Mrs.* Slammekin was so fond of.

*A dance à la ronde*⁴⁷ *in the French manner; near the end of it this song and chorus.*

Air 22. Cotillion.

Youth's the season made for joys;
　　Love is then our duty.
She alone who that employs
　　Well deserves her beauty.
　　　　Let's be gay,
　　　　While we may:
Beauty's a flower despised in decay.

[CHORUS.]
Youth's the season, etc.

Let us drink and sport today;
　　Ours is not tomorrow.

---

⁴⁶ "If … on."] opening line of Shakespeare's *Twelfth Night*
⁴⁷ dance à la ronde] a dignified and formal dance, an expression of aristocratic taste, further identified in the text as a cotillion

Love with youth flies swift away;
　　Age is naught but sorrow.
　　　　Dance and sing;
　　　　Time's on the wing:
　　Life never knows the return of spring.
CHORUS.
Let us drink, etc.
MACHEATH.
Now pray ladies, take your places.—Here fellow. (*Pays the harper.*) Bid the drawer bring us more wine.
Exit harper.
If any of the ladies choose gin, I hope they will be so free to call for it.
JENNY.
You look as if you meant me. Wine is strong enough for me. Indeed sir, I never drink strong waters, but when I have the colic.
MACHEATH.
Just the excuse of the fine ladies! Why, a lady of quality* is never without the colic. I hope, Mrs.* Coaxer, you have had good success of late in your visits among the mercers.
COAXER.
We have so many interlopers, yet with industry one may still have a little picking. I carried a silver flowered lutestring and a piece of black paduasoy to Mr. Peachum's lock but last week.
VIXEN.
There's Molly Brazen hath the ogle of a rattlesnake. She riveted a linen draper's eye so fast upon her that he was nicked of three pieces of cambric before he could look off.
BRAZEN.
Oh dear madam! But sure nothing can come up to your handling of laces! And then you have such a sweet deluding tongue! To cheat a man is nothing, but the woman must have fine parts* indeed who cheats a woman!
VIXEN.
Lace, madam, lies in a small compass and is of easy conveyance. But you are apt, madam, to think too well of your friends.
COAXER.
If any woman hath more art than another, to be sure 'tis Jenny Diver. Though her fellow be never so agreeable, she can pick his pocket as coolly as

if money were her only pleasure. Now that is a 80
command of the passions uncommon in a woman!

JENNY.

I never go to the tavern with a man but in the view
of business. I have other hours and other sort of men
for my pleasure. But had I your address, madam—

MACHEATH.

Have done with your compliments, ladies, and 85
drink about.—You are not so fond of me, Jenny,
as you use to be.

JENNY.

'Tis not convenient, sir, to show my fondness among
so many rivals. 'Tis your own choice and not the
warmth of my inclination that will determine you. 90

Air 23. "All in a misty morning," etc.

Before the barn door crowing,
　　The cock by hens attended,
His eyes around him throwing,
　　Stands for a while suspended. 95
Then one he singles from the crew
　　And cheers the happy hen
With how do you do, and how do you do,
　　And how do you do again.

MACHEATH.

Ah Jenny! thou art a dear slut. 100

TRULL.

Pray madam, were you ever in keeping?*

TAWDRY.

I hope, madam, I ha'nt been so long upon the
Town, but I have met with some good fortune as
well as my neighbors.

TRULL.

Pardon me, madam, I meant no harm by the 105
question; 'twas only in the way of conversation.

TAWDRY.

Indeed madam, if I had not been a fool, I might
have lived very handsomely with my last friend.

But upon his missing five guineas, he turned me
off. Now I never suspected he had counted them. 110

SLAMMEKIN.

Who do you look upon, madam, as your best sort
of keepers?*

TRULL.

That, madam, is thereafter as they be.

SLAMMEKIN.

I, madam, was once kept by a Jew, and bating their
religion, to women they are a good sort of people. 115

TAWDRY.

Now for my part, I own I like an old fellow, for
we always make them pay for what they can't do.

VIXEN.

A spruce prentice, let me tell you, ladies, is no ill
thing, they bleed freely. I have sent at least two or
three dozen of them in my time to the plantations.* 120

JENNY.

But to be sure, sir, with so much good fortune as
you have had upon the road, you must be grown
immensely rich.

MACHEATH.

The road, indeed, hath done me justice, but the
gaming table hath been my ruin. 125

Air 24. "When once I lay with another man's wife," etc.

JENNY.

The gamesters and lawyers are jugglers alike:
　　If they meddle, your all is in danger.
Like Gypsies, if once they can finger a souse,[48]
Your pockets they pick, and they pilfer your house 130
　　And give your estate to a stranger.
A man of courage should never put anything to
the risk but his life.[c]

She takes up his pistol. Tawdry takes up the other.

These are the tools of a man of honor. Cards and
dice are only fit for cowardly cheats who prey upon 135
their friends.

─────────────
48 souse] a sou, a trifling coin

Air 23

Air 24

TAWDRY.

This, sir, is fitter for your hand. Besides your loss of money, 'tis a loss to the ladies. Gaming takes you off from women. How fond could I be of you! but before company, 'tis ill bred. 140

MACHEATH.

Wanton hussies!

JENNY.

I must and will have a kiss to give my wine a zest.

They take him about the neck and make signs to Peachum and the constables, who rush in upon him.

Scene v.

To them, Peachum and constables.

PEACHUM.

I seize you, sir, as my prisoner.

MACHEATH.

Was this well done, Jenny? Women are decoy ducks. Who can trust them? Beasts, jades, jilts, harpies, furies, whores!

PEACHUM.

Your case, Mr. Macheath, is not particular. The 5 greatest heroes have been ruined by women. But to do them justice, I must own they are a pretty sort of creatures, if we could trust them. You must now, sir, take your leave of the ladies, and if they have a mind to make you a visit, they will be sure to find you at 10 home.—The gentleman, ladies, lodges in Newgate. —Constables, wait upon the captain to his lodgings.

Air 25. "When first I laid siege to my Chloris," etc.

MACHEATH.

At the tree I shall suffer with pleasure,
At the tree I shall suffer with pleasure;
Let me go where I will, 15
In all kinds of ill,
I shall find no such furies as these are.

PEACHUM.

Ladies, I'll take care the reckoning shall be discharged.

Exit Macheath, guarded with Peachum and Constables.

Scene vi.

The women remain.

VIXEN.

Look ye, Mrs.* Jenny, though Mr. Peachum may have made a private bargain with you and Suky Tawdry for betraying the captain, as we were all assisting, we ought all to share alike.

COAXER.

I think Mr. Peachum, after so long an acquaint- 5 ance, might have trusted me as well as Jenny Diver.

SLAMMEKIN.

I am sure at least three men of his hanging and in a year's time too (if he did me justice) should be set down to my account.

TRULL.

Mrs.* Slammekin, that is not fair. For you know 10 one of them was taken in bed with me.

JENNY.

As far as a bowl of punch or a treat, I believe Mrs.* Suky will join with me. As for anything else, ladies, you cannot in conscience expect it.

SLAMMEKIN.

Dear madam— 15

TRULL.

I would not for the world—

SLAMMEKIN.

'Tis impossible for me—

TRULL.

As I hope to be saved, madam—

SLAMMEKIN.

Nay, then I must stay here all night—

TRULL.

Since you command me. 20

Exeunt with great ceremony.

Scene vii. Newgate.

Lockit, turnkeys, Macheath, constables.

LOCKIT.

Noble Captain, you are welcome. You have not been a lodger of mine this year and half. You know the custom, sir: garnish, Captain, garnish.—Hand me down those fetters there.

MACHEATH.

Those, Mr. Lockit, seem to be the heaviest of the 5

whole set. With your leave, I should like the further pair better.

LOCKIT.

Look ye, Captain, we know what is fittest for our prisoners. When a gentleman uses me with civility, I always do the best I can to please him.—Hand 10 them down, I say.—We have them of all prices, from one guinea to ten, and 'tis fitting every gentleman should please himself.

MACHEATH.

I understand you, sir. (*Gives money.*) The fees here are so many and so exorbitant that few fortunes 15 can bear the expense of getting off handsomely or of dying like a gentleman.

LOCKIT.

Those, I see, will fit the captain better. Take down the further pair.—Do but examine them, sir. Never was better work. How genteelly they are made! 20 They will sit as easy as a glove, and the nicest* man in England might not be ashamed to wear them. (*He puts on the chains.*) If I had the best gentleman in the land in my custody I could not equip him more handsomely. And so, sir, I now leave you to 25 your private meditations.

[*Exeunt. Manet Macheath.*]

Scene viii.

Macheath.

Air 26. *"Courtiers, courtiers think it no harm," etc.*

[MACHEATH.]

Man may escape from rope and gun.
Nay, some have outlived the doctor's pill.
Who takes a woman must be undone;
    That basilisk is sure to kill. 5
The fly that sips treacle is lost in the sweets,
So he that tastes woman, woman, woman,
    He that tastes woman ruin meets.

To what a woeful plight have I brought myself! Here must I (all day long till I am hanged) be 10 confined to hear the reproaches of a wench who lays her ruin at my door. I am in the custody of her father, and to be sure, if he knows of the matter, I shall have a fine time on't betwixt this and my execution. But I promised the wench marriage. 15 What signifies a promise to a woman? Does not man in marriage itself promise a hundred things that he never means to perform? Do all we can, women will believe us, for they look upon a promise as an excuse for following their own 20 inclinations.—But here comes Lucy, and I cannot get from her. Would I were deaf!

Scene ix.

Macheath, Lucy.

LUCY.

You base man you, how can you look me in the face after what hath passed between us? See here, perfidious wretch, how I am forced to bear about the load of infamy you have laid upon me. Oh Macheath! thou hast robbed me of my quiet. To 5 see thee tortured would give me pleasure.

Air 27. *"A lovely lass to a friar came," etc.*

Thus when a good housewife sees a rat
    In her trap in the morning taken,
With pleasure her heart goes pit-a-pat 10
    In revenge for her loss of bacon.
        Then she throws him
        To the dog or cat
    To be worried, crushed, and shaken.

MACHEATH.

Have you no bowels, no tenderness, my dear Lucy, 15 to see a husband in these circumstances?

LUCY.

A husband!

MACHEATH.

In ev'ry respect but the form, and that, my dear, may be said over us at any time. Friends should not insist upon ceremonies. From a man of honor, his word is as good as his bond.   20

LUCY.

'Tis the pleasure of all you fine men to insult the women you have ruined.

Air 28. "'Twas when the sea was roaring," etc.

How cruel are the traitors   25
    Who lie and swear in jest
To cheat unguarded creatures
    Of virtue, fame, and rest!
Whoever steals a shilling
    Through shame the guilt conceals;   30
In love the perjured villain
    With boasts the theft reveals.

MACHEATH.

The very first opportunity, my dear (have but patience), you shall be my wife in whatever manner you please.   35

LUCY.

Insinuating monster! And so you think I know nothing of the affair of Miss Polly Peachum. I could tear thy eyes out!

MACHEATH.

Sure Lucy, you can't be such a fool as to be jealous of Polly!   40

LUCY.

Are you not married to her, you brute you?

MACHEATH.

Married! Very good. The wench gives it out only to vex thee and to ruin me in thy good opinion. 'Tis true, I go to the house; I chat with the girl; I kiss her; I say a thousand things to her (as all gentlemen do)   45

that mean nothing, to divert my self. And now the silly* jade hath set it about that I am married to her, to let me know what she would be at. Indeed my dear Lucy, these violent passions may be of ill consequence to a woman in your condition.   50

LUCY.

Come, come, Captain, for all your assurance, you know that Miss Polly hath put it out of your power to do me the justice you promised me.

MACHEATH.

A jealous woman believes everything her passion suggests. To convince you of my sincerity, if we can   55
find the ordinary, I shall have no scruples of making you my wife. And I know the consequence of having two at a time.

LUCY.

That you are only to be hanged, and so get rid of them both.   60

MACHEATH.

I am ready, my dear Lucy, to give you satisfaction—if you think there is any in marriage. What can a man of honor say more?

LUCY.

So then it seems, you are not married to Miss Polly.

MACHEATH.

You know, Lucy, the girl is prodigiously conceited.   65
No man can say a civil thing to her, but (like other fine ladies) her vanity makes her think he's her own forever and ever.

Air 29. "The sun had loosed his weary teams," etc.

The first time at the looking glass   70
    The mother sets her daughter,
The image strikes the smiling lass
    With self-love ever after.
Each time she looks, she, fonder grown,
    Thinks ev'ry charm grows stronger.   75
But alas, vain maid, all eyes but your own
    Can see you are not younger.

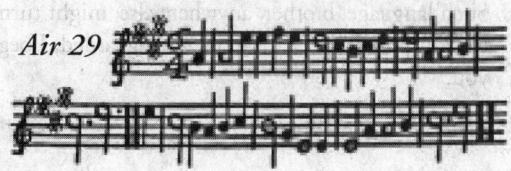

When women consider their own beauties, they are all alike unreasonable in their demands, for they expect their lovers should like them as long 80 as they like themselves.

LUCY.

Yonder is my father—perhaps this way we may light upon the ordinary, who shall try if you will be as good as your word. For I long to be made an honest woman. 85

[*Exeunt.*]

Scene x.

Peachum, Lockit with an account book.

LOCKIT.

In this last affair, brother Peachum, we are agreed. You have consented to go halves in Macheath.

PEACHUM.

We shall never fall out about an execution. But as to that article, pray how stands our last year's account? 5

LOCKIT.

If you will run your eye over it, you'll find 'tis fair and clearly stated.

PEACHUM.

This long arrear of the government is very hard upon us! Can it be expected that we should hang our acquaintance for nothing, when our betters 10 will hardly save theirs without being paid for it. Unless the people in employment pay better, I promise them for the future I shall let other rogues live besides their own.

LOCKIT.

Perhaps brother, they are afraid these matters may 15 be carried too far. We are treated too by them with contempt, as if our profession was not reputable.

PEACHUM.

In one respect indeed, our employment may be reckoned dishonest, because, like great statesmen, we encourage those who betray their friends. 20

LOCKIT.

Such language, brother, anywhere else, might turn to your prejudice. Learn to be more guarded, I beg you.

Air 30. "How happy are we," etc.

When you censure the age, 25
　　Be cautious and sage,
Lest the courtiers offended should be:
　　If you mention vice or bribe,
　　'Tis so pat to all the tribe,
Each cries, "That was leveled at me." 30

PEACHUM.

Here's poor Ned Clincher's name, I see. Sure brother Lockit, there was a little unfair proceeding in Ned's case: for he told me in the condemned hold that, for value received, you had promised him a session or two longer without molestation. 35

LOCKIT.

Mr. Peachum, this is the first time my honor was ever called in question.

PEACHUM.

Business is at an end if once we act dishonorably.

LOCKIT.

Who accuses me?

PEACHUM.

You are warm, brother. 40

LOCKIT.

He that attacks my honor attacks my livelihood. And this usage—sir—is not to be borne.

PEACHUM.

Since you provoke me to speak, I must tell you too that Mrs.* Coaxer charges you with defrauding her of her information-money for the apprehending of 45 Curl-pated Hugh. Indeed, indeed, brother, we must punctually pay our spies, or we shall have no information.[49]

LOCKIT.

Is this language to me, sirrah, who have saved you from the gallows, sirrah! 50

---

49 spies … information] This is one of many oblique references throughout the play to the chief minister, Robert Walpole. A grievance of Walpole's critics was his intelligence budget which funded secret methods of gaining damaging evidence against those he opposed.

Air 30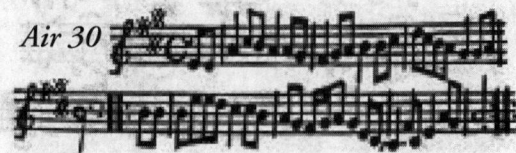

Collaring each other.

PEACHUM.

If I am hanged, it shall be for ridding the world of an arrant rascal.

LOCKIT.

This hand shall do the office of the halter you deserve and throttle you, you dog!

PEACHUM.

Brother, brother, we are both in the wrong. We 55
shall be both losers in the dispute. For you know we have it in our power to hang each other. You should not be so passionate.

LOCKIT.

Nor you so provoking.

PEACHUM.

'Tis our mutual interest, 'tis for the interest of the 60
world we should agree. If I said anything, brother, to the prejudice of your character, I ask pardon.

LOCKIT.

Brother Peachum, I can forgive as well as resent. Give me your hand. Suspicion does not become a friend. 65

PEACHUM.

I only meant to give you occasion to justify yourself. But I must now step home, for I expect the gentleman about this snuffbox that Filch nimmed two nights ago in the park. I appointed him at this hour. [*Exit.*] 70

Scene xi.

Lockit, Lucy.

LOCKIT.

Whence come you, hussy?

LUCY.

My tears might answer that question.

LOCKIT.

You have then been whimpering and fondling, like a spaniel, over the fellow that hath abused you.

LUCY.

One can't help love; one can't cure it. 'Tis not in 5
my power to obey you and hate him.

LOCKIT.

Learn to bear your husband's death like a reasonable woman. 'Tis not the fashion nowadays so much as

to affect sorrow upon these occasions. No woman would ever marry if she had not the chance of 10
mortality for a release. Act like a woman of spirit, hussy, and thank your father for what he is doing.

Air 31. "Of a noble race* was Shenkin."

LUCY.

Is then his fate decreed, sir?
　　Such a man can I think of quitting? 15
When first we met, so moves me yet,
　　Oh see how my heart is splitting!

LOCKIT.

Look ye, Lucy, there is no saving him. So I think you must even do like other widows: buy yourself weeds and be cheerful. 20

Air 32.

You'll think ere many days ensue
　　This sentence not severe;
I hang your husband, child, 'tis true,
　　But with him hang your care. 25
　　　　Twang dang dillo dee.

Like a good wife, go moan over your dying husband. That, child, is your duty. Consider, girl, you can't have the man and the money too, so make yourself as easy as you can by getting all you 30
can from him. [*Exit.*]

Scene xii.

Lucy, Macheath.

LUCY.

Though the ordinary was out of the way today, I
hope, my dear, you will upon the first opportunity
quiet my scruples. Oh sir! my father's hard heart is
not to be softened, and I am in the utmost despair.

MACHEATH.

But if I could raise a small sum, would not twenty   5
guineas, think you, move him? Of all the
arguments in the way of business, the perquisite
is the most prevailing. Your father's perquisites for
the escape of prisoners must amount to a
considerable sum in the year. Money well timed   10
and properly applied will do anything.

Air 33. "London Ladies."

If you at an office solicit your due
        And would not have matters neglected,
You must quicken the clerk with the perquisite too,   15
        To do what his duty directed.
Or would you the frowns of a lady prevent,
        She too has this palpable failing:
The perquisite softens her into consent;
        That reason with all is prevailing.   20

LUCY.

What love or money can do shall be done, for all
my comfort depends upon your safety.

Scene xiii.

Lucy, Macheath, Polly.

POLLY.

Where is my dear husband? Was a rope ever
intended for this neck! Oh let me throw my arms

about it and throttle thee with love! Why dost thou
turn away from me? 'Tis thy Polly, 'tis thy wife.

MACHEATH.

Was ever such an unfortunate rascal as I am!   5

LUCY.

Was there ever such another villain!

POLLY.

Oh Macheath! was it for this we parted? Taken!
imprisoned! Tried! Hanged! Cruel reflection! I'll
stay with thee till death; no force shall tear thy dear
wife from thee now. What means my love? Not   10
one kind word! not one kind look! Think what thy
Polly suffers to see thee in this condition.

Air 34. "All in the downs," etc.

Thus when the swallow, seeking prey,
        Within the sash is closely pent,   15
His consort, with bemoaning lay,
        Without sits pining for th'event.
Her chatt'ring lovers all around her skim;
She heeds them not (poor bird!), her soul's with him.

MACHEATH. (*Aside.*)

I must disown her.—The wench is distracted.   20

LUCY.

Am I then bilked of my virtue? Can I have no
reparation? Sure men were born to lie and women
to believe them! Oh villain! villain!

POLLY.

Am I not thy wife? Thy neglect of me, thy aversion
to me too severely proves it. Look on me. Tell me,   25
am I not thy wife?

LUCY.

Perfidious wretch!

POLLY.

Barbarous husband!

LUCY.

Hadst thou been hanged five months ago, I had
been happy.   30

POLLY.

And I too. If you had been kind* to me till death, it would not have vexed me—and that's no very unreasonable request (though from a wife) to a man who hath not above seven or eight days to live. 35

LUCY.

Art thou then married to another? Hast thou two wives, monster?

MACHEATH.

If women's tongues can cease for an answer, hear me.

LUCY.

I won't. Flesh and blood can't bear my usage. 40

POLLY.

Shall I not claim my own? Justice bids me speak.

Air 35. "Have you heard of a frolicsome ditty," etc.

MACHEATH.

How happy could I be with either,
    Were t'other dear charmer away!
But while you thus tease me together,
    To neither a word will I say, 45
        But tol de rol, etc.

POLLY.

Sure my dear, there ought to be some preference shown to a wife! At least she may claim the appearance of it.—He must be distracted with his misfortunes, or he could not use me thus! 50

LUCY.

Oh villain, villain! thou hast deceived me. I could even inform against thee with pleasure. Not a prude wishes more heartily to have facts against her intimate acquaintance than I now wish to have facts against thee. I would have her satisfaction, and they should all out. 55

Air 36. Irish trot.

POLLY.

I'm bubbled.[50]

LUCY.

                                I'm bubbled. 60

POLLY.

Oh how I am troubled!

LUCY.

Bamboozled, and bit!*

POLLY.

                    My distresses are doubled.

LUCY.

When you come to the tree, should the hangman refuse,
These fingers with pleasure could fasten the noose. 65

POLLY.

I'm bubbled, etc.

MACHEATH.

Be pacified, my dear Lucy. This is all a fetch of Polly's to make me desperate with you in case I get off. If I am hanged, she would fain have the credit of being thought my widow.—Really, Polly, this is no time 70 for a dispute of this sort, for whenever you are talking of marriage, I am thinking of hanging.

POLLY.

And hast thou the heart to persist in disowning me?

MACHEATH.

And hast thou the heart to persist in persuading 75 me that I am married? Why Polly, dost thou seek to aggravate my misfortunes?

---

50 bubbled] cheated; also refers to the South Sea Company stock bubble and crash of 1720, in which many, including Gay, lost money. In resolving the crisis, Walpole consolidated his ministerial power, using strong arm tactics to stabilize the government and shield the monarchy from investigation and scandal.

Air 35

Air 36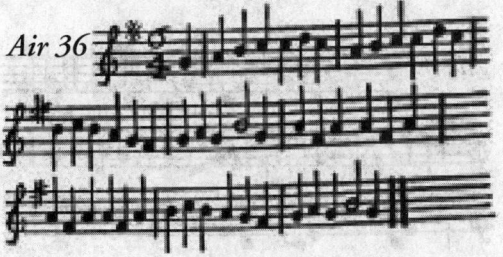

LUCY.

Really Miss Peachum, you but expose yourself. Besides, 'tis barbarous in you to worry a gentleman in his circumstances. 80

Air 37.

POLLY.

> Cease your funning;
> Force or cunning
> Never shall my heart trepan.
> All these sallies 85
> Are but malice
> To seduce my constant man.
> 'Tis most certain
> By their flirting
> Women oft have envy shown: 90
> Pleased to ruin
> Others wooing,
> Never happy in their own!

POLLY.

Decency, madam, methinks might teach you to behave yourself with some reserve with the 95 husband while his wife is present.

MACHEATH.

But seriously, Polly, this is carrying the joke a little too far.

LUCY.

If you are determined, madam, to raise a disturbance in the prison, I shall be obliged to send 100 for the turnkey to show you the door. I am sorry, madam, you force me to be so ill-bred.

POLLY.

Give me leave to tell you, madam, these forward airs don't become you in the least, madam. And my duty, madam, obliges me to stay with my 105 husband, madam.

Air 38. "Good morrow, Gossip Joan."

LUCY.

Why how now, Madam Flirt:
> If you thus must chatter
And are for flinging dirt, 110
> Let's try who best can spatter,
> > Madam
> Flirt!

POLLY.

Why how now, saucy jade:
> Sure the wench is tipsy! 115
(*To him.*)
> How can you see me made
> The scoff of such a Gypsy?
> > (*To her.*)
> Saucy jade!

> Scene xiv.

Lucy, Macheath, Polly, Peachum.

PEACHUM.

Where's my wench? Ah hussy! hussy! Come you home, you slut, and when your fellow is hanged, hang yourself to make your family some amends.

POLLY.

Dear, dear father, do not tear me from him. I must speak. I have more to say to him.—Oh! twist thy 5 fetters about me that he may not haul me from thee!

PEACHUM.

Sure all women are alike! If ever they commit the folly, they are sure to commit another by exposing themselves.—Away, not a word more. You are my prisoner now, hussy. 10

Air 39. Irish howl.

POLLY. (*Holding Macheath, Peachum pulling her.*)
No power on earth can e'er divide
The knot that sacred love hath tied.
When parents draw against our mind,

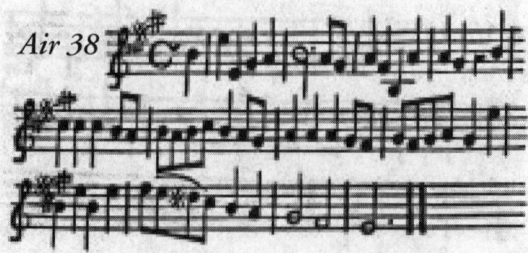

The true-love's knot they faster bind. 15
      Oh, oh ray, oh amborah—oh, oh, etc.

[Exeunt Polly and Peachum.]

Scene xv.

Lucy, Macheath.

MACHEATH.

I am naturally compassionate, wife, so that I could
not use the wench as she deserved, which made you
at first suspect there was something in what she said.

LUCY.

Indeed my dear, I was strangely puzzled.

MACHEATH.

If that had been the case, her father would never 5
have brought me into this circumstance. No Lucy,
I had rather die than be false to thee.

LUCY.

How happy am I, if you say this from your heart!
For I love thee so, that I could sooner bear to see
thee hanged than in the arms of another. 10

MACHEATH.

But couldst thou bear to see me hanged?

LUCY.

Oh Macheath, I can never live to see that day.

MACHEATH.

You see, Lucy, in the account of love you are in my
debt, and you must now be convinced that I rather
choose to die than be another's. Make me, if possi- 15
ble, love thee more, and let me owe my life to thee.
If you refuse to assist me, Peachum and your father
will immediately put me beyond all means of escape.

LUCY.

My father, I know, hath been drinking hard with
the prisoners, and I fancy he is now taking his nap 20
in his own room. If I can procure the keys, shall I
go off with thee, my dear?

MACHEATH.

If we are together, 'twill be impossible to lie concealed. As soon as the search begins to be a little cool,
I will send to thee. Till then my heart is thy prisoner. 25

LUCY.

Come then, my dear husband, owe thy life to me,
and though you love me not, be grateful. But that
Polly runs in my head strangely.

MACHEATH.

A moment of time may make us unhappy forever.

Air 40. "The lass of Patie's Mill," etc. 30

LUCY.

I like the fox shall grieve,
      Whose mate hath left her side,
Whom hounds, from morn to eve,
      Chase o'er the country wide.
Where can my lover hide? 35
      Where cheat the wary^d pack?
If Love be not his guide,
      He never will come back!

[Exeunt.]

      Act III, scene i. Newgate.

Lockit, Lucy.

LOCKIT.

To be sure, wench, you must have been aiding and
abetting to help him to this escape.

LUCY.

Sir, here hath been Peachum and his daughter
Polly, and to be sure they know the ways of
Newgate as well as if they had been born and bred 5
in the place all their lives. Why must all your
suspicion light upon me?

LOCKIT.

Lucy, Lucy, I will have none of these shuffling answers.

LUCY.

Well then, if I know anything of him, I wish I may be burnt![51]   10

LOCKIT.

Keep your temper, Lucy, or I shall pronounce you guilty.

LUCY.

Keep yours, sir, I do wish I may be burnt, I do. And what can I say more to convince you?   15

LOCKIT.

Did he tip handsomely? How much did he come down with? Come hussy, don't cheat your father, and I shall not be angry with you. Perhaps you have made a better bargain with him than I could have done. How much, my good girl?   20

LUCY.

You know, sir, I am fond of him and would have given money to have kept him with me.

LOCKIT.

Ah Lucy! thy education might have put thee more upon thy guard, for a girl in the bar of an alehouse is always besieged.   25

LUCY.

Dear sir, mention not my education, for 'twas to that I owe my ruin.

Air 41. "If love's a sweet passion," etc.

---

[51] burnt] Being burned to death was the punishment for women convicted of treason; alternatively, Lucy may be referring to the punishment for first offenders who, receiving the benefit of clergy, were branded on the thumb to ensure that they not use the plea again (LT).

When young at the bar you first taught me to score
And bid me be free of my lips and no more,   30
I was kissed by the parson, the squire, and the sot.
When the guest was departed, the kiss was forgot.
But his kiss was so sweet and so closely he pressed,
That I languished and pined till I granted the rest.
If you can forgive me, sir, I will make a fair   35
confession, for to be sure, he hath been a most
barbarous villain to me.

LOCKIT.

And so you have let him escape, hussy, have you?

LUCY.

When a woman loves, a kind look, a tender word can persuade her to anything. And I could ask no   40 other bribe.

LOCKIT.

Thou wilt always be a vulgar slut, Lucy. If you would not be looked upon as a fool, you should never do anything but upon the foot of interest. Those that act otherwise are their own bubbles.*   45

LUCY.

But love, sir, is a misfortune that may happen to the most discreet woman, and in love we are all fools alike. Notwithstanding all he swore, I am now fully convinced that Polly Peachum is actually his wife. Did I let him escape (fool that I was!) to go to her?   50 Polly will wheedle herself into his money, and then Peachum will hang him and cheat us both.

LOCKIT.

So I am to be ruined because, forsooth, you must be in love—a very pretty excuse!

LUCY.

I could murder that impudent, happy strumpet. I   55 gave him his life, and that creature enjoys the sweets of it. Ungrateful Macheath!

Air 42. "South Sea Ballad."

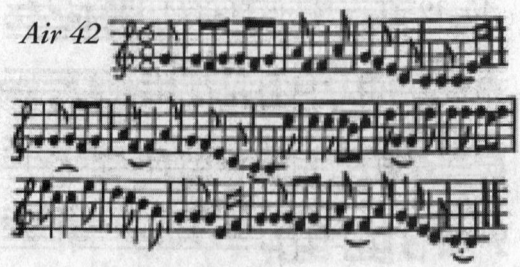

My love is all madness and folly:
   Alone I lie,   60
   Toss, tumble, and cry,
"What a happy creature is Polly!"
Was e'er such a wretch as I:
With rage I redden like scarlet
That my dear inconstant varlet,   65
   Stark blind to my charms,
   Is lost in the arms
Of that jilt, that inveigling harlot!
   Stark blind to my charms,
   Is lost in the arms   70
Of that jilt, that inveigling harlot!
This, this my resentment alarms.

LOCKIT.
And so, after all this mischief, I must stay here to be entertained with your caterwauling, mistress puss! Out of my sight, wanton strumpet! you shall 75 fast and mortify yourself into reason, with now and then a little handsome discipline to bring you to your senses. Go.

[Exit Lucy.]

      Scene ii.

LOCKIT.
Peachum then intends to outwit me in this affair, but I'll be even with him. The dog is leaky in his liquor, so I'll ply him that way, get the secret from him, and turn this affair to my own advantage. Lions, wolves, and vultures don't live together in herds, droves, or 5 flocks. Of all animals of prey, man is the only sociable one. Every one of us preys upon his neighbor, and yet we herd together. Peachum is my companion, my friend. According to the custom of the world, indeed, he may quote thousands of precedents for 10 cheating me. And shall not I make use of the privilege of friendship to make him a return?

Air 43. "Packington's Pound."

Thus gamesters united in friendship are found,
Though they know that their industry all is a cheat; 15
They flock to their prey at the dice box's sound
And join to promote one another's deceit.
   But if by mishap
   They fail of a chap,
To keep in their hands they each other entrap. 20
Like pikes, lank with hunger, who miss of their ends,
They bite their companions and prey on their
  friends.

Now Peachum, you and I, like honest tradesmen, are to have a fair trial which of us two can overreach the other.—Lucy. 25

Enter Lucy.

Are there any of Peachum's people now in the house?

LUCY.
Filch, sir, is drinking a quartern of strong-waters in the next room with Black Moll.

LOCKIT.
Bid him come to me. 30

[Exit Lucy.]

      Scene iii.

Lockit, Filch.

LOCKIT.
Why boy, thou lookest as if thou wert half starved, like a shotten herring.

FILCH.
One had need have the constitution of a horse to go through the business. Since the favorite child-getter was disabled by a mishap, I have picked up a little 5 money by helping the ladies to a pregnancy against their being called down to sentence. But if a man cannot get an honest livelihood an easier way, I am sure 'tis what I can't undertake for another session.

LOCKIT.
Truly, if that great man* should tip off, 'twould be 10 an irreparable loss. The vigor and prowess of a knight-errant never saved half the ladies in distress that he hath done. But boy, canst thou tell me where thy master is to be found?

FILCH.
At his lock, sir, at the Crooked Billet. 15

LOCKIT.

Very well, I have nothing more with you.

Exit Filch.

I'll go to him there, for I have many important affairs to settle with him, and in the way of those transactions, I'll artfully get into his secret so that Macheath shall not remain a day longer out of my clutches. 20

Scene iv. A gaming house.

Macheath in a fine, tarnished coat, Ben Budge, Matt of the Mint.

MACHEATH.

I am sorry, gentlemen, the road was so barren of money. When my friends are in difficulties, I am always glad that my fortune can be serviceable to them. (*Gives them money.*) You see, gentlemen, I am not a mere Court friend who professes 5 everything and will do nothing.

Air 44. "Lillibullero."

The modes of the Court so common are grown,
    That a true friend can hardly be met;
Friendship for interest is but a loan, 10
    Which they let out for what they can get.
        'Tis true, you find
        Some friends so kind,
Who will give you good counsel themselves to
    defend.
        In sorrowful ditty, 15
        They promise, they pity,
But shift you for money from friend to friend.
But we, gentlemen, have still honor enough to break through the corruptions of the world. And while I can serve you, you may command me. 20

Air 44

BEN.

It grieves my heart that so generous a man should be involved in such difficulties as oblige him to live with such ill company and herd with gamesters.

MATT.

See the partiality of mankind: one man may steal a horse better than another look over a hedge. Of 25 all mechanics, of all servile handicraftsmen, a gamester is the vilest. But yet, as many of the quality* are of the profession, he is admitted amongst the politest company. I wonder we are not more respected. 30

MACHEATH.

There will be deep play tonight at Marrabone,* and consequently money may be picked up upon the road. Meet me there, and I'll give you the hint who is worth setting.

MATT.

The fellow with a brown coat with a narrow gold 35 binding, I am told, is never without money.

MACHEATH.

What do you mean, Matt? Sure you will not think of meddling with him! He's a good, honest kind of a fellow and one of us.

BEN.

To be sure, sir, we will put ourselves under your 40 direction.

MACHEATH.

Have an eye upon the moneylenders. A rouleau or two would prove a pretty sort of an expedition. I hate extortion.

MATT.

Those rouleaus are very pretty things. I hate your* 45 bank bills. There is such a hazard in putting them off.

MACHEATH.

There is a certain man of distinction, who in his time hath nicked me out of a great deal of the ready. He is in my cash, Ben. I'll point him out 50 to you this evening, and you shall draw upon him for the debt.—The company are met; I hear the dice box in the other room. So gentlemen, your servant. You'll meet me at Marrabone.

[Exeunt.]

Scene v. Peachum's lock.

A table with wine, brandy, pipes and tobacco.
Peachum, Lockit.

LOCKIT.
The Coronation account,[52] brother Peachum, is
of so intricate a nature, that I believe it will never
be settled.

PEACHUM.
It consists indeed of a great variety of articles. It
was worth to our people, in fees of different kinds, 5
above ten installments.[53] This is part of the
account, brother, that lies open before us.

LOCKIT.
"A lady's tail[54] of rich brocade"—that, I see, is
disposed of.

PEACHUM.
To Mrs.* Diana Trapes, the tallywoman, and she 10
will make a good hand on't in shoes and slippers
to trick out young ladies upon their going into
keeping.*

LOCKIT.
But I don't see any article of the jewels.

PEACHUM.
Those are so well known, that they must be sent 15
abroad. You'll find them entered under the article
of exportation. As for the snuffboxes, watches,
swords, etcetera, I thought it best to enter them
under their several heads.

LOCKIT.
"Seven and twenty women's pockets complete with 20
the several things therein contained"—all sealed,
numbered, and entered.

PEACHUM.
But brother, it is impossible for us now to enter
upon this affair. We should have the whole day
before us. Besides, the account of the last half year's 25
plate* is in a book by itself, which lies at the other
office.

LOCKIT.
Bring us then more liquor. Today shall be for
pleasure, tomorrow for business. Ah brother, those
daughters of ours are two slippery hussies. Keep a 30
watchful eye upon Polly, and Macheath in a day
or two shall be our own again.

Air 45. "Down in the North Country," etc.

LOCKIT.
What gudgeons are we men!
    Ev'ry woman's easy prey. 35
Though we have felt the hook, again
    We bite, and they betray.
The bird that hath been trapped,
    When he hears his calling mate,
To her he flies, again he's clapped 40
    Within the wiry grate.

PEACHUM.
But what signifies catching the bird, if your
daughter Lucy will set open the door of the cage?

LOCKIT.
If men were answerable for the follies and frailties
of their wives and daughters, no friends could keep 45
a good correspondence together for two days. This
is unkind of you, brother, for among good friends,
what they say or do goes for nothing.

Enter a servant.

SERVANT.
Sir, here's Mrs.* Diana Trapes wants to speak with
you. 50

PEACHUM.
Shall we admit her, brother Lockit?

LOCKIT.
By all means. She's a good customer and a fine-
spoken woman—and a woman who drinks and
talks so freely, will enliven the conversation.

PEACHUM.
Desire her to walk in. 55

Exit Servant.

Air 45

---

52 Coronation account] account of goods stolen during the
   lavish coronation ceremonies of George II in October
   1727, three months before *The Beggar's Opera* opened
53 installment] public installation of the Lord Mayor of the
   City of London
54 tail] train

Scene vi.

Peachum, Lockit, Mrs.* Trapes.

PEACHUM.

Dear Mrs. Di, your servant. One may know by your kiss, that your gin is excellent.

TRAPES.

I was always very curious* in my liquors.

LOCKIT.

There is no perfumed breath like it. I have been long acquainted with the flavor of those lips, han't I, Mrs. Di? 60

TRAPES.

Fill it up. I take as large draughts of liquor, as I did of love. I hate a flincher in either.

Air 46. "A shepherd kept sheep," etc.

In the days of my youth I could bill like a dove, 65
    fa, la, la, etc.
Like a sparrow at all times was ready for love, fa,
    la, la, etc.
The life of all mortals in kissing should pass,
Lip to lip while we're young—then the lip to the
    glass, fa, etc.

But now, Mr. Peachum, to our business. If you have blacks[55] of any kind brought in of late, 70
mantuas, velvet scarves, petticoats—let it be what it will, I am your chap, for all my ladies are very fond of mourning.

PEACHUM.

Why, look ye, Mrs. Di, you deal so hard with us that we can afford to give the gentlemen who 75
venture their lives for the goods little or nothing.

TRAPES.

The hard times oblige me to go very near in my dealing. To be sure, of late years I have been a great sufferer by the Parliament. Three thousand pounds

---

55 blacks] mourning clothes

would hardly make me amends. The act for 80
destroying the Mint[56] was a severe cut upon our business: till then, if a customer stepped out of the way, we knew where to have her. No doubt you know Mrs.* Coaxer: there's a wench now (till today) with a good suit of clothes of mine upon her back, 85
and I could never set eyes upon her for three months together. Since the act too against imprisonment for small sums,[57] my loss there too hath been very considerable, and it must be so, when a lady can borrow a handsome petticoat or a clean gown and I 90
not have the least hank upon her! And o'my conscience, nowadays most ladies take a delight in cheating, when they can do it with safety.

PEACHUM.

Madam, you had a handsome gold watch of us t'other day for seven guineas. Considering we must 95
have our profit, to a gentleman upon the road a gold watch will be scarce worth the taking.

TRAPES.

Consider, Mr. Peachum, that watch was remarkable, and not of very safe sale. If you have any black velvet scarves, they are a handsome winter wear and take 100
with most gentlemen who deal with my customers. 'Tis I that put the ladies upon a good foot. 'Tis not youth or beauty that fixes their price. The gentlemen always pay according to their dress, from half a crown to two guineas. And yet those hussies make 105
nothing of bilking of me. Then too, allowing for accidents (I have eleven fine customers now down under the surgeon's hands), what with fees and other expenses, there are great goings-out, and no comings-in, and not a farthing to pay for at least a 110
month's clothing. We run great risks—great risks indeed.

PEACHUM.

As I remember, you said something just now of Mrs.* Coaxer.

TRAPES.

Yes sir, to be sure, I stripped her of a suit of my 115
own clothes about two hours ago and have left her

---

56 act … Mint] After 1722 debtors could be arrested in this former sanctuary.
57 act … sums] Parliament passed an act in 1725 against imprisonment of people for small debts.

as she should be, in her shift, with a lover of hers at my house. She called him upstairs as he was going to Marrabone in a hackney coach. And I hope, for her own sake and mine, she will persuade the captain to redeem her, for the captain is very generous to the ladies.

LOCKIT.

What captain?

TRAPES.

He thought I did not know him. An intimate acquaintance of yours, Mr. Peachum: only Captain Macheath, as fine as a lord.

PEACHUM.

Tomorrow, dear Mrs. Di, you shall set your own price upon any of the goods you like. We have at least half a dozen velvet scarves and all at your service. Will you give me leave to make you a present of this suit of nightclothes for your own wearing? But are you sure it is Captain Macheath?

TRAPES.

Though he thinks I have forgot him, nobody knows him better. I have taken a great deal of the captain's money in my time at second hand, for he always loved to have his ladies well dressed.

PEACHUM.

Mr. Lockit and I have a little business with the captain—you understand me—and we will satisfy you for Mrs. Coaxer's debt.

LOCKIT.

Depend upon it, we will deal like men of honor.

TRAPES.

I don't enquire after your affairs, so whatever happens, I wash my hands on't. It hath always been my maxim that one friend should assist another. But if you please, I'll take one of the scarves home with me. 'Tis always good to have something in hand.

[Exeunt.]

Scene vii. Newgate.

Lucy.

LUCY.

Jealousy, rage, love, and fear are at once tearing me to pieces. How I am weather-beaten and shattered with distresses!

Air 47. "One evening, having lost my way," etc.

I'm like a skiff on the ocean tossed,
    Now high, now low, with each billow borne,
With her rudder broke and her anchor lost,
    Deserted and all forlorn.
While thus I lie rolling and tossing all night,
That Polly lies sporting on seas of delight!
    Revenge, revenge, revenge,
Shall appease my restless sprite.
I have the ratsbane ready. I run no risk, for I can lay her death upon the gin,[58] and so many die of that naturally that I shall never be called in question. But say I were to be hanged, I never could be hanged for anything that would give me greater comfort than the poisoning that slut.

Enter Filch.

FILCH.

Madam, here's our Miss Polly come to wait upon you.

LUCY.

Show her in.

[Exit Filch.]

Scene viii.

Lucy, Polly.

LUCY.

Dear madam, your servant. I hope you will pardon my passion, when I was so happy to see you last. I was so overrun with the spleen that I was perfectly out of myself. And really, when one hath the spleen, everything is to be excused by a friend.

---

58 gin] The cheap gin sold in great quantities to Londoners in the 1720s was often so improperly distilled as to be poisonous.

Air 47

Air 48. "Now Roger, I'll tell thee, because thou'rt my son."

> When a wife's in her pout
> (As she's sometimes, no doubt),
> The good husband as meek as a lamb,
>> Her vapors to still   10
>> First grants her her will,
>> And the quieting draught is a dram.
> Poor man! And the quieting draught is a dram.
> I wish all our quarrels might have so comfortable
> a reconciliation.   15

POLLY.

I have no excuse for my own behavior, madam, but my misfortunes. And really madam, I suffer too upon your account.

LUCY.

But Miss Polly, in the way of friendship, will you give me leave to propose a glass of cordial to you?   20

POLLY.

Strong-waters are apt to give me the headache. I hope madam, you will excuse me.

LUCY.

Not the greatest lady in the land could have better in her closet* for her own private drinking. You seem mighty low in spirits, my dear.   25

POLLY.

I am sorry, madam, my health will not allow me to accept of your offer. I should not have left you in the rude manner I did when we met last, madam, had not my papa hauled me away so unexpectedly. I was indeed somewhat provoked   30 and perhaps might use some expressions that were disrespectful. But really madam, the captain treated me with so much contempt and cruelty that I deserved your pity, rather than your resentment.

LUCY.

But since his escape, no doubt all matters are made   35 up again. Ah Polly! Polly! 'tis I am the unhappy wife, and he loves you as if you were only his mistress.

POLLY.

Sure madam, you cannot think me so happy as to be the object of your jealously. A man is always afraid of a woman who loves him too well, so that   40 I must expect to be neglected and avoided.

LUCY.

Then our cases, my dear Polly, are exactly alike. Both of us indeed have been too fond.

Air 49. "Oh Bessy Bell."

POLLY.

> A curse attends that woman's love,
>> Who always would be pleasing.   45

LUCY.

> The pertness of the billing dove,
>> Like tickling, is but teasing.

POLLY.

> What then in love can woman do?

LUCY.

>> If we grow fond they shun us.   50

POLLY.

> And when we fly them, they pursue—

LUCY.

>> But leave us when they've won us.
> Love is so very whimsical in both sexes that it is
> impossible to be lasting. But my heart is particular
> and contradicts my own observation.   55

POLLY.

But really, Mistress Lucy, by his last behavior I think I ought to envy you. When I was forced from him, he did not show the least tenderness. But perhaps, he hath a heart not capable of it.

Air 50. "Would fate to me Belinda give—" 60

> Among the men coquets we find,
> Who court by turns all womankind,
> And we grant all their hearts desired,
> When they are flattered and admired.

The coquets of both sexes are self-lovers, and that 65
is a love no other whatever can dispossess. I fear,
my dear Lucy, our husband is one of those.

LUCY.

Away with these melancholy reflections. Indeed,
my dear Polly, we are both of us a cup too low.
Let me prevail upon you to accept of my offer. 70

Air 51. "Come, sweet lass," etc.

> Come, sweet lass,
> Let's banish sorrow
> Till tomorrow;
> Come, sweet lass,
> Let's take a chirping⁵⁹ glass. 75
> Wine can clear
> The vapors of despair
> And make us light as air;
> Then drink, and banish care.

I can't bear, child,* to see you in such low spirits. 80
And I must persuade you to what I know will do
you good. (*Aside.*) I shall now soon be even with
the hypocritical strumpet.

[*Exit.*]

---

59 chirping] cheering

Air 50

Air 51

Scene ix.

Polly.

POLLY.

All this wheedling of Lucy cannot be for nothing.
At this time too, when I know she hates me! The
dissembling of a woman is always the forerunner
of mischief. By pouring strong- waters down my
throat, she thinks to pump some secrets out of me. 5
I'll be upon my guard and won't taste a drop of
her liquor, I'm resolved.

Scene x.

Lucy, with strong-waters, Polly.

LUCY.

Come, Miss Polly.

POLLY.

Indeed child,* you have given yourself trouble to
no purpose. You must, my dear, excuse me.

LUCY.

Really Miss Polly, you are so squeamishly affected
about taking a cup of strong-waters as a lady before 5
company. I vow, Polly, I shall take it monstrously
ill if you refuse me. Brandy and men (though
women love them never so well) are always taken
by us with some reluctance—unless 'tis in private.

POLLY.

I protest, madam, it goes against me.——What do 10
I see! Macheath again in custody! Now every
glimmering of happiness is lost. (*Drops the glass of
liquor on the ground.*)

LUCY. (*Aside.*)

Since things are thus, I'm glad the wench hath
escaped, for by this event 'tis plain she was not 15
happy enough to deserve to be poisoned.

Scene xi.

Lockit, Macheath, Peachum, Lucy, Polly.

LOCKIT.

Set your heart to rest, Captain. You have neither
the chance of love or money for another escape,
for you are ordered to be called down upon your
trial immediately.

PEACHUM.

Away, hussies! This is not a time for a man to be
hampered with his wives. You see, the gentleman
is in chains already.

LUCY.

Oh Husband, Husband, my heart longed to see
thee, but to see thee thus distracts me!

POLLY.

Will not my dear husband look upon his Polly?
Why hadst thou not flown to me for protection?
with me thou hadst been safe.

Air 52. "The last time I went o'er the moor."

POLLY.

Hither, dear Husband, turn your eyes—

LUCY.

Bestow one glance to cheer me.

POLLY.

Think with that look thy Polly dies.

LUCY.

Oh shun me not but hear me.

POLLY.

'Tis Polly sues.

LUCY.

'Tis Lucy speaks.

POLLY.

Is thus true love requited?

LUCY.

My heart is bursting.

POLLY.

Mine too breaks.

LUCY.

Must I—

POLLY.

Must I be slighted?

MACHEATH.

What would you have me say, ladies? You see, this
affair will soon be at an end without my
disobliging either of you.

PEACHUM.

But the settling this point, Captain, might prevent
a lawsuit between your two widows.

Air 53. "Tom Tinker's my true love."

MACHEATH.

Which way shall I turn me? How can I decide?
Wives, the day of our death, are as fond as a bride.
One wife is too much for most husbands to hear,
But two at a time there's no mortal can bear.
This way and that way and which way I will,
What would comfort the one, t'other wife would
take ill.

POLLY.

But if his own misfortunes have made him
insensible to mine, a father sure will be more
compassionate.—Dear, dear sir, sink the material
evidence and bring him off at his trial. Polly upon
her knees begs it of you.

Air 54. "I am a poor shepherd undone."

When my hero in court appears
    And stands arraigned for his life,
Then think of poor Polly's tears,
    For ah! Poor Polly's his wife.

Like the sailor he holds up his hand,
　　Distressed on the dashing wave.
To die a dry death at land
　　Is as bad as a wat'ry grave.　　50
　　And alas, poor Polly!
　　Alack and well-a-day!
　　Before I was in love,
　　　　Oh! every month was May.

LUCY. (*Kneeling.*)

If Peachum's heart is hardened, sure you, sir, will　55
have more compassion on a daughter. I know the
evidence is in your power. How then can you be
a tyrant to me?

Air 55. "Ianthe the lovely," etc.

When he holds up his hand, arraigned for his life,　60
Oh think of your daughter, and think I'm his wife!
What are cannons or bombs or clashing of swords?
For death is more certain by witnesses' words.
Then nail up their lips, that dread thunder allay,
And each month of my life will hereafter be May.　65

LOCKIT.

Macheath's time is come, Lucy. We know our own
affairs; therefore, let us have no more whimpering
or whining.

Air 56. "A Cobbler there was," etc.

Ourselves, like the great, to secure a retreat,　70
When matters require it, must give up our gang:
　　And good reason why,
　　Or instead of the fry,
　　Ev'n Peachum and I,
Like poor petty rascals, might hang, hang,　75
Like poor petty rascals, might hang.ᵉ

PEACHUM.

Set your heart at rest, Polly. Your husband is to die
today; therefore, if you are not already provided,
'tis high time to look about for another. There's
comfort for you, you slut.　80

LOCKIT.

We are ready, sir, to conduct you to the Old Bailey.

Air 57. "Bonny Dundee."

MACHEATH.

The charge is prepared; the lawyers are met;
The judges all ranged (a terrible show!).
I go undismayed, for death is a debt,　85
A debt on demand. So, take what I owe.
Then farewell, my love, dear charmers, adieu.
Contented I die: 'tis the better for you.
Here ends all dispute the rest of our lives,
For this way at once I please all my wives.　90
Now gentlemen, I am ready to attend you.

[*Exeunt Peachum, Lockit, Macheath.*]

Scene xii.

Lucy, Polly, Filch.

POLLY.

Follow them, Filch, to the court. And when the
trial is over, bring me a particular account of his
behavior and of everything that happened. You'll
find me here with Miss Lucy.

Exit Filch.

But why is all this music?　5

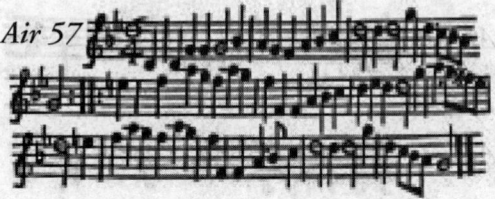

LUCY.

> The prisoners whose trials are put off till next session are diverting themselves.

POLLY.

> Sure there is nothing so charming as music! I'm fond of it to distraction! But alas, now all mirth seems an insult upon my affliction. Let us retire, 10 my dear Lucy, and indulge our sorrows. The noisy crew, you see, are coming upon us.

Exeunt.

A dance of prisoners in chains, etc.

Scene xiii. The condemned hold.

Macheath, in a melancholy posture.

Air 58. *"Happy Groves."*

> Oh cruel, cruel, cruel case!
> Must I suffer this disgrace?

Air 59. *"Of all the girls that are so smart."*

> Of all the friends in time of grief, 5
> When threat'ning death looks grimmer,
> Not one so sure can bring relief
> As this best friend, a brimmer. (*Drinks.*)

Air 60. *"Britons strike home."*

(Rises.)

> Since I must swing, I scorn, I scorn to wince or 10
> whine.

Air 61. *"Chevy Chase."*

> But now again my spirits sink;
> I'll raise them high with wine. (*Drinks a Glass of Wine.*)

Air 62. *"To old Sir Simon the King."*

> But valor the stronger grows, 15
> The stronger liquor we're drinking.
> And how can we feel our woes,
> When we've lost the trouble of thinking? (*Drinks.*)

Air 63. *"Joy to great Caesar."*

> If thus—a man can die 20
> Much bolder with brandy. (*Pours out a bumper of brandy.*)

Air 64. *"There was an old woman."*

> So I drink off this bumper, and now I can stand the test.
> And my comrades shall see that I die as brave as the best. (*Drinks.*)

Air 65. *"Did you ever hear of a gallant sailor."* 25

> But can I leave my pretty hussies
> Without one tear or tender sigh?

Air 66. "Why are mine eyes still flowing."

> Their eyes, their lips, their busses
> Recall my love. Ah must I die? 30

Air 67. "Green Sleeves."

> Since laws were made for ev'ry degree
>   To curb vice in others, as well as me,
>   I wonder we han't better company
>   Upon Tyburn* tree! 35
> But gold from law can take out the sting,
> And if rich men like us were to swing,
>   'Twould thin the land such numbers to string
>   Upon Tyburn tree!

[Enter jailer.]

JAILER.

> Some friends of yours, Captain, desire to be 40
> admitted. I leave you together.

[Exit.]

Scene xiv.

Macheath, Ben Budge, Matt of the Mint.

MACHEATH.

> For my having broke prison, you see, gentlemen,
> I am ordered immediate execution. The sheriff's
> officers, I believe, are now at the door. That Jemmy
> Twitcher should peach me, I own surprised me!
> 'Tis a plain proof that the world is all alike and 5
> that even our gang can no more trust one another
> than other people. Therefore, I beg you,
> gentlemen, look well to yourselves, for in all
> probability you may live some months longer.

MATT.

> We are heartily sorry, Captain, for your misfortune. 10
> But 'tis what we must all come to.

MACHEATH.

> Peachum and Lockit, you know, are infamous
> scoundrels. Their lives are as much in your power
> as yours are in theirs. Remember your dying friend.
> 'Tis my last request: bring those villains to the 15
> gallows before you, and I am satisfied.

MATT.

> We'll do't.

[Enter jailer.]

JAILER.

> Miss Polly and Miss Lucy entreat a word with you.

MACHEATH.

> Gentlemen, adieu.

[Exeunt Matt, Ben, jailer.]

Scene xv.

Lucy, Macheath, Polly.

MACHEATH.

> My dear Lucy, my dear Polly, whatsoever hath
> passed between us is now at an end. If you are fond
> of marrying again, the best advice I can give you is
> to ship yourselves off for the West Indies, where
> you'll have a fair chance of getting a husband apiece, 5
> or by good luck, two or three, as you like best.

POLLY.

> How can I support this sight!

LUCY.

> There is nothing moves one so much as a great
> man* in distress.

Air 68. "All you that must take a leap," etc. 10

[III.xv]

LUCY.
Would I might be hanged!
POLLY.
And I would so too!
LUCY.
To be hanged with you—
POLLY.
My dear, with you.
MACHEATH.
Oh leave me to thought! I fear! I doubt!   15
I tremble! I droop! See, my courage is out. (*Turns up the empty bottle.*)
POLLY.
No token of love?
MACHEATH.
See, my courage is out.
(*Turns up the empty pot.*)
LUCY.
No token of love?
POLLY.
Adieu.   20
LUCY.
Farewell.
MACHEATH.
But hark! I hear the toll of the bell.*
CHORUS.
Tol de rol lol, etc.

[Enter jailer.]

JAILER.
Four women more, Captain, with a child apiece!
See, here they come.   25

Enter women and children.

MACHEATH.
What, four wives more! This is too much. Here, tell the sheriff's officers I am ready.

Exit Macheath guarded.

Scene xvi.

To them, enter player and beggar.

PLAYER.
But honest friend, I hope you don't intend that Macheath shall be really executed.

BEGGAR.
Most certainly, sir. To make the piece perfect I was for doing strict poetical justice: Macheath is to be hanged, and for the other personages of the drama,   5
the audience must have supposed they were all either hanged or transported.
PLAYER.
Why then, friend, this is a downright deep tragedy. The catastrophe is manifestly wrong, for an opera must end happily.   10
BEGGAR.
Your objection, sir, is very just, and is easily removed. For you must allow, that in this kind of drama 'tis no matter how absurdly things are brought about.—So, you rabble there, run and cry a reprieve. Let the prisoner be brought back to his   15
wives in triumph.
PLAYER.
All this we must do to comply with the taste of the Town.*
BEGGAR.
Through the whole piece you may observe such a similitude of manners in high and low life that it   20
is difficult to determine whether (in the fashionable vices) the fine gentlemen imitate the gentlemen of the road, or the gentlemen of the road the fine gentlemen. Had the play remained as I at first intended, it would have carried a most   25
excellent moral: 'twould have shown that the lower sort of people have their vices in a degree as well as the rich: And that they are punished for them.

Scene xvii.

To them, Macheath with rabble, etc.

MACHEATH.
So it seems I am not left to my choice but must have a wife at last.—Look ye, my dears, we will have no controversy now. Let us give this day to mirth, and I am sure she who thinks herself my wife will testify her joy by a dance.   5
ALL.
Come, a dance, a dance.
MACHEATH.
Ladies, I hope you will give me leave to present a partner to each of you. And (if I may without

offence) for this time, I take Polly for mine. (*To Polly.*) And for life, you slut, for we were really married. As for the rest— But at present keep your own secret.

A dance.

Air 69. *"Lumps of pudding," etc.*

Thus I stand like the Turk with his doxies around;
From all sides their glances his passion confound;
For black,* brown, and fair, his inconstancy
    burns,
And the different beauties subdue him by turns:
Each calls forth her charms to provoke his desires;
Though willing to all, with but one he retires.
But think of this maxim, and put off your sorrow:
The wretch of today may be happy tomorrow.
CHORUS.
But think of this maxim, etc.

[Exeunt.]

FINIS.

Textual Notes

^a Copytext is the first edition, a 1728 octavo, which exists in two states (O1a, O1b). Also consulted were the second edition, another 1728 octavo (O2); the third edition, a 1729 quarto (Q); and modern editions of 1939, revised 1969 (Nettleton, Case, and Stone—NCS), of 1983 (Fuller), and of 1986 (Loughrey and Treadwell—LT).

^b glass of a most delicious cordial] Q, NCS, Fuller, LT; most delicious glass of a cordial O1-2

^c A man … life.] O2, Q, NCS, Fuller, LT; *om.* O1

^d wary] O2, Q, NCS; weary O1 and some copies of O2, Fuller, LT

^e Air 15a … hang] O1b, O2, Q, NCS, Fuller, LT; *om.* O1a

Corrective Satire

Corrective satire condemns aberrant behavior by exposing it to ridicule and lashing it with a rod clearly representing the violated standard of behavior. Most comedies contain satire. What makes a comical satire is the ending. Comedies end in centripetal celebration, even if some aspect behaves centrifugally (as in subversive comedies), even if the ending represents wish-fulfillment. Satires either end with nothing really resolved, the aberrant behavior to continue ad infinitum, or they end with draconian poetical justice. Corrective comical satires judge behavior as morally reprehensible. Aristophanes was the classic master; Ben Jonson the Jacobean. Restoration corrective comical satire attacks the libertinism of its hegemonic class of aristocrats, as well as the selfishness, ineptitude, and pusillanimity of its competing class of bourgeois cits. Post-Revolution satire attacks the failure of the Revolution to extend its principles to other classes and genders, to provide real relief to the oppressed, especially women trapped in bad marriages. At its best, it reveals the total bankruptcy of England's—and Europe's—supposed moral superiority.

The Princess of Clèves[a]

by Nathaniel Lee (ca. 1645/52-1692)

edited by Anthony Kaufman

In 1678, Marie-Madeleine de Lafayette caused a sensation with her pioneering psychological novel, *La Princesse de Clèves*. The novel is the story of a love triangle set in the court of Henri II in the sixteenth century. Based largely on historical figures, the novel concerns the tortured relation of three admirable, principled, self-consciously noble, people: the Princess and Prince of Clèves and her illicit suitor, the duke of Nemours, the best friend of her husband. The crux of the plot is the Princess's ingenuous confession of another lover lurking in her heart. The confession destroys her husband, but the Princess, now freed, finally rejects her lover and chooses instead a life of retirement and religious mortification. The novel was a great success and was quickly translated into English in 1679.

From this English translation, Nathaniel Lee, already known for his successful tragedies, *Sophinisba*, *The Rival Queens*, and *Lucius Junius Brutus*, offered his audience an unexpected and shocking revision of Lafayette's novel of courtly life. He alters the historical basis of the novel, adds and drops characters and events, and, although he retains the heroic tragedy of the noble Prince and Princess of Clèves, makes the duke of Nemours into an unprincipled, cynical rakehell. His ruthless pursuit of the Princess of Clèves, even as he attempts to seduce Marguerite, Princess of Jainsville, and toys sexually with Madame Tournon, jars uneasily with the tender and romantic love of the increasingly tormented Princess and Prince of Clèves. Lee adds a third plot concerning the farcical cuckolding of the would-be wits, Saint-André and Poltrot, by their witty, lusty wives, Celia and Elianor. And whereas in the French novel the Princess of Clèves seems resolute in her retirement from the world, Lee has his Princess acknowledge the possibility that in time her

passion for Nemours will overwhelm her desire to renounce the world. Nemour's musings late in the play on his own reformation are improbable, and the play ends on a note of uncertainty, if not cynicism.

Lee was aware of the novelty of his play. He noted in his dedication that, whereas the audience expected from their familiarity with the novel a tale of courtly love, he belied their expectations and gave them instead a drama of uncertain genre: "Farce, Comedy, Tragedy, or mere Play." It offered not the courtly, romantic Nemours of Mme. de Lafayette, but a rakehell reeking of the prostitute-riddled slums: "[W]hen they expected the most polished hero in Nemours, I gave 'em a ruffian reeking from Whetstone's-Park."

Lee altered *La Princesse de Clèves* in order to satirize the then fashionable libertinism of a group of courtiers who surrounded Charles II. Witty and wicked, they lived lives of brilliant dissipation. Foremost among them was John Wilmot, earl of Rochester, himself an accomplished satiric poet. Lee apparently had mixed feelings about Rochester, who had died in 1680 after uttering a deathbed repentance. He was able to admire Rochester's poetic accomplishments, his personal elegance, wit, and charm, in the figure of "Count Rosidore," whose death is referred to in Act I. But Lee was aware, as others were, of the ego and arrogance, the selfish, privileged immorality and destructive power of Rochester and his titled friends. Lee turned the gentlemanly Nemours of the novel into, as he says in his epilogue, "a bulling gallant in a wanton play."

The play was produced at the Dorset Garden Theater in December 1682 or January-February 1683, with the leading actor of the age, Thomas Betterton, as Nemours, and Elizabeth Barry as the

Princess of Clèves. The incongruity between the romantic plot of the Prince and Princess and the scenes of Nemour's wild libertinism, along with the ribald cuckolding plot and the bitterness of the satire, may have put off the London audience: the play was not successful. Until recently critics either ignored the play or deplored its "immorality." More recently the play has been revalued as a forceful and telling corrective satire. The play at times may shock, even disgust us, as does much good satire, but it is a ruthless attack on the pathological sexual aggression of arrogant men who thought themselves because of their wealth and privilege immune from any sort of constraint.

DRAMATIS PERSONAE

[MEN]

Prince of Clèves.
Duke Nemours.
Vidame[1] of Chartres, [uncle of the Princess of Clèves].
Bellamore, [Nemour's young intimate].
Jacques, [servant to Nemours].
Saint-André.
Poltrot, [cousin to Saint-André.]
[Pedro.]
[Boy, servant to Saint-André.]

[WOMEN]

Princess of Clèves.
Tournon, [a woman of the Court and agent of Queen Catherine de Medici.]
Marguerite, [Princess of Jainsville.]
Elianor, [wife to Saint-André.]
Celia, [wife to Poltrot.]
Irene, [confidante of the Princess of Clèves.]
La March, [a lady of the Court.]

---

[1] Vidame] One who held lands from a bishop as his representative and defender in temporal matters (*OED*)

SCENE: PARIS.

The Princess of Clèves.[b]

Act I, scene i. [Nemour's palace in Paris.]

Nemours, Bellamore, [and musicians]. Fiddles Playing.

NEMOURS.

Hold there you, Monsieur Devol. Prithee leave off
playing fine in consort and stick to time and tune.[2]
So, now the song: call in the eunuch.

Enter Singer.

Come my pretty stallion, hem and begin.
                    Song.
All other blessings are but toys   5
To his that in his sleep enjoys,
Who in his fancy can possess
The object of his happiness.
The pleasure's purer, for he spares
The pains, expenses, and the cares.   10
                    II.
Thus when Adonis got the stone,[3]
To Love the boy still made his moan;
Venus, the queen of fancy, came,
And as he slept, she cooled his flame.   15
The fancy charmed him as he lay,
And fancy brought the stone away.

[Exeunt singer and musicians.]

NEMOURS.   20

Sirrah, stick to clean pleasures, deep sleep,
moderate wine, sincere whores, and thou art
happy. Now by this damask cheek, I love thee.
Keep but this gracious form of thine in health, and
I'll put thee in the way of living like a man. What 25
I have trusted thee with—my love to the Princess
of Clèves—treasure it as thy life. Nor let the
Vidame of Chartres know it. For however I seem
to cherish him, because he has the knack of telling
a story maliciously and is a great pretender to   30

---

[2] fine in consort … time and tune] Nemours calls for the musicians to cease playing in harmony and to emphasize rhythm and melody.
[3] stone] painful erection

nature,[4] I cast him off here: 'tis too much for him. Besides, he is her uncle and has a sort of affected honor that would make him grin[5] to see me leap her.—Hey Jacques—

[Enter Jacques.]

When Madame Tournon comes, bring her in. And hark you, sir, whoever comes to speak with me while she is with me—   35

JACQUES.
What if the Dauphin comes?

NEMOURS.
What if his father comes! Dog, slave, fool! What if Paris were afire, the President and Council of Sixteen[6] at the door! I'm sick, I'm not within—   40
I'm a hundred mile off.

[Exit Jacques.]

My bosom dear—so young, and yet I trust thee too. But away, to the Princess of Clèves, thou art acquainted with her women. Watch her motions,   45
my sweet-faced pimp, and bring me word of her rising.

BELLAMORE.
She is a prize, my lord, and oh what a night of pleasure has Clèves had with her—the first too!

NEMOURS.
Anything but what makes such a pleasure would   50
I give for such another. But be gone, and no more of this provoking discourse, lest ravishing should follow thee at the heels and spoil my sober design.

Exeunt severally. Enter Tournon and La March with Jacques.

JACQUES.
Madam, my lord was just now asking for you.

TOURNON.
Go tell him I'm coming. Is he dressed?   55

JACQUES.
Yes, but your ladyship knows that's all one to him.

---

4 pretender to nature] declared practitioner of libertine naturalism
5 grin] grimace
6 Council of Sixteen] a political-religious faction that seized control of Paris between 1588 and 1590.

TOURNON.
Honest Jacques, 'tis pity such honesty should not be encouraged. [*Gives money.*]

JACQUES. [*Aside.*]
This comes of pimping, which she calls honesty.   60
(*Exit.*)

TOURNON.
Thus thou mayst see the method of the Queen.[7] We are the lucky sieves, where fond* men trust their hearts, and so she sifts 'em through us.

LA MARCH.
What of Nemours, whom you thus early visit?

TOURNON.
The Queen designs to rob him of a mistress,   65
Marguerite, the Princess of Jainsville, whom he keeps from the knowledge of the Court and, if the Queen be a judge, is contracted to her. The Dauphin loves her too, whereon the Queen, who works the Court quite round by womankind and   70
thinks this way to mould his supple soul, resolves, if possible, to gain her for him.

LA MARCH.
But how is it possible to work the princess from the Duke Nemours, who loves him as the Queen affects ambition?   75

TOURNON.
Why thus: She knows Nemours his* soul is bent upon variety; therefore, to gain her ends she has made me sacrifice my honor. Nay I'm become his bawd, and ply him every day with some new face to wean his heart from Marguerite's form. Nor   80
must you longer be without your part.

LA MARCH.
Employ me, for you know the Queen commands me.

TOURNON.
There was a letter dropped in the tennis court out of Nemours his* pocket, as I'm told, and read last   85
night in the presence. 'Tis your task slyly to insinuate with Marguerite this[c] note, which came from some abandoned mistress, is certainly the duke's.

LA MARCH.
Then jealousy's the ground on which you build.   90

---

7 The Queen] Catherine de Medici (1519-1589)

TOURNON.

Right: we must make 'em jealous of each other. Jealousy breeds disdain in haughty minds and so from the extremes of violent love proceeds to fiercest hate.

Enter Saint-André [and a boy].

But see, the gay, the brisk, the topping gallant, 95 Saint-André here, cousin to Poltrot, who arrived from England with a pretty wife last week and lodges in the palace of this his related fool; Saint-André has a wife too of my acquaintance: both for the duke, my dear. 100

[Enter Jacques.]

But haste, I'm called—

Exit La March.

JACQUES.

Madam—

TOURNON.

I go. (*Exit.*)

SAINT-ANDRÉ.

Monsieur Jacques, your most obliged, faithful, humble servant. What, his Grace continues the old 105 trade, I see, by the flux of bawds and whores that choke up his avenues. And I must confess, excepting my self, there's no man so built for whoring as his Grace: black,* sanguine, brawny, a Roman nose, long foot, and a stiff— calf of a leg. 110

JACQUES.

Your lordship has all these in perfection.

SAINT-ANDRÉ.

Sir, your most faithful, obliged, humble servant.— Boy?

BOY.

My lord?

SAINT-ANDRÉ.

How many bottles last night? 115

BOY.

Five, my lord.

SAINT-ANDRÉ.

Boy?

BOY.

My lord?

SAINT-ANDRÉ.

How many whores?

BOY.

Six my lord. 120

SAINT-ANDRÉ.

Boy?

BOY.

My lord?

SAINT-ANDRÉ.

What quarrels,* how many did I kill?

BOY.

Not one, my lord. But the night before you hamstrung a beadle and run a linkman in the back. 125

SAINT-ANDRÉ.

What, and no blood nor blows last night?

BOY.

Oh yes, my lord, now I remember me. You drew upon a gentleman that knocked you down with a bottle.

SAINT-ANDRÉ. [*To the boy, aside.*]

Not so loud, you urchin, lest I twist your neck 130 round.—Monsieur Jacques, is his Grace stirring?

JACQUES.

My lord, he's at Council.

SAINT-ANDRÉ.

'Od,* I beg his pardon. Pray give my duty to him and tell him, if he pleased to hear a languishing air or two, I am at the Princess of Clèves' with a 135 serenade. [*To the boy.*] Go rascal, go to Monsieur Poltrot, tell him he'll be too late.

Exit Boy.

Black,* airy shape— but then Madam Clèves is virtuous, chaste, cold. Gad, I'll write to her, and then she's mine directly, for 'tis but reason of course, that 140 he that has been yoked to so many duchesses should at last back a princess.—Sir, your most obliged, faithful, and very humble servant, sir.

Exeunt.

Scene ii. [The palace of Nemours.]

Nemours and Tournon.

TOURNON.

Undone, undone! Will your sinful Grace never give over? Will you never leave ruining of bodies and damning of souls? Could you imagine that I came for this? What have you done?

NEMOURS.

No harm, pretty rogue, no harm, nay, prithee leave blubbering. 5

TOURNON.

'Tis blubbering now, plain blubbering, but before you had your will 'twas another tone: "Why, madam, do you waste those precious tears? Each falling drop shines like an orient pearl and sets a 10 gaity on a face of sorrow."

NEMOURS.

Thou art certainly the pleasantest of womankind, and I'm the happiest of men. Dear, delightful rogue, let's have another main.* Like a winning gamester, I long to make it t'other hundred pound. 15

TOURNON.

Inconsiderate, horrid peer, will you damn your soul deeper and deeper? Can you be thus insensible of your crime?

NEMOURS.

Why there's it. I was as a man may be, very dry, and thou, kind soul, gav'st me a good draught of 20 drink. Now 'tis strange to me, if a man must be damned for quenching his thirst.

TOURNON.

Ha, Ha! Well, I'll swear you are such another[8] man. Who would have thought you could delude a woman thus, and a woman of honor too, that 25 resolved so much against it! Ah my lord, your Grace has a cunning tongue.

NEMOURS.

No cunning, Tournon. My way is downright, leaving body, state, and spirit, all for a pretty woman. And when gray hairs, gout, and 30 impotence come, no more but this: drink away pain and be gathered to my fathers.

TOURNON.

Oh thou dissembler! Give me your hand, this soft, this faithless, violating hand. Heaven knows what this hand has to answer for. 35

NEMOURS.

And for this hand, with these long, white, round, pretty bobbins, 't has the kindest grip, and I so love

---

8 such another] unique

it. Now God's blessing on't, that's all I say. But come tell me: What, no new game? For thou knowest I die directly, without variety. 40

TOURNON.

Certainly never woman loved like me, who am not satisfied with sacrificing my own honor, unless I rob my delights by undoing others'.

NEMOURS.

Come, come, out with it, I see thou art big with some new intrigue, and it labors for a vent. 45

TOURNON.

What think you of Saint-André's lady?

NEMOURS.

That I'm in bed with her, because thou dar'st befriend me.

TOURNON.

Nay, there's more: Monsieur Poltrot lodges in his house with a young English wife* of the true breed 50 and the prettier of the two.

NEMOURS.

Excellent creature! But command me something extravagant, as thy kindness,* state, life, and honor.

TOURNON.

Yet all this will be lost when you are married to Marguerite. 55

NEMOURS.

Never! By Heaven I'm thine with all the heat and vigorous inspiration of an unfleshed lover—and so will be while young limbs and lechery hold together, and that's a bond methinks should last till doomsday.

TOURNON.

But do you believe if Marguerite should know— 60

NEMOURS.

The question's too grave. When and where shall I see the gems thou hast in store?

TOURNON.

By noon or thereabouts. Take a turn in Luxembourg Garden,[9] and one, if not both, shall meet you.

NEMOURS.

And thou'lt appear in person? 65

TOURNON.

With colors flying, a handkerchief held out, and yet methinks it goes against my conscience.

---

9 Luxembourg Garden] the public gardens of the Luxembourg Palace above the left bank of the Seine in Paris

NEMOURS.

Away! That serious look has made thee old.
Conscience and consideration? In a young woman
too? It makes a bawd of thee before thy time. 70
Nay, now thou put'st me in poetic rapture,
And I must quote Ronsard[10] to punish thee.
"Call all your wives to council and prepare
To tempt, dissemble, flatter, lie and swear.

To make her mine use all your utmost skill. 75
Virtue! an ill-bred crossness in the will;
Honor a notion, piety a cheat!
Prove but successful bawds and you are great."
Come, thou wilt meet me.

TOURNON.

'Tis resolved I will. Till which time, thou dear man— 80

NEMOURS.

Thou pretty woman—

TOURNON.

Thou very dear man—

NEMOURS.

Thou very pretty woman—one kiss.

TOURNON.

Hey ho—

NEMOURS.

Now all the gods go with thee! 85

TOURNON.

A word, my lord: you are acquainted with these
fops. Set 'em in the modish way of abusing their
wives. They are turning already, and that will
certainly bring 'em about.

NEMOURS.

Bellamore shall do't with less suspicion. Farewell. 90

Exit Tournon.

Hey Jacques!

Enter Jacques with the Vidame. [Exit Jacques.]

Hah! My grave lord of Chartres! Welcome as

health, as wine, and taking whores! And tell me
now the business of the Court.

VIDAME.

Hold it, Nemours, forever at defiance: 95
Fogs of ill humor, damps of melancholy;
Old maids of fifty choked with eternal vapors
Stuff it with fulsome honor. Dozing virtue
And everlasting dullness husk it round,
Since he that was the life, the soul of pleasure, 100
Count Rosidore,[11] is dead.

NEMOURS.

Then we may say,
Wit was, and satire is a carcass now.
I thought his last debauch would be his death.
But is it certain? 105

VIDAME.

Yes, I saw him dust.
I saw the mighty thing a nothing made,
Huddled with worms and swept to that cold den,
Where kings lie crumbled just like other men.

NEMOURS.

Nay then, let's rave and elegize together: 110
Where Rosidore is now but common clay,
Whom every wiser emmet bears away
And lays him up against a winter's day.
He was the spirit of wit and had such an art in gilding
his failures that it was hard not to love his faults. He 115
never spoke a witty thing twice, though to different
persons. His imperfections were catching, and his
genius was so luxuriant that he was forced to tame it
with a hesitation in his speech to keep it in view. But
oh how awkward, how insipid, how poor and 120
wretchedly dull is the imitation of those that have all
the affectation of his verse and none of his wit.

Enter Jacques.

JACQUES.

My lord, Monsieur Poltrot desires to kiss your
Grace's hand.

NEMOURS.

Let's have him to drive away our melancholy. 125

VIDAME.

I wonder what pleasure you can take in such dull
dogs, asses, fools.

---

10 Ronsard] Pierre de Ronsard, 1524-85, outstanding
French Renaissance poet and a favorite of Rochester. But
the lines that follow echo Rochester's libertine drama,
Valentinian, where the decadent emperor sardonically
urges his followers to win advancement by prostituting
their wives.

11 Count Rosidore] suggestive of Rochester (see headnote)

NEMOURS.

But this is a particular fool, man, Fate's own fool, and perhaps it will never hit the like again. He's ever the same thing, yet always pleasing. In short, he's a finished fool, and has a fine wife. Add to this his late leaving the Court of France and going to England to learn breeding.[12] 130

Enter Poltrot.

POLTROT.

My lord Duke, your Grace's most obedient humble servant. My lord of Chartres, and Monsieur Jacques, yours monsieur. Saint-André desires your Grace's presence at a serenade of mine and his together. And I must tell your Grace by the way, he is a great master and the fondest thing of my labors. 135

NEMOURS.

And the greatest oaf in the world. 140

POLTROT.

How my lord!

VIDAME.

The whole Court wonders you will keep him company.

NEMOURS.

Such a passive rascal. He had his shins broke last night in the presence, and were it not feared you would second him, he would be kicked out of all society. 145

POLTROT.

I second him my lord! I'll see him damned ere I'll be second to any fool in Christendom. For, to tell your Grace the truth, I keep him company and lie at his house because I intend to lie with his wife— a trick I learned since I went into England, where, o'my conscience, cuckoldom is the destiny of above half the nation. 150

NEMOURS.

Indeed! 155

POLTROT.

Oh, there's not such another drinking, scouring, roaring, whoring nation in the world. And for little London, to my knowledge, if a bill* were taken of the weekly cuckolds, it would amount to more than the number of christenings and burials put together. 160

VIDAME.

What, and were you acquainted with the wits?

POLTROT.

Oh Lord sir, I lived in the City* a whole year together; my Lord Mayor and I and the Common Council[13] were sworn brothers. I could sing you twenty catches and drolls[14] that I made for their feast days, but at present I'll only hint you one or two. 165

NEMOURS.

Pray do us the favor, sir.

POLTROT.

Why look you, sir, this is one of my chief ones, and I'll assure your Grace, 'twas much sung at Court too. [*Sings.*] "Oh to bed to me—to bed to me" etc.[15] 170

NEMOURS.

Excellent, incomparable.

POLTROT.

Why, is it not, my lord? This is no kickshaw; there's substance in the air and weight in the words. Nay, I'll give your Grace a taste of another. The tune is, let me see—aye, aye— [*Sings.*] "Give me the lass that is true country bred."[16] But I'll present your Grace with some words of my own, that I made on my wife before I married her, as she sat singing one day in a low parlor and playing on the virginals. 175

180

NEMOURS. [*Tickling Poltrot.*]

For Heaven's sake oblige us, dear, pleasant creature.

POLTROT.

I'll swear I'm so ticklish you'll put me out, my lord, for I am as wanton as any little Bartholomew boar-pig.[17]

VIDAME.

Dear, soft, delicate rogue, sing! 185

---

12 Court of France … to England] from the more to the less sophisticated, cosmopolitan, fashionable center

13 my Lord Mayor … Common Council] The mayor and the aldermen of London were considered cits* not wits.

14 drolls] comic songs

15 "Oh to bed to me—to bed to me"] first line of a well-known ballad

16 "Give me the lass that is true country bred"] a line from another popular ballad of the period

17 Bartholomew boar-pig.] Bartholomew Fair, held in London in August, was the site of vulgar spectacles, often involving animals.

POLTROT.

Nay, I protest my lord, I vow and swear, but you'll make me run to a whore. Lord sir, what do you mean?

NEMOURS.

Come then, begin.

POLTROT. (*Sings.*)

Phillis is soft, Phillis is plump,   190
And Beauty made up this delicate lump.
Like a rosebud she looks, like a lily she smells,
And her voice is a note above sweet Philomel's.

Now a little smutty, my lord, is the fashion—
II.

Her breasts are two hillocks where hearts lie and pant,   195
In the herbage so soft, for a thing that they want.
But mum, sir, for that, though a notable jest,
For if I should name it, you'd call me a beast.

Enter Saint-André without his hat and wig.

SAINT-ANDRÉ.

My lord, the serenade is just begun, and if you   200
don't come just in the nick—I beg your Grace's
pardon for interrupting you, but if you have a
mind to hear the sweetest airs in the world—

NEMOURS.

With all my heart, sir.

POLTROT.

Nay, since your Grace has put my hand in, I'll sing   205
you, my lord, before you go, the softest thing—
composed in the nonage of my muse, yet such a
one as our best authors borrow from. Nay, I'll be
judged by your Grace, if they do not steal their
dying from my killing.[18]   210

SAINT-ANDRÉ.

Nay prithee, Poltrot, thou art so impertinent.

POLTROT.

No more impertinent than yourself, sir. Nor do I
doubt, sir, but my character* shall be drawn by the
poets for a man of wit and sense, sir, as well as
yourself, sir.   215

VIDAME.

Aye, I'll be sworn, shall it.

---

[18] dying ... killing] "Dying"* and "killing" are clichés of
    seventeenth-century love poetry.

POLTROT.

For I know how to repartee with the best, to rally
my wife, to kick her too if I please, sir, to make
similes as fast as hops, sir, though I lay a-dying—
slap-dash, sir—quickly off and quickly on, sir, and   220
as round as a hoop, sir.

SAINT-ANDRÉ.

I grant you, dear bully, all this. But let's have your
song another time, because mine are begun.

POLTROT.

Nay, look you dear rogue, mine is but a prologue
to your play, and by your leave his Grace has a   225
mind to hear it, and he shall hear it, sir.

NEMOURS.

Aye, and will hear it, sir, though the Great Turk
were at St. Dennis's Gate.[19] Come along, my
Orpheus, and then, sir, we'll follow you to the
Prince of Clèves'.   230

[POLTROT. *Sings.*]

"When Phoebus had fetched," etc.

Exeunt singing.

Scene iii. The Prince of Clèves' palace.

Music.

Song.[20]

In a room for delight, the landscape of love,
    Like a shady old lawn
    With the curtains half drawn,
My love and I lay in the cool of the day
    Till our joys did remove.[21]   5
II.
So fierce was our fight and so smart ev'ry stroke,
    That Love, the little scout,
    Was put to the rout:
His bow was unbent, ev'ry arrow was spent,
    And his quiver all broke.   10

---

[19] the Great Turk were at St. Dennis's Gate] The Great
    Turk was the Ottoman Sultan in Constantinople, an
    enemy of Christian Europe. St. Denis's Gate was the
    main northern entrance to Paris.

[20] Song] This is part of Poltrot's serenade, most likely
    played off-stage while the scene changes.

[21] remove] were satisfied

Enter Vidame and Nemours.

NEMOURS.

I have lost my letter, and by your description it must be that which the Queen read at Court. But are you sure the Princess of Clèves has seen it?

VIDAME.

Why are you so concerned? Does your wild love turn that way too? She is too grave.   15

NEMOURS.

Too grave? As if I could not laugh with this, and cry^d with that, and veer with every gust of passion. But has she seen it?

VIDAME.

She has the letter; the Queen Dauphin[22] sent it her.

NEMOURS.

Then you must own it on occasion, and whatever   20
else I shall put upon your person.

VIDAME.

Why?

NEMOURS.

Lest it should reach the ears of Marguerite. For oh my Vidame, 'tis such a ranting devil. If she believes this letter mine, when next we meet, beware my   25
locks and eyes. No more but this: remember that you own it. (*Exit.*)

Enter Saint-André and Poltrot.

SAINT-ANDRÉ. (*Singing with Poltrot.*)

"His Bow was unbent," etc. Come my lord, we'll have all over again.

Enter the Prince of Clèves.

VIDAME.

See, we have raised the Prince of Clèves.—My lord,   30
good morrow.

PRINCE OF CLÈVES.

Good morrow my good lord.^e

POLTROT.

Give you joy, my lord. What! A little blue under the eyes? Ha, ha!

SAINT-ANDRÉ.

Give you joy, my lord! Hah, my lord, hah! (*Holds   35
up three fingers.*)

POLTROT.

Hah, my lord, hah! (*Holding up five fingers.*)

PRINCE OF CLÈVES.

You are merry, gentlemen. I am not in the vein; therefore, dear Chartres, take these fingers hence.

SAINT-ANDRÉ.

My lord, you look a little heavy. Shall we dance,   40
sing, fence, take the air, ride?

VIDAME.

Come away, sir, the prince is indisposed.

SAINT-ANDRÉ.

Gad I remember now I talk of riding: at the tournament of Metz, as I was riding the great horse—   45

VIDAME.

Leave off your lying and come along.

SAINT-ANDRÉ.

With three pushes of pike and six hits of sword, I wounded the Duke of Ferrara, Duke of Milan, Duke of Parma, Prince of Clèves—

PRINCE OF CLÈVES.

My lord, I was not there—   50

SAINT-ANDRÉ.

My lord, I beg your lordship's pardon, I meant the Vidam of Chartres.

VIDAME.

You lie: I was then at Rome.

SAINT-ANDRÉ.

My lord—

POLTROT.

Ha, ha! Lord, lord, how this world is given to lying!   55
Hah! Come, come, you're damnably out.[23] Come away.

SAINT-ANDRÉ.

My lord, I beg your pardon. I see you are indisposed. Besides the Queen obliged me this morning to let 'em choose colors for my complexion.[24]   60

VIDAME.

Hark you, will you go, or shall I— (*Pulling him off by the nose.*)

SAINT-ANDRÉ.

My friend, my lord, you see, is a little familiar, but

---

22 Queen Dauphin] the dauphine, at this time, Mary Stuart, who became Mary Queen of Scots, 1542-87

23 out] mistaken, exposed

24 colors for my complexion] clothes or makeup that will flatter

I am ever your highness's most humble, faithful, obedient servant. 65

Exeunt [Vidame, Saint-André and Poltrot]. Manet Prince of Clèves.

PRINCE OF CLÈVES.
Full of himself, the happy man is gone.
Why was not I too cast in such a mold:
To think like him, or not to think at all?

Enter the Princess of Clèves [unobserved by the Prince].

Had he a bride like me, earth would not bear him.
But oh, I wish that it might cover me, 70
Since Chartres[25] cannot love me: Oh, I found it!
Last night I found it in her cold embraces,
Her lips too cold—cold as the dew of death.
And still* whene'er I pressed her in my arms,
I found my bosom all afloat with tears. 75

PRINCESS of CLÈVES. [*Aside.*]
He weeps, Oh heaven!—My lord, the Prince of
Clèves.

PRINCE OF CLÈVES.
My life, my dearest part!

PRINCESS OF CLÈVES.
Why sighs my lord?
What have I done, sir, thus to discompose you?

PRINCE OF CLÈVES.
Nothing. 80

PRINCESS OF CLÈVES.
Ah sir, there is a grief within,
And you would hide it from me.

PRINCE OF CLÈVES.
Nothing, my Chartres, nothing here but love.

PRINCESS OF CLÈVES.
Alas my lord, you hide that secret from me
Which I must know or think you never loved me. 85

PRINCE OF CLÈVES.
Ah princess! That you loved but half so well!

PRINCESS OF CLÈVES.
I have it then: you think me criminal
And tax my honor—

PRINCE OF CLÈVES.
Oh, forbid it Heaven!

But since you press me, madam, let me ask you 90
Why, when the Princess[26] led you to the altar,
Why caked the tears upon your bloodless face?
Why sighed you when your hand was clasped
with mine,
As if your heart, your heart refused to join?

PRINCESS OF CLÈVES.
Ah sir— 95

PRINCE OF CLÈVES.
Behold, you're dashed with the remembrance.
Why, when my hopes were fierce and joys grew
strong,
Why were you carried like a corpse along?
When like a victim by my side you lay,
Why did you gasp, why did you swoon away? 100
Oh speak!
You have a soul so open and so clear
That, if there be a fault, it must appear.

PRINCESS OF CLÈVES.
Alas, you are not skilled in beauty's cares,
For oh, when once the god[27] his wrath declares 105
And Stygian oaths[28] have winged the bloody dart
To make its passage through the virgin's heart,
She hides her wound, and hasting to the grove,
Scarce whispering to the winds her conscious love,
The touch of him she loves she'll not endure 110
But weeps and bleeds and strives against the cure.
So judge of me when any grief appears,
Believe my sighs are kind, and trust my tears.

PRINCE OF CLÈVES.
Vanish, my doubts, and jealousies be gone.
On thy loved bosom let me break my joy: 115
Oh, only sweets that fill but never cloy!
And was it, was it only virgin's fear?
But speak forever, and I'll ever hear.
Repeat, and let the echoes deal it round,
While listening angels bend to catch the sound. 120
Nay, sigh and weep, drain all thy precious store;
Be kind, as now, and I'll complain no more.
(*Exit.*)

25 Chartres] the princess, who before her marriage was Mlle. de Chartres

26 Princess] unidentified
27 god] Cupid
28 Stygian oaths] To swear by the river Styx was a powerful and irrevocable oath.

PRINCESS OF CLÈVES.

    Was ever man so worthy to be loved,

    So good, so gentle, soft a disposition,

    As if no gall had mixed with his creation;   125

    So tender and so fearful to displease,

    No barbarous heart but thine would stop his

        entrance.

    But thou, inhuman, banished him from his own,

    And while the lordly master lies without,

    Thou, traitress, riot'st with a thief within.   130

Enter Irene.

IRENE.

    Ah madam, what new grief?

PRINCESS OF CLÈVES.

                Alas Irene,

    Thou treasurer of my thoughts—

    What shall I do? How shall I chase Nemours,

    That robber, ravisher of my repose?   135

IRENE.

    For the great care you wish,[29] may I inquire

    Whether you think the duke insensible,

    Indifferent to the rest of womankind?

PRINCESS OF CLÈVES.

    I must confess I did not think him so,

    Though now I do—but would give half my blood   140

    To think him otherwise.

IRENE.

                Without the expense,

    There, take your wish: a letter which he dropped

    In the tennis court, given the Queen Dauphin

    By her page, and sent to you to read   145

    For your diversion.

PRINCESS OF CLÈVES.

            Alas! Irene—

    Why trembles thus my hand? Why beats my heart?

    But let us read—

    (*Reads.*) "Your affection has been divided betwixt   150

    me and another. You are false, a traitor to the truest

    love. Never see me more."

    Ah, 'tis too plain, I thought as much before.

    But oh, we are too apt to excuse the faults

    Of those we love, and fond of our own undoing.   155

    Support me, oh, to bear this dreadful pang,

---

29 wish] impose

This stab to all my gathered resolution.

IRENE.

    Read it again, and call Revenge to aid you.

PRINCESS OF CLÈVES.

    Perhaps he makes his boast too of the conquest,

    For oh, my heart he knows too well, my passion—   160

    But as thou hast inspired me, I'll revenge

    The affront and cast him from my poisoned breast

    To make him room that merits all my thoughts.

Enter the Prince of Clèves with Nemours.

PRINCE OF CLÈVES.

    Madam, there is a letter fallen by accident into

    your hands. My friend comes in behalf of the   165

    Vidame of Chartres to retrieve it.—When I am

    dismissed from the King, my lord, I'll wait you

    here again.

NEMOURS.

    My lord—

PRINCE OF CLÈVES.

    Not a step further. (*Exit.*)   170

NEMOURS.

    Madam, I come most humbly to inquire

    Whether the Dauphin Queen sent you a letter

    Which the Vidame lost?

PRINCESS OF CLÈVES.

                Sir, you had better

    Find the Queen Dauphin out, tell her the truth,   175

    For she's informed the letter is your own.

NEMOURS.

    Ah madam, I have nothing to confess

    In this affair—or if I had, believe me,

    Believe these sighs that will not be kept in,

    I should not tell it to the Dauphin Queen.   180

    But to the purpose. Know my lord of Chartres

    Received the note you saw from Madam Tournon,

    A former mistress. But the secret's this:

    The sister of our Henry long has loved him.

PRINCESS OF CLÈVES.

    I thought the King intended her for Savoy.[30]   185

NEMOURS.

    True madam, but the Vidame is beloved.

---

30 The sister … Savoy] Henry is Henri II, King of France.
    His sister is Marguerite de France (1523-74), who mar-
    ried the Duke of Savoy in 1559.

In short, he dropped the letter and desired,
For fear of her he loves, that I would own it;
I promised too to trace the business for him,
And, if 'twere possible, regain the letter.   190
PRINCESS OF CLÈVES.
　　The Vidame then has shown but small discretion,
　　Being engaged so high.
　　Why did he not burn the letter?
NEMOURS.
　　But madam, shall I dare presume to say,
　　'Tis hard to be in love and to be wise?   195
　　Oh, did you know like him—like him? like me,
　　What 'tis to languish in those restless fires.
PRINCESS OF CLÈVES.
　　Irene, Irene, restore the duke his* letter.

*[The Princess gives the letter to Irene, who hands it to
Nemours.]*

NEMOURS.
　　Madam, you've bound me ever to your service.
　　But I'll retire and study to repay,   200
　　If aught but death can quit the obligation. (*Exit.*)
PRINCESS OF CLÈVES.
　　Oh 'tis too much, I'm lost, I'm lost again!
　　The duke has cleared himself, to the confusion
　　Of all my settled rage and vowed revenge,
　　And now he shows more lovely than before.   205
　　He comes again to wake my sleeping passion,
　　To rouse me into torture. Oh the racks
　　Of hopeless love! It shoots, it glows, it burns,
　　And thou, alas, shalt shortly close my eyes.
IRENE.
　　Alas! you're pale already.   210
PRINCESS OF CLÈVES.
　　　　　　　　　　Oh Irene,
　　Methinks I see Fate set two bowls before me:
　　Poison and health, a husband and Nemours.
　　But see with what a whirl my passions move:
　　I loathe the cordial of my husband's love,   215
　　But when Nemours my fancy does recall,
　　The bane's so sweet that I could drink it all.

Exeunt.

Act II, scene i. [The Court.]

Tournon and La March.

TOURNON.
　　It works, my dear, it works beyond belief:
　　The letter which he lost has sprung a mine
　　That shatters all the Court. Each jealous duchess
　　Concludes her man concerned and straight employs
　　A confidant to find the mystery out.   5
　　But that which takes the Queen, and makes me die
　　With pleasure, is that Marguerite thinks,
　　Spite of the imprecations of Nemours,
　　The letter sent to him.
LA MARCH.
　　I see 'em move this way.   10
TOURNON.
　　Haste to Saint-André's palace. Watch their wives
　　till I appear. I have promised Nemours an
　　afternoon assignation with 'em in Luxembourg
　　Garden, but I will antedate the business, as he is
　　waiting, and set Marguerite upon him just as he   15
　　meets 'em, which will heighten the design. Be
　　gone, while I attend the business here.

*Exit La March. [Tournon retires to the rear of the
stage.] Enter Marguerite and Nemours [followed by]
the Vidame.*

MARGUERITE.
　　Away! You have combined to ruin me.
　　You have conspired the death of her you hate!
　　But tell me, oh confess, and I'll forgive thee;   20
　　Say it was thine. Nay, look not on the Vidame.
　　There is discourse in eyes, consent, denial,
　　All understood by looks. Say it was thine,
　　Confess, and lay this tempest with a word.
　　Not yet? Why then, I'll have it in despite   25
　　Of thee and him. I'll sell my soul to Hell—
　　If woman can be worth the Devil's purchase
　　After she has been blown upon by man—
　　That I may tell thee, as I sink forever,
　　Thou hast been false.   30
NEMOURS.
　　　　　　　　　　You have heard me more than once
　　Affirm: the Vidame, if you'll give him leave,
　　Will own it to your face.

MARGUERITE.
　　　　　　　Hear, hear him, Heaven.
—By all extremes, thou art false. Therefore be gone,　35
For if I look upon thee in this rage,
I shall do mischief. Speak not, but away.

*Nemours beckons the Vidame. They steal off. Tournon
[comes forward].*

TOURNON.
Madam, the duke has taken you at your word and is
gone with the Vidame. I made bold to overhear part
of your discourse, because I have more of his　40
infidelity to tell you. Betwixt one and two in Luxembourg Garden he has appointed some ladies—f

MARGUERITE.
Furies and Hell!

TOURNON.
Have patience for an hour. I'll bring you to the
place, where, if you please, you may flesh your　45
fingers in the blood of those young women whom
he meets to enjoy.

MARGUERITE.
No, no, I have a better cast, if I can conquer this
rising spleen. How long will it be ere you call me?

TOURNON.
An hour or thereabouts.　50

MARGUERITE.
And by that time I'll put on a disguise. Fail not—

TOURNON.
But what do you intend?

MARGUERITE.
I know not yet myself. Revenge—

TOURNON.
You had a lover once, Francis the Dauphin—

MARGUERITE.
Be that then the last card. I know not what—　55
The Dauphin shall—I'll do't, and openly affront
　him,
And as the little worshippers adore me,
Spy the duke out and, leaning on the Prince,
Inquire, "Who's that?" It shall be so, I will!
Revenge, revenge, and show thyself true woman.　60
Down then, proud heart; down woman, down.
　　I'll try—
I'll do't. I've sworn to curb my will or die.

Exeunt.

Scene ii. [Saint-André's palace.]

Saint-André, Poltrot, and Bellamore.

BELLAMORE.
Well gentlemen, good morrow, and remember my
counsel.

POLTROT.
What, to bear ourselves like men of wit and sense,
snub our wives, rally 'em, and be as witty as the
Devil?　5

SAINT-ANDRÉ.
With all my heart. 'Tis not my time of assignation
yet with my duchesses, and this is very fashionable.

BELLAMORE.
I've put you in the way—and so good morrow.
(*Exit.*)

POLTROT.
They come, they come.　10

Enter Elianor and Celia.

Walk by 'em. Take no notice, and repeat verses.
"Phillis did in so strange a posture lie:
Panting and breathless, languishing her eye,
She seemed to live and yet she seemed to die."

SAINT-ANDRÉ.
I grow sick of the wife. Prithee Poltrot, let's go.　15

POLTROT.
Whither thou wilt, so we get rid of 'em. S'life,* I am
as weary of mine as a modish lady of her old clothes.

CELIA.
What, does the maggot bite? You must be jogging
from this place of little ease? Yet I am resolved to
know some reason why a wife may not be as good　20
company as a wench.

POLTROT.
Prithee spouse, do not provoke me, for I'm in the
witty vein and shall repartee thee to the devil.

ELIANOR.
Pray Saint-André, leave tricing your curls, your
affected nods, grimaces, taking of snuff, and　25
answer me. Why are we not as pleasing as
formerly?

SAINT-ANDRÉ.
Why Nell—Gad 'tis special, this amarum[31] is very

31　amarum] sweet marjoram, taken like snuff by inhaling

pungent. Why Nell, I can give no more reason for my change of humor than for the turning of a weathercock. Only this: I love whoring, because I love whoring.

POLTROT.

Nay, since you provoke us, know I can give a reason: we run after whores, because you bar us from 'em, as some take pleasure to go a-deer-stealing that have fine parks of their own. Gad, and there I was with her! This itch of the blood, spouse, is nothing but a spice of the first great jilt, your grandmother Eve: we long for the fruit, because it is forbidden.

SAINT-ANDRÉ.

Nay, that's not all, for misses are really more pleasant than a wife can be. *Probatum est.** A wife dares not assume the liberty of pleasing like a miss, for fear of being thought one. A wife may pretend to dutiful affection and bustle below, but must be still at night. 'Tis miss alone may be allowed flame and rapture, and all that.

CELIA.

Yet how do you know but a wife may have flame and rapture and all that?

POLTROT.

'Tis impossible. 'Tis the nature of a wife to be as cold as a stone. There's slap-dash[32] for you.

CELIA.

Yet out of a stone a man of sense would strike fire. There's slap-dash for you.

ELIANOR.

Will you be constant to us if we make it appear by your own confession that we can please as well as the subtlest she that ever charmed you?

SAINT-ANDRÉ.

Till which miracle come to pass, since 'twas your own proposition, I Saint-André and thou Elianor come not between a pair of sheets.

ELIANOR.

How should they know then?

POLTROT.

Nor I Antony with thee Celia.

ELIANOR.

But we hope you are not in earnest. You cannot be so inhuman.

CELIA.

'Tis a curse beyond all curses to have a man that can and will not. 'Tis worse than teaching a fool or leading the blind.

ELIANOR.

To marry and live thus is to be like fish in frosty weather: have water but pine for want* of air.

CELIA.

Yet who knows but Heaven may send some kind, good man that in mere pity may break the ice and give us a breathing?

ELIANOR.

Can you be so hard-hearted?

POLTROT.

Come bully, let's away for fear we should melt.— Look ye, spouses of ours: if our wenches prove ill-humored, we'll come back to you.

SAINT-ANDRÉ.

Agreed. Rather than grow rusty, let our wives file us. But I thank Heaven 'tis not come to that yet. There's no such want.* I'll have you to know, Nell, there's no woman can resist me if she would. No duchess 'scapes me if I make it my business to compass her.

POLTROT.

Any man of wit and sense like us charms all women, as one key unlocks all doors at Court.[33] Nay, I'll say a bold word for myself: turn me to the sharpest shrew that ever bit or scratched; if I do not make her feed out of my hand like a tame pigeon, may I be condemned to lie with my wife.

ELIANOR.

Flesh and blood can endure no longer! You are the vainest lying fellows that ever lived. You compass a duchess! There's not a footman but would shame you.

SAINT-ANDRÉ.

S'death* and fury, if they should try!

---

32 slap-dash] pointed witticism delivered in a seemingly careless manner

33 one key unlocks all doors at Court] as did the Lord Chamberlain's passkey

CELIA.

You pitiful, sneaking, rascally cuckold-countenanced scoundrels, that dare bespatter ladies of honor thus! For Heaven sake, what are you? How do you live, and where do you spend your time? In tennis courts, taverns, eating houses, bawdy houses, where you quarrel in drink for your trulls, who, while you manfully fight their cause, they run away with your hats and belts. 95

ELIANOR.

Then you come home and swear you'll be revenged on this lord, or that duke, that assaulted you single with all his footmen.

CELIA.

And says my gentleman, "If I had not been the most skillful person alive, my body had been by this time like an old-fashioned suit, pinked all over and full of eyelet-holes!" 105

ELIANOR.

But did he not disarm my lord at last?

CELIA.

By all means, and made him beg his life. 110

ELIANOR.

When indeed he compounded with the constable for his own liberty.

CELIA.

You persons of quality!* What person of honor would keep company with such debauchees? S'life* madam, an orange wench* is above their ambition. 115

ELIANOR.

An orange wench! If they can but run in her debt and the poor creature comes dunning 'em to their lodgings, they'll swear they lay with her, when they dare not be known that they are within.

CELIA.

Sometimes lie lolling upon a long scarf in the playhouse, talking loud and affectedly, and swear at night they had the prettiest thing just come out of the country. 120

ELIANOR.

And wish themselves damned if she did not smell of the grass. 125

CELIA.

When in truth 'twas some disguised bawd that met 'em there according to assignation.

POLTROT.

Hark you, Potiphar's wife of mine. By Pharaoh's lean kine,[34] thou shalt starve for this!

SAINT-ANDRÉ.

And for thee, Nell, mark me: thou shalt dream and be tormented with imagination, like one that, having drunk hard, is thirsty in the night, dreams of vessels brimful, and drinks and drinks yet never is satisfied. 130

POLTROT.

For my part, I'll serve my damned wife as Tantalus was punished: the fruit shall bob at her lips, which she shall never enjoy. 135

Exeunt Saint-Andrè and Poltrot.

ELIANOR.

Very well. The world's come to a fine pass. If this be marrying, would I were a maid again. Men take wives now as they snatch up a gazette: look it over and then fling it by. 140

CELIA.

They forget us in a day or two, or if they read us over again, 'tis only to rub up remembrance, and commonly they fall asleep so.

ELIANOR.

What's to be done, child?* For rather than live thus— 145

CELIA.

Rather than live thus, let's do anything.

ELIANOR.

Anything, rogue? Why, cuckolds are things.

CELIA.

Perhaps they think we have no such thing as flesh and blood about us, but we'll make 'em know a young woman in the flower of her age is not like painted fruit in a glass, only to be looked on. Perhaps you are a more contemplative person, and will go farther about? 150

ELIANOR.

What, dear rogue, dost think I will leave thee? By this kiss not I. 155

---

34 Potiphar's wife … Pharaoh's lean kine] The stories of Joseph's interpretation of the Pharoah's dream of seven lean years and of Potiphar's wife's attempted seduction of Joseph are told in Genesis 41.

CELIA.

Thus then: we'll slip on long scarfs and black gowns, put on masks, and ramble about.

ELIANOR.

Rare rogue, let me kiss thee again. Certainly, intriguing is the pleasantest part of life. To meet a gallant abroad in a summer's evening and laugh away an hour or two in a garden bower, where nobody sees nor nobody knows—methinks 'tis so pretty and harmless. Lord, how it works in my fancy!

CELIA.

We must tell Madam Tournon by all means.

ELIANOR.

I believe her secret and know her very good-natured. But for all that, methinks she has the cant of a refined Florence bawd—

CELIA.

The better for our purpose.

Enter Tournon.

She comes as wished.

TOURNON.

Dear precious rosebuds, your servant! Now for all the world you look as you were new-blown. And how do ye, my pretty primroses? 'Tis a whole day since I saw ye.

CELIA.

Oh madam, we have a suit to your ladyship.

TOURNON.

I grant it, whate'er it be. Speak, my hyacinth.

ELIANOR.

Our husbands are worse than ever.

CELIA.

They use us as if we had neither beauty nor portion.

TOURNON.

What's this I hear? Oh ingrate and ignoble! Revenge yourselves, sweetings. 'Tis time to pule and put finger in eye when you are past propagation. But my lady-birds, you are in your prime. Let me touch your delicate hands. Well, and do not these humid palms claim a man? Nay, and your breasts! Lord, Lord! How swollen and hard they are! How they heave and pant now, by Cynthia, as if they were ready to burst! Look to't,

have a care of a cancer. Draw 'em down, draw 'em down, for let me tell you, jewels, it may be dangerous for you to go thus long without cultivation.

ELIANOR.

What would you have us do, madam?

TOURNON.

Do, violet? Why, do as all the world does beside: lose no time, catch him by the forelock[35]—get a man to your mind. I'll acquaint you with one that's as true as the day, that will fight like a lion, and love like a sparrow.[36] He has eyes as black as sloes—you can hardly look on 'em—and a skin so white and soft as satin with the grain. And for thee, tulip—

CELIA.

For me, madam?

TOURNON.

For thee, honysuckle, such a man. Well, I shall never forget him. Such a straight bole of a body, such a trunk, such a shape, such a quick strength. He will over anything he can lay his hand on, and vaults to admiration.

ELIANOR.

But madam, will you provide us lodgings on occasion?

TOURNON.

The richest in the town: the costliest hangings, great glasses,* china dishes, silver tables, silver stands, and silver urinals! And then these gallants are the closest lovers, so good at keeping a secret. Well, give me your man that says nothing but minds the business in hand, for a secret lover's like a gun charged with white powder: does execution but makes no noise.

CELIA.

Well, and let me tell you that's the point, madam.

TOURNON.

Aye, and 'tis a precious point, a feeling point, and a pleasing point. You shall know him. You must

---

35 catch him by the forelock] Time, in his manifestation of Occasion, is conventionally figured as bald but with a forelock; to catch him by the forelock is the only way to seize the present opportunity, lest it pass one by.

36 sparrow] proverbially sexually indefatigable

know him. I shall die if you don't know him. He
has the fling of a gentleman.

ELIANOR.

Pray madam, how's that?

TOURNON.

Why thus, apricot: into your arms, then stops your 225
mouth with a double-tongued English kiss, that
you can't be angry with him for your blood.

CELIA.

I know 'tis my filthy country way, but I'll assure
you, if he should serve me so, my blood would rise
at him. 230

TOURNON.

But then you'd repent and fall before him, for he
has the most particular, obliging way, and she
whom he particularly loves is so obliged with his
particular— Well, for my part, my twins of beauty,
I set an infinite value on their caresses, distresses, 235
and addresses. Nay, I could refuse a quilt imperial
to be obliged by them, though on the bare boards
or the cold stones.

ELIANOR.

But madam, are they in being?

TOURNON.

They are, my blossoms. Then they kiss beyond 240
imagination, just for all the world as when you cut
a pure, juicy China orange,* the goodness runs
over. Lord, now it comes in my cogitation! I'm just
now going to take a view of 'em in Luxembourg
Garden, where, if you please to walk, they shall sun 245
themselves in your smiles. Come my carnations,
nay, I protest I will not go before ye.

CELIA.

But madam, we're at home.

TOURNON.

Oh Lord, beauties, I know not the way.

ELIANOR.

Indeed Madam you must, or we shall use violence. 250

TOURNON.

Well ladies, since 'tis your command, I dare not
but obey.

Exeunt.

Scene iii. [The Princess of Clèves' palace.]

Nemours and Bellamore.

NEMOURS.

Thou dear, soft rogue, my spouse, my Hephestion,
my Ganymede!³⁷ Nay, if I die tonight, my
dukedom's thine. But art thou sure the Princess of
Clèves withdraws here after dinner?

BELLAMORE.

One of her women, whom I have debauched, tells 5
me 'tis her custom. You may slip into the closet*
and overhear all. And yet, methinks 'tis hard,
because the Prince of Clèves loves you as his life.

NEMOURS.

I saved his life, sweetheart, when he was assaulted
by a mistake in the dark. And shall he grudge me 10
a little fooling with his wife for so serious an
obligation?

Enter the Vidame.

A pox upon him, here comes the Vidame with his
sour morals.

VIDAME.

'Tis certain I like her. She's very pretty, and 15
Tournon shall help me to her—

NEMOURS.

In love, by my lechery! Aye, and she shall help thee
to her. But who, but who is't, my man of
principles?

VIDAME.

To tell your Grace, I am sure, were to be a man of 20
none for myself—you that are the whores'
engrosser. Let me see. There's Tournon your
ubiquitary whore, your bawd, your bawd-barber
or bawd-surgeon,³⁸ for you're ever under her
hands, and she plasters you every day with new 25
wenches. Then there's your domestic termagants,
Elianor and Celia, with something new in chase.

---

37 Hephestion, my Ganymede] legendary catamites, the
   former the intimate of Alexander the Great, the latter,
   a prince of Troy so beautiful Zeus carried him off to
   serve as cupbearer to the gods

38 bawd-barber or bawd-surgeon] a play on the barber surgeon, who in the seventeenth century treated venereal
   diseases

Why, you outdo Cesar himself in your way and dictate to more whores at once than he did to knaves. Believe me, sir, in a little time you'll be nicked the town-bull. 30

NEMOURS.

Why, there's the difference betwixt my sense and yours. Would I were, and your darkling mistress the first should come in my way. Jove and Europa, I'd leap her in thy face! Why, how now, Vidame, 35 what devil has turned thee grave—the devil of love, or the devil of envy?

VIDAME.

Friendship, mere* friendship and care of your soul. I thought it but just to tell you the whole town takes notice of your way. 40

NEMOURS.

Why, then the whole town does me wrong, because I take no notice of theirs. Thus t'other night I was in company with two or three well-bred fops that found fault with my obscenity and protested "'twas such a way." Why, 'tis the way of ye all! Only you 45 sneak with it under your cloaks like tailors and barbers, and I, as a gentleman should do, walk with it in my hand. For prithee observe, does not your* priest the same thing? Did not I see Father Patrick,[39] declaiming against flesh in Lent, strip up to the 50 elbow and, telling the congregation he had eat nothing but fish these twenty years, yet protest to the ladies that fat arm of his, which was a chopping one, was the least member about him?

VIDAME.

Faith, and it may be so too. 55

NEMOURS.

Does not your politician, your little great man of business, that sets the world together by the ears, after all his plotting, drudging and sweating at lying, retire to some little punk* and untap at night?

VIDAME.

I submit to the weight of your reasons and confess 60 the whole world does you injustice, wherefore I judge it fit that they bring your Grace their wives and daughters to make you amends.

NEMOURS.

Why, now thou talk'st like an honest fellow, for never let business flatter thee, Frank, into 65 nonsense. Women are the sole pleasure of the world. Nay, I had rather part with my whole estate, health and sense, than lose an inch of my love. I was t'other day at a pretty entertainment, where two or three grave, politic rogues were wondering 70 why women should be brought into plays. I as gravely replied, "The world was not made without 'em." He full pop upon me, "But sir, it had been better if it had."

VIDAME.

And then no doubt a gloomy smile arose. 75

NEMOURS.

These are your rogues, Frank, that would be thought critics, that are never pleased but with something new, as they call it, just, proper, and never as men speak: your out-of-the-way men, that hate us rogues with a way. 80

VIDAME.

But after all this they'll run you down and say your Grace is no scholar.

NEMOURS.

Why faith, nor would be, if learning must wrench a man's head quite round. I understand my mother tongue well enough, and some others, just as I do 85 women: not to be married to 'em but to serve my turn. What's good in 'em never 'scapes me, but as for points and tags,[40] for which those solemn fops are to be valued, I slight 'em, nor would remember 'em if I could. For he that once listens to jingling, 90 ten to one if ever he gets it out of his head while he lives. But prithee be gone and leave me to my musing. Find Tournon out, my Vidame, and bid her remember the handkerchief. Away! Thou art concerned in the business, therefore away! 95

Exeunt the Vidame and Bellamore. Enter the Princess of Clèves and Irene.

She comes, ye gods, with what a pompous state;
The stars and all Heaven's glories on her wait.

---

39 Father Patrick] a generic term for a priest, but perhaps the Anglican priest, Simon Patrick, satirized by Rochester

40 points and tags] would-be witty aphorisms and hackneyed quotations

That's out of the way too—but now for my closet.*
(*Exit.*)
PRINCESS OF CLÈVES.
  No, no, I charge thee pity me no longer,   100
  But on the earth let us consult our woes,
  For earth I shall be shortly. Sit and hear me,
  While on thy faithful bosom thus I lean
  My aching head and breathe my cruel sorrows.

[*They sit together on the ground.*]

IRENE.
  Speak madam, speak. They'll strangle if contained.   105
PRINCESS OF CLÈVES.
  As late I lay upon a flowery bank,
  My head a little heaved beyond the verge
  To look my troubles in the rockless stream,
  I slept and dreamt I saw
  The bosom of the flood unfold.   110
  I saw the naked nymphs ten fathom down,
  With all the crystal thrones in their green courts
      below,
  Where in their busy arms Nemours appeared,
  His head reclined, and swollen as he were drowned,
  While each kind goddess dewed his senseless face   115
  With nectar's drops to bring back life in vain.
  When on a sudden the whole synod rose
  And laid him to my lips. Oh, my Irene!
  Forgive me, Honor, Duty——Love, forgive me!
  I found a pleasure I ne'er felt before: 120
  Dissolving pains and swimming, shuddering joys,
  To which my bridal night with Clèves was dull.

Enter the Prince of Clèves.

IRENE.
  Behold him, madam. [*Exit.*]
PRINCE OF CLÈVES.
  Hah! My Chartres, how!
  Why on the earth?   125
PRINCESS OF CLÈVES.
              Because, my lord, it suits
  The humble posture of my sad condition.
PRINCE OF CLÈVES.
  These starts again. But why thy sad condition?
  Oh rise and tell me why this melancholy?
  Why fall those tears? Why heaves this bosom thus? 130
  Nay, I must then constrain thee with my arms.

[*Clèves helps the Princess to] rise [and embraces her].*
  Is't possible? Does then thy load of grief
  Oppress thee so, thou canst not speak for sighing?
  Ah Chartres, Chartres! Then thou didst but
      soothe me.
  There is some cause, too frightful to be told,   135
  And thou hast learnt the art too to dissemble.
PRINCESS OF CLÈVES.
  Oh heavens, dissemble? When I strip my soul,
  Show it all bare and trembling to your view,
  Can you suspect me, sir, for a dissembler?
PRINCE OF CLÈVES.
  By all my hopes, doubts, jealousies and fears,   140
  I know not what to think. I think thou show'st
  Thy inmost thought, and now I think thou dost not.
  I think there is a bosom secret still
  And have a dawn of it through all thy folds
  That hide it from my view. Oh trust me, Chartres!g 145
  Trust me, whate'er it be. I love thee more
  Than thou lov'st help for that which thus
      enthralls thee.
  Trust thy dear husband. Oh, let loose the pain
  That makes thee droop, though it should be my
      death!
  By thy dear self, I'll welcome it to ease thee.   150
PRINCESS OF CLÈVES.
  Thou best of all thy kind, why should you rack me,
  Who dare not, cannot speak? No more but this:
  Take me from Paris, from the Court.
PRINCE OF CLÈVES.
                            Hah, Chartres!
  How! What, from the Court of Paris? Why?   155
PRINCESS OF CLÈVES.
  Because—
  My mother's death-bed counsel so advised me,
  Because the Court has charms, because I love
  A grotto best, because 'tis best for you
  And me and all the world.   160
PRINCE OF CLÈVES.
                        Because, oh Heaven,
  Because there is some cursèd charm at Court,
  Which you love better than me and all the world.
  The reason's plain for which you would remove:
  To lose the mem'ry of some lawless love!   165
PRINCESS OF CLÈVES.
  Why then am I detained, if that's your fear?

PRINCE OF CLÈVES.

  It is, it ought, and shall, and oh! you must
Confess this horrid falsehood to my face.

PRINCESS OF CLÈVES.

  Never, my lord, never confess a lie.
By heavens, I love your life above my own.   170

PRINCE OF CLÈVES.

  Not that, not that. Speak home and fly not wide.
Swear by thyself, thou dearly purchased pleasure,
Swear by those chaster sweets thy mother left thee,
Swear that thy soul, which cannot hide a treason,
Prefers me ev'n to all the world hold precious.ʰ   175
Swear that thou lov'st him more—and only lov'st him,
And in such sense as not to love another.

PRINCESS OF CLÈVES.

  Ah sir, why will you sink me to your feet,
Where I must lie and groan my life away?

PRINCE OF CLÈVES.

  Speak, Chartres, speak. Nor let the name of husband   180
Sound terror to thy soul. For by my hopes
Of paradise, howe'er thou usest me,
I am thy creature, still* to make and mold me
Thy cringing, crawling slave and will adore
The hand that kills me.   185

PRINCESS OF CLÈVES.

               Oh you are too good!
And I must never hope for pardon. Yet
I could excuse it, but my lord, I will not.
Know then— I cannot speak.

PRINCE OF CLÈVES.

               Nor I, by Heav'n.   190

PRINCESS OF CLÈVES.

  I love—

PRINCE OF CLÈVES.

        Go on.

PRINCESS OF CLÈVES.

           I love you as my soul.

PRINCE OF CLÈVES.

  Hah—but the rest?

PRINCESS OF CLÈVES.

          Alas, alas, I dare not.   195

PRINCE OF CLÈVES.

  Why then, farewell forever.

PRINCESS OF CLÈVES.

            Stay and take it—
Take the extremist pang of tortured virtue;

Take all: I love, I love thee, Clèves, as life,
But oh! I love, I love another more.   200

PRINCE OF CLÈVES.

  Oh Chartres! Oh!

PRINCESS OF CLÈVES.

         Why did you rack me then?
You were resolved, and now you have it all.

PRINCE OF CLÈVES.

  All, Chartres! All! Why, can there then be more?
But rise and know, I by this kiss forgive thee.   205
Thou hast made me wretched by the clearest
   proof
Of perfect honor that e'er flowed from woman.
But crown the misery which you have begun,
And let me know who 'tis you would avoid,
Who is the happy man that had the power   210
To burn that heart which I could never warm.

PRINCESS OF CLÈVES.

  Forgive me, sir: in this, prudence commands
Eternal silence.

PRINCE OF CLÈVES.

         Hah! If silent now,
Why didst thou speak at all? If here thou stop'st,   215
I shall conclude that which I thought thy virtue
A start of passion which thou couldst not hide,
And now vexation gnaws thy guilty soul
With a too-late repentance for confessing.
His name?ⁱ   220

PRINCESS OF CLÈVES.

         You shall not know it. Yes my lord,
Now a too-late repentance tears my soul
And tells me I have done amiss to trust you.
Yet, by my hopes of ease at last by death,
I swear my love has never yet appeared   225
To any man but you—

PRINCE OF CLÈVES.

  Weep not, my Chartres, for howe'er my tongue
Upbraid thy fame, my heart still worships thee,
And by the blood that chills me round, I swear,
From this sad moment I'll ne'er urge thee more.   230
All that I beg of thee is not to hate me.

PRINCESS OF CLÈVES.

  The study of my life shall be to love you.

PRINCE OF CLÈVES.

  Never, oh never! I were mad to hope it.
Yet thou shalt give me leave to fold thy hand,

To press it with my lips, to sigh upon it,   235
And wash it with my tears—
PRINCESS OF CLÈVES.
    I cannot bear this kindness without dying.
PRINCE OF CLÈVES.
    Nay, we will walk and talk sometimes together.
Like Age, we'll call to mind the pleasures past—
Pleasures, like theirs, which never shall return.   240
For oh, my Chartres, since thy heart's estranged,
The pleasure of thy beauty is no more,
Yet I each night will see thee softly laid,
Kneel by thy side, and when thy vows are paid,
Take one last kiss, ere I to death retire,   245
Wish that the heav'ns had giv'n us equal fire,
Then sigh, "It cannot be," and so expire.

Exeunt. Enter Nemours.

NEMOURS.
    She loves, she loves, and I'm the happy man!
She has avowed it, past all precedent,
Before her husband's face—   250
Hah! But from love like hers, such daring virtue,
That, like a bleeding quarry lately chased,
Plunges among the waves or turns at bay,
What is there to expect? But, let it come,
The worst can happ'n, yet 'tis glorious still:*   255
To bring to such extremes so chaste a mind
And charm to love the wisest of her kind.

Enter the Vidame.

Ah Vidame! I could tell thee such a story of such
a friend of mine, the oddest, prettiest, out of the
way of business. But thou art so flippant there's   260
no trusting thee.
VIDAME.
    Tournon says the flag's held out.
NEMOURS.
    Tournon be damned! Know then, but be secret,
there is a friend of mine beloved, but by a soul so
virtuous—   265
VIDAME.
    That was too much.
NEMOURS.
    That, quite from the method of all womankind,
she told it to her husband!

VIDAME.
    That's strange indeed. And how did her husband
like it?   270
NEMOURS.
    Why, after a tedious, passionate discourse,
approved her carriage and swore he loved her more
than ever. So they cried and kissed and went away
most lovingly together.
VIDAME.
    Why then she cuckolds him to rights, nor can he   275
take the law of her, and I'll be judge by any bawd
in Christendom. And so my lord, farewell, I have
business of my own, and Tournon waits you.
NEMOURS.
    But hark you, Frank. I have occasion for you and
must press thee, I hope, to no unwelcome office—   280
only a second.
VIDAME.
    With all my heart, my lord. The time and place?
NEMOURS.
    Just now in Luxembourg Garden, betwixt one and
two: a challenge from a couple, the smartest,
briskest, prettiest tilting ladies.   285
VIDAME.
    Your servant, sir, and as you thrive, let me hear from
your Grace, and so fate speed your plow. (*Exit.*)

Enter Tournon with Marguerite, who wears a mask.

NEMOURS.
    And so fate speed your plow, an* you go to that.
And I shall tell you, sir, 'twas not handsomely
done, to leave me thus to the mercy of two   290
unreasonable women at once.
TOURNON.
    You have him now in view, and so I leave you.
(*Exit.*)
MARGUERITE.
    Stand, sir.
NEMOURS.
    To a lady, while I have breath.   295
MARGUERITE.
    Would you not fall to a lady too, if she should ask
the favor?
NEMOURS.
    Aye, Gad, any pretty woman may bring me upon
my knees at her pleasure.

MARGUERITE. [*Aside.*]

Oh, devil! 300

NEMOURS.

Prithee, my dear soft, warm rogue, let thee and I
be kind*—

MARGUERITE.

And kiss, you were going to say.

NEMOURS. [*Aside.*]

S'life,* how pat she hits me!—Why thou and I were
made for one another. Let's try how our lips fit. 305

MARGUERITE.

Is that your fitting?

NEMOURS. [*Aside.*]

'Fore Heaven she's wonderous quick!—Nay my
dear, an* you go to that, I can fit you every way.

MARGUERITE.

You are a notorious talker.

NEMOURS.

And a better doer. Prithee try. 310

MARGUERITE.

As if that were to do now.

NEMOURS.

Nay, then I'm sure of thee, for never was a woman
mine once but was mine always.

MARGUERITE.

Know then you are a heavy, sluggish fellow. But I
see there is no more faith in man than woman: 315
cork and feathers.

NEMOURS.

Make a shuttlecock—that's woman. Let me, if
you please, be battledore, and by Gad, for a day
and a night I'll keep up with any fellow in
Christendom. 320

MARGUERITE.

Come away then, and I'll keep count, I warrant
you. [*Aside.*] Monster! Villain!

NEMOURS. [*Aside.*]

Now is the devil and I as great as ever.—I come,
my dear.—But then what becomes of my other
dears, for whom I was primed and charged? 325

MARGUERITE.

Why don't you come, my dear?

NEMOURS.

There with that sweet word she cocked me.

MARGUERITE.

Lord, how you tremble!

NEMOURS.

There the pan flashed.

MARGUERITE.

I'll set my teeth in you. 330

NEMOURS.

Now I go off. Oh man! Oh woman! Oh flesh! Oh
devil!41

Exeunt.

Act III, scene i. [Luxembourg Garden.]

Vidame and Tournon.

TOURNON.

A woman in love with another and confess it to her
husband! What would I give to know her! Without
all question Nemours is the person beloved.

VIDAME.

That's plain by his eagerness in the discovery.* He
forced me to hear him, whether I would or no. Yet 5
what I so admire in his temper is, that for all the
former heat, I no sooner mentioned you, but he
flew from it and run upon another scent, as if the
first had never been.

TOURNON.

Where did you find him? 10

VIDAME.

At the Princess of Clèves', and my heart tells me
that's the lady that acquainted her husband how
she was determined to make him a cuckold—if he
pleased to give his consent.

TOURNON.

My judgment, which is most sagacious in these 15
matters, is most positive in your opinion, for by
his whitely cast, the Prince of Clèves must be the
man forked in the book of fate.

VIDAME.

And yet 'tis odd that Nemours, of all men, should
have such luck at this lottery. 20

TOURNON.

Oh, to choose,42 my lord! Because she's nice* and
precise. Your* demure ladies, that are so squab in

---

41 flesh … devil] Nemours plays off the Medieval formula
for the negative trinity of evil: "the world, the flesh, and
the devil."

42 to choose] to be chosen (by Luck)

company, are devils in a corner. They are a sort of
melancholy birds, that ne'er peep abroad by day
but they tu-whit, tu-woo it at night. Nay, to my   25
particular knowledge, all grave women love wild
men. And if they can but appear civil at first, they
certainly snap 'em. For mark their language: "The
man is a handsome man, if he had but grace";
"The man has wit, parts* and excellent gifts, if he   30
would but make a right use of 'em." Why, all these
ifs are but civil pimps to a most bawdy conclusion.
But see, I descry him with a mask* yonder.

VIDAME.

You'll remember Saint-André's lady for this
discovery?*   35

TOURNON.

If she be not yours tonight, never acquaint me with
a mystery again.

VIDAME.

Not a word to the duke. My gravity gets me a hank
over him. Therefore, if you tell him of any love
matters of mine, you must never hope for more   40
secrets.

TOURNON.

Trouble not your head, but away.

Exit the Vidame.

So. This gets me a diamond from the Queen, an
ambassador's merit at least.[43] Confess to her
husband! Alas poor princess.—See, they come. But   45
that which startles me is how a woman of
Marguerite's sex can contain all this while, as she
seems to do. But perhaps she designs to pump him
or has some further end, which I must learn.
(*Exit.*)   50

Enter Nemours and Marguerite.

MARGUERITE.

But did you never promise thus before?

NEMOURS.

Never. But why these doubts? Thou hast all the
wit in the world. Thou know'st I love thee without
protestations. Why then this delay?

---

[43] ambassador's merit] Ambassadors usually received gifts
at the end of their embassies, such as jewels, artwork,
etc.

MARGUERITE.

I have not conversed with you an hour, and you are   55
for running over me. No sir—but if you can have
patience till the ball— [*Aside.*] Oh, I shall burst!

NEMOURS.

Patience? I must. But if it were not for the clog*
of thy modesty, we might have been in the third
heaven by this and have danced at the ball beside.   60
Hah! You faint—take off your mask.

MARGUERITE.

Unhand me, or— but pray, ere we part, let me ask
you a serious question: What if you should have
picked up a devil incarnate?

NEMOURS.

Why, by your loving to go in the dark thus, I make   65
me begin to suspect you. But be a devil an* thou wilt.
If we must be damned together, who can help it?

MARGUERITE. [*Aside.*]

I shall not hold.

NEMOURS.

Yet, now I think on't, thou canst be no devil; thou
art so 'fraid of a sinner. For you refused me just   70
now, when I proffered to sell myself and seal the
bargain with the best of my blood.

MARGUERITE.

But if I should permit you, could you find in your
heart to engender with a damned spirit?

NEMOURS.

Yes marry,* could I, for all you ask the question   75
so seriously. For know, thou bewitching creature,
I have longed any time this seven years to be the
father of a succubus.

MARGUERITE.

Fiend, and no man!

NEMOURS.

Besides madam, don't you think a feat devil of   80
yours and my begetting would be a prettier sight
in a house than a monkey or a squirrel? Gad, I'd
hang bells about his neck and make my valet
spruce up his brush-tail every morning as duly as
he combed my head.[44]   85

MARGUERITE.

But is it possible—for I know you have a mistress,

---

[44] head] wig

a convenience as you call her—that you could leave
her for me, who may be ugly, diseased, or a devil
indeed, for ought you know?

NEMOURS.

Why, since you tax me with truth, I must answer 90
like a man of honor: I could leave her for thee or
any else of your tribe, so they were all like you.

MARGUERITE.

But in the name of reason, what is there in us
runners-at-all that a wife or a mistress of that
nature may not possess with more advantage? 95

NEMOURS.

Why, the freedom, wit and roguery, and all sort
of acting, as well as conversation.* In a domestic
she, there's no gaiety, no chat, no discourse but of
the cares of this world and its inconveniencies.
What we do we do, but so dully. By Gad, my thing 100
asked me once, when my breeches were down,
what the stuff cost a yard.

[Exit Marguerite.]

Hah! What now, upon the gog* again? Nay, then
have with you at all adventures—at least to put you
in mind of the ball. (*Exit.*) 105

Enter Tournon.

TOURNON.

Hah! Yonder she lost him. See— What can she
intend by keeping her self so close? But see, La
March has seized her, and now the mystery will
open of itself.

Reenter Marguerite with La March.

LA MARCH.

But have you found him false? 110

MARGUERITE.

Curses, damnation,
The racks of woman's wits, when her soul
Is balked of vengeance, wait on his desires.

LA MARCH.

Why did you leave him so upon the sudden?

MARGUERITE.

Because I found my passion move too strongly. 115
My foolish heart would not obey my will.
I found my eyes grow full, my sighs had choked me,
And I was dying* in his arms.

LA MARCH.

But now
You have got breath, what is your purpose, madam? 120

MARGUERITE.

To meet him as I promised, to enjoy him
With the last pang of revengeful pleasure
And let him know—
Then make him damn himself with thousand oaths
That he'll ne'er see forsak'n Marguerite more, 125
The curst, fond,* foolish, doting Marguerite.
For thus with an extorted gallantry
I'll force him to revile me to my face,
Then throw the mask away, and vent my rage:
Tell him he is a fiend, devil, devil, devil, 130
Or what is worse, a man—
And leave him to the horror of his soul. (*Exit.*)

TOURNON.

I've heard her rave and must applaud thy conduct.
To the next task: then when she has satisfied
This odd figary[45] of revenge and pleasure, 135
Take her in the height of her disdain
And ply her with the Dauphin. Then tell Nemours
Of her resolve to cast him further off.
Millions to one we carry the design.
But haste and scout, while I attend the duke, 140
That harps upon the loss of his new mistress.

[Exit La March.] Enter Nemours.

NEMOURS.

Death and the devil! We went talking along so
pleasantly, when of a sudden, whispering she would
not fail me at the ball, she sprung from me at yon
dark corner and vanished. Well, if she be a devil, hell 145
by her should be a merry place, or perhaps she has
not been there yet but fell this morning and took
earth in her way. My comfort is, I shall make a new
discovery if she keeps her word, and she has too
much wit to break it before she tries me. 150

TOURNON.

And where are you to make this new discovery?

NEMOURS.

At the ball in masquerade. Thus would I have time
roll still,* all in these lovely extremes, the
corruption of reason being the generation of wit,

---

45 figary] whim, eccentric prank

and the spirit of wit lying in the extravagance of 155
pleasure. Nay, the two nearest ways to enter the
closet* of the gods and lie even with the Fates
themselves are fury[46] and sleep. Therefore, the fury
of wine and fury of women possess me waking and
sleeping. Let me dream of nothing but dimpled 160
cheeks and laughing lips and flowing bowls. Venus
be my star and whoring my house, and Death, I
defy thee. Thus sung Rosidore[47] in the urn.—But
where and when with my fops' wives? be quick.
Thou know'st my appointment with this 165
unknown, and the minute's precious.

TOURNON.
Why, I have contrived you the sweetest wight in
the world, if you dare.

NEMOURS.
Dare, and in a woman's cause! Why, I have no drop
of blood about me but must out in their service, 170
and what matter is't which way?

TOURNON.
Know Poltrot's lady has informed me, how Saint-
André walks in his sleep, and that her husband last
night attempted to cuckold him, that she watched
and overheard the whole matter, but Poltrot could 175
not find the door before Saint-André returned. She
doubts not but he will try again tonight. Now, if
you can nick the time when Poltrot rises and steal
to her, ten to one but she'll be glad to be revenged.

NEMOURS.
Or she would not have told thee the business. 180
There wants* but speaking with her, taking her by
the hand, and 'tis a bargain.

*Enter Celia and Elianor, [both] masked; Poltrot and
Saint-André following.*

TOURNON.
Step, step aside. They are upon the hunt for you,
and their husbands have 'em in the wind. Stand by
a while to observe, and I'll turn you loose upon 'em. 185

[Exeunt Tournon and Nemours.]

---

46 fury] ecstatic frenzy
47 Rosidore] perhaps a reference to Rochester's poem,
   "Upon his Drinking a Bowl," but a general philosophical libertinism is the subject of this entire scene.

SAINT-ANDRÉ.
Hah, Tournon!—By my honor, a prize. Let's board
'em.

POLTROT.
Be not too desperate, my little frigate, for I am that
I am: a furious man of honor.

CELIA.
Now Heaven defend us. What, will you give us a 190
broadside?

ELIANOR.
Lord! how I dread the guns of the lower tier.

SAINT-ANDRÉ.
Such notable marksmen too—we never miss
hitting between wind and water.

CELIA.
I'll warrant they carry chain-shot.[48] Pray Heaven 195
they do not split us, sister!

POLTROT.
Yield then, yield quickly, or no mercy. We have
been so shattered today already by two she-pirates
that we are grown desperate.

ELIANOR.
But what alas have we done, that you should turn 200
your revenge upon us poor harmless innocents,
that never wronged you, never saw you before?

CELIA.
If you should deal unkindly with us, 'twould break
our hearts, for we are the gentlest things.

SAINT-ANDRÉ.
And we will use you so gently, so kindly, like little 205
birds, you shall never repent the loss of your liberty.

ELIANOR.
I'll warrant, sister, they'll put us in a cage or tie us
by the legs.

POLTROT.
No, upon the word of a man of honor, your legs
shall be at liberty. 210

CELIA.
What, will you pinion our wings then and let us
hop up and down the house?

SAINT-ANDRÉ.
Not in the house where we live, pretty soul, for
there's two ravenous sow-cats will eat you.

---

48 chain-shot] two cannonballs chained together

ELIANOR.

Your wives you mean.   215

POLTROT.

Something like—two melancholy things that sit purring in the chimney corner and, to exercise their spite, kill crickets.

CELIA.

Oh! For God-sake, keep us from your wives!

SAINT-ANDRÉ.

I'll warrant thee, little Rosamond, safe from my   220
jealous Elianor.[49]

POLTROT.

And if any wife in Europe dares but touch a hair of thee, I say not much, but that wife were better be a widow.

ELIANOR.

But are your wives handsome and well qualitied?*   225
For whatever you say to us, when you have had your will, you'll home at night, and for my part I cry, "All or none."

POLTROT.

And all thou shalt have, dear rogue. Never fear my wife's beauty or good nature. They are things to   230
her like saints and angels, which she believes never were nor never will be. She's a basin of water against lechery and looks so sharp whenever I see her, like vinegar she makes me sweat.

SAINT-ANDRÉ.

And mine's so fulsome, that a goat with the help   235
of cantharides would not touch her.

CELIA.

But then for their qualities—

SAINT-ANDRÉ.

Such scolds, like thunder they turn all the drink in the cellar.

POLTROT.

Such niggards, they eat kitchen-stuff and candles'   240
ends. Once indeed, raving mad, my wife seemed prodigal, for, a rat having ate his way through an old cheese, she baited a trap for him with a piece of paring. But having caught him, by the Lord she ate him up without mercy, tail and all.   245

ELIANOR. [Aside to Celia.]

Are they not even with us, sister?

SAINT-ANDRÉ.

'Tis hoped, though, the hangman will take 'em off of our hands, for they are shrewdly suspected for witches. Mine 'noints herself every night, sets a broomstaff in the chimney, and opens the window,   250
for what purpose but to fly?

POLTROT.

Gad, and my wife has teats in the wrong place. She's warted all over like a pumpled orange.

CELIA.

Yet sure, gentlemen, you told these hags another story once and made as deep protestations to them   255
as you do to us?

SAINT-ANDRÉ.

Never, by this hand, the salt* souls fell in lust with us and hauled us to matrimony like bears to the stake.

POLTROT.

Where they set a long black thing upon us that   260
cried, "Have and hold."

ELIANOR.

Put the question they had been handsome, brought you great portions, were pleasant and airy and willing to humor you—

Enter Nemours with the Vidame.

NEMOURS.

Nay, then I can hold no longer. 'Sdeath,* there's   265
it madam! Willing! That willingness spoils all, my dear, my honey, my jewel. It palls the appetite like sack* at meals. Give me the smart, disdainful she that, like brisk champagne or sprightly burgundy, makes me smack my lips after she's down and long   270
for t'other glass.

SAINT-ANDRÉ.

Nay, if your Grace come in, there's no dallying. I'll make sure of one! [Takes hold of Elianor.]

POLTROT.

Nay, and for my part I am resolved to secure another. Come madam, no striving, for I am like a   275
lion: when I lay hold, if the body come not willingly, I pull a whole limb away. [Takes hold of Celia.]

NEMOURS.

Yes madam, he speaks truth. Take it on my word

---

49 Rosamond] Rosamond Clifford was the subject of Henry's II's queen, Eleanor's, jealousy.

who am a rational creature: he is a great, furious, wild beast.   280

CELIA.

Pray Heaven he be not a horned* beast. Is the monster married?

VIDAME.

Yes ladies, they are both married.

ELIANOR.

Married! For Heaven sake, gentlemen, save us from the cattle.   285

POLTROT.

Why, what is the breeze[50] in your tails? 'Sdeath* ladies, we'll not eat you.

CELIA.

Say you so? But we'll not trust you. I am sure you both look hungrily.

VIDAME.

It may be their wives use 'em unkindly.   290

ELIANOR.

And the poor good-natured things take it to heart.

CELIA.

I swear 'tis pity. They have both promising looks.

NEMOURS.

Proceed, sweet souls, we'll defend you to death. Spare 'em not.

ELIANOR.

Or it may be we mistake all this while, and their   295
pitiful looks are caused by loving too much.

VIDAME.

Right madam, a little too uxorious. Ha, ha!

SAINT-ANDRÉ. [*Aside, to Poltrot.*]

Now have not I one word to say, but stand to endure all jerks* like a school-boy with my shirt up.   300

POLTROT.

I'll have one fling at 'em, though I die for't.—Why ladies, you'll overshoot yourselves at this rate. Must we only be the butts to bear all your raillery? Methinks you might spend one arrow at random and take off that daw that chatters so near you.—   305
Gad and I think I paid 'em there.

CELIA.

Butts and daw! Let me never laugh again, if they

be not witty too. Why, you pleasant rogues! 'Slife,* I could kiss 'em if they did not stink of matrimony.

SAINT-ANDRÉ. [*Aside to Poltrot.*]

Mum, mum, mum. Did not I tell you 'twas a   310
madness to speak to 'em?

ELIANOR.

They envy my friend too here, this pleasant companion.

CELIA.

This dear agreeable person.

NEMOURS.

Aye, damme madam, the rogues envy us.   315

ELIANOR.

What a gentle aspect!

CELIA.

How proper and airy![51]

ELIANOR.

See, here's blood in this face.

VIDAME.

Pure blood, madam, at your service.

CELIA.

Will you walk, dear sir? Give me your hand.   320

ELIANOR.

And me yours.

NEMOURS.

Come, you dear, ravishing rogues. Your servant, Mr. Butts.

VIDAME.

Gentle Mr. Butts.

ELIANOR.

Adieu, sweet Mr. Butts.   325

CELIA.

Witty Mr. Butts. Ha, ha, ha!

Exeunt Nemours, the Vidame, Celia, and Elianor.

SAINT-ANDRÉ.

Well, I'll to a duchess.

POLTROT.

Lord! Thou art always so high-flown. Hast thou never a cast* countess for me?

SAINT-ANDRÉ.

Come along to the ball and thou shalt see. The   330
Duke of Nemours is the gallant tonight and treats

---

[50] breeze] gadfly

[51] proper and airy] handsome and vivacious

at his palace, because 'tis the King's birthday. Let
me see. What new fancy for the masquerade? Oh!
I have it. Because the town is much taken with
fortune-telling, I'll act the dumb man, the   335
highlander that made such a noise,[52] and thou
shalt be my interpreter. Come along, and as we go
I'll instruct thee in the signs.

POLTROT.

Dear rogue, let's practice a little before we stir—
as, what sign for lechery, because we may nick our   340
wives?

SAINT-ANDRÉ.

Why thus: _____.* That's a glancing, squeezed eye.
Or thus ____,* for a moist hand. Or thus____,*
for a whore in a corner. Or thus _____,* for
downright cuckolding.   345

POLTROT.

Well, I swear this will be rare sport. And so, my
damned spouse, I am resolved to tickle her with a
squeezed eye and a moist hand and a whore in a
corner, till she confess her self guilty of downright
cuckoldom; then, in revenge for her last   350
impudence, sue for a divorce:[53]
And holding to her face the flying label,[54]
Call her in open court the Whore of Babel.

Exeunt.

Scene ii. [The Prince of Clèves' Palace.]

The Prince and Princess of Clèves.

PRINCE OF CLÈVES.

Madam, the King commands me to attend
His daughter into Spain and further adds,
Because no princess rivals you in fame,
You will oblige the Court in going with me.

PRINCESS OF CLÈVES.

My lord, I am prepared, and leave the Court   5
With such a joy as would admit no bounds.

---

[52] Highlander… noise] Perhaps an allusion to a real person, not identified. Highland Scots putatively could
forecast the future, as well as perform other supernatural feats.

[53] divorce] extremely difficult—and expensive—to obtain
in England; impossible in France

[54] flying label] brandished list of charges

PRINCE OF CLÈVES.

As would admit no bounds! And why? because
It takes you from the charms which you would shun.
This is a virtue of such height indeed
As none but you can boast, nor I deplore.   10
But madam, rumor says the King intends
To join another with me.

PRINCESS OF CLÈVES.

                Who, my lord?

PRINCE OF CLÈVES.

'Twas thought at first the Chevalier de Guise.

PRINCESS OF CLÈVES.

He is your friend, nor could the King choose better.   15

PRINCE OF CLÈVES.

I say, at first 'twas thought the Duke of Guise.
But I was since instructed by the Queen
That honor's fixed upon the Duke Nemours.

PRINCESS OF CLÈVES.

Nemours, my lord?

PRINCE OF CLÈVES.

              Most certain.   20

PRINCESS OF CLÈVES.

              For what reason?

PRINCE OF CLÈVES.

Because I moved the Dauphin Queen to gain him.

PRINCESS OF CLÈVES.

'Twas rashly done, against your interest moved.

PRINCE OF CLÈVES.

Perhaps 'tis not too late yet to supplant him.

PRINCESS OF CLÈVES.

Do't then, be quick. Nemours will share your honors,   25
Eclipse your glory.

PRINCE OF CLÈVES.

           Hah, I must confess
The soldiers love him, and he bears the palm
Already from the marshals of the field.[55]

PRINCESS OF CLÈVES.

And in the Court he's called the rising star.   30
You see each night at every entertainment
Where he moves, what troops of beauties follow;
How the queens praise him, and all eyes admire him.

PRINCE OF CLÈVES.

Hah! Chartres!

---

[55] he bears the palm … marshals of the field] He is more
esteemed than the generals already in command.

PRINCESS OF CLÈVES.

     Ah! my lord—what have I done? 35
PRINCE OF CLÈVES.

Nothing, my Chartres, but admire Nemours!
Oh, heaven and earth! And if I had but patience
To hear you out, how had you lost yourself
On that eternal object of your love?
No madam, no, 'tis false: 'tis not Nemours, 40
'Twas my invention to find out the truth.
Your trouble has convinced me 'tis Nemours,
Which curst discovery* in another woman
I should have made by her too eager joy.
Why speak you not? You're shocked with your 45
 own virtue.
The resolution of your justice awes you,
Which cannot, dares not give itself the lie.
PRINCESS OF CLÈVES.

My lord, my love, my life. Alas my Clèves! [Kneels.]
Oh pity me! I know not what to answer.
I'm mortally ashamed. I'm on the rack. 50
But spare this humble passion. Take me with you,
Where I may never see a man again.
PRINCE OF CLÈVES.

Oh, rise my Chartres! Rise! If possible
I'll force thee to be mine in spite of Fate.
My constant martyrdom and deathless kindness, 55
My more than mortal patience in these sufferings
Shall poise his noblest qualities. Oh Heaven!
No fear, my Chartres, though these sorrows fall,
That I suspect thy glory. Thou hast strength
To curb this passion in that else may end us. 60
All that I ask thee is to bend thy heart.
PRINCESS OF CLÈVES.

I'll break it.
PRINCE OF CLÈVES.

   Turn it from Nemours, Nemours—
But oh! that name presents thy danger greater.
Look to thy honor then, and look to mine. 65
I ask it as thy lover and thy husband.
I beg it as a man, whose life depends
Upon thy breath, that offers thee a heart
All bleeding with the wounds of mortal love,
All hacked and gashed and stabbed and mangled 70
 o'er—
And yet a heart so true, in spite of pain,
As ne'er yet loved nor ever shall again. (Exit.)

Enter Irene.

IRENE.

Hah! madam, speak. How is it with your heart?
PRINCESS OF CLÈVES.

As with a timorous slave, condemned to torments,
That still cries out, he cannot, will not bear it, 75
And yet bears on.
IRENE.

    Ah madam, I would speak,
If you could bear the dreadful news I bring.
PRINCESS OF CLÈVES.

Alas! thou canst not add to grief like mine.
IRENE.

May I demand then if you have not told 80
The secret to your husband?
PRINCESS OF CLÈVES.

     Hah! Irene—
Why dost thou ask?
IRENE.

Because—
But now Tournon, a lady of the Queen's, 85
Told me 'tis blazed at Court, Nemours confessed
He is beloved by one of such nice* virtue,
That, fearing lest the passion might betray her,
She owned, confessed, and told it to her husband.
PRINCESS OF CLÈVES.

Death and despair! But does Nemours avow it? 90
IRENE.

He owned it to the Vidame, who again
Told it to Madam Tournon, she to others.
'Tis true, Nemours told not the lady's name
Nor would confess himself to be the party,
But yet the Court in general does believe it. 95
PRINCESS OF CLÈVES.

I am undone: my fame is lost for ever,
And death, Irene, must be my remedy.
'Tis true, indeed, I laid my bosom op'n,
I showed my heart to that ungrateful Clèves,
Who since, in dangerous search of him I love, 100
To the eternal ruin of my honor
Has trusted a third person. But away.
I hear his tread and am resolved to tax him.

[Exit Irene.] Enter Prince of Clèves.

Ah sir, what have you done? If you must kill me,
Are there not daggers, poison? But the jealous 105

Are cruel still* and thoughtful in revenge,
And single death's too little. Must your will
Of knowing names my duty durst not tell you
Oblige you to betray me to another?
So to divulge the secret of my soul   110
That the whole Court must know it?

PRINCE OF CLÈVES.
                                        Hah! Know what?
Know my dishonor? Have you told it then?

PRINCESS OF CLÈVES.
No, 'tis yourself, 'tis you revealed it, sir,
To gain a confidant for more discovery.*   115
A lady of the Queen's just now declared it:
To your eternal shame you have divulged it.
She had it from the Vidame, sir, of Chartres,
And he—from the Duke Nemours.

PRINCE OF CLÈVES.
                                        Nemours!   120
How, madam, said you? What, Nemours! Nemours!
Does Nemours know you love him? Hell and Furies!
And that I know it, too, and not revenge it!

PRINCESS OF CLÈVES.
That's yet to seek. He will not own himself
To be concerned; he offers not at names.   125
But yet 'tis found, 'tis known, believed by all.
He cannot hold it; 'twill be shortly posted
That, Clèves, your wife's that curst dishonored she
You told him of.

PRINCE OF CLÈVES.
                                Is't possible I told him?   130
Peace, peace, and if it lies in human power
To reason calmly, tell me, murd'ress, tell me—
Compose that face of flushed hypocrisy,
And answer to a truth: Was it my interest
To speak of this? Was I not rather tied   135
To wish it buried in the grave in hell,
Whence it might never rise to blot my honor?
But you have seen him. By my hopes of heaven,
You have met and interchanged your secret souls;
On that complotted, since I bore so tamely   140
Your first confession, I should bear the latter.

PRINCESS OF CLÈVES.
Believe it if you please.

PRINCE OF CLÈVES.
                                I must believe it.
This last proceeding has unmasked your soul.

He sees you ev'ry hour and knows you love him.   145
Nay, for your greater freedom, you have joined
To make this loathed, detested Clèves your stale.[56]
Hah! I believed you might o'ercome this passion,
So well you knew to charm me with the show
Of seeming virtue 'till I lost my reason.   150

PRINCESS OF CLÈVES.
'Tis likely, sir, it was but seeming virtue,
And you did ill to judge so kindly of me.
I was mistaken too in that confession,
Because I thought that you would do me justice.

PRINCE OF CLÈVES.
You were mistaken when you thought I would.   155
Sure you forgot that I was desperate,
Sentenced and doomed by Fate, or rather damned
To love you to my grave—and could I bear
A rival? What, and when I was your husband,
And when you owned your passion to my face,   160
Confessed you loved me much, but loved him more?
Hah! Is not this enough to make me mad?

PRINCESS OF CLÈVES.
You have the power to set all right again:
Why do you not end me?

PRINCE OF CLÈVES.
                                No, I'll end my self.   165
My thoughts are grown too violent for my reason.
By this last usage, oh, thou hast undone me.
I know not what— This ought not to be thine:
I have offended and would sue for pardon.
But yet I blush; the treason is too gross.   170
After that most unnatural confession,
I wonder now that I have lived so long.
Confess and then divulge! Make me your bawd!
It scents too far; the God of Love flies wide,
He gets the wind and stops the nose at this.   175
No more—farewell. False Chartres, false Nemours,
False world, false all, since Chartres is not true!
But you your wish with loved Nemours shall have,
And shortly see your husband in the grave. (*Exit*.)

PRINCESS OF CLÈVES.
False world, false Clèves, false Chartres, false   180
    Nemours,
Farewell to all, a long and last farewell.

---

56 stale] laughingstock, a dupe

From all converse to deserts let me fly
And in some gloomy cave forgotten lie.
My bower at noon the shade of some old trees
With whistling winds t'indulge my pomp of ease   185
And lulling murmurs rolled from neighb'ring seas,
Where I may sometimes hasten to the shore
And to the rocks and waves my loss deplore,
Where when I feel my hour of fate draws on,
Lest the false world should claim a parting groan,   190
My mother's ghost may rise to fix my mind
And leave no thought of tenderness behind.

Exit.

    Act IV, scene i. [The palace of Nemours.]
      Music, songs, maskers, etc.

Enter Nemours with musicians, Celia.

NEMOURS.
He has confessed to me he intends to cuckold
Saint-André when he walks in his sleep. Therefore,
if Love should inspire me to nick the opportunity,
I hope you will not bar the door which your
husband opens.   5
CELIA.
Ingrateful monster!
NEMOURS.
Ingrateful, that's certain, and it lies in your power
to make him a monster.
CELIA.
I dare not—
NEMOURS.
What?   10
CELIA.
Trust you.
NEMOURS.
Nay then I am sure thou wilt. Let me but in to
show the power you have over me.
CELIA.
As how, my lord?
NEMOURS.
Why, when I have thee in my arms, by Heaven   15
I'll quit my joys at thy desire.
CELIA.
That will indeed be a perfect trial of your love. Come
then through the garden backstairs, and when you
see the candle put out, thrust open the door.

NEMOURS.
By Heaven I'll eat thy hand—thou dear, sweet   20
seducer, how it fires my fancy to steal into a
garden, to rustle through the trees, to stumble up
a narrow pair of back stairs, to whisper through
the hole of the door, to kiss it open, and fall into
thy arms with a flood of joy!   25
CELIA.
Farewell, the company comes. I must leave you
awhile, to engage with my husband. You'll fall
asleep before the hour.
NEMOURS.
If I do, the very transport of imagination shall
carry me in my sleep to thy bed, and I'll wake in   30
the act.

Exit Celia.

So there's one in the fern brake, and if she stir till
morning, I have lost my aim.

*Enter Tournon in the habit of a Huguenot,[57]
[Marguerite, masked, and others].*

But now, why what have we here? A Huguenot
whore by this light. Have I the forward,[k] brisk she   35
that promised me the ball assignation, that said there
was nothing like slipping out of the crowd into a
corner, breathing short an ejaculation, and returning
as if we came from church. Let me see. I'll put on my
mask, fling my cloak over my shoulder, and view   40
'em as they pass. Not thou, nor thou—
TOURNON.
Ah thou unclean person, have I hunted thee there
like a hart from the mountains to the valleys, and
thou wouldst not be found? Verily thou hast been
amongst the daughters of the Philistines. Nay, if   45
you are innocent, stand before me and reply to the
words of my mouth—
NEMOURS.
I shall truly.
TOURNON.
Say then, hast thou not defiled thyself with any

---

57 Huguenot] These French Protestants did not wear dis-
tinctive clothing; Lee here associates them with the English Puritans; thus Tournon wears plain, drab, and
decorous dress.

Delilah since last you fell upon my neck and loved 50
much?
NEMOURS.
Nay verily.
TOURNON.
Have you not overheated your body with
adulterate wines? Have you not been at a play nor
touched fruit after the lewd orange women?* 55
NEMOURS.
I am unpolluted.
TOURNON. (*Unmasking.*)
And yet methinks there is not the same color in
your cheeks, nor does the spirit dance in your eye
as formerly. Why do you not approach me?
NEMOURS.
Tournon turned heretic! Why thou dear rascal, this 60
is such a new frolic, that though I am engaged as deep
as damnation to another, thou shalt not 'scape me.

Marguerite comes forward and claps him on the shoulder.

MARGUERITE.
I love a man that keeps the commandment of his
word.
NEMOURS.
And I a woman that breaks hers with her husband, 65
yet loves her neighbor as herself. I would fain be
in private with you.

[Exit Tournon.]

MARGUERITE.
And I with you, because I am resolved never to
see you more.
NEMOURS.
Never to see me more? The reason? 70
MARGUERITE.
Because I hate you.
NEMOURS.
And yet I believe you love me too, because you are
precise to the minute.
MARGUERITE.
True, yet I hate you justly, heartily, and maliciously.
NEMOURS.
By Gad, and I'll love thee as heartily, justly, and 75
maliciously as thou canst love me, for thy blood.
Come away, riddle, and I'll unfold thee.

*Exeunt [Marguerite and Nemours]. Enter Poltrot and
Saint-André disguised, with Elianor and Celia coming
up to 'em.*

ELIANOR.
But is it true indeed, that your friend can tell all
the actions of our life past, present, and to come,
yet cannot speak one word? 80
POLTROT.
Oh he's infallible! Why what, did you never hear of
your* second-sight men, your dumb Highlanders
that tell fortunes? Why, you would think the Devil
in hell were in him, he speaks so exactly.
ELIANOR.
I thought you had said he was dumb? 85
POLTROT.
Right, but I am his interpreter, and when the fit
comes on him, he blows through me like a trunk,
and straight I become his speaking trumpet.
CELIA.
Pray sir, may not I have my fortune told me too?
POLTROT.
Aye, an* there were a thousand of you, he will run 90
you 'em over like the crisscross row58 and never
miss a tittle. He shall tell ye his name that cried,
"God bless you," when you sneezed last, tell you
when you winked last, when and where you
scratched last, and where you sate o'Saturday. 95
ELIANOR.
Pray let him tell us then—for we are sisters—our
tempers and conditions, whether married or
unmarried, with all the impertinences thereunto
belonging.
POLTROT.
I'll speak to him: Son of the Sun, and Emperor of 100
the Stars!
SAINT-ANDRÉ.
Hah, hah—
POLTROT.
Look ye, look ye, he's pleased to tell you. But you
must go near him, for he must look in your hand,
touch your face, breasts, and whereever else he 105
pleases.

---

58 crisscross row] hornbook (q.v.), whose first row was initiated by the sign of Christ's cross.

Saint-André makes horns with both his hands, puts his finger in his mouth, and laughs.

In nomine domine bomine.[59] I protest I am confounded. Well ladies, I could not have thought it had been in you. But 'tis certainly true, and I must out with it. First he says, you are both 110 married, you are both libidinous beyond example, and your husbands are the greatest cornutos^l in Christendom.

ELIANOR, CELIA.

Indeed.

POLTROT.

Aye indeed, indeed and indeed. He says you are a 115 couple of Messalinas, and the stews cannot satisfy you. He says your thoughts are swelled with a carnosity. Nay, you have the greensickness of the soul, which runs upon nothing but neighing^m stallions, churning boars, and bellowing bulls. 120

CELIA.

Oh! I confess, I confess. But for Heaven sake, dear sir, let it not take air, for then we are both undone.

ELIANOR.

Oh, undone, undone, sir, if our husbands should know it, for they are a couple of the jealousest, troublesome, impertinent cuckolds alive. 125

POLTROT. [*Aside.*]

Alack, alack! Oh Jezabel!* But I will have my eunuchs fling her from the window, and the dogs shall eat her.

CELIA.

But pray sir, ask him how many times.

POLTROT.

What, how many times you have cuckolded 'em? 130

ELIANOR.

Spare our modesty. You make the blood so flush in our faces.

POLTROT. [*Aside.*]

But by Jove I'll let it out, I'll hold her by the muzzle and stick her like a pig.

CELIA.

Will you speak to him, sir? 135

---

59 *In nomine domine bomine*] corruption of *in nomine domini*, in the name of the lord (Lat.), with "bomine" tacked on as gibberish

POLTROT.

See, he understands you without it. He says your iniquities are innumerable, your fornications like the hairs of your head, and your adulteries like the sands on the seashore; that you are all fish downward; that Lot's wife is fresh to you, and that 140 when you were little girls of seven, you were so wanton, your mothers tied your hands behind you.

ELIANOR.

All this we confess to be true. But we confess too, if Fate had found out any sort of tools but those leaden rogues, our husbands— 145

CELIA.

Whose wits are as dull as their appetites—

ELIANOR.

Mine such a utensil as is not fit to wedge a block—

CELIA.

Nor mine the beetle to drive him.

SAINT-ANDRÉ.

Nay then 'tis time to uncase and be revenged.

POLTROT.

Hark you, strumpet— 150

ELIANOR.

Ha, ha, ha! Are you not fitted* finely?

CELIA.

You must turn fortune-tellers, must you?

ELIANOR.

And think we could not know you?

CELIA.

Well gentlemen, shall homely Beck go down with you at last? 155

POLTROT.

But didst thou know me then indeed?

CELIA.

As if that sweet voice of yours could be disguised in any shape.

POLTROT.

Nay, I confess I have a whirl in my voice, a warble that is particular. 160

ELIANOR.

And what say you, sir? Shall musty wife come into grace again?

SAINT-ANDRÉ.

She shall, and here's my hand on't. All friends, Nell, and when I leave thee again, may I be cuckold in earnest. 165

POLTROT. [*Aside.*]

Certain as I live, all this proceeded from his lady; my dreaming-cuckold-wife could never think on't. Well, I am resolved this very night, when he rambles in his sleep, to watch him, slip to his wife, and say nothing.—Hey! Come, come, where are these dancers? A little diversion, and then for bed. 170

Dance. Enter Tournon.

TOURNON. (*To Elianor.*)

I have locked the Vidame in your closet,* who will be sure to watch your husband's rising. Therefore, be not surprised. (*Exit.*)

SAINT-ANDRÉ.

Come, well, let's away to bed. 175

ELIANOR.

And what then?

SAINT-ANDRÉ.

Nay, gad, that I can't tell, for what with dancing, singing, fencing, and my last duchess, I am very drowsy.

POLTROT.

And so am I. Perhaps our wives have given us 180 opium, lest we should disturb 'em in the night.

ELIANOR. [*Aside to Celia.*]

Don't these men deserve to be fitted?*

CELIA.

They do, and Fortune grant they may. Hear us, oh! hear us, good Heaven, for we pray heartily.

Exeunt [Poltrot, Saint-André, Celia and Elianor], as Nemours and Marguerite enter.

NEMOURS.

Was ever man so blest with such possession, 185
Thou ebbing, flowing, ravishing, racking joy!
A skin so white and soft, the yielding mold
Lets not the fingers stay upon the dint,
But from the beauteous dimples slips 'em down
To pleasures that must be without a name. 190
Yet hands and arms and breasts we may remember,
And that which I so love, no smelling art,
But sweet by nature, as just peeping violets
Or op'ning buds.

MARGUERITE.

    Then you do love me? 195

NEMOURS.

Oh! I could die methinks this very hour,
But for the luscious hopes of thousand more
And all like these. Yet when I must go out,
Let it be thus, with beauty laughing by me,
Songs, lutes, and canopies, while I sacrifice 200
To thee the last dear ebbing drop of love.
But show me now that face.

MARGUERITE.

No, you dissemble. You say the same thing to every one you meet. I thought once indeed to have fixed my heart upon you. But I'm off again and am 205 resolved you shall never see me.

NEMOURS.

You dally. Come, by all the kindness* past.

MARGUERITE.

Swear then.

NEMOURS.

What?

MARGUERITE.

Never to touch your dear domestic she, 210
That lives in shades to all the world but me.
Do you guess I know you now?

NEMOURS.

I do, and swear. But are these equal terms: that you shall never touch a man but me?

MARGUERITE.

I will. But how can you convince me? Oaths with 215 you libertines of honor are to little purpose.

NEMOURS.

But this must satisfy thee. There is more pleasure in thee after enjoyment than in her and all womankind before it. Thou hast inspiration, ecstasy, and transport, all these bewitching joys that 220 make men mad.

MARGUERITE. (*Unmasking.*)

And thou villain, treachery, perjury, all those monstrous, diabolical arts that seduce young virgins from their innocent homes to set 'em on the highway to hell and damnation. 225

NEMOURS.

Ha! Ha! My Marguerite, is't possible?

MARGUERITE.

Call me not yours nor think of me again.
I am convinced you're traitors all alike
And from this hour renounce you—

Not but I'll be revenged,   230
Yes, I will try the joys of life like you,
But not with men of quality,* you devils of honor.
No, I will satisfy
My pride, disdain, rage, and revenge more safely,
By all the powers of heaven and earth I will.   235
I'll change my loving, lying, tinsel lord
For an obedient, wholesome, drudging fool.

NEMOURS.
Why, this will make the matter easy to both:
Take you your ramble, madam, and I'll take mine.
But is't possible for one of your nice* taste   240
To bed a fool?

MARGUERITE.
                    To choose, to choose, my lord.
A fool! Now by my will and pride of heart,
There's freedom, fancy, and creation in't:
He truckles to the frown and cries, "Forgive me,"   245
Besides the molding of him without blushing.
And what would woman more? Now view the other,
Your man of sense, that vaunts despotic pow'r,
That reels precisely home at break of day,
Thunders the house, brains half the family,*   250
Cries, "Where's my whore? What, will she stew
    till doomsday?"
When she appears and kindly goes to help him,
Roars out, "A shop, a walking shop of scents,
Flavors of physic and the clammy bath,
The stench of orange flowers, the devil pulvillio:*   255
These, these," he cries, "are the blest husband's
    joys!"

NEMOURS.
I swear, most natural and unaffected. Ha, ha!

MARGUERITE.
But if he chance to use her civilly,
Take heed, there's covert malice in his smiles.
Millions to one the villain has been whoring   260
And comes to try experiments on her,
Besides a thousand underplots and crosses.
Prescribing silence still* where'er he comes,
"No chat," he cries, "of colors, points, or
    fashions."

NEMOURS.
Preach on, divine. Ha, ha!   265

MARGUERITE.
"Let me not hear you ask my sickly lady,

whether she found obstructions at the waters."[60]

NEMOURS.
Fie, that's obscene.

MARGUERITE.
Thus damns the affectation of our prattle
And swears he'll gag the clack, or what is worse—   270

NEMOURS.
Nay, hold!

MARGUERITE.
Send for the newfound lock.[61]

NEMOURS.
What, mad?

MARGUERITE.
Do, villain, traitor—
Contrive this mischief, if thou canst, for me.   275
Send thou the padlock, but I'll find the key. (*Exit.*)

NEMOURS.
Where goes the partridge on the purring wing?
Yet when I see my time, I must recall her. For she
has admirable things in her, such as, if I gain not
the Princess of Clèves, may[n] fix me to her, without   280
nauseating the vice of constancy.

Enter Bellamore.

Hah! Bellamore! What news, my dear, hah? Hast
thou found her? Speak!

BELLAMORE.
I have.

NEMOURS.
Where, how, when, and by what means?   285

BELLAMORE.
After I had inquired after the Prince's health, I
asked a woman of his lady, who told me she was
retired into the great bower in the garden.

NEMOURS.
The very place where first I saw and loved her,
When after I had saved the Prince's life,   290
He brought me late one ev'ning to the view.
There love and friendship first began.
My love remains and friendship, as
Much as man can have for his cuckold.

_____

60 obstructions of the waters] difficulty urinating
61 newfound lock] possibly to seal an iron mask or even a
    chastity belt of the latest design

Nay, I know not that man upon earth I love so 295
well or could take so much from as this hopeful
Prince of Clèves. Didst thou see her in the garden?
BELLAMORE.

My lord, I did, where she appeared like her that gave
Actaeon horns, with all her nymphs about her, busy
in tying knots which she took from baskets of 300
ribbons that they brought her. And methought she
tied and untied 'em so prettily, as if she had been at
cross-questions or knew not what she did. Her face,
her neck, and arms quite bare—
NEMOURS.

No more. If I live, I'll see her tonight, for the 305
heroic vein comes upon me. Death and the devil,
what shall become of the backstair lady then? Hark
thee, Bellamore: Take this key, dost thou hear,
rogue? Go to Saint-André's house, through the
garden up the backstairs, push open the door, and 310
be blest. Hell! Can't I be in two places at once?
Hark thee, give her this ____* and this ____* and
this ____,* and when thou bitest her with a
parting blow, sigh out "Nemours."
BELLAMORE.

I'll do't. 315

Enter the Prince of Clèves.

NEMOURS.

Go to Tournon for the rest. She'll instruct thee in
the management. Away!

Exit Bellamore.

Hah! He comes up but slowly, yet he sees me.
Perhaps he's jealous. Why then I'm jealous too.
Hypocrisy and softness, with all the arts of woman, 320
tip my tongue.
PRINCE OF CLÈVES.

I come, my lord, to ask you if you love me.
NEMOURS.

Love thee, my Clèves! By Heav'n, ere yet I saw thee
Thus were my prayers still* offer'd to the Fates,
If I must choose a friend, grant me, ye Powers, 325
The man I love may seize my heart at once.
Guide him the perfect temper of yourselves,
With every manly grace and shining virtue.
Add yet the bloom of beauty to his youth,
That I may make a mistress of him too— 330

PRINCE OF CLÈVES.

Oh Heav'n!
NEMOURS.

That at first view our souls may kindle
And like two tapers, kindly mix their beams.
I knelt and prayed and wept for such a blessing,
And they returned me more than I could ask, 335
All that was good or great or just in thee.
PRINCE OF CLÈVES.

You say you love me. I must make the proof,
For you have brought it to a doubt.*
NEMOURS.

In what?
PRINCE OF CLÈVES.

In this: you have not giv'n me all your heart. 340
You muse of late. Ev'n on my bridal day
I saw you sit with a too thoughtful brow.
You sighed and hung your head upon your hand.
Nay, in the midst of laughter,
You started, blushed, and cried 'twas wondrous 345
well,
And yet you knew not what. Speak like a friend.
What is the cause, my lord?
NEMOURS.

Shall I deal plainly with you? I'm not well.
PRINCE OF CLÈVES.

I do believe it.
How happ'ned the distemper? 350
NEMOURS.

It is too deep to search,
Nor can I tell you.
PRINCE OF CLÈVES.

Then you're no friend.
Should Clèves thus answer to Nemours, "I cannot"?
Say rather that you will not trust a man 355
You do not love.
NEMOURS.

By Heav'n I do.
PRINCE OF CLÈVES.

By Heav'n you do? Yet 'tis too deep to search
For such a shallow friend.
NEMOURS.

Of all mankind 360
You ought not—
PRINCE OF CLÈVES.

Nay, the rest.

NEMOURS.

                          It is not fit.
Be satisfied. I'll bear it to my grave   365
Whate'er it be.
PRINCE OF CLÈVES.

              You are in love, my lord,
And if you do not swear— But where's the need?
You start, you change, you are another man.
You blush, you're all constraint, you turn away.   370
NEMOURS.

Why take it then. 'Tis true, I am in love,
In torture, racks, in all the hells of love,
Of hopeless, restless, and eternal love.
PRINCE OF CLÈVES.

Her name, my lord?
NEMOURS.

                  Her name, my lord, to you?   375
PRINCE OF CLÈVES.

To me? Confusion, plagues, and death upon me!
Why not to me? And wherefore did you say,
Of all mankind I ought not? There you stopped,
But would have said, "to pry into this business."
Yet speak to ease the troubles of my soul.   380
By all our friendship, by the life thou gav'st me,
I do conjure thee: thunder in my ears.
'Tis Chartres that thou lov'st, Chartres, my wife.
NEMOURS.

Your wife, my lord?
PRINCE OF CLÈVES.

My wife, my lord, and I must have you own it.   385
NEMOURS.

I will not tell you, sir, who 'tis I love,
Yet think me not so base, were it your wife,
That all the subtlest wit of earth or hell
Should make me vent a secret of that nature
To any man on earth, much less to you.   390
PRINCE OF CLÈVES.

Yet you could basely tell it to the Vidame,
And he to all the Court. But I waste time.
By all the boiling venom of my passion,
I'll make you own it ere we part. Dispatch!
Say thou hast whored my wife! Damnation on   395
  me!
Pronounce me cuckold!
NEMOURS.

But then I give myself the lie,

Who told you just before, I would not speak,
Though I had done it—which I swear I have not.
Beside, I fear you are going mad.   400
PRINCE OF CLÈVES.

Draw then and make it up,
For if thou dost not own what I demand,
What you both know and have complotted on
  me,
Though neither will confess, I swear again,
That one of us must fall.   405
NEMOURS.

                      Then take my life.
PRINCE OF CLÈVES.

I will, by Heav'n, if thou refuse me justice.
Draw then, for if thou dost not, I will kill thee
And tell my wife thou basely didst confess
Thy guilt at last in hopes to save thy life.   410
NEMOURS.

That is a blast indeed that honor shrinks at.
Therefore I draw—-but oh, be witness, Heav'n,
With such a trembling hand and bleeding heart,
As if I were to fight against my father.
Therefore I beg thee by the name of friend,   415
Which once with half this suit would have
  dissolved thee,
I beg thee, gentle Clèves, to hold thy hand.
PRINCE OF CLÈVES.

I'm deaf as Death, that calls for one or both.

[They fight.] Clèves is disarmed. Nemours gives him his
sword again.

NEMOURS.

Then give it me, I arm thy hand again
Against my heart, against this heart that loves thee. 420
Thrust then, for by the blood that bears my life,
Thou shalt not know the name of her I love—
Not but I swear upon the point of death,
Your wife's as clear from me as Heav'n first made her.
PRINCE OF CLÈVES.

No more my lord, you've giv'n me twice my life.   425
NEMOURS.

Are you not hurt?
PRINCE OF CLÈVES.

                  Alas, 'tis not so well.
I have no wound but that which honor makes,
And yet there's something cold upon my heart.

I hope 'tis death, and I shall shortly pay you   430
With Chartres' love, for you deserve her better.

NEMOURS.
No sir, you shall not, you shall live, my lord,
And long enjoy your beauteous, virtuous bride.
You shall, dear prince—why are you then so cold?

PRINCE OF CLÈVES.
I cannot speak—   435
But thus and thus, there's something rises here.

NEMOURS.
I'll wait you home, nay, shake these drops away
And hang upon my arm—

PRINCE OF CLÈVES.
                              I will do anything,
So you will promise never to upbraid me.   440

NEMOURS.
I swear I will not.

PRINCE OF CLÈVES.
                        But will you love me too
As formerly?

NEMOURS.
                  I swear far more than ever.

PRINCE OF CLÈVES.
Thou know'st my nature soft. Yet oh, such love,   445
Such love as mine, and injured as I thought,
Would spleen the gall-less turtle,* would it not?

NEMOURS.
It would, by Heav'n. (*Weeping.*) You make a
    woman of me.

PRINCE OF CLÈVES.
Why, anything thou say'st to humor me,
Yet it is kind, and I must love these tears.   450
I hope my heart will break, and then we're ev'n.
Yet if this cruel love thy Clèves should kill,
Remember after death thou lov'st me still.

Exeunt.

Scene ii. [The palace of Saint-André.]

Tournon with the Vidame.

TOURNON.
So. Let that corner be your post, and as soon as
ever you see Saint-André come stalking in his
dream, slip to his lady, and when you have agreed
upon the writings, I'll be ready to bring you off
with a witness.   5

VIDAME.
Thou dear, obliging—

TOURNON.
No more o'that. Away!

[The Vidame hides himself.]

Mark but how easily those that are gifted with
discretion bring things about. In the name of
goodness, let men and women have their risks but   10
still* be careful of the main.* Here's a hot-headed
lord goes mad for a prating girl, treats her, presents
her, flames for her, dies for her, till the fool
complies for pure love and, when the business fails,
is forced to live at last by the love of his footmen.   15
But she that makes a firm bargain is commonly
thought a great soul, for my lord having considered
on't, thinks her a person of depth, and so resolves
to have it out of her. But why do I talk so myself,
when there's something to do? Certainly I should   20
have made a rare speaker in a parliament of
women, or a notable head to a female jury when
his lordship[62] gravely puts the question whither it
be *Satis* or *Non Satis* or *Nunquam Satis*, and we
bring it in *Ignoramus*.[63]—Hah, but who comes   25
here? I must attend for Bellamore. [*Exit.*]

Enter Poltrot [followed by] Celia over-hearing.

POLTROT.
My wife and I went to bed together, and I'll
warrant full she was of expectation, so white and
clean and much inclined to laugh, and lay at her
full length, as who would say, "Come eat me!"   30

CELIA. [*Aside.*]
Said she so, sweet sir?

POLTROT.
Not a bit, by the lord! Not I, not I.

CELIA. [*Aside.*]
Alas! Nice* gentleman!

---

62 lordship] The judge.
63 *Satis* or *Non Satis* or *Nunquam Satis*, and we bring it in
    Ignoramus] A grand jury may return a verdict of "suffi-
    cient" for a prosecution, "not sufficient," "not at all suf-
    ficient," or "We take no notice of it" (literally, "We do
    not know").

POLTROT.

A farmer would say this was barbarously done, because he loves beef, but I have plover[64] in reserve.—Hah, Saint-André! Hark, I hear him bustle. Oh Lord! How my heart goes pit-a-pat! Nay, I dreamt last night I was gelt.[65] 35

Enter Saint-André in his sleep.

'Tis he, 'tis he. By the twilight I see him.

The Vidame goes in [to the bedroom unseen by Poltrot].

Aye, now the politic head goes. It shall be branched by and by. What was that stop for? There's neither gate nor stile in your way. Now, by that sudden stretch, he seems as if he would take a jump or practice on the high rope. Oh your humble servant, sir. I'll but do a little business for you and be with you again. Nay, look you sir, I have as many bobs as Democritus when he cried, "Poor Jack." There's more pride in a Puritan's band, short hair, and cap pinched, than under a king's crown. Poor Jack! Citizens, citizens, look to your wives-the courtiers come. Look to 'em, they'll do 'em. Look to 'em, they'll do 'em. Poor Jack! [*Exit.*] 40 45 50

SAINT-ANDRE.

Ha! Ha! You'll tickle me to death. Nay, prithee, Pen,[66] your mistress will hear us. Thou art the wantonest rogue— 55

Enter Tournon with Bellamore.

TOURNON.

Madam.

CELIA.

Here's.

TOURNON.

Here's a thief I took in your chamber.

BELLAMORE.

Ah madam, retire for a moment, and I'll make you the whole confession. 60

CELIA.

Confess, and you know what follows.[67] However, I am resolved to hear what you can say for yourself.

Exeunt [Bellamore and Celia, Tournon severally].

SAINT-ANDRE.

"Nay pish, nay fie, sweetheart—
But I'll kiss you if I can." 65

"I did not take you for to be
Such a kind of a man.
But I'll go call my mother as loud as I can cry,
Why mother, mother, mother! Out upon you!
Fie!"[68]

Reenter Poltrot.

POLTROT.

Oh Lord! Oh Lord! I had like to have trod upon a serpent that would have bit me to death. I went to take up the clothes as gently as I could for my life, when a great, huge, hoarse voice flew in my face, with "Damme, you son of a whore, I'll cut your throat!" You may guess I withdrew, for, o'my conscience, the fright had almost made me unclean. But I'll to my own spouse, and if the Lord be pleased to bring me off safe this bout, I'll never, never go a-cuckold-making again while my eyes are open. (*Exit.*) 70 75 80

SAINT-ANDRE.

Hark, my wife's coming up stairs. Help up with my breeches. So, so smooth the bed. What damned luck's this! So, fall a-rubbing the room again.—Hark you, wife, Celia has been upon the hunt for you all this day. She's below in the garden. Go, go! We'll kiss when you come back.—Now sirrah, now you rogue, she's gone. Come, come, lose not your opportunity. I'll keep on my breeches for fear. Aye? no, no, not upon the bed——pish— against the back of this chair. Won't it? How can you tell? Try. I'll buy thee a new gown and a fan and a laced petticoat and pay thee double wages. Oh! Thou dear, pretty, soft, sweet, wriggling, rogue! What, wouldst thou dodge me? Gad but I'll 85 90

---

64 plover] a game fowl, noted for its delicious eggs; also, courtesan
65 gelt] gelded
66 Pen] probably his wife Elianor's maid

67 Confess ... follows] proverbially, "Confess and be hanged."
68 Nay pish ...fie!] Saint-André dreams a song in dialogue.

have thee—gad but I'll catch thee. Aye, and have 95
at thee again and again. (*Exit.*)

Reenter Poltrot.

POLTROT.
Was ever man of honor thus unfortunately met
with? I went into my chamber and trod as softly
as a half-starved mouse for fear of waking my cat,
when coming close to my bedside, methought it 100
rocked to and fro like a great cradle and the clothes
heaved as if some beast lay blowing there. But the
beast was by the bedside it seems! Yes, I am, and
who can help it, as very* a cornuto as e'er was
grafted. I heard my beloved wife too—the plagues 105
of Egypt[69] on her!—speak so lovingly and angrily
together: "Nay prithee, my dear, nay now you are
tiresome—I shall be ashamed to look you in the
face again!" Why, how will she look upon me then?
Oh Lord—Oh Lord—what shall I do? Shall I 110
stand thus like a cuckoldly son of a whore, with
my horns* in my pocket and not be revenged?

Enter Saint-André.

But here comes as very* a cuckold as myself. I am
resolved to wake him, and we'll fall upon 'em
together. Halloo, Saint-André! Saint-André! 115
SAINT-ANDRÉ.
Ti—ti 'ti 'tis im-im-im-possible I-I-I should be the
man, fo-fo—for I cannot speak a plain word.
POLTROT.
You're a cuckold, a cuckold, a cuckold!
SAINT-ANDRÉ.
Why lo-lo-look you, I said it co-co-could not be
me, for sir, I, all the world knows, I am no cu-cu- 120
cu-ckold.
POLTROT.
Wake, wake, I say, or I'll shake the bones out of
your body! Your horns are a-growing, your bed is
a-going, your heifer's a-plowing.
SAINT-ANDRÉ.
Why, let her plo-plo-plow on. If the se-se-seed be 125
well sown, we shall have a good cro-crop—

POLTROT.
Worse and worse. Why then I will roar out directly
and raise the neighbors: Help! Ho, help! Murder!
Murder! Fire! Fire! Fire! Cuckoldom! Cuckoldom!
Thieves! Murder! Rapes! Cuckoldom! 130

*Enter the Vidame and Bellamore. The Vidam comes up
to Poltrot, shoots off a pistol. Saint-André and Poltrot
fall down together. Tournon enters with [Elianor and
Ceila]. Tournon leads off the Vidame and Bellamore.*

CELIA.
Thieves, thieves! Ho! Jacques! Pedro! Thomas!

Enter servants.

ELIANOR.
Thieves! Thieves! Wake, wake, my lord!
SAINT-ANDRÉ. (*Waking.*)
Why, what a devil's the matter? Where am I?
ELIANOR.
Oh! you'll never leave this ill habit of walking in
your sleep. 'Tis a mercy we had not all been 135
murdered! You went down in your shirt, sir,
opened the door, and let in rogues that had like
to have cut all our throats. But for the future I am
resolved to tie you to me with the bed cord rather
than endure this. 140
SAINT-ANDRÉ.
Where's Poltrot?
CELIA.
Murdered sir! Here, here, here! One of the villains
discharged a pistol just in his belly.
SAINT-ANDRÉ.
Shot in the guts! Lord bless us!—Here Thomas, a
light! light! light!—Shot in the guts say you? 145
POLTROT.
Oh! oh—lower, lower, lower! Feel, feel, search me,
lower, lower!
SAINT-ANDRÉ.
Cold hereabouts! Let's bear him to his bed and
send for a surgeon.
POLTROT.
Softly, softly, softly! Come not near me crocodile.[70] 150
Oh! oh!

---

69 The plagues of Egypt] *Exodus*, 7-12, tells of the plagues
    visited upon the Egyptians.

---

70 crocodile] hypocrite, as in "crocodile tears" (q.v.)

SAINT-ANDRÉ.

Unhappy chance! Nowhere but just in the guts?

POLTROT.

Yes, yes, yes—in the head too. In the head, man,
in the head. Nay, and let me tell you, you had best
search your own. But bear me off or I shall swoon. 155
I feel something trickle, trickle in my breeches. Oh,
oh, oh!

Exeunt.

Scene iii. [The Prince of Clèves's palace.]

Enter Nemours, Pedro listening.

NEMOURS.

Alas! Poor prince. I protest, the violence of his
passion has cast him in a fever. He dies of it. And
how then? Shall I marry the Princess of Clèves or
stick to Marguerite as we are? For 'tis most certain
she has rare things in her, which I found by my 5
last experiment, and I love her more than ever,
almost to jealousy. Besides, Tournon tells me the
Dauphin begins to buzz about her again, and who
knows but in this heat of hers, as she says, she will
hang herself out to sale. But he may nick the time 10
and buy her. I like not that. No, I'll throw boldly,
clear the table if I can. If not, 'tis but at last
forswearing play, shake off my new acquaintance,
and be easy with my reserve. Hark, I am just upon
the bower. Music! 15

PEDRO. [*Aside.*]

I have hitherto obeyed my master's order, but I'm
resolved to dog him till he's lodged.

NEMOURS.

Now do I know the precise will call me damned
rogue for wronging my friend, especially such a
soft sweet-natured friend as this gentle prince. 20
Verily, I say they lie in their throats. Were the
gravest of 'em in my condition and thought it
should never be known, they would rouse up the
spirit, cast the dapper[71] cloak, leave off their
humming and hawing, and fall to like a man of 25
honor. (*Exit.*)

---

71 dapper] neat and trim

PEDRO.

I'll face him till he enters the bower and then call
my lord.

Exit.

Scene [iv. Draws to reveal] the Bower. Lights.

*[The Princess of Clèves and Irene discovered. *]*

Song.

Lovely Selina, innocent and free
From all the dangerous arts of love,
Thus in a melancholy grove
Enjoyed the sweetness of her privacy,
Till th'envious gods, designing to undo her, 5
Dispatched the swain, not unlike them, to woo her.
It was not long ere the design did take.
A gentle youth, born to persuade,
Deceived the too, too easy maid.
Her scrip and garlands soon she did forsake 10
And rashly told the secrets of her heart,
Which the fond* man would ever more impart:
"False Florimel, joy of my heart," said she,
"'Tis hard to love and love in vain,
To love and not be loved again. 15
And why should love and prudence disagree?
Pity ye Powers that sit at ease above,
If e'er you knew what 'tis to be in love."

PRINCESS OF CLÈVES.

Alas Irene, I do believe Nemours
The man thou represents him. Yet, oh Heav'n, 20
And oh my heart, in spite of my resolves,
Spite of those matchless virtues of my husband,
I love the man my reason bids me hate.
Yet grant me some few hours, ye saints, to live,
That I may try what innocence so armed 25
As mine with vows can do in such a cause!
The war's begun, the war of love and virtue,
And I am fixed to conquer or to die.

IRENE.

Your fate is hard, and since you honored me
With the important secret of your life, 30
I've labored for the remedy of love.

PRINCESS OF CLÈVES.

I must to death own thee my better angel.
Thou know'st the strugglings of my wounded soul,
Hast seen me strive against this lawless passion,

Till I have lain like slaves upon the rack, 35
My veins half burst, my weary eyeballs fixed,
My brows all covered with big drops of sweat,
Which strangling grief wrung from my tortured
    brain.

IRENE.

Alas, I weep to see you thus again.

PRINCESS OF CLÈVES.

Thou hast heard me curse the hour when first I saw 40
The fatal, charming face of loved Nemours,
Hast heard the deathbed counsel of my mother.
Yet what can this avail, spite of my soul,
The nightly warnings from her dreadful shroud?
I love Nemours, I languish for Nemours, 45
And when I think to banish him my breast,
My heart rebels, I feel a gorging pain
That chokes me up, tremblings from head to foot—
A shog of blood and spirits, madmen's fears,
Convulsions, gnawing griefs, and angry tears. 50

Enter Nemours.

Hah, but behold!—My lord!

NEMOURS.

               Oh! pardon me,
Spare me a minute's space and I am gone.

PRINCESS OF CLÈVES.

Is this a time, sir?

NEMOURS.

            Oh! I must speak or die. 55

PRINCESS OF CLÈVES.

Die, then, ere thus presume to violate
The honor of your friend, your own and mine.

NEMOURS.

Yet hear me, and I swear by all things sacred
Never to see you more.

PRINCESS OF CLÈVES.

Speak then—and keep your word. 60

[Enter Prince of Clèves above.]

PRINCE OF CLÈVES.

            Horror and death! [*Exit.*]

NEMOURS.

Did you but know what 'tis to love like me,
Without a dawn of bliss to dream all day,
To pass the night in broken sleeps away,
Tossed in the restless tides of hopes and fears, 65

With eyes forever running o'er with tears;
To leave my couch and fly to beds of flowers,
T'invoke the stars, to curse the dragging hours,
To talk like madmen to the groves and bowers.
Could you know this yet blame my tortured love 70
If thus it throws my body at your feet?
Oh! fly not hence.
Vouchsafe but just to view me in despair.
I ask not love but pity from the fair.

PRINCESS OF CLÈVES.

Oh heavens, inspire my heart. 75

NEMOURS.

               The heavenly Powers
Accept the poorest sacrifice we bring.
A slave to them's as welcome as a king.
Behold a slave that glories in your chains.
Ah, with some show of mercy view my pains. 80
Your piercing eyes have made their splendid way
Where lightning could not pass—
Even through my soul their pointed luster goes
And sacred smart upon my spirit throws.
Yet I your wounds with as much zeal desire 85
As sinners that would pass to bliss through fire.
Yes madam, I must love you to my death;
I'll sigh your name with my last gasp of breath.

PRINCESS OF CLÈVES.

No more, I have heard you, sir, as you desired.

Enter the Prince of Clèves [and Pedro unobserved].

Reply not, but withdraw, if possible. 90
Fix to your word, and let us trust our fates.
Be gone, I charge you. Speak not, but retire.

Exit Nemours.

PRINCE OF CLÈVES.

Excellent woman, and, oh! matchless friend!
Love, friendship, honor, poison, daggers, death—
(*Falls.*)

PRINCESS OF CLÈVES.

Oh Heaven! Irene, help! help the Prince my lord. 95
—My dearest Clèves, wake from this dream of death
And hear me speak—

PRINCE OF CLÈVES.

             Curse on my disposition,
That thus permits me bear the wounds of honor!

And oh! thou foolish, gentle, love-sick heart,　　　100
Why didst thou let my hand from stabbing both?

PRINCESS OF CLÈVES.

Behold, 'tis yet, my lord, within your power
To give me death.

PRINCE OF CLÈVES.

　　　　　　　　I do entreat thee, leave me.
I'm bound for death myself, and I would make　　　105
My passage easy, if you would permit me.
All that I ask thee for the heart I gave thee
And for the life I love in thy behalf
Is that thou'dst leave me to myself a while
And this poor, honest friend.　　　　　　　　110

PRINCESS OF CLÈVES.

　　　　　　　　　　I would obey you
But cannot stir. I know, I know, my lord,
You think that I designed to meet Nemours
This night, but by the Powers above I swear—

PRINCE OF CLÈVES.

Oh, do not swear, for, Chartres, credit me,　　　115
There is a Power that can and will revenge.
Therefore, dear soul, for I must love thee still,
If thou wilt speak, confess, repent thy fault,
And thou, perhaps, mayst find a door of mercy.
For me, by all my hopes of heav'n, I swear　　　120
I freely now forgive thee. Oh, my heart!
Pedro, thy arm, let me to bed—

PRINCESS OF CLÈVES.

And do you then refuse my help?

PRINCE OF CLÈVES.

In honor, Chartres, after such a fall,
I ought not to permit that thou shouldst touch　　　125
　me.

PRINCESS OF CLÈVES.

But sir, I will. Your arm? I'll hold you all
Thus in the closest, strictest, dearest clasps.
Nor shall you die believing my dishonor.
I swear I knew not of Nemours his* coming,
Nor had I spoke those words which yet were guiltless　　　130
Had he not vowed never to see me more.
By our first meeting, by our nuptial joys,
By my dead mother's ghost, by your own spirit,
Which, oh I fear, is taking leave forever,
I swear that this is true.　　　　　　　　135

PRINCE OF CLÈVES.

　　　　　　　　I do believe thee.

Thou hast such power, such charms in those dear
　lips,
As might persuade me that I am not dying.
—Off, Pedro.—By my most untimely fate
I swear, I'm reconciled. And hark thee, Chartres,°　　　140
If thou dost marry— hah! I cannot speak.
—Away to bed.—Yet love my memory—

PRINCESS OF CLÈVES.

To bed! And must we part then?

PRINCE OF CLÈVES.

　　　　　　　　　　Oh, we must.
Were I to live, I should not see thee more—　　　145
But since I am dying, by this kiss I beg thee—nay,
I command thee—part. Be gone and leave me.

PRINCESS OF CLÈVES.

I go, and leave this farewell prayer behind me:
For me, if all I've said be not most true,
True as thou think'st me false, all curses on me!　　　150
The whips of conscience and the stings of
　pleasure,
Sores and distempers, disappointments plague me!
May all my life be one continued torment,
And that more racking than a woman's labor.
In meeting death may my least trouble be　　　155
As great as now my parting is with thee.

Exeunt severally.

　　Act V, scene i. [The palace of Saint-André.]

Poltrot and Bellamore.

BELLAMORE.

Come, come, take her into grace again. 'Twas but
a slip.

POLTROT.

Take her into grace again? Why sure you would
have her bring me to that pass she did in England,
when my Lord Harebrain° used to keep me in awe,　　　5
stand biting my lips, twisting my hat, playing with
my thumbs while they were at it, and I durst not
look behind me.

BELLAMORE.

Mere jealousy! You say yourself you saw nothing.

POLTROT.

No sir, I thank you; I had more care of my throat.　　　10
Neither is this the first fault. For once upon a time,
a little while after we were married, at London—a

pox o'that cuckolding Trojan race[72]—she was talking to me one day out of her window more pleasantly than ordinary and acted with her head and body 15
wonderous prettily, butting at me like a little goat,
while I butted at her again. I, being glad to find her
in so good humor, what did I, sir, but stole away and
came softly up the backstairs, thinking to cry boo!
But oh Lord, how was I thunderstruck to find my 20
Lord Harebrain there, all in a sweat, kissing and
smacking, puffing and blowing so hard, you would
have sworn they had been at hot-cockles.*

BELLAMORE.

A little familiar perhaps, things of custom—

POLTROT.

Aye sir, kiss my wife and welcome, but for that zeal 25
in her shogging and butting—*noli me tangere,*[73] I
cry. I am sure it ran so in my imagination; I have
been horn*-mad ever since. Therefore spare your
pains, for I am resolute.

Enter Celia.

BELLAMORE.

See where she comes, my lord. But you are 30
resolved, you say. However, let me advise you: have
a care of making her desperate. (*Exit.*)

POLTROT.

Desperate! Damn her, polluter of my sheets—
damn her!

CELIA.

Seek⁹ not to shun me, for where'er you fly, 35
I'll follow, hang upon thy knees, and die.
Poltrot, behold. Ah, canst thou see me kneel
And yet no bowels of compassion feel?
Why dost thou bluster by me like a storm
And ruffle into frowns that godlike form? 40
Why dost thou turn away those eyes of thine,
In which love's glory and his conquests shine?

POLTROT.

What is this thing called woman? She is worse
Than all ingredients rammed into a curse.
Were she a witch, a bawd, a noseless* whore, 45
I could forgive her, so she were no more.

---

72 Trojan race] According to legend, the Britons were descendants of the Trojans—and therefore of Paris (q.v.).

73 *noli me tangere*] Touch me not (Lat., proverbial)

But she's far worse and will in time forestall
The devil and be the damning of us all.

CELIA.

Yet honor bids you sink with her you call
So foul, whose frailties you too sharply named. 50
Like Adam, you should choose with her to fall,
And in mere* generosity be damned.

POLTROT.

No! By thyself and all alone be cursed,
And by the winds thy venom dust be hurled.
For thou'rt a serpent equal to the first 55
And hast the will to damn another world.

CELIA.

But am I not thy wife? Let that atone.

POLTROT.

My dear, damned wife, I do confess thou art
Flesh of my flesh and bone* too of my bone:
Would mine had all been broke when first thou wert. 60

CELIA.

Why then I'll cringe no longer. Hark you, sir, leave
off your swelling and frowning and awkward
ambling and tell me, in fine, whether you'll be
reconciled or no, for I am resolved to stoop no
longer to an ungrateful person. 65

POLTROT.

To your husband, to your head, to your lord and
master, you will not, Goody Bathsheba?[74] But you
could stoop your swine's flesh, last night you could,
to your rank bravado, that would have struck his
tusks in my guts! He had you with a beck, a snort. 70
Nay, o'my conscience thou wouldst not give him
time to speak, but hunched him on the side like a
full-acorned boar, cried oh! and mounted![75]

CELIA.

Are you resolved, then, never to take me into grace
again for one slip? 75

---

74 Bathsheba] Bathsheba was seduced and impregnated by
   King David, who sent her husband, Uriah the Hittite,
   to certain death in battle and then David married her
   (2 Samuel 11: 2-27).

75 like … mounted] fully fed and thus lustful; an allusion
   to Shakespeare's *Cymbeline,* where Posthumous agonizes
   over his wife's presumed adulterous lover: "Perchance he
   spoke not, but / Like a full-acorned boar, a German one,
   / Cried, Oh! And mounted" (II.v.15-17).

POLTROT.

No, I'm the son of a carted bawd[76] if I do. A slip, do you call it? What, when I heard the bed crack with the violence of my cuckoldom! No, I will ascend the judge of my own cause, proceed to condemnation, and banish thee forever the confines of our benevolence.

CELIA.

What, here, before the Vidame here?[77]

POLTROT.

Yes Impudence, before the Vidame and the Duke Nemours. Nay, to thy eternal confusion, I will post thee in the marketplace.[78] But first I'll find out Saint-André and tell him the whole matter, that he may know too what a ram his blessed ewe has made him, and then—

CELIA.

And then I'll have your throat cut.

POLTROT.

Hah! Tigress! Cut my throat! Why, thou she-bear! Thou dam of lion's whelps, thou cormorant of cormorants! Why what, wilt thou devour me horns* and all?

CELIA.

He that missed your guts in the dark shall take better aim at your gullet by daylight. Nay, to thy terror of heart be it known, thou monster of ill nature, if I would have consented last night to have run his fortune, which is no small one, he would have murdered thee in thy bed. For I heard him speak these very words, "Let him lie *in mortuis— et in limbo patrum,*"[79] where I must have prayed for that unthankful soul, or thou wouldst have been damned to all eternity, dying suddenly and without repentance.

___

76 carted bawd] Prostitutes were brought by cart to be whipped.

77 Vidame here?] Celia is threatening to bring the Vidame back. See below.

78 post … marketplace] I will post a sign publishing the news of your infidelity.

79 *in mortuis—et in limbo patrum*] among the dead in the limbo of the fathers (Lat.); this limbo is the place where the souls of the righteous pagans resided before the coming of Christ. Celia's defensive rhetoric is theologically nonsensical.

POLTROT.

Oh Lord! Oh Lord! *In mortuis—et in limbo patrum.* What, to be tossed on burning pitchforks for my sins? Why, what a bloody-minded son of Belial is this?

CELIA.

In fine, since you will have the truth, he has long had a design upon both our bodies—to ravish mine, and rip open yours.

POLTROT.

Why then he's a cannibal! Lord, Lord, Lord, Lord! Why, what pleasure can it be to any man to rip me open? To ravish thee, indeed there's some sense in that. But there's none in ripping me open. Why, this is such a brutish cruelty!

CELIA.

Rogue, and so I told him. Therefore, when he found that nothing could make me consent to your murder, he swore, and caught me by the hair, if I stirred or made the least noise, he would murder us all, set the house o'fire, and so leave us to ourselves.

POLTROT.

And so thou wert forced to consent? Why then, by this kiss, I swear from my soul, which might have been damned as thou say'st, but for thee, I forgive thee. And what was he that cuckolded Saint-André? Such another Mephistopheles as this too?

CELIA.

Oh my dear, there are not such a pair of fiends upon earth again. Why, they look upon't as a favor to our sex if they ravish a woman, for you must know they were formerly heads of the banditti.

POLTROT.

Well, and I must praise thy discretion in sacrificing thy body. For o'my conscience, if they had seen this smock-face of mine, I had gone to pot[80] too before my execution.

CELIA.

They sent their pages this morning to know whether it was our pleasure to have your throats cut. But we answered 'em all was well and desired 'em, as ever they hoped to see us again, to stir no further in the matter.

___

80 gone to pot] cut in pieces

POLTROT.

Mum, mum. Dear, sweet soul, secure my life and thou shalt command me for the future with as full a swinge as thou canst desire. Only like those that use that exercise, let it be too and fro, sometimes at home and sometimes abroad, and we'll be as merry as the day is long. 145

CELIA.

Be thou but true to me, and like the Indian wives, I'll not outlive thee.[81]

POLTROT.

And I'll swear now, that was kindly said, as I hope for mercy. But it makes me weep. What, burn for me! And shall I not return? I will, I will, I will return when thou dost burn. 150

Enter Saint-André and Elianor.

Nay, when thy body in the fire appears,
My ghost shall rise and quench it with his tears.

SAINT-ANDRÉ.

All flesh is grass,[82] that's certain. We're all mortal; the Court's in mourning for the Prince of Clèves. The Vidame of Chartres is extremely grieved. Hark you, Poltrot, sure as I am alive he died of jealousy.—Well Nell, for this last care of thine, I swear to be constant to thy sheets, and as thou say'st, I think it will not be amiss to tie me to thee now and then for fear of the worst.—Hah, Poltrot— 155 160

POLTROT.

Hah, Bully, I heard your kind expressions to your Nell, and I'll swear I'll vie thee with who shall love most, for I'll swear these daily examples make my hair stand on end. Cut my throat and rip me open! He shall cuckold me all over first, like the man in the almanac,[83] nay, he shall ravish her while I hold the door to my own deflowering. 165 170

Exeunt.

---

81 Indian … thee] will commit suttee (q.v.)
82 All flesh is grass] 1 Peter 1: 24, slightly misquoted
83 man in the almanac] anatomized figure on the cover of almanacs

Scene ii. [The palace of Nemours.]

Tournon and Nemours.

NEMOURS.

Resolved never to see me more and give up her honor to the Dauphin, that puling, sniveling prince, that looks as if he sucked still or were always in a milk diet for the sins of his Florentine mother.

TOURNON.

Bless me! You are jealous. 5

NEMOURS.

I confess it. The last time I had her in disguise, she made such discoveries* as I shall never forget. Lose her I must not. No, I'll lose a limb first. Therefore go tell her—tell her the Prince of Clèves' death has wrought my conversion: I grow weary of my wild courses, repent of my sins, am resolved to leave off whoring and marry his wife. 10

TOURNON.

So the town talks indeed.

NEMOURS.

The town is as it always was and will be: a talk, a hum, a buzz, and a great lie. Do as I bid thee, and tell her, just as you left me, I was going to make my court to the Princess upon her husband's tomb, which is true too—I mean, a visit by the way of consolation. Not but I knew it the only opportunity to catch a woman in the undress of her soul. Nay, I would choose such a time for my life, and 'tis like the rest of those starts and one of the secrets of their nature. Why they melt. Nay, in plagues, fire, famine, war, or any great calamity—mark it—let a man stand but right before 'em, and like hunted hares they run into his lap. 15 20 25

TOURNON.

But who's the instrument to bring you to her?

NEMOURS.

Her uncle, the Vidame. She lies at his house immured in a dark room, with her husband's image in her view, and so resolves, he says, for death. However, I'll sound her in the ebb of her soul. If my boat run aground, 'tis but calling for Marguerite, and she'll weep a tide that shall set me afloat again—as thus: I'll lay the Dauphin in her dish, nose her in the tiptoe of her pride, railing, 30 35 lying, laming, hanging, drowning, dying, and she comes about again. (*Exit.*)

TOURNON.

Go thy ways, Petronius.[84] Nay, if he were dying too, with his veins cut, he would call for wine, fiddles, and whores and laugh himself into the other world. 40

Enter La March.

Where's Marguerite?

LA MARCH.

She follows like a wind, with swollen cheeks, ruffled hair, and glaring eyes. The Princess of Clèves has found her Fury, nor will she yet believe it. 45

Exeunt.

Scene iii. [The Vidame's house.]

Princess of Clèves, Irene in mourning. Song, as the Princess kneels at the state.[85]

I.

Weep, all ye nymphs, your floods unbind,
    For Strephon's now no more.
Your tresses spread before the wind
    And leave the hated shore.
See, see, upon the craggy rocks 5
    Each goddess stripped appears.
They beat their breasts and rend their locks
    And swell the sea with tears.

II.

The God of Love that fatal hour
    When this poor youth was born 10
Had sworn by Styx, to show his power,
    He'd kill a man ere morn.
For Strephon's breast he armed his dart
    And watched him as he came.
He cried, and shot him through the heart, 15
    "Thy blood shall quench my flame."

III.

On Stella's lap he laid his head
    And, looking in her eyes,
He cried, "Remember when I'm dead,
    That I deserve the prize." 20
Then down his tears like rivers ran;
    He sighed, "You love, 'tis true.
You love perhaps a better man,
    But ah, he loves not you."
        Chorus.
Why should all things bow to Love, 25
Men below and gods above?
Why should all things bow to Love?
Death and Fate more awful* move,
Death below and Fate above,
Death below and Fate above. 30
Mortals, mortals, try your skill,
Seeking good or shunning ill.
Fate will be the burden still,*
Will be the burden still,
Fate will be the burden still, 35
Fate will be the burden still.

PRINCESS OF CLÈVES.

Dead thou dear lord—yet from thy throne of bliss,
If any thing on earth be worth thy view,
Look down and hear me, hear my sighs and vows,
Till Death has made me cold and wax like thee. 40
Water shall be my drink and herbs my food,
The marble of my chapel be my bed,
The altar's steps my pillows, while all night
Stretched out, I groaning lie upon the floor,
Beat my swoll'n breasts, and thy dear loss deplore. 45

IRENE.

Ah Madam, what a life have you proposed!

PRINCESS OF CLÈVES.

Too little all for an offence like mine.
Yet death will shortly purge my dross away,
For oh Irene, where's the joy? I find it here.
Yes, I shall die without those violent means 50
That might have hazarded my soul. Oh Heaven,
Oh thou that seest my heart and know'st my terrors,
Wilt thou forgive those crimes I could not help
And would not hide?

IRENE.

        Doubt not but your account 55

---

84 Petronius] Roman sensualist, author of the *Satyricon*, who committed suicide by opening his veins while chatting with friends on amusing subjects, listening to music, and feasting.

85 state] The prince of Clèves's body lies in state.

Shall stand as fair in His eternal book
As any saints' above.
PRINCESS OF CLÈVES.
          Take, take me then
From this bad world. Quench these rebellious
    thoughts.
For oh, I have a pang, a longing wish   60
To see the luckless face of loved Nemours,
To gaze a while and take one last farewell,
Like one that is to lose a limb. 'Tis gone.
It was corrupt, a gangrene to my honor.
Yet I methinks would view the bleeding part, 65
Shudder a little, weep, and grudge at parting.
But by the soul of my triumphant saint,
I swear this longing is without a guilt,
Nor shall it ever be by my appointment.

Enter Nemours, [unobserved].

IRENE.
But if he should attempt this cruel visit,   70
How would your heart receive him?
PRINCESS OF CLÈVES.
                With such temper,
So clear and calm in height of my misfortune,
As thou thyself perhaps wouldst wonder at.
IRENE.
Hah! But he's here—   75
PRINCESS OF CLÈVES.
            Is't possible, my lord?
Has then my uncle thus betrayed my honor?
NEMOURS.
Start not, nor wonder, madam, but forgive
The Vidame, who has thus entrapped your virtue
To end a ling'ring wretch that dies for love.   80
PRINCESS OF CLÈVES.
For love, my lord? Is this a time for love,
In tears and blacks, the livery of death?
But what's your hope, if I should stay to hear you?
Ah, what can you expect from rigorous virtue,
From chastity as cold as Clèves himself,   85
You that are made, my lord, for other pleasures?
NEMOURS.
Is this then the reward of all my passion?
As if there could be any happiness
For this disconsolate, despairing wretch
But in your love alone?   90

PRINCESS OF CLÈVES.
             You're pleased, my lord,
That I should entertain you, and I will,
Before this dear remembrancer of Clèves;
We'll talk of murdered love, and you shall hear,
From this abandoned part of him that was,   95
How much you have been loved.
NEMOURS.
              Hah! Madam—
PRINCESS OF CLÈVES.
                  Yes,
Sighing I speak it, sir: you have inspired me
With something which I never felt before,   100
That pleased and pained the quick'nings of first
    Love,
Nor feared him then, when with his infant beams,
He dawned upon my chill and senseless blood.
But oh, when he had reached his fierce meridian,
How different was his form! That angel face,   105
With his short rays, shot to a glaring god.
I grew inflamed, burnt inward, and the breath
Of the grown tyrant parched my heart to ashes.
Nor need I blush to make you this confession,
Because, my lord, 'tis done without a crime.   110
NEMOURS.
Because for this most blest discovery,*
I am resolved to kneel an age before you.
PRINCESS OF CLÈVES.
Rise, I conjure you, rise. I've told you nothing
But what you knew, my lord, too well before;
Not but I always vowed to keep those rules   115
My duty should prescribe.
NEMOURS.
              Strike me not dead
With duty's name. By Heav'n, I swear you're free
As air, as waters, winds, or open wilds.
There is no form of obligation now.   120
Nay, let me say, for duty—oh forgive me—
'Tis utmost duty now to keep that love
You have confessed for me.
PRINCESS OF CLÈVES.
             'Tis duty's charge,
The voice of honor, and the cry of love,   125
That I should fly from Paris as a pest,[86]

---

[86] pest] plague

That I should wear these rags of life away
In sunless caves, in dungeons of despair,
Where I should never think of man again—
But more particularly that of you,   130
For reasons yet unknown.
NEMOURS.
                          Unknown they are,
And would to Heav'n they might be ever so,
Since 'tis impossible they should be just.
Nay madam, let me say, the ghost of Clèves—   135
PRINCESS OF CLÈVES.
Ah sir, how dare you mention that dear name
That drains my eyes and cries to Heav'n for
    blood?
Name it no more without the consequence.
For 'tis but too, too true, you were the cause
Of Clèves untimely death, I swear I think,   140
No less than if you had stabbed him through the
    heart.
NEMOURS.
Oh cruel princess! But why should I answer
When thus you raise the shadow of a reason
To ruin me forever? Is it a fault
To love? Then blame not me—no, madam, no—   145
But blame yourself, who told it to your husband.
But oh, you would not argue thus against me
If ever you had loved—
You have deceived yourself and flattered me.
Why am I thrown else from the glorious height,   150
Snatched in a moment from my blissful state,
And hurled like lightning by the hand of Fate?
PRINCESS OF CLÈVES.
Be satisfied, my lord, you are not flattered.
I have such love for you that duty's bar
Would prove too weak to hinder our engagement.   155
But there is more.
NEMOURS.
                More fancy, more chimera!
But let it come. I'll stand the stalking nothing,
And when the bladdered air would turn the balance,
I'll cast in love substantial, pond'rous love,   160
Eternal love, and hurl him to the beam.
But speak, and if a hell of separation
Must part my soul and body, do not rack me,
But let the poison steal into my veins
And damn me mildly, madam, as you can.   165

PRINCESS OF CLÈVES.
Hear then, my bosom thought. 'Tis the last time
I e'er shall see you, and 'tis a poor reward
For such a love. Yet sir, 'tis all I have,
And you must ask no more.
NEMOURS.
                        Be witness, Heav'n,   170
Of my obedience. I will ask her nothing.
PRINCESS OF CLÈVES.
Know then, my lord, you're free, and I am so,
Free for^r the eternal bond of marriage.
My heart too is inclined by love like yours,
Nor can I fear the censuring world should blame   175
    us.
But now, my lord, what power on earth can give
Security that bond shall prove eternal?
NEMOURS.
Hah! Madam—
PRINCESS OF CLÈVES.
               Silence, silence I command you.
No, no, Nemours, I know the world too well.   180
You have a sense too nice* for long enjoyment.
Clèves was the man that only could love long.
Nor can I think his passion would have lasted
But that he found I could have none for him.
'Tis obstacle, ascent, and lets and bars   185
That whet the appetite of love and glory.
These are the fuel for that fiery passion.
But when the flashy stubble we remove,
The god goes out, and there's an end of love.
NEMOURS.
Ah madam, I'm not able to contain   190
But must perforce break your commands to
    answer.
Once to be yours is to be forever yours,
Yours only, without thought of other women.
PRINCESS OF CLÈVES.
Why, this sounds well and natural till you're cloyed,
But oh, when one^s satiety has palled you,   195
You sicken at each view, and every glance
Betrays your guilty soul and says you loathe her.
I know it, sir, you have the well-bred cast
Of gallantry and parts* to gain success.
And do but think, when various forms have   200
    charmed you,
How I should bear the cross returns of love?

NEMOURS.

Ah madam, now I find you're prejudiced
To blast my hopes.

PRINCESS OF CLÈVES.

'Tis reason, all calm reason.
Nature affirms no violent thing can last.   205
I know't, I see't, ev'ry new face that came
Would charm you from me. Hah, and could I liveᵗ
To see that fatal day and see you scorn me,
To hear the ghost of Clèves each hour upbraid me?
No, 'tis impossible, with all my passion,   210
Not to submit to these almighty reasons.
For this I brave your noblest qualities.
I'll keep your form at distance, curb my soul,
Despair of smiles and tears, and prayers and
    oaths,
And all the blandishments of perjured love.   215
I will, I must, I shall, nay, now I can
Defy to death the lovely traitor, man.

NEMOURS.

No madam, think not you shall carry't thus.
'Tis not allowable, 'tis past example.
'Tis most unnatural, unjust, and monstrous.   220
And were the rest of women thus resolved,
You would destroy the purpose of creation.
What, when I have the happiness to please,
When heav'n and earth combine to make us
    happy,
Will you defeat the aim of destiny   225
By most unparalleled extremes of virtue,
Which therefore take away its very being?⁸⁷

PRINCESS OF CLÈVES.

Away! I must not answer but conjure you
Never to seek occasion more to see me.
Farewell. 'Tis past.   230

NEMOURS.

I cannot let you go.
I'll follow on my knees and hold your robe
Till you have promised me that I shall see you,
To show you how each day by slow degrees
I die away. This you shall grant, by Heav'n,   235
Or you shall see my blood let out before you.

PRINCESS OF CLÈVES.

Alas, Nemours! Oh Heav'n, why must it be
That I should charge you with the death of Clèves?
Alas, why met we not ere I engaged
To my dead lord? And why did Fate divide us?   240

NEMOURS.

Fate does not. No——
'Tis you that cross both Fortune, Heav'n, and Fate.
'Tis you obstruct my bliss. 'Tis you impose
Such laws as neither sense nor virtue warrant.

PRINCESS OF CLÈVES.

'Tis true, my lord, I offer much to duty,   245
Which but subsists in thought. Therefore, have
    patience.
Expect what time, with such a love as mine,
May work in your behalf. My husband's death
So bleeding fresh, I see him in the pangs—
Nay look, methinks I see his image rise   250
And point an everlasting separation.
Yet oh, it shall not be without a tear.

NEMOURS.

Oh, stay!

PRINCESS OF CLÈVES.

Let go. Believe, no other man
Could thus have wrought me, but yourself, to love—   255

NEMOURS.

Stay then.

PRINCESS OF CLÈVES.

I dare not. Think I love you still.*

NEMOURS.

I do—but stay and speak it o'er again.

PRINCESS OF CLÈVES.

Believe that I shall love you to my death.

NEMOURS.

I will. But live and love me.   260

PRINCESS OF CLÈVES.

Off, I charge you.
Believe this parting wounds me like the fate
Of Clèves or worse. Believe—but oh, farewell—

NEMOURS.

Believe—but what? That last thought I implore!

PRINCESS OF CLÈVES.

Believe that you shall never see me more. (*Exit.*)   265

Enter the Vidame.

---

87 extremes of virtue … being] According to Arisotle, vir-
    tue is the mean between extremes.

VIDAME.

Well, and how goes the game? What, on the knee, a gathered brow, and a large dew upon it? Nay, then you are a loser.

NEMOURS.

Didst thou see her pass?

VIDAME.

I did. She wrung me by the hand and sighed,   270
Then looked back twice,
And tottered on the threshold at the door.

NEMOURS.

"Believe that you shall never see me more." She lies. I'll wager my state I bed her eighteen months, three weeks hence, at half an hour past two in the   275
morning.

VIDAME.

Why faith, and that's as exact as e'er an astrologer of 'em all.

NEMOURS.

Give me thy hand, Vidame. I know the souls of
Women better than they know themselves.   280
I know the ingredients just that make 'em up,
All to loose grains, the subtlest volatile atoms
With the whole mish-mash of their composition.
Hark there without! The voice of Marguerite.
Now thou shalt see a battle worth the gazing.   285
Mark but how easily my reason flings her,
And yet at last I'll swing into friendship
Because I love her.

Enter Bellamore.

BELLAMORE.

The Princess! Shall I stop her?

NEMOURS.

                    No, let her come   290
With flying colors and with beat of drum,
Like the fanatic. I'll but rub me down
And then have at her.—Vidame, stay you here.
By Heaven, I'm jealous of this changeable stuff.
Therefore, the hits will be the livelier o'both sides.   295
The Dauphin, but no more—she comes, she
comes.

Enter Marguerite, pushing Bellamore.

MARGUERITE.

Be gone, villain, devil, fury, monster of a man!

NEMOURS.

But hear me but six words in private.

Enter Poltrot, Celia, [Saint-Andrè and Elianor].

POLTROT.

And I swear by this lascivious bit of beauty, I will
cleave to my Celia for better, for worse, in serge,   300
grogram, or crepe, though a queen should come
in my way in beaten gold.

NEMOURS.

What then, gentlemen, I perceive there have been
wars at home?

POLTROT.

Not a battle, my lord. Only a charge, a charge   305
sounded or so.

NEMOURS.

What, was it a trumpet or through a horn, sir?

POLTROT.

A horn, sir, a horn, sir? No sir, 'twas not a horn,
sir. Only my Celia was a little disdainful. But we
are friends again, sir. And what then, sir?   310

NEMOURS.

Come, come, all friends. Were Tournon here, I
would forgive her. A little scorn in a pretty woman,
so it be not too much affected, is a charm to new
friendship. Therefore, [*taking Marguerite's hand*] let
each man take his fair one by the hand, thus lay   315
it to his lips, and swear a whole life's constancy.

SAINT-ANDRÉ.

As I will to my Nell, though I haul cats at sea or
cry small-coal.[88] And for him that upbraids her,
I'll have more bobs than Democritus when he
cried, "Poor Jack." There's more pride in Diogenes   320
or under a Puritan's cap than in a king's crown.

NEMOURS.

For my part, the death of the Prince of Clèves,
upon second thoughts, has so truly wrought a
change in me, as nothing else but a miracle could.
For first, I see and loathe my debaucheries. Next,   325
while I am in health, I am resolved to give
satisfaction to all I have wronged—and first to this
lady, whom I will make my wife before all this

---

88 haul … small-coal] raising cat-anchors at sea or carrying and hawking coal through the city streets

company ere we part. This, I hope, whenever I die,
will convince the world of the ingenuity of my   330
repentance, because I had the power to go on.
He well repents that will not sin, yet can,
But deathbed sorrow rarely shows the man.[89]

[Exeunt.]

FINIS.

Textual Notes

a Copytext is the first edition, a 1689 quarto (Q); also
consulted were modern editions of 1955 (Stroup and
Cooke—SC) and of 1995 (Cordner). Many passages are
set as verse in the original, but only when they seem to
make an important point about character or rhetoric are
they retained as such.

b Clèves] Cordner; Cleve Q, SC. Lee used the English
translation of the novel (1679) as the source for his revision, and he used the title he found there, *The Princess of Cleve*, throughout his play. Modern scholars and
critics have returned, however, to an Anglicized French
title, *The Princess of Cleves*, as more accurate and appropriate. Here the French original, Clèves, is honored.

c Marguerite this] Marguerite. This Q, SC, Cordner (the
original begins another line with This)

d cry] Cordner; try Q, SC

e my good lord.] Cordner; my good lord—Save you my
dear Nemours! Q, SC (Nemours has exited.)

f Hear, hear him, Heaven … appointed some ladies"] Q
(some copies), SC, Cordner; *om.* Q (some copies)

g Chartres] Clèves Q, SC, Cordner

h world hold precious.] World; Hold Precious, Q, SC;
world. Hold, precious. Cordner

i for confessing. / His name?] Cordner; for confessing /
His name— Q, SC

j Rise! If possible / I'll force] Cordner; Rise if possible; /
I'll force Q, SC

k Have I the forward, brisk she] Cordner; Have I? For the
forward brisk, she Q, SC

l cornutos] cornutors Q, SC; cornutoes Cordner

m neighing] SC, Cordner; weighing. Q

n such as, if I gain not the Princess of Clèves, may]
Cordner; such as if I gain not, the Princess of Clèves
may Q, SC

o Chartres] Clèves Q, SC, Cordner

p Harebrain] Cordner; Hairbrain Q, SC

q CELIA. Seek] SC, Cordner; Seek, *Celia* Q

r for] Q; from SC, Cordner (following the emendation
of the second and all other editions)

s one] Q; once SC, Cordner

t live] SC, Cordner; love Q

---

89 deathbed sorrow rarely shows the man.] a skeptical reference to the deathbed repentance of Rochester

The Lucky Chance; or, An Alderman's Bargain[a]

by Aphra Behn (1640?-1689)

edited by Lori Snook

Aphra Behn, one of the most prolific playwrights in the late seventeenth century, is notable also as the first professional female playwright. *The Lucky Chance* came in 1686, sixteen years after her first play was produced, and was performed at Drury Lane by the United Company. In the roles of Sir Feeble and Sir Cautious were the great comedians Anthony Leigh and James Nokes; Thomas Betterton and Elizabeth Barry took the parts of Gayman and Lady Fulbank. While a success in 1686, after 1716 the play disappeared from the stage until Hannah Cowley adapted the material (cutting out the adultery) for *A School for Greybeards* (1786).

Unlike her full-fledged Spanish intrigue play, *The Rover*, *The Lucky Chance* is a Town comedy, set in London and containing an atmosphere of political and economic class conflict. Nevertheless, the convolutions of its high plot enable Behn to identify it specifically as "a comedy of intrigue" in her preface. The darkness of both high and low plots, however, sets this play apart, as does the figure of Lady Fulbank, the witty wife whose choices seem to disrupt the society of which she is a part. The ending in particular is rich in its ambiguity.

The Lucky Chance was controversial during its first run; discussed in Behn's preface was the charge of indecency, one which plagued her throughout her writing career. She defends herself against that charge mainly by objecting that she has written nothing but what was already popular on the stage, the only difference being that the other plays were written by men, who can, by an implicit double standard, get away with it: "But a devil on't, the woman damns the poet." She pleads, "All I ask is for the privilege for my masculine part, the poet in me (if any such you will allow me), to tread in those successful paths my predecessors have so long thrived in, to take those measures that both the Ancient and Modern writers have set me, and by which they have pleased the world so well." Apparently, however, it was not just the dialogue of the play that offended: on opening night Tony Leigh, in the role of Sir Feeble Fainwould, took the liberty of flashing by opening his dressing gown in front of the women in his bedchamber on his wedding night. Behn protests that if he did, "it was a jest of his own making, and which I never saw." She adds somewhat lamely, "I hope he has his clothes on underneath? And if so, where is the indecency?" Did Behn add the stage direction for Sir Feeble to throw open his gown before or after opening night?

DRAMATIS PERSONAE

[Men]

    Sir Feeble Fainwould, an old alderman to be
      married to Leticia.

    Sir Cautious Fulbank, an old banker married to
      Julia, [Lady Fulbank].

    Mr. Gayman, a spark of the Town,* lover of
      Julia.

    Mr. Belmour, contracted to Leticia, disguised,
      and passes for Sir Feeble's nephew.

    Mr. Bearjest, nephew to Sir Cautious, a fop.

    Captain Noisy, his companion.

    Mr. Bredwel, prentice to Sir Cautious and
      brother to Leticia, in love with Diana.

    Rag, footman to Gayman.

    Ralph, footman to Sir Feeble.

    Dick, footman to Sir Cautious.

    [Gingle, a musician.]

[Women]

    Lady Fulbank, in love with Gayman, honest*
      and generous.*

    Leticia, contracted to Belmour, married to Sir
      Feeble, young and virtuous.

    Diana, daughter to Sir Feeble, in love with
      Bredwel, virtuous.

    Pert, Lady Fulbank's woman.*

    Gammer Grime, landlady to Gayman, a smith's
      wife in Alsatia.[1]

    [Susan, a servant to Sir Feeble.]

    [Phillis, Leticia's woman.*]

    A parson, fiddlers, dancers, and singers,

    [nymphs, shepherds, a post-man, porters].

SCENE: LONDON.

The Lucky Chance; or, An Alderman's Bargain.

Act I, scene i. The street at break of day.

Enter Belmour disguised in a traveling habit.

BELMOUR.

Sure 'tis the day that gleams in yonder east,

The day that all but lovers blessed by shade
Pay cheerful homage to:
Lovers! and those pursued like guilty me
By rigid laws,[2] which put no difference   5
'Twixt fairly killing in my own defense
And murders bred by drunken arguments,
Whores, or the mean revenges of a coward.
This is Leticia's father's house (*Looking about.*)
And that the dear balcony   10
That has so oft been conscious of our loves,
From whence she's sent me down a thousand sighs,
A thousand looks of love, a thousand vows!
Oh thou dear witness of those charming hours,
How do I bless thee, how am I pleased to view   15
    thee
After a tedious age of six months' banishment.

Enter several with music.

FIDDLER.

But hark ye, Mr. Gingle, is it proper to play before
the wedding?

GINGLE.

Ever while you live, for many a time in playing
after the first night, the bride's sleepy, the   20
bridegroom tired, and both so out of humor that
perhaps they hate anything that puts 'em in mind
they are married.

They play and sing.

Rise, Cloris, charming maid, arise!
    And baffle breaking day,   25
Show the adoring world thy eyes
    Are more surprising gay.
The gods of love are smiling round
    And lead the bridegroom on,
And Hymen has the altar crowned,   30
    While all thy sighing lovers are undone.
To see thee pass they throng the plain;
    The groves with flowers are strown,
And every young and envying swain
    Wishes the hour his own.   35
Rise, then, and let the god of day,

---

1 Alsatia] disreputable area within the City* walls, also
  called Whitefriars, a "liberty" where debtors could not
  be arrested

2 rigid laws] The 1680 "Proclamation against Dueling"
  withdrew the possibility of royal pardon for this capital
  crime.

When thou dost to the lover yield,
Behold more treasure given away
Than he in his vast circle e'er beheld.

Enter Phillis in the balcony, throws them money.

BELMOUR.

Hah, Phillis, Leticia's woman!   40

GINGLE.

Fie Mrs.* Phillis, do ye take us for fiddlers that play
for hire? I came to compliment Mrs.* Leticia on
her wedding morning because she is my scholar.

PHILLIS.

She sends it only to drink her health.

GINGLE.

Come lads, let's to the tavern then.   45

Exit [Gingle and] musicians.

BELMOUR.

Hah! Said he Leticia?
Sure I shall turn to marble at this news;
I harden, and cold damps pass through my
    senseless pores.
—Hah, who's here?

Enter Gayman, wrapped in his cloak.

GAYMAN.

'Tis yet too early, but my soul's impatient, and I   50
must see Leticia. [*Goes to the door.*]

BELMOUR.

Death and the devil, the bridegroom!—Stay sir, by
Heaven you pass not this way. (*As [Gayman] is
knocking, pushes him away, and draws.*)

GAYMAN.

Hah! what art thou that durst forbid me entrance?   55
Stand off.

They fight a little, and closing, view each other.

BELMOUR.

Gayman!

GAYMAN.

My dearest Belmour.

BELMOUR.

Oh thou false friend, thou treacherous, base
deceiver!   60

GAYMAN.

Hah, this to me, dear Harry?

BELMOUR.

Whither is honor, truth, and friendship fled?

GAYMAN.

Why, there ne'er was such a virtue, 'tis all a poet's
dream.

BELMOUR.

I thank you, sir.   65

GAYMAN.

I am sorry for't, or that ever I did anything that
could deserve it. Put up your sword; an honest man
would say how he's offended before he rashly draws.

BELMOUR.

Are not you going to be married, sir?

GAYMAN.

No sir, as long as any man in London is so that   70
has but a handsome wife, sir.

BELMOUR.

Are not you in love, sir?

GAYMAN.

Most damnably and would fain lie with the dear,
jilting gypsy.

BELMOUR.

Hah, who would you lie with, sir?   75

GAYMAN.

You catechise me roundly. 'Tis not fair to name,
but I am no starter,[3] Harry: just as you left me,
you find me; I am for the faithless Julia still, the
old alderman's wife. 'Twas high time the City*
should lose their charter,[4] when their wives turn   80
honest.* But pray, sir, answer me a question or two.

BELMOUR.

Answer me first, what make you here this
morning?

GAYMAN.

Faith, to do you service. Your damned little jade
of a mistress has learned of her neighbors the art   85
of swearing and lying in abundance and is—

BELMOUR. (*Sighing.*)

To be married!

GAYMAN.

Even so, God save the mark, and she'll be a fair

---

3 starter] one who easily deserts a position
4 charter] In 1683 the City of London's charter (its governing document) had been revoked after Charles II clashed
   with the aldermen over the choice of City sheriffs.

one for many an arrow besides her husband's, though he be an old Finsbury hero[5] this threescore years.

BELMOUR.

Who mean you?

GAYMAN.

Why, thy cuckold that shall be, if thou be'st wise.

BELMOUR.

Away! Who is this man? Thou dalliest with me.

GAYMAN.

Why, an old knight and alderman, here, o'th'City, Sir Feeble Fainwould: a jolly old fellow, whose activity is all got into his tongue, a very excellent teaser, but neither youth nor beauty can grind his dudgeon to an edge.

BELMOUR.

Fie, what stuff's here.

GAYMAN.

Very excellent stuff, if you have but the grace to improve it.

BELMOUR.

You banter me. But in plain English tell me what made you here thus early, entering yon house with such authority?

GAYMAN.

Why, your mistress Leticia, your contracted wife, is this morning to be married to old Sir Feeble Fainwould, induced to't I suppose by the great jointure he makes her and the improbability of your ever gaining your pardon for your high duel. Do I speak English now, sir?

BELMOUR.

Too well. Would I had never heard thee.

GAYMAN.

Now I, being the confidant in your amours, the Jack-go-between—the civil pimp, or so—you left her in charge with me at your departure.

BELMOUR.

I did so.

GAYMAN.

I saw her every day, and every day she paid the tribute of a shower of tears, to the dear lord of all her vows, young Belmour, till faith, at last, for reasons manifold, I slacked my daily visits.

90

95

100

105

110

115

120

BELMOUR.

And left her to temptation: Was that well done?

GAYMAN.

Now must I afflict you and myself with a long tale of causes why, or be charged with want* of friendship.

BELMOUR.

You will do well to clear that point to me.

GAYMAN.

I see you're peevish, and you shall be humored. You know my Julia played me e'en such another prank as your false one is going to play you and married old Sir Cautious Fulbank, here, i'th'City, at which you know I stormed and raved and swore, as thou wilt now, and to as little purpose. There was but one way left, and that was cuckolding him.

BELMOUR.

Well, that design I left thee hot upon.

GAYMAN.

And hotly have I pursued it. Swore, wept, vowed, wrote, upbraided, prayed, and railed, then treated lavishly and presented high, till between you and I, Harry, I have presented the best part of eight hundred a year into her husband's hands in mortgage.

BELMOUR.

This is the course you'd have me steer, I thank you.

GAYMAN.

No, no, pox on't, all women are not jilts. Some are honest and will give as well as take, or else there would not be so many broke i'th'City. In fine, sir, I have been in tribulation, that is to say, moneyless, for six tedious weeks, without either clothes or equipage to appear withal, and so not only my own love affair lay neglected but thine too. And I am forced to pretend to my lady that I am i'th'country with a dying uncle, from whom if he were indeed dead, I expect two thousand a year.

BELMOUR.

But what's all this to being here this morning?

GAYMAN.

Thus have I lain concealed like a winter fly, hoping for some blest sunshine to warm me into life again and make me hover my flagging wings, till the news of this marriage (which fills the Town) made me crawl out this silent hour to upbraid the fickle maid.

125

130

135

140

145

150

155

---

5 Finsbury hero] Finsbury Fields was an archery range.

BELMOUR.

Didst thou? Pursue thy kind design. Get me to see her, and sure no woman, even possessed with a new passion, grown confident even to prostitution, but when she sees the man to whom she's sworn so very, very much, will find remorse and shame.

GAYMAN.

For your sake, though the day be broke upon us and I'm undone if seen, I'll venture in. (*Throws his Cloak over [his head].*)

Enter Sir Feeble Fainwould, Sir Cautious Fulbank, Bearjest, and Captain Noisy. [They] pass over the stage and go in.

Hah, see, the bridegroom! and with him my destined cuckold, old Sir Cautious Fulbank.— Hah, what ail'st thou, man?

BELMOUR.

The bridegroom! Like Gorgon's head he's turned me into stone.

GAYMAN.

Gorgon's head? a cuckold's head. 'Twas made to graft upon.

BELMOUR.

By Heaven, I'll seize her even at the altar and bear her thence in triumph!

GAYMAN.

Aye, and be borne to Newgate in triumph, and be hanged in triumph; 'twill be cold comfort celebrating your nuptials in the press yard[6] and be waked next morning like Mr. Barnardine in the play:[7] "Will you please to rise and be hanged a little, sir?"

BELMOUR.

What wouldst thou have me do?

GAYMAN.

As many an honest man has done before thee: cuckold him, cuckold him.

BELMOUR.

What, and let him marry her! She that's mine by

160

165

170

175

180

sacred vow already? By Heaven, it would be flat adultery in her!

GAYMAN.

She'll learn the trick, and practice it the better with thee.

BELMOUR.

Oh heavens! Leticia marry him! And lie with him!—Here will I stand and see this shameful woman, see if she dares pass by me to this wickedness.

GAYMAN.

Hark ye, Harry, in earnest have a care of betraying yourself and do not venture sweet life for a fickle woman, who perhaps hates you.

BELMOUR.

You counsel well.—But yet to see her married! How every thought of that shocks all my resolution.—But hang it, I'll be resolute and saucy, despise a woman who can use me ill, and think myself above her.

GAYMAN.

Why, now thou art thyself: a man again. But see, they're coming forth; now stand your ground.

Enter Sir Feeble, Sir Cautious, Bearjest, Captain Noisy, Leticia sad, Diana, Phillis. [They] pass over the stage.

BELMOUR.

'Tis she; support me, Charles, or I shall sink to earth. Methought in passing by she cast a scornful glance at me: such charming pride I've seen upon her eyes, when our love-quarrels armed 'em with disdain. I'll after 'em. If I live, she shall not 'scape me. (*Offers* to go. Gayman holds him.*)

GAYMAN.

Hold, remember you're proscribed and die if you are taken.

BELMOUR.

I've done, and I will live, but he shall ne'er enjoy her.—Who's yonder, Ralph, my trusty confidant?

Enter Ralph.

Now though I perish I must speak to him.— Friend, what wedding's this?

RALPH.

One that was never made in heaven, sir: 'tis Alderman Fainwould and Mrs.* Leticia Bredwel.

185

190

195

200

205

210

215

---

6 press yard] in a prison such as Newgate, the staging area for the trip to execution

7 Mr. Barnardine in the play] Shakespeare's *Measure for Measure*, adapted for the Restoration stage as Sir William Davenant's *Law against Lovers*

BELMOUR.

Bredwel? I've heard of her; she was mistress—

RALPH.

—To fine Mr. Belmour, sir. Aye, there was a gentleman, but rest his soul, he's hanged, sir. (*Weeps.*)

BELMOUR.

How! hanged?   220

RALPH.

Hanged, sir, hanged: at the Hague in Holland.

GAYMAN.

I heard some such news, but did not credit it.

BELMOUR.

For what, said they, was he hanged?

RALPH.

Why, e'en for high treason, sir: he killed one of their kings.   225

GAYMAN.

Holland's a commonwealth and is not ruled by kings.

RALPH.

Not by one, sir, but by a great many; this was a cheesemonger. They fell out over a bottle of brandy, went to snickersnee; Mr. Belmour cut his   230 throat, and was hanged for it, that's all, sir.

BELMOUR.

And did the young lady believe this?

RALPH.

Yes, and took on most heavily; the doctors gave her over, and there was the devil to do to get her to consent to this marriage. But her fortune was   235 small, and the hope of a ladyship and a gold chain at the spittle sermon[8] did the business. And so, your servant, sir. (*Exit.*)

BELMOUR.

So, here's a hopeful account of my sweet self now.

Enter Postman with letters.

POSTMAN.

Pray sir, which is Sir Feeble Fainwould's?   240

BELMOUR.

What would you with him, friend?

POSTMAN.

I have a letter from the Hague for him.

BELMOUR. [*Aside.*]

From the Hague! Now have I a curiosity to see it.—I am his servant, give it me.

[Postman] gives it him and exits.

Perhaps here may be the second part of my   245
tragedy.—I'm full of mischief, Charles, and have a mind to see this fellow's secrets. For from this hour I'll be his evil genius:* haunt him at bed and board, he shall not sleep nor eat; disturb him at his prayers, in his embraces; and tease him into   250
madness.—Help me, invention, malice, love, and wit. (*Opening the letter.*) Ye gods and little fiends, instruct my mischief. (*Reads.*) "Dear Brother, according to your desire I have sent for my son from St. Omer's,[9] whom I have sent to wait on   255
you in England. He is a very good accountant and fit for business, and much pleased he shall see that uncle to whom he's so obliged, and which is so gratefully acknowledged by—Dear Brother, your affectionate brother, Francis Fainwould." Hum.—   260
Hark ye, Charles, do you know who I am now?

GAYMAN.

Why, I hope a very honest friend of mine, Harry Belmour.

BELMOUR.

No sir, you are mistaken in your man.

GAYMAN.

It may be so.   265

BELMOUR.

I am, d'ye see, Charles, this very individual, numerical young Mr.—what-ye-call-um Fainwould, just come from St. Omer's into England, to my uncle the alderman. I am, Charles, this very man.

GAYMAN.

I know you are, and will swear't upon occasion.   270

---

8 ladyship … Spittle sermon] As the wife of an alderman, who wears a gold chain of office, Leticia would become a lady and attend the Easter sermons preached for the Lord Mayor and his entourage originally at St. Mary Spittle (hospital).

9 St. Omer's] a French city, with a Jesuit seminary; since it's unlikely that an alderman's son would attend it, the allusion may be to Titus Oates, the impostor central to the revelations of the Popish Plot, who claimed he'd studied there.

BELMOUR.

This lucky thought has almost calmed my mind.
And if I don't fit you, my dear uncle, may I never
lie with my aunt.

GAYMAN.

Ah rogue, but prithee what care have you taken
about your pardon? 'Twere good you should secure   275
that.

BELMOUR.

There's the devil, Charles: had I but that— But I
have had a very good friend at work, a thousand
guineas, that seldom fails, but yet in vain, I being the
first transgressor since the act against dueling. But I,   280
impatient to see this dear delight of my soul and
hearing from none of you this six weeks, came from
Brussels in this disguise—for the Hague I have not
seen, though hanged there.—But come, let's away
and complete me a right St. Omer's spark, that I may   285
present myself as soon as they come from church.

Exeunt.

Scene ii. Sir Cautious Fulbank's house.

*Enter Lady Fulbank, Pert, and Bredwel. Bredwel gives
her a letter.*

LADY FULBANK. (*Reads.*)

"Did my Julia know how I languish in this cruel
separation, she would afford me pity and write
oftener. If only the expectation of two thousand a
year kept me from you, ah! Julia, how easily would
I abandon that trifle for your more valued sight,   5
but that I know a fortune will render me more
agreeable to the charming Julia, I should quit all
my interest here to throw myself at her feet, to
make her sensible how am I entirely her adorer,
Charles Gayman." Faith Charles, you lie. You are   10
as welcome to me now, now when I doubt* thy
fortune is declining, as if the universe were thine.

PERT.

That, madam, is a noble gratitude. For if his
fortune be declining, 'tis sacrificed to his passion
for your ladyship. 'Tis all laid out on love.   15

LADY FULBANK.

I prize my honor more than life, yet I had rather
have given him all he wished of me than be guilty
of his undoing.

PERT.

And I think the sin were less.

LADY FULBANK.

I must confess such jewels, rings, and presents as   20
he made me must needs decay his fortune.

BREDWEL.

Aye madam, his very coach at last was turned into
a jewel for your ladyship. Then madam, what
expenses his despairs have run him on, as drinking
and gaming, to divert the thought of your   25
marrying my old master.

LADY FULBANK.

And put in wenching too.

BREDWEL.

No, assure yourself, madam—

LADY FULBANK. [*Aside.*]

Of that I would be better satisfied.—And you too
must assist me as e'er you hope I should be kind   30
to you in gaining you Diana.

BREDWEL.

Madam, I'll die to serve you.

PERT.

Nor will I be behind in my duty.

LADY FULBANK.

Oh, how fatal are forced marriages:
How many ruins one such match pulls on.   35
Had I but kept my sacred vows to Gayman,
How happy had I been, how prosperous he!
Whilst now I languish in a loathed embrace,
Pine out my life with age, consumptious coughs.
—But does thou fear that Gayman is declining?   40

BREDWEL.

You are my lady, and the best of mistresses;
therefore, I would not grieve you, for I know you
love this best but most unhappy man.

LADY FULBANK.

You shall not grieve me. Prithee on.

BREDWEL.

My master sent me yesterday to Mr. Crap, his   45
scrivener, to send to one Mr. Wasteall to tell him
his first mortgage was out, which is two hundred
pounds a year, and who has since engaged five or
six hundred more to my master. But if this first
be not redeemed, he'll take the forfeit on't, as he   50
says a wise man ought.

LADY FULBANK.

That is to say, a knave, according to his notion of a wise man.

BREDWEL.

Mr. Crap, being busy with a borrowing lord, sent me to Mr. Wasteall, whose lodging is in a nasty place, called Alsatia, at a blacksmith's. 55

LADY FULBANK.

But what's all this to Gayman?

BREDWEL.

Madam, this Wasteall was Mr. Gayman.

LADY FULBANK.

Gayman? Saw'st thou Gayman?

BREDWEL.

Madam, Mr. Gayman, yesterday. 60

LADY FULBANK.

When came he to Town?

BREDWEL.

Madam, he has not been out of it.

LADY FULBANK.

Not at his uncle's in Northamptonshire?

BREDWEL.

Your ladyship was wont to credit me.

LADY FULBANK.

Forgive me. You went to a blacksmith's— 65

BREDWEL.

Yes madam, and at the door encountered the beastly thing he calls a landlady, who looked as if she'd been of her own husband's making, composed of molded smith's dust. I asked for Mr. Wasteall, and she began to open and did so rail at 70 him, that what with her billingsgate, and her husband's hammers, I was both deaf and dumb. At last the hammers ceased, and she grew weary and called down Mr. Wasteall. But he not answering, I was sent up a ladder rather than a pair 75 of stairs. At last I scaled the top and entered the enchanted castle; there did I find him, spite of the noise below, drowning his cares in sleep.

LADY FULBANK.

Whom found'st thou? Gayman?

BREDWEL.

He, madam, whom I waked, and seeing me, 80 heavens, what confusion seized him! which nothing but my own surprise could equal. Ashamed, he would have turned away, but when he saw by my dejected eyes I knew him, he sighed and blushed, and heard me tell my business, then begged I would 85 be secret, for he vowed his whole repose and life depended on my silence. Nor had I told it now, but that your ladyship may find some speedy means to draw him from this desperate condition.

LADY FULBANK.

Heavens, is't possible! 90

BREDWEL.

He's driven to the last degree of poverty. Had you but seen his lodgings, madam!

LADY FULBANK.

What were they?

BREDWEL.

'Tis a pretty convenient tub, madam. He may lie along in't; there's just room for an old joined stool 95 besides the bed, which one cannot call a cabin,[10] about the largeness of a pantry bin or a usurer's trunk. There had been dornex[11] curtains to't in the days of yore, but they were now annihilated, and nothing left to save his eyes from the light but my 100 landlady's blue apron, tied by the strings before the window, in which stood a broken six-penny looking-glass, that showed as many faces as the scene in *Henry the Eighth*,[12] which could but just stand upright, and then the comb case filled it. 105

LADY FULBANK.

What a lewd description hast thou made of his chamber!

BREDWEL.

Then for his equipage, 'tis banished to one small monsieur, who (saucy with his master's poverty) is rather a companion than a footman. 110

LADY FULBANK.

But what said he to the forfeiture of his land?

BREDWEL.

He sighed and cried, "Why, farewell, dirty acres. It shall not trouble me, since 'twas all but for love!"

LADY FULBANK.

How much redeems it?

---

10 cabin] a room, more like an alcove, saving space with the bed built into the wall

11 dornex] dornick, a coarse damask material

12 *Henry the Eighth*] Shakespeare's play, noted for its crowd scenes.

BREDWEL.

Madam, five hundred pounds. 115

LADY FULBANK.

Enough. You shall in some disguise convey this money to him, as from an unknown hand. I would not have him think it comes from me for all the world; that nicety and virtue I've professed I am resolved to keep. 120

PERT.

If I were your ladyship, I would make use of Sir Cautious his* cash: pay him in his own coin.

BREDWEL.

Your ladyship would make no scruple of it if you knew how this poor gentleman has been used by my unmerciful master. 125

LADY FULBANK.

I have a key already to his countinghouse; it being lost, he had another made, and this I found and kept.

BREDWEL.

Madam, this is an excellent time for't, my master being gone to give my sister Leticia at church. 130

LADY FULBANK.

'Tis so. I'll go and commit the theft, whilst you prepare to carry it, and then we'll to dinner with your sister the bride.

Exeunt.

Scene iii. The house of Sir Feeble.

Enter Sir Feeble, Leticia, Sir Cautious, Bearjest, Diana, Captain Noisy. Sir Feeble sings and salutes* them.

SIR FEEBLE.

Welcome, Joan Sanderson[13], welcome, welcome. 'Ods* bobs, and so thou art, sweetheart.

Kisses the bride. So do the rest.

BEARJEST.

Methinks my lady bride is very melancholy.

SIR CAUTIOUS.

Aye, aye, women that are discreet are always thus upon their wedding day. 5

SIR FEEBLE.

Always by daylight, Sir Cautious.
But when bright Phoebus does retire
To Thetis' bed to quench his fire
And do the thing we need not name,
We mortals by his influence do the same. 10
Then, then[b] the blushing maid lays by
Her simpering and her modesty
And round the lover clasps and twines
Like ivy or the circling vines.
—Here Ralph, the bottle, rogue, of sack,* ye rascal. 15
Hadst thou been a butler worth hanging, thou wouldst have met us at the door with it.—'Ods bobs, sweetheart, thy health.

BEARJEST.

Away with it, to the bride's *Haunce in Kelder*.[14]

SIR FEEBLE.

Gots so, go to,* rogue, go to, that shall be, knave, 20
that shall be, by the morrow morning, hee.—'Ods bobs, we'll do't, sweetheart, here's to't. (*Drinks again.*)

LETICIA.

I die but to imagine it; would I were dead indeed.

SIR FEEBLE.

Hah—hum, how's this? Tears upon your wedding 25
day? Why, why, you baggage you, ye little ting, fools-face. Away, you rogue, you're naughty, you're naughty. (*Patting, and playing, and following her.*) Look, look, look now, buss it, buss it, and friends, did'ums, did'ums, beat its nown* silly baby—away, 30
you little hussy, away, and pledge me.

She drinks a little.

SIR CAUTIOUS.

A wise discreet lady, I'll warrant her; my lady would prodigally have took it off all.

SIR FEEBLE.

Dear's its nown* dear fubbs,* buss again, buss again, away, away. 'Ods bobs, I long for night.— 35
Look, look, Sir Cautious: what an eye's there.

---

13 Joan Sanderson] In the round-dance of that name, dancers would be invited into the pattern with the words "welcome Joan or John Sanderson" and then be kissed by the dancers of the opposite sex.

14 *Haunce in Kelder*] "Hans in the cellar"; pregnancy

SIR CAUTIOUS.

Aye, so there is, brother, and a modest eye too.

SIR FEEBLE.

Adod, I love her more and more.—Ralph, call old Susan hither.—Come, Mr. Bearjest, put the glass about. 'Ods bobs, when I was a young fellow, I would not let the young wenches look pale and wan but would rouse 'em and touse 'em and blowze[15] 'em till I put a color in their cheeks like an apple john,[16] i'facks.* Nay, I can make a shift still, and pupsey shall not be jealous.

Enter Susan; Sir Feeble whispers her; she goes out.

LETICIA.

Indeed not I, sir. I shall be all obedience.

SIR CAUTIOUS.

A most judicious lady. Would my Julia had a little of her modesty, but my lady's a wit.

Enter Susan with a box.

SIR FEEBLE.

Look here, my little puskin, here's fine playthings for its nown* little coxcomb. Go, get ye gone, get ye gone and off with this Saint Martin's trumpery,[17] these playhouse glass baubles, this necklace, and these pendants and all this false ware. 'Ods bobs, I'll have no counterfeit gear about thee, not I. See, these are right as the blushes on thy cheeks, and these as true as my heart, my girl. Go, put 'em on and be fine. (*Gives 'em her.*)

LETICIA.

Believe me, sir, I shall not merit this kindness.

SIR FEEBLE.

Go to—more of your love, and less of your ceremony. Give the old fool a hearty buss and pay him that way—hee, ye little wanton tit. I'll steal up and catch ye and love ye, adod I will. Get ye gone, get ye gone.

LETICIA. [*Aside.*]

Heavens, what a nauseous thing is an old man turned lover.

40

45

50

55

60

65

---

15 blowze] rumple the clothes of a woman

16 apple john] an apple which was kept for a long time, therefore probably wrinkled as well as red

17 Saint Martin's trumpery] fake jewelry, as made by the goldsmiths at St. Martin le Grand in Holborn

Exeunt Leticia and Diana.

SIR CAUTIOUS.

How, "steal up" Sir Feeble? I hope not so; I hold it most indecent before the lawful hour.

SIR FEEBLE.

Lawful hour! Why, I hope all hours are lawful with a man's own wife.

SIR CAUTIOUS.

But wise men have respect to times and seasons.

SIR FEEBLE.

Wise young men, Sir Cautious, but wise old men must nick their inclinations: (*Singing and dancing.*) "For it is not as 'twas wont to be, for it is not as 'twas wont to be."

Enter Ralph.

RALPH.

Sir, here's a young gentleman without would speak with you.

SIR FEEBLE.

Hum, I hope it is not that same Belmour come to forbid the banns. If it be, he comes too late. Therefore, bring me first my long sword and then the gentleman.

Exit Ralph.

BEARJEST.

Pray sir, use mine. It is a traveled blade, I can assure you, sir.

SIR FEEBLE.

I thank you, sir.

Enter Ralph, and Belmour disguis'd; [Belmour] gives [Sir Feeble] a letter; he reads.

How, my nephew Francis Fainwould? (*Embraces him.*)

BELMOUR. [*Aside.*]

I am glad he has told me my Christian name.

SIR FEEBLE.

Sir Cautious, know my nephew: 'tis a young St. Omer's scholar, but none of the witnesses.[18]

SIR CAUTIOUS.

Marry* sir, the wiser he, for they got nothing by't.

70

75

80

85

---

18 none of the witnesses] the (false) witnesses in the Popish Plot, brought from St. Omer's

BELMOUR.

Sir, I love and honor you because you are a traveler.   90

SIR FEEBLE.

A very proper young fellow and as like old Frank
Fainwould as the devil to the collier.[19] But Francis,
you are come into a very lewd town, Francis, for
whoring and plotting and roaring and drinking. But
you must go to church, Francis, and avoid ill com-   95
pany, or you may make damnable havoc in my cash,
Francis—what, you can keep merchants' books?

BELMOUR.

'T has been my study, sir.

SIR FEEBLE.

And you will not be proud but will be commanded
by me, Francis?   100

BELMOUR.

I desire not to be favored as a kinsman, sir, but as
your humblest servant.

SIR FEEBLE.

Why, thou'rt an honest fellow, Francis, and thou'rt
heartily welcome, and I'll make thee fortunate!—
But come, Sir Cautious, let you and I take a turn   105
i'th'garden, and beget a right understanding
between your nephew Mr. Bearjest and my
daughter Di.

SIR CAUTIOUS.

Prudently thought on, sir. I'll wait on you.

Exeunt Sir Feeble and Sir Cautious.

BEARJEST.

You are a traveler, sir, I understand—   110

BELMOUR.

I have seen a little part of the world, sir.

BEARJEST.

So have I, sir, I thank my stars, and have performed
most of my travels on foot, sir.

BELMOUR.

You did not travel far then, I presume, sir.

BEARJEST.

No sir, it was for my diversion indeed, but I assure   115
you I traveled into Ireland afoot, sir.

BELMOUR.

Sure sir, you go by shipping into Ireland?

BEARJEST.

That's all one, sir, I was still afoot, ever walking
on the deck.

BELMOUR.

Was that your farthest travels, sir?   120

BEARJEST.

Farthest? Why, that's the end of the world, and sure
a man can go no further.

BELMOUR.

Sure, there can be nothing worth a man's curiosity?

BEARJEST.

No sir, I'll assure you, there are the wonders of the
world, sir. I'll hint you this one: there is a harbour   125
which since the creation was never capable of
receiving a lighter, yet by another miracle the King
of France was to ride there with a vast fleet of ships,
and to land a hundred thousand men.[20]

BELMOUR.

This is a swingeing wonder, but are there store of   130
madmen there, sir?

BEARJEST.

That's another rarity, to see a man run out of his
wits.

NOISY.

Marry* sir, the wiser they, I say.

BEARJEST.

Pray sir, what store of miracles have you at St.   135
Omer's?

BELMOUR.

None, sir, since that of the wonderful Salamanca
doctor,[21] who was both here and there at the same
instant of time.

BEARJEST.

How, sir! Why, that's impossible.   140

BELMOUR.

That was the wonder, sir, because 'twas impossible.

---

19 devil to the collier] proverbial expression indicating simi-
larity, as both were traditionally black

20 There is a harbor....hundred thousand men] During the
Popish Plot, there were wild rumors of French forces
preparing to invade from Ireland, the absurdity of which
is here figured forth in the harbor's barely being able to
accommodate a lighter, a boat or barge with a shallow
draft.

21 Salamanca doctor] another reference to Titus Oates, who
had falsely claimed a doctorate from Salamanca

NOISY.

But 'twas a greater, sir, that 'twas believed.

Enter Lady Fulbank and Pert, Sir Cautious, and Sir Feeble.

SIR FEEBLE.

Enough, enough, Sir Cautious, we apprehend one another.—Mr. Bearjest, your uncle here and I have struck the bargain: the wench is yours with three thousand pound present and something more after death, which your uncle likes well. 145

BEARJEST.

Does he so, sir? I'm beholding to him; then 'tis not a pin matter whether I like or not, sir.

SIR FEEBLE.

How sir, not like my daughter Di? 150

BEARJEST.

Oh Lord, sir, die or live, 'tis all one for that, sir; I'll stand to the bargain my uncle makes.

PERT. (*Aside [to Bearjest].*)

Will you so, sir? You'll have very good luck if you do.

BEARJEST.

Prithee hold thy peace, my lady's woman.

LADY FULBANK.

Sir, I beg your pardon for not waiting on you to church; I knew you would be private. 155

Enter Leticia, fine in jewels.

SIR FEEBLE.

You honor us too highly now, Madam. (*Presents his wife, who salutes* her.*)

LADY FULBANK.

Give you joy, my dear Leticia!—I find, sir, you were resolved for youth, wit, and beauty. 160

SIR FEEBLE.

Aye madam, to the comfort of many a hoping coxcomb.—But Lette, rogue Lette, thou wouldst not make me free o'th'City a second time. Wouldst thou entice the rogues with the twire* and wanton leer? the amorous simper that cries "Come, kiss me"? Then the pretty round lips are pouted out; hee, rogue, how I long to be at 'em! Well, she shall never go to church more, that she shall not. 165

LADY FULBANK.

How sir, not to church, the chiefest recreation of a City lady? 170

SIR FEEBLE.

That's all one, madam, that tricking and dressing and prinking and patching is not your devotion to heaven but to the young knaves that are licked and combed and are minding you more than the parson. 'Ods bobs, there are more cuckolds destined at church than are made out of it. 175

SIR CAUTIOUS. (*To his lady.*)

Ha, ha, ha. He tickles ye, i'faith, ladies.

BELMOUR. [*Aside.*]

Not one chance look this way; and yet I can forgive her lovely eyes, because they look not pleased with all this ceremony. And yet methinks some sympathy[22] in love might this way glance their beams. I cannot hold.—Sir, is this fair lady my aunt? 180

SIR FEEBLE.

Oh Francis! Come hither, Francis.—Lette, here's a young rogue has a mind to kiss thee. 185

Puts them together; she starts back.

Nay, start not, he's my own flesh and blood, my nephew, baby.—Look how the young rogues stare at one another: like will to like, I see that.

LETICIA. [*Aside.*]

There's something in his face so like my Belmour it calls my blushes up and leaves my heart defenceless. 190

Enter Ralph.

RALPH.

Sir, dinner's on the table.

SIR FEEBLE.

Come, come, let's in then, gentlemen and ladies, And share today my pleasures and delight. But, 'Ods bobs, they must be all mine own at night. 195

Act II, scene i. Gayman's Lodging.

Enter Gayman in a nightcap and an old campaign coat tied about him, very melancholy.

GAYMAN.

Curse on my birth! Curse on my faithless fortune! Curse on my stars, and curst be all—but love!

———————————

22 sympathy] natural attraction, not compassion

That dear, that charming sin, though 't have pulled
Innumerable mischiefs on my head,
I have not, nor I cannot find repentance for.   5
No, let me die despised, upbraided, poor;
Let fortune, friends, and all abandon me,
But let me hold thee, thou soft smiling god,
Close to my heart while life continues there.
Till the last pantings of my vital blood   10
May the last spark of life and fire be Love's!

Enter Rag.

How now, Rag, what's o'clock?

RAG.

My belly can inform you better than my tongue.

GAYMAN.

Why you gourmandizing vermin you, what have
you done with the threepence I gave you a   15
fortnight ago.

RAG.

Alas sir, that's all gone, long since.

GAYMAN.

You gutling rascal, you are enough to breed a
famine in a land. I have known some industrious
footmen that have not only gotten their own   20
livings but a pretty livelihood for their masters too.

RAG.

Aye, till they came to the gallows, sir.

GAYMAN.

Very well, sirrah, they died in an honorable calling.
But hark ye, Rag: I have business, very earnest
business abroad this evening. Now were you a   25
rascal of docity,[23] you would invent a way to get
home my last suit that was laid in lavender[24] with
the appurtenances thereunto belonging, as periwig,
cravat, and so forth.

RAG.

Faith, master, I must deal in the black art then,   30
for no human means will do't. And now I talk of
the black art, master, try your power once more
with my landlady.

GAYMAN.

Oh! Name her not, the thought on't turns my

stomach. A sight of her is a vomit, but he's a bold   35
hero that dares venture on her for a kiss, and all
beyond that sure is hell itself. Yet there's my last,
last refuge, and I must to this wedding. I know not
what, but something whispers me this night I shall
be happy, and without Julia 'tis impossible!   40

RAG.

Julia, who's that? my Lady Fulbank, sir?

GAYMAN.

Peace sirrah, and call a—no—pox on't, come
back—and yet—yes, call my fulsome landlady.

Exit Rag.

Sir Cautious knows me not, by name or person, and
I will to this wedding. I'm sure of seeing Julia there, 45
and what may come of that— But here's old Nasty
coming: I smell her up.—Hah, my dear landlady.

Enter Rag and Gammer Grime.

Quite out of breath.—A chair there for my
landlady.

RAG.

Here's ne'er a one, sir.   50

GAMMER GRIME.

More of your money and less of your civility, good
Mr. Wasteall.

GAYMAN.

Dear landlady—

GAMMER GRIME.

Dear me no dears, sir, but let me have my money:
eight weeks' rent last Friday, besides taverns, ale   55
houses, chandlers, laundresses' scores, and ready
money out of my purse. You know it, sir.

GAYMAN.

Aye, but your husband does not; speak softly.

GAMMER GRIME.

My husband! What, do you think to fright me
with my husband? I'd have you to know I am an   60
honest* woman and care not this _____* for my
husband. Is this all the thanks I have for my
kindness: for patching, borrowing, and shifting for
you? 'Twas but last week I pawned my best
petticoat, as I hope to wear it again; it cost me six   65
and twenty shillings besides making. Then this
morning my new Norwich mantua followed, and
two 'postle spoons; I had the whole dozen when

---

23 docity] educability (from Lat. *docere*, to teach)
24 laid in lavender] stored with an aromatic sachet; a euphemism for being pawned

you came first, but they dropped and dropped till
I had only Judas left for my husband. 70
GAYMAN.
Hear me, good landlady—
GAMMER GRIME.
Then I've passed my word at the George Tavern[25]
for forty shillings for you, ten shillings at my
neighbour Squabs for ale, besides seven shillings
to Mother Suds for washing. And do you fob me 75
off with my husband?
GAYMAN. [Aside.]
Here Rag, run and fetch her a pint of sack;* there's
no other way of quenching the fire in her slobber
chops.

Exit Rag.

But my dear landlady, have a little patience. 80
GAMMER GRIME.
Patience? I scorn your words, sir. Is this a place to
trust in? Tell me of patience that used to have my
money beforehand. Come, come, pay me quickly,
or old Gregory Grime's house shall be too hot to
hold you. 85
GAYMAN.
Is't come to this, can I not be heard!
GAMMER GRIME.
No sir, you had good clothes when you came first,
but they dwindled daily, till they dwindled to this
old campaign, with tanned colored lining, once red
but now all colors of the rainbow, a cloak to skulk in 90
a-nights, and a pair of piss-burned shammy breeches. Nay, your very badge of manhood's gone too.
GAYMAN.
How landlady! Nay then, i'faith, no wonder if you
rail so.
GAMMER GRIME.
Your silver sword, I mean: transmogrified to this 95
two-handed basket hilt, this old Sir Guy of
Warwick,[26] which will sell for nothing but old
iron. In fine, I'll have my money, sir, or i'faith,
Alsatia shall not shelter you.

---

25 George Tavern] a tavern in Alsatia
26 two-handed ... Sir Guy of Warwick] a broadsword, requiring two hands, with a large protective hilt, nick-
named after the hero of a popularized medieval romance

Enter Rag.
GAYMAN.
Well landlady, if we must part, let's drink at 100
parting. Here landlady, here's to the fool that shall
love you better than I have done. (*Sighing, drinks.*)
GAMMER GRIME.
Rot your wine! D'ye think to pacify me with wine,
sir?

*She refusing to drink, he holds open her jaws; Rag
throws a glass of wine into her mouth.*

What, will you force me? No— Give me another 105
glass, I scorn to be so uncivil to be forced. My
service to you, sir.
She drinks, he embraces her.
But this shan't do, sir.
GAYMAN. (*Sings.*)
Ah Cloris, 'tis in vain you scold
Whilst your eyes kindle such a fire. 110
Your railing cannot make me cold,
So fast as they a warmth inspire.
GAMMER GRIME.
Well sir, you have no reason to complain of my
eyes nor my tongue neither, if rightly understood.
(*Weeps.*) 115
GAYMAN.
I know you are the best of landladies: as such I
drink your health. (*Drinks.*) But to upbraid a man
in tribulation, fie, 'tis not done like a woman of
honor. A man that loves you too.

She drinks.

GAMMER GRIME.
I am a little hasty sometimes, but you know my 120
good nature.
GAYMAN.
I do, and therefore trust my little wants with you.
I shall be rich again, and then, my dearest
landlady—
GAMMER GRIME.
Would this wine might ne'er go through me if I 125
would not go as they say through fire and water,
by night or by day for you. (*Drinks.*)
GAYMAN.
And as this is wine, I do believe thee. (*Drinks.*)

GAMMER GRIME.

Well, you have no money in your pocket now, I'll
warrant you. Here, here's ten shillings for you old   130
Gregory knows not of. (*Opens a great greasy purse.*)

GAYMAN.

I cannot in conscience take it, good faith I cannot;
besides, the next quarrel you'll hit me in the teeth
with it.

GAMMER GRIME.

Nay, pray no more of that, forget it, forget it. I   135
own I was to blame. Here sir, you shall take it.

GAYMAN.

Aye, but what should I do with money in these
damned breeches? No, put it up. I can't appear
abroad thus. No, I'll stay at home and lose my
business.   140

GAMMER GRIME.

Why, is there no way to redeem one of your suits?

GAYMAN.

None, none. I'll e'en lay me down and die.

GAMMER GRIME.

Die? marry,* heavens forbid! I would not for the
world— Let me see, hum, what does it lie for?

GAYMAN.

Alas! dear landlady, a sum, a sum—   145

GAMMER GRIME.

Well, say no more, I'll lay about me.

GAYMAN.

By this kiss, but you shall not. Asafetida, by this
light.

GAMMER GRIME.

Shall not? That's a good one, i'faith. Shall you rule,
or I?   150

GAYMAN.

But should your husband know it—

GAMMER GRIME.

Husband! marry* come up. Husbands know wives'
secrets? No, sure the world's not so bad yet. Where
do your things lie? And for what?

GAYMAN.

Five pound equips me. Rag can conduct you. But   155
I say you shall not go, I've sworn—

GAMMER GRIME.

Meddle with your matters.—Let me see, the caudle
cup that Molly's grandmother left her will pawn
for about that sum; I'll sneak it out.—Well sir, you

shall have your things presently.* Trouble not your   160
head, but expect me.

Exeunt Gammer Grime and Rag.

GAYMAN.

Was ever man put to such beastly shifts? 'Sdeath,*
how she stunk; my senses are most luxuriously
regaled.

Knocking of hammers on an anvil.

There's my perpetual music too. The ringing of   165
bells is an ass to't.

Enter Rag.

RAG.

Sir, there's one in a coach below would speak to
you.

GAYMAN.

With me, and in a coach: Who can it be?

RAG.

The Devil, I think, for he has a strange   170
countenance.

GAYMAN.

The Devil? Show yourself a rascal of parts,* sirrah,
and wait on him up with ceremony.

RAG.

Who, the Devil, sir?

GAYMAN.

Aye, the Devil, sir, if you mean to thrive.   175

Exit Rag.

Who can this be? But see, he comes to inform me.

Enter [Rag, leading] Bredwel, dressed like a devil.

[*To Rag.*] Withdraw.

BREDWEL.

I come to bring you this. (*Gives him a letter.*)

GAYMAN. (*Reads.*)

"Receive what Love and Fortune present you with.
Be grateful and be silent, or 'twill vanish like a   180
dream and leave you more wretched than it found
you. Adieu."

[Bredwel] gives him a bag of money.

Hah!

BREDWEL.

Nay, view it, sir, 'tis all substantial gold.

GAYMAN. (*Aside.*)

> Now dare not I ask one civil question for fear it 185
> vanish all.—But I may ask how 'tis I ought to pay
> for this great bounty.

BREDWEL.

> Sir, all the pay is secrecy.

GAYMAN.

> And is this all that is required, sir?

BREDWEL.

> No, you're invited to the shades below. 190

GAYMAN.

> Hum, shades below? I am not prepared for such a
> journey, sir.

BREDWEL. (*In feigned heroic tone.*)

> If you have courage, youth, or love, you'll follow me.
> When night's black curtain's drawn around the
>   world,
> And mortal eyes are safely locked in sleep, 195
> And no bold spy dares view when gods caress,
> Then I'll conduct thee to the banks of bliss.
> Durst thou not trust me?

GAYMAN.

> Yes, sure, on such substantial security. (*Hugs the
> bag.*) 200

BREDWEL.

> Just when the day is vanished into night,
> And only twinkling stars inform the world,
> Near to the corner of the silent wall
> In fields of Lincoln's Inn,[27] thy spirit shall meet
>   thee.
> Farewell. 205

(*Goes out.*)

GAYMAN.

> Hum. I am awake, sure, and this is gold I grasp.
> I could not see this devil's cloven foot,
> Nor am I such a coxcomb to believe
> But he was as substantial as his gold.
> Spirits, ghosts, hobgoblins, furies, fiends, and devils 210
> I've often heard old wives fright fools and children
>   with,
> Which, once arrived to common sense, they laugh at.
> No, I am for things possible and natural:

---

27 Fields of Lincoln's Inn] area around one of the Inns of
   Court*

Some female devil old and damned to ugliness
And past all hopes of courtship and address, 215
Full of another devil called desire,
Has seen this face, this shape, this youth,
And thinks it worth her hire. It must be so.
I must moil on in the damned dirty road,
And sure such pay will make the journey easy. 220
And for the price of the dull drudging night,
All day I'll purchase new and fresh delight.

Exit.

Scene ii. Sir Feeble's house.

Enter Leticia, pursued by Phillis.

PHILLIS.

> Why, madam, do you leave the garden for this
> retreat to melancholy?

LETICIA.

> Because it suits my fortune and my humor,
> And even thy presence would afflict me now.

PHILLIS.

> Madam, I was sent after you: my Lady Fulbank 5
> has challenged Sir Feeble at bowls and stakes a ring
> of fifty pound against his new chariot.*

LETICIA.

> Tell him I wish him luck in every thing,
>
> [*Aside.*] But in his love to me.
>
> —Go tell him I am viewing of the garden. 10

Exit Phillis.

> Blest be this kind retreat, this lone occasion,
> That lends a short cessation to my torments
> And gives me leave to vent my sighs and tears.
>   (*Weeps.*)

Enter Belmour at a distance behind her.

BELMOUR.

> And doubly blest be all the powers of love, 15
> That give me this dear opportunity.

LETICIA.

> Where were you, all ye pitying gods of love,
> That once seemed pleased at Belmour's flame and
>   mine
> And smiling joined our hearts, our sacred vows,
> And spread your wings and held your torches high? 20

BELMOUR.

Oh—

She starts, pauses.

LETICIA.

Where were you now when this unequal marriage
Gave me from all my joys, gave me from Belmour?
Your wings were flagged, your torches bent to
    earth,
And all your little bonnets veiled your eyes;   25
You saw not, or were deaf and pitiless.

BELMOUR.

Oh, my Leticia!

LETICIA.

Hah, 'tis there again; that very voice was Belmour's.
Where art thou, oh thou lovely charming shade?
For sure thou canst not take a shape to fright me.   30
What art thou? Speak! (*Not looking behind her yet
    for fear.*)

BELMOUR.

                              Thy constant true adorer,
Who all this fatal day has haunted thee
To ease his tortured soul. (*Approaching nearer.*)

LETICIA. (*Speaking with signs of fear.*)   35
My heart is well acquainted with that voice,
But oh, my eyes dare not encounter thee.

BELMOUR.

Is it because thou'st broken all thy vows?
Take to thee courage and behold thy slaughters.

LETICIA.

Yes, though the sight would blast me, I would   40
    view it. (*Turns.*)
'Tis he, 'tis very Belmour! or so like,
I cannot doubt but thou deserv'st this welcome.
    (*Embraces him.*)

BELMOUR.

Oh, my Leticia!

LETICIA.

I'm sure I grasp not air; thou art no phantom.
My arms return not empty to my bosom   45
But meet a solid treasure.

BELMOUR.

A treasure thou so easily threw'st away:
A riddle simple love ne'er understood.

LETICIA.

Alas I heard, my Belmour, thou wert dead.

BELMOUR.

And was it thus you mourned my funeral?   50

LETICIA.

I will not justify my hated crime.
But oh, remember I was poor and helpless
And much reduced and much imposed upon.

BELMOUR. (*Weeps.*)
And want* compelled thee to this wretched
    marriage, did it?

LETICIA.

'Tis not a marriage since my Belmour lives: 55
The consummation were adultery.
I was thy wife before. Wouldst thou deny me?

BELMOUR.

No, by those powers that heard our mutual vows,
Those vows that tie us faster than dull priests.[28]

LETICIA.

But oh, my Belmour, thy sad circumstances   60
Permit thee not to make a public claim.
Thou art proscribed and die'st if thou art seen.

BELMOUR.

Alas!

LETICIA.

Yet I would wander with thee o'er the world
And share thy humblest fortune with thy love.   65

BELMOUR.

Is't possible, Leticia, thou wouldst fly
To foreign shores with me?

LETICIA.

Can Belmour doubt the soul he knows so well?

BELMOUR.

Perhaps in time the king may find my innocence
And may extend his mercy.   70
Meantime I'll make provision for our flight.

LETICIA.

But how 'twixt this and that can I defend
Myself from the loathed arms of an impatient
    dotard,
That I may come a spotless maid to thee?

BELMOUR.

Thy native modesty and my industry   75

---

28 our mutual vows … dull priests] Under contemporary
canon law, vows exchanged constituted a pre-contract,
which would invalidate a later ceremony, provided it was
not consummated.

Shall well enough secure us.
Feign your nice* virgin-cautions all the day,
Then trust at night to my conduct to preserve thee.
—And wilt thou yet be mine? Oh, swear anew,
Give me again thy faith, thy vows, thy soul,   80
For mine's so sick with this day's fatal business
It needs a cordial of that mighty strength.
Swear, swear so, as if thou break'st,
Thou mayst be—anything but damned, Leticia.

LETICIA. (*Kneels.*)
Thus then, and hear me, Heaven!   85

BELMOUR. (*Kneels.*)
And thus I'll listen to thee.

Enter Sir Feeble, Lady Fulbank, Sir Cautious.

SIR FEEBLE.
Lette, Lette, Lette, where are you, little rogue,
Lette?—Hah! Hum, what's here?

Belmour snatches her to his bosom, as if she fainted.

BELMOUR.
Oh heavens, she's gone, she's gone!

SIR FEEBLE.
Gone, whither is she gone? It seems she had the   90
wit to take good company with her.

The women go to her, take her up.

BELMOUR.
She's gone to heaven, sir, for aught I know.

SIR CAUTIOUS.
She was resolved to go in a young fellow's arms, I
see.

SIR FEEBLE.
Go to,* Francis, go to.   95

LADY FULBANK.
Stand back, sir, she recovers.

BELMOUR.
Alas, I found her dead upon the floor. Should I
have left her so? If I had known your mind—

SIR FEEBLE.
Was it so, was it so? Gots so, by no means, Francis.

LETICIA.
Pardon him, sir, for surely I had died, but for his   100
timely coming.

SIR FEEBLE.
Alas poor pupsey, was it sick? Look here, here's a

fine thing to make it well again. Come, buss, and
it shall have it.—Oh, how I long for night.—
Ralph, are the fiddlers ready?   105

RALPH.
They are tuning in the hall, sir.

SIR FEEBLE.
That's well, they know my mind. I hate that same
twang, twang, twang, fum, fum, fum, tweedle,
tweedle, tweedle, then screw go the pins, till a
man's teeth are on an edge; then snap, says a small   110
gut, and there we are at a loss again. I long to be
in bed with a hey tredodle, tredodle, tredodle,—
with a hay tredool, tredodle, tredo. (*Dancing and
playing on his stick like a flute.*)

SIR CAUTIOUS.
A prudent man would reserve himself. Good   115
facks,* I danced so on my wedding day that when
I came to bed, to my shame be it spoken, I fell
fast asleep and slept till morning.

LADY FULBANK.
Where was your wisdom then, Sir Cautious? But
I know what a wise woman ought to have done.   120

SIR FEEBLE.
'Ods bobs, that's wormwood, that's wormwood. I
shall have my young hussy set agog too; she'll hear
there are better things in the world than she has
at home, and then, 'Ods bobs, and then they'll ha't,
adod they will, Sir Cautious. Ever while you live,   125
keep a wife ignorant, unless a man be as brisk as
his neighbors.

SIR CAUTIOUS.
A wise man will keep 'em from bawdy
christenings, then, and gossipings.

SIR FEEBLE.
Christenings and gossipings! Why, they are the   130
very schools that debauch our wives, as dancing
schools do our daughters.

SIR CAUTIOUS.
Aye, when the overjoyed good man invites 'em all
against that time twelve month: "Oh he's a dear
man," cries one; "Aye, marry,*" cries another, "here's 135
a man indeed. My husband, God help him—"

SIR FEEBLE.
Then she falls to telling of her grievance, till (half
maudlin) she weeps again. "Just my condition,"
cries a third. So the frolic goes round, and we poor

cuckolds are anatomized and turned the right side   140
outwards, 'Ods bobs, we are, Sir Cautious.

SIR CAUTIOUS.

Aye, aye, this grievance ought to be redressed, Sir
Feeble. The grave and sober part o'th'Nation are
hereby ridiculed, aye, and cuckolded too for aught
I know.   145

LADY FULBANK.

Wise men, knowing this, should not expose their
infirmities by marrying us young wenches, who,
without instruction, find how we are imposed upon.

Enter fiddles playing, Mr. Bearjest and Diana dancing;
Bredwel, Captain Noisy, et al.

LADY FULBANK.

So cousin, I see you have found the way to Mrs.*
Di's heart.   150

BEARJEST.

Who, I, my dear lady aunt? I never knew but one
way to a woman's heart, and that road I have not
yet traveled, for my uncle, who is a wise man, says
that matrimony is a sort of a—kind of a—as it
were, d'ye see, of a voyage, which every man of   155
fortune is bound to make one time or other, and,
madam, I am, as it were—a bold adventurer.

DIANA.

And are you sure, sir, you will venture on me?

BEARJEST.

Sure! I thank you for that—as if I could not believe
my uncle. For in this case a young heir has no   160
more to do but to come and see, settle, marry, and
use you scurvily.

DIANA.

How sir, scurvily?

BEARJEST.

Very scurvily, that is to say, be always fashionably
drunk, despise the tyranny of your bed, and reign   165
absolutely; keep a seraglio of women, and let my
bastard issue inherit; be seen once a quarter, or so,
with you in the Park* for countenance, where we
loll two several ways in the gilt coach like Janus
or a spread eagle.[29]   170

DIANA.

And do you expect I should be honest* the while?

_____

[29] spread eagle] The heraldic spread eagle often had two
heads and was a common street sign of the times.

BEARJEST.

Heaven forbid, not I, I have not met with that
wonder in all my travels.

LADY FULBANK.

How sir, not an honest woman?

BEARJEST.

Except my lady aunt. Nay, as I am a gentleman   175
and the first of my family, you shall pardon me.
(*Kneels.*) Here, cuff me, cuff me soundly.

Enter Gayman, richly dressed.

GAYMAN.

This love's a damned bewitching thing: now
though I should lose my assignation with my devil,
I cannot hold from seeing Julia tonight. Hah,   180
there, and with a fop at her feet?
Oh, vanity of woman! (*Softly pulls her.*)

LADY FULBANK.

Oh sir, you're welcome from Northamptonshire.

GAYMAN. (*Aside.*)

Hum, surely she knows the cheat.

LADY FULBANK.

You are so gay, you save me, sir, the labor of asking   185
if your uncle be alive.

GAYMAN. (*Aside.*)

Pray Heaven she have not found my circumstances!
But if she have, confidence must assist me.—And,
madam, you're too gay for me to inquire whether
you are that Julia which I left you?   190

LADY FULBANK.

Oh, doubtless, sir.

GAYMAN.

But why the devil do I ask? Yes, you are still the
same: one of those hoiting[30] ladies, that love
nothing like fool and fiddle, crowds of fops; had
rather be publicly, though dully, flattered, than   195
privately adored; you love to pass for the wit of
the company, by talking all and loud.

LADY FULBANK.

Rail on, till you have made me think my virtue at
so low ebb it should submit to you.

GAYMAN.

What, I'm not discreet enough? I'll babble all in   200

_____

[30] hoiting] flighty, thoughtless

my next high debauch, boast of your favors, and
describe your charms to every wishing fool?

LADY FULBANK.

Or make most filthy verses of me under the name
of Cloris, you Philander,[31] who in lewd rhymes
confess the dear appointment: what hour and 205
where, how silent was the night, how full of love
your eyes, and wishing, mine. Faith, no. If you can
afford me a lease of your love, till the old
gentleman my husband depart this wicked world,
I'm for the bargain. 210

SIR CAUTIOUS. (*Goes about 'em.*)

Hum, what's here, a young spark at my wife?

GAYMAN.

Unreasonable Julia, is that all my love, my
sufferings, and my vows must hope? Set me an age,
say when you will be kind,* and I will languish
out in starving wish. But this to gape for legacies 215
of love till youth be past enjoyment, the devil I will
as soon. Farewell. (*Offers* to go.*)

LADY FULBANK.

Stay, I conjure you stay.

GAYMAN. (*Aside.*)

And lose my assignation with my devil.

SIR CAUTIOUS.

'Tis so, aye, aye, 'tis so, and wise men will perceive 220
it; 'tis here, here in my forehead, it more than buds,
it sprouts, it flourishes.

SIR FEEBLE.

So, that young gentleman has nettled him, stung
him to th'quick. I hope he'll chain her up. The gad
bee's in his conundrum.[32] In charity I'll relieve 225
him.—Come my Lady Fulbank, the night grows
old upon our hands. To dancing, to jiggeting.
Come, shall I lead your ladyship?

LADY FULBANK.

No sir, you see I am better provided. (*Takes
Gayman's hand.*) 230

SIR CAUTIOUS.

Aye, no doubt on't, a pox on him for a young,
handsome dog.

---

31 Cloris … Philander] two of Behn's own favored names
for pastoral
32 the gad bee's in his conundrum] To have a gad bee (cf.
gadfly) in one's whimsy would mean he's out of his wits.

They dance all.

SIR FEEBLE.

Very well, very well, now the posset, and then—
'Ods bobs, and then—

DIANA.

And then we'll have t'other dance. 235

SIR FEEBLE.

Away, girls, away, and steal the bride to bed. They
have a deal to do upon their wedding nights, and
what with the tedious ceremonies of dressing and
undressing, the smutty lectures of the women, by
way of instruction, and the little stratagems of the 240
young wenches, 'Ods bobs, a man's cozened of half
his night.—Come gentlemen, one bottle, and
then, we'll toss the stocking.[33]

*Exeunt all but Lady Fulbank [and] Bredwel, who are
talking, and Gayman.*

LADY FULBANK.

But dost thou think he'll come?

BREDWEL.

I do believe so, madam. 245

LADY FULBANK.

Be sure you contrive it so he may not know
whither or to whom he comes.

BREDWEL.

I warrant you, madam, for our parts.

Exit Bredwel; Gayman stealing out.

LADY FULBANK.

How now, what, departing?

GAYMAN.

You are going to the bride chamber. 250

LADY FULBANK.

No matter, you shall stay.

GAYMAN.

I hate to have you in a crowd.

LADY FULBANK.

Can you deny me? Will you not give me one lone
hour i'th'garden?

GAYMAN.

Where we shall only tantalize each other with dull 255
kissing and part with the same appetite we met.
No, madam. Besides, I have business.

---

33 toss the stocking] a wedding-night ritual akin to tossing the bride's garter today

---

LADY FULBANK.

    Some assignation, is it so indeed?

GAYMAN.

    Away, you cannot think me such a traitor. 'Tis most important business. 260

LADY FULBANK.

    Oh, 'tis too late for business; let tomorrow serve.

GAYMAN.

    By no means, the gentleman is to go out of Town.

LADY FULBANK.

    Rise the earlier then.

GAYMAN.

    But madam, the gentleman lies dangerously— sick—and should he die— 265

LADY FULBANK.

    'Tis not a dying uncle, I hope, sir?

GAYMAN.

    Hum.

LADY FULBANK.

    The gentleman a-dying and to go out of Town tomorrow?

GAYMAN.

    Aye—a—he goes—in a litter—'tis his fancy, 270 madam; change of air may recover him.

LADY FULBANK.

    So may your change of mistress do me, sir. Farewell. (*Goes out.*)

GAYMAN.

    Stay, Julia! Devil be damned, for you shall tempt no more, I'll love and be undone.—But she is 275 gone, and if I stay, the most that I shall gain is but a reconciling look or kiss. No, my kind goblin, I'll keep my word with thee as the least evil: A tantalizing woman's worse than devil.

Exit.

      Act III, scene i. Sir Feeble's house.

        Song.[34]

No more, Lucinda, ah! expose no more
    To the admiring world those conqu'ring charms:

In vain all day unhappy men adore
    What the kind night gives to my longing arms.
Their vain attempts can ne'er successful prove 5
Whilst I so well maintain the fort of love.

Yet to the world with so bewitching arts
    Your dazzling beauty you around display
And triumph in the spoils of broken hearts,
    That sink beneath your feet and crowd your way. 10
Ah! suffer now your cruelty to cease,
And to a fruitless war prefer a peace.

Enter Ralph with light, Sir Feeble, and Belmour sad.

SIR FEEBLE.

    So, so, they're gone. Come Francis, you shall have the honor of undressing me for the encounter, but 'twill be a sweet one, Francis. 15

BELMOUR. [*Aside.*]

    Hell take him, how he teases me! (*Undressing [Sir Feeble] all the while.*)

SIR FEEBLE.

    But is the young rogue laid, Francis, is she stolen to bed? What tricks the young baggages have to whet a man's appetite? 20

BELMOUR.

    Aye, sir.—Pox on him, he will raise my anger up to madness, and I shall kill him to prevent his going to bed to her.

SIR FEEBLE.

    A pize* of those bandstrings:[35] the more haste, the less speed. 25

BELMOUR.

    Be it so in all things, I beseech thee, Venus!

SIR FEEBLE.

    Thy aid a little, Francis. (*[Belmour] pinches him by the throat.*) Oh, oh, thou chokest me. 'Sbobs, what dost mean?

BELMOUR.

    You had so hampered 'em, sir. (*Aside.*) The Devil's 30 very mischievous in me.

SIR FEEBLE.

    Come, come, quick, good Francis, adod, I'm as

---

34 Song] the "second song," with accompaniment, of the play, performed "before the entry" of the actors to begin Act III, and written by one "Mr. Cheek," i.e.,

Thomas Cheek, a contemporary musician who also wrote songs for Thomas Southerne's plays.

35 bandstrings] strings which tie a man's collar

yare as a hawk at the young wanton. Nimbly, good
Francis, untruss, untruss.

BELMOUR. [*Aside.*]

Cramps seize ye. What shall I do? The near   35
approach distracts me!

SIR FEEBLE.

So, so, my breeches, good Francis. But well,
Francis, how dost think I got the young jade my
wife?

BELMOUR.

With five hundred pounds a year jointure, sir.   40

SIR FEEBLE.

No, that would not do, the baggage was damnably
in love with a young fellow they call Belmour; a
handsome young rascal he was, they say, that's
truth on't, and a pretty estate, but happening to
kill a man, he was forced to fly.   45

BELMOUR.

That was great pity, sir.

SIR FEEBLE.

Pity! Hang him, rogue, 'sbobs, and all the young
fellows in the Town deserve it: we can never keep
our wives and daughters honest* for rampant
young dogs, and an old fellow cannot put in   50
amongst 'em, under being undone, with presenting
and the devil and all. But what dost think I did,
being damnably in love? I feigned a letter as from
the Hague, wherein was a relation of this same
Belmour's being hanged.   55

BELMOUR.

Is't possible, sir? Could you devise such news?

SIR FEEBLE.

Possible, man? I did it, I did it. She swooned at
the news, shut herself up a whole month in her
chamber, but I presented high; she sighed and wept
and swore she'd never marry; still I presented; she   60
hated, loathed, spit upon me; still adod I
presented, till I presented myself effectually in
church to her, for she at last wisely considered her
vows were cancelled, since Belmour was hanged.

BELMOUR.

Faith sir, this was very cruel to take away his fame   65
and then his mistress.

SIR FEEBLE.

Cruel! Thou'rt an ass, we are but even with the
brisk rogues, for they take away our fame, cuckold

us, and take away our wives. So, so, my cap,
Francis.   70

BELMOUR.

And do you think this marriage lawful, sir?

SIR FEEBLE.

Lawful! It shall be when I've had livery and seisin
of her body, and that shall be presently,* rogue.
Quick. Besides, this Belmour dares as well be
hanged as come into England.   75

BELMOUR.

If he gets his pardon, sir—

SIR FEEBLE.

Pardon! No, no, I have took care for that, for I
have, you must know, got his pardon already.

BELMOUR.

How sir! got his pardon, that's some amends for
robbing him of his wife.   80

SIR FEEBLE.

Hold, honest Francis: What, dost think 'twas in
kindness to him? No you fool, I got his pardon
myself that nobody else should have it, so that if he
gets anybody to speak to his Majesty for it, his Majesty cries he has granted it. But for want* of my ap-   85
pearance, he's defunct, trussed up, hanged, Francis.

BELMOUR.

This is the most excellent revenge I ever heard of.

SIR FEEBLE.

Aye, I learned it of a great politician of our times.

BELMOUR.

But have you got his pardon?

SIR FEEBLE.

I've done't, I've done't. Pox on him, it cost me five   90
hundred pounds, though. Here 'tis, my solicitor
brought it me this evening. (*Gives it him.*)

BELMOUR. [*Aside.*]

This was a lucky hit, and if it 'scape me, let me be
hanged by a trick indeed.

SIR FEEBLE.

So, put it into my cabinet. Safe, Francis, safe.   95

BELMOUR.

Safe, I'll warrant you, sir.

SIR FEEBLE.

My gown, quick, quick—t'other sleeve, man—so,
now my night-cap. Well, I'll in, throw open my
gown to fright away the women, and jump into
her arms. (*Exit.*)   100

BELMOUR.

He's gone. Quickly, oh Love, inspire me!

Enter a footman.

FOOTMAN.

Sir, my master, Sir Cautious Fulbank, left his watch
on the little parlor table tonight and bid me call for't.

BELMOUR.

Hah!—The bridegroom has it, sir, who is just gone
to bed; it shall be sent him in the morning.   105

FOOTMAN.

'Tis very well, sir, your servant. (*Exit.*)

BELMOUR.

Let me see. Here is the watch. I took it up to keep
for him, but his sending has inspired me with a
sudden stratagem that will do better than force to
secure the poor trembling Leticia, who, I am sure,   110
is dying with her fears.

Exit.

Scene [ii]. Bedchamber.

*Leticia in an undress, by the women at the table. Enter
to them Sir Feeble Fainwould.*

SIR FEEBLE.

What's here? What's here? The prating women*
still. 'Ods bobs, what, not in bed yet? For shame
of love, Leticia.

LETICIA.

For shame of modesty, sir. You would not have me
go to bed before all this company.   5

SIR FEEBLE.

What, the women? Why, they must see you laid,[36]
'tis the fashion.

LETICIA.

What, with a man? I would not for the world.
[*Aside.*] Oh Belmour, where art thou with all thy
promised aid?   10

DIANA.

Nay madam, we should see you laid indeed.

LETICIA.

First in my grave, Diana.

SIR FEEBLE.

'Ods bobs, here's a compact amongst the women:

---

36 laid] put to bed (alongside the groom)

high treason against the bridegroom.—Therefore,
ladies, withdraw, or adod, I'll lock you all in.   15

*Throws open his gown, they run all away. He locks the
door.*

So, so, now we're alone, Leticia, off with this foolish
modesty, and nightgown,* and slide into my arms.

She runs from him.

Hey, my little puskin, what, fly me, my coy
Daphne? (*Pursues her.*)

Knocking.

Hah, who's that knocks? Who's there?   20

BELMOUR. [*Within.*]

'Tis I, sir, 'tis I. Open the door presently.*

SIR FEEBLE.

Why, what's the matter, is the house o'fire?

BELMOUR. [*Within.*]

Worse, sir, worse.

*[Sir Feeble] opens the door; Belmour enters with the
watch in his hand.*

LETICIA.

'Tis Belmour's voice!

BELMOUR.

Oh sir, do you know this watch?   25

SIR FEEBLE.

This watch!

BELMOUR.

Aye sir, this watch.

SIR FEEBLE.

This watch! Why prithee, why dost tell me of a
watch? 'Tis Sir Cautious Fulbank's watch. What
then, what a pox dost trouble me with watches?   30
(*Offers* to put him out; he returns.*)

BELMOUR.

'Tis indeed his watch, sir, and by this token he has
sent for you to come immediately to his house, sir.

SIR FEEBLE.

What a devil, art mad, Francis, or is his worship
mad, or does he think me mad? Go, prithee tell him   35
I'll come to him tomorrow. (*Goes to put him out.*)

BELMOUR.

Tomorrow, sir! Why, all our throats may be cut
before tomorrow.

SIR FEEBLE.

What say'st thou, throats cut?

BELMOUR.

Why, the City's up in arms,[37] sir, and all the   40
aldermen are met at Guildhall.[38] Some damnable
plot, sir.

SIR FEEBLE.

Hah, plot, the aldermen met at Guildhall—hum—
why, let 'em meet, I'll not lose this night to save
the Nation.   45

LETICIA.

Would you to bed, sir, when the weighty affairs
of state require your presence?

SIR FEEBLE.

Hum, met at Guildhall? My clothes, my gown
again, Francis, I'll out. (*Putting on his gown,
pausing, pulls it off again.*) Out, what, upon my   50
wedding night? No, I'll in.

LETICIA.

For shame, sir, shall the reverend council of the
City debate without you?

SIR FEEBLE.

Aye, that's true, that's true. Come, truss again,
Francis, truss again. Yet now I think on't, Francis,   55
prithee run thee to the hall and tell 'em 'tis my
wedding night, d'ye see, Francis, and let somebody
give my voice for—

BELMOUR.

What, sir?

SIR FEEBLE.

Adod, I cannot tell. Up in arms, say you? Why,   60
let 'em fight dog, fight bear, mun, I'll to bed. Go.

LETICIA.

And shall his Majesty's service and his safety[39] lie
unregarded for a slight woman, sir?

SIR FEEBLE.

Hum, his Majesty! Come, haste, Francis, I'll away,
and call Ralph and the footmen and bid 'em arm: 65
each man shoulder his musket and advance his
pike. And bring my artillery implements quick and
let's away.—Pupsey, 'bye, pupsey, I'll bring it a fine
thing yet before morning, it may be.—Let's away:
I shall grow fond* and forget the business of the   70
Nation. Come, follow me, Francis. (*Exit.*)

Belmour runs to Leticia.

BELMOUR.

Now my Leticia, if thou e'er didst love,
If ever thou design'st to make me blest,
Without delay fly this adulterous bed!

SIR FEEBLE. (*Within.*)

Why Francis, where are you, knave?   75

BELMOUR.

I must be gone lest he suspect us. I'll lose him and
return to thee immediately. Get thyself ready.

LETICIA.

I will not fail, my love.

Exit Belmour.

Old man, forgive me: thou the aggressor art,
Who rudely forced the hand without the heart.   80
She cannot from the paths of honor rove
Whose guide's religion and whose end is love.

Exit.

Scene [iii]. A wash house or out house.[40]

*Enter with a dark lantern Bredwel, disguised like a
devil, leading Gayman.*

BREDWEL.

Stay here till I give notice of your coming. (*Exit,
leaving his lantern.*)

GAYMAN.

Kind light, a little of your aid. Now must I be peeping, though my curiosity should lose me all. Hah!
Zounds, what's here, a hovel or a hog sty? Hum, see   5
the wickedness of man, that I should find no time to
swear in, but just when I'm in the Devil's clutches.

Enter Pert, as an old woman, with a staff.

PERT.

Good even to you, fair sir.

---

37 City's up in arms] Riots often disturbed London's peace
   in the late 1670s and early 1680s; in 1686, the year of
   the play's debut, anti-Catholic riots occurred.

38 Guildhall] the seat of City government.

39 Majesty's … safety] The King's life had been threatened
   as recently as the Rye House Plot of 1683.

40 out house] structure away from the main house, not
   privy

GAYMAN.

Hah, defend me! If this be she, I must rival the
Devil, that's certain.

PERT.

Come, young gentleman, dare not you venture?

GAYMAN.

He must be as hot as Vesuvius that does. I shall
never earn my morning's present.

PERT.

What, do you fear a longing woman, sir?

GAYMAN.

The devil I do.—This is a damned preparation to   15
love.

PERT.

Why stand you gazing, sir? A woman's passion is
like the tide, it stays for no man when the hour is
come.

GAYMAN.

I'm sorry I have took it at the turning. I'm sure   20
mine's ebbing out as fast.

PERT.

Will you not speak, sir, will you not on?

GAYMAN.

I would fain ask a civil question or two first.

PERT.

You know, too much curiosity lost paradise.

GAYMAN.

Why, there's it now.   25

PERT.

Fortune and Love invite you if you dare follow me.

GAYMAN.

This is the first thing in petticoats that ever dared
me in vain. Were I but sure she were but human
now, for sundry considerations she might down.[41]
But I will on.   30

She goes, he follows; both go out.

Scene [iv]. A chamber in the
apartments of Lady Fulbank.

*Enter [Pert as] old woman, followed by Gayman in the
dark. Soft music plays; she leaves him.*

GAYMAN.

Hah, music, and excellent!

Song.[42]

Oh Love, that stronger art than wine,
Pleasing delusion, witchery divine,
Wont to be prized above all wealth,
Disease that has more joys than health.
Though we blaspheme thee in our pain   5
And of thy tyranny complain,
We all are bettered by thy reign.

What reason never can bestow,
We to this useful passion owe: 10
Love wakes the dull from sluggish ease
And learns a clown* the art to please,
Humbles the vain, kindles the cold,
Makes misers free and cowards bold.
'Tis he reforms the sot from drink   15
And teaches airy fops to think.

When full brute appetite is fed,
And choked the glutton lies and dead,
Thou new spirits dost dispense,
And fines the gross delights of sense: 20
Virtue's unconquerable aid,
That against nature can persuade,
And makes a roving mind retire
Within the bounds of just desire;
Cheerer of age, youth's kind unrest,   25
And half the heaven of the blest.

[GAYMAN.]

Ah Julia, Julia! if this soft preparation were but to
bring me to thy dear embraces, what different
motions would surround my soul from what
perplex it now.   30

*Enter Nymphs and Shepherds [and Pert as old
woman], and dance.*

*Then two dance alone. All go out but Pert and
Shepherd.*

If these be devils, they are obliging ones: I did not
care if I ventured on that last female fiend.

---

41 she might down] like a distasteful beverage

42 Song] lyrics by Robert Wolselely; music by John Blow;
sung in the 1686 production by John Bowman, who also
played Bredwel; however, Bowman does not sing as
Bredwel here (Todd).

SHEPHERD.^c (*Sings.*)
  Cease your wonder, cease your guess
  Whence arrives your happiness.
  Cease your wonder, cease your pain,   35
  Human fancy is in vain.

BOTH.^d
  'Tis enough you once shall find
  Fortune may to worth be kind,

Shepherd gives him gold.

  And love can leave off being blind.

PERT. (*Sings.*)
  You, before you enter here,   40
  On this sacred ring must swear: (*Puts it on his
      finger, holds his hand.*)
  By the figure which is round,
  Your passion constant and profound;
  By the adamantine stone,
  To be fixed to one alone.   45
  By the luster which is true,
  Ne'er to break your sacred vow;
  Lastly, by the gold that's tried,
  For love all dangers to abide.

*[Reenter nymphs and shepherds, who] all dance around
him, while these same two sing.*

SHEPHERD.
  Once about him let us move   50
  To confirm him true to love.
  (*Repeats.*)

PERT.
  Twice with mystic turning feet
  Make him silent and discreet.
  (*Repeats.*)

SHEPHERD.
  Thrice around him let us tread   55
  To keep him ever young in bed. (*Repeats, gives
      him another part [of gold].*)
  Forget Aminta's proud disdain;
  Taste here, and sigh no more in vain,
  The joy of love without the pain.

PERT.
  That god repents his former slights,   60
  And Fortune thus your faith requites.

BOTH.
  Forget Aminta's proud disdain;

  Then taste, and sigh no more in vain,
  The joy of love without the pain.
  The joy of love without the pain.   65

*Exeunt all dancers. [Gayman] looks on himself and
feels about him.*

GAYMAN.
  What the devil can all this mean? If there be a
  woman in the case— Sure I have not lived so bad
  a life to gain the dull reputation of so modest a
  coxcomb but that a female might down with me
  without all this ceremony. Is it care of her honor?   70
  That cannot be; this age affords none so nice.* Nor
  fiend nor goddess can she be, for these I saw were
  mortal! No, 'tis a woman, I am positive. Not young
  nor handsome, for the vanity had made her glory
  to've been seen. No, since 'tis resolved a woman,   75
  she must be old and ugly and will not balk my
  fancy with her sight but baits me more with this
  essential beauty.
  Well, be she young or old, woman or devil,
  She pays, and I'll endeavor to be civil.   80

Exit.

  Scene [v]. A hall in the same house.^43

*After a knocking, enter Bredwel in his masking habit
with his vizard in the one hand and a light in t'other,
in haste.*

BREDWEL.
  Hah, knocking so late at our gate—(*Opens the
  door.*)

*Enter Sir Feeble, dressed and armed cap-a-pie, with a
broad waist-belt stuck round with pistols, a helmet,
scarf, buffcoat and half pike.*

SIR FEEBLE.
  How now, how now, what's the matter here?

BREDWEL. [*Aside.*]
  Matter? What, is my lady's innocent intrigue found
  out?—Heavens, sir, what makes you here in this   5
  warlike equipage?

---

43 hall] a s.d. in Q identifies "The flat scene of the hall"—
  probably a reference to a stock flat or set of flats that
  could be drawn across to create the setting

SIR FEEBLE.

What makes you in this showing equipage, sir?

BREDWEL.

I have been dancing among some of my friends.

SIR FEEBLE.

And I thought to have been fighting with some of my friends. Where's Sir Cautious, where's Sir Cautious?   10

BREDWEL.

Sir Cautious—sir, in bed.

SIR FEEBLE.

Call him, call him, quickly, good Edward.

BREDWEL. [Aside.]

Sure my lady's frolic is betrayed and he comes to make mischief. However, I'll go and serve Mr.   15
Gayman. (Exit.)

Enter Sir Cautious and [Dick, his] boy with light.

DICK.

Pray sir, go to bed, here's no thieves; all's still and well.

SIR CAUTIOUS.

This last night's misfortune of mine, Dick, has kept me waking, and methought all night I heard a kind   20
of a silent noise. I am still* afraid of thieves. Mercy upon me, to lose five hundred guineas at one clap, Dick.—Hah, bless me! What's yonder? Blow the great horn, Dick. Thieves, murder, murder!

SIR FEEBLE.

Why, what a pox, are you mad? 'Tis I, 'tis I, man.   25

SIR CAUTIOUS.

I, who am I? Speak—declare—pronounce.

SIR FEEBLE.

Your friend, old Feeble Fainwould.

SIR CAUTIOUS.

How, Sir Feeble! At this late hour and on his wedding night.—Why, what's the matter, sir? Is it peace or war with you?   30

SIR FEEBLE.

A mistake, a mistake.[44] Proceed to the business, good brother, for time, you know, is precious.

---

44 peace or war … mistake] Sir Feeble's attire must include
    a remnant of his nightware, so that Sir Cautious ges-
    tures to it and then to his military accoutrements, and
    Sir Feeble waves him off.

SIR CAUTIOUS. (Aside.)

Some strange catastrophe has happened between him and his wife tonight that makes him disturb me thus.—Come sit, good brother, and to the   35
business, as you say.

They sit one at one end of the table, the other at the other;
Dick sets down the light and goes out. Both sit gaping
and staring and expecting when either should speak.

SIR FEEBLE.

As soon as you please, sir.—Lord, how wildly he stares! He's much disturbed in's mind.—Well sir, let us be brief.

SIR CAUTIOUS.

As brief as you please, sir—well, brother—(Pausing   40
still.)

SIR FEEBLE.

So, sir.

SIR CAUTIOUS.

How strangely he stares and gapes: some deep concern.

SIR FEEBLE.

Hum—hum—   45

SIR CAUTIOUS.

I listen to you, advance.

SIR FEEBLE.

Sir?

SIR CAUTIOUS. (Aside.)

A very distracted countenance: pray Heaven he be not mad, and a young wife is able to make an old fellow mad, that's the truth on't.   50

SIR FEEBLE. [Aside.]

Sure 'tis something of his lady, he's so loath to bring it out.—I am sorry you are thus disturbed, sir.

SIR CAUTIOUS.

No disturbance to serve a friend.

SIR FEEBLE.

I think I am your friend indeed, Sir Cautious, or I would not have been here upon my wedding night.   55

SIR CAUTIOUS. (Aside.)

His wedding night: there lies his grief, poor heart! Perhaps she has cuckolded him already.—Well come, brother, many such things are done—

SIR FEEBLE.

Done, hum. Come, out with it, brother: What troubles you tonight?   60

SIR CAUTIOUS. (*Aside.*)

Troubles me? Why, knows he I am robbed?

SIR FEEBLE.

I may perhaps restore you to the rest you've lost.

SIR CAUTIOUS.

The rest? Why, have I lost more since? Why, know
you then who did it? Oh, how I'd be revenged
upon the rascal! 65

SIR FEEBLE. (*Aside.*)

'Tis jealousy, the old worm that bites.—Who is it
you suspect?

SIR CAUTIOUS.

Alas, I know not whom to suspect, I would I did,
but if you could discover him, I would so swinge
him. 70

SIR FEEBLE.

I know him? What, do you take me for a pimp,
sir? I know him! (*Rises in rage.*) There's your watch
again, sir. I'm your friend, but no pimp, sir.

SIR CAUTIOUS.

My watch, I thank you, sir. But why pimp, sir?

SIR FEEBLE.

Oh, a very thriving calling, sir, and I have a young 75
wife to practice with. I know your rogues?

SIR CAUTIOUS. (*Aside.*)

A young wife: 'tis so, his gentlewoman has been at
hot-cockles* without her husband, and he's horn*
mad upon't. I suspected her being so close in with
his nephew: in a fit with a pox!—Come, come, Sir 80
Feeble, 'tis many an honest man's fortune.

SIR FEEBLE.

I grant it, sir, but to the business, sir, I came for.

SIR CAUTIOUS.

With all my soul—

*They sit gaping and expecting when either should
speak. Enter Bredwel and Gayman at the door.
Bredwel sees them and puts Gayman back again.*

BREDWEL.

Hah, Sir Feeble and Sir Cautious there. What shall
I do? For this way we must pass, and to carry him 85
back would discover* my lady to him, betray all,
and spoil the jest.—Retire, sir, your life depends
upon your being unseen.

[They] go out.

SIR FEEBLE.

Well sir, do you not know that I am married, sir?
And this my wedding night? 90

SIR CAUTIOUS.

Very good, sir.

SIR FEEBLE.

And that I long to be in bed!

SIR CAUTIOUS.

Very well, sir.

SIR FEEBLE.

Very good, sir, and very well, sir. (*Rises in a rage.*)
Why then, what the devil do I make here, sir! 95

SIR CAUTIOUS.

Patience, brother, and forward.

SIR FEEBLE.

Forward! Lend me your hand, good brother, let's
feel your pulse. How has this night gone with you?

SIR CAUTIOUS.

Ha, ha, ha! [*Aside.*] This is the oddest conundrum.
Sure he's mad—and yet now I think on't, I have 100
not slept tonight, nor shall I ever sleep again till I
have found the villain that robbed me. (*Weeps.*)

SIR FEEBLE. (*Aside.*)

So, now he weeps. Far gone. This laughing and
weeping is a very bad sign!—Come, let me lead
you to your bed. 105

SIR CAUTIOUS. [*Aside.*]

Mad, stark mad.—No, now I'm up 'tis no matter.
Pray ease your troubled mind. I am your friend.
Out with it: What, was it acted? Or but designed?

SIR FEEBLE.

How, sir?

SIR CAUTIOUS.

Be not ashamed; I'm under the same praemunire[45] 110
I doubt,* little better than a—but let that pass.

SIR FEEBLE.

Have you any proof?

SIR CAUTIOUS.

Proof of what, good sir?

SIR FEEBLE.

Of what! Why, that you're a cuckold, sir, a cuckold,
if you'll ha't. 115

SIR CAUTIOUS.

Cuckold, sir. Do ye know what ye say?

---

45 praemunire] forfeit

SIR FEEBLE.

What I say?

SIR CAUTIOUS.

Aye, what you say, can you make this out?

SIR FEEBLE.

I make it out—

SIR CAUTIOUS.

Aye sir, if you say it and cannot make it out, you're   120
a—

SIR FEEBLE.

What am I, sir? What am I?

SIR CAUTIOUS.

A cuckold as well as myself, sir, and I'll sue you
for *scandalum magnatum*.[46] I shall recover
swingeing damages with a City jury.   125

SIR FEEBLE.

I know of no such thing, sir.

SIR CAUTIOUS.

No, sir?

SIR FEEBLE.

No, sir.

SIR CAUTIOUS.

Then what would you be at, sir?

SIR FEEBLE.

I be at, sir? What would you be at, sir?   130

SIR CAUTIOUS.

Ha, ha, ha! Why, this is the strangest thing: to see
an old fellow, a magistrate of the city, the first night
he's married forsake his bride and bed and come
armed cap-a-pie, like Gargantua, to disturb
another old fellow and banter him with a tale of a   135
tub,[47] and all to be-cuckold him here. In plain
English, what's your business?

SIR FEEBLE.

Why, what the devil's your business, an* you go
to that?

SIR CAUTIOUS.

My business with whom?   140

SIR FEEBLE.

With me, sir, with me. What a pox do ye think I
do here?

---

46 *scandalum magnatum*] a statute protecting high-ranking
officials or persons against slander

47 a tale of a tub] a spurious story

SIR CAUTIOUS.

'Tis that I would be glad to know, sir.

Enter Dick.

SIR FEEBLE.

Here Dick, remember I've brought back your
master's watch. Next time he send for me o'er   145
night, I'll come to him in the morning.

SIR CAUTIOUS.

Ha, ha, ha. I send for you? Go home and sleep,
sir. 'Od, an* ye keep your wife waking to so little
purpose, you'll go near to being haunted with a
vision of horns.*   150

SIR FEEBLE.

Roguery, knavery to keep me from my wife. Look
ye, this was the message I received. (*Tells him
seemingly.*[48])

*Enter Bredwel to the door, in a white sheet like a ghost,
speaking to Gayman who stands within.*

BREDWEL.

Now sir, we are two to two, for this way you must
pass or be taken in the lady's lodgings. I'll first   155
adventure out to make you pass the safer. (*Aside.*)
And that he may not, if possible, see Sir Cautious,
whom I shall fright into a trance, I am sure. And
Sir Feeble, the devil's in't if he know him.

GAYMAN.

A brave,* kind fellow, this.   160

Enter Bredwel, stalking on as a ghost by them.

SIR CAUTIOUS.

Oh—undone—undone—help help—I'm dead,
I'm dead. (*Falls down on his face.*)

Sir Feeble stares and stands still.

BREDWEL. (*Aside.*)

As I could wish. (*Turns.*) Come on, thou ghastly
thing, and follow me.

Enter Gayman like a ghost, with a torch.

SIR CAUTIOUS.

Oh Lord, oh Lord!   165

---

48 seemingly] in dumb show

GAYMAN.

Hah, old Sir Feeble Fainwould. Why, where the devil am I? 'Tis he, and be it where it will, I'll fright the old dotard for cozening my friend of his mistress. (*Stalks on.*)

SIR FEEBLE. (*Trembling.*)

Oh guard me, guard me, all ye Powers!   170

GAYMAN.

Thou call'st in vain, fond* wretch, for I am
   Belmour,
Whom first thou rob'st of fame and life,
And then what dearer was—his wife. (*Goes out,
   shaking his torch at him.*)

SIR CAUTIOUS.

Oh Lord, oh Lord!

Enter Lady Fulbank in an undress, and Pert undressed.

LADY FULBANK.

Heavens, what noise is this?—So he's got safe out,   175
I see. (*Sees Sir Feeble armed.*) Hah, what thing art thou?

SIR FEEBLE.

Stay, madam, stay. 'Tis I, 'tis I, a poor trembling mortal.

LADY FULBANK.

Sir Feeble Fainwould! Rise. Are you both mad?   180

SIR CAUTIOUS.

No, no, madam, we have seen the Devil.

SIR FEEBLE.

Aye, and he was as tall as the Monument.[49]

SIR CAUTIOUS.

With eyes like a beacon and a mouth, Heaven bless us, like London Bridge at a full tide.

SIR FEEBLE.

Aye, and roared as loud.   185

LADY FULBANK.

Idle fancies. What makes you from your bed?—
And you, sir, from your bride?

Enter Dick with sack. *

SIR FEEBLE.

Oh! that's the business of another day, a mistake only, madam.

---

49 Monument] a column over 200 feet high commemorating the Great Fire of London in 1666

LADY FULBANK.

Away, I'm ashamed to see wise men so weak: the   190
phantoms of the night or your own shadows, the whimsies of the brain for want* of rest, or perhaps Bredwel, your man, who being wiser than his master, played you this trick to fright you both to bed.   195

SIR FEEBLE.

Hum—adod, and that may be, for the young knave, when he let me in tonight, was dressed up for some waggery.

SIR CAUTIOUS.

Ha, ha, ha, 'twas even so, sure enough, brother.

SIR FEEBLE.

'Ods bobs, but they frighted me at first basely, but   200
I'll home to Pupsey: there may be roguery, as well as here.——Madam, I ask your pardon, I see we're all mistaken.

LADY FULBANK.

Aye Sir Feeble, go home to your wife.

Exeunt severally.

Scene [vi]. The street.

Enter Belmour at the door, knocks; enter to him from the house Phillis.

PHILLIS.

Oh, are you come, sir? I'll call my lady down.

BELMOUR.

Oh haste, the minutes fly. Leave all behind,
And bring Leticia only to my arms.

A noise of people.

Hah, what noise is that? 'Tis coming this way. I tremble with my fears. Hah, death and the devil,   5
'tis he—

Enter Sir Feeble and his men armed, goes to the door, knocks.

Aye, 'tis he, and I'm undone. What shall I do to[50]
kill him now? Besides, the sin would put me past all hopes of pardoning.

SIR FEEBLE.

A damned rogue to deceive me thus—   10

---

50 What shall I do to ... ?] What would happen if I did ... ?

BELMOUR.

Hah, see, by Heaven, Leticia! Oh, we are ruined!

SIR FEEBLE.

Hum—what's here, two women? (*Stands a little off.*)

Enter Leticia and Phillis softly, undressed, with a box.

LETICIA.

Where are you, my best wishes? Lord of my vows and charmer of my soul? Where are you?

BELMOUR.

Oh, heavens! (*Draws his sword half-way.*)   15

SIR FEEBLE. (*Aside.*)

Hum, who's here? My gentlewoman. She's monstrous kind* of the sudden. But whom is't meant to?

LETICIA.

Give me your hand, my love, my life, my all—alas! where are you?   20

SIR FEEBLE.

Hum—no, no, this is not to me; I am jilted, cozened, cuckolded, and so forth.

LETICIA. (*Groping, she takes hold of Sir Feeble.*)

Oh, are you here? Indeed you frighted me with your silence. Here, take these jewels and let us haste away.   25

SIR FEEBLE. [*Aside.*]

Hum—are you thereabouts, mistress? Was I sent away with a sham-plot for this! She cannot mean it to me.

LETICIA.

Will you not speak? Will you not answer me? Do you repent already? Before enjoyment are you cold   30 and false?

SIR FEEBLE.

Hum, "before enjoyment"? That must be me. "Before enjoyment"— (*Merrily.*) Aye, aye, 'tis I. I see a little prolonging a woman's joy sets an edge upon her appetite.   35

LETICIA.

What means my dear? Shall we not haste away?

SIR FEEBLE. [*Aside.*]

Haste away? There 'tis again. No, 'tis not me she means. What, at your tricks and intrigues already? Yes, yes, I am destined a cuckold.

LETICIA.

Say, am I not your wife? Can you deny me?   40

SIR FEEBLE.

Wife! (*Merrily.*) Adod 'tis I she means, 'tis I she means.

LETICIA.

Oh, Belmour, Belmour!

Sir Feeble starts back from her hands.

SIR FEEBLE.

Hum, what's that? Belmour!

LETICIA.

Hah! Sir Feeble!—He would not, sir, have used me   45 thus unkindly.

SIR FEEBLE.

Oh, I'm glad 'tis no worse. "Belmour," quotha; I thought the ghost was come again.

PHILLIS.

Why did you not speak, sir, all this while? My lady weeps with your unkindness.   50

SIR FEEBLE.

I did but hold my peace to hear how prettily she prattled love. But facks,* you are naught* to think of a young fellow, 'Ods bobs, you are now.

LETICIA.

I only said he would not have been so unkind to me.

SIR FEEBLE.

But what makes ye out at this hour and with these   55 jewels?

PHILLIS.

Alas sir, we thought the City was in arms and packed up our things to secure 'em if there had been a necessity for flight. For had they come to plundering once, they would have begun with the   60 rich aldermen's wives, you know, sir.

SIR FEEBLE.

'Ods bobs, and so they would, but there was no arms nor mutiny.—Where's Francis?

BELMOUR.

Here sir.

SIR FEEBLE.

"Here sir." Why, what a story you made of a   65 meeting in the Hall and—arms, and—a—the devil of anything was stirring, but a couple of old fools that sat gaping and waiting for one another's business.

BELMOUR.

Such a message was brought me, sir.   70

SIR FEEBLE.

Brought! Thou'rt an ass, Francis. But no more.—
Come, come, let's to bed.

LETICIA.

To bed, sir! What, by daylight? for that's hasting
on. I would not for the world: the night would
hide my blushes, but the day would let me see 75
myself in your embraces.

SIR FEEBLE.

Embraces, in a fiddlestick. Why, are we not
married?

LETICIA.

'Tis true, sir, and time will make me more familiar
with you, but yet my virgin modesty forbids it. I'll 80
to Diana's chamber; the night will come again.

SIR FEEBLE.

For once you shall prevail, and this damned jaunt
has pretty well mortified me.—A pox of your
mutiny, Francis.—Come, I'll conduct thee to Diana
and lock thee in, that I may have thee safe, rogue. 85
We'll give young wenches leave to whine and blush
And fly those blessings which, 'Ods bobs, they wish.

Exeunt.

Act IV, scene i. Sir Feeble's house.

*Enter Lady Fulbank, and Gayman fine, gently pulling
her back by the hand; and Ralph meets 'em.*

LADY FULBANK.

How now, Ralph, let your lady know I am come
to wait on her.

Exit Ralph.

GAYMAN.

Oh, why this needless visit?
Your husband's safe, at least till evening safe.
Why will you not go back? 5
And give me one soft hour, though to torment me?

LADY FULBANK.

You are at leisure now, I thank you, sir.
Last night when I with all Love's rhetoric pleaded,
And Heaven knows what last night might have
produced,
You were engaged! False man, I do believe it, 10
And I am satisfied you love me not. (*Walks away
in scorn.*)

GAYMAN.

Not love you!
Why do I waste my youth in vain pursuit,
Neglecting interest and despising power,
Unheeding and despising other beauties? 15
Why at your feet is all my fortune laid,
And why does all my fate depend on you?

LADY FULBANK.

I'll not consider why you play the fool,
Present me rings and bracelets; why pursue me;
Why watch whole nights before my senseless door 20
And take such pains to show yourself a coxcomb.

GAYMAN.

Oh! why all this?
By all the Powers above! By this dear hand
And by this ring, which on this hand I place,
On which I've sworn fidelity to love, 25
I never had a wish or soft desire
To any other woman,
Since Julia swayed the empire of my soul!

LADY FULBANK. (*Aside.*)

Hah, my own ring I gave him last night.—Your
jewel, sir, is rich. Why do you part with things of 30
so much value so easily and so frequently?

GAYMAN.

To strengthen the weak arguments of love.

LADY FULBANK.

And leave yourself undone?

GAYMAN.

Impossible, if I am blessed with Julia.

LADY FULBANK.

Love's a thin diet nor will keep out cold. You 35
cannot satisfy your dunning tailor to cry, "I am in
love!" though possible you may your seamstress.

GAYMAN.

Does aught about me speak such poverty?

LADY FULBANK.

I am sorry that it does not, since to maintain this
gallantry, 'tis said you use base means, below a 40
gentleman.

GAYMAN.

Who dares but to imagine it's a rascal, a slave,
below a beating. What means my Julia?

LADY FULBANK.

No more dissembling, I know your land is gone.
I know each circumstance of all your wants;* 45

therefore, as e'er you hope that I should love you ever, tell me where 'twas you got this jewel, sir.

GAYMAN. (*Aside.*)

Hah, I hope 'tis no stolen goods.—Why on the sudden all this nice* examining?

LADY FULBANK.

You trifle with me, and I'll plead no more. 50

GAYMAN.

Stay—why—I bought it, madam.

LADY FULBANK.

Where had you money, sir? You see I am no stranger to your poverty.

GAYMAN.

This is strange—perhaps it is a secret.

LADY FULBANK.

So is my love, which shall be kept from you. 55
(*Offers* to go.*)

GAYMAN. (*Sighing.*)

Stay Julia, your will shall be obeyed,
Though I had rather die than be obedient,
Because I know you'll hate me when 'tis told.

LADY FULBANK.

By all my vows, let it be what it will, 60
It ne'er shall alter me from loving you.

GAYMAN.

I have—of late—been tempted—with presents,
jewels, and large sums of gold.

LADY FULBANK.

Tempted! By whom?

GAYMAN.

The Devil, for aught I know. 65

LADY FULBANK.

Defend me, Heaven! The Devil? I hope you have not made a contract with him?

GAYMAN.

No, though in the shape of woman it appeared.

LADY FULBANK.

Where met you with it?

GAYMAN.

By magic art I was conducted, I know not how, 70
to an enchanted palace in the clouds, where I was so attended—young, dancing, singing fiends innumerable.

LADY FULBANK.

Imagination all!

GAYMAN.

But for the amorous devil, the old Proserpine— 75

LADY FULBANK.

Aye, she, what said she?

GAYMAN.

Not a word! Heaven be praised, she was a silent devil, but she was laid in a pavilion, all formed of gilded clouds, which hung by geometry,[51] whither I was conveyed, after much ceremony, and laid in 80
bed with her; where with much ado and trembling with my fears, I forced my arms about her.

LADY FULBANK. (*Aside.*)

And sure that undeceived him.

GAYMAN.

But such a carcass 'twas, deliver me, so riveled,[52] lean, and rough, a canvas bag of wooden ladles 85
were a better bedfellow.

LADY FULBANK. [*Aside.*]

Now though I know that nothing is more distant than I from such a monster, yet this angers me.—
Death! could you love me and submit to this?

GAYMAN.

'Twas that first drew me in: the tempting hope of 90
means to conquer you would put me upon any dangerous enterprise.
Were I the lord of all the universe,
I am so lost in love,
For one dear night to clasp you in my arms 95
I'd lavish all that world—then die* with joy.

LADY FULBANK. [*Aside.*]

'Slife,* after all to seem deformed, old, ugly—
(*Walking in a fret.*)

GAYMAN.

I knew you would be angry when you heard it.
(*Pursues her in a submissive posture.*) 100

*Enter Sir Cautious, Bearjest, Captain Noisy, and
Bredwel.*

SIR CAUTIOUS.

How, what's here? My lady with the spark that courted her last night? Hum, with her again so soon?
Well, this impudence and importunity undoes more
City wives than all their unmerciful finery.

GAYMAN.

But madam— 105

---

51 by geometry] hung in a stiff, angular fashion
52 riveled] contracted into wrinkles, shriveled

LADY FULBANK. (*Angry.*)
Oh, here's my husband: you'd best tell him your story. [*Aside.*] What makes him here so soon?
SIR CAUTIOUS.
Me his story? I hope he will not tell me he has a mind to cuckold me!
GAYMAN. [*Aside.*]
A devil on him, what shall I say to him?   110
LADY FULBANK. (*Aside [to Gayman].*)
What, so excellent at intrigues and so dull at an excuse?
GAYMAN.
Yes, madam, I shall tell him—

Enter Belmour.

LADY FULBANK.
Is my lady at leisure for a visit, sir?
BELMOUR.
Always to receive your ladyship.   115

She goes out.

SIR CAUTIOUS.
With me, sir, would you speak?
GAYMAN.
With you, sir, if your name be Fulbank?
SIR CAUTIOUS.
Plain Fulbank: methinks you might have had a sir-reverence under your girdle, sir: I am honored with another title, sir. (*Goes talking to the rest.*)   120
GAYMAN.
With many, sir, that very well become you. (*Pulls him a little aside.*) I've something to deliver to your ear.
SIR CAUTIOUS. [*Aside.*]
So, I'll be hanged if he do not tell me I'm a cuckold now. I see it in his eyes.—My ear, sir? I'd have you   125
to know I scorn any man's secrets, sir; for aught I know you may whisper treason to me, sir. (*Aside.*) Pox on him, how handsome he is! I hate the sight of the young stallion.
GAYMAN.
I would not be so uncivil, sir, before all this   130
company.
SIR CAUTIOUS.
Uncivil? [*Aside.*] Aye, aye, 'tis so, he cannot be content to cuckold but he must tell me so too.

GAYMAN.
But since you will have it, sir, you are—a rascal—a most notorious villain, sir, d'ye hear?   135
SIR CAUTIOUS. (*Laughing.*)
Yes, yes, I do hear and am glad 'tis no worse.
GAYMAN.
Gripping as hell and as insatiable, worse than a brokering Jew: not all the twelve tribes harbors such a damned extortioner.
SIR CAUTIOUS.
Pray under favor, sir, who are you? (*Pulling off his*   140
hat.)
GAYMAN.
One whom thou hast undone—
SIR CAUTIOUS. (*Aside, smiling.*)
Hum, I'm glad of that, however.
GAYMAN.
Racking me up to a starving want* and misery, then took advantages to ruin me.   145
SIR CAUTIOUS. (*Aside, smiling.*)
So, and he'd revenge it on my wife.
GAYMAN.
Do not you know one Wasteall, sir?

Enter Ralph with wine, sets it on a table.

SIR CAUTIOUS.
Wasteall! Ha, ha, ha, if you are any friend to that poor fellow, you may return and tell him, sir—d'ye hear—that the mortgage of two hundred pound   150
a year is this day out, and I'll not bate him an hour, sir. Ha, ha, ha, what, do you think to hector civil magistrates?
GAYMAN.
Very well, sir, and is this your conscience?
SIR CAUTIOUS.
Conscience! What do you tell me of conscience?   155
Why, what a noise's here, as if the undoing a young heir were such a wonder. 'Ods so, I've undone a hundred without half this ado.
GAYMAN.
I do believe thee and am come to tell you: I'll be none of that number, for this minute I'll go and   160
redeem it and free myself from the hell of your indentures.
SIR CAUTIOUS. [*Aside.*]
How, redeem it? Sure the Devil must help him

then!—Stay sir, stay. Lord sir, what need you put yourself to that trouble? Your land is in safe hands, sir. Come, come, sit down, and let us take a glass of wine together, sir. 165

BELMOUR.

Sir, my service to you. (*Drinks to him.*)

GAYMAN.

Your servant, sir. [*Aside.*] Would I could come to speak to Belmour, which I dare not do in public, lest I betray him. I long to be resolved where 'twas Sir Feeble was last night—if it were he—by which I might find out my invisible mistress. 170

NOISY.

Noble Mr. Wasteall— (*Salutes* him; so does Bearjest.*)

BELMOUR.

Will you please to sit, sir? 175

GAYMAN.

I have a little business, sir, but anon I'll wait on you.—Your servant, gentlemen, I'll to Crap the scrivener's. (*Goes out.*)

SIR CAUTIOUS. (*To Noisy.*)

Do you know this Wasteall, sir?

NOISY.

Know him, sir? Aye, too well. 180

BEARJEST.

The world's well amended with him, Captain, since I lost my money to him and you at the George in Whitefriars.

NOISY.

Aye, poor fellow: he's sometimes up and sometimes down, as the dice favor him. 185

BEARJEST.

Faith, and that's pity, but how came he so fine o'th'sudden? 'Twas but last week he borrowed eighteen pence of me on his waist belt to pay his dinner in an ordinary.

BELMOUR.

Were you so cruel, sir, to take it? 190

NOISY.

We are not all one man's children; faith sir, we are here today and gone tomorrow.

SIR CAUTIOUS.

I say 'twas done like a wise man, sir. But under favor, gentlemen, this Wasteall is a rascal—

NOISY.

A very* rascal, sir, and a most dangerous fellow: 195

he cullies in your prentices and cashiers to play, which ruins so many o'th'young fry i'th'City.

SIR CAUTIOUS.

Hum, does he so?—Do hear that, Edward?

NOISY.

Then he keeps a private press and prints your Amsterdam and Leyden libels.53 200

SIR CAUTIOUS.

Aye, and makes 'em too, I'll warrant him: a dangerous fellow.

NOISY.

Sometimes he begs for a lame soldier with a wooden leg.

BEARJEST.

Sometimes, as a blind man, sells switches in Newmarket road.54 205

NOISY.

At other times he runs the country like a gypsy, tells fortunes, and robs hedges when he's out of linen.

SIR CAUTIOUS.

Tells fortunes too! Nay, I thought he dealt with the Devil. Well, gentlemen, you are all wide o' this matter, for to tell you the truth, he deals with the Devil, gentlemen. (*Aside.*) Otherwise he could never have redeemed his land. 210

BELMOUR.

How sir, the Devil?

SIR CAUTIOUS.

I say the Devil. Heaven bless every wise man from the Devil. 215

BEARJEST.

The Devil, pshaw! There's no such animal in nature. I rather think he pads.*

NOISY.

Oh sir, he has not courage for that, but he's an admirable fellow at your lock. 220

SIR CAUTIOUS.

Lock! my study lock was picked. I begin to suspect him.

---

53 Amsterdam and Leiden libels] These Dutch towns would have allowed the publication of works attacking the Stuart monarchy.

54 Newmarket road] Possibly a reference to the Rye House Plot, in which Charles II and James, duke of York, were to be assassinated as they returned from the Newmarket races.

BEARJEST.

I saw him once open a lock with the bone of a
breast of mutton and break an iron bar asunder
with the eye of a needle.   225

SIR CAUTIOUS.

Prodigious! Well, I say the Devil still.

Enter Sir Feeble.

[SIR FEEBLE].

Who's this talks of the Devil? A pox of the Devil,
I say, this last night's devil has so haunted me—

SIR CAUTIOUS.

Why, have you seen it since, brother?

SIR FEEBLE.

In imagination, sir.   230

BELMOUR.

How sir, a devil?

SIR FEEBLE.

Aye, or a ghost.

BELMOUR.

Where, good sir?

BEARJEST.

Aye, where? I'd travel a hundred mile to see a
ghost.   235

BELMOUR.

Sure sir, 'twas fancy.

SIR FEEBLE.

If 'twere a fancy, 'twas a strong one, and ghosts and
fancy are all one if they can deceive. I tell you, if
ever I thought in my life, I thought I saw a ghost.
Aye, and a damnable impudent ghost too: he said   240
he was a—a fellow here they call Belmour.

BELMOUR.

How sir!

BEARJEST.

Well, I would give the world to see the Devil,
provided he were a civil, affable devil, such a one
as Wasteall's acquaintance is.   245

SIR CAUTIOUS.

He can show him too soon, it may be. I'm sure as
civil as he is, he helps him to steal my gold, I
doubt,* and to be sure: gentlemen, you say he's a
gamester; I desire when he comes anon that you
would propose to sport a die or so, and we'll fall   250
to play for a tester or the like. And if he sets any
money, I shall go near to know my own gold by

some remarkable pieces amongst it, and if he have
it, I'll hang him, and then all his six hundred a year
will be my own, which I have in mortgage.   255

BEARJEST.

Let the captain and I alone to top upon[55] him.
Meantime sir, I have brought my music to
entertain my mistress with a song.

SIR FEEBLE.

Take your own methods, sir—they are at leisure—
while we go drink their healths within. Adod, I   260
long for night. We are not half in kilter. This
damned ghost will not out of my head yet.

Exeunt all but Belmour.

BELMOUR.

Hah, a ghost! What can he mean? A ghost, and
Belmour's.
—Sure my good angel, or my genius,*
In pity of my love, and of Leticia—   265
But see, Leticia comes, but still attended.

Enter Leticia, Lady Fulbank, Diana.

(*Aside to her, passing by.*) —Remember—oh,
remember to be true! (*Goes out.*)

LADY FULBANK.

I was sick to know with what Christian patience
you bore the martyrdom of this night.   270

LETICIA.

As those condemned bear the last hour of life: a
short reprieve I had, and by a kind mistake Diana
only was my bedfellow. (*Weeps.*)

DIANA.

And I wish for your repose you ne'er had seen my
father. (*Weeps.*)   275

LETICIA.

And so do I: I fear he has undone me—

DIANA.

And me, in breaking of his word with Bredwel.

LADY FULBANK.

So, as Trincolo says, would you were both hanged
for me, for putting me in mind of my husband.[56]

---

55 top upon] trick
56 as Trincolo says … my husband] Actually, Lady Fulbank
    paraphrases Stephano, not Trincolo, in the Dryden/
    Davenant adaptation of Shakespeare's *Tempest.*

For I have e'en no better luck than either of you.   280
Let our two fates warn your approaching one. I
love young Bredwel and must plead for him.

DIANA.

I know his virtue justifies my choice, but pride and
modesty forbids I should unloved pursue him.

LETICIA.

Wrong not my brother so, who dies for you.   285

DIANA.

Could he so easily see me given away
Without a sigh at parting?
For all the day a calm was in his eyes,
And unconcerned he looked and talked to me,
In dancing never pressed my willing hand   290
Nor with a scornful glance reproached my
    falsehood.

LETICIA.

Believe me, that dissembling was his masterpiece.

DIANA.

Why should he fear: Did not my father promise
him?

LETICIA.

Aye, that was in his wooing time to me. But now   295
'tis all forgotten.

*Music at the door, after which enter Bearjest and
Bredwel.*

LADY FULBANK.

How now, cousin! Is this high piece of gallantry
from you?

BEARJEST.

Aye madam, I have not traveled for nothing.

LADY FULBANK.

I find my cousin is resolved to conquer; he assails
with all his artillery of charms. We'll leave him to   300
his success, madam.

Exeunt Leticia and Lady Fulbank.

BEARJEST.

Oh Lord, madam, you oblige me.—Look Ned,
you had a mind to have a full view of my mistress,
sir, and—here she is.

[Bredwel] stands gazing.

Go, salute* her.—Look how he stands now: what   305
a sneaking thing is a fellow who has never traveled

and seen the world!—Madam, this is a very honest
friend of mine, for all he looks so simply.

DIANA.

Come, he speaks for you, sir.

BEARJEST.

He, madam, though he be but a banker's prentice,   310
madam, he's as pretty a fellow of his inches[57] as
any i'th'City: he has made love* in dancing schools
and to ladies of quality* in the middle gallery,[58]
and shall joke ye and repartee with any foreman
within the walls.—Prithee to her and commend   315
me, I'll give thee a new point cravat.

DIANA.

He looks as if he could not speak to me.

BEARJEST.

Not speak to you? Yes, gad madam, and do
anything to you too.

DIANA. (*In scorn.*)

Are you his advocate, sir?   320

BEARJEST.

For want* of a better. (*Stands behind [Bredwel],
pushing him on.*)

BREDWEL.

An advocate for love I am, and bring you such a
message from a heart—

BEARJEST.

Meaning mine, dear madam.   325

BREDWEL.

That when you hear it, you will pity it.

BEARJEST.

Or the Devil's in her.

DIANA.

Sir, I have many reasons to believe it is my fortune
you pursue, not person.

BEARJEST. [*Aside.*]

There is something in that, I must confess.—But   330
say what you will, Ned.

BREDWEL.

May all the mischiefs of despairing love fall on me
if it be.

---

57 of his inches] of his height, with a likely jest at the dis-
    parity in height between the tall Thomas Jevon, who
    played Bearjest, and the short John Bowman, who
    played Bredwel

58 middle gallery] theater area frequented by prostitutes

BEARJEST.

That's well enough—

BREDWEL.

No, were you born an humble village maid,   335
That fed a flock upon the neighbouring plain,
With all that shining virtue in your soul,
By heaven, I would adore you, love you, wed you,
Though the gay world were lost by such a nuptial.

Bearjest looks on him.

(*Recollecting.*) This I would do, were I my friend   340
the squire.

BEARJEST.

Aye, if you were me, you might do what you
pleased, but I'm of another mind.

DIANA.

Should I consent, my father is a man whom
interest sways, not honor, and whatsoever promise   345
he's made you, he means to break 'em all, and I
am destined to another.

BEARJEST.

How, another! His name, his name, madam. Here's
Ned and I fear ne'er a single man i'th'Nation. What
is he? What is he?   350

DIANA.

A fop, a fool, a beaten ass, a blockhead.

BEARJEST.

What a damned shame's this, that women should
be sacrificed to fools, and fops must run away with
heiresses, whilst we men of wit and parts* dress and
dance, and cock and travel, for nothing but to be   355
tame keepers.*

DIANA.

But I, by Heaven, will never be that victim,
But where my soul is vowed, 'tis fixed for ever.

BREDWEL.

Are you resolved, are you confirmed in this? (*Runs
to her, and embraces her.*)
Oh my Diana, speak it o'er again.   360
Bless me and make me happier than a monarch.

BEARJEST.

Hold, hold, dear Ned, that's my part, I take it.

BREDWEL.

Your pardon, sir, I had forgot myself.—But time
is short: What's to be done in this?

BEARJEST.

Done! I'll enter the house with fire and sword, d'ye   365

see, not that I care this ____* but I'll not be fobbed
off. What, do they take me for a fool, an ass?

BREDWEL.

Madam, dare you run the risk of your father's
displeasure and run away with the man you love?

DIANA.

With all my soul.   370

BEARJEST.

That's hearty, and we'll do't, Ned and I here. And
I love an amour with an adventure in't, like *Amadis
de Gaul*[59].—Hark ye, Ned, get a coach and six
ready tonight when 'tis dark at the back gate.

BREDWEL.

And I'll get a parson ready in my lodging, to which   375
I have a key through the garden, by which we may
pass unseen.

BEARJEST.

Good.—Mun,[60] here's company.

*Enter Gayman with his hat with money in't; Sir
Cautious in a rage; Sir Feeble, Lady Fulbank, Leticia,
Captain Noisy, Belmour.*

SIR CAUTIOUS.

A hundred pound lost already! Oh coxcomb, old
coxcomb, and a wise coxcomb, to turn prodigal at   380
my years. Why,[e] I was bewitched!

SIR FEEBLE.

Pshaw, 'twas a frolic, sir. I have lost a hundred
pound as well as you. My lady has lost, and your
lady has lost, and the rest— What, old cows will
kick sometimes. What's a hundred pound?   385

SIR CAUTIOUS.

A hundred pound! Why, 'tis a sum, sir, a sum.
Why, what the devil did I do with a box and dice?

LADY FULBANK.

Why, you made a shift to lose, sir. And where's the
harm of that? We have lost, and he has won. Anon
it may be your fortune.   390

SIR CAUTIOUS.

Aye, but he could never do it fairly, that's certain.
Three hundred pound!—Why, how came you to
win so unmercifully, sir?

---

59 *Amadis de Gaul*] hugely popular sixteenth-century chiv-
alric romance

60 Mun] rural variant of mon, man

GAYMAN.

Oh, the Devil will not lose a gamester of me, you see, sir.   395

SIR CAUTIOUS.

The Devil!—Mark that, gentlemen.

BEARJEST.

The rogue has damned luck sure, he has got a fly.[61]

SIR CAUTIOUS.

And can you have the conscience to carry away all our money, sir?

GAYMAN.

Most assuredly, unless you have the courage to   400
retrieve it. I'll set it at a throw, or any way. What say you, gentlemen?

SIR FEEBLE.

'Ods bobs, you young fellows are too hard for us every way, and I am engaged at an old game with a new gamester here, who will require all an old   405
man's stock.

LADY FULBANK.

Come cousin, will you venture a guinea?—Come, Mr. Bredwel.

GAYMAN.

Well, if nobody dare venture on me, I'll send away
my cash.   410

*They all go to play at the table, but Sir Cautious, Sir
Feeble, and Gayman.*

SIR CAUTIOUS. *(Aside.)*

Hum, must it all go? A rare sum: if a man were
but sure the Devil would stand but neuter now.—
Sir, I wish I had anything but ready money to
stake: three hundred pound, a fine sum!

GAYMAN.

You have moveables, sir, goods, commodities—   415

SIR CAUTIOUS.

That's all one, sir; that's money's worth, sir. But if
I had anything that were worth nothing—

GAYMAN.

You would venture it, I thank you, sir. I would
your lady were worth nothing.

SIR CAUTIOUS.

Why so, sir?   420

GAYMAN.

Then I would set all this against that nothing.

SIR CAUTIOUS.

What, set it against my wife?

GAYMAN.

Wife, sir! Aye, your wife.

SIR CAUTIOUS. *[Aside.]*

Hum, my wife against three hundred pounds?—
What, all my wife, sir?   425

GAYMAN.

All your wife. Why sir, some part of her would
serve my turn.

SIR CAUTIOUS. *(Aside.)*

Hum, my wife: why, if I should lose, he could not
have the impudence to take her.

GAYMAN.

Well, I find you are not for the bargain, and so I   430
put up—

SIR CAUTIOUS.

Hold sir, why so hasty? My wife? no, put up your
money, sir. What, lose my wife for three hundred
pounds!

GAYMAN.

Lose her, sir! Why, she shall be never the worse for   435
my wearing, sir. *[Aside.]* The old covetous rogue
is considering on't, I think.—What say you to a
night? I'll set it to a night; there's none need know
it, sir.

SIR CAUTIOUS. *[Aside.]*

Hum, a night! Three hundred pounds for a night!   440
Why, what a lavish whoremaster's this: we take
money to marry our wives, but very seldom part
with 'em and by the bargain get money.—For a
night, say you? *(Aside.)* Gad, if I should take the
rogue at his word, 'twould be a pure jest.   445

SIR FEEBLE.

You are not mad, brother.

SIR CAUTIOUS.

No, but I'm wise, and that's as good. Let me
consider—

SIR FEEBLE.

What, whether you shall be a cuckold or not?

SIR CAUTIOUS.

Or lose three hundred pounds, consider that. A   450
cuckold—why, 'tis a word, an empty sound, 'tis
breath, 'tis air, 'tis nothing—but three hundred

---

61 fly] an incubus as his familiar

pounds, Lord, what will not three hundred pounds do? You may chance to be a cuckold for nothing, sir.

SIR FEEBLE.

It may be so, but she shall do't discreetly then.

SIR CAUTIOUS.

Under favor, you're an ass, brother: this is the discreetest way of doing it, I take it.

SIR FEEBLE.

But would a wise man expose his wife?

SIR CAUTIOUS.

Why, Cato was a wiser man than I, and he lent his wife to a young fellow they called Hortensius, as story says, and can a wise man have a better precedent than Cato?[62]

SIR FEEBLE.

I say Cato was an ass, sir, for obliging any young rogue of 'em all.

SIR CAUTIOUS.

But I am of Cato's mind.—Well, a single night, you say?

GAYMAN.

A single night: to have, to hold, possess, and so forth, at discretion.

SIR CAUTIOUS.

A night.—I shall have her safe and sound i'th'morning?

SIR FEEBLE.

Safe, no doubt on't, but how sound?*

GAYMAN.

And for non-performance, you shall pay me three hundred pounds. I'll forfeit as much if I tell.

SIR CAUTIOUS.

Tell? Why, make your three hundred pounds six hundred and let it be put into the *Gazette*, if you will, man. But is't a bargain?

GAYMAN.

Done! Sir Feeble shall be witness, and there stands my hat.

Puts down his hat of money, and each of 'em take a box and dice, and kneel on the stage; the rest come about 'em.

SIR CAUTIOUS.

He that comes first to one and thirty wins.

They throw and count.

LADY FULBANK.

What are you playing for?

SIR FEEBLE.

Nothing, nothing—but a trial of skill between an old man and a young, and your ladyship is to be judge.

LADY FULBANK.

I shall be partial, sir.

SIR CAUTIOUS.

Six and five's eleven. (*Throws, and pulls the hat towards him.*)

GAYMAN.

Cater trey.[63] Pox of the dice.

SIR CAUTIOUS.

Two fives: (*Sets up,*[64] *pulls the hat nearer.*) one and twenty.

GAYMAN.

Now, Luck! Doubles of sixes: nineteen.

SIR CAUTIOUS.

Five and four: (*Draws the hat to him.*) thirty.

SIR FEEBLE.

Now if he wins it, I'll swear he has a fly indeed; 'tis impossible without doubles of sixes.

GAYMAN.

Now Fortune smile, and for the future frown. (*Throws.*)

SIR CAUTIOUS.

Hum, two sixes. (*Rises and looks dolefully around.*)

LADY FULBANK.

How now, what's the matter? You look so like an ass, what have you lost?

SIR CAUTIOUS.

A bauble, a bauble. 'Tis not for what I've lost, but because I have not won.

SIR FEEBLE.

You look very simply, sir. What think you of Cato now?

SIR CAUTIOUS.

A wise man may have his failings.

---

62 Cato] According to Plutarch's *Lives*, Cato the Younger passes his wife to Quintus Hortensius, receiving her back after the latter dies.

63 Cater trey] four and three

64 sets up] counts

LADY FULBANK.

    What has my husband lost? 505

SIR CAUTIOUS.

    Only a small parcel of ware that lay dead upon my hands, sweetheart.

GAYMAN.

    But I shall improve 'em, madam, I'll warrant you.

LADY FULBANK.

    Well, since 'tis no worse, bring in your fine dancer, cousin, you say you brought to entertain your 510 mistress with.

Bearjest goes out.

GAYMAN.

    Sir, you'll take care to see me paid tonight?

SIR CAUTIOUS.

    Well sir, but my lady, you must know, sir, has the common frailties of her sex and will refuse what she even longs for, if persuaded to't by me. 515

GAYMAN.

    'Tis not in my bargain to solicit her, sir. You are to procure her, or three hundred pounds, sir. Choose you whether.

SIR CAUTIOUS.

    Procure her? With all my soul, sir. Alas, you mistake my honest meaning: I scorn to be so unjust as not to 520 see you a-bed together, and then agree as well as you can, I have done my part. In order to this, sir, get you but yourself conveyed in a chest to my house with a direction upon't for me, and for the rest—

GAYMAN.

    I understand you. 525

SIR FEEBLE.

    Ralph, get supper ready.

Enter Bearjest with dancers; all go out but Sir Cautious.

SIR CAUTIOUS.

    Well, I must break my mind, if possible, to my lady. But if she should be refractory now and make me pay three hundred pounds— Why, sure she won't have so little grace— Three hundred pounds 530 saved is three hundred pounds got, by our account. Could all

    Who of this City privilege are free

    Hope to be paid for cuckoldom like me,

    Th'unthriving merchant, whom gray hair adorns, 535

    Before all ventures would insure his horns.*

    For thus, while he but lets spare rooms to hire,

    His wife's cracked[f] credit keeps his own entire.

Exit.

Act V, scene i. Sir Feeble's[g] house.

Enter Belmour alone, sad.

BELMOUR.

    The night is come, oh, my Leticia!

    The longing bridegroom hastens to his bed,

    Whilst she, with all the languishment of love

    And sad despair, casts her fair eyes on me,

    Which silently implore I would deliver her. 5

    But how? aye, there's the question— (*Pausing.*) Hah!

    I'll get myself hid in her bedchamber,

    And something I will do may serve us yet.

    If all my arts should fail, I'll have recourse (*Draws a dagger.*)

    To this—and bear Leticia off by force. 10

    —But see, she comes.

Enter Lady Fulbank, Sir Cautious, Sir Feeble, Leticia, Bearjest, Captain Noisy, Gayman. Exit Belmour.

SIR FEEBLE.

    Lights there, Ralph, and my lady's coach there.

Bearjest goes to Gayman.

BEARJEST.

    Well sir, remember you have promised to grant me my diabolical request in showing me the Devil.

GAYMAN.

    I will not fail you, sir. 15

[Enter Ralph with a light.]

LADY FULBANK.

    Madam, your servant.—I hope you'll see no more ghosts, Sir Feeble.

SIR FEEBLE.

    No more of that, I beseech you, madam.—Prithee, Sir Cautious, take away your wife.—Madam, your servant. 20

[Lady Fulbank, Sir Cautious, Bearjest, Captain Noisy, and Gayman] go out after [Ralph with] the light.

Come Lette, Lette, hasten, rogue, hasten to thy chamber, away, here be the young wenches coming.

Puts her out; he goes out. Enter Diana, puts on her hood and scarf.

DIANA.

So, they are gone to bed, and now for Bredwel: the coach waits, and I'll take the opportunity. Father, farewell: if you dislike my course, 25
Blame the old rigid customs of your force.

Goes out.

Scene [ii]. A bedchamber.

Enter Sir Feeble, Leticia, and Phillis.

LETICIA.

Ah, Phillis! I am fainting with my fears. Hast thou no comfort for me?

He undresses to his gown.

SIR FEEBLE.

Why, what art doing there, fiddle-faddling? Adod, you young wenches are so loath to come to, but when your hand's in, you have no mercy upon us 5
poor husbands.

LETICIA.

Why do you talk so, sir?

SIR FEEBLE.

Was it angered at the fool's prattle? Tum-a-me, tum-a-me, I'll undress it, i'facks, I will, roguy.

LETICIA.

You are so wanton, sir, you make me blush. I will 10
not go to bed unless you promise me—

SIR FEEBLE.

No bargaining, my little hussy. What, you'll tie my hands behind me, will you?

She goes to the table.

LETICIA.

What shall I do?—Assist me, gentle maid, thy eyes methinks puts on a little hope! 15

PHILLIS.

Take courage, madam, you guess right. Be confident.

SIR FEEBLE.

No whispering, gentlewoman, and putting tricks

into her head that shall cheat me of another night.

As she is at the toilet, he looks over her shoulder, and sees her face in the glass.*

Look on that silly* little round chitty-face; look on 20
those smiling, roguish, loving eyes there; look, look how they laugh, twire,* and tempt. Hee, rogue, I'll buss 'em there and here and everywhere. 'Ods bobs, away, this is fooling and spoiling of a man's stomach, with a bit here and a bit there. To bed, to bed. 25

LETICIA.

Go you first, sir, I will stay but to say my prayers. (*Aside.*) Which are that Heaven would deliver me.

SIR FEEBLE.

Say thy prayers? What, art thou mad, prayers upon thy wedding night? A short thanksgiving or so, but prayers, quotha! 'Sbobs, you'll have time enough 30
for that, I doubt.*

LETICIA.

I am ashamed to undress before you, sir. Go to bed.

SIR FEEBLE.

What, was it ashamed to show its little white foots, and its little round bubbies? Well, I'll go, I'll go. 35
(*Going towards the bed.*) I cannot think on't, no, I cannot.

Belmour comes forth from between the curtains, his coat off, his shirt bloody, a dagger in his hand, and his disguise off.

BELMOUR.

Stand!

SIR FEEBLE.

Hah!

LETICIA and PHILLIS. (*Squeak.*)

Oh, heavens! 40

LETICIA. (*Aside to Phillis.*)

Why, is it Belmour?

BELMOUR.

Go not to bed, I guard this sacred place,
And the adulterer dies that enters here.

SIR FEEBLE.

Oh, why do I shake? Sure I'm a man, what art thou? 45

BELMOUR.

I am the wronged, the lost and murdered Belmour.

SIR FEEBLE.

Oh Lord! It is the same I saw last night. Oh!—
Hold thy dread vengeance, pity me, and hear
me.—Oh! a parson, a parson! What shall I do? Oh!
where shall I hide myself?   50

BELMOUR.

I'th'utmost borders of the earth I'll find thee;
Seas shall not hide thee, nor vast mountains guard
  thee.
Even in the depth of Hell I'll find thee out
And lash thy filthy and adulterous soul.

SIR FEEBLE.

Oh! I am dead, I'm dead, will no repentance save   55
me? 'Twas that young eye that tempted me to sin.
Oh!

BELMOUR.

See, fair seducer, what thou'st made me do:
Look on this bleeding wound, it reached my heart,
To pluck thy^h dear tormenting image thence,   60
When news arrived that thou hadst broke thy
  vow.

SIR FEEBLE.

Oh Lord! Oh!—I'm glad he's dead though.

LETICIA.

Oh, hide that fatal wound; my tender heart faints
with a sight so horrid! (*Seems to weep.*)

SIR FEEBLE.

So, she'll clear herself and leave me in the devil's   65
clutches.

BELMOUR.

You've both offended Heaven and must repent or
die.

SIR FEEBLE.

Ah, I do confess I was an old fool, bewitched with
beauty, besotted with love, and do repent most   70
heartily.

BELMOUR.

No, you had rather yet go on in sin:
Thou wouldst live on and be a baffled cuckold.

SIR FEEBLE.

Oh, not for the world, sir. I am convinced and
mortified.   75

BELMOUR.

Maintain her fine, undo thy peace to please her,
And still* be cuckolded on.
Believe her, trust her, and be cuckolded still.*

SIR FEEBLE.

I see my folly and my age's dotage and find the
Devil was in me. Yet spare my age, ah, spare me   80
to repent.

BELMOUR.

If thou repent'st, renounce her, fly her sight,
Shun her bewitching charms, as thou wouldst Hell,
Those dark eternal mansions of the dead—
Whither I must descend.   85

SIR FEEBLE.

Oh, would he were gone!

BELMOUR.

Fly—be gone—depart, vanish forever
From her to some more safe and innocent
  apartment.

SIR FEEBLE.

Oh, that's very hard!

*He goes back trembling, Belmour follows in with his
dagger up; both go out.*

LETICIA.

Blest be this kind release, and yet methinks it   90
grieves me to consider how the poor old man is
frighted.

Belmour re-enters, puts on his coat.

BELMOUR.

He's gone, and locked himself into his chamber.
—And now, my dear Leticia, let us fly.
Despair till now did my wild heart invade,   95
But pitying love has the rough storm allayed.

Exeunt.

Scene [iii]. Sir Cautious his* garden.

*Enter two porters and Rag, bearing Gayman in a chest;
[they] set it down; [Gayman] comes forth with a dark
lantern.*

GAYMAN.

Set down the chest behind yon hedge of roses and
then put on those shapes I have appointed you.
And be sure you well-favoredly bang both Bearjest
and Noisy, since they have a mind to see the Devil.

RAG.

Oh sir, leave 'em to us for that, and if we do not   5
play the devil with 'em, we deserve they should

beat us. But sir, we are in Sir Cautious his* garden:
Will not he sue us for a trespass?

GAYMAN.

I'll bear you out. Be ready at my call.

Exeunt [Rag and porters].

Let me see, I have got no ready stuff to banter with, 10
but no matter, any gibberish will serve the fools. 'Tis
now about the hour of ten, but twelve is my
appointed lucky minute, when all the blessings that
my soul could wish shall be resigned to me.

Enter Bredwel.

Hah! Who's there? Bredwel? 15

BREDWEL.

Oh, are you come, sir? And can you be so kind to
a poor youth to favor his designs and bless his
days?

GAYMAN.

Yes, I am ready here with all my devils, both to
secure you your mistress and to cudgel your 20
captain and squire for abusing me behind my back
so basely.

BREDWEL.

'Twas most unmanly, sir, and they deserve it. I
wonder that they come not?

GAYMAN.

How durst you trust her with him? 25

BREDWEL.

Because 'tis dangerous to steal a City heiress, and
let the theft be his, so the dear maid be mine.—
Hark, sure they come.

Enter Bearjest, runs against Bredwel.

Who's there? Mr. Bearjest?

BEARJEST.

Who's that? Ned? Well, I have brought my 30
mistress. Hast thou got a parson ready and a
license?

BREDWEL.

Aye, aye, but where's the lady?

BEARJEST.

In the coach with the captain at the gate. I came
before to see if the coast be clear. 35

BREDWEL.

Aye sir, but what shall we do? Here's Mr. Gayman

come on purpose to show you the Devil, as you
desired.

BEARJEST.

Pshaw! A pox of the Devil, man: I can't intend to
speak with him now. 40

GAYMAN.

How, sir! D'ye think my devil of so little quality*
to suffer an affront unrevenged?

BEARJEST.

Sir, I cry his devilship's pardon: I did not know his
quality. I protest, sir, I love and honor him, but I
am now just going to be married, sir, and when 45
that ceremony's past, I'm ready to go to the devil
as soon as you please.

GAYMAN.

I have told him your desire of seeing him. And
should you baffle him?

BEARJEST.

Who, I, sir! Pray let his worship know I shall be 50
proud of the honor of his acquaintance, but sir,
my mistress and the parson wait in Ned's chamber.

GAYMAN.

If all the world wait, sir, the Prince of Hell will
stay for no man.

BREDWEL.

Oh sir, rather than the Prince of the Infernals shall 55
be affronted, I'll conduct the lady up and entertain
her till you come, sir.

BEARJEST.

Nay, I have a great mind to kiss his—paw, sir, but
I could wish you'd show him me by daylight, sir.

GAYMAN.

The Prince of Darkness does abhor the light. But 60
sir, I will for once allow your friend the captain to
keep you company.

Enter Captain Noisy and Diana.

BEARJEST.

I'm much obliged to you, sir.—Oh, Captain—
(*Talks to him.*)

BREDWEL.

Haste, dear, the parson waits,
To finish what the Pow'rs designed above. 65

DIANA.

Sure nothing is so bold as maids in love.

They go out.

NOISY.

Pshaw! He conjure? He can fly as soon.

GAYMAN.

Gentlemen, you must be sure to confine yourselves
to this circle and have a care you neither swear nor   70
pray.

BEARJEST.

Pray, sir? I dare say neither of us were ever that way
gifted.

A horrid noise.

GAYMAN.

Cease your horror, cease your haste
And calmly as I saw you last   75
Appear! Appear!
By thy pearls and diamond rocks,
By thy heavy money box,
By thy shining petticoat,
That hid thy cloven feet from note,   80
By the veil that hid thy face,
Which else had frightened human race:
Appear, that I thy love may see,

Soft music ceases.

Appear, kind fiends, appear to me.
—A pox of these rascals, why come they not.   85

*Four enter from the four corners of the stage, to music
that plays; they dance, and in the dance, dance 'round
[Bearjest and Captain Noisy], and kick, pinch, and
beat 'em.*

BEARJEST.

Oh, enough, enough! Good sir, lay 'em and I'll pay
the music.

GAYMAN.

I wonder at it. These spirits are in their nature kind
and peaceable. And you have basely injured
somebody. Confess,[i] and then they will be satisfied.   90

BEARJEST.

Oh good sir, take your Cerberuses off. I do confess
the captain here and I have violated your fame.

NOISY.

Abused you and traduced you, and thus we beg
your pardon.

GAYMAN.

Abused me! 'Tis more than I know, gentlemen.   95

BEARJEST.

But it seems your friend the Devil does.

GAYMAN. [*Aside.*]

By this time Bredwel's married.—Great
Pantamogan,[65] hold, for I am satisfied.

Exeunt devils.

And thus undo my charm.

*Takes away the circle; [Bearjest and Captain Noisy]
run out.*

So, the fools are going, and now to Julia's arms.   100

[*Exit.*]

Scene [iv]. Lady Fulbank's antechamber.

[*Lady Fulbank is*] *discovered** undressed at her glass.**
Sir Cautious undressed.*

LADY FULBANK.

But why tonight? Indeed you're wondrous kind,*
methinks.

SIR CAUTIOUS.

Why, I don't know, a wedding is a sort of an alarm
to love; it calls up every man's courage.

LADY FULBANK.

Aye, but will it come when 'tis called?   5

SIR CAUTIOUS. (*Aside.*)

I doubt* you'll find it, to my grief.—But I think 'tis
all one to thee, thou car'st not for my compliment;
no, thou'dst rather have a young fellow.

LADY FULBANK.

I am not used to flatter much: if forty years were
taken from your age, 'twould render you   10
something more agreeable to my bed, I must
confess.

SIR CAUTIOUS.

Aye, aye, no doubt on't.

LADY FULBANK.

Yet you may take my word without an oath: were
you as old as time, and I were young and gay as   15
April flowers, which all are fond to gather,
My beauties all should wither in the shade
E'er I'd be worn in a dishonest bosom.

---

65 Pantamogan] Gayman's own imaginary name for his
devil

SIR CAUTIOUS.

Aye, but you're wondrous free methinks,
sometimes, which gives shrewd suspicions.   20

LADY FULBANK.

What, because I cannot simper, look demure, and
justify my honor when none questions it?
Cry "fie" and "out upon the naughty women"
Because they please themselves—and so would I?

SIR CAUTIOUS.

How, "would"? What, cuckold me?   25

LADY FULBANK.

Yes, if it pleased me better than virtue, sir.
But I'll not change my freedom and my humor*
To purchase the dull fame of being honest.*

SIR CAUTIOUS.

Aye, but the world, the world—

LADY FULBANK.

I value not the censures of the crowd.   30

SIR CAUTIOUS.

But I am old.

LADY FULBANK.

That's your fault, sir, not mine.

SIR CAUTIOUS.

But being so, if I should be good-natured and give
thee leave to love discreetly?

LADY FULBANK.

I'd do't without your leave, sir.   35

SIR CAUTIOUS.

"Do't"! What, cuckold me?

LADY FULBANK.

No, love discreetly, sir, love as I ought, love
honestly.

SIR CAUTIOUS.

What, in love with anybody but your own husband?

LADY FULBANK.

Yes.   40

SIR CAUTIOUS.

"Yes," quotha! Is that your loving as you ought?

LADY FULBANK.

We cannot help our inclinations, sir,
No more than time or light, from coming on,
But I can keep my virtue, sir, entire.

SIR CAUTIOUS.

What, I'll warrant this is your first love, Gayman?   45

LADY FULBANK.

I'll not deny that truth, though even to you.

SIR CAUTIOUS.

Why, in consideration of my age and your youth,
I'd bear a conscience, provided you do things
wisely.

LADY FULBANK.

Do what thing, sir?   50

SIR CAUTIOUS.

You know what I mean—

LADY FULBANK.

Hah, I hope you would not be a cuckold, sir?

SIR CAUTIOUS.

Why, truly, in a civil way or so.

LADY FULBANK.

There is but one way, sir, to make me hate you,
and that would be tame suffering.   55

SIR CAUTIOUS. [Aside.]

Nay, an* she be thereabouts, there's no discovering.*

LADY FULBANK.

But leave this fond* discourse, and if you must,
let us to bed.

SIR CAUTIOUS.

Aye, aye, I did but try your virtue, mun. Dost
think I was in earnest?   60

Enter servant.

SERVANT.

Sir, here's a chest directed to your worship.

SIR CAUTIOUS. [Aside.]

Hum, 'tis Wasteall. Now does my heart fail me.—
A chest, say you, to me? So late: I'll warrant it
comes from Sir Nicholas Smuggle, some
prohibited goods that he has stolen the custom of,   65
and cheated his Majesty. Well, he's an honest man,
bring it in.

Exit servant.

LADY FULBANK.

What, into my apartment, sir, a nasty chest!

SIR CAUTIOUS.

By all means, for if the searchers come, they'll
never be so uncivil to ransack thy lodgings, and   70
we are bound in Christian charity to do for one
another. Some rich commodities, I am sure, and
some fine knickknack will fall to thy share, I'll
warrant thee. (*Aside.*) Pox on him for a young
rogue, how punctual he is!   75

Enter [men] with the chest.

Go, my dear, go to bed. I'll send Sir Nicholas a receipt for the chest and be with thee presently.

Exeunt severally. Gayman peeps out of the chest and looks round him, wondering.

GAYMAN.

Hah, where am I? By Heaven, my last night's vision! 'Tis that enchanted room and yonder the alcove! Sure 'twas indeed some witch, who, knowing of my infidelity, has by enchantment brought me hither. 'Tis so: I am betrayed. (*Pauses.*) Hah! or was it Julia, that last night gave me that lone opportunity? But hark, I hear some coming. (*Shuts himself in.*)

Enter Sir Cautious.

SIR CAUTIOUS. (*Lifting up the chest lid.*)

So, you are come, I see. (*Goes and locks the door.*)

GAYMAN. (*Aside.*)

Hah, he here! Nay, then I was deceived, and it was Julia that last night gave me the dear assignation.

Sir Cautious peeps into the bedchamber.

LADY FULBANK. (*Within.*)

Come, Sir Cautious. I shall fall asleep, and then you'll waken me.

SIR CAUTIOUS.

Aye my dear, I'm coming.—She's in bed. I'll go put out the candle, and then—

GAYMAN.

Aye, I'll warrant you for my part.

SIR CAUTIOUS.

Aye, but you may over-act your part and spoil all. But sir, I hope you'll use a Christian conscience in this business.

GAYMAN.

Oh doubt not, sir, but I shall do you reason.

SIR CAUTIOUS.

Aye sir, but—

GAYMAN.

Good sir, no more cautions. You, unlike a fair gamester, will rook me out of half my night. I am impatient.

SIR CAUTIOUS.

Good Lord, are you so hasty? If I please, you shan't go at all.

GAYMAN.

With all my soul, sir: pay me three hundred pound, sir.

SIR CAUTIOUS.

Lord sir, you mistake my candid meaning still. I am content to be a cuckold, sir, but I would have things done decently, d'ye mind me?

GAYMAN.

As decently as a cuckold can be made, sir. But no more disputes, I pray, sir.

SIR CAUTIOUS.

I'm gone, I'm gone. (*Going out, returns.*) But hark ye, sir, you'll rise before day?

GAYMAN.

Yet again—

SIR CAUTIOUS.

I vanish, sir, but hark ye, you'll not speak a word? But let her think 'tis I?

GAYMAN.

Be gone, I say, sir.

[Sir Cautious] runs out.

I am convinced last night I was with Julia. Oh, sot,* insensible and dull!

Enter softly Sir Cautious.

SIR CAUTIOUS.

So, the candle's out; give me your hand.

Leads him softly in.

Scene [v]. [Draws to reveal] a bedchamber.

Lady Fulbank supposed in bed. Enter Sir Cautious and Gayman by dark.

SIR CAUTIOUS.

Where are you, my dear? (*Leads [Gayman] to the bed.*)

LADY FULBANK.

Where should I be? In bed. What, are you by dark?

SIR CAUTIOUS.

Aye, the candle went out by chance.

Gayman signs to him to be gone; he makes grimaces as loath to go and exits.

Scene [vi]. Draws over, and represents another room in the same house.

Enter Parson, Diana, and Pert dressed in Diana's clothes.

DIANA.

I'll swear, Mrs.* Pert, you look very prettily in my clothes.—And since you, sir, have convinced me that this innocent deceit is not unlawful, I am glad to be the instrument of advancing Mrs. Pert to a husband she already has so just a claim to.   5

PARSON.

Since she has so firm a contract, I pronounce it a lawful marriage. But hark, they are coming sure.

DIANA.

Pull your hoods down and keep your face from the light. (*Runs out.*)

Enter Bearjest and Captain Noisy, disordered.

BEARJEST.

Madam, I beg your pardon. I met with a most   10
devilish adventure.—Your pardon too, Mr. Doctor, for making you wait. But the business is this, sir: I have a great mind to lie with this young gentlewoman tonight, but she swears if I do, the parson of the parish shall know it.   15

PARSON.

If I do, sir, I shall keep counsel.

BEARJEST.

And that's civil, sir. Come, lead the way;
With such a guide, the Devil's in't, if we can go astray.

Scene [vii]. The antechamber.

Enter Sir Cautious.

SIR CAUTIOUS.

Now cannot I sleep but am as restless as a merchant in stormy weather that has ventured all his wealth in one bottom. Woman is a leaky vessel. If she should like the young rogue now, and they should come to a right understanding—why then   5
am I a—wittol, that's all, and shall be put in print at Snow-Hill, with my effigies o'th'top like the sign of Cuckolds Haven.[66] Hum, they're damnable

---

66 in print at Snow Hill … Cuckolds Haven] Sir Cautious
     imagines his state will be known throughout London,

silent. Pray Heaven he have not murdered her and robbed her. Hum, hark, what's that? A noise: he   10
has broke his covenant with me and shall forfeit the money. How loud they are! Aye, aye, the plot's discovered, what shall I do? Why, the devil is not in her sure to be refractory now and peevish. If she be, I must pay my money yet, and that would be   15
a damned thing. Sure they're coming out; I'll retire and harken how 'tis with them. (*Retires.*)

Enter Lady Fulbank, undressed; Gayman half undressed, upon his knees, following her, holding her gown.

LADY FULBANK.

Oh! You unkind— What have you made me do?
Unhand me, false deceiver, let me loose.

SIR CAUTIOUS. (*Aside, peeping.*)

Made her do? So, so, 'tis done. I'm glad of that.   20

GAYMAN.

Can you be angry, Julia?
Because I only seized my right of love.

LADY FULBANK.

And must my honor be the price of it?
Could nothing but my fame reward your passion?
What, make me a base prostitute, a foul   25
   adulteress?
Oh, be gone, be gone, (*Weeping.*) dear robber of
   my quiet.

SIR CAUTIOUS.

Oh, fearful!

GAYMAN.

Oh! Calm your rage, and hear me: if you are so,
You are an innocent adulteress.
It was the feeble husband you enjoyed   30
In cold imagination and no more;
Shyly you turned away, faintly resigned.

SIR CAUTIOUS.

Hum, did she so—

GAYMAN.

Till my excess of love betrayed the cheat.

SIR CAUTIOUS.

Aye, aye, that was my fear.   35

---

from the Snow Hill site in Holborn, a western suburb where lampoons were printed, to Cuckolds Haven eastward on the Thames.

LADY FULBANK.

    Away—be gone, I'll never see you more.

GAYMAN.

    You may as well forbid the sun to shine.

    Not see you more! Heavens! I before adored you,

    But now I rave! And with my impatient love,

    A thousand mad and wild desires are burning!   40

    I have discovered now new worlds of charms

    And can no longer tamely love and suffer.

SIR CAUTIOUS.

    So, I have brought an old house upon my head,

    entailed cuckoldom upon myself.

LADY FULBANK.

    I'll hear no more.—Sir Cautious! Where's my   45

        husband?

    Why have you left my honor thus unguarded?

SIR CAUTIOUS.

    Aye, aye, she's well enough pleased, I fear, for all

    that.

GAYMAN.

    Base as he is, 'twas he exposed this treasure,

    Like silly* Indians, bartered thee for trifles.   50

SIR CAUTIOUS.

    Oh, treacherous villain!

LADY FULBANK.

    Hah, my husband do this?

GAYMAN.

    He, by Love, he was the kind procurer,

    Contrived the means and brought me to thy bed.

LADY FULBANK.

    My husband? My wise husband!   55

    What fondness in my conduct had he seen

    To take so shameful and so base revenge?

GAYMAN.

    None: 'twas filthy avarice seduced him to't.

LADY FULBANK.

    If he could be so barbarous to expose me,

    Could you who loved me be so cruel too?   60

GAYMAN.

    What, to possess thee when the bliss was offered,

    Possess thee too without a crime to thee?

    Charge not my soul with so remiss a flame,

    So dull a sense of virtue, to refuse it.

LADY FULBANK.

    I am convinced the fault was all my husband's.   65

(Kneels.)

And here I vow, by all things just and sacred,

    To separate forever from his bed.

SIR CAUTIOUS.

    Oh, I am not able to endure it!—Hold, oh, hold,

    my dear.

He kneels as she rises.

LADY FULBANK.

    Stand off, I do abhor thee.

SIR CAUTIOUS.

    With all my soul. But do not make rash vows.   70

    They break my very heart. Regard my reputation!

LADY FULBANK.

    Which you have had such care of, sir, already.

    Rise, 'tis in vain you kneel.

SIR CAUTIOUS.

    No, I'll never rise again. Alas! Madam, I was merely

    drawn in, I only thought to sport a die or so; I   75

    had only an innocent design to have discovered

    whether this gentleman had stolen my gold that

    so I might have hanged him.

GAYMAN.

    A very innocent design indeed.

SIR CAUTIOUS.

    Aye sir, that's all, as I'm an honest man.   80

LADY FULBANK.

    I've sworn, nor are the stars more fixed than I.

Enter servant.

SERVANT.

    How! My lady and his worship up?—Madam, a

    gentleman and a lady below in a coach knocked

    me up and say they must speak with your ladyship.

LADY FULBANK.

    This is strange!—Bring 'em up.   85

Exit servant.

    Who can it be at this odd time of neither night

    nor day?

Enter Leticia, Belmour, and Phillis.

LETICIA.

    Madam, your virtue, charity, and friendship to me

    has made me trespass on you for my life's security

    and beg you will protect me and my husband—   90

    (Points at Belmour.)

SIR CAUTIOUS.

So, here's another sad catastrophe!

LADY FULBANK.

Hah, does Belmour live, is't possible?

—Believe me, sir, you ever had my wishes

And shall not fail of my protection now.   95

BELMOUR.

I humbly thank your ladyship.

GAYMAN.

I'm glad thou hast her, Harry, but doubt* thou

durst not own her, nay, dar'st not own thyself.

BELMOUR.

Yes, friend, I have my pardon. But hark, I think

we are pursued already— But now I fear no force.   100

A noise of somebody coming in.

LADY FULBANK.

However, step into my bedchamber.

*Exeunt Leticia, Gayman, [Belmour,] and Phillis. Enter
Sir Feeble in an antic manner.*

SIR FEEBLE.

Hell shall not hold thee, nor vast mountains cover

thee, but I will find thee out, and lash thy filthy

and adulterous carcass. (*Coming up in a menacing

manner to Sir Cautious.*)   105

SIR CAUTIOUS.

How, lash my filthy carcass? I defy thee, Satan.

SIR FEEBLE.

'Twas thus he said.

SIR CAUTIOUS.

Let who's[67] will say it, he lies in's throat.

SIR FEEBLE.

How, the ghostly—hush, have a care—for 'twas the

ghost of Belmour—oh! Hide that bleeding wound,   110

it chills my soul! (*Runs to the Lady Fulbank.*)

LADY FULBANK.

What bleeding wound? Heavens, are you frantic,

sir?

SIR FEEBLE.

No, but for want of rest, I shall ere morning.

(*Weeps.*) She's gone, she's gone, she's gone— (*Weeps.*)   115

SIR CAUTIOUS.

Aye, aye, she's gone, she's gone indeed. (*Weeps.*)

---

67 who's] who as, a colloquialism

SIR FEEBLE.

But let her go, so I may never see that dreadful

vision.—Hark ye, sir, a word in your ear: have a

care of marrying a young wife.

SIR CAUTIOUS. (*Weeping.*)

Aye, but I have married one already.   120

SIR FEEBLE.

Hast thou? Divorce her—fly her, quick—depart,

be gone, she'll cuckold thee, and still she'll cuckold

thee.

SIR CAUTIOUS.

Aye brother, but whose fault was that? Why, are

not you married?   125

SIR FEEBLE.

Mum: no words on't, unless you'll have the ghost

about your ears. Part with your wife, I say, or else

the Devil will part ye.

LADY FULBANK.

Pray go to bed, sir.

SIR FEEBLE.

Yes, for I shall sleep now, I shall lie alone. (*Weeps.*)   130

Ah fool, old, dull, besotted fool: to think she'd love

me. 'Twas by base means I gained her, cozened an

honest gentleman of fame and life.

LADY FULBANK.

You did so, sir, but 'tis not past redress; you may

make that honest gentleman amends.   135

SIR FEEBLE.

Oh, would I could, so I gave half my estate—

LADY FULBANK.

That penitence atones with him and Heaven.

—Come forth, Leticia, and your injured ghost.

[Enter Leticia, Gayman, Belmour and Phillis.]

SIR FEEBLE.

Hah, ghost! Another sight would make me mad

indeed.   140

BELMOUR.

Behold me, sir, I have no terror now.

SIR FEEBLE.

Hah, who's that, Francis, my nephew Francis?

BELMOUR.

Belmour or Francis—choose you which you like,

and I am either.

SIR FEEBLE.

Hah, Belmour! and no ghost?   145

BELMOUR.

Belmour—and not your nephew, sir.

SIR FEEBLE.

But art alive? 'Ods bobs, I'm glad on't, sirrah—but are you real, Belmour?

BELMOUR.

As sure as I'm no ghost.

GAYMAN.

We all can witness for him, sir.   150

SIR FEEBLE.

Where be the minstrels? We'll have a dance, adod we will.—Ah, art thou there, thou cozening little chits-face? A vengeance on thee: thou madest me an old, doting, loving coxcomb, but I forgive thee and give thee all thy jewels.—And you your   155
pardon, sir, so you'll give me mine, for I find you young knaves will be too hard for us.

BELMOUR.

You are so generous, sir, that 'tis almost with grief I receive the blessing of Leticia.

SIR FEEBLE.

No, no, thou deserv'st her, she would have made an   160
old, fond* blockhead of me; and one way or other you would have had her, 'Ods bobs you would.

Enter Bearjest, Diana, Pert, Bredwel and Captain Noisy.

BEARJEST.

Justice, sir, justice! I have been cheated, abused, assassinated, and ravished!

SIR CAUTIOUS.

How, my nephew ravished!   165

PERT.

No sir, I am his wife.

SIR CAUTIOUS.

Hum, my heir marry a chambermaid!

BEARJEST.

Sir, you must know I stole away Mrs.* Di and brought her to Ned's chamber here to marry her.

SIR FEEBLE.

My daughter Di stolen—   170

BEARJEST.

But I being to go to the devil a little, sir, whip—what does he, but marries her himself, sir, and fobbed me off with my lady's cast petticoat.[68]

---

[68] cast petticoat] Ladies' maids like Pert often were given their mistresses' old clothes in payment.

NOISY.

Sir, she's a gentlewoman and my sister, sir.

PERT.

Madam, 'twas a pious fraud, if it were one, for I   175
was contracted to him before: see, here it is—
(*Gives it 'em.*)

ALL.

A plain case, a plain case.

SIR FEEBLE. (*To Bredwel, who with Diana kneels.*)

Hark ye, sir, have you had the impudence to marry my daughter, sir?   180

BREDWEL.

Yes, sir, and humbly ask your pardon, and your blessing.

SIR FEEBLE.

You will ha't, whether I will or not. Rise, you are still too hard for us.—Come sir, forgive your nephew.   185

SIR CAUTIOUS.

Well sir, I will, but all this while you little think the tribulation I am in: my lady has forsworn my bed.

SIR FEEBLE.

Indeed, sir, the wiser she.

SIR CAUTIOUS.

For only performing my promise to this   190
gentleman.

SIR FEEBLE.

Aye, you showed her the difference, sir; you're a wise man. Come, dry your eyes, and rest yourself contented; we are a couple of old coxcombs, d'ye hear, sir, coxcombs.   195

SIR CAUTIOUS. (*To Gayman.*)

I grant it, sir. And if I die, sir, I bequeath my lady to you, with my whole estate; my nephew has too much already for a fool.

GAYMAN.

I thank you, sir.—Do you consent, my Julia?

LADY FULBANK.

No sir, you do not like me: a canvas bag of wooden   200
ladles were a better bedfellow.

GAYMAN.

Cruel tormenter! Oh, I could kill myself with shame and anger!

LADY FULBANK.

Come hither, Bredwel. Witness for my honor that

I had no design upon his person but that of trying 205
of his constancy.

BREDWEL.

Believe me, sir, 'tis true. I feigned a danger near
just as you got to bed. And I was the kind devil,
sir, that brought the gold to you.

BEARJEST.

And you were one of the devils that beat me and 210
the captain here, sir?

GAYMAN.

No, truly, sir, those were some I hired to beat you
for abusing me today.

NOISY.

To make you 'mends, sir, I bring you the certain
news of the death of Sir Thomas Gayman, your 215
uncle, who has left you two thousand pounds a
year.

GAYMAN.

I thank you, sir, I heard the news before.

SIR CAUTIOUS.

How's this? Mr. Gayman, my lady's first lover? I
find, Sir Feeble, we were a couple of old fools 220
indeed to think at our age to cozen two lusty
young fellows of their mistresses. 'Tis no wonder
that both the men and the women have been too
hard for us; we are not fit matches for either, that's
the truth on't. 225
The warrior needs must to his rival yield
Who comes with blunted weapons to the field.

[Exeunt.]

FINIS.

Textual Notes

a The copytext is the first edition, a 1687 quarto (Q); also
consulted were the first collected edition of plays in 1702
(C1); the second collected edition of plays in 1724 (C2);
and modern editions of 1915 (Summers), of 1995
(Spencer), and of 1996 (Todd). Q frequently prints parts
of dialogue as verse full of half-lines, hexameters, and
even heptameters, perhaps (though inconsistently) to
suggest heroic status. Most of these here are printed as
prose. In Act V, however, a couple of Belmour's prose
speeches are printed as verse for consistency's sake.

b Then, then] Summers, Spencer, Todd; Then, thou Q,
C1-2

c SHEPHERD] Todd; MAN Q, C1-2, Summers, Spencer

d BOTH] Chorus, all editions consulted

e Why] whe Q; see *The Rover* n. c

f cracked] C2, Summers, Spencer, Todd; racked Q, C1

g Sir Feeble's] Sir Cautious his, all editions consulted

h thy] Spencer, Todd; my Q, C1-2, Summers

i Confess] C2, Summers, Spencer; *om.* Q, C1, Todd

The Relapse; or, Virtue in Danger,

Being the Sequel of The Fool in Fashion[a]

by John Vanbrugh (1664-1726)
edited by James E. Gill

The world of *The Relapse* was the politically and economically uncertain world of England in the 1690s—a world in which there were two contending kings of England and hence a world of divided and contending loyalties, of intriguing "double dealers," and of financial crisis brought on by debased coinage and war debt. The great families and important noblemen of the realm often followed their own interests and advancement rather than any single royal leader or national policy. Some toasted "the king across the water" (James II), some pursued liberal, quasi-republican ideals, and some were loyal to William III's pro-Dutch policies, but many served themselves. *The Relapse* also belonged to a world of attempted reform and answering skepticism. In this tense atmosphere John Vanbrugh, one of nineteen children born to a Dutch immigrant, struggled to make his way, first as a soldier and as a spy (perhaps), then as a playwright and theatrical manager, and finally as an architect who built two of the really impressive edifices of the day—Castle Howard and Blenheim Palace.

The play's occasion was the production of the young actor Colley Cibber's popular comedy *Love's Last Shift*, a comedy which, according to the droll Congreve, "had something like wit," and which has been described as containing four acts of bawdy and one act of reform, the conversion of Loveless to true love. Vanbrugh "continues" Cibber's play by lifting characters and some plot details and by transforming them into an original, intelligent comical satire, which exposes the instability and vanity of human desires. Loveless's conversion is portrayed as shallow, and he suffers the relapse of the title.

The Relapse's opening scenes poise the satiety and ennui of marriage against pernicious luxury and the prodigal's poverty, and thereafter the play exposes the callous treacheries of the characters in search of pleasure and money; it questions marital and familial stability; and it probes the desire for social position, the doubts and anxieties of sexual restlessness, the desire for vengeance, and even the retreat to moral rectitude. The play, having travelled back and forth from country to city and from fall to recuperation, ends with a satiric paean to fickleness in love and a dance featuring not the right couples of social comedy but the wrong couples of satire.

The Relapse seems to have been an instant success and quickly became part of the repertory, along with *Love's Last Shift*, of the Drury Lane company and its successor, where Cibber continued to play Sir Novelty Fashion and Lord Foppington until the 1730s.

DRAMATIS PERSONAE

MEN

Sir Novelty Fashion, newly created Lord
    Foppington.
Young Fashion, his brother.
Loveless, husband to Amanda.
Worthy, a gentleman of the Town.*
Sir Tunbelly Clumsey, a country gentleman.
Sir John Friendly, his neighbor.
Coupler, a matchmaker.
Bull, chaplain to Sir Tunbelly.
Syringe,[1] a surgeon.
Lory, servant to Young Fashion.
[La Vérole, servant to Lord Foppington.]
[Foretop,] a perriwigmaker.
[Mendlegs, a hosier.]
Shoemaker.
Tailor.
[Clerk.]
[Constable.]

WOMEN

Amanda, wife to Loveless.
Berinthia, her cousin, a young widow.
[Abigail, her maid.]
Miss Hoyden, a great fortune, daughter to Sir
    Tunbelly.
Nurse, her governess.
[Mrs. Callicoe, a sempstress.]

The Relapse.

Act I, scene i. [A room in
Amanda's country house.][2]

Enter Loveless reading.

LOVELESS.
  How true is that philosophy which says
  Our heaven is seated in our minds!

---

1 Syringe] at this time not a needle for administering injections but a device for giving clysters or enemas.

2 Amanda's country house] estate to which the couple has retired after their reconciliation at the end of *Love's Last Shift*. Loveless, having returned penniless to England after abandoning Amanda and spending several years abroad, now has Amanda's money and property at his disposal.

  Through all the roving pleasures of my youth
  (Where nights and days seemed all comsumed in
     joy,
  Where the false face of luxury*   5
  Displayed such charms
  As might have shaken the most holy hermit
  And made him totter at his altar),
  I never knew one moment's peace like this.
  Here, in this little soft retreat,   10
  My thoughts unbent from all the cares of life,
  Content with Fortune,
  Eased from the grating duties of dependence,[3]
  From envy free, ambition under foot,
  The raging flame of wild destructive lust   15
  Reduced to a warm pleasing fire of lawful love,
  My life glides on, and all is well within.

Enter Amanda.

LOVELESS. (*Meeting her kindly.*)
  How does the happy cause of my content,
  My dear Amanda?
  You find me musing on my happy state   20
  And full of grateful thoughts to Heaven and you.
AMANDA.
  Those grateful offerings Heaven can't receive
  With more delight than I do:
  Would I could share with it as well
  The dispensations of its bliss,   25
  That I might search its choicest favors out
  And shower 'em on your head forever.
LOVELESS.
  The largest boons that Heaven thinks fit to grant
  To things it has decreed shall crawl on earth
  Are in the gift of women formed like you.   30
  Perhaps, when time shall be no more,
  When the aspiring soul shall take its flight
  And drop this pond'rous lump of clay behind it,
  It may have appetites we know not of,
  And pleasures as refined as its desires—   35
  But till that day of knowledge shall instruct me,
  The utmost blessing that my thought can reach

(*Taking her in his arms.*)

  Is folded in my arms and rooted in my heart.

---

3 dependence] the state of being a kept man

AMANDA.

    There let it grow forever.

LOVELESS.

    Well said, Amanda—let it be forever—   40

    Would Heaven grant that—

AMANDA.

        'Twere all the heaven I'd ask.

    But we are clad in black mortality,

    And the dark curtain of eternal night

    At last must drop between us.[b]   45

LOVELESS.

                It must:

    That mournful separation we must see.

    A bitter pill it is to all, but doubles

    Its ungrateful taste when lovers swallow it.

AMANDA.

    Perhaps that pain may only be my lot;   50

    You possibly may be exempted from it:

    Men find out softer ways to quench their fires.

LOVELESS.

    Can you then doubt my constancy, Amanda?

    You'll find 'tis built upon a steady basis—

    The rock of reason now supports my love,   55

    On which it stands so fixed,

    The rudest hurricane of wild desire

    Would, like the breath of a soft slumbering babe,

    Pass by and never shake it.

AMANDA.

    Yet still 'tis safer to avoid the storm;   60

    The strongest vessels, if they put to sea,

    May possibly be lost.

    Would I could keep you here, in this calm port,

    Forever.

    Forgive the weakness of a woman:

    I am uneasy at your going to stay so long in   65

      Town;*

    I know its false insinuating pleasures;

    I know the force of its delusions;

    I know the strength of its attacks;

    I know the weak defence of nature;

    I know you are a man—and I—a wife.   70

LOVELESS.

    You know then all that needs to give you rest,

    For wife's the strongest claim that you can urge.

    When you would plead your title to my heart,

    On this you may depend; therefore, be calm,

    Banish your fears, for they are traitors to your peace;   75

    Beware of 'em, they are insinuating busy things

    That gossip to and fro and do a world of mischief

    Where they come:

    But you shall soon be mistress of 'em all;

    I'll aid you with such arms for their destruction,   80

    They never shall erect their heads again.

    You know the business is indispensible

    That obliges me to go to London,

    And you have no reason, that I know of,

    To believe I'm glad of the occasion.   85

    For my honest conscience is my witness,

    I have found a due succession of such charms

    In my retirement here with you,

    I have never thrown one roving thought that way.

    But since, against my will, I'm dragged once more   90

    To that uneasy theater of noise,

    I am resolved to make such use on't

    As shall convince you 'tis an old cast* mistress

    Who has been so lavish of her favors,

    She's now grown bankrupt of her charms   95

    And has not one allurement left to move me.

AMANDA.

    Her bow, I do believe, is grown so weak,

    Her arrows (at this distance) cannot hurt you,

    But in approaching 'em, you give 'em strength.

    The dart that has not far to fly will put   100

    The best armor to a dangerous trial.

LOVELESS.

    That trial past, and y'are at ease forever.

    When you have seen the helmet proved,

    You'll apprehend no more for him that wears it.

    Therefore, to put a lasting period to your fears,   105

    I am resolved, this once, to launch into

      temptation.

    I'll give you an essay of all my virtues:

    My former boon companions of the bottle

    Shall fairly try what charms are left in wine;

    I'll take my place amongst 'em,   110

    They shall hem me in,

    Sing praises to their god and drink his glory,

    Turn wild enthusiasts* for his sake

    And beasts to do him honor,

    Whilst I, a stubborn atheist,   115

    Sullenly look on

    Without one reverend glass to his divinity.

That for my temperance.
Then for my constancy—
AMANDA.
　　　　　　　　Ay, there take heed;
LOVELESS.
Indeed the danger's small.
AMANDA.
　　　　　　　　And yet my fears are great.
LOVELESS.   120
Why are you so timorous?
AMANDA.
　　　　　　　　Because you are so bold.
LOVELESS.
My courage should disperse your apprehensions.　125
AMANDA.
My apprehensions should alarm your courage.
LOVELESS.
Fie, fie, Amanda! It is not kind thus to distrust me.
AMANDA.
And yet my fears are founded on my love.
LOVELESS.
Your love then is not founded as it ought,
For if you can believe 'tis possible   130
I should again relapse to my past follies,
I must appear to you a thing
Of such an undigested composition
That but to think of me with inclination
Would be a weakness in your taste   135
Your virtue scarce could answer.
AMANDA.
'Twould be a weakness in my tongue
My prudence could not answer
If I should press you farther with my fears;
I'll therefore trouble you no longer with 'em.   140
LOVELESS.
Nor shall they trouble you much longer.
A little time shall show you they were groundless:
This winter shall be the fiery trial of my virtue,
Which, when it once has passed,
You'll be convinced 'twas of no false allay;[4]   145
There all your cares will end.
AMANDA.
　　　　　　　　Pray Heaven they may.
Exeunt hand in hand.

---

[4] allay] obsolete form of *alloy* necessary for the tag rhyme

Scene [ii]. [By the stairs* to
the Thames below] Whitehall.*

Enter Young Fashion, Lory, and waterman.[5]

FASHION.
Come, pay the waterman, and take the port-
manteau.
LORY.
Faith, sir, I think the waterman had as good take
the portmanteau and pay himself.
FASHION.
Why, sure there's something left in't!   5
LORY.
But a solitary old waistcoat, upon honor, sir.
FASHION.
Why, what's become of the blue coat, sirrah?
LORY.
Sir, 'twas eaten at Gravesend;[6] the reckoning came
to thirty shillings, and your privy purse was worth
but two half crowns.   10
FASHION.
'Tis very well.
WATERMAN.
Pray, master, will you please to dispatch me?
FASHION.
Aye, here, a—canst thou change me a guinea?
LORY. (*Aside.*)
Good!
WATERMAN.
Change a guinea, master! Ha! ha! your honor's   15
pleased to compliment.
FASHION.
Egad, I don't know how I shall pay thee then, for
I have nothing but gold about me.
LORY. (*Aside.*)
Hum, hum.
FASHION.
What dost thou expect, friend?   20
WATERMAN.
Why, master, so far against wind and tide is richly
worth half a piece.

---

[5] waterman] rower of a small boat transporting customers across the river

[6] Gravesend] port city east of London on the Thames

FASHION.

Why, faith, I think thou art a good conscionable fellow. Egad, I begin to have so good an opinion of thy honesty, I care not if I leave my portmanteau with thee, till I send thee thy money. 25

WATERMAN.

Hah! God bless your honor; I should be as willing to trust you, master, but that you are, as a man may say, a stranger to me, and these are nimble times; there are a great many sharpers stirring. 30 (*Taking up the portmanteau.*) Well, master, when your worship sends the money, your portmanteau shall be forthcoming: my name's Tug; my wife keeps a brandy shop in Drab Alley at Wapping.[7]

FASHION.

Very well. I'll send for't tomorrow. 35

Exit waterman.

LORY.

So. Now sir, I hope you'll own yourself a happy man, you have outlived all your cares.

FASHION.

How so, sir?

LORY.

Why, you have nothing left to take care of.

FASHION.

Yes, sirrah, I have myself and you to take care of 40 still.

LORY.

Sir, if you could but prevail with somebody else to do that for you, I fancy we might both fare the better for't.

FASHION.

Why, if thou canst tell me where to apply myself, 45 I have at present so little money and so much humility about me, I don't know but I may follow a fool's advice.

LORY.

Why then, sir, your fool advises you to lay aside all animosity and apply to Sir Novelty, your elder 50 brother.

FASHION.

Damn my elder brother.

LORY.

With all my heart, but get him to redeem your annuity, however.

FASHION.

My annuity? 'Sdeath,* he's such a dog, he would 55 not give his powder puff to redeem my soul.

LORY.

Look you, sir, you must wheedle him or you must starve.

FASHION.

Look you, sir, I will neither wheedle him nor starve. 60

LORY.

Why, what will you do then?

FASHION.

I'll go into the army.

LORY.

You can't take the oaths; you are a Jacobite.[8]

FASHION.

Thou mayst as well say I can't take orders because I'm an atheist. 65

LORY.

Sir, I ask your pardon. I find I did not know the strength of your conscience so well as I did the weakness of your purse.

FASHION.

Methinks, sir, a person of your experience should have known that the strength of the conscience 70 proceeds from the weakness of the purse.

LORY.

Sir, I am very glad to find you have a conscience able to take care of us, let it proceed from what it will. But I desire you'll please to consider that the army alone will be but a scanty maintenance for a 75 person of your generosity, at least as rents[9] now are paid. I shall see you stand in damnable need of some auxiliary guineas for your *menus plaisirs.*[10] I will therefore turn fool once more for your service, and advise you to go directly to your 80 brother.

---

7 Wapping] a shore-side suburb of London

8 oaths … Jacobite] As an adherent of James II in exile, Young Fashion was a non-juror, one who could not take the oath of loyalty to William III.

9 rents] incomes, in this instance army pay

10 *menus plaisirs*] little pleasures (Fr.)

FASHION.

Art thou then so impregnable a blockhead to believe he'll help with a farthing?

LORY.

Not if you treat him *de haut en bas*[11] as you use to do.

FASHION.

Why, how wouldst have me treat him?

LORY.

Like a trout, tickle* him.

FASHION.

I can't flatter.

LORY.

Can you starve?

FASHION.

Yes.

LORY.

I can't. (*Going.*) Good bye t'ye, sir.

FASHION.

Stay, thou wilt distract me. What wouldst thou have me say to him?

LORY.

Say nothing to him. Apply yourself to his favorites: speak to his periwig, his cravat, his feather, his snuff box, and when you are well with them, desire him to lend you a thousand pounds. I'll engage you prosper.

FASHION.

'Sdeath* and Furies! Why was that coxcomb thrust into the world before me? Oh Fortune, Fortune, thou art a bitch, by gad.

Exeunt.

Scene [iii]. A dressing room
[in Lord Foppington's Town* house].

Enter Lord Foppington in his nightgown. *

FOPPINGTON.

Page!—

Enter Page.

PAGE.

Sir.

FOPPINGTON.

Sir! Pray sir, do me the favor to teach your tongue

the title the King has thought fit to honor me with.[12]

PAGE.

I ask your lordship's pardon, my lord.

FOPPINGTON.

Oh, you can pronounce the word, then? I thought it would have choked you. D'ye hear?

PAGE.

My lord.

FOPPINGTON.

Call La Vérole.* I would dress.

Exit Page.

Well, 'tis an unspeakable pleasure to be a man of quality,* strike me dumb! My lord—your lordship—my Lord Foppington. *Ah, c'est quelque chose de beau, que le diable m'emporte.*[13] Why, the ladies were ready to puke at me whilst I had nothing but Navelty[14] to recommend me to 'em. Sure whilst I was but a knight, I was a very nauseous fellow. Well, 'tis ten thousand pawnd well given, stap my vitals.

Enter La Vérole.

LA VÉROLE.

Me lord, de shoemaker, de tailor, de hosier, de sempstress, de barber, be all ready if your lordship please to be dress.

FOPPINGTON.

'Tis well, admit 'em.

LA VÉROLE.

Hey, messieurs, entrez.

Enter tailor, etc.

FOPPINGTON.

So, gentlemen, I hope you have all taken pains to show yourselves masters in your professions.

---

11 *de haut en bas*] condescendingly, haughtily (Fr.)

12 title ... fit] Formerly Sir Novelty Fashion in Cibber's play, Lord Foppington, it is later noted, has purchased his barony. The sale of honors might have fallen off historically since the time of James I, but it was still an important trope in literature.

13 *Ah ... 'emporte*] Ah! it's beautiful, devil take me! (Fr.)

14 Navelty] Foppington's drawl allegedly is a court affectation; it represents the phonetic drift from close to open o.

TAILOR.

I think I may presume to say, sir—

LA VÉROLE.

"My lord," you clawn, you.

TAILOR.

Why, is he made a lord? My lord, I ask your lordship's pardon, my lord. I hope, my lord, your lordship will please to own I have brought your lordship as accomplished a suit of clothes as ever peer of England trod the stage in, my lord. Will your lordship please to try 'em now? 30

FOPPINGTON.

Aye, but let my people dispose the glasses* so, that I may see myself before and behind, for I love to see myself all raund. 35

Whilst he puts on his clothes, enter Young Fashion and Lory.

FASHION.

Hey-dey, what the devil have we here? Sure my gentleman's grown a favorite at Court,* he has got so many people at his levee. 40

LORY.

Sir, these people come in order to make him a favorite at Court; they are to establish him with the ladies.

FASHION.

Good God, to what an ebb of taste are women fallen that it would be in the power of a laced coat 45 to recommend a gallant to 'em.

LORY.

Sir, tailors and periwigmakers are now become the bawds of the Nation; 'tis they debauch all the women.

FASHION.

Thou say'st true, for there's that fop now has not 50 by nature wherewithal to move a cook-maid, and by that time these fellows have done with him, egad he shall melt down a countess.—But now for my reception: I'll engage it shall be as cold a one as a courtier's to his friend who comes to put him 55 in mind of his promise.

FOPPINGTON. (*To his tailor.*)

Death and eternal tartures, sir, I say the packet's too high by a foot.

TAILOR.

My lord, if it had been an inch lower, it would not have held your lordship's pocket handkerchief.

FOPPINGTON.

Rat* my pocket handkerchief! Have not I a page 60 to carry it? You may make him a packet up to his chin a-purpose for it, but I will not have mine come so near my face.

TAILOR.

'Tis not for me to dispute your lordship's fancy.

FASHION. (*To Lory.*)

His lordship! Lory, did you observe that? 65

LORY.

Yes sir, I always thought 'twould end there. Now I hope you'll have a little more respect for him.

FASHION.

Respect! Damn him for a coxcomb. Now has he ruined his estate to buy a title that he may be a fool of the first rate. But let's accost him.—Brother, 70 I'm your humble servant.

FOPPINGTON.

Oh Lard, Tam, I did not expect you in England. Brother, I am glad to see you. (*Turning to his tailor.*) Look you sir, I shall never be reconciled to this nauseous packet. Therefore, pray get me another suit 75 with all manner of expedition, for this is my eternal aversion. Mrs. Callicoe, are you not of my mind?

MRS. CALLICOE.

Oh, directly,[15] my lord, it can never be too low.

FOPPINGTON.

You are positively right on't, for the packet becomes no part of the body but the knee. 80

MRS. CALLICOE.

I hope your lordship is pleased with the steenkirk?*

FOPPINGTON.

In love with it, stap my vitals. Bring your bill, you shall be paid tomarrow.

MRS. CALLICOE.

I humbly thank your honor. (*Exit.*)

FOPPINGTON.

Hark thee, shoemaker, these shoes a'n't ugly, but 85 they don't fit me.

SHOEMAKER.

My lord, methinks they fit you very well.

---

15 directly] precisely (*OED*)

FOPPINGTON.

They hurt me just below the instep.

SHOEMAKER. (*Feeling his foot.*)

My lord, they don't hurt you there.

FOPPINGTON.

I tell thee they pinch me execrably. 90

SHOEMAKER.

My lord, if they pinch you, I'll be bound to be hanged, that's all.

FOPPINGTON.

Why, wilt thou undertake to persuade me I cannot feel?

SHOEMAKER.

Your lordship may please to feel what you think 95 fit, but that shoe does not hurt you. I think I understand my trade.

FOPPINGTON.

Now by all that's great and powerful, thou art an incomprehensible coxcomb, but thou makest good shoes, and so I'll bear with thee. 100

SHOEMAKER.

My lord, I have worked for half the people of quality* in town these twenty years, and 'twere very hard I should not know when a shoe hurts and when it don't.

FOPPINGTON.

Well, prithee be gone about thy business. 105

Exit Shoemaker.

(*To the hosier.*) Mr. Mendlegs, a word with you. The calves of the stockings are thickened a little too much; they make my legs look like a chairman's.*

MENDLEGS.

My lord, methinks^c they look mighty well.

FOPPINGTON.

Aye, but you are not so good a judge of these 110 things as I am; I have studied 'em all my life. Therefore, pray let the next be the thickness of a crawn piece less. (*Aside.*) If the Town* takes notice my legs are fallen away, 'twill be attributed to the violence of some new intrigue. 115

Exit hosier.

(*To the periwigmaker.*) Come, Mr. Foretop, let me see what you have done, and then the fatigue of the marning will be over.

FORETOP.

My lord, I have done what I defy any prince in Europe t'outdo; I have made you a periwig so long 120 and so full of hair, it will serve you for hat and cloak in all weathers.

FOPPINGTON.

Then thou hast made me thy friend to eternity. Come, comb it out.

FASHION.

Well Lory, what dost think on't? A very friendly 125 reception from a brother after three years' absence.

LORY.

Why sir, it's your own fault. We seldom care for those that don't love what we love. If you would creep into his heart, you must enter into his pleasures. Here have you stood ever since you came 130 in and have not commended any one thing that belongs to him.

FASHION.

Nor never shall, whilst they belong to a coxcomb.

LORY.

Then sir, you must be content to pick a hungry bone. 135

FASHION.

No sir, I'll crack it and get to the marrow before I have done.

FOPPINGTON.

Gad's curse! Mr. Foretop, you don't intend to put this upon me for a full periwig?

FORETOP.

Not a full one, my lord? I don't know what your 140 lordship may be pleased to call a full one, but I have crammed twenty ounces of hair into it.

FOPPINGTON.

What it may be by weight, sir, I shall not dispute, but by tale* there are not nine hairs of a side.

FORETOP.

Oh Lord, Oh Lord, Oh Lord! Why, as Gad shall 145 judge me, your honor's side face is reduced to the tip of your nose.

FOPPINGTON.

My side face may be in eclipse for aught I know, but I'm sure my full face is like the full moon.

FORETOP.

Heavens bless my eyesight. (*Rubbing his eyes.*) Sure 150 I look through the wrong end of the perspective,* for by my faith, an't* please your honor, the broadest place I see in your face does not seem to me to be two inches in diameter.

FOPPINGTON.

If it did, it would be just two inches too broad. 155
Far a periwig to a man should be like a mask to a woman nothing should be seen but his eyes.

FORETOP.

My lord, I have done. If you please to have more hair in your wig, I'll put it in.

FOPPINGTON.

Passitively, yes. 160

FORETOP.

Shall I take it back now, my lord?

FOPPINGTON.

Noh. I'll wear it today, though it show such a manstrous pair of cheeks. Stap my vitals, I shall be taken for a trumpeter.

Exit Foretop.

FASHION.

Now your people of business are gone, Brother, I 165
hope I may obtain a quarter of an hour's audience of you.

FOPPINGTON.

Faith Tam, I must beg you'll excuse me at this time, for I must away to the House of Lards immediately. My Lady Teaser's case[16] is to come on today, and I 170
would not be absent for the salvation of mankind.—
Hey, page, is the coach at the door?

[Enter Page.]

PAGE.

Yes, my lord.

FOPPINGTON.

You'll excuse me, Brother. (*Going.*)

FASHION.

Shall you be back at dinner? 175

FOPPINGTON.

As Gad shall jidge me, I can't tell, for 'tis passible I may dine with some of aur House at Lacket's.[17]

---

16 My Lady Teaser's case] perhaps a scandalous case of divorce, which among the nobility were tried in the House of Lords
17 Lackets] Lockets*

FASHION.

Shall I meet you there? For I must needs talk with you.

FOPPINGTON.

That I'm afraid mayn't be so praper, for the lards 180
I commonly eat with are people of nice* conversation, and you know, Tam, your education has been a little at large. But if you'll stay here, you'll find a family* dinner.—Hey fellow! What is there for dinner? There's beef, I suppose my 185
brother will eat beef.—Dear Tam, I'm glad to see thee in England, stap my vitals. (*Exit with his equipage.*)

FASHION.

Hell and Furies, is this to be borne?

LORY.

Faith sir, I could amost have given him a knock 190
o'th'pate, myself.

FASHION.

'Tis enough. I will now show thee the excess of my passion by being very calm. Come Lory, lay your loggerhead to mine, and in cool blood let us contrive his destruction. 195

LORY.

Here comes a head, sir, would contrive it better than us both, if he would but join in the confederacy.

Enter Coupler.

FASHION.

By this light, old Coupler alive still! Why, how now, matchmaker, art thou here still to plague the 200
world with matrimony? You old bawd, how have you the impudence to be hobbling out of your grave twenty years after you are rotten?

COUPLER.

When you begin to rot, sirrah, you'll go off like a pippin; one winter will send you to the devil. What 205
mischief brings you home again? Hah, you young, lascivious rogue, you. Let me put my hand in your bosom, sirrah.[d]

FASHION.

Stand off, old Sodom![18]

---

18 Sodom] a pun on a kind of apple and the biblical city destroyed for its vice, especially homosexuality

COUPLER.

Nay, prithee now, don't be so coy. 210

FASHION.

Keep your hands to yourself, you old dog you, or I'll wring your nose off.

COUPLER.

Hast thou been a year in Italy and brought home a fool at last? By my conscience, the young fellows of this age profit no more by their going abroad than 215 they do by their going to church. Sirrah, sirrah, if you are not hanged before you come to my years, you'll know a cock from a hen. But come, I'm still a friend to thy person, though I have contempt of thy understanding, and therefore, I would willingly 220 know thy condition, that I may see whether thou stand'st in need of my assistance, for widows swarm, my boy, the Town's infected with 'em.

FASHION.

I stand in need of anybody's assistance that will help me to cut my elder brother's throat without 225 the risk of being hanged for him.

COUPLER.

Egad, sirrah, I could help thee to do him almost as good a turn without the danger of being burned in the hand[19] for't.

FASHION.

Sayest thou so, old Satan? Show me but that, and 230 my soul is thine.

COUPLER.

Pox o'thy soul, give me thy warm body, sirrah. I shall have a substantial title to't when I tell thee my project.

FASHION.

Out with it then, dear dad, and take possession as 235 soon as thou wilt.

COUPLER.

Sayst thou so, my Hephestion?[20] Why then, thus lies the scene.—But hold, who's that? If we are heard, we are undone.

FASHION.

What, have you forgot Lory? 240

_____

19 burned in the hand] Branding the thumb or hand was usual for felons who escaped the gallows.

20 Hephestion] the military comrade—and lover—of Alexander the Great

COUPLER.

Who? Trusty Lory, is it thee?

LORY.

At your service, sir.

COUPLER.

Give me thy hand, old boy. Egad, I did not know thee again. But I remember thy honesty, though I did not thy face; I think thou hadst like to have 245 been hanged once or twice for thy master.

LORY.

Sir, I was very near once having that honor.

COUPLER.

Well, live and hope, don't be discouraged. Eat with him and drink with him and do what he bids thee, and it may be thy reward at last as well as 250 another's.—Well sir, you must know I have done you the kindness to make up a match for your brother.

FASHION.

Sir, I am very much beholden[e] to you, truly.

COUPLER.

You may be, sirrah, before the wedding day yet. 255 The lady is a great heiress: fifteen hundred pound a year and a great bag of money.[21] The match is concluded, the writings are drawn, and the pipkin's to be cracked[22] in a fortnight. Now, you must know, stripling (with respect to your mother), your 260 brother's the son of a whore.

FASHION.

Good.

COUPLER.

He has given me a bond of a thousand pounds for helping him to this fortune and has promised me as much more in ready money upon the day of 265 marriage, which I understand by a friend he ne'er designs to pay me. If, therefore, you will be a generous young dog and secure me five thousand pounds, I'll be a covetous old rogue and help you to the lady. 270

_____

21 heiress … money] heir to an estate worth fifteen hundred pounds a year in revenue, who would also bring to the marriage a good deal of ready money

22 pipkin … cracked] a small earthenware pot will be broken—part of a folk wedding ceremony, symbolic of the breaking of the maidenhead as well

FASHION.

Egad, if thou canst bring this about, I'll have thy statue cast in brass. But don't you dote, you old pander you, when you talk at this rate?

COUPLER.

That your youthful parts* shall judge of. This plump partridge that I tell you of lives in the country, fifty miles off, with her honored parents, in a lonely old house which nobody comes near. She never goes abroad nor sees company at home. To prevent all misfortunes she has her breeding within doors: the parson of the parish teaches her to play upon the bass viol, the clerk to sing, her nurse to dress, and her father to dance. In short, nobody can give you admittance there but I, nor can I do it any other way than by making you pass for your brother.

FASHION.

And how the devil wilt thou do that?

COUPLER.

Without the Devil's aid, I warrant thee. Thy brother's face not one of the family ever saw. The whole business has been managed by me, and all the letters go through my hands. The last that was writ to Sir Tunbelly Clumsey (for that's the old gentleman's name) was to tell him, his lordship would be down in a fortnight to consummate. Now you shall go away immediately, pretend you writ that letter only to have the romantic pleasure of surprising your mistress, fall desperately in love as soon as you see her, make that your plea for marrying her immediately, and when the fatigue of the wedding night's over, you shall send me a swingeing purse of gold, you dog you.

FASHION.

Egad, old dad, I'll put my hand in thy bosom now—

COUPLER.

Ah, you young, hot, lusty thief, let me muzzle you. (*Kissing.*) Sirrah, let me muzzle you.

FASHION. (*Aside.*)

Psha, the old lecher!

COUPLER.

Well, I warrant thou hast not a farthing of money in thy pocket now; no, one may see it in thy face.

FASHION.

Not a sou, by Jupiter.

COUPLER.

Must I advance then? Well sirrah, be at my lodgings in half an hour, and I'll see what may be done. We'll sign and seal and eat a pullet, and when I have given thee some farther instructions, thou shalt hoist sail and be gone. (*Kissing.*) T'other buss, and so adieu.

FASHION.

Um, psha!

COUPLER.

Ah, you young, warm dog you! What a delicious night will the bride have on't! (*Exit.*)

FASHION.

So Lory. Providence, thou seest at last, takes care of men of merit. We are in a fair way to be great people.

LORY.

Aye sir, if the Devil don't step between the cup and the lip as he uses to do.

FASHION.

Why faith, he has played me many a damned trick to spoil my fortune, and egad, I'm almost afraid he's at work about it again now. But if I should tell thee how, thou'dst wonder at me.

LORY.

Indeed sir, I should not.

FASHION.

How dost know?

LORY.

Because, sir, I have wondered at you so often, I can wonder at you no more.

FASHION.

No? What wouldst thou say if a qualm of conscience should spoil my design?

LORY.

I would eat my words and wonder more than ever.

FASHION.

Why faith, Lory, though I am a young rakehell and have played many a roguish trick, this is so full-grown a cheat I find I must take pains to come up to't. I have scruples.

LORY.

They are strong symptoms of death. If you find they increase, pray sir, make your will.

FASHION.

No, my conscience shan't starve me neither. But

thus far I will hearken to it before I execute this
project. I'll try my brother to the bottom: I'll speak
to him with the temper of a philosospher; my
reasons, though they press him home, shall yet be
clothed with so much modesty not one of all the
truths they urge shall be so naked to offend his
sight. If he has yet so much humanity about him
as to assist me, though with a moderate aid, I'll
drop my project at his feet and show him I can
do for him much more than what I ask he'd do
for me. This one conclusive trial of him I resolve
to make.

> Succeed or no, still victory's my lot;
> If I subdue his heart, 'tis well; if not,
> I shall subdue my conscience to my plot.

Exeunt.

Act II, scene i. [Loveless's lodgings in London.]

Enter Loveless and Amanda.

LOVELESS.
How do you like these lodgings, my dear? For my
part, I am so well pleased with 'em, I shall hardly
remove whilst we stay in town, if you are satisfied.
AMANDA.
I am satisfied with everything that pleases you, else
I had not come to town at all.
LOVELESS.
Oh, a little of the noise and bustle of the world
sweetens the pleasures of retreat. We shall find the
charms of our retirement doubled when we return
to it.
AMANDA.
That pleasing prospect will be my chiefest
entertainment whilst (much against my will) I am
obliged to stand surrounded with these empty
pleasures, which 'tis so much the fashion to be
fond of.
LOVELESS.
I own most of 'em are indeed but empty, nay, so
empty that one would wonder by what magic
power they act when they induce us to be vicious
for their sakes. Yet some there are we may speak
kindlier of. There are delights, of which a private
life is destitute, which may divert an honest man
and be a harmless entertainment to a virtuous

woman. The conversation* of the Town* is one,
and truly, with some small allowances, the plays,
I think, may be esteemed another.
AMANDA.
The plays, I must confess, have some small charms
and would have more, would they restrain that
loose, obscene encouragement to vice, which
shocks, if not the virtue of some women, at least
the modesty of all.
LOVELESS.
But till that reformation can be made, I would not
leave the wholesome corn for some intruding tares
that grow amongst it. Doubtless, the moral of a
well-wrought scene is of prevailing force. Last night
there happened one that moved me strangely.
AMANDA.
Pray what was that?
LOVELESS.
Why 'twas about—but 'tis not worth repeating.
AMANDA.
Yes, pray let me know it.
LOVELESS.
No, I think 'tis as well let alone.
AMANDA.
Nay, now you make me have mind to know.
LOVELESS.
'Twas a foolish thing. You'd perhaps grow jealous
should I tell you, though without cause, Heaven
knows.
AMANDA.
I shall begin to think I have cause if you persist in
making it a secret.
LOVELESS.
I'll then convince you have none by making it no
longer so. Know then, I happened in the play to
find my very character, only with the addition of
a *Relapse*, which struck me so, I put a sudden stop
to a most harmless entertainment, which till then
diverted me between the acts. 'Twas to admire the
workmanship of Nature in the face of a young lady
that sate some distance from me: she was so
exquisitely handsome.
AMANDA.
So exquisitely handsome?
LOVELESS.
Why do you repeat my words, my dear?

AMANDA.

Because you seemed to speak 'em with such pleasure I thought I might oblige you with their echo.

LOVELESS.

Then you are alarmed, Amanda?

AMANDA.

It is my duty to be so when you are in danger.   60

LOVELESS.

You are too quick in apprehending for me; all will be well when you have heard me out. I do confess I gazed upon her; nay, eagerly I gazed upon her.

AMANDA.

Eagerly? That's with desire.

LOVELESS.

No, I desired her not. I viewed her with a world   65
of admiration but not one glance of love.

AMANDA.

Take heed of trusting to such nice* distinctions.

LOVELESS.

I did take heed. For observing in the play that he who seemed to represent me there was by an accident like this unwarily surprised into a net in   70
which he lay a poor entangled slave and brought a train of mischiefs on his head, I snatched my eyes away. They pleaded hard for leave to look again, but I grew absolute, and they obeyed.

AMANDA.

Were they the only things that were inquisitive?   75
Had I been in your place, my tongue, I fancy, had been curious too; I should have asked her name and where she lived (yet still without design). Who was she, pray?

LOVELESS.

Indeed I cannot tell.   80

AMANDA.

You will not tell.

LOVELESS.

By all that's sacred, then, I did not ask.

AMANDA.

Nor do you know what company was with her?

LOVELESS.

I do not.

AMANDA.

Then I am calm again.   85

LOVELESS.

Why were you disturbed?

AMANDA.

Had I then no cause?

LOVELESS.

None, certainly.

AMANDA.

I thought I had.

LOVELESS.

But you thought wrong, Amanda. For turn the   90
case, and let it be your story. Should you come home and tell me you had seen a handsome man, should I grow jealous because you had eyes?

AMANDA.

But should I tell you he were exquisitely so, that I had gazed on him with admiration, that I looked   95
with eager eyes upon him, should you not think 'twere possible I might go one step farther and inquire his name?

LOVELESS. (*Aside.*)

She has reason on her side. I have talked too much, but I must turn it off another way.—Will you then   100
make no difference, Amanda, between the language of our sex and yours? There is a modesty restrains your tongues, which makes you speak by halves when you commend, but roving flattery gives a loose to ours, which makes us still speak   105
double what we think. You should not, therefore, in so strict a sense take what I said to her advantage.

AMANDA.

Those flights of flattery, sir, are to our faces only. When women once are out of hearing, you are as   110
modest in your commendations as we are. But I shan't put you to the trouble of farther excuses; if you please, this business shall rest here. Only give me leave to wish both for your peace and mine that you may never meet this miracle of beauty more.   115

LOVELESS.

I am content.

Enter Servant.

SERVANT.

Madam, there's a young lady at the door in a chair* desires to know whether you ladyship sees company. I think her name is Berinthia.

AMANDA.

Oh dear, 'tis a relation I have not seen these five 120
years.—Pray her to walk in.

Exit Servant.

—Here's another beauty for you. She was young
when I saw her last, but I hear she's grown
extremely handsome.

LOVELESS.

Don't you be jealous now, for I shall gaze upon her 125
too—

Enter Berinthia.

(*Aside.*) Hah! By heavens, the very woman!

BERINTHIA. (*Saluting* Amanda.*)

Dear Amanda, I did not expect to meet with you
in town.

AMANDA.

Sweet cousin, I'm overjoyed to see you.—Mr. 130
Loveless, here's a relation and a friend of mine I
desire you'll be better acquainted with.

LOVELESS. (*Saluting Berinthia.*)

If my wife never desires a harder thing, madam,
her request will be easily granted.

BERINTHIA.

I think, madam, I ought to wish you joy. 135

AMANDA.

Joy! Upon what?

BERINTHIA.

Upon your marriage. You were a widow[23] when I
saw you last.

LOVELESS.

You ought rather, madam, to wish me joy upon
that, since I am the only gainer. 140

BERINTHIA.

If she has got so good a husband as the world
reports, she has gained enough to expect the
compliments of her friends upon it.

LOVELESS.

Aye,[f] the world is so favorable to me to allow I
deserve that title; I hope 'tis so just to my wife to 145
own I derive it from her.

---

23 widow] In Cibber's play Amanda dresses as a widow
until the last act, when she disguises herself and seduces
Loveless.

BERINTHIA.

Sir, it is so just to you both to own you are (and
deserve to be) the happiest pair that live in it.

LOVELESS.

I'm afraid we shall lose that character, madam,
whenever you happen to change your condition. 150

Enter Servant.

SERVANT.

Sir, my Lord Foppington presents his humble
service to you and desires to know how you do.
He but just now heard you were in town. He's at
the next door, and if it be not inconvenient, he'll
come and wait upon you. 155

LOVELESS.

Lord Foppington! I know him not.

BERINTHIA.

Not his dignity, perhaps, but you do his person.
'Tis Sir Novelty; he has bought a barony in order
to marry a great fortune. His patent has not been
passed eight-and-forty hours, and he has already 160
sent how-do-ye's to all the Town to make 'em
acquainted with his title.

LOVELESS.

Give my service to his lordship, and let him know
I am proud of the honor he intends me.

Exit [servant].

Sure this addition of quality* must have so 165
improved his coxcomb he can't but be very good
company for a quarter of an hour.

AMANDA.

Now it moves my pity more than my mirth to see
a man whom Nature has made no fool to be so
very industrious to pass for an ass. 170

LOVELESS.

No, there you are wrong, Amanda; you should
never bestow your pity upon those who take pains
for your contempt. Pity those whom Nature
abuses, but never those who abuse Nature.

BERINTHIA.

Besides, the Town would be robbed of one of its 175
chief diversions if it should become a crime to
laugh at a fool.

AMANDA.

I could never yet perceive the Town inclined to

part with any of its diversions for the sake of their being crimes, but I have seen it very fond of some 180 I think had very little else to recommend 'em.

BERINTHIA.

I doubt,* Amanda, you are grown its enemy, you speak with so much warmth against it.

AMANDA.

I must confess I am not much its friend.

BERINTHIA.

Then give me leave to make you mine by not 185 engaging in its quarrel.

AMANDA.

You have many stronger claims than that, Berinthia, whenever you think fit to plead your title.

LOVELESS.

You have done well to engage a second, my dear, for here comes one will be apt to call you to an 190 account for your country principles.

Enter Lord Foppington.

FOPPINGTON.

Sir, I am your most humble servant.

LOVELESS.

I wish you joy, my lord.

FOPPINGTON.

O Lard, sir.—Madam, your ladyship's welcome to tawn. 195

AMANDA.

I wish your lordship joy.

FOPPINGTON.

Oh heavens, madam—

LOVELESS.

My lord, this young lady is a relation of my wife's.

FOPPINGTON. (*Saluting* *[Berinthia].*)

The beautifullest race* of people upon earth, rat* me! Dear Loveless, I'm overjoyed to see you have 200 braught your family to tawn again; I am, stap my vitals! (*Aside.*) Far I design to lie with your wife.— Far Gad's sake, madam, haw has your ladyship been able to subsist thus long under the fatigue of a country life? 205

AMANDA.

My life has been very far from that, my lord; it has been a very quiet one.

FOPPINGTON.

Why, that's the fatigue I speak of, madam. For 'tis

impossible to be quiet without thinking: now thinking is to me the greatest fatigue in the world. 210

AMANDA.

Does not your lordship love reading, then?

FOPPINGTON.

Oh passionately, madam. But I never think of what I read.

BERINTHIA.

Why, can your lordship read without thinking?

FOPPINGTON.

Oh Lard!—can your ladyship pray without 215 devotion, madam?

AMANDA.

Well, I must own I think books the best entertainment in the world.

FOPPINGTON.

I am so much of you ladyship's mind, madam, that I have a private gallery (where I walk sometimes) 220 is furnished with nothing but books and looking glasses.* Madam, I have gilded 'em and ranged 'em so prettily, before Gad, it is the most entertaining thing in the world to walk and look upon 'em.

AMANDA.

Nay, I love a neat library, too, but 'tis, I think, the 225 inside of the book should recommend it most to us.

FOPPINGTON.

That, I must confess, I am nat altogether so fand of. Far to mind the inside of a book is to entertain one's self with the forced product of another man's 230 brain. Naw I think a man of quality* and breeding may be much better diverted with the natural sprauts of his own. But to say the truth, madam, let a man love reading never so well, when once he comes to know this Tawn, he finds so many 235 better ways of passing the four-and-twenty hours that 'twere ten thousand pities he should consume his time in that. Far example, madam, my life: my life, madam, is a perpetual stream of pleasure that glides through such a variety of entertainments I 240 believe the wisest of our ancestors never had the least conception of any of 'em. I rise, madam, about ten-a-clock. I don't rise sooner, because 'tis the worst thing in the world for the complexion. Nat that I pretend to be a beau, but a man must 245 endeavor to look wholesome, lest he make so nauseous a figure in the side-box the ladies should be compelled to turn their eyes upon the play. So at ten a-clack, I say, I rise. Naw, if I find 'tis a good day, I resalve to take a turn in the Park* and see the fine women, so huddle on my clothes and get dressed by one. If it be nasty weather, I take a turn in the chocolate hause,24 where, as you walk, madam, you have the prettiest prospect in the world; you have looking glasses* all round you— But I'm afraid I tire the company.

BERINTHIA.

Not at all. Pray go on.

FOPPINGTON.

Why then, ladies, from thence I go to dinner at Lacket's, where you are so nicely* and delicately served that, stap my vitals, they shall compose you a dish no bigger than a saucer shall come to fifty shillings. Between eating my dinner (and washing my mauth, ladies) I spend my time till I go to the play, where till nine a-clack I entertain myself with looking upon the company and usually dispose of one hour more in leading25 'em aut. So there's twelve of the four-and-twenty pretty well over. The other twelve, madam, are disposed of in two articles: in the first four I toast myself drunk, and in t'other eight I sleep myself sober again. Thus, ladies, you see my life is an eternal raund O of delights.

LOVELESS.

'Tis a heavenly one, indeed.

AMANDA.

But I thought, my lord, you beaux spent a great deal of your time in intrigues: you have given us no account of them yet.

FOPPINGTON. (*Aside.*)

Soh, she would inquire into my amours—That's jealousy—She begins to be in love with me.— Why, madam—as to time for my intrigues, I usually make detachments of it from my other pleasures according to the exigency. Far your ladyship may please to take notice that those who intrigue with women of

250

255

260

265

270

275

280

quality* have rarely occasion far above half an hour at a time, people of that rank being under those decorums they can seldom give you a langer view than will just serve to shoot 'em flying. So that the course of my other pleasures is not very much interrupted by my amours.

LOVELESS.

But your lordship is now become a pillar of the state; you must attend the weighty affairs of the Nation.

FOPPINGTON.

Sir—as to weighty affairs, I leave them to weighty heads. I never intend mine shall be a burden to my body.

LOVELESS.

Oh but you'll find the House26 will expect your attendance.

FOPPINGTON.

Sir, you'll find the House will compound for my appearance.

LOVELESS.

But your friends will take it ill if you don't attend their particular causes.

FOPPINGTON.

Not, sir, if I come in time enough to give 'em my particular vote.

BERINTHIA.

But pray, my lord, how do you dispose of yourself on Sundays? For that, methinks, is a day should hang wretchedly upon your hands.

FOPPINGTON.

Why faith, madam—Sunday—is a vile day, I must confess. I intend to move for leave to bring in a bill that the players may work upon it, as well as the hackney coaches. Though this I must say for the government, it leaves us the churches to entertain us. But then again, they begin so abominable early a man must rise by candlelight to get dressed by the psalm.27

BERINTHIA.

Pray, which church does your lordship most oblige with your presence?

285

290

295

300

305

310

---

24 chocolate hause] Chocolate was a fashionable imported item of consumption; houses which dispensed it were as popular as coffee houses for social gathering, gossip, and politics.

25 leading] formally escorting especially the ladies

---

26 House] of Lords

27 psalm] part of the service, a fashionably late time to arrive at church

FOPPINGTON.

Oh, St. James's,[28] madam—there's much the best 315
company.

AMANDA.

Is there good preaching, too?

FOPPINGTON.

Why faith, madam—I can't tell. A man must have
very little to do there that can give an account of
the sermon. 320

BERINTHIA.

You can give us an account of the ladies at least?

FOPPINGTON.

Or I deserve to be excommunicated. There is my
Lady Tattle, my Lady Prate, my Lady Titter, my
Lady Leer, my Lady Giggle, and my Lady Grin.
These sit in the front of the boxes and all church- 325
time are the prettiest company in the world, stap
my vitals. (To Amanda) Mayn't we hope for the
honor to see your ladyship added to our society,
madam?

AMANDA.

Alas, my lord, I am the worst company in the 330
world at church: I'm apt to mind the prayers or
the sermon or—

FOPPINGTON.

One is indeed strangely apt at church to mind
what one should not do. But I hope, madam, at
one time or other, I shall have the honor to lead 335
your ladyship to your coach there. (Aside.)
Methinks she seems strangely pleased with
everything I say to her. 'Tis a vast pleasure to
receive encouragement from a woman before her
husband's face. I have a good mind to pursue my 340
conquest and speak the thing plainly to her at
once. Egad, I'll do't, and that in so cavalier a
manner she shall be surprised at it.—Ladies, I'll
take my leave; I'm afraid I begin to grow
troublesome with the length of my visit. 345

AMANDA.

Your lordhip's too entertaining to grow
troublesome anywhere.

FOPPINGTON. (Aside.)

That now was as much as if she had said—pray
lie with me. I'll let her see I'm quick of

apprehension.—Oh Lard, madam, I had like to 350
have forgot a secret I must needs tell your
ladyship.—Ned, you must not be so jealous now
as to listen.

LOVELESS.

Not I, my lord, I am too fashionable a husband
to pry into the secrets of my wife. 355

FOPPINGTON. (To Amanda, squeezing her hand.)

I am in love with you to desperation, strike me
speechless!

AMANDA. (Giving him a box o'th'ear.)

Then thus I return your passion.—An impudent
fool!

FOPPINGTON.

Gad's curse, madam, I'm a peer of the realm! 360

LOVELESS.

Hey, what the devil, do you affront my wife, sir?
Nay then—

They draw and fight. The women run shrieking for
help.

AMANDA.

Ah! What has my folly done? Help! Murder! Help!
Part 'em, for Heaven's sake.

FOPPINGTON. (Falling back and leaning upon his
sword.)

Ah—quite through the body—stap my vitals! 365

Enter servants.

LOVELESS. (Running to him.)

I hope I han't killed the fool, however.—Bear him
up! Where's your wound?

FOPPINGTON.

Just through the guts.

LOVELESS.

Call a surgeon there.—Unbutton him quickly.

FOPPINGTON.

Ay, pray make haste. 370

[Exit servant.]

LOVELESS.

This mischief you may thank yourself for.

FOPPINGTON.

I may so—love's the devil indeed, Ned.

Enter Syringe and Servant.

28 St. James's] new, fashionable church in Piccadilly

SERVANT.

Here's Mr. Syringe, sir, was just going by the door.

FOPPINGTON.

He's the welcomest man alive.

SYRINGE.

Stand by, stand by, stand by! Pray gentlemen, 375
stand by. Lord have mercy upon us! did you never
see a man run through the body before? Pray,
stand by!

FOPPINGTON.

Ah, Mr. Syringe—I'm a dead man!

SYRINGE.

A dead man and I by! I should laugh to see that, 380
egad!

LOVELESS.

Prithee don't stand prating, but look upon his
wound.

SYRINGE.

Why, what if I won't look upon his wound this
hour, sir? 385

LOVELESS.

Why, then he'll bleed to death, sir.

SYRINGE.

Why, then I'll fetch him to life again, sir.

LOVELESS.

'Slife,* he's run through the guts, I tell thee.

SYRINGE.

Would he were run through the heart: I should get
the more credit by his cure. Now I hope you're 390
satisfied? Come now, let me come at him; now let
me come at him. (*Viewing his wound.*) Oons,*
what a gash is here! Why sir, a man may drive a
coach and six horses into your body.

FOPPINGTON.

Ho— 395

SYRINGE.

Why, what the devil, have you run the gentleman
through with a scythe? (*Aside.*) A little prick
between the skin and the ribs, that's all.

LOVELESS.

Let me see his wound.

SYRINGE.

Then you shall dress it, sir, for if anybody looks 400
upon it, I won't.

LOVELESS.

Why, thou art the veriest coxcomb I ever saw.

SYRINGE.

Sir, I am not master of my trade for nothing.

FOPPINGTON.

Surgeon!

SYRINGE.

Well, sir. 405

FOPPINGTON.

Is there any hopes?

SYRINGE.

Hopes? I can't tell. What are you willing to give
for your cure?

FOPPINGTON.

Five hundred paunds, with pleasure.

SYRINGE.

Why, then perhaps there may be hopes. But we 410
must avoid farther delay.—Here, help the
gentleman into a chair* and carry him to my house
presently,* that's the properest place (*Aside.*)—to
bubble* him out of his money.—Come, a chair, a
chair quickly—there, in with him. 415

They put him into a chair.

FOPPINGTON.

Dear Loveless—adieu! If I die—I forgive thee, and
if I live—I hope thou'lt do as much by me. I'm
very sorry you and I should quarrel,* but I hope
here's an end on't, for if you are satisfied—I am.

LOVELESS.

I shall hardly think it worth my prosecuting any 420
farther, so you may be at rest, sir.

FOPPINGTON.

Thou art a generous* fellow, strike me dumb. (*Aside.*)
But thou hast an impertinent wife, stap my vitals.

SYRINGE.

So, carry him off, carry him off. We shall have him
prate himself into a fever by and by. Carry him off. 425

Exit with Lord Foppington.

AMANDA.

Now on my knees, my dear, let me ask your
pardon for my indiscretion; my own I never shall
obtain.

LOVELESS.

Oh, there's no harm done: you served him well.

AMANDA.

He did indeed deserve it. But I tremble to think 430

how dear my indiscreet resentment might have cost
you.

LOVELESS.

Oh no matter, never trouble yourself about that.

BERINTHIA.

For Heaven's sake, what was't he did to you?

AMANDA.

Oh, nothing: he only squeezed me kindly* by the   435
hand and frankly offered a coxcomb's heart. I know
I was to blame to resent it as I did, since nothing
but a quarrel* could ensue. But the fool so surpised
me with his insolence, I was not mistress of my
fingers.   440

BERINTHIA.

Now I dare swear, he thinks you had 'em at great
command, they obeyed you so readily.

Enter Worthy.

WORTHY.

Save you, save you, good people: I'm glad to find
you all alive; I met a wounded peer carrying off.
For Heaven's sake, what was the matter?   445

LOVELESS.

Oh, a trifle! He would have lain with my wife
before my face, so she obliged him with a box
o'th'ear, and I run him through the body: that was
all.

WORTHY.

Bagatelle on all sides. But pray, madam, how long   450
has this noble lord been an humble servant of
yours?

AMANDA.

This is the first I have heard on't. So I suppose 'tis
his quality* more than his love has brought him
into this adventure. He thinks his title an authentic   455
passport to every woman's heart below the degree
of a peeress.

WORTHY.

He's coxcomb enough to think anything. But I
would not have you brought into trouble for him.
I hope there's no danger of his life?   460

LOVELESS.

None at all. He's fallen into the hands of a roguish
surgeon I perceive designs to frighten a little money
out of him. But I saw his wound, 'tis nothing; he
may go to the play tonight if he pleases.

WORTHY.

I am glad you have corrected him without farther   465
mischief. And now, sir, if these ladies have no
farther service for you, you'll oblige me if you can
go to the place I spoke to you of t'other day.

LOVELESS.

With all my heart. (*Aside.*) Though I could wish,
methinks, to stay and gaze a little longer on that   470
creature. Good gods, how beautiful she is! But
what have I to do with beauty? I have already had
my portion and must not covet more.—Come sir,
when you please.

WORTHY.

Ladies, your servant.   475

AMANDA.

Mr. Loveless, pray one word with you before you
go.

LOVELESS. (*To Worthy.*)

I'll overtake you, sir.

Exit Worthy.

—What would my dear?

AMANDA.

Only a woman's foolish question: How do you like   480
my cousin here?

LOVELESS.

Jealous already, Amanda?

AMANDA.

Not at all, I ask you for another reason.

LOVELESS. (*Aside.*)

Whate'er her reason be, I must not tell her true.—
Why, I confess she's handsome. But you must not   485
think I slight your kinswoman if I own to you, of
all the women who may claim that character, she
is the last would triumph in my heart.

AMANDA.

I'm satisfied.

LOVELESS.

Now tell me why you asked?   490

AMANDA.

At night I will. Adieu.

LOVELESS. (*Kissing her.*)

I'm yours. (*Exit.*)

[AMANDA.] (*Aside.*)

I'm glad to find he does not like her, for I have a
great mind to persuade her to come and live with

me.—Now, dear Berinthia, let me inquire a little 495
into your affairs, for I do assure you, I am enough
your friend to interest myself in everything that
concerns you.

BERINTHIA.

You formerly have given me such proofs on't I
should be very much to blame to doubt it. I am 500
sorry I have no secrets to trust you with, that I
might convince you how entire a confidence I
durst repose in you.

AMANDA.

Why, is it possible that one so young and beautiful
as you should live and have no secrets? 505

BERINTHIA.

What secrets do you mean?

AMANDA.

Lovers.

BERINTHIA.

Oh, twenty! but not one secret one amongst 'em.
Lovers in this age have too much honor to do
anything underhand; they do all above board. 510

AMANDA.

That now, methinks, would make me hate a man.

BERINTHIA.

But the women of the Town are of another mind: for
by this means a lady may (with the expense of a few
coquette glances) lead twenty fools about in a string
for two or three years together. Whereas if she 515
should allow 'em greater favors and oblige 'em to
secrecy, she would not keep one of 'em a fortnight.

AMANDA.

There's something indeed in that to satisfy the
vanity of a woman, but I can't comprehend how
the men find their account in it. 520

BERINTHIA.

Their entertainment, I must confess, is a riddle to
me. For there's very few of 'em ever get farther than
a bow and an ogle. I have half a score for my share,
who follow me all over the Town and at the play,
the park, and the church do (with their eyes) say 525
the violentest things to me. But I never hear any
more of 'em.

AMANDA.

What can be the reason of that?

BERINTHIA.

One reason is, they don't know how to go farther.

They have had so little practice they don't 530
understand the trade. But besides their ignorance,
you must know there is not one of my half score
lovers but follows half a score of mistresses. Now,
their affections, being divided amongst so many,
are not strong enough for any one to make 'em 535
pursue her to the purpose. Like a young puppy in
a warren, they have a flirt to all and catch none.

AMANDA.

Yet they seem to have a torrent of love to dispose of.

BERINTHIA.

They have so. But 'tis like the rivers of a modern
philosopher[29] (whose works, though a woman, I 540
have read), it sets out with a violent stream, splits
in a thousand branches, and is all lost in the sands.

AMANDA.

But do you think this river of love runs all its
course without doing any mischief? Do you think
it overflows nothing? 545

BERINTHIA.

Oh yes. 'Tis true it never breaks into anybody's
ground that has the least fence about it, but it
overflows all the commons that lie in its way. And
this is the utmost achievement of those dreadful
champions in the field of love—the beaux. 550

AMANDA.

But prithee, Berinthia, instruct me a little farther,
for I'm so great a novice I am almost ashamed on't.
My husband's leaving me whilst I was young and
fond* threw me into that depth of discontent that
ever since I have led so private and recluse a life 555
my ignorance is scarce conceivable. I therefore fain
would be instructed. Not (Heaven knows) that
what you call intrigues have any charms for me;
my love and principles are too well fixed. The
practick[30] part of all unlawful love is— 560

BERINTHIA.

Oh, 'tis abominable! But for the speculative, that,
we must all confess, is entertaining. The
conversation of all the virtuous women in the
Town turns upon that and new clothes.

---

29 modern philosopher] Zimansky identifies as the natural historian, Thomas Burnet.

30 practick] practical as opposed to theoretical or Berinthia's
"speculative" below

AMANDA.

Pray be so just then to me to believe 'tis with a   565
world of innocency I would inquire whether you
think those women we call women of reputation
do really 'scape all other men, as they do those
shadows of 'em, the beaux.

BERINTHIA.

Oh no, Amanda: there are a sort of men make   570
dreadful work amongst 'em, men that may be
called the beaux' antipathy, for they agree in
nothing but walking upon two legs. These have
brains; the beau has none. These are in love with
their mistress; the beau with himself. They take   575
care of her reputation; he's industrious to destroy
it. They are decent; he's a fop. They are sound; he's
rotten.³¹ They are men; he's an ass.ᵍ

AMANDA.

If this be their character, I fancy we had here e'en
now a pattern of 'em both.   580

BERINTHIA.

His lordship and Mr. Worthy?

AMANDA.

The same.

BERINTHIA.

As for the lord, he's eminently so, and for the other,
I can assure you, there's not a man in town who
has a better interest with the women that are worth   585
having an interest with. But 'tis all private: he's like
a backstair minister at Court, who whilst the
reputed favorites are sauntering in the bedchamber, is ruling the roost in the closet.*³²

AMANDA.

He answers then the opinion I had ever of him.   590
Heavens, what a difference there is between a man
like him and that vain nauseous fop, Sir Novelty.
(*Taking her hand.*) I must acquaint you with a
secret, Cousin. 'Tis not that fool alone has talked
to me of love. Worthy has been tampering too. 'Tis   595
true, he has done't in vain: not all his charms or
art have power to shake me. My love, my duty, and

my virtue are such faithful guards I need not fear
my heart should e'er betray me. But what I wonder
at is this: I find I did not start at this proposal, as   600
when it came from one whom I contemned. I
therefore mention his attempt that I may learn
from you whence it proceeds. That vice (which
cannot change its nature) should so far change at
least its shape as that the self-same crime proposed   605
from one shall seem a monster gaping at your ruin,
when from another it shall look so kind as though
it were your friend and never meant to harm you.
Whence, think you, can this difference proceed?
For 'tis not love, Heaven knows.   610

BERINTHIA.

Oh no, I would not for the world believe it were.
But possibly, should there a dreadful sentence pass
upon you to undergo the rage of both their
passions, the pain you'd apprehend from one might
seem so trivial to the other the danger would not   615
quite so much alarm you.

AMANDA.

Fie, fie, Berinthia! you would indeed alarm me could
you incline me to a thought that all the merit of
mankind combined could shake that tender love I
bear my husband. No! he sits triumphant in my   620
heart, and nothing can dethrone him.

BERINTHIA.

But should he abdicate again, do you think you
should preserve the vacant throne ten tedious
winters more in hopes of his return?

AMANDA.

Indeed, I think I should. Though I confess, after   625
those obligations he has to me, should he abandon
me once more, my heart would grow extremely
urgent with me to root him thence and cast him
out forever.

BERINTHIA.

Were I that thing they call a slighted wife,   630
somebody should run the risk of being that thing
they call—a husband.

AMANDA.

Oh fie, Berinthia! No revenge should ever be taken
against a husband. But to wrong his bed is a
vengeance, which of all vengeance—   635

BERINTHIA.

Is the sweetest. Ha! ha! ha! Don't I talk madly?

---

31 sound ... rotten] healthy, diseased—particularly with
    venereal disease
32 backstair ... closet] a minister who has private access to
    the monarch, as opposed to those who pride themselves
    on access to his or her more public levee

AMANDA.

Madly, indeed.

BERINTHIA.

Yet I'm very innocent.

AMANDA.

That I dare swear you are. I know how to make allowances for your humor.* You were always very 640 entertaining company, but I find, since marriage and widowhood have shown you the world a little, you are very much improved.

BERINTHIA. (*Aside.*)

Alack-a-day, there has gone more than that to improve me, if she knew all. 645

AMANDA.

For Heaven's sake, Berinthia, tell me what way I shall take to persuade you to come and live with me?

BERINTHIA.

Why, one way in the world there is—and but one.

AMANDA.

Pray which is that?

BERINTHIA.

It is, to assure me—I shall be very welcome. 650

AMANDA.

If that be all, you shall e'en lie here tonight.

BERINTHIA.

Tonight?

AMANDA.

Yes, tonight.

BERINTHIA.

Why, the people where I lodge will think me mad.

AMANDA.

Let 'em think what they please. 655

BERINTHIA.

Say you so, Amanda? Why, then they shall think what they please, for I'm a young widow, and I care not what anybody thinks. Ah, Amanda, it's a delicious thing to be a young widow!

AMANDA.

You'll hardly make me think so. 660

BERINTHIA.

Phu! because you are in love with your husband. But that is not every woman's case.

AMANDA.

I hope 'twas yours, at least.

BERINTHIA.

Mine, say ye? Now have I a great mind to tell you

a lie, but I should do it so awkwardly you'd find 665 me out.

AMANDA.

Then e'en speak the truth.

BERINTHIA.

Shall I?—Then after all I did love him, Amanda— as a nun does penance.

AMANDA.

Why did not you refuse to marry him, then? 670

BERINTHIA.

Because my mother would have whipped me.

AMANDA.

How did you live together?

BERINTHIA.

Like man and wife, asunder. He loved the country, I the Town. He hawks and hounds, I coaches and equipage. He eating and drinking, I carding and play- 675 ing. He the sound of horn, I the squeek of a fiddle. We were dull company at table, worse a-bed. When- ever we met, we gave one another the spleen and never agreed but once, which was about lying alone.[h]

AMANDA.

But tell me one thing, truly and sincerely. 680

BERINTHIA.

What's that?

AMANDA.

Notwithstanding all these jars, did not his death at last—extremely trouble you?

BERINTHIA.

Oh yes. Not that my present pangs were so very violent, but the after-pains were intolerable. I was 685 forced to wear a beastly widow's band a twelvemonth for't.

AMANDA.

Women, I find, have different inclinations.

BERINTHIA.

Women, I find, keep different company. When your husband ran away from you, if you had fallen 690 into some of my acquaintance, 'twould have saved you many a tear. But you go and live with a grandmother, a bishop, and an old nurse—which was enough to make any woman break her heart for her husband. Pray Amanda, if ever you are a 695 widow again, keep yourself so, as I do.

AMANDA.

Why, do you then resolve you'll never marry?

BERINTHIA.

Oh no, I resolve I will.

AMANDA.

How so?

BERINTHIA.

That I never may.

AMANDA.

You banter me.

BERINTHIA.

Indeed I don't. But I consider I'm a woman and form my resolutions accordingly.

AMANDA.

Well, my opinion is, form what resolution you will, matrimony will be the end on't.

BERINTHIA.

Faith, it won't.

AMANDA.

How do you know?

BERINTHIA.

I'm sure on't.

AMANDA.

Why, do you think 'tis impossible for you to fall in love?

BERINTHIA.

No.

AMANDA.

Nay, but to grow so passionately fond that nothing but the man you love can give you rest.

BERINTHIA.

Well, what then?

AMANDA.

Why, then you'll marry him.

BERINTHIA.

How do you know that?

AMANDA.

Why, what can you do else?

BERINTHIA.

Nothing——but sit and cry.

AMANDA.

Psha!

BERINTHIA.

Ah, poor Amanda! you have led a country life, but if you'll consult the widows of this Town, they'll tell you you should never take a lease of a house you can hire for a quarter's warning.

Exeunt.

Act III, [scene i. A room in Lord Foppington's Town house.]

Enter Lord Foppington and servant.

FOPPINGTON.

Hey fellow, let the coach come to the door.

SERVANT.

Will your lordship venture so soon to expose yourself to the weather?

FOPPINGTON.

Sir, I will venture as soon as I can to expose myself to the ladies; though give me my cloak, however, for in that side-box, what between the air that comes in at the door on one side, and the intolerable warmth of the masks* on t'other, a man gets so many heats and colds 'twould destroy the canstitution of a harse.

SERVANT. (*Putting on his cloak.*)

I wish your lordship would please to keep house a little longer; I'm afraid your honor does not well consider your wound.

FOPPINGTON.

My wound? I would not be in eclipse another day, though I had as many wounds in my guts as I have had in my heart.

[Exit Servant.] Enter Young Fashion.

FASHION.

Brother, your servant. How do you find yourself today?

FOPPINGTON.

So well, that I have ardered my coach to the door: so there's no great danger of death this baut, Tam.

FASHION.

I'm very glad of it.

FOPPINGTON. (*Aside.*)

That I believe's a lie.——Prithee, Tam, tell me one thing: Did nat your heart cut* a caper up to your mauth when you heard I was run through the bady?

FASHION.

Why do you think it should?

FOPPINGTON.

Because I remember mine did so when I heard my father was shat through the head.

FASHION.

It then did very ill.

FOPPINGTON.

Prithee, why so?

FASHION.

Because he used you very well. 30

FOPPINGTON.

Well, naw strike me dumb! he starved me. He has let me want* a thausand women for want* of a thausand paund.

FASHION.

Then he hindered you from making a great many ill bargains, for I think no woman is worth money 35 that will take money.

FOPPINGTON.

If I were a younger brother, I should think so too.

FASHION.

Why, is it possible you can value a woman that's to be bought?

FOPPINGTON.

Prithee, why not as well as a padnag?33 40

FASHION.

Because a woman has a heart to dispose of; a horse has none.

FOPPINGTON.

Look you, Tam, of all things that belang to a woman, I have an aversion to her heart, far when once a woman has given you her heart—you can 45 never get rid of the rest of her body.

FASHION.

This is strange doctrine, but pray, in your amours, how is it with your own heart?

FOPPINGTON.

Why, my heart in my amours—is like my heart aut of my amours: *à la glace*.34 My bady, Tam, is 50 a watch, and my heart is the pendulum to it: whilst the finger runs raund to every hour in the circle, that still beats the same time.

FASHION.

Then you are seldom much in love?

FOPPINGTON.

Never, stap my vitals. 55

FASHION.

Why then did you make all this bustle about Amanda?

FOPPINGTON.

Because she was a woman of an insolent virtue, and I thought myself piqued[i] in honor to debauch her. 60

FASHION.

Very well. (*Aside.*) Here's a rare fellow for you to have the spending of five thousand pounds a year! But now for my business with him.—Brother, though I know to talk to you of business (especially of money) is a theme not quite so entertaining to 65 you as that of the ladies, my necessities are such I hope you'll have patience to hear me.

FOPPINGTON.

The greatness of your necessities, Tam, is the worst argument in the world for your being patiently heard. I do believe you are going to make me a 70 very good speech, but strike me dumb, it has the worst beginning of any speech I have heard this twelvemonth.

FASHION.

I'm very sorry you think so.

FOPPINGTON.

I do believe thau art. But come, let's know thy 75 affair quickly, far 'tis a new play, and I shall be so rumpled and squeezed with pressing through the crawd to get to my servant the women will think I have lain all night in my clothes.

FASHION.

Why then (that I may not be the author of so great 80 a misfortune), my case in a word is this: The necessary expenses of my travels have so much exceeded the wretched income of my annuity that I have been forced to mortgage it for five hundred pounds, which is spent; so that unless you are so 85 kind to assist me in redeeming it, I know of no remedy but to go take a purse.35

FOPPINGTON.

Why faith, Tam—to give you my sense of the thing, I do think taking a purse the best remedy in the world: for if you succeed, you are relieved 90 that way; if you are taken—you are relieved t'other.36

---

33 padnag] an ambling jade (*OED*); a broken-down, vicious, or worthless horse

34 *à la glace*] iced (Fr.)

35 take a purse] commit highway robbery

36 you are relieved t'other] by the gallows

FASHION.

    I'm glad to see you are in so pleasant a humor. I
hope I shall find the effects on't.

FOPPINGTON.

    Why, do you then really think it a reasonable thing   95
I should give you five hundred paunds?

FASHION.

    I do not ask it as a due, Brother; I am willing to
receive it as a favor.

FOPPINGTON.

    Thau art willing to receive it anyhaw, strike me
speechless! But these are damned times to give   100
money in: taxes are so great, repairs so exorbitant,
tenants such rogues, and periwigs so dear* that, the
devil take me, I am reduced to that extremity in
my cash I have been forced to retrench in that one
article of sweet pawder till I have braught it dawn   105
to five guineas a manth. Naw judge, Tam, whether
I can spare you five hundred paunds.

FASHION.

    If you can't, I must starve, that's all. (*Aside.*) Damn
him!

FOPPINGTON.

    All I can say is, you should have been a better   110
husband.*

FASHION.

    Oons,* if you can't live upon five thousand a year,
how do you think I should do't upon two
hundred?

FOPPINGTON.

    Don't be in a passion, Tam, far passion is the most   115
unbecoming thing in the world—to the face. Look
you, I don't love to say anything to you to make you
melancholy, but upon this occasion I must take leave
to put you in mind that a running horse does require
more attendance than a coach-horse. Nature has   120
made some difference 'twixt you and I.

FASHION.

    Yes, she has made you older. (*Aside.*) Pox take her!

FOPPINGTON.

    That is nat all, Tam.

FASHION.

    Why, what is there else?

FOPPINGTON. (*Looking first upon himself, then
upon his brother.*)

    Ask the ladies.   125

FASHION.

    Why, thou essence bottle! thou musk cat![37] dost
thou then think thou hast any advantage over me
but what Fortune has given thee?

FOPPINGTON.

    I do—stap my vitals!

FASHION.

    Now, by all that's great and powerful, thou art the   130
prince of coxcombs!

FOPPINGTON.

    Sir—I am praud of being at the head of so
prevailing a party.

FASHION.

    Will nothing then provoke thee? Draw, coward!

FOPPINGTON.

    Look you, Tam, you know I have always taken you   135
for a mighty dull fellow, and here is one of the
foolishest plats broke out that I have seen in a long
time. Your paverty makes your life so burdensome
to you, you would provoke me to a quarrel,* in
hopes either to slip through my lungs into my   140
estate or to get yourself run through the guts to
put an end to your pain. But I will disappoint you
in both your designs, far with the temper of a
philasapher and the discretion of a statesman—I
will go to the play with my sword in my scabbard.   145
(*Exit.*)

FASHION.

    Soh! Farewell, snuff-box! And now, conscience, I
defy thee.—Lory!

Enter Lory.

LORY.

    Sir.

FASHION.

    Here's rare news, Lory: his lordship has given me   150
a pill has purged off all my scruples.

LORY.

    Then my heart's at ease again. For I have been in
a lamentable fright, sir, ever since your conscience
had the impudence to intrude into your company.

FASHION.

    Be at peace, it will come there no more: my   155

---

[37] essence … cat] perfume bottle, civet cat (yielder of
musky scent)

brother has given it a wring by the nose, and I have
kicked it down stairs. So run away to the inn, get
the horses ready quickly, and bring 'em to old
Coupler's without a moment's delay.

LORY.

Then sir, are you going straight about the fortune?   160

FASHION.

I am. Away! Fly, Lory!

LORY.

The happiest day I ever saw. I'm upon the wing
already.

Exeunt several ways.

Scene [ii]. A garden [adjoining Loveless's lodgings].

Enter Loveless and servant.

LOVELESS.

Is my wife within?

SERVANT.

No, sir, she has been gone out this half hour.

LOVELESS.

'Tis well; leave me.

[Exit Servant.]

Sure Fate has yet some business to be done
Before Amanda's heart and mine must rest.   5
Else why amongst those legions of her sex
Which throng the world
Should she pick out for her companion
The only one on earth
Whom Nature has endowed for her undoing?   10
Undoing, was't I said? Who shall undo her?
Is not her empire fixed? Am I not hers?
Did she not rescue me, a grov'ling slave,
When chained and bound by that black tyrant, Vice,
I labored in his vilest drudgery?   15
Did she not ransom me and set me free?
Nay, more: When by my follies sunk
To a poor, tattered, despicable beggar,
Did she not lift me up to envied fortune?
Give me herself and all that she possessed   20
Without a thought of more return
Than what a poor, repenting heart might make her?
Han't she done this? And if she has,
Am I not strongly bound to love her for it?
To love her! Why, do I not love her then?   25

By earth and heaven I do.
Nay, I have demonstration that I do:
For I would sacrifice my life to serve her.
Yet hold—if laying down my life
Be demonstration of my love,   30
What is't I feel in favor of Berinthia?
For should she be in danger, methinks I could
Incline to risk it for her service too,
And yet I do not love her.
How then subsists my proof?—   35
Oh, I have found it out!
What I would do for one
Is demonstration of my love,
And if I'd do as much for t'other,
It[k] there is demonstration of my friendship—   40
Aye—it must be so. I find I'm very much her
    friend.
—Yet let me ask myself one puzzling question
    more:
Whence springs this mighty friendship all at once?
For our acquaintaince is of later date.
Now friendship's said to be a plant of tedious   45
    growth:
Its root composed of tender fibers, nice* in their
    taste,
Cautious in spreading, checked with the least
Corruption in the soil long ere it take
And longer still ere it appear to do so.
Whilst mine is in a moment shot so high   50
And fixed so fast it seems
Beyond the power of storms to shake it.
I doubt* it thrives too fast.[l] (*Musing.*)

Enter Berinthia.

Hah! she here! Nay, then take heed my heart,
For there are dangers towards.   55

BERINTHIA.

What makes you look so thoughtful, sir? I hope
you are not ill.

LOVELESS.

I was debating, madam, whether I was so or not,
and that was it which made me look so thoughtful.

BERINTHIA.

Is it then so hard a matter to decide? I thought all   60
people had been acquainted with their own bodies,
though few people know their own minds.

LOVELESS.

What if the distemper I suspect be in the mind?

BERINTHIA.

Why, then I'll undertake to prescribe you a cure.

LOVELESS.

Alas! you undertake you know not what. 65

BERINTHIA.

So far at least then allow me to be a physician.

LOVELESS.

Nay, I'll allow you so yet farther, for I have reason
to believe, should I put myself into your hands,
you would increase my distemper.

BERINTHIA.

Perhaps I might have reasons from the College not 70
to be too quick in your cure,[38] but 'tis possible I
might find ways to give you often ease, sir.

LOVELESS.

Were I but sure of that, I'd quickly lay my case
before you.

BERINTHIA.

Whether you are sure of it or no, what risk do you 75
run in trying?

LOVELESS.

Oh! a very great one.

BERINTHIA.

How?

LOVELESS.

You might betray my distemper to my wife.

BERINTHIA.

And so lose all my practice. 80

LOVELESS.

Will you then keep my secret?

BERINTHIA.

I will, if it don't burst me.

LOVELESS.

Swear.

BERINTHIA.

I do.

LOVELESS.

By what? 85

BERINTHIA.

By Woman.

LOVELESS.

That's swearing by my deity. Do it by your own,
or I shan't believe you.

BERINTHIA.

By Man, then.

LOVELESS.

I'm satisfied. 90
Now hear my symptoms and give me your advice.
The first were these:
When 'twas my chance to see you at the play,
A random glance you threw at first alarmed me;
I could not turn my eyes from whence the danger 95
    came.
I gazed upon you till you shot again,
And then my fears came on me.
My heart began to pant, my limbs to tremble,
My blood grew thin, my pulse beat quick, my eyes
Grew hot and dim, and all the frame of nature 100
Shook with apprehension.
'Tis true, some small recruits of resolution
My manhood brought to my assistance,
And by their help I made a stand a while
But found at last your arrows flew so thick 105
They could not fail to pierce me, so left the field
And fled for shelter to Amanda's arms.
What think you of these symptoms, pray?

BERINTHIA.

Feverish, every one of 'em.
But what relief, pray, did your wife afford you? 110

LOVELESS.

Why, instantly, she let me blood,[39]
Which for the present much assuaged my flame.
But when I saw you, out it burst again,
And raged with greater fury than before.
Nay, since you now appear, 'tis so increased 115
That in a moment, if you do not help me,
I shall, whilst you look on, consume to ashes.[m]
    (*Taking hold of her hand.*)

BERINTHIA. (*Breaking from him.*)

Oh Lard, let me go! 'Tis the plague, and we shall
all be infected.

LOVELESS. (*Catching her in his arms and kissing her.*)

Then we'll die together, my charming angel! 120

_____

38 College … cure] College of Physicians, who would
forego extra fees in the event of a rapid cure

39 let me blood] Draining blood (bloodletting) was state-
of-the-art therapy for many maladies.

BERINTHIA.

Oh Ged—the Devil's in you!—Lord, let me go, here's somebody coming.

Enter servant.

SERVANT.

Sir, my lady's come home and desires to speak with you. She's in her chamber.

LOVELESS.

Tell her I'm coming. 125

Exit servant.

—But before I go, one glass of nectar more to drink her health.

BERINTHIA.

Stand off, or I shall hate you, by heavens!

LOVELESS. (*Kissing her.*)

In matters of love, a woman's oath is no more to be minded than a man's. 130

BERINTHIA.

Um—

Enter Worthy.

WORTHY. [*Aside.*]

Hah! What's here? My old mistress, and so close, i'faith! I would not spoil her sport for the universe. (*He retires.*)

BERINTHIA.

Oh Ged!—Now do I pray to Heaven— 135

Exit Loveless running.

with all my heart and soul, that the Devil in hell may take me—if ever—I was better pleased in my life! This man has bewitched me, that's certain. (*Sighing.*) Well, I am condemned, but thanks to Heaven, I feel myself each moment more and more 140 prepared for my execution. Nay to that degree, I don't perceive I have the least fear of dying. No, I find, let the executioner be but a man, and there's nothing will suffer with more resolution than a woman. Well, I never had but one intrigue yet— 145 but I confess I long to have another. Pray Heaven it end as the first did though, that we may both grow weary at a time, for 'tis a melancholy thing for lovers to outlive one another.[n]

Enter Worthy.

WORTHY. (*Aside.*)

This discovery's a lucky one; I hope to make a 150 happy use on't. That gentlewoman there is no fool, so I shall be able to make her understand her interest.—Your servant, madam; I need not ask how you do, you have got so good a color.

BERINTHIA.

No better than I used to have, I suppose? 155

WORTHY.

A little more blood in your cheeks.

BERINTHIA.

The weather's hot.

WORTHY.

If it were not, a woman may have color.

BERINTHIA.

What do you mean by that?

WORTHY.

Nothing. 160

BERINTHIA.

Why do you smile then?

WORTHY.

Because the weather's hot.

BERINTHIA.

You'll never leave roguing, I see that.

WORTHY.

You'll never leave— (*Putting his finger to his nose.*[40]) I see that. 165

BERINTHIA.

Well, I can't imagine what you drive at. Pray tell me what you mean?

WORTHY.

Do you tell me; it's the same thing.

BERINTHIA.

I can't.

WORTHY.

Guess! 170

BERINTHIA.

I shall guess wrong.

WORTHY.

Indeed you won't.

BERINTHIA.

Psha! either tell or let it alone.

---

40 nose] The upper is often taken as the sign of the nether nose (penis).

WORTHY.

Nay, rather than let it alone, I will tell. But first I must put you in mind that, after what has passed 'twixt you and I, very few things ought to be secrets between us.

BERINTHIA.

Why, what secrets do we hide? I know of none.

WORTHY.

Yes, there are two: one I have hid from you, and t'other you would hide from me. You are fond of Loveless, which I have discovered, and I am fond of his wife—

BERINTHIA.

Which I have discovered.

WORTHY.

Very well, now I confess your discovery to be true, what do you say to mine?

BERINTHIA.

Why, I confess—I would swear 'twere false, if I thought you were fool enough to believe me.

WORTHY.

Now am I almost in love with you again. Nay, I don't know but I might be quite so, had I made one short campaign with Amanda. Therefore, if you find 'twould tickle your vanity to bring me down once more to your lure, e'en help me quickly to dispatch her business, that I may have nothing else to do but to apply myself to yours.

BERINTHIA.

Do you then think, sir, I am old enough to be a bawd?

WORTHY.

No, but I think you are wise enough to—

BERINTHIA.

To do what?

WORTHY.

To hoodwink Amanda with a gallant, that she mayn't see who is her husband's mistress.

BERINTHIA. (*Aside.*)

He has reason: the hint's a good one.

WORTHY.

Well madam, what think you on't?

BERINTHIA.

I think you are so much a deeper politician in these affairs than I am, that I ought to have a very great regard for your advice.

WORTHY.

Then give me leave to put you in mind: that the most easy, safe, and pleasant situation for your own amour is the house in which you now are, provided you keep Amanda from any sort of suspicion; that the way to do that is to engage her in an intrigue of her own, making yourself her confidante; and the way to bring her to intrigue is to make her jealous of her husband in a wrong place—which the more you foment, the less you'll be suspected. This is my scheme, in short, which if you follow as you should do, my dear Berinthia, we may all four pass the winter[41] very pleasantly.

BERINTHIA.

Well, I could be glad to have nobody's sins to answer for but my own. But where there is a necessity—

WORTHY.

Right as you say, where there is a necessity, a Christian is bound to help his neighbor. So, good Berinthia, lose no time, but let us begin the dance as fast as we can.

BERINTHIA.

Not till the fiddles are in tune, pray, sir. Your lady's strings will be very apt to fly, I can tell you that, if they are wound up too hastily. But if you'll have patience to screw 'em to their pitch by degrees, I don't doubt but she may endure to be played upon.

WORTHY.

Aye, and will make admirable music too, or I'm mistaken. But have you had no private closet* discourse with her yet about males and females and so forth, which may give you hopes in her constitution, for I know her morals are the devil against us?

BERINTHIA.

I have had so much discourse with her that I believe, were she once cured of her fondness for her husband, the fortress of her virtue would not be so impregnable as she fancies.

WORTHY.

What! she runs, I warrant you, into that common

41 winter] It was fashionable for the aristocracy, from nobility to gentry, to pass the winter in the Town and the summer in the country (away from the plague and other diseases).

mistake of fond* wives, who conclude themselves 240
virtuous because they can refuse a man they don't
like, when they have got one they do.

BERINTHIA.

True, and therefore I think 'tis a presumptuous
thing in a woman to assume the name of virtuous
till she has heartily hated her husband and been 245
soundly in love with somebody else. Whom, if she
has withstood—then—much good may it do her.

WORTHY.

Well, so much for her virtue. Now, one word of
her inclinations, and every one to their post. What
opinion do you find she has of me? 250

BERINTHIA.

What you could wish: she thinks you handsome
and discreet.

WORTHY.

Good, that's thinking half-seas over. One tide more
brings us into port.

BERINTHIA.

Perhaps it may, though still remember, there's a 255
difficult bar to pass.[42]

WORTHY.

I know there is, but I don't question I shall get well
over it by the help of such a pilot.

BERINTHIA.

You may depend upon your pilot—she'll do the
best she can; so weigh anchor and be gone as soon 260
as you please.

WORTHY.

I'm under sail already. Adieu! (*Exit*.)

BERINTHIA.

Bon voyage! So, here's fine work! What a business
have I undertaken! I'm a very pretty gentlewoman,
truly. But there was no avoiding it: he'd have 265
ruined me if I had refused him. Besides, faith, I
begin to fancy there may be as much pleasure in
carrying on another body's intrigue as one's own.
This at least is certain, it exercises almost all the
entertaining faculties of a woman. For there's 270
employment for hypocrisy, invention, deceit,
flattery, mischief, and lying.

---

42 half-seas over . . . pass] Half the journey is accomplished
. . . all one has to do is pass the sand bar at the harbor's
mouth at high tide.

Enter Amanda, her woman following her.

WOMAN.

If you please, madam, only to say whether you'll
have me buy 'em or not.

AMANDA.

Yes, no, go fiddle! I care not what you do. Prithee 275
leave me.

WOMAN.

I have done. (*Exit*.)

BERINTHIA.

What in the name of Jove's the matter with you?

AMANDA.

The matter, Berinthia! I'm almost mad, I'm
plagued to death. 280

BERINTHIA.

Who is it that plagues you?

AMANDA.

Who do you think should plague a wife but her
husband?

BERINTHIA.

Oh ho, is it come to that? We shall have you wish
yourself a widow by and by. 285

AMANDA.

Would I were anything but what I am! A base,
ungrateful man, after what I have done for him,
to use me thus!

BERINTHIA.

What, he has been ogling now, I'll warrant you?

AMANDA.

Yes, he has been ogling. 290

BERINTHIA.

And so you are jealous? Is that all?

AMANDA.

That all! Is jealousy then nothing?

BERINTHIA.

It should be nothing, if I were in your case.

AMANDA.

Why, what would you do?

BERINTHIA.

I'd cure myself. 295

AMANDA.

How?

BERINTHIA.

Let blood in the fond* vein: care as little for my
husband as he did for me.

AMANDA.

That would not stop his course.

BERINTHIA.

Nor nothing else, when the wind's in the warm
corner.[43] Look you, Amanda, you may build
castles in the air and fume and fret and grow thin
and lean and pale and ugly, if you please. But I
tell you, no man worth having is true to his wife
or can be true to his wife or ever was or ever will
be so.

AMANDA.

Do you then really think he's false to me? For I
did but suspect him.

BERINTHIA.

Think so? I know he's so.

AMANDA.

Is it possible? Pray tell me what you know.

BERINTHIA.

Don't press me then to name names, for that I have
sworn I won't do.

AMANDA.

Well, I won't, but let me know all you can without
perjury.

BERINTHIA.

I'll let you know enough to prevent any wise
woman's dying of the pip, and I hope you'll pluck
up your spirits and show upon occasion you can
be as good a wife as the best of 'em.

AMANDA.

Well, what a woman can do I'll endeavor.

BERINTHIA.

Oh, a woman can do a great deal, if once she sets her
mind to it. Therefore, pray don't stand trifling any
longer and teasing yourself with this and that and
your love and your virtue and I know not what. But
resolve to hold up your head, get a tip-toe, and look
over 'em all, for to my certain knowledge your
husband is a-pickering[44] elsewhere.

AMANDA.

You are sure on't?

BERINTHIA.

Positively. He fell in love at the play.

AMANDA.

Right, the very same. Do you know the ugly thing?

BERINTHIA.

Yes, I know her well enough, but she's no such an
ugly thing neither.

AMANDA.

Is she very handsome?

BERINTHIA.

Truly I think so.

AMANDA.

Hey ho!

BERINTHIA.

What do you sigh for now?

AMANDA.

Oh, my heart!

BERINTHIA. (*Aside.*)

Only the pangs of nature; she's in labor of her love.
Heaven send her a quick delivery, I'm sure she has
a good midwife.

AMANDA.

I'm very ill, I must go to my chamber. Dear
Berinthia, don't leave me a moment.

BERINTHIA.

No, don't fear. (*Aside.*) I'll see you safe brought to
bed, I'll warrant you.

Exeunt, Amanda leaning upon Berinthia.

Scene [iii. The gate of] a country house.

Enter Young Fashion and Lory.

FASHION.

So here's our inheritance, Lory, if we can but get
into possession. But methinks the seat of our
family looks like Noah's ark, as if the chief part on't
were designed for the fowls of the air and the beasts
of the field.

LORY.

Pray sir, don't let your head run upon the orders
of building[45] here; get but the heiress, let the Devil
take the house.

FASHION.

Get but the house, let the Devil take the heiress, I

---

43 when the wind's in the warm corner] when a comfortable situation is troubled (Tilley)

44 a-pickering] reconnoitering, maneuvering

45 orders of building] the Classical forms of architecture,
called orders, as in Doric, Ionic, and Corinthian columns

say, at least if she be as old Coupler describes her.
But come, we have no time to squander. Knock
at the door.

Lory knocks two or three times.

What the devil, have they got no ears in this house?
Knock harder.

LORY.
Egad, sir, this will prove some enchanted castle; we
shall have the giant come out by and by with his
club and beat our brains out.(*Knocks again.*)

FASHION.
Hush, they come.

[SERVANT.] (*From within.*)
Who is there?

LORY.
Open the door and see. Is that your country
breeding?

[SERVANT.] (*Within.*)
Aye, but two words to a bargain.—Tummas, is the
blunderbuss primed?

FASHION.
Oons,* give 'em good words, Lory; we shall be shot
here a fortune-catching.

LORY.
Egad, sir, I think y'are in the right on't.—Ho! Mr.
What-d'ye-call'um.

Servant appears at the window with a blunderbuss.

SERVANT.
Weall, naw what's yare business?

FASHION.
Nothing, sir, but to wait upon Sir Tunbelly, with
your leave.

SERVANT.
To weat upon Sir Tunbelly? Why, you'll find that's
just as Sir Tunbelly pleases.

FASHION.
But will you do me the favor, sir, to know whether
Sir Tunbelly pleases or not?

SERVANT.
Why, look you, do you see, with good words much
may be done.—Ralph, go thy weas, and ask Sir
Tunbelly if he pleases to be waited upon. And dost
hear? Call to Nurse that she may lock up Miss
Hoyden before the geat's open.

FASHION.
D'ye hear that, Lory?

LORY.
Aye sir, I'm afraid we shall find a difficult job on't.
Pray Heaven that old rogue Coupler han't sent us
to fetch milk out of the gunroom.

FASHION.
I'll warrant thee all will go well. See, the door
opens.

*Enter Sir Tunbelly, with his servants armed with guns,
clubs, pitchforks, scythes, etc.*

LORY. (*Running behind his master.*)
Oh Lord! O Lord! O Lord! We are both dead men!

FASHION.
Take heed, fool! Thy fear will ruin us.

LORY.
My fear, sir! 'Sdeath,* sir, I fear nothing. (*Aside*)
Would I were well up to the chin in a horsepond!

SIR TUNBELLY.
Who is it here has any business with me?

FASHION.
Sir, 'tis I, if your name be Sir Tunbelly Clumsey.

SIR TUNBELLY.
Sir, my name is Sir Tunbelly Clumsey whether you
have any business with me or not. So you see I am
not ashamed of my name—nor my face neither.

FASHION.
Sir, you have no cause that I know of.

SIR TUNBELLY.
Sir, if you have no cause neither, I desire to know
who you are, for till I know your name, I shall not
ask you to come into my house, and when I know
your name, 'tis six to four I don't ask you neither.

FASHION. (*Giving him a letter.*)
Sir, I hope you'll find this letter an authentic
passport.

SIR TUNBELLY.
Cod's my life! I ask your lordship's pardon ten
thousand times. (*To his servants.*) Here, run in a-
doors quickly. Get a Scotch-coal fire in the great
parlor; set all the Turkey-work chairs[46] in their
places; get the great brass candlesticks out, and be
sure stick the sockets full of laurel. Run!—My lord,

---

[46] Turkey-work chairs] chairs covered with Turkish tapestry

I ask your lordship's pardon. (*To other servants*) And do you hear, run away to Nurse, bid her let Miss Hoyden loose again, and if it was not shifting day,[47] let her put on a clean tucker quick. 70

Exeunt servants confusedly.

—I hope your honor will excuse the disorder of my family;* we are not used to receive men of your lordship's great quality* every day. Pray where are your coaches and servants, my lord? 75

FASHION.
Sir, that I might give you and your fair daughter a proof how impatient I am to be nearer akin to you, I left my equipage to folow me and came away post[48] with only one servant.

SIR TUNBELLY.
Your lordship does me too much honor. It was 80 exposing your person to too much fatigue and danger, I protest it was. But my daughter shall endeavor to make you what amends she can, and though I say it that should not say it—Hoyden has charms.

FASHION.
Sir, I am not a stranger to them, though I am to 85 her. Common fame has done her justice.

SIR TUNBELLY.
My lord, I am common fame's very grateful humble servant. My lord—my girl's young, Hoyden is young, my lord. But this I must say for her, what she wants* in art, she has by nature; what she wants in 90 experience, she has in breeding; and what's wanting in her age, is made good in her constitution. So pray, my lord, walk in; pray, my lord, walk in.

FASHION.
Sir, I wait upon you.

Exeunt.

Scene [iv. A room in Sir Tunbelly's house.]

Miss Hoyden sola.

[HOYDEN].
Sure never nobody was used as I am. I know well enough what other girls do, for all they think to make a fool of me. It's well I have a husband a-

coming, or, i'cod, I'd marry the baker, I would so. Nobody can knock at the gate but presently* I 5 must be locked up, and here's the young greyhound bitch can run loose about the house all day long, she can; 'tis very well.

NURSE. (*Without, opening the door.*)
Miss Hoyden, Miss, Miss, Miss! Miss Hoyden!

Enter nurse.

HOYDEN.
Well, what do you make such a noise for, hah? 10 What do you din a body's ears for? Can't one be at quiet for you?

NURSE.
What do I din your ears for? Here's one come will din your ears[49] for you.

HOYDEN.
What care I who's come. I care not a fig who 15 comes nor who goes, as long as I must locked up like the ale cellar.

NURSE.
That, Miss, is for fear you should be drank before you are ripe.

HOYDEN.
Oh, don't trouble your head about that; I'm as ripe 20 as you, though not so mellow.

NURSE.
Very well! Now have I a good mind to lock you up again and not let you see my lord tonight.

HOYDEN.
My lord? Why, is my husband come?

NURSE.
Yes, marry is he, and a goodly person too. 25

HOYDEN. (*Hugging nurse.*)
Oh my dear nurse, forgive me this once and I'll never misuse you again. No, if I do, you shall give me three thumps on the back and a great pinch by the cheek.

NURSE.
Ah the poor thing, see how it melts; it's as full of 30 good nature as an egg's full of meat.

HOYDEN.
But my dear nurse, don't lie now. Is he come, by your troth?

---

47 shifting day] when one changes linen
48 post] both in a hurry and on horseback

49 ears] ear was slang for female genitalia

NURSE.

Yes, by my truly, is he.

HOYDEN.

Oh Lord! I'll go put on my laced smock, though 35
I am whipped till the blood run down my heels
for't. (*Exit running*.)

NURSE.

Eh! The Lord succor thee, how thou art delighted!

Exit after her.

[Scene v. Another room in Sir Tunbelly's house.]

*Enter Sir Tunbelly and Young Fashion, a servant with
wine.*

SIR TUNBELLY.

My Lord, I am proud of the honor to see your
lordship within my doors, and I humbly crave
leave to bid you welcome in a cup of sack* wine.

FASHION.

Sir, to your daughter's health. (*Drinks*.)

SIR TUNBELLY.

Ah poor girl, she'll be scared out of her wits on 5
her wedding night, for honestly speaking, she does
not know a man from a woman but by his beard
and his britches.

FASHION.

Sir, I don't doubt but she has a virtuous education,
which with the rest of her merit makes me long 10
to see her mine. I wish you should dispense with
the canonical hour* and let it be this very night.

SIR TUNBELLY.

Oh not so soon neither, that's shooting my girl
before you bid her stand. No, give her fair warning;
we'll sign and seal tonight, if you please, and this 15
day seven-night—let the jade look to her quarters.

FASHION.

This day sennight? Why, what do you take me for,
a ghost, sir? 'Slife,* sir, I'm made of flesh and blood
and bones and sinews and can no more live a week
without your daughter—(*Aside*.) than I can a 20
month with her.

SIR TUNBELLY.

Oh, I'll warrant you, my hero, young men are hot,
I know, but they don't boil over at that rate neither;
besides, my wench's wedding gown is not come
home yet. 25

FASHION.

Oh, no matter, sir, I'll take her in her shift. (*Aside*.)
A pox of this old fellow; he'll delay the business
'till my damned star[50] finds me out and discovers
me.—Pray, sir, let it be done without ceremony,
'twill save money. 30

SIR TUNBELLY.

Money?—Save money when Hoyden's to be
married? Udswoons,* I'll give my wench a wedding
dinner though I go to grass with the King of
Assyria[51] for't, and such a dinner it shall be as is
not to be cooked in the poaching of an egg. 35
Therefore, my noble lord, have a little patience;
we'll go and look over our deeds and settlements
immediately, and as for your bride, though you
may be sharp[52] before she's quite ready, I'll engage
for my girl she stays your stomach at last. 40

Exeunt.

Act IV, scene i. [Another room
in Sir Tunbelly's house.]

Enter Miss Hoyden and nurse.

NURSE.

Well miss, how do you like your husband that is
to be?

HOYDEN.

Oh Lord, Nurse, I'm so overjoyed I can scarce
contain myself.

NURSE.

Oh, but you must have a care of being too fond, 5
for men nowadays hate a woman that loves 'em.

HOYDEN.

Love him! Why, do you think I love him, Nurse?
Ecod, I would not care if he were hanged so I were
but once married to him. No, that which pleases
me is to think what work I'll make when I get to 10
London, for when I am a wife and a lady both,
Nurse, ecod, I'll flaunt it with the best of 'em.

---

50 damned star] ill or evil planetary influence
51 King of Assyria] Nebuchadnezzar, ruler of Babylon, not
   Assyria, went mad and "did eat grass as oxen" (Daniel
   4:33).
52 sharp] hungry

NURSE.

Look, look, if his honor not be coming again to
you; now if I were sure you would behave yourself
handsomely and not disgrace me that have brought   15
you up, I'd leave you alone together.

HOYDEN.

That's my best nurse, do as you would be done by.
Trust us together this once, and if I don't show my
breeding from the head to the foot of me, may I
be twice married and die a maid.   20

NURSE.

Well, this once I'll venture you, but if you
disparage53 me—

HOYDEN.

Never fear. I'll show him my parts,* I'll warrant
him.

Exit Nurse.

These old women are so wise when they get a poor   25
girl in their clutches, but ere it be long, I shall
know what's what as well as the best of 'em.

Enter Young Fashion.

FASHION.

Your servant, madam. I'm glad to find you alone,
for I have something of importance to speak to you
about.   30

HOYDEN.

Sir—my lord, I meant—you may speak to me
about what you please, I shall give you a civil
answer.

FASHION.

You give me so obliging a one, it encourages me
to tell you in a few words what I think both for   35
your interest and mine. Your father, I suppose you
know, has resolved to make me happy in being
your husband, and I hope I may depend upon
your consent to perform what he desires.

HOYDEN.

Sir, I never disobey my father in anything but   40
eating of green gooseberries.

FASHION.

So good a daughter must needs make an admirable
wife; I am therefore impatient till you are mine and

---

53 disparage] bring discredit on

hope you will so far consider the violence of my
love that you won't have the cruelty to defer my   45
happiness so long as your father designs it.

HOYDEN.

Pray, my lord, how long is that?

FASHION.

Madam, a thousand year—a whole week.

HOYDEN.

A week! Why, I shall be an old woman by that
time.   50

FASHION.

And I an old man, which you'll find a greater
misfortune than t'other.

HOYDEN.

Why, I thought 'twas to be tomorrow morning, as
soon as I was up; I'm sure Nurse told me so.

FASHION.

And it shall be tomorrow morning still, if you'll   55
consent?

HOYDEN.

If I'll consent? Why, I thought I was to obey you
as my husband.

FASHION.

That's when we are married; till then, I am to obey
you.   60

HOYDEN.

Why then, if we are to take it by turns, it's the
same thing. I'll obey you now, and when we are
married you shall obey me.

FASHION.

With all my heart, but I doubt* we must get Nurse
on our side or we shall hardly prevail with the   65
chaplain.

HOYDEN.

No more we shan't indeed, for he loves her better
than he loves his pulpit and would always be a-
preaching to her, by his good will.

FASHION.

Why then, my dear little bedfellow, if you'll call   70
her hither, we'll try to persuade her presently.*

HOYDEN.

Oh Lord, I can tell you a way how to persuade her
to anything.

FASHION.

How's that?

HOYDEN.

Why, tell her she's a wholesome, comely woman— 75
and give her half a crown.

FASHION.

Nay, if that will do, she shall have half a score of
'em.

HOYDEN.

Oh jiminy,* for half that she'd marry you herself.
I'll run and call her. (*Exit.*) 80

FASHION.

So, matters go swimmingly. This is a rare girl,
i'faith; I shall have a fine time on't with her at
London. I'm much mistaken if she don't prove a
March hare all year round. What a scamp'ring
chase will she make on't when she finds the whole 85
kennel of beaux at her tail! Hey to the park and
the play and the church and the devil! She'll show
'em sport, I'll warrant 'em. But no matter: she
brings an estate will afford me a separate
maintenance.⁵⁴ 90

Enter Miss Hoyden and Nurse.

How do you do, good Mistress Nurse. I desired
your young lady would give me leave to see you,
that I might thank you for your extraordinary care
and conduct of her education. Pray accept of this
small acknowledgement for it at present, and 95
depend upon my farther kindness when I shall be
that happy thing her husband. [*Gives a purse.*]

NURSE. (*Aside.*)

Gold, by makings!⁵⁵—Your honor's goodness is
too great. Alas, all I can boast of is, I gave her pure
good milk, and so your honor would have said, an* 100
you had seen how the poor thing sucked it. Eh,
God's blessing on the sweet face on't, how it used
to hang at this poor teat, and suck and squeeze and
kick and sprawl it would, till the belly on't was so
full it would drop off like a leech. 105

HOYDEN. (*To Nurse, taking her angrily aside.*)

Pray one word with you. Prithee, Nurse, don't

---

54 separate maintenance] an arrangement whereby husband
   and wife agreed to live apart and receive support for
   separate living
55 by makings] a variant of "by mackins," an emphatic but
   otherwise meaningless phrase (Zimansky)

stand ripping up old stories to make one ashamed
before one's love. Do you think such a fine proper
gentleman as he cares for a fiddlecome⁵⁶ tale of a
draggle-tailed girl? If you have a mind to make him 110
have a good opinion of a woman, don't tell him
what one did then, tell him what one can do
now.—I hope your honor will excuse my
mismanners to whisper before you; it was only to
give some orders about the family.* 115

FASHION.

Oh, everything, madam, is to give way to business;
besides, good housewifery is a very commendable
quality in a young lady.

HOYDEN.

Pray, sir, are the young ladies good housewives at
London town? Do they darn their own linen? 120

FASHION.

Oh no, they study how to spend money, not to
save it.

HOYDEN.

I'cod, I don't know but that may be better sport
than t'other, hah, Nurse?

FASHION.

Well, then you shall have your choice when you 125
come there.

HOYDEN.

Shall I? Then by my troth I'll get there as fast as I
can.—His honor desires you'll be so kind as to let
us be married tomorrow.

NURSE.

Tomorrow, my dear madam? 130

FASHION.

Yes, tomorrow, sweet Nurse, privately. Young folks
you know are impatient, and Sir Tunbelly would
make us stay a week for a wedding dinner. Now
all things being signed and sealed and agreed, I
fancy there could be no great harm in practicing 135
a scene or two of matrimony in private, if it were
only to give us better assurance when we come to
play it in public.

NURSE.

Nay, I must confess stolen pleasures are sweet. But
if you should be married now, what will you do 140
when Sir Tunbelly calls for you to be wed?

---

56 fiddlecome] silly, absurd

HOYDEN.

Why then we'll be married again.

NURSE.

What, twice, my child?

HOYDEN.

I'cod, I don't care how often I'm married, not I.

FASHION.

Pray, Nurse, don't you be against your young lady's 145
good, for by this means she'll have the pleasure of
two wedding days.

HOYDEN. (*To Nurse softly.*)

And of two wedding nights, too, Nurse.

NURSE.

Well, I'm such a tender-hearted fool, I find I can
refuse nothing; so you shall e'en follow your own 150
inventions.

HOYDEN.

Shall I? (*Aside.*) Oh Lord, I could leap over the
moon.

FASHION.

Dear Nurse, this goodness of yours shan't go
unrewarded, but now you must employ your 155
power with Mr. Bull the chaplain that he may do
us his friendly office too, and then we shall all be
happy. Do you think you can prevail with him?

NURSE.

Prevail with him? Or he shall never prevail with
me, I can tell him that. 160

HOYDEN.

My lord, she has had him upon the hip this seven
year.

FASHION.

I'm glad to hear it; however, to strengthen your
interest with him, you may let him know I have
several fat livings in my gift and that the first that 165
falls shall be in your disposal.

NURSE.

Nay, then I'll make him marry more folks than
one, I'll promise him.

HOYDEN.

Faith do, Nurse. Make him marry you too; I'm
sure he'll do't for a fat living, for he loves eating 170
more than he loves his Bible, and I have often
heard him say, a fat living was the best meat in the
world.

NURSE.

Aye, and I'll make him commend the sauce too,
or I'll bring his gown to a cassock,[57] I will so. 175

FASHION.

Well, Nurse, whilst you go and settle matters with
him, then your lady and I will go take a walk in
the garden.

NURSE.

I'll do your honor's business in the catching up of
a garter. (*Exit.*) 180

FASHION. (*Giving her his hand.*)

Come, madam, dare you venture yourself alone
with me?

HOYDEN.

Oh dear, yes sir; I don't think you'll do anything
to me I need be afraid on.

Exeunt.

[Scene ii. Loveless's lodgings.]

Enter Amanda and Berinthia.

Song.

"I smile at love and all its arts,"
    The charming Cynthia cried;
"Take heed, for Love has piercing darts,"
    A wounded swain replied.
"Once free and blest as you are now, 5
    I trifled with his charms;
I pointed at his little bow
    And sported with his arms.
Till, urged too far, 'Revenge!' he cries;
    A fatal shaft he drew. 10
It took its passage through your eyes,
    And to my heart it flew.

II
"To tear it thence, I tried in vain,
    To strive I quickly found
Was only to increase the pain 15
    And to enlarge the wound.
Ah, much too well I fear you know
    What pain I'm to endure,
Since what your eyes alone could do,
    Your heart alone can cure. 20

---

57 bring his gown to a cassock] tear off the gown which a
clergyman wore over his cassock: to expose

And that (grant Heaven I may mistake)
    I doubt* is doomed to bear
A burden for another's sake
    Who ill rewards its care."

AMANDA.

Well, now Berinthia, I'm at leisure to hear what 25
'twas you had to say to me.

BERINTHIA.

What I had to say was only to echo the sighs and
groans of a dying lover.

AMANDA.

Phu, will you never learn to talk in earnest of
anything? 30

BERINTHIA.

Why, this shall be in earnest, if you please. For my
part, I only tell you matter of fact. You may take
it which way you like best, but if you'll follow the
women of the Town, you'll take it both ways, for
when a man offers himself to one of them, first 35
she takes him in jest, and then she takes him in
earnest.

AMANDA.

I'm sure there's so much jest and earnest in what
you say to me I scarce know how to take it, but I
think you have bewitched me, for I don't find it 40
possible to be angry with you, say what you will.

BERINTHIA.

I'm very glad to hear it, for I have no mind to
quarrel with you, for more reasons than I'll brag
of. But quarrel or not, smile or frown, I must tell
you what I have suffered upon your account. 45

AMANDA.

Upon my account?

BERINTHIA.

Yes, upon yours. I have been forced to sit still and
hear you commended for two hours together,
without one compliment to myself. Now don't you
think a woman had a blessed time of that? 50

AMANDA.

Alas, I should have been unconcerned at it; I never
knew where the pleasure lay of being praised by
the men. But pray, who was this that commended
me so?

BERINTHIA.

One you have a mortal aversion to, Mr. Worthy. 55
He used you like a text: he took you all to pieces

but spoke so learnedly upon every point one might
see the spirit of the church was in him; if you are
a woman, you'd have been in an ectasy to have
heard how feelingly he handled your hair, your 60
eyes, your nose, your mouth, your teeth, your
tongue, your chin, your neck, and so forth. Thus
he preached for an hour, but when he came to use
and application, he observed that all these without
a gallant were nothing. Now consider of what has 65
been said, and Heaven give you grace to put it in
practice.

AMANDA.

Alas Berinthia, did I incline to a gallant (which you
know I do not), do you think a man so nice* as
he could have the least concern for such a plain 70
unpolished thing as I am? It is impossible!

BERINTHIA.

Now have you a great mind to put me upon
commending you.

AMANDA.

Indeed that was not my design.

BERINTHIA.

Nay, if it were, it's all one, for I won't do't; I'll leave 75
that to your looking glass.* But to show you I have
some good nature left, I'll commend him, and
maybe that will do as well.

AMANDA.

You have a great mind to persuade me I am in love
with him. 80

BERINTHIA.

I have a great mind to persuade you, you don't
know what you are in love with.

AMANDA.

I am sure I am not in love with him nor never shall
be; so let that pass. But you were saying something
you would commend him for. 85

BERINTHIA.

Oh, you'd be glad to hear a good character* of him,
however.

AMANDA.

Psha!

BERINTHIA.

Psha! Well,'tis a foolish undertaking for women in
these kind of matters to pretend to deceive one 90
another. Have not I been bred a woman as well as
you?

AMANDA.

What then?

BERINTHIA.

Why then, I understand my trade so well that whenever I am told of a man I like, I cry, psha. 95 But that I may spare you the pains of putting me a second time in mind to commend him, I'll proceed and give you this account of him: that though 'tis possible he may have had women with as good faces as your ladyship's (no discredit to it 100 neither), yet you must know your cautious behavior, with that reserve in your humor,* has given him his death's wound; he mortally hates a coquette; he says 'tis impossible to love where we cannot esteem and that no woman can be 105 esteemed by a man who has sense if she makes herself cheap in the eye of a fool; that pride to a woman is as necessary as humility to a divine; and that far-fetched and dear-bought is meat for gentlemen as well as for ladies—in short, that every 110 woman who has beauty may set a price on herself and that by underselling the market they ruin the trade. This is his doctrine. How do you like it?

AMANDA.

So well that, since I never intend to have a gallant for myself, if I were to recommend one to a friend, 115 he should be the man.

Enter Worthy.

Bless me, he's here! Pray Heaven he did not hear me.

BERINTHIA.

If he did, it won't hurt your reputation; your thoughts are as safe in his heart as in your own. 120

WORTHY.

I venture in at an unseasonable time of night, ladies; I hope if I'm troublesome, you'll use the same freedom in turning me out again.

AMANDA.

I believe it can't be late, for Mr. Loveless is not come home yet, and he usually keeps good hours. 125

WORTHY.

Madam, I'm afraid he'll transgress a little tonight, for he told me about half an hour ago he was going to sup with some company he doubted* would keep him out till three or four o'clock in the morning and desired I would let my servant 130 acquaint you with it, that you might not expect him. But my fellow's a blunderhead, so lest he should make some mistake, I thought it my duty to deliver the message myself.

AMANDA.

I'm very sorry he should give you that trouble, sir. 135 But—

BERINTHIA.

But since he has, will you give me leave, madam, to keep him to play at ombre with us?

AMANDA.

Cousin, you know you command my house.

WORTHY. (*To Berinthia.*)

And, madam, you know you command me, 140 though I'm a very wretched gamester.

BERINTHIA.

Oh, you play well enough to lose your money, and that's all the ladies require. So, without any more ceremony, let us go into the next room and call for the cards. 145

AMANDA.

With all my heart.

Exit Worthy leading Amanda.

BERINTHIA.

Well, how this business will end, Heaven knows, but she seems to me to be in as fair a way—as a boy is to be a rogue when he's put as clerk to an attorney.

Exit.

Scene [iii.] Berinthia's chamber.

Enter Loveless cautiously in the dark.

LOVELESS.

So, thus far all's well. I'm got into her bedchamber, and I think nobody has perceived me steal into the house; my wife don't expect me home till four o'clock, so if Berinthia comes to bed by eleven, I shall have a chase of five hours. Let me see, where 5 shall I hide myself? Under her bed? No, we shall have her maid searching there for something or other. Her closet's* a better place, and I have a master key will open it; I'll e'en in there and attack her just when she comes to her prayers; that's the 10 most likely to prove her critical minute, for then the Devil will be there to assist me. (*He opens the closet, goes in, and shuts the door after him.*)

Enter Berinthia with a candle in her hand.

BERINTHIA.

Well, sure I am the best-natured woman in the world. I that love cards so well (there is but one thing 15 upon earth I love better) have pretended letters to write, to give my friends—a *tête-à-tête*. However, I'm innocent, for piquet is the game I set 'em to; at her own peril be it if she ventures to play with him at any other. But now what shall I do with myself? I don't 20 know how in the world to pass my time; would Loveless were here to *badiner*[58] a little. Well, he's a charming fellow; I don't wonder his wife's so fond of him. What if I should sit down and think of him till I fall asleep and dream of the Lord knows what? Oh, 25 but then if I should dream we were married, I should be frightened out of my wits. (*Seeing a book.*) What's this book? I think I had best go read. Oh, *splénétique*![59] It's a sermon. Well, I'll go into my closet and read *The Plotting Sisters*.[60] (*She opens the* 30 *closet, sees Loveless, and shrieks out.*) Oh Lord, a ghost, a ghost, a ghost, a ghost!

Enter Loveless running to her.

LOVELESS.

Peace, my dear, it's no ghost; take it in your arms, you'll find 'tis worth a hundred of 'em.

BERINTHIA.

Run in again; here's somebody coming. 35

[Loveless enters the closet.] Enter her Maid.

MAID.

Lord, madam, what's the matter?

BERINTHIA.

Oh heavens! I'm almost frighted out of my wits. I thought verily I had seen a ghost, and 'twas nothing but the white curtain with a black hood pinned up against it. You may be gone again. I am 40 the fearfull'st fool.

---

58 *badiner*] to banter, trifle (Fr.)
59 *splénétique*] causing spleen, depressing (Fr.)
60 *The Plotting Sisters*] Durfey's *A Fond Husband* (see below)

Exit Maid. Re-enter Loveless.

LOVELESS.

Is the coast clear?

BERINTHIA.

The coast clear! I suppose you are clear,[61] you'd never play such a trick as this else.

LOVELESS.

I am very well pleased with my trick thus far and 45 shall be so till I have played it out, if it ben't your fault. Where's my wife?

BERINTHIA.

At cards.

LOVELESS.

With whom?

BERINTHIA.

With Worthy. 50

LOVELESS.

Then we are safe enough.

BERINTHIA.

Are you so? Some husbands would be of another mind if he were at cards with their wives.

LOVELESS.

And they'd be in the right on't, too. But I dare trust mine. Besides, I know he's in love in another place, 55 and he's not one of those who court half a dozen at a time.

BERINTHIA.

Nay, the truth on't is, you'd pity him if you saw how uneasy he is at being engaged with us. But 'twas my malice. I fancied he was to meet his 60 mistress somewhere else, so did it to have the pleasure of seeing him fret.

LOVELESS.

What says Amanda to my staying abroad so late?

BERINTHIA.

Why, she's as much out of humor as he; I believe they wish one another at the devil. 65

LOVELESS.

Then I'm afraid they'll quarrel at play and soon throw up the cards. (*Offering to pull her into the closet.*) Therefore, my dear charming angel, let us make good use of our time.

BERINTHIA.

Heavens, what do you mean? 70

---

61 clear] drunk

LOVELESS.

Pray, what do you think I mean?

BERINTHIA.

I don't know.

LOVELESS.

I'll show you.

BERINTHIA.

You may as well tell me.

LOVELESS.

No, that would make you blush worse than t'other. 75

BERINTHIA.

Why, do you intend to make me blush?

LOVELESS.

Faith, I can't tell that, but if I do, it shall be in the dark. (*Pulling her.*)

BERINTHIA.

Oh heavens! I would not be in the dark with you for all the world. 80

LOVELESS.

I'll try that. (*Puts out the candles.*)

BERINTHIA.

Oh Lord! Are you mad? What shall I do for light?

LOVELESS.

You'll do as well without it.

BERINTHIA.

Why, one can't find a chair to sit down.

LOVELESS.

Come into the closet, madam; there's moonshine 85 upon the couch.

BERINTHIA.

Nay, never pull, for I will not go.

LOVELESS. (*Carrying her.*)

Then you must be carried.

BERINTHIA. (*Very softly.*)

Help, help, I'm ravished, ruined, undone! Oh Lord, I shall never be able to bear it. 90

[*Exeunt.*]

Scene [iv]. Sir Tunbelly's house.

Enter Miss Hoyden, Nurse, Young Fashion, and Bull.

FASHION.

This quick dispatch of yours, Mr. Bull, I take so kindly it shall give you a claim on my favor as long as I live, I do assure you.

HOYDEN.

And to mine, too, I promise you.

BULL.

I most humbly thank your honors, and I hope, 5 since it has been my lot to join you in the holy bands of wedlock, you will so well cultivate the soil which I have craved a blessing on that your children may swarm about you like bees about a honeycomb. 10

HOYDEN.

I'cod with all my heart, the more the merrier, I say. Hah, Nurse?

Enter Lory taking his master hastily aside.

LORY.

One word with you, for Heaven's sake.

FASHION.

What the devil's the matter?

LORY.

Sir, your fortune's ruined, and I don't think your 15 life's worth a quarter of an hour's purchase. Yonder's your brother arrived with two coaches and six horses, twenty footmen and pages, a coat worth fourscore pound, and a periwig down to his knees. So judge what will become of your lady's heart. 20

FASHION.

Death and Furies, 'tis impossible!

LORY.

Fiends and specters, sir, 'tis true.

FASHION.

Is he in the house yet?

LORY.

No, they are capitulating with him at the gate; the porter tells him, he's come to run away with Miss 25 Hoyden, and has cocked the blundrbuss at him; your brother swears, Gad damme, they are a parcel of clawns and he has a good mind to break off the match, but they have given the word for Sir Tunbelly, so I doubt* all will come out presently.* 30 Pray, sir, resolve what you'll do this moment, for egad, they'll maul you.

FASHION.

Stay a little.—My dear, here's a troublesome business my man tells me of, but don't be frightened, we shall be too hard for the rogue. 35 Here's an impudent fellow at the gate (not knowing I was come hither incognito) has taken my name upon him in hopes to run away with you.

HOYDEN.

Oh, the brazen-faced varlet! It's well we are 40 married, or maybe we might never a been so.

FASHION. (Aside.)

Egad, like enough!—Prithee dear doctor, run to Sir Tunbelly and stop him from going to the gate before I speak with him.

BULL.

I fly, my good lord. (Exit.) 45

NURSE.

An't* please your honor, my lady and I had best lock ourselves up till the danger be over.

FASHION.

Aye, by all means.

HOYDEN.

Not so fast! I won't be locked up any more. I'm married. 50

FASHION.

Yes, pray my dear, do, till we have seized this rascal.

HOYDEN.

Nay, if you pray me, I'll do anything.

Exeunt Hoyden and Nurse.

FASHION.

Oh, here's Sir Tunbelly coming.—Hark you, sirrah, things are better than you imagine; the wedding's over. 55

LORY.

The devil it is, sir.

FASHION.

Not a word, all's safe. But Sir Tunbelly don't know it, nor must not yet, so I am resolved to brazen the business out and have the pleasure of turning the imposter upon his lordship,62 which I believe 60 may be easily done.

Enter Sir Tunbelly, Bull, and servants armed.

Did you ever hear, sir, of so impudent an undertaking?

SIR TUNBELLY.

Never, by the mass! But we'll tickle* him, I warrant him. 65

FASHION.

They tell me, sir, he has a great many people with him disguised like servants.

SIR TUNBELLY.

Aye, aye, rogues enough, but I'll soon raise the posse upon 'em.

FASHION.

Sir, if you'll take my advice, we'll go a shorter way to 70 work. I find whoever this spark is, he knows nothing of my being privately here; so if you pretend to receive him civilly, he'll enter without suspicion, and as soon as he is within the gate, we'll whip up the drawbridge upon his back, let fly the blunderbuss to 75 disperse his crew, and so commit him to gaol.

SIR TUNBELLY.

Egad, your lordship is an ingenious person and a very great general. But shall we kill any of 'em or not?

FASHION.

No, no, fire over their heads only to fright 'em; 80 I'll warrant the regiment scours63 when the colonel's a prisoner.

SIR TUNBELLY.

Then come along, my boys, and let your courage be great—for your danger is but small.

Exeunt.

Scene [v]. The gate.

Enter Lord Foppington and followers.

FOPPINGTON.

A pax of these bumkinly people, will they open the gate, or do they desire I should grow at their moat-side like a willow? (*To the Porter.*) Hey, fellow, prithee do me the favor, in as few words as thou canst find to express thyself, to tell me whether thy 5 master will admit me or not, that I may turn about my coach and be gone.

PORTER.

Here's my master himself now at hand; he's of age, he'll give you his answer.

62 turning the imposter upon his lordship] making his lordship seem to be the imposter

63 scours] scurries, flees

Enter Sir Tunbelly and servants.

SIR TUNBELLY.

My most noble lord, I crave your pardon for   10
making your honor wait so long, but my orders
to my servants have been to admit nobody without
my knowledge for fear of some attempt upon my
daughter, the times being full of plots and
roguery.⁶⁴   15

FOPPINGTON.

Much caution, I must confess, is a sign of great
wisdom. But stap my vitals, I have got a cold
enough to destroy a porter—he, hem—

SIR TUNBELLY.

I am very sorry for't indeed, my lord, but if your
lordship please to walk in, we'll help you to some   20
brown-sugar candy. My lord, I'll show you the way.

FOPPINGTON.

Sir, I follow you with pleasure.

*Exeunt [Sir Tunbelly and Lord Foppington]. As Lord
Foppington's servants go to follow him him in, [Sir
Tunbelly's servants] clap the door against La Vérole.*

SERVANTS. (*Within.*)

Nay, hold you me there, sir!

LA VÉROLE.

Jernie die, qu'est-ce que veut dire ça?*⁶⁵

SIR TUNBELLY. (*Within.*)

Fire, Porter.

PORTER. (*Fires.*)   25

Have among ye, my masters!

LA VÉROLE.

*Ah, je suis mort!*⁶⁶

The servants all run off.

PORTER.

Not one soldier left, by the mass!

[Exit.]

---

64 the times being full of plots and roguery] There were
   ongoing plots to restore James II to the throne.

65 *qu'est-ce que veut dire ça?*] What's that he says? (Fr.)

66 *Ah, je suis mort!*] Oh, I am dead! (Fr.)

Scene [vi]. Changes to the hall.

*Enter Sir Tunbelly, Bull, and servants [including a
clerk and a constable], with Lord Foppington
disarmed.*

SIR TUNBELLY.

Come, bring him along, bring him along!

FOPPINGTON.

What the pax do you mean, gentlmen? Is it Fair
time, that you are all drunk before dinner?

SIR TUNBELLY.

Drunk, sirrah! Here's an impudent rogue for you.
Drunk or sober, bully, I'm a Justice of the Peace   5
and know how to deal with strollers.

FOPPINGTON.

Strollers!

SIR TUNBELLY.

Aye, strollers. Come, give an account of yourself:
What's your name? where do you live? do you pay
scot and lot? are you a Williamite or a Jacobite?⁶⁷   10
Come!

FOPPINGTON.

And why dost thou ask me so many impertinent
questions?

SIR TUNBELLY.

Because I'll make you answer 'em before I have
done with you, you rascal, you.   15

FOPPINGTON.

Before Gad, all the answer I can make thee to 'em
is that thou art a very extraordinary old fellow, stap
my vitals.

SIR TUNBELLY.

Nay, if you are for joking with deputy lieutenants,
we'st⁶⁸ know how to deal with you. Here, draw a   20
warrant for him immediately.

FOPPINGTON.

A warrant! What the devil is't thou wouldst be at,
old gentleman?

SIR TUNBELLY.

I would be at you, sirrah, if my hands were not
tied as a magistrate, and with these two double fists 25
beat your teeth down your throat, you dog you!

---

67 Williamite or a Jacobite] a follower of William III or of
   James II (see General Introduction)

68 we'st] obviously a dialectal variant of *we*

FOPPINGTON.

And why wouldst thou spoil my face at that rate?

SIR TUNBELLY.

For your design to rob me of my daughter, villain.

FOPPINGTON.

Rab thee of thy daughter!—[*Aside.*] Now do I
begin to believe I am abed and asleep and that all   30
this is but a dream. If it be, 'twill be an agreeable
surprise enough to waken by and by, and instead
of the impertinent company of a nasty country
justice, find myself, perhaps, in the arms of a
woman of quality.*—Prithee, old father, wilt thou   35
give me leave to ask thee one question?

SIR TUNBELLY.

I can't tell whether I will or not till I know what
it is.

FOPPINGTON.

Why, then it is whether thou didst not write to
my Lord Foppington to come down and marry thy   40
daughter?

SIR TUNBELLY.

Yes, marry,* did I, and my Lord Foppington is
come down and shall marry my daughter before
she's a day older.

FOPPINGTON.

Now give me thy hand, dear Dad, I thought we   45
should understand one another at last.

SIR TUNBELLY.

This fellow's mad. Here, bind him hand and foot.

They bind him.

FOPPINGTON.

Nay, prithee knight, leave fooling; thy jest begins
to grow dull.

SIR TUNBELLY.

Bind him, I say, he's mad. Bread and water, a dark   50
room, and a whip may bring him to his senses
again.

FOPPINGTON. (*Aside.*)

Egad, if I don't waken quickly, by all I can see this
is like to prove one of the most impertinent dreams
that ever I dreamt in my life.   55

Enter Miss Hoyden and Nurse.

HOYDEN. (*Going up to him.*)

Is this he that would have run away with me?

Faugh, how he stinks of sweets! Pray father, let him
be dragged through the horse pond.

FOPPINGTON. (*Aside.*)

This must be my wife by her natural inclination
to her husband.   60

HOYDEN.

Pray father, what do you intend to do with him,
hang him?

SIR TUNBELLY.

That at least, child.

NURSE.

Aye, and it's e'en too good for him too.

FOPPINGTON. (*Aside.*)

Madame la gouvernante, I presume. Hitherto this   65
appears to me to be one of the most extraordinary
families that ever man of quality* matched into.

SIR TUNBELLY.

What's become of my lord, daughter?

HOYDEN.

He's just coming, sir.

FOPPINGTON. (*Aside.*)

My lord—What does he mean by that now?   70

Enter Young Fashion and Lory.

(*Seeing him.*) Stap my vitals, Tam, now the dream's
out.

FASHION.

Is this the fellow, sir, that designed to trick me of
your daughter?

SIR TUNBELLY.

This is he, my lord. How do you like him? Is not   75
he a pretty fellow to get a fortune?

FASHION.

I find by his dress he thought your daughter might
be taken with a beau.

HOYDEN.

Oh jiminy!* Is this a beau? Let me see him again.
Hah, I find a beau's no such an ugly thing neither.   80

FASHION. [*Aside.*]

Egad, she'll be in love with him presently;* I'll e'en
have him sent way to gaol. (*To Lord Foppington.*)
Sir, though your understanding shows you are a
person of no extraordinary modesty, I suppose you
han't confidence enough to expect much favor   85
from me?

FOPPINGTON.

Strike me dumb, Tam, thou art a very impudent fellow.

NURSE.

Look if the varlet has not the 'frontery to call his lordship plain Thomas. 90

BULL.

The business is, he would feign himself mad to avoid going to gaol.

FOPPINGTON. (*Aside.*)

That must be the chaplain, by his unfolding of mysteries.

SIR TUNBELLY.

Come, is the warrant writ? 95

CLERK.

Yes, sir.

SIR TUNBELLY.

Give me the pen; I'll sign it. So, now constable, away with him.

FOPPINGTON.

Hold one moment. Pray, gentlemen.—My Lord Foppington, shall I beg one word with your 100 lordship?

NURSE.

Oh ho, it's my lord with him now; see how afflictions will humble folks.

HOYDEN.

Pray my lord, don't let him whisper too close, lest he bite your ear off. 105

FOPPINGTON.

I am not altogether so hungry as your ladyship is pleased to imagine.—Look you, Tam, I am sensible I have not been so kind to you as I ought, but I hope you'll forget what's past and accept of the five thousand pounds I offer; thou mayst live in 110 extreme splendor with it, stap my vitals.

FASHION.

It's a much easier matter to prevent a disease than to cure it. A quarter of that sum would have secured your mistress; twice as much won't redeem her. (*Leaving him.*) 115

SIR TUNBELLY.

Well, what says he?

FASHION.

Only the rascal offered me a bribe to let him go.

SIR TUNBELLY.

Aye, he shall go with a pox to him. Lead on, Constable.

FOPPINGTON.

One word more, and I have done. 120

SIR TUNBELLY.

Before Gad, thou art an impudent fellow to trouble the court at this rate after thou art condemned, but speak once and for all.

FOPPINGTON.

Why then once for all: I have at last luckily called to mind that there is a gentleman of this country, 125 who I believe cannot live far from this place, if he were here would satisfy you I am Navelty, Baron of Foppington, with five thousand pounds a year, and that fellow there, a rascal not worth a groat. 130

SIR TUNBELLY.

Very well. Now who is this honest gentleman you are so well acquainted with? (*To Young Fashion.*) Come sir, we shall hamper him.

FOPPINGTON.

'Tis Sir John Friendly.

SIR TUNBELLY.

So: he lives within half a mile and came down into 135 the country but last night; this bold-faced fellow thought he had been at London still and so quoted him. Now we shall display him in his colors; I'll send for Sir John immediately. Here, fellow, away presently* and desire my neighbor he'll do me the 140 favor to step over upon an extraordinary occasion—and in the meanwhile you had best secure this sharper in the gate house.

CONSTABLE.

An't* please your worship, he may chance to give us the slip thence. If I were worthy to advise, I 145 think the dog kennel's a surer place.

SIR TUNBELLY.

With all my heart, anywhere.

FOPPINGTON.

Nay, for Heaven's sake, sir, do me the favor to put me in a clean room, that I mayn't daub my clothes.

SIR TUNBELLY.

Oh, when you have married my daughter, her 150 estate will afford you new ones. Away with him.

FOPPINGTON.

A dirty country justice is a barbarous magistrate, stap my vitals!

Exit constable with Lord Foppington.

FASHION. (*Aside.*)

Egad, I must prevent this knight's coming, or the house will grow soon too hot to hold me.—Sir, I fancy 'tis not worth while to trouble Sir John upon this impertinent fellow's desire; I'll send and call the messenger back.

SIR TUNBELLY.

Nay, with all my heart, for to be sure he thought he was far enough off, or the rogue would never have named him.

Enter servant.

SERVANT.

Sir, I met Sir John just lighting at the gate; he's come to wait upon you.

SIR TUNBELLY.

Nay, then it happens as one could wish.

FASHION. (*Aside.*)

The devil it does! [*To Lory, apart.*] Lory, you see how things are: here will be a discovery presently,* and we shall have our brains beat out, for my older brother will be sure to swear he don't know me. Therefore, run into the stable, take the two first horses you can light on; I'll slip out at the back door, and we'll away immediately.

LORY.

What, and leave your lady, sir?

FASHION.

There's no danger in that; as long as I have taken possession, I shall know how to treat with 'em well enough, if once I am out of their reach. Away, I'll steal after thee.

Exit Lory, his master follows him out at one door as Sir John enters at t'other.

Enter Sir John.

SIR TUNBELLY.

Sir John, you are the wecomest man alive; I had just sent a messenger to desire you'd step over upon a very extraordinary occasion. We are all in arms here.

SIR JOHN.

How so?

SIR TUNBELLY.

Why you must know, a finical sort of tawdry fellow here (I don't know who the devil he is, not I), hearing, I suppose, that the match was concluded between my Lord Foppington and my girl Hoyden, comes impudently to the gate with a whole pack of rogues in liveries and would have passed upon me for his lordship. But what does I? I comes up to him boldly at the head of his guards, takes him by the throat, strikes up his heels, binds him hand and foot, dispatches a warrant, and commits him prisoner to the dog kennel.

SIR JOHN.

So, but how do you know but this was my lord? For I was told he set out from London the day before me with a very fine retinue and intended to come directly hither.

SIR TUNBELLY.

Why now, to show you how many lies people raise in that damned town, he came two nights ago post, with only one servant, and is now in the house with me. But you don't know the cream of the jest yet: this same rogue (that lies yonder neck and heels among the hounds), thinking you were out of the country, quotes you for his acquaintance and said, if you were here, you'd justify him to be Lord Foppington and I know not what.

SIR JOHN.

Pray will you let me see him?

SIR TUNBELLY.

Aye, that you shall presently.—Here, fetch the prisoner.

Exit servant.

SIR JOHN.

I wish there ben't some mistake in this business. Where's my lord? I know him very well.

SIR TUNBELLY.

He was here just now.—See for him, doctor, tell him Sir John is here to wait upon him.

Exit Bull.

SIR JOHN.

I hope, Sir Tunbelly, the young lady is not married yet.

SIR TUNBELLY.

No, things won't be ready this week. But why do you say you hope she is not married ? 215

SIR JOHN.

Some foolish fancies only; perhaps I'm mistaken.

Re-enter Bull.

BULL.

Sir, his lordship is just rid out to take the air.

SIR TUNBELLY.

To take the air! Is that his London breeding to go take the air when gentlemen come to visit him? 220

SIR JOHN.

'Tis possible he might want it; he might not be well, some sudden qualm perhaps.

Enter Constable, etc., with Lord Foppington.

FOPPINGTON.

Stap my vitals, I'll have satisfaction.

SIR JOHN. (*Running to him.*)

My dear Lord Foppington!

FOPPINGTON.

Dear Friendly, thou art come in the critical minute, strike me dumb. 225

SIR JOHN.

Why, I little thought I should have found you in fetters.

FOPPINGTON.

Why, truly, the world must do me the justice to confess I do use to appear a little more *dégagé*.[69] But this old gentleman, not liking the freedom of my air, has been pleased to skewer down my arms like a rabbit. 230

SIR TUNBELLY.

Is it then possible that this should be the true Lord Foppington at last? 235

FOPPINGTON.

Why, what do you see in his face to make you doubt of it? Sir, without presuming to have any extraordinary opinion of my figure, give me leave to tell you, if you had seen as many lords as I have done, you would not think it impossible a person 240

___

69 *dégagé*] nonchalant, at ease (Fr.)

of a worse *taille*[70] than mine might be a modern man of quality.*

SIR TUNBELLY.

Unbind him, slaves.—My lord, I'm struck dumb; I can only beg pardon by signs, but if a sacrifice will appease you, you shall have it.—Here, pursue this tartar, bring him back. Away, I say!—A dog, oons!* I'll cut off his ears and his tail, I'll draw out all his teeth, pull his skin over his head, and—and what shall I do more? 245

SIR JOHN.

He does indeed deserve to be made an example of. 250

FOPPINGTON.

He does deserve to be *chartré*,°[71] stap my vitals.

SIR TUNBELLY.

May I then hope I have your honor's pardon?

FOPPINGTON.

Sir, we courtiers do nothing without a bribe; that fair young lady might do miracles.

SIR TUNBELLY.

Hoyden, come hither, Hoyden. 255

FOPPINGTON.

Hoyden is her name, sir?

SIR TUNBELLY.

Yes, my lord.

FOPPINGTON.

The prettiest name for a song I ever heard.

SIR TUNBELLY.

My lord, here's my girl, she's yours: she has a wholesome body and a virtuous mind; she's a woman complete both in flesh and in spirit; she has a bag of milled crowns, as scarce as they are, and fifteen hundred a year stitched fast to her tail.[72] So go thy ways, Hoyden. 260

___

70 *taille*] figure, bearing (Fr.)

71 *chartré*] jailed, perhaps from *mis en chartre* (Fr.); modern editors who emend to *châtré* (castrated) do so in anticipation of Foppington's later threat to "qualify" Fashion for a "seraglio."

72 milled crowns … tail] Hoyden brings with her into a marriage both ready money—coins which retain their full value because they have not been clipped* or debased—and her father's estate, worth fifteen hundred pounds revenue per year, which etate will pass to her husband upon her father's death: thus it is entailed (with a sexual pun).

FOPPINGTON.

Sir, I do receive her like a gentleman. 265

SIR TUNBELLY.

Then I'm a happy man, I bless Heaven, and if your lordship will give me leave, I will, like a good Christian at Christmas, be very drunk by way of thanksgiving. Come, my noble peer, I believe dinner's ready; if your honor pleases to follow me, I'll 270 lead you on to the attack of a venison pasty. (*Exit.*)

FOPPINGTON.

Sir, I wait upon you.—Will your ladyship do me the favor of your little finger, madam?

HOYDEN.

My lord, I'll follow you presently; I have a little business with my nurse. 275

FOPPINGTON.

Your ladyship's most humble servant. Come Sir John, the ladies have *des affaires.*[73]

Exeunt Lord Foppington and Sir John.

HOYDEN.

So, Nurse, we are finely brought to bed. What shall we do now?

NURSE. (*Crying.*)

Ah, dear miss, we are all undone. Mr. Bull, you 280 were used to help a woman to a remedy.

BULL.

Alack-a-day, but it's past my skill now; I can do nothing.

NURSE.

Who would have thought that ever your invention should have been drained so dry? 285

HOYDEN.

Well, I have often thought old folks fools, and now I am sure they are so. I have found a way myself to secure us all.

NURSE.

Dear lady, what's that?

HOYDEN.

Why, if you two will be sure to hold your tongues 290 and not say a word of what's past, I'll e'en marry this lord too.

NURSE.

What! Two husbands, my dear?

_____

73 *des affaires*] their own concerns (Fr.)

HOYDEN.

Why you have had three, good Nurse; you may hold your tongue. 295

NURSE.

Aye, but not all together, sweet child.

HOYDEN.

Psha, if you had, you'd ne'er a-thought much on't.

NURSE.

Oh, but 'tis a sin, sweeting.

BULL.

Nay, that's my business to speak to, Nurse. I do confess, to take two husbands for the satisfaction 300 of the flesh is to commit the sin of exorbitancy, but to do it for the peace of the spirit is no more than to be drunk by way of physic; besides, to prevent a parent's wrath is to avoid the sin of disobedience, for when the parent's angry, the child 305 is froward. So that upon the whole matter, I do think, though miss should marry again, she may be saved.

HOYDEN.

I'cod, and I will marry again, then, and so there's an end of the story. 310

Exeunt.

Act V, scene [i]. London.

Enter Coupler, Young Fashion, and Lory.

COUPLER.

Well, and so Sir John coming in—

FASHION.

And so Sir John coming in, I thought it might be manners in me to go out, which I did, and getting on horseback as fast as I could, rid away as if the Devil had been at the rear of me. What has 5 happened since, Heaven knows.

COUPLER.

Egad, sirrah, I know as well as Heaven.

FASHION.

What do you know?

COUPLER.

That you are a cuckold.

FASHION.

The devil I am! By who? 10

COUPLER.

By your brother.

FASHION.

My brother! Which way?

COUPLER.

The old way: he has lain with your wife.

FASHION.

Hell and Furies, what dost thou mean?

COUPLER.

I mean plainly; I speak no parable.   15

FASHION.

Plainly! Thou dost not speak common sense; I cannot understand one word thou say'st.

COUPLER.

You will do soon, youngster. In short, you left your wife a widow, and she married again.

FASHION.

It's a lie.   20

COUPLER.

I'cod, if I were a young fellow, I'd break your head, sirrah.

FASHION.

Dear dad, don't be angry, for I'm as mad as Tom of Bedlam.[74]

COUPLER.

When I had fitted you with a wife, you should   25
have kept her.

FASHION.

But is it possible the young strumpet could play me such a trick?

COUPLER.

A young strumpet, sir, can play twenty tricks.

FASHION.

But prithee instruct me a little farther: Whence   30
comes thy intelligence?

COUPLER.

From your brother, in this letter. There, you may read it.

FASHION. (*Reads, pulling off his hat.*[75])

"Dear Coupler, I have only time to tell thee in three lines, or thereabouts, that here has been the   35
devil. That rascal Tam, having stole the letter thou hadst formerly writ for me to bring to Sir Tunbelly,

formed a damnable design upon my mistress and was in a fair way of success when I arrived. But after having suffered some indignities (in which I   40
have all daubed my embroidered coat), I put him to flight. I sent out a party of horse after him in hopes to have made him my prisoner, which if I had done, I would have qualified him for the seraglio,[76] stap my vitals!   45

"The danger I have thus narrowly 'scaped has made me fortify myself against further attempts by entering immediately into an association with the young lady by which we engage to stand by one another as long as we both shall live.   50

"In short, the papers are sealed and the contract is signed, so the business of the lawyers is *achevé*, but I defer the divine part of the thing till I arrive at London, not being willing to consummate in any other bed but my own.   55

"Postscript. 'Tis passible I may be in tawn as soon as this letter, far I find the lady is so violently in love with me I have determined to make her happy with all the dispatch that is practicable without disardering my coach harses." So here's   60
rare work, i'faith!

LORY.

Egad, Miss Hoyden has laid about her bravely.

COUPLER.

I think my country girl has played her part as well as if she had been born and bred in St. James's parish.   65

FASHION.

That rogue the chaplain—

LORY.

And then that jade the nurse, sir.

FASHION.

And then that drunken sot Lory, sir, that could not keep himself sober to be a witness to the marriage.

LORY.

Sir, with respect, I know very few drunken sots that   70
do keep themselves sober.

FASHION.

Hold your prating, sirrah, or I'll break your head.—Dear Coupler, what's to be done?

---

74 Tom of Bedlam] legendary wandering madman pursued by the devil: see Edgar's ruse in Shakespeare's *King Lear*.

75 *pulling off his hat*] in mock deference to Lord Foppington's dignity?

76 qualified … seraglio] Women in seraglios (harems) were guarded by eunuchs.

COUPLER.

Nothing's to be done till the bride and bridegroom come to town. 75

FASHION.

Bride and bridegroom! Death and Furies! I can't bear that thou shouldst call 'em so.

COUPLER.

Why, what shall I call 'em, dog and cat?

FASHION.

Not for the world, that sounds more like man and wife than t'other. 80

COUPLER.

Well, if you'll hear of 'em in no language, we'll leave 'em for the nurse and the chaplain.

FASHION.

The devil and the witch.77

COUPLER.

When they come to town—

LORY.

We shall have stormy weather. 85

COUPLER.

Will you hold your tongues, gentlemen, or not?

LORY.

Mum.

COUPLER.

I say, when they come, we must find what stuff they are made of, whether the churchman be chiefly composed of the flesh or the spirit. I 90 presume the former, for as chaplains now go, 'tis probable he eats three pound of beef to the reading of one chapter. This gives him carnal desires: he wants money, preferment, wine, a whore; therefore, we must invite him to supper, give him fat capons, 95 sack* and sugar, a purse of gold, and a plump sister.78 Let this be done, and I'll warrant thee, my boy, he speaks truth like an oracle.

FASHION.

Thou art a profound statesman, I allow it, but how shall we gain the nurse? 100

---

77 the devil and the witch] proverbially contending lovers; also a metaphor for thunder and lightning (cf. Lory's "stormy weather")

78 sister] member of the congregation, as in "bretheren and sisters."

COUPLER.

Oh, never fear the nurse if once you have got the priest, for the devil always rides the hag. Well, there's nothing more to be said of the matter at this time that I know of. So let us go and enquire if there's any news of our people yet; perhaps they 105 may be come. But let me tell you one thing by the way, sirrah, I doubt you have been an idle fellow; if thou hadst behaved thyself as thou shouldst have done, the girl would never have left thee.

Exeunt.

Scene [ii]. Berinthia's apartment.

Enter her maid, passing the stage, followed by Worthy.

WORTHY.

Hem, Mrs. Abigail, is your mistress to be spoken with?

ABIGAIL.

By you, sir, I believe she may.

WORTHY.

Why 'tis by me I would have her spoken with.

ABIGAIL.

I'll acquaint her, sir. (*Exit.*) 5

WORTHY.

One lift more I must persuade her to give me, and then I'm mounted. Well, a young bawd and a handsome one for my money, 'tis they do the execution; I'll never go to an old one but when I have occasion for a witch. Lewdness looks heavenly 10 to a woman when an angel appears in its cause, but when a hag is advocate, she thinks it comes from the Devil. An old woman has something so terrible in her looks that, whilst she is persuading your mistress to forget she has a soul, she stares 15 hell and damnation full in her face.

Enter Berinthia.

BERINTHIA.

Well, sir, what news bring you?

WORTHY.

No news, madam, there's a woman going to cuckhold her husband.

BERINTHIA.

Amanda? 20

WORTHY.

I hope so.

BERINTHIA.

Speed her well.

WORTHY.

Aye, but there must more than a Godspeed, or
your charity won't be worth a farthing.

BERINTHIA.

Why, han't I done enough already? 25

WORTHY.

Not quite.

BERINTHIA.

What's the matter?

WORTHY.

The lady has a scruple still, which you must
remove.

BERINTHIA.

What's that? 30

WORTHY.

Her virtue—she says.

BERINTHIA.

And do you believe her?

WORTHY.

No, but I believe it's what she takes for her virtue;
it's some relics of lawful love. She is not yet fully
satisfied her husband has got another mistress, 35
which unless I can convince her of, I have opened
the trenches in vain, for the breach must be wider
before I dare storm the town.

BERINTHIA.

And so I'm to be your engineer?*

WORTHY.

I'm sure you know best how to manage the battery. 40

BERINTHIA.

What do you think of springing a mine? I have a
thought just now come into my head, how to blow
her up at once.

WORTHY.

That would be a thought, indeed.

BERINTHIA.

Faith, I'll do't, and thus the execution of it shall 45
be: we are invited to my Lord Foppington's tonight
to supper; he's come to town with his bride and
makes a ball, with an entertainment of music. Now
you must know, my undoer here, Loveless, says he
must needs meet me about some private business 50

(I don't know what 'tis) before we go to the
company. To which end he has told his wife one
lie, and I have told her another. But to make her
amends, I'll go immediately and tell her a solemn
truth. 55

WORTHY.

What's that?

BERINTHIA.

Why, I'll tell her that to my certain knowldege her
husband has a rendezvous with his mistress this
afternoon and that, if she'll give me her word she'll
be satisfied with the discovery without making any 60
violent inquiry after the woman, I'll direct her to
a place where she shall see 'em meet. Now friend,
this I fancy may help you to a critical minute. For
home she must go again to dress. You (with your
good breeding) come to wait upon us to the ball, 65
find her alone, her spirit enflamed against her
husband for his treason and her flesh in heat from
some contemplations upon the treachery, her
blood on fire, her conscience in ice; a lover to draw,
and the devil to drive—ah, poor Amanda. 70

WORTHY. (Kneeling.)

Thou angel of light, let me fall down and adore
thee.

BERINTHIA.

Thou minister of darkness, get up again, for I hate
to see the Devil at his devotions.

WORTHY.

Well, my incomparable Berinthia, how I shall 75
requite you—

BERINTHIA.

Oh, ne'er trouble yourself about that: virtue is its
own reward. There's a pleasure in doing good
which sufficiently pays itself. Adieu.

WORTHY.

Farewell, thou best of women. 80

*Exeunt several ways. Enter Amanda, meeting Berinthia
[on her way out].*

AMANDA.

Who was that went from you?

BERINTHIA.

A friend of yours.

AMANDA.

What does he want?

BERINTHIA.

Something you might spare him and be ne'er the poorer. 85

AMANDA.

I can spare him nothing but my friendship; my love already's all disposed of. Though, I confess, to one ungrateful to my bounty.

BERINTHIA.

Why, there's the mystery: you have been so 90 bountiful you have cloyed him. Fond wives do by their husbands as barren wives do by their lapdogs, cram 'em with sweatmeats till they spoil their stomachs.

AMANDA.

Alas! Had you but seen how passionately fond he 95 has been since our last reconciliation, you would have thought it were impossible he ever should have breathed an hour without me.

BERINTHIA.

Aye, but there you thought wrong again, Amanda: you should consider that in matters of love men's 100 eyes are always bigger than their bellies. They have violent appetites, 'tis true, but they have soon dined.

AMANDA.

Well, there's nothing upon earth astonishes me more than men's inconstancy. 105

BERENTHIA.

Now, there's nothing upon earth astonishes me less, when I consider what they and we are composed of. For Nature has made them children and us babies.* Now Amanda, how we used our babies you may remember. We were mad to have 'em as 110 soon as we saw 'em, kissed 'em to pieces as soon as we got 'em, then pulled off their clothes, saw 'em naked, and so threw 'em away.

AMANDA.

But do you think all men are of this temper?

BERINTHIA.

All but one. 115

AMANDA.

Who is that?

BERINTHIA.

Worthy.

AMANDA.

Why, he's weary of his wife, too, you see.

BERINTHIA.

Aye, that's no proof.

AMANDA.

What can be a greater? 120

BERINTHIA.

Being weary of his mistress.

AMANDA.

Don't you think 'twere possible he might give you that, too?

BERINTHIA.

Perhaps he might if he were my gallant, not if he were yours. 125

AMANDA.

Why do you think he should be more constant to me than he would to you? I'm sure I'm not so handsome.

BERINTHIA.

Kissing goes by favor;[79] he likes you best.

AMANDA.

Suppose he does? That's no demonstration he 130 would be constant to me.

BERINTHIA.

No, that I'll grant you. But there are other reasons to expect it. For you must know after all, Amanda, the inconstancy we commonly see in men of brains does not so much proceed from the uncertainty of their 135 temper as from the misfortunes of their love. A man sees perhaps a hundred women he likes well enough for an intrigue, and away, but possibly, through the whole course of his life, does not find above one who is exactly what he could wish her; now her, 'tis a 140 thousand to one, he never gets. Either she is not to be had at all (though that seldom happens, you'll say) or he wants* those opportunities that are necessary to gain her. Either she likes somebody else much better than him, or uses him like a dog 145 because he likes nobody so well as her. Still* something or other fate claps in the way between them and the woman they are capable of being fond of, and this makes them wander about from mistress to mistress, like a pilgrim from town to town, who 150 every night must have a fresh lodging and's in haste to be gone in the morning.

---

79 Kissing goes by favor] We love as we are individually inclined.

AMANDA.

'Tis possible there may be something in what you say. But what do you infer from it as to the man we were talking of? 155

BERINTHIA.

Why, I infer that, you being the woman in the world the most to his humor, 'tis not likely he would quit you for one that is less.

AMANDA.

That is not to be depended upon, for you see Mr. Loveless does so. 160

BERINTHIA.

What does Mr. Loveless do?

AMANDA.

Why, he runs after something for variety I'm sure he does not like so well as he does me.

BERINTHIA.

That's more than you know, madam.

AMANDA.

No, I'm sure on't. I am not very vain, Berinthia, 165 and yet I'd lay my life, if I could look into his heart, he thinks I deserve to be preferred to a thousand of her.

BERINTHIA.

Don't be too positive in that neither; a million to one but she has the same opinion of you. What 170 would you give to see her?

AMANDA.

Hang her, dirty trull! though I really believe she's so ugly she'd cure me of my jealousy.

BERINTHIA.

All the men of sense about town say she's handsome. 175

AMANDA.

They are as often out in those things as any people.

BERINTHIA.

Then I'll give you farther proof: all the women about town say she's a fool. Now I hope you are convinced?

AMANDA.

Whate'er she be, I'm satisfied he does not like her 180 well enough to bestow anything more than a little outward gallantry upon her.

BERINTHIA.

Outward gallantry? (*Aside.*) I can't bear this.— Don't you think she's a woman to be fobbed off

so. Come, I'm too much your friend to suffer you 185 should be thus grossly imposed upon by a man who does not deserve the least part about you unless he knew how to set a greater value upon it. Therefore in one word, to my certain knowledge he is to meet her now, within a quarter of an hour, 190 somewhere about that Babylon of wickedness, Whitehall.* And if you'll give me your word that you'll be content with seeing her masked in his hand without pulling her head-clothes off, I'll step immediately to the person from whom I have my 195 intelligence and send you word whereabouts you may stand to see 'em meet. My friend and I'll watch 'em from another place and dodge[80] 'em to their private lodging. But don't you offer to follow 'em, lest you do it awkwardly and spoil all. I'll 200 come home to you again as soon as I have earthed 'em and give you an account in what corner of the house the scene of their lewdness lies.

AMANDA.

If you can do this, Berinthia, he's a villain.

BERINTHIA.

I can't help that; men will be so. 205

AMANDA.

Well! I'll follow your directions, for I shall never rest till I know the worst of this matter.

BERINTHIA.

Pray, go immediately and get yourself ready then. Put on some of your woman's clothes, a great scarf and a mask, and you shall presently receive orders. 210 (*Calls within.*) Here, who's there? Get me a chair* quickly.

SERVANT [*Without.*]

There are chairs at the door, madam.

BERINTHIA.

'Tis well, I'm coming.

AMANDA.

But pray, Berinthia, before you go, tell me how I 215 may know this filthy thing if she should be so forward (as I suppose she will) to come to the rendezvous first, for methinks I would fain view her a little.

BERINTHIA.

Why, she's about my height and very well shaped. 220

---

80 dodge] surreptitiously follow

AMANDA.

I thought she had been a little crooked.

BERINTHIA.

Oh no, she's as straight as I am. But we lose time; come away.

Exeunt.

[Act V, scene iii. Young Fashion's lodgings.]

Enter Young Fashion, meeting Lory.

FASHION.

Well, will the doctor come?

LORY.

Sir, I sent a porter to him as you ordered me. He found him with a pipe of tobacco and a great tankard of ale, which he said he would dispatch while I could tell three, and be here.   5

FASHION.

He does not suspect 'twas I that sent for him?

LORY.

Not a jot, sir; he divines as little for himself as for other folks.

FASHION.

Will he bring Nurse with him?

LORY.

Yes.   10

FASHION.

That's well. Where's Coupler?

LORY.

He's half way up the stairs taking breath; he must play his bellows a little before he can get to the top.

Enter Coupler.

FASHION.

Oh, here he is.—Well, old phthisic,[81] the doctor's   15
coming.

COUPLER.

Would the pox had the doctor—I'm quite out of wind. (*To Lory.*) Set me a chair, sirrah. Ah— (*Sits down. To Young Fashion.*) Why the plague canst not thou lodge upon the ground floor?   20

FASHION.

Because I love to lie as near heaven as I can.

COUPLER.

Prithee let heaven alone. Ne'er affect tending that way; thy center's downward.

FASHION.

That's impossible. I have too much ill luck in this world to be damned in the next.   25

COUPLER.

Thou art out in thy logic. Thy major is true but thy minor[82] is false, for thou art the luckiest fellow in the universe.

FASHION.

Make that out.

COUPLER.

I'll do it. Last night the Devil ran away with the   30
parson of Fatgoose living.

FASHION.

If he had run away with the parish too, what's that to me?

COUPLER.

I'll tell thee what it's to thee. This living is worth five hundred pound a year,[83] and the presentation   35
of it is thine if thou canst prove thyself a lawful husband to Miss Hoyden.

FASHION.

Say'st thou so, my protector? Then i'cad, I shall have a brace of evidences* here presently.*

COUPLER.

The nurse and the doctor?   40

FASHION.

The same; the Devil himself won't have interest enough to make 'em withstand it.

COUPLER.

That we shall see presently; here they come.

Enter Nurse and Bull; they start back, seeing Young Fashion.

NURSE.

Ah goodness, Roger, we are betrayed.

---

81 phthisic] asthmatic or consumptive

82 major … minor] premises, terms in logic; the argument goes: All those with bad luck here go to heaven. I have bad luck here. Ergo: I'll go to heaven.

83 five hundred pound a year] a very good living indeed since an annual income of as little as one hundred pounds might elevate one into the ranks of the lesser gentry

FASHION. (*Laying hold on 'em.*)

Nay, nay, ne'er flinch for the matter, for I have you 45
safe. Come, to your trials immediately; I have no
time to give you copies of your indictment. There
sits your judge—

NURSE, BULL. (*Kneeling.*)

Pray sir, have compassion on us.

NURSE.

I hope, sir, my years will move your pity; I am an 50
aged woman.

COUPLER.

That is a moving argument indeed.

BULL.

I hope, sir, my character will be considered; I am
Heaven's ambassador.

COUPLER. (*To Bull.*)

Are not you a rogue of sanctity? 55

BULL.

Sir (with respect to my function) I do wear a gown.

COUPLER.

Did not you marry this vigorous young fellow to
a plump, young, buxom wench?

NURSE. (*To Bull.*)

Don't confess, Roger, unless you are hard put to
it, indeed. 60

COUPLER.

Come, out with't.—Now is he chewing the cud of
his roguery and grinding a lie between his teeth.

BULL.

Sir—I cannot positively say—I say, sir—positively
I cannot say—

COUPLER.

Come, no equivocations, no Roman turns[84] upon 65
us. Consider thou standest upon Protestant
ground, which will slip from under thee like a
Tyburn* cart, for in this country we have always
ten hangmen for one Jesuit.

BULL. (*To Young Fashion.*)

Pray sir, then will you but permit me to speak one 70
word in private with Nurse?

FASHION.

Thou art always for doing something in private
with Nurse.

COUPLER.

But pray, let his betters be served before him for
once. I would do something in private with her 75
myself.—Lory, take care of this reverend gownman
in the next room a little. Retire, priest.

Exit Lory with Bull.

Now, virgin, I must put the matter home to you
a little: Do you think it might not be possible to
make you speak truth? 80

NURSE.

Alas! Sir, I don't know what you mean by truth.

COOUPLER.

Nay, 'tis possible thou mayst be a stranger to it.

FASHION.

Come Nurse, you and I were better friends when we
saw one another last, and I still believe you are a very
good woman in the bottom. I did deceive you and 85
your young lady, 'tis true, but I always designed to
make a very good husband to her and to be a very
good friend to you. And 'tis possible in the end, she
might have found herself happier and you richer
than ever my brother will make you. 90

NURSE.

Brother! Why, is your worship then his lordship's
brother?

FASHION.

I am, which you should have known if I durst have
stayed to have told you, but I was forced to take
horse a little in haste, you know. 95

NURSE.

You were indeed, sir; poor young man, how he was
bound to scour for't. Now won't your worship be
angry if I confess the truth to you; when I found
you were a cheat (with respect be it spoken), I
verily believed Miss had got some pitiful skip- 100
jack[85] varlet or other for her husband, or I had
ne'er let her think of marrying again.

COUPLER.

But where was your conscience all this while,
woman? Did not that stare in your face with huge
saucer eyes and a great horn upon the forehead? 105
Did not you think you should be damned for such
a sin? Hah?

---

84 Roman turns] Equivocation was associated with Roman
  Catholics, especially Jesuits, since Elizabethan times.

85 skip-jack] foolish, pert

FASHION.

Well said, divinity, press? that home upon her.

NURSE.

Why, in good truly, sir, I had some fearful thoughts on't and could never be brought to consent till Mr. Bull said it was a peccadillo and he'd secure my soul for a tithe pig.

FASHION.

There was a rogue for you.

COUPLER.

And he shall thrive accordingly; he shall have a good living. Come, honest Nurse, I see you have butter in your compound: you can melt. Some compassion you can have of this handsome young fellow.

NURSE.

I have indeed, sir.

FASHION.

Why then, I'll tell you what you shall do for me. You know what a warm living here is fallen and that it must be in the disposal of him who has the disposal of Miss. Now if you and the doctor will agree to prove my marriage, I'll present him to it upon condition he makes you his bride.

NURSE.

Naw the blessing of the Lord follow your good worship both by night and by day. Let him be fetched in by the ears; I'll soon bring his nose to the grindstone.

COUPLER. (*Aside.*)

Well said, old white-leather.[86]—Hey, bring in the prisoner there.

Enter Lory with Bull.

COUPLER.

Come, advance, holy man. Here's your duck does not think fit to retire with you into the chancel at this time but has a proposal to make to you in the face of the congregation. Come Nurse, speak for yourself; you are of age.

NURSE.

Roger, are not you a wicked man, Roger, to set your strength against a weak woman and persuade her it was no sin to conceal Miss's nuptials? My conscience flies in my face for it, thou priest of Baal, and I find by woeful experience thy absolution is not worth an old cassock. Therefore, I am resolved to confess the truth to the whole world, though I die a beggar for it. But his worship overflows with his mercy and his bounty; he is not only pleased to forgive us our sins but designs thou sha't squat thee down in Fatgoose living and, which is more than all, has prevailed with me to become the wife of thy bosom.

FASHION.

All this I intend for you, doctor. What you are to do for me, I need not tell you.

BULL.

Your worship's goodness is unspeakable. Yet there is one thing seems a point of conscience, and conscience is a tender babe. If I should bind myself, for the sake of this living, to marry Nurse and maintain her afterwards, I doubt it might be looked on as a kind of simony.

COUPLER. (*Rising up.*)

If it were sacrilege, the living's worth it. Therefore, no more words, good doctor. But with the parish (*Giving Nurse to him.*)—here—take the parsonage house. 'Tis true, 'tis a little out of repair; some dilapidations there are to be made good. The windows are broke, the wainscot warped, the ceilings are peeled, and the walls are cracked, but a little glazing, painting, whitewash, and plaster will make it last thy time.

BULL.

Well sir, if it must be so, I shan't contend; what Providence orders, I submit to.

NURSE.

And so do I, with all humility.

COUPLER.

Why, that now was spoke like good people. Come my turtle doves, let us go help this poor pigeon to his wandering mate again, and after institution and induction[87] you shall all go a-cooing together.

Exeunt.

---

86 white-leather] a bleached leather, indicating Nurse's complexion

87 institution and induction] The installation of a clergyman in a parish is parallelled to marriage and consummation.

[Act V, scene iv. Loveless's lodgings.]

Enter Amanda in a scarf, etc., as just returned, her woman following her.

AMANDA.

Prithee, what care I who has been here?

WOMAN.

Madam, 'twas my Lady Bridle and my Lady Tiptoe.

AMANDA.

My Lady Fiddle and my Lady Faddle. What dost stand troubling me with the visits of a parcel of 5
impertinent women? When they are well seamed with the smallpox they won't be so fond of show-ing their faces. There are more coquettes about this Town—

WOMAN.

Madam, I suppose they only came to return your 10
ladyship's visit, according to the custom of the world.

AMANDA.

Would the world were on fire and you in the middle on't.
Be gone; leave me. 15

Exit Woman.

　　　　　　　—At last I am convinced.
My eyes are testimonies of his falsehood.
The base, ungrateful, perjured villain—
Good gods—what slippery stuff are men
　　composed of?
Sure the account of their creation's false 20
And 'twas the woman's rib that they were formed of.
But why am I thus angry?
This poor relapse should only move my scorn.
'Tis true, the roving flights of his unfinished youth
Had strong excuses⁹ from the plea of nature; 25
Reason had thrown the reins loose on his neck
And slipped him to unlimited desire.
If therefore he went wrong, he had a claim
To my forgiveness, and I did him right.
But since the years of manhood rein him in, 30
And reason well digested into thought
Has pointed out the course he ought to run,
If now he strays,
'Twould be as weak and mean in me to pardon

As it has been in him t'offend. But hold: 35
'Tis an ill cause indeed, where nothing's to be said for't.
My beauty possibly is in the wane;
Perhaps sixteen has greater charms for him.
Yes, there's the secret. But let him know,
My quiver's not entirely emptied yet: 40
I still have darts, and I can shoot 'em too;
They're not so blunt but they can enter still—
The want's* not in my power but in my will.
Virtue's his friend, or through another's heart
I yet could find the way to make his smart. 45

Going off, she meets Worthy.

Hah! He here?
Protect me, Heaven, for this looks ominous.

WORTHY.

You seem disordered, madam. I hope there's no misfortune happened to you?

AMANDA.

None that will long disorder me, I hope. 50

WORTHY.

What e'er it be disturbs you, I would to Heaven 'twere in my power to bear the pain till I were able to remove the cause.

AMANDA.

I hope e'ere long it will remove itself.
At least, I have given it warning to be gone. 55

WORTHY.

Would I durst ask where 'tis the thorn torments you?
Forgive me if I grow inquisitive.
'Tis only with desire to give you ease.

AMANDA.

Alas! 'Tis in a tender part.
It can't be drawn without a world of pain. 60
Yet out it must,
For it begins to fester in my heart.

WORTHY.

If 'tis the sting of unrequited love,
Remove it instantly.
I have a balm will quickly heal the wound. 65

AMANDA.

You'll find the undertaking difficult.
The surgeon who already has attempted it
Has much tormented me.

WORTHY.
 I'll aid him with a gentler hand,
 If you will give me leave.   70
AMANDA.
 How soft soe'er the hand may be,
 There still is terror in the operation.
WORTHY.
 Some few preparatives would make it easy,
 Could I persuade you to apply 'em.
 Make home reflections, madam, on your slighted   75
   love,
 Weigh well the strength and beauty of your charms,
 Rouse up that spirit women ought to bear,
 And slight your god if he neglects his angel.
 With arms of ice receive his cold embraces,
 And keep your fire for those who come in flames.   80
 Behold a burning lover at your feet,
 His fever raging in his veins.
 See how he trembles, how he pants;
 See how he glows, how he consumes.
 Extend the arms of mercy to his aid.   85
 His zeal may give him title to your pity,
 Although his merit cannot claim your love.
AMANDA.
 Of all my feeble sex, sure I must be the weakest,
 Should I again presume to think on love.
 (Sighing.) Alas! my heart has been too roughly   90
   treated.
WORTHY.
 'Twill find the greater bliss in softer usage.
AMANDA.
 But where's that usage to be found?
WORTHY.
                             'Tis here,
 Within this faithful breast; which, if you doubt,
 I'll rip it up before your eyes,   95
 Lay all its secrets open to your view,
 And then you'll see 'twas sound.
AMANDA.
 With just such honest words as these
 The worst of men deceived me.
WORTHY.
                      He therefore merits   100
 All revenge can do; his fault is such,
 The extent and stretch of vengeance cannot reach it.
 Oh, make me but your instrument of justice;

You'll find me execute it with such zeal
 As shall convince you I abhor the crime.   105
AMANDA.
 The rigor of an executioner
 Has more the face of cruelty than justice,
 And he who puts the cord about the wretch's neck
 Is seldom known to exceed him in his morals.
WORTHY.
 What proof then can I give you of my truth?   110
AMANDA.
 There is on earth but one.
WORTHY.
 And is that in my power?
AMANDA.
                        It is.
 And one that would so thoroughly convince me,
 I should be apt to rate your heart so high   115
 I possibly might purchase't with a part of mine.
WORTHY.
 Then, Heav'n, thou art my friend, and I am blest,
 For if 'tis in my power, my will, I'm sure
 Will reach it—no matter what the terms may be—
 When such a recompense is offererd.   120
 Oh, tell me quickly what this proof must be.
 What is it will convince you of my love?
AMANDA.
 I shall believe you love me as you ought
 If from this moment you forbear to ask
 Whatever is unfit for me to grant.   125
 —You pause upon it, sir.—I doubt on such hard
   terms
 A woman's heart is scarcely worth the having.
WORTHY.
 A heart like yours on any terms is worth it.
 'Twas not on that I paused. But I was thinking
   (Drawing nearer to her.)
 Whether some things there may not be   130
 Which women cannot grant without a blush
 And yet which men may take without offense.
 (Taking her hand.) Your hand, I fancy, may be of
   the number:
 Oh, pardon me if I commit a rape
 Upon it (Kissing it eagerly.) and thus devour it   135
   with my kisses.
AMANDA.
 Oh heavens! Let me go.

WORTHY.

　　Never, whilst I have strength to hold you here.
　　(*Forcing her to sit down on a couch.*)
　　My life, my soul, my goddess, oh, forgive me!

AMANDA.

　　Oh, whither am I going? Help, Heaven, or I am lost.

WORTHY.

　　Stand neuter, gods, this once I do invoke you.　　140

AMANDA.

　　Then save me, virtue, and the glory's thine.

WORTHY.

　　Nay, never strive.

AMANDA.

　　　　　　　　I will, and conquer too.
　　My forces rally bravely to my aid, (*Breaking from
　　　　him.*)
　　And thus I gain the day.　　145

WORTHY.

　　Then mine as bravely double their attack,
　　(*Seizing her again.*) And thus I wrest it from you.
　　Nay, struggle not,
　　For all's in vain: or death or victory,
　　I am determined.　　150

AMANDA.

　　　　　　　　And so am I. (*Rushing from him.*)
　　Now keep your distance, or we part forever.

WORTHY. (*Offering again.*)

　　For Heaven's sake—

AMANDA. (*Going.*)

　　Nay then, farewell.

WORTHY. (*Kneeling and holding her by her clothes.*)

　　Oh stay, and see the magic force of love:　　155
　　Behold this raging lion at your feet,
　　Struck dead with fear, and tame as charms can
　　　　make him.
　　What must I do to be forgiven by you?

AMANDA.

　　Repent, and never more offend.

WORTHY.

　　Repentence for past crimes is just and easy,　　160
　　But sin no more's a task too hard for mortals.

AMANDA.

　　Yet those who hope for heaven
　　Must use their best endeavors to perform it.

WORTHY.

　　Endeavors we may use, but flesh and blood
　　Are got in t'other scale,　　165
　　And they are ponderous things.

AMANDA.

　　　　　　　　Whate'er they are,
　　There is a weight in resolution
　　Sufficient for their balance. The soul, I do
　　　　confess,
　　Is usually so careless of its charge,　　170
　　So soft, and so indulgent to desire
　　It leaves the reins in the wild hand of nature,
　　Who, like a Phaeton,[88] drives the fiery chariot
　　And sets the world on flame.
　　Yet still* the sovereignty is in the mind　　175
　　Whene'er it pleases to exert its force.
　　Perhaps you may not think it worth your while
　　To take such mighty pains for my esteem,
　　But that I leave to you.
　　You see the price I set upon my heart;　　180
　　Perhaps 'tis dear,* but spite of all your art,
　　You'll find on cheaper terms we ne'er shall part.
　　　　(*Exit.*)

WORTHY.

　　Sure there's divinity about her,
　　And sh'as dispensed some portion on't to me.
　　For what but now was the wild flame of love,　　185
　　Or (to dissect that specious term)
　　The vile, the gross desires of flesh and blood,
　　Is in a moment turned to adoration.
　　The coarser appetite of nature's gone,
　　And 'tis, methinks, the food of angels I require.　　190
　　How long this influence may last, Heaven knows,
　　But in this moment of my purity
　　I could on her own terms accept her heart.
　　Yes, lovely woman, I can accept it,
　　For now 'tis doubly worth my care.　　195
　　Your charms are much increased since thus adorned.
　　When truth's extorted from us, then we own
　　The robe of virtue is a graceful habit.
　　Could women but our secret counsels scan,
　　Could they but reach the deep reserves of man,　　200
　　They'd wear it on, that that of love might last,
　　For when they throw off one, we soon the other cast.

───────────────

88　Phaeton] son of Helios, the sun god, who won his fa-
　　ther's permission to drive the chariot of the sun and lost
　　control

Their sympathy is such—
The fate of one, the other scarce can fly;
They live together and together die. 205

Exit.

[Scene v. Lord Foppington's Town house.]

Enter Hoyden and Nurse.

HOYDEN.
But is it sure and certain, say you, he's my lord's
own brother?
NURSE.
As sure as he's your lawful husband.
HOYDEN.
I'cod, if I had known that in time, I don't know
but I might have kept him. For between you and 5
I, Nurse, he'd have made a husband worth two of
this I have. But which do you think you should
fancy most, Nurse?
NURSE.
Why truly, in my poor fancy, madam, your first
husband is the prettier gentleman. 10
HOYDEN.
I don't like my lord's shapes, Nurse.
NURSE.
Why, in good truly, as a body may say, he is but a
slam.[89]
HOYDEN.
What do you think now he puts me in mind of?
Don't you remember a long, loose, shambling sort 15
of a horse my father called Washy?
NURSE.
As like as two twin brothers.
HOYDEN.
I'cod, I have thought so a hundred times; faith,
I'm tired of him.
NURSE.
Indeed, madam, I think you had e'en as good 20
stand to your first bargain.
HOYDEN.
Oh but Nurse, we han't considered the main thing
yet. If I leave my lord, I must leave my lady too,
and when I rattle about the streets in my coach,

they'll only say, there goes Mistress—Mistress— 25
Mistress what? What's this man's name I have
married, Nurse?
NURSE.
Squire Fashion.
HOYDEN.
Squire Fashion is it? Well squire, that's better than
nothing. Do you think one could not get him 30
made a knight, Nurse?
NURSE.
I don't know but one might, madam, when the
King's in a good humor.
HOYDEN.
I'cod, that would do rarely. For then he'd be as
good a man as my father, you know. 35
NURSE.
By'r Lady, and that's as good as the best of 'em.
HOYDEN.
So 'tis, faith, for then I shall be my lady and your
ladyship at every word, and that's all I have to care
for. Hah, Nurse, but hark you me; one thing more,
and then I have done. I'm afraid, if I change my 40
husband again, I shan't have so much money to
throw about, Nurse.
NURSE.
Oh, enough's as good as a feast. Besides, madam,
one don't know but as much may fall to your share
with the younger brother as with the elder. For 45
though these lords have a power of wealth indeed,
yet as I have heard say, they give it all to their sluts
and their trulls, who joggle it about in their
coaches, with a murrain to 'em, whilst poor
madam sits sighing and wishing and knotting and 50
crying and has not a spare half-crown to buy her
a *Practice of Piety*.[90]
HOYDEN.
Oh but for that, don't deceive yourself, Nurse. For
this I must say for my lord, and a—(*Snapping her
fingers.*) for him. He's as free as an open house at 55
Christmas. For this very morning he told me I should
have two hundred a year to buy pins. Now Nurse, if
he gives me two hundred a year to buy pins, what do
you think he'll give me to buy fine petticoats?

---

89 a slam] an ill-shaped person (*OED* gives this as the only
instance of the word.)

90 *Practice of Piety*] an extremely popular devotional manual
by Lewis Bayley, appearing in over 100 editions

NURSE.

Ah my dearest, he deceives thee foully, and he's no
better than a rogue for his pains. These Londoners
have got a gibberish with 'em would confound a
Gypsy. That which they call pin money is to buy
their wives everything in the varsal[91] world, down
to their very shoe ties; nay, I have heard folks say
that some ladies, if they will have gallants, as they
call 'um, are forced to find them out of their pin
money too.

HOYDEN.

Has he served me so, say ye? Then I'll be his wife
no longer, so that's fixed. Look, here he comes,
with all the fine folk at's heels. I'cod, Nurse, these
London ladies will laugh till they crack again to
see me slip my collar and run away from my
husband. But d'ye hear? Pray take care of one
thing: when the busniess comes to break out, be
sure you get between me and my father, for you
know his tricks; he'll knock me down.

NURSE.

I'll mind him, never fear, madam.

*Enter Lord Foppington, Loveless, Worthy, Amanda,
and Berinthia.*

FOPPINGTON.

Ladies and gentlemen, you are all welcome.—
Loveless, that's my wife: prithee do me the favor
to salute* her, and dost hear—(*Aside to him.*) if
thau hast a mind to try thy fartune to be revenged
of me, I won't take it ill, stap my vitals.

LOVELESS.

You need not fear, sir; I'm too fond of my own wife
to have the least inclination to yours.

All salute Hoyden.

FOPPINGTON. (*Aside.*)

I'd give you a thausand paund he would make love
to her, that he may see she has sense enough to prefer
me to him, though his own wife has not. (*Viewing
him.*) He's a very beastly fellow, in my opinion.

HOYDEN. (*Aside.*)

What a power of fine men there are in this
London! He that kissed me first is a goodly

gentleman, I promise you. Sure those wives have
a rare time on't that live here always!

Enter Sir Tunbelly, with musicians, dancers, etc.

SIR TUNBELLY.

Come, come in, good people, come in; come, tune
your fiddles, tune your fiddles.—(*To the hautboys.*)
Bagpipes, make ready there. Come, strike up.
(*Sings.*)
For this is Hoyden's wedding day,
And therefore we keep holiday,
    And come to be merry.
Hah, there's my wench, i'faith! Touch and take, I'll
warrant her; she'll breed like a tame rabbit.

HOYDEN. (*Aside.*)

I'cod, I think my father's gotten drunk before
supper.

SIR TUNBELLY. (*To Loveless and Worthy.*)

Gentlemen, you are welcome. (*Saluting Amanda
and Berinthia.*) Ladies, by your leave.—Hah, they
bill like turtles.* Udsookers,* they set my old blood
afire; I shall cuckold somebody before morning.

FOPPINGTON. (*To Sir Tunbelly.*)

Sir, you being master of the entertainment, will
you desire the company to sit?

SIR TUNBELLY.

Oons,* sir, I'm the happiest man on this side the
Ganges.

FOPPINGTON. (*Aside.*)

This is a mighty unaccountable old fellow.—I said,
sir, it would be convenient to ask the company to
sit.

SIR TUNBELLY.

Sit? With all my heart! Come, take your places,
ladies, take your places, gentlemen. Come, sit
down, sit down; a pox of ceremony, take your
places.

They sit, and the masque begins.

Dialogue between Cupid and Hymen.

1

CUPID.

Thou bane to my empire, thou spring of contest,
Thou source of all discord, thou period to rest,
Instruct me, what wenches in bondage can see
That the aim of their life is still pointed to thee.

---

91 varsal] universal

2

HYMEN.

Instruct me, thou little impertinent god,   5
From whence all thy subjects have taken the mode
To grow fond of a change, to whatever it be,
And I'll tell thee why those would be bound who
    are free.

CHORUS.

For change, we're for change, to whatever it be,
We are neither contented with freedom nor thee.   10
    Constancy's an empty sound.
    Heaven and earth and all go round,
    All the works of nature move,
    And the joys of life and love
        Are in variety.   15

3

CUPID.

Were love the reward of a painstaking life,
Had a husband the art to be fond of his wife,
Were virtue so plenty, a wife could afford
These very hard times to be true to her lord,
Some specious account might be given of those   20
Who are tied by the tail to be led by the nose.

4

But since 'tis the fate of a man and his wife
To consume all their days in contention and strife;
Since whatever the bounty of Heaven may create
    her,
He's morally sure he shall heartily hate her;   25
I think 'twere much wiser to ramble at large,
And the volleys of love on the herd to discharge.

5

HYMEN.

Some color of reason thy counsel might bear,
Could a man have no more than his wife to his share,
Or were I a monarch, so cruelly just,   30
To oblige a poor wife to be true to her trust,
But I have not pretended, for many years past,
By marrying of people, to make 'em grow chaste.

6

I therefore advise thee to let me go on,
Thou'lt find I'm the strength and support of thy   35
    throne,
For hadst thou but eyes thou wouldst quickly
    perceive it,
        How smoothly thy dart

    Slips into the heart
    Of a woman that's wed,
    Whilst the shivering maid   40
Stands trembling and wishing, but dare not
    receive it.

CHORUS.

    For change, *etc.*

The masque ended, enter Young Fashion, Coupler, and Bull.

SIR TUNBELLY.

So, very fine, very fine, i'faith, this is something
like a wedding; now if supper were but ready, I'd
say a short grace, and if I had such a bedfellow as   45
Hoyden tonight—I'd say as short prayers. (*Seeing
Young Fashion.*) How now, what have we got here?
A ghost? Nay, it must be so, for his flesh and blood
could never have dared to appear before me. (*To
him.*) Ah, rogue—   50

FOPPINGTON.

Stap my vitals, Tam again.

SIR TUNBELLY.

My lord, will you cut his throat? Or shall I?

FOPPINGTON.

Leave him to me, sir, if you please.—Prithee, Tam,
be so ingenuous now as to tell me what thy
business is here?   55

FASHION.

'Tis with your bride.

FOPPINGTON.

Thau art the impudent'st fellow that Nature has
yet spawned into the warld, strike me speechless.

FASHION.

Why, you know my modesty would have starved
me; I sent it a-begging to you, and you would not   60
give a groat.

FOPPINGTON.

And dost thau expect by an excess of assurance to
extart a maintenance from me?

FASHION. (*Taking Hoyden by the hand.*)

I do intend to extort your mistress from you, and
that I hope will prove one.   65

FOPPINGTON.

I ever thaught Newgate or Bedlam would be his
fartune, and naw his fate's decided. Prithee,
Loveless, dost know of a mad-doctor hard by?

FASHION.

There's one at your elbow will cure you presently.*—Prithee doctor, take him in hand quickly. 70

FOPPINGTON.

Shall I beg the favor of you, sir, to pull your fingers out of my wife's hand.

FASHION.

His wife! Look you there, now I hope you are all satisfied he's mad. 75

FOPPINGTON.

Naw it is nat passible far me to penetrate what species of fally it is thau art driving at.

SIR TUNBELLY.

Here, here, here! Let me beat out his brains, and that will decide all.

FOPPINGTON.

No, pray sir hold, we'll destray him presently according to law. 80

FASHION. (*To Bull.*)

Nay then, advance, doctor. Come, you are a man of conscience; answer boldly to the questions I shall ask: Did not you marry me to this young lady, before ever that gentleman there saw her face? 85

BULL.

Since the truth must out, I did.

FASHION.

Nurse, sweet Nurse, were not you a witness to it?

NURSE.

Since my conscience bids me speak—I was.

FASHION. (*To Hoyden.*)

Madam, am not I your lawful husband?

HOYDEN.

Truly I can't tell, but you married me first. 90

FASHION.

Now I hope you are all satisfied?

SIR TUNBELLY. (*Offering to strike him, is held by Loveless and Worthy.*)

Oons* and thunder, you lie.

FOPPINGTON.

Pray sir, be calm, the battle is in disarder but requires more canduct than courage to rally our forces. Pray dactar, one word with you. (*To Bull, aside.*) Look you, sir, though I will not presume to calculate your notions of damnation fram the description you give us of hell, yet since there is 95

at least a passibility you may have a pitchfark thrust in your backside, methinks it should not be worth your while to risk your soul in the next world for the sake of a beggarly yaunger brather who is not able to make your bady happy in this. 100

BULL.

Alas, my lord, I have no worldly ends; I speak the truth, Heaven knows. 105

FOPPINGTON.

Nay, prithee never engage Heaven in the matter, far, by all I can see, 'tis like to prove a business for the Devil.

FASHION.

Come, pray sir, all above-board, no corrupting of evidences,* if you please. This young lady is my lawful wife, and I'll justify it in all the courts of England; so your lordship (who always had a passion for variety) may go seek a new mistress if you think fit. 110

FOPPINGTON.

I am struck dumb with his impudence and cannot passitively tell whether ever I shall speak again or nat. 115

SIR TUNBELLY.

Then let me come and examine the business a little; I'll jerk the truth out of 'em presently.* Here, give me my dog-whip.

FASHION.

Look you, old gentleman, 'tis in vain to make a noise; if you grow mutinous, I have some friends within call have swords by their sides above four foot long. Therefore, be calm, hear the evidence patiently, and when the jury have given their verdict, pass sentence according to law: here's honest Coupler shall be foreman and ask as many questions as he pleases. 120 125

COUPLER.

All I have to ask is whether Nurse persists in her evidence? The parson, I dare swear, will never flinch from his. 130

NURSE. (*To Sir Tunbelly, kneeling.*)

I hope in heaven your worship will pardon me; I have served you long and faithfully, but in this thing I was overreached; your worship, however, was deceived as well as I, and if the wedding dinner had been ready, you had put madam to bed to him with your own hands. 135

SIR TUNBELLY.

But how durst you do this without acquainting of me?

NURSE.

Alas! If your worship had seen how the poor thing begged and prayed and clung and twined about me like ivy to an old wall, you would say I, who had suckled it and swaddled it and nursed it both wet and dry, must have had a heart of adamant to refuse it.   140

SIR TUNBELLY.

Very well.   145

FASHION.

Foreman, I expect your verdict.

COUPLER.

Ladies and gentlemen, what's your opinions?

ALL.

A clear case, a clear case.

COUPLER.

Then, my young folks, I wish you joy.

SIR TUNBELLY. (*To Young Fashion.*)

Come hither, stripling. If it be true, then, that thou   150
hast married my daughter, prithee tell me who thou art.

FASHION.

Sir, the best of my condition is, I am your son-in-law, and the worst of it is, I am brother to that noble peer there.   155

SIR TUNBELLY.

Art thou brother to that noble peer? Why then that noble peer and thee and thy wife and the nurse and the priest—may all go and be damned together. (*Exit.*)

FOPPINGTON. (*Aside.*)

Now for my part, I think the wisest thing a man   160
can do with an aching heart is to put on a serene countenance, for a philosophical air is the most becoming thing in the world to the face of a person of quality;* I will therefore bear my disgrace like a great man and let the people see I am above an   165
affront.—Dear Tam, since things are thus fallen aut, prithee give me leave to wish thee jay. I do it *de bon coeur*,[92] strike me dumb; you have married a woman beautiful in her person, charming in her

airs, prudent in her canduct, canstant in her   170
inclinations, and of a nice* marality, split my windpipe.

FASHION.

Your lordship may keep up your spirits with your grimace if you please; I shall support mine with this lady and two thousand pound a year. (*Taking   175
Hoyden.*) Come, madam.
We once again, you see, are man and wife,
And now perhaps the bargain's struck for life;
If I mistake and we should part again,
At least you see you may have choice of men.   180
Nay, should the war[93] at length such havoc make
That lovers should grow scarce, yet for your sake
Kind Heaven always will preserve a beau—

(*Pointing to Lord Foppington*)

You'll find his lordship ready to come to.

FOPPINGTON.

Her ladyship shall stap my vitals, if I do.   185

[*Exeunt.*]

Epilogue
Spoken by Lord Foppington.

Gentlemen and Ladies,
These people have regaled you here today
(In my opnion) with a saucy play,
In which the author does presume to show
That coxcomb, *ab origine*—was beau.
Truly, I think the thing of so much weight   5
That, if some sharp chatisement ben't his fate,
Gad's curse! it may in time destroy the state.
I hold no one its friend, I must confess,
Who would discauntenance your men of dress.
Far, give me leave t'abserve, good clothes are   10
   things
Have ever been of great support to kings.
All treasons come from slovens; it is nat
Within the reach of gentle* beaux to plat:
They have no gall, no spleen, no teeth, no
   stings—
Of all Gad's creatures, the most harmless things.   15

---

92 *de bon coeur*] cheerfully (Fr.)

93 the war] England and Holland were at war with France
    from 1689 to 1697.

Through all recard, no prince was ever slain
By one who had a feather in his brain.
They're men of too refined an education
To squabble with a court—for a vile dirty nation.
I'm very very pasitive you never saw   20
A through⁹⁴ republican a finished beau.
Nor, truly, shall you very often see
A Jacobite much better dressed than he.
In shart, through all the courts that I have been
    in,
Your men of mischief—still are in faul linen.   25
Did ever one yet dance the Tyburn jig
With a free air ar a well-pawdered wig?
Did ever highwayman yet bid you stand
With a sweet bawdy snuff box⁹⁵ in his hand?
Ar do you ever find they ask your purse   30
As men of breeding do?—Ladies, Gad's curse!
This author is a dag, and 'tis not fit
You should allow him ev'n one grain of wit;
To which, that his pretence may ne'er be named,
My humble motion is—he may be damned.   35

FINIS.

Textual Notes

ᵃ Copytext is the first quarto edition in 1697 (Q1). Also consulted: a quarto edition in 1698 (Q2), a quarto edition of 1708 (Q3), a collected edition in 1719 (C), and modern editions in 1970 (Zimansky) and in 1971 (Harris).

ᵇ But … us] Q1 printed as prose. Sometimes hereafter speeches which read as poetry are printed as prose. Printing them as poetry—even when it produces hemstiches and hypermetric lines—seems authorized by other passages containing these features and clearly printed as poetry. I have scanned them without further comment as best I can.

ᶜ methinks] my thinks Q1, Q2, Q3, C, Zimansky, Harris

ᵈ When … sirrah] Q1 prints as verse.

ᵉ beholden] Q2, Q3, C; beholding Q1, Zimansky, Harris

ᶠ Aye,] Ay, Q2, Q3; I Q1; If C, Zimansky, Harris. Zimansky claims his copy of Q1 has space for a dropped letter after the I; ours does not, and I is common for Ay throughout the period.

ᵍ These have brains … ass] Q1 prints as verse.

ʰ Like man … alone] Q1 prints as verse.

ⁱ piqued] C, Zimansky, Harris; pickt Q1; prickt Q2, Q3

ʲ in] Zimansky; om. Q1, Q2, Q3, C, Harris

ᵏ It] C, Zimansky, Harris; If Q1, Q2, Q3

ˡ How then subsists … fast] Q1 prints as a hopeless jumble of verse and prose.

ᵐ I'm satisfied … ashes] Q1 has another hopeless jumble of verse and prose

ⁿ Oh Ged— … one another] Q1 prints as verse.

ᵒ chartré] Chartre Q1, Q2, Q3 C; châtré Zimansky, Harris (following some other modern editors). See also explanatory note.

ᵖ press] Zimansky, Harris; pass Q1, Q2, Q3, C

�q excuses] Zimansky (emending for the meter); excuse Q1, Q2, Q3, C, Harris

---

94 through] thorough-going (Harris)
95 bawdy snuff box] Snuff boxes could apparently have bawdy decorations or images within.

Polly: An Opera[a]

by John Gay (1685-1732)

edited by Rob Canfield

John Gay's *Polly*, written in 1728 as "the second part of" *The Beggar's Opera*, which had its first performance in the same year, immediately became a play that would test the authority of Walpole's power as the moral and cultural magistrate of the English theater. Banned from production, *Polly* was prohibited from enacting its political and discursive subversions that were, for Gay, the logical extensions of his earlier subversive comedy of Macheath and his Newgate gang. Macheath's disruption of both the aesthetic world of English opera and the social world of emergent bourgeois London made *The Beggar's Opera* an immediate theatrical hit. *Polly* would not enjoy such stage presence until almost fifty years later. Ironically, however, Gay's sequel became imitated by history itself. For just as Polly Peachum and Macheath both don disguises and exist throughout much of the play in counterfeit roles, so, too, did the script go underground and become pirated by presses defiant of Walpole's edicts, ensuring that it would enjoy enormous financial success and rival its predecessor in popularity. Like Polly, the play would survive and redefine the "virtue" of English drama through an act of piracy.

Hence, while students will discover significant connections between *The Beggar's Opera* and *Polly*, the more important developments of Gay's drama lie in the shift from Newgate criminals to New World colonials, from bourgeois hypocrisy to creole mimicry, and from Macheath and Polly as rogues to their transformation into pirates. Even the songs and melodies themselves that had provided the parodic center of *The Beggar's Opera* by mocking the foppish duplicities of the London middle class and their dependencies upon an equally pernicious lower-class parasitism, become supplanted by a range of sea chanteys and ballads culled from England's recent experience on the imperialist stage.

As Gay transfers Polly into the New World and transforms her into a pirate, he transfers his critique of mercantile capitalism from the Old to the New World and transforms it into a critique of imperialist ideologies of industry and inherent right to rule. Moreover, Polly's donning of male disguise and her sojourn in Jamaica as a pirate allow Gay to satirize both the heroic ideal of English adventurers since Sir Francis Drake and the very popular counter-role of the pirate (and the female pirate) created for London audiences by Defoe's *General History of the Pirates* (1724). Very likely drawn from Defoe's portraits of the folk heroes Anne Bonny and Mary Read, and from a plethora of other eighteenth-century fantasies of transvestite inversion in gender politics, Polly's role as female pirate provides Gay with an opportunity to critique even the ostensibly alternative social structures that piracy promised in the 1720s (the heyday of the Brethren of the Coast). While contemporary critics may attempt to vindicate the pirates of the Caribbean as a quasi-democratic community that resisted the ideals and evils of colonialism and capitalism, Gay condemns the pirates as complicitous in imperial rapacity, and the final death of Macheath seals Gay's rather dark vision of a world forever tainted, corrupted, and self-interested.

Most important, perhaps, in Gay's transference of his cast to the Caribbean is the addition of the figure of the noble savage. In the final alliance between Polly and the Arawak prince Gay's play moves beyond the subversion of *The Beggar's Opera* and becomes a corrective satire, appropriating out of bankrupt European morality the crucial virtue of honor and relocating it among the "savages."

DRAMATIS PERSONAE

[MEN]

    Ducat.
    Morano.[1]
    Vanderbluff.
    Capstern.[2]
    Hacker.
    Culverin.
    Laguerre.[3]
    Cutlass.
    Pohetohee.
    Cawwawkee.
    [Poet.]
    [Players.]
    Servants, Indians, pirates, guards, etc.

[WOMEN]

    Polly.
    Mrs. Ducat.
    [Diana] Trapes.[4]
    Jenny Diver.[5]
    Flimzy.
    Damaris.
    [Signora Crotchetta.]

SCENE. IN THE WEST INDIES.[6]

INTRODUCTION.

Poet. Player.

POET.

A sequel to a play is like more last words. 'Tis a kind of absurdity, and really, sir, you have prevailed upon me to pursue this subject against my judgment.

FIRST PLAYER.

Be the success as it will, you are sure of what you have contracted for, and upon the inducement of gain nobody can blame you for undertaking it.

POET.

I know I must have been looked upon as whimsical and particular if I had scrupled to have risked my reputation for my profit, for why should I be more squeamish than my betters? And so sir, contrary to my opinion I bring Polly once again upon the stage.

FIRST PLAYER.

Consider sir, you have prepossession on your side.

POET.

But then the pleasure of novelty is lost, and in a thing of this kind I am afraid I shall hardly be pardoned for imitating myself, for sure, pieces of this sort are not to be followed as precedents. My dependence, like a tricking bookseller's, is that the kind reception the first part met with will carry off the second be it what it will.

FIRST PLAYER.

You should not disparage your own works; you will have critics enough who will be glad to do that for you, and let me tell you, sir, after the success you have had, you must expect envy.

POET.

Since I have had more applause than I can deserve, I must, with other authors, be content if critics allow me less. I should be an arrant courtier or an arrant beggar indeed, if as soon as I have received one undeserved favor I should lay claim to another. I don't flatter myself with the like success.

FIRST PLAYER.

I hope sir, in the catastrophe you have not run into the absurdity of your last piece.

POET.

I know that I have been unjustly accused of having given up my moral for a joke, like a fine gentleman in conversation, but whatever be the event now, I will not so much as seem to give up my moral.

FIRST PLAYER.

Really sir, an author should comply with the customs and taste of the Town.* I am indeed afraid too that your satyr* here and there is too free. A

---

1 Morano] suggestive of *Maroon* (q.v.)
2 Capstern] shipping machinery used for lifting heavy weights by winding a rope around a vertical spindle-mounted drum
3 Laguerre] French for war; also the name of a contemporary actor (Fuller) and of an infamous pirate of the 17th century
4 Trapes] slattern
5 Diver] pickpocket
6 West Indies] more properly, Jamaica, ceded to England by Spain in 1655 and recolonized by Cromwell as part of his "Western Design," transforming the famous pirate ports and buccaneer communities into plantations and transporting indentured labor to cultivate them

man should be cautious how he mentions any vice 40
whatsoever before good company, lest somebody
present should apply it to himself.

POET.

The stage, sir, hath the privilege of the pulpit to
attack vice however dignified or distinguished, and
preachers and poets should not be too well bred 45
upon these occasions: nobody can overdo it when
he attacks the vice and not the person.

FIRST PLAYER.

But how can you hinder malicious applications?

POET.

Let those answer for 'em who make 'em. I aim at
no particular persons; my strokes are at vice in 50
general. But if any men particularly vicious are
hurt, I make no apology but leave them to the cure
of their flatterers. If an author write in character,
the lower people reflect on the follies and vices of
the rich and the great, and an Indian judges and 55
talks of Europeans by those he hath conversed
with, etcetera. And I will venture to own that I
wish every man of power or riches were really and
apparently virtuous, which would soon amend and
reform the common people who act by imitation. 60

FIRST PLAYER.

But a little indulgence and partiality to the vices
of your own country without doubt would be
looked upon as more discreet. Though your satyr,
sir, is on vices in general, it must and will give
offence; every vicious man thinks you particular, 65
for conscience will make self-application. And why
will you make yourself so many enemies? I say no
more upon this head. As to us I hope you are
satisfied we have done all we could for you, for you
will now have the advantage of all our best singers. 70

Enter second player.

SECOND PLAYER.

'Tis impossible to perform the opera tonight: all the
fine singers within are out of humor with their parts.
The tenor says he was never offered such indignity
and in a rage flung his clean lambskin gloves into the
fire; he swears that in his whole life he never did sing, 75
would sing, or could sing but in true kid.

FIRST PLAYER.

Music might tame and civilize wild beasts, but 'tis
evident it never yet could tame and civilize
musicians.

Enter third player.

THIRD PLAYER.

Sir, signora Crotchetta says she finds her character 80
so low that she had rather die than sing it.

FIRST PLAYER.

Tell her by her contract I can make her sing it.

Enter Signora Crotchetta.

CROTCHETTA.

Barbarous tramontane! Where are all the lovers of
virtu? Will they not all rise in arms in my defense?
Make me sing it! Good gods! Should I tamely 85
submit to such usage, I should debase myself
through all Europe.

FIRST PLAYER.

In the opera nine or ten years ago, I remember,
madam, your appearance in a character little better
than a fish. 90

CROTCHETTA.

A fish! monstrous! Let me inform you, sir, that a
mermaid or a siren is not many removes from a
sea goddess, or I had never submitted to be that
fish which you are pleased to call me by way of
reproach. I have a cold, sir; I am sick. I don't see 95
why I may not be allowed the privilege of sickness
now and then as well as others. If a singer may not
be indulged in her humors, I am sure she will soon
become of no consequence with the Town. And
so, sir, I have a cold; I am hoarse. I hope now you 100
are satisfied. (*Exit in a fury.*)

Enter fourth player.

FOURTH PLAYER.

Sir, the base voice insists upon pearl-colored
stockings and red-heeled shoes.

FIRST PLAYER.

There is no governing caprice. But how shall we
make our excuses to the house? 105

FOURTH PLAYER.

Since the Town was last year so good as to
encourage an opera without singers, the favor I was
then shown obliges me to offer myself once more,
rather than the audience should be dismissed. All

the other comedians upon this emergency are willing to do their best and hope for your favor and indulgence.

FIRST PLAYER.

Ladies and gentlemen, as we wish to do every thing for your diversion, and that singers only will come when they will come, we beg you to excuse this unforeseen accident and to accept the proposal of the comedians, who rely wholly on your courtesy and protection.

Exeunt.

Overture.

Polly: An Opera.

Raro antecedentem scelestum
Deseruit pede poena claudo. Hor.[7]

Act I, scene i. Ducat's house.

Ducat. Trapes.

TRAPES.

Though you were born and bred and live in the Indies, as you are a subject of Britain you should live up to our customs. Prodigality there is a fashion among all ranks of people. Why, our very younger brothers push themselves into the polite world by squandering more than they are worth. You are wealthy, very wealthy, Mr. Ducat, and I grant you, the more you have, the taste of getting more should grow stronger upon you. 'Tis just so with us. But then the richest of our lords and gentlemen, who live elegantly, always run out. 'Tis genteel to be in debt. Your luxury should distinguish you from the vulgar. You cannot be too expensive in your pleasures.

Air 1. "The disappointed widow."

The manners of the great affect;
    Stint not your pleasure:
If conscience had their genius checked,
    How got they their treasure?

---

7 *Raro* ... Hor.] Horace, *Odes* 3.2.31-32: "Rarely has punishment, even with lame foot, failed to overtake the wicked."

The more in debt, run in debt the more,
    Careless who is undone;
Morals and honesty leave to the poor,
    As they do at London.

DUCAT.

I never thought to have thrift laid to my charge. There is not a man, though I say it, in all the Indies who lives more plentifully than myself nor who enjoys the necessaries of life in so handsome a manner.

TRAPES.

There it is now: Who ever heard a man of fortune in England talk of the necessaries of life? If the necessaries of life would have satisfied such a poor body as me, to be sure I had never come to mend my fortune to the plantations.* Whether we can afford it or no, we must have superfluities. We never stint our expense to our own fortunes, but are miserable if we do not live up to the profuseness of our neighbors. If we could content ourselves with the necessaries of life, no man alive ever need be dishonest. As to woman now, why look ye, Mr. Ducat, a man hath what we may call everything that is necessary in a wife. 40

DUCAT.

Aye, and more!

TRAPES.

But for all that, d'ye see, your married men are my best customers. It keeps wives upon their good behaviors.

DUCAT.

But there are jealousies and family lectures, Mrs.* 45 Trapes.

TRAPES.

Bless us all! How little are our customs known on this side the herring-pond! Why, jealousy is out of fashion even among our common country gentlemen. I hope you are better bred than to be jealous. 50 A husband and wife should have a mutual complaisance for each other. Sure, your wife is not so unreasonable to expect to have you always to herself.

DUCAT.

As I have a good estate, Mrs. Trapes, I would willingly run into everything that is suitable to my 55 dignity and fortune. Nobody throws himself into the extravagancies of life with a freer spirit. As to conscience and musty morals, I have as few drawbacks upon my profits or pleasures as any man of quality* in England; in those I am not in 60 the least vulgar. Besides madam, in most of my expenses I run into the polite taste. I have a fine library of books that I never read; I have a fine stable of horses that I never ride; I build, I buy plate,* jewels, pictures, or anything that is valuable 65 and curious,* as your great men do, merely out of ostentation. But indeed I must own, I do still cohabit with my wife, and she is very uneasy and vexatious upon account of my visits to you.

TRAPES.

Indeed, indeed, Mr. Ducat, you should break 70 through all of this usurpation at once, and keep* _____.* Now too is your time, for I have a fresh cargo of ladies just arrived: nobody alive shall set eyes upon 'em till you have provided yourself. You should keep your lady in awe by her maid; place a handsome, 75

sprightly wench near your wife, and she will be a spy upon her into the bargain. I would have you show yourself a fine gentleman in everything.

DUCAT.

But I am somewhat advanced in life, Mrs. Trapes, and my duty to my wife lies very hard upon me; I 80 must leave keeping* to younger husbands and old bachelors.

TRAPES.

There it is again now! Our very vulgar pursue pleasures in the flush of youth and inclination, but our great men are modishly profligate when their 85 appetite hath left 'em.

Air 2. "The Irish ground."

Bass.

DUCAT.

What can wealth
When we're old?
Youth and health 90
Are not sold.

Treble.

TRAPES.

When love in the pulse beats low
  (As haply it may with you),
A girl can fresh youth bestow
  And kindle desire anew. 95
Thus numbed in the brake,
Without motion, the snake
  Sleeps cold winter away,
But in every vein
Life quickens again 100
On the bosom of May.

We are not here, I must tell you, as we are at London, where we can have fresh goods every week by the wagon. My maid is again gone aboard the vessel; she is perfectly charmed with one of the 105 ladies. 'Twill be a credit to you to keep* her. I have obligations to you, Mr. Ducat, and I would part with her to no man alive but yourself. If I had her at London, such a lady would be sufficient to make my fortune, but in truth, she is not impudent 110 enough to make herself agreeable to the sailors in a public house in this country. By all accounts, she hath a behavior only fit for a private family.*

DUCAT.

But how shall I manage matters with my wife?

TRAPES.

Just as the fine gentlemen do with us. We could 115
bring you many great precedents for treating a wife
with indifference, contempt, and neglect, but that,
indeed, would be running into too high life. I would
have you keep some decency and use her with
civility. You should be so obliging as to leave her to 120
her liberties and take them too yourself. Why, all our
fine ladies, in what they call pin money, have no
other views; 'tis what they all expect.

DUCAT.

But I am afraid it will be hard to make my wife
think like a gentlewoman upon this subject; so that 125
if I take her, I must act discreetly and keep the
affair a dead secret.

TRAPES.

As to that, sir, you may do as you please. Should
it ever come to her knowledge, custom and
education perhaps may make her at first think it 130
somewhat odd. But this I can affirm with a safe
conscience, that many a lady of quality* have
servants of this sort in their families,* and you can
afford an expense as well as the best of 'em.

DUCAT.

I have a fortune, Mrs. Trapes, and would fain make 135
a fashionable figure in life. If we can agree upon
the price, I'll take her into the family.*

TRAPES.

I am glad to see you fling yourself into the polite
taste with a spirit. Few, indeed, have the turn or
talents to get money, but fewer know how to spend 140
it handsomely after they have got it. The elegance
of luxury consists in variety, and love requires it
as much as any of our appetites and passions. And
there is a time of life when a man's appetite ought
to be whetted by a delicacy. 145

DUCAT.

Nay Mrs. Trapes, now you are too hard upon me.
Sure, you cannot think me such a clown* as to
really be in love with my wife! We are not so
ignorant here as you imagine. Why, I married her
in a reasonable way, only for her money. 150

Air 3. "Noel Hills."

He that weds a beauty
 Soon will find her cloy;
When pleasure grows a duty,
 Farewell love and joy.
He that weds for treasure 155
 (Though he hath a wife)
Hath chose one lasting pleasure
 In a married life.

Scene ii.

Ducat. Trapes. Damaris.

DUCAT. (*Calling at the door.*)

Damaris, Damaris, I charge you not to stir from
the door, and the instant you see your lady at a
distance returning from her walk, be sure to give
me notice.

TRAPES.

She is in a most charming rigging; she won't cost 5
you a penny, sir, in clothes at first setting out. But
alack-a-day! No bargain could ever thrive with dry
lips; a glass of liquor makes everything go so glibly.

DUCAT.

Here Damaris, a glass of rum for Mrs.* Di.

*Damaris goes out and returns with a bottle and a glass
[and exits].*

TRAPES.

But as I was saying, sir, I would not part with her 10
to anybody alive but yourself, for to be sure, I
could turn her to ten times the profit by jobs and
chance customers. Come sir, here's to the young
lady's health.

Scene iii.

Ducat. Trapes. Flimzy.

TRAPES.

Well Flimzy, are all the ladies safely landed and
have you done as I ordered you?

FLIMZY.

Yes madam. The three ladies for the run of the
house are safely lodged at home; the other is
without in the hall to wait your commands. She 5
is a most delicious creature, that's certain. Such
lips, such eyes, and such flesh and blood! If you

had her in London you could not fail of the custom of all the foreign ministers. As I hope to be saved, madam, I was forced to tell her ten thousand lies before I could prevail upon her to come with me.—Oh sir, you are the most lucky, happy man in the world! Shall I go call her in?

TRAPES.

'Tis necessary for me first to instruct her in her duty and the ways of the family.* The girl is bashful and modest, so I must beg leave to prepare her by a little private conversation, and afterwards, sir, I shall leave you to your private conversations.*

FLIMZY.

But I hope, sir, you won't forget poor Flimzy, for the richest man alive could not be more scrupulous than I am upon these occasions, and the bribe only can make me excuse it to my conscience. I hope, sir, you will pardon my freedom.

He gives her money.

Air 4. *"Sweetheart, think upon me."*

My conscience is of courtly mold,
  Fit for highest station.
Where's the hand, when touched with gold,
  Proof against temptation? (*Exit.*)

DUCAT.

We can never sufficiently encourage such useful qualifications. You will let me know when you are ready for me. [*Exit.*]

Scene iv.

Trapes.

TRAPES.

I wonder I am not more wealthy, for, o'my conscience, I have as few scruples as those that are ten thousand times as rich. But alack-a-day! I am forced to play at small game. I now and then betray and ruin an innocent girl. And what of that? Can I in conscience expect to be equally rich with those who betray and ruin provinces and countries? In troth, all their great fortunes are owing to situation; as for genius and capacity I can match them to a hair: were they in my circumstances they would act like me; were I in theirs, I should be

rewarded as a most profound, penetrating politician.

Air 5. *"'Twas within a furlong."*

In pimps and politicians
  The genius is the same:
Both raise their own conditions
  On others' guilt and shame;
With a tongue well-tipped with lies
Each the want* of parts* supplies
And with a heart that's all disguise
  Keeps his schemes unknown.
Seducing as the Devil,
  They play the tempter's part
And have, when most they're civil,
  Most mischief in their heart.
Each a secret commerce drives,
First corrupts and then connives,
And by his neighbor's vices thrives,
  For they are all his own.

Scene v.

Trapes. Flimzy. Polly.

TRAPES.

Bless my eyesight, what do I see? I am in a dream, or it is Miss Polly Peachum! Mercy upon me! Child,* what brought you on this side of the water?

POLLY.

Love, madam, and the misfortunes of our family. But I am equally surprised to find an aquaintance here. You cannot be ignorant of my unhappy story, and perhaps from you, Mrs. Di, I may receive some information that may be useful to me.

TRAPES.

You need not be much concerned, Miss Polly, at a sentence of transportation, for a young lady of your beauty hath wherewithal to make her fortune in any country.

POLLY.

Pardon me, madam, you mistake me. Though I was educated among the most profligate in low life, I never engaged in my father's affairs as a thief or thief-catcher, for indeed I abhorred his profession. Would my papa had never taken it up; he then still had been alive and I had never known Macheath!

Air 6. "Sortez des vos retraites."[8]

> She who hath felt a real pain 20
>> By Cupid's dart
> Finds that all absence is in vain
>> To cure her heart.
> Though from my lover cast
>> Far as from pole to pole, 25
> Still* the pure flame must last,
>> For love is in the soul.

You must have heard, madam, that I was unhappy in my marriage. When Macheath was transported all my peace was banished with him, and my papa's death hath now given me liberty to pursue my inclinations. 30

TRAPES.

Good lack-a-day! Poor Mr. Peachum! Death was so much obliged to him that I wonder he did not allow him a reprieve for his own sake. Truly, I think 35 he was obliged to nobody more except the physicians, but they die it seems too. Death is very impartial: he takes all alike, friends and foes.

POLLY.

Every monthly sessions-paper[9] like the apothecary's files (if I may make the comparison) was a record 40 of his services. But my papa kept company with gentlemen, and ambition is catching. He was in too much haste to be rich. I wish all great men would take warning. 'Tis now seven months since my papa was hanged. 45

TRAPES.

This will be a great check indeed to your men of enterprising genius, and it will be unsafe to push at making a great fortune if such accidents grow common. But sure, child,* you are not so mad as to think of following Macheath. 50

POLLY.

In following him I am in pursuit of my quiet. I love him and like a troubled ghost shall never be at rest till I appear to him. If I can receive any information of him from you, it will be a cordial to a wretch in despair. 55

TRAPES.

My dear Miss Polly, you must not think of it. 'Tis

now above a year and a half since he robbed his master, ran away from the plantation, and turned pirate. Then, too, what puts you beyond all possibility of redress is that since he came over he 60 married a transported slave, one Jenny Diver, and she is gone off with him. You must give over all thoughts of him, for he is a very* devil to our sex: not a woman of the greatest vivacity shifts her inclinations half so fast as he can. Besides, he 65 would disown you, for like an upstart he hates an old acquaintance. I am sorry to see those tears, child,* but I love you too well to flatter you.

POLLY.

Why have I a heart so constant? Cruel love!

Air 7. "Oh Waly, Waly, up the bank." 70

> Farewell, farewell, all hope of bliss!
> For Polly always must be thine.

Shall then my heart be never his,
Which never can again be mine?
Oh Love, you play a cruel part; 75
Thy shaft still festers in the wound.
You should reward a constant heart,
Since 'tis, alas, so seldom found!

TRAPES.

I tell you once again, Miss Polly, you must think
no more of him. You are like a child who is crying 80
after a butterfly that is hopping and fluttering
upon every flower in the field. There is not a
woman that comes in his way but he must have a
taste of; besides, there is no catching him. But my
dear girl, I hope you took care, at your leaving 85
England, to bring off wherewithal to support you.

POLLY.

Since he is lost, I am insensible of every other
misfortune. I brought indeed a sum of money with
me, but my chest was broke open at sea, and I am
now a wretched vagabond exposed to hunger and 90
want,* unless charity relieve me.

TRAPES.

Poor child! Your father and I have had great
dealings together, and I shall be grateful to his
memory. I will look upon you as my daughter. You
shall be with me. 95

POLLY.

As soon as I can have remittances from England,
I shall be able to acknowledge your goodness. I
have still five hundred pounds there which will be
returned to me upon demand, but I had rather
undertake any honest service that might afford me 100
a maintenance than be burthensome to my friends.

TRAPES.

Sure never anything happened so luckily! Madam
Ducat just now wants* a servant, and I know she will
take my recommendation. And one so tight and
handy as you must please her. Then too, her husband 105
is the civilest, best-bred man alive. You are now in her
house, and I won't leave it till I have settled you. Be
cheerful, my dear child,* for who knows but all these
misfortunes may turn to your advantage? You are in
a rich, creditable family, and I dare say your person 110
and behavior will soon make you a favorite. As to
Captain Macheath, you may now safely look upon
yourself as a widow, and who knows, if Madam

Ducat should tip off, what may happen? I shall
recommend you, Miss Polly, as a gentlewoman. 115

Air 8. "Oh Jenny, come tie me."

Despair is all folly;
Hence, melancholy.
Fortune attends you while youth is in flower.
By beauty's possession 120
Used with discretion,
Woman at all times hath joy in her power.

POLLY.

The service, madam, you offer me, makes me as
happy as I can be in my circumstance, and I accept
it with ten thousand obligations. 125

TRAPES.

Take a turn in the hall with my maid for a minute
or two, and I'll take care to settle all matters and
conditions for your reception. Be assured, Miss
Polly, I'll do my best for you.

Scene vi.

Trapes, Ducat.

TRAPES.

Mr. Ducat, sir, you may come in. I have had this
very* girl in my eye for you ever since you and I
were first acquainted, and to be plain with you,
sir, I have run great risks for her. I had many a
strategem, to be sure, to inveigle her away from 5
her relations! She, too, herself was exceeding
difficult. And I can assure you, to ruin a girl of
severe education is no small addition to the
pleasure of our fine gentlemen. I can be answerable
for it too, that you will have the first of her. I am 10
sure I could have disposed of her upon the same
account for at least a hundred guineas to an
alderman of London, and then too, I might have
had the disposal of her again as soon as she was
out of keeping.* But you are my friend, and I shall 15
not deal hard with you.

DUCAT.

But if I like her, I would agree upon terms
beforehand, for should I grow fond of her, I know
you have the conscience of other tradespeople and
would grow more imposing, and I love to be upon 20
a certainty.

TRAPES.

Sure you cannot think a hundred pistoles too much—I mean for me. I leave her wholly to your generosity. Why your* fine men, who never pay anybody else, pay their pimps and bawds well— always ready money. I ever dealt conscientiously and set the lowest price upon my ladies. When you see her, I am sure you will allow her to be as choice a piece of beauty as ever you laid eyes on. 25

DUCAT.

But dear Mrs.* Di, a hundred pistoles say you? Why, I could have half a dozen negro princesses for the price. 30

TRAPES.

But sure you cannot expect to buy a fine handsome Christian[10] at that rate. You are not used to see such goods on this side of the water. For the women, like the clothes, are all tarnished and half worn out before they are sent hither. Do but cast your eye upon her, sir; the door stands half open. See, yonder she trips in conversation with my maid Flimzy in the hall. 35

DUCAT.

Why truly I must own she is handsome. 40

TRAPES.

Bless me! You are no more moved by her than if she were your wife. Handsome! What a cold husband-like expression is that! Nay, there is no harm done. If I take her home, I don't question the making more money of her. She was never in anybody's house but your own since she was landed. She is pure as she was imported, without the least adulteration. 45

DUCAT.

I'll have her. I'll pay you down upon the nail. You shall leave her with me. Come, count your money, Mrs. Di. 50

TRAPES.

What a shape is there! She's of the finest growth.

DUCAT.

You make me mis-reckon. She even takes off my eyes from gold.

TRAPES.

What a curious pair of sparkling eyes! 55

---

10 Christian] synonymous with free (in contradistinction to slaves)

DUCAT.

As vivifying as the sun. I have paid you ten.

TRAPES.

What a racy flavor must breathe from those lips!

DUCAT.

I want* no provoking commendations. I'm in youth. I'm on fire! Twenty more makes it thirty, and this here makes it just fifty. 60

TRAPES.

What a most inviting complexion! How charming a color! In short, a fine woman has all the perfections of fine wine and is a cordial that is ten times as restorative.

DUCAT.

This fifty then makes it just the sum. So now, madam, you may deliver her up. 65

Scene vii.

Ducat, Trapes, Damaris.

DAMARIS.

Sir, sir, my mistress is just at the door. (*Exit*).

DUCAT.

Get you out of the way this moment, dear Mrs.* Di, for I would not have my wife see you. But don't stir out of the house till I am put in possession. I'll get rid of her immediately. 5

Exit Trapes.

Scene viii.

Ducat, Mrs. Ducat.

MRS. DUCAT.

I can never be out of the way for an hour or so, but you are with that filthy creature. If you were young, and I took liberties, you could not use me worse, you could not, you beastly fellow. Such usage might force the most virtuous woman to resentment. I don't see why the wives in this country should not put themselves upon as easy a foot as in England. In short, Mr. Ducat, if you behave yourself like an English husband, I will behave myself like an English wife.* 5 10

Air 9. "Red House."

I will have my humors, I'll please all senses,
I will not be stinted—in love or expenses.

I'll dress with profusion, I'll game without
  measure;
You shall have the business, I will have the   15
  pleasure:
    Thus every day I'll pass my life,
    My home shall be my least resort;
    For sure 'tis fitting that your wife
    Should copy the ladies of the Court.

DUCAT.
All these things, I know, are natural to the sex, my   20
dear. But husbands, like colts, are restive, and they
require a long time to break 'em. Besides, 'tis not
the fashion as yet for husbands to be governed in
this country. That tongue of yours, my dear, hath
not eloquence enough to persuade me out of my   25
reason. A woman's tongue, like a trumpet, only
serves to raise my courage.

Air 10. "Old Orpheus tickled," etc.

  When billows come breaking on the strand,
  The rocks are deaf and unshaken stand;   30
  Old oaks can defy the thunder's roar,
  And I can stand woman's tongue—that's more,
      With a twinkum, twankum, etc.
With that weapon, women, like pirates, are at war
with the whole world.[11] But I thought, my dear,   35
your pride would have kept you from being
jealous. 'Tis the whole business of my life to please
you, but wives are like children: the more they are
flattered and humored, the more perverse they are.
Here now have I been laying out my money, purely   40
to make you a present, and I have nothing but
these freaks and reproaches in return. You wanted
a maid, and I have bought you the handiest
creature.[12] She will indeed make a very creditable
servant.   45

MRS. DUCAT.
I will have none of your hussies about me. And
so, sir, you would make me your convenience, your
bawd. Out upon it!

---

11 at war … world] "A pyrate is *hostis humanis generis*" (the
     common enemy of mankind—Lat.), from Defoe's *General History of the Pyrates*.
12 bought … creature] A colonist could "buy" an inden-
     tured servant for a period of years.

DUCAT.
But I bought her on purpose for you, madam.

MRS. DUCAT.
For your own filthy inclinations, you mean. I won't   50
bear it. What, keep* an impudent strumpet under
my nose? Here's fine doings indeed!

DUCAT.
I will have the directions of my family.* 'Tis my
pleasure it shall be so. So madam, be satisfied.

Air 11. "Christchurch Bells."   55

  When a woman jealous grows,
    Farewell all peace of life!
MRS. DUCAT.
  But ere man roves, he should pay what he owes,
    And with her due content his wife.
DUCAT.
  'Tis man's the weaker sex to sway.   60

MRS. DUCAT.

   We too, whene'er we list, obey.

DUCAT.

    'Tis just and fit

    You should submit.

MRS. DUCAT.

   But sweet, kind husband—not today.

DUCAT.

   Let your clack be still. 65

MRS. DUCAT.

   Not till I have my will.

   If thus you reason slight,

   There's never an hour,

   While breath has power,

   But I will assert my right. 70

Would I had you in England, I should have all the
women there rise in arms in my defense. For the
honor and prerogative of the sex, they would not
suffer such a precedent of submission. And so Mr.
Ducat, I tell you once again, that you shall keep your 75
trollops out of the house, or I will not stay in it.

DUCAT.

Look'ee, Wife, you will be able to bring about
nothing by pouting and vapors. I have resolution
enough to withstand either obstinacy or stratagem.
And I will break this jealous spirit of yours before it 80
gets a head. And so my dear, I order that upon my
account you behave yourself to the girl as you ought.

MRS. DUCAT.

I wish you would behave yourself to your wife as
you ought, that is to say, with good manners and
compliance. And so sir, I leave you and your minx 85
together. I tell you once again that I would sooner
die upon the spot than not to be mistress in my
own house.

Exit in a passion.

Scene ix.

Ducat.

DUCAT.

If by these perverse humors I should be forced to
part with her and allow her a separate maintenance,* the thing is so common among people of
condition that it could not prove to my discredit.
Family divisions and matrimonial controversies are 5

a kind of proof of a man's riches, for the poor
people are happy in marriage out of necessity,
because they cannot afford to disagree.—Damaris,
saw you my wife?

Enter Damaris.

Is she in her own room? What said she? Which 10
way went she?

DAMARIS.

Bless me, I was perfectly frightened, she looked so
like a fury! Thank my stars, I never saw her look
so before in all my life, though mayhap you may
have seen her look so before a thousand times. Woe 15
be to the servants that fall in her way! I'm sure I'm
glad to be out of it.

Air 12. "Cheshire-rounds."

   When kings by their huffing

   Have blown up a squabble, 20

   All the charge and cuffing

   Light upon the rabble.

   Thus when man and wife

   By their mutual snubbing

   Kindle civil strife, 25

   Servants get the drubbing.

DUCAT.

I would have you, Damaris, have an eye upon your
mistress. You should have her good at heart and
inform me when she has any schemes afoot. It may
be the means to reconcile us. 30

DAMARIS.

She's wild, sir. There's no speaking to her. She's
flown into the garden! Mercy upon us all, say I!
How can you be so unreasonable to contradict a
woman, when you know we can't bear it?

DUCAT.

I depend upon you, Damaris, for intelligence. You 35
may observe her at a distance and, as soon as she
comes into her own room, bring me word. (*Aside.*)
There is the sweetest pleasure in the revenge that
I have now in my head! I'll this instant go and take
charge from Mrs.* Trapes.—Damaris, you know 40
your instructions.

Exit.

Scene x.

Damaris.

DAMARIS.

Sure all masters and mistresses, like politicians, judge of the conscience of mankind by their own and require treachery of their servants as a duty! I am employed by my master to watch my mistress and by my mistress to watch my master. Which party shall 5 I espouse? To be sure my mistress's. For in hers, jurisdiction and power, the common cause of the whole sex, are at stake. But my master I see is coming this way. I'll avoid him and make my observations.

Exit.

Scene xi.

Ducat, Polly.

DUCAT.

Be cheerful, Polly, for your good fortune hath thrown you into a family* where, if you rightly consult your own interest, as everybody nowadays does, you may make yourself perfectly easy. Those eyes of yours, Polly, are a sufficient fortune for any 5 woman, if she have but conduct and knew how to make the most of 'em.

POLLY.

As I am your servant, sir, my duty obliges me not to contradict you, and I must hear your flattery though 10 I know myself undeserving. But sure sir, in handsome women you must have observed that their hearts often oppose their interest, and beauty certainly has ruined more women than it has made happy.

Air 13. "The bush a boon traquair." 15

The crow or daw through all the year
    No fowler seeks to ruin,
But birds of voice or feather rare
    He's all day long pursuing.
Beware, fair maids, so 'scape the net 20
    That other beauties fell in,
For sure at heart was never yet
    So great a wretch as Helen!
If my lady, sir, will let me know my duty, gratitude
will make me study to please her. 25

DUCAT.

I have in mind a little conversation* with you, and I would not be interrupted. (*Bars the door.*)

POLLY.

I wish, sir, you would let me receive my lady's commands.

DUCAT.

And so Polly, by these downcast looks of yours you 30 would have me believe you don't know you are handsome and that you have no faith in your looking glass. Why, every pretty woman studies her face, and a looking glass to her is what a book is to a pedant: she is poring upon it all day long. In 35 troth, a man can never know how much love is in him by conversations* with his wife. A kiss on those lips would make me young again. (*Kisses her.*)

Air 14. "Bury Fair."

POLLY.

How can you be so teasing? 40

DUCAT.

    Love will excuse my fault.
How can you be so pleasing! (*Going to kiss her.*)

POLLY.

    I vow I'll not be naught.

DUCAT.

All maids I know at first resist. (*Struggling.*)
    A master may command. 45

POLLY.

You're monstrous rude, I'll not be kissed,
    Nay fie, let go my hand.

DUCAT.

'Tis foolish pride—

POLLY.

            'Tis vile, 'tis base
Poor innocence to wrong. 50

DUCAT.

I'll force you,

POLLY.

        Guard me from disgrace.
You find that virtue's strong. (*Pushing him away.*)
'Tis barbarous in you, sir, to take the occasion of
my necessities to insult me. 55

DUCAT.

Nay hussy, I'll give you money.

POLLY.

I despise it. No sir, though I was born and bred

in England, I can dare to be poor, which is the only thing nowadays men are ashamed of.

DUCAT.

I shall humble these saucy airs of yours, Mrs. 60
Minx. Is this language from a servant! From a slave!

POLLY.

Am I then betrayed and sold!

DUCAT.

Yes hussy, that you are, and as legally my property
as any woman is her husband's who sells herself
in marriage. 65

POLLY.

Climates that change constitutions have no effect
upon manners. What a profligate is that Trapes!

DUCAT.

Your fortune, your happiness depends upon your
compliance. What, proof against a bribe! Sure

hussy, you belie your country, or you must have 70
had a very vulgar education. 'Tis unnatural.

Air 15. "Bobbing Joan."

Maids like courtiers must be wooed;
Most by flattery are subdued;
Some capricious, coy* or nice,* 75
Out of pride protract the vice,
But they fall,
One and all,
When we bid up to their price.
Besides, hussy, your consent may make me your 80
slave; there's power to tempt you into the bargain.
You must be more than woman if you can stand
that too.

POLLY.

Sure you only mean to try me! But 'tis barbarous
to trifle with my distresses. 85

DUCAT.

I'll have none of these airs. 'Tis impertinent in a
servant to have scruples of any kind. I hire honor,
conscience, and all, for I will not be served by
halves. And so, to be plain with you, you obstinate
slut, you shall either contribute to my pleasure or 90
my profit, and if you refuse play in the
bedchamber, you shall go work in the fields among
the planters.[13] I hope now I have explained myself.

POLLY.

My freedom may be lost, but you cannot rob me
of my virtue and integrity, and whatever is my lot, 95
having that, I shall have the comfort of hope and
find pleasure in reflection.

Air 16. "A swain long tortured with disdain."

Can I or toil or hunger fear?
For love's a pain that's more severe. 100
The slave, with virtue in his breast,
Can wake in peace, and sweetly rest.
(*Aside.*) But love, when unhappy, the more
virtuous it is, the more it suffers.

DUCAT.

What noise is that? 105

DAMARIS. (*Without.*)

Sir, sir.

---

13 planters] slaves

DUCAT.

Step into the closet.* I'll call you out immediately
to present you to my wife. Don't let bashfulness
ruin your fortune. The next opportunity I hope
you will be better disposed.   110

Exit Polly.

DAMARIS.

Open the door, sir, this moment, this moment.

Scene xii.

Ducat, Damaris.

DUCAT.

What's the matter? Was anybody about to ravish
you? Is the house o'fire? Or my wife in a passion?

DAMARIS.

Oh sir, the whole country is in an uproar! The pirates
are all coming down upon us, and if they should raise
the militia,[14] you are an officer you know. I hope you   5
have time enough to fling up your commission.

Enter first footman.

FIRST FOOTMAN.

The neighbors, sir, are all frighted out of their wits;
they leave their houses and fly to yours for
protection. Where's my lady your wife? Heaven
grant they have not taken her!   10

DUCAT.

If they only took what one could spare.

FIRST FOOTMAN.

That's true, there were no great harm done.

DUCAT.

How are the muskets?

FIRST FOOTMAN.

Rusty, sir, all rusty and peaceable! For we never
clean 'em but against training day.   15

DAMARIS.

Then sir, your honor is safe, for now you have a
just excuse against fighting.

Enter second footman.

SECOND FOOTMAN.

The Indians, sir! with whom we are in alliance are all
in arms; there will be bloody work, to be sure. I hope
they will decide the matter before we can get ready.   20

Enter Mrs. Ducat.

MRS. DUCAT.

Oh dear husband! I'm frightened to death! What
will become of us all? I thought a punishment for
your wicked lewdness would light upon you at last.

DUCAT.

Presence of mind, my dear, is as necessary in
dangers as courage.   25

DAMARIS.

But you are too rich to have courage. You should
fight by deputy. 'Tis only for poor people to be
brave and desperate, who cannot afford to live.

Enter maids, etc. one after another.

FIRST MAID.

The pirates, sir, the pirates! Mercy upon us, what
will become of us poor helpless women!   30

SECOND MAID.

We shall all be ravished.

FIRST OLD WOMAN.

All be ravished!

SECOND OLD WOMAN.

Aye to be sure, we shall be ravished—all be
ravished!

FIRST OLD WOMAN.

But if fortune will have it so, patience is a virtue   35
and we must undergo it.

SECOND OLD WOMAN.

Aye for certain, bear it, Mrs. Damaris.

[Enter third footman.]

THIRD FOOTMAN.

A soldier, sir, from the Indian camp[15] desires
admittance. He's here, sir.

Enter Indian.

INDIAN.

I come, sir, to the English colony, with whom we   40

---

14 militia] Given the disproportion between owners and
slaves, militias were deemed necessary and participation
mandatory.

15 Indian] There was no indigenous community left on Jamaica.

are in alliance, from the mighty King Pohetohee, my lord and master, and address myself to you, as you are of the council, for succors. The pirates are ravaging and plundering the country, and we are now in arms, ready for battle, to oppose 'em.   45

DUCAT.

Does Macheath command the enemy?

INDIAN.

Report says he is dead. Above twelve moons are passed since we heard of him. Morano, a Negro villain, is their chief, who in rapine and barbarities is even equal to him.   50

DUCAT.

I shall inform the council, and we shall soon be ready to join you. So acquaint the king, your master.

Exit Indian.

Air 17. "March in Scipio.*"*[16]

(*To the men.*)
    Brave boys, prepare.
(*To [Mrs. Ducat].*)
    Ah! Cease, fond* wife, to cry.   55
SERVANT.
    For when the danger's near,
    We've time enough to fly.
MRS. DUCAT.
    How can you be disgraced?
    For wealth secures your fame.
SERVANT.
    The rich are always placed   60
    Above the sense of shame.
MRS. DUCAT.
    Let honor spur the slave
    To fight for fighting's sake.
DUCAT.
    But even the rich are brave
    When money is at stake.   65

Be satisfied, my dear, I shall be discreet. My servants here will take care that I be not over-rash, for their wages depend upon me. But before I go to council:—Come hither, Polly.

Enter Polly.

_____

16 *Scipio*] *Scipione*, opera by Händel in 1726

I entreat you, wife, to take her into your service   70
and use her civilly. Indeed my dear, your suspicions are very frivolous and unreasonable.

MRS. DUCAT.

I hate to have such a handsome wench about me. They are always so saucy!

DUCAT.

Women, by their jealousies, put one in mind of   75
doing that which otherwise we should never think of. Why, you are a proof, my dear, that a handsome woman may be honest.

MRS. DUCAT.

I find you can say a civil thing to me still.

DUCAT.

Affairs, you see, call me hence. And so I leave her   80
under your protection.

[Exeunt Ducat et alii; manent Mrs. Ducat, Polly, Damaris.]

Scene xiii.

MRS. DUCAT.

Away, into the other room again. When I want you, I'll call you.

Exit Polly.

Well Damaris, to be sure you have observed all that has passed. I will know all. I'm sure she's a hussy.

DAMARIS.

Nay madam, I can't say so much. But—   5

MRS. DUCAT.

But what?

DAMARIS.

I hate to make mischief.

Air 18. "Jig-it-o'foot."

    Better to doubt
    All that's doing   10
    Than to find out
    Proofs of ruin.
What servants hear and see
    Should they tattle,
Marriage all day would be   15
    Feuds and battle.

A servant's legs and hands should be under your command, but for the sake of quiet, you should leave their tongues to their own discretion.

MRS. DUCAT.

I vow, Damaris, I will know it. 20

DAMARIS.

To be sure, madam, the door was bolted, and I could only listen. There was a sort of bustle between 'em, that's certain. What passed I know not. But the noise they made, to my thinking, did not sound very honest.* 25

MRS. DUCAT.

Noises that did not sound very honest, said you?

DAMARIS.

Nay madam, I am a maid and have no experience. If you had heard them, you would have been a better judge of the matter.

MRS. DUCAT.

An impudent slut! I'll have her before me. If she be not a thorough profligate, I shall make a discovery by her behavior. Go call her to me. 30

Exit Damaris and returns.

Scene xiv.

Mrs. Ducat. Damaris. Polly.

MRS. DUCAT.

In my own house! Before my face! I'll have you sent to the house of correction, strumpet.—By that over-honest look, I guess her to be a horrid jade, a mere* hypocrite that is perfectly whitewashed with inno-cence. My blood rises at the sight of all strumpets, for they are smugglers in love, that ruin us fair traders in matrimony.—Look upon me, Mrs.* Brazen.—She has no feeling of shame. She is so used to impudence that she has not a blush within her.— Do you know, madam, that I am Mr. Ducat's wife? 10 5

POLLY.

As your servant, madam, I think myself happy.

MRS. DUCAT.

You know Mr. Ducat, I suppose.—She has beauty enough to make any woman alive hate her.

Air 19. Trumpet minuet.

Abroad after misses most husbands will roam, 15
Though sure they find woman sufficient at home.
To be nosed¹⁷ by a strumpet! Hence, hussy, you'd
best.

---

17 nosed] disdained, looked down (the nose) upon

Would he give me my due, I would give her the rest.
I vow I had rather have a thief in my house. For to be sure, she is that besides. 20

POLLY.

If you were acquainted with my misfortunes, madam, you could not insult me.

MRS. DUCAT.

What does the wench mean?

DAMARIS.

There's not one of these common creatures but, like common beggars, hath a moving story at her finger's ends, which they tell over, when they are maudlin, to their lovers. I had a sweetheart, madam, who was a rake, and I know their ways very well, by hearsay. 25

POLLY.

What villains are hypocrites! For they rob those of relief who are in real distress. I know what it is to be unhappy in marriage. 30

MRS. DUCAT.

Married!

POLLY.

Unhappily.

MRS. DUCAT.

When, where, to whom?

POLLY.

If woman can have faith in woman, may my words find belief. Protestations are to be suspected, so I shall use none. If truth can prevail, I know you will pity me. 35

MRS. DUCAT.

Her manner and behavior are so particular, that is to say, so sincere, that I must hear her story.— Unhappily married! That is a misfortune not to be remedied. 40

POLLY.

A constant woman hath but one chance to be happy; an inconstant woman, though she hath no chance to be very happy, can never be very unhappy. 45

DAMARIS.

Believe me, Mrs. Polly, as to pleasures of all sorts, 'tis a much more agreeable way to be inconstant.

Air 20. "Polwart on the green."

Love now is naught but art,
'Tis who can juggle best; 50
To all men seem to give your heart,

But keep it in your breast.
What gain and pleasure do we find,
  Who change whene'er we list!
The mill that turns with every wind   55
  Must bring the owner grist.

POLLY.

My case, madam, may in these times be looked
upon as singular, for I married a man only because
I loved him. For this I was looked upon as a fool by
all my acquaintance; I was used inhumanly by my   60
father and mother; and to complete my misfortunes,
my husband, by his wild behavior incurred the
sentence of the law and was separated from me by
banishment. Being informed he was in this country,
upon the death of my father and mother, with most   65
of my small fortune, I came here to seek him.

MRS. DUCAT.

But how then fell you into the hands of that
consummate bawd, Trapes?

POLLY.

In my voyage, madam, I was robbed of all I had.
Upon my landing in a strange country, and in
want,* I was found out by this inhuman woman   70
who had been an acquaintance of my father's. She
offered me at first the civilities of her own house.
When she was informed of my necessities, she
proposed to me the service of a lady, of which I
readily accepted. 'Twas under that pretence that   75
she treacherously sold me to your husband as a
mistress. This, madam, is in short the whole truth.
I fling myself at your feet for protection. By
relieving me, you make yourself easy.

MRS. DUCAT.

What is it you propose?   80

POLLY.

In conniving at my escape, you save me from your
husband's worrying me with threats and violence
and at the same time quiet your own fears and
jealousies. If it is ever in my power, madam, with
gratitude I will repay you my ransom.   85

DAMARIS.

Besides madam, you will effectually revenge
yourself upon your husband, for the loss of the
money he paid for her will touch him to the quick.

MRS. DUCAT.

But have you considered what you request? We are
invaded by the pirates, the Indians are in arms, the   90
whole country is in commotion, and you will
everywhere be exposed to danger.

DAMARIS.

Get rid of her at any rate. For such is the vanity
of man, that when once he has begun with a
woman, out of pride he will insist upon his point.   95

POLLY.

In staying with you, madam, I make two people
unhappy. And I choose to bear my own
misfortunes without being the cause of another's.

MRS. DUCAT.

If I let her escape before my husband's return, he
will imagine she got off by the favor of this bustle   100
and confusion.

POLLY.

May Heaven reward your charity.

MRS. DUCAT.

A woman so young and handsome must be

exposed to continual dangers. I have a suit of
clothes by me of my nephew's, who is dead. In a   105
man's habit you will run fewer risks. I'll assist you,
too, for the present with some money, and as a
traveller, you may with greater safety make
inquiries after your husband.

POLLY.
   How shall I ever make a return for so much   110
goodness?

MRS. DUCAT.
   May love reward your constancy. As for that
perfidious monster Trapes, I will deliver her into
the hands of the magistrate.—Come Damaris, let
this instant equip her for her adventures.   115

DAMARIS.
   When she is out of the house, without doubt,
madam, you will be more easy. And I wish she may
be so too.

POLLY.
   May virtue be my protection, for I feel within me
hope, cheerfulness, and resolution.   120

Air 21. "St. Martin's Lane."

      As pilgrims through devotion
   To some shrine pursue their way,
   They tempt the raging ocean
      And through deserts stray.   125
   With zeal their hope desiring,
   The saint their breast inspiring
      With cheerful air,
      Devoid of fear,
      They every danger bear.   130
   Thus equal zeal possessing,
   I seek my only blessing.
   Oh Love, my honest vow regard!
      My truth protect,
      My steps direct,   135
      His flight detect,
   A faithful wife reward.

Exeunt.

   Act II, scene i. The view of an Indian country.

Polly in boy's clothes.

Air 22. "La Villanella."

POLLY.
   Why did you spare him
   O'er seas to bear him
Far from his home and constant bride?
   When Papa peached him,   5
   If death had reached him,
I then had only sighed, wept, and died!
If my directions are right, I cannot be far from the
village. With the habit I must put on the courage
and resolution of a man, for I am everywhere   10
surrounded with dangers. By all I can learn of these
pirates, my dear Macheath is not of the crew.
Perhaps I may hear of him among the slaves of the
next plantation. How sultry is the day! The cool
of this shade will refresh me. I am jaded, too, with   15
reflection. How restless is love!

Music, two or three bars of the Dead March.

My imagination follows him everywhere. Would
my feet were as swift. The world, then, could not
hide him from me.   20

Two or three bars more.

Yet even thought is now bewildered in pursuing
him.

Two or three bars more.

I'm tired, I'm faint.

The symphony.

Air 23. "Dead March in Coriolanus."[18]

      Sleep, oh sleep,   25
   With thy rod of incantation,
   Charm my imagination.
   Then, only then, I cease to weep.
      By thy power,
   The virgin, by time o'ertaken,   30
   For years forlorn, forsaken,
   Enjoys the happy hour.
      What's to sleep?
   'Tis a visionary blessing,
   A dream that's past expressing.   35

18 Dead March in Coriolanus] concludes Shakespeare's play
   as Coriolanus's body is carried off

Our utmost wish possessing,
   So may I always keep. (*Falls asleep.*)

Scene ii.

Capstern, Hacker, Culverin, Laguerre, Cutlass, Polly
asleep in a distant part of the stage.

HACKER.
  We shall find but a cool reception from Morano,
  if we return without either booty or intelligence.
CULVERIN.
  A man of invention hath always intelligence ready.
  I hope we are not exempted from the privilege of
  travellers.   5
CAPSTERN.
  If we had got booty, you know we had resolved to
  agree in a lie. And, gentlemen, we will not have
  our dilligence and duty called in question for that
  which every common servant has at his finger's end
  for his justification.   10
LAGUERRE.
  Alack gentlemen, we are not such bunglers in love
  or politics, but we must know that either to get
  favor or keep it, no man ever speaks what he thinks
  but what is convenient.

Air 24. "Three Sheepskins."   15

CUTLASS.
  Of all the sins that are money-supplying,
  Consider the world, 'tis past all denying,
    With all sorts,
     In towns or courts,
  The richest sin is lying.   20
CULVERIN.
  Fatigue, gentlemen, should have refreshment. No
  man is required to do more than his duty. Let us
  repose ourselves awhile. A sup or two of our cag[19]
  would quicken invention.

They sit and drink.

ALL.
  Agreed.   25
HACKER.
  I had always a genius for ambition. Birth and

---

[19] cag] keg

education cannot keep it under. Our profession is
great, brothers. What can be more heroic than to
have declared war with the whole world?
CULVERIN.
'Tis a pleasure to me to recollect times past and to 30
observe by what steps a genius will push his fortune.
HACKER.
Now as to me, brothers, mark you me. After I had
rubbed through my youth with variety of
adventures, I was preferred to be footman to an
eminent gamester, where, after having improved 35
myself by his manners and conversation, I left him,
betook myself to his politer profession, and cheated
like a gentleman. For some time I kept a faro bank
with success, but unluckily in a drunken bout was
stripped by a more expert brother of the trade. I 40
was now, as 'tis common with us upon these
occasions, forced to have recourse to the highway
for a recruit to set me up. But making the

experiment once too often, I was tried and received sentence but got off for transportation. Which hath made me the man I am.

LAGUERRE.

From a footman I grew to be a pimp to a man of quality.* Considering I was for some time in that employment, I look upon myself as particularly unlucky that I then missed making my fortune. But to give him his due, only his death could have prevented it. Upon this, I betook myself to another service, where my wages not being sufficient for my pleasures, I robbed my master and retired to visit foreign parts.

CAPSTERN.

Now you must know, I was a drawer of one of the fashionable taverns and of consequence was daily in the politest conversations. Though I say it, nobody was better bred. I often cheated my master and, as a dutiful servant, now and then cheated for him. I had always my gallantries with the ladies that the lords and gentlemen brought to our house. I was ambitious too of a gentleman's profession and turned gamester. Though I had great skill and no scruples, my play would not support my extravagancies. So that now and then I was forced to rob with pistols, too. So I also owe my rank in the world to transportation.

CULVERIN.

Our chief, Morano, brothers, had never been the man he is had he not been trained up in England. He has told me that from his infancy he was the favorite page of a lady. He had a genius too above service and, like us, ran into higher life. And indeed, in manners and conversation, though he is black, nobody has more the air of a great man.*

HACKER.

He is too much attached to his pleasures. That mistress of his is a clog* to his ambition. She's an arrant Cleopatra.

LAGUERRE.

If it were not for her, the Indies would be our own.

Air 25. "Rigadoon."

> By women won,
> We're all undone,
> Each wench hath a siren's charms.

The lover's deeds
Are good or ill,
As whim succeeds
In woman's will:
Resolution is lulled in her arms.

HACKER.

A man in love is no more to be depended on than a man in liquor, for he is out of himself.

Air 26. "Ton humeur est Catharine."[20]

> Woman's like the flatt'ring ocean:
> Who her pathless ways can find?
> Every blast directs her motion:
> Now she's angry, now she's kind.*
> What a fool's the vent'rous lover,
> Whirled and tossed by every wind!
> Can the bark the port recover
> When the silly pilot's blind?

HACKER.

A good horse is never turned loose among mares till all his good deeds are over. And really your heroes should be served the same way, for after they take to women, they have no good deeds to come. That inviegling Gypsy, brothers, must be hauled from him by force. And then—the Kingdom of Mexico shall be mine. My lot shall be the Kingdom of Mexico.

CAPSTERN.

Who talks of Mexico?

All rise.

I'll never give it up. If you outlive me, brother, and I die without heirs, I'll leave it to you for a legacy. I hope now you are satisfied. I have set my heart upon it, and nobody shall dispute it with me.

LAGUERRE.

The island of Cuba, methinks, brother, might satisfy any reasonable man.

CULVERIN.

That I had allotted for you. Mexico shall not be parted with without my consent. Captain Morano, to be sure, will choose Peru. That's the country of gold, and all your great men love gold. Mexico hath only silver, nothing but silver. Governor of

---

20 *Ton humeur est Catharine*] Catharine is thy fancy (Fr.).

Cartegena,[21] brother, is a pretty snug employment. That I shall not dispute with you. 120

CAPSTERN.

Death, sir, I shall not part with Mexico so easily.

HACKER.

Nor I.

CULVERIN.

Nor I.

LAGUERRE.

Nor I. 125

CULVERIN.

Nor I.

HACKER.

Draw then, and let the survivor take it.

They fight.

POLLY.

Bless me, what noise was that! Clashing of swords and fighting! Which way shall I fly? How shall I escape? 130

CAPSTERN.

Hold, hold, gentlemen, let us decide our pretensions some other time. I see booty. A prisoner. Let us seize him.

CULVERIN.

From him we will extort both ransom and intelligence. 135

POLLY.

Spare my life, gentlemen. If you are the men I take you for, I sought you to share your fortunes.

HACKER.

Why, who do you take us for, friend?

POLLY.

For those brave spirits, those Alexanders, that shall soon by conquest be in possession of the Indies. 140

LAGUERRE.

A mettled young fellow.

CAPSTERN.

He speaks with respect, too, and gives us our titles.

CULVERIN.

Have you heard of Captain Morano?

POLLY.

I came hither in mere* ambition to serve under him. 145

Air 27. "Ye nymphs and sylvan gods."

I hate those coward tribes,
Who by mean and sneaking bribes,
By tricks and disguise,
By flattery and lies, 150
To power and grandeur rise.
    Like heroes of old,
    You are greatly bold,
The sword your cause supports.
    Untaught to fawn, 155
    You ne'er were drawn
    Your truth to pawn
    Among the spawn
Who practice the frauds of courts.

I would willingly choose a more honorable way of making a fortune. 160

HACKER.

The youth speaks well. Can you inform us, my lad, of the disposition of the enemy? Have the Indians joined the factory?[22] We should advance toward 'em immediately. Who knows but they may side with us? Mayhap they may like our tyranny better. 165

POLLY.

I am a stranger, gentlemen, and entirely ignorant of the affairs of this country. But in the most desperate undertaking, I am ready to risk your fortunes.

HACKER.

Who and what are you, friend? 170

POLLY.

A young fellow who has genteelly run out his fortune with a spirit and would now with more spirit retrieve it.

CULVERIN.

The lad may be of service. Let us bring him before Morano and leave him to his disposal. 175

POLLY.

Gentlemen, I thank you.

Air 28. Minuet.

---

21 Cartagena] in the 17th century site of a major fortress and a major port for the exportation of gold and the importation of slaves

22 factory] colonial center where factors, agents for absentee owners, did business

CULVERIN.

> Cheer up my lads, let us push on the fray,
> For battles, like women, are lost by delay.
> Let us seize victory while in our power. 180
> Alike war and love have their critical hour.
> > Our hearts bold and steady
> > Should always be ready,
> So think war a widow, a kingdom the dower.

Exeunt.

> Scene iii. Another country prospect.

Morano. Jenny.

MORANO.

Sure, hussy, you have more ambition and more vanity than to be serious in persuading me to quit my conquests. Where is the woman who is not fond of title? And one bold step more may make you a queen, you Gypsy. Think of that. 5

Air 29. "Mirleton."[23]

> When I'm great and flush of treasure,
> > Checked by neither fear or shame,
> You shall tread a round of pleasure,
> > Morning, noon, and night the same. 10
> > > With a mirleton, etc.
> Like a city wife or beauty
> > You shall flutter life away,
> And shall know no other duty
> > But to dress, eat, drink, and play. 15
> > > With a mirleton, etc.

When you are queen, Jenny, you shall keep your coach and six and shall game as deep as you please. So, there's the two chief ends of woman's ambition satisfied. 20

*Air 30. "Sawny was tall and of noble race."**

> Shall I not be bold when honor calls?
> You've a heart that would upbraid me then.

JENNY.

> But ah, I fear, if my hero falls,
> Thy Jenny shall ne'er know pleasure again. 25

MORANO.

> To deck their wives fond tradesmen cheat;
> I conquer but to make thee great.

JENNY.

> But if my hero falls, ah then
> Thy Jenny shall ne'er know pleasure again!

MORANO.

Insinuating creature! But you must own, Jenny, 30 you have had convincing proofs of my fondness, and if you were reasonable in your love, you should have some regard to my honor as well as my person.

JENNY.

Have I ever betrayed you since you took me to 35 yourself? That's what few women can say who ever were trusted.

MORANO.

In love, Jenny, you cannot outdo me. Was it not entirely for you that I disguised myself as a black to screen myself from women who laid claim to 40 me wherever I went? Is not the rumor of my death,

---

23 Mirleton] probably mirliton, a voice-activated musical instrument (e.g. kazoo)

which I purposely spread, credited through the whole country? Macheath is dead to all the world but you. Not one of the crew have the least suspicion of me. 45

JENNY.

But dear Captain, you would not, sure, persuade me that I have all of you. For though women cannot claim you, you now and then lay claim to other women. But my jealousy was never teasing or vexatious. You will pardon me, my dear. 50

MORANO.

Now you are silly, Jenny. Prithee—poh! Nature, girl, is not to be corrected at once. What do you propose? What would you have me do? Speak out, let me know your mind.

JENNY.

Know when you are well. 55

MORANO.

Explain yourself; speak your sentiments freely.

JENNY.

You have a competence in your power. Rob the crew and steal off to England. Believe me, Captain, you will be rich enough to be respected by your neighbors. 60

MORANO.

Your opinion of me startles me. For I never in my life was treacherous but to women, and you know men of the nicest* punctilio make nothing of that.

JENNY.

Look round among all the snug fortunes that are made, and you will find most of 'em were secured 65 by a judicious retreat. Why will you bar yourself from the customs of the times?

Air 31. "Northern Nancy."

How many men have found the skill
    Of power and wealth acquiring? 70
But sure there's a time to stint the will,
    And the judgment is in retiring.
        For to be displaced,
        For to be disgraced,
Is the end of too high aspiring. 75

Enter sailor.

SAILOR.

Sir, Lieutenant Vanderbluff wants to speak with

you. And he hopes your honor will give him the hearing. (*Exit.*)

MORANO.

Leave me, Jenny, for a few minutes. Perhaps he would speak with me in private. 80

JENNY.

Think of my advice before it is too late. By this kiss I beg it of you.

Exit.

Scene iv.

Morano, Vanderbluff.

VANDERBLUFF.

For shame, Captain, what, hampered in the arms of a woman when your honor and glory are all at stake! While a man is grappling with these jill-flirts* (pardon the expression, Captain), he runs his reason aground, and there must be a woundy[24] deal of labor to set it afloat again. 5

Air 32. "Amante fuggite cadente beltà."[25]

Fine women are devils, complete in their way;
They always are roving and cruising for prey.
When we flounce on their hook, their views they 10
    obtain;
Like those too their pleasure is giving us pain.

Excuse my plain speaking, Captain: a boatswain must swear in a storm, and a man must speak plain when he sees foul weather ahead of us.

MORANO.

D'you think me like the wheatear, only fit for 15 sunshine, who cannot bear the least cloud over him? No Vanderbluff, I have a heart that can face a tempest of dangers. Your blustering will but make me obstinate. You seem frightened, Lieutenant.

VANDERBLUFF.

From anybody but you, that speech should have 20 had another-guess answer than words. Death, Captain, are not the Indies in dispute? An hour's delay may make their hands too many for us. Give the word, Captain, this hand shall take the Indian

---

24 woundy] exceeding
25 *Amante fuggite cadente beltà*] Lovers, avoid declining beauty (It.).

king prisoner and keelhaul him afterwards till I 25
make him discover* his gold. I have known you
eager to venture your life for a less prize.

MORANO.

Are Hacker, Culverin, Capstern, Laguerre, and the
rest, whom we sent out for intelligence, returned,
that you are under this immediate alarm? 30

VANDERBLUFF.

No sir, but from the top of yon hill, I myself saw
the enemy putting themselves in order of battle.

MORANO.

But we have nothing at all to apprehend, for we
have still a safe retreat to our ships.

VANDERBLUFF.

To our woman, you mean. Furies! You talk like 35

one. If our captain is bewitched, shall we be
bedeviled and lose the footing we have got?
(*Draws.*)

MORANO.

Take care, Lieutenant. This language may provoke
me. I fear no man. I fear nothing, and that you 40
know. Put up your cutlass, Lieutenant, for I shall
not ruin our cause by a private quarrel.*

VANDERBLUFF.

Noble Captain, I ask pardon.

MORANO.

A brave man should be cool till action, Lieutenant;
when danger presses us, I am always ready. Be 45
satisfied, I'll take my leave of my wife and then
take the command.

VANDERBLUFF.

That's what you can never do till you have her
leave. She is but just gone from you, sir. See her
not; hear her not; the breath of a woman has ever 50
proved a contrary wind to great actions.

MORANO.

I tell you I will see her. I have got rid of many a
woman in my time, and you may trust me—

VANDERBLUFF.

With any woman but her. The husband that is
governed is the only man that never finds out that 55
he is so.

MORANO.

This then, Lieutenant, shall try my resolution. In
the meantime, send out parties and scouts to
observe the motions of the Indians.

Air 33. "Since all the world's turned upside down." 60

Though different passions rage by turns
    Within my breast fermenting,
Now blazes love, now honor burns;
    I'm here, I'm there consenting.
I'll each obey, so keep my oath, 65
    That oath by which I won her;
With truth and steadiness in both,
    I'll act like a man of honor.

Doubt me not, Lieutenant. But I'll now go with
you to give the necessary commands and after that 70
return to take my leave before the battle.

Scene v.

Morano, Vanderbluff, Jenny, Capstern, Culverin,
Hacker, Laguerre, Polly.

JENNY.

Hacker, sir, and the rest of the party are returned with
a prisoner. Perhaps from him you may learn some
intelligence that may be useful. See, here they are.
(*Aside.*) A clever, sprightly young fellow! I like him.

VANDERBLUFF.

What cheer, my lads? Has Fortune sent you a prize?   5

JENNY.

He seems some rich planter's son.

VANDERBLUFF.

In the common practice of commerce you should
never slip an opportunity, and for his ransom, no
doubt, there will be room for comfortable
extortion.   10

MORANO.

Hath he informed you of anything that may be of
service? Where picked you him up? Whence is he?

HACKER.

We found him upon the road. He is a stranger, it
seems, in these parts. And as our heroes generally
set out, extravagance, gaming, and debauchery   15
have qualified him for a brave* man.

MORANO.

What are you, friend?

POLLY.

A young fellow who hath been robbed by the world.
And I came on purpose to join you, to rob the world
by way of retaliation. An open war with the whole   20
world is brave and honorable. I hate the clandestine,
pilfering war that is practised among friends and
neighbors in civil societies. I would serve, sir.

Air 34. "Hunt the Squirrel."

The world is always jarring;   25
   This is pursuing
   T'other man's ruin;
Friends with friends are warring
   In a false cowardly way.
Spurred on by emulations,   30
   Tongues are engaging:
   Calumny, raging,
Murthers reputations;

Envy keeps up the fray.
Thus with burning hate   35
Each, returning hate,
Wounds and robs his friends.
   In civil life
   Each man and wife
Squabble for selfish ends.   40

JENNY. (*Aside.*)

He really is a mighty pretty man.

VANDERBLUFF.

The lad promises well and has just notions of the
world.

MORANO.

Whatever other great men do, I love to encourage
merit. The youth pleases me, and if he answers in   45
action (D'you hear me, my lad?), your fortune is
made.—Now Lieutenant Vanderbluff, I am for you.

VANDERBLUFF.

Discipline must not be neglected.

MORANO.

When everything is settled, my dear Jenny, I will
return to take my leave.—After that, young   50
gentleman, I shall try your mettle.—In the
meantime, Jenny, I leave you to sift him with
farther questions. He has lived in the world, you
find, and may have learnt to be treacherous.
[*Exeunt with other pirates.*]   55

Scene vi.

Jenny. Polly.

JENNY.

How many women have you ever ruined, young
gentleman?

POLLY.

I have been ruined by women, madam. But I
think, indeed, a man's fortune cannot be more
honorably disposed of, for those have always a kind   5
of claim to their protection who have been ruined
in their service.

JENNY.

Were you ever in love?

POLLY.

With the sex.

JENNY.

Had you never a woman in love with you?   10

POLLY.

All the women that I ever knew were mercenary.

JENNY.

But sure you cannot think all women so.

POLLY.

Why not as well as all men? The manners of courts are catching.

JENNY.

If you have found only such usage, a generous 15
woman can the more oblige you. Why so bashful, young spark? You don't look as if you would revenge yourself on the sex.

POLLY.

I lost my impudence with my fortune. Poverty keeps down assurance. 20

JENNY.

I am a plain-spoken woman, as you may find, and I own I like you. And let me tell you, to be my favorite may be your best step to preferment.

Air 35. "Young Damon once the loveliest swain."

In love and life, the present use. 25
One hour we grant, the next refuse.
    Who then would risk a nay?
Were lovers wise, they would be kind,*
And in our eyes the moment find,
    For only then they may. 30

Like other women I shall run to extremes. If you won't make me love you, I shall hate you. There never was a man of true courage who was a coward in love. Sure you are not afraid of me, stripling. (*Taking Polly by the hand.*) 35

POLLY.

I know you only rally me. Respect, madam, keeps me in awe.

JENNY.

By your expression and behavior, one would think I were your wife. If so, I may make use of her freedoms and do what I please without shame or 40
restraint. (*Kisses her.*) Such raillery as this, my dear, requires replication.

POLLY.

You'll pardon me then, madam. (*Kisses her.*)

JENNY.

What, my cheek! Let me die, if by your kiss I should not take you for my brother or my father. 45

POLLY. (*Aside.*)

I must put on more assurance, or I shall be discovered.—Nay then, madam, if a woman will allow me liberties, they are never flung away upon me. If I am too rude— (*Kisses her.*)

JENNY.

A woman never pardons the contrary fault. 50

Air 36. "Catharine Ogye."

We never blame the forward swain,
    Who puts us to the trial.

POLLY.

I know you first would give me pain,
    Then balk me with denial. 55

JENNY.

What mean we then by being tried?

POLLY.

With scorn and slight to use us.
Most beauties, to indulge their pride,
    Seem kind* but to refuse us.

JENNY.

Come then, my dear, let us take a turn in yonder   60
grove. A woman never shows her pride before
witnesses.

POLLY. (*Aside*.)

How shall I get rid of this affair?—Morano may
surprise us.

JENNY.

That is more a wife's concern. Consider, young   65
man, if I have put myself in your power, you are
in mine.

POLLY.

We may have more easy and safe opportunities.
Besides, I know, madam, you are not serious.

JENNY.

To a man who loses one opportunity, we never   70
grant a second.—Excuses! Consideration! He hath
not a spark of love in him. I must be his
aversion!—Go, monster, I hate you, and you shall
find I can be revenged.

Air 37. "Roger a Coverly."

My heart is by love forsaken,   75
    I feel the tempest growing.
A fury the place hath taken,
    I rage, I burn, I'm glowing.
Though Cupid's arrows are erring,
    Our indifference may secure ye;   80
When woman's revenge is stirring,
    You cannot escape that fury.
I could bear your excuses, but those looks of
indifference kill me.

Scene vii.

Jenny, Polly, Morano.

JENNY.

Sure never was such insolence! How could you leave
me with this bawdy-house bully? For if he had been
bred a page, he must have made his fortune. If I had
given him the least encouragement, it would not
have provoked me. Odious creature!   5

MORANO.

What-a-vengeance is the matter?

JENNY.

Only an attempt upon your wife. So ripe an
assurance! He must have sucked in impudence
from his mother!

MORANO.

An act of friendship only. He meant to push his   10
fortune with the husband. 'Tis the way of the
Town,* my dear.

Air 38. "Bacchus m'a dit."[26]

    By halves no friend
Now seeks to do you pleasure.   15
    Their help they lend
In every part of life:
    If husbands part,
The friend hath always leisure;
    Then all his heart   20
Is bent to please the wife.

JENNY.

I hate you for being so little jealous.

MORANO.

Sure Jenny, you know the way of the world better
than to be surprised at a thing of this kind. 'Tis a
civility that all you fine ladies expect, and upon the   25
like occasion, I could not have answered for myself.
I own, I have a sort of partiality to impudence. Perhaps, too, his views might be honorable. If I had been
killed in battle, 'tis good to be beforehand. You know
'tis a way often practised to make sure of a widow.   30

JENNY.

If I find you so easy in these affairs, you may make
my virtue less obstinate.

Air 39. "Health to Betty."

If husbands sit unsteady,
Most wives for freaks are ready.   35
    Neglect the rein,
    The steed again
Grows skittish, wild, and heady.
Your behavior forces me to say what my love for
you will never let me put in practice. You are too   40
safe, too secure, to think of pleasing me.

―――――――――

26 *Bacchus m'a dit*] Bacchus said to me (Fr.)

MORANO.

Though I like impudence, yet 'tis not so agreeable when put in practice upon my own wife, and jesting apart, young fellow, if I ever catch you thinking this way again, a cat-o'-nine-tails shall cool your courage.   45

Scene viii.

Morano, Jenny, Polly, Vanderbluff, Capstern, Laguerre, etc. with Cawwawkee, prisoner.

VANDERBLUFF.

The party, Captain, is returned with success. After a short skirmish, the Indian prince Cawwawkee here was made prisoner, and we want* your orders for his disposal.

MORANO.

Are all our troops ready and under arms?   5

VANDERBLUFF.

They wait but for your command. Our numbers are strong. All the ships' crews are drawn out, and the slaves that have deserted to us from the plantations are all brave, determined fellows, who must behave themselves well.   10

MORANO.

Look'ee, Lieutenant, the trussing up of this prince, in my opinion, would strike terror among the enemy. Besides, dead men can do no mischief. Let a gibbet be set up, and swing him off between the armies before the onset.   15

VANDERBLUFF.

By your leave, Captain, my advice blows directly contrary. Whatever may be done hereafter, I am for putting him first of all upon examination. The Indians, to be sure, have hid their treasures, and we shall want a guide to show us the best plunder.   20

MORANO.

The counsel is good. I will extort intelligence from him. Bring me word when the enemy are in motion, and that instant I'll put myself at your head.

Exit sailor.

Do you know me, Prince?   25

CAWWAWKEE.

As a man of injustice I know you, who covets and invades the properties of another.

MORANO.

Do you know my power?

CAWWAWKEE.

I fear it not.

MORANO.

Do you know your danger?   30

CAWWAWKEE.

I am prepared to meet it.

Air 40. 'Cap de Bonne Espérance.'[27]

The body of the brave may be taken,
    If chance bring on our adverse hour,
But the noble soul is unshaken,   35
    For that still* is in our power:
'Tis a rock whose firm foundation
    Mocks the waves of perturbation;
'Tis a never-dying ray,
    Brighter in our evil day.   40

MORANO.

Mere downright barbarians, you see, Lieutenant. They have our notional honor still in practice among 'em.

VANDERBLUFF.

We must beat civilizing into 'em to make 'em capable of common society and common   45
conversation.

MORANO.

Stubborn Prince, mark me well: Know you, I say, that your life is in my power?

CAWWAWKEE.

I know, too, that my virtue is in my own.

MORANO.

Not a mule or an old, out-of-fashioned   50
philosopher could be more obstinate. Can you feel pain?

CAWWAWKEE.

I can bear it.

MORANO.

I shall try you.

CAWWAWKEE.

I speak truth. I never affirm but what I know.   55

MORANO.

In what condition are your troops? What numbers

---

27 *Cap de Bonne Espérance*] Cape of Good Hope (Fr.)

have you? How are they disposed? Act reasonably and openly, and you shall find protection.

CAWWAWKEE.

What, betray my friends! I am no coward, European. 60

MORANO.

Torture shall make you squeak.

CAWWAWKEE.

I have resolution, and pain shall neither make me lie or betray. I tell thee once more, European: I am no coward.

VANDERBLUFF.

What, neither cheat nor be cheated! There is no 65 having either commerce or correspondence with these creatures.

JENNY.

We have reason to be thankful for our good education. How ignorant is mankind without it!

CAPSTERN.

I wonder to hear the brute speak. 70

LAGUERRE.

They would make a show of him in England.

JENNY.

Poh, they would only take him for a fool.

CAPSTERN.

But how can you expect anything else from a creature who hath never seen a civilized country? Which way should he know mankind? 75

JENNY.

Since they are made like us, to be sure, were they in England, they might be taught.

LAGUERRE.

Why we see country gentlemen grow into courtiers, and country gentlewomen, with a little polishing of the Town, in a few months become fine ladies. 80

JENNY.

Without doubt, education and example can do much.

POLLY. (Aside.)

How happy are these savages! Who would not wish to be in such ignorance.

MORANO.

Have done, I beg you, with your musty reflections. 85 You but interrupt the examination.—You have treasures, you have gold and silver among you, I suppose.

CAWWAWKEE.

Better it had been for us if that shining earth had never been brought to light. 90

MORANO.

That you have treasures then you own, it seems. I am glad to hear you confess something.

CAWWAWKEE.

But out of benevolence we ought to hide it from you. For as we have heard, 'tis so rank a poison to you Europeans that the very touch of it makes you 95 mad.

Air 41. "When bright Aurelia tripped the plain."

For gold you sacrifice your fame,
    Your honor, life, and friend;
You war, you fawn, you lie, you game, 100
And plunder without fear or shame.
    Can madness this transcend?

MORANO.

Bold savage, we are not to be insulted with your ignorance. If you would save your lives, you must, like the beaver, leave behind you what we hunt for, 105 or we shall not quit the chase.[28] Discover* your treasures, your hoards, for I will have the ransacking of 'em.

JENNY.

By his seeming to set some value upon gold, one would think that he had some glimmering of 110 sense.

Air 42. "Peggy's Mill."

When gold is in hand,
    It gives us command;
It makes us loved and respected. 115
    'Tis now, as of yore:
    Wit and sense, when poor,
Are scorned, o'erlooked, and neglected.
    Though peevish and old,
    If women have gold, 120
They have youth, good humor, and beauty.
    Among all mankind

---

28 beaver … chase] It was a classical misapprehension that the beaver gnawed off his own testicles (instead of the inquinal glands which are the source of a valuable drug) and left them for his hunters in order to save himself.

Without it we find
Nor love, nor favor, nor duty.
MORANO.
I will have no more of these interruptions. Since 125
women will be always talking, one would think
they had a chance now and then to talk in
season.—Once more I ask you, obstinate,
audacious savage, if I grant you your life, will you
be useful to us? For you shall find mercy upon no 130
other terms. I will have immediate compliance, or
you shall undergo the torture.
CAWWAWKEE.
With dishonor life is nothing worth.
MORANO.
Furies! I'll trifle no longer.

Recitative: "*Sia fuggetta la plebe Coriolan.*"29
Hence let him feel his sentence. 135
Pain brings repentance.
LAGUERRE.
You would not have us put him to death, Captain?
MORANO.
Torture him leisurely, but severely.—I shall stagger
your resolution, Indian.

Recitative.
Hence let him feel his sentence. 140
Pain brings repentance.
But hold, I'll see him tortured. I will have the
pleasure of extorting answers from him myself. So
keep him safe till you have my directions.
LAGUERRE.
It shall be done. 145
MORANO.
As for you, young gentleman, I think it not proper
to trust you till I know you farther.—Let him be
your prisoner too till I give order how to dispose
of him. *Exeunt Cawwawkee and Polly guarded.*

Scene ix.

Morano, Jenny, Vanderbluff.

VANDERBLUFF.
Come, noble Captain, take one hearty smack upon
her lips and then steer off, for one kiss requires
another, and you will never have done with her.
If once a man and woman come to grappling,
there's no hauling of 'em asunder. Our friends 5
expect us.
JENNY.
Nay Lieutenant Vanderbluff, he shall not go yet.
VANDERBLUFF.
I'm out of all patience. There is a time for all
things, madam. But a woman thinks all times must
be subservient to her whim and humor. We should 10
be now upon the spot.

---

29 *Sia fuggetta la plebe Coriolan*] The common people be
damned, Coriolanus (It.); probably from the opera *Cajo
Mario Coriolano* performed at the Haymarket and published in London in 1723, music by Attilio Ariosti, li-
bretto by Niccolà Francesco Haym

JENNY.

Is the captain under your command, Lieutenant?

VANDERBLUFF.

I know women better than so. I shall never dispute the command of any gentleman's wife. Come Captain, a woman will never take the last kiss; she will always want another. Break from her clutches. 15

MORANO.

I must go— But I cannot.

Air 43. "Excuse me."

(*To him.*)

Honor calls me from thy arms;
With glory my bosom is beating.
Victory summons to arms: then to arms 20
Let us haste, for we'er sure of defeating.

(*To her.*)

One look more—and then—
Oh, I am lost again!
What a power has beauty! 25

(*To him.*)

But honor calls, and I must away.

(*To her.*)

But love forbids, and I must obey.

Vanderbluff pulling him away.

(*To him.*)

You grow too bold;
Hence, loose your hold,

(*To her.*)

For love claims all my duty. 30
They will bring us word when the enemy is in motion. I know my own time, Lieutenant.

VANDERBLUFF.

Lose the Indies then, with all my heart. Lose the money, and you lose the woman, that I can tell you, Captain. Furies, what would the woman be at! 35

JENNY.

Not so hasty and choleric, I beg you, Lieutenant. Give me the hearing, and perhaps, whatever you may think of us, you may once in your life hear a woman speak reason.

VANDERBLUFF.

Dispatch then. And if a few words can satisfy you, 40
be brief.

JENNY.

Men only slight women's advice through an over-

conceit of their own opinions. I am against hazarding a battle. Why should we put what we have already got to the risk? We have money 45 enough on board our ships to secure our persons and can reserve a comfortable subsistence besides. Let us leave the Indies to our comrades.

VANDERBLUFF.

Sure you are the first of the sex that ever stinted herself in love or money.—If it were consistent with 50 our honor, her counsel were worth listening to.

JENNY.

Consistent with our honor! For shame, Lieutenant, you talk downright Indian. One would take you for the savage's brother or cousin-german at least. You may talk of honor, as other great men do, but 55 when interest comes in your way, you should do as other great men do.

Air 44. "Ruben."

Honor plays a bubble's* part,
Ever bilked and cheated; 60
Never in ambition's heart,
Int'rest there is seated.
Honor was in use of yore,
Though by want* attended,
Since 'twas talked of and no more— 65
Lord, how times are mended!

VANDERBLUFF.

What think you of her proposal, noble Captain?
We may push matters too far.

JENNY.

Consider, my dear, the Indies are only treasures in expectation. All your sensible men, nowadays, love 70 the ready. Let us seize the ships then and away for England while we have the opportunity.

VANDERBLUFF.

Sure you can have no scruple against treachery, Captain. 'Tis as common a money-getting vice as any in fashion, for who nowadays ever boggles at 75 giving up his crew?

MORANO.

But the balking of a great design—

VANDERBLUFF.

'Tis better balking our own designs than have 'em balked by others, for then our designs and our lives will be cut short together. 80

Air 45. "Troy Town."

When ambition's ten years' toils
Have heaped up mighty hoards of gold,
Amid the harvest of the spoils,
Acquired by fraud and rapine bold,   85
Comes justice. The great scheme is crossed:
At once wealth, life, and fame, are lost.
This is a melancholy reflection for ambition, if it
ever could think reasonably.

MORANO.
If you are satisfied, and for your security, Jenny.   90
For any man may allow that he has money enough,
when he hath enough to satisfy his wife.

VANDERBLUFF.
We may make our retreat without suspicion, for
they will readily impute our being missed to the
accidents of war.   95

Scene x.

Morano, Jenny, Vanderbluff, sailor.

SAILOR.
There is just now news arrived that the troops of
the plantation have intercepted the passage to our
ships, so that victory is our only hope. The Indian
forces too are ready to march, and ours grow
impatient for your presence, noble Captain.   5

MORANO.
I'll be with 'em. Come then, Lieutenant, for death
or the world.

JENNY.
Nay then, if affairs are desperate, nothing shall part
me from you. I'll share your dangers.

MORANO.
Since I must have an empire, prepare yourself,   10
Jenny, for the cares of royalty. Let us on to battle,
to victory.

Trumpet sounds.
Hark, the trumpet.

Air 46. "We've cheated the parson."

Despair leads to battle, no courage so great: 15
They must conquer or die who've no retreat.

VANDERBLUFF.
No retreat.

JENNY.
No retreat.

MORANO.
They must conquer or die who've no retreat.
Exeunt.

Scene xi. A room of a poor cottage.

Cawwawkee, in chains; Polly.

POLLY.
Unfortunate Prince! I cannot blame your disbelief
when I tell you that I admire your virtues and share
in your misfortunes.

CAWWAWKEE.
To be oppressed by an European implies merit. Yet   5
you are an European. Are you fools? Do you
believe one another? Sure speech can be of no use
among you.

POLLY.
There are constitutions that can resist a pestilence.

CAWWAWKEE.
But sure vice must be inherent in such   10
constitutions. You are ashamed of your hearts; you
can lie. How can you bear to look into yourselves?

POLLY.
My sincerity could even bear your examination.

CAWWAWKEE.
You have cancelled faith. How can I believe you?
You are cowards too, for you are cruel.   15

POLLY.
Would it were in my power to give you proofs of
my compassion.

CAWWAWKEE.
You can be avaricious. That is a complication of
all vices. It comprehends them all. Heaven guard
our country from the infection.   20

POLLY.
Yet the worst men allow virtue to be amiable, or
there would be no hypocrites.

CAWWAWKEE.
Have you then hypocrisy still among you? For all
that I have experienced of your manners is open
violence and barefaced injustice. Who that had   25
ever felt the satisfaction of virtue would ever part
with it?

Air 47. "T'amo tanto."[30]

> Virtue's treasure
> Is a pleasure,
> Cheerful even amid distress;   30
> Nor pain nor crosses,
> Nor grief nor losses,
> Nor death itself can make it less:
> Here relying,   35
> Suff'ring, dying,
> Honest souls find all redress.

POLLY.

My heart feels your sentiments, and my tongue longs to join in 'em.

CAWWAWKEE.

> Virtue's treasure   40
> Is a pleasure,

POLLY.

> Cheerful even amid distress;

CAWWAWKEE.

> Nor pain nor crosses,

POLLY.

> Nor grief nor losses,

CAWWAWKEE.

> Nor death itself can make it less: 45

POLLY.

> Here relying,

CAWWAWKEE.

> Suff'ring, dying,

POLLY.

> Honest souls find all redress.

CAWWAWKEE.

Having this, I want no other consolation. I am perpared for all misfortune.   50

POLLY.

Had you means of escape, you could not refuse it. To preserve your life is your duty.

CAWWAWKEE.

By dishonest means, I scorn it.

POLLY.

But stratagem is allowed in war, and 'tis lawful to use all the weapons employed against you. You 55
may save your friends from affliction and be the instrument of rescuing your country.

---

30 *T'amo tanto*] I love you so much (It.)

CAWWAWKEE.

Those are powerful inducements. I seek not voluntarily to resign my life. While it lasts, I would do my duty.   60

POLLY.

I'll talk with our guard. What induces them to rapine and murther, will induce 'em to betray. You may offer them what they want, and from no hands, upon no terms corruption can resist the temptation.

CAWWAWKEE.

I have no skill. Those who are corrupt themselves 65
know how to corrupt others. You may do as you please. But whatever you promise for me, contrary to the European custom, I will perform. For though a knave may break his word with a knave, an honest tongue knows no such distinctions.   70

Air 47

POLLY.

Gentlemen, I desire some conference with you, that may be for your advantage.

Scene xii.

Polly, Cawwawkee, Laguerre, Capstern.

POLLY.

Know you that you have the Indian prince in your custody?

LAGUERRE.

Full well.

POLLY.

Know you the treasures that are in his power?

LAGUERRE.

I know, too, that they shall soon be ours. 5

POLLY.

In having him in your possession they are yours.

LAGUERRE.

As how, friend?

POLLY.

He might well reward you.

LAGUERRE.

For what?

POLLY.

For his liberty. 10

CAWWAWKEE.

Yes European, I can and will reward you.

CAPSTERN.

He's a great man,* and I trust no such promises.

CAWWAWKEE.

I have said it, European, and an Indian's heart is always answerable for his words.

POLLY.

Think of the chance of war, gentlemen. Conquest 15 is not so sure when you fight against those who fight for their liberties.

LAGUERRE.

What think you of the proposal?

CAPSTERN.

The prince can give us places; he can make us all great men.* Such a prospect I can tell you, 20 Laguerre, would tempt our betters.

LAGUERRE.

Besides, if we are beaten, we have no retreat to our ships.

CAPSTERN.

If we gain our ends, what matter how we come by it? 25

LAGUERRE.

Every man for himself, say I. There is no being even with mankind, without that universal maxim. Consider, brother, we run no risk.

CAPSTERN.

Nay, I have no objections.

LAGUERRE.

If we conquered and the booty were to be divided 30 among the crews, what would it amount to? Perhaps this way we might get more than would come to our shares.

CAPSTERN.

Then, too, I always liked a place at court. I have a genius to get, keep in, and make the most of an 35 employment.

LAGUERRE.

You will consider, Prince, our own politicians would have rewarded such meritorious services. We'll go off with you.

CAPSTERN.

We want only to be known to be employed. 40

LAGUERRE.

Let us unbind him then.

POLLY. [*Aside.*]

'Tis thus one able politician outwits another, and we admire their wisdom.—You may rely upon the prince's word as much as if he was a poor man.

CAPSTERN.

Our fortunes then are made. 45

Air 48. "Down in a meadow."

POLLY.

The sportsmen keep hawks, and their quarry they gain;
Thus the woodcock, the partridge, the pheasant is slain.
What care and expense for their hounds are employed!
Thus the fox and the hare and the stag are destroyed. 50
The spaniel they cherish, whose flattering way
Can as well as their masters cringe, fawn, and betray.
Thus staunch politicians, look all the world round,

Love the men who can serve as hawk, spaniel, or
hound.

Exeunt.

Act III, scene i. The Indian camp.

Pohetohee, attendants, Ducat.

INDIAN.

Sir, a party from the British factory have joined us.
Their chief attends your majesty's orders for their
disposition.

POHETOHEE.

Let them be posted next my command, for I
would be witness of their bravery. But first let their   5
officer know I would see him.

Exit Indian. Enter Ducat.

DUCAT.

I would do all in my power to serve your majesty.
I have brought up my men, and now, sir, I would
fain give up. I speak purely upon your majesty's
account. For as to courage and all that—I have   10
been a colonel of the militia these ten years.

POHETOHEE.

Sure, you have not fear. Are you a man?

DUCAT.

A married man, sir, who carries his wife's heart about
him and that, indeed, is a little timorous. Upon
promise to her, I am engaged to quit in case of battle,   15
and her heart hath ever governed me more than my
own. Besides sir, fighting is not our business; we pay
others for fighting. And yet 'tis well known we had
rather part with our lives than with our money.

POHETOHEE.

And have you no spirit then to defend it? Your famil-   20
ies, your liberties, your properties are at stake. If these
cannot move you, you must be born without a heart.

DUCAT.

Alas sir, we cannot be answerable for human
infirmities.

Air 49. "There was an old man, and he lived."   25

What man can on virtue or courage repose
    Or guess if the touch 'twill abide?
Like gold, if intrinsic, sure, nobody knows
    Till weighed in the balance and tried.

POHETOHEE.

How different are your notions from ours! We   30
think virtue, honor, and courage as essential to
man as his limbs or senses, and in every man we
suppose the qualities of a man till we have found
the contrary. But then we regard him only as a
brute in disguise. How custom can degrade nature!   35

DUCAT.

Why should I have any more scruples about myself
than about my money? If I can make my courage
pass current, what matter is it to me whether it be
true or false? 'Tis time enough to own a man's
failings when they are found out. If your majesty   40
then will not dispense with my duty to my wife,
with permission, I'll to my post. 'Tis wonderful to
me that kings ever go to war, who have so much
to lose and nothing essential to get.

Exit.

Scene ii.

Pohetohee, attendants.

POHETOHEE.

My son a prisoner! Tortured perhaps and
inhumanly butchered! Human nature cannot bear
up against such afflictions. The war must suffer by
his absence. More then is required from me. Grief
raises my resolution and calls me to relieve him,   5
or to a just revenge.

Enter Indian.

What mean those shouts?

INDIAN.

The prince, sir, is returned. The troops are
animated by his presence. With some of the pirates
in his retinue, he waits your majesty's commands.   10

Scene iii.

Pohetohee, Cawwawkee, Polly, Laguerre, Capstern, etc.

POHETOHEE.

Victory then is ours. Let me embrace him.
Welcome, my son. Without thee my heart could
not have felt a triumph.

CAWWAWKEE.

Let this youth then receive your thanks. To him

are owing my life and liberty. And the love of 5
virtue alone gained me his friendship.

POHETOHEE.

This hath convinced me that an European can be
generous* and honest.

CAWWAWKEE.

These others, indeed, have the passion of their
country. I owe their services to gold, and my 10
promise is engaged to reward them. How it galls
honor to have obligations to a dishonorable man!

LAGUERRE.

I hope your majesty will not forget our services.

POHETOHEE.

I am bound for my son's engagements.

CAWWAWKEE.

For this youth, I will be answerable. Like a gem 15
found in rubbish, he appears the brighter among
these his countrymen.

*Air 50. 'Iris la plus charmante.'*31

Love with beauty is flying;
At once 'tis blooming and dying. 20
But all seasons defying,
Friendship lasts on the year.
Love is by long enjoying,
    Cloying;
Friendship, enjoyed the longer, 25
    Stronger.
Oh may the flame divine
Burn in your breast like mine!

POLLY.

Most noble Prince, my behavior shall justify the
good opinion you have of me, and my friendship 30
is beyond professions.

POHETOHEE.

Let these men remain under guard till after the
battle. All promises shall then be made good to
you. *Exeunt pirates guarded.*

Scene iv.

Pohetohee, Cawwawkee, Polly.

CAWWAWKEE.

May this young man be my companion in the war.

---

31 *Iris la plus charmante*] Most charming Iris (Fr.)

As a boon I request it of you. He knows our cause
is just, and that is sufficient to engage him in it.

POHETOHEE.

I leave you to appoint him his command. Dispose
of him as you judge convenient. 5

POLLY.

To fall into their hands is certain torture and death.
As far as my youth and strength will permit me,
you may rely upon my duty.

Enter Indian.

INDIAN.

Sir, the enemy are advancing toward us.

POHETOHEE.

Victory then is at hand. Justice protects us, and 10
courage shall support us. Let us then to our posts.
Exeunt.

Scene v. The field of battle.

Culverin, Hacker, pirates.

Air 51. "There was a jovial beggar."

FIRST PIRATE.

When horns with cheerful sound
Proclaim the active day,
Impatience warms the hound,
He burns to chase the prey. 5

CHORUS.

Thus to battle we will go, etc.

SECOND PIRATE.

How charms the trumpet's breath!
The brave, with hope possessed,
Forgetting wounds and death,
Feel conquest in their breast. 10

CHORUS.

Thus to battle, etc.

CULVERIN.

But yet I don't see, brother Hacker, why we should
be commanded by a Neger. 'Tis all along of him
that we are led into these difficulties. I hate this
land fighting. I love to have sea-room. 15

HACKER.

We are of the council, brother. If we ever get on
board again, my vote shall be for calling of him
to account for these pranks. Why should we be

such fools to be ambitious of satisfying another's
ambition?   20

CULVERIN.

Let us mutiny. I love mutiny as well as my wife.

FIRST PIRATE.

Let us mutiny.

SECOND PIRATE.

Aye, let us mutiny.

HACKER.

Our captain takes too much upon him. I am for
no engrosser of power. By our articles he hath no   25
command but in a fight or in a storm. Look'ee,
brothers, I am for mutiny as much as any of you,
when occasion offers.

CULVERIN.

Right, brother, all in good season. The pass to our
ships is cut off by the troops of the plantation. We   30
must fight the Indians first, and we have a mutiny
good[32] afterwards.

HACKER.

Is Morano still with his doxy?

CULVERIN.

He's yonder on the right, putting his troops in
order for the onset.   35

HACKER.

I wish this fight of ours were well over. For to be
sure, let soldiers say what they will, they feel more
pleasure after a battle than in it.

CULVERIN. (*Takes dice out of his pocket.*)

Does not the drumhead here, quartermaster, tempt
you to fling a merry main* or two?   40

HACKER.

If I lose my money, I shall reimburse myself from
the Indians. I have set.

CULVERIN. (*Flings.*)

Have at you. A nick.

HACKER.

Throw the dice fairly out. Are you at me again!

CULVERIN.

I'm at it. Seven or eleven. (*Flings.*) Eleven.[33]   45

---

32 good] an adverbial intensifier: well

33 set … eleven] From the game of hazard: Hacker has
    placed his bet; Culverin throws a nick or win with a
    seven, establishing seven as the main, and throws a win-
    ning eleven.

HACKER.

Furies! A manifest cog![34] I won't be bubbled,* sir.
This would not pass upon a drunken country
gentleman. Death, sir, I won't be cheated.

CULVERIN.

The money is mine. D'you take me for a sharper,
sir?   50

HACKER.

Yes sir.

CULVERIN.

I'll have satisfaction.

HACKER.

With all my heart.

Fighting.

Scene vi.

Hacker, Culverin, pirates, Morano, Vanderbluff, etc.

MORANO.

For shame, gentlemen! (*Parting them.*) Is this a time
for private quarrel?* What do I see! Dice upon the
drumhead! If you have not left off those cowardly
tools, you are unworthy your profession. The articles
you have sworn to prohibit gaming for money.   5
Friendship and society cannot subsist where it is
practiced. As this is the day of battle, I remit your
penalties. But let me hear no more of it.

CULVERIN.

To be called sharper, Captain, is a reproach that
no man of honor can put up.   10

HACKER.

But to be one is what no man of honor can
practice.

MORANO.

If you will not obey my orders, quartermaster, this
pistol shall put an end to the dispute. (*Claps it to
his head.*) The common cause now requires your   15
agreement. If gaming is so rife, I don't wonder that
treachery still subsists among you.

HACKER.

Who is treacherous?

MORANO.

Capstern and Laguerre have let the prince and the
stripling you took prisoner escape and are gone off   20

---

34 cog] trick

with them to the Indians. Upon your duty, gentlemen, this day depends our all.

CULVERIN.

Rather than have ill blood among us, I return the money. I value your friendship more. Let all animosities be forgot. 25

MORANO.

We should be Indians among ourselves and show our breeding and parts* to everyone else. If we cannot be true to one another and false to the world beside, there is an end of every great enterprise.

HACKER.

We have nothing to trust to but our death or victory. 30

MORANO.

Then hey for victory and plunder, my lads.

Air 52. "To you fair ladies."

By bolder steps we win the race.

FIRST PIRATE.

Let's haste where danger calls. 35

MORANO.

Unless ambition mend its pace,
It totters, nods, and falls.

FIRST PIRATE.

We must advance or be undone.

MORANO.

Think thus, and then the battle's won.

CHORUS.

With a fa la la, etc. 40

MORANO.

You see your booty, your plunder, gentlemen. The Indians are just upon us. The great must venture death some way or other, and the less ceremony about it, in my opinion, the better. But why talk I of death! Those only talk of it who fear it. Let us all live 45 and enjoy our conquests. Sound the charge.

Air 53. "Prince Eugene's[35] March."

When the tiger roams
And the timorous flock is in his view,
Fury foams, 50

---

35 Prince Eugene] Of Savoy: one of the greatest military strategists of the age, a great friend of Marlborough and later teacher of Frederick the Great

He thirsts for the blood of the crew.
His greedy eyes he throws;
Thirst with their number grows;
On he pours, with a wide waste pursuing,
Spreading the plain with a general ruin. 55
Thus let us charge and our foes o'erturn.

VANDERBLUFF.

Let us on one and all!

FIRST PIRATE.

How they fly, how they fall!

MORANO.

For the war, for the prize I burn.

VANDERBLUFF.

Were they dragons, my lads, as they sit brooding 60 upon treasure, we would fright them from their nests.

MORANO.

But see, the enemy are advancing to close engagement. Before the onset, we'll demand a parley and, if we can, obtain honorable terms: we are 65 overpowered by numbers, and our retreat is cut off.

Scene vii.

Enter Pohetohee, Cawwawkee, Polly, etc., with the Indian army drawn up against the pirates.)

POHETOHEE.

Our hearts are all ready. The enemy halts. Let the trumpets give the signal.

Air 54. "The marlborough."

CAWWAWKEE.

We the sword of justice drawing,
Terror cast in guilty eyes; 5
In its beam false courage dies;
'Tis like lightning keen and awing.
Charge the foe,
Lay them low,
On then and strike the blow. 10
Hark, victory calls us. See, guilt is dismayed:
The villain is of his own conscience afraid.
In your hands are your lives and your liberties held;
The courage of virtue was never repelled.

PIRATE.

Our chief demands a parley. 15

POHETOHEE.

Let him advance.

Art thou Morano, that fell man of prey?

That foe to justice?

MORANO.

Tremble and obey.

Art thou great Pohetohee styled?   20

POHETOHEE.

                                        The same.

I dare avow my actions and my name.

MORANO.

Thou know'st then, king, thy son there was my prisoner. Pay us the ransom we demand, allow us safe passage to our ships, and we will give you your   25 lives and liberties.

POHETOHEE.

Shall robbers and plunderers prescribe rules to

Air

right and equity? Insolent madman! Composition with knaves is base and ignominious. Tremble at the sword of justice, rapacious brute.   30

Air LV. '*Les rats.*'[36]

MORANO.

Know then, war's my pleasure.

Am I thus controlled?

Both thy heart and treasure

I'll at once unfold.   35

You, like a miser, scraping, hiding,

Rob all the world; you're but mines of gold.

Rage my breast alarms!

War is by kings held right-deciding;

Then to arms, to arms: 40

With this sword I'll force your hold.

By your obstinacy, king, thou hast provoked thy fate, and so expect me.

POHETOHEE.

Rapacious fool, by thy avarice thou shalt perish.

MORANO.

Fall on.   45

POHETOHEE.

For your lives and liberties.

Fight, pirates beat off.

                              Scene viii.

Ducat.

DUCAT.

A slight wound now would have been a good certificate, but who dares contradict a soldier? 'Tis your common soldiers who must content themselves with mere fighting, but 'tis we officers that run away with the most fame as well as pay. Of   5 all fools, the foolhardy are the greatest, for they are not even to be trusted with themselves. Why should we provoke men to turn again upon us after they are run away? For my own part, I think it wiser to talk of fighting than only to be talked of. The fame of a   10 talking hero will satisfy me, the sound of whose valor amazes and astonishes all peaceable men, women, and children. Sure a man may be allowed a little lying in his own praise when there's so much going

---

36 *Les rats*] either *the rats* or *the misers* (Fr.)

to his discredit. Since every other body gives a man 15
less praise than he deserves, a man, in justice to
himself, ought to make up deficiences. Without this
privilege, we should have fewer good characters* in
the world than we have.

Air 56. "Mad Robin." 20

How faultless does the nymph appear,
When her own hand the picture draws!
    But all others only smear
Her wrinkles, cracks, and flaws.
Self-flattery is our claim and right, 25
    Let men say what they will;
Sure we may set our good in sight,
    When neighbors set our ill.
So, for my own part, I'll no more trust my reputa-
tion in my neighbors' hands than my money but 30
will turn them both myself to the best advantage.

Scene ix.

Pohetohee, Cawwawkee, Ducat, Indians.

POHETOHEE.
    Had Morano been taken or slain, our victory had
    been complete.
DUCAT.
    A hare may escape from a mastiff. I could not be
    a greyhound too.
POHETOHEE.
    How have you disposed of the prisoners? 5
CAWWAWKEE.
    They are all under safe guard, till the king's justice,
    by their exemplary punishment, deters others from
    the like barbarities.
POHETOHEE.
    But all our troops are not as yet returned from the
    pursuit. I am too for speedy justice, for in that 10
    there is a sort of clemency. Besides, I would not
    have my private thoughts worried by mercy to
    pardon such wretches. I cannot be answerable for
    the frailties of my nature.
CAWWAWKEE.
    The youth who rescued me from these cruel men 15
    is missing, and amidst all our successes I cannot
    feel happiness. I fear he is among the slain. My
    gratitude interested itself so warmly in his safety

that you must pardon my concern. What hath
victory done for me? I have lost a friend. 20

Air 57. "Through the wood laddy."

As fits the sad turtle* alone on the spray
    His heart sorely beating,
    Sad murmur repeating,
Indulging his grief for his consort astray, 25
For force or death only could keep her away.
Now he thinks of the fowler and every snare:
    "If guns have not slain her,
    The net must detain her."
Thus he'll rise in my thoughts every hour with a tear, 30
If safe from the battle he do not appear.
POHETOHEE.
    Dead or alive, bring me intelligence of him, for I
    share in my son's affliction.

Exit Indian.

DUCAT.
    I had better too be upon the spot, or my men may
    embezzle some plunder which by right should be 35
    mine. (*Exit.*)

Enter Indian.

INDIAN.
    The youth, sir, with a party is just returned from the
    pursuit. He's here to attend your majesty's commands.

Scene x.

Pohetohee, Cawwawkee, Polly, Indians.

CAWWAWKEE.
    Pardon, sir, the warmth of my friendship, if I fly
    to meet him and for a moment intercept his duty.
    (*Embracing [Polly].*)

Air 58. "Clasped in my dear Melinda's arms."

POLLY.
    Victory is ours. 5
CAWWAWKEE.
                    My fond heart is at rest.
POLLY.
    Friendship thus receives its guest.
CAWWAWKEE.
    Oh what transport fills my breast!

POLLY.

    Conquest is complete,

CAWWAWKEE.

    Now the triumph's great.   10

POLLY.

    In your life is a nation blest.

CAWWAWKEE.

    In your life I'm of all possessed.

POHETOHEE.

The obligations my son hath received from you makes me take a part in his friendship. In your safety victory has been doubly kind to me. If 15 Morano hath escaped, justice only reserves him to be punished by another hand.

Air   **13**

POLLY.

In the rout, sir, I overtook him flying with all the cowardice of guilt upon him. Thousands have false courage enough to be vicious; true fortitude is 20 founded upon honor and virtue. That only can abide all tests. I made him my prisoner and left him without under strict guard, till I received your majesty's commands for his disposal.

POHETOHEE.

Sure this youth was sent me as a guardian.—Let 25 your prisoner be brought before us.

Scene xi.

Pohetohee, Cawwawkee, Polly, Morano, guarded.

MORANO.

Here's a treacherous dog now, who hangs the husband to come at the wife. There are wives in the world, who would have undertaken that affair to come at him. Your son's liberty, to be sure, you think better worth than mine; so that I allow you a good 5 bargain if I take my own for his ransom, without a gratuity. You know, king, he is my debtor.

POHETOHEE.

He hath the obligations to you of a sheep who hath escaped out of the jaws of the wolf, beast of prey!

MORANO.

Your great men* will never own their debts, that's 10 certain.

POHETOHEE.

Trifle not with justice, impious man. Your barbarities, your rapine, your murthers are now at an end.

MORANO.

Ambition must take its chance. If I die, I die in 15 my vocation.

Air 59. "Parson upon Dorothy."

The soldiers, who by trade must dare
    The deadly cannon's sounds,
You may be sure, betimes prepare   20
    For fatal blood and wounds.
The men, who with adventurous dance,
    Bound from the cord on high,
Must own they have the frequent chance
    By broken bones to die.   25

Since rarely then
  Ambitious men
Like others lose their breath,
  Like these, I hope,
  They know a rope   30
Is but their natural death.
We must all take the common lot of our
professions.

POHETOHEE.
Would your European laws have suffered crimes
like these to have gone unpunished?   35

MORANO.
Were all I am worth safely landed, I have
wherewithal to make almost any crime sit easy
upon me.

POHETOHEE.
Have ye notions of property?

MORANO.
Of my own.   40

POHETOHEE.
Would not your honest industry have been
sufficient to have supported you?

MORANO.
Honest industry! I have heard talk of it indeed
among the common people, but all great geniuses
are above it.   45

POHETOHEE.
Have you no respect for virtue?

MORANO.
As a good phrase, sir. But the practicers of it are
so insignificant and poor that they are seldom
found in the best company.

POHETOHEE.
Is not wisdom esteemed among you?   50

MORANO.
Yes sir, but only as a step to riches and power, a
step that raises ourselves and trips up our
neighbors.

POHETOHEE.
Honor and honesty, are not those distinguished?

MORANO.
As incapacities and follies.—How ignorant are   55
these Indians!—But indeed I think honor is of
some use: it serves to swear upon.

POHETOHEE.
Have you no consciousness? Have you no shame?

MORANO.
Of being poor.

POHETOHEE.
How can society subsist with avarice? Ye are but   60
the forms of men. Beasts would thrust you out of
their herd upon that account, and man should cast
you out for your brutal dispositions.

MORANO.
Alexander the Great was more successful. That's all.

Air 60. "The collier has a daughter."   65

When right or wrong's decided
In war or civil causes,
We by success are guided
To blame or give applauses.
Thus men exalt ambition,   70
In power by all commended,
But when it falls from high condition,
Tyburn* is well attended.

POHETOHEE.
Let justice then take her course; I shall not interfere
with her decrees. Mercy too obliges me to protect   75
my country from such violences. Immediate death
shall put a stop to your further mischiefs.

MORANO.
This sentence indeed is hard. Without the
common forms of trial! Not so much as the
counsel of a Newgate attorney! Not to be able to   80
lay out my money in partiality and evidence!* Not
a friend perjured for me! This is hard, very hard.

POHETOHEE.
Let the sentence be put in execution. Lead him to
death. Let his accomplices be witnesses of it, and
afterwards let them be securely guarded till farther   85
orders.

Air 61. "Mad Moll."

MORANO.
All crimes are judged like fornication;
  While rich we are honest* no doubt.
Fine ladies can keep reputation,   90
  Poor lasses alone are found out.
If justice had piercing eyes,
Like ourselves, to look within,
She'd find power and wealth a disguise
That shelter the worst of our kin.   95

Exit guarded.

Scene xii.

Pohetohee, Cawwawkee, Polly.

POHETOHEE.

How shall I return the obligations I owe you? Everything in my power you may command. In making a request, you confer on me another benefit. For gratitude is obliged by occasions of making a return. And every occasion must be agreeable, for a grateful 5 mind hath more pleasure in paying than receiving.

CAWWAWKEE.

My friendship too is impatient to give you proofs of it. How happy would you make me in allowing me to discharge that duty!

Air 62. "Prince George." 10

All friendship is a mutual debt,

POLLY.

The contract's inclination:

CAWWAWKEE.

We never can that bond forget
Of sweet retaliation.

POLLY.

All day and every day the same: 15
We are paying and still* owing;

CAWWAWKEE.

By turns we grant, by turns we claim
The pleasure of bestowing.

BOTH.

By turns we grant, etc.

POLLY.

The pleasure of having served an honorable man 20
is sufficient return. My misfortunes, I fear, are
beyond relief.

CAWWAWKEE.

That sigh makes me suffer. If you have a want,*
let me know it.

POHETOHEE.

If it is in a king's power, my power will make me 25
happy.

CAWWAWKEE.

If you believe me a friend, you are unjust in
concealing your distresses from me. You deny me
the privilege of friendship, for I have a right to
share them or redress them. 30

POHETOHEE.

Can my treasures make you happy?

POLLY.

Those who have them not think they can; those
who have them know they cannot.

POHETOHEE.

How unlike his countrymen!

CAWWAWKEE.

While you conceal one want* from me, I feel every 35
want* for you. Such obstinacy to a friend is
barbarity.

POLLY.

Let not my reflection interrupt the joys of your
triumph. Could I have commanded my thoughts,
I would have reserved them for solitude. 40

CAWWAWKEE.

Those sighs and that reservedness are symptoms of
a heart in love: a pain that I am yet a stranger to.

POLLY.

Then you have never been completely wretched.

Air 63. *"Blithe Jockey young and gay."*

Can words the pain express 45
    Which absent lovers know?
He only mine can guess
    Whose heart hath felt the woe.
'Tis doubt, suspicion, fear,
    Seldom hope, oft despair; 50
'Tis jealousy, 'tis rage; in brief,
    'Tis every pang and grief.

CAWWAWKEE.

But does not love often deny itself aid and comfort
by being too obstinately secret?

POLLY.

One cannot be too open to generosity. That is a sun 55
of universal benignity. In concealing ourselves from
it we but deny ourselves the blessings of its influence.

Air 64. *"In the fields in frost and snow."*

The modest lilly, like the maid,
    Its pure bloom defending, 60
Is of noxious dews afraid,
    Soon as even's descending.
Closed all night,
Free from blight,
It preserves the native white 65
But at morn unfolds its leaves
And the vital sun receives.

Yet why should I trouble your majesty with the
misfortunes of so inconsiderable a wretch as I am?

POHETOHEE.

A king's beneficence should be like the sun: the 70
most humble weed should feel its influence as well
as the most gaudy flower. But I have the nearest
concern in anything that touches you.

POLLY.

You see then at your feet the most unhappy of
women. 75

Kneels, he raises her.

CAWWAWKEE.

A woman! Oh my heart!

POHETOHEE.

A woman!

POLLY.

Yes sir, the most wretched of her sex. In love!
Married! Abandoned and in despair!

POHETOHEE.

What brought you into these countries? 80

POLLY.

To find my husband. Why had not the love of
virtue directed my heart? But alas, 'tis outward
appearance alone that generally engages a woman's
affections! And my heart is in the possession of the
most profligate of mankind. 85

POHETOHEE.

Why this disguise?

POLLY.

To protect me from the violences and insults to
which my sex might have exposed me.

CAWWAWKEE. (*Aside.*)

Had she not been married, I might have been
happy. 90

POLLY.

He ran into the madness of every vice. I detest his
principles, though I am fond of his person to
distraction. Could your commands for search and
inquiry restore him to me, you reward me at once
with all my wishes. For sure my love still might 95
reclaim him.

CAWWAWKEE.

Had you concealed your sex, I had been happy in
your friendship. But now, how uneasy, how restless
is my heart!

Air 65. *"Whilst I gaze on Chloe."* 100

Whilst I gaze in fond desiring,
    Every former thought is lost.
Sighing, wishing, and admiring,
    How my troubled soul is tossed!
Hot and cold my blood is flowing, 105
How it thrills in every vein!
Liberty and life are going,
    Hope can ne'er relieve my pain.

Enter Indian.

INDIAN.

The rest of the troops, sir, are returned from the
pursuit with more prisoners. They attend your 110
majesty's commands.

POHETOHEE.

Let them be brought before us.

Exit Indian.

(*To Polly.*) Give not yourself up to despair, for everything in my power you may command.

CAWWAWKEE.

And everything in mine. But alas, I have none, for 115 I am not in my own!

Scene xiii.

Pohetohee, Cawwawkee, Polly, Ducat, Jenny, guarded, etc.

JENNY.

Spare my husband. Morano is my husband.

POHETOHEE.

Then I have relieved you from the society of a monster.

JENNY.

Alas sir, there are many husbands who are furious monsters to the rest of mankind that are the tamest 5 creatures alive to their wives. I can be answerable for his duty and submission to your majesty, for I know I have so much power over him that I can even make him good.

POHETOHEE. 10

Why then had you not made him so before?

JENNY.

I was, indeed, like other wives, too indulgent to him, and as it was agreeable to my own humor, I was loath to balk his ambition. I must, indeed, 15 own too that I had the frailty of pride. But where is the woman who hath not an inclination to be as great and rich as she can be?

POHETOHEE.

With how much ease and unconcern these 20 Europeans talk of vices, as if they were necessary qualifications.

Air 66. "The Jamaica."

JENNY. 25

The sex, we find,
Like men, inclined
To guard against reproaches,
And none neglect
To pay respect 30
To rogues who keep their coaches.

Indeed sir, I had determined to be honest myself and to have made him so too, as soon as I had put myself upon a reasonable foot in the world, and that is more self-denial than is commonly practiced. 35

POHETOHEE.

Woman, your profligate sentiments offend me, and you deserve to be cut off from society with your husband. Mercy would be scarce excusable in pardoning you. Have done then. Morano is now 40 under the stroke of justice.

JENNY.

Let me implore your majesty to respite his sentence. Send me back again with him into slavery, from whence we escaped. Give us an occasion of being honest, for we owe our lives and liberties to another. 45

Air 66

DUCAT.

Yes sir, I find some of my runaway slaves among the crew, and I hope my services at least will allow me to claim my own again.

JENNY.

Morano, sir, I must confess hath been a free liver and a man of so many gallantries that no woman could escape him. If Macheath's misfortunes were known, the whole sex would be in tears.   50

POLLY.

Macheath!

JENNY.

He is no black, sir, but under that disguise, for my sake, screened himself from the claims and importunities of other women. May love intercede for him?   55

POLLY.

Macheath! Is it possible?—Spare him, save him, I ask no other reward.

POHETOHEE.

Haste, let the sentence be suspended.

Exit Indian.

POLLY.

Fly, a moment may make me miserable. Why could not I know him? All his distresses brought upon him by my hand! Cruel love, how couldst thou blind me so?   60

Air 67. "Tweed Side."

The stag, when chased all the long day   65
O'er the lawn, through the forest and brake,
Now panting for breath and at bay,
Now stemming the river or lake;
When the treacherous scent is all cold,
And at eve he returns to his hind,   70
Can her joy, can her pleasure be told?
Such joy and such pleasure I find.
But alas, now again reflection turns fear upon my heart. His pardon may come too late, and I may never see him more.   75

POHETOHEE.

Take hence that profligate woman. Let her be kept under strict guard till my commands.

JENNY.

Slavery, sir, slavery is all I ask. Whatever becomes of him, spare my life. Spare an unfortunate

woman. What can be the meaning of this sudden   80
turn! Consider, sir, if a husband be never so bad, a wife is bound to duty.

POHETOHEE.

Take her hence, I say. Let my orders be obeyed.

Exit Jenny guarded.

Scene xiv.

Pohetohee, Cawwawkee, Polly, Ducat etc.

POLLY.

What, no news yet? Not yet returned!

CAWWAWKEE.

If justice hath overtaken him, he was unworthy of you.

POLLY.

Not yet! Oh, how I fear.

Air 68. "One evening as I lay."   5

My heart forebodes he's dead.
That thought how can I bear?
He's gone, forever fled;
My soul is all despair!
I see him pale and cold;   10
The noose hath stopped his breath,
Just as my dream foretold.
Oh had that sleep been death!

Scene xv.

Pohetohee, Cawwawkee, Polly, Ducat, Indians.   5

POLLY.

He's dead, he's dead! Their looks confess it. Your tongues have no need to give it utterance to confirm my misfortunes! I know, I see, I feel it! Support me! Oh Macheath!

DUCAT.

Mercy upon me! Now I look upon her nearer, bless   10
me, it must be Polly.—This woman, sir, is my slave, and I claim her as my own. I hope, if your majesty thinks of keeping her, you will reimburse me and not let me be a loser. She was an honest* girl, to be sure, and had much virtue to thrive, for   15
to my knowledge, money could not tempt her.

POHETOHEE.

And if she is virtuous, European, dost thou think

I'll act the infamous part of a ruffian and force her? 'Tis my duty as a king to cherish and protect virtue.   20

CAWWAWKEE.

Justice has relieved you from the society of a wicked man. If an honest heart can recompense your loss, you would make me happy in accepting mine. I hope my father will consent to my happiness.   25

POHETOHEE.

Since your love of her is founded upon the love of virtue and gratitude, I leave you to your own disposal.

CAWWAWKEE.

What, no reply?

POLLY.

Abandon me to my sorrows. For in indulging them   30
is my only relief.

POHETOHEE.

Let the chiefs have immediate execution. For the rest, let 'em be restored to their owners and return to their slavery.

Air 69. "Buff coat."   35

CAWWAWKEE.

    Why that languish?

POLLY.

    Oh, he's dead! Oh, he's lost forever!

CAWWAWKEE.

    Cease your anguish and forget your grief.

POLLY.

                  Ah, never!

    What air, grace, and stature!   40

CAWWAWKEE.

    How false is his nature!

POLLY.

    To virtue my love might have won him.

CAWWAWKEE.

    How base and deceiving!

POLLY.

    But love is believing.

CAWWAWKEE.

    Vice, at length, as 'tis meet, hath undone him.   45

By your consent you might at the same time give me happiness and procure your own. My titles, my treasures, are all at your command.

Air 70. An Italian ballad.

POLLY.

Frail is ambition, how weak the foundation!   50
    Riches have wings as inconstant as wind;
My heart is proof against either temptation:
    Virtue, without them, contentment can find.

I am charmed, Prince, with your generosity and virtues. 'Tis only by the pursuit of those we secure   55
real happiness. Those that know and feel virtue in themselves, must love it in others. Allow me to give a decent time to my sorrows. But my misfortunes at present interrupt the joys of victory.

CAWWAWKEE.

Fair princess, for so I hope shortly to make you,   60
permit me to attend you, either to divide your grief or, by conversation,* to soften your sorrows.

POHETOHEE.

  'Tis a pleasure to me by this alliance to recompense
your merits.

Exeunt Cawwawkee and Polly.

  Let the sports and dances then celebrate our 65
victory. (*Exit.*)

Dance.

Air 71. "The temple."

FIRST INDIAN.

  Justice long forbearing,
  Power or riches never fearing,
  Slow, yet persevering, 70
  Hunts the villain's pace.

CHORUS.

  Justice long, etc.

SECOND INDIAN.

  What tongues then defend him?
  Or what hand will succour lend him?
  Even his friends attend him 75
  To foment the chase.

CHORUS.

  Justice long, etc.

THIRD INDIAN.

  Virtue, subduing,
  Humbles in ruin
All the proud wicked race. 80
  Truth, never-failing,
  Must be prevailing;
Falsehood shall find disgrace.

CHORUS.

  Justice long forbearing, etc. 85

[Exeunt.]

FINIS.

Textual Notes

a Copytext is the first edition, a 1729 quarto (Q). Other
editions consulted include modern editions of 1923 (the
Abbey Classics edition—AC), and of 1983 (Fuller).

Menippean Satire

Menippean satire presents a jumble of competing voices, with no clear standard by which to judge behavior aberrant. Lucian and Petronius Arbiter are the classic exemplars. Shakespeare's *Antony and Cleopatra* pulls the rug out from under any set of values. Restoration menippean satire does the same, presenting us with endings that not only make no sense but make nonsense of previous positioning. Post-Revolution menippean satire forces us to confront a world grown secular and materialist, where God himself may be nothing but another tyrannical force of sheer will-to-power. The ludic is all that is left.

The Rump; or, The Mirror of the Late Times[a]

by John Tatham (fl. 1632-1664)

edited by Judith Bailey Slagle

John Tatham appears to have succeeded John Taylor and Thomas Heywood in the office of laureate to the Lord Mayor's show in London in the middle of the seventeenth century. He wrote the city pageants regularly from 1657 to 1664. His main characteristics seem to have been an almost bigoted loyalty and a hatred of strangers, especially Scots. *The Rump* was first performed privately in Dorset Court perhaps as early as February 1660 as political events unfolded dissolving the Rump Parliament, dispatching the ruling generals, and preparing the way for the restoration of Charles II. Long before Charles II actually stepped ashore at Dover to claim the throne, the politics of drama extended into the London streets, and Tatham's play aimed at satire of the fallen leaders.

With the execution of Charles I in 1649 and Oliver Cromwell's ascent to power, England was governed until 1653 by the Rump Parliament, that fragment of the Long Parliament that accepted the regicide and assumed all legislative and executive power. Though many members tried to justify the Rump, it was in practice unorganized and unfunded. By the spring of 1653 the army was ready for a change, and with fresh victories over Scotland and Ireland and over Charles II, Cromwell expelled the Rump. Ruling through a Council of State under a new constitution probably drafted by Major General John Lambert, Cromwell placed each region of England under the supervision of a senior military commander, Major Generals responsible for security. After his death in 1658, Cromwell was succeeded as Lord Protector by his son Richard, who lacked any leadership qualities. A new Parliament was elected in April 1659 but proceeded to quarrel with the army, which forced Richard to dissolve it, invited back the old Rump, and then forced Richard himself to retire. Relations between the army and the Rump soured, and in October it was again dissolved. But elements chafed at army rule, and in the winter one section of the army under General George Monck swept past Lambert on its way toward London. Panicked, the generals restored the Rump yet once more. On 3 February 1660 Monck entered London. The Rump ordered Monck to arrest city officials and destroy city fortifications, but that once done, Monck ensconced himself in the City, ordered the final dissolution of the Rump, and made preparations for not only the election of a "free" parliament but for the Restoration. The citizens of London celebrated by roasting rumps of beef.

The Rump; or, The Mirror of the Late Times.

The Argument of the Play.
Fleetwood is fooled by Lambert to consent
To th'pulling out of the Rump Parliament;
Which done, another government they frame
In embryo, that wants* matter for a name.   5
In brief "by force fools supplant crafty men;
The bauble exits, enter knaves again."

DRAMATIS PERSONAE[b]

[MEN]
Lambert,[1] Fleetwood,[2] [generals and] competitors for the Protectorship.

---

[1] Lambert] Major General John Lambert (1619-1683) was one of Cromwell's leading generals, but they fell out over the question of Cromwell's being appointed king. In the late 1650s he became a member of the Committee of Safety which succeeded the Council of State. Lambert was later deprived of his commands and ordered to retire to his house in Yorkshire. The evident approach of the Restoration caused republicans to reconcile with Lambert in an attempt to employ him against Monck, but his soldiers refused to fight, and he was brought prisoner back to London. While Lambert had been politically more dangerous than many of his associates, he had not taken part in the king's trial and thus escaped with comparatively light punishment (*DNB*).

[2] Fleetwood] In December 1654 Charles Fleetwood (d. 1692) was appointed one of Cromwell's council and at once assumed a leading place in the Protector's court. His connection with the Cromwell family (Fleetwood's second wife was Cromwell's eldest daughter Bridget) prompted his elevation of Richard Cromwell, but there were rumors that Oliver Cromwell had actually appointed Fleetwood as his successor. Royalist agents, however, had for some time been soliciting Fleetwood on behalf of Charles II, and he was pressed by his brother Sir William Fleetwood and by Bulstrode Whitelocke to enter into negotiations with Charles and declare for a free parliament, but because of his commitment to Lambert he declined. He escaped prosecution at the Restoration only because he had taken no part in the king's trial and was not regarded as politically dangerous (*DNB*).

Wareston,[3] A Scotch Laird, President of the Committee [of Safety].
Whitelock,[4] a lawyer of the same Committee.[c]
Desborough,[5] Huson,[6] Cobbet,[7] Duckinfield,[8] colonels and of the same Committee.

---

[3] Wareston] or Lord Warriston, a courtesy title granted Scottish statesman Archibald Johnston (1611-1663) by Charles I, in effect, for resisting English oppression. When Charles I became a virtual prisoner with the Scots at Newcastle in 1646, he made Johnston king's advocate with an allowance of 3,000 pounds per year. After Charles I's execution, Johnston, though never friendly to the royal cause, was present officially when Charles II was proclaimed king at Edinburgh in February 1649. He is reported to have had several interviews with Cromwell after the battle of Dunbar in 1650, and though his Presbyterianism placed him in a preplexing situation with Cromwell, Johnston accepted his old office of lord clerk register in 1657 and became president of the Committee of Safety after the suppression of the Rump Parliament in 1659. At the Restoration, Charles II singled Johnston out for punishment, issuing a death warrant in May 1661. He was hanged in Edinburgh on 23 July 1663 (DNB).

[4] Whitelock] Bulstrode Whitelocke attempted a mediation between the army and Charles I and later became a commissioner of the Great Seal. As an ambassador to Sweden, Whitelock negotiated the Anglo-Swedish treaty of 1654 and rejected a viscountcy just before Cromwell's death. His *Memorials* are an important source for the period.

[5] Desborough] Major General John Desborough (1608-1680) was married to Oliver Cromwell's sister Jane. On Cromwell's death Desborough joined the party of officers who planned to make Fleetwood commander-in-chief independent of Richard Cromwell. Failing this, the officers sent Fleetwood and Desborough to force Richard to dissolve Parliament in April 1659. Successful, Desborough was elected one of the councils of state in May 1659, but on the second restoration of the Rump, he rusticated to his house "farthest off London." When the Restoration was inevitable, Desborough escaped to Holland. On threat of being charged with treason, he returned in 1666 and was imprisoned in the Tower but was eventually permitted to reside in England the rest of his life (*DNB*).

[6] Huson] John Hewson (d. 1662), originally a shoemaker, rose to a high rank as commander under Cromwell. Hewson was knighted by Cromwell in December 1657 and named one of the Committee of Safety. He escaped

Trotter,[9] secretary to Lord Lambert.
A Frenchman.
Four prentices.
Four soldiers.
Two clerks, and two doorkeepers to the
      Committee.
[WOMEN]
Lady Lambert, wife to Lord Lambert.
Mrs. Cromwell, Oliver's widow.
Lady Fleetwood.[10]
Three ladies.d
Prissilla, woman* to Lady Lambert.

The Rump; or, The Mirror of the Late Times.

Act I, scene i. [A field.]

Enter three or four soldiers severally.

FIRST SOLDIER.
   Ah, rogues, the business is done.

London at the Restoration and is said to have died at
Amsterdam in 1662 (*DNB*).

7 Cobbet] Miles Corbet, or Cobbet (d. 1662), was a lawyer and clerk of the Court of Wards in 1644. For his
part in the regicide, he was arrested for high treason in
January 1660 and, excluded from the act of indemnity,
was executed in April 1662 (*DNB*).

8 Duckinfield] Roundhead colonel, Robert Duckinfield
(1619-1689) was proprietor of a large estate in Cheshire, where he supported the popular party. He was deputed to sit on the trial of Charles I but declined the
appointment. Later he was associated with General Lambert in 1659 in suppressing Sir George Booth's "Cheshire Rising" in favor of the exiled king. Immediately after
the Restoration he was tried as one of the officers who
sat on the court-martial of the Earl of Derby, was released from custody but later imprisoned in the Tower
in 1665 for about a year. After this date he appears to
have lived quietly at Duckinfield Hall until his death
in 1689 (*DNB*).

9 Trotter] Since Tathum occasionally substitutes Walker
for Trotter in the text of Q1, he probably had in mind
not an historical character but a type.

10 Lady Fleetwood] Mrs. Cromwell's daughter Bridget was
first married to Roundhead Henry Ireton and second
to Fleetwood.

SECOND SOLDIER.
   In a dish, I warrant you.
FIRST SOLDIER.
   And thrown out o'th'windows. The town's our
   own, boys.
THIRD SOLDIER.
   And all the wealth in't.
FIRST SOLDIER.
   And wenches to boot, boys.   5
SECOND SOLDIER.
   Boot me no boots, 'tis bootless, 'till we have 'um.
FOURTH SOLDIER.
   Those are commodities, I confess, I fain would
   truck for.
FIRST SOLDIER.
   Thou shalt have them by the belly, lad.
FOURTH SOLDIER.
   Rare recruits after a long march!   10
FIRST SOLDIER.
   Gramercy Lambert.
SECOND SOLDIER.
   Heroic Lambert.
THIRD SOLDIER.
   The man of men and might.
FIRST SOLDIER.
   We were opposed and even at push a pike for't;
   though a wet morning, 'twould have been dry   15
   service had we gone to't.
SECOND SOLDIER.
   Dry blows would ne're have done't; some must
   have sweat blood for't, but 'tis prevented.
FIRST SOLDIER.
   The nail of Providence was in't.
SECOND SOLDIER.
   Or the parings rather; no matter which, 'tis done. 20
FIRST SOLDIER.
   Morley was a stubborn lad, yet Lambert fitted him,
   and in his kind too. His rhetoric silenced the
   mouth of his pistol; it had sent a bad report else,
   and a home one. But Lambert, brave Lambert! that
   carries charms on the tip of his tongue, acted the 25
   part both of a soldier and a courtier, an enemy and
   a friend, exposing his breast to danger, under the
   canopy of security; and all this for us, you knaves.
   He told 'um a fair tale, but means to trust them
   no further than he can fling 'um.   30

SECOND SOLDIER.

That's some out of commission.

FOURTH SOLDIER.

Or into prison, or both.

FIRST SOLDIER.

We may, lads, in time grow up to something.

SECOND SOLDIER.

Ill weeds grow apace, brother, and thou art one of them, and in time mayst reach the gallows. 35

FIRST SOLDIER.

Speak for yourself, brother, I need not your oratory; well, Lambert has wit at will; Fleetwood's an ass to him.

SECOND SOLDIER.

A mere milksop.

THIRD SOLDIER.

A whey-brained fellow. 40

FIRST SOLDIER.

And of courage as cold as a cucumber.

FOURTH SOLDIER.

A fool in folio.[11]

FIRST SOLDIER.

Ambitious puppet.

SECOND SOLDIER.

A general in the hangings, and no better.

THIRD SOLDIER.

What think you of Vane?[12] 45

FIRST SOLDIER.

As of a vain fellow.

THIRD SOLDIER.

And what of Haslerigge?[13]

FIRST SOLDIER.

A hangman for Haslerigge, I cry.

SECOND, THIRD, FOURTH SOLDIER.

One and all, one and all.

FIRST SOLDIER.

'Tis Lambert for my money, boys; he is our 50
general, our protector, our king, our emperor, our
Caesar, our Kaiser, our—even what he pleaseth
himself.

SECOND SOLDIER.

If he pleaseth himself, he shall please me.

FIRST SOLDIER.

He is our rising sun, and we'll adore him. 55

THIRD SOLDIER.

For the Speaker's[14] glory's set.

FIRST SOLDIER.

At nought, boy; how the slave looked when his
coach was stopped?

FOURTH SOLDIER.

Like a dog outlawed; the palate of his breech fell
down with fear.

FIRST SOLDIER. 60

He told us he was our general.

SECOND SOLDIER.

Of what? Bills, bonds, and obligations; or green-
sleeves[15] and pudding pies?

FIRST SOLDIER.

And we told him he was an old doting fool, and
bade him get him home and take a caudle of calves' 65
eggs[16] to comfort his learned coxcomb, for he
looked but faintly on't.

THIRD SOLDIER.

And what said he?

FIRST SOLDIER.

Said he! I prithee, what could he say that we would
admit for a reasonable answer? We were better 70

---

11 A fool in folio] referring to the large pages of a folio edition, a fool of the largest kind

12 Vane] Sir Henry Vane, the younger (1613-1662), statesman and author, was elected a member of every council of state chosen during the Commonwealth. On the Restoration Vane was considered dangerous and excluded from the Act of Indemnity; imprisoned in the Tower, he was later executed in June 1662 (DNB).

13 Haslerigge] Statesman Sir Arthur Hesilrige, or Haselrig (d. 1661), had been appointed one of the king's judges but refused to act, though he spoke approvingly of the king's execution in 1659. As a member of the Committee of Safety and Council of State, he was one of the most powerful men in government. He accused Lambert of attempting to set up the rule of "a single per-

son." At the Restoration, Hesilrige argued his innocence in the king's trial but passed the remainder of his life in the Tower (DNB).

14 Speaker's] Thomas Bamfield, last Speaker of the Rump Parliament, whose authority ceased with the current dissolution of Parliament by the generals

15 green-sleeves] inconstant lady-love or the ballad about one (OED)

16 eggs] testicles

principled than so; reason and our business were two things. What we did, we did; that was our will, and the word of command lodged in our hilts. Alas, poor worm, Cobbet and Duckinfield showed him cockpit law, and o're-ruled his rolls. He 75 understood not the soldier's dialect. The searching language of the sword puzzled his intellect; the keenness whereof would have proved too sharp for his wit had he been obstinate or persisted in the interpretation, and therefore very mannerly he 80 kissed his hand and wheeled about.

SECOND SOLDIER.

To the place from whence he came.

THIRD SOLDIER.

And ere long to the place of execution.

FIRST SOLDIER.

No, hang him, he will have his clergy.

SECOND SOLDIER.

Is he such an infidel to love them? 85

FIRST SOLDIER.

Yes, as we do barbers, that is, while they are trimming us: he'd fain go à la mode to heaven.

SECOND SOLDIER.

If his foot slip not, but if it do, his finery is spoiled, he will be so sootified.

FIRST SOLDIER.

He that deals with pitch must expect no better; 90 black will to black, quoth the devil to the collier. But, dost thou think there is a heaven or hell?

SECOND SOLDIER.

Why dost thou ask me that question? I am a soldier, and so art thou; let's ne're trouble our heads about it. A short life and a merry life, I cry; happy 95 man be his dole.

THIRD SOLDIER.

And so say I. While we are here, we are here; when we are gone, we are gone, for better or for worse, for rich or for poor; amongst the good or the bad, we shall find room, I warrant thee, lad, and our 100 general can expect no more.

SECOND SOLDIER.

And now you have put us in mind of our general, I mean Lambert (not Fleetwood, that son of a custard-maker, always quaking): let us as bravely spend his this day's benevolence as he nobly 105 intended it.

THIRD SOLDIER.

A good resolution.

FIRST SOLDIER.

Rather a proposition, brother, but where, how, and in what?

SECOND SOLDIER.

Not in rotgut beer, I will assure you, or muddy ale; 110 wine for my money.

FIRST SOLDIER.

Wine is the life of action, 'tis decreed.

SECOND SOLDIER.

And I obey.

FIRST SOLDIER.

Blood requires blood, then from the purple grape, I'll suck my fill, spite of you, jackanape'. 115 There's poetry for you, gentlemen.

SECOND SOLDIER.

A pin for your poetry! March upon't.

Exeunt.

[Scene ii. A tavern.]

They go out and come in again at the other end of the stage.

FIRST SOLDIER.

Bring us more wine there. Come, who sings?

THIRD SOLDIER.

He that best can, my comrade here.

FIRST SOLDIER.

Something on the times, or nothing.

A Song for the Soldiers.

SECOND SOLDIER.

Though the morning was wet,
     We are merrily met 5
In a house more dry than our skin, boys;
     We'll drink down the day,
     Ne're question our pay,
Let them heartily laugh out that win, boys.

CHORUS.

Then drink a full brimmer to him that intends 10
For the good of the soldier to labor his ends.

II.

Let him flatter and lie,
     What is't to thee or I?

And ape Noll[17] in ev'ry condition;
  If we thrive upon't,   15
  Let all the world want,*
And the city kneel down and petition.

CHORUS.
Then drink a full brimmer to him that intends
For the good of the soldier to labor his ends.

SOLDIERS.
Hey boys, come away.   20

Exeunt.

[Scene iii. Lambert's offices.]

Enter Lambert and Trotter his secretary.

LAMBERT.
Trotter.ᵉ

TROTTER.
My lord?

LAMBERT.
Has Whitelock been here yet?

TROTTER.
Not yet, my lord. Sir—

LAMBERT.
What wouldst thou have?   5

TROTTER.
Nothing, my lord, not I.

LAMBERT.
Thou hast not thy name for nothing; I see thy
tongue will keep pace with thy wit and still be
trotting. I prithee leave off thy impertinences; I
have told thee enough on't.   10

TROTTER.
Why my lord, an* it shall please you.

LAMBERT.
I tell thee it does not please me; 'tis my fear thou'lt
be my shame. I sent thee into France to learn some
breeding, and thou render'st me the poorest and
the pitifull'st account that ever porter gave on a   15
slight errand. Dost thou keep company?

TROTTER.
Yes, my lord.

LAMBERT.
What are they, of what sort?

TROTTER.
Of the better, sir.

LAMBERT.
'Tis strange! thy knowledge being so bad. Are they   20
men of intelligence?

TROTTER.
I think so, my lord.

LAMBERT.
You think so! sad, I profess 'tis very sad. Were it
my case, as it is yours, and it behooves you as you
assume the title of a secretary, I'd draw men's souls   25
out by inspeculation, and in the inquest of their
faculties cull out such matter as would yield
advantage to him I had relation to; and without
this, thou neither dost deserve the place thou hast,
nor art thou fit for company.   30

TROTTER.
My lord, I have done my endeavor.

LAMBERT.
A weak one. Let Thurloe[18] be your precedent.

TROTTER.
When your lordship is translated to your Highness,
and that you have command of the public purse,
I shall be as ready to waste it as he or the proudest   35
of 'um. But I am but a fool to explain myself.

LAMBERT.
That time is drawing near.

*He turns about in wrath with his dapper dagger at his
breech.*

TROTTER.
In the meantime I have not been idle; I have done
something.

LAMBERT.
What hast thou done that may deserve recording?   40

---

17 Noll] nickname for Oliver (Cromwell)

18 Thurloe] John Thurloe (1616-68), secretary of state during the Protectorate, who directed foreign intelligence
operations and played an important role in Richard
Cromwell's elevation. In the Parliament of early 1659
Thurloe was the official leader of government supporters and its recognized spokesman. After the return of
Charles II, Thurloe was accused of high treason but was
set free with the proviso of attending the secretaries of
state "for the service of the state [i.e. gathering foreign
intelligence] whenever they should require" (*DNB*).

TROTTER.

Why, I have endeavored to find how the common
cry of the town goes as to this day's business.

LAMBERT.

That's something indeed. And how do the people
relish it?

TROTTER.

Relish it! why truly, sir, it is thought—   45

LAMBERT.

Thou wilt return to thy vomit.

TROTTER.

Why truly, sir, it is thought, and if I may speak
my thoughts freely, the Rump was but a stinking
Rump, and scented so ill in the nostrils of the
people that they feared a sudden plague attended   50
the concavity, and with much joy blest the rue and
wormwood you brought to their conservation.

LAMBERT.

Dost thou know what thou sayest?

TROTTER.

I could say more, sir.

LAMBERT.

To as little purpose. Be gone! I would be private—   55
yet if Whitelock come, admit him.

TROTTER.

Nay my lord, I warrant here will be the whole fry
presently.

LAMBERT.

Thou a secretary, and talk so like a fisherman!
What fry, you fool?   60

TROTTER.

Fleetwood and the rest, sir.

LAMBERT.

My mind is not at rest while thou art here.
Be gone—

Exit Trotter.

I wonder Whitelock comes not? he's a man
Has run all hazards, with as good success,   65
Except Old Noll, as any man I know;
He was his creature, and he now is mine,
And hitherto he has performed his part
In my revenge upon that family
So home, even to their doors, that my disgrace   70
Lies buried in their infamy.

Enter Trotter and Whitelock.

—How now?

TROTTER.

My lord, he's come.

LAMBERT.

'Tis well, leave us.—My lord, how goes causes?

WHITELOCK.

They cannot go amiss, sir, whilst you are advocate.   75

LAMBERT.

The sword, thou meanest; that must decide all
controversies.

WHITELOCK.

It will do much, sir, but policy puts the best edge to't.

LAMBERT.

And that you have. Come my lord, be free. Where
shall we set up our rest? We have had tossing times.   80

WHITELOCK.

Indeed, my lord, time hath been tost in a blanket,
but I hope now we shall use time better than so.

LAMBERT.

As how?

WHITELOCK.

You may trim him, sir; you have him by the
foretop.   85

LAMBERT.

If I thought so, I'd hold him fast.

WHITELOCK.

Now or never: if you let slip your hold, you are
undone, *aut Caesar aut nullus.*[19]

LAMBERT.

But the *remora*[20] to that is Fleetwood.

WHITELOCK.

Alas! you know him, sir.   90

LAMBERT.

True, he's but of a softly nature.

WHITELOCK.

A fine commendation for a general, that should
be rough as war itself. But he has a soft place in
his head too, and that's worse. However, he's a fit
subject for our purpose, and therefore sir, let's use   95
him as Catiline did Lentulus:[21] drill him along

---

19 *aut Caesar aut nullus*] either Caesar or no one (Lat.)
20 *Remora*] hindrance (Lat.)
21 Cataline did Lentulus] After Cicero's exposure of his conspiracy, Catiline (q.v.) abandoned Rome and the other
conspirators, now led by Publius Cornelius Lentulus, who
was arrested, charged with treason, and executed.

with hope that all tends to his only advancement. Fools are soon persuaded, and believe me, my lord, that was the very engine* made him consent to th'blowing up of his brother, a gentleman in some sense better qualified.

LAMBERT.

Aye, but a small nutshell, I am confident, may with ease contain both their courages; yet I know Fleetwood will fleer, he dare not grin, after honor and is as greedy on't as a cat is of a dish of milk.

WHITELOCK.

'Twill be ill bestowed, sir, if it light on him.

LAMBERT.

What, a dish of milk?

WHITELOCK.

You misinterpret me; honor I meant, sir. If you make him groom of your closestool, 'twill draw more from your goodness than his merit, and keep his wife in smocks too, during pleasure. That will be, sir, your highness' pleasure.

LAMBERT.

It is not come to that yet.

WHITELOCK.

Oliver had it; his time is passed, and your time's coming on. Princes have power o'er the persons of both sexes.

LAMBERT.

Name him no more; I hate his memory.

WHITELOCK.

I confess, I do not much care for't, yet I hate nothing brought or brings me profit. I loved the father of the heroics,[22] while he had a power to do me good; that failing, my reason did direct me to that party then prevailing, the fag end of the Parliament. What though I took the oath of allegiance as Oliver, your lordship and others did, without the which I could not have sat there. Yet it conducing not to our advantage, it was an ill oath, better broke than kept, and so are all oaths in the stricter sense. Laws of nature and of nations do dispense with matters of divinity in such a case, for no man willingly would be an enemy to himself. The very beasts do by instinct of nature seek for self-preservation: Why not man, who is

the lord of reason? Oaths, what are they, but bubbles, that break with their own emptiness?

LAMBERT.

You say very right, my lord; I'm of that judgment too, and shall persist in't.

WHITELOCK.

Yet the pulpiteers belch forth fire and brimstone 'gainst it. But my lord, how could I have served my country by setting the Dane and Swede by the ears, while the thread for a Protectorian interest was spinning here? How could I have carried on, or rather promoted, the design for Jamaica,[23] though it went in Oliver's name? How could I have lopt off those ill branches to the Commonwealth, the Cavaliers and Essex,[24] his* discontented reformadoes? How could I have showed myself loyal to your interest, by fooling Fleetwood in the disseating of Dick[25] by his dissolving the honest Parliament, as they called it, and bringing in the odious Rump? How could I in my speech at the Council of State have raked up Oliver's ashes, by bespattering him and his family, and told Ireton[26] how Providence had brought things about and that the hand of the Lord was in't, when I meant nothing less? How could I, under favor, have advised you to this day's enterprise if I should have startled or scrupled at oaths, preferred honesty or divinity before temporal interest or human reason? I desire, my lord, in this case you will be my judge.

---

22 father of the heroics] Charles I, leader of the Cavaliers

23 Jamaica] The English took Jamaica from the Spaniards in 1655 for its sugar plantations.

24 Cavaliers and Essex] the effort to pursue the Civil War against the remaining loyalists and disgruntled followers of Robert Devereux, 3rd Earl of Essex, forced to resign their military commissions to remain in Parliament. Essex as early as 1644 had become an opponent of Cromwell.

25 Dick] Oliver Cromwell's son Richard (1626-1712)

26 Ireton] Lieutenant General Henry Ireton attempted an agreement between the army and Charles I but later signed the king's death warrant. Married to Cromwell's daughter Bridget, he died of plague at Limerick in November 1652 subduing the Irish. For his hand in the king's trial, his body was exhumed after the Restoration, along with Cromwell's and John Bradshaw's, and hanged at Tyburn* on the Triple Tree.

LAMBERT.

Nay my lord, you are your own judge in this case, but in my opinion you have done yourself but justice.   160

WHITELOCK.

And he that will not do justice to himself will never do it to another.

LAMBERT.

You advise well.

WHITELOCK.

My lord, take it from me: he that will live in this world must be endowed with these three rare qualities—DISSIMULATION, EQUIVOCATION, and MENTAL RESERVATION.   165

Enter Trotter.

LAMBERT.

How now, the news with you?

TROTTER.

The Lord Fleetwood, sir.   170

LAMBERT.

What of him?

TROTTER.

My lord, he is come, sir.

LAMBERT.

Prithee, thy wit and his may walk together, admit him.—I knew I should be troubled with him.

Exit Trotter.

WHITELOCK.

I doubt not but you have prepared yourself for the encounter.   175

Enter Fleetwood.

LAMBERT.

I am pretty well antidoted 'gainst the poison. He's here.—My lord, your most submissive servant.

WHITELOCK.

My lord, I cannot compliment, but I am in heart your creature, that is, at your disposal.   180

FLEETWOOD.

Seriously, I profess, I cannot reach your meaning, gentlemen.

LAMBERT.

You are not skilled then in mathematics, sir.g

FLEETWOOD.

Indeed, I profess I believe so, gentlemen. I hope things are now in the Lord's handling and will go on well and become the doings of Christians.   185

WHITELOCK.

The government has been all this while in the horrid hands of infidels, Jews, pagans, and Turks. (*Aside to Lambert.*) I must make them up a medley.

FLEETWOOD.

Yea, abomination hath been in the hands of iniquity.   190

LAMBERT.

But my lord, those hands are now cut off, and all our ambition is that your lordship would take the government into the white hands of your goodness.   195

FLEETWOOD.

Who, I? Gentlemen—seriously—I profess—indeed—and by yea and nay. Law, you shame me, so you do! I can say no more, alas! I!

WHITELOCK.

You. Why, my lord, if you knew yourself as well as I do, you would say more.   200

FLEETWOOD.

Truly, I think, I have been something in my time.

LAMBERT.

Something! You have been more than something.

WHITELOCK. (*Aside.*)

That's stark nought, my lord, but it shall pass.

VOICES. (*Within.*)

Where's my Lord Lambert, where's my Lord Lambert?   205

Enter Trotter.

LAMBERT.

What's the meaning of this?

TROTTER.

The Lord Wareston, the Lord Huson, Colonel Cobbet, Colonel Duckinfield, and others desire your favorable and courteous admittance, sir.

LAMBERT.

By all means, let them enter.—But my lord, be sparing of your speech, for these are catching fellows and will interpret strangely. Our aim is only to advance your interest.   210

FLEETWOOD.

You know, my lord, I can keep my tongue within my teeth, sometimes.   215

WHITELOCK.

'Tis a high point of wisdom in you, sir.

FLEETWOOD.

'Odd* so they are here, I cry mum—

Enter Wareston, Desborough, Huson, Cobbet, Duckinfield.

WHITELOCK.

The less you speak, the better 'twill be, sir.

LAMBERT.

My Lord Wareston.

WARESTON.

Many benisons light on you for this day's wark, 220
my geod loord.

DESBOROUGH.

How do you do my Lord Fleetwood? how do you
my Lord Lambert? how do you my Lord
Whitelock? and how do you all? Hah!

FLEETWOOD.

The better for your asking, sir. 225

DESBOROUGH.

Say you so, then, I'll ask again, and how? and how?

HUSON.

And what? and what?

COBBET.

Your language cannot be translated, brother.

HUSON.

Let them take me by the meaning then.

WARESTON.

By th' Members, hawd there my Loord, 'tis sere, 230
and faw27 pley, sirs.

DUCKINFIELD.

My lords, I have not been backward in this day's
business, nor any here, I think.

LAMBERT.

'Tis confessed, sir. What would you infer farther
upon't? 235

DUCKINFIELD.

And therefore requisite we should know how
things will go.

WHITELOCK.

As they may, sir: soft fire makes sweet malt. You
know that, Colonel.

DESBOROUGH.

And that I know very well too, and you have said 240
very well, as much as a man can say and no more.

HUSON.

And that's enough.

DUCKINFIELD.

But we are in a chaos, a confusion.

HUSON.

A mere* chaos, a confusion. 245

COBBET.

And the people expect suddenly* something from
us.

WHITELOCK.

Why gentlemen, Rome was not built in a day.

WARESTON.

Mickle wisdom, geod feath, in that, sirs, there's
mickle wisdom in that, I's 'sure ye. 250

LAMBERT.

At three a'clock we'll meet at Wallingford House28
and discuss the business further. What say you my
lord?

FLEETWOOD.

I profess, I say so too, at three a'clock be't,
gentlemen. What say you? 255

DUCKINFIELD, HUSON, COBBET.

We'll wait upon you, my lords. Your servants.

Exeunt Duckinfield, Huson, Cobbet.

DESBOROUGH.

I protest, I am glad of this with all my heart, for I
have business in Smithfield where my horse stands.
Now it comes in my mind, on my conscience, the
roguish ostler has not given him oats today, and 260
the knave's hay is musty too; well, my man is such
another ass. Farewell gentlemen, I'll see you anon.
If I come not soon enough, pray keep me a place
in the Council, or let my vote stand for one, no
matter how. (*Exit.*) 265

WARESTON.

Au geod rason too, my loord, he's a braw* mon
this, my leords, ye ken him weel enough.

---

27 hawd, faw] here and elsewhere (though not always) *aw*
represents *ol* or *oul* in Scottish dialect

28 Wallingford House] Fleetwood's home where council
and political strategy meetings were taking place prior
to the Restoration

WHITELOCK.

And you too, sir.

LAMBERT.

Come my Lord Wareston, we presume you are a
knowing man. To what kind of government stand 270
you affected?

WARESTON.

E'en tol[29] what ye plase, sir.

WHITELOCK.

What think you of a single person? here's my Lord
Fleetwood.

WARESTON.

Marry,* an' he's a braw* mon, sir, bet are ye in geod 275
earnest, sirs?

LAMBERT.

What else, my lord?

WARESTON.

Bread a' God, I's for him, than.

WHITELOCK.

You see, my lord, how Heaven does raise you
friends. 280

FLEETWOOD.

Seriously I profess, my lord, you know, 'tis none
of my seeking.

WHITELOCK. (Aside.)

Nor is like to be of your enjoying.—My lord, a
word with you: What if my Lord Lambert were
the man? 285

WARESTON.

Reight sir—ou'z,* in one word ya ha' spoken aw,
sir, he's a mon, indeed mon, gif Wareston ha' any
brains, sir.

WHITELOCK.

You will live, I see, sir.—My lord, he's your friend
now. 290

LAMBERT.

No matter whose, he's a required property and
must be used by somebody.—And why so
melancholy, my lord?

FLEETWOOD.

I profess, not I; I was thinking 'twas dinner time.

LAMBERT.

Will your lordship please to take part of our small 295
cheer?

———————

29 tol] to

FLEETWOOD.

No indeed, my lord, I thank you, not I. My wife,
I profess, stays for me. Adieu, Gentlemen all—
(Exit.)

OMNES.

Your servants, my lord. 300

LAMBERT.

Nor you, my Lord Wareston?

WARESTON.

Ne in geod feath, sir, pardon me. I's invited by a
gay mon, sirs, tol platters of bra'* capons, sirs, and
aw the fowles in the aerie, sirs, aye, an' marry,* sirs,
tol one a my nown* countrymen ta, geod feath 305
noow.

LAMBERT.

If you please to stay, my lord, y'are welcome.

WARESTON.

God's benison and mine light on you, sir, geod
feath, y'are like a bra' mon, 'twould brest mon's
hert to part fro ye. I's e'en yar humble servant, my 310
geod loord.

LAMBERT.

You'll stay then.

WARESTON.

Aye marry sir, wi' yar nown* sel' tol deeth, sir, gif
ye ta plase, sir.

FLEETWOOD.

I knew. A small hair would have drawn him to 315
your table, without this ado.

LAMBERT.

My Lord Whitelock lead the way.

WARESTON. (Speaking to the Lord Whitelock.)

Ater ye is geod manners, sir.

WHITELOCK. [Aside.]

That's more than you know.—My lord, I am your
servant. 320

LAMBERT.

I'll break off the compliment then.

A treatment, sometimes, proves a trap to men.

Exeunt.

Act II, scene i. [The Lamberts' house.]

Enter the Lady Lambert and Prissilla her woman.*

LADY LAMBERT.

Priss, Priss.

PRISSILLA.

Madam.

LADY LAMBERT.

Why how now, Priss, where hast thou left thy breeding, in thy other pocket? Art thou not read in times and seasons? 5

PRISSILLA.

I never was such a fool to put trust in almanac-makers yet, madam.

LADY LAMBERT.

What a wench art thou! and why "madam," prithee? There's a word indeed, as common as the cries about the town. 10

PRISSILLA.

Your ladyship hath used me to't.

LADY LAMBERT.

I'll break that custom; 'tis a rude one. Hast thou no wit, wench? canst thou pick out no better title for me?

PRISSILLA.

In sooth, I cannot reach it yet, madam.

LADY LAMBERT.

Reach a fool's head of thy own. Sure thou art mad, wench. 15

PRISSILLA.

The secretary indeed says I am a mad wench, but I thank my stars I can make a fool of twenty such as he is, madam.

LADY LAMBERT.

Again! Can flesh and blood endure this? I must new mold thy manners. Madam! there's a gammer's title, out upon't. 20

PRISSILLA.

Seriously, I know not by what other names or titles to distinguish you, madam.

LADY LAMBERT.

I profess thou art dull, abominable dull. Dost thou not know upon what score my dear and second self is gone to Wallingford House? 25

PRISSILLA.

How should I, madam? I cannot divine.

LADY LAMBERT.

Lord help thy head. Why, he is gone to be made a man, wench. 30

PRISSILLA.

Was he not so before? If not, your ladyship hath had but an ill time on't.

LADY LAMBERT.

The Prince of men, you baggage. Thou art such a dull one.

PRISSILLA.

I cannot help it, madam, while I remain in ignorance. 35

LADY LAMBERT.

I see I must open thy eyes by way of explanation: then know that from henceforth I will be called her Highness.

PRISSILLA.

Nay, now you tell me what you would be called, I shall obey your Highness. 40

LADY LAMBERT.

It will do well, and 'twill be but your duty. Prithee tell me, how dost think I shall behave myself in't? (*She struts it.*)

PRISSILLA.

Highly well, you cannot choose, you begin so soon, if it shall please your Highness. 45

LADY LAMBERT.

I think I am better shaped for't than Joan— (*She surveys herself.*) or what do you call her, Cromwell.[30]

PRISSILLA.

Abundantly, for at her best she was but a bundle of f___,* madam—Lord, I am so forgetful— Highness I should have said. 50

LADY LAMBERT.

That's the word. Con it, and be perfect in't, or I profess you and I shall part—

Prissilla repeats to herself, "Highness, Highness, Highness." Enter Trotter.

What's the news with you? Am I sent for to Wallingford House? 55

TROTTER.

No, madam.

LADY LAMBERT.

What a beetle-headed fellow's this.

PRISSILLA. (*Pulls him by the skirt.*)

Highness, you changeling, you must call her Highness. 60

---

30 Joan ... Cromwell] Oliver Cromwell married Elizabeth Bourchier in 1620, daughter of a London merchant; Joan is a conventionally peasant name.

TROTTER.

No, an* it shall please your Highness.

LADY LAMBERT.

It pleases me very well. (*She struts it, and surveys herself.*) What's your business?

TROTTER.

Gammer Cromwell would speak a word or two with your Highness. 65

LADY LAMBERT.

Bid the poor woman wait without; I'll do her what good I can for her poor children's sake.

PRISSILLA.

Or rather for husband's sake, if it shall please your Highness; good turns ought not to be forgotten.

LADY LAMBERT.

Thou say'st true. One good turn requires another. 70 He was, I confess, a man every inch of him.

PRISSILLA.

Aye, and though he was out with my lord many times, he would be in with you, as the saying is, an't please your Highness.

LADY LAMBERT.

Well, I care not if I go to her. 75

PRISSILLA.

Your Highness will decline much your state then.

LADY LAMBERT.

Say'st thou so, Priss?—Trotter, admit her. I'll hear what the sad creature can say for herself.

Exit Trotter. Enter Trotter and Mistress Cromwell the Elder.

MRS. CROMWELL.

I thought I should have staid at the door 'till midnight. Marry* come up, Mrs. Minks.[31] Is there 80 such a do to speak with you? No marvel indeed.

LADY LAMBERT.

Prithee woman, what wouldst have?

MRS. CROMWELL.

Thy husband by the throat, had I him here, and I could find in my heart in the meantime to claw thy eyes out and make thee wear black patches for 85 something, thou proud, imperious slut, thou.

LADY LAMBERT.

The woman sure is lately come from Billingsgate.* Priss, ask how oysters go there.

PRISSILLA.

She's very quick of hearing, an't please your Highness. 90

MRS. CROMWELL.

Highness! in the Devil's name, it is not come to that sure yet, is it? hah! Thy husband may be hanged first, like a crafty knave as he is. Did my husband make him a lord for this? to ruin our family? Or as the word is indeed, trepan 'um? 95 Curse on the time thy husband was born; he fooled my son-in-law to betray the innocent babe, my poor child Richard,[32] that our fames are now brought to the slaughter houses, and the very names of the Cromwells will become far more 100 odious than ever Needham[33] could make the Heroics: woe worth the time.

LADY LAMBERT.

Priss, I pity the creature, ne'er trust me. Alas, it weeps.

MRS. CROMWELL.

Thou liest, baggage. I scorn thy pity, my spirit is 105 above it. Let me come at her: as old as I am, I can spoil that fine face my dear, deceased lord did so much dote on. Let me come at her.

Priss holds her.

Hands off. I'll do't, thou Jezebel.*

LADY LAMBERT.

She begins to rave: send her to Bedlam among her 110 consorts.

TROTTER.

I promise you, you shall have clean straw, Mrs. Cromwell.

MRS. CROMWELL.

Out rogue, rascal, vagabond, a fellow raised from the horse heels. Dost thou upbraid me too? I'll be 115 the death of thee if thou com'st near me. (*Falls back into a chair.*) Oh Dick, Dick, hadst thou had but thy father's spirit, thy mother ne'er had come unto this shame.

---

31 Minks] a lewd or wanton woman (*OED*)

32 my poor child Richard] Cromwell's son-in-law Charles Fleetwood sided with Lambert in forcing Richard Cromwell to dissolve Parliament and retreat into exile.

33 Needham] Journalist Marchamont Needham (1620-78), Commonwealth pamphleteer who vilified the Cavaliers

LADY LAMBERT.

Priss, a cordial presently. 'Odds so, she faints.   120

Prissilla goes in and enters immediately.

PRISSILLA.

I run, an't please your Highness. I have it here.

LADY LAMBERT.

Prithee give it her. I would not for a hundred
pound she should die here; we should be put to
th'charge of burying her.

*Then Priss offers her the cordial; she starts up and with
her hand casts it on the ground.*

PRISSILLA.

'Tis a precious cordial water of my own making,   125
madam; I hope there's no offense in that.

MRS. CROMWELL.

I need it not, proud woman. I divine this scorn
will be revenged on thee and thine. (*Exit.*)

LADY LAMBERT.

Farewell, Naught,
Th'art better lost than sought.   130

PRISSILLA.

She has a notable spirit of her own.

LADY LAMBERT.

'Twill get her nothing. She beats against the wind.

PRISSILLA.

She's windfallen, an't please your Highness.

LADY LAMBERT.

'Tis an ill wind, they say, blows nobody good. Let
her rave and rail; my dearest second self will fare   135
the better for't.

PRISSILLA.

The fox fares best when he is curst.

TROTTER.

Priss, Priss, a word or two, sweet Priss.

As they are going off, Trotter pulls Priss by the sleeve.

PRISSILLA.

Why how now, sauce? Plain Priss? Am not I her
Highness' maid of honor?   140

TROTTER.

I know thou art a maid of honor, but the meaning
of this, dear Priss?

PRISSILLA.

The meaning of what, thou novice?

TROTTER.

That madam is so suddenly turned to Highness.
Is my lord made Protector?   145

PRISSILLA.

No, you dunce. Well, thou art the simplest Trotter!
What, must I find thee brains and understanding?
Know then and grow wise upon't: she will be
Protectoress whether he be Protector or not. If he
has any honor, it must come from her, for aught I   150
see. She is beforehand with him and hath installed
herself already. I'm sure my voice was herald to't.
Thou piteous thing, question the pride and
pleasure of a woman? I will have thee, scribe, to
know the time will come I shall have honor too   155
and be courted by the better sort.

TROTTER.

Have I been wanting* in that duty, Priss?

PRISSILLA.

Wanting? Why thou art always wanting, never
provided, still* behindhand, never beforehand to
a woman. This I profess, and to thy shame be it   160
spoken. And therefore walk upon't; I have no more
to say to thee.

TROTTER.

But I have something to say to thee, oh ungrateful
Priss!

PRISSILLA.

Ungrateful? and why ungrateful, pray?   165

TROTTER.

Hast thou forgot the small token I sent thee?

PRISSILLA.

It was a small one indeed if it came from thee.

TROTTER.

The tweezers[34] out of France.

PRISSILLA.

Did travail hither, but were as dull as he that sent   170
them; they would not cut a feather. Is that your
precious present? If thou hast no better, walk alone,
for Priss, she's not for thy company.

TROTTER.

Nay dear Priss, shall we be married?

PRISSILLA.

What, are you so hot, sir? There's a jest indeed,   175

---

34 tweezers] a set or case of small instruments, obviously
   containing a cutting instrument

marry, before your 'prenticeship is out?

TROTTER.

What dost thou mean, wench? Prithee kiss me.

PRISSILLA.

I'll see better clothes on your back first.

TROTTER.

Why, are not these good?

PRISSILLA.

Enough, had not a fool the wearing of 'um.   180

TROTTER.

Thou mayst say anything, Priss. I may have better.

PRISSILLA.

When that time comes, and thy wit is more
refined, I may say something to thee.

TROTTER.

Oh my dear Priss, in the meantime, let me but kiss
thy hand.   185

PRISSILLA.

That you may. But hear me, be not proud on't.
Nor take this as a punctual promise from me; I
love myself better than so.

TROTTER.

Yet I may live in hope.

PRISSILLA.

If it were not for hope, the heart would break, they   190
say. But 'odds so, I forget my duty to her Highness.

TROTTER.

And so do I. Thou hast transported me.

PRISSILLA.

Not to Jamaica yet.

Exeunt.

[Scene ii. The Fleetwoods' house.]

Enter Mrs. Cromwell and the Lady Fleetwood.

LADY FLEETWOOD.

Good Lady Mother, be patient.

MRS. CROMWELL.

Good Lady Fool, hold your prating. Was ever
mother so unhappy or children so senselessly
ungracious?

LADY FLEETWOOD.

I beseech you, think not so; things will make for   5
the best.

MRS. CROMWELL.

Oh fond* girl, what hope canst thou create unto
thyself can save us now from sinking? We must
perish, undoubtedly we must: though Lambert
carry a smooth tongue to thy husband, it speaks   10
not the language of his heart, for that is rugged.
It will deceive him as it did thy brother and the
late idolized Parliament which he set up, out of a
malice to thy father's memory, to make it odious
because he pulled the Babel down. Yet now he has   15
usurped that privilege himself. Let his pretense be
what it will, it bears no other weight but that of
his ambition, to which thy husband is a property.

Enter Fleetwood.

FLEETWOOD.

Mother, I profess I'm glad to see you here, ne'er
trust me, law. How do you, forsooth?   20

MRS. CROMWELL.

The worse for thee. I wish I ne'er had known the
time occasioned thee to call me Mother.

FLEETWOOD.

Why, forsooth, Mother, if it please your Highness?

MRS. CROMWELL.

Oh monstrous, not to be endured! I have been
tame too long. The fool hath found a way   25
t'upbraid my misery. She had a husband, dear
Ireton, my best of sons, had wit and by his counsel
stilted up our honors, which thou pull'st down as
fast by thy simplicity.

FLEETWOOD.

I profess, ne'er trust me, I speak ingeniously, ne'er   30
stir now. I am no such baby neither, as you take
me to be, Mother.

MRS. CROMWELL.

A mere stalking horse to Lambert's pride. His wife,
that minion, doth assume that title I once, and my
son Richard's wife, enjoyed. She will be called her   35
Highness with a horse pox, while I am called Old
Joan, Old Bess, Old Bedlam, Old Witch, Old Hag,
the Commonwealth's Nightmare. 'Tis well if any
have the modesty to call me Gammer, or old Mrs.
Cromwell, and leave out many other horrid   40
nicknames. This infamy and more thou hast
brought on us. (*Weeps.*)

LADY FLEETWOOD.

Good Mother, do not weep.

MRS. CROMWELL.

    Would I were dead. Nothing torments me more
than that thy father, who whilst he lived was called 45
the most serene, the most illustrious and most
puissant prince, whilst that the fawning poets'
panegyrics swelled[h] with ambitious epithets, is now
called th'firebrand of hell, monster of mankind,
regicide, homicide, murderer of piety, a rump[i] of 50
flesh soaked in a sea of blood, traitor to God and
goodness, an advancer of fiends and darkness. Such
as these and worse, could I but think on 'um, are
daily cast into my ears by every idle fellow.

FLEETWOOD.

    I pray, take their names; I profess, Mother, I'll 55
order them, as I am here.

MRS. CROMWELL.

    Thou order 'um! Alas, they value not so poor a
thing as thou art. Had Dick continued, he had
kept our fame up fair in the world; none durst have
blemished it. They tell me that the time is coming 60
I must make a stall my court and learn to thrive
by footing stockings, and if that won't do it, I must
be, what I ne'er was, a woman of carriage, either
for tubs of ale, as suiting best with my original
condition, or else for oysters. I was made for 65
burdens and am too old and ugly to cry oranges.*
If these trades fail me, then I must turn bawd.
They think me tough enough t'endure that
tempest and tell me there's a place called Sodom
will receive me and my retinue; I know it not, but 70
thus I am made a public scorn by all men. And in
that, thee nor thine nor any other that claim
relation to us are exempted—and all this by thy
foolery.

FLEETWOOD.

    I profess, Mother, I will be even with 'um; I know 75
what I know, and there's an end, as I am here.

MRS. CROMWELL.

    I would there were an end to our disgraces, which
I do prophesy is but beginning. What will become
of that fair monument thy careful father did erect
unto thy memory before, lest none should do't 80
after thy death, next to thy husband Ireton's? nay,
even of his, thy father's too, and all that living bore
a love to him and us? The raging malice of proud
Lambert is so irresistible, 'twill destroy all.

FLEETWOOD.

    I profess, Mother, my Lord Lambert is a very 85
honest gentleman, and he loves me well, I profess
now to you. Well, I know what I know, few words
are best, I am and must be the man when all is
done, as I am here.

MRS. CROMWELL.

    'Tis very likely, when all is done, thou'lt be the man 90
will prove their scorn and laughingstock.

FLEETWOOD.

    I profess now, Mother, in sober sadness, I scorn
the words, so I do.—You know what I told you,
sweetheart, as I am here.

LADY FLEETWOOD.

    Very well, and do believe't, though you, forsooth, 95
are so doubtful.*

MRS. CROMWELL.

    Doubtful, of what? of that I never heard.

FLEETWOOD.

    No more words, but mum, I say, I charge you,
sweetheart.

Enter a messenger from the Committee of Safety.

MESSENGER.

    My lord, the Council waits your coming. 100

FLEETWOOD.

    Why law ye now, as I am here, you thought, I
warrant, I should not be sent for neither. I profess,
forsooth Mother, you are very hard of belief.—Tell
the lords I'm coming.

MESSENGER.

    I shall, my lord; most honored lady, your most 105
humble servant. Your humble servant, madam.
(*Exit.*)

MRS. CROMWELL.

    I have seen this fellow's face before; methinks he
does retain something o'th'duty he paid me
formerly. 110

LADY FLEETWOOD.

    Be but patient, Mother; I'll warrant things will go
according to your wish.

FLEETWOOD.

    Aye, if you'll have some patience; if not, I profess,
Mother, I cannot tell how to help it, for I must to
coach, that's the truth on't.—Sweetheart, pray 115
make much of my Mother. (*Exit.*)

LADY FLEETWOOD.

Will you please to walk in, forsooth.

MRS. CROMWELL.

My heart was very heavy when I came hither; 'tis somewhat now at ease by the disburdening of my oppressing griefs.   120

LADY FLEETWOOD.

I hope, forsooth, you'll have no cause to create more of them.

Exeunt.

[Scene iii. The Lamberts' house.]

Enter Lady Lambert and Prissilla.

LADY LAMBERT.

Hast thou summoned those inferior things?

PRISSILLA.

What, the ladies of the last edition?

LADY LAMBERT.

Those whose husbands have been stigmatized by Noll and Dick, with the title of baronets.

PRISSILLA.

I gave order to Trotter to trot about it, an't* shall please your Highness.   5

Enter Trotter.

TROTTER.

The ladies are coming forth.

LADY LAMBERT.

They were not bound to their good behavior, but—'tis well they understand their duties. Set us our chair of state, and then admit 'um.   10

Enter ladies.

LADY LAMBERT.

Gentlewomen, for ladies we cannot call you, your obedience to our commands is well resented; if you persevere in't, you will oblige our favor. Priss, proceed.

PRISSILLA.

By what authority and from whom do you derive   15
your titles of "madams," I pray?

LADIES.

From our husbands.

PRISSILLA.

What are they? of what standing?

FIRST LADY.

Of no long standing, we confess.

PRISSILLA.

That's a common complaint and a general   20
grievance.

LADY LAMBERT.

And shall be taken into consideration for a thing we know. Priss, prick that down in your notebook. Who made your husbands knights?

LADIES.

Oliver the First.   25

LADY LAMBERT.

Of horrid memory, put that in your notebook, Priss.

LADIES.

And Richard.

PRISSILLA.

Of sottish memory, shall I put that down too? 'tis remarkable?   30

LADY LAMBERT.

By all means, put it down in the margin as a hand directing to the rest.

PRISSILLA.

Of the foolish families, 'tis done, an't please your Highness.

LADY LAMBERT.

What coats of arms do your husbands bear?   35

FIRST LADY.

Who? mine, madam?

LADY LAMBERT.

Aye, thine, woman.

PRISSILLA.

You a lady, and show so little manners. Forget her Highness!

LADY LAMBERT.

I pass by their dirty breeding.—Woman, we say,   40
what coat of arms does thy husband give?

FIRST LADY.

He bears argent upon a bend gules, three cuckolds' heads attired or.

PRISSILLA.

Three cuckolds' heads! Why, one is sufficient, in all conscience.   45

FIRST LADY.

'Tis a paternal coat belonging to the family of the Wittols.

PRISSILLA.
It may be they were founders of Cuckolds Haven.[35]

LADY LAMBERT.
No more of cuckolds, Priss; 'tis opprobrious and intrencheth much upon the honor of our sex. Put that down in your notebook as a public grievance, and it concerns us to look after and the Committee of Safety to remedy.

SECOND LADY.
'Tis a material and punctual point to a woman.

LADY LAMBERT.
And what does thy husband give, prithee?

SECOND LADY.
He bears three gantlets dexter or.

PRISSILLA.
Or again. Your Highness may perceive they have had golden times on't.

LADY LAMBERT.
Dexter Or. Well, we know he has been an ambidexter all his life time, and he shall now give another coat: a body without a head in a field sable.—And what's thine, prithee?

THIRD LADY.
Ours is but parte per pale.[36]

LADY LAMBERT.
Parte per pale. What's that?

PRISSILLA.
A motley coat of two colors.

LADY LAMBERT.
'Tis a wonder with what impudence those fellows Noll and Dick could knightify your husbands! For 'tis a rule in heraldry that none can make a knight but he that is a knight himself. 'Tis Zanca Panca's case in *Donquixott*.[37]

FIRST LADY.
If none can make a knight but he that is a knight, how shall our husbands receive honor from your husband, who is no knight himself?

LADY LAMBERT.
Let me alone to dub him.

PRISSILLA.
You have done that already, an't please your Highness.

FIRST LADY.
If dubbing[38] our husbands will carry it, we can do that ourselves.

LADY LAMBERT.
But ours is of greater honor and antiquity and therefore ought to take place. Receive that as a maxim from us; dispute no further.

LADIES.
We shall not.

LADY LAMBERT.
Since, being enfranchised through our grace and favor, you are become members of our Commonwealth, declare your grievances, and we'll hear 'em, whether public or private.

FIRST LADY.
Begin with the private first, sweet Mrs.* Priss.

PRISSILLA.
This lady complains her husband prays too much, and it takes him off his other business.

LADY LAMBERT.
There can be no charity in that man is remiss in his benevolence.—Receive that as another maxim, Priss. You mind us not.

PRISSILLA.
I'm pricking of it down, an't please your Highness.

LADY LAMBERT.
But it may be he prays when's zeal's on fire, as bells ring, backwards.

FIRST LADY.
And then he rails against the Whore of Babylon,* and the people think he calls me whore.

LADY LAMBERT.
That's gross and shows small breeding; we'll have it rectified, it concerns us.

SECOND LADY.
And my husband says I talk in my sleep and call on men to come to bed to me and discover* his infirmities.

---

35 Cuckolds Haven] a town downstream from London on the Thames

36 parte per pale] divided by a perpendicular stripe

37 Zanca Panca … *Donquixott*] Sancho Panza cannot be knighted in Cervantes' *Don Quixote* because Quixote himself is not a knight.

38 dubbing] Prisilla and the ladies are thinking of a secondary meaning, to strip the comb and wattles from a rooster.

LADY LAMBERT.

Oh! have a care of that.

SECOND LADY.

Have a care of what? Were he capable of more care of me, I should have less care of myself.   105

PRISSILLA.

I commend the lady's resolution.

LADY LAMBERT.

And what sayst thou?

THIRD LADY.

Why truly, I cannot say much. My husband is a man of reason and is willing I should satisfy myself; he knows the failings of women and imputes it to   110 the frailty of our sex.

LADY LAMBERT.

He's an honest man, I warrant him.

PRISSILLA.

Such a husband for my money.

LADY.

As you are a lover of women, let the act of the 24 of June against fornication[39] be repealed; methinks   115 it frights as there were a furnace in't.

LADY LAMBERT.

As there were conveniences in that act, which tied up men's tongues from babbling, so there were destructive inconveniences in't. For familiarity was not so frequently used between man and woman   120 as formerly, when, you must know, society is the life of Republics—Martin the First, and Peters the Second[40]—indeed things were rather done in fear than freedom.

FIRST LADY.

In a Free State who is not free?   125

SECOND LADY.

I beseech you, in the next place, that the Cavaliers may not be looked upon as monsters, for they are men.

FIRST LADY.

And that it may be imputed no crime to keep 'em company, for they are honest—   130

THIRD LADY.

And men that will stand to their tackling.

LADY LAMBERT.

Well, we'll have these amended. What have you more to say?

FIRST LADY.

Now Mrs. Priss, to the public, I pray.

PRISSILLA.

Whereas several abuses have lately crept in amongst   135 us—

LADY LAMBERT.

That's a small abuse: love must creep till it can go.

PRISSILLA.

Her Highness hath the feeling sense of it and gropes out the meaning already, you see.

FIRST LADY.

We could not go to Hyde Park* nor Spring   140 Garden[41] so much as with our own husbands.

LADY LAMBERT.

Why, what had you to do to go with them? Could you find no better company?

FIRST LADY.

Good men were scarce, and then to avoid suspicion.

PRISSILLA.

In my foolish opinion, that rather begat it. What,   145 walk with your own husband? How contrary to conscience and high breeding is that?

LADY LAMBERT.

When things are settled, we'll have an act that no lady or gentlewoman shall be put to that slavery, but shall have liberty to walk or—talk, with whom   150 they please.

SECOND LADY.

Now may a multitude of men's blessings light on you.

LADY LAMBERT.

Priss, proceed.

PRISSILLA.

Here's a lady desires a patent for painting.   155

LADY LAMBERT.

'Tis too great a grant for a subject. We intend it

---

39 act … fornication] The second offense of fornication was declared a capital crime around 1650.

40 Martin … Second] possibly a reference to Henry Martin, who signed the king's death warrant, and Hugh Peters, whose sermon denouncing Charles I on the eve of his execution focused on Isaiah's denunciation of the king of Babylon.

41 Spring Garden] London suburb

for ourself and to that end have employed several
persons as our agents in foreign parts to find out
the readiest and securest way for making it, that
it may not eat into the cheeks, beget wrinkles,   160
impair the eyesight, or rot the teeth.

THIRD LADY.
  I have found the woeful experience of that.

LADY LAMBERT.
  We have intelligence of a water that will in two
  hours time take the withered skin off the face, and
  a new one suddenly* shall supply the place, that   165
  no lady or gentlewoman, though she have out-
  worn sixty, shall appear above five and twenty years
  of age.

PRISSILLA.
  That makes your highness look so smooth upon't.

LADY LAMBERT.
  There's no invention for sleeking, glazing, or   170
  anointing but we have notice of, and for powders
  and perfumes, we may be scented a street off.

LADIES.
  Oh sweet woman!

LADY LAMBERT.
  Then for attiring, and to find out the mazes of
  fashions, there's no lady but must follow us.   175

LADIES.
  You are at a great charge, sure!

LADY LAMBERT.
  We are so, but 'tis princely. (Rises.)

FIRST LADY.
  We hope your Highness will remember the
  foregoing premises.

LADY LAMBERT.
  Priss, be it your care to mind us; we must to   180
  Wallingford House and have 'um confirmed.
  And in the meantime, let our music play,
  To celebrate the glory of this day.

Exeunt.

Act III, scene i. [Wallingford House.]

Enter one of the doorkeepers; he trims up the table, lays
the paper and standishes in their places. Then enter
two clerks to the Committee.

FIRST CLERK.
  The lords are coming.

DOORKEEPER.
  Are you sure on't?

[SECOND] CLERK.
  They are upon us already.

DOORKEEPER.
  That they are not, I'll assure you, gentlemen.
  However, I will attend my charge. Keep back there,   5
  keep back there, I say, keep back there, make room
  for the lords there.—God bless your Honors.

Enter Lambert, Fleetwood, Whitelock, and Wareston.
Enter [momentarily] Duckinfield and Cobbet; they
pass a complement to the rest, Cobbet takes Wareston by
the hand, Duckinfield and they walk together
whispering. Lambert, Fleetwood and Whitelock do the
like; after a turn or two Lambert speaks.

LAMBERT.
  It must be done, my lord; we have nothing else to
  take him off.

WHITELOCK.
  Scots, we know, generally are greedy of gain, and   10
  since we have made him President, and sensible of
  our secrets, 'tis requisite we do something to stop
  his mouth.

LAMBERT.
  For he's a gaping fellow; it must be done, my lord.j

FLEETWOOD.
  Say you so? I profess, seriously, if I thought good   15
  would ensue on't, with all my heart.

COBBET. (To Wareston.)
  My lord, believe us, all we can serve you in you
  may command.

DUCKINFIELD.
  And you shall find it so when occasion serves and
  the government's new molded.   20

WARESTON.
  Marry* sirs, and I's sa mold itt, 'twas neer so
  molded sen the dam bound the head on't.[42]

COBBET.
  I know there are some ambitious spirits would have
  it settled in a single person, but we are quite against
  it.   25

____

42 so molded … on't] plays off the practice of mothers
   binding the heads of infants to shape them

WARESTON.

The faw Deel,* split his pipe, will be for't than, for Archibald Johnston.

DUCKINFIELD.

But my Lord Lambert is a stirring man, you see.

WARESTON.

Lambert? let Lambert gang tol Bedlam in the Deel's nam, what ha' I to da with him? I's yeer humble servant, gentlemen.

Enter Desborough and Huson.

DESBOROUGH.

How do you, how do you, and how do you, my lords and gentlemen all, how do you?

HUSON.

And how do you, how do you?

WARESTON.

Ah my geod loords, ken ye me, sirs.

LAMBERT.

We shall make up our number anon. Will you please to assume the chair, my lord?

WARESTON.

Marry,* and I's your humble servant, my geod Loord Lambert.

DESBOROUGH.

Come, come, what government must we have? what government must we have?

HUSON.

Aye, Aye, Aye, what government? Let's know quickly. Come, you talk of *Conservetat, Conservetat,* 'tis a hard word, hang't, but there's "tors" in't, I'm sure of that.

DUCKINFIELD.

Conservator, my lord! Conservator.

HUSON.

Conservators[43] let it be then; when shall we have um, when shall we have um?

LAMBERT.

My lord, we'll think on that hereafter.

HUSON.

Hereafter comes not yet then, it seems.

DESBOROUGH.

But while the grass grows, the horse may starve.

COBBET.

Howe'er, gramercy horse, though't has no tail to't.

WARESTON.

Geod feath, sirs, and Ile tell you a blithe tale of a Scottish puddin will gar ye aw tell laugh, sirs.

LAMBERT.

That puddin will have no end to't, good my lord.

DESBOROUGH.

I love to hear of a puddin so it be a bag puddin.

HUSON.

So do I, if it be a good one.

WARESTON.

Bread a Goad, as geod a puddin as e'er was cut up, sirs.

FLEETWOOD.

I profess, my hair stands on end.

DUCKINFIELD.

No more swearing, my lord, 'tis not seasonable in this place.

WARESTON.

Hark ye me than, sirs, mind ye me now or ne'er. There was a poor woman, sirs, boged o'th'carl the Speaker, sirs, an he'd gee her nought whilke gard her to let a crack, sirs.[44] "Aye marry,"* quo the woman, quo, "now I see my rump has a speaker too." Haw lick ye my tayle noow, sirs?

OMNES.

Ha, ha, ha!

LAMBERT.

My lord, I know you have many of 'em, but pray let's mind our business.

DESBOROUGH.

Business, why there's the thing; I think every man ought to mind his business. I should go and bespeak a pair of mittens and shears for my shearer, a pair of cards for my thrasher, a scythe for my mower, hobnail shoes for my carter, a screen for my lady wife, and I know not what. My head is so full of business, I cannot stay, gentlemen.

---

43 *Conservetat* ... Conservators] Huson actually says in Latin "Let it be saved"; Duckinfield corrects to Conservator in the sense of "conservators of the peace," generally applied to the Lord Chancellor, Lord Treasurer, Justices of the King's Bench, etc. (*OED*).

44 woman ... sirs] the gist of the story is that she was sexually engaged by the Speaker until she farted

WHITELOCK.

Fie, fie, gentlemen, will you neglect the business of this day? We meet to gratify our friends. 80

DESBOROUGH.

Nay, then do what you will so I may rise time enough to see my horse at night.

WHITELOCK.

Is that it? Clerk, read what we passed the other day; I mean the heads of 'em. What papers and petitions remain in your hands referring to this day's business? 85

COBBET.

Forbid we should be backward in rewarding such have done service to the Commonwealth.

WHITELOCK.

There's money enough, gentlemen.

DUCKINFIELD.

If we knew where to find it. However, clerk, read.

[CLERK.]

"To Walter Walton,[45] draper, 6929 pounds, six 90 shillings, five pence for blacks[46] for his Highness."

LAMBERT.

For a halter. Put it down for Oliver Cromwell's burial. We'll have no record rise up in judgment against us for such a villain.

WHITELOCK.

But first let's consider whether that were good 95 service or not.

LAMBERT.

However, we'll give him a paper for't. Let him get his money when he can. Paper is not so dear, gentlemen, and the clerk's pains will be rewarded.

WARESTON.

Geod consideration, my geod loord. Bread sir, that 100 Cromwell was the veriest* limmer loon that e'er cam intol our country, the faw Deel* has tane him by th'lugs by this time for robbing so rich a country, bread sirs, aye.

FLEETWOOD.

I profess, my Lord Wareston, you are to blame, I 105 promise you, you are. Why do you swear so?

WARESTON.

Geod feath, I gi you thanks for your chastisement, I's fit ye, sir, au profess ta, anly gif you ha' me.

COBBET.

That may bring you profit indeed.—Clerk, proceed. 110

CLERK.

"To Walter Frost, Treasurer of the Contingencies,[47] five thousand pounds. To Mr. Edward Backwell,[48] 4600 pounds. To Mr. Hutchinson,[49] Treasurer of the Navy, two hundred thousand pounds."

WARESTON. 115

Ounds,* there's a sum! marry,* it came from a cannon sure.

CLERK.

"To Mr. Backwell more, three hundred twenty six pounds, sixteen shillings, five pence. To Mr. Ice,[50] four hundred pounds. To Mr. Thurloe, late Secretary to his—" 120

WHITELOCK.

"To Oliver Cromwell," say: leave out "Highness." You were ordered so before, where'er you find it.

CLERK.

"Secretary to O. Cromwell, 2999 pounds, five shillings, seven pence for intelligence, and trepanning the King's liege people." 125

WARESTON.

Marry,* sirs, an* ye gif so fast, yeel gi aw away fro poor Archibald Johnston.

WHITELOCK. (*Aside.*)

Oil the wheel, my lord, your engine* will go the better. Move for him first.

---

45 Walter Walton] unidentified

46 blacks] mourning clothes and/or funeral drapings

47 Walter Frost, Treasurer of the Contingencies] Frost unidentified, but the Contingencies were contracted troops

48 Edward Backwell] (d. 1683) a celebrated London goldsmith and the principal founder of the banking system in England. There is reason to believe that Backwell was the chief originator of the deposit system, which originated about the time of the Civil War, and he was the best known banker of his day (*DNB*).

49 Mr. Hutchinson] (1615-1664) parliamentary committee member from Nottinghamshire and regicide, Hutchinson was a member of the first two councils of state of the Commonwealth but did not take a very active part in public affairs. With the expulsion of the Long parliament in 1653, he retired to private life (*DNB*).

50 Mr. Ice] unidentified

LAMBERT.

Be it your business, I'll do as much for you.

WHITELOCK.

Content, Gentlemen, since we have set this day apart from other business, purposely to gratify our most concerned friends, let us consider the worth of the Lord Wareston, a person of eminent fidelity and trust.

WARESTON.

Geod feath, and I ha' been a trusty Trojan, sirs.

FLEETWOOD.

We know it very well, sir, I profess, my lord.

DUCKINFIELD.

And 'tis but reason you should be rewarded.

DESBOROUGH.

I'd scorn to let a dog go unrewarded.

HUSON.

And so would I, he fawns so prettily.

COBBET.

My lord, you are witty; I hope we shall have no more on't.

HUSON.

And performs his graces to a Scottish pipe so handsomely.

DUCKINFIELD.

You may content yourself with that, my lord, he is our friend.

WARESTON.

Geod feath, sirs, an sa I am. Wha denies it?

HUSON.

Nay my lord, we are not foes; I am for you.

DESBOROUGH.

And so am I, as I live.

WARESTON.

Geod feath, weel sed ye ken well enough I's sure; I's a man can serve ye aw, sirs. Sin ye are so kind, sirs.—Scribe, read my paper too.

WHITELOCK.

You have a petition then?

WARESTON.

Geod feath, I had been a very fool else.

LAMBERT.

Give us the substance of it.

CLERK.

"That your Honors would be pleased, in consideration of his faithful service and the constant charge he is at, both at home and abroad—"

HUSON.

That's his whores.

CLERK.

"To grant him some certain considerable sum of money for his present supply."

DUCKINFIELD.

Order him two thousand pound.

LAMBERT.

Seriously, let it be three thousand, gentlemen. You must understand he is much in debt.

WARESTON.

God's benison light on your saw, my geod Loord Lambert.

HUSON.

Three thousand pound! Why, half such a sum will buy all Scotland.

WARESTON.

Bread sir, ye leok but blindly on't, than.

LAMBERT.

Gramercy, my lord.

COBBET.

Well brother, the time was, a mite of it would have bought all the shoes in your shop. I will not say your stall for your honor's sake, though now you do abound in Irish lands.

WARESTON.

Y'are my geod friend, sir; geod feath, y'ave e'en hit him home. Clerk, gang a teeny bit farder.

CLERK.

"That your Honors would be pleased to confer some annual pension upon him."

LAMBERT.

Gentlemen, I think that but reason; he has been faithful, and I hold him a good Commonwealth's man and the rather because Haslerigge hath so bespattered him. Since you have consented to his present supply, let him not suffer for want* of a future one. What think you of four hundred pounds per an? 'Tis but small. Say are you willing to't, Gentlemen?

OMNES.

Aye, Aye, Aye.

LAMBERT.

Are you pleased, my lord?

WARESTON.

Bread, thar's a question indeed; ounz,* sir, ye ha'
won my heart.

LAMBERT.

Then, gentlemen, since my Lord Whitelock's
modesty is such he cannot speak for himself, give me
leave to become an humble suitor in his behalf: That
you will be pleased to make him Constable of
Windsor Castle, Warden of the Forests, etcetera;
Lieutenant of the Castle and Forests, with the rents,
perquisites, and profits thereof. Gentlemen, I need
not instance his faithfulness to us and our
designments hitherto. No man here, I presume, but
hath been, and is satisfied in himself of his reality,
and therefore, I am confident you cannot confer a
place of so great honor or trust upon a person more
deserving. But I submit to your wisdom.

OMNES.

'Tis granted.

WARESTON.

Bread my good lord, what can ye ask that we sall
not grant?

LAMBERT.

I have heard some say that honor without
maintenance is like a bluecoat without a badge.[51]

DESBOROUGH.

Or a pudding without suet.

LAMBERT.

You have made him Keeper of the Great Seal. 'Tis
honor, I confess, but no salary attends upon't, and
bribes, you know, are not now so frequent as they
were in Noll's time. Besides, my lord is a person
of that honor—

HUSON.

Well, my lord, let us be brief and tedious; let us
humor one another. I love my Lord Whitelock well.

LAMBERT.

I move for a salary, gentlemen. Scobel[52] and other
petty clerks have had five hundred pounds a year
apiece granted to them. I hope he merits more.

HUSON.

Let him have a thousand pound a year then? You

shall not want* my voice, my lord.

WHITELOCK.

'Tis a liberal one, my lord.

FLEETWOOD.

I profess soberly with all my heart.

LAMBERT.

Does that please your lordship?

WHITELOCK.

Your faithful servant, my lord, but if I may be so
bold to know from whence I shall receive it.

COBBET.

Out of the customs, the best place, I think.

WARESTON.

Sure pay my loord, bread a Goad. I's uphold you
now, gang your ways.—On scribe, let us mind
meere good warks; we sall prosper then, aw my
saw, sirs.

LAMBERT.

Clerk, proceed where you left off.

CLERK.

"John Bresley three thousand pounds, upon
account; Backwell for 9600 pounds, Worseley
Aubrey for 2500 pounds."

WARESTON.

Bread! Holt, for shame, where the Deel* sall they
ha' aw this siller, sirs?

WHITELOCK.

Ne'er trouble yourself for that, my lord.

LAMBERT.

These things must be granted; we know the
persons, they are our friends.

FLEETWOOD.

I profess, indeed brotherly love ought to go along
with us all, but when all is gone, when shall we
have more?

LAMBERT.

Pough, my lord, the City's* big with riches and
near her time, I hope, to be delivered.

HUSON.

I'll be the midwife, or what you will call me; I'll
undertake to do my office as well as Dr.
Chamberlyn[53] can do his.

---

[51] blue ... badge] livery of rank or office without its attendant signs of power

[52] Scobel] Henry Scobell (d. 1660), clerk of the Parliament

[53] Dr. Chamberlyn] probably physician and poet William
Chamberlayne (1619-1689), practicing in Dorsetshire
and distinguished for his loyalty to Charles I during the
civil wars.

DESBOROUGH.   250

   Well said, brother.—What's the matter there?

The Lady Lambert strives to enter; the doorkeeper goes to the Lord Lambert and whispers him; he riseth and goes to her.

LAMBERT.

   I'll wait on you immediately, gentlemen.

HUSON.

   Is the Lord Lambert gone?

FLEETWOOD.

   I profess, I know not.

LAMBERT.

   Why, how now, sweetheart, what make you here?

LADY LAMBERT.   255

   Nay, what make you here then?

LAMBERT.

   This is not a place for women.

LADY LAMBERT.

   How so, pray? While thou art here I have as much right to the place as thou hast, if I am John Lambert's lady,* and for ought I know, my advice may do as well here as thine, for all you perk it   260
so.

LAMBERT.

   Good sweetheart, return to thy coach.

LADY LAMBERT.

   Good sweetheart, tell me, am I her Highness or not her Highness, or what do you intend to make of me?   265

LAMBERT.

   Thou makest thyself seem to be mad, woman.

She strives; Lambert holds her.

LADY LAMBERT.

   Do I so, sir? I'll be madder yet then; I'll to the Board and know what they intend to do with me.

LAMBERT.

   Thou wilt not, sure.

LADY LAMBERT.   270

   But I will, and hear what they will say to me; I will be put off no longer.

LAMBERT.

   Be not so loud.

LADY LAMBERT.

   I'll be louder, sir, and they shall hear me; if I am

not her Highness, they shall not sit there.

LAMBERT.   275

   Thou shalt be as high as can be, if thou wilt be patient.

LADY LAMBERT.

   Patient, aye, thou knowst too well I am a patient fool. Pray, when will the time come I shall be styled Her Highness? For that I will be.

LAMBERT.   280

   I'll tell thee that anon. Prithee, sweetheart, take thy coach.

LADY LAMBERT.

   Aye, thou think'st with thy fine words to work me to anything, but if you defer the time too long, you'll find the contrary.—Call my man there, d'ye hear me? pray make haste home. (*Exit.*)   285

LAMBERT.

   Well, well.

HUSON.

   My lord, we thought you had been gone.

LAMBERT.

   No my lord, I am not so unkind to leave you in the heat and midst of business.

WHITELOCK.   290

   Nay, I think the heat of our business is over for this day.—Clerk, see, have you any more papers?

CLERK.

   Not any.

HUSON.

   Let us rise then. I think we have sate a pretty time by't.

DESBOROUGH.   295

   And my colon begins to cry out beans and bacon.

They rise.

FLEETWOOD.

   I profess, my lord, it is not I think fit to put you in mind; I hope I need not, I profess.

LAMBERT.

   Oh, to move concerning a single person.

WHITELOCK.

   By all means, for his lordship.

LAMBERT.   300

   Seriously, my lords, I hold it would have been unseasonable, but at the next sitting it will fall in course, my lord, and then, my lord—

WHITELOCK.

We are your creatures.

FLEETWOOD.

Say you so. I profess, let it be so then.

DESBOROUGH.   305

Come, let us go; I'm mad to be gone. What should we stay here for?

WARESTON.

Marry,* and ye speke right, sir.—Scribe, see aw theise orders be ready for my honds anenst morne; meere especially my none and my geod Loords' here, that they may gang to the Patent, scribe, heare ye me?   310

CLERKS.

They shall, my lord.

Exeunt.

FIRST CLERK.

Come sirrah, here be thriving times; some men rise with their breech upwards.

SECOND CLERK.

And 'tis very probable may be lasht for't. How they divide the kingdom's treasure!   315

FIRST CLERK.

I commend them: they make use of their time, make hay whilst the sun shines. I wonder my Lord Desborough missed that proverb at the table.

SECOND CLERK.

Was ever such language heard at a council table before? they are all made up of proverbs and old   320 sayings, *exceptis tamen semper*[54] Lambert and Whitelock.

FIRST CLERK.

Oh! these are two precious devils, but for a fawning and colloguing devil, give me the Scotch devil.

SECOND CLERK.   325

No more of this, the Doorkeeper has ears.

FIRST CLERK.

I would his ears were off; they are not worth the sense of hearing. But come, let's put up our trinkets. A pox on't, I did not think they would have sate so long.

SECOND CLERK.   330

Thou hast some baggage or other to go to, I'll be hanged else.

---

54 *exceptis tamen semper*] roughly, except as always (Lat.)

FIRST CLERK.

Thou mayst be hanged in time; however, we'll go.

DOORKEEPER.

Well, go your ways; you are a precious* couple.

Exeunt.

[Scene ii. The environs of the City of London.]

A noise within crying, "Tom, Will, Harry, Dick, have you a mind to be murdered in your beds?" Enter a corporal and soldiers after him in a confused manner, as from their several lodgings.

FIRST SOLDIER.

What's the matter, Corporal?

CORPORAL.

The City's up in arms.

FIRST SOLDIER.

I am glad on't.

SECOND SOLDIER.

And so am I. There's plunder enough. I am mad to be at it.

CORPORAL.   5

The Committee sate all this night about it. 'Tis said they are up everywhere.

FIRST SOLDIER.

I warrant that dog in a doublet Haslerigg is the ringleader.

CORPORAL.

'Tis likely, the news came but within this hour, and the danger that lurks in't hath called the Committee   10 together. Tomorrow the prentices intend to petition the Lord Mayor for a free Parliament.

FIRST SOLDIER.

Let 'em, 'tis good fishing in troubled waters.

SECOND SOLDIER.

Must the Rump come in again?

CORPORAL.   15

I know not, good lads. Make haste, the captain stays for us.

FIRST SOLDIER.

Pox on't, let's ne'er stand buttoning ourselves. We'll leave our doublets behind us.

CORPORAL.

No, by no means.

FIRST SOLDIER.   20

And is't come to that? Then hey for Lombard

Street: there's a shop that I have marked out for
mine already.

SECOND SOLDIER.

You must not think to have it all yourself, brother.

FIRST SOLDIER.

He that wins gold, let him wear gold, I cry.

CORPORAL.

Well, we shall have enough; 'tis a rich city. Never   25
came better news to the soldiery.

FIRST SOLDIER.

We'll cancel the prentices' indentures and bind
them to us in surer bonds.

SECOND SOLDIER.

And they shall ne'er be made free by my consent
till they have paid for their learning.   30

FIRST SOLDIER.

Methinks I see the town on fire and hear the
shrieks and cries of woman and children already,
the rogues running to quench the fire and we
following the slaughter. Here lies one without an
arm, and he cannot hold a hand against us;   35
another without a leg, and he shan't run for't;
another without a nose, he'll never smell us out;
another without a head, and his plotting's spoiled.
Here lies a rich curmudgeon burnt to ashes, who
rather than he would survive his treasure, perisheth   40
with his chests and leaves his better angels* to wait
on us, you knaves.

SECOND SOLDIER.

Oh, brave* Tom!

CORPORAL.

I know you have all mettle enough, but our captain
stays.   45

FIRST SOLDIER.

Not a minute longer. Hey for Lombard Street, hey
for Lombard Street!

OMNES.

Hey for Lombard Street, hey for Lombard Street!

Exeunt.

Act IV, scene i. [The City.]

Enter a company of prentices with clubs.

FIRST PRENTICE.

Come boys, come. As long as this club lasts, fear nothing; it shall beat out Huson's tother eye. I scorn to

take him on the blind side; I'm more a man than so.

SECOND PRENTICE.

Thou a man, a mere pigmy!

FIRST PRENTICE.

Children are poor worms. I would have you to
know that I am the City's champion.   5

SECOND PRENTICE.

Thou the City's champion!

FIRST PRENTICE.

Yes, and will spend life and limb for *Magna Charta*
and a free Parliament.

OMNES.

So we will all, so we will all!

FIRST PRENTICE.   10

Why then, you are my boys and true sons to the
City; cry up a free Parliament.

OMNES.

A free Parliament, a free Parliament!

FIRST PRENTICE.

Boys, this was done like men. But do you hear the
news? My intelligence is good.

SECOND PRENTICE.   15

What is't, Champion, what is't?

FIRST PRENTICE.

There's a proclamation come from the Committee
of No Safety.

OMNES.

For what, Champion?

FIRST PRENTICE.

To hang us all up if we depart not to our homes.
How like you that, gallants, how like you that?   20

SECOND PRENTICE.

This hanging is such a thing, I do not like it. Well,
I'll go home.

FIRST PRENTICE.

Why, now you show what a man you are. I was a
pigmy as you said but erewhile, but now I say and
will maintain it, thou hast not so much spirit or   25
spleen in thee as a wasp.

OMNES.

Oh brave Champion!

FIRST PRENTICE.

Will you like cowards forsake your petition and
have no answer to't? Rather let us die one and all.

OMNES.   30

One and all, one and all.

FIRST PRENTICE.

Why, this is bravely* said. Now I'll tell you what you shall do: when the sheriff begins to read the proclamation, every man enlarge his voice and cry, "No proclamation, no proclamation!"

OMNES.

Agreed, agreed: No proclamation, no proclamation, no proclamation!

Exeunt, wavering their clubs over their heads. Enter Huson and his myrmidons with their swords drawn.

HUSON.

Was ever such a sort of rogues seen in a city? Come follow me. I'll so order 'um.

SOLDIERS.

Oh brave Colonel!

Exeunt. Enter prentices at the other end of the stage crying, "Whoop cobbler, whoop cobbler," and he pursuing them.

HUSON.

Shoot, shoot, I charge you. Kill the rogues, leave not one of them alive!

A musket is let off within. Exeunt. Enter prentices again, crying, "Whoop cobbler."

FIRST PRENTICE.

Cain has killed his brother, Col. Cordwayner; he has spun a fine thread today.

SECOND PRENTICE.

It may bring him to his end.

FIRST PRENTICE.

St. Hugh's bones must go to th'rack, and there let him take his last, whoop cobbler.

OMNES.

Whoop cobbler, whoop cobbler!

Exeunt. Enter Huson again pursuing the prentices; they continuing their cry, "Whoop cobbler"; turnip tops are thrown at him as from house tops; boys run in.

HUSON.

From whence come these? Search that house and every house. I vow there's not a street free from these rogues.

Exeunt. Enter the prentices severally.

SECOND PRENTICE.

Where hast thou been, Champion?

FIRST PRENTICE.

Where none but a champion durst be.

SECOND PRENTICE.

Where's that? where's that?

FIRST PRENTICE.

Stand here and admire.* You are beholding to me; I have passed the pikes to meet you and sweat for't. I tell you I have been at Guildhall, and what I have done there, let histories record. I'll not be my own trumpet.

OMNES.

What didst thou do there?

FIRST PRENTICE.

Do you see this small engine?* (*Shows a pistol.*) 'Tis a good one and has been trusty to his master. I say no more.

OMNES.

Nay good Champion, what? what?

FIRST PRENTICE.

How dull you are! With this, I say, heartily charged and rammed, under my apron closely hid, *Latit anguis in herba,*[55] there's Latin for you, rogues, I got into the yard.

OMNES.

What then, what then?

FIRST PRENTICE.

By good fortune I espyed a very fine fellow, some officer no doubt, he did randan[56] so.

OMNES.

But prithee be plain and short.

FIRST PRENTICE.

No, it was home: the sting of my serpent hath either killed him or lamed him downright. I warrant he troubles us no more this day.

A drum is heard within.

Hark, the rogues are marching! Let them go and be hanged; they shall not abide here. I have given them an earnest penny already, and if they come again, I'll double it. Well, boys, when they are

---

55 *Latit anguis in herba*] "The snake lay hidden in the grass" (Lat.: should be *latuit*).
56 randan] act like a drunk (Partridge)

passed, we'll go and drink the King's health. Say, boys.   80

OMNES.

Viva le roy, viva le roy!

Exeunt.

[Scene ii. Wallingford House.]

Enter Lord Lambert and Lord Whitelock.

LAMBERT.

My lord, you will still endear me.

WHITELOCK.

A duty so obliged cannot be paid too often. My prayers go with you, my most honored lord.

LAMBERT.

If I return, my lord, command my heart; in the meantime, let not your friendship cool.   5

WHITELOCK.

My body shall be ice first.

Enter Lord Wareston.

LAMBERT.

My Lord Wareston, this is a high piece of kindness indeed.

WARESTON.

Marry,* I's come tol kiss your nown* hand, sir, ere ye gang anenst the limmer loon.   10

Enter Trotter and the Lady Lambert.

LAMBERT.

Your servant, my lord.—Trotter, are you ready?

TROTTER.

Yes, my lord.

LAMBERT.

Direct the Lord Wareston to the blue chamber, where I'll attend your lordship.

WARESTON.   15

Your very humble servant, my loords.

Exit Trotter and Wareston.

LAMBERT.

I know she's clogged with passion, and 'tis not fit a Scot should understand it.

WHITELOCK.

You have done wisely in that, my lord.

LADY LAMBERT.

Have I stayed long enough? may you be spoken with yet?   20

LAMBERT.

Why not, sweetheart?

LADY LAMBERT.

Am I a wife, or no wife? (*Weeps.*)

LAMBERT.

My only joy and comfort, why dost weep? There's not a tear but wounds me. Prithee leave. I'm sure th'ast no occasion for't.   25

LADY LAMBERT.

Did Noll do so by his wife Bess, that puss? He had some care of her and made her what her heart could wish, but I have nought but empty promises.

LAMBERT.

Will you believe me or this gentleman?

LADY LAMBERT.   30

He's a lawyer and may lie.

LAMBERT.

He's my friend.

LADY LAMBERT.

'Twas a by-compliment, I confess, but I believe he knows more than you do.—Pray sir, say, shall I be what I will be, as he says?

WHITELOCK.   35

The power is now in his own hands, and doubtless my lord's so wise he will not part with't.

LADY LAMBERT.

Say you so! Then prithee kiss me, John; ne'er stir, I shall so love thee.

LAMBERT.

But we forget the Lord Wareston.

WHITELOCK.   40

He's got a Scottish fog in's mouth[57] by this time.

LADY LAMBERT.

Hang him, 'tis such a boorish, stammering fellow; I can't endure him.

LAMBERT.

But he's a property, if I return victorious, I must make use of. Therefore, prithee sweet, be moderately sparing in thy language; let it not soar too high, lest   45 it prevent my towering thoughts of their fruition and clip those wings should hover thee to greatness.

---

57 Scottish fog … mouth] He's off smoking a pipe.

LADY LAMBERT.

I'll not tie my tongue up for no man's pleasure living. I think I am a free woman, no bondslave, sir.

WHITELOCK.   50

But under favor, madam, when you weigh the advancement—

LADY LAMBERT.

I weigh it not a rush, nor shall I fee you for your counsel, sir.

LAMBERT.

He's a good man, sweetheart.

LADY LAMBERT.   55

Let him be ne'er so good, I'll have my will.

LAMBERT.

I prithee do.

WHITELOCK.

I trust I have not angered you, madam.

LADY LAMBERT.

Again "madam"! let his goodness be what it will, I'm sure he hath but ill breeding.

Enter Trotter.   60

TROTTER.

My Lord Wareston is going, sir.

LAMBERT.

'Odds so, indeed, we have been too uncivil. Come sweetheart.—My lord, will you please to walk in?

Exeunt.

[Scene iii. Environs of the City.]

Enter two or three soldiers.

FIRST SOLDIER.

How now, gentlemen? You are upon the merry march, I hear.

SECOND SOLDIER.

Aye, a pox on't, we shall have little cause, I fear, to call it a merry one.

FIRST SOLDIER.

Well, I thank my stars our regiment stays here at the well head, you Rogues, where there is plenty   5
of all things.

SECOND SOLDIER.

What says Pluck? The worser knave, the better luck.

THIRD SOLDIER.

But do you hear me, sirrah? for all that, your colonel may be hanged for killing his brother   10
cobbler.

FIRST SOLDIER.

I hear no harm; I'm not to answer for him. But prithee tell me, d'ye think there will be bloody noses?

SECOND SOLDIER.   15

Those that have a mind to't, let 'em give or take 'em. Hang him that fights a stroke, for my part.

THIRD SOLDIER.

Or mine either; our company swear they'll all be hanged first.

FIRST SOLDIER.

The general is like to be well hoped up with such soldiers.   20

SECOND SOLDIER.

Why, what would you have us to do? If the generals cannot agree, let 'em fight it out themselves, and the Devil part 'em, I cry.

THIRD SOLDIER.

If they will fight, we'll make a ring for 'em.

FIRST SOLDIER.   25

They say that General Philagathus[58] is a gallant, stout man, an excellent soldier, and a marvelous honest man.

SECOND SOLDIER.

Then we have the less reason to fight against him.

THIRD SOLDIER.

Nor will we fight against him.

FIRST SOLDIER.   30

But brothers, let me advise you to have a care what you say, lest you make your words good and be hanged in earnest. There are rogues abroad.

SECOND SOLDIER.

Aye, too many. I thank you, brother, for your advice.

THIRD SOLDIER.   35

Alack, we talk away our time. Let's go, let's go.

---

58 Philagathus] "Lover of the good" (Gr.): General George Monck (1608-1670), who was marching from Scotland toward London; Lambert's army was marching to confront him as the coalition of generals began to disintegrate.

FIRST SOLDIER.

Nay sure, brother soldiers, we will not part with
dry lips.

SECOND SOLDIER.

What you intend to do, do quickly.

FIRST SOLDIER.

Come away then.

[Exeunt.]   40

[Scene iv. The Lamberts' house.]

Enter Trotter and Prissilla.

TROTTER.

Now Priss, what think you now?

PRISSILLA.

Why truly, Secretary, I think thou wilt be a brave*
fellow when my lord returns.

TROTTER.

You will let me kiss you now, I hope.

PRISSILLA.

No indeed, Secretary, I will not make you so bold   5
yet; if you return safe and sound and in good
plight, that is, my lord's brows circled with laurel,
and people smell you out to be a Secretary of State,
'tis very probable you may have admittance to my
lip, and something else in a lawful way.   10

TROTTER.

These words have comforted my heart; I'm
overjoyed, trust me now.

Calls within: "Trotter, Trotter."

'Odds so, my lord's upon taking horse. Ah! ah! dear
Priss.

PRISSILLA.

Sigh not, man, thou shalt have it. Come, take   15
livery and seisin, and adieu.

TROTTER. *(Kisses her.)*

Oh, so sweet as the honeycomb!

PRISSILLA.

Have a care you do not surfeit with't.

Calls within: "Trotter."

TROTTER.

I must be gone, dear Priss, once more.

PRISSILLA.

Why law you now, give you an inch and you will   20
take an ell. I shall be troubled with you——

Kisses.

TROTTER.

No, truly, Priss.

Calls within.

PRISSILLA.

Why, you are bold indeed!

TROTTER.

Oh heart! Oh Fates! Why should such lovers part?
(Exit.)   25

PRISSILLA.

Well, go thy ways for a modest ass. Thou might'st
have had something else, hadst thou pressed me
to't, but the fool will make a fine husband: when
he comes to taste the fruit, he'll so love the tree!
'Tis a sweet thing for a woman of knowledge to   30
meet with a man of ignorance, and better to keep
him in't. My secretary, I see, never read Arratine;*
if he had, he would have been furnished with more
audacity. Lord, how honor creeps upon me! I shall
be ladified, there's no doubt on't. How my ears will   35
be filled with "madams"! And, "Will your ladyship
be pleased? What will your Honor have to
breakfast? How do you, madam? I am come to give
you a visit, madam. Will you go to Hyde Park
today, madam? How does your good lord, madam?   40
Did you sleep well tonight, madam? Is your dog
recovered of his fit, madam? Your faithful servant,
madam. Have you any service to command me,
madam?" This her Highness despises. I am as
proud as she, and methinks it sounds very well.   45
"Madam"! Why, 'tis a word of state.

Enter scullion-boy.

SCULLION.

Mrs.* Priss, Mrs. Priss, you must come away to her
Highness presently!*

PRISSILLA.

Why how now, sauce?

SCULLION.

Sauce! Why, what are you, pray? Will you come   50
away? I'll tell her.

PRISSILLA.

I'll have you boxed anon, sirrah, for this.

Exeunt.

[Scene v. City streets.]

Enter prentices severally.

SECOND PRENTICE.
Champion, how now, Champion? What news, Champion?
FIRST PRENTICE.
Nay, what news do you say, then?
THIRD PRENTICE.
Lambert is gone.
FIRST PRENTICE.
The Devil and John a Cumber[59] go with him! 5
Well, I hope General Philagathus will so pay his jacket—
SECOND PRENTICE.
He will be forced to turn it.
FIRST PRENTICE.
That he hath done often enough already.
THIRD PRENTICE.
The rogues were well mounted. 10
FIRST PRENTICE.
May the horse founder and the foot[60] die in ditches! My prayers go along 'em.
SECOND, THIRD PRENTICE.
Oh brave* champion!
FIRST PRENTICE.
Come gentlemen, if you have any chink, go along with me; we'll drink Philagathus' health. How they 15
look at one another!
SECOND, THIRD PRENTICE.
Faith, Champion——
FIRST PRENTICE.
Speak no more; your countenances betray your meanings. I perceive your masters are not so 20
tenderhearted as mine; he's honest, lives in hope, allows me the merry sice[61] a day to spend till better times come.
SECOND, THIRD PRENTICE.
Thou art happy, Champion.

---

59 John a Cumber] derived from the Scottish word "coom," cumber means ashes or coal dust (*Scottish National Dictionary*).
60 horse … foot] cavalry and infantry
61 sice] a throw in which the dice turns up six; winnings from a gamble (*OED*)

FIRST PRENTICE.
You shall participate of that happiness! It were pity 25
such proper fellows as we are should part without drinking a health to noble Philagathus his* success.
SECOND PRENTICE.
Well Champion, we'll make you amends.
FIRST PRENTICE.
Let the mends make itself; come away.

Exeunt.

[Scene vi. The Fleetwoods' house.]

Enter Fleetwood, Mrs. Cromwell, and Lady Fleetwood.

FLEETWOOD.
How say you so forsooth, Mother, as I'm here?
MRS. CROMWELL.
I say thy folly will undo us all.
FLEETWOOD.
I profess, Mother, as I'm here, you always harp upon one string. Ne'er stir, as I'm here, and like the cuckoo have but one note. Ne'er stir now. 5
MRS. CROMWELL.
What dost make of me, a hooting-stock?
FLEETWOOD.
No, I profess not I. I know my duty, as I'm here.
MRS. CROMWELL.
Thou wouldst fain seem a soldier and a courtier, but thou art neither.
LADY FLEETWOOD.
Good Mother, be not so bitter; he's an honest man. 10
MRS. CROMWELL.
Hang honesty, 'tis mere foolery. Thy father had more wit than to be thought one of that needy crew. Could ever man have given the power out of his own hand, as he hath done, and to his enemy, a fellow as fierce as aqua fortis and will eat 15
into the very marrow of our families!
FLEETWOOD.
I profess, Mother, you may be mistaken for all this; he is in some sense but my servant.
MRS. CROMWELL.
And he'll become thy master to thy shame. Why didst not go thyself? 20
FLEETWOOD.
Why I profess, whether you believe it or not, Mother, I am the greatest man in the nation.

MRS. CROMWELL.

Until a greater come. How stupid art thou? Girl, prithee instruct him.

LADY FLEETWOOD.

'Twould ill become me, sure, to teach my lord. I   25
ne'er was guilty of that crime yet; he knows his own business best.

FLEETWOOD.

I profess, Mother, you are such a strange woman, I know not what to say to you. Had not General Philagathus, like a fool, made this disturbance, I   30
know what I had been ere this time.

MRS. CROMWELL.

Thou hadst been neither better nor worse than what thou art, the common-tavern and town table-talk.

FLEETWOOD.

Why? I profess, Mother, you are not so well spoken of neither, for all you look so.   35

MRS. CROMWELL.

That's long of such an idiot as thou art.

LADY FLEETWOOD.

Nay, Mother, indeed you do not well. He's my husband; I ought not to suffer this.

MRS. CROMWELL.

Good Lord! it seems he plays better at treytrip[62]
with thee than thy husband Ireton did. Thou   40
couldst find tongue enough for him. Well, there's foul liars if this marchpane fellow did not melt in your mouth in his lifetime.

LADY FLEETWOOD.

I thank you, Mother.

FLEETWOOD.

What's that, what's that she says, sweetheart?   45

LADY FLEETWOOD.

Nothing, my lord, worthy your notice.

MRS. CROMWELL.

Had not a fool rid thee, thou hadst known thy duty better. So much for that, farewell. (*Exit.*)

LADY FLEETWOOD.

Nay, good Mother.

FLEETWOOD.

Let her go, sweetheart; the house will be the   50
quieter, I profess.

---

62 treytrip] a game at dice in which success depends upon the trey, or three (*OED*)

LADY FLEETWOOD.

She is my mother, my lord.

FLEETWOOD.

And I'm your husband, my lady; as I'm here, I think so. I profess I know not anybody cares for her company.   55

LADY FLEETWOOD.

She does not come to trouble you, sir.

FLEETWOOD.

Yes she does, I profess, and very much. I was just thinking of state affairs, and she has put all out of my head. The Committee have no reason to thank her, to my knowledge.   60

LADY FLEETWOOD.

Why, my lord?

FLEETWOOD.

Why, the citizens are mad for a free Parliament; the counties are all up, and is it not time to look about us, I profess?

LADY FLEETWOOD.

Indeed my lord, you say right.   65

FLEETWOOD.

If a free Parliament sit once, what will become of us? I profess we must secure ourselves as well as we can. The Rump, as the wicked call it, must and shall come in again, I profess.

LADY FLEETWOOD.

What will become of your friend the Lord   70
Lambert, then?

FLEETWOOD.

I profess, I care not. Your mother takes me for a fool, but let me alone to deal my cards: the Speaker and I are reconciled. But sweetheart, I profess I must be gone; I say no more. Lambert, Wareston,   75
and Whitelock are knaves, downright knaves. I profess they have fooled me all this while; it will now turn to 'em, I profess. Let 'em suffer.

LADY FLEETWOOD.

I understood, my lord, they were your friends.

FLEETWOOD.

But I have found 'em out; say no more. Will you   80
go in, sweetheart? I profess I must be gone.

LADY FLEETWOOD.

I obey you, my lord.

Exeunt.

[Scene vii. The Lamberts' house.]

*Enter Lady Lambert and Prissilla, her waiting
gentlewoman.*

LADY LAMBERT.

I wonder, Priss, that none of the modern poets
have been here with their encomiums since thy
lord went!

PRISSILLA.

It may be the Helicon[63] is dried up, or their brains
are turned addle.   5

LADY LAMBERT.

Well, I'm resolved to make him that brings me the
first copy Poet Laureate, provided he sings victory
in't. I will dispose of my places myself and be Lord
Steward[64] myself, or it shall cost me a fall.
Whitelock for all his art shall never carry it.   10

PRISSILLA.

How? Her Highness become Lord Steward!

LADY LAMBERT.

No matter for that; profit and service will come
by't. I'll have the ordering of all places both above
and below stairs, and so give out to the people.

PRISSILLA.

And good reason too, by'r lady.   15

LADY LAMBERT.

A counselor, a foolish fellow, at every end he calls
me "madam."

PRISSILLA.

Truly, there was one called me "madam" too t'other
day. Lord, we women are so frail! I thought myself
to be a madam in good earnest.   20

LADY LAMBERT.

Aye Priss, thou might'st be called so and be proud
on't. But I, I think, am somewhat above that style
or title.

PRISSILLA.

A story to please your Highness.

LADY LAMBERT.

I will have eight gentlemen ushers. That puss Bess   25
had four. Two shall bear up my train.

PRISSILLA.

Rather four, an* it shall please your Highness, for
you have a long one, no peahen like you. That
pettifogger Thurloe's wife had one, and as I'm a
Christian, another foolish fellow went bare before   30
her. No Countess could have been better manned.
Well, it will come to my turn shortly, but that the
wicked Rump is sat. There lies my fear. Oh
Fleetwood, Fleetwood! thou art stark nought.

LADY LAMBERT.

What sayst thou, Priss?   35

PRISSILLA.

I was thinking, an* it please your Highness, what
a canary bird Fleetwood was, to settle the Rump,
the abominable Rump, and pretended so much
love to my lord and master.

LADY LAMBERT.

His love is not worth the inquiring after, wench. As   40
for the Rump, I smell 'tis stale already and must be
peppered when thy lord returns. Dost think, wench,
it shall have a sitting place then? No, I warrant thee,
he that jerked it when he came out of the west will
do the like when he comes out of the north.   45

PRISSILLA.

Aye, an* it shall please your Highness, if he return
with victory.

LADY LAMBERT.

Ne'er fear it, wench, I have sent for Lilly* and
wonder he stays so long; 'tis such a dreaming
fellow.   50

Enter a servant and Master Lilly.

SERVANT.

Here's Master Lilly, an't* please your Highness.

LADY LAMBERT.

How now, Lilly, hast thou done what I
commanded thee?

LILLY.

I have examined the Zodiac, searcht the twelve
houses, and by my powerful art put the whole   55
regiment of gods and goddesses out of order:
Saturn and Jupiter are by the ears, and Venus will
be rampant, assisted by Mars the god of battles.

PRISSILLA.

This makes for your Highness. I love mischief with
all my heart!   60

---

63 Helicon] mountain sacred to the Muses
64 Lord Steward] official of the royal household

LADY LAMBERT.

How stands my husband's fortune?

LILLY.

In the Alnathay[k] of Aries, or as some others have it, Salhay, being the head of Aries.[65]

LADY LAMBERT.

Aries, what is that Aries?

PRISSILLA.

A monster, I warrant it.   65

LILLY.

'Tis a sign, and signifies a ram.

LADY LAMBERT.

You rascal, do you put the horns upon my princely husband?

PRISSILLA.

It may be a new piece of heraldry.

LILLY.

He's subtle, politic, and crafty.   70

LADY LAMBERT.

Thou hit'st pretty well there.

LILLY.

Then in the Allothanie, or, as some have it, Alhurto, being the tail of Aries, I find him eloquent, prodigal in necessity, proud, inconstant, and deceitful.

LADY LAMBERT.

Dost thou abuse me, rascal?   75

LILLY.

No such matter.

PRISSILLA.

Alas! he means innocently, for these are virtues given to most of the male kind.

LILLY.

He's there denoted to be fortunate in warfare.

LADY LAMBERT.

Go on, fellow!

LILLY.   80

In Adoldaya, being the head of Taurus.

LADY LAMBERT.

Taurus, what's that?

LILLY.

A bull.

LADY LAMBERT.

Dar'st thou horn him again?

LILLY.

'Tis a sign.   85

PRISSILLA.

A very ill sign, the sign of the bull. But he does not mean, an* it shall please your Highness, the town-bull of Ely.[66]

LILLY.

Has your lord e'er a mark or mold upon his members? If he has, he vanquishes his enemies.   90

LADY LAMBERT.

He has that, Priss. I'm sure on't.

PRISSILLA.

You are best acquainted with his secrets.

LILLY.

For Mars being with the Moon in the sextile aspect encourages men of war, and in the trine promises success.   95

LADY LAMBERT.

I'll love that trine while I live for't.

PRISSILLA.

I wonder where the fellow got all these hard words.

LILLY.

Lose not an inch of your state, lest you diminish the luster of that planet predominates.

She struts it.

LADY LAMBERT.

Why, sirrah, you grow saucy.—Priss, let the   100
footboy pay the fellow for his pains.

LILLY.

I hope she does not mean to pay me with kicks. Is she angry?

PRISSILLA.

No, no, you have only put her in mind of her majesty; she loves you ne'er the worse for't. You   105
must flatter her.

LILLY.

I have been bred to't.—I take my leave of your Highness.

LADY LAMBERT.

But take thy reward with thee. Thou art sure of what thou sayest?   110

---

65 Alnathay … Aries] stars in the constellation of the ram, Alnath first in the horns

66 town-bull of Ely] Cromwell's family estate consisted of various properties around and in the town of Ely.

LILLY.

As sure as if I had the planets in my hand; a man
can say no more.

LADY LAMBERT.

Well, go thy ways, and if thy judgment falter,
To second thy gold chain expect a halter.

Exit Lilly.

Priss, what dost thou think now?   115

PRISSILLA.

How can I think amiss? He's a notable man. I'll
get him into the larder one time or other, and I'll
make him show me all.

LADY LAMBERT.

Show thee all, wench! Out upon't.

PRISSILLA.

What, the lily and the rose. I promise you, for   120
aught I see, the lily is the best flower in your
garden.

Enter a servant.

SERVANT.

Here's a letter from my lord to your Highness.

PRISSILLA.

Hast ne'er a one for me from the secretary?

SERVANT.

Yes, Mrs. Priss. (*Exit.*)   125

PRISSILLA.

So, this fellow is saucy; I must take him down a
buttonhole lower. Good news, no doubt on't, and
then we shall have such bonfiring. I'll read my
switter-com swatter-com's letter anon. But her
Highness begins to look pale upon't. I do not like   130
this changing countenance.

LADY LAMBERT.

Thy lord is murdered.

PRISSILLA.

Then my honor goes to the dunghill. A pox of
Lilly and his legion of devils.

LADY LAMBERT.

Murdered in his fame, his honor: the soldiery have   135
forsaken him.

PRISSILLA.

If that be all, no matter, madam.

LADY LAMBERT.

Even call me what thou wilt.

PRISSILLA.

I should have called you Highness, I confess, but
I hope you are not offended. Lilly is a mere rogue.   140
I'll never endure a lily hereafter: 'tis a flattering
flower and stinks abominably.

LADY LAMBERT.

He writes me word he'll be in town this night; he's
sent for by the Rump.

PRISSILLA.

Oh nasty Rump! But an't* shall please your   145
Highness, shall I seek out for eight proper striplings
to man your Highness, and four spring-gots to trick
up your train, a French tailor that has a yard thus—
long, a cook whose nose will not offend your sauce
by dropping in't, a gentlemen sewer that can dance   150
before your dishes, an able carver to cut up your
custards, a taster that hath a sweet breath and no
rotten teeth, a baker whose hand is not mangy? Who
shall be lord chamberlain, groom of the stool, your
maids of honor, your starcher, your tirer, yeoman of 155
your cellar, yeoman of your pantry, yeoman of your
pastry, clerk of your kitchen, clerk of the rolls? Lord,
I'm even out of breath with reckoning up your
servitors!

LADY LAMBERT.

How now, audaciousness!   160

PRISSILLA.

Why seriously, I dreamt last night, an't* please your
Highness, that we have been but princes in disguise
all this while and that our visors are now falling
off. And who would think that dreams should
come to light so?   165

LADY LAMBERT.

Now could I tear my flesh. All my hopes are lost.

PRISSILLA.

No, you say there's one a-coming.

LADY LAMBERT.

How this Fleetwood's wife will o'ertop me!

PRISSILLA.

Pull her eyes out and then let a dog lead her.

LADY LAMBERT.

Well, I'll do something.   170

PRISSILLA.

I'll be your second so good, an't* please your
Highness.

Exeunt.

[Scene viii. City streets.]

Enter three or four prentices.

FIRST PRENTICE.

Hy boys, the noble General Philagathus lay at Barnet last night.

SECOND PRENTICE.

Say'st thou so, Champion?

FIRST PRENTICE.

And the pitiful, pitiful Lambert, one of Don Quixot's lords, is in the Tower. He's been a whipster[67] all his 5 lifetime and now is become a staid gentleman.

SECOND PRENTICE.

Well said, Champion.

FIRST PRENTICE.

No more of that if you love me. Noble Philagathus must be the City's Champion; I'll resign my office and yet be loyal still. 10

OMNES.

Who will not? who will not?

FIRST PRENTICE.

Then you are my boys again. Do you not observe how the fanatics are trotting out of town? Some of the rogues begin to mutiny.

SECOND PRENTICE.

Hang 'em up then, I cry. 15

FIRST PRENTICE.

So say I, by thousands. Noble Philagathus enters with love, and they go out with curses, or like the snuff of a candle, stinkingly.

THIRD PRENTICE.

I'm sure they have eaten our masters up.

FIRST PRENTICE.

Even to their bowels, that trading is become a mere 20 skeleton.

SECOND PRENTICE.

Now, I hope we shall see better days.

FIRST PRENTICE.

Ne'er fear it, lads. Philagathus is right and sound to the very core.

SECOND PRENTICE.

What will become of our Exchange Merchant?[68] 25

---

67 whipster] a lively, smart, violent, or mischievous person (*OED*)

68 Exchange Merchant] This probably refers to banker/ goldsmith Edward Backwell; see above, n. 48.

FIRST PRENTICE.

What? he that turned part of the house of God into a den of thieves?

THIRD PRENTICE.

The very same, the very same.

FIRST PRENTICE.

Let him hang himself, and when he is cold meat, the Devil carbanado him for a breakfast. 30

Drums heard within.

But hark, they are marching out, and Philagathus his* honest soldiers are coming in. Oh, let's see 'um! let's see 'um.

OMNES.

By all means let's see 'um.

Exeunt, running.

Act V, scene i. [City streets.]

Enter Mrs. Cromwell and the Lady Lambert at several doors; they meet.

MRS. CROMWELL.

Bless my eyesight! what? her Highness without her train. Where is that precious bird thy husband, caged? His wings are clipt from flying. Faith now, this comes of treachery. Had he been true to my son Dick, he might have still continued honorable 5 and thou a lady. And now I know not what to call thee.

LADY LAMBERT.

Thy rudeness cannot move me. I impute it to thy want* of breeding.

MRS. CROMWELL.

My want of breeding, Mrs. Minx. 10

LADY LAMBERT.

We can't expect from dunghills odorous savors. Were our affections greater than they are, they merit not half the contempt and scorn pursues thy wretched family and the memory of thy abhorred husband. 15

MRS. CROMWELL.

How durst thou name him but with reverence. He that outdid all histories of kings or kaisers; was his own herald and could give titles of honor to the meanest peasants; made brewers, draymen, cobblers, tinkers, or anybody lords. Such was his 20 power; no prince ever did the like. Amongst the rest, that precious piece thy husband was one of his making.

LADY LAMBERT.

Would we had never known these painted titles that are so easily washt off.   25

Enter Fleetwood.

But yonder comes the cause of all our miseries.

FLEETWOOD.

Ne'er go, yonder's my mother; I profess, as I'm here, I'd rather meet, ne'er stir, a beggar in my dish, so I had, as I'm here.

MRS. CROMWELL.

And art thou there? Nay, ne'er hide thy face for't,   30
though thou mayst be ashamed of all thy actions.

FLEETWOOD.

Why I, forsooth, Mother? I profess, ne'er go, not I, Mother, as I'm here.

MRS. CROMWELL.

Call me not "Mother." Thou hast ruined my children and thyself too, like a fool as thou art.   35

LADY LAMBERT.

And me and my husband, like a knave as thou art.

MRS. CROMWELL.

Would ever coxcomb have committed such folly!

LADY LAMBERT.

Or ever changeling done the like! Jack Adams[69] is a man to thee.

FLEETWOOD.

I profess, indeed law, you are strange folks, I   40
profess, ne'er go, law. (*Walks about the stage, they following him.*) Cannot a man, as I'm here, pass the street, I profess, law?

LADY LAMBERT.

Hang thee, thou'rt good for nothing—

MRS. CROMWELL.

But fleering and fooling.   45

LADY LAMBERT.

And how do you, forsooth? I profess.

MRS. CROMWELL.

And truly, I know what I know, and there's an end.

LADY LAMBERT.

Of an old song, few words are best.

---

69 Jack Adams] a fool (*OED*)

MRS. CROMWELL.

Ne'er go, I'm the greatest man in the nation, I profess, ne'er stir now. Think you what you will,   50
forsooth, Mother, as I'm here.

FLEETWOOD.

I profess, ne'er stir, as I'm here, there's no enduring it, law now, as I'm here, and therefore farewell, as I'm here, for I'll be gone, ne'er stir now. (*Exit running.*)

MRS. CROMWELL.

Nay, we'll follow thee to thy very doors and ring   55
thee a peal on both sides thy head.

Exeunt.

[Scene ii. The same.]

Enter prentices with clubs.

SECOND PRENTICE.

Now Champion, what think you of your General Philagathus now?

FIRST PRENTICE.

A rope on't, I know not what to think on't. Was ever such a rape committed upon a poor she city before? Lay her legs open to the wide world, for   5
every rogue to peep in her breech.[70]

THIRD PRENTICE.

'Tis monstrous!

SECOND PRENTICE.

Is this the City's champion?

FIRST PRENTICE.

Well, on my conscience, he's honest for all this. The plaguy Rump has done this mischief. Well,   10
club stand stiff to thy master, somebody shall suffer for't. I say no more.

SECOND PRENTICE.

We shall be cooped up shortly for hawksmeat in our cellars, while they possess our shops and feast upon our mistresses.   15

FIRST PRENTICE.

Well, I'll warrant the soldiery will be honest for all this, and then we'll singe the maggots out of the lousy Rump, or else swinge me.

---

70 to peep in her breech] In February 1660 Monck was commanded by the Rump to destroy the gates and portcullios of London and pull up their posts and chains.

Enter fourth prentice.

FOURTH PRENTICE.

News, boys, news.

FIRST PRENTICE.

From whence, from Tripulo?[71]   20

FOURTH PRENTICE.

From Guildhall, you knaves. We shall have a free
Parliament.

OMNES. (*They make a shout.*)

Hy, hy, hy.

FOURTH PRENTICE.

The general and the City are agreed, and he has
promised it.   25

FIRST PRENTICE.

Oh noble Philagathus!

SECOND PRENTICE.

Brave* Philagathus!

THIRD PRENTICE.

Honorable Philagathus!

FOURTH PRENTICE.

Renowned Philagathus!

FIRST PRENTICE.

Now, you infidels, what think you now? Has your   30
fears and jealousies left you, or will you still dam
yourselves up with dirty suspicion. You that spoke
even now you should be cooped up for hawksmeat
shall be crammed up for capons; your cellars shall
become warehouses, your shops exchanges, and   35
your mistresses persons of honor.

OMNES.

And what shall we be?

FIRST PRENTICE.

Squires of the body. Honor sufficient enough for
men of our rank, gentlemen.

OMNES.

Oh brave* Champion!   40

FIRST PRENTICE.

I tell you, I will have no more of that. Where is
Lilly now?

SECOND PRENTICE.

In one of the twelve houses.

FIRST PRENTICE.

We'll fire him out of it.

THIRD PRENTICE.

How will the Man in the Moon drink claret then?   45

FIRST PRENTICE.

Claret is best burnt, sir, by your leave.

THIRD PRENTICE.

Aye, but Lilly has thirteen houses.

FIRST PRENTICE.

A baker's dozen. We'll fire the odd end first.

OMNES.

A match, a match; we'll do't.

FIRST PRENTICE.

But now I think on't, we must have no firing of   50
houses; there's a statute against it. Better once wise
than never.

OMNES.

Oh brave* sack!*

FIRST PRENTICE.

We'll be merry tonight, I'm resolved on't, or else
never let prentices presume to be honest again, and 55
therefore follow me. God bless the general!

Exeunt.

[Scene iii. The Lamberts' house.]

Enter Trotter and Prissilla.

PRISSILLA.

Now, Secretary, where's your titles now? Not so
much as a tittle of 'em remaining, all sunk in the
sandbox.

TROTTER.

I'm between Silla[72] and Carybdis, I must confess;
and thou hast graveled me, my dear Priss.   5

PRISSILLA.

Hang your dog poetry; it made my lord thrive so
ill as he did. I think thou didst infect him; he used
to have a serene brain and courage good enough.
Sure the vicar of fools was his ghostly father.[73] Be
beat without a blow: there's a mystery indeed!   10

TROTTER.

Truly Priss, my lord could not help it.

---

71 Tripulo] This may simply be a misspelling of Tripoli,
which was in the news at the time, but so was Triploe/
Triplow Heath, though the latter seems less likely. Since
tripular/tripulo means "to ship" in Spanish, this could
also be a place name like Tripulina in Argentina.

72 Silla] Scylla (q.v.)

73 ghostly father] spiritual advisor

PRISSILLA.

Not help it! There's a jest indeed. I'm sure he has helped himself into prison for't, let who will help him out again. What course wilt thou take now, Secretary? 15

TROTTER.

Not horse-coursing, Priss. I'd have thee know that.

PRISSILLA.

Why, thou'rt pretty well timbered for such an employment. Canst thou make pens?

TROTTER.

Yes, and ink too, Priss, I tell you but so.

PRISSILLA.

There will be a trade indeed for thee. 20

TROTTER.

Nay, and the worst come to the worst, I can teach to dance. (*Frisks about.*)

PRISSILLA.

I confess, thy sword is always dancing.

TROTTER.

That's the à la mode I learned in France.

PRISSILLA.

Come, if thou canst dance so well, let's have a frisk 25 if thou dar'st.

TROTTER.

Truly Priss, I have not my pumps in my pocket.

PRISSILLA.

'Tis well thy mother left thee wit enough for an excuse.

He draws.

TROTTER.

That is not all; look here, I can fence too— 30

PRISSILLA. (*Starts.*)

What dost thou mean to do!

TROTTER.

Set your right foot forward, keep a close guard, have an eye to your enemy's point, extend your arm thus.

She runs and he follows her.

PRISSILLA.

Lord, Lord, the man is mad, sure. 35

TROTTER.

Traverse your ground, sometimes reverse, as thus. Give back, then come on again, play with his

point. If he makes a pass, put it by; make a home thrust thus, run him through and he falls, I warrant you. 40

She screams.

PRISSILLA.

Put up thy fool's bauble there. I profess I'll call my lady else.

Puts up his sword.

TROTTER.

Why, did it fright thee, Priss? Seriously, I did but show thee what skill I had at my weapon.

PRISSILLA.

Thou wouldst make a rare fellow to fence before 45 the bears, if there were any.

TROTTER.

Why Priss! I dare say I can kill any man living that can't defend himself.

PRISSILLA.

Ha, ha, ha! I am of thy mind, that can't defend himself. 50

TROTTER.

Why Priss, such as fight must take all advantages.

PRISSILLA.

And I that do not fight will take the advantage to leave thee and thy foolery. (*Exit.*)

TROTTER.

Nay dear Priss, ne'er go. I'll follow thee.

Exit.

[Scene iv. City streets.]

Enter prentices with faggots upon their shoulders, they pass the stage whooping and holloing. Enter again, whooping and holloing with rumps of mutton upon spits.

OMNES.

Roast the rump, roast the rump. (*Exeunt.*)[1]

Enter a boy upon a colt-staff[74] carried by two, and others follow him whooping and holloing.

FIRST PRENTICE.

Silence, silence, I say.

---

74 colt-staff] pole used by two people to carry large, two-handled vat or colt

OMNES.

Silence, silence there.

FIRST PRENTICE.

Gentlemen all, I tell you plain, my rump does itch;
we shall have rain.   5

*Exeunt whooping and holloing. A piece of wood is set
forth painted like a pile of faggots and fire, and faggots
lying by to supply it. Enter prentices and soldiers.*

FIRST PRENTICE.

Come gentlemen, you are welcome, sit down.—
Bring some drink there, 'tis a night of jubilee; we'll
want* no drink while the rump roasts.

A form is set forth. Enter one with drink.

Here's a health to your noble general.

SOLDIER.

Thank you, young man.   10

Racks are set out, one turns the spit with rumps on't.

FIRST PRENTICE.

Baste the rump soundly.

SECOND PRENTICE.

It bastes itself; it has been well fed, a dog take it.
But pray give us some drink too; we are almost dry
roasted.

Enter Frenchman.

FRENCHMAN.

Begar,* dis be very light night: me can find my way   15
to my lodging, begar, very well, if me not take a
cup too mush by the way. Now, garsoone,[75] what
be de matter vitt you?

PRENTICES.

Some *larshan*[76] for the bonfire, Monsieur.

FRENCHMAN.

Bonfires! begar, me tinck de grand Divell be in the   20
bonfires. There, garsoone, what be you? *Vill-a vou
done larshan* to de bonfire?[77]

_____

75 garsoone] *garçon*, boy, young man (Fr.)
76 larshan] *l'argent*, silver, money (Fr.)
77 *Vill-a vou done larshan* to de bonfire?] corruption of
    Voulez-vous donner l'argent … —Do you want to give
    money to the bonfire? or perhaps of *Veuillez-vous donner
    l'argent* …—You give money to the bonfire, if you wish!

Enter musicians.

MUSICIANS.

We are musicians and will give you a lesson,
Monsieur.

FRENCHMAN.

A lesson, dat be very good, begar, me love itt vitt   25
all mine heart, *alle alle vic moy*[78] to de bonfire,
begar, fur boone company, de souldate de
Angletar.[79]

They go to the bonfire.

Me love dem vitt all min heart; play a lesson, or
begar, me vil brake-a your fiddells.   30

They play.

OMNES.

Oh brave* Monsieur!

FRENCHMAN.

Fur boone, begar, now give me de marry song, me
give you de larshan.

Musicians play a short lesson.

SOLDIER.

Have you this song, "We Came from Scotland"?

MUSICIANS.

Yes, sir.   35

FRENCHMAN.

Begar, me will have-a dat.

                      Song.

We came from Scotland with a small force,
    With a hey down, down, a-down-a,
But with hearts far truer than steel;
        We got, by my fay,   40
        The glory o'th' day,
Yet no man a hurt did feel.

All sing the tune, and throw their hats about their heads.

When Lambert first our army did face,
    With a hey down, down, a-down-a,

_____

78 *alle alle vic moy*] *allez, allez avec moi*—Go, go with me
    (Fr.)
79 fur … Angletar] very good company, the soldiers of
    Angleterre (England) (Fr.)

He looked as fierce as the Devil; 45
   We feared a rout,
   But he wheeled about,
The gentleman was so civil.

All sing the tune again.

Our general marched with the country's love,
  With a hey down, down, a-down-a, 50
All persons to him did address;
   Small money we spent,
   For we found as we went
Good friends, and here find no less.

Sing all again.

FRENCHMAN.
Fur boone, begar, fur boone, done moy be toder 55
cup, burn-a de rump.

FIRST PRENTICE.
That has been often done in your country,
Monsieur.

FRENCHMAN.
Begar, me vill dance about de bonfire, come vit
me, men. 60

They dance about the bonfire.

OMNES.
Oh brave Monsieur!

Enter Prissilla.

PRISSILLA.
Let my lady say what she will, I will see the
bonfire.

FRENCHMAN.
Begar, metress, you be a very fine, shentileve
man.[80] 65

She offers to get from him.

Begar, me dance one time vitt you, nay begar, you
noe serve-a me soe.

PRISSILLA.
I cannot dance indeed, sir.

FRENCHMAN.
Begar, me vill have on touch vitt you, metress.

FIRST PRENTICE.
What, before all this company, Monsieur? 70

FRENCHMAN.
Datt me vill, begar.

PRISSILLA.
Well, if I must dance, play "Fortune My Foe."

FIRST PRENTICE.
No, "Sellenger's Round,"[81] we are beginning the
world again.

FRENCHMAN.
Me vill have none of dat, me vill have a de 75
courante of de foot *ça, ça.* Come metress, lend-a
me your hand. (*Sings a tune.*) Courage, courage,
metress.

They dance.

PRISSILLA.
Well, now indeed I must be gone, sir.

FRENCHMAN.
Begar, me vill see you to your lodging, pardon-a 80
moy.

PRISSILLA.
By no means, I shall be knocked o'th' head then.

FRENCHMAN.
Mee no care for dat, par ma moy.[82] Adieu. *Je vous
remercie*[83] pour dis boone company.—Adieu, petit
garsoone. [*Exit.*] 85

OMNES.
Adieu, Monsieur.

SECOND PRENTICE.
What are you resolved to do? Every man to his
home, or shall we make a night on't?

OMNES.
A night on't, a night on't.

FIRST PRENTICE.
Come to the next bonfire. 90

OMNES.
To the next bonfire, to the next bonfire.

Exeunt, hooping and holloing.

---

80 shentileve man] fractured French for gentle-lipped man
(Prisilla, played probably by a boy, is dressed as one so
she can go to the bonfire; below the Frenchman calls
her "garsoone.")

81 "Sellenger's Round"] a maypole fertility dance
82 par ma moy] fractured French for "for my self"
83 *Je vous remercie*] I thank you (Fr.)

[Scene v. The same.]

Enter Whitelock, Wareston, Huson, and Desborough.

DESBOROUGH.

We have played our cards fair.

HUSON.

I deny it; we have not played our cards fair.

WARESTON.

Bread sirs, then yee have plaid them faw, and that's
faw play, geod feath, sirs.

WHITELOCK.

A fool had the shuffling of them; the game had   5
gone better else.

WARESTON.

The faw Deel* himself was trump, sirs. I think,
sirs, we ha' had nee geod luck, sirs, this bout.

WHITELOCK.

We are lost, sirs, utterly lost.

HUSON.

No sir, we are found, sir, catcht in a net of our own   10
making.

DESBOROUGH.

Thou wouldst give all the shoes in thy shop to be
out of 't.

HUSON.

Is there no remedy, my Lord Whitelock?

DESBOROUGH.

No remedy against the king's evil.   15

WARESTON.

Bread, hee's no doctor, sirs, hee's my noble liar, sirs.

HUSON.

Who's Keeper of the Great Seal now?

DESBOROUGH.

Where will you find your thousand pounds per
annum now?

WARESTON.

Bread sirs, doe ye give, do ye give? hee's gate nought,   20
sirs, nar I of any the gifts I had ge'en me, geod feath.

DESBOROUGH.

Hark you, Mr. Lawyer, have you e'er a *Habulus
Corpulus*[84] to remove us from the storm is coming?

HUSON.

With a razor scissors, or what a devil do you call it?

DESBOROUGH.

You are politic: Will you sell a pennyworth of   25
policy, sir?

WARESTON.

Bread, he had meer need buy some to save his crag,
sirs.

HUSON.

Come, let's leave the law in the lurch, and every
man shift for himself. Adieu, Mr. Lawyer!   30

DESBOROUGH.

Adieu, Mr. Lawyer!

WARESTON.

Adieu, Mr. Liar!

Exeunt [Wareston, Huson, Desborough].

WHITELOCK.

How monstrously have I exposed myself to the
dirty censure of the basest creatures, things never
mentioned but with scorn, and now I am become   35
the thesis unto theirs! The very* cobbler reads a
lecture to me, and I'm convinced I should amend
my manners and become loyal—dictates long
before divinity discovered! There's no sin like that
we know, and that we surfeit in.   40

Exit.

[Scene vi. The same.]

Enter Trotter.

TROTTER.

Do you want any pens or ink, pens or ink? Will
you fence, or will you dance? What pens and ink
do you want, gentlemen?

Enter Prissilla with her basket of oranges and lemons.

PRISSILLA.

Fine civil[85] oranges, fine lemons; fine civil oranges,
fine lemons.—Methinks it sounds very well. A pox   5
of her Tallness for me. No matter, ne'er repine,
wench, thy trade's both pleasant and profitable,
and if any gentleman take me up, I am still.—Fine
civil oranges, fine lemons.

TROTTER.

Pens or ink, pens, pens or ink?   10

---

84 *Habulus Corpulus*] habeas corpus (q.v.)

85 civil] probably Seville

PRISSILLA.

'Tis he.—Trotter.

TROTTER.

Priss, my dear Priss!

PRISSILLA.

Why how now, Secretary, thou see'st my words are
come to pass: I knew what a lord thou wouldst be.
But Fortune's a whore.   15

TROTTER.

A whip take her. But shall we meet now, Priss?

PRISSILLA.

I think we are met, Trotter, although unhappily.

TROTTER.

I mean upon equal terms.

Enter Wareston.

WARESTON.

Will you buy a geodly ballad, or a Scots spur, sirs;
will yee buy a geodly ballad, or a Scots spur, sirs?   20
Any thing to live in this world. Bread, gif I sud
gang intol my nown* country, my crag would be
stretcht two inches longer then 'tis.—Will ye buy
a geodly ballad, or a Scots spur,[86] sirs, will ye buy
a line, a Jack-line, a line, a Jack Lambert's line?   25

TROTTER.

'Tis the Lord Wareston.

PRISSILLA.

No more lord than thyself, Trotter. Let's have some
sport with him.—Fine civil oranges, fine lemons.
Will your lordship buy any lemons and oranges?
Fine civil oranges, fine lemons.   30

TROTTER.

Ink or pens, ink or pens, will your lordship buy
any ink or pens for the Committee of No Safety?

WARESTON.

Bread a Geod, what a whore and a knave is this.

Enter Desborough.

DESBOROUGH.

Turnips, turnips, turnips, ho.—Did ever lord cry
turnips before? But a pox of lordships; would I had   35
my old farm over my head again.—Turnips,
turnips, turnips ho, turn up mistress, and turn up
the maid, and who buys my long turnips, ho!

---

86 spur] a group of folded papers (?) (*OED*)

PRISSILLA.

He does it rarely well. Fine oranges, fine civil
oranges, fine lemons.   40

MRS. CROMWELL.

TROTTER.

Ink or pens, ink or pens for the Lord Desborough.

WARESTON.

Bread, 'tis he indeed. These are witches sure.—
How does your geod lady, sir?

DESBOROUGH.

What, my Lord Wareston?

WARESTON.

Ne, bread a Geod, I'm ne meer a loord then yer   45
neeneself. My honoor is in the dust, sir.

Enter one-eyed Huson.

HUSON.

Have you any old boots or shoes to mend?—I have
helped to underlay the government this twenty
years and have been upon the mending hand, but
I fear now I shall be brought to my last and   50
therefore ought to mind my end.—Will you buy
shoes for brooms, or brooms for shoes?

PRISSILLA.

Or a knave for a whip, or a whip for a knave?—
Fine civil oranges, fine lemons.

TROTTER.

Ink or pens, ink or pens.—How do you, my lord?   55

HUSON.

Dost mock me, fellow? Who are these?

WARESTON.

My geod friend.

DESBOROUGH.

Brother Huson, and how, and how?

HUSON.

And what, and what? and pox o'that, and that.
Let's embrace however.   60

Enter Mrs. Cromwell with boys after her.

MRS. CROMWELL.

What kitchen stuff have you, maids?—Was ever
princess brought to such a pass?—What kitchen
stuff have you, maids?

BOY.

Gammer Cromwell, our maid calls you.

MRS. CROMWELL.

Where, you rascal?   65

BOY.

In my_____.*

MRS. CROMWELL.

You rogue, do you abuse me? (*Flings down her tub and runs after him.*) I'll claw your eyes out. (*Exit. Enter again presently and takes up her tub.*)

MRS. CROMWELL.

Oh Dick! Oh Dick! Did ever I think to come to this?—What kitchen stuff have you, maids; maids, have you any kitchen stuff, maids? 70

PRISSILLA.

Fine civil oranges, fine lemons?—Will your ladyship buy any oranges and lemons?

MRS. CROMWELL.

Dost thou mock me, baggage? I'll be at thee presently.* 75

TROTTER.

No indeed she does not; 'tis Priss, my Lady Lambert's woman,* and I am Trotter, her secretary.

MRS. CROMWELL.

How? thou hast walked fair indeed. Where is her Highness now? 80

PRISSILLA.

They say she intends to cry fresh cheese and cream.

MRS. CROMWELL.

She has brought her hogs to a fair market.

HUSON.

And so we have all, methinks.

MRS. CROMWELL.

What, art thou there too?

WARESTON.

Bread, an' I's here ta, and my geod Loord Desborough. Bread a Geod, heer's e'en a jolly company. 85

MRS. CROMWELL.

It somewhat palliates my misery, that in afflictions you like sharers be.^m

PRISSILLA.

Come let's mind our business. Words are but wind.—Fine civil oranges, fine lemons. (*Exit.*) 90

TROTTER.

Ink or pens, ink or pens, will you buy any ink or pens? (*Exit.*)

WARESTON.

Will ye buy a geodly ballad, or a Scots spur, will ye buy a Jack-line, a Jack Lambert's line, or a line for a Jock-a-Lambert. (*Exit.*) 95

DESBOROUGH.

Turnips, turnips, turnips, ho! Turn-up mistress, and turn-up maid, and turn-up my cousin and be not afraid of a long, long, red, turn-up, ho. (*Exit.*)

HUSON.

Boots or shoes, boots or shoes to mend? (*Exit.*) 100

MRS. CROMWELL.

What kitchen stuff have you, maids? what kitchen stuff have you, maids? (*Exit.*)

Enter Whitelock.

WHITELOCK.

I am a poor lawyer, gentlemen, and can show you legerdemain for your money, no hocus-pocus like me. I have two hands, neither of them disabled from taking fees. Have you any causes to split? for that's my doom; my bag is a receptacle for them. I am for that cause brings me most profit, be it good or be it bad, but indeed have been better experienced in the bad and now would fain follow the good cause and turn honest. But a man shall hardly grow rich then, you'll say, and that would vex a man. 105 110

Howe'er, I'll try't, for to my grief I find

Riches ill got do scatter with the wind. 115

Have you any work for a poor honest lawyer, for a poor honest lawyer? I am your next man, gentlemen.

Ambition and base avarice, adieu!

Howe'er your glories seem, they are not true.

[*Exeunt.*]

THE END.

Textual Notes

a The copytext is the second edition, a 1661 quarto (Q2), corrected by Tatham. Also consulted was the first edition, a 1660 quarto (Q1). The second edition of *The Rump* appeared with names changed in the *Dramatis Personae* but not consistently in the text itself (i.e., Lambert for Bertlam, etc.), so names have been standardized herein to avert confusion. A modern edition of *The Rump* appeared in 1879 as part of *The Dramatic Works of John Tatham*, edited by James Maidment.

b Dramatis Personae is reproduced here exactly as it appears in the 1661 second edition. The 1660 first edition uses anagrams as follows: Bertlam, Woodfleet, Stoneware, Lockwhit, Lady Bertlam, Lady Woodfleet.

c Whitelock … Committee] Lockwhit … Committee Q1; *om.* Q2

d Three ladies] Q1; *om.* Q2

e Trotter] Q2; Walker Q1

f *aut Caesar aut*] Q1; *aut Caesar* Q2

g You are not skilled then in mathematics, sir.] Q2; Our meaning's not amiss, Sir; we know, Sir, what we say Q1.

h swelled] Q1; smelled Q2

i Rump] Q2; Lump Q1

j For he's a gaping fellow, it must be done] Q2; Lest he— No matter, it must be done Q1

k Alnathay] Q1; Alvathay Q2.

l *Enter … (Exeunt.)*] Q1; *om.* Q2

m Q2 contains the following impertinent character and speech: *Enter Kelsey.* Water, maids water, who buyes my sweet water? oh my dainty conduit water, three pales a penny.

A Fond Husband; or, The Plotting Sisters[a]

by Thomas Durfey (ca. 1653-1723)

edited by Heidi Hutner (with Tony Jarrells)

Thomas Durfey was extremely popular in his own time. He was one of the most prolific playwrights of the period, composing for the stage thirty-three works (twenty-three comedies, five tragedies, four operas, and one tragicomedy) over a period of fifty years. Durfey had his detractors (he was often called a plagiarist), including Gerald Langbaine, Jeremy Collier, Alexander Pope, and Jonathan Swift, but he was championed by Richard Steele and Joseph Addison, and he gained the patronage of Charles II, James II, King William, and Queen Anne. He became a prominent literary figure in their royal courts.

A Fond Husband (1677), Durfey's second play, debuted at the Duke's Theatre, and by all known accounts it was fairly successful. The cast had the benefit of the two greatest comic actors of the time, Nokes and Leigh, who played the comic dupes, Peregrine Bubble and Old Fumble, respectively. The roles of the plotting sisters of the subtitle were probably originally created for the Marshall sisters, Rebecca and Anne, two of the original—and two of the best—women actresses of the period. But Anne Marshall Quin was no longer with the Duke's company when the play came to the stage, and the role of Emilia was played instead by the brilliant Elizabeth Barry. Charles

II attended three of the first five nights it was performed, and the original production had an impressive nine-night run. Twenty-nine productions of *A Fond Husband* were staged by 1740, and significantly, the comedy was performed as a benefit to raise funds for the impoverished playwright in 1713.

A Fond Husband is a fine example of Durfey's talent for comical satire, a genre within which he excelled, for example in *The Fool Turned Critic* (1676), *Trick for Trick* (1678), and *A Fool's Preferment* (1688). Only Shadwell and Behn could match him in this genre. Most of his comical satires are corrective, but this one is menippean. The play seems headed toward a poetical justice for the outrageous sexual tricksters, Rashley and Emilia, but the ending undercuts any standard by which they might ultimately be judged, as Maria and Ranger, the apparent moralists in the play, undercut their righteousness by their own petty passions, and Ranger abruptly adopts a libertine ethic at the end. Rashley's brazen assertion that he wears a sword and therefore cannot be brought to justice by anyone seems positively Rochestrian. And Cordelia's name seems incredibly misapplied to this delightfully pragmatic trickstress. The fools are duped, but the world seems inherited by other fools and knaves.

DRAMATIS PERSONAE

[MEN]

Rashley, a gentleman, friend to Emilia.

Ranger, his rival.

Peregrine Bubble,* a credulous, fond* cuckold, husband to Emilia.

Old Fumble, a superannuated alderman, that dotes on black* women. He's very deaf and almost blind and, seeking to cover his imperfection of not hearing what is said to him, answers quite contrary.

Sir Roger Petulant, a jolly old knight of the last age.

Sneak, nephew to Sir Roger, a young raw student.[1]

Spatterdash, servant to Fumble.

Jeremy, servant to Rashley.

Apothecary.

Servants and Attendants.

[WOMEN]

Emilia, wife to Bubble.

Maria, sister to Bubble.

Cordelia, niece to Bubble.

Betty, woman to Emilia.

Governess [Lettice].

A Fond* Husband; or, The Plotting Sisters.

Haec, dum incipias, gravia sunt, dumque ignores, ubi cognoris, facilia. Terent.[2]

Act I, scene i. [Bubble's lodging.]

A dining room, a table, shuttlecock and battledores.[3]

Rashley and Emilia sitting, Betty singing.

BETTY.

In vain, cruel nymph, you my passion despise
And slight a poor lover that languishing dies.

---

1 raw] should perhaps read a young "law" student (Vaughn)

2 *Haec … Terent.*] Terence, *The Self-Tormentor* 1058-59: "These things are irksome at the start before you know about them: when you are come to know, they are easy" (Loeb); Mendemus gives this advice to Clitipho upon the advent of his marriage.

3 battledores] rackets for a parlor game similar to badminton

Though Fortune my name with no titles endowed,
Yet fierce is my passion and warm is my blood.
Delay in affection exalts an amour,   5
For he that loves often will soonest give o'er.

2.

But vigorous and young, I'll flee to thy arms,
Infusing my soul in Elysium of charms.
A monarch I'll be when I lie by thy side,
And thy pretty hand my scepter shall guide,   10
Till cloyed with delight, you confess with a joy,
No monarch so happy, so pleasant as I. [*Exit.*]

RASHLEY.

By Heaven, there's nothing so dear to a free and generous spirit as this roving and uncontrolled way of love. Methinks we live like angels, and every kiss   15
brings a new life of pleasure.

EMILIA.

You have reason to believe I think so for suffering this early visit from you in my husband's absence, who, poor man, went from me by break of day to see a horse race a mile beyond Highgate.[4]   20

RASHLEY.

Nay, I confess, 'tis a sign of your kind* resentment[5] of my passion. Oh Heaven! That happy thought has made me all rapture. I'll cherish it, madam, as I would my youth or the best of all my senses, the sense of feeling.   25

EMILIA.

Cherish it rather as the means of keeping our love from my husband's knowledge. Well! I swear the thought of my indirect plot sometimes makes me very melancholy.

RASHLEY.

Melancholy? Fie madam, banish such thoughts   30
forever from your breast. If you are melancholy now, what would you have done, if I had not known you, when the clog of your conscience (I mean your husband) would have been your perpetual plague and given you cause for more melancholy than the   35
contrivance of the plots you speak of?

EMILIA.

Aye, but to break a vow, sir, a vow! Little do you think what 'tis to break a vow.

---

4 Highgate] northern suburb of London

5 resentment] acknowledgement, return

RASHLEY.

Little do I think? Madam, I thought you had known me so much a gentleman to imagine I know what belongs to the breaking of a vow as well as another man. To undeceive you, I have broken twenty vows, that is, unnecessary vows (such as yours are!), nay, and without a scruple of conscience. I thank my stars I'm of a tougher constitution.

EMILIA.

Besides, you consider not the other inconveniences: you know my husband's sister Maria loves you and is of that untamed, malicious nature that she'll revenge my invading her propriety[6] in your heart by discovering* our love to my husband. I know she plots it hourly, and though her pretense is the honor of our family, her real design is through her love to you.

RASHLEY.

Never doubt* your husband, madam: he has so strange a confidence in my fidelity, that to possess him otherwise were utterly to take away the little sense is left him. You know he brought me to lodge in this house, which prudently I refused at first and seemingly fled from the heaven I desired to make him more importunate. Since I came here, you know how he has caressed me, and to color my design, and divert you, have I[b] feigned a mistress in this quarter of the Town,* and then, as if I spoke of her, have told him all that has passed between myself and you, at which the good-natured creature has laughed extremely and wished me good luck a thousand times. And can we now doubt further success? By Heaven, we cannot, madam.

EMILIA.

Then you know there's another great obstacle: Ned Ranger has long professed a passion for me and doubtless is not ignorant that my love for you is the cause of his no better success. A jealous man sees more than twenty others, and 'twill be very necessary for us to be careful of so dangerous an enemy.

RASHLEY.

Dangerous? Not at all, madam, never think him so. Success, which animates the hero and leads him on to greater enterprises than before he durst

40

45

50

55

60

65

70

75

attempt, has cherished hopes in me. Let me alone with him, and for thy part, egad, I'll turn thee loose to any female-devil on this side Lapland,[7] either for plot or repartee.

EMILIA.

Yet still I fear the worst.

RASHLEY.

Fear nothing, madam. Fear is the worst of passions, and incident to base, not noble hearts; besides, our love, considered rightly, is a second-rate innocence, where affection, not duty, bears prerogative; 'tis the great and primitive business of our souls, suspicion and fear came in by the by.

Enter Betty.

BETTY.

Madam, Mr. Ranger, in spite of my resistance, has rudely pressed into the house and is just coming hither.

EMILIA.

Call up the footmen. Lock the door.

Enter Ranger.

RANGER. (*To Betty.*)

Stand still, Mrs.* Jilt, or I shall spoil your door-keeping hereafter.—Jack[8] Rashley, here? Hell and the Devil!

[Exit Betty.]

EMILIA.

What insolence is this? Pray sir, your business?

RANGER.

Only my zeal, madam, to give you notice of an approaching danger: your husband has so entangled his horns* yonder in a hawthorn bush that 'tis to be feared without immediate help he will lose the decent and commodious ornament of his forehead.

EMILIA.

Most impudent of men! How dare you talk thus?

RANGER.

Most infamous of women! How dare you do thus?

80

85

90

95

100

---

6 propriety] property

7 Lapland] a fabled home to witches and magicians

8 Jack] may mean simply knave; Rashley is later called Tom.

RASHLEY.

Do what, sir?

EMILIA.

Hold, and as you love me, move no farther.— 105
Basest of men! Have you the folly to believe this
way can prove beneficial to your love? No, I hate
thee mortally, nor shall thy malice from henceforth
be successful. I'll disarm it, and when thou thinkest
thy plots are surest laid, be sure of a surprise. 110

RANGER.

Oh infamy! 'Sdeath,* is your forehead steel? And
is your skin of that obdurate temper you cannot
force a blush into your cheeks at the confession of
your obscene crime? How great a friend to hell is
impudence! 115

EMILIA.

Pray sir, forgive him, 'tis an insipid fellow that I
am often troubled with and believe his insolence
for the future shall be prevented. In the meantime,
to express my gratitude, give me leave to present
you with this necklace; this ring too will fit your 120
finger. Nay, and swear you shan't refuse 'em. My
husband gives me often such as these; 'tis all the
good I get by him.

RANGER.

Very well. The blessing of a wife let all men judge.
What envious fiend to plague me makes me love 125
this creature?

RASHLEY.

I will preserve your favors* as my life; your
memory shall possess my soul and all your charms
live ever in my sight. My kindest, sweetest,
dearest— (Kisses her hand.) 130

RANGER.

Death and damnation, must I stay and see this?—
Madam, this modest carriage before a jealous lover
makes—

EMILIA.

Little for your contentment I doubt not, sir. But
'tis a fate proper enough for such busy and 135
inquisitive persons.

RASHLEY. (Sings.)

Fa, la, la, la, la—

RANGER.

Go—you are a devil, so far from being a woman
that I begin to doubt whether Nature had any

hand in your creation. Is't not enough, vile 140
creature, that I know you abuse your husband, but
that you dare give me an ocular proof? dispense
your favors to the man that horns him before my
face? Oh unparalleled impudence!

EMILIA.

Incorrigible fool, thinkest thou to daunt my will? 145
The little ill I do can raise no infamy, nor will I
ever doubt* it.

RASHLEY.

Fa, la, la, la.
The joys of a lover in passion remains,
In passion that's fervent and free, etc.

Enter Betty.

BETTY.

Oh madam, my master's just come home and 150
coming up.

RANGER.

Blest minute! Now I hope his eyes will be unsealed
and through the right end of the perspective* see
you. Madam, assure yourself there shall want*
nothing in me. 155

EMILIA.

I know, sir, and am prepared for the worst of thy
malice. Here, take this battledore and let us play.
(*They play.*)

RASHLEY.

Out, out, madam—y'are out.

Enter Bubble.

BUBBLE.

Ha, ha, ha. Chicken, good morrow, Chicken.— 160
Morrow, Tom.—Chick, prithee let me kiss thee.
What, in the mumps?[9] This morning, pop—no
more of that.—Hoh, what, my old friend Ranger
too! Morrow, Ned. Faith! Would you had been
with me this morning; I have had the rarest sport 165
yonder at Highgate with two or three country
fellows.—Hark ye, Chick, I have invited 'em all
to dinner one day this week, good, blunt, course
fellows, faith, but damnable rich. As Gad jidge me,
I passed for a brave* fellow amongst 'em. 170

---

[9] in the mumps] out of sorts

EMILIA.

You need boast of applause from such clowns?*

BUBBLE.

Clowns? What, honest, tough, hard-fisted, plain-dealing farmers clowns? Pop I say, you are an inconsiderable varlet, Chicken, and know not what belongs to such good company. 175

RANGER.

She is so well-diverted at home, sir, that all rural society is distasteful to her.

EMILIA.

I guess 'em to be much of your humor,* sir, owners of a great deal of dull, insipid noise and very little or no sense. 180

BUBBLE.

Well said, Chicken.—Ned. To her. To her again, Ned. 'Tis a raging Turk at repartee. Invent, invent, strike her home; prithee try her wit. Thou art a scholar. For my part I dare not (as Gad jidge me!), she's always too hard for me. 185

RANGER.

And me too, I assure you, sir. But there's a gentleman that has the good fortune to be more intimate; his address is far more pleasing than mine.

BUBBLE.

Who, Tom! Come, I'll hold a guinea she's too hard 190 for him too; why, 'tis the readiest, wittiest, jeering'st, fleering'st quean—'Sbud,* she's one of the pearls of eloquence. And pop, by the way, let me tell you, there's ne'er an orator in Christendom has more tropes and figures, take her when her 195 hand's in—

RANGER.

Nor knows the art of wheedling better, I'll say that for her.

BUBBLE.

Gad, thou art in the right, she's a *non parelio*[10] at it. But now you talk of wheedling, prithee Tom, 200 how goes thy love affairs? Thou look'st but ill upon't? Any plots? adventures of late? Hah!

RASHLEY.

None that can make me frown, sir. My stars have allotted me so mild a destiny that I can caress my

friend with my wonted air without being 205 discouraged by my success in love affairs.

BUBBLE.

I'm glad on't, faith. Come, prithee let me be partaker of thy good fortune. When wert thou with her?

EMILIA.

Tell him, tell him, sir. Lord, you never used to be so cautious in these matters. Pray tell him and 210 tremble. (*To Ranger aside.*) Now observe.

RASHLEY.

Why sir, I was with her this morning.

BUBBLE.

So! And what success prithee?

RASHLEY.

Why, at my first coming she entertained me with a song, softly expressing the delights of love in an 215 excellent air, and added to it a thousand kind* words and kisses. I had all the privilege imaginable, and 'twas my good luck to come at a very happy hour, for her husband went out early i'th'morning a-fowling as far as Holloway.[11] 220

BUBBLE.

Holloway? a pox on't, what damned luck had I? If it had been Highgate, I should have met the fool, for I have been there all this morning.

RASHLEY.

Ah, 'tis no matter, sir, his company can add little to anyone's credit, for he is but a kind of a soft- 225 headed, a half-witted fellow—

BUBBLE.

A ninny, a fool, ha, ha, ha!

RASHLEY.

Aye, and the most credulous of all the cuckolds I ever met with.

BUBBLE.

Poor animal! Faith, I pity him, but there's a 230 number of 'em about Town i'faith. We men of wit should want* diversion else.

RANGER. [*Aside.*]

We men of wit, quotha! Damn him, he's duller than a justice's clerk. To be made a property all this while and not discern it. Oh insufferable stupidity! 235

EMILIA.

Observe, sir, observe.

---

10 *Non parelio*] bad Italian for Fr. *nonpareil*, without equal

11 Holloway] another northern suburb

RANGER.

Yes, devil, I do observe; I doubt not but my observation shall add little to your quiet. Oh curse of—

BUBBLE.

Why how now, Ned? What, grinning like a monkey eating of chestnuts? Prithee what art thou thinking on? As Gad jidge me, I think thou art grown insipid, as my wife says. How dost like Tom's intrigue, hah? Is it not pleasant?

RANGER.

Very pleasant, sir, and faith, in my judgment represents as nearly as any character* I ever saw—

BUBBLE.

Represents? Hoo, pox, you're at your quirks and quidits, your Cambridge-puns and Westminster-quibbles, are you?12

EMILIA.

Pray, forward, sir, methinks 'tis very divertive.

RANGER. [Aside.]

Very divertive! Damn her, she was sure the offspring of Beelzebub.

RASHLEY.

After a thousand other caresses intermixed with kisses and smiles and a world of happy thoughts and fancies extravagantly rendered upon so happy an occasion, she obliged me in a new and most sensible way, presenting me, with a sweet and incomparable grace, this gold watch and this diamond ring.

Ranger looks amazedly.

BUBBLE.

Prithee observe Ned there, he's grown a strange whimsical fellow. Ha, ha, ha, look how he stares.

RANGER.

Was ever such an impudence? Sure I dream and this is all delusion!—Hark ye sir, are you irrecoverably blind?

BUBBLE.

Blind? What, I blind?

RANGER.

Methinks that watch looks very like one I have seen your wife wear often.

240

245

250

255

260

265

12 quirks … quiddits … puns … quibbles] clever rhetorical tricks, such as would be employed by students (Cambridge) and lawyers (Westminster)

BUBBLE.

Hah! As Gad jidge me, and so it does. But much good do thy heart, Tom, I'll warrant it right.

RANGER.

Methinks that ring, too, much resembles yours.

BUBBLE.

The square is right, but I think my stones were a little bigger.

RANGER. (*Aside.*)

Now the devil take thee for a dull rogue.

RASHLEY.

But the best jest was, before she gave me these, there happened to come rudely into the room a wild young fellow, that I found afterwards to be my rival and one she hated for his ill nature and impertinence. But to see how pitiful he looked to see me so presented before his face would have made you die with laughing. Ha, ha, ha.

BUBBLE, EMILIA.

Ha, ha, ha.

RANGER.

Hell and Furies, what's this I hear? Am I made a property too? If I bear this, may I be posted for a coward and my infamy known to all nations.— Hark ye sir.

RASHLEY.

Well sir.

RANGER.

By your ridiculous, fleering behavior, I guess I was concerned in your last description, an affront that requires instant satisfaction, and believe, sir, you shall not carry it off so clearly as you imagined. Though he is such a fool to be bubbled out of his reason, I am not. Follow me, sir, if you dare.

RASHLEY.

Dare! Lead on, sir, you shall see how much I dare.

EMILIA.

Hold, sir, you shall not go.

RASHLEY.

Dare follow you?

RANGER.

Aye sir, 'twould be a doubtful question if your protection there were out of the way. (*Points to Emilia.*)

RASHLEY.

What's that? Protection?

270

275

280

285

290

295

BUBBLE.

How now? What, jokes? Hard words? What's the matter, Tom? I must have no quarrels* here.

EMILIA.

'Tis Mr. Ranger's ill humor. Prithee love, speak to him, he's always disturbing good company. Tell him he's impertinent.

BUBBLE.

Gad, and so I will.—What a pox, a man cannot be a little jocose in his own house but he must disturb him? You shall see me go and huff him.

RANGER.

His horns I am sure are large enough: horns of sufficient growth, substantial horns, horns visible, large, craggy-branched, rough horns, and yet he may not believe it.

BUBBLE.

Believe what, Ned?—Ha, ha, ha. He's mad. Downright out of his wits. 'Tis a thick-skulled fellow, God knows, but we were not all born to be wits.—What dost believe, Ned?

RANGER.

Why sir, I believe you are mad.

BUBBLE.

I mad? Damn Ned, you're an impertinent fellow.— Now observe, Chicken.

RANGER.

How, sir?

BUBBLE.

I say, sir, an impertinent fellow, sir, and deserve to be crammed into a powdering-tub.[13]

RANGER. [*Aside.*]

Damn this fool, how he tortures me! But my revenge lies another way: I'll instantly go to his sister Maria, who I know loves Rashley and will willingly join with me in my revenge. This must do, and I'll about it instantly. (*Exit.*)

BUBBLE.

Ah—he's gone. I thought when I began to roar once, he would quickly vanish. I warrant I have

---

13 powdering-tub] a tub in which the flesh of animals is "powdered," or salted and pickled; humorously applied to a sweating-tub used for the cure of venereal diseases (*OED*)

frighted him into an ague. Poor fool, he'll hardly trouble us again this good while.

RASHLEY.

An uncivil person, first to intrude into our company and then to hinder our discourse, especially of so pleasant a narration. Gad! 'twas too much.

BUBBLE.

Too much? Why 'twas the devil and all, and as Gad jidge me, he's the son of a whore, and I'll make him an example.

Enter footman.

FOOTMAN.

Sir Roger Petulant, with his nephew, and old Mr. Fumble are come to visit you.

BUBBLE.

Gads so! Sirrah! Wait on 'em up and call my niece down.—This is the man, Chicken, I told thee that I intend for Cordelia's husband. He's very rich, I am told, and his father's a knight and sheriff of the county.

EMILIA.

But who is the other, sir?

BUBBLE.

Why, dost not know him? 'Tis old Alderman Fumble. He's a little deaf, but i'faith very good company and will so fumble about the women. You shall see he's a very jolly fellow and repartees and talks and chats at all rates, but the devil a word he hears, for he always answers quite contrary. He'll make us all laugh, i'faith.

EMILIA.

I've heard he dotes on all the women he sees and is as passionate and inconstant at his age of seventy-three as the brisk sparks of our times are at five-and-twenty.

RASHLEY.

He says (the devil take him that believes him) nothing fails him but his eyes, which defect he has lately amended by a pair of Venetian spectacles.

BUBBLE.

Ha, ha, 'tis a pleasant old fellow.—But here they come.

Enter Sir Roger, Sneak, Fumble.

SIR ROGER.

Cob![14] Come, Cob, come! Along, I say, and hold
up thy head. Fie, fie, be not so bashful, child. Nay   360
Cob, what, dost thou think I'll forsake thee? Pish,
in verity I will not. Wipe thy eyes, I say.

Enter Cordelia.

BUBBLE.

He's a little moody-hearted, that's the worst on't.
But the young man will show his parts* by and
by, I warrant ye.—Come hither, niece.—Sir Roger,   365
your most humble servant.

*Old Fumble pulls out his spectacles, and looks on
Cordelia.*

SIR ROGER.

Yours, good Mr. Peregrine. You see, sir, I am as
good as my word: I have brought my nephew.—
Cob, here's your Mrs. Cob. Look, look up, and go
and salute* her. I'll show thee the way. Nay Cob,   370
still in thy dumps? Look upon me, man! I'll do it
first.

SNEAK.

Well, well! I'll follow you, Uncle. I am a little
bashful at present, but I shall come to't anon.

SIR ROGER.

Well said.—Madam, I am your humble servant.   375
(Kisses her.)

SNEAK.

And I likewise, madam!

FUMBLE.

I'fack, i'fack!* A pretty well-favored woman that
there! A good eye, good hair, and i'fack, I think
everything good.—Hah, hem, Mr. Peregrine,   380
prithee who is that there? The woman there?

BUBBLE.

Who, she yonder?

FUMBLE.

Hah!

BUBBLE. *(Aloud.)*

Why, she's a near friend of mine, sir.—What an
ignorant old fellow 'tis, not to know my niece?   385

FUMBLE.

A friend? Well I could have heard you, I could have
heard you without this exclamation. What, i'fack,
I am not deaf; I could have heard you. But if she
be a friend, I hope an old friend may salute her;
'tis a civility well paid. By your leave, sweet lady.   390
(Goes to kiss Cordelia and kisses Sneak.)

SNEAK.

What the devil does this old fellow mean? Uncle!
Did you ever see the like?

SIR ROGER.

Ha, ha, ha! A pleasant mistake, i'faith.

FUMBLE.

Hah! I'fack, I think I was mistaken, was I not,   395
gentlemen? Was I not? I doubt* my false light
guided me to the wrong person. Hah! But come, no
matter, I meant it right, madam, I meant it right.
Never the older for a mistake, i'fack! I meant it right.

CORDELIA.

I am glad I missed it for all that.   400

SIR ROGER.

Mr. Rashley, you are not merry; in troth, I fear I
have disturbed you, hah!

RASHLEY.

Not at all, sir: 'tis impossible your free humor* can
be troublesome to any one.

SIR ROGER.

You know my old way, sir, jovial and inoffensive.   405
Pray let me commend my nephew to you.—Cob,
come hither.—He's a little too modest, sir, but else
I think I may say, a youth of notable parts.*—
Come hither, Cob.

RASHLEY.

I can believe no less.—Sir, your humble servant.   410

SNEAK.

With all my heart, sir, and I am your servant in
like manner.

CORDELIA.

Bless me! What a figure of a husband shall I have?

SIR ROGER.

You know, sir, when I was a bachelor I delighted
much in merry songs and catches. Ah! Sawny   415
Broome,[15] rare fellow, and when a dozen of us

---

14 Cob] a huge, lumpish person (*OED*); also a possible pun
on "testicle"

15 Sawny Broome] Alexander Brome (1620–1666), Royalist songwriter and playwright

Royalists were met at the Miter[16] under the rose*
there, the leveler[17] went round, round, i'faith. I
hold out still, sir, as well as I can, and though I
cannot sing myself, I keep* those that can.
BUBBLE.
Aye, and so do I. My wife's maid shall sing you a   420
Scotch song.—Come, sing it, Betty.
BETTY. (*Sings.*)

A Scotch song.

In January last on Munnonday[18] at morne,
As along the fields I passed to view the winter
corn,*
I leaked[19] me behind, and saw come o'er the
knough[20]
Yen glenting[21] in an apron with a bonny brent[22]   425
brow.

2.

I bid, "Gud morrow, fair maid," and she right
courteously
Bekt lew[23] and sine,[24] "Kind sir," she said, "gud
day agen to ye."
I speard[25] o her, "Fair maid," quo I, "how far
intend you now?"
Quo she, "I mean a mile or twa to yonder bonny
brough."[26]

3.

"Fair maid, I'm weel contented to ha' sike[27]   430
company,
For I am ganging out the gate that you intend to
be."
When we had walkt a mile or twa, I said to her,
"My dow,[28]

---

16 Miter] a popular tavern, Durfey's favorite
17 leveler] bottle? perhaps a reference to a song lampooning the Levelers (q.v.)
18 Munnonday] Monday
19 leaked] looked
20 knough] knoll
21 Yen glenting] One moving
22 brent] smooth
23 bekt lew] curtseyed
24 sine] then
25 speard] asked
26 brough] bridge
27 sike] such
28 dow] dear

May I not light[29] your apron sine kiss your bonny
brow?"

4.

"Nea, gud sir, you are far mistean,[30] for I am
nean o those;
I hope you ha' more breeding than to light a   435
woman's clothes,
For I've a better chosen than any sike as you,
Who boldly may my apron light, and kiss your*
bonny brow."

5.

"Nay, gif[31] you are contracted, I have no more to
say;
Rather than be rejected, I will give o'er the play.
And I will choose yen o my own that shall not on   440
me rew,[32]
Will boldly let me light her apron, kiss her bonny
brow."

6.

"Sir, I see you are proud-hearted and leath[33] to be
said nay;
You need not 'tall ha' started for eaght[34] that I did
say.
You knaw wemun for modesty no at the first time
boo,[35]
But gif we like your company, we are as kind* as   445
you."
BUBBLE.
How d'ye like it?
SIR ROGER.
Oh, I have hundred such as this, sir.
FUMBLE.
A pretty matter, i'fack, a very pretty matter.
RASHLEY.
I doubt,* sir, you heard it not.
FUMBLE.
Aye, is it not, Mr. Rashley, is it not? I'fack, I like   450
it well.

---

29 light] lift
30 mistean] mistaken
31 gif] if
32 rew] rue, show scorn? (Vaughn)
33 leath] loath
34 eaght] aught
35 boo] bow

RASHLEY.

  With all my heart, sir.

FUMBLE.

  Right i'fack, it was sung well indeed.

OMNES.

  Ha, ha, ha!

BUBBLE.

  Well said, Grandsire Fumble.—Come, Sir Roger,   455
now let's in and toss a bumper about.

SIR ROGER.

  I wait upon you, sir.—Cob, lead in your mistress.

Exeunt all but Rashley and Emilia.

RASHLEY.

  So! Thus far all is well. But what's next to be done?
For I know Ranger and Maria are plotting mischief.

EMILIA.

  To prevent 'em we must counterfeit a falling out   460
by railing at you to my husband. I'll soon confirm
it in his opinion, but be sure you are melancholy
enough, and by this means their designs are
frustrated and we still safe in our intrigue.

RASHLEY.

  Excellent! And I'll warrant you, sweet, I'll play my   465
part well.

EMILIA.

  The better will be the success. But let's go in for
fear we are seen.

RASHLEY.

  Thus whilst we're equally involved in thought,
That side fares best that lays the wisest plot.   470

Exeunt.

Act II, [scene i. Ranger's lodging.]

Enter Ranger and Maria.

RANGER.

  Never was an intrigue carried with so much confidence: every word they spoke retained a double
meaning, but so evident that any animal but a dull
husband could not fail to understand it. For they
were so far from hiding their amour that they   5
openly confessed all, only speaking in a third
person for a slender security. He stood and heard
it and often would laugh heartily to hear himself
notoriously abused.

MARIA.

  An insipid fool! Oh that I had been there to have   10
changed the scene a little! But sir, could you be
idle on such an occasion? Why did you not play
your part cunningly and discover* 'em?

RANGER.

  Faith, I did what I could. But the cunning devil
your sister, still* as I was speaking something   15
towards the discovery, would interrupt me and in
a minute dash all my hopes by turning what was
said into raillery.

MARIA.

  Is she so politic? 'Tis very well: I once imagined I
could best design and thought my talent of wit   20
equal with any. But are they so intimate, say ye,
sir?

RANGER.

  As man and wife.

MARIA.

  Impudent fellow! Dares he insult over my love?
Baffle my passion with a sly pretence? I am not   25
fair enough! But he shall find my brain has wit
enough to ruin his design, fool as I am.

RANGER. (*Aside.*)

  Now the devil in her is working hard for me; we
shall have it anon.

MARIA.

  Fooled by a brother's wife! A creature that law   30
makes kin to me! No, 'twas tamely thought, and I
as tamely now should suffer wrongs had I a dastard
spirit. But in me Nature has shown her
masterpiece, and to a masculine person Providence
has bestowed an active soul so sensible of wrongs   35
that to forgive would argue me as base as is their
treachery.

RANGER. (*Aside.*)

  Now she thunders; the devil has been priming her
all this while, and now she scatters like a hand-
granado.   40

MARIA.

  My love refused! 'Tis death to the dull fool, death,
double death, damnation, too, 'tis likely. But why
did I name it love? There's no such word, for with
this breath I banish it forever and in my breast
receive obscure revenge, my heart's delightful   45
darling! Oh the pleasure in that slender word

revenge! I'll plague the fool her husband with a story shall make his gall flow upwards.

RANGER.

Plague him with doubts* and make his jealousy break into violent fits of rage and passion. I'll further all, madam; by Heaven I will not fail you. 50

MARIA.

Enough, and doubt not we'll soon turn the current.

RANGER.

We'll catch 'em in his lodging.

MARIA.

Entrap 'em there and bring him in to see it. 55

RANGER.

Right! What else? We'll shame 'em.

MARIA.

Slight 'em.

RANGER.

Laugh at 'em.

MARIA.

Vex 'em.

RANGER.

Ruin 'em. 60

MARIA.

Damn 'em.

RANGER.

Hey! By Heaven 'tis excellent! And now I see the sense of wrongs can arm a female spirit and make it vigorous. Oh I adore thy temper!

MARIA.

I'll instantly go to her and first charge her with the 65 fact, then upbraid her, for I am resolved never to let her rest till she deserts his passion.

And whilst she suffers that base wretch to woo her, I'll plot, and counter-plot, but I'll undo her.

(*Exit.*)

RANGER.

I am glad I met with her, for of all the persons I 70 am acquainted with, she only has enough of the devil to follow such a business closely, for she'll never rest till she has betrayed 'em, which still will further my revenge. And I am resolved to enjoy her sister, if it be but only for the dear pleasure of 75 boasting it hereafter. I'll straight to Bubble and once more infect him with my poison. Maria is my pilot, and her being thus slighted by Rashley

will still* augment her desire of revenge; 'tis natural to the sex: 80

For balk a woman once, and love rebate, Not all the devils shall reclaim her hate.

Exit.

Scene ii. [Bubble's lodging.]

Enter Rashley, Emilia.

EMILIA.

Manage it but carefully, you need not doubt the consequence. I have already possessed my husband with a belief of our variance, and I know he's coming up with an intent to reconcile us. I'll not be seen; the rest is your part: carry it but 5 handsomely, and Ranger's plots are fruitless. Maria has sent also to speak with him. I guess the business, and I am accordingly provided. But remember you are not tardy.

RASHLEY.

Never doubt me, madam: I am more a lover than to 10 be idle in a business that so nearly concerns us. Besides, 'tis so well contrived and so easy to be followed that to fail now would demonstrate me as defective in sense as your husband is. But what business can your sister have with you? The Devil and she 15 have been plotting together about this intrigue.

EMILIA.

Let 'em plot: I am so much her sister that my part shall never be wanting* to furnish the comedy. I'll go to her straight. In the meantime be you sure to play your part with him. 20

Noise within.

Hark! I hear him coming. (*Exit.*)

RASHLEY.

Well! I never thought a woman till now so necessary a creature. Intrigues are their masterpieces, and as readily they undertake 'em as a country lawyer a bad cause from a half-witted 25 client. 'Twould be excellent sport to hear the two she-wolves bark at one another, but since I cannot be there, I'll divert myself with entertaining the fool her husband.—Here he comes! Now to my studied posture. 30

Enter Bubble.

BUBBLE.

Why how now, Tom? What, all-a-mort?[36] In verity this is foppery, as Sir Roger says. Come, cheer up, cheer up, man, and hold up thy head; in troth thou makest me sad to see thee look so like—so like a—gammon of bacon.—There I was sharp 35 upon him. Ha, ha! A good jest, i'faith.

RASHLEY. (*Aside.*)

Damn him, what a simile the fool has found out!—Sir, it lies not within any man's power to banish serious thoughts at all times. Besides, I have some cause for my present melancholy. 40

BUBBLE.

The cause? Come, come, Tom, I know the cause, ha, ha. You thought, I warrant, to have carried matters so privately, but if I once go about such a business, there's ne'er a man in Christendom (though I say it) can find out a cause sooner 45 than I.

RASHLEY.

You may be mistaken in mine, sir, for all that.

BUBBLE.

Mistaken? Ha, ha! I see, Tom, thou knowest not what 'tis to be ingenious. I tell thee once more, I do know the cause, the very* cause. Aye, and more 50 than that, the cause of the cause. 'Sbud,* there's ne'er an attorney in the Inns of Court* knows more causes than I do.

RASHLEY.

I doubt not but in the end you'll be brought to confess yourself too positive in this particular. But 55 since you have such an excellent faculty and imagine yourself so well skilled in finding out secrets, come, what is't? what is't?

BUBBLE.

What is't? Why, ha, ha, ha! My wife, my wife, Tom, and you're fallen out, ha, ha, ha! Have I mumpt[37] 60 you now, i'faith?

RASHLEY.

I must confess you are in the right, sir.

BUBBLE.

Oh must you so, sir? What a pox! I warrant you

thought we husbands had no wit but what our wives lend us. But I would have you to know, Tom, 65 that I am a leviathan at these matters: to be plain, that is as much as to say, a whale.

RASHLEY.

I am sufficiently convinced of your excellent judgment, sir, and as I have confessed to you freely the cause of my sadness to be your wife's ill usage 70 of me, so I am continually tortured to guess the reason, for I am confident, sir, you know I always honored her and loved her.

BUBBLE.

Faith! So thou didst! I'll say that for thee. And by the Lord Harry,[38] she shall love and honor thee 75 too, or I'll be very sharp upon her: I'll pinch her severely, faith, for all she's my chicken. Nay, if she'll be still refractory, rather than fail thou shalt pinch her too, Tom. I am not like your surly-burly-waspish-cross-grained fellows that fall out and fight 80 about their wives. 'Sbud, I'll give my friend leave at any time to chastise my wife if she don't behave herself civilly.

RASHLEY.

You ever load me with your kind expressions, dear friend! 85

BUBBLE.

Dear Tom, faith, thou'rt an honest fellow. (*Embrace.*)

RASHLEY. (*Aside.*)

This ever is the fate of cuckolds.

BUBBLE.

Never doubt, I'll bring you together again with a vengeance. Nay, I can tell you the reason of her 90 anger too, if I thought 'twere convenient.

RASHLEY.

Convenient! Why sir, 'tis the only thing that conduces to my contentment, for I have long studied in vain and could never yet so much as guess at it. Let me beg it of you, sir. Come, I'm 95 sure you cannot deny so near a friend.

BUBBLE.

I'faith I cannot, that's the truth on't, and thou shalt have it. Why, you must know, Tom, one night

---

36 all-a-mort] dumfounded, in tragic aspect; from the French word for "dead," "mort"

37 mumpt] outguessed

38 by the Lord Harry] an antiquated oath, perhaps by King Harry (Henry V)

(when I was examining her about you) she told me
very seriously that the cause of her anger was that 100
you promised to give her a squirrel that night and
never kept your word, and she loves squirrels
passionately.

RASHLEY.

'Tis true, I confess I did promise her, but as the
devil would have it, I was disappointed utterly of 105
my squirrel that night myself, for I got very drunk,
and from thence sprung this fatal consequence.

BUBBLE.

Pugh! no matter, I'll warrant thee I'll bring all
about again.

RASHLEY.

Oh 'tis impossible; I am sure she'll ne'er be brought 110
to't.

BUBBLE.

Not brought to't? Yes, I'll lay my commands upon
her, and I'll have you know she shall be brought
to't. I'll lay a wager I'll reconcile you both before
night. 115

RASHLEY.

Done. Any wager.

BUBBLE.

What shall it be?

RASHLEY.

Why, five guineas to be spent in a treat of venison
and champagne.

BUBBLE.

Agreed i'faith, and we'll drink and sing tory rory.* 120
Not reconcile you! You shall be all one before
tomorrow morning. I have a spell for that. I'll do't,
I say. Come along, boy.

RASHLEY.

A petty friend for pimping we applaud,
But of all men a husband's the best bawd. 125

Scene iii. [Another room in Bubble's lodging.]

Enter Sir Roger, Cordelia, Sneak.

SIR ROGER.

Madam, you, as being the niece to Mr. Peregrine,
truly deserve the favor I intend you by this alliance.
You are a handsome woman, and in verity were I
a young man, none should be more forward than
I for a place in your affection. I like your air well, 5

and upon my faith, you have the right way on't.
Ah, madam, I once saw the days when such an eye
as yours—well, I say no more on't, 'tis for my
nephew now I make addresses. You see what he
is, madam. His face is none the worst, nor his 10
person I think any way defective. In brief madam,
I present him to you, nor shall he want* an estate
to make him worthy.

CORDELIA. [*Aside.*]

'Tis well he named an estate to candy over his
bitter pill; my squeamish stomach would else have 15
hardly digested it. Lord, how he looks!

SIR ROGER.

Cob! Go, prithee go and make your address to the
lady.—He's newly come from the college, madam,
and is as the rest of 'em are, a little bashful at first,
but by that time he's seen a play or two— 20

CORDELIA.

Methinks this silence becomes him very well, sir.
A student should always be contemplative; 'tis a
great sign of learning.

SIR ROGER.

'Tis a sign he thinks the more. But, madam, ladies
of this age are not to be won with imaginary 25
courtship; 'tis the practick[39] part they love. And
he that can sing well, dance well, talk well, rhyme
modishly, swear decently, and lie confoundedly, is
certainly the happy man, whilst others pass
unregarded. 30

CORDELIA.

I see, sir, you are well skilled in modish address, but
give me leave to tell ye, perhaps few other ladies are
of my humor.* I love words considerately spoken.

SIR ROGER.

And I too, faith madam.—Cob, d'ye hear that,
Cob? 35

SNEAK.

Aye, aye! 'tis a fine woman, by Jericho, and now I
begin to be a little in heart. I shall put up well
enough anon, Uncle.

SIR ROGER.

Well said! Why now I love thee.—And madam,
as to his interior virtues, I dare speak for 'em: his 40
wit is hereditary. Ah! His father, old Sir Jeremy

---

39 practick] practical

Sneak, had a notable headpiece, and troth, Cob comes very near him. You'll find it, madam, when he talks with you.

CORDELIA.

Your character* of him, sir, gives me the 45 satisfaction I should receive in his discourse. I imagine him to be one of those that hoard up wit for Plato's great year[40] and are very shy of using their talent for fear of diminishing the value in making it too common. 50

SIR ROGER.

In verity, madam, I always held him so.—Cob!

SNEAK.

Aye, madam, you may say of me what you please; I am your slave, your vassal, your pig, madam. But as for wit, as my nuncle says, I think I may compare with another, take the Court Cabal[41] 55 away. 'Tis a blessing thrown upon me. Besides, mine is none of your wheedling wits that cheat for a livelihood. I am no parasite, madam, I am a scholar, I!

SIR ROGER.

In troth, he's in the right. Did not I tell you, 60 madam, he would speak notably? Ah, 'tis a wag.

CORDELIA.

His disputes in the college have added extremely to his rhetoric; he speaks with good emphasis and gives a delightful period to every jest, of which I see he has many. But I would fain have the 65 gentleman speak himself; a little talk, I am sure, would become him.

SIR ROGER.

He shall do't, madam.—Cob, now's your time; she's wrought finely.—Madam, I'll take my leave for a minute. I know his temper, madam: he'll 70 speak the better for my absence. (*Exit.*)

CORDELIA.

Pray sir, what university was blessed with your presence?

SNEAK.

Cambridge, madam.

---

40 Plato's great year] a measurement of celestial time (ca. 30,000 years) when all planets return to their original relative positions

41 Court Cabal] Court party of wits

CORDELIA.

Will you not be angry if I ask you one question 75 more?

SNEAK.

Oh Lord, angry, madam? You do not know me. Angry! You mistake me clearly. We of the Round Cap[42] are not given to't; 'tis your graduates are the angry people. 80

CORDELIA.

Pray, what have you learned at Cambridge?

SNEAK.

Learned! What a plaguy question's that?—Where's my uncle now?—Learned, madam?

CORDELIA.

Yes sir, learned.

SNEAK.

Why, madam—I learned nothing. 85

CORDELIA.

Nothing, sir!

SNEAK.

No, but to wear a daggled[43] gown, as the rest do, and eat dry chops of rotten mutton. We fellow commoners don't go thither to learn, madam, we go for diversion, we. 90

CORDELIA.

I thought you had gone to learn the sciences.

SNEAK.

Right, madam, but not gentlemen. Your green, half-witted pupils, I confess, come thither for some such business; that is, madam, your prigs that would be parsons. But the sciences of your* 95 persons of quality*—I'll give you a description— hum?—'tis to wench immoderately, to be drunk hourly, to wear their clothes slovenly, to abuse the proctor damnably, and to be expelled the college triumphantly. There are seven,[44] but I contented 100 myself with these.

CORDELIA. [*Aside.*]

This is ever found: your* sly fool is in his nature more impudent than the greatest professors of debauchery. I must shift him off.

Enter Fumble.

---

42 Round cap] a Cambridge undergraduate

43 daggled] mudsplattered (Vaughn); unkempt, bedraggled

44 seven] liberal arts (q.v.)

FUMBLE.

Oh, here she is, and i'fack, I'll put up to her now 105
I have found her.—How dost thou do, girl? Hah!
How dost thou do? Give me thy hand. Ah, little
rogue! Well, I have been with my goldsmith about
the ring I promised thee; thou shalt have it, bird,
thou shalt have it.—How now, who is that there? 110

SNEAK.

Oh the devil! Now will the old, doting fellow
disturb us before I have told her half my mind.—
Who am I, sir? Why sir, I am one that cares as
little—

FUMBLE.

Thank you heartily, sir, i'fack, I am very well. Only 115
cold weather, cold weather. 'Tis Sir Roger's
nephew! A pretty fellow, a very pretty fellow.

SNEAK.

Very well, sir, would you were very sick, sir.—
'Ounds,* I must beat this fellow.

CORDELIA.

Here's like to be rare sport. 120

SNEAK.

Pray, old philosopher, depart in silence for fear of
further damage; this lady and I have business.

FUMBLE.

I'fack, and so she is, sir, very pretty, very pretty,
bona fide. Ah that black o'th top there! Well, I'll
say no more. But i'fack, black hair, black eyes, and 125
a black—Gad forgive me, what was I going to
say?—patch or two further generation more than
tissues[45] and embroideries.

SNEAK.

Generation? Oh Lord! Was ever such impudence?
An old, doting, impotent fellow, one that was 130
rotten in his minority and now has lost three of
his five senses, to talk of generation!—I am
impatient. Will you be gone, sir? 'Sbud,* I will so
swinge you else.

CORDELIA.

Hold, sir, and pray forbear this rudeness. I like his 135
company very well.

SNEAK.

How! Like him? Why, he has nothing, madam. A
lady can like no hearing, no smelling, no tasting,
no teeth, no strength, no—nothing I say that a
man should have? Besides, he's above four score 140
and by being a stallion in his youth has acquired
to be a baboon in his age, by Jericho. 'Sbud, like
him, quotha?

FUMBLE.

What does the wag say? Hah! What does he say?
He's a pretty, spruce fellow, madam, and i'fack, 145
knows a hawk from a handsaw,[46] as the saying is.
But here are those not far off that, i'fack, know as
much as he, if that were all. What think'st thou,
bird? Do they not? Do they not, rogue? Well, still
I say that hair of thine. Ah, rascal! 150

CORDELIA.

I am glad it pleases you, sir.

SNEAK.

But madam, when shall I begin? 'Sbud, methinks
we lose time.

CORDELIA.

Begin! What, sir?

SNEAK.

Why, my courtship. Pox o'this old chattering 155
fellow; if he had not come, I had been out of my
pain before now.—Hark ye, reverend sir, 'sbud,
what d'ye do prating here? Why don't you go and
chat to your granddaughter at home, if you love
women so well? 160

FUMBLE.

Hah! What does the wag say, madam?

CORDELIA.

He says, sir, he's extremely in love with your
granddaughter.

FUMBLE.

My granddaughter? And i'fack, she deserves it,
madam. She's a juicy, sprightly girl; she'll make a 165
pottle of water of a pint of ale, a chip o'the old block,
bona fide, and shall turn her back to ne'er a one in
Christendom of her inches, I'll say that for her.

Enter Betty.

BETTY.

Sir, there's one Mrs.* Snare below desires to speak
with you, 170

---

45 tissues] a rich kind of cloth, often interwoven with gold
or silver (*OED*)

46 handsaw] heron

SNEAK.

Snare! Oh Lord, what shall I do? How the devil came she to know I was here? Hark, prithee, sweetheart, tell her I am gone. Oh, I would not see her for the world.

BETTY.

Sir, she says she dogged you hither and swears and   175
rants yonder strangely.

SNEAK.

Oh damned quean! What shall I do?

BETTY.

And vows if you come not instantly, she'll go into the parlor to Sir Roger and discover* something to him, I know not what, but I saw she was a big-   180
bellied woman, and I was loath to discourage her.

SNEAK.

Well, well, tell her I'll come.

Exit Betty.

Why, how the devil could she get from Cambridge already?

CORDELIA.

What's the matter, sir? Not well?   185

SNEAK.

Yes, I thank you, madam, very well, only thinking of a little business I have; I must about it presently.* Madam, your servant. I'll wait upon you some other time. [*Aside.*] I must go and pacify this quean. This comes of learning the sciences,   190
with a pox. (*Exit.*)

CORDELIA.

Come sir, shall we go in?

FUMBLE.

I'fack, and so he is, madam. But the fellow has some pretty parts* and will grow better in time. But come, let's go in and see Sir Roger.   195

CORDELIA.

'Twas that I asked you.

FUMBLE.

Hah! Dost like me, sayst thou, i'fack? I'm glad on't. Shall we not have a word or two in private, my little Queen of Fairies? We must, I say, we must. Ah rogue! I'll warrant thou art a swinger. But   200
come, let's go.

Exeunt.

Scene iv. Emilia's bedchamber.

Enter Maria and Emilia severally.

EMILIA.

Now for my talent of women! I see by her looks I shall have occasion for it.

MARIA.

Sister!

EMILIA.

Sister!

MARIA.

The natural love I bear you, and my desire to   5
prevent your growing infamy, has brought me hither to give you counsel.

EMILIA.

The sense I have of your ill nature, and my knowledge of the little good it will do you, has brought me hither to give you advice.   10

MARIA.

Your reputation is loudly branded by all tongues, and I only as a sister have power to speak indifferently of your life in hopes of your reformation.

EMILIA.

Your malice and unexampled envy is mortally   15
hated by all people, I only as a sister retaining so much pity as to desire its utter dissolution.

MARIA.

Why do you echo me?

EMILIA.

Why do you question me? What have I done deserves it?   20

MARIA.

Done! Recollect your thoughts and then confess. For my part, shame ties up my tongue. I dare not speak it.

EMILIA.

Dare not! Nay, that I'm sure is false; you dare speak anything. Come, prithee don't fright me, what is't   25
you mean?

MARIA. (*Aside.*)

Excellent cunning! She has fitted* me.—Why would you seem ignorant? I confess, to a stranger you might be cautious of a nice confession. But this artifice to your sister, fie, Emilia.   30

EMILIA.

Now I'll lay my life your design is to wheedle something out of me to make yourself merry withal.

MARIA. [*Aside.*]

Rare still!—No madam, this is no such merry matter; the infamy of a family is not so to be jested with.

EMILIA.

Infamy! Nay, then I see 'tis time to be serious. Come, express it. I suppose 'tis the invention of your envy, some new stratagem to affront me with; I am no stranger to your temper.

MARIA.

This is an impudence beyond a prostitute. Do I not know you are false?

EMILIA.

False! How?

MARIA.

False to your husband, false with Rashley. I need not tell you; you best know that.

EMILIA.

I know you love him! and am sensible of the intrigues and assignations which you have had, which makes your meaning visible. But methinks this is so strange a design.

MARIA.

Design! What is't she means? I hope you can tax me with no such crime with him.

EMILIA.

Not I, 'tis not my business. I have only liberty to guess. Yet indeed your often private meetings were a little suspicious, and I suppose your late raillery was only a design. But you might have took a better way with your sister: I am not so talkative.

MARIA.

Exquisite devil! Death, I am incensed beyond all bounds of reason. I private with him! An intrigue with me! Fury! Thou knowest—

EMILIA.

I do, and to exasperate thy rage, will now confess all. I do love Rashley more than I love fame, nay, more than you could do, could you die for him. But why should that offend you?

MARIA.

Oh confusion! I am all o'er fire. Dare you be such a devil? Dare you love him?

EMILIA.

Yes, and to vex you more, dare make you of my counsel.

MARIA.

Can I endure this? Oh for a look now of a basilisk that I might kill thee.

EMILIA.

Thou art worse.

MARIA.

Expect to find me so, for if there be a stratagem of malice in all hell, I'll have it thence. Ah, I'll be a tender sister to thee.

EMILIA.

As ever woman yet was blessed withal.

MARIA.

Not all the infernals, clad in the secret, darkest robes of malice, did ever watch a soul they meant to ruin as I will thee. Thy very sleeps shall be discovered* to me, and every dream I'll trace with so much care that, if thou 'scapest, thou art the wiser sister and I a poor unthinking creature good for nothing.

EMILIA.

I slight thy threats and dare thee to persevere. Manage thy hate with such dexterity the world may wonder at thee and confess thou hadst the practick part of policy. Design thy plots so subtly that the Devil should own himself outdone in his own mystery, yet in the arms of him I love I'd laugh to see my wit outdo 'em.

MARIA.

Thy wit! Thy wit compare with mine, insipid fool?

EMILIA.

Yes, and my prosperous fate shall mount me far above thy shallow stratagems.

MARIA.

I'll pull thee down from that ambitious height and trample thee in ashes.

EMILIA.

Do.

MARIA.

Expect it.

EMILIA.

And from that low recess I'll forge a plot shall blow thee into air.

I'll make that devil in thy envy tame.

MARIA.

And if I fail thee, may I sink and damn.

Exeunt.

Act III. [Scene i. A room adjacent
to Emilia's chamber.]

Enter Sneak and Mrs. Snare.

SNEAK.

Nay! prithee, Pegg, have patience.

SNARE.

Tell not me of patience, sir, for my part I can stay
no longer. You see my condition. If you will
consider, so; if not, Sir Roger shall know that the
abuse of so innocent a person as I was deserves 5
better satisfaction.

SNEAK.

Innocent! 'Sbud,* she was a strumpet to the whole
college before I knew her. Innocent, with a pox!

SNARE.

Sir, do not grumble, nor say your* Devil's
Paternoster to me, but give me money. Fifty 10
pounds I demand, which I think is reasonable
enough, considering the charge of my journey.

SNEAK.

You might have stayed till I came back again; I was
not running away.

SNARE.

But I was, sir, and so might you for anything I 15
know. Come, come, sir, I am to be baffled no
more; I am grown older now, make me thankful.

SNEAK. [*Aside.*]

Aye, in impudence, by Jericho. She has been
snapped, it seems, formerly, but has now learnt
cunning. Ah, plague o'these sciences, I say still!*— 20
Come, wilt thou be civil? Wilt thou take twenty
pounds? Pox, use a little conscience in thy dealings;
thou wilt thrive the better for't.

SNARE.

I'll abate not a farthing, sir; don't tell me of
conscience. 25

SNEAK.

'Sbud, would she were in the sea and a millstone
about her neck. I must give it, for if my uncle
comes and sees her, I am undone.

Enter Betty.

BETTY.

Oh sir, what shall we do? Sir Roger and my master
are just coming. 30

SNEAK.

Oh unhappy minute! If he sees me, I am lost
forever. No hole nor corner to hide us in, my little
rogue? 'Sbud, here's a guinea for thee; do but
contrive handsomely.

BETTY.

Well sir, I see you are a gentleman; therefore, I'll 35
help you. This door opens to my lady's chamber.
There you may hide yourselves, and at night when
it begins to grow dark, I'll come and let you out.

SNEAK.

With all my heart! Oh, I've an ague on me.

Exeunt. Enter Ranger and Emilia.

RANGER.

Are you still resolved? 40

EMILIA.

Assure yourself I am and shall be ever.

RANGER.

Give me but hopes, and I'll forget all injuries and
ask your pardon.

EMILIA.

Fie, this from a man of wit, one that can plot so well?
'Tis impossible. What would you have me do? 45

RANGER.

Desert young Rashley. Come, I beg thee do it.

EMILIA.

Not for the world! Oh Heaven! Desert him! I love
him, sir.

RANGER.

Go on then, devil, and if I don't plague thee—

Enter Bubble, Sir Roger, Rashley, Fumble.

BUBBLE.

Now for the venison, Tom! You'll stand to your 50
bargain?

RASHLEY.

Firmly, sir, win it and 'tis yours.—Hah! what a
devil makes Ranger here?

SIR ROGER.

Madam, I hope you'll excuse my last, abrupt
departure. My nature, madam, is merry and, in 55
verity, careless sometimes. I have not since I came

to England achieved the polite method of
courtship and address, but if blunt actions, kind
behavior, and merry songs can do it, I think I have
shown an example, have I not, old signior?   60

FUMBLE.

I'fack sir, and 'tis right, let who will say the
contrary. What does he say now? Madam, you may
believe him.

EMILIA.

Anything, sir, rather than put you to the trouble
of an apology. (*Frowns on Rashley.*)   65

RASHLEY. [*Aside to Bubble.*]

What think you now, sir? Do you observe her
angry look? Do but see what an eye of indignation
she casts upon me!

BUBBLE.

Aye, aye, I'll put out her eye of indignation
presently;* I'll fetch her down with her haughty   70
looks in a moment; I'll make her look as I'd have
her, or I'll put her head into a pudding bag.

RANGER. [*Aside.*]

'Sdeath,* how she looks! Here's another plot a-
hatching.

BUBBLE.

Wife! I have brought honest Tom here to be   75
reconciled to thee, and to take away all manner of
distastes, he says he will give thee a squirrel at any
time, wouldst thou not, Tom?

RASHLEY.

Sir, and my heart into the bargain, if she please to
pardon me.   80

BUBBLE.

Why, look ye now, he's as honest a fellow as lives,
I'll say that for him.

EMILIA.

Sir, the affront he offered me was so contrary to
my nature, and his behavior so opposite to his duty
and character, that to forgive him would argue my   85
spirit as mean* as by his late deportment one
might guess his breeding.

BUBBLE.

What! Dare you be refractory? Hoh! Do it, or by
the Lord Harry I shall be very sharp upon you,
that's in short.   90

RANGER. [*Aside.*]

Now all the fiends that dwell beneath the center

And hourly study deeds subtle and horrid
To soothe and snare the souls ye mean to damn,
In favor of your commonwealth appear
And to be still more devilish copy her.   95

BUBBLE.

Still refractory? Then thus I break the truce and
sally out with my full power.

RANGER.

Sir, do you not see her artifice? This is nothing
what she intends; 'tis all feigned and you are
abused, by Heaven. Sir, there's nothing of this real.   100

BUBBLE.

Ah! would it were not. But Ned, thou canst talk
well, prithee go and try if thou canst reconcile 'em.
Faith, I'll do as much for thee. Prithee try.

RANGER.

Insufferable ignorance! No brains! No sense of
feeling! Sir, this is all dissimulation and to carry   105
on their design of abusing you.

BUBBLE.

Why peace, I say, not a word of this. 'Sbud,* I shall
lose my venison by this fool's prating, if I let him
alone a little longer.—Wife, I command you once
more, and instantly obey upon this summons, or   110
I'll turn you away like a vagabond for contempt
of my government.—Sir Roger, try you to
persuade her. 'Sbud, this Ned here had liked to
have spoiled all, but what says Scoggen?[47]

EMILIA.

'Tis hard to force lost friendship to the blood when   115
once 'tis banished.

RANGER.

Had she been bred a witch, she had lost half her
character.

SIR ROGER.

Come madam, forget and forgive. 'Tis necessary
your husband should be obeyed.—Mr. Rashley, I   120
am sorry to see you so deserted by the ladies you
used to be most in favor withal.

RASHLEY.

Not I, but you weigh my merits in your own scale,
Sir Roger.

---

47 Scoggen] coarse jester or buffoon; from John Skoggin,
court fool to Edward IV (*OED*)

SIR ROGER.

No faith, I am old now, but about some thirty 125
years ago I could have said something; I could have
fetched 'em about, with a horse-pox[48] i'faith. I
never flinched; I was a true knight-errant, I.

FUMBLE. [*Aside*.]

What is the meaning of all this? I'fack, I cannot
guess the matter. But mum, I must not discover* 130
my failing.

EMILIA.

Well sir, rather than be thought disobedient, I will
submit, but Heaven knows with what an ill will—

BUBBLE.

Why so, now all's well, and the venison's mine—
ha, ha, ha—I thought I should have it. Faith Tom, 135
be civil and kiss her, 'tis no confirmation else.

RANGER.

Oh damn him, damn him! Was ever such a
coxcomb?

RASHLEY. (*Aside [to Emilia].*)

'Tis now about five; at seven I will not fail ye.—
Madam, you have given me new life with this 140
favor.

RANGER. (*Aside*.)

At seven? (Good!) Thanks to my ear for that
discovery. I shall go near to spoil your assignation.

BUBBLE.

Go now, get you in and begin a set at ombre, and
I'll come and make one presently.* By the Lord 145
Harry, I am glad they are friends with all my heart.

*Exeunt Sir Roger, Fumble, Rashley, Emilia smiling.
Enter Maria.*

RANGER.

So Paris stole the wife of Menelaus, and Troy grew
bright with fire.

BUBBLE.

Hey day! Troy! Why what hast thou to do with
Troy? Ned, prithee let us talk of our own affairs. 150

MARIA.

And wisely too, for your reputation suspended one
hour will grow nauseous. The rabble will shout at
ye and point their fingers, and by your name you
will grow infamous.

---

48 horse-pox] a severe or virulent pox

Enter Betty at door.

BUBBLE.

My name, Sister! What dost mean? What name? 155

MARIA.

A cuckold. Can you bear it, sir? A cuckold-buzz.[49]

BUBBLE.

By the Lord Harry, 'tis but a scurvy name for a
man of honor, that's the truth on't. But what is't
to me?

RANGER.

Nothing, sir, nothing, only you are the man, that's 160
all.

BUBBLE.

That's all, quotha? What a pox does he mean?

MARIA.

Dull man! I blush to call ye brother, that kind name,
your want of sense taken from you: Can you see the
guilty love between Rashley and your wife, the 165
melting touches, and the glancing eyes? The often
pressings, sighs, and kind* caresses, and all the signs
of shame and burning lust, and yet be patient? Oh
the insipid dullness of a husband! A husband.

BUBBLE.

Rashley and my wife! Pish, why I reconciled 'em 170
but just now; she has been angry with him this
week for not giving her a squirrel he promised her.

RANGER.

A squirrel? Hah! A very fine present that, if you
understood all.

MARIA.

That anger was designed. You are abused, and I, 175
that have a share in all your ignominy, have now
resolved prevention. Oh that ever I should live to
be a witness of this shame! (*Weeps.*) Heaven knows
how I have loved her, instructed her, and told her
the duty of a wife was to obey and be constant, 180
yet all would not do. Therefore, I am resolved to
right myself and you in the discovery,* nor shall
our race* in future times be branded with any
spurious offspring.

RANGER.

I could not be believed; I was impertinent. But if 185
you knew what I have seen, sir.

---

49 cuckold-buzz] rumored to be a cuckold

BUBBLE.

Seen! Why prithee what hast thou seen, Ned?

RANGER.

Faith, 'twill be no secret long, therefore I'll tell you: I have seen her lie in Rashley's arms and kiss him, play with his nose and clap his cheeks and laugh 190 till her whole frame was shook with titillation; I guess, sir, 'twas at you, but will not swear it. She'd sing and breathe upon him, and with her hand locked fast in his and eyes with rapture gazing on his face, she'd tell him wanton stories of her love 195 and of her easy husband. He, to requite her, would display[50] her charms and betwixt every word imprint a kiss to prove his amorous argument.

BUBBLE.

And you have seen this?

RANGER.

More than this, sir: I have seen (but to tell you is 200 to be called impertinent!) such things, such monstrous things.

BUBBLE.

My head begins to ache; all is not well. Prithee Ned, out with 'em. Come, I am thy friend, and 'sbud, if I thought any thing were done in hugger- 205 mugger—

MARIA.

What would you do then?

BUBBLE.

Do! Why, I'd ask him civilly whether his meaning were good or no.

RANGER.

His meaning? 210

BUBBLE.

Aye. You know 'tis best to begin mildly, that afterwards, if occasion be, a man may cut his throat with greater assurance.

MARIA.

Stare on your infamy with eagle aspect! Behold the evidence of shame writ in their eyes and actions! 215 See every glance, each touch, each kind embrace, and when you have seen 'em in the very fact, stand coldly unconcerned and ask the meaning. Ah! curse upon all dullness.

RANGER.

Let Rashley smile and point his fingers at ye, tell 220 you a story of a quondam mistress (which is indeed your wife), how oft he has lain with her and pleasantly deceived the easy cuckold, yet as a president[51] of excellent nature, I could advise you still to ask his meaning, his meaning. 225

MARIA.

Watch all his actions, and when some kind genius* has, to undeceive you, made you a spectator of Rashley, full of hopes and all undressed, entering your bed with a glad lover's haste, step in and pull him back and ask his meaning, his meaning! 230

BUBBLE.

My bed! My bed is my castle, and by the Lord Harry, he that violates it but with a look my fist shall crush him into mummy.[52]

RANGER. (*Aside.*)

So, now he begins to take fire.

BUBBLE.

He's a son of a whore, a dog, a bitch, a succubus, 235 and if I find this true, I'll cut him piecemeal though he were swordproof and had a witch to call his mother.

MARIA.

Aye, this is meaning now! Go on and prosper.

RANGER.

These words display a revived sense of honor, nor 240 shall you want* encouragement to forward it. And since I see your eyes and understanding are opened, I, as your friend, will give this secret to you: 'twas my good fortune to hear an assignation appointed between 'em this night at seven o'clock. 245 I guess 'tis now very near the hour. You have a key to the chamber. Go thither at the time appointed, and then never trust your friend if you find her not the falsest of women.

BUBBLE.

If I do, I'll make her the ugliest in Christendom, 250 for I'll cut off her nose and send her to the Devil for a New Year's gift.

---

50 display] expound upon

51 president] a presiding deity, patron, or guardian (*OED*)

52 mummy] powdered parts of a dead body, used for medicinal purposes

MARIA.

Here she comes, we must not be seen, 'twill spoil all. Talk of going abroad and carry it handsomely, for fear she mistrusts. 255

BETTY. [*Aside.*]

Happy discovery! This shall to my lady immediately. [*Exit.*]

BUBBLE.

But where shall we meet?

RANGER.

At my lodging in the Strand,* about half an hour hence. 260

Exeunt [Ranger and Maria]. Enter Emilia.

EMILIA.

What, studying, my dear? Come, come, indeed you must not be so thoughtful. Did you not promise to come and make one at ombre?

BUBBLE. [*Aside.*]

Now if I might be hanged, cannot I speak an angry word, no.—I won't play, I am busy, I am going abroad for two or three hours. Farewell. (*Exit.*) 265

EMILIA.

'Tis so: our intrigue tonight is discovered* to him, I find by his actions. The infernal colleagues, Ranger and Maria, have been possessing him with some strange resolutions. But since 'tis but what I expect-ed, it gives me the less trouble, and 'tis ten to one but I have a counterplot left that shall undo their poli-cies, though the Devil made one in the invention. 270

Enter Rashley.

—Did you meet my husband?

RASHLEY.

Yes, but in a strange humor. He looked with so dull an aspect and returned my salute* so coldly and so far from his usual manner that I more than half fear our intrigue is discovered.* 275

EMILIA.

Without doubt it is. They have played their parts to discover, and it now belongs to us to study to repel. Come, summon your wits together and advise what's to be done in so critical a conjuncture; you had a contriving genius once. 280

RASHLEY.

Aye, 'tis true, madam, I had once, but this damned

champagne has so dulled it that, egad, 'tis now worth little or nothing. Madam, you know my talent in plot is insignificant, but if a rencontre or cutting Ranger's throat may do the business, I'll thrust my hand as far as any man. I'll spoil his plotting by Heaven, say you but the word. 285 290

EMILIA.

No! Fighting will do in any other business better than this. For instead of defending, it blasts my reputation.

RASHLEY.

The devil take me, if I had not like to have forgot that too. Well, I am a dull rogue, madam, that's the truth on't. 295

Enter Betty.

BETTY.

Oh madam, you are betrayed! Mr. Ranger, by what means Heaven knows, has been informed of your assignation. I accidentally overheard him telling it to my master, and Madam Maria coming in, seconded his story with an extravagant fury, and in conclusion 'twas designed that he should pretend business abroad, but privately return home and surprise ye. 300

EMILIA.

'Tis as I imagined, and I am glad of this caution. Now we may take breath again. 305

RASHLEY.

Gad and so am I. But is there no way to keep on the plot and deceive 'em still?

EMILIA.

'Tis in my head and will have birth presently.— Betty, you have Sneak still fast in my chamber? 310

BETTY.

Yes madam, he's securely locked in, and here's the key.

EMILIA.

Follow me then and do as I directed you.—In the meantime, sir, go to your chamber and put on your gown and nightcap as if you had been in bed, and when you hear me stamp, come out and wonder. Let me alone for the rest: I'll plague 'em with an after-plot. Away, the minute's near. 315

Exit Emilia and Betty.

RASHLEY.

What she intends I know not but am certain of
the success by the assurance she does it with. Hah!   320
'Tis a rare creature and, by Heaven, is mistress of
the sweetest nature and noblest trust and most
substantial good English principles of any woman
in Europe. Well, if cuckolding be a crime, 'tis the
sweetest crime in Christendom and has certainly   325
the most practicers. But let that pass; now to my
gown and nightcap. (*Exit.*)

Enter Sir Roger, Fumble, Cordelia, and servant.

SIR ROGER.

'Sdeath!* I have had confounded luck tonight: not
a good chance since I begun, nor no mirth neither,
there's the plague on't. Had I had the liberty to   330
have sung two or three merry catches and have lost
my money with a trolly lolly lo, it had been
nothing.—Here, hey, where's Cob? Call him hither
quickly, and let us go.

SERVANT.

Sir! I have not seen him these two hours; I believe   335
he's gone home. [*Exit.*]

SIR ROGER.

How! What, without taking leave of his mistress?
'Tis impossible.

FUMBLE.

Sir Roger, you are disturbed, methinks. What is
the matter? Hah! Your behavior seems to publish   340
that—

SIR ROGER.

No great matter, sir.—Pox o'this old fool.

CORDELIA.

Sir, it ill becomes a person of your gravity to be
angry on so small an occasion.

SIR ROGER.

Small! By Heaven, madam, 'tis a matter of   345
moment. What, run away without taking leave? In
verity 'tis barbarous and derogates from his birth
and breeding, nor can I, though his kinsman,
excuse—

FUMBLE.

What does Sir Roger say, madam? Does he rally?   350
Hah! He's a merry man, and a good fellow, and
i'fack, I love mirth. For my part I hate your drowsy,
insipid, phlegmatic fellows that sleep over a glass

and talk of nothing but state politics. But Sir Roger
is a man for the purpose, a merry jolly man, he.   355

SIR ROGER.

Sir, you may spare your commendations for them
that delight in 'em.—What an impertinent old
fellow 'tis!—Pray sir, no more of this, I am not
pleased with it.

FUMBLE.

Your song of Sir Thomas Fairfax[53] and the rest of   360
the brave old fellows was very fine, Sir Roger. Well!
I'll not be positive, but there was certainly a great
deal of judgment and sheer wit in some of those
Rump songs.[54]

SIR ROGER.

'Sdeath! This is the most insufferable old fellow.—   365
Pox, tell not me of Rump songs. Sir in verity,
would you had been hanged up instead of the
Rump, that I might have been free from the
noise.—But madam, as I was saying, upon my
honor I never knew Cob in such an error.   370

FUMBLE.

Then, Sir Roger, "Chevy Chase," and "The
Hunting of the Hare"[55] is finely penned! Finely
penned! I'fack it was—

SIR ROGER.

Oh the devil, is there no riddance of this clack?
Because he can hear nothing, he would speak all.   375

FUMBLE.

Aye, so it was, sir, so it was. But i'fack, that
"Hunting" was most excellently contrived. Ah, he
makes the dogs speak notably. Icod, and the hare
repartees again very well for an animal of her
magnitude.   380

SIR ROGER.

'Sbud,* I shall grow as deaf as he if I stay longer. I
must go seek my nephew.—Come madam, let's go
away and leave him; I am sure his eyes are so

---

53 song of Sir Thomas Fairfax] a song by Alexander Brome
    ridiculing Thomas, third Lord Fairfax (1612-1671), who
    led the Parliamentary Army against Charles I (Vaughn)
54 Rump-songs] songs ridiculing the Rump Parliament of
    the Commonwealth
55 Chevy Chase … Hunting of the Hare] popular ballad
    and song

defective he cannot miss us presently.* (*Exeunt [Sir Roger and Cordelia].*)   385

FUMBLE.

And though some petulant, insignificant, and disaffected persons have raised calumnies by calling it doggerel and fustian and such like, yet i'fack, the thing is really a witty, facetious, nay, and as some think, a moral satire. For mark me, Sir Roger, and   390
madam, pray give your attention, for the dogs were hieroglyphic characters of fanatics, as the hare was of the Quakers, and i'fack, I have often heard the sisters sing it, instead of an hymn or an anthem, for the conversion of unbelievers, and nay, and as   395
a greater rarity, I have heard it acted to the life betwixt a dog-fanatic and a coney-Quaker.[56] But i'fack, I think you mind me not. Hah, Sir Roger, madam—Sir Roger, madam— (*Pulls out spectacles.*) What, a vacuity? Gone? Well. I'll after and redeem   400
all, but icod, this was a little uncivil. (*Exit.*)

Enter Ranger, Betty with a candle, sets it on table.

BETTY.

Come sir, and with as little noise as you can for fear of discovery. I swear, were you not a man to whom I am sensibly obliged, I should not be drawn to this infidelity.   405

RANGER.

I will reward thy care. Are they together?

BETTY.

Yes sir, in that room there. (*Pointing to the little door.*)

RANGER.

Take this, and be gone, I have no further service for thee, and I would have her ignorant that this   410
is thy discovery.* Away.

BETTY. (*Aside.*)

The discovery will add little to your content. But since I have the profit, I care not. (*Exit.*)

Enter Bubble and Maria.

BUBBLE.

Ned! What says she? Are they met?

RANGER.

Securely and with a great deal of content they are   415
in that room in the dark. Met! Ah sir! They are both better practiced than ever to be tardy in a love intrigue.

MARIA. (*Aside.*)

Now I think I have trapped her finely. Oh my joy! I shall not be able to contain myself.   420

BUBBLE.

A man of wit and honor thus abused! 'Tis horrible! A cuckold! 'Sbud, 'tis a worse name than a conjurer and has more of the devil in't. But I'll be so revenged the world shall tremble at it. I'll first cut off her hair to affront her family; then the want   425
of a nose shall proclaim her a bawd, and the penny-pot-poets[57] shall make ballads on her. (*Exit.*)

RANGER.

So! this thrives as I would have it, and we have snapped 'em finely in the nick! Just when the   430
intrigue was at its best perfection! Oh revenge!

MARIA.

Ha, ha, ha! Nay, and at such a time when all help is denied 'em; when her blushes, sighs, entreaties are all fruitless; when her exasperated husband's rage flows high; and best of all, when Rashley is   435
defenseless. Oh Wit! I love thee for this stratagem!

RANGER.

She dared us to persevere, slighted our plots, and had the confidence to make descriptions of her kind* intrigue before her husband's face, then laughed at us.   440

MARIA.

'Tis now our time. Ha, ha, ha! I thought I could not fail.

RANGER.

No, and this happy minute brings me more perfect pleasure and more true delight than pristine ages. For she's one whom Hell designed for its chief   445
instrument. She will out-lie a siren, cheat the devil, and damn more souls to further her intrigue than Charon's boat has room for. (*Aside.*) Yet I own a kind of mongrel love, and must enjoy her though legions were her guard.   450

---

56 hieroglyphic … Quaker] Fumble reads the song as an allegory of battles among Dissenting sects of the time, who were on the Roundhead side of the Civil War.

57 penny-pot-poets] cheap balladeers

A shriek within.

MARIA.

Hark! He's as good as his word. Now I hope she'll own her sister's wit above her. Well! this was rarely plotted.

RANGER.

By Heaven it was, and fit to be chronicled, madam. Your wit surpasses human thought and should be spoken of with wonder. You plot with such assurance that— 455

Enter Emilia.

Hell, death, and confusion! Can I believe my eyes? She here!

MARIA.

I am confounded and have lost my senses. Sure sir, we dream. Are we awake, think you? 460

EMILIA.

No, nor shall never wake when I design to raise my wit above the poor weak creature's. I could laugh now, but I swear I pity ye. Wear out your tedious nights in dull design, and then in the morning hatch the abortive brood which ere night turns to nothing: 465 slender encouragement, Heaven knows, for wit.— And you, sir, plot and sweat and plot again for moonshine in the water: poor reward, sir, for one so well-skilled in intrigue as you are! 470

MARIA.

Oh that I had thy heart here in my hand! How pleasant were the diet! Fate and death! Was ever such a devil?

RANGER.

No, never! Therefore since thou art a devil, as I now am sure thou art, (*Kneels.*) have mercy on me, 475 and do not take my soul for my first crime, and I will plot no more. Thou art my conqueror; I'll honor thee. Good devil, do not hurt me.

Shrieking within. Enter Bubble dragging in Snare.

BUBBLE.

Strumpet! Whore! Witch! I'll spoil your curls, by the Lord Harry.—Oh Lord! My wife! and she that 480 I have beaten a stranger.

SNARE.

Oh Heaven, was ever poor sinner so abused? (*Weeps.*)

BUBBLE. (*Looks amazedly at his wife, then at Snare, then at a lock of black hair in his hand.*)

Madam, I beg your pardon, and am ashamed of my fault, but I'll make you amends presently.* 485

RANGER. (*To Emilia kneeling.*)

Well, nothing but the greatest devil could have brought this woman hither for this intrigue, and therefore once more I acknowledge thy power.

BUBBLE.

Aye, you had need ask her pardon; 'tis you have betrayed us.—Chicken! Dear chicken, don't frown 490 so. I confess I was a fool, but forgive me this once, and if ever I offend again, I'll give thee leave to cuckold me indeed.

EMILIA.

Indeed sir, your jealousy is a little severe; I wonder what I have done to deserve it. 495

BUBBLE.

Nothing, I know thou hast not, prithee forgive me.

EMILIA.

But to be disturbed thus when I was at my devotion.

BUBBLE.

Prithee forget it. Come Tom, you may come out now; here's none but friends. 500

EMILIA.

Who do you mean, sir? (*Stamps with her foot.*)

BUBBLE.

Tom Rashley. Poor fellow, I warrant now he'll be so bashful.

RANGER.

So, that's something yet, and I'll fetch him out or bleed for't. (*Exit.*) 505

Enter Rashley at the other side.

EMILIA.

Look, yonder he is!

MARIA.

I find it now, and this is all designed. Oh devil! Devil!

Enter Sir Roger after Rashley.

SIR ROGER.

What's the matter, Mr. Rashley? What's the matter?

BUBBLE.

Rashley here? Hey day! Who the devil is that 510 yonder then?

Enter Ranger dragging out Sneak.

RANGER.

Come sir, appear; I find you are now no Hercules.
Hah! Death, more miracles, Sneak!

SIR ROGER.

'Sdeath,* my Cob! and taken with a wench. Why
how now, sirrah?   515

EMILIA. [*Aside to Rashley.*]

Now it works to my wish; prithee observe how
they look.

RASHLEY.

Hush. I do.

SNEAK.

Oh Lord, Uncle, your mercy. I was betrayed,
seduced, as a man may say. (*To Snare.*) Go, go, be   520
gone, I'll speak with you tomorrow.—I say, Uncle,
I was seduced, choused, cheated.

SIR ROGER.

Catcht with a wench? Come sir, I'll talk with you.
Oh disgrace to the family. With a wench? A lewd
wench? Come along, sir, I'll watch you henceforth.   525

Exeunt Sir Roger, Sneak.

RASHLEY. (*Gapes.*)

Hah? hah? Why, here has been a great deal of
intrigue tonight I see, hah sir? I am sorry now I
went to bed so soon. But I have been in the
sweetest dream yonder.

BUBBLE.

Here has in troth been a great deal of intrigue, as   530
thou say'st, Tom. But no matter, now all's well.
And since it has happened so well, a day of jubilee
shall crown it. Tomorrow is my wedding day, and
in memory of that happy hour that conjoined me
and my sweet chicken there together, we'll have a   535
feast, and I'll sing and roar and drink *cum
privilegio.*[58] Go, wait on her in, Tom.—Chicken,
remember we are friends. Go, I'll be with you
presently.

*Exeunt [Emilia and] Rashley, bowing scornfully to
Ranger and Maria.*

RANGER.

Never was such a day, nor such a deed.   540

---

[58] *cum privilegio*] with privilege, unrestrained (Lat.)

BUBBLE.

Ned! Let me have no more of your doubts* nor
counsels. D'ye hear? 'Sbud, I say once more my
wife is the honestest woman in Christendom, and
you shall hear from me. (*Exit.*)

MARIA.

Was ever the like known?   545

RANGER.

Never since Adam, but she was a devil before the
creation.

MARIA.

I'll not give over thus.

RANGER.

Nor I.

MARIA.

Your hand on't.   550

RANGER.

Here, and may all the demons that have pow'r
In subtle plots help now, though never more.

MARIA.

I'll die but I'll perform it.
My slights shall with immortal wit be wrought,
And all my senses shall convert to thought.   555

Exeunt ambo.[59]

Act IV, [scene i. On the street
near Sir Roger's house.]

Enter Sir Roger and Sneak.

SIR ROGER.

Sirrah! Haunt me no more, I know thee not.

SNEAK.

Nay, Uncle.

SIR ROGER.

Go to your wench, and let her entertain* you; then
stock Sir Jeremy's manor house at home with
bastards, birds of night,[60] and teach 'em all to   5
know their father when you ha' done.

SNEAK.

Good Uncle, let me speak.

SIR ROGER.

No place to bring your cattle to but thither, under
your mistress's nose, thou most notorious ass?

---

[59] *Exeunt ambo*] Exit both.

[60] birds of night] prostitutes (Vaughn)

Mercy o'me, what will this world come to? Who 10
could imagine that sheep's face of thine, that
mouth, whence ne'er came anything that had
sense, that person that has as oft been thought a
Puritan as thou hast been a fool? Then that
hanging-dog look. I'll say no more, but the devil 15
is subtle.

SNEAK.

Uncle, you know 'tis an old saying, we cannot
appoint our own destinies, nor did I foresee this.
Besides, sir, if you knew her as well as I do, you'd
find the woman has some parts* that are not 20
contemptible. 'Sbud,* I know what's what; I am
not such a fool.

SIR ROGER.

Not such a fool! In verity, if thou wert but a grain
nearer to a natural,* I'd beg thee of the King[61] and
adopt another to inherit thy estate. Not such a fool! 25

SNEAK.

No, so I say, sir, since you go to that. Whoop!
What a pox, you have forgot since you were young
yourself?

SIR ROGER.

I young! Why sir, I hope I got no bastards.

SNEAK.

No. But you kept* whores, that you did, and that's 30
all one, bona fide.

SIR ROGER. [Aside.]

This rogue has heard all; I must stop his mouth.—
How, sirrah, I kept whores?

SNEAK.

It has been thought so, sir, since you go to that.
Nay, 'tis no such miracle nowadays; there's many 35
an old badger about Town* does the like; 'tis grown
a custom now.

SIR ROGER.

But 'tis not so customary with your uncle, sir. But
come, pray express yourself: What women do the
infamous world lay to my charge? 40

SNEAK.

What women! 'Sbud, are you ignorant? Hum,
Nan, Pegg, Joan of the Dairy, Sara, Jenny, Dorothy,
Mary, Bridgett.

SIR ROGER.

Hold! hold, I say.—'Sdeath,* he'll reckon the
whole country presently. I must quiet him; the 45
rogue has me upon the hip.—Hark ye, Cob.

SNEAK.

Then the parson's wife, sir, and the old hostess at
the Townsend. You see the fool has a good
memory.

SIR ROGER.

A waggish one I see thou hast. Hah, if thou couldst 50
remember law cases as well, thou wouldst be a
brave* fellow. Why Cob, thou think'st thou hast
paid me off now, dost not?

SNEAK.

I know not. If my wit flow too fast, sir, I cannot
help it; 'tis a good that's thrown upon me, 'tis not 55
my seeking. 'Tis true, I have an unhappy way with
me sometimes, but 'tis over presently; it never lasts
long, that's one comfort.

SIR ROGER.

In verity I see thou hast wit, and now I'll cherish
it. Why Cob, my instruction is for thy good, child. 60
What will thy mistress think when she hears of it?
Come, come, in verity, Cob, 'twas ill done, 'twas,
i'faith. But mum, no more words on't, I'll make
all well again.

SNEAK. [Aside.]

So, so, I have brought him about finely. 'Sbud, I 65
did not think I had so much wit, but I see a man
may be mistaken in his own parts.*

SIR ROGER.

But d'ye hear, Cob, not a word more of these
wenches, let the foolish world say what it will.
Thou art a good boy, in verity; I like thy wit well. 70
Thou know'st I have no heir, and when I die, Cob,
I will not say I'll give thee anything, lest I should
make thee proud, but expect, expect wonders may
fall, who knows?

SNEAK.

By Jericho, I would not have spoke on't now, but 75
that I had nothing else to say, and you know 'tis a
disgrace to a scholar to be silent in company.

SIR ROGER.

'Tis no matter, 'tis no matter. Prithee how cam'st
thou to know that Pegg and I were so intimate?

---

61 beg … king] petition the Court of Wards to take custody of him

SNEAK.

Ah, you'll be angry if I should tell you.　　　　80

SIR ROGER.

In verity not I. Angry? Come, come, out with it,
Cob, out with't.

SNEAK.

Why, the truth is, I lay with her one night, and
the quean told me all.

SIR ROGER.

Didst thou! God-a-mercy.—Damn him! What a　85
snake have I fostered?—Done like a cock
o'th'game, in verity. Ah, when I was of thy years, I
could have done as much myself.

SNEAK.

Yes, she told me you had done as much. But mum,
sir, not a word more. I know my cue.　　　　90

SIR ROGER.

'Sdeath, I shall be a byword to th'Town.

Enter a servant.

—How now?

SERVANT.

Sir Roger, I was just coming to your house for you;
my master desires yours and Mr. Sneak's company
immediately.

SIR ROGER.

What, the solemnity holds? This is his wedding　95
day?

SERVANT.

Yes sir.

SIR ROGER.

Tell him I am coming.

Exit servant.

—Come Cob, let us go, and mum, d'ye hear? You
understand me?　　　　100

SNEAK.

I warrant you, sir.

Exeunt.

Scene ii. [Bubble's house.]

*Bubble, Emilia, Maria, Rashley, Ranger, Cordelia,
Fumble sitting at a table.*

BUBBLE.

Come, come, another bumper about: my chicken's

health. Here, I am not wet through yet. Tom, what
say'st thou?

RASHLEY.

With all my heart, sir! Oh here comes Sir Roger
and his nephew.　　　　5

Enter Sir Roger and Sneak.

SIR ROGER.

Mr. Bubble and gentlemen, your most humble
servant.

BUBBLE.

Yours, good Sir Roger. I am glad to see you, i'faith,
and you, sweet Mr. Sneak. Well faith, Sir Roger, we
have been bumping it about here; we have been　10
dipped, as the saying is. Tom Rashley, send it round,
come, Sir Roger's a freshman, he'll drink an ocean.

RASHLEY.

Fill every man's glass there. Mr. Ranger, you want*
it. 'Tis Madam Emilia's health.

All drink.

RANGER.

I'll do you reason, sir. (*Aside.*) And ten to one but　15
I have a stratagem shall dash this mirth. [*To
Maria.*] Are they ready?

MARIA.

Hush! We are observed. They are.

BUBBLE.

So, so! Come, now the song and then the dance.
Look ye, gentlemen, you must know—　　　　20

FUMBLE.

Come, come, Mr. Bubble, let's have t'other soop,[62]
I say; i'fack, we lose time. Ah sirrah, are you there?
Gad I'll be with you presently.* Dust it about once
more, I say; the wine has a pretty smack with it,
it cherishes,[63] I like it well. Come, another soop,　25
and then do what you will.

BUBBLE.

Fill wine there!—Gentlemen (as I was saying), I
got this song made purposely; 'tis in praise of
marriage, and there was not one ready made of 'em
in Town. I searched it all over.　　　　30

RANGER.

Were you at the poet's lodging?

---

62 soop] drink
63 cherishes] cheers up, heartens

BUBBLE.

Yes, but they had none, for they told me 'twas a
song would not take. Besides, they were so busy
getting plays up for the next term that I could
hardly get one made.   35

SIR ROGER.

Sir, you needed not have troubled 'em; you once
had a very good vein that way yourself.

BUBBLE.

Yes, I was mightily given to rapture and flame
once. I writ "Tom Farthing." I had a hand too in
"Colly my Cow,"[64] a song that took well, I can   40
assure you. But this is of another kind in praise of
marriage, sir, and they told me the Town loved
nothing but satires against marriage, and the reason
was because they were afraid of being cuckolded—
when, alas, poor silly rogues, there's no such thing   45
in nature.

RANGER. (*Aside.*)

Well, of all stupid animals a drowsy husband is the
most notorious. But I shall change your note
presently, I doubt not, sir.

BUBBLE.

You shall hear, gentlemen.—Hey, the song there   50
and the dance?

Song.

Under the branches of a spreading tree,
Silvander sate, from care and danger free,
And his inconstant roving humor* shows
To his dear nymph, that sung of marriage vows.   55
But she with flowing graces, charming air
    Cried, "Fie, fie, my dear, give o'er,
    Ah, tempt the gods no more!
But thy offense with penitence repair.
For though vice in a beauty seem sweet in thy arms,   60
An innocent virtue has always more charms."
                     2.
"Ah Phillida!" the angry swain replied,
"Is not a mistress better than a bride?
What man that universal yoke retains,
But meets an hour to sigh and curse his chains?"   65
She smiling cried, "Change, change that impious
    mind;

---

64 "Tom Farthing" … "Colly my Cow"] folk songs

Without it we could prove
    Not half the joys of love.
'Tis marriage makes the feeling joys divine.
For all our life long we from scandal remove,   70
And at last fall the trophies of honor and love."

BUBBLE.

Well sung, i'faith. Look ye, gentlemen, is it not as
I told you?

SIR ROGER.

In verity, very well, very well, sir.

BUBBLE.

Come, now the dance.   75

A dance.
Enter servant.

SERVANT.

Sir, here's a letter for you; it was left by a porter,
who said it required no answer, and is gone.

RANGER. [*Aside.*]

So, now for a change of countenance. [*To Maria.*]
I think this will do.

MARIA.

If not, I've writ a letter that will. But let's observe.   80

BUBBLE.

What the devil has this fellow given me here? A
letter? Pray Heaven it be no challenge. How? What's
here? (*Reads.*) "Sir, that you are blind, I have heard;
that you are a fool, I know; and that you are a
cuckold, I believe. However, as a friend, though   85
unknown, I am bound in conscience to give you this
information: your wife is false; you are abused; the
author of your wrong you know as well as yourself,
if you know yourself as well as you know Rashley."
Oh Heaven, was ever such fate? But hush, I'll   90
smother my resentment till they are gone.—Come,
Sir Roger and gentlemen, there's a tongue in the next
room; pray go and eat. I'll be with you presently.

Exeunt all but Bubble, Ranger, and Maria.

RANGER. [*Aside.*]

So I see by this behavior it takes, and I'll away, lest
he should suspect me. Now for my t'other plot.   95
(*Exit.*)

BUBBLE.

Oh Sister, here's a new discovery: the Devil is come
abroad again.

MARIA.

How? The Devil?

BUBBLE.

Aye, in the likeness of a letter. Here, prithee read it; 'tis his character. I am sure it looks as if 'twere writ with a cloven hoof. Hah! What think'st thou? 100

MARIA.

Sir, he calls you fool here.

BUBBLE.

Aye, he's a little uncivil, that's the truth on't. But what's to be done, Sister? 105

MARIA.

A cuckold, too.

BUBBLE.

Aye, was ever such an impudence?

MARIA.

I never heard of any. But 'tis no more, sir, than I expected. Alas! 'tis nothing to be a cuckold now.

BUBBLE.

Oh unfortunate estate of marriage! By the Lord 110 Harry, if this be true, I have praised it to fine purpose. But Sister, thou wert wont to be kind; prithee advise me.

MARIA.

'Tis to no purpose, sir: you know I am envious; my words have double meaning. I did my sister wrong 115 in my last story. Pray let me offend no more.

BUBBLE.

Well, I confess I was to blame, but who the devil could have mistrusted her when the plot was carried so handsomely?

MARIA.

Oh you will find, sir, she has still more plots, and 120 I find you so credulous and so wedded to your infamy that for my part I am afraid to have anything to do with it.

BUBBLE.

Help me but this once, and if I fail thee again, may I be proved a cuckold to the whole county and my 125 case tried in Westminster Hall.*

MARIA.

Well! Once more, then, I'll assist you, and to confirm what that letter has informed, know, sir, she is false, and though she frustrated our last plot by her waiting woman's means, she certainly met 130 Rashley that night. I am glad you credit a stranger's letter; for my part I love her so well, I should have hardly caused a second breach between ye else. But since 'tis out, and you desire my assistance, follow me, and ere night I doubt not but to give you 135 sufficient proof of your misfortune.

BUBBLE.

With all my heart, dear Sister. 'Sbud, a cuckold? 'Tis impossible, I ha' no cuckold's face. But I'll be resolved immediately.

Exeunt. Enter Ranger and governess.

RANGER.

Do this, thou shalt command me. 140

GOVERNESS.

In truth, sir, I am afraid 'twill be discovered, and I would not have my lady know it for the world.

RANGER.

I swear she never shall. What, dost thou doubt me? Besides, I'll be so grateful to thee, thou shalt never 145 have cause to repent this courtesy.

GOVERNESS.

Sir, you know you always might command me in any reasonable thing. Pray speak it again, sir: What would you have me do?

RANGER.

Why only plant me in or near her chamber for a 150 design I have; she shall be ignorant why or by what means I got thither. I'll still* be careful of thy reputation. Come, take this purse, and prithee, do it willingly.

GOVERNESS.

Well sir, what you mean I know not, but Heaven 155 direct all for the best. I can deny you nothing, sir; I lie in a closet* that joins to her chamber, where you may both overhear and speak to her.

RANGER.

That above all things! Prithee let's go.

GOVERNESS.

But for Heaven's sake take care she knows not that 160 I brought ye thither; I would not be seen in such a business for the world.

RANGER.

Ne'er doubt, I warrant thee I'll be careful.

GOVERNESS.

Follow me then, sir.

Exeunt.

Scene iii. [Another room in Bubble's house.]

Enter Fumble and Spatterdash.

FUMBLE.

Spat! Sirrah!

SPATTERDASH.

Here sir, here.

FUMBLE.

Whither is this rascal gone? Well i'fack, I am too
full of clemency. I must swinge this rogue, or he'll
never be good for anything. He's at nine-holes[65]
now, I'll lay my life. A damned villain, that
spends[66] me three-pence a day I know not how.

SPATTERDASH.

Oh Lord, who, I, sir?

FUMBLE.

Who's within there? What, will nobody hear me?
Am I left desolate? I have not the plague, I think,
hah!

SPATTERDASH.

Why, here I am, sir; I have been here all this while.

FUMBLE.

Oh sirrah, are you come? Where have you been,
hah? I say, where have you been, rogue?

SPATTERDASH.

Nowhere, sir, not I.

FUMBLE.

Sirrah! I must be left alone, must I! And when I
have message to send, go myself, hah! Sirrah, Mr.
Little-Pox has a boy, that though he was stinted
at nurse and is not above pocket high, can run and
frisk and jump upon occasion, sirrah, know a
bayly[67] by his nose and a wench by her buttocks,
ye rogue, and a good linguist and a pretty pimp,
sirrah, and can hold the door with a steady hand,
ye rogue. But thou, a rascal, a drone, art good for
nothing.

SPATTERDASH.

Anything, sir, I warrant you. Try me and you shall
find I can hold a door as well as he.

FUMBLE.

Why, how now, sirrah? What, make mouths at me?

5

10

15

20

25

---

65 nine-holes] a game like billiards
66 spends] costs
67 bayly] baliff

Is your master grown your mirth? (*Beats him.*)
Hah, this will teach you better, this will new mold
you. I'll fetch you out of your damned looks, i'fack.
French grimaces, rogue, French grimaces?

SPATTERDASH.

Oh Lord, what shall I do? Because he's deaf and
cannot hear me, he thinks I mock him. (*Aloud.*)
Hold sir, for Heaven's sake. Upon my faith, I don't
mock you. 'Tis all a mistake, and sir, you have
beaten me for nothing.

FUMBLE.

What a noise the rogue makes! Why sirrah, cannot
you speak temperately, but you must roar thus? I am
not so deaf, but I can hear without this thunderclap.
But you do it in contempt, do you, sirrah? Bless us,
to what an impudence this age has grown! But I'll
fetch the devil out, lest he should grow in ye—thus.
(*Beats him.*) I should be loath to see thee hanged till
you come to years of discretion.

SPATTERDASH.

Mercy o'me, what a master have I! If I stay long
here, I shall be beaten into mummy.

FUMBLE.

Come sir, now I have performed the part of a
master and a friend in your castigation, I have now
a word or two by way of instruction. Mark me,
sirrah, nothing exasperates more than scorn, nor
nothing pleases more than observance. A master
should be strict in finding occasion to beat his
servant, and a servant should be careful in avoiding
the beatings of his master.

SPATTERDASH.

So he has taught me; now I shall be careful of
avoiding it hereafter if my legs will carry me.

FUMBLE.

What, mouths again, sirrah, mouths again?

SPATTERDASH.

Umph. (*Makes a low congé, says nothing.*)

FUMBLE.

Oh this submission pacifies. Come hither, I have
a message for ye, and let me see how you can
behave yourself. 'Tis a matter of moment.

SPATTERDASH.

I'll do my best to please ye, sir.

FUMBLE.

What dost thou say now?—Look, look! Was ever

30

35

40

45

50

55

60

such a rascal as this? This rogue knows well enough 65
that I cannot hear him.—Sirrah, come and lay
your mouth to my ear and then speak, if you
would have me understand ye.

SPATTERDASH.

Yes sir, I shall be very careful to remember it
hereafter. 70

FUMBLE.

Rafters? What rafters, rogue?

SPATTERDASH. (*Aloud.*)

Sir, I shall be careful to remember it hereafter.

FUMBLE.

Oh shall you so, sir? and 'twill become you, i'fack.
For look ye, sirrah, 'tis my humor as long as I am
healthy and jovial to cover failings and imperfections 75
in nature as well as I can; 'tis a wise-man's virtue, and
I have patterns for't every day. Ah, here are a sort of
jolly, brisk, ingenious, old signiors about Town, that
with false calves,[68] false bellies, false teeth, false
noses, and a false, fleering face upon the matter fill 80
up society as well as e'er a masquerading fop of 'em
all. But to the matter: sirrah, you must carry this ring
to Cordelia and possess her with my love in an
elegant manner. Stand there, and let me see how you
can carry yourself in such a business. 85

SPATTERDASH.

Thus, sir. I had my honors from the dancing
school.

FUMBLE.

Oh damned rogue! What a bow's there? 'tis worse
than a country counselor's to a client that has no
money. Sirrah, pull me your hat off thus, with a 90
grace. Ah! I could have done it rarely twenty years
ago, but i'fack, time and gravity defaces all things.
Come, sirrah.

SPATTERDASH.

Madam! My master, too well knowing the charms
of your wit and beauty are too sharp at all times 95
to be opposed, has by me sent this ring and
humbly desires—

FUMBLE.

Well, that last honor was pretty well. But come
now, let's hear what you can say?

---

68 false calves] padded hose for gentlemen with less than
shapely legs

SPATTERDASH.

'Sdeath!* he has not heard me all this while. What 100
shall I do?

Knocking.

Oh somebody knocks; this was happy. (*Aloud.*) Sir,
there's somebody at door to speak with you.

FUMBLE.

Go see who 'tis, I'll follow.—This is a plaguy dull
rogue, but I must have patience and take pains 105
with him. Nor should he do any thing in this
business had I not a design in't, and i'fack, I like
the woman well. She's young and plump, free in
her nature, and of a sanguine complexion[69] and
bona fide; I never see her but some secret motions 110
in my blood seem to imply that she is the cause.
What? I am not bedrid. I can dance yet, aye, and
run and jump too if occasion be, and why not the
t'other thing? Come, come, it must, it must: mine
was ever a stirring family. It must, I say, and she 115
shall know it suddenly.*

Exit.

Scene iv. [A hallway in Bubble's house.]

Enter Maria and Bubble.

MARIA.

Come softly, sir, and plant yourself here at this
back door. I have already made a discovery.

BUBBLE.

Are they together?

MARIA.

I believe so. They seldom miss such an opportunity, especially when they think you absent. 5

BUBBLE.

No, they are politic, with a pox to 'em. Sister, what
revenge, hah? I am resolved to be a tyrant. 'Sbud,*
I'll pinch her to death with a pair of tongs.

MARIA.

Oh fie, that will be too cruel.

BUBBLE.

Cruel! By the Lord Harry, 'tis justice, palpable 10
justice! Why, should she live, she'd cuckold the
whole nation.

---

69 sanguine complexion] of an easy-going temperament
(humours theory)

MARIA.

Consider better on't. 'Tis but a venial crime and
deserves not much rigor. But come, meditate of no
revenge till you are certain of the fault. Keep close 15
at that door; be sure you discover* not yourself till
I come to you. I'll go and observe.

BUBBLE.

I'll try my patience, but 'tis a damned cause.

Exeunt.

Scene [v.] A bedchamber.

Enter Rashley and Emilia.

EMILIA.

Our intrigue as yet goes well.

RASHLEY.

I swear, to admiration. And had I not seen each
passage, I should have thought 't had been
impossible. Oh my dearest! How shall I gratify
thee? My love's too poor and my desert too mean* 5
ever to equal it. (*Kisses her hand.*)

Enter Ranger.

RANGER. [*Aside.*]

I'm glad I've got air again. This damned old gib-
cat[70] has mewed me this half hour into such a hole
that, had I stayed a minute longer, I had certainly
been smothered. It stinks worse than a 'pothecary's 10
shop and is furnished with nothing but gallipots
full of nasty oil, into which, groping about, I often
thrust my fingers. Faugh! asafoetida, as I live! A
most intolerable stink! Ah, the devil grind her old
chops.—Stay, this is sure Emilia's chamber, and if 15
I am not mistaken, I heard a whispering here; it
may be they're together. I'll be still and listen.

RASHLEY.

Our love shall last whole ages, and each kiss add
new and fierce desires. Death shall want* power
to separate us, and Envy droop and pine itself away 20
to see its stratagem succeed no better.

RANGER.

By Heaven, 'tis so: they are here. Blest minute!
Now I shall make a rare discovery.

---

70 gib-cat] a castrated tom cat, but gib is also a term of
reproach, especially for an old woman (*OED*).

EMILIA.

I am confirmed and will proceed in loving. A
husband is a dull insipid thing, palled and grown 25
stale within a week. But a lover appears still new
and gay and is to perpetuity the same he was at
first—all mirth, all pleasure.

RANGER.

A most excellent theme. Oh that that property,
that fool her husband, stood now to hear this devil 30
of a wife make out this free confession!

RASHLEY.

He, dull creature, Heaven knows, is blind to all
your charms. Marriage acts only the decrees of
duty; love has the least share in't. In this age a
husband with a wife is like a bully in a church: the 35
only pleasure he takes is to sleep away the hours
should be employed in conjugal duty.

EMILIA.

Well! I am very glad our plots succeed so well. I
swear I was half frighted t'other day when my
sister-in-law Maria discovered us. Was it not done 40
subtly? Did I not fetch all off again with an
excellent invention?

RANGER.

Good! Rarely good! This devil cannot sure have so
much impudence to deny this again.

RASHLEY.

Ha, ha, ha! By Heaven I'm ready to die with 45
laughing when I think what asses we made of 'em.
Ranger too, that busy coxcomb, what a fretting
and plotting and sweating did he make for
nothing! Alas, poor fool! Ha, ha, ha!

EMILIA.

Ha, ha, ha! 50

RANGER.

Oh the devil, fleer you? 'Sdeath,* am I still their
property? I shall have a slice at your nose ere long.
I doubt not, my young gallant, I shall dash your
mummery.

RASHLEY.

Come, we lose time. Let talk be our diversion 55
when we are old and can reap nothing else; our
minutes now should all be spent in rapture. Thus,
thus, my sweet! Oh that we could live thus ever!—
How now, what noise is that?

BUBBLE. (*Within.*)

　Bawds! Strumpets! Whores! Witches! Break open 60
the door there, break open the door.

MARIA. [*Within.*]

　Fetch a lever, or call the smith over the way
presently.*

EMILIA.

　Oh Heaven, my husband and Maria! We are
undone. 65

RANGER.

　'Tis Bubble's voice, sure! This completes my joy.
Now let Beelzebub, if he owes her any kindness,
fetch her from hence. I'll guard this passage.

RASHLEY.

　What! What shall I do, madam?

EMILIA.

　Here quickly, run into this closet,* sir, and jump 70
out of the window into the garden. If you were
gone, let me alone for the rest.

RANGER.

　Who steps a foot this way, steps on his death; his
soul shall not be his a minute.

EMILIA.

　Hah! Ranger here? I am lost in my amazement. 75

RASHLEY.

　Death and hell! And I defenseless too! Oh cursed
minute!

RANGER.

　No madam, I'll secure you from this stratagem.
This window shall be no bawd to th' intrigue now,
that I'll be sure on. (*Exit into the closet.*) 80

BUBBLE. (*Within.*)

　Quickly, quickly! A lever, a lever!

RASHLEY.

　No way t'escape? Can I not climb the chimney?
Anything to get free this once. Oh fate, taken
i'th'midst of our security, when we least thought
of it! What shall we do? 85

EMILIA.

　I have it: come hither, get ye under this table and
diligently listen to what I say. 'Tis ten to one he
never searches here. Come, in, in, quickly, and pray
the rest may prosper.

RASHLEY.

　I never had more need of prayers. I'll try. (*Goes* 90
under table.)

Enter Ranger from the closet.

RANGER.

　So, that conveyance is fast enough. Now madam,
what think ye of a fleering jest upon the fool
Ranger, the coxcomb, the ass Ranger, and your
jolly spleen to laugh, ha, ha? I think the dice are 95
mine now. Now, devil, I have trapped ye.

Knock within.

EMILIA. [*Aside.*]

　This key may add to my design. (*Takes out the key
from the door.*)

BUBBLE. (*Within.*)

　Down, down with it, break it open there.

RANGER.

　What think you of that, madam? Does your 100
husband's voice refresh you extremely?

EMILIA.

　Now help me, wit, or I am lost. (*She goes and puts
the key into his coat pocket, and then lays hold of him,
and cries out.*) Help, help there, for Heaven's sake.
I am undone, ruined forever. A rape, a rape! Help, 105
help!

RANGER.

　Hell and the devil, what does she mean?

EMILIA.

　Ah, cruel man, cannot these tears prevail? Will
nothing stop barbarity? What have I done could
deserve this usage? Oh most unfortunate of 110
women.

RANGER.

　Damn her, I shall be finely catched if this hold. I
must get away. (*Struggles, she holds him.*)

EMILIA.

　A rape, a rape! Help there, for Heaven's sake, help.

*Enter Bubble and Maria with a light. They stand
amazed.*

RANGER.

　By Heaven, I am snapped again, catched in my 115
own snare.

EMILIA.

　Has my husband been so much thy friend and
wouldst abuse him thus, thou base man? But
Heaven forgive thee.

BUBBLE.

'Sbud, what's this I see? Ranger? 120

MARIA.

Ranger here, and Rashley absent. I have plotted finely. 'Tis plain now that traitor loves her and has only made me an engine* to work his design with more facility.

RANGER.

Rashley gone too? Now has the devil to spite me conveyed him away in a mist. Here's like to be fine work towards, but I must stand the brunt now I am entered. 125

BUBBLE.

Now sir, what a pox make you here with my wife? Hah? 130

RANGER.

So, it begins rarely! Oh this subtle devil!—Why sir, as I am a gentleman, and upon my honor—

EMILIA.

Oh my dear, a thousand thanks for this deliverance, and by all our love I charge thee, by our marriage vows, by all our pleasures since and joys to come, I charge you, revenge me upon that traitor there. He would have ravished me! Oh Heaven, that ever I should live to be so put to't! 135

BUBBLE.

'Sbud! Ravish my chicken? Ranger, you are the son of a whore, and I shall presume to cut your throat. 140

RANGER.

Sir, do but hear me: upon my honor all this is false.

MARIA. (*Aside.*)

It must be true! What should he come hither for but upon some ill intent? I am resolved I'll be revenged on him however. 145

RANGER.

'Sdeath! She against me too? This is worse and worse.

BUBBLE.

Discover* the matter, that I may do justice on both sides.

EMILIA.

Sir, know then, Ranger long has loved me, often solicited me unlawfully. But finding something in my virtue that shook his designs, his recourse was to make you jealous of me and Rashley, who, poor 150

man, has often told me with sighs how deeply he has resented your unkind suspicions. 155

BUBBLE.

Alas, poor fellow!

RANGER.

Oh confusion! He begins to believe her again.

EMILIA.

At last, sir, finding his suit to be too troublesome for me to bear and being loath to vex you with such fooleries, I told Rashley, who promised all assistance imaginable. I desired him also to be careful and watch lest I should be surprised—as tonight (Heaven knows) I was. 160

RANGER.

Damn her, what a lie is this!—Pray sir, let me speak. 165

BUBBLE.

Not in my house, sir, you have talked too much already, and by the Lord Harry, I'll talk with you anon. But let that pass.—Go on, Chicken.

EMILIA.

At last, sir, this unhappy night coming hither as I used to do to my devotions, he, it seems, having corrupted some of my servants, got into the closet* and thence came and surprised me, first locking the door and putting the key into his pocket. 170

RANGER.

I, a key? Sir, as I live, I saw none. This is the most notorious lie— 175

EMILIA.

Oh wretched man! Was it not crime enough to make such an attempt but you must persist in falsehood?—Sir, he has it now about him there in that pocket; I saw him put it in.

RANGER.

This pocket? Why, thou devil! (*Puts his hand in his pocket, pulls out a key.*) Hah! 'Sdeath, how came it here? Magic, witchcraft, the Devil and all combine against me! Would I were well out. If ever I plot again— 180

MARIA.

'Tis evident now he would have ravished her! Locked her in for that purpose. Perfidious traitor, see me no more. 185

RANGER.

A very fine business this!

BUBBLE.

Is it so, sir? I'll do your business for you. (*Goes to run at Ranger and overthrows the table.*) 190

EMILIA.

Discovered? I am lost again.

BUBBLE.

'Sbud, Rashley!

RASHLEY.

'Sdeath and hell, what will become of me now?

RANGER.

How! Rashley under the table? Then fate is mine again. Now sir, do you perceive anything yet? 195

MARIA.

Stranger and stranger! What can this mean? or what could they both do here?

BUBBLE. (*To Emilia.*)

'Sdeath! How came he here? Hoh!

RANGER.

Aye, examine that point closely. Sure this will make for me. 200

BUBBLE.

As Gad jidge me, and so I will. Speak, I say, how came he here?

EMILIA.

Nay, Heaven knows, not I. I believe for the same design with Ranger.

RASHLEY.

'Sdeath, she'll betray me too. 205

EMILIA.

Tell him, tell him, sir. (*Softly.*) Speak for yourself, say anything.

RASHLEY.

Speak? Why—'sbud madam, have I not done as you commanded me? Have I not watched here this two hours to frustrate Ranger's design? What, d'ye think to make an ass of me? 210

RANGER.

How sir, my design? Damn me, this must not pass upon me, sir.

RASHLEY.

Nor shall you not pass upon my friend here neither, sir. I heard you this evening when you corrupted one 215 of the women to get you into that closet* that you might accomplish with more ease, sir. But madam, this is a little unnatural, to make me suspected as his colleague, when my design was so far different.

BUBBLE.

'Sbud, I cannot find the meaning of this. 220

RASHLEY.

The meaning! Why sir, she hid me under the table as a defense against Ranger's insolence. But when she heard you at the door and knew you were coming in, she conjured me by all the love I bore her to sit still and not discover* myself, and all her 225 excuse was your jealousy (jealousy with a pox!), a very fine slight for the abuse she intended to me.— 'Sdeath madam, my service deserved a better reward if you consider it. [*Aside.*] Pray Heaven this lie prosper. 230

EMILIA.

Ha, ha, ha! I knew I should vex him, but I confess 'tis all true. For (my dear rogue!) I am so hourly tormented with fear of thy naughty jealousy that I dare not tell thee anything. Prithee desert it, do, my dear sweet; i'fads,* thou wouldst be the best 235 husband in the world if thou wouldst but leave it. (*Kisses him.*)

BUBBLE.

Well! it must be so; this cannot be feigned. Come hither to me; I will forsake it. By the Lord Harry, thou art the best wife in Christendom, and I the 240 most ungrateful husband. But forgive, my dear, forgive. (*Kisses her.*) We have all failings, thou knowest. Prithee, forgive me.

RANGER.

So! now may I hang myself. 'Sdeath! All the fiends are asses to her. I'll be gone for shame, lest worse 245 befall me.

—Succubus, farewell;

There is not such a sorceress in hell. (*Exit.*)

BUBBLE.

Come! Hast thou sealed my pardon?

EMILIA.

You know the softness of my temper, but your 250 unkind jealousy will kill me one day.

BUBBLE.

Egad, I'll kill myself first. Come, prithee no more.—Tom, thy hand too, come, I know thou canst bear with my frailty.

RASHLEY.

Aye sir, I can bear well enough! But methought 255 'twas a little strange to tax me.

BUBBLE.

Come, come, all shall be well, faith, we'll go in and frolic. Oh my dear, suspect thee! Well, I am a fool, that's the truth on't.

Exeunt Bubble and Emilia.

MARIA.

The Devil helps her, sure, for this was certainly an 260 assignation. I'll after Ranger and know the truth on't. (*Exit.*)

RASHLEY.

Ha, ha, ha! Was ever plot carried thus? Sure never! Her wit has more supplies than I have thoughts, and happily they end still.* And Gad for my own 265 part I shall love lying the better as long as I live for the success of this. Once more all is well, and he the cuckold still, ha, ha, ha! I must go in and laugh with her.

Intrigue's her masterpiece, and all may see, 270
A woman's wit's best in extremity.

Exit.

Act V, [scene i. A room in Bubble's house.]

Enter Cordelia.

CORDELIA.

Well, of all creatures that vex mortality, a superannuated lover is certainly the most troublesome, especially to one of my years. Our inequality is so preposterous, and his address so unnatural, that I always entertain rather hate for 5 his person than compliance for his love. From fourscore and five, Heaven deliver me: 'tis an age of doting.—Here he comes; I knew I could not be quiet one hour.

Enter Fumble.

FUMBLE.

Sirrah, sirrah! Rogue, rogue! And how and how! 10 Hah! Art thou jolly, blithe, like a bird in a tree? I'fack, I was impatient till I came to see thee. Well, and how fits the ring? Does it shine? Does it glitter? Hah! Little black rogue! I'fack, I bought it of the best goldsmith in Cheapside,* a man of 15 good reputation, a cuckold too, and they are always the honestest fellows.

CORDELIA.

From henceforth let me desire you, sir, to bestow your presents on somebody else. I sent your ring back by your man; he can best give you an account 20 of it.

FUMBLE.

Hah! What say'st thou? Counterfeit? I'fack, thou art mistaken, bird, thou art, bona fide. They are as well cut as any in Christendom and of the right black-water.[71] What, dost thou think I'll put any 25 false stones upon thee, i'fack? I am more civil, icod. [*Aside.*] There I was waggish, but she's a witty rogue, she'll apprehend the jest.

CORDELIA.

Was ever such an insipid piece of antiquity? Pray sir, forbear these impertinences and assure yourself 30 I hate an old fellow for a husband as much as an old gown or an old piece of wit that after forty years' oblivion with a new name is published for a new Lenten play.[72]

FUMBLE.

What does she say now? But no matter, I'll go 35 on.—Well said, bird, well said. Bona fide, thou hast wit in abundance; that color, and such a sort of nose, never fail. But come, we lose time. I know 'tis ordained I must marry thee. I am the man that must gather the rosebuds. Ah rogue! I'll warrant 40 thou'rt a swinger, and i'fack, that black atop there fires me strangely. I am all flame, and bona fide, methinks as youthful and mercurial as any spark of 'em all.

Song.

And he took her by the middle small 45
And laid her on the plain,
With a hey down derry down, come diddle,
With a ho down derry, etc.
What think you, madam? Am I old?

---

71 black-water] Water, perhaps from an Arabic word meaning lustre, is a measure of the purity of a diamond, the highest being white, descending through colors such as blue, yellow, brown, which are called "colored" (*OED*).

72 *Lenten* play] a play performed by young actors on Wednesdays or Fridays during Lent, days traditionally closed to established actors—and plays

CORDELIA.

So old that your presence is more terrible than a   50
death's-head at supper. For my part I tremble all
over. There's a kind of horror in all your antic
gestures, 'specially those that you think become
you, that fright worse than the Devil, (*Aloud.*) than
the Devil, sir.   55

FUMBLE.

The Devil! What of him, bird? Pish, the Devil's
an ass, I ha' seen't in a play,[73] and i'fack, we lose
time in talking about so worthless a matter. Lovers
should never be slow in their affairs, for as my
good friend Randolph tells me, nothing is like   60
opportunity taken in the nick, in the nick,
sweetheart!—Icod, I was waggish again, I was
waggish again, i'fack.—Come, bird, come.

CORDELIA.

What will you do, sir?—Heaven, how he tortures
me!   65

FUMBLE.

Come along then, I have got a priest ready and
paid for the license and all. Prithee let me kiss thee;
I long to practice something that might please
thee. Never was a man so altered! Never! Come,
prithee bird, come, i'fack, I have not patience.   70

Enter governess and Sir Roger.

GOVERNESS.

Here's Sir Roger Petulant, my dear mouse, desires
to speak a word or two with you.

CORDELIA.

Oh here's some hope of deliverance!—Sir Roger,
your humble servant. Come hither, Lettice, and
stand just in my place. I am so tortured with this   75
old fellow, prithee be kind to him and follow him
whither he'd have thee; it may be a husband in thy
way and a good estate.

GOVERNESS.

A husband! Marry,* that's fine! I warrant you, sweet
mouse, I'll be very punctual.   80

CORDELIA.

So, now let us slip aside and observe; 'twould be
an excellent revenge if he should marry her.

---

73 Devil's an ass … play] could refer to Ben Jonson's play
of that name (1616)

They step aside.

He's coming to her already, and his eyes are so old
and dim that he perceives not his mistake.

FUMBLE.

Delays, sweetheart, are dangerous, i'fack. I have   85
considered it. The time I have lived in the world
has given me the benefit of knowing more than
another of fewer minutes. Along, along, I say, thou
shalt be my queen, my paramour, my Cleopatra,
and I will live another age in love, and then   90
farewell, old Simon, i'fack. Come, come along.

GOVERNESS.

Oh sadness! What happy fortune's this? Well, I'll
go with him. Pray Heaven he be blind enough,
that's all I fear.

FUMBLE.

She seems kinder than usual; i'fack, I have wrought   95
her finely.—Come, poor rogue, come.

GOVERNESS.

I am ready, sir.—This was a happy hour,
And if it hit but right, I'm made forever.

*Exeunt [Fumble and governess]. Sir Roger and
Cordelia re-enter.*

CORDELIA.

Ha, ha, I am glad I am rid of him any way. But
now, Sir Roger, to your business. I hear your   100
nephew is sick.

SIR ROGER.

In verity, madam, most dangerously sick, and the
cause of my giving you this trouble was, in verity,
to give you information of it, for by his melancholy
I find love is the cause. Ah madam, your last   105
indifference was very prejudicial to him. 'Tis true,
he denies it, but I am old enough to judge of the
contrary and, therefore, have found out 'tis passion,
nay passion for you has laid him thus low, and
nothing but your smiles can raise him, 'tis gone   110
so far, in verity.

CORDELIA.

I am sorry, sir, I have the misfortune to be
th'occasion of such a disaster. But is there any
remedy? What would you have me do?

SIR ROGER.

Madam, my suit to you is that you would be   115
pleased to go with me and give him a visit; the

surprise of your presence, I am confident, will dissipate his melancholy and perhaps totally banish his distemper.

Enter Maria.

But I see we are interrupted. Let's retire, madam, 120 and if you please, now will be a very good time to visit him.
CORDELIA.
Softly, sir, I would not have my cousin Maria know anything of it. But if that can do him any good, I'll not be so cruel to deny it. 'Tis an act of charity. 125 Come sir, I'll go with you.
SIR ROGER.
Madam, you oblige us both—

Exeunt [Sir Roger and Emilia].

MARIA.
Still baffled! Sure this cannot last long; the Devil will be weary of obliging her in a little time. I have been yonder sifting Ranger about the last plot, and 130 by all circumstances find what he said was true. And shall I leave off thus poorly? Pish, I cannot for shame. I have truth and honesty on my side; she's only cunning, and 'tis impossible that should last ever. Once more then have at 'em. I have by 135 several false messages buzzed it again into my brother's ears; he believes, and will once more follow my counsel. Besides, I have here a false key to her chamber and can surprise 'em when they least suspect. This, if Ranger be at all diligent, must 140 needs effect it, for I am resolved not to rest till 'tis done for the satisfaction of my revenge on that false man.

Exit.

[Scene ii. Sir Roger's lodging.]

Enter apothecary and Sneak in a nightgown.

SNEAK.
Uh! Uh!
APOTHECARY.
Nay sir, if you would have the effects answer your expectation, you must suffer, sir, and be patient.
SNEAK.
'Ounds!* I cannot have patience. Sure a civil clap

might be cured without all this stir. 'Tis not a 5 miracle in this age. Oh Lord!

Enter Sir Roger and Cordelia.

SIR ROGER.
Oh horrible! What's this I see?
SNEAK.
My uncle! Oh I am undone, lost forever.
APOTHECARY.
But sir, your civil clap might ha' been an uncivil pox in time. 10
CORDELIA.
How, Sir Roger? Was it fit to make me a spectator of this object?
SIR ROGER. (*Aside.*)
The pox? In verity I have brought his mistress to fine purpose. Ah damned rascal! The pox? What shall I do? I am disgraced forever. 15
CORDELIA.
Hark ye, sir, pray what is that there? (*Pointing to a sweating-chair*[74] *within [upstage].*)
SIR ROGER. [*Aside.*]
What shall I say? Death, she has found out his sweating-chair!—Why, madam, 'tis—umph—'tis a mathematical engine* they use at Cambridge. Cob 20 was always addicted to study.
CORDELIA.
'Twere a fault to hinder him then, sir, being so well employed. Farewell. (*Exit.*)
SIR ROGER.
She has found it out.—Sirrah, see my face no more. From this hour I abhor thee, a damned 25 rascal!
SNEAK.
Good Uncle!
SIR ROGER.
The pox! A sneaking, sniveling rogue! Heavens, was ever the like seen? But 'tis now a general maxim, and your* sandy,[75] sheep's-face, unthink- 30 ing villain, is always the greatest whoremaster.
SNEAK.
Why, by Jericho, it was by chance, Uncle; hab-

---

74 sweating-chair] an implement thought to cure syphilis through the inducement of sweating
75 sandy] shifty, unreliable (Vaughn)

nab,[76] as a man may say. As I hope to be saved,
'twas against my will.

APOTHECARY.

Sir, your anger makes an addition to his distemper. 35

SIR ROGER.

What, you are his pander, sir, are you? But I think
you may be the devil for your honesty; so may ye
all; such as you soothe 'em in vices. I warrant you
are tired with such customers, hah sir, are you not?

APOTHECARY.

In troth, sir, my rotten patients are so loath to die, 40
and my sound* ones, which for my art's improvement I would make rotten, so hasty to recover, that
I confess I am often weary, but not tired, sir.

SIR ROGER.

So sir, in verity, you are all a company of rascals,
and as for his part, I'll instantly write to his father 45
to disinherit him that I may revenge my disgrace
and punish his folly. The pox! A son of a whore!
The pox! (*Exit.*)

APOTHECARY.

A mad old fellow, but your penitence will recover
all. 50

SNEAK.

Would you were hanged, by Jericho, for leaving
the door open. Oh what shall I do? This comes of
learning the sciences, in the devil's name.

APOTHECARY.

Patience, sir, have patience.

*Scene shuts [on Sneak in sweating-chair]. Exit
[apothecary].*

[Scene iii. Emilia's chamber.]

Enter Rashley, Emilia, and Betty.

RASHLEY.

A trapdoor, say you, madam?

EMILIA.

Yes, we happily discovered it yesterday looking for
a ring accidentally dropped; it opens upon the
stairs the backside of the kitchen. I am sure 'twill
be very necessary in our intrigue.—Here, take the 5
candle, you, and go and watch, and when I give
the sign, be sure be ready.

_____

76 hab-nab] by chance; hit or miss

BETTY.

I'll not fail, madam. [*Exit.*]

EMILIA.

'Tis good to be secure, for I know Maria has still
an eye over us, and my husband's new jealousy 10
gives me fresh cause of doubt.*

RASHLEY.

Egad, 'tis unnecessary. This trapdoor must needs
be very useful. I see Fortune is ours still and will
not leave us. Let us doubt* when we see danger;
there is none now, nor can be whilst our love 15
continues.

EMILIA.

Which I fear will be but a short time: for what is
indirect is seldom permanent; therefore, let us
consider on't.

RASHLEY.

Damn consideration: 'tis a worse enemy to mankind 20
than malice. Let impotent age consider, that is fit for
nothing but dull, tame thoughts of what he has been
formerly; let the lawyer and physician consider what
quibbles and what potions are most necessary; and
let the sly fanatic think his time out and consider 25
how to be securely factious. But let the lover love on,
still* transported, whilst all his thoughts and senses
are employed in the dear joys of rapture, endless
passion, without a grain of dull consideration.

EMILIA.

I swear the softness of our tempers abuses half our 30
sex; we should not else be won so easily. But we
are such kind* fools!

RASHLEY.

Aye, we are all fools, madam, that's the truth on't,
but how shall we help it?

EMILIA.

Resolve upon a remedy: love no more. 35

RASHLEY.

Resolve upon the contrary: love forever. Gad, the
world would be at a fine pass if all were of your
mind.—How now?

Noise of a lock. Enter Maria with a light.

MARIA. [*To Bubble, outside.*]

Stand there till I fetch you in. I'm sure they're here.

EMILIA.

My sister, as I live! Malicious accident! 40

RASHLEY.

Hah, with a light too! How the devil got she in?

EMILIA.

Heaven knows, unless with a false key.

MARIA.

Nay, y'are caught, and finely too. I'm cozened else. What plot now, madam, to convey you hence? Now show your mighty skill, and if there is a devil at your service, employ him now; you never had more cause. Methinks you are melancholy. Why d'ye not laugh? Smile at your wit and great security? You, I know, have a thousand ways to get off still, or if you want, that gentleman can supply you.

RASHLEY.

I supply! A plague o'your damned jest!

EMILIA.

Hush, and leave me to her.—Nay, Sister, this is barbarous to triumph o'er our misfortunes. You know yourself what love is and what inconveniences it brings poor women too.

MARIA.

You can confess now, and here's a gentleman not far off, your husband, madam. I know this cannot choose but be grateful to him. I'll call him to hear it.

EMILIA.

Ah, be not so cruel to undo me quite! I'll confess all to thee and from this minute be converted. Ah, had I taken thy counsel before, I had been happy.

MARIA.

Aye, but you would persist, and now see what comes on't.

EMILIA.

Oh! I am miserable! Forgive me, dear Maria! (*Weeps.*)

MARIA.

Nay, Heaven forgive you. But come, will you confess? (*Aside.*) I have her at a rare advantage.

EMILIA.

Most faithfully. But let me do't in the dark; let no light see my guilty blushes: it is enough my tongue dares utter it. Dear sister, let me not be too much ashamed. Oh misery! Misery! (*Weeps.*)

MARIA.

Well, here is a light not far off, and thus much I'll

comply with you. Now begin. (*Puts out the light.*)

RASHLEY. [*Aside.*]

By Heaven I grow cheerful. We shall 'scape, I am sure we shall. Oh this dear devil!

EMILIA.

My grief ties up my tongue.

MARIA.

'Tis time to grieve. But come, when d'ye begin?

EMILIA.

This cruel man seduced me: cruel Rashley. (*Aside.*) Where are you, sir?

RASHLEY. (*Softly.*)

Here, sweet, here!

EMILIA.

First won upon me with his comely presence, handsome demeanor, every several grace my soul admired. (*To Rashley.*) Give me your hand.—But when he came to speak, his tongue, his charming tongue, oh Heaven, that I shall live to utter it! so ensnared me, that I no longer knew my liberty but as his victim gloried in my passion.

MARIA.

With shame you live to speak it.

RASHLEY.

'Twas my misfortune too. [*Aside.*] But Heaven forgive me, I shall laugh out; I am not able to hold.

EMILIA.

Down, quickly down.

Both sink in the trap.

MARIA.

Now could I laugh till my heart ached again to think how I have caught 'em. I knew 'twas impossible she should 'scape always, and I will tyrannize more than a Turk over his slave.—For my part I am sorry for your infamy, and were it not that by the laws of nature I have a great concern in any of my brother's injuries, you might love on for me, but since my blood runs in his veins, I dare not see his infamy and let it pass unquestioned. Therefore, either swear from this hour to desert Rashley and never see him more, or your disgrace I will this instant publish or call your husband to be spectator of his shame and yours. What, are ye dumb? Not answer me! It seems you dislike this proposal, but do not provoke me. Not yet? Nay then—Within there, Brother, here they are. A light, a light, quickly.   110

Enter Bubble with a light and long sword.

BUBBLE.

Where? Where is this traitor? This strumpet? By Scanderbeg,[77] I am ready for a charge. I'll push him with a vengeance. Where is he?

MARIA.

Here, here! How now? What, are you got under the table again? or into a corner?—Give me the candle,   115
Brother, I am sure I have 'em fast. (*Looks about.*)

BUBBLE.

Here's nothing, another mistake, as Gad jidge me.

MARIA.

She is a devil, and I lose my labor. Gone! What, both gone? Oh I could tear myself. Which way? How? by what means could they escape?   120

BUBBLE.

'Scape? 'Sbud!* 'tis impossible they should escape if they were here. Pish, this is only one of your maggots, Sister; you do but fancy you saw 'em.

MARIA.

Fancy? Eternal light forsake me if I did not both see and speak to 'em two minutes since, heard her   125
confess the crime and vow repentance, here, in this very place. But by what means they 'scaped, I can only admire,* not imagine.

BUBBLE.

Prithee hold thy peace. I say once more 'tis only a maggot. Sleep, fool, and purge thy head from   130
fancies. How now, Ned?

Enter Ranger and Betty behind.

RANGER.

Sir, I know not whether the news I bring may please you, but I have made a strange discovery yonder.

BUBBLE.

Discovery! Of what, prithee?   135

RANGER.

Sir, I saw Rashley and your wife going laughing arm in arm through the entry the backside of the

kitchen into the parlor, where, if you please to give yourself the trouble, you may find 'em.

BETTY. [*Aside.*]

This is as my mistress suspected, and I'll inform   140
her immediately. [*Exit.*]

BUBBLE.

Hey day! My wife and Rashley? Art sure on't, Ned?

RANGER.

As sure, sir, as I live, I saw 'em there. Nay, what's more, my curiosity inducing me to peep through the keyhole, I saw his head lie in her lap, whilst   145
she with a fond passion stroked his cheeks and dallied with his hair. Faith, sir, I could not see this and be silent. But you, I fear, will think the worse of me for't.

BUBBLE.

In the parlor, say'st thou? 'Sbud, was ever such a   150
confusion? Why, my sister says that within these two minutes she saw and spoke to 'em here in this chamber. They are here, there, and everywhere, and yet I can find 'em nowhere! What a pox should a man think of this?   155

RANGER.

They are there this instant, sir, upon my honor.

MARIA.

Sure, I have not dreamt all this while! Did I not see her? By Heaven, I saw the Devil in her likeness then.

BUBBLE.

Why peace, I say, if you are mad, offend no one but yourself with it. What a pox, shall I not believe   160
my eyes? The house is not haunted that I know of, unless it be with fools. There's a bob for you by way of conclusion.

MARIA.

Yes, cuckolds too! There's a bob for you by way of repartee.   165

BUBBLE.

Cuckold? I'd have you to know I scorn your words, and were you not my sister, I'd fetch you out with your repartees. What, because you are a fool, you guess all persons are alike? Do you but conceive me, Mrs. Juniper?[78] I am a Turk at matter of fact   170
when I see occasion.

---

77 Scanderbeg] Iskender Bey, an Albanian hero who defeated the Ottoman Turks

78 Mrs. Juniper] a contemptuous epithet, especially for a
prostitute (Vaughn)

RANGER.

Good sir, no more of this, but go down and satisfy
yourself in the truth of my story. If I tell you a lie,
call me fool, horse, anything. Do but go and see.

BUBBLE.

'Sbud, I know not what to do: one brings me up,   175
another carries me down; one jilts me, another
abuses me; a third laughs at me; and yet I find
nothing, nor see nothing, nor know nothing, and
you are nothing but fools to make all this stir about
nothing. But come, I'll go with thee, Ned.   180

MARIA.

And I, that I may say once in my life I saw a
miracle.

RANGER.

I have her once more in the noose of the slip; now
the Devil hold her fast in th'other world. 'Tis above
mortal power!—Come, sir.   185

Exeunt.

Scene iv. [The parlor.]

Enter Rashley and Emilia in nightgowns, Betty,
Jeremy.

EMILIA.

Here, here, quickly, take my nightgown and put
it on. You are sure they are coming?

BETTY.

Very sure, madam, I stood at the door and heard
all.

RASHLEY.

What must I do, sweet? Prithee, do not let us be   5
surprised again.

EMILIA.

Uncase, uncase, sir, and let your man represent you
as Betty does me.—Jeremy, be sure you play your
part well and court her to the life.

[Betty and Jeremy] put on the gowns.

RASHLEY.

D'ye hear, sirrah!   10

JEREMY.

I'll warrant you, sir.—Come, Mrs.* Betty.

EMILIA.

Stay, a word more in thy ear: I see this fellow is
but a blockhead and therefore am afraid of trusting

him too far. Keep him as ignorant of our intrigue
as thou canst, and if my husband ask where I am,   15
tell him I am gone to visit my Lady Courtly. I'll
be in my chamber, and when they are all gone,
bring me word what Ranger and Maria are doing.

BETTY.

Yes madam, I'll be very careful.

RASHLEY.

I will reward thy care, my pretty little—   20

Noise.

EMILIA.

Hark! I hear 'em coming. Now to your postures.

Exit Rashley and Emilia.

JEREMY.

Now Mrs. Betty, we having so fit an occasion, let
us make love* in some heroic vein.

BETTY.

No, I am for the plain-dealing way.

JEREMY.

Pish! t'other's a great deal better, as thus: 25
Your eyes with so bright charms are decked about,
That I could kiss 'em till I kissed 'em out.

BETTY.

Oh I hate that, I vow, 'tis very silly.

Enter Ranger, Bubble, and Maria.

RANGER.

There, there, sir. D'ye see 'em now? Will you
believe next time?   30

BUBBLE.

Oh dismal object! I am a cuckold then.

MARIA.

This is miraculous! How was it possible they could
get hither? But I am glad they are here however.

BUBBLE.

Now for a good full blow at his head before he sees
me: 'tis a cuckold's way of revenge, I'm sure. Have   35
at him! (*Offers* to strike.)

JEREMY.

Oh Lord, what mean you, sir, what mean you?

BUBBLE.

Traitor! Rogue! Rascal! I'll—Hah, Jeremy?

JEREMY.

Aye sir, 'tis I, poor Jeremy, sir.

MARIA.

And Betty in her mistress's nightgown. 40

RANGER. (*Amazed.*)

Their old friend the Devil has fetched 'em away again.

BUBBLE.

What make you here in their nightgowns?

BETTY.

Only, sir, through an ambition to make love* as genteelly as we could. 45

BUBBLE.

Go, go, and find your mistress out and tell her, her humble servant and husband desires to speak with her.—Look ye, Ned, you are a fool, I see.

RANGER.

I am so, sir, I acknowledge it.

BUBBLE.

And you, madam, are a little leaning that way, are 50 ye not?

MARIA.

I can say nothing for myself, sir.

BUBBLE.

Then I can say y'are a couple of fools. Did I not tell you what all of this would come to? Ha, ha, ha! It makes me laugh to think how busy you two 55 asses have been about nothing, and I am no better than a third fool for believing you. But from henceforth, he that speaks against my chicken's virtue is the son of a whore, for 'uds* bood, she's the honestest* woman in Christendom, and he 60 that denies it I will immediately invade him with battle-ax, poniard, and pistol.

RANGER.

She is a very saint, sir.

MARIA.

A very devil, sir! Oh death, is there no remedy?

BUBBLE.

I'll go instantly and reconcile myself to her, with 65 a strict vow never to doubt* her more.—Oh Sir Roger! Welcome.

Enter Sir Roger and Cordelia.

Faith! I was wishing for some good company to be witness of my reconcilement to my dear chicken. You are melancholy, sir. I heard your 70 nephew was sick; I suppose that's the cause.

SIR ROGER. [*Aside.*]

If he has heard of what, I am disgraced forever.

BUBBLE.

Come sir, cheer up, cheer up; he will be well again, doubt not.

SIR ROGER.

I hope so, sir. [*Aside to Cordelia.*] Madam, this 75 generous act of concealing the infamy of our family has so wrought upon me that if I could requite—

CORDELIA.

No more, sir: your nephew's forbearance is all I desire. You are sensible now that I have some reason to request that. 80

SIR ROGER.

I am, madam, and am extremely bound to your generosity, and Gad, I have another nephew whom I'll make better by two hundred pound a year to make you amends.—Well, Mr. Bubble, I am glad to come at so good a time, when mirth is going 85 forward. You are a merry man, sir, and in verity, I like your company.

BUBBLE.

And I yours, Sir Roger, for I am very merry for some private reason best known to myself. We'll toss a bumper about by and by, faith! 90

Enter Fumble pushing in governess.

FUMBLE.

An old crone, a sorceress! What i'fack, and in the Devil's name, am I to be popped in the mouth with fourscore and twelve? A beldame, a witch, that expects next winter to be turned into a gib-cat, thought fit to be yoked with me! No, no, some 95 wiser than some, and I'll have her know within this week that I am as fit for two and twenty as two and twenty is for me. In the mean time, avaunt Jezebel, I like thee not, icod; thou hast no black o'top, i'fack; thou art not for my turn. 100

BUBBLE.

What, old signior Fumble? What's the matter, man?

FUMBLE.

Yes marry,* I am, sir, and choused damnably too, and some shall know't when I can find 'em.

CORDELIA.

He's groping for his spectacles; now I expect to be rated. 105

FUMBLE.

Ah, are you there, rogue, are you there! Why, you very* wag, would you offer* to serve me so? But hang thee, thou'rt a rogue, and come, i'fack, though 'twas a knavish trick, I am pleased with the wit on't. Give me thy hand, and come and kiss me, 110 and all shall be well again.

CORDELIA.

Upon condition you never trouble me more, there 'tis.

FUMBLE.

Icod, she has a pretty touch with her, she has, i'fack. I forgive thee with all my heart.—Well, old woman, depart in peace, old woman, I say, depart, 115 and trouble me no more. I am busy and cannot dispense with the fopperies of age now.

GOVERNESS.

Well, this comes of eating sweetmeats when I was young. He had never found out the trick, if my want* of teeth had not discovered* me. 120

BUBBLE.

Ha, ha! Here had like to have been fine sport, i'faith. But would I knew where my wife is, that we might all go and address, now I am in this good humor.

GOVERNESS.

Sir, just as I came in, I saw her go up into her chamber. 125

BUBBLE.

Didst thou? I am glad on't, i'faith. Come, let's all go.

Enter Betty.

BETTY.

Sir, I cannot find her, but I heard her say about an hour since she intended to go and visit my Lady Courtly. 130

BUBBLE.

No, no, I know where she is now. Poor creature! I warrant she sits so melancholy above now. Well, I dare proudly say I have the best wife in Christendom, for i'faith, I have been very jealous of her, but I was wrought upon, when, o'my 135 conscience, the innocent wretch would not hurt a worm. But come, we'll all go to her, and be sure, Sir Roger, you plead for me. In troth, my heart aches to think how I have used her.

BETTY. [*Aside.*]

I must prevent their going up, or we are undone. 140 (*Is running; Maria stops her.*)

MARIA.

Whither are you running? I have some business with you.

BETTY.

Good madam, I'll wait on you immediately.

MARIA.

Ye shall not stir till I have spoke to you. [*Aside.*] 145 Here must be something in this, I find, by her eagerness to be gone.

SIR ROGER.

Well Mr. Bubble, in verity, I'll do my best in your behalf; my tongue is at your service at any time.

BUBBLE.

Sir Roger, you will oblige me in't. She is the most 150 innocent, sweetest, and most virtuous person in the whole world, and I shall never be able to make her amends. Come, let us go.

RANGER.

Now will I see how she behaves herself and wonder at the prosperous impudence Hell has endowed her 155 with, though it lies not in my power to repel it.

MARIA.

Now I think better on't, I'll defer my business till another time. You may go where you please.

Exeunt [omnes, except Betty].

BETTY.

This cunning devil has undone 'em, nor lies it now in my power to hinder it. Oh I could curse—— 160

Exit.

Scene [v. Emilia's chamber.]

Enter Rashley and Emilia.

EMILIA.

The plague of living with such a husband, you must imagine, is very disagreeable to my temper, and were it not for the happy hours I have the good fortune to enjoy in thy society, my life would be wholly uncomfortable. But my dear, thou wilt 5 forget me. One day I shall grow cheap to thee, shall I not?

RASHLEY.

No, never, never, my sweet! Thou hast more charms each hour added to thee, rather than one diminished. Forget thee! I sooner shall forget to feed myself or that the sun ere shone in midst of summer than thy more precious favors. Thou bring'st each new hour sweets, and every minute a thousand thousand graces throng about thee, my dear, (*Kisses her.*) dear, charming, sweet, precious—

Enter Bubble, Sir Roger, Fumble, Ranger, Maria, Cordelia.

BUBBLE. (*Entering.*)

Softly, softly, Sir Roger. Poor soul, I warrant she's at prayers.—Hah! What's this I see? Gad jidge me—

RANGER.

By Heaven, they're here a-kissing! Oh happy minute!

EMILIA.

Ah, who could have the heart to leave thy blisses for such a fool, such a beast, such a dull, sordid, filthy, insipid creature as my husband?

BUBBLE.

How's that? Oh devil!

RASHLEY.

I am smothered with thy charms, oh for some air! (*Starts.*) Hah! Oh horror, cursed minute! Taken thus?

EMILIA.

My husband! Nay then, I am lost forever.

BUBBLE.

Ah cursed creature! Is this thy virtue? But I'll— (*Goes to wound her.*)

SIR ROGER.

Hold sir, in verity, that must not be. No swords against women in my company.

BUBBLE. [*To Rashley.*]

Then here let my vengeance light. Traitor! Have I obliged thee so often for this? Have at thee!

RANGER.

Your pardon, sir, I must hinder dishonorable proceedings; in the field you may do what you please.

BUBBLE.

Speak, witch, speak! What reason hadst thou to use me thus? Thou limb of the Devil, speak I say.

EMILIA.

Use you thus? Why sir, your rage makes you suggest strange thoughts without cause. My kindness to Mr. Rashley was only because—he promised to be my friend in urging my reconcilement with you—and because I knew he was your friend, I therefore—I say, because I knew you loved him, I desired him to—to—I was very urgent with him—about—about—no, I mistake, 'twas he was urgent with me to entreat you to do me the favor—no—to do him the favor—I mean, hum—to—to—

BUBBLE.

Pox! What a story's here? Oh strumpet! Witch!

MARIA.

To cuckold him, was that it, Sister?

RANGER.

Madam, methinks your speech fails you exceedingly.

EMILIA.

All will not do. Oh spiteful minute! Taken thus at last? Shame ties my tongue, and absence is most necessary. (*Exit.*)

BUBBLE.

Oh farewell in the Devil's name! Oh horns!* Horns! found a cuckold at last! I have spun a fair thread, by the Lord Harry. A cuckold at last!

RASHLEY.

A cuckold! Why sir, have I done anything but by your directions? Why do you suggest such things to yourself? Well sir, if I have injured you, I wear a sword, sir—and so—farewell. (*Exit.*)

SIR ROGER.

In verity, this was a strange discovery, but such things will happen—sometimes.

CORDELIA.

So it seems, yet this, methinks, is wonderful.

BUBBLE.

Oh unfortunate husband! Well, I'll go instantly and get a divorce and spend the remainder of my life in penning a satire against women. I'll call it, *A Caution for Cuckolds*, where I will deplorably set down my own case, and as a warning-piece for rash young men and for the benefit of my country: *Felix quem faciunt aliena cornua cautum.*79 (*Exit.*)

79 *Felix … cautum*] "Happy is he whom another's horns make cautious." (Lat.)

[V.v]

FUMBLE.

Something is the matter now, if I could guess. But mum! I must not yet discover* my failing.

RANGER.

Now the mighty sophistress[80] is o'erthrown!

MARIA.

Thank chance for that, but no wit of our own. 75

RANGER.

Right, madam, and by this a man may see how unnecessary a thing it is to strive to turn the current of a woman's fancy when it is bent to another. 'Tis a damned thing this wenching, if a man considers seriously on it, and yet 'tis such a 80
damnable age we live in that, Gad, he that does not follow it is either accounted sordidly unnatural or ridiculously impotent. Well for my part, henceforward this shall be my resolution:

I'll love for interest, court for recreation, 85
Change still* a mistress to be still* in fashion.
I'll aid all women in an amorous league,
But from this hour ne'er balk a love-intrigue.

Exeunt omnes.

FINIS.

Textual Notes

a The copytext is the first edition, a 1677 quarto (Q1). Also consulted were quarto editions of 1678 (Q2), 1685 (Q3), and 1711 (Q4), as well as the modern edition of 1976 (Vaughn).
b Have I] Q3, Vaughn; have feigned, Q1, Q2, Q4

---

80 Sophistress] a woman practiced in the art of sophistry (q.v.)

Venice Preserved; or, A Plot Discovered[a]

by Thomas Otway (1652-1685)

edited by Jessica Munns

Venice Preserved was first performed at the Duke's playhouse in February 1682. The Whig political ascendancy of the Exclusion Crisis had been broken by Charles II's dissolution of the Parliament he called in Oxford in March 1681. This event was swiftly followed by the arrest of the earl of Shaftesbury. *Venice Preserved*, probably written and certainly performed during the time of the "Tory revenge," seems to have been taken by its first audiences as a triumphant Tory play. And Otway's dedication to Louise Kéroualle, the duchess of Portsmouth and Charles II's chief mistress at the time, and his prologue and epilogue (included below) are certainly royalist. However, the play's political sympathies are notoriously unclear.

Set in the Republic of Venice, a state much admired by Whig ideologues and detested by Tories, the play depicts a conspiracy against the Senate. Were the conspiracy royalist, or were the senators noble, a clear political reading could emerge, either condemning or endorsing republicanism, or endorsing or condemning political revolt. However, the Senate and conspiracy are equally morally and politically bankrupt. Neither of the groups can be admired, and their conflict is acted out with both savage and comic intensity. Otway intensifies the sense of equality between the two groups and constantly undercuts his tragic materials with scenes of perverse comedy. Belvidera pleads with her harsh father for the lives of the conspirators, and in the scene immediately following the courtesan Aquilina similarly pleads with the perverse senator, Antonio, while he lies at her feet begging her to kick him. Politics in general emerge as an absurd, degrading, and corrupting activity.

Apart from contemporary politics, Otway's main source was a novella by César Vischard, l'abbé de Saint Réal, *La Conjuration des Espagnols contre la République de Vénise* (1674), translated into English as *A Conspiracy of the Spaniards Against the State of Venice* in 1675 and reissued in 1679. Saint Réal's narrative is also ambiguous, depicting the Senate as corrupt and the conspirators as debased yet touched by moments of nobility. Otway drew on Saint Réal's material, collapsing the timescale and adding in the characters of Belvidera, the sensual wife of Jaffeir, and the perverse senator Antonio. He greatly expanded the role of Aquilina, and the famous "Nicky Nacky" scenes[1] between Aquilina and Antonio are all his own.

Otway had the benefit of the great actors of the Duke's Company in their prime. Thomas Betterton and William Smith played Jaffeir and Pierre, respectively, and Elizabeth Barry played Belvidera. But the actors who perhaps stole the show were Tony Leigh as Antonio and Elizabeth Currer as Aquilina. And although the play entered the permanent repertoire and remained one of the half-dozen most popular tragedies in the eighteenth century, outside of Shakespeare's, it was only as a version sanitized by the excision of the Nicky-Nacky scenes.

Venice Preserved is an unusual form, a tragic political satire. In Jaffeir and Belvidera, Otway created passionate and confused lovers who are destroyed even as Venice is "preserved," but for whose benefit? The only surviving major characters are Antonio and Aquilina.

---

[1] Nicky Nacky scenes] these scenes were very popular with Tories, and an anonymous Whig "Satyr," c. 1682, complained they were more popular than Shadwell's comedies. In the eighteenth century the scenes came to be regarded as obscene (indeed, nicky-nacky was a slang term for female sexual organs) and pointless and were excised.

PROLOGUE

In these distracted times, when each man dreads
The bloody stratagems of busy heads;
When we have feared three years we know not what,[2]
Till witnesses begin to die o'th'rot,
What made our poet meddle with a plot?   5
Was't that he fancied, for the very sake
And name of plot, his trifling play might take?
For there's not in't one inch-board evidence,[3]
But 'tis, he says, to reason plain and sense,
And that he thinks a plausible defense.   10
Were truth by sense and reason to be tried,
Sure all our swearers might be laid aside:
No, of such tools our author has no need
To make his plot or make[b] his play succeed;
He of black bills has no prodigious tales[4]   15
Or Spanish pilgrims cast ashore in Wales;[5]
Here's not one murthered magistrate at least,
Kept rank like venison for a city feast,
Grown four days stiff, the better to prepare
And fit his pliant limbs to ride in chair:*[6]   20
Yet here's an army raised, though under ground,
But no man seen nor one commission found;
Here is a traitor too, that's very old,
Turbulent, subtle, mischievous and bold,
Bloody, revengeful, and to crown his part,   25
Loves fumbling with a wench with all his heart,[7]

---

[2] three years] from the Popish Plot through the Exclusion Crisis (1678-81)

[3] inch-board evidence] "to swear through an inch-board" is to "swear home and hard," presumably hard enough to go through a board an inch thick (*OED*)

[4] black bills ... tales] Oates's testimony included reference to raising an army in Ireland armed with black bills (q.v.).

[5] Spanish pilgrims ... Wales.] William Bedloe, a Popish Plot informer, claimed evidence of a plot to land Irish soldiers, disguised as Spanish pilgrims, in Wales.

[6] murthered magistrate ... chair] Sir Edmund Berry Godfrey, whose body, it was alleged, was removed to Somerset House in a sedan chair* and kept there for tfour days

[7] traitor ... all his heart] the character Renault (probably based on Anthony Ashley Cooper, first earl of Shaftesbury and leader of the movement to exclude James Stuart)

Till after having many changes passed,
In spight of age (thanks Heaven) is hanged at last.
Next is a Senator that keeps a whore;[8]
In Venice none a higher office bore.   30
To lewdness every night the lecher ran;
Show me, all London, such another man,
Match him at Mother Creswold's if you can.[9]
Oh Poland, Poland! had it been thy lot
T'have heard in time of this Venetian plot,   35
Thou surely chosen hadst one king from thence
And honored them as thou hast England since.[10]

DRAMATIS PERSONAE

[MEN]
    Duke of Venice.
    Priuli, father to Belvidera, a senator.
    Antonio, a fine speaker in the Senate.
    Jaffeir.
    Pierre.
    Renault,
    Bedamar,
    Spinosa,
    Theodore,
    Eliot,
    Revillido,
    Durand,
    Mezzana,
    Bramveil,
    Ternon,
    Brabe,
    [Retrossi,] conspirators.
    The Council of Ten.
    Officer.
    Guards.
    Friar.
    Executioner and rabble.

---

[8] Senator that keeps a whore] the character Antonio (perhaps also based on Shaftesbury, whose first name was Anthony; however, this was also the name of the famous comic actor who created the role, Anthony Leigh)

[9] Mother Creswold's] also spelled Creswell, a notorious London procuress

[10] Poland ... since] Poland had an elective monarchy in the seventeenth century, and Tory satires claimed that Shaftesbury had put himself forward for the election of 1675.

[WOMEN]
>   Belvidera.
>   Aquilina.
>   Two women, attendants on Belvidera.
>   Two women, servants to Aquilina.

Venice Preserved; or, A Plot Discovered.

Act I.

Enter Priuli and Jaffeir.

PRIULI.
>   No more! I'll hear no more. Be gone and leave.

JAFFEIR.
>   Not hear me! By my sufferings but you shall!
>   My lord, my lord, I'm not that abject wretch
>   You think me. Patience! Where's the distance throws
>   Me back so far, but I may boldly speak   5
>   In right, though proud oppression will not hear me!

PRIULI.
>   Have you not wronged me?

JAFFEIR.
>   Could my nature e'er
>   Have brooked injustice or the doing wrongs,
>   I need not now thus low have bent myself   10
>   To gain a hearing from a cruel father!
>   Wronged you?

PRUILI.
>   Yes! wronged me, in the nicest* point:
>   The honor of my house. You have done me
>   wrong.
>   You may remember (for I now will speak,   15
>   And urge its baseness) when you first came home
>   From travel with such hopes as made you looked on
>   By all men's eyes, a youth of expectation,
>   Pleased with your growing virtue, I received you,
>   Courted, and sought to raise you to your merits.   20
>   My house, my table, nay my fortune too,
>   My very self, was yours. You might have used me
>   To your best service. Like an open friend,
>   I treated, trusted you, and thought you mine,
>   When in requital of my best endeavors   25
>   You treacherously practiced to undo me,
>   Seduced the weakness of my age's darling,
>   My only child, and stole her from my bosom.
>   Oh Belvidera!

JAFFEIR.
>   'Tis to me you owe her,   30
>   Childless you had been else and in the grave,
>   Your name extinct nor no more Priuli heard of.
>   You may remember, scarce five years are past
>   Since in your brigantine you sailed to see
>   The Adriatic wedded by our Duke,[11]   35
>   And I was with you. Your unskillful pilot
>   Dashed us upon a rock, when to your boat
>   You made for safety, entered first yourself.
>   The affrighted Belvidera following next,
>   As she stood trembling on the vessel side,   40
>   Was by a wave washed off into the deep,
>   When instantly I plunged into the sea,
>   And buffeting the billows to her rescue,
>   Redeemed her life with half the loss of mine.
>   Like a rich conquest in one hand I bore her   45
>   And with the other dashed the saucy waves
>   That thronged and pressed to rob me of my prize.
>   I brought her, gave her to your despairing arms.
>   Indeed you thanked me, but a nobler gratitude
>   Rose in her soul: for from that hour she loved me, 50
>   Till for her life she paid me with herself.

PRIULI.
>   You stole her from me, like a thief you stole her,
>   At dead of night; that cursèd hour you chose
>   To rifle me of all my heart held dear.
>   May all your joys in her prove false like mine;   55
>   A sterile fortune and a barren bed
>   Attend you both; continual discord make
>   Your days and nights bitter and grievous; still*
>   May the hard hand of a vexatious need
>   Oppress and grind you till at last you find   60
>   The curse of disobedience all your portion.

JAFFEIR.
>   Half of your curse you have bestowed in vain:
>   Heav'n has already crowned our faithful loves
>   With a young boy, sweet as his mother's beauty.
>   May he live to prove more gentle than his   65
>   grandsire
>   And happier than his father!

---

11 Adriatic wedded … Duke] On Ascension Day, August
   15, the Doge would cast a ring into the Adriatic Sea to
   signify the marriage of Venice to the source of its wealth
   and maritime empire.

PRIULI.

                    Rather live
To bait thee for his bread and din your ears
With hungry cries whilst his unhappy mother
Sits down and weeps in bitterness of want.*   70

JAFFEIR.

You talk as if it would please you.

PRIULI.

                   'Twould, by Heav'n.
Once she was dear indeed: the drops that fell
From my sad heart when she forgot her duty,
The fountain of my life was not so precious.   75
But she is gone, and if I am a man,
I will forget her.

JAFFEIR.

Would I were in my grave.

PRIULI.

              And she too with thee.
For living here, you're but my cursed remembrancers 80
I once was happy.

JAFFEIR.

You use me thus because you know my soul
Is fond of Belvidera. You perceive
My life feeds on her; therefore, thus you treat me.
Oh! could my soul ever have known satiety.   85
Were I that thief, the doer of such wrongs
As you upbraid me with, what hinders me
But I might send her back to you with contumely
And court my fortune where she would be kinder!

PRIULI.

You dare not do't.   90

JAFFEIR.

           Indeed my lord, I dare not.
My heart that awes me is too much my master.
Three years are past since first our vows were
    plighted,
During which time, the world must bear me
    witness,
I have treated Belvidera like your daughter,   95
The daughter of a senator of Venice:
Distinction, place, attendance, and observance,
Due to her birth, she always has commanded.
Out of my little fortune I have done this
Because (though hopeless e'er to win your nature) 100
The world might see I loved her for herself,
Not as the heiress of the great Priuli—

PRIULI.

No more!

JAFFEIR.

           Yes! all, and then adieu forever.
There's not a wretch that lives on common charity 105
But's happier than me, for I have known
The luscious sweets of plenty, every night
Have slept with soft content about my head
And never waked but to a joyful morning,
Yet now must fall like a full ear of corn,   110
Whose blossom 'scaped yet's withered in the
    ripening.

PRIULI.

Home and be humble; study to retrench;
Discharge the lazy vermin of thy hall,
Those pageants of thy folly;
Reduce the glittering trappings of thy wife   115
To humble weeds, fit for thy little state;
Then to some suburb cottage both retire;
Drudge to feed loathsome life; get brats; and
    starve—
Home, home, I say. (*Exit.*)

JAFFEIR.

          Yes, if my heart would let me— 120
This proud, this swelling heart—home I would go,
But that my doors are hateful to my eyes,
Filled and dammed up with gaping creditors,
Watchful as fowlers when their game will spring.
I have now not fifty ducats in the world,   125
Yet still I am in love and pleased with ruin.
Oh Belvidera! oh she's my wife,
And we will bear our wayward fate together
But ne'er know comfort more.

Enter Pierre.

PIERRE.

          My friend, good morrow! 130
How fares the honest partner of my heart?
What, melancholy! not a word to spare me?

JAFFEIR.

I'm thinking, Pierre, how that damned starving
    quality
Called honesty got footing in the world.

PIERRE.

Why, pow'rful villainy first set it up   135
For its own ease and safety. Honest men

Are the soft, easy cushions on which knaves
Repose and fatten. Were all mankind villains,
They'd starve each other; lawyers would want*
   practice,
Cut-throats rewards; each man would kill his brother 140
Himself, none would be paid or hanged for murder.
Honesty was a cheat invented first
To bind the hands of bold deserving rogues
That fools and cowards might sit safe in power
And lord it uncontrolled above their betters. 145

JAFFEIR.
   Then honesty is but a notion.

PIERRE.
               Nothing else:
Like wit, much talked of, not to be defined;
He that pretends to most, too, has least share in't;
'Tis a ragged virtue. Honesty! No more on't. 150

JAFFEIR.
   Sure thou art honest?

PIERRE.
           So indeed men think me.
But they're mistaken, Jaffeir: I am a rogue
As well as they——
A fine, gay, bold-faced villain,[12] as thou seest me. 155
'Tis true, I pay my debts when they're contracted;
I steal from no man, would not cut a throat
To gain admission to a great man's purse
Or a whore's bed; I'd not betray my friend
To get his place or fortune; I scorn to flatter 160
A blown-up fool above me or crush the wretch
   beneath me,
Yet Jaffeir, for all this, I am a villain!

JAFFEIR.
   A villain?

PIERRE.
         Yes, a most notorious villain:
To see the suff'rings of my fellow creatures 165
And own myself a man; to see our senators
Cheat the deluded people with a show
Of liberty which yet they ne'er must taste of.
They say, by them our hands are free from fetters,
Yet whom they please they lay in basest bonds, 170

Bring whom they please to infamy and sorrow,
Drive us like wracks down the rough tide of power
Whilst no hold's left to save us from destruction.
All that bear this are villains, and I one,
Not to rouse up at the great call of Nature 175
And check the growth of these domestic spoilers
That make us slaves and tell^c us 'tis our charter.

JAFFEIR.
   Oh Aquilina! Friend, to lose such beauty,
The dearest purchase of thy noble labors:
She was thy right by conquest, as by love. 180

PIERRE.
   Oh Jaffeir! I'd so fixed my heart upon her,
That wheresoe'er I framed a scheme of life
For time to come, she was my only joy
With which I wished to sweeten future cares.
I fancied pleasures, none but one that loves 185
And dotes as I did can imagine like 'em.
When in the extremity of all these hopes,
In the most charming hour of expectation,
Then when our eager wishes soar the highest,
Ready to stoop and grasp the lovely game, 190
A haggard owl, a worthless kite of prey,
With his foul wings sailed in and spoiled my quarry.

JAFFEIR.
   I know the wretch and scorn him as thou hat'st
   him.

PIERRE.
   Curse on the common good that's so protected,
Where every slave that heaps up wealth enough 195
To do much wrong becomes a lord of right.
I, who believed no ill could e'er come near me,
Found in embraces of my Aquilina
A wretched old but itching senator,
A wealthy fool that had bought out my title, 200
A rogue that uses beauty like a lambskin,
Barely to keep him warm. That filthy cuckoo too
Was in my absence crept into my nest
And spoiling all my brood of noble pleasure.

JAFFEIR.
   Didst thou not chase him thence? 205

PIERRE.
              I did and drove
The rank old bearded hirco[13] stinking home.

---

12 villain] Throughout this scene, Pierre plays off both
   meanings of *villain*, base-born villager (even slave) and
   scoundrel (his *noblesse* should *oblige*).

---

13 hirco] he-goat

The matter was complained of in the Senate,
I summoned to appear and censured basely
For violating something they call privilege—   210
This was the recompense of my service.
Would I'd been rather beaten by a coward!
A soldier's mistress, Jaffeir, 's his religion.
When that's profaned, all other ties are broken,
That even dissolves all former bonds of service,   215
And from that hour I think my self as free
To be the foe as e'er the friend of Venice—
Nay, dear Revenge, whene'er thou call'st, I am
    ready.

JAFFEIR.
I think no safety can be here for virtue
And grieve, my friend, as much as thou to live   220
In such a wretched state as this of Venice
Where all agree to 'spoil the public good
And villains fatten with the brave man's labors.

PIERRE.
We have neither safety, unity, nor peace,
For the foundation's lost of common good;   225
Justice is lame as well as blind amongst us;
The laws (corrupted to their ends that make 'em)
Serve but for instruments of some new tyranny
That every day starts up to enslave us deeper.
Now could this glorious cause but find out friends   230
To do it right! oh Jaffeir ! then might'st thou
Not wear these seals of woe upon thy face;[14]
The proud Priuli should be taught humanity
And learn to value such a son as thou art.
I dare not speak! But my heart bleeds this   235
    moment!

JAFFEIR.
Curst be the cause, though I thy friend be part on't.
Let me partake the troubles of thy bosom,
For I am used to misery and perhaps
May find a way to sweeten't to thy spirit.

PIERRE.
Too soon it will reach thy knowledge—   240

JAFFEIR.
                              Then from thee
Let it proceed. There's virtue in thy friendship
Would make the saddest tale of sorrow pleasing,
Strengthen my constancy, and welcome ruin.

---

14 seals of woe] as in the imprint of a signet; marks or signs

PIERRE.
Then, thou art ruined!   245

JAFFEIR.
                          That I long since knew,
I and ill fortune have been long acquaintance.

PIERRE.
I passed this very moment by thy doors
And found them guarded by a troop of villains;
The sons of public rapine were destroying.   250
They told me, by the sentence of the law,
They had commission to seize all thy fortune,
Nay more, Priuli's cruel hand hath signed it.
Here stood a ruffian with a horrid face
Lording it o'er a pile of massy plate*   255
Tumbled into a heap for public sale;
There was another, making villainous* jests
At thy undoing. He had ta'en possession
Of all thy ancient, most domestic ornaments:
Rich hangings, intermixed and wrought with gold;   260
The very bed which on thy wedding night
Received thee to the arms of Belvidera,
The scene of all thy joys, was violated
By the coarse hands of filthy dungeon villains
And thrown amongst the common lumber.*   265

JAFFEIR.
Now thanks, Heav'n—

PIERRE.
Thank Heav'n! For what?

JAFFEIR.
                          That I am not worth a ducat.

PIERRE.
Curse thy dull stars and the worse fate of Venice,
Where brothers, friends, and fathers, all are false; 270
Where there's no trust, no truth; where innocence
Stoops under vile oppression, and vice lords it.
Hadst thou but seen, as I did, how at last
Thy beauteous Belvidera, like a wretch
That's doomed to banishment, came weeping   275
    forth,
Shining through tears, like April suns in showers
That labor to o'ercome the cloud that loads 'em,
Whilst two young virgins, on whose arms she
    leaned,
Kindly looked up and at her grief grew sad,
As if they catched the sorrows that fell from her.   280
Even the lewd rabble that were gathered round

To see the sight stood mute when they beheld her,
Governed their roaring throats, and grumbled pity.
I could have hugged the greasy rogues; they
    pleased me.

JAFFEIR.

I thank thee for this story from my soul,   285
Since now I know the worst that can befall me.
Ah Pierre! I have a heart that could have born
The roughest wrong my fortune could have done
    me,
But when I think what Belvidera feels,
The bitterness her tender spirit tastes of,   290
I own myself a coward. Bear my weakness,
If, throwing thus my arms about thy neck,
I play the boy and blubber in thy bosom.
Oh! I shall drown thee with my sorrows!

PIERRE.

                        Burn!   295
First burn and level Venice to thy ruin!
What, starve like beggars' brats in frosty weather
Under a hedge and whine our selves to death!
Thou or thy cause shall never want* assistance
Whilst I have blood or fortune fit to serve thee.   300
Command my heart: thou art every way its
    master.

JAFFEIR.

No: there's a secret pride in bravely dying.

PIERRE.

Rats die in holes and corners; dogs run mad;
Man knows a braver remedy for sorrow:
Revenge, the attribute of gods! They stamped it   305
With their great image on our natures. Die?
Consider well the cause that calls upon thee,
And if thou art base enough, die then. Remember,
Thy Belvidera suffers. Belvidera!
Die? Damn first! What, be decently interred   310
In a churchyard and mingle thy brave* dust
With stinking rogues that rot in dirty winding
    sheets,
Surfeit-slain fools, the common dung o'th soil?

JAFFEIR.

Oh!

PIERRE.

          Well said, out with't, swear a little—   315

JAFFEIR.

                        Swear!

By sea and air! by earth, by heaven and hell,
I will revenge my Belvidera's tears!
Hark thee, my friend: Priuli—is—a senator!

PIERRE.

A dog!   320

JAFFEIR.

        Agreed.

PIERRE.

              Shoot him.

JAFFEIR.

                      With all my heart.
No more. Where shall we meet at night?

PIERRE.

                    I'll tell thee: 325
On the Rialto every night at twelve
I take my evening's walk of meditation.
There we two will meet and talk of precious*
    Mischief.

JAFFEIR.

Farewell.

PIERRE.

           At twelve.   330

JAFFEIR.

                At any hour, my plagues
Will keep me waking.

Exit Pierre.

Tell me why, good Heav'n,
Thou mad'st me what I am, with all the spirit,
Aspiring thoughts, and elegant desires   335
That fill the happiest man? Ah rather, why
Did'st thou not form me sordid as my fate,
Base minded, dull, and fit to carry burdens?
Why have I sense to know the curse that's on me?
Is this just dealing, Nature?—Belvidera!   340

Enter Belvidera [with two women attending her].

Poor Belvidera!

BELVIDERA.

           Lead me, lead me, my virgins!
To that kind voice.—My lord, my love, my refuge!
Happy my eyes when they behold thy face.
My heavy heart will leave its doleful beating   345
At sight of thee and bound with sprightful joys.
Oh smile, as when our loves were in their spring,
And cheer my fainting soul.

JAFFEIR.
As when our loves
Were in their spring? Has then my fortune   350
    changed?
Art thou not Belvidera, still the same,
Kind, good, and tender, as my arms first found
    thee?
If thou art altered, where shall I have harbor?
Where ease my loaded heart? Oh! where
    complain?

BELVIDERA.
Does this appear like change or love decaying   355
When thus I throw my self into thy bosom
With all the resolution of a strong truth?
Beats not my heart as 'twould alarm thine
To a new charge of bliss? I joy more in thee
Than did thy mother when she hugged thee first   360
And blessed the gods for all her travail past.

JAFFEIR.
Can there in woman be such glorious faith?
Sure all ill stories of thy sex are false.
Oh woman! lovely woman! Nature made thee
To temper man: we had been brutes without you;   365
Angels are painted fair to look like you;
There's in you all that we believe of Heav'n,
Amazing brightness, purity and truth,
Eternal joy and everlasting love.

BELVIDERA.
If love be treasure, we'll be wondrous rich: 370
I have so much, my heart will surely break with't.
Vow's cannot express it when I would declare
How great's my joy. I am dumb with the big
    thought:
I swell and sigh and labor with my longing.
Oh lead me to some desert wide and wild,   375
Barren as our misfortunes, where my soul
May have its vent, where I may tell aloud
To the high heavens and every list'ning planet
With what a boundless stock my bosom's fraught;
Where I may throw my eager arms about thee,   380
Give loose to love with kisses, kindling joy,
And let off all the fire that's in my heart.

JAFFEIR.
Oh Belvidera! double I am a beggar,
Undone by fortune and in debt to thee.
Want!* worldly want! that hungry, meager fiend   385

Is at my heels and chases me in view.
Canst thou bear cold and hunger? Can these
    limbs,
Framed for the tender offices of love,
Endure the bitter gripes of smarting poverty?
When banished by our miseries abroad   390
(As suddenly we shall be) to seek out
(In some far climate where our names are strangers)
For charitable succor, wilt thou then,
When in a bed of straw we shrink together
And the bleak winds shall whistle round our   395
    heads,
Wilt thou then talk thus to me? Wilt thou then
Hush my cares thus and shelter me with love?

BELVIDERA.
Oh I will love thee, even in madness love thee:
Though my distracted senses should forsake me,
I'd find some intervals when my poor heart   400
Should 'suage itself and be let loose to thine.
Though the bare earth be all our resting place,
Its roots our food, some cleft our habitation,
I'll make this arm a pillow for thy head,
As thou sighing ly'st and swelled with sorrow,   405
Creep to thy bosom, pour the balm of love
Into thy soul, and kiss thee to thy rest,
Then praise our God, and watch thee till the
    morning.

JAFFEIR.
Hear this, you heavens, and wonder how you
    made her!
Reign, reign, ye monarchs that divide the world.   410
Busy rebellion ne'er will let you know
Tranquility and happiness like mine.
Like gaudy ships, th'obsequious billows fall
And rise again to lift you in your pride;
They wait but for a storm and then devour you.   415
I, in my private bark, already wrecked,
Like a poor merchant driven on unknown land,
That had by chance packed up his choicest
    treasure
In one dear casket and saved only that,
Since I must wander further on the shore,   420
Thus hug my little but my precious store,
Resolved to scorn and trust my fate no more.

Exeunt.

Act II, [scene i. Aquilina's house.]

Enter Pierre and Aquilina.

AQUILINA.
  By all thy wrongs, thou art dearer to my arms
  Than all the wealth of Venice. Prithee stay,
  And let us love tonight.
PIERRE.
                        No. There's fool,
  There's fool about thee. When a woman sells   5
  Her flesh to fools, her beauty's lost to me.
  They leave a taint, a sully where they've passed;
  There's such a baneful quality about 'em
  Even spoils complexions with their own
      nauseousness;
  They infect all they touch. I cannot think   10
  Of tasting anything a fool has palled.
AQUILINA.
  I loathe and scorn that fool thou mean'st, as much
  Or more than thou canst, but the beast has gold
  That makes him necessary, power too,
  To qualify my character and poise me   15
  Equal with peevish virtue that beholds
  My liberty with envy: in their hearts
  Are loose as I am, but an ugly power
  Sits in their faces and frights pleasures from 'em.
PIERRE.
  Much good may't do you, madam, with your senator. 20
AQUILINA.
  My senator! Why, canst thou think that wretch
  E'er filled thy Aquilina's arms with pleasure!
  Think'st thou, because I sometimes give him leave
  To foil himself at what he is unfit for;
  Because I force myself to endure and suffer him, 25
  Think'st thou I love him? No, by all the joys
  Thou ever gav'st me, his presence is my penance;
  The worst thing an old man can be's a lover,
  A mere *memento mori* to poor woman.
  I never lay by his decrepit side,   30
  But all that night I pondered on my grave.
PIERRE.
  Would he were well sent thither.
AQUILINA.
                        That's my wish too,
  For then, my Pierre, I might have cause with pleasure
  To play the hypocrite. Oh! how I could weep   35

Over the dying dotard and kiss him too
In hopes to smother him quite. Then, when the time
Was come to pay my sorrows at his funeral,
For he has already made me heir to treasures
Would make me out-act a real widow's whining,
How could I frame my face to fit my mourning!   40
With wringing hands attend him to his grave;
Fall swooning on his hearse; take mad possession
Even of the dismal vault where he lay buried;
There like the Ephesian matron[15] dwell, till thou,
My lovely soldier, comest to my deliverance;   45
Then throwing up my veil, with open arms
And laughing eyes run to new dawning joy.
PIERRE.
  No more! I have friends to meet me here tonight
  And must be private. As you prize my friendship,
  Keep up your coxcomb. Let him not pry nor listen 50
  Nor fisk[16] about the house as I have seen him
  Like a tame, mumping* squirrel with a bell on;
  Curs will be abroad to bite him, if you do.
AQUILINA.
  What friends to meet? may I not be your council?
PIERRE.
  How! A woman ask questions out of bed?   55
  Go to your senator, ask him what passes
  Amongst his brethren, he'll hide nothing from
      you,
  But pump me not for politics. No more!
  Give order that whoever in my name
  Comes here receive admittance. So good night.   60
AQUILINA.
  Must we ne'er meet again! Embrace no more!
  Is love so soon and utterly forgotten!
PIERRE.
  As you henceforward treat your fool, I'll think
  on't. [*Exit.*]
AQUILINA.
  Cursed be all fools and doubly cursed myself,
  The worst of fools. I die if he forsakes me.   65
  And now to keep him, Heaven or Hell instruct me.

Exit.

---

15 Ephesian matron] In the *Satyricon* of Petronius Arbiter, an
   Ephesian matron mourned her husband's death until seduced in his very mausoleum by a handsome soldier.
16 fisk] to jump about

Scene [ii.] The Rialto.

Enter Jaffeir.

JAFFEIR.
I am here, and thus, the shades of night around me,
I look as if all hell were in my heart
And I in hell. Nay, surely 'tis so with me,
For every step I tread, methinks some fiend
Knocks at my breast and bids it not be quiet.   5
I've heard how desperate wretches, like myself,
Have wandered out at this dead time of night
To meet the Foe of mankind in his walk.
Sure I am so curst that, though of Heav'n
     forsaken,
No minister of darkness cares to tempt me.   10
Hell! Hell! why sleepest thou?

Enter Pierre.

PIERRE.
Sure I have stayed too long:
The clock has struck, and I may lose my proselyte.
—Speak, who goes there?
JAFFEIR.
                         A dog that comes to howl   15
At yonder moon. What's he that asks the question?
PIERRE.
A friend to dogs, for they are honest creatures
And ne'er betray their masters, never fawn
On any that they love not. Well met, friend.
Jaffeir!   20
JAFFEIR.
The same. Oh Pierre! Thou art come in season,
I was just going to pray.
PIERRE.
                         Ah that's mechanic,
Priests make a trade on't and yet starve by it too.
No praying, it spoils business, and time's precious.   25
Where's Belvidera?
JAFFEIR.
                         For a day or two
I've lodged her privately, till I see farther
What Fortune will do with me. Prithee friend,
If thou wouldst have me fit to hear good counsel,
Speak not of Belvidera—   30
PIERRE.
          Speak not of her?

JAFFEIR.
Oh no!
PIERRE.
          Nor name her? May be I wish her well.
JAFFEIR.
Who well?   35
PIERRE.
          Thy wife, thy lovely Belvidera,
I hope a man may wish his friend's wife well
And no harm done!
JAFFEIR.
          Y'are merry, Pierre!
PIERRE.
                         I am so.   40
Thou shalt smile too, and Belvidera smile,
We'll all rejoice. Here's something to buy pins;
Marriage is chargeable.
JAFFEIR.
          I but half wished
To see the Devil, and he's here already.   45
Well!
What must this buy, rebellion, murder, treason?
Tell me which way I must be damned for this.
PIERRE.
When last we parted, we had no qualms like these
But entertained each other's thoughts like men   50
Whose souls were well acquainted. Is the world
Reformed since our last meeting? What new miracles
Have happened? Has Priuli's heart relented?
Can he be honest?
JAFFEIR.
          Kind Heav'n! Let heavy curses   55
Gall his old age; cramps, aches, rack his bones;
And bitterest disquiet wring his heart.
Oh let him live till life become his burden!
Let him groan under't long, linger an age
In the worst agonies and pangs of death,   60
And find its ease but late.
PIERRE.
          Nay, couldst thou not
As well, my friend, have stretched the curse to all
The Senate round, as to one single villain?
JAFFEIR.
But curses stick not. Could I kill with cursing,   65
By Heav'n I know not thirty heads in Venice
Should not be blasted. Senators should rot

Like dogs on dunghills, but their wives and daughters
Die of their own diseases. Oh for a curse
To kill with!   70

PIERRE.

          Daggers, daggers are much better!

JAFFEIR.

  Hah!

PIERRE.

      Daggers.

JAFFEIR.

          But where are they?

PIERRE.

                     Oh, a thousand   75
May be disposed in honest hands in Venice.

JAFFEIR.

  Thou talk'st in clouds.

PIERRE.

             But yet a heart half wronged
As thine has been would find the meaning, Jaffeir.

JAFFEIR.

  A thousand daggers, all in honest hands,   80
And have not I a friend will stick one here?

PIERRE.

  Yes, if I thought thou wert not to be cherished
To a nobler purpose, I'd be that friend.
But thou hast better friends, friends whom thy
    wrongs
Have made thy friends friends worthy to be called so.   85
I'll trust thee with a secret: there are spirits
This hour at work. But as thou art a man,
Whom I have picked and chosen from the world,
Swear that thou wilt be true to what I utter,
And when I have told thee that which only gods   90
And men like gods are privy to, then swear
No chance or change shall wrest it from thy bosom.

JAFFEIR.

  When thou wouldst bind me, is there need of oaths?
(Greensickness girls lose maidenheads with such
    counters.)
For thou art so near my heart that thou mayst see   95
Its bottom, sound its strength and firmness to thee:
Is coward, fool, or villain in my face?
If I seem none of these, I dare believe
Thou wouldst not use me in a little cause,
For I am fit for honor's toughest task   100
Nor ever yet found fooling was my province;

And for a villainous, inglorious enterprise,
I know thy heart so well, I dare lay mine
Before thee, set it to what point thou wilt.

PIERRE.

  Nay, it's a cause thou wilt be fond of, Jaffeir.   105
For it is founded on the noblest basis:
Our liberties, our natural inheritance.
There's no religion, no hypocrisy in't;
We'll do the business and ne'er fast and pray for't,
Openly act a deed the world shall gaze   110
With wonder at and envy when it is done.

JAFFEIR.

  For liberty!

PIERRE.

          For liberty my friend.
Thou shalt be freed from base Priuli's tyranny,
And thy sequestered fortunes healed again.   115
I shall be freed from opprobrious wrongs
That press me now and bend my spirit downward.
All Venice free and every growing merit
Succeed to its just right. Fools shall be pulled
From wisdom's seat; those baleful unclean birds,   120
Those lazy owls,* who (perched near Fortune's top)
Sit only watchful with their heavy wings
To cuff down new-fledged virtues that would rise
To nobler heights and make the grove harmonious.

JAFFEIR.

  What can I do?   125

PIERRE.

          Canst thou not kill a senator?

JAFFEIR.

  Were there one wise or honest, I could kill him
For herding with that nest of fools and knaves.
By all my wrongs, thou talk'st as if revenge
Were to be had, and that brave* story warms me.   130

PIERRE.

  Swear then!

JAFFEIR.

          I do, by all those glittering stars
And yond great ruling planet of the night!
By all good Pow'rs above and ill below!
By love and friendship, dearer than my life!   135
No pow'r or death shall make me false to thee.

PIERRE.

  Here we embrace, and I'll unlock my heart.
A council's held hard by, where the destruction

Of this great empire's hatching. There I'll lead thee!
But be a man, for thou art to mix with men   140
Fit to disturb the peace of all the world
And rule it when it's wildest—
JAFFEIR.
                                    I give thee thanks
For this kind warning. Yes, I will be a man
And charge thee, Pierre, whene'er thou seest my fears   145
Betray me less, to rip this heart of mine
Out of my breast and show it for a coward's.
Come, let's be gone, for from this hour I chase
All little thoughts, all tender, human follies
Out of my bosom. Vengeance shall have room.   150
Revenge!
PIERRE.
                    And liberty!
JAFFEIR.
                    Revenge! Revenge!

Exeunt.

Scene [iii.] Aquilina's house, the Greek Courtesan.

Enter Renault.

RENAULT.
Why was my choice ambition, the worst^d ground
A wretch can build on? It's indeed at distance
A good prospect, tempting to the view;
The height delights us, and the mountain top
Looks beautiful because it's nigh to heav'n,   5
But we ne'er think how sandy's the foundation,
What storm will batter and what tempest shake us!
—Who's there?

Enter Spinosa.

SPINOSA.
Renault, good morrow! for by this time
I think the scale of night has turned the balance   10
And weighs up morning. Has the clock struck
    twelve?
RENAULT.
Yes, clocks will go as they are set. But man,
Irregular man's ne'er constant, never certain.
I've spent at least three precious hours of darkness
In waiting dull attendance; 'tis the curse   15
Of diligent virtue to be mixed, like mine,
With giddy tempers, souls but half resolved.

SPINOSA.
Hell seize that soul amongst us it can frighten.
RENAULT.
What's then the cause that I am here alone?
Why are we not together?   20
Enter Eliot.
                                    Oh sir, welcome!
You are an Englishman: when treason's hatching
One might have thought you'd not have been
    behindhand.
In what whore's lap have you been lolling?
Give but an Englishman his whore and ease,   25
Beef and sea-coal fire,[17] he's yours forever.
ELIOT.
Frenchman, you are saucy.
RENAULT.
                                    How!

*Enter Bedamore the Ambassador, Theodore, Brainveil,
Durand, Brabe, Revellido, Mezzana, Ternon, Retrosi,
Conspirators.*

BEDAMORE.
                                    At difference? Fie,
Is this a time for quarrels?* Thieves and rogues   30
Fall out and brawl. Should men of your high calling,
Men separated by the choice of Providence
From the gross heap of mankind and set here
In this great assembly as in one great jewel
T'adorn the bravest purpose it e'er smiled on,   35
Should you like boys wrangle for trifles?
RENAULT.
                                    Boys!
BEDAMORE.
Renault, thy hand!
RENAULT.
                    I thought I'd given my heart
Long since to every man that mingles here   40
But grieve to find it trusted with such tempers
That can't forgive my froward age its weakness.
BEDAMORE.
Eliot, thou once hadst virtue. I have seen

---

17 sea-coal fire] In the seventeenth century, mineral coal
    mined in the north of England (mostly in the Newcas-
    tle area) was transported to London along the west coast
    by ship.

Thy stubborn temper bend with godlike goodness
Not half thus courted: 'tis thy nation's glory 45
To hug the foe that offers brave* alliance.
Once more embrace, my friends—we'll all
   embrace—
United thus, we are the mighty engine
Must twist this rooted empire from its basis!
Totters it not already? 50

ELIOT.
               Would it were tumbling.

BEDAMORE.
   Nay it shall down; this night we seal its ruin.

Enter Pierre.

Oh Pierre! thou art welcome!
Come to my breast, for by its hopes thou look'st
Lovelily dreadful, and the fate of Venice 55
Seems on thy sword already. Oh my Mars!
The poets that first feigned a God of War
Sure prophesied of thee.

PIERRE.
             Friends! was not Brutus
(I mean that Brutus who in open senate 60
Stabbed the first Caesar that usurped the world)
A gallant man?

RENAULT.
         Yes, and Catiline too,
Though story wrong his fame: for he conspired
To prop the reeling glory of his country; 65
His cause was good.

BEDAMORE.
         And ours as much above it
As Renault thou art superior to Cethegus[18]
Or Pierre to Cassius.

PIERRE.
          Then to what we aim at 70
When do we start? Or must we talk forever?

BEDAMORE.
No Pierre, the deed's near birth: Fate seems to
   have set
The business up and given it to our care.
I hope there's not a heart nor hand amongst us
But is firm and ready. 75

---

[18] Cethegus] a member of the Catiline conspiracy

ALL.
   All! We'll die with Bedamore.

BEDAMORE.
              Oh men,
Matchless as will your glory be hereafter.
The game is for a matchless prize, if won;
If lost, disgraceful ruin. 80

RENAULT.
            What can lose it?
The public stock's a beggar; one Venetian
Trusts not another. Look into their stores
Of general safety: empty magazines,[19]
A tattered fleet, a murmuring unpaid army, 85
Bankrupt nobility, a harassed commonalty,
A factious, giddy, and divided Senate
Is all the strength of Venice. Let's destroy it.
Let's fill their magazines with arms to awe them,
Man out their fleet, and make their trade maintain it; 90
Let loose the murmuring army on their masters
To pay themselves with plunder; lop their nobles
To the base roots whence most of 'em first sprung;
Enslave the rout, whom smarting will make humble;
Turn out their droning Senate; and possess 95
That seat of empire which our souls were framed for.

PIERRE.
Ten thousand men are armèd at your nod,
Commanded all by leaders fit to guide
A battle for the freedom of the world.
This wretched state has starved them in its service, 100
And by your bounty quickened,* they're resolved
To serve your glory and revenge their own!
They've all their different quarters in this city,
Watch for th'alarm, and grumble 'tis so tardy.

BEDAMORE.
I doubt not, friend, but thy unwearied diligence 105
Has still* kept waking, and it shall have ease.
After this night it is resolved we meet
No more till Venice own us for her lords.

PIERRE.
How lovely the Adriatic whore,
Dressed in her flames, will shine! Devouring flames! 110
Such as shall burn her to the watery bottom
And hiss in her foundation.

---

[19] magazines] buildings where ammunition is stored

BEDAMORE.

       Now if any
Amongst us that owns this glorious cause
Have friends or interest he'd wish to save,   115
Let it be told. The general doom is sealed,
But I'd forgo the hopes of a world's empire
Rather than wound the bowels of my friend.

PIERRE.

I must confess you there have touched my weakness:
I have a friend, hear it, such a friend   120
My heart was ne'er shut to him. Nay, I'll tell you,
He knows the very business of this hour,
But he rejoices in the cause and loves it.
We've changed a vow to live and die together,
And he's at hand to ratify it here.   125

RENAULT.

How! All betrayed?

PIERRE.

     No—I've dealt nobly with you;
I've brought my all into the public stock:
I had but one friend, and him I'll share amongst
 you!
Receive and cherish him, or if, when seen   130
And searched, you find him worthless, as my
 tongue
Has lodged this secret in his faithful breast,
To ease your fears I wear a dagger here
Shall rip it out again and give you rest.
—Come forth, thou only good I e'er could boast of. 135

Enter Jaffeir with a dagger.

BEDAMORE.

His presence bears the show of manly virtue.

JAFFEIR.

I know you'll wonder all that, thus uncalled,
I dare approach this place of fatal counsels.
But I am amongst you, and by Heaven it glads me,
To see so many virtues thus united   140
To restore justice and dethrone oppression.
Command this sword, if you would have it quiet,
Into this breast. But if you think it worthy
To cut the throats of reverend rogues in robes,
Send me into the cursed assembled Senate;   145
It shrinks not, though I meet a father there.
Would you behold this city flaming? Here's
A hand shall bear a lighted torch at noon

To the Arsenal[20] and set its gates on fire.

RENAULT.

You talk this well, sir.   150

JAFFEIR.

      Nay, by Heav'n I'll do this.
Come, come, I read distrust in all your faces.
You fear me a villain, and indeed it's odd
To hear a stranger talk thus at first meeting
Of matters that have been so well debated.   155
But I come ripe with wrongs as you with counsels.
I hate this Senate, am a foe to Venice,
A friend to none but men resolved like me
To push on mischief. Oh did you but know me,
I need not talk thus!   160

BEDAMORE.

     Pierre! I must embrace him.
My heart beats to this man as if it knew him.

RENAULT.

I never loved these huggers.

JAFFEIR.

     Still I see
The cause delights me not.[21] Your friends survey me 165
As I were dangerous, but I come armed
Against all doubts* and to your trust will give
A pledge worth more than all the world can pay for.
—My Belvidera! Ho! my Belvidera!

BEDAMORE.

What wonder next?   170

JAFFEIR.

     Let me entreat you,
As I have henceforth hopes to call ye friends,
That all but the ambassador, this
Grave guide of councils, with my friend that owns
 me,
Withdraw a while to spare a woman's blushes.   175

Exeunt all but Bedamore, Renault, Jaffeir, Pierre.

BEDAMORE.

Pierre, whither will this ceremony lead us?

JAFFEIR.

My Belvidera! Belvidera!

Enter Belvidera.

---

20 Arsenal] the state-run shipyard in Venice
21 delights me not] takes no delight in me

BELVIDERA.

             Who?

Who calls so loud at this late peaceful hour?

That voice was wont to come in gentler whispers   180

And fill my ears with the soft of breath of love.

Thou hourly image of my thoughts, where art
thou?

JAFFEIR.

Indeed, 'tis late.

BELVIDERA.

           Oh! I have slept, and dreamt,

And dreamt again. Where hast thou been, thou   185
loiterer?

Though my eyes closed, my arms have still* been
opened,

Stretched every way betwixt my broken slumbers

To search if thou wert come to crown my rest.

There's no repose without thee. Oh the day

Too soon will break and wake us to our sorrow.   190

Come, come to bed and bid thy cares good night.

JAFFEIR.

Oh Belvidera! we must change the scene

In which the past delights of life were tasted.

The poor sleep little: we must learn to watch

Our labors late, and early every morning,   195

Midst winter frosts, then clad and fed with sparing,

Rise to our toils and drudge away the day.

BELVIDERA.

Alas! where am I? Whither is't you lead me?

Methinks I read distraction in your face!

Something less gentle that the fate you tell me.   200

You shake and tremble too! Your blood runs cold!

Heavens guard my love and bless his heart with
patience.

JAFFEIR.

That I have patience, let our fate bear witness,

Who has ordained it so that thou and I

(Thou the divinest good man e'er possessed,   205

And I the wretched'st of the race of man)

This very hour, without one tear, must part.

BELVIDERA.

Part! Must we part? Oh! am I then forsaken?

Will my love cast me off? Have my misfortunes

Offended him so highly that he'll leave me?   210

Why drag you from me? Whither are you going?

My dear! my life! my love! [*Falling to the ground.*]

JAFFEIR.

Oh friends!

BELVIDERA.

        Speak to me.

JAFFEIR.

              Take her from my heart,   215

She'll gain such hold else I shall ne'er get loose.

I charge thee take her, but with tender'st care

Relieve her troubles and assuage her sorrows.

RENAULT.

Rise, madam, and command amongst your
servants!

JAFFEIR.

To you, sirs, and your honors, I bequeath her,   220

And with her this when I prove unworthy—

(*Gives a dagger.*)

You know the rest: then strike it to her heart

And tell her, he, who three whole happy years

Lay in her arms and each kind night repeated

The passionate vows of still increasing love,   225

Sent that reward for all her truth and sufferings.

BELVIDERA.

Nay, take my life, since he has sold it cheaply,

Or send me to some distant clime your slave,

But let it be far off, lest my complainings

Should reach his guilty ears and shake his peace.   230

JAFFEIR.

No Belvidera, I've contrived thy honor.

Trust to my faith, and be but Fortune kind

To me, as I'll preserve that faith unbroken

When next we meet, I'll lift thee to a height

Shall gather all the gazing world about thee   235

To wonder what strange virtue placed thee there.

But if we ne'er meet more—

BELVIDERA.

              Oh thou unkind one,

Never meet more! Have I deserved this from you?

Look on me, tell me, tell me, speak, thou dear   240
deceiver:

Why am I separated from thy love?

If I am false, accuse me, but if true,

Don't, prithee don't in poverty forsake me,

But pity the sad heart that's torn with parting.

Yet hear me! yet recall me—   245

Exeunt Renault, Bedamore, and Belvidera.

JAFFEIR.

                Oh my eyes!
Look not that way but turn your selves a while
Into my heart and be weaned altogether.
—My friend, where art thou?

PIERRE.

               Here, my honor's brother.   250

JAFFEIR.

  Is Belvidera gone?

PIERRE.

             Renault has led her
Back to her own apartment, but by Heav'n!
Thou must not see her more till our work's over.

JAFFEIR.

  No?   255

PIERRE.

        Not for your life.

JAFFEIR.

           Oh Pierre, wert thou but she,
How I could pull thee down into my heart,
Gaze on thee till my eye-strings cracked with love,
Till all my sinews with its fire extended   260
Fixed me upon the rack of ardent longing;
Then swelling, sighing, raging to be blest,
Come like a panting turtle* to thy breast,
On thy soft bosom, hovering, bill and play,
Confess the cause why last I fled away,   265
    Own 'twas a fault, but swear to give it o'er,
    And never follow false ambition more.

Exeunt.

      Act III. [Aquilina's house.]

Enter Aquilina and her Maid.

AQUILINA.

  Tell him I am gone to bed; tell him I am not at
home; tell him I've better company with me, or
anything; tell him in short I will not see him, the
eternal troublesome, vexatious fool. He's worse
company than an ignorant physician. I'll not be   5
disturbed at these unseasonable hours.

MAID.

  But madam! He's here already, just entered the
doors.

AQUILINA.

  Turn him out again, you unnecessary, useless,

giddy-brained ass! If he will not be gone, set the   10
house afire and burn us both. I had rather meet a
toad in my dish than that old hideous animal in
my chamber tonight.

Enter Antonio.

ANTONIO.

  Nacky, Nacky, Nacky—how dost do Nacky? Hurry
durry. I am come, little Nacky. Past eleven o'clock,   15
a late hour, time in all conscience to go to bed,
Nacky—Nacky did I say? Aye, Nacky, Aquilina,
lina, lina, quilina, quilina, quilina, Aquilina,
Naquilina, Naquilina, Acky, Acky, Nacky, Nacky,
Queen Nacky. Come let's to bed, you fubbs,* you   20
pug[22] you, you little puss—puree tuzzey—I am a
Senator.

AQUILINA.

  You are a fool, I am sure.

ANTONIO.

  May be so too, sweetheart. Never the worse senator
for all that. Come Nacky, Nacky, let's have a game   25
at rump, Nacky.

AQUILINA.

  You would do well, signor, to be troublesome here
no longer but leave me to myself, be sober, and
go home, sir.

ANTONIO.

  Home, Madonna!   30

AQUILINA.

  Aye, home, sir. Who am I?

ANTONIO.

  Madonna, as I take it you are my—you are—thou
art my little Nicky Nacky—that's all!

AQUILINA.

  I find you are resolved to be troublesome, and so
to make short of the matter in few words, I hate   35
you, detest you, loathe you; I am weary of you,
sick of you. Hang you, you are an old, silly,
impertinent, impotent, solicitous coxcomb, crazy
in your head and lazy in your body, love to be
meddling with everything, and if you had not   40
money, you are good for nothing.

ANTONIO.

  Good for nothing! Hurry durry, I'll try that

---

22 pug] a small animal

presently. Sixty-one years old [23] and good for
nothing? That's brave.* (*To the Maid.*) Come,
come, come, Mistress Fiddle-Faddle, turn you out 45
for a season. Go turn out I say, it is our will and
pleasure to be private some moments—out, out,
when you are bid to— (*Puts her out and locks the
door.*) Good for nothing, you say.

AQUILINA.

Why, what are you good for? 50

ANTONIO.

In the first place, madam, I am old, and
consequently very wise, very wise, Madonna, d'ye
mark that? In the second place, take notice, if you
please, that I am a senator and, when I think fit,
can make speeches, Madonna. Hurry durry, I can 55
make a speech in the Senate House now and then
would make your hair stand on end, Madonna.

AQUILINA.

What care I for your speeches in the Senate House?
If you would be silent here, I should thank you.

ANTONIO.

Why, I can make speeches to thee too, my lovely 60
Madonna; for example, "My cruel fair one, (*Takes
out a purse of gold, and at every pause shakes it.*)
since it is my fate that you should with your
servant angry prove, though late at night—I hope
'tis not too late with this to gain reception for my 65
love."—There's for thee, my little Nicky Nacky—
take it, here take it—I say take it, or I'll throw it
at your head—how now, rebel!

AQUILINA.

Truly, my illustrious senator, I must confess your
Honor is at present most profoundly eloquent 70
indeed.

ANTONIO.

Very well. Come, now let's sit down and think
upon't a little—come sit I say—sit down by me a
little, my Nicky Nacky, hah— (*Sits down.*) hurry
durry—good for nothing— 75

AQUILINA.

No sir, if you please, I can know my distance and
stand.

---

23 Sixty-one years old] this was also the age of the earl of
   Shaftesbury.

ANTONIO.

Stand? how, Nacky up and I down! Nay then let
me exclaim with the poet:

> Show me a case more pitiful who can: 80
> A standing woman and a falling man.

Hurry durry—not sit down—"see this ye Gods"—
You won't sit down?

AQUILINA.

No sir.

ANTONIO.

Then look you now, suppose me a bull, a Basan- 85
bull,[24] the bull of bulls, or any bull. Thus up I get
and with my brows thus bent—I broo, I say I broo,
I broo, I broo. You won't sit down will you?—I
broo— (*Bellows like a Bull, and drives her about.*])

AQUILINA.

Well sir, I must endure this. (*She sits down.*) Now 90
your Honor has been a bull, pray what beast will
your Worship please to be next?

ANTONIO.

Now I'll be a senator again and thy lover, little
Nicky Nacky! (*He sits by her.*) Ah toad, toad, toad,
toad! Spit in my face a little, Nacky—spit in my 95
face, prithee, spit in my face, never so little: spit
but a little bit—spit, spit, spit, spit, when you are
bid I say; do, prithee spit—now, now, now, spit.
What, you won't spit, will you? Then I'll be a dog.

AQUILINA.

A dog, my lord? 100

ANTONIO.

Aye, a dog—and I'll give thee this t'other purse to let
me be a dog—and to use me like a dog a little.
Hurry durry—I will—here 'tis. (*Gives the purse.*)

AQUILINA.

Well, with all my heart. But let me beseech your
Dogship to play your tricks over as fast as you can, 105
that you may come to stinking the sooner and be
turned out of doors as you deserve.

ANTONIO.

Aye, aye—no matter for that— (*He gets under the
table.*) That shan't move me. Now, bough waugh
waugh, bough waugh— (*Barks like a dog.*) 110

---

24 Basan-bull] See Psalms 22:12-13; "Many bulls have
   compassed me; strong bulls of Bashan have beset me
   round."

AQUILINA.

Hold, hold, hold, sir, I beseech you. What is't you
do? If curs bite they must be kicked, sir. Do you
see, kicked thus.

ANTONIO.

Aye with all my heart. Do kick, kick on, now I
am under the table, kick again—kick harder— 115
harder yet, bough waugh waugh, waugh, bough—
'Odd,* I'll have a snap at thy shins—bough waugh
wough, waugh, bough.—'Odd, she kicks bravely.*

AQUILINA.

Nay then, I'll go another way to work with you
and I think here's an instrument fit for the 120
purpose. (*Fetches a whip and bell.*) What, bite your
mistress, sirrah! Out, out of doors, you dog, to
kennel and be hanged—bite your mistress by the
legs, you rogue. (*She whips him.*)

ANTONIO.

Nay prithee Nacky, now thou art too loving. Hurry 125
durry, 'Odd, I'll be a dog no longer.

AQUILINA.

Nay, none of your fawning and grinning, but be
gone, or here's the discipline. What, bite your
mistress by the legs, you mongrel? Out of doors—
hout, hout, to kennel, sirrah! Go! 130

ANTONIO.

This is very barbarous usage, Nacky, very
barbarous. Look you, I will not go—I will not stir
from the door, that I resolve—hurry durry, what,
shut me out?

She whips him out.

AQUILINA.

Aye, and if you come here any more tonight I'll 135
have my footmen lug you, you cur. What, bite
your poor Mistress Nacky, sirrah!

Enter Maid.

MAID.

Heavens, madam! What's the matter?

He howls at the door like a dog.

AQUILINA.

Call my footmen hither presently.*

Enter two footmen.

MAID.

They are here already, madam, the house is all 140
alarmed with a strange noise that nobody knows
what to make of.

AQUILINA.

Go all of you and turn that troublesome beast in
the next room out of my house. If I ever see him
within these walls again without my leave for his 145
admittance, you sneaking rogues, I'll have you
poisoned all, poisoned, like rats. Every corner of
the house shall stink of one of you. Go, and learn
hereafter to know my pleasure.—So now for my
Pierre: 150

Thus when godlike lover was displeased,
We sacrifice our fool, and he's appeased.

Exeunt.

Scene ii. [Another room in Aquilina's house.]

Enter Belvidera.

BELVIDERA.

I'm sacrificed! I am sold! betrayed to shame!
Inevitable ruin has enclosed me!
No sooner was I to my bed repaired,
To weigh and (weeping) ponder my condition,
But the old, hoary wretch, to whose false care 5
My peace and honor was entrusted, came
(Like Tarquin) ghastly with infernal lust.
Oh thou Roman Lucrece!25
Thou couldst find friends to vindicate thy wrong;
I never had but one, and he's proved false: 10
He that should guard my virtue has betrayed it,
Left me! undone me! Oh that I could hate him!
Where shall I go! Oh whither, whither wander?

Enter Jaffeir.

JAFFEIR.

Can Belvidera want* a resting place

---

25 Tarquin … Lucrece] Sextus Tarquinius, son of the tyrannical last king of Rome, raped the chaste matron
Lucretia, who begged husband and father to revenge her
and committed suicide. Their vengeance led to the expulsion of the Tarquins from Rome and the establishment of republican government (see Lee, *Lucius Junius
Brutus,* above).

When these poor arms are open to receive her? 15
Oh 'tis in vain to struggle with desires
Strong as my love to thee, for every moment
I am from thy sight, the heart within my bosom
Moans like a tender infant in its cradle
Whose nurse had left it. Come, and with the 20
    songs
Of gentle love persuade it to its peace.

BELVIDERA.

I fear the stubborn wanderer will not own me,
'Tis grown a rebel to be ruled no longer,
Scorns the indulgent bosom that first lulled it,
And like a disobedient child, disdains 25
The soft authority of Belvidera.

JAFFEIR.

There was a time—

BELVIDERA.

        Yes, yes, there was a time
When Belvidera's tears, her cries, and sorrows
Were not despised; when if she chanced to sigh 30
Or look but sad, there was indeed a time
When Jaffeir would have ta'en her in his arms,
Eased her declining head upon his breast,
And never left her till he found the cause.
But let her now weep seas, 35
Cry till she rend the earth, sigh till she burst
Her heart asunder, still* he bears it all,
Deaf as the wind, and as the rocks unshaken.

JAFFEIR.

Have I been deaf? Am I that rock unmoved
Against whose root tears beat and sighs are sent 40
In vain? Have I beheld thy sorrows calmly?
Witness against me, heavens, have I done this?
Then bear me in a whirlwind back again,
And let that angry dear one ne'er forgive me!
Oh thou too rashly censur'st of my love! 45
Couldst thou but think how I have spent this
    night,
Dark and alone, no pillow to my head,
Rest in my eyes, nor quiet in my heart,
Thou wouldst not, Belvidera, sure thou wouldst
    not
Talk to me thus but, like a pitying angel 50
Spreading thy wings, come settle on my breast
And hatch warm comfort there ere sorrows freeze
    it.

BELVIDERA.

Why then, poor mourner, in what baleful corner
Hast thou been talking with that witch, the
    Night?
On what cold stone hast thou been stretched 55
    along,
Gathering the grumbling winds about thy head
To mix with theirs the accents of thy woes?
Oh now I find the cause my love forsakes me!
I am no longer fit to bear a share
In his concernments: my weak female virtue 60
Must not be trusted; 'tis too frail and tender.

JAFFEIR.

Oh Porcia! Porcia! What a soul was thine!

BELVIDERA.

That Porcia was a woman, and when Brutus,
Big with the fate of Rome (Heav'n guard thy
    safety!)
Concealed from her the labors of his mind, 65
She let him see her blood was great as his,
Flowed from a spring as noble and a heart
Fit to partake his troubles as his love.26
Fetch, fetch that dagger back, the dreadful dower
Thou gav'st last night in parting with me; strike it 70
Here to my heart; and as the blood flows from it,
Judge if it run not pure as Cato's daughter's.

JAFFEIR.

Thou art too good, and I indeed unworthy,
Unworthy so much virtue. Teach me how
I may deserve such matchless love as thine, 75
And see with what attention I'll obey thee.

BELVIDERA.

Do not despise me; that's the all I ask.

JAFFEIR.

Despise thee! Hear me—

BELVIDERA.

        Oh thy charming tongue
Is but too well acquainted with my weakness, 80
Knows, let it name but love, my melting heart
Dissolves within my breast, till with closed eyes
I reel into thy arms, and all's forgotten.

---

26 Porcia … love] Portia was the daughter of Cato Uticensis
    and wife of Marcus Junius Brutus. She cut her thigh to
    prove she could keep the secret of the conspiracy against
    Julius Caesar.

JAFFEIR.

What shall I do?

BELVIDERA.

              Tell me! Be just, and tell me   85

Why dwells that busy cloud upon thy face?

Why am I made a stranger? Why that sigh,

And I not know the cause? Why when the world

Is wrapped in rest, why chooses then my love

To wander up and down in horrid darkness,   90

Loathing his bed and these desiring arms?

Why are these eyes bloodshot with tedious watching?

Why starts he now and looks as if he wished

His fate were finished? Tell me, ease my fears,

Lest when we next time meet, I want* the power   95

To search into the sickness of thy mind

But talk as wildly then as thou look'st now.

JAFFEIR.

Oh Belvidera!

BELVIDERA.

Why was I last night delivered to a villain?

JAFFEIR.

Hah, a villain!   100

BELVIDERA.

Yes! To a villain! Why at such an hour

Meets that assembly all made up of wretches

That look as Hell had drawn 'em into league?

Why, I in this hand and in that a dagger,

Was I delivered with such dreadful ceremonies?   105

"To you, sirs, and to your honor I bequeath her,

And with her this. Whene'er I prove unworthy,

You know the rest, then strike it to her heart."

Oh! Why's that "rest" concealed from me? Must I

Be made the hostage of a hellish trust?   110

For such I know I am, that's all my value!

But by the love and loyalty I owe thee,

I'll free thee from the bondage of these slaves:

Straight to the Senate, tell 'em all I know,

All that I think, all that my fears inform me!   115

JAFFEIR.

Is this the Roman virtue! This the blood

That boasts its purity with Cato's daughter!

Would she have e'er betrayed her Brutus?

BELVIDERA.

              No:

For Brutus trusted her. Wert thou so kind,   120

What would not Belvidera suffer for thee?

JAFFEIR.

I shall undo myself and tell thee all.

BELVIDERA.

Look not upon me as I am a woman

But as a bone,* thy wife, thy friend, who long

Has had admission to thy heart and there   125

Studied the virtues of thy gallant nature:

Thy constancy, thy courage, and thy truth

Have been my daily lesson. I have learnt them,

Am bold as thou, can suffer or despise

The worst of fates for thee and with thee share them.   130

JAFFEIR.

Oh you divinest Powers! Look down and hear

My prayers! Instruct me to reward this virtue!

Yet think a little, ere thou tempt me further:

Think I have a tale to tell will shake thy nature,

Melt all this boasted constancy thou talkst of   135

Into vile tears and despicable sorrows.

Then if thou shouldst betray me!

BELVIDERA.

              Shall I swear?

JAFFEIR.

No, do not swear. I would not violate

Thy tender nature with so rude a bond.   140

But as thou hop'st to see me live my days

And love thee long, lock this within thy breast:

I've bound myself by all the strictest sacraments,

Divine and human—

BELVIDERA.

              Speak!   145

JAFFEIR.

              To kill thy father—

BELVIDERA.

My father!

JAFFEIR.

          Nay, the throats of the whole Senate

Shall bleed, my Belvidera. He amongst us

That spares his father, brother, or his friend   150

Is damned. How rich and beauteous will the face

Of Ruin look, when these wide streets run blood:

I and the glorious partners of my fortune

Shouting and striding o'er the prostrate dead,

Still to new waste, whilst thou, far off in safety   155

Smiling, shalt see the wonders of our daring

And, when night comes, with praise and love

   receive me.

BELVIDERA.

  Oh!

JAFFEIR.

  Have a care, and shrink not even in thought!

  For if thou dost—   160

BELVIDERA.

              I know it, thou wilt kill me.

  Do, strike thy sword into this bosom, lay me

  Dead on the earth, and then thou wilt be safe.

  Murder my father! Though his cruel nature

  Has persecuted me to my undoing,   165

  Driven me to basest wants,* can I behold him

  With smiles of vengeance, butchered in his age?

  The sacred fountain of my life destroyed?

  And canst thou shed the blood that gave me being?

  Nay, be a traitor too and sell thy country?   170

  Can thy great heart descend so vilely low,

  Mix with hired slaves, bravoes, and common

     stabbers,

  Nose-slitters, alley-lurking villains! join

  With such a crew, and take a ruffian's wages

  To cut the throats of wretches as they sleep?   175

JAFFEIR.

  Thou wrong'st me, Belvidera! I've engaged

  With men of souls, fit to reform the ills

  Of all mankind. There's not a heart amongst them

  But's as stout as death, yet honest as the nature

  Of man first made ere fraud and vice were fashions. 180

BELVIDERA.

  What's he, to whose curst hands last night thou

     gav'st me?

  Was that well done? Oh! I could tell a story

  Would rouse thy lion heart out of its den

  And make it rage with terrifying fury.

JAFFEIR.

  Speak on I charge thee!   185

BELVIDERA.

              Oh my love! If e'er

  Thy Belvidera's peace deserved thy care,

  Remove me from this place. Last night, last night!

JAFFEIR.

  Distract me not, but give me all the truth.

BELVIDERA.

  No sooner wert thou gone and I alone,   190

  Left in the pow'r of that old son of mischief;

  No sooner was I lain on my sad bed,

But that vile wretch approached me, loose,

    unbuttoned,

Ready for violation. Then my heart

Throbbed with its fears. Oh how I wept and sighed, 195

And shrunk and trembled, wished in vain for him

That should protect me. Thou, alas, wert gone!

JAFFEIR.

  Patience, sweet Heav'n, till I make vengeance sure.

BELVIDERA.

  He drew the hideous dagger forth thou gav'st him,

  And with upbraiding smiles he said, "Behold it,   200

  This is the pledge of a false husband's love."

  And in my arms then pressed and would have

    clasped me,

  But with my cries I scared his coward heart

  Till he withdrew and muttered vows to Hell.

  These are thy friends! With these thy life, thy   205

    honor,

  Thy love, all's staked, and all will go to ruin.

JAFFEIR.

  No more. I charge thee keep this secret close,

  Clear up thy sorrows, look as if thy wrongs

  Were all forgot, and treat him like a friend,

  As no complaint were made. No more, retire,   210

  Retire, my life, and doubt not of my honor:

  I'll heal its failings and deserve thy love.

BELVIDERA.

  Oh, should I part with thee, I fear thou wilt

  In anger leave me and return no more.

JAFFEIR.

  Return no more! I would not live without thee   215

  Another night to purchase the creation.

BELVIDERA.

  When shall we meet again?

JAFFEIR.

              Anon at twelve!

  I'll steal myself to thy expecting arms,

  Come like a traveled dove and bring thee peace.   220

BELVIDERA.

  Indeed?

JAFFEIR.

        By all our loves!

BELVIDERA.

              'Tis hard to part,

  But sure no falsehood e'er looked so fairly.

  Farewell—remember, twelve. (*Exit.*)   225

JAFFEIR.

                    Let Heav'n forget me
When I remember not thy truth, thy love.
How curst is my condition, tossed and jostled
From every corner, Fortune's common fool,
The jest of rogues, an instrumental ass   230
For villains to lay loads of shame upon
And drive about just for their ease and scorn.

Enter Pierre.

PIERRE.
    Jaffeir!

JAFFEIR.
            Who calls!

PIERRE.
                   A friend, that could have wished 235
T'have found thee otherwise employed. What,
   hunt
A wife on the dull foil?[27] Sure a staunch husband
Of all hounds is the dullest. Wilt thou never,
Never be weaned from caudles and confections?
What feminine tale hast thou been listening to 240
Of unaired shirts, catarrhs and toothache got
By thin-soled shoes? Damnation! that a fellow
Chosen to be a sharer in the destruction
Of a whole people should sneak thus in corners
To ease his fulsome lusts and fool his mind. 245

JAFFEIR.
May not a man then trifle out an hour
With a kind* woman and not wrong his calling?

PIERRE.
Not in a cause like ours.

JAFFEIR.
                 Then, friend, our cause
Is in a damned condition, for I'll tell thee, 250
That cankerworm called lechery has touched it,
'Tis tainted vilely. Wouldst thou think it, Renault
(That mortified, old, withered winter rogue)
Loves simple fornication like a priest:
I found him out for watering at my wife; 255
He visited her last night like a kind guardian.
Faith, she has some temptations, that's the truth
   on't.

PIERRE.
He durst not wrong his trust!

JAFFEIR.
                   'Twas something late, though,
To take the freedom of a lady's chamber. 260

PIERRE.
Was she in bed?

JAFFEIR.
             Yes faith, in virgin sheets
White as her bosom, Pierre, dished neatly up,
Might tempt a weaker appetite to taste.
Oh how the old fox stunk, I warrant thee, 265
When the rank fit was on him.

PIERRE.
                  Patience guide me!
He used no violence?

JAFFEIR.
               No, no! Out on't, violence!
Played with her neck, brushed her with his gray 270
   beard,
Struggled and toused, tickled her till she squeaked
   a little,
Maybe, or so—but not a jot of violence—

PIERRE.
Damn him.

JAFFEIR.
         Aye, so say I. But hush, no more on't.
All hitherto is well, and I believe 275
Myself no monster[28] yet, though no man knows
What fate he's born to! Sure 'tis near the hour
We all should meet for our concluding orders.
Will the Ambassador be here in person?

PIERRE.
No: he has sent commission to that villain, 280
Renault, to give the executing charge.
I'd have thee be a man if possible
And keep thy temper, for a brave* revenge
Ne'er comes too late.

JAFFEIR.
             Fear not, I am cool as patience: 285
Had he completed my dishonor, rather
Than hazard the success our hopes are ripe for,
I'd bear it all with mortifying virtue.

---

27 dull foil] "Foil" means track of a hunted animal (Ghosh)
    and "dull" an unimportant animal.

28 monster] cuckold

PIERRE.

   He's yonder coming this way through the hall;

   His thoughts seem full. 290

JAFFEIR.

               Prithee, retire and leave me

   With him alone. I'll put him to some trial,

   See how his rotten part will bear the touching.

PIERRE.

   Be careful then. (*Exit.*)

JAFFEIR.

              Nay never doubt, but trust me. 295

   —What, be a devil! Take a damning oath

   For shedding native blood! Can there be a sin

   In merciful repentance?—Oh this villain.

Enter Renault.

RENAULT.

   Perverse! and peevish! What a slave is man!

   To let his itching flesh thus get the better of him! 300

   Dispatch the tool her husband, that were well.

   —Who's there?

JAFFEIR.

         A man.

RENAULT.

             My friend, my near ally!

   The hostage of your faith, my beauteous charge, 305

   Is very well.

JAFFEIR.

         Sir, are you sure of that?

   Stands she in perfect health? Beats her pulse even?

   Neither too hot nor cold?

RENAULT.

           What means that question? 310

JAFFEIR.

   Oh, women have fantastic constitutions,

   Inconstant as their wishes, always wavering,

   And ne'er fixed. Was it not boldly done

   Even at the first sight to trust the thing I loved

   (A tempting treasure too!) with youth so fierce 315

   And vigorous as thine? But thou art honest.

RENAULT.

   Who dares accuse me?

JAFFEIR.

          Curst be him that doubts

   Thy virtue. I have tried it and declare,

   Were I to choose a guardian of my honor, 320

I'd put it into thy keeping: for I know thee.

RENAULT.

   Know me!

JAFFEIR.

        Aye, know thee: there's no falsehood in thee;

   Thou look'st just as thou art. Let us embrace.

   Now wouldst thou cut my throat or I cut thine? 325

RENAULT.

   You dare not do't.

JAFFEIR.

         You lie, sir.

RENAULT.

         How!

JAFFEIR.

         No more.

   'Tis a base world and must reform, that's all. 330

Enter Spinosa, Theodore, Eliot, Revellido, Durand,
Brainveil, and the rest of the conspirators.]

RENAULT.

   Spinosa! Theodore!

SPINOSA.

   The same.

RENAULT.

   You are welcome!

SPINOSA.

   You are trembling, sir.

RENAULT.

   'Tis a cold night indeed, I am aged, full of decay 335

   and natural infirmities. We shall be warm, my

   friend, I hope tomorrow.

Pierre reenters, [talks aside to Jaffeir].

PIERRE.

   'Twas not well done, thou shouldst have stroked

   him and not galled him.

JAFFEIR.

   Damn him, let him chew on't. 340

   —Heav'n! where am I? Beset with cursèd fiends

   That wait to damn me. What a devil's man

   When he forgets his nature? Hush my heart.

RENAULT.

   My friends, 'tis late. Are we assembled all? Where's

   Theodore?

THEODORE.

   At hand. 345

RENAULT.
  Spinosa.
SPINOSA.
  Here.
RENAULT.
  Brainveil.
BRAINVEIL.
  I am ready.
RENAULT.
  Durand and Brabe.
DURAND.   350
  Command us, we are both prepared!
RENAULT.
  Mezzana, Revellido, Ternon, Retrosi:
  Oh you are men I find
  Fit to behold your fate, and meet her summons,
  Tomorrow's rising sun must see you all   355
  Decked in your honors!—Are the soldiers ready?
ALL.
  All, all.
RENAULT.
  You, Durand, with your thousand must possess
  St. Marks. You, Captain, know your charge already:
  'Tis to secure the ducal palace. You,   360
  Brabe, with a hundred more must gain the Secque.
  With the like number Brainveil to the
    Procuralle.29
  Be all this done with the least tumult possible,
  Till in each place you post sufficient guards:
  Then sheath your swords in every breast you meet. 365
JAFFEIR. [Aside.]
  Oh reverend cruelty, damned bloody villain!
RENAULT.
  During this execution, Durand, you
  Must in the midst keep your battalia fast,
  And Theodore be sure to plant the canon
  That may command the streets, whilst Revellido, 370
  Mezzana, Ternon, and Retrosi guard you.
  This done, we'll give the general alarm,
  Apply petards, and force the Ars'nal gates;
  Then fire the city round in several places,

29 St. Marks … Procuralle] St. Marks, the central piazza
  in Venice; the Secque, the Mint; the Procuralle, the residence of the Procurators, most important men in Venice after the Doge

  Or with our canon (if it dare resist)   375
  Batter't to ruin. But above all I charge you:
  Shed blood enough, spare neither sex nor age,
  Name nor condition. If there live a senator
  After tomorrow, though the dullest rogue
  That e'er said nothing, we have lost our ends.   380
  If possible, let's kill the very name
  Of senator and bury it in blood.
JAFFEIR. [Aside.]
  Merciless, horrid slave! Aye, blood enough!
  Shed blood enough, old Renault: how thou
    charm'st me!
RENAULT.
  But one thing more, and then farewell till Fate 385
  Join us again or separate us ever:
  First, let's embrace, Heav'n knows who next shall
    thus
  Wing ye together. But let's all remember
  We wear no common30 cause upon our swords.
  Let each man think that on his single virtue   390
  Depends the good and fame of all the rest,
  Eternal honor or perpetual infamy.
  Let's remember, through what dreadful hazards
  Propitious Fortune hitherto has led us,
  How often on the brink of some discovery*   395
  Have we stood tottering and yet still kept our ground
  So well, the busiest searchers ne'er could follow
  Those subtle tracks which puzzled all suspicion.
  —You droop, sir.
JAFFEIR.
              No. With a most profound attention   400
  I've heard it all and wonder at thy virtue.
REANULT.
  Though there be yet few hours 'twixt them and ruin,
  Are not the Senate lulled in full security,
  Quiet and satisfied, as fools are always!
  Never did so profound repose forerun   405
  Calamity so great. Nay, our good fortune
  Has blinded the most piercing of mankind,
  Strengthened the fearfull'st, charmed the most
    suspectful,
  Confounded the most subtle: for we live,
  We live my friends, and quickly shall our life   410
  Prove fatal to these tyrants. Let's consider

30 common] vulgar

That we destroy oppression, avarice,
A people nursed up equally with vices
And loathsome lusts, which Nature most abhors
And such as without shame she cannot suffer.

JAFFEIR. [*Aside.*]
Oh Belvidera, take me to thy arms   415
And show me where's my peace, for I've lost it.
 (*Exit.*)

RENAULT.
Without the least remorse then let's resolve
With fire and sword t'exterminate these tyrants,
And when we shall behold those curst tribunals
Stained by the tears and sufferings of the   420
 innocent,
Burning with flames rather from Heav'n than ours,
The raging, furious, and unpitying soldier
Pulling his reeking dagger from the bosoms
Of gasping wretches, death in every quarter,
With all that sad Disorder can produce   425
To make a spectacle of horror, then,
Then let's call to mind, my dearest friends,
That there's nothing pure upon the earth,
That the most valued things have most alloys,
And that, in change of all those vile enormities   430
Under whose weight this wretched country labors,
The means are only in our hands to crown them.

PIERRE.
And may those Powers above that are propitious
To gallant minds record this cause and bless it.

RENAULT.
Thus happy, thus secure of all we wish for,   435
Should there, my friends, be found amongst us one
False to this glorious enterprise, what fate,
What vengeance were enough for such a villain?

ELIOT.
Death here without repentance, hell hereafter.

RENAULT.
Let that be my lot: If as here I stand   440
Lifted by fate amongst her darling sons,
Though I had one only brother, dear by all
The strictest ties of Nature; though one hour
Had given us birth, one fortune fed our wants,*
One only love, and that but of each other,   445
Still* filled our minds; could I have such a friend
Joined in this cause and had but ground to fear
Meant foul play, may this right hand drop from me

If I'd not hazard all my future peace
And stab him to the heart before you.   450
Who would not do less? Wouldst not thou Pierre
 the same?

PIERRE.
You have singled me, sir, out for this hard question,
As if 'twere started only for my sake!
Am I the thing you fear? Here, here's my bosom,
Search it with all your swords! Am I a traitor?   455

REANULT.
No. But I fear your late commended friend
Is little less. Come sirs, 'tis now no time
To trifle with our safety. Where's this Jaffeir?

SPINOSA.
He left the room just now in strange disorder.

REANULT.
Nay, there is danger in him. I observed him   460
During the time I took for explanation:
He was transported from most deep attention
To a confusion which he could not smother.
His looks grew full of sadness and surprise,
All which betrayed a wavering spirit in him,   465
That labored with relunctancy and sorrow.
What's requisite for safety must be done
With speedy execution; he remains
Yet in our power. I for my own part wear
A dagger.   470

PIERRE.
   Well.

RENAULT.
    And I could wish it—

PIERRE.
      Where?

RENAULT.
Buried in his heart.

PIERRE.
    Away! we're yet all friends.   475
No more of this, 'twill breed ill blood amongst us.

SPINOSA.
Let us all draw our swords and search the house,
Pull him from the dark hole where he sits brooding
O'er his cold fears, and each man kill his share of
 him.

PIERRE.
Who talks of killing? Who's he'll shed the blood   480
That's dear to me? Is't you? or you? or you, sir?

What, not one speak? How you stand gaping all
On your grave oracle, your wooden god there,
Yet not a word? (*To Renault.*) Then, sir, I'll tell
   you a secret:
Suspicion's but at best a coward's virtue!   485

RENAULT.

A coward— (*Handles his sword.*)

PIERRE.

              Put, put up thy sword, old man,
Thy hand shakes at it. Come, let's heal this breach,
I am too hot. We may yet live friends.

SPINOSA.

Till we are safe, our friendship cannot be so.   490

PIERRE.

Again! Who's that?

SPINOSA.

             'Twas I.

THEODORE.

                  And I.

REVELLIDO.

                     And I.

ELIOT.

And all.   495

RENAULT.

        Who are on my side?

SPINOSA.

                Every honest sword.
Let's die like men, and not be sold like slaves.

PIERRE.

One such word more, by Heav'n I'll to the Senate
And hang ye all like dogs in clusters.   500
Why peep your coward swords half out their shells?
Why do you not all brandish them like mine?
You fear to die and yet dare talk of killing?

RENAULT.

Go to the Senate and betray us, hasten,
Secure thy wretched life; we fear to die   505
Less than thou dar'st be honest.

PIERRE.

               That's rank falsehood,
Fear'st not thou death? Fie, there's a knavish itch
In that salt* blood, an utter foe to smarting.
Had Jaffeir's wife proved kind,* he had still been   510
   true.
Faugh—how that stinks!
Thou die! Thou kill my friend! or thou, or thou,

Or thou, with that lean, withered, wretched face!
Away! Disperse all to your several charges
And meet tomorrow where your honor calls you.
I'll bring that man whose blood you so much   515
   thirst for,
And you shall see him venture for you fairly.
Hence, hence, I say.

Exit Renault angrily.

SPINOSA.

I fear we have been to blame and done too much.

THEODORE.

'Twas too far urged against the man you loved.

REVILLIDO.

Here, take our swords and crush 'em with your feet.   520

SPINOSA.

Forgive us, gallant friend.

PIERRE.

             Nay, now y'have found
The way to melt and cast me as you will.
I'll fetch this friend and give him to your mercy.
Nay, he shall die if you will take him from me;   525
For your repose I'll quit my heart's jewel
But would not have him torn away by villains
And spiteful villainy.

SPINOSA.

            No. May you both
Forever live and fill the world with fame!   530

PIERRE.

Now you are too kind. Whence rose all this discord?
Oh what a dangerous precipice have we 'scaped!
How near a fall was all we had long been building!
What an eternal blot had stained our glories,
If one the bravest and the best of men   535
Had fallen a sacrifice to rash suspicion,
Butchered by those whose cause he came to cherish!
Oh could you know him all as I have known him,
How good he is, how just, how true, how brave,
You would not leave this place till you had seen him,   540
Humbled your selves before him, kissed his feet,
And gained remission for the worst of follies.
   Come, but tomorrow all your doubts shall end
   And to your loves me better recommend,
   That I've preserved your fame and saved my   545
   friend.

Exeunt omnes.

Act IV, [scene i.]

Enter Jaffeir and Belvidera.

JAFFEIR.
Where dost thou lead me? Every step I move,
Methinks I tread upon some mangled limb
Of a racked friend. Oh my dear charming ruin!
Where are we wand'ring?

BELVIDERA.
                              To eternal honor,   5
To do a deed shall chronicle thy name
Among the glorious legends of those few
That have saved sinking nations. Thy renown
Shall be the future song of all the virgins,
Who by thy piety have been preserved   10
From horrid violation; every street
Shall be adorned with statues to thy honor
And at thy feet this great inscription written,
"Remember him that propped the fall of Venice."

JAFFEIR.
Rather, remember him, who after all   15
The sacred bond of oaths and holier friendship
In fond* compassion to a woman's tears
Forgot his manhood, virtue, truth, and honor,
To sacrifice the bosom that relieved him.
Why wilt thou damn me?   20

BELVIDERA.
                              Oh inconstant man!
How will you promise, how will you deceive!
Do, return back, replace me in my bondage,
Tell all thy friends how dangerously thou lov'st me,
And let thy dagger do its bloody office.   25
Oh that kind dagger, Jaffeir, how 'twill look
Stuck through my heart, drenched in my blood to
     th'hilts!
Whilst these poor dying eyes shall with their tears
No more torment thee; then thou wilt be free.
Or if thou think'st it nobler, let me live   30
Till I am a victim to the hateful lust
Of that infernal devil, that old fiend
That's damned himself and would undo mankind.
Last night, my love!

JAFFEIR.
                              Name, name it not again.   35
It shows a beastly image to my fancy
Will wake me into madness. Oh the villain!

That durst approach such purity as thine
On terms so vile. Destruction, swift destruction
Fall on my coward head and make my name   40
The common scorn of fools if I forgive him.
If I forgive him? if I not revenge
With utmost rage and most unstaying fury
Thy sufferings, thou dear darling of my life, love.

BELVIDERA.
Delay no longer then, but to the Senate   45
And tell the dismal'st story e'er was uttered,
Tell 'em what bloodshed, rapines, desolations
Have been prepared, how near's the fatal hour!
Save thy poor country, save the reverend blood
Of all its nobles, which tomorrow's dawn   50
Must else see shed. Save the poor, tender lives
Of those little infants which the swords
Of murtherers are whetting for this moment.
Think thou already hear'st their dying screams;
Think that thou seest their sad distracted mothers   55
Kneeling before thy feet and begging pity
With torn disheveled hair and streaming eyes,
Their naked, mangled breasts besmeared with blood
And even the milk with which their fondled babes
Softly they hushed dropping in anguish from 'em.   60
Think thou seest this, and then consult thy heart.

JAFFEIR.
Oh!

BELVIDERA.
          Think too, if thou lose this present minute,
What miseries the next day bring upon thee.
Imagine all the horrors of that night: 65
Murther and rapine, waste and desolation
Confusedly ranging. Think what then may prove
My lot! The ravisher may then come safe
And midst the terror of the public ruin
Do a damned deed, perhaps too lay a train   70
May catch thy life. Then where will be revenge,
The dear revenge that's due to such a wrong?

JAFFEIR.
By all Heaven's powers, prophetic truth dwells in
     thee,
For every word thou speak'st strikes through my heart
Like a new light and shows it how't has wandered.   75
Just what th'hast made me, take me, Belvidera,
And lead me to the place where I'm to say
This bitter lesson, where I must betray

My truth, my virtue, constancy, and friends.
Must I betray my friends? Ah take me quickly, 80
Secure me well before that thought's renewed.
If I relapse once more, all's lost forever.
BELVIDERA.
Hast thou a friend more dear than Belvidera?
JAFFEIR.
No, th'art my soul itself, wealth, friendship, honor;
All present joys and earnest of all future 85
Are summed in thee. Methinks when in thy arms
Thus leaning on thy breast, one minute's more
Than a long thousand years of vulgar hours.
Why was such happiness not given me pure?
Why dashed with cruel wrongs and bitter wantings? 90
Come, lead me forward now like a tame lamb
To sacrifice: thus in his fatal garlands,
Decked fine and pleased, the wanton skips and plays,
    Trots by the enticing, flattering priestess' side
    And, much transported with his little pride, 95
    Forgets his dear companions of the plain,
    Till by her, bound, he's on the altar lain
Yet then too hardly bleats, such pleasure's in the pain.

Enter officer and six guards.

OFFICER.
Stand, who goes there?
BELVIDERA.
Friends. 100
JAFFEIR.
Friends, Belvidera! hide me from my friends.
By Heaven, I'd rather see the face of Hell
Than meet the man I love.
OFFICER.
But what friends are you?
BELVIDERA.
Friends to the Senate and the state of Venice. 105
OFFICER.
My orders are to seize on all I find
At this late hour and bring 'em to the Council,
Who now are sitting.
JAFFEIR.
                     Sir, you shall be obeyed.
Hold, brutes, stand off, none of your paws upon me. 110
—Now the lot's cast, and Fate do what thou wilt.

Exeunt guarded.

Scene [ii]. The Senate House.

*Where appear sitting, the Duke of Venice, Priuli,
Antonio, and eight other senators.*

DUKE.
Antony, Priuli, Senators of Venice,
Speak. Why are we assembled here this night?
What have you to inform us of concerns
The state of Venice' honor or its safety?
PRIULI.
Could words express the story I have to tell you, 5
Fathers, these tears were useless, these sad tears
That fall from my old eyes. But there is cause
We all should weep, tear off these purple robes,
And wrap our selves in sackcloth, sitting down
On the sad earth and cry aloud to Heaven. 10
Heaven knows if yet there be an hour to come
Ere Venice be no more!
ALL SENATORS.
                      How!
PRIULI.
                            Nay, we stand
Upon the very brink of gaping ruin: 15
Within this city's formed a dark conspiracy
To massacre us all, our wives, and children,
Kindred and friends, our palaces and temples
To lay in ashes. Nay, the hour, too, fixed;
The swords, for aught I know, drawn even this 20
    moment
And the wild waste begun. From unknown hands
I had this warning. But if we are men,
Let's not be tamely butchered but do something
That may inform the world in after ages,
Our virtue was not ruined though we were. 25
[VOICE.] (*Without.*)
Room, room, make room for some prisoners.
SENATOR.
Let's raise the city.

Enter officer and guard.

PRIULI.
                     Speak there, what disturbance?
OFFICER.
Two prisoners have the guard seized in the streets,
Who say they come to inform this reverend Senate 30
About the present danger.

Enter Jaffeir and Belvidera guarded.

ALL.
                              Give 'em entrance—

[DUKE.]
    Well, who are you?

JAFFEIR.
                    A villain.

ANTONIO.
                              Short and pithy.   35
    The man speaks well.

JAFFEIR.
                    Would every man that hears me
    Would deal so honestly and own his title.

DUKE.
    'Tis rumored that a plot has been contrived
    Against this state, that you have a share in't too.   40
    If you are a villain, to redeem your honor,
    Unfold the truth and be restored with mercy.

JAFFEIR.
    Think not that I to save my life come hither,
    I know its value better, but in pity
    To all those wretches whose unhappy dooms   45
    Are fixed and sealed. You see me here before you
    The sworn and covenanted foe of Venice.
    But use me as my dealings may deserve,
    And I may prove a friend.

DUKE.
                              The slave capitulates,   50
    Give him the tortures.

JAFFEIR.
                    That you dare not do,
    Your fears won't let you nor the longing itch
    To hear a story which you dread the truth of:
    Truth which^e the fear of smart shall ne'er get from   55
      me.
    Cowards are scared with theatenings; boys are
      whipped
    Into confessions; but a steady mind
    Acts of itself, ne'er asks the body counsel.
    "Give him the tortures"? Name but such a thing
    Again, by Heaven I'll shut these lips forever.   60
    Not all your racks, your engines, or your wheels
    Shall force a groan away that you may guess at.

ANTONIO.
    A bloody minded fellow I'll warrant, a damned
      bloody minded fellow.

DUKE.
    Name your conditions.

JAFFEIR.
                    For my self full pardon,   65
    Besides the lives of two and twenty friends
      (*Delivers a list.*)
    Whose names are here enrolled. Nay, let their crimes
    Be ne'er so monstrous, I must have the oaths
    And sacred promise of this reverend Council,
    That in a full assembly of the Senate   70
    The thing I ask be ratified. Swear this,
    And I'll unfold the secrets of your danger.

ALL.
    We'll swear.

DUKE.
                    Propose the oath.

JAFFEIR.
                              By all the hopes   75
    Ye have of peace and happiness hereafter,
    Swear—

ALL.
                    We all swear.

JAFFEIR.
                    To grant me what I've asked,
    Ye swear.   80

ALL.
                    We swear.

JAFFEIR.
                    And as ye keep the oath,
    May you and your posterity be blest
    Or curst forever.

ALL.
                    Else be curst forever.   85

JAFFEIR.
    Then here's the list, and with't the full disclose
      (*Delivers another paper.*)
    Of all that threatens you.—Now Fate, thou hast
      caught me.

ANTONIO.
    Why, what a dreadful catalogue of cutthroats is
    here! I'll warrant you not one of these fellows but
    has a face like a lion. I dare not so much as read   90
    their names over.

DUKE.
    Give orders that all diligent search be made
    To seize these men. Their characters* are public.

The paper intimates their rendezvous
To be at the house of a famed Grecian courtesan   95
Called Aquilina: see that place secured.
ANTONIO. [Aside.]
What, my Nicky Nacky, hurry durry, Nicky Nacky
in the plot? I'll make a speech.—Most noble
Senators,
What headlong apprehension drives you on,
Right noble, wise, and truly solid Senators,   100
To violate the laws and right of nations?
The lady is a lady of renown.
'Tis true, she holds a house of fair reception,
And though I say't myself, as many more
Can say as well as I.   105
SENATOR.
                    My lord, long speeches
Are frivolous here when dangers are so near us.
We all well know your interest in that lady,
The world talks loud on't.
ANTONIO.
                              Verily I have done,   110
I say no more.
DUKE.
                    But since he has declared
Himself concerned, pray Captain, take great caution
To treat the fair one as becomes her character,
And let her bedchamber be searched with decency.   115
You, Jaffeir, must with patience bear till morning
To be our prisoner.
JAFFEIR.
                    Would the chains of death
Had bound me fast e'er I had known this minute.
I've done a deed will make my story hereafter   120
Quoted in competition with all ill ones.
The history of my wickedness shall run
Down through the low traditions of the vulgar
And boys be taught[f] to tell the tale of Jaffeir.
DUKE.
Captain, withdraw your prisoner.   125
JAFFEIR.
                              Sir, if possible,
Lead me where my own thoughts themselves may
     lose me,
Where I may doze out what I've left of life,
Forget myself and this day's guilt and falsehood.
Cruel remembrance, how shall I appease thee!   130
     (Exit guarded.)

[VOICE.] (Without.)
More traitors, room, room, make room there.
DUKE.
                              How's this? Guards,
Where are our guards? Shut up the gates, the treason's
Already at our doors.

Enter Officer.

OFFICER.
                    My lords, more traitors,   135
Seized in the very act of consultation,
Furnished with arms and instruments of mischief.
Bring in the prisoners.

Enter Pierre, Renault, Theodore, Elliot, Revellido and
other conspirators, in fetters, guarded.

PIERRE.
                    You, my lords and fathers
(As you are pleased to call your selves) of Venice,   140
If you sit here to guide the course of justice,
Why these disgraceful chains upon the limbs
That have so often labored in your service?
Are these the wreaths of triumphs ye bestow
On those that bring you conquests home and   145
     honors?
DUKE.
Go on, you shall be heard, sir.
ANTONIO.
                    And be hanged too, I hope.
PIERRE.
Are these the trophies I've deserved for fighting
Your battles with confederated powers,
When winds and seas conspired to overthrow you   150
And brought the fleets of Spain to your own harbors?
When you, great Duke, shrunk trembling in your
     palace
And saw your wife, th'Adriatic, ploughed
Like a lewd whore by bolder prows than yours,
Stepped not I forth and taught your loose Venetians   155
The task of honor and the way to greatness,
Raised you from your capitulating fears
To stipulate the terms of sued for peace,
And this my recompense? If I am a traitor,
Produce my charge, or show the wretch that's base   160
     enough
And brave enough to tell me I am a traitor.

DUKE.

    Know you one Jaffeir?

All the conspirators murmur.

PIERRE.

                      Yes, and know his virtue.

    His justice, truth, his general worth, and sufferings

    From a hard father taught me first to love him.   165

DUKE.

    See him brought forth.

Enter Jaffeir guarded.

PIERRE.

                 My friend too bound? Nay then,

    Our fate has conquered us, and we must fall.

    Why droops the man whose welfare's so much mine

    They're but one thing? These reverend tyrants, Jaffeir,   170

    Call us all traitors. Art thou one, my brother?

JAFFEIR.

    To thee I am the falsest, veriest* slave

    That e'er betrayed a generous trusting friend

    And gave up honor to be sure of ruin:

    All our fair hopes which morning was to have   175
      crowned

    Has this curst tongue o'erthrown.

PIERRE.

                    So, then all's over:

    Venice has lost her freedom, I my life.

    No more, farewell.

DUKE.

               Say, will you make confession   180

    Of your vile deeds and trust the Senate's mercy?

PIERRE.

    Curst be your Senate, curst your constitution.

    The curse of growing factions and division

    Still* vex your councils, shake your public safety,

    And make the robes of government you wear   185

    Hateful to you as these base chains to me.

DUKE.

    Pardon or death?

PIERRE.

            Death, honorable death.

REANULT.

    Death's the best thing we ask or you can give.

ALL CONSPIRATORS.

    No shameful bonds, but honorable death.   190

DUKE.

    Break up the Council. Captain, guard your prisoners.

    Jaffeir, y'are free, but these must wait for judgment.

Exeunt all the Senators [and Belvidera].

PIERRE.

    Come, where's my dungeon? Lead me to my straw:

    It will not be the first time I've lodged hard

    To do your Senate service.   195

JAFFEIR.

                  Hold one moment.

PIERRE.

    Who's he disputes the judgment of the Senate?

    Presumptuous rebel—on— (*Strikes Jaffeir.*)

JAFFEIR.

               By Heaven you stir not.

    I must be heard, I must have leave to speak: 200

    Thou hast disgraced me, Pierre, by a vile blow.

    Had not a dagger done thee nobler justice?

    But use me as thou wilt, thou canst not wrong me,

    For I am fallen beneath the basest injuries.

    Yet look upon me with an eye of mercy,   205

    With pity and with charity behold me;

    Shut not thy heart against a friend's repentance,

    But as there dwells a godlike nature in thee,

    Listen with mildness to my supplications.

PIERRE.

    What whining monk art thou? What holy cheat   210

    That wouldst encroach upon my credulous ears

    And cant'st thus vilely? Hence. I know thee not.

    Dissemble and be nasty. Leave me, hypocrite.

JAFFEIR.

    Not know me, Pierre?

PIERRE.

             No, know thee not. What art thou?   215

JAFFEIR.

    Jaffeir, thy friend, thy once loved, valued friend,

    Though now deservedly scorned and used most
      hardly.

PIERRE.

    Thou Jaffeir! Thou my once loved, valued friend!

    By Heavens thou ly'st: the man so called, my friend,

    Was generous, honest, faithful, just, and valiant,   220

    Noble in mind, and in his person lovely,

    Dear to my eyes and tender to my heart,

    But thou a wretched, base, false, worthless coward,

Poor even in soul, and loathsome in thy aspect.
All eyes must shun thee, and all hearts detest thee.   225
Prithee avoid, nor longer cling thus round me
Like something baneful that my nature's chilled at.

JAFFEIR.
I have not wronged thee, by these tears I have not,
But still am honest, true, and, hope too, valiant,
My mind still full of thee, therefore still noble.   230
Let not thy eyes then shun me nor thy heart
Detest me utterly. Oh look upon me,
Look back and see my sad, sincere submission!
How my heart swells as even 'twould burst my
    bosom,
Fond of its gaol and laboring to be at thee!   235
What shall I do? What say to make thee hear me?

PIERRE.
Hast thou not wronged me? Dar'st thou call
    thyself
Jaffeir, that once loved, valued friend of mine,
And swear thou hast not wronged me? Whence
    these chains?
Whence the vile death, which I may meet this   240
    moment?
Whence this dishonor, but from thee, thou false one?

JAFFEIR.
All's true, yet grant one thing, and I've done asking.

PIERRE.
What's that?

JAFFEIR.
                    To take thy life on such conditions
The Council have proposed. Thou and thy friends   245
May yet live long and to be better treated.

PIERRE.
Life! Ask my life! Confess! Record my self
A villain for the privilege to breathe
And carry up and down this cursèd city
A discontented and repining spirit,   250
Burdensome to itself a few years longer,
To lose, it may be, at last in a lewd quarrel*
For some new friend, treacherous and false as
    thou art!
No, this vile world and I have long been jangling
And cannot part on better terms than now   255
When only men like thee are fit to live in't.

JAFFEIR.
By all that's just—

PIERRE.
                    Swear by some other powers,
For thou has broke that sacred oath too lately.

JAFFEIR.
Then by that hell I merit, I'll not leave thee   260
Till to thyself, at least, thou'rt reconciled,
However thy resentments deal with me.

PIERRE.
Not leave me!

JAFFEIR.
                    No, thou shalt not force me from thee.
Use me reproachfully and like a slave,   265
Tread on me, buffet me, heap wrongs on wrongs
On my poor head: I'll bear it all with patience,
Shall weary out thy most unfriendly cruelty,
Lie at thy feet and kiss 'em though they spurn me,
Till, wounded by my sufferings, thou relent   270
And raise me to thy arms with dear forgiveness.

PIERRE.
Art thou not—

JAFFEIR.
                    What?

PIERRE.
                    A traitor?

JAFFEIR.
                                        Yes.   275

PIERRE.
                    A villain?

JAFFEIR.
Granted.

PIERRE.
                    A coward, a most scandalous coward,
Spiritless, void of honor, one who has sold
Thy everlasting fame for shameless life?   280

JAFFEIR.
All, all, and more, much more: my faults are
    numberless.

PIERRE.
And wouldst thou have me live on terms like thine?
Base as thou art false—

JAFFEIR.
                    No, 'tis to me that's granted;
The safety of thy life was all I aimed at   285
In recompense for faith and trust so broken.

PIERRE.
I scorn it more because preserved by thee,

And as when first my foolish heart took pity
On thy misfortunes, sought thee in thy miseries,
Relieved thy wants,* and raised thee from thy state 290
Of wretchedness in which thy fate had plunged thee
To rank thee in my list of noble friends,
All I received in surety for thy truth
Were unregarded oaths. And this, this dagger,
Given with a worthless pledge, thou since hast stol'n; 295
So I restore it back to thee again,
Swearing by all those powers which thou hast
    violated
Never from this curst hour to hold communion,
Friendship, or interest with thee, though our years
Were to exceed those limited the world. 300
Take it—farewell—for now I owe thee nothing.

JAFFEIR.
Say thou wilt live then.

PIERRE.
                        For my life, dispose it
Just as thou wilt, because 'tis what I'm tired with.

JAFFEIR.
Oh, Pierre! 305

PIERRE.
        No more.

JAFFEIR.
            My eyes won't lose the sight of thee
But languish after thine and ache with gazing.

PIERRE.
Leave me—Nay, then thus, thus, I throw thee
    from me.
And curses, great as is thy falsehood, catch thee. 310
    [Exit.]

JAFFEIR.
Amen.—He's gone, my father, friend, preserver,
And here's the portion he has left me, (Holds the
    dagger up.)
This dagger, well remembered. With this dagger
I gave a solemn vow of dire importance,
Parted with this and Belvidera together. 315
Have a care, mem'ry, drive that thought no farther—
No, I'll esteem it as a friend's last legacy,
Treasure it up in this wretched bosom,
Where it may grow acquainted with my heart,
That when they meet, they start not from each other. 320
So, now for thinking: a blow, called traitor, villain,
Coward, dishonorable coward, faugh!

Oh for a long, sound sleep and so forget it!
Down, busy devil—

Enter Belvidera.

BELVIDERA.
                    Whither shall I fly? 325
Where hide me and my miseries together?
Where's now the Roman constancy I boasted?
Sunk into trembling fears and desperation!
Not daring now to look up to that dear face
Which used to smile even on my faults, but down 330
Bending these miserable eyes to earth,
Must move in penance and implore much mercy.

JAFFEIR.
Mercy! Kind Heaven has surely endless stores
Hoarded for thee of blessings yet untasted.
Let wretches loaded hard with guilt as I am 335
Bow with the weight and groan beneath the burden,
Creep with a remnant of that strength they've left
Before the footstool of that Heaven they've injured.
Oh Belvidera! I'm the wretchedest creature
E'er crawled on earth. Now if thou hast virtue, 340
    help me,
Take me into thy arms and speak the words of peace
To my divided soul that wars within me
And raises every sense to my confusion.
By Heav'n, I am tottering on the very brink
Of peace, and thou art all the hold I've left. 345

BELVIDERA.
Alas! I know thy sorrows are most mighty;
I know th'hast cause to mourn: to mourn, my
    Jaffeir,
With endless cries and never ceasing wailings.
Th'hast lost—

JAFFEIR.
            Oh I have lost what can't be counted. 350
My friend too, Belvidera, that dear friend,
Who, next to thee, was all my health rejoiced in,
Has used me like a slave, shamefully used me.
'Twould break thy pitying heart to hear the story.
What shall I do? Resentment, indignation, 355
Love, pity, fear, and mem'ry how I've wronged him
Distract my quiet with the very thought on't
And tear my heart to pieces in my bosom.

BELVIDERA.
What has he done?

JAFFEIR.

            Thou'dst hate me, should I tell thee.   360

BELVIDERA.

  Why?

JAFFEIR.

      Oh he has used me—yet by Heaven I bear it—
He has used me, Belvidera—but first swear
That, when I've told thee, thou'lt not loath me
    utterly,
Though vilest blots and stains appear upon me,   365
But still at least with charitable goodness
Be near me in the pangs of my affliction,
Not scorn me, Belvidera, as he has done.

BELVIDERA.

  Have I then e'er been false that now I am doubted?
Speak, what's the cause I am grown into distrust,   370
Why thought unfit to hear my love's complainings?

JAFFEIR.

  Oh!

BELVIDERA.

  Tell me.

JAFFEIR.

       Bear my failings, for they are many,
Oh my dear angel! In that friend I've lost   375
All my soul's peace, for every thought of him
Strikes my sense hard and deads it in my brains.
Wouldst thou believe it?

BELVIDERA.

           Speak.

JAFFEIR.

             Before we parted,   380
Ere yet his guards had led him to his prison,
Full of severest sorrows for his suff'rings,
With eyes o'erflowing and a bleeding heart,
Humbling myself almost beneath my nature,
As at his feet I kneeled and sued for mercy,   385
Forgetting all our friendship, all the dearness
In which we've lived so many years together,
With a reproachful hand, he dashed a blow;
He struck me, Belvidera, by Heaven, he struck me,
Buffeted, called me traitor, villain, coward.   390
Am I a coward? Am I a villain? Tell me:
Th'art the best judge and mad'st me, if I am so.
Damnation. Coward!

BELVIDERA.

       Oh! forgive him, Jaffeir.

And if his sufferings wound thy heart already,   395
What will they do tomorrow?

JAFFEIR.

             Hah!

BELVIDERA.

               Tomorrow,
When thou shalt see him stretched in all the agonies
Of a tormenting and a shameful death,   400
His bleeding bowels and his broken limbs
Insulted o'er by a vile, butchering villain.
What will thy heart do then? Oh sure 'twill stream
Like my eyes now.

JAFFEIR.

          What means thy dreadful story?   405
Death, and tomorrow? broken limbs and bowels?
Insulted o'er by a vile, butchering villain?
By all my fears I shall start out to madness
With barely guessing if the truth's hid longer.

BELVIDERA.

  The faithless senators, 'tis they've decreed it: 410
They say according to our friends' request
They shall have death and not ignoble bondage,
Declare their promised mercy all as forfeited,
False to their oaths, and deaf to intercession:
Warrants are passed for public death tomorrow.   415

JAFFEIR.

  Death! Doomed to die! Condemned unheard!
    Unpleaded!

BELVIDERA.

  Nay, cruelest racks and torments are preparing
To force confessions from their dying pangs.
Oh do not look so terribly upon me:
How your lips shake and all your face disordered!   420
What means my love?

JAFFEIR.

  Leave me, I charge thee leave me—strong
    temptations
Wake in my heart.

BELVIDERA.

         For what?

JAFFEIR.

           No more, but leave me.   425

BELVIDERA.

  Why?

JAFFEIR.

      Oh! by Heaven I love thee with that fondness

I would not have thee stay a moment longer
Near these curst hands: Are they not cold upon thee?

BELVIDERA.

No, everlasting comfort's in thy arms;   430

[Jaffeir] pulls the dagger half out of his bosom and puts it back again.

To lean thus on thy breast is softer ease
Than downy pillows decked with leaves of roses.

JAFFEIR.

Alas thou thinkest not of the thorns 'tis filled with.
Fly ere they gall^h thee. There's a lurking serpent
Ready to leap and sting thee to thy heart: 435
Art thou not terrified?

BELVIDERA.

                                No.

JAFFEIR.

                                        Call to mind
What thou hast done and whither thou hast
    brought me.

BELVIDERA.

    Hah!   440

JAFFEIR.

Where's my friend? my friend, thou smiling mischief?
Nay, shrink not, now 'tis too late, thou shouldst
    have fled
When thy guilt first had cause, for dire Revenge
Is up and raging for my friend. He groans,
Hark how he groans, his screams are in my ears   445
Already. See, they've fixed him on the wheel,
And now they tear him— Murther! Perjured Senate!
Murther! Oh hark thee, traitress, thou hast done this.
Thanks to thy tears and false persuading love—
    (*Fumbling for his dagger.*)
How her eyes speak! Oh thou bewitching creature!   450
Madness cannot hurt thee. Come, thou little
    trembler,
Creep even into my heart and there lie safe;
'Tis thy own citadel— Hah! yet stand off,
Heaven must have justice, and my broken vows
Will sink me else beneath its reaching mercy.   455
I'll wink and then 'tis done—

BELVIDERA.

                                What means the lord
Of me, my life and love? What's in thy bosom
Thou grasp'st at so? Nay, why am I thus treated?

[He] draws the dagger, offers* to stab her.

What wilt thou do? Ah, do not kill me, Jaffeir,   460
Pity these panting breasts and trembling limbs,
That used to clasp thee when thy looks were milder,
That yet hang heavy on my unpurged soul,
And plunge it not into eternal darkness.

JAFFEIR.

No Belvidera, when we parted last   465
I gave this dagger with thee as in trust
To be thy portion if I e'er proved false.
On such condition was my truth believed,
But now 'tis forfeited and must be paid for.
    (*Offers* to stab her, again.*

BELVIDERA. (*Kneeling.*)

Oh, mercy!   470

JAFFEIR.

                Nay, no struggling.

BELVIDERA.

                                Now then kill me,
    (*Leaps upon his neck and kisses him.*)
While thus I cling about thy cruel neck,
Kiss thy revengeful lips and die in joys
Greater than any I can guess hereafter.   475

JAFFEIR.

I am, I am a coward: witness't, heaven,
Witness it, earth, and every being witness.
'Tis but one blow yet— By immortal love,
I cannot longer bear a thought to harm thee,
    (*Throws away the dagger and embraces her.*)
The seal of Providence is sure upon thee,   480
And thou wert born for yet unheard of wonders.
Oh thou wert either born to save or damn me!
By all the power that's given thee o'er my soul,
By thy resistless tears and conquering smiles,
By the victorious love that still* waits on thee,   485
Fly to thy cruel father, save my friend,
Or all our future quiet's lost forever:
Fall at his feet, cling round his reverend knees,
Speak to him with thy eyes, and with thy tears
Melt the^i hard heart and wake dead nature in him,   490
Crush him in th'arms, and torture him with thy
    softness,
    Nor, till thy prayers are granted, set him free
    But conquer him, as thou hast vanquished me.

Exeunt.

Act V[, scene i. Priuli's house.]

Enter Priuli solus.

PRIULI.

Why, cruel Heaven, have my unhappy days
Been lengthened to this sad one? Oh! dishonor
And deathless infamy is fall'n upon me.
Was it my fault? Am I a traitor? No.
But then, my only child, my daughter, wedded: 5
There my best blood runs foul, and a disease
Incurable has seized upon my memory
To make it rot and stink to after ages.
Curst be the fatal minute when I got her,
Or would that I'd been anything but man   10
And raised an issue which would ne'er have
          wronged me.
The miserablest creatures (man excepted)
Are not the less esteemed though their posterity
Degenerate from the virtues of their fathers;
The vilest beasts are happy in their offsprings,   15
While only man gets traitors, whores, and villains.
Curst be the names, and some swift blow from
          Fate
Lay his head deep, where mine may be forgotten.

Enter Belvidera in a long mourning veil.

BELVIDERA.

He's there, my father, my inhuman father,
That for three years has left an only child   20
Exposed to all the outrages of Fate
And cruel Ruin—Oh!—

PRIULI.

                    What child of sorrow
Art thou that com'st thus wrapped in weeds of
          sadness
And mov'st as if thy steps were towards a grave?   25

BELVIDERA.

A wretch, who from the very top of happiness
Am fallen into the lowest depths of misery
And want* your pitying hand to raise me up again.

PRIULI.

Indeed thou talk'st as thou hadst tasted sorrows.
Would I could help thee.   30

BELVIDERA.

                    'Tis greatly in your power,
The world, too, speaks you charitable, and I,

Who ne'er asked alms before, in that dear hope
Am come a-begging to you, sir.

PRIULI.

                              For what?   35

BELVIDERA.

Oh, well regard me: Is this voice a strange one?
Consider too, when beggars once pretend*
A case like mine, no little will content 'em.

PRIULI.

What wouldst thou beg for?

BELVIDERA.

                    Pity and forgiveness.   40
          (*Throws up her veil.*)
By the kind, tender names of child and father,
Hear my complaints and take me to your love.

PRIULI.

My daughter?

BELVIDERA.

                    Yes, your daughter, by a mother
Virtuous and noble, faithful to your honor,   45
Obedient to your will, kind to your wishes,
Dear to your arms. By all the joys she gave you,
When in her blooming years she was your treasure,
Look kindly on me, in my face behold
The lineaments of hers y'have kissed so often   50
Pleading the cause of your poor, cast-off child.

PRIULI.

Thou art my daughter.

BELVIDERA.

                    Yes—and y'have oft told me,
With smiles of love and chaste, paternal kisses,
I'd much resemblance of my mother.   55

PRIULI.

                    Oh!
Hadst thou inherited her matchless virtues,
I'd been too blessed.

BELVIDERA.

                    Nay, do not call to memory
My disobedience, but let pity enter   60
Into your heart and quite deface the impression,
For could you think how mine's perplexed, what
          sadness,
Fears, and despairs distract the peace within me,
Oh, you would take me in your dear, dear arms,
Hover with strong compassion o'er your young one   65
To shelter me with a protecting wing

From the black, gathered storm that's just, just
   breaking.

PRIULI.
Don't talk thus.

BELVIDERA.
        Yes, I must, and you must hear too.
I have a husband. 70

PRIULI.
        Damn him.

BELVIDERA.
           Oh, do not curse him!
He would not speak so hard a word towards you
On any terms, howe'er he deal with me.

PRIULI.
Hah! What means my child? 75

BELVIDERA.
        Oh there's but this short moment
'Twixt me and fate, yet send me not with curses
Down to my grave, afford me one kind blessing
Before we part: just take me in your arms
And recommend me with a prayer to Heaven 80
That I may die in peace, and when I'm dead—

PRIULI.
How my soul's catcht!

BELVIDERA.
        Lay me, I beg you, lay me
By the dear ashes of my tender mother.
She would have pitied me, had Fate yet spared her. 85

PRIULI.
By Heaven, my aching heart forebodes much
   mischief.
—Tell me thy story, for I'm still thy father.

BELVIDERA.
No, I'm contented.

PRIULI.
      Speak.

BELVIDERA.
        No matter. 90

PRIULI.
          Tell me.
By you, blest Heaven, my heart runs o'er with
   fondness.

BELVIDERA.
Oh!

PRIULI.
   Utter't

BELVIDERA.
      Oh my husband, my dear husband 95
Carries a dagger in his once kind bosom
To pierce the heart of your poor Belvidera.

PRIULI.
Kill thee?

BELVIDERA.
      Yes, kill me. When he passed his faith
And covenant against your state and senate, 100
He gave me up as hostage for his truth,
With me a dagger and a dire commission:
Whene'er he failed, to plunge it through this bosom.
I learned the danger, chose the hour of love
T'attempt his heart and bring it back to honor. 105
Great love prevailed and blessed me with success:
He came, confessed, betrayed his dearest friends
For promised mercy. Now they're doomed to suffer,
Galled with remembrance of what then was sworn.
If they are lost, he vows t'appease the gods 110
With this poor life and make my blood
   th'atonement.

PRIULI.
Heavens!

BELVIDERA.
      Think you saw what passed at our last parting;
Think you beheld him like a raging lion,
Pacing the earth and tearing up his steps, 115
Fate in his eyes, and roaring with the pain
Of burning fury; think you saw his one hand
Fixed on my throat, while the extended other
Grasped a keen threat'ning dagger. Oh 'twas thus
We last embraced, when, trembling with revenge, 120
He dragged me to the ground and at my bosom
Presented horrid death, cried out, "My friends,
Where are my friends?" swore, wept, raged,
   threatened, loved,
For he yet loved, and that dear love preserved me
To this last trial of a father's pity. 125
I fear not death but cannot bear a thought
That that dear hand should do th'unfriendly office.
If I was ever then your care, now hear me:
Fly to the Senate, save the promised lives
Of his dear friends, ere mine be made the 130
   sacrifice.

PRIULI.
Oh, my heart's comfort!

[V.i]

BELVIDERA.

                       Will you not, my father?
Weep not but answer me.

PRIULI.

                     By Heaven, I will.
Not one of 'em but what shall be immortal.   135
Canst thou forgive me all my follies past?
I'll henceforth be indeed a father, never,
Never more thus expose but cherish thee
Dear as the vital warmth that feeds my life,
Dear as these eyes that weep in fondness o'er thee. 140
Peace to thy heart. Farewell.

BELVIDERA.

                  Go, and remember,
'Tis Belvidera's life her father pleads for.

Exeunt severally.

        [Scene ii. Aquilina's house.]

Enter Antonio.

ANTONIO.

Hum, hum, hah: "Seignor Priuli, my Lord Priuli,
my lord, my lord, my lord—" Now, we lords love
to call one another by our titles. "My lord, my
lord, my lord—" Pox on him, I am a lord as well
as he, and so let him fiddle. I'll warrant him, he's 5
gone to the Senate House, and I'll be there too,
soon enough for somebody. 'Odd,* here's a tickling
speech about the plot; I'll prove there's a plot with
a vengeance— Would I had it without book. Let
me see: "Most Reverend Senators, that there is 10
plot, surely by this time no man that hath eyes or
understanding in his head will presume to doubt,
'tis as plain as the light in the cucumber—" No,
hold there, cucumber does not come in yet—"'tis
as plain as the light in the sun or as the man in 15
the moon even at noonday. It is indeed a
pumpkin-plot,[31] which, just as it was mellow, we
have gathered. And now we have gathered it,

---

[31] cucumber … pumpkin-plot] Otway hits at both scientific
experiment by the Royal Society and at details of the Popish Plot: actual experiments were being conducted to discover the relationship between sunlight and vegetables;
one of the putative conspirators in the Plot was said to
have hidden important papers in a pumpkin.

prepared and dressed it, shall we throw it like a
pickled cucumber* out at the window? No. That 20
it is not only a bloody, horrid, execrable, damnable,
and audacious plot, but it is, as I may so say, a
saucy plot. And we all know, most Reverend
Fathers, that what is sauce for a goose is sauce for
a gander; therefore, I say, as those blood-thirsty 25
ganders of the conspiracy would have destroyed us
geese of the Senate, let us make haste to destroy
them. So I humbly move for hanging." Hah, hurry
durry, I think this will do, though I was something
out, at first, about the sun and the cucumber. 30

Enter Aquilina.

AQUILINA.

Good morrow, Senator.

ANTONIO.

Nacky, my dear Nacky, 'morrow, Nacky, 'Odd, I
am very brisk, very merry, very pert, very jovial—
haaaaa—kiss me, Nacky. How dost thou do, my
little tory rory* strumpet, kiss me, I say, hussy, kiss 35
me.

AQUILINA.

"Kiss me, Nacky." Hang you, Sir Coxcomb, hang
you, sir.

ANTONIO.

Hayty tayty, is it so indeed, with all my heart,
faith— (*Sings.*) "Hey then up go we," faith, "hey 40
then up go we, dum dum derum dump."

AQUILINA.

Signor.

ANTONIO.

Madonna.

AQUILINA.

Do you intend to die in your bed?

ANTONIO.

About threescore years hence, much may be done, 45
my dear.

AQUILINA.

You'll be hanged, Signor.

ANTONIO.

Hanged, sweetheart? Prithee be quiet, hanged
quotha, that's a merry conceit, with all my heart,
why thou jok'st, Nacky, thou art given to joking, 50
I'll swear; well I protest, Nacky, nay, I must protest,
and will protest that I love joking dearly, man. And

I love thee for joking, and I'll kiss thee for joking,
and touse thee for joking, and 'Odd, I have a
devilish mind to take thee aside about that business   55
for joking too, 'Odd I have, and "Hey then up go
we, dum dum derum dump."

AQUILINA.

See you this, sir? (*Draws a dagger.*)

ANTONIO.

Oh Laud, a dagger! Oh Laud! it is naturally my
aversion, I cannot endure the sight on't, hide it,   60
for Heaven's sake, I cannot look that way till it be
gone—hide it, hide it, oh, oh, hide it!

AQUILINA.

Yes, in your heart I'll hide it.

ANTONIO.

My heart, what, hide a dagger in my heart's blood!

AQUILINA.

Yes, in thy heart, thy throat, thou pampered devil.   65
Thou hast helped to spoil my peace, and I'll have
     vengeance
On thy curst life for all the bloody Senate,
The perjured, faithless Senate: Where's my lord,
My happiness, my love, my god, my hero?
Doomed by thy accursèd tongue, amongst the   70
     rest,
T'a shameful rack? By all the rage that's in me,
I'll be whole years in murthering thee.

ANTONIO.

Why, Nacky, wherefore so passionate? What have
I done? What's the matter, my dear Nacky? Am
not I thy love, thy happiness, thy lord, thy hero,   75
thy senator, and everything in the world, Nacky?

AQUILINA.

Thou! Think'st thou, thou art fit to meet my joys,
To bear the eager clasps of my embraces?
Give me my Pierre, or—

ANTONIO.

Why, he's to be hanged, little Nacky, trussed up   80
for treason, and so forth, child.*

AQUILINA.

Thou ly'st, stop down thy throat that hellish
     sentence,
Or 'tis thy last. Swear that my love shall live,
Or thou art dead.

ANTONIO.

                    Ahhhh.   85

AQUILINA.

                    Swear to recall his doom,
Swear at my feet and tremble at my fury.

ANTONIO.

I do.—Now if she would but kick a little bit, one
kick now. Ahhhh.

AQUILINA.

Swear, or—   90

ANTONIO.

I do, by these dear fragrant foots and little toes,
sweet as, eeee my Nacky Nacky Nacky.

AQUILINA.

How!

ANTONIO.

Nothing but untie thy shoestring a little, faith and
troth, that's all, that's all, as I hope to live, Nacky,   95
that's all.

AQUILINA.

Nay, then—

ANTONIO.

Hold, hold, thy love, thy lord, thy hero shall be
preserved and safe.

AQUILINA.

Or may this poniard rust in thy heart.   100

ANTONIO.

With all my soul.

AQUILINA.

Farewell— (*Exit.*)

ANTONIO.

Adieu. Why what a bloody-minded, inveterate,
termagant, strumpet have I been plagued with!
Ohhh yet more! Nay then I die,* I die—I am dead   105
already. (*Stretches himself out.*)

Enter Jaffeir.

JAFFEIR.

Final destruction seize on all the world:
Bend down, ye heavens, and shutting round this
     earth,
Crush the vile globe into its first confusion,
Scorch it with elemental flames to one curst cinder,   110
And all us little creepers in't, called men,
Burn, burn to nothing. But let Venice burn
Hotter than all the rest; here kindle hell
Ne'er to extinguish, and let souls hereafter
Groan here in all those pains which mine feels now.   115

Enter Belvidera, meeting him.

BELVIDERA.
My life—
JAFFEIR. (*Turning from her.*)
                 My plague—
BELVIDERA.
                       Nay then I see my ruin,
If I must die!
JAFFEIR.
                 No, Death's this day too busy: 120
Thy father's ill-timed mercy came too late.
I thank thee for thy labors, though, and him too,
But all my poor, betrayed, unhappy friends
Have summons to prepare for Fate's black hour.
And yet I live.   125
BELVIDERA.
             Then be the next my doom.
I see thou hast passed my sentence in thy heart,
And I'll no longer weep or plead against it,
But with the humblest, most obedient patience
Meet thy dear hands and kiss 'em when they   130
     wound me.
Indeed I am willing, but I beg thee do it
With some remorse, and when thou giv'st the blow,
View me with eyes of a relenting love
And show me pity, for 'twill sweeten justice.
JAFFEIR.
Show pity to thee?   135
BELVIDERA.
               Yes, and when thy hands,
Charged with my fate, come trembling to the deed,
As thou hast done a thousand thousand dear times
To this poor breast, when kinder* rage has
     brought thee;
When our stinged hearts have leaped to meet each   140
     other
And melting kisses sealed our lips together;
When joys have left me gasping in thy arms,
So let my death come now, and I'll not shrink
     from't.
JAFFEIR.
Nay, Belvidera, do not fear my cruelty
Nor let the thoughts of death perplex thy fancy,   145
But answer me to what I shall demand
With a firm temper and unshaken spirit.

BELVIDERA.
I will when I've done weeping—
JAFFEIR.
                      Fie, no more on't.
How long is't since the miserable day   150
We wedded first?
BELVIDERA.
               Ohhh.
JAFFEIR.
                Nay, keep in thy tears,
Lest they unman me too.
BELVIDERA.
                   Heaven knows I cannot;   155
The words you utter sound so very sadly
These streams will follow—
JAFFEIR.
                   Come, I'll kiss 'em dry then.
BELVIDERA.
But, was't a miserable day?
JAFFEIR.
                     A curst one.   160
BELVIDERA.
I thought it otherwise, and you've oft sworn
In the transporting hours of warmest love,
When sure you spoke the truth, you've sworn you
     blessed it.
JAFFEIR.
'Twas a rash oath.
BELVIDERA.
               Then why am I not curst too?   165
JAFFEIR.
No Belvidera, by th'eternal truth,
I dote with too much fondness.
BELVIDERA.
                   Still so kind?
Still then do you love me?
JAFFEIR.
                 Nature, in her workings,   170
Inclines not with more ardor to creation
Than I do now towards thee; man ne'er was blessed,
Since the first pair first met, as I have been.
BELVIDERA.
Then sure you will not curse me.
JAFFEIR.
                   No, I'll bless thee.   175
I came on purpose, Belvidera, to bless thee.

'Tis now, I think, three years we've lived together.

BELVIDERA.

And may no fatal minute ever part us
Till, reverend grown for age and love, we go
Down to one grave, as our last bed, together,   180
There sleep in peace till an eternal morning.

JAFFEIR. (*Sighing.*)

When will that be?

BELVIDERA.

I hope long ages hence.

JAFFEIR.

Have I not hitherto (I beg thee tell me
Thy very fears) used thee with tenderest love?   185
Did e'er my soul rise up in wrath against thee?
Did I e'er frown when Belvidera smiled
Or, by the least unfriendly word, betray
A bating passion? Have I ever wronged thee?

BELVIDERA.

No.   190

JAFFEIR.

Has my heart, or have my eyes e'er wandered
To any other woman?

BELVIDERA.

Never, never—
I were the worst of false ones should I accuse thee.
I own I've been too happy, blessed above   195
My sex's charter.

JAFFEIR.

Did I not say I came
To bless thee?

BELVIDERA.

Yes.

JAFFEIR.

Then hear me, bounteous Heaven,   200
Pour down your blessings on this beauteous head,
Where everlasting sweets are always springing.
With a continual giving hand, let peace,
Honor, and safety always hover round her;
Feed her with plenty; let her eyes ne'er see   205
A sight of sorrow, nor her heart know mourning;
Crown all her days with joy, her nights with rest
Harmless as her own thoughts, and prop her virtue
To bear the loss of one that too much loved
And comfort her with patience in our parting.   210

BELVIDERA.

How, parting, parting!

JAFFEIR.

Yes, forever parting:
I have sworn, Belvidera, by yon Heaven,
That best can tell how much I lose to leave thee,
We part this hour forever.   215

BELVIDERA.

Oh, call back
Your cruel blessings, stay with me, and curse me!

JAFFEIR.

No, 'tis resolved.

BELVIDERA.

Then hear me too, just Heaven,
Pour down your curses on this wretched head   220
With never-ceasing vengeance; let despair,
Danger, or infamy, nay all surround me;
Starve me with wantings;* let my eyes ne'er see
A sight of comfort, nor my heart know peace,
But dash my days with sorrow, nights with horrors   225
Wild as my own thoughts now, and let loose fury
To make me mad enough for what I lose,
If I must lose him. If I must? I will not.
Oh turn and hear me!

JAFFEIR.

Now hold, heart, or never.   230

BELVIDERA.

By all the tender days we have lived together,
By all our charming nights and joys that crowned
'em,
Pity my sad condition, speak, but speak.

JAFFEIR.

Ohhh.

BELVIDERA.

By these arms that now cling round thy neck,   235
By this dear kiss and by ten thousand more,
By these poor streaming eyes—

JAFFEIR.

Murther! unhold me.
By th'immortal destiny that doomed me
(*Draws his dagger.*)
To this curst minute, I'll not live one longer.   240
Resolve to let me go or see me fall—

BELVIDERA.

Hold, sir, be patient.

Passing-bell tolls.*

JAFFEIR.

Hark, the dismal bell

Tolls out for death. I must attend its call too,
For my poor friend, my dying Pierre, expects me: 245
He sent a message to require I'd see him
Before he died and take his last forgiveness.
Farewell forever.
BELVIDERA.
              Leave thy dagger with me.
Bequeath me something. Not one kiss at parting?   250
—Oh my poor heart, when wilt thou break?
JAFFEIR. (*Going out, looks back at her.*)
                         Yet stay:
We have a child, as yet a tender infant.
Be a kind mother to him when I am gone,
Breed him in virtue and the paths of honor,   255
But let him never know his father's story;
I charge thee guard him from the wrongs my fate
May do his future fortune or his name.
Now—nearer yet—

Approaching each other.

Oh that my arms were riveted   260
Thus round thee ever!—But my friends, my oath!
—This and no more. (*Kisses her.*)
BELVIDERA.
                 Another, sure another
For that poor little one you've ta'en care of,
I'll giv't him truly.   265
JAFFEIR.
            So, now farewell.
BELVIDERA.
                  Forever?
JAFFEIR.
Heaven knows, forever. All good angels guard
    thee. [*Exit.*]
BELVIDERA.
All ill ones sure had charge of me this moment!
Curst be my days and doubly curst my nights,   270
Which I must now mourn out in widowed tears;
Blasted be every herb and fruit and tree;
Curst be the rain that falls upon the earth;
And may the general curse reach man and beast.
Oh give me daggers, fire, or water.   275
How I could bleed, how burn, how drown the waves
Huzzing and booming round my sinking head
Till I descended to the peaceful bottom!
Oh there's all quiet, here all rage and fury;

The air's too thin and pierces my weak brain.   280
I long for thick substantial sleep. Hell, hell,
Burst from the center, rage, and roar aloud,
If thou art half so hot, so mad as I am.

Enter Priuli and servants.

Who's there?
PRIULI.
             Run, seize and bring her safely home,   285

They seize her.

Guard her as you would life. Alas poor creature!
BELVIDERA.
What? to my husband then conduct me quickly.
Are all things ready? Shall we die most gloriously?
Say not a word of this to my old father:
Murmuring streams, soft shades, and springing   290
    flowers,
Lutes, laurels, seas of milk, and ships of amber.

Exeunt.

[Scene iii.] Scene opening discovers* a scaffold
and a wheel prepared for the executing of Pierre.

*Enter officers, Pierre and guards, a friar, executioner
and a great rabble.*

OFFICER.
Room, room there—stand all by, make room for
    the prisoner.
PIERRE.
My friend not come yet?
FRIAR.
                 Why are you so obstinate?
PIERRE.
Why are you so troublesome, that a poor wretch
Cannot die in peace?   5
But you, like ravens, will be croaking round him—
FRIAR.
Yet, Heaven—
PIERRE.
             I tell thee Heaven and I are friends;
I ne'er broke peace with't yet by cruel murthers,
Rapine, or perjury or vile deceiving,   10
But lived in moral justice towards all men
Nor am a foe to the most strong believers,
Howe'er my own shortsighted faith confine me.

FRIAR.
   But an all-seeing Judge—
PIERRE.
                              You say my conscience 15
   Must be mine accuser. I have searched that
      conscience
   And find no records there of crimes that scare me.
FRIAR.
   'Tis strange you should want* faith.
PIERRE.
                              You want to lead
   My reason blindfold, like a hampered lion, 20
   Checked of its nobler vigor then, when baited,
   Down to obedient tameness, make it couch
   And show strange tricks which you call signs of
      faith.
   So silly* souls are gulled and you get money.
   Away, no more.—Captain, I would hereafter 25
   This fellow write no lies of my conversion
   Because he has crept upon my troubled hours.

Enter Jaffeir.

JAFFEIR.
   Hold. Eyes, be dry; heart, strengthen me to bear
   This hideous sight and humble me to take
   The last forgiveness of a dying friend, 30
   Betrayed by my vile falsehood to his ruin.
   Oh Pierre!
PIERRE.
                  Yet nearer.
JAFFEIR.
                           Crawling on my knees
   And prostrate on the earth, let me approach thee. 35
   How shall I look up to thy injured face,
   That always used to smile with friendship on me?
   It darts an air of so much manly virtue
   That I, methinks, look little in thy sight
   And stripes are fitter for me than embraces. 40
PIERRE.
   Dear to my arms, though thou hast undone my
      fame,
   I cannot forget to love thee. Prithee Jaffeir,
   Forgive that filthy blow my passion dealt thee.
   I am now preparing for the land of peace
   And fain would have the charitable wishes 45
   Of all good men like thee to bless my journey.

JAFFEIR.
   Good! I am the vilest creature, worse than e'er
   Suffered the shameful fate thou art going to taste of.
   Why was I sent for to be used thus kindly?
   Call, call me villain, as I am, describe 50
   The foul complexion of my hateful deeds,
   Lead me to the rack, and stretch me in thy stead:
   I've crimes enough to give it its full load
   And do it credit. Thou wilt but spoil the use on't,
   And honest men hereafter bear its figure 55
   About 'em as a charm from treacherous friendship.
OFFICER.
   The time grows short, your friends are dead already.
JAFFEIR.
   Dead!
PIERRE.
         Yes, dead, Jaffeir, they've all died like men too,
   Worthy their character. 60
JAFFEIR.
                           And what must I do?
PIERRE.
   Oh, Jaffeir!
JAFFEIR.
               Speak aloud thy burthened soul
   And tell thy troubles to thy tortured friend.
PIERRE.
   Friend! Couldst thou yet be a friend, a generous 65
      friend,
   I might hope comfort from thy noble sorrows.
   Heaven knows I want* a friend.
JAFFEIR.
                              And I a kind one,
   That would not thus scorn my repenting virtue
   Or think, when he is to die, my thoughts are idle. 70
PIERRE.
   No! live, I charge thee, Jaffeir.
JAFFEIR.
                              Yes, I will live,
   But it shall be to see thy fall revenged
   At such a rate as Venice long shall groan for.
PIERRE.
   Wilt thou? 75
JAFFEIR.
            I will, by Heav'n.
PIERRE.
                        Then still thou'rt noble,
   And I forgive thee, oh—yet—shall I trust thee?

JAFFEIR.

No: I've been false already.

PIERRE.

       Dost thou love me?   80

JAFFEIR.

Rip up my heart and satisfy thy doubtings.

PIERRE.

Curse on this weakness. (*Weeps.*)

JAFFEIR.

       Tears! Amazement! Tears!

I never saw thee melted thus before

And know there's something lab'ring in thy bosom   85

That must have vent. Though I'm a villain, tell me.

PIERRE.

Seest thou that engine? (*Pointing to the wheel.*)

JAFFEIR.

Why?

PIERRE.

Is't fit a soldier who has lived with honor,

Fought nation's quarrels,* and been crowned with   90

  conquest,

Be exposed a common carcass on a wheel?

JAFFEIR.

Hah!

PIERRE.

   Speak! is't fitting?

JAFFEIR.

      Fitting?

PIERRE.

        Yes, is't fitting?   95

JAFFEIR.

What's to be done?

PIERRE.

     I'd have thee undertake

Something that's noble to preserve my memory

From the disgrace that's ready to attaint it.

OFFICER.

The day grows late, sir.   100

PIERRE.

     I'll make haste!—Oh Jaffeir,

Though thou'st betrayed me, do me some way

  justice.

JAFFEIR.

No more of that. Thy wishes shall be satisfied:

I have a wife, and she shall bleed, my child too

Yield up his little throat, and all t'appease thee—   105

Going away Pierre holds him.

PIERRE.

No—this—no more! (*Whispers Jaffeir.*)

JAFFEIR.

     Hah! is't then so?

PIERRE.

        Most certainly.

JAFFEIR.

I'll do't.

PIERRE.

  Remember.   110

OFFICER.

     Sir.

PIERRE.

       Come, now I am ready.

He and Jaffeir ascend the scaffold.

Captain, you should be a gentleman of honor,

Keep off the rabble, that I may have room

To entertain my fate and die with decency.   115

Come!

Takes off his gown. Executioner prepares to bind him.

FRIAR.

Son!

PIERRE.

  Hence, tempter.

OFFICER.

     Stand off, priest.

PIERRE.

       I thank you, sir. (*To Jaffeir.*)   120

You'll think on't.

JAFFEIR.

   'Twon't grow stale before tomorrow.

PIERRE. (*Executioner having bound him.*)

Now, Jaffeir! Now I am going. Now—

JAFFEIR.

        Have at thee,

Thou honest heart, then—here— (*Stabs him.*)   125

And this is well too. (*Then stabs himself.*)

FRIAR.

Damnable deed!

PIERRE.

    Now thou hast indeed been faithful.

This was done nobly—we have deceived the Senate.

JAFFEIR.

    Bravely.   130

PIERRE.

               Ha ha ha—oh oh— (*Dies.*)

JAFFEIR.

                         Now ye curst rulers,

Thus of the blood y'have shed I make libation

And sprinkle't mingling: may it rest upon you

And all your race. Be henceforth peace a stranger 135

Within your walls; let plagues and famine waste

Your generations— Oh poor Belvidera!

Sir, I have a wife, bear this in safety to her,

A token that with my dying breath I blessed her

And the dear little infant left behind me. 140

I am sick—I am quiet— (*Dies.*)

OFFICER.

                     Bear this news to the Senate

And guard their bodies till there's farther order.

—Heaven grant I die so well.

Scene shuts upon them.

[Scene iv. Priuli's house.]

*Soft Music. Enter Belvidera distracted, led by two of
her women, Priuli, and servants.*

PRIULI.

    Strengthen her heart with patience, pitying Heav'n.

BELVIDERA.

    Come, come, come, come, come. Nay, come to bed!

Prithee my love. The winds! hark how they whistle!

And the rain beats. Oh how the weather shrinks me!

You are angry now, who cares? Pish, no indeed. 5

Choose then, I say you shall not go, you shall not;

Whip your ill nature; get you gone then! Oh,

Jaffeir's ghost rises.

Are you returned? See father, here he's come again,

Am I to blame to love him! Oh thou dear one.

Ghost sinks.

Why do you fly me? Are you angry still then? 10

Jaffeir! where art thou? Father, why do you do thus?

Stand off, don't hide him from me. He's here

    somewhere.

Stand off I say! What, gone? Remember't, tyrant!

I may revenge my self for this trick one day.

Enter Officer and others.

I'll do't—I'll do't. Renault's a nasty fellow. 15

Hang him, hang him, hang him.

PRIULI.

              News, what news?

Officer whispers Priuli.

OFFICER.

               Most sad, sir.

Jaffeir upon the scaffold, to prevent

A shameful death, stabbed Pierre and next himself. 20

Both fell together.

PRIULI.

            Daughter.

*The ghosts of Jaffeir and Pierre rise together both
    bloody.*

BELVIDERA.

               Hah, look there!

My husband bloody, and his friend too! Murther!

Who has done this? Speak to me, thou sad vision, 25

Ghosts sink.

On these poor trembling knees I beg it.—

    Vanished—

Here they went down. Oh I'll dig, dig the den up.

You shan't delude me thus. Hoa, Jaffeir, Jaffeir.

Peep up and give me but a look. I have him!

I've got him, Father. Oh now how I'll smuggle him! 30

My love! my dear! my blessing! Help me, help me!

They have hold on me and drag me to the bottom.

Nay—now they pull so hard—farewell— (*Dies.*)

MAID.

                 She's dead.

Breathless and dead. 35

PRIULI.

             Then guard me from the sight on't.

Lead me into some place that's fit for mourning,

Where the free air, light, and the cheerful sun

May never enter. Hang it round with black,

Set up one taper that may last a day, 40

As long as I've to live, and there all leave me.

    Sparing no tears when you this tale relate,

But bid all cruel fathers dread my fate.

Curtain falls, exeunt omnes.

EPILOGUE

The text is done, and now for application,
And, when that's ended, pass your approbation.
Though the conspiracy's prevented here,
Methinks I see another hatching there,
And there's a certain faction fain would sway,[32]   5
If they had strength enough, and damn this play,
But this the author bade me boldly say:
If any take his plainness in ill part,
He's glad on't from the bottom of his heart;
Poets in honor of the truth should write   10
With the same spirits brave men for it fight,
And though against him causeless hatreds rise
And daily where he goes of late he spies
The scowls of sullen and revengeful eyes,
'Tis what he knows with much contempt to bear   15
And serves a cause too good to let him fear.
He fears no poison from an incensed drab,
No ruffian's five-foot-sword, nor rascal's stab,
Nor any other snares of mischief laid:
Not a Rose Alley cudgel ambuscade,[33]   20
From any private cause where malice reigns,
Or general pique all blockheads have to brains.
Nothing shall daunt his pen when truth does call,
No, not the picture-mangler at Guildhall.[34]
The rebel tribe, of which that vermin's one,   25
Have now set forward and their course begun.
And while that prince's figure they deface,
As they before had massacred his name,
Durst their base fears but look him in the face,
They'd use his person as they've used his fame;   30
A face, in which such lineaments they read
Of that great martyr's[35] whose rich blood they
     shed

That their rebellious hate they still retain
And in his son would murther him again.
With indignation then, let each brave heart   35
Rouse and unite to take his injured part,
Till royal love and goodness call him home[36]
And songs of triumph meet him as he come;
Till Heaven his honor and our peace restore,
And villains never wrong his virtue more.   40

FINIS.

Textual Notes

[a] Copytext is the first edition, a 1682 quarto (Q1). Also consulted were the second edition, a 1696 quarto (Q2); the third edition, a 1704 quarto (Q3); the first collected edition in 1712 (C); and modern editions of 1932 (Ghosh) and of 1969 (Kelsall).
[b] make] Q3, C, Ghosh, Kelsall; may Q1-2
[c] make … tell] Q3, C, Ghosh, Kelsall; makes … tells Q 1-2
[d] worst] Q3, C, Ghosh; first Q1-2, Kelsall
[e] which] Q3, C, Ghosh, Kelsall; with Q1-2
[f] taught] Q3, C, Ghosh, Kelsall; thought Q1-2
[g] with] Q3, C, Ghosh, Kelsall; om. Q1-2
[h] gall] C, Ghosh, Kelsall; call Q1-3
[i] the] Ghosh, Kelsall; thy Q1-2; his Q3, C
[j] to] Ghosh, Kelsall; om. Q1-3, C

---

[32] certain faction] Whigs, supporters of the bill to exclude the duke of York from the succession
[33] Rose Alley cudgel ambuscade] refers to an assault on John Dryden on the evening of 18 December 1679; neither the motive nor the assailants are known, though some contemporaries—and some modern scholars—suspect Whigs.
[34] picture-mangler] A marginal note reads, "The rascal that cut the Duke of York's picture." The incident took place at Guildhall, City office building, in January 1682, shortly before the play's first performance.
[35] great martyr] Charles I

---

[36] call him home] To avoid the provocation of his presence in England during the Exclusion Crisis, Charles II sent James, duke of York, out of the country repeatedly between 1679 and 1682; he was currently in Scotland.

Amphitryon; or, the Two Sosias[a]

by John Dryden (1631-1700)

edited by Robert Markley and Jeannie Dalporto

First acted in October 1690 by the United Company at Drury Lane, John Dryden's *Amphitryon* was an instant success and enjoyed numerous productions before and after his death in 1700. Among his plays, it ranks second only to *The Spanish Fryar* in eighteenth-century revivals.

As a convert to Catholicism and an ardent supporter of the deposed James II, Dryden found himself out of favor at court after the ascension of William III to the English throne in 1689. Deprived of his posts as Poet Laureate and Historiographer Royal, Dryden late in his career turned once again to the theater to support himself. The classical myth of Jupiter's seduction of Alcmene by disguising himself as her husband, the Theban general, Amphitryon, was a popular topic for classical dramatists; the most enduring and best-known of ancient versions of this tale was Plautus's *Amphitruo*. The basic outlines of this Roman comedy were reworked by several European playwrights in the seventeenth century. Molière's 1668 *Amphitryon* was the most successful and the most influential for Dryden.

Dryden's comedy differs from Molière's in several important ways: its satire is aimed more directly at British politics in the aftermath of the Glorious Revolution; its humor, in keeping with British audiences' appetite for sexual farce, is bawdier; and its portrayal of Alcmena (Dryden and his age's spelling) is more extensive and sympathetic. Rather than a passive dupe of Jove's disguise, Alcmena voices her anger and indecision when she is confronted by the seemingly arbitrary changes in her husband's behavior. Her predicament, in some respects, mirrors the dilemmas that Dryden and many members of his audience faced with William's arrival. The new monarchy put Dryden in a difficult position, both professionally and politically; in *Amphitryon* he walks a fine line between satirizing the Whiggish emphasis on the rights of subjects to check the exercise of monarchical power and endorsing the Jacobite belief that the authority of kings was absolute. Although James II adhered fervently to the theory that a king should be able to wield unquestioned authority, his supporters were quick to accuse William of acting as a tyrant in dragging England into wars on the European continent against Louis XIV of France. As one might expect, Dryden ridicules the idea that the usurpation of lawful authority can be justified, but implies that a sovereign's exercise of royal prerogative (particularly when that sovereign has just deposed a rightful monarch) can have destructive effects.

It is significant, then, that one of Dryden's main concerns in the play is the effect of absolute power on individuals. The gods' arbitrary and selfish manipulation of Amphitryon, Alcmena, and Sosia compels the mortals to confront—however comically—the ironies of social and moral identity: we are individuals precisely to the extent that others recognize us as such. The mortals' sense of self-identity becomes increasingly—and comically—ambiguous as Jove's and Mercury's plans unfold. Tellingly, Amphitryon and Alcmena offer no response at the end of the play when Jove declares that he has brought no shame to either of them by impregnating her with the future Hercules. In one respect, their silence captures effectively the ambiguities of Dryden's reaction to the compromises that he and his contemporaries had to make to survive the revolutions of their times.

Dryden's version differs from Molière's in one other important respect: it may call divine justice itself into question. If God himself exemplifies power rather than justice, then where can humans appeal? This is the question Mercury (played by the irrepressible Tony Leigh) repeatedly asks.

DRAMATIS PERSONAE

[MEN]

Jupiter.
Mercury.
Phoebus.
Amphitryon.
Sosia.
Gripus.
Polidas.
Tranio.

[WOMEN]

Alcmena.
Phaedra.
Bromia.
Night.

THE SCENE: THEBES.

Amphitryon; or, The Two Sosias.
Egregiam vero laudem, et spolia ampla refertis;
Una dolo divum si femina victa duorum est. Virg.[1]

Act I, scene i.

Mercury and Phoebus descend in several machines.

PHOEBUS.

Know you the reason of this present* summons?
'Tis neither council day, nor is this heaven.
What business has our Jupiter on earth?
Why more at Thebes than any other place?
And why we two of all the herd of gods   5
Are chosen out to meet him in consult?
They call me the god of wisdom,
But Mars and Vulcan, the two fools of heaven,
Whose wit lies in their anvil and their sword,
Know full as much as I.   10

MERCURY.

And Venus may know more than both of us,
For 'tis some petticoat affair, I guess.
I have discharged my duty, which was to summon
you, Phoebus. We shall know more anon when the
Thunderer comes down. 'Tis our part to obey our   15

---

[1] *Egregiam … Virg.]* Virgil, *Aeneid* IV:93, 95: "High
praises, endless honors, you have won, … / Two gods a
silly woman have undone" (Dryden IV.134, 136).

father, for, to confess the truth, we two are little
better than sons of harlots.[2] And if Jupiter had not
been pleased to take a little pains with our
mothers, instead of being gods, we might have
been a couple of linkboys.   20

PHOEBUS.

But know you nothing farther, Hermes? What
news in court?

MERCURY.

There has been a devilish quarrel, I can tell you,
betwixt Jupiter and Juno. She threatened to sue
him in the spiritual court[3] for some matrimonial   25
omissions, and he stood upon his prerogative.
Then she hit him on the teeth of all his bastards,
and your name and mine were used with less
reverence than became our godships. They were
both in their cups, and at the last the matter grew   30
so high that they were ready to have thrown stars
at one another's heads.

PHOEBUS.

'Twas happy for me that I was at my vocation,
driving daylight about the world. But I had rather
stand my father's thunderbolts than my   35
stepmother's railing.

MERCURY.

When the tongue battle was over, and the
championess had harnessed her peacocks to go for
Samos[4] and hear the prayers that were made to
her—   40

PHOEBUS.

By the way, her worshippers had a bad time on't;
she was in a damnable humor for receiving
petitions.

MERCURY.

Jupiter immediately beckons me aside and charges
me that, as soon as ever you had set up your horses,   45

---

[2] sons of harlots] Both Mercury and Phoebus are illegiti-
mate, since neither one is a son of Juno, Jupiter's wife.
Mercury's mother was Maia, and Phoebus's mother was
Leto.

[3] spiritual court] The Church of England's ecclesiastical
court, which maintained jurisdiction over adultery and
other matrimonial offenses

[4] Samos] Greek island in the Aegean, reported to be Juno's
birthplace, where she was worshipped

you and I should meet him here at Thebes. Now, putting the premises together, as dark as it is, methinks I begin to see daylight.

PHOEBUS.

As plain as one of my own beams. She has made him uneasy at home, and he is going to seek his 50 diversion abroad. I see heaven itself is no privileged place for happiness, if a man must carry his wife along with him.

MERCURY.

'Tis neither better nor worse, upon my conscience. He is weary of hunting in the spacious forest of a 55 wife and is following his game incognito in some little purlieu here at Thebes. That's many an honest man's case on earth too, Jove help 'em, as indeed he does to make 'em cuckolds.

PHOEBUS.

But if so, Mercury, then I, who am a poet, must 60 indict his love letter, and you, who are by trade a porter, must convey it.

MERCURY.

No more. He's coming down souse upon us and hears as far as he can see too. He's plaguey hot upon the business; I know it by his hard driving. 65

Jupiter descends.

JUPITER.

What, you are descanting upon my actions? Much good may do you with your politics: All subjects will be censuring their kings. Well, I confess I am in love, what then?

PHOEBUS.

Some mortal, we presume, of Cadmus' blood, 70 Some Theban beauty, some new Semele, Or some Europa.

MERCURY.

I'll say that for my father, he's constant to an handsome family. He knows when they have a good smack with 'em and snuffs up incense so 75 savorly, when 'tis offered him by a fair hand.

JUPITER.

Well, my familiar sons, this saucy carriage I have deserved, for he who trusts a secret Makes his own man his master. I read your thoughts; Therefore, you may as safely speak as think. 80

MERCURY.

Mine was a very homely thought. I was considering into what form your almightyship would be pleased to transform yourself tonight— whether you would fornicate in the shape of a bull, or a ram, or an eagle, or a swan;[5] what bird or 85 beast you would please to honor by transgressing your own laws in his likeness; or, in short, whether you would recreate yourself in feathers or in leather.

PHOEBUS.

Any disguise to hide the King of Gods. 90

JUPITER.

I know your malice, Phoebus. You would say That when a monarch sins it should be secret To keep exterior show of sanctity, Maintain respect, and cover bad example: For kings and priests are in a manner bound, 95 For reverence' sake, to be close hypocrites.

PHOEBUS.

But what necessitates you to this love, Which you confess a crime, and yet commit? For to be secret makes not sin the less— 'Tis only hidden from the vulgar view— 100 Maintains, indeed, the reverence due to princes, But not absolves the conscience from the crime.

JUPITER.

I love because 'twas in the fates I should.

PHOEBUS.

With reverence be it spoke—a bad excuse. Thus every wicked act in heav'n or earth 105 May make the same defense. But what is Fate? Is it a blind contingence of events? Or sure necessity of causes linked That must produce effects? Or is't a Pow'r That orders all things by superior will, 110 Foresees his work, and works in that foresight?

JUPITER.

Fate is what I, By virtue of omnipotence, have made it, And power omnipotent can do no wrong—

---

5 bull ... swan] Jupiter took the form of a bull during his liaison with Europa, the form of a ram with Theophane, the form of an eagle with Asterie, and the form of a swan with Leda.

Not to myself, because I willed it so,   115
Nor yet to men, for what they are is mine.
This night I will enjoy Amphitryon's wife:
For when I made her, I decreed her such
As I should please to love. I wrong not him
Whose wife she is, for I reserved my right   120
To have her while she pleased me. That once past,
She shall be his again.

MERCURY.

Here's omnipotence with a vengeance—to make
a man a cuckold and yet not to do him wrong.
Then I find, Father Jupiter, that when you made   125
Fate, you had the wit to contrive a holy-day[6] for
yourself now and then. For you kings never enact
a law, but you have a kind of an eye to your own
prerogative.

PHOEBUS.

If there be no such thing as right and wrong   130
Of an eternal being, I have done.
But if there be—

JUPITER.

                    Peace, thou disputing fool.
Learn this: if thou couldst comprehend my ways,
Then thou wert Jove, not I. Yet thus far know,   135
That, for the good of humankind, this night
I shall beget a future Hercules,
Who shall redress the wrongs of injured mortals,
Shall conquer monsters, and reform the world.

MERCURY.

Aye brother Phoebus, and our father made all   140
those monsters for Hercules to conquer and
contrived all those vices on purpose for him to
reform too—there's the jest on't.

PHOEBUS.

Since arbitrary power will hear no reason, 'tis
wisdom to be silent.   145

MERCURY.

Why, that's the point: this same arbitrary power is
a knock-down argument; 'tis but a word and a
blow. Now methinks our father speaks out like an
honest bare-faced god, as he is; he lays the stress
in the right place, upon absolute dominion. I   150
confess if he had been a man, he might have been
a tyrant, if his subjects durst have called him to

---

6 holy-day] both holy day and holiday

account. But you, brother Phoebus, are but a mere
country gentleman that never comes to court, that
are abroad all day on horseback, making visits   155
about the world, are drinking all night, and in your
cups are still* railing at the government. Oh these
patriots, these bumpkin patriots are a very silly sort
of animal.

JUPITER.

My present purpose and design you heard: 160
T'enjoy Amphitryon's wife, the fair Alcmena.
You two must be subservient to my love.

MERCURY. (To Phoebus.)

No more of your grumbletonian* morals, brother.
There's preferment coming; be advised and pimp
dutifully.   165

JUPITER.

Amphitryon, the brave Theban general,
Has overcome his country's foes in fight,
And in a single duel slain their king.
His conquering troops are eager on their march,
Returning home, while their young general,   170
More eager to review his beauteous wife,
Posts on before, winged with impetuous love,
And by tomorrow's dawn will reach this town.

MERCURY.

That's but short warning, Father Jupiter. Having
made no former advances of courtship to her, you   175
have need of your omnipotence and all your
godship, if you mean to be beforehand with him.

PHOEBUS.

Then how are we to be employed this evening?
Time's precious, and these summer nights are
short;
I must be early up to light the world.   180

JUPITER.

You shall not rise; there shall be no tomorrow.

MERCURY.

Then the world's to be at an end, I find.

PHOEBUS.

Or else a gap in nature of a day.

JUPITER.

A day will well be lost to busy man.
Night shall continue sleep, and care shall cease.   185
So, many men shall live and live in peace,
Whom sunshine had betrayed to envious sight,
And sight to sudden rage, and rage to death.

Now, I will have a night for love and me,
A long luxurious night, fit for a God   190
To quench and empty his immortal heat.

MERCURY.

I'll lay on the woman's side for all that—that she
shall love longest tonight, in spite of your
omnipotence.

PHOEBUS.

I shall be cursed by all the lab'ring trades   195
That early rise, but you must be obeyed.

JUPITER.

No matter for the cheating part of man.
They have a day's sin less to answer for.

PHOEBUS.

When would you have me wake?   200

JUPITER.

Why, when Jove goes to sleep. When I have
    finished,
Your brother Mercury shall bring you word.

Exit Phoebus on his chariot.

(To Mercury.)

Now, Hermes, I must take Amphitryon's form
T'enjoy his wife.
Thou must be Sosia, this Amphitryon's slave,   205
Who all this night is travelling to Thebes
To tell Alcmena of her lord's approach
And bring her joyful news of victory.

MERCURY.

But why must I be Sosia?

JUPITER.

Dull god of wit, thou statue of thyself!   210
Thou must be Sosia to keep out Sosia,
Who by his entrance might discover* Jove,
Disturb my pleasures, raise unruly noise,
And so distract Alcmena's tender soul.
She would not meet my warmth when I dissolve   215
Into her lap, nor give down half her love.

MERCURY.

Let me alone; I'll cudgel him away.
But I abhor so villainous* a shape.

JUPITER.

Take it. I charge thee on thy duty, take it,
Nor dare lay it down till I command.   220
I cannot bear a moment's loss of joy.
Night appears above in her chariot.

Look up. The night is in her silent chariot,
And rolling just o'er Thebes. Bid her drive slowly,
Or make a double turn about the world,   225
While I drop Jove and take Amphitryon's dress,
To be the greater, while I seem the less. (*Exit.*)

MERCURY.

Madam Night, a good even to you. Fair and softly,
I beseech you, madam, I have a word or two to
you, from no less a god than Jupiter.   230

NIGHT.

Oh, my nimble-fingered god of theft, what make
you here on earth at this unseasonable hour? What
banker's shop is to be broken open tonight? Or
what clippers* and coiners⁷ and conspirators have
been invoking your deity for their assistance?   235

MERCURY.

Faith, none of those enormities, and yet I am still
in my vocation, for you know I am a kind of jack-
of-all-trades. At a word, Jupiter is indulging his
genius tonight with a certain noble sort of
recreation called wenching. The truth on't is,   240
adultery is its proper name.

NIGHT.

Jupiter would do well to stick to his wife, Juno.

MERCURY.

He has been married to her above these hundred
years, and that's long enough, in conscience, to
stick to one woman.   245

NIGHT.

She's his sister too, as well as his wife. That's a
double tie of affection to her.

MERCURY.

Nay, if he made bold with his own flesh and blood,
'tis likely he will not spare his neighbors'.

NIGHT.

If I were his wife, I would raise a rebellion against   250
him for the violation of my bed.

MERCURY.

Thou are mistaken, old Night. His wife could raise
no faction. All the deities in heaven would take the
part of the cuckold-making god, for they are all
given to the flesh most damnably. Nay, the very   255
goddesses would stickle in the cause of love. 'Tis
the way to be popular—to whore and love. For

---

7 coiners] counterfeiters

what dost thou think old Saturn was deposed,[8] but that he was cold and impotent and made no court to the fair ladies? Pallas and Juno themselves, as chaste as they are, cried shame on him. I say unto thee, old Night, woe be to the monarch that has not the women on his side.

NIGHT.

Then by your rule, Mercury, a king who would live happily must debauch his whole nation of women.

MERCURY.

As far as his ready money will go, I mean, for Jupiter himself can't please all of 'em. But this is beside my present commission. He has sent me to will and require you to make a swingeing long night for him, for he hates to be stinted in his pleasures.

NIGHT.

Tell him plainly, I'll rather lay down my commission. What, would he make a bawd of me?

MERCURY.

Poor ignorant! Why, he meant thee for a bawd when he first made thee. What art thou good for, but to be a bawd? Is not daylight better for mankind, I mean as to any other use but only for love and fornication? Thou hast been a bawd too—a reverend, primitive, original bawd from the first hour of thy creation. And all the laudable actions of love have been committed under thy mantle. Prithee, for what dost thou think that thou art worshipped?

NIGHT.

Why, for my stars and moonshine.

MERCURY.

That is, for holding a candle to iniquity. But if they were put out, thou woudst be double worshipped by the willing bashful virgins.

NIGHT.

Then for my quiet and the sweetness of my sleep.

MERCURY.

No, for thy sweet waking all the night, for sleep comes not upon lovers till thou art vanished.

NIGHT.

But it will be against nature to make a long winter's night at midsummer.

MERCURY.

Trouble not yourself for that. Phoebus is ordered to make a short summer's day tomorrow, so in four-and-twenty hours all will be at rights again.

NIGHT.

Well, I am edified by your discourse, and my comfort is that, whatever work is made, I see nothing.

MERCURY.

About your business, then. Put a spoke into your chariot wheels and order the seven stars[9] to halt, while I put myself into the habit of a serving man and dress up a false Sosia to wait upon a false Amphitryon. Good night, Night.

NIGHT.

My service to Jupiter. Farewell, Mercury.

Night goes backward. Exit Mercury.

Scene ii. Amphitryon's palace.

Enter Alcmena alone.

ALCMENA.

Why was I married to the man I love!
For had he been indifferent to my choice
Or had been hated, absence had been pleasure,
But now I fear for my Amphitryon's life.
At home in private and secure from war,   5
I am amidst an host of armèd foes,
Sustaining all his cares, pierced with his wounds,
And, if he falls (which, oh ye gods, avert),
Am in Amphitryon slain. Would I were there,
And he were here; so might we change our fates,   10
That he might grieve for me, and I might die for him.

Enter Phaedra, running.

PHAEDRA.

Good news, good news, madam. Oh such admirable news, that if I kept it in a moment, I should burst with it!

ALCMENA.

Is it from the army?   15

PHAEDRA.

No matter.

---

8 Saturn] king of the gods, overthrown by his son, Jupiter

9 seven stars] the constellation Pleiades, visible during the summer months

ALCMENA.

From Amphitryon?

PHAEDRA.

No matter neither.

ALCMENA.

Answer me, I charge thee, if thy good news be
anything relating to my lord; if it be, assure thyself
of a reward.

PHAEDRA.

Aye madam, now you say something to the matter.
You know the business of a poor waiting woman
here upon earth is to be scraping up something
against a rainy day, called the day of marriage—
everyone in our vocation. But what matter is it to
me if my lord has routed the enemies, if I get
nothing of their spoils?

ALCMENA.

Say, is my lord victorious?

PHAEDRA.

Why, he is victorious. Indeed, I prayed devoutly
to Jupiter for a victory, by the same token, that you
should give me ten pieces of gold if I brought you
news of it.

ALCMENA.

They are thine, supposing he be safe too.

PHAEDRA.

Nay, that's a new bargain, for I vowed to Jupiter
that then you should give me ten pieces more. But
I do undertake for my lord's safety, if you will
please to discharge his godship Jupiter of the debt
and take it upon you to pay.

ALCMENA.

When he returns in safety, Jupiter and I will pay
your vow.

PHAEDRA.

And I am sure I articled with Jupiter, that if I
brought you news that my lord was upon return,
you should grant me one small favor more that will
cost you nothing.

ALCMENA.

Make haste, thou torturer. Is my Amphitryon
upon return?

PHAEDRA.

Promise me that I shall be your bedfellow tonight
as I have been ever since my lord's absence—unless
I shall be pleased to release you of your word.

ALCMENA.

That's a small request. 'Tis granted.

PHAEDRA.

But swear by Jupiter.

ALCMENA.

But why by Jupiter?

PHAEDRA.

Because he's the greatest. I hate to deal with one
of your little baffling[10] gods that can do nothing
but by permission. But Jupiter can swinge you off
if you swear by him and are foresworn.

ALCMENA.

I swear by Jupiter.

PHAEDRA.

Then I believe he is victorious, and I know he is
safe, for I looked through the keyhole and saw him
knocking at the gate, and I had the conscience to
let him cool his heels there.

ALCMENA.

And wouldst thou not open to him? Oh, thou
traitress!

PHAEDRA.

No, I was a little wiser. I left Sosia's wife to let him
in, for I was resolved to bring the news and make
my pennyworths out of him—as time shall show.

*Enter Jupiter in the shape of Amphitryon, with Sosia's
wife, Bromia. He kisses and embraces Alcmena.*

JUPITER.

Oh, let me live forever on those lips!
The nectar of the gods to these is tasteless.
I swear that, were I Jupiter, this night
I would renounce my heav'n to be Amphitryon.

ALCMENA.

Then, not to swear beneath Amphitryon's oath
(Forgive me, Juno, if I am profane),
I swear I would be what I am this night,
And be Alcmena rather than be Juno.

BROMIA.

Good my lord, what's become of my poor
bedfellow, your man Sosia? You keep such a billing
and colling[11] here to set one's mouth a-watering.
What, I say, though I am a poor woman, I have a

10 baffling] trifling and ineffectual
11 colling] caressing, hugging

husband as well as my lady and should be as glad 80
as she of a little honest recreation.

PHAEDRA.
And what have you done with your old friend and
my old sweetheart, Judge Gripus? Has he brought
me home a crammed purse that swells with bribes?
If he be rich, I'll make him welcome like an 85
honorable magistrate, but if he has not had the wit
to sell justice, he judges no causes in my court, I
warrant him.

ALCMENA.
My lord, you tell me nothing of the battle.
Is Thebes victorious, are our foes destroyed? 90
For now I find you safe, I should be glad
To hear you were in danger.

JUPITER. (Aside.)
A man had need be a god to stand the fury of three
talking women. I think, in my conscience, I made
their tongues of thunder. 95

BROMIA. (Pulling him on one side.)
I asked the first question. Answer me, my lord.

PHAEDRA. (Pulling him on t'other side.)
Peace. Mine's a lover, and yours is but a husband.
And my judge is "my lord" too; the title shall take
place, and I will be answered.

JUPITER.
Sosia is safe; Gripus is rich; both coming. 100
I rode before 'em with a lover's haste.
(Aside.)
Was e'er poor god so worried! But for my love,
I wish I were in heav'n again with Juno.

ALCMENA.
Then I, it seems, am last to be regarded?

JUPITER.
Not so, my love. But these obstreperous tongues 105
Have snatched their answers first—they will be
heard.
And surely Jove would never answer prayer
That women made, but only to be freed
From their eternal noise. Make haste to bed;
There let me tell my story in thy arms. 110
There, in the gentle pauses of our love,
Betwixt our dyings,* ere we live again,
Thou shalt be told the battle and success,
Which I shall oft begin and then break off.
For love will often interrupt my tale 115

And make so sweet confusion in our talk
That thou shalt ask, and I shall answer, things
That are not of a piece, but patched with kisses
And sighs and murmurs and imperfect speech.
And nonsense shall be eloquent in love. 120

BROMIA. (To Phaedra.)
My lord is very hot upon't. This absence is a great
friend to us poor neglected wives; it makes us new
again.

ALCMENA.
I am the fool of love and find within me
The fondness of a bride without the fear. 125
My whole desires and wishes are in you.

PHAEDRA. (Aside.)
My lady's eyes are pinking[12] to bedward too. Now
is she to look very sleepy, counterfeiting yawning,
but she shall ask me leave first.

ALCMENA.
Great Juno, thou whose holy care presides 130
Over the nuptial bed, pour all thy blessings
On this auspicious night.

JUPITER.
Juno may grudge, for she may fear a rival
In those bright eyes, but Jupiter will grant
And doubly bless this night. 135

PHAEDRA. (Aside.)
But Jupiter should ask my leave first, were he here
in person.

ALCMENA.
Bromia, prepare the bed.
The tedious journey has disposed my lord
To seek his needful rest. 140

Exit Bromia.

PHAEDRA.
'Tis very true, madam. The poor gentleman must
needs be weary, and therefore, 'twas not ill
contrived that he must lie alone tonight to recruit
himself with sleep and lay in enough for tomorrow
night, when you may keep him waking. 145

ALCMENA. (To Jupiter.)
I must confess I made a kind of promise—

PHAEDRA. (Almost crying.)
A kind of promise, do you call it? I see you would

---

12 pinking] winking in a sleepy or sly manner

fain be coming off. I am sure you swore to me by
Jupiter that I should be your bedfellow, and I'll
accuse you to him too, the first prayers I make. 150
And I'll pray a-purpose too, that I will, though I
have not prayed to him this seven years.

JUPITER.

Oh, the malicious hilding!

ALCMENA.

I did swear indeed, my lord.

JUPITER.

Foreswear thyself, for Jupiter but laughs 155
At lovers' perjuries.

PHAEDRA.

The more shame for him if he does. There would
be a fine god indeed for us women to worship, if
he laughs when our sweethearts cheat us of our
maidenheads. No, no, Jupiter is an honester 160
gentleman than you make of him.

JUPITER.

I'm all on fire and would not lose this night
To be the master of the universe.

PHAEDRA.

Aye my lord, I see you are on fire, but the devil a 165
bucket shall be brought to quench it without my
leave. You *may* go to bed, madam, but you shall
see how heaven will bless your night's work if you
foreswear yourself. [*Aside.*] Some fool, some mere
elder brother,13 or some blockheadly hero, Jove, I 170
beseech thee, send her.

JUPITER. (*Aside.*)

Now I could call my thunder to revenge me,
But that were to confess myself a god,
And then I lost my love.—Alcmena, come,
By heav'n, I have a bridegroom's fervor for thee, 175
As I had ne'er enjoyed.

ALCMENA. (*Sighing.*)

          She has my oath,
And sure she may release it if she please—

PHAEDRA.

Why truly madam, I am not cruel in my nature
to poor distressed lovers, for it may be my own case 180

---

13 mere elder brother] Although eldest sons inherited the
    family estate, they were proverbially dullards, while their
    younger brothers had to have the intelligence to live by
    their wits.

another day. And therefore, if my lord pleases to
consider me—

JUPITER.

Anything, anything, but name thy wish and have
it.

PHAEDRA.

Aye, now you say "anything, anything," but you 185
would tell me another story tomorrow morning.
Look you, my lord, here's a hand open to receive—
you know the meaning of it. I am for nothing but
the ready.

JUPITER.

Thou shalt have all the treasury of heav'n. 190

PHAEDRA.

Yes, when you are Jupiter to dispose of it.

JUPITER. (*Aside.*)

I had forgot and showed myself a god.
This love can make a fool of Jupiter.

PHAEDRA.

You have got some part of the enemy's spoil, I
warrant you; I see a little trifling diamond upon 195
your finger, and I am proud enough to think it
would become mine too.

JUPITER. (*Taking a ring off his finger and giving it.*)

Here, take it. This is a very* woman.
Her sex is avarice, and she, in one,
Is all her sex. 200

PHAEDRA.

Aye, aye, 'tis no matter what you say of us. What,
would you have your money out of the treasury
without paying the officers their fees? Go, get you
together, you naughty couple, till you are both
weary of worrying one another, and then 205
tomorrow morning, I shall have another fee for
parting you.

Phaedra goes out before Alcmena with a light.

JUPITER. (*Alone.*)

Why, now I am indeed the lord of all,
For what's to be a god, but to enjoy?
Let humankind their sovereign's leisure wait. 210
Love is, this night, my great affair of state.
Let this one night, of providence be void;
All Jove, for once, is on himself employed.
Let unregarded altars smoke in vain,
And let my subjects praise me or complain. 215

Yet if betwixt my intervals of bliss
Some am'rous youth his orisons address,
His prayer is in a happy hour preferred.
And when Jove loves, a lover shall be heard.

Act II. Night scene of [Amphitryon's] palace.

*Sosia with a dark lantern [and] Mercury in Sosia's
shape with a dark lantern also.*

SOSIA. [*To himself, not seeing Mercury.*]

Was not the devil in my master to send me out in
this dreadful dark night to bring the news of his
victory to my lady? And was not I possessed with
ten devils for going on his errand without a convoy
for the safeguard of my person? Lord, how am I   5
melted into sweat with fear! I am diminished of
my natural weight above two stone. I shall not
bring half myself home again to my poor wife and
family. I have been in an ague fit ever since shut
of evening, what with the fright of trees by the   10
highway, which looked maliciously like thieves by
moonshine, and what with bulrushes by the
riverside that shaked like spears and lances at me.
Well, the greatest plague of a serving man is to be
hired to some great lord. They care not what   15
drudgery they put upon us while they lie lolling
at their ease abed and stretch their lazy limbs in
expectation of the whore which we are fetching for
them.

MERCURY. (*Aside.*)

He is but a poor mortal that suffers this. But I,   20
who am a god, am degraded to a footpimp, a
waiter without doors[14]—a very civil employment
for a deity!

SOSIA.

The better sort of 'em will say "upon my honor"
at every word. Yet ask 'em for our wages, and they   25
plead the privilege of their honor and will not pay
us, nor let us take our privilege of the law upon
them. These are a very hopeful sort of patriots* to
stand up as they do for liberty and property of the
subject—there's conscience for you!   30

MERCURY. (*Aside.*)

This fellow has something of the republican spirit
in him.

SOSIA. (*Looking about him.*)

Stay. This, methinks, should be our house. And I
should thank the gods now for bringing me safe
home. But I think I had as good let my devotions   35
alone till I have got the reward for my good news,
and then thank 'em once for all. For if I praise 'em
before I am safe within doors, some damned
mastiff dog may come out and worry me, and then
my thanks are thrown away upon 'em.   40

MERCURY. (*Aside.*)

Thou art a wicked rogue and wilt have thy bargain
beforehand; therefore, thou get'st not into the
house this night—and thank me accordingly as I
use thee.

SOSIA.

Now am I to give my lady an account of my lord's   45
victory; 'tis good to exercise my parts* beforehand
and file my tongue into eloquent expressions to
tickle her ladyship's imagination.

MERCURY. (*Aside.*)

Good! And here's the god of eloquence[15] to judge
of thy oration.   50

SOSIA. (*Setting down his lantern.*)

This lanthorn, for once, shall be my lady, because
she is the lamp of all beauty and perfection.

MERCURY. (*Aside.*)

No rogue, 'tis thy lord is the lanthorn[16] by this
time, or Jupiter is turned fumbler.

SOSIA.

Then thus I make my addresses to her. (*Bows.*)   55
Madam, my lord has chosen me out as the most
faithful, though the most unworthy, of his followers,
to bring your ladyship this following account of our
glorious expedition. Then she (*In a shrill tone.*): "Oh
my poor Sosia, how am I overjoyed to see thee!" She   60
can say no less. [*Turning to the lantern.*] Madam, you
do me too much honor, and the world will envy me
this glory.—Well answered on my side.—"And how
does my lord Amphitryon?"—Madam, he always

---

[14] waiter without doors] an inferior servant who works
outside

[15] god of eloquence] Mercury also was the god of wit and
rhetoric.

[16] lanthorn] with pun on horns*

does like a man of courage when he is called by 65
honor.—There, I think I nicked it.—"But when
will he return?"—As soon as possibly he can, but not
so soon as his impatient heart could wish him with
your ladyship.
MERCURY. (*Aside.*)
When Thebes is an university, thou deservest to 70
be their orator.[17]
SOSIA.
"But what does he do and what does he say?
Prithee, tell me something more of him."—He
always says less than he does, madam, and his
enemies have found it to their cost.—Where the 75
devil did I learn these elegancies and gallantries?
MERCURY. [*Aside.*]
So, he has all the natural endowments of a fop and
only wants* the education.
SOSIA. (*Staring up to the sky.*)
What, is the devil in the night! She's as long as two
nights. The seven stars are just where they were 80
seven hours ago. High day[18]—high night, I mean,
by my favor. What, has Phoebus been playing the
goodfellow[19] and overslept himself that he forgets
his duty to us mortals?
MERCURY. [*Aside*].
How familiarly the rascal treats us gods! But I shall 85
make him alter his tone immediately. (*Comes nearer
and stands just before him.*)
SOSIA. (*Seeing him and starting back, aside.*)
How now? What, do my eyes dazzle, or is my dark
lanthorn false to me? Is not that a giant before our
door? Or a ghost of somebody slain in the late 90
battle? If he be, 'tis unconscionably done to fright
an honest man thus, who never drew weapon
wrathfully in all my life. Whatever wight he be, I
am devilishly afraid, that's certain. But 'tis
discretion to keep my own counsel; I'll sing, that 95
I may seem valiant.

---

17 orator] an official position at the universities of Cambridge and Oxford that required speaking at ceremonial
   functions
18 High day] a variation of "hey-day," an exclamation of
   surprise
19 goodfellow] jovial and reveling companion, perhaps with
   a hint of Robin Goodfellow (q.v.)

*Sosia sings, and as Mercury speaks, by little and little
drops his voice.*

MERCURY.
What saucy companion is this that deafens us with
his hoarse voice? What midnight ballad singer have
we here? I shall teach the villain* to leave off
caterwauling. 100
SOSIA. [*Aside.*]
I would I had courage for his sake, that I might teach
him to call my singing caterwauling. An illiterate
rogue—an enemy to the muses and to music.
MERCURY.
There is an ill savor that offends my nostrils, and
it wafteth this way. 105
SOSIA. [*Aside.*]
He has smelt me out; my fear has betrayed me into
this savor. I am a dead man. The bloody villain is
at his fee, fa, fum already.
MERCURY.
Stand. Who goes there?
SOSIA.
A friend. 110
MERCURY.
What friend?
SOSIA.
Why, a friend to all the world that will give me
leave to live peaceably.
MERCURY.
I defy peace and all its works. My arms are out of
exercise—they have mauled nobody these three 115
days. I long for an honorable occasion to pound a
man and lay him asleep at the first buffet.
SOSIA. (*Aside.*)
That would almost do me a kindness, for I have
been kept waking without tipping one wink of
sleep these three nights. 120
MERCURY.
Of what quality are you, fellow?
SOSIA.
Why, I am a man, fellow. [*Aside.*] Courage, Sosia.
MERCURY.
What kind of man?
SOSIA.
Why, a two-legged man. What man should I be?
(*Aside.*) I must bear up to him; he may prove as 125
arrant a milksop as myself.

MERCURY.

Thou art a coward, I warrant thee. Do not I hear thy teeth chatter in thy head?

SOSIA.

Aye, aye, that's only a sign they would be snapping at thy nose. (*Aside.*) Bless me, what an arm and fist he has, with great thumbs too, and gols[20] and knuckle bones of a very* butcher.

MERCURY.

Sirrah, from whence come you and wither go you? Answer me directly upon pain of assassination.

SOSIA.

I am coming from whence I came and am going wither I go. That's directly home, though this is somewhat an uncivil manner of proceeding at the first sight of a man, let me tell you.

MERCURY.

Then to begin our better acquaintance, let me first make you a small present of this box o'the ear. (*Strikes him.*)

SOSIA.

If I were as choleric a fool as you now, here would be fine work betwixt us two. But I am a little better bred than to disturb the sleeping neighborhood, and so good night, friend. (*Is going.*)

MERCURY. (*Stopping him.*)

Hold, sir, you and I must not part so easily. Once more, wither are you going?

SOSIA.

Why, I am going as fast as I can to get out of the reach of your clutches. Let me but only knock at that door there.

MERCURY.

What business have you at that door, sirrah?

SOSIA.

This is our house. And when I am got in, I'll tell you more.

MERCURY.

Whose house is this, sauciness, that you are so familiar with to call it "ours"?

SOSIA.

'Tis mine in the first place. And next, my master's, for I lie in the garret, and he lies under me.

---

20 golls] hands

MERCURY.

Have your master and you no names, sirrah?

SOSIA.

His name is Amphitryon—hear that and tremble.

MERCURY.

What, my lord general?

SOSIA.

Oh, has his name mollified you! I have brought you down a peg lower already, friend.

MERCURY.

And your name is—

SOSIA.

Lord, my friend, you are so very troublesome. What should my name be but Sosia?

MERCURY.

How? Sosia, say you? How long have you taken up that name, sirrah?

SOSIA.

Here's a fine question. Why, I never took it up, friend. It was born with me.

MERCURY.

What, was your name born "Sosia"? Take this remembrance for that lie. (*Beats him [with a cudgel].*)

SOSIA.

Hold, friend. You are so very flippant with your hands, you won't hear reason. What offence has my name done you that you should beat me for it? S-O-S-I-A. They are as civil, honest, harmless letters as any are in the whole alphabet.

MERCURY.

I have no quarrel to the name, but that 'tis e'en too good for you, and 'tis none of yours.

SOSIA.

What, am not I Sosia, say you?

MERCURY.

No.

SOSIA.

I should think you are somewhat merrily disposed if you had not beaten me in such sober sadness. You would persuade me out of my heathen name, would you?

MERCURY.

Say you are Sosia again at your peril, sirrah.

SOSIA.

I dare say nothing, but thought is free. But whatever I am called, I am Amphitryon's man, and

the first letter of my name is "S" too. You had best
tell me that my master did not send me home to
my lady with news of his victory.   190

MERCURY.

I say he did not.

SOSIA.

Lord, lord, friend. One of us two is horribly given
to lying—but I do not say which of us, to avoid
contention.

MERCURY.

I say my name is Sosia and yours is not.   195

SOSIA.

I would you could make good your words, for then
I should not be beaten and you should.

MERCURY.

I find you would be Sosia if you durst, but if I
catch you thinking so—

SOSIA.

I hope I may think I was Sosia, and I can find no   200
difference between my former self and my present
self, but that I was plain Sosia before, and now I
am laced Sosia.

MERCURY.

Take this for being so impudent to think so. (*Beats
him.*)   205

SOSIA. (*Kneeling.*)

Truce a little, I beseech thee! I would be a stock or a
stone now, by my good will, and would not think at
all for self preservation. But will you give me leave to
argue the matter fairly with you? And promise me to
depose that cudgel if I can prove myself to be that   210
man that I was before I was beaten?

MERCURY.

Well, proceed in safety. I promise you I will not
beat you.

SOSIA.

In the first place then, is not this town called
Thebes?   215

MERCURY.

Undoubtedly.

SOSIA.

And is not this house Amphitryon's?

MERCURY.

Who denies it?

SOSIA.

I thought you would have denied that too, for all

hangs upon a string. Remember then, that those   220
two preliminary articles are already granted. In the
next place, did not the foresaid Amphitryon beat
the Teleboans, kill their king, Pterelas,[21] and send
a certain servant—meaning somebody that for
sake-sake shall be nameless—to bring a present to   225
his wife with news of his victory and of his
resolution to return tomorrow?

MERCURY.

This is all true to a very tittle. But who is that
certain servant? There's all the question.

SOSIA.

Is it peace or war betwixt us?   230

MERCURY.

Peace.

SOSIA.

I dare not wholly trust that abominable cudgel, but
'tis a certain friend of yours and mine that had a
certain name before he was beaten out of it. But
if you are a man that depend not altogether upon   235
force and brutality, but somewhat also upon
reason, now do you bring better proofs that you
are that same certain man, and in order to it,
answer me to certain questions.

MERCURY.

I say I am Sosia, Amphitryon's man. What reason   240
have you to urge against it?

SOSIA.

What was your father's name?

MERCURY.

Davus, who was an honest husbandman, whose
sister's name was Harpagè, that was married and
died in a foreign country.   245

SOSIA.

So far you are right, I must confess. And your
wife's name is—

---

21 Pterelas] the son of Poseidon who, leading the Teleboans,
tried to usurp the kingdom of Mycenae from Electryon,
Alcmene's father; during his campaign to help Electryon
defeat Pterelas, Amphitryon married Alcmene, with the
understanding that the marriage could not be consummated until Pterelas and his followers were crushed. According to legend, Jupiter seduced Alcmene, disguised
as Amphitryon, before the marriage had been consummated.

MERCURY.

Bromia—a devilish shrew of her tongue and a vixen of her hands that leads me a miserable life, keeps me to hard duty abed, and beats me every morning when I have risen from her side without having first— 250

SOSIA.

I understand you by many a sorrowful token. (*Aside.*) This must be I.

MERCURY.

I was once taken upon suspicion of burglary and was whipped through Thebes and branded for my pains. 255

SOSIA. [*Aside.*]

Right—me again.—But if you are I, as I begin to suspect, that whipping and branding might have been passed over in silence for both our credits. 260 [*Aside.*] And yet now I think on't, if I am I (as I am I), he cannot be I. All these circumstances he might have heard, but I will now interrogate him upon some private passages.—What was the present that Amphitryon sent by you or me—no 265 matter which of us—to his wife, Alcmena?

MERCURY.

A buckle of diamonds consisting of five large stones.

SOSIA.

And where are they now?

MERCURY.

In a case, sealed with my master's coat of arms. 270

SOSIA.

This is prodigious, I confess. (*Aside.*) But yet 'tis nothing now I think on't, for some false brother may have revealed it to him.—But I have another question to ask you, of somewhat that passed only betwixt myself and me. If you are Sosia, what were 275 you doing in the heat of battle?

MERCURY.

What a wise man should that has a respect for his own person. I ran into our tent and hid myself amongst the baggage.

SOSIA. (*Aside.*)

Such another cutting answer and I must provide 280 myself of another name.—And how did you pass your time in that same tent? You need not answer to every circumstance so exactly now. You must lie

a little, that I may think you the more me.

MERCURY.

That cunning shall not serve your turn to 285 circumvent me out of my name. I am for plain naked truth. There stood a hogshead of old wine, which my lord reserved for his own drinking.

SOSIA. (*Aside.*)

Oh, the devil! As sure as death, he must have hid himself in that hogshead or he could never have 290 known that.

MERCURY.

And by that hogshead, upon the ground, there lay the kind inviter and provoker of good drinking—

SOSIA.

Nay, now I have caught you; there was neither inviter nor provoker, for I was all alone. 295

MERCURY.

A lusty gammon of—

SOSIA. (*Sighing.*)

Bacon. [*Aside.*] That word has quite made an end of me. Let me see—this must be I, in spite of me. But let me view him nearer. (*Walks about Mercury with his dark lantern.*) 300

MERCURY.

What are you walking about me for with your dark lanthorn?

SOSIA.

No harm, friend. I am only surveying a parcel of earth here that I find we two are about to bargain for. [*Aside.*] He's damnable like me, that's certain. 305 Imprimis: there's the patch upon my nose,[22] with a pox to him. Item: a very foolish face with a long chin at end on't. Item: one pair of shambling legs with two splay feet belonging to them. And, *summa totalis*: from head to foot, all my bodily apparel. (*To 310 Mercury.*) Well, you are Sosia; there's no denying it. But what am I, then? For my mind gives me I am somebody still, if I knew but who I were.

MERCURY.

When I have a mind to be Sosia no more then thou mayst be Sosia again. 315

SOSIA.

I have but one request more to thee: that, though

---

22 patch … nose] a covering of a sore, with a suggestion of venereal disease

not as Sosia, yet as a stranger, I may go into that
house and carry a civil message to my lady.

MERCURY.

No, sirrah. Not being Sosia, you have no message
to deliver, nor no lady in this house.   320

SOSIA.

Thou canst not be so barbarous to let me lie in
the streets all night after such a journey and such
a beating. And therefore, I am resolved to knock
at the door in my own defense.

MERCURY.

If you come near the door, I recall my word and   325
break off the truce. And then expect—(*Holds up
his cudgel.*)

SOSIA.

No, the devil take me if I do expect. I have felt
too well what sour fruit that crab tree bears. I'll
rather beat it back upon the hoof to my lord   330
Amphitryon to see if he will acknowledge me for
Sosia; if he does not, then I am no longer his slave.
There's my freedom dearly purchased with a sore
drubbing. If he does acknowledge me, then I am
Sosia again; so far 'tis tolerably well. But then I   335
shall have a second drubbing for an unfortunate
ambassador as I am, and that's intolerable. (*Exit.*)

MERCURY.

I have fobbed off his excellency pretty well. Now let
him return and make the best of his credentials. I
think too I have given Jupiter sufficient time for his   340
consummation.—Oh, he has taken his cue, and
here he comes as leisurely and as lank as if he had
emptied himself of the best part of his almightyship.

[*Mercury stands aside.*] *Enter Jupiter leading Alcmena,
followed by Phaedra, pages with torches before them.*

JUPITER. (*To the pages.*)

Those torches are offensive. Stand aloof,
(*To [Alcmena].*)

For, though they bless me with thy heavenly sight,   345
They may disclose the secret I would hide.
The Thebans must not know I have been here.
Detracting crowds would blame me that I robbed
These happy moments from my public charge
To consecrate to thy desired embrace.   350
And I could wish no witness but thyself,
For thou thyself art all I wish to please.

ALCMENA.

So long an absence and so short a stay!
What, but one night? One night of joy and love
Could only pay one night of cares and fears,   355
And all the rest are an uncancelled sum.
Curse on this honor and this public fame.
Would you have less of both and more of love.

JUPITER.

Alcmena, I must go.

ALCMENA.

                                   Not yet, my lord.   360

JUPITER.

Indeed, I must.

ALCMENA.

                       Indeed, you shall not go.

JUPITER.

Behold the ruddy streaks o'er yonder hill.
Those are the blushes of the breaking morn
That kindle daylight to this nether world.   365

ALCMENA.

No matter for the day, it was but made
To number out the hours of busy men.
Let 'em be busy still* and still* be wretched,
And take their fill of anxious, drudging day.
But you and I will draw our curtains close,   370
Extinguish daylight, and put out the sun.
Come back, my lord; in faith, you shall retire.
You have not yet lay long enough in bed
To warm your widowed side.

PHAEDRA. (*Aside.*)

I find my lord is an excellent schoolmaster, my lady   375
is so willing to repeat her lesson.

MERCURY. (*Aside.*)

That's a plaguey little devil. What a roguish eye
she has! I begin to like her strangely. She's the
perquisite of my place too, for my lady's waiting
woman is the proper fees of my lord's chief   380
gentleman. I have the privilege of a god too; I can
view her naked through all her clothes. Let me see,
let me see. I have discovered something that pleases
me already.

JUPITER.

Let me not live, but thou art all enjoyment.   385
So charming and so sweet that not a night,
But whole eternity, were well employed
To love thy each perfection as it ought.

ALCMENA. (*Kissing him.*)

  I'll bribe you with this kiss to stay a while.

JUPITER.

  A bribe indeed that soon will bring me back.   390

  But, to be just, I must restore your bribe. (*Kissing*
    her.)

  How I could dwell forever on those lips!

  Oh, I could kiss 'em pale with eagerness!

  So soft, by heav'n, and such a juicy sweet

  That ripened peaches have not half the flavor.   395

ALCMENA.

  Ye niggard gods! You make our lives too long.

  You fill 'em with diseases, wants,* and woes,

  And only dash 'em with a little love,

  Sprinkled by fits and with a sparing hand.

  Count all our joys from childhood ev'n to age,   400

  They would but make a day of ev'ry year.

  Take back your sev'nty years (the stint of life),

  Or else be kind and cram the quintessence

  Of sev'nty years into sweet sev'nty days:

  For all the rest is flat, insipid being.   405

JUPITER.

  But yet one scruple pains me at my parting:

  I love so nicely* that I cannot bear

  To owe the sweets of love, which I have tasted,

  To the submissive duty of a wife.

  Tell me, and soothe my passion ere I go,   410

  That in the kindest moments of the night,

  When you gave up yourself to love and me,

  You thought not of a husband but a lover.

ALCMENA.

  But tell me first why you would raise a blush

  Upon my cheeks by asking such a question.   415

JUPITER.

  I would owe nothing to a name so dull

  As husband is, but, to a lover, all.

ALCMENA.

  You should have asked me then, when love and
    night

  And privacy had favored your demand.

JUPITER.

  I ask it now because my tenderness   420

  Surpasses that of husbands for their wives.

  Oh, that you loved like me! Then you would find

  A thousand, thousand niceties in love.

  The common love of sex to sex is brutal,

But love refined will fancy to itself   425

  Millions of gentle cares and sweet disquiets.

  The being happy is not half the joy;

  The manner of the happiness is all!

  In me, my charming mistress, you behold

  A lover that disdains a lawful title,   430

  Such as of monarchs to successive thrones.

  The generous* lover holds by force of arms

  And claims his crown by conquest.

ALCMENA.

  Methinks you should be pleased. I give you all

  A virtuous and a modest wife can give.   435

JUPITER.

  No, no, that very name of wife and marriage

  Is poison to the dearest sweets of love.

  To please my niceness* you must separate

  The lover from his mortal foe, the husband.

  Give to the yawning husband your cold virtue,   440

  But all your vigorous warmth, your melting sighs,

  Your amorous murmurs, be your lover's part.

ALCMENA.

  I comprehend not what you mean, my lord.

  But only love me still* and love me thus,

  And think of me such as best may please your   445

    thought.

JUPITER.

  There's mystery of love in all I say.

  Farewell, and when you see your husband next,

  Think of your lover then.

*Exeunt Jupiter and Alcmena severally. Phaedra follows
her.*

MERCURY.

  Now I should follow him, but love has laid a lime-
twig for me and made a lame god of me. Yet why   450
should I love this Phaedra? She's interessèd[23] and
a jilt into the bargain. Three thousand years hence
there will be a whole nation of such women in a
certain country that will be called France, and
there's a neighbor island, too, where the men of   455
that country will be all interest. Oh, what a
precious* generation will that be, which the men
of the island shall propagate out of the women of
the continent.

---

23 interessèd] looking out only for her own best interests

Phaedra re-enters.

And so much for prophecy, for she's here again, 460
and I must love her in spite of me. And since I
must, I have this comfort, that the greatest wits
are commonly the greatest cullies because neither
of the sexes can be wiser than some certain parts
about 'em will give 'em leave. 465

PHAEDRA.

Well Sosia, and how go matters?

MERCURY.

Our army is victorious.

PHAEDRA.

And my servant,* Judge Gripus?

MERCURY.

A voluptuous gourmand.

PHAEDRA.

But has he gotten wherewithal to be voluptuous? 470
Is he wealthy?

MERCURY.

He sells justice as he uses, fleeces the rich rebels,
and hangs up the poor.

PHAEDRA.

Then while he has money he may make love to
me. Has he sent me no token?

MERCURY.

Yes, a kiss, and by the same token, I am to give it 475
you as a remembrance from him.

PHAEDRA.

How now, impudence! A beggarly serving man
presume to kiss me?

MERCURY.

Suppose I were a god and should make love to
you? 480

PHAEDRA.

I would first be satisfied whether you were a poor
god or a rich god.

MERCURY.

Suppose I were Mercury, the god of merchandise?

PHAEDRA.

What, the god of small wares and fripperies, of
peddlers and pilferers? 485

MERCURY. (*Aside.*)

How the gypsy despises me!

PHAEDRA.

I had rather you were Plutus, the god of money,
or Jupiter in a golden shower[24]—there was a god
for us women! He had the art of making love. Dost
thou think that kings, or gods either, get mistresses 490
by their good faces? No, 'tis the gold and the
presents they can make. There's the prerogative
they have over their fair subjects.

MERCURY.

All this notwithstanding, I must tell you, pretty
Phaedra, I am desperately in love with you. 495

PHAEDRA.

And I must tell thee, ugly Sosia, thou hast not
wherewithal to be in love.

MERCURY.

Yes, a poor man may be in love, I hope?

PHAEDRA.

I grant a poor rogue may be in love, but he can never
make love.* Alas Sosia, thou hast neither face to 500
invite me, nor youth to please me, nor gold to bribe
me. And besides all this, thou hast a wife, poor
miserable Sosia. [*Calling out.*] What ho, Bromia!

MERCURY.

Oh, thou merciless creature, why dost thou
conjure up that sprite of a wife? 505

PHAEDRA.

To rid myself of that devil of a poor lover. Since
you are so lovingly disposed, I'll put you together
to exercise your fury upon your own wedlock.—
What, Bromia, I say, make haste! Here's a vessel
of yours, full freighted, that's going off without 510
paying duties.

MERCURY.

Since thou wilt not let me steal custom, she shall
have all the cargo I have gotten in the wars. But
thou might'st have lent me a little creek to smuggle
in. 515

PHAEDRA.

Why, what have you gotten, good gentleman
soldier, besides a legion of—(*Snaps her fingers.*)

MERCURY.

When the enemy was routed, I had the plundering
of a tent.

24 Jupiter ... shower] In order to reach the sequestered
Danae, daughter of the King of Argos, Jupiter transformed himself into a golden shower of sunlight, spilling himself into her lap.

PHAEDRA.

That's to say a house of canvas with movables of 520
straw.—Make haste, Bromia!

MERCURY.

But it was the general's own tent.

PHAEDRA.

You durst not fight, I'm certain, and therefore
came last in when the rich plunder was gone
beforehand.—Will you come, Bromia? 525

MERCURY.

Prithee, do not call so loud—a great goblet that
holds a gallon.

PHAEDRA.

Of what was that goblet made? Answer quickly, for
I am just calling very loud: Bro—

MERCURY.

Of beaten gold. Now call aloud, if thou dost not 530
like the metal.

PHAEDRA. (Very softly.)

Bromia.

MERCURY.

That struts in this fashion, with his arms akimbo
like a city magistrate, and a great bouncing belly
like an hostess with child of a kilderkin of wine. 535
Now what say you to that present, Phaedra?

PHAEDRA.

Why, I am considering—

MERCURY.

What, I prithee?

PHAEDRA.

Why, how to divide the business equally—to take
the gift and refuse the giver. Thou art so damnably 540
ugly and so old.

MERCURY. (Aside.)

Now the devil take Jupiter for confining me to this
ungodly shape today!—But Gripus is as old and
as ugly, too.

PHAEDRA.

But Gripus is a person of quality* and my lady's 545
uncle, and if he marries me, I shall take place of
my lady.—Hark, your wife! She has sent her
tongue before her. I hear the thunderclap already;
there's a storm approaching.

MERCURY.

Yes, of thy brewing, I thank thee for it. Oh, how 550
I should hate thee now if I could leave loving thee!

PHAEDRA.

Not a word of the dear golden goblet, as you hope
for you-know-what, Sosia.

MERCURY.

You give me hope then—

PHAEDRA.

Not absolutely hope neither, but gold is a great 555
cordial in love matters, and the more you apply
of it, the better. (Aside.) I am honest,* that's
certain, but when I weigh my honesty against the
goblet, I am not quite resolved on which side the
scale will turn. (Exit.) 560

MERCURY. (Loudly.)

Farewell, Phaedra. Remember me to my wife and
tell her—

Enter Bromia.

BROMIA.

Tell her what, traitor? That you are going away
without seeing her?

MERCURY.

That I am doing my duty and following my 565
master.

BROMIA.

Umph—so brisk, too. Your master did his duty to
my lady before he parted. He could leave his army
in the lurch and come galloping home at midnight
to have a lick at the honey pot and steal to bed as 570
quietly as any mouse, I warrant you. My master
knew what belonged to a married life. But you,
sirrah—you trencher-carrying rascal, you worse-
than-dunghill-cock that stood clapping your wings
and crowing without doors when you should have 575
been at roost, you villain*—

MERCURY.

Hold your peace, Dame Partlet,25 and leave your
cackling. My master charged me to stand sentry
without doors.

BROMIA.

"My master"? I dare swear thou beliest him. My 580
master's more a gentleman than to lay such an
unreasonable command upon a poor, distressed

---

25 Dame Partlet] the shrewish hen in Chaucer's *The Nun's
Priest's Tale*

married couple, and after such an absence too. No, there's no comparison between my master and thee, thou sneaksby.²⁶

MERCURY.

No more than there is betwixt my lady and you, Bromia. You and I have had our time in a civil way, spouse, and much good love has been betwixt us, but we have been married fifteen years, I take it, and that hoity-toity business ought, in conscience, to be over.

BROMIA.

Marry* come up, my saucy companion! I am neither old nor ugly enough to have that said to me.

MERCURY.

But will you hear reason, Bromia? My lord and my lady are yet in a manner bride and bridegroom; they are in honeymoon still. Do but think in decency what a jest it would be to the family to see two venerable old married people lying snug in a bed together and sighing out fine tender things to one another.

BROMIA.

How now, traitor, dar'st thou maintain that I am past the age of having fine things said to me?

MERCURY.

Not so, my dear. But certainly I am past the age of saying 'em.

BROMIA.

Thou deserv'st not to be yoked with a woman of honor, as I am, thou perjured villain.*

MERCURY.

Aye, you are too much a woman of honor to my sorrow. Many a poor husband would be glad to compound for less honor in his wife and more quiet. Prithee, be but honest and continent in thy tongue, and do thy worst with everything else about thee.

BROMIA.

Thou wouldst have a woman of the Town,* wouldst thou? To be always speaking my husband fair to make him digest his cuckoldom more easily. Wouldst thou be a wittol with a vengeance to thee?

I am resolved I'll scour thy hide for that word. (*Holds up her ladle at him.*)

MERCURY.

Thou wilt not strike thy lord and husband, wilt thou?

BROMIA.

Since thou wilt none of the meat, 'tis but justice to give thee the bastings of the ladle. (*She courses him about.*)

MERCURY. (*Running about, aside.*)

Was ever poor deity so henpecked as I am? Nay, then 'tis time to charm her asleep with my enchanted rod before I am disgraced or ravished. (*Plucks out his caduceus²⁷ and strikes her upon the shoulder with it.*)

BROMIA.

What, art thou rebelling against thy anointed wife? I'll make thee—how now—what, has the rogue bewitched me? I grow dull and stupid* on the sudden. I can neither stir hand nor foot. I am just like him; I have lost the use of all my—members. (*Yawning.*) I can't so much as wag my tongue—neither, and that's the last liv—ing part about a—woman. (*Falls down. [Scene closes on Bromia.]*)

MERCURY.

Lord, what have I suffered for being but a counterfeit married man one day? If ever I come to this house as a husband again, then—and yet that "then" was a lie too, for while I am in love with this young gypsy, Phaedra, I must return. But lie thou there, thou type of Juno, thou that want'st* nothing of her tongue but the immortality. If Jupiter ever let thee set foot in heaven, Juno will have a rattling second of thee, and there will never be a fair day in heaven or earth after it.

For two such tongues will break the poles asunder
And, hourly scolding, make perpetual thunder.

Exit.

---

26 sneaksby] mean-spirited person

27 caduceus] Mercury's famous wand—intertwined with two serpents—that could put people to sleep by its touch

Act III. Before Amphitryon's palace.

Amphitryon and Sosia.

AMPHITRYON.

Now sirrah, follow me into the house; thou shalt be convinced at thy own cost, villain.* What horrible lies hast thou told me! Such improbabilities, such stuff, such nonsense, that the monster with two long horns that frighted the great King and the devil at the stone-cutter's[28] are truths to these!

SOSIA.

I am but a slave and you are master, and a poor man is always to lie when a rich man is pleased to contradict him. But as sure as this is our house— 10

AMPHITRYON.

So sure, 'tis thy place of execution. Thou art not made for lying neither.

SOSIA.

That's certain, for all my neighbors say I have an honest face, or else they would never call me cuckold, as they do. 15

AMPHITRYON.

I mean thou hast not wit enough to make a lie that will hang together. Thou hast set up a trade that thou hast not stock enough to manage. Oh, that I had but a crab-tree cudgel for thy sake!

SOSIA.

How, a cudgel, said you? The devil take Jupiter for 20 inventing that hard-hearted, merciless, knobby wood.

AMPHITRYON.

The bitterness is yet to come. Thou hast had but a half dose of it.

SOSIA.

I was never good at swallowing physic, and my 25 stomach wambles at the very thought of it, but if I must have a second beating, in conscience, let me strip first that I may show you the black and blue streaks upon my sides and shoulders. I am sure I suffered them in your service. 30

---

28 monster … stone-cutter's] contemporary stories about pacts with the devil, one involving, supposedly, Louis XIV of France, the other a stone-cutter and a wealthy widow

AMPHITRYON.

To what purpose wouldst thou show them?

SOSIA.

Why, to the purpose that you may not strike me upon the sore places, and that as he beat me last night crossways, so you would please to beat me longways to make clean work on't, that at least my 35 skin may look like checker work.

AMPHITRYON.

This request is too reasonable to be refused. But that all things may be done in order, tell me over again the same story with all the circumstances of thy commission, that a blow may follow in due form for 40 every lie. To repetition, rogue, to repetition.

SOSIA.

No, it shall be all a lie if you please, and I'll eat my words to save my shoulders.

AMPHITRYON.

Aye sirrah, now you find you are to be disproved. But 'tis too late—to repetition, rogue, to repetition. 45

SOSIA.

With all my heart, to any repetition but the cudgel. But would you be pleased to answer me one civil question? Am I to use complaisance to you, as to a great person that will have all things said your own way? or am I to tell you the naked truth alone, 50 without the ceremony of a farther beating?

AMPHITRYON.

Nothing but the truth and the whole truth, so help thee cudgel.

SOSIA.

That's a damned conclusion of a sentence. But since it must be so—back and sides at your own 55 peril. I set out from the port in an unlucky hour. The dusky canopy of night enveloping the hemisphere—

AMPHITRYON. (*Strikes him.*)

Imprimis for fustian. Now proceed.

SOSIA.

I stand corrected. In plain prose then, I went 60 darkling and whistling to keep myself from being afraid, mumbling curses betwixt my teeth for being sent at such an unnatural time of night.

AMPHITRYON.

How sirrah, cursing and swearing against your lord and master? Take— (*Going to strike.*) 65

SOSIA.

Hold, sir—pray consider if this be not unreasonable
to strike me for telling the whole truth when you
commanded me. I'll fall into my old dogtrot of lying
again, if this must come of plain dealing.

AMPHITRYON.

To avoid impertinences, make an end of your   70
journey and come to the house. What found you
there, a-God's name?

SOSIA.

I came thither in no god's name at all, but in the
devil's name, I found before the door a swingeing
fellow with all my shapes and features and   75
accoutred also in my habit.

AMPHITRYON.

Who was that fellow?

SOSIA.

Who should it be, but another Sosia? A certain
kind of other me, who knew all my unfortunate
commission precisely to a word as well as I, Sosia,   80
as being sent by yourself from the port upon the
same errand to Alcmena.

AMPHITRYON.

What gross absurdities are these?

SOSIA.

Oh lord, oh lord, what absurdities? As plain as any
packstaff.²⁹ That other me had posted himself   85
there before me-me. You won't give a man leave
to speak poetically now, or else I would say that I
was arrived at the door before I came thither.

AMPHITRYON.

This must either be a dream or drunkenness or
madness in thee. Leave your buffooning and lying;   90
I am not in humor to bear it, sirrah.

SOSIA.

I would you should know I scorn a lie and am a
man of honor in everything, but just fighting. I
tell you once again in plain sincerity and simplicity
of heart that, before last night, I never took myself   95
but for one single individual Sosia, but coming to
our door, I found myself, I know not how, divided
and, as it were, split into two Sosias.

---

29 As plain … packstaff] version of the proverbial phrase,
   "as plain as any pikestaff"; a packstaff was the traditional
   walking stick of itinerant peddlers

APMHITRYON.

Leave buffooning. I see you would make me laugh,
but you play the fool scurvily.   100

SOSIA.

That may be. But if I am a fool, I am not the only
fool in this company.

AMPHITRYON.

How now, impudence! I shall—

SOSIA.

Be not in wrath sir. I meant not you. I cannot
possibly be the only fool, for if I am one fool, I   105
must certainly be two fools because, as I told you,
I am double.

AMPHITRYON.

That one should be two is very probable!

SOSIA.

Have you not seen a six pence split into two halves
by some ingenious schoolboy, which bore on either   110
side the impression of the monarch's face? Now as
those moieties were three pences, and yet in effect
but one six pence—

AMPHITRYON.

No more of your villainous* tropes and figures.

SOSIA.

Nay, if an orator must be disarmed of his   115
similitudes—

AMPHITRYON.

A man had need of patience to endure this
gibberish. Be brief and come to a conclusion.

SOSIA.

What would you have, sir? I came thither, but the
t'other I was there before me. For that there was   120
two I's is as certain as that I have two eyes in this
head of mine. This I, that am here, was weary. The
t'other I was fresh. This I was peaceable, and
t'other I was a hectoring bully I.

AMPHITRYON.

And thou expect'st I should believe thee?   125

SOSIA.

No, I am not so unreasonable, for I could never
have believed it myself, if I had not been well-
beaten into it. But a cudgel, you know, is a
convincing argument in a brawny fist. What shall
I say, but that I was compelled at last to   130
acknowledge myself? I found that he was very* I,
without fraud, cozen, or deceit. Besides, I viewed

myself as in a mirror from head to foot. He was handsome, of a noble presence, a charming air, loose and free in all his motions—and saw he was so much I, that I should have reason to be better satisfied with my own person, if his hands had not been a little of the heaviest.

AMPHITRYON.

Once again to a conclusion. Say you passed by him and entered into the house.

SOSIA.

I am a friend to truth and say no such thing. He defended the door, and I could not enter.

AMPHITRYON.

How, not enter?

SOSIA.

Why, how should I enter, unless I were a sprite to glide by him and shoot myself through locks and bolts and two-inch boards?

AMPHITRYON.

Oh coward! Didst thou not attempt to pass?

SOSIA.

Yes, and was repulsed and beaten for my pains.

AMPHITRYON.

Who beat thee?

SOSIA.

I beat me.

AMPHITRYON.

Didst thou beat thyself?

SOSIA.

I don't mean I, here, but the absent me beat me here, present.

AMPHITRYON.

There's no end to this intricate piece of nonsense.

SOSIA.

'Tis only nonsense because I speak it who am a poor fellow, but it would be sense, and substantial sense, if a great man said it that was backed with a title and the eloquence of ten thousand pounds a year.

AMPHITRYON.

No more, but let us enter.—Hold. My Alcmena is coming out and has prevented* me. How strangely will she be surprised to see me here so unexpectedly!

Enter Alcmena and Phaedra.

ALCMENA. (*To Phaedra.*)

Make haste after me to the temple that we may thank the gods for this glorious success which Amphitryon has had against the rebels. (*Seeing him.*) Oh heavens!

AMPHITRYON. (*Saluting* her.*)

Those heav'ns and all their blest inhabitants
Grant that the sweet rewarder of my pains
May still be kind, as on our nuptial night.

ALCMENA.

So soon returned!

APMHITRYON. (*Stepping back.*)

"So soon returned"? Is this my welcome home?
"So soon returned" says I am come unwished.
This is no language of desiring love.
Love reckons hours for months and days for years,
And every little absence is an age.

ALCMENA.

What says my lord?

AMPHITRYON.

No, my Alcmena, no.
True love by its impatience measures time,
And the dear object never comes too soon.

ALCMENA.

Nor ever came you so, nor ever shall.
But you yourself are changed from what you were,
Palled in desires and surfeited of bliss.
Not so I met you at your last return
When, yesternight, I flew into your arms
And melted in your warm embrace.

AMPHITRYON.

How's this?

ALCMENA.

Did not my soul ev'n sparkle at my eyes
And shoot itself into your much-loved bosom?
Did not I tremble with excess of joy?
Nay, agonize with pleasure at your sight
With such inimitable proofs of passion
As no false love could feign?

AMPHITRYON.

What's this you tell me?

ALCMENA.

Far short of truth, by heav'n!
And you returned those proofs with usury
And left me with a sigh at break of day.
Have you forgot?

AMPHITRYON.

            Or have you dreamt, Alcmena?
Perhaps some kind, revealing deity   200
Has whispered in your sleep the pleasing news
Of my return, and you believed it real.
Perhaps too, in your dream, you used me kindly,
And my preventing* image reaped the joys
You meant awake to me.   205

ALCMENA.

Some melancholy vapor, sure, has seized
Your brain, Amphitryon, and disturbed your
    sense,
Or yesternight is not so long a time
But you might yet remember and not force
An honest blush into my glowing cheeks   210
For that which lawful marriage makes no crime.

AMPHITRYON.

I thank you for my melancholy vapor.

ALCMENA.

'Tis but a just requital for my dream.

*Amphityron and Alcmena walk by themselves and
frown at each other as they meet.*

PHAEDRA. [*Aside.*]

I find my master took too much of the creature30
last night and now is angling for a quarrel that no   215
more may be expected from him tonight when he
has no assets.

AMPHITRYON.

You dare not justify it to my face.

ALCMENA.

Not what?

AMPHITRYON.

      That I returned before this hour.   220

ALCMENA.

You dare not, sure, deny you came last night
And stayed till break of day?

AMPHITRYON.

Oh impudence!—Why, Sosia!

SOSIA.

Nay, I say nothing, for all things here may go by
enchantment, as they did with me, for aught I   225
know.

---

30 too much of the creature] to have too much alcohol/
  sex

ALCMENA.

Speak, Phaedra. Was he here?

PHAEDRA.

You know, madam, I am but a chambermaid and,
by my place, I am to forget all that was done
overnight in love matters—unless my master please   230
to rub up my memory with another diamond.

AMPHITRYON.

Now in the name of all the gods, Alcmena,
A little recollect your scattered thoughts
And weigh what you have said.

ALCMENA.

I weighed it well, Amphitryon, ere I spoke.   235
And she and Bromia, all the slaves and servants,
Can witness they beheld you when you came.
If other proof were wanting,* tell me how
I came to know your fight, your victory,
The death of Pterelas in single combat,   240
And farther, from whose hands I had a jewel,
The spoils of him you slew.

AMPHITRYON.

            This is amazing!
Have I already given you those diamonds,
The present I reserved?   245

ALCMENA.

            'Tis an odd question.
You see I wear 'em—look.

AMPHITRYON.

      Now answer, Sosia.

SOSIA.

Yes, now I can answer with a safe conscience as to
that point; all the rest may be art magic, but as   250
for the diamonds, here they are under safe custody.

ALCMENA. (*To Sosia.*)

Then what are these upon my arm?

SOSIA.

Flints or pebbles or some such trumpery of
enchanted stones.

PHAEDRA. [*Aside.*]

They say the proof of a true diamond is to glitter   255
in the dark. I think my master had best take my
lady into some by-corner and try whose diamond
will sparkle best.

SOSIA. [*To Alcmena*].

Yet now I think on't, madam, did not a certain
friend of mine present 'em to you?   260

ALCMENA.

What friend?

SOSIA.

Why, another Sosia, one that made himself Sosia
in my despite and also unsociated me.

AMPHITRYON.

Sirrah, leave your nauseous nonsense. Break open
the seal and take out the diamonds.   265

SOSIA.

More words than one to a bargain, sir, I thank you.
That's no part of prudence for me to commit
burglary upon the seals. Do you look first upon
the signet and tell me in your conscience whether
the seals be not as firm as when you clapped the   270
wax upon them.

AMPHITRYON. (*Looking.*)

The signature is firm.

SOSIA. (*Giving him the casket.*)

Then take the signature into your own custody and
open it, for I will have nothing done at my proper
peril.   275

AMPHITRYON. (*Breaking open the seal.*)

Oh heavens! Here's nothing but an empty space,
the nest where they were laid.

SOSIA.

Then if the birds are flown, the fault's not mine.
Here has been fine conjuring work, or else the
jewel, knowing to whom it should be given, took   280
occasion to steal out by a natural instinct and tied
itself upon that pretty arm.

AMPHITRYON.

Can this be possible?

SOSIA.

Yes, very possible. You, my lord Amphitryon, may
have brought forth another you, my lord   285
Amphitryon, as well as I, Sosia, have brought forth
another me, Sosia, and our diamonds may have
procreated these diamonds, and so we are all three
double.

PHAEDRA. (*Aside.*)

If this be true, I hope my goblet has gigged[31]   290
another golden goblet, and then they may carry
double upon all four.

ALCMENA.

My lord, I have stood silent out of wonder
What you could wonder at.

AMPHITRYON.(*Aside.*)

A chilling sweat, a damp of jealousy,   295
Hangs on my brows and clams upon my limbs.
I fear, and yet I must be satisfied,
And to be satisfied, I must dissemble.

ALCMENA.

Why muse you so and murmur to yourself?
If you repent your bounty, take it back.   300

AMPHITRYON.

Not so. But if you please, relate what passed
At our last interview.

ALCMENA.

That question would infer you were not here.

AMPHITRYON.

I say not so.
I only would refresh my memory   305
And have my reasons to desire the story.

PHAEDRA.

So. This is as good sport for me as an examination
of a great belly before a magistrate.[32]

ALCMENA.

The story is not long. You know I met you,
Kissed you, and pressed you close within my arms   310
With all the tenderness of wifely love.

AMPHITRYON. (*Aside.*)

I could have spared that kindness. (*To her.*) And
    what did I?

ALCMENA.

You strained me with a masculine embrace,
As you would squeeze my soul out.

AMPHITRYON.

                                                        Did I so?   315

ALCMENA.

You did.

AMPHITRYON. (*Aside.*)

                    Confound those arms that were so kind.

(*To her.*)

Proceed, proceed.

---

31 gigged] spun out smaller repetitions of itself, as a spinning top opens up for a smaller top (*OED*)

32 examination … magistrate] legal inquiry concerning the
circumstances of an unmarried woman's pregnancy, usually in public

ALCMENA.

You would not stay to sup but, much complaining
Of your drowsiness and want of natural rest—   320

AMPHITRYON.

Made haste to bed. Hah, was't not so? Go on—
(*Aside.*)
And stab me with each syllable thou speak'st.

PHAEDRA.

So, now 'tis coming, now 'tis coming.

ALCMENA.

I have no more to say.

AMPHITRYON.

Why, went we not to bed?   325

ALCMENA.

Why not?
Is it a crime for husband and for wife
To go to bed, my lord?

AMPHITRYON.

                              Perfidious woman!

ALCMENA.

Ungrateful man!   330

AMPHITRYON.

                    She justifies it, too!

ALCMENA.

I need not justify. Of what am I accused?

AMPHITRYON.

Of all that prodigality of kindness
Giv'n to another and usurped from me.
So bless me heav'n, if since my first departure   335
I ever set my foot upon this threshold.
So am I innocent of all those joys
And dry of those embraces.

ALCMENA.

Then I, it seems, am false?

AMPHTIRYON.

As surely false as what thou say'st is true.   340

ALCMENA.

I have betrayed my honor and my love?
And am a foul adultress?

AMPHITRYON.

                        What thou art
Thou stand'st condemned to be by thy relation.

ALCMENA.

Go, thou unworthy man, forever go,   345
No more my husband. Go, thou base imposter
Who tak'st a vile pretense to taint my fame

And, not content to leave, wouldst ruin me.
Enjoy thy wished divorce. I will not plead
My innocence of this pretended crime;   350
I need not. Spit thy venom, do thy worst.
But know, the more thou wouldst expose my virtue,
Like purest linen laid in open air,
'Twill bleach the more and whiten to the view.

AMPHITRYON.

'Tis well thou art prepared for thy divorce.   355
For know thou, too, that after this affront,
This foul indignity done to my honor,
Divorcement is but petty reparation.
But since thou hast with impudence affirmed
My false return and bribed my slaves to vouch it,   360
The truth shall in the face of Thebes be cleared.
Thy uncle, the companion of my voyage,
And all the crew of seamen shall be brought
Who were embarked and came with me to land,
Nor parted till I reached this cursèd door.   365
So shall this vision of my late return
Stand a detected lie, and woe to those
Who thus betrayed my honor.

SOSIA.

Sir, shall I wait on you?

AMPHITRYON.

No, I will go alone. Expect me here. (*Exit.*)   370

PHAEDRA. (*To Alcmena.*)

Please you—that I—

ALCMENA.

                    Oh, nothing now can please me.
Darkness and solitude and sighs and tears
And all th'inseparable train of grief
Attend my steps forever. (*Exit.*)   375

SOSIA. (*Aside.*)

What if I should lie now and say we have been here
before? I never saw any good that came of telling
truth.

PHAEDRA. (*Aside.*)

He makes no more advances to me. I begin a little
to suspect that my gold goblet will prove but   380
copper.

SOSIA. (*Aside.*)

Yes, 'tis resolved: I will lie abominably against the
light of my own conscience. For suppose the t'other
Sosia has been here. Perhaps that strong dog has not
only beaten me, but also has been predominate   385

upon my wife and most carnally misused her. Now,
by asking certain questions of her with a side-wind,
I may come to understand how squares go and
whether my nuptial bed be violated.

PHAEDRA. (*Aside.*)

Most certainly he has learned impudence of his
master and will deny his being here, but that shall
not serve his turn, to cheat me of my present.—
Why Sosia, what, in a brown study?

SOSIA.

A little *cogitabund*[33] or so concerning this dismal
revolution in our family.

PHAEDRA.

But that should not make you neglect your duty
to me, your mistress.

SOSIA.

Pretty soul, I would thou wert—upon condition
that old Bromia were six foot underground.

PHAEDRA.

What? Is all your hot courtship to me dwindled
into a poor unprofitable wish? You may remember
I did not bid you absolutely despair.

SOSIA.

No, for all things yet may be accommodated in an
amicable manner betwixt my master and my lady.

PHAEDRA.

I mean to the business betwixt you and me.

SOSIA.

Why, I hope we two never quarreled.

PHAEDRA.

Must I remember you of a certain promise that you
made me at our last parting?

SOSIA.

Oh, when I went to the army—that I should still
be praising thy beauty to Judge Gripus and keep
up his affections to thee.

PHAEDRA.

No, I mean the business betwixt you and me this
morning that you promised me.

SOSIA.

That I promised thee— (*Aside.*) I find it now. That
strong dog, my bother Sosia, has been here before
me and made love* to her.

PHAEDRA.

You are considering whether or no you should keep
your promise.

SOSIA.

That I should keep my promise— (*Aside.*) The
truth on't is, she's another-guess morsel than old
Bromia.

PHAEDRA.

And I had rather you should break it in a manner
and, as it were, in some sense—

SOSIA.

"In a manner, and as it were, and in some sense,"
thou say'st? (*Aside.*) I find the strong dog has only
tickled up her imagination and not enjoyed her so
that with my own limbs I may perform the sweetness of his function with her.—No, sweet creature,
the promise shall not be broken, but what I have
undertaken I will perform like a man of honor.

PHAEDRA.

Then you remember the preliminaries of the
present—

SOSIA.

Yes, yes, in gross I do remember something, but
this disturbance of the family has somewhat
stupefied my memory. Some pretty *quelque
chose*,[34] I warrant thee, some acceptable toy of
small value.

PHAEDRA.

You may call a gold goblet a toy, but I put a greater
value upon your presents.

SOSIA.

A gold goblet, say'st thou! Yes, now I think on't, it
was a kind of a gold goblet—as a gratuity after
consummation.

PHAEDRA.

No, no. I had rather make sure of one bribe
beforehand than be promised ten gratuities.

SOSIA.

Yes, now I remember, it was, in some sense, a gold
goblet by way of earnest, and it contained—

PHAEDRA.

One large—

SOSIA.

How, one large—

---

33 *cogitabund*] *cogitabunt*, literally, they shall think (Lat.);
 deep thought or meditation

34 *quelque chose*] something (Fr.)

PHAEDRA.

   Gallon.

SOSIA.

   No, that was somewhat too large, in conscience. 450
It was not a whole gallon, but it may contain,
reasonably speaking, one large thimbleful. But
gallons and thimblefuls are so like that, in
speaking, I might easily mistake them.

PHAEDRA.

   Is it come to this? Out, traitor! 455

SOSIA.

   I had been a traitor, indeed, to have betrayed thee
to the swallowing of a gallon. But a thimbleful of
cordial water is easily sipped off, and then this
same goblet is so very light, too, that it will be no
burden to carry it about with thee in thy pocket. 460

PHAEDRA.

   Oh apostate to thy love! Oh perjured villain!

Enter Bromia.

   What, are you here Bromia? I was telling him his
own.[35] I was giving him a rattle for his treacheries
to you, his love. You see, I can be a friend upon
occasion. 465

BROMIA.

   Aye chicken, I never doubted of thy kindness, but
for this fugitive, this rebel, this miscreant—

SOSIA.

   A kind welcome to an absent lover, as I have been.

BROMIA.

   Aye, and a kind greeting you gave me at your
return when you used me so barbarously this 470
morning.

SOSIA. (*Aside.*)

   The t'other Sosia has been with her too and has
used her barbarously—barbarously, that is to say,
uncivilly—and uncivilly, I am afraid, that means
too civilly. 475

PHAEDRA.

   You had best deny you were here this morning!
And by the same token—

SOSIA.

   Nay, no more tokens, for heaven's sake, dear
Phaedra. (*Aside.*) Now must I ponder with myself

_____
35 his own] the truth about his behavior

a little, whether it be better for me to have been 480
here or not to have been here this morning.

Enter a servant.

SERVANT.

   Phaedra, my lord's without and will not enter till
he has first spoken with you. (*Exit.*)

PHAEDRA. (*To [Sosia] in private.*)

   Oh, that I could stay to help worry thee for this
abuse! But the best on't is I leave thee in good 485
hands. Farewell, thimble.—To him, Bromia. (*Exit.*)

BROMIA.

   No, you did not beat me and put me into a
swound and deprive me of the natural use of my
tongue for a long half hour. You did not beat me
down with your little wand. But I shall teach you 490
to use your rod another time, I shall.

SOSIA. (*Aside.*)

   Put her into a swound with my little wand and so
forth. That's more than ever I could do. These are
terrible circumstances that some Sosia or another
has been here. Now, if he has literally beaten her, 495
gramercy, brother Sosia, he has but done what I
would have done if I had durst. But I am afraid it
was only a damned love-figure, and that the wand
that laid her asleep might signify the peacemaker.

BROMIA.

   Now you are snuffling upon a cold scent for some 500
pitiful excuse. I know you—twenty to one but you
will plead a drunkenness. You are used to be pot-
valiant.

SOSIA. [*Aside*].

   I was pumping, and I thank her; she has invented
for me.—Yes Bromia, I must confess I was exalted 505
and possibly I might scour upon thee, or perhaps
be a little more familiar with thy person by the way
of kindness than if I had been sober. But prithee,
inform me what I did that I may consider what
satisfaction I am to make thee. 510

BROMIA.

   Are you there at your dog tricks? You would be
forgetting, would you? Like a drunken bully that
affronts overnight and, when he is called to
account the next morning, remembers nothing of
the quarrel and asks pardon to avoid fighting. 515

SOSIA.

By Bacchus, I was overtaken, but I should be loath
that I committed any folly with thee.

BROMIA. (*Crying.*)

I am sure I kept myself awake all night, that I did,
in expectation of your coming.

SOSIA.

But what amends did I make thee when I came?   520

BROMIA.

You know well enough, to my sorrow, but that you
play the hypocrite.

SOSIA.

I warrant, I was monstrous kind to thee.

BROMIA.

Yes, monstrous kind indeed. You never said a truer
word, for when I came to kiss you, you pulled   525
away your mouth and turned your cheek to me.

SOSIA.

Good.

BROMIA.

How, good? Here's fine impudence. He justifies!

SOSIA.

Yes, I do justify that I turned my cheek like a
prudent person that my breath might not offend   530
thee, for now I remember, I had eaten garlic.

BROMIA.

Aye, you remember and forget, just as it makes for
you or against you. But to mend the matter, you
never spoke one civil word to me, but stood like a
stock without sense or motion.   535

SOSIA. (*Aside.*)

Yet better.

BROMIA.

After which, I lovingly invited you to take your
place in your nuptial bed as the laws of matrimony
oblige you, and you inhumanly refused me.

SOSIA.

Aye, there's the main point of the business. Art   540
thou morally certain that I refused thee? Look me
now in the face and say I did not commit
matrimony with thee.

BROMIA.

I wonder how thou canst look me in the face after
that refusal.   545

SOSIA.

Say it once again, that I did not feloniously come
to bed to thee.

BROMIA.

No, thou cold traitor, thou know'st thou didst not.

SOSIA. [*Aside*].

Best of all.—'Twas discreetly done of me to
abstain.   550

BROMIA.

What, do you insult upon me, too?

SOSIA.

No, I do not insult upon you, but—

BROMIA.

But what? How was it discreetly done then? Hah?

SOSIA.

Because it is the received opinion of physicians that
nothing but puling-chits and booby fools are   555
procreated in drunkenness.

BROMIA.

A "received opinion," snivel-guts? I'll be judged by
all the married women of this town if anyone of
'em has received it. The devil take the physicians
for meddling in our matters. If a husband be ruled   560
by them, there are five weeks of abstinence in dog
days, too, for fear a child that was got in August
should be born just nine months after and be
blear-eyed like a May kitten.[36]

SOSIA.

Let the physicians alone; they are honest men,   565
whatever the world says of 'em. But for a certain
reason (that I best know) I am glad that matter
ended so fairly and peaceably betwixt us.

BROMIA.

Yes, 'twas very fair and peaceable to strike a woman
down and beat her most outrageously.   570

SOSIA.

Is it possible that I drubbed thee?

BROMIA.

I find your drift. You would fain be provoking me
to a new trial now, but i'faith, you shall bring me
to no more handy blows. I shall make bold to trust
to my tongue hereafter. You never durst have   575
offered to hold up a finger against me till you went
a-trooping.

---

36 May kitten] Progeny born in May were said to be physically inferior or defective, therefore needing special nur-
turing.

SOSIA. (*Strutting.*)

Then I am a conqueror, and I laud my own courage.
This renown I have achieved by soldiership and
stratagem. Know your duty, spouse, henceforward, 580
to your supreme commander.

*Enter Jupiter and Phaedra attended by musicians and
dancers.*

PHAEDRA.

Indeed, I wondered at your quick return.

JUPITER.

Even so, almighty Love will have it, Phaedra,
And the stern goddess[37] of sweet-bitter cares
Who bows our necks beneath her brazen yoke. 585
I would have manned my heart and held it out,
But when I thought of what I had possessed—
Those joys that never end but to begin—
Oh, I am all on fire to make my peace
And die, Jove knows, as much as I can die, 590
Till I am reconciled.

PHAEDRA.

I fear 'twill be in vain.

JUPITER.

                              'Tis difficult.
But nothing is impossible to love,
To love like mine, for I have proved his force, 595
And my Alcmena too has felt his dart.
If I submit, there's hope.

PHAEDRA.

'Tis possible I may solicit for you.

JUPITER.

But wilt thou promise me to do thy best?

PHAEDRA. (*Curtsying.*)

Nay, I promise nothing—unless you begin to 600
promise first.

JUPITER.

I would not be ungrateful.

PHAEDRA.

Well, I'll try to bring her to the window. You shall
have a fair shoot at her; if you can bring her down,
you are a good marksman. 605

JUPITER.

That's all I ask;
And I will so reward thee, gentle Phaedra—

_____

37 Love … goddess] Cupid and his mother Venus

PHAEDRA.

What, with cats' guts and rosin! This sol-la is but
a lamentable, empty sound.

JUPITER. (*Throwing her a purse.*)

Then there's a sound will please thee better. 610

PHAEDRA.

Aye, there's something of melody in this sound. I
could dance all day to the music of "chink, chink."
(*Exit.*)

JUPITER.

Go, Sosia, round our Thebes
To Polydas, to Tranio, and to Gripus, 615
Companions of our war; invite 'em all
To join their prayers to smooth Alcmena's brow
And, with a solemn feast, to crown the day.

SOSIA. (*Taking Jupiter about the knees.*)

Let me embrace you, sir. (*Jupiter pushes him away.*)
Nay, you must give me leave to express my 620
gratitude. I have not eaten, to say eating, nor
drunk, to say drinking, never since our villainous
encamping so near the enemy. 'Tis true I 'scaped
the bloody flux because I had so little in my bowels
to come out, and I durst let nothing go, in 625
conscience, because I had nothing to swallow in
the room on't.

JUPITER.

You, Bromia, see that all things be prepared
With that magnificence, as if some god
Were guest or master here. 630

SOSIA.

Or rather as much as if twenty gods were to be
guests or masters here.

BROMIA.

That you may eat for today and tomorrow.

SOSIA.

Or rather again, for today and yesterday and as
many months backwards as I am indebted to my 635
own belly.

JUPITER.

Away, both of you.

Exeunt Sosia and Bromia severally.

JUPITER.

Now I have packed him hence, thou, other Sosia
(Who, though thou art not present, hear'st my
voice),

Be ready to attend me at my call   640
And to supply his place.

Enter Mercury to Jupiter. Alcmena and Phaedra
appear above.

JUPITER. (*Seeing Alcmena.*)
                              See, she appears.
This is my bribe to Phaedra. When I made
This gold, I made a greater god than Jove
And gave my own omnipotence away.   645

Jupiter signs to the musicians [who play a song while
dancers dance.]

                    Song.
                      I.
Celia, that I once was blest
Is now the torment of my breast,
Since to curse me, you bereave me
Of the pleasures I possessed.
Cruel creature to deceive me!   650
First to love and then to leave me!
                     II.
Had you the bliss refused to grant,
Then I had never known the want.*
But possessing once the blessing
Is the cause of my complaint.   655
Once possessing is but tasting;
'Tis no bliss that is not lasting.
                    III.
Celia now is mine no more,
But I am hers and must adore,
Nor to leave her will endeavor.   660
Charms that captived me before
No unkindness can dissever.
Love that's true is love forever.

Alcmena withdraws, frowning.

JUPITER.
Oh, stay.
MERCURY.
            She's gone, and seemed to frown at parting.   665
JUPITER.
Follow, and thou shalt see her soon appeased,
For I, who made her, know her inward state.
No woman once well pleased can throughly hate.
I gave 'em beauty to subdue the strong

(A mighty empire, but it lasts not long);   670
I gave 'em pride to make mankind their slave,
But in exchange, to men I flattery gave.
Th'offending lover when he lowest lies,
Submits to conquer and but kneels to rise.

[Exeunt.]

                Act IV. [The same.]

Enter Jupiter following Alcmena; Mercury and
Phaedra.

JUPITER.
Oh stay, my dear Alcmena, hear me speak.
ALCMENA.
No. I would fly thee to the ridge of earth
And leap the precipice to 'scape thy sight.
JUPITER.
For pity—
ALCMENA.
                      Leave me, thou ungrateful man.   5
JUPITER.
I cannot leave you, no, but like a ghost
Whom your unkindness murdered, will I haunt you.
ALCMENA.
Once more, be gone. I'm odious to myself
For having loved thee once.
JUPITER.
Hate not the best and fairest of your kind,   10
Nor can you hate your lover, though you would.
Your tears, that fall so gently, are but grief.
There may be anger, but there must be love.
The dove that murmurs at her mate's neglect
But counterfeits a coyness to be courted.   15
ALCMENA.
Courtship from thee after such affronts!
JUPITER.
Is this that everlasting love you vowed
Last night, when I was circled in your arms?
Remember what you swore—
ALCMENA.
Think what thou wert, and who could swear too   20
    much?
Think what thou art, and that unswears it all.
JUPITER.
Can you forsake me for so small a fault?
'Twas but a jest, perhaps too far pursued.

'Twas but at most a trial of your faith,
How you could bear unkindness.   25
'Twas but to get a reconciling kiss,
A wanton stratagem of love.

ALCMENA.
See how he doubles like a hunted hare.
A jest, and then a trial and a bait—
All stuff and daubing!   30

JUPITER.
                              Think me jealous, then.

ALCMENA.
Oh that I could, for that's a noble crime
And which a lover can, with ease, forgive.
'Tis the high pulse of passion in a fever—
A sickly draught, but shows a burning thirst.   35
Thine was a surfeit, not a jealousy,
And in that loathing of thy full-gorged love,
Thou saw'st the nauseous object with disdain.

JUPITER.
Oh think not that, for you are ever new.
Your fruits of love are like eternal spring   40
In happy climes, where some are in the bud,
Some green, and ripening some, while others fall.

ALCMENA.
Aye, now you tell me this,
When roused desires and fresh recruits of force
Enable languished love to take the field.   45
But never hope to be received again.
You would again deny you were received
And brand my spotless fame.

JUPITER.
I will not dare to justify my crime,
But only point you where to lay the blame.   50
Impute it to the husband, not the lover.

ALCMENA.
How vainly would the sophister divide
And make the husband and the lover two!

JUPITER.
Yes, 'tis the husband is the guilty wretch.
His insolence forgot the sweets of love   55
And, deeming them his due, despised the feast.
Not so the famished lover could forget.
He knew he had been there and had been blest
With all that hope can wish or sense can bear.

ALCMENA.
Husband and lover—both alike I hate.   60

JUPITER.
And I confess I have deserved that hate.
(*Kneeling.*)
Too charming fair, I kneel for your forgiveness;
I beg by those fair eyes,
Which gave me wounds that time can never cure,
Receive my sorrows and restore my joys.   65

ALCMENA.
Unkind and cruel! I can speak no more.

JUPITER.
Oh give it vent, Alcmena, give it vent.
I merit your reproach; I would be cursed.
Let your tongue curse me while your heart forgives.

ALCMENA.
Can I forget such usage?   70

JUPITER.
                              Can you hate me?

ALCMENA.
I'll do my best, for sure I ought to hate you.

JUPITER.
That word was only hatched upon your tongue;
It came not from your heart. But try again,
And if once more you can but say, "I hate you,"   75
My sword shall do you justice.

ALCMENA.
                              Then I hate you.

JUPITER.
Then you pronounce the sentence of my death.

ALCMENA.
I hate you much, but yet I love you more.

JUPITER.
To prove that love, then say that you forgive me,   80
For there remains but this alternative:
Resolve to pardon or to punish me.

ALCMENA.
Alas, what I resolve appears too plain:
In saying that I cannot hate, I pardon.

JUPITER.
But what's a pardon worth without a seal?   85
Permit me, in this transport of my joy—(*Kisses her
hand.*)

ALCMENA. (*Putting him gently away with her hand.*)
Forbear. I am offended with myself
That I have shown this weakness. Let me go
Where I may blush alone. (*Going, and looking
back on him.*) But come not you,   90

Lest I should spoil you with excess of fondness,*
And let you love again. (*Exit.*)

JUPITER. (*Aside.*)

Forbidding me to follow, she invites me.
This is the mold of which I made the sex:
I gave 'em but one tongue to say us nay,   95
And two kind* eyes to grant. (*To Mercury.*) Be
    sure that none
Approach to interrupt our privacy. (*Exit after
    Alcmena.*)

MERCURY.

Your lady has made the challenge of reconciliation
to my Lord. Here's a fair example for us two,
Phaedra.   100

PHAEDRA.

No example at all, Sosia, for my lady had the
diamonds aforehand, and I have none of the gold
goblet.

MERCURY.

The goblet shall be forthcoming, if thou wilt give
me weight for weight.   105

PHAEDRA.

Yes, and measure for measure, too, Sosia—that is,
for a thimbleful of gold, a thimbleful of love.

MERCURY. (*Pulling out the goblet in a case from
    under his cloak.*)

What think you now, Phaedra? Here's a weighty
argument of love for you.

PHAEDRA. (*Taking it in both hands.*)

Now Jupiter, of his mercy, let me kiss thee. Oh   110
thou dear metal!

MERCURY.

And Venus, of her mercy, let me kiss thee, dear,
dear Phaedra.

PHAEDRA.

Not so fast, Sosia! There's a damned proverb in
your way: "Many things happen betwixt the cup
and the lips," you know.   115

MERCURY.

Why, thou wilt not cheat me of my goblet?

PHAEDRA.

Yes—as sure as you would cheat me of my
maidenhead. I am yet but just even with you for
the last trick you played me. And besides, this is
but a bare retaining fee. You must give me another 120
before the cause is opened.

MERCURY.

Shall I not come to your bedside tonight?

PHAEDRA.

No, nor tomorrow night neither. But this shall be
my sweetheart in your place. 'Tis a better bedfellow
and will keep me warmer in cold weather. (*Exit.*) 125

MERCURY.

Now, what's the god of wit in a woman's hand?
This very goblet I stole from Gripus, and he got
it out of bribes, too. But this is the common fate
of ill-gotten goods, that as they came in by
covetousness, they go out by whoring.   130

Enter Amphitryon.

Oh, here's Amphitryon again, but I'll manage him
above in the balcony. (*Exit.*)

AMPHITRYON.

Not one of those I looked for to be found!
As some enchantment hid 'em from my sight.
Perhaps, as Sosia says, 'tis witchcraft all: 135
Seals may be opened, diamonds may be stolen.
But how I came in person yesterday
And gave that present to Alcmena's hands—
That which I never gave, nor ever came—
Oh, there's the rock on which my reason splits.   140
Would that were all! I fear my honor, too.
I'll try her once again. She may be mad,
A wretched remedy, but all I have
To keep me from despair.

[Enter Mercury above.]

MERCURY. (*Aside.*)

This is no very charitable action of a god to use   145
him ill who has never offended me, but my planet
disposes me to malice, and when we great persons
do but a little mischief, the world has a good
bargain of us.

AMPHITRYON.

How now? What means this locking up of my   150
doors at this time of day? (*Knocks.*)

MERCURY.

Softly, friend, softly. You knock as loud and as
saucily as a lord's footman that was sent before him
to warn the family of his Honor's visit. Sure you
think the doors have no feeling. What the devil   155
are you that rap with such authority?

AMPHITRYON.

Look out and see. 'Tis I.

MERCURY.

You? What you?

AMPHITRYON.

No more, I say, but open.

MERCURY.

I'll know to whom first.   160

AMPHITRYON.

I am one that can command the doors open.

MERCURY.

Then you had best command 'em and try whether
they will obey you.

AMPHITRYON.

Dost thou not know me?

MERCURY.

Prithee, how should I know thee? Dost thou take   165
me for a conjurer?

AMPHITRYON.

What's this? Midsummer moon?[38] Is all the world
gone a-madding? Why, Sosia!

MERCURY.

That's my name indeed. Didst thou think I had
forgot it?   170

AMPHITRYON.

Dost thou see me?

MERCURY.

Why, dost thou pretend to go invisible? If thou
hast any business here, dispatch it quickly. I have
no leisure to throw away upon any such prattling
companions.   175

AMPHITRYON.

Thy companion, slave? How dar'st thou use this
insolent language to thy master!

MERCURY.

How! Thou my master? By what title? I never had
any other master but Amphitryon.

AMPHITRYON.

Well, and for whom dost thou take me?   180

MERCURY.

For some rogue or other, but what rogue I know not.

AMPHITRYON.

Dost thou not know me for Amphitryon, slave?

---

38 Midsummer moon] lunacy associated both with the
moon and midsummer nights

MERCURY.

How should I know thee when I see thou dost
not know thyself? Thou Amphitryon? In what
tavern hast thou been? And how many bottles   185
did thy business to metamorphose thee into my
lord?

AMPHITRYON.

I will so drub thee for this insolence!

MERCURY.

How now, impudence! Are you threatening your
betters? I should bring you to condign punishment   190
but that I have a great respect for the good wine,
though I find it in a fool's noddle.

AMPHITRYON.

What, none to let me in? Why, Phaedra! Bromia!

MERCURY.

Peace, fellow. If my wife hears thee, we are both
undone. At a word, Phaedra and Bromia are very   195
busy—one in making a caudle for my lady, and
the other in heating napkins to rub down my lord
when he rises from bed.

AMPHITRYON.

Amazement seizes me.

MERCURY.

At what art thou amazed? My master and my lady   200
had a falling out and are retired, without seconds,
to decide the quarrel.* If thou wert not a
meddlesome fool, thou wouldst not be thrusting
thy nose into other people's matters. Get thee
about thy business, if thou hast any, for I'll hear 205
no more of thee. (*Exit from above.*)

AMPHITRYON.

Braved by my slave, dishonored by my wife,
To what a desp'rate plunge am I reduced,
If this be true the villain* says! But why
That feeble "if"? It must be true. She owns it.   210
Now, whether to conceal or blaze th'affront?
One way, I spread my infamy abroad,
And t'other hide a burning coal within
That preys upon my vitals. I can fix
On nothing but on vengeance.   215

Enter to him Sosia, Polydas, Gripus, Tranio.

GRIPUS.

Yonder he is, walking hastily to and fro before his
door like a citizen* clapping his sides before his

shop in a frosty morning. 'Tis to catch a stomach, I believe.

SOSIA.

I begin to be afraid that he has more stomach to my sides and shoulders than to his own victuals. How he shakes his head and stamps! And what strides he fetches! He's in one of his damned moods again. I don't like the looks of him.

AMPHITRYON.

Oh, my mannerly, fair-spoken, obedient slave, are you there? I can reach you now without climbing. Now we shall try who's drunk and who's sober.

SOSIA.

Why, this is as it should be. I was somewhat suspicious that you were in a pestilent humor. Yes, we will have a crash at the bottle when your lordship pleases. I have summoned 'em, you see, and they are notable topers, especially Judge Gripus.

GRIPUS.

Yes, faith. I never refuse my glass in a good quarrel.

AMPHITRYON. (*To Sosia.*)

Why, thou insolent villain!* I'll teach a slave how to use his master thus.

SOSIA.

Here's a fine business towards. I am sure I ran as fast as ever my legs could carry me to call 'em. Nay, you may trust my diligence in all affairs belonging to the belly.

GRIPUS.

He has been very faithful to his commission. I'll bear him witness.

AMPHITRYON.

How can you be witness where you were not present? The balcony, sirrah, the balcony!

SOSIA.

Why, to my best remembrance, you never invited the balcony.

AMPHITRYON.

What nonsense dost thou plead for an excuse of thy foul language and thy base replies!

SOSIA.

You fright a man out of his senses first and blame him afterwards for talking nonsense. But 'tis better for me to talk nonsense than for some to do nonsense. I will say that whate'er comes on't. Pray

sir, let all things be done decently. What, I hope when a man is to be hanged he is not trussed upon the gallows, like a dumb dog,[39] without telling him wherefore.

AMPHITRYON.

By your pardon, gentlemen, I have no longer patience to forbear him.

SOSIA.

Justice, justice, my lord Gripus. As you are a true magistrate, protect me. Here's a process of beating going forward without sentence given.

GRIPUS.

My lord Amphitryon, this must not be. Let me first understand the demerits of the criminal.

SOSIA.

Hold you to that point, I beseech your Honor, as you commiserate the case of a poor, innocent malefactor.

AMPHITRYON.

To shut the door against me in my very face, to deny me entrance, to brave me from the balcony, to laugh at me, to threaten me! What proofs of innocence call you these? But if I punish not this insolence—(*Going to beat him and is held by Polydas and Tranio.*) I beg you let me go.

SOSIA.

I charge you in the King's name, hold him fast, for you see he's bloodily disposed.

GRIPUS.

Now, what hast thou to say for thyself, Sosia?

SOSIA.

I say, in the first place, be sure you hold him, gentlemen, for I shall never plead worth one farthing while I am bodily afraid.

POLYDAS.

Speak boldly. I warrant thee.

SOSIA.

Then, if I may speak boldly, under my lord's favor, I do not say he lies neither—no, I am too well-bred for that. But his lordship fibs most abominably.

AMPHITRYON.

Do you hear his impudence? Yet will you let me go?

---

39 gallows … dog] Mad and vicious dogs were hanged in the seventeenth century.

SOSIA.

No impudence at all, my lord, for how could I, 285
naturally speaking, be in the balcony and affronting
you when, at the same time, I was in every street in
Thebes inviting these gentlemen to dinner?

GRIPUS.

Hold a little. How long since was it that he spoke
to you from the said balcony? 290

AMPHITRYON.

Just now—not a minute before he brought you
hither.

SOSIA.

Now speak, my witnesses.

GRIPUS.

I can answer for him for this last half hour.

POLYDAS.

And I. 295

TRANIO.

And I.

SOSIA.

Now judge equitably, gentlemen, whether I was
not a civil, well-bred person to tell my lord he fibs
only.

AMPHITRYON.

Who gave you that order to invite 'em? 300

SOSIA.

He that best might—yourself. By the same token,
you bid old Bromia provide an* 'twere for a god,
and I put in for a brace or a lease. No, now I think
on't, it was for ten couple of gods to make sure of
plenty. 305

AMPHITRYON.

When did I give thee this pretended commission?

SOSIA.

Why, you gave me this pretended commission
when you were just ready to give my lady the
fiddles and a dance, in order, I suppose, to your
second bedding. 310

AMPHITRYON.

Where? In what place did I give this order?

SOSIA.

Here, in this place, in the presence of this very
door and of that balcony, and if they could speak
they would both justify it.

AMPHITRYON.

Oh heaven! These accidents are so surprising that 315
the more I think of 'em, the more I am lost in my
imagination.

GRIPUS.

Nay, he has told us some passages as he came along
that seem to surpass the power of nature.

SOSIA.

What think you now, my lord, of a certain twin 320
brother of mine, called Sosia? 'Tis a sly youth. Pray
heaven you have not just such another relation
within doors, called Amphitryon. It may be it was
he that put upon me in your likeness, and perhaps
he may have put something upon your lordship, 325
too, that may weigh heavy upon the forehead.⁴⁰

AMPHITRYON. (*To those who hold him.*)

Let me go. Sosia may be innocent, and I will not
hurt him.

[*They release him.*]

Open the door. I'll resolve my doubts immediately.

SOSIA.

The door is peremptory that it will not be opened 330
without keys, and my brother, on the inside, is in
possession and will not part with 'em.

AMPHITRYON.

Then 'tis manifest that I am affronted. Break open
the door there.

GRIPUS.

Stir not a man of you to his assistance. 335

AMPHITRYON.

Dost thou take part with my adulteress, too,
because she is thy niece?

GRIPUS.

I take part with nothing but the law, and to break
the doors open is to break the law.

AMPHITRYON.

Do thou command 'em, then. 340

GRIPUS.

I command nothing without my warrant, and my
clerk is not here to take his fees for drawing it.

AMPHITRYON. (*Aside.*)

The devil take all justice-brokers. I curse him, too,
when I have been hunting him all over the town
to be my witness! But I'll bring soldiers to force 345
open the doors by my own commission. (*Exit.*)

---

40 something ... forehead] horns*

SOSIA.

Pox o'these forms of law, to defeat a man of a dinner when he's sharp set. 'Tis against the privilege of a freeborn stomach and is no less than a subversion of fundamentals.

Enter Jupiter above in the balcony.

JUPITER.

Oh, my friends, I am sorry I have made you wait so long. You are welcome, and the door shall be opened to you immediately. (*Exit.*)

GRIPUS.

Was that not Amphitryon?

SOSIA.

Why, who should it be else?

GRIPUS.

In all appearance it was he. But how he got he thither?

POLYDAS.

In such a trice, too.

TRANIO.

And after he had just left us.

GRIPUS.

And so much altered for the better in his humor.

SOSIA.

Here's such a company of foolish questions when a man's a-hungry. You had best stay dinner till he has proved himself to be Amphitryon in form of law. But I'll make short work of that business, for I'll take mine oath 'tis he.

GRIPUS.

I should be glad it were.

SOSIA.

How, "glad it were"? with your damned interrogatories when you ought to be thankful that so it is.

GRIPUS. (*Aside.*)

That I may see my mistress Phaedra and present her with my great gold goblet.

SOSIA.

If this be not the true Amphitryon, I wish I may be kept without doors, fasting and biting my own fingers, for want of victuals—and that's a dreadful imprecation! I am for the inviting, and eating, and treating Amphitryon. I am sure 'tis he that is my lawfully begotten lord, and if you have an ounce of true justice in you, you ought to have laid hold

on t'other Amphitryon and committed him for a rogue and an impostor and a vagabond.

The door is opened.

MERCURY. (*From within.*)

Enter quickly, masters. The passage on the right hand leads to the gallery where my lord expects you, for I am called another way.

Gripus, Tranio, and Polydas go into the house.

SOSIA.

I should know that voice by a secret instinct. 'Tis a tongue of my family and belongs to my brother Sosia. It must be so, for it carries a cudgeling kind of sound in it. But put the worst; let me weigh this matter wisely. Here's a beating and a bellyful, against no beating and no bellyful. The beating is bad, but the dinner is good. Now, not to be beaten is but negatively good, but not to fill my belly is positively bad. Upon the whole matter, my final resolution is to take the good and the bad as they come together.

[Sosia] is entering; Mercury meets him at the door.

MERCURY.

Whither now, you kitchen scum? From whence this impudence to enter here without permission?

SOSIA.

Most illustrious sir, my ticket is my hunger. Show the full bowels of your compassion to the empty bowels of my famine.

MERCURY.

Were you not charged to return no more? I'll cut you into quarters and hang you upon the shambles.

SOSIA.

You'll get but little credit by me. Alas sir, I am but mere carrion. Brave Sosia, compassionate coward Sosia, and beat not thyself in beating me.

MERCURY.

Who gave you that privilege, sirrah, to assume my name? Have you not been sufficiently warned of it? And received part of the punishment already?

SOSIA.

May it please you, sir, the name is big enough for both of us, and we may use it in common like a strumpet. Witness heaven that I would have obeyed you and quitted my title to the name, but

wherever I come, the malicious world will call me 410
"Sosia" in spite of me. I am sensible there are two
Amphitryons, and why may not there be two
Sosias? Let those two cut one another's throats at
their own pleasure, but you and I will be wiser, by
my consent, and hold good intelligence together.[41] 415

MERCURY.

No, no. Two Sosias would but make two fools.

SOSIA.

Then let me be the fool, and be you the prudent
person and choose for yourself some wiser name. Or
you shall be the elder brother, and I'll be content to
be the younger, though I lose my inheritance. 420

MERCURY.

I tell thee, I am the only son of our family.

SOSIA.

Then let me be your bastard brother and the son
of a whore. I hope that's but reasonable.

MERCURY.

No. Thou shalt not disgrace my father, for there
are few bastards nowadays worth owning. 425

SOSIA.

Ah, poor Sosia! What will become of thee?

MERCURY.

Yet again profanely using my proper name?

SOSIA.

I did not mean myself. I was thinking of another
Sosia, a poor fellow, that was once of my
acquaintance, unfortunately banished out of doors 430
when dinner was just coming upon the table.

Enter Phaedra.

PHAEDRA.

Sosia, you and I must—Bless me! What have we
here? A couple of you, or do I see double?

SOSIA.

I would fain bring it about that I might make one
of 'em. But he's unreasonable and will needs 435
incorporate me and swallow me whole into
himself. If he would be content to be but one and
a half, 'twould never grieve me.

MERCURY.

'Tis a perverse rascal. I kick him and cudgel him
to no purpose, for he's still obstinate to stick to me, 440

---

41 hold … together] understand each other

and I can never beat him out of my resemblance.

PHAEDRA.

Which of you two is Sosia? For t'other must be
the devil.

SOSIA.

You had best ask him that has played the devil with
my back and sides. 445

MERCURY.

You had best ask him who gave you the gold
goblet.

PHAEDRA.

No, that's already given. But he shall be my Sosia
that will give me such another.

MERCURY.

I find you have been interloping, sirrah. 450

SOSIA.

No indeed, sir. I only promised her a gold thimble,
which was as much as comes to my proportion of
being Sosia.

PHAEDRA.

This is no Sosia for my money. Beat him away,
t'other Sosia. He grows insufferable. 455

SOSIA. (*Aside.*)

Would I were valiant that I might beat him away
and succeed him at the dinner, for a pragmatical
son of a whore as he is!

MERCURY.

What's that you are muttering betwixt your teeth
of a "son of a whore," sirrah? 460

SOSIA.

I am sure I meant you no offense, for if I am not
Sosia, I am the son of a whore, for aught I know.
And if you are Sosia, you may be the son of a
whore for aught you know.

MERCURY.

Whatever I am, I will be Sosia as long as I please, 465
and whenever you visit me, you shall be sure of
the civility of the cudgel.

SOSIA.

If you will promise to beat me into the house, you
may begin when you please with me. But to be
beaten out of the house at dinnertime—flesh and 470
blood can never bear it.

*Mercury beats him about, and Sosia is still making
towards the door. But Mercury gets betwixt, and at
length drives him off the stage.*

PHAEDRA.

In the name of wonder, what are you that are Sosia and are not Sosia?

MERCURY.

If thou wouldst know more of me, my person is freely at thy disposing. 475

PHAEDRA.

Then I dispose of it to you again, for 'tis so ugly 'tis not for my use.

MERCURY.

I can be ugly or handsome, as I please, go to bed old and rise young. I have so many suits of persons by me that I can shift 'em when I will. 480

PHAEDRA.

You are a fool, then, to put on your worst clothes when you come a-wooing.

MERCURY.

Go to.* Ask no more questions. I am for thy turn, for I know thy heart and see all thou hast about thee.

PHAEDRA.

Then you can see my backside, too; there's a 485 bargain[42] for you.

MERCURY.

In thy right pocket—let me see—three love letters from Judge Gripus, written to the bottom, on three sides, full of fustian passion and hearty nonsense; as also, in the same pocket, a letter of thine 490 intended to him, consisting of nine lines and a half, scrawled and false-spelled, to show thou art a woman, and full of fraudulence and equivocations and shoeing-horns of love to him, to promise much and mean nothing—to show 495 over and above that thou art a mere* woman.

PHAEDRA.

Is the devil in you to see all this? Now, for heaven's sake, do not look into t'other pocket.

MERCURY.

Nay, there's nothing there but a little godly prayer book, and a bawdy lampoon, and— 500

PHAEDRA. (Giving a great frisk.)

Look no farther, I beseech you.

MERCURY.

And a silver spoon—

---

42 bargain] an obscene retort, from the verbal game of "selling bargains"

PHAEDRA. (Shrieking.)

Ah!

MERCURY.

Which you purloined last night from Bromia.

PHAEDRA. (Holding up her hands to him.)

Keep my counsel or I am undone forever. 505

MERCURY.

No. I'll mortify thee, now I have a handle to thy iniquity, if thou wilt not love me.

PHAEDRA.

Well, if you promise me to be secret, I will love you—because indeed I dare do no other.

MERCURY.

'Tis a good girl. I will be secret, and further I will 510 be assisting thee in thy filching, for thou and I were born under the same planet.

PHAEDRA.

And we will come to the same end too, I'm afraid.

MERCURY.

No, no. Since thou hast wit enough already to cozen a judge, thou needst never fear hanging. 515

PHAEDRA.

And will you make yourself a younger man and be handsome too and rich? For you that know hearts must needs know that I shall never be constant to such an ugly old Sosia.

MERCURY.

Thou shalt know more of that another time. In 520 the meanwhile, here's a cast of my office for thee.

He stamps upon the ground. Some dancers come from underground and others from the sides of the stage. A song and a fantastic dance.

Mercury's song to Phaedra.

I.

Fair Iris I love and hourly I die,
But not for a lip nor a languishing eye.
She's fickle and false, and there we agree,
For I am as false and as fickle as she. 525
We neither believe what either can say,
And neither believing, we neither betray.

II.

'Tis civil to swear and say things of course;
We mean not the taking for better, for worse.
When present, we love; when absent agree: 530
I think not of Iris, nor Iris of me.

The legend of love no couple can find
So easy to part or so equally joined.

After, the dance.

PHAEDRA.

This power of yours makes me suspect you for
little better than a god. But if you are one, for more
certainty, tell me what I am just now thinking.

MERCURY.

Why, thou art thinking—let me see. For thou art a
woman, and your minds are so variable that it's very
hard even for a god to know them. But to satisfy
thee, thou art wishing now for the same power I
have exercised, that thou mightest stamp, like me,
and have more singers come up for another song.

PHAEDRA.

Gad, I think the devil's in you. Then I do stamp
in somebody's name, but I know not whose.
(*Stamps.*) Come up, gentlefolks from below, and
sing me a pastoral dialogue where the woman may
have the better of the man, as we always have in
love matters.

New singers come up and sing a song.

A pastoral dialogue betwixt Thrysis and Iris.[b]

I.

Fair Iris and her Swain
Were in a shady bower,
Where Thrysis long in vain
Had sought the shepherd's hour.[43]
At length, his hand advancing upon her snowy
    breast,
He said, "Oh kiss me longer,
And longer yet and longer,
If you will make me blest."

II.

"An easy, yielding maid
By trusting is undone.
Our sex is oft betrayed,
By granting love too soon.
If you desire to gain me, your suff'rings to redress,
Prepare to love me longer,
And longer yet and longer,
Before you shall possess."

III.

"The little care you show
Of all my sorrows past
Makes death appear too slow
And life too long to last.
Fair Iris, kiss me kindly,* in pity of my fate,
And kindly still and kindly,
Before it be too late."

IV.

"You fondly* court your bliss
And no advances make.
'Tis not for maids to kiss,
But 'tis for men to take.
So you may kiss me kindly,* and I will not rebel,
And kindly still and kindly,
But kiss me not and tell."

V.

A rondeau.[44]

CHORUS.

Thus at the height we love and live
And fear not to be poor;
We give and give and give and give,
Till we can give no more.
But what today will take away
Tomorrow will restore.
Thus at the height we love and live,
And fear not to be poor.

[Exeunt performers.]

PHAEDRA.

Adieu. I leave you to pay the music. Hope well,
Mr. Planet; there's a better heaven in store for you.
I say no more, but you can guess. (*Exit.*)

MERCURY.

Such bargain-loves as I with Phaedra treat
Are all the leagues and friendships of the great.
All seek their ends, and each would other cheat.
They only seem to hate and seem to love,
But int'rest is the point on which they move.
Their friends are foes, and foes are friends again
And, in their turns, are knaves and honest men.

---

43 shepherd's hour] moment of dominance, here sexual

44 rondeau] Dryden uses the term loosely to indicate a
    musical shift (CE).

Our iron age is grown an age of gold:[45]
'Tis who bids most, for all men would be sold.

Exit.

Act V. [Courtyard within Amphitryon's palace.]

Enter Gripus, Phaedra. Gripus has the goblet in his hand.

PHAEDRA.
You will not be so base to take it from me?
GRIPUS.
'Tis my proper chattel, and I'll seize my own in
whatever hands I find it.
PHAEDRA.
You know I only showed it you to provoke your
generosity that you might outbid your rival with   5
a better present.
GRIPUS.
My rival is a thief, and I'll indict you for a receiver
of stolen goods.
PHAEDRA.
Thou hidebound lover!
GRIPUS.
Thou very mercenary mistress!   10
PHAEDRA.
Thou most mercenary magistrate!
GRIPUS.
Thou seller of thyself!
PHAEDRA.
Thou seller of other people! Thou weathercock of
government, that when the wind blows for the
subject point'st to privilege, and when it changes   15
for the sovereign veers to prerogative![46]
GRIPUS.
Will you compound, and take it as my present?
PHAEDRA.
No, but I'll send thy rival to force it from thee.
GRIPUS.
When a thief is rival to his judge, the hangman
will soon decide the difference.   20

---

[45] iron … gold] According to pagan historians, such as
Polybius, the iron age was the most recent and degenerate of the four ages of civilization's degeneration—from
gold, to silver, to brass, to iron.

[46] privilege … prerogative] rights of Parliament, rights of
the monarch—terms of great contention in the seventeenth century

Exit Phaedra. Enter Mercury, with two swords.

MERCURY. (*Bowing.*)
Save your good lordship.
GRIPUS.
From an impertinent coxcomb. I am out of humor
and am in haste. Leave me.
MERCURY.
'Tis my duty to attend on your lordship and to
ease you of that undecent burden.   25
GRIPUS.
Gold was never any burden to one of my
profession.
MERCURY.
By your lordship's permission, Phaedra has sent me
to take it from you.
GRIPUS.
What, by violence?   30
MERCURY. (*Still bowing.*)
No, but by your honor's permission, I am to
restore it to her and persuade your lordship to
renounce your pretensions to her.
GRIPUS.
Tell her flatly I will neither do one nor t'other.
MERCURY.
Oh my good lord, I dare pass my word for your   35
free consent to both. Will your honor be pleased
to take your choice of one of these?
GRIPUS.
Why, these are swords. What have I to do with
them?
MERCURY.
Only to take your choice of one of them, which   40
your lordship pleases, and leave the other to your
most obedient servant.
GRIPUS.
What, one of these ungodly weapons? Take notice.
I'll lay you by the heels,* sirrah. This has the
appearance of an unlawful bloody challenge.   45
MERCURY.
You magistrates are pleased to call it so, my lord.
But with us swordsmen 'tis an honorable invitation
to the cutting of one another's throats.
GRIPUS.
Be answered: I have no throat to cut. The law shall
decide our controversy.   50

MERCURY.

By your permission, my lord, it must be dispatched this way.

GRIPUS.

I'll see thee hanged before I give thee any such permission to dispatch me into another world.

MERCURY.

At the least, my lord, you have no occasion to 55 complain of my want* of respect to you. You will neither restore the goblet nor renounce Phaedra. I offer you the combat; you refuse it. All this is done in the forms of honor. It follows that I am to affront, cudgel you, or kick you, at my own 60 arbitrement, and I suppose you are too honorable not to approve of my proceeding.

GRIPUS.

Here's a new sort of process that was never heard of in any of our courts.

MERCURY.

This, my good lord, is law in shorthand, without 65 your long preambles and tedious repetitions that signify nothing but to squeeze the subject. Therefore, with your lordship's favor, I begin. (*Fillips him under the chin.*)

GRIPUS.

What's this for? 70

MERCURY.

To give you an occasion of returning me a box o'th'ear. That so, all things may proceed methodically.

GRIPUS.

I put in no answer, but suffer a nonsuit.

MERCURY.

No my lord, for the costs and the charges are to 75 be paid. Will you please to restore the cup?

GRIPUS.

I have told thee, no.

MERCURY.

Then from your chin I must ascend to your lordship's ears.

GRIPUS.

Oh, oh. Oh, oh. Wilt thou never leave lugging me 80 by the ears?

MERCURY. (*Pulling again.*)

Not till your lordship will be pleased to hear reason.

GRIPUS.

Take the cup, and the devil give thee joy on't.

MERCURY. (*Still holding him.*)

And your lordship will farther be graciously pleased 85 to release all claims, titles, and actions whatsoever to Phaedra. You must give me leave to add one small memento, for that too. (*Pulling him again.*)

GRIPUS.

I renounce her. I release her.

Enter Phaedra.

MERCURY. (*To her.*)

Phaedra, my lord has been pleased to be very 90 gracious, without pushing matters to extremity.

PHAEDRA.

I overheard it all. But give me livery and seisin of the goblet, in the first place.

MERCURY.

There's an Act of Oblivion[47] should be passed, too.

PHAEDRA.

Let him begin to remember quarrels when he 95 dares. Now I have him under my girdle, I'll cap verses[48] with him to the end of the chapter.

Enter Amphitryon and Guards.

AMPHITRYON. (*To Gripus.*)

At the last I have got possession without your lord-ship's warrant.—Phaedra, tell Alcmena I am here.

PHAEDRA.

I'll carry no such lying message. You are not here, 100 and you cannot be here, for to my knowledge, you are above with my lady in the chamber.

AMPHITRYON.

All of a piece and all witchcraft! Answer me precisely: Dost thou not know me for Amphitryon?

PHAEDRA.

Answer me first: Did you give me a diamond and 105 a purse of gold?

AMPHITRYON.

Thou know'st I did not.

---

47 Act of Oblivion] amnesty, such as those offered after the Restoration and the Revolution

48 cap verses] a game in which one replies to a verse with another beginning with the final or first letter of that verse

PHAEDRA.

Then by the same token, I know you are not the
true Amphitryon. If you are he, I am sure I left
you in bed with your own wife. Now you had best 110
stretch out a leg and feel about for a fair lady.

AMPHITRYON.

I'll undo this enchantment with my sword and kill
the sorcerer. (*To the guards.*) Come up, gentlemen,
and follow me.

PHAEDRA.

I'll save you the labor and call him down to 115
confront you, if you dare attend him. (*Exit.*)

MERCURY. (*Aside.*)

Now the spell is ended, and Jupiter can enchant no
more, or else Amphitryon had not entered so easily.

Gripus is stealing off.

Whither now, Gripus? I have business for you. If 120
you offer to stir, you know what follows.

Enter Jupiter, followed by Tranio and Polydas.

JUPITER.

Who dares to play the master in my house?
What noise is this that calls me from above,
Invades my soft recess and privacy,
And, like a tide, breaks in upon my love? 125

AMPHITRYON.

Oh heav'ns, what's this I see?

TRANIO.

What prodigy!

POLYDAS.

How, two Amphitryons?

GRIPUS.

I have beheld th'appearance of two suns,
But still the false was dimmer than the true. 130
Here both shine out alike.

AMPHITRYON.

This is a sight that, like the Gorgon's head,
Runs through my limbs and stiffens me to stone.
I need no more inquire into my fate,
For what I see resolves my doubts too plain. 135

TRANIO.

Two drops of water cannot be more alike.

POLYDAS.

They are two very sames.

MERCURY. (*Aside.*)

Our Jupiter is a great comedian; he counterfeits

most admirably. Sure his priests have copied their
hypocrisy from their master. 140

AMPHITRYON. (*Drawing his sword.*)

Now, I am gathered back into myself.
My heart beats high and pushes out the blood
To give me just revenge on this impostor.
(*To the guards.*)
If you are brave, assist me.—Not one stirs. 145
What, are all bribed to take th'enchanter's part?
'Tis true. The work is mine, and thus—(*Going to
rush upon Jupiter and is held by Tranio and
Polydas.*)

POLYDAS.

It must not be. 150

JUPITER.

Give him his way. I dare the madman's worst.
But still take notice that it looks not like
The true Amphitryon to fly out at first
To brutal force. It shows he doubts his cause
Who dares not trust his reason to defend it. 155

AMPHITRYON. (*Struggling.*)

Thou base usurper of my name and bed!
No less than thy heart's blood can wash away
Th'affronts I have sustained.

TRANIO.

We must not suffer
So strange a duel as Amphitryon 160
To fight against himself.

POLYDAS.

Nor think we wrong you, when we hold your hands.
We know our duty to our general.
We know the ties of friendship to our friend.
But who that friend or who that gen'ral is, 165
Without more certain proofs betwixt you two,
Is hard to be distinguished by our reason,
Impossible by sight.

AMPHITRYON.

I know it and have satisfied myself:
I am the true Amphitryon. 170

JUPITER.

See again.
He shuns the certain proofs and dares not stand
Impartial judgment and award of right.
But since Alcmena's honor is concerned,
Whom, more than heav'n and all the world, I love, 175
This I propose as equal to us both:

Tranio and Polydas, be you assistants;
The guards be ready to secure th'impostor,
When once so proved, for public punishment;
And Gripus, be thou umpire of the cause.   180
AMPHITRYON.
I am content; let him proceed to examination.
GRIPUS. (*Aside to Mercury.*)
On whose side would you please that I should give
the sentence?
MERCURY. (*Aside to him.*)
Follow thy conscience for once, but not to make
a custom of it neither, nor to leave an evil   185
precedent of uprightness to future judges. (*Aside.*)
'Tis a good thing to have a magistrate under
correction. Your old fornicating judge dare never
give sentence against him that knows his haunts.
POLYDAS.
Your lordship knows I was master of Amphitryon's   190
ship and desire to know of him what passed in
private betwixt us two at his landing when he was
just ready to engage the enemy.
GRIPUS.
Let the true Amphitryon answer first.
JUPITER, AMPHITRYON. (*Together.*)
My lord, I told him—   195
GRIPUS.
Peace, both of you. 'Tis a plain case they are both
true, for they both speak together. But for more
certainty, let the false Amphitryon speak first.
MERCURY.
Now they are both silent.
GRIPUS.
Then it's as plain on t'other side that they are both   200
false Amphitryons.
MERCURY.
Which Amphitryon shall speak first?
GRIPUS.
Let the choleric Amphitryon speak, and let the
peaceable hold his peace.
AMPHITRYON. (*To Polydas.*)
You may remember that I whispered you not to   205
part from the stern one single moment.
POLYDAS.
You did so.
GRIPUS.
No more words then. I proceed to sentence.

JUPITER.
'Twas I that whispered him, and he may remember
I gave him this reason for it—that if our men were   210
beaten, I might secure my own retreat.
POLYDAS.
You did so.
GRIPUS.
Now again he's as true as t'other.
TRANIO.
You know I was paymaster. What directions did
you give me the night before the battle?   215
GRIPUS.
To which of the yous art thou speaking?
MERCURY. (*Aside.*)
It should be a double U, but they have no such
letter in their tongue.[49]
AMPHITRYON.
I ordered you to take particular care of the great bag.
GRIPUS.
Why this is demonstration.   220
JUPITER.
The bag that I recommended to you was of tiger's
skin and marked "beta."
GRIPUS.
In sadness, I think they are both jugglers. Here's
nothing, and here's nothing, and then *hictius
doctius*,* and they are both here again.   225
TRANIO.
You, peaceable Amphitryon, what money was there
in that bag?
JUPITER.
That sum in gross amounted to just fifty Attic
talents.[50]
TRANIO.
To a farthing.   230
GRIPUS.
Paugh! Obvious, obvious.
AMPHITRYON.
Two thousand pieces of gold were tied up in a
handkerchief by themselves.
TRANIO.
I remember it.   235

---

49 double U] pun on the letter "w," which is not part of
  the Greek alphabet
50 fifty Attic talents] well over a ton of gold or silver

GRIPUS.

Then 'tis dubious again.

JUPITER.

But the rest was not all silver, for there were just
four thousand brass halfpence.

GRIPUS.

Being but brass, the proof is inconsiderable. If they
had been silver, it had gone on your side.   240

AMPHITRYON. (*To Jupiter.*)

Death and hell! You will not persuade me that I
did not kill Pterelas?

JUPITER.

Nor you me that I did not enjoy Alcmena?

AMPHITRYON. (*Aside.*)

That last was poison to me.
—Yet there's one proof thou canst not counterfeit.   245
In killing Pterelas, I had a wound
Full in the brawny part of my right arm
Where still the scar remains. Now blush, impostor,
For this thou canst not show. (*Bares his arm and
shows the scar, which they all look on.*)

OMNES.

This is the true Amphitryon.   250

JUPITER.

May your lordship please—

GRIPUS.

No sirrah, it does not please me. Hold your
tongue, I charge you, for the case is manifest.

JUPITER.

By your favor, then, this shall speak for me. (*Bares
his arm and shows it.*)   255

TRANIO.

'Tis just in the same muscle.

POLYDAS.

Of the same length and breadth, and the scar of
the same bluish color.

GRIPUS. (*To Jupiter.*)

Did not I charge you not to speak? 'Twas plain
enough before, and now you have puzzled it again.   260

AMPHITRYON.

Good gods, how can this be?

GRIPUS.

For certain there was but one Pterelas, and he must
have been in the plot against himself too, for he was
killed first by one of them, and then rose again out of
respect to t'other Amphitryon to be killed twice over.   265

Enter Alcmena, Phaedra, and Bromia.

ALCMENA. (*Turning to Phaedra and Bromia.*)

No more of this; it sounds impossible
That two should be so like, no difference found.

PHAEDRA.

You'll find it true.

ALCMENA.

Then where's Alcmena's honor and her fame?
Farewell my needless fear. It cannot be.   270
This is a case too nice* for vulgar sight.
But let me come; my heart will guide my eyes
To point and tremble to its proper choice. (*Seeing
Amphitryon, goes to him.*)
There neither was, nor is, but one Amphitryon,
And I am only his. (*Goes to take him by the hand.*)   275

AMPHITRYON. (*Pushing her away from him.*)
                                        Away, adulteress!

JUPITER.

My gentle love, my treasure and my joy,
Follow no more that false and foolish fire[51]
That would mislead thy fame to sure destruction.
Look on thy better husband and thy friend,   280
Who will not leave thee liable to scorn,
But vindicate thy honor from that wretch
Who would by base aspersions blot thy virtue.

ALCMENA. (*Going to him, who embraces her.*)

I was indeed mistaken. Thou art he!
Thy words, thy thoughts, thy soul is all Amphitryon.   285
Th'impostor has thy features, not thy mind.
Thy face might have deceived me in my choice;
Thy kindness is a guide that cannot err.

AMPHITRYON.

What, in my presence to prefer the villain!
Oh execrable cheat! I break the truce   290
And will no more attend your vain decisions.
To this [*Unsheathes his sword.*]—and to the
gods—I'll trust my cause. (*Is rushing upon
Jupiter, and is held again.*)

JUPITER.

Poor man. How I contemn those idle threats!
Were I disposed, thou might'st as safely meet
The thunder launched from the red arm of Jove   295
(Nor Jove need blush to be Alcmena's champion),
But in the face of Thebes she shall be cleared,

---

51 false … fire] ignis fatuus (q.v.)

And what I am and what thou art be known.
Attend, and I will bring convincing proof.

AMPHITRYON.

Thou wouldst elude my justice and escape. 300
But I will follow thee through earth and seas,
Nor hell shall hide thee from my just revenge.

JUPITER.

I'll spare thy pains; it shall be quickly seen,
Betwixt us two, who seeks and who avoids.
—Come in, my friends, and thou who seem'st 305
Amphitryon,
That all who are in doubt may know the true.

Jupiter re-enters the house; with him Amphitryon,
Alcmena, Polydas, Tranio, and guards.

MERCURY. (*To Gripus and Bromia, who are following.*)
Thou, Gripus, and you, Bromia, stay with Phaedra.
Let their affairs alone, and mind we ours.
Amphitryon's rival shall appear a god.
But know before hand, I am Mercury, 310
Who want* not heav'n while Phaedra is on earth.

BROMIA.

But an't* please your lordship, is my fellow Phaedra
to be exalted into the heavens and made a star?

PHAEDRA.

When that comes to pass, if you look up a-nights,
I shall remember old kindness and vouchsafe to 315
twinkle on you.

Enter Sosia, peeping about him, and seeing Mercury, is
starting back.

SOSIA.

Here he is again, and there's no passing by him
into the house, unless I were a sprite to glide
through the keyhole. I am to be a vagabond, I find.

MERCURY.

Sosia, come back. 320

SOSIA.

No, I thank you. You may whistle me long enough;
a beaten dog has always the wit to avoid his master.

MERCURY.

I permit thee to be Sosia again.

SOSIA.

'Tis an unfortunate name, and I abandon it. He
that has an itch to be beaten, let him take it up 325
for Sosia. What have I said now? I mean for me,
for I neither am nor will be Sosia.

MERCURY.

But thou mayst be so in safety, for I have
acknowledged myself to be God Mercury.

SOSIA.

You may be a god, for aught I know, but the devil 330
take me if ever I worship you, for an unmerciful
deity as you are.

MERCURY.

You ought to take it for an honor to be drubbed
by the hand of a divinity.

SOSIA.

I am your most humble servant, good Mr. God. But 335
by the faith of a mortal, I could well have spared the
honor that you did me. But how shall I be sure that
you will never assume my shape again?

MERCURY.

Because I am weary of wearing so villainous* an
outside. 340

SOSIA.

Well, well. As villainous as it is, here's old Bromia
will be contented with it.

BROMIA.

Yes, now I am sure that I may chastize you safely
and that there's no god lurking under your
appearance. 345

SOSIA.

Aye, but you had best take heed how you attempt
it, for as Mercury has turned himself into me, so
I may take the toy into my head to turn myself
into Mercury that I may swinge you off condignly.

MERCURY.

In the meantime, be all my witnesses that I take 350
Phaedra for my wife of the left hand[52]—that is,
in the nature of a lawful concubine.

PHAEDRA.

You shall pardon me for believing you, for all you
are a god, for you have a terrible ill name below,
and I am afraid you'll get a footman instead of a 355
priest to marry us.

MERCURY.

But here's Gripus shall draw up the articles betwixt us.

PHAEDRA.

But he's damnably used to false conveyancing.

---

52 wife of the left hand] in a morganatic marriage (q.v.), so
called because of such a ceremony performed by Gypsies

Well, be it so, for my counsel shall overlook 'em before I sign. Come on, Gripus, that I may have him under black and white.

Here Gripus gets ready pen, ink, and paper.

MERCURY.

With all my heart, that I may have thee under black and white hereafter.

PHAEDRA. (*To Gripus.*)

Begin, begin: "Heads of articles to be made, etcetera, betwixt Mercury, god of thieves—"

MERCURY.

"And Phaedra, queen of Gypsies. Imprimis: I promise to buy and settle upon her an estate, containing nine thousand acres of land, in any part of Boeotia to her own liking."

PHAEDRA.

"Provided always that no part of the said nine thousand acres shall be upon or adjoining to Mount Parnassus," for I will not be fobbed off with a poetical estate.53

MERCURY.

"Memorandum: that she be always constant to me and admit no other lover."

PHAEDRA.

"Memorandum: unless it be a lover that offers more, and that the constancy shall not exceed the settlement."

MERCURY.

"Item: that she shall keep no male servants in her house. Item: no rival lapdog for a bedfellow. Item: that she shall never pray to any of the gods."

PHAEDRA.

What, would you have me an atheist?

MERCURY.

No devotion to any he-deity, good Phaedra.

BROMIA.

Here's no provision made for children yet.

PHAEDRA.

Well remembered, Bromia. I bargain that my eldest son shall be a hero and my eldest daughter a king's mistress.

MERCURY.

That is to say a blockhead and a harlot, Phaedra.

PHAEDRA.

That's true. But who dares call 'em so? Then for the younger children—but now I think on't, we'll have no more but Mass and Miss, for the rest would be but chargeable and a burden to the nation.

MERCURY.

Yes, yes. The second shall be a false prophet. He shall have wit enough to set up for a new religion and too much wit to die a martyr for it.

PHAEDRA.

Oh, what had I forgot? There's pin money, and alimony, and separate maintenance,* and a thousand things more to be considered that are all to be tacked to this Act of Settlement.54

SOSIA.

I am a fool, I must confess, but yet I can see as far into a millstone as the best of you. I have observed that you women wits are commonly so quick upon the scent that you often overrun it. Now I would ask of Madame Phaedra that, in case Mr. Heaven there should be pleased to break these articles, in what court of judicature she intends to sue him.

PHAEDRA.

The fool has hit upon't. Gods and great men are never to be sued, for they can always plead privilege of peerage.55—And therefore for once, monsieur, I'll take your word, for as long as you love me, you'll be sure to keep it, and in the meantime, I shall be gaining experience how to manage some rich cully, for no woman has ever made her fortune by a wit.

It thunders, and the company within-doors— Amphitryon, Alcmena, Polydas, and Tranio—all come running out and join with the rest.

---

53 Parnassus … estate] Mountain in Greece sacred to Apollo and the Muses. Because poets were notoriously poor, "poetical" has the sense of imaginary.

54 Act of Settlement] cf. the act passed by Parliament to legitimize William III as King of England and settle the crown on his heirs

55 privilege of peerage] titled nobility could avoid trials in ordinary courts by claiming a trial by their peers—that is, other members of the House of Lords and their immediate families.

AMPHITRYON.

Sure 'tis some god. He vanished from our sight,   415
And told us we should see him soon return.

ALCMENA.

I know not what to hope, nor what to fear.
A simple error is a real crime,
And unconsenting innocence is lost.

*A second peal of thunder, after which Jupiter appears
in a machine.*

JUPITER.

Look up, Amphitryon, and behold above   420
Th'impostor god, the rival of thy love.
In thy own shape see Jupiter appear,
And let that sight secure thy jealous fear.
Disgrace and infamy are turned to boast;
No fame in Jove's concurrence[56] can be lost.   425
What he enjoys, he sanctifies from vice,
And, by partaking, stamps into a price.[57]
'Tis I who ought to murmur at my fate,
Forced by my love my godhead to translate,
When on no other terms I could possess   430
But by thy form, thy features, and thy dress.
To thee were given the blessings that I sought,
Which else not all the bribes of heav'n had bought.
Then take into thy arms thy envied love,
And in his own despite triumph over Jove.   435

MERCURY. (*Aside.*)

Amphitryon and Alcmena both stand mute and
know not how to take it.

SOSIA. (*Aside.*)

Our sovereign lord Jupiter is a sly companion; he
knows how to gild a bitter pill.

JUPITER.

From this auspicious night shall rise an heir,   440
Great like his sire and like his mother fair.
Wrongs to redress and tyrants to disseise,
Born for a world that wants* a Hercules.
Monsters and monster-men he shall engage,
And toil and struggle through an impious age.   445
Peace to his labors shall at length succeed,
And murm'ring men, unwilling to be freed,
Shall be compelled to happiness by need.

---

[56] in Jove's concurrence] in being a rival to Jove
[57] stamps ... price] increases its value

Jupiter is carried back to heaven.

OMNES.

We all congratulate Amphitryon.

MERCURY.

Keep your congratulations to yourselves,   450
gentlemen. 'Tis a nice* point, let me tell you that,
and the less that is said of it, the better. Upon the
whole matter, if Amphitryon takes the favor of
Jupiter in patience, as from a god, he's a good
heathen.   455

SOSIA.

I must take a little extraordinary pains tonight that
my spouse may come even with her lady and
produce a squire to attend on young Hercules
when he goes out to seek adventures—that when
his master kills a man, he may stand ready to pick   460
his pockets and piously relieve his aged parents. Ah
Bromia, Bromia, if thou hadst been as handsome
and as young as Phaedra—I say no more, but
somebody might have made his fortunes as well
as his master, and never the worse man neither.   465
For let the wicked world say what they please,
The fair wife makes her husband live at ease.
The lover keeps him too, and but receives,
Like Jove, the remnants that Amphitryon leaves.
'Tis true the lady has enough in store   470
To satisfy those two and eke two more.
In fine, the man who weighs the matter fully
Would rather be the cuckold than the cully.

[*Exeunt.*]

FINIS.

Textual Notes

a Copytext is the first edition, a 1690/91 quarto (Q1.)
Also consulted: the second edition, a 1692 quarto (Q2)
and modern editions of 1976 (the California edition—
CE), and of 1995 (Cordner).
b pastoral dialogue] Q1 etc. mark the stanzas with the
characters' names, but since Thyrsis does not actually
start speaking until the middle of the first stanza, quo-
tation marks have been employed until the choric stanza.

The Author's Farce[a]

by Henry Fielding (1707-1754)
edited by Jill Campbell

Debuting at the New Theater in the Haymarket on March 30, 1730, *The Author's Farce* is a play about the relation between art and money. Its first two acts, employing a fairly conventional "realistic" mode of representation, depict the struggles of an impecunious author whose efforts are rejected in turn by a theater manager and a bookseller, both of whom are only concerned with catering to popular tastes in order to maximize profit. In desperation, the aspiring author, Luckless, decides that he "would rather eat by his nonsense than starve by his wit," and the result is a radical transformation of Fielding's play in its third act: there, as we watch a performance of the absurd theatrical hodgepodge Luckless has created to make money, we see the consequences of the control wielded over literary culture by facile popular tastes and mercenary middle-men. In the presentation of the play-within, the representational mode of the play has suddenly become fantastic and emblematical, as live actors perform the parts of puppets emblematizing various "pleasures of the town" (opera, pantomime, heroic tragedy, etc.).

While the use of ballad tunes in the play is indebted to Gay's *The Beggar's Opera*, the action and satiric perspective of Act III are clearly influenced by Pope's 1728 *Dunciad*, in which Lewis Theobald is elevated to the position of Head Dunce, presiding over the inverted world of the reign of Nonsense or Dullness. Fielding shares Pope's bitterly satiric view of the English culture of their time, and many of the specific targets of *The Author's Farce* appear in *The Dunciad* as well. Fielding's dramatic mode, however,

allows him to both exemplify directly the art forms he treats and frame them critically; throughout the play-within, Luckless, who has practiced the debased art forms of his time with no illusions about their value, sits on the side of the stage, commenting ironically on its absurdities. If Luckless has "sold out," Fielding himself can claim that he only exploits the popular entertainments of his day in order to expose them satirically, seeking, like a court jester, to achieve reform through laughter.

The play's concluding scenes, however, unsettle this controlled satiric relation between the two levels of representation in the play. In the end, fantastic good fortune enters the realistic framing play, and an accelerating series of discoveries reveals unsuspected relationships between "real" people, puppet-characters, and the players who represent them. The collapse of distinctions between realistic and fantastic modes of representation extends Fielding's experimentation with "alienation effects" in this play in a manner proleptic of modern playwrights such as Pirandello and Brecht. With forty-one performances during the spring and summer of 1730, this innovative play enjoyed the success on stage for which needy authors such as Luckless—and the young Henry Fielding himself—must hope. Fielding had discovered his metier in a form of satiric, experimental theater that he would practice fruitfully until 1737, when a Licensing Act passed partly in response to Fielding's own increasingly pointed political satire on stage, would force him to turn from playwriting to the career as a novelist for which he is most widely known.

Prologue

Too long the Tragic Muse hath awed the stage
And frightened wives and children with her rage.
Too long Drawcansir roars, Parthenope weeps,[1]
While ev'ry lady cries and critic sleeps.
With ghosts, rapes, murders, tender hearts they 5
   wound
Or else, like thunder, terrify with sound.
When the skilled actress to her weeping eyes
With artful sigh the handkerchief applies,
How grieved each sympathizing nymph appears,
And box and gallery both melt in tears. 10
Or when in armor of Corinthian brass
Heroic actor stares you in the face
And cries aloud with emphasis that's fit on
Liberty, Freedom, Liberty, and Briton;[2]
While frowning, gaping for applause he stands, 15
What generous Briton can refuse his hands?
Like the tame animals designed for show,
You have your cues to clap, as they to bow.
Taught to commend, your judgments have no
   share:
By chance you guess aright, by chance you err. 20
    But handkerchiefs and Britain laid aside,
Tonight we mean to laugh and not to chide.
    In days of yore, when fools were held in
   fashion,
Though now, alas! all banished from the nation,
A merry jester had reformed his lord, 25
Who would have scorned the sterner Stoic's word.
    Bred in Democritus his* laughing schools,

Our author flies sad Heraclitus' rules:
No tears, no terror plead in his behalf;
The aim of farce is but to make you laugh. 30
Beneath the tragic or the comic name,
Farces and puppet shows ne'er miss of fame.
Since then in borrowed dress they've pleased the
   Town,*
Condemn them not, appearing in their own.
    Smiles we expect from the good-natured few; 35
As ye are done by, ye malicious, do,
And kindly laugh at him who laughs at you.

DRAMATIS PERSONAE

MEN
    Luckless, the author and master of the show.
    Witmore, his friend.
    Marplay,
    Sparkish, comedians.
    Bookweight, a bookseller.
    Scarecrow,
    Dash,
    Quibble,
    Blotpage, scribblers.
    Jack, servant to Luckless.
    Jack-Pudding.
    Bantomite.

WOMEN
    Mrs. Moneywood, the author's landlady.
    Harriot, her daughter.

PERSONS IN THE PUPPET SHOW
    Player.
    Constable.
    Murdertext, a Presbyterian parson.
    Goddess of Nonsense.
    Charon.
    Curry, a bookseller.
    A poet.
    Signior Opera.
    Don Tragedio.
    Sir Farcical Comic.
    Dr. Orator.
    Monsieur Pantomime.
    Mrs. Novel.
    Robgrave, the sexton.
    Sailor.
    Somebody.

---

1 Drawcansir, Parthenope] examples of the overblown
tragic hero and heroine, as named in Buckingham's *The
Rehearsal* (1671), which burlesqued the inflated rhetoric and melodramatic events of the heroic tragedies of
Dryden and others. The reference to Buckingham's characters obliquely acknowledges Fielding's debt to his use
of the "rehearsal" structure, in which an author-charac-
ter and visitors watch and comment upon a performance of a play.

2 Liberty … Briton] "British Liberty" was a standard patriotic rallying-cry throughout the eighteenth century;
Fielding alludes to the frequent appeals to patriotism in
serious drama of the period. "Briton"—rather than "Britain"—is dictated by the rhyme.

Nobody.
Punch.
Joan.
Lady Kingcall.
Mrs. Cheat'em.
Mrs. Glassring.

An Author's Farce.
Written by Scriblerus Secundus.[3]
—*Quis iniquae*
Tam patiens urbis, tam ferreus, ut teneat se?
Juv. Sat. I.[4]

Act I, scene i. Luckless's room
in Mrs. Moneywood's house.

Mrs. Moneywood, Harriot, Luckless.

MONEYWOOD.
Never tell me, Mr. Luckless, of your play, and your
play. I say, I must be paid. I would no more
depend on a benefit night[5] of an unacted play than
I would on a benefit ticket in an undrawn lottery.
Could I have guessed that I had a poet in my   5
house? Could I have looked for a poet under laced
clothes?
LUCKLESS.
Why not, since you may often find poverty under
them?
MONEYWOOD.
Do you make a jest of my misfortune, sir?   10
LUCKLESS.
Rather, my misfortune. I am sure I have a better
title to poverty than you. You wallow in wealth,
and I know not where to dine.

---

3 Scriblerus Secundus] Fielding's choice of pseudonym
affiliates him with the satiric project of the Scriblerus
Club, a group formed in 1713-14 by Pope, Swift,
Arbuthnot, Gay, Parnell, and Harley, earl of Oxford, to
satirize learned follies, abuses of writing, and the political abuses of the Whig government.
4 *Quis* ... Sat. I] Juvenal, *Satires* I.30-31: "Who can be
so tolerant of this city, who so iron of soul, as to contain himself."
5 benefit night] Playwrights often received payment in the
uncertain form of profits from every third night of a
play's run.

MONEYWOOD.
Never fear that; you'll never want* a dinner till you
have dined at all the eating houses round. No one   15
shuts their doors against you the first time—and
I think you are so kind never to trouble them a
second.
LUCKLESS.
No, and if you will give me leave to walk out of
your doors, the Deel* take me if ever I come into   20
them again.
MONEYWOOD.
Whenever you please, sir—leaving your movables
behind.
LUCKLESS.
All but my books, dear madam; they will be of no
service to you.   25
MONEYWOOD.
When they are sold, sir, and that's more than your
other effects would, for I believe you may carry
away everything else in your pockets—if you have
any.
HARRIOT.
Nay, Mamma, it is barbarous to insult him.   30
MONEYWOOD.
No doubt you'll take his part. Pray, get about your
business. I suppose he intends to pay me by
ruining you. Get you in—and if ever I see you
together again, I'll turn you out of doors,
remember that.   35

[Exit Harriot.]

Scene ii.

Luckless, Mrs. Moneywood.

LUCKLESS.
Discharge all your ill-nature on me, madam, but
spare poor Miss Harriot.
MONEYWOOD.
Oh! then it is plain. I have suspected your
familiarity a great while. You are a base man. Is it
not enough to stay three months in my house   5
without paying me a farthing, but you must ruin
my child?
LUCKLESS.
I love her as I love my soul. Had I the world, I'd
give it her all—

MONEYWOOD.

But as you happen to have nothing in the world, I desire you would have nothing to say to her. I suppose you would have settled all your castles in the air. Oh! I wish you had lodged in one of them, instead of my house. Well, I am resolved, when you are gone away (which I heartily hope will be very soon), I'll hang over my door in great red letters, "*No Lodgings for Poets.*" Sure, never was such a guest as you have been. My floor is all spoiled with ink, my windows with verses, and my door has been almost beat down with duns.

LUCKLESS.

Would your house had been beaten down and everything but my dear Harriot crushed under it. Must I be your scolding-stock every morning? And because my pocket is empty, must my head be filled with noise and impertinence? Naturalists say that all creatures, even the most venemous, are of some use in the creation, but I'm sure a scolding old woman is of none—unless she serves in this world, as the Devil will in the other, to torment us. And if our torment were to lie in noise, I defy the Devil to invent a worse.

MONEYWOOD.

Sir, sir—

LUCKLESS.

Madam, madam! I will attack you at your own weapon. I'll pay you in your own coin—

MONEYWOOD.

I wish you would pay me in any coin, sir.

LUCKLESS.

Pay you! That word is always uppermost in your mouth, as gelt is in a Dutchman's.[6] Look you, madam, I'll do as much as a reasonable woman can require: I'll show you all I have—and give you all I have too, if you please to receive it. (*Turns his pockets inside out.*)

MONEYWOOD.

I will not be used in this manner. No sir, I will be paid, if there be any such thing as law.

LUCKLESS.

By what law you will put money into my pocket, I don't know, for I never heard of any one who got money by the law but the lawyers. I have told you already, madam, and I tell you again, that the first money I get shall be yours, and I have great expectations from my play. In the meantime, your staying here can be of no service, and you may possibly drive some fine thoughts out of my head. I must write a love scene, and your daughter would be properer company on that occasion than you.

MONEYWOOD.

You would act a love scene, I believe, but I shall prevent you, for I intend to dispose of myself before my daughter.

LUCKLESS.

Dispose of yourself! to whom? to the tallow-chandler? You will never have anything to do with matrimony till Hymen turns his torch into a tallow candle; then you may be of as much use to him as a fine lady's eyes to Cupid and may serve to light young people to bed together.

MONEYWOOD.

You are a vile slanderer. I am not so old nor so fat nor so ugly as you would make me. And 'tis very well known that I have had very good offers since my last dear husband died, if I would have accepted them. I might have had an attorney of New Inn[7] or Mr. Fillpot the exciseman; yes, I had my choice of two parsons or a doctor of physic—and yet I slighted them all. Yes, I slighted them for you—

LUCKLESS.

For me!

MONEYWOOD.

Yes, you have seen too visible marks of my passion —too visible for my reputation.

LUCKLESS.

I have heard very loud tokens of your passion, but I rather took it for the passion of anger than of love.

MONEYWOOD.

Oh! it arose from love! Do but be kind,* and I'll forgive thee all.

---

6 gelt … Dutchman's] Leading the way in the development of institutions of finance and trade, the Dutch were frequently typed by the English in this period as mercenary and materialistic.

7 New Inn] an Inn of Chancery in Drury Lane

LUCKLESS.

Death! Madam, stand off. If I must be plagued 80
with you, I had rather you should afflict my eyes
than my touch: at a distance, you offend but one
sense, but nearer, you offend them all—and I
would sooner lose them all than undergo you.

MONEYWOOD.

You shall repent this, sir, remember that—you shall 85
repent it. I'll show you the revenge of an injured
woman.

LUCKLESS.

I shall never repent anything that rids me of you,
madam, I assure you.

[Exit Moneywood.]

Scene iii.ᵇ

Luckless, Harriot.

HARRIOT.

My dear Harry, I have been waiting an opportunity
to return to you.

LUCKLESS.

My dear Harriot—come to my arms, and let me
lay my aching, sick head on thy tender bosom.

HARRIOT.

What's the matter, my dear? 5

LUCKLESS.

I am sick of the most abominable distemper.

HARRIOT.

Heaven forbid! What is it?

LUCKLESS.

Poverty, my love—and your mother is a most
excellent nurse.

HARRIOT.

What shall I do for you? My money is all gone and 10
so are my clothes, which, when my mother finds
out, I shall have as much need of a surgeon as you
can have now of a doctor.

LUCKLESS.

No, I would sooner starve or beg or steal or die
than one hair of my dear Harriot should be hurt. 15
I am armed against her utmost rage, but for you I
fear, for such a spirit as your mother no Amazon
ever possessed before. So, if my present design
succeeds, we will leave her together.

HARRIOT.

But if it should fail— 20

LUCKLESS.

Say then, my Harriot, would my charmer fly
To the cold climes beneath the polar sky?
Or armed with love, could she endure to sweat
Beneath the sultry, dry equator's heat?
Thirst, hunger, labor, hardship, could she prove, 25
From conversation* of the world remove,
And only know the joys of constant love?

HARRIOT.

Oh more than this, my Luckless, would I do:
All places are a heaven when with you.
Let me repose but on that faithful breast; 30
Give me thy love—the world may take the rest.

LUCKLESS.

My dear Harriot! By Heaven, thy lips are sweeter
than the honey, and thy temper is yet sweeter than
them.

HARRIOT.

(*Sighs.*) 35

LUCKLESS.

Why do you sigh, my sweet?

HARRIOT.

I only wish I were assured of the sincerity of your
love.

*Air 1. "Buttered Pease."*⁸

8 "Buttered Pease."] Fielding uses popular ballad tunes for
the songs in his play, indicating the tune in most cases
by the name or first line of its ballad source (as here,
"Buttered Pease"). Many of these tunes were recorded
for his readers in collections of songs, such as *Wit and
Mirth: or Pills to Purge Melancholy*, compiled by Thomas Durfey in 1719-20.

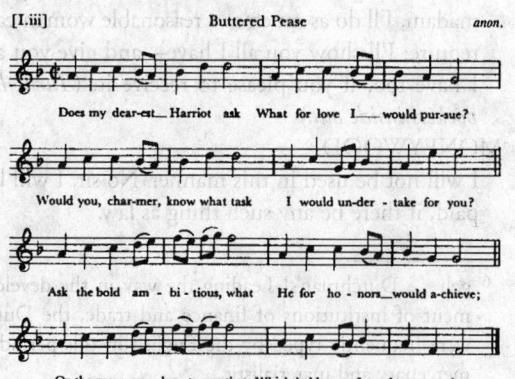

[I.iii]   Buttered Pease   *anon.*

Does my dear-est Harriot ask What for love I would pur-sue?

Would you, char-mer, know what task I would un-der - take for you?

Ask the bold am - bi - tious, what He for ho - nors would a-chieve;

Or the gay vo - lup - tuous, that Which he'd not for plea-sures give.

LUCKLESS.
> Does my dearest Harriot ask 40
>> What for love I would pursue?
> Would you, charmer, know what task
>> I would undertake for you?

> Ask the bold ambitious what
>> He for honors would achieve 45
> Or the gay voluptuous that
>> Which he'd not for pleasures give.

> Ask the miser what he'd do
>> To amass excessive gain
> Or the saint what he'd pursue 50
>> His wished heav'n to attain.

> These I would attempt, and more,
>> For oh! my Harriot is to me
> All ambition, pleasure, store,
>> Or what heav'n itself can be. 55

HARRIOT.
> Would my dearest Luckless know
>> What his constant Harriot can,
> Her tender love and faith to show,
>> For her dear, her only man?

> Ask the vain coquette what she 60
>> For men's adoration would
> Or from censure to be free
>> Ask the vile censorious prude.

> In a coach and six to ride,
>> What the mercenary jade, 65
> Or the widow, to be bride
>> To a brisk, broad-shouldered blade.

> All these I would attempt for thee,
>> Could I but thy passion fix;
> Thy tongue my sole commander be 70
>> And thy arms my coach and six.

LUCKLESS.
It is unkind in you to doubt it. I wish it was in my power to give you greater proofs, but I will give you the greatest in my power—which is, to marry you this instant. 75

HARRIOT.
Then I am easy. But it is better to delay that till our circumstances alter. For, remember what you have yourself said in the song you taught me:
> Would you the charming Queen of Love
>> Invite with you to dwell, 80
> No want* your poverty should prove,
>> No state your riches tell.

> Both her and happiness to hold
>> A middle state must please;
> They shun the house that shines with gold 85
>> And that which shines with grease.

MONEYWOOD. (*Within.*)
Harriot! Harriot!

HARRIOT.
Hear the dreadful summons. Adieu, my dear. I will take the first opportunity of seeing you again. [*Exit.*] 90

LUCKLESS.
Adieu to my pretty charmer!—Go thy ways, for the first of thy sex. What fool would dangle after and make himself a slave to the insolent pride of a mistress, when he may find another with as much good nature as he would wish? 95

Scene iv.

Luckless, Jack.

LUCKLESS.
So! What news bring you?

JACK.
An't* please your honor, I have been at my lord's, and his lordship thanks you for the favor you have offered of reading your play to him, but he has such a prodigious deal of business, he begs to be 5 excused. I have been with Mr. Keyber,[9] too; he made me no answer at all. Mr. Bookweight will be here immediately.

---

9 Keyber] a derogatory distortion of Colley Cibber's last name, Germanicizing it to mock his support for the Hanoverian royal family, which would make him Poet Laureate in December, 1730. Cibber (1671-1757) reappears in the figure of Marplay in Act II and again as Sir Farcical Comic in Act III. While he was also a

LUCKLESS.

Jack!

JACK.

Sir.

LUCKLESS.

Fetch my hat hither.

JACK.

It is here, sir.

LUCKLESS.

Carry it to the pawnbroker's. And in your way home, call at the cook's shop. Make haste.

[Exit Jack.]

So, one way or other, I find, my head must always 15
provide for my belly.

Scene v.

Luckless, Witmore.

LUCKLESS.

I am surprised—dear Witmore!

WITMORE.

Dear Harry!

LUCKLESS.

This is kind, indeed, but I do not more wonder at finding a man in this age who can be a friend to adversity than that Fortune should be so much 5
my friend as to direct you to me, for she is a lady I have not been much indebted to lately.

WITMORE.

She who told me, I assure you, is one you have been indebted to a long while.

LUCKLESS.

Whom do you mean? 10

WITMORE.

One who complains of your unkindness in not visiting her—Mrs.* Lovewood.

LUCKLESS.

Dost thou visit there still, then?

___

successful playwright, actor, and public personality, Cibber appears here and in Act II as one of the three managers of Drury Lane Theater; Jack has sought reward for Luckless's writings from the old system of patronage (at "my lord's"), from the newer system of marketing through booksellers, and from the theater.

WITMORE.

I throw an idle hour away there sometimes. When I am in an ill humor, I go there and rail, where I 15
am sure to feed it with all the scandal in Town.* No news writer is more diligent in procuring intelligence, no bawd in looking after girls with an uncracked maidenhead, than she in searching out women with cracked reputations. 20

LUCKLESS.

The much more infamous office of the two.

WITMORE.

Thou art still a favorer of the women, I find.

LUCKLESS.

Aye, the women and the Muses—the high roads to beggary.

WITMORE.

What, art thou not cured of scribbling yet? 25

LUCKLESS.

No, scribbling is as impossible to cure as the gout.

WITMORE.

And as sure a sign of poverty as the gout of riches. 'Sdeath!* In an age of learning and true politeness, where a man might succeed by his merit, it would be an encouragement. But now, when party and 30
prejudice carry all before them, when learning is decried, wit not understood, when the theaters are puppet shows, and the comedians ballad singers— when fools lead the Town—would a man think to thrive by his wit? If you must write, write 35
nonsense, write operas, write entertainments, write *Hurlothrumbos,** set up an oratory and preach nonsense,[10] and you may meet with encouragement enough. If you would receive applause, deserve to receive sentence at the Old 40
Bailey—and if you would ride in your coach, deserve to ride in a cart.[11]

___

[10] oratory … nonsense] Oratories—entertainments featuring sermons and orations—were popularized by the eccentric preacher John "Orator" Henley, who appears in Act III as Dr. Orator. Witmore rapidly lists several of the popular forms of entertainment that Luckless will both satirize and exploit in his puppet show.

[11] applause … cart] Criminals often gave speeches on the gallows, to which they rode in a cart; the Old Bailey Sessions House functioned as London's central criminal court.

LUCKLESS.

You are warm, my friend.

WITMORE.

It is because I am your friend. I cannot bear to hear the man I love ridiculed by fools and idiots—to see 45 a fellow who, had he been born a Chinese, had been some low mechanic, toss up his empty noddle with a scornful disdain of what he has not understood, and women abusing what they have neither seen nor read from an unreasonable prejudice to an honest 50 fellow whom they have not known. If thou wilt write against all these reasons, get a patron, be pimp to some worthless man of quality,* write panegyrics on him, flatter him with as many virtues as he has vices—and don't pretend to stand thyself against a 55 tide of prejudice and ill nature which would have overwhelmed a Plato or a Socrates.

LUCKLESS.

I own thy advice is friendly, and I fear too much truth is on your side. But what would you advise me to do? 60

WITMORE.

Thou art a vigorous young fellow—and there are rich widows in Town.

LUCKLESS.

But I am already engaged.

WITMORE.

Why don't you marry then? For I suppose you are not so mad to have any engagement with a poor 65 mistress.

LUCKLESS.

Even so, faith, and so heartily that I would not change her for the widow of a Croesus.[12]

WITMORE.

Now thou art undone, indeed. Matrimony clenches ruin beyond retrieval. What unfortunate stars wert 70 thou born under! Was it not enough to follow those nine ragged jades the Muses, but you must fasten on some earth-born mistess as poor as them?

LUCKLESS.

Fie Witmore, thou art grown a churl.

WITMORE.

While thou wert happy, I could bear these flights; 75

---

12 Croesus] the last king of Lydia, whose wealth was legendary

while thy rooms were furnished and thy clothes whole, I could bear thee. But for a man to preach up love and the Muses in a garret, it would not make me more sick to hear honesty talked of at Court, conscience at Westminster,[13] politeness at 80 the university. Nay, I had rather hear women disputing on the mathematics—

Scene vi.c

Luckless, Witmore, Bookweight.[14]

LUCKLESS.

Mr. Bookweight, your very humble servant.

BOOKWEIGHT.

I was told, sir, you had particular business with me.

LUCKLESS.

Yes, Mr. Bookweight, I have something to put into your hands. I have a play for you, Mr. Bookweight.

BOOKWEIGHT.

Is it accepted, sir? 5

LUCKLESS.

Not yet.

BOOKWEIGHT.

Oh, sir! When it is, it will be then time enough to talk about it. A play, like a bill, is of no value before it is accepted, nor indeed when it is very often. This too is a plentiful year of plays—and 10 they are like nuts: in a plentiful year they are commonly very bad.

LUCKLESS.

But suppose it were accepted (as you term it), what would you give me for it? Not that I want* money, sir— 15

BOOKWEIGHT.

No sir, certainly. But before I can make any answer I must read it. I cannot offer anything for what I do not know the value of.

WITMORE.

That I imagine granted by the players' approbation. For they are, you know, very great 20 judges.

---

13 Westminster] either the Abbey or the Hall*
14 Bookweight] partly based on the notorious publisher and bookseller Edmund Curll (1675-1747), who also appears in the figure of "Curry" in Act III

BOOKWEIGHT.

Yes sir, that they are, indeed—that they must be allowed to be, as being men of great learning. But a play which will do for them, will not always do for us. There are your acting plays, and your reading plays. 25

WITMORE.

I do not understand that distinction.

BOOKWEIGHT.

Why sir, your acting play is entirely supported by the merit of the actor, without any regard to the author at all: in this case, it signifies very little 30 whether there be any sense in it or no. Now your reading play is of a different stamp and must have wit and meaning in it. These latter I call your* substantive, as being able to support themselves. The former are your* adjective, as what require the 35 buffoonery and gestures of an actor to be joined to them to show their signification.

LUCKLESS.

Very learnedly defined, truly, Mr. Bookweight.

BOOKWEIGHT.

I hope I have not had so much learning go through my hands without leaving some in my head. 40

LUCKLESS.

Well—but Mr. Bookweight, I hope you will advance something—

BOOKWEIGHT.

Why, had you a great reputation, I might venture. But truly, for young beginners it is a very great hazard, for indeed, the reputation of the author 45 carries the greatest sway in these affairs. The Town have been so fond of some authors that they have run them up to infallibility and would have applauded them even against their senses.

WITMORE.

And who but a madman would write in such an age? 50

LUCKLESS.

'Sdeath,* Witmore! 'Tis cruel to insult my misfortunes.

WITMORE.

I would cure them—and that is not to be done by lenitives.

BOOKWEIGHT.

I am of that gentleman's opinion: I do think 55 writing the silliest thing a man can undertake.

LUCKLESS.

'Tis strange you should say so, who live by it.

BOOKWEIGHT.

Live by it! Ah, if you had lost as much by writers as I have done, you would be of my opinion.

LUCKLESS.

But we are losing time. Will you advance fifty 60 guineas on my play?[15]

BOOKWEIGHT.

No—nor fifty shillings, I assure you.

LUCKLESS.

'Sdeath, sir, do you beat me down at this rate?

BOOKWEIGHT.

Sir, I would not give you fifty farthings. Fifty guineas, indeed! Your name is well worth that. 65

LUCKLESS.

Jack—

Jack enters.

Take this worthy gentleman and kick him downstairs.[16]

BOOKWEIGHT.

Sir, I shall make you repent this—

JACK.

Come sir, will you please to brush[17]— 70

BOOKWEIGHT.

Help! Murder! I'll have the law of you, sir.

LUCKLESS.

Ha, ha, ha!

[Exeunt Bookweight, Jack.]

Scene vii.

Luckless, Witmore, Mrs. Moneywood.

MONEYWOOD.

What noise is this? It is a very fine thing truly, Mr. Luckless, that you will make these uproars in my house.

---

15 fifty guineas] "an exorbitant demand, since few established playwrights could hope to realize as much from a single work" (Woods)

16 kick him downstairs] recalls several well-known episodes in which Curll had suffered humiliating physical violence from individuals whose rights or dignity had been violated by his publications

17 brush] to be gone, decamp, make off (*OED*)

LUCKLESS.

If you dislike it, it is in your power to drown a
much greater. Do you but speak, madam, and I
am sure no one will be heard but yourself.

MONEYWOOD.

Very well, indeed! Fine reflections on my character!
Sir, sir, all the neighbors know that I have been as
quiet a woman as any in the parish. I had no noises
in my house till you came. We were the Family of
Love.[18] But you have been a nuisance to the whole
neighborhood. While you had money my doors
were thundered at every morning at four and five,
and since you have had none, my walls have
echoed nothing but your noise and your poetry.
Then there's the rascal your man—but I'll pay the
dog—I'll scour him—. (*To Witmore.*) Sir, I am glad
you are a witness to his abuses of me—

WITMORE.

I am a witness indeed, madam, how unjustly he
has abused you.

Jack [enters and] whispers.

LUCKLESS.

Witmore, you'll excuse me a moment.

[Exeunt Luckless, Jack.]

Scene viii.

Mrs. Moneywood, Witmore.

MONEYWOOD.

Yes sir, and sir, a man that has never shown one
the color of his money.

WITMORE.

Very hard, truly. How much may he be in your
debt, pray? Because he has ordered me to pay you.

MONEYWOOD.

Ah sir, I wish he had.

WITMORE.

I am serious, I assure you.

MONEYWOOD.

I am very glad to hear it, sir. Here is the bill as we

settled it this very morning. I always thought
indeed Mr. Luckless had a good deal of honesty
in his principles. Any man may be unfortunate—
but I knew when he had money I should have it.
I never was in any fear for my money, for my part.

WITMORE.

There, madam, is your money on the table. Please
to write a receipt only.

MONEYWOOD.

Sir, I give you a great many thanks. There, sir, is the
receipt. Well, if Mr. Luckless was but a little soberer,
I should like him for a lodger exceedingly, for I must
say I think him a very pleasant good-natured man.

Scene ix.

[Witmore, Mrs. Moneywood,] Luckless.

LUCKLESS.

Those are words I never heard out of that mouth
before.

MONEYWOOD.

Ha, ha, ha! You are pleased to be merry.

LUCKLESS.

Why Witmore, thou hast the faculty opposite to
that of a witch and canst lay a tempest. I should have
as soon imagined one man could have stopped a
cannon ball in its full force as her tongue, and I
believe she may be heard as far. Were she to roar
forth a summons to a town, it would have more
effect on the governor than a volley of artillery.

MONEYWOOD.

Ha, ha, ha!

WITMORE.

Luckless, good morrow. I will see you again soon.

LUCKLESS.

Witmore, I am yours.

[Exit Witmore.]

Scene x.

Luckless, Mrs. Moneywood.

MONEYWOOD.

Well Mr. Luckless, you are a comical man, to give
one such a character* to a stranger.

LUCKLESS.

The company is gone, madam, and now, like true

18 Family of Love] the name of a sect, originating in Holland and gaining many adherents in England in the 16th
and 17th centuries, which held that religion consists
chiefly of the exercise of love

man and wife, we may fall to abusing one another as fast as we please.

MONEYWOOD.

Abuse me as you will, so you pay me, sir.

LUCKLESS.

'Sdeath! Madam, I will pay you.

MONEYWOOD.

Nay sir, I do not ask it before it is due. I don't question your payment at all: if you were to stay in my house this quarter of a year, as I hope you will, I should not ask you for a farthing.

LUCKLESS.

Tol, lol, lol. [Aside.] But I shall have her begin with her passion immediately, and I had rather feel the highest effects of her rage, than the lightest of her love.

MONEYWOOD.

But why did you choose to surprise me with my money? Why did you not tell me you'd pay me?

LUCKLESS.

Why have I not told you?

MONEYWOOD.

Yes, you told me of a play and stuff—but you never told me you would order a gentleman to pay me. Well, you have comical ways with you, but you have honesty in the bottom, and I'm sure the gentleman himself will own I gave you that character.*

LUCKLESS. [Aside.]

Oh! I smell you now.——You see, madam, I am better than my word to you. Did he pay it you in gold or silver?

MONEYWOOD.

All pure gold.

LUCKLESS.

I have a vast deal of silver within. Will you do me the favor of taking it in silver? That may be of use to you in the shop, too.

MONEYWOOD.

Anything to oblige you, sir!

LUCKLESS.

Jack, bring out the great Bag Number One. Please to tell the money, madam, on that table.

MONEYWOOD. (Tells the money.)

It's easily told—Heaven knows there's not so much on't.

Enter Jack. Luckless gets between Mrs. Moneywood and the table.

JACK.

Sir, the bag is so heavy, I cannot bring it in.

LUCKLESS.

Why then, come and help to thrust a heavier bag out.

MONEYWOOD.

What do you mean, sir?

LUCKLESS.

Only to pay you in my bedchamber.

MONEYWOOD.

Villain, dog, I'll swear a robbery and have you hanged! Rogues, villains!

LUCKLESS. (Shuts the door.)

Be as noisy as you please.—Jack, call a coach, and d'ye hear, get up behind it and attend me.

[Exeunt.]

Act II, scene i.d A tavern.

Luckless, Marplay, Sparkish.[19]

LUCKLESS. (Reads.)

"Then hence my sorrows, hence my every fear;
No matter where, so we are blessed together.
With thee, the barren rocks, where not one step
Of human race lies printed in the snow,
Look lovely as the smiling infant spring."

MARPLAY. (Yawning.)

Will you please to read that again, sir?

LUCKLESS. (Reads again.)

MARPLAY.

"Then hence my sorrow——" Horror is a much better word, in my opinion. And then in the second line—will you please to read it again?

---

19 Marplay, Sparkish] Under the name of Marplay, Colley Cibber appears in this scene in his role as leader of the "triumvirate" managing Drury Lane Theater, here accompanied by Robert Wilks as Sparkish (the third manager, Barton Booth, was on good terms with Fielding). Cibber's treatment of aspiring playwrights was famously imperious and capricious: if, with great difficulty, an author was able to arrange a reading of his play with all three managers, Cibber was likely at the reading to insist on absurd "corrections" to the piece, and then abruptly to dismiss the author with the pronouncement that "This will not do at all!"

LUCKLESS.

"No matter where, so we are blessed together." 10

MARPLAY.

In my opinion it would be better so:
No matter where, so somewhere we're together.
"Where" is the question, "somewhere" is the
answer. Read on, sir.

LUCKLESS. (*Reads on.*)

"With thee," etc. 15

MARPLAY.

I could alter those lines to a much better idea:
With thee, the barren blocks—that is, trees—
    where not a bit
Of human face is painted on the bark,
Look green as Covent Garden* in the spring.

LUCKLESS.

Green as Covent Garden! 20

MARPLAY.

Yes, Covent Garden Market—where they sell
greens.

LUCKLESS.

Monstrous!—Sir, I must ask your pardon, I cannot
consent to such an alteration. It is downright
nonsense. 25

MARPLAY. (*Rising from the table.*)

Sir, it will not do—and so I would not have you
think any more of it.

SPARKISH.

No, no, no. It will not do.[20]

LUCKLESS.

What faults do you find?

MARPLAY.

Sir, there is nothing in it that pleases me, so I am 30
sure there is nothing in it that will please the Town.

SPARKISH.

There is nothing in it that will please the Town.

LUCKLESS.

Methinks you should find some particular fault.

MARPLAY.

Truly sir, it is so full of faults—that the eye of my
judgment is so distracted with the variety of objects 35
that it cannot fix on any.

SPARKISH.

No, no, no—cannot fix on any.

MARPLAY.

In short, there is not one good thing in it from
the beginning to the end.

LUCKLESS.

Some who have read it think otherwise. 40

MARPLAY.

Let them think as they please—I'm sure we are the
best judges.

SPARKISH.

Yes, yes, we are the best judges.

LUCKLESS.

Could you convince me of any fault, I would
amend it. But you argue in plays as the Pope does 45
in religion or the Aristotelists in philosophy: you
maintain your hypothesis by an *ipse dicit*.[21]

MARPLAY.

I don't understand your hard words, sir, but I think
it is very hard if a man who has been so long in a
trade as I have should not understand the value 50
of his merchandise—should not know what goods
will best please the Town.—Come Sparkish, will
you go to Tom's?[22]

LUCKLESS.

Fare ye well, gentlemen. May another play do you
more service. 55

[*Exit.*]

Scene ii.[e]

Marplay, Sparkish.

MARPLAY.

Ha, ha, ha!

SPARKISH.

What dost think of the play?

MARPLAY.

It may be a very good one, for aught I know, but
I know the author has no interest.[23]

---

20 No … not do] Though a co-manager of Drury Lane,
   Wilks was said merely to follow Cibber's decisive lead
   in responding to authors.

---

21 *ipse dicit*] The Latin phrase, *ipse dixit*, meaning "he himself [the master] said it" (Fielding's Latin changes the
   tense to present), denotes an unproved assertion that
   rests on the bare authority of a speaker.

22 Tom's] a fashionable coffee house in Covent Garden

23 interest] influence due to personal connection; the term
   was often used to describe the means by which many
   attained appointments in the government or at court.

SPARKISH.

Give me interest, and rat[24] the play—

MARPLAY.

Rather rat the play which has no interest. Interest sways as much in the theater as at court. And you know it is not always the companion of merit in either.

SPARKISH.

But pray, Mr. Marplay, what was the reason of that extraordinary demand of yours upon the office?

MARPLAY.

Truly sir, it was for the good of the office. Some of it was given to puffs, to cry up our new plays— and one half guinea to Mr. Scribbler for a panegyrical essay in the newspaper, with some other such services. But have you seen my new entertainment practiced, *Cuckolds All a Row*?[25]

SPARKISH.

No.

MARPLAY.

I will affirm this, that it is the best thing that has ever appeared on the stage. I don't know whether I shall not lay the pit and boxes together,[26] at half a guinea a seat.

SPARKISH.

I would not advise that, for the Town grumbles at our raising the prices as we have done.

MARPLAY.

Rat the Town. Let them grumble, I'm sure they will not stay away. For their hisses, they have no more effect on me than music would have on an owl* or the curses of an undone client on an attorney. I have been used to them, and any man who loves hissing may have his three shillings' worth at me whenever he pleases.

[Exeunt.]

Scene iii. A room in Mr. Bookweight's house.[27]

Dash, Blotpage, Quibble, writing at several tables.

DASH.

Pox on't, I'm as dull as an ox, though I have not a bit of one within me. I have not dined these two days, and yet my head is as heavy as any alderman's or lord's. I carry about me symbols of all the elements: my head is as heavy as water, my pockets are light as air, my appetite is as hot as fire, and my coat is as dirty as earth.

BLOTPAGE.

Lend me your *Bysshe*,[28] Mr. Dash; I want a rhyme for wind.

---

24 rat] probably an exaggerated open-vowel pronunciation of "rot" (as in Cibber's Foppington roles and others)

25 *Cuckolds All a Row*] Fielding alludes to Cibber's uneven career as a playwright and portrays him using his power as a theater manager to promote his own play. Here, a phrase from an old song substitutes for the title of his pastoral ballad opera, *Love in a Riddle* (1729), which was hissed off the stage in two performances. The audience's antagonism to Cibber's play had a political edge: it resented the appearance of an imitation of Gay's *Beggar's Opera* by the pro-government Cibber when Gay's own sequel, *Polly*, had been banned from the stage by the government. On this occasion, Cibber exhibited his characteristic imperviousness to ridicule by addressing the hissing crowd from the stage himself, successfully placating them.

26 lay ... together] charge the same price for entrance to the pit as to the boxes, a frequent practice when high demand for seats was expected; "usually this would mean a price of 5 *s.* (as for *The Author's Farce* after its success was assured), though the half guinea Marplay suggests was sometimes charged" (Woods).

27 Bookweight's house] Some booksellers kept stables of impoverished "hack" writers who were given writing assignments to fulfill; at the worst, these writers labored in a kind of sweatshop servitude of the pen. Curll was accused by Pope of starving one of his writers to death; Richard Savage, who had written for Curll, claimed that, after he had escaped Curll's clutches, "he arrested me for several months board, brought me back to my garret, and made me drudge on in my old dirty work." Savage confessed that in Curll's service he "wrote Obscenity and profaneness, under the names of Pope and Swift.... abridged histories and travels, translated from the French what they never wrote, and was expert at finding out new titles for old books."

28 *Bysshe*] Edward Bysshe, *The Art of English Poetry* (1702), which includes a handy "Dictionary of Rhymes"; the entry for words rhyming on "ind" contains wind and all the words suggested by Dash.

DASH.

Why there! blind and kind and behind and find 10
and mind—it is one of the easiest terminations
imaginable; I have had it four times in a page.

BLOTPAGE.

Devil take the first inventor of rhyming, I say. Your
business is much easier, Mr. Dash. Well, of all the
places in my master's gift, I should most like to 15
be Clerk of the Ghosts and Murders. You have
nothing to do but to put a set of terrible words
together in the title page.

DASH.

The business is easy enough, but it is at a very low
ebb now. No, Mr. Quibble there, as Clerk of the 20
Libels, would have the best place, were it not that
few men ever sat in his chair long without standing
on an odd sort of a stool in the street[29] to be gaped
at an hour or two by the mob.

QUIBBLE.

We act on different principles, Mr. Dash: 'tis your 25
business to promise more than you perform, and
mine to promise less.

BLOTPAGE.

Pshaw! Thy business is to perform nothing at all.

DASH.

It becomes an author to be diffusive in his title page.
A title page is to a book what a fine neck is to a 30
woman—therefore ought to be the most regarded as
it is the part which is viewed before the purchase.

Air 2. Ye Commons and Peers.[30]

BLOTPAGE.

How unhappy's the fate
To live by one's pate
And be forced to write hackney for bread![31] 35
An author's a joke
To all manner of folk,

Wherever he pops up his head, his head,
Wherever he pops up his head. 40

Though he mount on that hack,
Old Pegasus' back
And of Helicon[32] drink till he burst,
Yet a curse of those streams,
Poetical dreams, 45
They never can quench one's thirst, etc.

Ah, how should he fly
On fancy so high
When his limbs are in durance and hold?
Or how should he charm 50
With genius so warm
When his poor naked body's a-cold, etc.

Scene iv.

To them, Bookweight.

BOOKWEIGHT.

Fie upon it, gentlemen! What, not at your pens? Do
you consider, Mr. Quibble, that it is above a fortnight since your Letter from a Friend in the
Country[33] was published? Is it not high time for an
Answer to come out? At this rate, before your Answer 5

---

29 an odd … street] the pillory, to which authors and booksellers might be condemned for publishing libels or obscenity; Curll himself had stood in the pillory in 1728.

30 "Ye Commons and Peers"] reproduced in Durfey, the
original praises an English victory over the French.

31 write hackney] write as a hireling; the term "hack writer"
derives from an analogy to hackney horses

32 Helicon] mountains sacred to Apollo and the Muses,
whence sprung fountains believed to inspire those who
drank of them

33 Letter … Country] Political polemics were often presented in the form of "letters" composed by landown-
ing patriots residing at a distance from the political fray.

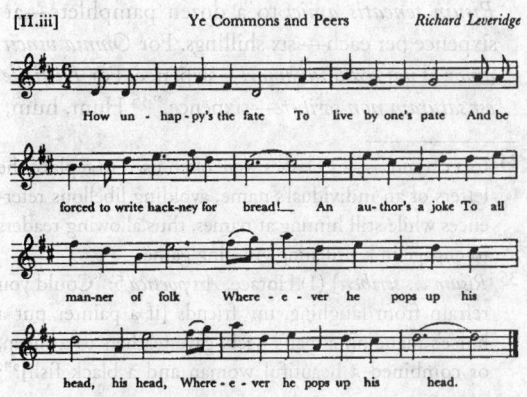

[II.iii]   Ye Commons and Peers   *Richard Leveridge*

How un-hap-py's the fate   To   live by one's pate   And be
forced to write hack-ney for   bread!__   An   au-thor's a joke   To all
man-ner of   folk   Where-e-ver he   pops up his
head, his head,   Where-e-ver he pops up his   head.

is printed your Letter will be forgot. I love to keep a controversy up warm—I have had authors who have writ a pamphlet in the morning and answered it in the afternoon and compromised the matter at night.

QUIBBLE.

Sir, I will be as expeditious as possible.   10

BOOKWEIGHT.

Well Mr. Dash, have you done that murder yet?

DASH.

Yes sir, the murder is done. I am only about a few moral reflections to place before it.

BOOKWEIGHT.

Very well, then let me have the ghost finished by this day sevennight.   15

DASH.

What sort of a ghost would you have, sir? The last was a pale one.

BOOKWEIGHT.

Then let this be a bloody one.—Mr. Blotpage, what have your lucubrations produced? (*Reads.*) "Poetical Advice to a certain —— from a certain   20 —— on a certain —— from a certain ——."34 Very good! I will say, Mr. Blotpage writes as good a dash as any man in Europe.

Scene v.

To them, Index.

BOOKWEIGHT.

So, Mr. Index, what news with you?

INDEX.

I have brought my bill, sir.

BOOKWEIGHT.

What's here? [*Reads.*] "For adapting the motto of *Risum teneatis amici* to a dozen pamphlets—at sixpence per each— six shillings. For *Omnia vincit*   5 *amor et nos cedamus amori*—sixpence. For *Difficile est saturam non scribere*—sixpence."35 Hum, hum,

hum. Ah. "A sum total, for thirty-six Latin mottoes, eighteen shillings; ditto English, seven, one shilling and ninepence; ditto Greek, four, one   10 shilling." Why, friend, are your Latin mottoes dearer than your Greek?

INDEX.

Yes, marry are they, sir, for as nobody now understands Greek, so I may use any sentence in that language to whatsoever purpose I please.   15

BOOKWEIGHT.

You shall have your money immediately. And pray remember that I must have two Latin sedition mottoes and one Greek moral motto, for pamphlets, by tomorrow morning.

QUIBBLE.

I want* two Latin sentences, sir, one for page the   20 fourth in praise of virtue, and the other for page the tenth in the praise of beauty.

BOOKWEIGHT.

Let me have those too.

INDEX.

Sir, I shall take care to provide them.

[*Exit.*]

Scene vi.

Bookweight, Dash, Blotpage, Quibble, Scarecrow.

SCARECROW.

Sir, I have brought you a libel against the ministry.36

BOOKWEIGHT.

Sir, I shall not take anything against them (*Aside.*) for I have two in the press already.

SCARECROW.

Then sir, I have another in defense of them.   5

BOOKWEIGHT.

Sir, I never take anything in defense of power.

---

34 to a certain ——] Dashes were often used to replace the letters of an individual's name, avoiding libellous references while still hinting at names, thus allowing readers to engage in a titillating guessing-game.

35 *Risum … scribere*] (1) Horace, *Ars poetica* 5: "Could you refrain from laughing, my friends [if a painter put a horse's mane on a man's neck, gave feathers to a sheep, or combined a beautiful woman and a black fish]?";

(2) Virgil, *Eclogues* X.69: "Love conquers all, and we must yield to love" (Dryden's translation); (3) Juvenal, *Satires* I.30: "It is hard not to write satire [when one sees the abuses of sense and order in this city]"—a line that precedes the play's epigraph.

36 libel … ministry] Sir Robert Walpole's unprecedented political power as the "prime minister" of England (not yet an official position) from 1721 to 1742 provoked considerable opposition in the press.

SCARECROW.

I have a translation of Virgil's *Aeneid*, with notes on it.

BOOKWEIGHT.

That, sir, is what I do not care to venture on. You may try by subscription, if you please, but I would not advise you, for that bubble is almost down: people begin to be afraid of authors, since they have writ and acted like stockjobbers. So to oblige a young beginner, I don't care if I print it at my own expense.

SCARECROW.

But pray, sir, at whose expense shall I eat?

BOOKWEIGHT.

That's an empty question.

SCARECROW.

It comes from an empty stomach, I'm sure.

BOOKWEIGHT.

From an empty head, I'm afraid. Are there not a thousand ways for a man to get his bread by?

SCARECROW.

I wish you would put me into one.

BOOKWEIGHT.

Why then, sir, I would advise you to come and take your seat at my tables. Here will be everything that is necessary provided for you. I am as great a friend to learning as the Dutch are to trade; no one can want* bread with me who will earn it. Besides, a translator will be of use to me, for my last is in Newgate for shoplifting. The rogue had gotten a trick of translating out of the shops as well as out of the languages.

SCARECROW.

I prefer anything to starving.

BOOKWEIGHT.

Then sir, if you please to throw by your hat, which you will have no more use for, and take up your pen.

SCARECROW.

But sir, I am afraid I am not qualified for a translator.

BOOKWEIGHT.

How, not qualified?

SCARECROW.

No sir, I understand no language but my own.

BOOKWEIGHT.

What, and translate Virgil?

SCARECROW.

Alas sir, I translated him out of Dryden.

BOOKWEIGHT.

Not qualified! If I was an emperor, thou shouldst be my prime minister. Thou art as well versed in thy trade as if thou hadst labored in my garret these ten years. Let me tell you, friend, you will have more occasion for invention than learning here: you will be sometimes obliged to translate books out of all languages (especially French) which were never printed in any language whatsoever.

SCARECROW.

Your trade abounds in mysteries.

BOOKWEIGHT.

The study of bookselling is as difficult as the law, and there are as many tricks in the one as the other. Sometimes we give a foreign name to our own labor, and sometimes we put our own names to the labor of others. Then as the lawyers have John-a-Nokes and Tom-a-Stiles, so we have Messieurs Moore near St. Paul's and Smith near the Royal Exchange.[37]

Scene vii.

To them, Luckless.

LUCKLESS.

Mr. Bookweight, your servant. Who can form to himself an idea more amiable than of a man at the head of so many patriots working for the benefit of their country?

BOOKWEIGHT.

Truly sir, I believe it is an idea more agreeable to you—than that of a gentleman in the Crown Office[38] paying thirty or forty guineas for abusing an honest tradesman.

LUCKLESS.

Pshaw, that was only jocosely done, and a man

---

37 John-a-Nokes … Exchange] Just as lawyers use fictitious names in warrants, so does Bookweight employ fictitious publishers' imprints on title pages as screens to avoid prosecution.

38 Crown Office] an office at which an individual could bring suit for offences and misdemeanors at common law, such as private batteries; Bookweight threateningly recalls Luckless's violent ejection of him in I.vi.

who lives by wit must not be angry at a jest; 10
besides, the law has been your enemy,39 and you
would not fly to an enemy for succor.

BOOKWEIGHT.

Sir, I will use my enemy as I would my friend, for
my own ends. But pray, sir, what has brought you
hither? If you have a mind to compromise the 15
matter, I had rather have a little of your money
than that the lawyers should have a great deal.

LUCKLESS.

Hast thou dealt in paper so long and talk of money
to a modern author? You might as well have talked
Latin or Greek to him. I have brought you paper, sir. 20

BOOKWEIGHT.

That is not bringing me money, I own—but it
shall not be taking away money, sir, for I will have
nothing to do with your paper or you either.

LUCKLESS.

Why prithee, man, I have not brought you a play
nor a sermon. 25

BOOKWEIGHT.

Have you brought me an opera?

LUCKLESS.

You may call it an opera if you will, but I call it a
puppet show.

BOOKWEIGHT.

A puppet show!

LUCKLESS.

Aye, a puppet show, and is to be played this night 30
in the Haymarket playhouse.40

BOOKWEIGHT.

A puppet show in a playhouse!

LUCKLESS.

What have been all the playhouses a long time but
puppet shows?

BOOKWEIGHT.

Why, I don't know but it may succeed; at least, I 35
had rather venture on a thing of that nature than

---

39 law … enemy] Curll's unscrupulous publishing practices
led to several scrapes with the law.

40 Haymarket playhouse] the New (or Little) Theater in
the Haymarket, one of several playhouses in London
offering alternatives in the early 1730's to the patent
theaters at Drury Lane and Covent Garden. *The Author's
Farce* itself first played at the Little Haymarket.

a regular play. So if you please to come in, if I can
make a bargain with you I will.—Gentlemen, you
may go to dinner.

[Exeunt.]

Scene viii. The street.

*Enter Jack-Pudding,*41 *drummer, and mob. The drum
ceasing—*

[JACK PUDDING.]

This is to give notice to all gentlemen, ladies, and
others, that at the playhouse opposite to the Opera
in the Haymarket, this evening will be performed
the whole puppet show called *The Pleasures of the
Town*, in which will be shown the whole Court of 5
Dullness, with abundance of singing and dancing,
and several other entertainments; also the comical
and diverting humors of Somebody and Nobody;
Punch and his wife Joan; to be performed by living
figures—some of them six foot high— beginning 10
exactly at seven o'clock. God save the King!

Drum beats.

[Exeunt.]

Scene ix.

Witmore with a paper, Luckless meeting.

WITMORE.

Oh Luckless, I am overjoyed at meeting you. Here,
take this paper, and you will be discouraged from
writing, I warrant you.

LUCKLESS.

What is it? Oh! one of my playbills.

WITMORE.

One of thy playbills! 5

LUCKLESS.

Even so, sir. I have taken the advice you gave me
this morning.

WITMORE.

Explain.

LUCKLESS.

Why, I had some time since given this puppet
show of mine to be rehearsed, and the actors were 10

---

41 Jack-Pudding] "a buffoon, clown, or merry-andrew, esp.
one attending on a mountebank" (*OED*)

all perfect in their parts, but we happened to
dissent about some particulars, and I had a design
to have given it over, till having my play refused
by Marplay and Sparkish, I sent for the managers
of the house in a passion, joined issue with them,   15
and this very evening it is to be acted.
WITMORE.
Well, I wish you success—
LUCKLESS.
Where are you going?
WITMORE.
Anywhere but to hear you damned, which I must
if I were to go to your puppet show. I tell you the   20
Town is prejudiced against you, and they will
damn you, whether you deserve it or no. If they
should laugh till they burst—the moment they
knew you were the author, they would change their
faces and swear they never laughed at all.   25
LUCKLESS.
Pshaw, I can't believe thee.
WITMORE.
'Sdeath!* I have heard sense run down and seen
idiotism, downright idiotism, triumph so often
that I could almost think of wit and folly as Mr.
Hobbes[42] does of moral good and evil, that there   30
are no such things.
LUCKLESS.
Well, indulge me in this trial, and I assure thee, if
it be successless, it shall be the last.
WITMORE.
On that condition I will. But should the torrent
run against you, I shall be a fashionable friend and   35
hiss with the rest.
LUCKLESS.
No, a man who could do so unfashionable and so
generous a thing as Mr. Witmore did this morning—
WITMORE.
In return, will you grant me a favor?
LUCKLESS.
Do you doubt it?   40

---

42 Hobbes] the philosopher Thomas Hobbes, author of *The
   Leviathan* (1651), who scandalized his contemporaries
   by arguing against the existence of any absolute bases,
   other than relations of power, for moral law or political
   rule

WITMORE.
Never mention it to me more. I will now to the
pit—
LUCKLESS.
And I behind the scenes.

[Exeunt.]

Scene x. Mrs. Moneywood's.

Mrs. Moneywood, Harriot.

HARRIOT.
It is very hard, madam, that you will not suffer me
at least to indulge myself in grief; that it is not
enough to tear me from the man I love, but I must
have my ears eternally cursed with hearing him
abused—   5
MONEYWOOD.
Oh monstrous! Love a puppet-show fellow!
HARRIOT.
His misfortunes may lessen him in the eye of the
world, but they shall never lessen him in mine.
Nay, I love him for them.
MONEYWOOD.
You have not a drop of my blood in you. Love a   10
man for his misfortune! Hussy, to be poor and
unfortunate are crimes. Riches are the only
recommendations to people of sense of both sexes,
and a coach and six is one of the cardinal virtues.
HARRIOT.
I despise it, and the fool who was born to it. No,   15
give me the man who, thrown naked upon the
world, like my dear Luckless, can make his way
through it by his merit and virtuous industry.
MONEYWOOD.
Virtuous industry! A very virtuous, industrious gentleman, truly. He hath robbed me of a few guineas   20
today or so, but he is a very virtuous man, no doubt.
HARRIOT.
He hath only borrowed what you know he will
repay: you know he is honest.
MONEYWOOD.
I am no more satisfied of his honesty than you can
be of his love.   25
HARRIOT.
Which I am sure he hath given me sufficient
proofs of.

MONEYWOOD.

Proofs! Oh, the villain! Hath he given you proofs of love?

HARRIOT.

All that a modest woman can require. 30

MONEYWOOD.

If he hath given you all a modest woman can require, I am afraid he has given you more than a modest woman should take. Because he hath been so good a lodger, I suppose I shall have some more of the family to keep: it is probable I may live to 35 see half a dozen grandsons of mine in Grub Street.[43]

Scene xi.

Enter Jack.

MONEYWOOD.

So, rascal, what's become of your master?

JACK.

Oh madam! I am frightened out of my wits.

MONEYWOOD, HARRIOT.

What's the matter?

JACK.

There's the strangest sort of man below inquiring after my master that ever was seen. 5

MONEYWOOD.

What, I suppose a sort of bailiff?

JACK.

Oh madam, I fancy it is the Man in the Moon or some monster. There are five hundred people at the door looking at him—he is dressed up in nothing but ruffles and cabbage nets. 10

MONEYWOOD.

This is either some trick of his to catch me or some trick of a bailiff to catch him. However, I'll go sift out the bottom of it. Come, show me where he is.

HARRIOT.

Heavens protect my dear Luckless. 15

[Exeunt.]

---

43 Grub Street] a street in London associated with the life of the needy author or literary hack

Act III,[f] scene i. The playhouse.

Enter Luckless as Master of the Show, and Player.

LUCKLESS.

It's very surprising, that after I have been at all this expense and trouble to set up my things in your house, you should desire me to recant and now too, when the spectators are all assembled and will either have the show or their money. 5

PLAYER.

It is beneath the dignity of the stage.

LUCKLESS.

That may be; so is all farce, and yet you see a farce brings more company to a house than the best play that ever was writ, for this age would allow Tom Durfey a better poet than Congreve or Wycherley.[44] 10 Who would not then rather eat by his nonsense than starve by his wit? The lodgings of wits have long been in the air, and air must be their food nowadays.

PLAYER.

I am not the first indeed that has disgraced the stage. 15

LUCKLESS.

And I heartily wish you may be the last and that my puppet show may expel farce and opera as they have done tragedy and comedy.

PLAYER.

But hark you, friend, how came you to call this performance of yours a puppet show? 20

LUCKLESS.

You must know, sir, that it was originally designed to be played by real puppets till a friend of mine, observing the success of some things in Town, advised me to bring it on the stage.[45] I had offered it to the old house, but they say nothing but your 25

---

44 Durfey … Wycherley] playwrights represented in this volume (q.v.)

45 real puppets … the stage] Woods comments: "Since it was often charged that actors had become mere puppets, it is hardly unexpected to find them taking puppet parts: live Punches turned up [in several early eighteenth-century plays, including Thomas Sheridan's 1721 *Punch Turned School-Master*. Fielding] probably instructed his actors to mimic the sounds and movements of puppets, as Sheridan had done."

fine sense, such plays as *Caesar in Egypt*,[46] will go down there.

PLAYER.

But what is the design or plot? For I could make neither head nor tail of it, for my part.

LUCKLESS.

Why sir, the Goddess of Nonsense is to fall in love with the ghost of Signior Opera.g [47]

PLAYER.

Fall in love with a ghost, ha, ha, ha!

LUCKLESS.

Aye sir, you must know that the scene is laid on the other side of the River Styx, so all the people of the play are ghosts.

PLAYER.

This marrying of ghosts is a new doctrine, friend.

LUCKLESS.

So much the likelier to please—though I can't say but I took the hint of this thing from the old house, who observing that everyone could not see the real coronation, brought a representation of it upon their stage.[48] So sir, since everyone has not time or opportunity to visit all the diversions of the Town, I have brought most of them together in one. But come, it is time to begin. I think we will have an overture, though ours be not a regular opera.

PLAYER.

By all means, an overture.

———————

46 *Caesar in Egypt*] an unsuccessful attempt at solemnity by Cibber offered at Drury Lane ("the old house") for two nights in 1724.

47 fall in love … Opera] Castrato singers from Italy were the great operatic celebrities in England in this period; they were particularly adored by many women in their audiences. Satirists commented searingly on the preference for sound over "sense" inherent in English audiences' devotion to opera sung in Italian, and they associated that preference with what they saw as women's perverse infatuation with castrated men.

48 real coronation] Following the coronation of George II on October 11, 1727, a revival of Shakespeare's *Henry VIII* at Drury Lane emphasized the play's enactment of the coronation of Queen Anne Bullen; *The Daily Post* praised the magnificence of this scene and "the extraordinary Grandeur of the Decorations."

LUCKLESS.

If you please, sir, you shall sit down by me. Play away.[49]

[Music begins.]

LUCKLESS.

Gentlemen, the first thing I present you with is Punchinello.

The curtain drawn discovers* Punch in a great chair.

Air 1. "Whilst the Town's Brimful of Folly."

PUNCH.

Whilst the Town's brimful of farces,
Flocking whilst we see her asses
> Thick as grapes upon a bunch,
Critics, whilst you smile on madness
And more stupid, solemn sadness,
> > Sure you will not frown on Punch.

———————

49 Play away] Luckless as author and "master" of a show, sitting beside and commenting upon a play-within-the-play, recalls such predecessors as Leatherhead in Ben Jonson's *Bartholomew Fair* (1614) and Bayes in Buckingham's *The Rehearsal* (1671). Unlike the latter, he is fully aware of the absurdity of the performance he offers.

AIR I.   Whilst the Town's Brimful of Folly   *George Monro*

Whilst the town's brim-ful of far-ces, Flock-ing whilst we see her as-ses Thick as grapes up-on a bunch, Crit-ics, whilst you smile on mad-ness, And more stu-pid sol-em sad-ness, Sure you will not frown on Punch. Crit-ics whilst you smile on mad-ness, And more stu-pid sol-em sad-ness, Sure you will not frown on Pu——nch. Sure you will not frown on Punch.

LUCKLESS.

The next is Punch's wife Joan.

Enter Joan.

JOAN.

What can ail my husband? He is continually 60
humming tunes, though his voice be only fit to
warble at Hog's Norton,[50] where the pigs would
accompany it with organs. I was in hopes death
would have stopped his mouth at last—but he keeps
his old harmonious humor* even in the shades. 65

PUNCH.

Be not angry, dear Joan, Orpheus obtained his wife
from the shades by charming Pluto with his music.

JOAN.

Sirrah, sirrah, should Pluto hear you sing, you
could expect no less punishment than Tantalus
has—nay, the waters would be brought above your 70
mouth, to stop it.

PUNCH.

Truly madam, I don't wish the same success
Orpheus met with. Could I gain my own liberty,
the Devil might have you with all my heart.

Air 2. "The First of August."[h] 75

PUNCH.

Joan, Joan, Joan has a thundering tongue,
And Joan, Joan, Joan is a bold one.
　　How happy is he

---

50 Hog's Norton] "Hock Norton, a village in Oxfordshire
proverbial for boorishness and for the music of its pigs"
(Woods)

Who from wedlock is free:
For who'd have a wife to scold one? 80

JOAN.

Punch, Punch, Punch, prithee think of your
　　hunch,
Prithee look at your great strutting belly:
　　Sirrah, if you dare
　　War with me declare,
I will beat your fat guts to a jelly. 85

Here they dance.

Air 3. "Bobbing Joan."

PUNCH.

Joan, you are the plague of my life;
A rope[51] would be welcomer than such a wife.

JOAN.

Punch, your merits had you but shared,
Your neck had been longer by half a yard. 90

PUNCH.

　　Ugly witch—

JOAN.

　　Son of a bitch—

BOTH.

Would you were hanged or drowned in a ditch.

Here they dance again.

PUNCH.

Since we hate, like people in vogue,

---

51 rope] A standard Punch and Joan plot culminates in
Punch's murder of his wife, his attempt to bargain with
the Devil, and the prospect of his death by hanging.

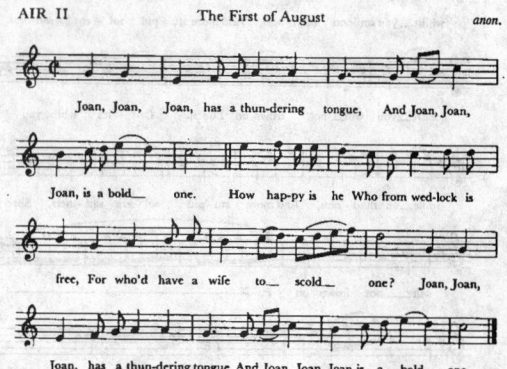

AIR II　　The First of August　　*anon.*

Joan, Joan, Joan, has a thun-dering tongue, And Joan, Joan, Joan, is a bold__ one. How hap-py is he Who from wed-lock is free, For who'd have a wife to__ scold__ one? Joan, Joan, Joan, has a thun-dering tongue, And Joan, Joan, Joan is a bold one.

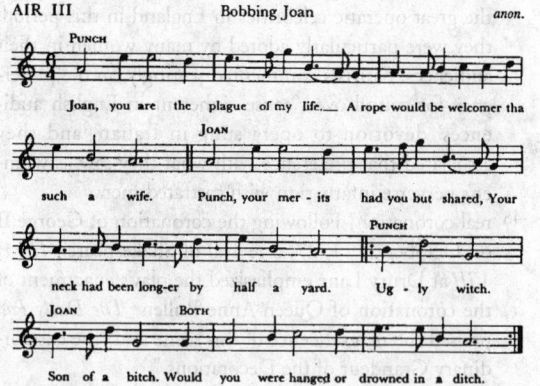

AIR III　　Bobbing Joan　　*anon.*

PUNCH
Joan, you are the plague of my life.__ A rope would be welcomer tha such a wife. JOAN Punch, your mer-its had you but shared, Your neck had been long-er by half a yard. PUNCH Ug-ly witch. JOAN BOTH Son of a bitch. Would you were hanged or drowned in a ditch.

Let us call not bitch and rogue: 95
Gentler titles let us use,
Hate each other, but not abuse.

JOAN.

Pretty dear!

PUNCH.

Ah! ma chère!

BOTH.

Joy of my life and only care. 100

Dance and exeunt [Punch and Joan].

LUCKLESS.

Gentlemen, the next is Charon and a poet. They are disputing about an affair pretty common with poets: going off without paying.

Enter Charon and a poet.

CHARON.

Never tell me, sir. I expect my fare.—I wonder what trade these authors drive in the other world: I would 105 with as good a will see a soldier aboard my boat. A tattered redcoat and a tattered black one have bilked me so often that I am resolved never to take either of them up again unless I am paid beforehand.

POET.

What a wretched thing it is to be poor. My body lay 110 a fortnight in the other world before it was buried. And this fellow has kept my spirit a month, sunning himself on the other side of the river, because my pockets were empty.—Wilt thou be so kind as to show me the way to the Court of Nonsense? 115

CHARON.

Ha, ha, ha! the Court of Nonsense! Why pray, sir, what have you to do there? These rags look more like the dress of one of Apollo's people than of Nonsense's.

POET.

Why fellow, didst thou never carry rags to 120 Nonsense?

CHARON.

Truly sir, I cannot say but I have, but it is a long time ago, I assure you. If you are really bound thither, I'll set your name down in my pocketbook, and I don't question your honor's payment. 125 Nonsense is the best deity to me in the shades. Look at that account, sir.

POET. (*Reads.*)

"Spirits imported for the Goddess of Nonsense since October, in the year _____*: five people of great quality; seven ordinary courtiers; nineteen 130 attorneys; eleven counselors; twenty-six justices of the peace; and one hundred Presbyterian parsons." These courtiers and people of quality* pay swingingly, I suppose?

CHARON.

Not always: I have wafted over many a spirit in a 135 laced coat who has been forced to leave it with me.

LUCKLESS.

Gentlemen, the next is one of Charon's men with a prisoner.

Enter sailor and sexton.

CHARON.

How now?

SAILOR.

We have caught the rogue at last—this is Mr. 140 Robgrave the Sexton, who has plundered so many spirits.

CHARON.

Are you come at last, sir? What have you to say for yourself? Hah! what's become of all the jewels and other valuable things you have stolen? Where 145 are they, sirrah? Hah!

SEXTON.

Alackaday, I am an unfortunate poor rogue. The churchwardens and clerks have had them all; I had only a small reward for stealing them.

CHARON.

Then you shall have another reward here, sir. Carry 150 him before Justice Minos immediately—away with him.

Exeunt sailor and sexton.[i]

POET.

Who knows whether this rogue has not robbed me too. I forgot to look in upon my body before I came away. 155

CHARON.

Had you anything of value buried with you?

POET.

Things of inestimable value: six folios of my own works.

LUCKLESS.

Most poets of this age will have their works buried
with them.   160

Enter sailor.

SAILOR.

There is a great number of passengers arrived from
England, all bound to the Court of Nonsense.

CHARON.

Some plague, I suppose, or a fresh cargo of
physicians come to Town from the universities. Or
perhaps a war broke out.   165

SAILOR.

No, no, these are all authors, and a war never sends
any of them hither.

LUCKLESS.

Now gentlemen, I shall produce such a set of
figures as I may defy all Europe, except our own
playhouses, to equal.—Come, put away.   170

*Enter Don Tragedio, Sir Farcical Comic, Dr. Orator,
Signior Opera, Mounsieur Pantomine, and Mrs. Novel.*[52]

POET.

Hah! Don Tragedio, your most obedient servant. Sir
Farcical. Dr. Orator, I am heartily glad to see you.
Dear Signior Opera. Monsieur Pantomine. Mrs.
Novel in the shades too! What lucky distemper can
have sent so much good company hither?   175

TRAGEDIO.

A tragedy occasioned me to die;
That perishing the first day, so did I.[53]

---

52 Don Tragedio … Mrs. Novel] Each of the ghost-pup-
pets who enters in this group represents one of the
"pleasures of the town" or popular entertainments that
satirists of the time saw as debasements of art and reason (several of them cannot strictly be termed "authors,"
though the sailor introduces them all thus). With vary-
ing extents of satiric specificity, the characters may also
be identified with living individuals, as noted below.

53 TRAGEDIO … I] Don Tragedio recalls Lewis Theobald
(1688-1744) and other authors of those overblown heroic tragedies which the prologue complains have come
to dominate the English stage. Tragedio's opening lines
and later dialogue emphasize Theobald's early and unsuccessful efforts in the genre. Less overtly, some of
Theobald's other literary activities are relevant to the

FARCICAL.

An entertainment sent me out of the world: my
life went out in a hiss, stap my breath![54]

Air 4. "Silvia, my Dearest."   180

---

entire Act. He and John Rich (here appearing as Pantomime) collaborated on a series of "operas," in which
Theobald's retelling in verse and song of some classical
tale, often set in the underworld, alternated with Rich's
"grotesque" antics; this peculiar form of entertainment
provides the general structure for Luckless's puppet show.
Theobald's editing of Shakespeare is glanced at in
Tragedio's verbal mannerisms. He had also been associated with Curll (here seen as Curry) as one of his literary hacks. Finally, he held the ignominious position of
Head Dunce in Pope's 1728 *Dunciad*, which provided
Fielding with the general satiric model of a competition
for Nonsense's laurels.

54 FARCICAL … breath!] Colley Cibber, referred to as
"Mr. Keyber" in Act I and satirized as Marplay in Act
II, here reappears as both comic actor and playwright,
with a satiric emphasis on his infamous abuses of lan-
guage and his impudent public personality. Sir Farcical
Comic's name and speech recall Cibber's popularity in
the role of foppish characters prone to mannered excla-
mations (here with exaggeratedly open vowels) such as
"Stap my vitals!" or "Stap my breath!" (See *Love's Last
Shift* and *The Relapse*, above.) Cibber's *Love in a Riddle*

AIR IV   Silvia, My Dearest   G. F. Handel

Claps un-i-ver-sal, Ap-plau-ses re-sound-ing, His-ses con-
found-ing At-tend-ing my song.__ My sen-ses drowned__ And I fell
down dead, Whilst I was sing-ing,__ ding, dang, dong. Claps un-i-
ver-sal, Ap-plau-ses re-sound-ing, His-ses con-found-ing At-
tend-ing__my song.__ My sen-ses drowned And I fell down dead,
Whilst I__was__ sing-ing,__ ding,__ dang, dong.

OPERA.

Claps universal,
Applauses resounding,
Hisses confounding
Attending my song:
My senses drownèd, 185
And I fell down dead
Whilst I was singing, Ding, dang, dong.[55]

POET.

Well, Monsieur Pantomine, how came you by your
fate?

PANTOMIME. (*Makes signs to his neck.*)[56]

POET.

Broke his neck. Alas, poor gentleman!—And you, 190
Madam Novel?

---

had recently been hissed off the stage. He would be
made Poet Laureate by George II in December, 1730,
and would replace Theobald as Head Dunce in Pope's
final version of *The Dunciad*.

55 OPERA ... song] Signior Opera recalls most specifically
Francesco Bernardi Senesino, the most famous castrato
singer in England from 1720-35, who received both wild
adulation and severe ridicule and attack.

56 PANTOMIME ... neck] John Rich (c. 1682-1761),
appearing as Harlequin under the stage name of Lun,
developed English pantomime out of entertainments in
the Italian style in 1716-17, and thereafter produced a
pantomime annually at Lincoln's Inn Fields, where he
also served as manager (see n. 53 on his collaborations
with Theobald).

AIR V   'Twas When the Seas Were Roaring   G. F. Handel

Oh! Pit-y all a maid-en Con-demned hard fates to
prove; I ra-ther would have laid in Than
thus have died for love. 'Twas hard t'en-count-er
death-a Be-fore the brid-al bed. Ah! Would I had kept my
breath-a And lost my maid-en-head.

NOVEL.

Mine was a hard case indeed.[57]

Air 5. "'Twas When the Seas were Roaring."

Oh! Pity all a maiden,
Condemned hard fates to prove; 195
I rather would have laid-in[58]
Than thus have died for love!
'Twas hard t'encounter death-a,
Before the bridal bed;
Ah! would I had kept my breath-a, 200
And lost my maidenhead.

POET.

Poor lady!

LUCKLESS.

'Twas a hard fate indeed, in this age.

CHARON.

Well my masters, I wish you well. I must take leave
of you. If you follow that path, you'll arrive at the 205
Court of Nonsense. (*Exit.*)

POET.

Gentlemen, if you please I'll show you the way.

Exeunt [puppet characters].

LUCKLESS.

The next, gentlemen, is a blackamoor lady, who
comes to present you with a saraband and
castanets. 210

A dance.

LUCKLESS.

Now, gentlemen and ladies, I shall produce a
bookseller who is the Prime Minister of Nonsense,
and the poet.

Enter Curry and poet.

POET.

'Tis strange, 'tis wondrous strange!

---

57 NOVEL ... indeed] Mrs. Novel has been identified as
Eliza Haywood (c. 1693-1756), the most popular and
prolific novelist of the 1720's, known particularly for her
ability to represent erotic passion. Pope and others associated the erotic content of her novels with a licentious personal life.

58 laid-in] be "confined," or brought to bed for childbirth

CURRY.

And yet 'tis true. Did you observe her eyes? 215

POET.

Her ears rather, for there she took the infection.
She saw the Signior's visage in his voice.

CURRY.

Did you not mark how she melted when he sung?

POET.

I saw her like another Dido. I saw her heart rise
up to her eyes and drop down again to her ears.[59] 220

CURRY.

That a woman of so much sense as the Goddess
of Nonsense should be taken thus at first sight! I
have served her faithfully these thirty years as a
bookseller in the upper world and never knew her
guilty of one folly before. 225

POET.

Nay certainly, Mr. Curry, you know as much of
her as any man.

CURRY.

I think I ought; I am sure I have made as large
oblations to her as all Warwick Lane and
Paternoster Row.[60] 230

POET.

But is she this night to be married to Signior
Opera?

CURRY.

This is to be the bridal night. Well, this will be
the strangest thing that has happened in the shades
since the rape of Proserpine.[61] But now I think 235
on't, what news bring you from the other world?

POET.

Why, affairs go much in the same road there as
when you were alive: authors starve and booksellers
grow fat; Grub Street harbors as many pirates as
ever Algiers did; they have more theaters than are 240
at Paris and just as much wit as there is at
Amsterdam; they have ransacked all Italy for
singers and all France for dancers.

CURRY.

And all hell for conjurers.

POET.

My Lord Mayor has shortened the time of 245
Bartholomew Fair in Smithfield, and so they are
resolved to keep it all the year round at the other
end of the Town.[62]

CURRY.

I find matters go swimmingly, but I fancy I am
wanted. If you please, sir, I will show you the way. 250

POET.

Sir, I follow you.

*Exeunt [poet and Curry]. Enter Joan, Lady Kingcall,
Mrs. Glassring, and Mrs. Cheat'em.]*

JOAN.

I ask leave.

ALL.

With you, madam.

JOAN.

Clubs, and the king of hearts.

GLASSRING.

Sure never was anything so provoking as this; you 255
always put me out of a great game.

They play.

KINGCALL.

There's your king, madam; you have called very

---

59 Dido … ears] Virgil's Dido, like Shakespeare's
Desdemona, falls in love with a man as he relates his
heroic exploits.

60 Warwick … Row] "The booksellers who had their shops
in these streets near St. Paul's seem to have done a thriving business in pamphlets and other inexpensive publications" (Woods).

61 rape of Proserpine] Theobald's *The Rape of Proserpine*
(1727) was one of the most popular of his operatic collaborations with Rich. As in their other operas, high
drama and antic pantomime were placed in shameless
proximity in this work.

62 shortened … Town] The poet echoes the contention of
the opening lines of *The Dunciad*, which Pope glosses,
"Smithfield is the place where Bartholomew Fair was
kept, whose Shews, Machines, and Dramatical Entertainments, formerly agreeable only to the Taste of the
Rabble, were, by the Hero of this Poem [Theobald] and
others of equal Genius, brought to the Theatres of
Covent-Garden, Lincolns-inn-Fields, and the Hay-Mar-
ket, to be the reigning Pleasures of the Court and Town.
This happened in the Year 1725 [the year of Theobald's
first pantomime collaborations with Rich] …" In 1717
the length of Bartholomew Fair had been shortened
from two weeks to three days.

luckily this time. Spadille, there's basto; we have won our game.

JOAN.

I say nothing.

KINGCALL.

I'll play it.

GLASSRING.

Then you have lost it: there is the best diamond.[63]

JOAN.

Was ever such play seen? I would not play with Lady Kingcall for farthings.

KINGCALL.

I have seen your ladyship make greater mistakes.

JOAN.

I wish you'd name when, madam.

KINGCALL.

I have not so good a memory, madam.

JOAN.

I am sorry for it, madam, for you seem to want* one; it might be of use to you.

KINGCALL.

I wish you had a better, madam, it might be of use to others.

JOAN.

What do you mean, madam?

KINGCALL.

I mean, that you owe me a guinea.

JOAN.

I believe, madam, you forget you owe me two.

KINGCALL.

Madam, I deny it.

JOAN.

And I deny yours.

GLASSRING, CHEAT'EM.

Oh fie, ladies!

KINGCALL.

It's happy for your enemies that your ladyship's character is so well known.

JOAN.

It would become anybody to say so, better than you—I never stole china.

KINGCALL.

You are an impudent sow.

JOAN.

You are an old ugly sow, and I'll make you know it.

They fight. Enter Punch.

PUNCH.

Have I caught you, madam? I'll put an end to your quadrille, I am resolved. Get you home, strumpet.—And you are the fine ladies who bring her to this. I'll drive all of you. (*Kicks them out and overturns the table.*)

LUCKLESS.

Very uncivilly done, truly, Master Punch.

PUNCH.

Uncivilly! Why sir, since this game of quadrille has been in fashion, she has never looked after my family; she does nothing but eat, drink, sleep, dress, and play at quadrille.

Air 6. "To You Fair Ladies."

To all you husbands and you wives,
    This Punchinello sings;
For reformation of your lives
    This good advice he brings:
That if you would avoid all ill,
You should leave off the dear quadrille.

No tyrant on the earth his slaves
    With greater terror awes,
With force more absolute behaves,
    Nor gives severer laws.
Unequal though his taxes fall,
They're with a smile received by all.

---

63 Joan … diamond] Fielding stages a quick game of qua-drille, the four-handed card game that began to take the place of ombre in 1726 and quickly became wildly fash-ionable. Lady Kingcall's name derives from a player's option in quadrille to "ask leave" (as Joan does) to "call for a king." If permission is granted, the bidder names trumps and calls for a king of another suit; the player who holds the called-for king (in this case, Lady Kingcall) becomes the bidder's partner. The game goes well for Joan and Lady Kingcall, who win a series of tricks, including one with the ace of spades ("spadille") and one with the ace of clubs ("basto"). Lady Kingcall, however, then blunders in deciding to "play it"; her part-ner Joan is forbidden by the rules of the game to dis-courage her from doing so, and the two women therefore lose their chance to make a vole (or slam).

How many beauties, rich in charms,
    Are subject to his will!
The bride, when in the bridegroom's arms,
    Still thinks on dear quadrille: 310
Her spouse her body may enroll,
Quadrille is master of her soul.

The China people (sailors say)
    When they have lost their pence,
Their family and selves will play;   315
    Heaven keep that custom hence!
For beauties of the first degree
May so be slaves to some marquis. (*Exit.*)

LUCKLESS.
Gentlemen, the next figures are Somebody and
Nobody,[64] who come to present you with a dance. 320

---

64 Somebody and Nobody] The puppet Nobody recalls a
tradition of witticisms in which the term "nobody" is
given substance and used as a proper noun, naming, for
example, the person who is responsible for some mishap around the house: "Nobody did it." Variations on
this joke appear in *The Odyssey*, in medieval Latin commentaries on the Bible, in sixteenth-century German
humor, and in an English folk tradition. As Woods comments, the pun worked differently in different languages;
in English, it generated a visual image of a figure with
almost no "body" or trunk, the legs coming up almost

AIR VI   To You Fair Ladies   anon.

To all you hus - bands and you wives This Punch-i-nel-lo
sings, For re-form-a - tion of your lives This good advice he brings: That if you would a - void all ill, You
should leave off the dear quad - rille. With a fa, la, la, la
la. That if you would a - void all ill, You should leave
off the dear Quad-rille. With a fa, la, la, la la.

Enter Somebody and Nobody. They dance.

Air 7. "Black Joke."

SOMEBODY.
Of all the men in London town,
Or knaves or fools, in coat or gown,
    The representative am I.
NOBODY.
Go through the world, and you will find,   325
In all the classes of humankind,
    Many a jolly Nobody.
For him a Nobody sure we may call
Who during his life does nothing at all
    But eat and snore   330
    And drink and roar

---

to the neck. When "Somebody" appeared as Nobody's
complement, he was represented with a very large trunk
and stunted legs, and the two characters became associated with general social types: the "Somebody" who
flaunts his rank or position, though he lacks personal
substance, and the "Nobody" who lacks position and
purpose altogether.

AIR VII   Black Joke   anon.

SOMEBODY
Of all the men in Lon-don town, Or knaves or fools, in
coat or gown, The rep-re-sen-ta-tive am I. NOBODY Go
through the world and you will find In all the clas-ses of
hu-man kind Man-y a jol-ly No-bod-y. For
him a No-bod-y sure we may call Who dur-ing his life does
noth-ing at all But eat and snore And drink and roar, From
whore to the tav-ern, from tav-ern to whore, With
a laced coat, and that is all.

From whore to the tavern, from tavern to whore,
With a laced coat and that is all.

[Exeunt Somebody and Nobody.]

LUCKLESS.
Gentlemen, this is the end of the first interlude.

[The curtain closes.]

Now gentlemen, I shall present you with the most 335
glorious scene that has ever appeared on the stage:
it is the Court of Nonsense. Play away, soft music,
and draw up the curtain.

The curtain drawn up to soft music, discovers the
Goddess of Nonsense on a throne; the Orator in a
tub;*[65] *Tragedio, etc., attending.*

NONSENSE.
Let all my votaries prepare
To celebrate this joyful day. 340
LUCKLESS.
Gentlemen, observe what a lover of recitativo
Nonsense is.
NONSENSE.
Monsieur Pantomine, you are welcome.
PANTOMIME. (*Cuts a caper.**)
NONSENSE.
Alas, poor gentleman! He is modest. You may 345
speak. No words offend that have no wit in them.
LUCKLESS.
Why, Madam Nonsense, don't you know that Mon-
sieur Pantomine is dumb? And yet, let me tell you, he
has been of great service to you: he is the only one of
your votaries that sets people asleep without talking. 350
But here's Don Tragedio will make noise enough.
TRAGEDIO.
Yes, Tragedio is indeed my name,
Long since recorded in the rolls of fame
At Lincoln's Inn and eke at Drury Lane.
Let everlasting thunder sound my praise 355
And forked lightning in my scutcheon blaze.
To Shakespeare, Jonson, Dryden, Lee, or Rowe,

I not a line, no, not a thought, do owe.
Me, for my novelty, let all adore,
For, as I wrote, none ever wrote before.[66] 360
NONSENSE.
Thou art doubly welcome, welcome.
TRAGEDIO.
That welcome, yes, that welcome is my due,
Two tragedies I wrote, and wrote for you,
And had not hisses, hisses me dismayed,[67]
By this, I'd writ two score, two score, by jayed. 365
LUCKLESS.
By jayed! Aye, that's another excellence of the Don's:
he does not only glean up all the bad words of other
authors but makes new bad words of his own.
FARCICAL.
Nay, egad, I have made new words and spoiled old
ones too, if you talk of that. I have made foreigners 370
break English, and Englishmen break Latin. I have
as great a confusion of languages in my play as was
at the building of Babel.
LUCKLESS.
And so much the more extraordinary because the
author understands no language at all. 375
FARCICAL.
No language at all! Stap my vitals!
LUCKLESS.
But Sir Farcical, I hear you had once an intention
to introduce a set of marrowbones and cleavers
upon the stage.[68]

---

65 tub] "applied contemptuously or jocularly to a pulpit,
    especially of a nonconformist preacher" (*OED*); Henley
    preached from a "gilt Tub" that was "covered with vel-
    vet, and adorned with gold" (*Dunciad* II).

66 Yes, … before] Theobald's first play, *The Persian Princess*
    (1708), was performed at Drury Lane, and in 1727 Drury
    Lane was also the venue for Theobald's presentation of
    Double Falshood, a play which he claimed was written by
    Shakespeare. His collaborations with Rich were per-
    formed at Lincoln's Inn Fields. In his role as editor of
    Shakespeare, Theobald highlighted certain characteristics
    of Shakespeare's style, including the custom of repeating
    a word to give force; Fielding imitates this mannerism in
    Tragedio's speeches and in Nonsense's response.

67 Two tragedies … dismayed] Theobald's first two failed.

68 marrowbones … stage] In Act IV of Cibber and
    Vanbrugh's *The Provok'd Husband*, the Landlady responds
    to a hungry guest: "Good lack! here's Company, Sir; will
    you give me leave to get you a broil'd Bone, or so, till the
    Ladies come home, Sir?" This and other "low" scenes, at-
    tributed to Cibber but in fact written by Vanbrugh, be-
    came a perennial jest at Cibber's expense.

FARCICAL.

'Tis true, and I did produce one bone, but it stuck so confoundedly in the stomach of the audience that I was obliged to drop the project.   380

NONSENSE.

Dr. Orator, I have heard of you.

ORATOR.

Aye, and you might have heard me too; I bawled loud enough, I'm sure.[69]   385

LUCKLESS.

She might have heard you, but if she had understood your advertisements, I will believe Nonsense to have more understanding than Apollo.

ORATOR.

Have understood me, sir! What has understanding to do? My hearers would be diverted, and they are so—which could not be, if understanding were necessary—because very few of them have any.   390

NONSENSE.

You've all deserved my hearty thanks. (*To Signior Opera.*) But here my treasure I bestow.

Air 8. *"Lillibolera."*[70]   395

OPERA.

Let the foolish philosopher strive in his cell
  By wisdom or virtue to merit true praise,
The soldier in hardship and danger still* dwell
    That glory and honor may crown his last days,
        The patriot* sweat   400
          To be thought great,
  Or beauty all day at the looking glass toil,
          That popular voices

May ring their applauses,
While a breath is the only reward of their coil.   405

But would you a wise man to action incite,
  Be riches proposed the reward of his pain.
In riches is centered all human delight;
  No joy is on earth but what gold can obtain.   410
        If women, wine,
          Or grandeur fine
Be most your delight, all these riches can.
        Would you have men to flatter?
        To be rich is the matter.
When you cry he is Rich, you cry a Great Man.*   415

NONSENSE. (*Repeating in an ecstasy.*)

When you cry he is Rich, you cry a Great Man. Bravissimo! I long to be your wife.

NOVEL.

If all my romances ever pleased the ear of my goddess, if I ever found favor in her sight, oh, do not rob me thus!   420

---

[69] ORATOR ... sure] John "Orator" Henley (1692-1756) offered sermons and orations from an outdoor pulpit in Newport Market three times a week, heavily advertising both his orations and his publications. His rhetorical style was embellished with bursts of singing and chanting, extravagant hand gestures, and rapid series of fantastic comparisons (particularly of men to various kinds of birds, fish, or animals). He also served Walpole's ministry in print by ridiculing the political opposition.

[70] Lillibolera] "Lillibullero" was said to have been the watchword of the Irish Roman Catholics during their 1641 massacre of Protestants; the word (variously spelt) was later taken up by Protestants as the refrain of a very popular nonsense song used to ridicule Irish Papists.

AIR VIII   Lillibolera   Henry Purcell (?)

Let the fool-ish phil-o-soph-er strive in his cell, By wis-dom or vir-tue to mer-it true praise, The sol-dier in hard-ship and dang-er still dwell That glo-ry and hon-or may crown his last days, The pa-triot sweat To be thought great, Or beau-ty all day at the look-ing glass toil, That pop-u-lar voic-es May ring their ap-plaus-es, While a breath is the on-ly re-ward of their coil.

NONSENSE.

What means my daughter?

NOVEL.

Alas, he is my husband!

CURRY.

But though he were your husband in the other world, death solves that tie, and he is at liberty now to take another. And I never knew any one instance of a 425 husband here who would take the same wife again.

Air 9. "Whilst I Gaze on Cloe Trembling."

NOVEL.

May all maids from me take warning
    How a lover's arms they fly,
Lest the first kind offer scorning, 430
    They without a second die.

How unhappy is my passion!
    How tormenting is my pain!
If you thwart my inclination,
    Let me die for love again. 435

CURRY.

Again! What, did you die for love of your husband?

NOVEL.

He knows he ought to have been so. He swore he would be so. Yes, he knows I died for love, for I died in childbed.

AIR IX   Whilst I Gaze on Cloe Trembling   *Lewis Ramonden*

May all maids from me take warn-ing

How a lov-er's arms they fly; Lest the first kind

of - fer scorn-ing, They, with-out a sec-ond, die.

How un-hap-py is my pas-sion! How tor-ment-ing

is my pain! If you thwart my in-clin-a-tion,

Let me die for love a-gain.

ORATOR.

Why, madam, did you not tell me all the road 440 hither that you was a virgin?

Air 10. "Highland Laddy."

[OPERA.]

I was told in my life,
Death forever
Did dissever 445
Men from every mortal strife
And that greatest plague, a wife.

For had the priests possessed men
    That to Tartarus
    Wives came after us, 450
Their Devil would be a jest then,
    And our Devil a wife.

NONSENSE.

Avaunt, polluted wretch, begone!
Think not I'll take pollution to my arms.
No, no,—no no,—no no, no. 455

OPERA.

Well, since I can't have a goddess, I'll e'en prove a man of honor.—I was always in love with thee, my angel.

NOVEL.

Now I am happy, verily.

OPERA.

My long-lost dear! 460

NOVEL.

My new-found bud!

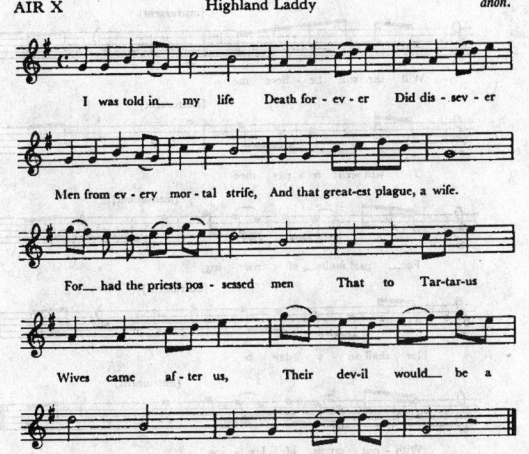

AIR X   Highland Laddy   *anon.*

I was told in my life Death for - ev - er Did dis - sev - er

Men from ev - ery mor - tal strife, And that great-est plague, a wife.

For had the priests pos - sessed men That to Tar-tar-us

Wives came af - ter us, Their dev - il would be a

jest then, And our dev - il a wife.

Air 11. "Dusty Miller."

[OPERA.]

Will my charming creature
  Once again receive me?
Though I proved a traitor,
  Will she still believe me? 465
I will well repay thee
  For past faults of roving,
Nor shall any day be
  Without proofs of loving.

On that tender lily breast 470
  Whilest I lie panting,
Both together blest,
  Both with transports fainting.
Sure no human hearts
  Were ever so delighted! 475
Death, which others parts,
  Hath our souls united.

Air 12. "Over the Hills and Far Away."[71]

OPERA.

Were I laid on Scotland's coast
  And in my arms embraced my dear, 480
Let scrubado[72] do its most,
  I would know no grief or fear.

---

[71] "Over the Hills and Far Away"] Fielding's use of this ballad tune gave the air two layers of parodic resonance: his puppet lovers sing of their devotion in comically unromantic terms to a popular Scottish ballad tune that had already been used memorably by Gay for Macheath and Polly's duet at the end of Act I of *The Beggar's Opera*.

[72] scrubado] "the itch"

NOVEL.

Were we cast on Ireland's soil,
  There confined in bogs to dwell,
For thee potatoes I would boil;   485
  No Irish spouse should feast so well.

OPERA.

And though we scrubbed it all the day,

NOVEL.

We'd kiss and hug the night away;

OPERA.

Scotch and Irish both should say,

BOTH.

Oh, how blest! how blest are they!   490

ORATOR.

Since my goddess is disengaged from one lover,
may the humblest yet not the least diligent of her
servants hope she would smile on him?

LUCKLESS.

Master Orator, you had best try to charm the
Goddess with an oration.   495

ORATOR.

The History of a Fiddle and a Fiddlestick is going
to be held forth: A fiddle is a statesman: why?
because it's hollow. A fiddlestick is a drunkard:
why? because it loves rosening.[73]

LUCKLESS.

Gentlemen, observe how he balances his hands: his   500
left hand is the fiddle, and his right hand is the
fiddlestick.

ORATOR.

A fiddle is like a beau's nose,* because the bridge
is often down; a fiddlestick is like a mountebank,
because it plays upon a crowd.* A fiddle is like a   505
stockjobber's tongue, because it sounds different
notes; and a fiddlestick is like a stockjobber's wig,
because it has a great deal of horsehair in it.

LUCKLESS.

And your oration is like yourself, because it has a
great deal of nonsense in it.   510

NONSENSE.

In vain you try to charm my ears, unless by music.

ORATOR.

Have at you then.

---

73 rosening] "rubbing with rosin, and (dialectal) indulging
in drink" (Woods)

LUCKLESS.

Gentlemen, observe how the doctor sings in his
tub—here are no wires—all alive, alive, ho!

ORATOR.

Chimes of the Times, to the tune of Moll Pately.[74]   515

Air 13. *"Moll Pately."*

All men are birds by nature, sir,
  Though they have not wings to fly;
On earth a soldier's a creature, sir,
  Much resembling a kite in the sky;   520
The physician is a fowl, sir,
Whom most men call an owl,* sir,
    Who by his hooting,
    Hooting, hooting,
    Hooting, hooting,   525
    Hooting, hooting,
  Tells us that death is nigh.

The usurer is a swallow, sir,
  That can swallow gold by the jorum;
A woodcock is Squire Shallow, sir,   530

---

74 Chimes of the Times] a regular feature of Henley's pro-
grams after 1728 (Woods).

AIR XIII   Moll Pately   anon.

All men are birds by na - ture,
sir, Though they have not wings — to fly; On earth a sol - dier's a
crea - ture, sir, Much re - sem - bling a
kite in the sky; The phy - si - cian is a
fowl, sir, Whom most — men call an owl, sir, Who —
by his hoot-ing, Hoot-ing, hoot - ing, Hoot-ing, hoot - ing,
Hoot - ing, hoot - ing, Tells us that death — is nigh.

And a goose is oft of the quorum;
The gamester is a rook, sir;
The lawyer, with his Coke,[75] sir,
  Is but a raven,
   Croaking, croaking,   535
   Croaking, croaking,
   Croaking, croaking
  After the ready rhinorum.[76]

Young virgins are scarce as rails, sir;
  Plenty as bats the nightwalkers go;   540
Soft Italians are nightingales, sir;
  And a cock-sparrow mimics a beau.
Like birds men are to be caught, sir;
Like birds men are to be bought, sir.
   Men of a side,   545
   Like birds of a feather,
   Will flock together,
   Will flock together,
  Both sexes like birds will ____* too.

NONSENSE.
 'Tis all in vain.   550
TRAGEDIO.
 Is Nonsense of me then forgetful grown,
 And must the Signior be preferred alone?
 Is it for this, for this, ye gods! that I
 Have in one scene made some folks laugh, some
  cry?
 For this does my low blustering language creep,   555
 At once to wake you and to make you sleep?
FARCICAL.
 And so all my puns and quibbles and conundrums
 are quite forgotten, stap my vitals! But surely your
 Goddess-ship will remember a certain thing called
 a Pastoral.   560
ORATOR.
 More Chimes of the Times, to the tune of
 "Rogues, Rogues, Rogues."

*Air 14. "There Was a Jovial Beggar."*k

The stone that all things turns at will
  To gold, the chemist craves,   565
But gold without the chemist's skill
  Turns all men into knaves.
   For a-cheating they will go, etc.

The merchant would the courtier cheat,
  When on his goods he lays   570
Too high a price—but faith he's bit,*
  For a courtier never pays.
   For a-cheating they will go, etc.

The lawyer, with a face demure,
  Hangs him who steals your pelf;   575
Because the good man can endure
  No robber but himself.
   For a-cheating, etc.

Betwixt the quack and highwayman
  What difference can there be?   580
Though this with pistol, that with pen,
  Both kill you for a fee.
   For a-cheating, etc.

The husband cheats his loving wife
  And to a mistress goes,   585
While she at home, to ease her life,
  Carouses with the beaus.
   For a-cheating, etc.

The tenant doth the steward nick
  (So low this art we find);   590
The steward doth his lordship trick,

AIR XIV   There Was a Jovial Beggar   anon.

The stone that all things turns at will to gold, the chem-ist
craves; But gold, with-out the chem-ist's skill, Turns
all men in-to knaves. For a-cheat-ing they will
go, will go, will go, For a-cheat-ing they will go.

---

75 Coke] Sir Edward Coke's *The Institutes of the Lawes of
 England, or a Commentarie Upon Littleton* (1628), the
 standard reference on the English common law
76 rhinorum] from "the ready Rhino," a slang expression
 for money

My lord tricks all mankind.
    For a-cheating, etc.

One sect there are to whose fair lot
    No cheating arts do fall, 595
And those are parsons called, God wot:
    And so I cheat you all.
        For a-cheating, etc.

Enter Charon.

CHARON.

An't* please your Majesty, there is an odd sort of
a man o' t'other side the water says he's 600
recommended to you by some people of quality.*
Egad, I don't care to take him aboard, not I. He
says his name is Hurloborumbo—rumbo—
Hurloborumbolo,* I think he calls himself. He
looks like one of Apollo's people in my opinion; 605
he seems to me mad enough to be a real poet.

NONSENSE.

Take him aboard.

CHARON.

I had forgot to tell your ladyship, I hear rare news:
they say you are to be declared Goddess of Wit.

CURRY.

That's no news, Mr. Charon. 610

CHARON.

Well, I'll take Hurloborumbo aboard. (*Exit.*)

ORATOR.

I must win the Goddess before he arrives, or else
I shall lose her forever.—A Rap at the Times:

Air 15. "When I Was a Dame of Honor."

Come all who've heard my cushion beat, 615
    Confess me as full of dullness
As any egg is full of meat
    Or full moon is of fullness.
Let the justice and his clerk both own
    Than theirs my dullness greater, 620
And tell how I've harangued the Town,
    When I was a bold orator.

The lawyer wrangling at the bar,
    While the reverend bench is dozing,
The scribbler in a pamphlet war 625
    Or Grub Street bard composing,

The trudging quack in scarlet cloak
    Or coffeehouse politic prater
Can none come up to what I have spoke,
    When I was a bold orator. 630

The well-bred courtier telling lies
    Or levee hunter believing,
The vain coquette that rolls her eyes,
    More empty fops deceiving,
The parson of dissenting gang 635
    Or flattering dedicator
Could none of them like me harangue,
    When I was a bold orator.

Enter Punch.

PUNCH.

You, you, you.

LUCKLESS.

What's the matter, Punch? 640

PUNCH.

Who is that?

LUCKLESS.

That's an orator, Master Punch.

PUNCH.

An orator—what's that?

LUCKLESS.

Why, an orator is—is—egad, I can't tell what; he
is a man that nobody dares dispute with. 645

AIR XV   When I Was a Dame of Honor   *Thomas Durfey*

Come all who've heard my cush-ion beat, Confess me as full of dull-ness As an-y egg is
full of meat Or full moon is of full-ness.
Let the jus-tice and his clerk both own, Than
theirs my dull-ness great-er, And tell how I've harangued the town When I was a bold or-a-tor.

PUNCH.

Say you so, I'll be with him presently.* Bring out
my tub there.—I'll dispute with you, I'll warrant,
I am a Muggletonian.[77]

ORATOR.

I am not.

PUNCH.

Then you are not of my opinion.   650

ORATOR.

Sirrah, I know that you and your whole tribe would
be the death of me, but I am resolved to proceed to
confute you as I have done hitherto, and as long as
I have breath, you shall hear me, and I hope I have
breath enough to blow you all out of the world.   655

PUNCH.

If noise will.

ORATOR.

Sir, I—

PUNCH.

Hear me, sir.

NONSENSE.

Hear him—hear him—hear him.

Air 16. "Hey Barnaby, Take it for Warning."   660

PUNCH.

No tricks shall save your bacon.
Orator, Orator, you are mistaken:
Punch will not be thus confuted;
Bring forth your reasons or you are nonsuited.
    Heigh ho.   665

No tricks shall save your bacon.
Orator, Orator, you are mistaken.

ORATOR.

Instead of reasons advancing,
Let the dispute be concluded by dancing.
Ti, to.   670

They dance.

---

77 Muggletonian] a member of the radical sect founded *c.*
1651 by Lodowicke Muggleton and John Reeve, who
claimed to be the "two witnesses" of *Revelation* xi.3-6.
Henley's manuscripts included four volumes of lectures
from 1728-29 against the sect, which still had adherents among the lower classes.

NONSENSE.

'Tis all in vain: a virgin I will live. And oh, great
Signior, prithee take this chaplet and still wear it
for my sake.

TRAGEDIO.

And does great Nonsense then at length determine
To give the chaplet to that singing vermin?   675

NONSENSE.

I do.

TRAGEDIO.

Then, Opera, come on, and let us try
Whether shall wear the chaplet, you or I.

Air 17. "Be Kind and Love."

NOVEL.

Oh, spare to take his precious life away;   680
So sweet a voice must sure your passion lay.
Oh hear his gentle murmurs first, and then,
If you can kill him, I will cry Amen.

TRAGEDIO.

Since but a song you ask, a song I'll hear;

AIR XVII   Be Kind and Love   anon.

But tell him that last song is his last prayer.   685
[*Draws his sword.*]

Air 18.

OPERA.
    Barbarous cruel man,
I'll sing thus while I'm dying, I'm dying like a swan,
    I'm dying like a swan,
        A swan,   690
        A swan,
With my face all pale and wan.
More fierce art thou than pirates,
    Than pirates,
Whom the sirens' music charms,   695
    Alarms,
    Disarms;
More fierce than men on the high roads,
    On the high - - - - - roads,
    On the high - - - - - roads.   700
More fierce than men on the high roads,
Whom Polly Peachum[78] warms.
    The Devil
    Was made civil
By Orpheus' tuneful charms;   705
    And ca - - - - -
    - - - - - - n,
He gentler prove than man?

TRAGEDIO.
    I cannot do it— (*Sheathes his sword.*)
    Methinks I feel my flesh congealed to bone   710
    And know not when I'm flesh and blood, or stone.

PANTOMIME. (*Runs several times round the stage.*)

NONSENSE.
    Alas, what means Monsieur Pantomine?

CURRY.
    By his pointing to his head, I suppose he would
    have the chaplet.   715

NONSENSE.
    Pretty youth!

NOVEL.
    Oh my dear, how shall I express the trouble of my
    soul?

OPERA.
    If there be sympathy in love, I'm sure I felt it—
    for I was in a damnable fright too.   720

NOVEL.
    Give me a buss, then.

---

78 Polly Peachum] heroine of *The Beggar's Opera* and *Polly*,
in love with the highwayman Macheath

Air 19. "Under the Greenwood Tree."

In vain a thousand heroes and kings
    Should court me to their arms,
In vain should give me a thousand fine things.   725
    For thee I'd reserve my charms.
On that dear breast, entranced in joys,
    Oh, let me ever be.
OPERA.
    Oh, how I will kiss thee,
    How I'll embliss thee,   730
    When thou art abed with me.
NONSENSE. (*Repeats.*)
    Oh, how I will kiss thee, etc.
FARCICAL.
    Since nothing but a song will do, I will have my
    song too.
LUCKLESS.
    Gentlemen, pray observe and take notice how Sir   735
    Farcical's song sets Nonsense asleep.

Air 20. "Hunt the Squirrel."

[FARCICAL.]
    Can my Goddess then forget
        Paraphonalia,
        Paraphonalia?[79]   740
    Can she the crown on another head set
        Than of her Paraphonalia?
        If that had not done too,
        Remember my bone too,
    My bone, my bone, my bone.   745
    Sure my Goddess never can
        Forget my marrowbone.
CURRY.
    Nonsense is asleep.
TRAGEDIO.
    Oh, ye immortal Powers!
FARCICAL.
    If anything can wake her, 'tis a dance.   750
OMNES.
    A dance, a dance, a dance!

Enter Charon.

---

[79] Paraphonalia] In his Preface to *The Provok'd Husband*,
    while praising the actress Anne Oldfield in extravagant
    terms, Cibber had spelled "paraphernalia" thus.

LUCKLESS.
    How now, Charon? You are not to enter yet.

CHARON.

To enter, sir! Alackaday! We are all undone: here is a constable, and Mr. Murdertext the Presbyterian parson, coming in. 755

Enter Murdertext[1] and Constable.

CONSTABLE.

Are you the master of the puppet show?

LUCKLESS.

Yes, sir.

CONSTABLE.

Then you must along with me, sir; I have a warrant for you, sir.

LUCKLESS.

For what? 760

MURDERTEXT.

For abusing Nonsense, sirrah.

CONSTABLE.

People of quality* are not to have their diversions libeled at this rate.

MURDERTEXT.

No, sirrah, nor the Saints* are not to be abused neither. 765

LUCKLESS.

Of what do you accuse me, gentlemen?

MURDERTEXT.

Verily, I smell a great deal of a—bomination[80] and profaneness—a smell of brimstone offendeth my nostrils, a puppet show is the Devil's house, and I will burn it. Shall you abuse Nonsense, when the 770 whole Town supports it?

LUCKLESS.

Pox on't, had this fellow stayed a few moments longer till the dance had been over, I had been easy.—Hark you, Mr. Constable, shall I only beg your patience for one dance and then I'll wait on 775 you?

MURDERTEXT.

Sirrah, don't try to corrupt the magistrate with thy bribes. Here shall be no dancing; verily, it is a profane mystery, and hath in it a super—fluity of abomination. 780

---

80 a—bomination] The punctuation of Murdertext's speeches in the original texts seems to signal either a speech impediment or a tendency to overwrought sputtering.

NOVEL.

What does this fellow of a constable mean by interrupting our play?

Air 21. "Fair Dorinda."

Oh Mr. Constable,
   Drunken rascal,
Would I had thee at the Rose.[81] 785
   May'st thou be beaten,

---

81 the Rose] a famous—and dangerous—tavern in Covent Garden*

Hanged up and eaten,
May'st thou be eaten, eaten,
  Eaten, eaten,
 May'st thou be eaten by the carrion crows. 790

The filth that lies in common shores,[82]
 May it ever lie in thy nose,
  May it ever
  Lie in thy nose, 795
 Oh may it lie in thy nose.

LUCKLESS.

Mollify yourself, madam.

MURDERTEXT. (*Aside.*)

Verily that is a pretty creature. It were a piece of
charity to take her to myself for a handmaid.

CONSTABLE.

Very pretty, very pretty truly. If magistrates are to be 800
abused at this rate, the Devil may be a constable for
me.—Harkee, madam, do you know who we are?

NOVEL.

A rogue, sir.

CONSTABLE.

Madam, I'm a constable by day and a justice of
peace by night. 905

NOVEL.

That is, a buzzard by day and an owl by night.

Air 22. "Newmarket."

CONSTABLE.

Why, madam, do you give such words as these
To a constable and justice of peace?
I fancy you'll better know how to speak 910
By that time you've been in Bridewell a week,
 Have beaten good hemp and been
  Whipped at a post.
 I hope you'll repent, when some skin
  You have lost. 915
But if this makes you tremble, I'll not be severe;
Come down a good guinea, and you shall be clear.

NOVEL.

Oh Mr. Murdertext, you, I am sure, are the commander in this enterprise. If you will prevent the rest
of our show, let me beg you will permit the dance. 920

Air 23. "Charming Betty."

---

82 common shores] open sewers: channels full of refuse in
 the London streets

AIR XXII   Newmarket   anon.

Why, madam, do you give such words as these To a constable and justice of peace? I fancy you'll better know how to speak By that time you've been in Bridewell a week, Have beaten good hemp and been Whipped at a post; I hope you'll repent when some skin You have lost. But if this makes you tremble, I'll not be severe, Come down a good guinea and you shall be clear.

AIR XXIII   Charming Betty   Henry Carey (?)

Gentle preacher, Non-con teacher, Prithee let us take a dance. Leave your canting, Zealous ranting, Come and shake a merry haunch. Motions firing, Sounds inspiring, We are led to softer joys. Where in trances, Each soul dances, Music then seems only noise.

Gentle preacher,
Non-con[83] teacher,
   Prithee let us take a dance.
Leave your canting, 925
Zealous ranting,
   Come and shake a merry haunch.
Motions firing,
Sounds inspiring,
   We are led to softer joys; 930
Where in trances
Each soul dances,
   Music then seems only noise.

MURDERTEXT.

Verily, I am conquered. Pity prevaileth over severity, and the flesh hath subdued the spirit. I feel a motion 935 in me, and whether it be of grace or no, I am not certain.—Pretty maid, I cannot be deaf any longer to your prayers. I will abide the performing a dance and will myself, being thereto moved by an inward working, accompany you therein, taking for my 940 partner that reverend gentleman.

LUCKLESS.

Then strike up.

Enter Witmore, Mrs. Moneywood, Harriot, and Bantomite.

HARRIOT.

My dear Harry!

WITMORE.

Long live His Majesty of Bantam![84]

MONEYWOOD.

Heaven preserve him. 945

BANTOMITE.

Your gracious father, sir, greets you well.

LUCKLESS.

What, in the devil's name, is the meaning of this?

BANTOMITE.

I find he is entirely ignorant of his father.

---

83 Non-con] nonconformist: member of a religious body separate from the Church of England

84 Bantam] As Bantam in Java was both exotically remote and understood to be a place of incredible wealth, the notion of becoming the "king of Bantam" had become a comic cliché for good fortune beyond one's wildest dreams.

WITMORE.

Aye sir, it is very common in this country for a 950 man not to know his father.

LUCKLESS.

What do you mean?

BANTOMITE.

His features are much altered.

LUCKLESS.

Sir, I shall alter your features if you proceed.

BANTOMITE.

Give me leave to explain myself. I was your tutor in 955 your earliest years, sent by your father, his present Majesty Francis IV, King of Bantam, to show you the world. We arrived at London, when one day among other frolics our ship's crew shooting the bridge, the boat overset, and of all our company, I 960 and your royal self were only saved by swimming into Billingsgate. But though I saved my life, I lost for some time my senses and you, as I then feared, forever. When I recovered, after a long fruitless search for my royal master, I set sail for Bantam but 965 was driven by the winds on far distant coasts and wandered several years till at last I arrived once more at Bantam. Guess how I was received. The King ordered me to be imprisoned for life. At last, some lucky chance brought thither a merchant, who 970 offered this jewel as a present to the King of Bantam.

LUCKLESS.

Hah! It is the same which was tied upon my arm, which by good luck I preserved from every other accident till want* of money forced me to pawn it.

BANTOMITE.

The merchant, being strictly examined, said he had 975 it of a pawnbroker, upon which I was immediately dispatched to England and the merchant kept close prisoner till my return, then to be punished with death or rewarded with the government of an island.

LUCKLESS.

Know then, that at that time when you lost your 980 senses, I also lost mine. I was taken up half dead by a waterman and conveyed to his wife, who sold oysters, by whose assistance I recovered. But the waters of the Thames, like those of Lethe, had caused an entire oblivion of my former fortune. But 985 now it breaks in like light upon me, and I begin to recollect it all. Is not your name Gonsalvo?

BANTOMITE.

It is.

LUCKLESS.

Oh, my Gonsalvo!

BANTOMITE.

Oh, my dearest lord!

} *They embrace.*

990

LUCKLESS.

But say by what lucky accident you discovered me.

BANTOMITE.

I did intend to have advertised you in the *Evening Post* with a reward,[85] but being directed by the merchant to the pawnbroker, I was accidentally there inquiring after you when your boy brought your nab.[86] (Oh, sad remembrance, that the son of a king should pawn a hat!) The woman told me that was the boy that pawned the jewel, and of him I learnt where you lodged.

995

LUCKLESS.

Prodigious fortune!

1000

A post horn without. Enter Messenger.

MESSENGER.

An express is arrived from Bantam with the news of His Majesty's death.

BANTOMITE.

Then, sir, you are king. Long live Henry I, King of Bantam!

OMNES.

Long live Henry I, King of Bantam!

1005

LUCKLESS.

Witmore, I now may repay your generosity.

WITMORE.

Fortune has repaid me, I am sure more than she owed, by conferring this blessing on you.

LUCKLESS.

My friend— But here I am indebted to the golden goddess for having given me an opportunity to

1010

---

aggrandize the mistress of my soul and set her on the throne of Bantam; so once more repeat your acclamations: Long live Henry and Harriot, King and Queen of Bantam!

OMNES.

Huzza!

1015

Air 24. "Gently Touch the Warbling Lyre."

HARRIOT.

Let others fondly court a throne,
All my joy's in you alone.
Let me find a crown in you,
Let me find a sceptre too.
Equal in the court or grove,
I am blest, do you but love.

1020

LUCKLESS.

Were I not with you to live,
Bantam would no pleasure give.
Happier in some forest I
Could upon that bosom lie.
I would guard you from all harms
While you slept within my arms.

1025

HARRIOT.

Would an Alexander rise,
Him I'd view with scornful eyes.

1030

AIR XXIV   Gently Touch the Warbling Lyre   *Francesco Geminiani*

Let o-thers fond-ly court a throne, All my joy's in you a-lone; Let me find a crown in you, Let me find a scep-ter too; E-qual in the court or grove, I am blest, do you but love.

---

85 advertised ... reward] Newspaper advertising was a relatively new and rapidly growing phenomenon in early eighteenth-century England; advertising columns indiscriminately mixed notices of runaway apprentices, lost animals, lost family members, or lost parcels with commercial advertisements, especially for books, theater performances, and quack medicines.

86 nab] slang term for a loose-brimmed hat

LUCKLESS.

   Would Helen with thy charms compare,
   Her I'd think not half so fair:
   Dearest shalt thou ever be.

HARRIOT.

   Thou alone shalt reign in me.

CONSTABLE.

   I hope your Majesty will pardon a poor, ignorant con- 1035
stable: I did not know your worship, I assure you.

LUCKLESS.

   Pardon you? Aye, more: you shall be Chief Constable
of Bantam. You, Mr. Murdertext, shall be my Chaplain; you, sir, my Orator; you, my Poet Laureate; you,
my Bookseller; you, Don Tragedio, Sir Farcical, and 1040
Signior Opera, shall entertain the city of Bantam
with your performances. Mrs. Novel, you shall be a
romance writer. And to show my generosity, Marplay
and Sparkish shall superintend my theaters—all
proper servants for the King of Bantam. 1045

MONEYWOOD.

   I always thought he had something more than
ordinary in him.

LUCKLESS.

   This gentlewoman is the Queen's mother.

MONEYWOOD.

   For want* of a better, gentlemen.

AIR XXV   Oh Ponder Well   anon.

MONEYWOOD

A - lack how al - tered is my fate, What
chan - ges have I seen. For I, who lodg - ings
let of late, Am now a - gain a queen. And
I, who in this pup - pet show Have
played Punch - in - el - lo, Will now let all the
aud - ience know I am no com - mon fel - low.

Air 25. "Oh Ponder Well." 1050

   Alack how altered is my fate!
   What changes have I seen!
   For I, who lodgings let of late,
   Am now again a queen.

PUNCH.

   And I, who in this puppet show 1055
   Have play'd Punchinello,
   Will now let all the audience know
   I am no common fellow.

   If his Majesty of Bantam will give me leave, I can
make a discovery* which will be to his satisfaction. 1060
You have chose for a wife, Henrietta, Princess of
Old Brentford.[87]

OMNES.

   How!

PUNCH.

   When the King of Old Brentford was expelled by
the King of the New, the Queen flew away with 1065
her little daughter, then about two years old, and
was never heard of since. But I sufficiently recollect
the phiz of my mother, and thus I ask her blessing.

MONEYWOOD.

   Oh, my son!

HARRIOT.

   Oh, my brother! 1070

PUNCH.

   Oh, my sister!

MONEYWOOD.

   I am sorry, in this pickle, to remember who I am.
But alas! too true is all you've said: though I have
been reduced to let lodgings, I was the Queen of
Brentford, and this, though a player, is a king's son. 1075

Enter Joan.

JOAN.

   Then I am a king's daughter, for this gentleman is
my husband.

MONEYWOOD.

   My daughter!

---

87 Old Brentford] One of the most famous features of
Buckingham's *The Rehearsal* was the comic doubling in-
volved in its invention of "the two Kings of Brentford."
Durfey had already posed the question of those kings'
consorts when he titled an unacted burlesque *The Two
Queens of Brentford* (1721).

HARRIOT, LUCKLESS.
  My sister!
PUNCH.
  My wife!   1080
LUCKLESS.
  Strike up kettledrums and trumpets.—Punch, I will
  restore you into your kingdom at the expense of my
  own. I will send an express to Bantam for my army.
PUNCH.
  Brother, I thank you.—And now, if you please, we
  will celebrate these happy discoveries* with a dance.   1085

A dance.

LUCKLESS.
  Taught by my fate, let never bard despair,
  Though long he drudge and feed on Grub Street air,
  Since him (at last) 'tis possible to see
  As happy and as great a king as me.

[Exeunt.][88]

FINIS.

Textual Notes

a Copytext is the first edition, a 1730 octavo (O1),which
   exists in two states; another octavo was published the same
   year, the "second" edition; there are no substantive variants
   among them. There was an unauthorized Dublin edition
   in 1730 as well (Dublin). Also consulted, a 1750 octavo,
   based on Fielding's 1734 revisions (O3); and a modern
   edition of the original version in 1966 (Woods). Fielding
   revised *The Author's Farce* for performance at Drury Lane
   in 1734, making many small revisions throughout the play.
   He also substantially recast several scenes to adapt the play's
   topical references to changes in the contemporary scene, or
   to make the most of his new cast. Unlike Gay, he did not
   publish the scores of his songs along with the play.
b Scene iii] In the revised version of this scene, Fielding gave
   the talented actress Kitty Clive as Harriot a greater emo-

tional range by having Luckless initially pretend that he
plans to marry Mrs. Moneywood for her money.
c Scene vi] In 1734 a new scene is inserted here, in which
   Marplay, Jr., visits Luckless to boast that authors' plays are
   nothing until theater managers "lick them into form" with
   their "alterations." Marplay, Jr., is a new character in the
   play, a satiric depiction of Colley Cibber's son Theophilus,
   who had served as his father's deputy at Drury Lane and
   then, after his father sold his share in Drury Lane, led a
   revolt of the actors against the new management.
d scene i] After the death of Robert Wilks, on whom
   Sparkish was based, Marplay, Jr., replaces him in the 1734
   version of this and the following scene. Fielding also expanded this scene in revision by allowing Luckless to read
   more passages of hackneyed and overblown poetry from
   the tragedy he offers for consideration.
e scene ii] In the 1734 revision of this scene, Marplay, Sr.,
   offers fatherly advice to his son about how to thrive in the
   theater through professional impudence and literary thefts.
f Act III] Fielding replaced the Player with the Manager as
   Luckless's interlocutor in his 1734 revision of Act III. He
   also incorporated into the opening scene an exchange with
   Mr. Seedo, the musical director of the Drury Lane staff,
   playing himself; when Luckless requests an overture from
   Mr. Seedo, he responds, "I have composed one," and the
   overture begins.
g Goddess of Nonsense … Signior Opera] When Fielding
   revised his play in 1734, he shifted the emphasis from
   Nonsense's love for Signior Opera to her choice of an
   Archpoet (already implicit in 1730 in her awarding of the
   chaplet).
h "The First of August."] Dublin; *om.* O1, O2, Woods
i *Exeunt … sexton*] In 1734, Fielding responded to a recent
   scandal involving the misconduct of the directors of the
   Charitable Corporation by bringing in a new character at
   this point in the Act: a "Director" who arrives with two
   wagon loads of treasure and who hopes to cheat the devil.
j Fielding eliminated the on-stage game of quadrille in his
   1734 revision, substituting an account of it by Punch and
   an exchange between Punch and Luckless about Punch's
   search for a trade; the exchange concludes with Punch's
   decision that he will "turn great man"* because "that requires no qualification whatsoever."
k "There … Beggar] In 1734, Fielding added another stanza
   to this song, responding to current scandals, about cheating by the directors of charitable corporations.
l *Murdertext*] In the 1734 revision, Fielding replaced
   Murdertext with Sir John Bindover (possibly a satiric portrait of Sir John Gonson, "the harlot-hunting Justice of
   Peace"), thus reducing the religious satire in the play.

---

88 Original productions of the play followed Luckless's triumphant final lines with a return to the scene of struggling authorship: the play's epilogue consisted of four
   poets at a table, trying unsuccessfully to write an epilogue. The poets are only released from their task by the
   appearance of an actress in the dress of a cat, who then
   "metamorphoses" into a woman and addresses the audience in epilogue form.

Laughing Comedy

Laughing comedy is a later Georgian attempt to eschew sentimental comedy and melodrama, which portray, as Goldsmith put it, the "distresses" of the middle and lower classes—about which we do not care, as Aristotle insisted—and to return to earlier satirical comedy, which portrays the vices and follies of the members of those classes, leaving the upper classes to tragedy. But the values remain Revolutionary, bourgeois: good nature and generosity. And the satire within the comedies has not the bite of earlier comedy, much less that of earlier comical satire. Benevolence still reigns, and the sentimental still prevails. England as imperial metropolis basks in its newfound wealth and patronizingly disciplines its wayward sons and daughters—at home if not abroad.

The Belle's Stratagem[a]

by Hannah Cowley (1743-1809)

edited by Linda R. Payne

Like a stock character type in the plays of the period, including her own, Hannah Parkhouse Cowley was raised in the rural environs of Tiverton, Devonshire, and was brought to London when she married. Her husband went to India, however, leaving her on her own in London with three children and her writing career, through which she became an acute observer and satirist of English society.

The Belle's Stratagem enjoyed a particularly profitable run of twenty-eight nights beginning February 22, 1780. The role of Letitia Hardy, originated by Elizabeth Younge, drew the best actresses of subsequent generations, most notably Ellen Terry, playing opposite Henry Irving as Doricourt in the late nineteenth century. The original audience enjoyed John Quick, as Mr. Hardy, reprising his role of Isaac Mendoza from *The Duenna* (1779).

The play follows the "laughing comedy" revival popularized by Goldsmith and Sheridan in the 1760s and '70s. Cowley foregrounds a courtship plot involving the witty couple Letitia and Doricourt, backed with a sentimental subplot in which the doting but misguided Touchwoods are educated into a right relationship. The more original features of these plots include Letitia as the blocking figure who subverts her own arranged marriage to a rich, handsome man she adores unrequitedly in order to gamble at re-establishing the relationship on a more equal footing; and the role of Saville, the agent of the subplot who protects the virtue and marriage of a woman he loves without hope of return.

The portrayal of Letitia's unwillingness to settle for a conventionally advantageous marriage, along with the emphasis given her intelligence and courage, can certainly be viewed as a feminist perspective, although complicated by more traditional characteristics. And both of the play's chief strategists triumph from traditionally powerless positions: Letitia as woman and marriage pawn, Saville as second son or descendant of a decayed family who lacks the economic status to marry within the class he deserves.

Both plots build on errors in discerning appearance from reality. There are also strong nationalistic themes inspired by the revolt of the American colonies and tensions with France. Yet the play outlasted its times. Acted 118 times in London by 1800, ranking fourth of full-length plays written between 1776 and 1800, it continued to be frequently produced in both England and America through the nineteenth century.

DRAMATIS PERSONAE

MEN

    Doricourt.

    Hardy.

    Sir George Touchwood.

    Flutter.

    Saville.

    Villers.

    Courtall.

    Silvertongue.

    Crowquill.

    First Gentleman.

    Second Gentleman.

    Mountebank.

    French Servant.

    Porter.

    Dick.

    [Mask.]

WOMEN

    Letitia Hardy.

    Mrs. Racket.

    Lady Frances Touchwood.

    Miss Ogle.

    Kitty Willis.

    Lady.

    [Mrs. Fagg.]

    Masqueraders, tradesmen, servants, etc.

The Belle's Stratagem.

Act I, scene i. Lincoln's Inn.[1]

Enter Saville followed by a servant at the top of the stage, looking round as if at a loss.

SAVILLE.

Lincoln's Inn! Well, but where to find him, now I am in Lincoln's Inn? Where did he say his master was?

SERVANT.

He only said in Lincoln's Inn, sir.

SAVILLE.

That's pretty! And your wisdom never enquired at whose chambers? 5

SERVANT.

Sir, you spoke to the servant yourself.

SAVILLE.

If I was too impatient to ask questions, you ought to have taken directions, blockhead!

Enter Courtall singing.

Hah, Courtall!—Bid him keep the horses in motion and then enquire at all the chambers round. 10

Exit servant.

What the devil brings you to this part of the Town?* Have any of the long robes[2] handsome wives, sisters, or chambermaids?

COURTALL.

Perhaps they have, but I came on a different errand, and had thy good fortune brought thee here half an hour sooner, I'd have given thee such a treat, ha, ha, ha! 15

SAVILLE.

I'm sorry I missed it. What was it?

COURTALL.

I was informed a few days since that my cousins Fallow were come to Town and desired earnestly to see me at their lodgings in Warwick-Court, Holborn.[3] Away drove I, painting them all the way as so many Hebes. They came from the farthest part of Northumberland, had never been in Town, and in course were made up of rusticity, innocence, and beauty. 20 25

SAVILLE.

Well!

COURTALL.

After waiting thirty minutes, during which there was a violent bustle, in bounced five sallow damsels, four of them maypoles; the fifth, Nature, by way of variety, had bent in the Aesop style.[4] But they all opened at once like hounds on a fresh scent: "Oh cousin Courtall! How do you do, cousin Courtall! Lord, cousin, I am glad you are come! We want you to go with us to the Park* and 30 35

---

1 Lincoln's Inn] one of the Inns of Court*

2 long robes] judges

3 Holborn] a small district of central London sandwiched between the City* and the Town* and dominated by the Inns of Court

4 Aesop style] deformed, as was Aesop, legendarily

the plays and the opera and Almack's[5] and all the fine places!" The devil, thought I, my dears, may attend you, for I am sure I won't. However, I heroically stayed an hour with them and discovered the virgins were all come to Town with the hopes of leaving it—wives: their heads full of knight-baronights,[6] fops, and adventures.

SAVILLE.

Well, how did you get off?

COURTALL.

Oh, pleaded a million engagements. However, conscience twitched me, so I breakfasted with them this morning and afterwards squired them to the gardens here as the most private place in Town and then took a sorrowful leave, complaining of my hard, hard fortune that obliged me to set off immediately for Dorsetshire, ha, ha, ha!

SAVILLE.

I congratulate your escape! Courtall at Almack's with five awkward country cousins! Ha, ha, ha! Why, your existence as a man of gallantry could never have survived it.

COURTALL.

Death and fire! Had they come to Town like the rustics of the last age to see Paul's, the Lions, and the Waxwork[7]—at their service. But the cousins of our days come up ladies, and with the knowledge they glean from magazines and pocket books, fine ladies; laugh at the bashfulness of their grandmothers; and boldly demand their entrées in the first circles.

SAVILLE. [Aside.]

Where can this fellow be!—Come, give me some news. I have been at war with woodcocks and partridges these two months and am a stranger to all that has passed out of their region.

COURTALL.

Oh! enough for three gazettes. The ladies are going to petition for a bill that, during the war,[8] every man may be allowed two wives.

SAVILLE.

'Tis impossible they should succeed, for the majority of both Houses know what it is to have one.

COURTALL.

Gallantry was blackballed at the coterie last Thursday, and Prudence and Chastity voted in.

SAVILLE.

Aye, that may hold till the camps break up. But have ye no elopements? no divorces?

COURTALL.

Divorces are absolutely out and the commons-doctors[9] starving, so they are publishing trials of crim. con.[10] with all the separate evidences at large, which they find has always a wonderful effect on their trade, actions tumbling in upon them afterwards like mackerel at Gravesend.

SAVILLE.

What more?

COURTALL.

Nothing—for weddings, deaths, and politics I never talk of but whilst my hair is dressing. But prithee, Saville, how came you in Town, whilst all the qualified gentry are playing at popgun on Coxheath and the country overrun with hares and foxes?[11]

SAVILLE.

I came to meet my friend Doricourt, who, you know, is lately arrived from Rome.

COURTALL.

Arrived! Yes faith, and has cut us all out! His carriage, his liveries, his dress, himself are the rage

---

5 Almack's] popular assembly rooms on King St., St. James, London, exclusive marriage mart for eligible daughters of fashionable London

6 baronights] play off of baronet, whose title of address, like that of knights, was "Sir"

7 Paul's, the Lions, and the Waxwork] typical tourist attractions: St. Paul's Cathedral, the lions of the royal menagerie housed in the Tower of London, exhibits or sales of wax figures, the most famous and popular in the eighteenth century being Mrs. Salmon's Waxwork in Fleet Street, established in 1693.

8 war] the American Revolution and concomitant colonial skirmishes with France and Spain

9 commons-doctors] lawyers at Doctors Commons*

10 crim. con.] criminal conversation

11 playing at popgun ... foxes] Country squires neglected their hunting as they drilled their militia at Coxheath, a village in Kent, its heath the site of encampments where George III reviewed the troops in 1778.

of the day! His first appearance set the whole *ton*[12] in a ferment, and his valet is besieged by levees of tailors, habit-makers, and other ministers of fashion to gratify the impatience of their customers for becoming *à la mode de Doricourt*. Nay, the beautiful Lady Frolic t'other night, with two sister countesses, insisted upon his waistcoat for muffs, and their snowy arms now bear it in triumph about Town, to the heartrending affliction of all our *beaux garçons*.[13]

SAVILLE.

Indeed! Well, those little gallantries will soon be over; he's on the point of marriage.

COURTALL.

Marriage! Doricourt on the point of marriage! 'Tis the happiest tidings you could have given, next to his being hanged. Who is the bride elect?

SAVILLE.

I never saw her, but 'tis Miss Hardy, the rich heiress. The match was made by the parents and the courtship begun on their nurses' knees; Master used to crow at Miss, and Miss used to chuckle at Master.

COURTALL.

Oh! then by this time they care no more for each other than I do for my country cousins.

SAVILLE.

I don't know that; they have never met since thus high and so, probably, have some regard for each other.

COURTALL.

Never met! Odd!

SAVILLE.

A whim of Mr. Hardy's: he thought his daughter's charms would make a more forcible impression if her lover remained in ignorance of them till his return from the continent.

Enter Saville's servant.

SERVANT.

Mr. Doricourt, sir, has been at Counsellor Pleadwell's and gone about five minutes. (*Exit.*)

SAVILLE.[b]

Five minutes! Zounds![c] I have been five minutes too late all my lifetime!—Good morrow, Courtall, I must pursue him. (*Going.*)

COURTALL.

Promise to dine with me today. I have some honest fellows. (*Going off on the opposite side.*)

SAVILLE.

Can't promise, perhaps I may.—See there, there's a bevy of female Patagonians coming down upon us.

COURTALL.

By the Lord, then, it must be my strapping cousins. I dare not look behind me. Run, man, run.

Exeunt on the same side.

Scene ii. A hall at Doricourt's.

A gentle knock at the door. Enter the porter.

PORTER.

Tap! What sneaking devil art thou? (*Opens the door.*)

Enter Crowquill.[d]

So! I suppose *you* are one of monsieur's customers, too? He's above stairs, now, overhauling all his honor's things to a parcel of 'em.

CROWQUILL.

No sir, it is with you, if you please, that I want to speak.

PORTER.

Me! Well, what do you want with me?

CROWQUILL.

Sir, you must know that I am—I am the gentleman who writes the tête-à-têtes in the magazines.

PORTER.

Oh, oh! What, you are the fellow that ties folks together in your sixpenny cuts[14] that never meet anywhere else?

CROWQUILL.

Oh dear sir, excuse me! We always go on *foundation*, and if you can help me to a few anecdotes of your master, such as what marchioness he lost money to

---

12 *ton*] the *bon ton*, beautiful Town, fashionable society (Fr.)

13 *beaux garçons*] handsome young men; men of fashion (Fr.)

14 sixpenny cuts] cheap tabloids

in Paris, who is his favorite lady in Town, or the
name of the girl he first made love* to at college, or
any incidents that happened to his grandmother or
great aunts—a couple will do, by way of 20
supporters—I'll weave a web of intrigues, losses, and
gallantries between them that shall fill four pages,
procure me a dozen dinners and you, sir, a bottle of
wine for your trouble.

PORTER.

Oh, oh! I heard the butler talk of you when I lived 25
at Lord Tinket's. But what the devil do you mean
by bottle of wine! You gave him a crown for a
retaining fee.

CROWQUILL.

Oh sir, that was for a lord's amours; a commoner's
are never but half. Why, I have had a baronet's for 30
five shillings, though he was a married man and
changed his mistress every six weeks.

PORTER.

Don't tell me! What signifies a baronet or a bit of
a lord, who maybe was never further than fun and
fun round London? *We* have traveled, man! My 35
master has been in Italy and over the whole island
of Spain, talked to the Queen of France and
danced with her at a masquerade. Aye, and such
folks don't go to masquerades for nothing, but
mum—not a word more. Unless you'll rank my 40
master with a lord, I'll not be guilty of blabbing
his secrets, I assure you.

CROWQUILL.

Well sir, perhaps you'll throw in a hint or two of
other families where you've lived that may be
worked up into something, and so, sir, here is one, 45
two, three, four, five shillings.

PORTER.

Well, that's honest. (*Pocketing the money.*) To tell
you the truth, I don't know much of my master's
concerns yet, but here comes Monsieur and his
gang, I'll pump them; they have trotted after him 50
all round Europe from the Canaries to the Isle of
Wight.

*Enter several foreign servants and two tradesmen. The
porter takes one of them aside.*

TRADESMAN.

Well then, you have showed us all?

FRENCHMAN.

All, *en vérité, messieurs*! you *avez* seen every ting.
Serviteur, serviteur. 55

Exeunt tradesmen.

Ah, here comes one *autre* curious Englishman, and
dat's one *autre* guinea *pour moi.*

Enter Saville.

Allons,[15] monsieur, dis way; I will shew you tings,
such tings you never see, begar,* in England!—
velvets by Le Mosse, suits cut by Verdue, 60
trimmings by Grossette, embroidery by
Detanville[16]—

SAVILLE.

Puppy!* Where is your master?

PORTER.

Zounds! You chattering, frog-eating, dunderhead,
can't you see a gentleman? 'Tis Mr. Saville. 65

FRENCHMAN. [*Aside.*]

Monsieur Saville! *Je suis mort de peur.*[17]—Ten
tousand pardons! *Excuser mon erreur*, and permit
me you conduct to Monsieur Doricourt; he be too
happy *à vous voir.*[18]

Exeunt Frenchman and Saville.

PORTER.

Step below a bit. We'll make it out somehow! I 70
suppose a slice of sirloin won't make the story go
down the worse.

Exeunt Porter and Crowquill.

Scene iii. An apartment at Doricourt's.

Enter Doricourt.

DORICOURT. (*Speaking to a servant behind.*)

I shall be too late for St. James's.* Bid him come
immediately.

Enter Frenchman and Saville.

---

15 *Allons*] Let's go (Fr.)
16 LeMosse, Verdue, Grossette, Detanville] popular French
   merchants
17 *Je suis mort de peur*] I am dead with fear (Fr.)
18 *à vous voir*] to see you (Fr.)

FRENCHMAN.

Monsieur Saville. (*Exit.*)

DORICOURT.

Most fortunate! My dear Saville, let the warmth
of this embrace speak the pleasure of my heart.   5

SAVILLE.

Well, this is some comfort, after the scurvy
reception I met with in your hall. I prepared my
mind, as I came upstairs, for a bonjour, a grimace,
and an adieu.

DORICOURT.

Why so?   10

SAVILLE.

Judging of the master from the rest of the family.*
What the devil is the meaning of that flock of
foreigners below, with their parchment faces and
snuffy whiskers? What! can't an Englishman stand
behind your carriage, buckle your shoe, or brush   15
your coat?

DORICOURT.

Stale, my dear Saville, stale! Englishmen make the
best soldiers, citizens, artisans, and philosophers in
the world, but the very worst footmen. I keep
French fellows and Germans as the Romans kept   20
slaves, because their own countrymen had minds
too enlarged and haughty to descend with a grace
to the duties of such a station.

SAVILLE.

A good excuse for a bad practice.

DORICOURT.

On my honor, experience will convince you of its   25
truth. A Frenchman neither hears, sees, nor breathes
but as his master directs, and his whole system of
conduct is comprised in one short word, *obedience*!
An Englishman reasons, forms opinions, cogitates,
and disputes. He is the mere creature of your will,   30
the other, a being conscious of equal importance in
the universal scale with yourself and is therefore your
judge, whilst he wears your livery and decides on
your actions with the freedom of a censor.

SAVILLE.

And this in defense of a custom I have heard you   35
execrate, together with all the adventitious manners
imported by our traveled gentry.

DORICOURT.

Aye, but that was at eighteen; we are always *very*
wise at eighteen. But consider this point: we go
into Italy where the sole business of the people is   40
to study and improve the powers of music; we
yield to the fascination and grow enthusiasts in the
charming science. We travel over France and see
the whole kingdom composing ornaments and
inventing fashions; we condescend to avail   45
ourselves of their industry and adopt their modes.
We return to England and find the nation intent
on the most important objects: polity, commerce,
war, with all the liberal arts, employ her sons. The
latent sparks glow afresh within our bosoms; the   50
sweet follies of the continent imperceptibly slide
away whilst senators, statesmen, patriots, and
heroes emerge from the virtu of Italy and the
frippery of France.

SAVILLE.

I may as well give it up! You had always the art of   55
placing your faults in the best light, and I can't help
loving you, faults and all. So, to start a subject
which must please you, when do you expect Miss
Hardy?

DORICOURT.

Oh, the hour of expectation is past. She is arrived,   60
and I this morning had the honor of an interview
at Pleadwell's. The writings were ready, and in
obedience to the will of Mr. Hardy, we met to sign
and seal.

SAVILLE.

Has the event answered? Did your heart leap or   65
sink when you beheld your mistress?

DORICOURT.

Faith, neither one nor t'other. She's a fine girl, as
far as mere flesh and blood goes, but—

SAVILLE.

But what?

DORICOURT.

Why, she's *only* a fine girl: complexion, shape, and   70
features—nothing more.

SAVILLE.

Is not that enough?

DORICOURT.

No! she should have spirit! fire! *l'air enjoué*[19] that
something, that nothing, which everybody feels

---

19 *l'air enjoué*] a playful nature (Fr.)

and which nobody can describe in the resistless charmers of Italy and France. 75

SAVILLE.

Thanks to the parsimony of my father that kept me from travel! I would not have lost my relish for true, unaffected English beauty to have been quarreled for by all the belles of Versailles and Florence. 80

DORICOURT.

Faugh! thou has no taste. *English* beauty! 'Tis insipidity; it wants* the zest, it wants* poignancy, Frank! Why, I have known a Frenchwoman, indebted to nature for no one thing but a pair of decent eyes, reckon in her suite as many counts, marquises, and *petits maîtres*[20] as would satisfy three dozen of our first-rate toasts. I have known an Italian *marquizina*[21] make ten conquests in stepping from her carriage and carry her slaves from one city to another, whose real intrinsic beauty would have yielded to half the little grisettes that pace your Mall* on a Sunday. 85 90

SAVILLE.

And has Miss Hardy nothing of this?

DORICOURT.

If she has, she was pleased to keep it to herself. I was in the room half an hour before I could catch the color of her eyes, and every attempt to draw her into conversation occasioned so cruel an embarrassment that I was reduced to the necessity of news, French fleets, and Spanish captures with her father. 95 100

SAVILLE.

So Miss Hardy, with only beauty, modesty, and merit, is doomed to the arms of a husband who will despise her.

DORICOURT.

You are unjust. Though she has not inspired me with violent passion, my honor secures her felicity. 105

SAVILLE.

Come, come, Doricourt, you know very well that when the honor of a husband is *locum-tenens*[22] for his heart, his wife must be as indifferent as himself, if she is not unhappy.

DORICOURT.

Faugh! never moralize without spectacles. But as we are upon the tender subject, how did you bear Touchwood's carrying Lady Frances? 110

SAVILLE.

You know I never looked up to her with hope, and Sir George is every way worthy of her.

DORICOURT.

Á la mode Angloise, a philosopher even in love. 115

SAVILLE.

Come, I detain you, you seem dressed at all points and of course have an engagement.

DORICOURT.

To St. James. I dine at Hardy's and accompany them to the masquerade in the evening. But breakfast with me tomorrow, and we'll talk of our old companions, for I swear to you, Saville, the air of the continent has not effaced one youthful prejudice or attachment. 120

SAVILLE.

With an exception to the case of ladies and servants. 125

DORICOURT.

True, there I plead guilty, but I have never yet found any man whom I could cordially take to my heart and call friend who was not born beneath a British sky and whose heart and manners were not truly English. 130

Exeunt Doricourt and Saville.

Scene iv. An apartment at Mr. Hardy's.

Villers^e seated on a sofa, reading. Enter Flutter.

FLUTTER.

Hah, Villers, have you seen Mrs. Racket? Miss Hardy, I find, is out.

VILLERS.

I have not seen her yet. I have made a voyage to Lapland since I came in. (*Flinging away the book.*) A lady at her toilet* is as difficult to be moved as a Quaker.[23] (*Yawning.*) What events have happened in the world since yesterday? Have you heard? 5

---

20 *petits maîtres*] lesser gentry (Fr.)
21 *marquizina*] *marchesina*, lesser marchioness (It.)
22 *locum-tenens*] representative or placeholder (Lat.)

23 as difficult … Quaker] Quakers have services without ministers, where members sit silently until an individual feels "moved" to speak.

FLUTTER.

Oh yes, I stopped at Tattersall's[24] as I came by, and there I found Lord James Jessamy, Sir William Wilding, and Mr. _____.* But now I think of it, you shan't know a syllable of the matter, for I have been informed you never believe above one-half of what I say. 10

VILLERS.

My dear fellow, somebody has imposed upon you most egregiously! Half! Why, I never believe one tenth part of what you say, that is, according to the plain and literal expression. But as I understand you, your intelligence is amusing. 15

FLUTTER.

That's very hard now, very hard. I never related a falsity in my life, unless I stumbled on it by mistake. And if it were otherwise, your dull matter-of-fact people are infinitely obliged to those warm imaginations which soar into fiction to amuse you. For positively, the common events of this little dirty world are not worth talking about unless you embellish 'em!—Hah! here comes Mrs. Racket: adieu to weeds, I see! All life! 20 25

Enter Mrs. Racket.

Enter, madam, in all your charms! Villers has been abusing your toilet* for keeping you so long, but I think we are much obliged to it, and so are you. 30

MRS. RACKET.

How so, pray? Good morning t'ye both. Here, here's a hand apiece for you. (*They kiss her hands.*)

FLUTTER.

How so! Because it has given you so many beauties.

MRS. RACKET.

Delightful compliment! what do you think of that, Villers? 35

VILLERS.

That he and his compliments are alike: showy, but won't bear examining. So you brought Miss Hardy to Town last night?

MRS. RACKET.

Yes, I should have brought her before, but I had a fall from my horse that confined me a week. I 40

___

24 Tattersall's] an auction establishment specializing in horses

suppose in her heart she wished me hanged a dozen times an hour.

FLUTTER.

Why?

MRS. RACKET.

Had she not an expecting lover in Town all the time? She meets him this morning at the lawyer's. I hope she'll charm him; she's the sweetest girl in the world. 45

VILLERS. [*Aside.*]

Vanity, like murder, will out.—You have convinced me you think yourself more charming.

MRS. RACKET.

How can that be? 50

VILLERS.

No woman ever praises another unless she thinks herself superior in the very perfections she allows.

FLUTTER.

Nor no man ever rails at the sex unless he is conscious he deserves their hatred.

MRS. RACKET.

Thank ye, Flutter, I'll owe ye a bouquet for that. I am going to visit the new-married Lady Frances Touchwood. Who knows her husband? 55

FLUTTER.

Everybody.

MRS. RACKET.

Is there not something odd in his character?

VILLERS.

Nothing but that he is passionately fond of his wife, and so petulant is his love that he opened the cage of a favorite bullfinch and sent it to catch butterflies because she rewarded its song with her kisses. 60

MRS. RACKET.

Intolerable monster! Such a brute deserves— 65

VILLERS.

Nay, nay, nay, nay, this is your sex now. Give a woman but one stroke of character,* off she goes like a ball from a racket, sees the whole man, marks him down for an angel or a devil, and so exhibits him to her acquaintance. This "monster"! this "brute"! is one of the worthiest fellows upon earth—sound sense and a liberal mind—but dotes on his wife to such excess that he quarrels with everything she admires and is jealous of her tippet and nosegay. 70

MRS. RACKET.

Oh, less love for me, kind Cupid! I can see no 75
difference between the torment of such an
affection and hatred.

FLUTTER.

Oh pardon me, inconceivable difference,
inconceivable: I see it as clearly as your bracelet.
In the one case the husband would say, as Mr. 80
Snapper said t'other day, "Zounds! madam, do you
suppose that *my* table and *my* house and *my*
pictures—" *À propos des bottes*,25 there was the
divinest *Plague of Athens* sold yesterday at
Langford's!26 The dead figures so natural you 85
would have sworn they had been alive! Lord
Primrose bid five hundred. "Six," said Lady
Carmine. "A thousand," said Ingot the Nabob.
Down went the hammer. "A rouleau for your
bargain," said Sir Jeremy Jingle. And what answer 90
do you think Ingot made him?

MRS. RACKET.

Why, took the offer.

FLUTTER.

"Sir, I would oblige you, but I buy this picture to
place in the nursery: the children have already got
Whittington and his Cat;27 'tis just this size, and 95
they'll make good companions.

MRS. RACKET.

Ha, ha, ha! Well, I protest that's just the way now.
The nabobs and their wives outbid one at every
sale, and the creatures have no more taste—

VILLERS.

There again! You forget this story is told by Flutter, 100
who always remembers everything but the
circumstances and the person he talks about: 'twas
Ingot who offered a rouleau for the bargain, and
Sir Jeremy Jingle who made the reply.

FLUTTER.

Egad, I believe you are right. Well, the story is as 105
good one way as t'other, you know. Good
morning. I am going to Mrs. Crotchet's concert

25 *À propos des bottes*] by way of nothing (Fr.)
26 Langford's] a popular auction house
27 *Whittington and his Cat*] painting of legendary poor boy
whose cat is sold for a fortune and who becomes Lord
Mayor of London

and in my way back shall make my bow at Sir
George's. (*Going*.)

VILLERS.

I'll venture every figure in your tailor's bill you 110
make some blunder there.

FLUTTER. (*Turning back*.)

Done! My tailor's bill has not been paid these two
years, and I'll open my mouth with as much care
as Mrs. Bridget Button, who wears cork plumpers
in each cheek and never hazards more than six 115
words for fear of showing them. (*Exit*.)

MRS. RACKET.

'Tis a good-natured, insignificant creature! let in
everywhere and cared for nowhere.—There's Miss
Hardy returned from Lincoln's Inn. She seems
rather chagrined. 120

VILLERS.

Then I leave you to your communications.

Enter Letitia followed by her maid.

Adieu!—I am rejoiced to see you so well, madam,
but I must tear myself away.

LETITIA.

Don't vanish in a moment.

VILLERS.

Oh inhuman! you are two of the most dangerous 125
women in Town. Staying here to be cannonaded
by four such eyes is equal to a rencontre with Paul
Jones or a midnight march to Omoa!28 (*Aside*.)
They'll swallow the nonsense for the sake of the
compliment. (*Exit*.) 130

LETITIA. (*Gives her cloak to her maid*.)

Order Du Quesne never to come again; he shall
positively dress my hair no more.

Exit maid.

And this odious silk, how unbecoming it is! I was
bewitched to choose it. (*Throwing herself on a sofa
and looking in a pocket glass,* * *Mrs. Racket staring at* 135
her.) Did you ever see such a fright as I am today?

MRS. RACKET.

Yes, I have seen you look much worse.

28 Omoa] fortification on the Bay of Honduras, site of a
grueling 5-month invasion of Honduras in 1780 with
disastrous results to British troops

LETITIA.

How can you be so provoking? If I do not look this morning worse than ever I looked in my life, I am naturally a fright. You shall have it which way you will.

MRS. RACKET.

Just as you please. But pray, what is the meaning of all this?

LETITIA. (*Rising.*)

Men are all dissemblers! flatterers! deceivers! Have I not heard a thousand times of my air, my eyes, my shape—all made for victory! and today, when I bent my whole heart on one poor conquest, I have proved that all those imputed charms amount to nothing—for Doricourt saw them unmoved. A husband of fifteen months could not have examined me with more cutting indifference.

MRS. RACKET.

Then you return it like a wife of fifteen months and be as indifferent as he.

LETITIA.

Aye, there's the sting! The blooming boy who left his image in my young heart is, at four and twenty, improved in every grace that fixed him there. It is the same face that my memory and my dreams constantly painted to me, but its graces are finished and every beauty heightened. How mortifying to feel myself at the same moment his slave and an object of perfect indifference to him!f

MRS. RACKET.

How are you certain that was the case? Did you expect him to kneel down before the lawyer, his clerks, and your father to make oath of your beauty?

LETITIA.

No, but he should have looked as if a sudden ray had pierced him! He should have been breathless! speechless! For oh, Caroline, all this was I.

MRS. RACKET.

I am sorry you was such a fool. Can you expect a man who has courted and been courted by half the fine women in Europe to feel like a girl from a boarding school? He is the prettiest fellow you have seen and in course bewilders your imagination. But he has seen a million of pretty women, child,* before he saw you, and his first feelings have been over long ago.

LETITIA.

Your raillery distresses me, but I will touch his heart or never be his wife.

MRS. RACKET.

Absurd and romantic! If you have no reason to believe his heart pre-engaged, be satisfied; if he is a man of honor, you'll have nothing to complain of.

LETITIA.

Nothing to complain of! Heavens! shall I marry the man I adore with such an expectation as that?

MRS. RACKET.

And when you have fretted yourself pale, my dear, you'll have mended your expectation greatly.

LETITIA. (*Pausing.*)

Yet I have one hope. If there is any power whose peculiar care is faithful love, that power I invoke to aid me.

Enter Mr. Hardy.

HARDY.

Well now, wasn't I right? Aye, Letty! Aye, cousin Racket! Wasn't I right? I knew 'twould be so. He was all agog to see her before he went abroad and, if he had, he'd have thought no more of her face, maybe, than his own.

MRS. RACKET.

Maybe not half so much.

HARDY.

Aye, maybe so, but I see into things: exactly as I foresaw, today he fell desperately in love with the wench, he! he! he!

LETITIA.

Indeed, sir! how did you perceive it?

HARDY.

That's a pretty question! How do I perceive everything? How did I foresee the fall of corn* and the rise of taxes? How did I know that if we quarreled with America, Norway deals would be dearer? How did I foretell that a war would sink the funds? How did I forewarn Parson Homily that if he didn't some way or other contrive to get more votes than Rubrick, he'd lose the lectureship? How did I—but what the devil makes you so dull, Letitia? I thought to have found you popping about as brisk as the jacks of your harpsichord.

LETITIA.

Surely sir, 'tis a very serious occasion.　210

HARDY.

Faugh, faugh! girls should never be grave before marriage. How did you feel, cousin, beforehand? Aye!

MRS. RACKET.

Feel! why, exceedingly full of cares.

HARDY.

Did you?　215

MRS. RACKET.

I could not sleep for thinking of my coach, my liveries, and my chairmen;* the taste of clothes I should be presented in distracted me for a week; and whether I should be married in white or lilac gave me the most cruel anxiety.　220

LETITIA.

And is it possible that you felt no other care?

HARDY.

And pray, of what sort may your cares be, Mrs.* Letitia? I begin to foresee now that you have taken a dislike to Doricourt.

LETITIA.

Indeed sir, I have not.　225

HARDY.

Then what's all this melancholy about? Ain't you going to be married? And what's more, to a sensible man? And what's more to a young girl, to a handsome man? And what's all this melancholy for, I say?

MRS. RACKET.

Why, because he *is* handsome and sensible, and　230
because she's over head and ears in love with him; all which, it seems, your foreknowledge had not told you a word of.

LETITIA.

Fie, Caroline!

HARDY.

Well come, do you tell me what's the matter then?　235
If you don't like him, hang the signing and sealing, he shan't have ye—and yet I can't say that, neither, for you know that estate that cost his father and me upwards of fourscore thousand pounds must go all to him if you won't have him; if he won't　240
have you, indeed, 'twill be all yours. All that's clear, engrossed upon parchment, and the poor dear man set his hand to it whilst he was a-dying. "Ah!" said

I, "I foresee you'll never live to see 'em come together, but their first son shall be christened　245
Jeremiah after you, that I promise you." But come, I say, what is the matter? Don't you like him?

LETITIA.

I fear, sir—if I must speak—I fear I was less agreeable in Mr. Doricourt's eyes than he appeared in mine.　250

HARDY.

There you are mistaken, for I asked him, and he told me he liked you vastly.—Don't you think he must have taken a fancy to her?

MRS. RACKET.

Why really I think so, as I was not by.

LETITIA.

My dear sir, I am convinced he has not. But if　255
there is spirit or invention in woman, he shall.

HARDY.

Right, girl, go to your toilet—*

LETITIA.

It is not my toilet* that can serve me. But a plan has struck me, if you will not oppose it, which flatters me with brilliant success.　260

HARDY.

Oppose it! not I indeed! What is it?

LETITIA.

Why sir, it may seem a little paradoxical, but as he does not like me enough, I want him to like me still less and will at our next interview endeavor to heighten his indifference into dislike.　265

HARDY.

Who the devil could have foreseen that?

MRS. RACKET.

Heaven and earth! Letitia, are you serious?

LETITIA.

As serious as the most important business of my life demands.

MRS. RACKET.

Why endeavor to make him dislike you?　270

LETITIA.

Because 'tis much easier to convert a sentiment into its opposite than to transform indifference into tender passion.

MRS. RACKET.

That may be good philosophy, but I am afraid you'll find it a bad maxim.　275

[II.i]

LETITIA.

I have the strongest confidence in it. I am inspired with unusual spirits and on this hazard willingly stake my chance for happiness. I am impatient to begin my measures. (*Exit.*)

HARDY.

Can you foresee the end of this, cousin? 280

MRS. RACKET.

No sir, nothing less than your penetration can do that, I am sure, and I can't stay now to consider it. I am going to call on Miss Ogleᵍ and then to Lady Frances Touchwood's and then to an auction and then—I don't know where—but I shall be at 285 home time enough to witness this extraordinary interview. Goodbye. (*Exit.*)

HARDY.

Well, 'tis an odd thing—I can't understand it—but I foresee Letty will have her way, and so I shan't give myself the trouble to dispute it. 290

Exit.

Act II, scene i. Sir George Touchwood's.

Enter Doricourt and Sir George.

DORICOURT.

Married, ha, ha, ha! you, whom I heard in Paris say such things of the sex, are in London a married man.

SIR GEORGE.

The sex is still what it has ever been since *la petite morale*[29] banished substantial virtues, and rather than have given my name to one of your high-bred 5 fashionable dames, I'd have crossed the line[30] in a fire ship and married a Japanese.

DORICOURT.

Yet you have married an English beauty, yea, and a beauty born in high life.

SIR GEORGE.

True, but she has a simplicity of heart and manners 10 that would have become the fair Hebrew damsels toasted by the patriarchs.

DORICOURT.

Ha, ha! Why, thou art a downright matrimonial

Quixote. My life on't, she becomes as mere* a Town lady in six months as though she had been 15 bred to the trade.

SIR GEORGE. (*Contemptuously.*)

Common, common. No sir, Lady Frances despises high life so much from the ideas I have given her that she'll live in it like a salamander in fire.

DORICOURT.

Oh, that the circle *dans la Place Victoire*[31] could 20 witness thy extravagance! I'll send thee off to St. Évreux[32] this night, drawn at full length and colored after nature.

SIR GEORGE.

Tell him then, to add to the ridicule, that Touchwood glories in the name of husband, that 25 he has found in one Englishwoman more beauty than Frenchmen ever saw and more goodness than Frenchwomen can conceive.

DORICOURT.

Well, enough of description. Introduce me to this phoenix.[33] I came on purpose. 30

SIR GEORGE.

Introduce! oh, aye, to be sure—I believe Lady Frances is engaged just now—but another time— (*Aside.*) How handsome the dog looks today!

DORICOURT.

Another time! but I have no other time. 'Sdeath!* this is the only hour I can command this fortnight! 35

SIR GEORGE. (*Aside.*)

I am glad to hear it, with all my soul.—So then, you can't dine with us today? That's very unlucky.

DORICOURT.

Oh yes, as to dinner, yes I can, I believe, contrive to dine with you today.

SIR GEORGE.

Psha! I didn't think on what I was saying; I meant 40 supper—you can't sup with us?

---

[29] *la petite morale*] small details of politeness and courtesy (Fr.)
[30] line] equator

[31] *dans la Place Victoire*] in the Place de la Victoire (Victory Square), on the right bank in Paris
[32] St. Évreux] The cathedral at Évreux in Normandy was famous for its stained-glass windows from the 12th to the 17th centuries; the "him" in the next line may be a personification or someone from St. Évreux.
[33] phoenix] Only one of these mythical birds existed at any given time.

THE BELLE'S STRATAGEM 1837

DORICOURT.

Why, supper will be rather more convenient than dinner. But you are fortunate: if you had asked me any other night, I could not have come.

SIR GEORGE.

Tonight—Gad, now I recollect, we are particularly 45 engaged tonight—but tomorrow night—

DORICOURT.

Why look ye, Sir George, 'tis very plain you have no inclination to let me see your wife at all; so here I sit. (*Throws himself on a sofa.*) There's my hat, and here are my legs. Now I shan't stir till I have 50 seen her, and I have no engagements: I'll breakfast, dine, and sup with you every day this week.

SIR GEORGE. [*Aside.*]

Was there ever such a provoking wretch!—But to be plain with you, Doricourt, I and my house are at your service. But you are a damned agreeable fellow 55 and ten years younger than I am, and the women, I observe, always simper when you appear. For these reasons I had rather, when Lady Frances and I are together, that you should forget we are acquainted further than a nod, a smile, or a how-d'ye. 60

DORICOURT.

Very well.

SIR GEORGE.

It is not merely yourself in propria persona that I object to, but if you are intimate here, you'll make my house still more the fashion than it is, and it is already so much so that my doors are of no use 65 to me. I married Lady Frances to engross her to myself, yet such is the blessed freedom of modern manners that, in spite of me, her eyes, thoughts, and conversation are continually divided amongst all the flirts and coxcombs of fashion. 70

DORICOURT.

To be sure, I confess that kind of freedom is carried rather too far. 'Tis hard one can't have a jewel in one's cabinet but the whole Town must be gratified with its luster. (*Aside.*) He shan't preach me out of seeing his wife, though. 75

SIR GEORGE.

Well now, that's reasonable. When you take time to reflect, Doricourt, I always observe you decide right, and therefore I hope—

Enter servant.

SERVANT.

Sir, my lady desires—

SIR GEORGE.

I am particularly engaged. 80

DORICOURT. (*Leaping from the sofa.*)

Oh Lord, that shall be no excuse in the world. Lead the way, John. I'll attend your lady. (*Exit, following the servant.*)

SIR GEORGE.

What devil possessed me to talk about her!—Here, Doricourt! (*Running after him.*) Doricourt! 85

Enter Mrs. Racket and Miss Ogle, followed by a servant.

MRS. RACKET.

Acquaint your lady that Mrs. Racket and Miss Ogle are here.

Exit servant.

MISS OGLE.

I shall hardly know Lady Frances, 'tis so long since I was in Shropshire.

MRS. RACKET.

And I'll be sworn you never saw her out of 90 Shropshire. Her father kept her locked up with his caterpillars and shells and loved her beyond anything—but a blue butterfly and a petrified frog!

MISS OGLE.

Ha, ha, ha! Well, 'twas a cheap way of breeding her: you know he was very poor, though a lord, 95 and very high-spirited, though a virtuoso. In Town, her pantheons,* operas, and *robes de cour*,34 would have swallowed his seaweeds, moths, and monsters in six weeks. Sir George, I find, thinks his wife a most extraordinary creature: he has taught her to 100 despise everything like fashionable life and boasts that example will have no effect on her.

MRS. RACKET.

There's a great degree of impertinence in all that. I'll try to make her a fine lady to humble him.

MISS OGLE.

That's just the thing I wish. 105

Enter Lady Frances.

---

34 *robes de cour*] fashionable attire to wear at Court (Fr.)

LADY FRANCES.

I beg ten thousand pardons, my dear Mrs. Racket.—Miss Ogle, I rejoice to see you. I should have come to you sooner, but I was detained in conversation by Mr. Doricourt.

MRS. RACKET.

Pray make no apology; I am quite happy that we have your ladyship in Town at last. What stay do you make? 110

LADY FRANCES.

A short one! Sir George talks with regret of the scenes we have left and, as the ceremony of presentation[35] is over, will, I believe, soon return. 115

MISS OGLE.

Sure he can't be so cruel! Does your ladyship wish to return so soon?

LADY FRANCES.

I have not the habit of consulting my own wishes, but I think, if they decide, we shall not return immediately. I have yet hardly formed an idea of London. 120

MRS. RACKET.

I shall quarrel with your lord and master if he dares think of depriving us of you so soon. How do you dispose of yourself today?

LADY FRANCES.

Sir George is going with me this morning to the mercer's to choose a silk, and then— 125

MRS. RACKET.

Choose a silk for you! Ha, ha, ha! Sir George chooses your laces, too, I hope, your gloves and your pincushions!

LADY FRANCES.

Madam! 130

MRS. RACKET.

I am glad to see you blush, my dear Lady Frances. These are strange, homespun ways! If you do these things, pray keep them secret. Lord bless us, if the Town should know your husband chooses your gowns! 135

MISS OGLE.

You are very young, my lady, and have been brought up in solitude. The maxims you learnt among the wood nymphs in Shropshire won't pass

current here, I assure you.

MRS. RACKET.

Why my dear creature, you look quite frightened! Come, you shall go with us to an exhibition and an auction. Afterwards, we'll take a turn in the Park* and then drive to Kensington;* so we shall be at home by four to dress, and in the evening I'll attend you to Lady Brilliant's masquerade. 140

LADY FRANCES.

I shall be very happy to be of your party, if Sir George has no engagements.

MRS. RACKET.

What! Do you stand so low in your own opinion that you dare not trust yourself without Sir George? If you choose to play Darby and Joan,[36] my dear, you should have stayed in the country; 'tis an exhibition not calculated for London, I assure you! 150

MISS OGLE.

What! I suppose, my lady, you and Sir George will be seen pacing it comfortably round the canal,[37] arm and arm, and then go lovingly into the same carriage, dine tête-à-tête, spend the evening at piquet, and so go soberly to bed at eleven! Such a snug plan may do for an attorney and his wife, but for Lady Frances Touchwood, 'tis as unsuitable as linsey-woolsey or a black bonnet at the festino![38] 155 160

LADY FRANCES.

These are rather new doctrines to me! But my dear Mrs. Racket, you and Miss Ogle must judge of these things better than I can. As you observe, I am but young and may have caught absurd opinions. Here is Sir George! 165

Enter Sir George.

SIR GEORGE. (*Aside.*)

'Sdeath!* another room full!

35 ceremony of presentation] formal introduction at Court

36 Darby and Joan] John Darby (d. 1730) and wife Joan, originals for characters of Henry Woodfall's ballad "Darby and Joan; or, The Happy Old Couple"

37 the canal] A system of canals linking London with the rest of the country was begun in the late eighteenth century.

38 festino] a feast and party, sometimes including a masquerade

LADY FRANCES.

My love! Mrs. Racket and Miss Ogle.

MRS. RACKET.

Give you joy, Sir George. We came to rob you of
Lady Frances for a few hours. 170

SIR GEORGE.

A few hours!

LADY FRANCES.

Oh yes! I am going to an exhibition and an auction
and the Park* and Kensington and a thousand
places! It is quite ridiculous, I find, for married
people to be always together. We shall be laughed at! 175

SIR GEORGE.

I am astonished!—Mrs. Racket, what does the dear
creature mean?

MRS. RACKET.

Mean, Sir George! what she says, I imagine.

MISS OGLE.

Why, you know, sir, as Lady Frances had the
misfortune to be bred entirely in the country, she 180
cannot be supposed to be versed in fashionable life.

SIR GEORGE.

No, Heaven forbid she should! If she had, madam,
she would never have been my wife!

MRS. RACKET.

Are you serious?

SIR GEORGE.

Perfectly so. I should never have had the courage 185
to have married a well-bred, fine lady.

MISS OGLE. (Sneeringly.)

Pray sir, what do you take a fine lady to be, that
you express such fear of her?

SIR GEORGE.

A being easily described, madam, as she is seen
everywhere but in her own house. She sleeps at 190
home, but she lives all over the Town. In her mind,
every sentiment gives place to the lust of conquest
and the vanity of being particular. The feelings of
wife and mother are lost in the whirl of dissipation.
If she continues virtuous, 'tis by chance, and if she 195
preserves her husband from ruin, 'tis by her
dexterity at the card table! Such a woman I take
to be a perfect fine lady!

MRS. RACKET.

And you I take to be a slanderous cynic of two-and-
thirty. Twenty years hence, one might have forgiven 200

such a libel! Now sir, hear my definition of a fine
lady: she is a creature for whom nature has done
much and education more; she has taste, elegance,
spirit, understanding. In her manner she is free, in
her morals nice.* Her behavior is undistinguishingly 205
polite to her husband and all mankind; her
sentiments are for their hours of retirement. In a
word, a fine lady is the life of conversation, the spirit
of society, the joy of the public! Pleasure follows
wherever she appears, and the kindest wishes attend 210
her slumbers.—Make haste, then, my dear Lady
Frances, commence fine lady and force your
husband to acknowledge the justness of my picture!

LADY FRANCES.

I am sure 'tis a delightful one. How can you dislike
it, Sir George? You painted fashionable life in 215
colors so disgusting that I thought I hated it, but
on a nearer view, it seems charming. I have
hitherto lived in obscurity; 'tis time that I should
be a woman of the world. I long to begin; my heart
pants with expectation and delight! 220

MRS. RACKET.

Come then, let us begin directly. I am impatient
to introduce you to that society which you were
born to ornament and charm.

LADY FRANCES.

Adieu, my love! We shall meet again at dinner.
(Going.) 225

SIR GEORGE.

Sure, I am in a dream!—Fanny!

LADY FRANCES. (Returning.)

Sir George?

SIR GEORGE.

Will you go without me?

MRS. RACKET.

Will you go without me! Ha, ha, ha! What a
pathetic address! Why, sure you would not always 230
be seen side by side, like two beans upon a stalk.
Are you afraid to trust Lady Frances with me, sir?

SIR GEORGE.

Heaven and earth! with whom can a man trust his
wife in the present state of society? Formerly there
were distinctions of character amongst ye: every 235
class of females had its particular description.
Grandmothers were pious, aunts discreet, old
maids censorious. But now aunts, grandmothers,

girls, and maiden gentlewomen are all the same creature; a wrinkle more or less is the sole difference between ye. 240

MRS. RACKET.

That maiden gentlewomen have lost their censoriousness is surely not in your catalogue of grievances.

SIR GEORGE.

Indeed it is, and ranked amongst the most serious grievances. Things went well, madam, when the tongues of three or four old virgins kept all the wives and daughters of a parish in awe. They were the dragons that guarded the Hesperian fruit,[39] and I wonder they have not been obliged, by act of Parliament, to resume their function. 245 250

MRS. RACKET.

Ha, ha, ha! And pensioned, I suppose, for making strict enquiries into the lives and conversations* of their neighbors.

SIR GEORGE.

With all my heart, and empowered to oblige every woman to conform her conduct to her real situation. You, for instance, are a widow: your air should be sedate, your dress grave, your deportment matronly, and in all things an example to the young women growing up about you; instead of which, you are dressed for conquest, think of nothing but ensnaring hearts, are a coquette, a wit, and a fine lady. 255 260

MRS. RACKET.

Bear witness to what he says! A coquette! a wit! and a fine lady! Who would have expected a eulogy from such an ill-natured mortal? Valor to a soldier, wisdom to a judge, or glory to a prince is not more than such a character* to a woman. 265

MISS OGLE.

Sir George, I see, languishes for the charming society of a century and a half ago, when a grave squire and a still graver dame, surrounded by a sober family, formed a stiff group in a moldy old house in the corner of a park. 270

---

39 dragons … Hesperian fruit] In Greek mythology, Hera had to place a dragon who never slept to protect her tree of golden apples from the Hesperides, the singing daughters of Atlas.

MRS. RACKET.

Delightful serenity! Undisturbed by any noise but the cawing of rooks and the quarterly rumbling of an old family coach on a state visit, with the happy intervention of a friendly call from the parish apothecary or the curate's wife. 275

SIR GEORGE.

And what is the society of which you boast? A mere* chaos in which all distinction of rank is lost in a ridiculous affectation of ease and every different order of beings huddled together as they were before the creation. In the same *select party*, you will often find the wife of a bishop and a sharper, of an earl and a fiddler. In short, 'tis one universal masquerade, all disguised in the same habits and manners. 280 285

[Enter servant.]

SERVANT.

Mr. Flutter. (*Exit.*)

SIR GEORGE.

Here comes an illustration. Now I defy you to tell from his appearance whether Flutter is a privy counselor or a mercer, a lawyer, or a grocer's prentice. 290

Enter Flutter.

FLUTTER.

Oh, just which you please, Sir George, so you don't make me a Lord Mayor.—Ah, Mrs. Racket!—Lady Frances, your most obedient, you look—now hang me, if that's not provoking—had your gown been of another color, I should have said the prettiest thing you ever heard in your life. 295

MISS OGLE.

Pray give it us.

FLUTTER.

I was yesterday at Mrs. Bloomer's. She was dressed all in green; no other color to be seen but that of her face and bosom. So says I, "My dear Mrs. Bloomer! you look like a carnation just bursting from its pod." 300

SIR GEORGE.

And what said her husband?

FLUTTER.

Her husband! Why, her husband laughed and said a cucumber* would have been a happier simile. 305

SIR GEORGE.

But there *are* husbands, sir, who would rather have corrected than amended your comparison. I, for instance, should consider a man's complimenting my wife as an impertinence. 310

FLUTTER.

Why, what harm can there be in compliments? Sure they are not infectious, and, if they were, you, Sir George, of all people breathing, have reason to be satisfied about your lady's attachment. Everybody talks of it: that little bird there that she 315 killed out of jealousy, the most extraordinary instance of affection that ever was given.

LADY FRANCES.

I kill a bird through jealousy! Heavens! Mr. Flutter, how can you impute such a cruelty to me?

SIR GEORGE.

I could have forgiven you, if you had. 320

FLUTTER.

Oh, what a blundering fool! No, no—now I remember—it was your bird, Lady Frances—that's it, your bullfinch, which Sir George, in one of the refinements of his passion, sent into the wide world to seek its fortune. He took it for a knight 325 in disguise.

LADY FRANCES.

Is it possible! Oh Sir George, could I have imagined it was you who deprived me of a creature I was so fond of?

SIR GEORGE.

Mr. Flutter, you are one of those busy, idle, 330 meddling people who, from mere* vacuity of mind are the most dangerous inmates in a family. You have neither feelings nor opinions of your own but, like a glass in a tavern, bear about those of every blockhead who gives you his. And because you 335 *mean* no harm, think yourselves excused though broken friendships, discords, and murders are the consequences of your indiscretions.

FLUTTER. (*Taking out his tablets.*)

Vacuity of mind!—What was the next? I'll write down this sermon; 'tis the first I have heard since 340 my grandmother's funeral.

MISS OGLE.

Come Lady Frances, you see what a cruel creature your loving husband can be. So let us leave him.

SIR GEORGE.

Madam, Lady Frances shall not go.

LADY FRANCES.

Shall not, Sir George? This is the first time such 345 an expression— (*Weeping.*)

SIR GEORGE.

My love! my life!

LADY FRANCES.

Don't imagine I'll be treated like a child, denied what I wish and then pacified with sweet words.

MISS OGLE. (*Apart.*)

The bullfinch! that's an excellent subject; never let 350 it down.

LADY FRANCES.

I see plainly you would deprive me of every pleasure, as well as of my sweet bird, out of pure love! Barbarous man!

SIR GEORGE.

'Tis well, madam: your resentment of that 355 circumstance proves to me what I did not before suspect, that you are deficient both in tenderness and understanding. Tremble to think the hour approaches in which you would give worlds for such a proof of my love. Go madam, give yourself 360 to the public, abandon your heart to dissipation, and see if, in the scenes of gaiety and folly that await you, you can find a recompense for the lost affection of a doting husband. (*Exit.*)

FLUTTER.

Lord! what a fine thing it is to have the gift of speech! 365 I suppose Sir George practices at Coachmakers-hall[40] or the Black Horse in Bond Street.[41]

LADY FRANCES.

He is really angry. I cannot go.

MRS. RACKET.

Not go! Foolish creature! You are arrived at the moment which some time or other was sure to 370

---

[40] Coachmakers Hall] The hall for the coachmakers guild, in 1780 the site of a fiery speech by Lord George Gordon commencing the Gordon Riots in response to a Parliamentary act granting more tolerance to Roman Catholics

[41] Black Horse on Bond Street] The pubs often hosted weekly oratorical events with announced topics, at which all were free to speak.

happen, and everything depends on the use you make of it.

MISS OGLE.

Come, Lady Frances! Don't hesitate: the minutes are precious.

LADY FRANCES.

I could find in my heart—and yet I won't give up 375 neither. If I should in this instance, he'll expect it forever.

Exeunt Lady Frances and Mrs. Racket.

MISS OGLE.

Now you act like a woman of spirit. (*Exit.*)

FLUTTER.

A fair tug, by Jupiter*—between Duty and Pleasure! Pleasure beats and off we go, *Iö* 380 *triumphe!*[42] (*Exit.*)

　　　Scene [ii].[h] An auction room,
　　　　with busts, pictures, etc.

Enter Silvertongue with [Mrs. Fagg, Mask, and another] puffer.[43]

SILVERTONGUE.

Very well, very well. This morning will be devoted to curiosity; my sale begins tomorrow at eleven. But Mrs. Fagg, if you do no better than you did in Lord Fillagree's sale, I shall discharge you. You want* a knack terribly. And this dress: why, 5 nobody can mistake you for a gentlewoman.

MRS. FAGG.

Very true, Mr. Silvertongue, but I can't dress like a lady upon half-a-crown a day, as the saying is. If you want me to dress like a lady, you must double my pay. Double or quits, Mr. Silvertongue. 10

SILVERTONGUE.

Five shillings a day! what a demand! Why woman, there are a thousand parsons in the Town who don't make five shillings a day, though they preach, pray, christen, marry, and bury for the good of the community. Five shillings a day! Why, 'tis the pay 15 of a lieutenant in a marching regiment, who keeps a servant, a mistress, a horse; fights, dresses, ogles, makes love,* and dies upon five shillings a day.

MRS. FAGG.

Oh as to that, all that's very right. A soldier should not be too fond of life, and forcing him to do all 20 these things upon five shillings a day is the readiest way to make him tired on't.

SILVERTONGUE.

Well, Mask, have you been looking into the antiquaries? Have you got all the terms of art in a string, aye? 25

MASK.

Yes, I have: I know the age of a coin by the taste and can fix the birthday of a medal, anno mundi or anno Domini, though the green rust should have eaten up every character. But you know, the brown suit and the wig I wear when I personate 30 the antiquary are in limbo.

SILVERTONGUE.

Those you have on may do.

MASK.

These! Why, in these I am a young traveled cognoscente. Mr. Glib bought them of Sir Tom Totter's valet, and I am going there directly. You 35 know his picture sale comes on today, and I have got my head full of Parmegiano, Sal Rosa, Metzu, Tarback, and Vandermeer.[44] I talk of the relief of Woovermans, the spirit of Teniers, the coloring of the Venetian School, and the correctness of the 40 Roman.[45] I distinguish Claude by his sheep and

---

42　*Iö triumphe*] hurrah, triumph: the cry of soldiers and spectators greeting a triumphal procession in ancient Rome (Lat.)

43　puffers] bidders hired by auctions to exaggerate the value and pretend interest in items in order to drive up the bidding

44　Parmegiano … Vandermeer] Parmigianino (real name Francesco Mazzola, 1503-1540), Italian artist; Sal Rosa: Salvatore Rosa (1615-1673), Neopolitan artist; Metzu: Gabriel Metsu (1629-1667), Dutch artist; Tarbaek: Gerard Terborch (1617-1667), Dutch artist; and Vandermeer: Jan Vermeer (1632-75), Dutch genre painter

45　Woovermans … Roman] Phillips Wouwermans (1619-68), Dutch Baroque painter; Teniers: David Teniers the Younger (1610-90), Flemish Baroque painter; the Venetian School: school of painting in Venice in the later 15th century, exploring color, light, and the sensuous rendering of surface texture; the Roman: Counter-

Ruysdael by his water.[46] The rapidity of Tintoret's pencil strikes me at the first glance, whilst the harmony of Vandyke and the glow of Correggio point out their masters.[47]   45

Enter company.

FIRST LADY.
Heyday, Mr. Silvertongue! what, nobody here?

SILVERTONGUE.
Oh my lady, we shall have company enough in a trice; if your carriage is seen at my door, no other will pass it, I am sure.

FIRST LADY. (*Aside.*)
Familiar monster!—That's a beautiful Diana, Mr.   50
Silvertongue, but in the name of wonder, how came Actaeon to be placed on the top of a house?

SILVERTONGUE.
That's a David and Bathsheba,[48] ma'am.

FIRST LADY.
Oh, I crave their pardon! I remember the names but know nothing of the story.   55

More company enters.

FIRST GENTLEMAN.
Was not that Lady Frances Touchwood coming up with Mrs. Racket?

SECOND GENTLEMAN.
I think so—yes, it is, faith. Let us go nearer.

Enter Lady Frances, Mrs. Racket, and Miss Ogle.

Reformation style developed in Rome synthesizing Renaissance, Michelangelesque, Mannerist, and Baroque elements and stressing down-to-earth subjects

[46] Claude ... water] Claude Lorrain (1600-82), French landscape painter, noted for pastorals; Ruysdael: Jacob van Ruisdael (1628-82), Dutch landscape painter, noted for waterfalls and marshes

[47] Tintoret] Jacopo Robusti Tintoretto (1518-94), Italian Mannerist painter; Vandyke: Anthony van Dyck (1599-1641), Flemish religious and narrative painter who spent much of his career in England as artist to Charles I; Correggio: Antonio Allegri Correggio (1489-1534), Italian painter of the high Renaissance

[48] David and Bathsheba] Hebrew King David spied from his roof the beautiful bathing Bathsheba, wife of Uriah the Hittite, lusted after her, had her husband killed in battle, and married her (2 Samuel 11: 2-27).

SILVERTONGUE.
Yes sir, this is to be the first lot: the model of a city in wax.   60

SECOND GENTLEMAN.
The model of a city! What city?

SILVERTONGUE.
That I have not been able to discover, but call it Rome, Peking, or London, 'tis still a city: you'll find in it the same jarring interests, the same passions, the same virtues and the same vices,   65
whatever the name.

[FIRST] GENTLEMAN.
You may as well present us a map of terra incognita.

SILVERTONGUE.
Oh pardon me, sir! a lively imagination would convert this waxen city into an endless and interesting amusement. For instance, look into this little   70
house on the right hand; there are four old prudes in it taking care of their neighbors' reputations. This elegant mansion on the left, decorated with Corinthian pillars: Who needs to told that it belongs to a Court lord and is the habitation of patriotism,   75
philosophy, and virtue? Here's a City Hall: the rich steams that issue from the windows nourish a neighboring workhouse. Here's a church: we'll pass over that, the doors are shut. The parsonage-house comes next; we'll take a peep here, however. Look at   80
the doctor! He's asleep on a volume of Toland,[49] whilst his lady is putting on rouge for the masquerade. Oh! oh! this can be no English city; our parsons are all orthodox and their wives the daughters of modesty and meekness.   85

Lady Frances and Miss Ogle come forward, followed by Courtall.

LADY FRANCES.
I wish Sir George was here. This man follows me about and stares at me in such a way that I am quite uneasy.

MISS OGLE.
He has traveled and is heir to an immense estate,

---

[49] Toland] John Toland (1670-1722), English deistic philosopher, offered a purely rational defense of God's existence.

so he's impertinent by patent. 90

COURTALL.

You are very cruel, ladies. Miss Ogle, you will not let me speak to you. As to this little scornful beauty, she has frowned me dead fifty times.

LADY FRANCES. (*Confused.*)

Sir—I am a married woman.

COURTALL. (*Aside.*)

A married woman! a good hint.—'Twould be a 95 shame if such a charming woman was not married. But I see you are a Daphne just come from your sheep and your meadows, your crook and your waterfalls. Pray now, who is the happy Damon[50] to whom you have vowed eternal truth and constancy? 100

MISS OGLE.

'Tis Lady Frances Touchwood, Mr. Courtall, to whom you are speaking.

COURTALL. (*Aside.*)

Lady Frances! By Heaven, that's Saville's old flame.— —I beg your ladyship's pardon. I ought to have believed that such beauty could belong only to 105 your name, a name I have long been enamored of because I knew it to be that of the finest woman in the world.

Mrs. Racket comes forward.

LADY FRANCES. (*Apart.*)

My dear Mrs. Racket, I am so frightened! Here's a man making love* to me, though he knows I am 110 married.

MRS. RACKET.

Oh, the sooner for that, my dear. Don't mind him.—Was you at the Casino last night, Mr. Courtall?

COURTALL.

I looked in. 'Twas impossible to stay. Nobody there 115 but antiques. You'll be at Lady Brilliant's tonight, doubtless?

MRS RACKET.

Yes, I go with Lady Frances.

LADY FRANCES. (*To Miss Ogle.*)

Bless me! I did not know this gentleman was acquainted with Mrs. Racket. I behaved so rude 120 to him!

―――――――――

50 Daphne ... Damon] stereotypical pastoral names

MRS. RACKET. (*Looking at her watch.*)

Come ma'am, 'tis past one. I protest, if we don't fly to Kensington we shan't find a soul there.

LADY FRANCES.

Won't this gentleman go with us?

COURTALL. (*Looking surprised.*)

To be sure. You make me happy, madam, beyond 125 description.

MRS. RACKET.

Oh, never mind him, he'll follow.

Exeunt Lady Frances, Mrs. Racket, and Miss Ogle.

COURTALL.

Lady *Touchwood*! with a vengeance! But 'tis always so: your reserved ladies are like ice, egad, no sooner begin to soften than they melt. 130

[Exit following.]

Act III, scene i. Mr. Hardy's.

Enter Letitia and Mrs. Racket.

MRS. RACKET.

Come, prepare, prepare, your lover is coming.

LETITIA.

My lover! Confess now that my absence at dinner was a severe mortification to him.

MRS. RACKET.

I can't absolutely swear it spoilt his appetite; he ate as if he was hungry and drank his wine as though 5 he liked it.

LETITIA.

What was the apology?

MRS. RACKET.

That you were ill. But I gave him a hint that your extreme bashfulness could not support his eye.

LETITIA.

If I comprehend him, awkwardness and 10 bashfulness are the last faults he can pardon in a woman, so expect to see me transformed into the veriest malkin.

MRS. RACKET.

You persevere then?

LETITIA.

Certainly. I know the design is a rash one and the 15 event important. It either makes Doricourt mine by all the tenderest ties of passion or deprives me of him forever, and never to be his wife will afflict me less than to be his wife and not be beloved.

MRS. RACKET.

So you won't trust to the good old maxim, "Marry first, and love will follow?" 20

LETITIA.

As readily as I would venture my last guinea that good fortune might follow. The woman that has not touched the heart of a man before he leads her to the altar has scarcely a chance to charm it when 25 possession and security turn their powerful arms against her.—But here he comes. I'll disappear for a moment. Don't spare me. (*Exit.*)

Enter Doricourt (not seeing Mrs. Racket).

DORICOURT. (*Looking at a picture.*)

So, this is my mistress, I presume. Ma foi, the painter has hit her off: the downcast eye, the 30 blushing cheek, timid, apprehensive, bashful. A tear and a prayer book would have made her *La Bella Magdalena.*[51]

Give *me* a woman in whose touching mien
A mind, a soul, a polished art is seen, 35
Whose motion speaks, whose poignant air can move.
Such are the darts to wound with endless love.

MRS. RACKET. (*Touching him on the shoulder with her fan.*)

Is that an impromptu?

DORICOURT. (*Starting.*)

Madam! (*Aside.*) Finely caught!—Not absolutely, it struck me during the dessert as a motto for your 40 picture.

MRS. RACKET.

Gallantly turned! I perceive, however, Miss Hardy's charms have made no violent impression on you. And who can wonder? The poor girl's defects are so obvious. 45

DORICOURT.

Defects!

MRS. RACKET.

Merely those of education. Her father's indulgence ruined her. *Mauvaise honte,*[52] conceit, and ignorance—all unite in the lady you are to marry.

DORICOURT.

Marry! I marry such a woman? Your picture, I 50 hope, is overcharged. I marry *mauvaise honte,* pertness, and ignorance!

MRS. RACKET.

Thank your stars that ugliness and ill temper are not added to the list. You must think her handsome?

DORICOURT.

Half her personal beauty would content me, but 55 could the Medicean Venus[53] be animated for me and endowed with a vulgar soul, *I* should become the statue and my heart transformed to marble.

MRS. RACKET.

Bless us! We are in a hopeful way then!

DORICOURT. (*Aside.*)

There must be some envy in this! I see she is a 60 coquette.—Ha, ha, ha! And you imagine I am persuaded of the truth of your character?* Ha, ha, ha! Miss Hardy, I have been assured, madam, is elegant and accomplished. But one must allow for a lady's painting. 65

MRS. RACKET. (*Aside.*)

I'll be even with him for that.—Ha, ha, ha! And so you have found me out! Well, I protest I meant no harm; 'twas only to increase the éclat of her appearance that I threw a veil over her charms.— Here comes the lady; her elegance and accomplish- 70 ments will announce themselves.

Enter Letitia, running.

LETITIA.

La, cousin, do you know that our John— Oh, dear heart!—I didn't see you, sir. (*Hanging down her head and dropping behind Mrs. Racket.*)

MRS. RACKET.

Fie, Letitia! Mr. Doricourt thinks you a woman of 75

---

51 *La Bella Magdalena*] The character type-and favorite trope in Renaissance painting—of the penitent Magdalen derives from a confusion of three figures in the Gospels, one of them the sinner who washes Jesus's feet in Luke 7:37-38.

52 *mauvaise honte*] extreme bashfulness (Fr.)
53 Medicean Venus] Venus de Medici, classical statue discovered in many pieces during the 17th century near Tivoli

elegant manners. Stand forward and confirm his
opinion.

LETITIA.

No, no, keep before me. He's my sweetheart, and
'tis impudent to look one's sweetheart in the face,
you know.

MRS. RACKET.

You'll allow in future for a lady's painting, sir. Ha,
ha, ha!

DORICOURT.

I am astonished!

LETITIA.

Well hang it, I'll take heart. Why, he is but a man,
you know, cousin, and I'll let him see I wasn't born in
a wood to be scared by an owl. (*Half apart, advances,
and looks at him through her fingers.*) He, he, he!

*Goes up to him and makes a very stiff formal curtsy.
He bows.*

You have been a great traveler, sir, I hear?

DORICOURT.

Yes madam.

LETITIA.

Then I wish you'd tell us about the fine sights you
saw when you went oversea. I have read in a book
that there are some countries where the men and
women are all horses.[54] Did you see any of them?

MRS. RACKET.

Mr. Doricourt is not prepared, my dear, for these
enquiries; he is reflecting on the importance of the
question and will answer you—when he can.

LETITIA.

When he can! Why, he's as slow in speech as Aunt
Margery when she's reading Thomas Aquinas and
stands gaping like mumchance.[55]

MRS. RACKET.

Have a little discretion.

LETITIA.

Hold your tongue! Sure I may say what I please
before I am married, if I can't afterwards. Do ye
think a body does not know how to talk to a
sweetheart? He is not the first I have had.

DORICOURT.

Indeed!

LETITIA.

Oh Lud!* he speaks!—Why, if you must know—
there was the curate at home. When Papa was a-
hunting, he used to come a-suitoring and make
speeches to me out of books. Nobody knows what
a *mort* of fine things he used to say to me—and
call me Venis, and Jubah, and Dinah![56]

DORICOURT.

And pray, fair lady, how did you answer him?

LETITIA.

Why, I used to say, "Look you, Mr. Curate, don't
think to come over me with your flimflams, for a
better man than ever trod in your shoes is coming
oversea to marry me." But i'fags!* I begin to think
I was out. Parson Dobbins was the sprightfuller
man of the two.

DORICOURT.

Surely this cannot be Miss Hardy!

LETITIA.

Laws! Why, don't you know me! You saw me
today—but I was daunted before my father and
the lawyer and all them, and did not care to speak
out, so, maybe, you thought I couldn't. But I can
talk as fast as anybody when I know folks a little,
and now I have shown my parts,* I hope you'll like
me better.

Enter Hardy.

HARDY.

I foresee this won't do!—Mr. Doricourt, maybe
you take my daughter for a fool, but you are
mistaken. She's a sensible girl as any in England.

DORICOURT.

I am convinced she has a very uncommon
understanding, sir. (*Aside.*) I did not think he had
been such an ass.

LETITIA. [*Aside.*]

My father will undo the whole.—Laws, Papa, how
can you think he can take me for a fool, when
everybody knows I beat the potecary[57] at conun-

---

54 men … horses] allusion to *Gulliver's Travels*, pt. 4

55 mumchance] a game of dice where silence is indispensable

56 Venis, Jubah, Dinah] probably corrupted versions of Venus, Jubal, and Diana

57 potecary] corruption of apothecary

drums last Christmastime? and didn't I make a string of names, all in riddles, for the lady's diary? There was a little river and a great house: that was Newcastle. There was what a lamb says and three letters: that was *Ba*, and *k-e-r*, ker, Baker. There was— 140

HARDY.

Don't stand ba-a-ing there. You'll make me mad in a moment!—I tell you, sir, that for all that, she's devilish sensible.

DORICOURT.

Sir, I give all possible credit to your assertions.

LETITIA.

Laws, Papa, do come along. If you stand watching, 145 how can my sweetheart break his mind and tell me how he admires me?

DORICOURT.

That would be difficult, indeed, madam.

HARDY.

I tell you, Letty, I'll have no more of this. I see well enough— 150

LETITIA.

Laws! don't snub me before my husband-that-is-to-be. You'll teach him to snub me, too. And I believe, by his looks, he'd like to begin now. So, let us go.—Cousin, you may tell the gentleman what a genus[58] I have: how I can cut watch 155 papers[59] and work catgut, make quadrille baskets[60] with pins, and take profiles in shade,[61] aye, as well as the lady at No. 62, South Moulton Street, Grosvenor Square.*

Exit Hardy and Letitia.

MRS. RACKET.

What think you of my painting now? 160

DORICOURT.

Oh, mere watercolors, madam! The lady has caricatured your picture.

---

58 genus] corruption of genius
59 watch papers] small circles, cut from pretty paper, silk, or satin, which replaced the ordinary papers that kept the dust out of pocket watches; often intricately ornamented love tokens
60 quadrille baskets] baskets quadrilled, marked with squares
61 take profiles in shade] make silhouettes

MRS. RACKET.

And how does she strike you on the whole?

DORICOURT.

Like a good design, spoilt by the incapacity of the artist. Her faults are evidently the result of her 165 father's weak indulgence. I observed an expression in her eye that seemed to satirize the folly of her lips.

MRS. RACKET.

But at her age, when education is fixed, and manner becomes nature, hopes of improvement—

DORICOURT.

Would be as rational as hopes of gold from a 170 juggler's[62] crucible. Doricourt's wife must be incapable of improvement, but it must be because she's got beyond it.

MRS. RACKET.

I am pleased your misfortune sits no heavier.

DORICOURT.

Your pardon, madam, so mercurial was the hour 175 in which I was born that misfortunes always go plump to the bottom of my heart like a pebble in water and leave the surface unruffled. I shall certainly set off for Bath, or the other world, tonight, but whether I shall use a chaise with four 180 swift coursers, or go off in a tangent from the aperture of a pistol, deserves consideration. So I make my adieus. (*Going.*)

MRS. RACKET.

Oh but I entreat you, postpone your journey till tomorrow. Determine on which you will—you 185 must be this night at the masquerade.

DORICOURT.

Masquerade!

MRS. RACKET.

Why not? If you resolve to visit the other world, you may as well take one night's pleasure first in this, you know. 190

DORICOURT.

Faith, that's very true; ladies are the best philosophers, after all. Expect me at the masquerade. (*Exit.*)

MRS. RACKET.

He's a charming fellow. I think Letitia shan't have him. (*Going.*) 195

---

62 juggler] trickster, in this case an alchemist

Enter Hardy.

HARDY.

What, 's he gone?

MRS. RACKET.

Yes, and I am glad he is. You would have ruined us! Now I beg, Mr. Hardy, you won't interfere in this business; it is a little out of your way. (*Exit.*)

HARDY.

Hang me, if I don't though. I foresee very clearly   200
what will be the end of it if I leave ye to yourselves.
So I'll e'en follow him to the masquerade and tell
him all about it. Let me see. What shall my dress
be? A great mogul? No. A grenadier? No, no, that,
I foresee, would make a laugh. Hang me, if I don't   205
send to my favorite little Quick,[63] and borrow his
Jew Isaac's[64] dress. I know the dog likes a glass of
good wine, so I'll give him a bottle of my forty-
eight[65] and he shall teach me. Aye, that's it: I'll
be cunning little Isaac! If they complain of my   210
want* of wit, I'll tell 'em the cursed Duenna wears
the breeches[66] and has spoilt my parts.

Exit.

Scene ii. Courtall's.

Enter Courtall, Saville, and three others from an apartment in the back scene. (The last three tipsy.)

COURTALL.

You shan't go yet. Another catch and another
bottle!

FIRST GENTLEMAN.

May I be a bottle, and an empty bottle, if you
catch me at that! Why, I am going to the
masquerade. Jack ____,* you know who I mean,   5
is to meet me, and we are to have a leap at the
new lusters.

---

63 Quick] John Quick (d.1831), character actor at Covent
Garden Theatre, originated the part of Hardy, and so
spoke this line about himself

64 Jew Isaac] the character of Isaac Mendoza in *The Duenna*
by Richard Brinsley Sheridan, also played by John Quick

65 forty-eight] vintage of his best wine

66 cursed Duenna wears the breeches] in the play, Mendoza
is tricked into marrying Margaret, the old duenna (chap-
erone), instead of her beautiful young charge

SECOND GENTLEMAN.

And I am going, too—a Harlequin—(*Hiccups.*)
Am not I in a pretty pickle to make
Harlequinades? And Tony, here—he is going in the   10
disguise—in the disguise—of a gentleman!

FIRST GENTLEMAN.

We are all very disguised;* so bid them draw up.
Do ye hear! (*Exeunt the three gentlemen.*)

SAVILLE.

Thy skull, Courtall, is a lady's thimble. No, an
eggshell.   15

COURTALL.

Nay, then you are gone too; you never aspire to
similes but in your cups.

SAVILLE.

No, no, I am steady enough, but the fumes of the
wine pass directly through thy eggshell and leave
thy brain as cool as— Hey! I am quite sober: my   20
similes fail me.

COURTALL.

Then we'll sit down here and have one sober
bottle.—Bring a table and glasses.

SAVILLE.

I'll not swallow another drop, no, though the juice
should be the true Falernian.[67]   25

COURTALL.

By the bright eyes of her you love, you shall drink
her health.

SAVILLE.

Ah! (*Sitting down.*) Her I loved is gone. (*Sighing.*)
She's married!

COURTALL.

Then bless your stars you are not her husband! I   30
would be husband to no woman in Europe who
was not devilish rich and devilish ugly.

SAVILLE.

Wherefore ugly?

COURTALL.

Because she could not have the conscience to exact
those attentions that a pretty wife expects. Or if   35
she should, her resentments would be perfectly
easy to me; nobody would undertake to revenge
her cause.

---

67 Falernian] choice Italian wine celebrated in classical literature

SAVILLE.

Thou art a most licentious fellow!

COURTALL.

I should hate my own wife, that's certain. But I 40
have a warm heart for those of other people, and
so here's to the prettiest wife in England—Lady
Frances Touchwood.

SAVILLE.

Lady Frances Touchwood! I rise to drink her.
(*Drinks.*) How the devil came Lady Frances in your 45
head? I never knew you give[68] a woman of chastity
before.

COURTALL.

That's odd, for you have heard me give half the
women of fashion in England. But pray now,
(*Sneeringly.*) what do you take a woman of chastity 50
to be?

SAVILLE.

Such a woman as Lady Frances Touchwood, sir.

COURTALL.

Oh, you are grave, sir. I remember you was an
adorer of hers. Why didn't you marry her?

SAVILLE.

I had not the arrogance to look so high. Had my 55
fortune been worthy of her, she should not have
been ignorant of my admiration.

COURTALL.

Precious fellow! What, I suppose you would not
dare tell her now that you admire her?

SAVILLE.

No, nor you. 60

COURTALL.

By the Lord, I have told her so.

SAVILLE.

Have! impossible!

COURTALL.

Ha, ha, ha! Is it so?

SAVILLE.

How did she receive the declaration?

COURTALL.

Why, in the old way: blushed and frowned and 65
said she was married.

SAVILLE.

What amazing things thou art capable of! I could

___

68 give] toast

more easily have taken the Pope by the beard than
profaned her ears with such a declaration.

COURTALL.

I shall meet her at Lady Brilliant's tonight, where 70
I shall repeat it. And I'll lay my life, under a mask,
she'll hear it all without blush or frown.

SAVILLE. (*Rising.*)

'Tis false, sir! She won't.

COURTALL. (*Rising.*)

She will! Nay, I'd venture to lay a round sum that
I prevail on her to go out with me—only to taste 75
the fresh air, I mean.

SAVILLE.

Preposterous vanity! From this moment I suspect
that half the victories you have boasted are false and
slanderous as your pretended influence with Lady
Frances. 80

COURTALL.

Pretended! How should such a fellow as you, now,
who never soared beyond a cherry-cheeked daughter
of a ploughman in Norfolk, judge of the influence
of a man of my figure and habits? I could show thee
a list in which there are names to shake thy faith in 85
the whole sex! And to that list I have no doubt of
adding the name of Lady—

SAVILLE.

Hold, sir! My ears cannot bear the profanation. You
cannot, dare not approach her! For your soul you
dare not mention love to her! Her look would freeze 90
the word whilst it hovered on thy licentious lips!

COURTALL.

Hoo hoo! Well, we shall see. This evening, by
Jupiter, the trial shall be made. If I fail, I fail.

SAVILLE.

I think thou darest not! But my life, my honor on
her purity. (*Exit.*) 95

COURTALL.

Hotheaded fool! (*Musing.*) But since he has
brought it to this point, by Gad I'll try what can
be done with her ladyship.[i] (*Rings.*) She's frostwork,
and the prejudices of education yet strong; ergo,
passionate professions will only inflame her pride 100
and put her on her guard. For other arts then!

Enter Dick.

Dick, do you know any of the servants at Sir
George Touchwood's?

DICK.

Yes sir, I knows the groom and one of the
housemaids; for the matter o'that, she's my own 105
cousin. And it was my mother that helped her to
the place.

COURTALL.

Do you know Lady Frances's maid?

DICK.

I can't say as how I know she.

COURTALL.

Do you know Sir George's valet? 110

DICK.

No sir, but Sally is very thick with Mr. Gibson,
Sir George's gentleman.

COURTALL.

Then go there, directly, and employ Sally to
discover* whether her master goes to Lady
Brilliant's this evening. And if he does, the name 115
of the shop that sold his habit.

DICK.

Yes sir.

COURTALL.

Be exact in your intelligence and come to me at
Boodle's.[69]

Exit Dick.

If I cannot otherwise succeed, I'll beguile her as 120
Jove did Alcmene, in the shape of her husband.
The possession of so fine a woman, the triumph
over Saville, are each a sufficient motive––and
united they shall be resistless.

Exit.

Scene iii. The street.

Enter Saville.

SAVILLE.

The air has recovered me! What have I been doing!
Perhaps my petulance may be the cause of her ruin,
whose honor I asserted. His vanity is piqued, and
where women are concerned, Courtall can be a
villain. 5

Enter Dick. Bows and passes hastily.

Hah! That's his servant!––Dick!

---

69 Boodle's] gentlemen's club on St James's Street

DICK. (*Returning.*)

Sir.

SAVILLE.

Where are you going, Dick?

DICK.

Going! I am going, sir, where my master sent me.

SAVILLE.

Well answered. But I have a particular reason for 10
my enquiry, and you must tell me.

DICK.

Why then sir, I am going to call upon a cousin of
mine that lives at Sir George Touchwood's.

SAVILLE.

Very well. (*Gives him money.*) There, you must
make your cousin drink my health. What are you 15
going about?

DICK.

Why sir, I believe 'tis no harm, or elseways I am
sure I would not blab. I am only going to ax if Sir
George goes to the masquerade tonight and what
dress he wears. 20

SAVILLE.

Enough! Now Dick, if you will call at my lodgings
in your way back and acquaint me with your
cousin's intelligence, I'll double the trifle I have
given you.

DICK.

Bless your honor, I'll call, never fear. (*Exit.*) 25

SAVILLE.

Surely the occasion may justify the means; 'tis
doubly my duty to be Lady Frances's protector.
Courtall, I see, is planning an artful scheme, but
Saville shall outplot him.

Exit.

Scene iv. Sir George Touchwood's.

Enter Sir George and Villers.

VILLERS.

For shame, Sir George! You have left Lady Frances
in tears. How can you afflict her?

SIR GEORGE.

'Tis I that am afflicted; my dream of happiness is
over. Lady Frances and I are disunited.

VILLERS.

The devil! Why, you have been in Town but ten 5

days. She can have made no acquaintance for a Commons* affair yet.

SIR GEORGE.

Faugh! 'Tis our minds that are disunited. She no longer places her whole delight in me; she has yielded herself up to the world! 10

VILLERS.

Yielded herself up to the world! Why did you not bring her to Town in a cage? Then she might have taken a peep at the world! But after all, what has the world done? A twelvemonth since you was the gayest fellow in it. If anybody asked, "Who dresses 15 best?" Sir George Touchwood. "Who is the most gallant man?" Sir George Touchwood. "Who is the most wedded to amusement and dissipation?" Sir George Touchwood. And now Sir George is metamorphosed into a sour censor and talks of 20 fashionable life with as much bitterness as the old crabbed fellow in Rome.[70]

SIR GEORGE.

The moment I became possessed of such a jewel as Lady Frances, everything wore a different complexion: that society in which I lived with so 25 much éclat became the object of my terror, and I think of the manners of polite life as I do of the atmosphere of a pesthouse. My wife is already infected; she was set upon this morning by maids, widows, and bachelors who carried her off in 30 triumph, in spite of my displeasure.

VILLERS.

Aye, to be sure, there would have been no triumph in the case if you had not opposed it. But I have heard the whole story from Mrs. Racket, and I assure you, Lady Frances didn't enjoy the morning 35 at all. She wished for you fifty times.

SIR GEORGE.

Indeed! Are you sure of that?

VILLERS.

Perfectly sure.

SIR GEORGE.

I wish I had known it. My uneasiness at dinner

was occasioned by very different ideas. 40

VILLERS.

Here then she comes to receive your apology. But if she is true woman, her displeasure will rise in proportion to your contrition, and till you grow careless about her pardon, she won't grant it. However, I'll leave you. Matrimonial duets are 45 seldom set in the style I like. (*Exit.*)

Enter Lady Frances.

SIR GEORGE. (*Embracing her.*)

The sweet sorrow that glitters in these eyes, I cannot bear. Look cheerfully, you rogue.

LADY FRANCES.

I cannot look otherwise, if you are pleased with me. 50

SIR GEORGE.

Well Fanny, today you made your entrée in the fashionable world. Tell me honestly the impressions you received.

LADY FRANCES.

Indeed Sir George, I was so hurried from place to place that I had not time to find out what my 55 impressions were.

SIR GEORGE.

That's the very spirit of the life you have chosen.

LADY FRANCES.

Everybody about me seemed happy—but everybody seemed in a hurry to be happy somewhere else. 60

SIR GEORGE.

And you like this?

LADY FRANCES.

One must like what the rest of the world likes.

SIR GEORGE.

Pernicious maxim!

LADY FRANCES.

But my dear Sir George, you have not promised to go with me to the masquerade. 65

SIR GEORGE.

'Twould be a shocking indecorum to be seen together, you know.

LADY FRANCES.

Oh no. I asked Mrs. Racket, and she told me that we might be seen together at the masquerade without being laughed at. 70

---

[70] old crabbed fellow in Rome] perhaps Cato the Elder (the Censor), associated with simple life, severe morals, self-denying habits, strict justice, brusque manners, blunt speech

SIR GEORGE.

Really?

LADY FRANCES.

Indeed, to tell you the truth, I could wish it was the fashion for married people to be inseparable, for I have more heartfelt satisfaction in fifteen minutes with you at my side than fifteen days of amusement could give me without you.

SIR GEORGE.

My sweet creature! How that confession charms me! Let us begin the fashion.

LADY FRANCES.

Oh impossible! We should not gain a single proselyte, and you can't conceive what spiteful things would be said of us. At Kensington today a lady met us whom we saw at Court when we were presented. She lifted up her hands in amazement! "Bless me!" said she to her companion, "here's Lady Francis without Sir Hurlo Thrumbo!"* —My dear Mrs. Racket, consider what an important charge you have! For Heaven's sake take her home again, or some enchanter on a flying dragon will descend and carry her off." "Oh," said another, "I dare say Lady Frances has a clue at her heel, like the peerless Rosamond:[71] her tender swain would never have trusted her so far without such a precaution."

SIR GEORGE.

Heaven and earth! How shall Innocence preserve its luster amidst manners so corrupt?—My dear Fanny, I feel a sentiment for thee at this moment tenderer than love, more animated than passion. I could weep over that purity exposed to the sullying breath of fashion and the *ton*, in whose latitudinary vortex Chastity herself can scarcely move unspotted.

Enter Gibson.

GIBSON.

Your honor talked, I thought, something about going to the masquerade?

SIR GEORGE.

Well.

GIBSON.

Isn't it?—hasn't your honor?—I thought your honor had forgot to order a dress.

LADY FRANCES.

Well considered, Gibson.—Come, will you be Jew, Turk, or heretic; a Chinese emperor or a ballad-singer; a rake or a watchman?

SIR GEORGE.

Oh neither, my love, I can't take the trouble to support a character.

LADY FRANCES.

You'll wear a domino then. I saw a pink domino trimmed with blue at the shop where I bought my habit. Would you like it?

SIR GEORGE.

Anything, anything.

LADY FRANCES.

Then go about it directly, Gibson. A pink domino trimmed with blue and a hat of the same.—Come, you have not seen my dress yet. It is most beautiful; I long to have it on.

Exeunt Sir George and Lady Frances.

GIBSON.

A pink domino trimmed with blue and a hat of the same. What the devil can it signify to Sally, now, what his dress is to be? Surely the slut has not made an assignation to meet her master!

Exit.

Act IV, scene i. A masquerade [at Lady Brilliant's].

A party dancing cotillions in front—a variety of characters pass and repass. Enter Folly on a hobbyhorse, with cap and bells.

MASK.[72]

Hey! Tom Fool! what business have you here?

FOLLY.

What sir! Affront a prince in his own dominions! (*Struts off.*)

MOUNTEBANK.

Who'll buy my nostrums? Who'll buy my nostrums?

---

71 peerless Rosamond] Rosamond Clifford, beloved by King Henry II, was hidden away at the end of a maze so intricate that a clue was needed to find the end.

72 MASK] a reveler at a masquerade who simply covers the face without being in full costume

MASK.

What are they?

They all come round him.

MOUNTEBANK.

Different sorts and for different customers. Here's a liquor for ladies: it expels the rage of gaming and gallantry. Here's a pill for members of Parliament: good to settle consciences. Here's an eye-water for jealous husbands: it thickens the visual membrane through which they see too clearly. Here's a decoction for the clergy: it never sits easy if the patient has more than one living. Here's a draught for lawyers: a great promoter of modesty. Here's a powder for projectors:* 'twill rectify the fumes of an empty stomach and dissipate their airy castles. 10

15

MASK.

Have you a nostrum that can give patience to young heirs whose uncles and fathers are stout and healthy?

MOUNTEBANK.

Yes, and I have an infusion for creditors: it gives resignation and humility when fine gentlemen break their promises or plead their privilege. 20

MASK.

Come along! I'll find you customers for your whole cargo.

Enter Hardy in the dress of Isaac Mendoza.

HARDY.

Why, isn't it a shame to see so many stout, well-built young fellows masquerading and cutting courantes here at home, instead of making the French cut* capers to the tune of your cannon or sweating the Spaniards with an English fandango? I foresee the end of all this. 25

30

MASK.

Why, thou little testy Israelite! back to Duke's Place,[73] and preach your tribe into a subscription for the good of the land on whose milk and honey ye fatten. Where are your Joshuas and your Gideons, aye? What, all dwindled into stock-brokers, peddlers, and ragmen? 35

---

73 Duke's Place] mansion once owned by the Duke of Norfolk, became a center for settling Jews in 1650 and in 1682 became the site for the Great Synagogue

HARDY.

No, not all. Some of us turn Christians and by degrees grow into all the privileges of Englishmen! In the second generation we are patriots, rebels, courtiers, and (*Puts his fingers to his forehead [making horns*].*) husbands. 40

Two other masks advance.

THIRD MASK.

What, my little Isaac! How the devil came you here? Where's your old Margaret?

HARDY.

Oh, I have got rid of her.

THIRD MASK.

How? 45

HARDY.

Why, I persuaded a young Irishman that she was a blooming, plump beauty of eighteen, so they made an elopement. Ha, ha, ha! and she is now the toast of Tipperary. [*Aside.*] Hah! there's Cousin Racket and her party; they shan't know me. (*Puts on his mask.*) 50

Enter Mrs. Racket, Lady Frances, Sir George, and Flutter.

MRS. RACKET.

Look at this dumpling Jew; he must be a Levite by his figure. You have surely practiced the flesh-hook[74] a long time, friend, to have raised that goodly presence.

HARDY.

About as long, my brisk widow, as you have been angling for a second husband, but my hook has been better baited than yours. (*Pointing to Flutter.*) You have only caught gudgeons, I see. 55

FLUTTER.

Oh! this is one of the geniuses they hire to entertain the company with their *accidental* sallies.—Let me look at your commonplace book, friend. I want* a few good things. 60

HARDY.

I'd oblige you, with all my heart, but you'll spoil them in repeating. Or if you should not, they'll gain you no reputation, for nobody will believe they are your own. 65

---

74 flesh-hook] a hook for removing meat from the pot

SIR GEORGE.

He knows ye, Flutter; the little gentleman fancies himself a wit, I see.

HARDY.

There's no depending on what *you* see; the eyes of the jealous are not to be trusted. Look to your lady. 70

FLUTTER.

He knows ye, Sir George.

SIR GEORGE. (*Aside.*)

What, am I the Town talk?

HARDY. [*Aside.*]

I can neither see Doricourt nor Letty. I must find them out. (*Exit.*)

MRS. RACKET.

Well Lady Frances, is not all this charming? Could 75 you have conceived such a brilliant assemblage of objects?

LADY FRANCES.

Delightful! The days of enchantment are restored; the columns glow with sapphires and rubies. Emperors and fairies, beauties and dwarfs, meet me 80 at every step.

SIR GEORGE.

How lively are first impressions on sensible minds! In four hours, vapidity and languor will take place of that exquisite sense of joy which flutters your little heart. 85

MRS. RACKET.

What an inhuman creature! Fate has not allowed us these sensations above ten times in our lives, and would you have us shorten them by anticipation?

FLUTTER.

Oh Lord! your* wise men are the greatest fools upon earth: they reason about their enjoyments 90 and analyze their pleasures whilst the essence escapes. Look, Lady Frances, do ye see that figure strutting in the dress of an emperor? His father retails oranges in Botolph Lane.[75] That gypsy is a maid of honor, and that ragman a physician. 95

LADY FRANCES.

Why, you know everybody.

FLUTTER.

Oh, every creature. A mask is nothing at all to me.

I can give you the history of half the people here. In the next apartment there's a whole family who, to my knowledge, have lived on watercresses this 100 month to make a figure here tonight. But to make up for that, they'll cram their pockets with cold ducks and chickens for a carnival tomorrow.

LADY FRANCES.

Oh, I should like to see this provident family.

FLUTTER.

Honor me with your arm. 105

Exeunt Flutter and Lady Frances.

MRS. RACKET.

Come Sir George, you shall be *my* beau. We'll make the tour of the rooms and meet them. Oh! your pardon, you must follow Lady Frances or the wit and fine parts* of Mr. Flutter may drive you out of her head. Ha, ha, ha! (*Exit.*) 110

SIR GEORGE.

I was going to follow her, and now I dare not. How can I be such a fool as to be governed by the *fear* of that ridicule which I despise! (*Exit.*)

Enter Doricourt, meeting a mask.

DORICOURT.

Hah, my lord! I thought you had been engaged at Westminster[76] on this important night. 115

MASK.

So I am. I slipped out as soon as Lord Trope got upon his legs; I can *badiner*[77] here an hour or two and be back again before he is down.

Enter Letitia.

There's a fine figure! I'll address her.—Charity, fair lady! Charity for a poor pilgrim. 120

LETITIA.

Charity! If you mean my prayers, Heaven grant thee wit, pilgrim.

MASK.

That blessing would do from a devotee; from you I ask other charities—such charities as Beauty should bestow: soft looks, sweet words, and kind 125 wishes.

---

75 Botolph Lane] street and area surrounding and named for St. Botolph Billingsgate Church

76 Westminster] site of the houses of Parliament

77 *badiner*] to jest, banter (Fr.)

LETITIA.

Alas! I am bankrupt of these and forced to turn beggar myself. [*Aside.*] There he is! How shall I catch his attention?

MASK.

Will you grant me no favor?   130

LETITIA.

Yes, one: I'll make you my partner—not for life, but through the soft mazes of a minuet. Dare you dance?

DORICOURT.

Some spirit in that.

MASK.

I dare do anything you command.

DORICOURT.

Do you know her, my lord?   135

MASK.

No, such a woman as that would formerly have been known in any disguise, but Beauty is now common. Venus seems to have given her cestus[78] to the whole sex.

A minuet.

DORICOURT. (*During the minuet.*)

She dances divinely.   140

When ended.

Somebody must know her! Let us enquire who she is. (*Exit.*)

Enter Saville and Kitty Willis, habited like Lady Frances.

SAVILLE.

I have seen Courtall in Sir George's habit, though he endeavored to keep himself concealed. Go and seat yourself in the tearoom, and on no account   145 discover* your face. Remember too, Kitty, that the woman you are to personate is a woman of virtue.

KITTY.

I am afraid I shall find that a difficult character; indeed, I believe it is seldom kept up through a whole masquerade.   150

SAVILLE.

Of that *you* can be no judge. Follow my directions, and you shall be rewarded.

―――――――――

78 Venus … cestus] Venus's girdle (sash), a metonym for her irresistible sexual attraction

Exit Kitty. Enter Doricourt.

DORICOURT.

Hah! Saville! Did you see a lady dance just now?

SAVILLE.

No.

DORICOURT.

Very odd. Nobody knows her.   155

SAVILLE.

Where is Miss Hardy?

DORICOURT.

Cutting watch papers and making conundrums, I suppose.

SAVILLE.

What do you mean?

DORICOURT.

Faith, I hardly know. She's not here, however, Mrs. 160 Racket tells me. I asked no further.

SAVILLE.

Your indifference seems increased.

DORICOURT.

Quite the reverse: 'tis advanced thirty-two degrees towards hatred.

SAVILLE.

You are jesting?   165

DORICOURT.

Then it must be with a very ill grace, my dear Saville, for I never felt so seriously. Do you know the creature's almost an idiot?

SAVILLE.

What?

DORICOURT.

An idiot. What the devil shall I do with her? Egad! 170 I think I'll feign myself mad, and then Hardy will propose to cancel the engagements.

SAVILLE.

An excellent expedient. I must leave you; you are mysterious, and I can't stay to unravel ye. I came here to watch over Innocence and Beauty.   175

DORICOURT.

The guardian of Innocence and Beauty at three and twenty! Is there not a cloven foot under that black gown, Saville?

SAVILLE.

No, faith. Courtall is here on a most detestable design. I found means to get a knowledge of the   180 lady's dress and have brought a girl to personate her whose reputation cannot be hurt. You shall know the result tomorrow. Adieu. (*Exit.*)

DORICOURT. (*Musing.*)

Yes, I think that will do. I'll feign myself mad, see the doctor to pronounce me incurable, and when the parchments are destroyed— 185

As he stands in a musing posture, Letitia enters and sings.

Song.

Wake, thou Son of Dullness, wake!
    From thy drowsy senses shake
All the spells that Care employs,
    Cheating mortals of their joys. 190
II.
Light-winged spirits, hither haste,
    Who prepare for mortal taste
All the gifts that Pleasure sends,
    Every bliss that youth attends.
III.
Touch his feelings, rouse his soul, 195
    Whilst the sparkling moments roll,
Bid them wake to new delight,
    Crown the magic of the night.

DORICOURT.

By Heaven, the same sweet creature!

LETITIA.

You have chosen an odd situation for study. 200 Fashion and taste preside in this spot; they throw their spells around you; ten thousand delights spring up at their command—and you, a stoic, a being without senses, are wrapped in reflection.

DORICOURT.

And you, the most charming being in the world, 205 awake me to admiration. Did you come from the stars?

LETITIA.

Yes, and I shall reascend in a moment.

DORICOURT.

Pray show me your face before you go.

LETITIA.

Beware of imprudent curiosity; it lost paradise. 210

DORICOURT.

Eve's curiosity was raised by the Devil; 'tis an angel tempts mine. So your allusion is not in point.

LETITIA.

But *why* would you see my face?

DORICOURT.

To fall in love with it.

LETITIA.

And what then? 215

DORICOURT.

Why then— (*Aside.*) Aye, curse it! there's the rub.

LETITIA.

Your mistress will be angry—but perhaps, you have no mistress?

DORICOURT.

Yes, yes, and a sweet one it is!

LETITIA.

What, is she old? 220

DORICOURT.

No.

LETITIA.

Ugly?

DORICOURT.

No.

LETITIA.

What then?

DORICOURT.

Faugh! don't talk about *her*, but show me your face. 225

LETITIA.

My vanity forbids it; 'twould frighten you.

DORICOURT.

Impossible! Your shape is graceful, your air bewitching, your bosom transparent, and your chin would tempt me to kiss it, if I did not see a pouting red lip above it that demands— 230

LETITIA.

You grow too free.

DORICOURT.

Show me your face then, only half a glance.

LETITIA.

Not for worlds.

DORICOURT.

What, you will have a little gentle force? (*Attempts to seize her mask.*) 235

LETITIA.

I am gone forever! (*Exit.*)

DORICOURT.

'Tis false; I'll follow to the end. (*Exit.*)

Flutter, Lady Frances, and Saville advance.

LADY FRANCES.

How can you be thus interested for a stranger?

SAVILLE.

Goodness will ever interest; its home is heaven. On earth 'tis but a wanderer. Imprudent lady! why have you left the side of your protector? Where is your husband? 240

FLUTTER.

Why, what's that to him?

LADY FRANCES.

Surely it can't be merely his habit; there's something in him that awes me. 245

FLUTTER.

Faugh! 'tis only his grey beard.—I know him; he keeps a lottery-office on Cornhill.[79]

SAVILLE.

My province as an enchanter lays open every secret to me. Lady! there are dangers abroad—beware! (*Exit.*) 250

LADY FRANCES.

'Tis very odd. His manner has made me tremble. Let us seek Sir George.

FLUTTER.

He is coming towards us.

Courtall comes forward habited like Sir George.

COURTALL.

There she is! If I can but disengage her from that fool Flutter, crown me, ye schemers, with immortal wreaths. 255

LADY FRANCES.

Oh my dear Sir George! I rejoice to meet you. An old conjuror has been frightening me with his prophecies. Where's Mrs. Racket?

COURTALL.

In the dancing room.—I promised to send you to her, Mr. Flutter. 260

FLUTTER.

Ah! she wants me to dance. With all my heart. (*Exit.*)

LADY FRANCES.

Why do you keep on your mask? 'Tis too warm.

COURTALL.

'Tis very warm—I want* air—let us go. 265

---

[79] Cornhill] highest hill in London

LADY FRANCES.

You seem quite agitated. Shan't we bid our company adieu?

COURTALL.

No, no, there's no time for forms. I'll just give directions to the carriage and be with you in a moment. (*Going, steps back.*) Put on your mask. I have a particular reason for it. (*Exit.*) 270

Saville advances with Kitty.

SAVILLE.

Now Kitty, you know your lesson. (*Takes off his mask.*) Lady Frances, let me lead you to your husband.

LADY FRANCES.

Heavens! is Mr. Saville the conjuror? Sir George is just stepped to the door to give directions. We are going home immediately. 275

SAVILLE.

No madam, you are deceived: Sir George is this way.

LADY FRANCES.

This is astonishing!

SAVILLE.

Be not alarmed: you have escaped a snare and shall be in safety in a moment. 280

Exit Saville and Lady Frances.

Enter Courtall and seizes Kitty's hand.

COURTALL.

Now!

KITTY.

'Tis pity to go so soon.

COURTALL.

Perhaps I may bring you back, my angel, but go now, you must. 285

Exeunt [Courtall and Kitty].

Music. Doricourt and Letitia come forward.

DORICOURT.

By heavens! I never was charmed till now. English beauty, French vivacity, wit, elegance. Your name, my angel! tell me your name, though you persist in concealing your face.

LETITIA.

My name has a spell in it. 290

DORICOURT.

I thought so; it must be *Charming*.

LETITIA.

But if revealed, the charm is broke.

DORICOURT.

I'll answer for its force.

LETITIA.

Suppose it Harriet or Charlotte or Maria or—

DORICOURT.

Hang Harriet and Charlotte and Maria—the name   295
your father gave ye!

LETITIA.

That can't be worth knowing, 'tis so transient a
thing.

DORICOURT.

How transient?

LETITIA.

Heaven forbid my name should be *lasting* till I am   300
married.

DORICOURT.

Married! The chains of matrimony are too heavy and
vulgar for such a spirit as yours. The flowery wreaths
of Cupid are the only bands you should wear.

LETITIA.

They are the lightest, I believe, but 'tis possible to   305
wear those of marriage gracefully: throw 'em
loosely round and twist 'em in a true lover's knot
for the bosom.

DORICOURT.

An angel! but what will you be when a wife?

LETITIA.

A woman. If my husband should prove a churl, a   310
fool, or a tyrant, I'd break his heart, ruin his
fortune, elope with the first pretty fellow that asked
me—and return the contempt of the world with
scorn, whilst my feelings preyed upon my life.

DORICOURT. (*Aside.*)

Amazing!—What if you loved him and he were   315
worthy of your love?

LETITIA.

Why, then I'd be anything—and all: grave, gay,
capricious, the soul of whim, the spirit of variety;
live with him in the eye of fashion or in the shade
of retirement; change my country, my sex; feast   320
with him in an Eskimo's hut or a Persian pavilion;
join him in the victorious war dance on the
borders of Lake Ontario or sleep to the soft
breathings of the flute in the cinnamon groves of
Ceylon; dig with him in the mines of Golconda   325
or enter the dangerous precincts of the Mogul's
seraglio, cheat him of his wishes, and overturn his
empire to restore the husband of my heart to the
blessings of liberty and love.

DORICOURT.

Delightful wildness. Oh, to catch thee and hold   330
thee forever in this little cage! (*Attempting to clasp
her.*)

LETITIA.

Hold, sir! Though Cupid must give the bait that
tempts me to the snare, 'tis Hymen must spread
the net to catch me.   335

DORICOURT.

'Tis in vain to assume airs of coldness: Fate has
ordained you mine.

LETITIA.

How do you know?

DORICOURT.

I feel it *here*. I never met with a woman so perfectly
to my taste, and I won't believe it formed you so   340
on purpose to tantalize me.

LETITIA. (*Aside.*)

This moment is worth a whole existence.

DORICOURT.

Come, show me your face and rivet my chains.

LETITIA.

Tomorrow you shall be satisfied.

DORICOURT.

Tomorrow! and not tonight?   345

LETITIA.

No.

DORICOURT.

Where then shall I wait on you tomorrow? Where
see you?

LETITIA.

You shall see me in an hour when you least expect
me.   350

DORICOURT.

Why all this mystery?

LETITIA.

I like to be mysterious. At present be content to
know that I am a woman of family and fortune.
Adieu!

Enter Hardy.

HARDY. (*Aside.*)

Adieu! Then I am come at the fag end.   355

DORICOURT.

Let me see you to your carriage.

LETITIA.

As you value knowing me, stir not a step. If I am
followed, you never see me more. (*Exit.*)

DORICOURT.

Barbarous creature! She's gone! What, and is this
really serious? am I in love? Faugh! it can't be.   360

Enter Flutter.

Oh, Flutter! do you know that charming creature?

FLUTTER.

What charming creature? I passed a thousand.

DORICOURT.

She went out at that door as you entered.

FLUTTER.

Oh, yes, I know her very well.

DORICOURT.

Do you, my dear fellow? Who?   365

FLUTTER.

She's kept* by Lord George Jennet.

HARDY. (*Aside.*)

Impudent scoundrel!

DORICOURT.

Kept!!!

FLUTTER.

Yes, Colonel Gorget had her first, then Mr.
Loveill—then—I forget exactly how many—and   370
at last she's Lord George's. (*Talks to other masks.*)

DORICOURT.

I'll murder Gorget, poison Lord George, and shoot
myself.

HARDY.

Now's the time, I see, to clear up the whole.—Mr.
Doricourt! I say—Flutter was mistaken. I know   375
who you are in love with.

DORICOURT.

A strange rencontre! Who?

HARDY.

My Letty.

DORICOURT.

Oh, I understand your rebuke. 'Tis too soon, sir,
to assume the father-in-law.   380

HARDY.

Zounds! what do you mean by that? I tell you that
the lady you admire is Letitia Hardy.

DORICOURT.

I am glad *you* are so well satisfied with the state of
my heart. I wish *I* was. (*Exit.*)

HARDY.

Stop a moment—stop, I say! What, you won't? Very   385
well, if I don't play you a trick for this, may I never
be a grandfather! I'll plot *with* Letty now and not
against her, aye, hang me if I don't. There's
something in my head that shall tingle in his heart.
He shall have a lecture upon impatience that I fore-   390
see he'll be the better for as long as he lives. (*Exit.*)

Saville comes forward with other masks.

SAVILLE.

Flutter, come with us. We're going to raise a laugh
at Courtall's.

FLUTTER.

With all my heart. "Live to live" was my father's
motto; "Live to laugh" is mine.   395

Exeunt.

Scene [ii]. Courtall's.

Enter Kitty and Courtall.

KITTY.

Where have you brought me, Sir George? This is
not our home.

COURTALL. (*Kneels and takes off his mask.*)

'Tis *my* home, beautiful Lady Frances! Oh, forgive
the ardency of my passion which has compelled
me to deceive you.   5

KITTY.

Mr. Courtall! what will become of me?

COURTALL.

Oh, say but that you pardon the wretch who
adores you. Did you but know the agonizing
tortures of my heart since I had the felicity of
conversing with you this morning—or the despair   10
that now—

Knock.

KITTY.

Oh! I'm undone!

COURTALL.

Zounds! my dear Lady Frances. [*To servant.*] I am not at home. Rascal! do you hear? Let nobody in; I am not at home.

SERVANT. (*Without.*)

Sir, I told the gentlemen so.

COURTALL.

Eternal curses! they are coming up. Step into this room, adorable creature, *one* moment; I'll throw them out of the window if they stay three.

Exit Kitty through the back scene. Enter Saville, Flutter, and masks.

FLUTTER.

Oh jiminy!* Beg the petticoat's pardon. Just saw a corner of it.

FIRST MASK.

No wonder admittance was so difficult. I thought you took us for bailiffs.

COURTALL.

Upon my soul, I am devilish glad to see you, but you perceive how I am circumstanced. Excuse me at this moment.

SECOND MASK.

Tell us who 'tis then.

COURTALL.

Oh, fie!

FLUTTER.

We won't blab.

COURTALL.

I can't, upon honor. Thus far: she's a woman of the first character and rank. Saville (*Takes him aside.*), have I influence, or have I not?

SAVILLE.

Why sure, you do not insinuate—

COURTALL.

No, not insinuate, but swear that she's now in my bed chamber! By Gad, I don't deceive you. There's generalship, you rogue! Such an humble, distant, sighing fellow as thou art, at the end of a six-month siege would have *boasted* of a kiss from her glove. I only give the signal and—pop—she's in my arms.

SAVILLE.

What, Lady Fran—

COURTALL.

Hush! You shall see her name tomorrow morning in red letters at the end of my list.—Gentlemen, you must excuse me now. Come and drink chocolate at twelve, but—

SAVILLE.

Aye, let us go, out of respect to the lady—'tis a person of rank.

FLUTTER.

Is it? Then I'll have a peep at her. (*Runs to the door in the back scene.*)

COURTALL.

This is too much, sir. (*Trying to prevent him.*)

FIRST MASK.

By Jupiter, we'll all have a peep.

COURTALL.

Gentlemen, consider—for Heaven's sake—a lady of quality.* What will be the consequences?

FLUTTER.

The consequences! Why, you'll have your throat cut, that's all. But I'll write your elegy. So, now for the door!

Part open the door, whilst the rest hold Courtall.

Beg your ladyship's pardon, whoever you are. (*Leads her out.*) Emerge from darkness like the glorious sun and bless the wondering circle with your charms. (*Takes off her mask.*)

SAVILLE.

Kitty Willis! ha, ha, ha!

OMNES.

Kitty Willis! ha, ha, ha! Kitty Willis!

FIRST MASK.

Why, what a fellow you are, Courtall, to attempt imposing on your friends in this manner! A lady of quality—an earl's daughter—your ladyship's most obedient—ha, ha, ha!

SAVILLE.

Courtall, have you influence, or have you not?

FLUTTER.

The man's moonstruck.

COURTALL.

Hell and ten thousand furies seize you all together!

KITTY.

What! me, too, Mr. Courtall? me, whom you have knelt to, prayed to, and adored?

FLUTTER.

That's right, Kitty, give him a little more.

COURTALL.

Disappointed and laughed at!

SAVILLE.

Laughed at and despised. I have fulfilled my design, which was to expose your villainy and laugh at your presumption. Adieu, sir! Remember how you again boast of your influence with women of rank. And when you next want amusement, dare not to look up to the virtuous and to the noble for a companion. (*Exit, leading Kitty.*)

FLUTTER.

And Courtall, before you carry a lady into your bedchamber again, look under her mask, d'ye hear? (*Exit.*)

COURTALL.

There's no bearing this! I'll set off for Paris directly.

Exit.

Act V, scene i. Hardy's.

Enter Hardy and Villers.

VILLERS.

Whimsical enough! Dying for her and hates her; believes her a fool and a woman of brilliant understanding.

HARDY.

As true as you are alive. But when I went up to him last night at the masquerade, out of downright good nature to explain things, my gentleman whips round upon his heel and snapped me as short as if I had been a beggar woman with six children and he overseer of the parish.

VILLERS.

Here comes the wonder-worker.

Enter Letitia.

Here comes the enchantress who can go to masquerades and sing and dance and talk a man out of his wits! But pray, have we morning masquerades?

LETITIA.

Oh no, but I am so enamored of this all-conquering habit that I could not resist putting it on the moment I had breakfasted. I shall wear it on the day I am married and then lay it by in spices, like the miraculous robes of St. Bridget.[80]

VILLERS.

That's as most brides do. The charms that helped to catch the husband are generally *laid by*, one after another till the lady grows a downright wife and then runs crying to her mother because she has transformed her *lover* into a downright husband.

HARDY.

Listen to me. I han't slept tonight for thinking of plots to plague Doricourt. And they drove one another out of my head so quick that I was as giddy as a goose and could make nothing of 'em. I wish to goodness you could contrive something.

VILLERS.

Contrive to plague him! Nothing so easy. Don't undeceive him, madam, till he is your husband. Marry him whilst he possesses the sentiments you labored to give him of Miss Hardy, and when you are his wife—

LETITIA.

Oh heavens! I see the whole—that's the very thing. My dear Mr. Villers, you are the divinest man.

VILLERS.

Don't make love* to me, hussy.

Enter Mrs. Racket.

MRS. RACKET.

No, pray don't, for I design to have Villers myself in about six years. There's an oddity in him that pleases me. He holds women in contempt, and I should like to have an opportunity of breaking his heart for that.

VILLERS.

And when I am heartily tired of life, I know no woman whom I would with more pleasure make my executioner.

HARDY.

It cannot be. I foresee it will be impossible to bring it about. You know the wedding wasn't to take place this week or more, and Letty will never be able to play the fool so long.

VILLERS.

The knot shall be tied tonight. I have it all here.

---

80 robes of St. Bridget] Healing powers were attributed to St. Bridget's cloak, which became a relic.

(*Pointing to his forehead.*) The license is ready. Feign yourself ill, send for Doricourt, and tell him you can't go out of the world in peace except you see the ceremony performed.   55

HARDY.

I feign myself ill! I could as soon feign myself a Roman ambassador. I was never ill in my life, but with the toothache. When Letty's mother was a-breeding, I had all the qualms.

VILLERS.

Oh, I have no fears for *you*.—But what says Miss   60
Hardy? Are you willing to make the irrevocable vow before night?

LETITIA.

Oh heavens! I—I— 'Tis so exceeding sudden, that really—

MRS. RACKET.

That really she is frightened out of her wits—lest   65
it should be impossible to bring matters about. But *I* have taken the scheme into my protection, and you shall be Mrs. Doricourt before night. (*To Mr. Hardy.*) Come, to bed directly: your room shall be crammed with phials and all the apparatus of   70
death. Then heigh presto! for Doricourt.

VILLERS. (*To Letty.*)

You go and put off your conquering dress and get all your awkward airs ready. (*To Hardy.*) And you practice a few groans. (*To Mrs. Racket.*) And you—
if possible—an air of gravity. I'll answer for the   75
plot.

LETITIA.

Married in jest! 'tis an odd idea! Well, I'll venture it.

Exeunt Letitia and Mrs. Racket.

VILLERS.

Aye, I'll be sworn! (*Looks at his watch.*) 'Tis past three. The budget's to be opened this morning. I'll   80
just step down to the House. Will you go?

HARDY.

What! with a mortal sickness?

VILLERS.

What a blockhead! I believe if half of us were to stay away with mortal sicknesses, it would be for the health of the nation. Good morning. I'll call   85
and feel your pulse as I come back. (*Exit.*)

HARDY.

You won't find 'em over brisk, I fancy. I foresee some ill happening from this making believe to die before one's time. But hang it, ahem! I am a stout man yet, only fifty-six. What's that? In the last yearly bill*   90
there were three lived to above a hundred. Fifty-six! Fiddle-de-dee! I am not afraid, not I.

Exit.

Scene ii. Doricourt's.

Doricourt in his robe de chambre. Enter Saville.

SAVILLE.

Undressed so late?

DORICOURT.

I didn't go to bed till late; 'twas late before I slept, late when I rose. Do you know Lord George Jennet?

SAVILLE.

Yes.

DORICOURT.

Has he a mistress?   5

SAVILLE.

Yes.

DORICOURT.

What sort of a creature is she?

SAVILLE.

Why, she spends him three thousand a year with the ease of a duchess and entertains his friends with the grace of a Ninon.[81] Ergo, she is handsome,   10
spirited, and clever.

Doricourt walks about disordered.

In the name of caprice, what ails you?

DORICOURT.

You have hit it: *elle est mon caprice.* The mistress of Lord George Jennet is my caprice. Oh, insufferable!   15

SAVILLE.

What, you saw her at the masquerade?

DORICOURT.

Saw her, *loved* her, *died* for her—without knowing her. And now the curse is, I can't hate her.

---

81 Ninon] nickname for Anne de Lenclos (1620-1705), witty French courtesan noted for her prominent liaisons and salon

SAVILLE.

Ridiculous enough! All this distress about a kept woman whom any man may have, I dare swear, in a fortnight. They've been jarring some time. 20

DORICOURT.

Have her! The sentiment I have conceived for the witch is so unaccountable that, in that line, I cannot bear her idea. Was she a woman of honor, for a wife I could adore her. But I really believe, if she should 25 send me an assignation, I should hate her.

SAVILLE.

Heyday! This sounds like love. What becomes of poor Miss Hardy?

DORICOURT.

Her name has given me an ague. Dear Saville, how shall I contrive to make old Hardy cancel the 30 engagements? The moiety of the estate which he will forfeit shall be his the next moment by deed of gift.

SAVILLE.

Let me see. Can't you get it insinuated that you are a devilish wild fellow, that you are an infidel 35 and attached to wenching, gaming, and so forth?

DORICOURT.

Aye, such a character* might have done some good two centuries back. But who the devil can it frighten now? I believe it must be the mad scheme, at last. There, will that do for a^k grin? 40

SAVILLE.

Ridiculous! But how are you certain that the woman who has so bewildered you belongs to Lord George?

DORICOURT.

Flutter told me so.

SAVILLE.

Then fifty to one against the intelligence. 45

DORICOURT.

It must be so. There was a mystery in her manner for which nothing else can account.

A violent rap.

Who can this be?

SAVILLE. (*Looking out.*)

The proverb[82] is your answer: 'tis Flutter himself.

Tip him a scene of the madman and see how it takes. 50

DORICOURT.

I will—a good way to send it about Town. Shall it be of the melancholy kind or the raving?

SAVILLE.

Rant! Rant! Here he comes.

DORICOURT.

Talk not to me who can pull comets by the beard and overset an island! 55

Enter Flutter.

There! this is he! This is he who hath sent my poor soul, without coat or breeches, to be tossed about in ether like a duck feather!—Villain, give me my soul again!

FLUTTER. (*Exceedingly frightened.*)

Upon my soul I haven't got it. 60

SAVILLE.

Oh Mr. Flutter, what a melancholy sight! I little thought to have seen my poor friend reduced to this.

FLUTTER.

Mercy defend me! What, 's he mad?

SAVILLE.

You see how it is. A cursed Italian lady—Jealousy—gave him a drug, and every full of the moon— 65

DORICOURT.

Moon! Who dares talk of the moon? The patroness of genius—the rectifier of wits—the—Oh! here she is!—I feel her—she tugs at my brain—she has it—she has it—Oh! (*Exit.*)

FLUTTER.

Well! this is dreadful! exceeding dreadful, I protest. 70 Have you had Monro?[83]

SAVILLE.

Not yet. The worthy Miss Hardy—what a misfortune!

FLUTTER.

Aye, very true. Do they know it?

SAVILLE.

Oh no, the paroxysm seized him but this morning. 75

FLUTTER.

Adieu! I can't stay. (*Going in great haste.*)

---

82 proverb] "Speak of the devil and he's sure to appear."

83 Monro] John Monro, MD (1715-1791), first physician to Bethlem Hospital, second of five generations of Monros who were eminent mad-doctors

SAVILLE.

But you must. (*Holding him.*) Stay and assist me: perhaps he'll return again in a moment, and when he is in this way, his strength is prodigious.

FLUTTER.

Can't indeed—can't upon my soul. (*Exit[ing].*) 80

SAVILLE.

Flutter, don't make a mistake now. Remember, 'tis Doricourt that's mad.

FLUTTER.

Yes—you mad.

SAVILLE.

No, no: Doricourt.

FLUTTER.

Egad, I'll say you are both mad, and then I can't 85
mistake.

Exeunt severally.

Scene iii. Sir George Touchwood's.

Enter Sir George and Lady Frances.

SIR GEORGE.

The bird is escaped. Courtall is gone to France!

LADY FRANCES.

Heaven and earth! Have ye been to seek him?

SIR GEORGE.

Seek him! Aye.

LADY FRANCES.

How did you get his name? I should never have told it you. 5

SIR GEORGE.

I learned it at the first coffeehouse I entered. Everybody is full of the story.

LADY FRANCES.

Thank Heaven, he's gone! But I have a story for you. The Hardy family are forming a plot upon your friend Doricourt, and we are expected in the 10
evening to assist.

SIR GEORGE.

With all my heart, my angel, but I can't stay to hear it unfolded. They told me Mr. Saville would be at home in half an hour, and I am impatient to see him. The adventure of last night— 15

LADY FRANCES.

Think of it only with gratitude. The danger I was in has overset a new system of conduct that,

perhaps, I was too much inclined to adopt. But henceforward, my dear Sir George, you shall be my constant companion and protector. And when they 20
ridicule the unfashionable monsters, the felicity of our hearts shall make their satire pointless.

SIR GEORGE.

Charming angel! You almost reconcile me to Courtall. Hark! here's company. (*Stepping to the door.*) 'Tis your lively widow. I'll step down the 25
back stairs to escape her. (*Exit.*)

Enter Mrs. Racket.

MRS. RACKET.

Oh Lady Frances! I am shocked to death. Have you received a card from us?

LADY FRANCES.

Yes, within these twenty minutes.

MRS. RACKET.

Aye, 'tis of no consequence. 'Tis all over. Doricourt 30
is mad.

LADY FRANCES.

Mad!

MRS. RACKET.

My poor Letitia! Just as we were enjoying ourselves with the prospect of a scheme that was planned for their mutual happiness, in came Flutter, 35
breathless, with the intelligence. I flew here to know if you had heard it.

LADY FRANCES.

No indeed, and I hope it is one of Mr. Flutter's dreams.

Enter Saville.

Apropos, now we shall be informed.—Mr. Saville, 40
I rejoice to see you, though Sir George will be disappointed: he's gone to your lodgings.

SAVILLE.

I should have been happy to have prevented* Sir George. I hope your ladyship's adventure last night did not disturb your dreams? 45

LADY FRANCES.

Not at all, for I never slept a moment. My escape, and the importance of my obligations to you, employed my thoughts. But we have just had shocking intelligence. Is it true that Doricourt is mad? 50

SAVILLE. (*Aside.*)

So, the business is done.—Madam, I am sorry to say that I have just been a melancholy witness of his ravings; he was in the height of a paroxysm.

MRS. RACKET.

Oh, there can be no doubt of it. Flutter told us the whole history. Some Italian princess gave him a drug in a box of sweetmeats sent to him by her own page, and it renders him lunatic every month. Poor Miss Hardy! I never felt so much on any occasion in my life.   55

SAVILLE.

To soften your concern, I will inform you, madam, that Miss Hardy is less to be pitied than you imagine.   60

MRS. RACKET.

Why so, sir?

SAVILLE.

'Tis rather a delicate subject, but he did not love Miss Hardy.   65

MRS. RACKET.

He did love Miss Hardy, sir, and would have been the happiest of men.

SAVILLE.

Pardon me, madam, his heart was not only free from that lady's chains but absolutely captivated by another.   70

MRS. RACKET.

No, sir, no. It was Miss Hardy who captivated him. She met him last night at the masquerade and charmed him in disguise. He professed the most violent passion for her and a plan was laid, this evening to cheat him into happiness.   75

SAVILLE.

Ha, ha, ha! Upon my soul, I must beg your pardon. I have not eaten of the Italian princess's box of sweetmeats sent by her own page, and yet I am as mad as Doricourt, ha, ha, ha!

MRS. RACKET.

So it appears. What can all this mean?   80

SAVILLE.

Why madam, he is at present in his perfect senses, but he'll lose 'em in ten minutes through joy. The madness was only a feint to avoid marrying Miss Hardy, ha, ha, ha! I'll carry him the intelligence directly. (*Going.*)   85

MRS. RACKET.

Not for worlds. I owe him revenge, now, for what he has made us suffer. You must promise not to divulge a syllable I have told you. And when Doricourt is summoned to Mr. Hardy's, prevail on him to come, madness and all.   90

LADY FRANCES.

Pray do. I should like to see him showing off, now I am in the secret.

SAVILLE.

You must be obeyed, though 'tis inhuman to conceal his happiness.

MRS. RACKET.

I am going home, so I'll set you down at his   95
lodgings and acquaint you, by the way, with our whole scheme. *Allons!*

SAVILLE.

I attend you. (*Leading her out.*)

MRS. RACKET.

You won't fail us?

Exeunt Saville and Mrs. Racket.

LADY FRANCES.

No, depend on us.   100

Exit.

Scene iv. Doricourt's.

Doricourt seated, reading.

DORICOURT. (*Flings away the book.*)

What effect can the morals of fourscore have on a mind torn with passion? (*Musing.*) Is it possible such a soul as hers can support itself in so humiliating a situation? A kept woman! (*Rising.*) Well, well—I am glad it is so—I am glad it is so!   5

Enter Saville.

SAVILLE.

What a happy dog you are, Doricourt! I might have been mad or beggared or pistoled myself without its being mentioned. But you, forsooth! the whole female world is concerned for. I reported the state of your brain to five different women: the   10
lip of the first trembled; the white bosom of the second heaved a sigh; the third ejaculated and turned her eye—to the glass;* the fourth blessed

herself; and the fifth said, whilst she pinned a curl, "Well, now, perhaps, he'll be an amusing companion. His native dullness was intolerable."

DORICOURT.

Envy! sheer envy, by the smiles of Hebe! There are not less than forty pair of the brightest eyes in Town will drop crystals when they hear of my misfortune.

SAVILLE.

Well, but I have news for you: poor Hardy is confined to his bed. They say he is going out of the world by the first post, and he wants to give you his blessing.

DORICOURT.

Ill! So ill! I am sorry from my soul. He's a worthy little fellow—if he had not the gift of foreseeing so strongly.

SAVILLE.

Well, you must go and take leave.

DORICOURT.

What! To act the lunatic in the dying man's chamber?

SAVILLE.

Exactly the thing, and will bring your business to a short issue: for his last commands must be that you are not to marry his daughter.

DORICOURT.

That's true, by Jupiter! And yet, hang it, impose upon a poor fellow at so serious a moment! I can't do it.

SAVILLE.

You must, faith. I am answerable for your appearance, though it should be in a strait waistcoat. He knows your situation and seems the more desirous of an interview.

DORICOURT.

I don't like encountering Racket. She's an arch little devil and will discover the cheat.

SAVILLE.

There's a fellow! Cheated ninety-nine women and now afraid of the hundredth.

DORICOURT.

And with reason—for that hundredth is a widow.

Exeunt.

Scene v. Hardy's.

Enter Mrs. Racket and Miss Ogle.

MISS OGLE.

And so Miss Hardy is actually to be married tonight?

MRS. RACKET.

If her fate does not deceive her. You are apprised of the scheme, and we hope it will succeed.

MISS OGLE. (*Aside.*)

Deuce take her! She's six years younger than I am.—Is Mr. Doricourt handsome?

MRS. RACKET.

Handsome, generous, young, and rich. There's a husband for ye! Isn't he worth pulling caps[84] for?

MISS OGLE. (*Aside.*)

I'my conscience, the widow speaks as though she'd give cap, ears, and all for him.—I wonder you didn't try to catch this wonderful man, Mrs. Racket!

MRS. RACKET.

Really Miss Ogle, I had not time. Besides, when I marry, so many stout young fellows will hang themselves that out of regard to society, in these sad times, I shall postpone it for a few years. (*Aside.*) This will cost her a new lace:[85] I heard it crack.

Enter Sir George and Lady Frances.

SIR GEORGE.

Well, here we are. But where's the Knight of the Woeful Countenance?[86]

MRS. RACKET.

Here soon, I hope. For a woeful night it will be without him.

SIR GEORGE.

Oh fie! do you condescend to pun?

MRS. RACKET.

Why not? It requires genius to make a good pun. Some men of bright parts* can't reach it. I know

---

84 pulling caps] quarreling like two women who pull each other's caps

85 lace] corset lacing

86 Knight of the Woeful Countenance] nickname for Cervantes' Don Quixote

a lawyer who writes them on the back of his briefs and says they are of great use in a dry cause.

Enter Flutter.

FLUTTER.

Here they come! Here they come! Their coach stopped as mine drove off.

LADY FRANCES.

Then Miss Hardy's fate is at a crisis. She plays a hazardous game, and I tremble for her.

SAVILLE.

(*Without.*) Come let me guide you! This way, my poor friend! Why are you so furious?

DORICOURT.

The house of death—to the house of death!

Enter Doricourt and Saville.

Ah! this is the spot!

LADY FRANCES.

How wild and fiery he looks!

MISS OGLE.

Now, I think, he looks terrified.

FLUTTER.

Poor creature, how his eyes work!

MRS. RACKET.

I never saw a madman before. Let me examine him. Will he bite?

SAVILLE.

Pray keep out of his reach, ladies, you don't know your danger. He's like a wildcat if a sudden thought seizes him.

SIR GEORGE.

You talk like a keeper of wildcats. How much do you demand for showing the monster?

DORICOURT. [*Aside.*]

I don't like this. I must rouse their sensibility.— There! there she darts through the air in liquid flames! Down again! Now I have her—oh, she burns, she scorches!—oh! she eats into my very heart!

OMNES.

Ha, ha, ha!

MRS. RACKET.

He sees the apparition of the wicked Italian princess.

FLUTTER.

Keep her highness fast, Doricourt.

MISS OGLE.

Give her a pinch, before you let her go.

DORICOURT.

I am laughed at!

MRS. RACKET.

Laughed at, aye, to be sure. Why, I could play the madman better than you.—There! there she is! Now I have her! Ha, ha, ha!

DORICOURT. (*Aside.*)

I knew that devil would discover me.—I'll leave the house; I'm covered with confusion. (*Going.*)

SIR GEORGE.

Stay, sir. You must not go. 'Twas poorly done, Mr. Doricourt, to affect madness rather than fulfil your engagements.

DORICOURT.

Affect madness!—Saville, what can I do?

SAVILLE.

Since you are discovered, confess the whole.

MISS OGLE.

Aye, turn evidence and save yourself.

DORICOURT.

Yes, since my designs have been so unaccountably discovered, I will avow the whole. I cannot love Miss Hardy—and I will never—

SAVILLE.

Hold, my dear Doricourt! Be not so rash. What will the world say to such—

DORICOURT.

Damn the world! What will the world give me for the loss of happiness? Must I sacrifice my peace to please the world?

SIR GEORGE.

Yes, everything, rather than be branded with dishonor.

LADY FRANCES.

Though *our* arguments should fail, there *is* a pleader whom you surely cannot withstand: the dying Mr. Hardy supplicates you not to forsake his child.

Enter Villers.

VILLERS.

Mr. Hardy requests you to grant him a moment's conversation, Mr. Doricourt, though you should persist to send him miserable to the grave. Let me conduct you to his chamber.

DORICOURT.

Oh, aye, anywhere, to the antipodes, to the moon 85
carry me, do with me what you will.

MRS. RACKET.

Mortification and disappointment, then, are
specifics in a case of stubbornness. I'll follow, and
let you know what passes.

Exeunt Villers, Doricourt, Mrs. Racket, and Miss Ogle.

FLUTTER.

Ladies, ladies, have the charity to take me with 90
you, that I may make no blunder in repeating the
story. (*Exit.*)

LADY FRANCES.

Sir George, you don't know Mr. Saville? (*Exit.*)

SIR GEORGE.

Ten thousand pardons, but I will not pardon
myself for not observing you. I have been with the 95
utmost impatience at your door twice today.

SAVILLE.

I am concerned you had so much trouble, Sir
George.

SIR GEORGE.

Trouble! what a word!—I hardly know how to
address you. I am distressed beyond measure, and 100
it is the highest proof of my opinion of your honor
and the delicacy of your mind that I open my heart
to you.

SAVILLE.

What has disturbed you, Sir George?

SIR GEORGE.

Your having preserved Lady Frances in so 105
imminent a danger. Start not, Saville. To protect
Lady Frances was my right. You have wrested from
me my dearest privilege.

SAVILLE.

I hardly know how to answer such a reproach. I
cannot apologize for what I have done. 110

SIR GEORGE.

I do not mean to reproach you; I hardly know
what I mean. There is one method by which you
may restore peace to me: I cannot endure that my
wife should be so infinitely indebted to any man
who is less than my brother. 115

SAVILLE.

Pray explain yourself.

SIR GEORGE.

I have a sister, Saville, who is amiable—and you are
worthy of her. I shall give her a commission to steal
your heart out of revenge for what you have done.

SAVILLE.

I am infinitely honored, Sir George, but— 120

SIR GEORGE.

I cannot listen to a sentence which begins with so
unpromising a word. You must go with us into
Hampshire, and if you see each other with the eyes
I do, your felicity will be complete. I know no one
to whose heart I would so readily commit the care 125
of my sister's happiness.

SAVILLE.

I will attend you to Hampshire with pleasure, but
not on the plan of retirement. Society has claims
on Lady Frances that forbid it.

SIR GEORGE.

Claims, Saville! 130

SAVILLE.

Yes, claims: Lady Frances was born to be the
ornament of courts. She is sufficiently alarmed not
to wander beyond the reach of her protector. And
from the British court, the most tenderly anxious
husband could not wish to banish his wife. Bid her 135
keep in her eye the bright example who presides
there,[87] the splendor of whose rank yields to the
superior luster of her virtue.

SIR GEORGE.

I allow the force of your argument. Now for
intelligence! 140

*Enter Mrs. Racket, Lady Frances, [Miss Ogle], and
Flutter.*

MRS. RACKET.

Oh heavens! do you know—

FLUTTER.

Let me tell the story—as soon as Doricourt—

MRS. RACKET.

I protest you shan't—said Mr. Hardy—

FLUTTER.

No, 'twas Doricourt spoke first. Says he—no, 'twas
the parson—says he— 145

---

87 bright example who presides there] Queen Charlotte
(1744-1818), consort of George III (1738-1820)

MRS. RACKET.

Stop his mouth, Sir George, he'll spoil the tale.

SIR GEORGE.

Never heed circumstances, the result, the result.

MRS. RACKET.

No, no, you shall have it in form. Mr. Hardy performed the sick man like an angel. He sat up in his bed and talked so pathetically that the tears stood in Doricourt's eyes.

FLUTTER.

Aye, stood—they did not drop, but stood. I shall, in future, be very exact. The parson seized the moment; you know, they never miss an opportunity.

MRS. RACKET.

"Make haste," said Doricourt. "If I have time to reflect, poor Hardy will die unhappy."

FLUTTER.

They were got as far as the "day of judgement," when we slipped out of the room.

SIR GEORGE.

Then by this time they must have reached "amazement,"[88] which, everybody knows, is the end of matrimony.

MRS. RACKET.

Aye, the reverend fathers ended the service with that word prophetically, to teach the bride what a capricious monster a husband is.

SIR GEORGE.

I rather think it was sarcastically to prepare the bridegroom for the unreasonable humors and vagaries of his helpmate.

LADY FRANCES.

Here comes the bridegroom of tonight.

Enter Doricourt and Villers. Villers whispers Saville, who goes out.

OMNES.

Joy! joy! joy!

MISS OGLE.

If *he's* a sample of bridegrooms, keep me single! A younger brother from the funeral of his father could not carry a more fretful countenance.

FLUTTER.

Oh! now he's melancholy mad, I suppose.

LADY FRANCES.

You do not consider the importance of the occasion.

VILLERS.

No, nor how shocking a thing it is for a man to be forced to marry one woman whilst his heart is devoted to another.

MRS. RACKET.

Well, now 'tis over, I confess to you, Mr. Doricourt, I think 'twas a most ridiculous piece of quixotism to give up the happiness of a whole life to a man who perhaps has but a few moments to be sensible of the sacrifice.

FLUTTER.

So it appeared to me. But thought I, Mr. Doricourt has traveled; he knows best.

DORICOURT.

Zounds! Confusion! Did ye not all set upon me! Didn't ye talk to me of honor, compassion, justice?

SIR GEORGE.

Very true. You have acted according to their dictates, and I hope the utmost felicity of the married state will reward you.

DORICOURT.

Never, Sir George! To felicity I bid adieu, but I will endeavor to be content. Where is my—I must speak it—where is my *wife*?

Enter Letitia, masked, led by Saville.

SAVILLE.

Mr. Doricourt, this lady was pressing to be introduced to you.

DORICOURT. (*Starting.*)

Oh!

LETITIA.

I told you last night you should see me at a time when you least expected me, and I have kept my promise.

VILLERS.

Whoever you are, madam, you could not have arrived at a happier moment. Mr. Doricourt is just married.

LETITIA.

Married! Impossible! 'Tis but a few hours since he

---

88 "day of judgment" … "amazement"] phrases near the beginning and the end of the Church of England wedding ceremony

swore to me eternal love. I believed him, gave him up my virgin heart—and now!—ungrateful sex! 205

DORICOURT.

Your virgin heart! No, lady, my fate, thank Heaven, yet wants* that torture. Nothing but the conviction that you was another's could have made me think one moment of marriage to have saved the lives of half mankind. But this visit, madam, 210 is as barbarous as unexpected. It is now my duty to forget you, which, spite of your situation, I found difficult enough.

LETITIA.

My situation! What situation?

DORICOURT.

I must apologize for explaining it in this company. 215 But madam, I am not ignorant that you are the companion of Lord George Jennet, and this is the only circumstance that can give me peace.

LETITIA.

I—a companion! Ridiculous pretense! No sir, know to your confusion that my heart, my honor, 220 my name is unspotted as hers you have married, my birth equal to your own, my fortune large. That, and my person, might have been yours. But, sir, farewell! (*Going.*)

DORICOURT.

Oh, stay a moment. [*To Flutter.*] Rascal! is she 225 not—

FLUTTER.

Who, she? Oh, Lard no! 'Twas quite a different person that I meant. I never saw that lady before.

DORICOURT.

Then never shalt thou see her more. (*Shakes Flutter.*) 230

MRS. RACKET.

Have mercy upon the poor man! Heavens! He'll murder him.

DORICOURT.

Murder him! Yes, you, myself, and all mankind. Sir George, Saville, Villers, 'twas you who pushed me on this precipice, 'tis you who have snatched 235 from me joy, felicity, and life.

MRS. RACKET.

There! Now, how well he acts the madman! This is something like! I knew he would do it well enough when the time came.

DORICOURT.

Hard-hearted woman! enjoy my ruin, riot in my 240 wretchedness.

Hardy bursts in.

HARDY.

This is too much. You are now the husband of my daughter, and how dare you show all this passion about another woman?

DORICOURT.

Alive again! 245

HARDY.

Alive! aye, and merry. Here, wipe off the flour from my face. I was never in better health and spirits in my life. I foresaw 'twould do. Why, my illness was only a fetch, man, to make you marry Letty.

DORICOURT.

It was! Base and ungenerous! Well sir, you shall be 250 gratified. The possession of my heart was no object either with you or your daughter. My fortune and name was all you desired, and these—I leave ye. My native England I shall quit, nor ever behold you more.—But lady, that in my exile I may have 255 one consolation, grant me the favor you denied last night: let me behold all that mask conceals, that your whole image may be impressed on my heart and cheer my distant solitary hours.

LETITIA.

This is the most awful* moment of my life. Oh 260 Doricourt, the slight action of taking off my mask stamps me the most blessed or miserable of women!

DORICOURT.

What can this mean? Reveal your face, I conjure you. 265

LETITIA.

Behold it.

DORICOURT.

Rapture! Transport! Heaven!

FLUTTER.

Now for a touch of the happy madman.

VILLERS.

This scheme was mine.

LETITIA.

I will not allow that. This little stratagem arose 270 from my disappointment in not having made the impression on you I wished. The timidity of the English character threw a veil over me you could not penetrate. You have forced me to emerge in some measure from my natural reserve and to throw off the veil that hid me.   275

DORICOURT.

I am yet in a state of intoxication. I cannot answer you. Speak on, sweet angel!

LETITIA.

You see I *can* be anything. Choose then my character. Your taste shall fix it. Shall I be an *English* wife? Or, breaking from the bonds of   280 nature and education, step forth to the world in all the captivating glare of foreign manners?

DORICOURT.

You shall be nothing but yourself; nothing can be captivating that you are not. I will not wrong your penetration by pretending that you won my heart   285 at the first interview. But you have now my whole soul. Your person, your face, your mind I would not exchange for those of any other woman breathing.

HARDY.

A dog! How well he makes up for past slights!—   290 Cousin Racket, I wish you a good husband with all my heart.—Mr. Flutter, I'll believe every word you say this fortnight.—Mr. Villers, you and I have managed this to a "T." I never was so merry in my life. 'Gad, I believe I can dance! (*Footing.*)   295

DORICOURT.

Charming, charming creature!

LETITIA.

Congratulate me, my dear friends! Can you conceive my happiness?

HARDY.

No, congratulate me, for mine is the greatest.

FLUTTER.

No, congratulate me that I have escaped with life,   300 and give me some sticking plaster. This wildcat has torn the skin from my throat.

SIR GEORGE.

I expect to be among the first who are congratulated, for I have recovered one angel while Doricourt has gained another.   305

HARDY.

Faugh! Faugh! don't talk of angels, we shall be happier by half as mortals. Come into the next room! I have ordered out every drop of my forty-eight, and I'll invite the whole parish of St. George's[89] but what we'll drink it out—except one   310 dozen which I shall keep under three double locks for a certain christening that I foresee will happen within this twelvemonth.

DORICOURT.

My charming bride! It was a strange perversion of taste that led me to consider the delicate timidity   315 of your deportment as the mark of an uninformed mind or inelegant manners. I feel now it is to that innate modesty *English* husbands owe a felicity the married men of other nations are strangers to. It is a sacred veil to your own charms; it is the surest   320 bulwark to your husband's honor. And cursed be the hour, should it ever arrive, in which *British* ladies shall sacrifice to *foreign graces* the grace of modesty!

[*Exeunt.*]

FINIS.

---

89 St. George's] another prominent church on Botolph Lane

a Copytext is the first authorized edition, a 1782 quarto (Q1). Also consulted were the 1780 manuscript presented for registration (A), housed in the Larpent collection of the Henry E. Huntington Library and published in *Three Centuries of English Drama*; the second edition, a 1787 quarto (Q2), and the 1813 *Collected Works* (W). I have followed Frederick Link in the 1979 Garland facsimile edition of Q1 in accepting Q1 and Q2 as authoritative over W and have shown only representatives of the many changes made in that posthumously published edition revised by the author in her old age.

b SAVILLE] SERV. A, Q1, Q2, W

c Zounds] In W, oaths such as zounds, 'sdeath, begar, etc., are eliminated.

d Crowquill] In W, I.ii is severely curtailed, with the character of Crowquill excised and the lines about the gossip column eliminated.

e Villers] In W the characters of Villers and Saville are collapsed into one character named Saville.

f It is the same ... beauty heightened] a typical example of the cosmetic tinkering of W: It is the same face that my memory, or my fancy, constantly painted, its expression more heightened, its graces more finished.

g Miss Ogle] the Ogles, A, Q1, Q2, W; one of three references in the published editions to a plurality of Misses Ogle—a holdover from the ms (A); there is only one Miss Ogle in the published play.

h Scene ii] A includes nine lines omitted Q1, Q2, and W, in which Silvertongue educates the puffers on their trade.

i W gives Courtall a brief moment of contrition: "But softly!—softly—a moment— crise conscience! Wilt thou attempt to blemish her character for virtue—merely to keep up thy own for vice!" But with a "psha" he quickly dismisses his "qualm."

j masquerade] Pantheon A, Q1, Q2, W

k a] Q2, W; the A, Q1

She Stoops to Conquer; or, The Mistakes of a Night[a]

by Oliver Goldsmith (1730-74)
edited by Richard A. Barney

Oliver Goldsmith's *She Stoops to Conquer* has been one of the most beloved English comedies since it was first staged in March 1773. The events leading to its production, however, were anything but promising. Goldsmith had no abiding interest in theater per se, since this play was only the second one he ever wrote, the first being *The Good Natured Man*, which was staged with moderate success in 1768. As with that play, *She Stoops to Conquer* was the brainchild of financial necessity, because Goldsmith wrote it with the hope of a windfall to get himself out of extreme debt, a chronic condition that dogged him most of his life. Moreover, because Goldsmith's play departed from the theatrical fashions of the times, it was initially rejected for production by the managers of the two key London theaters, George Colman of Covent Garden and David Garrick of Drury Lane. Despite his misgivings, Colman later agreed to take on Goldsmith's play, but problems persisted: Colman insisted on several controversial changes to the script; at least two better actors were lost because of the play's staging so late in the season; Goldsmith wrestled with three versions of the epilogue before settling on one that served; and the play's title was decided only at the last minute. Beginning with its opening night, however, *She Stoops to Conquer* proved a blazing success, as if confirming the peculiar logic by which its characters also ultimately thrive despite—or because of—their mutually chaotic lives.

Goldsmith's play seemed risky because, as one eighteenth-century critic explained, it was "taking the field against that monster called Sentimental Comedy." Goldsmith saw his play as an attempt to revive the edgier wit of Restoration comedy in the face of what the Prologue calls the "mawkish drab" of senti-mental moralizing. Diggory's clownish antics, Tony Lumpkins' rambunctious capers, and Kate Hard-castle's disguising herself as a barmaid were all "low" elements intended not only for laughs, but also for the purpose of undermining the confident gentility of many of its characters—or of the audience. Hence Charles Marlow's and George Hastings' inability to distinguish Mr. Hardcastle from an innkeeper—the initial "mistake" producing a cascade of comic misrecognitions throughout the play—is part of a larger dynamic in which the usual markers of class distinction become disoriented or fluid at best.

Ultimately, Goldsmith's play did not slay that theatrical dragon, since the genre flourished well into the nineteenth century, partly under the guise of melodrama. What is more, on its own terms, his play does not so much reject sentimental elements as it does juxtapose them with characters' other, venal propensities, usually with a twist of dramatic irony that links the "high" and "low" inextricably to each other. Such a dual perspective is fitting for Goldsmith's aim that comedy should be, as he put it, "perfectly satirical yet perfectly goodnatured." That capacious, comic vision seems to account for the play's enormous success, even during its premiere, when Goldsmith reintegrated the role of individuals who had been initially unhelpful. In a conciliatory gesture for having rejected the play earlier, Garrick ended up contributing the prologue, and Henry Woodward, a leading comic actor who had declined to play Tony Lumpkin, delivered that prologue during the first run. Since then, *She Stoops to Conquer* has been one of the most restaged and reproduced of English comedies, appearing in more than 300 editions since the 1770s.

PROLOGUE

Enter Mr. Woodward, dressed in black and holding a handkerchief to his eyes.

Excuse me, sirs, I pray—I can't yet speak—
I'm crying now—and have been all the week!
'Tis not alone this mourning suit, good masters;
I've that within[1]—for which there are no plasters!
Pray would you know the reason why I'm crying?   5
The comic muse, long sick, is now a-dying!
And if she goes, my tears will never stop,
For as a player, I can't squeeze out one drop.
I am undone, that's all—shall lose my bread—
I'd rather, but that's nothing—lose my head.   10
When the sweet maid is laid upon the bier,
Shuter and I shall be chief mourners here.
To her a mawkish drab of spurious breed
Who deals in sentimentals[2] will succeed!
Poor Ned[3] and I are dead to all intents;   15
We can as soon speak Greek as sentiments!
Both nervous grown, to keep our spirits up
We now and then take down a hearty cup.
What shall we do? If Comedy forsake us,
They'll turn us out, and no one else will take us![4]   20
But why can't I be moral?—Let me try—
My heart thus pressing—fixed my face and eye
With a sententious look that nothing means
(Faces are blocks,[5] in sentimental scenes).
Thus I begin: "All is not gold that glitters;   25
Pleasure seems sweet but proves a glass of bitters;
When ign'rance enters, folly is at hand;
Learning is better far than house and land;
Let not your virtue trip, who trips may stumble,
And virtue is not virtue, if she tumble."   30
      I give it up—morals won't do for me;
To make you laugh I must play tragedy.
One hope remains: hearing the maid was ill,

---

1 'Tis not ... within] allusion to *Hamlet* I.ii.77, 85
2 sentimentals] the currently popular dramas, whose pious moralizing is parodied in the lines below
3 Shuter ... Ned] Edward Shuter, the fine comic actor who played Mr. Hardcastle
4 They'll ... take us] slightly misquoted from Buckingham's *The Rehearsal* (1671), II.iv.67-68
5 blocks] wooden heads used as wig stands

A doctor[6] comes this night to show his skill.
To cheer her heart and give your muscles motion,   35
He in five draughts prepared presents a potion:
A kind of magic charm—for be assured,
If you will swallow it, the maid is cured.
But desperate the Doctor and her case is,
If you reject the dose and make wry faces!   40
This truth he boasts, will boast it while he lives:
No pois'nous drugs are mixed in what he gives.
Should he succeed, you'll give him his degree;
If not, within he will receive no fee!
The college, you, must his pretensions back,   45
Pronounce him regular, or dub him quack.

DRAMATIS PERSONAE

MEN

  Sir Charles Marlow.
  Young Marlow, his son.
  Hardcastle.
  Hastings.
  Tony* Lumpkin.
  Diggory.
  [Roger.]
  [Jeremy]
  Landlord, servants, etc.

WOMEN

  Mrs. Hardcastle.
  Miss Hardcastle.
  Miss Neville.
  Maid.

She Stoops to Conquer; or, The Mistakes of a Night.

Act I, scene i. A chamber in an old-fashioned house.

Enter Mrs. Hardcastle and Mr. Hardcastle.

MRS. HARDCASTLE.

  I vow, Mr. Hardcastle, you're very particular. Is there a creature in the whole country but ourselves that does not take a trip to Town* now and then to rub off the rust a little? There's the two Miss Hoggs and our neighbor, Mrs. Grigsby, go to take   5
a month's polishing every winter.

---

6 A doctor] Goldsmith, who used the title after 1763 (including on the titlepage of this play)

HARDCASTLE.

Aye, and bring back vanity and affectation to last them the whole year. I wonder why London cannot keep its own fools at home. In my time, the follies of the Town crept slowly among us, but now they travel faster than a stagecoach. Its fopperies come down not only as inside passengers but in the very basket.[7]

MRS. HARDCASTLE.

Aye, *your* times were fine times, indeed; you have been telling us of *them* for many a long year. Here we live in an old rumbling[8] mansion that looks for all the world like an inn, but that we never see company. Our best visitors are old Mrs. Oddfish, the curate's wife, and little Cripplegate, the lame dancing master, and all our entertainment your old stories of Prince Eugene and the Duke of Marlborough.[9] I hate such old-fashioned trumpery.

HARDCASTLE.

And I love it. I love everything that's old: old friends, old times, old manners, old books, old wine. And I believe, Dorothy, (*Taking her hand.*) you'll own I have been pretty fond of an old wife.

MRS. HARDCASTLE.

Lord, Mr. Hardcastle, you're forever at your Dorothy's and your old wife's. You may be a Darby, but I'll be no Joan,[10] I promise you. I'm not so old as you'd make me, by more than one good year. Add twenty to twenty, and make money of that.

HARDCASTLE.

Let me see, twenty added to twenty, makes just fifty and seven.

MRS. HARDCASTLE.

It's false, Mr. Hardcastle: I was but twenty when I was brought to bed of Tony, that I had by Mr. Lumpkin, my first husband, and he's not come to years of discretion yet.

HARDCASTLE.

Nor ever will, I dare answer for him. Aye, you have taught *him* finely.

MRS. HARDCASTLE.

No matter, Tony Lumpkin has a good fortune. My son is not to live by his learning. I don't think a boy wants* much learning to spend fifteen hundred a year.

HARDCASTLE.

Learning, quotha! A mere composition of tricks and mischief.

MRS. HARDCASTLE.

Humor,* my dear, nothing but humor. Come, Mr. Hardcastle, you must allow the boy a little humor.

HARDCASTLE.

I'd sooner allow him a horsepond.[11] If burning the footmen's shoes, frighting the maids, and worrying the kittens be humor, he has it. It was but yesterday he fastened my wig to the back of my chair, and when I went to make a bow, I popped my bald head in Mrs. Frizzle's face.

MRS. HARDCASTLE.

And am I to blame? The poor boy was always too sickly to do any good. A school would be his death. When he comes to be a little stronger, who knows what a year or two's Latin may do for him?

HARDCASTLE.

Latin for him! A cat and fiddle. No, no, the alehouse and the stable are the only schools he'll ever go to.

MRS. HARDCASTLE.

Well, we must not snub the poor boy now, for I believe we shan't have him long among us. Anybody that looks in his face may see he's consumptive.

HARDCASTLE.

Aye, if growing too fat be one of the symptoms.

MRS. HARDCASTLE.

He coughs sometimes.

HARDCASTLE.

Yes, when his liquor goes the wrong way.

MRS. HARDCASTLE.

I'm actually afraid of his lungs.

---

7 basket] the outside back seat or baggage carrier of a stagecoach

8 rumbling] rambling; apparently an old-fashioned usage by 1773

9 Eugene … Marlborough] leaders (q.v.) during the War of the Spanish Succession (1701-14).

10 Darby … Joan] old married couple whose happiness is proverbial

11 horsepond] a pond for watering horses

HARDCASTLE.

And truly so am I, for he sometimes whoops like a speaking trumpet— 70

Tony hallooing behind the scenes.

Oh there he goes—a very consumptive figure, truly.

Enter Tony, crossing the stage.

MRS. HARDCASTLE.

Tony, where are you going, my charmer? Won't you give papa and I a little of your company, lovey?

TONY.

I'm in haste, mother, I cannot stay. 75

MRS. HARDCASTLE.

You shan't venture out this raw evening, my dear: you look most shockingly.

TONY.

I can't stay, I tell you. The Three Pigeons expects me down every moment. There's some fun going forward. 80

HARDCASTLE.

Aye, the alehouse, the old place: I thought so.

MRS. HARDCASTLE.

A low, paltry set of fellows.

TONY.

Not so low neither. There's Dick Muggins the exciseman, Jack Slang the horse doctor, Little Aminadab that grinds the music box,[12] and Tom 85 Twist that spins the pewter platter.

MRS. HARDCASTLE.

Pray my dear, disappoint them for one night at least.

TONY.

As for disappointing *them*, I should not so much mind, but I can't abide to disappoint *myself*. 90

MRS. HARDCASTLE. (*Detaining him.*)

You shan't go.

TONY.

I will, I tell you.

MRS. HARDCASTLE.

I say you shan't.

---

12 Dick Muggins … box] A muggins is a fool; Dick is a tax collector; slang meant "humbug, nonsense"; Aminadab was a Jew, the father-in-law of Aaron in the Bible (Davis).

TONY.

We'll see which is strongest, you or I.

Exit, hauling her out.

HARDCASTLE.

Aye, there goes a pair that only spoil each other. 95 But is not the whole age in a combination to drive sense and discretion out of doors? There's my pretty darling Kate; the fashions of the times have almost infected her too. By living a year or two in Town, she is as fond of gauze and French frippery 100 as the best of them.

Enter Miss Hardcastle.

Blessings on my pretty innocence! Dressed out as usual, my Kate. Goodness! What a quantity of superfluous silk hast thou got about thee, girl! I could never teach the fools of this age that the 105 indigent world could be clothed out of the trimmings of the vain.

MISS HARDCASTLE.

You know our agreement, sir. You allow me the morning to receive and pay visits and to dress in my own manner, and in the evening, I put on my 110 housewife's dress to please you.

HARDCASTLE.

Well, remember I insist on the terms of our agreement. And by the bye, I believe I shall have occasion to try your obedience this very evening.

MISS HARDCASTLE.

I protest, sir, I don't comprehend your meaning. 115

HARDCASTLE.

Then to be plain with you, Kate, I expect the young gentleman I have chosen to be your husband from Town this very day. I have his father's letter, in which he informs me his son is set out and that he intends to follow himself shortly after. 120

MISS HARDCASTLE.

Indeed! I wish I had known something of this before. Bless me, how shall I behave? It's a thousand to one I shan't like him. Our meeting will be so formal and so like a thing of business that I shall find no room for friendship or esteem. 125

HARDCASTLE.

Depend upon it child, I'll never control your choice, but Mr. Marlow, whom I have pitched upon, is the son of my old friend, Sir Charles Marlow, of whom you have heard me talk so often. The young gentleman has been bred a scholar and is designed for an employment in the service of his country. I am told he's a man of an excellent understanding. 130

MISS HARDCASTLE.

Is he?

HARDCASTLE.

Very generous.

MISS HARDCASTLE.

I believe I shall like him. 135

HARDCASTLE.

Young and brave.

MISS HARDCASTLE.

I'm sure I shall like him.

HARDCASTLE.

And very handsome.

MISS HARDCASTLE.

My dear papa, say no more. (*Kissing his hand.*) He's mine, I'll have him. 140

HARDCASTLE.

And to crown all, Kate, he's one of the most bashful and reserved young fellows in all the world.

MISS HARDCASTLE.

Eh! You have frozen me to death again. That word "reserved" has undone all the rest of his accomplishments. A reserved lover, it is said, always 145 makes a suspicious husband.

HARDCASTLE.

On the contrary, modesty seldom resides in a breast that is not enriched with nobler virtues. It was the very feature in his character that first struck me.

MISS HARDCASTLE.

He must have more striking features to catch me, 150 I promise you. However, if he be so young, so handsome, and so everything, as you mention, I believe he'll do still. I think I'll have him.

HARDCASTLE.

Aye Kate, but there is still an obstacle. It's more than an even wager he may not have *you*. 155

MISS HARDCASTLE.

My dear papa, why will you mortify one so? Well, if he refuses, instead of breaking my heart at his indifference I'll only break my glass* for its flattery, set my cap to some newer fashion, and look out for some less difficult admirer. 160

HARDCASTLE.

Bravely* resolved! In the meantime, I'll go prepare the servants for his reception; as we seldom see company, they want* as much training as a company of recruits the first day's muster. (*Exit.*)

MISS HARDCASTLE.

Lud,* this news of Papa's puts me all in a flutter. 165 Young, handsome: these he put last, but I put them foremost. Sensible,[13] good-natured: I like all that. But then, reserved and sheepish: that's much against him. Yet can't he be cured of his timidity by being taught to be proud of his wife? Yes, and 170 can't I— But I vow I'm disposing of the husband before I have secured the lover.

Enter Miss Neville.

I'm glad you're come, Neville, my dear. Tell me, Constance, how do I look this evening? Is there anything whimsical about me? Is it one of my well 175 looking days, child?* Am I in face today?

MISS NEVILLE.

Perfectly, my dear. Yet now I look again—bless me!—sure no accident has happened among the canary birds or the goldfishes. Has your brother or the cat been meddling? Or has the last novel 180 been too moving?

MISS HARDCASTLE.

No, nothing of all this. I have been threatened—I can scarce get it out—I have been threatened with a lover.

MISS NEVILLE.

And his name— 185

MISS HARDCASTLE.

Is Marlow.

MISS NEVILLE.

Indeed!

MISS HARDCASTLE.

The son of Sir Charles Marlow.

MISS NEVILLE.

As I live, the most intimate friend of Mr. Hastings, *my* admirer. They are never asunder. I believe you 190 must have seen him when we lived in Town.

MISS HARDCASTLE.

Never.

---

13 Sensible] having sensibility; capable of delicate or tender feeling (*OED*)

MISS NEVILLE.

 He's a very singular character, I assure you. Among women of reputation and virtue, he is the modestest man alive, but his acquaintance give him 195 a very different character* among creatures of another stamp: you understand me.

MISS HARDCASTLE.

 An odd character, indeed. I shall never be able to manage him. What shall I do? Pshaw, think no more of him but trust to occurrences for success. But how 200 goes on your own affair, my dear? Has my mother been courting you for my brother Tony as usual?

MISS NEVILLE.

 I have just come from one of our agreeable tête-à-têtes. She has been saying a hundred tender things and setting off her pretty monster as the very pink 205 of perfection.

MISS HARDCASTLE.

 And her partiality is such that she actually thinks him so. A fortune like yours is no small temptation. Besides, as she has the sole management of it, I'm not surprised to see her 210 unwilling to let it go out of the family.

MISS NEVILLE.

 A fortune like mine, which chiefly consists in jewels, is no such mighty temptation. But at any rate, if my dear Hastings be but constant, I make no doubt to be too hard for her at last. However, I let her suppose 215 that I am in love with her son, and she never once dreams that my affections are fixed upon another.

MISS HARDCASTLE.

 My good brother holds out stoutly. I could almost love him for hating you so.

MISS NEVILLE.

 It is a good-natured creature at bottom and, I'm 220 sure, would wish to see me married to anybody but himself. But my aunt's bell rings for our afternoon's walk round the improvements. Allons.[14] Courage is necessary, as our affairs are critical.

MISS HARDCASTLE.

 Would it were bedtime and all were well. 225

Exeunt.

---

14 Allons] "Let's go"; an anglicized version of the French, "Allons y"

Scene [ii]. An alehouse room.

Several shabby fellows, with punch and tobacco. Tony at the head of the table, a little higher than the rest: a mallet in his hand.

OMNES.

 Hurrah, hurrah, hurrah, bravo.

FIRST FELLOW.

 Now gentlemen, silence for a song. The squire is going to knock himself down for a song.

OMNES.

 Aye, a song, a song.

TONY.

 Then I'll sing you, gentlemen, a song I made upon 5 this alehouse, the Three Pigeons.

Song.

Let schoolmasters puzzle their brain
 With grammar and nonsense and learning;
Good liquor, I stoutly maintain,
 Gives genus[15] a better discerning. 10
Let them brag of their heathenish gods,
 Their Lethes, their Styxes, and Stygians,
Their *quis*, and their *quaes*, and their *quods*,[16]
 They're all but a parcel of pigeons.
  Toroddle, toroddle, toroll. 15
When Methodist preachers come down,
 A-preaching that drinking is sinful,
I'll wager the rascals a crown,
 They always preach best with a skinful.
But when you come down with your pence, 20
 For a slice of their scurvy religion,
I'll leave it to all men of sense,
 But you my good friend are the pigeon.
  Toroddle, toroddle, toroll.
Then come, put the jorum about, 25
 And let us be merry and clever;
Our hearts and our liquors are stout;
 Here's the Three Jolly Pigeons forever.
Let some cry up woodcock or hare,
 Your bustards, your ducks, and your widgeons 30

---

15 genus] a Lumpkinism for "genius" in the sense of natural capacity or quality of mind

16 *quis … quods*] the nominative forms of Latin relative pronouns, Latin being a sign of a learned education

But of all the birds in the air,
    Here's a health to the Three Jolly Pigeons.
               Toroddle, toroddle, toroll.

OMNES.
  Bravo, bravo.

FIRST FELLOW.
  The squire has got spunk in him.   35

SECOND FELLOW.
  I loves to hear him sing, bekeays he never gives us
  nothing that's *low*.

THIRD FELLOW.
  Oh damn anything that's *low*, I cannot bear it.

FOURTH FELLOW.
  The genteel thing is the genteel thing at any time.
  If so be that a gentleman bees in a concatenation   40
  ackoardingly.[b]

THIRD FELLOW.
  I like the maxum[17] of it, Master Muggins. What,
  though I am obligated to dance a bear, a man may be
  a gentleman for all that. May this be my poison if my
  bear ever dances but to the very genteelest of tunes.   45
  "Water Parted"[18] or the minuet in *Adriadne*.[19]

SECOND FELLOW.
  What a pity it is the squire is not come to his own.
  It would be well for all the publicans within ten
  miles round of him.

TONY.
  Ecod and so it would, Master Slang. I'd then show   50
  what it was to keep choice of company.

SECOND FELLOW.
  Oh he takes after his own father for that. To be sure,
  old Squire Lumpkin was the finest gentleman I ever
  set my eyes on. For winding the straight horn or
  beating a thicket for a hare or a wench, he never had   55
  his fellow. It was a saying in the place that he kept
  the best horses, dogs, and girls in the whole county.

TONY.
  Ecod, and when I'm of age I'll be no bastard I
  promise you. I have been thinking of Bett Bouncer
  and the miller's grey mare to begin with. But come,   60

my boys, drink about and be merry, for you pay
no reckoning.

Enter landlord.

  Well Stingo, what's the matter?

LANDLORD.
  There be two gentlemen in a post chaise at the
  door. They have lost their way upo'the forest, and   65
  they are talking something about Mr. Hardcastle.

TONY.
  As sure as can be one of them must be the
  gentleman that's coming down to court my sister.
  Do they seem to be Londoners?

LANDLORD.
  I believe they may. They look woundily[20] like   70
  Frenchmen.

TONY.
  Then desire them to step this way, and I'll set them
  right in a twinkling.

Exit landlord.

  Gentlemen, as they mayn't be good enough
  company for you, step down for a moment, and   75
  I'll be with you in the squeezing of a lemon.

Exeunt mob.

TONY.
  Father-in-law[21] has been calling me whelp and
  hound this half year. Now if I pleased, I could be
  so revenged upon the old grumbletonian.* But
  then, I'm afraid—afraid of what! I shall soon be   80
  worth fifteen hundred a year, and let him frighten
  me out of *that* if he can.

Enter landlord, conducting Marlow and Hastings.

MARLOW.
  What a tedious, uncomfortable day have we had
  of it! We were told it was but forty miles across
  the country, and we have come above threescore.   85

HASTINGS.
  And all, Marlow, from that unaccountable reserve
  of yours, that would not let us enquire more
  frequently on the way.

---

17 maxum] maxim
18 "Water Parted"] an aria from Thomas Augustine Arne's
    opera *Artaxerxes* (1762)
19 minuet … *Adriadne*] The minuet forms part of the over-
    ture of Händel's opera *Arianna in Creta* (1734).

---

20 woundily] extremely
21 Father-in-law] stepfather

MARLOW.

I own, Hastings, I am unwilling to lay myself under an obligation to everyone I meet and often stand the chance of an unmannerly answer.　90

HASTINGS.

At present, however, we are not likely to receive any answer.

TONY.

No offense, gentlemen. But I'm told you have been enquiring for one Mr. Hardcastle in these^c parts. Do you know what part of the country you are in?　95

HASTINGS.

Not in the least, sir, but should thank you for information.

TONY.

Nor the way you came?

HASTINGS.

No sir, but if you can inform us—　100

TONY.

Why gentlemen, if you know neither the road you are going, nor where you are, nor the road you came, the first thing I have to inform you is that— you have lost your way.

MARLOW.

We wanted* no ghost to tell us that.[22]　105

TONY.

Pray gentlemen, may I be so bold as to ask the place from whence you came?

MARLOW.

That's not necessary towards directing us where we are to go.

TONY.

No offense, but question for question is all fair, you know. Pray gentlemen, is not this same Hardcastle a cross-grained, old-fashioned, whimsical fellow, with an ugly face, a daughter, and a pretty son?　110

HASTINGS.

We have not seen the gentleman, but he has the family you mention.　115

TONY.

The daughter, a tall traipsing,[23] trolloping, talkative maypole; the son, a pretty, well-bred, agreeable youth, that everybody is fond of.

MARLOW.

Our information differs in this. The daughter is said to be well-bred and beautiful; the son, an awkward booby, reared up and spoiled at his mother's apron string.　120

TONY.

He-he-hem— Then gentlemen, all I have to tell you is that you won't reach Mr. Hardcastle's house this night, I believe.　125

HASTINGS.

Unfortunate!

TONY.

It's a damned long, dark, boggy, dirty, dangerous way.—Stingo, tell the gentlemen the way to Mr. Hardcastle's. (*Winking upon the landlord.*) Mr. Hardcastle's of Quagmire Marsh, you understand me.　130

LANDLORD.

Master Hardcastle's! Lock-a-daisy, my masters, you're come a deadly deal wrong! When you came to the bottom of the hill, you should have crossed down Squash Lane.　135

MARLOW. (*Noting it down.*)^d

Cross down Squash Lane!

LANDLORD.

Then you were to keep straight forward till you came to four roads.

MARLOW. (*Still noting.*)^e

Come to where four roads meet!

TONY.

Aye, but you must be sure to take only one of them.　140

MARLOW.

Oh sir, you're facetious.

TONY.

Then keeping to the right, you are to go sideways till you come upon Crackskull Common: there you must look sharp for the track of the wheel and go forward till you come to Farmer Murrain's[24] barn. Coming to the farmer's barn, you are to turn to the right, and then, to the left, and then to the right about again, till you find out the old mill—　145

---

22 We … that] adapted from *Hamlet* I.v.125-26

23 traipsing] going about in a slovenly manner (*OED*)

24 Murrain] a pestilence or plague affecting domestic plants or animals

MARLOW. (*Who had been noting.*)f

Zounds, man! we could as soon find out the 150
longitude!25

HASTINGS.

What's to be done, Marlow?

MARLOW.

This house promises but a poor reception, though
perhaps the landlord can accommodate us.

LANDLORD.

Alack master, we have but one spare bed in the 155
whole house.

TONY.

And to my knowledge, that's taken up by three
lodgers already. (*After a pause, in which the rest seem
disconcerted.*) I have hit it. Don't you think, Stingo,
our landlady could accommodate the gentlemen 160
by the fireside, with—three chairs and a bolster?

HASTINGS.

I hate sleeping by the fireside.

MARLOW.

And I detest your three chairs and a bolster.

TONY.

You do, do you?—then let me see—what if you
go on a mile further, to the Buck's Head, the old 165
Buck's Head on the hill, one of the best inns in
the whole county?

HASTINGS.

Oh ho! so we have escaped an adventure for this
night, however.

LANDLORD. (*Apart to Tony.*)

Sure, you ben't sending them to your father's as an 170
inn, be you?

TONY.

Mum, you fool you. Let *them* find that out. (*To
them.*) You have only to keep on straight forward,
till you come to a large old house by the roadside.
You'll see a pair of large horns over the door. That's 175
the sign. Drive up the yard and call stoutly about
you.

HASTINGS.

Sir, we are obliged to you. The servants can't miss
the way?

TONY.

No, no, but I tell you, though, the landlord is rich 180
and going to leave off business, so he wants to be
thought a gentleman, saving your presence, he! he!
he! He'll be for giving you his company, and ecod
if you mind him, he'll persuade you that his
mother was an alderman and his aunt a justice of 185
peace.

LANDLORD.

A troublesome old blade to be sure, but 'a* keeps
as good wines and beds as any in the whole
county.g

MARLOW.

Well, if he supplies us with these, we shall want* 190
no further connection. We are to turn to the right,
did you say?

TONY.

No, no, straight forward. I'll just step myself and
show you a piece of the way. (*To the landlord.*)
Mum. 195

LANDLORD.

Ah, bless your heart, for a sweet, pleasant—
damned mischievous son of a whore.

Exeunt.

Act II, scene i. An old-fashioned house.

*Enter Hardcastle, followed by three or four awkward
servants.*

HARDCASTLE.

Well, I hope you're perfect in the table exercise I
have been teaching you these three days. You all
know your posts and your places and can show
that you have been used to good company without
ever stirring from home. 5

OMNES.

Aye, aye.

HARDCASTLE.

When company comes, you are not to pop out and
stare, and then run in again, like frighted rabbits
in a warren.

OMNES.

No, no. 10

---

25 we could … longitude] Since 1713, Parliament had offered a £20,000 reward for an invention that could determine the longitude at sea. After John Harrison had
claimed the prize for his marine chronometer in 1761,
the reward was tardily granted in 1773.

HARDCASTLE.

You, Diggory, whom I have taken from the barn, are to make a show at the side table, and you, Roger, whom I have advanced from the plough, are to place yourself behind *my* chair. But you're not to stand so, with your hands in your pockets. Take your hands from your pockets, Roger—and from your head, you blockhead you. See how Diggory carries his hands. They're a little too stiff, indeed, but that's no great matter.

DIGGORY.

Aye, mind how I hold them. I learned to hold my hands this-aways[h] when I was upon drill for the militia. And so being upon drill—

HARDCASTLE.

You must not be so talkative, Diggory. You must be all attention to the guests. You must hear us talk, and not think of talking; you must see us drink, and not think of drinking; you must see us eat, and not think of eating.

DIGGORY.

By the laws, your worship, that's parfectly unpossible. Whenever Diggory sees yeating going forward, ecod he's always wishing for a mouthful himself.

HARDCASTLE.

Blockhead! Is not a bellyful in the kitchen as good as a bellyful in the parlor? Stay your stomach with that reflection.

DIGGORY.

Ecod, I thank your worship, I'll make a shift to stay my stomach with a slice of cold beef in the pantry.

HARDCASTLE.

Diggory, you are too talkative. Then if I happen to say a good thing or tell a good story at table, you must not all burst out a-laughing, as if you made part of the company.

DIGGORY.

Then ecod, your worship must not tell the story of Auld Grouse in the gun room: 'I can't help laughing at that—he! he! he!—for the soul of me. We have laughed at that these twenty years—ha! ha! ha!

HARDCASTLE.

Ha! ha! ha! The story is a good one. Well, honest Diggory, you may laugh at that—but still

remember to be attentive. Suppose one of the company should call for a glass of wine, how will you behave? "A glass of wine, sir, if you please." Eh, why don't you move?

DIGGORY.

Ecod, your worship, I never have courage till I see the eatables and drinkables brought upo'the table, and then I'm as bauld as a lion.

HARDCASTLE.

What, will nobody move?

FIRST SERVANT.

I'm not to leave this pleace.

SECOND SERVANT.

I'm sure it's no pleace of mine.

THIRD SERVANT.

Nor mine, for sartain.

DIGGORY.

Wauns,[26] and I'm sure it canna be mine.

HARDCASTLE.

You numbskulls! and so while, like your betters, you are quarreling for places, the guests must be starved. Oh you dunces! I find I must begin all over again.—But don't I hear a coach drive into the yard? To your posts, you blockheads. I'll go in the meantime and give my old friend's son a hearty reception at the gate. (*Exit.*)

DIGGORY.

By the elevens,[27] my pleace is gone quite out of my head.

ROGER.

I know that my pleace is to be everywhere.

FIRST SERVANT.

Where the devil is mine?

SECOND SERVANT.

My pleace is to be nowhere at all, and so I's go about my business.

Exeunt servants, running about as if frighted, different ways. Enter servant with candles, showing in Marlow and Hastings.

SERVANT.

Welcome, gentlemen, very welcome. This way.

---

26 Wauns] (God's) wounds; a mild oath

27 By the elevens] obscure exclamation. Davis speculates: "'Heavens'? 'Apostles' (minus Judas)?"

HASTINGS.

After the disappointments of the day, welcome once more, Charles, to the comforts of a clean room and a good fire. Upon my word, a very well-looking house—antique but creditable. 75

MARLOW.

The usual fate of a large mansion. Having first ruined the master by good housekeeping, it at last comes to levy contributions as an inn. 80

HASTINGS.

As you say, we passengers are to be taxed to pay all these fineries. I have often seen a good sideboard or a marble chimney piece, though not actually put in the bill, inflame a reckoning confoundedly.

MARLOW.

Travelers, George, must pay in all places. The only 85 difference is, that in good inns, you pay dearly for luxuries; in bad inns, you are fleeced and starved.

HASTINGS.

You have lived pretty much among them. In truth, I have been often surprised that you, who have seen so much of the world, with your natural good 90 sense and your many opportunities could never yet acquire a requisite share of assurance.

MARLOW.

The Englishman's malady. But tell me, George, where could I have learned that assurance you talk of? My life has been chiefly spent in a college or 95 an inn,[28] in seclusion from that lovely part of the creation that chiefly teach men confidence. I don't know that I was ever familiarly acquainted with a single modest woman—except my mother. But among females of another class, you know— 100

HASTINGS.

Aye, among them you are impudent enough of all conscience.

MARLOW.

They are of *us* you know.

HASTINGS.

But in the company of women of reputation I never saw such an idiot, such a trembler; you look 105 for all the world as if you wanted an opportunity of stealing out of the room.

MARLOW.

Why man, that's because I *do* want to steal out of the room. Faith, I have often formed a resolution to break the ice and rattle away at any rate. But I don't 110 know how, a single glance from a pair of fine eyes has totally overset my resolution. An impudent fellow may counterfeit modesty, but I'll be hanged if a modest man can ever counterfeit impudence.

HASTINGS.

If you could but say half the fine things to them 115 that I have heard you lavish upon the barmaid of an inn or even a college bedmaker—

MARLOW.

Why George, I can't say fine things to them. They freeze, they petrify me. They may talk of a comet or a burning mountain or some such bagatelle. But to 120 me, a modest woman, dressed out in all her finery, is the most tremendous object of the whole creation.

HASTINGS.

Ha! ha! ha! At this rate, man, how can you ever expect to marry!

MARLOW.

Never, unless as among kings and princes, my 125 bride were to be courted by proxy. If indeed, like an Eastern bridegroom, one were to be introduced to a wife he never saw before, it might be endured. But to go through all the terrors of a formal courtship, together with the episode of aunts, 130 grandmothers, and cousins, and at last to blurt out the broad, staring[29] question, of, "Madam, will you marry me?"—no, no, that's a strain much above me I assure you.

HASTINGS.

I pity you. But how do you intend behaving to the 135 lady you are come down to visit at the request of your father?

MARLOW.

As I behave to all other ladies: bow very low, answer yes or no to all her demands. But for the rest, I don't think I shall venture to look in her face 140 till I see my father's again.

HASTINGS.

I'm surprised that one who is so warm a friend can be so cool a lover.

---

28 inn] one of the Inns of Court*

29 staring] obvious, conspicuous

MARLOW.

To be explicit, my dear Hastings, my chief inducement down was to be instrumental in forwarding 145
your happiness, not my own. Miss Neville loves
you; the family don't know you; as my friend you
are sure of a reception, and let honor do the rest.

HASTINGS.

My dear Marlow! But I'll suppress the emotion.
Were I a wretch, meanly seeking to carry off a 150
fortune, you should be the last man in the world
I would apply to for assistance. But Miss Neville's
person is all I ask, and that is mine, both from her
deceased father's consent and her own inclination.

MARLOW.

Happy man! You have talents and art to captivate any 155
woman. I'm doomed to adore the sex and yet to
converse with the only part of it I despise. This
stammer in my address and this awkward
prepossessing[30] visage of mine can never permit me
to soar above the reach of a milliner's prentice or one 160
of the duchesses of Drury Lane.[31]—Pshaw! this
fellow here to interrupt us.

Enter Hardcastle.

HARDCASTLE.

Gentlemen, once more you are heartily welcome.
Which is Mr. Marlow? Sir, you're heartily welcome.
It's not my way, you see, to receive my friends with 165
my back to the fire. I like to give them a hearty
reception in the old style at my gate. I like to see
their horses and trunks taken care of.

MARLOW. (*Aside.*)

He has got our names from the servants already.
(*To him.*) We approve your caution and hospitality, 170
sir. (*To Hastings.*) I have been thinking, George, of
changing our traveling dresses in the morning. I
am grown confoundedly ashamed of mine.

HARDCASTLE.

I beg, Mr. Marlow, you'll use no ceremony in this
house. 175

HASTINGS.

I fancy, Charles, you're right: the first blow is half
the battle. I intend opening the campaign with the
white and gold.

HARDCASTLE.

Mr. Marlow—Mr. Hastings—gentlemen—pray be
under no constraint in this house. This is Liberty 180
Hall, gentlemen. You may do just as you please
here.

MARLOW.

Yet, George, if we open the campaign too fiercely
at first, we may want* ammunition before it is
over. I think to reserve the embroidery to secure a 185
retreat.

HARDCASTLE.

Your talking of a retreat, Mr. Marlow, puts me in
mind of the Duke of Marlborough, when we went
to besiege Denain.[32] He first summoned the
garrison. 190

MARLOW.

Don't you think the *ventre d'or*[33] waistcoat will do
with the plain brown?

HARDCASTLE.

He first summoned the garrison, which might
consist of about five thousand men—

HASTINGS.

I think not: brown and yellow mix but very poorly. 195

HARDCASTLE.

I say, gentlemen, as I was telling you, he
summoned the garrison, which might consist of
about five thousand men—

MARLOW.

The girls like finery.

HARDCASTLE.

Which might consist of about five thousand men, 200
well appointed with stores, ammunition, and other
implements of war. "Now," says the Duke of
Marlborough to George Brooks, that stood next

---

30 prepossessing] Marlow is using this word in its older
sense of "creating prejudice." He may be alluding to his
propensity to blush.

31 duchesses of Drury Lane] women of dubious repute,
including prostitutes, who frequented the theater on
Drury Lane, often claiming to be nobility

32 Marlborough … Denain] During the War of the Spanish Succession the French defeated the Allies (England,
Netherlands, and Prussia) in Denain, France in 1712.
It was Lord Albemarle who led the Allies during that
battle, rather than Marlborough, who was not even
present because he had been dismissed in 1711.

33 *ventre d'or*] gold-fronted

to him—you must have heard of George Brooks—
"I'll pawn my dukedom," says he, "but I take that   205
garrison without spilling a drop of blood." So—

MARLOW.

What, my good friend, if you gave us a glass of
punch in the meantime? It would help us to carry
on the siege with vigor.

HARDCASTLE.

Punch, sir! (*Aside.*) This is the most unaccountable   210
kind of modesty I ever met with.

MARLOW.

Yes sir, punch. A glass of warm punch after our
journey will be comfortable. This is Liberty Hall,
you know.

HARDCASTLE.

Here's cup,34 sir.   215

MARLOW. (*Aside.*)

So this fellow, in his Liberty Hall, will only let us
have just what he pleases.

HARDCASTLE. (*Taking the cup.*)

I hope you'll find it to your mind. I have prepared
it with my own hands, and I believe you'll own
the ingredients are tolerable. Will you be so good   220
as to pledge me, sir? Here, Mr. Marlow, here is to
our better acquaintance. (*Drinks.*)

MARLOW. (*Aside.*)

A very impudent fellow this! But he's a character,
and I'll humor him a little.—Sir, my service to you.
(*Drinks.*)   225

HASTINGS. (*Aside.*)

I see this fellow wants to give us his company and
forgets that he's an innkeeper before he has learned
to be a gentleman.

MARLOW.

From the excellence of your cup, my old friend, I
suppose you have a good deal of business in this   230
part of the country. Warm work now and then at
elections, I suppose.

HARDCASTLE.

No sir, I have long given that work over. Since our
betters have hit upon the expedient of electing each
other, there's no business for us that sell ale.35   235

34 cup] flavored, sweetened wine
35 us … ale] referring to the practice of electoral candidates
giving free drinks to voters

HASTINGS.

So then you have no turn for politics, I find.

HARDCASTLE.

Not in the least. There was a time, indeed, I fretted
myself about the mistakes of government, like other
people, but finding myself every day grow more
angry and the government growing no better, I left   240
it to mend itself. Since that, I no more trouble my
head about Hyder Ali,36 or Ali Kahn,37 than about
Ally Croaker.38 Sir, my service to you.

HASTINGS.

So that with eating above stairs, and drinking
below, with receiving your friends without, and   245
amusing them within,k you lead a good pleasant
bustling life of it.

HARDCASTLE.

I do stir about a great deal, that's certain. Half the
differences of the parish are adjusted in this very
parlor.   250

MARLOW. (*After drinking.*)

And you have an argument in your cup, old
gentleman, better than any in Westminster Hall.*

HARDCASTLE.

Aye, young gentleman, that, and a little
philosophy.

MARLOW. (*Aside.*)

Well, this is the first time I ever heard of an   255
innkeeper's philosophy.

HASTINGS.

So then, like an experienced general, you attack
them on every quarter. If you find their reason
manageable, you attack it with your philosophy; if
you find they have no reason, you attack them with   260
this. Here's your health, my philosopher. (*Drinks.*)

HARDCASTLE.

Good, very good, thank you, ha! ha! Your
Generalship puts me in mind of Prince Eugene,
when he fought the Turks at the Battle of
Belgrade.39 You shall hear.   265

36 Hyder Ali] maharaja of Mysore in India, who defeated
the English in 1767
37 Ali Khan] the subahdar of Bengal known for his cruelty
38 Ally Croker] a figure in a popular Irish ballad
39 Prince Eugene … Belgrade] Eugene led the military of
Holy Roman Emperor Charles VI in assisting Venice

MARLOW.

Instead of the Battle of Belgrade, I believe it's almost time to talk about supper. What has your philosophy got in the house for supper?

HARDCASTLE.

For supper, sir! (*Aside.*) Was ever such a request to a man in his own house! 270

MARLOW.

Yes sir, supper sir. I begin to feel an appetite. I shall make devilish work tonight in the larder, I promise you.

HARDCASTLE. (*Aside.*)

Such a brazen dog sure never my eyes beheld. (*To him.*) Why really, sir, as for supper I can't well tell. 275 My Dorothy and the cook maid settle these things between them. I leave these kind of things entirely to them.

MARLOW.

You do, do you?

HARDCASTLE.

Entirely. By the bye, I believe they are in actual 280 consultation upon what's for supper this moment in the kitchen.

MARLOW.

Then I beg they'll admit *me* as one of their privy council. It's a way I have got. When I travel, I always choose to regulate my own supper. Let the 285 cook be called. No offence I hope, sir.

HARDCASTLE.

Oh no, sir, none in the least, yet I don't know how, our Bridget, the cook maid, is not very communicative upon these occasions. Should we send for her, she might scold us all out of the house. 290

HASTINGS.

Let's see your list of the larder, then. I ask it as a favor. I always match my appetite to my bill of fare.

MARLOW. (*To Hardcastle, who looks at them with surprise.*)

Sir, he's very right, and it's my way too.

HARDCASTLE.

Sir, you have a right to command here.—Here, Roger, bring us the bill of fare for tonight's supper. 295 I believe it's drawn out.—Your manner, Mr.

---

during the Turkish War of 1715-18. He took Belgrade in 1717.

Hastings, puts me in mind of my uncle, Colonel Wallop. It was a saying of his, that no man was sure of his supper till he had eaten it.

Enter Roger, who gives a bill of fare[1] *[and exits].*

HASTINGS. (*Aside.*)

All upon the high ropes![40] His uncle a Colonel! 300 We shall soon hear of his mother being a justice of peace. But let's hear the bill of fare.

MARLOW. (*Perusing.*)

What's here? For the first course; for the second course; for the dessert. The devil, sir, do you think we have brought down the whole Joiners 305 Company or the Corporation of Bedford[41] to eat up such a supper? Two or three little things, clean and comfortable, will do.

HASTINGS.

But, let's hear it.

MARLOW. (*Reading.*)

For the first course at the top, a pig's face and 310 prune sauce.

HASTINGS.

Damn your pig's face, I say.

MARLOW.

And damn your prune sauce, say I.

HARDCASTLE.

And yet, gentlemen, to men that are hungry, a pig's face[m] with prune sauce is very good eating. 315

MARLOW.

At the bottom, a calf's tongue and brains.

HASTINGS.

Let your brains be knocked out, my good sir, I don't like them.

MARLOW.

Or you may clap them on a plate by themselves. I do. 320

HARDCASTLE. (*Aside.*)

Their impudence confounds me. (*To them.*) Gentlemen, you are my guests, make what

---

40 All ... ropes!] on his high horse

41 Joiners Company ... Corporation of Bedford] The Joiners Company was a guild of woodworkers; the Corporation was either the city council or an organization of merchants. All three groups sponsored well-known banquets.

alterations you please. Is there anything else you wish to retrench or alter, gentlemen?

MARLOW.

Item: a pork pie, a boiled rabbit and sausages, a florentine,[42] a shaking pudding,[43] and a dish of tiff—taff—taffety cream![44]

HASTINGS.

Confound your made dishes,[45] I shall be as much at a loss in this house as at a green and yellow dinner at the French ambassador's table. I'm for plain eating.

HARDCASTLE.

I'm sorry, gentlemen, that I have nothing you like, but if there be anything you have a particular fancy to—

MARLOW.

Why really, sir, your bill of fare is so exquisite that any one part of it is full as good as another. Send us what you please. So much for supper. And now to see that our beds are aired and properly taken care of.

HARDCASTLE.

I entreat you'll leave all that to me. You shall not stir a step.

MARLOW.

Leave that to you! I protest, sir, you must excuse me, I always look to these things myself.

HARDCASTLE.

I must insist, sir, you'll make yourself easy on that head.

MARLOW.

You see I'm resolved on it. (*Aside*.) A very troublesome fellow this, as ever I met with.

HARDCASTLE.

Well sir, I'm resolved at least to attend you. (*Aside*.) This may be modern modesty, but I never saw anything look so like old-fashioned impudence.

---

42 florentine] a deepdish pie or tart made of meat and spices
43 shaking pudding] eggs, cream, and flour boiled with flavorings
44 taffety cream] a dish of cream made with ground spices and sugar
45 made dishes] dishes made by combining several ingredients, considered by the English as either refined eating or the stuff of excessive foreign appetites

Exeunt Marlow and Hardcastle.

HASTINGS.

So I find this fellow's civilities begin to grow troublesome. But who can be angry at those assiduities which are meant to please him?—Hah! what do I see? Miss Neville, by all that's happy!

Enter Miss Neville.

MISS NEVILLE.

My dear Hastings! To what unexpected good fortune, to what accident am I to ascribe this happy meeting?

HASTINGS.

Rather let me ask the same question, as I could never have hoped to meet my dearest Constance at an inn.

MISS NEVILLE.

An inn! Sure you mistake! My aunt, my guardian, lives here. What could induce you to think this house an inn?

HASTINGS.

My friend Mr. Marlow, with whom I came down, and I, have been sent here as to an inn, I assure you. A young fellow whom we accidentally met at a house hard by directed us hither.

MISS NEVILLE.

Certainly it must be one of my hopeful cousin's tricks, of whom you have heard me talk so often, ha! ha! ha! ha!

HASTINGS.

He whom your aunt intends for you? he of whom I have such just apprehensions?

MISS NEVILLE.

You have nothing to fear from him, I assure you. You'd adore him if you knew how heartily he despises me. My aunt knows it too and has undertaken to court me for him and actually begins to think she has made a conquest.

HASTINGS.

Thou dear dissembler! You must know, my Constance, I have just seized this happy opportunity of my friend's visit here to get admittance into the family. The horses that carried us down are now fatigued with their journey, but they'll soon be refreshed, and then if my dearest girl will trust in her faithful Hastings, we shall soon be landed in France, where even among slaves the laws of marriage are respected.[46]   385

MISS NEVILLE.

I have often told you that, though ready to obey you, I yet should leave my little fortune behind with reluctance. The greatest part of it was left me by my uncle, the India Director,[47] and chiefly consists in jewels. I have been for some time   390 persuading my aunt to let me wear them. I fancy I'm very near succeeding. The instant they are put into my possession you shall find me ready to make them and myself yours.

HASTINGS.

Perish the baubles! Your person is all I desire. In   395 the meantime, my friend Marlow must not be let into his mistake. I know the strange reserve of his temper is such that, if abruptly informed of it, he would instantly quit the house before our plan was ripe for execution.   400

MISS NEVILLE.

But how shall we keep him in the deception? Miss Hardcastle is just returned from walking. What if we still continue to deceive him?—This, this way— (They confer.)

Enter Marlow.

MARLOW.

The assiduities of these good people tease me   405 beyond bearing. My host seems to think it ill manners to leave me alone, and so he claps not only himself but his old-fashioned wife on my back. They talk of coming to sup with us too, and then, I suppose, we are to run the gauntlet through   410 all the rest of the family.—What have we got here!

---

46 the laws of marriage] a reference to the unpopular Royal Marriage Act of 1772, which prohibited relations of the monarch from marrying at will. William Henry, Duke of Gloucester and brother to George III, had been partly responsible for provoking this law because of his marriage to Lady Waldegrave; when he attended the play's first performance, the audience enthusiastically applauded this line, perceiving it as an attack on the recent legislation.

47 the India Director] Director of the East India Company

HASTINGS.

My dear Charles! Let me congratulate you! The most fortunate accident! Who do you think is just alighted?

MARLOW.

Cannot guess.   415

HASTINGS.

Our mistresses, my boy,[n] Miss Hardcastle and Miss Neville. Give me leave to introduce Miss Constance Neville to your acquaintance. Happening to dine in the neighborhood, they called, on their return to take fresh horses, here.   420 Miss Hardcastle has just stepped into the next room and will be back in an instant. Wasn't it lucky, eh?

MARLOW. (Aside.)

I have just been mortified enough of all conscience, and here comes something to complete my   425 embarrassment.

HASTINGS.

Well! but wasn't it the most fortunate thing in the world?

MARLOW.

Oh yes! Very fortunate—a most joyful encounter—but our dresses, George, you know, are   430 in disorder. What if we should postpone the happiness till tomorrow? Tomorrow at her own house? It will be every bit as convenient—and rather more respectful—tomorrow let it be. (Offering* to go.)   435

MISS NEVILLE.

By no means, sir. Your ceremony will displease her. The disorder of your dress will show the ardor of your impatience. Besides, she knows you are in the house and will permit you to see her.

MARLOW.

Oh! the devil! how shall I support it? Hem! hem!   440 Hastings, you must not go. You are to assist me, you know. I shall be confoundedly ridiculous. Yet, hang it! I'll take courage. Hem!

HASTINGS.

Pshaw, man! it's but the first plunge, and all's over. She's but a woman, you know.   445

MARLOW.

And of all women, she that I dread most to encounter!

Enter Miss Hardcastle as returned from walking, with a bonnet, etc.

HASTINGS. (*Introducing them.*)

Miss Hardcastle, Mr. Marlow, I'm proud of bringing two persons of such merit together, that only want* to know, to esteem each other.   450

MISS HARDCASTLE. (*Aside.*)

Now, for meeting my modest gentleman with a demure face and quite in his own manner. (*After a pause, in which he appears very uneasy and disconcerted.*) I'm glad of your safe arrival, sir. I'm told you had some accidents by the way.   455

MARLOW.

Only a few madam. Yes, we had some. Yes madam, a good many accidents, but should be sorry— madam—or rather glad of any accidents—that are so agreeably concluded. Hem!

HASTINGS. (*To him.*)

You never spoke better in your whole life. Keep it   460
up, and I'll insure you the victory.

MISS HARDCASTLE.

I'm afraid you flatter, sir. You that have seen so much of the finest company can find little entertainment in an obscure corner of the country.

MARLOW. (*Gathering courage.*)

I have lived, indeed, in the world, madam, but I   465
have kept very little company. I have been but an observer upon life, madam, while others were enjoying it.

MISS NEVILLE.

But that, I am told, is the way to enjoy it at last.

HASTINGS. (*To him.*)

Cicero never spoke better. Once more, and you are   470
confirmed in assurance forever.

MARLOW. (*To him.*)

Hem! Stand by me, then, and when I'm down, throw in a word or two to set me up again.

MISS HARDCASTLE.

An observer, like you, upon life, were, I fear, disagreeably employed, since you must have had   475
much more to censure than to approve.

MARLOW.

Pardon me, madam. I was always willing to be amused. The folly of most people is rather an object of mirth than uneasiness.

HASTINGS. (*To him.*)

Bravo, bravo. Never spoke so well in your whole   480
life.—Well! Miss Hardcastle, I see that you and Mr. Marlow are going to be very good company. I believe our being here will but embarrass the interview.

MARLOW.

Not in the least, Mr. Hastings. We like your   485
company of all things. (*To him.*) Zounds! George, sure you won't go? How can you leave us?

HASTINGS.

Our presence will but spoil conversation, so we'll retire to the next room. (*To him.*) You don't consider, man, that we are to manage a little tête-   490
à-tête of our own.

Exeunt [Hastings and Miss Neville].

MISS HARDCASTLE. (*After a pause.*)

But you have not been wholly an observer, I presume, sir: the ladies I should hope have employed some part of your addresses.

MARLOW. (*Relapsing into timidity.*)

Pardon me, madam, I—I—I—as yet have°   495
studied—only—to—deserve them.

MISS HARDCASTLE.

And that some say is the very worst way to obtain them.

MARLOW.

Perhaps so, madam. But I love to converse only with the more grave and sensible part of the sex.—   500
But I'm afraid I grow tiresome.

MISS HARDCASTLE.

Not at all, sir, there is nothing I like so much as grave conversation myself; I could hear it forever. Indeed, I have often been surprised how a man of *sentiment* could ever admire those light, airy   505
pleasures where nothing reaches the heart.

MARLOW.

It's—a disease—of the mind, madam. In the variety of tastes there must be some who, wanting* a relish—for—um—a—um—

MISS HARDCASTLE.

I understand you, sir. There must be some who,   510
wanting* a relish for refined pleasures, pretend to despise what they are incapable of tasting.

MARLOW.

My meaning, madam, but infinitely better expressed. And I can't help observing—a—

MISS HARDCASTLE. (*Aside.*)

Who could ever suppose this fellow impudent 515 upon some occasions? (*To him.*) You were going to observe, sir—

MARLOW.

I was observing, madam—I protest, madam, I forget what I was going to observe.

MISS HARDCASTLE. (*Aside.*)

I vow and so do I. (*To him.*) You were observing, 520 sir, that in this age of hypocrisy—something about hypocrisy, sir.

MARLOW.

Yes, madam. In this age of hypocrisy there are few who upon strict enquiry do not—a—a—a—

MISS HARDCASTLE.

I understand you perfectly, sir. 525

MARLOW. (*Aside.*)

Egad! and that's more than I do myself.

MISS HARDCASTLE.

You mean that in this hypocritical age there are few that do not condemn in public what they practice in private and think they pay every debt to virtue when they praise it. 530

MARLOW.

True, madam. Those who have most virtue in their mouths have least of it in their bosoms. But I'm sure I tire you, madam.

MISS HARDCASTLE.

Not in the least, sir. There's something so agreeable and spirited in your manner, such life and force— 535 pray sir, go on.

MARLOW.

Yes, madam. I was saying—that there are some occasions—when a total want* of courage, madam, destroys all the—and puts us—upon a—a—a—

MISS HARDCASTLE.

I agree with you entirely, a want* of courage upon 540 some occasions assumes the appearance of ignorance and betrays us when we most want to excel. I beg you'll proceed.

MARLOW.

Yes, madam. Morally speaking, madam— But I see Miss Neville expecting us in the next room. I 545

would not intrude for the world.

MISS HARDCASTLE.

I protest, sir, I never was more agreeably entertained in all my life. Pray go on.

MARLOW.

Yes, madam. I was— But she beckons us to join her. Madam, shall I do myself the honor to attend you? 550

MISS HARDCASTLE.

Well then, I'll follow.

MARLOW (*aside.*)

This pretty smooth dialogue has done for me. (*Exit.*)

MISS HARDCASTLE.

Ha! ha! ha! Was there ever such a sober, sentimental interview? I'm certain he scarce looked 555 in my face the whole time. Yet the fellow, but for his unaccountable bashfulness, is pretty well too. He has good sense, but then so buried in his fears, that it fatigues one more than ignorance. If I could teach him a little confidence, it would be doing 560 somebody that I know of a piece of service. But who is that somebody?—that, faith, is a question I can scarce answer. (*Exit.*)

Enter Tony and Miss Neville, followed by Mrs. Hardcastle and Hastings.

TONY.

What do you follow me for, Cousin Con? I wonder you're not ashamed to be so very engaging. 565

MISS NEVILLE.

I hope, Cousin, one may speak to one's own relations and not be to blame.

TONY.

Aye, but I know what sort of a relation you want to make me, though, but it won't do. I tell you, Cousin Con, it won't do, so I beg you'll keep your 570 distance, I want no nearer relationship. (*She follows coquetting him to the back scene.*)

MRS. HARDCASTLE.

Well! I vow, Mr. Hastings, you are very entertaining. There's nothing in the world I love to talk of so much as London, and the fashions, 575 though I was never there myself.

HASTINGS.

Never there! You amaze me! From your air and manner, I concluded you had been bred all your life either at Ranelagh,[48] St. James's,* or Tower Wharf.[49] 580

MRS. HARDCASTLE.

Oh, sir! you're only pleased to say so. We country persons can have no manner at all. I'm in love with the Town, and that serves to raise me above some of our neighboring rustics. But who can have a manner that has never seen the Pantheon,* the 585 Grotto Gardens, the Borough,[50] and such places where the nobility chiefly resort? All I can do is to enjoy London at second hand. I take care to know every tête-à-tête from the *Scandalous Magazine*[51] and have all the fashions, as they come 590 out, in a letter from the two Miss Rickets of Crooked Lane. Pray, how do you like this head,[52] Mr. Hastings?

HASTINGS.

Extremely elegant and dégagé, upon my word, madam. Your friseur is a Frenchman, I suppose? 595

MRS. HARDCASTLE.

I protest I dressed it myself from a print in the *Ladies Memorandum Book*[53] for the last year.

HASTINGS.

Indeed. Such a head in a side box at the playhouse would draw as many gazers as my Lady Mayoress at a city ball. 600

MRS. HARDCASTLE.

I vow, since inoculation began,[54] there is no such thing to be seen as a plain woman; so one must dress a little particular, or one may escape in the crowd.

---

48 Ranelagh] highly fashionable center for the upper classes
49 Tower Wharf] a hangout of the lower classes
50 Grotto Gardens … Borough] the former a rendezvous for the "vulgar" classes and, by 1773, the latter (in Southwark) for wealthy tradesmen
51 tête … *Magazine*] a reference to the monthly articles in the *Town and Country Magazine* about scandals, accompanied by engravings of the heads of a well-known man and his mistress
52 this head] this hairstyle, probably shaped around an internal frame
53 *Ladies Memorandum Book*] a magazine of fashions that first appeared in January 1773
54 inoculation began] 1721 in England and typically available only for the well off

HASTINGS.

But that can never be your case, madam, in any 605 dress. (*Bowing.*)

MRS. HARDCASTLE.

Yet, what signifies *my* dressing when I have such a piece of antiquity by my side as Mr. Hardcastle: all I can say will never argue down a single button from his clothes. I have often wanted him to throw 610 off his great flaxen wig and, where he was bald, to plaster it over, like my Lord Pately, with powder.

HASTINGS.

You are right, madam, for as among the ladies, there are none ugly, so among the men, there are none old. 615

MRS. HARDCASTLE.

But what do you think his answer was? Why, with his usual Gothic vivacity, he said I only wanted him to throw off his wig to convert it into a tête for my own wearing.

HASTINGS.

Intolerable! At your age you may wear what you 620 please, and it must become you.

MRS. HARDCASTLE.

Pray Mr. Hastings, what do you take to be the most fashionable age about Town?

HASTINGS.

Some time ago, forty was all the mode, but I'm told the ladies intend to bring up fifty for the 625 ensuing winter.

MRS. HARDCASTLE.

Seriously? Then I shall be too young for the fashion.

HASTINGS.

No lady begins now to put on jewels till she's past forty. For instance, Miss there, in a polite circle, 630 would be considered as a child, as a mere maker of samplers.

MRS. HARDCASTLE.

And yet Mrs.* Niece thinks herself as much a woman, and is as fond of jewels, as the oldest of us all. 635

HASTINGS.

Your niece, is she? And that young gentleman, a brother of yours, I should presume?

MRS. HARDCASTLE.

My son, sir. They are contracted to each other.

Observe their little sports. They fall in and out ten
times a day, as if they were man and wife already. 640
(*To them.*) Well Tony, child, what soft things are
you saying to your cousin Constance this evening?
TONY.

I have been saying no soft things, but that it's very
hard to be followed about so. Ecod! I've not a place
in the house now that's left to myself but the stable. 645
MRS. HARDCASTLE.

Never mind him, Con, my dear. He's in another
story behind your back.
MISS NEVILLE.

There's something generous in my cousin's manner.
He falls out before faces to be forgiven in private.
TONY.

That's a damned, confounded—crack.⁵⁵ 650
MRS. HARDCASTLE.

Ah! he's a sly one. Don't you think they're like each
other about the mouth, Mr. Hastings? The
Blenkinsop mouth to a T. They're of a size too.—
Back to back, my pretties, that Mr. Hastings may
see you. Come Tony. 655
TONY.

You had as good not make me, I tell you.
(*Measuring.*)
MISS NEVILLE.

Oh Lud!* he has almost cracked my head.
MRS. HARDCASTLE.

Oh the monster! For shame, Tony. You a man, and
behave so! 660
TONY.

If I'm a man, let me have my fortin.⁵⁶ Ecod! I'll
not be made a fool of no longer.
MRS. HARDCASTLE.

Is this, ungrateful boy, all that I'm to get for the pains
I have taken in your education? I that have rocked
you in your cradle and fed that pretty mouth with a 665
spoon! Did not I work that waistcoat to make you
genteel? Did not I prescribe for you every day and
weep while the receipt* was operating?
TONY.

Ecod! you had reason to weep, for you have been
dosing me ever since I was born. I have gone 670

through every receipt in the *Complete Houswife*⁵⁷
ten times over, and you have thoughts of coursing
me through *Quincy*⁵⁸ next spring. But ecod! I tell
you, I'll not be made a fool of no longer.
MRS. HARDCASTLE.

Wasn't it all for your good, viper? Wasn't it all for 675
your good?
TONY.

I wish you'd let me and my good alone then.
Snubbing this way when I'm in spirits. If I'm to
have any good, let it come of itself, not to keep
dinging it, dinging it into one so. 680
MRS. HARDCASTLE.

That's false: I never see you when you're in spirits.
No Tony, you then go to the alehouse or kennel.
I'm never to be delighted with your agreeable, wild
notes, unfeeling monster!
TONY.

Ecod! Mamma, your own notes are the wildest of 685
the two.
MRS. HARDCASTLE.

Was ever the like? But I see he wants to break my
heart, I see he does.
HASTINGS.

Dear madam, permit me to lecture the young
gentleman a little. I'm certain I can persuade him 690
to his duty.
MRS. HARDCASTLE.

Well! I must retire.—Come, Constance, my
love.—You see, Mr. Hastings, the wretchedness of
my situation. Was ever poor woman so plagued
with a dear, sweet, pretty, provoking, undutiful 695
boy!

Exeunt Mrs. Hardcastle and Miss Neville.

TONY. (*Singing.*)

"There was a young man riding by, and fain would
have his will. Rang do didlo dee." Don't mind her.
Let her cry. It's the comfort of her heart. I have

---

⁵⁵ crack] a lie; an antiquated expression by the 1770s
⁵⁶ fortin] fortune

⁵⁷ *Complete Houswife*] a popular handbook of cooking
recipes and medical treatments used in eighteenth-century households
⁵⁸ *Quincy*] Dr. John Quincy's *Compleat English Dispensatory*, first published in 1718 and reissued numerous times
thereafter

seen her and sister cry over a book for an hour together, and they said they liked the book the better the more it made them cry. 700

HASTINGS.

Then you're no friend to the ladies, I find, my pretty young gentleman?

TONY.

That's as I find 'um. 705

HASTINGS.

Not to her of your mother's choosing, I dare answer? And yet she appears to me a pretty, well-tempered girl.

TONY.

That's because you don't know her as well as I. Ecod! I know every inch about her, and there's not 710 a more bitter, cantankerous toad in all Christendom.

HASTINGS. (Aside.)

Pretty encouragement this for a lover!

TONY.

I have seen her since the height of that. She has as many tricks as a hare in a thicket or a colt the first 715 day's breaking.

HASTINGS.

To me she appears sensible and silent!

TONY.

Aye, before company. But when she's with her playmates, she's as loud as a hog in a gate.

HASTINGS.

But there is a meek modesty about her that charms 720 me.

TONY.

Yes, but curb her never* so little, she kicks up, and you're flung in a ditch.

HASTINGS.

Well, but you must allow her a little beauty. Yes, you must allow her some beauty. 725

TONY.

Bandbox! She's all a made up thing, mun. Ah! could you but see Bet Bouncer of these parts, you might then talk of beauty. Ecod, she has two eyes as black as sloes and cheeks as broad and red as a pulpit cushion. She'd make two of she. 730

HASTINGS.

Well, what say you to a friend that would take this bitter bargain off your hands?

TONY.

Anon?[59]

HASTINGS.

Would you thank him that would take Miss Neville and leave you to happiness and your dear Betsy? 735

TONY.

Aye, but where is there such a friend, for who would take *her*?

HASTINGS.

I am he. If you but assist me, I'll engage to whip her off to France, and you shall never hear more of her.

TONY.

Assist you! Ecod I will, to the last drop of my 740 blood. I'll clap a pair of horses to your chaise that shall trundle you off in a twinkling and may beget you a part of her fortin beside, in jewels, that you little dream of.

HASTINGS.

My dear squire, this looks like a lad of spirit. 745

TONY.

Come along then, and you shall see more of my spirit before you have done with me. (*Singing.*) "We are the boys that fears no noise where the thundering cannons roar."

Exeunt.

Act III, scene i.

Enter Hardcastle.

HARDCASTLE.

What could my old friend Sir Charles mean by recommending his son as the modestest young man in Town? To me he appears the most impudent piece of brass that ever spoke with a tongue. He has taken possession of the easy chair 5 by the fireside already. He took off his boots in the parlor and desired me to see them taken care of. I'm desirous to know how his impudence affects my daughter. She will certainly be shocked at it.

Enter Miss Hardcastle, plainly dressed.

Well my Kate, I see you have changed your dress 10 as I bid you, and yet, I believe, there was no great occasion.

---

59 Anon?] Say that again?

MISS HARDCASTLE.

I find such a pleasure, sir, in obeying your
commands that I take care to observe them
without ever debating their propriety.   15

HARDCASTLE.

And yet, Kate, I sometimes give you some cause,
particularly when I recommended my *modest*
gentleman to you as a lover today.

MISS HARDCASTLE.

You taught me to expect something extraordinary,
and I find the original exceeds the description.   20

HARDCASTLE.

I was never so surprised in my life! He has quite
confounded all my faculties!

MISS HARDCASTLE.

I never saw anything like it: and a man of the
world too!

HARDCASTLE.

Aye, he learned it all abroad. What a fool was I to   25
think a young man could learn modesty by
traveling. He might as soon learn wit at a
masquerade.

MISS HARDCASTLE.

It seems all natural to him.

HARDCASTLE.

A good deal assisted by bad company and a French   30
dancing master.

MISS HARDCASTLE.

Sure you mistake, Papa! A French dancing master
could never have taught him that timid look, that
awkward address, that bashful manner—

HARDCASTLE.

Whose look? whose manner? child!   35

MISS HARDCASTLE.

Mr. Marlow's: his *mauvaise honte*,[60] his timidity,
struck me at the first sight.

HARDCASTLE.

Then your first sight deceived you, for I think him
one of the most brazen first sights that ever
astonished my senses.   40

MISS HARDCASTLE.

Sure, sir, you rally! I never saw any one so modest.

HARDCASTLE.

And can you be serious! I never saw such a

bouncing, swaggering puppy since I was born.
Bully Dawson[61] was but a fool to him.

MISS HARDCASTLE.

Surprising! He met me with a respectful bow, a   45
stammering voice, and a look fixed on the ground.

HARDCASTLE.

He met me with a loud voice, a lordly air, and a
familiarity that made my blood freeze again.

MISS HARDCASTLE.

He treated me with diffidence and respect; censured
the manners of the age; admired the prudence of   50
girls that never laughed; tired me with apologies for
being tiresome; then left the room with a bow, and,
"Madam, I would not for the world detain you."

HARDCASTLE.

He spoke to me as if he knew me all his life before;
asked twenty questions, and never waited for an   55
answer; interrupted my best remarks with some silly
pun; and when I was in my best story of the Duke
of Marlborough and Prince Eugene, he asked if I
had not a good hand at making punch. Yes Kate, he
asked your father if he was a maker of punch!   60

MISS HARDCASTLE.

One of us must certainly be mistaken.

HARDCASTLE.

If he be what he has shown himself, I'm
determined he shall never have my consent.

MISS HARDCASTLE.

And if he be the sullen thing I take him, he shall
never have mine.   65

HARDCASTLE.

In one thing then we are agreed—to reject him.

MISS HARDCASTLE.

Yes. But upon conditions. For if you should find
him less impudent, and I more presuming; if you
find him more respectful, and I more
importunate—I don't know—the fellow is well   70
enough for a man. Certainly we don't meet many
such at a horse race in the country.

HARDCASTLE.

If we should find him so—but that's impossible.
The first appearance has done my business. I'm
seldom deceived in that.   75

---

60 *mauvaise honte*] shamefacedness, awkward shyness

61 Bully Dawson] a notorious ruffian of the early eighteenth century

MISS HARDCASTLE.

And yet there may be many good qualities under that first appearance.

HARDCASTLE.

Aye, when a girl finds a fellow's outside to her taste, she then sets about guessing the rest of his furniture. With her, a smooth face stands for good sense and a genteel figure for every virtue.

MISS HARDCASTLE.

I hope, sir, a conversation begun with a compliment to my good sense won't end with a sneer at my understanding?

HARDCASTLE.

Pardon me, Kate. But if young Mr. Brazen can find the art of reconciling contradictions, he may please us both, perhaps.

MISS HARDCASTLE.

And as one of us must be mistaken, what if we go to make further discoveries?

HARDCASTLE.

Agreed. But depend on't, I'm in the right.

MISS HARDCASTLE.

And depend on't, I'm not much in the wrong.

Exeunt. Enter Tony running in with a casket.

TONY.

Ecod! I have got them. Here they are. My cousin Con's necklaces, bobs[62] and all. My mother shan't cheat the poor souls out of their fortune neither. Oh! my genus,* is that you?

Enter Hastings.

HASTINGS.

My dear friend, how have you managed with your mother? I hope you have amused her with pretending love for your cousin and that you are willing to be reconciled at last? Our horses will be refreshed in a short time, and we shall soon be ready to set off.

TONY.

And here's something to bear your charges by the way. (*Giving the casket.*) Your sweetheart's jewels. Keep them, and hang those, I say, that would rob you of one of them.

HASTINGS.

But how have you procured them from your mother?

TONY.

Ask me no questions, and I'll tell you no fibs. I procured them by the rule of thumb. If I had not a key to every drawer in mother's bureau, how could I go to the alehouse so often as I do? An honest man may rob himself of his own at any time.

HASTINGS.

Thousands do it every day. But to be plain with you, Miss Neville is endeavoring to procure them from her aunt this very instant. If she succeeds, it will be the most delicate way at least of obtaining them.

TONY.

Well, keep them, till you know how it will be. But I know how it will be well enough: she'd as soon part with the only sound tooth in her head.

HASTINGS.

But I dread the effects of her resentment when she finds she has lost them.

TONY.

Never you mind her resentment, leave *me* to manage that. I don't value her resentment the bounce of a cracker.[63]—Zounds! here they are. Morris.[64] Prance.

Exit Hastings. Enter Mrs. Hardcastle and Miss Neville.

MRS. HARDCASTLE.

Indeed, Constance, you amaze me. Such a girl as you want jewels? It will be time enough for jewels, my dear, twenty years hence, when your beauty begins to want* repairs.

MISS NEVILLE.

But what will repair beauty at forty will certainly improve it at twenty, madam.

MRS. HARDCASTLE.

Yours, my dear, can admit of none. That natural blush is beyond a thousand ornaments. Besides, child, jewels are quite out at present. Don't you see, half the ladies of our acquaintance, my Lady Killdaylight and Mrs. Crump[65] and the rest of them, carry their jewels to Town and bring nothing but paste and marcasites back.

---

62 bobs] pendants, earrings

63 bounce of a cracker] bang of a firework

64 Morris] Get going.

65 Crump] hunchback (*OED*)

MISS NEVILLE.

But who knows, madam, but somebody that shall be nameless would like me best with all my little finery about me? 140

MRS. HARDCASTLE.

Consult your glass,* my dear, and then see, if with such a pair of eyes, you want* any better sparklers.—What do you think, Tony, my dear, does your cousin Con want* any jewels, in your eyes, to set off her beauty? 145

TONY.

That's as thereafter may be.

MISS NEVILLE.

My dear aunt, if you knew how it would oblige me.

MRS. HARDCASTLE.

A parcel of old-fashioned rose- and table-cut things.[66] They would make you look like the court of King Solomon at a puppet show. Besides, I believe I can't readily come at them. They may be missing for aught I know to the contrary. 150

TONY. (*Apart to Mrs. Hardcastle.*)

Then why don't you tell her so at once, as she's so longing for them. Tell her they're lost. It's the only way to quiet her. Say they're lost, and call me to bear witness. 155

MRS. HARDCASTLE. (*Apart to Tony.*)

You know, my dear, I'm only keeping them for you. So if I say, they're gone, you'll bear me witness, will you? He! he! he! 160

TONY.

Never fear me. Ecod! I'll say I saw them taken out with my own eyes.

MISS NEVILLE.

I desire them but for a day, madam, just to be permitted to show them as relics, and then they may be locked up again. 165

MRS. HARDCASTLE.

To be plain with you, my dear Constance, if I could find them, you should have them. They're missing, I assure you. Lost, for aught I know. But we must have patience wherever they are.

MISS NEVILLE.

I'll not believe it; this is but a shallow pretense to 170

deny me. I know they're too valuable to be so slightly kept, and as you are to answer for the loss.

MRS. HARDCASTLE.

Don't be alarmed, Constance. If they be lost, I must restore an equivalent. But my son knows they are missing and not to be found. 175

TONY.

That I can bear witness to. They are missing, and not to be found, I'll take my oath on't.

MRS. HARDCASTLE.

You must learn resignation, my dear, for though we lose our fortune, yet we should not lose our patience. See me, how calm I am. 180

MISS NEVILLE.

Aye, people are generally calm at the misfortunes of others.

MRS. HARDCASTLE.

Now, I wonder a girl of your good sense should waste a thought upon such trumpery. We shall soon find them, and in the meantime, you shall make use of my garnets till your jewels be found. 185

MISS NEVILLE.

I detest garnets.

MRS. HARDCASTLE.

The most becoming things in the world to set off a clear complexion. You have often seen how well they look upon me. You *shall* have them. (*Exit.*) 190

MISS NEVILLE.

I dislike them of all things. You shan't stir— Was ever anything so provoking to mislay my own jewels and force me to wear her trumpery?

TONY.

Don't be a fool. If she gives you the garnets, take what you can get. The jewels are your own already. 195 I have stolen them out of her bureau, and she does not know it. Fly to your spark, he'll tell you more of the matter. Leave me to manage *her*.

MISS NEVILLE.

My dear cousin.

TONY.

Vanish. She's here and has missed them already. 200

[*Exit Miss Neville.*]

Zounds! how she fidgets and spits about like a Catherine wheel.[67]

---

[66] rose- and table-cut things] two modes of cutting lesser stones, the better kind being reserved for a brilliant-cut

[67] Catherine wheel] a pinwheeled firework, named after St.

Enter Mrs. Hardcastle.

MRS. HARDCASTLE.

Confusion! thieves! robbers! We are cheated, plundered, broke open, undone.

TONY.

What's the matter, what's the matter, mamma? I hope nothing has happened to any of the good family! 205

MRS. HARDCASTLE.

We are robbed. My bureau has been broke open, the jewels taken out, and I'm undone.

TONY.

Oh! is that all? Ha! ha! ha! By the laws, I never saw it better acted in my life. Ecod, I thought you was ruined in earnest, ha! ha! ha! 210

MRS. HARDCASTLE.

Why boy, I *am* ruined in earnest. My bureau has been broke open and all taken away.

TONY.

Stick to that, ha! ha! ha! Stick to that. I'll bear witness, you know, call me to bear witness. 215

MRS. HARDCASTLE.

I tell you, Tony, by all that's precious, the jewels are gone, and I shall be ruined forever.

TONY.

Sure I know they're gone, and I am to say so. 220

MRS. HARDCASTLE.

My dearest Tony, but hear me. They're gone, I say.

TONY.

By the laws, mamma, you make me for to laugh, ha! ha! I know who took them well enough, ha! ha! ha!

MRS. HARDCASTLE.

Was there ever such a blockhead that can't tell the difference between jest and earnest.—I tell you, I'm not in jest, booby. 225

TONY.

That's right, that's right: you must be in a bitter passion, and then nobody will suspect either of us. I'll bear witness that they are gone.

MRS. HARDCASTLE.

Was there every such a cross-grained brute that won't hear me! Can you bear witness that you're no better 230

than a fool? Was ever poor woman so beset with fools on one hand and thieves on the other?

TONY.

I can bear witness to that.

MRS. HARDCASTLE.

Bear witness again, you blockhead you, and I'll turn you out of the room directly. My poor niece, what will become of *her*? Do you laugh, you unfeeling brute, as if you enjoyed my distress? 235

TONY.

I can bear witness to that.

MRS. HARDCASTLE.

Do you insult me, monster? I'll teach you to vex your mother, I will. 240

TONY.

I can bear witness to that.

He runs off; she follows him. Enter Miss Hardcastle and maid.

MISS HARDCASTLE.

What an unaccountable creature is that brother of mine to send them to the house as an inn, ha! ha! I don't wonder at his impudence. 245

MAID.

But what is more, madam, the young gentleman, as you passed by in your present dress, asked me if you were the barmaid? He mistook you for the barmaid, madam. 250

MISS HARDCASTLE.

Did he? Then as I live, I'm resolved to keep up the delusion. Tell me, pimple, how do you like my present dress? Don't you think I look something like Cherry[68] in *The Beaux' Stratagem*?

MAID.

It's the dress, madam, that every lady wears in the country but when she visits or receives company. 255

MISS HARDCASTLE.

And are you sure he does not remember my face or person?

MAID.

Certain of it.

MISS HARDCASTLE.

I vow I thought so, for though we spoke for some 260

Catherine of Alexandria (4th century AD), who was famously martyred on a breaking wheel

68 Cherry] the landlord's daughter in Farquhar's comedy of 1707 (see above)

time together, yet his fears were such that he never
once looked up during the interview. Indeed, if he
had, my bonnet would have kept him from seeing
me.

MAID.

But what do you hope from keeping him in his 265
mistake?

MISS HARDCASTLE.

In the first place, I shall be *seen*, and that is no
small advantage to a girl who brings her face to
market. Then I shall perhaps make an acquaintance, and that's no small victory gained over 270
one who never addresses any but the wildest of her
sex. But my chief aim is to take my gentleman off
his guard and, like an invisible champion of
romance, examine the giant's force before I offer*
to combat. 275

MAID.

But are you sure you can act your part and disguise
your voice so that he may mistake that, as he has
already mistaken your person?

MISS HARDCASTLE.

Never fear me. I think I have got the true bar cant:
Did your honor call? Attend the Lion there. Pipes 280
and tobacco for the Angel. The Lamb[69] has been
outrageous this half hour.

MAID.

It will do, madam. But he's here. (*Exit.*)

Enter Marlow.

MARLOW.

What a bawling in every part of the house. I have
scarce a moment's repose. If I go the best room, 285
there I find my host and his story. If I fly to the
gallery, there we have my hostess with her curtsy
down to the ground. I have at last got a moment
to myself, and now for recollection. (*Walks and
muses.*) 290

MISS HARDCASTLE.

Did you call, sir? Did your honor call?

MARLOW. (*Musing.*)

As for Miss Hardcastle, she's too grave and
sentimental for me.

---

69 Lion … Angel … Lamb] Rooms at inns were often assigned fanciful names.

MISS HARDCASTLE.

Did your honor call? (*She still* places herself before
him, he turning away.*) 295

MARLOW.

No, child.* (*Musing.*) Besides, from the glimpse I
had of her, I think she squints.

MISS HARDCASTLE.

I'm sure, sir, I heard the bell ring.

MARLOW.

No, no. (*Musing.*) I have pleased my father, however,
by coming down, and I'll tomorrow please myself by 300
returning. (*Taking out his tablets and perusing.*)

MISS HARDCASTLE.

Perhaps the other gentleman called, sir.

MARLOW.

I tell you, no.

MISS HARDCASTLE.

I should be glad to know, sir. We have such a parcel
of servants. 305

MARLOW.

No, no, I tell you. (*Looks full in her face.*) Yes, child,
I think I did call. I wanted—I wanted—I vow,
child, you are vastly handsome.

MISS HARDCASTLE.

Oh la, sir, you'll make one ashamed.

MARLOW.

Never saw a more sprightly, malicious eye. Yes, yes, 310
my dear, I did call. Have you got any of your—
a—what d'ye call it in the house?

MISS HARDCASTLE.

No sir, we have been out of that these ten days.

MARLOW.

One may call in this house, I find, to very little
purpose. Suppose I should call for a taste, just by 315
way of trial, of the nectar of your lips; perhaps I
might be disappointed in that too.

MISS HARDCASTLE.

Nectar! nectar! that's a liquor there's no call for in
these parts. French, I suppose. We keep no French
wines here, sir. 320

MARLOW.

Of true English growth, I assure you.

MISS HARDCASTLE.

Then it's odd I should not know it. We brew all
sorts of wines in this house, and I have lived here
these eighteen years.

MARLOW.

Eighteen years! Why, one would think, child, you 325
kept the bar before you were born. How old are you?

MISS HARDCASTLE.

Oh! sir, I must not tell my age. They say women
and music should never be dated.

MARLOW.

To guess at this distance, you can't be much above
forty. (*Approaching.*) Yet nearer I don't think so 330
much. (*Approaching.*) By coming close to some
women they look younger still, but when we come
very close indeed— (*Attempting to kiss her.*)

MISS HARDCASTLE.

Pray sir, keep your distance. One would think you
wanted to know one's age as they do horses, by 335
mark of mouth.

MARLOW.

I protest, child, you use me extremely ill. If you
keep me at this distance, how is it possible you and
I can be ever acquainted?

MISS HARDCASTLE.

And who wants to be acquainted with you? I want 340
no such acquaintance, not I. I'm sure you did not
treat Miss Hardcastle that was here awhile ago in
this obstropalous[70] manner. I'll warrant me, before
her you looked dashed and kept bowing to the
ground and talked, for all the world, as if you was 345
before a justice of peace.

MARLOW. (*Aside.*)

Egad! She has hit it, sure enough. (*To her.*) In awe
of her, child? Ha! ha! ha! A mere, awkward,
squinting thing, no, no. I find you don't know me.
I laughed and rallied her a little, but I was 350
unwilling to be too severe. No, I could not be too
severe, *curse me*!

MISS HARDCASTLE.

Oh! then, sir, you are a favorite, I find, among the
ladies?

MARLOW.

Yes my dear, a great favorite. And yet, hang me, I 355
don't see what they find in me to follow. At the Ladies
Club[71] in Town, I'm called their agreeable Rattle.

Rattle, child, is not my real name, but one I'm
known by. My name is Solomons. Mr. Solomons,
my dear, at your service. (*Offering* to salute* her.*) 360

MISS HARDCASTLE.

Hold, sir, you were introducing me to your club,
not to yourself. And you're so great a favorite there,
you say?

MARLOW.

Yes, my dear. There's Mrs. Mantrap, Lady Betty
Blackleg,[72] the Countess of Sligo, Mrs. 365
Longhorns,P old Miss Biddy Buckskin,[73] and your
humble servant, keep up the spirit of the place.

MISS HARDCASTLE.

Then it's a very merry place, I suppose.

MARLOW.

Yes, as merry as cards, suppers, wine, and old
women can make us. 370

MISS HARDCASTLE.

And their agreeable Rattle, ha! ha! ha!

MARLOW. (*Aside.*)

Egad! I don't quite like this chit. She looks
knowing, methinks.—You laugh, child!

MISS HARDCASTLE.

I can't but laugh to think what time they all have
for minding their work or their family. 375

MARLOW. (*Aside.*)

All's well, she don't laugh at me. (*To her.*) Do *you*
ever work, child?

MISS HARDCASTLE.

Aye, sure. There's not a screen or a quilt in the
whole house but what can bear witness to that.

MARLOW.

Odso!* Then you must show me your embroidery. 380
I embroider and draw patterns myself a little. If
you want a judge of your work, you must apply
to me. (*Seizing her hand.*)

MISS HARDCASTLE. (*Struggling.*)

Aye, but the colors don't look well by candlelight.
You shall see all in the morning. 385

---

70 obstropalous] illiterate variant of obstreperous (*OED*)

71 Ladies Club] a fashionable club that met in London's
Albemarle Street and often invited men to visit

72 Blackleg] A turf swindler; also, a swindler in other species of gambling (*OED*)

73 Biddy Buckskin] "Biddy" was originally "Rachel" (in the
Larpent ms.), an allusion to Rachel Lloyd, one of the
leading women of the Albemarle club.

MARLOW.

And why not now, my angel? Such beauty fires beyond the power of resistance.—Pshaw! the father here! My old luck: I never nicked seven that I did not throw ambsace three times following. (*Exit.*)

Enter Hardcastle, who stands in surprise.

HARDCASTLE.

So, madam! So I find *this* is your *modest* lover. This 390 is your humble admirer that kept his eyes fixed on the ground and only adored at humble distance. Kate, Kate, art thou not ashamed to deceive your father so?

MISS HARDCASTLE.

Never trust me, dear papa, but he's still the modest 395 man I first took him for; you'll be convinced of it as well as I.

HARDCASTLE.

By the hand of my body, I believe his impudence is infectious! Didn't I see him seize your hand? Didn't I see him haul you about like a milkmaid? 400 And now you talk of his respect and his modesty, forsooth!

MISS HARDCASTLE.

But if I shortly convince you of his modesty, that he has only the faults that will pass off with time and the virtues that will improve with age, I hope 405 you'll forgive him.

HARDCASTLE.

The girl would actually make one run mad! I tell you I'll not be convinced. I am convinced. He has scarcely been three hours in the house, and he has already encroached on all my prerogatives. You 410 may like his impudence and call it modesty, but my son-in-law, madam, must have very different qualifications.

MISS HARDCASTLE.

Sir, I ask but this night to convince you.

HARDCASTLE.

You shall not have half the time, for I have 415 thoughts of turning him out this very hour.

MISS HARDCASTLE.

Give me that hour, then, and I hope to satisfy you.

HARDCASTLE.

Well, an hour let it be then. But I'll have no trifling with your father. All fair and open, do you mind me?

MISS HARDCASTLE.

I hope, sir, you have ever found that I considered 420 your commands as my pride, for your kindness is such that my duty as yet has been inclination. (*Exeunt.*)

Act IV, scene i.

Enter Hastings and Miss Neville.

HASTINGS.

You surprise me! Sir Charles Marlow expected here this night? Where have you had your information?

MISS NEVILLE.

You may depend upon it. I just saw his letter to Mr. Hardcastle, in which he tells him he intends setting out a few hours after his son. 5

HASTINGS.

Then, my Constance, all must be completed before he arrives. He knows me, and should he find me here, would discover* my name, and perhaps my designs, to the rest of the family.

MISS NEVILLE.

The jewels, I hope, are safe. 10

HASTINGS.

Yes, yes. I have sent them to Marlow, who keeps the keys of our baggage. In the meantime, I'll go to prepare matters for our elopement. I have had the squire's promise of a fresh pair of horses and, if I should not see him again, will write him further 15 directions. (*Exit.*)

MISS NEVILLE.

Well! success attend you. In the meantime, I'll go amuse my aunt with the old pretense of a violent passion for my cousin. (*Exit.*)

Enter Marlow, followed by a servant.

MARLOW.

I wonder what Hastings could mean by sending 20 me so valuable a thing as a casket to keep for him, when he knows the only place I have is the seat of a post coach at an inn door.—Have you deposited the casket with the landlady, as I ordered you? Have you put it into her own hands? 25

SERVANT.

Yes, your honor.

MARLOW.

She said she'd keep it safe, did she?

SERVANT.

Yes, she said she'd keep it safe enough; she asked me how I came by it, and she said she had a great mind to make me give an account of myself. (*Exit.*) 30

MARLOW.

Ha! ha! ha! They're safe, however. What an unaccountable set of beings have we got amongst! This little barmaid, though, runs in my head most strangely and drives out the absurdities of all the rest of the family. She's mine, she must be mine, 35 or I'm greatly mistaken.

Enter Hastings.

HASTINGS.

Bless me! I quite forgot to tell her that I intended to prepare at the bottom of the garden.—Marlow here, and in spirits too!

MARLOW.

Give me joy, George! Crown me, shadow me with 40 laurels! Well George, after all, we modest fellows don't want* for success among the women.

HASTINGS.

Some women, you mean. But what success has your honor's modesty been crowned with now, that it grows so insolent upon us? 45

MARLOW.

Didn't you see the tempting, brisk, lovely little thing that runs about the house with a bunch of keys to its girdle?

HASTINGS.

Well! and what then?

MARLOW.

She's mine, you rogue you. Such fire, such motion, 50 such eyes, such lips—but egad! she would not let me kiss them, though.

HASTINGS.

But are you so sure, so very sure of her?

MARLOW.

Why man, she talked of showing me her work above-stairs,[74] and I am to improve the pattern. 55

HASTINGS.

But how can *you*, Charles, go about to rob a woman of her honor?

MARLOW.

Pshaw! pshaw! we all know the honor of the

_____

74 above-stairs] upstairs

barmaid of an inn. I don't intend to *rob* her; take my word for it, there's nothing in this house I 60 shan't honestly *pay* for.

HASTINGS.

I believe the girl has virtue.

MARLOW.

And if she has, I should be the last man in the world that would attempt to corrupt it.

HASTINGS.

You have taken care, I hope, of the casket I sent 65 you to lock up? It's in safety?

MARLOW.

Yes, yes. It's safe enough. I have taken care of it. But how could you think the seat of a post coach at an inn door a place of safety? Ah! numbskull! I have taken better precautions for you than you did 70 for yourself. I have—

HASTINGS.

What!

MARLOW.

I have sent it to the landlady to keep for you.

HASTINGS.

To the landlady!

MARLOW.

The landlady. 75

HASTINGS.

You did.

MARLOW.

I did. She's to be answerable for its forthcoming, you know.

HASTINGS.

Yes, she'll bring it forth, with a witness.

MARLOW.

Wasn't I right? I believe you'll allow that I acted 80 prudently upon this occasion?

HASTINGS. (*Aside.*)

He must not see my uneasiness.

MARLOW.

You seem a little disconcerted though, methinks. Sure nothing has happened?

HASTINGS.

No, nothing. Never was in better spirits in all my 85 life. And so you left it with the landlady, who, no doubt, very readily undertook the charge?

MARLOW.

Rather too readily. For she not only kept the casket

but, through her great precaution, was going to
keep the messenger too. Ha! ha! ha!   90

HASTINGS.

He! he! he! They're safe, however.

MARLOW.

As a guinea in a miser's purse.

HASTINGS. (*Aside.*)

So now all hopes of fortune are at an end, and we
must set off without it. (*To him.*) Well Charles, I'll
leave you to your meditations on the pretty   95
barmaid, and, he! he! he! may you be as successful
for yourself as you have been for me. (*Exit.*)

MARLOW.

Thank ye, George! I ask no more. Ha! ha! ha!

Enter Hardcastle.

HARDCASTLE.

I no longer know my own house. It's turned all
topsy-turvy. His servants have got drunk already.   100
I'll bear it no longer, and yet, from the respect for
his father, I'll be calm. (*To him.*) Mr. Marlow, your
servant, I'm your very humble servant. (*Bowing
low.*)

MARLOW.

Sir, your humble servant. (*Aside.*) What's to be the 105
wonder now?

HARDCASTLE.

I believe, sir, you must be sensible, sir, that no man
alive ought to be more welcome than your father's
son, sir. I hope you think so?

MARLOW.

I do from my soul, sir. I don't want* much   110
entreaty. I generally make my father's son welcome
wherever he goes.

HARDCASTLE.

I believe you do, from my soul, sir. But though I
say nothing to your own conduct, that of your
servants is insufferable. Their manner of drinking   115
is setting a very bad example in this house, I assure
you.

MARLOW.

I protest, my very good sir, that's no fault of mine.
If they don't drink as they ought, *they* are to blame.
I ordered them not to spare the cellar. I did, I   120
assure you. (*To the side scene.*) Here, let one of my
servants come up. (*To him.*) My positive directions

were, that as I did not drink myself, they should
make up for my deficiencies below.

HARDCASTLE.

Then they had your orders for what they do! I'm   125
satisfied!

MARLOW.

They had, I assure you.9 You shall hear from one
of themselves.

Enter [Jeremy] drunk.

You, Jeremy! Come forward, sirrah! What were my
orders? Were you not told to drink freely and call   130
for what you thought fit for the good of the house?

HARDCASTLE. (*Aside.*)

I begin to lose my patience.

JEREMY.

Please your honor, liberty and Fleet Street
forever!75 Though I'm but a servant, I'm as good
as another man. I'll drink for no man before   135
supper, sir, damme! Good liquor will sit upon a
good supper, but a good supper will not sit upon—
(*Hiccups.*) upon my conscience, sir.

MARLOW.

You see, my old friend, the fellow is as drunk as
he can possibly be. I don't know what you'd have   140
more, unless you'd have the poor devil soused in a
beer barrel.

HARDCASTLE. [*Aside.*]

Zounds! He'll drive me distracted if I contain
myself any longer.—Mr. Marlow. Sir, I have
submitted to your insolence for more than four   145
hours, and I see no likelihood of its coming to an
end. I'm now resolved to be master here, sir, and
I desire that you and your drunken pack may leave
my house directly.

---

75 liberty and Fleet Street forever!] This is an ambiguous
reference to the slogans of the 1760s in support of John
Wilkes, the politician, journalist, and agitator whose vi-
tuperative attacks on the government produced severe
judicial retaliation and in turn his martyrdom for the
cause of a free press. Goldsmith may be citing Fleet
Street in its late eighteenth-century capacity as London's
center for journalism, but he may also be using it here
as an emblem of the metropolis–or as the area in London that had numerous taverns.

MARLOW.

Leave your house!—Sure you jest, my good friend? 150
What, when I'm doing what I can to please you?

HARDCASTLE.

I tell you, sir, you don't please me, so I desire you'll
leave my house.

MARLOW.

Sure you cannot be serious? At this time o'night,
and such a night. You only mean to banter me? 155

HARDCASTLE.

I tell you, sir, I'm serious, and now that my
passions are roused, I say this house is mine, sir,
this house is mine, and I command you to leave
it directly.

MARLOW.

Ha! ha! ha! A puddle in a storm. I shan't stir a step, 160
I assure you. (*In a serious tone.*) This, your house,
fellow! It's my house. This is my house. Mine, while
I choose to stay. What right have you to bid me leave
this house, sir? I never met with such impudence,
curse me, never in my whole life before. 165

HARDCASTLE.

Nor I, confound me if ever I did. To come to my
house, to call for what he likes, to turn me out of
my own chair, to insult the family, to order his
servants to get drunk, and then to tell me "This
house is mine, sir." By all that's impudent, it makes 170
me laugh. Ha! ha! ha! Pray sir, (*Bantering.*) as you
take the house, what think you of taking the rest
of the furniture? There's a pair of silver
candlesticks, and there's a fire screen, and here's a
pair of brazen-nosed bellows, perhaps you may 175
take a fancy to them?

MARLOW.

Bring me your bill, sir, bring me your bill, and let's
make no more words about it.

HARDCASTLE.

There are a set of prints too. What think you of
the *Rake's Progress*[76] for your own apartment? 180

MARLOW.

Bring me your bill, I say, and I'll leave you and
your infernal house directly.

---

76 *Rake's Progress*] a famous series of paintings (and later, engravings) by William Hogarth that charted the downward
spiral of the life of a profligate young man in London

HARDCASTLE.

Then there's a mahogany table that you may see
your own face in.

MARLOW.

My bill, I say. 185

HARDCASTLE.

I had forgot the great chair, for your own particular
slumbers after a hearty meal.

MARLOW.

Zounds! bring me my bill, I say, and let's hear no
more on't.

HARDCASTLE.

Young man, young man, from your father's letter 190
to me I was taught to expect a well-bred, modest
man as a visitor here, but now I find him no better
than a coxcomb and a bully. But he will be down
here presently and shall hear more of it. (*Exit.*)

MARLOW.

How's this! Sure I have not mistaken the house! 195
Everything looks like an inn. The servants cry, "Coming"; the attendance is awkward; the barmaid, too, to
attend us. But she's here and will further inform
me.—Whither so fast, child?* A word with you.

Enter Miss Hardcastle.

MISS HARDCASTLE.

Let it be short, then. I'm in a hurry. (*Aside.*) I 200
believe he begins to find out his mistake, but it's
too soon quite to undeceive him.

MARLOW.

Pray child, answer me one question! What are you,
and what may your business in this house be?

MISS HARDCASTLE.

A relation of the family, sir. 205

MARLOW.

What, a poor relation?

MISS HARDCASTLE.

Yes sir, a poor relation appointed to keep the keys
and to see that the guests want* nothing in my
power to give them.

MARLOW.

That is, you act as the barmaid of this inn. 210

MISS HARDCASTLE.

Inn! Oh law, what brought that in your head? One
of the best families in the county keep an inn! Ha!
ha! ha! Old Mr. Hardcastle's house an inn!

MARLOW.

Mr. Hardcastle's house! Is this house Mr. Hardcastle's house, child? 215

MISS HARDCASTLE.

Aye, sure. Whose else should it be?

MARLOW.

So then all's out, and I have been damnably imposed on. Oh, confound my stupid head, I shall be laughed at over the whole Town. I shall be stuck up in caricatura in all the print shops: The 220 Dullissimo Macaroni. To mistake this house of all others for an inn and my father's old friend for an innkeeper. What a swaggering puppy must he take me for. What a silly puppy do I find myself. There again, may I be hanged, my dear, but I mistook 225 you for the barmaid.

MISS HARDCASTLE.

Dear me! dear me! I'm sure there's nothing in my *behaviour* to put me upon a level with one of that stamp.

MARLOW.

Nothing, my dear, nothing. But I was in for a list 230 of blunders and could not help making you a subscriber. My stupidity saw everything the wrong way. I mistook your assiduity for assurance and your simplicity for allurement. But it's over: this house I no more show *my* face in. 235

MISS HARDCASTLE.

I hope, sir, I have done nothing to disoblige you. I'm sure I should be sorry to affront any gentleman who has been so polite and said so many civil things to me. I'm sure I should be sorry (*Pretending to cry.*) if he left the family upon my account. I'm 240 sure I should be sorry people said anything amiss, since I have no fortune but my character.ᵣ

MARLOW. (*Aside.*)

By Heaven, she weeps. This is the first mark of tenderness I ever had from a modest woman, and it touches me. (*To her.*) Excuse me, my lovely girl, 245 you are the only part of the family I leave with reluctance. But to be plain with you, the difference of our birth, fortune, and education make an honorable connection impossible, and I can never harbor a thought of seducing simplicity that 250 trusted in my honor or bringing ruin upon one whose only fault was being too lovely.

MISS HARDCASTLE. (*Aside.*)

Generous man! I now begin to admire him. (*To him.*) But I'm sure my family is as good as Miss Hardcastle's, and though I'm poor, that's no great 255 misfortune to a contented mind, and until this moment, I never thought that it was bad to want* fortune.

MARLOW.

And why now, my pretty simplicity?

MISS HARDCASTLE.

Because it puts me at a distance from one that, if 260 I had a thousand pound, I would give it all to.

MARLOW. (*Aside.*)

This simplicity bewitches me, so that if I stay, I'm undone. I must make one bold effort and leave her. (*To her.*) Your partiality in my favor, my dear, touches me most sensibly, and were I to live for 265 myself alone, I could easily fix my choice. But I owe too much to the opinion of the world, too much to the authority of a father, so that—I can scarcely speak it—it affects me. Farewell. (*Exit.*)

MISS HARDCASTLE.

I never knew half his merit till now. He shall not go, 270 if I have power or art to detain him. I'll still preserve the character in which I stooped to conquer but will undeceive my papa, who, perhaps, may laugh him out of his resolution. (*Exit.*)

Enter Tony, Miss Neville.

TONY.

Aye, you may steal for yourselves the next time. I 275 have done my duty. She has got the jewels again, that's a sure thing, but she believes it was all a mistake of the servants.

MISS NEVILLE.

But my dear cousin, sure you won't forsake us in this distress. If she in the least suspects that I am 280 going off, I shall certainly be locked up or sent to my aunt Pedigree's, which is ten times worse.

TONY.

To be sure, aunts of all kinds are damned bad things. But what can I do? I have got you a pair of horses that will fly like Whistlejacket,⁷⁷ and I'm 285 sure you can't say but I have courted you nicely

---

77 Whistlejacket] a famous racehorse

before her face.—Here she comes. We must court a bit or two more, for fear she should suspect us.

They retire and seem to fondle. Enter Mrs. Hardcastle.

MRS. HARDCASTLE.

Well, I was greatly fluttered, to be sure. But my son tells me it was all a mistake of the servants. I shan't be easy, however, till they are fairly married, and then let her keep her own fortune.—But what do I see! Fondling together, as I'm alive. I never saw Tony so sprightly before. Ah! have I caught you, my pretty doves! What, billing, exchanging stolen glances and broken murmurs. Ah! 290 295

TONY.

As for murmurs, mother, we grumble a little now and then, to be sure. But there's no love lost between us.

MRS. HARDCASTLE.

A mere sprinkling, Tony, upon the flame, only to make it burn brighter. 300

MISS NEVILLE.

Cousin Tony promises to give us more of his company at home. Indeed, he shan't leave us anymore. It won't leave us, Cousin Tony, will it?

TONY.

Oh! it's a pretty creature. No, I'd sooner leave a hare in her form,[78] the dogs in full cry, or⁵ my horse in a pound than leave you when you smile upon one so. Your laugh makes you so becoming. 305

MISS NEVILLE.

Agreeable cousin! Who can help admiring that natural humor,* that pleasant, broad, red, thoughtless—(*Patting his cheek.*) ah! it's a bold face. 310

MRS. HARDCASTLE.

Pretty innocence.

TONY.

I'm sure I always loved cousin Con's hazel eyes and her pretty long fingers, that she twists this way and that over the haspicholls,[79] like a parcel of bobbins. 315

MRS. HARDCASTLE.

Ah, he would charm the bird from the tree. I was never so happy before. My boy takes after his father, poor Mr. Lumpkin, exactly.—The jewels,

---

78 form] the nest or lair in which a hare crouches (*OED*)
79 haspicholls] Lumpkin for harpsichord

my dear Con, shall be yours incontinently. You shall have them. Isn't he a sweet boy, my dear? You shall be married tomorrow, and we'll put off the rest of his education, like Dr. Drowsy's sermons, to a fitter opportunity. 320

Enter Diggory.

DIGGORY.

Where's the squire? I have got a letter for your worship. 325

TONY.

Give it to my mamma. She reads all my letters first.

DIGGORY.

I had orders to deliver it into your own hands.

TONY.

Who does it come from?

DIGGORY.

Your worship mun[80] ask that o'the letter itself. [*Exit.*] 330

TONY.

I would wish to know, though. (*Turning the letter and gazing on it.*)

MISS NEVILLE. (*Aside.*)

Undone, undone. A letter to him from Hastings. I know the hand. If my aunt sees it, we are ruined forever. I'll keep her employed a little if I can. (*To Mrs. Hardcastle.*) But I have not told you, madam, of my cousin's smart answer just now to Mr. Marlow. We so laughed—you must know, madam—this way a little, for he must not hear us. (*They confer.*) 335

TONY. (*Still gazing.*)

A damned cramp piece of penmanship, as ever I saw in my life. I can read your print-hand very well. But here there are such handles and shanks and dashes that one can scarce tell the head from the tail. "To Anthony Lumpkin, Esquire." It's very odd, I can read the outside of my letters, where my own name is, well enough. But when I come to open it, it's all—buzz. That's hard, very hard, for the inside of the letter is always the cream of the correspondence. 340 345

MRS. HARDCASTLE.

Ha! ha! ha! Very well, very well. And so my son was too hard for the philosopher. 350

---

80 mun] must

MISS NEVILLE.

Yes, madam, but you must hear the rest, madam. A little more this way, or he may hear us. You'll hear how he puzzled him again.

MRS. HARDCASTLE.

He seems strangely puzzled now himself, methinks. 355

TONY. (*Still gazing.*)

A damned up and down hand, as if it was disguised* in liquor. (*Reading.*) "Dear Sir." Aye, that's that. Then there's an "M" and a "T" and an "S," but whether the next be an "izzard"[81] or an "R," confound me, I cannot tell. 360

MRS. HARDCASTLE.

What's that, my dear. Can I give you any assistance?

MISS NEVILLE.

Pray, aunt, let me read it. Nobody reads a cramp hand better than I. (*Twitching the letter from her.*) Do you know who it is from? 365

TONY.

Can't tell, except from Dick Ginger the feeder.[82]

MISS NEVILLE.

Aye, so it is. (*Pretending to read.*) "Dear Squire, Hoping that you're in health, as I am at this present. The gentlemen of the Shake-bag[83] club has cut the gentlemen of Goose-green quite out 370 of feather. The odds"—um—"odd battle"—um— "long fighting"—um—here, here, it's all about cocks and fighting; it's of no consequence, here, put it up, put it up. (*Thrusting the crumpled letter upon him.*) 375

TONY.

But I tell you, miss, it's of all the consequence in the world. I would not lose the rest of it for a guinea. (*Giving Mrs. Hardcastle the letter.*) Here, mother, do you make it out.—Of no consequence!

MRS. HARDCASTLE.

How's this! (*Reads.*) "Dear Squire, I'm now waiting 380 for Miss Neville with a post chaise and pair at the bottom of the garden, but I find my horses yet unable to perform the journey. I expect you'll assist us with a pair of fresh horses, as you promised.

Dispatch is necessary, as the *hag* (aye, the hag) your 385 mother, will otherwise suspect us. Yours, Hastings." Grant me patience. I shall run distracted. My rage chokes me.

MISS NEVILLE.

I hope, madam, you'll suspend your resentment for a few moments and not impute to me any 390 impertinence or sinister design that belongs to another.

MRS. HARDCASTLE. (*Curtseying very low.*)

Fine spoken, madam, you are most miraculously polite and engaging and quite the very pink of courtesy and circumspection, madam. (*Changing* 395 *her tone.*) And you, you great ill-fashioned oaf, with scarce sense enough to keep your mouth shut. Were you, too, joined against me? But I'll defeat all your plots in a moment.—As for you, madam, since you have got a pair of fresh horses ready, it 400 would be cruel to disappoint them. So, if you please, instead of running away with your spark, prepare, this very moment, to run off with *me*. Your old aunt Pedigree will keep you secure, I'll warrant me.—You too, sir, may mount your horse 405 and guard us upon the way.—Here, Thomas, Roger, Diggory.—I'll show you that I wish you better than you do yourselves. (*Exit.*)

MISS NEVILLE.

So now I'm completely ruined.

TONY.

Aye, that's a sure thing. 410

MISS NEVILLE.

What better could be expected from being connected with such a stupid fool, and after all the nods and signs I made him.

TONY.

By the laws, miss, it was your own cleverness and not my stupidity that did your business. You were 415 so nice* and so busy with your Shake-bags and Goose-greens that I thought you could never be making believe.

Enter Hastings.

HASTINGS.

So sir, I find by my servant that you have shown my letter and betrayed us. Was this well done, 420 young gentleman.

---

81 izzard] an old name for the letter *z*
82 feeder] trainer of fighting cocks
83 Shake-bag] large fighting cock

TONY.

Here's another. Ask miss there who betrayed you.
Ecod, it was her doing, not mine.

Enter Marlow.

MARLOW.

So I have been finely used here among you:
rendered contemptible, driven into ill manners,   425
despised, insulted, laughed at.

TONY.

Here's another. We shall have old Bedlam broke
loose presently.

MISS NEVILLE.

And there, sir, is the gentleman to whom we all
owe every obligation.   430

MARLOW.

What can I say to him, a mere boy, an idiot, whose
ignorance and age are a protection?

HASTINGS.

A poor contemptible booby, that would but
disgrace correction.

MISS NEVILLE.

Yet with cunning and malice enough to make   435
himself merry with all our embarrassments.

HASTINGS.

An insensible cub.

MARLOW.

Replete with tricks and mischief.

TONY.

Baw! damme, but I'll fight you both one after the
other—with baskets.[84]   440

MARLOW.

As for him, he's below resentment. But your
conduct, Mr. Hastings, requires an explanation. You
knew of my mistakes yet would not undeceive me.

HASTINGS.

Tortured as I am with my own disappointments,
is this a time for explanations? It is not friendly,   445
Mr. Marlow.

MARLOW.

But sir—

MISS NEVILLE.

Mr. Marlow, we never kept on your mistake till it
was too late to undeceive you. Be pacified.

---

84 baskets] basket hilts (q.v.)

Enter servant.

SERVANT.

My mistress desires you'll get ready immediately,   450
madam. The horses are putting to. Your hat and
things are in the next room. We are to go thirty
miles before morning. (*Exit.*)

MISS NEVILLE.

Well, well, I'll come presently.

MARLOW. (*To Hastings.*)

Was it well done, sir, to assist in rendering me   455
ridiculous? To hang me out for the scorn of all my
acquaintance? Depend upon it, sir, I shall expect
an explanation.

HASTINGS.

Was it well done, sir, if you're upon that subject,
to deliver what I entrusted to yourself to the care   460
of another, sir?

MISS NEVILLE.

Mr. Hastings. Mr. Marlow. Why will you increase
my distress by this groundless dispute? I implore,
I entreat you—

Enter servant.

SERVANT.

Your cloak, madam. My mistress is impatient.   465
[*Exit.*]

MISS NEVILLE.

I come.—Pray be pacified. If I leave you thus, I
shall die with apprehension.

Enter servant.

SERVANT.

Your fan, muff, and gloves, madam. The horses are
waiting. [*Exit.*]   470

MISS NEVILLE.

Oh, Mr. Marlow! if you knew what a scene of
constraint and ill nature lies before me, I'm sure
it would convert your resentment into pity.

MARLOW.

I'm so distracted with a variety of passions that I
don't know what I do. Forgive me, madam.—   475
George, forgive me. You know my hasty temper
and should not exasperate it.

HASTINGS.

The torture of my situation is my only excuse.

MISS NEVILLE.

Well my dear Hastings, if you have that esteem for me that I think, that I am sure you have, your constancy for three years will but increase the happiness of our future connection. If— 480

MRS. HARDCASTLE. (*Within.*)

Miss Neville! Constance, why Constance, I say!

MISS NEVILLE.

I'm coming.—Well, constancy. Remember, constancy is the word. (*Exit.*) 485

HASTINGS.

My heart! How can I support this? To be so near happiness, and such happiness.

MARLOW. (*To Tony.*)

You see now, young gentleman, the effects of your folly. What might be amusement to you is here disappointment and even distress. 490

TONY. (*From a reverie.*)

Ecod, I have hit it. It's here. Your hands: yours and yours, my poor Sulky.—My boots there, ho.—Meet me two hours hence at the bottom of the garden, and if you don't find Tony Lumpkin a more good-natured fellow than you thought for, I'll give you 495 leave to take my best horse, and Bet Bouncer into the bargain.ᵗ Come along. My boots, ho.

Exeunt.

Act V, scene i. Scene continues.

Enter Hastings and servant.

HASTINGS.

You saw the old lady and Miss Neville drive off, you say?

SERVANT.

Yes, your honor. They went off in a post coach, and the young squire went on horseback. They're thirty miles off by this time. 5

HASTINGS.

Then all my hopes are over.

SERVANT.

Yes, sir. Old Sir Charles is arrived. He and the old gentleman of the house have been laughing at Mr. Marlow's mistake this half hour. They are coming this way. 10

HASTINGS.

Then I must not be seen. So now to my fruitless

appointment at the bottom of the garden. This is about the time.

Exeunt. Enter Sir Charles and Hardcastle.

HARDCASTLE.

Ha! ha! ha! The peremptory tone in which he sent forth his sublime commands. 15

SIR CHARLES.

And the reserve with which I suppose he treated all your advances.

HARDCASTLE.

And yet he might have seen something in me above a common innkeeper, too.

SIR CHARLES.

Yes Dick, but he mistook you for an uncommon 20 innkeeper, ha! ha! ha!

HARDCASTLE.

Well, I'm in too good spirits to think of anything but joy. Yes my dear friend, this union of our families will make our personal friendships hereditary, and though my daughter's fortune is 25 but small—

SIR CHARLES.

Why Dick, will you talk of fortune to *me*? My son is possessed of more than a competence already and can want* nothing but a good and virtuous girl to share his happiness and increase it. If they 30 like each other, as you say they do—

HARDCASTLE.

If, man? I tell you they *do* like each other. My daughter as good as told me so.

SIR CHARLES.

But girls are apt to flatter themselves, you know.

HARDCASTLE.

I saw him grasp her hand in the warmest manner 35 myself.—And here he comes to put you out of your "ifs," I warrant him.

Enter Marlow.

MARLOW.

I come, sir, once more to ask pardon for my strange conduct. I can scarce reflect on my insolence without confusion. 40

HARDCASTLE.

Tut boy, a trifle. You take it too gravely. An hour or two's laughing with my daughter will set all to rights again. She'll never like you the worse for it.

MARLOW.

Sir, I shall be always proud of her approbation.

HARDCASTLE.

Approbation is but a cold word, Mr. Marlow; if I   45
am not deceived, you have something more than
approbation thereabouts. You take me?

MARLOW.

Really sir, I have not that happiness.

HARDCASTLE.

Come boy, I'm an old fellow and know what's what
as well as you that are younger. I know what has   50
passed between you, but mum.

MARLOW.

Sure sir, nothing has passed between us but the most
profound respect on my side and the most distant
reserve on hers. You don't think, sir, that my impudence has been passed upon all the rest of the family?   55

HARDCASTLE.

Impudence! No, I don't say that—not quite
impudence—though girls like to be played with
and rumpled a little, too, sometimes. But she has
told no tales, I assure you.

MARLOW.

I never gave her the slightest cause.   60

HARDCASTLE.

Well, well, I like modesty in its place well enough.
But this is overacting, young gentleman. You *may* be
open. Your father and I will like you the better for it.

MARLOW.

May I die, sir, if I ever—

HARDCASTLE.

I tell you, she don't dislike you, and as I'm sure   65
you like her—

MARLOW.

Dear sir—I protest, sir—

HARDCASTLE.

I see no reason why you should not be joined as
fast as the parson can tie you.

MARLOW.

But hear me, sir—   70

HARDCASTLE.

Your father approves the match, I admire it, every
moment's delay will be doing mischief, so—

MARLOW.

But why won't you hear me? By all that's just and
true, I never gave Miss Hardcastle the slightest mark

of my attachment or even the most distant hint to   75
suspect me of affection. We had but one interview,
and that was formal, modest, and uninteresting.

HARDCASTLE. (*Aside.*)

This fellow's formal, modest impudence is beyond
bearing.

SIR CHARLES.

And you never grasped her hand, or made any   80
protestations?

MARLOW.

As Heaven is my witness, I came down in
obedience to your commands. I saw the lady
without emotion and parted without reluctance.
I hope you'll exact no further proofs of my duty   85
nor prevent me from leaving a house in which I
suffer so many mortifications. (*Exit.*)

SIR CHARLES.

I'm astonished at the air of sincerity with which
he parted.

HARDCASTLE.

And I'm astonished at the deliberate intrepidity of   90
his assurance.

SIR CHARLES.

I dare pledge my life and honor upon his truth.

HARDCASTLE.

Here comes my daughter, and I would stake my
happiness upon her veracity.

Enter Miss Hardcastle.

Kate, come hither, child. Answer us sincerely and   95
without reserve: Has Mr. Marlow made you any
professions of love and affection?

MISS HARDCASTLE.

The question is very abrupt, sir! But since you
require unreserved sincerity, I think he has.

HARDCASTLE. (*To Sir Charles.*)

You see.   100

SIR CHARLES.

And pray, madam, have you and my son had more
than one interview?

MISS HARDCASTLE.

Yes sir, several.

HARDCASTLE. (*To Sir Charles.*)

You see.

SIR CHARLES.

But did he profess any attachment?   105

MISS HARDCASTLE.

A lasting one.

SIR CHARLES.

Did he talk of love?

MISS HARDCASTLE.

Much, sir.

SIR CHARLES.

Amazing! And all this formally?

MISS HARDCASTLE.

Formally.   110

HARDCASTLE.

Now my friend, I hope you are satisfied.

SIR CHARLES.

And how did he behave, madam?

MISS HARDCASTLE.

As most professed admirers do: said some civil
things of my face, talked much of his want* of
merit and the greatness of mine, mentioned his   115
heart, gave a short tragedy speech, and ended with
pretended rapture.

SIR CHARLES.

Now I'm perfectly convinced, indeed. I know his
conversation among women to be modest and
submissive. This forward, canting, ranting manner   120
by no means describes him, and I am confident
he never sate for the picture.

MISS HARDCASTLE.

Then what, sir, if I should convince you to your face
of my sincerity? If you and my papa in about half an
hour will place yourselves behind that screen, you   125
shall hear him declare his passion to me in person.

SIR CHARLES.

Agreed. And if I find him what you describe, all
my happiness in him must have an end. (*Exit.*)

MISS HARDCASTLE.

And if you don't find him what I describe—I fear
my happiness must never have a beginning.   130

Exeunt.

Scene ii. The back of the garden.

Enter Hastings.

HASTINGS.

What an idiot am I to wait here for a fellow who
probably takes a delight in mortifying me. He
never intended to be punctual, and I'll wait no

longer.—What do I see? It is he, and perhaps with
news of my Constance.   5

Enter Tony, booted and spattered.

HASTINGS.

My honest squire! I now find you a man of your
word. This looks like friendship.

TONY.

Aye, I'm your friend, and the best friend you have
in the world, if you knew but all. This riding by
night, by the bye, is cursedly tiresome. It has shook   10
me worse than the basket of a stagecoach.

HASTINGS.

But how? Where did you leave your fellow
travelers? Are they in safety? Are they housed?

TONY.

Five and twenty miles in two hours and a half is
no such bad driving. The poor beasts have   15
smoked[85] for it: rabbit me,[86] but I'd rather ride
forty miles after a fox than ten with such varmint.

HASTINGS.

Well, but where have you left the ladies? I die with
impatience.

TONY.

Left them? Why, where should I leave them but   20
where I found them?

HASTINGS.

This is a riddle.

TONY.

Riddle me this then: What's that goes round the
house and round the house and never touches the
house?   25

HASTINGS.

I'm still astray.

TONY.

Why that's it, mon. I have led them astray. By
jingo, there's not a pond or slough within five miles
of the place but they can tell the taste of.

HASTINGS.

Ha! ha! ha! I understand; you took them in a   30
round, while they supposed themselves going

---

85 smoked] The horses have steamed from the sweat of gal-
    loping at top speed.

86 rabbit me] an expletive the equivalent of "darn me" or
    "drat me"

forward. And so you have at last brought them home again.

TONY.

You shall hear: I first took them down Feather-bed Lane, where we stuck fast in the mud; I then 35 rattled them crack over the stones of Up-and-down Hill; I then introduced them to the gibbet on Heavy-tree Heath; and from that, with a circumbendibus,[87] I fairly lodged them in the horse-pond at the bottom of the garden. 40

HASTINGS.

But no accident, I hope.

TONY.

No, no. Only mother is confoundedly frightened. She thinks herself forty miles off. She's sick of the journey, and the cattle can scarce crawl. So if your own horses be ready, you may whip off with 45 cousin, and I'll be bound that no soul here can budge a foot to follow you.

HASTINGS.

My dear friend, how can I be grateful?

TONY.

Aye, now it's dear friend, noble squire. Just now, it was all idiot, cub, and run me through the guts. 50 Damn *your* way of fighting, I say. After we take a knock in this part of the country, we kiss and be friends. But if you had run me through the guts, then I should be dead, and you might go kiss the hangman. 55

HASTINGS.

The rebuke is just. But I must hasten to relieve Miss Neville. If you keep the old lady employed, I promise to take care of the young one. (*Exit.*)

TONY.

Never fear me.—Here she comes. Vanish. She's got from the pond and draggled up to the waist like a 60 mermaid.

Enter Mrs. Hardcastle.

MRS. HARDCASTLE.

Oh Tony, I'm killed. Shook. Battered to death. I shall never survive it. That last jolt that laid us against the quickset hedge has done my business.

---

[87] circumbendibus] a roundabout route (bogus Lat.)

TONY.

Alack Mama, it was all your own fault. You would 65 be for running away by night without knowing one inch of the way.

MRS. HARDCASTLE.

I wish we were at home again. I never met so many accidents in so short a journey: drenched in the mud, overturned in a ditch, stuck fast in a slough, 70 jolted to a jelly, and at last to lose our way. Whereabouts do you think we are, Tony?

TONY.

By my guess we should be upon Crackskull Common, about forty miles from home.

MRS. HARDCASTLE.

Oh Lud!* Oh Lud! the most notorious spot in all 75 the country. We only want* a robbery to make a complete night on't.

TONY.

Don't be afraid, Mama, don't be afraid. Two of the five that kept here are hanged, and the other three may not find us. Don't be afraid.—Is that a man 80 that's galloping behind us? No, it's only a tree. Don't be afraid.

MRS. HARDCASTLE.

The fright will certainly kill me.

TONY.

Do you see anything like a black hat moving behind the thicket? 85

MRS. HARDCASTLE.

Oh death!

TONY.

No, it's only a cow. Don't be afraid, Mama, don't be afraid.

MRS. HARDCASTLE.

As I'm alive, Tony, I see a man coming towards us. Ah! I'm sure on't. If he perceives us we are undone. 90

TONY. (*Aside.*)

Father-in-law, by all that's unlucky, come to take one of his night walks. (*To her.*) Ah, it's a highwayman, with pistols as long as my arm. A damned ill-looking fellow.

MRS. HARDCASTLE.

Good Heaven defend us! He approaches. 95

TONY.

Do you hide yourself in that thicket, and leave me to manage him. If there be any danger I'll cough and cry "hem." When I cough be sure to keep close.

Mrs. Hardcastle hides behind a tree in the back scene. Enter Hardcastle.

HARDCASTLE.

I'm mistaken, or I heard voices of people in want* of help. Oh Tony, is that you? I did not expect you 100 so soon back. Are your mother and her charge in safety?

TONY.

Very safe, sir, at my aunt Pedigree's. Hem!

MRS. HARDCASTLE. (*From behind.*)

Ah death! I find there's danger.

HARDCASTLE.

Forty miles in three hours; sure, that's too much, 105 my youngster.

TONY.

Stout horses and willing minds make short journeys, as they say. Hem!

MRS. HARDCASTLE. (*From behind.*)

Sure he'll do the dear boy no harm.

HARDCASTLE.

But I heard a voice here; I should be glad to know 110 from whence it came.

TONY.

It was I, sir, talking to myself, sir. I was saying that forty miles in four hours was very good going. Hem! As to be sure it was. Hem! I have got a sort of cold by being out in the air. We'll go in, if you 115 please. Hem!

HARDCASTLE.

But if you talked to yourself, you did not answer yourself. I am certain I heard two voices and am resolved (*Raising his voice.*) to find the other out.

MRS. HARDCASTLE. (*From behind.*)

Oh! he's coming to find me out. Oh! 120

TONY.

What need you go, sir, if I tell you? Hem! I'll lay down my life for the truth—hem!—I'll tell you all, sir. (*Detaining him.*)

HARDCASTLE.

I tell you, I will not be detained. I insist on seeing. It's in vain to expect I'll believe you. 125

MRS. HARDCASTLE. (*Running forward from behind.*)

Oh Lud, he'll murder my poor boy, my darling. Here, good gentleman, whet your rage upon me.

Take my money, my life, but spare that young gentleman, spare my child, if you have any mercy.

HARDCASTLE.

My wife, as I'm a Christian! From whence can she 130 come, or what does she mean?

MRS. HARDCASTLE. (*Kneeling.*)

Take compassion on us, good Mr. Highwayman. Take our money, our watches, all we have, but spare our lives. We will never bring you to justice, indeed we won't, good Mr. Highwayman. 135

HARDCASTLE.

I believe the woman's out of her senses. What, Dorothy, don't you know *me*?

MRS. HARDCASTLE.

Mr. Hardcastle, as I'm alive! My fears blinded me. But who, my dear, could have expected to meet you here, in this frightful place, so far from home? 140 What has brought you to follow us?

HARDCASTLE.

Sure, Dorothy, you have not lost your wits. So far from home, when you are within forty yards of your own door. (*To Tony.*) This is one of your old tricks, you graceless rogue you. (*To her.*) Don't you 145 know the gate and the mulberry tree? and don't you remember the horsepond, my dear?

MRS. HARDCASTLE.

Yes, I shall remember the horsepond as long as I live, I have caught my death in it. (*To Tony.*) And is it to you, you graceless varlet, I owe all this? I'll 150 teach you to abuse your mother, I will.

TONY.

Ecod, mother, all the parish says you have spoiled me, and so you may take the fruits on't.

MRS. HARDCASTLE.

I'll spoil you, I will.

Follows him off the stage and exeunt.

HARDCASTLE.

There's morality, however, in his reply. (*Exit.*) 155

Enter Hastings and Miss Neville.

HASTINGS.

My dear Constance, why will you deliberate thus? If we delay a moment, all is lost forever. Pluck up a little resolution, and we shall soon be out of the reach of her malignity.

MISS NEVILLE.

I find it impossible. My spirits are so sunk with 160
the agitations I have suffered that I am unable to
face any new danger. Two or three years' patience
will at last crown us with happiness.

HASTINGS.

Such a tedious delay is worse than inconstancy. Let
us fly, my charmer. Let us date our happiness from 165
this very moment. Perish fortune. Love and
content will increase what we possess beyond a
monarch's revenue. Let me prevail.

MISS NEVILLE.

No, Mr. Hastings, no. Prudence once more comes
to my relief, and I will obey its dictates. In the 170
moment of passion, fortune may be despised, but
it ever produces a lasting repentance. I'm resolved
to apply to Mr. Hardcastle's compassion and justice
for redress.

HASTINGS.

But though he had the will, he has not the power 175
to relieve you.

MISS NEVILLE.

But he has influence, and upon that I am resolved
to rely.

HASTINGS.

I have no hopes. But since you persist, I must
reluctantly obey you. 180

Exeunt.

Scene iii.

Enter Sir Charles and Miss Hardcastle.

SIR CHARLES.

What a situation am I in. If what you say appears,
I shall then find a guilty son. If what he says be
true, I shall then lose one that, of all others, I most
wished for a daughter.

MISS HARDCASTLE.

I am proud of your approbation, and to show I 5
merit it, if you place yourselves as I directed, you
shall hear his explicit declaration.—But he comes.

SIR CHARLES.

I'll to your father and keep him to the
appointment. (*Exit.*)

Enter Marlow.

MARLOW.

Though prepared for setting out, I come once 10
more to take leave, nor did I, till this moment,
know the pain I feel in the separation.

MISS HARDCASTLE. (*In her own natural manner.*)

I believe these sufferings cannot be very great, sir,
which you can so easily remove. A day or two
longer, perhaps, might lessen your uneasiness by 15
showing the little value of what you now think
proper to regret.

MARLOW. (*Aside.*)

This girl every moment improves upon me. (*To
her.*) It must not be, madam. I have already trifled
too long with my heart. My very pride begins to 20
submit to my passion. The disparity of education
and fortune, the anger of a parent, and the
contempt of my equals begin to lose their weight,
and nothing can restore me to myself but this
painful effort of resolution. 25

MISS HARDCASTLE.

Then go, sir. I'll urge nothing more to detain you.
Though my family be as good as hers you came
down to visit and my education, I hope, not
inferior, what are these advantages without equal
affluence? I must remain contented with the slight 30
approbation of imputed merit; I must have only
the mockery of your addresses, while all your
serious aims are fixed on fortune.

Enter Hardcastle and Sir Charles from behind.

SIR CHARLES.

Here, behind this screen.

HARDCASTLE.

Aye, aye, make no noise. I'll engage my Kate covers 35
him with confusion at last.

MARLOW.

By heavens, madam, fortune was ever my smallest
consideration. Your beauty at first caught my eye,
for who could see that without emotion. But every
moment that I converse with you, steals in some 40
new grace, heightens the picture, and gives it
stronger expression. What at first seemed rustic
plainness now appears refined simplicity. What
seemed forward assurance now strikes me as the
result of courageous innocence and conscious 45
virtue.

SIR CHARLES.

What can it mean? He amazes me!

HARDCASTLE.

I told you how it would be. Hush!

MARLOW.

I am now determined to stay, madam, and I have too good an opinion of my father's discernment, when he sees you, to doubt his approbation. 50

MISS HARDCASTLE.

No, Mr. Marlow, I will not, cannot detain you. Do you think I could suffer a connection in which there is the smallest room for repentance? Do you think I would take the mean advantage of a transient passion to load you with confusion? Do you think I could ever relish that happiness which was acquired by lessening yours? 55

MARLOW.

By all that's good, I can have no happiness but what's in your power to grant me. Nor shall I ever feel repentance but in not having seen your merits before. I will stay, even contrary to your wishes, and though you should persist to shun me, I will make my respectful assiduities atone for the levity of my past conduct. 60 65

MISS HARDCASTLE.

Sir, I must entreat you'll desist. As our acquaintance began, so let it end, in indifference. I might have given an hour or two to levity, but seriously, Mr. Marlow, do you think I could ever submit to a connection where *I* must appear mercenary and *you* imprudent? Do you think I could ever catch at the confident addresses of a secure admirer? 70

MARLOW. (*Kneeling.*)

Does this look like security? Does this look like confidence? No, madam, every moment that shows me your merit only serves to increase my diffidence and confusion. Here let me continue— 75

SIR CHARLES.

I can hold it no longer. Charles, Charles, how hast thou deceived me! Is this your indifference, your uninteresting conversation?

HARDCASTLE.

Your cold contempt, your formal interview? What have you to say now? 80

MARLOW.

That I'm all amazement! What can it mean?

HARDCASTLE.

It means that you can say and unsay things at pleasure; that you can address a lady in private and deny it in public; that you have one story for us and another for my daughter. 85

MARLOW.

Daughter! this lady your daughter!

HARDCASTLE.

Yes sir, my only daughter, my Kate. Whose else should she be?

MARLOW.

Oh, the devil. 90

MISS HARDCASTLE.

Yes sir, that very* identical tall, squinting lady you were pleased to take me for. (*Curtesying.*) She that you addressed as the mild, modest, sentimental man of gravity, and the bold forward agreeable Rattle of the Ladies Club. Ha! ha! ha! 95

MARLOW.

Zounds, there's no bearing this; it's worse than death.

MISS HARDCASTLE.

In which of your characters, sir, will you give us leave to address you? As the faltering gentleman, with looks on the ground, that speaks just to be heard and hates hypocrisy, or the loud, confident creature, that keeps it up with Mrs. Mantrap and old Miss Biddy Buckskin till three in the morning; ha! ha! ha! 100

MARLOW.

Oh, curse on my noisy head. I never attempted to be impudent yet that I was not taken down. I must be gone. 105

HARDCASTLE.

By the hand of my body, but you shall not. I see it was all a mistake, and I am rejoiced to find it. You shall not stir,[u] I tell you. I know she'll forgive you.—Won't you forgive him, Kate? We'll all forgive you. Take courage, man. 110

They retire, she tormenting him to the back scene.
Enter Mrs. Hardcastle and Tony.

MRS. HARDCASTLE.

So, so, they're gone off. Let them go, I care not.

HARDCASTLE.

Who gone?

MRS. HARDCASTLE.

My dutiful niece and her gentleman, Mr. Hastings, from Town. He who came down with our modest visitor here. 115

SIR CHARLES.

Who, my honest George Hastings? As worthy a fellow as lives, and the girl could not have made a more prudent choice. 120

HARDCASTLE.

Then, by the hand of my body, I'm proud of the connection.

MRS. HARDCASTLE.

Well, if he has taken away the lady, he has not taken her fortune; that remains in this family to console us for her loss. 125

HARDCASTLE.

Sure, Dorothy, you would not be so mercenary?

MRS. HARDCASTLE.

Aye, that's my affair, not yours.

HARDCASTLE.ᵛ

But you know if your son, when of age, refuses to marry his cousin, her whole fortune is then at her own disposal. 130

MRS.ʷ HARDCASTLE.

Aye, but he's not of age, and she has not thought proper to wait for his refusal.

Enter Hastings and Miss Neville.

(*Aside.*) What, returned so soon? I begin not to like it.

HASTINGS. (*To Hardcastle.*)

For my late attempt to fly off with your niece, let my present confusion be my punishment. We are now come back to appeal from your justice to your humanity. By her father's consent, I first paid her my addresses, and our passions were first founded in duty. 135

MISS NEVILLE.

Since his death, I have been obliged to stoop to dissimulation to avoid oppression. In an hour of levity, I was ready even to give up my fortune to secure my choice. But I'm now recovered from the delusion and hope from your tenderness what is denied me from a nearer connection. 140

145

MRS. HARDCASTLE.

Pshaw, pshaw, this is all but the whining end of a modern novel.

HARDCASTLE.

Be it what it will, I'm glad they're come back to reclaim their due.—Come hither, Tony boy. Do you refuse this lady's hand whom I now offer you? 150

TONY.

What signifies my refusing? You know I can't refuse her till I'm of age, Father.

HARDCASTLE.

While I thought concealing your age, boy, was likely to conduce to your improvement, I concurred with your mother's desire to keep it secret. But since I find she turns it to a wrong use, I must now declare you have been of age these three months. 155

TONY.

Of age! Am I of age, Father?

HARDCASTLE.

Above three months. 160

TONY.

Then you'll see the first use I'll make of my liberty. (*Taking Miss Neville's hand.*) Witness all men by these presents, that I, Anthony Lumpkin, Esquire, of _____* place, refuse you, Constantia Neville, spinster, of no place at all, for my true and lawful wife. So Constance Neville may marry whom she pleases, and Tony Lumpkin is his own man again. 165

SIR CHARLES.

Oh brave* squire.

HASTINGS.

My worthy friend.

MRS. HARDCASTLE.

My undutiful offspring. 170

MARLOW.

Joy, my dear George, I give you joy sincerely. And could I prevail upon my little tyrant here to be less arbitrary, I should be the happiest man alive if you would return me the favor.

HASTINGS. (*To Miss Hardcastle.*)

Come madam, you are now driven to the very last scene of all your contrivances. I know you like him, I'm sure he loves you, and you must and shall have him. 175

HARDCASTLE. (*Joining their hands.*)

And I say so too. And Mr. Marlow, if she makes as good a wife as she has a daughter, I don't believe you'll ever repent your bargain. So now to supper; 180

tomorrow we shall gather all the poor of the parish about us, and the Mistakes of the Night shall be crowned with a merry morning. So, boy, take her, and as you have been mistaken in the mistress, my wish is, that you may never be mistaken in the wife. 185

[Exeunt.]

FINIS.

Textual Notes

ᵃ Copytext is the first edition corrected, a 1773 octavo (Oc). Also consulted: first edition uncorrected, a 1773 octavo (Ou); Larpent ms. in the Huntington Library, the earliest surviving text of the play (not Goldsmith's holograph), prepared before the first performance for the licenser for the theater and used as the basis for some performances up through the 19th century (L); modern editions of 1939, rev. 1969 (Nettleton, Case, Stone—NCS); 1966 (Friedman); 1979 (Davis). If the modern scholarly editions (Friedman and/or Davis) do not incorporate substantive and/or interesting variants from L, they are not noted here.

ᵇ ackoardingly] L, Friedman; accordingly Oo, NCS, Davis

ᶜ these] L, NCS, Friedman, Davis; those Oo

ᵈ (*Noting it down.*)] L, Davis; *om.* Oo, NCS, Friedman

ᵉ (*Still noting.*)] L, Davis; *om.* Oo, NCS, Friedman

ᶠ (*Who had been noting.*) L, Davis; *om.* Oo, NCS, Friedman

ᵍ county] L, Friedman; country Oo, NCS, Davis

ʰ this-aways] L, Friedman; this way Oo, NCS, Davis

ⁱ prepossessing] Oo, NCS, Friedman; professing L, Davis

ʲ Charles] L, NCS, Friedman, Davis; George Oo

ᵏ without … within] L, Friedman, Davis; within … without Oo, NCS

ˡ *Enter Roger … fare.*] L, Friedman, Davis; *om.* Oo; *Re-enter Roger* NCS

ᵐ a pig's face … pig's face … pig's face] L, Davis; pig Oo, Friedman, NCS

ⁿ my boy] L, Davis; boy Oo, NCS, Friedman

ᵒ I–I–I–as yet have] Oo, NCS, Friedman; I-I-I- MISS HARDCASTLE. Then why take such pains to study and observe them? MARLOW. As yet I have L, Davis

ᵖ Longhorns,] L, Davis; Langhorns Oo, NCS, Friedman

ᵠ you] L, NCS, Friedman, Davis; *om.* Oo

ʳ fortune but my character.] Oo, NCS, Davis; fortin but my charackter L, Friedman

ˢ a hare … cry, or] L, Davis; *om.* Oo, NCS, Friedman

ᵗ to take … the bargain.] Oo, NCS, Friedman; to run me through the guts with a shoulder of mutton L, Davis

ᵘ not stir,] L, Davis; not, Sir, Oo, NCS, Friedman

ᵛ HARDCASTLE.] L, NCS, Friedman, Davis; *om.* Oo

ʷ MRS.] L, NCS, Friedman, Davis; *om.* Oo

The School for Scandal[a]

by Richard Brinsley Sheridan (1751-1816)

edited by Mita Choudhury

Richard Brinsley Sheridan wrote many plays, including *The Rivals, The Critic, A Trip to Scarborough, The Duenna*, but none was as successful as *The School for Scandal* (premiere at Drury Lane, Thursday, May 8, 1777). On the eighteenth-century London stage, only John Gay's *Beggar's Opera* (1728) came close to this play's performance record. In addition to writing plays, Sheridan was the principal manager of Drury Lane Theater from 1776 on—right after David Garrick withdrew from the theater on grounds of poor health.

The central message of *The School for Scandal* is that appearances are deceptive, so much so that the man of true sentiment and virtue may not necessarily appear to be so. The play deals with the machinations of half a dozen delightfully dubious characters that caricature the late eighteenth-century London society newly invigorated by social mobility, trade, and commerce. Dressing rooms and tea parlors, libraries and picture galleries provide the right blend of settings for gossip and a variety of social schemes. Sir Oliver Surface, the moral arbiter in the play, returns from India with ample means to satisfy the whims of his nephews, only one of whom turns out to have the right values to deserve the uncle's support. While Joseph Surface appears to be a man of sentiment, it is his brother, Charles, who wins the support of their rich uncle and the theater audiences when he reveals his benevolence and compassion, his truly sentimental nature. The two most memorable scenes in the play—the picture and the screen scenes—are also two of the most effective "discovery"* scenes in the history of English drama, designed specifically to reveal the contrasting characters of Oliver Surface's nephews.

Sheridan created most of the characters with specific actors in mind. It is not surprising that William Smith—genteel, debonaire, and charismatic—would be cast, at age forty-seven, as Charles Surface. He looked twenty years younger than his age, and he was able to carry off that role with as much panache much later at age sixty-eight. Likewise, John Palmer, who was cast as Joseph Surface, had a reputation for being hypocritical and unfaithful to his wife. A good friend of Garrick's, Thomas King had become the principal comedian at Drury Lane theater circa mid 1770s. He was the original Sir Peter Teazle, playing opposite Frances Abington as Lady Teazle. Abington was one of the greatest comediennes of her time, and Lady Teazle was her most successful part, following, among many others, Lucy in *The Beggar's Opera* and Mrs. Sullen in *The Beaux' Stratagem*. Richard Yates, the versatile actor and one-time manager of the Birmingham theater, was about seventy when he played the original Sir Oliver Surface.

Good casting alone cannot account for the success of *The School for Scandal*, however. The tone and texture of Sheridan's characters and dialogue add depth to our understanding of a metropolitan public culture at the dawn of London's dynamic role as the imperial capital, the metropolis to which her adventuring colonists, like Sir Oliver, returned with increasing wealth and power.

DRAMATIS PERSONAE

[MEN]

Sir Peter Teazle.
Sir Oliver Surface.
Joseph Surface.
Charles Surface.
Snake.
Rowley.
Moses.
Careless.
Sir Toby Bumper.
Trip.
Sir Benjamin Backbite.
Crabtree.
[Servants.]

[WOMEN]

Lady Teazle.
Lady Sneerwell.
Mrs. Candor.
Maria.

The School for Scandal.

Act I, scene i. [Lady Sneerwell's house.]

Lady Sneerwell at the dressing table; Mr. Snake drinking chocolate.

LADY SNEERWELL.

The paragraphs you say, Mr. Snake, were all inserted?

SNAKE.

They were, madam, and as I copied them myself in a feigned hand, there can be no suspicion whence they came.

LADY SNEERWELL.

Did you circulate the report of Lady Brittle's intrigue with Captain Boastall?

SNAKE.

That is in as fine a train as your ladyship could wish; in the common course of things, I think it must reach Mrs. Clackit's ears within four-and-twenty hours, and then you know the business is as good as done.

LADY SNEERWELL.

Why truly, Mrs. Clackit has a very pretty talent and a great deal of industry.

SNAKE.

True, madam, and has been tolerably successful in her day. To my knowledge she has been the cause of six matches being broken off and three sons being disinherited, of four forced elopements, as many close confinements,[1] nine separate maintenances,* and two divorces. Nay, I have more than once traced her causing a tête-à-tête in the *Town and Country Magazine*[2] when the parties perhaps had never seen each others' faces before in the course of their lives.

LADY SNEERWELL.

She certainly has talents, but her manner is gross.

SNAKE.

'Tis very true: she generally designs well, has a free tongue and a bold invention, but her coloring is too dark and her outline often extravagant. She wants* that delicacy of hint and mellowness of sneer which distinguishes your ladyship's scandal.

LADY SNEERWELL.

Ah! You are partial, Snake.

SNAKE.

Not in the least: everybody allows that Lady Sneerwell can do more with a word or a look than many can with the most labored detail, even when they happen to have a little truth on their side to support it.

LADY SNEERWELL.

Yes, my dear Snake, and I am no hypocrite to deny the satisfaction I reap from the success of my efforts. Wounded myself in the early part of my life by the envenomed tongue of slander, I confess I have since known no pleasure equal to the reducing others to the level of my own reputation.[b]

SNAKE.

Nothing can be more natural. But Lady Sneerwell, there is one affair in which you have lately employed me wherein I confess I am at a loss to guess your motives.

---

1 close confinements] hushed-up childbirths
2 *Town and Country Magazine*] a monthly periodical, an early-modern equivalent of today's print tabloid. Celebrities' identities were indicated by pseudonyms or initials; their portraits often accompanied these anecdotes (Price).

LADY SNEERWELL.

I conceive you mean with respect to my neighbor, Sir Peter Teazle, and his family?

SNAKE.

I do. Here are two young men to whom Sir Peter has acted as a kind of guardian since their father's death: 50 the eldest possessing the most amiable character and universally well spoken of; the youngest the most dissipated and extravagant young fellow in the kingdom, without friends or character. The former an avowed admirer of your ladyship's and apparently 55 your favorite; the latter attached to Maria, Sir Peter's ward, and confessedly beloved by her. Now on the face of these circumstances, it is utterly unaccountable to me why you, the widow of a City* knight with a good jointure, should not close with 60 the passion of a man of such character and expectation as Mr. Surface, and more so, why you should be so uncommonly earnest to destroy the mutual attachment between his brother Charles and Maria. 65

LADY SNEERWELL.

Then at once to unravel this mystery, I must inform you that love has no share whatever in the intercourse between Mr. Surface and me.

SNAKE.

No!

LADY SNEERWELL.

His real attachment is to Maria or her fortune, but 70 finding in his brother a favored rival, he has been obliged to mask his pretensions and profit by my assistance.

SNAKE.

Yet still I am more puzzled why you should interest yourself in his success. 75

LADY SNEERWELL.

Heavens, how dull you are! Cannot you surmise the weakness which I hitherto through shame have concealed even from you? Must I confess that Charles, that libertine, that extravagant, that bankrupt in fortune and reputation, that he it is 80 for whom I am thus anxious and malicious and to gain whom I would sacrifice everything.

SNAKE.

Now, indeed your conduct appears consistent, but how came you and Mr. Surface so confidential?

LADY SNEERWELL.

For our mutual interest. I have found him out a 85 long time since. I know him to be artful, selfish, and malicious—in short, a sentimental knave— while with Sir Peter, and indeed with all his acquaintance, he passes for a miracle of prudence, good sense, and benevolence.[c] 90

SNAKE.

Nay, Sir Peter vows he has not his equal in England, and above all he praises him as a Man of Sentiment.

LADY SNEERWELL.

True, and with the assistance of sentiments and hypocrisy, he has brought him entirely into his 95 interest with regard to Maria, while poor Charles has no friend in the house, though I fear he has a powerful one in Maria's heart, against whom we must direct our schemes.

Enter servant.

SERVANT.

Mr. Surface. 100

LADY SNEERWELL.

Show him up.

Exit servant.

He generally calls about this time; I don't wonder at people's giving him to me for a lover.

Enter Joseph Surface.

JOSEPH SURFACE.

My dear Lady Sneerwell, how do you do to day? Mr. Snake, your most obedient. 105

LADY SNEERWELL.

Snake has just been arraigning me on our mutual attachment, but I have informed him of our real views. You know how useful he has been to us, and believe me, the confidence is not ill placed.

JOSEPH SURFACE.

Madam, it is impossible for me to suspect a man 110 of Mr. Snake's sensibility and discernment.

LADY SNEERWELL.

Well, well, no compliments now, but tell me when you saw your mistress, Maria, or what is more material to me, your brother.

JOSEPH SURFACE.

I have not seen either since I left you, but I can 115

inform you that they never meet. Some of your
stories have taken a good effect on Maria.

LADY SNEERWELL.
Ah my dear Snake, the merit of this belongs to
you.—But do your brother's distresses increase?

JOSEPH SURFACE.
Every hour. I am told he has had another execution[3]   120
in his house yesterday; in short, his dissipation and
extravagance exceed everything I ever heard of.

LADY SNEERWELL.
Poor Charles!

JOSEPH SURFACE.
True, madam, notwithstanding his vices, one cannot
help feeling for him. Aye, poor Charles indeed. I am   125
sure I wish it was in my power to be of any essential
service to him. For the man who does not share in
the distresses of a brother, even though merited by
his own misconduct, deserves—

LADY SNEERWELL.
Oh Lud!* You are going to be moral and forget   130
that you are among friends.

JOSEPH SURFACE.
Egad that's true. I'll keep that sentiment till I see
Sir Peter. However, it is certainly a charity to rescue
Maria from such a libertine, who, if he is to be
reclaimed, can be so only by one of your ladyship's   135
superior accomplishments and understanding.

SNAKE.
I believe, Lady Sneerwell, here's company coming;
I'll go and copy the letter I mentioned to you.—
Mr. Surface, your most obedient. (*Exit.*)

JOSEPH SURFACE.
Sir, your very devoted— Lady Sneerwell, I am very   140
sorry you have put any further confidence in that
fellow.

LADY SNEERWELL.
Why so?

JOSEPH SURFACE.
I have lately detected him in frequent conference
with old Rowley, who was formerly my father's   145
steward and has never, you know, been a friend of
mine.

LADY SNEERWELL.
And do you think he would betray us?

JOSEPH SURFACE.
Nothing more likely, take my word for it, Lady Sneerwell, that fellow has not virtue enough to be faithful   150
or constant even to his own villainy.—Hah, Maria!

Enter Maria.

LADY SNEERWELL.
Maria, my dear, how do you do? What's the
matter?

MARIA.
Oh, there's that disagreeable lover of mine, Sir
Benjamin Backbite, has just called at my guardian's   155
with his odious uncle Crabtree, so I slipped out
and ran hither to avoid them.

LADY SNEERWELL.
Is that all?

JOSEPH SURFACE.
If my brother Charles had been of the party,
madam, perhaps you would not have been so   160
much alarmed.

LADY SNEERWELL.
Nay now, you are severe, for I dare swear the truth
of the matter is, Maria heard you were here.—But
my dear, what has Sir Benjamin done that you
should avoid him so?   165

MARIA.
Oh, he has done nothing, but 'tis for what he has
said. His conversation is a perpetual libel on all his
acquaintance.

JOSEPH SURFACE.
Aye, and the worst of it is, there is no advantage
in not knowing him, for he'll abuse a stranger just   170
as soon as his best friend, and his uncle is as bad.

LADY SNEERWELL.
Nay, but we should make allowance: Sir Benjamin
is a wit and a poet.

MARIA.
For my part I own, madam, wit loses its respect
with me when I see it in company with malice.—   175
What do you think, Mr. Surface?

JOSEPH SURFACE.
Certainly, madam, to smile at the jest which plants
a thorn in another's breast is to become a principal
in the mischief.

LADY SNEERWELL.
Pshaw! There's no possibility of being witty   180

without a little ill nature; malice of a good thing is the barb which makes it stick.—What's your opinion, Mr. Surface?

JOSEPH SURFACE.

To be sure, madam, that conversation where the spirit of raillery is suppressed will ever appear 185 tedious and insipid.

MARIA.d

Well, I'll not debate how far scandal may be allowable, but in a man I am sure it is always contemptible. We have pride, envy, rivalship, and a thousand little motives to depreciate each other, 190 but the male slanderer must have the cowardice of a woman before he can traduce one.

Enter servant.

SERVANT.

Madam, Mrs. Candor is below and, if your ladyship's at leisure, will leave her carriage.

LADY SNEERWELL.

Beg her to walk in. 195

[Exit servant.]

Now Maria, however, here is a character to your taste, for though Mrs. Candor is a little talkative, everybody allows her to be the best natured and best sort of woman.

MARIA.

Yet with a very gross affectation of good nature and 200 benevolence, she does more mischief than the direct malice of old Crabtree.

JOSEPH SURFACE.

I'faith, 'tis very true, Lady Sneerwell. Whenever I hear the current running against the characters* of my friends, I never think them in such danger as 205 when Candor undertakes their defence.

LADY SNEERWELL.

Hush! Here she is.

Enter Mrs. Candor.

MRS. CANDOR.

My dear Lady Sneerwell, how have you been this century? Mr. Surface, what news do you hear, though indeed it is no matter, for I think one hears 210 nothing else but scandal.

JOSEPH SURFACE.

Just so indeed, madam.

MRS. CANDOR.

Ah! Maria, child,* is the whole affair off between you and Charles? His extravagance, I presume; the Town* talks of nothing else. 215

MARIA.

I am very sorry, ma'am, the Town have so little to do.

MRS. CANDOR.

True, true, child, but there is no stopping people's tongues. I own I was hurt to hear it, as indeed I was to learn from the same quarter that your guardian, Sir Peter, and Lady Teazle have not 220 agreed lately so well as could be wished.

MARIA.

'Tis strangely impertinent for people to busy themselves so. I'm sure such reports are—

MRS. CANDOR.

Very true, child, but what's to be done? People will talk, there's no preventing it. Why it was but 225 yesterday I was told that Miss Gadabout had eloped with Sir Filagree Flirt—but Lord, there is no minding what one hears—though to be sure I had this from very good authority.

MARIA.

Such reports are highly scandalous. 230

MRS. CANDOR.

So they are, child—shameful! shameful! But the world is so censorious no character* escapes. Lord now! Who would have suspected your friend Miss Prim of an indiscretion? Yet such is the ill nature of people that they say her uncle stopped her last 235 week just as she was stepping into the York Diligence with her dancing master.

MARIA.

I'll answer for it, there are no grounds for the report.

MRS. CANDOR.

Oh, no foundation in the world, I dare swear, no more probably than for the story circulated last 240 month of Mrs. Festino's affair with Colonel Cassino, though to be sure that matter was never rightly cleared up.

JOSEPH SURFACE.

The license of invention some people take is monstrous indeed! 245

MARIA.

'Tis so, but in my opinion those who report such things are equally culpable.

MRS. CANDOR.

To be sure they are: tale bearers are as bad as tale makers; 'tis an old observation and a very true one. But what's to be done, as I said before? How will you 250 prevent people from talking? Today Mrs. Clackit assured me Mr. and Mrs. Honeymoon were at last become mere man and wife like the rest of her acquaintance. She likewise hinted that a certain widow in the next street had got rid of her dropsy and 255 recovered her shape in a most surprising manner, and the same time Miss Tattle, who was by, affirmed that Lord Buffalo had discovered his lady at a house of no extraordinary fame and that Sir Harry Bouquet and Tom Saunter were to measure swords on a similar 260 provocation. But Lord, do you think I would report these things? No, no, tale-bearers, as I said before, are just as bad as tale-makers.

JOSEPH SURFACE.

Oh Mrs. Candor, if everybody had your forbearance and good nature! 265

MRS. CANDOR.

I confess, Mr. Surface, I cannot bear to hear people attacked behind their backs, and when ugly circumstances come out against one's acquaintances, I own I always love to think the best. By the bye, I hope 'tis not true that your 270 brother is absolutely ruined.

JOSEPH SURFACE.

I am afraid his circumstances are very bad indeed, madam.

MRS. CANDOR.

Ah, I heard so, but you must tell him to keep up his spirits: Sir Thomas Splint,e Captain Quinzes, 275 and Mr. Nickit, all up, I hear, within this week, so if Charles is undone, he will find half his acquaintances ruined too, and that, you know, is a consolation.

JOSEPH SURFACE.

Doubtless, ma'am, a very great one. 280

Enter servant.

SERVANT.

Mr. Crabtree and Sir Benjamin Backbite. [*Exit.*]

LADY SNEERWELL.

So Maria, you see your lover pursues you. Positively you shan't escape.

Enter Crabtree and Sir Benjamin Backbite.

CRABTREE.

Lady Sneerwell, I kiss your hands.—Mrs. Candor, I don't believe you are acquainted with my nephew, 285 Sir Benjamin Backbite. Egad ma'am, he has a pretty wit and is a pretty poet too.—Isn't he, Lady Sneerwell?

SIR BENJAMIN.

Oh fie, Uncle!

CRABTREE.

Nay, egad 'tis true: I'll back him at a rebus or a 290 charade against the best rhymer in the kingdom. Has your ladyship heard the epigram he wrote last week on Lady Frizzle's feather catching fire! Do, Benjamin, repeat it, or the charade you made last night extempore at Mrs. Drowzy's conversazione. 295 Come now, your first is the name of a fish, your second a great naval commander—and—

SIR BENJAMIN.

Uncle—now—prithee!

CRABTREE.

I'faith, madam, 'twould surprise you to hear how ready he is at these things. 300

LADY SNEERWELL.

I wonder, Sir Benjamin, you never publish anything.

SIR BENJAMIN.

To say truth, ma'am, 'tis very vulgar to print, and as my little productions are mostly satires and lampoons on particular people, I find they circulate more by giving copies in confidence to the friends 305 of the parties; however, I have some love elegies which, when favored with this lady's smiles, I mean to give to the public.

CRABTREE.

Fore Heaven, ma'am, they'll immortalize you; you'll be handed down to posterity like Petrarch's Laura or Waller's Sacharissa.[4] 310

SIR BENJAMIN.

Yes madam, I think you will like them when you shall see them on a beautiful quarto page, where a neat rivulet of text shall murmur through a meadow of margin. Fore gad, they will be the most elegant things of their kind— 315

---

4 Waller's Sacharissa] Edmund Waller (1606-87) wrote verses to Sacharissa, Lady Dorothy Sidney.

CRABTREE.

But ladies, that's true. Have you heard the news?

MRS. CANDOR.

What, sir, do you mean the report of—

CRABTREE.

No ma'am, that's not it. Miss Nicely* is going to be married to her own footman.

MRS. CANDOR.

Impossible!   320

CRABTREE.

Ask Sir Benjamin.

SIR BENJAMIN.

'Tis very true, ma'am: everything is fixed and the wedding livery bespoke.

CRABTREE.

Yes, and they do say there were pressing reasons for it.   325

LADY SNEERWELL.

Why, I have heard something of this before.

MRS. CANDOR.

It can't be, and I wonder anyone should believe such a story of so prudent a lady as Miss Nicely.

SIR BENJAMIN.

Oh Lud* ma'am, that's the very reason 'twas believed at once. She has always been so cautious   330
and so reserved that everybody was sure there was some reason for it at bottom.

MRS. CANDOR.

Why, to be sure a tale of scandal is as fatal to the credit of a prudent lady of her stamp as a fever is generally to those of the strongest constitutions.   335
But there is a sort of puny, sickly reputation that is always ailing yet will outlive the robuster character of a hundred prudes.

SIR BENJAMIN.

True madam, there are valetudinarians in reputation as well as constitution, who, being conscious of their   340
weak part, avoid the least breath of air and supply their want* of stamina by care and circumspection.

MRS. CANDOR.

Well, but this may be all a mistake. You know, Sir Benjamin, very trifling circumstances often give rise to the most injurious tales.   345

CRABTREE.

That they do, I'll be sworn, ma'am. Did you ever hear how Miss Piper came to lose her lover and

her character* last summer at Tunbridge? Sir Benjamin, you remember it?

SIR BENJAMIN.

Oh, to be sure! The most whimsical circum-   350
stance—

LADY SNEERWELL.

How was it pray?

CRABTREE.

Why, one evening at Mrs. Ponto's assembly the conversation happened to turn on the difficulty of breeding Nova Scotia sheep in this country; says a   355
lady in company, "I have known instances of it, for Miss Laetitia Piper, a first cousin of mine, had a Nova Scotia sheep that produced her twins." "What!" cries the Dowager Lady Dundizzy (who you know is as deaf as a post) "has Miss Laetitia   360
Piper had twins?" This mistake, as you may imagine, threw the whole company into a fit of laughter; however, 'twas the next day reported, and in a few days believed by the whole Town, that Miss Letitia Piper had actually been brought to bed of a fine boy   365
and a girl, and in less than a week there were people who could name the father and the farmhouse where the babies were put out to nurse.

LADY SNEERWELL.

Strange indeed.

CRABTREE.

Matter of fact, I assure you.—Oh Lud, Mr.   370
Surface, pray is it true that your Uncle Sir Oliver is coming home?

JOSEPH SURFACE.

Not that I know of, indeed sir.

CRABTREE.

He has been in the East Indies a long time; you can scarcely remember him, I believe. Sad comfort   375
whenever he returns to hear how your brother has gone on.

JOSEPH SURFACE.

Charles has been imprudent, sir, to be sure, but I hope no busy people have already prejudiced Sir Oliver against him; he may reform.   380

SIR BENJAMIN.

To be sure he may. For my part I never believed him so utterly void of principle as people say, and though he has lost all his friends, I am told nobody is better spoken of by the Jews.

CRABTREE.

That's true, egad Nephew. If the old Jewry was a 385
ward, I believe Charles would be an alderman. No
man more popular there. Fore gad, I hear he pays
as many annuities as the Irish tontine[5] and that
whenever he's sick they have prayers for the
recovery of his health in the synagogue. 390

SIR BENJAMIN.

Yet no man lives in greater splendor. They tell me
when he entertains his friends, he can sit down to
dinner with a dozen of his own securities, have a
score of tradesman in the anti-chamber and an
officer behind every guest's chair. 395

JOSEPH SURFACE.

This may be entertainment to you, gentlemen, but
you pay very little regard to the feelings of a
brother.

MARIA. [*Aside.*]

Their malice is intolerable.—Lady Sneerwell, I
must wish you a good morning—I'm not very 400
well. (*Exit.*)

MRS. CANDOR.

Oh dear, she changes color very much.

LADY SNEERWELL.

Do Mrs. Candor follow her, she may want*
assistance.

MRS. CANDOR.

That I will with all my soul, ma'am. Poor dear 405
creature, who knows what her situation may be?
(*Exit.*)

LADY SNEERWELL.

'Twas nothing but that she could not bear to hear
Charles reflected on, notwithstanding their
difference. 410

SIR BENJAMIN.

The young lady's penchant is obvious.

CRABTREE.

But Benjamin, you mustn't give up the pursuit for
that. Follow her and put her into good humor,
repeat her some of your verses. Come, I'll assist you.

SIR BENJAMIN.

Mr. Surface, I did not mean to hurt you, but 415
depend on't, your brother is utterly undone.

CRABTREE.

Oh Lud! Aye! undone as ever man was, can't raise
a guinea.

SIR BENJAMIN.

Everything sold, I am told, that was moveable.[6]

CRABTREE.

I have seen one that was at his house: not a thing 420
left but some empty bottles that were overlooked
and the family pictures, which I believe are framed
in the wainscot.

SIR BENJAMIN.

And I am very sorry to hear also some bad stories
against him. (*Going.*) 425

CRABTREE.

Oh, he has done many mean* things, that's certain.

SIR BENJAMIN.

But however, as he's your brother— (*Going.*)

CRABTREE.

We'll tell you all another opportunity.

Exeunt Sir Benjamin and Crabtree.

LADY SNEERWELL.

Ha, ha, ha! 'tis very hard for them to leave a subject
they have not quite run down. 430

JOSEPH SURFACE.

And I believe their abuse was no more acceptable
to your ladyship than Maria.

LADY SNEERWELL.

I doubt* her affections are further engaged than
we imagined. But the family are to be here this
evening, so you may as well dine where you are, 435
and we shall have an opportunity of observing
further; in the meantime, I'll go and plot mischief,
and you shall study sentiments.

Exeunt.

Scene ii. Sir Peter Teazle's house.

Enter Sir Peter.

SIR PETER.

When an old bachelor takes a young wife, what is he
to expect? 'Tis now six months since Lady Teazle
made me the happiest of men, and I have been the

---

5 Irish tontine] The Anglo-Irish government had set up a
   tontine to help pay off its debts (Price).

6 moveable] admitting of being removed or displaced; applied to 'personal' as opposed to 'real' property (*OED*)

miserablest dog ever since. We tiffed a little going to church and came to a quarrel before the bells were done ringing. I was more than once nearly choked with gall during the honeymoon and had lost all comfort in life before my friends had done wishing me joy. Yet I chose with caution: a girl bred wholly in the country, who never knew luxury beyond one silk gown nor dissipation above the annual gala of a race ball. Yet now she plays her part in all the extravagant fopperies of the fashion and the Town with as ready a grace as if she had never seen a bush nor a grass plot out of Grosvenor Square.* I am sneered at by my old acquaintance, paragraphed in the newspapers; she dissipates my fortune and contradicts all humors. Yet the worst of it is, I doubt* I love her, or I should never bear all this; however, I'll never be weak enough to own it.

Enter Rowley.

ROWLEY.
Oh Sir Peter, your servant. How is it with you, sir?
SIR PETER.
Very bad, Master Rowley, very bad. I meet with nothing but crosses and vexations.
ROWLEY.
What can have happened to trouble you since yesterday?
SIR PETER.
A good question to a married man.
ROWLEY.
Nay, I'm sure Sir Peter, your lady can't be the cause of your uneasiness.
SIR PETER.
Why, has anyone told you she was dead?
ROWLEY.
Come, come, Sir Peter, you love her, notwithstanding your tempers don't exactly agree.
SIR PETER.
But the fault is entirely hers, Master Rowley. I am myself the sweetest tempered man alive and hate a teazing temper, and so I tell her an hundred times a day.
ROWLEY.
Indeed!
SIR PETER.
Aye, and what is very extraordinary, in all our

disputes she is always in the wrong. But Lady Sneerwell and the set she meets at her house encourage the perverseness of her disposition. Then to complete my vexations, Maria, my ward, whom I ought to have the power of a father over, is determined to turn rebel too and absolutely refuses the man whom I have long resolved on for her husband, meaning, I suppose, to bestow herself on his profligate brother.
ROWLEY.
You know, Sir Peter, I have always taken the liberty to differ with you on the subject of these two young gentlemen. I only wish you may not be deceived in your opinion of the elder; for Charles, my life on't, he will retrieve his errors yet. Their worthy father, once my honored master, was at his years nearly as wild a spark, but when he died, he did not leave a more benevolent heart to lament his loss.
SIR PETER.
You are wrong, Master Rowley. On their father's death you know I acted as a kind of guardian to them both 'till their uncle Sir Oliver's eastern liberality gave them an early independence. Of course, no person could have more opportunities of judging of their hearts, and I was never mistaken in my life. Joseph is indeed a model for the young men of the age: he is a man of sentiment and acts up to the sentiments he professes. But for the other, take my word for't, if he had any grains of virtue by descent, he has dissipated them with the rest of his inheritance. Ah, my old friend Sir Oliver will be deeply mortified when he finds how part of his bounty has been misapplied.
ROWLEY.
I am sorry to find you so violent against the young man because this may be the most critical period of his fortune; I came hither with news that will surprise you.
SIR PETER.
What? let me hear.
ROWLEY.
Sir Oliver is arrived and at this moment in Town.
SIR PETER.
How! You astonish me! I thought you did not expect him this month.

ROWLEY.

I did not, but his passage has been remarkably quick.

SIR PETER.

Egad, I shall rejoice to see my old friend; 'tis sixteen 80 years since we met. We have had many a day together. But does he still enjoin us not to inform his nephews of his arrival?

ROWLEY.

Most strictly. He means before it is known to make some trial of their dispositions. 85

SIR PETER.

Ah, there needs no art to discover their merits; however, he shall have his way. But pray, does he know I am married?

ROWLEY.

Yes, and will soon wish you joy.

SIR PETER.

What, as we drink health to a friend in a consump- 90 tion? Ah! Oliver will laugh at me. We used to rail at matrimony together, but he has been steady to his text. Well, he must be at my house though. I'll in-stantly give orders for his reception. But Master Row-ley, don't drop a word that Lady Teazle and I disagree. 95

ROWLEY.

By no means—

SIR PETER.

For I should never be able to stand Noll's jokes, so I'd have him think, Lord forgive me, that we are a very happy couple.

ROWLEY.

I understand you. But then you must be very 100 careful not to differ while he's in the house with you.

SIR PETER.

Egad, and so we must—and that's impossible. Ah Master Rowley, when an old bachelor marries a young wife, he deserves—no, the crime carries the 105 punishment along with it.

Exeunt.

Act II, scene i. Sir Peter Teazle's house.

Enter Sir Peter and Lady Teazle.

SIR PETER.

Lady Teazle, Lady Teazle, I'll not bear it.

LADY TEAZLE.

Sir Peter, Sir Peter, you may bear it or not, as you please, but I ought to have my own way in everything, and what's more, I will too. What, though I was educated in the country, I know very 5 well that women of fashion in London are accountable to nobody after they are married.

SIR PETER.

Very well, ma'am, very well, so a husband is to have no influence, no authority?

LADY TEAZLE.

Authority! No, to be sure. If you wanted authority 10 over me, you should have adopted me and not married me; I am sure you were old enough.

SIR PETER.

Old enough! Aye, there it is, well, well, Lady Teazle, though my life may be made unhappy by your temper, I'll not be ruined by your 15 extravagance.

LADY TEAZLE.

My extravagance? I'm sure I'm not more extravagant than a woman of fashion ought to be.

SIR PETER.

No, no, madam, you shall throw away no more sums on such unmeaning luxury. 'Slife,* to spend 20 as much to furnish your dressing room with flowers in winter, as would suffice to turn the Pantheon* into a greenhouse and give a fête champêtre at Christmas.

LADY TEAZLE.

Lord, Sir Peter, am I to blame because flowers are 25 dear* in cold weather; you should find fault with the climate and not with me. For my part I am sure I wish it were spring all the year round and that roses grew under our feet.

SIR PETER.

'Oons* madam! If you had been born to this, I 30 should not wonder at your talking thus, but you forget what your situation was when I married you.

LADY TEAZLE.

No, no, I don't: 'twas a very disagreeable one, or I should never have married you.

SIR PETER.

Yes, yes, madam, you were then somewhat in an 35 humbler style: the daughter of a plain country squire. Recollect, Lady Teazle, when I first saw you sitting at your tambour in a pretty figured linen gown, with a bunch of keys by your side, your hair combed smoothly over a roll, and your apartment hung round with fruits in worsted of your own working.

LADY TEAZLE.

Oh yes, I remember it very well, and a curious life I led! My daily occupation: to inspect the dairy, superintend the poultry, make extracts from the family receipt* book, and comb my aunt Deborah's lapdog.

SIR PETER.

Yes, yes, madam, 'twas so indeed.

LADY TEAZLE.

And then you know my evening amusements: to draw patterns for ruffles which I had not the materials to make, to play Pope Joan[7] with the curate, read a sermon[f] to my aunt, or be stuck down to an old spinnet to strum my father to sleep after a fox chase.

SIR PETER.

I am glad you have so good a memory. Yes madam, these were the recreations I took you from. But now you must have your coach, vis-à-vis,[8] and three powdered footmen before your chair*—and in summer a pair of white cats[9] to draw you to Kensington Gardens.* No recollection I suppose when you were content to ride double behind the butler on a docked coach horse?

LADY TEAZLE.

No, I swear I never did that, I deny the butler and the coach horse.

SIR PETER.

This, madam, was your situation, and what have I not done for you? I have made you a woman of fashion, of fortune, of rank; in short, I have made you *my wife*.

LADY TEAZLE.

Well then, and there is but one thing more you can make me to add to the obligation—and that is—

SIR PETER.

My widow, I suppose?

LADY TEAZLE.

Hem, hem!

SIR PETER.

Thank you, madam, but don't flatter yourself, for though your ill conduct may disturb my peace, it shall never break my heart, I promise you; however, I am equally obliged to you for the hint.

LADY TEAZLE.

Then why will you endeavor to make yourself so disagreeable to me and thwart me in every little elegant expense?

SIR PETER.

'Slife* madam, I say, had you any of these elegant expenses when you married me?

LADY TEAZLE.

Lord, Sir Peter, would you have me be out of fashion?

SIR PETER.

The fashion indeed! What had you to do with the fashion when you married me?

LADY TEAZLE.

For my part I should think you would like to have your wife thought a woman of taste.

SIR PETER.

Aye, there again—taste—Zounds, Madam! You had no taste when you married me.

LADY TEAZLE.

That's very true indeed, Sir Peter, and after having married you, I should never pretend to taste again, I allow. But now Sir Peter, if we have finished our daily jangle, I presume I may go to my engagement at Lady Sneerwell's?

SIR PETER.

Aye, there's another precious* circumstance, a charming set of acquaintance you have made there.

LADY TEAZLE.

Nay Sir Peter, they are people of rank and fortune, and remarkably tenacious of reputation.

SIR PETER.

Yes, egad, they are tenacious of reputation with a vengeance! For they don't choose anybody should have a character* but themselves. Such a crew! Ah! Many a wretch has rid on a hurdle who has done less mischief than these utterers of forged tales,

7 Pope Joan] a three-handed card game, named after the infamous female pope

8 vis-à-vis] a light carriage for two persons sitting face-to-face (*OED*)

9 cats] ponies (NCS)

coiners of scandal, and clippers* of reputation.

LADY TEAZLE.

What, would you restrain the freedom of speech? 105

SIR PETER.

Oh, they have made you just as bad as any one of the society.

LADY TEAZLE.

Why I believe I do bear a part with a tolerable grace, but I vow I have no malice against the people I abuse. When I say an ill-natured thing, 110 'tis out of pure good humor, and I take for granted they'll deal exactly in the same manner with me. But Sir Peter, you know you promised to come to Lady Sneerwell's too.

SIR PETER.

Well, well, I'll call in just to look after my own 115 character.*

LADY TEAZLE.

Then, indeed, you must make haste after me or you'll be too late. So goodbye to you. (*Exit*.)

SIR PETER.

So! I have gained much by my intended expostulations. Yet with what a charming air she 120 contradicts everything I say and how pleasingly she shows her contempt of my authority. Well, though I can't make her love me, there is great satisfaction in quarrelling with her, and I think she never appears to such advantage as when she's doing 125 everything in her power to plague me.

Exit.

Scene ii. Lady Sneerwell's house.

Lady Sneerwell, Mrs. Candor, Crabtree, Sir Benjamin Backbite, and Joseph Surface discovered; servants attending with tea.*

LADY SNEERWELL.

Nay, positively we will have it.

JOSEPH SURFACE.

Yes, yes, the epigram, by all means.

SIR BENJAMIN.

Oh plague on't, Uncle, 'tis mere nonsense.

CRABTREE.

No, no, fore gad, very clever for an extempore.

SIR BENJAMIN.

But ladies, you should be acquainted with the 5

circumstance. You must know that one day last week, as Lady Betty Curricle was taking the dust in Hyde Park* in a sort of duodecimo phaeton, she desired me to write some verses on her ponies, upon which I took out my pocket book and in one 10 moment produced the following:

Sure never were seen two such beautiful ponies,
Other horses are clowns, and these macaronies;
Nay, to give them this title I'm sure is not wrong,
Their legs are so slim, and their tails are so long. 15

CRABTREE.

There ladies, done in the smack of a whip and on horseback too.

JOSEPH SURFACE.

A very Phoebus mounted indeed, Sir Benjamin.

SIR BENJAMIN.

Oh dear sir, trifles, trifles!

Enter Lady Teazle and Maria.

MRS. CANDOR.

I must have a copy. 20

LADY SNEERWELL.

Lady Teazle, I hope we shall see Sir Peter.

LADY TEAZLE.

I believe he'll wait on your ladyship presently.

LADY SNEERWELL.

Maria my dear, you look grave. Come, you shall sit down to piquet with Mr. Surface.

MARIA.

I take very little pleasure in cards; however, I'll do 25 as your ladyship pleases.

LADY TEAZLE. [*Aside.*]

I am surprised Mr. Surface should sit down with her. I thought he would have embraced this opportunity of speaking to me before Sir Peter came. 30

MRS. CANDOR.

Now, I'll die but you are so scandalous, I'll foreswear your society.

LADY TEAZLE.

What's the matter, Mrs. Candor?

MRS. CANDOR.

They'll not allow our friend, Miss Vermillion, to be handsome. 35

LADY SNEERWELL.

Oh surely, she's a pretty woman.

CRABTREE.

I'm very glad you think so, madam.

MRS. CANDOR.

She has a charming, fresh color.

LADY TEAZLE.

Yes, when it is fresh put on.

MRS. CANDOR.

Oh fie! I'll swear her color is natural. I have seen 40
it come and go.

LADY TEAZLE.

I dare swear you have, ma'am; it goes off at night
and comes again in the morning.

MRS. CANDOR.

Ha, ha, ha! How I hate to hear you talk so. But
surely now, her sister *is* or *was* very handsome. 45

CRABTREE.

Who, Mrs. Evergreen? Oh Lord! She's six-and-fifty
if she's an hour.

MRS. CANDOR.

Now positively you wrong her, fifty-two or fifty-
three is the utmost, and I don't think she looks
more. 50

SIR BENJAMIN.

Oh there's no judging by her looks, unless one
could see her face.

LADY SNEERWELL.

Well, well, if Mrs. Evergreen does take some pains
to repair the ravages of time, you must allow she
effects it with great ingenuity, and surely that's 55
better than the careless manner in which the
Widow Ochre caulks her wrinkles.

SIR BENJAMIN.

Nay now Lady Sneerwell, you are severe upon the
widow. Come, come, it is not that the widow
paints so ill, but when she has finished her face, 60
she joins it on so badly to her neck that she looks
like a mended statue in which the connoisseur
discovers at once that the head is modern though
the trunk's antique.

CRABTREE.

Ha, ha, ha! Well said, Nephew. 65

MRS. CANDOR.

Well, you make me laugh, but I vow I hate you
for't. What do you think of Miss Simper?

SIR BENJAMIN.

Why, she has very pretty teeth.

LADY TEAZLE.

Yes, and on that account when she is neither
speaking nor laughing, which very seldom 70
happens, she never absolutely shuts her mouth but
leaves it always on ajar as it were.

MRS. CANDOR.

How can you be so ill-natured?

LADY TEAZLE.

I'll allow that's better than the pains Mrs. Prim takes
to conceal her losses in front. She draws her mouth 75
till it positively resembles the aperture of a poor box,
and all her words appear to slide out edgeways.

LADY SNEERWELL.

Very well, Lady Teazle, I see you can be a little
severe.

LADY TEAZLE.

In defense of a friend it is but justice.—But here 80
comes Sir Peter to spoil our pleasantry.

Enter Sir Peter.

SIR PETER.

Ladies, your most obedient— Mercy on me, here
is the whole set: a character* dead at every word,
I suppose.

MRS. CANDOR.

I am rejoiced you are come, Sir Peter; they have been 85
so censorious, they'll allow good qualities to nobody,
not even good nature to our friend, Mrs. Pursey.

LADY TEAZLE.

What, the fat dowager who was at Mrs. Codille's
last night?

MRS. CANDOR.

Nay, her bulk is her misfortune, and when she 90
takes such pains to get rid of it, you ought not to
reflect on her.

LADY SNEERWELL.

That's very true, indeed.

LADY TEAZLE.

Yes, I know she almost lives upon acids and small
whey, laces herself by pullies, and often in the 95
hottest noon in summer you may see her on a
little, squat pony with her hair plaited up behind
like a drummer and puffing around the Ring* in
a full trot.

MRS. CANDOR.

I thank you, Lady Teazle, for defending her. 100

SIR PETER.

Yes, a good defense, truly.

MRS. CANDOR.

But Sir Benjamin is as censorious as Miss Sallow.

CRABTREE.

Yes, and she is a curious being to pretend to be censorious, an awkward gawky without any one good point under heaven. 105

MRS. CANDOR.

Positively you shall not be so severe. Miss Sallow is a relation of mine by marriage, and as for her person, great allowance is to be made, for let me tell you, a woman labors under many disadvantages who tries to pass for a girl at six-and- 110 thirty.

LADY SNEERWELL.

Though surely she *is* handsome still, and for the weakness in her eyes, considering how much she reads by candlelight, it is not to be wondered at.

MRS. CANDOR.

True, and then as to her manner, upon my word I 115 think it is particularly graceful, considering she never had the least education, for you know her mother was a Welsh milliner and her father a sugar baker at Bristol.

SIR BENJAMIN.

Ah, you are both of you too good-natured. 120

SIR PETER.

Yes, damn'd good-natured—this is their own relation, mercy on me!

SIR BENJAMIN.

And Mrs. Candor is of so moral a turn.

MRS. CANDOR.g

Well, I will never join in ridiculing a friend. And so I constantly tell my cousin Ogle, and you well know 125 what pretensions she has a to be critical in beauty.

CRABTREE.

Oh, to be sure, she has herself the oddest countenance that ever was seen; 'tis a collection of features from all the different countries of the globe.

SIR BENJAMIN.

She has indeed an Irish front. 130

CRABTREE.

Caledonian locks.

SIR BENJAMIN.

Dutch nose.

CRABTREE.

Austrian lip.

SIR BENJAMIN.

Complexion of a Spaniard.

CRABTREE.

And teeth *à la chinoise*.[10] 135

SIR BENJAMIN.

In short, her face resembles a table d'hôte at Spa, where no two guests are of a nation.

CRABTREE.

Or a congress at the close of a general war, where all the members, even to her eyes, appear to have a different interest, and her nose and chin are the 140 only parties likely to join issue.

MRS. CANDOR.

Ha, ha, ha!

SIR PETER.

Mercy on my life! A person they dine with twice a week.

MRS. CANDOR.

Nay, but I vow you shall not carry the laugh off 145 so, for give me leave to say that Mrs. Ogle—

SIR PETER.

Madam, madam, I beg your pardon, there is no stopping these good gentlemen's tongues, but when I tell you, Mrs. Candor, that the lady they are abusing is a particular friend of mine, I hope you'll 150 not take her part.

LADY SNEERWELL.

Well said, Sir Peter, but you are a cruel creature: too phlegmatic yourself for a jest and too peevish to allow it in others.

SIR PETER.

Ah madam, true wit is more nearly allied to good 155 nature than your ladyship is aware of.

LADY TEAZLE.

True, Sir Peter, I believe they are so near of kin they can never be united.

SIR BENJAMIN.

Oh! Rather, ma'am, suppose them man and wife, 160 because one so seldom sees them together.

LADY TEAZLE.

But Sir Peter is such an enemy to scandal, I believe he would have it put down by Parliament.

---

10 *à la chinoise*]of a Chinese woman: stereotypically black

SIR PETER.

Fore Heaven, madam, if they were to consider the sporting with reputation of as much importance 165 as the poaching on manors and pass an Act for the Preservation of Fame, I believe many would thank them for the bill.

LADY SNEERWELL.

Oh Lud!* Sir Peter, would you deprive us of our privileges? 170

SIR PETER.

Aye madam, and then no person should be permitted to kill characters* or run down reputations but qualified old maids and disappointed widows.

LADY SNEERWELL.

Go, you monster!

MRS. CANDOR.

But sure you would not be quite so severe on those 175 who only report what they hear?

SIR PETER.

Yes madam, I would have law-merchant[11] for them too, and in all cases of slander currency, whenever the drawer of the lie was not to be found, the injured party should have a right to 180 come on any of the endorsers.

CRABTREE.

Well, for my part, I believe there never was a scandalous tale without some foundation.

LADY SNEERWELL.

Come ladies, shall we sit down to cards in the next room? 185

Enter servant, who whispers to Sir Peter.

SIR PETER.

I'll be with them directly.

[Exit servant.]

[Aside.] I'll get away unperceived. (*Going.*)

LADY SNEERWELL.

Sir Peter, you are not leaving us?

SIR PETER.

Your ladyship must excuse me; I'm called away by particular business—but I'll leave my character 190 behind me. (*Exit.*)

---

11 law-merchant] a special system of rules for the regulation of trade and commerce, differing in some respects from the Common Law (*OED*)

SIR BENJAMIN.

Well certainly, Lady Teazle, that lord of yours is a strange being. I would tell you some stories of him that would make you laugh heartily, if he wasn't your husband. 195

LADY TEAZLE.

Oh pray don't mind that, come, do, let's hear them.

They retire. Joseph Surface and Maria come forward.

JOSEPH SURFACE.

Maria, I see you have no satisfaction in this society.

MARIA.

How is it possible I should? If to raise malicious smiles at the infirmities and misfortunes of those 200 who have never injured us be the province of wit or humor, Heaven grant me a double portion of dullness.

JOSEPH SURFACE.

Yet they appear more ill-natured than they are; they have no malice at heart. 205

MARIA.

Then is their conduct more inexcusable, for in my opinion, nothing but a depravity of heart could tempt them to such practices.[h]

JOSEPH SURFACE.

But can you, Maria, feel thus for others and be unkind to me alone; is hope to be denied the 210 tenderest passion?

MARIA.

Why will you distress me by renewing the subject?

JOSEPH SURFACE.

Ah Maria! You would not treat me thus and oppose your guardian's, Sir Peter's will but that I see that profligate Charles is still a favored rival. 215

MARIA.

Ungenerously urged! But whatever my sentiments of that unfortunate young man are, be assured I shall not feel more bound to give him up because his distresses have lost him the regard even of a brother.

Lady Teazle returns.

JOSEPH SURFACE. *[Kneeling.]*

Nay but Maria, do not leave me with a frown. By 220 all that's honest, I swear— (*Aside.*) Gad's life, here is Lady Teazle.—You must not, no, you shall not, for though I have the greatest regard for Lady Teazle—

MARIA.

Lady Teazle! 225

JOSEPH SURFACE.

Yet were Sir Peter once to suspect—

LADY TEAZLE. [*Aside.*]

What's this, pray? Does he take her for me?— Child,* you are wanted in the next room.

Exit Maria.

What's all this, pray?

JOSEPH SURFACE.

Oh, the most unlucky circumstance in nature. 230 Maria has somehow suspected the tender concern which I have for your happiness and threatened to acquaint Sir Peter with her suspicions, and I was just endeavoring to reason with her when you came.

LADY TEAZLE.

Indeed! But you seemed to adopt a very tender 235 method of reasoning: Do you usually argue on your knees?

JOSEPH SURFACE.

Oh, she's a child, and I thought a little bombast— But Lady Teazle, when are you to give me your judgment on my library as you promised? 240

LADY TEAZLE.

No, no, I begin to think it would imprudent, and you know I admit you as a lover no further than fashion requires.

JOSEPH SURFACE.

True, a mere platonic cicisbeo, what every wife¹ is entitled to. 245

LADY TEAZLE.

Certainly, one must not be out of the fashion; however, I have so many of my country prejudices left that though Sir Peter's ill humor may vex me ever so, it shall never provoke me to—

JOSEPH SURFACE.

The only revenge in you power. Well, I applaud 250 your moderation.

LADY TEAZLE.

Go, you are an insinuating wretch. But we shall be missed; let us join the company.

JOSEPH SURFACE.

But we had best not return together.

LADY TEAZLE.

Well, don't stay, for Maria shan't come to hear any 255 more of your reasoning, I promise you. (*Exit.*)

JOSEPH SURFACE.

A curious dilemma, truly, my politics have run me into: I wanted at first only to ingratiate myself with Lady Teazle that she might not be my enemy with Maria, and I have, I don't know how, become her 260 serious lover! Sincerely, I begin to wish I had never made such a point of gaining so very good a character,* for it has led me into so many rogueries that I doubt* I shall be exposed at last.

Exit.

Scene iii. Sir Peter Teazle's house.

Enter Rowley and Sir Oliver.

SIR OLIVER.

Ha, ha, ha! and so my old friend is married, hey! A young wife out of the country, ha, ha, ha! That he should have stood bluff¹² to old bachelor so long, and sink into husband at last.

ROWLEY.

But you must not rally him on the subject, Sir 5 Oliver; 'tis a tender point I assure you, though he has been married only seven months.

SIR OLIVER.

Then he has been just half a year on the stool of repentance. Poor Peter! But you say he has entirely given up Charles? Never sees him, hey? 10

ROWLEY.

His prejudice against him is astonishing and, I'm sure, greatly increased by a jealousy of him with Lady Teazle, which he has been industriously led into by a scandalous society in the neighborhood, who have contributed not a little to Charles's ill 15 name, whereas the truth is, I believe, if the lady is partial to either of them, his brother is the favorite.

SIR OLIVER.

Aye, I know there is a set of malicious, prating, prudent gossips, both male and female, who murder characters* to kill time and will rob a 20 young fellow of his good name before he has years to know the value of it. But I am not to be

---

12 stood bluff] stood firm or stiff (*OED*)

prejudiced against my nephew by such, I promise you; no, no, if Charles has done nothing false or mean,* I shall compound for his extravagance. 25

ROWLEY.

Then my life on't, you will reclaim him. Ah sir, it gives me new life to find that your heart is not turned against him and that the son of my good old master has one friend, however, left.

SIR OLIVER.

What, shall I forget, Master Rowley, when I was at his years myself? Egad, my brother and I were nei-ther very prudent youths, and yet I believe you have not seen many better men than your old master was. 30

ROWLEY.

Sir, 'tis this reflection gives me assurance that Charles may yet be a credit to his family.—But here comes Sir Peter. 35

SIR OLIVER.

Egad, so he does. Mercy on me! he's greatly altered and seems to have a settled, married look! One may read husband in his face at this distance.

Enter Sir Peter.

SIR PETER.

Hah! Sir Oliver, my old friend, welcome to England a thousand times. 40

SIR OLIVER.

Thank you, thank you, Sir Peter. And i'faith, I'm as glad to find you well, believe me.

SIR PETER.

Ah! 'Tis a long time since we met: sixteen years, I doubt,* Sir Oliver, and many a cross accident in the time. 45

SIR OLIVER.

Aye, I have had my share. But what, I find you are married, hey, my old boy! Well, well, it can't be helped, and so I wish you joy with all my heart.

SIR PETER.

Thank you, thank you, Sir Oliver. Yes, I have entered into the happy state—but we'll not talk of that now. 50

SIR OLIVER.

True, true, Sir Peter, old friends should not begin on grievances at first meeting, no, no, no.

ROWLEY. (*To Sir Oliver.*)

Take care, pray sir. 55

SIR OLIVER.

So, one of my nephews I find is a wild, extravagant young rogue, hey!

SIR PETER.

Wild! Ah my old friend, I grieve for your disappointment there: he's a lost young man indeed. However, his brother will make you amends; Joseph is indeed what a youth should be. Everybody in the world speaks well of him. 60

SIR OLIVER.

I am sorry to hear it: he has too good a character* to be an honest fellow. Everybody speaks well of him! Pshaw! Then he has bowed as low to knaves and fools as to the honest dignity of genius or virtue. 65

SIR PETER.

What, Sir Oliver, do you blame him for not making enemies?

SIR OLIVER.

Yes, if he has merit enough to deserve them.

SIR PETER.

Well, well, you'll be convinced when you know him. 'Tis edification to hear him converse. He possesses the noblest sentiments. 70

SIR OLIVER.

Oh plague of his sentiments! If he salutes* me with a scrap of morality in his mouth, I shall be sick directly. But, however, don't mistake me, Sir Peter, I don't mean to defend Charles's errors, but before I form my judgment of either of them, I intend to make a trial of their hearts, and my friend Rowley and I have planned something for the purpose. 75

ROWLEY.

And Sir Peter shall own he has been for once mistaken. 80

SIR PETER.

Oh, my life on Joseph's honor.

SIR OLIVER.

Well, come, give us a bottle of good wine, and we'll drink your lady's good health and tell you all our scheme. 85

SIR PETER.

Allons[13] then.

SIR OLIVER.

And don't, Sir Peter, be so severe against your old

---

13 *Allons*] Let's go (Fr.)

friend's son. 'Odd's* my life! I'm not sorry that he
has run out of the course a little. For my part, I
hate to see prudence clinging to the green suckers   90
of youth. 'Tis like ivy round a sapling and spoils
the growth of the tree.

Exeunt.

    Act III, scene i. Sir Peter Teazle's house.

Enter Sir Peter, Sir Oliver, and Rowley.

SIR PETER.

Well then, we will see this fellow first and have our
wine afterwards. But how is this, Master Rowley?
I don't see the gist of your scheme.

ROWLEY.

Why sir, this Mr. Stanley, whom I was speaking
of, is nearly related to them by their mother. He   5
was once a merchant in Dublin but has been
ruined by a series of undeserved misfortunes. He
has applied by letter since his confinement both
to Mr. Surface and Charles. From the former he
has received nothing but evasive promises of future   10
service, while Charles has done all that his
extravagance has left him power to do, and he is
at this time endeavoring to raise a sum of money,
part of which in the midst of his own distresses, I
know, he intends for the service of poor Stanley.   15

SIR OLIVER.

Ah! He is my brother's son.

SIR PETER.

Well, but how is Sir Oliver personally to—

ROWLEY.

Why sir, I will inform Charles and his brother that
Stanley has obtained permission to apply in person
to his friends, and as they have neither of them ever 20
seen him, let Sir Oliver assume the character, and he
will have a fair opportunity of judging at least of the
benevolence of their dispositions. And believe me,
sir, you will find in the youngest brother one, who
in the midst of folly and dissipation, has still, as our 25
immortal bard expresses it,

    A tear for pity and a hand
  Open as day for melting charity.[14]

---

[14] A tear ... charity] Shakespeare, *2 Henry IV*, IV.iv.31-32.

SIR PETER.

Pshaw! What signifies his having an open hand or
a purse either when he has nothing left to give?   30
Well, well, make the trial if you please, but where
is the fellow whom you brought for Sir Oliver to
examine relative to Charles's affairs?

ROWLEY.

Below, waiting his commands, and no one can give
him better intelligence.—This, Sir Oliver, is a   35
friendly Jew, who to do him justice, has done
everything in his power to bring your nephew to
a proper sense of his extravagance.

SIR PETER.

Pray, let us have him in.

ROWLEY.

Desire Mr. Moses to walk upstairs.   40

SIR PETER.

But pray, why should you suppose he will speak
the truth?

ROWLEY.

Oh, I have convinced him he has no chance of
recovering certain sums advanced to Charles but
through the bounty of Sir Oliver, who he knows   45
is arrived, so that you may depend on his fidelity
to his own interest. I have also another evidence*
in my power, one Snake, whom I have detected
in a matter little short of forgery, and shall shortly
produce him to remove some of *your* prejudices,   50
Sir Peter, relative to Charles and Lady Teazle.

SIR PETER.

I have heard too much on that subject.

ROWLEY.

Here comes the honest Israelite.

Enter Moses.

ROWLEY.

This is Sir Oliver.

SIR OLIVER.

Sir, I understand you have lately had great dealings   55
with my nephew, Charles?

MOSES.

Yes, Sir Oliver. I done all my power for him, but
he was ruined before he came to me for assistance.

SIR OLIVER.

That was unlucky, truly, for you have had no
opportunity of showing your talents.   60

MOSES.

None atal. I had not the pleasure of knowing his distresses till he was some thousands worse than nothing.

SIR OLIVER.

Unfortunate indeed! But I suppose you have done all in your power for him, honest Moses? 65

MOSES.

Yes, he knows that. This very evening I was to have brought him a gentleman from the City,* who does not know him and will, I believe, advance him some money.

SIR PETER.

What, one Charles never had money from before? 70

MOSES.

Yes, Mr. Premium, of Crutched Friars,[15] formerly a broker.

SIR PETER.

Egad, Sir Oliver, a thought strikes me.—Charles, you say, doesn't know Mr. Premium?

MOSES.

Not atal. 75

SIR PETER.

Now then, Sir Oliver, you may have an opportunity of satisfying yourself better than by an old romancing tale of a poor relation.—Go with my friend, Moses, and present Mr. Premium.—And then I'll answer for't, you will see 80 your nephew in all his glory.

SIR OLIVER.

Egad, I like this idea better than the other, and I may visit Joseph afterwards as old Stanley.

SIR PETER.

True, so you may.

ROWLEY.

Well, this is taking Charles at a disadvantage to be 85 sure; however, Moses, you understand Sir Peter and will be faithful.

MOSES.

You may depend upon me. This is near the time I was to have gone.

SIR OLIVER.

I'll accompany you as soon as you please, Moses, 90

---

15 Crutched Friars] a continuation of Jewry Street, running
from Aldgate to Mark Lane (Price)

but hold, I forgot one thing: How the plague shall I be able to pass for a Jew?

MOSES.

There is no need: the principal is Christian.

SIR OLIVER.

Is he? I am sorry to hear it. But then again, an't I too smartly dressed to look like a moneylender? 95

SIR PETER.

Not atal. 'Twould not be out of character if you went in your own carriage, would it, Moses?

MOSES.

Not in the least.

SIR OLIVER.

Well, but how must I talk? There's certainly some cant of usury and mode of treating that I ought 100 to know.

SIR PETER.

Oh, there's not much to learn. The great point, as I take it, is to be exorbitant enough in your demands, hey Moses?

MOSES.

Yes, that's a very great point. 105

SIR OLIVER.

I'll answer for't; I'll not be wanting* in that. I'll ask him eight, or ten percent, upon the loan, at least.

MOSES.

If you ask him no more as dat,[k] you'll be discovered immediately. 110

SIR OLIVER.

Hey, what a plague! How much then?

MOSES.

That depends upon circumstances; if he appears not very anxious for the supply, you should require only forty or fifty percent, but if you find him in great distress and want the monies very bad, you 115 may ask him double.

SIR PETER.

A good, honest trade you are learning, Sir Oliver.

SIR OLIVER.

Truly, I think so, and not unprofitable.

MOSES.

Then, you know, you haven't the monies yourself but are forced to borrow them for him of a friend. 120

SIR OLIVER.

Oh! I borrow it of a friend, do I?

MOSES.

Yes, and your friend is an unconscionable dog, but
you can't help it.

SIR OLIVER.

My friend is an unconscionable dog, is he?

MOSES.

Yes, and he himself has not the monies by him but   125
is forced to sell stock at a great loss.

SIR OLIVER.

He's forced to sell stock at a great loss, is he? Well,
that's very kind of him.

SIR PETER.

I'faith, Sir Oliver, Mr. Premium I mean, you'll
soon be master of the trade.   130

SIR OLIVER.

Right, right!^{l} Well, Moses shall give me further
instructions as we go together.

SIR PETER.

You will not have much time, for your nephew
lives hard by.

SIR OLIVER.

Oh, never fear, my tutor appears so able that,   135
though Charles lived in the next street, it must be
my own fault if I'm not a complete rogue before I
turn the corner.

Exeunt Sir Oliver and Moses.

SIR PETER.

So now I think Sir Oliver will be convinced you
are partial, Rowley, and would have prepared   140
Charles for the other plot.

ROWLEY.

No, upon my word, Sir Peter.

SIR PETER.

Well, go bring me this Snake, and I'll hear what
he has to say presently.—I see Maria and want to
speak with her.   145

Exit Rowley.

I should be glad to be convinced my suspicions of
Lady Teazle and Charles were unjust. I have never
yet opened my mind on this subject to my friend
Joseph; I am determined I will do it: he will give
me his opinion sincerely.   150

Enter Maria.

SIR PETER.

So child,* has Mr. Surface returned with you?

MARIA.

No sir, he was engaged.

SIR PETER.

Well Maria, do you not reflect the more you
converse with that amiable young man what return
his partiality for you deserves?   155

MARIA.

Indeed, Sir Peter, your frequent importunity on
this subject distresses me extremely; you compel
me to declare that I know no man who has ever
paid me a particular attention whom I would not
prefer to Mr. Surface.   160

SIR PETER.

So, here's perverseness! No, no, Maria, 'tis Charles
only whom you would prefer; 'tis evident his vices
and follies have won your heart.

MARIA.

This is unkind, sir. You know I have obeyed you
in neither seeing nor corresponding with him. I   165
have heard enough to convince me that he is
unworthy my regard, yet I cannot think it culpable
if, while my understanding severely condemns his
vices, my heart suggests some pity for his distresses.

SIR PETER.

Well, well, pity him as much as you please, but give   170
your heart and hand to a worthier object.

MARIA.

Never to his brother.

SIR PETER.

Go, perverse and obstinate! But take care, madam,
you have never yet known what the authority of a
guardian is; do not compel me to inform you of it.   175

MARIA.

I can only say you shall not have just reason. 'Tis
true, by my father's will I am for a short period
bound to regard you as his substitute but must
cease to think you so when you would compel me
to be miserable. (*Exit.*)   180

SIR PETER.

Was there ever man so crossed as I am! Everything
conspiring to fret me. I had not been involved in
matrimony a fortnight before her father, a hale and
hearty man, died, on purpose, I believe, for the
pleasure of plaguing me with the care of his   185

daughter. But here comes my helpmate. She appears
in great good humor. How happy I should be if I
could tease her into loving me, though but a little.

Enter Lady Teazle.

LADY TEAZLE.
Lud!* Sir Peter, I hope you haven't been quarreling
with Maria? It isn't using me well to be ill-humored   190
when I'm not by.
SIR PETER.
Ah! Lady Teazle, you might have the power to
make me good-humored at all times.
LADY TEAZLE.
I am sure I wish I had, for I want you to be in a
charming, sweet temper at this moment. Do be   195
good-humored now and let me have two hundred
pounds, will you?
SIR PETER.
Two hundred pounds! What, an't I to be in a good
humor without paying for it? But speak to me thus,
and i'faith, there's nothing I would refuse you. You   200
shall have it but seal me a bond for the repayment.
LADY TEAZLE.
Oh no! There's my note of hand will do as well.
SIR PETER.
And you shall no longer reproach me with not
giving you an independent settlement—I mean
shortly to surprise you—but shall we always live   205
thus, hey?
LADY TEAZLE.
If you please. I'm sure I do not care how soon we
leave off quarreling, provided you'll own you were
tired first.
SIR PETER.
Well then, let our future contest be who shall be   210
most obliging.
LADY TEAZLE.
I assure you, Sir Peter, good nature becomes you;
you look now as you did before we were married!
When you used to walk with me under the elms
and tell me stories of what a gallant you were in   215
your youth, and chuck me under the chin, you
would, and ask me if I thought I could love an old
fellow who would deny me nothing, didn't you?
SIR PETER.
Yes, yes, and you were as kind and attentive—

LADY TEAZLE.
Aye, so I was and would always take your part   220
when my acquaintance used to abuse you and turn
you into ridicule.
SIR PETER.
Indeed!
LADY TEAZLE.
Aye, and when my cousin Sophy called you a stiff,
peevish old bachelor and laughed at me for   225
thinking of marrying one who might be my father,
I have always defended you and said I didn't think
you so ugly by any means.
SIR PETER.
Thank you!
LADY TEAZLE.
And that I dared say you would make a very good   230
sort of a husband.
SIR PETER.
And you prophesied right, and we shall certainly
now be the happiest couple—
LADY TEAZLE.
And never differ again.
SIR PETER.
No, never—though at the same time indeed, my   235
dear Lady Teazle, you must watch your temper very
narrowly, for in all our little quarrels, my dear,—if
you recollect, my love, you always began first.
LADY TEAZLE.
I beg pardon, my dear Sir Peter, indeed you always
gave the provocation.   240
SIR PETER.
Now see my angel, contradicting isn't the way to
keep friends.
LADY TEAZLE.
Then don't you begin it, my love.
SIR PETER.
There now—you—you are going on, you don't
perceive, my life, that you are just doing the very   245
thing which you know always makes me angry.
LADY TEAZLE.
Nay, you know if you will be angry without any
reason—
SIR PETER.
There now, you want to quarrel again.
LADY TEAZLE.
No, I'm sure I don't, but if you will be so peevish—   250

SIR PETER.

There, *now* who begins first?

LADY TEAZLE.

Why, you, to be sure. I said nothing, but there's no bearing your temper.

SIR PETER.

No, no, madam, the fault is in your own temper.

LADY TEAZLE.

Aye, you are just what my cousin Sophy said you 255
would be—

SIR PETER.

Your cousin Sophy is a forward, impertinent Gypsy.

LADY TEAZLE.

And you a great bear to abuse my relations.

SIR PETER.

Now may all the plagues of marriage be doubled 260
on me if ever I try to be friends with you any more.

LADY TEAZLE.

So much the better.

SIR PETER.

No, no, madam, 'tis evident you never cared a pin for me, and I was a madman to marry you: a pert, rural coquette that had refused half the honest 265
squires in the neighborhood.

LADY TEAZLE.

And I am sure I was a fool to marry you: an old, dangling bachelor, who was single at fifty only because he never could meet with anyone who would have him. 270

SIR PETER.

Aye, aye, madam, but you were pleased enough to listen to me: you never had such an offer before.

LADY TEAZLE.

No! Didn't I refuse Sir Tivy Terrier, who everybody said would have been a better match? For his estate is just as good as yours, and he has broke his neck 275
since we have been married.

SIR PETER.

Oh, oh, oh! I have done with you, madam. You are unfeeling, ungrateful—but there is an end of everything. I believe you capable of anything that's bad. Yes madam, I now believe the report relative 280
to you and Charles, madam. Madam—yes, madam, you and Charles, not without grounds.

LADY TEAZLE.

Take care, Sir Peter. You had better not insinuate any such thing. I'll not be suspected without a cause, I promise you. 285

SIR PETER.

Very well, madam, very well, a separate maintenance* as soon as you please—yes madam, or a divorce. I'll make an example of myself for the benefit of all old bachelors. Let us separate, madam.

LADY TEAZLE.

Agreed, agreed. And now my dear Sir Peter, we are 290
of a mind once more; we may be the happiest couple and never differ again, you know, ha, ha! Well, you are going to be in a passion, I see, and I shall only interrupt you, so bye bye. (*Exit.*)

SIR PETER.

Plagues and tortures! Can't I make her angry either? 295
Oh, I am the miserablest fellow! But I'll not bear her presuming to keep her temper. No, she may break my heart, but she shall not keep her temper.

Exit.

Scene ii. A chamber in Charles's house.

Enter Trip, Moses, and Sir Oliver.

TRIP.

Here master, master, if you will stay a moment, I'll try whether—what's the gentleman's name?

SIR OLIVER. [*Aside.*]

Mr. Moses, what is my name?

MOSES.

Mr. Premium.

TRIP.

Premium—very well. (*Exit taking snuff.*) 5

SIR OLIVER.

To judge by the servants, one would believe the master was ruined. But what! Sure this was my brother's house!

MOSES.

Yes sir, Mr. Charles bought it of Mr. Joseph, with the furniture, pictures, etcetera, just as the old 10
gentleman left it. Sir Peter thought it a great piece of extravagance in him.

SIR OLIVER.

In my mind the other's economy in selling it him was more reprehensible by half.

Enter Trip.

TRIP.

My master says you must wait, gentleman, he has   15
company and can't speak with you yet.

SIR OLIVER.

If he knew who it was wanted to see him, perhaps
he wouldn't have sent such a message.

TRIP.

Yes, yes, sir, he knows you are here; I didn't forget
little Premium, no, no, no.   20

SIR OLIVER.

Very well, and I pray sir, what may be your name?

TRIP.

Trip, sir, my name is Trip, at your service.

SIR OLIVER.

Well then Mr. Trip, you have a pleasant sort of
place here I guess?

TRIP.

Why yes, here are three or four of us pass our time   25
agreeably enough, but then our wages are
sometimes a little in arrear, and not very good
either, but fifty pounds a year and find our own
bags and bouquets.[16]

SIR OLIVER.

Bags and bouquets! Halters and bastinadoes.   30

TRIP.

But apropos, Moses! Have you been able to get me
that little bill* discounted?

SIR OLIVER. [*Aside.*]

Wants to raise money too—mercy on me—has his
distresses, I warrant, like a lord, and affects
creditors and duns.   35

MOSES.

'Twas not to be done indeed, Mr. Trip.

TRIP.

Good lack! You surprise me. My friend Brush has
endorsed it, and I thought, when he puts his mark
to the back of the bill, 'twas as good as cash.

MOSES.

No, 'twouldn't do.   40

TRIP.

A small sum—but twenty pounds. Harkee, Moses,
do you think you could get it me by way of annuity?

___

16 bags and bouquets] extras or perks, including food and
clothing

SIR OLIVER. [*Aside.*]

An annuity! Ha, ha, ha! A footman raise money
by annuity! Well done, luxury, egad!

MOSES.

But you must insure your place.   45

TRIP.

Oh, with all my heart I'll insure my place—and
my life too if you please.

SIR OLIVER. [*Aside.*]

It's more than I would your neck.[m]

MOSES.

But is there nothing you could deposit?

TRIP.

Why nothing capital of my master's wardrobe has   50
dropped lately, but I could give you a mortgage
on some of his winter clothes, with equity and
redemption before November, or you shall have
the reversion of the French velvet or a post-obit
on the blue and silver—these, I should think,   55
Moses, with a few pair of point ruffles, as a
collateral security, hey my little fellow?

MOSES.

Well, well—

Bell rings.

TRIP.

Egad, I heard the bell. I believe, gentlemen, I can
now introduce you.—Don't forget the annuity,   60
little Moses.—This way, gentlemen.—Insure my
place, you know!

SIR OLIVER. [*Aside.*]

If the man be the shadow of the master, this is the
temple of dissipation indeed!

Exeunt.

Scene iii.

Charles, Careless, Sir Toby Bumper, etc. discovered at
a table drinking wine.*

CHARLES.

Fore Heaven 'tis true, there's the great degeneracy
of the age: many of our acquaintance have taste,
spirit, and politeness, but plague on't, they won't
drink.

CARELESS.

It is so indeed, Charles; they give into all the   5

substantial luxuries of the table and abstain from
nothing but wine and wit.

CHARLES.

Oh certainly, society suffers by it intolerably, for
now instead of the social spirit of raillery that used
to mantle over a glass of bright burgundy, their   10
conversation is become just like the spa-water they
drink, which has all the pertness and flatulence of
champagne without its spirit or flavor.

FIRST GENTLEMAN.

But what are they to do, who love play better than
wine?   15

CARELESS.

True, there's Harry diets himself for gaming and
is now under a hazard regimen.

CHARLES.

Then he'll have the worst of it. What! You wouldn't
train a horse for the course by keeping him from
corn?* For my part, egad, I am now never so   20
successful as when I am a little merry; let me throw
on a bottle of champagne, and I never lose, at least
I never feel my losses, which is exactly the same
thing.

SECOND GENTLEMAN.

Aye, that I believe.   25

CHARLES.

And then, what man can pretend to be a believer
in love who is an abjurer of wine? 'Tis the test by
which the lover knows his own heart. Fill a dozen
bumpers to a dozen beauties, and she that floats
at top is the maid that has bewitched you.   30

CARELESS.

Now then, Charles, be honest and give us your real
favorite.

CHARLES.

Why, I have withheld her only in compassion to
you; if I toast her, you must give a round of her
peers, which is impossible on earth.   35

CARELESS.

Oh, then we'll find some canonized vestals or
heathen goddesses that will do, I warrant.

CHARLES.

Here then, bumpers, you rogues, bumpers. Maria,
Maria!

FIRST GENTLEMAN.

Maria who?   40

CHARLES.

Oh damn the surname, 'tis too formal to be
registered in love's calendar.—But now, Sir Toby,
beware, we must have beauty's superlative.

CARELESS.

Nay, never study, Sir Toby; we'll stand to the toast
though your mistress should want* an eye, and you   45
know you have a song will excuse you.

SIR TOBY.

Egad, so I have, and I'll give him the song instead
of the lady.

Song and Chorus.

Here's to the maiden of bashful fifteen;
    Here's to the widow of fifty;   50
Here's to the flaunting, extravagant quean,
    And here's to the housewife that's thrifty.
        Chorus.
      Let the toast pass,
      Drink to the lass,
I'll warrant she'll prove an excuse for the glass.   55

Here's to the charmer whose dimples we prize;
    Now to the maid who has none, sir;
Here's to the girl with a pair of blue eyes,
    And here's to the nymph with but one, sir.
        Let the toast pass, etc.   60

Here's to the maid with a bosom of snow;
    Now to her that's as brown as a berry;
Here's to the wife with her face full of woe,
    And now for the damsel that's merry.
        Let the toast pass, etc.   65

For let them be clumsy or let them be slim,
    Young or ancient I care not a feather;
So fill a pint bumper quite up to the brim,
    And let us e'en toast them together.
        Let the toast pass, etc.   70

ALL.

Bravo, Bravo!

Enter Trip, who whispers Charles.

CHARLES.

Gentlemen, you must excuse me a little.—
Careless, take the chair, will you?

CARELESS.

Nay prithee Charles, what now? This is one of your peerless beauties, I suppose, has dropped in by chance. 75

CHARLES.

No, faith, to tell you the truth, 'tis a Jew and a broker who are come by appointment.

CARELESS.

Oh damn it, let's have the Jew in.

FIRST GENTLEMAN.

Aye, and the broker too, by all means. 80

SECOND GENTLEMAN.

Yes, yes, the Jew and the broker.

CHARLES.

Egad, with all my heart.—Trip, bid the gentlemen walk in,

Exit Trip

though there's one of them a stranger, I can assure you. 85

CARELESS.

Charles, let us give them some generous burgundy, and perhaps they'll grow conscientious.

CHARLES.

Oh hang 'em, no, wine does but draw forth the natural qualities of a man, and to make them drink would only be to whet their knavery. 90

Enter Trip, Sir Oliver, and Moses.

CHARLES.

So, honest Moses, walk in, walk in pray, Mr. Premium. That's the gentleman's name, isn't it, Moses?

MOSES.

Yes sir.

CHARLES.

Set chairs, Trip.—Sit down, Mr. Premium.— 95
Glasses, Trip.—Sit down, Moses.—Come, Mr. Premium, I'll give you a sentiment: here's success to usury.—Moses, fill the gentleman a bumper.

MOSES.

Success to usury.

CARELESS.

Right, Moses, usury is prudence and industry and 100
deserves to succeed.

SIR OLIVER.

Then here's all the success it deserves.

CARELESS.

No, no, that won't do, Mr. Premium. You have demurred to the toast and must drink it in a pint-bumper. 105

FIRST GENTLEMAN.

A pint bumper at least.

MOSES.

Oh pray sir, consider Mr. Premium's a gentleman.

CARELESS.

And therefore loves good wine.

SECOND GENTLEMAN.

Give Moses a quart-glass; this is mutiny and a high contempt of the chair. 110

CARELESS.

Here now for 't. I'll see justice done to the last drop of my bottle.

SIR OLIVER.

Nay, pray gentlemen, I did not expect this usage.

CHARLES.

No, hang it, Careless, you shan't. Mr. Premium's a stranger. 115

SIR OLIVER. [*Aside.*]

'Odd,* I wish I was well out of their company.

CARELESS.

Plague on them, then. If they won't drink, we'll not sit down with them. Come Harry, the dice are in the next room. Charles, you'll join us when you've finished your business with these gentlemen. 120

Exeunt Sir Toby and gentlemen.

CHARLES.

I will, I will. Careless!

CARELESS.

Well.

CHARLES.

Perhaps I may want you.

CARELESS.

Oh, you know I am always ready; word, note, or bond, 'tis all the same to me. (*Exit.*) 125

MOSES.

Sir, this is Mr. Premium, a gentleman of the strictest honor and secresy and always performs what he undertakes. Mr. Premium, this is—

CHARLES.

Pshaw! Have done.—Sir, my friend Moses is a very honest fellow but a little slow at expression; he'll 130 be an hour giving us our titles. Mr. Premium, the plain state of the matter is this: I am an extravagant young fellow who wants money to borrow; you I take to be a prudent old fellow who has got money to lend. I am blockhead enough to give fifty per cent sooner than not have it, and *you*, I presume, are rogue enough to take an hundred if you can get it. Now sir, you see we are acquainted at once and may proceed to business without any further ceremony.

SIR OLIVER. [*Aside.*]

Exceeding frank, upon my word.—I see, sir, you are not a man of many compliments.

CHARLES.

Oh no, sir, plain dealing in business I always think best.

SIR OLIVER.

Sir, I like you the better for't. However, you are mistaken in one thing: I have no money to lend. But I believe I could procure some of a friend, but then he's an unconscionable dog, isn't he, Moses? and must sell stock to accommodate you, mustn't he, Moses?

MOSES.

Yes indeed. You know I always speak the truth and scorn to tell a lie.

CHARLES.

Right! People that speak the truth generally do.— But these are trifles, Mr. Premium. What, I know money isn't to be bought without paying for't.

SIR OLIVER.

Well, but what security could you give? You have no land, I suppose?

CHARLES.

Not a mole-hill nor a twig but what's in beau-pots[17] out at the window.

SIR OLIVER.

Nor any stock, I presume?

CHARLES.

Nothing but livestock, and that's only a few pointers and ponies. But pray, Mr. Premium, are you acquainted at all with any of my connections?

SIR OLIVER.

Why to say truth, I am.

---

17 beau-pots] large ornamental vases for cut flowers (*OED*)

CHARLES.

Then you must know that I have a devilish rich uncle in the East Indies, Sir Oliver Surface, from whom I have the greatest expectations.

SIR OLIVER.

That you have a wealthy uncle, I have heard, but how your expectations will turn out is more, I believe, than you can tell.

CHARLES.

Oh no! There can be no doubt; they tell me I'm a prodigious favorite and that he talks of leaving me everything.

SIR OLIVER.

Indeed! This is the first I have heard of it.

CHARLES.

Yes, yes, 'tis just so. Moses knows 'tis true, don't you, Moses?

MOSES.

Oh yes, I'll swear to it.

SIR OLIVER. [*Aside.*]

Egad, they'll persuade me presently I'm at Bengal.

CHARLES.

Now I propose, Mr. Premium, if it is agreeable to you, to grant you a post-obit on Sir Oliver's life, though at the same time the old fellow has been so liberal to me that I give you my word I should be very sorry to hear anything had happened to him.

SIR OLIVER.

Not more than I should, I assure you. But the bond you mention happens to be just the worst security you could offer me, for I might live to an hundred and never recover the principal.

CHARLES.

Oh, yes you would, the moment Sir Oliver dies you know you would come on me for the money.

SIR OLIVER.

Then I believe I should be the most unwelcome dun you ever had in your life.

CHARLES.

What, I suppose you are afraid Sir Oliver is too good a life?

SIR OLIVER.

No indeed, I am not though I have heard he is as hale and healthy as any man of his years in Christendom.

CHARLES.

There again you are misinformed; no, no, the

climate has hurt him considerably. Poor Uncle
Oliver! Yes, he breaks apace, I am told, and so
much altered lately that his nearest relations would
not know him.   200
SIR OLIVER.
No? Ha, ha, ha! So much altered lately that his
relations would not know him, ha, ha, ha! That's
droll, egad, ha, ha, ha!
CHARLES.
Ha, ha, ha! You're glad to hear that, little Premium?
SIR OLIVER.
No, no, I am not.   205
CHARLES.
Yes, yes, you are, ha, ha, ha! You know that mends
your chance.
SIR OLIVER.
But I'm told Sir Oliver is coming over; nay, some
say he is actually arrived.
CHARLES.
Pshaw! Sure I must know better than you whether   210
he's coming or not; no, no, rely on't, he is at this
moment at Calcutta, isn't he, Moses?
MOSES.
Yes, certainly.
SIR OLIVER.
Very true, as you say, you must know better than
I, though I have it from pretty good authority,   215
haven't I, Moses?
MOSES.
Yes, most undoubted.
SIR OLIVER.
But sir, as I understand you want a few hundreds
immediately, is there nothing you would dispose of?
CHARLES.
How do you mean?   220
SIR OLIVER.
For instance, now, I have heard that your father
left behind him a great quantity of massy old
plate.*
CHARLES.
Oh, Lud!* That's gone long ago; Moses can tell you
how better than I.   225
SIR OLIVER. [*Aside.*]
Good lack! All the family race-cups and
corporation bowls!—Then it was also supposed his
library was one of the most valuable and complete.

CHARLES.
Yes, yes, so it was, vastly too much so for a private
gentleman; for my part I was always of a   230
communicative disposition, so I thought it was a
shame to keep so much knowledge to myself.
SIR OLIVER. [*Aside.*]
Mercy on me! Learning that had run in the family
like an heirloom.—Pray, what are become of the
books?   235
CHARLES.
You must inquire of the auctioneer, Master
Premium, for I don't believe even Moses can direct
you there.
MOSES.
I know nothing of books.
SIR OLIVER.
So, so, nothing of the family property left, I   240
suppose?
CHARLES.
Not much indeed, unless you have a mind to the
family pictures. I have got a room full of ancestors
above, and if you have taste for old paintings, egad,
you shall have them a bargain.   245
SIR OLIVER.
Hey, the devil! Sure you won't sell your forefathers,
would you?
CHARLES.
Every man of them to the best bidder.
SIR OLIVER.
What, your great uncles and aunts?
CHARLES.
Yes, and my grandfathers and grandmothers too.   250
SIR OLIVER. [*Aside.*]
Now I give him up.—What the plague, have you
no bowels for your kindred? 'Odd's* life! Do you
take me for Shylock in the play, that you would
raise money of me on your own flesh and blood?
CHARLES.
Nay, my little broker, don't be angry. What need   255
you care, if you have your money's worth?
SIR OLIVER.
Well, I'll be the purchaser; I think I can dispose
of the family canvas. [*Aside.*] Oh! I'll never forgive
him this—never.

Enter Careless.

CARELESS.

Come Charles, what keeps you? 260

CHARLES.

I can't come yet, i'faith; we are going to have a sale above. Here's little Premium will buy all my ancestors.

CARELESS.

Oh, burn your ancestors!

CHARLES.

No, he may do that afterwards, if he pleases. Stay, 265 Careless, we want you; egad, you shall be auctioneer, so come along with us.

CARELESS.

Oh, have with you, if that's the case; I can handle a hammer as well as a dice-box. A-going, a-going, etcetera. 270

SIR OLIVER. [*Aside.*]

Oh the profligates!

CHARLES.

Come, Moses. You shall be appraiser, if we want one.—Gad's life, little Premium, you don't seem to like the business?

SIR OLIVER.

Oh, yes, I do vastly, ha, ha! Yes, yes, I think it a 275 rare joke to sell one's family by auction, ha, ha! (*Aside.*) Oh the prodigal!

CHARLES.

To be sure! When a man wants* money, where the plague should he get assistance if he can't make free with his own relations? 280

SIR OLIVER. [*Aside.*]

I'll never forgive him! Never, never!

Exeunt.

Act IV, scene i. Picture room at Charles's house.

Enter Charles, Sir Oliver, Moses, and Careless.

CHARLES.

Walk in, gentlemen, walk in pray. Here they are, the family of the Surfaces up to the Conquest.[18]

SIR OLIVER.

And in my opinion, a goodly collection.

CHARLES.

Aye, aye, they are done in the true spirit of portrait painting, no volunteer grace or expression, not like 5

---

18 Conquest] Norman Conquest in 1066

the works of your* modern Raphael, who gives you the strongest resemblance yet contrives to make your own portrait independent of you, so that you may sink the original and not hurt the pictures. No, no, the merit of these is the inveterate likeness: all stiff and awkward as the originals and like nothing in human nature beside. 10

SIR OLIVER.

Ah! We shall never see such figures of men again.

CHARLES.

I hope not. Well, you see, Master Premium, what a domestic character I am; here I sit of an evening 15 surrounded by my family. But come, go to your pulpit, Mr. Auctioneer. Here's an old, gouty chair of my grandfather's will answer the purpose.

CARELESS.

Aye, aye, this will do, but Charles, I have ne'er a hammer, and what's an auctioneer without his 20 hammer?

CHARLES.

Egad, that's true. What parchment do we have here? Richard, heir to Thomas[19]— Oh, our genealogy in full.—Here Careless, you shall have no common bit of mahogany; here's the family tree for you, you 25 rogue. This shall be your hammer, and now you may knock down my ancestors with their own pedigree.

SIR OLIVER. [*Aside.*]

What an unnatural rogue! An ex post facto parricide!

CARELESS.

Yes, yes, here's a list of your generation, indeed. 30 'Faith, Charles, this is the most convenient thing you could have found for the business, for 'twill serve not only as a hammer but a catalog into the bargain. But come, begin, a-going, a-going, a-going—

CHARLES.

Bravo, Careless! Well, here's my great uncle, Sir 35 Richard Raveline, a marvellous good general in his day, I assure you; he served in all the Duke of Marlborough's wars and got that cut over his eye at the Battle of Malplaquet.[20] What say you, Mr.

---

19 Richard, heir to Thomas] Richard Brinsley Sheridan was the son of Thomas Sheridan.

20 Battle of Malplaquet] 1709 battle in the War of the Spanish Succession

Premium, look at him, there's a hero: not cut out 40
of his feathers as your modern clipped captains are
but enveloped in wig and regimentals as a general
should be. What do you bid?

SIR OLIVER. (*Aside to Moses.*)

Bid him speak.

MOSES.

Mr. Premium would have you speak. 45

CHARLES.

Why, then he shall have him for ten pounds, and
I'm sure that's not dear* for a staff officer.

SIR OLIVER. [*Aside.*]

Heaven deliver me! His famous uncle Richard for
ten pounds!—Very well, sir, I take him at that.

CHARLES.

Careless, knock down my Uncle Richard. Here now 50
is a maiden sister of his, my great aunt Deborah,
done by Kneller in his best manner and esteemed a
very formidable likeness; there she is, you see, a
shepherdess feeding her flock. You shall have her at
five pounds ten; the sheep are worth the money. 55

SIR OLIVER. [*Aside.*]

Ah, poor Deborah! A woman who set such a value
on herself.—Five pounds ten, she is mine.

CHARLES.

Knock down my Aunt Deborah. This[n] now is a
grandfather of my mother's, a learned judge, well-
known on the western circuit. What do you rate 60
him at, Moses?

MOSES.

Four guineas.

CHARLES.

Four guineas! Gad's life, you don't bid me the price
of his wig.—Mr. Premium, you have more respect
for the woolsack. Do let us knock his lordship 65
down at fifteen.

SIR OLIVER.

By all means.

CARELESS.

Gone.

CHARLES.

And there are two brothers of his, William and
Walter Blunt, Esquires, both members of 70
Parliament and noted speakers, and what's very
extraordinary, I believe this is the first time they
were ever bought and sold.

SIR OLIVER.

That is very extraordinary indeed! I'll take them
at your own price for the honor of Parliament. 75

CARELESS.

Well said, little Premium; I'll knock them down
at forty.

CHARLES.

Here's a jolly fellow. I don't know what relation,
but he was Mayor of Norwich. Take him at eight
pounds. 80

SIR OLIVER.

No, no, six will do for the mayor.

CHARLES.

Come, make it guineas, and I'll throw you the two
aldermen into the bargain.

SIR OLIVER.

They are mine.

CHARLES.

Careless, knock down the mayor and aldermen. 85
But plague on't, we shall be all day retailing in this
manner. Do let us deal wholesale. What say you,
Premium, give me three hundred pounds, and take
all that remains on each side in the lump.

SIR OLIVER.°

Well, well, anything to accommodate you; they are 90
mine. But there is one portrait which you have
always passed over.

CARELESS.

What! That little ill-looking fellow over the settee?

SIR OLIVER.

Yes sir, I mean that, though I don't think him so
ill-looking a little fellow by any means. 95

CHARLES.

What, that! Oh, that's my Uncle Oliver; 'twas done
before he went to India.

CARELESS.

Your Uncle Oliver! Gad, then you'll never be friends,
Charles. That now to me is as stern a looking rogue
as ever I saw: an unforgiving eye and a damned 100
disinheriting countenance. An inveterate knave,
depend on't. Don't you think so, little Premium?

SIR OLIVER.

Upon my soul, sir, I do not. I think it as honest a
looking face as any in the room, dead or alive.—
But I suppose your Uncle Oliver goes with the rest 105
of the lumber.*

CHARLES.

No, hang it, I'll not part with poor Noll; the old fellow has been very good to me, and egad, I'll keep his picture while I've a room to put it in.

SIR OLIVER. [*Aside.*]

The rogue's my nephew after all!—But sir, I have somehow taken a fancy to that picture. 110

CHARLES.

I'm sorry for't, for you certainly will not have it. 'Oons!* Haven't you got enough of 'em.

SIR OLIVER. [*Aside.*]

I forgive him everything!—But sir, when I take a whim in my head, I don't value money. I'll give you as much for that as for all the rest. 115

CHARLES.

Don't tease me, Master Broker, I tell you I'll not part with it, and there's an end on't.

SIR OLIVER. [*Aside.*]

How like his father the dog is. Well, well, I have done. I did perceive it before, but I never saw such a resemblance.—Well sir, here's a draft for the sum. 120

CHARLES.

Why, 'tis for eight hundred pounds.

SIR OLIVER.

You will not let Oliver go?

CHARLES.

Zounds! No, I tell you once more.

SIR OLIVER.

Then never mind the difference; we'll balance another time. But give me your hand on the bargain. You are an honest fellow, Charles. I beg pardon for being so free.—Come, Moses. 125

CHARLES. [*Aside.*]

Egad, this is a whimsical old fellow!—But harkee, Premium, you'll prepare lodgings for these gentlemen? 130

SIR OLIVER.

Yes, yes, I'll send for them in a day or two.

CHARLES.

But hold, do now send a genteel conveyance for them, for I assure you they were most of them used to ride in their own carriages. 135

SIR OLIVER.

I will, I will, for all but—Oliver.

CHARLES.

Aye, all but the little nabob.

SIR OLIVER.

You're fixed!

CHARLES.

Peremptorily.

SIR OLIVER. [*Aside.*]

A dear extravagant rogue.—Good day. Come, Moses, let me hear now who dares call him profligate. 140

Exeunt Sir Oliver and Moses.

CARELESS.

Why this is the oddest genius of the sort I ever saw.

CHARLES.

Egad, he's the prince of brokers, I think. I wonder how the devil Moses got acquainted with so honest a fellow? But hark! Here's Rowley. Do, Careless, say that I'll join the company in a moment. 145

CARELESS.

I will. But don't now let that old blockhead persuade you to squander any of that money on old musty debts or any such nonsense, for tradesmen, Charles, are the most exorbitant fellows. 150

CHARLES.

Very true, and paying them is only encouraging them.

CARELESS.

Nothing else.

CHARLES.

Aye, aye, never fear. 155

Exit Careless.

So, this was an odd fellow indeed—let me see—two thirds of this, five hundred and thirty odd pounds are mine by right. Fore Heaven, I find one's ancestors are more valuable relations than I took them for! Ladies and gentlemen, your most obedient and very grateful humble servant. 160

Enter Rowley.

Hah! Old Rowley, egad, you are just come in time to take leave of your old acquaintance.

ROWLEY.

Yes, I heard they were going, but I wonder you can have such spirits under so many distresses. 165

CHARLES.

Why, there's the point: my distresses are so many that I can't afford to part with my spirits. But I shall be rich and splenetic all in good time; however, I

suppose that you are surprised that I am not more 170
sorrowful at parting with so many near relations. To
be sure, 'tis very affecting, but rot 'em, you see they
never move a muscle, so why should I?

ROWLEY.

There's no making you serious a moment.

CHARLES.

Yes, faith I am so now. Here, my honest Rowley, 175
here, get me this changed directly and take a
hundred pounds of it immediately to old Stanley.

ROWLEY.

A hundred pounds! Consider only—

CHARLES.

Gad's life, don't talk about. Poor Stanley's wants*
are pressing, and if you don't make haste, we shall 180
have someone call that has a better right to the
money.

ROWLEY.

Ah! there's the point. I never will cease dunning
you with the old proverb—

CHARLES.

"Be just before you're generous." Hey! Why, so I 185
would if I could, but justice is an old, lame,
hobbling beldam, and I can't get her to keep pace
with generosity for the soul of me.

ROWLEY.

Yet Charles, believe me, one hour's reflection—

CHARLES.

Aye, aye, it is very true, but harkee, Rowley, while 190
I have, by heaven I will give. So damn your
economy and now for hazard.

Exeunt.

Scene ii. The parlor.

Enter Sir Oliver and Moses.

MOSES.

Well sir, I think, as Sir Peter said, you have seen
Mr. Charles in high glory; 'tis great pity he's so
extravagant.

SIR OLIVER.

True, but he wouldn't sell my picture.

MOSES.

And loves wine and women so much. 5

SIR OLIVER.

But he wouldn't sell my picture.

MOSES.

And game so deep.

SIR OLIVER.

But he wouldn't sell my picture.—Oh, here's
Rowley.

Enter Rowley.

ROWLEY.

Oh Sir Oliver, I find you have made a purchase. 10

SIR OLIVER.

Yes, yes, our young rake has parted with his
ancestors like old tapestry.

ROWLEY.

And here has he commissioned me to redeliver you
a part of the purchase money, I mean, though, in
your necessitous character of Old Stanley. 15

MOSES.

Ah! There is the pity of all, he's so damned
charitable.

ROWLEY.

And I left a hosier and two tailors in the hall, who
I'm sure won't be paid, and this hundred would
satisfy them. 20

SIR OLIVER.

Well, well, I'll pay his debts and his benevolence
too. But now I'm no more a broker, and you shall
introduce me to the brother as Old Stanley.

ROWLEY.

Not yet a while. Sir Peter, I know, means to call
there about this time. 25

Enter Trip.

TRIP.

Oh gentlemen, I beg pardon for not showing you
out. This way, gentlemen.—Moses, a word—

Exeunt Trip and Moses.

SIR OLIVER.

There's a fellow for you. Would you believe it, that
puppy intercepted the Jew on our coming and
wanted to raise money before he got to his master. 30

ROWLEY.

Indeed!

SIR OLIVER.

Yes, they are now planning an annuity business. Ah
Master Rowley, in my days servants were content

with the follies of their masters when they were worn
a little threadbare, but now they have their vices like   35
their birthday* clothes, with the gloss on.

Exeunt.

               Scene. iii. A library.

Enter Joseph Surface and servant.

JOSEPH SURFACE.
  No letter from Lady Teazle?
SERVANT.
  No sir.
JOSEPH SURFACE.
  I am surprised she has not sent if she is prevented
  from coming. Sir Peter certainly does not suspect
  me, yet I wish I may not lose the heiress through   5
  the scrape I have drawn myself in with the wife.
  However, Charles's imprudence and bad character*
  are great points in my favor.

[*Knock within.*]

SERVANT.
  Sir, I believe that must be Lady Teazle.
JOSEPH SURFACE.
  Hold! See whether it is or not before you go to   10
  the door; I have a particular message for you if it
  should be my brother.
SERVANT.
  'Tis her ladyship, sir, she always leaves her chair*
  at the milliner's in the next street.
JOSEPH SURFACE.
  Stay, stay, draw that screen before the window; that   15
  will do. My opposite neighbor is a maiden lady of
  a curious temper.

Servant draws the screen, and exit.

  I have a difficult hand to play in this affair. Lady
  Teazle has lately suspected my views on Maria, but
  she must by no means be let into that secret, at   20
  least till I have her more in my power.

Enter Lady Teazle.

LADY TEAZLE.
  What, sentiment in soliloquy! Have you been very
  impatient now? O Lud,* don't pretend to look
  grave. I vow I couldn't come before.

JOSEPH SURFACE.
  Oh madam! Punctuality is a species of constancy—   25
  very unfashionable quality in a lady.
LADY TEAZLE.
  Upon my word, you ought to pity me. Do you
  know that Sir Peter is grown so ill-natured of late
  and so jealous of Charles too? That's the best of
  the story, isn't it?   30
JOSEPH SURFACE. (*Aside.*)
  I am glad my scandalous friends keep that up.
LADY TEAZLE.
  I'm sure I wish he would let Maria marry him, and
  then perhaps he would be convinced. Don't you,
  Mr. Surface?
JOSEPH SURFACE. (*Aside.*)
  Indeed I do not.—Oh, certainly I do, for then my   35
  dear Lady Teazle would also be convinced how
  wrong her suspicions were of my having any design
  on the silly girl.
LADY TEAZLE.
  Well, well, I'm inclined to believe you, but isn't it
  provoking to have the most ill-natured things said   40
  to one. There is my friend Lady Sneerwell has
  circulated I don't how many scandalous tales of
  me—and all without any foundation too. That's
  what vexes me.
JOSEPH SURFACE.
  Aye madam, that is the provoking circumstance—   45
  without foundation; yes, yes, there's the
  mortification indeed. For when a scandalous story is
  believed against one, there certainly is no comfort
  like the consciousness of having deserved it.
LADY TEAZLE.
  No, to be sure. Then I'd forgive their malice. But   50
  to attack *me*, who am really so innocent and who
  never says an ill-natured thing of anybody, that is,
  of my friends—and then Sir Peter too to have him
  so peevish and so suspicious—when I know the
  integrity of my own heart—indeed 'tis monstrous.   55
JOSEPH SURFACE.
  But my dear Lady Teazle, 'tis your own fault if you
  suffer it. When a husband entertains a groundless
  suspicion of his wife and withdraws his confidence
  from her, the original compact is broke, and she
  owes it to the honor of her sex to endeavor to   60
  outwit him.

LADY TEAZLE.

Indeed! So that if he suspects me without cause, it follows that the best way of curing his jealousy is to give him reason for't?

JOSEPH SURFACE.

Undoubtedly, for your husband should never be 65 deceived in you, and in that case it becomes *you* to become frail in compliment to his discernment.

LADY TEAZLE.

To be sure what you say is very reasonable, and when the consciousness of my own innocence—

JOSEPH SURFACE.

Ah, my dear madam, there is the great mistake; 'tis 70 this very conscious innocence that is of the greatest prejudice to you. What is it makes you negligent of forms and careless of the world's opinion? Why, the consciousness of your innocence. What makes you thoughtless in your conduct and apt to run into a 75 thousand little imprudences? Why, the consciousness of your innocence. What makes you impatient of Sir Peter's temper, and outrageous at his suspicions? Why, the consciousness of your own innocence.

LADY TEAZLE.

'Tis very true. 80

JOSEPH SURFACE.

Now my dear Lady Teazle, if you would but once make a trifling faux-pas, you can't conceive how cautious you would grow and how ready to humor and agree with your husband.

LADY TEAZLE.

Do you think so? 85

JOSEPH SURFACE.

Oh, I'm sure on't. And then you'd find all scandal would cease at once, for in short, your character at present is like a person in a plethora: absolutely dying of too much health.

LADY TEAZLE.

Why, if* my understanding were once convinced— 90

JOSEPH SURFACE.

Oh certainly, madam. Your understanding *should* be convinced—yes, yes. Heaven forbid I should persuade you to do anything you thought wrong— no, no. I have too much honor to desire it.

LADY TEAZLE.

Don't you think we may as well leave honor out 95 of the argument.

JOSEPH SURFACE.

Ah! The ill effects of your country education I see still remain with you.

LADY TEAZLE.

I doubt* they do, indeed, and I will fairly own to you that, if I could be persuaded to do wrong, it 100 would be Sir Peter's ill usage sooner than your honorable logic after all.

JOSEPH SURFACE.

Then by this hand which he is unworthy of—

Enter Servant

'Sdeath,* you blockhead, what do you want?

SERVANT.

I beg pardon, sir, but I thought you wouldn't 105 choose Sir Peter's coming upstairs without announcing him.

JOSEPH SURFACE.

Sir Peter, 'oons,* and the devil!

LADY TEAZLE.

Sir Peter! Oh Lud,* I'm ruined! I'm ruined!

SERVANT.

Sir, 'twasn't I let him in. 110

LADY TEAZLE.

Oh! I'm undone. What will become of me now, Mr. Logic? Oh mercy, he's on the stairs! I'll get behind here, and if ever I'm so imprudent again! (*Goes behind the screen.*)

JOSEPH SURFACE.

Give me a book. 115

Enter Sir Peter.

SIR PETER.

Aye, ever improving himself.—Mr. Surface! Mr. Surface!

JOSEPH SURFACE.

Oh my dear Sir Peter, I beg your pardon, (*Gaping and throwing away the book.*) I have been dozing over a stupid* book. Well, I am much obliged to 120 you for this call. You have not been here, I believe, since I fitted up this room. Books, you know, are the only things I am a coxcomb in.

SIR PETER.

'Tis very neat indeed. Well, well, that's proper, and you make even your screen a source of knowledge: 125 hung, I perceive, with maps.

JOSEPH SURFACE.

Oh yes, I find great use in that screen.

SIR PETER.

I dare say you must, certainly, when you want to find anything in a hurry.

JOSEPH SURFACE. (*Aside.*)

Aye, or to hide anything in a hurry either. 130

SIR PETER.

Well, I have a little private business.

JOSEPH SURFACE.

You needn't stay.

SERVANT.

No sir. (*Exit.*)

JOSEPH SURFACE.

Here's a chair, Sir Peter. I beg—

SIR PETER.

Well now we are alone, there is a subject, my dear 135 friend, on which I wish to unburden my mind to you, a point of greatest moment to my peace—in short, my good friend, Lady Teazle's conduct of late has made me very unhappy.

JOSEPH SURFACE.

Indeed, I am sorry to hear it. 140

SIR PETER.

Yes, 'tis but too plain she has not the least regard for me, but what's worse, I have pretty good authority to suppose that she must have formed an attachment to another.

JOSEPH SURFACE.

Indeed! You astonish me! 145

SIR PETER.

Yes, and between ourselves, I think I have discovered the person.

JOSEPH SURFACE.

How! You alarm me exceedingly!

SIR PETER.

Ah my dear friend, I knew you would sympathize with me! 150

JOSEPH SURFACE.

Yes, believe me, Sir Peter, such a discovery would distress me just as much as it would you.

SIR PETER.

I am convinced of it. Ah, it is a happiness to have a friend whom one can trust even with one's family secrets. But have you no guess who I mean? 155

JOSEPH SURFACE.

I haven't the most distant idea. It can't be Sir Benjamin Backbite?

SIR PETER.

Oh, no. What say you to Charles?

JOSEPH SURFACE.

My brother! Impossible!

SIR PETER.

It's very true. 160

JOSEPH SURFACE.

Oh no, Sir Peter, you must not credit the scandalous insinuation you hear. No, no, Charles, to be sure, has been charged many things of this kind, but I can never think he could mediate so gross an injury.

SIR PETER.

Ah, my dear friend! The goodness of your own 165 heart misleads you; you judge of others by yourself.

JOSEPH SURFACE.

Certainly, Sir Peter, the heart that is conscious of its own integrity is ever slow to credit another's baseness.ᴘ

SIR PETER.

True, but your brother has no sentiment; you never 170 hear him talk so.

JOSEPH SURFACE.

Yet I can't but think that Lady Teazle herself has too much principle.

SIR PETER.

Aye, but what's her principle against the flattery of a handsome, lively, young fellow. 175

JOSEPH SURFACE.

That's very true.

SIR PETER.

And then you know the difference of our ages makes it highly improbable that she should have any violent affection for me, and if she were to be frail, and I were to make it public, why the Town 180 would only laugh at me, the foolish old bachelor who had married a girl.

JOSEPH SURFACE.

That's true. To be sure, they would laugh.

SIR PETER.

Laugh, aye, and make ballads and paragraphs and the devil knows what of me. 185

JOSEPH SURFACE.

No, you must never make it public.

SIR PETER.

But then again, that the nephew of my old friend, Sir Oliver, should be the person to do such a wrong hurts one more nearly.

JOSEPH SURFACE.

Aye, there's the point: When ingratitude barbs the 190 dart of injury, the wound has double danger in it.

SIR PETER.

Aye, I that was in a manner left his guardian, in whose house he has been so often entertained, who never in my life denied him——my advice.

JOSEPH SURFACE.

Oh 'tis not to be credited. There may be a man 195 capable of such baseness to be sure, but for my part, till you can give me positive proofs, I cannot but doubt it; however, if this should be proved on him, he is no longer a brother of mine. I disclaim kindred with him. For the man who can break through the 200 laws of hospitality and attempt the wife of his friend deserves to branded as the pest of society.

SIR PETER.

What a difference there is between you! What noble sentiments!

JOSEPH SURFACE.

Yet I cannot suspect Lady Teazle's honor. 205

SIR PETER.

I am sure I wish to think well of her and to remove all ground of quarrel between us. She has lately reproached me more than once with having made no settlement on her, and in our last quarrel she almost hinted that she would not break her heart 210 if I was dead. Now as we seem to differ in our ideas of expense, I have resolved she shall be her own mistress in that respect for the future, and if I were to die, she shall find that I have not been inattentive to her interests while living. Here, my 215 friend, are the drafts of two deeds which I wish to have your opinion on: by one, she will enjoy eight hundred a year, independent, while I live, and by the other, the bulk of my fortune after my death.

JOSEPH SURFACE.

This conduct, Sir Peter, is indeed truly generous! 220 (*Aside.*) I wish it may not corrupt my pupil.

SIR PETER.

Yes, I am determined she shall have no cause to complain, though I would not have her acquainted

with the latter instance of my affection yet awhile.

JOSEPH SURFACE. [*Aside.*]

Nor I, if I could help it. 225

SIR PETER.

And now, my dear friend, if you please, we will talk over the situation of your hopes with Maria.

JOSEPH SURFACE. [*Softly.*]

No, no, Sir Peter, another time if you please.

SIR PETER.

I am sensibly chagrined at the little progress you seem to make in her affections—— 230

JOSEPH SURFACE. (*Softly.*)

I beg you will not mention it, sir. What are my disappointments when your happiness is in debate. [*Aside.*] 'Sdeath,* I shall be ruined every way.

SIR PETER.

And though you are so averse to my acquainting Lady Teazle with your passion, I am sure she is not 235 your enemy in the affair.

JOSEPH SURFACE.

Pray Sir Peter, oblige me—I am really too much affected by the subject we have been talking to bestow a thought on my own concerns. The man who is entrusted with his friend's distresses—can 240 never—— Well, sir——

Enter Servant.

SERVANT.

Your brother, sir, is speaking to a gentleman in the street and says he knows you are within.

JOSEPH SURFACE.

'Sdeath! Blockhead, I am not within; I am out for the day. 245

SIR PETER.

Stay, hold, a thought has struck me: you shall be at home.

JOSEPH SURFACE.

Well, well, let him up.

Exit Servant.

(*Aside.*) He'll interrupt Sir Peter, however.

SIR PETER.

Now my good friend, oblige me, I entreat you: be- 250 fore Charles comes, let me conceal myself some- where; then do you tax him on the point we have been talking on, and his answers may satisfy me at once.

JOSEPH SURFACE.

Oh fie, Sir Peter! Would you have me join in so 255
mean* a trick—to trepan my brother too—

SIR PETER.

Nay, you tell me you are sure he's innocent; if so,
you do him the greatest service in giving him an
opportunity to clear himself, and you will set my
heart at rest. Come, you shall not refuse me. Here 260
behind this screen will be— Hey! What the devil!
There seems to be one listener already. I'll swear I
saw a petticoat.

JOSEPH SURFACE.

Ha, ha, ha! Well, this is ridiculous enough. I'll tell
you, Sir Peter, though I hold a man of intrigue to 265
be a most despicable character, yet you know it
does not follow that one is to be an absolute Joseph
either. Harkee, 'tis a little French milliner, a silly*
rogue that plagues me, and having some character,
on your coming in she ran behind the screen. 270

SIR PETER.

Ah, you rogue. But egad, she has overheard all I
have been saying of my wife.

JOSEPH SURFACE.

Oh, 'twill never go any farther, you may depend on't.

SIR PETER.

No! Then 'ifaith, let her hear it out. Here's a closet
will do as well. 275

JOSEPH SURFACE.

Well, go in then.

SIR PETER.

Sly rogue, sly rogue! (*Goes into the closet.*)

JOSEPH SURFACE.

A narrow escape indeed, and a curious situation I
am in, to part man and wife in this manner.

LADY TEAZLE. (*Peeping out.*)

Couldn't I steal off? 280

JOSEPH SURFACE.

Keep close, my angel.

SIR PETER. (*Peeping out.*)

Joseph, tax him home.

JOSEPH SURFACE.

Back, my dear friend.

LADY TEAZLE.

Couldn't you lock Sir Peter in?

JOSEPH SURFACE.

Lie still, my life. 285

SIR PETER.

You are sure the little milliner won't blab?

JOSEPH SURFACE.

In, in, my dear Sir Peter. Foregad, I wish I had a
key to the door.

Enter Charles.

CHARLES.

Holla, brother! What has been the matter? Your
fellow wouldn't let me up at first. What, have you 290
had a Jew or a wench with you?

JOSEPH SURFACE.

Neither brother, I assure you.

CHARLES.

And what has made Sir Peter steal off? I thought
he had been with you.

JOSEPH SURFACE.

He was, brother, but hearing you were coming, he 295
did not choose to stay.

CHARLES.

What! Was the old gentleman afraid I wanted to
borrow money of him?

JOSEPH SURFACE.

No, sir. But I am sorry to find, Charles, that you
have lately given that worthy man grounds for 300
great uneasiness.

CHARLES.

Yes, yes, they tell me I do that to a great many
worthy men, but how so pray?

JOSEPH SURFACE.

To be plain with you, brother, he thinks you are endeavoring to gain Lady Teazle's affections from him. 305

CHARLES.

Who I? Oh Lud!* Not I, upon my word. Ha, ha,
ha! So the old fellow has found out that he has got
a young wife, has he?ʳ

JOSEPH SURFACE.

This is no subject to jest upon, brother. He who
can laugh— 310

CHARLES.

True, true, as you were going to say—then
seriously, I never had the least idea of what you
charge me with, upon my honor.

JOSEPH SURFACE.

Well, well, it will give Sir Peter great satisfaction
to hear it. 315

CHARLES.

To be sure, I once thought the lady seemed to have taken a fancy to me, but upon my soul, I never gave the least encouragement; besides, you know my attachment to Maria.

JOSEPH SURFACE.

But sure brother, if Lady Teazle had betrayed the 320 fondest partiality for you—

CHARLES.

Why, look ye Joseph, I hope I shall never deliberately do a dishonorable action—but if a pretty woman were purposely to throw herself in my way—and that pretty woman married to a man 325 old enough to be her father—

JOSEPH SURFACE.

Well!

CHARLES.

Why, I believe I should be obliged to borrow a little of your morality, that's all. But brother, do you know now that you surprise me exceedingly 330 by naming me with Lady Teazle, for 'faith, I always understood *you* were her favorite.

JOSEPH SURFACE.

For shame, Charles, this retort is foolish.

CHARLES.

Nay, I swear I have seen you exchange such significant glances. 335

JOSEPH SURFACE.

Nay, nay sir, this is no jest.

CHARLES.

Egad, I'm serious, don't you remember one day when I called here—

JOSEPH SURFACE.

Nay prithee Charles—

CHARLES.

And found you together— 340

JOSEPH SURFACE.

Zounds sir! I insist—

CHARLES.

And another time when your servant—

JOSEPH SURFACE.

Brother, brother, a word with you. (*Aside.*) Gad I must stop him.

CHARLES.

Informed me, I say, that— 345

JOSEPH SURFACE.

Hush! I beg your pardon, but Sir Peter has overheard all we have been saying; I knew you would clear yourself, or I should not have consented.

CHARLES.

How! Sir Peter! Where is he?

JOSEPH SURFACE.

Softly—there. (*Points to the closet.*) 350

CHARLES.

Oh! Fore Heaven, I'll have him out.—Sir Peter, come forth.

JOSEPH SURFACE.

No, no.

CHARLES.

I say, Sir Peter, come into court. (*Pulls in Sir Peter.*) What, my old guardian! What! Turned inquisitor, 355 and taking evidence incog?

SIR PETER.

Give me your hand, Charles, I believe I have suspected you wrongfully. But you mustn't be angry with Joseph—'twas my plan.

CHARLES.

Indeed! 360

SIR PETER.

But I acquit you. I promise you, I don't think near so ill of you as I did. What I have heard has given me great satisfaction.

CHARLES.

Egad then! 'twas lucky you didn't hear any more.— Wasn't it, Joseph? 365

SIR PETER.

Ah! You would have retorted on him.

CHARLES.

Aye, aye, that was a joke.

SIR PETER.

Yes, yes, I know his honor too well.

CHARLES.

But you might as well have suspected *him* as me in this matter for all that.—Mightn't he, Joseph? 370

SIR PETER.

Well, well, I believe you.

JOSEPH SURFACE. (*Aside.*)

I wish they were both well out of the room.

SIR PETER.

And in future perhaps we may not be such strangers.

Enter servant who speaks to Joseph Surface.

SERVANT.

Sir, Lady Sneerwell is below and says she will come 375
up.

JOSEPH SURFACE. (*To the servant.*)

Lady Sneerwell—Gad's life! She mustn't come
here.—Gentlemen, I beg pardon—I must wait on
you downstairs—here is a person come on
particular business. 380

CHARLES.

Well, well, you can see him in another room; Sir
Peter and I have not met for a long time, and I
have something to say to him.

JOSEPH SURFACE. [*Aside.*]

They must not be left together. I'll send Lady
Sneerwell away directly.—Sir Peter, not a word of 385
the French milliner.

SIR PETER.

Oh not for the world!

Exit Joseph Surface [and servant].

Ah Charles, if you associated more with your
brother, one might indeed hope for your
reformation. He is a man of sentiment. Well, 390
there's nothing so noble as a man of sentiment.

CHARLES.

Pshaw, he is too moral by half and so apprehensive
of his good name, as he calls it, that I suppose he
would as soon let a priest into his house as a wench.

SIR PETER.

No, no, come, come, you wrong him. No, no, 395
Joseph is no rake, but he is no such saint in that
respect either. (*Aside.*) I have a great mind to tell
him; we should have such a laugh.

CHARLES.

Oh, hang him! He's a very anchorite—a young
hermit! 400

SIR PETER.

Hark ye, you must not abuse him; he may chance
to hear of it again, I promise.

CHARLES.

Why, you won't tell him?

SIR PETER.

No—but—this way— [*Aside.*] Egad, I'll tell
him.—Hark ye, have you a mind to have a good 405
laugh against Joseph?

CHARLES.

I should like it of all things.

SIR PETER.

Then, faith, we will. [*Aside.*] I'll be quit with him
for discovering* me. (*Whispers.*) He had a girl with
him when I called. 410

CHARLES.

What, Joseph! You jest.

SIR PETER.

Hush! A little French milliner—and the best of the
jest is—she's in the room now.

CHARLES.

The devil she is! (*Looking at the closet.*)

SIR PETER.

Hush I tell you! (*Points to the screen.*) 415

CHARLES.

Behind the screen? 'Odd's* life! Let us unveil her.

SIR PETER.

No, no, he's coming, you shan't indeed.

CHARLES.

Oh egad, we'll have a peep at the little milliner!

SIR PETER.

No, not for the world—Joseph will never forgive
me. 420

CHARLES.

I'll stand by you.

SIR PETER.

'Odd's life! Here he is.

Joseph enters as Charles throws down the screen.

CHARLES.

Lady Teazle, by all that's wonderful!

SIR PETER.

Lady Teazle, by all that's damnable!ˢ

CHARLES.

Sir Peter, this is one of the smartest French milliners 425
I ever saw. Egad, you seem all to have been diverting
yourselves at hide and seek. And I don't see who is
out of the secret.—Shall I beg your ladyship to
inform me? Not a word!—Brother, will you please
to explain this matter? What, is morality dumb 430
too?—Sir Peter, though I found you in the dark,
perhaps you are not so now. All mute! Well, though
I can make nothing of this affair, I suppose you
perfectly understand one another, so I shall leave you
to yourselves. (*Going.*) Brother, I am sorry to find 435

you have given that worthy man grounds for so much uneasiness.—Sir Peter, there's nothing in the world so noble as a man of sentiment! (*Exit.*)

JOSEPH SURFACE.

Sir Peter, notwithstanding I confess that appearances are against me, if you will afford me your patience, I make no doubt but I shall explain everything to your satisfaction. 440

SIR PETER.

If you please, sir.

JOSEPH SURFACE.

The fact is, sir—that Lady Teazle, knowing my pretensions to your ward, Maria—I say, sir, Lady Teazle being apprehensive of the jealousy of your temper and knowing my friendship to the family—she, sir, I say, called here, in order that I might explain those pretensions—but on your coming, being apprehensive as I said of your jealousy—she withdrew—and this, you may depend on't, is the whole truth of the matter. 445 450

SIR PETER.

A very clear account upon my word, and I dare swear the lady will vouch for every article of it.

LADY TEAZLE.

For not one word of it, Sir Peter. 455

SIR PETER.

How! Don't you think it worthwhile to agree in the lie?

LADY TEAZLE.

There is not one syllable of truth in what that gentleman has told you.

SIR PETER.

I believe you, upon my soul, madam. 460

JOSEPH SURFACE.

'Sdeath,* madam, will you betray me?

LADY TEAZLE.

Good Mr. Hypocrite, by your leave, I will speak for myself.

SIR PETER.

Aye, let her alone, sir; you'll find she'll make a better story than you without prompting. 465

LADY TEAZLE.

Hear me, Sir Peter, I came hither on no matter relating to your ward and even ignorant of this gentleman's pretensions to her. But I came here seduced by his insidious arguments, at least to listen to his pretended passion, if not to sacrifice your honor to his baseness. 470

SIR PETER.

Now I believe the truth is coming indeed.

JOSEPH SURFACE.

The woman's mad.

LADY TEAZLE.

No sir, she has recovered her senses, and your own arts have furnished her with the means.—Sir Peter, I do not expect you to credit me, but the tenderness you expressed for me, when I'm sure you could not think I was a witness to it, has penetrated so to my heart that, had I left the place without the shame of the discovery, my future life should have spoken the sincerity of my gratitude. As for that smoothed-tongue hypocrite, who would have seduced the wife of his too credulous friend while he affected honorable addresses to his ward, I behold him now in a light so truly despicable that I never again shall respect myself for having listened to him. (*Exit.*) 475 480 485

JOSEPH SURFACE.

Notwithstanding all this, Sir Peter, Heaven knows—

SIR PETER.

That you are a villain, and so I leave you to your conscience. 490

JOSEPH SURFACE.

You are too rash, Sir Peter—you shall hear me— the man who shuts out conviction by refusing to—

SIR PETER.

Oh, damn your sentiment!^t

Exeunt.

Act V, scene. i. A library.

Enter Joseph Surface and servant.

JOSEPH SURFACE.

Mr. Stanley! and why should you think I would see him? You must know he comes to ask something.

SERVANT.

Sir, I should not have let him in, but that Mr. Rowley came to the door with him. 5

JOSEPH SURFACE.

Pshaw! Blockhead! To suppose that I should now

be in a temper to receive visits from poor relations! Well, why don't you show the fellow up?

SERVANT.

I will, sir. Why sir, it wasn't my fault that Sir Peter discovered my lady. (*Exit.*) 10

JOSEPH SURFACE.

Go, fool. Sure, Fortune never played a man of my policy such a trick before. My character* with Sir Peter, my hopes with Maria, destroyed in a moment! I am in a rare humor to listen to other people's distresses! I shan't be able to bestow even a benevo- 15 lent sentiment on Stanley.—Oh, here he comes, and Rowley with him. I must try to recover myself and put a little charity into my face, however. (*Exit.*)

Enter Sir Oliver and Rowley.

SIR OLIVER.

What, does he avoid us? That was he, was it not?

ROWLEY.

It was, sir, but I doubt* you are come a little^u too 20 abruptly. His nerves are so weak that the sight of a poor relation may be too much for him. I should have gone first to break you to him.

SIR OLIVER.

A plague of his nerves! Yet this is he whom Sir Peter extols as a man of the most benevolent way 25 of thinking.

ROWLEY.

As to his way of thinking, I cannot pretend to decide, for to do him justice, he appears to have as much speculative benevolence as any private gentleman in the kingdom, though he is seldom so 30 sensual as to indulge himself in the exercise of it.

SIR OLIVER.

Yet has a string of charitable sentiments, I suppose, at his fingers' ends.

ROWLEY.

Or rather at his tongue's end, Sir Oliver, for I believe there is no sentiment he has more faith in 35 than that "Charity begins at home."

SIR OLIVER.

And his, I presume, is of that domestic sort, it never stirs abroad at all.

ROWLEY.

I doubt* you'll find it so. But he's coming. I must not seem to interrupt you, and you know, 40 immediately as you leave him, I come in to announce your arrival in your real character.

SIR OLIVER.

True, and afterwards you'll meet me at Sir Peter's.

ROWLEY.

Without losing a moment. (*Exit.*)

SIR OLIVER.

So! I don't like the complaisance of his features. 45

Enter Joseph Surface.

JOSEPH SURFACE.

Sir, I beg you ten thousand pardons for keeping you a moment waiting. Mr. Stanley, I presume?

SIR OLIVER.

At your service, sir.

JOSEPH SURFACE.

Sir, I beg you will do me the honor to sit down. I entreat you, sir. 50

SIR OLIVER.

Dear sir, there's no occasion. (*Aside.*) Too civil by half.

JOSEPH SURFACE.

I have not the pleasure of knowing you, Mr. Stanley, but I am extremely happy to see you look so well. You were nearly related to my mother, Mr. 55 Stanley, I think?

SIR OLIVER.

I was, sir, so nearly that my present poverty, I fear, may do discredit to her wealthy children, else I should not have presumed to trouble you.

JOSEPH SURFACE.

Dear sir, there needs no apology. He that is in 60 distress, though a stranger, has a right to claim kindred with the wealthy. I'm sure I wish I was of that class and had it in my power to offer you even a small relief.

SIR OLIVER.

If your uncle Sir Oliver was here, I should have a 65 friend.

JOSEPH SURFACE.

I wish he was, sir, with all my heart. You should not want* an advocate with him, believe me Sir.

SIR OLIVER.

I should not need one; my distresses would recommend me. But I imagined his bounty had 70 enabled you to become the agent of his charity.

JOSEPH SURFACE.

My dear sir, you are strangely misinformed. Sir
Oliver is a worthy man, a very worthy sort of a man,
but avarice, Mr. Stanley, is the vice of the age. I will
tell you, my good sir, in confidence, what he has   75
done for me has been a mere nothing, though
people, I know, have thought otherwise, and for my
part, I never chose to contradict the report.

SIR OLIVER.

What! Has he never transmitted you bullion,
rupees, pagodas?²¹   80

JOSEPH SURFACE.

Oh dear sir! Nothing of the kind. No, no, a few presents now and then, china, shawls, congou tea, avadavats,²² and India crackers, little more, believe me.

SIR OLIVER. [*Aside.*]

Here's gratitude for twelve thousand pounds!
Avadavats and India crackers!   85

JOSEPH SURFACE.

Then, my dear sir, you have heard, I doubt not,
of the extravagance of my brother; there are very
few would credit what I have done for that
unfortunate young man.

SIR OLIVER. (*Aside.*)

Not I, for one.   90

JOSEPH SURFACE.

The sums I have lent him— Indeed I have been exceedingly to blame. It was an amiable weakness, however. I don't pretend to defend it, and now I feel it
doubly culpable since it has deprived me of the power
of serving you, Mr. Stanley, as my heart directs.   95

SIR OLIVER. [*Aside.*]

Dissembler!—Then, sir, you cannot assist me.

JOSEPH SURFACE.

At present it grieves me to say I cannot, but
whenever I have the ability, you may depend upon
hearing from me.

SIR OLIVER.

I am extremely sorry—   100

JOSEPH SURFACE.

Not more than I am, believe me; to pity without

the power to relieve is still* more painful than to
ask and be denied.

SIR OLIVER.

Kind sir, your most obedient humble servant.

JOSEPH SURFACE.

You leave me deeply affected, Mr. Stanley—   105
William, be ready to open the door.

SIR OLIVER.

Oh dear sir, no ceremony!

JOSEPH SURFACE.

Your very obedient.

SIR OLIVER.

Sir, your most obsequious.

JOSEPH SURFACE.

You may depend upon hearing from me, whenever   110
I can be of service.

SIR OLIVER.

Sweet sir, you are too good.

JOSEPH SURFACE.

In the meantime, I wish you health and spirits.

SIR OLIVER.

Your ever grateful and perpetual humble servant.

JOSEPH SURFACE.

Sir, yours as sincerely.   115

SIR OLIVER.

Now I'm satisfied. (*Exit.*)

JOSEPH SURFACE.

This is one of the bad effects of a good character.*
It invites application from the unfortunate, and
there needs no small degree of address to gain the
reputation of benevolence without incurring the   120
expense. The silver ore of pure charity is an
expensive article in the catalog of a man's good
qualities, whereas the sentimental French plate I
use instead of it makes just as good a show and
pays no tax.   125

Enter Rowley.

ROWLEY.

Mr. Surface, your servant. I was apprehensive of
interrupting you, though my business demands
immediate action, as this note will inform you.

JOSEPH SURFACE.

Always happy to see Mr. Rowley. (*Aside.*) A
rascal!ᵛ—How! Sir Oliver Surface, my uncle,   130
arrived!

---

21 pagodas] gold (less commonly silver) coins formerly current in Southern India (*OED*)

22 avadavats] corruption of amadavats, Indian song-birds
(*OED*)

ROWLEY.

He is indeed—we have just parted—quite well
after a speedy voyage, and impatient to embrace
his worthy nephew.

JOSEPH SURFACE.

I am astonished!—William, stop Mr. Stanley if he's   135
not gone.

ROWLEY.

Oh he's out of reach, I believe.

JOSEPH SURFACE.

Why didn't you let me know this when you came
in together?

ROWLEY.

I thought you had particular business, but I must   140
be gone to inform your brother and appoint him
here to meet his uncle. He will be with you in a
quarter of an hour.

JOSEPH SURFACE.

So he says. Well, I'm strangely overjoyed at his
coming. (*Aside.*) Never was anything, to be sure,   145
so damned unlucky.

ROWLEY.

You will be delighted to see how well he looks.

JOSEPH SURFACE.

Oh, I am rejoiced to hear it. (*Aside.*) Just at this time.

ROWLEY.

I will tell him how impatient you expect him.
(*Exit.*)   150

JOSEPH SURFACE.

Do, do, pray give my best duty and affection.—
Indeed, I cannot express the sensations I feel at the
thought of seeing him. Certainly his coming just
at this time is the cruellest piece of ill fortune.

Exit.

Scene ii. Sir Peter Teazle's house.

Enter Mrs. Candor and maid.

MAID.

Indeed, ma'am, my lady will see nobody at present.

MRS. CANDOR.

Did you tell her it was her friend, Mrs. Candor?

MAID.

Yes ma'am, but she begs you will excuse her.

MRS. CANDOR.

Do go again. I shall be glad to see her only for a

moment, for I'm sure she must be in great distress.   5

Exit maid.

Dear heart, how provoking! I'm not mistress of half
the circumstances. We shall have the whole affair
in the newspapers with the names of the parties
at full length before I have dropped the story at a
dozen houses.   10

Enter Sir Benjamin Backbite.

Oh dear, Sir Benjamin! You have heard I
suppose—

SIR BENJAMIN.

Of Lady Teazle and Mr. Surface.

MRS. CANDOR.

And Sir Peter's discovery.

SIR BENJAMIN.

Oh, the strangest piece of business, to be sure!   15

MRS. CANDOR.

Well, I never was so surprised in my life. I am sorry
for all parties indeed!

SIR BENJAMIN.

Now, I don't pity Sir Peter at all; he was so
extravagantly partial to Mr. Surface.

MRS. CANDOR.

Mr. Surface! Why, 'twas with Charles Lady Teazle   20
was detected.

SIR BENJAMIN.

No such thing. Mr. Surface is the gallant.

MRS. CANDOR.

No, no, Charles is the man. 'Twas Mr. Surface
brought Sir Peter on purpose to discover them.

SIR BENJAMIN.

I tell you I have it from one—   25

MRS. CANDOR.

And I have it from one—

SIR BENJAMIN.

Who had it form one—who had it—

MRS. CANDOR.

From one immediately—but here's Lady Sneerwell;
perhaps she knows the whole affair.

Enter Lady Sneerwell.

LADY SNEERWELL.

So my dear Mrs. Candor, here's a sad affair of our   30
friend Teazle.

MRS. CANDOR.

Aye, my dear friend, who could have thought it.

LADY SNEERWELL.

Well, there's no trusting to appearances, though indeed she was always too lively for me.

MRS. CANDOR.   35

To be sure, her manners were a little too free, but she was very young.

LADY SNEERWELL.

And had indeed some good qualities.

MRS. CANDOR.

She had indeed—but have you heard the particulars?   40

LADY SNEERWELL.

No, but everybody says that Mr. Surface—

SIR BENJAMIN.

Aye, there I told you, Mr. Surface was the man.

MRS. CANDOR.

No, no indeed, the assignation was with Charles.

LADY SNEERWELL.

With Charles! You alarm me, Mrs. Candor.

MRS. CANDOR.

Yes, yes, he was the lover; Mr. Surface, to do him   45
justice, was only the informer.

SIR BENJAMIN.

Well, I'll not dispute with you, Mrs. Candor. Be it which it may, I hope that Sir Peter's wound will not—

MRS. CANDOR.

Sir Peter's wound! Oh mercy, I did not hear a word of their fighting.   50

LADY SNEERWELL.

Nor I a syllable.

SIR BENJAMIN.

No! What, no mention of the duel!

MRS. CANDOR.

Not a word.

SIR BENJAMIN.

Oh Lord! Yes, yes, they fought before they left the room.   55

LADY SNEERWELL.

Pray, let us hear.

MRS. CANDOR.

Aye, do oblige us with the duel.

SIR BENJAMIN.

"Sir," says Sir Peter, immediately after the discovery, "you are a most ungrateful fellow"—

MRS. CANDOR.

Aye, to Charles.   60

SIR BENJAMIN.

No, no, to Mr. Surface—"a most ungrateful fellow, and old as I am, sir," says he, "I insist on immediate satisfaction."

MRS. CANDOR.

Aye, that must have been to Charles, for 'tis very unlikely Mr. Surface should go fight in his own   65
house.

SIR BENJAMIN.

Gad's life, madam, not at all—"giving me immediate satisfaction"—on this, madam, Lady Teazle, seeing Sir Peter in such danger, ran out of the room in strong hysterics and Charles after her,   70
calling for hartshorn and water; then madam, they began to fight with swords—

Enter Crabtree.

CRABTREE.

With pistols, Nephew, I have it from undoubted authority.

MRS. CANDOR.

Oh Mr. Crabtree, then it's all true.   75

CRABTREE.

Too true indeed, ma'am, and Sir Peter is dangerously wounded.

SIR BENJAMIN.

By a thrust in segoon,[23] quite through his left side.

CRABTREE.

By a bullet lodged in the thorax.

MRS. CANDOR.

Mercy on me, poor Sir Peter!   80

CRABTREE.

Yes ma'am, though Charles would have avoided the matter if he could.

MRS. CANDOR.

I knew Charles was the person.

SIR BENJAMIN.

My uncle, I see, knows nothing of the matter.

CRABTREE.

But Sir Peter taxed him with the basest ingratitude.   85

SIR BENJAMIN.

That I told you, you know.

---

23 segoon] seconde, a fencing term for the second of the seven classic thrusts (*OED*)

CRABTREE.

Do, Nephew, let me speak—and insisted on immediate satisfaction.

SIR BENJAMIN.

Just as I said.

CRABTREE.

'Odd's* life! Nephew, allow others to know 90 something too—a pair of pistols lay on the bureau (for Mr. Surface, it seems, had come the night before late from Salt Hill where he had been to see the Montem[24] with a friend who has a son at Eton), so unluckily the pistols were left charged. 95

SIR BENJAMIN.

I heard nothing of this.

CRABTREE.

Sir Peter forced Charles to take one, and they fired, it seems, pretty nearly together; Charles's shot took place as I tell you, and Sir Peter's missed. But what is very extraordinary, the ball struck against a little 100 bronze Shakespeare[w] that stood over the chimneypiece, grazed out of the window at a right angle, and wounded the postman, who was just coming to the door with a double letter[25] from Northamptonshire. 105

SIR BENJAMIN.

My uncle's account is more circumstantial, I must confess—but I believe mine is the true one for all that.

LADY SNEERWELL. [*Aside.*]

I am more interested in this affair than they imagine and must have better information. (*Exit.*) 110

SIR BENJAMIN.

Ah! Lady Sneerwell's alarm is very easily accounted for.

CRABTREE.

Yes, yes, they certainly *do* say— but that's neither here nor there.

MRS. CANDOR.

But pray, where is Sir Peter at present? 115

CRABTREE.

Oh, they brought him home, and he is now in the house, though the servants are ordered to deny it.

MRS. CANDOR.

I believe so, and Lady Teazle, I suppose, attending him.

CRABTREE.

Yes, yes, I saw one of the Faculty[26] enter just before 120 me.

SIR BENJAMIN.

Hey! Who comes here?

CRABTREE.

Oh this is he! Physician, depend on't.

MRS. CANDOR.

Oh certainly, it must be the physician—and now we shall know. 125

Enter Sir Oliver.

CRABTREE.

Well, Doctor, what hopes?

MRS. CANDOR.

Aye Doctor, how's your patient?

SIR BENJAMIN.

Now Doctor, isn't it a wound with a small sword?

CRABTREE.

A bullet lodged in the thorax, for a hundred.

SIR OLIVER.

Doctor! A wound with a small sword and a bullet 130 in the thorax! What, are you mad, good people?

SIR BENJAMIN.

Perhaps, sir, you are not a doctor?

SIR OLIVER.

Truly, I am to thank you for my degrees if I am.

CRABTREE.

Only a friend of Sir Peter's then, I presume. But sir, you must have heard of his accident? 135

SIR OLIVER.

Not a word.

CRABTREE.

Not of his being dangerously wounded?

SIR OLIVER.

The devil he is!

---

24 Montem] festival wherein the scholars of Eton would go in fancy costumes to "Salt Hill," a mound near Slough, and there collect money from the bystanders (*OED*)

25 double letter] a letter written on two sheets and charged double postage (*OED*)

26 Faculty] of the medical profession (in popular language 'The Faculty') (*OED*)

SIR BENJAMIN.

Run through the body!

CRABTREE.

Shot in the breast. 140

SIR BENJAMIN.

By one Mr. Surface.

CRABTREE.

Aye, by the younger.

SIR OLIVER.

Hey! What the plague! You seem to differ strangely in your accounts. However, you agree that Sir Peter is dangerously wounded? 145

SIR BENJAMIN.

Oh yes, we agree in that.

CRABTREE.

Yes, yes, I believe there can be no doubt of that.

SIR OLIVER.

Then upon my word, for a person in that situation, he is the most imprudent man alive, for here he comes walking as if nothing at all was the 150 matter.

Enter Sir Peter.

'Odd's* heart! Sir Peter, you are come in good time, I promise you, for we had just given you over.

SIR BENJAMIN.

Egad Uncle, this is the most sudden recovery—

SIR OLIVER.

Why man, what do you do out of your bed, with 155 a small sword through your body and a bullet lodged in your thorax?

SIR PETER.

A small sword and a bullet?

SIR OLIVER.

Aye, these gentlemen would have killed you without law or physic and wanted to dub me a 160 doctor to make me an accomplice.

SIR PETER.

Why, what is all this?

SIR BENJAMIN.

We rejoice, Sir Peter, that the story of the duel is not true and are sincerely sorry for your other misfortunes. 165

SIR PETER. [*Aside.*]

So, it's all over the Town already.

CRABTREE.

Though, Sir Peter, you were certainly vastly to blame to marry at all at your years.

SIR PETER.

What business is that of yours, sir?

MRS. CANDOR.

Though indeed, as Sir Peter made so good a 170 husband, he's very much to be pitied.

SIR PETER.

Plague on your pity, ma'am, I desire none of it.

SIR BENJAMIN.

However, Sir Peter, you mustn't mind the laughing and jests you will meet with on the occasion.

SIR PETER.

Sir, I desire to be master of my own house. 175

CRABTREE.

'Tis no uncommon case—that's one comfort.

SIR PETER.

I insist on being left to myself; without ceremony, I insist on your leaving my house directly.

MRS. CANDOR.

Well, well, we are going—and depend on't, we'll make the best report of you we can. 180

SIR PETER.

Leave my house.

CRABTREE.

And tell how hard you have been treated.

SIR PETER.

Leave my house.

SIR BENJAMIN.

And how patiently you bear it.

SIR PETER.

Leave my house— 185

Exeunt Mrs. Candor, Sir Benjamin, and Crabtree.

Fiends! Vipers! Furies! Oh that their own venom would choke them.

SIR OLIVER.

They are very provoking indeed, Sir Peter.

Enter Rowley.

ROWLEY.

I heard high words. What has ruffled you, Sir Peter? 190

SIR PETER.

Pshaw! What signifies asking? Do I ever pass a day without my vexations?

SIR OLIVER.

Well, I'm not inquisitive. I come only to tell you that I have seen both my nephews in the manner we proposed. 195

SIR PETER.

A precious* couple they are!

ROWLEY.

Yes, and Sir Oliver is convinced that your judgement was right, Sir Peter.

SIR OLIVER.

Yes, I find Joseph is indeed the man after all.

ROWLEY.

Aye, as Sir Peter says, he's a man of sentiment. 200

SIR OLIVER.

And acts up to the sentiments he professes.

ROWLEY.

It's certainly edification to hear him talk!

SIR OLIVER.

Oh, he's a model for the young men of the age! But how's this, Sir Peter? You don't join in your friend Joseph's praise, as I expected. 205

SIR PETER.

Sir Oliver, we live in a damned, wicked world, and the fewer we praise, the better.

ROWLEY.

What, do you say so, Sir Peter, who never were mistaken in your life?

SIR PETER.

Pshaw! Plague on you both. I see by your sneering 210 you have heard the whole affair. I shall go mad among you.

ROWLEY.

Then, to fret you no longer, Sir Peter, we are indeed acquainted with it all. I met Lady Teazle coming from Mr. Surface's so humbled that she 215 deigned to request me to be her advocate with you.

SIR PETER.

And does Sir Oliver know all too?

SIR OLIVER.

Every circumstance.

SIR PETER.

What, of the closet—and the screen, hey?

SIR OLIVER.

Yes, yes, and the little French milliner! Oh, I have 220 been vastly diverted with the story—ha, ha!

SIR PETER.

'Twas very pleasant.

SIR OLIVER.

I never laughed more in my life, I assure you, ha, ha, ha!

SIR PETER.

Oh, vastly diverting, ha, ha, ha! 225

ROWLEY.

To be sure, Joseph with his sentiments—ha, ha, ha!

SIR PETER.

Yes, yes, his sentiments—ha, ha, ha! A hypocritical villain!

SIR OLIVER.

Aye, and that rogue Charles to pull Sir Peter out 230 of the closet—ha, ha, ha!

SIR PETER.

Ha, ha!—'twas devilish entertaining, to be sure.

SIR OLIVER.

Ha, ha! Egad, Sir Peter, I should like to have seen your face when the screen was thrown down—ha, ha, ha! 235

SIR PETER.

Yes, yes, my face when the screen was thrown down—ha, ha! Oh, I must never show my head again.

SIR OLIVER.

But come, come, it isn't fair to laugh at you neither, my old friend, though upon my soul I can't help it. 240

SIR PETER.

Oh pray, don't restrain your mirth on my account; it doesn't hurt me at all. I laugh at the whole affair myself. Yes, yes, I think being a standing jest for all one's acquaintances a very happy situation. Oh yes, and then of a morning to read the paragraphs 245 about Lady T. and Sir P.ˣ will be so entertaining. I shall certainly leave town tomorrow and never look mankind in the face again.ʸ

ROWLEY.

Without affectation, Sir Peter, you may despise the ridicule of fools. But I see Lady Teazle going 250 towards the next room; I am sure you must desire a reconciliation as much as she does.

SIR OLIVER.

Perhaps my being here prevents her coming to you. Well, I'll leave honest Rowley to mediate between

you—but he must bring you all presently to Mr. 255
Surface's, where I am now returning, if not to
reclaim a libertine, at least to expose hypocrisy.
(*Exit.*)

SIR PETER.

Ah! I'll be present at your discovering* yourself
there with all my heart, though 'tis a vile, unlucky 260
place for discoveries.

ROWLEY.

We'll follow.

SIR PETER.

She's not coming here, you see, Rowley.

ROWLEY.

No. But she has left the door of that room open,
you perceive. She's in tears. 265

SIR PETER.

Certainly a little mortification appears very
becoming in a wife. Don't you think 'twill do her
good to let her pine a little?

ROWLEY.

Oh! This is ungenerous in you.

SIR PETER.

Well, I know not what to think. You remember, 270
Rowley, the letter I found of hers evidently
intended for Charles.

ROWLEY.

Oh mere forgery, Sir Peter, laid in your way on
purpose; this is one of the points I intend Snake
shall give you conviction on. 275

SIR PETER.

I wish I was once satisfied of that.—She looks this
way. What a remarkably elegant turn of the head
she has.—Rowley, I'll go to her.

ROWLEY.

Certainly.

SIR PETER.

Though when 'tis known we are reconciled, people 280
will laugh at me ten times more.

ROWLEY.

Let them laugh, and retort their malice only by
showing you are happy in spite of it.

SIR PETER.

I'faith, so I will, and if I am not mistaken we may
be the happiest couple in the country. 285

ROWLEY.

Nay Sir Peter, he who once lays aside suspicion—

SIR PETER.

Hold, Master Rowley! If you have any regard for
me, never let me hear you utter anything like a
sentiment. I have had enough of *them* to serve me
the rest of my life. 290

Exeunt.

Scene iii. The library.

Enter Joseph Surface and Lady Sneerwell.

LADY SNEERWELL.

Impossible! Will not Sir Peter immediately be
reconciled to Charles and of consequence no
longer oppose his union with Maria? The thought
is distraction to me.

JOSEPH SURFACE.

Can passion furnish a remedy? 5

LADY SNEERWELL.

No, nor cunning either. Oh, I was a fool! an idiot!
to league with such a blunderer.

JOSEPH SURFACE.

Sure Lady Sneerwell, I am the greatest sufferer, yet
you see I bear the accident with calmness.

LADY SNEERWELL.

Because the disappointment doesn't reach your 10
heart; your interest only attached you to Maria.
Had you felt for her what I have felt for that
ungrateful libertine, neither your temper nor
hypocrisy could prevent your showing the
sharpness of your vexation. 15

JOSEPH SURFACE.

But why should your reproaches fall on me for this
disappointment?

LADY SNEERWELL.

Are you not the cause of it? What had you to do to
bate in your pursuit of Maria, to pervert Lady Teazle
by the way? Had you not a sufficient field for your 20
roguery in blinding Sir Peter and supplanting your
brother? I hate such an avarice of crimes; 'tis an
unfair monopoly and never prospers.

JOSEPH SURFACE.

Well, I admit I have been to blame. I confess I have
deviated from the direct road of wrong, but I don't 25
think we are so totally defeated either.

LADY SNEERWELL.

No?

JOSEPH SURFACE.

You tell me you have made a trial of Snake since we met and that you still believe him faithful to us? 30

LADY SNEERWELL.

I do believe so.

JOSEPH SURFACE.

And that he has undertaken, should it be necessary, to swear and prove that Charles is at this time contracted by vows and honor to your ladyship, which some of his former letters to you will serve 35 to support.

LADY SNEERWELL.

This indeed might have assisted.

JOSEPH SURFACE.

Come, come, it is not too late yet.

Knocking.

But hark! This is probably my uncle, Sir Oliver. Retire to that room and we'll consult farther when 40 he's gone.

LADY SNEERWELL.

I have^z no diffidence of your abilities, only to be constant to one roguery at a time. (*Exit.*)

JOSEPH SURFACE.

I will, I will— So, 'tis confounded hard after such bad fortune to be baited by one's confederate in 45 evil. Well, at all events my character is so much better than Charles's that I certainly— Hey! What! This is not Sir Oliver but old Stanley again. Plague on't that he should return to tease me just now. We shall have Sir Oliver come and find him here 50 and—

Enter Sir Oliver.

Gad's life, Mr. Stanley, you have come back to plague me at this time? You must not stay, upon my word.

SIR OLIVER.

Sir, I hear your uncle Sir Oliver is expected here, 55 and though he has been so penurious to you, I'll try what he will do for me.

JOSEPH SURFACE.

Sir, 'tis impossible for you to stay now. So I must beg you, come any other time, and I promise you, you shall be assisted. 60

SIR OLIVER.

No. Sir Oliver and I must be acquainted.

JOSEPH SURFACE.

Zounds sir, then I insist on your quitting the room directly.

SIR OLIVER.

Nay sir—

JOSEPH SURFACE.

Sir, I insist on't.—Here William, show this 65 gentleman out.—Since you compel me, sir—not one moment—this is such insolence—

Enter Charles.

CHARLES.

Heyday! What's the matter? What the devil, have you got hold of my little broker here? Zounds, don't hurt little Premium! What's the matter, my 70 little fellow?

JOSEPH SURFACE.

So he has been with you too, has he?

CHARLES.

To be sure he has. Why, 'tis as honest a little— But sure, Joseph, you have not been borrowing money too, have you? 75

JOSEPH SURFACE.

Borrowing! No. But Brother, you know here we expect Sir Oliver every—

CHARLES.

Oh gad! That's true. Noll musn't find the little broker here, to be sure.

JOSEPH SURFACE.

Yet Mr. Stanley insists— 80

CHARLES.

Stanley! Why, his name is Premium.

JOSEPH SURFACE.

No, no, Stanley.

CHARLES.

No, no, Premium.

JOSEPH SURFACE.

Well, no matter which—but—

CHARLES.

Aye, aye, Stanley or Premium, 'tis the same thing, as 85 you say, for I suppose he goes by half an hundred names, besides A and B at the coffee house.

Knocking.

JOSEPH SURFACE.

'Sdeath!* Here's Sir Oliver at the door. Now I beg, Mr. Stanley—

CHARLES.

Aye, aye, and I beg, Mr. Premium—   90

SIR OLIVER.

Gentlemen—

JOSEPH SURFACE.

Sir, by Heaven you shall go.

CHARLES.

Aye, out with him certainly.

SIR OLIVER.

This violence—

JOSEPH SURFACE.

'Tis your own fault.   95

CHARLES.

Out with him to be sure.

Both forcing Sir Oliver out. Enter Sir Peter, Lady Teazle, Maria and Rowley.

SIR PETER.

My old friend, Sir Oliver, hey! What in the name of wonder! Here are dutiful nephews! assault their uncle at the first visit.

LADY TEAZLE.

Indeed, Sir Oliver, 'twas well we came in to rescue   100
you.

ROWLEY.

Truly it was, for I perceive, Sir Oliver, the character of Old Stanley was not a protection to you.

SIR OLIVER.

No, nor of Premium either: the necessities of the   105
former couldn't extort a shilling from that benevolent gentleman, and with the other I stood a chance of faring worse than my ancestors and being knocked down without being bid for.

JOSEPH SURFACE.

Charles!   110

CHARLES.

Joseph!

JOSEPH SURFACE.

'Tis now complete.

CHARLES.

Very.

SIR OLIVER.

Sir Peter, my friend, and Rowley too, look on that

elder nephew of mine. You know what he has   115
already received from my bounty, and you know also how gladly I would have regarded half my fortune as held in trust for him. Judge then my disappointment in discovering him to be destitute of truth, charity, and gratitude.   120

SIR PETER.

Sir Oliver, I should be more surprised at this declaration if I had not myself found him to be selfish, treacherous, and hypocritical.

LADY TEAZLE.

And if the gentleman pleads not guilty to these, pray let him call me to his character.*   125

SIR PETER.

Then I believe we need add no more. If he knows himself, he will consider it as the most perfect punishment that he is known by the world.

CHARLES. [*Aside.*]

If they talk this way to honesty, what will they say to me by and by?   130

SIR OLIVER.

As for that prodigal his brother there—

CHARLES. [*Aside.*]

Aye, now comes my turn—the damned family pictures will ruin me.

JOSEPH SURFACE.

Sir Oliver! Uncle! If you will honor me with a hearing.   135

SIR OLIVER. (*Turns from him with contempt.*)

Psha!

CHARLES. (*Aside.*)

Now if Joseph would make one of his long speeches, I might recollect myself a little.

SIR OLIVER.

I suppose you would undertake to justify yourself entirely.   140

JOSEPH SURFACE.

I trust I could.

SIR OLIVER.

Pshaw. Nay, if you desert your roguery in its distress and try to be justified, you have even less principle than I thought you had.aa (*To Charles.*) Well sir, and you could justify yourself yourself too,   145
I suppose.

CHARLES.

Not that I know of, Sir Oliver.

SIR OLIVER.

What, little Premium has been let too much into the secret, I presume.

CHARLES.

True, sir, but they were family secrets and should never be mentioned again, you know. 150

ROWLEY.

Come, Sir Oliver, I know you cannot speak of Charles's follies with anger.

SIR OLIVER.

'Odd's* heart! No more I can, nor with gravity either.—Sir Peter, do you know the rogue 155 bargained with me for all his ancestors: sold me judges and generals by the foot, and maiden aunts as cheap as broken china.

CHARLES.

To be sure, Sir Oliver, I did make free with the family canvas, that's the truth on't; my ancestors 160 may certainly rise in evidence against me, there's no denying. But believe me sincere when I tell you, and upon my soul I would not say it if it was not, that, if I do not appear mortified at the exposure of my follies, it is because I feel at this moment 165 the warmest satisfaction in seeing *you*, my liberal benefactor.

SIR OLIVER.

Charles, I believe you, give me your hand: the ill-looking little fellow over the settee has made your peace. 170

CHARLES.

Then sir, my gratitude to the original is still increased.

LADY TEAZLE.

Yet I believe, Sir Oliver, there is one whom Charles is still more anxious to be reconciled to.

SIR OLIVER.

Oh, I have heard of his attachment there, and with 175 the young lady's pardon, if I construe right that blush—

SIR PETER.

Well, child,* speak your sentiments.

MARIA.

Sir, I have little to say but that I shall rejoice to hear that he is happy; for me, whatever claim I had 180 to his attention,bb I willingly resign it to one who has a better title.

CHARLES.

How Maria!

SIR PETER.

Heyday! What's the mystery now? While he appeared an incorrigible rake, you would give your 185 hand to no one else, and now that he's likely to reform, I warrant you won't have him.

MARIA.

His own heart and Lady Sneerwell's knows the cause.

CHARLES.

Lady Sneerwell! 190

JOSEPH SURFACE.

Brother, it is with great concern I am obliged to speak on this point, but my regard to justice obliges me, and Lady Sneerwell's injuries can no longer be concealed. (*Goes to the door.*)

Enter Lady Sneerwell.

ALL.

Lady Sneerwell!!!cc 195

SIR PETER.

So! Another French milliner. Egad, he has one in every room in the house, I suppose.

LADY SNEERWELL.

Ungrateful Charles! Well may you be surprised and feel for the indelicate situation which your perfidy has forced me into. 200

CHARLES.

Pray, Uncle, is this another plot of yours, for as I have life, I don't understand it.

JOSEPH SURFACE.

I believe, sir, there is but the evidence of one person more necessary to make it extremely clear.

SIR PETER.

And that person, I imagine, is Mr. Snake.— 205 Rowley, you were perfectly right to bring him with us, and pray let him appear.

ROWLEY.

Walk in, Mr. Snake.

Enter Snake.

I thought his testimony might be wanted;* however, it happens unluckily that he comes to 210 confront Lady Sneerwell and not to support her.

LADY SNEERWELL.

A villain! treacherous to me at last. Speak fellow, have you conspired against me?

SNAKE.

I beg your ladyship ten thousand pardons: You paid me extremely liberally for the lie in question, but I have unfortunately been offered double the sum to speak the truth. 215

SIR PETER.

Plot and counterplot.dd

LADY SNEERWELL.

The torments of shame and disappointment on you all. 220

LADY TEAZLE.

Hold, Lady Sneerwell, before you go, let me thank you for the trouble you and that gentleman have taken in writing letters to me from Charles and answering them yourself. And let me also request you to make my respects to the Scandalous 225 College, of which you are president, and inform them that Lady Teazle, licentiate, begs leave to return the diploma they granted her—as she leaves off practice and kills characters* no longer.

LADY SNEERWELL.

You too, madam—provoking—insolent—may 230 your husband live these fifty years. (*Exit*.)ee

LADY TEAZLE.

What a malicious creature it is!

SIR PETER.

Hey! What, not for her last wish?

LADY TEAZLE.

Oh, no.

SIR OLIVER.

Well sir, what have you to say now? 235

JOSEPH SURFACE.

Sir, I am so confounded that Lady Sneerwell could be guilty of suborning Mr. Snake in this manner to impose on us all that I know not what to say; however, lest her revengeful spirit should prompt her to injure my brother, I had certainly better 240 follow her directly. (*Exit*.)

SIR PETER.

Moral to the last drop.

SIR OLIVER.

Aye, and marry her, Joseph, if you can, oil and vinegar, egad you'll do very well together.

ROWLEY.

I believe we have no more occasion for Mr. Snake 245 at present.

SNAKE.

Before I go, I beg pardon once for all for whatever uneasiness I have been the humble instrument of causing to the parties present.

SIR PETER.

Well, well, you have made atonement by a good 250 deed at last.

SNAKE.

But I must request of the company that it shall never be known.

SIR PETER.

Hey! What the plague, are you ashamed of having done a right thing once in your life. 255

SNAKE.

Ah sir, consider I live by the badness of my character. I have nothing but my infamy to depend on, and if it were once known that I had been betrayed into an honest action, I should lose every friend I have in the world. (*Exit*.) 260

SIR PETER.

Here's a precious* rogue.ff

SIR OLIVER.

Well, well, we'll not traduce you by saying any thing to your praise, never fear.

LADY TEAZLE.

See, Sir Oliver, there needs no persuasion now to reconcile your nephew and Maria. 265

SIR OLIVER.

Aye, aye, that's as it should be, and egad, we'll have the wedding tomorrow morning.

CHARLES.

Thank you, my dear uncle.

SIR PETER.

What, you rogue! Don't you ask the girl's consent first? 270

CHARLES.

I have done that a long time—a minute—ago, and she looked—yes.

MARIA.

For shame, Charles.—I protest, Sir Peter, there has not been a word.

SIR OLIVER.

Well then, the fewer the better. May your love for 275

each other never know abatement.

SIR PETER.

And may you live as happily together as Lady Teazle and I—intend to do.

CHARLES.

Rowley, my old friend, I am sure you congratulate me, and I suspect that I owe you much.   280

SIR OLIVER.

You do indeed, Charles.

ROWLEY.

If my efforts to serve you had not succeeded, you would have been in my debt for the attempt, but deserve to be happy, and you overpay me.

SIR PETER.

Aye! Honest Rowley always said you would reform.   285

CHARLES.

Why as to reforming, Sir Peter, I'll make no promises—and that I take to be a proof that I intend to set about it. But here shall be my monitor, my gentle guide. Ah! can I leave the virtuous path those eyes illumine? (*To the*   290
audience.)

For thou, dear maid, shouldst waive thy beauty's sway.

Thou still* must rule because I will obey.

An humbled fugitive from folly view—

No sanctuary near but love and you.

You can indeed each anxious fear remove,   295

For even scandal dies if you approve.

[*Exeunt.*]

THE END.

Textual Notes

a Because of the complicated publishing history of the play, resulting from Sheridan's refusal to publish it, the copytext chosen is the 1799 Dublin edition (Du), which is generally regarded as being both accurate and complete. Also consulted were modern editions of 1939, revised 1969 (Nettleton, Case, and Stone—NCS) and of 1973 (Price), which is based on the Frampton Court, the Georgetown Crewe, the Second Crewe, the Buckinghamshire, and the Powell mss.

b reputation] Du; injured reputation NCS, Price

c while with Sir Peter … benevolence] Du; *om.* NCS, Price

d MARIA] Du, NCS; LADY SNEERWELL Price.

e his spirits: Sir Thomas Splint] Du; his Spirits—every body almost is in the same way—Lord Spindle, Sir Thomas Splint NCS, Price

f sermon] Du; novel NCS, Price

g turn. MRS. CANDOR.] Du; turn—she can sit for an hour to hear Lady Stucco talk sentiment. LADY TEAZLE. Nay, I vow Lady Stucco is very well with the dessert after dinner for she's just like the French fruit one cracks for mottoes—made up of paint and proverb. MRS. CANDOR. NCS, Price

h opinion … practices.] Du; opinion—nothing could—excuse the intemperance of their tongues but a natural and ungovernable bitterness of mind. NCS, Price

i every wife] Du; every London wife NCS, Price

j I … him] Du; I have done all I could for him NCS, Price

k If … dat] Du; If you ask him no more than that NCS, Price; only the Dublin edition has such speech patterns for Moses.

l trade. SIR OLIVER. Right, right!] Du; trade—but Moses—wouldn't you have him run out a little against the annuity Bill? That should be in character, I should think. MOSES. Very much. ROWLEY. And lament that a young man now must be at years of discretion before he is suffered to ruin himself? MOSES. Aye, great pity. SIR PETER. And abuse the public for allowing merit to an act whose only object is to snatch misfortune and imprudence from the rapacious relief of usury, and give the minor a chance of inheriting his estate without being undone by coming into possession. SIR OLIVER. So, so NCS, Price.

m neck. MOSES. But] Du; neck. TRIP. But then, Moses, it must be done before this d——d register takes place—one wouldn't like to have one's name made public you know. MOSES. No, certainly, but NCS, Price

n Deborah. This] Du; Deborah! Here now are two that were a sort of cousins of theirs.—You see, Moses, these pictures were done some time ago, when beaux wore wigs, and the ladies wore their own hair. SIR OLIVER. Yes, truly, head-dresses appear to have been a little lower in those days. CHARLES. Well, take that couple for the same. MOSES. 'Tis good bargain. CHARLES. Careless!—This NCS, Price

o pounds and take … in the lump. SIR OLIVER.] Du; pounds, for the rest of the family in the lump. CARELESS. Aye—aye—that will be the best way. SIR OLIVER. NCS, Price

p health. LADY TEAZLE. Why, if] health. LADY TEAZLE. So, so; then I perceive your prescription is, that I must sin in my own defence and part with my virtue to preserve my reputation? JOSEPH SURFACE. Exactly so, upon my credit, ma'am. LADY TEAZLE. Well, certainly this is the oddest doctrine, and the newest receipt for avoiding calumny? JOSEPH SURFACE. An infallible one, believe me. *Prudence*, like *experience*, must be paid for. LADY TEAZLE. Why, if NCS, Price

q baseness] Du; treachery NCS, Price

r has he?] Du; has he? Or what's worse has her ladyship discovered that she has an old husband? NCS, Price

s damnable] Du; horrible NCS, Price

t damn … sentiment!] Du; *om.* NCS, Price

u are … little] NCS, Price; Du illegible

v (*Aside.*) a rascal!] Du; *om.* NCS, Price

w Shakespeare] Du; Pliny NCS, Price

x Lady T. and Sir P.] Du; Mr. S—, Lady T—, and Sir P— NCS, Price

y I shall … again] Du; *om.* NCS, Price

z gone. LADY SNEERWELL. I have] Du; gone. LADY SNEERWELL. Well!—but if *he* should find you out too— JOSEPH SURFACE. Oh I have no fear of that. Sir Peter will hold his tongue for his own credit sake—and you may depend on't I shall soon discover Sir Oliver's weak side! LADY SNEERWELL. I have NCS, Price

aa nay … you had.] Du; *om.* NCS, Price

bb attention] Du; affection NCS, Price

cc ALL… . Sneerwell!!!] Du; *om.* NCS, Price

dd counterplot. LADY SNEERWELL.] Du; counterplot. Egad—I wish your ladyship joy of the success of your negotiation. LADY SNEERWELL. NCS, Price

ee years. (*Exit.*)] Du; years. Oons what a fury—] NCS, Price

ff rogue. SIR OLIVER.] Du; rogue—yet that fellow is a writer and a critic! SIR OLIVER. NCS, Price

Glossary

_____] blanks for actors to fill in, sometimes with words, sometimes with gestures, such as snapping their fingers, sometimes at their peril

'a] he

admire(ation)] wonder at, wonder; not: esteem

an, an if, an't] if, if it; not: the article

angel] angel noble, gold coin stamped with archangel Michael, worth about a half pound

Arratine/Aretino] Pietro Aretino (1492–1556), Italian poet, whose "Lewd Sonnets" (1524) were accompanied by scandalously erotic illustrations.

art] human contrivance, artifice; opposed to nature

awful] awe inspiring; not: terrible

baby] doll; not: infant

basset] card game, resembling faro; not: bandy-legged hound dog

Bear Garden] any of several sites for bear-baiting and other rough sports, also associated with theatrical performances, esp. on the South Bank of the Thames; lower-class folk were often in attendance, like butchers, but fashionable folk frequented them as well

begar] by god, "not a polite use" (*OED*)

bell] A church bell rings the morning of execution, when criminals—including traitors—are carted to the scaffold.

bill₁] bill of exchange

bill₂] list; bills were published (usually weekly) of all deaths in a parish, along with bills of births and baptisms.

Billingsgate] one of the gates to the city of London and the fish market thereby, known for its abusive language

birthday] referring to the monarch's birthday and its attendant celebration, at which ladies and gentlemen wore fine, new clothes

bite] cheat, flimflam; not: injure with teeth

black] usually dark haired, sometimes dark-skinned; not: racial category

bona roba] compliant woman, courtesan (literally, good gown)

bone] a reference to Eve's creation from Adam's rib; thus he calls her "bone of my bones, and flesh of my flesh" (Gen. 2:21–23)

brave(ly), braw(ly)] excellent(ly); not: courageous(ly)

brutal] animal; not: cruel

bubble] to cheat; victim of a cheat

bug] bogey; not: insect

canonical hours] hours when marriages could be legally performed (before noon)

cast] discarded

Cause (Good Old)] the effort to establish a commonwealth in mid-seventeenth-century England

chair, etc.] sedan, a portable chair borne by chairmen

Change] v. Exchange, New

character] description, as in a character sketch

chariot] light 4-wheel vehicle; not: ancient 2-wheel cart

Chateline's] a fashionable ordinary in Covent Garden*

Cheapside] a business district within the walls of London

Chedreux] fashionable Parisian wig-maker—or one of his products

chemist] alchemist (q.v.); also apothecary

child] term of affection for a young, usually noble, person; not: youngster

China orange] sweet, thin-skinned orange, a delicacy originally from China

cit(s), citizen(s)] inhabitant(s) of the City, usually derogatory

City] the old part of London within the walls, housing the financial district

clip] to shave edges of unmilled coins for the gold or silver

clog] shackles or encumbrance; not: shoe

closet] inner chamber of one's lodgings; not: a wardrobe

clown(ish)] rustic; not: comic pantomime

Commons, Doctors] College of Doctors of Civil Law in London, whose lawyers practiced both canon and civil law; they handled cases of separation and divorce in the ecclesiastical courts; also, where wills were registered

conversation] interchange with company, sometimes sexual intercourse; not limited to talk

corn] grain, e.g. wheat; not: maize

Covent Garden] during the Restoration, a fashionable residential area of the Town*; later, a somewhat disreputable area, haven to prostitutes; also location for a market

coy] shy; not: coquettish

crossbite] outcheat

crowd] fiddle

crown] English coin

cucumber] considered inedible by people in the eighteenth century and discarded

curious] skillfully made, precisely accurate; not: odd

cut (a caper)] to spring from the ground and, while in the air, to twiddle the feet one in front of the other alternately with great rapidity (*OED*)

dear] expensive; not: lovable

decide] figure out; not: come to a decision

Deel] Devil

demean] behave; not: lower (oneself)

despise] to regard as negligible, worthless; not: to loathe

die] to suffer *la petite mort* of sexual orgasm; not: to expire

discover] reveal; not: find

disguised] drunk; not: in masquerade

doubt] suspect or fear; not: call into question

Drawing Room] reception room at the royal palace

ears] Perjury and other offenses were sometimes punished by cutting off one or both of the perpetrator's ears.

en cavalier] in the manner of a fashionable gentleman, gallantly

engine] a tool, mechanical or human, often suspected to be sinister; not: motor

engineer] one who works with engines, often mines planted beneath walls to blow them up, usually with sexual connotations

English wife] proverbially (sexually) liberated

entertain] maintain, receive, or show hospitality to; not: amuse

enthusiasm, etc.] religious frenzy; not: eager interest

evidence] witness; not: material support of a case or testimony

Exchange, New] a meeting place for bankers and merchants, as well as a gallery of fashionable shops located on the Strand in London. The original Exchange burned down in the fire of 1666.

fack(s), fads, fags, fackins] colloquial for "faith"

family] servants or whole household; not: relatives

favor] token gift of remembrance, sometimes sexual; not: help

fit] pay back; not: make appropriate

Flanders] Part of the Spanish Netherlands in the seventeenth century, Flanders was nibbled at by other countries, especially France; noted for elegant lace and expensive coach horses.

fond(ness)] foolish(ness); not: amorous(ness)

fubb(s)] small, chubby person, term of endearment

furniture] livery; not: movables

geese] According to Roman legend, the cackling of the geese in Juno's temple saved the Capitol from invaders by warning the guards.

generous] highborn, demonstrating nobility; not: openhanded

gentle] of birth and its attendant worth; not: soft, kind

genius] attendant spirit, often associated with place (as in *genius loci*); not: inclination, penchant, or creative brilliance

glass] mirror; not: a receptacle for liquid or liquor

go to] a mild oath

gog] eagerness

great man] ironic epithet applied to Robert Walpole by his political opponents

groom-porter's] Until the office was abolished under George III, the groom-porter was a royal officer responsible for regulating gaming.

Grosvenor Square] large square, an eighteenth-century extension of the Town*

grumbletonian] derogatory nickname given to the Country Party by their adversaries at Court

half-seas-over] more than half drunk

heels, lie (lay one) by] manacle or put one in the stocks

hictius doctius] standard part of the magician's (juggler's) repertoire; perhaps from *hicce est doctus*—this is the doctor (Lat.).

his] a spurious spelling out of the meaning of *'s* noting possession

hogoe(s)] piquant, strong-smelling (dishes)—from French *de haut goût*, spicy

honest, -ty] chaste/chastity; not: truthfulness

horns] sign of a cuckold, supposedly sprouting from his forehead

hot-cockles] A game in which a player lay down blindfolded and then guessed who had hit him. Cockle is also a slang term for vagina.

humor, humorous, humorsome] (subject to) a permanent characteristic (from humours theory); not: a temporary state of mind or an ability to laugh

Hurlothumbro] eponymous hero of ridiculous farce by Samuel Johnson of Cheshire in 1729

husband] manager of economic affairs; not: spouse

Hyde Park] large fashionable park and promenade, with a track ("the Ring") for coaches; northwest of the more accessible Park* and Mall*

i'facks, etc.] v. facks

ill] unpropitious; not: sick

influence] specifically astrological influence

Inns of Court] Lincoln's, Middle Temple, Inner Temple, and Gray's: the residences of law students preparing for the bar

jerk] lash or cutting jibe; not: spasmodic motion (or foolish person)

jernie] a mild oath, from the much more profane French oath, *je renie dieu*: I renounce God

Jesuit's Powder] quinine

Jezabel] The shameless wife of King Ahab. In 2 Kings 9: 30–37, eunuchs throw her out of a window, her body eaten by dogs.

jill-flirt(ing)] a familiar, contemptuous term for a young woman or her dismissive behavior

jiminy] a mild oath, perhaps a corruption of *jesu domine*

joy] a term of endearment, often used by the Irish

keep(er)] support(er), especially a mistress; not: take custody of

Kensington] fashionable section west of London during the eighteenth century, noted for large mansions and private schools and Kensington Gardens, a large park that provided a fashionable promenade for wealthy citizens; until the reign of George III (1762) Kensington Palace was the center of court life.

kind, -ness] affection(ate)—often to the point of indulging sexual favors; not: sympathetic or helpful

lady] woman of title, not just gentlewoman

lie, give the] to *give the lie direct* was to call someone a liar unambiguously and thus to invite a duel

Lilly] William Lilly, popular astrologer

Locket's, Long's] fashionable ordinaries

lousy or lousey] have lice; not: inferior

Lucrece] virtuous Roman matron, was raped by Sextus Tarquinius and subsequently committed suicide; therefore, the emblem of marital chastity (her story is told in Lee's *Lucius Junius Brutus*)

Lud] euphemism for Lord; mild oath

lumber] surplus or disused articles; not: building material

luxury] lust and free living; not: rich abundance

Machiavel] unscrupulous villain, named after Niccolò Machiavelli for his *Prince*

main (chance)] term from hazard, a contemporary dice game similar to modern craps: used metaphorically to signify playing the odds

make love] pay court; not: copulate

Mall] v. Pall Mall

Marrabone] a corruption of Marylebone, an area northwest of London notorious for gambling and bowling

marry] a mild oath, by St. Mary; not: to wed

mask] woman wearing a visor, often a prostitute

mean] low; not: nasty

mere] no less than; not: no more than

millstone, see into] a proverbial (and ironic) claim to acuteness

month's mind] strong desire or inclination (of considerable duration)

mother, fit of the] hysteric attack

motion] acting or puppetry; not: movement

Mrs.] "Mistress," used for both married and unmarried women

mumping] moving the mouth spasmodically, as in nibbling, gumming

natural] *noun* fool or mistress; *adj.* illegitimate

naught] unworthy, bad, vile, naughty; not: nothing

never] ever

nightgown] robe or dressing gown; not: lingerie

nice, etc.] fastidious, delicate, or picky, sometimes foolish, wanton; not: the generalized term of approval

nose] damage to the nose (both upper and nether) was a common effect of syphilis

nouns] v. 'ouns

nown] contraction of mine own or just baby talk

obnoxious to] exposed to something extremely harmful or distasteful

'Od(d), 'Ud] corruption of God, a mild oath; used often in combination (v. 'sbud)

offer] threaten or gesture or start; not: propose

orange women, wenches] women who sell oranges, especially at plays—and often act as bawds

'oun(d)s ('oons, ou'z)] by Christ's wounds (a mild oath)

owl] proverbially stupid bird; not: wise

pad; padder, footpad] to steal; highway robber

Pall Mall] the Mall, a fashionable promenade in the Town*

Pantheon] In imitation of the temple at Rome, a pantheon was built in London in 1772 for musical entertainments.

Park] St. James's Park, the royal park adjacent to St. James's Palace, a fashionable place to walk

parole] promise; not: criminal surveillance

parts] personal qualities, talents; not: bodily members

patriot] honorific and self-righteous self-identification for Whigs

person] appearance; not: individual

perspective] telescope; not: point of view

pit] area on the "ground" in front of the stage, by this time having benches, notorious for noise, bawdry, assignations

pize] a softened version of "pox"

plantation] entire settlement in a new region (like the New World); not: individual estate

plate] silver (plated); not: dish

play] game, sport, gaming, gambling, or a gambit therein

postures] v. Arratine/Aretino

precious] notorious; not: valuable

prefer] advance; not: choose

present(ly)] instant(ly) or immediate(ly); not: near or soon

pretend] venture, aspire; not: feign

prevent] to come before or to anticipate; not: to keep from

probatum (est)] tried and tested (literally, it is approved [Lat.]), usually written on prescriptions

profession] religious belief; not: occupation

project(or)] scheme(r), generally elaborate and unfeasible

pulvillio(ed)] (treated with) powdered perfume

punk] prostitute; not: hoodlum

pupp(e)y] doll or toy; not: young dog

quality] gentry or nobility; not: value

quarrel] violent fight; not: verbal disagreement

quick] alive, lively, or when referring to a fetus, moving; not: fast

race] family, lineage; not: ethnic identity

receipt] recipe or prescription; not: proof of purchase

resty] restive, stubborn

rib] v. bone

Ring] a circular drive in Hyde Park*

rook] a cheat, con man; not: a chesspiece or a crow

Rosamond's Pond] favorite trysting place, put into St. James's Park and surrounded by trees by Charles II; named after the (in)famous mistress of Henry II

rose, under the] sub rosa, in secret

Rowland...Oliver] tit for tat; Roland and Olivier were two of Charlemagne's Twelve Peers, inseparable heroes of the Medieval chanson de geste, *La Chanson de Roland (The Song of Roland)*.

sack] wine; not: bag

Saint] Puritan (often hypocritical); not: truly holy person

St. James's] St. James's Palace, Park, and Square, at the western end of Pall Mall, near Westminster: a very fashionable district in the Town*

salt] lusty

salute] to greet, often with a kiss or embrace; not: to hold hand to eyebrow or over heart

satyr] satire, incorrectly thought to be derived from the Greek word, rather than from Latin *satura* (mixed dish)

'sbud, 'sdeath, 'slife, 'sheart, 'slid(s)] by God's (Christ's) blood/death/life/heart/(eye)lids

scour] in 17th-18th century slang: to roam about at night uproariously, breaking windows, beating the watch, and molesting wayfarers (*OED*)

separate maintenance] money allotted to a wife separated from her husband

servant] courtly-love term for a professed lover; not: domestic employee

shock] shaggy dog

shore] open sewer

silly] innocent, plain, unsophisticated, usually rustic; not: foolish, frivolous snuff] charred part of a candlewick; not: tobacco product

sophisticate(d)] adulterated, falsified; not: cosmopolitan

sot] fool; not: drunkard

sound] healthy, but especially, free from venereal disease

stairs] steps down the embankment of the Thames; not: steps between stories

steenkirk] lace-trimmed neckcloth, worn tied or twisted through a loop or ring

still] always; not: yet

Strand] major thoroughfare connecting the City* of London with the Town* and the Court, a site of popular, public celebrations like erecting a maypole (for example, the one erected after the Restoration)

stum] wine artificially aged; hence, as a verb, to pass off such bad wine or to impair one with it

stupid(ity)] (of people) torpid, (of things) tiresome, boring; not: unintelligent

sudden(ly)] prompt(ly); not: abrupt(ly)

tale] count, tally; not: story

Teague] A pejorative name for any native Irishman (Tadhg is the Irish for the name Timothy.)

teeth] defiance, opposition; not: dental appurtenances

Temple] one of the Inns of Court*

tickle trout] to seduce a trout into one's hand by rubbing its belly

toilet] dressing table or the act of dressing; not: commode

Toledo] sword made in Toledo, Spain, famous for their fine—and long—steel blades

Tony] a foolish person; a simpleton. (*OED*)

tory rory] boisterous

Tower] main garrison for the City of London, often used as a prison

Town] fashionable area west of the City of London; not: a big village in the country

turtle] dove; not: reptile in a shell

twire] to look at covertly, coyly

Tyburn] Middlesex Gallows, west of the Tyburn River (near the northeast corner of modern Hyde Park)

'ud] v. 'od

unsound] see sound

Vérole] French for syphilis

very] genuine, or legitimate, actual; not: extremely

vile] of little worth or account; not: despicable

villain] lowborn, uncouth; not: deliberate scoundrel

visor, vizard] metonymy for masked prostitute

want] lack or (in) need (of); not: desire

watch waters] to scrutinize conduct closely, often used literally, to examine urine for medical diagnosis, especially pregnancy

Westminster Hall] the law court at Westminster (q.v.)

Whitehall] the English royal palace and the area around it in Westminster

whore of Babylon] in the Christian tradition, second only to Satan in her distance from God (see Revelations 17:1–6); in the Restoration, a figure for the corruption of the Roman Church.

willow] symbol of grief for unrequited love or loss of a mate

woman] waiting-woman, usually of gentry, not peasant, status

your] almost equivalent to "the"; not to be taken personally

'zbud] see 'sbud

Index of Authors and Titles